THE HOLY BIBLE,

CONTAINING

THE OLD AND NEW TESTAMENTS,

WITH THE APOCRYPHAL BOOKS,

IN THE EARLIEST ENGLISH VERSIONS

MADE FROM THE LATIN VULGATE BY

JOHN WYCLIFFE AND HIS FOLLOWERS;

EDITED BY

THE REV JOSIAH FORSHALL, F R S ETC

LATE FELLOW OF EXETER COLLEGE,

AND

SIR FREDERIC MADDEN, K H F R S ETC

KEEPER OF THE MSS IN THE BRITISH MUSEUM

VOLUME II

OXFORD,
AT THE UNIVERSITY PRESS
M DCCC L

I. KINGS.

IN this book of Kingis the first is contened, how Anna, the wijf of Helchana, that was longe tyme bareyn, axide of God to haue a sone, and God ȝaf to her axing; which sone Anna ȝaf in to the seruyse of the Lord, in the tabernacle of boond of pees, vndur Heli the heiȝeste prest   And God chees Samuel, and spak to him alle thingis, and forsook Heli and hise sones, for wickidnesse that the sones diden, wherfore thei perischiden alle in o dai   And Samuel anoyntide Saul in to king on Israel; and whanne Saul fulfillide not the bestis of God, God forsook him; and Samuel anoyntide Dauith in to king, whanne he kepte hise fadris scheep; wherfor Saul hatide Dauith, and pursuwide him, til to the dai of veniaunce of the Lord cam; and Saul perischide, and hise sones, and al his hous

---

Here bigynneth the prolog of the foure bokis of Kyngis[a]

THE tunge forsothe of Syrus, and of Caldeis, witnessith to ben anentis the[b] Ebrewis two and twenti lettris, the whiche of a[c] greet parti[d] miȝ coostieth to Ebrew; for and thei two and twenti elementis han in the same sown, but in dyuerse printis   Samarytans also the fyue[e] bokis of Moyses wiyten in as feele lettris, oonli in figuris and printis dyuersynge, and it is certeyn Esdras, the scribe and the doctour of the lawe, after Jerusalem takun, and the restorynge of the temple vndur Zorobabel, to han foundun other lettris, the whiche we nowe vsen, whanne vnto that tyme weren the same printis of Samarytanys and of E-brews. Forsothe in the book of Noum-bris this same noumbrynge[f] vnder the noumbre of Leuitis and prestis mistih is

[Prologue to the four books of Kings[b]]

THE langage of men Sirus, and of Cal-deis also, witnessith that there ben two an twenty lettris, the which of a greet partie is acordynge to Ebrew, for also thei han two and twenti elementis in the same sown, and in dyuerse pryntis   Also Samaritans writen the fyue bokis of Moyses with so many lettris, oonly dyuersynge in the figuris and prentis; and it is certeyn, that Esdras, the scribe and a doctour of the lawe, foond other lettris, which we vsen now, aftir that Jerusalem was taken, and aftir restorynge of the temple vndur Zoro-babel, for vnto that tyme weren the same lettris and fyguris of Samarytans and of Ebrews vsid   Also in book of Numeri the same noumbrynge is mistily schewid vndir the noumbre of dekenes and prestis, and we han founden the hie name of the

---

shewid, and the name of the Lord Tetragramaton in summe Grece volyms vnto this day we han founden with oold lettris expressyd But and the Salmys sixe and threttis[g], and the hundrid tenthe, and the hundryd enleueth, and the hundrid eiȝtenth[h], and the hundrid foure and fourtithe, albeit that thei ben wryten with dyuerse metre, neuertheluter thei ben weuyd[i] with[k] the abece of the same noumbre, and the Lamentaciouns of Jeremye, and the Preier of hym, and forsothe the Prouerbis of Salomon, in the eend, fro that place in whiche he seith, A strong womman who shal fynde, with the same abicees or markyngis ben noumbrid Forsothe fyue dowble lettrys ben anentis the Ebrewis, Caph, Men, Nun, Phe, Sade; forsothe other wise thei writen bi thes the bigynningis and the mydils of wordis, other wise the eendis Wherfore and fyue bokis, Samuel, Malachym, Dabreiamyn, Esdras, Jeremye with Cynoth, that is, his Lamentaciouns, ben eymyd of sum men dowble bookis What maner wise therfor two and twenti elymentis ben, bi the whiche we wryten Ebrewly al that we speken, and mannus voyce with the bigynnyngis of hem is takun, so two and twenti volyms ben noumbrid, bi the whiche as bi lettris and bigynnyngis the tendre and the ȝit sowkynge childhod of the riȝtwise man is tauȝt in the doctrine of God The first book anentis hem is clepid[l] Bresith, which we Genesis seyn, the secounde, Ellesmoth, 'the which[m] Exodus is clepid[n], the thridde is Vagetra, that is Leuytik, the ferth, Vagedaber, 'the which[o] we clepen[p] Noumbre, the fifthe Abdabarym, 'the which[o] is before notid Deutronomy Thes ben the fyue bokis of Moyses, 'the whiche[o] thei clepen[q] proprely Thorath, that is, the lawe The secounde ordre of the prophetis thei maken, and bigynnen fro Jesu[r], the sone of Naue, 'the which[s] anentis hem is seid Josue Bennum

Lord Tetragramaton in summe bookes of Grew expressid with olde lettris vnto this day But also the salmes of the Sauter, as the xxxvj. salm, and the hundrid and x salm, and the hundrid and aleuene salm, and the hundrid and xviij salm, and the hundrid and xliiij. salm, al be it that thei ben writen with dyuerse metre, netheles thei ben writen and wouen to gideris with the abece of the same noumbre; and the Lamentaciouns of Jeremye, and the Preier of him, and also the Prouerbis of Salamon, in the ende, fro that place in which he seith, Who shal fynde a strong womman, be noumbryd with the same abeces of merkyngis Forsothe the fyue double lettris anentis the Ebrews ben thes, Caph, Men, Num, Phe, Sade, for bi these lettris thei writen other while the bygynnyngis and the myddes of wordes, and in anothir maner the endis Wherfor these fyue bookes, Samuel, Malachim, Dabre Jamyn, Esdras, and Jeremye with Cynnoth, that is, his Lamentaciouns, ben gessid of sum men to be dowble bookes Therfor as there ben xxij lettris, by which we writen in manere of Ebrews alle thingis that we speken, and mannes vois taken with the bigynnynges of hem, so xxij volyms ben noumbrid, by the whiche as by lettris and bygynnynges the ȝonge tendre and ȝit soukynge childhod of the riȝtwise man is enformed in the doctryne of God The first book anentis hem is clepid Bresith, whiche we clepen Genesis; the secounde, Elesmoth, which is clepid Exodi, the thridde, Vagetra, that is, the book of Leuyticy, the fourthe, Vagetaber, which we clepen Noumbre, the fyfte, Addabarim, the which is bifore notid Deutronomye. These ben the fyue bookes of Moyses, the whiche thei clepen propurly Thorath, what is to seie, the lawe Thanne thei maken the secunde ordre of profetis, and bygynnen at Jhesu, the sone of Naue, that anentis hem is seid Josue Benum Fro thennus thei ioyneden yn

[g] threttithe *CHI* [h] eiȝtene *I* [i] wouen *c* [k] of *I* [l] callid *CEI* [m] that *c* [n] cald *I* [o] that *c* [p] cal *I* [q] callen *I* [r] Josue *A* [s] that *c*

Fro thens thei vndurweuydent Sophym, that is, the book of Jugis; and intoᵘ the same thei puttenᵛ in Ruth, for in the dayes of Jugis don is toold hir storye The thridde folowith Samuel, the which we seyn the Firste and the Secounde of Rewmys; the ferthe, Malachim, that is, of Kyngis, the which is conteyned in the thridde and the ferthe volym of Rewmys; and mych betere it is to seye Malachym, that is, of Kyngis, thanne Malathot, that is, of Rewmes; forsothe not of many folk he discriueth rewmes, but of oon Yrael puple, that is conteyned in twelue lynagis The fifthe is Ysay; the sixt Jeremye, the seuenthe Ezechiel; theʷ eiʒtith the book of the twelue prophetis, 'the whichˣ anentis hem is clepidʸ Thariasra The thridde ordre weeldith Agiogropha, that ben holi wryten ensaumplis² And the first book bigynneth fro Job; the secounde fro Dauyd, the which men holden in fyue dyuysiouns, and in o volym of Psalmys; the thridde is of Salomon, hauynge thre bokis, Prouerbis, that thei clepenᵃ Parablis, that is, Masloth; the ferthe Ecclesiasten, that is, Coelech; the fifthe is Soonge of Songis, whom theiᵇ before noten bi title Syrassyrym; the sixte is Danyel; the seuentheᶜ Dabreiamyn, that is, the wordis of days, the whiche more nameli we mowen clepeᵈ theᵉ Cronycle of al Goddis story, the which book anentis vs is wryten Paralypomynonᶠ the First and the Secounde, the eiʒtthe Esdras, the which and heᵍ lijk maner, anentis Grekis and Latyns, in two bokis is dyuydid; the nynthe Ester And so ben maad togidre the bokis of the oold lawe two and twenti, that is, of Moyses fyue, of Prophetis eiʒte, of Agiografis, that ben expresse exsaumplis to holynesse, nyne; al be it that summe wryten Ruth and Synoth among the Agiographis, and thes bookis in her noumbre thei wenen to be toʰ noumbrid, and bi that to ben of the

Sophim, that is, the book of Juges; and in to the same thei putten in Ruth, for in the dayes of Juges her storie is teeld to be fulfillid The thridde book folewith, that is clepid Samuel, which we seyn the Firste and the Secounde book of Kynges The fourthe is Malachim, that is, of Kyngis, which is conteyned in the thridde and the iiij volym of Rewmes, and myche betere it is to seie Malachym, that is, of Kynges, than Maletoch, that is, of rewmes; for he discryueth not the rewmes of many folkis, but the rewme of o puple of Israel, that is conteyned in xij lynagis. The fifte is Isaie; the sixte Jeromye, the seuenthe Ezechiel; the eiʒte in the book of xij. profetis, that anentis hem is clepid Thariasrai The thridde ordre weldith Agiografa, *that ben hooly writen ensaumplis*, and the firste book bygynneth fro Job, the secounde fro Dauith, which men holden in fyue dyuysiouns, and in o volym of Salmes; the thridde is of Salomon, hauynge iij. bookes, as Prouerbis *or Parablis*, that is clepid Maloth; the iiij. Ecclesiasten, that is clepid Coelech, the fyfethe is the Song of Songis, whom thei biforen seien bi title Sirassirym, the sixte is Daniel, the seuenthe Debraiamyn, that is to seie, the wordis of daies, the which more kouthly may be clepid the Cronycle of Goddis stories; the which book anentis vs is writen Paralipomenon the Firste and the Secounde; the eiʒtthe book is Esdias, the which also in lijk maner, bothe anentis Grekis and Latynes, is departid in to twey bookis, the nynthe is the book of Ester And that is to seie, fyue booke of Moyses, and eiʒte bookes of the profitis, and neyne of Agiogrofis, that is to seie, of expresse ensaumplis of holynesse, al be it that sum men writun Ruth and Synoth among the Agiografis, and thei weenen that thes bookes shulden be rekened in her noumbre, and be that to ben xxiiij. bookes of olde lawe; which the Apocalips of Joon bryngeth yn, vndur the noumbre of xxiiij

---

ᵗ vnderwouen c   ᵘ in ɪ   ᵛ puttiden ɪ   ʷ and the ɪ   ˣ that c   ʸ cald ɪ   ᶻ exsaumplis cʀ
ᵃ callen ɪ   ᵇ we ɪ   ᶜ seuenthe is ɪ.   ᵈ calle ɪ.   ᵉ Om. ɪ   ᶠ in Paralypomynon ʙɪ   ᵍ the ɪ   ʰ Om c

oold lawe foure and twenti bokis; the whiche vndre noumbre of foure and twenti eldris the Apocalips[j] of Joon bryngith yn, honourynge the loomb, and offrynge her crownes, the cheerys born doun, hem stondynge betore the foure beestis eyed before and behynde, that is, biholdynge into that that is passid, and into that that is to comen, and criynge with contynuel voyce, Holy, Holy, Holi, Lord God Almyȝti, that was, and that is, and that is to comen! This prologe of[k] Scripturis as an helmyd bigynnynge to al the bokis 'the whiche[l] fro Ebrewe we han turned into Latyn, may acoorde, that we mowen knowe that what euere thing out of thes is, it is to be put among the Apographase, that is, among tho thingis whos autor is not knowun of al holi chirch Therfore Sapiens, that comounli is wryten in of Salomon, and of Jesu, the sone of Syrak, and the book of Judith, and Toby, and Pastor, ben not in the canoun I foond the Fyrst book of Machabeis Ebrewe, the Secounde is Greke, that may be proued of that settynge The whiche thingis whanne thei so han hem, thou reder, Y biseche thee, ne eyme thou my traueyle the repreuynge of oold men In the tabernacle of God ech man offreth that he may, other men gold, and siluer, and precious stones, other men bise, and purpur, and cocko[m] offren, and iacynct With vs is wel doon, if we offren skynnys and heeris of she geet, and neuerthelater[n] the Apostle oure more[o] contemptible thingis shewith more nedeful Wherfor and al the[p] fayrnesse of the tabernacle, and the distinccioun of the present, and of the chirche to comen, bi eche spicis is coueied with skynnys, and with herys; tho that ben fowler thingis letten the brennynge of the sunne, and the harme of wederis Thanne rede thow first Samuel, and myn[q] Malachym, myn forsothe, myn[r], what euere thing forsothe ofter[s] turnynge and in amend-

eldris onourynge the lomb, and offrynge her crownes, with her cheiris cast doun, and stondynge bifor the foure beestis that weren iȝed bifore and bihynde, that is to seie, biholdynge in to the tyme that is passid, and in to the tyme that is to come, and criynge with contynuel vois, without feyntise, Hooly, Holi, Holy, Lord God Almyȝti, that was, and that is, and that is to comen! This prologe of Scripturis as an helmed principle mai acorde to alle the bookes which we han turned fro Ebrew in to Latyn, that we moun knowun that what euere wrytynge is out of these, is to be put amonge the Apocrifas, that is, amonge thilke wrytynges whos auctours ben vnknowe of alle hooly chirche Therfore the book of Sapience, that comynly is writen to be the book of Salomon, and the book of Jhesu, the sone of Sirak, and the book of Judith, and Thobie, and Pastor, be not in the canoun I found the Firste book of Makabeus of Ebrews langage; the Secounde book is Grew, that may be preued of the sittinge and of the speche The which thingis, siththe thei han in sich manere, thou reder, I byseche thee, deeme thou not my trauayle to be maad in repreuynge of old men For ech man offrith in to the tabernacle of God that he mai, aftir his power, sum men offren gold, and siluer, and precious stoonys, othere men offren biys, and purpur, and scarled, and iacynt With vs it is weel, if we offren skynnes, and the heeris of geet, and netheles the Postle schewith opynly, that oure foule thingis and contemptible ben more needful than sum faire thingis Wherfore al the fairnesse of the tabernacle, that was distinccioun and figure of hooly chirche that is now, and that is aftir to comynge, by alle her semelynesses is kyuerid with skynnes, and with heeris, and tho thingis that ben foulere letten the brennynge of the sunne, and the dispitousnesse of reynes and stormes Thanne rede thou first Samuel, and my book Ma-

[j] Apocalipsis E [k] to I [l] that c [m] cocce E cok c cocke I [n] nerthelatere c [o] moste I
[p] that BCFFHI [q] Om E pr m [r] Om A [s] ouer I

ynge more bisili and we han lernyd, and we holden, oure is, oure is. And whanne thou vndurstoondist that bifore hoond thou knewe not, or eyme thou me a remenour, if thou art kynde, or a leeyer bisiden, if thow art vnkynde; al be it that Y haue no conscience to myself, me to haue chaungid eny thing fro Ebrews trewth. Certeyne, if thow ert[t] of hard bileue, rede Greke[u] bokis and Latyns, and ley[w] togidre with thes litil werkis, the whiche[x] aboue we han out[y] toold; and where euere thow see bitwix[z] hemself to[a] discorde, ask eny of the Ebrews, to whom more thou owist to ȝeue feith, and if oure thingis be stable, I trowe that thou shalt not eyme hym a lyer, for in the same place with me lijk maner he dyuyne. But and ȝow, wymmen seruauntis of Crist, Y preye, the whiche anoynten the heed of the Lord, doun syttynge with the[b] moost precyous myrre of bileue, the whiche sechen not the Saueour in sepulcre[c], for[d] whom nowe Crist hath stied vp to the fader, that aȝens the berkynge houndis that aȝens me with wood mouth waxen cruel, and goon about the cytee, and in that demen hem self wyse, if to other they bacbiten, that ȝe aȝen putten the targetis of ȝoure preyers. I, knowynge my lownes, of that sentence euere more Y shal recorde, I seyde, I shal kepe my weyes, that I trespasse not in my tunge; Y haue put to my mouth warde, whanne the synful stood aȝens me; Y bicam dowmbe, and[e] am lowid, and heelde[f] my pees fro good thingis.

Here endith the prolog of the foure bokis of Kyngis, and nowe bygynneth the first book[g].

lachim, ȝhe, myn forsothe, myn; fore what euere we han lerned in ofte turnynge of bookes, and in more bisily amendynge, if we holden it in oure hertis, it is ouris, it is ouris. And whanne thou vndurstondist that biforn hond thou knewe not, thanne or deme thou me to be a trewe drawere out of hooly writ, if thou art kynde, or ellis a false spekere, if thou art vnkynde; al be it that I haue no conscience to my silf, me to haue chaungid ony thing fro Ebrews treuthe. Certis, if thou art hard of byleeue, rede the bookis of Grew and of Latyn, and leie hem to gideris with these litil werkes, whiche we han teld aboue; and where euer thou seest hem discorde bitwixe hem silf, axe thou ony mon of the Ebrewis, to whom thou shuldist ȝyue more feith to, and if he conferneth oure writyngis, I trowe thou shalt not deeme him a coniecture of lesyngis, that he hath dyuyned in the same place in lijk manere with me. But also I preye ȝou, Paula and Eustochie, seruauntis of Crist, which anoynten the heed of the Lord, sittinge doun with the moost preciouse myrre of bileeue, the whiche seken not oure Sauyour in the sepulcre, to whos bileeue Crist hath stied vp to his fadir, I preie ȝou, that ȝe putte the scheeldis of ȝoure good preieris aȝens the berkynge houndis that wexen cruel aȝens me with wood mouth, and gon aboute the citee, and in that demen hem to be wise, whanne thei bacbiten othir men. Therfor I, knowynge my lownesse, shal euermore haue mynde of that sentence, [I] seid, I shal kepe my weies that I trespasse not [in] my tonge; I haue ordeyned a warde to my mouth, whan the synful trespasour stood aȝenus me; I bicame doumbe, and was lawid, and held my pees fro good thingis.

---

[t] be *1.* [u] Grekis *ci.* [w] leȝe *hem 1.* [x] that *c.* [y] ouȝte *11.* not *1.* [z] betwe *c.* bytwen *BEFH.* [a] Om. *1.* [b] Om. *1.* [c] the sepulcre *1.* [d] fro *E pr.m.* from *1.* [e] and I *1.* [f] heuld *1.* [g] *Here endith the prolog and bigynneth the firste book of Kingis. E. Here endeth the prolog. se now the firste book of Kingis. 1.* No final rubric in *BCFH.*

The firste of Kyngis[a].

CAP. I.

1 THERE was a man of Ramathaym of Sophym, of the hil of Effraym, and the name of hym Elchana, the sone of Jeroboam, sone[b] of Elyuth, sone of Thau, 2 sone of Suph, Eufrate. And he hadde two wyues; name to the toon Anna, and name to the secounde Phenenna; and there weren of Phenenne sonys; forsothe of Anne there weren noon free children. 3 And that man stiede fro his cytee vp the ordeynd days, for to honour and sacrifie to the Lord of oostis in Sylo. Forsothe there weren the two sonys of Hely, Ophny and Phynees, preestis of the Lord. 4 The day thanne cam, and Elchana offerde, and ȝaf to Phenenne his wijf, and to alle 5 his children and douȝtren[c] parties; forsothe to Anne he ȝaf o party drerye, for he louede Anne; forsothe the Lord hadde 6 closid hir wombe. Forsothe hir enemye tourmentide hir, and hugely angwishide, in so mych that she putte to reproue, that 7 the Lord hadde closid hir wombe. And so she dyde bi ech ȝeer, whanne, turnynge aȝen the tyme, thei styeden vp into the hows of the Lord; and she so terryde hyr. Forsothe she wepte, and took no 8 meete. Thanne seide to hyr Helchana, hir man, Anna, whi wepist thow, and whi etist thow nouȝt, and for what cause is tourmentid thin herte? Whether am Y not betere to thee than ten sones? 9 Forsothe Anna roos, after that she hadde eetyn in Silo and dronken. And Hely the preest sittynge vpon a litil seete, before the postis of the hows of the Lord, 10 whanne Anna was in bitter[d] inwit, she

Here biginnith the firste book of Kingis[a].

CAP. I.

1 'A man was[b] of 'Ramathym of[c] Sophym, of the hil of Effraym, and his name was Elchana, the sone of Jeroboam, sone of Thau, sone of Suph, of Effraym †. And Helchana hadde twei 2 wyues; the name 'to oon[d] was Anna, and the[e] 'name of the[f] secounde was[g] Fenenna; and sones weren to Feuenna; forsothe[h] fre children 'weren not to Anna[i]. And 3 thilke[k] man styede[l] fro his citee in daies[m] ordeyned, to worschipe and offre[n] sacrifice to the Lord of oostis in Silo. Forsothe[o] twei sones of Heli weren there, Ophym[p] and Fynees, preestis of the Lord. Ther-4 for[q] the dai cam, and Helcana offride, and ȝaf[r] partis to Fenenna, his wijf, and to alle hise sones and douȝtris; forsothe[s] he ȝaf soreufulyǂ o part to Anna, for he louyde Anna; forsothe[t] the Lord hadde closid hir wombe. And hir[u] enemy turmentide 'hir, and angwischide[w] greetly, in so myche that sche vpbreidide[x], that the Lord hadde closid hir wombe. And so 7 sche[y] dide 'bi alle ȝeeris[z], whanne 'in tyme comynge aȝen[a], thei stieden[b] in to the hows of the Lord; and so sche terride Anna. Forsothe[c] Anna[d] wepte, and took not[e] mete‖. Therfor Helcana, hir hose-8 bonde, seide to hir, Anna, whi wepist thou, and whi etist thou[f] not, and whi is thin herte turmentid? Whether[ff] Y am not betere to thee than ben ten sones? 'Sotheli Anna[g] roos, aftir that sche hadde 9 ete and drunke in Silo. 'And the while Hely was on his greet seete, bifor[h] the postis of the 'hows of the Lord[i], whanne[k] 10 Anna[l] was in bittere soule[m], sche preyede

† *Effraym; for he dwellide in the hil of Effraym, not for he was of the lynage of Effraym, for he was a dekene of the sones of Chore, as it is had in thre book of Paral. vi. c°. Lire here. c.*

ǂ *he ȝaf soreufulȝ; Helcana was not soreuful of the ȝyuyng, but for he hadde not fre children of Anna, to whiche children partis schulden be ȝouun. In Ebreu it is had o part either double, of which the resoun sueth, for he louyde Anna; and in this he wolde onoure hir. Lire here. c.*

‖ *mete, that is, took litil of mete. Lire here. c.*

---

a From D. *Here bygynneth the first bok of Kyngis.* P. No initial rubric in ACEH.   b the sone E pr. m. c douȝtris CE.   d betere A.

a From MP. No initial rubric in the other MSS.   b Ther was a man I.   c Ramatha in DGIKMNOQXB. d of that oon I. to the toon K.   e Om. DKM.   f name to the *plures.* Om. I.   g hiȝte I.   h but Anna hadde none I.   i Om. I.   k that I.   l stiede up I.   m the daies *that weren* I.   n to offre I.   o And I. P Ofny I. Ophny nb.   q Thanne I.   r he ȝaf I.   s and I.   t and I.   u *Fenenna* hir I.   w and noiede hir I.   x vpbreidide hir I.   y Fenenna I.   z eche ȝeer I.   a the tyme came that I.   b stieden up I. c And I.   d thanne sche I.   e no I.   f Om. I.   ff Wher *ceteri passim.*   g Anna forsothe I.   h Hely sittinge upon his sete I.   i Lordis hows I.   k and whanne I.   l sche I.   m *seroue* of soule I.

11 preiede the Lord, wepynge largeli , and
a vowe she vowide, seiynge, Lord God of
oostis, if biholdynge thow see the tourmentynge of thi seruaunt, and were recordid of me, ne forȝetiste thin hoond-
maydyn, and ȝyuest to thi seruaunt maal
kynde, I shal ȝyue hym to the Lord alle
the days of his lyjf, and rasour shal not
12 stie vpon his heed Forsothe it is doon,
that whanne she multipliede preieis before the Lord, that Heli weytide hir
13 mouth. Forsothe Anna spak in hir
herte, and oonli the lippis of hir weren
meued, and the vois of hire was not fulli
herd. Heli therfor eymyde hir dronken,
14 and seide to hyr, Howe long shalt thou
be dronken ? Defye a litil wiȝt the wyn,
15 bi the which thou art dronken Anna
answerynge, Nay, she seith, my loid, for
a womman wel mych wretcheful Y am ;
for wyn and al that may make dronken
Y dranke not, but I haue held out my
16 soule in the siȝt of the Lord ; ne hoold
thou thin handwomman as oon of the
douȝtres of Belial, for of the multitude
of sorwe and of my mournynge Y haue
17 spokun vnto nowe Thanne Heli seith
to hir, Go in pees, and God of Yrael
ȝeue to thee the askynge that thou hast
18 preied hym And she seide, Wolde God
thin handwoman fynde grace in thin
eyen And the womman ȝede into hir
weye, and eete , and the cheeris off hir
ben not more ouere into dyuerse thingis
19 chaungid And thei arysen eerly, and
anowredeng before the Lord ; and ben
turned aȝen, and camen into her hows
in Ramatha Forsothe Helchana knewe
Anne his wyjf , and the Lord is re-
20 cordid of hir And doon it is after the
cercle of dais, Anna conceyuede, and beer
a child, and clepide his name Samuel ;

the Lord, and wepte largeli ; and madeⁿ a 11
vowo, and seide, Lord God of oostis, if
thou biholdist, and seest the turment of
thi seruauntesse, and hastᵖ mynde of me,
and forȝetist not thin handmayde, and
ȝyuest toʳ thi seruauntesse 'a male kyndeˢ,
Y schal ȝyue hym to the Lord inᵗ alle
daiesᵘ of his lyjf, and a rasour schal not
stieᵛ on his heed Forsotheʷ itˣ was doon, 12
whanne sche multipliede preierisʸ bifor
the Lord, that Elyᶻ aspiede hir mouth.
Forsotheᵃ Anna spak in hir herte, and 13
oneli hir lippis weren mouyd, and outerly
hir vois was not herd. Therfor Helyᵇ
gesside hir drunkun, and he seide to hyr, 14
Hou longe schalt thou be drunkun ? Ditye
thou a litil theᶜ wyn, 'bi whichᵈ thou art
moistᵉ Anna answeride, and seide, Nay†, 15
my lord, for Y am 'a wietchidf womman
greethᵍ , Y 'drank notʰ wyn 'and al thingⁱ
that may make drunkun, but Y scheddeᵏ
out my soule in the 'siȝt of the Lordˡ ;
gesse thou not thin handmaide as oon of 16
the douȝtris of Belyal, for of the multitude of my sorewe and morenyngᵐ Y
spakⁿ 'til in too present tyme Thanne 17
Hely seide to hir, Go thou in pees, and
God of Israel ȝyue‡ to thee the axyng
whichᵖ thou preiedistq hym And scheʳ 18
seide, 'Y woldeˢ that thin hondmayde fynde
grace in thin 13en And the womman ȝedeᵗ
in to hir weie, and eet ; and hir cheris
weren no more chaungid dyuersly And 19
'thei rysedenᵘ eerly, andᵛ worschipiden bifore the Lord , and thei turneden aȝen,
and camen in to hir hows in Ramatha
Forsotheʷ Helchana knew *fleischli*ˣ Anna,
his wyjf ; and the Lord thouȝte on hir
And it was doon after the cumpas of daies, 20
Anna conseyuede, and childide a sone, and
scheʸ clepide his name Samuel‖, for sche
hadde axid hym of the Lord. Forsotheᶻ 21

† *Nay, that
m, Y am not
drunkun* c

‡ *ȝyue, in E-
breu it is, schal*
18 *ȝyue* c

‖ *Samuel is in
terpretid axid
of God. I ire
here* c

ᵉ forȝeten BCEFn   f in E pr m   ᵍ honouredyn EC

ⁿ sche made I   o vow to the Lord I   ᵖ if thou hast I   q ȝyue c   ʳ a sone to I   ˢ Om I   ᵗ Om I
ᵘ the daies I   ᵛ come up I   ʷ And I   ˣ whanne it c   ʸ hir preieris I   ᶻ Ely the prest I   ᵃ Sotheli I
ᵇ Hely the prest I   ᶜ and a lytil the I   ᵈ that I   ᵉ maad moist with I   f an vnhappy I   ᵍ Om I
ʰ haue not drunken I   ⁱ nether ony thing I   ᵏ haue helde I   ˡ Lordis siȝt I   ᵐ of my morenyng
ᵃ haue spoken I   o vnto this I   ᵖ that I   q hast preied I   ʳ Anna I   ˢ Wolde God I   ᵗ ȝede forth I
ᵘ *Helcana and his meyne* arisen up I   ᵛ and thei I   ʷ And I   ˣ Om IKo   ʸ Om s.   ᶻ And I

foithi that she hadde askid hym of the
21 Lord   Forsothe hir man Helchana stiede
vp, and al his hows, for to offre to the
Lord a solempne oost, and his vowe
22 And Anna assendide not ; forsothe she
seide to hir man, Y shal not goo, to the
tyme that the child be wened, and I
brynge hym, and he apere^h before the
si3t of the Lord, and dwelle there con-
23 tynuely   And Helchana, hir man, seith
to hir, Do that is seen to thee good, and
dwel to the tyme that thow wene hym ,
and I preye, that the Lord fulfille his
word   Thanne the woman abood, and
3af hir sone mylk, to the tyme that he
shulde meue hym awey fro the mylk
24 And she biou3te hym with hir, after that
she hadde wened hym, with thre calues,
and thre bushelis of meele, and a vessel
of wyn , and she brou3te him to the
hows of the Lord in Sylo   Forsothe the
25 child 3it was a lytil faunt   And thei
slewen a calf, and offreden the child to
26 Hely   And Anna seith, I biseche, my
lord, thi soule lyueth , Y am that womman that stood before thee here, prey-
27 inge to the Lord , for this child I
pieyede, and the Lord hath 3euen to me
28 the askynge that I askyde hym ; therfor
and I haue lent hym to the Lord alle
the dais, in the whiche he were lent to
the Lord   And there thei honourden the
Lord   And Anna honourde, and seith,

hir hosebonde Helcana stiede^a, and al his
hows^b, to offie a solempne sacrifice, and his
avow to the Lord   And Anna stiede not^c, 22
for sche hadde seid to hir hosebonde, Y
schal not go, til the 3onge child be wenyd,
and til Y lede hym^d, and he appere bifor
the 'si3t of the Lord^e, and dwelle there
contynueli†   And Helcana, hir hosebonde, 23
seide to hir, Do thou that that semeth
good to thee, and dwelle thou^f til thou
wene^g hym ; and Y biseche, that the Lord
fille^h his word   Therfor the womman
dwellideⁱ, and 3af mylk to hir sone, til^k
sche iemouyde hym fro^l mylk   And sche^m 24
biou3te hym with hir, aftir that sche
hadde wened hym, with thre caluys, and
thre buyschelis of mele, and amfoieⁿ, 'ether
a pot^o, of wyn , and sche brou3te hym to
the hows of the Lord in Silo   Forsothe^p
the child was 3it ful 3onge   And thei 25
sacrifieden^q a calf, and thei offriden the
child to Hely. And Anna seide, My lord, 26
Y biseche^r, that is^s, that this^t child be thi^u
'disciple and^v seruaunt^w, thi soule lyueth,
Y am that^x womman, that stood bifor
thee here, and preiede the Lord , for this 27
child Y^y preiede, and the Lord 3af to
me myn axyng which^z Y axide hym ,
therfoi^a Y haue 3oue hym to the Lord 'in 28
alle^b daies, in whiche he is 3ouun to the
Lord   And thei worschypiden theie the
Lord.

† contynuely.
in Ebreu it is,
til in to the
world, that is,
til to the fifithe
3eer   Lire
here c

CAP II

1   Gladid out isⁱ myn heite in the Lord,
and aieryd^k is myn horn in my God ,
maad large is my mouth vpon myn ene-
myes, foi Y am glade in thin^l 3yuer of
2 heelth   There is noon holy as is the
Loid , forsothe ne there is othei with
out thee, and there is not strong as our

CAP II.

And Anna worschipide, and seide, Myn 1
heite fulli ioiede in the Lord, and myn
horn is reisid in my God , my mouth is
alaigid on^e myn enemyes, for Y was^d glad
in thin helthe^e   Noon is hooli as the Lord 2
is ; 'foi noon other is, outakun^f thee, and
noon is strong as^g oure God   Nyle 3e 3

h aperide A   i Om EFCH   k rerid c   l the E pr m

a stiede up I   b meynee I   c not up to that solempnytee I   d hym thidere I   e Lord s si3t I   f thou
stille I   g haue wened I   h fulfille I   i abode I   k til the tyme I   l fro the I   m Anna I   n a
mesure I an amfore K   O Om I   P And I   q sacrifisiden plures   r biseche thee I   s Om AGKLMO
t thi FGMNPQSb   u Om c   v Om DGMNPQXb   w the whole gloss omitted in I   x the I   y and Y A
z that I   a therfor and BCKI GKLMN FQRSU W xb   b alle the I   c upon I   d am I   e helthe 3iuer I, f neither
certis ther is an other withoute I   g as is I

3 God Wole ȝe not multiplie to spcke
heiȝe thingis, gloriynge; go there awey
oold thingis fro ȝoure mouthe; foɪ the God
of sciencis[l] Lord is, and to hym ben be-
4 fore maad redi thouȝtis   The boowe of
stronge men is ouercomen, and feble[m]
5 ben gird with strength   The fillid be-
foɪe for looues han leyd hem self, and
the hungri ben fulfillid, to the tyme that
the bareyn bere wel many, and she that
6 many sones hadde, is feblid   The Lord
mortifieth, and quykeneth; bryngith doun
7 to hellis, and aȝen bryngith   The Lord
makith pore, and richeth, and[n] mekith,
8 and vndurrerith   He bryngith vp fro
powdre the nedye, and fro diyt he heueth
vp the pore, that he sitte with princis,
and the seet of glorie he holde, of the
Lord forsothe ben the vttermoost parties
of the erthe, and he hath put vpon hem
9 the woild   The feet of his halowis he
shal kepe, and vnpyteuous men in derknessis shulen waxe stille; for in his owne
strength shal not be strengthid a man
10 The Lord shulen drede the aduersaries
of hym, and vpon hem in heuenes he
shal thondre, the Lord shal deme the
eendis of erthe[o], and he shal ȝyue empyre to his kyng, and he shal hieȝ the
11 horn of his Crist   And Helchana wente
in Ramatha, into his hows, forsothe the
child was seruaunt in the siȝt of the
Lord before the face of Hely the preest
12 Forsothe the sones of Hely the sones of
13 Belial, not knowynge the Lord, ne the
office of preestis to the puple; but who
so euere hadde offerd the slayn sacrifyce,
the child of the preest cam, while the
flesh were sothen, and hadde a flesh hook
14 thre tothid in his hoond, and he putte
it into the leede, or into the cawdroun,
or into the pot, or into the greet panne;
and al that the fleshook reryde, the preest

multiplie to speke hiȝe thingis, and haue
glorie[h], elde thingis go awey fro ȝoure
mouth; for God is Lord of kunnyngis,
and thouȝtis ben maad redi to hym   The 4
bouwe of stɪong men is ouercomun, and
sijk[i] men ben giid with strengthe. Men 5
fillid[k] bifore settiden hem silf to hire for
looues, and hungri men ben fillid; while[l]
the bareyn womman childide[m] ful manye,
and sche that hadde many sones, was
sijke[n] The Lord sleeth, and quikeneth; ɪ 6
he[o] ledith forth to hellis[oo], and bryngith
aȝen The Lord makith pore, and[p] makith 7
riche; he makith low, and[p] reisith[q]   He 8
reisith[r] a nedi man fɪo poudur, and 'he
reisith[s] a pore man fɪo dryt, that he sitte
with princes, and holde the secte of glorie;
for the endis of erthe[t] ben of the Lord,
and he hath set the woɪld on[u] tho   He 9
schal kepe 'the feet of hise seyntis[v], and
wickid men schulen be stille to gidere in
deɪknessis; for a man schal not be maad
strong in his owne strengthe   Aduersa- 10
ries of the Lord schulen diede hym, and
in[w] heuenes he schal thundre on[x] hem,
the Loɪd schal deme the endis of erthe,
and he schal ȝyue lordschip to his kyng,
and he schal enhaunse the horn, 'that is,
power[y], of his Ciɪst   And Helcana ȝede 11
in to Ramatha, in to his hows, foɪsothe[z]
the child was seruant in the siȝt of the
Lord bifor the face of Ely the pɪeest
Forsothe the sones of Hely weren sones[a] 12
of Belial, and knewen[b] not the Lord, ne- 13
theɪ the office of pɪeestis to the puple; but
who euer hadde offɪid sacrifice, the child
of the preest cam, while the fleɪschis weren
in sething, and he hadde a fleɪschhook with
thre teeth in his hond; and he sente[c] it 14
in to the 'grete vessel of stoon[d], ethir in to
the candrun, etbɪr in to the pot, ethir[e] in
to the[f] 'panne, and what euer thing[g] the
fleɪschhook[h] reiside[i], the preest took[k] to

[l] siencis A.   [m] feble men E pr m   [n] he EC   [o] the erthe BDFH

[h] glorie theryn I   [i] feble I   [k] fulfillid I   [l] til BCDFGLMNOPQRSUWXb vnto I to EL   [m] childe GQN
[n] maad sijk I   [o] and A   [oo] hillis A. [p]and he I   [q] reisith up I   [r] upreisith I   [s] upreisith I   [t] the erthe I
[u] upon I   [v] hise seyntis feet I   [w] fro I   [x] upon I   [y] Om x pr m   [z] and I   [a] the sones I   [b] theɪ
knewen I   [c] putte c sec m N   putide I   [d] stonen vessel I   [e] or I   [f] Om cNo a K   [g] flesh I
[h] hook I   [i] cauȝte I   [k] took that I

took to hym self; so thei diden to al
15 Irael of men comynge in Silo Also or
that thei brenten the fat, the child of the
preest cam, and seide to the offreie, Ʒif
to me flesh, that I seethe to the pieest;
I shal not take forsothe sothen flesh, but
16 rawe And the offreie seide to hym, Be
brent first after the maner to day the
talwʒ, and tak to thee as mych as thi
soule desireth The which answerynge
seide to hym, Nay, forsothe nowe thow
shalt ʒyue; ellis I shal tak bi forse
17 Therfor the synne of the children was
gieet wel mych before the Loid; for thei
drowen awey men fro the sacrifice of
18 the Lord Forsothe Samuel sei uede be-
toie the face of the Loid, a child gud
19 with a surplesse And a litil coote his
modei made to hym, the which she
brouʒt the oideyned days, stiynge vp
with hir man for to offre a solempne
20 oost, and hii vowe And Hely blesside
to Elchana and to his wijf, and he seide
to hym, The Loid ʒeelde to thee seed of
this womnnan, for the enciees that thou
hast lent to the Lord And thei wenten
21 into her place Thanne the Loid visitide
Anne, and she conseyuede, and bare thre
sones and two douʒtren And the child
Samuel is magnyfied anentis the Lord
22 Forsothe Hely was wel oold, and he
heide alle thingis that his sones diden
in al Yrael, and what maner wise thei
slepten with wymmen, the whiche weyt-
23 eden at the dore of the tabernacle And
he seide to hem, Whi doon ʒe siche maner
thingis, the which I here werst thingis of
24 al the puple? Wole ʒe not, my sones, it is
not good loos that Y here, that ʒe maken
25 to trespas the puple of the Lord If a
man synneth in a man, God may be plesid
to him, forsothe if in to the Loid a man

hym silf[1]; so them diden to al Israel of
men comynge in to Silo Ʒhe bifor that 15
'the sones of Hely' brenten the ynnere
fatnesse, the 'child of the preest' cam, and
seyde to the offerere, Ʒyue 'thou fleisch to
me', that Y sethe to the preest; for Y
schal not take of thee sodun fleisch, but
raw And 'the offrerei seide to hym, The 16
ynnere fatnesse be' brent first' to day bi'
the custom, and take thou to' thee hou
myche euer thi soule desirith Whiche
answeride, and seide to hym, Nay, for
thou schalt ʒyue' now; ellis' Y schal take
bi violence Therfoi the synne of the chil- 17
dren' was ful gieuouse bifoi the Lord, for
thei withdrowen men fio the 'sacrifice of
the Lord' 'Foisothe Samuel, a child' 18
gird with a lynnun clooth, mynystride'
bifor the face of the Loid And his moder 19
made to hym a litil coote, whichg scheb
brouʒte in' daies ordeyned', and stiede'
with hir hosebonde, that he schulde' offre
a solempue offiyng, and his auow And 20
Heh blesside Helcana and his wijf; and
Heh' seide 'to hym', The Lord ʒelde to
thee seed of this woinman, tor the ʒifte
which' thou hast ʒoue to the Lord And
thei ʒeden in to her place' Therfor the 21
Loid visitide Anna, and sche conseyuede,
and childide thie sones and twei douʒtiis
And the child Samuel was 'magnyfied at'
the Lord. Forsothe' Hely was ful eld, 22
and he herde alle 'thingis whiche' hise
sones diden in al Israel, and hou thei
slepten with wymmen, that awaitiden' at
the dore of the tabernacle And he' seide 23
to hem', Whi doen ʒe siche thingis, the
worste thingis whiche' Y here ot al the
puple? Nyle ʒe, my sones', it is not good' 24
fame, which' Y here, that ʒe make the
'puple of the Loid' to do tiespas If a 25
man synneth aʒeus a man, God may be

P er BCEFH   q doʒtris CE

1 Om 1   m the prestis 1   n thei 1   o prestis child 1   P to me the fleisch 1   q seke it 1   r he that
offnde 1   s He first the 1.   t Om. 1   u Om 1   v aftir 1   w thanne to 1   x the whiche 1   y but 1
z ʒyue it 1   a for ellis 1   b take it 1   c sones of Hely prestis 1   d Lordis sacrifice 1   e Certis the
child Samuel 1   f seruyde 1   g the which 1   h he 1   i to him in the 1   k ordeyned to offre 1   l sche
stiede up 1   m wolde 1   n Om 1   o that 1.   P place oʒen 1   q maad wondurful gret anentis 1   r And 1
s the thingis that 1   t waitiden 1   u Hely 1   v his sones 1   w that 1   x puple of Israel 1   y sones,
do so 1   z a good 1   a that 1   b Lordis puple 1

synneth, who shal preye for hym? And
thei herden not the voyce of her fader,
26 for God wold sleen hem Forsothe Samuel the child profitide, and wexe; and
27 he pleside both to God and to men. Forsothe there cam a man of God to Heli,
and seith to hym, Thes thingis seith the
Lord, Whether not apertly Y am shewid
to the hows of thi fader, whanne thei
weren in Egipt, in the hows of Pharao?
28 And I cheese him of alle the lynagis of
Yrael to me in to preest, that he shulde
stie vp to myn auter, and brenne to me
encense, and beer befoie me ephot, and
I haue 3ouen to the hows of thi fadei
alle thingis of the sacrifices of the sones
29 of Yrael. Whi with the heele 3e han
throwen awey my slayn sacrifice, and
my 3iftis, that I haue comaundid to be
offred in the temple; and more thou
hast honourede thi sones than meq, that
3e my3ten eete the cheefe thingis of al
30 the sacrifice of Yrael, my puple? Therfoi seith the Lord God of Yrael, Spekynge
I haue spoken, that thin hows and the
hows of thi fader serue in my si3t intor
with out ende; forsothe nowe seith the
Lord, Awey be that fro me, but who so
euere honourith me, Y shal glorifie hym,
forsothe who dispisen me, shulen be vn-
31 noble Loo! the dais comen, and I shal
kut of thin arme, and the aime of the
hows of thi fadre, that there be not an
32 oold man in thin hows And thou shalt
see thin enemye in the temple, in alle the
welsum thingis of Yrael, and there shal
not be an oold man in thin hous alle dais
33 Neuerthelater I shal not doo awey fulli
fro thee a man fro myn auter, but that
thin eyen faylen, and thi lyf fayle; and a
greet parti of thin hows shal die, whanne
34 to mannus age it shal come Forsothe
this shal be the tokne, that is to come to

plesid to himt, forsothec if a man synneth a3ens the Lord, who schal preye for
hymt? And theid herden not the vois of
her fadir, for God wolde sle hem For-26
sothe the child Samuel profitide, and en-
creessyde, and pleside bothe God and men
Sotheli e a man of God cam to Hely, and 27
seide to hym, The Lord seith these thingis,
Whether Y was not schewid apertli to the
hows of thi fadir, whanne he was in E-
gipt, in the hows of Farao? And Y chees 28
hym of alle lynagisf of Israel 'in tog preest
to me, that he schulde stieh to myn auter,
and schulde brenne encense to me, and
that he schulde beie bifor me preestis'
cloth, and Y 3af to 'the hows of thi fadirk
alle thingis|| of thel sacrifices of the sones
of Israel Whi hast thou cast awey with 29
them heele my sacrificen, and my 3iftis,
whicheo Y comaundide to be offrid in the
temple; and thou onouridstp more thi
sones than me, that 3e eeten the principal
partis of ech sacrifice of 'Israel, my pupleq?
Therfor the Loid God of Israel seith these 30
thingis, Y spekynge spak, that thin hows
and 'the hows of thi fadirr schulde my-
nystres in my si3t til in to with outen
ende, 'now forsothet the Lord seith, Fei
be this fro me; but who euere onourith
me, Y schal glorifie hym; forsotheu thei
that dispisen me, schulen be vnnoble Lo!31
daies comen, and Y schal kitte awei thin
armv, and the arm of the hows of thi
fadir, that an eld mann be not in thin
hows And thou schalt se thin enemyx in 32
the temple, in alle prosperiteesy of Israel;
and an eld man schal not be in thin hows
in alle daies Netheles Y schal not outerli 33
take awei of thee a man fro myn auter,
but that thin i3en faile, and thi soulez
failea; and greetb pait of thin hows schal
die, whanne it schal come to mannus nge
Forsothec this schal be signed, that schal 34

t *be plesid to him*, bi prayeris and sacrifices c.

‡ *who schal preie for him*, that is, it schal not be for3ouun to him bi suche thingis, nethe-les it may be for3ouun *Lire here* c

|| *alle thingis pertevininge to hem*, for sum part was breut to God, and sum part perteynede to the offereris *Lire here* c,

q men ꞇ   r vnto BCEFH

c but ꞇ   d his sones ꞇ   e Certis ꞇ   f the lynagis ꞇ   g to be a ꞇ   h stie up ꞇ   i a preestis ꞇ   k thi fadris hous ꞇ   l Om ꞇ   m thin ꞇ   n sacrifices ꞇ   o the whiche ꞇ   p hast honourid ꞇ   q my puple of Israel ꞇ   r thi fadris hous ꞇ   s haue myny3trid ꞇ   t certis now ꞇ   u certis ꞇ   v arm or thi power ꞇ
w prest or ny3se   x enemyes ꝃ   y the prosperitees ꞇ   z lyf ꞇ text or soule marg   a langwishe ꞇ
b greet ꞇ   c Certis ꞇ   d the tokene ꞇ

thi two sonys, Ophny and Phynees, in
35 o day thei shulen die bothe. And I shal
rere to me a trewe preest, that after myn
herte and soule shal doo; and I shal bilde
to hym a trewe hows, and he shal goo
36 before my Crist alle days. Forsothe it
is to come, that who so euere abidith^s stil
in thin hows, he come that it be preyed
for hym, and he offre a silueren peny,
and a round kaak of breed, and seye,
Lete me, Y biseche, to o preeste^t paarte,
that I eete a morsel^u of breed.

CAP. III.

1   Child forsothe Samuel mynystrede to
the Lord before Hely, and the sermoun
of the Lord was precious; in tho dais
2 was noon opyn visioun. It was maad
thanne on a day, Heli leye in his place,
and his eyen daswiden, and he my3te not
see the lanterne of God, before it were
3 quenchid. Forsoth Samuel slepte in the
temple of the Lord, where was the arke
4 of God. And the Lord clepide Samuel;
the which answerynge seith, Loo! I.
5 And he ranne to Hely, and seide to hym,
Loo! Y; thou hast clepid forsothe me.
The which seide, I haue not clepid thee;
turn a3en and sleep. And he 3ede and
6 slept. And the Lord eft leyde to to^v clepe
Samuel; and Samuel rysynge 3ede to
Heli, and seide, Loo! Y; for thou hast
clepid me. The which answeryde, Y
haue not clepid thee, sone myn; turn
7 a3en and sleep. Forsothe Samuel 3it not
knewe the Lord, ne the sermoun of the
8 Lord was openyd to hym. And the
Lord leide to, and 3it clepide Samuel the
thridde tyme; the which rysynge 3ede
9 to Hely, and seith, Loo! Y; for thou
hast clepid me. Thanne Hely vndurstood, that the Lord clepide the child;
and he seith to Samuel, Go and sleep;

come to thi twei sones Ophym^e and Fynees, bothe^f schulen die in o dai. And 35
Y schal reise to me a feithful preest, that
schal do bi^g myn herte and my soule; and^h
Y schal bilde to hym a feithful hows, and
he schal go bifore my Crist in alle daies.
Forsotheⁱ it schal come, that who euer 36
dwellith^k in thin hows, he come† that 'me
preie^l for him, and that he offre a peny of
siluer, and a cake of breed, and seie, Y
biseche, suffre thou me to o 'part of the
preest^m, that Y ete a musselⁿ of breed.

CAP. III.

Forsothe the child Samuel 'mynystride 1
to^o the Lord bifor Heli, and the word of
the Lord was precious‡; in tho daies was
noon opyn reuelacioun. Therfor^p it was 2
doon in a dai, Heli lay in his bed, and
hise i3en dasewiden, and he my3te not se
the lanterne of God‖, bifor that it was
quenchid. Forsothe Samuel slepte in the 3
temple§ of the Lord, where the ark of
God was. And the Lord clepide Samuel; 4
and he answeride and seide, Lo! Y^r. And 5
he ran to Heli, and seide to hym, Lo! Y;
for thou clepidist me. Which^s Hely seide,
Y clepide not thee; turne thou^t a3en and
slepe. And he^u 3ede and slepte. And the 6
Lord addide eft to clepe Samuel; and Samuel roos, and 3ede to Hely, and seide,
Lo! Y^v; for thou clepidist me. And Heli
answeride, Y clepide not thee, my sone;
turne thou a3en and slepe. Forsothe^w 7
Samuel knew not 3it the Lord††, nether
the 'word of the Lord^x was shewid to
hym. And the Lord addide, and clepide^y 8
3it Samuel the thridde tyme; 'which Sa-
muel^z roos^a and 3ede^b to Heli, and seide, 9
Lo! Y; for thou clepidist me. Therfor^c
Heli vndirstood, that the Lord clepide^d
the child; and Heli^e seide to Samuel, Go^f
and slepe; and if he clepith thee aftir-

† he come. In Ebreu it is, the he come to bow for hir silf, in an halpeny of siluer; Ebrewis expownen tho, that preestis dwellinge of the generacioun of Hely, ou3ten to make hem silf bifor the hi3este preest, and to praye, that they my3ten serue in the temple for the priys of an halpeny of siluer, and of a cake of breed in the day, and the lettre that meeth, semeth acorde, whanne it seeth, and he seye, and so forth. Lire here. c.

‡ was precious. In Ebreu it is, was forbedun ethir maad derk. c.

‖ the lanterne of God. Comyn Latyn biblis han thus, and hise i3en dasewiden, and he my3te not se the lanterne of God, bifor that it was quenchid, but certis this lettre is corrupt, as the Maistre of Stories and Lire here witnessen, and the book of Ebreu questiouns; therfor in Ebreu it is had thus, and hise i3en dasewiden, and he my3te not se; the lanterne of God was not 3it quenchid. He my3te not se the lanterne of God, bifor that it was quenchid. c.

§ slepte in the temple; that is, in a chaumbir bisidis the temple, where dekenes weren that kepten the temple. Lire here. c.

†† knewe not 3it the Lord; that is, the maner of speking of the Lord with profecis. Lire here. c.

^s abytt DFH. abit EC.   ^t prestis EC.   ^u mussel CE.   ^v Om. DE.

^e Ofni EIP.   ^f bothe thei I.   ^g aftir I.   ^h Om. K.   ⁱ Sothly I.   ^k schal dwelle I.   ^l men
preie DGMNOPQRSUX. it be preied I.   ^m prestis part I.   ⁿ morsel I.   ^o seruyde I.   ^p Thanne I.   ^q And I.
^r Y am redi I.   ^s And I.   ^t Om. DGIKMNOW sec. m.   ^u Samuel I.   ^v Y here I.   ^w Sothly I.   ^x Lordis
word I.   ^y he clepide I.   ^z the which I.   ^a roos up I.   ^b wente I.   ^c Thanne I.   ^d had clepid I.   ^e he I.
^f Go thou I.

and if heiafter he clepe^w thee, thou shalt
seye, Spek, Loid, for thi seruaunt herith
Thanne Samuel wente and slept in his
10 place And the Lord cam, and stood,
and clepide as he clepide the secounde
tyme, Samuel, Samuel And Samuel
seith, Spek, Lord, foi thi seruaunt herith
11 And the Lord seide to Samuel, Loo ' Y
doo a word in Yiael, the which who so
euere herith, bothe his eeris shulen tyn-
12 clen In that day I shal arere⸍ aȝens
Hely alle thingis, the whiche I haue
spokun vpon the hows of hym ; Y shal
13 bigynne, and fulfille Forsothe I seide
before to hym, that I was to deme his
hows withont ende for wickidnes , for thi
that he knewe his sonys vnworthili to
14 doon, and vndurnam hem not Therfore
Y swore to the hows of Hely, that the
wickidnes of hys hows shal not be doon
a seeth before^y with slayn sacrifices and
15 ȝiftis vnto with out· ende Forsothe
Samuel slept vnto the morwe, and he
openyde the dorys of the hows of the
Lord , and Samuel dredde to shewe the
16 visyoun to Hely Thanne Hely clepide
Samuel, and seide, Samuel, my sone The
17 which answerynge seith, Y am redy And
he askide hym, What is the woid that
the Lord hath spoken to thee ? Y preye
thee, ne hele thou fro me ; thes thingis
do to thee God, and thes thingis adde, if
thou hidist fro me a word of alle the
18 wordis that ben seyd to thee And Samuel shewide to hym alle the wordis,
and hidde not fro hym And he an-
sweide, A Lord he is , that good is in his
19 eyen, do he Forsothe Samuel wexe, and
the Lord was with hym, and there felle
not into the erthe of alle the wordis of
20 hym And alle Yiael knewȝ fro Dan
vnto Bersabee, that Samuel was the feith-

ward, thou schalt seie, Speke thou, Lord,
for thi seruaunt herith Therfor^g Samuel
ȝede and slepte in his place. And the 10
Lord cam, and stood, and clepide as he
hadde clepid the secunde tyme, Samuel,
Samuel And Samuel seide, Speke thou,
Lord, for thi seruaunt heiith And the 11
Lord seide to Samuel, Lo ' Y make a
word† in^h Israel, whichⁱ woid who euei
schal here, bothe hise eeris schulen iyngek†
In that dai Y schal ieise^l aȝens Heli alle 12
thingis, whiche^m Y spakⁿ on his hows ,
Y schal bigynne, and Y schal ende Foi 13
Y biforseide to hym, that Y schulde deme
his hows with outen ende for wickid-
nesse^o, for he^p knew, that hise sones diden
vnworthili, and he chastiside not hem
Therfor Y swoor^q to the hows of Heli, 14
that the wickidnesse of his hows^r schal
not be clensid‖ bi^s sacrifices and ȝiftis til
in to with outen ende Forsothe^t Samuel 15
slepte til the morewtid, and he openyde
the doris of the hows of the Lord ; and
Samuel dredde to schewe the reuelacioun
to Heli Theifoi Heli clepide Samuel, 16
and seide, Samuel, my sone And he answeride and seide, Y am redi And Heli 17
axide hym, What is the word which^u the
Lord spak^v to thee ? Y preye thee, hide
thou^w not fro me ; God do to thee 'these
thingis^x, and encreesse^y these thingis, if
thou hidist fro me a woid of alle wordis^z
that ben seid to thee And Samuel schew- 18
ide to hym^a alle the wordis, and 'hidde
not^b fio hym And Heli answeride, He is
the^c Lord , do he that^d, that is good in hise
iȝen. Forsothe^e Samuel encreeside, and the 19
Lord was with hym, and noon of alle hise^f
wordis felde^g in to erthe§ And al Israel 20
fro Dan to Bersabee knew, that feithful
Samuel was a profete of the Lord And 21
the Loid addide 'that he schulde^h appeie

*† a word , that
is, a thing sig-
nched in a
word c*

*† rynge that
is, he schal be
astonved for
wundur and
dredi Lire
here c*

*‖ schal not be
clensid, as to
peyne ordeyn-
ed, thouȝ it
were clensid as
to synne and
euerlastinge
peyne, in hem
that repent
iden verily
Lire here c*

*§ in to erthe,
that is, in veyn,
for al was
fillid Lire
here c*

^w clepeth ce   ^x reren c   ^y fore bcefh   ^z knee ᴀ   kne c *pr m* f

^g Thanne 1. ^h to be *knowen* in 1 ⁱ the which 1 ^k tyncle 1 ^l reise up 1 ^m that 1 ⁿ haue spoken
up 1 ^o the wickidnesse theroff 1 ^p Hely 1 ^q haue swore 1 ^r meyree *or hows* 1 ^s with 1 ^t And
thanne 1 ^u that 1 ^v hath spoke 1 ^w it 1 ^x alle these *yuelis* 1 ^y encresse he 1 ^z the
wordis 1 ^a Hely 1 ^b he hidde noon 1 ^c Om 1 ^d Om c ^e Certis 1 ^f the 1 ^g felle *voide* 1
^h to 1.

21 ful^a prophet of the Lord And the Lord addide that he shulde apeie in Sylo, for the Loid was shewid to Samuel in Sylo after the woid of the Lord; and the woid of Samuel felle 'into^b al Yiael

in^l Silo, for the Lord was schewid to Samuel in Silo bi the 'word of the Lord^k, and the word of Samuel cam to al Israel

CAP IV

1 And it is doon in tho days Philistien camen togidre into fi3t, forsothe and Yrael wente out into batayl to meet Phylistien, and he sette tentis bisyde the stoon of help Forsothe Philistien 2 camen into Aphet, and maden shilti oun^c a3ens Yrael Foisothe, the striif bigun^d, Yiael turnede backis to the^e Philistiens^f; and there ben slayn in that striif pasmele bi feeldis as fome thowsandys of 3 men; and the puple is turnede a3en to the tentis And the moie thur3 biith of Yrael seyden, Whi hath the Lord smyten vs to day before Philistien ? Biynge we forth to vs fro Sylo the aike of the boond of pees of the Lord, and come it in the myddil of vs, that it saue vs fro the 4 hoond of oure enemyes Thanne the puple senten into Sylo, and token thens the arke of the boond of pees of the Lord of oostis, sittynge vpon cherubym. And the two sones of Hely, Ophny and Phynees, weren with the arke of the 5 boond of pees of the Lord And whanne the arke of the boond of pees of the Lord was comen into the tentis, al Yrael cryede out with a greet ciye, and the 6 erth thur3 sownede And Philistien herden the voys of the ciye, and seiden, Forsothe what is this vois of greet crye in the tentis of Ebrewis ? And thei knewen, that the aike of the boond of pees of the Lord was comen into the 7 tentis And Philistien dredden, seiynge,

CAP IV

And it was doon in tho daies Filisteis 1 camen to gideie in to batel; for^l Israel 3ede out a3ens Filisteis^m in to batel, and settiden^n tentis bisidis the stoon of help Forsothe^o Filisteis camen in to Aphet, and maden redi scheltrun a3ens Israel 2 Sotheli^p whanne the batel was bigunnun, Israel turned backis^q to Filisteis, and as^r foure thousynde of^s men^t weren slayn in that batel 'euery where^u bi feeldis^v, and the puple of Israel turnede a3en to tentis^w. And the grettere men in birthe of Israel seiden, Whi hath the Lord smyte vs to dai bifore Filisteis^x ? Biynge we to vs fro Silo the aike of boond^y of pees of the Loid, and come it in to the myddis of vs, that it saue vs fro the hond of oure enemyes. Therfor the puple sente in to 4 Silo, and thei token fro thennus the arke of boond^z of pees of the Lord of oostis, 'that sat on^a cherubyn And Ophym^b and Fynees, twei^c sones of Heli, weren with the arke of boond^d of pees of the Lord And whanne the arke of boond of pees of 5 the Lord hadde come in to the castels^e, al Israel criede^f with grete cry, and the erthe sownede. And Filisteis^g herden the vois of 6 cry^h, and seiden, What^k is this vois of greet cry in the castels^l of Ebrews ? And thei knewen, that the arke of boond of pees of the Lord hadde come in to castels^m And Filisteis^n dredden, and seiden, 7 God is come in to 'the castels^o; and thei^p weihden, and seiden, Wo to vs^! for so s

---

^a trewe c pr m   ^b to ncEH   ^c schetrome E passim   ^d gon in E pr m begunnen sec m   ^e Om cE
^f Filisteis c passim

^i eft in i   ^k Lordis word i   ^l forsothe i.   ^m the Filisteis i   ^n Israel sette i   ^o And the i   ^p And i
^q the backis i   ^r as a i   ^s Om i   ^t men of Israel i   ^u oner al i   ^v the feeldis i   ^w her tentis i
^x the Filisteis i   ^y the boond i   ^z the boond i   ^a sittinge upon i   ^b Ophny DIX sec m PE   ^c the
two i   ^d the boond i   ^e tentis i   ^f for joie criede i   ^g the Filisteis i   ^h her cry i   ^i thei seiden i
^k And what i   ^l tentis i   ^m the castels CDEI PQSUWX the tentis of Israel i   ^n the Filisteis i   ^o her
tentis i   ^p the Philistees i

God is comen into the tentis, and in-
8 wardly thei weiliden, seiynge, Woo to
vs! forsothe there was not so mych
gladynge ȝisterday[g], ne before ȝisturday[g],
woo to vs! who shal kepe vs fro the
hoondis[h] of thes heiȝe goddis? thes ben
the goddis that smyten Egipt bi al ven-
9 iaunce in deseert Takith coumfort, and
'be ȝe[i] men of Philistien, ne serue ȝe to
Ebrewis, as thei serueden to vs, takith
10 coumfort, and fiȝtith Thanne Philystien
fouȝten, and Yrael is hewen down, and
echon fleeȝ[k] into his tabernacle, and there
is doon a wel greet veniaunce, and there
fellen of Yrael thretti thowsandis of foot
11 men And the arke of God is taken, and
the two sones of Hely ben deed, Ophny
12 and Phynees. Forsothe rennynge a man
of Beniamyn fro the sheltroun cam into
Sylo in that day, rent the clooth, and
13 spreynt[l] with powdre the heed, and
whan he was comen, Hely sat vpon
the litil seet aȝens the weye abidynge;
forsothe his herte was dredynge for the
arke of the Lord Forsothe that man
after that he is goon yn, toolde to the
14 cytee, and al the cytee ȝellide And
Hely herde the sown of the crye, and
seide, What is this sown of this noyse?
And he hiede, and cam, and toold to
15 Hely Forsothe Hely was of nynty and
eiȝt ȝeer, and his eyen dasweden, and he
16 myȝt not se And he seyde to Hely, Y
am that am comen fro the batayl, and
Y that haue flowen fro the shiltroun to
day To whom he seith, What is doon,
17 sone myn? Answerynge forsothe he that
toold, seith, Yrael hath flowen before the
Philistiens, and a greet fallynge is doo
in the puple, also and thi two sones been
deed, Ophny and Phynees, and the arke
18 of God is takun And whanne he hadde

greet ful[q] ioiyng was not[r] ȝistirdai, and
the thridde day passid; wo to vs! who
schal kepe vs fro the hond[s] of 'these hiȝe[t]
goddis? these ben the goddis, that smytiden[u] Egipt with al veniaunce† in deseert
Filisteis[v], be ȝe coumfortid, and be ȝe men, 9
serue ȝe not[w] Ebrews, as thei serueden[x]
vs[y]; be ȝe coumfortid, and fiȝte ȝe[z] Ther- 10
for[a] Filisteis[b] fouȝten, and Israel was
slayn[c], and ech man fled[d] in to his tabernacle, and a ful greet veniaunce was maad,
and thretti thousynde of foot men of Israel
felden doun. And the arke of God was 11
takun; and, twei[e] sones of Heli, Ophym[f]
and Fynees, weren deed. Sotheli[g] a man 12
of Beniamyn ran fro the scheltrun, and
cam in to Silo in that dai, with his cloth
torent and his[h] heed bispreynt with dust;
and whanne he was comen, Heli sat 'on an[i] 13
hiȝe[k] seete, 'and bihelde[l] aȝens the[m] weie,
for his herte was dredyng for the arke of
the Lord Sotheli[n] aftir that thilke man
entride[o], he telde to the[p] citee, and al the
citee ȝellide. And Heli herde the soun of 14
cry[q], and seide[r], What is this[s] sown of
this noise? And he[t] hastide, and cam, and
telde to Heli Forsothe[u] Heli was of foure 15
score ȝeer and eiȝtene, and hise iȝen dasi-
widen[v], and he myȝte not se And he[w] 16
seide to Heli, Y am[x] that cam fro batel[y],
and Y am[z] that fled[a] to dai fro the scheltrun To whom Ely seide, My sone, what
is doon[b]? Forsothe[c] he that telde an- 17
sweride, and seide, Israel fled[d] bifor Filisteis[e], and a greet fal[f] is maad in the
puple[g], ferthermore and thi twey sones,
Ophym[h] and Fynees, ben deed, and the
arke of God is takun And whanne he 18
hadde[i] nemyd[k] the arke of God, Hely felde
fro 'the hiȝe[l] seete bacward bisidis the
dore, and 'was deed; for the nollis‡[m]
weren brokun[n] For he was an eld man,

† *with al ven-iaunce*, as if they seyde, these goddis dide thenne al her myȝt, and therfor they moun not now anoye vs *Lire here* c

‡ *for the nollis* In Ebreu it is, for his necke was brokun. c.

[g] ȝistai c ȝistay E [h] hondo BCEFH [i] beth CE [k] fleth E [l] sprengd CE

[q] out I. [r] not there I [s] hondis K [t] the L [u] smyten I [v] *and it was seid,* Filisteis I [w] not to the I [x] han serued I [y] to ȝou I [z] ȝe *aȝens Israel* I [a] Thanne I [b] the Filisteis I. [c] ouercomen I [d] fledde I [e] the two I [f] Ophny EIPX *sec m* [g] And I [h] with his I [i] on his c upon a I [k] Om I [l] abidynge I [m] Om QR *sec m* [n] And I [o] hadde entrid I [p] men of the I [q] the cry I [r] he seide I [s] the I [t] the man I [u] And I [v] derkeden I [w] the man I [x] am *he* I [y] the batel I [z] am *he* I [a] fledde I [b] ther don I [c] And I [d] hath fled I [e] the Filisteis I [f] fallyng I [g] puple *of Israel* I [h] Ophny PIPX *sec. m* [i] Om I [k] nempned CEILMPUW namid R [l] his I [m] *his* skulles I [n] broke and he was deed I

nemnyd the arke, he felle fro the litil
seet backward biside the dore, and the
scullis brokun, he is deed Forsothe an
oold man he was, and of greet age, and
19 he demyde Yrael fourti¹ 3eer His dou3-
tre in lawe torsothe, the wijf of Phynees,
was with child, and ny3 to the berynge;
and the messager heide that the arke
of God was takun, and hir fader in lawe
deed, and hir man, she bowide hii self,
and bare child torsothe there fellen in
20 hir sodeyn sorwis Forsothe in that moment of hei deeth seiden to hir, that
stoden about hii, Ne drede thow, for a
sone thow hast born The which answerde not to hem, forsothe ne took hede
21 And she clepide the child Hicaboth, seiynge, Translatid is the glorye of the Lord
fro Irael, for takun is the ark of God;
and for hii fader in lawe and for hir
22 man she seith, Translatid is the glorie
of God fro Yrael, forthi that the aike
of God was takun

and of greet age, and he demyde Israel
bi⁰ fourti 3eer. Forsothe^p his dou3ter in 19
lawe, 'the wijf of Finees^q, was with childe,
and ni3 the child bering, and whanne 'the
message was herd^r that the aike of God
was takun, and that hii fadir in lawe was
deed, and hir hosebonde, sche bowide hir
silf^s, and childide; for sodeyn sorewis
telden in to hir. Sotheli^t in that moment 20
of hir deeth, *wymmen*^{u} that stoden aboute
hir, seiden to hir, Drede thou not, for thou
hast childid a sone And sche answeride
not to hem, for^v nether 'sche perseyuede^w.
And sche clepide the child Ichaboth†, and 21
seide, The glorie of the Lord is translatid
fro Israel, for the arke of God is takun^x,
and for hii fadir in lawe and for hii hosebonde sche seide, The glorie of God is 22
translatid^y fro Israel, for the arke of God
is^z takun

† *Icaboth*, that
is, withoute
glorie *Lire*
here c

CAP. V

1 Philistien forsothe token the arke of
God, and beien it fro the stoon of help
2 into Azoth And Philistien token the
arke of God, and brou3ten it into the
temple of Dagon, and setten it beside
3 Dagon And whanne Azothis weren
rysen eeili the tother day, loo! Dagon
lay redi in the ceith before the ark of
the Lord And thei token Dagon, and
4 setten it a3en in his place And eft,
eeili the tother day 1ysynge, thei fonden
Dagon hynge vpon his face in the erthe
before the aike of the Lord Forsothe
the heed of Dagon, and the two palmys
of his hoondis weren knt awey vpon the
5 thresshwold, forsothe the stok of Dagon
aloone lafte in his place For this cause
the preestis of Dagon, and alle that goon
into his temple, treden not vpon the
thresshwold of Dagon in Azoth into the

CAP. V

Forsothe^a Filistes token the arke of 1
God, and baren^b awey it fro the stoon of
help in to Azotus And Filisteis^c tokun 2
the aike of God, and brou3ten it to^d the
temple of Dagon, and settiden it bisidis
Dagon And whanne men of Azotus had- 3
den rise eeili in^e the todir dai, lo! Dagon
lay low in the erthe bifor the aike of the
Lord And thei token Dagon, and re-
storiden hym in^f his place. And eft thei 4
risiden^g eeili in the tothir day, and found-
en^h Dagon liggynge on his face on^i the
erthe bifor the aike of the Lord For-
sothe^k the heed of Dagon, and twei^l
pawmes of his hondis weren knt^m of^n on^o
the threisfold, certis^p the stok aloone of 5
Dagon lefte in his place For this cause
the picestis of Dagon, and alle that entren
in to his temple, treden not on^q the threis-
fold^r of Dagon in Azotus til^s in to^t this

1 forurti A

° Om 1 P And 1 q Finees wijf 1 r sche herde bi the messangere 1 s silf doun 1 t And 1
u *thei* 1 v Om 1 w toki heede 1 x taken awei 1 y takun awei 1 z was *plures* a And the 1
b baren it 1 c the Filisteis 1 d into DEFGIKLMNOPX e into o f into 1 g risen 1 h thei founden 1
i upon 1 k And 1 l the two 1 m broken 1 kutte K. n off 1 o upon 1 p and 1 q upon 1
r threxhold L s Om 1 t into 1

ᵸday that is nowe Forsothe the hoond of the Lord is greggid vpon the Azothis, and he wastide hem, and he smoot A-zothe and his coostis in the more priue party of the arsis, and the towns and feeldis booyleden out in the mydil of thatᵐ regioun, and myis ben born; and there is doon a greet confusioun of deeth in the 7 cytee Men forsothe of Azoth seynge siche a manei veniaunce seiden, Dwel not the arke of God of Yrael anentis vs; for hard is his hoond vpon vs, and vpon 8 Dagon oure god. And seendynge thei gedreden to hem self alle the maystris of Philistiens, and seiden, What shulen we doo of the arke of God of Yrael? And Gethey answerden, The arke of God of Yrael be tuined about; and thei turn-eden about the arke of God of Yrael. 9 Forsothe hem turnynge it about, the hoond of the Lord of a greet slauȝter wel mych was doon vpon alle the cytees; and he smoot the men of ech cytee fro litil vnto more, and the arsroppis of hem goynge out stonken; and Gethey wenten into counseil, and maden to hem letheren 10 seetis Thanne thei senten the arke of the Lord into Acharon And whanne the arke of the Lord was comen into Acharon, Acharonytis cryeden out, sei-ynge, Thei han brouȝt to vs the arke of God of Yrael, that he sle vs and ouie 11 puple Thei senten thanne, and gedriden togidre alle the maystrys of Philistiens; the which seiden, Leeue ȝe the arke of God of Yrael, and be it turned aȝen into his place, and sle it not vs with oure 12 puple Forsothe dreed of deth was maad in alle the cytees, and moost greuous was greetli the hoond of the Lord Forsothe the men, that weren not deed, weren smyten in the priuyer party of the arsis, and the ȝellynge of ech cytee stiede ⱱp into heuene

dai Forsothe the hond of the Lord was 6 maad greuouse onⁿ men of Azotus, and heᵛ distriede hem, and he smoot Azotusᵗ† and the coostis therof in the priuyereʷ part of buttokisˣ; and townesʸ‡ and feeldis in theᶻ myddis of that cuntrey buyliden outᵃ, and myis camen foith; and greet confusioun of deth was maad in the citee Sotheliʰ men of Azotus sien siche a ven- 7 iaunce, and seidenᶜ, The arke of God of Israel dwelle not atᵈ vs: for hisᵉ hondᶠ is hard ouˢ vs, and on Dagon oure god And 8 thei senten, and gaderidenʰ alle the wise men, ῾ether princes῾, of Filisteis ῾to hemʰ, and seiden, What schulen we do of the arke of God of Israel? And menˡ of Geth answeriden, The arke of God of Israel be led aboute, and thei ledden aboute the arke of God of Israel Forsotheᵐ while 9 thei ledden it aboute, the hond of the Lord ῾of ful greet sleyngⁿ was maad onᵒ alle citeesᵖ, and he smoot men of ech citee fro a litil manᑫ tilʳ to ῾the moreˢ, and the lowereᵗ entraylis ῾of hemᵘ wexiden rotun, and camen forth · and men of Geth token counsel, and madenᵛ to hemʷ seetis of skynnes, ethir cuyschuns Therfor thei 10 senten the arke of the Lord in to Acco-ron And whanne the arke of the Lord hadde come in to Accoron, men of Acco-ron crieden, and seiden, Thei han brought to ⱱs the arke of God of Israel, that he sle ⱱs and ouie puple Therforˣ thei senten, 11 and gaderidenʸ alle the wise men, ῾ethir princesᶻ, of Filisteis; whicheᵃ seiden, De-lyuere ȝe the arke of God of Israel, and turne it aȝen in to his place, and sle notʰ ⱱs with oure puple For dreed of deeth 12 was maad in alle citees, and the hond of the Lord was ῾greuouse greetliᶜ Alsoᵈ the men, that weren not deed, weren smytun in the priuyᵉ partᶠ of buttokisᵍ, and the ȝelling of ech citee stiedeʰ in to heuene

† he smoot Azotus, that is, men dwelling there ᴄ ‡ and tounes, al this vers is not in Ebrew, til thᶦdur, Sothely men of Azotus Lire here ᴄ

ᵐ the ₐ

ᵘ upon ı   ᵛ the Lord ı   ʷ more priuee ı   ˣ her tail eandis ı   ʸ the townes ı   ᶻ Om. ı   ᵃ out myis ı   ᵇ And ı   ᶜ thei seiden ı   ᵈ anentis ı   ᵉ the ı   ᶠ hond of God ı   ᵍ upon ı   ʰ gaderiden to hem ı   ˡ Om ᴄᴅɢɪᴍɴᴏsx pr m   ᵏ Om ı   ˡ the men ı   ᵐ And ı   ⁿ Om ı   ᵒ upon ı   ᵖ the citees aboute of ful gret slauȝtere ı   ᑫ child ı   ʳ Om ı   ˢ a more man ı   ᵗ her priuey nether ı   ᵘ Om ı   ᵛ thei maden ı   ʷ hem self ı   ˣ Thanne ı   ʸ gaderiden togidere ı   ᶻ Om ɴᴅɪᴍɴᴏqsx pr m   ᵃ the whiche ı   ᵇ not the Lord ı   ᶜ ful greuouse ı   ᵈ And ı   ᶜ priuuer ɴᴄw   ᶠ parties ı   ᵍ her but-tokis ı.   ʰ stiede up ı

CAP. VI.

1 Was thanne the arke of the Lord in the regioun of the Philistiens seuen 2 monethes; and after thes thingis Philistiens clepiden the preestis and dyuynours, seiynge, What shal we doon with the arke of God? Shewe ȝe vs, what maner wyse we shulen sende it aȝen 'in 3 to[u] his place. The whiche seiden, If ȝe senden aȝen the arke of God of Yrael, wole ȝe not leeue it voyde, but that ȝe owen, ȝeldeth to hym for the synne; and thanne ȝe shulen be heelid, and ȝe shulen knowe, whi that his hoond goth not a wey 4 fro ȝow. The whiche seiden, What is that for the trespasse we owen to ȝeeld to 5 it? And thei answerden[o], After noumbre of prouyncis of Philistiens fyue golden arsis ȝe shulen make, and fyue golden myis; for o plage was to ȝow alle and to ȝoure maistris. And ȝe shulen make a licnesse of ȝoure arsis, and a licnesse of the myis that han wastid the loond; and ȝe shulen ȝyue to the God of Yrael glorye, if[p] perauenture he releue his hoond fro ȝou, and fro ȝoure goddis, and 6 fro ȝoure loond. Whi agreggen ȝe ȝoure hertis, as Egipt agreggide, and Pharao his hert? Whether not after he is smyten, thanne he lafte hem, and thei 7 ȝeden a wey? Nowe thanne takith, and makith a newe weyn, and ioyneth two kyen that han calued late, in the weyn, to whom is not put on ȝok; and reclosith 8 her calues at home. And ȝe shulen take the arke of the Lord, and putte in the weyn; and the goldun vessels that ȝe han payed out to it for the trespas, ȝe shulen put in a litle cofre at the side of it; and 9 leeue ȝe it, that it goo. And ȝe shulen biholden, forsothe and if bi the weye of her coostis it stie vp aȝen Bethsames, it

CAP. VI.

Therfor the arke of the Lord was in[i] 1 the cuntrei of Filisteis bi[i] seuene monethis; and aftir these thingis Filisteis[k] clepiden[l] 2 preestis and false dyuynours, and seiden, What schulen we do of the arke of God? Shewe ȝe to vs, hou we schulen sende it[m] in to his place[n]. Whiche[o] seiden, If ȝe 3 senden aȝen the arke of God of Israel, nyle ȝe delyuere it voide, but ȝelde ȝe to hym that[p], that ȝe owen for synne; and thanne ȝe schulen be heelid, and[q] ȝe schulen wite, whi 'his hond[r] goith not awei fro ȝou. And thei seiden, What[s] is it, that 4 we owen to ȝelde to hym[t] for trespas[n]? And thei answeriden to hem, Bi the[s] noumbre of prouynees[v] of Filisteis ȝe schulen make fyue goldun ersis, and fyue goldun myis; for o veniaunce was to alle ȝou and to ȝoure 'wise men, ether princes[w]. And ȝe schulen make the licnesse of ȝoure ersis, and the licnesse of myis that distriede ȝoure lond; and ȝe schulen ȝyue glorie to God of Israel, if in hap he withdrawe his hond[x] fro ȝou, and fro ȝoure goddis, and fro youre lond. Whi maken[6] ȝe heuy ȝoure hertis, as Egipt, and Farao 'made heuy[y] his[z] herte? Whether not after that he was smytun, thanne he delyuerede hem[a], and thei ȝeden forth? Now ther- 7 for take ȝe, and make[b] o[c] newe wayn, and ioyne ȝe[d] twei kien hauynge caluys, on[e] whiche kyen no ȝok was put; and close ȝe her calues at hoome. And ȝe schulen 8 take the arke of the Lord, and ȝe schulen sette in the wayn; and ȝe schulen put in a panyere[f] at the side therof[g] the goldun vessels, whiche ȝe[h] payeden[i] to hym[k] for trespas[l]; and delyuere ȝe the arke, that it go[m]. And ȝe schulen biholden[n], and so- 9 theli if it stieth[o] aȝens Bethsames[p] bi the weie of 'hise coostis[q], 'he dide[r] to ȝou this

---

n to E.   o answerden to them E pr. v.   p lest E pr. m.

i Om. 1.   k the Filisteis 1.   l clepiden *togidere* 1.   m it aȝen 1.   n place of it 1.   o The whiche 1. p that thing 1.   q and so 1.   r the hond of God 1.   s What thing 1.   t God 1.   u oure trespas 1.   v the prouynces 1.   w princes c. wise men DGMNOQX.   x wrath 1.   y grenyde 1.   z her 1.   a Goddis peple 1. b make ȝe A. maketh 1.   c a IR.   d ȝe theryn 1.   e upon the 1.   f litil coffre 1.   g of the ark 1. h thei ELPRU.   i han paied DGIKMNOQSXb.   k the Lord 1.   l ȝoure trespas 1.   m go forth 1.   n biholde *it* 1.   o goth up 1.   p Bethsames A.   q tho 1.   r the Lord hath thanne do 1.

hath doo to ȝou this greet yuel; forsothe if not, we shulen wyte that the hoond of it hath not towchid vs, but by hap it 10 hath fallun. Thanne thei diden this wise; and takynge two kyen that ȝauen calues sowke, thei ioyneden to the wayn; forsothe the calues of hem thei elosiden at 11 home. And thei putten the arke of God vpon the wayn, and the litle coofre that hadde the golden myis, and the licnes of 12 arsis. Forsothe the kyen ȝeden euen ryȝt bi the weye that ledith to Bethsames; and in o weye thei wenten goynge and loowynge, and thei boweden not asyde ne to the ryȝt ne to the left; but and the maystris of Philistyens folweden vnto 13 the teermys of Bethsames. Forsothe Bethsamytis repiden whete in the valey, and rerynge vp the eyen thei seen the arke, and thei ioyeden, whanne thei had- 14 den seen. And the wayn cam into the feeld of Josue Bethsamyte, and stood there. Forsothe a greet stoon was there; and thei heweden⁹ the trees of the wayn, and the kien thei putten vpon, the brent 15 sacrifice to the Lord. Forsothe Leuytis putten down the arke of God, and the litil coofre that was biside it, in the which weren the golden vessels; and thei putten vpon the greet stoon. Forsothe Bethsamytis men offreden brent sacrifice, and slewen sacrifices in that day to the 16 Lord. And the fyue maystris of Phi- listiens seen, and ben turned aȝen into 17 Acharon in that day. Forsothe thes ben the golden arsis, the whiche Philistiens for the trespas ȝolden to the Lord; Aȝot oon, Gaza oon, Ashalon oon, Geth oon, 18 Acharon oon; and goldun myis after the noumbre of Philistiens cytees, of the fyue prouyncis, fro wallid cytee vnto toun that was with outen wal, and vnto greet Abel,

greet yuel; but if nayˢ, we schulen wite 'for his' hond" touchide not vs, but 'if it bifelde⁰ bi hap. Therfor" thei diden in 10 this manere; and thei token twei kien that ȝauen mylk to caluys˟, and ioyneden⁰ to the wayn; and thei closiden her caluys at hoome. And thei puttiden˟ the arke of 11 God on" the wayn, and 'thei puttiden⁰ the panyere⁰, that hadde the goldun myis, and the licnesse of ersis 'on the wayn⁰. Sotheli⁰ 12 the kien ȝeden streiȝtli bi the weie that ledith to Bethsames; and tho' ȝeden⁰ in o weie goynge and lowynge, and bowiden" not nether to the riȝt side nether¹ to the left side; but also the wise men of Filis- teis sueden 'til to˟ the termes¹ of Beth- sames. Forsothe" men of Bethsames rep- 13 iden whete in the" valey, and thei reisiden⁰ the⁰ iȝen, and sien the arke, and thei weren ioyful, whanne thei hadden sien 'the arke⁹. And the wayn cam in to the feelde of 14 Josue of Bethsames, and stood' there". Forsothe' a greet stoon was there; and thei" kittiden⁰ 'the trees of" the wayn, and puttiden˟ the⁰ kien 'on tho trees˟, a brent sacrifice to the Lord. Sotheli⁰ de- 15 kenes⁰ token doun the arke of God, and the panyere⁰, that was bisidis it, where ynne the goldun vessels weren; and thei settiden⁰ on⁰ the greet stoon. Forsothe' the men of Bethsames offriden brent sacri- fices, and offriden⁰ slayn sacrifices in that dai 'to the Lord". And fyue¹ princes˟ of 16 Filisteis sien, and turneden¹ aȝen in to Accoron in that dai. Sotheli" these ben 17 the goldun" ersis, whiche the Filisteis ȝeldiden to the Lord for trespas⁰; Azotus ȝeldide oon; Gaza ȝeldide⁰ oon; Ascolon ȝeldide⁰ oon; Geth ȝeldide⁰ oon; Acca- ron ȝeldide⁰ oon; and Filisteis⁹ ȝeldiden 18 golden myis bi' the noumbre of 'citees of Filisteis˟ of fyue prouynces, fro a wallid

ˢ it go not thider 1.   ᵗ that tho 1.   ᵘ hond of the Lord 1.   ᵛ if it fel L. it bifelde D. this thing hath fallen to us 1.   ʷ Thanne 1.   ˟ her caluys 1.   ʸ thei ioyneden hem 1.   ˣ putten 1.   ᵃ upon 1.   ᵇ Om. 1. ᶜ litil coffre 1.   ᵈ Om. 1.   ᵉ And 1.   ᶠ thilke kijn 1.   ᵍ wenten 1.   ʰ thei bowiden 1.   ⁱ ne 1.   ᵏ vnto 1. ˡ coostis 1.   ᵐ And 1.   ⁿ a 1.   ⁰ lifte up 1.   ᵖ her 1.   ⁹ it 1.   ʳ it stood 1.   ˢ there stille 1.   ᵗ And 1. ᵘ men of Bethsames 1.   ᵛ hewiden 1.   ʷ Om. 1.   ˟ upon that wode thei puttiden 1.   ʸ tho 1.   ˣ Om. 1. ᵃ And 1.   ᵇ the dekenes 1.   ᶜ litil coffre 1.   ᵈ puttiden tho 1.   ᵉ upon 1.   ᶠ And 1.   ᵍ Om. 1.   ʰ Om. 1. ⁱ the fyue 1.   ᵏ satrapis 1.   ˡ thei turneden 1.   ᵐ And 1.   ⁿ mennus goldun 1.   ⁰ her trespas 1. ᵖ Om. 1.   ⁹ the Filisteis 1.   ʳ aftir 1.   ˢ her citees 1.

vpon the which he putte the ark of the
Lord, that was vnto that day in the
19 feeld of Josue Bethsamyte. Forsothe he
smoot of the men of Bethsamyte, for that
thei hadden seen the arke of the Lord,
and he smoot of the puple seuenti men,
and fifti thowsandis of the raskeyl. And
the puple weyliden, whanne the Lord
hadde smyten with a greet veniaunce the
20 comoun puple. And the men of Bethsamyte seiden, Who shal mowe stoond
in the siȝt of this holy Lord God, and
21 to whom shal he stye vp fro vs? And
thei senten messagerys to the dwellers of
Caryathyarym, seiynge, Philistiens han
brouȝt aȝen[r] the arke of the Lord; cometh doun, and bryngeth it aȝen to ȝow.

CAP. VII.

1 Thanne the men of Caryathyarym
camen, and brouȝten aȝen the arke of
the Lord, and beren it into the hows of
Amynadab in Gabaa. And thei halweden
Eleazer his sone, for he shulde kepe the
2 arke of the Lord. And it is doon, fro
what day the arke of the Lord dwellide in
Caryathiarym, multiplied ben the days;
forsothe nowe was the twentithe ȝeer;
and al the hows of Yrael restide after
3 the Lord. Forsothe Samuel seith to al
the hows of Yrael, seiynge, If in al ȝoure
herte ȝe turnen to the Lord, doth awey
alien goddis fro the mydil of ȝow, Baalym and Astaroth; and makith redi
ȝoure hertis to the Lord, and serueth to
hym alone; and he shal delyuere ȝow
4 fro the hond[s] of Philistyens. Thanne the
sones of Yrael token awey Baalym and
Astaroth, and serueden to the Lord alone.
5 Forsothe Samuel seide, Gederith al Yrael
in to Masphat, that Y preye the Lord for
6 ȝou. And thei camen togidre in Masphat,

citee 'til to[t] 'a town that was with out
wal[u], and 'til to[v] the greet Abel†[w], 'on
which[x] thei puttiden the arke of the Lord,
that[y] was there 'til in[z] that dai in the
feeld of Josue of Bethsames. Forsothe 19
the Lord smoot of the men of Bethsames,
for thei hadden seyn the arke of the Lord,
and he smoot of the puple seuenti men‡,
and fifty thousynde of the porail. And
the puple morenyde, for the Lord hadde
smyte 'the puple[a] with greet veniaunce.
And men of Bethsames seiden, Who schal 20
now stonde in the siȝt of the Lord God
of this hooli thing, and to whom schal it
stie[b] fro vs? And thei senten messan- 21
geris to the dwelleris of Cariathiarym,
and seiden, Filisteis[c] han brouȝt aȝen the
arke of the Lord; come ȝe doun, and lede[d]
it aȝen to ȝou.

CAP. VII.

Therfor men of Cariathiarym camen, 1
and ledden aȝen the arke of the Lord, and
brouȝten[e] it in to the hows of Amynadab
in Gabaa. Sotheli[f] thei halewiden Eleazar
his sone, that he schulde kepe the ark of
the Lord. And it was doon, fro which[g] 2
dai 'the arke of the Lord[h] dwellide in
Caryathiarym, daies[i] weren multiplied‖;
for[k] the twentithe ȝeer was[l] now[m], *after
that Samuel bigan to teche the puple;*
and al Israel restide[n] aftir the Lord. For- 3
sothe[o] Samuel spak to al the hows of Israel, and seide, If in al ȝoure herte ȝe
turnen aȝen to the Lord, do ȝe awei alien
goddis, Balym and Astaroth, fro the myddis
of ȝou; and make ȝe redi ȝoure hertis to
the Lord, and serue ȝe hym aloone; and
he schal delyuere ȝou fro the hond of Filisteis[p]. Therfor the sones of Israel diden 4
awey Baalym and Astoroth, and serueden[q]
the[r] Lord aloone. Forsothe[s] Samuel seide, 5
Gadere ȝe[t] al Israel[u] in to Masphat, that
Y preie the Lord for ȝou. And thei camen 6

† *greet Abel,* that is, a stoon, and is interpretid morenyng. *Lire here.* c.

‡ *and he smoot of the peple seuenti men;* for foure causis the Lord smoot the peple; for vnresonable gladnesse, that cam of the liȝtnesse of heed, and not of du reuerence; and for brent sacrifice offrid vnduly of kyn, for femalis schulden not be offrid in to brent sacrifice to the Lord, as it is seid in i. c°. of Leuyt.; and for they weren stirid bi curiouste to se the nakid arke, whiche thing is forbodun undur the peyne of deth in foure c°. of Numeri; and for they suffriden the arke to dwelle out of hows, and with out liȝt and du religioun. Ebrews understonden thus the noumbre of men slayn here; they seyen that onely seuenti men weren smytun, whiche weren of so greet reputacioun, that they weren comparisound to one thousinde of the comyn peple; for therfor the principal men of the peple weren smytun, for they ouȝten ordeyne the peple, and bifore be war of the forseid offensis. *Lire here.* c.

‖ *daies were multiplied,* in whiche Samuel excitide the puple to good. *Lire here.* c.

[r] aȝens *A*. Om. B. [s] hoondis *A*.

[t] vnto I. [u] an vnwalled town I. [v] vnto I. [w] *ston that hiȝte* Abel I. tabel K *sec. m.* [x] upon whom I. [y] the which ston I. [z] vnto I. til into K *pr. m.* X *sec. m.* in to E. [a] it I. [b] stie up I. [c] the Filisteis I. [d] ledeth I. [e] thei brouȝten I. [f] And I. [g] that I. [h] that the Lordis arke I. [i] the daies I. [k] and I. [l] Om. D. [m] thanne I. [n] restide *in pes* I. [o] And I. [p] the Filisteis I. [q] thei serueden I. [r] to the I. [s] And I. [t] ȝe togidere I. [u] the peple of Israel I.

and thei drewen water, and heelden out in the siȝt of the Lord , and thei fastiden in that day, and seiden, To thee we han synned, Lord　And Samuel demyde the 7 sones of Yrael in Masphat　And Philistiens herden that the sones of Yrael weren gediyd in Masphat; and the satrapis of Philistiens stieden vp to Yrael The which thing whanne the sones of Yrael hadden herd, thei diedden fro the 8 face of Philistiens　And thei seiden to Samuel, Ne ceese thow for vs to crye to the Lord oure God, that he saue vs 9 fro the hondt of Philistyens　Forsothe Samuel took o sowkynge loomb, and offrede it into hool brent sacrifice to the Lord　And Samuel criede to the Lord for Yrael , and the Lord herde hym 10 Forsothe it is doon, whanne Samuel offrede brent sacryfice, Philistiens to-goon into batayl aȝens Yrael　Forsothe the Lord thundryde with greet crakkynge in that day vpon the Philistiens, and he feeride hem , and thei ben slayn fro the 11 face of Yrael.　And the sones of Yrael goon out fro Masphat, pursueden Philistiens, and smyten hem vnto the place 12 that was vndur Bethaai.　Forsothe Samuel took au stoon, and putte it betwixv Masphat and betwixw Sen; and he clepide the name of that place The stoon of help　And he seide, Hidir to the Lord 13 hath holpen to vs　And Philistiens ben mekid, and no more ouer thei leiden to that thei camen into the teermys of Yrael　And so is doon the hoond of the Lord vpon Philistyens alle the days of 14 Samuel　And the cytees that the Philistiens token fro Yrael, ben ȝolden aȝen to Yrael, fro Accharon vnto Geth and his teermys , and he delyueride Yrael fro the hoond of Philistyens, and pees was bi-

togidere in to Masphat, and thei drowen watir, and shedden w out in the siȝt of the Loidx; and thei fastiden in that day, and seiden, Lord, we synnedeny to thee　And Samuel demyde the sonesz of Israel in Masphat　And Filisteisa herden that the 7 sones of Israel weren gaderidb in Masphat; and the princes of Filisteis stiedenc to Israel　And whanne the sones of Israel hadden herd this, thei dredden of the face of Filisteis　And thei seidend to Samuel, Ceesse thou not to crye for vs to oure 8 Lord God, that he saue vs fro the hoond of Filisteise　Forsothef Samuel took o 9 soukynge lomb, and offiide thatg hool in to brent sacrifice to the Lord　And Samuel criede to the Lord for Israel; and the Lord herde hym　Forsotheh it was 10 doon, whanne Samuel offryde brent sacrifice, thatk Filisteisl bigunnen batel aȝens Israel　Sothelim the Lord thundride with greet thundurn in that dai ono Filisteis, and madep hem afeid; and thei weren slayn of the sones of Israel　And thei 11 sones of Israel ȝedenq out ofr Masphat, and pursueden Filisteiss, and smytident hem 'til tou the place that was vndur Bethachai　Forsothev Samuel took o stoon, 12 and puttidew it bitwixe Masphat, and bitwixex Sen; and he clepide the name of that place The stoon of help　And he seide, Hidir to the Lord helpidev vs.　And 13 Filisteisz weren maad low, and addidena no more to come in to the termes of Israel　And so the 'hond of the Lordb was maad onc Filisteis in alle the daies of Samuel　And the citees whiched the Filis- 14 teis tokene fro Israel, weren ȝoldunf to Israel, fro Accaron 'til tog Geth and 'hise termesh; and the Lord delyuerede Israel fro the hond of Filisteis, and pees was bitwixe Israel and Ammorrey†　Also 15 i

---

t hoondis *A*　u oon BE oo II　v bytwene BF　betwen E　betwe C　w bytwene BFH　betwen CA

y Om DK　w holden it I　x Lordis siȝt I　y han synned I　z hous I　a the Filisteis I　b gaderid to gidere I　c stieden up I　d Israel criede I　e Philistees hoond I　f And I　g it I　h And I　i the brent I　k Om DGKMNOQSXb　l the Filisteis I　m And I　n thundring KX　o upon the I　p he made I　q wenten I　r fro I　s the Filisteis I　t smoten I　u vnto I　v And I　w putte I　x Om I　y hath helpid I　z the Filisteis I　a thei addiden I　b Lordis hond I　c upon the I　d that I　e hadden take I　f ȝoldun aȝen I　g vnto I　h the coostis of Geth I　i And I

† *Amorey*, for Ammore.s serueden to Israel vndur tribut *I ire here* C

15 twix^x Yrael and Ammorre. Forsothe Samuel demyde Yrael alle the days of
16 his lijf; and wente bi eche ʒeer enuy-ronnynge Bethel, and Galgal, and Mas-phat, and he demyde Yrael in the forseid
17 placis; and turned aʒen in to Ramatha, forsothe there was his hows; and there he demyde Yrael, and he bildide vp there also an auter to the Lord.

CAP. VIII.

1 Forsothe it is doon whanne Samuel wexe oold, he putte his sones domesmen
2 of Yrael. And the name of his first geten sone was Joel, the name of the secounde Abya, domysmen in Bersabe.
3 And the sones of hym wenten not in his weyes, but boweden aside after aueryce, and thei token ʒiftis, and thei peruert-
4 iden doom. Thann alle the more thurʒ birth of Yrael gedrid, camen to Samuel
5 in Ramatha. And thei seiden to hym, Loo! thou art waxen oold, and thi sones goon not in thi weyes; ordeyn to vs a kyng, that he deme vs, and as alle na-
6 cyouns han. And the word displeside in the eyen of Samuel, forthi that thei had-den seid, ʒif to vs a kyng, that he deme vs. And Samuel preide to the Lord.
7 Forsothe the Lord seide to Samuel, Here the voys of the puple in alle thingis that thei speken to thee; forsothe thei han not throwun awey thee, but me, lest Y
8 regne vpon hem. Aftir alle her werkis that thei han doo, fro the day that Y ladde hem out of Egipt vnto this day, as thei forsoken me, and serueden to alien
9 goddis, so thei doon also to thee. Nowe thanne here the voyce of hem; neuer-thelater take hem togidre to witnesse; and sey before to hem the riʒt of a kyng,

Samuel demyde Israel in^k alle the daies of his lijf †, *that is, 'til to^l the ordeynyng 'and confermyng^m of Saul^n*; and he ʒede^o‡ bi 'alle ʒeeris^p, and cumpasside Bethel, and Galgal, and Masphat, and he demyde Is-rael in the forseid places. And he turnede 17 aʒen in to Ramatha, for his hows was there; and he demyde Israel there, and he bildide there also an auter to the Lord.

CAP. VIII.

Forsothe^q it was don, whanne Samuel 1 hadde^r wexide^s eld, he settide^t hise sones iugis^u on^v Israel. And the name of his 2 firste gendrid^w sone was Johel, and the name of the secounde was^x Abia, iugis^y in Bersabee. And hise sones ʒeden^z not in 3 'the weies of hym^a, but thei bowiden after aueryce, and thei token ʒiftis, and per-uertiden^b doom. Therfor alle the grettere 4 men in birthe of Israel weren gaderid^c, and camen to Samuel in to Ramatha. And 5 thei seiden to hym^d, Lo! thou hast wexide^e eld, and thi sones goen not in thi weies; ordeyne thou a kyng to vs, 'that he deme vs^f, as also alle naciouns^g han. And the 6 word displeside in the iʒen^h of Samuel, for thei hadden seid, ʒyue thou to vs a kyng, that he deme vs. And Samuel preiede to the Lord. Forsothe^i the Lord seide to 7 Samuel, Here thou the vois of the puple in alle thingis whiche^k thei speken to thee; for^l thei han not caste awey thee^m, but me, that Y regne not on^n hem. Bi alle her^o 8 werkis whiche^p thei diden^q, fro the day in whiche Y ledde hem out of Egipt 'til to^r this dai, as thei forsoken^s me, and seruyden^t alien goddis, so thei doon also to thee. Now therfor here thou her vois; 9 nctheles^tt witnesse^u thou to^v hem^w; bifor-seie^x thou to hem^y the riʒt of^z the kyng,

† *of his lijf; that is, til to the ordeynyng and conferm-yng of Saul. c.*
‡ *and he ʒede, etc. til his owne trauel and contin-to deme the peple in couen-able places, as it seid in xii. c^o. Lire here. c.*

---

k Om. i. l *in to* E. m Om. N. n gloss omitted in GIQSX *pr. m.* b. o wente i. P ech ʒeer i. q And i.
r Om. i. s waxen EKL. t sette i. u *to be* iugis i. v *of* DEIKLMOX. w goten i. x Om. i. y that weren iugis i. z wenten i. a his weies i. b misturneden i. c gaderid togidere i. d Samuel i. e wexe i. f Om. K. g *othere* naciouns i. h siʒt i. i And i. k that i. l forsothe i. m thee fro hem i. n vpon i. o the i. P that i. q han do i. r vnto i. s han forsake i. t thei han serued i. tt and notheles b. u take i. v Om. i. w hem togidere and witnesse thou to hem i. x and biforseie IL. y hem and witnesse thou to hem KX. z on K.

10 the which is to regne vpon hem And so Samuel seide alle the wordis of the Lord to the puple, that askiden of him a kyng,
11 and seith, This shal be the ri3t of a kyng, that is to comaunde to 3ou; 3ou1e sonys he shal take, and putte in his charys, and he shal make to hym ryders, and before
12 renners of his long cartis, and he shal ordeyn to hym rewlers of thowsandis, and rewlers of hundridis, and ereies of his feeldis, and repers of cornys, and smythis of aarmys, and of his chaiis
13 Forsothe 3oure dou3tres he shal make to him oynement makers, and fier makers,
14 and clothmakers Forsothe 3oure feeldis and vynes and olyues, the best he shal
15 take, and 3yue to his seruauntis But and 3oure cornys, and the rentis of vynes he shal tithe, that he 3yue to geldyngis
16 and to his seruauntis. Forsothe 3oure seruauntis and hoondwymmen, and the best 3onge men and assis he shal take
17 awey, and putte in his werk Forsothe 3oure flockis he shal tithe, and 3e shulen
18 be to him seruauntis And 3e shulen crye in that day fro the face of 3oure kyng, whom 3e han chosun to 3ow, and the Lord shal not here 3ou in that day,
19 for 3e han askid to 3ou a kyng Forsothe the puple wolden not here the vois of Samuel, but seiden, Nay, forsothe a kyng
20 shal be vpon vs· and we forsothe shulen be as other folk of kynde, and oure kyng shal deme vs, and he shal go out before vs, and he shal fi3t oure batayl for vs
21 And Samuel herde alle the wordis of the puple, and spak hem in the eeiis of the
22 Lord Forsothe the Lord seide to Samuel, Here thow the voys of hem, and set vpon hem a kyng And Samuel seith to the men of Yrael, Goo ech man into his cytee

that schal regne on^a hem Therfor^b Sa-
10 muel seide alle the wordis of the Lord to the puple, that hadde axid of him a king; and he seide, This schal be the 'ri3t of the
11 kyng^c†, that schal comaunde to 3ou, he schal take 3oure sones, and schal^d sette^e in hise charis, and he schal make hem
12 'to hym silf^f rideris, and bifoiegoeris of hise cartis; and he schal ordeyne to hym tribunes, 'that is, souereyns of a thou-synd^g, and centuriouns, 'that is, soue-reyns of an hundrid^h, and eereris^i of hise feeldis, and reperis of cornes^k, and smythis of hise armeris, and chaiis^l
13 Also he schal make 3oure dou3tris makeris of 'oynementis to hym silf^m, and fueris^n, and bakeris^o And he schal take 3oure
14 feeldis and vyneris^p and the beste places of olyues, and schal^q 3yue^r to hise ser-uauntis But also he schal take the
15 tenthe pait of 3oure cornes, and rentis^s of vyneris^t, that he 3yue^u to his chaum-berleyns and seruauntis Sothel^v he schal
16 take awey 3oure seruauntis and^w hand-maydes^x, and beste^y 3ong men, and assis^z, and schal^a sette^b in his werk. Also he
17 schal take the tenthe part of 3oure flockis, and 3e schulen be 'seruauntis to hym^c.
18 And 3e schulen ciye in that dai fro the face of 3oure kyng, whom 3e han chose to 3ou; and the Lord schal not here 3ou in that dai, foi 3e axiden a kyng to 3ou.
19 Sothel^d the puple nolde^e here the vois of Samuel, but thei seiden, Nay, for^f a kyng schal be on^g vs, and we also^h schulen be
20 as alle folkis^i, and oure kyng schal deme vs, and he schal go out^k bifor vs, and he schal fi3te oure batel^l for vs And Samuel
21 herde alle the wordis of the puple, and 'spak hem^m in the eeris of the Lord. For-
22 sothe^n the Lord seide to Samuel, Heie thou 'the vois of hem^o, and ordeyne thou a kyng on^p hem And Samuel seide to the inen of Israel, Ech man go in to his citee.

10 † This schal be the ri3t of the kyng Alle thingis teld here of Samuel ben of the ri3t of rewme and kyng set in nede for comyn good of the rewme, for in sich a caas alle goodis of the rewme ben the kingis, netheles tho schulen be set forth and spendid for commyn profit and good If the ri3t of the king is takun in an other maner out of nede, so ful many thingis hen expressid of Samuel, that perteynen not to the ri3t of a kyng, as alle tho thingis that maken the puple suget seruyle eithir thral, and whiche thingis bhold en not comyn good, but more singuler man set in the rewme, and Samuel bifor seide siche things to hem, to withdrawe hem that they schulden not axe a kyng, for it was not spedeful to hem And for gouernail is turned li3tly in to tirauntrie, for greetnesse of power grauntid to kyngis, therfor it sueth and 3e schulen be seruauntis to him, that is, if the gouernail is turned in to tirauntrie, whiche thing is doon li3tly, nameli in parti for the greet power of the king Therfor in xvij c^o of Deut^o a kyng is comaundid to kepe him silf fro pride, couetyse and tyranntrie Lire here c

‡ Nay, that is, the Lord schal not forsake to here vs, if we han a kyng Lire here c

---

a upon 1   b Thanne 1   c kyngis ri3t 1   d he schal 1   e sette hem 1   f Om 1   g or souereyns on thousandis 1 Om x pr m   h Om ix pr m   i tiheris 1   k his cornes 1   l of his charis 1   m his oyne-mentis 1   n his fire makers 1   o his makers of bred 1   p 3oure vyneris 1   q he schal 1   r 3yue tho 1
s the rentis 1   t 3oure vyneris 1   u 3yue tho 1   v and 1   w and 3oure 1   x handmaydens DEI   y 3oure beste 1   z 3oure assis 1   a he schal 1   b sette these 1   c his seruauntis   d And 1   e wolde not 1.
f certis 1   g upon 1   h Om 1   i folkis hen 1   k forth 1   l batels nciw   m he spak hem 1   n And 1
o her voices 1   p upon 1

CAP. IX.

1 And there was a man of Beniamyn, Cys bi name, the sone of Abyel, sone[y] of Seor, sone[y] of Bethor, sone[y] of Aphya, sone[y] of the man of Gemyny, stronge bi 2 strength. And ther was to hym a sone, Saul bi name, chosyn and good; and there was not a man of the sones of Israel betere than he; fro the shuldre and aboue 3 he peeryde aboue al the puple. Forsothe the shee assys of Cys, fadre[z] of Saul, weren lost. And Cys seide to Saul his sone, Tak with thee oon of the children, and rysynge go, and seche the she assis. The which whanne thei hadden 4 passid bi the mount of Effraym, and bi the loond of Saliza, and thei hadden not foundun, thei passiden also bi the loond of Salym, and there was noon; bot and by the loond of Gemyny, and thei founden 5 not. Forsothe whanne thei weren comen into the loond of Suph, and hadden not foundun, Saul seide to his chijld that was with hym, Come, and turne we aзen; lest perauenture my fadre leeue the she assis, 6 and be bysie for vs. The which seith to hym, Loo! the man of God is in this cytee, a noble man; al that he spekith, with out dout it cometh. Now thanne goo we thidre, if perauenture he shewe to vs of oure weye, for the which we ben 7 comen. And Saul seyde to his child, Loo! we shulen go; what shulen we brynge to the man of God? Breed faylith in oure sackis, and a lepe we han not, that we зuen to the man of God, ne eny other 8 thing. Eft the child answerde to Saul, and seith, Loo! there is founden in myn hoond the feerth part of a sicle of siluer; and зue we to the man of God, that he 9 shewe to vs oure weye. Sumtyme in

CAP. IX.

And 'a man was[q] of Beniamyn, 'Cys bi 1 name[r], the sone of Abiel, sone[s] of Seor, sone[s] of Bethor, sone[s] of Aphia, sone[t] of the[t] man Gemyny[u], strong[v] in bodili myзt. And to hym was a sone, Saul bi name, 2 chosun and good†; and no man‡ of the sones of Israel was betere than he; fro the schuldur and aboue[w] he apperide ouer al[x] the puple. Stotheli[y] the femal[z] assis of 3 Cys, the fadir of Saul, perischyden[a]‖. And Cys seide to Saul his sone, Take with thee oon of the children, and rise thou, and go, and[b] seke the femal[c] assis. And whanne thei hadden go[d] bi the hil of Effraym, and 4 bi the lond of Salisa, and hadden[e] not foundun[f], thei passiden[g] also bi the lond of Salyn, and tho[h] weren not there; but also 'thei passiden[i] bi the lond of Gemyny, and foundun[k] not. Sotheli[l] whanne thei 5 hadden come in to the lond of Suph, and hadden[m] not founde, Saul seide to his child that was with hym, Come thou, and turne we aзen; lest perauenture my fadir hath[n] lefte[o] the[p] femal[q] assis, and is bisy[r] for vs. Which[s] child seide to hym, 6 Lo! the[t] man of God is in this citee, a noble man; a thing that he spekith, cometh with out doute. Now therfor go we thidir, if perauenture he schewe to vs[u] of oure weie, for which we camen. And Saul 7 seide to his child, Lo! we schulen go; what schulen we bere to the man of God? Breede failide[v] in oure scrippis, and we han no present[w], that we зyue to the man of God, 'nether ony othir thing[x]. Eft the child 8 answeride to Saul, and seide, Lo! the fourthe part of 'a stater, that is, a cicle, of sileur[y] is foundun in myn hond; зyue we[z] to the man of God, that he schewe to vs oure weie[a]. Sumtyme in Israel ech man 9

Margin notes:

† chosun and good, with out notable wem of vices; good, bi resoun of goodes maneris and of vertues. c.

‡ no man, and so forth, not onely he was good, but also of excellent goodnesse. Lire here. c.

‖ perischiden, that is, strayeden, for tho perischiden not outirly, that weren foundun aftirward. Lire here. c.

---

y the sone ε *pr. v.*   z the fadre ε *pr. v.*

q ther was a man 1.   r that hiзte Cys 1.   s the sone 1.   t a 1. Om. n.   u of Gemyny cx *pr. m. that hiзt* Gemyny 1.   v a strong man 1.   w upward 1.   x Om. 1.   y And 1.   z sche 1.   a weren lost 1. b Om. 1.   c sche 1.   d gon forth 1.   e thei hadden 1.   f foundun hem 1.   g passiden forth 1.   h thei 1. i Om. 1.   k зit thei founden 1.   l Forsothe *plures.* And 1.   m thei hadden 1.   n haue 1.   o lefte *to charge* 1. p thes ε. his κ. Om. l.   q Om. 1.   r bisy in herte *or careful* 1.   s And the 1.   t a 1.   u vs *the cause* 1. v hath faild 1.   w present monei neither ony other thing 1.   x Om. 1.   y a siluern sicle 1.   z we *it* 1. a *wher we schul go ferther or no* 1 marg.

Yrael thus spak echon goynge to counseyle God, Cometh, and goo we to the
seer; forsothe he, that to day is seid a
10 prophet, sumtyme was clepid seer. And
Saul seide to his child, Altherbest is thi
word; com, go^a we. And thei wenten
into the cyte, in the which was the man
11 of God. And whanne thei stieden vp the
hil of the citee, thei founden children
wymmen goynge out to drawe watir, and
thei seiden to hem, Whether here is the
12 seer? The which answerynge seiden to
hem, Here he is, loo! before thee; hye
nowe, forsothe to day he cam into the
cytee; for to day is sacrifice of the puple
13 in the heiʒe. Goynge into the cyte anoon
ʒe shulen fynde hym, or he stie vp into
the hiʒe for to eete; forsothe ne the puple is to eete to the tyme that he come,
for he shal blesse to the oost, and there
after shulen eete that ben clepid. Nowe
thanne stieth vp, for to day ʒe shulen
14 fynde hym. And thei stieden vp into the
cytee. And whanne thei wenten in^b the
mydil of the cyte, Samuel aperyde goynge out metynge to hem, that he stye
15 vp into the heiʒ. Forsothe the Lord
hadde toold the litil eer of Samuel before
16 o day, that Saul cam, seiynge, This same
our that nowe is to morwe, Y shal seende
to thee a man of the loond of Beniamyn,
and thow shalt anoynt hym duyk vpon
my puple Yrael, and he shal saue my
puple fro the hoond of Philistyens; for
I haue biholden my puple, forsothe the
17 crye of hem is comen to me. And
whanne Samuel hadde beholden Saul, the
Lord seide^c to hym, Loo! the man that
I seide to thee; this shal lordship to my^d
18 puple. Forsothe Saul neiʒede to Samuel
in the mydil of the ʒate, and seith, Shewe
to me, Y preye, where is the hows of the
19 seer? And Samuel answerde to Saul, sci-

goynge to counsel God^b spak thus, Come
ʒe, and go we to the seere; for he, that
is seid 'to dai^c a profete, was clepid sumtyme a seere. And Saul seide to his child, 10
'Thi word is the beste^d; come thou, go
we^e. And thei ʒeden in to the citee, 'in
which^f the man of God was^g. And whanne 11
thei stieden^h in to the hiʒnesse of the citee,
thei founden damesels goynge out to drawe
watir, and thei seiden to the dameselis,
Whether the seere is here? Whicheⁱ dame- 12
selis answeriden, and seiden to hem, He is
here; lo! he is bifor thee; 'haste thou^k
now^l, for to day he cam in to the citee;
for to dai is sacrifice of the puple in the
hiʒ place. ʒe schulen entre^m in to the 13
citee, and anoon ʒe schulen fynde hym,
bifor that he stieⁿ in to the hiʒ place to
ete; for the puple schal not ete til^o he
come, for he schal blesse the sacrifice,
and afterward thei schulen ete that ben
clepid. Now therfor stie ʒe^p, for to day
ʒe schulen fynde hym. And thei stieden^q 14
in to the citee. And whanne thei ʒeden in^r
the^s myddis of the citee, Samuel apperide
goynge out aʒens hem, that he schulde
stie^t in to the hiʒ place. Forsothe^u the 15
Lord 'hadde maad^v reuelacioun in the eere
of Samuel 'bifor o dai, that Saul cam^w,
and seide, In this same our which^x is now 16
to morewe, Y schal sende to thee a man of
the lond of Beniamyn, and thou schalt
anoynte hym duyk on^y my puple Israel,
and he schal saue my puple fro the hond
of Filisteis; for Y haue biholde my puple†,
for^z 'the cry of hem^a cam^b to me. And 17
whanne Samuel hadde biholde Saul, the
Lord seide to Samuel, Lo! the man, whom
Y seide to thee; this man schal be lord of
my puple. Forsothe^c Saul neiʒede to Sa- 18
muel in the myddis of the ʒate, and seide,
Y preye^d, schewe thou to me, where is
the hows of the seere? And Samuel an- 19

† *Y haue bi-
holde, etc.; that
is, with iʒe of
mercy. Lire
here. c.*

---

^a and go CE. ^b into A. ^c seith CE. ^d the E pr. m.

^b with God I. ^c now I. ^d Ful good is thi word I. ^e we *to him* I. ^f that I. ^g was ynne I. ^h stieden
up I. ⁱ And the I. ^k and haste c. haste thee D. haste ʒou E. hie thee I. ^l Om. GQ. forsothe I. ^m entre
forth I. ⁿ wende up I. ^o til that I. ^p ʒe up I. ^q wenten up I. ^r in to A *pr. m.* ^s Om. EIL. ^t stie
up I. ^u And the dai before that Saul came I. ^v made I. ^w Om. I. ^x that I. ^y upon I. ^z forsothe I.
^a her cry. ^b hath come I. ^c And I. ^d preye thee I.

ynge, Y am the seer; sty vp before me into the hei3, that thou eete with me to day, and Y shal leeue thee the morwe-tide, and alle thingis that ben in thin 20 herte Y shal shewe to thee. And of the assis 'the which^e thre days hens thou lostist, ne be thow bysy, for thei ben foundun; and of whom shulen be alle the best thingis of Yrael, whether not to thee, and to al the hows of thi fader? 21 Forsothe Saul answerynge seith, Whe-ther not the sone of Gemyny Y am, of the leest lynage of Yrael, and my kyn-rede the last among alle the meynees of the lynage of Beniamyn? Whi thanne hast thou spoken to me thes^f wordis^g? 22 And so Samuel takynge Saul, and hys child, brou3te hem into the hows of thre benchis, and he 3af to hem a place in the cheefe^h of hem that weren bodenⁱ to meet; forsothe there weren as thretti 23 men. And Samuel seide to the cook, 3if thow the part that I 3af to thee, and co-maundide, that thow shulde lay aside 24 anentis thee. And the cook reryde the shuldre, and putte before Saul. And Sa-muel seide, Loo! that is laft, put before thee, and ete; for of purpos it is kept to thee, whanne Y clepide the puple. And 25 Saul eet with Samuel in that day. And thei wenten down fro the hei3 into the bur3 town; and he spak with Saul in the solere, and he beddide Saul in the solere, 26 and he slepte. And whanne eerly thei weren rysen, and nowe the day wexe li3t, Samuel clepide Saul into the solere, sey-ynge, Ryse, that^k Y leeue^l thee. And Saul roos, and bothe thei wenten oute, 27 he, that is, and Samuel. And whanne thei weren goo down in the vttermost parti of the cytee, Samuel seide to Saul, Sey^m to the child, that he goo before vs,

sweride to Saul, and seide, Y am the seere; stie thou^e bifor me in to the hi3 place, that thou ete with me to dai, and Y schal delyuere thee in the morewtid, and Y schal schewe to thee alle thingis that ben in thin herte. And be thou not 20 bisy of the femal^f assis, whiche^g thou lostist the^h thridde dai agoon, for thoⁱ ben foundun; and whose schulen be alle the beste thingis of Israel, whether not to thee, and to al the hows of thi fader†? Sotheli^k Saul answeride, and seide, Whe- 21 ther Y am not a^l sone of Gemyny, of the leeste lynage of Israel, and my kynrede is the laste among alle the meynees of the lynage of Beniamyn? Whi therfor hast thou spoke to me this word? Therfor^m 22 Samuel took Saul, and his child, and leddeⁿ hem in to the^o chaumbur of thre ordris^p, and he 3af to hem a place in the bigyn-nyng of hem that weren clepid^q; for^r thei weren as thretti^s men^t. And Samuel 23 seide to the cook, 3yue thou^u the part, which^v Y 3af to thee, and comanndide, that thou schuldist kepe bi it silf anentis thee. Sotheli^w the cook reiside^x the^y 24 schuldir, and settide^z bifor Saul. And Samuel scide, Lo! that, that lefte^a, 'sette thou^b bifor thee, and ete; for of purpos it was kept to thee, whanne Y clepide the puple^c. And Saul eet with Samuel in^d that dai. And thei camen doun fro the 25 hi3 place in to the citee; and Samuel spak with Saul in the^e soler, and Saul 'araiede a bed in the soler^f, and slepte. And whanne thei hadden rise eerli, and 26 'now it^g bigan to be cleer, Samuel clepide Saul in to the^h soler, and seide, Rise thouⁱ, that Y delyuere thee. And Saul roos^k, and bothe 3eden out, that is, he, and Sa-muel. And whanne thei 3eden doun in 27 the laste part of the citee, Samuel seide

† to the hous of thy fadir; for Saul was kyng, and alle the beste thinges of the peple ben the kingis in nede, and Abner, prince of the kny3[t]hod, and othere my3ty men of the hows of Saul, hadden the beste thingis of the rewme; and so schulden her eyris hane had, if Saul hadde stonde in his good-nesse. Lire here. c.

^e that c pr. m.   ^f this CEH.   ^g worde B. woord CF. word FH.   ^h heuyd E.   ⁱ byden BCF. bedyn EH.   ^j shepte A.   ^k thou E pr. m.   ^l schal leeue E pr. m. exp. s. m.   ^m Seide A.

^e thou up I.   ^f Om. I.   ^g whom I.   ^h in the I.   ⁱ thei I.   ^k And I.   ^l the I.   ^m And so I.   ⁿ he ledde I.   ^o a I.   ^p seetis I.   ^q boden to the mete I.   ^r and I.   ^s a thretti I.   ^t men at mete I.   ^u thou him I.   ^v that I.   ^w And I.   ^x toke up I.   ^y a I.   ^z he sette it I.   ^a hath left I.   ^b take I.   ^c puple hidere I.   ^d Om. I.   ^e a I.   ^f beddide him there I.   ^g the day I.   ^h a I.   ⁱ thou up I.   ^k roos up I.

and passe forth; forsothe thow stoond
stil a litil, while that Y shewe to thee the
word of the Lord.

to Saul, Seie thou to the¹ child, that he
go bifor vs, and passe^m; forsothe^n stonde
thou° a litil, that Y schewe to thee the
word of the Lord.

CAP. X.

1 Samuel forsothe took a 'litil brytil^n
vessel of oyle, and heelde out on his heed,
and he kisside hym, and seith, Loo! the
Lord hath anoyntide thee vp on his erytage into a prince; and thow schalt delyuer his puple fro the hoondis of her
enemyes, 'the which° ben in enuyroun^p
of it. And this to thee a tokne, for the
Lord hath anoyntide thee into a prince;
2 whanne thow gost to dai fro me, thow
shalt fynde two men byside the sepulcre
of Rachel, in the coostis of Beniamyn, in
the myddday^q, feermynge^r greet dichis;
and thei shulen seye to thee, The she
assis ben foundun, to the whiche to be
sou3t thou wentist; and thi fader, the
meen while the assis laft, is bisy for 3ow,
and seith, What shal Y do of my sone?
3 And whanne thou gost thens, and ferther passist, and comest to the ook of
Thabor, thre men shulen fynde thee
there, stiynge vp to God into Bethel,
oon^s berynge thre kyddis, and another
berynge thre^t kakis of breed, and another
4 berynge a galoun of wyn. And whanne
thei saluten thee, thei shulen 3yue to thee
two looues, and thow schalt take of^u the
5 hoond of hem. After thes thingis thou
shalt come into the hil of the Lord,
where is the stacioun of Phylistynes;
and whanne thow were goon into the
cytee, there thow shalt haue metynge a
floc^v of prophetis comynge doun fro the
hee3, and before hem a sawtrye, and a
tymbre, and a trompe, and an harp, and
6 hem propheciynge. And the Spyrit of

CAP. X.

Forsothe Samuel took 'a vessel of oyle^p, 1
and schedde^q out on the heed of Saul, and
kisside^r hym, and seide, Lo!† the Lord
hath anoyntid thee in to prince^s on hys
eritage; and thou schalt delyuere his puple fro the hond of his enemyes, that ben
'in his cumpas'. And this^u a tokene to thee,
that the Lord hath anoyntid thee in to
prince^v; whanne thou schalt go fro me to 2
day, thou schalt fynde twei men bisidis
'the sepulcre of Rachel^w, in 'the endis of
Beniamyn^x, in myddai^y, clensynge grete
dichis‡; and thei schulen seie to thee, The
femel^z assis ben foundun, whiche^a thou
3edist to seke; and while^b the assis ben^c
lefte, thi fadir is bisy for 3ou, and seith^d,
What schal Y do of my sone? And whanne 3
thou hast go fro thennus, and hast passid
ferthere^e, and hast come to the ook of
Tabor, thre men, stiynge^f to God in to
Bethel, schulen fynde thee there, o man^g
berynge thre kydis, and another man
berynge thre kakis of breed, and an other
man berynge a galoun of wyn. And 4
whanne thei han gret thee, thei schulen
3yue to thee twei loues, and thou schalt
take^h of 'the hond of hem^i. After these 5
thingis thou schalt come in to the 'hil of
the Lord), where is the stondyng^k, *that is,
forselet* ^l, of Filisteis; and whanne thou
schalt entre in to the citee, there thou
schalt haue metynge thee the^m flok^n of
prophetis|| comynge doun fro the hi3 place,
and a sautree, and tympane°, and pipe^p, and
harpe^q bifor hem, and hem prophesiynge.
And the Spirit of the Lord schal skippe^r 6

†Fro this
word *in til thi-
dur in to prince*
is not in Ebreu.
Lire here. c.

‡ This word
*clensyng grete
dichis,* is not
in Ebreu, ne-
ther in bokis
amendid.
Lire here. c.

|| *profetis;* pro-
fetis ben clepid
here deuout
men and reli-
giouse, whiche
Samuel gader-
ide to preise
God; and with
this they had-
den spirit of
profesie,
namely summe
of hem. *Lire
here.* c.

^n Om. E pr. m. ° that c pr. m. ^p the enuyroun cE. ^q south E pr. m. ^r lepynge E pr. m. ^s oon be A.
^t Om. A. ^u fro E pr. m. ^v folk A.

^l thi I. ^m passe forth I. ^n and I. ° thou *stille* I. ^p an oile vessel I. ^q he helde it I. ^r he kisside I.
^s a prince I. ^t aboute *hem* I. ^u *be* this I. this is K. ^v a prince I. ^w Rachels biriel I. ^x Beniamyns
coostis I. ^y the myddai I. ^z sche I. ^a whom I. ^b Om. I. ° Om. I. ^d he saith I. ^e fertheremore I.
^f stiynge up I. ^g man *of hem* I. ^h take *tho* I. take *hem* K. ^i her hond I. ^j Lordis hil I. ^k stondyng
place I. ^l *the forselet* wx sec. m. gloss omitted in IX *pr. m.* ^m a I. ^n flok *or a cumpanye* I. ° a tympane I. ^p a pipe I. ^q an harpe I. ^r unoon falle I.

the Lord shal leep into thee, and thow
shalt prophecye with hem, and thow shalt
7 be chaungid into another man. Whanne
thanne alle thes toknes comen to thee, do
what euere thingis fyndith thin hoond,
8 for the Lord is with thee. And thow
shalt goo doun before me in Galgala; forsothe Y shal come down to thee, that
thow offre an offrynge, and offre pesible
slayn sacrificis; seuen days thow shalt
abide, to the tyme that Y come to thee,
9 and shewe to thee what thow doo. And
so whanne he hadde turned his shuldre,
that he ʒede fro Samuel, God with ynne
chaungide to hym another herte, and alle
10 thes toknes camen in that day. And thei
camen to the forseyd hil, and loo! a companye of prophetis metynge to hym; and
the Spyryt of the Lord leepe yn vpon
hym, and he propheciede in the mydil of
11 hem. Forsothe seynge alle, that knewen
hym ʒistyrday ᵂ and the thridde day hens,
that he was with prophetis, and prophe-
cide, seiden togidre, What nowe thing
fallith to the sone of Cys? Whether and
12 Saul among the prophetis? And another
answerde to the tothir, seiynge, And who
is the fadre of hym? Therfor it is turnyd
into a prouerbe, Whether and Saul among
13 the prophetis? Forsothe he ceside to pro-
14 phecie, and cam to the heiʒ. And the
brother of the fader of Saul saide to
hym, and to .his child, Whidre ʻwenten
ʒe ˣ? The whiche answerde, To seche the
she assis; the whiche whanne we hadden
15 not founde, we camen to Samuel. And
his fader brother seide to him, Shewe to
16 me what Samuel seide to thee. And Saul
seith to his fader ʸ brothir, He shewide
to vs, for the she assis weren founden.
Forsothe of the word of the kyngdam he
shewide not to hym, the which Samuel
17 spak to hym. And Samuel clepide togidre the puple to the Lord in Masphat;

in to thee, and thou schalt prophecie with
hem, and thou schalt be chaungid in to
another man. Therfor whanne alle thesse 7
signes ˢ bifallen to thee, do thou, what euer
thingis thin hond fyndith, ʻthat is, dispose
thee to regne comelili ᵗ and myʒtily ᵘ, for
the Lord is with thee. And thou schalt 8
go doun bifor me in to Galgala; for Y schal
come doun to thee, that thou ʻoffre† an
offryng, and offre ᵛ pesible sacrifices; bi
seuene daies thou schalt abide, til I come
to thee, and shewe to ᵂ thee what thou
schal do. Therfor whanne Saul hadde 9
turnede awei his schuldre to go fro Samuel, God chaungide another herte to
Saul, and alle these signes ˣ camen in that
dai. And thei ʸ camen to the forseid hil, 10
and lo! a cumpeny of prophetis metynge ˣ
hym; and the Spirit of the Lord ʻscippide
on hym ᵃ, and he propheciede in the myddis
of hem ᵇ. Sotheli ᶜ alle men, that knewen 11
hym ᵈ ʒisterdai and the thrid dai ago, sien
that he was with the prophetis, and that
he prophesiede, and thei seiden togidere,
What thing bifelde ᵉ to the sone of Cys?
Whether also Saul is among ᶠ prophetis?
And o man answeride to another man ᵍ, 12
and seide, And who is ʻhis fadir ʰ ‡? Therfor it was turned in to a prouerbe, Whether also Saul is among prophetis ⁱ? For- 13
sothe ᵏ Saul ceside to prophesie, and he
cam to an hiʒ place. And the brothir of 14
ʻthe fadir of Saul ˡ seide to hym, and to
his child, Whidur ʒeden ᵐ ʒe? And thei
answeriden, To seke the ⁿ female assis;
and whanne we ᵖ founden ʻnot thoo ᑫ, we
camen to Samuel. And the brother of his ʳ 15
fadir seide to hym, Schewe thou to me
what Samuel seide to thee. And Saul 16
seide to ʻthe brother of hys fadir ˢ, He ᵗ
schewide to vs, that the femal ᵘ assis weren
foundun. Sotheli ʸ Saul ᵂ schewide not to
hym ˣ of the word of rewme ʸ, ʻwhich word ᶻ
Samuel spak to hym. And Samuel cle- 17

† that thou
offre; in E.
breu it is to
offre an of-
fring, that is,
with me for
thyn helthe;
and thus oure
translacioun is
expouned of
oure doctours,
that thou offre
and make sacri-
fice, not bi thee
but by me, as
the peple of-
fride bi thee
preestis. Lire
here. c.

‡ who is his fa-
dir; in Ebreu
it is, who is the
fadir of hem,
that is, of the
profetis; as if
he seide, pro-
fesie is not bi
eritage of fa-
dris, but God
ʒyueth profesie
bi his grace, to
whom he wole.
Lire here. c.

ᵂ ʒistai c. ʒistay E.   ˣ hast thou gon E pr. m.   ʸ fadris CE.

ˢ thingis ı.   ᵗ comeli G.   ᵘ gloss omitted in ıx pr. m.   ᵛ sacrifie ı.   ᵂ Om. ı.   ˣ tokens ı.   ʸ Saul and
his child ı.   ᶻ weren metynge with ı.   ᵃ felle anoon upon Saul ı.   ᵇ the prophetis ı.   ᶜ And ı.   ᵈ Saul ı.
ᵉ hath bifalle ı.   ᶠ chosen among the ı.   ᵍ Om. ı.   ʰ the fadir of Saul ı.   ⁱ the prophetis ı.   ᵏ And ı.
ˡ Saulis fadir ı.   ᵐ wenten ı.   ⁿ Om. ı.   ᵒ sche ı.   ᵖ thei A.   ᑫ hem not ıN.   ʳ Sauls ı.   ˢ his uncle ı.
ᵗ Samuel ı.   ᵘ sche ı.   ᵛ But ı.   ᵂ he ı.   ˣ his uncle ı.   ʸ the rewme ı.   ᶻ that ı.

18 and seith to the sones of Yrael, Thes
thingis seith the Lord God of Yrael, Y
haue ladde out Yrael fro Egipt, and Y[z]
haue delyuerde ȝow fro the hoond of
Egipciens, and fro the hoond of alle
19 kyngis that tourmentiden ȝow. Forsothe
ȝe to day han throwun awey ȝoure God,
the which alone saueth ȝow fro alle
yuels, and ȝoure tribulaciouns; and ȝe
han seiden, Nay, but a kyng ordeyn
vpon vs. Nowe thanne stondith before
the Lord bi ȝoure lynagis, and by mey-
20 nees. And Samuel appliede alle the lynagis of Yrael, and the lot felle vpon the
21 lynage of Beniamyn. And he apliede
the lynage of Beniamyn, and the kynredis of hym; and lot felle vpon the kynrede of Metry, and cam vnto Saul, the
sone of Cys. Thanne thei souȝten hym,
22 and he is not founden there. And thei
counseilden after thes thingis the Lord,
forsothe[a] whether he were to come thidre.
And the Lord answerde, Loo! he is hidde
23 at home. And so thei runnen, and token
hym thens; and he stood in the mydil of
the puple, and he was heiȝer than al the
24 puple fro the shuldres and aboue. And
Samuel seith to al the puple, Certis ȝe
seen whom the Lord hath chosun; for
there is noon lijk to hym in al the puple.
And al the puple criede, and seith, Lyue
25 the kyng! Forsothe Samuel spak to the
puple the lawe of the rewme, and wroot
in the book, and leyde vp before the
Lord. And Samuel laft al the puple, eche
26 into her hows; but and Saul wente into
his hows in Gabaath; and wente with
hym a paart of the oost, of whom God
27 hadde towchid the hertis. Forsothe the
sones of Belial seiden, Whether this shal
mowe saue vs? And thei dispysiden
hym, and brouȝten not to hym ȝiftis;
forsothe he feynde, as thouȝ he herde
not.

pide togidere the puple to the Lord in
Masphat; and he seide to the sones of Is- 18
rael, The Lord God of Israel seith these
thingis, Y ledde Israel out of the lond of
Egipt, and Y delyuerede ȝou fro the hond
of Egipcians, and fro the hond of alle
kyngis[a] that turmentiden ȝou. Forsothe[b] 19
to day ȝe han caste awei ȝoure Lord God,
which[c] aloone sauyde ȝou fro alle ȝoure
yuelis and tribulaciouns; and ȝe seiden,
Nay, but ordeyne thou a kyng on[d] vs.
Now therfor stonde ȝe bifor the Lord bi
ȝoure lynagis, and bi[e] meynees. And Sa- 20
muel settide[f] to gidere alle the lynages[ff]
of Israel, and lot felde on[g] the lynage of
Beniamyn. And he settide[h] togidere the 21
lynage of Beniamyn, and the meynees
therof; and lot felde on[i] the meynees[k] of
Mathri †, and it cam 'til to[l] Saul, the son
of Cys. Therfor[m] thei souȝten hym[n], and
he was not foundun there. And aftir 22
these thingis thei counseliden the[o] Lord,
whether Saul schulde come thidur. And
the Lord answeride, Lo! he[p] is hid at
hoom ‡. Therfor thei runnen, and token 23
hym fro thennus; and he[q] stood in the[r]
myddil[s] of the puple, and was[t] hiȝere than
al the puple fro the schulder and 'aboue[u].
And Samuel seide to al the puple, Certis 24
ȝe seen[v] whom the Lord hath chose; for
noon in al the puple is lijk hym. And al
the puple cryede, and seide, Lyue the kyng!
Forsothe[w] Samuel spak to the puple the 25
lawe of rewme[x], and wroot[y] in a book,
and puttide[yy] vp bifor the Lord. And Samuel[z] dilyuerede al the puple, ech man in
to his hows; but also Saul ȝede in to his[a] 26
hous in to[b] Gabaath; and the[c] part of the
oost ȝede with hym, whose hertis God
hadde touchid. Forsothe[d] the sones of 27
Belyal seiden, Whether this man may saue
vs? And thei dispisiden hym, and brouȝten[e]
not ȝiftis, '*that is, preisyngis*[f], to him; forsothe[g] he 'dissymelide hym to here[h].

† *Mathari*, that is, of archeris schetinge to a signe. *Lire here.* C.

‡ *he is hid at hoome;* not in Gabaa, but in the hows in which he was ynned. In Ebreu it is, he is hid among vessels, that is, armeris, ether what euer othere vessels thei puttiden in the yn, for keping. *Lire here.* C.

[z] Om. BCEFH. [a] now E *pr. m.*

[a] the kyngis I. [b] And I. [c] the which I. [d] upon I. [e] Om. I. [f] sette I. [ff] lynage A. [g] upon I. [h] sette I. [i] upon I. [k] meynee I. [l] vnto EIL. [m] Thanne I. [n] Saul I. [o] with the I. [p] Saul I. [q] Saul I. [r] Om. I. [s] myddis I. [t] he was I. [u] upward I. [v] han seen I. [w] And I. [x] the rewme EIKLX. [y] he wroot it I. [yy] putte it I. [z] he I. [a] Om. A. [b] Om. I. [c] a I. [d] And I. [e] thei brouȝten I. [f] *that is, presentis* BNW. Om. CIX *pr. m.* [g] and I. [h] lete as thouȝ he herde not I.

CAP. XI.

1 And it is doon as after a moneth, Naas
Amonite stiede vp, and bigan to fiȝt
aȝens Jabes Galaath. And alle the men
of Jabes seiden to Naas, Haue thow vs
boundun in pees, and we shulen serue to
2 thee. And Naas Amonyte answerde to
hem, In this I shal smyte with ȝou boond
of pees, that I drawe out the riȝt eyen
of ȝow alle, and Y put ȝou reproue in al
3 Yrael. And the eldres of Jabes seiden
to hym, Graunt to vs seuen days, that
we senden messagers to alle the[b] teermes
of Yrael; and if there weren not the
which defende vs, we shulen goon out to
4 thee. Thanne messagers camen inuto Gabaath of Saul, and speken the wordis,
herynge the puple; and al the puple
5 reryde her[c] voys, and wepte. And, loo!
Saul cam, folowynge the oxen fro the
feeld; and seith, What hath the puple,
that he wepith? And thei toolden to
hym the wordis of the men of Jabes.
6 And the Spyrit of the Lord leepe into
Saul, whanne he hadde herd thes wordis,
and the woodnesse of hym wraththid wel
7 mych. And takynge to either oxe he
hewȝ into gobetis, and sente into alle the
teermys of Yrael, bi the hoond of the
messageers, seiynge, Who so euere goth
not out, and hath not folwid Saul and
Samuel, thus shal be doo to the oxen of
hym. Thanne the dreed of the Lord
cauȝte the puple, and thei wenten out as
8 o man. And he noumbrede hem in Be-
seth[d]; and of the sones of Yrael weren
thre hundrid thowsandis; of the men for-
9 sothe of Juda thretti thowsandis. And
thei seiden to the messagers that camen,
So ȝe shulen seie to the men that ben in
Jabes of Galaath, To morwe shal be to
ȝow helth, whanne the sunne hetith.
Thanne the messagerys camen, and

CAP. XI.

1 And it was don as[l] aftir a monethe,
Naas of Amon stiede[k], and bigan[l] to fiȝte
aȝens Jabes of Galaad. And alle the men
of Jabes[m] seiden to Naas, Haue thou vs
boundun in pees, and we schulen serue
thee. And Naas of Amon answeride to
2 hem, In this[n] Y schal smyte boond of pees
with ȝou, that Y putte out the riȝt iȝen of
alle ȝou, and that Y sette[o] ȝou schenschip[p]
in al Israel. And the eldere men of Jabes
3 seiden to him, Graunte thou to vs seuene
daies, that we senden messangeris to alle
the termes[q] of Israel; and if noon be that
defende vs, we schulen go out to thee.
4 Therfor[r] messangeris camen in to Gabaad
of Saul, and spaken these wordis, 'while[s]
the puple herde[t]; and al the puple reiside
her vois, and wepte. And lo! Saul cam,
5 'and suede oxis[u] fro the feeld[v]; and he
seide, What hath the puple, for it wepith?
And thei telden to hym the wordis of
men[w] of Jabes. And the Spirit of the
6 Lord† skippide[x] in to Saul, whanne he
hadde herd these wordis, and his woodnesse[y] was 'wrooth greetli[z]. And he took
7 euer either oxe, and kittide[a] in to gobetis,
and sente[b] in to alle the termes[c] of Israel,
bi the hondis of messangeris; and seide[d],
Who euer goith not out, and sueth not
Saul and Samuel, so it schal be don to
hise oxun. Therfor the drede of the Lord
asailide[e] the puple, and thei ȝeden out as
8 o man. And he[f] noumbride hem in Besech; and thre hundrid thousynd weren[g]
of the sones of Israel; forsothe[h] of the
men of Juda weren thretti thousynde.
And thei seiden to the messangeris that
9 camen, Thus ȝe schulen seie to the men
that ben in Jabes of Galand, To morew‡
schal be helthe to ȝou, whanne the sunne
is hoot. Therfor[i] the messangeris camen,
and telden to the[k] men of Jabes; whiche[l]

† the Spirit of the
Lord, etc.; that
is, the stiring
of strengthe
and of stide-
fastnesse, to
delyuere the
peple bisegid.
Lire here. c.

‡ to morewe;
that is, in tyme
to comynge of
next. Lire
here. c.

b Om. R.   c his E pr. m.   d Reseth A.

i as it were I.   k stiede up I.   l he bigan I.   m the citee Jabes I.   n this thing I.   o putte I.   p to be
reproff I.   q coostis I.   r Thanne I.   s which c.   't heringe the puple I.   u Om. I.   v feild and he suede
oxen I.   w the men I.   x fel anoon I.   y feers wrath I.   z greetli stirid I.   a he kitte hem I.   b he
sente tho I.   c coostis I.   d he seide I.   e wonte into I.   f Saul I.   g weren there I.   h and I.
i Thanne I.   k Om. plures.   l the whiche I. whiche men K.

toolden to the men of Jabes; the whiche
10 weren glad, and seiden, To morwe we
shulen goo out to 3ow, and 3e shulen doo
11 to vs al that shal plese to 3ow And it
is doon, whanne the moiwe was comen,
Saul sette the puple in thre paities, and
he wente into the mydil tentis in the
morwetide watche, and he smoot Amon
'vnto the tyme that the day hetide; forsothe the tother ben scatrid, so that there
weren not laft in hem tweyn togidre
12 And the puple seith to Samuel, Who is
he this, that seide, Saulf shal not regne
vpon vs ? 3if 3e the men, and we shulen
13 slee hem And Saul seith, There shal
not be slayn eny man in this day, for to
day the Lord hath doon helth in Yrael
14 Forsothe Samuel seide to the puple,
Cometh, and goo we into Galgala, and
15 renewe we there the rewme And al the
puple 3ede to Galgala, and thei maden
there Saul a kyng before the Loid in
Galgala; and thei offreden pesyble slayn
saciifice to the Lord And Saul gladdide
theie, and alle the men of Yrael wel
mych

weren glad, and seiden, Eerli we schulen 10
go out to 3ou, and 3e schulen do to vs† al
that plesith 3oun And it was don, whanne 11
the morewe dai cam, Saul ordeynede the
puple in to thre partis, and he entride
in to the myddil tentis 'in the wakyng
of the morewtid, and he smoot Amon til
the dai 'was hoot, 'forsothe the residues
weren scateiid, so that tweyne togidere
weien not left in hem. And the puple 12
seide to Samuel, Who is this, that seide,
Saul schal not regne on vs ? 3yue 3e the
men, and we schulen sle hem And Saul 13
seide, No man schal be slayn in this dai,
for to dai the Lord made helthe in Isiael.
Forsothe Samuel seide to the puple, Come 14
3e, and go we in to Galgala, and ienule we
there the rewme And al the puple 3ede 15
in to Galgala, and there thei maden Saul
kyng bifor the Lord 'in Galgala; and
thei offriden pesible sacrifices bifor the
Lord And Saul was glad there, and alle
the men of Israel greeth

†and 3e schulen do to vs, etc thei seiden this in scorn, for thei wisten that help schal come to hem in the morewe Iire here

CAP XII

1 Forsothe Samuel seide to alle Yrael,
Loo! I haue herd 3oure voys aftir alle
thingis that 3e han spokun to me, and I
2 haue ordeynd vpon 3ou a kyng; and nowe
the kyng goth before 3ow Forsothe Y
haue celdid, and waxen hoor; forsothe
my sones ben with 3ow; also conuer-
saunt before 3ou fro my 3ongth vnto this
3 day Loo! Y am redi; spek 3e to me
before the Lord, and before the crist of
hym, whether oxe of eny man Y took,
or asse, if eny man Y chalengide, if Y
oppresside eny man, if of the hoond of
eny man Y took 3ift, and Y shal dispise
4 it to day, and restore to 3ow And thei

CAP. XII.

Forsothe Samuel seide to al Israel, Lo! 1
Y herde 3oure vois bi alle thingis whiche
3e spaken to me, and Y ordeynede a kyng
on 3ou, and now the kyng goith bifor 2
3ou Sotheli Y wexide eld and hoor;
forsothe my sones ben with 3ou; thei foi
Y lyuyde bifor 3ou fro my 3ong wexynge
age 'til to this dai And lo! Y am redi, 3
speke 3e to me bifoi the Lord, and bifor
'the crist of hym, whether Y took 'the
oxe of ony man, ethei the oxe of ony man, ass; if Y
falsly chalengide ony mou, yf Y oppresside ony man, if Y took 3iftei of 'the hond
of ony man, and Y schal 'dispise it to
dai, and Y schal restore to 3ou And thei 4

‡ if Y took 3ifte, etc, of this it is opin, that hi hise owne costis and trauils, he fillide the office of iuge, as it was seid in vii e Lire here

e al the while F pr m   f the puple A

m seiden to Amon 1   n to 3ou 1   o tijd 1   P in the morewe tijd wacche Saul 1   q tentis of Amon 1
r Om 1   s wexide 1   t and thei that weren left aliue 1   u two men 1   v upon 1   w thoi 1   x men
hidere 1   y hath maad 1   z And 1   a renel EL   b there therinne L   c Om c   d Om 1   e offriden
there 1   f upon 1   g And 1   h haue wexe 1   i and 1   k also 1   l haue lyued 1   m vnto 1   n his
anoyntid or kyng 1   o haue take 1   P ony mans oxe 1   q his 1   r haue falsly 1   s haue oppressid 1
t haue take 1   u ony mans hond 1   v Om plures   w be despised L

seiden, Thow hast not chalengid vs, ne
oppressid, ne takyn eny thing of the
5 hoond of eny man. And he seide to
hem, Witnesse is the Lord aȝens ȝow,
and witnesse the crist of hym in this
day; for ȝe han not founden in myn
hoond eny thing. And thei seiden, Wit-
6 nesse. And Samuel seith to the puple,
The Lord, that made Moysen and Aaron,
and ladde ȝoure fadres fro the loond of
7 Egipt, is nyȝ; now thanne stondith, that
in doom I stryue aȝens ȝow before the
Lord, of alle the mercyes of the Lord,
that he hath done with ȝow, and with
8 ȝoure fadres. What maner wise Jacob
wente into Egipt, and ȝoure fadres crieden to the Lord; and the Lord sente
Moyses and Aaron, and ladde ȝoure fadres out of Egipt, and sette hem in this
9 place. The whiche forȝeten of the Lord,
her God; and he took hem in the hoond
of Cysar[g], mayster[h] of the knyȝthod of
Asor, and in the hoond of Philistiens,
and in the hond of the king of Moab;
10 and thei fouȝten aȝens hem. Forsothe
aftyrward thei cryeden to the Lord, and
seiden, We han synned, for we han forsakun the Lord, and serueden to Baalym
and Astaroth; nowe thanne delyuer vs
fro the hoond of oure enemyes, and we
11 shulen serue to thee. And the Lord sente
Jeroboal, and Bedan, and Barach, and
Jepte, and Samuel; and he delyuerde
ȝow fro the hoond of ȝoure enemyes bi
enuyroun; and ȝe han dwellid trustily.
12 Forsothe seynge that Naas, the kyng of
the sones of Amon, was comen aȝens ȝow,
ȝe seiden to me, Nay, but the kyng shal
comaunde to vs; whanne the Lord ȝour
13 God shulde regne in ȝow. Nowe thanne
ȝoure kyng is redi, whom ȝe han chosen
and askid; loo! the Lord hath ȝeuen to
14 ȝow a kyng. If ȝe dreden the Lord, and

seiden, Thou hast not falsly chalengid vs,
nether hast[x] oppressid *vs*[y], nether hast[z]
take ony thing of 'the hond of ony man[a].
And he[b] seide to hem, The Lord is wit- 5
nesse aȝens ȝou, and his crist[c] is witnesse
in this day; for ȝe han not founde ony
thing in myn hond. And thei seiden†,
Witnesse[d]. And Samuel seide to the 6
puple, The Lord, that made Moises and
Aaron, and ledde[e] ȝoure fadris out of the
lond of Egipt, is present; now therfor 7
stonde ȝe[f], that Y stryue bi doom aȝens
ȝou bifor the Lord, of alle the mercyes of
the Lord, whiche[g] he dide[h] with ȝou, and
with ȝoure fadris. Hou[i] Jacob entride in 8
to Egipt, and ȝoure fadris crieden to the
Lord; and the Lord sente Moises and
Aaron, and ledde ȝoure fadris out of
Egipt, and settide[k] hem in this place.
Whiche[l] forȝaten[m] her Lord God; and he 9
bitook hem in[n] the hond of Sisara, maystir[o] of the chyualrie of Asor, and in the
hond of Filisteis, and in the hond of the[p]
kyng of Moab; and thei[q] fouȝten aȝens
hem. Sotheli[r] afterward[s] thei[t] crieden to 10
the Lord, and seiden, We synneden[u], for
we forsoken the Lord, and seruyden Baalym and Astroth; now therfor delyuere
thou vs fro 'the hond of oure enemyes[v],
and we schulen serue thee. And the Lord 11
sente Gerobaal[w], and 'Bedan, *that is*[x],
Sampson, 'and Barach, and Jepte, and
Samuel, and delyuerede[y] ȝou fro the hond
of ȝoure enemyes bi cumpass; and ȝe[z]
dwelliden tristili[a]. Forsothe[b] ȝe sien, that 12
Naas, kyng[c] of the sones of Amon, cam
aȝens ȝou; and ȝe seiden to me, *counseilynge*[d] *to axe noon other kyng than God,*
Nay, but a kyng schal comaunde to vs;
whanne 'ȝoure Lord God[e] regnede[f] in ȝou.
Now therfor ȝoure kyng is redi, whom ȝe 13
han chose and axid; lo! the Lord ȝaf[g]
to ȝou a kyng. If ȝe dreden the Lord, 14

† *and thei seiden;* in Ebreu it is, *and he seide, Witnesse.* Ebrews expownen thus, that aftir the witnessing of the puple declaringe the innocence of Samuel, he axide herwith Goddis witnessing, and seide, *the Lord is witnesse*, that is, Y preye that he be witnesse; and thanne a voys cam sent fro the Lord, and seide, *Witnesse*, in witnessinge the innocence of Samuel. *Lire here.* C.

g Syȝare E. h the mayster E *pr. m.*

x thou hast EIL. y Om. *plures.* z thou hast EIL. a ony mans hond I. b Samuel I. c crist *or king* I. d He is witnesse I. e that ledde I. f ȝe *forth* I. g that I. h hath do I. i Hou that I. k hath sett I. l The whiche I. m han forȝete I. n in to I. o the maystir I. p Om. DFKOXb. q these I. r And I. s aftir this I. t ȝoure faders I. u han synned I. v our enemyes hond I. w Gerobaal, *that is Gedeon* B *text.* C *marg.* x Om. C. y he delyuerede I. z thanne ȝe I. a sikirly I. b And I. c the kyng I. d *counseilinge ȝou* I. e the Lord ȝoure God I. f schulde regne I. g hath ȝoue I.

serueth to hym, and herith the voys of hym, and whettith not the mouth of the Lord; and ȝe shulen ben, and the kyng that comaundith to ȝow, folowynge the 15 Lord ȝoure God. Forsothe if ȝe heren not the voys of the Lord, but whettith[i] out the word of hym, the hoond of the Lord shal be vpon ȝow, and vpon ȝoure 16 fadres. But nowe stondith, and seeth this greet thing that the Lord is to doo 17 in ȝoure siȝt. Whether not repynge tyme of whete is to day? Y shal inwardly clepe the Lord, and he shal ȝyue voicis, and reynes; and ȝe shulen wite, and seen, for greet yuel ȝe han doo to ȝow in the siȝt of the Lord, askynge vpon ȝow a 18 kyng. And Samuel criede to the Lord, and the Lord ȝaf voicis and reynes in 19 that day. And al the puple dredde wel mych the Lord and Samuel; and al the puple seide to Samuel, Prey for thi ser-uauntis to the Lord thi God, that we dyen not; forsothe we han addid to alle oure synnes yuel, that we asken to vs a 20 kyng. Forsothe Samuel seide to the pu-ple, Wole ȝe not drede; ȝe han doon alle this yuel; neuerthelater[j] wole ȝe not goo awey fro the bak of the Lord, but serueth to the Lord in al ȝoure herte; 21 and wole ȝe not bowe aside after veyn thingis, that shulen not profyt ȝou, ne shulen delyuer ȝou; for veyn thingis thei 22 ben. And the Lord shal not forsake his puple for his greet name; for the Lord hath sworn to make ȝow to hym a puple. 23 Forsothe God sheelde the synne fro me in the Lord, that I ceese to prey for ȝow; and I shal teche ȝow a riȝt weye and 24 good. Therfor dredith the Lord, and serueth to hym in treuth, and of al ȝoure herte; forsothe ȝe han seen the greet dedis, the whiche[k] he hath doon in ȝow; 25 and if ȝe ben stedfast in malice, and ȝe and ȝoure kyng to gidre shulen perishe.

and seruen hym, and heren his vois, and wraththen not the mouth of the Lord[h]†; ȝe and ȝoure kyng, that comaundith to ȝou, schulen sue ȝoure Lord God. For-15 sothe[i] if ȝe heren not the vois of the Lord[k], but wraththen his word, the hond of the Lord schal be on ȝou‡, and on ȝoure fadris. But also now stonde ȝe, and se 16 this gret thing which[l] the Lord schal make[m] in ȝoure siȝt. Whether heruest[n] of 17 whete is not to dai[o]? I schal inwardli clepe the Lord, and he schal ȝyue voices, that is, thundris[p], and reynes; and ȝe schulen wite, and schulen[q] se, for[r] ȝe axynge a kyng on[s] ȝou han[t] do greuouse yuel to ȝou[u] in the siȝt of the Lord. And 18 Samuel criede to the Lord, and the Lord ȝaf voices[v] and reynes in that dai. And 19 al the puple dredde greetli the Lord and Samuel; and al the puple seide to Sa-muel, Preye thou for thi seruauntis to thi Lord God, that we die not; for[w] we addiden[x] yuel to alle oure synnes, that we axiden a kyng to vs. Forsothe[y] Sa-20 muel seide to the puple, Nyle ȝe drede[z]; ȝe han do al this yuel; netheles nyle ȝe go[a] awey fro the bak of the Lord, but serue ȝe the Lord in al ȝoure herte; and 21 nyle ȝe bowe aftir veyn thingis‖, that schulen not profite to[b] ȝou, nether schulen[c] delyuere ȝou; for tho ben veyn thingis. And[d] the Lord schal not forsake his puple 22 for his grete name; for the Lord swoor[e] to make ȝou a puple to hym silf. For-23 sothe[f] this synne be fer fro me in[g] the Lord, that Y ceesse to preye for ȝou; and Y schal teche ȝou a riȝtful weie and good[h]. Therfor drede ȝe the Lord, and serue ȝe[i] 24 hym in treuthe, and of al ȝoure herte; for ȝe sien tho grete thingis, whiche[k] he dide in[l] ȝou; that if ȝe contynuen in malice, 25 bothe ȝe and ȝoure kyng schulen perische togidere.

† that is, the trewe speker of his word. s.

‡ on ȝou; that is, it schal be on ȝou in tyme to comynge, as it was on ȝoure fadris in tyme passid. Lire here. c.

‖ veyn thingis; that is, idols in worschipinge tho, for no myȝt is in tho to saue ȝou. Lire here. c.

i whetten c. j nerthelatere c passim. k that c.

h Lordis mouth 1. i And 1. k ȝoure Lord God 1. l that 1. m do 1. n the heruest 1. o now 1. p or thundris 18. Om. x pr. m. q Om. 1. r that nx. s upon 1. t ȝe han 1. u ȝou silf 1. v thundres 1. w forsothe 1. x han eechid 1. y And 1. z Drede ȝe not 1. a go ȝe not 1. b Om. 1. c thei schulen 1. d And thanne 1. e hath swore 1. f And 1. g aȝens 1. h a good 1. i serueth 1. k that 1. l hath do to 1.

CAP. XIII.

1 A sone of o ȝeer was Saul whanne he began to regne; forsothe two ȝeer he 2 regnede vpon Irael. And Saul chees to hym thre thowsandis of Yrael, and there weren 'in Machynas¹ with Saul two thowsandis¹¹, in the hil of Bethel; forsothe a thowsand with Jonatha in Gabaa Beniamyn; forsothe the tother puple he sente 3 aȝen echon into her tabernaclis. And Jonathas smoot the stacioun of Philistiens, that was in Gabaa. The which thing whanne Philistyens hadden herd, Saul criede with a trompe in al the loond, 4 seiynge, Heren the Ebrewis. And al Yrael herde siche a maner loos, Saul hath smyten the stacioun of Philistiens; and Yrael arcride him aȝens the Philistiens; thanne the puple criede after Saul 5 in Galgala. And Philistiens ben gedrid to fiȝt aȝens Yrael; thretti thousandis of charys, and sexe thousandis of horsmen, and the tother comoun, as mych grauel that is in brenk of the see; and thei stiynge vp setten tentis 'in Machynasᵐ, at 6 the este of Bethauen. The which thing whanne the men of Yrael hadden seen, hem seluen in streit set, forsothe the puple was tourmentid, and thei hiddenᵐᵐ hem self in dennys, and in hidils, in stonys forsothe, and in dichis, and in cysternes. 7 Forsothe Hebrewis passiden Jordanⁿ, the loond of Gad, and of Galaad. And whanne ȝit Saul was in Galgala, al the puple is 8 feerd thatⁿⁿ folwide hym. And he abood Samuel seuen days 'after the conenauntᵒ, and Samuel cam not in Galgala; and theᵖ 9 puple is slyden fro hym. Thanne seith Saul, Bryngith to me brent sacrifice and

CAP. XIII.

Saul was a childᵐ of o ȝeer† whanne he 1 bigan to regne; forsotheⁿ he regnede onᵒ Israel twei ȝeer‡. And Saul chees to 2 hym thre thousyndeᵖ of Israel, and twei thousyndeᵠ weren with Saul in Machynas, in the hil of Bethel; forsotheʳ a thousynde weren with Jonathas in Gabaath of Beniamyn; sotheliˢ heᵗ sente aȝen the tother puple ech man in toᵘ 'hise tabernaclisᵛ. And Jonathas smoot the staciounʷ‖ 3 of Filisteis, that was in Gabaa. And whanne Filisteisˣ hadden herd thisʸ, Saul sownede with a clarioun in al the lond, and seide, Ebreysᶻ hereᵃ. And al Israel herde 4 siche a fame, Saul smootᵇ the staciounᶜ of Filisteis; and Israel reisideᵈ hym silf aȝens Filisteisᵉ; therforᶠ the puple criede after Saul in Galgala. And Filisteisᵍ 5 weren gaderidʰ to fiȝte aȝens Israel; 'of Filisteis werenⁱ thretti thousyndeᵍ of charisʲ, and sixe thousyndeᵏ of knyȝtisˡ, and the tother comyn puple, asᵐ grauelⁿ 'which is fulᵒ myche in the brynke of the see; and thei stiedenᵖ, and settiden tentisᵠ in Machynas, at the eestʳ of Bethauen. And 6 whanne men of Israel hadden seyn thisˢ, that thei weren set in streiȝtnesseᵗ, forᵘ the puple was turmentid, thei hidden hem silf in dennes, and in priuey places, and in stonys, and in dychis, and in cisternes. Sotheliᵛ Ebreisʷ passidenˣ Jordan in toᵞ 7 the lond of Gad and of Galaad. And whanne Saul was ȝit in Galgala, al the puple was aferd that suede hym. And 8 seuene daies heʸ abood Samuel bi couenaunt, and Samuel cam not in to Galgala; and the puple ȝede awei fro Saul. Therfor 9 Saul seide, Brynge ȝe to me brent sacri-

† a child of o ȝeer; that is, so innocent and cleene of synne [as] a child of o ȝeer. c.

‡ regnede on Israel by it. ȝeer; that is, in his goodnesse and innocence, thouȝ he regnede in mo ȝeris whille he was in malice; ether aftir ii. ȝeer of Saul, Dauyth was chosun of God in to kyng, and anoyntyd of Samuel, as it is had in xvi. c°., and fro that tyme Saul regnede not biriȝt, but onely bi tyrauntrie, and therfor the ȝeris seyng ben kit awey here fro his rewme. Lire here. c.

‖ stacioun, that is, forselet, ether strong hold. c.

§xxx. thousinde, that is, of men fiȝtinge in charis. Lire here. c.

---

l in to engines E *pr. m.*   ll thousende c.   m in to engines E *pr. m.*   mm hadden B.   n *Sic codd. omnes.* nn and *ABFH.*   o aftyr Samuel plesid E *pr. m.*   p al the E *pr. m.*

m sone I.   n and I.   o upon I.   p thousynde *men* K.   q thousynde *of hem* I.   r and I.   s and I. t Saul I.   u Om. D.   v his tabernacle K *sec. m.* EL.   w standurt I.   x the Filisteis I.   y that I.   z ȝe men of Ebrewe I.   a here ȝe I.   b hath smyten I.   c standart I.   d reiside up I.   e the Filisteis I.   f thanne I. g the Filisteis I.   h gaderid to gidre I.   i Om. I.   j charis, that is, of men fiȝtinge in charis B. k hundrid thousynde I.   l horsmen I.   m *was* as the I.   n grauel of the see I.   o Om. I.   p stieden up I. q her tentis I.   r eest coost I.   s Om. I.   t the streiȝtnesse o.   u and that I.   v And I.   w the men of Ebrew I.   x passiden ouer I.   y Saul I.

pesible*q*; and he offrede brent sacrifice.
10 And whanne offrynge he hadde fulfillid the brent sacrifice, loo! Samuel cam; and Saul wente out to mete hym, for to
11 salute hym. And Samuel spak to hym, What hast thou doon? Saul answerde, For I saw3 that the puple shulde slyde awey fro me, and thou cam not after the couenauntid*r* dais; forsothe the Philistyens weren gedryd into Machy-
12 nas*s*; Y seide, Nowe Philistiens shulen come to me in Galgala, and the face of the Lord I haue not plesid; thur3 nede constreined Y haue offrid*t* brent sacry-
13 fice to the Lord. And Samuel seide to Saul, Folily thow hast doon, ne thou hast kept the heestis of the Lord thi God, the whiche he hath comaundid to thee; the which thing if thou haddist not doon, ri3t nowe the Lord hadde maad redi thi kyngdom vpou Yrael into with-
14 outen ende; but thi kyngdom shal no more ryse togidre. Thanne the Lord sou3te a man after his herte; and the Lord hath comaundid to hym, that he were a duyk vpon his puple, forthi that thou hast not kept the thingis that the
15 Lord comaundide. Forsothe Samuel roos, and stiede vp fro Galgalis in Gabaa of Beniamyn; and the tother puple stieden vp after Saul, metynge to the puple that ouercamen hem; comynge fro Galgala in Gabaa, in the hil of Beniamyn. And Saul noumbrede the puple, that weren foundun with hym as sixe hundryd men.
16 And Saul, and Jonathas his sone, and the puple that was foundun with hem, was in Gabaa of Beniamyn; forsothe Philistiens seeten togidre 'into aspijs*n*, for
17 to fi3ten. And there wenten out for to fi3te fro the tentys of Philistiens thre cumpanyes; o cumpanye wente a3ens the weye of Effraym to the loond of Saul;

fice, and pesible sacrifices*z*; and he offride brent sacrifice. And whanne he hadde
10 endid offrynge brent*a* sacrifice, lo! Samuel cam; and Saul 3ede out a3ens hym*b*, to greete Samuel*c*. And Samuel spak*d* to
11 hym*e*, What hast thou do? Saul an- sweride, For*f* Y si3 that the puple 3ede awei fro me, and thou camest not bi the daies of couenaunt; certis*g* Filisteis weren gaderid*h* in Machynas; Y seide, Now Fi-
12 listeis schulen come doun to me in to Gal- gala, and Y haue not plesyd the face of the Lord; Y was compellid bi nede, and Y offryde brent sacrifice to the Lord. And
13 Samuel seide to Saul, Thou hast do folili, and thou 'keptist not*i* the heestis of thi Lord God, whiche he comaundide to thee; and if thou haddist not do this thing, ri3t now the Lord hadde maad redi thi rewme on*k* Israel with outen ende†; but thi
14 rewme schal not rise*l* ferthere*m*. The Lord hath sou3t a man to hym silf after his herte; and the Lord comaundide*n* to hym, that he schulde be duyk on his puple, for thou keptist not tho thingis whiche the Lord comaundide. Forsothe*o* Samuel roos,
15 and stiede*p* fro Galgala in to Gabaa of Beniamyn; and the 'residue puplis*q* sti- eden*r* after Saul a3ens the puple which*s* fou3ten a3ens hem; and thei camen fro Galgala in to Gabaa, in the hil of Benia- myn. And Saul noumbride the puple, that weren foundun with hym as sixe*t* hundrid men. And Saul, and Jonathas
16 his sone, and the puple that was foundun with hem, was in Gabaa of Beniamyn; forsothe*u* Filisteis*v* saten togidere in Ma- chynas. And thre cumpanyes 3eden out
17 of the 'castels of Filisteis*w* to take prey; o cumpany 3ede a3ens the weie of Effraym‡ to the lond of Saul; sothely*x* an other
18 cumpeny entride bi the weie of Bethoron; forsothe*y* the thridde cumpenye turnede it

14 † with outen ende; that is, if thou haddist not do a3enus Goddis heest, and haddist stonde in the goodnesse in which thou were, whanne thou bigannst to regne, thou were disposid, that the rewme schulde be con- fermed to thee and to thi sones; netheles this confermy- yng schal be vndurstodun vndur a condi- cioun, if Saul and hise diris stoden in good-*16* nesse, which is chaungeable. Lire here. c.

‡ of Effraym; in Ebreu it is, a3enus the weye of Effmta to the lond of Saul. c.

q pesible thyngus E pr. m.　　*r* desirid E pr. m.　　*s* fi3tys E pr. m.　　*t* Om. A.　　*u* into aspies B pr. m. in Machinas sec. m. correxit eadem manus in to aspies.

z offringis 1.　*a* the brent 1.　*b* Samuel 1.　*c* him 1.　*d* seide 1.　*e* Saul 1.　*f* Lo! for 1.　*g* and the 1. *h* gaderid to gidre 1.　*i* hast not kept 1.　*k* upon 1.　*l* rise to gidre 1.　*m* ferthermore with thee, for thou hast lost iust tijtle 1.　*n* hath comaundid 1.　*o* And 1.　*p* stiede up 1.　*q* peple that lefte 1.　*r* wenten up 1.　*s* that 1.　*t* a sixe 1.　*u* and 1.　*v* the Filisteis 1.　*w* Filisteis tentis 1.　*x* and 1.　*y* and 1.

18 forsothe another wente bi the weye of Betheron; forsothe the thridde turnede hem to the weye of the teerme in^v the loond of Saba, 'stondynge nyȝ to the^w 19 valey of Seboym aȝens the deseert. Forsothe there was not an yren smith foundun in al the loond of Yrael; forsothe Philistiens shunneden, lest perauenture the Hebrews maden swerd or speer. 20 Thanne al Yrael descendide to Philistiym, that echon sharpe his shaar, and diggyng 21 yren, and axe, and purgyng hook; for eggys of the sharis, and of diggynge^x yrens, and of forkis, and of the axis 22 weren blunt, vnto a prik to menden. And whanne the day of the batayl was comen, there is not founden swerd and speer in hoond of the^y puple that was with Saul and Jonatha, out takun Saul, and 23 Jonatha hys sone. Forsothe the stacioun of Philistym^z wente out, for to stye ouer into aspijs to fiȝt.

CAP. XIV.

1 And it felle on a day, that Jonathas, the sone of Saul, seide to the ȝong man his squyer, Com, and goo we to the stacioun of Philistyens, that is biȝonde that place; to his fader forsothe that same 2 thing he shewide not. Forsothe Saul dwellide in the vttermoost parti of Gabaa, vndur a poomgarnet tree, that was in 'the feeld of Gabaa^a; and there was a puple with hym as of sexe hundred men. 3 And Achias, the sone of Achitob, the brother of Ychabod, the sone of Phynees, that was comen of Hely, the preest of the Lord in Silo, beere the prestis coope; but and the puple knewe not whider Jona- 4 thas was goon. Forsothe there weren bytwixe^b the stiyngis vp, bi the whiche

---

silf to the weie of the terme in the lond of Sabaa; and that^z terme neiȝeth^a to the valey of Seboym aȝens the deseert. For- 19 sothe^b 'no smyȝth of yrun^c was foundun in al the lond of Israel; for Filisteis^d 'weren war, *ether*^e *eschewiden*, lest perauenture Ebreis^f maden a^g swerd ether a^h spere. Therfor al Israel ȝede doun to Fi- 20 listeisⁱ, that ech man schulde scharpe his schar, and picoise^k, and ax^l, 'and sarpe^m; 'and soⁿ alle egis^o weren bluntid^p 'of 21 scharris^q, and of picoisis^r, and of 'forkis of thre teeth^s, and of axis, 'til to^t a pricke to be amendid. And whanne the dai of 22 batel cam, no swerd andⁿ spere was foundun in the hond of al the puple that was with Saul and Jonathas, outakun Saul^v, and Jonathas his sone. Forsothe^w 23 the stacioun^x of Filisteis^y ȝede out, that it schulde passe in to Machynas.

CAP. XIV.

And it bifelde in a day, that Jonathas, 1 the sone of Saul, seide to his squyer, a ȝong man, Come thou, and passe we^z to the staciouns^a of the Filisteis, which^b is biȝende that place; 'sotheli he^c schewide not this same thing to his fadir. Sotheli^d 2 Saul dwellide in the laste part of Gabaa, vndur a pumgarnarde tre, that was in the feeld of Gabaa; and the puple as of sixe^e hundrid men was with^f hym. And Achias, 3 sone^g of Achitob, brother of Icaboth, sone^g of Fynees, that was gendrid of Ely, preest^h of the Lord in Silo, bar ephodⁱ, 'that is^k, the^l preestis cloth^m; but also the puple wiste not whidur Jonathas haddeⁿ go. Sotheli^o bitwixe the stiyngis^p, bi whiche^q 4 Jonathas enforside to passe to the sta-

---

^v of E pr. m.   ^w of the heȝe E pr. m.   ^x the diggynge CE.   ^y al the CE.   ^z Filisteys c.   ^a Magron E pr. m.   ^b bytween BFH. between E. betwe c. pass.

^z the ABC.   ^a neiȝede I. noiyed L.   ^b And I.   ^c noon yren smith I.   ^d the Filisteis I.   ^e Om. I.   ^f the Ebreis I.   ^g Om. DIKOXb.   ^h Om. DEIKLOPSX.   ⁱ the Filisteis I.   ^k his picoise I.   ^l his ax I.   ^m Om. DGKMNOSXb. and his kuttinge hook I.   ⁿ for I.   ^o the egis of her scharris I.   ^p blunt I.   ^q Om. I.   ^r her picoises I.   ^s her thre tothid forkis I.   ^t vnto I.   ^u ne CEIO pr. m.   ^v Sauls I.   ^w And I.   ^x standart I.   ^y the Filisteis I.   ^z we forth I.   ^a standart I.   ^b that I.   ^c and Jonathas I.   ^d And I.   ^e a sixe I.   ^f there with I.   ^g the sone I.   ^h the preest I.   ⁱ the ephod I.   ^k or I.   ^l Om. M.   ^m cope I. the whole gloss omitted in X.   ⁿ was I.   ^o And I.   ^p stiyngis up I.   ^q the whiche I.

Jonathas enforside to goo to the sta-
cyouns of Philistiens, hei3e stonys on
either side, and as in maner of teeth litle
rochis hens and thens before brokun;
name to the oon Boosez, and to the
5 tother the name Sene; o litil roche ful
hee3 at the north a3ens Machynas° to
fi3ten, and another at the south a3ens
6 Gabaa. Jonathas forsothe seide to the
3oug man his squyer, Come, and passe
we to the stacioun of thes vncercumci-
dide, if perauenture the Lord do for vs;
for it is not to the Lord hard to saue, or
7 in many or in fewe. And his squyer
seide to hym, Do alle thingis that plesen
to thin inwit; go whider thow coueytist,
I shal be with thee where euere thou
8 wolt. And Jonathan seith, Loo! we goon
to thes men; and whanne we aperen to
9 hem, if this maner thei spoken to vs,
Dwel 3e, to the tyme that we comen to
3ou; stondeᵈ weᵉ in oureᶠ place, ne stye
10 we vp to hem. Forsothe if thei seyn,
Stye 3e vp to vs; stye we vp, for the Lord
hath takun hem in oure hoondis; this
11 shal be to vs a tokne. And so eitherᵍ
aperide to the stacioun of Philistiens;
and Philistiens seiden, Loo! the Hebrewis goon out fro the caues, in the
12 whiche thei weren hid. And the men
speken fro the stacioun to Jonathan and
to his squyer, and seiden, Stieth vp to vs,
and we shulen shewe 3ou a thing. And
Jonathas seith to his squier, Stie we,
folwe me; forsothe the Lord hath taken
13 hem into the hoondis of Yrael. Forsothe
Jonathas styede crepynge with hoondis
and feet, and his squyer after hym; and
whanne thei hadden seen the face of
Jonathan, other fellen before Jonathan,
other his squyer slow3, folowynge hym.
14 And the first veniaunce is doon, the
which smoot Jonathas and the squyer of

cioun of Filisteis, weren stonys stondynge forth on euer either side, and scarris
brokun bifore bi the maner of teeth on
ech syde; name to oonʳ was Boses, and
name to 'the totherˢ was Sene; o scarre⁵
was stondynge forth to the north a3ens
Machynas, and the tother scarre to the
south a3ens Gabaa. Forsotheᵗ Jonathas⁶
seide to his 3ong squyer, Come thou, passe
we to the stacioun of theseᵘ vncircumcisid
men, if in hap the Lord do for vs; for it
is not hard to the Lord to saue, ethir in
manye ethir in fewe. And his squyer⁷
seide to hym, Do thou alle thingis that
plesenᵛ thi soule; go whidur thou coueitist, Y schal be with thee, where euer
thou wolt. And Jonathas seide, Lo! we⁸
passen to these men; and whanne we apperen to hem, if thei speken thus to vs,⁹
Dwelle 3eʷ, til we comen to 3ou; stonde
we in oure place, and stie we not toˣ
hem. Sotheliʸ if thei seien, Stye 3eᶻ to vs;¹⁰
stie weᵃ, for the Lord hath bitake hem inᵇ
oure hondis; this schal be a signeᶜ to vs.
'Therfor euerᶜᶜ either apperide to the sta-¹¹
ciounᵈ of Filisteisᵉ; and Filisteisᵉ seiden,
Lo! Ebreisᶠ goen out of caues, in whiche
thei weren hid. And men of the staciounᵍ¹²
spaken to Jonathas and to his squyer, and
seiden, Stie 3eʰ to vs, and we schulen
schewe to 3ou a thing. And Jonathas
seide to his squyer, 'Stie weⁱ, sue thou
me; for the Lord hath bitake hem in to
the hondis of Israel. Forsotheᵏ Jonathas¹³
stiedeˡ crepynge on hondis and feet, and
his squyer after hym; and whanne theiᵐ
hadden seyn the face of Jonathas, summe
felden doun bifor Jonathas, hisⁿ squier
killed othere, and suedeᵒ hym. And the¹⁴
firste woundeᵖ was maadᵈ, whichʳ Jonathas
and his squyer smootˢ, as of twentiᵗ menᵘ,
in 'the myddil part of lond whichᵛ a peire
of oxun was wont to ere in theʷ dai. And¹⁵

° the aspies ε pr. m.   ᵈ and stonde ε pr.m.   ᵉ 3e ε pr.m.   ᶠ 3oure ε pr.m.   ᵍ he ε pr.m.

ʳ that oon ɪ. the toon ᴋ.   ˢ that other ɪ.   ᵗ And ɪ.   ᵘ this ᴄ.   ᵛ plesith ᴀ.   ʷ 3e
stille ɪ.   ˣ up to ɪ.   ʸ And ɪ.   ᶻ 3e up ɪ.   ᵃ we up to hem ɪ.   ᵇ in to ᴋ.   ᶜ token ɪ.   ᶜᶜ And so ɪ.
Therfor ᴋ.   ᵈ standart ɪ.   ᵉ the Filisteis ɪ.   ᶠ the Ebreis ɪ.   ᵍ stacioun of Philistees ɪ.   ʰ 3e up ɪ.
ⁱ Wende we up to hem ɪ.   ᵏ And ɪ.   ˡ stiede up ɪ.   ᵐ the Philistees ɪ.   ⁿ and his ɪ.   ᵒ he suede ɪ.
ᵖ veniaunce ɪ.   ᵈ don ɪ.   ʳ the which ɪ.   ˢ killide ɪ.   ᵗ Om. ᴄ.   ᵘ thousynd men ᴅ pr. m. ɪᴋᴍɴᴏǫxb.
Om. ᴄ.   ᵛ space of the erthe that ɪ.   ʷ o ɪ.

hym as of twenti thousand[h] men, in the half party of an akir that a peyre of
15 oxen in a day is wont to ere. And a myracle is doon in the tentis, bi the feeldys, but and al the puple of the stacioun of hem that weren at robbynge, wexe astonyed, and the tentis ben disturblid; and it felle as a myracle fro
16 God. And the weyters of Saul, that weren in Gabaa of Beniamyn, bihelden, and, loo! a multitude throwun doun, and
17 hidir and thider down fleynge. And Saul seith to the puple that weren with hym, Enserchith, and lokith, who ȝede awey fro vs. And whanne thei hadden souȝt, it is founden not[i] to be neeȝ Jona-
18 thas and his squyer. And Saul seith to Achyam, Applye the arke of 'the Lord[k]; forsothe the arke of God was there in
19 that day with the sonys of Israel. And whanne Saul spak to the preest, greet noyse is out sprongen in the tentis of Philistyen; and it wexe litilmele, and cleerliker it sownyde. And Saul seith to the preest, Withdrawe thin hoond.
20 Thanne Saul and the puple that was with hym criede togidre; and thei camen to the place of the strijf, and, loo! the swerd of echon was turned to his neiȝbour, and a greet slauȝter wel
21 mych. But and the Hebrewis that weren with Philistiens ȝistirday[l] and bifore ȝisterdai, and[m] stieden vp with hem in the tentis, ben turned for to ben with Yrael, that weren with Saul and Jonatha.
22 Forsothe alle the[nm] Iraelitis, the whiche hadden hid hem silf in the hil of Effraym, herynge that Philistiens weren flowen, felawshipten hem seluen with hem[n] in the batayl, and weren with Saul as twenti
23 thousandis of men. And the Lord sauyde Irael in[o] that day. Forsothe the fiȝt camen

a myracle was don in the castels[x], and bi the[y] feeldis, but also al the puple of the[z] 'stacioun of hem[a] that ȝeden out to take prey, dredde, and 'the castels[b] weren disturblid; and it bifelde as a myracle of God. And aspyeris[c] of Saul bihelden[d],
16 that weren in Gabaa of Beniamyn, and lo! a multitude cast[e] doun, and fleynge
17 awei hidur and thidur. And Saul seide to the puple that weren with hym, Seke ȝe, and se ȝe, who ȝede awei fro vs. And whanne thei hadden souȝt, it was foundun, that Jonathas and his squyer weren not present. And Saul seide to Achias,
18 Brynge[f] the arke of the Lord; for the arke of God was there in that dai[g] with the sones of Israel. And whanne Saul
19 spak to the preest, a grete noise roos in the castelis[h] of Filisteis[i]; and it encresside litil and litil, and sownede[k] cleerliere[j]. And Saul seide to the preest, Withdraw thin hond. Therfor[m] Saul criede, and al the
20 puple[n] that was with hym; and thei camen 'til to[o] the place of batel, and, lo! the swerd of ech man[p] was turned to his neiȝbore, and a ful grete sleynge[q] was. But also Ebreis[r] that weren with Filisteis
21 ȝistirday and the thridde dai ago, and hadde stied[s] with hem in[t] castels[u], turneden aȝen to be with Israel[v], that weren with Saul and Jonathas. Also alle men[w]
22 of Israel, that hadden hid hem silf in the hil of Effraym, herden that Filisteis[x] hadden fled; and thei felouschipiden hem silf with her men in batel, and as ten[y] thousynde of men weren with Saul. And the
23 Lord sauyde Israel in that day. Sotheli[z] the batel cam til[a] to Bethauen. And men[b] of Israel weren felouschipid[c] to hem silf in that dai; forsothe[d] Saul swoor† to the puple, and seide, Cursid be the man, that etith breed 'til to[e] euentid[f], tils 'Y venge

h Om. b sec. m.   i Om. abfii.   k God b.   l ȝistai ce.   m thei a.   mm Om. a.   n theiris c.
o and in e.

x Philistees tentis i.   y her i.   z Om. gqb.   a Philistees stacioun i.   b her tentis i.   c the aspyeris i.
d bihelden this doyng i.   e of Philistees was cast i.   f Bryng hidere i.   g tyme i.   h tentis i.   i the Filisteis i.   k it sownede i.   l more clerly i.   m Thanne i.   n multitude i.   o vnto i. into el.
p mannes i.   q slauȝtere ther i.   r the Ebreis i.   s stied up i.   t in to k.   u her tentis i.   v the men of Israel i.   w the men cr.   x the Filisteis i.   y a ten i.   twenti kxeq.   z And i.   a in el.   b the men i.   c socied i.   d and i.   e vnto i. into el.   f the euentid i. euetide e.   g til the tyme that i.

24 vnto Bethauen. And men of Yrael ben
felawshipt to hem seluen in that day;
forsothe Saul swore to the puple, sey-
ynge, Cursid be^p the man that etith breed
vnto euen, to the tyme that I be vengid
25 of myn enemyes. And al the puple eete
no breed. And alle the comouns of the
loond camen into a^q wast wody place,
in the which was hony on the face of
26 the feeld. And so al the puple wente
into the place of hei3e trees, and there
apperide flowyng hony; and no man
appliede the hond^r to his mouth; for-
27 sothe the puple dredde the ooth. Forsothe Jonathas herde not, whanne his
fadre swore to the puple; and he strau3t
out the cop of the 3eerde, that he hadde
in the hoond, and he wette into the hony
combe; and he turnede his hoond to his
mouth, and the eyen of hym ben li3tned.
28 And answerynge oon of the puple seith,
Thi fader hath constreynyd the puple
with ooth, seiynge, Cursid be^s the man
that etith breed to day. Forsothe the
29 puple faylide. And Jonathas seide, My
father hath disturblid the loond; 3oure
self han seen, for myn eyen ben li3tned,
forthi that Y taastide a litil of this hony;
30 myche more if the puple hadde eeten of
the prei3e of her enemyes, that thei
foonden; whether not more veniaunce
31 hadde be doo in Philistees^t? Thanne thei
smyten in that day the Philistees^{tt} fro
32 the place of engynes vnto Hailon. Doun
weried is the puple wel miche; and
turned to the praye, took sheep, and oxen,
and calues, and slewen in the lond; and
33 the puple eete with blood. And thei
toolden to Saul, seiynge, that the puple
hadde synned to the Lord, etynge with
blood. The which seith, 3e han trespasside; turneth to me ry3t nowe a greet

me^h of myn enemyes. And al the puple 25
ete notⁱ breed^k. And al the comyn puple
of the lond cam in to a forest, in which
was hony^l on the 'face of ^m erthe. And 26
so the puple entride in to the forest, and
flowynge^o hony apperide^p; and no man
puttide^q hond^r to his mouth^s, for the puple dredde the ooth. Forsothe^t Jonathas 27
herde not, whanne his fadir swoor^u to the
puple; and he^v helde forth the ende of a
litil 3erde, whiche^w he hadde^x in the^y hond,
and dippide^z in to 'a coomb of hony^a; and
he turnede his hond to his mouth, and
hise i3en weren li3tned. And oon of the 28
puple answeride, and seide, Thi fader boond
the puple with an ooth, and seide, Cursid
be the man that etith breed to dai. For-
sothe^b the puple was feynt. And Jonathas 29
seide, My fadir hath^c disturblid the lond;
3e sien, that myn i3en ben li3tned, for Y
tastide a litil of this hony; hou myche 30
more if the puple hadde ete the^d prey of
hise^e enemyes, which^f 'prey it^g foond;
whether not gretter veniaunce hadde be
maad in Filisteis? Therfore thei smyt- 31
iden^h Filisteis in that dai fro Machynas
'til in toⁱ Hailon. Forsothe^k the puple was
maad ful wery; and the puple turnede 32
to prey^l, and took^m scheep and oxun, and
calues; and thei killiden inⁿ the erthe;
and the puple eet^o with blood. And thei^p 33
telden to Saul, and seiden, that the puple
etynge with blood hadde synned to the
Lord. And Saul seide, 3e han trespassid;
walewe 3e^q to me 'ri3t now^r a greet stoon.
And Saul seyde, 'Be 3e spred^s abrood in to 34
the comyn puple, and seie 3e to hem, that
ech man brynge to me his oxe and ram^t;
and sle 3e on^u this stoon, and ete 3e^v, and
3e schulen not do synne to the Lord, 'and
ete^w with blood. Therfor^x al the puple
brou3te ech man an oxe in his hond 'til

---

p Om. BCEFH.   q Om. ABFH.   r hony ABFH.   s Om. BCEFH.   t the Philistees BCEFH.   tt Phistees A.

h Y be vengid I.   i no ELO pr. m.   k breed til that tyme I.   l hony aboue I.   m Om. I.
o Om. I.   p apperide there flowynge I.   q putte I.   r his hond I.   s mouth therof I.   t And I.   u forbede
this I.   v Jonathas I.   w that I.   x heelde I.   y his I.   z he dippide it I.   a an honycombe I.   b And I.
c bi this heest hath I.   d of the DGIKMNOQSWXb.   e her I.   f that I.   g thei I.   h smytyn c. smeten LP.
smitten E.   i vnto L.   into L.   k And I.   l take prey I.   m it took I.   n these beestis vpon I.   o eet the
fleishe I.   p men I.   q 3e anoon I.   r Om. I.   s Go 3e forth I.   t his wether I.   u tho vpon I.   v 3e
hem I.   w etynge hem I.   x And so I.

34 stoon. And Saul seide, Beth ȝe scatered
into the comouns, and seyeᵘ ȝe to hem,
that echon brynge to me his oxe and
wether; and sleeth vpon it, and etith,
and ȝe shulen not synne to the Lord,
etynge with blood. And so al the puple
brouȝte echon an oxe in his hoond vnto
35 nyȝt, and thei slowen there. And Saul
bildide vp an auter to the Lord; and
thanne first he bigan to bilde an auter
36 to the Lord. And Saul seide, Falle we
vpon the Philistyens bi nyȝt, and waste
we hem vnto the morwetide liȝt; ne
leeue we of hem a man. And the puple
seide, Al that good is seen to thee in
thin eyen, do. And the preest seith,
37 Neiȝ we hider to God. And Saul coun-
seylide the Lord, seiynge, Whether shal
Y pursue Philistiym, if thou taake hem
into the hoondis of Yrael? And he an-
38 swerde not to hym in that day. And
Saul seide, Aplieth hidir alle the corners
of the puple, and witith, and seeth, bi
39 whom fallith this synne to day. The
Lord the saueour of Yrael lyueth; for
if bi Jonathan my sone it is doon, with
out aȝen drawynge he shal die. To the
which no man aȝen seide to hym of al
40 the puple. And he seide to al Yrael, Be
ȝe seuerd into o parti, and Y with Jonathan my sone shal be in o parti. And
the puple answerde to Saul, That good
41 is seen in thin eyen, do. And Saul seide
to the Lord God of Irael, Lord God of
Yrael, ȝyue dom, what is, that thou an-
swerst not to thi seruaunt to day? If
in me, or in Jonathan my sone, is this
wickidnes, ȝyf shewynge; and if this
wickidnes is in thi puple, ȝif holynes.
And Jonathas and Saul benᵛ taken; for-
42 sothe the puple ȝede out. And Saul seith,
Leyeth lot betwixᵂ me and Jonathan my
43 sone. And Jonathas is taken. Forsothe

toʸ nyȝt, and thei killidenᶻ there. Sotheliᵃ 35
Saul bildideᵇ an auter to the Lord; and
thanne firste he bigan to bilde an auter to
the Lord. And Saul seide, Falle we onᶜ 36
the Filisteis in the nyȝt, and wasteᵈ we
hem til the morewtid schyne; and leeue
we not of hem a man. And the puple
seide, Do thou al thing that semeth good
to thee in thin iȝen. And the preest seide,
Neiȝe we hidur to God. And Saul coun- 37
selideᵉ the Lord, and seide, Whether Y
schal pursue Filisteisᶠ? whether thou schalt
bitake hem in to the hondis of Israel?
And the Lord answeride not to him in
that dai. And Saul seide, Brynge ȝe 38
hidur alle the cornerisᵍ of the puple, and
wite ȝe, and seʰ, bi whom this synne
bifeldeⁱ to dai. The Lord sauyourᵏ of Is- 39
rael lyueth; for if 'it isˡ don bi Jonathas
my sone, he schal die with out aȝen drawyng. At whichᵐ *ooth* no man of al the
puple aȝenseide hymⁿ. And he seide to al 40
Israel, Be ȝe departid in to o part, and Y
with my sone Jonathas schal be in the
tothir part. And the puple answeride to
Saul, Do thou that, that semeth good in
thin iȝen. And Saul seide to the Lord 41
God of Israel, Lord God of Israel, ȝyue
thou doom, what isᵒ, that thou answerist
not to dai to thi seruaunt†? If this wickid-
ness is in me, etherᵖ in Jonathas my
sone, ȝyueᑫ thou schewyngʳ; ether if this
wickidnesse is in thiˢ puple, ȝyue thou
hoolynesse. And Jonathas was takun,
and Saulᵗ; forsotheⁿ the puple ȝede out.
And Saule seide, Sende ȝe lot bitwixe me 42
and Jonathas my sone. And Jonathas
was takun 'bi lotᵛ. Forsotheᵂ Saul seide 43
to Jonathas, Schewe thou to me, what
thou didist. And Jonathas schewide to
hym, and seide, Y tastynge tastide a litil
ofˣ hony 'in the ende of the ȝerdeʸ, that
was in myn hond; and lo! Y dieǂ. And 44

† Fro this word, to thi seruaunt, al that sooth till aftir this word, ȝyue thou hoolynesse, is not in Ebreu, nether is of the text. Lire here. c.

‡ lo Y die; with out resonable cause. Lire here. c.

ᵘ seith BEFII.   ᵛ is BCEFII.   ᵂ betwen BEFII. betwe c.

ʸ vnto the I. into EL.   ᶻ killiden hem I.   ᵃ And I.   ᵇ bildide there I.   ᶜ upon I.   ᵈ destrie I.
ᵉ counselide with I.   ᶠ the Filisteis I.   ᵍ corneris, or *the vttermeste parties* I.   ʰ se ȝe DIKO.   ⁱ hath
fallen I.   ᵏ the sauyour I.   ˡ this synne be I.   ᵐ the which I.   ⁿ Saul I.   ᵒ is it I.   ᵖ other EL.
ᑫ make I.   ʳ schewyng *therof* I.   ˢ the A.   ᵗ Saul *bi lott* I.   ⁿ and I.   ᵛ Om. I.   ᵂ And I.   ˣ Om. I.
ʸ with my ȝerdis eende I.

Saul seide to Jonathan, Shewe to me what thow hast doon. And Jonathas shewide to hym, and seith, Taastynge Y tastide in the cop of the ȝeerd that was in myn hoond a litil of hony, and 44 loo! Y dye. And Saul seith, Thes thingis do to me God, and thes thingis adde, for 45 bi deeth thou shalt dye, Jonathas. And the puple seide to Saul, Thanne whether Jonathas shulde dye, that hath doo this greet helth in Yrael? that is felony; the Lord lyueth, oon heer of the heed of hym shal not fal into the erthe, for with God he hath wrouȝt to day. Thanne the puple delyuerd Jonathan, that he diede 46 not. And Saul wente a wey, and pur- suede not Philistiym; forsothe Philisteis 47 wenten a wey into her placis. And, the rewme stablid vpon Yrael, Saul fauȝt bi enuyroun aȝens alle his enemyes, aȝens Moab, and the sones of Amon, and Edom, and the kyngis of Saba, and the Philis- teis; and whidir euerᵂ he turnede hym silf, 48 he venkusede. And, the oost gedrid, he smoot Amalech, and heˣ delyuerde Yrael 49 fro the hoond of his wastours. Therˣˣ weren forsothe the sones of Saul, Jonathas, and Jesuy, and Melchisona; names of his twoʸ douȝtersᶻ, name of the first goten Merob, and name of the lasse Mycol. 50 And name of the wijf of Saul Achy- noem, the douȝter of Achymaas; and the name of the prince of his chiualrye Ab- ner, the sone of Ner, cosyn germeyn of 51 Saul. Forsothe Cys was the fader of Saul, and Ner, the fader of Abner, the 52 sone of Abyel. Forsothe there was strong batail aȝens Philisties alle the days of Saul; wherfor whom euere Saul sawȝ a strong man and able to bateil, he felaw- shipide him to him silf.

Saul seide, God do to me these thingis, and adde ʻthese thingisᶻ, forᵃ thou, Jona- thas, schaltᵇ dieᶜ bi deeth. And the puple 45 seide to Saul, ʻTherfor whethirᵈ Jonathas schal die, that dide this greet helthe in Israel? thisᵉ is vnleuefulᶠ; the Lord lyueth; noonᵍ heer of his heed schal falleʰ in toⁱ ertheᵏ; for he wrouȝteˡ with God to dai. Therforᵐ the puple delyueredeⁿ Jonathas, that he diede not. And Saul ȝede a wey, 46 and pursuedeⁿⁿ not Filisteisᵒ; sotheliᵖ Fi- listeysᑫ ȝeden in to her places. And Saul, 47 whanne theʳ rewme was ʻconfermyd onˢ Israel, fauȝtᵗ bi cumpas aȝens alle hise enemyes, aȝens Moab, and the sones of Amon, and Edom, and aȝens the kyngis of Soba, and aȝens Filisteisᵘ; and whidur euer he turnede hym, he ouercam†. And 48 whanne theᵛ oost was gaderidᵂ, he smoot Amalech; and delyueredeˣ Israel fro the hond of hise distrieris. Forsotheʸ the 49 sones of Saul weren Jonathas, and Jesuy, and Melchisua; the names of hise twei douȝtrisʸʸ, nameᶻ of theᵃ firste gendrid douȝter was Merob, and nameᵇ ʻof theᶜ lesseᵈ douȝtereᵉ was Mycol. And nameᶠ of 50 ʻthe wijf of Saulᵍ was Achynoem, the douȝtir of Achymaas; and the name of the prince of his chyualrye was Abner, soneʰ of Ner, brotherⁱ of the fadir of Saul. Forsotheᵏ Cys was the fadir of Saul; and 51 Ner, the sone of Abiel, was fadirˡ of Ab- ner. Sotheliᵐ myȝtiⁿ batel was aȝens Fi- 52 listeisᵒ in alle the daies of Saul; for whom euere Saul siȝ a strong man and schapli toᵖ batel, Saulᑫ felouschipide to him silf that man.

† *he ouercam.* In Ebreu it is thus, dide vn- feithfully, ether was vnfeithful; and the lettre suynge acord- ith, where he fauȝte aȝenus Amalech. *Lire here.* C.

ᵂ eue *A*.   ˣ Om. *CE*.   ˣˣ that *A*.   ʸ Om. *A*.   ᶻ douȝtren *BFII*.

ᶻ this to 1.   ᵃ if 1.   ʰ Om. 1.   ᶜ die not 1.   ᵈ Wher thanne 1.   ᵉ it 1.   ᶠ vnleueful *that he dye* 1. ᵍ for no 1.   ʰ perishe 1.   ⁱ Om. 1.   ᵏ the erthe KM.   ˡ hath wrouȝt 1.   ᵐ Thanne 1.   ⁿ deluyede *A*. ⁿⁿ he pursuede 1.   ᵒ the Filisteis 1.   ᵖ and 1.   ᑫ the Filisteis 1.   ʳ his 1.   ˢ stablid vpon 1.   ᵗ he fauȝt 1. ᵘ the Filisteis 1.   ᵛ his 1.   ᵂ gaderid togidere 1.   ˣ he delyuerede 1.   ʸ And 1.   ʸʸ douȝtris *ben these* 1. ᶻ the name 1.   ᵃ his c.   ᵇ the name 1.   ᶜ to his c.   ᵈ ȝounger 1.   ᵉ Om. 1.   ᶠ the name 1.   ᵍ Sauls wijf 1.   ʰ the sone 1.   ⁱ the brothir 1.   ᵏ And 1.   ˡ the fadir 1.   ᵐ And 1.   ⁿ strong 1.   ᵒ the Filisteis 1. ᵖ in 1.   ᑫ he 1.

CAP. XV.

1 And Samuel seide to Saul, The Lord sente me, that I anoynte thee into kyng vpon his puple Yrael; nowe thanne here 2 the voys of the Lord. Thes thingis seith the Lord of oostis, I haue remembrid alle thingis that Amalech dide to Yrael; what maner wyse he withstood to hym in the weye, whanne he shulde stye vp fro Egipt. 3 Nowe thanne go, and smyte Amalech, and destruy alle the thingis of hym; ne spare thou to hym, ne coueyt thou eny thing of his[a] thingis; but sle fro man vnto womman, and litil child, and soukynge, 4 oxe, and sheep, and camel, and asse. And so Saul comaundide to the puple, and noumbrede hem as loombs two hundrid thousandis of foot men, and ten thow-5 sandis of the men of Juda. And whanne Saul was comen vnto the cyte of Ama-lech, he leyde out aspies in the streem. 6 And Saul seide to Cynee, Goth hens, goth awey, and departith fro Amalech, lest perauenture I enwrappe thee with hem; forsothe thou didist mercy with alle the sones of Yrael, whanne thei sti-eden vp fro Egipt. And Cynee wente 7 awey fro the mydil of Amalech. And Saul smoot Amalech fro Euila, to the tyme that he cam to Sur, that is fro the 8 regioun of Egipt. And he took Agage, the kyng of Amalech, on lyue; forsothe al the comoun he slew₃ in the mouth of 9 swerd. And Saul sparide, and the puple, to Agag, and to the best flockis of sheep, and of drouys, and to clothis, and to wetheris, and to alle thingis that weren fayre; ne thei wolden scatere hem; for-sothe what thing was foul and reprouable, 10 that thei destruyden. Forsothe the word of the Lord is doon to Samuel, seiynge,

CAP. XV.

And Samuel seide to Saul, The Lord 1 sente me, that Y schulde anoynte thee in to 'kyng on[r] his puple Israel; now therfor here thou the vois 'of the Lord[s]. The 2 Lord of oostis seith thes thingis, Y haue rikenyd[t] what euer thingis Amalech dide[u] to Israel; hou Amalech a₃enstood Israel in the weic, whanne he[v] stiede[w] from E-gipt. Now therfor go thou, and sle Ama-3 lech, and distruye thou alle 'thingis of hym[x]; spare thou not hym, and[y] coueyte thou not[z] ony thing of hise thingis; but sle thou fro man 'til to[a] womman, and a[b] litil child, and soukynge, an[c] oxe, and scheep, and camel, and asse. Therfor[d] 4 Saul comaundide to[e] the puple[f], and he noumbride hem as lambren twei hundrid thousynde of foot men, and ten thousynde of men of Juda. And whanne Saul cam 5 to the citee of Amalech, he made redi buyschementis in the stronde. And Saul 6 seide to Cyney[g]†, Go ₃e[h], departe ₃e[i], and go ₃e awei[k] fro Amalech, lest perauen-ture Y wlappe thee in with hem; for thou didist mercy with alle the sones of Israel, whanne thei stieden[l] fro Egipt. And Cyney departide fro the myddis of Amalech. And Saul smoot Amalech fro 7 Euila, til[m] thou[n] come[o] to Sur[n], which is a₃ens[q] Egipt. And he[r] took Agag quyke[s], 8 the kyng of Amalech; sotheli[t] he killide bi the[u] scharpnesse of swerd alle the comyn puple. And Saul and the[v] puple sparide 9 Agag, and the[v] beste flockis of scheep, and of grete beestis, and clothis, and rammes, and alle thingis that weren faire; and thei nolden[w] destrie tho; sotheli[x] what euer thing was vijl, and repreuable, thei dis-trieden this[y]. Forsothe[z] the word of the 10 Lord was maad to Samuel, and seide, It 11

† *Saul seide to Cyney, that is, to hem that camen of Jetro, and weren with the sones of Israel. Lire here. c.*

ª this ᴅ.

r a kyng upon ɪ.   s Om. ɪ.   t brou₃t to mynde ɪ.   u hath do ɪ.   v Israel ɪ.   w stiede up ɪ.   x his thingis ɪ.   y ne ɪ.   z Om. ɪ.   ª vnto ᴇʟ.   b Om. ꜰ *sec. vice.* ᴇɪꜰxʙ.   c Om. ꜰ *sec. vice.* ᴅᴇɪꜰxʙ.   d And so ɪ.   e Om. ɪ.   f puple *to be gadrid togidre* ɪ.   g the peple of Cyney ɪ.   h ₃e henns ɪ.   i ₃e awey ɪ.   k forth ɪ.   l stieden up ɪ.   m to ᴇ. tho ʟ.   n he ᴀ *sec. m.* x *sec. m.* ᴇɪꜰʙ.   o came ɪ. cam ᴘ.   p Assur ꜰ *sec. m.* ᴇɢᴋʟɴꜰQʀʙx *sec. m.*   q euen a₃ens ɪ.   r Saul ɪ.   s aliyue ɪ.   t and ɪ.   u Om. ɪ.   v his ɪ.   w wolden not ɪ.   x but ɪ.   y that thing ɪ. it ᴇʟ.   z Sothly ɪ.

11 It othinkith me, that I haue ordeyned Saul a kyng; for he hath forsokyn me, and my wordis he hath not fulfillid in dede. And Samuel is sory, and crycde 12 to the Lord al ny3t. And whanne fro ni3t Samuel was rysen that he go to Saul eerli, it is toold to Samuel, for Saul was comen into Carmeel, and hadde arerid to hym an out shynynge tokne of victory in maner of a bow, and turned was passid, and goon doun into Galgala. Thanne Samuel cam to Saul, and Saul offred brent sacrifice to the Lord of the cheef of the preiys, that he brou3te fro Ama-13 lech. And while Samuel was comen to Saul, Saul seide to hym, Thou blessid of^b the Lord, Y haue^c fulfillid the word of 14 the Lord. And Samuel seide, And what is this voys of flockis that rengith in myn eeris, and of droues that I here? 15 And Saul seith, Fro Amalech men han brou3t thes thingis, forsothe the puple sparede to the betre sheep and drouys, for thei shulden be offrid to the Lord thi God; the tother forsothe we slewen. 16 And Samuel seide to Saul, Suffre me, and I shal shewe to thee what thingis the Lord hath spoken to me to ny3t. And 17 he seid to hym, Spek. And Samuel seith, Whether not, whanne thou were a litil child in thin owne^{cc} eyen, and thou art maad heed in the lynage of Yrael, and the Lord anoyntide thee into kyng vpon 18 Yrael; and the Lord sente thee into the weye, and seith, Go, and sle the synful men of Amalech, and thou shalt fi3t 19 a3ens hem vnto the slau3ter of hem. Whi thanne hast thow not herd the voys of the Lord, but turnedist to the preye, and didist yuel in the eyen of the Lord? 20 And Saul seith to Samuel, If I haue herd the voys of the Lord, and haue

repentith me†, that Y made Saul kyng^a; for he forsook^b me, and fillide^c not my wordis in werk. And Samuel was sory, and he criede to the Lord in al the^d ny3t. And whanne Samuel hadde rise^e bi ny3t 12 to go eerly to Saul, it was teld to Samuel that Saul hadde come in to Carmel, and hadde reisid^f to hym a signe of victorye; and that^g he hadde turned a3en^h, and hadde passidⁱ, and hadde go doun in to Galgala. Therfor^k Samuel cam to Saul, and Saul offride brent sacrifice to the Lord of the cheef thingis of preies, whiche he hadde brou3t fro Amalech. And the while 13 Samuel cam to Saul, Saul seide to hym, Blessid be thou of the Lord, Y haue fillid^l the 'word of the Lord^m. And Samuel 14 seide, Andⁿ what is the^o vois of flockis, that sowneth in myn eeris, and of grete beestis, whiche Y here? And Saul seide, 15 Thei^p brou3ten tho fro Amalech, for the puple sparide the betere^q schcep and grete beestis, that tho schulden be offrid to thi^r Lord God; sotheli^s we killiden the tothere beestis. Forsothe^t Samuel seide to Saul, 16 Suffre thou me, and Y schal schewe to thee what thingis the Lord spak^u to me in the^v ny3t. And he^w seide to Samuel, Speke thou. And Samuel seide, Whether 17 not, whanne thou were litil in thin^x i3en, thou were maade heed in the lynages of Israel, and the Lord anoyntide thee in to kyng^y on^z Israel; and the Lord sente^a 18 thee in to the weie, and seide, Go thou, and sle the synneris of Amalech, and thou schalt fi3te a3ens hem 'til to^b sleyng^c of hem. Whi therfor herdist thou not the 19 vois of the Lord, but thou were turned to prey^d, and didist yuel in the 'i3en of the Lord^e? And Saul seide to Samuel, 3his^f, 20 Y herde^g the 'vois of the Lord^h, and Y 3edeⁱ in the weie, bi which the Lord sente^k

† It repentith me. Repentinge, whanne it berith chaungeablete, may not be in God, netheles God is seid to repente, for he hath him at the maner of a man repentinge, whanne he distrieth that that he made; so it is in this poynt, for he derayde Saul to be cast awey, whom he reiside biforr; netheles thilke chaungeablete, is onely in creaturis, for God bi vnchaungenble wille, makith chaungeable thingis. Lire here, c.

^b bi ᴇ pr. m.　　^c ha c.　　^{cc} ownth ᴇ.

^a a kyng c pr. m.　^b hath forsaken ɪ.　^c hath not fulfillid ɪ.　^d that ɪ.　^e rise up ɪ.　^f reisid up ɪ. ^g Om. c.　^h a3en fro Amalech ɪ.　ⁱ passid forth ɪ.　^k Thanne ɪ.　^l fulfillid ɪ.　^m Lordis word ɪ. ⁿ Om. ᴅꜰ pr. m. ɢᴍɴǫᴡx.　^o this ᴅᴄɪ.　^p Men ɪ.　^q beste ɪ.　^r the ᴀ pr. m. ɪ.　^s and ɪ.　^t And ɪ.　^u hath spoke ɪ.　^v this ɪ.　^w Saul ɪ.　^x thin owne ɪ.　^y a kyng ɪ.　^z upon ɪ.　^a sende ɪ.　^b vnto ɪ. into ᴇʟ. ^c the sleyng plures.　^d the prey ɪ.　^e Lordis si3t ɪ.　^f This ᴇɪʟ.　^g haue herd ɪ.　^h Lordis vois ɪ. ⁱ haue go ɪ.　^k sende ɪ.

goon in the weye bi the which the Lord sente me, and haue brouȝt Agag, the kyng of Amalech, and Amalech Y slewe.

21 Forsothe the puple took of the praye, sheep and oxen, the cheef of hem that ben slayn, that thei offren to the Lord 22 her God in Galgalis. And Samuel seith, Whether wole the Lord brent sacrifices or slayn offryngis, and not more that it be obeishid to the voice of the Lord? Forsothe betre is obeishaunce than slayn sacrificis, and to take heed more than to 23 offre the fatnes of wetheris; for as synne of denyynge bi deuelis is to repugne, and as hidows trespas of mawmetrye to wiln not assent. Forthi thanne that thow hast throwen aweye the word of the Lord, the Lord hath throwen awey thee, that 24 thow be not kyng. And Saul seide to Samuel, Y haue synned, for[d] I haue broken the word of the Lord, and thi wordis, dredynge the puple and obeish-25 ynge to the voyce of hem; but nowe, Y biseche, bere my synne, and turne aȝen 26 with me, that I honoure the Lord. And Samuel seith to Saul, Y shal not turne aȝen with thee, for thow hast throwen awey the word of the Lord, and the Lord hath throwen awey thee, that thow 27 be not kyng vpon Irael. And Samuel turnede forto goo awey; forsothe he cauȝte the cop of the mantil of hym, the 28 which also is rent. And Samuel seide to hym, The Lord hath kyt the kyngdam of Yrael fro thee to day, and hath takyn 29 it to thi neiȝbore beter than thow; for-sothe to the ouercomer in Yrael he shal not spare, and thurȝ athenkynge he shal not be bowid; forsothe ne a man he is 30 that he do othenkynge. And he seith, Y haue synned; bot nowe honour me[e] before the eldren of my puple, and be-

me, and Y haue brouȝt Agag, the kyng of Amalech, and Y killide[l] Amalech. For-21 sothe[m] the puple took[n] of the prey, scheep and oxun, the firste[o] fruytis of tho thingis, that ben slayn, that thei make sacrifice to her Lord God in Galgalis. And Samuel 22 seide, Whether wole the Lord brent sacri-fices, ethir slayn sacrifices, and not more[p] that me obeie to the vois of the Lord? For[q] obedience[r] is betere than sacrifices, and to 'herkene Goddis[rr] word is more than to offre the ynnere fatnesse of rammes; for 23 it is as the synne of mawmetrie to 'fiȝte aȝens Goddis heest[s]†, and it is as the wickidnesse of ydolatrie to nyle[t] 'ascente to Goddis heest[u]. Therfor for that[v], that thou castidist[w] awey the word of the Lord, the Lord castide[x] thee awei, that thou be not kyng. And Saul seide to Samuel, Y 24 synnede[y], for Y brak[z] the word of the Lord, and thi wordis; 'and Y dredde[a] the puple, 'and obeiede[b] to 'the vois of hem[c]; but now, Y bisech[d], bere thou my synne, 25 and turne thou aȝen with me, that Y wor-schipe the Lord. And Samuel seide to 26 Saul, Y schal not turne aȝen with thee, for thou castidist[e] awey the word of the Lord, and the Lord castide[f] awei thee, that thou be not king on[g] Israel. And 27 Samuel turnede[h] to go a wey; sotheli[i] Saul took the eude[k] of the mentil of Sa-muel, which[l] also was to-rent. And Sa-28 muel seide to hym[m], The Lord hath kit the rewme of Israel fro thee to dai, and ȝaf[n] it to thi neiȝbore betere than thou; certis the ouercomere in Israel schal not 29 spare[o], and[p] he schal[q] not be bowid bi re-pentaunce; for he is not man[r], 'that is, chaungeable[s], that he do repentaunce. And Saul seide, Y synnede[t]; but now 30 onoure thou me bifor the eldere men of my puple, and bifor Israel, and turne thou

---

d and ⅄.   e Om. ⅄.

l haue killid ɪ. m And ɪ. n hath take ɪ. o cheef ɪ. p more rather ɪ. q forsothe ɪ. r obedience to him ɪ. rr take heede to his ɪ. s repugne the word of God ɪ. fiȝte aȝens Goddis heestis ⅄. t nat ɪ. u consente to it ɪ. v thi ɪ. w hast throwen ɪ. x hath throwe ɪ. y haue synned ɪ. z haue broke ɪ. a dredinge ɪ. Y dredde ⅄. b obeiynge ɪ. c her vois ɪ. d biseche thee ɪ. e hast throwen ɪ. f hath cast ɪ. g upon ɪ. h turnede him ɪ. i and ɪ. k hemme ɪ. l the which ɪ. m Saul ɪ. n he hath ȝouen ɪ. o spare hem that wil not obeie to him ɪ. p for c. q wil ɪ. r a man ɪ. s Om. ɪ. t haue synned ɪ.

fore Yrael; turne aȝen with me, that I
31 honour the Lord thi God. Thanne Samuel, turned aȝen, folwide Saul, and Saul
32 honourede the Lord. And Samuel seide,
Bringith to me Agag, the king of Amalech. And offrid is to him Agag alther-
fattest tremblynge. And Agag seide, So
33 whether 'not seuereth[f] bitter deth? And
Samuel seith, As thi swerd hath maad
wymmen withouten free children, so thi
moder shal be with out free children
among wymmen. And Samuel hewide[g]
hym into gobbetis before the Lord in
34 Galgalis. Forsothe Samuel ȝede into Ramatha; forsothe Saul stiede vp into his
35 hows in Gabaa. And Saul sawȝ no more
Samuel vnto the day of his deth; neuerthelater Samuel weilide Saul, for it
othouȝt[gg] the Lord, that he hadde ordeynyd Saul kyng vpon Irael.

CAP. XVI.

1 And the Lord seide to Samuel, How
long thow weilist Saul, whanne Y haue
thrown hym a ferre, that he regne not
vpon Irael; fil thin horn with oyle, and
come, that Y sende thee to Ysaye Bethlamyte; forsothe Y haue purueyd in the
2 sonys of hym a kyng to me. And Samuel seith, Howe shal Y goo? forsothe
Saul shal here, and he shal slee me.
And the Lord seith, A calf of the droue
thow shalt take in thin hoond, and sey,
3 To offre to the Lord Y am comen. And
thou shalt clepe Ysaye to the slayn sacrifice, and I shal shewe to thee what thou
doo; and thou shalt anoynt whom euer
4 Y shal shewe to thee. Thanne Samuel
dide, as the Lord spak to hym; and he
cam into Bethleem, and the eldrys of the
cytee aȝen comynge to hym wondriden,
and seiden, Whether pesible is thin yn-
5 comynge? And he seith, Pesible; to offre
to the Lord Y am comen; be ȝe halowid,
and cometh with me, that I offre. Thanne

aȝen with me, that Y worschipe thi Lord
God. Therfor Samuel turnede aȝen[t], and 31
suede Saul, and Saul worschipide the Lord.
And Samuel seide, Brynge ȝe to me Agag, 32
the kyng of Amalech. And Agag 'moost
fat[u] tremblynge was brouȝt to hym. And
Agag seide, Whether thus departith[v] bitter
deeth? And Samuel seide, As thi swerd 33
made[w] wymmen with out fre children, so
thi modir schal be with out fre children
among wymmen. And Samuel kittide[x]
hym[y] in to gobetis bifor the Lord in Galgalis. Forsothe[z] Samuel ȝede in to Ra-34
matha; sotheli[a] Saul stiede[b] in to his hows
in[c] Gabaa. And Samuel siȝ no more Saul‡35
'til to[d] the dai of his deeth; netheles Samuel biweilide Saul‖, for it repentide the
Lord, that he hadde ordeyned Saul kyng
on[e] Israel.

CAP. XVI.

And the Lord seide to Samuel, Hou 1
long biweilist thou Saul, sithen[f] Y castide[g]
hym awey, that he regne not on[h] Israel;
fille thin horn with oile, and come, that
Y sende thee to Ysay of Bethleem; for
among hise sones Y haue purueide a king
to me. And Samuel seide, Hou schal Y 2
go? for[i] Saul schal here[k], and he schal
sle me. And the Lord seide, Thou schalt
take a calf of the droue in thi hond, and
thou schalt seye, Y cam to make sacrifice
to the Lord. And thou schalt clepe Ysay 3
to the sacrifice, and Y schal schewe to
thee, what thou schalt do; and thou schalt
anoynte, whom euere Y schal schewe to
thee. Therfor[l] Samuel dide, as the Lord 4
spak to hym; and he cam in to Bethleem,
and the eldere men of the citee wondriden,
and camen[m] to hym, and seiden, Whether
thin entryng[n] is[o] pesible? And he seide, 5
It is pesible; Y cam to make sacrifice to
the Lord; be ȝe halowid, and come ȝe with
me, that Y make sacrifice. Therfor[p] he[q]

† *Samuel turn-*
ede aȝen; he
wolde do wor-
schip to Saul,
as long as he
was suffrid of
God in the
rewme, and that
he schulde sle
Agag, that was
kept ȝit quyk.
Lire here. c.

‡ *Samuel siȝ*
no more Saul,
in the kingis
cloth and
comyn staat.
Lire here. c.
‖ *Samuel bi-*
weilide Saul,
not that the
sentence of the
Lord schulde
be chaungid
aȝenus him, but
Samuel hadde
compassioun
of his soule,
lest it were
dampned with-
outen ende,
and Samuel
dredde, lest the
puple of Israel
schulde be
punyschid for
the synnes of
Saul. Lire
here. c.

---

[f] ne seuere E pr. m.   [g] hewȝ E.   [gg] othorȝt A.

[u] the moost fat man I.   [v] departe E. departid L.   [w] hath made I.   [x] hewide I.   [y] Agag I.   [z] And I.
[a] and I.   [b] wente up I.   [c] in to *plures*.   [d] vnto I. into L.   [e] upon I.   [f] sith I.   [g] haue cast I.   [h] upon I.
[i] certis I.   [k] here *therof* I.   [l] Thanne I.   [m] ther camen I.   [n] entree I.   [o] be I.   [p] Thanne t.
[q] Samuel I.

he halowid Ysaye, and hys sones, and
6 clepide hem to the sacrifice. And whanne
thei weren comen yn, he saw3 Elyab,
and seith, Nowe before the Lord is the
7 crist of hym. And the Lord seide to
Samuel, Ne behold thou the cheere of
hym, ne the hei3te of his stature; for Y
haue throwun hym aweye, ne aftir the
lokynge of men Y deme; forsothe a man
seeth tho thingis that ben opyn, forsothe
8 the Lord lokith the herte. And Ysaye
clepide Amynadab, and brou3te hym before Samuel; the which seide, Ne this
9 the Lord hath chosun. Forsothe Ysaye
brou3te forth Sama; of whom he seith,
Also this the Lord hath not chosun.
10 And so Ysaye brou3te forth his seuen
sones before Samuel; and Samuel seith
to Ysaye, The Lord hath not chosen of
11 thes. And Samuel seide to Ysaye, Whether nowe fulfillid ben the sones? The
which answerde, 3it another there is, a
litil child, and fedith sheep. And Samuel
seith to Ysaye, Send, and bryng forth
hym; forsothe ne we shulen sitte, before
12 that he come hidir. Thanne he sente,
and brou3te hym forth; forsothe he was
rodi^h, and fayr in si3t, and sembli^i in
face. And the Lord seith, Rise, and
13 anoynt^k hym; forsothe he it is. Thanne
Samuel took an horn of oyle, and anoyntide hym in the myddis of the britheren of hym; and the Spirit of the
Lord is ful sent into Dauyd fro that
day and therafter. And Samuel rysynge
14 wente into Ramatha. And so the Spyrit
of the Lord wente awey fro Saul, and
the shrewid spyryt fro the Lord 'shook
15 hym^l. And the seruauntis of Saul seiden
to hym, Loo! the ynel spiryt of the Lord
16 shakith^m thee; comaunde the lord oure
kyng, and thi seruauntis that before thee
ben, sechen a man kunnynge to pleye

halewide Ysai, and hise sones, and clepide^r
hem to the sacrifice. And whanne thei 6
hadden entrid, he^s si3 Eliab^t, and seide^u†,
Whether bifor the Lord is his crist^v? And 7
the Lord seide to Samuel, Biholde thou
not his cheer, nethir hi3nesse^w of his stature; for Y castide^x hym awei‡, and Y
demyde^y not bi 'the si3t of man^z; for a^a
man seeth tho thingis that ben opyn, but
the Lord biholdith the herte. And Ysai 8
clepide Amynadab, and brou3te hym bifor
Samuel; which^b seide, Nether the Lord
hath chose this. Forsothe^c Isay brou3te^d 9
Samma; of whom Samuel seide, Also the
Lord hath not chose this. Therfor^e Isai 10
brou3te^f hise seuene sones bifor Samuel;
and Samuel seide to Ysai, The Lord hath
'not chose^g of these. And Samuel seide to 11
Isai, Whether thi sones ben now fillid^h?
And Isai answeride, 3it 'another is, a^i litil
child, and lisewith^k scheep. And Samuel
seide to Isai, Sende thou^l, and brynge
hym^m; for we schulen not sitte to mete,
bifor that he come hidur. Therfor^n Ysai 12
sente, and brou3te hym; sotheli he was
rodi, and fair in si3t, and of semely face.
And the Lord seide, Rise thou, and
anoynte hym; for^o it is he. Therfor Sa- 13
muel took the horn of oyle, and anoyntid
hym in the myddis of his britheren; and
the Spirit of the Lord† was dressid in to
Dauid fro that day 'and afterward^p. And
Samuel roos^q, and 3ede^r in to Ramatha.
And so the Spirit of the Lord 3ede^s awei 14
fro Saul, and a^t wickid spirit of the Lord
trauelide Saul. And the seruauntis of Saul 15
seiden to hym, Lo! an'yuel spirit‡ of the
Lord traueilith thee; oure lord the kyng 16
comaunde, and thi seruauntis that ben
bifore thee, schulen seke a man, that kan
synge with an harpe, that^u whanne the
yuel spirit of the Lord takith thee, he^v
harpe with his hond, and thou bere esi-

† and seide, in
his herte. Lire
here. c.

‡ for Y castide
him awey, that
he regne not.
Lire here. c.

|| the Spirit of
the Lord; that
is, the spirit of
strengthe and
of stidefast-
nesse, to dely-
uere the puple;
wherfor it is
seid in xvii. c°.
that Dauid vn-
armed 3ede
stidefastly and
wilfuly, to fi3te
a3ens the Fi-
listey. Sothely
Jerom seith,
that fro that
day the spirit
of profecie was
in Dauyth, and
fro that tyme
he began to
singe salmes,
and this ac-
cordith to the
seiyng of hem,
whiche seyen
that salm, Do-
minus illumi-
natio mea, in
his anoynting.
Lire here. c.
¶ Lo an yuel
spirit; the
feend is seid the
spirit of the
Lord, for the
good kynde of
hym is of God
bi creacioun
either making of
nou3t, but he
was maad yuel
bi his owne
pride. Lire
here. c.

h brown E pr. m.   i semely C&U.   k anoyntide A.   l waggide hym out E pr. m.   m out waggeth E pr. m.

r he clepide 1.   s Samuel 1.   t Eliab a sone of Ysai 1.   u he seide 1.   v crist whom I anoynte 1.
w the hi3nesse FGIKLNOPQRSUW.   x haue cast 1.   y deme 1.   z mans si3t 1.   a Om. 1.   b and he 1.
c And 1.   d brou3te forth 1.   e And so 1.   f brou3te forth 1.   g chose noon 1.   h fulfillid 1.   i ther is
anothir 1.   k he pasturith 1.   l 3e 1.   m hym hidere 1.   n Thanne 1.   o forsothe 1.   p forth 1.   q roos
up 1.   r wente 1.   s wente 1.   t the 1.   u and c.   v the man 1.

with harpe, that whanne the yuel spyrit of the Lord takith[n] thee, he pleye with 17 his hoond, and li3ter[o] thou bere. And Saul seith to his seruauntis, Purueieth to me sum man wel harpynge, and 18 bryngith hym to me. And answerynge oon of the children seith, Loo! I saw3 the sone of Ysaye Bethlemyte, kunnynge to harpe, and moost my3ti bi strength, a man curaiows in batayl, and wyse[p] in wordis, and a fayre man; and the Lord 19 is with hym. Thanne Saul sente messagers to Ysaye, seiynge, Send to me Dauith thi sone, the which is in the 20 lesewis. And so Ysay took an asse ful of loouys, and a galoun of wyn, and o kyd of the she geet; and he sente bi the 21 hoond of Dauid his sone to Saul. And Dauid cam to Saul, and stood before hym; and he louyde hym ful mych, and 22 is made a squyer of hym. And Saul sente to Ysaye, seiynge, Stoond Dauyd in my si3t, forsothe he hath foundun 23 grace in myn eyen. Thanne whanne euere the yuel spyryt of the Lord cau3te Saul, Dauid took arf harp, and smoot with hys hoond, and Saul was refourmyd, and li3ter he hadde; forsothe the yuel spiryt wente awey fro hym.

1 Forsothe Philisteis gedrynge her cumpanyes into batayl camen to gidre in Socoth of Judee, and thei setten tentis betwix[r] Socoth and Azecha, in the coostis 2 of Domyn. Forsothe Saul and the men of Yrael gedrid camen in the valey of Therebynt, and dressiden sheltrom to 3 fi3t a3ens the Phylisteis. And Philisteis stoden vpon the hil on this partye, and Irael stood vpon an hil, and on the tother 4 perty a valey that was bitwix[s] hem. And

liere[w]. And Saul seide to hise seruauntis, 17 Puruey 3e to me sum man syngynge wel, and brynge 3e hym to me. And oon of 18 the[x] children answeride and seide, Lo! Y si3 the[y] sone of Ysai of Bethlcem, kunnynge to synge, and 'strongeste in my3t[z], and 'a man able[a] to batel, and prudent in wordis, and a feir man; and the Lord is with hym. Therfor Saul sente messan- 19 geris to Ysay, and seide, Sende thou to me Dauid thi sone, 'which is in the lesewis[b]. Therfor[c] Isni took an asse 'ful of[d] 20 loouest, and a galoun of wyn, and a 'kyde of geet[e]; and sente[f] bi the hond of Dauid his sone to Saul. And Dauid cam to Saul, 21 and stood bifor hym; and Saul louyde hym greetli[g], and he[h] was maad 'his squyer[i]. And Saul sente to Isay, and 22 seide, Dauid stonde in my si3t, for he foond[k] grace in myn i3en. Therfor[l] 23 whanne euer the wickid[m] spirit of the Lord took[n] Saul, Dauid took the[o] harpe, and smoot[p] with his hond, and Saul was coumfortid, and he hadde li3tere[q]; for the wickid[r] spirit 3ede[s] awey fro hym.

Forsothe[t] Filisteis gaderiden[u] her cum- 1 penyes in to batel, and camen[v] togidere in[w] Socoth of Juda, and settiden[x] tentis bitwixe Socoth and Azecha, in the coostis of Domyn. Sotheli[y] Saul and the men 2 of Israel weren gaderid[z], and camen[a] in to the valey of Terebynte, and dressiden[b] scheltrun to fi3te a3ens Filisteis. And Fi- 3 listeis[c] stoden aboue the hil on this part, and Israel stood on the hil on the tother part of the valey, that was bitwixe hem.

† an asse ful of
looues, that is,
chargid with
looues. Lire
here. c.

[n] take EFH.   [o] li3tliere CE.   [p] a wyse E orig.   [r] bitwene DFH. betwen E. betwe C. in E pr.m.
[s] bytwene BEFH. betwe C.

[w] it more esely I.   [x] his I.   [y] a I.   [z] moost strong man I.   [a] an able man I.   [b] that is kepinge thi
bestes I.   [c] And so I.   [d] chargid with I.   [e] geet kyde I.   [f] he sente tho I.   [g] myche I.   [h] Dauid I.
[i] squyer of Saul I.   [k] hath founde I.   [l] Thanne I.   [m] yuel I.   [n] traueilide I.   [o] his I.   [p] harpide I.
[q] li3tliere plures. it more li3tly I.   [r] yuel I.   [s] wente I.   [t] Sotheli the I.   [u] gaderiden to gidere I.
[v] thei camen I.   [w] in to I.   [x] thei settiden I.   [y] And I.   [z] gaderid to gidre I.   [a] thei camen I.   [b] thei
dressiden I.   [c] the Filisteis I.

a bastard man wente out fro the tentis
of Philistiens, Goliath of Geth bi name,
5 in heiȝte of sexe cubitis and a span; and
a stelyn helm vpon his heed; and he was
clothid with a maylid hawberioun; forsothe the weiȝt of his hawberioun was of
6 fyue thousand siclys of steel; and stelyn
legharneis he hadde in the hipis, and
a stelyn sheeld couerde the shuldris of
7 hym. The shaft of his speer was as the
beem of websters; forsothe that yren of
his speer hadde sexe hundrid siclis of
yren; and his squyer wente before him.
8 And stondinge he criede aȝenst the cumpanyes of Israel, and he seide to hem,
Whi ben ȝe comyn redi to hatail? Whether Y am not a Philistee, and ȝe the
seruauntis of Saul? Chesith of ȝou a
man, and come he doun to a synguler
9 strijf; if he may fiȝt with me, and
smytith me, we shulen be to ȝou seruauntis; forsothe if Y shal haue the
maystrye, and smyte hym, ȝe shulen be
10 seruauntis, and serue to vs. And the
Philistee seide, I haue ȝeue reproof to
the cumpanyes of Yrael to day; ȝyueth
to me a man, and go he yn with me a
11 synguler strijf. Forsothe Saul herynge
and alle the Yraelitis the wordis of this
maner Philistee, thei weren stonyed, and
12 dradden ful mych. Forsothe Dauyd was
the sone of an Effratee man, of the
which it is aboue seid, of Bethlem Juda,
to whom the name was Ysaye, the
which hadde eiȝt sonys; and he was a
man in the days of Saul olde, and of
13 greet age amonge men. Forsothe the
thre more sonys of hym wenten after
Saul into batayl; and the names of the
thre sonys of hym, that wenten to
batayl, Heliab, the first goten, and the
secounde, Amynadab, forsothe the thridde,

And a man[d], 'sone of a widewe†, whos 4
fadir was vncerteyn[e], ȝede[f] out of the
'castels of[g] Filisteis[h], Goliath bi name of
Geth, of sixe cubitis heiȝ and a spanne;
and a brasun basynet on[i] his heed; and 5
he was clothid[ii] with 'an haburioun
hokid[k], ether mailid[l]; forsothe[m] the weiȝte
of his haburioun was fyue thousynde siclis[n] of bras; and he hadde 'bootis of bras 6
in the hipis[o], and a 'scheld of bras[p] hilide[q]
hise schuldris. Forsothe[r] 'the schaft of his 7
spere[s] was as the beem of webbis[t]; forsothe[u] thilke[v] yrun of his spere hadde[w]
sixe hundrid siclis of yrun; and his squier
ȝede bifor hym. And he[x] stood, and cried 8
aȝens the cumpenyes[y] of armed men of
Israel, and seide[z] to hem, Why camen ȝe
redi to batel? Whether Y am not a Filistei, and ȝe ben the seruauntis of Saul?
Chese ȝe a man of ȝou, and come he doun
to syngulere[a] batel; if he may fiȝte with 9
me, and sleeth[b] me, we schulen be 'seruauntis to ȝou[c]; forsothe[d] if Y haue the
maystry, and sle hym, ȝe schulen be
boonde, and 'ȝe schulen[e] serue vs. And 10
'the Filistei[f] seide, Y haue 'seyd schenschip[g] to dai to the cumpenyes of Israel;
ȝyue[h] ȝe a man[i], and bigynne he 'synguler
batel[ii] with me[k]. Sotheli Saul and alle 11
men[l] of Israel herden[m] siche wordis of
'the Filistey[n], and[o] thei weren astonyed,
and dredden greetli. Forsothe[p] Dauid was 12
'the sone of a man[q] of Effrata, of whom
it is 'biforseid[r], of Bethleem of Juda, to
'which man[s] the name was Isay, which[t]
hadde eiȝte sones; and 'the man was eld
in the daies of Saul[u], and of greet age
among men. Sotheli[v] thre grettere[w] sones 13
of Ysai ȝeden after Saul in to batel; and
the names of hise thre sones, that ȝeden[ww]
to batel, Heliab[x], the[y] firste gendryd[z], and
the secounde[a], Amynadab, and the thridde,

d bastard man GIKNob. man bastard MOQSWX.   e Gloss omitted in DGIKOQSWXb.   f wente I.   g Om. I.
h Filisteis tentis I.   i of A.   ii closid b.   k a mailed haburioun I.   l nailed b. gloss omitted in I.   m and I.
n siclis A.   o on his thies brasen bootis I.   p brasen scheld I.   q hilide with c.   r And I.   s his spere
schaft I.   t websters I.   u and I.   v the I.   w weiede I.   x Goliath I.   y cumpanye I.   z he seide I.
a a syngulere I.   b sle RIL.   c ȝoure seruauntis I.   d and I.   e Om. I.   f Goliath I.   g put repreef I.
h sende I.   i man to me I.   ii to fiȝte I.   k me aloone I.   l the men I.   m herynge I.   n Goliath I.
o Om. I.   p And I.   q a mannes sone I.   r seid bifore I.   s whom I.   t and he I.   u in the daies of Saul
Ysay was an olde man I.   v And the I.   Sotheli the K.   w eldeste I.   ww wenten I.   x weren Heliab I.
y his I.   z bigoten I.   a secounde hiȝte I.

14 Samma. Forsothe Dauyd was the leest. Thanne the thre more folwynge Saul, 15 Dauyd wente, and turnede aȝen fro Saul, for to fede the flok of his fadre in Beth- 16 leem. Forsothe the Philistee cam forth eerli, and at euen 'stondynge repreuyde 17 the children† of Yrael" fourti days. For- sothe Ysaye seide to Dauyd his sone, Tak to thi bretheren powned corn, of the mesure of ephi, and thes ten loouys, and renne into the tentis to thi britheren; 18 and ten chesis thes thou shalt bere to the tribune; and thi britheren thou shalt visite, if thei ryȝt doon, and with whom 19 thei ben ordeynyd, lern. Forsothe Saul, and thei, and alle the sonys of Yrael in the valey of Therebynt fouȝten aȝens 20 Philisteis. And so Dauid roos eerli, and commendide the flok to the keper, and chargyd ȝeed, as Ysay comaundide to hym; and cam to the place of Magala, and to the oost, that, goon out to fiȝt, 21 criede out in the strijf. Forsothe Irael hadde dressid sheltroun; but and aȝens 22 hem Philisteis weren redy. Thanne Dauid leuynge the vessels, the whiche he brouȝte, vndre the hoond of a keper at the fardels, he ran to the place of the strijf, and he askide, if alle thingis riȝt 23 weren doon anentys his britheren. And whanne ȝit he spak to hem, aperyde thatᵛ bastard man, Goliath bi name, Phi- listee of Geth, stiynge fro the tentis of Philisteis; and hym spekynge thes same 24 wordis, Dauyd herde. Forsothe alle the Ysraelitis whanne thei hadden seen the man, thei flowen fro his face, dredynge 25 hym greetli. And echon of Irael seide to other, Whether thou hast seen this man that styeth vp? forsothe to ȝyue reprofe to Yrael he stieth vp; therfor the man

Samma. Forsothe[b] Dauid was the leeste[c]. 14 Therfor[d] while thre[e] grettere[f] sueden Saul, Dauid ȝede, and turnede aȝen fro Saul, that 15 he schulde[g] kepe the floc of his fadir in Bethleem. Forsothe[h] the Filistey cam[i] 16 forth in the morewtid, and euentid; and stood 'bi fourti daies[k]. Sotheli[l] Ysai seide 17 to Dauid his sone, Take thou to thi bri- theren meete maad of meele, the[m] mesure of ephi[n], and these ten looues, and renne thou in to the castels[o] to thi britheren; and thou schalt bere to the tribune these 18 ten 'litil † formes of chese[p]; and thou schalt visite thi britheren, whether thei doon riȝtli[q], and lurne[r] thou, with whiche[s] men thei ben ordeyned. Forsothe[t] Saul, 19 and thei, and alle the sones of Israel in the valei of Terebynte fouȝten aȝens Fi- listeis[u]. Therfor[v] Dauid roos eerli, and 20 bitook[w] the floc to the[x] kepere, and he ȝede[y] chargid, as Ysai 'hadde comaundid to[z] hym; and he cam to the place Ma- gala[a], and to the oost, which[b] oost ȝede out to the batel[c], and criede[d] in 'the batel[dd]. For Israel hadde dressid[e] scheltrun; 'but 21 also[f] Filisteis[g] weren maad[h] redi 'euen aȝens[i]. Therfor[k] Dauid lefte the vessels, 22 whiche[l] he hadde brouȝt, vndur the hond of a kepere 'at the[m] fardels, and he ran to the place of batel, and he axyde, if alle thingis weren 'doon riȝtli[n] anentis hise britheren. And whanne he spak ȝit to 23 hem, thilke bastard apperide, Goliath bi name, a[o] Filistei of Geth, and stiede[p] fro the castels[q] of Filisteis[r]; and 'while he spak[s] these same wordis, Dauid herde. And whanne alle men[t] of Israel hadden 24 seyn 'the man[u], thei fledden fro his face[v], and dredden hym greetli. And ech man 25 of Israel seide[w], Whether thou hast seyn this man that stiede[x]? for[y] he stiede[z] to

† ten litle, etc. that is, x. litle chesis formed. Lire here.

---

† childre CE.   'º and stood E pr. m.   ᵛ the ilke E pr. m. the F.

b Therfor A. And I.   c ȝoungist I.   d Thanne I.   e the thre IK. the o.   f eldist sones I.   g wolde I. b And bi fourti daies I.   i ȝede I.   k into repreef of Israel I.   l And I.   m at the I.   n thre bushels I. o tentis I.   P smale cheeses I.   q iustly I.   r knowe I.   s what I.   t Certis I.   u the Filisteis I. v And so I. And therfor K.   w he bitook I.   x a I.   y ȝede forth I.   z comaundide I.   a of Magala I.   b the which I.   c fiȝt I.   d it criede I.   dd fiȝtyng I.   e ordeyned I.   f and euen aȝens hem I. g the Filisteis I.   h Om. DIB.   i also I.   k Thanne I.   l that I.   m atte EL.   n iustly doon I.   o the I. P he wente up I.   q tentis I.   r the Filisteis I.   s him spekynge I.   t the men IM.   u Goliath I.   v siȝt I. w seide to oother I.   x hath stied up I.   y forsothe I.   z ȝede up I.

that smytith hym, the kyng shal make
riche with greet ricchessis; and his douȝter he shal ȝyue to hym, and the hows
of his fadre he shal make with out tri-
26 bute in Yrael. And Dauid seide^w to the
men that stoden with hym, seiynge,
What shal it be ȝouun^x to the man that
smytith this Philistee, and bereth awey
reprofe fro Irael? forsothe who is he^y
this Philistee vncircumcidid, the which
reproueth the shiltrouns of the God lyu-
27 ynge? Forsothe the puple toolde to hym
the same word, seiynge, Thes thingis
shulen be ȝeue to the man that smitith
28 hym. The which thing whanne Heliab,
his more brother, hadde herd, hym spekynge with other, is wrooth aȝens Dauid,
and seith, Whi art thou comen, and whi
hast thow forsaken thes^z fewe sheep in
deseert? I haue knowen thi pride, and
the shrewidnesse of thin herte; for that
thou myȝtist se the bateil, thou art comen
29 doun. And Dauid scith^a, What haue I
30 doon? Whether is it not a word? And
he bowide a syde a litil fro hym to an
other; and he seide the same word, and
the puple answerde to hym word as bi-
31 fore. Forsothe the wordis that Dauid
spak, ben herd, and toold in the siȝt of
32 Saul. To whom whanne he was brouȝt,
he spak to hym, Ne falle^b not doun the
herte of eny man in hym, and thi seruaunt shal goo, and fiȝt aȝen the Philistee.
33 And Saul seith to Dauid, Thou mayst
not withstoond to this Philistee, ne fiȝte
aȝens hym, for a child thou art; forsothe this man is a fiȝter fro his ȝongth.
34 And Dauid seide to Saul, Thi seruaunt
fedde the flok of his fader, and there
cam a lioun or a beere, and took a wether
35 fro the mydil of the flok; I pursuede
hem, and smoot, and delyuerde fro the

seie schenship^a to Israel; therfor the kyng
schal make^b riche with greet richessis 'the
man^c that sleeth thilke Filistei; and the
kyng schal ȝyue his douȝter to that man,
and schal^d make the hows of his fader
with out 'tribut in Israel^e. And Dauyd 26
spak to the men that stoden with hym,
and seide, What schal be ȝouun to the
man that sleeth this Filistei, and doith
awei schenschip fro Israel? for^f who is^g
this Filistei vncircumcidid, that dispiside^h
the scheltruns of God lyuynge? Forsotheⁱ 27
the puple tolde to hym^k the same word,
and seide, These thingis schulen be ȝouun
to the man that sleeth hym^l. And whanne 28
Heliab, 'his more brother^m, had herd this,
while heⁿ spak with othere men, he was
wrooth aȝens Dauid, and seide, Whi camest
thou^o, and whi 'leftist thou^p tho fewe
scheep in deseert? Y knowe thi pride,
and the wewardnesse of thin herte; for
thou camest doun to se the batel. And 29
Dauid seide, What haue Y do^q? Whether
it is not a^r word? And Dauid bowide^s a 30
litil fro hym to another man; and Dauid
seide the same word, and the puple an-
sweride to hym al^t word as bifore^u. For- 31
sothe^v these^w wordis weren herd, whiche^x
Dauid spak, and weren^y teld 'in the siȝt
of^z Saul. And whanne Dauyd was brouȝt 32
to Saul, Dauyd spak to hym^a, The herte
of ony man falle not doun^b for 'that Fi-
listei^c, Y thi seruaunt schal go, and 'Y
schal^d fiȝte aȝens the Filistei. And Saul 33
seide to Dauid, Thou maist not aȝenstonde
this Filistei, nether fiȝte aȝens hym, for
thou art a child; forsothe^l this man is a
werriour fro his ȝong wexynge age. And 34
Dauid seide to Saul, Thi seruaunt kepte
'the floc of his fadir^m, and a lioun cam,
etherⁿ a bere, and took^o awei^p 'a ram fro
the myddis^q of the floc; Y pursuede, and 35

^w seith BCEFH.   ^x ȝeue DH. ȝiue c. ȝiuen E.   ^y Om. A.   ^z thos B. thoo CE sec. m. thulke E. pr. m.
^a seide CE.   ^b falle thou D.

^a repreef I.   ^b make that man I.   ^c Om. I.   ^d in Israel he schal I.   ^e paiyng of tribut I.   ^f and I.
^g is he I.   ^h dispisith I.   ⁱ And I.   ^k Dauid I.   ^l Goliath I.   ^m the eldre brother of Dauid I.   ⁿ Dauid I.
^o thou hidere I.   ^p hast thou lefte I.   ^q mysdo I.   ^r but a I.   ^s ȝede thenns I.   ^t the I.   ^u thei diden
bifore I.   ^v And I.   ^w the I.   ^x that I.   ^y thei weren I.   ^z bifore I.   ^a hym thus I.   ^b down in him I.
^c Om. I.   ^d Om. I.   ^l but I.   ^m his fadirs floc I.   ⁿ also I. other L.   ^o tooken A. sec. m. I.   ^p Om. EL.
^q myddil I.

mouth of hem; and thei rysen aȝens me,
and I cauȝte the chaul of hem, and
36 straunglide, and slowȝ hem. Forsothe
and a lioun and a beere slewe Y thi seruaunt; therfore shal he and this Philistee
vncircumcidid as oon of thes. Now Y
shal goo, and take awey the shenship of
the puple; for who is this Philistee
vncircumcidid, that is hardy to myssey
37 to the oost of the lyuynge God? And
Dauid seith, The Lord that hath delyuerd me fro the mouth of the lioun, and
fro the hoond of the beere, he shal delyuer me fro the hoond of this Philistee.
Forsothe Saul seide to Dauid, Go, and
38 the Lord be with thee. And Saul
clothide Dauid with his clothis, and
putte on a stelen helm vpon his heed,
and clothide hym with an hawberioun.
39 Thanne Dauid gyrd with his swerd vpon
his clothinge, began to asaye if armyd
he myȝte goo; forsothe he hadde not the
custome. And Dauid seide to Saul, I
may not thus goo, for and[c] vse I haue
not. And he putte doun tho thingis,
40 and he took his staf, that euermore he
hadde in hondis. And he cheese to hym
fyue moost cleer stonus of the streem;
and he putte hem into the sheepherdis
scrip that he hadde with hym; and he
took a slynge in hoond, and ȝeed forth
41 aȝens the Philystee. Forsothe the Philistee ȝeed, comynge and neiȝynge aȝens
42 Dauyd; and his squyer before hym. And
whanne the Philistee hadde inwardly beholden hym, and seen Dauyd, he despiside hym; forsothe he was a ȝong
43 man, rodi[d], and fayre in siȝt. And the
Philistee seide to Dauyd, Whethir I am[dd]
a dog, that thou comest to me with a
staf? And the Philistee curside Dauid in
44 his goddis; and seide to Dauyd, Com to
me, and Y shal ȝeue thi flesh to the

killide[r] hem, and rauyschide[s] fro 'the
mouth of hem[t]; and thei risiden[u] aȝens
me, and I took the[v] nether chaule 'of
hem[w], and Y stranglide, and killide hem.
For[x] Y thi seruaunt killide bothe a[y] lioun 36
and a[y] bere; therfor and this Filistei vncircumcidid schal be as oon of hem. Now
Y schal go, and Y schal do awey the
schenschip[z] of the puple; for who is this
Filistei vncircumcidid, that was hardi to
curse the oost of God lyuynge? And[a] 37
Dauid seide, The Lord that delyuerede me
fro the 'mouth of the lioun[b], and fro the
'hond, *that is*[c], *power*, of the bere, he schal
delyuere me fro the hond of this Filistei.
Forsothe[d] Saul seide to Dauid, Go thou,
and the Lord be with thee†. And Saul 38
clothide Dauid with hise clothis, and puttide[e] a brasun basynet on his heed, and
clothide hym with an haburioun. Therfor[f] 39
Dauid was gird with his[g] swerd on his
cloth, and bigan[h] to asaie if he myȝte go
armed; for[i] he hadde not custom[k]. And
Dauid seide to Saul, Y may not go so[l],
for Y haue not vss[m]. And Dauid puttide[n]
awei tho, and he took his staaf, which[o] he 40
hadde euere in the[p] hondis. And he chees
to hym fyue clereste[q] stonys, *that is, harde,*
pleyn, and rounde, of the stronde; and he
sente[r] tho in to the[s] schepherdis scrippe,
which[t] he hadde with hym; and he took
the[u] slynge in the[v] hond, and ȝede[w] forth
aȝens the Filistei. Sotheli[x] the Filistei 41
ȝede[y], 'goynge and neiȝyng aȝens Dauid[z];
and his squyer ȝede[a] bifor hym[b]. And 42
whanne 'the Filistei[c] hadde biholde Dauid,
and hadde[d] seyn hym, he dispiside Dauid;
forsothe[e] Dauid was a ȝong wexynge man,
rodi, and feir in siȝt. And 'the Filistei[f], 43
seide to Dauid, Whether Y am a dogge,
for thou comest to me with a staf? And
'the Filistei[g] curside Dauid in hise goddis;
and he seide to Dauid, Come thou to me, 44

† *the Lord be with thee;* bi this summe seyen, that Saul hadde reuelacioun, that Dauith schulde ouercome the Filistey, for Goddis reuelaciouns ben maad summtyme ȝhe to yuele men, for comyn good. *Lire here.* c.

[c] in B. [d] broun E *pr. m.* [dd] ham A.

[r] I killide I. [s] I rauyschide it I. [t] her mouth I. [u] risen ELP. reriden hem up I. [v] her I. Om. EL. [w] Om. I. [x] Certis I. [y] the I. [z] repreef I. [a] And eft I. [b] liouns mouth I. [c] Om. I. [d] And I. [e] he sette I. [f] Thanne I. [g] a I. [h] he bigan I. [i] forsothe I. [k] the custom *theroff* I. [l] thus I. [m] the uss *of it* I. [n] putte I. [o] that I. [p] his I. [q] ful clere *rounde* I. [r] putte IM. [s] his I. a X. Om. E. [t] that I. [u] a I. [v] his I. [w] he ȝede I. [x] And I. [y] ȝede forth I. [z] Om. I. [a] Om. I. [b] hym, comynge niȝ aȝens Dauid I. [c] Goliath I. [d] Om. I. [e] and I. [f] Goliath I. [g] Goliath I.

fowlis of heuene, and to the beestis of
45 the erthe. Forsothe Dauid seide to the
Philistee, Thou comest to me with swerd,
speer, and sheeld; forsothe Y come to
thee in the name of the Lord God of
oostis, God of the cumpanyes of Irael,
to whom thou hast reprouyd to day.
46 And the Lord shal ʒeue thee in myn
hoond, and I shal smyte thee, and take
awey thin heed fro thee; and I shal ʒyue
the careyns of the tentis of Philisteis to
day to the fowlis of heuene, and to the
beestis of the erthe; that al the erthe
47 wyte, for the Lord God is in Yrael, and
al this chirche knewe, for not in swerd
ne in speer saueth the Lord; forsothe of
hym is the batayl, and he shal take ʒou
48 in to oure hoondis. Thanne whanne the
Philistee was rysen, and cam, and neiʒede
aʒens Dauid, Dauid hyede, and aʒen cam
to the fiʒt forn aʒens of the Philistee.
49 And he putte his hoond into the scrip,
and took a stoon, and leyde in the slynge,
and, berynge it about, he smoot hym in
the forcheed; and the stoon is piʒt in the
forhed of hym, and he felle into his face
50 vpon the erthe. And Dauid hadde the
maystrie aʒens the Philistee in slynge
and stoon, and the smyten Philistee he
slewʒ. And whanne Dauid hadde no swerd
51 in the hoond, he ran, and stood vpon the
Philistee, and took his swerd, and drewʒ
it out of his sheeth; and he slewʒ hym,
and girde of his heed. Forsothe seynge
the Philisteis that the strengest of hem
52 was deed, thei flowen. And rysynge the
men of Yrael, and of Juda criden out, and
pursueden the Philisteis, for to the while
that thei camen into the valey, and vnto
the ʒate of Acharon. And there fellen
woundid of the Philisteis, in the weye of
Sarym, and vnto Geth, and vnto Acha-

and Y schal ʒyue thi fleischis to the volatilis of heuene, and to the beestis of
45 erthe. Sotheli Dauid seide to the Filistei, Thou comest to me with swerd,
and spere, and scheeld†; but Y come to
thee in the name of the Lord God†‡ of
oostis, of God of the cumpanyes of Israel, to whiche thou seidist schenschip
to dai. And the Lord schal ʒyue‖ thee in 46
myn hond, and Y schal sle thee, and Y
schal take awey thin heed fro thee; and
I schal ʒyue the deed bodies of the castels
of Filisteis to day to the volatils of heuene, and to the beestis of erthe; that al
47 the erthe wite, that the Lord God is in
Israel, and that al this chirche knowe,
that the Lord saueth not in swerd nether
in spere; for the batel is his, and he schal
bitake ʒou in to oure hondis. Therfor 48
whanne the Filistei hadde rise, and cam,
and neiʒede aʒens Dauid, Dauid hastide,
and ran to batel aʒens the Filistei. And 49
Dauid putte his hond in to his scrippe,
and he took o stoon, and he castide
with the slynge, and ledde aboute, and
smoot the Filistei in the forheed, and
the stoon was fastned in his forheed, and
he felde doun in to his face on the erthe.
And Dauid hadde the maistrie aʒens the 50
Filistei in a slyng and stoon, and he
killide the Filistei smytun. And whanne
Dauid hadde no swerd in the hond, he 51
ran, and stood on the Filistei, and took
his swerd; and Dauid drow out the swerd
of his schethe, and killide him, and kittide awei his heed. Forsothe the Filisteis sien, that the strongeste of hem
was deed, and thei fledden. And the sones 52
of Israel and of Juda risiden to gidere,
and crieden, and pursueden Filisteis, 'til
the while thei camen in to the valei, and
'til to the ʒate of Accaron. And woundid

† and scheeld; that is, tristinge in thyn armeris and virtu. Lire here. c.
‡ of the Lord God, etc.; that is, tristinge of Goddis virtu. Lire here. c.
‖ the Lord schal ʒyue, etc. Dauyth seid this bi Goddis reuelacioun, for he bifor tellith certenly thing to comynge, vn certeyn to mannus knowing. Lire here. c.

h fleishe I. i foulis of the eir I. k Om. I. l the erthe I. m And I. n Goliath I. o a swerd E.
p Om. IK. q Om. EILP. r Om. I. s Om. I. t Om. EL. u whom I. v hast seld I. w repreff I.
x Om. DIMXb. y and to dai I. z tentis I. a Om. I. b foulis I. c the erthe b. d Om. plures.
e sothely I. f Thanne I. g risen up I. h fiʒte I. i Golie I. k puttide Brb. l in D. m the plures.
n took out EIL. o a IL. p Dauid I. q whirlide I. castide it EL. r Om. I. s his EL. t slynge aboute I.
u and keste out therof a stoon I. v he smoot I. w Golie I. x the DL. Om. E. y Golie I.
z vpon I. a erthe, in a slynge and a stoon I. b Golie I. c in a slyng and a stoon KL. Om. I. d Golie I.
e whanne he hadde smytun him doun I. f his I. g vpon I. h Gobie I. i his A. that I. k the I.
l he killide therwith Golie I. m kitte I. n off I. o And I. p strengeste man I. q resen up I. risen ELP.
r thei crieden I. s the Filisteis I. t til the tyme I. vnto that EL. u vnto I. into EL. v the woundid I.

53 ron. And the sonis of Yrael turnynge aȝen, after that thei hadden pursued the Philisteis, thei asseilden the tentis of
54 hem. Forsothe Dauyd takynge the heed of the Philistee, brouȝte it into Jerusalem; forsothe the armys of hym he putte
55 in his tabernacle. Forsothe that tyme that Saul sawȝ Dauyd goynge out aȝens the Philistee, he seith to Abner, the prynce of his chyualrie, Abner, of what stok descendide this ȝong man? And Abner seide, Lyueth thi soule, kyng, I
56 knewȝ not. And the kyng seith, Ask
57 thou, whos sone ise this child. And whanne Dauyd was comen aȝen, the Philistee smyten, Abner took hym, and brouȝte hym yn before Saul, hauynge in
58 the hoond the heed of the Philistee. And Saul seith to hym, Of what progenye art thou, O thou ȝong man? And Dauid seide, The sone of thi seruaunt, Ysaye Bethlemyte, Y am.

men of Filisteisʷ feldenˣ in the weye of Sarym, and 'til toʸ Geth, and 'til toʸ Acca-
53 ron. And the sones of Israel turneden aȝen, aftir that thei hadden pursuede Filisteisʳ, and thei assailiden 'the tentis of
54 hemᵃ. Forsotheᵇ Dauid took the heed of 'the Filisteiᶜ, and brouȝte it in to Jerusalem; sotheliᵈ heᵉ puttide hiseᶠ armerisᵍ in
55 the 'tabernacle of the Lordʰ. Forsotheⁱ in that tyme in which Saul siȝ Dauid goynge out aȝens 'the Filisteiᵏ, he seide to Abner, princeˡ of his chiualrieᵐ, Abner, of what generacioun 'cam forthⁿ this ȝong wax-yngeᵒ man? And Abner seide, Kyng, thi soule lyueth, I knoweᵖ not. And the kyng
56 seide, Axe thou, whos sone this child is.
57 And whanne Dauid haddeq come aȝen, whanne 'the Filisteiʳ was slayn, Abnerˢ took Dauid, and brouȝteᵗ hym inᵘ, hauynge in theᵛ hond the heed of 'the Filisteiʷ, 'bi-for Saulˣ. And Saul seide to hymʸ, Of
58 what generacioun art thou, ȝong waxyngeᶻ man? And Dauid seide, Y am the sone of thi seruaunt, Isai of Bethleem.

CAP. XVIII.

1 And it is doon, whanne he hadde endid to speke to Saul, the soule of Jonathas is glewid to gidre to the soul of Dauid, and Jonathas louyde hym as his owne lijf.
2 And Saul took hym in that day, and grauntide not to hym, that he turne aȝen
3 into the hows of his fadre. Forsothe Jonathas and Dauid wenten into thef couenaunt of pees; forsothe he louyde
4 hym as his lijf; forwhi Jonathas spuylide hym self the coote, that he was clothid, and ȝaf it to Dauid, and his other clothis, vntoᵍ his 'bowe and swerdʰ, and vnto the
5 knyȝtis girdil. Forsothe Dauyd wente out to alle thingis, what euere Saul sente

CAP. XVIII.

1 And it was doon, whanne Dauid 'hadde endidᵃ to speke to Saul, the soule of Jona-thasᵃᵃ was glued† togidre to the soule of Dauid, and Jonathas louyde hymᵇ as his owne soule. And Saul tookᶜ Dauid in
2 that dai, and grauntideᵈ not 'to hymᵉ, 'that he schuldeᶠ turneᵍ aȝen in to 'the
3 hows of his fadirʰ. Forsotheⁱ Jonathas and Dauid maden boondᵏ of pees, 'that isˡ, swerynge euerlasiyngeᵐ frenschipⁿ; for Jonathas louyde Dauid as his owne souleᵒ;
4 for whi Jonathas dispuylideᵖ him silf fro the coote 'in whichq he was clothidʳ, and ȝafˢ it to Dauid, and hise othere clothis, 'til toᵗ his swerd and bouweᵘ, and 'til toᵗ

ᵉ be ᴅᴄᴇꜰʜ. ꜰ Om. ᴅᴄᴇꜰʜ. ᵍ into ᴀ. ʰ swerd and his bowe ᴇ pr. m.

ʷ the Filisteis ɪ. ˣ fellen doun ɪ. ȝellen ᴇʟᴘ. ʸ vnto ɪ. into ᴇʟ. ᶻ the Filisteis ɪ. ᵃ her tentis ɪ.
ᵇ And ɪ. ᶜ Golie ɪ. ᵈ and ɪ. ᵉ Dauid ɪ. ᶠ the ɪ. ᵍ armeris of Golie ɪ. ʰ Lordis tabernacle ɪ.
ⁱ And ɪ. ᵏ Golie ɪ. ˡ the prince ɪ. ᵐ chiualrie, seiynge ɪ. ⁿ is ɪ. ᵒ Om. ɪ. ᵖ wot ɪ. q was ɪ.
ʳ Golie ɪ. ˢ and Abner ɪ. ᵗ he brouȝte ɪ. ᵘ in bifore Saul ɪ. ᵛ his ɪ. ʷ Filistei plures. Golie ɪ.
ˣ Om. ɪ. ʸ Dauid ɪ. ᶻ Om. ɪ. ᵃ ent ᴇʟ. hadde end ᴘ. ᵃᵃ Jonathanas ᴀ. ᵇ Dauid ɪ. ᶜ took to him ɪ.
ᵈ he grauntide ɪ. ᵉ leeue to Dauid ɪ. ᶠ Om. ɪ. ᵍ to turne ɪ. ʰ his faders hows ɪ. ⁱ And ɪ. ᵏ a
boond ɪ. ˡ in that ᴅ. ᵐ of euerlastynge ᴇʟ. ⁿ The whole gloss omitted in ɪ. ᵒ lijf ɪ. ᵖ vnclothide ɪ.
q that ɪ. ʳ clothid ynne ɪ. ˢ he ȝaf ɪ. ᵗ vnto ɪ. into ᴇʟ. ᵘ his bouwe ɪ.

him, and wiseli he gouernde[i] hym self[k];
and Saul putte hym vpon men of batayl,
and he was acceptid in the eyen of al the
puple, and moost in the siȝt of the ser-
6 uauntis of Saul. Forsothe whanne Dauid
turnede aȝen, the Philistee smyten, and
beer the heed of hym into Jerusalem, the
wymmen wenten out fro alle the cytees
of Yrael, syngynge, and dauncis ledynge,
into aȝencomynge of Saul the kyng, in
7 tymbers of gladnes, and in trumpis. And
the wymmen songen before, pleiynge, and
seyynge, Saul hath smyten a thousand,
8 and Dauyd ten thowsandis. And Saul
is wrooth ful mych, and this word displeside in the eyen of hym; and seide,
Thei han ȝouun to Dauid ten thousandis,
and to me a thousand thei han ȝouun;
what to hym is more ouere but oneli the
9 rewme? Thanne not with riȝt eyen Saul
bihelde Dauid, fro that day and therafter.
10 Forsothe after the tother day the yuel
spiryt of God aseilide Saul, and he
straungeli spak in the myddis of his
hows. Forsothe Dauid harpide with his
hoond, as bi eche days; and Saul heelde
11 a speer, and kest it, wenynge that he
myȝt pitche to gidre Dauid with the wal;
and Dauyd bowide a side fro the face
12 of hym the secounde tyme. And Saul
dredde Dauid, forthi that the Lord was
with hym, and fro hym goon awey.
13 Thanne Saul moued hym a wey fro hym,
and made hym a leder vpon a thousand
men; and he wente out and cam yn in
14 the siȝt of the puple. Forsothe in alle
his weyes Dauid wiseli dide, and the
15 Lord was with hym; and so Saul sawȝ
that he was wel mych wiys, and began
16 to shunne hym. Forsothe al Yrael and
Juda louyde Dauyd; forsothe he ȝede

the[v] girdil. Also[w] Dauid ȝede out[x] to alle 5
thingis, to what euer thingis Saul 'hadde
sent[y] hym, and he gouernede hym silf
prudentli; and Saul settide[z] hym ouer the
men of batel[a], and 'he was[b] acceptid[c], '*ether
plesaunt*[d], in the iȝen[e] of al[f] the puple[g],
and moost in the siȝt of 'the seruauntis of
Saul[h]. Forsothe[i] whanne Dauid turnede 6
aȝen, whanne[k] 'the Filistei[l] was slayn, and
bar the heed of 'the Filistei[m] in to Jerusalem, wymmen ȝeden out of alle the
citees of Israel, and sungen[n], and ledden
queris[o], aȝens the comyng of king Saul, in
tympans of[p] gladnesse, and in[q] trumpis.
And the wymmen sungen, pleiynge[r], and 7
seiynge, Saul smoot[s] a thousynde, and
Dauid *smoot*[t] ten thousynde. Saul[u] was 8
wrooth greetli, and this word displeside
'in his iȝen[v]; and he seide, Thei ȝauen[w]
ten thousynde to Dauid, and 'thei ȝauen
a[x] thousynde to me; what leeueth to hym[y],
no but the rewme aloone? Therfor[z] Saul 9
bihelde Dauid not with 'riȝtful iȝen[a], 'fro
that dai and afterward[b]. Sotheli[c] aftir 10
the tother dai a[d] wickid[e] spirit of God
asailide Saul, and he propheciede† in the
myddis of his hows[f]. Forsothe[g] Dauid 11
harpide with his hond, as bi alle daies[h];
and Saul helde a spere, and caste[i] it, and[k]
gesside that he myȝte prene[l] Dauid with[m]
the wal, *that is, perse with the spere, so
that it schulde passe*[n] *til*[o] *to the wal*[p]; and
Dauid bowide 'fro his face[q] the secounde
tyme. And Saul dredde Dauid, for the 12
Lord was with hym[r], and hadde go awei
fro him silf[s]. Therfor[t] Saul remouide 13
Dauid fro hym silf, and made hym tribune[u]‡ on[v] a thousynde men; and Dauid
ȝede[w] out and entride[x] in 'the siȝt of[y] the
puple. And Dauid dide warli[z] in alle hise 14
weies, and the Lord was with hym; and 15

† *profesiede*; not propirly, but he spak alien thingis, as a man trauelid of a fend. *Lire here.* c.

‡ *and made him tribune, etc.*; Saul dide this, not for the onour of Dauyth, but that Dauyth schulde go out to batels, and schulde be slayn; but the Lord turnede this in to the good of Dauyth as it is opin of the lettre suynge. *Lire here.* c.

[i] dide E *pr.m.* [k] sel E *sec.m.*

[v] his I. [w] And I. [x] forth I. [y] sente I. [z] sette I. [a] his batel I. [b] Om. I. [c] accept *plures.* Om. I. [d] Om. CI. [e] siȝt I. [f] Om. E. [g] puple Dauid was alowid I. [h] Sauls seruauntis I. [i] And I. [k] and I. [l] Golie I. [m] Golie I. [n] wymmen sungen I. [o] daunces A *sec.m.* squeris L. [p] and K *sec.m.* [q] Om. I. [r] pleynge A *sec.m.* fleyng DEGLMNOPQRSUWb. [s] hath sley I. [t] Om. I. [u] And Saul I. [v] bifore him I. [w] han ȝouen I. [x] but o I. [y] Dauith heroff I. [z] Thanne fro that dai forth I. [a] blythe chere I. [b] Om. I. [c] And I. [d] the I. [e] yuel I. [f] meynee I. [g] And I. [h] daies *bifore* I. [i] he threwe I. castide M. sente DEKLOPXb. [k] for he I [l] haue perschid I. [m] thorouȝ to I. [n] *prene* G. [o] *in* E. [p] The whole gloss omitted in CI. [q] aside fro Saul I. [r] Dauid I. [s] Om. DIb. [t] Thanne I. [u] chefteyn I. [v] upon I. [w] wente I. [x] he came I. [y] bifore I. [z] wisely I.

17 yn and 3ede out before hem. And Saul seide to Dauid, Loo! my more dou3ter Merob, hir Y shal 3eue to thee a wijf; oneli be a strong man, and fi3t the bateils of the Lord. Forsothe Saul trowide, sei- ynge, Be not myn hoond in hym, but be 18 vpon hym the hoond of Philisteis. For- sothe Dauyd seide to Saul, Who am Y, or what is my lijf, or the kynrede of my fadre in Irael, that Y be maad the sone 19 in lawe of the kyng? It is doon forsothe the tyme whanne Merob, the dou3ter of Saul, shulde be 3euen to Dauid, 3euen is 20 Hadriel Molatite wijf. Forsothe Dauyd louyd Mychol, the tother dou3ter of Saul; and it is toold to Saul, and it pleside to 21 hym. And Saul seide, Y shal 3yue hir to hym, that it be maad to hym into sclaundre, and be vpon hym the hoond of Philisteis. Thanne seide Saul to Dauyd, In two thingis thow shalt be my 22 sone in lawe to day. And Saul co- maundide to his seruauntis, Spek 3e to Dauith¹ pryuely fro me, seiynge, Loo! thou plesist to the kyng, and alle the seruauntis of hym louen thee; now thanne be thow the sone in lawe of 23 the kyng. And the seruauntis of Saul speken in the eeris of Dauid alle thes wordis. And Dauid seith, Whether litil it seme to 3ow to be the^m sone in lawe of the kyng? Forsothe Y am a pore 24 man, and a thinne. And the seruauntis of Saul toolden a3en, seiynge, Sich maner 25 wordis spak Dauid. Forsothe Saul seide, Thus spekith to Dauid, The kyng nedith no^n sposeilis, but oonli an hundrid tersis of Philisteis, that veniaunce be doon of the enemyes of the kyng. Forsothe Saul thou3te to betray Dauid into the hoondis 26 of Philisteis. And whanne his seruauntis hadden a3en toold to Dauid the wordis that Saul hadde seid, the word pleside

so Saul si3 that Dauid was ful prudent^a, and he bigan to be war of Dauid. For-16 sothe^b al Israel and Juda louyden Dauid; for he entride^c and 3ede^d out bifor hem. And Saul seide to Dauid, Lo! 'my more^e 17 dou3tir Merob, Y schal 3iue her wijf to thee; oneli be thou a strong man, and fi3te thou the 'batels of the Lord^f. For- sothe^g Saul 'arettide, and^h seide^i, Myn hond be not in hym^k, but the hond of Filisteis be on hym. Sotheli^l Dauid seide 18 to Saul, Who am Y, ether what is my lijf, ether the^m meynee^n of my fadir in Israel, that Y be maad the 'sone in lawe of the kyng^o? Forsothe^p the tyme 'was maad^q 19 whanne^r Merob, the dou3ter of Saul, 'ou3te to^s be 3ouun^t to Dauid, sche was 3ouun wijf to Hadriel Molatite. Forsothe^u Dauid 20 louide Mychol, the dou3tir of Saul; and it was teld to Saul, and it pleside hym. And 21 Saul seide, Y schal 3yue hir to hym, that it be to hym in to sclaundir, and the hond of Filisteis be on^v hym. Therfor^w Saul seide to Dauid, In 'twei dou3tris^x† thou schalt be my sone in lawe to dai. And 22 Saul comaundide to hise seruauntis, Speke 3e^y to Dauid, while^z it 'is hid fro me^a, and seie 3e^b, Lo! thou plesist the king, and alle hise seruauntis louen thee; now ther- for be thou hosebonde of the 'dou3tir of the kyng^c. And the seruauntis of Saul 23 spaken alle these wordis in the eeris^d of Da- uid. And Dauid seide, Whether it semeth^e litil to 3ou 'to be sone in lawe of the kyng^f? Forsothe^g Y am a pore man, and a feble. And the seruauntis telden to Saul, 24 and seiden, Dauid spak siche wordis. So- 25 theli^h Saul seide, Thus speke 3e to Dauid, The kyng hath no nede to 3iftis for spow- sails†, no^i but onely to an hundrid pre- pucies^k, 'that is, mennus 3erdis vncircum- cidid^l, 'of Filisteis^m, that veniaunce be maad of the kyngis enemyes. Certis Saul

† dou3tris; in summe bokis it is addid thingis, but it is not in Ebreu, nether it is of the text. Lire here. c.

† spousails; that is, pre- ciouse 3iftis of gold ether of siluer, that ben wont to be 3ouun to kingis, whanne thei 3yuen her dou3tris to hosebondis. Lire here. c.

¹ day a. ^m Om. b. ^n not E sup. ras.

^a wijs 1. ^b And 1. ^c 3ede vn 1. ^d Om. 1. ^e myn eldre 1. ^f Lordis batels 1. ^g And 1. ^h Om. 1. ^i seide withynne him self 1. ^k Dauid 1. ^l And 1. ^m what is the 1. ^n kynrede 1. ^o kyngis sone in lawe 1. ^p And whanne 1. ^q came 1. ^r that 1. ^s schulde haue 1. ^t 3ouun wijf 1. ^u Certis 1. ^v vpon 1. ^w Thanne 1. ^x two thingis 1. ^y 3e priuely 1. ^z as if 1. ^a were me vnwitinge 1. ^b 3e to him 1. ^c kingis dou3tir 1. ^d heringe 1. ^e seme 1. ^f me to be the kyngis sone in lawe 1. ^g Sothli 1. ^h And 1. ^i Om. 1. ^k Om. 1. ^l Om. 1. ^m Filisteis prepucies 1.

in the eyen of Dauyd, that he were maad
27 the sone in lawe of the kyng. And after
a fewe days Dauyd rysynge wente into
Acharon, with the men that with hym
weren, and smoot of the Philisteis two
hundrid men; and brou3te the 3erdis of
hem, and noumbride hem to the kyng,
that he were the sone in lawe of the
kyng. And so Saul 3af to hym Mychol,
28 his dou3ter, wijf. And Saul saw3, and
vndurstood, that the Lord was with
29 Dauid. Forsothe Mychol, the dou3ter of
Saul, louid hym, and Saul began more to
drede Dauyd; and Saul is maad the ene-
30 mye of Dauyd alle days. And the princis
of Philisteis wenten out; forsothe fro the
bigynnynge of the goynge out of hem
Dauyd wiselyer beer hym self than alle
the men of Saul; and solempne is maad
the name of hym ful myche.

thou3te to bitake Dauid in to the hondis
of Filisteis[n]. And whanne the seruauntis 26
of Saul hadden teld to Dauid the wordis,
whiche[o] Saul hadde seid, the word pleside
'in the i3en of[p] Dauid, that he schulde be
maad the kyngis son in lawe. And aftir 27
a fewe daies Dauid roos[q], and 3ede in to
Acharon, with the[r] men that weren with
hym, and he killide of Filisteis twei hundrid men; and brou3te[s] 'the prepucies of
hem[t], and noumbride[u] tho to the kyng,
that he schulde be the kyngis sone in
lawe. And so Saul 3af Mycol, his dou3ter,
wiif to hym[v]. And Saul si3, and vndir- 28
stood, that the Lord was with Dauid.
Forsothe[w] Mychol, 'the dou3ter of Saul[x], 29
louide Dauid, and Saul bigan more to drede
Dauid; and Saul was maad enemye to
Dauid in alle daies. And the princes of 30
Filisteis 3eden out[y]; forsothe[z] fro the bigynnyng of her goyng out Dauyd bar
hym silf more warli[a] than alle the[b] men
of Saul; and the name of Dauid was
maad ful solempne.

CAP. XIX.

1 Saul spak to Jonathan, his sone, and
to alle his seruauntis, that thei shulden
slee Dauid; forsothe Jonathas, the sone
2 of Saul, louid Dauyd mych. Jonathas
shewide to Dauid, seiynge, Saul, my
fader, sechith to slee thee, wherfor keep
the wel; Y biseche[o], dwel; and thou shalt
3 dwel priueli, and be hyd. Forsothe Y
goynge out shal stoond biside my fadre
in the feeld, where euer he were; and I
shal spek of thee to my fadre, and what
euere thing Y shal see, Y shal telle to
4 thee. Thanne Jonathas spak good thingis
of Dauid to Saul, his fader, and seide to
hym, Ne synne thou, kyng, into thi seruaunt Dauid, for he hath not synned to
5 thee, and the werkis of hym ben goode
to thee mych; and he hath put his lijf

CAP. XIX.

Forsothe[c] Saul spak to Jonathas, his 1
sone, and to alle hise seruauntis, that thei
schulden sle Dauid; certis Jonathas, the
sone of Saul, louyde Dauid greetli. And 2
Jonathas schewide to Dauid, and seide,
Saul, my fadir, sekith to sle thee, wherfor,
Y biseche, kepe 'thou thee[d] eerli[e]; and
thou schalt dwelle priueli[f], and thou schalt
be hid. Sotheli[g] Y schal go out, and 3
stonde bisidis my fadir in the feeld, where
euer he schal be; and Y schal speke of
thee to my fadir, and what euer thing Y
shal se[h], Y schal telle to[i] thee. Therfor[k] 4
Jonathas spak good thingis of Dauid to
Saul, his fadir, and seide to hym, Kyng,
do thou not synne a3ens thi seruaunt
Dauid, for he 'synnede not[l] to thee, and
hise werkis ben ful good to thee; and he 5

---

o biseche thee ε pr. m.

---

n the Filisteis 1. o that 1. p bifore 1. q roos up 1. r Om. 1. s Dauith brou3te 1. t her prepucies 1.
u he noumbride 1. v Dauid 1. w Certis 1. x Sauls dou3tir 1. y out to fi3te 1. z but 1. a wisely 1.
b Om. M. c Sotheli 1. d thi self 1. e to morowe eerly 1. f priueli in the feeld 1. g And 1. h vndirstonde of him 1. i Om. 1. k Thanne 1. l hath not synned 1.

in thin hoond, and smoot the Philistee.
And the Lord hath doo greet helth[p] to
al Yrael; thou hast seen and gladidist;
whi thanne synnest thou in the giltles
blood, sleynge Dauyd, that is with out
6 blame? The which thing whanne Saul
hadde herd, pleside bi the voys of Jonathe, swore, The Lord lyueth, for he
7 shal not be slayn. And so Jonathas clepide Dauid, and shewide to hym alle thes
wordis. And Jonathas brouȝte yn Dauid
to Saul, and he was before hym, as he
was ȝistirday and the thridde day before.
8 Forsothe eft is moued batayl; and Dauyd
goon out fauȝt aȝens[q] Philisteis[r], and he
smoot hem bi a greet veniaunce, and thei
9 flowen fro the face of hym. And the yuel
spirit of the Lord is doon in Saul; forsothe
he sat in his hows, and helde a spere; for-
10 sothe Dauid harpid in his hoond. And Saul
enforside to fitche to gidre with a spere
Dauid in[s] the wal; and Dauid bowide a
side fro the face of Saul; forsothe the
speer, the wound pryued, is born into the
wal; and Dauid fleȝe, and is saued that
11 nyȝt. Thanne Saul sente his cruel seruauntis the nyȝt into the hows of Dauid,
that thei myȝten kepe hym, and sleen in
the morwe. The which thing whanne
Mychol, his wijf, hadde toold to Dauide,
seiynge, But if thou saue thee this nyȝt,
12 to morwe thou shalt die; she putte hym
down bi the wyndowe. Forsothe he ȝede
13 a wey, and fleiȝe, and is sauid. Forsothe
Michol took an ymage, and putte it vpon
the bed, and an heery skyn of the she
geet she putte vpon the heed of it, and
14 couerde it with clothis. Forsothe Saul
sente seruauntis that shulden taak Dauyd,
and it is answerd, that he was sike.

puttide[m] his lijf† in his[n] hond, and he
killide the Filistei. And[o] the Lord made[p]
greet heelthe[q] to al Israel; thou siȝ[r], and
were[s] glad; whi therfor synnest thou in
giltles blood, and sleest[t] Dauid, which[u] is
with out gilt? And whanne Saul hadde 6
herd this, he was plesid with the vois[v] of
Jonathas, and swoor[w], 'The Lord lyueth[x],
'*that is*[y], *bi the Lord lyuynge*[z], for Dauid
schal not be slayn. Therfor[a] Jonathas 7
clepide Dauid, and schewide to hym alle
these wordis. And Jonathas brouȝte in
Dauid to Saul, and he was bifor hym[b] as
'ȝistirdai and the thridde dai ago[c]. For- 8
sothe[d] batel was moued eft; and Dauyd
ȝede out, and fauȝt aȝens Filisteis[e], and he
smoot hem with a[f] greet wounde[g], and
thei fledden fro his face. And the yuel 9
spirit of the Lord was maad on[h] Saul;
sotheli[i] he sat in his hows, and helde a
spere; certis Dauid harpide in[k] his hond.
And Saul enforside[l] to prene[m] with the 10
spere[n] Dauid in the wal; and Dauid
bowide[o] fro 'the face of Saul[p]; forsothe[q]
the spere 'with voide wounde[r] was borun[s]
in to the wal; and Dauid fledde, and[t] was
saued in that niȝt. Therfor[u] Saul sente 11
hise knyȝtis[v] in the[w] nyȝt in to the hows
of Dauid, that thei schulden kepe hym,
and that he 'schulde be[x] slayn in the
morewtide. And whanne[y] Mychol, the
wijf of Dauid, hadde teld this to Dauid,
and seide, If thou sauest not thee in this
nyȝt, thou schalt die to morew; sche[z] 12
puttide[a] hym doun bi a wyndow. Forsothe[b] he[c] ȝede, and fledde[d], and was[e]
sauyd. Sotheli[f] Mychol took an ymage, 13
and puttide[g] it on the bed[h], and puttide[i]
'an heeri skyn of geet[k] at the heed therof,
and hilide it with clothis. Forsothe[l] Saul 14

† *he puttide his lijf;* that is, puttide forth his liyf to perel, as myche as it semyde to mannus doom; for he ȝede vnarmed to fiȝte aȝenus the Filistey, as it is seide in xvii. c°. *Lire here.* c.

[p] liȝt E *pr. m.* [q] aȝens the DEF. [r] Philistee CE. [s] and A.

[m] hath put I. [n] thin I. [o] And so I. [p] hath maad I. [q] helpe EL. [r] sauȝst this I. [s] thou were I. [t] wilt sle I. [u] that I. [v] spekyng I. [w] he swoor I. [x] Om. I. [y] Om. CI. [z] Om. C. [a] And so I. [b] Saul I. [c] he was wont bifore I. [d] Certis I. [e] the Filisteis I. [f] Om. I. [g] feersnesse I. [h] upon I. [i] and I. [k] with I. [l] enforside hym I. [m] prenede U. *that is, peerse* K *marg.* [n] spere to stike togidre I. [o] bowide awey I. [p] Sauls siȝt I. [q] and I. [r] with oute hurt *of Dauid* I. [s] ficchid I. [t] and so he I. [u] Thanne I. [v] cruel seruauntis I. [w] that I. [x] were I. [y] Om. I. [z] and sche I. [a] lete I. [b] And I. [c] Dauid I. [d] fledde thenns I. [e] he was I. [f] And I. [g] leide I. [h] bed of Dauid I. [i] sche putte I. [k] a rouȝ geet skin I. [l] And I.

15 And eft Saul sente messagers, that thei seen Dauid, seiynge, Brynge⁸⁸ ȝe hym to 16 me in the bed, that he be slayn. And whanne the messagers weren comen, it is foundun a simulacre vpon the bed, and skynnys of she geet at the heed of it. 17 And Saul seide to Mychol, Whi hast thou thus bigilid me, and hast laft myn enemye, that he flee? And Mychol answerde to Saul, For he spak to me, seiynge, Let me goon, ellis Y shal slee thee. 18 Forsothe Dauid fleynge is sauyd; and he cam to Samuel in Ramatha, and he toolde to hym alle thingis that Saul dide to hym; and he and Samuel wenten 19 a wey, and dwelten in Naioth. Forsothe it is toold to Saul of seicres, Loo! Dauyd 20 in Naioth in Ramatha. Thanne Saul sente catchepollis forto take Dauid; the whiche whanne thei hadden seen the companye of prophetis propheciynge, and Samuel stondynge vpon hem, the Spirit of the Lord is doon in hem, and also 21 thei bigunnen to prophecien. The whiche whanne was toold to Saul, he sente and other messagers; also thei propheciden. And eft Saul sente the thridde messageris*, the whiche and thei propheciden. 22 And Saul, wrooth with wrathfulnes, he ȝede also into Ramatha; and he cam vnto the greet cistern that is in Sochoth, and askide, and seide, In what place ben Samuel and Dauid? And it is seyd to hym, Loo! in Naioth thei ben in Ramatha. 23 And he ȝede into Naioth in Ramatha; and⁺⁺ is doon also vpon hym the Spirit of the Lord; and goynge yn he wente, and propheciede, for to he cam in Naioth in 24 Ramatha. And also he spuylide hym self his clothis, and propheciede with other before Samuel, and he propheciede

sente sergeauntis^m, 'that schulden^n rauysche Dauid^o, and it was answeride^p, that he^q was sijk. And eft Saul sente messangeris, 15 that thei schulden se^r Dauid, and he^s seide, Brynge ȝe hym^t to me^u in the^v bed, that he be slayn. And whanne the messangeris 16 hadden come^w, 'a symylacre^x was foundun on the^y bed, and 'skynnes of geet^z at^a the heed therof. And Saul seide to Mychol, 17 Whi scornedist^b thou me so, and 'delyneredist^c myn enemy, that he fledde^d? And Mychol answeride to Saul, For he^e spak to me, and seide, Delyuere thou me, ellis Y schal slee thee. Forsothe^f Dauid 18 fledde, and was sauyd; and he cam to Samuel in to Ramatha, and telde^g to hym alle thingis which^h Saul hadde do to hym; and he^i and Samuel ȝeden, and dwelliden in Naioth. Forsothe^k it was teld to Saul 19 of men, seiynge^l, Lo! Dauid is in Naioth in Ramatha. Therfor Saul sente^m sleeris, 20 that thei schulden rauysche^n Dauid; and whanne thei hadden seyn the^o cumpeny of profetis† profeciynge, and Samuel stondynge ouer hem, the Spirit of the Lord, 'that is, the spirit of deuocioun^p, was maad in hem, and thei also bigunnen to prophecie‡. And whanne this was teld 21 to Saul, he sente also othere messangeris; 'sotheli and^q thei profesieden. And eft Saul sente the thridde messangeris, and thei prophecieden. And^r Saul was wrooth 'with irefulnesse^s; and he also ȝede in to 22 Ramatha, and he cam 'til to^t the^u greet cisterne, which^v is in Socoth, and he axide, and seide, In what place ben Samuel and Dauid? And it was seid to hym, Lo! thei ben in Naioth in Ramatha. And he^w 23 ȝede in 'to Naioth^x in^y Ramatha; and the Spirit of the Lord was maad also on him; and he^z ȝede, and^a entride^b, and prophe-

† *profetis; that is, the felouschipe of religiouse men preisinge God. Lire here.* c.

‡ *in profesie; that is, to preise God, and ceessiden to pursue Dauith. Lire here.* c.

---

⁸⁸ bryngith ʙ.   * massageris ᴀ.   ⁺⁺ and it ᴀ.

---

^m his seruauntis ɪ.   ^n to ɪ.   ^o Dauid thenns ɪ.   ^p answeride *to Saul* ɪ.   ^q Dauid ɪ.   ^r slee ᴋ. ^s Saul ɪ.   ^t Om. ɪ.   ^u me Dauid ɪ.   ^v his ɪ.   ^w come to Dauid ɪ.   ^x an ymage *lijk to Dauid* ɪ.   ^y his ɪ. ^z geet skynnes ɪ.   ^a on ɪ.   ^b scornest ɪ.   ^c hast delyuered ɪ.   ^d fle awey ɪ.   ^e Dauid ɪ.   ^f Certis ɪ. ^g he telde ɪ.   ^h that ɪ.   ^i Dauid ɪ.   ^k And ɪ.   ^l seiynge *to him* ɪ.   ^m sente men ɪ.   ^n rauysche *thenns* ɪ. ^o ᴀ ɪ.   ^p Om. ɪ.   ^q and certis ɪ.   ^r And with wrathfulnesse ɪ.   ^s Om. ɪ.   ^t into ɪ. vnto ᴇʟ.   ^u ᴀ ɪ. ^v that ɪ.   ^w Saul ɪ.   ^x Om. ʙ.   ^y in to ᴀᴇꜰ.   ^z Saul ɪ.   ^a goynge yn ɪ.   ^b wente ɪ.

nakid al that day and nyƷt. Wherof Ʒede out a prouerbe, Whether and Saul among the prophetis?

ciede, 'til the while^c he cam 'in to^d Naioth in^e Ramatha. And 'he also^f dispuylide^g† him silf^h of hise clothis, and^i propheciede with othere men bifor Samuel, and he profeciede nakid in^k al that dai and nyƷt. Wherfor 'a prouerbe, *that is^l, a comyn word^m*, Ʒede out, Whether and Saul^n among prophetis‡?

† *dispuylide;* not that he lefte nakid, but for he dide awey the ournementis of kyng, that he schulde take clothis liyk religiouse men, preisinge God, as Danyth dide bifor the arke. *Lire here.* c.

‡ *wher and Saul among profetis;* this is seide of him, in whom sum denoclonn apperith sodeynly at an our, as whanne a man of dissolute liyf schewith ony signe of denocioun, it is seid of him, Bernard is maad a munk, so and thanne it was seid of siche men, wher and Saul among profetis, as if he seide thilke denocioun is transitorie and at an our, and is not stidefast. *Lire here.* c.

CAP. XX.

1 Forsothe Dauid fleiƷ fro Naioth, that is in Ramatha, and comynge spak before Jonatha, What haue I doon, what haue I doon? what is my wickidnes, and what 2 my synne into thi fader, for he sechith my lijf? The which seide to hym, A wey be it fro thee, thou shalt not die, forsothe ne my fader shal^u do eny thing greet or litil, but before he shewe to me; thanne 3 this word oonli my fader hath heelid fro me, forsothe this shal not be. And eft he swore to Dauid. And he seith, Sotheli thi fadre woot, that I haue foundun grace in thin eyen, and he shal seye, Jonathas wite not this, lest perauenture he be sory; but also the Lord lyueth, and lyueth thi soule, for in o degree oonli, that I so seye, Y and deeth ben dyuydid. 4 And Jonathas seith to Dauid, What euere thing thi soule seith to me, I shal 5 doo to thee. And Dauid seide to Jonathan, Loo! kalendis ben to morwe, and I of maner am wont to sitte biside the kyng to eete; leete me thanne, that I be 6 hid in the feeld vnto the euen of the thridde day. And if biholdynge thi fader aske me, thou shalt answere to hym, Dauid preide me for to goo swiftly into Bethlem, his citee, for solempne slayn sacrifices ben there to alle the men of his 7 lynage. And if he seye, Wel, pees shal be to thi seruaunt; forsothe if he were wrooth, wite thou, that fulfillid is the

CAP. XX.

1 Forsothe^o Dauid fledde fro Naioth, which^p is in Ramatha, and cam^q and spak bifor Jonathas, What haue Y do? what is my wickidnesse, and what is my synne aƷens thi fadir, for he sekith^r my lijf? 2 And Jonathas seide to hym^s, Fer be it fro thee, thou schalt not die, for my fadir schal not do ony thing greet ether litil, 'no but^t he schewe firste to me; therfor my fadir^u kepte^v preuy fro me this word oneli^w, forsothe^x it schal not be. And eft 3 he^y swoor to Dauid. And Dauid seide, Treuli^z thi fadir woot, that Y haue founde grace 'in thin Ʒen^a, and^b he schal^c seie, Jonathas wite not this, lest perauenture he be sory; certis the Lord lyueth, 'and thi soule lyueth^d, for^e, that Y seie so, Y and deeth ben departid oneli bi o degree. 4 And Jonathas seide to Dauid, What euer thing thi soule schal seie to me, Y schal 5 do^f to thee. And Dauid seide to Jonathas, Lo†! calendis ben to morewe, and bi custom Y am wont to sitte bi the kyng to ete; therfor suffre thou me, 'that YƷ be hid in the feeld 'til to^h euentid of the 6 thridde dai. If^i thi fadir biholdith, and axith me^k, thou schalt answere to hym, Dauid preiede me, that he schulde^l go swiftli^m into Bethleem, his citee, for solempne sacrifices ben^n there to alle the^o men of his lynage. If he^p seith^q, Wel, pees 7 schal be to thi seruaunt; forsothe^r if he is wrooth, wite thou, that his malice is

† *Lo! calendis;* that is, the feeste of newe moone. *Lire here.* c.

^u schulde B.

^c unto the while E. for to I. ^d to A. ^e in to ADEF. ^f Saul also I. ^g vnclothide I. ^h Om. I. ^i and he I. ^k Om. I. ^l Om. I. ^m seiynge I. ^n Saul be I. ^o Certis I. ^p that I. ^q he cam I. ^r sekith to lese I. ^s Dauid I. ^t but if I. ^u fadir oonli I. ^v hath kept I. ^w Om. I. ^x certis I. ^y Jonathas I. ^z Sotheli I. ^a bifore thee I. ^b and *therfor* I. ^c wil I. ^d Om. I. ^e forthi I. ^f do it I. ^g to I. ^h vnto I. ^i and if I. ^k after me I. ^l myƷte I. ^m anoon I. ^n ben *nowe* I. ^o Om. I. ^p thi fadir I. ^q sey I. ^r and I.

8 malice of hym. Do thanne mercy vnto thi seruaunt, for thow hast maad me thi seruaunt to goo in couenaunt of pees of the Lord with thee; forsothe if in me is eny wickidnes, thou sle me, and ne lede 9 thou me into thi fader. And Jonathas seith, God sheelde this fro me, forsothe ne it may be doon, that if certeynli I knowe to be fulfillid the malice of my fadre aȝens thee, Y telle not to thee. 10 And Dauid answerde to Jonathas, Who shal telle aȝen to me, if eny thing per- auenture thi fader shal answere to thee 11 hard of me? And Jonathas seide[v] to Dauid, Come, and goo we out into the feelde. And whanne bothe weren goon 12 into the feelde, Jonathas seith to Dauid, Lord God of Yrael, if I serche[w] the sen- tence of my fader to morwe, or other morwe, and eny thing of good were vpon Dauid, and anoon sende not to thee, and 13 make knowun to thee, this God doo to Jonatha, and thes thingis adde. For- sothe if the malice of my fader dwelle stedfastly aȝens thee, Y shal telle thin eer, and leete thee, that thou go in pees; and the Lord be with thee, as he was 14 with my fader. And if Y shal lyue, thou do to me the mercies of the Lord; for- 15 sothe if I shal dye, thou shalt not do awey thi mercy fro myn hows vnto with outen eende; othere if I shal not doo, whanne the Lord shal drawe out bi the rotis the enemyes of Dauid, echon fro the erthe, do he awey Jonathan fro his hows, and seche the Lord fro[x] the 16 hoond of the enemyes 'of Dauid[y]. Thanne Jonathas couenauntide a couenaunt of pees with the hows of Dauid, and the Lord souȝte[z] fro the hoond of the ene- 17 myes 'of Dauid[a]. And Jonathas addide to myche bynde Dauid bi ooth, forthi that

fillid. Therfor do thou mercy in to thi 8 seruaunt, for thou madist[s] me thi seruaunt to make with thee the[t] boond of pees of the Lord; sotheli[u] if ony wickidnesse is in me, sle thou me, and brynge thou not in me to thi fadir. And Jonathas seide, 9 Fer be this fro me, for[v] it mai not be doon, that Y telle not to thee, if Y knowe certeynli, that the malice of my fadir is fillid aȝens thee. And Dauid answeride to 10 Jonathas, Who schal telle to[c] me, if in caas thi fadir answerith[d] harde ony thing[e] of me? And Jonathas seide to Dauid, 11 Come thou, and go we forth in to the feeld. And whanne[f] bothe hadden go in to the feeld, Jonathas seide to Dauid, 12 Lord[g] God of Israel, if Y enquere the sentence of my fadir to morewe, ether in the nexte dai aftir, and ony 'thing of good[h] is[i] of Dauid[k], and Y sende not anoon to thee, and make[l] knowun to thee, God do[m] 13 these thingis to Jonathas, and 'adde these thingis[n]. Forsothe[o] if the malice of my fadir contynueth[p] aȝens thee, Y schal schewe[q] to thin eere, and Y schal delyuere thee, that thou go in pees; and the Lord be with thee, as he was with my fadir. And if Y lyue[r], do thou the mercies of the 14 Lord to me; forsothe[s] if Y am[t] deed, 'thou 15 schalt not take[u] awei thi mercy fro myn hows 'til in to[v] with outen ende; 'and ȝif Y do it not[w], whanne the Lord schal drawe out bi the roote the enemyes of Dauid, ech man fro the lond[x], take he awei Jonathas fro his hows, and seke the Lord of the hond of the enemyes of Dauid. Therfor 16 Jonathas made boond of pees with the hows of Dauid, and the Lord souȝte[y] of the hond of enemyes[z] of Dauid. And Jo- 17 nathas addide to swere stedfastli to Dauid, for he louyde Dauid[a]; for he louyde so Dauid, as his owne soule[b]. And Jonathas 18

---

v seith CE.   w aserche R. enserche c.   x Dauyd fro E pr. m.   y Om. E pr. m.   z souȝte Dauyd E pr. m.
a Om. E pr. m.

s hast maad I.   t Om. I.   u but I.   v certis I.   c Om. I.   d answere I.   e thingis I.   f whanne thei I.
g thou, Lord I.   h good thing I.   i be seid I.   k thee I.   l make it I.   m do ellis I.   n do he mo yuel
thingis to me I.   o And I.   P contynue I.   q schewe it I.   r schal lyue I.   s and I.   t be I.   u take
thou not I.   v vnto I. into E.   w Om. A pr. m. EFFb. cither if I schal not do to thee as I haue bihiȝt I.
forsothe Dauid seide, if I do not K sup. ras. ether if I do not DOMSW. or if I do not X.   x erthe I.
y souȝte out wreeche I.   z the enemyes I.   a him I.   b lijf I.

he louide hym; forsothe as his lijf, so he
18 louyde hym. And Jonathas seide to hym,
19 To morwe ben kalendis, and thou shalt
ben askid after; forsothe thi syttynge
schal be askid after vnto after to morwe.
Thanne thou shalt come doun hastily,
and come into the place, where thou art
to be hid in the day, whanne it is leueful
to worche; and thou shalt sitte biside
20 the stoon, to whom name is Ezel. And
Y shal sende thre arowis biside it, and
shal throwe as bauntynge me to a prik.
21 Forsothe and Y shal sende a child, seiynge to hym, Go, and bryng to me the
22 arowis. If I seye to the child, Loo! the
arowis ben with ynne thee, tak hem;
com thou to me, for pees is to thee, and
no thing is of yuel, lyueth the Lord.
Forsothe if thus Y shal speke to the
child, Loo! the arowis ben beȝonde thee;
goo in pees, for the Lord hath laft thee[b].
23 Of the word forsothe that we han spokun,
Y and thou, the Lord be bitwix[c] me and
24 thee vnto with outen eende. Thanne
Dauid is hid in the feelde; and the kalendis camen, and the kyng sat to eete
25 breed. And whanne the kyng hadde sitten vpon his chayer after the consuetude,
that was beside the wal, Jonathas roos,
and sat, and Abner on the side of Saul,
and voyde aperyde the place of Dauid.
26 And Saul spak not eny thing in that day;
forsothe he thouȝte, that perauenture was
comen to hym, that he was not cleen ne
27 purified. And whanne the secounde day
after the kalendis hadde liȝtid, eft aperide
void the place of Dauid. And Saul seide
to Jonathas hys sone, Why cometh not
the sone of Ysaye, ne ȝisterday[d], ne 'to
28 day for[e] to eete? And Jonathas answerde to Saul, He preide me enteerly,
29 that he myȝte goo into Bethleem; and

seide to hym[e], 'Calendis ben[d] to morewe',
and thou schalt be souȝt; for[f] thi sittyng 19
schal be souȝt[g] til after to[h] morewe. Therfor thou schalt go doun hastili, and thou
schalt come in to the[i] place, where thou
schalt be hid in the day, whanne it is
leueful to worche; and thou schalt sitte
bisidis the stoon, 'to which the name is[k]
Ezel†. And Y schal sende[l] thre[m] arowis 20
bisidis that stoon, and Y schal caste[n] as
'excercisynge ether pleiynge me at a
signe[o]. Y schal sende also and my[p] child, 21
and Y schal seie to hym, Go thou, and
brynge to me the[q] arewis. If Y seie[r] to 22
the child, Lo! the arewis ben 'with ynne[s]
thee, take thou tho; come[t] thou to me,
for pees is to thee, and no thing is of yuel,
the Lord lyueth. Sotheli[u] if Y speke thus
to the child, Lo! the arowis ben biȝende
thee; go thou[v] in pees, for the Lord deliuerede[w] thee. Forsothe[x] of the word†, 23
which[y] thou and Y han[z] spoke, the Lord
be[a] bitwixe me and thee til[b] in to with
outen ende. Therfor Dauid was hid in 24
the feeld; and the 'calendis camen[c], and
the kyng sat to ete breed. And whanne 25
the kyng hadde seete[d] on[e] his chaier bi
custom, 'which chaier[f] was[g] bisidis the
wal, Jonathas roos, and sat 'aftir Abner[h],
and Abner sat at the side of Saul, and the
place of Dauid apperide voide. And Saul 26
spak not ony thing in that dai[i]; for he[k]
thouȝte, that 'in hap[l] it bifelde[m] to hym[n],
that he was not clene 'nether[o] purified[p].
And whanne the secounde dai aftir the 27
calendis[q] hadde schyned[r], eft aperide the
place of Dauid apperide voide. And Saul seide to
Jonathas his sone, Whi cometh[s] not the
sone of Isai, nether ȝisterdai, nether[t] to dai
to ete? And Jonathas answeride to Saul, 28
He preide me mekeli, that he schulde go
in to Bethleem; and he seide, Suffre thou 29

20 † is Ezel; that
is, of walking.
Lire here. c.

23 : of the word,
ete.; that is,
of the bond
of pees bitwixe
vs and oure
eiris. Lire
here. c.

---

b Om. ABH.   c bytwene BFH. betwen E. betwe c.   d ȝistai CE.   e for to day AB. to day c.

c Dauid I.   d Om. I.   e morewe is the first day of the monthe, that is solempne I.   f and I.   g axld I.
h the I.   i a I.   k that hiȝt I.   l schete I.   m thee K.   n caste tho I.   o it were vsynge me to throwe at
a marke I.   P Om. I.   q tho I.   r schal seie I.   s on this side I.   t thanne come I.   u But I.   v thou
thanne forth I.   w hath delyuered I.   x certis I.   y that I.   z haue I.   a be witnesse I.   b Om. KL.
c solempne feest came I.   d sett him I.   e upon I.   f that I.   g was stondynge I.   h Om. I.   i dai of
Dauid I.   k Saul I.   l perauenture I.   m hadde bifalle I.   n Dauid I.   o ne I. ether K.   P purified as
her custom was I.   q firste solempne dai I.   r comen I.   s came I.   t ne I.

seith, Lete me, for solempne sacrifice is
yn my citee; oon of my britheren hath^f
clepid me; nowe thanne if Y haue
foundun grace in thin eyen, Y shal goo
soone, and se my britheren; for this
cause he cam not to the bord of the
30 kyng. Forsothe Saul, wrooth a3ens Jonathan, seide to hym, Thou sone of a womman wilfuli catchinge a man, whether I
knowe not, that thou louest the sone of
Ysay into thi^g confusioun, and into the
31 confusyoun of thi shenful moder? Forsothe alle the days in whiche the sone of
Ysay shal lyue vpon the erthe, shal not
be stable thou ne thi rewme; and so
nowe send, and bryng hym to me, for
32 the sone of deeth he is. Forsothe Jonathas answerynge to Saul his fader seith,
Whi shal he dye? what hath he doon?
33 And Saul cau3te a speer forto smyte
hym, and Jonathas vndurstood, that it
was fulli termyned of his fader, that
34 Dauyd shulde be slayn. Thanne Jonathas roos fro the bord in wraththe of
woodnes, and eete not breed in the secounde day of kalendis; forsothe he
sorowide vpon Dauid, forthi that his
35 fader hadde shent hym. And whanne
the morwetide hadde li3tid, Jonathas cam
into the feeld, after the couenaunt^h of
36 Dauid, and a litil child with him. And
he seith to his child, Go, and bryng to
me the arowis that I threwe. And
whanne the child hadde runnen, he
threwe an other arowe ouer the child.
37 And so the child cam to the place of the
dartisⁱ that Jonathas sente; and Jonathas
criede bihynde the bak of the child, and
seith, Loo! there is not the arowe, but
38 bi3onde thee. And Jonathas criede eft
bihynde the bak of the child, seiynge,
Hi3e swiftli, ne stoond thou. Thanne
the child of Jonathas gedride the arowis,

me, for solempne sacrifice is in my citee;
oon of my britheren clepide me; now
therfor^u if Y foond^v grace 'in thin i3en^w,
Y schal go soone^x, and 'Y schal^y se my
britheren; for this cause he^z cometh not
to the 'table of the kyng^a. Forsothe^b Saul 30
was wrooth a3ens Jonathas, and seide to
hym, Thou sone of a^c womman 'rauyschynge at her owne wille^d a man, whether
Y woot not, that thou louest the sone of
Ysay in to thi confusioun, and in to the
confusioun of thi schendful modir? For 31
in alle the daies in whiche the sone of
Isai lyueth on erthe, thou schalt not be
stablischid, nether thi rewme; therfor 'ri3t
now^e sende thou, and brynge hym to me,
for he is the sone of deeth. Sotheli^f Jona- 32
thas answeride to Saul his fadir, and seide,
Whi schal he^g die? what hath he do?
And Saul took the^h spere, that he schulde 33
smyte hym, and Jonathas vndirstood, that
it was determyndⁱ of his fadir, that Dauid
schulde be slayn. Therfor^k Jonathas roos 34
fro the table in 'the ire of woodnesse^l, and
he ete not breed in the secounde dai of
calendis^m; for he was sori onⁿ Dauid, for
his fadir hadde schent him. And whanne 35
the morewtid 'hadde schyned^o, Jonathas
cam in to the feeld, and a litil child with
hym, bi the couenaunt of^p Dauid. And 36
Jonathas seide to his child, Go thou, and
brynge to me the arowis whiche^q Y caste^r.
And whanne the child hadde runne^s, he
castide^t another arowe bi3ende the child.
Therfor^u the child cam to the place of the 37
arowe which^v Jonathas hadde sent^w; and
Jonathas criede bihynde the 'bak of the
child^x, and seide, Lo! the arowe is not
there, certis it is bi3ende^y thee. And Jo- 38
nathas criede eft bihynde the bak of the
child, 'and seide^z, Haste thou swiftli, stonde
thou not. Therfor^a the child gaderide^b
the arowis of Jonathas, and brou3te^c to his

---

^f han *ABFH*.   ^g thyn owne *E pr. m.*   ^h desyr *E pr. m.*   ⁱ darte *CE.*

^u therfor *he seide* i.   ^v haue founde i.   ^w bifore thee i.   ^x soone thidere i.   ^y Om. i.   ^z Dauid i.
^a kyngis table i.   ^b And i.   ^c the i.   ^d wilfully rauyschynge i.   ^e anoon i.   ^f And i.   ^g Dauid i.   ^h a i.
ⁱ purposid fulli i.   ^k Thanne i.   ^l ful feers wraththe i.   ^m that solempnytee i.   ⁿ for i.   ^o wexe cler i.
^p maad of i.   ^q that i.   ^r haue schotte i.   ^s runne forth i.   ^t schotte i.   ^u And so whanne i.   ^v that i.
^w schott i.   ^x childis bak i.   ^y bihynde i.   ^z Om. i.   ^a Sothely i.   ^b gaderide up i.   ^c brou3te *hem* i.

39 and brouȝte to his lord, and what shulde be doo vtterli he knewe not; forsothe oonli Jonathas and Dauyd knewen the 40 thing. Thanne Jonathas ȝaf his armis to the child, and seyde to hym, Go, and 41 bere into the cytee. And whanne the child was goon, Dauid roos fro the place that bowith to the south; and fallynge redi into the erthe, honourde the thridde tyme, and kissynge hem seluen either othir, thei wepten togidre; forsothe Dauid 42 more largeli. Thanne Jonathas seide to Dauid, Go in pees; what euer thing we han sworn bothe in the name of the Lord, seiynge, The Lord be bitwix^k me and thee, and bitwix^k my seed and thi 43 seed vnto with outen eende. And Dauid roos, and wente a wey, but and Jonathas wente into the cytee.

CAP. XXI.

1 Dauid forsothe cam into Nobe to Achymalech the preest; and Achymalech was astonyed, forthi that Dauid was comen; and he roos aȝens hym^l, and seide to hym, Whi thou alone, and no man is 2 with thee? And Dauid seith to Achymalech the preest, The kyng comaundide to me a word, and seide, No man knowe the thing, for the whych thou art sent fro me, and what maner heestis I haue ȝouen^m to thee; for and to the children I haue ordeynd also 'into that^n and that 3 place; nowe thanne if eny thing thou hast at hoond, or fyue looues, ȝif to me, or 4 what euer thou fyndist. And answerynge the preest to Dauid seith to hym, I haue not leeuyd loouys at hoond, but oonli hooli breed; if cleen be the children^o, 5 moost fro wymmen, eete thei. And Dauyd answerde to the preest, and seide to hym, Forsothe and if of wymmen it is

lord, and outerli he^d wiste not what was 39 doon; for oonli Jonathas and Dauid knewen the thing. Therfor^e Jonathas ȝaf 40 hise armeris^f to the child, and seide to hym, Go thou, bere^g in to the citee. And 41 whanne the child hadde go^h, Dauid roos^i fro the place that 'ȝede to^k the south; and he felde low 'in to^l the^m erthe, and worschipide^n the thridde tyme, and thei kissiden hem silf togidere, and 'wepten to gidere^o; forsothe^p Dauid wepte more. Therfor^q Jonathas seide to Dauid, Go 42 thou in pees; what euer thingis we bothe han swoore in^r the 'name of the Lord', 'and seiden^t, 'The Lord be^u bitwixe me and thee, and bitwixe my seed and thi seed til^v in to with outen ende, 'be stidfast^w. And Dauid roos^x, and ȝede^y, but also^z 43 Jonathas entride^a in to the citee.

CAP. XXI.

Forsothe Dauid cam in to Nobe to 1 Achimelech preest^b; and Achymelech wondrid, for Dauid 'hadde come^c; and^{cc} he seide to Dauid, Whi art thou aloone, and no man is with thee†? And Dauid seide 2 to Achymelech preest^d, The kyng comaundide^e to me a word, and seide, No man wite the thing, for which thou art sent fro me, and what maner comaundementis^f Y ȝaf^g to thee; for Y seide also to children^h, that thei schulden go in to that 'and that^i place; now^k therfor if thou 3 hast ony thing^l at hond, ether fyue looues, ȝyue thou^m to me, ether what euer thing thou fyndist^n. And the preest answeride 4 to Dauid, and seide to hym, Y haue 'not lewid^o, 'that is, comyn^o, looues at hoond^p, but oneli hooli breed; whether^{pp} the children ben clene‡, and moost^q of wymmen^r? And Dauid answeride to the preest, and 5 seide to hym, And sotheli if it is doon of

† and no man is with thee; sum men weren in his company, as it is seid with ȝame, but few in comparisoun of hem that weren wont to go with him. Lire here. c.

‡ wher the children ben clene; as if he seide, 'tho looues moun be ȝouun to hem in nede. Lire here. c.

---

^{k} bytwene DFH. betwe c. betwen EF.　　^{l} Om. E pr. m.　　^{m} ȝifyn E.　　^{n} hym E pr. m.　　^{o} childre DEFH. childer c.

^{d} the child I.　^{e} Thanne I.　^{f} bowe and arowis I.　^{g} bere these I.　^{h} go thenns I.　^{i} roos up I.　^{k} was towardis I.　^{l} upon I.　^{m} Om. plures.　^{n} he worschipide him I.　^{o} euer either wepten I.　^{p} but I. ^{q} Thanne I.　^{r} and seid in I.　^{s} Lordis name I.　^{t} Om. I.　^{u} Be the Lord witnesse therof I.　^{v} Om. EL. ^{w} Om. I.　^{x} roos up I.　^{y} ȝede forth I.　^{z} and I.　^{a} ȝede I.　^{b} the preest I.　^{c} came thidere I.　^{cc} also and M.　^{d} the preest I.　^{e} hath comaundid I.　^{f} heestis I.　^{g} haue ȝoue I.　^{h} my children I.　^{i} Om. I. ^{k} and that now I.　^{l} thing to ete I.　^{m} thou it I.　^{n} fyndist of mete I.　^{o} not rody lewid brede I.　^{p} that is, bred for lewid men I marg.　^{pp} if I.　^{q} namely I.　^{r} wymmen, ete thei I.

askid, we han conteyned vs fro ʒisterday[p]
and before ʒisterday[p], whanne we wenten
out, and the vessels of the children[q]
weren holy; forsothe[r] this weye is po-
lute, but and it to day shal be halowid
6 in the vessels. Thanne the preest ʒaf to
hym halwid breed, forsothe ne there was
breed, but oonly loouys of proposicioun,
the whiche weren born awey fro the
face[s] of the Lord, that there ben set hoot
7 loouys. Forsothe there was ther[t] a maner
man of the seruauntis of Saul in that day
with ynne in the tabernacle of the Lord;
this fedde the mulis of Saul; and the
name of hym Doech Ydume, moost myʒti
8 of the sheepherdis of Saul. Forsothe
Dauyd seide to Achymalech, If thou hast
here at hoond speer, or swerd, ʒif to me;
for my swerd and myn aarmys Y took
not with me; forsothe the word of the
9 kyng constreynede me. And the preest
seyde, Loo! heere the swerd of Goliath
Philistee, whom thou smoot[u] in the valey
of Therebynt, it is wrappid with a pal
after the preestis coope; if this thou wolt
take, tak; forsothe ne here is othere with
outen that. And Dauid seith, There is not
10 another lijk to this, ʒif to me it. And so
Dauid roos, and fleiʒ in that day fro the
face of Saul, and cam to Achis, the kyng
11 of Geth. And the seruauntis of Achis
seiden to hym, whanne thei seen Dauid,
Whether not this is Dauid, kyng[v] of the
loond? Whether not to this sungen bi
dauncys seiynge, Saul smoot o thousand,
12 and Dauid ten thousandis? Forsothe
Dauid putte thes wordis in his herte,
and dredde ful mych fro the face of
13 Achis, the kyng of Geth. And he
chaungyde hys mouth before Achis, and
he hurlide hidir and thider bitwix[w] the
hoondis of hem, and he aʒen[x] put into

wymmen, we absteyneden[s] vs fro ʒistirdai
and the thridde dai ago, whanne we ʒeden
out, and[t] the 'vessels, that is[u], bodies, of
the children weren cleene[v]'; forsothe[w] this
weie is defoulyd*, but also[x] that[y] schal be
halewid to dai in the vessels. Therfor[z] 6
the preest ʒaf to hym[a] halewid breed, for
noon other breed was there, no but[b] oneli
loouus of settyng forth, that weren[c] takun
awey fro the face of the Lord, that hoote
loouus schulen be set[c]. Forsothe[d] sum[e] 7
man of the seruauntis of Saul was there[f]
with ynne in the tabernacle† of the Lord;
and his name was Doech of Ydumee‡, the
myʒtiest[g] of the scheepherdis[h], 'that is,
iugis[i], of Saul[k]. Forsothe[l] Dauid seide to[s]
Achymelech, If thou hast 'here at hond[m]
spere, ether swerd, ʒyue[n] to me; for Y
took not with me my swerd and[o] myn
armeris; for[p] the 'word of the kyng[q] constreynede me[r]. And the preest seide, Lo! 9
here[s] the swerd of Goliath Filistei, whom
thou killidst in the valey of Terebynte, is
wlappid[t] in a cloth aftir[u] ephoth; if thou
wolt take this, take thou[v]; for here is
noon other outakun that. And Dauid
seide, Noon other is lijk this, ʒyue thou
it to me. Therfor[w] Dauid roos[x], 'and 10
fledde[y] in that dai fro the face of Saul,
and cam[x] to Achis, the kyng of Geth.
And the seruauntis of Achis seiden to 11
hym, whanne thei hadden seyn Dauid,
Whether this is not Dauid, kyng of the
lond[a]? Whether thei[b] sungen not to hym
bi queeris[c], and seiden, Saul smoot a thousynde, and Dauid smoot ten thousynde?
Sotheli[d] Dauid puttide[e] these wordis 'in 12
his[f] herte, and he dredde greetli of the
face of Achis, kyng of Geth. And Dauid 13
chaungide his mouth bifor Achis, and
felde doun bitwixe her hondis, and he
hurtlide aʒens the doris§ of the ʒate, and

* this weye is
defoulid; that
is, we myʒten
drawe vnclen-
nesse in the
weye; but also
that schal be
halewid in the
vessels; that is,
siche vnclen-
nesse schal be
excusid in vs
for the con-
tynence fro
wymmen.
Ether thus, this
weye is de-
foulid; that is,
this proces is
vnleueful of
comyn cours,
that halewid
breed be ʒouun
to lewid men,
but it schal be
excusid for
oure nede.
Lire here. c.
† in the taber-
nacle; that is,
in the campas
of the taber-
nacle, where
lewid men
weren res-
ceyued for
offryng ether
preyer. Lire
here. c.
‡ and his name
was Doech of
Ydume; this
that sueth in
summe bokis,
and he kepte
the mulis of
Saul, is not in
Ebreu, nether
is of the text.
Lire here. c.

§ and he hurt-
lide aʒenus the
doris; in Ebreu
it is, and he
peyntide on the
doris, in mak-
ing there
summe figuris,
as foolis ben
wont to make.
Lire here. c.

---

[p] ʒistai CE.   [q] childre BEFH. childer c.   [r] if forsothe E pr. m.   [s] place B sec. m.   [t] Om. A.   [u] smyte CE.
[v] the kyng E pr. m.   [w] bytwene BFH. betwen E. betwe c.   [x] aʒeynst B. aʒenst E.

[s] han absteyned I.   [t] Om. I.   [u] Om. I.   [v] cleene therof I.   [w] certis I.   [x] and I.   [y] it I.   [z] Thanne I.
[a] Dauid I.   [b] Om. I.   [c] set forth I.   [d] And I.   [e] a I.   [f] there that dai I.   [g] myʒtiest man Ib.
[h] heerdes I.   [i] Om. I.   [k] Saul, and he kepte the mulis of Saul IL.   Saul, he fedde the mules of Saul E.
[l] And I.   [m] redy here I.   [n] ʒyue it I.   [o] neither I.   [p] for why I.   [q] kyngis word I.   [r] me to go in
haaste I.   [s] Om. I.   [t] wrappid K.   [u] next after I.   [v] it I.   [w] And so I.   [x] roos up I.   [y] Om. I.   [z] he
cam I.   [a] lond of Israel I.   [b] wymmen I.   [c] carouls DEF sec. m. GIKLMNOPQRSWXb.   [d] And I.   [e] toke I.
[f] to I.

the doris of the ȝate, and his spotils
14 floweden doun into the beerd. And
Achis seith to his seruauntis, Han ȝe
seen a woode man? whi han ȝe brouȝt
hym to me? whether faylen to ȝou woode
men? whi han ȝe brouȝt hym yn, that
he wexe woode, me present? Letith hym
goon hens, lest he goo into myn hows.

CAP. XXII.

1 Dauid thanne ȝeed thens, and fleiȝ into
the spelunk of Odallam; the which thing
whanne the britheren of hym hadden
herd, and al the hows of his fadre, thei
2 camen doun to hym thidir. And camen
to gidre to hym alle that weren in
angwish set, and oppressid for other
mennus monee, and for bitter inwit; and
he is maad the prince of hem, and there
weren with hym as foure hundrid men.
3 And Dauid wente thens into Masphat,
that is of Moab; and seide to the kyng of
Moab, Dwelle, Y preye, my fader and
my moder with ȝow, to the tyme that
4 Y wite what God doo to me. And he
laft hem before the face of the kyng of
Moab; and thei dwelten anentis hym alle
days, in the whiche Dauid was in strong
5 socour. And Gad, the prophet, seide to
Dauid, Wole thow not dwelle in the
place of strong socour; weend forth, and
goo into the loond of Juda. And Dauid
wente, and cam into the wijlde wode of
6 Areth. And Saul herde, that Dauyd ap-
peryde, and men that with hym weren.
Forsothe Saul whanne he dwelt in Gabaa,
and was in the wode that is in Rama,
a speer in hoond holdynge, and alle his
7 seruauntis stoden about hym, he seith to
his seruauntis that stoden nyȝ to hym,
Herith me nowe, the sones of Gemyny;
whethir to alle ȝou the sone of Ysay
shal ȝyue feeldis and vynes, and alle ȝou
shal make lederys of thousandis and

his drauelis, 'that is, spotelis[z], flowiden
doun in to the beerd. And Achis seide 14
to hise seruauntis, Seen ȝe the wood man?
why brouȝten ȝe hym to me? whether
wood men failen to vs? whi han ȝe brouȝt
in hym, that he schulde be wood, while
Y am present? Delyuere ȝe hym fro
hennus, lest he entre in to myn hows.

CAP. XXII.

1 Therfor Dauid ȝede fro thennus, and
fledde[h] in to the denne of Odollam; and
whanne hise britheren, and al the hows
of his fadir hadden herd this, thei camen
doun thidur to hym. And alle men that 2
weren set in angwisch, and oppressid
with[i] othere mennus[k] dette[l], and in bittir
soule[m], camen togidere to hym[n]; and he
was maad the[o] prince 'of hem[p], and as
foure[q] hundrid men weren with hym.
And Dauid ȝede forth fro thennus in to 3
Masphat, which[r] is of[s] Moab; and he seide
to the kyng of Moab, Y preye, dwelle my
fadir and my modir with ȝou, til Y wite
what thing God schal do to me. And he 4
lefte hem[t] bifor the face of the kyng of
Moab; and thei dwelliden at hym in alle
daies[u], 'in whiche[v] Dauid was in 'the forselet,
ether[w] stronghold. And Gad, the profete, 5
seide to Dauid, Nyle thou dwelle[x] in 'the
forselet[y]; go thou forth, and go[z] in to the
lond of Juda. And Dauid ȝede forth, and
cam[a] in to the forest of Areth. And Saul 6
herde, that Dauid apperide, and the men
that weren with hym. Forsothe[b] whanne
Saul dwellide in Gabaa, and was in the[c]
wode which[d] is in Rama, and[e] 'helde a
spere[f] in the[g] hond, and alle hise seruauntis stoden aboute hym, he seide to 7
hise seruauntis that stoden nyȝ hym, The[h]
sones of Gemyny[i], here[k] me now; whether
the sone of Ysai schal ȝyue to alle ȝou
feeldis and vyneris, and schal[l] make alle
ȝou tribunes[m] and centuriouns[n]? For alle 8

---

[g] Om. 1.　[h] he fledde 1.　[i] with the dett of 1.　[k] men 1.　[l] Om. 1.　[m] sorowe of herte 1.　[n] Dauid 1.
[o] her 1.　[p] Om. 1.　[q] a foure 1.　[r] that 1.　[s] in 1.　[t] him there 1.　[u] the daies 1.　[v] that 1.　[w] Om. 1.
[x] dwelle still 1.　[y] oo strong hold 1.　[z] wende 1.　[a] he cam 1.　[b] And 1.　[c] a 1.　[d] that 1.　[e] and he 1.
[f] led a preste E. helid a preste L.　[g] his 1.　[h] ȝe AI.　[i] that is, ȝe that be my britheren 1 marg.　[k] here
ȝe 1.　[l] he schal 1.　[m] chefteyns upon thousyndis 1.　[n] upon hundridis of men 1.

8 leders of hundredis? For ȝe alle han sworn togidre aȝens me, and there is not that aȝen telle to me; moost whanne and my sone hath ioyned couenaunt of pees with the sone of Ysay; there is not that sorwith my while of ȝou, ne that telle to me, forthi that my sone hath reride my seruaunt aȝens^y me, weytynge to me vnto 9 to^z day. Forsothe answerynge Doech Ydume, that stood nyȝ, and was the fyrst amonge the seruauntis of Saul, I sawȝ, he seith, the sone of Ysay in Nobe, at Achimalech, the sone of Achitob, the 10 preest; the which counseilede the Lord for hym, and ȝaf meetis to hym, but and the swerd of Goliath Philistee he ȝaf to 11 hym. Thanne the kyng sente to cleepe Achymalech, the sone of Achitob, the preest, and al the hows of his fader, of the prestys that waren in Nobe; the whiche alle to the kyng ben comen. 12 And Saul seith to Achymalech, Here, thou sone of Achitob. The which an-13 swerde, I am prest^a, lord. And Saul seide to hym, Whi han ȝe sworn togidre aȝens_s me, thou, and the sone of Ysay, and thou hast ȝeuen to hym loonys and a swerd, and thou hast counseild for hym the Lord, that he ryse aȝens me, dwel-14 lynge a spye vnto to day? And Achymalech answerynge to the kyng seith, And who in alle thi seruauntis trewe as Dauid, and the sone in lawe of the kyng, and goynge at thin heest, and gloryous in 15 thin hows? Whether to day I haue begun for hym to counseil the Lord? A wey be that fro me, ne trowe the kyng aȝens his seruaunt sich a maner thing in al the hows of my fader; forsothe thi seruaunt wiste not eny thing vpon this nede, othere 16 litil or greet. And the kyng seide, Bi deth shal dye, Achymalech, thou, and al

ȝe han swore^o, *ether^oo conspirid^p*, togidere aȝens me, and noon is that tellith to me; moost sithen also my sone hath ioyned boond of pees with the sone of Ysai; noon is of ȝou, that sorewith 'for my stide^q, nether that tellith to me, for my sone hath reisid my seruaunt aȝens me, settynge tresoun to me 'til to^r dai^s. Sotheli^t Doech of^ȝ Ydumye answeride, that stood nyȝ, and was the firste^u among 'the seruauntis of Saul^v, and seide, Y siȝ 'the sone of Ysai^w in Nobe, at Achymelech, preest^x, the sone of Achitob; which^y counseilide^z the Lord 10 for Dauid, and ȝaf^a meetis 'to hym^b, but also he ȝaf to Dauid the swerd of Goliath^c Filistei. Therfor^d the kyng sente to clepe 11 Achymelech, the preest, 'the sone of Achitob^e, and al the hows^f of his fadir, of preestis that weren in Nobe; whiche^g alle camen to the kyng. And Saul seide to 12 Achymelech, Here^h, thou sone of Achitob. Which^i answeride, Lord, Y am redi. And 13 Saul seide to hym, Whi hast thou conspirid aȝens me, thou, and the sone of Ysai, and ȝauest^k looues and a swerd to hym, and councelidist^l the Lord for hym, that he schulde rise aȝens me, and he dwellith a tretour 'til to^m dai? And Achy-14 melech answeride to the kyng, and seide, And^n who among alle thi seruauntis is^o as Dauid feithful^p, and the^q sone in lawe 'of the kyng^r, and goynge at thi^s comaundement^t, and gloriouse in^u thin hows? Whe-15 ther Y bigan to dai to counsele the Lord for hym^v? Fer be this fro me; suppose not the kyng^w aȝens his seruaunt 'siche a thing^x in al 'the hows of my fadir^y; for thi seruaunt knew not ony thing, ether litil ethir greet, of this cause. And the kyng 16 seide, Achymelech, thou schalt die bi deeth, thou, and al^z the hows of thi fadir. And the kyng seide to men able to be 17

---

^y aȝeynst вн. aȝen c.   ^z Om. ⌐н.   ^a preest ⌐.

^o Om. ⌐.   ^oo Om. c⌐.   ^p Om. c.   ^q my while ⌐.   ^r vnto ⌐.   ^s this dai ⌐.   ^t But ⌐.   ^u cheef ⌐.   ^v Sauls seruauntis ⌐.   ^w Ysais sone ⌐.   ^x the preest ⌐.   ^y and Achimelech ⌐.   ^z counseilide with ⌐.   ^a ȝaf him ⌐.   ^b Om. ⌐.   ^c Golie ⌐.   ^d Thanne ⌐.   ^e Achitobs sone ⌐.   ^f meynee ⌐.   ^g the whiche ⌐.   ^h Here me ⌐.   ^i The which ⌐.   ^k hast ȝoue ⌐.   ^l hast counseilid with ⌐.   ^m vnto this ⌐.   ^n Om. ⌐.   ^o is so feithful ⌐.   ^p Om. ⌐.   ^q he is thi ⌐.   ^r Om. ⌐.   ^s Om. в⌐.   ^t heest ⌐.   ^u in al ⌐.   ^v Dauid ⌐.   ^w kyng sich thing ⌐.   ^x or aȝens ony other ⌐.   ^y my fadir hous ⌐.   ^z Om. c.

17 the hows of thi fader. And the kyng seith to the outgoers in his nedis, that stooden about hym, Turneth, and sleeth the preestis of the Lord, for the hoond of hem is with Dauid ; wytynge that he was flowen, and thei sheweden not to me. Forsothe the seruauntis of the kyng wolden not streeche out her hoond into 18 the preestis of the Lord. And the kyng seith to Doech, Turn thou, and fal into the preestis of the Lord. And Doech Ydume turnede, felle into the preestis, and hewȝ doun fyue and eiȝtith^aa men in 19 that day, clothid with surplees. Also he smoot Nobee, the citee of preestis, in mouth of swerd, men and wymmen, litil children and sowkynge, and oxe, and 20 asse, and sheep, in mouth of swerd. Forsothe oon ascapynge, sone of Achymalech, the sone of Achitob, whos name 21 was Abiathar, fleeȝ to Dauid, and toolde to hym, that Saul hadde slayn the prestis 22 of the Lord. And Dauid seith to Abiathar, Forsothe I wist in that day, that whanne there was Doech Ydume, with out dout he wold telle to Saul; I am 23 gilti of alle the soulis of thi fader. Dwel with me, ne drede thou; if eny man sechith^b my lijf, shal seche and thi lijf, and with me thou shalt be kept.

sent out, that stoden aboute hym, Turne ȝe, and sle the preestis of the Lord, for the hond of hem is with Dauid ; and thei wisten that he fledde, and thei schewiden not to me. Sotheli the seruauntis of the kyng nolden^a holde forth her houd† in to the preestis of the Lord. And the kyng 18 seide to Doech, Turne thou, and hurle^aa in to the preestis of the Lord. And Doech of Ydumee turnede, and hurlide^b in to the preestis, and stranglide in that dai foure score and fyue men, clothid with `ephoth‡ of lynnun cloth^c. Forsothe^d he^e smoot^f 19 Nobe, the citee of preestis^g, by the scharp- nesse of swerd, men and wymmen, litle children and soukynge, and oxe, and asse, and sheep, bi^h the scharpnesse of swerd. Forsothe^i o sone of Achymelech, sone^k of 20 Achitob, ascapide, of which sone the name was Abiathar; and he fledde to Dauid, and telde to^l hym that Saul hadde slayn 21 the preestis of the Lord. And Dauid 22 seide to Abiathar, Sotheli^m Y wiste, `that is, Y coniectide, ether dredde^n, in that dai, that whanne Doech of Ydumee was there, he wolde telle with out doute to Saul; Y am gilti of alle the lyues^o of thi fadir^p. Dwelle thou with me, drede thou 23 not; if ony man sekith thi lijf, he schal seke also my lijf, and thou schalt be kept with me. ..

† the ser-
uauntis of the
kyng nolden
holde forth her
houd ; these
men able to be
sent out, weren
Abner and
Amasa, that
weren sent out
to the nedis of
the rewme,
they nolden
sle the prestis
of the Lord,
for they wisten
that it was not
to obeye to the
king, in the
thingis that
ben aȝenus God;
and they token
this of that
word in t. e^o.
of Josue, as we
obeyeden in
alle thingis to
Moyses, so we
schulen obeie
also to thee,
oneli thi Lord
God be with
thee; that is,
in the thingis
in whiche is
acordinge
with Goddis
wille, we schu-
len obeye, and
in noon othere.
Lire here. c.
‡ clothid with
ephoth ; for
they camen to
the king in
the clothis in
whiche they
mynistriden
bifor God, that
thei schulden
bowe more his
wraththid soule
to pitee. Lire
here. c.
‖ telden, that
is, men of Seila
telden perel
neiȝinge to
hem. Lire
here. c.

CAP. XXIII.

1 And men toolden to Dauid, seiynge, Loo ! Phylisteis fiȝten aȝens Seyla, and 2 struyen the floris of cornys. Thanne Dauid counseilde the Lord, seiynge, Whe- ther I shal goo, and smyte thes Philisteis ? And the Lord seith to Dauid, Go, and thou shalt smyte Philisteis, and^bb saue Seylam. 3 And men seiden, that weren with Dauid, to hym, Loo ! we here beynge in Juda dreden ; myche more if we goon into

CAP. XXIII.

And thei^q telden‖ to Dauid, and seiden, 1 Lo ! Filisteis^r fiȝten aȝens Seila, and ra- uyschen^s the corn floris. Therfor^t Dauid 2 councelide^u the Lord, and seide, Whether Y schal go^v, and smyte Filisteis^w ? And the Lord seide to Dauid, Go thou^x, and thou schalt smyte Filisteis^y, and thou schalt saue Seila. And men, that weren with 3 Dauid, seiden to him, Lo ! we ben heere in Judee, and dredden^z; hou myche more,

aa eiȝtety cɛ.　　b shal seche ᴀ.　　bb Om. ᴀʙʜ.

a wolden not ɪ.　aa hurtle x.　b hurtlid ᴅʟx sec. m.　c lynnun prestes copis ɪ.　d Certis ɪ.
e Doech ɪ.　f destriede ɪ.　g the preestis ɪ.　h he slewȝe bi ɪ.　i But ɪ.　k the sone ɪ.　l Om. ɪ.
m Certis ɪ.　n Om. cɪ.　o lyues that be sleyn ɪ.　p fadir hous ɪ.　q men ɪ.　r the Filisteis ɪ.　s strien ɪ.
t Thanne ɪ.　u counseilde with ɪ.　v go out ɪ.　w these Filisteis ʙc. the Filisteis ɪ.　x forth ɪ.　y the
Filisteis ɪ.　z han dred ɪ.

Seilam a3ens the companyes of Philisteis.
4 Eft thanne Dauid counseilde the Lord;
the which answerynge seith to hym,
Ryse, and go into Seilam; forsothe I shal
5 take the Philisteis in thin hoond. Thanne
wente Dauid and his men into Seilam,
and fau3t a3ens the Philisteis; and
droue a wey the beestis of hem, and
smoot hem with a greet veniaunce; and
Dauid sauyde the dwellers of Seilam.
6 Forsothe that tyme, the which Abiathar,
the sone of Achymalech, flee3, he descendide to Dauid into Seylam, hauynge
7 with hym the preestis coope. Forsothe
it is toold to Saul, that Dauid was comen
into Seylam; and Saul seith, The Lord
hath taken hym into myn hoondis, and
closid is goon into the cytee, in the which
8 ben 3atis and lockis. And Saul comaundide to al the puple, that to the fi3t thei
shulden descende to Seilam, and bisege
9 Dauid and his men. The which thing
whanne Dauid a3en knewe, for Saul made
redy to hym priueli yuel, he seide to
Abiathar, the preest, Clothe thee the^bb
10 preestis coope. And Dauid seith, Lord
God of Yrael, thi seruaunt hath herd the
fame, that Saul hath disposid to come to
Seyla, that he turne vpsedoun for me the
11 cyte; if the men of Seyla shulen take me
into his hoondis, and if Saul shal come
doun, as thi seruaunt hath herd, Lord
God of Yrael, shewe to thi seruaunt? And
12 the Lord seith, He shal come doun. And
Dauid eft seyde, If the men of Seila shulen take me, and the men that ben with
me, into the hoondis of Saul? And the
13 Lord seide, Thei shulen take. Thanne
Dauid roos, and his men, as sex hundrid;
and, goon out fro Seyla, hidir and thider weren vagaunt vncerteyn. And it is
toold to Saul, that Dauid hadde flowen
fro Seila, and was sauid; for what skyl
14 he laft to goon out. Forsothe Dauid

if we schulen go in to Seila a3ens the
cumpanyes of Filisteis. Therfor eft Dauid 4
conncelide^a the Lord; which^b answeride,
and seide to Dauid, Rise thou^c, and go 'in
to^d Seila; for Y schal bitake Filisteis^e in^f
thin hond. Therfor^g Dauid 3ede^h, and hise 5
men, in to Seila, and fau3t a3ens Filisteis^i;
and he^k droof awey her werk beestis, and
smoot hem with greet wounde; and Dauid
sauyde the dwelleris of Seila. Forsothe 6
in that tyme, 'wher ynne^m Abiathar, sone^n
of Achymelech^o, fledde to Dauid in to
Seile, he^p cam doun^q, and hadde^r with
hym 'ephoth, *that is^s, the cloth^t of the
hi3este preest*^tt †. Forsothe^u it was teld 7
to Saul, that Dauid hadde come in to
Seila; and Saul seide, The Lord hath
take hym in to myn hondis, and he 'is
closid, and^w entride in to a^x citee, in^y
which^z ben 3atis and lockis. And Saul 8
comaundide to al the puple, that it schulde
go doun to batel in to Seila, and bisege^a
Dauid and hise men. And whanne Dauid 9
perceyuede, that Saul made redi yuel
priueli to hym, he seide to Abiathar,
preest^h, Brynge hidur ephoth^c †. And 10
Dauid seide, Lord God of Israel, thi seruaunt 'herde fame^d, that Saul disposith to
come to Seila, that he distrie the citee for
me; if the men of Seila schulen bitake me 11
in to hise hondis, and if Saul schal come
doun, as thi seruaunt herde^e, thou Lord
God of Israel schewe^f to thi seruaunt?
And the Lord seide, He schal come doun‖.
And Dauid seide eft, Whether the men of 12
Seila schulen bitake me, and the men that
ben with me, in to the hondis of Saul?
And the Lord seide, Thei schulen bitake,
'that is, if thou dwellist in the citee, and
Saul come^ff thidur^g. Therfor Dauid roos, 13
and hise men, as^h sixe hundrid; and thei
3eden out of Seila, and wandriden vncerteyn hidur and thidur. And it was telde
to Saul, that Dauid hadde fledde fro Seila,

Marginal glosses:

† prest; wher-ynne was the racional of doom, in whiche the answering of the Lord apperide. *Lire here.* c.

‡ ephoth; that is, clothe thee with ephoth, to conseele the Lord. *Lire here.* c.

‖ he schal come doun; that is, if thou dwellist in the citee, he schal come doun. *Lire here.* c.

bb with the s pr. m.

a conncelide with 1. b the which 1. c thou up 1. d in A. e the Filisteis 1. f in to EL. g Thanne 1.
h wente 1. i the Filisteis 1. k Dauid 1. l And 1. m in whiche 1. n the sone 1. o Abimelech ELP.
p Abiathar 1. q down thidere 1. r he hadde 1. s Om. 1. t coope 1. tt The whole gloss omitted in x.
u And 1. w Om. 1. x the 1. y is closid with ynne in 1. z the which 1. a bisege 3e 1. b the preest 1.
c the prestis coope 1. d hath herd sey 1. e hath herd 1. f schewe it 1. ff comith c. g Om. x. *thee to
Saul, if thou abijdist him there* 1. h as a 1.

dwellide in deseert, in moost defensable placis, and abood[c] in the hil of wildirnes of Ziph, in the derk[d] hil; neuerthelater[e] Saul souȝte hym alle days, and the Lord took hym not into the hoondis of hym. 15 And Dauid sawȝ, that Saul was goon out, for to seche his lijf. Forsothe Dauid was 16 in the deseert of Ziph, in a wode. And Jonathas, the sone of Saul, roos, and wente to Dauid into the wode, and coumfourtide the hoondis of hym in God. 17 And he seide to hym, Ne drede thou; forsothe ne the hoond of Saul my fader shal fynde thee, and thou shalt regne vpon Yrael, and I shal be to thee the secounde; but and Saul my fader woot 18 this. Thanne either smoot couenaunt of pees before the Lord. And Dauid abood[f] in the wode; forsothe Jonathas turnede 19 aȝen[g] into his hows. Forsothe Zipheis stieden vp to Saul in Gabaa, seiynge, Loo! whether not Dauid lurkith anentis vs in moost siker placys of a wode, in the hil of Achille, that is at the riȝt party 20 of deseert? Nowe thanne, as thi soule hath desyrid for to come doun, com doun; forsothe 'our shal be[h], that we taken hym 21 into the hoondis of the kyng. And Saul seide, Blessid be[i] ȝe of the Lord, for ȝe 22 han sorewid my while. Goth thanne, I praye, and more bisily makith redy beforn, and slelyer doth, and weitith swiftly the place, where be the foot of hym, or who sawȝ hym there, where ȝe han seid; forsothe he aȝen thenkith of me, that I 23 felli aspye hym. Biholdith, and seeth alle the hidils of hym, in whiche he is hid, and turneth to me at certeyn thing, that I goo with ȝou; that if also into the erthe he hide hym self, I shal thurȝ serche hym in alle the thousandis of 24 Juda. And thei rysynge wenten into Ziph before Saul. Forsothe Dauid and

and was saued; wherfor Saul dissymylide[i] to go out. Forsothe[k] Dauid dwellide in 14 the[l] descert, in strongeste[m] places, and he dwellide in the hil of wildirnesse of Ziph, in a derk hil[n]; netheles Saul souȝte hym in alle daies, and the Lord bitook not hym in to the hondis of Saul. And Dauid 15 siȝ, that Saul ȝede out, that he schulde[o] seke his lijf. Forsothe[p] Dauid was in the[q] descert of Ziph, in a wode. And Jonathas, 16 the sone of Saul, roos[r], and ȝede to Dauid in to the wode, and coumfortide[s] hise hondis in God. And he seide to Dauid, Drede 17 thou not; for the hond of Saul my fadir schal not fynde thee, and thou schalt regne on Israel, and Y schal be the secounde to thee; but also Saul my father woot this. Therfor euer eithir smoot boond of pees 18 bifor the Lord. And Dauid dwellide in the wode; forsothe[t] Jonathas turnede aȝen in to his hows. Forsothe[u] men of Ziph 19 stieden[v] to Saul in Gabaa, and seiden, Lo! whether not[w] Dauid is hid at[x] vs in the sikireste[y] placcs of[z] the wode[a], in the hille of Achille, which[b] is at the riȝt syde of deseert? Now therfor come thou doun, 20 as thi soule desiride, that thou schuldist come doun; forsothe it schal be oure[c], that we bitake hym[d] in to the hondis of the kyng. And Saul seide, Blessid be ȝe of 21 the Lord, for ȝe sorewiden[e] 'for my stide[f]. Therfor, Y preie[g], go ȝe, and make[h] redi 22 more diligentli, and do ȝe more curiousli ether intentifli, and biholde ȝe swiftly, where his foot is, ethir who siȝ hym there, where ȝe seiden; for he thenkith on me, that felli Y aspie hym. Biholde ȝe, and 23 se[i] alle his hidyng places, in whiche he is hid, and[k] turne ȝe aȝen to me at a certeyn thing, that Y go with ȝou; that if he closith[l] hym silf ȝhe in to[m] erthe, Y schal seke hym with[n] alle the thousyndis of Juda. And thei risiden[o], and ȝeden in to 24

---

c bode BFH. bod c. boid E. ᵈ thicke E pr. m. ᵉ nerthelater c passim. ᶠ boode BF. bod c. hood EH. ᵍ aȝeen c. acen E. ʰ he schal ben oure E pr. m. ⁱ Om. BCEFH.

ⁱ feynede I. ᵏ But I. ˡ Om. EIKL. ᵐ ful stronge I. ⁿ hil of wode I. ᵒ wolde I. ᵖ And I. ۹ Om. EL. ʳ roos up I. ˢ he coumfortide I. ᵗ and I. ᵘ Certis I. ᵛ stieden up I. ʷ Om. D. now EL. ˣ in D. anentis I. ʸ ful siker I. ᶻ in I. ᵃ thicke wode I. ᵇ that I. ᶜ oure doyng I. ᵈ Dauid I. ᵉ han screwid I. ᶠ my while I. ᵍ preie ȝou I. ʰ makith I. ⁱ se ȝe I. ᵏ and thanne I. ˡ schal close I. ᵐ the I. Om. DKMOSB. ⁿ in I. ᵒ resen up I. risen ELP.

his men weren in the deseert of Maon,
in the wijld feeldis, at the riȝt side of
25 Jesymith. Thanne Saul wente and his
felawis to seche hym, and it is toold to
Dauid; and anoon he wente doun to a
stoon, and abood in the deseert of Maon;
the whiche thinge whanne Saul had
herde, he pursuede Dauith in the de-
26 serte of Maon. And Saul wente and his
men at the side of the hil on the o partye; forsothe Dauid and his men weren
in the side of the hil on the tother party;
wherfor Dauid dispeyryde hym self to
mowe askaap fro the face of Saul. And
so Saul and his men in maner of a coroun
girdiden Dauid and his men, for to take
27 hem. And a messager cam to Saul, seiynge,
Hyȝe, and come, for the Philisteis han
28 held hem seluen vpon the loond. Thanne
Saul turnede aȝen, cesynge to pursue Dauid; and he wente into the aȝen comynge
of the Philisteis. For that thei clepen that
place the Dyuydynge Stoone.

CAP. XXIV.

1 Thanne Dauid stiede vp thens, and
dwelte in moost siker placis of Engaddi.
2 And whanne Saul was turned aȝen, after
that he hadde pursued the Philisteis, thei
toolden to hym, seiynge, Loo! Dauid is
3 in the descert of Engaddi. Thanne Saul,
takynge to thre thousandis of chosen
men of al Yrael, wente to aserche Dauid
and his men, vpon moost heiȝ rochis, that
oneli to wijlde capretis ben thurȝ weyes.
4 And he cam to the fooldys of sheep, the
which offrede hemself to the weye goer.
And a spelunk[k] was there, the which
Saul wente yn, that he purge the wombe;
forsothe Dauid and his men lurkeden in
5 the innere[l] parti of the denne. And the
seruauntis of Dauyd seiden to hym, Loo!

Ziph bifor Saul. Forsothe[p] Dauid and
hise men weren in the deseert of Maon, in
the[q] feldi places, at the riȝt half of Jesy-
myth. Therfor Saul ȝede and hise felowis 25
to seke Dauid, and it was teld to Dauid;
and anoon he[r] ȝede doun to the stoon, and
lyuyde in the deseert of Maon; and whanne
Saul hadde herd this, he pursuede Dauid
in the deseert of Maon. And Saul ȝede 26
and hise men at the side of the hil 'on o[s]
part; forsothe[t] Dauid and hise men weren[u]
in[v] the side of the hil on the tother part;
sotheli[w] Dauid dispeiride†, that he myȝte
ascape fro the face of Saul. And so Saul
and hise men cumpassiden bi the maner
of a coroun[x] Dauid and hise men, that
thei schulden take hem. And a messanger 27
cam to Saul, and seide, Haste thou, and
come, for Filisteis[y] han spred hem silf on
the lond. Therfor Saul turnede aȝen, and 28
ccesside to pursue Dauid; and ȝede[z] aȝens
the comyng of Filisteis. For this thing‡
thei clepen[a] that place the Stoon Departynge[b].

CAP. XXIV.

Therfor Dauid stiede[c] fro thennus, and 1
dwellide in the sykireste[d] places of Engaddi. And whanne[e] Saul turnede aȝen, 2
aftir that he pursuede Filisteis[f], thei[g]
telden to hym, and seiden, Lo! Dauid is
in the[h] descert of Engaddi. Therfor Saul 3
took thre thousinde of[i] chosun men of al
Israel, and ȝede[k] to seke Dauid and hise
men, ȝhe on[l] moost brokun rochis, that[m]
ben 'able to weie[n] to wield geet aloone.
And he[o] cam to the fooldis of scheep, that[p] 4
offriden[q] hem silf to the wei goere. And
there was a denne[r], in to which[s] denne[t]
Saul entride, that he schulde[u] purge the[v]
wombe; forsothe[w] Dauid and hise men
weren hid in the ynnere part of the[x]
denne. And the seruauntis of Dauid 5

† Dauyth dis-
peiride; Da-
uyth dispeiride
not to ascape
in his owne
persoone, for
he was certeyn
of the filling of
Goddis bihest,
that he schulde
be kyng aftir
Saul, but he
despeiride to
ascape with out
batel with Saul,
of which batel
he hadde hi-
dousnesse and
dredde, for the
deth of hise
men, and of
summen that
weren with
Saul, and ju-
eden him more
aȝenus her wille,
than wilfuly.
Lire here. c.
‡ for this thing;
that is, for the
cost of Saul
was departid
there, fro the
pursuyng of
Dauyth. Lire
here. c.

k spelunk or denne A pr. m.   l nyȝ ABFH.

p And I.   q Om. IK.   r Dauid I.   s the too K.   t and I.   u wenten I.   v at I.   w forsothe BC.
x coroun round aboute I.   y the Filisteis I.   z he ȝede I.   a clepiden DEFGIKLMNOPQRSUWXb.   b of
Departyng ÆIPX.   c stiede up I.   d most sikir I.   e whanne that I.   f the Filisteis I.   g men I.
b Om. EL.   i Om. I.   k he ȝede I.   l upon the I.   m the whiche I.   n weies DK sec. m. X sec. m.
thorouȝ weies I. able weie MX pr. m. able to weies o.   o Saul I.   p the whiche I.   q profreden I.
r canne I.   s the whiche I.   t Om. DIKMXb.   u wolde I.   v his I.   w certis I.   x that I.

the day of which the Lord spak to thee, I shal take to thee thin enemy, that thou doo to hym as it plesith in thin eyen. Thanne Dauid roos, and kyttide[m] of the hemme of the mantil of Saul 6 stilly[n]. After thes thingis the herte of Dauid smoot hym, forthi that he hadde kut a wey the hemme of the mantil of 7 Saul. And he seide to his men, Merciful be to me the Lord, that I doo not this thing to my lord, the crist of the Lord, that I putte myn hoond into hym, for the crist of the Lord he is. The Lord lyueth, for but the Lord smyte hym, other the day of hym come, that he dye, other comynge doun into batayl perish, merciful be to me the Lord, that I putte not myn hoond into the crist of the 8 Lord. And Dauid brak togidre his men with thes wordis, and suffrede hem not, that thei rysen into Saul; forsothe Saul rysynge fro the denne, wente in the weye 9 begun. Forsothe Dauid roos after hym, and wente out of the denne, and criede after the bak of Saul, seiynge, My lord kyng! And Saul beheelde bihynde hym; and Dauyd bowynge hym self redi into 10 the erthe honourede. And he seide to Saul, Whi herist thou wordis of men spekynge, Dauid sechith yuel aȝens thee? 11 Loo! to dai thin eyen seen, that the Lord took thee in myn hoond in the denne, and I thouȝt for to slee thee, but myn eye sparide to thee; forsothe I seide, I shal not stretche out myn hoond in my lord, 'for the° crist of the Lord he is. 12 But more ouere, fader myn, se, and know the hemme of thi mantil in myn hoond, for whanne I kut the coope[p] of thi man- til, I wold not stretch out myn hoond into thee; inwardly tak hede, and se, for there is not in myn hoond euel ne wick- idnes, ne I haue synned in thee; forsothe

seiden to hym, Lo! the dai of which the Lord spak to the, Y schal bitake to thee thin enemy, that thou do to hym as it plesith in thin iȝen. Therfor Dauid roos[y], and kittide the hemme of the mentil of Saul priuely. Aftir these thingis Dauid 6 smoot his herte[z]†, for he hadde kit awei the hemme of the mentil of Saul. And 7 Dauid seide to hise men, The Lord be merciful to me, lest Y do this thing to my lord, the crist[a] of the Lord, that[b] Y sende[c] myn hond 'in to[d] hym, for he is the crist of the Lord. The Lord lyueth, for no[e] but the Lord smyte hym[f], ether his dai come, that he die, ether he go doun in to batel and perische[g], the Lord be merciful to me, that Y sende[h] not[i] myn hond in to the crist[k] of the Lord†. For- 8 sothe[l] Saul roos out of the denne, and ȝede in the weie bigunnun. Sotheli[m] Dauid roos[n] 9 aftir hym, and he ȝede out of the denne, and criede aftir the bak of Saul, and seide, My lord, the° kyng! And Saul bihelde bihinde him silf[p]; and Dauid bowide hym silf lowe to the erthe, and worschipide[q]. And he[r] seide to Saul, Whi herist thou 10 the wordis of men spekynge, Dauid sckith yuel aȝens thee? Lo! to dai thin iȝen siȝen, 11 that the Lord bitook thee in myn hond in the denne, and Y thouȝte that Y wolde sle[s] thee, but myn iȝe[t] sparide thee; for Y seide, Y schal not holde forth myn hond in to my lord, which[u] is† the crist[w], 'that is, anoyntid[x], of the Lord. But rathere, my 12 fadir, se thou, and knowe the hemme of thi mentil in myn hond, for whanne Y kittide aweie the hemme of thi mentil, Y nolde[y] holde forth myn hond in[z] thee; perseyue thou, and see, for nether yuel nether wickidnesse is in myn hond, nether Y synnede[a] aȝens thee; but thou aspiest my lijf, that thou do it awei. The Lord 13 deme bitwixe me and thee, and the Lord

Marginal notes (right column):

† smoot his herte; that is, his conscience repreuyde him. Lire here. c.

† crist of the Lord; in summe bokis it sueth, and Dauyth brak his men bi siche wordis, and suffride not hem, that they risiden aȝenus Saul, but this lettre is not in Ebrou, nether in bokis amendid. Lire here. c.

‡ which is the crist; that is, anoyntid. c.

---

^m kytt BFH. kitte E. cutte c.   ⁿ stilleli CE.   ° that is E pr.m.   ^p cop E.

^y roos up I.   ^z herte, or repentide him I.   ^a anoyntid I. crist, that is, anoyntid K.   ^b and that A pr.m. CEGKLMNOPQRSUWXb. or that I. ^c putte MW.   ^d on I.   ^e Om. I.   ^f Saul I.   ^g perische so I.   ^h putte M. ⁱ Om. I.   ^k anoyntid I.   ^l And I.   ^m And I.   ⁿ roos up I.   ° Om. I.   ^p Om. I.   ^q worschipide him I. ^r Dauid I.   ^s haue slawe I.   ^t iȝen BC.   ^u for he I.   ^w anoyntid I.   ^x Om. INX.   ^y wolde not I.   ^z aȝens I. ^a haue synned I.

thou aspyist my lijf, that thou doo it
13 awey. The Lord deme bitwix^q me and
thee, and the Lord wreke me on thee;
14 forsothe myn hoond be not in thee, as
in the oold prouerbe it is seid, Fro vnpiteuous men goth out vnpiteuousnesse;
myn hoond forsothe be not in thee.
15 Whom pursuyst thou, kyng of Yrael?
whom pursuist thou? A deed dog thou
16 pursuist, and a quyk fly3e. The Lord
be domesman, and the Lord deme bitwix
me and thee, and see, and deme my
cause, and delyuere me fro thin hoond.
17 Forsothe whanne Dauid hadde ful cendid
spekynge siche maner wordis to Saul,
Saul seide, Whether this is thi voys, sone
myn Dauyd? And Saul reryde vp a voys,
18 and wepte. And to Dauid he seide, More
ri3twise thou art than Y; forsothe thou
hast 3oldun to me gode thingis; forsothe
I haue 3oldun a3eu to thee yuel thingis.
19 And thow hast shewid to me to day,
what goode thingis thou hast doo to me,
what maner wise the Lord took me in
20 thin hoond, and thou slew3 not me. Forsothe who, whanne he fyndith his enemy,
leeueth hym in a good weie? But the
Lord 3eelde to thee this while, for that,
21 that to day thou hast wrou3t in me. And
'now, for^r I knowe, that moost certeynli
thou art to regne, and to haue in thin
22 hoond the kyngdom of Yrael, swere to
me in the Lord, that thou do not a wey
my seed after me, ne doo a wey my name
23 fro the hows of my fader. And Dauid
swore to Saul. Thanne Saul wente into
his hows, and Dauid and his men stieden
vp to more sykyr placis.

venge me of thee; but myn hond be not
in^b thee, as it is seid also^c in eld prouerbe, 14
Wickidnesse schal go out of wickid men;
therfor myn hond be not in^d thee. 'Whom 15
pursuest^e thou, kyng of Israel, whom pursuest thou? Thou pursuest a deed hound,
and a quyk fle. The Lord be iuge, and 16
the Lord deme bitwixe me and thee, and
se, and deme my cause, and delyuere^f me
fro thin hond. Sotheli^g whanne Dauid hadde 17
fillid^h spekynge sicheⁱ wordis to Saul, Saul
seide, Whether this is thi vois, my sone
Dauid? And Saul reiside^k his vois, and
wepte. And he seide to Dauid, Thou art 18
more iust than Y; for thou 3auest goodis^l
to me; forsothe^m Y 3eldideⁿ yuelis to thee.
And thou schewidist^o to me to dai, what 19
goodis thou hast do to me, how the Lord
bitook me in thin hond, and thou killidist
not me. For who, 'whanne he fyndith 20
his enemy^p, schal delyuere hym^q in^r good
weie^s? But the Lord 3elde to thee this while,
for that, that^t thou wrou3tist^u to dai in
me. And now, for Y woot, that thou 21
schalt regne moost^v certeynli, and schalt
haue in thin hond the rewme of Israel,
swere thou to me in the Lord, that thou 22
do not a wei my seed aftir me, nether take
a wey my name fro the hows of my fadir.
And Dauid swoor to Saul. Therfor Saul 23
3ede in to his hows, and Dauid and hise
men stieden^w to sikire^x placis.

CAP. XXV.

1 Samuel forsothe diede; and al Yrael
is gaderid, and biweilide^s hym^t ful myche,
and biryeden hym in his hows in Ra-
matha. And Dauid risynge wente doun

CAP. XXV.

Forsothe Samuel was deed; and al Israel 1
was gaderid to gidere, and thei biweiliden
hym greetly, and birieden hym in his
hows in Ramatha. And Dauid roos^y, and

q bytwene BFH passim. betwen E passim. betwe c passim.   r these thyngis E pr. m.   s weylden BFH.
weiledyn CE.   t Om. BCEFH.

b a3ens I.   c Om. I.   d a3ens I.   e Om. I.   f delyuere he I.   g And I.   h fillid or endid I.   i siche
maner I.   k reiside up I.   l gode thingis I.   m but I.   n haue 3olden I.   o hast schewid I.   p Om. I.
q his enny I.   r in to K.   s weie, whanne he fyndith him I.   t Om. I.   u hast wrou3t I.   v ful I.
w stieden up I.   x sikerer BCKO.   y roos up I.

2 into the deseert of Pharan. Forsothe
there was a maner man in the wildernesse of Maon, and the possessioun of
hym was[u] in Carmele, and that man ful
myche greet, and there weren to hym
sheep thre thousandis, and a thousand
goot; and it felle that his flok shulde be
3 clippid in Carmele. Forsothe the name
of that man was Naabal, and the name
of his wijf Abigail; and that womman
was moost wyis and feyr, forsothe hir
man hard and werst and malicious; forsothe he was of the kynrede of Caleph.
4 Whanne thanne Dauid in deseert hadde
5 herd, that Naabal clippide his flok, he
sente ten ʒonge men, and seide to hem,
Stieth vp into Carmele, and ʒe shulen
come to Naabal, and ʒe shulen salute
6 hym in my name pesibly; and thus ʒe
shulen seye, Pees be to my britheren
and to thee, and pees to thin[v] hows, and
to alle, what euere thingis thou hast, be
pees; of many ʒeeris be thou maad saaf,
7 thou, and thin hows, and alle thin. I
haue herd that thi sheepherdis clippiden
thi flockis, that weren with vs in deseert;
neuere to hem we weren heuy, ne eny
tyme faylide to hem eny thing of the
flok, al the tyme that thei weren with vs
8 in Carmele; ask thi children[w], and thei
shulen shewe to thee. Nowe therfor
fynden thi children[w] grace in thin eyen;
in a good day forsothe we ben comen to
thee; what euere thing thin hoond fyndith[x], ʒif to thi seruauntis, and to thi sone
9 Dauid. And whanne the children[y] of
Dauid weren comen, thei speken to Naabal alle thes wordis in the name of
10 Dauid, and helden her pees. Forsothe
Naabal, answerynge to the children[z] of
Dauid, seith, Who is Dauid? and who is

---

3 ede[z] doun in to descert[a] of Faran. For-2
sothe[b] a[c] 'man was[d] in Maon[e]†, and[f] his
possessioun was in Carmele, and thilke[g]
man was ful greet, and thre[h] thousynde
scheep and a thousynde geet[i] 'weren to
hym[k]; and it bifelde that his flocke was
clippid[l] in Carmele. Forsothe[m] the name 3
of that man was Nabal, and the name of
his wijf was Abigail; and thilke womman
was moost prudent and fair; forsothe[n] hir
hosebond was hard and ful wickid and
malicious; sotheli[o] he was of the kyn of
Caleph. Therfor whanne Dauid hadde 4
herde in deseert, that Nabal clippide his
floc, he sente ten ʒonge men, and seide to 5
hem, Stie ʒe[p] in to Carmele, and ʒe schulen
come to Nabal, and ʒe schulen grete hym
of my name pesibli; and ʒe schulen seie 6
thus, Pees be to my britheren and to thee,
and pees be to thin hows, and pees be to
alle thingis, 'what euer thingis thou hast[q].
Y[r] herde[s] that thi scheepherdis, that weren 7
with vs in deseert, clippiden[t] thi flockis;
we weren neuere diseseful to hem, nether
ony tyme ony thing of the floc failide to
hem, in al time[u] in which thei weren with
vs in Carmele; axe thi children, and thei 8
schulen schewe to thee. Now therfor thi
children fynde[v] grace in thin iʒen; for in
a good dai we camen[w] to thee; what euer
thing thin hond fyndith[x], ʒyue[y] to thi seruauntis, and to thi sone Dauid. And 9
whanne the children of Dauid hadden
come[z], thei spaken to Nabal[a] alle these
wordis in the name of Dauid, and helden
pees. Forsoth[b] Nabal answeride to the 10
children of Dauid, and seide, Who is
Dauith? and who is the sone of Isai? To
dai seruauntis encreesiden[c] that fleen[d] her
lords. Therfor schal Y take my looues‡ 11
and my watris, and the fleischis[e] of beestis,

† in Maon; in
summe bokis ys
in the wildir-
nesse of Maon,
but this word
wildirnesse, is
not in Ebreu,
nether is of the
text; for bi the
book of Ebreu
questiouns he
dwellide in a
gretter citee,
but hise beestis
weren in Car-
mele. Lire
here. c.

‡ schal Y take
my looues; as
if he seye, Y
owe not to do,
and my watris,
that is, my
drynkis, for
ofte in scrip-
ture, ech drynk
is vndurstodun
bi the name of
water, as bi the
name of breed
is understond-
un ech mete.
Lire here. c.

---

    u Om. BCEFH.   v her A.   w childre BEFH. childer c.   x fynde BCEFH.   y childre E. childer c.
z childre E. childer c.

    z wente I.   a the deseert I.   b And I.   c sum BCDEFGKLNOPQRSUXb. Om. I.   d Om. I.   e the desert of
Maon rb marg.   f ther was a man, and I.   g that I.   h ther weren to him thre I.   i of geet I.   k Om. I.
l schore I.   m And I.   n but I.   o and I.   p ʒe up I.   q whateuer thou hast DIKOQSXb. thingis whiche thou
hast G. thingis whateuer thou hast N.   r which manie ʒeres hath maad sauf thi seruauntes and alle thi
godes, Y. A sec. m. rb sec. m.   s haue herd I.   t han schore I.   u the time BCEFGIKLMNOPQRSUWXb.
v we fynde I.   w ben comen I.   comen plures.   x fyndith or plesith to thee I.   y ʒyue it I.   z come to
Nabal I.   a him I.   b Certis I.   c han encressid I.   d han fled I.   e fleishe I.

the sone of Ysay? To day han sprungun
11 yn seruauntis that fleen her lordis. Shal
I thanne take my loouys, and my watris,
and flesh of beestis, that I haue slayn to
my clippers, and ȝife to men, whom I
12 knowe not whennus thei ben? And so
the children^a of Dauid wenten aȝen bi her
weye; and aȝen turned thei camen aȝen,
and toolden to hym alle the wordis that
13 Naabal hadde seid. Thanne Dauid seith
to his children, Echon be gyrd with his
swerd. And echon ben gird with her
swerdis, and Dauid is gird with his
swerd; and there folweden Dauid as
foure hundrid men, forsothe two hun-
14 dryd abiden stil at the fardels. Forsothe
to Abigail, the wijf of Naabal, oon of
hir children toold, seyynge, Loo! Dauid
sente messagers fro deseert, for thei wol-
15 stoode hem; these men weren good
ynow^b 'to vs^c, and not heuy, ne eny thing
that eny tyme perishid al the tyme we^d
16 han dwellid with hem in deseert; for a
wal thei weren to vs, as wel in nyȝt as
in day, alle days the whiche we fedden
17 flockis anentis hem. Wherfor behold,
and bithenk, what thou doo; for determyned is the malice aȝens thi man, and
aȝens thin hows; and he is the sone of
Belial, so that no man may speke to him.
18 Thanne Abigail hiȝede, and took two
hundryd loouys, and two botels of wyn,
and fyue wetheris sothen, and fyue busshellis of brayid corn, and an hundrid
busshellis of dryed grape, and two hundrid peyse of dryed figis; and she putte
19 vpon the assis, and seide to hir children,
Gooth before me; loo! after the bak Y
shal folwe ȝou. To Naabal forsothe hir
20 man she shewide it not. Whanne thanne
she was goon vpon the asse, and cam

whiche^f Y haue slayn to my schereris,
and schal Y ȝyue to men, whiche^g Y knowe
not of whennus thei ben? Therfor the 12
children of Dauid ȝeden aȝen bi her weie;
and thei turneden aȝen, and camen, and
telden to hym^h alle wordisⁱ whiche^k Nabal
hadde seid^l. Thanne Dauid seide to hise 13
children, Ech man be gird with his swerd.
And alle men weren gird with her swerdis,
and Dauid also was gird with his swerd;
and as foure^m hundrid men sueden Dauid,
forsotheⁿ two hundrid leften at the fardels.
Forsothe^o oon of hise^p children telde to 14
Abigail, wijf^q of Nabal, and seide, Lo!
Dauid sente^r messangeris fro deseert, that
thei schulden blesse oure lord†^s, and he
turnede^t hem awey; these men weren 15
good ynow, and not diseseful to vs, and
no thing^u perischide 'in ony tyme^v in al
the tyme in which we lyueden^w with hem
in deseert; thei weren to vs for a wal, 16
bothe in niȝt and in^x dai, in^y alle daies^z
in whiche we lesewiden flockis at^a hem.
Wherfor biholde thou, and thenke, what 17
thou schalt do; for malice is fillid^b aȝens
thin hosebonde, and aȝens 'thin hows^c; and
he^d is the sone of Belial, so that no man
may speke to him. Therfor Abigail hast- 18
ide, and took two hundrid looues, and two
vessels of wyn, and fyue whetheris sodun,
and seuene buyschelis and an half of flour,
and an hundrid bundles of dried grape^e,
and two hundrid gobetis^f of dried figus;
and puttide^g on^h assis, and seide to hir 19
children, Go ȝe bifor me; lo! Y schal sue
ȝou 'aftir theⁱ bak. Forsothe^k sche schewide not^l to hir hosebonde Nabal. Therfor 20
whanne sche hadde stied^m on theⁿ asse,
and cam doun 'at the roote^o of the hil,
and^p Dauid and hise men camen doun in
to the^q comyng 'of hir^r; whiche^s also^t sche
mette. And Dauid seide, Verili in veyn 21

† blesse oure
lord, in gret-
ynge hym cur-
teysly, and in
axinge mekly
his benefice.
Lire here. c.

---

^a childre E. childer c.   ^b a nowȝ cE.   ^c Om. A.   ^d that we E sec. m.

^f the whiche 1.   ^g that 1.   ^h Dauid 1.   ⁱ the wordis 1.   ^k that 1.   ^l seid to hem 1.
^m a foure 1.   ⁿ for 1.   ^o And 1.   ^p the 1.   ^q the wijf 1.   ^r hath sent 1.   ^s lord Nabal 1.   ^t hath
turned 1.   ^u thing of oure 1.   ^v Om. 1.   ^w weren 1.   ^x Om. plures.   ^y and L.   ^z the daies 1.   ^a anentis 1.
^b fulfillid 1.   ^c thi meynee 1.   ^d Nabal 1.   ^e grapes ELM. grapis or reisynns 1.   ^f peis 1.   ^g sche putte 1.
^h al this upon 1.   ⁱ bihynde ȝoure 1.   ^k And 1.   ^l not this 1.   ^m stied up 1.   ⁿ an 1.   ^o to the foot 1.
^p Om. 1.   ^q hir 1.   ^r Om. 1.   ^s the whiche 1.   ^t Om. 1.

doun at the roote of the hil, Dauid and
his men camen doun into a3en metynge
of hyre; to whom and sche a3en cam.
21 And Dauid seith, Verreili in veyn I haue
kept alle thingis that of this man weren
in descert, and there perishid not eny
thing of alle thingis that to hym per-
teyneden^e, and he hath 3oldun to me
22 yuel for good. Thes thingis do the
Lord to the enemyes of Dauid, and thes
thingis adde, if Y shal leeue of alle
thingis that to hym pertenen vnto the
23 morwe tide a pisser to the wal. Forsothe
whanne Abigail hadde seen Dauid, she
hi3ede, and wente doun of the asse, and
felle doun before Dauid vpon hir face,
24 and honourde vpon the erthe. And she
felle at the feet of hym, and seyde, My
lord, in me be this wickidnes; speke, My
biseche, thin hoondseruaunt in thin eeris,
25 and here the wordis of thi seruaunt; ne
put, Y preye, my lord kyng, his herte
vpon this^f wickid^g man Naabal, for after
his name he is a fool, and foli is with
hym; forsothe I, thin hoond womman,
saw3 not thi children^h, whom, my lord,
26 thou sentist. Now thann, my lord, lyueth
the Lord and lyueth thi soule, that hath
defendid thee, that thou cam not into
blood, and hath sauyd thin hoond to
thee; and now as Naabal thin enemyes
ben maad, and that sechen to my lord
27 yuel. Wherfor tak this blessynge, that
thin hoond womman hath brou3t to thee,
my lord, and 3yue to the children that
28 folowen thee, my lord. Do awey the
wickydnes of thi seruaunt; forsothe the
Lord makynge shal make to thee, my
lord, a trewe hows, for the batayls of
the Lord, my lord, thou fi3tist; malice
thanne be there not founden in thee alle
29 the days of thi lijf. Forsothe if there
arise any tyme a man pursuynge thee,

Y haue kept alle thingis^u that weren of
this Nabal in the^v descert, and no thing
perischide of alle thingis that perteyneden
to hym, and he hath 3olde to me yuel for
good. The Lord do these thingis, and 22
adde^w these thingis to the enemyes of
Dauid, if Y schal leeue^x of alle thingis
that perteynen to him til the^y morewe a
pisser to the^z wal. Sotheli^a whanne Abi-23
gail si3 Dauid, sche hastide, and 3ede doun
of the asse; and sche fel doun bifor Dauid
on hir face, and worschipide^b on the erthe.
And sche felde doun to hise feet, and seide, 24
My lord the^c kyng, this wickydnesse be
in^d me; Y biseche^e, speke thin handmayden^f
in thin eeris, and here thou the wordis of
thi seruauntesse; Y preie, my lord the^g 25
kyng, sette^h not his herte onⁱ this wickid
man Nabal, for bi his name he is a fool,
and foli is with hym; but, my lord, Y
thin handmayde si3 not thi children, whiche
thou sentist^k. Now therfor, my lord, the 26
Lord lyueth†, and thi soule lyueth, which^l
Lord forbeed^m thee, lestⁿ thou schuldist
come in to blood, and he^o saude thi soule^p
to thee‡; and now thin enemyes, and thei
that seken yuel to^q my lord, be^r maad as
Nabal. Wherfor resseyue thou this bless-27
yng, which^s thin handmaide brou3te^t to
thee, my lord, and 3yue^u thou^v to the children that suen thee, my lord. Do thou 28
awey the wickidnesse^{vv} of thi seruauntesse;
for the Lord makynge schal make a feith-
ful hows to thee, my lord, for thou, my
lord, fi3tist the batels of the Lord; therfor
malice be not foundun in thee in alle dais^w
of thi lijf. For if a man risith ony tyme, 29
and pursueth thee, and sekith thi lijf, the
lijf of my lord schal be kept‖ as in a
bundel of lyuynge *trees*, at thi Lord God;
forsothe^x the soule of thin enemyes schal
be hurlid round aboute as in feersnesse,
and sercle of a slynge. Therfor whanne 30

† *the Lord
lyueth*; *on if
sche seide, as
it is soth, that
the Lord lyu-
eth, and thou
lyuest, so it is
doon bi Goddis
mersy, that Y
cam a3enus thee
to lette. lest
thou schuldist
come in to
blood, that is,
to schede out
blood. Lire
here.* c.
‡ *he sauyde thi
soule innocent.
Lire here.* c.

‖ *schal be
kepte, etc.;
that is, schal
be defendid
a3enus alle tre-
souns of yuel
men. Lire
here.* c.

^e pertenen c.   ^f his A F II.   ^g wicke c.   ^h childre B E F H *passim.* childer c *passim.*

^u these thingis K.   ^v Om. E I L N P X.   ^w adde he I.   ^x leeue *vndestried* I.   ^y to I.   ^z a I.   ^a And I.
^b worschipide *him* I.   ^c Om. I.   ^d at I.   ^e biseche thee I.   ^f handmaide I.   ^g Om. I.   ^h that he sette I.
ⁱ upon I.   ^k sentist *to him* I.   ^l the which I.   ^m hath forbodun I.   ⁿ that I.   ^o the Lord I.   ^p lijf I.
^q to thee I b *sec. m.*   ^r be thei I.   ^s that I.   ^t hath brou3t I.   ^u 3yue *it* I.   ^v Om. I.   ^{vv} wickenesse E.
^w the daies I.   ^x but I.

and sechynge thi lijf, the lijf of my lord
shal be kept, as in a litil knytche of lyuynge men, anentis the Lord thi God;
forsothe the lijf of thin enemyes shal be
turned about as in the birre, and the
30 cercle of a slynge. Whanne thanne[i] the
Lord shal do to thee, my lord, alle thes
gode thingis, that he hath spokyn of
thee, and settith thee a duyk vpon Yrael,
31 this shal not be to thee, my lord, into
ʒoxynge and into scripil of herte, that
thou hast shed giltlesse blood, or thi self
thou hast vengid. And whanne the Lord
shal wel doo to thee, my lord, thow shalt
recorde of thin hoond womman, and thou
32 shalt wel doo to hir. And Dauid seide
to Abigayl, Blissid be[k] the Lord God of
Yrael, that sente thee to day into myn
aʒencomynge, and blessid thi[l] speche;
33 and blessid thou art[m], that hast defendid
me, that I ʒede not to day to the blood,
34 and vengide me bi myn hoond; ellis the
Lord God of Yrael lyueth, that hath defendide me, that Y dide not yuel to thee,
but soone thow haddist comen into aʒencomynge to me, there shulde not[n] han
laft to Naabal vnto the morwetide liʒt a
35 pisser to the wal. Thanne Dauid took
of the hoond of hir alle thingis that she
brouʒte to hym; and he seide to hir, Go
in pees into thin hows; loo! I haue herd
36 thi voys, and honourde thi face. Forsothe Abigail cam to Naabal; and loo!
there was to hym a feest in his hows, as
a feest of a kyng; and the herte of Naabal myri, forsothe he was drunken ful
myche; and she shewide not to hym
37 word litil or greet vnto the morwe. Forsothe eerli, whanne Naabal[o] hadde defied
the wyn, his wijf shewide to him thes
wordis; and the herte of hym with yn
forth is deed[p], and he is maad as a stoone.
38 And whanne ten days weren passid, the

the Lord hath do to thee, my lord, alle
these goode thingis, whiche he spak[y] of
thee, and hath ordeyned thee duyk on[z]
Israel, this schal not be in to siʒyng† and 31
in to doute of herte to thee, my lord, that
thou hast sched out giltles blood, ether
that thou hast vengid thee[a]. And whanne
the Lord hath do wel to thee, my lord,
thou schalt haue mynde on[b] thin handmaide, and thou schalt do wel to hir.
And Dauid seide to Abigail, Blessid be 32
the[c] Lord God of Israel, that sente[d] thee
to dai in to my comyng, and blessid be
thi speche; and blessid be thou, that hast 33
forbede[n] me, lest Y ʒede[f] to blood, and
vengide[g] me with myn hond; ellis the 34
Lord God of Israel lyueth, which[h] forbeed[i]
me, 'lest Y dide[k] yuel to thee, if thou
haddist not soone come in to 'metyng to
me[l], a pissere to the wal schulde not haue
left to Nabal til to the[m] morewe liʒt.
Therfor Dauid resseyuede of hir hond 35
alle thingis whiche sche hadde brouʒt to
hym[n]; and he seide to hir, Go thou in pees
in to thin hows; lo! Y herde[o] thi vois,
and Y onouride thi face. Forsothe Abi- 36
gail cam to Nabal; and, lo! a feeste was
to him in his hows, as the feeste of a
kyng; and the herte of Nabal was
iocounde[p], for[q] he was 'drunkun greetli[r];
and sche schewide not to hym a word
litil ether[s] greet til the morewe. Forsothe[t] 37
in the morewtid, whanne Nabal hadde
defied the wiyn, his wijf schewide to hym
alle these wordis; and his herte was almest
deed with ynne, and he was maad as a
stoon. And whanne ten daies hadden 38
passid, the Lord smoot Nabal, and he was
deed. Which[u] thing whanne Dauid hadde 39
herd, Nabal deed[r], he seide, Blessid be the
Lord God, that vengide[w] the cause of my
schenschip of the hond of Nabal, and
kepte[x] his seruaunt fro yuel, and the

† in to siʒyng; that is, in to morenyng of soule and in to remors of conscience. Lire here. c.

---

[i] Om. _A._   [k] Om. _BCEFH._   [l] the _ABFH._   [m] Om. _BCEFH._   [n] Om. _AFH._   [o] he _E_ orig.   [p] deadyd _BF._ deadid _E._ dedid _H._

[y] hath spoke 1.   [z] upon 1.   [a] thi silff 1.   [b] of 1.   [c] Om. c.   [d] hath sent 1.   [e] forbede L.   [f] ʒide to day 1.   [g] had vengid 1.   [h] that 1.   [i] hath forboden 1.   [k] Y schulde not do 1.   [l] my metyng 1.   [m] Om. 1.   [n] Dauid 1.   [o] haue herd 1.   [p] merye 1.   [q] certis 1.   [r] ful drunkun 1.   [s] ne BL. or P.   [t] But 1.   [u] The which 1.   [v] to be deed 1.   [w] hath vengid 1.   [x] hath kept 1.

39 Lord smoot Naabal, and he is deed. The
which thing whanne Dauid hadde herd,
Naabal deed, he seith, Blissid is[q] the
Lord, that hath vengid the cause of my
reproof fro the hoond of Naabal, and his
seruaunt hath kept fro yuel, and the
malice of Naabal the Lord hath ȝolden
into his heed. Than Dauid sente, and
spak to Abigail, that he take hir to hym
40 into wijf. And the children of Dauid
camen to Abigail into Carmele, and
speken to hir, seiynge, Dauid sente vs
to thee, that he take thee into wijf to
41 hym. The which arysynge honourde
redi into the erthe, and seith, Loo! thi
seruaunt be in to an hond womman, that
she wasshe the feet of the seruauntis of
42 my lord. And Abigail hiȝede, and roos,
and stiede vpon the asse; and fyue child-
wymmen, hir feet folowers, wenten with
hir, and she folowide the messagers of
43 Dauid, and is maad to hym a wijf. But
and Dauid took Achynoem fro Jezrael,
44 and either was the wijf of hym; forsothe
Saul ȝaf Mychol his douȝter, the wijf of
Dauid, to Phalti, the sone of Lays, that
was of Gallym.

CAP. XXVI.

1 And Ziphei camen to Saul in Gabaa,
seiynge, Loo! Dauid is hid in the hil of
Achille, the which is fro aȝens of the
2 wildernesse. And Saul roos, and cam
doun into the deseert of Ziph, and with
hym thre thousandis of men of the chosun
of Yrael, that he seche Dauid in the de-
3 seert of Ziph. And Saul sette tentis in
Gabaa of Achille, that was fro aȝens of
the wildernesse in the weye. Forsothe
Dauid dwellide in deseert. Forsothe
seynge that Saul was comen after hym
4 into deseert, he sente aspies, and lernyde
moost certeynli, that thidre he was
5 comyn. And Dauyd roos pryueli, and

Lord ȝeldide[y] the malice of Nabal in to
the heed of hym. Therfor Dauid sente,
and spak to Abigail, that he wolde take
hir wijf to hym. And the children of 40
Dauid camen to Abigail in to Carmele,
and spaken to hir, and seiden, Dauid sente
vs to thee, that he take thee in to wijf to
hym. And sche roos[z], and worschipide 41
lowe to erthe[a], and seide, Lo! thi seruauntesse be[b] in to an handmayde, that
sche waische the feet of the seruauntis of
my lord. And Abigail hastide[c], and roos[d], 42
and stiede[e] on an[f] asse; and fyue damesels,
sueris of hir feet, ȝeden[g] with hir, and sche[h]
suede the messangeris of Dauid, and was[i]
maad wijf to hym. But also Dauid took 43
Achynoem of Jezrael, and euer eithir was
wijf to hym; forsothe[k] Saul ȝaf Mycol his 44
douȝtir, wijf of Dauid, to Phalti †, the sone
of Lais, that was of Gallym.

† *to Phalti*; Ebreys seyen, that this Phalti was a doctour of the lawe, and therfor thouȝ he took Mychol, to obeye to Saul, and that he schulde be onourid as the hosebonde of the kingis douȝter, netheles he knew not hir fleisly, for he wiste that sche was the veri wiyf of Dauyth, for he hadde not forsake hir, and therfor Dauyth resseyuede hir aftirward, and netheles he hadde not take hir aftirward, if sche hadde be knowun fleisly of Phalti, as he entride no more to hise wyues, whiche Absolon knew, as it is had in ii. book xx. c°. *Lire here*. c.

CAP. XXVI.

And Zipheis[l] camen to Saul in to Ga- 1
baa, and seiden, Lo! Dauid is hidde in the
hille of Achille, which[m] is euene aȝens[n]
the wildirnesse. And Saul roos[o], and ȝede 2
doun in to deseert[p] of Ziph, and with hym
thre thousynde of men of the chosun of
Israel, that he schulde seke Dauid in the
desert of Ziph. And Saul settide tentis[q] 3
in Gabaa of Achille, that was euen aȝens
the wildirnesse in the weie. Sotheli[r]
Dauid dwellide in deseert[s]. Forsothe Dauid siȝ‡ that Saul hadde come aftir hym
in to deseert; and Dauid[t] sente aspieris, 4
and lernede[u] moost certeynli, that Saul
hadde come thidur. And Dauid roos[v] 5

‡ *Dauyth siȝ*, that is, knew bi a messanger. *Lire here*. c.

[q] Om. BCEFH.

[y] hath ȝoulde I. [z] roos up I. [a] the erthe I. [b] be sche I. [c] hastide hir I. [d] roos up I. [e] sche stiede up I. [f] the CDEFGKLMNOPQRSUWXb. [g] ȝeden forth I. [h] Abigail I. [i] sche was I. [k] and I. [l] men of Zephei I. [m] that I. [n] anentis I. [o] roos up I. [p] the deseert I. [q] his tentis I. [r] And I. [s] the deseert CI. [t] he I. [u] he lernede I. [v] roos up I.

cam to^r the place where Saul was. And
whanne he hadde seen the place, in the
whiche Saul slepte, and Abner, the sone
of Ner, prince of his chiualrye, and Saul
slepynge in the tent, and the tother
6 comouns bi the enuyroun of hym, Dauid
seith to Achymalech, Ethee, and to Abisay, the sone of Saruye, the brother of
Joab, seiynge, Who shal come doun with
me to Saul into the tentis? And Abisai
7 seide, Y shal goo doun with thee. Thanne
Dauid and Abisai camen to the puple the
ny3t, and founden Saul liynge, and slepynge in the tent, and a speer pi3t at his
heed in the erthe; forsothe Abner and
the puple slepynge in the enuyroun of
8 hym. And Abisai seide to Dauid, God
hath closid to dai thin enemye into thin
hoondis; now thanne I shal stike hym
with a speer in the erthe oonys, and the
9 secounde shal be no nede. And Dauid
seide to Abisai, Thou shalt not sle hym,
forsothe who shal stretche his hoond into
the crist of the Lord, and shal be inno-
10 cent? And Dauid seide, The Lord lyuith,
for but the Lord smyte hym, other the
day of hym come that he die, other into
11 batail comynge doun he perisshe; merciful be to me the Lord, that I stretche
not out myn hoond into the crist of the
Lord; now thanne tak the speer, that is
at his heed, and the cup of water, and go
12 wee. Dauid took the speer, and the cup
of water, that was at the heed of Saul,
and thei wenten awey, and there was not
eny man that saw3, and vndurstood, and
awook, but alle thei slepten; for the
13 sleep of the Lord felle vpon hem. And
whanne Dauid was goon fro a3ens, and
stood in the cop of the hil fro a fer, and
there was a greet myddil valey bitwix^s
14 hem, Dauid criede to the puple, and to
Abner, the sone of Ner, seiynge, Whether, Abner, thou shalt not answere?

priueli, and cam to the place where Saul
was. And whanne Dauid hadde seyn the
place, wher ynne Saul slepte, and Abner,
the sone of Ner, the prince of his chyualrye, and Saul slepynge in the^w tente, and
the tother comyn puple bi his cumpas,
Dauid seide to Achymelech, Ethey, and to 6
Abisai, sone^x of Saruye, the brother of Joab,
'and seide^y, Who schal go doun with me to
Saul in to 'the castels^z? And Abisai seide,
Y schal go doun with thee. Therfor Da-7
uid and Abisai camen to the puple in the
ny3t, and thei founden Saul lyggynge and
slepynge in 'the tente^a, and a spere sette
faste in the erthe at his heed; 'forsothe
thei founden^b Abner and the puple slepynge in his cumpas. And Abisay seide 8
to Dauid, God hath closid to dai thin
enemy in to thin hondis; now therfor Y
schal peerse hym with a^c spere onys in
the erthe, and 'no nede^d schal be in the
seconde tyme. And Dauid seide to Aby-9
sai, Sle thou not hym, for who schal holde
forth his hond into the crist of the Lord,
and schal be innocent? And Dauid seide, 10
The Lord lyueth, for no^e but the Lord
smyte hym^f, ether his dai come that he
die, ether he go doun in to batel and
perische; the Lord be merciful to me, 11
that Y holde not forth myn hond in to
the crist of the Lord; now^g therfor take
thou the spere, which^h is at his heed, and
'take thou^i the cuppe of watir, and go we
awei. Dauid^k took the spere, and the 12
cuppe of watir, that was at the heed of
Saul, and thei 3eden forth, and no man
was that si3, and vndirstood, and wakide,
but alle men slepten; for the sleep of the
Lord† 'hadde feld^l on hem. And whanne 13
Dauid hadde passid^m euene a3ens^n, and
hadde stonde on^o the cop of the^p hil afer^q,
and a greet space was bitwixe hem, Dauid 14
criede to the puple, and to Abner, the sone
of Ner, and seide, Abner, whether thou

† the sleep of the Lord; that is, a greuouse sleep sent of God. hadde feld on hem, that so Dauyth schulde go awey with out perel, and that bi the spere takun, and the ressel of water, he schulde declare his innocence anentis Saul, and schulde connycte ether ateynte him of wickidnesse. Lire here. c.

---

r into E pr. m.   s bytwene DF. betwen E. betwe c,

---

w his I.   3 the sone I.   y seijng K.   z his tentis I.   a his tentis I.   b and also I.   c the I.   d mouyd BC.
e Om. I.   f Saul I.   g Om. I.   h that I.   i Om. I.   k Thanne Dauid I.   l was fallen I. hadde fallen L.
hadde falle EMP.   m passid forth I.   n ouer a3ens hem I.   o afer upon I.   P an I.   q Om. I.

And Abner answerynge seith, Who art thou that criest, and vnrestist the kyng?

15 And Dauid seith to Abner, Whether ert thou not a man, and who other lijk thee in Yrael? whi thanne hast thou not kept thi lord the kyng? Forsothe there wente yn a man of the folk, for he wolde

16 sleye thi[t] lord the[u] kyng; it is not good, this that thou hast doo; the Lord lyuith, for sonys of deeth ʒe ben, for ʒe hán not kept ʒoure lord, crist of the Lord. Now thanne se, where be the speer of the kyng, and where be the cup of water, that

17 weren at the heed of hym. Forsothe Saul knewe the voys of Dauid, and seide, Whether is this thi vois, my sone Dauid? And Dauid seith, My vois, my lord kyng.

18 And he seith, For what cause pursueth my lord his seruaunt? What haue I doo,

19 or what yuel is in myn hoond? Nowe thanne here, I preye, my lord kyng, wordis of thi seruaunt; if the Lord stirith thee aʒens me, sacrifice be smellid; forsothe if the sones of men, cursid be thei in the siʒt of the Lord, that han throwun me out to day, that I dwelle not in the heritage of the Lord, seiynge,

20 Go, and serue to alien goddis. And now be not shed out my blood in the erthe before the Lord; for the kyng of Yrael is goon out that he seche a quyk fliʒe,

21 as a partritch is pursued in hillis. And Saul seith, Y haue synned; turne aʒen, my sone Dauid, namore forsothe I shal mysdoo to thee, forthi that my lijf was precious in thin eyen to day; forsothe it semeth that folili I haue doo, and many thingis to myche I haue vnknowen.

22 And Dauid answerynge seith, Loo! the speer of the kyng, go oon of the chil-dren[v] of the kyng, and take it; forsothe the Lord shal ʒeeld to ech man after his

23 riʒtwisnes and feith; forsothe the Lord

schalt[r] not answere? And Abner answeride, and seide, Who art thou, that criest, and disesist the kyng? And Dauith

15 seide to Abner, Whether thou art not a man, and what other man is lijk thee in Israel? whi therfor 'kepist thou not[s] thi lord the kyng? 'For o[t] man of the cumpanye entride, that he schulde sle thi lord the kyng; this that thou hast doon, is not

16 good; the Lord lyueth, for ʒe ben sones of deeth, that kepten not ʒoure lord, the crist[u] of the Lord. Now therfor se thou, where is the spere of the kyng, and where is the cuppe of watir, that weren[w] at his heed. Forsothe Saul knew the vois of

17 Dauid, and seide, Whether this vois is thin, my sone Dauid? And Dauid seide, My lord the[x] kyng, it is my vois. And

18 Dauid seide[y], For what cause pursueth my lord his seruaunt? What haue Y do, ether what yuel is in myn hond? Now

19 therfor, my lord the[z] kyng, Y preye, here the wordis of thi seruaunt; if the Lord stirith thee aʒens me, the sacrifice be smellid†; forsothe[a] if sones of men stiren thee, thei ben cursid in the siʒt of the Lord, whiche han cast me out 'to dai[b], that Y dwelle not in the erytage of the

20 Lord, and seien, Go thou, serue thou alien goddis. And now my blood be not sched out[c] in the erthe bifor the Lord; for the kyng of Israel ʒede[d] out, that he seke a quike fle, as a partrich is pursuede in

21 hillis. And Saul seide, Y synnede[e]; turne[f] aʒen, my sone Dauid, for[g] Y schal no more do yuel to thee, for my lijf[h] was precious to day in thin iʒen; for[i] it semeth[k], that[l] Y dide[m] folili, and Y vnknew[n] ful many

22 thingis. And Dauid answeride and seide, Lo! the spere of the kyng, oon of the 'children of the kyng[o] passe[p], and take it; forsothe the Lord schal ʒelde to ech man

23 bi[q] his riʒtfulnesse and feith[r]; for[s] the

† the sacrifice be smellid; that is, my pacience in this pursuyng be acceptid bifor God, as if Y offrede brent sacrifice at his auter. if the sones of men, bringe thee herto, as Doech and hise felowis doen. thei ben cursid, whiche han cast me out to day, that is, in present tyme. that Y dwelle not, etc.; that is, that Y dwelle not posibly in the lond of bihceste, where Goddis worchiping was quyk, that Y myʒte go thidur, and offre due sacrifices. and seyen, in dede. go thou, serue thou alien goddis, for thei that ben compellid for persecucioun, to entre in to a lond suget to idolatrie, be set forth to the synne of idolatrie, for liʒtly they ben enclyned herto of idolatrours, and sum tyme they ben compellid bi violence of peyne. Lire here. c.

† the ABFH.   u the ABFH.   v childre BEFH passim. childer c passim.

r wolt i.   s hast thou not kept i.   t Certis a i.   u anoyntid i.   w was i.   x Om. i.   y seide est i.   z Om. i.   a and i.   b now i.   c ouʒte L.   d hath gon i.   e haue synned i.   f turne thou i.   g forsothe i.   h lord G.   i Om. i.   k apperith BCDFGHKLMNOPQRSUWb. .   l forsothe that i.   m haue don i. die N. do M.   n haue unknowe i.   o kyngis children i.   p passe ouer hidere i.   q aftir i.   r his feith i.   s certis i.

hath takun thee to day into myn hoond, and I wold not stretche out myn hoond 24 in the crist of the Lord; and as thi lijf is maad greet to day in myn eyen, so my lijf be maad greet in the eyen of the Lord, and delyuer he me fro al angwish. 25 Thanne Saul seith to Dauid, Blessid thou, sone myn Dauid; forsothe and doynge thou shalt doo, and my3ti thou shalt mowe. Thanne Dauid wente into his weye, and Saul turnede a3en into his place.

CAP. XXVII.

1 And Dauid seith in his herte, Sumtyrne on a day I shal falle in the hoond of Saul; whether is it not beter, that I flee, and be sauid in the lond^w of Philisteis, that Saul dispeire, and ceese to seche me in alle the coostis of Yrael; 2 thanne flee we the hoondis of hym. And Dauid roos, and wente, he and sexe^x hundryd men with hym, to Achis, the sone 3 of Maoth, the kyng of Geth. And Dauid dwellide with Achis in Geth, he, and his men, and his hows; Dauid, and his two wyues, Achynoem Jezralite, and Abigail, 4 the wijf of Naabal Carmele. And it is toold to Saul, that Dauid was flowen into Geth; and he addide no more for to seche 5 hym. Forsothe Dauid seide to Achis, If I haue founden grace in thin eyen, a place be 3ouun to me in oon of the citees of this regioun, that I dwelle there; forsothe whi thi seruaunt dwellith in the 6 citee of the kyng with thee? And so Achis 3af to hym in that day Sichelech, for the which cause Sichelech is maad of 7 the kyngis of Juda vnto this day. Forsothe the noumbre of the dais, in the whiche Dauid dwellide in the regioun of 8 Philisteis, was of foure monethis. And Dauid stiede vp, and his men, and brou3ten prayes of Gethsury, and of Gethry, and of Amalachitis; forsothe

Lord bitook thee to dai in to myn hond, and Y nolde^t holde forth myn hond in to the crist of the Lord; and as thi lijf is 24 magnyfied to dai in myn i3en, so my lijf be magnyfied in the i3en of the Lord^u, and delyuere he me fro al angwisch. Therfor Saul seide to Dauid, Blessid be 25 thou, my sone Dauid; and sotheli thou doynge schalt do, and thou my3ti schalt be my3ti. Therfor^v Dauid 3ede^w in to his weie, and Saul turnede a3en in to his place.

CAP. XXVII.

And Dauid seide in his herte, Sumtyme 1 Y schal falle in o dai in the hond of Saul; whether it is not^x betere, that Y fle, and be sauyd in the lond of Filisteis, that Saul dispeire†, and cesse to seke me in alle the endis of Israel; therfor fle we hise hondis. And Dauid roos^y, and 3ede^z, he and sixe 2 hundrid men with hym, to Achis, the sone of Maoth, kyng of Geth. And Dauid 3 dwellide with Achis in Geth, he, and hise men, and his hows; Dauid^a, and hise twei wyues, Achynoem of Jezrael, and Abigail, the wijf of Nabal of Carmele. And it was 4 teld to Saul, that Dauid fledde in to Geth; and he^b addide^c no more that he schulde^d seke Dauid. Forsothe Dauid seide to 5 Achis, If Y haue founden grace in thin i3en, a place be 3ouun to me in oon of the citees of this cuntrey, that Y dwelle there; for whi dwellith thi seruaunt in the citee of the kyng with thee? Therfor Achis 6 3af to^e hym Sichelech in that dai, for which^f cause Sichelech was maad in to the^g possessioun of the kyngis of Juda 'til in to^h this dai. Forsothe the noumbre of 7 daies, in whiche Dauid dwellide in the cuntrei of Filisteis, was of foure monethis‡. And Dauid stiede^k, and hise men, and 8 token^l preies of Gethsuri, and of Gethri, and of men of Amalech; for these townes weren enhabitid bi eld tyme in the lond,

† *that Saul dispeire; that is, of my taking. Lire here.* c.

‡ *was foure monethis; in Ebreu it is, dayes and foure monethis, a 3eer ether 3eeris moun be vndurstondun by dayes, and so it schal be takun here, as it semeth. Lire here.* c.

w hoond AB.　x the sexe BCEFH.

t wolde not 1. u Lord God 1. v Thanne 1. w 3ede forth 1. x Om. c. y roos up 1. z 3ede forth 1. a *that is*, Dauid 1. b Saul 1. c addide to 1. d for to 1. e Om. 1. f the which 1. g Om. 1. h vnto 1. i And 1. k stiede up 1. l thei token 1.

thes hethen dwelliden in the loond bi oold tyme citees of Sur, vnto the loond 9 of Egipt. And Dauid smoot al the loond of hem, and he lafte not a lyuynge man and womman; and takynge sheep, and oxen, and assis, and camelis, and clothis, 10 he turnede aʒen, and cam to Achis. Forsothe Achis seide to hym, In whom felle thou on to dai? Dauid answerde, Aʒens the south of Jude, and aʒens the south of Yranyel, and aʒens the south of Ceny. 11 Man and womman Dauid lafte not on lyue, ne brouʒte into Geth, seiynge, Lest perauenture thei speken aʒens vs. These thingis dide Dauid, and this was the dom of hym, alle they dais 'the whiche² he dwellide in the regioun of Philisteis. 12 Thanne Achis leuyde to Dauid, seiynge, Forsothe manye yuels he hath wrouʒte aʒens his puple Yrael, therfor a seruaunt he shal be to me for euere more.

to men goynge to Sur, 'til to^m the lond of Egipt. And Dauid smoot al the lond of 9 hem, and lefteⁿ not man 'lyuynge and womman^o; and he took scheep, and oxun, and assis, and camels, and clothis, and turnede^p aʒen, and cam to Achis. Sotheli^r 10 Achis seide to hym, 'In to^s whom 'hurliden ʒe^t to dai? Dauid^u answeride, Aʒens the south of Juda, and aʒens the south of Hiramel, and aʒens the south of Ceney. Dauid left not^v quik man and^w womman, 11 nether brouʒte 'in to^x Geth^y, and² se ide, Lest perauenture thei speken aʒens vs. Dauid dide these thingis, and this was his doom, in alle daies in whiche he dwellide in the cuntrei of Filisteis. Therfor Achis 12 bileuyde to Dauid, and seide, Forsothe^a he^b wrouʒte^c many yuelis aʒens his puple Israel, therfor he schal be euerlastynge^d seruaunt to me^e.

CAP. XXVIII.

1 In the dais forsothe it is doon, Philisteis gadreden her companyes, that thei weren redi before aʒens Yrael at batail. And Achis seide to Dauid, Witynge now wite thou, for with me thou shalt goon 2 out in the tentis, thou and thi men. And Dauid seide to Achis, Now thou shalt knowe what thi seruaunt is to doo. And Achis seith to Dauid, And I shal putte 3 thee keper of myn heed alle dais. Forsothe Samuel is deed, and al Yrael biweilide^a hym, and biryede hym in Ramatha, his^b cytee. And Saul took awey the dyuynours and clepers of deuels fro the loond, and slewʒ hem that hadden 4 chaarmers^c of deuels in the wombe. And Philisteis ben gadrid, and camen, and setten tentis in Siccymam; forsothe and Saul gadrede al Yrael, and cam into

CAP. XXVIII.

Forsothe it was doon in tho daies, 1 Filisteis^f gaderiden^g her cumpenyes, that thei schulden be maad redi aʒens Israel to batel. And Achis seide to Dauid, Thou witynge 'wite now^h, for thou schalt go out with me inⁱ castels^k, thou and thi men. And Dauid seide to Achis, Now thou 2 schalt wyte what thingis thi seruaunt schal do. And Achis seide to Dauid, And Y schal sette thee kepere of myn heed in alle dayes. Forsothe^l Samuel was deed, 3 and al Israel biweilide hym, and thei birieden hym in Ramatha, his citee. And Saul dide awey fro the lond witchis and fals dyuynours†, 'and he slouʒ hem that hadden^m 'charmers ofⁿ deuelis^o 'in her wombe^p. And Filisteis weren gaderid, 4 and camen, and settiden tentis in Sunam; sotheli and Saul gaderide al Israel, and

† *false dyvynours; this that sueth, and he killide hem that hadden fendis spekinge in the wombe, is not in Ebreu, nether ls of the text. Lire here. c.*

y Om. BCEFH. z that c. a weylyde DH. weilede E. weylyden F. b in his E pr. m. c chaarmes A.

m vnto I. n he lefte I. o ne womman lyuynge I. q turneden A. he turnede I. r And I. s Aʒens I. t han ʒe hurlid I. u And Dauid c. v not in these I. w ne I. x in A. y Gethony I. z but he I. a Certis I. b we x pr. m. c pr. m. EGKLMNOPQRSU pr. m. WXb. c hath wrouʒt I. d a I. e me for euermore I. f the Filisteis I. g gaderiden to gidre I. h schalt knowe I. i in to K. k tentis I. l Certis I. m Om. A pr. m. BCEFLNPRU. n Om. A pr. m. BCDEFGIKLMNOPQRSUWX. charmers and b. o Om. A pr. m. BCEFLNPRU. fendis spekinge DIKMOSWX. p in the wombe DGKMOQSWX. Om. A pr. m. BCEFLNPRU.

5 Gelboe. And Saul saw3 the tentis of Philisteis, and dradde, and his herte 6 quauyde[d] ful myche. And he counseilde the Lord ; and he answerde hym not, ne bi prestis, ne bi sweuens[e], ne bi pro-7 phetis. And Saul seide to his seruauntis, Sechith to me a womman hauynge a charmynge goost; and I shal goo to hir, and ,aske bi hir. And his seruauntis seiden to hym, There is a womman hauynge a dyuynynge spirite in Endore. 8 Thanne he chaungide his abite, and is clothid with othere clothis; and he 3ede, and two men with hym; and thei camen to the womman bi ny3t. And he seith, Dyuyne to me in a chaarmynge spyrite, and rere to me whom Y shal seye to 9 thee. And the womman seith to hym, Loo! thou hast knowen how greet[f] thingis Saul dide, and what maner wyse he hath putte out dyuynours, and clepers of deuels fro the loond; whi thanne weytist thou to my lijf, that I be slayn? 10 And Saul swore to hyre in the Lord, seiynge, The Lord lyuith; for there shal not come to thee eny thing of yuel for 11 this thing. And the womman seide to him, Whom shal I rere to thee? The 12 which seith, Rere to me Samuel. For-sothe whanne the womman hadde seen Samuel, she cryede with a greet voys, and seide to Saul, Whi hast thou putte this to me? forsothe thou ert Saul. 13 And the kyng seide to hyr, Wole thou not drede; what hast thou seen? And the womman seith to Saul, I saw3 goddis 14 stiynge vp fro the erthe. And he seith to hir, What maner is the fourm of hym? The which seith, An oold man stiede vp, and he is clothid with a mantil. And Saul vndurstood that it was Samuel; and he bowide hym self vpon his face in 15 the erthe, and honourde. Forsothe Sa-muel seide to Saul, Whi hast thou vn-

cam in to Gelboe. And Saul si3 the cas-5 tels of Filisteis, and he dredde, and his herte dredde greetli. And he counselide 6 the Lord ; and the Lord answeride not to hym, nether bi preestis, nether[q] bi dremes, nether[q] bi profetis. And Saul seide to hise 7 seruauntis, Seke 3e to me a womman hau-ynge a feend spekynge in the[r] wombe ; and Y schal go to hir, and Y schal axe[s] bi hir. And hise seruauntis seiden to hym, A womman hauynge a feend spekynge in the wombe is in Endor. Therfor Saul 8 chaungide his clothing, and he was clothid with othere clothis ; and he 3ede[t], and twei men with hym ; and thei camen to the womman in the ny3t. And he[u] seyde, Dy-uyne thou to me in[v] a fend spekynge in the wombe, and reise thou to[w] me whom Y schal seie to thee. And the womman 9 seide to hym, Lo! thou woost hou grete thingis Saul hath do, and hou he dide[x] awei fro the lond witchis, and fals dyuyn-ours ; whi therfor settist thou tresoun to my lijf, that Y be slayn? And Saul swoor 10 to hir in the Lord,. and seide, The Lord lyueth ; for no thing of yuel schal come to thee for this thing. And the womman 11 seide to hym, Whom schal Y reise[y] to thee? And he[z] seide, Reise thou Samuel to[a] me. Sotheli whanne the womman hadde seyn 12 Samuel, sche criede with greet vois, and seide to Saul, Whi hast thou disseyued me? for[b] thou art Saul. And the kyng 13 seide to hir, Nyl thou drede ; what hast thou seyn? And the womman seide to Saul, Y si3 goddis stiynge[c] fro erthe[d]. And 14 Saul seide to hir, What maner forme is of hym? And sche seide, An eld man stieth[e], and he is clothid with a mentil. And Saul vndirstood that it was Samuel† ; and Saul bowide hym silf on his face to the erthe, and worschipide. Sotheli[f] Sa-15 muel seide to Saul, Whi hast thou disesid me, that Y schulde be reisid? And Saul

† *Saul endur-stood that it was Samuel, Seynt Austin in his Pistle to Simplycian, rehersith tweyne opyny-ouns: oon seith, that Samuel ap-peride verili in soule if Goddis ordenaunce, to telle to Saul his deth and the scateryng of the puple of Israel ; the tother opyny-oun seith, that the deuel ap-peride in the licnesse of Samuel ; and Austyn enclyn-eth more to this opynyoun, as it is told in Decrees, in xxvi, cause, v. ques-tioun, c[e]. nec myrum. For the deuel trans-figurith him-silf in to an aungel of li3t, as Poul seith, and bi the maner of spek-ing of scrip-ture, a licnesse takith the name of a thing, whos licnesse it berith, and the euydensis for the con-trarie part moun li3tly be asoilid. Lire here. c.*

d quakide n.   e swenes c.   f myche 3 pr. m.

q ne EILP.   r Om. 1.   s enquere 1.   t 3ede forth 1.   u Saul 1.   v Om. c.   w up to 1.   x hath do 1.
y reise up 1.   z Saul 1.   a up to 1.   b certis 1.   c stiynge up 1.   d the erthe 1.   e stieth up 1.
f And 1.

restid me, that I be rerid? And Saul seith, I am artid to myche; forsothe Philisteis fiȝten aȝens me, and God is goon a wey fro me, and wol not here me, ne bi the hoond of prophetis, ne bi sweuens; therfor I haue clepid thee, that 16 thou shewe to me what I shal doo. And Samuel seith, What askist thou me, sith God hath goon a wey fro thee, and goon 17 to thin enemye? Forsothe the Lord shal doo to thee as he spak in myn hoond, and he shal kut thi kyngdam fro thin hoond, and ȝyue it to thi neiȝbor Dauid; 18 for thou hast not obeishid to the vois of the Lord, ne thou didist the wraththe of his woodnes in Amalech. Therfor that that thou suffrist the Lord hath doo to 19 thee to day; and the Lord also shal ȝeue Irael with thee in the hoond of Philisteis. Forsothe to morwe thou and thi ſones shal be with me; but and the Lord shal take the tentis of Yrael in the 20 hoond of Philisteis. And Saul anoon felle straȝt into the erthe; he dradde forsothe the wordis of Samuel, and miȝt was not in hym, for he hadde not eten breed al 21 that dai and al niȝt. And so that womman wente yn to Saul, and saith; forsothe he was disturblid greetli; and she seide to hym, Loo! thin hoond womman hath obeishid to thi vois, and I haue put my lijf in myn hoond, and I haue herd thi 22 wordis, that thou speek to me. Now thanne here thou the vois of thin hoond womman, and I shal putte before thee a morsel[g] of breed, and etynge thou wexe 23 hool, and mowe goon the weye. The which forsoke, and seith, I shal not ete. Forsothe his seruauntis and the womman constreyneden; and at the last, the vois of hem herd, he roos fro the erthe, and 24 sat vpon the bedde. Forsothe that womman hadde a foddred calf in the hows, and she hiȝede, and slewȝ it; and takynge

seide, Y am constreyned greetli; for Filisteis[g] fiȝten aȝens me, and God ȝede[h] awei fro me, and he nolde[i] here me, nether bi the hond of profetis[k], nether[l] bi dremes; therfor Y clepide thee, that thou schuldist schewe to[m] me what Y schal do. And 16 Samuel seide, What axist thou me, whanne God hath go awei fro thee[n], and passide[nn] to thin enemy? For[o] the Lord schal do 17 to thee as he spak[p] in myn hond, and he schal kitte awey thi rewme fro thin hond, and he schal ȝyue it to Dauid, thi neiȝbore; for thou obeiedist not to[q] the vois 18 of the Lord, nether didist[r] the ire of hys strong veniaunce[s] in Amalech. Therfor the Lord hath do to thee to day that that thou suffrist; and the Lord schal ȝyue 19 also Israel with thee in the hond of Filisteis. Forsothe to morewe thou and thi sones schulen be with me; but also the Lord schal bitake the castels of Israel in the hond of Filistiym[t]. And anoon Saul 20 felde[u] stretchid[v] forth to[vv] erthe; for he dredde the wordis of Samuel, and strengthe was not in hym, for he hadde not ete breed in al that dai and al[w] nyȝt. Therfor thilke 21 womman entride to Saul, and seide; for he was disturblid greetli; and sche seide to hym, Lo! thin handmayde obeiede[x] to thi vois, and Y haue put my lijf in myn[y] hond†, and Y herde thi wordis, whiche 22 thou spakist to me. Now[z] therfor and[a] thou here the vois of thin handmaide, and Y schal sette a mussel[b] of breed bifor thee, and that[c] thou etynge wexe strong, and maist do the[d] iourney. And he forsook[e], 23 and seide, Y schal not ete. Sothely[f] hise seruauntis and the womman compelliden hym‡; and at the laste, whanne the vois of hem was herd, he roos[g] fro the erthe, and sat on the[h] bed. Sotheli[i] thilke wom- 24 man hadde a fat calf in the[k] hows, and sche hastide[l], and killide hym[m]; and sche took mele, and meddlide it[n], and made

† in myn hand; that is, Y dide at thyn axyng a werk forbedun vndur the peyne of deth. Lire here. c.

‡ compelliden him; that is, bi bisi preyeris, and so he was counfortid in party, and assentide to hem. Lire here. c.

ᵍ mussel E.

ᵍ the Filisteis I. ʰ hath gon I. ⁱ wolde not I. ᵏ prestys ELP. dyuynours I sed expunxit sec. m. ˡ ne ELP. ᵐ Om. I. ⁿ the A. ⁿⁿ hath passid I. ᵒ Sothli I. ᵖ hath spoke I. �q Om. I. ʳ thou didist I. ˢ feers wraththe of the Lord I. ᵗ Philistees I. ᵘ felle doun I. ᵛ and was stretchid I. ᵛᵛ vpon the I. ʷ al that I. ˣ hath obeied I. ʸ thin OKX sup. ras. ᶻ And now I. ᵃ Om. I. ᵇ morsel I. ᶜ Om. c. ᵈ thi I. ᵉ forsook it I. ᶠ But I. ᵍ roos up I. ʰ a I. ⁱ And I. ᵏ hir I. ˡ hee hastide E. hee castid L. ᵐ it I. ⁿ it togidre I.

floure she mengide it, and boke[h] therf
25 looues; and putte before Saul and his
seruauntis, the which whanne thei hadden eten, risen, and wenten thur3 out al
that[i] ny3t.

CAP. XXIX.

1 Thanne alle the companyes of Philisteis ben gadred in Aphech, but and
Irael sette tentis vpon the welle that was
2 in Jezrael. Forsothe and the maistris of
Philisteis wenten in hundredis and thousandis; forsothe Dauid and his men
weren in the last companye with Achis.
3 And the princis of Philisteis seiden to
Achis, What to hem self wolen thes
Ebrews? And Achis seith to the princys
of Philisteis, Whether knowe 3e not Dauid, that was seruaunt to Saul, kyng of
Irael? and is anentis me manye days or
3eeris, and I founde not in hym eny
thing, fro the dai that he ouer flei3 to
4 me vnto this dai. Forsothe the princis
of Philisteis ben wrooth a3ens hym, and
seiden to hym, The man turne a3en, and
sitt in his place, in the which I haue sett
hym, and dessende he not with vs into
batail, lest he be maad to vs aduersarye,
whanne we bigynnen to fi3te; forsothe
what maner wise other wise he shal
mowe plese his lord, but in oure heedis?
5 Whether is not this Dauid, to whom
thei syngen in dauncis, seiynge, Saul
hath smyten in his thousandis, and Dauid
6 in his ten thousandis? Thanne Achis
clepide Dauid, and seide to hym, The
Lord lyueth; for ri3t thou ert, and good
in my si3t, and thi goynge out and thin
incomynge with me is in the tentis, and
I haue not founden in thee eny thing of
yuel, fro the dai that thou cam to me
vnto this dai; but to the maistris thou
7 plesist not. Turn thanne a3en, and go in
pees, and offend thou not the eyen of the

therf breed; and settide[o] bifor Saul and 25
bifor hise seruauntis, and whanne thei
hadden ete, thei risiden[p], and walkiden
bi[q] al that[r] ny3t.

CAP. XXIX.

Therfor alle the cumpenyes of Filisteis[s] 1
weren gaderid in[t] Aphec, but also Israel
settide tentis aboue the welle that was in
Jezrael. And sotheli the princis of Fi- 2
listcis[u] 3eden in cumpenyes of an hundrid,
and in thousyndis; forsothe[v] Dauid and
hise men weren in the laste cumpenye
with Achis. And the princes of Filisteis 3
seiden to Achis, What wolen these Ebreis
to hem silf? And Achis scide to the
princes of Filisteis, Whether 3e knowen
not Dauid, that was the seruaunt of Saul,
kyng of Israel? and he was with me in[w]
many daies, ether 3eeris[x], and Y foond not
in hym ony thing†, fro the dai, in which
he fledde to me[y] 'til to[y] this dai. Sotheli[z] 4
the princes of Filisteis weren wrooth a3ens
hym[a], and seiden[b] to hym, The man turne
a3en, and sitte[c] in his place, in which thou
hast ordened hym, and come he not doun
with vs in to batel, lest he be maad aduersarie to vs, whanne we han bigunne to
fi3te; for hou mai he plese his lord in
other maner, no[e] but in oure heedis?
Whether this is not Dauid, to whom thei 5
sungen in daunsis, and seiden, Saul smoot
in thousyndis, and Dauid smoot in hise
ten thousyndis? Therfor Achis clepide 6
Dauid, and seide to hym, The Lord
lyueth; for thou art ri3tful, and good in
my si3t, and thi goyng out and 'thin
entryng[f] is with me in castels[g], and Y
'foond not[h] in thee ony thing of yuel, fro
the day[i] in which thou camest to me
til to this dai; but thou plesist not the
princis[k]. Therfor turne thou a3en, and 7
go in pees, and offende thou not the i3en

† ony thing;
of ymagynyng
to yuel, which
schulde be per-
seyued in so
long tyme, if it
hadde be verily
in him. Lire
here. c.

h booc ᴇ. boc c.   i the ᴀᴄ pr. m.

o sche sette forth ɪ.   p rosin ᴇᴘ. resen up ɪ.   q in ɪ.   r the ɪ.   s the Filisteis ɪ.   t jn to ɪ.
u Philistee ɪ.   v but ɪ.   w Om. ɪ.   x Om. c.   y vnto ɪ.   z Certis ɪ.   a Achis ɪ.   b thei sciden ɪ.
c abide he ɪ.   e Om. ɪ.   f thi comyng yn ɪ.   g tentis ɪ.   h haue not founden ɪ.   i tyme ᴀ.   k princis
or satrapis ɪ.

8 maistris of Philisteis. And Dauid seid
to Achis, Forsothe what haue I doo, and
what hast thou founden in me thi seruaunt, fro the dai that I was in thi si3t
vnto this dai, that I come not, and[k] fi3t
a3ens the enemyes of my lord the kyng?
9 Forsothe Achis answerynge spak to Dauid, I woot for thou art good, and in myn
eyen as the aungel of God; but the princis
of Philisteis seiden, He shal not stie vp
10 with vs into batail. Therfor rise eerli,
thou, and thi seruauntis that camen with
thee; and whanne fro ni3t 3e shulen rise,
and it bigynneth to 'li3te day[l], gooth.
11 And so Dauid roos fro ni3t, he and his
men, that he mi3t goo forth eerli to the
loond of Philisteis, and turne a3en; forsothe Philisteis stieden vp into Jezrael.

CAP. XXX.

1 Whanne Dauid and his men weren
comen into Sichelech the thridde dai,
Amalechites maden a bure fro the south
partie into Sichelech; and thei smyten
Sichelech, and thei brenten it with fier.
2 And caitifis thei ladden wymmen fro it,
fro the leest vnto the greet; and thei
slewen not eny man, but ladden with
3 hem, and wenten her weye. Thanne
whanne Dauid was comen, and his men,
to the citee, and thei founden it brent
with fier, and her wyues, and her sonys,
4 and dou3tris[m] to be ladde caitifes[n], Dauid and the puple that was with hym
rereden vp her voices, and weiliden, to
the tyme that teeris failleden in hem.
5 Forsothe and the two wyues of Dauid
weren ladde caitife, Achynóem Jezraelite,
and Abigail, the wijf of Naabal of Car-
6 mele. And Dauid sorowide greetli; forsothe al the puple wold stoone hym, for
bitter was the lyif of eche man vpon her
sones and dou3tres. Forsothe Dauid is

of princis[l] of Filisteis[m]. And Dauid seide 8
to Achis, Forsothe[n] what 'dide Y[o], and
what hast thou founde in me thi seruaunt,
fro the dai in which Y was in thi si3t til
in to this dai, that Y come not, and fi3te
a3ens the enemyes of my lord the kyng?
Forsothe[p] Achis answeride, and spak to 9
Dauid, Y woot that thou art good, and as
the aungel of God in my i3en; but the
princes of Filisteis seyden, He[q] schal not
stie[r] with vs in to batel. Therfor rise thou[s] 10
eerli, thou, and thi seruauntis that camen
with thee; and whanne 3e han ryse bi ny3t,
and it bigynneth to be cleer[t], go 3e[u].
Therfor Dauid roos[v] bi ny3t, he and hise 11
men, that thei schulden go forth eerli, and
turne a3en to the lond of Fylisteis; sotheli[w]
Filisteis stieden[x] in to Jezrael.

CAP. XXX.

And whanne Dauid and hise men hadden 1
come 'in to[y] Sichelech in the thridde dai,
men of Amalech hadden maad asau3t on[z]
the south part in[a] Sichelech; and thei[b]
smytiden[c] Sichelech, and brenten[d] it bi[e]
fier. And thei ledden the wymmen pri- 2
soneris fro thennus, fro the leeste 'til to[f]
the grete[g]; and thei hadden not slayn ony,
but thei ledden[h] with hem, and 3eden[i] in
her weie. Therfor whanne Dauid and 3
hise men hadde come to the citee, and
hadden founde it brent bi[k] fier, and that
her[l] wyues, and her sones, and dou3tris
weren led[m] prisoneris, Dauid[n] and the 4
puple that was with hym reisiden her
voices, and weiliden, til teeris[o] failiden in
hem. Forsothe[p] also twei[q] wyues of Dauid 5
weren led[r] prisoneris, Achynoem of Jezrael, and Abigail, the wijf of Nabal of
Carmele. And Dauid was ful sori; for- 6
sothe[a] al the puple wold stone[t] hym[u], for
the soule of ech man was bittir on her
sones and dou3tris. Forsothe Dauid was

k in *ADFH*.   l dai li3ten *CE*.   m dou3tren *BFH*.   n caytyfe *FH*.

l the princis *CKFL*. the satrapis I.   m the Filisteis I.   n And I.   o haue I. do I.   p And I.   q Dauid I.
r stie up I.   s thou up I.   t cleer *day* I.   u 3e forth I.   v roos up I.   w but the I.   x stieden up I.
y in A.   z fro I.   a of DC. a3ens I.   b Om. EL.   c smoten I. smeten L. smetyn EF.   d thei brenten I.
e with I.   f til A. vnto I. to *o sec. m.*   g moost I.   h ledden hem forth I.   i thei 3eden I.   k with I.
l menns I.   m led awey I.   n thanne Dauid I.   o the teeris I.   p And I.   q the two I.   r led awey I.
s certis I.   t haue stoned I.   u Dauid I.

7 coumfortid in the Lord his God. And
he seith to Abiathar, the preest, the sone
of Achimalech, Aplie to me the preestis
coope. And Abiathar apliede to Dauid
8 the preestis coope; and Dauid counseilde
the Lord, seiynge, Shal I pursue, or naye,
these theues, and take hem? And the
Lord seide to hym, Pursue; forsothe out
of dout thou shalt take hem, and shake
9 out the praye. Thanne Dauid wente, he
and sexe hundred men that weren with
hym, and camen to the streem of Besor;
10 and summe wery stoden stille. Forsothe
Dauid pursuede, he and foure hundrid
men; for there stoden stille two hundred, that weri my3ten not goon ouere
11 the streem of Besor. And thei founden
an Egipcien man in the feeld, and thei
brou3ten hym to Dauid; and thei 3euen
hym breed for to eete, and drynke water;
12 but and the relif of a wei3t of dried figis,
and two bundels of dried grapis. The
whiche thingis whanne he hadde eten,
the spiryt of hym is turned a3en, and he
is refresshid; forsothe he hadde not eten
breed, ne drunken water thre dais and
13 thre ni3tes. And so Dauid seide to hym,
Whos ert thou, or whens and whidir
gost thou? The which seith, An Egipcien child I am, and the seruaunt of an
Amalechite man; forsothe my lord laft
me, for I bigan to sikynyn⁰ the thridde
14 dai hens. Forsothe we wenten out of
the south coost of Cerethi, and a3ens
Judam, and to the south of Caleph, and
15 Sichilich we han brent vp with fier. And
Dauid seide to hym, Maist thou lede me
to this cumpanye? The which seith,
Sweer to me bi God, that thou shalt not
slee me, and not take me into the hoondis
of my lord; and I shal lede thee to this
companye. And Dauid swore to hym.
16 The which whanne he hadde ladde hym,

coumfortid in his Lord God. And he 7
seide to Abiathar, preest^v, the sone of
Achymelech, Bringe thou^w ephoth^x to me.
And Abiathar brou3te ephoth^y to Dauid;
and Dauid councelide^z the Lord, and seide, 8
Schal Y pursue^a, ether nay^b, 'these
theues^c? and schal Y take hem? And
the Lord seide to hym^d, Pursue thou; for
with out doute thou schalt take hem, and
thou schalt take awey the^e prey. Therfor 9
Dauid 3ede^f, he and sixe hundrid men that
weren with hym, and thei camen 'til to^g
the stronde of Besor; and sotheli^h the
wery men^i abididen^k. Forsothe^l Dauid pur- 10
suede^m, he and foure hundrid men; for
twei hundrid abididen^n, that weren weeri,
and my3ten not passe the stronde of Besor.
And thei founden a man of Egipte in the 11
feeld, and thei brou3ten hym to Dauid;
and thei 3auen 'breed to hym⁰, that he
schulde ete, and 'schulde drynke watir^p;
but also *thei 3auen to hym* a gobet of a^q 12
bundel of drye^r figis, and twei byndyngis^s
of dried grapis. And whanne he^t hadde
ete tho, his spirit turnede a3en^u, and he
was coumfortid; for he hadde not ete breed,
nether hadde^v drunk watir in thre daies
and thre ny3tis. Therfor^w Dauid seide 13
to hym, Whos *man* art thou, ethir fro
whennus and whidur goist thou? And
he seide, Y am a child of Egipt, the
seruaunt of a man of Amalech; forsothe^x
my lord forsook me, for Y bigan to be
sijk the thridde dai ago. Sotheli^y we 14
braken out to^z the south coost of Cerethi,
and a3ens Juda, and to^a the south of
Caleb, and we brenten Sichelech bi^b fier.
And Dauid seide to hym, Maist thou lede 15
me to this cumpeny? Which^c seide, Swere
thou to me bi God, that thou schalt not
sle me, and schalt^d not bitake me in to the
hondis of my lord; and Y schal lede thee
to this cumpeny. And Dauid swoor to

⁰ seeke ᴀ. seeken ʙᴇꜰ. syken ɴ.

---

^v the preest ɪ.   ^w thou the prestis coope *or* ɪ.   ^x ephoth, *that is, the cloth of the hi3est prest* ᴋ.   ^y the ephoth s.   ^z councelide with ɪ.   ^a pursue these theues ɪ.   ^b no ɪ.   ^c Om. ɪ.   ^d Dauid ɪ.   ^e fro hem her ɪ.   ^f 3ede forth ɪ.   ^g vnto ɪ.   ^h *there* ɪ.   ^i men *of the oost of Dauid* ɪ.   ^k abiden ᴄᴇʟᴘᴜ. abiden bihynde ɪ.   ^l And ɪ.   ^m pursuede forth ɪ.   ^n abiden ʙɪ.   ^o hym bred ɪ.   ^p watir to drinke ɪ.   ^q Om. *plures*.   ^r dried ɪ.   ^s clustris ɪ.   ^t the man ɪ.   ^u a3en *to him* ɪ.   ^v he hadde ɪ.   ^w Thanne ɪ.   ^x but ɪ.   ^y For ɪ.   ^z at ɪ.   ^a at ɪ.   ^b with ɪ.   ^c The which ɪ.   ^d that thou schalt ɪ.

loo! thei seeten vpon the face of al the
erthe, etinge and drinkynge, and as ha-
lowynge a feest dai, for al the pray and
spoilis that thei token fro the loond of
Philisteis, and fro the loond of Juda.
17 And Dauid smoot hem fro euen 'unto
euen^p of the tother dai, and there scapide not of hem eny man, but foure hundrid ȝonge men, that stieden vp^q camelis,
18 and flowen. Forsothe Dauid delyuerde
alle thingis that Amalachitis token, and
19 his two wyues he dilyuerde; ne there
failide eny man fro litil vnto miche, as
wel of sonys as of douȝtris^r, and of
spoilys; and what eure thingis thei had-
20 den robbid, alle Dauid brouȝte aȝen; and
took all the flockis and drouys, and droue
before his face. And thei seiden, This
21 is the praye of Dauid. Forsothe Dauid
cam to the two hundrid men, that wery
stoden stille, and myȝten not folowe
Dauid; and he hadde comaundid hem to
sitte stille biside the streem of Besor;
the whiche wenten out to mete Dauid,
and the puple that was with hym. Forsothe Dauyd comynge nyȝ to the puple,
22 salutede hem pesibli. And o man answerynge, werst and wickid of the men
that weren with Dauid, seide, For thei
camen not with vs, we shulen not ȝyue
to hem eny thing of the praye, that we
han delyuerde, but suffice to echon his
wijf and sonis; the whiche whanne thei
23 han takun, goo thei a weye. Forsothe
Dauid seide, Not so ȝe shulen doo, britheren myn, of these thingis that the
Lord hath taken to vs, and hath kepte
vs, and hath^s ȝeuen the theuys, that
breken out aȝens vs, into oure hoondis,
24 ne eny man shal here vs vpon this word.
Forsothe euen part shal be of the goynge
down to batail, and of the abidynge stille
at the fardels; and lijk maner thei shulen

hym. And whanne the child hadde ledde 16
hym^e, lo! thei saten at the mete, on^f the
face of al the erthe, etynge and drynkynge,
and as halewynge a feeste^g, for al the prey
and spuylis whiche thei hadden take of
the lond of Filisteis, and of the lond of
Juda. And Dauid smoot hem fro euentid^h 17
'til to^i euentid of the tothir dai, and not
ony^k of hem escapide, no^l but foure hundrid ȝonge^m men, that stieden on^n camels,
and fledden. Forsothe Dauid delyuerede 18
alle thingis whiche the men of Amalech
token, and he delyuerede hise twei wyues;
nether ony^o of hem failide fro litil^p 'til to^q 19
greet^r, as wel of sones as of douȝtris, and
of spuylis; and what euer thingis thei
hadden rauyschid, Dauid ledde aȝen alle^s
thingis; and he took alle flockis^t and grete 20
beestis, and droof^u bifor his face. And thei^v
seiden, This is the prey of Dauid. For- 21
sothe Dauid cam to twei^w hundrid men,
that weren weeri, and abididen^x, and
myȝten not sue Dauid; and he hadde^y
comaundid hem to sitte in^z the stronde
of Besor; whiche^a ȝeden out aȝens Dauid,
and the^b puple that was with hym. For-
sothe^c Dauid neiȝede to the puple, and
grette^d it pesibli. And o man, the werste^e 22
and vniust^f of the men that weren with
Dauid, answeride, and seide, For thei
camen not with vs, we schulen not ȝyue
to hem ony thing of the prey, which^g we
rauyschiden^h, but^i his wijf and children^k
'suffice to ech man^l; and whanne thei han
take hem, go thei awei. Forsothe^m Dauid 23
seide, My britheren, ȝe schulen not do so^n
of these thingis, whiche the Lord ȝaf^o to
vs, and kepte^p vs, and ȝaf^q the theues,
that braken out aȝens vs, in to oure
hondis; nether ony man^r schal here vs on^s 24
this word. For euene part schal be of him
that goith doun to batel, and of hym that
dwellith at the fardelis; and in lijk maner

P Om. A.   q bi A.   r douȝtren BFH.   s Om. CEFH.

e hym *thidere* I.   f upon I.   g feeste day *plures*.   h the euentid I.   i vnto the I.   k ony thing I.
l Om. I.   m of ȝonge I.   n upon I.   o ony *man* I.   P the litil I.   q vnto I.   r the greet I.   s Om. G.
t the flockis I.   u droof hem I.   v men I.   w his two I.   x abidin EP. abididen bihynde I.   y Om. I.
z at I.   a the whiche I.   b aȝens the I.   c Certis I.   d he grett I.   e werste man I.   f wickid I.
g that I.   h han rauischid I.   i but suffice it to eche man I.   k his children I.   l Om. I.   m And I.   n so
as ȝe speken I.   o hath ȝouen I.   P he hath kept I.   q hath ȝouen I.   r Om. I.   s *stryue* on I.

25 departe. And this is maad fro that day,
and there aftir a statute, and a decree,
and as a lawe in Yrael vnto this day.
26 Thanne Dauid cam into Sichelech, and
sente ʒiftis of the praye to the eldris of
Juda, his neiʒbours, seiynge, Takith blessynge of the praye of the enemyes of the
27 Lord; to hem that weren in Bethel, and
that in Ramoth, at the south, and that in
28 Gether, and that in Aroer, and that in
29 Sephamoth, and that in Eschama, and
that in Rethala, and that in the citees of
Hierameli, and that in the citees of Ceny,
30 and that in Arama, and that in Lautua-
31 saam, and that in Athech, and that in
Ebron, and to other, that weren in thes
places, in the whiche Dauid hadde dwellid
and his men.

thei schulen departe[t]. And this was maad 25
a constitucioun and doom[u] fro that dai
and afterward[†], and as a lawe in Israel til-
in to this dai. Therfor[v] Dauid cam in to 26
Sichelech, and sente[w] ʒiftis of the prey to
the eldere men of Juda, hise neiʒboris, and
seide, Take ʒe blessyng of the prey of
enemyes of the Lord; to[x] hem that weren 27
in Bethel, and that weren in Ramoth, at
the south, and that weren in Jether, and 28
that weren in Aroer, and that weren in
Sephamoth, and that weren in Escama,
and that weren in Rethala, and that weren 29
in the citees of Jeramel, and that weren in
the citees of Ceny, and that weren[y] in 30
Arama, and that weren in Lautuasam, and
that weren in Athec, and that weren in 31
Ebron, and to othere men, that weren in
these places, in whiche Dauid dwellide and
hise men.

[† fro that day and oftirward; in Ebreu it is, in that day and fro bifore, that is, fro the tyme of Abraham; but this was ordeyned stide-fastliere bi Dauyth, and a doom of lawe bi the kyngis power, that it schulde be kept aftirward outirly. Lire here. c.]

CAP. XXXI.

1   Forsothe Philisteis fouʒten aʒens Irael,
and the men of Yrael flowen before the
face of Philisteis, and thei slayn fellen in
2 the hyl of Gelboe. And Philisteis fallen
into Saul, and into[t] the sonys of hym,
and thei smyten Jonathan, and Amynadab, and Melchisue, the sonys of Saul.
3 And al the charge of the batayl is turned
into Saul; and there folweden hym men
sheters, and he is woundid hydowsly of
4 the archers.   And Saul seide to his
squyer, Drawe out thi swerd, and smyit
me, lest perauenture thes vncircumcidid
men[u] comen, and sleen me, scornynge to
me. And his squier wolde not; forsothe
he was agaist with to mych gaistnes;
and so Saul cauʒte his swerd, and felle
5 vpon it. The which thing whanne his
squyer hadde seen, that is, that Saul was
deed, also he felle on his swerd, and is
6 deed with hym.   Thanne Saul is deed,
and his three sonys, and his squyer, and

CAP. XXXI.

Forsothe Filisteis[z] fouʒten aʒens Israel, 1
and the men of Israel fledden bifor the
face of Filisteis, and felden[a] slayn in the
hil of Gelboe.   And Filisteis[b] hurliden on[c] 2
Saul, and on[d] hise sones, and smytiden[e]
Jonathas, and Amynadab, and Melchisua,
sones of Saul. And al the weiʒte[f] of batel[g] 3
was turned 'in to[h] Saul; and men archeris
pursueden hym[i], and he was woundid
greetli of the archeris.   And Saul seide to 4
his squyer, Drawe out thi swerd, and sle
me, lest perauenture these vncircumcidid
men come, and sle me, and scorne me.
And his squyer nolde[k], for he was aferd bi
ful grete drede; therfor Saul took his
swerd, and felde theronne[l].   And whanne 5
his squyer hadde seyn this, 'that is[m], that
Saul was deed, also he felde on[n] his swerd
and was deed with hym.   Therfor[nn] Saul 6
was deed, and hise thre sones, and his
squyer, and alle his men in that dai togidere. Forsothe[o] the sones of Israel, that 7

t Om. E pr. m.   u Om. CEFH.

' departe *the preie* 1.   u a doom 1.   v Thanne 1.   w he sente 1.   x *he sente* to 1.   y weren *to hem* 1.
z the Filisteis 1.   a thei fellen doun 1.   b the Filisteis 1.   c feersly into 1.   d into 1.   e thei killiden 1.
smyten EFL. smetin P.   f charge 1.   g the batel 1.   h aʒens 1.   i Saul 1.   k wolde not 1.   l therupon 1.
m Om. AO pr. m.   n upon 1.   nn And so 1.   o And 1.

7 alle his men in that dai togidir. Forsothe seynge the sonys of Yrael, that
weren biȝonde the valey, and beȝonde
Jordan, that the men of Yrael hadden
flowen, and that Saul was deed, and his
sones[v], thei laften her citees, and flowen;
and Philisteis camen, and dwelliden there.
8 Forsothe the tother dai doon, Philisteis
camen for to spoyl out the slayn men,
and thei fonden Saul, and his thre sones,
liggynge[w] in the hil of Gelboe; and thei
girden of the heed of Saul, and thei
spoileden hym out of the aarmys. And
thei senten into the loond of Philisteis bi
enuyroun, that it were toold in the temple
10 of mawmettis, and in puplis. And thei
setten his aarmys in the temple of As-
charoth; forsothe the bodi of hym thei
11 hengen in the wal of Bethsan. The
which thing whanne the dwellers of
Jabes Galaad hadden herd, alle thingis
12 that Philisteis hadden doo to Saul, alle
the moost stronge men rysen, and wenten
al nyȝt, and token the careyns of Saul,
and the careyns of his sonis fro the wal
of Bethsan; and the men of Jabes Galaad camen, and brenten hem with fier.
13 And thei token the boonys of hem, and
biryeden in the wode of Jabes, and fastiden seuen days.

Here endith the first book of Kyngis, and now bigynneth the secounde[x].

weren biȝendis[p] the valei, and biȝendis
Jordan, sien that the[q] men of Israel hadden
fled, and that Saul was deed, and hise
sones, and thei leften her citees and fledden;
and Filisteis[r] camen, and dwelliden there.
Forsothe[s] in[t] the tother dai maad[u], Filisteis 8
camen, that thei schulden[v] dispuyle the
slayn men, and thei founden Saul, and hise
thre sones, liggynge in the hil of Gelboe;
and thei kittiden awei the heed of Saul, 9
and dispuyliden hym of armeris[w]; and
senten[x] in to the lond of Filisteis bi cumpas, that it schulde be teld in the temple[y]
of idols, and in the puplis. And thei put- 10
tiden hise armeris in the temple of Astoroth; sotheli[z] thei hangiden his bodi in
the wal of Bethsan. And whanne the 11
dwellers of Jabes of[a] Galaad hadden herd
this, what[b] euer thingis[c] Filisteis[d] hadden
do to Saul, alle[e] the strongeste[f] men ri- 12
siden[g], and ȝeden[h] in[i] al that nyȝt, and
token[k] the deed bodi of Saul, and the deed
bodies of hise sones fro the wal of Bethsan;
and the[l] men of Jabes of Galaad camen,
and brenten tho *deed bodies* bi[m] fier.
And thei token the boonus of hem, and 13
biriedeu[n] in the wode of Jabes, and fastiden[o] bi seuene daies.

Here endith the firste book of Kyngis, and here bigynneth the secounde[p].

[v] sone ABCEF. [w] liynge EFH, liende C. [x] *Here eendith the first boke of Kyngus, and bigynneth the secounde.* B. *Explicit liber primus Regum. Here endith the firste book of Kingis, and bigynneth the secounde.* E. No final rubric in CH.

[p] biȝonde I. [q] Om. I. [r] the Filisteis I. [s] And I. [t] Om. I. [u] aftir the I. [v] wolden I. [w] his armeris I. [x] thei senten I. [y] templis C. [z] but I. [a] Om. A. [b] and what I. [c] Om. A. thing M. [d] the Filisteis I. [e] and alle I. [f] mooste stronge I. [g] risiden up I. risen EP. [h] ȝeden forth I. [i] Om. I. [k] thei token I. [l] Om. K sec. m. [m] with I. [n] birieden hem I. [o] thei fastiden I. [p] *Here endith the firste book of Kyngis, and here bygynneth the secounde book.* DOQUWb. *Here endith the firste book, and here byggynneth the secounde book of Kyngis.* F. *Here endith the firste book of Kyngis, and bigynneth a prolog on the ij. book.* G. *Heere endith the firste book of Kyngis.* I. *Here endeth the firste book of Kinges; see now the seconde.* K. *Here endith the firste book of Kingis, and here bigyuneth a prologe on the secounde.* M. *Heere eendith the firste of Kinges and bigynneth the ij[e].* R. *Here eendith the firste book of Kyngis, and bigynneth the secounde book of Kyngis.* SXÇ. No final rubric in ELP.

II. KINGS.

[*Prologue on the Second book of Kings*[a].]

THIS secounde book of Kingis makith mencioun of the coronacioun of Dauith, first in Ebron bi the men of Juda, and aftirward in Jerusalem of al the peple of Israel; and of his werres; and how the Lord punischide Dauith with grete angwischis and disesis for the deeth of Vrie his seruaunt, and for the rauyschinge of Bersabee, the wijf of Vrie, and seide to him bi the profete, that werris scholden not ceese fro him in alle hise daies. Neuertheles the Lord louede Dauith, and ʒaf victorie to him of alle hise enemyes.

The secounde boke of Kynges[a].

CAP. I.

1 Forsothe it is doon, after that Saul is
deed, that Dauid is[b] turned aʒen fro the
slauʒter of Amalech, and dwellide in Si-
2 chelech two days. Forsothe in the thridde
day aperide a ʒong man, of the tentis of
Saul, with to-rent clooth, and sprengid
the heed with powdre; and as[c] he came
to Dauid, he[d] felle vpon his face, and
3 lowtide. And Dauid seide to hym, Whens
comyst thou? The which seith to Dauid,
4 Fro the tentis of Yrael I fleiʒ. And Dauid seide to hym, What is the word that
is doon; shewe to me. The which seith,
The puple fleiʒ fro the batail, and many
fallynge of the puple ben deed; but and
Saul, and Jonathas, his sone, han died.
5 And Dauid seide to the ʒong man, that
toolde to hym, Wherbi wost thou, that
6 Saul is deed, and Jonathas, his sone? And

Heere bigynnith the secunde book of Kyngis[b].

CAP. I.

Forsothe[c] it was doon, after that Saul 1
was deed, that Dauid turnede aʒen fro the
sleyng of Amalech, and dwellide[d] twei
daies in Sichelech. Forsothe[e] in the thridde 2
dai a man apperide, comynge fro the
castels[f] of Saul with the[g] cloth to-rent, and
his heed spreynt with dust; and as he
cam to Dauid, he felde on[gg] his face, and
worschipide[h]. And Dauid seide to hym, 3
Fro whennus comest thou? Which[i] seide to
Dauid, Y fledde fro the castels[k] of Israel.
And Dauid seide to hym, What is the 4
word which[l] is doon[m]; schewe thou[n] to me.
And he seide, The puple[o] fledde[p] fro the
batel, and many of the puple felden[q], and
ben deed; but also Saul, and Jonathas, his
sonne, perischyden[r]. And Dauid seide to 5
the ʒong man, that telde to hym[s], Wherof
woost thou, that Saul is deed, and Jo-

[a] From H. No initial rubric in the other Mss. [b] was CE. [c] Om. E *pr. m.* [d] and E *pr. m.*

[a] This Prologue is from M. [b] From IM. *The secounde of Kinges.* LP. *Here bigynneth the secunde book.* O. No initial rubric in the other Mss. [c] And I. [d] he dwellide I. [e] And I. [f] tentis I. [g] a I. [gg] upon I. [h] worschipide *him* I. [i] And he I. [k] tentis I. [l] that I. [m] doon there I. [n] thou it I. [o] puple of Israel I. [p] hath fled I. [q] fledden IOU. [r] han perischid I. [s] hym this I.

the ȝong man seith, that toolde to hym,
Bi hap I cam into the hil of Gelboe, and
Saul lenyde vpon his speer; forsothe
7 chaaris and horsis neiȝeden to^e hym; and
turned bihynde his ᾿rigge, and seynge
clepide me. To whom whanne I hadde an-
8 swerde, I am niȝ; he seide to me, Forsothe who art thou? And I seide^f to
9 hym, Amalechite I am. And he spak to
me, Stoond vpon me, and sle me; for
anguyshis holden me, and ȝit al my soule
10 is in me. And stondynge vpon hym I
slewȝ hym; forsothe I wiste that he
myȝte not lyue after the fallynge; and I
took the diademe that was in his heed,
and the beeȝ fro his arm, and I^g haue
11 brouȝte it^h to thee, my lord, hidyr. Forsothe Dauid takynge his clothis kitte,
and alle the men that weren with hym;
12 and thei weileden, and wepten, and fastiden vnto theⁱ euen, vpon Saul, and Jonathan, his sone, and vpon the puple of the
Lord, and vpon the hows of Irael, forthi
13 that thei weren faln with swerd. And
Dauid seide to the ȝonge man, that toolde
to hym, Whens ert thou? The which
answerde, I am the sone of an Amalechit
14 man comlynge. And Dauid seith to hym,
Whi draddist thou not to putte thin hoond
15 for to slee the crist of the Lord? And
Dauid clepynge oon of his children^k seith,
Goynge nyȝ fal into hym. The which
16 smoot hym, and he is deed. And Dauid
seith to hym, Thi blood vpon thin heed;
forsothe thi mouth hath spoken aȝens
thee, seiynge, I slewȝ the crist of the
17 Lord. Forsothe Dauyd weilide this maner
a weilynge vpon Saul, and vpon Jonathas,
18 his sone. And he comaundide, that thei
techen the sones of Juda weilynge, as it
is writen in the Book of Riȝtwise Men;
and seith, Bihold, Irael, for, thes that ben
deed, vpon thin heiȝe thingis woundide;

nathas, his sonne? And the ȝong man^c
seide, that telde to hym, Bi hap Y cam in
to the hil of Gelboe, and Saul lenyde on^t
his spere; forsothe^u charis and knyȝtis^v
neiȝiden to hym; and he turnede^w bihynde 7
his bak,᾿and siȝ me, and^x clepide. To whom
whanne Y hadde answeride, Y am present;
he seide to me, Who art thou? And Y 8
seide to hym, Y am a man of Amalech.
And he spak to me, Stonde thou on^y me, 9
and sle me; for angwischis holden me, and
ȝit al my lijf is in me. And Y stood on^y 10
hym, and Y killide^x hym; for Y wiste that
he myȝte not lyue aftir the fallyng; and Y
took the diademe, that was in^a his heed,
and the bye fro his arm, and Y brouȝte^b
hidur to thee, my lord. Forsothe^c Dauid 11
took and to-rente hise clothis, and^f the men
that weren with hym; and thei weiliden, 12
and wepten, and fastiden ᾿til to^g euentid^h, on
Saul, and Jonathas, his sone, and on the
puple of the Lord, and on the hows of
Israel, for thei hadden feldⁱ bi swerd.
And Dauid seide to the ȝong man, that 13
telde to him, Of whennus art thou? And
he answeride, Y am the sone of a man
comelyng, of a man of Amalech. And 14
Dauid seide to him, Whi dreddist thou not
to sende^k thine hond, that thou schuldist
sle the crist of the Lord? And Dauid 15
clepide oon of hise children, and seide, Go
thou, and falle on hym. Which^l smoot that
ȝong man, and he was deed. And Dauid 16
seide to hym, Thi blood be on thin heed;
for thi mouth spak aȝens thee, and seide,
Y killide the crist^m of the Lord. For- 17
sooth Dauid biweilide sych a weilyng on
Saul, and on Jonathas, his sone; and 18
comaundideⁿ, that thei^o schulden teche the
sones of Juda weilyng†^p, as it is^q writun
in the Book of Just Men. And Dauid
seyde, Israel, biholde thou, for these men^r
that ben deed, woundid^s on thin hiȝe

† *weiling;* in
Ebreu it is,
that thei
schulden teche
the sones of
Juda the
bouwe, that
is, the craft of
scheting; thus
it is in Ebreu,
and in bokis
amendid. *Lire
here.* c.

^e vnto E pr.m.　^f sey BF. seic CE.　^g Om. BCEFH.　^h Om. BCEFH.　ⁱ Om. E.　^k childre BEFH. passim.
childer c passim.

^t upon I.　^u and I.　^v horse men I.　^w yturned I.　^x and seynge me I.　^y upon I.　^z slowe I.
^a on I.　^b haue brouȝt hem I.　^c Certis I.　^f and cke I.　^g vnto I.　^h the euentid IK.　ⁱ falle doun I.
falle ELM.　^k putte c scc. m, M. putte forth I.　^l And he I.　^m anoyntid I.　ⁿ he comaundide I.
^o men I.　^p the weilyng I.　^q was A.　^r Om. I.　^s ben woundid I.

19 the noble men of Yrael vpon thin hillis ben slayn. What maner wise fellen the 20 strengthful? woleth¹ ʒe not telle in Geth, ne telle ʒe in the gedryngis togidre of the many weyes of Aschalon; lest perauenture the douʒtres of Philisteis gladen, ne ioyen the douʒtris of the vncircumcidid. 21 Hillis of Gelboe, ne dewe ne reyn come vpon ʒow, ne be thei feeldis of first fruytis; for there is throwen a wey the sheelde of stronge men, the sheelde of Saul, as thouʒ he hadde not ben 22 anoyntid with oyle. Fro^m the blood of the slayn, fro the talwʒ of stronge men, the arowe of Jonathas neuer turnede aʒen bacward, and the swerd of Saul is not 23 turned aʒen in ydel. Saul and Jonathas loueli, and feyr in her lyif, forsothe in deeth thei ben not deuydide; swifter than 24 eglis, stronger than liouns. Douʒtris of Yrael, vpon Saul wepith, the which cloth- ide ʒou with reed in delicis, the which ʒaf golden ournementis to ʒoure wor- 25 shipynge. What maner fellen strong men in batayl? Jonathas in thin heiʒ 26 thingis is slayn. I sorwe vpon thee, brother myn Jonatha, ful myche feir, and loueli ouere the loue of wymmen; as a moder louith hir^n oneli sone, so Y 27 louede thee. What maner wise fellen stronge men, and pershiden aarmes to fiʒten with in batayl?

CAP. II.

1 Therfor after thes thingis Dauid coun- seilde the Lord, seiynge, Whether I shal goon vp into oon of the cytees of Juda? And the Lord seith to hym, Go vp. And Dauid seide to hym, Whedir shal I go vp? And he answerde to hym, Into 2 Ebron. Thanne Dauid ʒede vp, and his two wyues, Achynoem Jezraelite, and Abigail, 3 the wijf of Naabal of Carmele. But and the men that weren with hym, Dauid

placis; the noble men of Israel ben slayn 19 on^t thin hillis. Hou felden^u stronge men†? 20 nyle ʒe telle^v in Geth, nether telle ʒe in the^w weilottis of Ascolon; lest perauenture the douʒtris of Filisteis be glad, lest the douʒtris of vncircumcidid men 'be glad^x. Hillis of Gelboe, neither dew nethir reyn 21 come on^y you, nether the^z feeldis of firste fruytis be^a; for the scheeld of stronge men was cast awey there, the scheeld of Saul, as 'if he were not anoyntid^b with oileʒ. Of the blood of slayn men, of^c the fatnesse 22 of strong men, the arewe of Jonathas ʒede neuer abak, and the swerd of Saul turnede not aʒen void. Saul and Jonathas amy- 23 able, and fair in her lijf, weren not de- partid also in deeth^d; thei weren swiftere than eglis, strongere than liouns. Douʒtris 24 of Israel, wepe ʒe on Saul, that clothide‖ ʒou with fyn reed colourid^e in^f delicis, that ʒaf goldun ournementis to ʒoure atyre. Hou 'felden doun stronge men^g in batel? 25 Jonathas was slayn in the^h hiʒe places. Y 26 make sorewe on^i thee, my brother Jonathas, ful fair, 'and amyable more than the^k loue of wymmen; as a modir loueth oon^l aloone^m sone, so Y louyde thee. Hou therfor 27 'felden doun stronge men^n, and armeris of batel perischide^o?

CAP. II.

Therfor aftir these thingis Dauid coun- 1 seilide^p the Lord, and seide, Whether Y schal stie^q in to oon of the citees of Juda? And the Lord seide to hym, Stie thou^r. And Dauid seide to the Lord, Whidur schal Y stie^s? And the Lord answeride to hym, In to Ebron. Therfor Dauid 2 stiede, and hise twei wyues, Achynoem of Jezrael, and Abigail, the wijf of Nabal of Carmele. But also Dauid ledde the men 3

† hou felden stronge men; as if he seide, it semeth not mannus victo- rie, but Goddis veniaunce, for the synnes of Saul and of his felawis; and therfor it is to eschewe souereynly fro slehe synnes. nyle ʒe telle and so forth, that is, if this myʒte be that

22 it were not teld, Y wolde that bi al the desir of soule. Lire here. c.

‡ with oile, that is, of con- secracioun of the king bi Samuel. Lire here. c.

‖ clothide ʒou, etc.; that is, with colourid and preciouse clothis, takun of the prey of enemyes. Lire here. c.

l wile CE.   m For A.   n Om. E pr. m.

t upon I.   u han falle I.   v telle this I.   w Om. C.   x ioyen I.   y upon I.   z be thei the I.   a Om. I. b if he hadde not ben anoyntid I. it were not anoynted X.   c and of I.   d her deeth EIL.   e Om. BC. colourid clothing I.   f and in A pr. m. CEFLMPRSU.   g han stronge men falle doun I.   h Om. I.   i upon I. k ouer the I.   l hir I.   m only I.   n han stronge men falle doun I.   o han perischid I.   p counseilide with I.   q stie up I.   r thou up I.   s stie up I.

ladde echon with her hows; and thei dwelliden in the burȝ touns of Ebron. 4 And the men of Juda camen, and anoyntiden there Dauid, for he shulde regne vpon the hows of Juda. And it is toold to Dauid, that the men of Jabes Galaad 5 hadden biryede Saul. Thanne Dauid sente messangeris to the men of Jabes Galaad, and he seide to hem, Blessid be⁰ ȝe of the Lord, the whiche diden this mercy with ȝoure lord Saul, and biryeden hym. 6 Forsothe and nowe the Lord shal ȝeelde to ȝou merci and treuth, but and Y shal ȝeelde grace, forthi that ȝe diden this 7 word. Be ȝoure hoondis coumfortid, and be ȝe sones of strength; forsothe thouȝ ȝoure lord Saul be deed, neuerthelater the hows of Juda hath anoyntid me into a 8 kyng to hem. Abner forsothe, the sone of Ner, prince of the oost of Saul, took Hisboseth, the sone of Saul, and ladde 9 hym about bi the tentis, and sette hym kyng vpon Galaad, and vpon Jethsuri, and vpon Jezrael, and vpon Effraym, and 10 vpon Beniamyn, and vpon al Yrael. Of fourti ȝeer was Hisboseth, the sone of Saul, whanne he bigan to regne vpon Irael; and two ȝeer he regnede. Forsothe oneli the hows of Juda folwide 11 Dauid. And the noumbre of dais, the which Dauid dwellide comaundynge in Ebron vpon the hows of Juda, was of 12 seuen ȝeris and of sexeᴾ monethis. And Abner, the sone of Ner, wente out, and the children of Hisboseth, theᑫ sone of Saul, 13 fro the tentis into Gabaon. Forsothe Joab, the sone of Saruye, and the children of Dauid wenten out, and aȝen camen to hem biside the fishpoond in Gabaon. And whanne thei weren comen 'togidir in oon forn aȝensʳ other, these seeten on the tooˢ parti of the fishpoond, 14 and thei on the tother. And Abner seide to Joab, Rise children, and pleye thei

that weren with hym, ech man with his hows; and thei dwelliden in the townes of Ebron. And the men of Juda camen, and 4 anoyntiden† there Dauid, that he schulde regne onᵗ the hows of Juda. And it was teld to Dauid, that men of Jabes of Galaad hadden biried Saul. Therfor Dauid 5 sente messangeris to the men of Jabes of Galaad, and seide to hem, Blessid be ȝe of the Lord, that diden this mercy with ȝourᵗᵗ lord Saul, and birieden hym. And now 6 sotheli the Lord schal ȝelde to ȝou merci and treuthe, but also Y schal ȝelde thankyng, for ȝe diden this word. Ȝoure hondis 7 be coumfortid, and be ȝe sonesⁿ of strengthe; for thouȝ ȝoure lord Saul isᵛ deed, netheles the hows of Juda anoyntideᵂ me kyng to 'hym silfˣ. Forsotheʸ Abner, the sone of 8 Ner, prince of the oost of Saul, took Isbosech, the sone of Saul, and leddeᵍ hym aboute bi theⁿ castels, and madeᵇ himᶜ 9 kyng on Galaad, and on Gethsury, and on Jezrael, and on Effraym, and on Beniamyn, and on al Israel. Isbosech, theᵈ 10 sone of Saul, was of fourti ȝeer, whanne he began to regne onᵉ Israel; and he regnede twei ȝeer. Sotheliᶠ the hous aloone of Juda suede Dauid. And the noumbre 11 of daies, bi whiche Dauid dwellide regnynge in Ebron on the hows of Juda, was of seuene ȝeer and sixe monethis. And Ab- 12 ner, the sone of Ner, ȝede out, and the children of Isbosech, soneᵍ of Saul, fro the castels inʰ Gabaon. Forsotheⁱ Joab, the 13 sone of Saruye, and the children of Dauid ȝeden out, and camenᵏ to hem bisidis the cisterne inˡ Gabaon. And whanne thei hadden come togidere in to o place euene aȝensᵐ, these saten on o part of the cisterne, and thei on theⁿ tother. And Abner 14 seide to Joab, 'The children rise⁰, and pleiᴾ befor us†. And Joab answeride, Rise theiᑫ. Therforʳ thei risidenˢ, and passidenᵗ 15 twelue in noumbre of Beniamyn, of the

† and anoyntiden there Dauyth; Dauyth was anoyntid thries; first in the hows, in the firste book of Kingis xvi. cᵉ.; the ii. tyme here of the hows of Juda; the thridde tyme on al Israel, in v. cᵒ.; in signe that a man owith to haue anoyntyng of the Hooly Goost, in herte bi veri feith, in mouth bi knouleching therof, and in the hond bi good worching. Lire here. c.

‡ pleye bifor uṣ; that is, schewe her strengthe and nobley; and here pleie is set for sle ethir fiȝte. Lire here. c.

⁰ Om. CEFH.　ᴾ seuene E pr. m.　ᑫ Om. CE sec. m.　ʳ in oon fro the regiown E pr. m.　ˢ o C. ton E.

† in A, upon I.　ᵗᵗ ȝou A.　ᵘ the sones I.　ᵛ be I.　ᵂ hath anoyntid I.　ˣ hym I.　ʸ Certis I.　ᶻ he ledde I. ⁿ Om. I.　ᵇ he made I.　ᶜ Om. plures.　ᵈ Om. KX.　ᵉ upon I.　ᶠ And I.　ᵍ the sone I.　ʰ of A. Om. D. ⁱ And I.　ᵏ thei camen I.　ˡ of I.　ᵐ aȝens either other I.　ⁿ that I.　⁰ Rise these children up I.　ᴾ plei thei I.　ᑫ thei up I.　ʳ Thanne I.　ˢ resen up I.　ᵗ passiden forth I.

before vs. And Joab answerde, Risen.
15 Thanne rysen and wenten twelue bi
noumbre of Beniamyn, of the parti of
Hysboseth, the sone of Saul; and twelue
16 of the children of Dauid. And taken of
echon the heed of his peere, he piȝte doun
a swerd in the side of the contrarie; and
thei fellen doun to gidre. And the name
of that place is clepid The Feelde of
17 stronge men in Gabaon. And there is
sprongen an hard⁰ batail ynowȝ in that
day; and Abner is dryuen, and the men
18 of Yrael, of the children of Dauid. Forsothe there weren there the thre sones of
Saruye, Joab, and Abisay, and Asahel;
ceertis Asahel was a moost swift renner,
as oon of the caprettis that dwellen in
19 wodis. Forsothe Asahel pursuede Abner,
and bowide not aside, ne fro the riȝt ne
fro the left, leeuynge to pursue Abner.
20 And so Abner bihelde bihynde his bak,
and seith, Whether art thou not Asahel?
21 The which answerde, Y am. And Abner
seide to hym, Go to the riȝt, or to the
left; and tak oon of the ȝonge men, and
tak to thee the⁰ spoilis of hym. Forsothe
Asahel wolde not leeue, but he con-
22 streynede hym. And eft Abner spak to
Asahel, Go a wey, and wole thou not
sue me, lest I be constreyned to stike
thee into the erthe, and I shal not mowe
23 rere my face to Joab, thi brother. The
which dispiside to here, and wolde not
bowe aside. Thanne Abner, the speer
turned a wey, smoot hym in the sheer,
and stikide hym thurȝ, and he is deed in
the same place; and alle that wenten bi
the place, in the which Asahel hadde
24 fallen, and was deed, biden stille. Forsothe Joab and Abisay pursuynge Abner
fleynge, the sunne wente doun; and thei
camen to the hil of the water kundit,

part of Isbosech, sone⁰ of Saul; and twelue
of the children⁰ of Dauid. And ech man, 16
whanne 'the heed of his felowe was takun⁰,
fastnede˟ tho⁰ swerde in to the side of 'the
contrarye˟; and thei felden doun togidere.
And the name of that place was clepid
The Feeld of stronge men† in Gabaon. And 17
'batel hard ynow⁰ roos in that dai; and
Abner⁰ and the sones of Israel 'weren
dryuun⁰ of the children⁰ of Dauid. For- 18
sothe thre sones of Saruye weren there,
Joab, and Abisai, and Asahel; forsothe⁰
Asahel was a 'rennere moost swift⁰, as oon
of the capretis that dwellen in woodis.
Forsothe⁰ Asahel pursuede Abner, and 19
bowide⁰ not¹, nether to the riȝt side nether˟
to the left side, ceessynge to pursue Abner.
Therfor Abner bihelde bihynde his bac, 20
and seide, Whether thou art Asahel?
Which¹ answeride, Y am. And Abner 21
seide to hym, Go⁰ to the riȝtside, ether to
the lefte side; and take oon of the ȝonge
men, and take to thee hise spuylis. Sotheli⁰
Asahel nolde⁰ ceesse, that ne he⁰ pursuede
hym⁰. And eft Abner spak to Asahel, Go 22
thou awei; nyle thou pursue me, lest Y be
compellid to peerse⁰ thee in to erthe⁰, and
Y schal not mowe reise⁰ my face to Joab,
thi brother. And Asahel dispiside to here, 23
and nolde⁰ bowe awey. Therfor⁰ Abner
smoot him 'with the spere turned awei⁰‡
in the schar, and roof˟ thorouȝ, and he
was deed in the same place; and alle men
that passiden bi the⁰ place, in which *place*⁰
Asahel felde doun, and was deed, stoden⁰
stille. Forsothe⁰ while Joab and Abisai 24
pursueden Abner fleynge, the sunne ȝede
doun; and thei camen til⁰ to the litil hil of
the⁰ water cundiyt, which⁰ is euene aȝens
the valey, and the weie of descert in Gabaon. And the sones of Beniamyn weren 25
gaderid⁰ to Abner, and thei weren gaderid

Right margin notes:

17 † *the feeld of stronge men:* in Ebreu it is, the feeld of men slayn

18 togidere. *Lire here.* c.

‡ *turned awey;* that is, turned aȝenus him, in the schar; in Ebreu it is, smoot him bihinde the mawe in the fyuethe rib, vndur which ben the membris of lyf. *Lire here.* c.

ᵃ herd ᴀ.   ᵗ Om. ᴅ.

ᵘ the sone ɪ.   ᵛ seuauntis ɪ.   ʷ he hadde take his felowe bi the heede ɪ.   ˟ fiechide ɪ.   ʸ his ɪ.
ᶻ his aduersarie ɪ.   ᵃ ful harde batel ɪ.   ᵇ Abner was dryuen awei ɪ.   ᶜ Om. ɪ.   ᵈ seuauntis ɪ.   ᵉ and ɪ.
ᶠ ful swifte rennere ɪ.   ᵍ Sotheli *plures.* And ɪ.   ʰ he bowide ɪ.   ⁱ Om. ɪ.   ᵏ ne ᴇʟ.   ˡ The which ɪ.
ᵐ Go thou ɪ.   ⁿ But ɪ.   ᵒ wolde not ɪ.   ᵖ Om. ᴀ.   ۹ Abner ɪ.   ʳ stike ɪ.   ˢ the erthe ᴋ.   ᵗ reise
thanne ɪ.   ᵘ he wolde not ɪ.   ᵛ therfor the spere of Azahel yturned awey ɪ.   ʷ Om. ɪ.   ˟ stikide him ɪ.
ʸ roof him ˟ *sec. m.*   ʸ that ɪ.   ᶻ Om. ɪ.   ᵃ abiden ɪ.   ᵇ And ɪ.   ᶜ Om. ᴇɪʟˣ. in ᴍ.   ᵈ a ɪ.   ᵉ that ɪ.
ᶠ gaderid togidre ɪ.

that is fro aȝens of the valey, and of the
25 weye of deseert in Gabaon. And the
sones of Beniamyn ben gederid to Abner,
and clustrid togidir in o cumpanye thei
26 stoden in the cop of a litil hil And
Abner criede to Joab, and seith, Whether
vnto slauȝter thi swerd shal be cruel?
Whether knowist thou not, that perilous
be despeir? How long thou seist not to
the puple, that he leeue to pursue his
27 britheren? And Joab seith, The Lord
lyueth, for if thou haddist spoken eerli,
the puple pursuynge his britheren hadde
28 goon awey Thanne Joab fulsownede
with the trompe, and al the oost stood;
and nomore thei pursueden Yrael, ne
29 wenten in stryf. Forsothe Abner and
his men wenten awey bi the wylde
feeldis of Moab al that niȝt, and thei
wenten ouer Jordan , and, passid alle
30 Bethoron, thei camen to the tentis. But
Joab turned aȝen, Abner laft, gederide al
the puple; and there failiden of the children of Dauid ten and nyn men, out
31 taken Asahel Forsothe the seruauntis
of Dauid smyten of Beniamyn, and of the
men that weren with Abner, thre hundred
32 and sexti, and the whiche ben deed And
thei token Asahel, and biryeden hym in
the biriels of his fader in Bethleem And
Joab, and the men that weren with hym,
wenten al niȝt, and in that bigynnynge
of day thei camen into Ebron

CAP III

1   There is maad thanne a longe stryu-
ynge togidre bitwixe[n] the hows of Dauid
and the hows of Saul, Dauid profitynge
and[v] euermore strenger than hym self,
forsothe the hows of Saul decresynge
2 eche dai And there ben born sones of
Dauid in Ebron , and his first geten was
3 Amon, of Achinoem Jezraelite; and after
hym ȝeliab, of Abigail, the[w] wijf of
Naabal Carmeel; forsothe the thridde[x],

togideie in to o cumpeny, and stoden[h] in
the hiȝnesse[i] of oon[k] heep of erthe. And 26
Abner criede to Joab, and seide, Whether
thi swerd schal be feers 'til to[l] sleyng?
Whether thou knowist not, that disperr†
is perelouse? Hou longe seist thou not to
the puple, that it ceesse to pursue hise
britheren? And Joab seyde, The Lord 27
lyueth, for if thou haddist spoke[m] eerli,
the puple pursuynge his brother hadde
go awey And Joab sownede with a cla-28
rioun, and al the oost stood[n], and thei
pursueden no ferthere Israel, nether bigunnen batel Forsothe[o] Abner and hise 29
men ȝeden[p] by the feeldi places of Moab
in al that nyȝt, and passiden[q] Jordan ,
and whanne al Bethoron was compassid,
thei camen to the castels Sotheli[r] whanne 30
Abner was left, Joab turnede aȝen, and
gaderide togideie al the[s] puple; and ten
men and nyne, outakun[t] Asahel, failiden
of the children[u] of Dauid Forsothe the 31
seruanntis of Dauid smytiden[v] of Beniamyn, and of the men that weren with
Abner, thre hundrid men and sixti, whiche[w]
also weren deed And thei token Asahel, 32
and birieden hym in the sepulcre of his
fadir in Bethleem. And Joab, and the
men that weren with hym, ȝeden in al
that nyȝt, and in thilke morewtid thei
camen in to Ebron

•

CAP III

Therfor long[x] stryf was maad bitwixe 1
the hows of Dauid and 'bitwixe[y] the hows
of Saul , and Dauid profitide and euere
was strongeie than hym silf‡, forsothe the
hows of Saul decrecsside ech dai. And 2
sones weren borne to Dauid in Ebron ,
and his firste gendrid[a] sone was Amon, of
Achynoem of Jezrael; and aftir hym was 3
Celeab, of Abigail, wijf[b] of Nabal of Carmele, sotheli[c] the thrydde was Absolon,

† that disperr,
etc., of fiȝt
without batel
for bi such
part settith al
for al I vre
here c

‡ than hun
silf, in com-
parisoun of
tyme passid,
for his power
encreessidt
euere Lire
here c

---

[u] bytwene NFII betwen E betwe C   [v] Om AF   [w] Om CE sec m   [x] thridde day A

[h] thei stoden I   [i] hiȝte I   [k] an I   [l] vnto I   [m] spoke thus I   [n] stood stille I   [o] And I.   [p] ȝeden
thenns I   [q] thei passiden I   [r] And I   [s] his I   [t] withoute I   [u] seruauntis I   [v] smeten DIL   [w] the
whiche I   [x] a long I   [y] Om. EI   [z] but I   [a] bigoten I   [b] the wyf I   [c] and I forsothe K

Absolon, the sone of Maacha, the^y douȝter
4 of Tholomay, the^z kyng Jethsure^a; forsothe the feerthe, Adonyas, the sone of
Agith; and the fifthe, Saphacias, the sone
5 of Abital; forsothe the sexte, Jethraam
of Egla, the wijf of Dauid. Thes ben
6 born to Dauid in Ebron. Thanne whanne
there was a^aa batail bytwixe the hows of
Saul and the hows of Dauid, Abner, the
sone of Ner, gouernde the hows of Saul.
7 Forsothe there was to Saul a secoundarie
wijf, Respha bi name, the doȝter of
Achay; and Abner wente into hir. And
8 Hisboseth seide to Abner, Whi wentist^b
thou in to the secoundarie wijf of my
fader? The which, ful miche wrooth for
the wordis of Hisboseth, seith, Whether
the heed of a dog Y am aȝens Juda to
day, the which haue doon merci vpon the
hows of Saul, thi fadre, and vpon britheren, and the next kyn of hym, and I
haue not takyn thee into the hondis of
Dauid, and thou hast aȝen souȝt in me
that thou vndurnyme for a womman to
9 day? Thes thingis doo God to Abner, and
thes thingis adde to hym, but what maner
wise the Lord hath swore to Dauid, so
10 shal I doo with hym, that the kyngdom
be ouerborn fro the hows of Saul, and the
trone of Dauid be rerid vpon Irael and
11 vpon Juda, fro Dan vnto Bersabe. And
he myȝte not answere to hym eny thing,
12 for he dradde hym. Thanne Abner sente
messageris to Dauid for hym self, seiynge,
Whos is the loond? and for thei shulden
speke, Mak with me frenships, and myn
hoond shal be with thee, and I shal
13 brynge aȝen to thee al^c Irael. The which
seith, Altherbest I shal doo with thee
frenships, but o thing I aske of thee,
seiynge, Thou shalt not se my face, before
that thou brynge Mychol, the douȝter of
Saul, and so thou shalt come, and se me.
14 Thanne Dauid sente messagers to His-

the sone of Maacha, douȝtir^d of Tholomay,
kyng of Gessur; forsothe^e the fourthe was 4
Adonyas, the sone of Agith; and the
fynethe was Saphacias, the sone of Abi-
tail; and^f the sixte was Gethraam of Egla†, 5
the wijf of Dauid. These weren borne to
Dauid in Ebron. Therfor whanne batel 6
was bytwixe the hows of Saul and the
hows of Dauid, Abner, the sone of Ner,
gouernyde the hows of Saul. Sotheli^g a^h 7
concubyn, *that is, a^i secoundarie wijf,*
Respha bi name, the douȝtir of Achia, was
to Saul^k; and Abner entride to hir. And 8
Isbosech seide to Abner, Whi 'entridist
thou^l to the concubyn of my fadir?
Which^m was wrooth greetli for the wordis
of Isbosech, and seide^n, Whether Y am^o
the heed of a dogge aȝens Juda to dai,
and Y haue do merci on the hous of Saul,
thi fadir, and on hise britheren, and neiȝboris, and Y bitook not thee in to the
hondis of David, and thou hast souȝt in
me that, that thou schuldist repreue me^p
for a womman to dai? God do these thingis 9
to Abner, and adde these thingis to hym‡,
no^q but as^r the Lord swoor to Dauid^s, 'so
Y do with hym^t, that the rewme be trans-10
latid fro the hous of Saul, and the trone
of Dauid be reisid on^u Israel and on Juda,
fro Dan 'til to^v Bersabee. And Isbosech 11
myȝte not answere ony thing to Abner,
for he dredde Abner. Therfor Abner sente 12
messangeris to Dauid, and thei seiden 'for
hym^w, Whos is the lond? and that the
messangeris schulden speke^x, Make thou
frenschipis with me, and myn hond schal
be with thee, and Y schal brynge al Israel
to thee. And Dauid seide, Best^y Y schal 13
make frenschipis^z with thee, but Y axe of
thee o thing, and seie^a, Thou schalt not
se my face, bifore that thou brynge^b Mycol,
the douȝter of Saul, and so thou schalt
come, and schalt se me. Therfor Dauid 14
sente|| messangeris to Isbosech, the sone

† of Egla, that was the douȝter of Saul, and sche was clepid speciali the wijf of Dauyth, for sche was first weddid. Lire here. c.

‡ and adde these thingis to him; that is, so many yuels and mo, than to ony wrecche, nobut Y fille the word of the Lord, that the rewme be translatid to Dauyth. Lire here. c.

|| therfor Dauyth sente, etc.; for Abner wroot aȝen to Dauyth, that he myȝte not bringe Mychol, no but of the wille of Isbosech hir brother, and therfor Dauyth axide hir of Isbosech. Lire here. c.

Y Om. CE sec. m. Z Om. CE sec. m. a of Jessure c. aa Om. BE. b wentis E. c to al E pr. m.

d the douȝter I. e and I. f Om. ELP. g And I. h to Saul was a I. i Om. CF. k Om. I.
l hast thou entrid I. m And Abner I. n he seide I. o am not C. be EL. P Om. plures. q Om. I.
r if I do so wth Dauid, as I. s him I. t Om. I. u upon I. v til AO sec. m. to EIL. w to hym a pr. m.
for Abner I. x speke thus I. y Om. I. z ful gode frenschipis I. a I seie I. b brynge to me I.

boseth, the sone of Saul, seiynge, 3eeld
my wijf Mychol, that I weddide to me for
15 an hundrid tersis^e of Philisteis. Thanne
Hisbotseth sente, and took hir 'fro hir^d
16 man, Faltiel, the sone of Lais; and hir
man folwide hir wepynge vnto Bahurym.
And Abner seide to hym, Go and turn
17 a3en; the which turnede a3en. Forsothe Abner brou3te in _a word_ to the
eldris of Irael, seiynge, Both 3isterday^e
and the thridde dai hens 3e sou3ten
18 Dauyd, that he regne vpon 3ou. Nowe
thanne doth; for the Lord spak to Dauid,
seiynge, In the hoond of my seruaunt
Dauid I shal saue my puple Yrael fro
the hoond of Philisteis, and of alle his
19 enemyes. Forsothe Abner spak also to
Beniamyn, and wente, for to speke to
Dauid, in Ebron, alle thingis that plesiden
20 to Irael and to al Beniamyn. And he
cam to Dauid, in Ebron, with twenti men.
And Dauid made to Abner, and to^f his
21 men that camen with hym, a feest. And
Abner seide to Dauid, Y shal ryse, that I
gedre to thee, my lord kyng, al Yrael,
and I goo in with the boond of pees, and
thou comaunde to al, as thi soule desirith. Thanne whanne Dauid hadde
ladde out Abner, and he was goon in
22 pees, anone the children of Dauid and of
Joab camen, the theuis slayn, with ful
miche greet pray; forsothe Abner was
not with Dauid, in Ebron, for nowe he
hadde laft hym, and he was goon forth
23 in pees. And Joab, and the oost that
was with hym, aftirward camen; and so
it is toold to Joab of tellers, Abner, the
sone of Ner, cam to the kyng, and he
lafte hym, and he wente awey in pees.
24 And Joab wente yn to the kyng, and
seith, What hast thou doon? Loo! Abner cam to thee; whi hast thou laft hym,
25 and he 3ede, and wente awey? Knowist
thou not Abner, the sone of Ner, for to

of Saul, and seide, 3elde thou my wijf
Mycol^c, whom Y spouside to me for an
15 hundryd prepucies of Filisteis. Therfor
Isbosech sente, and took hir fro hir hose-
bonde†, Faltiel, son^d of Lais; and hir hosebonde suede hir and wepte^ee‡ til^ee Bahurym. And Abner seide to hym, Go thou,
and turne a3en; and he^f turnede a3en.
17 Also Abner brou3te in a word to the
eldere men of Israel, and seide, Bothe
3istirdai and the thridde dai ago 3e
sou3ten Dauid, that he schulde regne on^g
3ou. Now therfor do 3e; for the Lord
18 spak to Dauid, and seide, In the hond of
my seruaunt Dauid Y schal saue my puple
Israel fro the hond of Filisteis, and of alle
19 his enemyes. Forsothe^h Abner spak also^i
to Beniamyn, and he 3ede, that he schulde
speke to^k Dauid, in Ebron, alle thingis that
plesiden Israel and al Beniamin. And he
20 cam to Dauid in Ebron with twenti men.
And Dauid made a feeste to Abner, and
to the^l men that camen with hym. And
21 Abner seide to Dauid, Y schal rise^m, that
Y gadere al Israel to thee, my lord the
kyng, and that Y make boond of pees
with thee, and that thou regne on alle, as
thi soule desirith. Therfor whanne Dauid
hadde ledde forth Abner, and he^n hadde
22 go in pees, anoon the children of Dauid
and Joab .camen with a ful grete prey,
whanne theues^o weren slayn; sotheli^p Abner was not^q with Dauid, in Ebron, for
Dauid hadde left hym, and he 3ede forth
23 in pees. And Joab, and the oostis that
weren with hym, camen aftirward; therfor it was teld to Joab of telleris, Abner,
the sone of Ner, cam to the kyng, and the
kyng lefte hym, and he 3ede^r in pees. And
24 Joab entride to the kyng, and seide, What
hast thou do? Lo! Abner cam to thee;
whi leftist^s thou hym, and^t he 3ede, and
25 departide^u? Knowist thou^v not Abner,
the sone of Ner, for herto he cam to thee,

16 † therfor Isbo-
sech sente, and
took hir fro hir
hosebonde; he
was not hir
hosebonde in
truthe, but in
17 gessing of the
peple, for in
truthe, sche
was the wijf of
Dauyth, and it
was neuere
leueful to a
18 womman, to
haue tweyue
hosebondis to
gidere. c.
‡ wepte; our
doctouris seyen
comynly that
19 he wepte for
loye, for sche
was brou3t a3en
to hir hose-
bonde, and he
20 touchide not
hir fleisly, but
kepte hir as a
sister; sunne
Ebrew doc-
tours seyen that
21 he wepte for
sorewe, for
excercise of
greet perfec-
cioun 3ede
awey fro him,
for he arettide
excercise of
greet perfec-
cioun to kepe
siche a ladi so
fair and noble,
22 as a sistir, with
out fleisly cou-
pling. _Lire
here._ c.

---

e prepucies κ _sup. ras._   d Om. 4.   e 3istai CE.   f Om. BCEFH.

c Mycol to me 1.   d the son 1.   e wente G.   ee til to BKLMPX.   f Lais 1.   g upon 1.   h And also 1.
i Om. 1.   k with BL.   l Om. CK.   m rise up 1.   n Abner 1.   o the theues 1.   p and 1.   q not thanne 1.
r 3ede forth 1.   s leetist 1.   t that 1.   u departide fro thee 1.   v Om. A.

that he cam to thee, that he desseyue thee, and knowe thin outgoynge and thin incomynge, and he shal knowe alle thingis 26 that thou dost? And so Joab, goon out fro Dauid, sente messageris after Abner; and brouȝte hym aȝen fro the cistern 27 Cyra, vnknowynge Dauid. And whanne Abner was turned aȝen into Ebron, Joab ladde hym aside to the mydil of the ȝaat, that he speke to hym in trecherye; and he smoot hym there in the sheer, and he is deed, into wreche of the blood of his 28 brother Asahel. That whanne Dauid hadde herd the thing doon, seith, Clene I am and my kyngdam anentis God vnto with outen ende fro the blood of Abner, 29 the sone of Ner; and come it vpon the heed of Joab, and vpon al the hows of his fader; ne fail there fro the hows of Joab oon suffrynge flux of seed, and a leprous, holdynge a spyndle, and a fall-ynge with swerd, and a nedi breed. 30 Therfor Joab, and Abisay, his brother, slewen Abner, forthi that he hadde slayn Asahel, the brother of hem, in Gabaon, in 31 the batail. And Dauid seide to Joab, and to al the puple that was with hym, Kit-tith ȝoure clothis, and beth gird with sackis, and weileth before the exequies of Abner. Forsothe Dauid folwide the 32 beere. And whanne thei hadden biryden Abner in Ebron, kyng Dauyd reride his voys, and wepte vpon the toumbe of Abner; forsothe and al the puple wepte. 33 And the kyng, weilynge and mournynge Abner, seith, Not as slow men ben went 34 to dye, thou diedist, Abner. Thin hoondis ben not boundun, and thi feet ben not greued with fettris, but as men ben wont to fal before the sonys of wickidnes thou felle. And doublynge togidre al the pu-35 ple wepte vpon hym. And whanne al the multitude was comen to taak meet with Dauid, ȝit cleer day, Dauid swore, sei-

that he schulde disseyue thee, and that he schulde knowe thi going out and thin entryng^w, and schulde^x knowe alle thingis whiche^y thou doist? Therfor Joab ȝede 26 out fro Dauid, and sente messageris aftir Abner; and ʻledde hym^z aȝen fro the cis-terne of Cyrie†, ʻwhile Dauid knew not^a. And whanne Abner hadde come aȝen in 27 to Ebron, Joab ledde hym asidis half to ʻthe myddil^b of the ȝate, that he schulde spoke to hym in gile; and he^c smoot Ab-ner there in the schar, and he was deed, in to the^d veniaunce of the blood of his brother Asahel. That whanne Dauid hadde 28 herd the^e thing doon, he seide, Y am clene and my rewme anentis God til^f in to with outen ende fro^g the blood of Abner, sone^h of Ner; and come it on the heed of Joab, 29 and on^i al the hows of his fadir; a^k man suffrynge flux^l of seed, and a leprouse man, holdynge spyndil^m, and fallynge^n bi swerd, and hauynge nede to^o breed, ʻthat is, suffrynge hungur^p, ʻfaile not of the hows of Joab^q. Therfor Joab, and Abisay, his 30 brother, killiden Abner, for he hadde slayn Asahel, her brother, in Gabaon, in batel. Forsothe^r Dauid seide to Joab, and to al 31 the puple that was with hym, To rende ȝe ȝour clothis, and be ȝe gird with sackis, and biweile^s ȝe bifor the heersis, ʻether dirige^t, of Abner. Forsothe^u kyng Dauid suede the beere. And whanne thei hadden 32 biried Abner in Ebron, kyng Dauid reiside his vois, and wepte^v on the biriel of Abner; ʻforsothe and^w al the puple wepte. And the kyng biweilide, and bymoren-33 yde Abner, and seide, Abner, thou diedist not as dredeful men, ʻethir cowardis^x, ben wont to die. Thin hondis weren not 34 boundun, and thi feet weren not greuyd with stockis, but thou feldist^y doun, as men ben wont to falle bifor the sones of wickidnesse. And al the puple doublide togidere, and wepte on^z hym^a. And whanne 35

† fro the cis-terne of Cirie; that place was clepid so, for thilke cisterne was in sum weye that lay toward Sirie, as sum men seyen; in Ebren it is, fro the cisterne of thorn, for a notable thorn and greet was there. Lire here. c.

---

w goyng yn i.   x that he schulde i.   y that i.   z Joab brouȝte Abner i.   a vnwitinge Dauid i.
b myddis i.   c Joab i.   d Om. i.   e this i.   f Om. i.   g of i.   h the sone i.   i upon i.   k and faile ther not fro the hous of Joab a i.   l flowyng i.   m a spyndil iK.   n a man fallinge i.   o of EL.   p Om. BI.
q Om. i.   r And i.   s weile plures.   t Om. i.   u Certis i.   v he wepte i.   w and certis i.   x Om. CI.
y last falle i.   z upon i.   a Abner i.

ynge, Thes thingis doo to me God, and thes thingis adde, it before the sunne goynge doun I shal taast breed or eny 36 other thing. And al the puple herde; and alle thingis plesiden to hem that the kyng dide in the si3t of al the puple; 37 and al the comoun knewe, and al Irael in that dai, for it was not doon of the kyng, that Abner, the sone of Ner, were slayn 38 And the kyng seide to his seruauntis, Whether 3e knowen not, for a prince and the moost to dai in Irael hath fall- 39 en ? Forsothe I 3it delicate and anoyntid kyng; greeth thes men, sonis of Saruye, ben hard to me; the Lord 3eeld to the doynge yuel after his malice

al the multitude cam to take mete with Dauid, while the dai was 3it cleer, Dauid swoor, and seide, God do to me these thingis, and adde these thingis[b], if Y schal taast breed ethir ony othir thing bifor the going doun of the sune And al the puple 36 herde[c]; and alle thingis which the kyng dide in the si3t of al the puple plesiden hem, and al the comyn puple and al Israel 37 knewe in that day, that it was not doon of the kyng, that Abner, the sone of Nei, was slayn Also the kyng seide to hise 38 seruauntis Whether 3e witen not, that the prince and gretteste[d] felde[e] doun to dai in Israel ? Forsothe[f] Y am 'delicat†, ether 39 tendirs[g], 3it[h] and anoyntid kyng; sotheli[i] these sones of Saruye ben hard to me, the Lord 3elde to hym that doith yuel bi[k] his malice

† Y am deli-
cat in Ebreu
it is tendir c

CAP IV

1 Forsothe Hisboseth, the sone of Saul, herde that Abner hadde faln in Ebron; and the hondis of hym ben feblid, and al 2 Irael is disturblid. Forsothe two men, princis of theuys, weien to the sone of Saul; name to the toon Baana, and name to the tothir Reechab, the sones of Rem- mon Berothit, of the sonys of Beniamyn, forsothe and Beroth is told into Benia- 3 myn. And Berothitis flowen into Je- thaym, and thei weren there comelyngis 4 into that tyme Forsothe theie was to Jonathe, the sone of Saul, a sone feble in feete[g]; forsothe he was fyue 3eer oolde, whanne a messager cam fro Saul and Jonatha, of Jezrael And so his nurish takynge hym flei3; and whanne she hiede foi to flee, he felle, and is maad halt; and 5 he hadde name Myphibosech Comynge thanne the sones of Remmon Berothit, Reechab and Baana, wenten in, the bren- nynge dai, the hows of Hisboseth, that

CAP IV

Forsothe[l] Isbosech, the sone of Saul, 1 herde that Abnei hadde falde[m] doun in Ebron, and 'hise hondis[n] weren discoum- fortid, and al Israel was disturblid[o] For- 2 sothe[p] twei men, princes of theues‡, weren to[q] the sone[r] of Saul; name[rr] to oon[s] was Baana, and name to the tother was Rechab, the sones of Remmon Beiothite, of the sones of Beniamyn, foi also Beroth is arettid[t] into Beniamyn And men of Be- 3 roth fledden in to Gethaym, and thei weren comelyngis there 'til to[v] that tyme Forsothe[w] a sone feble in feet[x] was to 4 Jonathas, the sone of Saul, forsothe[y] he was fyue 3eer eld, whanne the messanger cam fio Saul and Jonathas[z], fro Jezrael[a] Therfor his nurse took hym, and fledde, and whanne sche hastide to fle, sche felde doun, and the child was maad lame, and 'he hadde a name[b] Myphibosech Therfor 5 Rechab and Baana, sones[c] of Remmon of Beroth, camen, and entriden in the[d] hoot

‡ of theuys,
in Lbreu it is
of cumpenves
c

g fi3t ı

b thingis to 1   c herde this 1   d the gretteste 1   e hath fallen 1   f And 1   g Om 1   h 3it tendre 1 i and 1   k after 1   l And 1   m falle 1   n the hondis of Isbosech 1   o troublid 1   P And 1   q with 1 r sones 1,   rr the name 1   s the toon K   t rikened 1   u in the lynage of 1   v vnto 1   W And 1   x his feet 1   y and 1   z fro Jonathas 1   a Jezrael, tellinge that thei weren dede 1   b the name of the child was 1   c the sones 1   d a 1

o 2

slepte vpon his bed the myddai; and the womman that kepte the doris of the 6 hows purgynge whete, slepte fast. Forsothe thei wenten into the hows vnwityngly, takynge ecris of whete; and Reechab, and Bana, his brother, smyten 7 hym in the sheer, and flowen^{gg}. Forsothe whanne thei weren goon into the hows, he slepte vpon his bed in the priue chaumbre; and smytynge thei slewen hym; and his heed taken of, thei wenten 8 bi the weie of deseert al ny3t. And thei brou3ten the heed of Hisboseth to Dauid, in Ebron, and thei seiden to the kyng, Loo! the heed of Hisboseth, the sone of Saul, thin enemye, that sou3te thi lijf; and the Lord hath 3yuen to oure lord the kyng veniaunce to dai of Saul and of his 9 seed. Forsothe Dauid answerynge to Reechab, and Bana, his brothir, sones of Remmon Berothei, seide to hem, The Lord lyueth, that hath delyuerd my soule 10 fro al angwissh; for hym that toolde to me and seide, Deed is Saul, the whych wende hym self welsum thingis to telle, I heelde, and slew3 hym in Sichelech, to whom it hadde behouid me to 3eue meede 11 for the message; miche more nowe, whanne wickid men han slayn a giltles man in his hows vpon his bed, now I shal seche his blood fro 3oure hoond, and 12 doo awey 3ou fro the erthe. And so Dauid comaundide to his children, and thei slewen hem; and kyttynge of the hoondis and the feet of hem, thei hougeden hem ouer the fish poond in Ebron. Forsothe the heed of Hisboseth thei token, and biryeden it in Ebron, in the sepulcre of Abner.

dai in to the hows of Isbosech, that slepte on^e his bed in^f myd dai†, and the womman oischer^g of the hous clensynge^h wheete, slepteⁱ stronglik. Forsothe^l thei entriden 6 into the hows pryueli, and token^m eeris of whete; and Rechab, and Baana, his brother, smytidenⁿ Isbosech in the schar, and fledden^o. Sotheli^p whanne thei hadden 7 entrid in to the hous, he^q slepte on^r his bedde in a closet; and thei smytiden^s and killiden hym; and whanne 'his heed was takun^t, thei 3eden bi the weie of deseert in al the^u ny3t. And thei brou3ten the heed 8 of Isbosech to Dauid, in^v Ebron, and thei seiden to the kyng, Lo! the heed of Isbosech, sone^w of Saul, thin enemy, that sou3te thi lijf; and the Lord 3af^x to dai to oure lord the^y kyng veniaunce of Saul and of his seed. Forsothe^z Dauid au- 9 sweride to Rechab, and Baana, his brother, the sones of Remmon of Beroth, and seide^a to hem, The Lord lyueth, that delyueride^b my lijf fro al angwisch; for Y helde hym 10 that telde to me, and seide, Saul is deed, which man gesside hym silf to telle^c prosperitees^d, and^e Y killide hym in Sichelech, to whom it bihofte‡ me 3yue^f meede for message^g; hou myche more now, 11 whanne wickid men han slayn a giltles man in his hows on^h his bed, schal I not seke his blood fro 3oure hond, and schalⁱ Y do awey 3ou fro erthe^k? Therfor Dauid 12 comaundide to his children^l, and thei killiden hem; and thei kittiden^m aweiⁿ the^o hondis and 'feet of hem^p, and hangiden^q hem ouer the^r cisterne in Ebron. Forsothe^s thei token the heed of Isbosech, and birieden^t in the sepulcre of Abner, in Ebron.

† in mydday; this that sueth, and the womman kepere of the dore of the hows purgide wheete and slepte, is not in Ebreu. Forsothe they entriden; in Ebreu it is, and thei camen til to the myddis of the hows, and token whete. c.

‡ it bihofte, etc.; that is, bi gessing of the puple. Liue here. c.

CAP. V.

1 And alle the lynagis of Irael camen to Dauid, in Ebron, seiynge, Loo! we ben

CAP. V.

And^q alle the lynagis of Israel camen 1 to Dauid, in^v Ebron, and sciden, Lo! we

gg slowen ADII.

e upon 1. f at 1. g seruaunt G. that kepte the doris 1. h makynge cleene GQ. purgynge 1. i The whole passage is omitted in AEFLNFRUB pr. m. k Om. AEFGLNFQRUB pr. m. faste Ib sec. m. l And 1. m thei token 1. n smoten 1. smeten ELP. smyten F. o thei fledden 1. p But 1. q Isbosech 1. r upon 1. s smoten 1. smeten ELP. smyten F. t thei hadden take his heed 1. u that EIKLM. v in to 1. w the sone 1. x hath 3oue 1. y Om. 1. z And 1. a he seide 1. b hath delyuered 1. c haue told 1. d prosperitees to himselff 1. e but 1. f to haue 3oue 1. g his message 1. h upon 1. i schal not 1. k the erthe 1. l seruauntis 1. m kitten 1. n off 1. o her 1. p her feet 1. q thei hangiden 1. r a 1. s And 1. t thei birieden it 1. u Forsothe 1. v into 1.

2 thi boon and thi flesh. But and ȝistirdai[h] and before ȝisterdai[h], whanne Saul was kyng vpon vs, thou were ledynge out and bryngynge aȝen Yrael; forsothe the Lord seide to thee, Thou shalt fede my puple Irael, and thou shalt be duyk vpon 3 Irael. Forsothe and the eldris of Irael camen to the kyng, in Ebron; and kyng Dauid smoot with hem couenaunt of pees in Ebron, before the Lord; and thei anoyntiden Dauid into kyng vpon Irael. 4 A sone of thretti ȝeer was Dauid, whanne he bigan to regne, and fourti ȝeer he 5 regnede in Ebron; he regnyde vpon Juda seuen ȝeer and sixe monethis; forsothe in Jerusalem he regnede thretti and three 6 ȝeer, vpon al Irael and Juda. And the kyng ȝeede, and al the men that weren with hym, into Jerusalem, to Jebuse, dweller of the loond. And it is seid to Dauid of hem, Thou shalt not go in hidre, but if thou take a wey the blynde and the halt, seiynge, Dauid shal not goo 7 yn hidre. Forsothe Dauid took the tote[i] 8 hil Syon; that is the citee of Dauid. Forsothe he purposide in that dai mede to hym that smoot Jebuse, and touchide the goters of the 'hows eues[k], and took a wey the halt and the blynde, hatynge the lijf of Dauid. Therfore it is seid in prouerbe, The blynde and the halt shulen not goon 9 into the temple. Forsothe Dauid dwellide in the tote[l] hil, and clepide it the citee of Dauid; and he bieldide hi enuy- 10 roun fro Mello, and with in forth. And he wente profitynge and vndre grow- ynge; and the Lord God of oost was 11 with hym. Forsothe Yram, the kyng of Tiry, sente messangers to Dauid, and ce- dre trees, and 'crafty men[m] of trees, and crafti men of stonys to the wallys; and 12 thei beeldiden the hows of Dauid. And Dauid knewe, for the Lord hadde con- fermyd hym kyng vpon Irael, and for

ben thi boon and thi fleisch. But also 2 ȝistirdai and the thridde day ago, whanne Saul was kyng on[z] vs, thou leddist out, and leddist aȝen Israel; forsothe[a] the Lord seide to thee, Thou schalt fede my puple Israel, and thou schalt be duyk on[b] Israel. Also and the eldere men of Israel 3 camen to the kyng, in[c] Ebron; and kyng Dauid smoot with hem boond of pees in Ebron, bifor the Lord; and thei anoynt- iden Dauid in to kyng on[d] Israel. Dauid 4 was a sone of thretti ȝeer, whanne he bigan to regne, and he regnyde fourti ȝeer in Ebron; he regnede on[e] Juda 5 seuene ȝeer and sixe monethis; forsothe[f] in Jerusalem he regnede thretti[g] and thre ȝeer, on[h] al Israel and Juda. And the 6 kyng ȝede, and alle men that weren with hym, in to Jerusalem, to Jebusei, dweller[i] of the lond. And it was seide of hem to Dauid, Thou schalt not entre hidur, no[k] but thou do awei blynde men and lame, seiynge[l], Dauid schal not entre hydur. Forsothe[m] Dauid took the tour of Syon; 7 this is the citee of Dauid. For Dauid 8 hadde 'sette forth meede[n] in that dai to[o] hym, that hadde smyte Jebusei, and hadde[p] touchid the goteris of roouys[q], and hadde[r] take awey lame men and blynde, hatynge the lijf of Dauid. Therfor it is seid in prouerbe[s], A blynde man and lame[t] schulen not entre in to the temple. For- 9 sothe[u] Dauid dwellide in the tour, and clepide[v] it the citee of Dauid; and he bildide bi cumpas fro Mello†, and with 10 ynne. And he entride profitynge and en- creessynge; and the Lord God of oostis was with hym. Also Hyram, kyng[w] of 11 Tire, sent messangeris to Dauid, and cedre trees, and crafti men of trees, and crafti men of stoonus to wallis; and thei bildiden the hows of Dauid. And Dauid 12 knew, that the Lord hadde confermed hym kyng on[x] Israel, and that he hadde

† *Mello* was a swolew that was bifor that tour. *Lire here.* c.

h ȝistai c *passim.* ᴇ *passim.* i toot cᴇ. tute ꜰɪɪ. k houses ʙᴄᴇꜰɪɪ. l toot cᴇ. tute ꜰʜ. m craftis men ᴄᴇ.

z upon ɪ. a certis ɪ. b upon ɪ. c into ɪ. d upon ɪ. e upon ɪ. f and ɪ. g thretti ȝeer ɪ. h upon ɪ. i the dweller ʟ. k Om. ɪ. l that seiden ɪ. m Certis ɪ. n purposid ɪ. o to haue ȝoue mede to ɪ. p that hadde ɪ. q the hous roouys ɪ. r that hadde ɪ. s comoun speche ɪ. t a lame ɪᴋ. u And ɪ. v he clepide ɪ. w the kyng ɪ. x upon ɪ. of ᴋ.

he hadde arerid out his kyngdam vpon
13 his puple Yrael. Thanne Dauid took ʒit
secundarye wyues, and wyues of Jerusalem, after that he was comyn fro
Ebron; and there ben born to Dauid
14 and ⁿ other sones and douʒtris. And
thes the names of hem that ben born to
hym in Jerusalem; Samua, and Sobah,
15 and Nathan, and Salomon, and Jobaar,
16 and Elisua, and Repheg, and Japhia, and
Elizama, and Helida, and Heliphelech.
17 Thanne Philisteis herden, that thei hadden anoyntid Dauid kyng vpon Yrael,
and thei alle stieden vp for to seche
Dauid. The which thing whanne Dauid
hadde herd, wente doun in to a strength.
18 Forsothe Philisteis comynge ben heeld
19 out in the° valey of Raphaym. And
Dauid counseilde the Lord, seiynge, If
I shal stie vp to Philisteis, and if thou
shalt ʒyue hem in myn hoond? And the
Lord seide to Dauid, Sty, for takyng I
shal ʒyue Philisteis in thin hoond.
20 Thanne Dauid cam in Baal Pharasym,
and smoot hem there, and seide, The
Lord hath dyuidid myn enemyes before
me, as watris ben dyuidid. Therfor
the name of that place is clepid Baal
21 Pharasym. And thei laften there her
grauen thingis, the whiche Dauid took,
22 and his men. And ʒit the Philisteis
addiden for to stie vp, and thei° ben held
23 out in the valey of Raphaym. Forsothe
Dauid counseilde the Lord, seiynge, If
I shal stye aʒens the Philisteis, and if
thou shalt take hem into myn hoondis?
The which answerde, Thou shalt not
stye vp aʒens hem, but goo about bihynde
the bak of hem, and comynge to hem fro
24 aʒens of the peer trees. And whanne
thou herist noise of cry goynge in the
cop of the peer trees, thanne thou shalt

enhaunsid his rewme onʸ his puple Israel.
Therfor Dauid took ʒit concubyns, and 13
wyuest of Jerusalem, after that he cam fro
Ebron; and also othere sones and douʒtris weren borun to Dauid. And these 14
ben the names of hem that weren borun
to hym in Jerusalem; Samua, and Sobab,
and Nathan, and Salomon, and Jobaar, 15
and Helisua, and Repheg, and Japhia, 16
and Helysama, and Holida, and Heliphelech. Therforᶻ Filisteisᵃ herden, that thei 17
hadden anoyntid Dauid kyng onᵇ Israel,
and alle Filisteisᶜ stiedenᵈ to seke Dauid.
And whanne Dauid hadde herd this, he
ʒedeᵉ doun into a strong hold. Forsotheᶠ 18
Filisteisᵍ camen, aud werenʰ spred abrood
in the valei of Raphaym. And Dauid 19
counseilideⁱ the Lord, and seide, Whether
Y schal stieᵏ to Filisties, and whether
thou schalt ʒyue hem in myn hond? And
the Lord seide to Dauid, Stie thouˡ, for
Y schal bitakeᵐ, and Y schal ʒyue Filisteisⁿ
in thin hond. Therfor Dauid cam in to 20
Baal Farasym, and smoot° hemᵖ there, and
seide, The Lord departideᵠ myn enemyes
bifor me, as watris ben departid. Therfor
the name of that place was clepid Baal
Farasym‡. And theiʳ leften there her 21
sculptilsˢ, whiche Dauid took‡, and hise
men. And Filisteisᵗ addidenᵘ ʒit, that 22
thei schuldenᵛ stieʷ, and thei weren spred
abrood in the valei of Raphaym. Sotheliˣ 23
Dauid councelideʸ the Lord, and seide,
Whether Y schal stieᶻ agens Filistiesᵃ, and
whether thou schalt bitake hem in to myn
hondis? Whichʰ answeride, Thou schalt
not stieᶜ aʒens hem, but cumpasse thouᵈ
bihynde her bak, and thou schalt come to
hem on the contrarie side of the pere
trees. And whanne thou schalt here the 24
sown of cryᵉ goynge inᶠ the cop of ʿpere
treesᵍ‖, thanne thou schalt biginne batel;

† and vyues; this word and is set here for that is, for tho weren verily hise wyues, but thei ben seid here with concubyns, for they weren secundarie wyues, and not pryncipal. Lire here. c.

‡ Baal Farasym; that is, the feeld ether pleyn of departing. Lire here. c.

‡ Dauyth took; in Ebreu it is brente. c.

‖ pere trees; this was a signe of aungels comynge in to the help of Dauyth to fiʒte aʒenes aduersaries. Lire here. c.

ⁿ Om. ᴀ.   ° Om. ᴃ.   ᴘ to ᴇ pr. m.

ʸ upon ɪ.   ᶻ Thanne ɪ.   ᵃ the Philistees ɪ.   ᵇ upon ɪ.   ᶜ the Philistees ɪ.   ᵈ ʒeden up ɪ.   ᵉ wente ɪ.   ᶠ And ɪ.
ᵍ the Philistees ɪ.   ʰ thei weren ɪ.   ⁱ counseilide with ɪ.   ᵏ stie up ɪ.   ˡ thou up ɪ.   ᵐ bitake the
Philistees ɪ.   ⁿ hem ɪ.   ° he smoot ɪ.   ᵖ the Philistees ɪ.   ᵠ hath departid ɪ.   ʳ the Philistees ɪ.
ˢ grauen ymagis ɪ.   ᵗ the Philistees ɪ.   ᵘ addiden to ɪ.   ᵛ wolden ɪ.   ʷ wende up ɪ.   ˣ And ɪ.   ʸ counselide with ᴛ.   ᶻ stie up ɪ.   ᵃ the Philistees ɪ.   ᵇ And the Lord ɪ.   ᶜ stie up ᴛ.   ᵈ thou hem ᴛ.   ᵉ a crier ɪ.
ᶠ into ɪ.   ᵍ the pere trees ɪ.

goo into batail; for thanne the Lord shal
goo out before thi face, that he smyte the
25 tentis of Philisteis. And so Dauid dide
as the Lord comaundide to hym; and he
smoot Philisteis fro Gabaa vnto thou
come to Jezer.

CAP. VI.

1 Forsothe Dauid eft gedrede alle the
chosen men of Irael, thretti thousandis.
2 And Dauid roos, and wente, and al the
puple that was with him of the men of
Juda, for to brynge the arke of God,
vpon the which is inwardli clepid the
name of the Lord of oostis, sittynge in
3 cherubyn vpon it. And thei puttiden[q]
the arke of God vpon a newe wayn, and
thei token it fro the hows of Amynadab,
that was in Gabaa. Forsothe Oza and
Hayon, the sones of Amynadab, dryuen
4 the newe wayn. And whanne thei hadden
den taken it fro the hows of Amynadab,
that was in Gabaa, Hayon kepynge the
5 arke of God, wente before the arke. Forsothe
Dauid and al Yrael pleiden before
the Lord, in alle forgid trees, and harpis,
and syngynge instrumentis, and tymbris,
6 and trumpis, and cymbalis. Forsothe
after that thei camen to the corn flore of
Nachor, Oza strauȝte out the hoond to
the arke of God, and heelde it, for[r] the
7 oxen wynseden, and boweden it. And
the Lord is wrooth bi indignacioun aȝens
Ozam, and he smoot hym vpon the fool
hardynes; the which is there deed biside
8 the arke of God. Forsothe Dauid sorwide,
forthi that the Lord hadde smyten
Ozam; and the name of that place is
clepid the Smytynge of Oze into this dai.
9 And Dauid dradde the Lord in that dai,
seiynge, What maner wise shal goon into
10 me the arke of the Lord? And he wolde
not[s] turne aside to hym the arke of the

for thanne the Lord schal go out befor
thi face, that he smyte the castels[h] of
Filisteis. Therfor Dauid dide as the Lord 25
comaundide to hym; and he smoot Fi-
listeys[i] fro Gabaa til ⸢the while⸣[j] thei
camen to Jezer.

CAP. VI.

Forsothe Dauid gaderide eft alle the 1
chosun men of Israel, thritti thousynde.
And Dauid roos[k], and ȝede, and al the 2
puple that was with hym of the men of
Juda, to brynge the arke of God, on[l]
which[m] the name of the Lord of oostis,
sittynge in cherubyn on[n] that[o] arke, was
clepid[p]. And thei puttiden the arke of 3
God on a newe wayn, and thei token it
fro the hows of Amynadab, that was in
Gabaa. Forsothe[q] Oza and Haio, the
sons of Amynadab, dryueden[r] the newe
wayn. And whanne thei hadden take it 4
fro the hows of Amynadab, that was in
Gabaa, and[s] kepte the arke of God[t], Haio
ȝede bifor the arke. Forsothe[u] Dauid and 5
al Israel pleieden† byfor the Lord, in alle
⸢trees maad craftili[v], and harpis[w], and
sitols, and tympans, and trumpis, and
cymbalis. Forsothe[x] after that thei camen[y] 6
to the corn floor of Nachor, Oza helde
forth the[z] hond to the arke of God, and
helde it, for the oxun kikiden[a], and bowiden it[b]. And the Lord was wrooth bi 7
indignacioun aȝens Oza‡, and smoot[c] hym
on[d] ⸢the folie[e]; and he was deed there
bisidis the arke of God[f]. Forsothe[g] Dauid 8
was sori‖, for the Lord hadde smyte[h]
Oza; and the name of that place was
clepid the Smytyng of Oza ⸢til in to[i] this
dai. And Dauid dredde the Lord in that[k] 9
dai, and seide[l], Hou schal the arke of the
Lord entre to me? And he nolde[m] turne 10
the arke of the Lord to hym silf in to the
citee of Dauid, but he turnede it in to

† *pleieden*; not bi pley of dissolucioun, but of deuocioun. *Lire here.* c.

‡ *Oza* was smytun, for he ordeynede the arke to be put on vnresonable beestis in the wayn, for it schulde be borun on the schuldris of dekenes, as it is seid in vii. c°. of Numeri and in many mo places; and Oza knew this, ether ouȝte to knowe this; netheles he was smytun, whanne he touchide the arke bowid, for thanne it was opin, that it schulde not be borun so, but in the schuldris of resonable men. *Lire here.* c.

‖ *Dauyth was sori*; not of Goddis riȝtfulnesse, but more of the offence of Oza, for which he disseruede to be smytun; and of this dede Dauyth dredde, lest he were vnworthi to bringe the arke to his hows. c.

[q] putten BC. puttyn E. [r] the whiche E *pr. m.* [s] Om. AF.

[h] tentis I. [i] the Philistees I. [j] Om. I. [k] roos up I. [l] upon I. [m] the which I. [n] upon I. [o] the I.
[p] inwardly clepid I. [q] And I. [r] dreuen I. drywen E. dreuin P. [s] that I. [t] the Lord I. [u] And I.
[v] treen instrumentis of melodie I. [w] in harpis I. [x] But I. [y] hadden come I. [z] his I. [a] wynsiden I.
[b] the arke aside I. [c] he smoot I. [d] upon I. [e] his fool hardynesse I. [f] the Lord I. [g] And I. [h] sleyn I.
[i] vnto I. [k] al that EL. [l] he seide I. [m] wolde not I.

Lord in the cite of Dauid, but he turnede it aside into the hows of Obethedon
11 Jethei. And the arke of the Lord dwellid
in the hows of Obethedon Jethei thre
monethis; and the Lord blesside Obeth-
12 edon[t], and al his hows. And it is toold
to the kyng Dauid, that the Lord hadde
blessid Obethedon, and alle thingis of
hym, for the arke of God. And Dauid
seide, I shal goo, and brynge aȝen with
blessynge into myn hows. Thanne Dauid
wente, and brouȝte the arke of God fro
the hows of Obethedon into[u] the cytee
of Dauid with ioy; and there weren
with Dauid seuen holi companyes, and
13 the slayn sacrifice of a calf. And whanne
thei hadden stied ouer, that baren the
arke of the Lord, sexe paas[v], thei offreden
an oxe and a wether. And Dauid smoot
14 in orgayns bounden to the shuldres; and
he lepe with al his strength before the
Lord; forsothe Dauid is gird with a
15 surplees. And Dauid, and al the hows
of Irael, brouȝten the arke of the testament of the Lord in ioy, and in sown of
16 trompe. And whanne the arke of the
Lord was comen into the cite of Dauid,
Mychol, the douȝter of Saul, biholdynge
bi the wyndow, sawȝ the kyng vndur-
goynge and lepynge before the Lord;
17 and she dispiside hym in hir herte. And
thei brouȝten in the arke of the Lord,
and thei puttiden[w] it in his place, in the
myddis of the tabernacle, that Dauid
hadde strauȝt out to hym; and Dauid
offrede brent sacrifice and pesible before
18 the Lord. And whanne offrynge brent
sacrifice and pesible he hadde ful endid
hem, he blesside to the puple in the
19 name of the Lord of oostis. And he
partide to al the multitude of Yrael, as
wel to man as to womman, to echon o
kanke of breed, and o rostid gobet of oxe
flesh, and tried floure fried with oyle;

the hows of Obethedom of Geth. And 11
the arke of the Lord dwellide in the hows
of Obethedom† of Geth thre monethis; and
the Lord blessid Obethedom, and al his
hows. And it was teld to kyng Dauid, 12
that the Lord hadde blessid Obethedom,
and alle 'thingis of hym[n], for the arke of
God. And Dauid seide, Y schal go, and
brynge the arke with blessyng in to myn
hows. Therfor Dauid ȝede, and brouȝte
the arke of God fro the hows of Obethedom in to the citee of Dauid with ioye;
and ther weren with Dauid seuen cumpanyes[nn], and the slain[o] sacrifice of a
calff[oo]. And whanne thei, that baren the 13
arke of the Lord, hadden stied[p] six paaces[q],
thei offriden an oxe and a ram. And Dauid
smoot in organs boundun[r] to the[s] arm;
and daunside[t] with alle strengthis[u] bifor 14
the Lord; sotheli[v] Dauid was clothid with
a lynnun surplis. And Dauid, and al the 15
hows of Israel, ledden forth the arke of
testament[w] of the Lord in hertli[x] song,
and in sown of trumpe. And whanne the 16
arke of the Lord hadde[xx] entride in to the
citee of Dauid, Mychol, the douȝtir of
Saul, bihelde bi[y] a wyndow, and sche siȝ
the kyng skippynge[z] and daunsynge bifor the Lord; and sche dispiside hym in
hir herte. And thei brouȝten in the arke 17
of the Lord, and settiden it in his[a] place[b],
in the[c] myddis[d] of tabernacle[e], which[f]
tabernacle Dauid hadde maad 'redy therto[g]; and Dauid offride brent sacrifices
and pesible bifor the Lord. And whanne 18
Dauid hadde endid tho, and hadde offrid
brent sacrifices and pesible, he blesside the
puple in the name of the Lord of oostis.
And he ȝaf to al the multitude of Israel, 19
as wel to man as to womman, to ech 'o
thinne loof[h], and o part rostid of bugle
fleisch, and flour of wheete fried with oile;
and al the puple ȝede[i], ech man[k] in to his
hows. And Dauid turnede aȝen to blesse 20

† *Obethedom*
was of the de-
kenes, as it is
seid in 3 book of
Paralipomenon,
vi. c°.; and
he is seid of
Geth, for he
was in Geth,
with Dauyth
fleynge Saul.
Lire here, c.

---

[t] to Obethedon E *pr. m.*   [u] in E *pr. m.*   [v] paththis A.   [w] putten BCE.

[n] his thingis I.   [nn] mesures b *sec. m.*   [o] offrid b.   [oo] This passage is omitted in AEFGLNPWb. *pr. m.*
[p] stied up I.   [q] paas I.   [r] fastned I.   [s] his I.   [t] the daunside I.   [u] *his* strengthis I.   [v] and I.   [w] witnessyng I.
[x] hertily I.   [xx] Om. A.   [y] forth at I.   [z] hoppinge I.   [a] the I.   [b] place theroff I.   [c] Om. I.   [d] myddil I.
[e] the tabernacle EIX *sec. m.*   [f] the which I.   [g] therfore EL.   [h] a kake of bred I.   [i] ȝede forth I.   [k] Om. I.

and al the puple wente echon into his
20 hows And Dauid turned a3en, that he
blesse to his hows, and Mychol, the
dou3ter of Saul, goon out into a3en comynge of Dauid, seith, How glorious was
the kyng of Irael to dai discouerynge
hym self before the hoond wymmen of
his seruauntis, and is maad nakid as if[x]
21 were maad nakid oon of the knauys? And
Dauid seide to Mychol, The Lord lyueth,
for I shal pleye before the Lord, that
hath chosen me rather than thi fader,
and than al the hows of hym, and he
hath comaundid to me, that Y were a
ledere vpon the puple of the Lord of
22 Irael, and I shal pleye, and fowlere Y
shal be maad more than I am maad, and
I shal be meke in myn eyen, and with
'hoond wymmen[y], of the whiche thou
hast spoken, more glorious Y shal apere.
23 Therfor to Mychol, the dou3ter of Saul,
is not born a sone vnto the day of hir
deeth

CAP VII

1 Forsothe it is doon, whanne the kyng
hadde seeten in his hows, and the Lord
hadde 3euen to hym rest on al side fro
2 alle his enemyes, he seide to Nathan the
prophete, Seest thou not, that I dwelle in
a cedre hows, and the ark of God is put
3 in the mydil of skynnes? And Nathan
seide to the kyng, Al that is in thin
herte goo and do, for the Lord is with
4 thee Forsothe it is doon in that ny3t,
and[z] loo' the word of the Lord to Na-
5 than, seiynge, Go, and spek to my seruaunt Dauid, Thes thingis seith the
Lord, Whether thou shalt bilde to me
6 an hows to dwelle yn? Forsothe ne in
an hows I haue dwellid fro the day that
I ladde out the sones of Yrael fro the
loond of Egipt vnto this dai; but I wente
7 in tabernacle and in tente, thur3 out alle

his hows and Mychol, the dou3tir of Saul,
3ede out in to the comyng of Dauid, and
seide[l], Hou glorious was[m] the kyng of
Israel to[n] day vnhilynge hym silf bifor -
the handmaidis[o] of hise seruauntis, and he
was maad nakid, as if oon of the harlotis[p]
be[q] maad nakid? And Dauid seide to My- 21
chol, The Lord lyueth, for Y schal pley
bifor the Lord, that chees[r] me rathere
than thi fadir, and than[s] al the hows of
hym, and comaundide[t] to me, that Y
schulde be duyk on[u] the[v] puple 'of the
Lord of[w] Israel; and Y schal pleie, and 22
Y schal be maad 'vilere more[x] than Y
am[y] maad, and Y schal be meke in myn
i3en, and Y schal appere gloriousere[z] with
the[a] handmaydys[b], of whiche thou spakist[c]. Therfor a sone was not borun to 23
Mychol, the dou3tir of Saul, til in to the
dai of hir deeth

CAP. VII

1 Forsothe it was doon, whanne[d] the[e]
kyng Dauid hadde sete in his hows, and
the Lord hadde 3oue reste to hym on ech
side fro alle hise enemyes, he seyde to 2
Nathan the prophete, Seest thou not, that
Y dwelle in an hows of cedre, and the
arke of God is put in the myddis of
skynnys[f]? And Nathan seide† to the 3
kyng, Go thou, and do al thing which[g]
is in thin herte, for the Lord is with thee
Forsothe[h] it was don in that ni3t, and lo' 4
the word of the Lord, seiynge[i] to Nathan,
Go thou, and speke to my servaunt Dauid, 5
The Lord seith these thingis, Whether
thou schalt bilde to me an hows to dwelle
ynne? For[k] Y 'dwellide not[l] in an hows 6
fro the dai in which Y ledde the sones of
Israel out of the lond of Egipt til in to
this dai; but Y 3ede[m] in tabernacle[n] and

† Nathan
seide, not in
spirit of pro-
fesie, but in
spirit of man,
as it is open
afurward *Lire*
here c.

[x] it AFH   [y] the hoondwymmen BCE   [z] Om E pr i

[l] sche seide I   [m] hath I   [n] be to I   [o] handmaidvns I   [p] knaues I   [q] had be I   [r] hath chose I
[s] rather than I   [t] he hath comaundid I   [u] upon I   [v] his I   [w] Om I   [x] more vile I   [y] am 3it I
[z] more glorious I   [a] tho I.   [b] handmaidens I   [c] hast spoke I   [d] that whanne I   [e] Om IK sec. m.
[f] or *kyuered with lethir* I marg   [g] that I   [h] And I   [i] was maad I   [k] Sothly I   [l] haue not dwellid I
[m] haue go I.   [n] a tabernacle I

placis, to the whiche I passide with alle
the sones of Irael? Whether spekynge
I haue spokyn to oon of the lynagis of
Irael, to whom I haue comaundid, that
he fede my puple Irael, seiynge, Whi
hast thou not bildid^a to me a cedre
8 hows? And now thes thingis thow shalt
seye to my seruaunt Dauid, Thes thingis
seith the Lord of oostis, I took thee fro
the lesews folwynge flockis, that thou
9 were a duyk vpon my puple Irael, and
I was with thee 'in alle thingis^b, whidir
euere thou wentist, and I slew; alle thin
enemyes fro thi face, and I made to thee
a greet name after the name of greet
10 men that ben in erthe; and Y shal putt
a place to my puple Irael, and I shal
plaunte hym, and I shal dwelle with
hym, and he shal namore be disturblid,
ne the sones of wickidnes shulen adde
11 that thei tourmenten hym as before, fro
the day that I ordeynede iugis vpon my
puple Irael; and I shal ;yue rest to thee
fro alle thin enemyes. And the Lord
before seith to thee, that the Lord shal
12 make to thee an hows; and whanne thi
dais weren ful endyd, and thou slepist
with thi fadris, Y shal rere thi seed after
thee, that shal go out of thi wombe, and^c
13 Y shal fastne the kyngdom of hym. And
he shal beelde an hows to my name, and
Y shal stable the troon of his rewme vnto
14 eueremore; I shal be to hym into a fader,
and he shal be to me into a sone; the
which if eny thing wickidli shal doo, I
shal vndirnymme hym in the ;eerd of
men, and in the veniaunces of the sonys
15 of men. Forsothe my mercy I shal not
take a weye fro hym, as I took a weye
fro Saul, whom I mcuyde a weye fro my
16 face. And thin hows shal be feithful,
and thi kyngdam vnto with outen eende
before my face, and thi troon shal be

in^o tent^p, bi alle places, to whiche Y 7
passyde with alle the sones of Israel?
Whether Y spekynge spak^q to oon of the
lynagis of Israel, to whom Y comaundyde,
that he schulde feede my puple Israel, and
seide^r, Whi 'bildidist thou not^s an hows
of cedre to me? And now thou schalt seie 8
these thingis to my seruaunt Dauid, The
Lord of oostis seith these thingis, Y took^t
thee fro lesewis^u suynge flockis, that thou
schuldist be duyk on^v my puple Israel,
and Y was^w with thee in alle thingis, 9
where euere thou ;edist^x, and Y killide^y
alle thin enemyes fro thi face, and Y
made^z to thee a greet name bi the name
of grete men that ben in erthe; and Y 10
schall sette a place to my puple Israel,
and Y schal plaunte hym, and Y schal
dwelle with hym, and he schal no more
be troblid, and the sones of wickidnesse
schulen not adde^a, that thei turmente
hym as bifor, fro the dai in which Y or- 11
denede iugis on^b my puple Israel; and
Y schal ;yue reste to thee fro alle thin
enemyes. And the Lord biforseith to thee,
that 'the Lord^c schal mak an hows to
thee; and whanne thi daies be fillid^d, and 12
thou hast slept with thi fadris, Y schal
reyse^e thi seed aftir thee, which^f schal go
out of thi wombe, and Y schal make
'stidfast his rewme^g. He schal bilde an 13
hows to my name, and Y schal make
stable the troone of his rewme til in to
with outen ende† ; Y schal be to hym in 14
to fadir^h, and he schal be to me in to a
sone; and if he schal do ony thing wick-
idli, Y schal chastise hym in theⁱ ;erde of
men, and in the woundis of the sones of
men. Forsothe Y schal not do awey my 15
mercy fro hym, as Y dide^j awei fro Saul,
whom Y remouede^k fro my face. And 16
thin hows schal be feithful, and thi rewme
schal be til^l in to with outen ende bifor

+ with outen ende; that is, in to long tyme, as in Salomon, hilis ben seid euerlastinge, for the rewme of Salomon failide, in the caytifte of Isshiloyne, ether namell in the dayes of Erotide, that was an allen. Lire here. c.

^a bilde bc.   ^b Om. e pr. m.   ^c Om. a.

^o Om. c.   ^p a tent i.   ^q haue spoke i.   ^r I seide i.   ^s hast thou not bildid i.   ^t haue take i.   ^u the lesewis i.   ^v upon i.   ^w haue be i.   ^x hast gn i.   ^y haue killid i.   ^z haue made i.   ^a adde to i.
^b upon i.   ^c he i.   ^d fulfillid i.   ^e reyse up i.   ^f the which i.   ^g his rewme stable i.   ^h a fadir ix sec. m.
ⁱ Om. i.   ^j dide it i.   ^k haue remoued i.   ^l Om. a.

17 stedefast contynuli. After alle thes
wordis, and after al this visioun, thus
18 spak Nathan to Dauid. Forsothe Dauid
the kyng wente in, and sat before the
Lord, and seide, Who am I, Lord God,
and what myn hows, for thou hast
19 brouȝt me hidir to? But and this litil
is seen in thi siȝt, Lord my God; 'that
hast louyd me^d, but thou speke also of
the hows of thi seruaunt into ferre hens.
Forsothe this is lawe fro Adam, Lord
20 God; what thanne ȝit Dauid shal mowe
adde, that he speke to thee? Forsothe
thow knowist thi seruaunt, Lord God;
21 for thi word, and aftir thin herte, thou
hast doon alle thes greet thingis, so that
thou shuldist make knowen to thi ser-
22 uaunt. Therfor thou art magnified,
Lord God, for there is not lijk^e of thee,
ne there is God with out thee, in alle
thingis 'the whiche^{ee} we han herd with
23 oure eeris.' Forsothe what is there folk
of kynde as the puple of Irael in the
loond, for^f the which God wente, that he
bie it to hym into a puple, and sette to
hym a name, and make to hym greet
thingis, and orrible vpon thes^g erthe, fro
the face of thi puple, whom thou hast
bouȝt to thee fro Egipt folk and the god
24 of it? And thow hast fastned to thee thi
puple Irael into a puple euermore, and
thou, Lord, art maad to hem into a God.
25 Nowe thanne, Lord God, the word that
thou hast spoken vpon thi seruaunt and
vpon his hows, rere vnto euermore, and
26 do as thou hast spoken; and thi name
be magnyfied vnto euermore, and be it
seid, Lord of oostis God vpon Irael; and
the hows of thi seruaunt Dauid shal be
27 stablid before the Lord; for thou, Lord
of oostis, God of Irael, hast openyd the
eer of thi seruaunt, seiynge, An hows I
shal bilde to thee; therfor thi seruaunt

my face, and thi trone schal be stidfast
contynueli. By alle these wordys, and bi 17
al this reuelacioun, so^m Nathan spak to
Dauid. Forsothe Dauid the kyng entrideⁿ, 18
and satt^o bifor the Lord, and seide, Who
am Y, my^p Lord God, and what is myn
hows, that thou brouȝtist^q me hidur to?
But also this is seyn litil in thi siȝt, my 19
Lord God; no but thou schuldist speke
also of the hows of thi seruaunt in to
long tyme. Forsothe^r this is the lawe of
Adam†, Lord God; what therfor may 20
Dauid adde^s ȝit, that he speke to thee?
For^t thou, Lord God, knowist thi
seruaunt; thou hast do alle these grete^u
thingis, for thi word, and bi^v thin herte, 21
so that thou madist^w knowun to thi seruaunt. Herfor, Lord God, thou art mag- 22
nyfied^x, for noon is lijk thee, ne there is
no God outakun thee, in alle thingis
whiche we herden^y with oure eeris. Sotheli 23
what folk in erthe is as the puple of Is-
rael, for which‡ the Lord God ȝede, that
he schulde aȝenbie^z it to him in to a
puple, and schulde^a sette to hym silf a
name, and schulde do to it^b grete thingis,
and orible on^c erthe, in^{cc} *castinge out*
therof^d the folk^e and^f 'goddis therof^g fro
the face of thi puple, which^h thou 'aȝen
bouȝtistⁱ to thee fro Egipt? And thou 24
confermidist^k to thee thi puple Israel in
to a puple euerlastynge, and thou, Lord,
art maad in to God to hem. Now ther- 25
for, Lord God, reise^l thou^m withouten
ende the word that thou hast spoke onⁿ
thi seruaunt and on^o his hows, and do as
thou hast spoke; and thy name be mag- 26
nyfied^p til^q in to withouten ende, and he
it seid, The Lord of oostis is God on^r Israel; and the hows of thi seruaunt Dauid
schal be stablischid byfor the Lord; for 27
thou, Lord of oostis, God of Israel, hast
maad reuelacioun to the eere of thi ser-

† *lawe of A-
dam ; that ech
man be bisy
and desiringe
the prosperite
of hise eiris.
Lire here.* c.

‡ *for which,
etc. ; in Ebreu
it is, for which
Goddis ȝede,
that is, thre
persoones in
the Trinyte,
that ben o God
in substaunce,
therfor it sueth
in singuler
noumbre, thet
he schulde aȝen
bie it to him
silf. Lire here.*
c.

^d Om. E *pr. m.*　^e the lijk *A.*　^{ee} that c *pr. m.*　^f fro *A.*　^g Om. *A.*

^m thus I.　ⁿ entride *in to the tabernacle* I.　^o he satt I.　^p Om. I.　^q hast brouȝt I.　^r for I.　^s adde to I.
^t Therfor FGIKLNOQRSUW. herfor P.　^u Om. I.　^v aftir I.　^w madist *tho* I.　^x maad greet I.　^y han herd I.
^z aȝenbiȝgge K.　^a that he schulde I.　^b his puple I.　^c upon I.　^{cc} *and* b.　^d Om. A *sec. m.* therfore EL.
^e folkis E. folk of kynde I.　^f of E.　^g her goddis I.　^h the which I.　ⁱ hast aȝen bouȝt I.　^k hast con-
fermyd I.　^l reise up I.　^m Om. I.　ⁿ upon I.　^o upon I.　^p maad greet I.　^q Om. I.　^r upon I.

hath founden[h] his herte, that he preye
28 thee bi this preyer. Now thanne, Lord
God, thou ert verrey God, and thi wordis
shulen be sooth; forsothe thou hast spokyn
29 to thi seruaunt these good thingis; bigyn therfor, and blesse to the hows of thi
seruaunt, that it be[l] before thee into
euermore; for thou, Lord God, spakist[k]
thes thingis, and bi[l] thi blessynge the
hows of thi seruaunt shal be blessid into
euermore.

uaunt, and seidist, Y schal bilde an hows
to thee; therfor thi seruaunt foond[s] his
herte, that he schulde preie thee bi this
preier. Now therfor, Lord God, thou art 28
veri God, and thi wordis schulen be trewe;
for thou hast spoke these goodis[t] to thi
seruaunt; therfor bigynne thou, and blesse 29
the hows of thi seruaunt, that it be[u] withouten ende bifor thee; for thou, Lord God,
hast spoke these thingis, and bi[v] thi blessyng the hows of thi seruaunt schal be
blessid withouten ende.

CAP. VIII.

1 Forsothe it is doon after thes thingis,
Dauid smoot Philisteis, and mekide hem;
and Dauid took a bridil of tribut of
2 the hoond of Philisteis. And he smoot
Moab, and he metide[m] hem with a litil
coord euenynge to the erthe; forsothe
he metid two litil coordis, oon to slee,
and another to quykne. And Moab is
maad to Dauid seruynge vndir tribute.
3 And Dauid smoot Adadezer, the sone of
Roob, the kyng of Soba, whanne he
wente forth that he take[n] lordship vpon
4 the flood of Effraten. And take to Dauyd
on his partye a thousand and seuene
hundrid horsmen, and twenti thousand
of feet men, kut of bi the knee alle the
5 hem an hundrid charis. Forsothe Ciria
of Damasc cam to bere socour to Adadezer, the kyng of Soba; and Dauid smoot
of Ciria two and twenti thousand of men.
6 And Dauid putte a strength in Cirya of
Damask, and Cirya is maad to Dauid
seruynge vndir tribute. And the Lord
kepte Dauid in alle thingis, to what euere
7 thingis he wente forth. And Dauid took
goldun aarmys and beeȝis, that hadden the
seruauntis of Adadezer, and brouȝte hem
8 into Jerusalem. And Dauid the kyng
took fro Bethe, and fro Beroth, citees

CAP. VIII.

Forsothe[w] it was doon aftir these 1
thingis, Dauid smoot Filisteis[x], and made
low hem; and Dauid took awei the bridil
of tribute fro the hond of Filisteis†. And 2
Dauid smoot Moab, and mat[y] hem with
a coorde[z], and made[a] euene to the erthe;
forsothe 'he mat[b] twey[c] cordis, oon to
sle, and oon[d] to quikene. And Moab
seruyde Dauid vndur tribute. And Dauid 3
smoot Adadezer, sone[e] of Roob, kyng of
Soba, whanne he ȝede forth to be lord
ouer the flood Eufrates. And whanne a 4
thousynde and seuene hundrid kniȝtis[f] of
his part weren takun, and twenti thousynde of foot men, Dauid hoxide[g] alle
'drawynge beestis[h] in charis; but Dauid
lefte of tho an hundrid charis, *that is, the
horsis of an hundrid charis.* Also Sirie 5
of Damask cam, that it[i] schulde bere help
to Adadezer, kyng of Soba; and Dauid
smoot of Sirie two and twenti thousynde
of men. And Dauid settide strenghe‡ in 6
Sirie of Damask, and Sirie was maad
seruynge Dauid vndur tribute. And the
Lord kepte Dauid in alle thingis, to what
euer thingis he ȝede forth. And Dauid 7
took goldun armeris and bies, whiche the
seruauntis of Adadezer hadden, and he
brouȝte tho in to Jerusalem. And of 8
Bethe, and of Beroth, citees[k] of Adadezer,

h Om. E.   i Om. A.   k speeke BCEFH.   l be E.   m mat BCEFH.   n Om. CEFH.

a hath founden bi I.   t gode thingis I.   u be in to I.   v thorouȝ I.   w And I.   x the Filisteis I.
y he metide I.   z litil coorde I.   a he made hem I.   b Dauid metide hem bi I.   c two litil I.   d another I.
e the sone I.   f horse men I.   g kitte the hoxes of I.   h the beestis drawynge I.   i he I.   k the
citees I.

of Adadezer, ful myche brasse; of the
which Salomon made alle the brasen
vessels in the temple, and the brasen see,
9 and pilers, and auter. Forsothe Thou,
the kyng of Emath, herde that Dauid
hadde smyten al the strength of Adad-
10 ezer. And Thou sente Joram, his sone,
to kyng Dauid, that he salute hym,
thankynge to gidre, and he doo gracis,
forthi that he hath ouercomen Adadezer,
and smyten hym; forsothe Thou was
enemye to Adadezer; and in his hoond
weren silueren vessels, and golden vessels,
11 and brasen vessels. The whiche and thoo
halwide kyng Dauid to the Lord, with
the siluer and gold, 'the whiche[n] he
hadde halwid of alle the gentils, the
12 whiche he hadde dreuen out of Cyrie,
and Moab, and the sones of Amon, and
of Philisteis, and Amalech, and of the
spoylis of Adadezer, the[o] sone of Roob,
13 kyng[p] of Soba. Forsothe Dauid made to
hym a name, whanne he turnyde aȝen,
Cirye taken, in the valey of wodis slayn
eiȝteen thousandis, and in Jebelem, at[q]
14 thre and twenti thousand. And he putte
in Ydume kepers, and sette a strength,
and al Ydume is maad seruynge to Dauid;
and the Lord kept Dauid in alle thingis,
to what euer thingis he wente forth.
15 And Dauid regnyd vpon al Yrael, and
Dauid dide dome, and riȝtwysnes to al
16 the[r] puple. Forsothe Joab, the sone of
Saruye, was vpon the oost; aftirward
Josaphat, the sone of Achilud, was chaun-
17 seleer; and Sadoch, the sone of Achitob,
and Achimalech, the sone of Abiathar,
18 weren prestis; and Saraias a scribe. Forsothe Banaias, the sone of Joiade, was
vpon archeris and alblasters, 'that ben
clepid Cerethi and Pherethi[s]; forsothe
the sones of Dauid weren prestes.

Dauith the[l] kyng took ful myche metal[m];
'of the[n] whiche Salomon made alle the[o]
brasen vessels in the temple, and[p] the
brasen see, and the[q] pilers, and the auter[r].
Forsothe[s] Thou, kyng[t] of Emath, herde 9
that Dauid hadde smyte al the strengthe
of Adadezer. And Thou sente Joram, his 10
sone, to 'kyng Dauid[u], that he schulde
grete hym, and thanke, and do thankyngis, for he hadde ouercome Adadezer,
and hadde smyte[v] hym; for Thou was
enemy to[w] Adadeser; and vessels of sil-
ver, and vessels of gold, and vessels of
bras weren in his hond. And the same 11
vessels kyng Dauid halewid 'to the Lord,
with the siluer and gold, whiche he
hadde[x] halewid[y] of alle hethene men,
whiche '*hethene men*[z] he made[a] suget
of Sirye, and Moab[b], and the[c] sones 12
of Amon, and Filisteis[d], and Amalech[e],
and of the spuylis of Adadezer, sone[f] of
Roob, kyng of Soba. Also Dauid made 13
to hym a name, whanne he turnede aȝen,
whanne Sirie was takun, for eiȝtene thousynde[g] weren slayn in the valey, where
salt is[h] maad, and in Gebelem, to thre
and twenti thousynde. And he[i] settide[k] 14
keperis in Ydumee, and ordeinede strong
hold, and al Ydumee was maad seruynge
to Dauid; and the Lord kepte Dauid in
alle thingis, to whateuer thingis he ȝede
forth. And Dauid regnede on[l] al Israel, 15
and Dauid dide doom, and riȝtfulnesse[m] to
al his puple. Forsothe[n] Joab, the sone of 16
Saruy, was ouer the oost[o]; sotheli[p] Josaphat, sone[q] of Achilud, was chauncelerꝉ;
and Sadoch, sone[r] of Achitob, and Achy- 17
melech, sone[r] of Abiathar, weren preestis;
and Saraye was scryuyn[s]. Forsothe[t] Ba- 18
nanye, sone[u] of Joiada, was ouer Cerethi
and Pherethi, *that is, ouer archeris and
arblasteris*[v]; sotheli[w] the sones of Dauid
weren prestis‡.

† *chaunceler*; in Ebreu it is, recordour. c.
‡ *the sones of Dauyth weren prestis*; that is, grettere men in dignete, ether the firste to onours; for it may not be seid that thei weren prestis propirly, mynystringe in the tabernacle, for thei weren not of the kyn of Aaron. *Lire here*. c.

[n] that c *pr. m.* [o] Om. c. [p] the kyng E *pr. v.* [q] and A. [r] his CE. [s] E *in marg.*

[l] Om. I. [m] bras I. [n] Om. QSWbç. [o] Om. DMQSWXbç. [p] Om. KX. [q] Om. QXb. [r] The whole passage from the word *of* omitted in AELPRU. [s] And I. [t] the kyng I. [u] Dauid the kyng I. [v] sleyn I. [w] of I. [x] Om. A. [y] Om. AI. [z] Om. I. [a] had maad I. [b] of Moab I. [c] of the I. [d] of Filisteis I. [e] of Amalech I. [f] the sone I. [g] thousynde men I. [h] was I. [i] Dauid I. [k] sette I. [l] upon I. [m] riȝtwisnesse I. [n] And I. [o] oost *of Dauid* I. [p] and I. [q] the sone I. [r] the sone I. [s] a scribe I. [t] But I. [u] the sone I. [v] arowblasters ELP. [w] and I.

CAP. IX.

1 And Dauid seide, Whether wenist thou
that there be eny man, that is laft of the
hows of Saul, that I do with hym mercy
2 for Jonatha? Forsothe there was of the
hows of Saul a seruaunt, Cyba bi name;
whom whanne the kyng hadde clepid to
hym silf, seide to hym, Ert thou not
Cyba? And he answerde, Y am thi ser-
3 uaunt. And the kyng seith, Whether is
there on lyue eny man of the hows of
Saul, that I doo with hym merci† of
God? And Ciba seide to the kyng, The
sone of Jonatha is on lyue, feble the feet.
4 Where, he seith, is he? And Ciba seide[u]
to the kyng, Loo! he seith, he is in the
hows of Machir, the sone of Amyel, in
5 Lodobar. Thanne kyng Dauid sente,
and took hym fro the hows of Machir,
6 the sone of Amyel, fro Lodobar. Forsothe whanne Myphibosech, the sone of
Jonathan, the sone of Saul, was comen
to Dauid, he felle into his face, and
lowtide. And Dauid seide, Myphibosech!
The which answerde, I am ny3, thi ser-
7 uaunt. And Dauid seith to hym, Ne
dreed thow, for doynge I shal do with
thee merci for Jonathan, thi fader; and
I shal restore to thee alle the feeldis of
Saul, thi fader, and thou shalt eete breed
8 in my bord euermore. The which honouringe him seith, Who am I, thi seruaunt,
whom thou hast biholdyn vpon a deed
9 hownd lijk of me? And so the king
clepide Cibam, the child of Saul; and
seide to hym, Alle thingis, what euere
weren of Saul and al his hous, I haue
10 3euen to the sone of thi lord; wyrk
thanne the erthe to hym, thou, and thi
sones, and thi seruauntis, and thou shalt
brynge yn meetis to the sone of thi lord,
that he be nurshid; Myphibosech forsothe, the sone of thi lord, shal eete
euermore breed vpon my bord. Forsothe

CAP. IX.

And Dauid seide, Whether ony man is, 1
that lefte of the hows of Saul, that Y do
mercy with hym for Jonathas? Forsothe[x] 2
a seruaunt, Siba bi name, was[y] of the hous
of Saul; whom whanne the kyng hadde
clepid to hym silf, 'the kyng[z] seide to hym,
Whethir thou art not Siba? And he answeride, Y am thi seruaunt. And the 3
kyng seide, Whether ony man lyueth of
the hows of Saul, that Y do with hym
the mercy of God? And Siba seide to the
kyng, A sone of Jonathas lyueth, feble[a]
in the feet. The[b] kyng seide, Where is 4
he? And Siba seide to the kyng, Lo! he
is in the hows of Machir, sone[c] of Amyel,
in Lodabar. Therfor 'Dauid the kyng[d] 5
sente, and took hym[e] fro the hows of
Machir, sone[f] of Amyel, fro Lodobar.
Forsothe[g] whanne Myphibosech, the sone 6
of Jonathas, sone of Saul, hadde come to
Dauid, he felde in to his face, and worschipide[gg]. And Dauid seide, Myphibosech!
Which[h] answeride, Y am present, thi seruaunt. And Dauid seide to hym, Drede 7
thou not, for Y doynge schal do mersi to
thee for Jonathas, thi fadir; and Y schal
restore to thee alle the[i] feeldis of Saul, thi
fadir, and thou schalt ete breed in my
boord[k] euere. Which[l] worschipide him, and 8
seide, Who am Y, thi seruaunt, for thou
hast biholde on[m] a deed dogge[n] lijk me?
Therfor the kyng clepide Siba, the child 9
of Saul; and seide to hym, Y haue 3oue
to the sone of thi lord alle thingis, which
euer weren of Saul, and al the hows of
hym; therfor worche thou the lond to 10
hym, thou, and thi sones, and thi seruauntis, and thou schalt brynge in meetis
to the sone† of thi lord, that he be fed;
forsothe[o] Myphibosech, sone[p] of thi lord,
schal ete euer breed on[q] my bord. Sotheli[r]
fiftene sones and twenti seruauntis weren
to Siba. And Siba seyde to the kyng, As 11

† to the sone,
etc.; that is, to
Myca, sone of
Myphiboseth,
who is now thi
lord. Lire
here. c.

t the merci BCEH.   u Om. CEH.

x And ther was I.   y Om. I.   z he I.   a the whiche is sijk I.   b And the I.   c the sone I.   d kyng
Dauid I.   e Jonathas sone I.   f the sone I.   g And I.   gg worschipe A.   h And he I.   i Om. I.   k table I.
l The which I.   m upon I.   n hound I.   o but I.   p the sone I.   q of I.   r And I.

there weren of Ciba fifteen sonys and
11 twenti seruauntis. And Ciba seide to
the kyng, As thou hast comaundid, my
lord kyng, to thi seruaunt, so thi seruaunt shal doo; and Myphibosech shal
eete vpon thi bord, as oon of the sonys
12 of the kyng. Forsothe Myphibosech
hadde a litil sone, Mycha bi name; forsothe al the kynrede of the hows of Ciba
13 seruede to Myphibosech. But Myphibosech dwellide in Jerusalem; for of the
bord of the kyng contynueli he eete, and
he was halt either foot.

thou, my lord kyng, hast comaundid to
thi seruaunt, so thi seruaunt schal do;
and Myphibosech, as oon of the sones of
the kyng, schal ete on[s] thi boord. For- 12
sothe[t] Myphibosech hadde a litil sone,
Mycha bi name; sotheli[u] al the meyne of
the hows of Siba scruyde Myphibosech.
Forsothe[v] Myphibosech dwellide in Jeru- 13
salem; for he eet contynueli of the kingis
boord, and was[w] crokid[x] on either foot.

CAP. X.

1. Forsothe it is doon after thes thingis,
that Naas, the kyng of the sonys of
Amon, diede; and Anon, his sone, regn-
2 ede for hym. And Dauid seide, I shal
doo mercy with Anon, the sone of Naas,
as his fader dide merci with me. Thanne
sente Dauid comfortynge hym bi his seruauntis vpon the fader deth. Forsothe
whanne the seruauntis of Dauid weren
comen into the loond of the sonis of
3 Amon, the princis of the sones of Amon
seiden to Anon, her lord, Wenyst thou
that for the worship of thi fader Dauid
hath sente to thee coumfortours; and
not therfor that he aspie, and serche the
citee, and turne it vpsedoun, Dauid hath
4 sente his seruauntis to thee? And so
Anon took the seruauntis of Dauid, and
shooue the half part of the beerd of
hem, and he kittide[v] of the mydil clothis
of hem vnto the arsis; and he lafte hem.
5 The which whanne was toold to Dauid,
he sente into aȝen comynge of hem, forsothe thei weren men ful foul confoundid.
And Dauid sente to hem, Dwellith in
Jericho, to the tyme that ȝoure beerd
6 growe, and thanne turneth aȝen. Forsothe the sones of Amon, seynge that
thei hadden doo wronge to Dauid, thei
senten, and hireden bi mede Cyrie of

CAP. X.

Forsothe it was doon aftir these thingis, 1
that Naas, kyng of the sones of Amon, diede;
and Anoon, his sone, regnede for hym. And
Dauid seide, Y schal do mercy with Anon, 2
the sone of Naas, as his fadir dide mercy
with me. Therfor Dauid sente coumfort-
ynge hym by hise seruauntis on[y] the deeth
of the fadir. Sotheli[z] whanne the seruauntis of Dauid hadden come in to the
lond of the sones of Amon, princes[a] of the 3
sones of Amon seiden to Anon, her lord,
Gessist thou that for the onour of thi fadir
Dauid sente[b] coumfortouris to thee; and
not[c] herfor David sente hise seruauntis to
thee, that he schulde aspie, and enserche
the citee, and distrie it? Therfor Anoon 4
took the seruauntis of Dauid, and schauyde[d] half the part of the beerd of hem[e], and
he kittide[f] awey the myddil clothis of hem
'til to[g] the buttokis[h]; and[i] lefte hem. And 5
whanne this was teld to Dauid, he sente
in to the comyng of hem, for the men
weren schent ful vilensly. And Dauid comaundide to hem, Dwelle ȝe in Jerico, til
ȝoure beerd wexe, and thanne turne ȝe aȝen.
Sotheli[k] the sones of Amon sien†, that 6
thei hadden do wrong to Dauid, and thei
senten, and hiriden bi[l] meede Roob[m] of
Sirye, and Soba[n] of Sirie, twenti thousynde of foot men, and of kyng Maacha, a

† the sones of
Amon sien; for
thei knewen
that not bi
fraude, but of
veri frenschip,
Dauyth sente
messangeris;
and netheles
thei knoulech-
iden not gilt,
nether axiden
forȝyuenesse,
but thei maden
hem redi to
defende her
foli, in clepinge
othere men into
her help aȝenus
Dauyth, and
this doyng
agreggide
notably ether
gretly her gilt.
Lire here. C.

v kutt BCEFH.

s upon I.　t And I.　u And I.　v And I.　w he was I.　x halt I.　y upon I.　z And I.　a the princis I.
b hath sent I.　c not rather I.　d he schauyde I.　e her beerd I.　f kitte I.　g vnto I.　h hipes I.　i and
so I.　k And I.　l with I.　m of Roob I.　n of Soba I.

Roob, and Cirye of Soba, twenty thousandis of foot men, and of the kyng
of Maacha a thousand men, and of
7 Istob twelue thousandis of men. The
which thing whanne Dauid hadde herd,
he sente Joab and al the oost of fiȝters.
8 Thanne the sonys of Amon wenten out,
and dressiden sheltrun before hym in the
entree of the ȝate. Forsothe Cire of
Soba, and Roob, and Istob, and Maacha
9 weren aside in the feeld. Thanne Joab
seynge that a batail was maad redi aȝens
hym, and fro aȝens and bihynde the bac,
he cheese to hym of alle the chosen of Irael,
10 and ordeynde sheltrun aȝens Cyre. Forsothe the tother partye of the puple he
took to Abisai, his brothir, the which
dresside sheltrun aȝens the sones of
11 Amon. And Joab seith, If Cyres han
the ouerhoond aȝens me, thou shalt be to
me into help ; forsothe if the sones of
Amon han the ouerhoond aȝens thee, I
12 shal help to thee ; be thou a strong man,
and fiȝte we for oure puple, and for the
citee of oure God ; forsothe the Lord shal
13 do that is good in his siȝt. And so Joab
wente yn, and his puple that was with
hym, strijf aȝens Cyres, the whiche anoon
14 flowen fro the face of hym. Forsothe
the sones of Amon, seynge that the Cyres
weren flowen, and thei flowen fro the
face of Abisai, and wenten into the citee ;
and Joab is turned aȝen fro the sonis of
15 Amon, and cam into Jerusalem. Forsothe seynge the Cires that thei hadden
fallen before Irael, ben gadrid togidre[w].
16 And Adidazer sente, and brouȝte out the
Cirys that weren beȝonde the flood, and
brouȝte forth the oost of hem ; forsothe
Sabath, the maistre of chyualrye[x] of
17 Adadezer, was the prince of hem. And
whanne it was toold to Dauid, he drewȝ
togidre al Irael, and passide ouere Jordan, and cam into Helama. And the

thousynde men, and of Istob twelue thousynde of men. And whanne Dauid hadde 7
herd this, he sent[o] Joab and al the oost
of fiȝteris. Therfor the sones of Amon 8
ȝeden out, and dressiden scheltrun bifor
hem in the entryng of the ȝate. Forsothe[p] Soba, and Roob of Sirie, and Istob,
and Maacha weren asidis half in the feeld.
Therfor Joab siȝ, that batel[q] was maad 9
redi aȝens hym, bothe euene aȝens[r] and
bihynde the[s] bak ; and he chees to hym silf
of alle the chosun men of Israel, and
ordeynede[t] scheltrun aȝens Sirus[u]. For- 10
sothe[v] he[w] bitook to Abisai, his brothir,
the tother part of the puple, which[x] dresside scheltrun aȝens the sones of Amon.
And Joab seide, If men of Sirie han the 11
maistrie aȝens me, thou[y] schalt be to me
in to help ; sotheli[z] if the sones of Amon
han the maistrie aȝens thee, Y schal helpe
thee ; be thou a strong man, and fiȝte we 12
for oure puple, and for the citee of oure
God ; forsothe[a] the Lord schal do that,
that is good in his siȝt. Therfor Joab 13
and his[b] puple that was with hym, bigan
batel aȝens men of Sirie, whiche[c] fledden
anoon fro his face. Forsothe[d] the sones 14
of Amon sien, that men of Sirie hadden
fled ; and thei fledden also fro the face of
Abisai, and entriden[e] in to the citee ; and
Joab turnede aȝen fro the sones of Amon,
and cam in to Jerusalem. Forsothe[f] men 15
of Sirye sien that thei hadden feld[h] bifor
Israel, and thei weren gaderid to gidere.
And Adadezer sente, and ledde out men of 16
Sirie that weren biȝende the flood, and he
brouȝte[i] the oost of hem ; sotheli[k] Sobach,
mayster of the chyualrie of Adadezer, was
the prince of hem. And whanne this 17
was teld to Dauid, he drow togidere al
Israel, and passide[l] Jordan, and cam in
to Helama. And men of Sirie dressiden
scheltrun aȝens Dauid, and fouȝten aȝens
hym. And Sireis fledden fro the face of 18

---

w Om. ɢ pr. m.   x the chyualrye cᴇ.

o sente forth ɪ.   p and ɪ.   q the batel ɪ.   r aȝens hym ɪ.   s his ɪ.   t he ordeynede ɪ.   u Sirie ɪ.   v And ɪ.
w Joab ɪ.   x the which ɪ.   y thou, Abisay ɪ.   z and ɪ.   a for ɪ.   b the ɪ.   c the whiche ɪ.   d And ɪ.
e thei entriden ɪ.   f And ɪ.   g the men ɢꞯ.   h fled ꜰᴋᴏꜱ sup. ras. w. falle ᴇɪʟᴍᴘ.   i brouȝte forth ɪ.
k and ɪ.   l he passide ouer ɪ.

Cires dresseden sheltrun fro aȝens Dauid,
18 and fouȝten aȝens hym. And Cyres
flowen fro the face of Irael; and Dauid
slowȝ of Cires seuen hundrid chares, and
fourti thousandis[y] of horsmen; and he
smoot Sobach, the prynce of chyualrye,
19 the which anoon is deed. Forsothe
seynge alle the kyngis, that weren in the
strength of Adadezer, hem to be ven-
cusshid of Yrael, maden pees with Irael,
and serueden to hem; and Cires dradden
to ȝeue help to the sones of Amon.

CAP. XI.

1 Forsothe it is doon, turnynge the ȝeer
that tyme the which kyngis ben wont to
goo forth to batails, Dauid sente[z] Joab,
and with hym his seruauntis, and al Irael;
and thei wastiden the sones of Amon, and
bisegeden Raba; forsothe Dauid abood
2 stille in Jerusalem. While these thingis
weren doo, it felle, that Dauid roos on a
dai fro his bed aftir mydday, and wente
in the solere of the kyngis hows; and he
sawȝ a womman wasshynge hir fro aȝens
vpon hir solere; forsothe she was a ful
3 feyr womman. Than Dauid sente, and
aserchede, what was the womman; and it
is toold to hym, that she was Bersabee,
the douȝter of Elyam, the[a] wijf of Vrye
4 Ethei. And so Dauid sente messagers,
and[b] took hir; the which whanne she
was goon in to hym, he slepte with hir,
and anoon she is halwid fro hir vn-
5 clennes. And she turnede aȝen to hir hows,
the fruyt of hir wombe conseyued; and
she sendynge toold to Dauid, and seith,
6 I haue conseyued. Forsothe Dauid sente
to Joab, seiynge, Send to me Vrie Ethee;
7 and Joab sente Vrye to Dauid. And
Vrye cam to Dauid; and Dauid askide,
how riȝt dide Joab and the puple, and
what maner wise the batail was serued[c].
8 And Dauid seide to Vrye, Go into thin

Israel; and Dauid killide of Sireis[m] seuene
hundrid charis, and fourti thousynde of
knyȝtis[n]; and he smoot Sobach, the prince
of chyualrie[o], which[p] was deed anoon.
Forsothe[q] alle kyngis[r], that weren in the[s] 19
help of Adadezer, siȝen that thei weren
ouercomun of Israel, and thei maden pees
with Israel, and serueden hem; and Sireis[t]
dredden to ȝyue help to the sones of
Amon.

CAP. XI.

Forsothe[u] it was doon, whanne the ȝeer 1
turnede aȝen in that tyme wherynne[v]
kyngis ben wont to go forth to batels,
Dauid sente[w] Joab, and with hym hise
seruauntis, and al Israel; and thei distrieden the sones of Amon, and bisegiden
Rabath; forsothe[x] Dauid dwellide in
Jerusalem†. While these thingis weren 2
doon, it befelde, that Dauid roos in a dai
fro his bed after mydday, and walkide[y]
in the soler of the kyngis hows; and he
siȝ a womman‡ waischynge hir silf euen
aȝens[z] on[a] hir soler; sotheli[b] the womman
was ful fair. Therfor the kyng sente, 3
and enqueride, what womman it was; and
it was teld to hym, that sche was Bersabee,
the douȝtir of Heliam, *and was*[c] the wijf
of Vrye Ethei. Therfor[d] bi messangeris 4
sent Dauid took hir; and whanne sche
entride to hym, he slepte with hir, and
anoon sche was halewid fro hir vnclenesse[e]‖. And sche turnede aȝen in to 5
hir hows, with child[f] conseyued; and sche
sente, and telde[g] to Dauid, and seide, Y
haue conseyued. Forsothe[h] Dauid sente 6
to Joab, and seide, Sende thou Vrye Ethei
to me; and Joab sente Vrye to Dauid.
And Vrie cam to Dauid; and Dauid axide, 7
hou riȝtfuli Joab dide and the puple, and
hou[i] the batel was mynystrid[k]. And 8

† *Dauyth dwellide in Jerusalem;* whanne othere men ȝedon forth to batel, Dauyth dwellide as idil in Jerusalem, and therfor he was drawun to do auoutrie; wherfor the poete seith, If thou takist awey idilnesse, the craftis of coueitise, that is, of leccherie, perischiden; and in xxxiii. c°. Eccl. ydilnesse tauȝte myche malice. c.

‡ *And he siȝ a womman;* vnchast siȝt is ful perelouse, for Dauyth that was so hooly and good, was drawun herbi to auowtrie, and aftirward to procure mansleyng bi tresoun, and at the laste to parforme it in werk. *Lire here.* c.

‖ *halewid fro hir vnclennesse;* that is, fro flux of vncleene blood that schulde come til to the child bering, for sche conseyuede in that ligging bi, and vncleene blood renneth no more aftir conseyuyng of child, for thilke blood goith in to the formyng and mete of the child. *Lire here.* c.

[y] thousand BCEFH. [z] sente to E *pr.m.* [a] Om. E *pr.m.* [b] Om. BCEFH. [c] seuerd A.

[m] the Sireis I. [n] horsmen I. [o] the chyualrie I. [p] the which I. [q] And I. [r] the kyngis I. [s] Om. I. [t] the Sireis I. [u] And I. [v] in whiche I. [w] sente forth I. [x] and I. [y] he walkide I. [z] aȝens *him* I. [a] upon I. [b] and I. [c] *sche was* I. [d] Thanne I. [e] *bareyn wymmen weren seid vnclene* I. *marg.* [f] a child I. [g] schewide I. [h] And I. [i] what maner wise I. [k] serued I.

hows, and wassh thi feet. And Vrye wente out of the kyngis hows, and hym 9 folwide the kyngis meet. Forsothe Vrye slepte before the ʒate of the kyngis hows with othere seruauntis of his lord, and 10 he wente not down to his hows. And it is toold to Dauid of seieris, Vrye wente not to his hows. And Dauid seith to Vrye, Whether not fro 'a ferre[d] weye thou cam? whi desendist[e] thou[f] not into 11 thin hows? And Vrie seith to Dauid, The arke of God, and[g] Yrael and Juda dwellen in tentis, and my lord Joab, and the seruauntis of my lord biden vpon the face of the erthe, and I shal go[h] 'in to[i] myn hous, that I ete, and drinke, and slepe with my wijf? Bi thin helth, and bi the helth of thi soule, I shal not doo 12 this thing. Thanne Dauid seith to Vrie, Bijd here also to dai, and to morwe Y shal leeue thee. Vrye bode in Jerusalem that 13 day and the tothere. And Dauyd clepide hym, that he eete before hym and drynk, and he made hym drunke; the which goon out at euen, slepte in his bedde with the[k] seruauntis of his lord; and he desendide 14 not into his hows. And it is doon thanne eerli, and Dauid wroot a lettre to Joab, 15 and seute bi the hoond of Vrye, wrytynge in the lettre, Puttith Vrie fro aʒens of the batail, where the batail is moost strong, and forsakith hym, that he 16 smyten die. Thanne whanne Joab bisegide the citee, he putte Vrye in the place where he wiste moost stronge men 17 to ben. And the men gon out fro the cite, fouʒten aʒen Joab, and thei slewen of the puple of[l] the seruauntis of Dauid, 18 and also Vrie Ethee is deed. ˙ And so Joab sente, and toolde alle thes wordis of 19 the batail; and comaundide to the messageer, seiynge, Whanne thou hast ful endid alle the wordis of the batail to the 20 kyng, if thou seest hym to han indig-

Dauid seide to Vrye, Go in to thin hows, and waische thi feet. Vryc ʒede out[l] fro the hows of the kyng, and the kyngis mete suede hym. Sotheli[m] Vrye slepte 9 bifor the ʒate of the kyngis hows with othere seruauntis of his lord, and ʒede[n] not doun to his hows. And it was teld to 10 Dauid of men, seiynge, Vrye 'ʒede not[o] to his hows. And Dauid seide to Vrye, Whether[p] thou camest not fro the weye? whi ʒedist thou not doun in to thin hows? And Vrie seide to Dauid, The arke of 11 God, Israel[q] and Juda dwellen in tentis, and my lord Joab, and the seruauntis of my lord dwellen on[r] the face of erthe[s], and schal Y go in to myn hows, to ete and drynke, and slepe with my wijf? Bi thin helthe, and bi the helthe of thi soule, Y schal not do this thing. Therfor Dauid 12 seide to Vrye, Dwelle thou here also to dai, and to morewe Y schal delyuere thee. Vrie dwellide in Jerusalem in that day and the tothir. And Dauid clepide hym, 13 that he schulde ete and drynke bifor hym, and Dauid made druukun Vrye†; and he ʒede out in the euentid, and slepte in his bed with the seruauntes of his lord; and ʒede[t] not doun in to his hows. Therfor[u] 14 the morewtid was maad, and[uu] Dauid wroot epistle to Joab, and sente[v] bi the hond of Vrye, and wroot[w] iu the pistle[x], Sette[y] ʒe 15 Vrye euene aʒens the batel, where the batel is strongeste, 'that is, where the aduersaries ben stronge[z], and forsake[a] ʒe hym, that he be smitun and perische. Therfor whanne Joab bisegide the citee, 16 he settide[b] Vric in the[c] place where he wiste that strongeste men[d] weren. And 17 men ʒeden out of the citee, and fouʒten aʒens Joab, and thei killiden of the puple of seruauntis[e] of Dauid, and also Vrye Ethei was deed[f]. Therfor[g] Joab sente, and 18 telde alle the[h] wordis of the batel; and he 19 comaundyde to the messanger, and seide,

d the E pr.m.   e descendedest c.   f Om. E.   g of E pr.m.   h go out A.   i in AFH.   k Om. A.   l Om. A.

l forth I.   m And I.   n he ȝede I.   o hath not go I.   P For EL.   q of Israel I pr.m. w sup. ras.   r upon I.   s the erthe I.   t he ȝede I.   u Therfor whanne A sec. m. Thanne I.   uu Om. A sec. m.   v he sente it I.   w he wroot I.   x epistle CE.   y Putte I.   z Om. DCIX.   a leeue I.   b sette I.   c that I.   d enmyes I.   e the seruauntis BCIMUç.   f deed there I.   g And so I.   h these I.

nacioun, and seye, Whi neȝeden ȝe to the
wal for to fiȝte? whether knewen ȝe not,
that aboue fro the wal ben sent manye
21 dartis? who smoot Achymalech, the sone
of Jeroboal? whether not a womman
sente vpon hym a gobet of a myln stoon
fro the wal, and slewȝ hym in Thebes?
whi biside the wal ȝe wenten to? thow
shalt seye, Also thi seruaunt, Vrye Ethee,
22 is slayn. Thanne the messager wente,
and cam, and toolde to Dauid alle thingis
23 that Joab comaundide to hym. And the
messager seide to Dauid, The men hadden
the ouer hoond aȝens vs, and thei wenten
out to vs into the feeld; forsothe we, the
bure made, pursueden hem vnto the ȝate
24 of the citee. And the sheeters dresseden
dartis to thi seruauntis fro the wal aboue,
and there ben deed of the seruauntis of
the kyng; but also Vrie Ethee, thi seru-
25 aunt, is deed. And Dauid seide to the
messager, Thes thingis thou shalt seye
to Joab, This thing breke thee not; forsothe dyuerse is the hap of batail, and
now this, now hym wastith the swerd;
coumfort thi fiȝters aȝens the cytee, that
26 thou distroye it, and enhurte hem. Forsothe the wijf of Vrye herde, that Vrie
her houseboond was deed, and she wei-
27 lide hym. And the weilynge ouere doon,
Dauid sente, and brouȝte hir into his
hows; and she is maad wijf to hym,
and she bare to hym a sone. And the
word that Dauid dide displeside before
the Lord.

Whanne thou hast fillid[k] alle wordis[l] of
the batel to the kyng, if thou seest, that 20
he is wrooth, and seith, Whi neiȝiden ȝe
to the wal to fiȝte? whether ȝe wisten not,
that many dartis ben sent[m] fro aboue fro
the wal[n]? who smoot Abymelech, sone[o] 21
of Gerobaal? whether not a womman
sente[p] on[q] hym a gobet of a mylnestoon
fro the[r] wal[s], and killide[t] hym in Thebes?
whi neiȝiden ȝe bisidis the wal? thou
schalt seie[u], Also thi seruaunt, Vrye Ethei,
diede[v]. Therfor[w] the messanger ȝede[x], 22
and telde to Dauid alle thingis whiche
Joab hadde comaundid to hym. And the 23
messanger seide to Dauid, 'Men hadden[y]
the maistri aȝens us, and thei ȝeden out
to vs in to the feeld; sotheli[z] bi[a] 'fersnesse maad[b] we pursueden hem 'til to[c] the
ȝate of the citee. And archeris[d] senten[e] 24
dartis to thi seruauntis fro the wal
aboue, and summe of the 'kyngis seruauntis[f] ben deed; forsothe[g] also thi
seruaunt, Vrye Ethei, is deed. And Dauid 25
seide to the messanger, Thou schalt seie
these thingis to Joab, This thing breke
not thee; for the bifallyng[h] of batel is
dyuerse, and swerd wastith[i] now this
man, now that man; coumforte thi fiȝteris
aȝens the citee, that thou distrye it, and
excite[k] thou hem[l]. Forsothe[m] the wijf 26
of Vrye herde, that Vrye hir hosebond
was deed, and sche biweilide hym†. And 27
whanne the morenyng was passid, Dauid
sente, and brouȝte hir in to his hows;
and sche was maad wijf to hym, and sche
childide a sone to hym. And this word
which[n] Dauid hadde do displeside bifor
the Lord.

† and sche
biweilide him;
oneli bi feyn-
yng, and bi
mppering, for
sche desiride
his deth, that
hi this sche
schulde ascape
atonyng, and
be maad the
wijf of the
kyng, and for
this entent sche
procuride
Dauyth to hir
hosebondis
deth. Lire
here. c.
‡ The riche
man; this riche
man is vndur-
stondun Dauyth,
hauyng many
wyues; the pore
man is vndur-
stondun Vrie,
that hadde oonely
o wijf, whom
he hadde bouȝt,
in ȝyaȝynge
dower for hir,
and whom he
hadde murschid,
a Heill damesel.
Sche eet of his
breed, for sche
comynede with
hym in mete
and bed. This
pilgrym that
cam to the riche
man, is the
deuel, which is
alienyd fro the
comynyng of
heuenly cyte-
seyns, for
hardnesse in
synne; to which
pilgrym Da-
uyth made a
feeste bi consent
in to auountrie,
and manaleyng
brouȝt forth in
to dede, for the
deuel delitith
in syche synnes.
Dauyth seide,
he schal ȝelde
the scheep in to
the fourthe fold,
and so it was
doon to him, for
hise iiii. sones
weren deed,
for the deeth of
Vrie; the firste,
the sone of
Bersabee, the
ii. Amon, the
iii. Absolon, the
iiii. Adonye.
And Dauyth
seide, bi herte
and mouth, I
hawe synned to
the Lord; he
defendide not
his synne, but
knowlechede

CAP. XII.

1 Thanne the Lord sente Nathan to
Dauid; the which whanne he was
comen to hym, seide to hym, Answere
to me doom; two men weren in o cytee;
2 oon ryche, and another pore. The riche
3 hadde sheep and oxen ful manye; for-

CAP. XII.

Therfor the Lord sente Nathan to 1
Dauid; and whanne he hadde come to
Dauid, he seide to Dauid°, Answere thou
doom[p] to me; twei men weren in o[q] citee;
o[r] man was riche, and the tother was[s]
pore. The riche man‡ hadde ful many 2

[k] fulfillid 1. [l] the wordis IX sec. m. ç. [m] sent out 1. [n] fro the wal aboue 1. [o] the sone 1. [p] lete falle 1.
[q] upon 1. [r] a 1. [s] wal an hiȝe 1. [t] sche killide 1. [u] seie thanne 1. [v] was sleyn 1. [w] Thanne 1. [x] ȝede
forth 1. [y] Enmyes han had 1. [z] and 1. [a] with 1. [b] gret fersnesse 1. [c] vnto 1. [d] scheters 1. [e] senten
out 1. [f] seruauntis of the kyng 1. [g] and 1. [h] happe 1. [i] fordoith 1. [k] stire 1. [l] hem therto 1.
[m] And 1. [n] that 1. [o] him 1. [p] a doom 1. [q] a 1. [r] the oo 1. the too K. [s] Om. 1.

sothe the pore hadde no thing vtterly, saaf o litil sheep, the which he bou3te^m, and norshide, and the which wexe anentis hym with his sonys, togidre of his breed etinge, and of his cup drynkynge, and in his bosum slepynge; and 4 it was to hym as a dou3ter. Forsothe whanne a maner pylgrym was comen to the riche man, he sparynge to take of the sheep and of his oxen, that he 3eue a meetshipe to that pilgrym, that cam to hym, took the sheep of the pore man, and maade redi meetis to the man that 5 cam to hym. Forsothe Dauid wrooth ful myche bi indignacioun a3ens that man, seide to Nathan, The Lord lyueth, for the sone of deeth is the man, the 6 which dide that; the sheep he shal 3eelde into foure foold, forthi that he hath doo this word, and hath not sparyd. 7 Forsothe Nathan seide to Dauid, Thou ert thilk man, that didist this thing. Thes thingis seith the Lord God of Irael, I haue anoyntid thee into kyng vpon Irael, and I haue delyuerde thee fro 8 the hoond of Saul, and 3eue to thee the hows of thi lord, and the wyues of thi lord in thi bosum, and 3euen to thee the hows of Irael, and of Juda; and if thes thingis ben litil, I shulde adde to thee 9 myche more. Whi thanne hast thou dispisid the word of the Lord, that thou doo yuel thingis in my si3t? Vrye Ethei thou hast smyten with swerd, and the wijf of hym thou hast takyn to thee into wijf, and thou hast slayn hym bi the 10 swerd of the sones of Amon. For what thing swerd of thin hows shal not goo a wey fro thee vnto with outen ende; forthi that thou hast dispised me, and took the wijf of Vrie Ethei, that she 11 were thi wijf. And so thes thingis seith the Lord, Loo! I shal rere vpon thee yuel of thin hows, and I shal taak awey

scheep, and oxun; sotheli^t the pore man 3 hadde vttirli no thing, outakun o litil scheep, which ^u he hadde bou3t, and nurschid, and which^v 'hadde wexid^w at^x hym with hise sones, and eet togidere^y of his breed, and drank of his cuppe, and slepte in his bosum; and it was as a dou3ter to hym. Forsothe^z whanne a 4 pilgrym 'hadde come^a to the^b riche man, he sparide to take of hise^c scheep and oxun, that he schulde make a feeste to that pilgrym, that cam to hym; and he took the scheep of the pore man, and 'made redi^d metis to the man that cam to hym. Forsothe^e Dauid was ful wrooth with 5 indignacioun a3ens that man, and seide^f to Nathan, The Lord lyueth, for the man that dide this^g is the sone of deeth†; he 6 schal 3elde the scheep in to foure folde, for he dide this word, and sparide not. For- 7 sothe^h Nathan seide to Dauid, Thou art thilkeⁱ man, that hast do this thing. The Lord God of Israel seith these thingis, Y anoyntide^k thee 'in to^l kyng on^m Israel, and Y delyuerede thee fro the hond of Saul, and Y 3af to thee the hows 8 of thi lord, and the wyues of thi lord in thi bosum, and Y 3af to thee the hows of Israel, and of Juda; and if these thingis ben litil, Y schalⁿ adde^o to thee myche grettere thingis. Whi therfor hast 9 thou dispisid the word of the Lord, that thou didist yuels in my si3t? Thou hast smyte^p by swerd Vrye Ethei, and thou hast take his wijf in to wijf to thee, and thou hast slayn hym with the swerd of the sones of Amon. Wherfor swerd^q 10 schal not go awey fro thin hows‡ til in to with outen ende; for thou dispysidist^r me, and tokist^s the wijf of Vrye Ethei, that sche schulde be thi wijf. Therfor 11 the Lord seith these thingis, Lo! Y schal reise on^t thee yuel^u of thin hows, and Y schal take thi wyues in 'thin i3en^v, and Y

mekely, wherfor it sueth, *also the Lord hath turned awey thi synne*, as to the gilt, in for3yuynge it for thi penaunce, and as to the peyne, in temperinge it; for thou3 thou art a mansquellere and worthi the deth, netheles *thou schalt not die in thi propir persoone, but in thi sone born.* Of whiche the cause sueth, *for thou hast maad the enemyes to blasfeme the name of the Lord*; for yuele men and vnkunnynge blasfemeden bi this the priuy domes of God, and seiden, that he dide vniustly in repreuynge Saul, and in chesinge Dauyth, that dide synnes more worse than Saul hadde do. *Lire here.* c.

† is *the sone of deeth*; that is, worthi of deth, for the hidousnesse of the dede. *Lire here.* c.

‡ *fro thin hows, etc.*; for the brother killide the brother, as Absolon killide Amon, in xiii. c°., and Salomon killide Adonye, in iii. book ii. c°., and Absolon roos a3enus Dauyth his fadir, in this book xv. c°. c.

^t and 1. ^u the which 1. ^v the which 1. ^w wexide 1. ^x anentis 1. ^y bothe 1. ^z But 1. ^a came 1. ^b this 1. ^c his owne 1. ^d greithide 1. ^e Certis 1. ^f he seide 1. ^g this thing 1. ^h And 1. ⁱ that E.I. ^k haue anoyntid 1. ^l Om. 1. ^m upon 1. ⁿ schulde 1 pr. m. ^o thanne do 1. ^p killid 1. ^q a swerd K. ^r hast dispisid 1. ^s hast take 1. ^t upon 1. ^u the yuel 1. ^v thi si3t 1.

thi wyues in thin eyen, and ȝyue to thin neiȝbour, and he shal sleepe with thi 12 wyues in the eyen of this sunne. Forsothe thou didist hidyngli; forsothe I shal doo this word in siȝt of al Irael, 13 and in the siȝt of this sunne. And Dauid seide to Nathan, I haue synued to the Lord. And Nathan seide to Dauid, Forsothe the Lord hath ouerborn thi 14 synne; thou shalt not die. Neuerthelater for thou hast maad the enemyes to blaspheme the name of the Lord, for that word the sone that is born to thee bi 15 deeth shal die. And Nathan is turned aȝen into his hows. And the Lord smoot the litil child, whom the wijf of Vrye bare to Dauid, and he is dispeyrid. 16 And Dauid preyde the Lord for the litil child; and Dauid fastide with fastynge, and wente in aside, and laye vpon the 17 erthe. Forsothe the eldris of his hows camen, constreynynge hym that he shulde ryse fro the erthe; the whiche wolde 18 not, and eete not with hem meete. Forsothe it felle the seuenthe dai, that the child diede; and the seruauntis of Dauid dradden to telle to hym, that the child was deed; thei seiden forsothe, Loo! whanne the lityl child lynede, we speken to hym, and he herde not oure voys; how mych more if we seyn the child is deed, he shal turment hym 19 self? Whanne thanne Dauid hadde herd his seruauntis musynge, he vndirstood that the lytyl faunt was deed; and he seide to his seruauntis, Whether the child is deed? The whiche answerden 20 vnto hym, He is deed. Thanne Dauid roos fro the erthe, and was wasshid, and anoynt; and whanne he hadde chaungid clothinge, he wente into the hows of the Lord, and honourde, and cam into his hows; and he askyde, that thei shulden 21 sette to hym breed, and he eete. For-

schal ȝyue to thi neiȝbore, and he schal slepe with thi wyues in the iȝen of this sunne, 'that is, opynli bifor alle men, as in æv. chapitre. For thou hast do priueli; 12 forsothe Y schal do this word in the siȝt of al Israel, and in the siȝt of this sunne. And Dauid seide to Nathan, Y haue 13 synned to the Lord. And Nathan seide to Dauid, Also the Lord hath turned awei thi synne; thou schalt not die. Neteles for thou madist enemyes to 14 blasfeme the name of the Lord, for this word the child which is borun to thee schal die bi deeth. And Nathan turnede 15 aȝen in to his hows. And the Lord smoot the litil child, whom the wijf of Vrye childide to Dauid, and he dispeiride t. And Dauid preiede the Lord for the litil 16 child; and Dauid fastide bi fastyng, and entride asidis half, and lai on the erthe. Sotheli the eldere men of his hows 17 camen, and constreyneden hym 'bi meke preieris, that he schulde rise fro the erthe; and he nolde, nethir he eet mete with hem. Forsothe it bifelde in the 18 seuenthe dai, that the ȝong child diede; and the seruauntis of Dauid dredde to telle to hym, that the litil child was deed; for thei seiden, Lo! whanne the litil child lynede ȝit, we spaken to hym, and he herde not oure vois; hou myche more, if we seien the child is deed, he schal turment himsilf? Therfore whanne 19 Dauid hadde herd his seruauntis spekynge priueli, 'ether moterynge, he vnderstood that the ȝong child was deed; 'and he seyde to his seruauntis, Whether the child is deed? Whiche answeriden to hym, He is deed. Therfor Dauid 20 roos fro the erthe, and was waischid, and anoyntid; and whanne he hadde chaungid cloth, he entride in to the hows of the Lord, and worschipide, and cam in to his hows; and he axide, that

† he dispeiride; Dauyth dispeiride of the helthe of the child bi weye of kynde, not of myracle, and therfor he preyede, for he wiste not, wher God spak bi determynacioun, ether bi manassing. Lire here. c.

Om. E.   to BCEFH.   wasshen c.

ȝyue hem I.   Gloss omitted in I. chapitre bifore K.   haue I.   certis I.   Certis I.   hast made I.   that I.   Dauid I.   dispeiride of the liif of it I.   preiede to c.   he ȝede I.   he lai I.   upon I.   And I.   Om. I.   rise up I.   wolde not I.   And I.   while I.   seen I.   children I.   to speke I.   Om. A.   Om. EFRU.   The whiche I.   roos up I.   weischen I.   his clothis I.

sothe his seruauntys seiden to hym,
What is the word that thou hast doon?
For the litil faunt, whanne he ȝit lyuede,
thou fastidist and weptist; forsothe the
child deed, thou roos and eete breed?
22 The which seith, For the faunt whanne
he ȝit lyuede I fastide and wepte; forsothe I seide, Who woot, if perauenture
the Lord ȝyue hym to me, and the faunt
23 lyue? Forsothe now for he is deed, whi
fast I? whether shal I mowe more ouer
clepe hym aȝen? I shal more goo to
hym, forsothe he shal not turne aȝen to
24 me. And Dauid coumfortide Bersabe, his
wijf, and wente into hir, and slepte with
hir. The which gat a sone, and clepide
the name of hym Salomon; and the
25 Lord louyde hym. And he sente hym
in the hoond of Nathan, the prophet; and
he clepide the name of hym Loueli to
the Lord, forthi that the Lord shulde
26 loue hym. Thanne Joab fauȝt aȝens
Rabath, kyng of the sones of Amon,
and he hath ouercomen the kyngis citee.
27 And Joab sente messagers to Dauid,
seiynge, I haue fouȝten aȝens Rabath,
and the citee of watres is to be taken.
28 Now thanne gadre the tother parti of
the puple, and bisege the citee, and tak
it, lest whanne the citee were wastid of
me, to my name the victorie be ascriued.
29 And so Dauid gadride al the puple, and
wente forth aȝens Rabath; and whanne
30 he hadde fouȝten, he took it. And he
took the diademe fro the mawmet, that is
clepid the kyng of hem, fro his heed, in
weiȝt of gold a talent, hauynge moost
precious gemmys; and it is put vpon the
heed of Dauid; but and ful myche praye
31 of the cyte he bare out. And bryngynge
forth sawede[o] the puple of it, and ladde
about vpon hem boostful yren carris, and
he dyuydide with sharys, and he piȝt
thurȝ in the shap of the sidis; thus he

thei schulden sette breed to hym, and he
eet. Sothely[z] his seruauntis seiden to hym, 21
What is the word which[a] thou hast do?
Thou fastidist[b], and weptist[c] for the ȝong
child, whanne[d] he lyuede ȝit; sotheli[e]
whanne the child was deed, thou risidist[f]
and etist breed? And Dauid seide, Y fast- 22
ide and wepte for the ȝong child, whanne
he lyuyde ȝit; for Y seide†, Who woot, if
perauenture the Lord ȝyue hym to me,
and the ȝong child lyue? 'Now forsothe[g] 23
for he is deed, whi 'fast Y[h]? whether Y
schal mow aȝen clepe hym more? Y schal
'go more to[i] hym, but he schal not turne[k]
aȝen to me. And Dauid coumfortid Ber- 24
sabee, his wijf; and he entride to hir,
and slepte[l] with hir. And sche gendride
a sone, and *Dauid* clepide his name Sa-
lomon‡; and the Lord louyde hym. And 25
he sente Salomon[m] in the hond of Nathan,
the prophete; and he clepide his name
Amyable[n] to the Lord, for the Lord louyde
hym. Therfor[o] Joab fauȝt aȝens Rabath§, 26
of[p] the sones of Amon, and he fauȝt aȝens
the 'kyngis citee[q]. And Joab sente mes- 27
sangeris to Dauid, and seide, Y fauȝte[r]
aȝens Rabath, and the citee of watris
schal be takun. Now therfor gadere thou 28
the tother part of the puple, and bisege
thou the citee, and take thou it, lest
whanne the citee is[s] wastid of me, the
victorie be arettid to my name. Therfor 29
Dauid gaderide[t] al the puple, and he ȝede
forth aȝens Rabath; and whanne he hadde
fouȝte[u], he took it. And he[v] took the dia- 30
deme of the kyng‖ of hem[w] fro his heed,
bi weiȝte[x] a talent of gold, hauynge pre-
ciouseste[y] peerlis; and it was put on[z] the
heed of Dauid, '*that is*[a], *aftir that it was
weldid*[b] *and purgid bi fier*[c]; but also
Dauid bar awey ful myche prey of the[d]
citee. Also[e] he ledde forth the puple ther- 31
of¶, and sawide[f], and 'dide aboute[g] hem
'yrun instrumentis of turment[h], and de-

† *for I seide*; that is, Y thouȝte in myn herte. *Lire here.* c.

‡ *Salomon* is interpretid pesible; and this was of Goddis ordenaunce, for it was schewid to Dauyth, that Salomon schulde regne aftir him, and that he schulde lyue in so greet pees, that he schulde bilde a temple to the Lord, as the Lord bihiȝte to Dauyth, in vii. c°. bifore. *Lire here.* c.

§ *Rabath*; that was the principal citee and the kingis citee, and therfor the king and hise werriours putiden hem silf therinne. *Lire here.* c.

‖ *diademe of the king*; that is, of the idol of hem, which is clepid Melchon, that is interpretid the king of hem. *Lire here.* c.

¶ *the puple, etc.*; that is, not al the puple, but onely hem that ȝauen councel, that dispit schulde be doon to hise messangeris. *Lire here.* c.

[o] sauede *A*.

[z] And I. [a] that I. [b] hast fastid I. [c] wept I. [d] while I. [e] but I. [f] hast risen up I. [g] But now I. [h] schal I faste *for him* I. [i] more rathir go to I. [k] come I. [l] he slepte I. [m] him I. [n] Louely I. [o] Thanne I. [p] the kyng of I. [q] citee of the kyng I. [r] haue fouȝte I. [s] be I. [t] gaderide to gidre I. [u] fouȝte *aȝens that citee* I. [v] Dauid I. [w] Amon I. [x] the weiȝte of I. [y] preciouse ADb. [z] upon I. [a] Om. KX. [b] wellid CDEFGKLMNOPQRSUWXbç. '[c] Gloss omitted in I. [d] that I. [e] And I. [f] he sawide it I. [g] cumpasside I. [h] with iren bounde cartis I.

dide to alle the citees of the sonys of
Amon. And Dauid is turned aȝen, and
alle the oost of hym, into Jerusalem.

CAP. XIII.

1 Forsothe it is doon after thes thingis,
that Amon, the sone of Dauid, louede
the sister of Absolon, the sone of Da-
2 uid, moost fayre, Thamar by name ; and
'peyrede for^p hir ful myche, so that for
the loue of hir he wexe sijk. The which
for she was a mayde, hard to hym it
semede, that eny thing vnhonestly he
3 shulde do with hir. Forsothe there was
to Amon a freende, Jonadab bi name, the
sone of Semaa, brother^q of Dauid, a ful
4 sleiȝ man. The which seide to hym,
Whi thus ert thou waastid bi leenesse,
thou sone of the kyng, bi ech dai ? whi
shewist thou not to me? And Amon
seide to hym, I loue Thamar, the sister
5 of my brother Absolon. To whom answerde Jonadab, Ly vpon thi bedde,
and feyn sijknes ; and whanne thi fader
cometh, that he visite thee, sey to hym,
Come^r, I preye, Thamar^s, my sister^t, that
she ȝyue to me meet, and make sowil^u,
6 that I eete of hyr hoond. And so Amon
laye doun, as thouȝ he wexe sijk. And
whanne the kyng was comen to visite
hym, Amon seith to the kyng, Come,
I preye, Thamar, my sister, that she
make in myn eyen two maner of potagis,
and the^v meet maad redi I take of hir
7 hoond. Thanne Dauid sente to the hous
of Thamar, seiynge, Go in to the hows
of Amon, thi brothir, and mak to hym
8 potage. And Thamar cam into the
hows of Amon, hir brothir. Forsothe he
laye ; the which takynge meele mengide

partideⁱ with knyues, and 'ledde ouer bi
the licnesse of tijl stoonus^k ; so^l he dide
to alle the citees of the sones of Amon.
And Dauid turnede aȝen, and al his oost,
in to Jerusalem.

CAP. XIII.

Forsothe^m it was doon aftir these 1
thingis, that Amon, the sone of Dauid,
louyde the fairesteⁿ sistir, Thamar bi
name, of Absolon, sone^o of Dauid. And 2
Amon perischide^p greetli for hir, so that
he was sijk for 'the loue of hir^q. For
whanne^r she was a virgyn, it semyde hard
to hym, that he schulde do ony thing
vnonestli with hir. Forsothe^s a freend^t, 3
Jonadab bi name, sone^u of Semmaa, bro-
ther^v of Dauid, 'was to Amon^w ; Jonadab^x
was a ful prudent man. Which^y seide to 4
Amon, Sone of the kyng, whi art thou
maad feble so bi leenesse bi alle daies ?
whi schewist thou not to me^z? And
Amon seide to him, Y loue Thamar, the
sister of my brother Absolon. And Jona- 5
dab answeride to hym, Li thou on^a thi
bed, and feyne thou sikenesse ; and whanne
thi fadir cometh, that he visyte thee, seie
thou to hym, Y preye^b, come Thamar, my
sister, that sche ȝyue mete to me, and
make^{bb} a seew, that Y ete^c of hir hond.
Therfor^d Amon lay doun, and 'bigan as^e 6
to be sijk. And whanne the kyng hadde
come to visite him, Amon seide to the
kyng, Y biseche, come Thamar, my sistir,
that sche make twei^f soupyngis bifor my
iȝen, and that Y take of hir hond meete^g
maad redi. Therfor Dauid sente to the 7
hows of Thamar, and seide, Come thou
in to the hows of Amon, thi brother, and
make thou^h seewⁱ to hym. And Thamar 8
cam in to the hows of Amon^k, hir brother.
Sotheli^l he lai^m; and sche took mele, and

p spillede in to E pr. m.   q the brothir E pr. m.   r Om. A.   s that Thamar A.   t sister come A.
u sowfful II.   v Om. A. me B.

1 he departide hem 1.   k in the schapp of her sidis he stikide hem thorouȝ 1.   l thus 1.   m And 1.   n ful
fair 1.   o the sone CDIKMOWXç.   p peiride 1.   q hir loue 1.   r sith 1.   s But ther was 1.   t freend to Amon 1.
u the sone 1.   v the brothir 1.   w Om. 1.   x and Jonadab 1.   y The which 1.   z me thin herte 1.   a upon 1.
b biseeche 1.   bb make sche 1.   c ete it 1.   d Thanne 1.   e feynede 1.   f two maner 1. two L.   g the
meete 1.   h Om. A.   i a seew 1.   k Om. 1.   l And 1.   m lai doun 1.

togidir, and meltynge in his eyen she
9 sethide^w the supettis ; and takynge that
she hadde sothen, she helte out, and sette
before hym, and he wolde not eete. And
Amon seide, Doo ȝe^x a wey alle men^y fro
me. And whanne alle weren doon awey,
10 Amon seide to Thamar, Beer yn the
meet in the priue chaumbre, that I eete
of thin hoond. Thanne Thamar took the
sewis that she hadde maad, and brouȝte
to Amon, hir brother, in the priue chaum-
11 bre. And whanne she hadde brouȝte hym
meet, he cauȝte hir, and seith, Come, ly
12 with me, my sister. The which answerde
to hym, Wole thou not, my brother, wole
thou not oppresse me, ne forsothe it is
leeueful in Irael; wole thou not doo this
13 foli. Forsothe I shal not mowe bere my
reproof, and thou shalt be as oon of the
vnwise men in Irael; but rather spek
to the kyng, and he shal not denye me
14 to thee. Forsothe he wolde not assent to
the preyers of hir, but more myȝti bi
strengthis oppresside hir, and laye with
15 hir. And ful haatsum Amon hadde hir
with to myche greet haate, so that the
haat was more, that he hatide hir, thanne
the loue that he louede hir before. And
16 Amon seide to hir, Ryse, and goo. The
whych answerde to hym, This yuel is
more that thou now dost aȝens me, castynge me out, 'than that^z thou didist be-
17 fore. And he wolde not here hir; but
the child clepide, that seruede to hym, he
seide, Throw out this fro me, and close
18 the dore after hir. The which was
clothid with a coote doun to the heele;
forsothe sich maner clothis vseden the
douȝtris of the kyng maydens. And so
his seruaunt putte hyre out, and closide
19 the dore after hire. The which spryng-
ynge asshen^a to hire heed, the heele coot

medlide^n, and made^o moist bifor hise iȝen,
and sethide^p soupyngis^q; and sche took 9
that, that sche hadde sode, and helde^r out,
and settide^s byfor hym, and he nolde^t ete.
And Amon seide, Putte ȝe out alle men
fro me. And whanne thei hadden put out
alle men, Amon seide to Thamar, Bere the 10
mete in to the closet, that Y ete of thin
hond. Therfor Thamar took the soup-
ingis^u whiche^v sche hadde maad, and
brouȝte in to Amon, hir brother, in the
closet. And whanne sche hadde proferid 11
mete^w to hym, he took hir, and seide,
Come thou, my sistir, liȝ^x thou with me.
And sche answeride to hym, My brother, 12
nyle thou, nyle thou oppresse me, for^y this^z
is not leueful in Israel; nyle thou do this
foli. For^a Y schal not mow bere my schen- 13
schip, and thou schalt be as oon of the
vnwise men in Israel; but rather speke
thou to the kyng, and he schal not denye†
me to thee. Sotheli^b he nolde^c assente 14
to hir preieris; but he was strengere in
myȝtis, and oppresside^d hir, and lay with
hir. And 'Amon hadde hir hateful bi ful 15
grete haterede^e, so that the hatrede was
gretter, bi which he hatide hir, than the
loue bi which he louyde hir bifor. And
Amon seide to hir, Rise thou, and go^f.
And sche answeride to hym, This yuel is 16
more which^g thou doist now aȝens me,
and puttist me out, than that, that thou
didist bifore. And he nolde^h here hir;
but whanne the child was clepide, that 17
mynystride^i to hym, he seide, Putte thou
out this womman fro me, and close thou
the dore aftir hir. And sche was clothid 18
with a coote doun to the heele; for the
kyngis douȝtris virgyns vsiden siche
clothis. Therfor^k the mynystre^l of Amon
puttide^m hir out^n, and closide the dore
aftir hir. And sche spreynte aische^o to 19

† he schal not
denye, etc.
Rabi Salomon
seith, that sche
was not the
kyndly douȝter
of Dauyth, for
whanne Da-
uyth took in
batel hir modir,
sche was with
childe bi hir
formere hose-
bonde, and
aftirward Da-
uyth weddide
hir, bi licence
of the lawe,
therfor Thamar
myȝte be wed-
did to Amon.
Lire here. c.

---

^w seth c.   ^x Om. E pr. m.   ^y Om. E pr. m.   ^z than A. and than BFH.   ^a askes BCEFH.

---

^n medlide to gidre I.   ^o sche made it I.   ^p sche sethide I.   ^q soupinge metis I.   ^r heelde it I.   ^s sette
it I. sette E.   ^t wolde not I.   ^u soupynge mete I.   ^v that I.   ^w the mete I.   ^x and lie A pr. m. I.   ^y certis I.
^z this thing I.   ^a Forsothe I.   ^b But I.   ^c wolde not I.   ^d he oppresside I.   ^e thanne with ful grete
hatred Amon hatide hir I.   ^f go henns I.   ^g that I.   ^h wolde not I.   ^i seruide I.   ^k Thanne I.
^l seruaunt I.   ^m putte IX.   ^n forth I.   ^o asken EL. aiȝashis K.

kyt, and[b] the hoondis put on hire heed,
20 she ȝede goynge yn and criynge. Forsothe Absolon, hir brother, seide to hyre,
Whether Amon, thi brother, hath lyen
with thee? And now, sister, hold thi
pees; thi brothir he is, ne turment thin
herte for this thing. And so[c] Thamar
aboode[d] languysshynge there with ynne
21 the hows of Absolon, hir brothir. Forsothe whanne Dauid hadde herd thes
wordis, he greetli sorwide, and he wolde
not make sori the spirite of Amon, his
sone; for he louide hym, for he was the
22 firste goten of[e] hym. Forsothe Absolon
spak not to Amon, ne yuel ne good; but
Absolon hatide Amon, forthi thnt he
23 hadde defoulid Thamar, his sister. Forsothe it is doon after the tyme of two
ȝeer, that the sheep of Absolon weren
clippid in Baalassor, that is biside Effraym. And Absolon clepide alle the
24 sonys of the kyng. And he cam to the
kyng, and seith to hym, Loo! the sheep
of thi seruaunt ben clippid; come, I
preye, the kyng with his seruauntis to
25 his seruaunt. And the kyng seide to
Absolon, Wole thou not, sone myn, preye,
wole thou not, that we comen alle, and
greuen thee. Forsothe whanne he constreynede him, and wolde not come, he
26 blesside to hym. And Absolon seith to
Dauid, If thou wolt not come, come algate
with vs, I biseche, Amon, my brother.
And the kyng seide to hym, It is no
27 nede, that he goo with thee. And so
Absolon constreynede hym; and he lafte
with hym Amon, and alle the sones of
the kyng. And Absolon made a feest a
28 the feest of a kyng. Forsothe Absolon
hadde comaundid to his children, seiynge, Weitith wel, whanne Amon were
dronken with wyn, and I shal seye to
ȝou, Smitith hym, and sleeth. Wole ȝe
not drede, forsothe I am that comaunde

hir heed, whanne the coote to 'the heele[p]
was to-rent, and whanne[q] the[r] hondis
weren[s] put on hir heed, and[t] sche ȝede
entrynge and criynge. Forsothe[u] Absolon, 20
hir brother, seide to hir, Whether Amon,
thi brothir, hath leyn with thee? But
'now, sister, be stille[v]; he is thi brother,
and turmente[w] not thin herte for this
thing. Therfor Thamar dwellide morenynge in the hows of Absolon, hir brothir.
Forsothe[x] whanne 'kyng Dauid[y] hadde 21
herd these wordis, he was ful sori, and
he nolde[z] make sore the spyrit of Amon†,
his sone; for he louyde Amon, for he was
the[a] firste gendrid[b] 'to hym[c]. Forsothe[d] 22
Absolon spak not to Amon, nether yuel
nether[e] good; for Absolon hatide Amon,
for he hadde defoulid Thamar, his sistir.
Forsothe[f] it was doon aftir the tyme of 23
twei ȝeer, that the scheep of Absolon
weren shorun in Baalasor, which[g] is bisidis Effraym. And Absolon clepide alle
the sones of the kyng. And he cam to 24
the kyng, and seide to hym, Lo! the
scheep of thi seruaunt ben schorun; Y
preye, come the king with hise seruauntis
to his seruaunt. And the kyng seide to 25
Absolon, Nyle thou, my sone, nyle thou
preye, that alle we come, and greeue[h] thee.
Forsothe[i] whanne he constreynede‡ Dauid,
and he nolde[k] go, he blesside Absolon.
And Absolon seide to Dauid, If thou nylt[l] 26
come, Y byseche[m], come nameli Amon, my
brother, with vs. And the kyng seide to
hym, It is no nede, that he go with thee.
Therfor Absolon constreynede hym[n]; and 27
he delyuerede with him Amon, and alle
the sones of the kyng. And Absolon
hadde maad a feeste as the feeste of a
kyng. Sotheli[o] Absolon comaundide to 28
hise children, and seide, Aspie ȝe, whanne
Amon is drunkun of wyn, and Y[p] seie to
ȝou, Smyte ȝe, and slo[q] hym. Nyle ȝe drede,
for Y am that comaunde§ to ȝou; be ȝe

† he nolde
make sori the
spirit of Amon;
for that tyme,
for he was
feble, slyk, and
soreuful for the
dede, but he
repreuyde
Amon afftir-
ward in due
tyme; and he
killide not
Amon for this
violence, for
it was not
preued, and
he compellide
not Amon to
wedde hir, for
the hatrede, and
for drede of
deth. Lire
here. c.

‡ he constreyn-
ede, etc.; that
is, mekely
preyede his
fadir. Lire
here. c.

§ Y am that
comaunde; us
if he seide, Y
take the dede
on me, and
Y schal de-
fende ȝou.
Lire here. c.

b Om. A.　　c loo BEF.　　d bod c. boid E. boode BFH.　　e to BCEFH.

p hir long coote I.　　q Om. I.　　r hir I.　　s Om. I.　　t Om. I.　　u And I.　　v thou now stille, sistir I.
w turmente thou I.　　x And I.　　y the kyng Dauid I.　　z wolde not I.　　a his I.　　b bygoten sone I.　　c Om. I.
d And I.　　e ne KILP.　　f And I.　　g that I.　　h charge I.　　i And I.　　k wolde not I.　　l wilt not I.
m byseche thee I.　　n Dauid I.　　o And I.　　p whanne Y I.　　q sleeth I.

to 30u; be 3e maad stronge, and beth
29 stronge men. Thanne the children[f] of
Absolon diden a3ens Amon, as Absolon
hadde comaundid to hem; and alle the
sones of the kyng rysynge, eche styede
30 vpon her mulis, and flowen. And whanne
3it thei wenten in the weye, fame cam
fulli to Dauyd, seiynge, Absolon hath
smytyn alle the sones of the kyng, and
31 there lafte not of hem nameli oone. And
so the kyng roos, and kytte his clothis,
and felle vpon the erthe; and alle his
seruauntis that stoden ny3 to hym, cut-
32 ten her clothis. Forsothe Jonadab, the
sone of Semmaa, brother[g] of Dauid, answerynge seide, Ne eyme, my lord the
kyng, that alle the children, sones of the
kyng, ben deed; Amon alone is deed, for
in haat Absolon was sett, fro the day that
33 he oppresside Thamar, his sister. Now
thanne, my lord kyng, sette not on his
herte this word, seiynge, Alle the sones
of the kyng ben slayn; for Amon aloon
34 is deed. Forsothe Absolon flei3. And
the child weyter heuede vp his eyen, and
bihelde, and loo! myche puple cam bi
the out weye fro the side of the hil.
35 And Jonadab seide to the kyng, Loo!
the sones of the kyng ben ny3; after the
36 word of thi seruaunt, so it is doon. And
whanne he hadde cesside to speke, 'aperiden and the sones of the kyng[h]; and
comynge yn thei rereden her vois, and
wepten; but and the kyng and alle his
seruauntis wepten with ful myche greet
37 wepynge. Forsothe Absolom fleynge
wente to Tholamay, sone of Amyur,
kyng of Gethsur. Thanne Dauid weyl-
38 ide Amon, his sone, manye daies. Forsothe Absolon, whanne he was flowen,
and comen into Gethsur, he was there
39 thre 3eer. And kyng Dauid cesede to
pursue Absolon, forthi that he was
coumfortid vpon the deeth of Amon.

strengthid, and be 3e stronge men. Ther-29
for the children of Absolon diden a3ens
Amon, as Absolon hadde comaundide to
hem; and alle the sones of the kyng
risiden[r], and stieden ech on[s] his mule,
and fledden. And whanne thei 3eden 3it 30
in the weie, fame cam[t] to the kyng, and
seide[u], Absolon hath kild[v] alle the sones
of the king, and 'nameli not oon lefte[w] of
hem. Therfor the kyng roos[x], and to-31
rente hise clothis, and felde doun on[y] the
erthe; and alle hise seruauntis that stoden
ny3 to hym, to-renten her clothis. Sotheli[z] 32
Jonadab, sone[a] of Semmaa, brother of Dauid, answeride and seide, My lord the[b]
kyng, gesse[c] not, that alle the children, and
sones of the kyng, ben slayn; Amon aloone
is deed, for he was set in hatrede to Absolon, fro the day in which he oppresside
Thamar, his sistir. Now therfor, my lord 33
the[d] kyng, set[e] not this word on[f] his
herte, and seie, Alle the sones of the
kyng ben slayn; for Amon aloone is deed.
Forsothe[g] Absolon fledde. And a child 34
aspiere[h] reiside[i] hise i3en, and bihelde, and
lo! myche puple cam bi a weye out of the
comyn weie bi the side of the[k] hil. And 35
Jonadab seide to the kyng, Lo! the sones
of the kyng comen; bi[l] the word of thi
seruaunt, so it is doon. And whanne he 36
hadde ceessid to speke, also the sones of
the kyng apperiden; and thei entriden,
and reisiden[m] her vois, and wepten; but
also the kyng and alle his seruauntis
wepten bi[n] ful greet wepyng. Forsothe[o] 37
Absolon fledde, and 3ede[p] to Tholmai,
sone[q] of Amyur, the kyng of Gessur.
Therfor Dauid biweilide his sone Amon
in many daies. Forsothe[r] Absolon, whanne 38
he hadde fled, and hadde come in to[s] Gessur, was[t] there thre 3eer. And Dauid 39
ceesside to pursue Absolon, for he was
coumfortid on[u] the deeth of Amon.

---

[f] childer cE.   [g] the brother E pr. m.   [h] the sones of the kyng aperiden A.

[r] resen up I. resen E.   [s] upon I.   [t] cam therof I.   [u] it was seid I.   [v] sleyn I.   [w] he hath not left
nameli oon I.   [x] roos up I.   [y] upon I.   [z] But I.   [a] the sone I.   [b] Om. I.   [c] gesse thou I.   [d] Om. I.
[e] set he I.   [f] upon I.   [g] Certis I.   [h] spiere A pr. m. DIMPX sec. m. b5.   [i] reiside up I.   [k] an I.   [l] aftir I.
[m] reisiden up I.   [n] with I.   [o] And I.   [p] he 3ede I.   [q] the sone I.   [r] And I.   [s] Om. I.   [t] he was I.
[u] upon I.

CAP. XIV.

1 Forsothe Joab, the sone of Saruy, vndurstondynge, that the herte of the 2 kyng was turned to Absolon, he sente to Thekuam, and took thens a wise womman, and he seide to hir, Feyne thee to weil, and be clothid with the weilynge clooth, and be thou not anoynt with oyle, that thou be as a womman now myche tyme weilynge the deed. 3 And thou shalt goo in to the kyng, and thou shalt speek to hym thes maner wordis. Forsothe Joab putte the wordis 4 in hire mouth. And so whanne the Thekuyd womman was goon out to the kyng, she felle before hym vpon the erthe, and lowtide, and seide, Keep me, thou king. 5 And the kyng seide to hire, What hast thou of cause? The which answerde, Alas! a womman widewe I am, forsothe 6 my man is deed; and of thin hoond womman weren two sones, the whiche wraththeden aȝens hem self in the feeld, and no man was that hem myȝte defende, and the toon[i] smoot the tother, 7 and slowȝ hym. And loo! al the kynrede risynge aȝens thin hoond womman seith, Tak hym that hath smytyn his brothir, that we sleen hym for the lijf of his brother whom he slowȝ, and the eyr doo we a wey; and thei sechen to quench my spark that is laft, that there be not laft name to my man, and relikis 8 vpon erthe. And the kyng seith to the womman, Go into thin hows, and I shal 9 ordeyn for thee. And the Thekuyt womman seide to the kyng, In me, my lord kyng, be this wickidnes, and into the hows of my fader; forsothe the kyng 10 and his trone be innocent. And the king seith, Who so[k] aȝen seith[l] thee, bryng hym to me, and he shal no more 11 adde that he touche thee. The which seith, The kyng recoorde of the Lord

CAP. XIV.

Forsothe Joab, the sone of Saruye, 1 vndirstood, that the herte of the kyng was turned to Absolon; and he sente to 2 Thecua, and took[v] fro thennus a wise womman, and he seide to hir, Feyne thee to morene, and be thou clothid with clooth[w] of duyl[x], and be thou anoyntid[xx] with oile, that thou be[y] as a womman by morenynge[z] 'now in[a] ful myche tyme a deed man. And thou schalt entre to the kyng, 3 and thou schalt speke to hym siche[b] wordis. Sotheli[c] Joab puttide[d] the wordis in hir mouth. Therfor whanne the wom- 4 man of Thecua hadde entrid to the kyng, sche felde bifor hym on the erthe, and worschipide, and seide, A[e]! kyng, kepe[f] me. And the kyng seide to hir, What hast 5 thou of[g] cause? And sche answeride, Alas! Y am a womman widewe, for[h] myn hosebonde is deed; and tweyne sones 6 weren of[i] thin handmayde, whiche[k] debatiden aȝens hem silf in the feeld, and 'noon was[l] that myȝte forbede hem, and oon[m] smoot 'the tother[n], and killide hym. And lo! al the kynrede risith aȝens thin 7 handmayde, and seith, Ȝyue thou hym[o] that killide his brothir, that we sle hym for the lijf of his brother whom he killide, and that we do awei the eir; and thei seken to quenche my sparcle whych[p] is lefte, that name[q] dwelle not to myn hosebonde, and relikis[r], 'ethir remenauntis[s], be not to him on erthe. And the kyng seide 8 to the womman, Go in to thin hows, and Y schal comaunde for thee. And the 9 womman of Thecua seide to the kyng, My lord the kyng, this wickidnesse be on met, and on the hows of my fadir; forsothe the kyng and his trone be innocent[t]. And the kyng seide, Brynge thou hym to 10 me, that aȝenseith thee, and he schal no more adde[u] that he touche thee. And 11 sche seide, The kyng haue mynde on[v] his

† *this wickidnesse be on me;* Ebrews seyen thus, and wel as it semeth, My lord the kyng, for many causis and harde, thou mayst forȝete this cause, and thanne this wickidnesse schal be in me and in myn hows, and my sone schal be slayn of men sekinge his blood, and thou schalt be innocent, for this schal be doon with out thyn entent; as if she seide, Plese it more to thee to conferme this with an ooth, and to make sikur me and my sone, therfor the kyng seide at the laste, *the Lord lyueth, that is,* Y swere to thee bi the Lord *lyuynge for noon of the heeris, etc.* Lire here c.

i tother DCEFH. k Om. DCEFH. l seith to c.

v he took I. w a clooth I. x deyl K. deol L. doel M. deel K. xx not anoyntid c sec. m. y he now I. z mournynge I. a Om. I. b siche manere I. c And I. d putte I. e O I. f kepe thou I. g Om. I. h Certis I. i to I. k the whiche I. l ther was no man I. m the oon I. the toon K. n that other I. o hym to us I. p that I. q the name I. r that remenauntis I. s Om. I. t thei gitlees I. u adde to I. v of I.

his God, and be there not multiplied 'the kyn^m of the blood to wreche, and thei shulen not sle my sone. The which seith, The Lord lyueth, for there shal not falle of the erys of thi sone 12 vpon the erthe. Thanne the womman seyde, Spek thin hoond womman to my lord kyng a word. And he seith, Spek. 13 And the womman seide, Whi hast thou thou3t siche a maner thing a3ens the puple of God? and the kyng hath spoken this word, that he synne, and that he brynge 14 not a3en his casten out? Alle we dyen, and as watres we sliden into the erthe, that shulen not be turned a3en; and God wole not perishe the lijf, but withdraw-ith, thenkynge lest fulli he perishe, that 15 is cast^n awey. Now thanu come, that I spek to my lord kyng this word, pre-sent the puple; and thin hondwomman seide, I shal speke to the kyng, if eny maner the kyng doo the word of his 16 hoond womman. And the kyng herde 'the word^o, that he delyuer his hond-womman fro the hoond of alle, that wolden fro the erytage of the Lord doo 17 me awey, and my sone togidre. Sey thanne thin hondwomman, that the word of my lord the kyng be maad as sacri-fice; forsothe as the aungel of the Lord, so is my lord kyng^p, that nether bi blessynge ne bi cursynge he be meuyd. Wherfor and the Lord thi God is with 18 thee. And the kyng answerynge seide to the womman, Ne hijd thou fro me the word that I aske. And the wom-man seide to hym, Spek, my lord kyng. 19 And the kyng seith, Whether the hoond of Joab is with thee in alle these? The womman answerde, and seith, Bi the helth of thi soule, my lord kyng, ne at the left ne at the ri3t he is of alle thes thingis, the whiche my lord kyng^p hath spoken. Forsothe thi seruaunt Joab he comaundide to me, and he putte in the

Lord God, and the nexte men of blood to take veniaunce be^w not multiplied, and 'thei schulen not sle^y my sone. And the kyng seide, The Lord lyueth, for noon of the heeris of thi sone schal falle on^z the^a erthe. Therfor the womman seide, Thin 12 handmayde speke a word to^b my lord the^c kyng. And the kyng seide, Speke thou. And the womman seide, Whi 13 'thou3tist thou^d sich a thing a3ens the puple of God? and the^e kyng spak^f this word, that he do synne, and brynge not a3en his *sone* cast^g out? Alle we dyen, 14 and as watris that schulen not turne a3en, we sliden in to erthe^h; and God nyl^i that a soule perische, but he withdrawith, and thenkith lest he perische outirly, which^k is cast awey. Now therfor come thou, 15 that Y speke to my lord the^l kyng this word, while the puple is present†; and thin handmaide seide, Y schal speke to the kyng, if in ony maner the kyng do the word of his handmayde. And the 16 kyng herde the wordis, that he schulde delyuere his handmayde fro the hondis of alle men, that wolden do awei me, and my sone togidere^m, fro the eritage of the Lord. Therfor thin hand mayde seie, 17 that the word of my lord the kyng be maad as sacrifice, '*that is, that the sen-tence 3onun of hym be plesaunt to God, as sacrifice plesith^n God^o*; for as an aungel of the Lord, so is my lord the kyng, that he be not mouyd bi blessyng nether bi cursyng. Wherfor and thi Lord God is with thee. And the kyng 18 answeride, and seide to the womman, Hide thou not fro me the word which Y axe thee. And the womman seide to hym, Speke thou, my lord the^p kyng. And the kyng seide, Whether the hond 19 of Joab is with thee in alle these thingis? The womman answeride, and seide, Bi the helthe of thi soule, my lord the kyng, nether to the left side nether to the ri3t

† *while the pu-ple is present;* that is, that the sentence 3onun for me and for my sone, which is couferned bi thyn ooth, be puppßschid bi-for the puple, and that it haue the same effect, in thee and in thi sone. *Lire here.* c.

^m ne3ebores E *pr. m.* ^n past A.   ^o Om. E *pr. m.*   ^p the kyng CE.

^w be thei I. ^y sle thei not I. ^z upon I. ^a Om. KX *pr.m.* ^b to thee I. ^c Om. I. ^d hast thou thou3t I. ^e whi hath the I. ^f spoke I. ^g throwen I. ^h the erthe I. ^i wil not I. ^k that I. ^l Om. I. ^m bothe I. ^n *plesith to* GQb. '^o Gloss omitted in I. ^p Om. I.

mouth of thin hoond womman alle thes
20 wordis, that I turne the figure of this
word; forsothe thi seruaunt Joab comaundide this. Forsothe thou, my lord
kyng, ert wise, as the aungel of God
hath wisdom, that thou vndirstonde alle
21 thingis vpon erthe. And the kyng seith
to Joab, Loo! plesid I haue doo thi
word; go thanne, and cleep aȝen the
22 child Absolon. And Joab fallynge vpon
his face into the erthe, honourde, and
blisside to the kyng; and Joab seide, To
dai hath thi seruaunt vndurstonde, for I
haue foundun grace in thin eyen, my
lord kyng; forsothe thou hast doon the
23 word of thi seruaunt. Thanne Joab
roos, and wente into Gethsur, and
24 brouȝte Absolon into Jerusalem. Forsothe the kyng seide, Turne he aȝen into
25 his hows, and se he not my face. And
so Absolon is turned aȝen into his hows,
and the face of the kyng he sawȝ not.
Forsothe there was not a man as feyr
as Absolon in al Irael, and ful miche
semeli; fro the stap of the foot vnto the
top, there was not in hym eny spot;
26 and the more that he doddide the heeris,
so mych more thei wexen; forsothe
onys in the ȝeer he was doddid, for the
heere heuyde hym. He weiede the heeris
of his heed with two hundred siclis bi
27 the comoun weiȝt. Forsothe there been
born to Absolon thre sones, aud o douȝter, Thamar bi name, of sembli shap.
28 And Absolon dwellide in Jerusalem two
ȝeer, and sawȝ not the face of the kyng.
29 And so he sente[r] to Joab, that he shulde
sende hym to the kyng; the which
wolde not come to hym. And whanne
the secounde he hadde sent, and he wold
30 not come, he seide to his seruauntis, Ȝe
knowen the feelde of Joab biside my
feelde hauynge barli corn; gooth thanne,
and brenneth it vp with fier. Thanne

side is *ony thing* of alle these thingis,
whiche my lord the kyng spak[q]. For thi
seruaunt Joab hym silf comaundide to me,
and he puttide[r] alle these wordis in to the
mouth of thin handmaide, that Y schulde 20
turne the figure of this word; for thi
seruaunt Joab comaundide this thing[s].
Forsothe[t] thou, my lord the[u] kyng, art
wijs, as an aungel of God hath[v] wisdom,
that thou vnderstonde alle thingis on[w]
erthe. And the kyng seide to Joab, Lo! 21
Y am plesid, and Y haue do thi word;
therfor go thou, and aȝen clepe thou the
child Absolon. And Joab felde on[x] his 22
face to erthe[y], and worschipide[z], and
blesside the kyng; and Joab seide, Thi
seruaunt hath vndirstonde to dai, that
Y foond[a] grace in thin iȝen, my lord the[b]
kyng, for thou hast do the word of thi
seruaunt. Therfor Joab roos[c], and ȝede 23
in to Gessur, and brouȝte Absolon in to
Jerusalem. Forsothe[d] the kyng seide, 24
Turne he aȝen in to his hows, and se not
he my face. Therfor Absolon turnede 25
aȝen in to his hows, and siȝ not the face
of the kyng. Sotheli no man in al Israel
was so fair as Absolon, and ful comeli; fro
the step of the foot 'til to[e] the top, 'no
wem was[f] in hym; and in as myche as 'he 26
clippide[g] more the[h] heeris, bi so myche[i]
thei[k] wexiden more[l]; forsothe[m] he was
clippid onys in the ȝeer†, for the[n] heer
greuede him. And whanne he clippide
the heeris[o], he weiȝide 'the heeris of his
heed[p] bi[q] twei hundrid siclis with[r] comyn
weiȝte. Forsothe[s] thre sones, and a douȝ- 27
ter, Thamar bi name, of 'excellent forme[t]
weren borun to Absolon. And Absolon 28
dwellide in Jerusalem twei ȝeer, and he
siȝ not the face of the kyng. Therfor he 29
sente to Joab, that he schulde sende
hym to the kyng; which[u] Joab nolde[v]
come to hym. And whanne he[w] hadde
sent the secounde tyme, and Joab nolde[x]

† *onys in the ȝeer*, in Ebreu it is, in tyme determynd. c.

[r] wente B.

[q] hath spoke I. [r] hath put to I. [s] thing *to me* I. [t] Certis I. [u] Om. I. [v] that hath I. [w] upon I. [x] upon I. [y] the erthe I. [z] he worschipide I. [a] haue founden I. [b] Om. I. [c] roos up I. [d] And I. [e] vnto I. [f] ther was no wem I. [g] thei clippiden G. [h] his I. [i] myche the more I. [k] tho nc. [l] Om. I. [m] but I. [n] his I. [o] heeris of his heed I. [p] hem I. [q] with I. [r] bi AX *pr.m.* [s] And I. [t] semely schap I. [u] and I. [v] wolde not I. [w] Absolon I. [x] wolde not I.

the seruauntis of Absolon brenten the
corn with fier. And the seruauntis of
Joab comynge, her clothis kut, seiden,
The seruauntis of Absolon han brent vp a
31 partie of the feelde with fier. And Joab
roos, and cam to Absolon into his hows,
and seide, Whi han thi seruauntis brente
32 vp my corn with fier? And Absolon
answerde to Joab, I haue sente to thee,
preiynge that thou come to me, and I
sende thee to the kyng, that thou seie
to hym, Whi cam I fro Gethsur? Betere
it was to me to be there; I biseche
thanne, that I see the face of the kyng,
that if he haue mynde of my shrewidnes,
33 he slee me. Joab goon yn to the kyng
tolde to hym. And Absolon clepid
wente yn to the kyng, and he lowtide
upon the face of the erthe before hym,
and the kyng kisside Absolon.

CAP. XV.

1 Thanne after thes thingis Absolon
made to hym a chaar, and horsmen,
and fifti men that shulden goo before
2 hymª. And eerli risynge Absolon stood
biside the entre of the ʒate in the weye;
and eche man, that hadde a neede that
he com to the dom of the kyng, Absolon
clepide to hym self, and seide, Of what
citee ert thou? The which answerynge seide, Of aᵗ lynage of Yrael I am,
3 thi seruaunt. And Absolon answerde
to hym, To me thi wordis semen good
and iust, but there is not ʼthe whichᵘ ʼthee
heere ordeynedᵛ of the kyng. And Abso-
4 lon seide, Who ordeyneth me domesman
vpon the loond, that to me comen alle
that han neede, and riʒtwisly Y deme?
5 But whanne a man neiʒede to hym for to
salute hym, he strauʒte out his hoond,
6 and takynge he kisseᵂ hym; and that

come, Absolon seide to hise seruauntis, ʒe 30
knowen the feeld of Joab bisidis my feeld
hauynge ripe barli; therfor go ʒe, and
brenne ʒe it with fier. Therfor the ser-
uauntis† of Absolon brenten the corn with
fier. And the seruauntis of Joab camen
with her clothis to-rent, and seiden, The seruauntis of Absolon han brent theⁱ part of 31
feeldᶻ biª fier. And Joab roosᵇ, and cam to
Absolon in to his hows, and seide, Whi
han thi seruauntis brent my corn biᶜ fier? 32
And Absolon answeride to Joab, Y sente
to thee, and bisouʒte that thou schuldist
come to me, and that Y schulde sende
thee to the kyng, that thou schuldist
seie to hym, Whi cam Y fro Gessur?
It was betere to me to beᵈ there; therfor
Y biseche, that Y se the face of the kyng,
that if he is myndeful of my wickidnesse,
sle he me. Joab entride to the kyng, 33
and telde to hym. And Absolon was
clepid, and entrydeᵉ to the kyng, and
worschipideᶠ on the face of ertheᵍ bifor
hym, and the kyng kisside Absolon.

CAP. XV.

Therfor aftir these thingis Absolon 1
made a chaar to hym, and knyʒtis, and
fifti men, that schulden go bifor hym.
And Absolon roos eerli, and stood bisidis 2
the entryng of the ʒate in the weie; and
Absolon clepide to hym ech man, that
hadde a cause that he schulde come to
the doom of the kyng, and Absolon seide,
Of whatʰ citee art thou? Which answeride, and seide, Of oⁱ lynage of Israel Y
am, thi seruaunt. And Absolon answer- 3
ide to hym, Thi wordis semen to me good
and iust, but noon is ordeyned of the
kyng to here thee. And Absolon seide, 4
Who schal ordeyne me iuge on the lond,
that alle men that han cause come to me,
and Y deme iustly? But whanne a man cam 5
to Absolon to greete hym, he helde forth
theᵏ hond, and took, and kisside that
man; and Absolon dide this to al Israel, 6

† and the seru-
auntis, etc.;
this vers til
thidur and Joab
roos, is not in
Ebreu. c.

ª Om. D.　ᵗ oon DEF. o c. one II.　ᵘ that c pr.m.　ᵛ ordeyn thee heere A.　ᵂ kiste E.

ⁱ a I.　ᶻ the feeld c. thi feeld I.　ª with I.　ᵇ roos up I.　ᶜ with I.　ᵈ haue be I.　ᵉ he entryde K.
ᶠ he worschipide I.　ᵍ the erthe I.　ʰ which A.　ⁱ a I.　ᵏ his I.

he dide to al Yrael, the which cam to dom that he were herd of the king; and he biside the hertis of the men of Yrael. 7 Forsothe aftir fourti ʒeer Absolon seide to kyng Dauid, I shal go, and ʒeelde my vowis, that I vowide to the Lord in 8 Ebron; forsothe vowynge thi seruaunt vowide, whanne he was in Gethsur of Syrie, seiynge, If the Lord brynge me aʒen into Jerusalem, I shal sacrifie^x to 9 the Lord. And the kyng seide to hym, Goo in pees. And he roos, and wente 10 into Ebron. Forsothe Absolon sente a-spies into alle the lynagis of Yrael, seiynge, Anoon^y that ʒe heren the noyse of the trumpe, seith, Absolon shal regne 11 in Ebron. Forsothe with Absolon wenten two hundred men clepid of Jerusalem^yy, goynge with symple herte, and the cause 12 fulli vnknowynge. Forsothe Absolon clepide Achitophel Gilonyte, the coun-selour of Dauid, fro his cite Gilo. And whanne he hadde offrid slayn sacrifice, there is maad a strong coniurysoun, and the puple rennynge togidre encreside 13 with Absolon. Thanne cam a messager to Dauid, seiynge, With al the herte al 14 Yrael folowith Absolon. And Dauid seith to his seruauntis that weren with hym in Jerusalem, Risith, and flee we; forsothe ne there shal be to vs fliʒt fro the face of Absolon; hieth to goon out, lest perauenture he comynge ocupie vs, and fulfille vpon vs fallynge, and smyte the 15 cite in mouth^z of swerd^a. And the ser-uauntis of the kyng seiden to hym, Alle thingis, what euere comaundith oure lord the kyng, gladli we folowen out, 16 thi seruauntis. Thanne the kynge wente out, and al hys hows, on her feet; and the kyng lafte ten sccoundarie wyues to 17 the hows to be kept. And the kyng goon out, and al Yrael, on her feet, stoode 18 afer fro the hows. And alle his ser-uauntis wenten biside hym, and the

that cam to doom to be herd of the kyng; and Absolon drow^l aweit^m the hertis of men of Israel. Forsothe^n aftir foure ʒeer‡7 Absolon seide to kyng Dauid, Y schal go, and Y^o schal ʒelde my vowis, whiche Y vowide to the Lord in Ebron§; for this 8 seruaunt vowynge vowide, whanne he was in Gessur of Sirie, and seide^p, If the Lord bryngith aʒen me in to Jerusalem, Y schal make sacrifice to the Lord. And 9 the kyng seide to hym, Go thou in pees. And Absolon roos^q, and ʒede in to Ebron. Forsothe^r Absolon sente aspieris in to al 10 the lynage of Israel, and seide, Anoon as ʒe heren the sown of clarioun, seye ʒe, Absolon schal regne in Ebron. Forsothe^s 11 twei hundrid men clepid of Jerusalem ʒeden ^t with Absolon, and ʒede with sym-ple herte, and outirli thei knewen not the cause. Also Absolon clepide Achitofel 12 of Gilo, the councelour of Dauid, fro his citee Gilo. And whanne he^u offride^v sacri-fices^w a strong swerynge togidere was maad, and the puple rennynge togidere was encreessid with Absolon. Therfor 13 a messanger cam to Dauid, and seide, With al herte al Israel sueth Absolon. And Dauid seide to hise seruauntis that 14 weren with hym in Jerusalem, Rise ʒe^x, and flee we‖; for noon ascaping schal be to us fro the face of Absolon¶; therfor^y haste ʒe to go out, lest he come, and ocupie vs, and fille^z on^a vs fallynge^b, and smyte the citee bi^c the^d scharpnesse of swerd. And the seruauntis of the kyng 15 seiden to hym, We thi seruauntis schulen performe gladli alle thingis, what euer thingis^e oure lord the^f kyng schal com-aunde. Therfor^g the kyng ʒede out, and 16 al his hous, on^h her feet; and the king lefte ten^i wymmen concubyns^k, *that is*, *secundarie wyues*^m, to kepe the^n hous. And the king ʒede out, and al Israel, on^o her 17 feet, and the kyng stood fer fro the^p hous. And alle hise seruauntis ʒeden bisidis 18

x sacrificen DCFII. y Anoon forsothe E pr. v. yy the Jerusalem A. z the mouth H. a the swerd E.

l to him I. m Om. I. n But I. o Om. EC. p I seide I. q roos up I. r And I. s And I. t ʒeden forth I. u Absolon I. v had offrid I. w sacrifice I. x ʒe up I. y sothely I. z fulfille I. a Om. A. upon I. b his fallynge I. c with I. d Om. I. e Om. I. f Om. I. g Thanne I. h upon I. i his ten I. k Om. I, l Om. EIPX. m Om. EPX. n his I. o upon I. p his I.

legiouns Cerethi and Pherethi, and al Gethei stronge fiȝters, the sexe hundrid men, that hadden folwid hym fro Geth 19 on foot, wenten before the kyng. Forsothe the kyng seide to Ethei Gethee, Whi comyst thou with vs? Turn aȝen, and dwel with the kyng for a pilgrime thou art, and wentist out fro thi place. 20 ȝisterday[b] thou cam, and to day thou ert compellid to goo out with vs. Forsothe I shal goo, whider I am to goo; turn aȝen, and leede aȝen with thee thi britheren, and the Lord doo with thee merci and trewth, for thou hast shewid grace and 21 feith. And Ethei answerde to the kyng, seiynge, The Lord lyueth, and my lord the kyng lyueth, for in what euere place thou were, my lord kyng, other in deeth or in lijf, there shal be thi seruaunt. 22 And Dauid seith to Ethai, Come, and passe forth. And Ethei Gethee passide forth, and the kyng, and alle the men that with hym weren, and the tother 23 multitude. And alle thei wepten with a greet voys, and al the puple passide forth; the kyng forsothe wente ouer the streem of Cedron, and al the puple wente aȝens the weye of the olyne, that bihold- 24 ith to deseert. And Sadoch the preest cam, and alle the Leuytis with hym, berynge the arke of the boond of pees of God, and thei setten doun the arke of God; and Abiathar stiede vp, to the tyme that alle the puple weren[c] ful comen that 25 was goon out fro the citee. And the kyng seide to Sadoch, Beer aȝen the arke of God into the citee; if I shal fynde grace in the eyen of the Lord, he shal leede me aȝen, and shewe to me it and 26 his tabernacle. Forsothe if he shal seye, Thou plesist not to me; prest I am, do 27 he that is good before hym. And the kyng seide to Sadoch the preest, O seere[d], turne aȝen into the cite in pees, and

him, and the legiouns of Cerethi[q] and of[r] Ferethi[s], and alle men[t] of Geth 'strong fiȝters[u], sixe hundrid men, that sueden him fro Geth, ȝeden on foote bifor the 19 kyng†. Forsothe[v] the kyng seide to Ethai of Geth, Whi comest thou with vs? Turne thou aȝen, and dwelle with the kyng, for thou art a pilgrym, and thou[w] 20 ȝedist out fro thi place. Thou camest ȝis- tirdai, and to dai thou art compellid to go out with vs. Sotheli[x] Y schal go, whi- dur Y schal go; turne aȝen, and lede aȝen thi britheren with thee, and the Lord do mercy and treuthe with thee, for thou 21 schewidist[y] grace and feith. And Ethai answeride to the kyng, and seide, The Lord lyueth, and my lord the kyng lyueth, for in what euer place thou schalt be, my lord the[z] kyng, ether in deeth ethir in lijf, 22 there thi seruaunt schal be. And Dauid seide to Ethay, Come thou, and passe[a]. And Ethai of Geth passide[b], and the kyng, and alle men that weren with hym, 23 and the tother multitude. And alle men wepten with greet vois, and al the puple passide[c]; and the kyng ȝede ouer the stroud of Cedron, and al the puple ȝede aȝens the weie of the olyue tree, that bi- 24 holdith to deseert[d]. Forsothe[e] and Sadoch the preest cam[f], and alle the dekenes with hym, and thei baren[g] the arke of hoond of pees of God, and thei diden[h] doun the arke of God; and Abiathar stiede[i], til al the puple was passid[k] that ȝede out of the 25 citee. And the kyng seide to Sadoch, Bere aȝen the arke of God in to the citee; if Y schal fynde grace in the iȝen of the Lord, he schal lede me aȝen, and he schal schewe to me that arke and his taber- 26 nacle. Sotheli if the Lord seith[l], Thou plesist not me[m]; Y am redi‡, do he that, 27 that is good bifor hym silf. And the kyng seide to Sadoch, preest[n], Ao! thou seere, 'that is, profete[p], turne aȝen in to

of Absolon; not for the vertu of him, but of God, whose scourge he was, to the punysching of Dauyth. Lire here. c.

† bifor the king; Dauyth made al his puple to go bifor him, that he schulde putte him silf in the grettere perel, if Absolon pursuede him; he dide this, for he was in synne, and othere men suffriden not, no but for him. Lire here. c.

‡ Y am redi; that is, to resseyue fleing, exiling and deth, that the good plesaunce of God be fillid. Lire here. c.

b ȝistai c et e passim.   c was a.   d sire a. seare c. sere fii.

q archers i.   r Om. cqxb.   s alblasters i.   t the stronge fiȝtinge men i.   u Om. i.   v And i.   w Om. i. x certis i.   y hast schewid to me i.   z Om. i.   a passe forth i.   b passide forth i.   c passide forth i. d the deseert i.   e Certis i.   f cam forth i.   g baren forth with hem i.   h settiden i.   i stiede up i. k passid forth i.   l schal sey i.   m Om. d.   n the preest i.   o O i.   p Om. i. that is, a profete k.

Achymaas, thi sone, and Jonathan, the
sone of Abiathar, ʒoure two sonys, be thei
28 with ʒou. Loo! I shal be hid in the
wijlde feeldis of deseert, to the tyme that
the word come from ʒou, shewynge to me.
29 Thanne Sadoch and Abiathar beren aʒen
the arke of God into Jerusalem, and
30 dwelliden there. But Dauid stiede vp
the hil of olyues, stiynge and wepynge,
the heede couerde, and the feet nakid
goynge; but and al the puple that was
with hym, the heed couerde, stieden vp
31 wepynge. Forsothe it is toold to Dauid,
that Achitophel was in the coniurynge
with Absolon; and Dauid seide, Lord,
I biseche, mak foli the counseil of Achi-
32 tophel. And whanne Dauid stiede vp the
cop of the hil, in the which he was to
preye the Lord, loo! Cusy Arachites aʒen
cam to hym, the clothing kut, and the
33 heed ful of erthe. And Dauid seide to
hym, If thou comyst with me, thou shalt
34 be to me to^e chargynge^f; forsothe if thou
turnest aʒen into the citee, and seist to
Absolon, Thi seruaunt I am, kyng, suffre me to lyue; as I was the seruaunt of
thi fadre, so I shal be thi seruaunt; thou
shalt scatyr the counseyl of Achitophel.
35 Forsothe thou hast with thee Sadoch
and Abiathar, preestis; and eche word,
what euere thou herist in the hows of
the kyng, thou shalt shewe to the
36 prestis, Sadoch and Abiathar. Forsothe there ben with hem her two sonys,
Achymaas, the sone of Sadoch, and Jonathan, the sone of Abiathar; and ʒe
shulen seende bi hem to me al the word
37 that ʒe shulen here. Thanne comynge
Chusa, the freend of Dauid, into the
citee, forsothe Absolon is comen into
Jerusalem.

the citee, with pees; and Achymaas, thi
sone, and Jonathas, the sone of Abiathar,
ʒoure twei sones, be with ʒou. Lo! Y 28
schal be hid in the^q feeldi places of de-
seert^r, til word come fro ʒou, and schewe
to me. Therfor Sadoch and Abiathar 29
baren aʒen the arke of God in to Jerusalem, and dwelliden ^{t} there. Forsothe 30
Dauid stiede on^u the hil of olyue trees,
stiynge^v and wepynge, with the ^{w} heed
hilyd, and 'goynge with nakid feet^y; but
also^z al the puple^a that was with hym,
stiede^b with the^c heed hilid, and wepte.
Forsothe^d it was teld to Dauid, that 31
Achitofel was in the sweryng togidere
with Absolon; and Dauid seide, Lord, Y
byseche, make thou fonned the counsel of
Achitofel. And whanne Dauid stiede^e in 32
to the^f hiʒenesse of the hil, in which he
schulde worschipe the Lord, lo! Cusi of
Arath, with the^g cloth to-rent, and with
the^g heed ful of erthe, cam to hym^h. And 33
Dauid seide to hym, If thou comest with
me, thou schalt be to to^i charge;
sotheli if thou turnest aʒen in^k to the citee, 34
and seist to Absolon, Y am thi seruaunt,
kyng^l, suffre thou me to lyue; as Y was
the seruaunt of thi fadir, so Y schal be
thi seruaunt†; thou schalt distrye the
counsel of Achitofel. Forsothe^m thou hast 35
with thee Sadoch and Abiathar, preestis^n;
and 'thou schalt schewe ech word^o, what
euer word thou schalt here in the hows
of the kyng^p, to^q Sadoch and Abiathar,
preestis^r. Sotheli^s twei sones 'of hem^t ben^u 36
with hem, Achymaas, sone^v of Sadoch,
and Jonathan, sone^w of Abiathar; and ʒe
schulen sende bi hem to me ech word
which^x ʒe schulen here. Therfor whanne 37
Chusi, freend of Dauid, cam in to the
citee, also Absolon entryde in to Jerusalem.

^{e} Om. c. ^{f} charge BEF.

Om. 1. ^{r} the deseert 1. ^{t} thei dwelliden 1. ^{u} up upon 1. ^{v} goynge up 1. ^{w} his 1. ^{y} with bare
feet passynge forth 1. ^{z} and 1. ^{a} puple also 1. ^{b} stiede up 1. ^{c} her 1. ^{d} And 1. ^{e} stiede up 1.
^{f} Om. 1. ^{g} his 1. ^{h} Dauid 1. ^{i} Om. 1. ^{k} Om. 1. ^{l} O kyng 1. ^{m} And 1. ^{n} the preestis 1.
^{o} Om. 1. ^{p} kyng, thou schalt schewe it to the prestis 1. ^{q} Om. 1. ^{r} Om. 1. ^{s} And her 1. ^{t} Om. 1.
^{u} beeth L. ^{v} the sone 1. ^{w} the sone 1. ^{x} that 1.

CAP. XVI.

1 And whanne Dauid hadde goon a litil
the cop of the hil, Ciba, the child of
Myphibosech, aperide into aȝen comynge of hym, with two assis, that weren
chargid with two hundrid loouys, and
an hundred bundels of dried grapis, and
an hundred peysis of fijgis^g pressid, and
2 with two botels of wyn. And the kyng
seide to Cyba, What to hem wolen thes
thingys? And Ciba answerde, My lord
kyng, the assis, that the hoomli men of
the kyng sitten on; the loouis and the
fijgis, to thi children for to eete; forsothe
the wyn, that he drynke, who so failith in
3 deseert. And the kyng seith, Where is
the sone of thi lord? And Ciba an-
swerde to the kyng, He abood^h stille in
Jerusalem, seiynge, To day shal the 'hows
of Yrael restore to meⁱ the kyngdam of
4 my fader. And the kyng seith to Cyba,
Alle thingis^k that weren of Miphibosech
ben thin. And Cyba seide, I preye,
fynde I grace before thee, my lord kyng.
5 Thanne kyng Dauid cam into Bahurym,
and loo! there wente out a man thens of
the kynrede of the hows of Saul, Semei
bi name, the sone of Gera; and he wente
6 forth goynge out, and cursyde. And he
sente stonus aȝens Dauid, and aȝens alle
the seruauntis of king Dauid; forsothe
al the puple, and alle the fiȝters fro the
riȝt and fro the left side of the kyng
7 wenten. Forsothe thus spak Semei,
whanne he curside to the kyng, Go out,
go out, thou man of bloodis, and man of
8 Belial! The Lord hath ȝoldyn to thee al
the blood of the hows of Saul, for thou
hast reued the kyngdam fro^l hym; and
the Lord hath ȝouun the kyngdam in
the hoond of Absolon, thi sone; and loo!
thin euels beren thee doun, for a man

CAP. XVI.

And whanne Dauid hadde passid a litil 1
the cop of the^y hil, Siba, the child of
Mysphobosech, apperide in to his comyng,
with tweyne assis, that weren chargid
with twei hundrid looues, and with^z an
hundri bundels of dried grapis, and with
an hundrid gobetis^a of pressid figus, and
with twei vessels of wyn. And the kyng 2
seide to Siba, What wolen these thingis
to hem silf? And Siba answeride, My
lord the kyng, the assis ben to the mey-
neals of the kyng, that thei sitte^b; the^c
looues and 'figis pressid^d ben to thi children to ete; forsothe^e the wyn is, that if
ony man faile in deseert, he drynke. And 3
the kyng seide, Where is the sone of thi
lord? And Siba answeride to the kyng,
He dwellide^f in Jerusalem, 'and seide^g, To
dai the Lord of the hows of Israel schal
restore to me the rewme of my fadir.
And the kyng seide to Siba, Alle thingis† 4
that weren of Mysphibosech ben thine.
And Siba seide, Y preye, fynde Y grace
bifor thee, my lord the^h kyng. Therforⁱ 5
kyng Dauid cam 'til to^k Bahurym, and lo!
a man of the meynee of the hows of Saul,
Semey bi name, sone of Gera, ȝede out fro
thennus; he ȝede forth goynge out, and
curside. And he sente stoonys aȝens Da- 6
uid, and aȝens alle seruauntis^l of kyng
Dauid; forsothe^m al the puple, and alle
fiȝterisⁿ ȝeden at the riȝtside and at the
left side of the king. Sotheli^o Semey spak 7
so^p, whanne he curside the kyng, Go out,
go out, thou man of bloodis‡, and man of
Belial! The Lord hath ȝolde to thee al 8
the blood of the hows of Saul, for thou
rauyschedist^q the rewme fro^{qq} hym; and
the Lord ȝaf^r the rewme in to the hond
of Absolon, thi sone; and lo! thin yuels
oppressen thee, for thou art a man of

† alle thingis,
etc.; this was
seid yuele, vn-
auysely and
vniustly, for
this Siba seide
fals. Lire here.
c.

‡ man of
bloodis; that is,
schedere out of
myche gilteles
blood. Lire
here. c.

g dried figgis E pr. m.　h bood BEFH. bod. c.　i Lord restoren to me the housis of Israel and E pr. m.
k Om. CEFH.　l for HCEF.

y an I.　z Om. A.　a peisis I.　b sitte on hem I.　c and the I.　d the pressid figis I.　e certis I.
f dwellide stille I.　g seyynge I.　h Om. I.　i Thanne I.　k vnto I. to EL.　l the seruauntis I.　m and I.
n the fiȝtinge men I.　o And I.　p thus I.　q hast rauischid I.　qq for DEMPX sec. m. bç.　r hath ȝouen I.

9 of blodis thou art. Forsothe Abisai, the sone of Seruye, seide to the kyng, Whi cursith this dog to diynge^m to my lord kyng^n? I shal goo, and girde of his 10 heed. And the kyng seith, What is to me and to 3ou, 3e sonys of Saruye? Letith hym, that he curse; forsothe the Lord comaundide to hym that he curse Dauid; and who is that dar seie, Whi 11 thus he doth? And the kyng seith to Abisai, and to alle his seruauntis, Loo! my sone, that is goon out fro my wombe, sechith my lijf; mych more now this sone of Geminy `cursith to me^o? Letith hym, that he curse after the heest of the 12 Lord; if perauenture the Lord beholde my tourmentynge, and 3eelde to me good 13 for this cursynge to dai. And so Dauid wente, and his felawis, bi the weie with hym; forsothe Semei wente cursynge a3ens hym bi the cop^p of the hil aside, and^q sendynge stoonus a3ens bym, and 14 the erthe sprengynge. And so kyng Dauid cam, and al the puple with hym 15 wery, and there thei ben refreshid. Forsothe Absolon, and al the puple of Irael wenten into Jerusalem, but and Achi- 16 tophel with hym. Forsothe whaun Cusay Arachites^qq, the freend of Dauid, was comen to Absolon, he spak to hym, Heil, kyng^r! 17 heil, kyng! To whom Absolon, This is, he seith, thi grace to thi freend; whi hast 18 thou not goo with thi freend? And Cusai answerde to Absolon, Nay, for of hym I shal be, whom the Lord chesith, and al this puple, and al Yrael; and with 19 hym Y shal dwelle. `But and this I shal brynge^s yn, to whom am I to serue? whether not to the sone of the kyng? as I obeysshide to thi fadir, so and I shal 20 obeishe to thee. Forsothe Absolon seide to Achithophel, Goo 3e into counseyl, what 21 we owen to doon. And Achithophel seith to Absolon, Go into the secundarye wyues

blodis. Forsothe^s Abisay, the sone of 9 Saruye, seide to the kyng, Whi cursith this dogge, that schal die, my lord the kyng? Y schal go, and Y schal girde of his heed. And the kyng seide, 3e sones 10 of Saruye, what is to me and to 3ou? Suffre ye hym, that he curse; for^t the Lord comaundide^u to hym †, that he schulde curse Dauid; and who is be that dare seie, Whi dide he so? And the kyng 11 seide to Abysay, and to alle hise ser- uauntis, Lo! my sone, that 3ede out of my wombe, sekith my lijf; hou myche more now this sone of Gemyny? Suffre 3e hym, that he curse bi comaundement of the Lord; if in hap the Lord biholde 12 my turmentyng, and 3elde good to me for this `cursyng of this dai^v. Therfor Dauid 13 3ede^w, and hise felowis, hi the weie with hym; forsothe^x Semey 3ede^y bi the slade of the hil `bi the side^z a3ens hym^a; and curside^b, and sente^c stoonus a3ens him, and spreynte erthe. And so `Dauid the 14 king^d cam, and al the puple weery with hym, and thei weren refreischid there. Forsothe^e Absolon, and al the puple of 15 Israel entriden in to Jerusalem, but also Achitofel with hym^f. Sotheli^g whanne 16 Chusi of Arath, the frend of Dauid, hadde come to Absolon, he spak^h to Absolon^i, Heil, kyng! heil, kyng! To whom Ab- 17 solon seide, This is thi grace to thi freend^k; whi 3edist thou not^l with thi freend? And Chusi answeride to Abso- 18 lon, Nay ‡, for Y shal be seruaunt^m of hym, whom the Lord hath chose, and al this puple, and al Israel; and Y schal dwelle with him. But that Y seie also 19 this, to whom schal Y serue? as Y obeiede to thi fadir, so^n Y schal obeie to thee. Forsothe^o Absolon seide to Achitofel, Take 20 3e counsel, what we owen to do. And 21 Achytofel seide to Absolon, Entre thou

† for the Lord comaundide to him; Semey synnede in thie cursing, for he curside [bi wickid] wille. Dauyth si3 that Semey, aloone and vnarmed, dide wrong to Dauyth stide. fastly and with out drede, and opinly bifor many wer- riours, most stronge and most hardy, and most redi to venge the wrong doon to the king; and Dauyth per- seyuede that this was not of thilke Semey ouely, but of God doinge there specialy; and Danyth clepide this the comaundement of God; nethe- les God is not autour nether cause of synne, in as myche as it is synne. God is autour of the power, bi which me syenneth; this power is fre wille. Also God is autour of the stiring of fre wille in to consent to dire poweris of execucioun, but God is not au- tour of defor- myte ether de- faute, which is in vari3[t]ful dede; and this defaute of rhyt- fulnesse mak- ith synne. So here the stide- fastnesse and hardynesse of Semey in assail- inge Dauyth, and the sub- staunce of the doyng, was of God, that Da- uyth were punyschid herhy, and his pacience were preued, but the defaute, that is, that he dide this bi wickid wille, was not of God, but in the defaute ether errour of fre wille. Lire here. c. ‡ nay; that is, Y ouate not go with Da- uyth. Lire here. c.

---

m dien c.   n the kyng c.   o Om. E pr. m.   p 3ok E pr. m.   q and he E pr. m.   qq Arehites A.   r Om. H. s That and these thingus I brynge E pr. m.

s And I.   t forsothe I.   u hath comaundid I.   v daies cursyng I.   w 3ede forth I.   x but I.   y 3ede aside I.   z Om. I.   a Dauid I.   b curside Dauid I.   c threwe I.   d kyng Dauid I.   e And I.   f Absolon I. g And I.   h seyde I.   i him I.   k freend Dauid I.   l not forth I.   m the seruaunt I.   n so and I. o And I.

of thi fadre, 'the whiche[t] he hath laft at
the hows to be kept; that whanne al
Yrael herith, that thou hast defoulid thi
fader, the hoondis of hem ben strengthid
22 with thee. Thanne thei strau3ten out to
Absolon a tabernacle in the solere, and
he wente into the secundarye wyues of
23 his fader before al Irael. Forsothe the
counseil that Achithophel 3af in thoo dais,
as if a man counseilde God; so was al the
counseil of Achithophel, and whanne he
was with Dauid, and whanne he was
with Absolon.

CAP. XVII.

1 　Thanne seide Achitophel to Absolon,
I shal chese to me twelue thousandis of
men, and rysynge I shal pursue Dauid
2 this ni3t. And fallynge forsothe vpon
hym that is wery, and the hoondis feblid, I shal smyte hym; and whanne al
the puple fleeth that is with hym, I shal
3 smyte the kyng desolate. And I shal
brynge a3en al the puple, what maner o
man is wont to be turned a3en; forsothe
o man thou sechist, and al the puple shal
4 ben in pees. And his word pleside to
Absolon, and to alle the more thur3 birth
5 of Yrael. Forsothe Absolon seith, Clepe
3e and Cusai Arachite, and here we what
6 also he seith. And whan Cusai was
comen to Absolon, Absolon seith to hym,
Siche a maner word spak Achitophel;
shul we doo, or nay? what counseil 3yuest
7 thou? And Cusay seide to Absolon, It
is not good this counseil, that Achithophel
8 hath 3ouun at this tyme. And eft Cusay
brou3te yn, Thou hast knowen thi fader,
and the men that with hym ben, to ben
moost stronge, and in bitter wil, as if a
she bere wexe feers in the wijlde wode,
rauysshid the whelpis; but and thi fader
is a man fi3ter, and he shal not dwelle
9 with the puple. Perauenture now he

to the concubyns[P] of thi fadir, whiche he
lefte[q] to kepe the[r] hows; that whanne al
Israel herith, that thou hast defoulid thi
fadir[s], the hondis of hem be strengthid
with thee. Therfor thei tildeden[t] Abso- 22
lon a tabernacle in the soler, and he entride to the concubyns of his fadir bifor
al Israel. Sotheli[u] the counsel of Achito- 23
fel, which[v] he 3af in tho daies, was as if
a man counselide[w] God; so[x] was al the
counsel of Achitofel, bothe whanne he was
with Dauid, and whanne he was with
Absolon.

CAP. XVII.

　Therfor[y] Achitofel seide to Absolon, Y 1
schal chese[z] twelue thousynde of men 'to
me[a], and Y schal rise[b], and pursue Dauid
in this ny3t. And Y schal falle on hym, 2
for he is wery, and with vnboundun hondis
Y schal smyte hym. And whanne al the
puple fleeth which[c] is with hym, Y schal
smyte the kyng 'desolat, ether[d] left aloone.
And Y schal lede a3en al the puple, as o 3
man is wont to turne[e] a3en; for[f] thou
sekist o man, and al the puple schal be in
pees. And the word of him[g] plesyde Ab- 4
solon, and alle the grete[h] men in birthe of
Israel. Forsothe[i] Absolon seide, Clepe 3e 5
also Chusy of Arath, and here we what
also he seith. And whanne Chusi hadde 6
come to Absolon, Absolon seide to hym,
Achitofel spak[k] siche a word; owen we
do[l], ethir nay? what counsel 3yuest thou?
And Chusi seide to Absolon, This is not 7
good counsel, which[m] Achitofel 3af[n] in this
tyme. And eft Chusi seide, Thou knowist, 8
that thi fadir, and the men that ben with
him, ben moost[o] stronge, and in bitter
soule[p], as if a femal[q] bere is fers in the[r]
forest, whanne the[s] whelpis ben rauyschid[t];
but also thi fader is a man werriour, and
he schal not dwelle with the puple. In 9
hap now he is hid[u] in the[v] dichis, ethir in

---

[t] that c pr. m.

[P] secundarie wyues I.　　[q] hath left I.　　[r] his I.　　[s] fadir bed I.　　[t] strei3ten out I.　　[u] And I.
[v] that I.　　[w] had counseilid with I.　　[x] and so I.　　[y] Thanne I.　　[z] chese to me I.　　[a] Om. I.　　[b] rise up I.
[c] that I.　　[d] Om. I.　　[e] be turned I.　　[f] for Absolon I.　　[g] Achitofel I.　　[h] grettere nc.　　[i] And I.　　[k] hath
spoke I.　　[l] do theraftir I.　　[m] that I.　　[n] hath 3oue I.　　[o] ful I.　　[p] will I.　　[q] schue I.　　[r] a I.　　[s] hir I.
[t] rauyschid fro hir I.　　[u] ether lurketh I. x sec. m. marg.　　[v] Om. plures.

lurkith in dichis, or in a[u] place where he
wole; and whanne oon fallith, eche in the
bigynnynge shal here, who so euere herith,
and shal seye, There is maad veniaunce
10 in the puple that pursuede Absolon. And
eche moost strong, whos is the herte as
of a lioun, shal be feblid for drede;
forsothe al the puple of Yrael woot thi
fader to be strong, and alle stronge, that
11 with hym ben. But this semeth to me to
be riȝt counseil; be gedrid to thee al the
puple, fro Dan vnto Bersabe, vnnoumbrable as the grauel of the see; and thou
12 shalt be in the myddis of hem. And we
shulen falle vpon him, in what euer place
he were foundun, and we shulen couer
hym, as dewe is wont to falle on the
erthe; and we shulen not leeue of the
men that with hym ben, forsothe not
13 oone. And if he were goon in eny citee,
al Yrael shal wyynde aboute that citee
coordis, and we shulen drawe it into the
streem, that there be not foundun for-
14 sothe of it not a litil stoon. And
Absolon seide, and alle the men of Irael,
Betere is the counseil of Cusai Arachite
thanne the counseil of Achithophel; forsothe thurȝ[w] the wil of the Lord is
scaterid the[x] profitable counseil of Achithophel, that the Lord brynge yn yuel
15 vpon Absolon. And Cusay seith to the
preestys, Sadoch and Abiathar, This and
this maner Achithophel ȝaf counseil to
Absolon, and to the eldres of Yrael,
16 and I ȝaf sich counseil and sich. Now
thanne sendith soone, and tellith to
Dauid, seiynge, Ne abide thou this niȝt
in the wijlde feeldis of desert, but with
out tariynge weende ouer; lest perauenture the kyng be soopen awey, and al
17 the puple that is with hym. Forsothe
Jonathan and Achymas stoden biside the
welle of Rogel; an hondwomman ȝede,

o place, in which he wole[w]; and whanne
ony man fallith in the bigynnyng, who
euer schal here[x], he schal here, and schal[y]
seie, Wounde[z] is maad[a] in the puple that
suede Absolon. And ech strongeste[b] man, 10
whos herte is as 'the herte[c] of a lioun,
schal be discoumfortid for drede; for al the
puple of Israel knowith, that thi fadir
is strong, and that alle men[d] ben stronge,
that ben with him. But this semeth to me 11
to be riȝtful counsel; al Israel be gaderid
to thee, fro Dan 'til to[e] Bersabee, vnnoumbrable as the[f] soonds[g] of the see; and thou
schalt be in the myddis of hem. And we 12
schulen falle on[h] hym, in what euer place
he is foundun, and we schulen hile hym,
as dew is wont to falle on[h] the[i] erthe; and[k]
we schulen not leeue of[l] the men that ben
with hym[m], 'sotheli not oon[n]. 'That if 13
he[o] entrith in to ony citee, al Israel schal
cumpasse that citee† with roopis, and we
schulen drawe it in to the stronde, that[p]
no thing be foundun, sotheli[q] not a litil
stoon therof[r]. And Absolon seide, and 14
alle the men of Israel, The counsel of
Chusi of Arath is betere than the counsel
of Achitofel; sotheli[s] the profitable counsel‡
of Achitofel was destried bi Goddis wille,
that the Lord schulde brynge in yuel on
Absolon. And Chusi seide to Sadoch and 15
to Abiathar, preestis[t], Achitofel ȝaf counsel to Absolon, and to the eldere men of
Israel in this and this maner, and Y ȝaf
sich and sich counsel. Now therfor 16
sende ȝe soone, and telle ȝe to Dauid, and
seie ȝe, Dwelle thou not this[u] nyȝt in the[v]
feeldi places of deseert[w], but passe thou[x]
with out delay[y]; lest perauenture the kyng
be destried‖, and al the puple which[z]
is with hym. Forsothe[a] Jonathas and 17
Achymaas stoden bisidis the welle of
Rogel; an[b] handmaide ȝede[c], and telde to
hem, and thei ȝeden forth to telle the

† *al Israel schal cumpasse that citee*; Chusi spekith bi figuratiyf speche, and this is the sentence; we schulen so distrie al that citee, that noon aȝen standing schal be; wherfor in Ebreu it is had thus, al Israel schal ȝyue felouschipis of armed men aboute that citee, to distrie al. *Lire here.* c.

‡ *the profitable counsel*; that is, spedeful for the entent of Absolon. c.

‖ *the kyng be distried*; Dauyth be sopun vp bi the councel of Achitofel, parformed of Absalon in absence of Chusi; and therfor in Ebreu it is, *lest it be councelid to the king*, that is, to Absolon, that he do the councel of Achitofel. *Lire here.* c

[u] oon *BEF.* o *C.* one *H.* [w] thour *A.* [x] to *B.*

[w] wole *hide him* I. [x] here *it* I. [y] Om. I. [z] Veniaunce I. *ether vengeaunce* X *sec. m. marg.* [a] don I. [b] ful strong I. [c] Om. I. [d] the men I. [e] vnto I. til K. [f] Om. I. [g] soont A. [h] upon I. [i] Om. KX. [k] and sothely I. [l] oon of I. [m] Dauid I. [n] Om. I. [o] And if he that I. [p] ȝhe that I. [q] Om. I. [r] be founden therof I. [s] and I. [t] the preestis I. [u] in this C. [v] Om. I. [w] the deseert I. [x] thou forth I. [y] tariyng I. [z] that I. [a] And I. [b] and an I. [c] ȝede forth I.

and toolde to hem, and thei wenten forth,
that thei tellen to kyng[y] Dauid the message; forsothe thei my3ten not be seen,
18 or go[z] into the cytee. Forsothe a maner
child saw3 hem, and toolde to Absolon;
forsothe thei wenten in a swift paase in[a]
the hows of a maner man in Bahurym,
that hadde a pit in his vestiarye, and
19 thei descendiden into[b] it. Forsothe a
womman took, and strau3te out a couerynge vpon the mouth of the pit, as
driynge pild barli, and so the thing is
20 hid. And whanne the seruauntis of Absolon weren comen into the hows, thei
seiden to the womman, Where is Achymas and Jonathan? And the womman
answerde to hem, Thei wenten hiyngli,
a litil wi3t water taastid. And thes
that sou3ten, whanne thei founden not,
21 thei turneden a3en into Jerusalem. And
whanne thei weren goon, they stieden
vp fro the pit; and goynge toolden to
kyng Dauid, and seiden, Ryseth, and
soone goth ouer the flood, for sich maner
22 counseil 3af Achithophel a3ens 3ou. Thanne
Dauid roos, and al the puple that was
with hym, and thei passiden Jordan, to
the tyme that the dai were li3tid[c], or
the word were puplishid; and not oone
forsothe was laft, that passide not the
23 flood. Forsothe Achitophel seynge, that
his counseil was not doon, made redi his
asse, and roos, and wente into hys hows,
and into his citee; and his hows disposid,
he diede bi hoongynge, and is biried in
24 the sepulcre of his fader. Forsothe
Dauid cam into stronge placis, and Absolon passide ouer Jordan, and alle
25 the men of Yrael with hym. Forsothe
Absolon sette Amasan for Joab vpon
the oost; forsothe Amasan was the sone
of a man that was clepid Gethra of
Jezreli, that wente into Abigayl, the

message to kyng Dauid; for[d] thei my3ten
not be seyn, nether entre in to the citee.
Forsothe[e] a child si3 hem, and he schew- 18
ide[f] to Absolon; sotheli[g] thei entriden with
swift goyng in to the hows of sum man[h] in
Bahurym, that hadde a pit in his place,
and thei 3eden doun in to that pit. For- 19
sothe[k] a womman took, and spred abrood
an hilyng of[l] the mouth of the pit as
driynge barli with the pile takun a wey[m],
and so the thing was hid. And whanne 20
the seruauntis of Absolon hadde come in
to the hows, thei seiden to the womman,
Where is Achymaas and Jonathas? And
the womman answeride to hem, Thei[n]
passiden[o] hastily, whanne watir[†] was
tastid a litil[p]. And whanne thei that
sou3ten hem hadden not founde[q], thei
turneden a3en in to Jerusalem. And 21
whanne thei that sou3ten[r] hadden go[s],
thei stieden[t] fro the pit; and thei 3eden,
and telden to kyng Dauid, and seiden,
Rise 3e, passe 3e[u] soone the flood, for
Achitofel 3af[v] sich counsel a3ens 3ou.
Therfor Dauid roos[w], and al the puple 22
that was with hym, and thei passiden
Jordan, til it was cleer dai, bifor that the
word was pupplischid; and sotheli not
oon[x] was left, that passide not[y] the flood.
Forsothe[z] Achitofel si3, that his counsel 23
was not doon, and he sadlide his asse, and
roos[a], and 3ede in to his hows, and in to
his citee; and whanne his hows was disposid, he perischide bi hangyng[b][‡], and he
was biried in the sepulcre of his fadir.
Sotheli[c] Dauid cam in to the[d] castels, and 24
Absolon passide Jordan, he and alle the[e]
men of Israel with hym. Forsothe[f] Ab- 25
solon ordeynede Amasan for Joab on[g]
the[h] oost; forsothe[i] Amasan was the sone
of a man that was clepid Jethra of
Je3rael, which[k] entride to Abigail, dou3-
ter[l] of Naas, the sistir of Saruye, that was

† whanne
watir, etc., in
Ebreu it is,
they passiden
the ryuer of
watris, that is,
Jordan, as
Ebrews seyen.
Lire here. c.

‡ bi hangyng;
by him silf he
hangide him
silf for indigna-
cioun, that his
counsel was
not doon, and
for by the fuly
of Absolon and
of his puple, he
perseyuede and
helde for cer-
teyn, that Da-
uyth schulde
haue the mais-
try, and turne
a3en in to the
rewme; wher-
for he dredde
to be slayn of
him bi foul deth
and peyneful,
and therfor he
wolde haste his
deth bi an other
weye. Lire
here. c.

[y] the kyng E pr. m.   [z] to go E pr. m.   [a] Om. CEFH.   [b] in E pr. m.   [c] li3tede CE.

[d] certis I.   [e] And I.   [f] schewide it I.   [g] and I.   [h] a man IM.   [i] putt I.   [k] And I.   [l] ouer I.   [m] pild
barli I.   [n] And thei K.   [o] passidin forth I.   [p] thei hadden taasted a litil watir I.   [q] founde hem I.
[r] Om. I.   [s] go forth I.   [t] stieden up I.   [u] 3e up and passeth I.   [v] hath 3oue I.   [w] roos up I.   [x] oo man I.
[y] ne he passide I.   [z] And I.   [a] roos up I.   [b] hangyng him self I.   [c] And I.   [d] Om. I.   [e] Om. I.   [f] And I.
[g] upon I.   [h] his I.   [i] and I.   [k] the which I.   [l] the dou3tir I.

douȝter of Naas, sister of Saruye, that
26 was the moder of Joab.   And Irael
sette[d] tentis with Absolon in the loond
27 of Galaad.   And whanne Dauid was
comen into the defensable placis, Sobi,
the sone of Naas of Rabath[dd], of the sonys
of Amon, and Machir, the sone of Amyel,
of Lodobar, and Berzellay Galadite, of
28 Rogelym, offreden to hym coucrynge
clothis, and tapetis, and erthen vessels,
whete, and barli, and meele, and powned
corn, and benen, and potage, and fryed
'gederynge of corns, that is clepid cycer[e],
29 and hony, and bottre, and sheep, and
fatte calues.   And thei ȝynen to Dauid,
and to the puple that was with hym, for
to ete ; forsothe thei ouertroweden the
puple to be feyntid[f] in the[g] deseert bi
hungre and threst.

the modir of Joab.   And Israel settide 26
tentis with Absolon in the lond of Galaad.
And whanne Dauid hadde come in to cas- 27
tels[m], Sobi, the sone of Naas of Rabath,
of the sones of Amon, and Machir, the
sone of Amyel, of Lodobar, and Berzellai,
of Galaad, of Rogelym, brouȝten to hym[n] 28
beddyngis[o], and tapitis, and erthun vessels,
wheete[p], and barli, and mele, and flour,
and benys, and lente[q], and fried chichis[r],
and hony, and botere, and scheep, and 29
fatte calues.   And thei ȝauen[s] to Dauid, and
to the puple that weren with hym, to ete ;
for thei supposiden the puple to be maad
feynt for hungur and thirst in deseert.

CAP. XVIII.

1   Dauid thanne, his[h] puple biholden[i],
ordeynde vpon hem leders of thousandis,
2 and leders of hundridis.   And he ȝaf the
thridde parti of the puple vndir the
hoond of Joab ; and the thridde vndur
the hoond of Abisai, the sone of Seruye,
the brothir of Joab ; and the thridde
vndur the hoond of Ethay, that was of
Geth.   And the kyng seide to the puple,
3 And I shal goon out with ȝou.   And the
puple answerde, Thou shalt not goo out ;
forsothe whether we fleen, it shal not
perteyne to hem in greet forse of vs ; or
the half partie falle fro vs, thei shulen
not retche[j] anow, for thou oone for ten
thousandis ert[k] countyd ; beter it is
thanne, that thou be to vs in the cytee to
4 socour.   To whom seith the kyng, That
to ȝou semeth riȝt, that I shal doo.
Thanne the kyng stoode biside the ȝaate,
and the puple wente out bi her cumpanyes, bi[l] hundredis and thousandis.

CAP. XVIII.

Therfor Dauid, whanne the[t] puple 'was 1
biholdun[u], ordeynde tribunes[v] and centuriouns[w] on[x] hem.   And he ȝaf the thridde 2
part of the puple vndur the hond of Joab ;
and the thridde part vndur the hond of
Abisai, sone[y] of Saruye, brother[z] of Joab ;
and the thridde part vndur the hond of
Ethai, that was of Geth.   And the kyng
seide to the puple, Also Y schal go out †
with ȝou.   And the puple answeride, 3
Thou schalt not go out ; for whether we
fleen, it schal not perteyne to hem bi
greet werk[a] of vs ; whether half the part
fallith[b] doun of vs, thei schulen not recke
ynow[c], for thou[d] art rekynyd for ten
thousynde ; therfor it is betere, that thou
be to vs in the citee in stronge hold[e].   'To 4
whiche[f] the kyng seide[g], Y schal do this[h],
that semeth riȝtful to ȝou.   Therfor the
kyng stood bisidis the ȝate, and the puple
ȝede out bi her cumpenyes, bi hundridis
and bi thousyndis.   And the king co- 5

† Y schal ȝo
out, etc., for he
wolde be of the
firste to trauel
in perel. Lire
here. c.

---

[d] sente A.   [dd] Babath ABH.   [e] chichis E pr.m.   [f] weri E pr.m.   [g] Om. CEFH.   [h] the E pr.m.   [i] byholdynge H.   [j] recche CH.   [k] schalt ben E pr.m.   [l] Om. BCEFH.

[m] the castels I.   [n] Dauid I.   [o] beddyng I.   [p] and wheete I.   [q] fetchis I.   [r] thing that is clepid cycer I.
fried chichis, that is, gaderyng of cornys that is clepid cicer x sec.m. marg.   [s] ȝauen tho I.   [t] his A sec. m.
he had biholde his I.   [u] Om. I.   [v] chefteyns of thousyndis I.   [w] of hundridus I.   [x] upon I.   [y] the sone I.
[z] the brothir I.   [a] foors I.   [b] falle I.   [c] myche I.   [d] thou oon I.   [e] socour I.   [f] And I.   [g] seide to hem I.
[h] that I.

s And the kyng comaundide to Joab, and
Abisai, and Ethay, seiynge, Kepith to
me the child Absolon. And al the puple
herde the kyng comaundynge to alle the
5 princis for Absolon. And so the puple
wente into the feelde a3ens Yrael; and
a batail is doon in the wijld wode of
7 Effraym. And the puple of Irael is
there hewen doun of the oost of Dauid,
and there is doon a greet slau3ter in that
8 day of twenti thousand. Forsothe there
was the batail sparpoild vpon the face of
al the loond, and manye mo weren whom
the wijlde wode waastide of the puple,
than thei whom the swerd deuowrede[m]
9 in that day. Forsothe it felle, that Absolon a3encam to the seruauntis of Dauid,
sittynge vpon[n] a muyl; and whanne the
muyle wente yn vndur a thik ook, and a
greet, the heed of hym cleuyde to the
ook; and hym hongid bitwix heuene and
erthe, the muyle, to the which he satte in,
10 passide forth. Forsothe a maner man
saw3 that, and toolde to Joab, seiynge,
I saw3 Absolon hongynge fro an ook.
11 And Joab seith to the man that toolde
hym, If thou saw3, whi stikist thou not
hym with the erthe, and I shulde haue
3yue to thee ten ciclis of siluer, and a
12 kny3tis girdil? The which seide to Joab,
If thou peysedist in myn hoondis a thousand silueren platis, I shulde not putte
myn hoond into the sone of the kyng;
forsothe herynge vs, the kyng comaundide to thee, and to Abisai, and to Ethai,
seiynge, Kepith to me the child Absolon.
13 But and if I hadde doon a3ens my soul
foolhardili, that my3te not the kyng vnknowe, and thou shuldist stoond forn
14 a3ens. And Joab seith, Not as thou
wolt, but I shal goo to hym before thee.
Thanne Joab took three speris in his
hoond, and pi3te hem in the herte of
Absolon. And whanne 3it he qwappide

maundide to Joab, and to Abisai, and
Ethai[i], and seyde, Kepe 3e to me the child
Absolon. And al the puple herde the kyng
comaundinge to alle the princes for Absolon. Therfor the puple 3ede out in to 6
the feeld a3ens Israel; and the[k] batel was
maad in the forest of Effraym. And the 7
puple of Israel was slayn there of the oost
of Dauid, and a greet sleyng[l] of twenti
thousunde was maad in that dai. For- 8
sothe[m] the[n] batel was scaterid[nn] there on[o]
the face of al erthe[p], and many mo weren
of the puple whiche the forest wastide,
than thei whiche the swerd deuourid in
that dai. Sotheli it bifeld, that Absalon 9
sittinge on[q] a mule, cam a3ens the seruauntis of Dauid; and whanne the mule
hadde entrid vndur a thicke ook, and greet[r],
the heed of Absolon cleuyde to the ook;
and whanne he was hangid bitwixe
heuene and erthe, the mule, on[s] which[t] he
sat, passide[u]. Sotheli[v] 'sum man[w] si3 this, 10
and telde[x] to Joab, and seide, Y si3 Absolon hange on an ook. And Joab seide 11
to the man that 'hadde telde[y] to hym, If
thou si3est[z], whi persidist[a] thou not hym[b]
to the erthe, and Y schulde haue 3oue 'to
thee[c] ten siclis of siluer, and a girdil?
And he seide to Joab, Thou3 thou paiedist 12
in myn hondis a thousynde platis of siluer,
Y nolde[d] sende myn hond in to the sone
of the king; for thee[e] while we herden,
the kyng comaundide to thee, and to
Abisai, and to Ethai, and seide, Kepe 3e
to me the child Absolon. But and if[f] Y 13
hadde do[g] a3ens my lijf hardili[h], this my3te
not be[i] hid fro the kyng, and thou woldist
stonde on the contrarye side. And Joab 14
seide, Not as thou wolt[k], 'Absolon schal
be kept[l], but Y schal assaile hym bifor
thee. Therfore Joab took thre speris in his
hond, and fitchide[m] tho in the herte of
Absolon. And whanne he spraulide, 3it
cleuynge in the ook, ten 3onge squieris of 15

[m] vowrede CEFH.   [n] on E.

[i] to Ethai 1.   [k] a 1.   [l] slau3ter 1.   [m] And 1.   [n] Om. c.   [nn] sparpuylid 1.   [o] upon 1.   [p] the loond 1.
[q] upon 1.   [r] a greet 1.   [s] upon 1.   [t] whom 1.   [u] passide forth 1.   [v] And 1.   [w] a man 1M.   [x] tolde it 1.
[y] tolde 1KL.   [z] si3e *him* 1.   [a] perschidist 1.   [b] hym thorou3 1.   [c] Om. G.   [d] wolde not 1.   [e] Om. 1.
[f] thou3 1.   [g] do fool hardily 1.   [h] Om. 1.   [i] haue be 1.   [k] woldest EL.   [l] Om. 1.   [m] he fitchide 1.

15 cleuynge in the ook, ten ȝonge squyers of
Joab runnen, and smytynge slowen hym.
16 Forsothe Joab sownede with the trumpe,
and with heelde the puple, that he pursuede not Irael fleynge, wyluynge to
17 spare to the multitude. And thei token
Absolon, and casten hym in the wijld
wode in to a greet diche, and thei beren
togidir vpon hym a greet heep of stoonus
ful myche ; forsothe al Irael fleeȝ into her
18 tabernaclis. Forsothe Absolon hadde
arerede vp to hym, whanne he ȝit lyuede,
a title, that is in the valey of the kyng ;
he seide forsothe, I haue not a sone, and
this shal be in° mynde of my name; and
he clepide the title bi his name, and it is
clepid the Hoond of Absolon into this
19 day. Forsothe Achymas, the sone of
Sadoch, seith, I shal renne and telle to
the kyng, for the Lord dide doom to
hym fro the hoond of the enemyes of
20 hym. To whom Joab seide, Thou shalt
not be messager in this dai, but thou
shalt telle in the tother ; to day I wole not
thee to telle, forsothe the sone of the
21 kyng is deed. And Joab seith to Cusi,
Go, and tel to the kyng what thou hast
22 seen. Cusi lowtide to Joab, and ranne.
Eft Achymas, the sone of Sadoch, seide
to Joab, What lettith, if I also renne
after Cusi ? And Joab seide to hym,
What wolt thou renne, sone myn ? Come
hidir, thou shalt not be berer of good
23 message. The which answerde, What
forsothe if I shal renne ? And he seith
to hym, Renn. Thanne Achymaas rennynge bi the weye of the good short weye
24 ouerpasside Cusai. Dauid forsothe sat
bitwix two ȝatis ; the weyter forsothe,
that was in the heiȝt of the ȝate vpon
the walle, rerynge vp the eyen, sawȝ a
25 man aloone rennynge ; and cryinge out
shewide to the kyng. And the kyng
seide to hym, If he is aloone, gode mes-

Joab runnen, and smytiden°, and killiden
hym. Sotheli° Joab sownede° with a 16
clarioun, and withhelde° the puple, lest it
pursuede Israel fleynge, and he wolde
spare the multitude. And thei° token 17
Absolon, and castiden° forth him in to a
greet dich in the forest, and baren° togidere a ful greet heep of stoonys on°
hym ; forsothe° al Israel fledde in to his°
tabernaclis. Forsothe° Absolon, while 18
he lyuyde ȝit, hadde reisid to hym a memorial, which° is in the valey of the
kyng ; for he seide, Y haue no sone, and
this schal be the mynde of my name ; and
he clepide 'the memorial° bi his name, and
it is clepid the Hond, 'that is, werk°, of Absolon 'til to° this dai. Forsothe° Achy- 19
maas, sone° of Sadoch, seide, Y schal
renne, and Y schal telle to the kyng, that
the Lord hath maad doom to hym of the
hond of hise enemyes. To whom Joab 20
seide, Thou schalt not be messanger° in
this dai, but thou schalt telle° in° another
dai ; I nyle° that thou telle° to dai, for the
sone of the kyng is deed. And Joab seide 21
to Chusi†, Go thou, and telle to the kyng
tho thingis that thou hast seyn. Chusi
worschypide Joab, and ran. Eft° Achy- 22
maas, sone° of Sadoch, seide to Joab,
What lettith, if also Y renne aftir Chusi ?
And Joab seide to hym, What wolt thou
renne, my sone ? Come thou hidur, thou
schalt not be berere of good message.
Which¹ answeride, 'What sotheli if° Y 23
schal renne ? And Joab seide to hym,
Renn thou. Therfor Achymaas ran bi
the weie of schortnesse, 'and sped°, and
passide° Chusi. Forsothe° Dauid sat bi- 24
twixe twei ȝatis ; sotheli° the spiere°, that
was in the hiȝnesse of the ȝate on the
wal, reiside° the° iȝen, and siȝ° a man
aloone rennynge ; and the spiere° criede, 25
and schewide to the kyng. And the kyng
seide to hym, If he is aloone, good mes-

*† Joab seide
to Chusi ; this
Chusy was a
simple man of
the puple, and
was not that
Chusi that was
frend and
counceloure of
Dauyth, of
whom it is seid
in xv. and xvii.
c°. Lire here. c.*

° the *c E.*

ⁿ smoten ɪ. smiten ᴇ. ° And ɪ. ᴘ trumpide ɪ. q helde with him ɪ. ʳ men ɪ. ˢ threwen ɪ. ᵗ thei
baren ɪ. ᵘ upon ɪ. ᵛ and ɪ. ʷ her ɪ. ˣ And ɪ. ʸ that ɪ. ᶻ that token of mynde ɪ. ᵃ Om. ɪ.
ᵇ vnto ɪ. ᶜ And ɪ. ᵈ the sone ɪ. ᵉ a messanger ᴀ *sec. m.* ᶠ telle this ɪ. ᵍ wil not ɪ. ʰ telle this ɪ.
ⁱ forth. And eft ɪ. ᵏ the sone ɪ. ˡ The which ɪ. ᵐ But what ɪ. ⁿ Om. ɪ. ° he passide ɪ. ᵖ And ɪ.
q and ɪ. ʳ waiter ɪ. ˢ reiside up. ᵗ his ɪ. ᵘ he sawȝe ɪ. ᵛ biholder ɪ.

T

26 sage is in the mouth of hym. Forsothe hym goynge and neiȝynge nerre, the wayter sawȝ anothir man rennynge; and criynge out in the cop seith, There semeth to me another man rennynge aloone. And the kyng seide to hym, 27 And this is a good messager. Forsothe the weyter seith, I biholde the rennynge of the former, as the rennynge of Achymaas, the sone of Sadoch. And the kyng seith, A good man he is, and cometh 28 berynge good mesage. Forsothe the Achymaas criynge, seide to the kyng, Hail kyng! And lowtynge the kyng before hym bowide into the erthe, seith, Blessid beᵖ the Lord thi God, that hath concludid the men, that rereden her hoondis 29 aȝens my lord the kyng. And the kyng seith, Is there not pees to the child Absolon? And Achymaas seide, I sawȝ a greet towmbe, whanne Joab thi seruaunt sente me, O kyng, thi seruaunt; other 30 thing I knowe not. To whom the kyng, Passe, he seith, and stoond here. And 31 whanne he was passid, and stoode, Cusi aperide; and comynge seith, I brynge good message, my lord king; forsothe the Lord hath demyde for thee to day fro the hoond ʳof alleq that risen aȝens 32 thee. The kyng forsothe seide to Cusi, Is there not pees to the child Absolon? To whom answerynge Cusi, Be thei maad, he seith, as the child, the enemyes of my lord theʳ kyng, and alle that risen 33 aȝens hym into yuel. And so the kyng cauȝt with sorwe, stiede vp toˢ the sowpynge place of the ȝante, and wepte, and thus he spak goynge, Sone myn, Absolon! Absolon, sone myn! who to me ȝyueth, that I dye for thee? Absolon, sone myn! sone myn, Absolon!

26 sage is in his mouth. Sotheliʷ while he hastide, and neiȝede neer, the spiereˣ siȝ another man rennyngeʸ; and the spiere criede 'in the hiȝnesseᶻ, and seide, Another man rennynge aloone apperith to me. And the kyng seide to hym, And this man is a good messanger. Sotheliᵃ the spiereᵇ 27 seide, Y biholde the rennyng of the formere, as the rennyng of Achymaas, soneᶜ of Sadoch. And the kyng seide, He is a good man, and he cometh bryngynge aᵈ good message. Forsotheᵉ Achymaas 28 criede, and seide to the kyng, Heil kyng! And he worschipide the kyng lowli bifor hym to ertheᶠ, and seide, Blessid be thiᵍ Lord God, that closideʰ togidere the men, that reisydenⁱ her hondis aȝens my lord theʲ kyng. And the kyng seide, Whe- 29 ther pees is to the child Absolon? And Achymaas seide, Y siȝᵏ, 'that is, Y herde, a great noiseˡ, whanne Joab, thi seruaunt, thouᵐ kyng, senteⁿ me thi seruauntᵒ; Y kanᵖ noon othir thing. To whom the 30 kyng seide, Passe thouq, and stonde here. And whanne he hadde passid, and stood, Chusi apperide; and he cam and seide, 31 My lord theʳ kyng, Y brynge good message; forˢ the Lord hath demed to dai for thee of the hond of alle men that risenᵗ aȝens thee. Forsotheᵘ the kyng seide to 32 Chusi, Whether pees is to the child Absolon? To whom Chusi answeride, and seide, The enemyes of my lord theᵛ kyng, and alle men that risenʷ aȝens hym in to yuel, beˣ maad as the child. Therfor the 33 kyng was sory, and stiedeʸ in to the soler of the ȝate, and wepteᶻ, and spak thus goynge†, My sone, Absolon! Absolon, my sone! who ȝyueth to me, that Y die for thee? Absolon‡, my sone! my sone, Absolon!

† and wepie, and spak thus goyng; Dauith biwailide the goostly deth of Absolon, for he diede in dedly synne, in pursuynge in dede his fadir; and therfor this word Absolon my sone, is set six sithis here, and in xix. cᵒ. for vi. condiciouns of the peyne of helle; for peyne of harm, that is, of wantyng of blis, and the peyne of feelyng is there, gnasting of teeth and weping, outermere derknessis, and during with outen ende, ben in helle. *Lire here.* c.

‡ *Absolon*; goostly: Absolon that pursueth Dauyth and hise men, signefieth a tiraunt oppressere of simple men; whos heed cloueth to an ook, in desiringe liye thingis of the world; he is perisid with lil speris, in assentinge to thre maner coneitise; he is cast forth in to a dich, in goinge doun to helle. *Lire here.* c.

ᵖ Om. BCEFH.   q Om. ᴀ.   ʳ Om. BFH.   ˢ Om. BCEFH.

ʷ But ɪ.   ˣ waiter an hiȝe ɪ.   ʸ come rennynge ɪ.   ᶻ an hiȝe ɪ.   ᵃ And ɪ.   ᵇ waiter ɪ.   ᶜ the sone ɪ. ᵈ Om. ɪ.   ᵉ And ɪ.   ᶠ the erthe ɪ.   ᵍ the ᴀ.   ʰ hath closid ɪ.   ⁱ reisiden to gidre ɪ.   ʲ Om. ɪ.   ᵏ siȝ a gret biriel ᴀ *sec. m. marg.* sawȝe a biriel ɪ.   ˡ Om. ɪ.   ᵐ oo ɪ.   ⁿ sende ɪ.   ᵒ seruaunt to thee ɪ. ᵖ knowe ɪ.   q ouer ɪ.   ʳ Om. ɪ.   ˢ certis ɪ.   ᵗ risen ᴇ. han risen ɪ.   ᵘ And ɪ.   ᵛ Om. ɪ.   ʷ resen ɪʟᴘ. risen ᴇ.   ˣ be thei ɪ.   ʸ stiede up ɪ.   ᶻ he wepte ɪ.

CAP. XIX.

1 Forsothe it is toold to Joab, that the
2 kyng wept, and weilide his sone; and the
victorye is turned in that dai into weilynge to al the puple; forsothe the puple
herde in that day to be seid, The kyng
3 sorwith vpon his sone. And the puple
bowide aside in that dai to goo in to the
citee, what maner wise a puple turnede
and fleynge fro the batail is wont to
4 bowe aside. Forsothe the kyng couerde
his heed, and criede with a greet vois,
Sone myn, Absolon! Absolon, sone myn!
5 Thanne goon yn Joab to the kyng into
the hows, seide, Thou hast confoundid
to day the cheeris of alle thi seruauntis,
and that han maad saaf thi lijf, and the
lijf of thi sonys aud of thi douȝtris, and
the lijf of thi wyues, and the lijf of thi
6 secoundarye wyues. Thou louest the
hatynge thee, and thou hast in^t haate
the louynge thee; and thou hast shewid
to day, for thou reckist not of thi leeders
and of thi seruauntis; and verreily I
haue knowen now, that if Absolon lyuede, and alle we hadden diede, thanne it
7 shulde plese to thee. Now than ryse, and
go forth, and spekynge do^u asecthe to
thi seruauntis; forsothe I swere to thee
bi the Lord, that if thow gost not out,
that oon forsothe be not to abidynge still
with thee this nyȝt; and werse shal be
to thee this, than alle the yuels that
camen vpon thee fro thi ȝongth^v vnto
8 the tyme that is now. Thanne the kyng
roos, and satte in the ȝate; and to al
the puple it is toold, that the king satte
in the ȝate, and al the multitude cam
9 before the king. Forsothe Irael fleeȝ into
her tabernaclis. And al the puple stroof
in^w alle the lynagis of Irael, seiynge, The
kyng hath delyuerd vs fro the hoond of
oure enemyes, and he hath saued vs fro

CAP. XIX.

Forsothe it was teld to Joab, that the 1
kyng wepte, and biweilide his sone; and 2
the victorie in that dai was turned in to
morenyng to al the puple; for the puple
herde, that it was seid in that dai, The
kyng makith sorewe on his sone. And 3
the puple eschewide^a to entre in to the
citee in that dai, as the puple turned and
fleynge fro batel^b is wont to bowe awey.
Sotheli^c the kyng hilide his heed, and 4
criede with greet vois, My sone, Absolon!
Absolon, my sone! Therfor Joab entride 5
to the kyng in to the hows, and seide,
Thou hast schent to dai the cheris^d of alle
thi seruauntis, that han maad saaf thi lijf,
and the lijf of thi sones and of thi douȝtris, and the lijf of thi wyues, and the
lijf of thi^e secoundarie wyues. Thou louest 6
hem that haten thee, and thou hatist hem
that louen thee; and thou schewidist^f to
dai that thou reckist not of thi duykis
and of thi seruauntis; and verily Y haue
knowe now, that^g if Absolon lyuede, and
alle we hadden be deed, thanne it schulde
plese thee. Now therfor ryse^h thouⁱ, and 7
go^k forth, and speke thou, and make satisfaccioun to this eruauntis; for Y swere to
thee bi the Lord, that if thou schalt not
go out^l, sotheli^m not o man schal dwelle
with thee in this nyȝt; and this schal be
worse to thee, than alle yuelsⁿ that camen
on thee fro thi ȝong wexynge age til in to
present^o tyme. Therfor the kyng roos^p, 8
and sat in the ȝate; and it was teld to al
the puple, that the kyng sat in the ȝate,
and al the multitude cam bifor the kyng.
Forsothe Israel^{pp} fledde in to hise^q tabernaclis. And al the puple struede in al 9
the lynagis of Israel, and seide, The kyng
delyuerede^r vs fro the hond of alle oure
enemyes, and he sauede vs fro the hond of
Filisteis; and now'he fleeth^s fro the lond†

† he fleeth fro
the lond; that
is, fro the
kingis citee, as
if they seiden,
that the king
fle for Absolon.
Lire here. c.

† to BCEFII. ᵘ to do E pr. v. ᵛ ȝouthe CEFII. ʷ and ADII.

ᵃ etchewide I. ᵇ the batel A pr. m. ᶜ And I. ᵈ cheer KX. cheere O. ᵉ the ADM. ᶠ hast schewid I.
ᵍ for plures. ʰ ryse up I. ⁱ Om. I. ᵏ go thou I. ˡ forth I. ᵐ and I. ⁿ the yuels I. ᵒ this
present IK. ᵖ roos up I. ᵖᵖ al Israel E. ᵠ her IEL. ʳ hath delyuered I. ˢ hath fled I.

the hoond of Philisteis ; and now he flee3
10 fro the loond for Absolon. Forsothe Absolon, whom we anoyntiden kyng vpon
vs, is deed in batail; how long be 3e
stille, and 3e bren3en not a3en the kyng?
And the counseil of al Irael cam to the
11 king. Forsothe kyng Dauid sente to Sadoch and to Abiathar, preestis, seiynge,
Speke 3e to the more thur3 birth of Juda,
seiynge, Whi ben 3e comen last to brynge
a3en the kyng into his hows? Forsothe
the word of al Irael is ful comen to the
kyng, that thei brengen hym a3en into
his hows. For the kyng seide, Thes
12 thingis 3e shulen seye to the puple, My
britheren 3e, my boon and my flesh 3e ;
13 whi last brengen 3e a3en the kyng? And
to Amasa seye 3ee, Whether ert thou not
my boon and my flesh ? Thes thingis God
do to me, and thes thingis adde, if thou
were not maister of chiualrye after Joab
14 before me al tyme. And he bowide the
herte of alle the men of Juda as of o
man ; and thei senten to the king, seiynge, Turn a3en, thou and alle thi ser-
15 uauntis. And the kyng turnede a3en,
and cam vnto Jordan ; and al Juda cam
forth into Galgala, that he a3en come to
the kyng, and thei shulden brynge hym
16 ouer Jordan. Forsothe Semei, the sone
of Gera, the sone of Gemyny, of Bahurym, hi3ede, and cam doun with the men
of Juda into a3en comynge of kyng Da-
17 uid, with a thousand men of Beniamyn ;
and child Ciba of the hows of Saul, and
his fifteen sonys, and twenti seruantis
weren with hym ; and brekynge Jordan
18 before the kyng, passeden the forthis,
that^w thei brengen ouer the hows of the
kyng, and doon after his comaundynge.
Forsothe Semei, the sone of Gera, faln
doun before the kyng, whanne now he
19 hadde passid Jordan, seide to hym^x, My

for Absolon. Forsothe^t Absolon, whom we 10
anoyntiden on^u vs, is deed in batel; hou
longe ben 3e stille, *that is*^v, *fro*^w *know-*
lechyng of synne, and fro axyng of
for3yuenesse^x, and bryngen not a3en the
kyng ? And the counsel of al Israel cam
to the kyng. Forsothe^y kyng Dauid sente 11
to Sadoch and to^z Abiathar, preestis^a, and
seide, Speke 3e to the grettere men in
birthe of Juda, and seie 3e, Whi camen 3e
the^b laste to brynge a3en the kyng in to
his hows? Sotheli^c the word of al Israel
cam to the kyng, that thei wolden brynge
hym a3en in to his hows. For the kyng
seide, 3e schulen seie these thingis to the
puple, 3e ben my britheren†, 3e ben my 12
boon and my fleisch; whi the laste bryngen
3e a3ens the kyng ? And seie 3e to Amasa, 13
Whether thou art not my boon and my
fleisch ? God do these thingis to me, and
adde these thingis^d‡, if thou schalt not be
maistir of chyualrye bifore me in al tyme
aftir Joab‖. And Dauid bowide^e the herte 14
of alle men of Juda as of o man ; and thei
senten to the kyng, and seiden, Turne
thou a3en, and alle thi seruauntis. And 15
the kyng turnede a3en, and cam 'til to^f
Jordan ; and al Juda cam til in to Galgala
to mete the kyng, and lede^g hym ouer
Jordan. Forsothe^h Semei, the sone of 16
Gera, soneⁱ of Gemyny, of Bahurym, hastide, and cam doun with the men of Juda
in to the metyng of kyng Dauid, with a 17
thousynde men of Beniamyn ; and Siba,
a^k child of the hows of Saul, and fiftene
sones of hym, and twenti seruauntis weren
with hym ; and thei braken in to Jordan,
bifor the kyng, and passide^l the forthis^m, 18
that thei schulden lede ouer the hows of
the kyng, and schuldenⁿ do bi the co-
maundement^o of the kyng. Sotheli^p Semei, the sone of Gera, knelide bifor the
king, whanne he hadde passid now Jor-

† 3e ben my
britheren;
Dauyth sente
to the men of
Juda, that
weren with
Absolon, that
they schulden
be of the firste
to lede him
a3en, for of this
that thei weren
of Juda, they
weren ascham-
ed to appere in
his si3t, for
they hadden
forfetid a3enus
him more than
straungeris ;
and therfor
Dauyth per-
seyuede this,
and sente for
hem, that they
schulden come
sikirly, for he
was redy to
for3yue. *Lire*
here. c.
‡ *adde these*
thingis; that is,
grettere 3uels
than Y suffride
in the persecu-
cioun of Abso-
lon. *Lire here.*
c.
‖ *aftir Joab;*
summe bokis
han aftir Joab;
that is, vndur
Joab, for the
Ebreu word
here, is set
sum tyme for
vndur, and
sum tyme it
signefieth for;
and the same
sentence is,
for Dauyth pur-
poside not to
remoue Joab
fro his office,
but that Amasa
schulde fille
his while in
tyme and
places where it
semyde spede-
ful. *Lire here.*
c.

^w that and A.   ^x the kyng A.

^t Certis I. ^u upon I. ^v Om. DKMSXÇ. ^w in R. Om. KS. ^x Gloss omitted in I. ^y And I. ^z Om. C.
^a the preestis I. ^b Om. I. ^c And I. ^d thingis to I. ^e bowide *to him* I. ^f vnto I. ^g to lede I. ^h But I.
ⁱ the sone I. ^k the I. ^l thei passide I. ^m foordis IKR. fordes L. ⁿ Om. DKMXÇ. ^o heest I.
^p Certis I.

lord, ne wiyt thou to me the wickidnes,
ne haue thou mynde of the wrongis of
thi seruaunt in the dai, the which thou
wentist out, my lord kyng, fro Jerusalem, ne set thou, kyng, in thin herte ;
20 forsothe I thi seruaunt knowe my synne ;
and therfor to dai first I cam of al the
hows of Joseph, and cam doun into aȝen-
21 comynge of my lord the kyng. Forsothe
answerynge Abisai, the sone of Saruye,
seide, Whether for thes wordis Semei
shal not be slayn, that curside to the
22 crist of the Lord? And Dauid seith,
What to me and to ȝou, ȝe sonys of Saruye? Whi ben ȝe maad to me to day
into Sathan? Thanne whether to dai
shal not be slayn a man in Irael? Whether I knowe not me to day maad kyng
23 vpon Irael? And the kyng seith to Semei, Thou shalt not die; and he swore
24 to hym. Forsothe Myphibosech, the sone
of Jonathan, the sone of Saul, cam doun
into the aȝencomynge of the kyng, the
feet vnwasshen, and the beerd vnshauen.
And his clothis he hadde not washen, fro
the day that the kyng wente out vnto
the day of his turnynge aȝen in pees.
25 And whanne he hadde aȝen comen to the
kyng, the kyng seide to hym, Whi cam
26 thou not with me, Myphibosech? And
answerynge he seith, My lord kyng, my
seruaunt dispiside me ; and I thi seruaunt seide to hym, that he shulde make
to me redi an asse, and stiynge vp I myȝte
goo with the kyng; forsothe I thi ser-
27 uaunt am halt. Also and he accuside me,
thi seruaunt, to thee, my lord kyng; forsothe thou, my lord kyng, ert as the
aungel of God; do that is plesynge to
28 thee. Forsothe ne the hows of mi fader
was but gilti to the deth to my lord
kyng; forsothe thou puttist me thi seruaunt among thi meetfelawis of thi bord ;
what thanne haue I of ryȝtwise playnt,
or what may I more be spoken of to the

dan, and seide to the kyng, My lord the[q] 19
kyng, arette thou not wickidnesse to me,
nether haue thou mynde of the wrongis of
thi seruaunt in the dai, in which thou, my
lord the[q] kyng, ȝedist out of Jerusalem,
nether sette thou, kyng, in[r] thin herte;
for Y thi seruaunt knoleche my synne; 20
and therfor to dai Y cam the firste of al
the hows of Joseph, and Y cam doun in
to the meetyng of my lord the[s] kyng.
Forsothe[t] Abisai, the sone of Saruye, an- 21
sweride and seide, Whether Semei, that
curside the crist of the Lord, schal not be
slayn for these wordis? And Dauid seide, 22
What is to me and to ȝou, ȝe[u] sones of
Saruye? Whi ben ȝe maad to me to dai
in to Sathan†? Therfor whether a man
schal be slayn to dai in Israel? Whether
Y knowe not me maad kyng to dai on[v]
Israel? And the kyng seide to Semey, 23
Thou schalt not die‡; and the kyng swoor
to hym. Also Myphibosech, sone[w] of Jo- 24
nathas, sone[w] of Saul‖, cam doun with
vnwaischun feet, and with berd[x] vnclip-
pid, in to the comyng of the kyng. And
Mysphibosech hadde not waische hise
clothis, fro the dai in which the kyng
ȝede out of Jerusalem til to the dai of his
turnyng[y] aȝen in pees. And whanne at 25
Jerusalem he hadde come to the kyng,
the kyng seide to him, Myphibosech, whi
camest thou not[z] with me? And he an- 26
sweride and seide, My lord the[a] kyng, my
seruaunt dispiside me; and Y thi seruaunt
seide to hym, that he schulde sadle[b] the[c]
asse to me, and Y schulde stie[d], and Y
schulde[e] go with the king; for[f] Y thi seruaunt am crokid[g]. More ouer and he 27
accuside me, thi seruaunt, to thee, my
lord the[h] kyng; forsothe[i] thou, my lord
'the kyng[k], art as the aungel of God; do
thou that, that is plesaunt to thee. For[l] 28
the hows of my fadir was not[m] no but
gilti of[n] deeth to my lord the kyng; sotheli[o] thou hast set me thi seruaunt among

† in to Sathan; that is, aduersarie. c.

‡ thou schalt not die; for if Dauyth hadde suffrid Semey to be slayn anoon, othere men that weren with Absolon in purueynge Dauyth, wolden haue drad to hem silf, and thei that hadden not come ȝit, wolden haue go ahak, and in hap summen that hadden come thanne, wolden haue go awey priuely; and so the sleyng of Semey myȝte haue be occasioun of greet dissencioun, and of greet ȝuel aȝenus Dauyth. Lire here. c

‖ sone of Saul; summe bokis han here, the sone of Jonathas, sone of Saul, but the truthe of Ebreu and oure bokis amendid, han not so. Lire here. c

Y Om. BCEFH.

q Om. 1. r tho wrongis in 1. s Om. 1. t And 1. u the 1. v in no. upon 1. w the sone 1. x his berd 1. y comyng 1. z not forth 1. a Om. 1. b haue sadlid 1. c an 1. d haue stied up 1. e haue 1. f Om. 1. g halt 1. h Om. 1. i but 1. k Om. 1. l Certis ne ther 1. m Om. 1. n to 1. o and 1.

29 kyng? Forsothe the kyng seith to hym, What more shalt thou speke? stedefast it is that I haue spoken; thou and Siba,
30 dyuyde ȝe possessiouns. And Myphibosech answerde to the kyng, Also al take he, aftir that my lord the kyng is turned
31 aȝen pesibli[x] into his hows. Forsothe Berzellay Galadite, a[a] ful olde man, comynge down fro Rogelym, ladde the kyng ouer Jordan, redi also for to folwe hym
32 biȝonde the flood. Forsothe Berzellai Galadite was ful ooolde, that is, of fourscore ȝeer, and he ȝaf food to the kyng, whanne he dwellid in the defensable placis; forsothe he was a ful mych riche
33 man. And so the kyng seide to Berzellai, Come with me, that thou reste sikir with
34 me in Jerusalem. And Berzellai seith to the kyng, How feele ben the dayes of the ȝeeris of my lijf, that I stye vp with the
35 kyng to Jerusalem? Of foure scoore ȝeer I am to dai; whether my wittis thryuen to deme swote or bittir, or meet and drynk may delite thi seruaunt, or I may here forthermore the vois of men syngers and of wymmen syngers? Whi thi seruaunt be to charge to my lord kyng?
36 A litil I shal goo forth thi seruaunt fro Jordan with thee, ne I nede this while
37 ȝeeldynge; but I biseche, that I turne aȝen thi seruaunt, and die in my citee, and be biried bisyde the sepulcre of my fader and of my moder; forsothe ˌthere is thi seruaunt Chamaan; he go with thee, my lord kyng, and do to hym that
38 semeth to thee good. And so the kyng seide to hym, Chamaan goo with me; and I shal doo to hym what euer thing shal pleese to thee, and al that thou
39 askist of me, thou shalt geete. And whanne al the puple, and the kyng was passid ouer Jordan, he resteiede[b]; and the king kisside Berzellai, and blesside to hym; and he turnede aȝen into his
40 place. Thanne the kyng wente into Gal-

the gestis of thi boord[p]; what therfor haue Y of iust pleynt, ether what may Y more crye to the kyng? Sotheli[q] the 29 kyng seide to hym, What spekist thou more? that that Y haue spoke is stidefast; thou and Siba depart possessyouns[r]†.
And Myphibosech answeride to the kyng, 30 ȝhe, take he alle thingis, aftir that my lord the[s] kyng turnede[t] aȝen pesibli in to his hows. Also Berzellai of Galaad, 31 a ful eld man, cam doun fro Rogelym, and ledde the kyng ouer Jordan, redi also to sue hym ouer[u] the flood. Forsothe[w] 32 Berzellai of Galaad was ful eld, that is, of foure score ȝeer, and he ȝaf metis to the kyng, whanne the kyng dwellyde in castels; for Berzellai was a ful riche man.
Therfor[x] the kyng seide to Berzellai, 33 Come thou with me, that thou reste sikirli with me in Jerusalem. And Ber- 34 zellai seide to the kyng, Hou manye ben the daies‡ of ȝeeres of my lijf, that Y stie[y] with the kyng in to Jerusalem? Y am 35 of foure score ȝeer to dai; whether my wittis ben quike to deme swete thing ethir bittir, ether mete[z] and drynk may delite thi seruaunt, ether may Y here more the vois of syngeris ether of syngsters? Whi is thi seruaunt to charge to my lord the[a] kyng? Y thi seruaunt schal 36 go forth a litil fro Jordan with thee, Y haue no nede to this ȝeldyng; but Y bi- 37 seche[b], that Y thi seruaunt turne aȝen, and die in my citee, and be biried bisidis the sepulcre of my fadir and of my modir; forsothe[c] Chamaam is[d] thi seruaunt, my lord the[e] kyng, go he with thee, and do thou to hym that semeth good to thee. Therfor the kyng seide to hym[ee], 38 Chamaam passe[f] with me; and Y schal do to hym what euer thing plesith thee, and thou schalt gete al thing, which[g] thou axist of me. And whanne al the puple 39 and the kyng hadden passid Jordan, the kyng abood; and 'the kyng[h] kisside Ber-

† thou and Ciba, departe possessiouns; here Danyth grauntide vniustly to the seruaunt of Myphibosech, the half of the eritage of Myphibosech, wherfor the rewme was departid aftirward, in the tyme of Roboam sone of his sone, as it was seide pleynliere in 1. book xx. c°. Here it is to perseyue, hou myche flaterers and bachiteris ben perelouse to princes, for Danyth so booly and lust, was taknn and disseyued bi the wordis of Ciba, flaterere and bachitere, that he grauntide to Siba the eritage of Myphibosech his lord, in the absence of Myphiboseche, and while he herde not; and that is worse, aftir that he herde Myphiboseche, verily excusinge him silf, he withdrow not al his vniust seiyng, but he made the worste seruaunt euene with his lord, and netheles he auȝte to haue hanged thilke seruaunt, for the fals accusing of his lord of tresoun aȝenus the kingis mageste. Lire here. c.

‡ hou many ben the dages, etc.: as if he seyde, it is tyme that Y thenke of deth, not of onours ether of delices, and this is aȝenus elde now that preessen forth hem silf to the courtis of grete men. Lire here. c.

---

[z] pesibleli ᴇ. [a] Om. ᴇ pr. m. [b] resteȝede cᴇ. restide ᴇ.

[p] table 1. [q] And 1. [r] the possessyouns 1.
so 1. [y] stie up 1. [z] wher mete 1. [a] Om. 1. [b] biseche thee 1. [c] but 1. [d] Om. 1. [e] Om. 1. [ee] Barzellay 1. [f] go forth 1. [g] that 1. [h] Om. EL.

galan, and Chamaan with hym. Forsothe
al the puple of Juda brou3te ouer the
kyng, and of the puple of Irael oonli the
41 half parti was at. And so alle the men
of Irael rennynge to the kyng, seiden to
hym, Whi oure britheren, the men of
Juda, han stoln thee, and han brou3t ouer
Jordan the kyng and his hows, and alle
42 the men of Dauid with hym? And alle
the men of Juda answerden to the men
of Irael, For to me nerre is the kyng;
whi wraththist thou vpon this thing?
Whether we han eten eny thing of the
43 kyng, or 3iftis to vs ben 3euen? And the
man of Irael answerde to the men of
Juda, and seith, Bi ten parties more I
am anentis the kyng, and more to me
perteneth Dauid than to thee; whi hast
thou doo to me wronge, and it is not
toold to me former, that I brynge a3en
my kyng? Forsothe harder answerden the
men of Juda than the men of Irael.

zellai, and blesside hym; and he turnede
a3en in to his place. Therfor[i] the kyng 40
passide[k] in to Galgala, and Chamaam with
hym. Sotheli[l] al the puple of Juda hadde
ledde the kyng ouer, and the half part
oneli of the puple of Israel was present.
Therfor alle the men of Israel camen to- 41
gidere to the king, and seiden to hym,
Whi han oure britheren, the men of Juda,
stole thee, and han led[m] the kyng and his
hows ouer Jordan, and alle the men of
Dauid with hym? And ech man of Juda 42
answeride to the men of Israel, For the
kyng is neer to me; whi art thou wrooth
on[n] this thing? Whether we han ete ony
thing of the kyng, ether 3iftis ben 3ouun
to vs? And a man of Israel answeride to 43
the men of Juda, and seide, Y am grettere
bi ten partis at[o] the kyng, and Dauith
perteyneth more to me than to thee; whi
hast thou do wrong to me, and 'it was[p] not
teld[q] to 'me the formere[r], that Y schulde
brynge a3en my kyng? Forsothe[s] the
men of Juda answeryden hardere to the
men of Israel.

CAP. XX.

1 It felle forsothe, that there was a man
of Belial, Syba bi name, the sone of
Botry, a 'man of Gemyny[c]; and he songe
with a trumpe, and seith, There is not
to vs paart in Dauid, ne heritage in the
sone of Isay; turn a3en into thi taber-
2 naclis[d], Irael. And al Irael ys seuered
fro Dauid, and folwide Ciba, the sone of
Botri; the men forsothe of Juda cleueden
to her kyng, fro Jordan vnto Jerusalem.
3 And whanne the kyng was comen into
his hows into Jerusalem, he took the
wymmen, and his ten secoundarie wyues,
the whiche he hadde laft to the hows to
be kept, and he took hem into waard,
3yuynge foodis to hem; and he wente not
into hem, but thei weren closid vnto the
dai of her[e] deth, lyuynge in widewheed.

CAP. XX.

Also it bifelde, that a man of Belial 1
was there, Siba bi name, the sone of
Bothri, a man of the generacioun of Gemyny; and he sownede with a clarioun[t],
and seide, No part is to vs in Dauid,
nether eritage in the sone of Ysai; thou,
Israel, turne a3en in to thi tabernaclis.
And al Israel was departid fro Dauid[†],2
and suede Siba, the sone of Bothri; forsothe[u] the men of Juda clenyden to her
kyng, fro Jordan 'til to[w] Jerusalem. And 3
whanne the kyng hadde come in to his
hows in Jerusalem, he took ten wymmen,
hise secundarie wyues, whiche he hadde
left to kepe the[x] hous, and he bitook[y] hem
in to keping, and 3af mete to hem; and he[z]
entride not to hem; but thei weren closid
'til to[a] the dai of her deeth, and lyueden

† and Israel
was departid
fro Dauyth;
at a tyme that
Dauyth were
punyschid so;
for tresoun
a3enus Urie,
and that Siba
schulde be
slayn for his
malice. Lire
here. c.

---

c double man E pr. m.   d tabernacle A.   e his E pr. m.

1 Thanne I.   k passide forth I.   l And I.   m led forth I.   n upon I.   o to I.   p whi was it I.
q schewid I.   r me that I am formere I.   s And I.   t trumpe I.   u and I.   w vnto I.   x his I.   y took A.
z Dauid I.   a vnto I.

4 Forsothe the kyng seide to Amase, Cleep to me alle the men of Juda into the thridde dai, and thou be to present. 5 Thanne Amasa wente for to clepe Juda; and he dwelte out of the couenaunt f tyme that the kyng ordeynde to hym. 6 Forsothe Dauid seith to Abisai, Now more Siba, the sone of Botri, is to tourment vs than Absolon; tak therfor the seruauntys of thi lord, and pursue hym, lest perauenture he fynde the citee strengthid, and 7 flee awey fro vs. Thanne wente out with hym the men of Joab, Cerethi forsothe and Pherethi, and alle the stroonge men wenten out of Jerusalem to pursue 8 Siba, the sone of Botri. And whanne thei weren biside the greet stoon, that is in Gabaon, Amasa comynge aȝen cam to hem; forsothe Joab was clothid with a strait coote at the mesure of his shap, and there aboue gird with a knyif hongynge vnto the reyn gottys in the sheethe, the which forgid with liȝt meuynge myȝt 9 goon out, and smyte. And so Joab seide to Amasan, Heyl, my brother! And he heelde with the riȝt hoond the chyn of 10 Amase, as kyssynge hym. Forsothe Amasa weytide not wel the knyif that Joab hadde, the which smoot hym in the side, and shedde out the gottis of hym into the erthe, and is deed; ne the secounde wounde he putte to. Forsothe Joab and Abisay, his brother, pursueden Siba, the 11 sone of Botry. There among sum men of the children of Dauid, whanne thei hadden 'seen and ff stonden biside the careyn of Amase, of the felawis of Joab, seiden, Loo! that wolde be for Joab, leder of 12 Dauid. Forsothe Amasa spreynd g with blood laye in the myddil weye. That sawȝ a man, that al the puple stood stille to seen hym, and meuede a wey Amasa fro the weye into the feelde, and couerde hym with a clooth, lest the goers shulden

in widewehed. Forsothe b Dauid seide to 4 Amasa, Clepe thou to gidere to me alle the men of Juda in to the thridde dai, and be thou present. Therfor Amasa ȝede e, 5 that he clepe to gidere the puple of Juda; and he dwellide ouer the couenaunt d, which e the kyng hadde set to hym. So-6 theli f Dauid seide to Abisai, Now Siba, the sone of Botri, schal turmente vs more than Absolon dide g; therfor take h the seruauntis of i thi lord, and pursue hym, lest in hap he fynde strengthid citees, and ascape vs. Therfor the men of Joab 7 ȝeden k † out with Abisai, and Cerethi and Ferethi l, and alle stronge m men ȝeden out of Jerusalem to pursue Siba, the sone of Bochry. And whanne thei weren bisidis 8 the greet stoon, which n is in Gabaon, Amasa cam, and ran to hem; forsothe o Joab was clothid with a streit coote at the mesure of his abit p, and was q gird aboue with a swerd, 'ether dagger r', hangynge doun 'til to s the t entrayls in a schethe, 'which swerd u maad 'craftily myȝte go out v ‡ bi liȝt touchyng, and smyte w. Ther-9 for x Joab seide to Amasā, Heil, my brother! And he y helde with the z riȝt hond the chyn of Amasa, as kissinge him. For-10 sothe a Amasa took not b kepe of c the swerd d, 'which swerd e Joab hadde, and Joab smoot Amasa in the side, and schedde out his entraillis in to the erthe, and Amasa was deed; and Joab addide not 'the secounde f wounde. Forsothe g Joab and Abisai, his brother, pursueden Siba, the sone of Bochri. In the meene tyme whanne 11 'sum men h of the children of Dauid, of the felowis of Joab, hadden i stonde bisidis the deed bodi of Amasa, thei seiden, Lo! he that wolde k be the felowe of Dauid for Joab. Forsothe l Amasa was bispreynt 12 with blood, and lay in the myddil of the weie. Sum m man siȝ this, that al the puple abood to se Amasa, and he remouyde

† men of Joab ȝeden, etc.; that is, that weren went to go out with Joab, and obeye to him. Lire here. c.

‡ myȝte go out; in Ebren it is, and it ȝede out, and felde doun; Raby Salomon seith, that Joab disposide so of purpos, that it felde doun to the erthe fro the schethe, that Amasa schulde bileue so, that Joab reisede the swerd fro erthe to putte aȝen in the schethe, and not to smyte him; therfor it sueth, forsothe Amasa kepte not the swerd, that is, kepte not him silf, for smytyng of the swerd. Lire here. c.

f plesid E pr. m. couenauntid CE sec. m. ff Om. E pr. m. g sprengd CE.

b And 1. c ȝede forth 1. d couenaunt tyme 1. e that 1. f And 1. g Om. 1. h take thou 1. i of Joab 1. k wenten 1. l arblasters and archers 1 marg. m the stronge o. n that 1. o and 1. p schap 1. q he was 1. r Om. 1KX. s vnto 1. t his 1. u and it was 1. which swerd ether dagger K. v to drawe out 1. w to smyte 1. x And so 1. y Joab 1. z his 1. a And 1. b no 1. c to 1. d knyif 1. e that 1. f to an other 1. g And 1. h summe L. i hadde k wolde haue 1. l And 1. m A 1.

13 abide stille for hym. Thanne hym meued
fro the weie, eche man folowynge Joab
wente to pursue Siba, the sone of Botri.
14 But he passide thur3 out alle the lynagis
of Yrael vnto Hebelam, and into Bethmacha; and alle the chosen men weren
15 gedrid to hym. And so thei camen, and
setten a3ens hym in Habela, and in Bethmacha, and ennyrounden the citee with
strengthis; and the citee is bisegid. Forsothe al the puple, that was with Joab,
16 enforside to destrie the wallis. And a
wyse womman criede out fro the citee,
Herith! herith! seith[h] to Joab, Nei3
17 hidir, and I shal speke with thee. The
whych whanne he hadde nei3id to hire,
she seide to hym, Thou ert Joab? And
he answerde, I. To whom thus she
spake, Here the wordis of thin hoond
womman. The which answerde, I here.
18 And eft she, A word, she seith, was seide
in olde prouerbe, Who[i] aske, asken thei
19 in Habela; and so thei profiteden[k]. Whether I am not, the which answere the
trewthe of Yrael? and thou sechist to
turne vpsedoun the citee, and to doon
awey the moder of citees in Irael? whi
berist thou doun the herytage of the
20 Lord? And Joab answerynge seith,
Aweie be, aweie be this fro me; I bere
21 not doun, ne destrie. Not so the thing
hath hym; but a man of the hil of Effraym, bi name Siba, the sone of Botri,
reride his hoond a3ens kyng Dauid;
takith hym aloue, and we shulen goo
awey fro the citee. And the womman
seith to Joab, Loo! his heed shal be sente
22 to thee bi the walle. Thanne she wente
into al the puple, and spak to hem wiseli;
the which the gird of heed of Siba, the
sone of Botri, casten forth to Joab. And
he songe with the trompe, and thei
wenten awey fro the citee, echon into her
tabernaclis; forsothe Joab turnyde a3en

Amasa fro the weie in to the feeld, and
he hilide Amasa with a cloth, lest men
passynge schulden abide for hym. Therfor 13
whanne he was remouyd fro[n] the weie,
ech man passide[o] suynge Joab to pursue
Siba, the sone of Bochri. Forsothe[p] Siba 14
hadde passide bi alle the lynagis[†] of Israel
til in to Habela, and in to Bethmacha; and
alle chosun[q] men weren gaderid to hym.
Therfor thei[r] camen, and fou3ten a3ens 15
hym[s] in Habela, and in Bethmacha, and
cumpassiden the citee with strengthingis;
and the citee was bisegid. Sotheli[t] al the
cumpany, that was with Joab, enforside
to distrie the wallis. And a wijs wom- 16
man of the citee criede an[u] hi3, Here 3e!
here 3e! seie 3e to Joab, Nei3e thou hidur,
and Y schal speke with thee. And whanne 17
he hadde nei3ed to hir, sche seide to hym,
Art thou Joab? And he answeride, Y am.
To whom sche spak thus, Here thou the
wordis[v] of thin handmayde. Which[w] Joab
answeride, Y here. And eft sche seide, 18
A word was seid in eld prouerbe, Thei
that axen, axe in Habela; and so thei pro-
fitiden. Whethir Y am[†] not, that answere 19
treuthe to Israel? and sekist thou to distrie a citee, and to distrie[x] a modir citee
in Israel[‡]? whi castidist[y] thou doun the
eritage of the Lord? And Joab answeride, 20
and seide, Fer be[z], fer be this fro me; Y
`caste not doun[a], nether Y distrye[b]. The 21
thing hath not so it silf; but a man of
the hil of Effraym, Siba, sone[c] of Bochri,
bi surname, reiside his hond a3ens kyng
Dauid; bitake 3e him aloone[d], and we
schulen go awei fro the citee. And the
womman seide to Joab, Lo! his heed schal
be sent to thee bi the wal. Therfor[e] the 22
womman entride[f] to al the puple, and sche
spak to hem wiseli; whiche[g] `castiden forth[h]
to Joab the heed of Siba, sone[i] of Bochri,
gird of. And Joab sownede with a trumpe,
and thei departiden fro the citee, ech man

† li alle the
lynagis; and
he excitide
hem to make
him silf king.
Lire here. c.

‡ wher Y am;
the womman
spekith in the
persoone of the
cytee, as if sche
seide, This citee
holdis euere
truthe and
feith to the
king; and ther-
for in Ebreu
it is thus, Y
am oon of pe-
sible and trewe,
that is, oon of
the noumbre of
citees pesible
and trewe to
the kyng. Lire
here. c.
‡ a modir citee
in Israel; for
ech citee is mo-
dir of the pu-
ple boruu and
nurschid there.
In sum bokis
it is set in, of
citees, but it is
not of the text;
for nether it is
in Ebreu, ne-
ther in bokis
amendid. Lire
here. c.

h she seith A.　i Whoso E pr. m.　k wentyn forth E.

a for EC.　o passide forth I.　p Certis I.　q the chosun I.　r the oost of Joab I marg.　s Siba I.
t And I.　u on K. a EL.　v word CE.　w Om. I.　x do awey I.　y throwist I.　z be this fro me I.
a destrie not the citee I.　b waste it I.　c the sone I.　d aloone to us I.　e Thanne I.　f weote yn I.
g and thei I.　h threwen I.　i the sone I.

23 to Jerusalem to the kyng. Thanne Joab was vpon al the oost of Irael ; forsothe Bananyas, the sone of Joiade, vpon Cere-
24 theis and Pheretheis ; Adhuram forsothe vpon the tributis ; but Josaphat, the
25 sone of Achilud, the chaunselere ; Siba forsothe a scribe ; forsothe Sadoch and
26 Abiathar prestis ; forsothe Hira Hiracte was the preest of Dauid.

CAP. XXI.

1 Forsothe there is doon hungre in the dais of Dauid, thre ȝeer contynueli. And Dauid counseilde the heuenli answere of the Lord ; and the Lord seide, For Saul, and the hows of hym, and the blood, for
2 he slewȝ Gabanytes. Thanne the Gabanytis clepid, the kyng seide to hem ; forsothe Gabanytis ben not of the sonys of Irael, but the relikis of Ammoreis ; forsothe the sonys of Yrael hadden sworn to hem, that thei shulen not slee hem, and Saul wolde smyte hem bi enuye, as for the sonys of Irael and of Juda ;
3 thanne Dauid seide to Gabanitis, What shal I doo to ȝou, and what shal be ȝoure amendys, that ȝe blissen to the heritage
4 of the Lord ? And Gabanytis seiden to hym, There is no questioun to vs vpon gold and siluer, but aȝens Saul, and the hows of hym ; and we wolen not, that there be slayn a man of Irael. To whom the kyng seith, What thanne wolen ȝe,
5 that I doo to ȝow ? The whiche seiden to the kyng, The man that hath defowlid vs, and oppressid wickidli, so we owen to doon awey, ne oon forsothe be laft of the lynage of hym in alle the coostis of
6 Yrael. Be there ȝouun to vs seuen men of the sonys of hem, that we crucifien hem to the Lord in Gabaa of Saul, sum-

in to hise tabernaclis ; forsothe Joab turnede aȝen to Jerusalem to the kyng. Therfor Joab was on al the oost of Is- 23 rael ; forsothe Benanye, sone of Joiada, was on Cerethiȝ and Ferethi ; forsothe 24 Adhuram was on tributis ; forsothe Josaphat, sone of Achilud, was chaunceler ; forsothe Siba was scryueyn ; forsothe 25 Sadoch and Abiathar weren preestis† ; forsothe Hira of Hiarith was preest of 26 Dauid.

CAP. XXI.

Also hungur was maad in the lond of 1 Israel in the daies of Dauid‡, bi thre ȝeer contynueli. And Dauid counseilde the answere of the Lord^c ; and the Lord seide, For Saul, and his hows, and blood, for he killide men of Gabaon. Therfor whanne 2 Gabaonytis weren clepid, the kyng seide to hem ; sotheli Gabaonytis ben not of the sones of Israel, but thei ben the relikys of Ammorreis ; and the sones of Israel hadden swore to hem, 'that is, that thei schulden not 'be slayn°§, and Saul wolde smyte hem for feruent loue, as for the sones of Israel and of Juda ; therfor Da- 3 uid seide to Gabaonytis, What schal Y do to ȝou, and what schal be ȝoure amendis, that ȝe blesse the eritage of the Lord ? And Gabaonytis seiden to hym, No ques- 4 tioun is to vs on gold and siluer, but aȝens Saul, and aȝens his hows ; nether we wolen, that a man of Israel be slayn. To whiche the kyng seide, What therfor wolen ȝe, that Y do to ȝou ? Whiche 5 seiden to the king, We owen to do awei so the man, that 'al to brak ethir defoulide vs, and oppresside wickidli, that not oon sotheli be residue of his generacioun in alle the coostis of Israel. Seuene 6 men of hise sones be ȝouun to vs, that we 'crucifie hem to the Lord ‖ in Gabaa of

† prestis of Dauyth ; that is, a greet man among lugis and princes anentis Dauyth. Lire here. c.

‡ in the daies of Dauyth ; for he was necligent to panysche the opyn synne of Saul, that killide Gabaonytis for conceise of her eritage, aȝenus the ooth of Josue, and of the princes of Israel. Lire here. c.

§ that thei schulden not be slayn ; summe bokis han here, that they schulden not panysche ether not sle hem, but this is not in Ebreu, nether in bokis amendid, nethelees it is vndurstondun ; wherfor sum man settide it first bi the maner of a glos, and aftirward it was set in the text bi the ignoraunce of writeres. Lire here. c.

‖ to the Lord ; that is, to the declaring of Goddis riȝtfulnesse. Lire here.

^k and 1.   ^l And so 1.   ^m upon 1.   ⁿ and 1.   ^o the sone 1.   ^p upon 1.   ^q scheeters 1.   ^r up arblasters 1.   ^s and 1.   ^t upon 1.   ^u the tributis 1.   ^v and 1.   ^w the sone 1.   ^x and 1.   ^y but 1.
^z and 1.   ^a the preest 1.   ^b And c.   ^c that is, aȝide counsel of the Lord in the answering place κ marg.
^d it is for 1.   ^e for his 1.   ^f for blood 1.   ^g the men 1.   ^h men of Gabony 1.   ⁱ men of Gabony 1.
^k Om. 1.   ^l leeuyngis 1.   ^m Ammorey 1.   ⁿ Om. c1.   ^o sle hem 1.   ^p the men of Gabonye 1.   ^q Om. c.
^r upon 1.   ^s and nethir κ.   ^t whom 1.   ^u And thei 1.   ^v owen so 1.   ^w Om. 1.   ^x Om. 1.   ^y Om. c1.
^z Om. c.   ^a Om. 1.   ^b oppresside us 1.   ^c left 1.   ^d do hem on crosse 1.

tyme the chosen of the Lord. And the
7 kyng seith, I shal ȝeue. And the kyng
sparide to Myphibosech, the sone of
Jonathan, the sone of Saul, for the ooth
of the Lord, that was betwix Dauid and
8 Jonathan, the sone of Saul. And so the
kyng took two sonys of Respha, the
dowȝter of Ahia, whom she bare to Saul,
Armoony, and Myphibosech; and 'of
Mychol fyue sones, of the[l] douȝter of
Saul, whom she gat to Adriel, the sone
9 of Berzellay, that was of Demolati. And
he ȝaf hem into the hoondis of Gabanytis, the which crucifieden hem in the
hil before the Lord; and thes seuen
slayn togidir fellen in the dais of the
fyrst rijp, begynnynge the repynge of
10 barli. Forsothe takynge Respha, the
douȝter of Ahia, spradde abrood an
heyre to hire on a stoon, fro the bigynnynge of the ryp to the tyme that watir
droppide vpon hem fro heuene; and she
suffride not breddis to teren hem bi the
11 day, ne beestis[m] bi the nyȝt. And these
thingis ben toold to Dauid, the whiche
dide Respha, the douȝter of Ahia, the
12 secoundarye wijf of Saul. And Dauid
ȝede, and took the boonus of Saul, and
the boonus of Jonathan, his sone, of[n] the
men of Jabes Galaad; 'the which[o] hadden
stoln hem fro the streete of Bethsan, in
the which Philisteis hadden hongid hem,
13 whanne thei slewen Saul in Gelboe. And
bare a wey thens the boonus of Saul,
and the boonus of Jonathan, his sone;
and thei gederynge togidir the boonus of
hem that weren piȝt[p], birieden hem with
the boonus of Saul and Jonathan, his
sone, in the loond of Beniamyn, in the
side in the sepulcre of Cys, his fader.
14 And thei diden alle thingis, that the
kyng comaundide; and the Lord dide
mercy aȝen to the loond after thes

Saul, sum tyme the chosun man of the
Lord. And the kyng seide, Y schal ȝyue[e].
And the kyng sparide Myphibosech, sone[f] 7
of Jonathas, sone[f] of Saul, for the ooth of
the Lord, that was bitwixe Dauid and bitwixe[g] Jonathas, sone[h] of Saul. Therfor[i] 8
the kyng took twei sones of Respha, douȝter[j] of Ahira, whiche sche childide to Saul,
Armony, and Mysphibosech; and *he took*
fyue sones† of Mychol, douȝter[k] of Saul,
whiche sche gendride to Adriel, sone[l] of
Berzellai, that was of Molaty. And hem[m] 9
ȝaf hem in to the hondis of Gabaonytis[n],
whiche[o] crucifieden[p] tho sones[q] in[r] the[s] hil
bifor the Lord; and these seuene felden[t]
slayn togidere in the daies of the firste
rep[u], whanne the repyng of barli bigan.
Forsothe Respha, douȝtir[v] of Ahia, took[w] 10
an heire, and 'araiede to hir silf *a place*
aboue the[x] stoon, fro the bigynnyng of
heruest til[y] watir droppide 'on hem[z] fro
heuene; and sche suffride not briddis to
tere hem bi dai, nether beestis bi nyȝt. And 11
tho thingis whiche Respha, secoundarie[a]
wijf of Saul, douȝtir[b] of Ahia, hadde do,
weren teld to Dauid. And Dauid ȝede, and 12
took the boonys of Saul, and the boonys
of Jonathas, his sone, of[c] the men of Jabes
of Galaad; that[d] hadden stole tho boonys
fro the street of Bethsan, in which street[e]
the[f] Filisteis hadden hangid hem, whanne
thei hadden slayn[g] Saul in Gelboe. And 13
Dauid bar out fro thennus the boonys of
Saul, and the boonys of Jonathas, his sone;
and thei gaderiden[h] the boonys of hem
that weren crucified, and birieden[i] tho
with the boonys of Saul and of Jonathas,
his sone, in the lond of Beniamyn, in the
side of the sepulcre of Cys, fadir[k] of Saul.
And thei diden al thingis, what euer 14
thingis[l] the kyng comaundide[m]; and the
Lord dide mercy to the lond aftir these
thingis. Forsothe batel of Filisteis[n] was 15

† *fyue sones;* these weren the kyndly sones of Merob, sister of Mychol, but Mychol nurschide hem, and purchaside in to sones afterward, for sche hadde no kyndly sones; therfor thei ben seid hir sones, and by this, sche is said to haue gendrid to Adriel, not for sche was his wiyf, but for Merob, hir sister, was his wiyf. *Lire here.* c.

[l] the fiue sones of Michol, the ᴇ *pr. m.*   [m] the beestis ᴀ.   [n] fro ʙᴄᴇꜰʜ.   [o] that c *pr. m.*   [p] piȝt to ᴇ *pr. m.*

[e] ȝyue hem to ȝou ι.   [f] the sone ι.   [g] Om. ι.   [h] the sone ι.   [i] And so ι.   [j] the douȝter cι.   [k] the douȝter ι.   [l] the sone ι.   [m] Dauid ι.   [n] the men of Gabonye ι.   [o] and thei ι.   [p] diden ι.   [q] seuen sones ι.   [r] upon crosse in ι.   [s] an ι.   [t] fellen doun ι.   [u] ripp ι.   [v] the douȝtir ι.   [w] took to hir ι.   [x] leide it vndir hir upon ᴀ ι.   [y] til that ι.   [z] Om. ι.   [a] the secoundarie ι.   [b] the douȝtir ι.   [c] fro ι.   [d] whiche ι.   [e] Om. ι.   [f] Om. ᴇι.   [g] slawe ι.   [h] gaderiden to gidre ι.   [i] thei birieden ι.   [k] the fadir ι.   [l] Om. ι.   [m] comaundide hem ι.   [n] the Philistees ι.

15 thingis. Forsothe there is doon eft
bateil of the Philisteis aȝens Irael; and
Dauid cam doun, and his seruauntis
with hym, and thei fauȝten aȝens Phi-
16 listeis. Forsothe Dauid failynge, Jesbi-
denob, that was of the kynrede of
Arapha, whose yren of the specre peiside
thre hundrid vnncis, and he was gird
with a newe swerd, 'enforside^q to smyte
17 Dauid. And Abisay, the sone of Saruye,
was to hym a^r socour; and the Philistee
smyten he slewȝ. Thanne the men
sworen to Dauid, seiynge, Now thow
shalt not goo out with vs in to bateil,
lest thou quenche the lanterne of Yrael.
18 The secounde bateil forsothe^s was in
Gob aȝens Philisteis^t; thanne he smoot
Sobochai of Huzachizaph, of the lynage
of Arapha, of the kynrede of geauntis.
19 The thridde bateil forsothe was in Gob
aȝens the Philisteis; in the which Adeo-
datis, the sone of the wijlde wode, leyer
of dyuerse colours, Bethlamyte, smoot
Goliath Gethee, whos shaft of the speere
20 was as a beem of websters. The ferthe
bateyl was in Geth; in the which was an
heeȝ^u man, that hadde sexe fyngris in the
hoondis and feet, that is, foure and twenti;
21 and he was of the kyn of Arapha; and he
blasphemyde in^v Yrael; forsothe Jonathan, the sone of Samaa, the brother of
22 Dauid, smoot hym. These foure ben
born of Arapha in Jeth, and thei fellen
in the hoond of Dauid, and of his seruauntis.

maad eft aȝens Israel; and Dauid ȝede
doun, and hise seruauntis with hym, and
fouȝten aȝen Filisteis^n. Sotheli^o whanne 16
Dauid failide, Jesbydenob†, that was of
the kyn of Arapha, *that is, of*^p *giauntis*^q,
and the yrun of his^r spere peiside thre
hundrid ouncis, and he was gird with a
newe swerd‡, enforside^s to smyte Dauid^t.
And Abisai, sone^u of Saruye, was in help 17
to Dauid; and he smoot and killide the
Filistei. Than the men of Dauid sworen,
and seiden, Now^v thou schalt not go out
with vs in to batel, lest thou quenche the
lanterne of Israel. Also the secounde batel 18
was in Gob aȝens Filisteis; thanne Sobothai of Osothai smoot Zephi, of the generacioun of Arapha, of the kyn of giauntis.
Also the thridde batel was in Gob aȝens 19
Filisteis; in which batel a man ȝouun of
God‖, the sone of forest^w, a^x broiderer, a
man of Bethleem, smoot Golyath of Geth,
whos 'schaft of spere^y was as a^z beem of
webbis. The fourthe batel was in Geth; 20
where ynne was an hiȝ man, that hadde
sixe fyngris in the^a hondis and feet^b, that
is, foure and twenti; and he was of the
kyn of Arapha; and he blasfemyde Is- 21
rael; sotheli^c Jonathan, sone^d of Samaa,
brother^e of Dauid, killide hym. These 22
foure^f weren borun of Arapha in Geth,
and thei felden doun in the hond of Dauid,
and of hise seruauntis.

† *Jesbedenov*;
this is al o
word bi the
Ebren. *Lire*
here. c.

‡ *a newe swerd*;
this word
swerd, is not
in Ebreu, but
thus it is in
Ebreu; and he
was gird of the
newe, that is,
as Ebreis sey-
en, in that day
he was knyt
of the newe.
Lire here. c.

‖ *a man ȝouun*
of God; that is,
Dauyth, that
was chosun of
God, and ȝouun
to the gouer-
nail of the peo-
ple, as in 1.
book xvi. c^o.
the sone of fo-
rest; for he
dwellide longe
in wodis fle-
ynge fro the
face of Saul.
a broiderer;
for he cam of
the kyn of
Beseleel, that
was principal
in the werk of
broiderie of the
tabernacle. The
firste batel here
teld, was the
laste, and the
iii. batel was
the firste. *Lire*
here. c.

CAP. XXII.

1 Forsothe Dauid spak to the Lord the
wordis of this ditee, in the day in the
which the Lord delyuerde him fro the
hoond of alle his enemyes, and fro the
2 hoond of Saul. And seith, The Lord
my stoon, and my strength, and my
3 saueour; my God, my strong, and^w I

CAP. XXII.

Forsothe^g Dauid spak to the Lord the 1
wordis of this song, in the dai in which
the Lord delynerede hym fro the^h hond
of alle hise enemyes, and fro the hond
of Saul. And Dauid seide, The Lord 2
is my stoon, and my strengthe, and my
sauyour; my God, my stronge^i, I schal 3

---

^q he is seen E *pr. m.*　　^r to BCEFH.　　^s Om. A.　　^t the Philisteis BCEFII.　　^u heis A.　　^v to CE.
^w Om. E *pr. m.*

^n the Philistees I.　^o Forsothe c.　^p Om. c.　^q *the giauntis* EL.　^r whos I.　^s enforside *him* I.　^t Dauid, whanne
he feilide I.　^u the sone I.　^v Now, *Dauid* I.　^w a forest I.　^x and a K.　^y spere schaft I.　^z the c.　^a his I.
^b in his feet I.　^c and I.　^d the sone I.　^e the brother I.　^f foure geauntis I.　^g Sothely I.　^h Om. c.
^i stronge *helper* I. strengthe ELb.

shal hoop in hym ; my sheeld, and the
horn of myn heelth, my rerer, and my
refute ; my saueour, fro wickidnes thou
4 shalt delyuer me.   I shal inwardli clepe
the preysable Lord ; and fro myn ene-
5 myes I shal be saaf.   For there han
enuyround me the defoulyngis of deeth ;
6 the stremys of Belial fereden me.   The
coordis of helle enuryrounden me ; there
wenten before me the gnaris^{ww} of deeth.
7 In tribulacioun I shal inwardli clepe the
Lord, and to my God I shal crye ; and he
herde fro his hooli temple my vois, and
8 my crye shal come to his eeris.   The
erthe is togidir meued, and tremblide ;
the foundementis of hillis ben togidir
smyten and squat, for he wraththide to
9 hem.   Smook stiede vp fro the neesth-
rillis of hym, and fier fro his mouth shal
deuowre ; the colis ben brent vp of it.
10 And he bowide heuenes, and cam doun ;
11 and mystynes^{x} vndur his feet.   And he
stiede^{y} vpon cherubyn, and flow3 ; and
slood^{z} vpon the pennys of 'the wynd^{a}.
12 He putte derknessis an hidlis in 'his
enuyroun^{b}, wynnowynge watris of the
13 cloudis of heuenes ; for the li3tynge in
the si3t of hym ben brent vp the coolis
14 of fier.   The Lord shal thundre fro
heuene ; and the Hei3 shal 3eue his voys.
15 He sente his arowis, and scatrede hem ;
16 leytis, and wanstid hem.   And there
apperide the out heeldyngis of the see,
and ben opened the foundementis of the
world ; fro the blamynge of the Lord,
fro the inbrethinge of the spiryt of his
17 woodnes.   He sente fro an hei3, and took
me ; and drou3 out me fro manye watris.
18 He delyuerde me fro myn enemye moost
my3ti, and fro hem that hatiden me ;
19 for thei weren stronger than I.   Thei
camen before me in the day of my tourmentynge ; and the Lord is maad my
20 fastnynge.   And he ladde me into

hope in to hym ; my scheeld, and the
horn of myn helthe, 'my reisere^{k}, and my
refuyt ; my sauyour, thou schalt delyuere
me fro wickidnesse†.   Y schal inwardly 4
clepe the Lord worthi to be preisid ; and
Y schal be saaf fro myn enemyes.   For 5
the sorewis of deeth cumpasside^{l} me ; the
strondis of Belial‡ maden^{m} me aferd.   The 6
coordis of helle§ cumpassiden^{n} me ; the
snaris of deeth camen^{o} bifor me.   In 7
tribulacioun Y schal clepe^{p}, 'that is, Y
clepide^{q} thee^{r}, Lord, and Y schal crie to
my God ; and he herd^{s} fro his holi temple
my vois, and my crye schal come to hise
eeris.   The erthe was mouyd, and trem- 8
blide ; the foundementis of hillis weren
smytun and schakun togidere, for the
Lord was wrooth to hem.   Smoke stiede^{t} 9
fro hise nosethirlis^{u}, and fier of his mouth‖
schal deuoure ; colis weren kyndlid of it.
And he bowide heuenes, and cam doun ; 10
and myist vndur hise feet.   And he stiede 11
on^{v} cherubyn, and fli3 ; and he slood on
the^{w} pennys^{x} of wyndy.   He puttide^{z} 12
derknessis^{a} hidyng^{b} place in his cumpas,
and riddlide^{c} watris fro the cloudis of
heuenes ; for bri3tnesse in his si3t colis of 13
fier weren kyndelid.   The Lord schal 14
thundur fro heuene ; and hi3 God schal
3yue his vois.   He sente hise arowis, and 15
scateride hem ; he^{d} sente leitis, and wastide hem.   And the schedyngis out of the 16
see apperiden, and the foundementis of the
world weren schewid ; fro^{e} the blamyng
of the Lord, fro the brething of the spirit
of his strong veniaunce.   He sente fro 17
heuene, and took me ; and drow me out of
manye watris.   He delyuerede me fro my 18
my3tiest^{f} enemy, and fro hem that hatid-
en me ; for thei weren strongere than Y.
Thei camen bifore me in the dai of my 19
turmentyng ; and the Lord was maad my
stidfastnesse.   And he ledde me out in to 20
largenesse, and he delyuerede me ; for Y

† thou schalt
delyuere me fro
wickidnesse ;
that is, hast de-
lyuerid. Wick-
idnesse of Da-
uyth is clepid
here, in the
doynge of Ber-
sabee, fro
whiche wickid-
nesse he was
delyuerid, as to
gilt, bi veri
contricioun and
knowleching,
and as to peyne,
bi Goddis veu-
iaunce. Lire
here. c.
‡ the strondis of
Belial ; that is,
the fersnessis of
persecucioun
of Saul, that
was with out
3ck of chastis-
ing, and of God-
dis lawe. Lire
here. c.
§ the cordis of
helle ; in Ebreu
it is, the felou-
schipis of helle,
that is, sendis
excitinge Saul
to pursue me.
Lire here. c.
‖ fyer of his
mouth ; that is,
siche punysch-
ing was maad
of his wille and
comaundement.
Lire here. c.

^{ww} grynnys II sec.m.   ^{x} derknesse E pr.m.   ^{y} sty3id vp F.   ^{z} flow3 J.   ^{a} wyndis A. wynde II.
^{b} enuyroun of hym c.

^{k} myn upreiser I.   ^{l} han cumpassed I.   ^{m} han maad I.   ^{n} han enuyround I.   ^{o} han go I.   ^{p} ynwardly
clepe I.   ^{q} that is, I haue clepid B marg. Om. I.   ^{r} the IX sec.m. b.   ^{s} hath herd I.   ^{t} stiede up I.
^{u} nesethirles c.   ^{v} upon I.   ^{w} Om. L sec.m.   ^{x} federys EL.   ^{y} the wynd I.   ^{z} hath put I. putte DE.
^{a} derknesse E.   ^{b} an hidyng I.   ^{c} he hath wynewid I.   ^{d} and I.   ^{e} for c.   ^{f} ful my3ti I.

widnes, and delyuerde me; for I pleside
21 to hym. The Lord shal ȝeelde to me
after my riȝtwisnes; and after the
clennesse of myn hoondis he shal quyit
22 to me. For I haue kept the weyes of
the Lord; and I dide not vnpiteuousli fro
23 my God. Forsothe alle the domys of
hym in my siȝt; and his heestis I mouede
24 not awey fro me. And I shal be parfijt
with hym; and I shal kepe me fro my
25 wickidnes. And the Lord shal restore
to me after my riȝtwisnes; and after the
clennesse of myn hoondis^c in the siȝt of
26 his eyen. With the hooli hooli thou
shalt be, and with the stronge parfite;
27 and with the chosun chosun thou shalt
be, and with the peruertid thou shalt be
28 peruertid. And the pore puple thou
shalt make saaf; and to thin eyen heiȝ
29 thou shalt make meke. For thou, Lord,
my lantern, and thou, Lord, shalt liȝtne
30 my derkenessis. Into thee forsothe I
shall renne, gird vp; and in my God I
31 shal ouerleep the wal. God, the weye
of hym vndefoulid; the speche of the
Lord examynyd bi fier, a shelde is of alle
32 the hopers in hym. For who is a God,
saaf the Lord; and who strong saaf
33 oure Lord? God, that girdide me with
strength, and planede perfyte^d my wey;
34 euenynge my feet to hertis, and vpon my
35 heiȝ thingis settynge me; techynge myn
hoondis to bateil, and settynge togider as
36 a brasen boow myn armys. Thou ȝaf
to me a target of thin helth; and myn
37 hoomlynes multipliede me. Thou shalt
enlaarge^e my goyngis vndur me; and
38 myn heelis^f shulen not fayle. I shal
pursue myn enemyes, and treden; and I
shal not^g turne aȝen, to the tyme that I
39 waast hem. I shal waast hem, and
breek togidir, that thei togidre risen not;
40 thei shulen falle vndur my feet. Thou
girdist me with strengthe to batail; thow

pleside hym. The Lord schal ȝelde to me 21
vp^g my riȝtfulnesse^h; and he schal ȝelde
to me vpⁱ, '*ethir aftir*^k, the clennesse of
myn hondis. For Y kepte the weies of 22
the Lord; and Y dide not wickidli fro my
God. For alle hise domes *weren* in my 23
siȝt; and Y dide not awei fro me hise
heestis. And Y schal be perfit with hym; 24
and Y schal kepe me fro my wickidnesse.
And the Lord schal restore to me vpe^l 25
my riȝtfulnesse^m; and vpⁿ the clennesse of
myn hondis in the siȝt of hise iȝen. With 26
the hooli thou schalt be hooli, and with
the stronge, '*that is, to suffre aduersitees
pacientli*^o, thou schalt be perfit†; and 27
with a chosun man '*to blis*^p thou schalt be
chosun, and with a weiward man thou
schalt be maad weiward, '*that is, in ȝeld-
ynge iustli peyne to hym vpe*^q *his weiwardnesse*^r‡. And thou schalt make saaf 28
a pore puple; and with thin iȝen thou
schalt make lowe hem that ben hiȝe.
For thou, Lord, art my lanterne, and 29
thou, Lord^s, schalt liȝtne my derknessis^{ss}§.
For Y gird, '*that is, maad redi to batel*^t,
schal renne in^u thee, '*that is, in thi vertu*; 30
and in my God Y schal '*scippe ouer*^w the
wal. 'God his weie^x is 'with out wem^y; 31
the speche of the Lord is examynyd bi^z
fier, '*that is, is*^a *pure and clene as metal
preuyd*^b *in the furneys*^c; he is a scheeld
of alle men hopynge in hym. For who 32
is God, outakun the Lord; and who is
strong, outakun oure God? God, that 33
hath gird me with strengthe, and hath
maad pleyn my perfit weie; and he made^d 34
euene my feet with hertis, and settide^e me
on^f myn hiȝe thingis; and he tauȝte^{ff} myn 35
hondis to batel, and made^s myn armes|| as
a brasun bouwe. Thou hast ȝoue to me 36
the sheeld of thin heelthe; and my mylde-
nesse¶ multipliede^h me. Thou schalt alarge 37
my steppis vndur me; and myn heelis
schulen not faile. Y schal pursue myn 38

† *perfit*; in ȝyuynge to him grace to suffre aduersitees, bothe paciently and ioyfuly, as uartris ioyeden in passiouns. *Lire here.* c.

‡ *weiward-nesse*; ether thus, with a weiward man thou schalt be maad weiward, bi his errour; for whanne weyward men ben iustly punyschid of God, they seyen that God doith weiwardly with hem. c.

§ *liȝtne my derkneses*; that is, moodeful werkis quenchid bi ûedly synne comynge aboue, that ben quyk-enyd and liȝt-nyd bi grace rekyuerid. *Lire here.* c.

|| *and made myn armes, etc.*; in Ebreu it is, and a brasun bowe was gri[a]untid to myn armes for as Raby Salomon seith, he bente liȝtly a brasun bowe. *Lire here.* c.

¶ *and my myldenesse*; in Ebreu it is, thi myldenesse multipliede me, that is, of God dis good wille, and not of my merit, multi-pliyng in chil-dren, in tempo-ral goodis and goostly, cam to me. *Lire here.* c.

^c hoond A.   ^d perfijtli A.   ^e laargen BCEFH.   ^f heelthis A.   ^g no E.

^g vp *ether aftir* D. aftir EIL.   ^h riȝtwisnesse E.   ⁱ aftir IKN.   ^k *or vp* K. *ether vpe* N. Om. IRW. ^l aftir I.   ^m riȝtwisnesse EL.   ⁿ aftir I.   ^o Om. I.   ^p Om. I.   ^q is G.   ^r wickednesse E. The whole gloss omitted in I.   ^s Om. c.   ^{ss} derknesse E.   ^t Om. I.   ^u to I.   ^v Om. I.   ^w ouerpasse I.   ^x The weie of God I.   ^y vndefoulid I.   ^z with I.   ^a Om. FG.   ^b purid EGB.   ^c Gloss omitted in CI.   ^d hath maad I. ^e hath sett I.   ^f upon I.   ^{ff} hath tauȝt I.   ^g he hath maad I.   ^h hath multiplied I.

fulli bowedist the aȝenstondynge to me
41 vndur me. Myn enemyes thou ȝaf to
me the bak, hatynge me; and I shal
42 scatere hem. Thei shulen crye, and there
shal not be that saue; to the Lord, and
43 he shal not here hem. I shal do hem
awey as powdre of the erthe; and as
cleye of streetis I shal breek hem, and
44 to-flappe. Thou shalt saue me fro the
aȝenseiyngis of my puple; thou shalt
kepe me into the heed of folkis[1] of
kynde; the puple, whom I knowe[k] not,
45 shal serue to me. Alyen sones shulen
with stoonde to me; in herynge of the
46 eer thei shulen obeishe to me. Alien
sones floweden doun; and thei shulen be
47 drawen togidre in her angwishe. The
Lord lyueth, and blesside my God; and
the strong God of myn heelth shal be
48 enhaunsid. God, that ȝeuest veniaunces
to me; and threwe doun puplis vndur
49 me. The which ledist out me fro myn
enemyes, and fro the withstoondynge to
me arerist[1] me; fro a wickid[m] man thou
50 shalt delyuer me. Therfor I shal knowlech to thee in folk of kynde, Lord; and
51 to thi name I shal synge. Magnifiynge
heelthis of his kyng; and doynge mercies
to his crist Dauid, and into[n] his seed
euermore[o].

enemyes, and Y schal al to-breke hem; and
Y schal not turne aȝen, til Y waste hem.
Y schal waste hem, and Y schal breke[i], 39
that thei rise not; thei schulen falle
vndur my feet. Thou hast gird me with 40
strengthe to batel; thou hast bowid vnder
me hem that aȝenstoden[k] me. Thou hast 41
ȝoue myn enemyes abac to me, men hatynge me; and Y schal distrie hem. Thei 42
schulen crye, `that is, to ydols ether to
mennus help', and noon schal be that
schal saue[m]; `thei schulen[n] crie to the
Lord, and he schal not here hem. Y schal 43
do awei hem as the dust of erthe; Y schal
`powne hem[nn], and Y schal do[o] awei as the
clei[p] of stretis. Thou schalt saue me fro 44
aȝenseiyngis of my puple; thou schalt kepe
me in to the heed of folkis; the puple,
whom Y knowe not, schal serue me. Alien 45
sones schulen aȝenstonde me; bi heryng
of eere thei schulen obeie to me. Alien 46
sones fletiden awei; and thei schulen be
drawun togidere in her angwischis†.
The Lord lyueth, and my God is blessid; 47
and the stronge God of myn helthe schal
be enhaunsid. God, that ȝyuest veniauncis 48
to me; and hast cast doun puplis vndur
me. Which ledist me out fro myn ene- 49
myes, and reisist me fro men aȝenstond-
inge me; thou schalt deliuere me fro the
wickid man. Therfor, Lord, Y schal know- 50
leche to thee in hethene men; and Y schal
synge to thi name. And[q] he magnyfieth[r] 51
the helthis of his kyng; and doith mercyes[s]
to his crist Dauid, and to his seed til in to
withouten ende‡.

*† in her an-
gwischis; in
Ebreu it is, in
her closingis. c.*

*‡ til in to with
outen ende; for
the sones of
Dauyth regned-
en til to the
caitifte of Baby-
loyne; and aftir
the turning
aȝen fro Babi-
loyne, Zoroba-
bel, that cam
doun of Da-
nyth, hadde the
duchee, ether
leding, on the
puple, and othere
men suyngly
of the lynage of
Dauyth, til to
Eroude, an ali-
en, vndur whom
Crist was borun
of the seed of
Dauyth, bi
fleisch, of which
Crist the rewme
dwellith, in to
worldis of
worldis. Lire
here. c.*

CAP. XXIII.

1 Forsothe thes ben the last wordis, that
Dauid, the sone of Ysay, seide. A man
seide, to `whom there[p] is ordeynd of the
Crist of God of Jacob, a solempne salm
2 maker of Yrael; The spirite of the Lord
is spokyn bi me, and his word bi my
3 tonge. He seyde, God of Yrael to me

CAP. XXIII.

Forsothe these ben the laste wordis, 1
whiche Dauid, the sone of Ysai, seide. The
man seide, to whom it is ordeyued of
Crist, of the[t] God of Jacob, the noble salm
makere of Israel; The spiryt of the Lord 2
spak bi me, and his word bi my tunge.
Dauid[u] seide, God of Israel spak to me, 3

[1] folk BCEFH. [k] knewe A. [1] rerist c. [m] wyke BCEFH. [n] vnto BFH. to cE. [o] vnto euermore c.
[p] thee E pr. m.

[i] breke hem I. [k] stoden aȝens K. [1] Om. I. [m] saue hem I. [n] Om. IL. [nn] do hem to gidre I.
[o] do hem I. [p] fenne I. [q] That I. [r] maketh greet I. [s] mercy EI. [t] Om. I. [u] Om. I.

hath spokyn, the strong of Yrael, the lordshipper of men, the riȝtwise lord-4shipper in the dreed of God. As liȝt of morwtide, springinge the sunne eerli with out clowdis, gliterith; and as bi reynes buriouneth the eerbe of the erthe. 5And not so mych is myn hows anentis God, that euerlastynge couenaunt he shulde goo yn with me, stable in alle thingis and warnysshit; forsothe al myn heelth and al wil, ne there is eny thing 6of it, that ne buriowneth. Brekers of the lawe forsotheq as thornys shulen be pullid vp alle, the whiche ben not takyn 7withr hoondis. Andrr if eny man wolde touche hem, he shal be aarmyd with yren, and speer tree; and with fier tend vp, thei shulen be brent vnto nouȝt. 8Thes the names of the strong men of Dauid. Dauid sittynges in the chayer, moost wise prynce among three; he is a moost tendre litil werme of a tree, the which eiȝt hundrid slewȝ with a bure. 9Aftir this Eliazar, the sone of his vncless Abohy; among the three stronge, that weren with Dauid, whanne thei re-proueden to Philisteym, and thei ben 10gederid thidir into bateil. And whanne the men of Yrael hadden stiede vp, he stood, and smoot the Philisteis, to the tyme that his hoond failide, and wexe heuy with the swerd. And the Lord dide greet heelth in that day; and the puple that fleiȝ is turned aȝen to the spoilis of the sleyn men to be with-11drawen. After this Semma, the sone of Age, oft Arary. And Philisteis ben gedrid in the stacioun; forsothe there was thereu a feelde ful of corn; and whanne the puple hadde flowen fro the face of Phi-12listeis, he stood in the mydil of the feeld, and rescuwid it; and he smoot the Phi-listeis, and the Lord made a greet heelth. 13Also and before wenten doun the three,

the strongev of Israel, the `iust Lordw of men, `is Lordx in the drede of God. As4 the liȝt of the morewtid, whanne the sunne risith eerli, is briȝt with out cloudis; and as an erbe cometh forth of the erthe bi reynes. And myn hows is not so greet5 anentis God, that he schulde make with me euerlastynge couenaunt, stidefast and maad strong in alle thingis; for al myn helthe hangithy ofz him, and al thea wille `that is, al my desir, goith in to hymb, and no thing is therof, that makith not fruyt†. Forsothe alle trespassouris schulen be6 drawun out as thornes, that ben not takun with hondis. And if ony man wole touche7 tho, he schal be armed with irun, and with trec formed in to spered; and thee thornes schulen be kyndlid, and schulen be brent `til tof nouȝt. These ben the8 names of the stronge men of Dauid. Dauid sittith in the chaier, the wiseste prince among thre; he is as a moost tendir worm of treeg‡, that killide eiȝte hundrid with o fersnesse. Aftir hym was Eleazar,9 the sone of his fadirsh brother Abohi; among thre stronge men, that weren with Dauid, whanne thei seiden schenschip to Filisteisi, and weren gaderid thidir in to batel. And whanne the men of Israel10 hadden stiedk, hel stood§, and smoot Filisteism, tiln his hond failide, and was starke with the swerd. And the Lord made greet helthe in that dai; and the puple that fledde turnede aȝen to drawe awei the spuylis of slayn men. And aftir11 hymo was Semna, the sone of Age, of Arari. And Filisteis weren gaderid in the stacioun; forsothep there was a feeld ful of lenteq; and whanne the puper fledde fro the face of Filisteis, hes stood in the12 myddis of the feeld, and bihelde it‖; and he smoot Filisteist, and the Lord made greet helthe. Also and thre men ȝeden13 doun bifore, thatv weren princes among

† that makith not fruyt; and this is doon, whanne al thing that cometh forth of the wille, ether of anysement, is doon ya to the glorie of God. Lire here. c.

‡ he is as a moost tendir worm of tre; for thouȝ this worm in him silf is moost tendir, nethele he persith the harde tree; so Dauyth moost benygne and most mylde, was moost strong aȝenus enemyes rebellinge, ether as most tendir worm, that is, ful swee and anyȝable entis hise men, and hard aȝenus aduersaries. Lire here. c.

§ he stood, etc.; in batel, whanne hise felowis ȝeden abak. Lire here. c.

‖ and bihelde it; for he defendide the feeld. Lire here. c.

q or E pr. m.   r and with E pr. m.   rr Om. E pr. m.   s sitt E pr. m.   ss gem E pr. m.   t the sone of E pr. m.   u Om. A.

v stronge help I.   w lordschipere I.   x the riȝtwise lordschiper I.   y is I.   z on EKL.   a my I.   b Om. I. c a tre I.   d a spere I.   e tho I.   f vnto I.   g a tree I.   h fadir I.   i the Philistees I.   k stied up I. l Eleazar I.   m the Philisteis I.   n til that I.   o Eleazar I.   p and I.   q lentes or fetchis I.   r puple of Israel I.   s Semma I.   t the Philistees I.   u there greet I.   v whiche I.

that weren princis amonge thretti, and camen in tyme of rijp to Dauid into the spelunk of Odollam. Forsothe the tentis of Philisteis weren sett in the valey of 14 geauntis. And Dauid was in the strength; forsothe the stacioun^v of Philistees thanne 15 was in Bethlem. Dauid desiride thanne the watir of the laak, and seith, If eny man wolde 3yue to me drynke of the watir of the systern, that is in Bethleem, 16 biside the 3ate. Thanne breken out three stronge men the tentis of Philisteis, and drewen water of the sistern of Bethleem, that was biside the 3aat, and brou3ten to Dauid; and he wolde not drynke, but offride it to the Lord, 17 seiynge, Merciful be to me the Lord, lest Y doo this; whether the blood of thes men, that ben goon forth, and the perile of lyues I shal drynke? Thanne he wolde not drynke. Thes thingis 18 diden the three moost stronge. Forsothe Abisay, the brother of Joab, the sone of Saruye, was prince of the three; he is that reride his spere a3ens thre hundrid, whom he slew3, nemned in the 19 three, and amonge the three the nobler, and he was the prince of hem; but vnto 20 the three first men he ful cam not. And Banayas, the sone of Joiade, man moost strong of greet werkes, of Capseel, he smoot the two lyouns of Moab; and he cam doun, and smoot a lioun in the 21 mydil cistern in the dais of snow3. Forsothe he slew3 an Egipcian man worthi beholdynge, hauynge in the hoond a spere; and so whanne he was comyn doun to hym in a 3erd, bi force he pullide out the spere fro the hoond of the Egipcien, and he slew3 hym with his^w 22 speere. Thes thingis dide Banayas, the 23 sone of Joiade; and he namyd among the three stronge, that weren amonge

thretti^w, and camen^x to Dauid in the tyme of reep^y in to the denne of Odollam. Forsothe^z the castels^a of Filisteis weren set in the valei of giauntis. And Dauid was 14 in a strong hold; sotheli^b the stacioun of Filisteis was thanne in Bethleem. Ther-16 for^c Dauid desiride water of the lake, and seide, If ony man wolde 3yue to me drynk† of watir^d of the cisterne, which^e is in Bethleem, bisidis the 3ate. Therfor thre 16 stronge men braken in to the castels^f of Filisteis, and drowen watir of the cisterne of Bethleem, that was^g bisidis the 3ate, and brou3ten^h to Dauid; and he nolde^i drinke, but offride it to the Lord, and 17 seide, The Lord be merciful to me, that Y do not this; whether Y schal drynke the blood of these men, that 3eden forth, and the perel of soulis^k? Therfor he nolde^l drynke. Thre strongeste^m men diden 18 thes thingis. Also Abisay, brother^n of Joab, the sone of Saruye, was prince of thre^o; he it is that reiside his schaft^p a3ens thre hundrid men, whiche^q he killide; 'he was^r nemid^s among thre^t, and was^u the 19 noblere among thre^v, and he was the prince of hem; but he cam not to the thre firste men. And Banaye, the sone of 20 Joiada, strongeste^w man of grete werkis, of Capseel, he smoot twei liouns of Moab, 'that is, twei kny3tis hardi as liouns^x'; and he 3ede doun, and smoot a lioun in the myddil cisterne in the daies of snow. Also he^y killide a man of Egipt, a man 21 worthi of spectacle^z, hauynge a spere in the^a bond; therfor^b whanne he hadde come doun with a 3erde to that man, bi mi3t^c he wrooth^d out the spere fro the hond of the man of Egipt, and killide hym with his owne spere. Banaye, sone^e 22 of Joiada, dide these thingis; and he was 23 nemyed among thre stronge men, that weren among the thretti noblere men;

† if ony man wolde 3yue to me drynke, etc.; Dauyth seide this, not for coueitise of the watir, but for he wolde a3ye the hardynesse of hem; and therfor it seith, and he nolde drynke, but offride it to the Lord; he schewide hi this, that he that seith forth him silf to perels a3ens vnfeithful men, makith most acceptable sacrifice to God. Lire here. c.

---

^v staciouns A pr.m. ^w the B.

^w thretti *men* I. ^x thei camen I. ^y ripp I. ^z And I. ^a tentis I. ^b And I. ^c Thanne I. ^d the watir I. ^e that I. ^f tentis I. ^g is K. ^h thei brou3ten it I. ^i wolde not I. ^k her lyues I. ^l wolde not I. ^m ful stronge I. ^n the brother I. ^o the thre *men* I. ^p spere I. ^q the whiche I. ^r Om. I. ^s nempnyd I. named K. nemmed L. ^t *tho* thre I. ^u he was I. ^v hem thre I. ^w the strongeste I. ^x *that is, two stronge hardi kny3tis* I marg. ^y Banaye I. ^z biholdyng I. ^a his I. ^b and so I. ^c strengthe KMOX. ri3t strengthis s. ry3t strong D. ni3t ELPB. ^d wrong L. ^e the sone I.

the thretti nobler; neuerthelater vnto
the three he ful cam not. And Dauid
made hym^x to hym a secretarie of
24 pryuete. Asahel, the brother of Joab,
among the thretti; Elianan, the sone of
25 his eem^y, of Bethleem; Seruma, of Arary;
26 Elka, of Arodi; Helias, of Phelu; Hyra,
27 the sone of Aches, of Thekua; Abiazer,
28 of Anathoth; Nobanay, of Vsathi; Selmon
29 Acothes^z; Macharoy Nethophatites; E-
led, the sone of Baana, and he Netho-
phatite; Hitai, the sone of Rabai, of Je-
30 beeth, of the sonis of Beniamyn; Banai
Affrotonyte; Heddai, of the streem of
31 Gaas; Albiabon Arbachite; Asmanech, of
32 Berromy; Elyala, of Sobony; the sones of
33 Jonathan, and Jeson; Semma, of Horodi;
34 Hayam, the sone of Saray, Saratite; Eli-
pheleth, the sone of Saasbai, the sonys
of Maachati; Heliam, the sone of Achi-
35 tophel, Gilonyte; Esrai, of Carmeel; Pha-
36 rai, of Arbi; Igaal, the sone of Natha,
37 of^a Soba; Bony, of Gaddi; Selech, of Am-
mony; Naamy Berothite, the squyer of
38 Joab, the sone of Saruye; Ira Yatrite;
39 Gareb, and he Yatrite; Vrie Ethee; alle,
scuen and thretti.

CAP. XXIV.

1 And the woodnes of the Lord addide
to be wrooth a3ens Irael, and stiride Dauid in hem, seiynge to Joab, Go, and
2 noumbre Yrael and Juda. And the kyng
seide to Joab, prince^b of his oost, Go thur3
alle the lynagis of Irael fro Dan vnto
Bersabe, and noumbreth^c the puple, that
3 I knowe the noumbre of it. And Joab
seide to the kyng, The Lord thi God
eeche to thi puple, as myche as it is now,
and eft encrees it to the hundred so
myche in the si3t of my lord the kyng;
but^d what to hym wole my lord the kyng
4 in siche a maner thing? Forsothe the
word of the kyng hadde the ouer hoond
a3ens the wordis of Joab, and of the

netheles he cam not til^f to the thre3. And
Dauid made hym a counselour of priuyte^h
to hym silf. Asahel, the brother of Joab, 24
was among thretti^i men; Eleanan, the
sone of his fadris brother, of Bethleem;
Semma, of Arari; Elcha, of Arodi; Helas, 25
of Phelti; Hira, sone^k of Aches, of Thecua;
Abiezer, of Amatoth; Mobannoy, of Co- 27
sathi; Selmon, of Achotes; Macharai, of 28
Nethophath; Heled, the sone of Baana, 29
and he was of Netophath; Hiray, sone^l of
Rabai, of Gebeeth, of the sones of Beniamyn; Banay, of Effrata; Hedday, of the 30
stronde of Gaas; Abiabon, of Arbath; As- 31
maneth, of Berromy; Eliaba, of Sabony; 32
sones^m of Assen, Jonathan, and Jasan;
Semma, of Herodi; Hayam, sone^l of Sa- 33
rai, of Zaroth; Eliphelech, sone^l of Saal- 34
bai, the sone of Maachati; Heliam, sone^l
of Achitofel, of Gilo; Esrai, of Carmele; 35
Pharai, of Arbi; Ygaal, sone^l of Nathan, 36
of Soba; Bonny, of Gaddi; Silech, of Am- 37
mony; Naarai, of Beroth, the squyer of
Joab, the sone of Saruye; Haray, of Jethri; 38
Gareb, and he was of Gethri; Vrye, of E- 39
thei; alle^n weren seuene and thretti men.

CAP. XXIV.

And the strong veniaunce of the Lord 1
addide to be wrooth a3ens Israel†, and he
stiride in^o hem Dauid, seiynge to Joab,
Go thou, and noumbre thou Israel and
Juda. And the kyng seide to Joab, the 2
prince of his oost, Go thou bi alle lynagis^p
of Israel fro Dan 'til to^q Bersabee, and
noumbre thou the puple, that Y wite the
noumbre therof. And Joab seide to the 3
kyng, Thi Lord God encresse to this^r puple, 'hou greet^s it is now, and eft multiplie
he^t an hundrid fold in the si3t of my lord
the kyng; but what wole my lord the^u
kyng to hym silf in sich a thing? Sotheli^v 4
the word of the kyng ouer cam the wordis
of Joab, and of the princes of the oost;

† and the strong veniaunce of the Lord addide to be wrooth a3enus Israel; of this that the Lord wolde punysche the puple, he suffride Dauyth to be reisid bi pride to the noumbring of the puple; wherfor the gloss of Gregre on this place seith thus, The dedis of gouernours ben disposid for the maneris of suggetis, that ofte for the ynel of the floc, the lijf þe of a good schepparde trespassith, for Dauyth was preisid bi God witnesse, and he was blowun with the bolnyng of sudeyn pride, and synnede in noumbringe puple, and the puple resseyuede peyne; for the hertis of gouernours ben disposid, vp the meritis of the puplis. The synne of the puple for which it was punyschid, is not expressid in the text, but in the book of Ebreu questiouns it is seid, that this was berfor, for the puple a3en stood not Dauyth as it ou3te, in the dede of Vrie, but for this dede was priuy til it was al doon; the puple my3te not withstonde Dauyth in the synne to he lettid, and aftir that this synne cam in to the knowing of the puple, the puple ou3te not to punysche it, for the peyne was determynd thanne of God, as it is opin in xii. c°. bi the

---

x Om. A.   y gem. E.   z of Acothes B.   a Om. A.   b the prince E pr. m.   c nowmbre CE pr. m.

f Om. I.   g firste thre I.   h prince L.   i the thretti I.   k the sone I.   l the sone I.   m the sones I.
n alle these I.   o a3ens I.   p the lynagis I.   q vnto I.   r thi I.   s as myche as I.   t 3e A. he it I.
u Om. I.   v But I.

princis of the oost; and Joab wente
out, and the princis of kny3tis, fro the
face of the kyng; 'and thei noum-
5 brene the puple 'of Yrael'. Whanne thei
hadden passid ouer Jordan, thei camen
into Aroer, at the ri3t half of the citee
6 that is in the valey of Gad; and bi Jaser
thei passiden into Galaad, and into the
nether loond of Odsi, and camen into the
wodi placis of Dan; and goynge about
7 beside Sidon thei passiden ny3 the walles
of Tyri, and al the loond of Euey, and
of Chananei; and thei camen intos the
8 sowth of Juda, into Bersabe. And passid
al the loond, thei weren after nyne
monethis and twenty dais comen into
9 Jerusalem. Thanne Joab 3af the noumbre of the discryuynge of the puple to
the kyng. And there ben founden of
Yrael nyn hundrid thousandis of stronge
men, 'the whicheh my3ten drawe out
swerd; and of Juda fyue hundrid thou-
10 sandis of fi3tynge men. Forsothe the
herte of Dauid smoot hym, aftir that the
puple is noumbred; Dauid seide to the
Lord, I haue synned greetli in this deede;
but I preye, Lord, that thou bere ouer
the wickidnes of thi seruaunt, for foleli
11 I haue doo to myche. And so Dauid
roos eerli, and the word of the Lord is
maad to Gad, the prophete and seear,
12 seiynge, Go, and spek to Dauid, Thes
thingis seith the Lord, Of three thingis
to thee is 3ouun choys; chees oon, that
thou wolt of thes, that I doo to thee.
13 And whanne Gad was comen to Dauid,
he toold to hym, seiynge, Outher seuen
3eer shal come to thee hungre in thi loond;
or three monethis thou shalt flee thin aduersaries, and thei shulen pursue thee;
or certeyn three days pestilence shal be
in thi loond; now thanne delyuer, and
see, what word I shal answere to hym
14 that sente me. Forsothe Dauid seide to

and Joab 3ede out, and the princes of thew
kny3tis, fro the face of the kyng, that thei
schulden noumbre the puple of Israel. And5
whanne thei hadden passid Jordan, thei
camen in to Aroer, to the ri3t side of the
citee whichx is in the valei of Gad; and6
thei passideny bi Jazer in to Galaad, and
in to the lowere lond of Odsi, and camenz
in to the wodi places of Dan; and thei
cumpassidena bisidis Sidon, and passiden7
ny3 the wallis of Tire, and ny3 al the lond
of Euei, aud of Chananei; and thei camen
tob the south of Juda, in Bersabee. And8
whanne al the loud was cumpassid, thei
camen aftir nyne monethis and twenti
daies in to Jerusalem. Therforc Joab 3af9
the noumbre of discriuyng of the puple
to the kyng. And of Israel weren foundun
nyne hundryd thousyndt of stronge men,
that drewen out swerd; and of Juda fyue
hundrid thousynde of fi3teris. Forsothe10
the herte of Dauid smoot hym, 'that is,
his concience repreuyde hyme, aftir that
the puple was noumbrid; and Dauid seide
to the Lord, Y synnedef greetli‡ in this
dede; but, Lord, Y preye that thou turne
awei the wickidnesse of thi seruaunt, for
Y dides ful folili. Therfor Dauid roos11
eerli, and the word of the Lord was maad
to Gad, the prophete and seere, and seide,
Go thou, and speke to Dauid, The Lord12
seith these thingis, The chesyngh of thre
thingis is 3ouun to thee; chese thou oon,
which thou wolt of these, that Y do to
thee. And whanne Gad hadde come to13
Dauid, he telde to Dauidi, and seide, Ether
hungur schal come to thee in thi lond seuene 3eer; ethir thre monethis thou schalt
fle thin aduersaries, and thei schulen pursue thee; ether certis thre daies pestilence
schal be in thi lond; now therfor delyuere thou, 'ether anyse thouj, and se,
what word Y schal answere to hym that
sente me. Forsothek Dauid seide to Gad,14

e and thei nowmbriden E pr. m. that thei noumbren cE sec. m.　f Om. E pr. m.　g to BCEFII.
h that c pr. m.

w Om. plures.　x that I.　y passiden forth I.　z thei camen I.　a 3eden aboute I.　b in to K.
c And so I.　d And I.　e Om. I.　f haue synned I.　g haue do I.　h chois I.　i him I.　j ether examyne
thou B marg. Om. I.　k And I.

Gad, I am constreyned ful myche 'on alle sides[i]; but[k] beter it is that I falle into the hoondis of the Lord, forsothe manye ben the mercies of hym, than in the 15 hoondis of men. And the Lord sente yn pestilence into Irael fro eerli vnto the set tyme; and there ben deed of the puple fro Dan vnto Bersabec seuenti thou-16 sandis of men. And whanne the aungel of the Lord hadde stranȝt out his hoond vpon Jerusalem, that he scater it, the Lord hadde rewth vpon the tourment-ynge; and he seith to the aungel smyt-ynge the puple, Yt suffisith now; with-hoold thin hoond. Forsothe the aungel of the Lord was beside the corn flore of 17 Arewna of Jebusei. And Dauid seide[l] to the Lord, whanne he hadde seen the aungel sleynge the puple, I am that haue synnede, and I wykidli dide; thes that ben sheep, what diden thei? I biseche, be thin hoond turned aȝens me, and aȝens 18 the hows of my fader. Forsothe Gad, the prophete, cam to Dauid in that day, and seide to hym, Stye vp, and ordeyn an auter to the Lord in the corn flore of 19 Arewna of Jebusei. And Dauid stiede vp, after the word of Gad, the which the 20 Lord hadde comaundide to hym. And beholdynge Arewne vndurstoode the kyng and his seruauntis to comen ouer to hym; 21 and, goon out, he honourde the kyng, bowid the cheere into the erthe; and seith, What of cause is, that my lord the kyng cometh to his seruaunt? To whom Dauid seith, That I byc of thee the corn flore, and bilde an auter to the Lord, and cees the slauȝter, that is ful plenteuous in 22 the puple. And Arewna seith to Dauid, Tak, and offre my lord kyng, as it plesith to him; hast thou oxen into brent sacrifice, and a wayn, and ȝockis of oxen into 23 the vse of trees? Arewna ȝaf alle thingis to the king. And Arewna seide to the

Y am constreyned on ech side greetli; but it is betere that Y falle in to the hondis of the Lord†, for his emercies ben manye, than in[i] the[k] hondis of men. And the 15 Lord sente pestilence in to Israel fro the morewtid 'til to[l] the tyme ordeyned‡; and seuenti thousynde of men weren deed of the puple fro Dan 'til to[m] Bersabec. And 16 whanne the aungel of the Lord hadde holde[n] forth his hond ouer Jerusalem, that he schulde distrie it, the Lord hadde mercy on the turmentyng; and seide[o] to the aungel smytynge the puple, It sufficith now; withholde thin hond. Forsothe[p] the aungel of the Lord was bisidis the corn floor of Areuna Jebusey. And Dauid seide to 17 the Lord, whanne he hadde seyn the aungel sleynge the puple, Y am[q] he[r] that 'haue synned[s], and Y dide[t] wickidli; what han these do, that ben scheep? Y biseche, thin hond be turned aȝens me, and aȝens the hows of my fadir. Forsothe[v] Gad, the pro-18 phete, cam to Dauid in that dai, and seide to hym, Stic thou[w], and ordeyne an auter to the Lord in the corn floor of Areuna Jebusei. And Dauid stiede, vpe[x] the word 19 of Gad, which the Lord hadde comaundid to hym. And Areuna bihelde, and per-20 seyuede[y], that the kyng and hise seruauntis passiden[z] to hym; and he ȝede out, and 21 worschipide the kyng bi[a] low cheer to the erthe; and seide, What 'cause is[b], that my lord the[c] kyng cometh to his seruaunt? To whom Dauid seide, That Y bie of thee the corn floor, and bilde an auter to the Lord, and the sleynge ceesse, which[d] is cruel in the puple. And Areuna seide to 22 Dauid, My lord the[e] kyng take, and offre, as it plesith hym[f]; thou hast oxis[g] in to brent sacrifice, and a wayn and ȝockis of oxis[h] in to vss[i] of wode. Areuna ȝaf alle thingis‖ to the king. And Areuna seide to the king, Thi Lord God reseyue thi 24 vow. To whom the king answeride, and

† in to the hondis of the Lord; if Dauyth hadde chose hungur of vit. ȝeer, he and riche men wolden haue purneyed to hem silf of Hyflode, and pore men schulden haue be turmencid gredy; and if he hadde chose fliȝt bifor enemyes, he and myȝty men schulden haue be defendid and pore men slayn, therfor 17 he chees pestilence, comyn peyne to alle, for he tristide in Goddis mersi. Lire here. c.

‡ to the tyme ordeyned; that is, til to the oure of sacrifice 18 of euentid; the ii. laste dayes of pestilence, weren seid bi mannasing, and weren releessid 19 for the penaunce of Dauyth. Lire here. c.

‖ Areuna ȝaf 23 alle thingis, etc.; that is, wolde ȝyue. Lire here. c.

[l] Om. E pr. m.   [k] Om. B.   [l] seith B.

[i] into IKb.   [k] Om. K.   [l] vnto I.   [m] vnto I.   [n] helde I.   [o] he seide I.   [p] And I.   [q] it am I. [r] Om. plures.   [s] synnede I.   [t] haue do I.   [v] Certis I.   [w] thou up I.   [x] up, aftir I.   [y] vndirstode I. [z] passiden ouer I.   [a] with I.   [b] is the cause I.   [c] Om. I.   [d] that I.   [e] Om. I.   [f] to hym I.   [g] oxen IG. [h] oxun AMB.   [i] the vss I.

king, The Lord thi God take thi vowe.
24 To whom answeringe the king seith,
Not as thou wolt, but I shal bye bi prijs
of thee, and I shal not offre to the Lord
my God brent sacrifice freeli ȝeuen. Than
Dauid bouȝte the corn flore *for sexe hun-*
drid siclis of gold, and the oxen for fifti
25 siclis of siluer. And Dauid bilde there
an auter to the Lord, and he offride brent
sacrifices and pesible; and the Lord is
plesid aȝen to the loond, and the veniaunce is forfendyd fro^m Yrael.

Here endith the secounde book of
Kingis, and bigynneth the thridde
book ⁿ.

seide, Not as thou wolt, but Y schal bie^k
of thee for prijs, and Y schal not offre to
'my Lord^l God brent sacrifices ȝouun freli.
Therfor Dauid bouȝte the corn floor†, and
'*he bouȝte*^m oxisⁿ for fifti siclis of siluer.
And Dauid bildide there an auter to the 25
Lord, and offride brent sacrifices and pesible sacrifices; and the Lord dide merci
to the lond, and the veniaunce was refreyned fro Israel.

Here endith the secounde book of
Kyngis, and here bigynneth the thridde^o.

† *bouȝte the corn floor ; for* vi. hundrid siclis of gold, in the firste book of Paralip. xxi. c°. Lire here. c.

^m of n.   ⁿ From E. *Here endith the secounde bok of Kyngis, and here bygynneth the thrid bok.* F. No final rubric in ABCH.

^k bie *it* I.   ^l the Lord my I.   ^m Om. I.   ⁿ the oxen I.   ^o *Here endith the secounde book of Kyngis, and bigynneth a prolog on the iii. book of Kynges.* G. *Here endith the secounde book of Kyngis, and bigynneth the thridde.* IQ. *Here endith the secounde book of Kingis, se now the thridde.* K. *Here endith the secounde book of Kingis, and here bigynneth a prologe on the thridde.* M. *Here eendith the secunde book of Kyngis, and bygynneth the thridde book of Kyngis.* NRSX. *Here endith the secounde book of Kingis, and here bigynneth the thridde.* O. *Here endeth the secounde book, and bigynneth the thridde.* b. *Here endith the secunde book of Kyngis.* ç. No final rubric in ELP.

III. KINGS.

IN this thridde book of Kingis is contened the ending of Dauith, and the coronacioun of Salomon, ʒit lyuynge Dauith ; and how the Lord magnyfied Salomon with wisdom, and richessis, and in al prosperite, for the loue of Dauith his fadir, aboue alle kingis that weren bifor him and after, and ʒaf to hym pees on ech side. Also how the rewme was departid in the daies of Roboam, sone of Salomon, in to tweie kyngdoms, but the Lord reseruede the kyngdom of Juda to the generacioun of Dauith, for the merit of Dauith ; and of alle kingis that weren afterward on Juda and on Israel, in to the transmygracioun of Babiloyne.

Here bigynneth the thridde book of Kyngis[a]*.*

CAP. I.

1 AND kyng Dauid hadde eeldid, and he hadde of age manye dais ; and whanne he was couerd with clothis, he was not maad 2 hoot. Thanne his seruauntis seiden to hym, Seche we to oure lord[b] kyng[c] a ʒong wexen[d] mayden ; and stonde she before the kyng, and fede she hym, and sleep in his bosum, and make she hoot 3 oure lord kyng[e]. Thanne thei souʒten a fayre ʒong womman in alle the coostis of Irael ; and thei founden Abisaag Sunamytem, and brouʒten hir to the 4 kyng. Forsothe she was a child womman fayr ful mych, and she slepte with the kyng, and seruede to[f] hym ; forsothe 5 the kyng knewe hyre not. Forsothe Adouyas, the sone of Agith, was reryd vp, seiynge, I shal regne. And he made to hym a chaar, and horsmen, and fifti

Here beginneth the thridde book of Kyngis[b]*.*

CAP. I.

AND kyng Dauid wax[c] eld[cc], and hadde 1 ful many daies of age ; and[d] whanne he was hilid with clothis, he was not maad hoot†. Therfor hise seruauntis seiden to 2 hym, Seke we to oure lord the[e] kyng a ʒong wexynge virgyn ; and stonde sche bifor the kyng, and nursche sche hym, and slepe in his bosum, and make hoot[f] oure lord the[g] kyng. Therfor thei souʒten a 3 ʒong wexyng virgyn, fair in alle the coostis of Israel ; and thei founden Abisag of Sunam[h], and thei brouʒten hir to the kyng. Forsothe[i] the damysel was ful 4 fair, and sche slepte with the kyng†, and mynystride to hym ; forsothe the king knew not hir fleischli[j]. Sotheli[k] Adonye, 5 sone[l] of Agith, was reisid[m], and seide, Y schal regne. And he made to hym a chare, and knyʒtis[n], and fifti men, that

† *he was not made hoot ; for he was a werriour fro his ʒong age, and for he was hugely agast in the siʒt of the aungel. Lire here.* c.

‡ *sche slepte with the king ; Abisag was weddid to Dauyth. Lire here.* c.

---

[a] From A. *The thridde of Kyngis* B. No initial rubric in CFH.   [b] Om. H.   [c] the kyng CE pr. m.   [d] wexe H.   [e] the kyng CE pr. m. H.   [f] Om. B.

[a] This Prologue is from M.   [b] From AN. *The thridde of Kynges* L. *The iii. of Kinges* P. No initial rubric in the other Mss.   [c] wexide I. waxide EKLb.   [cc] ful old L.   [d] Om. S.   [e] Om. I.   [f] sche hoot I. [g] Om. I.   [h] Sunamye S.   [i] And I. [j] Om I.   [k] And I.   [l] the sone I.   [m] reisid up I.   [n] ordeynede kniʒtis I.

men, that before him shulden renne.
6 And his fadir vndurnam not hym eny
tyme, seiynge, Whi thus diddist thou?
Forsothe and he was ful fayr, the se-
7 cound born after Absolon; and the word
of hym with Joab, the sone of Saruye,
and with Abiathar, preest, that helpiden
8 the parties of Adonye. Forsothe Sadoch, the preest, and Banayas, the sone
of Joiade, and Nathan, the prophete, and
Semei, and Cerethi, and Pherethi, and al
the strength of the oost of Dauid, was
9 not with Adonye. Thanne wethers, and
calues, and alle the fat offrid biside the
stoon of Zoelech, that was ny3 to the
welle of Rogel, Adonyas clepede alle his
britheren, the sones of the kyng, and alle
the men of Juda, seruauntis of the kyng.
10 Forsothe Nathan, the prophet, and Banaye, and alle the stronge men, and Salo-
11 mon, his brother, he clepide not. And
so Nathan seide to Bersabe, the modir
of Salomon, Whether hast thou herd,
that Adonyas, the sone of Agith, 'hath
regnyd^g, and oure lord Dauid thes
12 thingis vnknowith? Now thanne come,
and tak counseil of me, and saue thi lijf,
13 and of thi sone Salomon. Go, and weend
in to kyng Dauid, and sey to him, Whether not thou, lord, my kyng, swore to
me thin hoond womman, seiynge, that
Salomon thi sone shal regne aftir me,
and he shal sitte in my see? Whi thanne
14 regneth Adonyas? And 3it there thee
spekynge with the kyng, I shal come
15 after thee, and fulfil thi wordis. And so
Bersabe is goon yn to the kyng in the
bedplace^h; forsothe the kyng hadde eeldid
ful myche, and Abisaag Sunamyte seru-
16 ede to him. Bersabe bowid hir, and
honourede the king; to whom the king,
17 he seith, What wolt thou to thee? The
which answerynge seith, My lord kyng,
thou swore bi the Lord thi God to thin

runnen bifor hym. Nether^o his fadir re- 6
preuyde hym ony tyme, and^p seide, Whi
'didist thou^q this? Forsothe^r also he was
ful fair, the secounde child aftir Absolon;
and his word was with Joab, sone^t of 7
Saruye, and with 'Abiathar, preest^u, that^v
helpiden the partis of Adonye. Sotheli^w 8
Sadoch, the preest, and Banaie, sone^x of
Joiada, and Nathan, the prophete, and
Semey, and Cerethi, and Ferethi, and al
the strengthe of the oost of Dauid, weren
not with Adonye. Therfor whanne 9
rammes weren offrid, and caluys, and alle
fatte thingis, bisidis the stoon Zoelech†,
that was ny3 the welle of Rogel, Adonye
clepide alle hise britheren, sones^y of the
kyng, and alle the^z men of Juda, seruauntis of the kyng. Sotheli^a 'he clepide 10
not^b Nathan, the profete, and Banaie, and
alle stronge men, and Salomon, his bro-
thir^c. Therfor^d Nathan seide to Bersa- 11
bee, modir^e of Salomon, Whether^f thou
herdist^{ff}, that Adonye, sone^g of Agith,
regnede^h, and oure lord Dauid knoweth
not this? Now therfor come thou, take 12
thou counsel of me, and saue thi lijf, and
of Salomon thi sone. Go thou, and entre 13
to kyng Dauid, and seie thou to hym,
Whether not thou, my lord the kyng,
hast swore to me, thin handmaide, and
seidist, that Salomon thi sone schal regne
aftir me, and he schal sitte in my trone?
Whi therfor regneth Adonye? And 3it 14
while thou schalt speke there with the
kyng, Y schal come aftir thee, and 'Y
schal fille^i thi wordis. Therfor Bersabee 15
entride to the kyng in the closet^k; for-
sothe^l the kyng was ful eeld, and Abisag
of Sunam 'mynystride^m to hym. Ber- 16
sabee^n bowide hir silf, and worschipide
the kyng; to whom the kyng seide, What
wolt thou to thee? And sche answeride, 17
and seide, My lord the^o kyng, thou hast
swore to thin handmaide bi thi Lord

† *bisidis the stoon Zoeleth;* Ebreys seyen, the stoon drawun, for stronge men asayeden her strengthe at it; also Ebreys seyen, *bisidis the welle of a fullere. Lire here. c.*

^{g} schal regnen E pr. m. ^{h} bed E pr. m.

^{o} Nethir *Dauid* I. ^{p} ne I. ^{q} hast thou do I. ^{s} But I. ^{t} the sone I. ^{u} the preest Abiathar I.
^{v} whiche I. ^{w} But I. ^{x} the sone I. ^{y} the sones I. ^{z} Om. I. ^{a} But I. ^{b} Om. I. ^{c} brothir he clepide
not I. ^{d} And so I. ^{e} the modir I. ^{f} wher *ceteri passim.* ^{ff} hast herd I. ^{g} the sone I. ^{h} hath regnyd I.
^{i} fulfille I.   bed place I. ^{l} and I. ^{m} seruyde I. ^{n} And Bersabee I. ^{o} Om. I.

hoond womman, Salomon thi sone shal
regne after me, and shal sitte in my see;
18 and loo! now Adonye hath regned, thee,
19 my lord kyng, vnknowynge; he hath
slayn oxen, and alle the fatte, and manye
wethers; and clepide alle the sones of the
kyng, and Abiathar, the preest, and
Joab, the prince of the chyualrie; forsothe Salomon, thi seruaunt^b, he clepide
20 not. Neuerthelater^i, my lord kyng, in
thee the eyen of al Yrael beholden, that
thou deme to hem, who owith to sit in
21 thi see, my lord kyng, aftir thee; and
it shal be, whanne my lord kyng shal
sleep with his faders, I and my sone
22 Salomon shulen be synful. ʒit she spekynge with the kyng, Nathan, the pro-
23 phete, cam. And men toolden to the
kyng, seiynge, Nathan, the prophete,
is nyʒ. And whanne he was comen in the
siʒt of the kyng, and hadde honourde
24 hym redi into the erthe, Nathan seide,
My lord kyng, hast thow seide, Adonye
regne after me, and he sitte vpon my
25 trone? For he cam doun to day, and
offride oxen, and fatte thingis, and
manye wethers; and clepide alle the
sonys of the kyng, and the prince of the
oost, and Abiathar, the preest; and hem
etynge, and drynkynge before hym, and
26 seiynge, Lyue the kyng Adonye, me, thi
seruaunt, and Sadoch, the preest, and
Benanye, the sone of Joiade, and Salo-
27 mon, thi sone, he clepide not. Whether
of my lord the kyng wente out this
word, and to me, thi seruaunt, thou
shewedist not, who shulde be to sitte
vpon the trone of my lord kyng after
28 hym? And kyng Dauid answerde, seiynge, Clepith to me Bersahe. The
which whanne was goon in before the
kyng, and hadde stoonden before hym,
29 the king swore, and seith, The Lord
lyueth, that hath delyuerd my soule fro

God, Salomon thy^p sone schal regne aftir
me, and he schal sitte in my trone; and 18
lo! Adonye hath regnede now, 'while
thou, my lord the kyng, knowist not^q; he 19
hath slayn oxis^r, and alle fatte thingis,
and ful many rammes; and he clepide^s
alle the^t sones of the king, also 'Abiathar
preest^u, and Joab, the prince of chyualri^v;
but he clepide not Salomon, thi seruaunt.
Netheles, my lord the^w kyng, the iʒen of 20
al Israel biholden in to thee, that thou
schewe to hem, who owith to sitte in thi
trone, my lord the^x kyng, aftir thee; and 21
it schal be, whanne my lord the^y kyng
hath slepte with hise fadris, Y and my
sone Salomon schulen be synneris†.
'While sche spak^z ʒit with the king, Na- 22
than, the prophete, cam. And thei telden 23
to the kyng, and seiden, Nathan, the prophete, is present. And whanne he hadde
entrid in the siʒt of the kyng, and hadde
worschipide hym lowli to^a erthe^b, Nathan 24
seide, My lord the kyng, seidist thou,
Adonye regne^c aftir me, and sitte he on
my trone? For he cam^d doun to dai, and 25
offride oxis^e, and fatte thingis, and ful
many wetheris; and he clepide alle the
sones of the kyng, also^f Abiathar, preest;
and whanne thei eten, and drunken bifor
hym, and seiden, Kyng Adonye lyue; he 26
clepide not me, thi seruaunt, and Sadoch,
preest^g, and Banaie, sone^h of Joiada, and
Salomon, thi sone. Whether this word 27
ʒede out fro my lord the^i kyng, and thou
schewidist not to me, thi seruaunt, who
schulde sitte on^k the trone of my lord the^l
king after hym? And kyng Dauid an- 28
sweride, and seide, Clepe ʒe Bersabee to
me. And whanne sche hadde entrid bifor
the kyng, and hadde stonde bifor hym,
the kyng swoor, and seide, The Lord 29
lyueth, that delyueryde^m my lijf fro al angwisch; for as Y swore to thee bi the 30
Lord God of Israel, and seide, Salomon,

† I' and my sone Salomon schulen be synneris; that is, Adonye schal putte on vs crymes, to prine vs fro liyf. Lire here. CK.

ʰ sone A.   ˡ Nerthelatere c passim.

P thy A sec; m.   q thee my lord kyng, vnwitynge I.   r oxen I.   s hath clepid I.   t Om. s.   u the preest Abiathar I.   v the chyualri I.   w Om. I.   x Om. I.   y Om. I.   z Bersabee spekynge I.   a in to I.   b the erthe EIKLP.   c regne he I.   d hath come I.   e oxen I.   f and also I.   g the preest I.   h the sone I.   i Om. I.   k upon I. in I.   l Om. I.   m hath delyuered I.

30 al angwish ; for as I swore to thee bi the Lord God of Irael, seiynge, Salomon, thi sone, shal regne after me, and he shal sitte vpon my see after me, so I shal do 31 to day. And Bersabe, the cheere put doun into the erthe, honourde the kyng, seiynge, Lyue my lord kyng Dauid 32 with outen eende. And kyng Dauid seide, Clepith to me Sadoch, the preest, and Nathan, the prophete, and Ba- nayam, the sone of Joiade. The whiche whanne thei weren comyn yn before 33 the kyng, the king seide to hem, Takith with ʒou the seruauntis of ʒoure lord, and puttith my sone Salomon vpon my 34 mule, and ledith hym into Gion. And anoynte hym there Sadoch, the preest, and Nathan, the prophete, into kyng vpon Yrael ʻand Juda¹; and ʒe shulen synge with trompe, and seye, Lyue the 35 king Salomon ! And ʒe shulen stye vp after hym, and come to Jerusalem ; and he shal sitte vpon my see, and he shal regne for me ; and to hym I shal com- aunde, that he be duyk vpon Irael and 36 upon Juda. And Banayas, the sone of Joiade, answerde to the kyng, seiynge, Amen ; thus speke the Lord God of my 37 lord the kyng. What maner wise the Lord was with my lord the kyng, so be he with Salomon, and heiʒer make he the see of hym fro the see of my lord 38 kyng Dauid. Thanne Sadoch, ·the preest, wente doun, and Nathan, the prophete, and Banayas, the sone of Joyade, and Cerethi, and Pherethi ; and putten Salo- mon vpon the mule of Dauid, the kyng, 39 and brouʒten hym into Gion. And Sa- doch, the preest, took an horn of oyle fro the tabernacle, and anoyntide Salomon ; and thei sungen with the trompe ; and al the puple seide, Lyue the kyng Salo- 40 mon ! And al the multitude steyede vp after hym, and the puple of men syng-

thi sone, schal regne after me, and he schal sitte on my trone for me, so Y schal do to dai. And Bersabee, with theⁿ cheer castº 31 doun in to ertheᵖ, worschipide the kyng, and seide, My lord theᑫ kyng Dauid lyue with outen ende†. And kyng Dauid 32 seide, Clepe ʒe Sadoch, the preest, to me, and Nathan, the prophete, and Banaie, soneʳ of Joiada. And whanne thei hadden entrid bifor the kyng, the kyng seide to 33 hem, Take with ʒou the seruauntis of ʒoure lord, and putte ʒe my sone Salomon onˢ my mule, and lede ʒe hym in to Gyon. And Sadoch, the preest, and Nathan, the 34 profete, anoynteᵗ hym in to kyng onᵘ Israel and Juda ; and ʒe schulen synge with a clariounᵛ, and ʒe schulen seie, Lyue kyng Salomon ! ʒe schulen stieʷ aftir hym, 35 and ʒe schulen come to Jerusalem ; and he schal sitte onˣ my trone, and he schal regne for me ; and Y schal comaunde to hym, that he be duyk onʸ Israel and onᶻ Juda. And Banaie, soneᵃ of Joiada, answeride 36 to the kyng, and seide, Amen, ʻthat is, so be itᵇ, etherᶜ verili, ether feithfuliᵈ ; so speke the Lord God of my lord the kyng. As the Lord was with my lord theᵉ kyng, 37 so be he with Salomon, and make he the trone of Salomon heiʒere than the trone of my lord theᶠ kyng Dauid. Ther- 38 forᵍ Sadoch, the preest, ʒede doun, and Nathan, the prophete, and Banaie, soneʰ of Joiada, and Cerethi, and Ferethi ; and thei puttiden Salomon onⁱ the mule of Dauid, the kyng, and thei brouʒten hym in to Gion. And Sadoch, the preest, took 39 an horn of oile of the tabernacle, and anoyntide Salomon ; and thei sungen with a clarioun ; and al the puple seide, Lyue kyng Salomon ! And al the multitude 40 stiedeᵏ after hym, and the puple of men syngynge with pipis, and ʻof menˡ beynge glad with greet ioye, ʻstiede aftir hymᵐ ; and the erthe sownede of the cry of hem.

† with outen ende ; that is, in blisful lyf, which is euer- lastinge. Lire here. c.

ˡ Om. E pr.m.

ⁿ hir ı.   ᶜ bowid ı.   ᵖ the erthe ı.   ᑫ Om. cı.   ʳ the sone ı.   ˢ upon ı.   ᵗ anoynte thei ı.   ᵘ upon ı. ᵛ trumpe ı.   ʷ stie up ı.   ˣ upon ı.   ʸ upon ı.   ᶻ Om. ı.   ᵃ the sone ı.   ᵇ it doon n.   ᶜ Om. as. ʻᵈ The gloss omitted in cı.   ᵉ Om. ı.   ᶠ Om. ı.   ᵍ Thanne ı.   ʰ the sone ı.   ⁱ upon ı.   ᵏ stiede up ı. ˡ Om. ı.   ᵐ Om. ı.

ynge with trompis, and 'of gladynge with[m] greet ioye; and the erthe 'with
41 ynne[n] sownede of the crye of hem. For-sothe Adonyas herde, and alle that weren beden 'to mete[o] of hym; and now the feest was eendid. But and Joab, the voys herd of the trompe, seith, What to hym wole the crye of the citee makynge
42 noys? 3it hym spekynge, Jonathan, the sone of Abiathar, the preest, cam; to whom seide Adonyas, Go yn, for a strong man thou ert, and good thingis
43 tellynge. And Jonathan answerde to Adonye, Nay; forsothe the lord oure kyng Dauid hath ordeyned Salomon
44 kyng; and sente with hym Sadoch, the preest, and Nathan, the prophete, and Banayam, the sone of Joyade, and Cere-thi, and Pherethi; and putten hym vpon
45 the mule of the kyng. And Sadoch, the preest, and Nathan, the prophet, anoynt-iden hym kyng in Gion; and gladynge thei stieden thens, and the cite with ynne sownede; this is the voys that 3e
46 herden. But and Salomon sitte vpon
47 the see of the rewme; and the ser-uauntis of the kyng goon yn, blessiden to oure lord kyng Dauid, seiynge, God more large the name of Salomon vpon thi name, and magnifie the trone of hym vpon thi trone. And kyng Dauid
48 honourde[p] in his bed; and ferthermore thes thingis spak[q], Blessid the[r] Lord God of Yrael, that 3af to day a sitter in my
49 see, seynge myn eyen. Thanne thei ben agaist, and alle risen, that weren bodyn 'to meete[s] of Adonye, and echon 3eede
50 into his weie. Forsothe Adonyas, dred-ynge Salomon, roos, and 3eed into the tabernacle of the Lord, and heelde the
51 horn of the auter. And thei toolden to Salomon seyynge, Loo! Adonyas dredynge kyng Salomon, holdith[t] the horn of the

Forsothe[n] Adonye herde, and alle that 41 weren clepid of hym to feeste[o]; and thanne the feeste was endid. But also Joab seide, whanne the vois of trumpe[p] was herd, What wole it[q] to it silf the cry of the citee[qq] makynge noise? 3it the[r] 42 while he spak, Jonathan, sone[s] of Abia-thar, the preest, cam; to whom Adonye seide, Entre thou, for thou art a strong man, and tellynge goode thingis. And 43 Jonathan[t] answeride to Adonye, Nay; for oure lord the[u] kyng Dauid hath or-deyned Salomon kyng; and Dauid sente[v] 44 with Salomon Sadoch, the preest, and Na-than, the prophete, and Banaie, sone[w] of Joiada, and Cerethi, and Ferethi; and thei puttiden[x] Salomon on[y] the mule of the kyng. And Sadoch, the preest, and 45 Nathan, the prophete, anoyntiden[z] hym kyng in Gion; and thei camen doun fro thennus beynge glad, and the citee sown-ede; this is the vois which[a] 3e herden. But also Salomon sittith on[b] the trone of 46 rewme[c]; and the seruauntis of the kyng 47 entriden[d], and blessiden[f] oure lord the[g] kyng Dauid, and seiden, God make large the name of Salomon aboue thi name, and magnyfye[h] his trone aboue thi trone. And kyng Dauid worschipide in his bed; and 48 ferthermore he spak these thingis, Blessid be the Lord God of Israel, that 3af[k] to dai a sittere in my trone, while myn i3en seen[l]. Therfor alle, that weren clepid of 49 Adonye to feeste[m], weren aferd, and ri-siden[n], and ech man 3ede in to his weie. Sotheli[o] Adonye dredde Salomon, and 50 roos[p], and 3ede in to the tabernacle of the Lord, and helde[q] the horn[r] of the auter. And thei telden to Salomon, and seiden, 51 Lo! Adonye dredith the kyng Salomon, and holdith[s] the horn[t] of the auter, and seith, Kyng Salomon swere to me to dai, that he schal not sle his seruaunt bi[u] swerd.

---

[m] verne glad and maden n recens manus.   [n] Om. n rec. m.   [o] Om.˙ε pr. m.   [p] smellede ε pr. m.
[q] spak, and the kyng seid n rec. m.   [r] be A.   [s] Om. ε pr. m.   [t] halt BCEFH.

[n] And 1.   [o] the feeste IKM.   [p] the trumpe K.   [q] Om. A sec. m.   [qq] Om. s.   [r] Om. L   [s] the sone 1.   [t] Jona-thas 1.   [u] Om. 1.   [v] hath sent 1.   [w] the sone 1.   [x] han putt 1.   [y] upon 1.   [z] han anoyntid 1.   [a] that 1.
[b] upon 1.   [c] the rewme 1.   [d] han entrid 1.   [f] han blessid 1.   [g] Om. 1.   [h] make greet 1.   [k] hath 3oue 1.
[l] seynge it 1.   [m] the feeste IKLP.   [n] risen E. resen up 1. resen P.   [o] And 1.   [p] roos up 1.   [q] he helde 1.
[r] horn or corner 1.   [s] he holdith 1.   [t] cornere 1.   [u] with 1.

auter, seiynge, Swere to me to dai kyng
Salomon, that he shal not sle his ser-
52 uaunt bi swerd. And Salomon seide, If
he were a good man, there shal not falle
forsothe an heere of hym in to the erthe;
forsothe if yuel were foundun in hym, he
53 shal die. Thanne kyng Salomon sente,
and brouȝte hym out fro the auter; and
goon yn, he honourde king Salomon;
and Salomon seide to hym, Go into thin
hows.

And Salomon seide, If he is a good man†, 52 † *if he is a*
sotheli not oon^v heer of hym schal falle in *good man ; not*
to erthe^w; but if yuel be foundun in hym, *sekinge aftir-*
ward ynngy-
he schal die. Therfor kyng Salomon sente, 53 *neciouns, to*
and ledde 'hym out^x fro the auter; and *gete the rewme.*
he entride, and worschipide kyng Salo- *Lire here. c.*
mon; and Salomon seide to hym, Go in
to thin hows.

CAP. II.

1   Forsothe the days of Dauid neiȝiden
that he shulde die; and he comaundide
2 to Salomon, his sone, seiynge, Loo! I
weende into the weye of al erthe; tak
3 coumfort, and be a strong man^u. And^v
keep wel the waardis and the heestis of
the Lord thi God, that thou goo in the
weyes of hym, and kepe the cerymonyes
of hym, and the heestis of hym, and
domys, and witnessyngis, as it is writyn
in the lawe of Moyses; that thou vndurstonde al that thou dost, and whidir euer
4 thou turne thee. That the Lord conferme
his wordis, 'the whiche^{vv} the Lord spak
of me, seiynge, If thi sonys kepen my
weyes^w, and goon before me in treuth,
and in al her hert, and in al her soule,
there shal not be doon awey to thee a
5 man fro the kyngis seete^x of Israel. Forsothe thou hast knowun what thingis^y
Joab, the sone of Saruye, dide to me;
what he dide to the^z two princis of the
oost of Irael, to Abner, the sone of Ner,
and to Amasi, the sone of Gether, whom
he slewȝ, and shadde the blood of the
batayl in pees; and putte the blood of the
batail in his girdyl, that was about his
6 leendis, and in his shoo, that was in his
6 feet. Thanne thou shalt do after thi
wisdam, and thou shalt not brynge doun
7 the hoornes of hym pesibli to hellis. But
and to the sones of Berzellay Galadite

CAP. II.

Forsothe the daies of Dauid neiȝiden, 1
that he schulde die; and he comaundide
to Salomon, his sone, and seide, Lo! Y 2
entre in to the weie of al erthe^y; be thou
coumfortid, and be thou a strong man.
And kepe thou the kepyngis and heestis^z 3
of thi Lord God, that thou go in hise
weies, and kepe hise cerymonyes, and hise
heestis, and hise domes, and witnessyngis,
as it is writun in the lawe of Moises;
that thou vndurstonde alle thingis whiche
thou doist, and whidur euer thou schalt
turne thee. That the Lord conferme hise 4
wordis, whiche the Lord spak of me, and
seide, If thi sones kepen my weies, and
goen bifor me in treuthe, in al her herte,
and in al her soule, a man schal not be
takun awei of thee fro the trone of Israel.
Also thou knowist what thingis Joab, 5
the sone of Saruye, dide^a to me‡; what
thingis he dide to twey princis of the
oost of Israel, to Abner, sone^b of Ner, and
to Amasa, sone^b of Jether, whiche he
killide, and schedde the blood of batel§ in
pees; and puttide^c the blood of batel in
his girdil, that was aboute hise leendis,
and in^d his scho^e, that was in hise feet.
Therfor thou schalt do by thi wisdom, 6
and thou schalt not lede forth his hoor-
nesse pesibli to hellis‖. But also thou 7
schalt ȝelde grace to the sones of Bersellai
of Galaad, and thei schulen be eetynge

‡ *dide to me ;*
Rabi Salomon
seith, that Joab
schewide to
othere men the
priuy lettris of
Dauyth to sle
Vrie. Lire
here. c.
§ *the blood of*
batel ; that is,
he schedde out
in the tyme of
pees mannus
blood, that owith
not to be sched
out no but in
batel. Lire
here. c.
‖ *to hellis ;*
Ebreys seyen,
to a dich, ether
sepulcre, for
Dauyth pur-
poside not, that
Joab schulde go
doun to the
helle of damp-
ned men ; ther-
for that was o
cause whi Da-
uyth wolde, that
he were pu-
nyschid here,
lest he were
punyschid in
helle, as Rabi
Salomon seith ;
as it was seid
of Achar in
vii. c°. of Josue.
Lire here. c.

^u Om. F.   ^v Om. *ABII.,*   ^{vv} that c *pr. m.*   ^w hestes E *pr. m.*   ^x citee *A.*   ^y thing *A.*   ^z Om. *A.*

^v an I.   ^w the erthe I.   ^x out Adonye I.   ^y erthe, *that is, to deth* I.   ^z the heestis I.   ^a hath do I.
^b the sone I.   ^c he hath putt I.   ^d Om. I.   ^e schoyng I.

Y 2

thou shalt ȝeelde grace, and thei shulen
be etynge in thi bord; forsothe thei
camen aȝen to me, whanne I fleiȝ fro the
8 face of Absolon, thi brother. And thou
hast anentis thee Semei, the sone of Gera,
the sone of Gemyny, of Bahurym, that
curside to me bi the werst cursynge,
whanne I wente to the defensable placys;
but for he cam doun to me into aȝen
comynge, whanne I shulde passe Jordan,
and I swore to hym bi the Lord, seiynge,
9 I shal not sle thee bi swerd, thou wole
not suffre hym to be harmles; forsothe
a wise man thou art, and thou shalt
knowe what thou shalt doo to hym, and
thou shalt lede doun his hoor heeris with
10 blood to helle. Forsothe Dauyd slepte
with his faders, and is biried in the citee
11 of Dauid. Forsothe the days, in the
whiche Dauid regnede vpon Yrael, ben
fourti ȝeer; in Ebron he regnede seuen
ȝeer, and in Jerusalem three and thretti.
12 Salomon forsothe sat vpon the troone of
Dauid, his fader, and the rewme of hym
13 is fastned ful mych. And Adonyas, the
sone of Agith, ȝeede into Bersabe, the
moder of Salomon; the which seide to
hym, Whether pesible thin yncomynge?
14 The which answerde, Pesible. And he
addide, A word to me is to thee. To
15 whom she seith, Spek. And he, Thou,
he seith, knewe[a] for the rewme was with
me, and al Irael purposide to make me
into a kyng to hym; but the rewme is
translatid, and is maad of my brother;
of the Lord forsothe it is ordeynd to
16 hym. Now thanne oon askyng Y preye
of thee; ne confounde thou my face. The
17 which seide to hym, Spek. And he seith,
Y preye that thou seye to Salomon the
kyng; forsothe ne to thee he may eny
thing denye; that he ȝyue to me Abi-
18 saag Sunamyte wijf. And Bersabe seith,
Wel, Y shal speke for thee to the kyng.

in thi boord; for thei metten me, whanne
Y fledde fro the face of Absolon, thi brother. Also thou hast anentis thee Semey, 8
sone[f] of Gera, sone[f] of Gemyny, of Bahurym, which[g] Semei curside me bi the
worste cursyng, whanne Y ȝede to 'the
castels[h]; but for[i] he cam doun to me in to
metyng[k], whanne Y passide Jordan, and
Y swoor to him bi the Lord, and seide, Y
schal not slee thee bi[l] swerd, nyle thou 9
suffre hym to be vnpunyschid; forsothe
thou art a wise man, and thou schalt wite
what thou schalt do to hym, and thou
schalt lede forth hise hoor heeris with
blood to hellis. Sotheli[m] Dauid slepte 10
with hise fadris, and was biriede in the
citee of Dauid. Forsothe[n] the daies, in 11
whiche Dauid regnede on[o] Israel, ben
fourti ȝeer; in Ebron he regned seuene
ȝeer, in[p] Jerusalem[q] thre and thretti ȝeer.
Forsothe Salomon sat on[qq] the trone of 12
Dauid, his fadir, and his rewme was maad
stidfast greetli. And Adonye, sone[r] of 13
Agith, entride to Bersabee, modir[s] of
Salomon; and sche seide to hym, Whether
thin entryng is pesible? And he answeride, It is pesible. And he addide[t], A word 14
of me is to thee. 'To whom[u] sche seide,
Speke thou. And he seide, Thou knowist 15
that[v] the rewme was myn, and al Israel
purposide to make me in to king to hem;
but the rewme is translatid, and is maad
my brotheris; for[w] of the Lord it is ordeyned to hym. Now therfor Y preye of 16
the oon axyng; schende[x] thou not my
face. And sche seide to hym, Speke thou.
And he seide, Y preie, that thou seie to 17
Salomon the king; for he may not denye
ony thing to thee; that he ȝyue to[y] me
Abisag of Sunam wijf[z]. And Bersabee 18
seide, Wel, Y schal speke for thee to the
kyng. Therfor Bersabee cam to kyng[a] 19
Salomon, to speke to hym for Adonye;
and the kyng roos aȝens the comyng of

[a] knowe A.

[f] the sone I. [g] the which I. [h] defensable placis I. [i] for thi I. [k] my metyng I. [l] with I. [m] And I. [n] And I. [o] upon I. [p] and in CI. [q] Israel N. [qq] upon I. [r] the sone I. [s] the modir I. [t] addide to I. [u] And I. [v] for BC. [w] for whi I. [x] confounde I. [y] Om. I. [z] to wijf I. [a] the kyng I.

19 Thanne Bersabe cam to kyng Salomon, that she speke to hym for Adonye; and the kyng roos into the^b aȝencomynge of hire, and he^c honourde hire, and he satte vpon his troone; and there is sett a troone to the modci of the kyng, the 20 which sat at the riȝt side of hym And sche seide to hym, Oon litil askynge I preye of thee; ne confounde thou my face And the kyng seide to hue, Ask, moder myn, forsothe ne leeueful it is 21 that I turne awey thi face The which seith, Abisnag Sunamyte be ȝouen to 22 Adonye, thi brother, a wijf And kyng Salomon answerde, and seide to his moder, Whi askist thou Abisaag Sunamyte to Adonye? Ask 'to hym^d and the kyngdam; forsothe he is my brother more than I, and hath Abiathar, the pieest, 23 and Joab, the sone of Saruye. And so kyng Salomon swore bi the Lord, seiynge, These thingis do to me God, and thes thingis adde, foi aȝens his lijf Adonye hath spoken this word And now 24 lyueth the Lord, that confermyde me, and sette me vpon the see of Dauid, my fader, and that made to me an hows, as he spak, foi to day Adonye shal be 25 slayn. And kyng Salomon sente bi the hoond of Banaye, the sone of Joiade; 26 the which slewȝ hym, and is deed Forsothe the kyng seide to Abiathar, the preest, Go into Anathot, to thi feelde, and forsothe a man of deeth thou art; but to day I shal not sle thee, for thou bere the arke of the Lord God before Dauid, my fader, and thou susteynedist tiaueyle in alle thingis, in the whiche 27 traueilde my fader Thanne Salomon made Abiathar, that he was not the^e preest of the Lord, that the word of the Lord were fulfillid, the whch he spak 28 vpon the hows of Hely, in Silo. Forsothe theie cam a messager to Salomon, that

hir^b, and worschipide hir, and 'sat on^c his trone; and a trone was set to the modir of the kyng, and sche sat at his riȝt side. And 20 sche seide to hym, Y preie of thee o litil axyng; schende^d thou not my face And the kyng seide to hir, My modir, axe thou; for^e it is not leueful that Y tuine awei thi^f face. And sche seide, Abisag 21 of Sunam† be ȝouun wijf to Adonye, thi brother. And kyng Salomon answeride, 22 and seide to his modir, Whi axist thou Abisag of Sunam to Adonye? Axe thou to hym also the rewme; foi^g he is 'my gretter^h brothir, and he hath Abiathar, preest, and Joab, sone^l of Saruye Ther-23 for kyng Salomon swoor bi the Lord, and seide, God do to me these thingis, and adde these thinges^k, for Adonie spak^l this word aȝens his lijf. And now the Lord 24 lyueth, that confermede^m me, and hath set me on^n the trone of my fadir, and that hath maad to me an hows, as he spak, for Adonye schal be slayn to dai And kyng Salomon sente bi the hond of 25 Banaie, sone^o of Joiada, which^p Banaie killide^q Adonye, and he was deed Also 26 the kyng seide to Abiathar, preest^r, Go thou in to Anatot, to thi feeld‡, and^s sothcli thou art a man of deeth, '*that is, worthi the^t deeth, for conspirying aȝens me, and the ordynaunce of God, and of my fadir^u*; but to dai Y schal not sle thee, for thou barist^v the arke of the Lord God bifor Dauid, my fadi, and thou suffridist tiauele in alle thingis, in whiche my fadi trauelide. Therfor Salomon puttide out 27 Abiathar, that he schulde not be preest^w of the Lord, that the word of the Lord were fillid^x, which^y he spak on^z the hows of Heli, in Silo§ Forsothe^a a messagei 28 cam to Salomon, that^h Joab hadde bowid aftii Adonye, and that he hadde not bowid after Salomon Therfoi Joab fledde in to the tabernacle of the Lord, and took

† *Abisag of Sunam*, sche was wijf of Danyth, and therbi the queen, and so bi hir he hadde weye to come to the rewme, bi the help of Joab and of Abia har,and of othere men fauoiinge him And Salomon, that was of scharpere wit than his modir, perseuuede this, and answeride, *axe thou to hun also the rewme*, as [if] he seide, by this he purposith to come to the rewme For *Adonye spak this word aȝenus his lijf*, for he vinagyned, aȝenus the kyng, and for he axide the wijf of his fadir aȝenus the lawe, m xv iii c^e of Leuyticy Lire here c : *to thi faeld*, that is, to the place of thi possessioun, for prestis hadden citees assigned foi her dwelling in xxxv c^e of Numeri and xxi. c^e of Josue. Lire here c. § *in Silo*, that he schulde be cast out iiro presthod, as in i book ii c^e Lire here Aaron was maad h ieste prest bi Goddis chesing, m xxviii c^e of Exodi and in xvii c^e of Numeri And he hadde ii sones, Eliazar and Xthamar, that dwelliden, whanne ii othere weren deed bifor the Lord, m x c^e of Leuitici, and thanne, bi Goddis wille, the presthod pass ide to Eleazar and hise sones, in xx c^e of Numeri, of

---

b Om. E. c Om. CE d forsothe E pr m e Om. A.

b his modir I c he sat upon I d confounde I e forsothe I f my I g certis I h myn eldir I i the sone I k thingis to I. l hath spoke I m hath confermed I n upon I o the sone I p aud I q slewȝe I r the preest I s Om A t to EL u that is, worthi of deth, foi conspiring aȝens me and *Dauid my fadir* I marg. v hast bore I. w the preest A see m I x fulfillid I y that I. z upon s a And I b and seide that I

Joab was bowid doun after Adonye, and after Salomon hadde not bowid. Thanne Joab fleiȝ into the tabernacle of the Lord, 29 and cauȝte the horn of the auter. And it is toold to kyng Salomon, that Joab hadde flowen into the tabernacle of the Lord, and was biside the auter; and Salomon sente Banaye, the sone of Joiade, 30 seiynge, Go, and sle hym. And Banaye cam to the tabernacle of the Lord, and seide to hym, Thes thingis seith the kyng, Go out. The which seith, I shal not goo out, but here I shal die. Banayas toolde aȝen to the kyng the word, seiynge, Thes thingis spak Joab, and thes 31 thingis answerde he to me. And the kyng seide to hym, Do as he spak, and sle hym, and birye; and thou shalt doo awey the innocent blood, that is shad of Joab, fro me, and fro the hows of my 32 fader. And the Lord ȝeelde vpon his heed the blood of hym, for he slewȝ two riȝtwise men betere than hym self, and he killide hem bi swerd, Dauid, my fader, vnknowynge, Abner, the sone of Ner, the prince of the chyualrie of Irael, and Amasam, the sone of Gether, prince 33 of the oost of Juda. And the blood of hem shal turne aȝen into the heed of Joab, and into the heed of the seed of him in to euermore; forsothe to Dauid, and to his seed, and to the hows of hym, and to the troone of hym be pees of the Lord 34 into withouten eende. And so Banaye, the sone of Joiade, steied vp, and wente to, and slewȝ hym; and he is biryed in 35 his hows in desert. And the kyng ordeynede for hym Banaye, the sone of Joiade, vpon the oost; and Sadoch he 36 sette preest for Abiathar. Forsothe the kyng sente, and clepide Semei, and seide to hym, Bild vp to thee howsis in Jerusalem, and dwel there, and thou shalt 37 not goo out thens hidir and thider; for-

the horn of the auter. And it was teld to 29 kyng Salomon, that Joab hadde fledde in to the tabernacle of the Lord, and was bisidis the auter; and Salomon sente Banaie, sone of Joiada, and seide, Go thou, and sle hym. And Banaie cam to the 30 tabernacle of the Lord, and seide to Joab, The kyng seith these thingis, Go thou out. And he seide, Yschal not go out, but Yschal die here. Banaie telde the word to the kyng, and seide, Joab spak thes thingis, and answeride these thingis to me. And the kyng 31 seide to Banaie, Do thou as he spak, and sle thou hym, and birie *him*; and thou schalt remoue the innocent blood, that was sched out of Joab, fro me, and fro the hows of my fadir. And the Lord 32 ȝelde on his heed his blood, for he killide twei iust men, and betere than hym silf, and he killide hem bi swerd, while Dauid, my fadir, wiste not, Abner, the sone of Ner, the prince of the chyualrie of Israel, and Amasa, sone of Jether, the prince of the oost of Juda. And the blood 33 of hem schal turne aȝen in to the heed of Joab, and in to the heed of his seed with outen ende; forsothe pees be of the Lord til in to with outen ende to Dauid, and to his seed, and to the hous and trone of hym. Therfor Banaie, sone of Joiada, 34 stiede, and asailide, and killide Joab; and Joab was biried in his hows in desert‡. And the kyng ordeynede Banaie, 35 sone of Joiada, on the oost for hym; and the kyng puttide Sadoch preest for Abiathar. Also the kyng sente, and cle-36 pide Semey, and seide to hym, Bilde to thee an hows in Jerusalem, and dwelle thou there, and thou schalt not go out fro thennus hidur and thidur; sotheli in 37 what euer dai thou goist out, and passist the stronde of Cedron, wite thou thee worthi to be slayn; thi blood schal be on thin heed. And Semei seide to the kyng, 38

f Om. CE.   g Om. E pr. m.   h Om. ABFH.

c the sone 1. d Joab 1. e hath spoke 1. f Om. 18. g is 1. h upon 1. i Joabs 1. k Om. 1. l with 1. m Om. 1. n vnwiting *it* 1. o the sone 1. p Om. 1. q but 1. r the sone 1. s stiede up 1. t asailide Joab 1. u him 1. v the sone 1. w upon 1. x Joab 1. y putte 1. z the preest 1. a Jerusalem 1. b for 1.

sothe whateuere day thou were goon out, and passist ouer the streem of Cedron, wite thou thee to be slayn; thi 38 blood shal be vpon thin heed   And Semei seide to the king, Good is the word of the kyng; as my lord kyng hath spokyn, so thi seruaunt shal doo And so Semei dwellide in Jerusalem manye dais. 39 It is doon forsothe after three ȝeer, that the seruauntis of Semei flowen to Achis, the sone of Macha, the kyng of Geth; and it is toold to Semei, that his ser-40 uauntis weren goon in to Geth. And Semei roos, and greithide his asse[l], and wente to Achis, into Geth, to his seruauntis to be souȝt; and he brouȝte hem 41 aȝen fro Geth. It is toold forsothe to kyng Salomon, that Semei was goon to . Geth fro Jerusalem, and was turned aȝen 42 And sendynge he clepide hym, and seide to hym, Whether Y witnesside not to thee bi the Lord, and before seide to thee, What euer dai thou were goon out hidir and thidir, wite thou thee to be to 43 die; and thou answerdist to me, Good is the word that I herde ? Whi thanne kepist[k] thou not the ooth of the Lord, and the heest that I comaundide to thee ? 44 And the kyng seide to Semei, Thou hast knowun al the yuel, of the which thin herte is gilti to thee, the which thou diddist to Dauid, my fader; the Lord hath 45 ȝolden thi malice into thin heed And kyng Salomon blisside, and the troone of Dauid shal be stable before the Lord 46 vnto euermore And so the kyng comaundide to Banaye, the sone of Joiade; the which stert to, smoot hym, and he is deed.

CAP III.

1 Thanne the rewme is confermyd into the hoondis of Salomon, and bi affynyte he is joyned to Pharao, the kyng of Egipt, forsothe he took his douȝter, and

The word of the kyng is good; as my lord the[c] kyng spak, so thi seruaunt schal do. Therfor[d] Semey dwellide in Jerusalem in[e] many daies Forsothe[f] it was 39 doon after thre ȝeer, that the seruauntis of Semei fledden to Achis, sone[g] of Maacha, the[h] kyng of Geth; and it was teld to Semey, that hise seruauntis hadden[i] go in to Geth. And Semey roos[k], and sadhde 40 his asse, and ȝede to Achis, in to Geth, to seke hise seruauntis; and brouȝte[l] hem aȝen fro Geth. Forsothe[m] it was teld to 41 kyng Salomon, that Semey hadde go[n] to Geth fro Jerusalem, and hadde come aȝen. And Salomon sente, and clepide hym, and 42 seide to hym, Whether Y witnessede not to thee bi the Lord, and bifor seide to thee, In what euer dai thou schalt go out hidur and thidur, wite thou that thou schalt die; and thou answerdist to me, The word is good, which[o] Y herde[p] ? Whi 43 therfor keptist thou not the ooth of the Lord, and the comaundement[q] which[r] Y comaundide to thee ? And the kyng seide 44 to Semei, Thou knowist al the yuel, of which[s] thin herte is gilti to thee[t], which yuel thou didist[u] to my fadir, the Lord hath ȝolde thi malice in to thin heed And 45 kyng Salomon *schal be* blessid; and the trone of Dauid schal be stable bifor the Lord til in to with outen ende Therfor 46 the kyng comaundide[v] to Banaie, sone[w] of Joiada, and he assailide[x], and smoot Semey[y], and he was deed

CAP. III.

Therfor the rewme was confermyd in 1 to the hondis of Salomon; and bi affynyte, '*ether aliaunce*[z], he was ioyned to Pharao, kyng of Egipt; for he[a] took[b] the douȝter

[l] assis A.   [k] keptist cF.

[c] Om 1   [d] And so 1   [e] Om 1   [f] But 1   [g] the sone 1   [h] Om 1   [i] weren 1   [k] roos up 1.   [l] he brouȝte 1   [m] And 1   [n] goon out 1   [o] that 1   [p] haue herd *of thee* 1   [q] heest 1   [r] that 1.   [s] the which 1   [t] thi self 1   [u] hast do 1.   [v] comaunde A   [w] the sone 1s   [x] assailede Semey 1   [y] him 1.   [z] Om. c1   [a] Salomon 1   [b] took *to myf* 1.

brouȝte into the cite of Dauid, to the tyme that he hadde fulfillid beeldynge his hows, and the hows of the Lord, and the wal of Jerusalem bi enuyroun. 2 Neuerthelater the puple offride in heiȝ placis; forsothe the temple was not beildid to the name of the Lord vnto 3 that dai. Forsothe Salomon louede the Lord, goynge in the heestis of Dauid, his fader, out taak that in heiȝ placis he offrede, and tende vp the maad encense. 4 And so Salomon wente into Gabaon, that he offre there; forsothe that was the moost heiȝ place. Salomon offride a thousand oostis into brent sacrifice vpon that 5 auter in Gabaon. Forsothe the Lord aperide to Salomon biᴶ sleepe theᵐ nyȝt, seiynge, Ask that thou wolt, that I ȝyue 6 to thee. And Salomon seith, Thou didist with thi seruaunt, my fader Dauid, greet mercy, as he wente in thi siȝt, in treuth and in riȝtwisnes, and in riȝt herte with thee; thou hast kept to hym thi greet merci, and hast ȝeuen to hym a sone, sittynge vpon his troone, as it is to dai. 7 And now, Lord God, thou hast maad thi seruaunt to regne for Dauid, my fader; forsothe I am a litil child, and vnknowynge the goynge out and myn yncom-8 ynge. And thi seruaunt is in the mydil of the puple, whom thou hast chosun, of a puple with out eende, that may not be noumbred and gessid, for multitude. 9 Thanne thou shalt ȝyue to thi seruaunt an able herte to lore, that he may deme thi puple, and knowe betwix good and yuel; forsothe who may deme this puple, 10 thi puple thus myche? Thanne the word pleside before the Lord, that Salomon 11 hadde askid siche a maner thing. And the Lord seide to Salomon, For thou askedist this word, and askidist not to thee manye dais, ne ritchessis, othereⁿ

of Faraot, and brouȝteᶜ in to the citee of Dauid, tilᵈ he 'fillide bildyngeᵉ his 'hows, and the hows of the Lord, and theᵉᵉ wal of Jerusalem bi cumpas. Netheles the 2 puplᶠ offrideᵍ in hiȝe placis; forᵇ the temple was not bildid toᶦ the name of the Lord til in to that dai. Forsotheᵏ Salo-3 mon louyde the Lord, and ȝede in the comaundementisᶦ of Dauid, his fadir, out takun that Salomon offride in hiȝe placis‡, and brente encense 'in hiȝe placesᵐ. Ther-4 forⁿ Salomon ȝedeᵒ in to Gabaon, to offre there; forᵖ thilkeᑫ was the moost hiȝ placeᶂ. Salomon offride onʳ that auter in Gabaon a thousynde offryngis in to brent sacrifice. Sotheli the Lord apperide 5 to Salomon bi sleep in the nyȝt, and seide, Axe thou 'that, thatˢ thou wolt, that Y ȝyueᵗ to thee. And Salomon seide, Thou 6 hast do greet merci with thi seruaunt Dauid, my fadir, as he ȝede in thi siȝt, in treuthe, and riȝtfulnesseⁿ, and riȝtfulᵛ herte with thee; thou hast kepte to hym thi greet merci, and hast ȝouun to hym a sone, sittynge onᵂ his trone, as it is to dai. And now, Lord God, thou hast maad 7 thi seruaunt to regne for Dauid, my fadir; forsothe Y am a litil child, and not knowynge myn outgoynge and entryngʳ. And 8 thi seruaunt is in the myddis of the puple, which thou hast chose, of puple with outen noumbre, that may not be noumbrid and rikened, for multitude. Therfor thou 9 schalt ȝyue to thi seruaunt an herte able to be tauȝt, 'that is, liȝtned of theeˢ, that he may deme theᵗ puple, and iugeⁿ bitwixe good and yuel; for who may deme this puple, thi puple, thisᵛ miche puple‖? Therfor the word pleside bifore the Lord, 10 that Salomonᵂ hadde axid sich a thing. And the Lord seide to Salomon, For thou 11 axidist this word, and axidist not to thee many daies, nether richessis, nether the

Marginal notes:

† *the douȝter of Farao; Salomon synnede not in this, for this wommman forsook hethenesse, and was conuertid to the feith of o veri God. Lire here. c.*

‡ *offride in hiȝe placis; this was leueful thanne, netheles it was lesse good than to offre in the place, where the arke of God was. Bifor the bilding of the temple, whanne the arke hadde not stable abiding, it was leueful to offre in othere places than bifor the arke; but aftir the bilding of the temple, this was not leueful, no but [bi] special stiring of God, as Elie dide, in III. book of Kingis, xviii. cᵒ. Lire here. c.*

§ *hiȝe place; not in greetnesse of erthe, but of reuerence and onour; for the tabernacle and the auter of brent sacrifice, whiche Moyses made, weren there; in I. book of Paral. xxi. cᵒ. Lire here. c.*

‖ *this myche puple; as if he seye, no man may, with out thi special liȝtnyng. Lire here. c.*

ᶦ in ᴅ rec. m.   ᵐ bi ᴅ rec. m.   ⁿ neither ᴮ rec. m.

ᶜ brouȝte hir ɪ.   ᵈ til that ɪ.   ᵉ bildynge hadde fulfillid ɪ.   ᵉᵉ Om. s.   ᶠ puple of the citee ᴋ.
ᵍ offride ȝit ᴋ.   ᵇ forsothe ɪ.   ᶦ in ɪ.   ᵏ Sotheli ɪ.   ᶦ heestis ɪ.   ᵐ Om. ɪ.   ⁿ And so ɪ.   ᵒ wente ɪ.
ᵖ certis ɪ.   ᑫ that ᴇɪʟ.   ʳ upon ɪ.   ˢ what that ᴇ. that what ʟ.   ᵗ ȝyue it ɪ.   ⁿ riȝtwisnesse ɪ.   ᵛ in
riȝtful ɪ.   ᵂ upon ɪ.   ʳ myn yn comyng ɪ.   ˢ Om. ɪ.   ᵗ thi ɪ.   ᵘ discryue ɪ.   ᵛ thus ɪ.   ᵂ he ɪ.

the[o] lyues of thin enemyes, but thou
askedist to thee wisdam to knowe doom,
12 loo! I haue doon to thee after thi wordis,
and ȝeuen to thee a wise herte and an
vndurstondynge, in so myche that noon
before thee were[p] lijk thee, ne aftir thee
13 ben to ryse. But and[q] thes thingis, 'the
whiche[r] thou askydist not, I haue ȝeuen
to thee, that is, ritchessis, and glorie, that
noon were lijk to thee in kyngis alle
14 dais after. Forsothe if thou gost in my
weies, and kepist myn heestis, and my
comaundementis[rr], as wente thi fader, long
15 I shal make thi dais. Thanne Salomon
wook vp, and vndurstood that it was a
sweuen. And whanne he was comen to
Jerusalem, he stood before the arke of
the boond of pees of the Lord, and offride
brent sacrifices, and made slayn pesible
sacrifices, and a greet feste to alle his
16 seruauntis. Thanne camen two wymmen
strompettis to the kyng, and stoden be-
17 fore hym; of the whiche oon seith, I
biseche, my lord, I and this womman
dwelliden in oon hows, and I bare child[s]
18 anentis hire in the bed. The thridde forsothe day after that I bare, bare[t] and[u]
this; and we[v] weren togidir, and noon
othere in the hows with vs, out takun vs
19 two. Forsothe the sone of this womman
is deed to nyȝt, for slepynge she ouerlaye
20 hym; and risynge with silence of the
vnkouenable niȝt, she took my sone fro
myn syde, of thin hond womman slepinge, and leide it in hir bosum; hir sone
forsothe, that was deed, she put in to my
21 bosum. And whan I was risyn eerli, for
to ȝyue milk to my sone, he semyde deed;
whom bisier[w] lokinge bi the cleer liȝt, I
perseyuede not be myn, whom Y gat.
22 The tother womman answerde, It is not
so as thou seist, but thi sone is deed;

lyues of thin enemyes, but thou axidist to
thee wisdom to deme doom, lo! Y haue 12
do to thee vpe[x] thi wordis, and Y haue
ȝoue to thee a wyse herte and vndirstondynge[y], in so myche that no man† bifor
thee was lijk thee[z], nether schal rise aftir
thee. But also Y haue ȝoue to thee these 13
thingis, whiche thou axidist not, that is,
richessis, and glorie, that no man be lijk
thee in kyngis in alle tymes aftirward.
Forsothe if thou goist in my weies, and 14
kepist my biddyngis and comaundementis[a],
as thi fadir ȝede[b], Y schal make thi daies
long. Therfor Salomon wakide, and vn- 15
dirstood[c]‡ what the sweuen was. And
whanne he hadde come to Jerusalem, he
stood bifor the arke of boond of pees of
the Lord, and he offride brent sacrifices[d],
and made[e] pesible sacrifices, and a greet
feeste to alle hise meynees. Thanne twei 16
wymmen hooris[f] camen to the kyng, and
stoden bifor hym; of whiche[g] oon seide, 17
My lord, Y biseche, Y and this womman
dwelliden in oon[h] hows, and Y childide at
hir in a couche. Sotheli[i] in the thridde 18
dai aftir that Y childide[k], also[l] this womman childide; and we weren togidere in
the hows, and noon other was with vs in
the[m] hows, outakun vs tweyne. Forsothe[n] 19
the sone of this womman was deed in the
nyȝt, for sche slepte, and oppresside[o]
hym; and sche roos[p] in the fourthe part 20
of the nyȝt in silence, and took[q] my sone
fro the side of me, thin handmaide slepynge, and settide[r] in hir bosum; forsothe[s]
sche puttide[t] in my bosum hir sone, that
was deed. And whanne Y hadde ryse 21
eerli, to ȝyue mylk to my sone, he apperide deed; whom Y bihelde diligentlier[u]
bi cleer liȝt, and Y perseyuede, that he
was not myn, whom Y hadde gendrid.
The tother womman answeride, It is not 22

† *that no man*; this is vndurstondun, in comparisoun of kingis that weren bifor him and aftir, for bothe Adam maad in the fulnesse of kunning in iii. c°. of Genesis, and Moises that spak to God, face to face, in xxxiii. c°. of Exodi, weren wisere than Salomon, and the postlis weren more liȝtned, than ony othere in the elde testament. *in kingis*; this schal be vndurstondun in these thre to gidere, that is, wisdom, glorie, and riches, for grete Alisaundre and emperours of Rome, weren myȝtiere and gloriousere than Salomon, and summe weren richere, as Octouyan, netheles thei failiden in wisdom, in which they weren not liyk Salomon. *Lire here*. c.

‡ *vndurstood, etc.*; therfor it was propirly a reuelacioun of God which is maad ofte in sleep. *Lire here*. c.

[o] Om. F. [p] was B *rec. m.* [q] Om. H. [r] that C. [rr] maundementis E. [s] Om. E *pr. m.* a child H. [t] bare child B *rec. m.* [u] and she A. [v] Y B *rec. m.* [w] bisilyer BCEFH.

[x] aftir I. [y] an vndirstondynge I. [z] Om. C. [a] myn heestis I. [b] ȝede *in hem* I. [c] he vndirstood I. [d] sacrifice I. [e] he made I. [f] strumpetis I. [g] the whiche I. [h] an I. [i] And I. [k] had childid I. [l] also and I. [m] that I. [n] And I. [o] ouerlay I. [p] roos up I. [q] sche took I. [r] sche leide it I. sette EL. [s] and I. [t] putte L. [u] diligentli A. more diligently I.

forsothe myn lyueth. And aȝenward she seide, Thou lieȝst; forsothe my sone lyneth, and thi sone is deed. And so in this maner thei stryuen before the kyng. 23 Thanne the kyng seith, This seith, My sone lyueth, and thi sone is deed; and she answerde, Nay, but thi sone is deed; 24 'myn forsothe^x lyneth. Thanne the kyng seide, Bryngith to me a swerd. And whanne thei hadden brouȝt a swerd be-25 fore the kyng, Denydith, he seith, the quyk child in two parties, and ȝyneth the half part to the toon, and the half part^y 26 to the tothir. Forsothe^z the womman, whos was the quyk child, seith to the kyng; for the bowels of her ben stiryd vpon hire sone; Lord, I biseche, ȝife^a to hir the quyk child, and wolith not sle hym. Aȝenward she seide, Ne to me, ne 27 to thee be he, but be he deuydide. The kyng answerde, and seith, Ȝyneth to this womman^b the quik child, and be he not 28 slayn; forsothe this is his modir. And so al Yrael herde the dome, that he hadde demyde; and thei dradden the kyng, se-ynge the wisdam of God to ben in hym, 'to do^c doom.

CAP. IV.

1 Forsothe kyng Salomon was regnynge 2 vpon al Yrael. And thes ben the princis that he hadde; Azarias, the sone of Sa-3 doch, the preest; Elyoreb, and Ahia, sones of Sila, scribe; Josaphat, the sone of 4 Achilud, chaunselere; Banayas, the sone of Joiade, vpon the oost; forsothe Sadoch 5 and Abiathar, preestis; Azarias, the sone of Nathan, vpon hem that stoden nyȝ to the kyng; Zabul, the sone of Nathan, a 6 preest, freend of the kyng; Ahiazar, pro-uost of the hows; and Adonyram, the 7 sone of Adda, vpon the tributis. For-

---

so as thou seist, but thi sone is deed; for-sothe^v 'my sone^w lyueth. Aȝenward sche seide, Thou liest; for my sone lyneth, and thi sone is deed. And bi this maner thei stryueden^x bifore the kyng. Thanne the 23 kyng seide, This womman seith, My sone lyueth, and thi sone is deed; and this womman answerith, Nay, but thi sone is deed; forsothe^y my sone lyueth. Therfor 24 the kyng seide, Brynge ȝe to me a swerd. And whanne thei hadden brouȝt a swerd bifor the kyng, he seide, Departe ȝe the 25 quyk ȝong child in to^z twei partis, and ȝyue ȝe the half part to oon^a, and the^b half part to the tother. Forsothe^c the 26 womman, whos sone was quik, seide to the kyng; for her entrailis weren mouyd on hir sone; Lord, Y biseche, ȝyue ȝe to hir the quik child, and nyle ȝe sle hym. Aȝenward sche seide, Be he^d nethir to me, nether^e to thee, but be he departid. The 27 kyng answeride, and seide, Ȝyue ȝe to this womman the ȝong child quyk, and be he not slayn; forsothe^f this is 'his modir^g. Therfor al Israel herde the doom, which^h 28 the kyng hadde demyd; and thei dredden the kyng, and sien, that the wisdom of God† was in hym, to make doom.

CAP. IV.

'Forsothe kyng Salomonⁱ was regnynge 1 on^k al Israel. And these weren the princes 2 which he hadde; Azarie, sone^l of Sadoch, preest^m‡; Helioreb, and Haia, sonesⁿ of 3 Sila, 'weren scryueyns^o; Josophat, sone^p of Achilud, was chaunseler; Banaie, sone^q 4 of Joiada, was on^r the oost; forsothe^s Sa-doch and Abiathar§ weren preestis; Azarie, 5 sone^t of Nathan, was on^u hem that stoden niȝ the kyng; Zabul, the sone of Nathan, was preest, 'that is, greet and worschip-ful^v, a freend of the kyng; and Ahiasar 6 was stiward of the hows; and Adonyram,

† wisdom of God; that is, ȝouun to him of God; was in him; aboue the maner of othere men, and ther-for they dred-den him, more than bifore. Lire here. c.
‡ preest; in Ebreu it is, was vndur his fadir, that was the hiȝeste prest. Lire here. c.
§ and Abia-thar; Salomon clepide him aȝen in to the temple, that he schulde lyue of the auter, ne-theles not to the hiȝeste presthod. Lire here. c.

^x and myn B rec. m.   ^y partie E   ^z But B rec. m.   ^a ȝeuyth BCEFH.   ^b Om. BCEFH.   ^c for this B rec. m.

^v and I.   ^w myn I.   ^x streuen EIL. streuyn P.   ^y and I.   ^z Om. I.   ^a the toon I. the oon K. ^b Om. I.   ^c And I.   ^d the child I.   ^e Om. EILP.   ^f for I.   ^g the modir of him I.   ^h that I.   ⁱ Kyng Salomon sothly I.   ^k vpon I.   ^l the sone I.   ^m the preest I.   ⁿ the sone I.   ^o the writer I.   ^p the sone I. ^q the sone I.   ^r prince upon I.   ^s and I.   ^t the sone I.   ^u upon I.   ^v Om. I.

sothe Salomon hadde twelue ouerseers vpon al Yrael, that ȝeuen corn to the kyng, and to his hows; forsothe bi the monethis arowe in the ȝeer, thei a rowe 8 mynystreden necessarijs. And thes the names of hem; Benhur, in the mount of 9 Effraym; Bendekar, in Maetes, and in Salebbym, and in Bethsames, and in He-10 lon, and in Bethanan; Benesech, and in Araboth; of hym forsothe was Socco, 11 and al the loond of Eefer; Benabidanab, of whom al Neptad; Dorthafaed, the^d douȝter of Salomon, he hadde to^e wijf. 12 Bena, the sone of Achilud, gouernede Thaneth, Amageddo, and al Bethsan, that is beside Sarthana, vndur Jezrael, fro Bethsan vnto Abelmeula, 'forn aȝens^f Sel-13 maan. Bengaber in Ramoth Galaad hadde Anothiair, of the sone of Manasse, in Galaad; he gouernede in al the regioun of Argob, that is in Basan, to sexti greet citees and wallid, that hadden brasen 14 lockis. Achymadab, the sone of Addo, 15 rewlide in Manahym; Achymaas, in Neptalym, but and he hadde Bachsemath, the 16 douȝter of Salomon, in mariage; Bena, the sone of Husi, in Aser, and in Balod; 17 Josaphat, the sone of Pharue, in^g Ysa-18 char; Semei, the sone of Hela, in Benia-19 myn; Gaber, the sone of Sury, in the loond of Galaad, and in the loond of Seon, kyng of Amorrey, and of Og, the kyng of Basan, vpon alle thingis^h that 20 weren in that loond. Juda and Yrael ben vnnoumbrable, as the grauel of the see in multitude, etynge, and drynkynge, 21 and gladynge. Forsothe Salomon was in his power, hauynge alle the rewmes, as fro the flood of the loond of Philisteis vnto the eende of Egipt, of men offryng to hym ȝiftis, and of seruynge to hym 22 alle the days of his lijf. Forsothe the meet of Salomon was bi eche day, thretti choris of tried floure, and sexti choris of

sone^w of Adda, was on^x the tributis. For-7 sothe Salomon hadde twelue 'prefectis, ether^y cheef minystrys^z, on^a al Israel, that^b ȝauen lijflode to the kyng, and to his hows; sotheli bi ech monethe bi it silf in the ȝeer, ech prefect^c bi hym silf mynystride necessaries. And these ben 8 the names of hem; Benhur, in the hil of Effraym; Bendechar, in Maeces, and in 9 Salebbym, and in Bethsames, and in He-lon, and in Bethanan; Beneseth, in Ara-10 both; forsothe^d Socco, and al the lond of Epher was his; Benabidanab, whos was 11 al Neptad, hadde Dortaphaed, 'Solomons douȝter^e, to wijf. Bena, sone^f of Achilud, 12 gouernyde Thaneth, and Mageddo, and al Bethsan, which^g is bisidis Sarthana, vndur Jezrael, fro Bethsan 'til to^h Abelmeula, euene aȝens Zelmaan. Bengaber in Ra-13 moth of Galaad hadde Anothiair, of the sone of Manassos, in Galaad; he was souereyn in al the cuntrey of Argob, whichⁱ is in Basan, to sixti greet citees and wallid, that^k hadden brasun lockis. Achymadab, sone^l of Addo, was souereyn 14 in Manaym; Achymaas was in Neptalym, 15 but also he hadde Bachsemath, douȝter^m of Salomon, in wedloc; Banaa, soneⁿ of 16 Husy, was^o in Aser, and in Balod; Jose-17 phat, sone^p of Pharue, was in Ysachar; Semey, sone^q of Hela, was^r in Beniamyn; 18 Gaber, sone^s of Sury, was^t in the lond of 19 Galaad, and in the lond of Seon, kyng of Amorrey, and of Og, kyng of Basan, on^u alle thingis, that weren in that lond. Juda 20 and Israel weren vnnoumbrable, as the soond of the see in multitude, etynge, and drynkynge, and beynge glad. For-21 sothe Solomon was in his lordschip, and hadde alle rewmes^v, as fro the flood of the lond of Filisteis 'til to^w the laste part of Egipt, of men offrynge ȝiftis† to hym, and seruynge to hym, in alle the daies of his lijf. Forsothe the mete of 22

† ȝiftis; that is, tributis. Lire here. c.

---

^d Om. b.   ^e Om. befh.   ^f fro the regioun of e pr. m.   ^g and in a.   ^h Om. e pr. m.

^w the sone i.   ^x upon i.   ^y Om. i.   ^z maistris i.   ^a upon i.   ^b the whiche i.   ^c cheef maister i.
^d and i.   ^e the douȝter of Salomon i.   ^f the sone i.   ^g that i.   ^h vnto i.   ⁱ that i.   ^k the whiche i.
^l the sone i.   ^m the douȝtir i.   ⁿ the sone i.   ^o Om. i.   ^p the sone i.   ^q the sone i.   ^r Om. i.   ^s the
sone   ^t Om. i.   ^u and upon i.   ^v the rewmes i.   ^w vnto i.

23 meele, ten fatte oxen, twenti 'lesewed oxen[i], and an hundrid wetheris, 'out taak[k] huntynge of hertis, and of goot, 24 and of buglis, and of fed foulis. Forsothe he helde al the regioun that was beȝonde the flood, as fro Capsa vnto Gasan, and alle the kingis of that regioun; and he hadde pees on al side in 25 enuyroun.   And Juda dwellide and[l] Yrael with outen eny drede, echon vndur his vyn, and vndur his fiyg tree, fro Dan vnto Bersabee, alle the dais of Salomon. 26 And Salomon hadde fourti thousand cratchis of chaare hors, and twelue thousand of ridynge hors; and the forseid ouerseers of the kyng norisheden hem. 27 But and the necessarijs of kyng Salomon[m] bord thei ȝauen with greet bisynes 28 in her[n] tyme; forsothe barli, and chaf of hors, and of beestis thei brouȝten into the place, where the kyng was, aftir the 29 settynge to hem. Forsothe God ȝaf wisdam to Salomon, and myche prudence ful greetli, and laargenesse of herte, as grauel that is in the brenk of the see. 30 And the wisdam of Salomon wente before the wisdam of alle the eest men, and 31 of Egipciens[o]; and he was wiser than alle men; wiser than Ethan Esrayte, and than Eman, and than Cacal, and than Dorda, the sones of Maol; and he was nemned in alle the[p] gentylis bi 32 enuyroun.   And Salomon spak thre thousand parablis, and the ditees of hym 33 weren fyue thousand; and he disputide vpon the[pp] trees, fro[q] the cedar that is in Liban, vnto the ysoop that goth out of the wal; and he tretyde of the beestis, and foulis, and of crepynge beestis, and 34 of fisshis. And there camen of alle puplis to the wysdam of Salomon to be herde, and of alle kyngis of erthe[r], the whiche herden the wisdam of hym.

Salomon was bi ech day, thritti chorus* of clene flour of whete, and sixti chorus of mele, ten fatte oxis[x], and twenti oxis[x] of 23 lesewe[y], and an hundrid wetheris, outakun huntyng of hertys, of geet, and of buglis, and of briddis maad fat. For he 24 helde al the cuntrei that was biȝende the flood, as fro Caphsa 'til to[z] Gasa, and alle the kyngis of tho[a] cuntreis; and he hadde pees bi ech part in cumpas. And Juda 25 and Israel dwelliden withouten ony drede, ech man vndur his vyne, and vndur his fige tree, fro Dan 'til to[b] Bersabe, in alle the daies of Salomon. And Salomon 26 hadde fourty thousynd cratchis† of horsis for charis, and twelue thousynde of roode[c] horsis; and the forseid prefectis[d] nurshiden tho horsis. But also with greet 27 bisynesse thei ȝauen necessaries to the boord of kyng Salomon in her tyme; also 28 thei brouȝten barli, and forage of horsis and werk[e] beestis, in to the place where the king was, 'bi ordenaunce[f] to hem. Also God ȝaf to Salomon wisdom, and 29 prudence ful myche, and largenesse‡ of herte, as the soond which [h] is in the brenke of the see. And the wisdom of 30 Solomon passide the wisdom of alle eest men, and Egipcians; and he was wisere 31 than alle men; he[l] was wisere than Ethan Esraite, and than Eman, and than Cacal, and than Dorda, the sones of Maol; and he[k] was named[l] among alle folkis bi cumpas. And Salomon spak thre thousynde 32 parablis, and hise songis weren fyue thousynde‖; and he disputide of trees fro a 33 cedre which[n] is in the[o] Lyban, 'til to[p] the ysope that goith out of the wal; he disputide of werk beestis, and briddis, and crepynge[q] beestis, and fischis[r]. And 34 thei[s] camen fro alle puplis to here the wisdom of Salomon, and fro alle kyngis[t] of erthe, that herden his wisdom.

* Chorus counteyneth thretti buschellis. *Lire here.* c. et plures.

† bi Ebreys a cracche is takun here for a place departid for ech hors bi him silf. *Lire here.* c.

‡ largenesse of herte; to spende in greet worschip. *Lire here.* c.

‖ fyue thousynde; in Ebreu it is, a thousinde and v. c.

[i] foddrid scheep A pr. m. BCBFH.   [k] without B rec. m.   [l] in AFH.   [m] Salomonys CEH.   [n] his E pr. m.   [o] the Egipciens BCEFH.   [p] Om. H.   [pp] Om. c.   [q] of B.   [r] the erthe E pr. v.

[x] oxen I.   [y] the lesewe I.   [z] vnto I.   [a] the A pr. m. CEGLMPQRSUbç.   [b] vnto I.   [c] rode D. rood P. reed R. reede Mb. reade Q. rede F pr. m. w.   [d] cheef maistris of the kyng I.   [e] of werk I.   [f] aftir that it was ordeyned I.   [h] that I.   [i] and he DKMX.   [k] Salomon I.   [l] losid I.   [n] that I.   [o] Om. GKLNOSbç.   [p] vnto I.   [q] of crepynge I.   [r] of fischis I.   [s] men I.   [t] the kyngis I.

CAP. V.

1 Forsothe Iram, the kyng of Tiry, sente his seruauntis to Salomon; forsothe he herde that men hadden anoyntid hym kyng for his fader; for Yram 2 was freend[s] of Dauid al tyme. Forsothe and Salomon sente to Yram, seiynge, 3 Thou wost the wil of my fader Dauid[t], and for he my3te not bilde vp an hows to the name of his God, for the batailis oncomynge bi enuyroun, to the tyme that the Lord 3af hem vndur the step of 4 his feet. Forsothe now the Lord my God hath 3ouen rest to me bi enuyroun, and there is not Sathan, ne yuel a3en-5 comynge; for what thing I thenke to beeld a temple to the name of the Lord my God, as God spak to my fader, sei-ynge, Thi sone, whom I shal 3yue to thee for thee vpon thi seete, he shal beelde to 6 my name an hows. Thanne comaund, that thei hewen to me cedrys of Liban; and my seruauntis ben with thi seruauntis; forsothe the mede of thi seruauntis I shal 3yue to thee, what euer thou askist[u]; forsothe thou wost that there is not in my puple a man, that 7 kan hewe trees, as[v] Sidonys[w]. Whanne thanne Iram hadde herd the wordis of Salomon, he gladide greetli, and seith, Blessid be[x] the Lord God to day, that 3af to Dauid a moost wise sone vpon this 8 myche[y] puple. And Yram sente to Salomon, seiynge, I haue herd alle thingis that thou sentist to me; I shal doo al thi wil, in cedre trees, and in firris. 9 My seruauntis shulen doo hem down fro the wode to the see, and I shal make hem togidre in shippis in the see, vnto the place the which thou shalt signyfye to me; and I shal leye hem to thee, that thou take hem; and thou shalt 3yue necessaryes to me, that meete be 3ouen

CAP. V.

Also Hiram, kyng[n] of Tire, sente hise 1 seruauntis to Salomon; for he herde that thei[v] hadden anoyntide hym kyng for his fadir; for Hiram was frend of Dauid in al time. Sotheli[w] also Salomon seute to 2 Hiram, and seide, Thou knowist the wille 3 of Dauid, my fadir, and for he mi3te not bilde an hows to the name of his God, for batels[x] nei3ynge bi cumpas, til the Lord 3af hem vndur the step of hise feet. Now[y] 4 forsothe[z] my Lord God 3af[a] reste to me bi cumpas, and noon aduersarie is, nethir yuel asailyng; wherfor Y thenke to 5 buylde a temple to the name of my Lord God, as God spak to Dauid, my fadir, and seide, Thi sone, whom Y schal 3yue to thee for thee on[b] thi trone, he schal bilde an hows to my name. Therfor comaunde 6 thou, that thi seruauntis hewe doun to me cedris of the Liban; and my seruauntis be with thi seruauntis; sotheli[c] Y schal 3yue to thee the meede of thi seruauntis, what euere meede[d] thou schalt axe; for thou woost, that in my puple is not a man that kan hewe trees, as Sidonyes[e] kunnen[f]. Therfor whanne Hiram hadde herde the 7 wordis of Salomon, he was ful glad, and seide, Blessid be the Lord God to dai, that 3af[g] to Dauid a[h] sone moost wijs on[i] this puple ful myche. And Hiram sente 8 to Salomon, and seide, Y haue herde what euer thingis[k] thou sentist[l] to me; Y schal do al thi wille, in trees of cedres, and of beechis[m][†]. My seruauntis schulen putte 9 doun tho[n] trees fro the Liban[o] to the see, and Y schal araye tho trees in schippis in the see, 'til to[p] the place which[q] thou schalt signyfie to me; and Y schal dresse tho there, that thou take tho; and thou schalt 3yue necessaries[r] to me, that mete be 3ouun to myn hows. Therfor[s] Hiram 10 3af to Salomon 'trees of cedres[t], and 'trees

† of beechis: Ebreys seyn, in trees of box, where oure translacioun hath, of beechis. c.

---

[s] the freend CE. [t] Om. E pr. m. [u] aske BCEFH. [v] of A. [w] Sidoyns A. [x] Om. CEFH. [y] mychil B. mychel CEH.

[u] the kyng I. [v] Israel I. [w] And I. [x] his batels I. [y] But now I. [z] Om. I. [a] hath 3ouen I. [b] upon I. [c] and I. [d] Om. I. [e] men of Sydonye I. [f] Om. I. [g] hath 3oue I. [h] the I. [i] upon I. [k] thing I. [l] hast sent I. [m] beeche I. [n] the I. [o] hil of Liban I. [p] vnto I. [q] that I. where I. [r] necessarie S. [s] And so I. [t] cedre trees I.

10 to myn hows. And so Yram ȝaf to
Salomon cedre trees and firre trees, after
11 al the wil of hym ; forsothe Salomon ȝaf
to Yram twenti thousand choris of whete
into mete to his hows, and twenti choris
of moost pure oyle ; thes thingis Salo-
12 mon ȝaf to Yram bi ech ȝeer. And the
Lord ȝaf wisdam to Salomon, as he spak
to hym ; and there was betwix Iram and
Salomon pees, and bothe smyten coue-
13 nant of pees. And king Salomon chees
werkmen of al[y] Israel ; and[z] the moustre
14 was thretti thousandis of men. And he
sente hem into the wode, ten thousand[a]
bi eche moneth whilmele, so that two
moncthis whilmele thei weren in her
howsis ; and Adonyram was vpon siche
15 a maner gedrynge of men. And so to
Salomon weren seuenti thousandis of hem,
that beren birthens, and eiȝti thousandis
16 of masouns in the hyl, with outen the
prouostis, that reuliden[b] to alle the
werkis, in noumbre of thre thousand and
thre hundrid, comaundinge to the puple,
17 and to hem that dyden werke[c]. And
the kyng comaundide, that thei shulden
take the greet stoonns, and the precious
stoonus, in to the foundement of the
temple, and thei shulden square hem ;
18 the whiche the masouns of Salomon, and
the masouns of Yram, han ouerscorchide[d].
Forsothe the cyteseynys of Biblis maden
redi the trees and stonus, to the hows to
be beeldid.

CAP. VI.

1 It is doo forsothe the foure hundrid
and eiȝti[e] ȝeer of the goynge out of the
sones of Irael fro the loond of Egipt, in
the ferth ȝeer, the moneth Zio ; he is the
secounde moneth of the regue of Salomon vpon Irael ; he began to beelde an
2 hows to the Lord. Forsothe the hows
that kyng Salomon beeldide to the Lord,

of beechis[u], bi al his wille ; forsothe[v] 11
Salomon ȝaf to Hiram twenti thousynde
chorus of wheete, in to meete to[w] his
hows, and twenti chorus of pureste[x] oile ;
Salomon ȝaf these thingis to Hiram bi
alle ȝeeris. Also the Lord ȝaf wisdom to 12
Salomon, as he spak to hym ; and pees
was bitwixe Hiram and Salomon, and
bothe[y] smytiden[z] boond of pees. And 13
kyng Salomon chees werk men of al
Israel ; and the summe was thretti thousynde of men. And 'Salomon sente hem 14
in to the Liban[a], ten thousynde[b] bi ech
monethe bi whilis, so that in twei monethis
bi whilis thei weren in her howsis ; and
Adonyram was on[c] sich a summe. Ther- 15
for[d] seuenti thousynde of hem[cc], that baren
burthuns, weren to Salomon, and foure
score thousynde of masouns in the hil,
with out the souereyns, that weren mais- 16
tris of alle werkis[e], bi the noumbre of thre
thousynde and thre hundrid, comaundynge
to the puple, and to hem that maden
werk. And the kyng comaundide, that 17
thei schulden take greete stonys, 'and preciouse stonys[f]†, in to[g] the foundement of
the temple, and that thei schulden make
tho square ; whiche stoonys the masouns 18
of Salomon, and the masouns of Hyram,
hewiden. Forsothe[h] Biblies[i] maden redi
trees and stonus, to the hows to[j] be bildid.

CAP. VI.

Forsothe it was doon in the fourthe[k] 1
hundrid and fourescore ȝeer‡ of the goynge
out of the sones of Israel fro the lond of
Egipt, in the fourthe ȝeer§, in the monethe
Zio ; thilke[l] is the secounde monethe‖ of
the rewme of Salomon on[m] Israel ; he
bigan to bilde an hows[n] to the Lord. For- 2
sothe[o] the hows which[p] kyng Salomon

† *precious stonys ; Ebreys seyen hauye stonys, for siche stonys ben able for the foundement. Lire here. c.*

‡ *Moises gouernede the puple bi xl. ȝeer, in xvi. c^e. of Exodi, Josue bi xl. ȝeer in iij. c^e. of Judicum, Othonyel bi xl. ȝeer, in fij. c^e. of Judicum, Aloth bi xl. ȝeer, in iij. c^e. of Judicum, Delbora bi xl. ȝeer, in v. c^e. of Judicum, Gedeon bi xl. ȝeer, in viij. c^e. of Judicum, Abymelech bi iij. ȝeer, in ix. c^e. of Judicum, Thola bi xxiij. ȝeer, in x. c^e. of Judicum, Jair bi xxij. ȝeer, in x. c^e. of Judicum, with out domesman bi xviii., in x. c^e. of Judicum, Jepte bi sixe ȝeer, in xij. c^e. of Judicum, Abessan bi vij. ȝeer, in xij. c^e. of Judicum, Abilon bi x. ȝeer, in xii. c^e. of Judicum, Abdon bi viij. ȝeer, in xij. c^e. of Judicum, Sampson bi. xx. ȝeer, in xvi. c^e. of Judicum, Hely bi xl. ȝeer, in I. book of Kingis iiij. c^e., Samuel and Saul bi xl. ȝeer, in xiij. c^e. of Dedis, Dauyth bi xl. ȝeer, in III. book of Kingis ii. c^e. Salomon bi iij. ȝeer, here in this text ; thus the noumbre teld here, is proued bi Scripture. Lire here. c.*

§ *in the fourthe ȝeer, of the rewme of Salomon. Lire here. c.*

‖ *thilke is the secounde monethe, of the iiij. ȝeer of the rewme of Salomon. Lire here. c.*

---

y Om. A.   z Om. A.   a thousandis E.   b reuliden hem A.   c werkis A.   d slascht E pr. vice.   e eiȝtith DF. eiȝtetithe E.

u beeche trees I.   v and I.   w into A pr. m. DEIMsbç.   x moost pure I.   y bothe thei I.   z smoten togidre I. smiten EL.   a into Liban Salamon sente I.   b thousynde men I.   c upon I. in K.   cc hors A rec. m.
d And so I.   e the werkis I.   f Om. K.   g Om. X.   h And I.   i men of Biblies I.   j Om. S.   k foure I.
l that I.   m upon I.   n the temple of Salamon K marg.   o And I.   p that I.

hadde sexti cubitis in length, and twenti in brede, and thretti cubitis in heiȝt. 3 And a ȝaat hows was before the temple of twenti cubitys in length, aftir the mesure of the brede of the temple ; and hadde ten cubitis of brede before the face of the 4 temple.   And he made in the temple 5 side wyndows.   And he bildide vpon the wal of the temple table beeldyngis bi enuyroun, in the wallis of the hows, bi enuyroun of the temple, and of Goddis answerynge place; and he made the 6 sidis in enuyroun.   The table beeldynge, that was aboue, hadde fyue cubitis of brede ; and the mydil table beeldynge of sexe cubitis of brede ; and the thridde table beeldynge hauing seuen cubitis of brede.   Forsothe beemys he putte in the hows bi enuyroun with ontforth, that[f] thei shulden not cleue to the wallis of 7 the temple.   Forsothe the hows, whanne it shulde be beeldid vp, is beeldid of stonus ouer scorchid and parfite ; and hamer, and axe, and al yren, ben not herd in the hows, whanne it was beeldid. 8 The door of the mydil side in the wal was of the hows of the riȝt side ; and bi a vyce thei stieden vp into the mydil sowpynge place, and fro the mydil into 9 the thridde.   And he beeldide vp the 10 hows, and endide it.   And he made the hows with cedre couplis, and bildide a table beeldynge vpon al the hows bi fyue cubitis of heiȝt, and couerde the hows 11 with cedre trees.   And the word of the 12 Lord is maad to Salomon, seyynge, This hows that thou beeldist ; if thou gost in myn hestis, and dost my domys, and kepist alle my comaundementis[g], goynge bi hem, I shal fastne my word to thee, that I haue spoken to Dauid, thi fader ; 13 and I shal dwelle in the mydil of the sonys of Yrael, and I shal not forsaak 14 my puple Yrael.   Thanne Salomon beeldide vp the hows, and eendide it ;

bildide to the Lord, hadde sexti cubitis in lengthe, and twenti cubitis[p] in breede, and thretti cubitis in heiȝthe.   And a 3 porche was bifor the temple of twenti cubitis of lengthe, by the mesure of the breed of the temple ; and the porche hadde ten cubitis of breede, bifor the face of the temple.   And Salomon made in 4 the temple 'wyndows streyte[q] withoutforth, and large with ynne.   And he bild- 5 ide on[r] the wal of the temple bildyngis of tablis bi cumpas, in the wallis of the hows, 'bi cumpas of[s] the temple, and of[t] Goddis answeryng place ; and he made sidis in the cumpas.   The bildyng of tablis, that 6 was vndur, hadde fyue cubitis of breede ; and the myddil bildyng of tablis was of sixe cubits of breede ; and the thridde bildyng of tablis was hauynge seuene cubitis of breede.   Sotheli[u] he puttide[v] beemys in the hous bi cumpas with outforth, that tho cleuiden not† to the wallis of the temple.   Forsothe[w] whanne the 7 hows was bildid, it was bildid[x] of 'stoonys hewid and perfit[y] ; and an[z] hamer, and ax, and al thing maad of yrun, weren not herd in the hows, while it was in bildyng. The doré of the myddil side was in the 8 wal of the riȝthalf hows[a] ; and bi a vijs thei[b] stieden[c] in to the myddil soler, and fro the myddil soler in to the thridde soler.   And Salomon bildide the hows, 9 and endide it.   Also[d] Salomon hilide the hows with couplis of cedre[e], and bildide[f] 10 a bildyng of tablis ouer al the hows, bi fyue cubitis of heiȝthe, and hilide[g] the hows with 'trees of cedre[h].   And the word 11 of the Lord was maad to Salomon, and seide, This is the hows, which[i] thou 12 bildist[k] ; if thou gost in myn heestis, and dost my domes, and kepist alle my comaundementis, and goist bi tho, Y schal make stidefast my word to thee, 'which word[l] Y spak to Dauid, thi fadir ; and Y 13 schal dwelle in the myddis of the sones of

f and A.   g maundementis DCE FII.

p Om. I.   q narowe wyndows I.   r upon I.   s aboute I.   t Om. I.   u And I.   v putte I.   w And I. x bild I.   y perfit hewyn stoonys I.   z Om. I.   a of the hows I.   b men I.   c stieden up I.   d And DKX.   e cedre trees I.   f he bildide I.   g he hilide I.   h cedre trees I.   i that I.   k bildidist K.   l that I.

15 and beeldide vp the wallis of the hows with ynforth with cedre table beeldyngis, fro the pawment of the hows vnto the heiȝest of the wal, and vnto the cowplis; and he couerde with cedre trees with inforth; and he couerde the pawment of 16 the hows with firre bordis. And he beeldide vp cedre table beeldingis of twenti cubitis at the hynder more parti of the temple, fro the pawment vnto the ouer parties; and he made an innermore hows of the heuenli answerynge place, 17 into the holy of halewis[h]. Forsothe of fourti cubitis was that[i] temple before[k] the ȝatis of Goddis answerynge place. 18 And with cedre al the hows with ynforth was clothid, hauynge his turnours, and his iuncturis[l] forgid, and grauyngis ouerbeynge; alle with cedre tablis thei weren clothid, ne algatis a stoone myȝte 19 apere in the wal. Goddis answerynge place forsothe he made in the mydil of the hows, in the inner more partie, that he putte there the arke of the boond of 20 pees of the Lord. Forsothe Goddis answerynge place hadde twenti cubitis of length, and twenti cubitis of brede, and twenti cubitis of heiȝt; and he couerde it, and clothide with moost pure gold; but and the auter he clothide with 21 cedre. Forsothe the hows before Goddis answerynge place he couerde with moost pure gold, and naylide platis to with 22 golden nailis. No thing was in the temple that was not couerde with gold; but and al the auter of Goddis answer-23 ynge place he couerde with gold; and made in Goddis answerynge place two cherubyn of the trees of olyues, of ten 24 cubitis of heiȝt; the too weenge of cherub of fyue cubitis, and the[m] tother weenge of cherub of fyue cubitis, that is, hauyng ten cubitis, fro the cop of the wenge vnto the cop of the tother weenge. 25 Forsothe of ten cubitis was the secounde

Israel, and Y schal not forsake my puple Israel. Therfor Salomon bildide the 14 hows, and endide it; and he bildide the 15 wallis of the hows with ynne with tablis of cedre, fro the pawment of the hows 'til to[m] the heiȝnesse of the wal, and 'til to[m] the couplis; and hilide[n] with trees of cedre with ynne; and he hilide the pawment of the hows with tablis of beeche. And he bildide a wal of tablis of cedre of 16 twenti cubitis at the hyndrere[o] part of the temple, fro the pawment 'til to[p] the hiȝere partis; and he made the ynnere hows of Goddis answeryng place, in to the hooli of hooli thingis. Sotheli[q] thilke[r] temple 17 bifor the doris of Goddis answering place was of·fourti cubitis. And al the 18 hows with ynne was clothid with cedre, and hadde hise smethenessis, and hise ioyuyngis maad suteli, and grauyngis apperynge[s] aboue; alle thingis weren clothid with tablis[t] of cedre, and outirli a stoon miȝte not appere in the wal. Forsothe[u] 19 Salomon made Goddis answeryng place in the myddis of the hows, in the ynnere part, that he schulde sette there the arke of boond of pees of the Lord. Sotheli[v] 20 Goddis answeryng place hadde twenti cubitis of lengthe, and twenti cubitis of breede, and twenti cubitis of hiȝte; and he hilide, and clothide it with pureste[w] gold; but also he clothide the auter with cedre. Also he hilide[x] with pureste 21 gold the[xx] hows bifor 'Goddis answeryng place[y], and fastnyde[z] platis with goldun nailis. No thing was in the temple, 22 'which thing[a] was not hilid with gold; but also he hilid with gold al the auter of Goddis answeryng place. And he made 23 in 'Goddis answeryng place[b] twey cherubyns of the[c] trees of olyues, of ten cubits of heiȝte; o wynge of cherub was of fyue 24 cubitis, and the tother wynge of cherub was of fyue cubitis, that is, hauynge ten cubitis, fro the heiȝnesse of 'the o[d] wynge

h holowis A.   i the F.   k for E pr. m.   l vynctours A.   m Om. A.

m vnto I.   n he hilide hem I.   o hyndir EILNç. hindere K.   p vnto I.   q And I. Forsothe EL.   r that EL.   s semynge I.   t bordis I.   u And I.   v And I.   w moost pure I.   x hilide it I.   xx an D.   Y or the oracle I marg.   z he fastnyde the I.   a that I.   b the oracle I.   c Om. c.   d that oon I. the too K. the DENXb. Om. ç.

cherub in the same mesure; and o werk
26 was in the two cherubyn, that is, o cherub hadde hei3t of ten cubitis, and lijk
27 maner the secounde cherub. And he
putte the cherubyn in the mydil of the
inner temple; forsothe the cherubyn
strau3ten out her weengis, and the too
weenge towchide the wal, and the weenge
of the secounde cherub touchyde the
tothere wal; forsothe the tothere weenges
in the mydyl[n] part of the temple towch-
28 eden hem self to gidre. And he couerde
29 cherubyn with gold, and alle the wallis
of the temple bi enuyroun; and grauyde
with dyuerse grauyngis and turnynge;
and made in hem cherubyn, and palmes,
and dyuerse peynturis, as ferre stond-
30 ynge[o] fro the wal in goynge out. But
and the pawment of the hows he couerde
with gold, with inforth and with outforth.
31 And in the goynge yn of Goddis answerynge place he made two litil dorys of the
trees of olyues; and fyue postis of the
32 corners, and the two dorys of the trees
of olyues; and he grauede in hem peynture of cherubyn, and[p] the lickenes of
palmes, and the ouermore grauyngis ful
fer stoondynge[q] out; and couerde hem
with gold; and both he couerde cherubyn, and the palmes, and other with gold.
33 And he made in the entre of the temple
postis of the trees of olyues foure cor-
34 nerd; and the two doris of firre trees,
either to other; and either dore was dowble, and holdynge hem self togidre was
35 opnyde. And he grauyde cherubyn, and
the palmys, and grauyngis myche semynge out; and alle he couerde with
goldyn platis, with squaryd werk at
36 rewle. And he bildide the porch with
ynforth, with three ordres of polshid
stonus, and with oon ordre of the trees
37 of cedre. The firthe 3eer the hows of the
Lord is foundid, in the moneth of Zio;

'til to[n] the hi3nesse of the tother wynge.
And the secunde cherub was of ten cubitis 25
in euene mesure; and o werk was in the
twey cherubyns, that is, o cherub hadde 26
the hi3the of ten cubitis, and in lijk maner
the tother cherub. And he[f] settide[g] che- 27
rubyns[h] in the myddis of the ynnere temple; forsothe[i] the cherubyns helden forth
her wyngis, and o wenge touchide the
wal[k], and the wynge of the secunde cherub touchide the tother wal; forsothe[l] the
othere[m] wyngis in the middil part of the
temple touchiden hem silf togidere. And 28
he hilide the cherubyns with gold, and 29
alle the wallis of the temple 'bi cumpas[n];
and grauyde[o] with dyuerse grauyngis and
smethenesse; and he made in tho wallys
cherubyns, and palmes, and dyuerse peynturis, as stondinge forth and goynge out
of the wal. But also he hilide with gold 30
the pawment of the hows, withynne[p] and
with outforthe. And in the entryng of 31
'Goddis answering place[q] he made twei
litil doris of the[r] trees of olyues; and he
made postis of fyue corneris, and twei 32
doris of the trees of olyues; and grauyde[s]
in tho the peynture of cherubyns, and the
licnessis of palmes, and grauyngis aboue
stondynge forth gretli; and he hilide tho
with gold; and he hilide as wel the cherubyns, as palmes, and othere thingis with
gold. And in the entring of the temple 33
he made postis foure cornerid of the[t] trees
of olyues; and he made twei doris of the[t] 34 † of beech;
trees of beech†, ech a3ens other; and euer   Ebreys seyen
either dore was double, and it was openyd   of box. c.
holdynge it silf togidere. And he grauyde 35
cherubyns, and palmes, and grauyngis apperynge greetli; and he hilide alle thingis
with goldun platis, bi square werk at reule.
And he bildide a large street[u] with ynne, 36
bi thre ordris of stoonys maad fair, and bi
oon ordre of trees of cedre. The hows of 37 ‡ in the fourthe
the Lord was foundid in the fourthe 3eer‡,   3eer; of the
                                              rewme of Salo-
                                              mon. Lire
                                              here. c

---

[n] Om. E pr. m.   [o] semynge E pr. m.   [p] in AH.   [q] seemynge E pr. m.

---

[e] vnto I.   [f] Salomon I.   [g] sette EIL.   [h] the cherubyns I.   [i] and I.   [k] oon wal I.   [l] and I.   [m] tothere
EKL_S.   [n] aboute I.   [o] he grauyde hem   I.   [p] with ynne forth I.   [q] the oracle I.   [r] Om. I.   [s] he grauyde I.
[t] Om. I.   [u] street, or an alure I.

38 and in the enleueth ȝeer, the moneth of
Ebul; he is the eiȝt moneth; the hows is
perfourmed in al his werk, and in alle
his necessaries; and he bildide it vp in
seuen ȝeer

in the monethe Zio; and the hows was 38
maad perfit[v] in al his werk, and in alle[w]
vessels, *ether* 'purtenauncis[x], in the eleuenthe ȝeer, in the monethe Zebul, thilke[xx]
is the eiȝthe monethe, and he bildide that
hows in seuene ȝeer.

CAP VII

1 Forsothe Salomon beeldide his hows
in thretene ȝeer, and vnto parfite brouȝte
2 forth And he bildide the hows of the
wiȝld wode of Liban, of an hundrid cubitis of length, and of fifti cubitis of
brede, and of thretti cubitis of heiȝt; and
foure aluris betwixe the cedre pilers; forsothe the cedre trees he hewȝ into pilers
3 And he clothide al the chaumbre with
cedre table beeldyngis, the which chaumbre was born vp with fyue and fourti
pilers The too ordre forsothe hadde
4 fifteen pilers, sette togidre aȝens hem
5 self, and 'for aȝen[r] hem self beholdynge,
with euen space betwixe the pilerys;
and vpon the pilers foure cornerd trees,
6 in alle thingis euen And the chaumbre
of pilers he made of fifti cubitis of
length, and of thretti cubitis of brede,
and another chaumbre into the face of
the more chaumbre; and pilers, and the
7 heedis vpon the pilers he made Forsothe the chaumbre of the see, in the
which is the chayer of dom, he made,
and couerde with cedre trees, fro the
8 pawment vnto the cop And the litil
hows, in the which he sat to deme, was
in the mydil chaumbre, lijk maner werk
Forsothe he made an hows to the douȝter of Pharao, whom Salomon weddide,
9 siche maner werk as this chaumbre Alle
thingis with precious stoonus, 'the whiche[s]
at a maner rewle and mesure, both with
ynforth and with outforth, weren loken,
fro the foundement vnto the cop of the

CAP VII

Forsothe Salomon bildide his owne hows 1
in thrittene[y] ȝeer, and brouȝte *it*[z] til to
perfeccioun[a] He bildide an hows of the 2
forest of Liban, of an hundrid cubitis of
lengthe, and of fifti cubitis of breede, and
of thretti cubitis of hiȝthe, and *he bildide*
foure aleis bitwixe the pilers of cedre; for
he hadde hewe doun trees of cedres in to
pilers And he clothide al the chaumbir 3
with wallis[b] of cedris[c]; which[d] chaumbir
was susteyned[e] with fyue and fourti pileris. Sotheli[f] oon ordre hadde fiftene pileris, set aȝens hem silf togidere, and bi- 4 5
holdynge hem silf[g] euene aȝens, bi[h] euene
space bitwixe the pilers; and on[i] the
pileris *weren*[k] foure square trees, euene in
alle thingis And he made a porche of 6
pilers of fifti cubitis of lengthe, and of
thritti cubitis of breede; and '*he made*[l] an
other porche in the face of the gretter
porche; and he made pileris, and pomels
on the pileris Also he[m] maad a porche 7
of the kyngis seete, in which[n] the seete of
doom was[o], and he[p] hilide[q] with trees of
cedre, fro the pawment 'til to[r] the hiȝnesse And a litil hows, in which he[s] sat 8
to deme, was in the myddil porche, bi lijk
werk Also Salomon made an hows to
the douȝter of Farao, whom he hadde
weddid, bi sich werk, bi what maner werk
he made and this porche. He made alle 9
thingis of preciouse stoonys, that weren
sawid at sum[t] reule and mesure, bothe
with ynne and with outforth, fro the
foundement 'til to[u] the hiȝnesse of wallis,

[r] fro the regioun E *pr m* forn aȝen E *sec m* [s] that C *pr m*

[v] perfit *or eendid* I [w] alle his I [x] *purtynaunce* W. [xx] that EL [y] the threttenethe K.
[z] Om DEGIMNPbq [a] perfeccioun *or perfit eend* I [b] tablis A *sec m* b [c] cedre I [d] the which I
[e] born up I [f] And I [g] silf eche I [h] *other* bi I [i] upon I [k] Om I [l] Om I [m] Salomon I.
[n] whiche *porche* was I [o] Om I [p] Om K [q] hilide it I [r] vnto I [s] Salomon I [t] a I [u] vnto I

wallis, and with ynforth and vnto the
10 more halle. The foundementis[t] forsothe
of precious stoonus, the greet stoonus of
11 ten, or of ei3t cubitis; and there aboue
precious stoonus of euen mesure weren
12 hewen[u]; and[uu] lijk maner of cedre. And
the more halle rownd, of thre ordres of
hewen stonus, and of oon ordre of planed
cedre; also and in[v] the innermore porche
of the hows of the Lord, and in the 3aat
13 hows of the hows of the Lord. And
14 kyng Salomon sente, and took Yram, the
sone of the widowe womman, fro Tyro,
of the lynage of Neptalym, fader of the
cuntre of Tyre, a crafti man of metal,
and ful of wisdom, and vndurstondynge,
and of lore, to doo al werk of metal.
Which whanne he was comen to kyng
Salomon, he made al the werk of hym;
15 and made two brasen pilers, of ei3teen
cubitis of hei3t o piler; and a liyn
of twelue cubitis wente[w] about either
16 piler. And two heed coueryngys he
made, that shulden be putte vpon the
heedis of the pilers, 3oten of bras; of
fyue cubitis of hei3t oon heed couerynge,
and of fyue cubitis of hei3t another heed
17 couerynge; and as in maner of a nette,
and of cheynys wouyn togidre to hem
self, in o werk. And either heed couerynge of the pilers was 3oten; seuen litil
nettis of verse in the toon heed couerynge, and seuen lytil nettis in the tothir
18 heed couerynge. And he fulfillide the
pilers, and the two ordris bi enuyroun
of alle the litil nettis, that thei coueren
the heed coueryngis, that weren vpon the
cop of the powmgarnettis; and the same
wise he made to the secounde heed couer-
19 ynge. Forsothe the heed coueryngis, that
weren vpon the heedis of the pilers, as in
werk of a lilye weren forgid, in the 3aat-
20 hows, of foure cubitis; and eft other heed
coueryngis in the cop of the pilers aboue,

and with ynne and 'til to[u] the gretter[v]
street, ethir court. Sotheli[w] the founde- 10
mentis weren of preciouse stoonys, grete[x]
stoonys of ten, ethir of[y] ei3te cubitis; and 11
preciouse stoonys hewun of euene mesure
weren aboue; in lijk maner and of cedre.
And the gretter court, 'ethir voide space[z], 12
was round, of thre ordris of hewun stonus,
and of oon ordre of hewun cedre[A]; also
and in the[aa] ynnere large strete of the
hows of the Lord, and in the porche of
the hows of the Lord. Also kyng Salo- 13
mon sente, and brou3te fro Tire Hiram,
the sone of a womman widewe, of the 14
lynage of Neptalym, of the fadir a[b] man
of Tyre, Hiram[c], a crafty man of brasse,
and ful of wisdom, and vndirstondynge[d],
and doctryn[e], to make al werk of bras.
And whanne he hadde come to kyng Salomon, he made al hys werk[f]. And he 15
made twey pilers of bras, o piler of ei3tene
cubitis of hi3the; and a lyne of twelue
cubitis cumpasside euer either piler. Also 16
he[g] made twei pomels, 3otun of bras, that[h]
weren set on the heedis of the pilers; o
pomel of fyue cubitis of hi3the, and the
tothir pomel of fyue cubitis of hei3the;
and bi the maner of a net, and of chaynes 17
knyt to gidere to hem[i], bi wonderful werk.
Euer either pomel of the pilers was 3otun;
seuen werkis lijk nettis of orders weren
in o pomel, and seuen werkis lijk nettis
weren[k] in the tother pomel. And he made 18
perfitli the pilers, and twei ordris 'bi cumpas of[l] alle werkis[m] lijk nettis, that tho
schulden hile the pomels, that[n] weren on[o]
the hi3nesse of pumgarnadis; in the same
maner he dide also to the secounde pomel.
Sotheli[p] the pomels, that weren on[q] the 19
heedis of the pilers in the porche, weren
maad as bi the[r] werk of lilye, of foure
cubitis; and eft othere pomels in the 20
hi3nesse of pilers aboue, bi the mesure of
the piler, a3ens[s] the werkis lijk nettis;

---

[t] foundement A.　[u] dyuydid E pr. m.　[uu] Om. A.　[v] Om. AFH.　[w] and wente A.

[u] vnto I.　[v] grett K.　[w] And I.　[x] of grete I.　[y] Om. I.　[z] Om. I.　[a] cedre trees I.　[aa] Om. S.　[b] of a I.
[c] Om. I.　[d] of vndirstondynge I.　[e] of techyng I.　[f] brasen werk I.　[g] Hiram I.　[h] whiche I.　[i] hem self I.
[k] Om. I.　[l] aboute I.　[m] the werkis I.　[n] whiche I.　[o] upon I.　[p] And I.　[q] upon I.　[r] Om. I.
[s] sett a3ens I.

aftir the mesure of the piler aȝens the litil nettis; forsothe two hundryd ordres of powmgarnettis weren in enuyroun of
21 the secounde heed coueErynge. And he sette two pilers in the ȝaat hows of the temple; and whanne he hadde sette the riȝt piler, he clepide it bi name Jachym; lijk maner he reride the secounde piler,
22 and clepide the name of it Booz. And vpon the heedis of the pilers he sette a werk in maner of a lilye; and fulfillid is
23 the werke of the pilers. He made forsothe the ȝoten see, of ten cubitis fro lippe vnto lippe, rounde in enuyroun; the heiȝt of hym of fyue cubitis; and the littil nette of thretti cubitis girdide
24 it by enuyroun. And the grauynge vndur the lippe wente about it bi ten cubitis, goynge about the see; two ordris
25 of storye grauyngis weren ȝoten, and stoden vpon twelue oxen; of the whiche three beheelden to the north, and three to the weste, and three to the south, and thre to the este; and the see was there aboue vpon hem, whos alle the hyndir-
26 more parties lurkiden with ynforth. The greetnes forsothe of the watyr vessel was of three ouncis, and the lippe of it as the lippe of a chalice, and as a leef of a lilye to be 'aȝen bowid; it conteynede two thousand mesuris of thre quartis, thre thousand mesuris neeȝ of a potel.
27 And he made ten brasen feet, eche foot of foure cubitis of length, and of foure cubitis of brede, and of foure cubitis of
28 heiȝt. And that werk of the feet was betwix grauyngis playn; and grauyngis
29 betwix the ioynturis. And betwix the litil crownes and wyndyngis, liouns, and oxen, and cherubin; and in the ioynturis lijk maner aboue; and vndur the lyouns and oxen as bridils of brasse hongynge.
30 And foure whelis bi eche feet, and brasen

forsothe twey hundrid ordris of pumgarnadis weren in the cumpas of the secounde pomel. And he settide the twey pilers in 21 the porche of the temple; and whanne he hadde set the riȝthalf pilere, he clepide it bi name Jachym; in lijk maner he reiside the secounde pilere, and he clepide the name therof Booz. And he settide 22 on the heedis of the pilers aȝ werk bi the maner of a lilie; and the werk of the pilers was maad perfit. Also he made 23 a ȝotun see, *that is, a waisching vessel for preestis,* round in cumpas, of ten cubitis fro brynke til to the brinke; the heiȝnesse therof was of fyue cubitis; and a corde of thretti cubitis ȝede aboute it bi cumpas. And grauyng vndir the brynke 24 cumpasside it, and cumpasside the see bi ten cubitis; tweyne ordris of grauyngis conteynynge summe stories weren ȝotun, and stoden on twelue oxis; of whiche 25 oxis thre bihelden to the north, and thre to the west, and thre to the south, and three to the eest; and the see was aboue on the oxis, of whiche alle the hyndere thingis weren hid 'with ynne. Sotheli 26 the thicknesse of the see was of thre ouncesꝉ, and the brynke therof was as the brynke of a cuppe, and as the leef of a lilie crokid aȝen; the see took twei thousynde bathusꝉ, threꝉ§ thousynde metretis¶. And he made ten brasun foundementes, 27 ech foundement of foure cubites of lengthe, and of foure cubitis of brede, and of thre cubitis of hiȝnes. And thilke werk of 28 foundementis was rasid bitwixe; and grauyngis weren bitwixe the ioynturis. And bitwixe the litil corouns and serclis 29 weren liouns, oxis, and cherubyns; and in the ioynturis in lijk maner aboue; and vndir the lyouns and oxis weren as reynes of bridels of bras hangynge doun. And bi ech foundement weren foure 30

ꝉ thre ounces; in Ebru it is here of iiij. fyngris; and bi Ebreys a pawm is as myche as iiij. fingris. Lire here. c.

ȝ bathus is a mesure of thre buschelis, and metreta conteineth two quartis and an haiff. 1.

§ this word iij. thousynde metretis, is not in Ebrew, nether in bokis amendid, but it was first a glos to schewe what is signefied bi bathus. and aftirward bi ignoraunce of writeris, it was set in the text. A metrete conteyneth ij. quartis and an half; and Id this the see conteynede xi. tunnes and an half, and iij. sextaries. Bi Isidore the see conteynede lxv. tunnes and x. sextaries. A sextarie is as a chopyn of Pariys, but for lengthe and variyng of mesuris in tymes and cuntreys, we han no certeynte of Ebrew mesuris. Lire here. c.

¶ a metrete conteyneth twei quartis and an half. Lire here. c. et plures.

ᵂ Om. E pr. m.   ˣ Om. A.   ʸ hym E pr. m.   ᶻ aparailid E pr. m.   ᵃ and it AF.   ᵇ Om. AII.

ᵗ and I.   ᵘ sette I.   ᵛ Jachym, that is, stidefastnesse c marg. K.   ᵂ reiside up I.   ˣ Booz, that is, strengthe c marg. K.   ʸ sette I.   ᶻ upon I.   ᵃ the c.   ᵇ Om. EL.   ᶜ up fully I.   ᵈ Hiram I.   ᵉ Om. IX.   ᶠ Om. KXϛ.   ᵍ the grauyng I.   ʰ it came aboute I.   ⁱ upon I.   ᵏ oxen I.   ˡ upon I.   ᵐ oxen I.   ⁿ whiche oxen I.   ⁿⁿ hyndrere A sec. m.   ᵒ withynne the see I.   ᴾ And I.   q conteynede I.   ʳ and thre K.   ˢ that EL.   ᵗ the foundementis I.   ᵘ raasid I.   ᵛ bitwene I.   ᵂ the serclis I.   ˣ oxen I.   ʸ the oxen I.

axtrees; and bi foure partyes as litil shuldres vndur the water vessel ʒoten, aʒens
31 hem self beholdynge. And the mouth
of the watir vessel with ynforth was in
the cop of the heed, and that, that with
outforth aperide, was of o cubite, and alle
round, and togidre hadde o cubite and an
half; in^e the corners forsothe of the pilers^d
weren dyuers grauyngis, and the mene
pilers^e betwix squaar^f, and not round.
32 Forsothe the foure whelis, that weren bi
the foure corners of the foot, cleueden togidre to hem self vndir the foot; o whele
33 hadde of heiʒt a cubite and an half. Forsothe the whelis weren siche, as ben wont
to be maad in a chaar; and the axtres
of hem, and the spokys, and the felijs^h,
34 and the naue, alle ʒoten. For thoo ilke^i
foure^k litil shuldres, bi alle the corners
of o foot, fro that foot weren ʒoten, and
35 ioyned. In the cop forsothe of the foot
was a maner roundnes, of a cubite and a
half, so forgid, that the watir vessel myʒte
be sette there aboue, hauynge his dyuerse endentyngis, and grauyngis of hym^l
36 self. Forsothe he grauede in the table
beeldyngis, that weren of brasse, and in
the corners, cherubyn, and liouns, and
palmys, as into the^m lickenesse of a man
stondynge, that thei shulen be seen not
37 grauen, but leid to bi enuyroun. And
in this maner he made ten feet, bi o ʒet-
ynge and mesure, and with lijk maner
38 grauynge. Forsothe he made ten brasen
water vessels; o water vessel heelde fourti
mesuris of thre quaartis, and was of foure
cubitis; and alle the water vessels he
putte vpon alle the feet, that is, vpon ten
39 feet. And he ordeynde the^n ten feet, fyue
at the ryʒt partie of the temple, and fyue
at the left; forsothe the see he putte at
the riʒt parti of the temple, aʒens the este
40 at the south. And Iram made cawdrones, and fier pannys, and wyn violis;
and he parformede al the werk of kyng

wheelis, and brasun extrees; and bi foure
partis weren as litle schuldryngis vndir
the waischyng vessel, `the schuldryngis^z†
ʒotun, and biholdynge aʒens hemsilf to-
31 gidere. And the mouth of the waischyng
vessel with ynne was in the hiʒnesse of
the heed‡, and that, that apperide with
outforth, was of o cubit, and it was al
round, and hadde togidere o cubit and an
half; sotheli^a dyuerse grauyngis weren in
the corneris of pilers, and the mydil piler
bitwixe^b was square, not^bb round. And
32 the foure wheelis, that^c weren bi foure
corneris of the foundement, cleuyden togidere to hem silf vndir the foundement;
o wheele hadde o cubit and an half of
33 hiʒthe. Sotheli^d the wheelis weren siche,
whiche maner wheelis ben wont to be
maad in a chare; and the extrees, and
the `naue stockis^e, and the spokis, and^f
dowlis^g of tho wheelis, alle thingis
34 weren ʒotun. For also the foure litle
schuldryngis, bi alle the corners of o
foundement, weren ioyned to gidere, and
35 ʒotun § of that foundement. Sotheli^h in
the hiʒnesse of the foundement was sum^i
roundenesse, of o cubite and an half, so
maad craftili, that the waischyng vessel
myʒte be set aboue, hauynge his purtrei-
yngis, and dyuerse grauyngis of it silf.
36 Also he^k grauyde in tho wallis^l, that
weren of bras, and in the corneris, cherubyns, and liouns, and palmes, as bi the
licnesse of a man stondynge, that tho
semeden not grauun, but put to bi cum-
37 pas. Bi this maner he made ten foundementis, bi o ʒetyng and mesure^m, and lijk
grauyng. Also he made ten waischyng
38 vessels of bras; o waischyng vessel took
fourti bathus, and it was of foure cubitis;
and he puttide^n ech waischyng vessel bi
it silf bi ech foundement bi it silf, that is,
ten. And he made ten foundementis, fyue
39 at the riʒt half of the temple, and fyue at
the left half; sotheli^o he settide^p the see

c and in ALL. ᵈ piler E sec. m. ᵉ piler E sec. m. ᶠ quarre BC pr. m. F. ᵍ axtrees CE. ʰ felys E sup. ras.
ᶦ Om. CE sec. m. ᵏ Om. E pr. m. ˡ hem A. ᵐ Om. AFH. ⁿ tho A.

ᶻ Om. I. ᵃ and I. ᵇ bitwene I. ᵇᵇ and not B. ᶜ whiche I. ᵈ And I. ᵉ nauelstockis L. ᶠ and the KOX.
ᵍ felies I. ʰ And I. ᶦ a I. ᵏ Hiram I. ˡ tablis c. ᵐ oo mesure I. ⁿ putte I. ᵒ and I. ᵖ sette I.

† schuldryngis;
that is, schorte
pileris to sus-
teyne the
waschyng ves-
sel. Lire here.
c.

‡ of the heed;
this word heed,
is not in E-
breu, but for
as this lettre
is had thus
in Ebreu, and
the mouth ther-
of was round
above, bi o cu-
bit; for on the
hiʒnesse that
was of o cubit,
was a sercle
that was clepid
the mouth,
hauynge half
a cubit in
heʒthe. Lire
here. c.

§ and ʒotun;
that is, weren
ʒotun to gidere
with that foun-
dement, and
maden o body.
Lire here. c.

41 Salomon in the temple of the Lord. Two
pilers, and two lytil cordis of the heed
coueryngis vpon the heedis of the pilers,
and two litil nettis, that thei coueren the
two litil coordis, that weren vpon the
42 heedis of the pilers. And foure hundrid
powmgarnettis in the two litil nettis;
two vers of powmgarnettis inⁿ eche litil
nettis, to the litil coordis to be couerd of
the heed coueryngis, that weren vpon the
43 heedis of the pilers. And the ten feet,
and the ten water vessels vpon the feet;
44 and oon see, and twelue oxen vndir the
45 see; and cawdrones, and fijr pannys, and
wyn vyolis. Alle the vessels, that Iram
made to kyng Salomon in the hows of
46 the Lord, weren of latoun. And in the
wijld feeldy regioun of Jordan the kyng
ʒetide hem, in the cleyyeⁿⁿ erthe, betwix
47 Socoht and Sarcham. And Salomon
putte alle the vessels in the hows; for the
mych multitude forsothe there was no
48 weiʒt of the brasse. And Salomon made
alle the vessels in the hows of the Lord;
forsothe a golden auter, and a golden
bord, on^o the^p which shulden be leyd the
49 looues of proposicioun; and fyue golden
candelstickis at the riʒt side, and fyue at
the left, aʒens Goddis answerynge place,
of moost pure gold; and as flouris of
lilie, and golden lanterns there aboue,
50 and golden snytters; and stenys, and
flesh hookis, and vyolis, and morters,
and censerys, of moost pure gold; and the
heengis of doris of the ynnermore hows
of the holy of halowis, and of the dorys
of the hows of the temple, weren of gold.
51 And he parfourmede al the werk, that
Salomon made in the hows of the Lord;
and he brouʒte in the thingis that Dauid,
his fader, hadde halowid; siluer, and
gold, and vessels; and he leide vp in the
tresours of the hows of the Lord.

at the riʒt half of the temple, aʒens the
eest, at the south^q. Also Hiram made 40
cawdrouns, and pannes, and wyn vessels;
and he made perfitli al the werk of kyng
Salomon in the temple of the Lord. *He* 41
made twey pilers, and twei cordis† of
pomels^r on^s the pomels of pilers^t, and
twei werkis lijk nettis, that tho schulden
hile twey^u cordis, that weren on^v the
heedis of pileris^w. And '*he made*^x pum- 42
garnadis foure hundrid in twey werkis
lijk nettis; '*he made*^x tweyne^y ordris of
pumgarnadis in^z ech werk^a lijk a net,
to hile the cordis of the pomels, that weren
on the heedis of pilers. And *he made* ten 43
foundementis, and ten waischyng vessels
on^b the foundementis; and o se, '*that is*, 44
a waischyng vessel for preestis^c, and
twelue oxis^d vndur the see; and '*he made*^e 45
cawdruns, and pannys, and wyn vessels.
Alle vessels^f, whiche Hiram made to kyng
Salomon ‡ in the hows of the Lord, weren
of latoun. And the kyng ʒetide tho ves- 46
sels in the feeldi cuntrey of Jordan, in
cleyi lond, bitwixe Sochot and Sarcham.
And Salomon settide^g alle the vessels^h; 47
forsotheⁱ for greet^k multitude no weiʒte
was of bras^l, '*that is, it passide al comyn
weiʒte*^m. And Salomon made alle vesselsⁿ 48
in the hows of the Lord; sotheli^o he made
the golden auter, '*that is, the auter of
encense, that was with ynne the temple*^p,
and the goldun boord, on^q whych the
loouys of settynge forth weren set; and 49
he made^r goldun candilstikis, fyue at the
riʒt half, and fyue at the left half, aʒens
Goddis answerynge place, 'of purest gold^s;
and *he made* as the flouris of a lilie, and^{ss}
goldun lanterns aboue, and goldun tongis;
and pottis, and hokis, and violis, and 50
morteris, and censeris of pureste gold; and
the herris, *ether heengis*, of the doris of the
ynnere hows of the hooli of hooli thingis,
and of the doris of the hows of the temple

† *cordis; that
is, serclis cum-
passinge the
pomels, at the
maner of cordis.
Lire here. c.*

‡ *Salomon; for
he made sichu
thingis to be
maad; ether the
kyng, that is,
Hiram,that was
seid king of
crafty men, for
the excellence
of craft. Lire
here. c.*

ⁿ and *AHF.*   ⁿⁿ cleye *AB.*   ^o vpon *BEFCH.*   ^p Om. *c.*

^q south coost I.   ^r the pomels I.   ^s upon I.   ^t the pilers I.   ^u the two I.   ^v upon I.   ^w the pileris I.
^x Om. I.   ^y and two I.   ^z on c.   ^a a werk B.   ^b upon I.   ^c Om. CI.   ^d oxen I.   ^e Om. I.   ^f the vessels I.
^g sette I.   ^h vessels *in a hous* I.   ⁱ but I.   ^k the greet I.   ^l the bras I.   ^m Om. I.   ⁿ the vessels I.
^o certis I.   ^p Om. I.   ^q upon I.   ^r *made* of moost pure golde I.   ^s Om. I.   ^{ss} Om. I.

weren of gold. And Salomon performyde 21 al the werk, which[t] he made in the hows of the Lord ; and he brou3te ynne the thingis, whiche Dauid, his fadir, hadde halewid ; siluer, and gold, and vessels ; and he kepte[u] in the tresours of the hows of the Lord.

CAP. VIII.

1 Thanne alle the more thur3 birth of Yrael ben gadryd, with the princis of lynagis, and the duykis of the meynees of the sones of Yrael, to king Salomon, in to Jerusalem, that thei bryngen the arke of the boond of pees of the Lord fro the cite 2 of Dauid, that is, frò Syon. And al Irael cam togidre to kyng Salomon, in the moneth of Bethanym, in a solempne 3 day ; he is the seuenth moneth. And alle the eldris of Irael camen ; and 4 preestis token the arke, and beren the arke of the Lord, and the tabernacle of the couenaunt of pees, and alle the vessels of the seyntuarie, that weren in the tabernacle ; and preestis and Leuytis 5 beren hem. Forsothe kyng Salomon, and al the multitude of Yrael, that was comen to hym, wenten with hym before the arke, and offreden sheep and oxen, 6 with out eymynge and noumbre. And the preestis brou3ten yn the arke of the boond of pees of the Lord into his place, into Goddis answerynge place of the temple, into the holi of halowis, vnder 7 the weengis of cherubyn. Forsothe cherubyn spradden out the weengis vpon the place of the arke ; and thei couerden the ark, and his clothis ther 8 aboue. And whanne the berynge stauys semeden out, and the hei3est of hem apereden with out the seyntuarie, before Goddis answerynge place, thei apereden no more with out forth ; and the whiche weren there vnto the day that is now. 9 Forsothe in the arke was noon othere

CAP. VIII.

Thanne[v] alle the gretter men in birthe 1 in Israel, with the[w] princes of lynagis[x], and the[y] duykis of meynees[z] of the sones of Israel, weren gaderid to kyng Salomon, in to Jerusalem, that thei schulden bere the arke of boond of pees of the Lord fro the citee of Dauid, that is, fro Syon. And 2 al Israel cam to gidere in the moneth Bethanym†[a], in the solempne dai ; thilke[b] is the seuenthe moneth. And alle the 3 elde men of Israel camen ; and the preestis token the arke, and baren[c] the arke of the[cc] 4 Lord, and the tabernacle of boond of pees, and alle vessels[d] of the seyntuarye, that weren in the tabernacle ; and the preestis and dekenes baren tho. Sotheli[e] kyng 5 Salomon, and al the multitude of Israel, that camen togidere to hym, 3ede with hym bifor the arke ; and thei offriden scheep and oxis[f], with out gessyng‡ and noumbre. And prestis brou3ten the arke 6 of boond of pees of the Lord in to his place, in to Goddis answerynge place of the temple, in to the hooli of hooli thingis, vndur the wengis of cherubyns[g]. For-7 sothe[h] cherubyns[i] spredden forth wengis[k] ouer the place of the arke ; and hiliden[l] the arke, and the barris therof aboue. And whanne the barris stoden forth, and 8 the hi3nesse[m] of tho apperiden with out the seyntuarye, bifor 'Goddis answerynge place[n], tho° apperyden no ferther with out-forth ; whiche[p] barris also weren there 'til, in to[q] present[r] day. Forsothe[s] in the 9 arke is[t] noon other thing§, no but twei tablis of stoon, whiche tablis[u] Moyses in

† that is, Septembre. Lire here. c. et plures.
‡ with out gessing ; this is seid bi figuratif speche, clepid íperbole, to signefie the multitude of sacrifices. Lire here. c.
§ in the arke is noon other thing ; the contrarie of this semeth in ix. c°. to Ebreys, where Poul seith thus, that the 3erde of Aaron, and a goldun vessel hauynge manna, weren there with the tablis. This is solid in double maner, first thus, that the tablis a-loone weren there principaly, for herfor the arke was maad. The 3erde of Aaron was there bi occasioun, to putte awey rebellioun of presthod ; and the goldun vessel with manna was there, to the mynde of meete 3ouun fro heuene. In the secounde maner thus, that the 3erde of Aaron and the goldun vessel weren not withynne the arke, but with-outforth in a cofere maad therto, and put in the side of the arke. Lire here. c.

t that 1.   u kepte thoo 1.   v Whanne A.   w Om. 1.   x the lynagis 1.   y with 1.   z the meynees 1.   a of Bethanym c.   b which EL.   c thei baren 1.   cc Om. A.   d the vessels 1.   e And 1.   f oxen 1.   g the cherubyns 1.   h And 1.   i the cherubyns 1.   k her wengis 1.   l thei hiliden 1.   m hi3nesses xx.   n the oracle 1 text. that is, Goddis answerynge place 1 marg.   o tho barrus 1.   p the whiche 1.   q vnto 1.   r this present 1.   s And 1.   t was 1.   u Om. 1.

thing but the two stonen tablis, the whiche Moyses hadde sette in it in Oreb, whanne the Lord couenauntide couenaunt of pees with the sones of Irael, whanne thei shulden goo out of the 10 loond of Egipt. It is doon forsothe whanne the preestis weren goon out of the seyntuarie, a litil clowde fulfillide 11 the hous of the Lord; and the preestis my3ten not stoond and mynystre, for the litil clowde; forsothe the glorie of the Lord hadde fulfillid the hous of the 12 Lord. Thanne seith Salomon, The Lord seide, that he shulde dwelle in a litil 13 clowde. Beeldynge I haue beeldid an hows in to thi 'dwellynge place9, thi 14 moost fast see into euermore. And the kyng turnede his face, and blisside to al the chirch in Irael; forsothe al the 15 chirch of Irael stood. And Salomon seith, Blessid isʳ the Lord God of Irael, that spak in his mouth to Dauid, my fader, and in the hondisˢ of hym per- 16 fourmyde, seiynge, Fro the day that I ladde out my puple Irael fro Egipt, I chees not a citee of alle the lynagis of Irael, that an hows shulde be beeldid vp, and my name were there; but Y chees, that I were vpon my puple 17 Irael. And Dauid, my fader, wolde beeld vp an bows to the name of the 18 Lord God of Yrael. And the Lord seith to Dauid, my fader, That thou thou3tist in thin herte to beelde vp an hows to my name, thou didist wel, that same thing 19 tretynge in mynde; neuerthelater thou shalt not beelde to me an hows, but thi sone, that shal goon out of thi reynes, he shal beelde an hows to my name. 20 The Lord hath confermyd his word, that he spak; and I stood for Dauid, my fader, and satte upon the trone of Irael, as the Lord spak; and I haue beeldᵗ an hows to the name of the Lord God of Yrael. 21 And I haue sette there a place of the arke, in the which is the couenaunt of

Oreb hadde put in the ark, whanne the Lord made boond of pees with the sones of Israel, whanne thei 3eden out of the loond of Egipt. Forsotheᵘ it was doon 10 whanne the preestis hadden go out of the seyntuarie, a cloude fillide the hows of the Lord; and the preestis my3ten not 11 stonde and mynystre, for the cloude; for whi the glorye of the Lord hadde fillid the hows of the Lord. Thanne Salomon 12 seide, The Lord seide, that he wolde dwelle in a cloude†. Y bildynge haue 13 bildid an hows in to thi dwelling place, in to thi moost stidefast trone with outen ende. And the kyng turnede his face, 14 and blesside al the chirche in Israel; for al the chirche of Israel stoodᵛ. And Sa- 15 lomon seide, Blessid be the Lord God of Israel, that spak with his mouth to Dauid, my fadir, and performyde in hise hondis, and seide, Fro the dai in which Y ledde 16 my puple Israel out of Egipt, Y chees not a citee of alle the lynagis of Israel, that an hows schulde be bildid, and my name schulde be there; but Y chees Dauid, that he schulde be ouer my puple Israel. And 17 Dauid, my fadir, wolde bildeʷ an hows to the name of the Lord God of Israel. And the Lord seide to Dauid, my fadir, 18 That thou thou3tist in thin herte to bilde an hows to my name, thou didist wel, tretynge this same thing in souleˣ; nethe- 19 les thou schalt not bilde an hows to me, but thi sone, that schal go out of thi reynes, he schal bilde an hows to my name. The Lord hathʸ confermyd his 20 word, whichᶻ he spak; and Y stood for Dauid, my fadir, and Y sat onᵃ the trone of Israel, as the Lord spak; and Y haue bildid an hows to the name of the Lord God of Israel. And Y haue ordeyned 21 there a place of the arke, in which arke the boond of pees of the Lord is, which he smoot with oure fadris, whanne thei 3eden out of the lond of Egipt. Forsotheᵇ 22 Salomon stood bifoor the auter‡ of the

† in a cloude; in Ebreu it is in a myist, and so it is in 11. book of Paralip. vi. cᵒ. Lire here. c.

‡ Salomon stood bifore the auter; of brent sacrifices, for preestis aloone entriden to the auter of encense. Lire here. c.

---

9 tabernacle ᴇ pr.m.   ʳ Om. ᴄᴇғɪɪ.   ˢ hows ᴀғʜ.   ᵗ beeldide ʙғʜ.

ᵘ And ɪ.   ᵛ stood *there* ɪ.   ʷ haue bildid ɪ.   ˣ thi soule ɪ.   ʸ hath *now* ɪ.   ᶻ that ɪ.   ᵃ upon ɪ.
ᵇ And ɪ.

pees of the Lord, the whiche he smoot with oure faders, whanne thei wenten 22 out of the loond of Egipt. Forsothe Salomon stood before the auter of the Lord, in the siȝt of the chyrch of Yrael; and he spradde ont his hoondis into 23 heuene, and seith, Lord God of Yrael, there is not lijk of᠎ᵘ thee, God in heuene aboue, and upon erthe beneeth, the which kepist couenaunt and mercy to thi seruauntis, that goon before thee in al her 24 herte; the which keptist to Dauid, my fader, thi seruaunt, that thou speke to hym; with mouth thou speke, and with hoondis thou hast fulfillid, as this dai 25 proueth. Now thanne, Lord God of Irael, kepe to thi seruaunt Dauid, my fader, that thou speke to hym, seiynge, There shal not be doon awey a man before me of thee, that sitte vpon the trone of Irael, so neuerthelater if thi sonis kepen thi weye, that thei goon before me, as thou wentist in my siȝt. 26 And now, Lord God of Irael, thi wordis ben thei fastned, that thou speke to thi 27 seruaunt Dauid, my fader. Thanne whethir it is to trowe, that vereli God dwelle vpon erthe; forsothe if heuene, and heuenes of heuens mowen not take thee, myche more this hows, that I haue 28 beeldid to thee. But behold to the orisoun of thi seruaunt, and to the preiers of hym, Lord my God; here the ympne, and the orysoun, that thi seruaunt 29 preieth before thee to day; that thin eyen ben openyd vpon this hows niȝt and day, vpon the hows, of the which thou seydyst, My name shal be there; that thou here the orisoun, that thi ser- 30 uaunt preieth to thee in this place; that thou here the preier of thi seruaunt, and of thi puple Irael, what euere thing be shal preye in this place, and thou here in the stede of thi dwellynge place in heuene; and whanne thou herist, thou

Lord, in the siȝt of the chirch of Israel; and he helde forth hise hondis aȝens heuene, and seide, Lord God of Israel, no 21 God in heuene aboue, netherᶜ onᵈ erthe bynethe, is lijk thee, which kepist coue- naunt and mercy to thi seruauntis, that goon bifor thee in al her herte; and thou 24 kepist to Dauid, my fadir, thi seruaunt, tho thingis whiche thou hast spoke to him; bi mouth thou hast spoke, and bi hondis thou hast fillidᵉ, as this day preu- eth. Now therfor, Lord God of Israel, 25 kepe thou to thi seruaunt Dauid, my fadir, tho thingis whiche thou spakist to hym, and seidist, A man of thee schal not be taken awei bifor me, which man schal sitte onᶠ the trone of Israel, so netheles if thi sones kepen thi weye, that thei go bifor me, as thou ȝedist in my siȝt. And 26 now, Lord God of Israel, thi wordisᵀ be maad stidfast, whiche thou spakist to thi seruaunt Dauid, my fadir. Therfor whe- 27 ther it is to gesse, that God dwellith verili onᵍ ertheᵗ; for if heuene, and heuene of heuenes moun not take thee, how myche more this hows, whichʰ Y bildidⁱ to thee, 'mai not take theeᵏ. But, my Lord God, 28 biholde thou to the preiereᵇ of thi ser- uaunt, and to the bisechyngis of hym; here thou the 'ympne, etherˡ preysing, and preiereᵐ, whichⁿ thi seruaunt preieth bifor thee to day; that thin iȝen be openyd onᵒ 29 this hows bi niȝt and dai, onᵒ the hows, ofᵖ which thou seidist, My name schal be there; that thou here the preier, whichᑫ thi seruaunt preieth to thee in this place; that thou here the bisechyng of thi ser- 30 uaunt, and of thi puple Israel, what euer thing he preiethʳ in this place, and here thouˢ in the place of thi dwellyng in heuene; and whanne thou hast herd, thou schalt be mercyful. If a man synneth 31 aȝens a man, and hath ony ooth, bi which he is holdun boundun, and comethᵗ for the ooth in to thin hows, bifor thin auter,

---

† thi wordis, etc. Not ony chaungeable- nesse is signe- fied herbi in God, but in men, to whiche the benefices of God ben bihiȝt vndur condi- cioun, that they here wel hem silf; therfor this is the sentence, thi wordis ben maad stidefast, that is, ȝyue thou to me and to othere girls of Danyth, stidefastnesse of soule in good abiding, that they be not defraudid fro the biheest. Lire here. c.

‡ that God dwellith verily on erthe; bi this, he exclud- ith the errour of hem, that gessiden that God bi the Godhed hath manns forme. Lire here. c.

§ biholde thou to the preier, etc., as if he seide, this hows is not bildid, that thou dwelle there, as a man dwellith in his hows, but that prey- eris maad there be more able to be herd than in an other place, for the excercise of Goddis wor- schiping. Lire here. c.

ᵘ Om. ᴇ pr. m.   ᵛ kepist ʙᴄᴇꜰʜ.

ᶜ ne ᴇʟ. ᵈ upon ɪ. in ᴇᴋʟx. ᵉ fulfillid ɪ. ᶠ upon ɪ. ᵍ upon ɪ. ʰ that ɪ. ⁱ haue bildid ɪ. ᵏ Om. ɪ. ˡ Om. ɪ. ᵐ the preiere ɪ. ⁿ that ɪ. ᵒ upon ɪ. ᵖ Om. ᴄ. ᑫ that ɪ. ʳ preie ᴋx. ˢ thou it ɪ. ᵗ he come ɪ.

31 shalt be merciful. If a man synneth into his nei3bour, and haue eny ooth, bi the which streyned he be holdyn, and come for the ooth before thi^w auter, into 32 thin hows, thou shalt here in heuen, and doon, and thou shalt deme thi seruauntis; condempnynge the wickid, and 3eeldynge his weye vpon his heed, iustifiynge the ri3twise, and 3eeldynge to hym after his 33 ri3twisnes. If thi puple Irael shul flee his enemyes, for he is to synne to thee, and doynge penaunce, and knowlechynge to thi greet name, comen, and honouren, 34 and preyen thee in this hows, here thou in heuene, and for3if the synne of thi puple Irael; and thou shalt lede hem a3en into the loond, that thou 3af to the 35 fadres of hem. If heuene were closid, and shal not reyne for the synnes of hem, and preiynge in this place, penaunce doon to thi name, and fro her^x synnes 36 weren conuertid for her affliccioun, here thou hem in heuene, and for3if the synnes of thi seruauntis, and of thi puple Irael, and shew to hem a good weye, bi the which thei goon, and 3if reyne vpon the loond, that thou hast 3ouun to thi puple 37 in to possessioun. 'If that hungre^y were growen 'vp on^z the erthe, or were pesti- lence, or corrupt eyr, or fretynge, or locust, or rust, and turmentith hym, and his enemy besegynge the 3atis, al ven- 38 iaunce, al infirmyte, al cursynge, and wisshynge, that shall falle to eny man of thi puple Yrael, if a man knowe the wounde of his herte, and stretche out his 39 hoondis in this hows, thou shalt here in heuene, in the place of thi dwellynge, and thou shalt be a3en plesid, and thou shalt doo that thou 3yue to echon after alle her weyes, as thou shalt seen the^a herte of hym; for thou alone hast knowun the 40 herte of alle the sonys of men, that thei dreden thee alle days in the which thei

thou schalt here^u in heuene, and thou 32 schalt do^v, and thou schalt deme thi ser- uauntis; and thou schalt condempne the wickid man, and schalt^w 3elde his weie on^x his heed, and thou schalt iustifie the iust man, and schalt^y 3elde to hym vp^z his ri3tfulnesse^a. If thi puple Israel fleeth 33 hise enemyes, for he schal do synne to thee †, and thei doen penaunce^b, and knoulechen to thi greet name, and comen, and worschipen, and bisechen thee in this hows, here thou in heuene, and for3yue 34 thou the synne of thi puple; and thou schalt lede hem a3en in to the lond, which^c thou hast 3oue to the fadris of hem. If 35 heuene is closid, and reyneth not for the synnes of hem^d, and thei preyen in this place, and doen penaunce to thi name, and ben conuertid^e fro her synnes for her turment, here thou hem in heuene, and 36 for3yue thou the synnes of thi seruauntis, and of thi puple Israel, and schewe thou to hem good^f weie, bi which thei schulen go, and 3yue thou reyn to hem on^g the lond, which^h thou hast 3oue to hem in to possessioun. If hungur risith in the 37 lond, ether pestilence is, ether corrupt eyr is, ether rust, ether locuste^i, ether myldew, and his^k enemy turmentith hym, and bi- segith the 3atis^l, al^m wounde^n, al sike- nesse^o, al cursyng, and wichyng^p of 3uel, 38 that bifallith to ech man of thi puple Israel, if^q ony man knowith the wounde of his herte, and holdith forth hise hondis. in this hows, thou schalt here^r in heuene, 39 in the place of thi dwellyng, and thou schalt do mercy, and thou schalt do that thou 3yue to ech man vpe^s alle hise weies, as thou seest his herte; for thou aloone knowist the herte of alle the sones of men, that thei drede thee in alle daies in 40 whiche thei lyuen on^t the face of the lond, which^u thou hast 3oue to oure fadrys. Ferthermore and whanne an alien, which^v 41

† do synne to thee ; that is, the synne to comynge, schal be cause of flijt suynge. Lire here. c.

w the *AFH.*   x Om. *E pr.m.*   y hungir if yt *CE.*   z vp in *CE.*   a in *A.*

u here *him* I.   v do *iustly* I.   w thou schalt I.   x upon I.   y thou schalt I.   z aftir I.   a ri3twisnesse I. b penaunce, *or forthinken her synne* I.   c that I.   d men I.   e altogidre turned I.   f a good I.   g upon I. h that I.   i a locuste A.   k if his I.   l 3atis of him I.   m and al I.   n veniaunce I.   o sikenesse, al denour- ing L.   p al wischyng I.   q and if I.   r here it I.   s aftir I.   t upon I.   u that I.   v that I.

lyuen vpon the face of the erthe, that thou
41 hast ȝeuen to oure fadris. Forthermore
and an alyen, that is not of thi puple
Irael, whanne he cometh fro a ferre loond
for thi name; forsothe thi greet name
shal be herd, and thi strong hoond, and
42 thi strauȝt out arme ouer al; whanne
thanne he shal come, and preye in this
43 place, thou shalt here in heuene, in the
firmament of thi dwellynge place, and
thou shalt doo alle thingis, for the whiche
the alien hath inwardli clepid thee, that
alle puplis of erthis lernen to drede thi[b]
name, as thi puple Yrael, and proue thei,
for thi name is inwardly clepid vpon this
44 hows, that I haue beeldid. If thi puple
were goon out to batail aȝens his enemyes, bi the weye whidir euere thou
shalt seende hem, thei shulen preye thee
aȝen the weye of the citee that thou hast
chosun, and aȝens the hows that I haue
45 beeldid to thi name, and thou shalt here
in heuene the orysouns of hem, and the
preyers of hem, and doon the doom of
46 hem. That yf thei synnen to thee, there
is not a man that synneth not, and
wrooth thou shalt take hem to her enemyes, and caytife were lad into the loond
47 of enemyes, ferre or niȝ, and doon penaunce in her herte, in the place of caitifte, and turned han preyed in her caytifte, seiynge, We han synned, wickidly
we han doon, vnpitously we han born
48 vs; and weren turned to thee in al her
herte, and in al her soule, in the loond
of her enemyes, to the which catife thei
weren lad, and preyen thee aȝens the
weie of her loond that thou hast ȝouen
to the faders of hem, and of the citee
that thou hast chosun, and of the temple
49 that I haue beeldid to thi name, thou
shalt here in heuen, in the firmament of
thi see, and the orysouns of hem, and
the preiers of hem, and thou shalt[c] doon

is not of thi puple Israel, cometh fro a fer
lond for thi name; for[w] thi grete name,
and thi strong hond, and thin arm ʼholdun 42
forth[x] schal be herd euery where; therfor whanne he cometh, and preieth in
this place, thou schalt here in heuene, in[y] 43
the firmament of thi dwellyng place, and
thou schalt do alle thingis, for whiche[x] the
alien clepith thee, that alle puplis of londis
lerne to drede thi name, as thi puple Israel doith, and preue[a], that thi name is
clepid[b] on[c] this hows, which[d] Y bildide[e].
If thi puple goith out to batel aȝens hise 44
enemyes, bi the weie whidir euer thou
sendist hem, thei schulen preye thee aȝens
the weie of the citee which thou hast
chose, and aȝens[f] the hows which[g] Y bildide[h] to thi name, and thou schalt here in 45
heuene the preyeris of hem, and the bisechyngis of hem, and thou schalt make
the doom of hem. That if thei synnen to 46
thee, for no man is that synneth not, and
thou art wrooth, and[i] bitakist hem to her
enemyes, and thei ben led prisoneris in to
the lond[k] of enemyes, fer ether niȝ, and thei 47
doon penaunce in her herte in the place of
prisonyng[l], and ben conuertid[m], and bisechen in her prisonyng, and seien, We
han[n] synned, we han[n] do wickidli, we
han[n] do vnfeithfuli; and[nn] thei turnen 48
aȝen to thee in al her herte and al[o] her
soule, in the lond of her enemyes, to which[p]
thei ben led prisoneris, and thei preyen
thee aȝens[q] the weie of her lond which[r]
thou hast ȝoue to her fadris, and of[s] the
citee which[t] thou hast chose, and of[u] the
temple which[v]. Y bildide[w] to thi name,
thou schalt here in heuene, in the firma- 49
ment of thi secte, the preiers of hem, and
the bisechingis of hem, and thou schalt
make the doom of hem; and thou schalt 50
be merciful to thi puple, that synnede[x]
to thee, and to alle the wickidnessis, bi
whiche thei trespassiden[y] aȝens thee; and

---

w forsothe I.   x streiȝt out I.   y and in KX.   z the whiche I.   a preue thei I.   b inwardly clepid I.
c upon I.   d that I.   e haue bildid I.   f forn aȝens I.   g that I.   h haue bildid I.   i therfore and I.
k hond A.   l her prisonyng I.   m al to gidre turned I.   n haue I.   nn and if s.   o in al I.   p the which I.
q forn aȝens I.   r that I.   s aȝens I.   t that I.   u aȝens I.   v that I.   w haue bildid I.   x hath synned I.
y han trespassid I.

50 the doom of hem ; and thou shalt haue
merci to thi puple, that hath synned to
thee, and to alle the wickidnesses bi the
whiche thei han trespassid in thee ; and
thou shalt ȝue merci before hem, that
hadden hem caitife, that thei doon merci
51 to hem. Forsothe thi puple he is, and
thin heritage, whom thou hast brought
out of the loond of Egipte, fro the mydil
52 of the yren furneis; that thin eyen ben
opened to the preyer of thi seruaunt, and
of thi puple Yrael ; and thou shalt here
hem in alle thingis, for the whiche thei
53 inwardly shulen clepe thee. Forsothe
thou hast seuerde hem to thee in to
herytage of alle puplis of thee^c erthe, as
thou speke bi^d Moysen, thi seruaunt,
whanne thou laddist out oure fadris fro
54 Egipt, Lord God. It is doon forsothe,
whanne Salomon hadde ful eendid, preiynge the Lord al the orysoun, and this
preier, he aroos^e fro the siȝt of the auter
of the Lord ; forsothe either knee he
hadde piȝt into the erthe, and the
hoondys he hadde sprad out to heuene.
55 Thanne he stood, and blesside to al the
chirche 'of Yrael^f with a greet voys, sey-
56 ynge, Blessid is^g the Lord God, that ȝaf
rest to his puple Irael, after alle thingis
that he spak ; there felle not of^h a word,
forsothe not oon, of alle the wordis that
57 he spak bi Moyses, his seruaunt. Be the
Lord oure God with vs, as he was with
oure faders, not forsakynge vs, ne throw-
58 ynge a ferre ; but bowe he oure hertis to
hym, that we goon in alle the weys of
hym, and kepe the maundements of hym,
and cerymonyes, and domes, what euere
59 he comaundide to oure fadres. And ben
thes myn wordis, in the whiche I haue
preied before the Lord, neiȝynge to thee
Lord oure God day and nyȝt, that he do,
doom to his seruaunt, and to his puple
60 Irael bi eche days ; and witen alle pu-

thou schalt do merci bifor tho men, that
hadden hem prisoneris, that tho men do
mercy to hem. For it is thi puple, and 51
thin erytage, whiche thou leddist out of
the lond of Egipt, fro the myddis of yronc^z
furneis† ; that thin yȝen be opyn to the 52
bisechyng of thi seruaunt, and of thi puple Israel ; and thou schalt here hem in
alle thingis, for whiche^a thei clepen^b thee.
For thou hast departid hem to thee in to 53
heritage fro alle the puplis of erthe, as
thou spakist bi Moyses, thi seruaunt,
whanne thou, Lord God, leddist oure fadris out of Egipt. Forsothe it was don, 54
whanne Salomon, preiynge the Lord, hadde
fillid al this preier and bisechyng, he roos^c
fro the^d siȝt of the auter of the Lord ; for^e
he hadde set fast euer either kne to the
erthe, and hadde^f holde forth the^g hondis
to heuene. Therfor he stood, and bless- 55
ide al the chirche of Israel, and seide with
greet vois, Blessid be the Lord God of Is- 56
rael, that ȝaf^h reste to his puple Israel,
bi alle thingis whiche he spak ; a word
felde not doun, sotheli nether^i oon^k, of alle
goodis^l whiche he spak bi Moises, his seruaunt. Oure Lord God be with vs, as he 57
was with oure fadris, and forsake not vs,
nether caste^m awey ; but bowe he oure 58
hertis, to hym silf, that we go in alle hise
weies, and kepe hise comaundementis^n, and
cerymonyes, and domes, whiche euere he
comaundide^o to oure fadris. And these 59
wordis of me, bi whiche Y preiede^p bifor
the Lord, be^q neiȝynge‡ to oure Lord God
bi dai and niȝt, that he make doom to^r
his seruaunt, and to his puple Israel bi
alle daies ; and alle the puplis of erthe 60
wite, that the Lord hym silf is God, and
noon^s 'is ouer^t 'with out^u hym. Also oure 61
herte be perfit with oure Lord God, that
we go in hise domes, and kepe hise co-
maundementis^v, as and^w to dai. Therfor 62
the kyng, and al Israel with hym, offriden

Right margin notes:
† *irone furneis ; that is,* hard at the maner of irun. *Lire here.* c.

‡ *be neiȝynge, etc.; that is,* worthi to be herd bifor God. *Lire here.* c.

---

c Om. ᴀᴄ.   d to ᴀꜰʜ.   e rose ʙᴄᴇꜰʜ.   f Om. ᴇ pr. m.   g Om. ʙᴄᴇꜰʜ.   h Om. ᴀʜ.

z the yrone 1.   a the whiche 1.   b schulen clepe ᴋx pr. m.   c roos up 1.   d Om. 1.   e sothely 1.
f he hadde 1.   g his 1.   h hath ȝoue 1.   i Om. 1.   k Om. ᴄ1.   l the gode thingis 1.   m caste us 1.
n hestis 1.   o hath comaundid 1.   p haue preied 1.   q be thei 1.   r to me 1.   s noon other ᴄꜰ pr. m. ɢ1ᴍQ.
t Om. ᴄɢᴍ.   u Om. 1.   v hestis 1.   w also 1.

plis of the erthe, for the Lord he is[l] God[k], and there is noon more with out 61 hym. Forsothe be oure herte parfite with the Lord oure God, 'that we goon[l] in the domys of hym, and kepen[m] the 62 heestis of hym, as and to day. Thanne the kyng, and al Yrael with hym, offreden slayn sacrifices before the Lord. 63 And Salomon slew3 pesible oostis, that he offrede to the Lord; two and twenti thousand[n] of oxen, and an hundryd and twenti thousand[n] of sheep; and the kyng and the sones of Yrael halweden the 64 temple of the Lord. In that day the kyng halwide the mydil of the porche, that was before the hows of the Lord; forsothe he dide brent offryngis there, and sacrifice, and the talw3 of the pesible thingis; for the brasen auter that was before the Lord was to litil, and my3te not take the brent offrynge, and the sacrifice, and the talw3 of pesible thingis. 65 Thanne Salomon made in that tyme a solempne feest day, and al Irael with hym, a greet multitude, fro the entre of Emath vnto the ryuer of Egipt, before the Lord oure God, seuen days and senen 66 dais, that is, fourteen dais. And in the ei3t[o] day he lafte the puple, the which blessynge to the kyng wente into her tabernaclis, gladynge and with myrye herte vpon alle the goodis that God hadde doon to Dauid, his seruaunt, and to Irael, his puple.

sacrifices bifor the Lord. And Salomon 63 killide[x] pesible sacrifices, whiche he offride to the Lord; of oxis[y] two[z] and twenti thousynde, and of scheep sixe score thousynde; and the king and the sones of Israel halewiden the temple of the Lord. In that dai the kyng halewide† the myddil 64 of the greet street, that was bifor the hows of the Lord; for he made there brent sacrifice, and sacrifice[a], and the innere fatnesse of pesible thingis; for the brasun auter that was bifor the Lord, was to litil, and my3te[b] not take the brent sacrifice, and the sacrifice[c], and the ynnere fatnesse of pesible thingis. Therfor Salo- 65 mon made in that tyme a solempne feeste, and al Israel with hym, a grete multitude, fro the entryng of Emath 'til to[d] the stronde of Egipt, bifor oure Lord God, in seuene daies and seuene daies, that is, fourteen daies. And in the ei3the day he[e] 66 delyueryde the puplis, whiche[f] blessiden the kyng, and 3eden forth in to her tabernaclis, and weren[g] glade and of ioyful herte on[h] alle the goodis whiche[i] God hadde do to Dauid, his seruaunt, and to Israel, his puple.

64 † the kyng halewide; that is, made to be halewid, and to be maad redy, that sacrifices shulden be brent there, that my3ten not be brent on the auter: this halewing was maad bi the bischop, 65 to whos office this perteyniede, and for this was doon at the stiring of the kyng, the kyng is seid to haue do this. Lire here. c.

CAP. IX.

1 It is doon forsothe, whanne Salomon hadde perfourmed the beeldynge of the hows of the Lord, and the beeldynge of the kyng, and al that he desyryde, and 2 wolde make, the Lord aperide to hym the secounde tyme, as he aperyde to hym 3 in Gabaon. And the Lord seide to hym, I haue herd thin orisoun, and thi preyer, that thou preiedist before me; I haue

CAP. IX.

Forsothe[k] it was doon, whanne Salo- 1 mon had perfourmed the bildyng of the hows of the Lord, and the bildyng of the kyng, and al thing that he conceitide, and wolde make, the Lord apperide to Salo- 2 mon[l] the secunde tyme, as he apperide to hym[m] in Gabaon. And the Lord seide to 3 hym, Y haue herd thi preier, and thi bisechyng, which[n] thou bisou3tist[o] bifor

[i] Om. ε pr. m.   [k] a God cε.   [l] go we ε pr. m.   [m] kepe we ε pr. m.   [n] thousendis ε.   [o] ei3tethe cε.

[x] slew3 I.   [y] oxen I.   [z] he offride two I.   [a] offryng I.   [b] it my3t I.   [c] offryng I.   [d] vnto I. [e] Salomon I.   [f] the whiche I.   [g] thei weren cI.   [h] of I.   [i] that I.   [k] And I.   [l] hym A.   [m] Salomon A. [n] that I.   [o] hast bisou3t I.

halwid this hows, that thou hast beeld[p],
that I putte my name there into euermore; and myn eyen and myn herte
4 shulen be there alle days. Forsothe thou,
if thou gost before me, as thi fader ȝede,
in symplenes of herte, and enennesse, and
dost alle thingis that I haue comaundid
to thee, and my domys, and my lawful
5 thingis kepest, I shal sette the trone of
thi rewme vpon Irael in to euermore, as I
spak to Dauid, thi fader, seiynge, There
shal not be doon awey a man of thi kyn-
6 rede fro the see of Iracl. Forsothe if bi
turnynge awey ȝe and ȝoure sonys weren
turned aweye, not folwynge me, ne kepynge myn heestis and cerymonyns, that
I purposide to ȝow, but ȝe goon awey,
and herein alyen goddis, and honouren
7 hem, I shal doo awey Irael fro the vttermoost of the erthe that I haue ȝeuen to
hem; and the temple that I haue halwid
to my name, I shal throwe awey fro my
siȝt; and Irael shal be into prouerbe
8 and into fable[q], to alle puplis. And this
hows shal be into exsaumple; alle that
passen bi it, shulen wondre, and whistlen,
9 and seyn, Whi dide the Lord thus to
this[r] loond, and to this hows? And thei
shulen answere, For thei forsoken the
Lord her God, that ladde out the faders
of hem fro the loond of Egipt; and thei
folweden alien goddis, and herieden hem,
and honourden hem; therfor the Lord
10 brouȝte yn vpon hem al this yuel. Forsothe fulfillid twenti ȝeer, after that Salomon hadde beeldid two howsis, that is,
the hows of the Lord, and the hows of
11 the kyng, Iram, the kyng of Tire, ȝeu-
ynge to kyng Salomon cedre and firre
trees, and gold, after al that he hadde
nede; thanne Salomon ȝaf to Iram twenti
12 burȝ touns in the loond of Galilee. And
Yram wente out fro Tyro for to se the
burȝ touns, that Salomon hadde ȝeuen to
13 hym, and thei plesiden not to hym; and
he seith, Whether thes ben the citees that

me; Y haue halewid this hows, which[p]
thou bildidist[q], that Y schulde sette there
my name with outen ende; and myn iȝen
and myn herte schulen be there in alle
4 daies. Also if thou goist bifore me, as
thi fadir ȝede, in simplenesse of herte, and
in equite, and doist alle thingis whiche Y
comaundide[r] to thee, and kepist my domes,
and my lawful thingis, Y schal sette the
5 trone of thi rewme on[s] Israel with outen
ende, as Y spak to Dauid, thi fadir, and
seide, A man of thi kyn schal not be takun
awei fro the trone of Israel. Forsothe if
6 bi turnyng awei ȝe and ȝoure sones turnen
awey, and suen not me, and kepen not
myn hestis and cerymonyes, whiche Y settide[t] forth to ȝou, but ȝe goen, and wor-
schipen alien goddis, and onouren hem 'bi
outward[u] reuerence[v], Y schal do awei Is-
7 rael fro the face of the lond which[w] Y ȝaue
to hem; and Y schal caste awei fro my
siȝt the temple†, which Y halewid to my
name; and Israel schal be in to a prouerbe and in to a fable, to alle puplis. And
8 this hows schal be in to ensaumple of
Goddis offence; ech man that schal passe
bi it, schal wondre, and schal hisse, and
schal seye, Whi hath the Lord do thus to
this lond, and to this hows? And thei[x]
9 schulen answere, For thei forsoken her
Lord God, that ladde the fadris of hem
out of Egipt; and thei sueden alien goddis, and worschipiden hem, and onouriden
hem; therfor the Lord brouȝte[y] in on[z]
hem al this yuel. Sotheli whanne twenti
10 ȝeer weren fillid[a], aftir that Salomon hadde
bildid tweyne housis, that is, the hows of
the Lord, and the hows of the kyng,
while Hiram, kyng of Tire, ȝaf to Salo-
11 mon trees of cedre, and of beech[b], and
gold, bi al thing that he hadde nedeful;
thanne Salomon ȝaf to Hiram twenti citees
12 in the lond of Galile. And Hiram ȝede
out of Tyre that he schulde se the citees,
whiche Salomon hadde ȝoue to hym, and
tho plesiden not hym; and he seide, Whe-
13

† the temple;
in distriynge it,
as it was doon
bi Nabugodo-
nosor. Lire
here. c.

p bildide DEFH.   q fablis A.   r thi AFH.

p that 1.   q hast bildid 1.   r haue comaundid 1.   s upon 1.   t haue sett 1. sette BL.   u uttirward K.
v Om. 1.   w that 1.   x men 1.   y hath brouȝt 1.   z upon 1.   a fulfillid 1.   b firr 1.

thou hast ʒeuen to me, brother? And he clepide hem the loond of Chabul, vnto this 14 day. Forsothe Iram sente to kyng Salomon an hundrid and twenti talentis of 15 gold. This is the summe of the expensis, that kyng Salomon offrede to beelde the hows of the Lord, and his hows of Mello, and the wal of Jerusalem, and Ezer, and 16 Magedo, and Gazer. Pharao, the kyng of Egipt, stiede vp, and took Gazer, and brente it vp with fier; and Chanane that dwellide in the citee he slewʒ, and ʒaf it into dower to his douʒter, Salomons wijf. 17 Thanne Salomon beeldide vp Gazer, and 18 the nethir Bethron, and Balaad, and Pal- 19 myram in the loond of wildirnes, and alle the touns that to hym perteyneden, and weren withouten wal; and he made sikir the citees of charis, and the cytees of horsmen, and what euere thing to hym pleside for to beelde in Jerusalem, and in Liban, and in al the loond of his power. 20 Al the puple that abood stylle of Amorreis, Ethees, and Pherezeis, Euees, and Jebuseis, that ben not of the sones of 21 Irael, of thes the sones that abiden stille in the loond, that is, whom the sones of Irael myʒten not throwe out, Salomon 22 made tributaries into this day. Of the sones forsothe of Irael kyng Salomon ordeynde not eny man to serue, but thei weren men fiʒters, and the seruauntis of hym, and princis, and duykis, and pre- 23 fectis of charis and of hors. Forsothe thei weren princis vpon alle the werkis of Salomon, prouostis fyue hundrid and fifti, that hadden the puple subiect, and 24 to the ordeynd werkis comaundiden. The douʒter forsothe of Pharao stiede vp fro the citee of Dauid in to hir hows, that Salomon hadde beeldid to hire; thanne 25 he bieldide Mello. Forsothe Salomon offride three sithes bi eche ʒeer brent sa-

thir thes ben the citees, whiche thou, brother, hast ʒoue to me? And he clepide tho citees the lond of Chabul†, 'til in to this dai. Also Hiram sente to king Salomon sixe score talentis of gold. This is 15 the summe of 'costis‡, which summe Salomon the kyng ʒaf to bilde the hows of the Lord, and his house Mello, and the wal of Jerusalem, and Ezer, and Mag- 16 geddo, and Gazer. Farao, kyng of Egipt, stiede, and took Gazer, and brente it bi fier; and he killide Chananei, that dwellide in the citee, and ʒaf it in to dower to his douʒtir, the wijf of Salomon. Ther- 17 for Salomon bildide Gazer, and the lower Bethoron, and Balaath, and Palmyra in 18 the lond of wildirnesse; and he made 19 strong alle the townes, that perteyneden to hym, and weren with out wal, and the citees of chaaris, and the citees of knyʒtis, and what euer thing pleside hym to bilde in Jerusalem, and in the Liban, and in al the lond of his power. Salomon made tri- 20 butaries 'til to this dai al the puple, that lefte of Ammorreis, Etheis, and Fereseis, and Eueys, and Jebuseys, that ben not of the sones of Israel, the sones of these 21 hethen men, that dwelliden in the lond, that is, whiche the sones of Israel myʒten not distrye. Sotheli kyng Salomon or- 22 deynede not ony man of the sones of Israel to serue, but thei weren men werriours, and mynystris of him, and princes, and dukis, and prefectis of his chares and horsis. Sotheli fyue hundrid and fifti 23 'souereynes weren princes ouer alle the werkis of Salomon, whiche princes hadden the puple suget, and comaundiden to werkis ordeyned. Sotheli the douʒter of 24 Farao stiede fro the citee of Dauid in to hir hows, which hows Salomon hadde bildid to hir; thanne he bildide Mello. Also Salomon offride in thre tymes bi 25

Side notes (right margin):

† lond of Chabul; that is, of displesyng ethir of foulnesse. Lire here. c.

‡ this is the summe of costis; in Ebreu it is, this is the reute, which Salomon biside; and this is not referrid to the lettre goynge next bifore, but to this that sueth aftirward of aliens, which Salomon made tributaries. Lire here. c.

§ to serue; that is, in vile werkis, and of the feeldis. Lire here. c.

a tourys E pr. m.

d Hiram 1. e Chabul, that is, displesing K. f vnto 1. g the expencis that kyng Salomon offride 1. h his owne 1. i And Farao 1. k stiede up 1. l to brente c. m Farao ʒaf 1. n that citee 1. o the dower A pr. m. DEFIKLMOSbç. p of DEFIKLMOXbç. q whiche 1. r Om. 1. s vnto 1. into s. t whiche 1. u and the 1. w whiche 1. the whiche sones 1. x Om. 1. y of werre 1. z seruauntis 1. a maistris 1. b And 1. c princes weren souereyns 1. d the whiche 1. e suget to hem 1. f And 1. g stiede up 1. h that 1. i bildid it s.

crifices and pesible slayn^t sacrifices^u, vpon the auter that he hadde beeldid to the Lord; and he brente the maad encense^v before the Lord, and perfite is the temple. 26 Forsothe kyng Salomon made a nauee in Aziongaber, that is besyde Haylam, in the brenk of the Reed see, in Ydume 27 loond. And Yram sente in that nauee his seruauntis, shipmen, and wise of the 28 see, with the^w seruauntis of Salomon; the whiche whanne thei weren comen in to Oofer, thens the taken gold of foure hundrid and twenti talentis thei brou3ten to kyng Salomon.

CAP. X.

1 But and queen Sabaa, the loos of Salomon herd in the name of the Lord, she 2 cam to asaye hym in derk sentensis. And she goon out with greet companye to Jerusalem, and ritchessis, and chamels berynge swote spices^x, and gold vnnoumbrid ful myche, and precious iemmys, cam to kyng Salomon, and spak to hym alle thingis that she hadde in hire herte. 3 And Salomon tau3te hire alle the wordis that she purposyde^y; and there was not a word that my3te be vnknowun fro the kyng, and that he answerde not to hire. 4 Forsothe queen Sabaa seynge al the wisdam of Salomon, and the hows that he 5 hadde beeldid vp, and the metis of his bord, and the dwellynge placis of the seruauntis, and the ordris of the seruytours, and the clothis of hem, and the botelers, and the brent sacrificis the whiche he offride in the hows of the 6 Lord, she hadde no more spirite. And she seide to the kyng, Sooth is the word 7 that I herde in my loond, vpon thi wordis, and vpon thi wisdam; and I trowide not to the tellers to me, to the tyme that I my self cam; and I haue seen with myn eyen, and proued that the half partye 8 was not toold to me; more is thi wisdam and thi werkis, than the loos that

alle 3eeris brent sacrifices and pesible sacrifices, on^i the auter which^k he hadde bildid to the Lord; and he brente encense† bifor the Lord, and the temple was performed. Also king Salomon made 'o 26 schip^l in Asiongaber, which^m is bisidis Haila, in the brenke of the Reed sea, and^n in the lond of Idumee. And Iram sente 27 in that schip^o hise seruauntis, schipmen, and kunnynge of the see, with the seruauntis of Salomon; and whanne thei 28 hadden come in to Ophir, thei brou3ten fro thennus gold of foure hundrid and twenti talentis to kyng Salomon.

CAP. X.

But also the queen of Saba, whanne 1 the fame of Salomon was herd, cam in the name of the Lord‡ to tempte^p hym in derk and douti questiouns. And sche entride 2 with myche felouschipe and richessis in to Jerusalem, and with camels berynge swete smellynge thingis, and gold greetli with out noumbre, and preciouse stoonys; and sche cam to king Salomon, and spak to hym alle thingis whiche sche hadde in hir herte. And Salomon tau3te hir alle 3 wordis whiche sche hadde put forth; no word was, that my3te be hid fro the kyng, and *which* he answeryde not to hir. For-4 sothe^q the queen of Saba si3 al the wisdom of Salomon, and the hows which^r he hadde bildid, and the metis of his table, and the 5 dwellyng places of hise seruauntis, and the ordris of mynystris^s, and the clothis of hem, and the boteleris, and the brent sacrifices whiche he offride in the hows of the Lord; and sche hadde no more spirite. And sche seide to the kyng, The 6 word is trewe, which^t Y herde in my lond, of thi wordis, and of thi wisdom; and Y 7 bileuyde not to men tellynge to me, til Y^u my silf cam, and si3^v with myn i3en, and preuede that the half part was not teld to me; thi wisdom is more and thi werkis, than the tale^w which^x Y herde. Thi men 8

Marginal notes:

† he brente encense; not bi him silf, but bi the bischops to whos office it perteynede. Lire here. c.

‡ cam in the name of the Lord; sche bileuyde in God and worschipide him, thou3 sche kepte not Moyses lawe, for sche was not beundun therto. Lire here. c.

---

† Om. F.   u Om. E pr. m. F.   v cense E.   w Om. A.   x oynementis E pr. m.

i upon E.   k that E.   l a nauey ELP sup. ras.   m that E.   n Om. IS.   o naueye ELP.   P assaye E.
q And E.   r that E.   s the men seruynge him E.   t that E.   u Om. M.   v si3 c.   w fame E.   x that E.

I haue herd. Blessid ben[y] thi men, and blessid ben[y] thi seruauntis, thes that stonden[yy] before thee euermore, and heren 9 thi wisdam. The Lord thi God be blessid, to whom thou hast plesid, and hath putte thee vpon the troone of Yrael; forthi that the Lord shal loue Yrael into euermore, and he hath sette thee a kyng, that thou 10 doo doom and ry3twisnes. Thanne she 3af to the kyng an hundrid and twenti talentis of gold, and many swote spicis[z] ful myche, and precious iemmys; there ben no more brou3t spicis[e] so manye, as[a] thoo 'the whiche[b] queen Sabaa 3af to 11 kyng Salomon. But and the nauee of Yram, 'the which[e] bare gold of Oofer, brou3te to[d] of Oofer manye tyyn[e] trees 12 ful myche, and precious iemmys. And the kyng made of the tyme[e] trees beddis, and of the hous of the Lord, and of the kyngis hows, and harpis, and syngynge instrumentis to syngers; there ben not brou3t syche maner tyme[e] trees ne seen, 13 vnto the day that is now. Forsothe kyng Salomon 3af to the queen Sabaa alle thingis that she wold, and axed[f] of hym, out take thes thingis the whiche freeli he 3af to hire in the kyngis 3ift; the which is turned a3en, and wente into 14 hire loond with hire seruauntis. Forsothe the peyse of gold, that was offrid to Salomon bi eche 3eer, was of sex hundrid and sexe and sexti talentis of gold, 15 out take that men offreden, that weren vpon tollis, and marchaundis, and alle the sellynge sheeldis, and alle kyngis of Ara-16 bye, and duykis of the loond. And kyng Salomon made two hundrid sheeldis of moost pure gold; sexe hundrid ouncis of 17 gold he 3af in[g] a plate of o sheeld; and thre hundrid bokelers of moost proued gold; thre hundrid pound of gold clotheden o bokelere. And the kyng putte hem in the hows of the wijlde wode of

ben blessid, and thi seruauntis ben blessid, these that stonden bifor thee euere, and heren thi wisdom. Blessid be thi Lord 9 God, whom thou plesedist, and hath set thee on the trone of Israel; for the Lord louyde Israel with outen ende, and hath ordeynyd thee kyng, that thou schuldist do doom and ri3tfulnesse. Therfor sche 10 3af to the kyng sixe score talentis of gold, and ful many swete smellynge thingis, and precious stoonus; so many swete smellynge thingis weren no more brou3t, as tho which the queen of Saba 3af to kyng Salomon. But also the schip of Hi-11 ram, that brou3te gold fro Ophir, brou3te fro Ophir ful many trees of tyme, and precioue stoonys. And kyng Salomon 12 made of the trees of tyme vndir set-tyngis† of the hows of the Lord, and of the kyngis hows, and harpis, and sitols to syngeris; siche trees of tyme weren not brou3t nether seyn, til in to present[y] dai. Sotheli kyng Salomon 3af to the 13 queen of Saba alle thingis whiche sche wolde[z], and axide of hym, outakun these thingis whiche he hadde 3oue to hir bi the kyngis 3ifte wilfuli; and sche turnede a3en, and 3ede in to hir lond with hir seruauntis. Forsothe[a] the we3te of gold, 14 that was offrid to Salomon bi ech 3eer, was of sixe hundrid and sixe and sixti talentis of gold, outakun[b] that which[c] men[d] that[e] 15 weren on[f] the talagis, 'that is, rentis for thingis borun aboute in the lond[g], and marchauntis[h], and alle men sillynge scheeldys, and alle[i] the kyngis of Arabie, and dukis[k] of erthe[l] 3auen. And kyng 16 Salomon made two hundrid scheeldis of purestem gold‡; he 3af sixe hundrid siclis of gold in to the[n] platis of oo scheeld; and he made[o] thre hundrid of[o] bokeleris 17 of preued gold; thre hundrid talentis of gold clothiden[p] o bokeler. And the kyng puttide[q] tho[r] in the hows of the forest of

† vndersettingis; Rabi Salomon seith, that he made therof grees, to stie fro the kingis hows in to the hows of the Lord, and in the sidis weren siche trees, that men schulden leue hem there. Lire here. c.

‡ of pureste gold; without forth, but withynne tho weren of other mater. Lire here. c.

18 Liban. Also kyng Salomon made a greet
trone of yuer, and he clothide it with ful
19 myche ȝalowȝ gold ; the which hadde
sexe grees ; and the cop of the trone was
round in the hyndermore[h] partie[i] ; and
two hoondis hens and thens, holdynge
the sittynge place, and two liouns stoden
20 beside eche hondis; and twelue litil liouns
stoondynge vpon the sexe grees hens and
thens ; there is not maad siche a werk
21 in alle rewmes. But and alle the vessels,
of the whiche kyng Salomon drank, weren
golden, and al the necessarie of the hows
of the wijlde wode of Liban of moost
pure gold ; and[k] there was not siluer, ne
of eny prijs was holden in the dais of
22 Salomon. For the nauee of the kyng bi
the see with the nauee of Yram onys bi
thre ȝeer wente into Tharsis, bryngynge
thens gold, and siluer, and olefauntis
23 teeth, and apis, and pokokis. Thanne
kyng Salomon is magnified vpon alle the
kyngis of erthe[l] in richesses[m] and wis-
24 dam. And al erthe desiride to se the
cheer of Salomon, that it here the wisdam of hym, that God hadde[n] ȝeuen in his
25 herte. And alle thei brouȝten to him ȝiftis,
golden vessels, and siluercn, clothis, and
batayl aarmys, swote spicis[o] forsothe, and
26 hors, and mulis, bi alle ȝeeris. And Salomon gedride charis, and horsmen ; and
there ben maad to hym a thousand and
foure hundrid charis, and twelue thousand of horsmen ; and he disposide hem
bi the strengthid citees, and with the
27 king in Jerusalem. And he made, that
there was as myche plente of siluer in
Jerusalem, as of stoonus ; and he ȝaf the
multitude of cedres as mulberie trees,
28 that growen in wijld feeldis. And the
hors of Salomon weren brouȝt out of
Egipt, and of Choa ; forsothe marchauntis of the kyng bouȝten of Choa,

Lyban. Also kyng Salomon made a greet 18
trone of yuer, and clothide[s] it with ful
fyn gold ; which[t] trone hadde sixe grees ; 19
and the hiȝnesse of the trone was round
in the hynderere[u] part ; and tweine hondis
on[v] this side and on that side, holdynge
the seete, and twei lyouns stoden bisidis
ech hond ; and twelue litil liouns stond- 20
ynge on[w] sixe[x] grees on this side and on
that side ; siche a werk was not maad in
alle rewmes. But also alle the vessels, 21
of which kyng Salomon drank, weren of
gold, and alle the purtenaunce of the hows
of the forest of Liban was of pureste gold ;
siluer wás not, nether it was arettid of[y]
ony prijs† in the daies of Salomon. For 22
the schip of 'the kyng[z] wente[a] onys bi[b]
thre ȝeer with the schip of Hiram in to
Tharsis, and brouȝte fro thennus gold,
and siluer, and teeth of olifauntis, and
apis, and pokokis[c]. Therfor kyng Salo- 23
mon was magnified aboue alle kyngis of
erthe[d] in richessis and wisdom. And al 24
erthe desiride to se the cheer of Salomon,
to[e] here the wisdom of him, which wisdom God hadde ȝoue in[f] his herte. And 25
alle men brouȝten ȝiftis to hym, vessels of
gold, and of siluer, clothis, and armeris of
batel, and swete smellynge thingis, and
horsis, and mulis, bi ech ȝeer. And Salo- 26
mon gaderide togidere charis, and knyȝtis[g] ;
and a thousinde and foure hundrid charis
weren maad to hym, and twelue thousynde 'of knyȝtis[h] ; and he disposide hem
bi strengthid citees, and with the kyng in
Jerusalem. And he[i] made, that so greet 27
aboundaunce of siluer was in Jerusalem,
how greet was also of stoonys ; and he
ȝaf the multitude of cedris as sicomoris[k],
that[l] growen in feeldy places. And the 28
horsis of Salomon weren led out of Egipt,
and of Coa ; for the[m] marchauntis of the
kyng bouȝten[n] of Coa, and brouȝten for[o]

+ of ony priys ;
that is, of litil
priys in com-
parisoun. Lire
here. c.

---

[h] innermore *AFH*. [i] part *c*. [k] ne *A*. [l] the erthe *E pr. m*. [m] ritchesse *ABFH*. [n] hath *ABH*. [o] oynementis *E pr. m*.

[s] he hilide I. [t] and the I. [u] hinder *EKLX*. hyndir I. [v] *weren* on I. [w] upon I. [x] the sixe I.
[y] to *A*. [z] Salomon I. [a] ȝede I. [b] in I. [c] pecokis I. [d] men I. [e] and to I. [f] in to I. [g] horsmen I.
[h] horsmen I. [i] Salomon I. [k] sicomoris trees I. [l] the whiche I. [m] Om. I. [n] bouȝten hem I. [o] hem
to him for I.

29 and the prijs set, brou3ten. Forsothe there was bou3t a foure whelid cart of Egipt for sexe hundrid ouncis of siluer, and an hors an hundrid and fifti; and in this maner alle the kyngis of Ethees and of Cyrye soolden hors.

prijs ordeyned. Forsotheᵖ a charet 3ede out of Egipt for sixe hundrid siclis of siluer, and an hors for an hundrid and fiftiᑫ siclisʳ; and bi this maner alle the kyngis of Etheis and of Sirye seelden horsis.

29 + a chare; that is, iiij. horsis of a chare. c. 3ede out: that is, was bou3t. Lire here. c.

CAP. XI.

1 Forsothe kyng Salomon to bren-nyngly louede many hethen wymmen, the dou3ter forsothe of Pharao, and Moabitis, and Amonytis, and Ydumees, 2 and Cidonees, and Ethees; of the gentils, on the whiche the Lord seide to the sones of Yrael, 3e shulen not goon into hem, ne of hem shulen goon out to 3ou; moost certeynli forsothe thei shulen turne aweie 3oure hertis, that 3e folwen the goddis of hem. And so to thes is couplid kyng Salomon, bi moost brennynge loue. 3 And there weren to hym wiues as queens seuen hundrid, and secoundarie wiues thre hundrid; and wymmen turn- 4 eden awey the herte of hym. And whanne now he was oold, the herte of hym is beshrewid bi wymmen, that he folwide alien goddis; and the herte of hym was not parfit with the Lord his God, as the 5 herte of Dauid, his fadre. But Salomon heryede Astertem, the goddesse of Sydo-nyes, and Chamos, the god of Moabitis, and Moloch, the mawmet of Amonytees; 6 and Salomon dide that was not plesynge beforeᵖ the Lord, and he fulfillide not that he folwe the Lord, as Dauid, his 7 fader. Thanne Salomon beeldideᑫ vp the temple of Chamos to the mawmet of Moab, in the hil that is a3ens Jerusalem, and to Moloch, the mawmet of the sones 8 of Amon. And in this maner he dide to alle his heythen wyues, that brenden en-9 cense, and offreden to her goddis. Ther-for the Lord wraththid toʳ Salomon, forthi that his mynde was turned aweie fro the Lord God of Irael; the which aper-

CAP. XI.

Forsothe kyng Salomon louyde bren-1 nyngliˢ many alien wymmen, andᵗ the dou3tir of Pharao, and wymmen of Moab, and Amonytisᵘ, and Ydumeisᵛ, and Sydo-neisʷ, and Etheisˣ; of the folkis of whiche 2 the Lord seide to the sones of Israel, 3e schulen not entre to tho folkis, nether ony of hem schulen entre to 3ou; for most cer-teynli thei schulen turne awei 3oure hertis, that 3e sue the goddis of hem. Therforʸ kyng Salomon was couplid to these wym-men, bi moost brennyng loue. And wyues 3 as queenys weren seuene hundrid to hym, and thre hundrid secundarie wyues; and the wymmen turneden awey‡ his herte. And whanne he was thanne eld, his herte 4 was bischrewid bi wymmen, that he suede alien goddis; and his herte was not perfit with his Lord God, as the herte of Dauid, his fadir, 'was perfitᶻ. But Salomon wor-5 schipide Astartes§, the goddesse of Sido-neis, and Chamos, the god of Moabitis, and Moloch, the idol of Amonytis; and 6 Salomon dide that, that pleside not bifor the Lord, and he fillideᵃ not that he suede the Lord, as Dauid, his fadir, dideᵇ. Thanne Salomon bildide a temple to Cha-7 mos, the idol of Moab, in theᶜ hil‖ whichᵈ is a3ensᵉ Jerusalem, and to Moloch, the idol of the sones of Amon. And bi this 8 maner he dide to alle hise alien wyues, thatᶠ brenten encencis, and offriden to her goddis. Therfor the Lord was wrooth to 9 Salomon, for his soule was turned awei fro the Lord God of Israel; that apperide toᵍ Salomonᶜ the secounde tyme, and co-10 maundide of thisʰ word, that he schulde

‡ turneden awey, etc., fro the loue of God, and fro keping of his heestis. Lire here. c.
§ Salomon worschipide Astartes, etc.: Salomon was not so fonned, that he bi-leuyde ony thing of God-hed to be in the idols, but he worschipide idols, for he nolde offende hise wyues. So Adam eet of the tre for-bedun at the tising of his wyif, lest he schulde make her sory, as Austyn seith. For as Poul seith in 1 Piete to Tyme. ii. c°. Adam was not disseyued, that he bileuyde, that by eting of that tre he schulde haue kunnyng of good and of yuel, as the serpent bihi3te. Lire here. c.
‖ in the hil; that is, of Olyuete. Lire here. c.

ᵖ to forn ᴇ.   ᑫ bilde c.   ʳ Om. ʙ.

ᵖ For ɪ.   ᑫ sixti ᴋ.   ʳ siclis of siluer ᴋᴍx pr. m.   ˢ ful myche ɪ.   ᵗ also he louyde ɪ.   ᵘ of Amon ɪ.
ᵛ of Ydumee ɪ.   ʷ of Sidonye ɪ.   ˣ of Ethey ɪ.   ʸ And so ɪ.   ᶻ Om. ɪ.   ᵃ fulfillide ɪ.   ᵇ Om. ɪ.
ᶜ an ɪ.   ᵈ that ɪ.   ᵉ forn a3ens ɪ.   ᶠ the whiche ɪ.   ᵍ him ɪ.   ʰ his ɪ.

10 ide to hym the secounde, and hadde comaundid of this word, that he shulde not
folwe alyen goddis; and he kepte not that,
11 that the Lord comaundyde to hym. And
so the Lord seide to Salomon, For thou
haddist this anentis thee, and keptist not
my couenant, and myn heestis, the whiche
I comaundide to thee, brekynge I shal
kitte thi^r rewme, and ȝeuen it to thi ser-
12 uaunt. Neuerthelater in thi days I shal
not doon, for Dauid, thi fader; fro the
13 hoond of thi sone I shal kutte it; and al
the rewme I shal not doon awey, but o
lynage I shal ȝyue to thi sone, for Dauid,
my seruaunt, and Jerusalem, that I haue
14 chosen. The Lord forsothe reride an ad-
uersary to Salomon, Adad Ydume, of the
15 kyngis seed, that was in Edom. Forsothe
whanne Dauid was in Ydume, and Joab,
the prince of chyualrie, hadde styed vp
to byrye hem that weren slayn, and
16 hadde slayn al maal in Ydume; forsothe
sexe monethis there dwellide Joab, and
al Irael, to the tyme that thei hadden
17 slayn al maal in Ydume; he Adad fleeiȝ,
and Ydume men, of the seruauntis of his
fadir, with hym, that he goo into Egipt;
18 forsothe Adad was a litil child. And
whanne thei hadden rysen fro Madian,
thei camen into Pharan; and thei token
with hem men of Pharan, and wenten
into Egipt, to Pharao, the kyng of Egipt;
the which ȝaf to hym an hows, and ordeynde meetis, and a loond asignede.
19 And Adad foonde grace before Pharao
ful myche, in so myche that he ȝaf to
hym a wijf, the sister germayn of his
20 wiif Taphnes, the queen. And the sister
of Taphnes gat to hym Jenebath, a sone;
and Taphnes norishide hym in the hows
of Pharao; and Jenebath was dwellynge
21 before Pharao, with his sones. And
whanne Adad hadde herd in Egipt, Dauid to haue slept with his fadris, and

not sue alien goddis; and he kepte not
tho thingis, whiche the Lord comaundide
to hym. Therfor the Lord seide to Salo-11
mon, For thou haddist this thing anentis
thee, and keptist not my couenaunt, and
myn heestis, whiche Y comaundide to thee,
Y schal breke, and Y schal departe thi
rewme, and Y schal ȝyue it to thi seruaunt. Netheles Y schal not do in^k thi 12
daies, for Dauid, thi fadir; Y schal kitte
it fro the hond of thi sone; nether Y schal 13
do awey al the rewme, but Y schal ȝyue
o lynage to thi sone, for Dauid, my ser-
uaunt, and for Jerusalem, which^l Y chees^m.
Forsothe the Lord reiside to Solomon an 14
aduersarie, Adad Ydumey, of the kyngis
seed, that was in Edom. For whanne 15
Dauid was in Ydumee, and Joab, the
prince of chyualrieⁿ, hadde stied^o to birie
hem that weren slayn, and he hadde slayn
ech male kynde in Ydumee; for Joab, and 16
al Israel dwelliden there bi sixe^p monethis,
til thei killiden^q ech male kynde in Ydumee; Adad hym silf fledde, and men of 17
Ydumee, of^r 'the seruauntis of his fadir^s,
with hym, that he schulde entre in to
Egipt; sotheli^t Adad was a litil child.
And whanne thei hadden rise fro Madian, 18
thei camen in to Faran; and thei token
with hem men of Faran, and entriden in
to Egipt, to Pharao, kyng of Egipt;
which^u Farao ȝaf an hows to hym, and
ordeynede^v metis, and assignede^w lond.
And Adad foond grace bifor Farao greetli, 19
in so myche that Farao ȝaf to hym a wijf,
the sister of his wijf, sister^x of the^{xx} queen,
of Taphnes. And the sistir of Taphnes 20
gendrid to hym^y a sone, Genebath; and
Taphnes nurschide hym in the hows of
Farao; and Genebath dwellide bifor Farao,
with hise^z sones^a. And whanne Adad 21
hadde herd in Egipt, that Dauid slepte†
with hise fadris, and that Joab, the prince
of chyualrie^b, was deed‡, he seide to Farao,

^r the A.

^k bi EL.   ^l whom I.   ^m haue chosen I.   ⁿ his chyualrie I.   ^o stied up I. stie S.   ^p six-
tene EL.   ^q hadden killid I.   ^r and men of I.   ^s his fadris seruauntis I.   ^t and I.   ^u and I.   ^v ordeynede
to him I.   ^w assignede to him I.   ^x the sistir KX.   ^{xx} his X.   ^y Adad I.   ^z the I.   ^a sones of Farao I.
^b Dauid chyualrie I.

† slepte; for
he diede bi
kindly deth.
Lire here. c.
‡ was deed;
for he was
slayn bi swerd.
Lire here. c.

Joab, prynce of chyualrie, to be deed, he seide to Pharao, Lete me, that I goo into 22 my loond. And Pharao seide to hym, What thing forsothe anentis me nedist thow, that thou seche to goo to thi loond? And he answerde, Noon; but I 23 preye thee, that thou lete me. Forsothe God reryde to hym an aduersarie, Rason, sone of Eliadan, that fleiȝ Adadezer, kyng 24 of Soba, his lord; and he gadride aȝens hym men, and he is maad prince of theues, whanne Dauid shulde haue slayn hem; and thei wenten to Damasch, and dwelliden there; and thei ordeyneden 25 hym a kyng in Damasch. And he was an aduersarie to Irael alle the days of Salomon; and this is the yuel of Adad, and haat aȝen Yrael; and he regnede in 26 Cyrye. Forsothe Jeroboam, the sone of Nabath, Eufrate of Seredera, seruaunt of Salomon, whos moder was a womman widwe, Serua bi name; and he reride 27 the hoond aȝens the kyng. And this the cause of the rebellioun aȝeus hym; for Salomon beeldide Mello, and euenede the swelwȝ of the citee of Dauid, his fader. 28 Forsothe Jeroboam was a myȝti man, and a strong; and Salomon seynge the ȝonge waxynge man of good witte, and able to be tauȝt, he made hym a prefect vpon the tributis^s of al the hows of Joseph. 29 It is doon thanne in that tyme, that Jeroboam shulde goon out fro Jerusalem; and Ahyas Silonyte, prophete, foonde him in the weye, couerde with a newe mantil; forsothe thei two weren alone in the 30 feelde. And Ahyas takynge hys newe mantil, with the which he was couerde, 31 kitte into twelue parties. And he seith to Jeroboam, Tak to thee ten kyttyngis; thes thingis forsothe seith the Lord God of Yrael, Loo! I shal kitte the rewme fro the hoond of Salomon, and I shal 32 ȝyue to thee ten lynagis; but o lynage

Suffre thou me, that Y go in to my lond. And Farao seide to hym, For^c of what 22 thing hast thou nede at^d me, that thou sekist to go to thi lond? And he answeride, Of no thing; but Y biseche thee, that thou 'delyuere me^e. Also God reiside 23 an^f aduersarie to Salomon, Rason, sone^g of Eliadam, that fledde Adadezer, kyng of Soba, his lord; and gaderide men aȝens 24 hym, and was maad the prince of theuys, whanne Dauid killide hem; and thei ȝeden to Damask, and dwelliden there; and thei maden hym^h kyng in Damask. And he 25 was aduersarie† of Israel in alle the daies of Salomon; and this is the yuel of Adad, and the^i hatrede aȝens Israel; and he regnede in Sirie. Also Jeroboam, sone^k of 26 Nabath, of Effraym of Saredera, the seruaunt of Salomon, of which^l Jeroboam, a womman widewe, Serua bi name, was modir, reisyde^m hond^n aȝens the kyng. And this was cause of rebelte aȝens the 27 kyng; for Salomon bildide Mello, and made euene the swolowe of the citee of Dauid, his fadir. Forsothe^o Jeroboam 28 was a miȝti man and strong^p; and Salomon siȝ the ȝong wexynge man of good kynrede, and witti in thingis to be doon, and Salomon made hym^q 'prefect, ether^r souereyn, on^s the tributis of al the hows of Joseph. Therfor it was doon in that 29 tyme, that Jeroboam ȝede out of Jerusalem; and Ahias of Sylo, a profete, hilid with a newe mentil, foond hym^t in the weie; sotheli^n thei tweyne weren oneli^v in the feeld. And Ahias took his newe 30 mentil, with which he was hilid, and kittide^w in to twelue partis; and seide to 31 Jeroboam, Take to thee ten kyttyngis^x; for the Lord God of Israel seith these thingis, Lo! Y schal kytte the rewme fro the hond of Salomon, and Y schal ȝyue to thee ten lynagis; forsothe^y o lynage schal 32 dwelle to hym, for Dauid, my seruaunt,

† was aduersarie; thouȝ he was aduersarie la wille of anoying, he noyede not myche to Israel to lette the pees of the puple. Lire here. C.

^{c} And I. ^{d} anentis I. ^{e} lete me go I. ^{f} an other I. ^{g} the sone I. ^{h} Razon I. ^{i} his I. ^{k} the sone I. ^{l} the which I. ^{m} he reisyde I. ^{n} his hond IKMOSX sec. m. ^{o} And I. ^{p} a strong I. ^{q} Jeroboam I. ^{r} Om. I. ^{s} upon I. in EL. ^{t} Jeroboam I. ^{u} and I. ^{v} aloone I. ^{w} he kitte it I. ^{x} kyttyngis of the mantel I. ^{y} but I.

shal leeue to hym, for my seruaunt Dauid, and Jerusalem, the citee that I haue
33 chosen of alle the lynagis of Irael; forthi
that he forsook me, and honourde Astar-
tem, goddesse of Sydonees, and Chamos,
god of Moab, and Moloch, god of the
sonys of Amon; and he wente not in my
weyes, that he dide riȝtwisnesse before
me, and my heestis, and my domys, as
34 Dauid, his fader. Ne I shal not doo
aweye al the rewme fro his hoond, but
I shal putte hym a duyk alle the days of
his lijf, for Dauid, my seruaunt, whom I
chees, the which kepte myn heestis, and
35 my maundementis. I shal doo aweye
forsothe the rewme fro the hoond of his
sone, I shal ȝyue to thee the ten lynagys;
36 to his sone forsothe I shal ȝyue o lynage,
that there abyde stille a lantern to Dauid, my seruaunt, alle dais before me in
Jerusalem, citee that I chees, that there
37 were my name. Forsothe thee I shall
take, and thou shalt regne vpon alle
thingis that thi soule desyrith, and thou
38 shalt be kyng vpon Yrael. If thanne
thou herist alle thingis that I shal comaunde to thee, and gost in my weies,
and dost that is riȝt before me, kepynge
my maundementis, and myn heestis, as
Dauid, my seruaunt, dide, I shal be with
thee, and beelde to thee a trewe hows,
what maner wise I beeldide to Dauid an
hows, and I shal take to thee Yrael;
39 and I shal tourmente the seed of Dauid
vpon this, neuerthelater not alle dais.
40 Thanne Salomon wolde slee Jeroboam, the
whiche roos, and fleiȝ into Egipt, to Su-
saach, the kyng of Egipt; and he was
in Egipt vnto the deeth of Salomon.
41 Forsothe the remnaunt of the wordis of
Salomon, and alle thingis that he dide,
and the wisdom of him, loo! alle thei
ben writyn in the boke of the wordis of
42 the dais of Salomon. Forsothe the dais
the whyche Salomon regnede in Jerusa-

and for Jerusalem, the citee which Y chees
of alle the lynagis of Israel; *this kittyng*[s] 33
schal be; for Salomon forsook me, and
worschipide Astartes, goddesse[t] of Sido-
neis[u], and Chamos, the god of Moab, and
Moloch, the god of the sones of Amon;
and ȝede[v] not in my weies, that he dide
riȝtwisnesse[w] bifor me, and[x] myn heestis,
and my domes, as Dauid, his fadir, dide[y].
And Y schal not take awey al the rewme 34
fro 'his hond[z], but Y schal putte hym
duyk in alle the daies of his lijf, for
Dauid, my seruaunt, whom Y chees, that
Dauid[a] kepte myn heestis, and my comaundementis. Sotheli[b] Y schal take awey 35
the rewme fro the hond of 'his sone[c], and
Y schal ȝyue ten lynagis to thee[d]; for- 36
sothe[e] Y schal ȝyue o lynage to 'his sone[f],
that a lanterne dwelle to Dauid, my seruaunt, in alle daies bifor me in Jerusalem,
the citee which[g] Y chees, that my name
schulde be there. Forsothe[h] Y schal take 37
thee[i], and thou schalt regne on[k] alle thingis
whiche thi soule desirith, and thou schalt
be kyng on[l] Israel. Therfor if thou schalt 38
here alle thingis whiche Y schal comaunde
to thee, and if thou schalt go in my weies,
and if thou schalt do that, that is riȝtful
bifore me, and if thou schalt kepe my
comaundementis, and myn heestis, as Dauid, my seruaunt, dide, Y schal be with
thee, and Y schal bilde a feithful hows to
thee, as Y bildide an hows to Dauid, and
Y schal ȝyue Israel to thee; and Y schal 39
turmente the seed of Dauid on this thing,
netheles not in alle daies. Therfor Salo- 40
mon wolde sle[m] Jeroboam, which[n] roos,
and fledde in to Egipt, to Susach, kyng of
Egipt; and he was in Egipt 'til to[o] the
deeth of Salomon. Forsothe the residue 41
of the wordis of Salomon, and alle thingis
whiche he dide, and his wisdom, lo! alle
thingis[p] ben writun in the book of wordis
of daies of Salomon. Sotheli[q] the daies bi[r] 42
whiche Salomon regnede in Jerusalem on[s]

---

43 lem vpon al Yrael, ben fourti ʒeer. And
Salomon slept with his faders, and is
biried in the citee of Dauid, his fader;
and Roboam, his sone, regnede for him.

CAP. XII.

1 Roboam forsothe cam into Sichym;
thider forsothe was gedrid al Irael to
2 ordeyn hym a kyng. Forsothe but Jeroboam, the sone of Nabath, whanne ʒit he
was in Egipt, ferre flowen fro the face
of Salomon the kyng, the deeth of hym
3 herd, he turnede aʒen fro Egipt; and
thei senten, and clepeden hym. Thanne
Jeroboam and al the multitude of Irael
cam, and thei speken to Roboam[t], sei-
4 ynge, Thi fader putte to vs moost hard
ʒok, and so thou now mak lasse a lytil
of the heest of thi fader moost hard, and
of the[u] moost greuous ʒok that he hath
putte on to vs, and we shulen serue to
5 thee. The which seith to hem, Gooth
vnto the thridde day, and turneth aʒen
6 to me. And whanne the puple was goon,
kyng Roboam[v] wente in counseil with
the eldris, that stoden nyʒ before Salomon, his fader, whil that he ʒit lyuede;
and seith, What counseil ʒeuen ʒe to me,
7 that I answere to the puple? The whiche
seiden to hym, If thou obesshe to this
puple to dai, and seruest to this puple,
and to the askynge of hem ʒeuest stede,
and spekist to hem liʒt wordis, thei shu-
8 len be to thee seruauntis alle dais. The
which forsook the counseil of the oold
men, that thei ʒauen to hym, and he
took to hym the ʒonge men, that weren
norishid with hym, and stoden nyʒ to
9 hym; and he seide to hem, What counseil ʒeuen ʒe to me, that Y answere to
this puple, that seiden to me, Mak liʒter
the ʒok that thi fader putte vpon vs?
10 And the ʒonge men seiden to hym, that
weren norishid with hym, Thus spek to
this puple, that speken to thee, seiynge,

al Israel, ben fourti ʒeer. And Salomon 43
slepte with hise fadris, and was biriede
in the citee of Dauid, his fadir; and Roboam, his sone, regnede for hym.

CAP. XII.

Forsothe[t] Roboam cam in to Sichem; 1
for al Israel was gaderid thidur to make
hym kyng. 'And sotheli[u] Jeroboam, sone[v] 2
of Nabath, whanne he was ʒit in Egipt,
and fledde fro the face of kyng Salomon,
turnede aʒen fro Egipt, for the deeth of
Salomon was herd; and thei[w] senten, and 3
clepiden hym. Therfor Jeroboam cam, and
al the multitude of Israel, and thei spaken
to Roboam, and seiden, Thi fadir puttide 4
hardeste[x] ʒok on[y] vs, therfor abate thou a
litil now of the hardest comaundement of
thi fadir, and of the greuousiste[z] ʒok which[a]
he puttide[b] on[c] vs, and we schulen serue
to thee. Which[d] Roboam seide to hem, 5
Go ʒe 'til to[e] the thridde dai, and turne ʒe
aʒen to me. And whanne the puple hadde 6
go, kyng[f] Roboam took counsel with the
eldere men, that[g] stoden bifor Salomon,
his fadir, while he lyuyde ʒit; and Roboam seide, What counsel ʒyue ʒe to me,
that Y answere to the puple? Whiche[h] 7
seiden to hym, If thou obeiest to dai to
this puple, and seruest this puple, and
ʒyuest stide to her axyng, and spekist to
hem liʒte[i] wordis, thei schulen be seruauntis to thee in alle daies. Which[k] Ro- 8
boam forsook the counsel of elde men,
which[l] thei ʒauen to hym, and took[m]
ʒonge† men, that weren nurschid with
hym, and stoden nyʒ him; and he seide 9
to hem, What counsel ʒyue ʒe to me, that
Y answere to this puple, that seiden to
me, Make thou esyere the ʒok which[n] thi
fadir puttide[o] on vs? And the ʒonge men, 10
that weren nurschid with hym, seiden to
hym, Thus speke thou to this puple, that
spaken to thee, and seiden, Thi fadir made
greuouse oure ʒok, releeue thou[p] vs; thus

† ʒonge: more
ʒonge in ver-
tues and kun-
nyng, than in
age. Lire
here. c.

t Jeroboam a.   u Om. a.   v Jeroboam a.

t Sothely i.   u But and i.   v the sone i.   w men of Israel i.   x the most hard i.   y upon i.
z greuouste Dкobç. ful greuous i.   a that i.   b hath put i.   c upon i.   d And i.   e vnto i.   f the kyng i.
g the whiche i.   h The whiche i.   i esie i.   k And i.   l that i.   m he took i.   n that i.   o hath put
up i.   p thus a.

Thi fader agregide oure ȝok, thou releue vs; thus thou shalt speke to hem;
My leest fyngre is gretter than the bak
11 of my fader; and now my fader putte
vpon ȝow a greuous ȝok, forsothe I shal
adde vpon ȝoure ȝok; my fader bette
ȝow with scourgis, forsothe I shal bete
12 ȝou with scorpiouns. Thanne Jeroboam
cam, and al the puple, to Roboam the
thridde day, as the kyng spak, seiynge,
Turneth aȝen to me the thridde dai.
13 And the kyng answerde to the puple
hard, forsakid the counseil of the eldres,
14 that thei hadden ȝeuen to hym; and he
spak to hem aftir the counseil of the
ȝonge men, seiynge, My fader agregide
ȝoure ȝok, and I forsothe shal adde to
ȝoure ȝok; my fader bette ȝou with
scourgis, Y shal bete ȝou with scor-
15 piouns. And the kyng assentide not to
the puple, for the Lord was aȝens hym,
that he rere his word, that the Lord
spak in the hoond of Ahye Silonyte to
16 Jeroboam, sone[w] of Nabath. And so the
puple seynge, that the kyng wolde not
here hem, answerde[x] to hym, seiynge,
What to vs part in Dauid, or what heritage in the sone of Ysaye? Turne aȝen
into thi tabernaclis, Irael; now se thin
hows, Dauid. And Yrael wente into her
17 tabernaclis. Vpon the sonys forsothe of
Irael, whiche euere dwelliden in the citees
18 of Juda, regnede Roboam. Thanne kyng
Roboam sente to Vram, that was vpon
the tributis; and al the puple stoneden
19 hym, and he is deed. Forsothe kyng
Roboam hastijf steiede vp in a chare, and
fleiȝ into Jerusalem; and Irael wente
a wey fro the hows of Dauid, vnto the
20 day that is now. It is doon forsothe
whanne al Irael hadde seen[y] that Jeroboam was[z] turned aȝen, thei senten, and
clepeden hym, the oost gadryd, and thei
ordeyneden hym kyng vpon al the rewme

thou schalt speke to hem, My leest fyngur
is gretteret than the bak of my fader;
and now my fadir puttide on[p] ȝou a gre-11
uouse ȝok, forsothe Y schal adde[q] on[r] ȝoure
ȝok; my fadir beet[s] ȝou with scourgis,
forsothe[t] Y schal bete ȝou with scor-
piouns‡. Therfor Jeroboam, and al the 12
puple, cam to Roboam, in the thridde dai,
as the kyng spak, seiynge, Turne ȝe aȝen
to me in the thridde dai. And the kyng 13
answeride harde thingis to the puple,
while the counsel of eldere men was forsakun, which[u] thei hadden ȝoue to hym;
and he spak to hem bi the counsel of 14
ȝonge men, and seide, My fadir made
greuouse ȝoure ȝok, forsothe[v] Y schal adde[w]
to ȝoure ȝok; my fadir beet ȝou with
scourgis, forsothe[x] Y schal bete ȝou with
scorpiouns. And the kyng assentide not 15
to the puple[y], for the Lord hadde turned[z]
awey, 'ether hadde wlatid[a] hym[b], that
the Lord schulde reise[c] his word, which[d]
he hadde spoke in the hond of Ahias[e] of
Silo to Jeroboam, sone[f] of Nabath. Ther-16
for[g] the puple siȝ, that the kyng nolde[h]
here hem; and the puple answeride to the
kyng, and seide, What part is to vs in
Dauid, ether what eritage in the sone of
Ysay? Israel, turne thou aȝen in to thi
tabernaclis; now, Dauid, se thou thin
hows. And Israel ȝede in to hise tabernaclis. Forsothe Roboam regnede on[i] the 17
sones of Israel, whiche[k] euere[kk] dwelliden
in the citees of Juda. Therfore kyng Ro-18
boam sente Adhuram§, that was on the
tributis; and al the puple of Israel stonyde
hym, and he was deed. Forsothe kyng 19
Roboam stiede[l] hastili on[m] the[n] chare, and
fledde in to Jerusalem; and Israel departide fro the hows of Dauid, til in to present[o] dai. Forsothe it was doon, whanne 20
al Israel hadde herd that Jeroboam turnede aȝen, thei senten, and clepiden hym,
whanne the cumpany was gaderid togi-

† is grettere: that is, is myche myȝ-tiere. Lire here. c.

‡ a scorpioun here is seilde a kynde of hard-este scourge, that hath knottis of lede ether of irun in the ende of cordis. Lire here. c et plures.

§ Roboam sente Adhuram; that he schulde peese the pu-ple and seye, that thilke word of Ro-boam was liȝtly seid, and they onȝten not go awey fro the kyng for this. And al the puple of Israel stonyde him; for deȝpit of his lord, for the puple hadde him suspect, lest he hadde be in the counsel of the king in answer-inge so to hem, for they that ben on tributis, ben wonnt to connnele of encrcessing of tho. Lire here. c.

[w] the sone E pr. m. [x] he answerde E pr. m. [y] Om. A. [z] hadde A.

[p] upon I. [q] ley to more I. [r] upon I. [s] betide I. beot K. [t] but I. [u] that I. [v] but I.
[w] leye to I. [x] but I. [y] puplis I. [z] turned him I. [a] Om. BI. [b] Om. I. [c] reise up I. [d] that I. [e] the
prophete Ahias I. [f] the sone I. [g] Thanne I. [h] wolde not I. [i] upon I. [k] the whiche I. [kk] Om. Is.
[l] stiede up I. [m] upon I. [n] his I. [o] this present I.

of Ysrael ; ne eny man folwide the hous of Dauid, saue the lynage of Juda alone.
21 Forsothe Roboam cam to Jerusalem, and he gadride al the hows of Juda, and the lynage of Beniamyn, an hundrid and four score thousand of chosen men and[a] fiȝters, that thei fiȝten aȝens the hows of Irael, and bryuge aȝen the rewme to Ro-
22 boam, the sone of Salomon. Forsothe the word of the Lord is don to Semeyam,
23 a man of God, seiynge, Spek to Roboam, the sone of Salomon, kyng of Juda, and to al the Hous of Juda and of Beniamyn, and to the tothere of the puple, seiynge,
24 Thes thingis seith the Lord, ȝe shulen not stie up, ne fiȝt aȝens ȝoure bretheren, the sones of Irael ; turne aȝen a man into his hows, of me forsothe is doon this word. Thei herden the word of the Lord, and thei ben turned aȝen fro the weye, as the Lord comaundide to hem.
25 Forsothe Jeroboam beeldide[b] vp Sichem, in the hil of Effraym, and dwellide there ; and goon out thens, he beeldide[c] vp Pha-
26 nuel. And Jeroboam seide in his herte, Now the kyngdam shal turne aȝen to the
27 hows of Dauid, if this puple stie vp, that he doo sacrifices in the hows of the Lord in Jerusalem ; and the herte of this puple shal be turned to her lord, Roboam, kyng of Juda ; and thei shulen slee me, and
28 turnen aȝen to hym. And the counseil out thouȝt, he made two golden calues, and seide to hem, Wole ȝe no more stye vp in to Jerusalem ; loo ! thi goddis, Irael, that ladden thee out of the loond
29 of Egipt. And he putte oon in Bethel,
30 and another in Dan. And doon is this word to Irael into synne ; forsothe the puple wente to honoure the calf, into Dan.
31 And he maande templis in heiȝtis, and preestis of the eendis of the puple, that
32 weren not of the sones of Leuy. And he ordeyned a solempne dai in the eiȝtithe

dere, and thei maden hym kyng on[q] al Israel ; and no man suede the hows of Dauid, outakun the lynage aloone of Juda.
21 Forsothe[r] Roboam cam to Jerusalem, and gaderide[s] al the hows of Juda, and the lynage of Beniamyn, an hundrid and fourescore thousynde of chosun men and weriours, that thei schulden fiȝte aȝens the hows of Israel, and schulden brynge aȝen the rewme to Roboam, sone[t] of Solomon.
22 Forsothe the word of God was made to Semeia, the man of God, and seide, Speke thou to Roboam, sone[u] of Sa-
23 lomon, the[v] kyng of Juda, and to al the hows of Juda and of Beniamyn, and to the residue of the puple, and seie thou, The Lord seith thes thingis, ȝe schulen
24 not stie[w], nether ȝe schulen fiȝte aȝens ȝoure britheren, the sones of Israel ; `a man[x] turne[y] aȝen in to his hows, for this word is doon of me. Thei herden the word of the Lord, and thei turneden aȝen fro the iurney, as the Lord comaundide to hem. Forsothe[z] Jeroboam bildide Sichem,
25 in the hil of Effraym, and dwellide there ; and he ȝede out fro thennus, and bildide Phanuel. And Jeroboam seide in his herte,
26 Now the rewme schal turne aȝen to the hows of Dauid, if this puple stieth[a] to
27 Jerusalem, that it make sacrifices[b] in the hows of the Lord in Jerusalem ; and the[c] herte of this puple schal turne[d] to her lord, Roboam, kyng of Juda ; and thei schulen sle me, and schulen turne aȝen to hym. And by counsel thouȝt out, he[e]
28 made tweyne goldun caluys, and seide[f] to hem[g], Nyle ȝe stie[h] more in to Jerusalem ; Israel, lo ! thi goddis, that[i] ledden thee out of the lond of Egipt. And he[k] set-
29 tide[l] oon[m] in Bethel, and the tother in Dan. And this word was maad to Israel
30 in to synne ; for the puple ȝede til[n] in to Dan, to worschipe the calf. And Jero-
31 boam made templis in hiȝe placis, and `he

---

a Om. B.   b bilde c passim.   c bilde CE.

q upon I.   r And I.   s gaderide togidre I.   t the sone I.   u the sone I.   v Om. I.   w stie up I.   x Om. I.   y turne eche man I.   z And I.   a schal stie up I.   b sacrifice I.   c thanne the I.   d turne aȝen I.   e Jeroboam I.   f he seide I.   g the peple I.   h wende up I.   i whiche I.   k Jeroboam I.   l sette EIL.   m oo calff I.   n Om. I.

moneth, the fiftenthe dai of the moneth, into the likues of the solempnete^c that is halwid in Juda. And stiynge vp, lijk maner he made an auter in Bethel, that he offre to the calues, the whiche he hadde forgid ; and he sette in Bethel preestis of the heiȝ thingis, that he hadde 33 maad. And he stiede vp vpon the auter, that he hadde maad in Bethel, the fifteenthe day of^d the eiȝtithe^e moneth, the which he feynede of his owne herte ; and he made a solempnete to the sonys of Yrael, and he stiede vp vpon the auter, that he brenne encense.

made^o preestis of the laste men† of the puple, that^p weren not of the sones of Leuy. And he^q ordeynede a solempne dai 32 in the eiȝthe monethe, in the fiftenthe dai of the monethe, bi the^r licnesse of solempnyte^s which^t was halewid in Juda. And he^u stiede^v, and made in lijk maner an auter in Bethel, that he schulde offre to the calues, whiche he hadde maad ; and he ordeynede in Bethel preestis of the^w hiȝe places, whiche he hadde maad. And 33 he styede on^x the auter, which^y he hadde bildid in Bethel, in the fiftenthe day of the eiȝthe monethe, which he^z hadde feyned of his herte ; and he made solempnyte^a to the sones of Israel, and he stiede on^b the auter, that he schulde brenne encence‡.

† *of the laste men ; that is, of ech lynage with out difference, for the kynrede of Leuy nolde assente to him. Lire here.* c.

‡ *brenne encence ; so he mystook to him preesthod. Lire here.* c.

CAP. XIII.

1 And loo ! a man of God cam fro Juda, in the word of the Lord, into Bethel, Jeroboam stoondynge vpon the auter, and 2 leiynge encense. And he criede out aȝens the auter, in the word of the Lord, and seith, Auter ! auter ! thes thingis seith the Lord, Loo ! a sone shal be born to the hows of Dauid, Jozias bi name ; and he shal offre vpon thee the preestis of heiȝ thingis, ʻthe whiche^f now in thee encensis brennen vp, and the boonys of 3 men vpon thee he shal brenne. And he ȝaf in that day a tokne, seiynge, This shal be the tokne that the Lord spak, Loo ! the auter shal be kyt, and the askis 4 shulen be shed out, that in hym is. And whanne the kyng hadde herde the word of the man of God, that criede aȝens the auter in Bethel, he strauȝte out his hoond fro the auter, seiynge, Takith him. And his hoond, that he strauȝte out aȝens hym, wex drye, and he myȝte not drawe 5 it aȝen to hym self. The auter forsothe is kit, and the askis ben shed out of the

CAP. XIII.

And lo ! a man of God cam fro Juda, 1 bi the word of the Lord, in to Bethel, while Jeroboam stood on^c the auter, ʻand castide^d encence. And ʻ*the man of God*^e 2 criede aȝens the auter, bi the word of the Lord, and seide, Auter ! auter ! the Lord seith these thingis, Lo ! a sone, Josias by name, shal be borun to^f the hows of Dauid ; and he schal offre on^g thee the preestis§ of hiȝe thingis, that^h brennen now encensisⁱ yn thee, and he schal brenne the bonys of men on^k thee. And he ȝaf³ a signe^l in that dai, ʻand seide^m, This schal be ʻthe signeⁿ that the Lord spak, Lo ! the auter schal be kit, and the aische which^o is ʻthere ynne^p, schal be sched out. And whanne the kyng hadde herd the 4 word of the man of God, which word^q he hadde cried aȝens the auter in Bethel, the kyng helde forth his hond fro the auter, and seide, Take ȝe hym. And his hond driede, which^r he hadde holde forth, and he myȝte not drawe it aȝen to hym silf. Also the auter was kit, and the aische was 5

§ *offre on thee the preestis, etc. ; for abhomynacioun of idolatrie, and this was accept, ether pleasaunt, to God, as sacrifice. Lire here.* c.

c solempte *A*.   d Om, E *pr. m*.   e eyȝte BF.   f that c *pr, m*.

o Om. 1.   p the whiche 1.   q the kyng 1.   r Om. 1.   s the solempnyte 1.   t that 1.   u the king 1.   v wente up 1.   w Om. c.   x up upon 1.   y that 1.   z the kyng 1.   a a solempnyte 1.   b upon 1.   c upon 1.   d castinge 1.   e he 1.   f of K.   g upon 1.   h the whiche 1.   i encense 1.   k upon 1.   l token t.   m seiynge 1.   n a token *to ȝou* 1.   o that 1.   p in the auter 1.   q Om. 1.   r that 1.

auter, after the tokne that the man of God hadde seid before, in the word of the 6 Lord. And the kyng seith to the man of God, Besech the face of the Lord thi God, and preye for me, that myn hoond be restorid to me. And the man of God preiede the face of God; and the hoond of the kyng is turned a3en bi to hym, and 7 is maad as it was before. Forsothe the kyng spak to the man of God, Cumme with me hoom, that thou eete, and I 8 shal 3yue to thee 3iftis. And the man of God seide to the kyng, If thou shuldist 3yue to me the half parti of thin hows, I shal not come with thee, and I shal not eete breed, ne drynke water in this 9 place; forsothe so it is comaundid to me in the word of the Lord, comaundynge, Thou shalt not eete breed, ne drynke water, ne thou shalt turne a3en bi the 10 waye that thou cam. Thanne he wente bi another weye, and he is not turned a3en bi the weie, bi the which he cam in 11 to Bethel. A maner prophete forsothe, an oold man, dwellide in Bethel, to whom camen his sonys, and toolden to hym alle the werkis that the man of God hadde doon in that day in Bethel; and the wordis that he hadde spoken to the kyng 12 thei toolden to her fader. And her fader seide to hem, Bi what weie wente he? His sones sheweden to hym the weye, bi the which the man of God hadde goon, 13 that cam fro Juda. And he seith to his sones, Makith redi to me an asse. The which whanne thei hadden maad redi, he 14 stiede vp, and wente aftir the man of God, and he foonde hym sittynge vndir a therebynt. And he seith to hym, Whether thou art the man 'of God', that cam fro Juda? He answerde to hym, I am. 15 And he seide to hym, Come with me 16 hoom, that thou eete breed. The which seith, I may not turne a3en, ne come with thee, and I shal not eete breed, ne

sched out of the auter, bi the signes which the man of God bifor seide, in the word of the Lord. And the kyng seide to the 6 man of God, Biseche thou the face of thi Lord God, and preie thou for me, that myn hond be restorid to me. And the man of God preiede the face of God; and the hond of the king turnede a3en to hym, and it was maad as it was bifore. 7 Sotheli the kyng spak to the man of God, Come thou hoom with me, that thou ete, and Y schal 3yue 3iftis to thee. And the 8 man of God seide to the kyng, Thou3 thou schalt 3yue to me the half part of thin hows, Y schal not come with thee, nether Y schal ete breed, nether Y schal 9 drynke watir in this place; 'for so' it is comaundid to me bi the word of the Lord, comaundinge, Thou schalt not ete breed, nether thou schalt drynke water†, nether thou schalt turne a3en bi the weie 10 bi which thou camest. Therfor he 3ede bi another weie, and turnede not a3en bi the weie, bi which he cam in to Bethel. 11 Forsothe sum elde profete dwellide in Bethel, to whom hise sones camen, and telden to hym alle the werkis whiche the man of God hadde do in that dai in Bethel; and thei telden to her fader the wordis 12 whiche he spak to the kyng. And the fadir of hem seide to hem, Bi what weie 3ede he? Hise sones schewiden to hym 13 the weie, bi which the man of God 3ede, that cam fro Juda. And he seide to hise 14 sones, Sadle 3e an asse to me. And whanne thei hadden sadlid, he stiede, and 3ede 15 after the man‡ of God, and foond hym sittyng vndur a terebynte. And he seide to the man of God, Whether thou art the man of God, that camest fro Juda? He 16 answeride, Y am. And he seide to hym, Come thou with me hoom, that thou ete breed. And he seide, Y may not turne a3en, nether come with thee, nether Y schal ete breed, nether Y schal drynke water in

† drynke watir; with idola-trours in this place. c.

‡ aftir the man, etc.; that he schulde dis-selue hym, and make to abide, that herbi he schulde preie voide. Lire here. c.

---

g Om. g pr. m.

s token I. t that I. u the I. v thi God I. w the Lord A sec. m. x And I. y for-sothe I. z was K. a boden I. b biddynge I. c an I. d dwellide thanne I. e the man of God I. f sadlid the asse I. g stiede up I. h answeride to hym plures. answeride hym E. i it am I.

17 drynke water in this place; for the Lord spak to me in the word of the Lord, seiynge, Thow shalt not ete breed, and thou shalt not drynke watir there[a], ne thou shalt turne aȝen bi the weye that 18 thou wentist. The which seith to hym, And I am a prophete lijk thee; and the aungel spak to me in the word of the Lord, seiynge, Bryng hym aȝen with thee into thin hous, that he eete breed, and drynke water. He[b] bigyilde hym, 19 and brouȝte aȝen with hym. Thanne he eete breed in his hous, and drank water. 20 And whanne he satte at the bord, the word of the Lord is doon to the prophete 21 that brouȝte hym aȝen; and he criede out to the man of God that cam fro Juda, seiynge, Thes thingis seith the Lord, For thou were not obeishynge[bb] to the mouth of the Lord, and keptist not the maundement that the Lord thi God 22 comaundide to thee, and turnedest aȝen, and eete breed, and dranke water in the place in the which I comaundide to thee, that thou shuldist not eete breed, ne drynke water, thi careyn shal not be born into the sepulcre of thi faders. 23 And whanne he hadde eeten and drunken, the prophete, whom he hadde brouȝt aȝen, 24 made redi his asse. The which whanne he was goon, a lioun foond hym in the weye, and slewȝ[c]. And the careyn of hym was throwun forth in the weye; forsothe the asse stood biside hym, and 25 the lioun stood biside the careyn. And loo! men goynge seen the careyn throwen in the weie, and a lioun stoondynge beside the careyn; and thei camen, and openeden into the citee, in the which 26 that ilke olde prophete dwellide. The which thing whanne the[cc] prophete hadde herd, that ladde him aȝen fro the weye, seith, The man of God he is, that was vnobeshynge[d] to the mouth of God;

this place; for the Lord spak to me in the 17 word of the Lord, and seide, Thou schalt not ete breed, and thou schalt not drynke water there, nether thou schalt turne aȝen bi the weie bi which[j] thou ȝedist[k]. Which[l] 18 seide to hym, And Y am a profete lijk thee; and an aungel spak to me bi the word of the Lord, and seide, Lede aȝen hym in to thin hows, that he ete breed, and drynke watir. He disseyuede the man of God, and brouȝte him[m] aȝen with 19 hym. Therfor he ete breed in his hows, and drank watir. And whanne he sat at 20 the table, the word of the Lord was maad to the prophete† that brouȝte hym aȝen; and he criede to the man of God that cam 21 fro Juda, and seide, The Lord seith these thingis, For thou obeidist not to the mouth of the Lord, and keptist not the comaunde-ment which[n] thi[o] Lord God comaundide to thee, and thou turnedist aȝen, and etist 22 breed, and drankist watir in the place in which Y comaundide to thee, that thou schuldist not ete breed, nether schuldist[p] drynke watir, thi deed bodi schal not be borun in to the sepulcre of thi fadris. And 23 whanne he hadde ete and drunke, the pro-phete, whom he hadde brouȝt aȝen, sadlide his asse. And whanne he hadde go[q], a 24 lioun foond hym in the weye, and killide‡ hym[r]. And his deed bodi was cast forth in the weie; sotheli the[s] asse stood bisydis hym, and the lioun[t] stood bisidis the deed bodi. And lo! men passynge sien the 25 deed bodi cast forth in the weye, and the lyoun stondynge bisidis the deed bodi; and thei camen, and pupplischiden[u] in the citee, in which thilke[v] eeld prophete dwell-ide. And whanne thilke prophete, that 26 brouȝte hym aȝen fro the weye, hadde herd this, he seide, It is the man of God, that was vnobedient to the mouth of God; and the Lord bitook[w] hym to the[x] lioun, that brak[y] hym, and killide hym[z], bi the word

† to the pro-fete; reuela-cioun of pro-fesie is ȝouun sum tyme to yuele men, as to Balaam, in xxii. c°. of Nu-meri. Lire here. c.

‡ and killide; hou myȝbe schal God pu-nysche the greuouse synnes of wick-id men, sithen die hil synne of an hooly man by deth. Lire here. c.

---

[a] Om. B.   [b] And he A.   [bb] obeyschaunt BCEFH.   [c] slewȝ hym A.   [cc] that CE.   [d] vnobeschaunt BCEFH.

[j] the whiche s.   [k] ȝedist thidre I.   [l] And he I.   [m] Om. plures.   [n] that I.   [o] the R.   [p] thou schuldist I. [q] go forth I.   [r] Om. plures.   [s] his I.   [t] lioun also I.   [u] pupplischiden it I.   [v] the I. that EL.   [w] hath bitake I.   [x] a I.   [y] hath broken I.   [z] Om. I.

and the Lord took hym to a lyoun, that brusside hym, and slew3 hym, after the word of the Lord that he[d] spak to hym. 27 And he seide to hys sonys, Makith redi to me an asse. The which whanne thei 28 hadden maad redi, and he is goon, he foond the careyn of hym throwun forth in the weye, and an asse and a lioun stondynge beside the careyn; and the lyoun eete not of the careyn, ne hurte 29 not the asse. Thanne the prophete took the careyn of the man of God, and putte it vpon the asse; and turned a3en, he brou3te it in to the citee of the oold pro-30 phete, that he weyle hym. And he putte the careyn of hym in his sepulcre, and thei weileden hym, Allas! allas! my bro-31 there! And whanne thei hadden weilid hym, he seide to hys sonys, Whanne I shal be deed, birieth me in the sepulcre, in the which the man of God is biried; beside the bonys of hym putte 3e my 32 bonys. For forsothe the word shal come, that he before seide in the word of the Lord, a3ens the auter that is in Bethel, and a3ens alle[e] the temples[f] of the3 hei3 thingis[gg], that ben in the citees of Sa-marye. Aftir thes wordis Jeroboam ys not turned awey fro his werst weye, but a3enward he made of the last puplis preestis of hei3 thingis[gg]; who so euer wolde, fulfillid[h] his hoond, and was maad 33 a preest of hei3 thingis. And for this cause the hows of Jeroboam synnede, and is turned vpsedoun, and doon awei fro the vttermoost of the erthe.

of the Lord which[a] he spak to hym. And[b] 27 he seide to hise sones, Sadle 3e an asse to me. And whanne thei hadden sadlid, and 28 he hadde go, he foond his deed bodi cast forth in the weie, and the asse and the[c] lioun stondinge bisidis the deed bodi; and the lioun eet not† the deed bodi, nether hirtide the asse. Therfor the profete took 29 the deed bodi of the man of God, and put-tide[d] it on[e] the asse; and he turnede a3en, and brou3te it in to the cyte of the eeld prophete, that he schulde biweile hym. And he puttide[f] his deed bodi in his se-30 pulcre, and thei biweiliden him, Alas![g] alas! my brother! And whanne thei had-31 den biweilid hym, he seide to hise sones, Whanne Y schal be deed, birie 3e[h] me in the sepulcre, in which the man of God is biried; putte 3e my bonys bisidis hise bonys. For sotheli the word schal come, 32 which[i] he bifor seide in the word of the Lord, a3ens the auter which[j] is in Bethel, and a3ens alle the templis of hi3 placis, that[k] ben in the citees of Samarie. After these wordis Jeroboam turnede not a3en[l]† fro his werste[m] weie, but a3enward of the laste puplis[n] he made preestis of hi3e places; who euer wolde, fillide[o] his[oo] hond§, and[p] he was maad preest of hi3 placis. And for this cause the hows of 33 Jeroboam synnede, and it was distried, and doon awey fro the face of erthe[pp].

CAP. XIV.

1 In that tyme Abya, the sone of Jero-2 boam, wexe sijke. And Jeroboam seide to his wijf, Ryse, and chaunge abijt, that thou be not knowun, that thow be the wijf of Jeroboam; and go in to Silo, where Ahya, the prophet, is, the which

CAP. XIV.

In that tyme Abia, sone of Jeroboam, 1 was sijk. And Jeroboam seide to his wijf, 2 Rise thou[q], and chaunge clothing[r], that thou be not knowun, that thou art the wijf of Jeroboam; and go thou in to Silo, where Ahia, the prophete, is, which[s] spak

[d] Om. AFH.　　[e] al AFH.　　[f] temple AFH.　　[g] Om. CE sec. m.　　[gg] Om. E pr. m.　　[h] he fulfillid E pr. m.

[a] that I.　　[b] And thanne I.　　[c] a I.　　[d] putte EL.　　[e] upon I.　　[f] putte I.　　[g] and seiden, Alas I.　　[h] Om. s. [i] that I.　　[j] that I.　　[k] whiche I.　　[l] awey IKLMOSX.　　[m] ful wickid I.　　[n] of the puple A sec. m. men DFG IKMNOQSWbç.　　[o] fille AELPb. fille ful D. he fillide I. fulfille KSç. fulfilide M.　　[oo] the kyngis I.　　[p] Om. D. [pp] the erthe IK.　　[q] thou up I.　　[r] the clothing DIKMOX sec. m. ç.　　[s] thut I.

† eet not, etc.; bi this it ap-perith, that he was sauyd, for he acceptide Goddis sen-tence, and purgide the synne of vn-obedience by bodily deth.
Lire here. c.
‡ Jeroboam turnede not a3en, etc.; for theu3 Jero-boam si3 the forseid signes in the auter kit, and in his hond dried, netheles he 3ede not awey fro his malice. Josephus touchith the cause therof. and seith, that the false pro-fete tau3te Jero-boam, that the forseid signes schewiden not Goddis vertu, for he that 3af the signe, was slayn of a lioun, a fals spekere; also he seide that the auter was brokun, for the birthun of sa-crifices put theronne, and that the kyngis hond was dry-ed, for the trauel of of-fring; and whanne he restide fro that trauel, his hond turnede a3en to the fermere staat, bi the vertu of kynde. Lire here. c.
§ fille his hond; in offringe a solempne sacri-fice, as Aaron dide, and bi this he was maad prest; ether this is referrid to Je-roboam, that selde presthod, and therfor he that 3af more prijs to Jero-boam, gat the presthod. Lire here. c.

spak to me, that I was to regne vpon this
3 puple. Tak forsothe in thin hoond ten
looues, and a litil kake, and a vessel of
hony, and go to hym; forsothe he shal
shewe to thee, what hen to come to this
4 child. The wijf dide as Jeroboam seide,
and arysynge she wente into Silo, and
cam into the hows of Ahye; and he myȝte
not se, for the eyen of hym hadden da-
5 sewide for eeld. Forsothe the Lord seide
to Ahyam, Loo! the wijf of Jeroboam is
comen in, that she counsele thee vpon
hire sone, that is sijk; thes thingys and
thes thou shalt speke to hire. Thanne
whanne she was comen yn, and hadde
vnlikned hire self to be that she was,
6 Ahias herde the soun of the feet of hire
comynge in bi the dore, and seith, Cum
in, wijf of Jeroboam; whi anothir thow
feynest thee to be? Forsothe I am sent to
7 thee an hard messagere. Go, and sey to
Jeroboam, These thingis seith the Lord
God of Irael, For I haue enhaunsid thee
fro the myddis of the puple, and ȝaf thee
8 duyk vpon my puple Irael, and kytte the
rewme of the hows of Dauid, and ȝaf it
to thee, and thow was not as my seruaunt Dauid, that kepte myn heestis,
and folwide me in al his herte, doynge
9 that was plesynge in my siȝt; but thou
hast wrouȝt euil, ouere alle that weren
before thee, and thou hast maad alien
goddis to thee, and ȝoten, that thou
terre me to wraththe, forsothe thou hast
10 throwen me behynde thi bak. Therfor
loo! I shal brynge yn yuels vpon the
hows of Jeroboam, and I shal smyte fro
Jeroboam vnto a pissere at the wal, and
closide, and last in Yrael; and I shal
clense the relikis of the hows of Jeroboam, as is wont to be clensid muk vnto
11 the pure; forsothe thoo that weren deed
of Jeroboam in the citee, houndis shulen
eete hem; forsothe thoo that weren deed
in the feeld, briddes of heuene shulen de-
12 uowre hem; for the Lord spak. Thou

to me, that Y schulde regne on[t] this puple.
Also take thou in the[u] hond ten looues, 3
and a cake, and a vessil of hony, and go
thou to hym; for he schal schewe to thee,
what schal bifalle to this child. The wijf 4
of Jeroboam dide as he seide, and sche
roos[v], and ȝede in to Silo, and cam in to
the hows of Ahia; and he[w] miȝte not se,
for hise iȝen dasewiden for eelde. For- 5
sothe the Lord seide to Ahia, Lo! the
wijf of Jeroboam entrith, that sche counsele thee[x] on[y] hir sone, which[z] is sijk;
thou schalt speke these and these thingis
to hir. Therfor whanne sche hadde entrid, and hadde feyned hir silf to be *that*
`*womman* which[a] sche was not, Ahia herde 6
the soune of the feet of hir entrynge bi
the dore, and he seide, Entre thou, the
wijf of Jeroboam; whi feynest thou thee
to bee an other *womman*[b]? Forsothe Y
am sent an hard messanger† to thee. Go 7
thou, and seie to Jeroboam, The Lord
God of Israel seith these thingis, For Y
enhaunside[c] thee fro the myddis of the
puple, and Y ȝaf thee duyk on[d] my puple
Israel, and Y kittide[e] the rewme of the 8
hows of Dauid, and Y ȝaf it to thee, and
thou were not as my seruaunt Dauid, that
kepte myn heestis, and suede me in al his
herte, and dide that that was plesaunt in
my siȝt; but thou wrouȝtist[f] yuel‡, ouer 9
alle men that weren bifore thee, and
madist to thee alien goddis, and wellid[g]
to gidere, that thou schuldist excite[h] me
to wrathfulnesse, sotheli thou hast cast
forth me bihyndis thi[i] bak. Therfor lo! 10
Y schal brynge in yuels on[k] the hows of
Jeroboam, and Y schal smyte of[l] Jeroboam `til to[m] a pissere§ *to the wal*, and
prisoned[n], and the laste in Israel; and Y
schal clense the relikis[o] of the hows of
Jeroboam, as dung‖ is wont to be clensid
`til to[p] the[q] purete, `*ether clennesse*[r]; so- 11
theli doggis schulen ete hem, that schulen
die of the hows of Jeroboam in citee[s];
forsothe[t] briddis of the eyr schulen de-

† *hard messanger*; that is, tellinge harde thingis. *Lire here*. c.

‡ *wrouȝtest yuel, etc.*; in gouernail of the puple. *Lire here*. c.

§ *Y schal smyte of Jeroboam til to a pissere, etc.*; that is, if a dogge is smytun, ether a feble man, that ouȝte to be sparid, myche more othere men of the hous of Jeroboam schulen be districd. *Lire here*. c.

‖ *as dung*; dung is not clensid in it silf, but the place in which the dung is, is clensid, whanne the dung is cast out; and bi this it is vndurstondun, that they of the hows of Jeroboam schulden not be clensid in hem silf, but the rewme of Israel schulde be clensid, bi the casting out and distriyng of hem. *Lire here*. c.

[t] upon I. [u] thin I. [v] roos up I. [w] Ahia I. [x] with thee I. [y] of I. [z] that I. [a] Om. I. [b] Om. I. [c] haue enhaunsid I. [d] upon I. [e] haue kitt I. [f] hast wrouȝt I. [g] wellid thoo I. [h] stire I. [i] the CN. [k] upon I. [l] the hous of I. [m] vnto I. [n] vnto him that is prisoned I. [o] relikis *or releffis* I. [p] vnto I. [q] Om. IR. [r] Om. I. [s] the citee CI. [t] and I.

therfor ryse, and go into thin hows; and in that goynge in of thi feet in to the 13 cytee the child shal dye. And al Yrael shal beweile hym, and berye; forsothe he alone shal be brou3t yn of Jeroboam in to the sepulcre, for there is founden vpon hym a good word of the Lord God 14 of Yrael, in the hows of Jeroboam. The Lord forsothe shal ordeyne to hym a kyng vpon Irael, that smyte the hows of Jeroboam, in this day and in this tyme; 15 and the Lord God of Irael shal smyit, as a reede in water is wont to be moued; and he shal pulle vp Irael fro this good loond, that he 3af to the faders of hem, and he shal wyndowe hem be3onde the flood, for thei maden to hem mawmet 16 wodis[i], that thei terren the Lord. And the Lord God shal take Irael ʼto her ene-myes[k], for the synnes[l] of Jeroboam, the which synnede, and made Irael to synne. 17 And so the wijf of Jeroboam roos, and wente, and cam into Tharsa; and whanne she wente in the threshwold of the hows, 18 the child dyede. And thei birieden hym; and al Irael weylide hym, aftir the word of the Lord, the which he spak in the hoond of his seruaunt, Ahye the prophete. 19 The remenaunt forsothe of the wordis of Jeroboam, how he fau3t, and how he regnede, loo! thei ben writen in the book of the wordis of the dais of the kyngis of 20 Yrael. The dais forsothe, in[m] ʼthe whiche[n] regnede Jeroboam, ben two and[o] twenti 3eer; and Jeroboam slepte with his fa-dres, and Naadab, his sone, regnede for 21 hym. Forsothe Roboam, the sone of Sa-lomon, regnede in Juda; of oon and fourti 3eer was Roboam whanne he began to regne, and seuenteen[p] 3eer he regnede vpon Jerusalem, the citee that the Lord chees, that he putte his name there, of alle the lynagis of Irael. The name forsothe of his moder, Naama Amanyte.

uoure hem, that schulen die in the feeld; for the Lord spak. Therfor rise thou, 12 and go in to thin hows; and in thilke en-tryng of thi feet in to the citee the child schal die. And al Israel schal biweile 13 him[u], and schal birie[v]; for this *child* aloone of Jeroboam schal be borun in to sepul-cre[w], for a good word is foundun on[x] hym of the Lord God of Israel, in the hows of Jeroboam. Forsothe the Lord 14 schal ordeyne to hym a kyng on[y] Israel, that schal smyte the hows of Jeroboam, in this dai and in this tyme†; and the 15 Lord God of Israel schal smyte, as a reed in the water is wont to be mouyd; and he schal drawe out Israel fro this good lond, which[z] he 3af to her fadris, and he schal wyndewe[a] hem ouer the flood, for thei maden to hem woodis[b]‡, that thei schulden terre the Lord to ire. And the 16 Lord God schal bitake Israel to[c] hise[d] enemyes[e], for the synnes[f] of Jeroboam, that synnede, and made Israel to do synne. Therfor the wijf of Jeroboam 17 roos, and 3ede, and cam in to Thersa; whanne[g] sche entride in to the thresch-fold of the hows, the child was deed. And 18 thei[h] birieden hym; and al Israel biweilide hym, bi the word of the Lord, which[i] he spak in the hoond of his seruaunt, Ahia the prophet. Forsothe, lo! the residue of 19 wordis[k] of Jeroboam, how he fau3t, and how he regnede, ben writun in the book of wordis of the daies of kyngis of Israel. Forsothe the daies, in whiche Jeroboam 20 regnede, ben two and twenti 3eer; and Jeroboam slepte with hise fadris, and Nadab, his sone, regnede for hym. For-21 sothe Roboam, the sone of Salomon, regnede in Juda; Roboam was of oon and fourti 3eer, whanne he bigan to regne, and he regnede seuentene 3eer in[l] Jerusalem, the citee which[m] the Lord chees of alle the lynagis of Israel, that he schulde sette his

† *in this tyme; that is, of ny3. Lire herre. c.*

‡ *maden to hem wodis; that is, diden idolatrie and lecherie in wodis. Lire here. c.*

i templis E pr. m. k Om. E pr. m. l synne ABFH. m Om. BCEFH. n that C. o Om. E. p ei3te-tene E pr. m.

u Om. A. v birie *him* A. w a sepulcre I. the sepulcre KOB. x upon I. y upon I. z that I. a winewe I. b marvmet woodis I. c Om. BCEF pr. m. d Om. BCEFOP pr. m. e Om. BCEP pr. m. f synne KB. g and whanne IK. h men I. i that I. k the wordis I. l whanne in s. m that I.

22 And Juda dide yuel before the Lord,
and thei terreden hym vpon alle thingis,
that the faders of him diden in her
23 synnes, that thei synneden. Forsothe and
thei beeldiden[p] vp to hem self auterys,
and ymagis, and mawmet wodis[q], vpon
al hei3 hil, and vndur eche tree ful of
24 braunchis. But men maad wommanlich[r]
weren in the loond, and thei diden alle
the abhomynaciouns of hethen[s] men, the
whiche the Lord al to-trade before the
25 face of the sonys of Irael. Forsothe in
the fifthe 3eer of the regne of Roboam,
Sesac, the kyng of Egipt, stiede vp into
26 Jerusalem; and he took the tresours of
the hous of the Lord, and the kyngis
tresours, and alle thingis he brak in[t] two,
and the golden sheeldis that Salomon
27 made. For the whiche kyng Roboam
made brasen sheeldis, and took hem in
the hoond of the duykis sheeldberers,
and of hem that watchiden before the
28 doore of the hows of the kyng. And
whanne the kyng wente into the hows
of the Lord, thei beeren hem, that hadden
the office of goynge before, and afterward
thei brou3ten a3en to the armerye place
29 of the sheeldberers. The remnaunt forsothe of the wordis of Roboam, and alle
thingis that he dide, loo! ben writen in
the book of the wordis of the dais of the
30 kyngis of Juda. And there batayl was
bitwix Roboam and Jerobuam alle dais.
31 And Roboam slepte with his faders, and
is biried with hem[u] in the citee of Dauid. Forsothe name of his moder, Naama
Amanyte; and Abya, his sone, regnede
for hym.

CAP. XV.

1 Thanne in the ei3tetenthe[v] 3eer of the
regne of Jeroboam, the sone of Naabath,
2 regnede Abya vpon Judam. Thre 3eer
he regnede in Jerusalem; name of his

---

name there. Sotheli[m] the name of his
moder was Naama Amanyte. And Juda 22
dide yuel bifor the Lord, and thei terriden
hym to ire on alle thingis, whiche her
fadris diden in her synnes, bi whiche thei
synneden. For also thei bildiden to hem 23
silf auters, and ymagis†, and wodis, on
eche li3 hil, and vndur ech tree ful of
bowis. But also 'men of wymmens con- 24
diciouns[n]‡ weren in the lond, and thei
diden alle abhominaciouns[o] of hethene
men, whiche the Lord al to-brak bifor
the face of the sones of Israel. Forsothe 25
in the fifthe 3eer of the rewme of Roboam,
Sesach, the kyng of Egipt, styede[p] in to
Jerusalem; and he took the tresouris of 26
the hows of the Lord, and the kyngis
tresouris, and he rauischide[q] alle thingis;
also 'he rauischide[r] the goldun scheeldis,'
whiche[s] Salomon made. For whiche[t] kyng 27
Roboam made brasun scheeldis, and 3af[u]
tho in the hondis of duykis of scheeld
makeris, and of hem that wakiden[v] bifor
the dore of the hows of the Lord. And 28
whanne the kyng entride in to the hows
of the Lord, thei that hadden office to go
bifore, baren tho, and baren[w] a3en to the
place of armer of scheeld makeris. For- 29
sothe, lo! the residue of wordis[x] of Roboam, and alle thingis whiche he dide,
ben writun in the book of wordis of daies
of kyngis of Juda. And hatel was bitwixe 30
Roboam and Jeroboam, in alle daies. And 31
Roboam slepte with hise fadris, and was
biried with hem in the citee of Dauid.
Forsothe[y] the name of his modir *was*
Naama Amanyte; and Abia, his sone,
regnede for hym.

CAP. XV.

Therfor in the ei3tenthe 3eer of the 1
rewme of Jeroboam, sone[z] of Nabath,
Abia regnede on[a] Juda. Thre 3eer he 2
regnede in Jerusalem; the name of his

---

† *vuteris and ymagis;* for idolatrie. *Lire here.* c.
and wodis, etc.; that is, thicke wodis aboute the places of idolis, to vse lecherie there. *Lire here.* c.
‡ *men of wymmens condiciouns; that is,* men geldid ether maad weren ordeyned in the worschiping of sum goddesse, as sum men seyen. Sothely the Ebreu word, which is set here, signefieth an hoorelling; and here bi men of wymmens condiciouns semen to be vndurstonden faire 3onge men set in hoore howsis, to haunte the synne of Sodom, as in II. book of Machabi. iiij. c°. Jason settide 3onge men in hoore housis, vndur the hi3 tour. *Lire here.* c.

p beelden *A*.　q templis *E pr. m.*　r wommannysch *BCEFH.*　s the hethen *E pr. m. II.*　t on *CE.*
u Om. *E pr. m.*　v nynteethe *A.* nynteenth *BFH.*

m And I.　n men of wymmen condiciouns A. wommanysche men I.　o the abhomynaciouna I.　p styede up I.　q rauischide *thenns* I.　r Om. I.　s also the whiche I.　t the whiche I.　u he 3af I.　v walkiden KB.
makeden L.　w thei baren thoo I.　x the wordis I.　y And I.　z the sone I.　a upon I.

moder Macha, the douȝter of Abessalon.
3 And he wente in alle the synnes of his
fader, the whiche he hadde doon before
hym; ne the herte of hym was parfite
with the Lord his God, as the herte of
4 Dauid, his fader. But for Dauid the
Lord his God ȝaf to hym a lanterne in
Jerusalem, that he rere his sone aftyr
5 hym, and stoonde in^u Jerusalem; for thi
that Dauid hadde doo riȝt in the eyen of
the Lord, and hadde not bowid awey fro
alle thingis that he hadde comaundide to
hym, alle days of his lijf, out tank the
6 word of Vrie Ethei. Neuerthelater there
was batail betwix Abyam and Jeroboam,
7 al tyme of his lijf. The remnaunt forsothe of the wordis of Abye, and alle
thingis that he dide, whethir not thes
ben writen in the book of the wordis of
the days of the kyngis of Juda? And
there was batail betwix Abyam and Jero-
8 boam. And Abya slepte with his faders;
and thei biryden hym in the cite of Dauid; and Asa, his sone, regnede for hym.
9 Forsothe in the twentithe ȝeer of Jeroboam, kyng of Irael, regnede Asa, kyng
10 of Juda; and oon and fourti ȝeer he
regnede in Jerusalem. Name of his moder, Macha, the douȝter of Abessalon.
11 And Asa dide riȝt in the siȝt of the
12 Lord, as Dauid, his fader; and he took
awey the wommannysh maad men of the
loond, and he purgide alle the^v filthis of
the mawmettis, 'the whiche^{vv} his fadris
13 maden. Ferthermore and his moder Ma-
chan he 'putte awey^w, that she were not
prince in the heriyng thingis of the
mawmet of mannus ȝeerde, and in^x his
'mawmet wode^y that she hadde halowide;
and he turnede vpsodoun the den of hym,
and he to-brak the foulest licnes, and
14 brente in the steem of Cedron; forsothe
the heiȝ thingis he dide not awey; neuerthelater the herte of Asa was perfijt with
15 the Lord his God, alle his dais. And he

modir was Maacha, douȝter^b of Abessalon.
And he ȝede in alle the synnes of his fadir, 3
which he dide bifor hym; and his herte
was not perfit with his Lord God, as the
herte of Dauid, his fadir, 'was perfit^c. But 4
for Dauid his Lord God ȝaf to hym a lan-
terne in Jerusalem, that he schulde reise
his sone after hym, and that he schulde
stonde in Jerusalem; for Dauid hadde do 5
riȝtfulnesse^d in the iȝen of the Lord, and
hadde not bowid fro alle thingis whiche^e
the Lord hadde comaundid to him, in alle
the daies of his lijf, outakun the word of
Urie Ethei†. Netheles batel was bitwix 6
Abia and Jeroboam, in al the tyme of his
lijf. Sotheli the residue of^f wordis^g of 7
Abia, and alle thinges whiche^h he dide,
whether these ben not writun in the book
of wordis of daies of the kyngys of Juda?
And batel was bitwixe Abia and Jeroboam. And Abia slepte with his fadris; 8
and thei birieden hym in the citee of
Dauid; and Asa, his sone, regnede for
hym. Sotheliⁱ Asa, king of Jude, regnede 9
in the twentithe ȝeer of Jeroboam, kyng
of Israel; and Asa regnede oon and fourti 10
ȝeer in Jerusalem. The^k name of his modir
was Maacha, douȝter^l of Abessalon. And 11
Asa dide riȝtfulnesse^m in the siȝt of the
Lord, as Dauid, his fadir, dide; and he 12
took awey fro the loond men of wymmens
condiciouns, and he purgide alle the filthis
of idols, whiche his fadris maden. Fer- 13
thermore and he remouyde Maacha, his
modir, that sche schulde not be princesse
in the solempne thingis of Priapusⁿ‡, and
in his wode^o which^p sche hadde halewid;
and he distriede the denne§ of hym, and
he brak the foulest symylacre, and brente^q
in the stronde of Cedron; sotheli he dide 14
not awei hiȝ^r thingis‖; netheles the herte
of Asa was perfit with hys Lord God, in
alle hise daies. And he brouȝte in to the 15
hous of the Lord tho thingis, whiche^s his
fadir hadde halewid and auowid, siluer^t,

† the word of
Vrie Ethei:
Dauyth syn-
nede in the
noumbring of
the puple, and
in sentence
ȝcuun aȝenus
Myphiboseth,
as it is teld in
ij. book, but
these synnes
weren ful litle,
in comparisoun
of the synne in
the dede of
Vrie, and ther-
for these ben
not arettid; for
a litil thing is
arettid as no-
thing, as the
Filosofore seith
in ij. book of
Fisikis. Lire
here. c.

‡ Priapus;
that is, an idol
liyk a man,
with outra-
giouse menabre
of man. c et
plures.
§ he distriede
the den; in
which the
wymmen
hauntiden lec-
cherie, for the
worschipe of
the idol. Lire
here. c.
‖ hiȝe thingis;
that is, hiȝe
places, in
whiche the
sones of Israel
maden sacrifice
to God, bifor
that the temple
was bildid;
and for that
tyme it was
leeueful, not
aftirward. Lire
here. c.

^u at E pr. m.   ^v Om. c pr. m.   ^{vv} that ć pr. m.   ^w amonestede E pr. m.   ^x Om. A.   ^y temple E.

^b the douȝter I.   ^c Om. I.   ^d riȝtwisnesse I.   ^e that I.   ^f Om. c.   ^g the wordis DI.   ^h that I.   ⁱ And I.
^k Om. c.   ^l the douȝter I.   ^m riȝtwisnesse I.   ⁿ the ydol Priapus I.   ^o mawmett wode I.   ^p that I.
^q brente it I.   ^r the hiȝ I.   ^s that I.   ^t and siluer I.

brou3te in tho thingis, the whiche his fader hadde halowid and vowede, into the hows of the Lord, siluer, and gold, and 16 vessels. Forsothe batayl there was betwix Asa and Baasa, kyng of Irael, alle 17 the dais of hem. Forsothe Baasa, the᙮ kyng of Yrael, stiede vp into Juda, and he beeldide Rama, that no man my3te goon out, or goon yn, fro the parti of 18 Asa, kyng of Juda. And so Asa takinge al the siluer and gold, that lafte in the tresours᙮ of the hows of the Lord, and in the tresours of the kyngis hows, 3af into the hoondis of hise seruauntis; and sente to Benadab, the sone of Trabemnon, the sone of Osyon, kyng of Cyrye, 19 that dwellide in Damasch, seiynge, Couenaunt of pees is betwix me and thee, and betwix my fader and thi fader, and therfor to thee I haue sent 3iftis, gold, and siluer; and I aske, that thou come, and make at nou3t the boond of pees, that thou hast with Baasa, the kyng of Irael, 20 and he goo awey fro me. Assentynge Benadab to kyng Asa, sente᙮ the princis of his oost into the citees of Yrael; and thei smiten Ahion, and Dayr, and Abel, and the hows of Maacha, and al Seneroth, that is, al the loond of Neptalym. 21 The which thing, whanne Baasa hadde herd, he lafte to beelde vp Rama, and 22 he turnede a3en into Tharsa. Forsothe kyng Asa sente a messager into al Juda, seiynge, No man be excusid. And thei token the stoonus of Rama, and the trees of it, with the whiche Baasa hadde beeldid; and kyng Asa made out of the same Gabaa of Beniamyn, and Maspha. 23 The remnaunt forsothe of alle the wordis of Asa, and of al᙮ his᙮ strength, and alle thingis that he dide, and the citees that he made vp, whethir not thes ben writen in the book of the wordis of the days of the kyngis of Juda? Neuerthelater in the tyme of his eelde he akide the feet.

and gold, and vessel᙮. Forsothe batel was 16 bitwixe Asa and Baasa, kyng of Israel, in alle the daies of hem. And Baasa, 17 kyng of Israel, stiede᙮ in to Juda, and bildide Rama, that᙮ no man of the part of Aza, kyng of Juda, my3te go out, ether go᙮ yn. Therfor Asa took al the siluer 18 and gold, that lefte in the tresouris of the hows of the Lord, and in the tresouris of the kyngis hows, and 3af it in to the hondis of hise seruauntis; and sente᙮ to Benadab, sone᙮ of Tabrennon, sone of Ozion, the kyng of Sirie, that dwellide in Damask, and seide, Boond᙮ of pees is bitwixe 19 me and thee, and bitwixe my fadir and thi fadir, and therfor Y sente to thee 3iftis, gold, and siluer; and Y axe, that thou come, and make voide the boond of pees, which᙮ thou hast with Baasa, kyng of Israel, and that he go awey fro me. Bena- 20 dab assentide to kyng Asa, and sente the princes of his oost in to the citees of Israel; and thei smytiden᙮ Ahion, and Dan, and Abel, the᙮ hows of Maacha, and al Cenoroth, that is, al the lond of Neptalym. And whanne Baasa hadde herd this thing, 21 he lefte to bilde Rama, and turnede a3en in to Thersa. Forsothe kyng Asa sente 22 message in to al Juda, and seide, No man be excusid. And thei token the stoonys of Rama, and the trees therof, bi whiche Baasa hadde bildid; and kyng Asa bildide of the same `stoonys and trees᙮ Gabaa of Beniamyn, and Maspha. Sotheli the re- 23 sidue of alle wordis᙮ of Asa, and of al his strengthe, and alle thingis whiche᙮ he dide, and the citees whiche he bildide, whether these ben not writun in the book of wordis of daies of kingis of Juda? Netheles Asa hadde ache in feet᙮†, in the tyme of his eelde. And Asa slepte with 24 hise fadris, and he was biried with hem in the citee of Dauid, his fader; and Josophat, his sone, regnede for him. Forsothe 25 Nadab, the sone of Jeroboam, regnede on᙮

† _Asa hadde ache in feet_: for he co- maundide Ana- nye the pro- fete to be sent in to stockis, that repreuyde him, for he tristide more in men than in God, as it is seid in II. book of Paralip. xvi. c᙮. _Lire here._ c.

᙮ Om. _A._   ᙮ tresories _CE._   ᙮ he sente _E pr. m._   ᙮ Om. _A._   ᙮ the _AFH._

᙮ vessels I.   ᙮ wente up I.   ᙮ and c.   ᙮ Om. I.   ᙮ he sente it I.   ᙮ the sone I.   ᙮ A boond I.   ᙮ that I.   ᙮ smeten EI. smiten L.   ᙮ and the I.   ᙮ _thingis_ I.   ᙮ the wordis I.   ᙮ that I.   ᙮ _his_ feet I.   ᙮ upon I.

24 And Asa slepte with his faders, and is biryed with hem in the citee of Dauid his fader; and Josaphath, his sone, regnede 25 for hym. Nadab forsothe, the sone of Jeroboam, regnede vpon Irael, the secounde ȝeer of Asa, the kyng of Juda; and he regnede vpon Yrael two ȝeer. 26 And he dide that is yuel in the siȝt of the Lord, and wente in the weies of his fader, and in the synnes of hym, in the 27 whiche he made Irael to synne. Forsothe Baasa, the sone of Ahia, of the hows of Ysachar, weytide to hym, and smoot hym in Jebethon, that is the citee of Philisteis; forsothe Naadab and al 28 Yrael besegiden Jebothon. Thanne Baasa slewȝ hym, in the thridde ȝeer of Asa, the kyng of Juda, and regnede for hym. 29 And whanne he hadde regned, he smoot al the hows of Jeroboam; and he laft not forsothe not oon lijf of his seed, to the tyme that he dide awey hym, after the word of the Lord, that he spak in the hoond of his seruaunt, Ahye Silonyte, 30 prophete, for the synnes of Jeroboam, the whiche he hadde synned, and with whiche he haddeᶠ made Irael to synnen, and for the trespas, in the which he hadde terred the Lord God of Yrael. 31 The remnaunt forsothe of the wordis of Naadab, and alle thingis that he wrouȝte, whether not thes ben wrytyn in the book of the wordis of the dais of the kyngis 32 of Yrael? And there was batail betwixe Asa and Baasa, king of Yrael, alle the 33 dais of hem. The thridde ȝeer of Asa, kyng of Juda, regnede Baasa, the sone of Ahia, vpon al Yrael, in Tharsa, foure 34 and twenti ȝeer. And he dide yuel before the Lord, and he wente in the weyesᵍ of Jeroboam, and in the synnes of hym, in the whiche he made Irael to synne.

Israel, inᵏ the secunde ȝeer of Asa, kingˡ of Juda; and he regnede on Israel two ȝeer. And he dide that, that was yuel in 26 the siȝt of the Lord, and he ȝede in the weies of his fadir, and in the synnes of hym, in whiche he máde Israel to do synne. Forsotheᵐ Baasa, the sone of 27 Ahia, of the hows of Ysachar, settide tresoun to hym, and smootⁿ him in Gebethon †, whichᵒ is a citee of Filisteis; sothelyᵖ Nadab and al Israel bisegiden Gebethon. Therfor Baasa killide hym�q, 28 in the thridde ȝeer of Asa, kingʳ of Juda, and regnede for hym. And whanne heᵗ 29 hadde regnede, he smoot al the hows of Jeroboam; heᵗ lefte notᵘ sotheliᵛ not o man of his seed, til he dide awei hym, bi the word of the Lord, whichʷ he spak in the hond of his seruaunt, Ahia of Silo, a profete, for the synnes of Jeroboam whicheˣ 30 he synnede, and in whiche he made Israel to doʸ synne, and for the trespas, bi which he wraththide the Lord God of Israel. Sotheli the residue of wordisᶻ of Nadab, 31 and alle thingis whiche he wrouȝte, whether these ben not writun in the book of wordis of daies of the kyngis of Israel? And batel was bitwixe Asa and Baasa, 32 kyng of Israel, in al the daies of hem. In the thridde ȝeer of Asa, kyng of Juda, 33 Baasa, soneᵃ of Ahia, regnede onᵇ al Israel, in Thersa, foure and twenti ȝeer. And he dide yuel bifor the Lord, and he 34 ȝede in the weies of Jeroboam, and in hise synnes, bi whiche he made Israel to do synne.

† in Gebethon; this was a citee in the lynage of Dan, but Filisteis occupieden it, a ȝenus which citee Nadab ȝede to rekenere it. Lire here. c.

ᶠ Om. A. ᵍ weye A.

ᵏ Om. c. ˡ the king I. ᵐ And I. ⁿ he smoot I. ᵒ that I. ᵖ and I. q Nadab I. ʳ the king I. ˢ Baasa I. ᵗ and he ᴋᴍᴡxç. and o. ᵘ Om. ᴅɪᴋᴍᴏꜱxç. ᵛ Om. oꜱᴡç. ʷ that I. ˣ the whiche I. ʸ Om. I. ᶻ the wordis I. ᵃ the sone cI. ᵇ upon I.

CAP. XVI.

1 Forsothe the word of the Lord is doon to Yau, the sone of Anany, aȝens Baasa,
2 seiynge, Forthi that I haue enhaunsid thee fro powdre, and sette thee duyk vpon Yrael, my puple; forsothe thow hast goon in the weie of Jeroboam, and hast maad my puple Irael to synne, that thow
3 terre me in the synnes of hem; and lo! I shal kitte of the hyndirmore of Baasa, and the hyndirmores of the hows of hym, and I shal make thin hows as the hows
4 of Jeroboam, the sone of Naabath. Who were deed of Baasa in[h] the citee, houndis shulen eete hym, and who were deed of hym in the regioun, the foulis of heuen
5 shulen ecte hym. Forsothe the remnaunt of the wordis of Baasa, and what euer thingis he dide, and the batayls of hym, whether not thes ben writyn in the bokis of the wordis of the dais of the kyngis of
6 Irael? Thanne Baasa slepte with his faders, and is biryed in Tharsa; and Hela
7 his sone, regnede for hym. Forsothe whanne in the hond[i] of Yau, the sone of Anany, the prophete, the word of the Lord was maad aȝens Baasa, and aȝens the hows of hym, and aȝens al the yuel that he hadde doon before the Lord, to terren hym in the werkis of his hondis, that he were maad as the hows of Jeroboam, for this cause he slewȝ hym, that is, Yau, the sone of Anany, the prophete.
8 The sixe and twentithe ȝeer of Asa, the kyng of Juda, regnede Hela, the sone of Baasa, vpon Yrael, in Tharsa, two ȝeer.
9 And aȝens hym rebellid Zamry, his seruaunt, duyk of the half partie of the horsmen; forsothe Hela was in Tharsa, drynkynge and drunken in the hows of
10 Arsa, prefect of Tharsa. Thanne Zamry fallinge on smoot, and slewȝ hym, the seuen and twentith ȝeer of Asa, kyng of

CAP. XVI.

Forsothe the word of the Lord was 1 maad to Hieu, sone[c] of Anany, aȝens Baasa, and seide, For that that Y reiside[d] thee 2 fro dust, and settide[e] thee duyk ou[f] Israel, my puple; sotheli thou ȝedist in the weie of Jeroboam, and madist[g] my puple Israel to do synne, that thou schuldist terre me to ire, in the synnes of hem; lo[h]! Y schal 3 kitte awey the hyndrere thingis of Baasa, and the hyndrere thingis of ʼhis hows[i], and Y schal make thin hows as the hows of Jeroboam, sone[k] of Nabath. Doggis[l] 4 schulen ete that man of Baasa, that schal be deed in citee[m], and briddis of the eyr schulen ete that man of Baasa, that schal die in the feeld. Sotheli the residue of 5 wordis[n] of Baasa, and what euer thingis he dide, and hise batels, whether these ben not writun in the book of wordis of daies of the kynges of Israel? Therfor[o] 6 Baasa slepte with hise fadris, and he was biried in Thersa; and Hela, his sone, regnede for hym. Forsothe whanne the 7 word of the Lord was maad in the hond of Hieu, sone[p] of Anany, aȝens Baasa, and aȝens his hows, and aȝens al yuel[q] which he dide bifor the Lord, to terre hym to ire in the werkis of hise hondis, that he schulde be as the hows of Jeroboam, for this cause he[r] killide hym, that is, Hieu†, the prophete, the sone of Anany. In the sixe and twentithe ȝeer of Aza, 8 kyng of Juda, Hela, the sone of Baasa, regnyde on[s] Israel, in Thersa, twei ȝeer. And Zamry, ʼhis seruaunt[t], duyk of the 9 half part of knyȝtis[u], rebellide aȝens hym; sotheli Hela was in Thersa, and drank, and was drunkun in the hows of Arsa, prefect[v] of Thersa. Therfor Zamri felde 10 in, and smoot[w], and killide hym, in the seuene and twentithe ȝeer of Asa, kyng of Juda; and regnede for hym. And whanne 11

† that is, Hieu, etc.; this sentence is not in Ebreu; it is a glos. In Ebreu it is, and for he killide Nadab, his lord, hi tresoun, as Rabi Salomon seith. Lire here. c.

h into E sec. m.　i loond ABFII.

c the sone I.　d haue upreisid I.　e sette I.　f upon I.　g thou hast made I.　h lo *herfore* I.　i the hows of him I.　k the sone I.　l houndis I.　m the citee CKL. a citee I.　n the wordis I.　o And so I. p the sone I.　q the yuel I.　r Baasa I.　s upon I.　t the seruaunt of Hela I.　u *his* knyȝtis I.　v a cheef officer I.　w smoot Hela I.

11 Jude; and he regnyde for hym. And whanne he hadde regned, and sitten vpon his see, he smoot al the hows of Baasa, and he lafte not of yt a pisser to the wal, and 'the kynne, and the freendis^k of hym. 12 And Zamri dide aweye al the hows of Baasa, after the word of the Lord, that he hadde spoken to Baasa, in the hoond 13 of Yau, the prophete, for alle the synnes of Baasa, and the synnes of Hela, his sone, the whiche synneden, and maden Israel to synne, terrynge the Lord God 14 of Israel in her vanitees. The remenaunt forsothe of the wordis of Hela, and alle thingis that he dide, whether not thes ben writin in the boke of the wordis of 15 the dais of the kyngis of Israel? The seuen and twentithe ȝeer of Asa, kyng of Juda, regnede Zamri seuen dais in Tharsa; forsothe an oost besegide Je-16 bethon, the citee of Philistees. And whanne it hadde herde Zamri to han rebellid, and to^l han sleyn the king, al Israel made to hem a kyng Amry, that was prince of the chyualri vpon Israel, in 17 that dai, in the tentis. Thanne Amri stiede vp, and al Israel with hym, fro 18 Jebethon, and segiden Tharsa. Forsothe Zamri seynge, that the cite was to be ouercomen, he wente in to the paleis, and brende vp him self with the kingis 19 hous; and is deed in his synnes that he synnede, doynge yuel before the Lord, and goynge in the weye of Jeroboam, and in the synnes of hym, by the whiche 20 he made Yrael to synne. The remnaunt forsothe of the wordis of Zamry, and of the spies of him, and of the tyraundise, whethir thes ben not writyn in the book of the wordis of the dais of the kyngys 21 of Yrael? Thanne the puple of Irael is deuydid^m in two parties; the half partye of the puple folwide Thebny, the sone of

he^x hadde regned, and hadde^y setun on^z his trone, he smoot al the hows of Baasa, and he^zz lefte not therof a pissere to the wal, and hise kynnesmen, and frendis. And^a 12 Zamri dide awey al the hows of Baasa, bi the word of the Lord, which^b he spak to Baasa, in the hond of Hieu, the pro- phete, for alle the synnes of Baasa, and 13 for the synnes of Hela, his sone, whiche^c synneden, and maden Israel to do^d synne, and wraththiden the Lord God of Israel in her vanytees. Sotheli the residue of 14 the wordis of Hela, and alle thingis whiche he dide, whether these ben not writun in the book of wordis of daies of the kyngis of Israel? In the seuene and twentithe 15 ȝeer of Aza, kyng of Juda, Zamri regnede seuene daies in Tharsa; forsothe the oost^e bisegide Gebethon, the citee of Philisteis. And whanne it^f hadde herd, that Zamri 16 hadde rebellid, and hadde slayn the kyng, al Israel made Amry kyng to hem^g, that was prince of^h the chyualrye, on^i Israel, in that dai, in 'the castels^k. Therfor Amry 17 stiede^l, and al Israel with hym, fro Gebe- thon, and bisegide Thersa. Sothely^m Zamri 18 siȝ, that the citee schulde be ouercomun, and he entride in to the palis, and brente hym silf with the kyngis hows; and he 19 was deed in hise synnes whiche he syn- nede, doynge yuel bifor the Lord, and goynge^n in the weie of Jeroboam, and in hise synnes, bi whiche he made Israel to do synne. Sotheli the residue of wordis^o 20 of Zamri, and of his tresouns, and tyraun- trie, whether these ben not writun in the book of wordis of daies of the kyngis of Israel? Thanne the puple of Israel was 21 departid in to twei partis; the half part of the^p puple suede Thebny, sone^q of Ge- neth, to make hym kyng, and the half^r part suede Amry. Sotheli^s the puple that 22 was with Amry, hadde maystry^t ouer the

---

k the neeȝ freendis *E pr. m.*   l Om. *A.*   m deuyd *A.*

x Zamry 1.   y Om. 1.   z upon 1.   zz Om. c.   a *Also* and 1.   b that 1.   c the whiche 1.   d Om. 1.
e oost of Israel 1.   f the Philistees 1.   g *the* oost 1.   h on A.   i upon 1.   k her tentis 1.   l stiede
up 1.   m And 1.   n in goynge 1.   o the wordis 1.   p Om. 1.   q the sone 1.   r *oother* half 1.   s And 1.
t the maystry 1.

Jeneth, that he ordeyne hym kyng, and 22 the half parti Amry. Forsothe the puple that was with Amry hadde the ouerhoond ouer the puple that folwide Thebny, the sone of Jeneth; and Thebny 23 is deed, and Amry regnede. The oon and threttyⁿ ʒeer of Asa, kyng of Juda, regnede Amry vpon Yrael, twelue ʒeer; 24 in Tharsa he regnede sixe ʒeer. And he bouʒte the hille of Samarye of Somer for two talentis of siluer, and he beeldide^o it; and he clepide the name of the citee, that he bieldide^o vp, by the name of Somer, that is, the hil of the Lord, or 25 the hil of Samarye. Forsothe Amry dide yuel in the siʒt of the Lord, and he wroʒte wickidly, ouer alle that weren 26 before hym. And he wente in al the weye of Jeroboam, the sone of Nabath, and in the synnes of hym, bi the whiche he made Irael to synne, that he terre the 27 Lord God of Irael in his vanitees. The remnaunt forsothe of the wordis of Amry, and the batailis of hym, that he dide, whether not thes ben wryten in the book of the wordis of the dais of the kyngis 28 of Irael? And Amry slepte with his faders, and is biried in Samarye; and 29 Achab, his sone, regnede for hym. Achab forsothe, the sone of Amry, regnede on Irael the eiʒt and thrittithe ʒeer of Asa, kyng of Juda; and Achab, the sone of Amry, regnede vpon Irael, in Samarie, 30 two and twenti ʒeer. And Achab, the sone of Amry, dide yuel in the siʒt of the Lord, ouer alle that weren before 31 hym; ne it suffiside to hym that he ʒede in the synnes of Jeroboam, the sone of Naaboth, but 'more ouere^{oo} he weddide a wijf, Jezabel, the douʒter of Methaal, kyng of Sydonyes; and he wente, and 32 seruede to Baal, and honourde hym. And he sette an auter of Baal in the temple of Baal, that he hadde beeldid^p vp in Sa-

puple that suede Thebny, the sone of Geneth; and Thebny was deed, and Amri regnede. In the oon and thrittithe ʒeer 23 of Aza, kyng of Juda, Amri regnede on^u Israel, twelue ʒeer; in Thersa he regnede sixe ʒeer. And he bouʒte of Soomeer, for 24 twei talentis of siluer, the hil of Samarie, and 'bildide that hil^v; and he clepide the name of the citee, which^w he hadde bildid, bi the name of Soomer, lord of the hil of Samarie. Forsothe Amri dide yuel in 25 the siʒt of the Lord, and wrouʒte wei-wardli^x, ouer^y alle men that weren bifor hym. And he ʒede in al the weie of Jero- 26 boam, sone^z of Nabath, and in hise synnes, bi whiche he made Israel to do synne, that he schulde terre to ire, in his vany-tees, the Lord God of Israel. Forsothe 27 the residue of wordis^a of Amry, and hise batels, which he dide, whether these ben not writun in the book of wordis of daies of the kyngis of Israel? And Amry slepte 28 with hise fadris, and was biried in Samarie; and Achab, his sone, regnede for hym. Forsothe Achab, the sone of Amry, regn- 29 ede on^b Israel, in the 'eiʒte and thrittithe ʒeer^c of Asa, kyng of Juda; and Achab, sone^d of Amry, regnede on^e Israel, in Samarie, two and twenti ʒeer. And Achab, 30 sone^f of Amry, dide yuel in the siʒte of the Lord, ouer alle men that weren bifor hym; and it suffiside not to hym that he 31 ʒede in the synnes of Jeroboam, sone^g of Nabath, ferthermore and he weddide a wijf, Jezabel, the douʒter of Methaal, kyng of Sydoneis; and he^h ʒede, and seruyde Baal, and worschipide hym. And he set- 32 tideⁱ an auter to Baal in the temple of Baal, which^k he hadde bildid in Samarie; and he plauntide a wode^l; and Achab add- 33 ide^m in his werk, and terride to ire the Lord God of Israel, more^o thanne alle kyngis^o of Israel that weren bifor hym. Forsothe in hise daies Ahiel of Bethel 34

ⁿ thrittithe BCEFH.　^o bilde c passim.　^{oo} oueremore BEF.　^p bild c passim.

^u upon I.　^v he bildide it I.　^w that I.　^x wickidly I.　^y bifore I.　^z the sone I.　^a the wordis BCI.　^b upon I,　^c eiʒthe and thretti K.　^d the sone I.　^e upon I.　^f the sone I.　^g the sone I.　^h Achab I.　ⁱ sette up I,　^k that I.　^l mawmet wode I.　^m addide to I.　ⁿ ouer I.　^o the kyngis I.

33 marye, and he plauntide a maumet
wode; and Achab addide in his werke,
terrynge the Lord God of Yrael, ouer
alle the kyngis of Irael that weren before
34 hym. In the dais forsothe of hym Ahiel
of Bethel beeldide vp Jericho; in Abiram,
his fyrst goten, he foundide it, and in
Segub, his last, he sette the ʒatis of it,
after the word of the Lord, that he hadde
spokyn in the hoond of Josue, the sone
of Nun.

bildide Jerico; in[o] Abiram, his[p] firste *sone*†, he foundide it, in[q] Segub, his[r] laste *sone*, he settide ʒatis[s] therof, bi the word of the Lord, which[t] he hadde spoke in the hond of Josue, sone[u] of Nun.

CAP. XVII.

1 And Helias Tesbites, of the dwellers
of Galaad, seide to Achab, The Lord God
of Yrael lyueth, in whos siʒt Y stond[q],
if there shal be thes ʒeeris dewe and
reyn, but after the wordis of my mouth.
2 And the word of the Lord is maad to
3 hym, seynge, Go aweye hens, and go
aʒens the est, and be hidde in the streem
4 of Carith, that is aʒens Jordan, and there
thou shalt drynke of the streem; and to
the crowis I haue comaundide, that thei
5 feden thee there. Thanne he wente, and
dide after the word of the Lord; and
whanne he hadde gon, he sat in the
streem of Carith, that is aʒens Jordan.
6 And the crowis brouʒten to hym breed
and flesh erly; also at euen; and he
7 dranke of the streem. Forsothe after
summe days the streem is dryed; forsothe it hadde not reyned vpon erthe[r].
8 Thanne the word of the Lord is do to
9 hym, seiynge, Ryis, and go 'into[rr] Sarept
of Sidonyes, and thow shalt dwelle there;
forsothe I haue comaundid there to a
womman widowe, that she fede thee.
10 And he roos, and wente into Serept of
Sydonyes; and whanne he was comyn to
the ʒate of the citee, a womman widowe
aperide to hym gederynge stickis; and
he clepide hire, and seide to[s] hir, ʒif to
me a litil of water in a vessel, that I
11 drynke. And whanne she wente, that

CAP. XVII.

And Elie 'of Thesbi[v], of the dwelleris 1
of Galaad, seide to Achab, The Lord God
of Israel lyueth, in whos siʒt Y stonde,
deeu and reyn schal not be in these ʒeeris,
no but bi the wordis of my mouth. And 2
the word of the Lord was maad to hym[w],
and seide, Go thou awey fro hennus‡, and 3
go aʒens the eest, and be thou hid in the
stronde of Carith, which[x] is aʒens Jordan, and there thou schalt drynke of the 4
stronde; and Y comaundide[y] to crowis,
that thei feede thee there. Therfor he[z] 5
ʒede, and dide bi the word of the Lord;
and whanne he hadde go, he sat in the
stronde of Carith, which[a] is aʒens Jordan.
And crowis baren to hym breed and fleisch 6
eerli; in[b] lijk maner in the euentid; and
he drank of the stronde. Forsothe[c] after 7
summe daies the stronde was dried; for it
hadde not reynede on the erthe. Therfor 8
the word of the Lord was maad to hym[d],
and seide, Rise thou, and go in to Serepta 9
of Sydoneis, and thou schalt dwelle there;
for Y comaundide[e] to a womman, widewe
there, that sche feede thee. He[f] roos, 10
and ʒede in to Sarepta of Sidoneis; and
whanne he hadde come to the ʒate of
the citee, a womman widewe gaderynge
stickis apperide to hym; and he clepide
hir, and seide to hir, ʒyue thou to me a
litil of water in a vessel, that Y drynke.
And whanne sche ʒede to bringe[g], he 11

† *in Abiram his firste sone*; that is, whanne he settide the foundementis, Abiram, his firste gendrid sone, diede, and whanne he ʒede forth in bildinge, hise sones dieden ech aftir other, til to the laste sone, that was deed in the filling of the werk. *Lire here.* c.

‡ *go thou awei fro hennes*; fro the face of Achab and of Jezabel; and herbi it is leueful to hooli men, to fle persecucioun of her persoones. *Lire here.* c.

[q] stood *A*. [r] the erthe BEFH. [rr] in E *pr. m.* [s] Om. *A*.

[o] and A *pr. m.* DEFGLMNPQRSUWXbç. [p] to his K *sec. m.* [q] and CGIK. [r] to his K *sec. m.* [s] the ʒatis I. [t] that I. [u] the sone I. [v] Thesbithes I. [w] Hely I. [x] that I. [y] haue comaundid I. [z] Hely I. [a] that I. [b] and in I. [c] And I. [d] Hely I. [e] haue comaundid I. [f] Hely I. [g] bringe it I. bringe *him watir* K.

she brynge to, he criede bihynde the bak
of hir, seiynge, Bryng to me, I beseche,
and a morsel of breed in thin hoond.
12 The which answerde, The Lord thy God
lyueth, for I haue not breed, but as myche
as an handful may take of mele in a
stene, and a litil of oyle in an oyle vessel; loo¹ I gedre stikkis, that I goo yn,
and make it to me, and to my sone, that
13 we eten and dien   To whom seith Helias, Wole thou not drede, but go, and
do as thow hast seid, neuerthelater to
me first make of that litil mele a litil loof,
baken vndre the*t* asshen*u*, and bryng to
me; forsothe to thee and to thi sone
14 thou shalt make afterward Thes thingis
forsothe seith the Lord God of Irael,
The stene of mele shal no3t fayle, ne the
vessel of oyle shal not be mynushid, vnto
the day in the which the Lord is to 3yue
15 reyn vpon the face of the erthe. The
which wente, and dide after the word of
Helye, and he ete, and she, and hir*v*
16 howis And fro that dai the steen of mele
failide not, and the vessel of oile is not
mynushid, after the word of the Lord,
that he hadde spokyn in the hoond of
17 Helye It is doon forsothe after thes
wordis, the sone of an huswijf womman
wexe sijk, and the langour was moost
strong, so that there lafte not in hym
18 breeth Thanne she seide to Helias,
What to me and to thee, thou man of
God? Thou wentist into me, that my
wickidnesses shulden be remembrid, and
19 thou shuldist slee my sone   And Helias
seith to hire, 3if to me thi sone   And
he took him fro hir bosum, and bare
in to the sowping place, where he dwellide, and putte hym vpon his litil bed
20 And he criede to the Lord, and seide,
Lord, my God, also whether*w* the widowe,
anentis whom Y 3it am susteyned, thou
hast tourmentid, that thow slee the sone
21 of hire? And he sprade out hym self,

criede bihynde hir bac, and seide, Y biseche, bringe thou to me also a mussel of
breed in thin hond   And sche answeride, 12
Thi Lord God lyueth, for Y haue no
breed, no but as myche of mele in a pot,
as a fist may take, and a litil of oile in a
vessel; lo¹ Y gadere twei stickis, that Y
entre, and make it to me, and to my sone,
that*h* we ete and die   And Elie seide to 13
hir, Nyle thou drede, but go, and make
as thou seidist, netheles make thou firste
to me of that litil mele a litil loof, bakun
vndur the' aischis*J*, and brynge thou*k* to
me, sotheli thou schalt make afterward
to thee and to thi sone Forsothe the 14
Lord God of Israel seith thes thingis,
The pot of mele schal not faile, and the
vessel of oile schal not be abatid, til to
the dai in which the Lord schal 3yue reyn
on the face of erthe*l* And sche 3ede, and 15
dide bi the word of Elie; and he*m* eet,
and sche, and hir howis And fro that dai 16
the pot of mele failide not, and the vessel
of oile was not abatid, bi the word of the
Lord, which*n* he hadde spoke in the hond
of Elie Forsothe it was doon aftir these 17
wordis, the sone of a womman hosewijf
was sijk, and the syknesse was moost*o*
strong, so that breeth*p* dwellide not in
hym Therfor sche seide to Elie, What 18
to me and to thee, thou man of God?
Entridist*q* thou to me, that my wickidnessis*qq* schulden be remembrid, and that
thou schuldist sle my sone? And Elie 19
seide to hir, 3yue thi sone to me   And
he took 'that *sone*r fro hir bosum, and bar*s*
in to the soler, where he dwellide; and he
puttide*t* hym on his bed And he criede 20
to the Lord, and seide, My Lord God,
whether thou hast turmentid also the widewe, at*u* whom Y am susteyned in al
maner, that thou killidist hir sone? He*v* 21
spiad abrood hym silf, and mat*w* on the
child bi thre tymes; and he cryede to the
Lord, and seide, My Lord God, Y biseche,

' Om *cefii*   *u* ashes c   *v* his A   *w* lest E pi m.

---

b and I   *i* Om DGIKNNOQwbç   J aisshen G   *k* thou it I   *l* the erthe I   *m* Hely I   *n* that I
o ful I   P the breeth I   q Hast thou entrid I   qq wickidnesse CL   *r* it I   *s* bar it I   *t* putte I
u anentis I   *v* Hely I   *w* was metid up I   maat L

and mesurede vpon the child thre sithis, and criede to the Lord, and seith, Lord my God, the soule of this child, Y beseche, be turned aȝen into the bowels of 22 hym. And the Lord herde the voys of Helias, and the soule of the child is turned aȝen with ynne hym, and he aȝen 23 quikenyde. And Helias took the child, and putte it doun fro the sowpyng place in to the nedre hows, and took to his moder; and he seith to hire, Lo! thi 24 sone lyueth. And the womman seide to Helias, Now in this Y haue knowe, for the man of God thow ert, and the word of God in thi mouth is sothe.

CAP. XVIII.

1 Aftir manye dais the word of the Lord is doo to Helias, in the thridde ȝeer, seiynge, Go, and shewe thee to Achab, that I ȝeue reyn vpon the face of the erthe. 2 Thanne Helias wente that he shewe hym to Achab; forsothe there was hidows 3 hungre in Samarye. And Achab clepide Abdiam, the stiward of his hows; forsothe Abdias dradde the Lord God of 4 Yrael myche. For whanne Jesabel shulde slee the prophetis of the Lord, he took an hundrid prophetis, and hidde hem, fifti and fifti, in dennys, and he fedde 5 hem with breed and water. Thanne Achab seide to Abdias, Go in to the loond, to alle the welles of watris, and into alle valeis, if peradventure we mowen fynde herbe, and saue hors and mulis; 6 and the beestis fulli dien not. And thei deuydeden the regiouns to ˣ hem self, that thei goon about hem; Achab wente bi o weye, and Abdias bi another, aside. 7 And whanne Abdias was in the weie, Helias aȝen cam to hym; the which whanne he hadde knowen hym, he felle vpon his face, and seith, Whethir thou 8 art my lord Helias? To whom he answerde, Y. And he seide, Go, and sey

the soule of this child turne aȝen in to the entrailis of hym. The Lord herde the 22 vois of Elie, and the soule of the child turnede aȝen with ynne hym, and he lyuede aȝen. And Elie took the child, 23 and puttideˣ hym doun of the soler in to the lower hows, and bitook himʸ to his modir; and he seide to hir, Lo! thi sone lyueth. And the womman seide to Elie, 24 Now in this Y haue knowe, that thou art theˣ man of God, and the word of Godᵃ is soth in thi mouth.

CAP. XVIII.

Aftir many daies the word of the Lord 1 was maad to Elie, in the thridde ȝeer†, and seide, Go, and schewe thee to Achab, that Y ȝyue reyn onᵇ the face of ertheᶜ. Therfor Elie ȝede to schewe hym silfᵈ to 2 Achab; forsotheᵉ greetᶠ hungur was in Samarie. And Achab clepide Abdie, dis- 3 pendereᵍ, etherʰ stiward, of his hows; forsothe Abdie dredde greetli the Lord God of Israel. For whanne Jezabel killide the 4 prophetis of the Lord, he took an hundrid prophetis, and hidde hem, bi fifties and fifties, in dennes, and fedde hem with breed and watir. Therforˡ Achab seide 5 to Abdie, Go thou in to the lond, to alle wellisᵏ of watris, and in to alle valeis, if in hap we moun fynde gras, and saue horsis and mulis; and werk beestis perische not outirli. Therforˡ thei depart- 6 iden the cuntreis to hem silf, that thei schulden cumpasse tho; Achab ȝede bi o weye, and Abdie ȝede bi another weie, 'bi hym silfᵐ. And whanne Abdie was in 7 the weie, Elie mette hym; and whanne he hadde knowe Elie, he felde on his face, and seide, Whethir thou art my lord Elie? To whom he answeride, Y am. And Elie 8 seide, Go thou, and seie to thi lord, Elie

† in the thridde ȝeer; this tyme is rekenyd fro the goyng out of Elie fro the lond of Israel; and fro the forbedding of reyn, til to his goyng out, passiden vi. monethis and more; for he was hid longe in the stronde of Sarith, so that of the drienesse of tyme the stronde was dried, bifor that he ȝede awey, as it is seid in xvij. cᵒ. bifore. For James seith in v. cᵒ. that Elie preiede, and it reynede not til iii. ȝeer and vi. monethis. Lire here. c.

ˣ of A.

x putte 1. y Om. plures. z a 1. ᵃ the Lord A. ᵇ upon 1. ᶜ the erthe 1. ᵈ Om. oɪκмɴosþç. ᵉ certis 1. ᶠ a greet x. ᵍ the dispendere 1. Om. c. ʰ Om. c. ˡ Thanne 1. ᵏ the wellis 1. ˡ And 1. ᵐ aside halff 1.

9 to thi lord, Helias is neeȝ. And he, What haue I synned, he seith, for thou takist me, thi sernaunt, in the hoond of 10 Achab, that he slee me? The Lord thi God lyueth, for there is not folk or rewme, in the whiche my lord hath not sent, sechynge thee; and alle men answer-ynge, He is not here, he hath adiurid alle rewmes 'and folkis^y, for thi that thou art 11 not foundun; and now thou seist to me, Go, and sey to thi lord, Helie is neiȝ. 12 And whanne I shal goo aweye fro me, the Spiryt of the Lord shal bere thee aweye into a^z place that I knowe not; and Y goon yn, shal telle to Achab, and not fyndynge thee, he shal slee me; thi seruaunt forsothe dredith the Lord fro 13 his ȝongth. Whethir is it^zz not shewid to thee, my lord, what I haue doon, whanne Jesabel shulde slee the prophetis of the Lord, that I hidde of the prophetis of the Lord an hundrid men, fifti and fifti, in dennys, and fedde hem with breed 14 and water? And now thow seist, Go, and sey to thi lord, Helye is neiȝ, that 15 he slee me. And Helyas seide, The Lord of oostis lyueth, before whos cheer I stonde, for to day Y shal apere to hym. 16 Thanne Abdias wente into the^a aȝen comynge of^b Achab, and shewide to hym; and Achab cam into the^c aȝen comynge 17 to Helye. And whanne he hadde seen hym, seith, Whether art thou not he, that 18 disturblist Irael? And he seith, I haue not disturblid Irael, but thow, and the hows of thi fader, that hast forsakyn the hestis^d of the Lord, and ȝe han folowid 19 Baalym. Neuerthelater now send, and gadre to me al Yrael, in the hil of Car-mele, and the prophetis of Baal foure hundrid and fifti, and the prophetis of mawmet wodis foure hundrid, that eten 20 of the bord of Jezebel. Achab sente to alle the sonys of Yrael, and gaderide the 21 prophetis in the hil of Carmele. For-

is present. And Abdie seide, What 'syn-9 nede Y^n, for thou bitakist me in the hond of Achab, that he sle me? Thi Lord God 10 lyueth, for no folk ethir rewme is, whidur my lord, sekynge thee, sente not; and whanne alle men answeriden, He is not here, he^o chargide^p greetli alle rewmes† and folkis, for thou were not foundun; and now thou seist to me, Go^q, and seie to 11 thi lord, Elie is present^r. And whanne 12 Y schal departe fro thee, the Spirit of the Lord schal bere thee awey in to a place which^s Y knowe not; and Y schal entre, and 'Y schal^t telle to Achab, and he schal not fynde thee, and he schal sle me; for-sothe^u thi seruaunt dredith the Lord fro his ȝong childhod. Whether it is not 13 schewid to thee, my lord, what Y dide, whanne Jesabel killide the prophetis of the Lord, that Y hidde of the^uu prophetis of the Lord an hundrid men, bi fifty and bi^v fifti, in dennes, and Y fedde hem with breed and watir? And now thou seist, 14 Go, and seie to thi lord, Elie is present^w, that he sle me. And Elie seide, The Lord 15 of oostis lyueth, bifor whos siȝt Y stonde, for to dai Y schal appere to hym^x. Ther-16 for Abdie ȝede in to the metyng of Achab, and schewide^y to hym; and Achab cam in to the meetyng of Elie. And whanne 17 he hadde seyn Elie, he seide, Whether thou art he, that disturblist Israel? And 18 he^z seide, Not Y disturble Israel, but thou, and the hows of thi fadir‡, whiche^a han forsake the comaundementis of the Lord, and sueden^b Baalym, 'disturbliden Israel^c. Netheles now sende thou, and gadere to 19 me al Israel, in^d the hil of Carmele, and foure^c hundrid and fifti prophetis of Baal, and foure hundrid prophetis of woodis^f§, that eten of the table of Jezabel. ·Achab 20 sente to alle the sones of Israel, and ga-deride prophetis^g in the hil of Carmele. Forsothe Elie neiȝede to al the puple of 21 Israel, and seide, Hou long halten ȝe in

† all rewmes; this is vndir-stondun of rewmes nyȝ him; and Achab chargide hem gretly, that if Elie were foundun in the lond, he schulde be takun, and sent to him. Lire here. c.

‡ thou and the hows of thi fadir; for the Lord sente this veniaunce, for thi malice. Lire here. c.

§ profetis of woodis; that is, of idols in the woodis. Lire here. c.

y Om. E pr. m.   z the A.   zz Om. B.   a Om. CE.   b to CE.   c Om. BCEFH.   d hest ABFII.

n haue I synned I.   o the kyng I.   p hath chargid I.   q Go thou C.   r nyȝ I.   s that I.   t Om. I.   u certis I.   uu tho C.   v Om. IKORUX.   w nyȝ I.   x Achab I.   y schewide it I.   z Hely I.   a the whiche I.   b suen I.   c Om. I.   d into I.   e the foure I.   f mawmet woodis I.   g togidre the prophetis I.

sothe Helie comynge ny3 to al the puple
of Yrael, seith, How long halt 3e into
two parties? If the Lord is God, folwith
hym; forsothe if Baal, folwith hym.
And the puple answerde not to hym a
22 word. And eft Elias seith to the puple,
I am laft a prophet of the Lord alone;
the prophetis forsothe of Baal foure hundryd and fifti, and the prophetis of maw-
23 mete wodis ben foure hundrid. Be there
3ouen to vs two oxen; and chese thei oon
oxe, and hewynge in gobetis thei shulen
leye vpon trees, forsothe fier vndurputen
thei not; and Y shal make anothir oxe,
and putten vpon trees, and fier I shal
24 not putte vndur. Inwardly clepe 3e the
name of 3owre goddis, and I shal inwardly
clepe the name of my God; and God that
herith bi the fier, he be God. Al the
puple answerynge seith, Best the propo-
25 sicioun, that Helias spac. Thanne Helias
seide to the prophetis of Baal, Chesith
to 3ou an oxe, and doth first, for 3e ben
moo; and inwardli clepith the namys of
3oure goddis, and puttith not vndir fier.
26 The whiche whanne thei hadden take
the oxe, that he 3af hem, thei diden, and
inwardli clepiden the name of Baal, fro
erly vnto myddai, seiynge, Baal, here vs!
And there was not voys that shulde answere; and thei skipten ouer the auter,
27 that thei maden. And whanne now was
myddai, Helye scornyde to hem, seiynge,
Crieth with a more voys, forsothe 3oure
god is, and perauenture with another he
spekith, or in a turnynge in place, or in
the weye, or certis he slepith, that he be
28 wakid. Thanne thei crieden with a greet
voys, and thei cuttiden hem self, after
her rijt, with sheeris and litil launcis, to
the tyme that thei weren alle beshed
29 with blood. Forsothe aftir that mydday
was passid, and hem propheciynge, the

to twey partis? If the Lord is God†, sue
3e hym; forsothe if Baal is God, sue 3e
hym. And the puple answeride not o
word to hym. And Elie seide eft to the 22
puple, Y dwellide aloone a prophete of
the Lord; sotheli the prophetis of Baal
ben foure hundrid and fifti, and the prophetis of woodis ben foure hundrid men.
Tweyne oxis be 3ouun to us; and chese 23
thei oon oxe, and thei schulen kitte in to
gobetis, and schulen putte on trees, but
putte thei not fier vndur; and Y schal
make the tother oxe in to sacrifice, and Y
schal putte on the trees, and Y schal
not putte fier vnder. Clepe 3e the name 24
of 3oure goddis, and Y schal clepe the
name of my God; and the God that herith
bi fier†, be he God. And al the puple
answeride, and seide, The resoun is best,
'which resoun' Elie spak. Therfor Elie 25
seide to the prophetis of Baal, Chese 3e
oon oxe to 3ou, and make 3e first, for 3e
ben the mo; and clepe 3e the names of
3oure goddis, and putte 3e not fier vnder.
And whanne thei hadden take the oxe§, 26
whom Elie 3af to hem‖, thei maden sacrifice, and clepiden the name of Baal, fro
the morewtid 'til to' myddai, and seiden,
Baal, here vs! And no vois was, nether
ony that answerd; and thei skippiden
ouer the auter, which thei hadden maad.
And whanne it was thanne myddai, Elie 27
scornede hem, and seide, Crie 3e with
gretter vois, for Baal is 3oure god, and
in hap he spekith with an other, ethir he
is in a herborgerie, ether in weie, ether
certis he slepith, that he be reisid. Ther- 28
for thei crieden with greet vois, and thei
kerueden hem silf with knyues and laun-
cetis, bi her custom, til thei weren bisched
with blood. Sotheli after that mydday 29
passide, and while thei prophesieden, the
tyme cam, in which the sacrifice is wont

Side notes (right margin):
† if the Lord is God; that is, if it is proued to 3ou by a visible myracle, that God of Is-rael is veri God, and not Baal. Sue 3e him; in wor-schipinge him, and noon other. Lire here. c.

‡ bi fier; 3ouun fro heuene, to waste the sacri-fice. Lire here. c.

§ and whanne thei hadden take the oxe; the false pro-fetis token the setting forth of Elye, for thei weren compellid of the puple to do this, which ap-preueden the resoun set forth of Elie, and for they tristiden in the power of the feend, which may do siche thingis, whanne he is suffrid of God. Wherfor and in the tyme of auntecrist, he schal make fier to come doun fro heuene, as it is had in xiii, cᵒ. of Apoc, and in hap at the cleping of hem, the feend dide lijk thing in another tyme. Lire here. c.

‖ whom Elie 3af to hem; for the oxe chosun for the prestis of Baal, fledde fro hem, and hidde him vn-dur the mentel of Elie, for the wlating of idolatrie; and thanne Elie 3af to hem, to conuyctyng of falsnesse of idolatrie, and to schewing of truthe of Goddis wor-schiping. Lire here. c.

c is besye A.

e and 1. f haue dwellid 1. g and 1. b the mawmet woodis 1. i Om. 1L. k putte it 1. l wode 1. m putte it 1. n vpon 1. o wode 1. p 3e thanne 1. PP names 1. q fier fallinge doun 1. r that 1. s lmth spoken 1. t an 1. u first 3oure sacrifice 1. v the prophetis 1. w that 1. x ynwardly clepiden 1. y vnto 1. z the mydday 1. a herde A pr. m. ncv. b the prophetis 1. c that 1. d forsothe 1. e the weie 1. f reisid vp 1. g kitten 1. h after 1. i But 1. k prophesieden, or preicden 1.

tyme was[f] comen, the which is wont sacrifice to be offrid, and vois is not herd, ne eny man answerde, ne took heed to 30 the praiynge. And Helye seide to al[g] the puple, Cometh to me. And the puple neiȝynge to hym, he curede the auter of 31 the Lord, that was destruyed. And he took twelue stonus, after the noumbre of the lynagis of the sonys of Jacob, to whom the word of the Lord is maad, 32 seiynge, Yrael shal be thi name. And he beeldide vp an auter of stonus, in name of the Lord, and he made a water cundid, as by two litil forwis in enuy- 33 roun of the auter. And he putte togidre the wode, and he deuydide bi membris 34 the oxe, and leide vpon the wode, and seith, Fillith foure stenys with water, and heeldith vpon the brent sacrifice, and vpon the wode. And eft he seide, Also the secounde doth this. The which whanne thei hadden doo the secounde, he seith, Also the thridde that same thing doth; and thei diden the thridde. 35 And the watris runnen aboute the auter, and the dijch of the water cundid is 36 fillid. And whanne now was tyme, that brent sacrifice shulde be offred[h], the pro- phete Helias comynge nyȝ seith, Lord God of Abraham, and of Ysaac, and of Yrael, to day shew for thow art God of Yrael, and Y thi seruaunt, and after thin 37 heest haue[i] doon alle thes wordis. Here me, Lord; here me, Lord; that this pu- ple lerne, for thou art Lord God, and thou hast conuertid the herte of hem eft- 38 sonys. Forsothe the[k] fijr of the Lord felle, and deuowride[l] the brent sacrifice, and the wode, and the stonus, forsothe the powdre, and the water that was in 39 the water cundid lickynge. The which thing whanne al the puple hadde seen,

to be offrid, nether vois was herd 'of her goddis[1], nether ony answeride, nether per- ceyuede hem preiynge. Elie seide to al 30 the puple, Come ȝe to me. And whanne the puple cam to him, he arrayede the auter of the Lord, that was distried. And 31 he took twelue stonys, bi the noumbre of[m] lynagis of sones[n] of Jacob[o], to which[p] Jacob the word of the Lord was maad, and seide, Israel schal be thi name. And 32 he[q] bildide an auter of stonys[r], in the name of the Lord, and he made a ledyng to[s] of watir, 'ether a dich[w], as bi[x] twei litle dichis[y]† in the cumpas of the auter. And he dresside trees[z], and he departide 33 the oxe bi membris, and puttide[a] on[b] the trees[c], and seide, Fille ȝe foure pottis with 34 watir, and schede[d] ȝe[e] on[f] the brent sacri- fice, and on[g] the trees[h]. And eft he seide, Also the secounde tyme do ȝe this. 'And thei diden[i] the secounde tyme. And[k] he seide, Do ȝe the same thing[l] the thridde tyme; and thei diden the thridde tyme. And the watris runnen aboute the auter, 35 and the dich[m] of ledyng to[n] 'of watir[o] was fillid. And whanne the tyme was thanne, 36 that the brent sacrifice schulde be offrid, Elye the prophete neiȝede, and seide, Lord God of Abraham‡, of Isaac, and of Israel, schewe thou to dai that thou art God of Israel, and that Y am thi seruaunt, and haue do alle these wordis bi thi comaunde- ment. Lord, here thou me; Lord, here 37 thou me; that this puple lerne, that thou art the Lord God, and that[p] thou hast conuertid eft the herte of hem. Sotheli 38 fier of the Lord felde doun[q], and deuouride brent[r] sacrifice, and[s] trees[t], and stonus[u], and lickide[v] vp also the poudre, and the water that was in the 'leding of watir[w]. And whanne al the puple hadde seyn this, 39 it[x] felde in to his face, and seide, The Lord

† twey litle dichis, etc.; in Ebreu it is thus, and he made a forow of iii. buyschelis of seed, that is, so myche seed myȝte be sowun withynne the cumpas of the forow, as Rabi Salomon seith. Lire here. c.

‡ Lord God of Abraham, etc.; me bileueth that Elie made this preyer an hiȝ, that the puple myȝte here, to the onour of God, and to the conuersioun of the puple. Bi thi comaundement; in offringe in hiȝe placis with out Jerusalem, aftir the bild- ing of the temple; which thing was vn- leueful, no but of special dis- pensacioun of God, which thing Elie dide in this poynt, and the Lord schewide this, bi fier comynge doun on the brent sacrifice of him. Lire here. c.

---

[f] is ᴀ. [g] Om. ᴀ. [h] brent ᴀ. [i] Y haue ᴇ pr. m. [k] Om. ᴀ. [l] rowrede ᴄᴇ.

[1] Om. ɪ. [m] and ᴀ. of the ɪ. [n] the sones ᴄᴇɪᴋʟᴍb. [o] Israel ᴍ. [p] the which ɪ. [q] Hely ɪ. [r] thilke stonys ɪ. [s] Om. ᴀᴇᴏ pr. m. [w] Om. ɪ. [x] Om. ɪ. [y] forowis ɪ. dikis s. [z] wode ɪ. [a] putte it ɪ. [b] upon ɪ. [c] wode ɪ. [d] heelde ɪ. [e] ȝe it ɪ. [f] upon ɪ. [g] upon ɪ. [h] wode ɪ. [i] Whiche whanne thei hadden do ɪ. [k] Om. ɪʟ. [l] thing also ɪ. [m] ridde ɪ. [n] Om. ᴀᴇʟ. [o] Om. ɢɪᴋqb. [p] Om. ᴀᴇʟᴘ. [q] doun thanne ɪ. [r] the brent ɪ. [s] Om. ɪ. [t] the wode ɪ. [u] the stonus ɪ. [v] it lickide ɪ. [w] watir ridde ɪ. [x] the peple ɪ marg.

he felle in to his face, and seith, The Lord he is God; the Lord he is God. 40 And Helias seide to hem, Takith the^m prophetys of Baal; ne oon forsothe flee aweye of hem. Whom whanne thei hadden cau3t, Helie ladde hem to the streem 41 of Syson, and slow3 hem there. And Helie seith to Achab, Sty vp, and eet, and dryuk, for sown of myche reyn is. 42 Achab stiede up, that he eete and drynke; Helyas^n forsothe stye3ede up into the hil of Carmel, and bowede into the erthe, 43 putte his face betwixe his knees. And he seide to hys child, Stye vp, and behold a3ens the see. The whiche whanne he hadde styed vp, and lokid, seith, Ther is no thing. And eft he seith to hym, 44 Turn a3en seuen sithis. Forsothe in the seuenthe sijth, loo! a litil clowde as the step of a man stiede vp fro the see. The which seith, Sty vp, and sey to Achab, Ioyn thi chare, and cum down, lest reyn 45 before ocupye thee. And whanne thei hadden turned hem self hidir and thidir, loo! heuenes ben derkid, and clowde, and wynde, and there is maad a greet reyn. And so Achab stiynge vp wente into 46 Jezrael; and the hoond of the Lord was vpon Helias, and the reynys gird, he ranne before Achab, to the tyme that he cam into Jezrael.

CAP. XIX.

1 Achab forsothe toolde to Jezabel alle thingis that Helias hadde doon, and what maner wise he hadde slayn alle the pro- 2 phetis of Baal bi swerd. And Jezabel sente a messager to Helias, seiynge, Thes thingis doon to me goddis, and thes^o adden, but this our to morwe I shal putte 3 thi lijf as the lijf of oon of hem. Thanne Helias dradde, and risynge wente whidir euer the wil bare hym; and he cam into Bersabe of Juda, and lafte his child 4 there; and wente into desert, the weye

---

he is God; the Lord he is God. And 40 Elie seide to hem, Take 3e the prophetis of Baal†; not oon sotheli ascape of hem. And whanne thei hadden take hem, Elie ledde hem to the stronde of Cison, and 41 killide hem there. And Elie seide to Achab, Stie thou^y, ete, and drynke, for the sown of myche reyn is^z. Achab stiede^a 42 to ete and drynke; forsothe^b Elie stiede^c in to the hil of Carmele, and he settide^d lowli his face to the erthe, bitwixe hise knees; and seide to his child, Stie thou^r, 43 and biholde^f a3ens the see. And whanne he hadde stied^g, and hadde^h biholde, he seide, No thing is. And eft Elie seide to hym, Turne thou a3en bi^i seuene tymes. Sotheli^k in the seuenthe tyme, lo! a litil 44 cloude as the step of a man stiede^l fro the see. And Elie seide, Stie thou^m, and seie to Achab, Ioyne thi chare, and go doun, lest the reyn byfor ocupie thee. And 45 whanne thei^n turneden^o hem^p hidur and thidur, lo! heuenes weren maad derk, and cloud^q, and wynd, and greet reyn was maad. Therfor Achab stiede^r, and 3ede in to Jezrael; and the hond of the Lord 46 was maad on^s Elie, and whanne the^t leendis weren gird, he ran bifor Achab, til he cam in to Jezrael.

CAP. XIX.

1 Forsothe Achab telde to Jezabel alle thingis whiche^u Elie hadde do, and how he hadde slayn by^v swerd alle the pro- phetis of Baal. And Jezabel sente a mes- 2 sanger to Elie, and seide, Goddis do these thingis to me, and adde these thingis^w, no but to morewe in this our Y schal putte thi lijf as the lijf of oon of hem. Therfor 3 Elie dredde‡, and roos, and 3ede whidur euer wille^x bar hym; and he cam in to Bersabe of Juda, and he lefte there his child; and 3ede in to deseert, the weie of 4

† take 3e the profetis of Baal; Elie sij the puple feruent to the onour of God, for the reuerence of myracle seyi, 42 therfor he wolde haste the deth of the prestis, that disseyueden the puple, lest Jezabel schulde 43 Induce the kyng, hir hosebond, and the king the puple, to kepe the lijf of hem. Lire here, c.

‡ Elf dredde; God suffride him for to drede, by mannus freelte, lest he were reuid euer myche, of the stidefastnesse bifor goinge. Lire here, c.

m alle the E pr. m.   n and Helyas A sce. m.   o thes thingis D pr. m.

y thou up, and I.   z is my3 I.   a 3ede up I.   b but I.   c 3ede up I.   d sette I.   e thou up I.   f biholde thou I.   g stied up I.   h Om. I.   i Om. I.   k And I.   l stiede up I.   m thou up I.   n men I.   o hadden turned I.   p hemselff I.   q a cloud I.   r stiede up I.   s upon I.   t his I.   v that I.   v with I.   w thingis to I.   x his wille I.

of o day. And whanne he was comen, and satte vndir an yue tree, he askide to his soule, that he die; and seith, Lord, it suffisith to me, tak awey my lijf; forsothe ne I am betere than my faders. 5 And he threwe hym self doun, and slepte in the shadew of the yue tree. And loo! the aungel of the Lord touchide hym, 6 and seide to hym, Rijs, and eet. He bihcelde, and loo! at his heed a loof bakyn vndur asshen, and a vessel of water. Thanne he ete, and drank, and 7 eft he slepte. And the aungel of the Lord is turned azen the secounde, and touchide hym; and he^p seide to hym, Rijs, and eet; forsothe a greet weye 8 fallith to thee. The which whanne he hadde rysen, ete, and drank; and he wente in the strength of that meete fourti dayes and fourti nyztis^q, vnto the 9 hil of God, Oreb. And whanne he was comen thidir, he dwellide in the denne; and loo! the word of the Lord to hym, and seide to hym, What dost thow here, 10 Helyas? And he answerde, Bi loue I haue loued, for the Lord God of oostis; for the sonys of Yrael han forsaken the couenaunt of the Lord; thin auters thei han distruyed, and thi prophetis thei han slayn bi swerd; and I am laft alone, and thei sechen my lijf, that thei doon it 11 aweye. And he seith to hym, Go out, and stoond in the hil, before the Lord. And loo! the Lord passith, and a greet wynde, and a^r stroong, and turnynge vpsedoun hillis, and togidre broosynge stonus before the Lord; not in the wynde the Lord. Also after the wynde quauynge; 12 not in the quauyng the Lord. And aftir the quauynge fijr; not in the fier the Lord. And after the fier whistlynge of 13 a thinne blast; there the Lord. The which thing whanne Helias hadde herd, he couerde his cheer with a mantil, and goon out, he stode in the dore of the

o dai. And whanne he cam, and^y sat vndir o iunypere tre, he axide to his soule, that he schulde die; and he seide, Lord, it suffisith to me, take my soule; for^z Y am not betere than my fadris. And 5 he castide forth hym silf, and slepte in the schadewe of the iunypere tree†. And lo! the aungel of the Lord touchide hym, and seide to hym, Rise thou, and ete. He 6 bihelde, and, lo! at his heed *was* a loof bakun vndur aischis^a, and a vessel of watir. Therfor he^b ete, and drank, and slepte eft. And the aungel of the Lord 7 turnede azen the secounde tyme, and touchide hym; and 'the *aungel*^c seide to hym, Rise thou, and ete; for a greet weie is to thee. And whanne he hadde rise, he ete, 8 and drank; and he^d zede in the strengthe of that mete bi^e fourti dayes and fourti nyztis, 'til to^f Oreb, the hil of God. And 9 whanne he hadde come thidur, he dwellide in a denne; and lo! the word of the Lord 'was maad^g to him, and seide to hym, Elie, what doist thou here? And 10 he answeride, Bi feruent loue‡ Y louede^h feruentli, for the Lord God of oostis; for the sones of Israel forsoken^i the couenaunt of the Lord; thei destrieden^k‡ thin auters, and killiden^l bi^m swerd thi prophetis; and Y am left aloone, and thei seken my lijf, that thei do it awei. And he^n seide to 11 Elie, Go thou out, and stonde in the hil, bifor the Lord. And lo! the Lord passith, and a greet wynde, and strong^o, turnynge vpsodoun hillis, and al to brekinge stonys bifor^p the Lord; not in the wynde ys the Lord. And aftir the wynd is a stirynge; not in the stiryng is the Lord. And^pp aftir the stiryng is fier^q; not in the 12 fier is the Lord. And aftir the fier is the^r issyng of thinne wynd^s; there is the Lord. And whanne Elie hadde herd this, he 13 hilide his face with a mentil, and he zede out, and stood in the dore of the denne. And a vois spak to hym, and seide, Elie,

† *the iunypere tre*, which is a tre wexynge in desert, whos schadewe serpentis fleen, as Plyneus seith. *Lire here. c.*

‡ *feruent loue*; that is, of al the herte. *Lire here. c.*

P Om. *A.*   q nyzt *CE.*   r Om. *CEFH.*

y he 1.   z certis 1.   a askys L.   b Hely 1.   c he 1.   d Hely 1.   e Om. DGIKMNOQSWBç.   f vnto 1.   g Om. *plures.*   h haue loued 1.   i han forsake 1.   k han destried 1.   l killid 1.   m with 1.   n the Lord 1.   o a strong 1.   P blowith before 1.   pp Om. s.   q a fier 1.   r an 1.   s wynd, *or brethinge softly* 1.

denne. And a vois seith to hym, seiynge, 14 What dost thou here, Helias? And he answerde, Bi loue I haue loued, for the Lord God of oostis; for the souys of Yrael han forsakyn thi couenaunt; thin auters thei han distruyed, and thi prophetis thei han slayn with swerd; and Y am lafte alone, and thei sechen my 15 lijf, that thei don it awey. And the Lord seith to hym, Go, and turn aȝen in to thi weye, bi deseert, into Damasch; and whanne thou comest thidre, thow shalt anoynte Azael kyng vpon Syrye; 16 and Hieu, the sone of Nampsy, thou shalt anoynt kyng vpon Yrael; Helisee forsothe, the sone of Saphat, that is of Abel Mewla, thow shalt anoynte⁸ prophete 17 for thee. And it shal be, who so euere fleeth the swerd of Azael, Hyeu shal sle hym; and who so euere shal flee the swerd of Hieu, Helisee shal slee hym. 18 And I shal leeue to me in Yrael seuen thousand of men, of whom the knees ben not bowid before Baal, and al mouth that hath⁴ not honourde hym, kyssynge 19 the hoond. Thanne Helias goon forth thens, foonde Helisee, the sone of Saphath, erynge in twelueⁿ ȝockis of oxen; and he in the twelue ȝockis of oxen erynge was oon. And whanne Helias was comen to 20 hym, he putte his mantil vpon him. The which anoon, the oxen laft, ranne aftir Helias, and seith, Kysse Y, I preye thee, my fader and my moder, and so I shal folwe thee. And he seide to hym, Go, and turn aȝen; forsothe that that was 21 myn I haue doon to thee. And turned aȝen forsothe fro hym, he took a peyr oxen, and slewȝ it; and in the plowȝ of oxen he sethide flesh, and ȝaf to the puple, and thei eten; and rysynge he wente, and folwide Helyas, and scruede to hym.

what doist thou here? And he answeride, 14 Bi⁴ feruent loue Y louede⁴ feruentli, for the Lord God of oostis; for the sones of Israel forsoken⁴ thi couenaunt; thei distrieden⁴ thin auteris, and thei killiden⁴ biʸ swerd thi prophetis; and Y am left aloone, and thei seken my lijf, that thei do it awey. And the Lord seide to hym, 15 Go, and turne aȝen in to thi weie, bi the deseert, in to Damask; and whanne thou schalt come thidur, thou schalt anoynte Asahel kyng onᶻ Sirie; and thou schalt 16 anoynte kyng onᵃ Israel Hieu, the sone of Namsi; sotheliᵇ thou schalt anoynte propheteᶜ for thee, Elise, soneᵈ of Saphat, whicheᵉ is of Abelmeula. And it schal 17 be, who euer schal fle the swerd of Asahel, Hieu schal sle hym; and who euer schal fle the swerd of Hieu, Elise schal sle hym. And Y schal leeue to me in 18 Israel seuene thousynde of men, of whiche the knees ben not bowid bifor Baal, and ech mouth that worschipide not hym, and kisside hondᶠ†. Therfor Elie ȝede forth 19 fro thennus, and foond Elise, soneᵍ of Saphat, erynge in twelue ȝockis of oxisʰ; and he was oon in the twelue ȝockis of oxysⁱ, erynge. And whanne Elie hadde come to hym, Elie castide his mentil onᵏ hym. Whichˡ ran anoon after Elie, whanne the 20 oxisᵐ weren left, and seide, Y preie thee, kysse Y my fadir and my modir, and so Y schal sue thee. And Elie seide to hym, Go thou, and turne aȝen, forⁿ Y haue do to thee that that was myn. Sotheli heᵒ 21 turnede aȝen fro Elie, and took tweineᵖ oxisᑫ, and killide hem‡; and with the plow of oxisʳ he sethide the fleischisˢ, and ȝafᵗ to the puple, and thei eeten; and heᵘ roosᵛ, and ȝede, and suede Elie, and mynystride toʷ hym.

ˢ noyntyn ᴇ.   ᵗ han ᴀ.   ⁿ the twelue ᴀʙꜰʜ.

ᵗ With ɪ.   ᵘ haue loued ɪ.   ᵛ han forsake ɪ.   ʷ han destried ɪ.   ˣ han killid ɪ.   ʸ with ɪ.   ᶻ upon ɪ. ᵃ upon ɪ.   ᵇ and ɪ.   ᶜ a prophete ɪ.   ᵈ the sone ᴄɪ.   ᵉ that ɪ.   ᶠ not his hond ɪ.   ᵍ the sone ɪ.   ʰ oxen ɪ. ⁱ oxen ɪ.   ᵏ upon ɪ.   ˡ And he ɪ.   ᵐ oxen ɪ.   ⁿ certis ɪ.   ᵒ And Helisee ɪ.   ᵖ the two ɪ.   ᑫ oxen ɪᴋ. ʳ the oxen ɪ. oxen ᴋ.   ˢ fleish ɪ.   ᵗ ȝaf hem ɪ.   ᵘ Helisee ɪ.   ᵛ roos up ɪ.   ʷ seruyde ɪ.

CAP. XX.

1 Benadab forsothe, kyng of Cyrye, gederide al his oost, and two and thretti kyngis with him, and hors, and charris; and stiynge vp aȝens Samarye fauȝt, and 2 besegide it. And sendynge messageris to Achab, kyng of Yrael, in to the citee, 3 seith, Thes thingis seith Benadab, Thi siluer and thi gold is myyn, and thi wyues, and thi sones altherbest ben 4 myyn. And the kyng of Irael answerde, Aftir thi word, my lord kyng, I am 5 thin, and alle miyn. And the messagers turnynge aȝen seiden, Thes thingis seith Benadab, that sente vs to thee, Thi siluer, and thi gold, and thi wyues, and thi 6 sonys thou shalt ȝyue to me. To morwe thanne, this same hour, I shal sende my seruauntis to thee, and thei shulen aserchen thin hows, and the hows of thi seruauntis; and al thing that to hem shal plese, thei shulen putte in her 7 hoondis, and taken aweye. The kyng of Yrael forsothe clepide alle the eldrys of the loond, and seith, Takith hede, and seeth, for he aspieth to vs; forsothe he sente to me for my wyues, and sonys, and for siluer, and gold, and I forsooke 8 not. And alle the more thurȝ birth seiden, and al the puple to hym, Here thou 9 not, ne assent thou to hym. And he answerde to the messageris of Benadab, Seith to my lord the kyng, Alle thingis for the whiche thou hast sent to me, thi seruaunt, in the bigynnynge I shal do; 10 forsothe this thing I may not doo. And the messagers turned aȝen, tolden alle thingis to hym. The which sente aȝen, and ᵛ seith, Thes thingis doon to me goddis, and thes thingis adden thei, if the powdre of Samarye suffisith to the handfulles 11 of al the puple that folwith me. And answerynge the kyng of Yrael seith, Seith to hym, Ne glorye euenly the gird 12 as the vngird. It is doo forsothe, whanne Benadab hadde herd this word, he drank,

CAP. XX.

Forsotheˣ Benadab, kyng of Sirye, gaderide ʸ al his oost, and two and thritti kyngis with hym, and horsis, and charis; and he stiede ᶻ aȝens Samarie, and fauȝt, and bisegide it. And he sente messangerist to Achab, kyng of Israel, in to the ᵃ citee, and seide, Benadab seith these thingis, Thi siluer and thi gold is myn, and thi wyues, and thi beste sones ben myn. And the kyng of Israel answeride, Bi thi word, my lord the ᵇ kyng, Y am thin, and alle my thingis *ben thine*ᶜ. And the messangeris turneden aȝen, and seiden, Benadab, that sente vs to thee, seith these thingis, Thou schalt ȝyue to me thi siluer, and thi gold, and thi wyues, and thi sones. Therfor to morewe, in this same our, Y schal sende my seruauntis to thee, and thei schulen seke thin hows, and the hows of thi seruauntis; and thei schulen putte in her hondis, and take awey al thing that schal plese hem. Forsothe the kyng of Israel clepide alle the eldere men of the ᵈ lond, and seide, Perseyue ȝe, and se, that he settith tresoun to vs; for he sente to me for my wyues, and sones, and ᵈᵈ for siluer, and gold, and Y forsook not. And alle the gretter men in birthe, and al the puple seiden to hym, Here thou not, nether assente thou to hym. And he ᵉ answeride to the messangeris of Benadab, Seie ȝe to my lord the ᶠ kyng, Y schal do alle thingis, for whiche thou sentist in the bigynnyng to me, thi seruaunt; forsothe ᵍ Y may not do this thing. And the messangeris turneden aȝen, and telden alle thingis to hym. Which ʰ sente aȝen, and seide, Goddis do these thingis to me, and adde these thingis ⁱ, if the dust of Samarie schal suffice to the fistis of al the puple that sueth me. And the kyng of Israel answeride, and seide, Seie ȝe to hym, A gird man, *that is, he that goith to batel*ᵏ, haue not glorie euenli as a man vngird‡. Forsothe ˡ it was doon, whanne Benadab

1
2
3
4
5
6
7
8
9
10
11
12

† messangeris; for Achab sente first messangeris to Benadab, to seke pees, and he answeride as it sueth. Lire here. c.

‡ vngird; that is, as be that hath the victorie, and hath put of hise armeris. Lire here. c.

ᵛ Om. ᴀ.

ˣ Certis ɪ.   ʸ gaderide togidere ɪ.   ᶻ stiede up ɪ.   ᵃ his ɪ.   ᵇ Om. ɪ.   ᶜ Om. ɪ.   ᵈ that ɪ.   ᵈᵈ Om. ɪ.   ᵉ Achab ɪ.   ᶠ Om. ɪ.   ᵍ but ɪ.   ʰ The which ɪ.   ⁱ thingis to ɪ.   ᵏ Om. ɪ.   ˡ And ɪ.

and the kyngis, in hiletis ; and he seith to his seruauntis, Enuyrounith the citee. 13 And thei enuyrounden it. And loo! a prophet comynge nyȝ to Achab, kyng of Yrael, seith to hym, Thes thingis seith the Lord God, Certis thow hast seen al this multitude ful myche ; loo! I shal take it into thin hoond to day, that thow 14 wite for I am a Lord. 'And Achab seith, Bi whom ? And he seide to hym, Thes thingis seith the Lord, Bi the foot folowers of the pryncis of prouyncis. And he seith, Who shal bigynne to fiȝte. And 15 he seide, Thow. Thanne he noumbride the children of the princis of ᵛ prouyncis, and he founde the noumbre of two hundryd and two and thretti ; and he toolde after hem the puple, alle the 16 sones of Yrael, seuen thousand. And thei wenten out at mydday. Benadab forsothe drank drunken in his hilet, and kyngis two and thretti with hym, 'the whiche ᵂ weren comen to the help of hym. 17 Forsothe the children of the princis of prouyncis ben goon out in the first frount. And so Benadab sente, the which toolden to hym, seiynge, Men ben goon 18 out fro Samarye. And he seith, Whether for pees thei comen, nymmeth hem on lyue ; whethir that thei fiȝten, takith 19 hem on lyue. Thanne the children of the pryncis of prouyncis wenten out, and 20 the tother oost folwide ; and echon ˣ smoot the man that aȝens hym cam. And Cyris floowen, and Irael pursuede hem ; Benadab forsothe, kyng of Cyrye, fleiȝ in hors 21 with his horsmen. Also the kyng of Irael goon out smoot hors and chaarys, and smoot Cyrye with a ful mych greet 22 veniaunce. Forsothe a prophete neiȝynge to the kyng of Irael, seide to hym, Go, and tak coumfort, and wite, and se, what thow dost ; forsothe the ȝeer folowynge the kyng of Cyrye shal steyȝe vp aȝens 23 thee. The seruauntis forsothe of the

hadde herd this word, he drank, and ᵐ the kyngis, in schadewyng places ; and he seide to hise seruauntis, Cumpasse ȝe the citee. And thei cumpassiden it. And lo! o pro- 13 phete neiȝede to Acab, kyng of Israel, and seide to hym, The Lord God seith these thingis, Certis thou hast seyn al this multitude ful greet ; lo! Y schal bitake it in to thin hond to dai, that thou wite that Y am the ⁿ Lord†. And Achab seide, Bi whom ? And he seide to Achab, The Lord seith these thingis, Bi the squyeris ᵒ of the princes‡ of prouynces. And Achab seide, Who schal bigynne to fiȝte ? And 15 the prophete seide, Thou. Therfor he noumbryde the children of the princes of prouynces, and he foond the noumbre of twei hundrid and two and thretti ; and aftir hem he ᵒᵒ noumbride the puple, alle 16 the sones of Israel, seuene thousynde. And thei ȝeden out in myddai. Forsothe Benadab drank, and was drunkun in his schadewyng place, and two and thretti kyngis with hym, that camen to the help of hym. Sotheli ᴾ the children of princes ᑫ 17 of prouynces ȝeden out in the firste frount. Therfor Benadab sente men, whiche ʳ telden to hym, and seide, Men ȝeden out of Samarie. And he seide, Whether thei comen 18 for pees, take ȝe hem quyke ; whether to fiȝte, take ȝe hem quyke. Therfor the 19 children of pryncees ˢ of prouynces ȝeden out, and the residue oost suede ; and ech 20 smoot the man that cam aȝens hym. And men of Sirie fledden, and Israel ˢˢ pursuede hem ; also Benadab, kyng ᵗ of Sirie, fledde on an hors with his kniȝtis. Also the 21 king of Israel ȝede out, and smoot horsis and charis, and he smoot Sirie with a ful greet veniaunce. Forsothe a prophete 22 neiȝede ᵘ to the kyng of Israel, and seide, Go thou, and be ᵛ coumfortid§, and wyte, and se, what thou schalt do ; for the kyng of Sirie schal stie ᵂ aȝens thee in the ȝeer suynge. Sotheli the seruauntis of the 23

14 † the Lord, and that thou tarne awey fro Idolatrie. Lire here. c.

‡ bi the squyeris of the princes ; that is, bi the squyeris of princes of the lond of Israel, as it is expowned comynly. Rabi Salomon seith, that herbi ben vndarstondun the children of noble men that weren not of the sones of Israel, but weren ioxun ostachin to Achab; wherfor in Ebreu it is had thus, bi the children of princes of prouynces. Lire here. c.

§ be coumfortid ; in taking trist in God, to defende thee in batel to coumpge. Lire here. c.

ᵛ of the ADSII. ᵂ that c pr. m. ˣ eche c.

ᵐ and also 1. ⁿ Om. DGIKMNOQSWX sec. m. b. ᵒ squyeris, or the footmen 1. ᵒᵒ Om. 8. ᴾ And 1. ᑫ the princes 1. ʳ to wite who these weren the whiche 1. ˢ the prynces 1. ˢˢ al Israel K. ᵗ the kyng 1. ᵘ neiȝede nyȝ 1. ᵛ be thou K. ᵂ weende up 1.

kyng of Cyrye seiden to hym, The
Goddis of hillis ben the[y] Goddis of hem,
therfor thei han ouercomen vs; but betere it is that we fiȝten aȝens hem in the
wijlde feeldis, and we shulen weelde hem.
24 Thow thanne do this word; remeue alle
the kyngis fro thin oost, and put princis
25 for hem; and restore the noumbre of
knyȝtis, that fellen of thin, and the hors
aftir the hors before hadde, and the
chaaris after the chaarys that thou haddist before; and we shulen fiȝte aȝens
hem in the wilde feeldis, and thou shalt
seen, that we shulen weelde hem. He
trowide to the counseil of hem, and dide
26 so. Thanne after that ȝeer was passid,
Benadab noumbride Cyros, and stieȝede
vp in to Affeth, that he fiȝte aȝens Yrael.
27 Forsothe the sones of Yrael ben noumbrid; and metis takyn, wenten forth euen
aȝens, and thei setten tentis aȝens hem,
as two litil flockis of geet. Ciries for-
28 sothe fulfilliden the erthe. And neiȝynge
oo man of God seide to the kyng of
Yrael, Thes thingis seith the Lord God,
For Cyries seiden, God of hillis is the
Lord of hem, and he is not God of
valeys, I shal ȝyue al this greet multitude in thin hoond, and ȝe shulen wite
29 for I am a Lord. Dresseden seuen days
forn aȝens thes and thei sheltruns; forsothe the seuenthe day the batail is doon,
and the sones of Yrael smyten of Cyryes
an hundrid thousand of foot men in o day.
30 Forsothe tho that laften flowen in to Affeth into the citee, and the wal felle vpon
scuen and twenti thousand of men that
laften. Forsothe Benadab fleynge wente
in to the citee, into the cowch that was
31 beside the bed place; and his seruauntis
seiden to hym, Loo! we han herd that
the kyngis of the hous of Yrael ben
mercyable, and so putte we sackis in oure
reens, and litil coordis in oure heedis,

kyng of Sirie seiden to hym, The Goddis
of hillis ben the Goddis of the sones of
Israel, therfor thei ouercamen vs; but it
is betere that we fiȝte aȝens hem in feeldi
placis, and we schulen geet hem[x]. Ther-24
for do thou this word[y]; remoue thou alle
kyngis fro thin oost, and sette thou princis
for hem; and restore thou the noumbre 25
of knyȝtis, that felden[z] of thine, and
horsis[a] bi[b] the formere[c] horsis, and restore
thou[d] charis, bi the charis whiche[e] thou
haddist bifore; and we schulen fiȝte aȝens
hem in feeldy places, and thou schalt se,
that we schulen gete hem. He[f] bileuyde
to the counsel of hem, and dide so. Ther-26
for after that the ȝeer hadde passid, Benadab noumbride men of Sirie, and he
stiede[g] in to Affech, to fiȝte aȝens Israel.
Forsothe the sones of Israel weren noum-27
brid; and whanne meetis weren takun,
thei ȝeden[h] forth euene aȝens, and thei,
twey litle flockis of geet, settiden tentis
aȝens men of Sirie. Forsothe men of Sirie filliden the erthe[i]. And o prophete of 28
God neiȝede†, and seide to the kyng of
Israel, The Lord God seith these thingis,
For men of Sirie seiden, God of hillis is
the Lord of hem, and he is not God of
valeis, Y schal ȝyue al this greet multitude in thin hond, and ȝe schulen wite
that Y am the[k] Lord. In[l] seuene daies 29
these and thei dressiden scheltruns euene
aȝens[m]; forsothe[n] in the seuenthe dai the
batel was joyned togidere, and the sones
of Israel smytiden[o] of men[p] of Syrie an
hundrid thousynde of[q] foot men in o dai.
Forsothe[r] thei that leften fledden in to the 30
citee of Affech, and the wal felde doun on[s]
seuene and twenti thousynde of men that
leften. Forsothe Benadab fledde, and entride in to the citee, in to a closet that was
with ynne a closet; and hise seruauntis 31
seiden to him, We herden[t] that the kyngis
of the hows of Israel ben merciful, therfor

† And o profete
of God neiȝide ;
thouȝ this pro-
fete is not
nemyd here,
doctours bothe
Latyns and
Ebreys seyen,
that he was
Mycheas, sone
of Romula.
God of hillis,
etc.; men of
Sirie weren
ouercomun, for
they blasfem-
eden God, and
the profete
seide that
Achab schulde
not spare Ben-
adab and his
puple, but sle
hem, for they
blasfemeden
God. Lire
here. c.

y Om. B.

x hem there 1.   y word or counseil 1.   z felden or weren sleyn 1.   a the horsis c.   b aftir 1. be s.
c forme DEGMNQSW. forme of o.   d the 1.   e that 1.   f Benadab 1.   g stiede up 1.   h wenten 1.   i lond 1.
k Om. GIKMNbṣ.   l And 1.   m aȝens ech oother 1.   n and 1.   o smoten 1. smeten EL.   p the men 1.
q Om. A.   r And 1.   s upon 1.   t han herd 1.

and goo we out to the kyng of Yrael;
perauenture he shal saue oure lyues.
32 Thei girdeden her reenes with sackis,
and puttiden litil coordis in her heedis,
and thei camen to the kyng of Yrael,
and seiden to hym, Thi seruaunt Benadab seith, I preye thee, lyue my lijf.
And he seith, If ȝit he lyue[z], my brother
33 he is. The which the men token for the
happi good word, and hastily thei ra-
uyshiden the word of his mouth, and
seiden, Thi brothir Benadab lyueth. And
he seide to hem, Goth, and bryngith hym
to me. Thanne Benadab wente out to
hym, and he[a] reryde hym into his chaare.
34 The which seide to hym, The citees that
my fader took fro thi fader I shal ȝeeld,
and streetis make to thee in Damask, as
my fader made in Samarye; and I
boundun to pees shal goo aweye fro thee.
Thanne he couenauntide a boond of pees,
35 and lafte hym. Thanne a maner man of
the sones of prophetis seide to his felawe,
in the word of the Lord, Smyit me. And
36 he wolde not smyte. To whom he seith,
For thow woldist not here the voys of
the Lord, loo! thou shalt goon a weye
fro me, and a lioun shal smyte thee. And
whanne he was goon a weye a litil fro
hym, a lioun foond hym, and smoot hym[b].
37 But and another man fyndynge he seide
to hym, Smyit me. The which smoot
38 hym, and woundide. Thanne the prophete wente, and aȝen cam to the kyng
in the weye; and he chaungide, bi spreng-
ynge of powdre, the mouth and his eyen.
39 And whanne the king was passid, he
criede to the kyng, and seith, Thi seruaunt wente out 'fro nyȝ[c] to fiȝte, and
whanne o man was flowen, a maner man
brouȝte hym to me, and seith, Keep this
man; the which if were slyden aweye,
thi lijf shal be for the lijf of hym, or a

putte we sackis in oure leendis, and cordis
in oure heedis, and go we out to the kyng
of Israel; in hap he schal saue oure lyues.
Thei[u] girdiden[v] her leendis with sackis, 32
and puttiden[w] coordis in her heedis, and
thei camen to the kyng of Israel, and
seiden to hym, Thi seruaunt Benadab
seith, Y preye thee, *lete*[x] 'my soule lyue[y].
And he[z] seide, If Benadab lyueth ȝit, he
is my brother†. Which[a] thing[b] the[c] men 33
of Sirie token for a graciouse word, and
rauyschiden[d] hastily the word of his mouth,
and seiden, Thi brother Benadab lyueth.
And Achab seide to hem, Go ȝe, and
brynge ȝe hym to me. Therfor Benadab
ȝede out to hym, and he reiside[e] Benadab
in to his chare. 'Which Benadab[f] seide 34
to hym[g], Y schal ȝelde the citees whiche
my fadir took fro thi fadir, and make
thou stretis to thee in Damask, as my
fadir made in Samarie; and Y schal be
boundun to pees, and Y schal departe fro
thee. Therfor he[h] made boond of pees[i],
and delyuerede hym. Thanne sum[k] man 35
of the sones of prophetis seide to his felowe, in the word of the Lord, Smyte thou
me. And he nolde[l] smyte. To 'whiche 36
felowe[m] he[n] seide, For thou noldist[o] here
the vois of the Lord, lo! thou schalt go
fro me, and a lioun schal smyte thee. And
whanne he hadde go a litil fro hym[p], a
lioun foond hym, and slowȝ *hym*[q]. But 37
also the prophete foond another man, and
he seide to that man, Smyte thou me.
Which[r] smoot him, and woundide *him*[s].
Therfor the prophete ȝede[t], and mette the[u] 38
kyng[v] in the weie; and he chaungide his
mouth and iȝen[w], by sprynging[x] of dust‡.
And whanne the kyng hadde passid, he 39
criede to the kyng, and seide, Thi seruaunt ȝede out to fiȝte anoon, and whanne
o man hadde fledde, sum[y] man brouȝte
hym to me, and seide, Kepe thou this

† *he is my brother*; that is, Y wole make pees with him. *Lire here*. c.

‡ *bi sprynging of dust*; in Ebreu it is, he chaungide with a cloth, that is, bi wlapping of a cloth. *Lire here*. c.

[z] lyueth CEF. [a] Om. E *pr. m.* [b] Om. BCEFH. [c] in comun E *pr. m.* afer *sec. m.* fro neeȝ *sec. vice*.

[u] *Thanne* thei I. [v] girden C. [w] putten L. puttend E. [x] Om. *plures*. that EL. [y] lyue my lijf I. [z] Achab I. [a] The which I. [b] seiyng I. [c] Om. EI. [d] thei rauyschiden I. [e] reiside up I. [f] And he I. [g] Achab I. [h] Achab I. [i] pees *with him* I. [k] a I. [l] wolde not I. [m] whom I. [n] the prophet I. [o] woldist not I. [p] the prophet I. [q] Om. *plures*. [r] And he I. [s] Om. *plures*. [t] wente I. [u] Om. I. [v] kyng *Achab* I. [w] his iȝen I. [x] sprengyng I. [y] a I.

40 talent of siluer thou shalt ȝeelde. Forsothe while Y disturblid hidir and thidyr
turnede me, feerly he aperide not. And
the kyng of Yrael seith to hym, This is
41 thi dome that thi self hast demyd. And
he anoon wipide aweye the powdre froᵈ
his face, and the kyng of Irael knewe
42 him, that he was of the prophetis. The
whiche seith to hym, Thes thingis seith
the Lord, For thou hast laft a man worthi the deeth fro thin hoond, thi lijf shal
be for the lijf of hym, and thi puple for
43 his puple. Thanne the kyng of Irael
turnede aȝen 'in toᵉ his hows, dispisynge
to here, and ful of woodnes cam in to
Samarie.

CAP. XXI.

1 Aftir thes wordis forsothe, in that
tyme, there was a vyn toᶠ Naboth Jezraelite, that was in Jezrael, biside the
paleys of Achab, kyng of Samarye.
2 Thanne spak Achab to Naboth, seiynge,
ȝif to me thi vyn ȝerd, that I make to me
a wort ȝerd, for it is niȝ, andᵍ biside myn
hows; and I shal ȝyue to thee for it a
betere vyn ȝerd; or if more profitable
thow wenyst to thee, of siluer the prijs
3 as myche as it is worth, I shal ȝeue. To
whom answerde Naboth, Merciful be to
me the Lord, that I ȝyue not the heri-
4 tage of my fadres to thee. Thanne
Achab cam into his hows, endeynynge,
andʰ grutchynge vpon the word that
Naboth Jezraelite hadde spoken to hym,
seiynge, I shal not ȝyue to thee the hori-
tage of my faders; and throwynge hym
5 self into his bed turnede aweye his face
to the wal, and eete not breed. Forsothe
Jezabel, his wijf, wente into hym, and
seide to hym, What is that, wherof thi
soule is drery? and whi etist thou not
6 breed? The which answerde to hire, I
spak to Naboth Jezraelite, and seide to

man; and if he aschapithᶻ, thi lijf schal be
for his lijf*, ether thou schalt paye a
talent of siluere. Sotheli while Y was tro- 40
blid, and turnede me hidur and thidur,
sodeynly he apperide not. And the kyng
of Israel seide to hym, This is thi doom
whichᵃ thou hast demed. And anoon he 41
wipideᵇ aweyt the dust fro his face, and
the kyng of Israel knew him, that he was
of the prophetis. Whichᶜ seide to the kyng, 42
The Lord seith these thingis, For thou
deliueridist fro thin hond a man worthi
theᵈ deeth, thi lijf schal be for his lijf, and
thi puple 'schal beᵉ for his puple. Therfor 43
the kyng of Israel turnede aȝen in to his
hows, and dispiside to hereᶠ, and camᵍ
wod in to Samariet.

CAP. XXI.

Forsothe after these wordis, in that 1
tyme, the vyner of Naboth of Jezrael,
'that was in Jezraelʰ, was bisidis the paleis of Achab, kyng of Samarye. Therfor 2
Achab spak to Naboth, and seide, ȝyue
thou to me theˡ vynerᵏ, that Y make to
meˡ a gardyn of wortis, for it is nyȝᵐ,
and nyȝ myn hows; and Y schal ȝyue to
thee a betere vyner for it; ethir if thou
gessist it more profitable to thee, Y schall
ȝyueⁿ the prijs of siluer, as myche as it is
worth. To whom Naboth answeride, The 3
Lord be mercifnl to me, that Y ȝyue not
to thee the eritage of my fadris§. Ther- 4
for Acab cam in to his hows, hauynge
indignacioun, and gnastyng on the word
whichᵒ Naboth of Jezrael hadde spoke to
him, and seide, Y schal not ȝyue to thee
the eritage of my fadirs. And Achab
castide doun him silf in to his bed‖, and
turnede awei his face to the wal, and ete
not breed. Forsotheᵖ Jezabel, his wijf, 5
entride to hym, and seide to hym, What
is this thing, wherof thi soule is maad
sory? and whi etist thou not breed?
Whichq answeride to hir, Y spak to Na- 6

* thi lijf schal be for his lijf, and Y resseyuede him in this condicioun. Lire here. C.

t and anoon he wipte awey, etc.; in Ebreu it is, remouyde the cloth, ether binding, fro his face. Lire here. C.

ȶ and cam wood in to Samarie; Josephus seith, that he killide the profete. Lire here. C.

§ the eritage of my fadris; for prijs, ether for other eritage, for the lond of Israel was propirly Goddis himsilf, and it myȝte not be seeld for euere, but onely til to the iubile in xxv. cᵒ. of Leuitici; and therfor nether that was grauntid in the lawe, no but in nede, but Naboth was riche, and therfor he was not compellid to sille his eritage; forsothe the king wolde haue it, for euerlastinge tyme. Lire here. C.

‖ in to his bed; for indignacioun and vnpacience, and bi this it is opin, that the kyng myȝte not take for his wille, the feeldis of hise sugetis. Lire here. C.

ᵈ of A.   ᵉ to A.   ᶠ in ABFH.   ᵍ Om. A.   ʰ the A.

ᶻ aschapith awey 1.   ᵃ that 1.   ᵇ wipte DEKLMSXbç.   ᶜ The which 1.   ᵈ Om. 1.   ᵉ O m. 1.   ᶠ here Goddis word 1.   ᵍ he cam 1.   ʰ Om. 1.   ˡ thi IK.   ᵏ vynȝeerd 1. vyne D.   ˡ me theroff 1.   ᵐ nyȝ to me 1.   ⁿ ȝyue thee 1.   ᵒ that 1.   ᵖ And 1.   q The which 1.

hym, 3if to me thi vyn 3erd, the monee takyn, or if to thee it plese, I shal 3yue to thee a betere vyn 3erd for it. And he seith, I shal not 3yue to thee my vyn 7 3erd. Thanne Jesabel, his wijf, seide to hym, Of greet autoryte thou art, and wel thou gouernyst the rewme of Yrael; rijs, and eet breed, and in[t] euen yuwit be thow; I shal 3yue to thee the vyn 3erd of 8 Naboth Jezraelite. And so she wroot lettris of the name of Achab, and signede hem with his rynge; and sente to the more thur3 birth, and to the best, that weren in his cytee, that dwelliden with 9 Naboth. Of the lettris forsothe this was the sentence; Preche 3e fastynge, and makith Naboth to sitte among the first 10 of the puple; and vndirleye 3ee two men, sonys of Belial, a3ens hym, and fals witnes seye thei, Naboth hath blessid God and the kyng; and ledith hym out, and 11 stonith, and so dye he. Thanne his citeseens more thur3 birth, and the best that dwelliden with hym in the citee, diden as Jesabel hadde comaundid to hem, and as it was writen in the lettris, that she 12 sente to hem. Thei prechiden fastynge, and maden Naboth to sitte among the 13 first of the puple; and two men brou3ten forth, sonys of the deuel, thei maden hem to sitte a3ens hym, and thei, that is, as deuels men, seiden a3ens hym witnes before al the multitude, Naboth blesside God and the kyng; for what thing thei ledden hym out of the citee, and with 14 stonus slowen[k]. And thei senten to Jesabel, seiynge, Naboth is stoned, and is 15 deed. It is doo forsothe, whanne Jesabel hadde herd Naboth stoned and deed, she spak to Achab, Rijs, weeld the vyn 3erd of Naboth Jezraelite, that wold not to thee assente, and 3yue it, the monee taken; forsothe Naboth lyueth not, but 16 he is deed. The which thing whanne

both of Jezrael, and Y seide to hym, 3yue thi vyner[r] to me for money takun, ethir if it plesith thee, Y schal 3yue to thee a betere vyner for it. And he seide, Y schal not 3yue to thee my vyner[s]. Therfor Je-7 zabel, his wijf, seide to hym, Thou art of[t] greet auctorite, and thou gouernest wel Israel; rise thou, and ete breed, and be thou `pacient, *ethir coumfortid*[u]; Y schal 3yue to thee the vyner of Naboth of Jezrael. Therfor sche[v] wroot lettris† in the 8 name of Achab, and seelide tho with the ryng of hym; and sche sente to the grettere men in birthe, and to the beste men, that weren in the citee of hym[w], and dwelliden with Naboth[x]. Botheli[y] this 9 was the sentence of the lettre; Preche 3e fastyng, and make 3e Naboth to sitte among the firste men of the puple; and 10 sende 3e prineli twei men, the sones of Belial, a3ens hym, and sey thei fals witnessyng, Naboth blesside[z] God and the kyng[a]‡; and lede 3e out hym, and[b] stoun 3e *him*[e], and die he so. Therfor hise cite-11 seyns, the grettere men in birthe, and the beste men that dwelliden with hym in the citee, diden as Jezabel hadde comaundid, and as it was writun in the lettris, whiche[d] sche hadde sent to hem. Thei prechiden 12 fastyng, and maden Naboth to sitte among the firste men of the puple; and whanne 13 twey men, sones of the deuel, weren brou3t, thei maden hem to sitte a3ens hym[e], and thei, that is[f], as men of the deuel, seiden witnessyng a3ens him bifor al the multitude, Naboth blesside God and the kyng; for which thing thei ledden hym with out the citee, and killiden *him*[g] with stoonys. And thei senten to Jezabel, and seiden, 14 Naboth is stoonyd, and is deed. Forsothe 15 it was doon, whanne Jezabel hadde herd Naboth stonyd and deed, sche spak to Achab, Rise thou, take thou[h] in possessioun the vyner of Naboth of Jezrael,

† *sche wroot lettris, etc.;* bi the wille and knowing of Achab. *Lire here. c.*

‡ *Naboth blesside God and the king;* that is, curside, as in li. c[o]. of Job, Blesse thou God, and die thou; for the errour of cursing, Jewis signefieden is bi the contrarie name. *Lire here. c.*

r vyn3erd I. s vyn3erd I. t a L. u coumfortid *ether pacient* CFMW. pacient *or of euen ynwill* I.
v Jezabel I. w Naboth I. x him I. y And I. z hath blessid I. a kyng, *that is, hath cursid* I. b Om. c.
c Om. *plures.* d that I. e Naboth I. f is *to wite* I. g Om. *plures.* h Om. I.

Achab hadde herd, that Naboth[l] is deed,
he roos, aud cam doun into the vyn ȝerd
of Naboth Jezraelite, that he weelde it.
17 Thanne the word of the Lord is doon to
18 Helias Thesbites, seiynge, Rijs, and come
down iuto aȝen comynge to Achab, kyng
of Irael, that is in Samarye; loo! to the
vyn ȝerd of Naboth he dessendide, that lie
19 weelde it. And thou shalt speke to hym,
seiynge, Thes thingis seith the Lord God,
Thow hast slayn, and furthermore[m] thou
hast weeldid; and after thes thingis thow
shalt adde, Thes thingis seith the Lord,
In this place, in the which houndis lickiden the blood of Naboth, shulen lick and
20 thi blood. And Achab seith to Helyas,
Whether thow hast foundun me thin
enemy? The which scide, I haue found-
en, forthi that thou be solde that thou
21 doo yuel in the siȝt of the Lord. Therfor thes thingis seith the Lord, Loo! I
shal brynge yn yuel vpon thee, and I
shal hewe of thin hyndirmoris, and slee
fro Achab a pisser to the wal, and the
22 closid, and the last in Irael; and I shal
ȝyue thin hows as the hows of Jeroboam,
the sone of Nabath, and as the hows of
Baasa, the sone of Achia; for thou hast
doon that thou terre me to wrath, and
23 thou hast maad Irael to synne. But and
of Jesabel the Lord hath spokyn, seiynge,
Houndis shulen eete Jezabel in the feelde
24 of Jezrael; if Achab were deed in the
citee, houndis shulen ete hym; forsothe
if he were deed in the feelde, foulis of
25 heuene shulen ete hym. Therfor there
was non other siche as Achab, that is
sold that he do yuel in the siȝt of the
Lord; forsothe Jezabel, his wijf, stiryde
26 hym; and abomynable is maad, inso-
miche that he folwide the mawmettis
that Amorreis maden, whom the Lord
destruyde fro the face of the sonis of

which[i] nolde[k] assente to thee, and ȝyue it
for money takun; for Naboth lyueth not,
but is deed. And whanne Achab hadde 16
herd this, that is, Naboth deed[l], he roos,
and ȝede doun in to the vyner of Naboth
of Jezrael, to haue it† in[m] possessioun.
Therfor the word of the Lord was maad 17
to Elie of Thesbi, and seide, Rise thou, 18
go doun in to the comyng of Achab, kyng
of Israel, which[n] is in Samarie; lo! he
goith doun to the vyner of Naboth, that
he haue it in possessioun. And thou 19
schalt speke to hym, and 'thou schalt° seie,
The Lord God[p] seith these thingis, Thou
hast slayn[q]‡, ferthermore and thou hast
take[r] in possessioun; and aftir these
thingis thou schalt adde[s], In this place,
wherynne doggis lickiden the blood of
Naboth, thei schulen licke also thi blood.
And Achab seyde to Elie, Whether thou 20
hast founde me thin enemy? Which[t] Elie[u]
seide, Y haue founde[v], for thou art seeld[w]§
that thou schuldist do yuel in the siȝt of
the Lord. Therfor the Lord seith these 21
thingis, Lo! Y schal brynge yn[x] on[y] thee
yuel, and Y schal kitte awey thin[yy] hyndrere[z] thingis, and Y schal sle of Achab
a pissere to the wal, and prisoned[a], and
the laste in Israel; and Y schal ȝyue thin 22
hows as[b] the hows of Jeroboam, sone[c] of
Naboth, and as the hows of Baasa, sone[d]
of Abia; for thou didist[e] to excite me to
wrathfulnesse, and madist Israel to do
synne. But also the Lord spak of[f] Jeza- 23
bel, and seide, Doggis schulen ete Jezabel
in the feeld of Jesrael; if Achab schal 24
die in the citee, doggis schulen ete hym;
sotheli if he schal die in the feeld, briddis
of the eyr schulen ete hym. Therfor noon 25
other was sich as Achab‖, that was seeld
to do yuel in the siȝt of the Lord; for
Jezabel his wijf excitide hym[g]; and he 26
was maad abhomynable, in so myche that

Marginal notes (right):

† to haue it, etc.; for hise goodis weren forfetid bi mannus dooth. Lire here. c.

‡ thou hast slayn; for the lettris of the deth of Naboth weren maad and sent bi the knowing and will of Achab. Lire here. c.

§ for thou art seeld; as a thing seeld passith in to the lordschip and possessioun of the biere, so Achab semyde al suget to idols, and seruynge to idols. madist Israel to do synne: not onely in the worschiping of calues, as othere kyngis bifor goyng diden, but also in the worschiping of Baal. Lire here. c.

‖ I was sich as Achab; that is, in kingis bifor goynge him, for he brouȝte in to his rewme the worschiping of Baal, at exciting of his wiyf. Lire here. c.

---

[l] Naboth Jezraelite E pr. m.   [m] therfor ABFH.

[i] that I.   [k] wolde not I.   [l] to be deed I.   [m] in to co pr. m.   [n] that I.   [o] Om. I.   [p] Om. CEL.   [q] slayn Naboth I.   [r] take his vynȝerd I.   [s] adde to mo yuelis I.   [t] And I.   [u] Om. C.   [v] founde thee so I.   [w] sold to the deuel I.   [x] Om. C.   [y] upon I.   [yy] the D.   [z] hyndere IXC.   [a] the prisoned I.   [b] to be as I.   [c] the sone I.   [d] the sone I.   [e] didist yuel I.   [f] to I.   [g] hym therto I.

27 Yrael. And so whanne Achab hadde herd thes wordis, he kitte his clooth, and couerde his flesh with an heire, and he fastide, and slepte in a sak, and wente, 28 the heed leyd doun. And the word of the Lord is maad to Helye Thesbite, sciynge, Whether hast thou not seen Achab mekyd before me? Thanne for he is mekid bi chesoun of me, I shal not brynge yn the yuel in the days of hym, but in the dais of his sone I shal brynge yn the yuel to the hows of hym.

CAP. XXII.

1 Three 3eer thanne passiden ouer with outen batail bitwixe Cirye and Irael. 2 Forsothe in the thridde 3eer Josaphat, kyng of Juda, cam doun to the kyng of 3 Irael. And the kyng of Irael seyde to his seruauntis, Vnknowe 3e, that Ramoth Galaad[m] is[n] oure, and we ben negligent to take it fro the hoond of the kyng of 4 Cyrye? And he seith to Josaphath, Shalt thou not come with me to fi3t in Ramoth 5 Galaad? And Josaphath seide to the kyng of Irael, As Y am, so and thow; my puple and thi puple ben oon, and mi horsmen and thi horsmen. And Josaphath seide to the kyng of Irael, Seche, I praye thee, the word of the Lord to 6 day. Thanne the kyng of Irael gaderide the prophetis about foure hundrid men, and seith to hem, Shal I goo into Ramoth Galaad to fi3te, or reste? The whiche answerden, Sty vp, and the Lord shal 7 3eue it in the hoond of the kyng. Josaphath forsothe seide, Is there not here eny man a prophete of the Lord, that 8 we asken bi hym? And the kyng of Irael seith to Josaphat, There is laft o man, bi the which we mowen aske the Lord; but and I haue hatid hym, for he

he suede the ydols that Ammorreis[h] maden, which Ammorreis[l] the Lord wastide fro the face of the sones of Israel. Therfor 27 whanne Achab hadde herd these wordis, he to-rente his cloth, and hilide his fleisch with an hayre, and he fastide, and slepte in a sak, and 3ede with the heed cast doun. The word of the Lord was maad 28 to Elie of Thesbi, and seide, Whethir thou hast not seyn Achab maad low bifor me? Therfor for he is maad low† for the[k] cause of me, Y schal not brynge yn yuel in hise daies, but in the daies of his sone Y schal bryng yn yuel to his hows.

CAP. XXII.

Therfor thre 3eeris[l] passiden with out batel bitwixe Sirie and Israel. Forsothe[m] 2 in the thridde 3eer Josephat, king of Juda, 3ede doun to the kyng of Israel. And the 3 kyng of Israel seide to hise seruauntis, Witen 3e not, that Ramoth of Galaad is oure, and we ben necgligent to take it fro the hoond of the kyng of Sirie? And he[n] 4 seide to Josaphat[o], Whether thou schalt come with me to fi3te in to Ramoth of Galaad? And Josophat seide to the kyng 5 of Israel, As Y am, so and thou; my puple and thi puple ben oon; and my kny3tis and thy kny3tis 'ben oon[p]. And Josephat seide to the kyng of Israel, Y preie thee, axe thou to dai the word of the Lord. Therfor[q] the 6 kyng of Israel gaderide[r] prophetis aboute foure hundrid men, and he seide to hem, Owe Y to go in to Ramoth of Galaad to fi3te, ethir to[s] reste? Whiche[t] answeriden, Stie thou[u], and the Lord schal 3yue it in the hond of the kyng[v]. Forsothe Jose- 7 phat seide, Is[w] not here ony profete of the Lord, that we axe bi hym? And the 8 kyng of Israel seide to Josephat, O man, Mychee[x], sone[y] of Hiemla, is left, bi whom we moun axe the Lord; but Y hate hym, for he prophesieth not good[z] to me, but

† he is maad low; this penatunce was for dreede of deth, as it is seid comynly, and therfor it disseruede not grace and moddeing of euerlastinge peyne, thou3 it disseruede delaiyng of temperal peyne; othere men seyen, that this was verl penaunce onely at an our, for he turnede a3en to yuele passid. Lire here. c.

m of Galaad a pr. m.   n be BCEFH.

h men of Ammorey 1.   i men 1.   j And the 1.   k Om. 1.   l 3eer 1. 3er EL.   m And 1.   n Achab 1.   o Johasaphat, king of Juda 1.   p Om. 1.   q And DKM¢.   r gaderide to gidre 1.   s owe I to 1.   t The whiche 1.   u thou up 1.   v kyng of Israel 1.   w Is ther 1.   x Mychee bi name 1.   y the sone 1.   z good thing 1.

prophesieth not to me good, but yuel,
Mycheas, the sone of Hyemla. To whom
Josaphath seith, Spek thou not so, kyng.
9 Thanne the kyng of Irael clepide[o] a
maner geldyng, and seide to hym, Hy
to brynge to Mychie, the sone of Hyemla.
10 The kyng of Irael forsothe, and Josaphath, kyng of Juda, seeten, echon in her
see, clothid with kyngis[p] ournynge, in
the corn floore biside the dore of the ȝaat
of Samarie; and alle the prophetis pro-
11 phecieden in the siȝt of hem. Forsothe
Sedechias, the sone of Chanaan, maade
to hym yren horns, and seith, Thes
thingis seith the Lord God, With thes
thou shalt wyndowe Cyrye, to the tyme
12 that thou doo it aweye. And alle the
prophetis lijc maner prophecieden, seiynge, Sty vp into Ramoth Galaad, and
goo welsumli; the Lord shal take in
the hoond of the kyng thin enemyes.
13 The messager forsothe, that was goon
for to clepe Mychie, spak to hym, seiynge,
Loo! the wordis of the prophetis with
oon mouth to the kyng good thinges
prechen; thanne be thi word lijc of[q]
14 hem, and speke good thingis. To whom
Mychie seith, The Lord lyueth, for what
euer thing the Lord seye to me, that I
15 shal speke. And so he cam to the kyng.
And the kyng seith to hym, Mychie,
shulen we goo in to Ramoth Galaad to
fiȝte, or ceese? To whom he answerde,
Sty, and go welsumli; and the Lord shal
16 take it in the hoond of the kyng. Forsothe the kyng seide to hym, Eft and eft
I adiure thee, that thou speke not to me,
but that is soth in name of the Lord.
17 And he seith, I sawȝ al Irael to scaterde
in hillis, as sheep not hauynge sheep-
herd; and the Lord seith, Thes han not
a lord, echon turn aȝen into his hows in
18 pees. Thanne the kyng of Irael seide to
Josaphat, Whether I seide noȝt to thee,
for he prophecyede not to me good, but

yuel. To whome Josephat seide, Kyng,
spek thou not so. Therfor the kyng of 9
Israel clepide summe[a] chaumburleyn[b], and
seide to hym, Haste thou[c] to brynge Mychee, sone[d] of Hiemla. Forsothe the kyng 10
of Israel, and Josephat, kyng of Juda,
saten, ech in his trone, clothid with kyngis
ournement[e], in the[f] large hows bisidis the
dore[g] of the ȝate of Samarie; and alle
prophetis[h] prophecieden in the siȝt of hem.
Also Sedechie, sone[i] of Chanaan, made to 11
hym silf hornes of yrun, and seide, The
Lord God seith these thingis, With these[k]
thou schalt scatere[l] Sirye, til thou do awei
it. And alle prophetis prophecieden in 12
lijk maner, and seiden, Stye thou in to
Ramoth of Galaad, and go thou with
prosperite; and the Lord schal bitake thin
enemyes in the hond of the kyng. So- 13
theli the messanger, that ȝede to clepe
Mychee, spak to hym, and seide, Lo! the
wordis of prophetis[m] with o mouth prechen
goodis to the kyng; therfor thi word be
lijk hem, and speke thou goodis. To 14
whom Mychee seide, The Lord lyueth,
for what euer thing the Lord schal seie
to me, Y schal speke this. Therfor he 15
cam to the kyng. And the kyng seide to
hym, Mychee, owen we go[n] in to Ramoth
of Galaad to fiȝte, ether ceesse? To which
kyng he answeride, Stie thou, and go in
prosperite†; and the Lord schal bitake it
in to[o] the hond of the kyng. Forsothe the 16
kyng seide to hym, Eft and eft Y coniure
thee, that thou speke not to me, no but
that that is soth in the name of the Lord.
And he seide, Y siȝ al Israel scaterid in 17
the hillis, as scheep not hauynge a scheepherde; and the Lord seide, These han no
lord, ech man turne aȝen in to his hows
in pees. Therfor the kyng of Israel seide 18
to Josaphat, Whethir Y seide not to thee,
that he prophecieth not good to me, but
euere yuel? Sotheli thilke Mychee addide, 19
and seide, Therefore here thou the word

† *go in prosperite*; he seide not this for certeyn, but more bi denying, ether bi desiring; and the kyng perseyuede this by signes, therfor he coniouride hym to speke truthe. *Lire here.* C.

[o] callede CE. [p] dynerse E *pr. m.* [q] to ABFH.

[a] a I. [b] chaumburleyn *of his* I. [c] thou *thee* I. [d] the sone I. [e] ournment A. [f] a I. [g] wikett I. [h] the prophetis CGINO. [i] the sone I. [k] these *hornes* I. [l] scatere abrood I. [m] the prophetis EL. [n] to go ELbç. [o] in BC *sec. m.*

19 euermore euyl? Forsothe he addynge seith, Therfor here the word of the Lord; I saw₃ the Lord vpon his see sittynge, and al the oost of heuene stondynge nee₃ 20 to hym, fro the ri₃t and fro the left. And the Lord seith, Who shal desseyue Achab, kyng of Yrael, that he stie vp, and falle in Ramoth Galaad? And oon seide siche maner wordis, and another otherwise. 21 Forsothe a spirit wente out, and stood before the Lord, and seith, I shal desseyue hym. To whom the Lord spak, 22 In what? And he seith, I shal goon out, and I shal be a spirit lee₃er in the mouth of alle the prophetis of hym. And the Lord seide, Thou shalt desseyue, and haue the ouerhoond; go out, and do so. 23 Now thanne, loo! the Lord hath ₃euen a spirit of lesynge in the mouth of alle thi prophetis that here ben; and the Lord 24 spak a₃ens thee yuel. Forsothe Sedechias, the sone of Chanaan, cam ny₃, and smoot Mychie in to the cheeke, and seith, Whethir thanne the Spirite of the Lord hath 25 laft me, and spoken to thee? And Mychie seith, Thou art to seen in that day, whanne thou shalt goon into the bed place with ynne the bedde, that thou be 26 hidde. And the kyng of Irael seith, Takith Mychie, and dwel he anentis Amon, the prynce of the citee, and 27 anentis Joas, the sone of Amalech; and seith to hem, Thes thingis seith the kyng, Puttith this man into prisoun, and susteyneth hym with breed of tribulacioun, and with water of angwishe, to 28 the tyme that[r] I turne a₃en in pees. And Mychie seide, If thow turne a₃en in pees, the Lord hath not spoken in me. And 29 he seith, Here ₃e, alle puplis. And so the kyng of Irael stieth vp, and Josaphath, kyng of Juda, into Ramoth Ga- 30 laad. And so the king of Yrael seide to Josaphath, Tak aarmys, and goo into batail, and be thou clothid[s] with thi clothis. But the kyng of Irael chaungide 31 his habite, and wente into batayl. The

of the Lord; Y si₃ the Lord sittynge on his trone, and Y si₃ al the oost of heuene stondynge ny₃ hym, on the ri₃t side and on the left side. And the Lord seide, 20 Who schal disseyue Achab, kyng of Is- rael, that he stye, and falle in Ramoth of Galaad? And oon seide siche wordis, and another in anothir maner. Sotheli a spi- 21 rit ₃ede out, and stood bifor the Lord, and seide, Y schal disseyue hym. To whom the Lord spak, In what thing? And he 22 seide, Y schal go out, and Y schal be a spirit of leesyng in the mouth of alle hise prophetis. And the Lord seide, Thou schalt disseyue†, and schalt haue the may- stry; go thou out, and do so. Now ther- 23 for, lo! the Lord ₃af a spirit of leesyng in the mouth of alle prophetis that ben here; and the Lord spak yuel a₃ens thee. For- 24 sothe Sedechie, sone of Canaan, nei₃ede, and smoot Mychee on the cheke, and seide, Whether the Spirit of the Lord forsook 25 me, and spak to thee? And Mychee seide, Thou schalt se in that dai, whanne thou schalt go in to closet[n] with ynne closet, that thou be hid. And the kyng of Israel 26 seide, Take ₃e[o] Mychee, and dwelle he at Amon, prince of the citee, and at Joas, the[p] sone of Amalech; and seie ₃e to hem, 27 The kyng seith these thingis, Sende ₃e this man in to prisoun, and susteyne ₃e hym with breed of tribulacioun, and with watir of angwisch, til Y turne a₃en in pees. And Mychee seide, If thou schalt 28 turne a₃en in pees, the Lord spak not in me. And he seide, Here ₃e, alle puplis. Therfor the kyng of Israel stiede, and 29 Josaphat, kyng of Juda, in to Ramoth of Galaad. Therfor the kyng of Israel seide 30 to Josephat, Take thou armeris, and entre thou in to batel, and be thou clothid in thi clothis, that is, noble[q] signes of the kyng. Certis the kyng of Israel chaung- ide hise clothing‡, and entride in to batel. Sotheli the kyng of Sirie hadde comaundid 31 to two and thritti princes of charis, and seide, ₃e schulen not fi₃te a₃ens ony man

† thou schalt disseyue; not that falsumme is shewid of the Lord, rther of his comaundemetis, but God suffrith bi iust doom, that ₃uele men be disseyuede of fendis, that han not power to do ony thing no but as he suffrith. Lire here. c.

‡ his clothing; that is, aray of king. Lire here. c.

r Om. CE.   s clad BCFFH.

n a closet CW. the closet K.   o Om. S.   p Om. S.   q in noble places.

VOL. II.   H h

kyng forsothe of Cirye comaundide to
the princis of the chaaris, two and
thretti, seiynge, 3e shulen not fi3te a3ens
the lasse, and a3ens any^t more, but oonli
32 a3ens the kyng of Irael. Whanne thanne
the pryncis hadden seen the chaar of
Josaphath, thei ouertroweden^u that he
hadde ben kyng of Irael, and the birre
maad thei fou3ten a3ens hym. And Jo-
33 saphath cried out; and the princis of the
charis vndirstoden, that it was not the
kyng of Irael, and thei ceseden fro hym.
34 A maner man bente a boowe, into vncerteyn dressynge an arowe, and bi hap he
smoot the kyng of Irael bytwixe the
lunge and the stomak. And he seide to
hys charyeter, Turn thin hond, and cast
out me fro the oost, for greuousli Y am
35 woundid. Thanne the batail is don in
that dai, and the kyng of Irael stood in
his chaar a3ens Cyryes, and is deed at
euen. Forsothe the blood of the wound
flowide in to the bosum of the chaar.
36 And the bedel fulsouned in al the oost,
before the sunne wente doun, seiynge,
Echon turne a3en into the citee, and into
37 his loond. The kyng forsothe is deed,
and is born into Samarye; and thei biry-
38 eden the kyng in Samarie. And thei
wasshen his chaar in the fish poond of
Samarye, and houndis lickeden his blood,
and thei lickeden the bridils, after the
word of the Lord that was spokyn.
39 The remnaunt forsothe of the wordis of
Achab, and al that he dide, and the yuer
hows that he beeldide^v, and of al the
citees that he made vp, whether not thes
ben wryten in the book of the wordis of
40 the days of the kyngis of Yrael? Thanne
Achab slept with his faders, and Ocho-
41 zias, his sone, reguede for hym. Josaphat forsothe, the sone of Asa, began to
regne vpon Juda, the ferth 3eer of Achab,
42 kyng of Yrael. Of fyue and thretti 3eer
he was, whanne he began to regne, and
fyue and twenti 3eer he regnede in Jerusalem; the name of his moder Azuba,

lesse, ethir more, no^p but a3ens the kyng
of Israel oonli. Therfor whanne the 32
princes of charis hadden seyn Josephat,
thei suposiden that he was king of Israel,
and bi feersnesse maad thei fou3ten a3ens
hym. And Josephat criede†; and the 33
princis of charis vndurstoden, that it was
not the king of Israel, and thei ceessiden
fro hym. Sotheli sum man bente a bowe, 34
and dresside an arowe in to vncerteyn,
and bi hap he smoot the kyng of Israel
bitwixe the lunge and the stomak. And
the kyng seide to his charietere, Turne
thin hond, and cast me out of the oost‡,
for Y am woundid greuousli. Therfor 35
batel was ioyned in that dai, and the
kyng of Israel stood in his chare a3ens
men of Sirie, and he was deed at euentid.
Forsothe the blood of the wounde fletide
doun in to the bothome of the chare. And 36
a criere sownede in al the oost, before that^q
the sunne 3ede doun, and seide, Ech man
turne a3en in to his citee, and in to his
lond. Forsothe the kyng was deed, and 37
was borun in to Samarie; and thei birieden
the kyng in Samarie. And thei waisch- 38
iden his chare in the cisterne of Samarie,
and doggis lickiden his blood, and thei
wayschiden the reynes§, bi the word of the
Lord whiche he hadde spoke. Sotheli 39
the residue of wordis of Achab, and alle
thingis whiche he dide, and the hows of
yuer which he bildide, and of alle citees
whiche he bildide, whether these ben not
writun in the book of wordis of daies of
the kyngis of Israel? Therfor Achab 40
slepte with hise fadris, and Ocozie, his
sone, regnede for hym. Forsothe Jose- 41
phat, sone of Asa, bigan to regne on Juda
in the fourthe 3eer of Achab, kyng of Israel. Josephat was of fyue and thretti 42
3eer, whanne he bigan to regne, and he
regnede fyue and twenti 3eer in Jerusalem; the name of his modir was^r Azuba,
dou3ter of Salai. And he 3ede in al the 43
weye of Asa, his fadir, and bowide not fro
it; and he dide that, that was ri3tful in

† Josephath eriede; clepinge Goddis help, and declaringe his honer. Lire here. c.

‡ cast me out of the oost; not fully, but he was cast out of that scheltrun in to another. Lire here. c.

§ and they waischiden the reynes; in Ebreu it is thus, and thei waischiden the armeris, fro the blood of Achab. Bi the word of the Lord, etc.; that is, bisidis the place, wherynne Naboth was stonyd, vpe this that the Lord seide bi Elie, for Achab hadde the hows of his armer in Jezrael, and therfor hise armeris in whiche he was woundid, weren brou3t thidur, and waschun there fro blood of Achab, and doggis lickiden it in that same place, where Naboth was slayn. Lire here. c.

---

t the ABFII.   u ortroweden c.   v bilde CE.

p Om. c.   q Om. A.   r Om. s.

43 the dou3ter of Salai. And he wente in
al the weye of Asa, his fader, and he
bowide not aside fro it; and he dide that
44 is ri3t in the si3t of the Lord. Neuerthelater the hei3e thingis he dyde not
aweye, 3it forsothe the puple sacrifiede,
45 and brente encense in he3tis. And Josaphath hadde pees with the kyng of Irael.
46 The remnaunt forsothe of the wordis of
Josaphath, and his werkis that he dide,
and batails, whether not thes ben wryten
in the book of the wordis of the days of
47 'the kyngis of w Juda? But and the relikis of the wommannysh maad men, that
laften in days of Asa, his fader, he dide
48 aweye fro the loond. And there was not
49 thanne a kyng ordeynyd in Edom. Forsothe kyng Josaphath made nauees in the
see, 'the whiche x saileden in to Oofer for
gold, and thei my3ten not goon, for thei
50 ben broken in Aziongober. Thanne Ochozias, the sone of Achab, seith to Josaphath, My seruauntis goon with thi seruauntis in shippis. And Josaphat wold
51 not. And Josaphath slepte with his faders, and is biried with hem in the citee
of Dauid, his fader; and Joram, hys sone,
52 regnede for hym. Forsothe Ochozias, the
sone of Achab, began to regne vpon Yrael,
in Samarye, the seuentynthe y 3eer of Josaphath, kyng of Juda; and he regnede
53 vpon Yrael two 3eer. And he dide yuel
in the si3t of the Lord, and he wente in
the weye of his fader, and of his moder,
and in the weye of Jeroboam, sone z of
54 Nabath, that made Irael to synne. Forsothe he seruede to Baal, and honourde
hym, and he terrede the Lord God of Irael,
aftir alle thingis that his fader dide.

*Here eendith the thridde book of
Kyngis, and now bigynneth the
fourthe a.*

the si3t of the Lord. Netheles he dide not 44
aweye hi3 thingis, for 3it the puple made
sacrifice, and brente encense in hi3 places.
And Josephat hadde pees with the king 45
of Israel. Sotheli the residue of wordis 46
of Josephat, and the werkis and batels,
whiche he dide, whethir these ben not
writun in the book of wordis of daies of
the kyngis of Juda? But also he took 47
awey fro the loond the relikis of men
turned in to wymmens condiciouns, that
leften in the daies of Aza, his fadir. Ne- 48
thir a kyng was ordeyned thanne in Edom.
Forsothe r king Josephat made schippis in 49
the see, that schulden seile in to Ophir
for gold, and tho my3ten not go, for thei
weren brokun† in Asiongaber. Thanne 50
Ocozie, sone of Achab, seide to Josephat,
My seruauntis go with thine in schippis.
And Josephat nolde‡. And Josephat slepte 51
with hise fadris, and was biried with hem
in the citee of Dauid, his fadir; and Joram, his sone, regnede for hym. Forsothe 52
Ocozie, sone of Achab, bigan to regne on
Israel, in Samarie, in the seuenetenthe 3eer
of Josephat, kyng of Juda; and Ocozie
regnede on Israel twei 3eer. And he dide 53
yuel in the si3t of the Lord, and 3ede in
the wey of his fadir, and of his modir,
and in the weie of Jeroboam, sone of Nabath, that made Israel to do synne. And 54
he seruyde Baal, and worschipide hym,
and wraththide the Lord God of Israel, bi
alle thingis whiche his fadir hadde do.

*Here endith the thridde book of
Kyngis, and here bigynneth the
fourthe s.*

50 † tho weren
brakun; bi
Goddis doom,
for he hadde
homelynesse
and felowschipe
with Ocozie,
king of Israel,
in ij. book of
Paral. xx. c°.
Lire here. c.
52 ‡ and Josephat
nolde; that is,
he assentid
with him the
ij. tyme in
nauey. Lire
here. c.

w Om. ANFH. x that c pr. m. y seuentythe b. z the sone CE. a Here eendith the thrydde boke of
Kyngis, and bigynneth the fourth boke of Kyngis. u. Explicit tertius liber Regum. E. Here endith the thrid
bok of Kyngis, and here bigynneth the fourth bok. F. No final rubric in CH.

r Sotheli PGKLNOPQRSUWQ. s Here endith the thridde book of Kyngis, and bigynneth the fourthe
book. BNQ. Here endith the thridde book of Kyngis, and byggynnethe the fourthe book of Kyngis. CSX. Here
endith the thridde book of Kyngis, and bigynnith a prolog on the iv. book. GM. Heere endeth the thridde book
of Kinges, se now the fourthe. K. Heere eendith the iije. book, and bigynneth the iiije. book of Kynges. N.
Here eendith the thrydde book of Kyngis. q. No final rubric in ELP.

IV. KINGS.

[*Prologue on the Fourth book of Kings*ᵃ.]

THIS Fourthe book of Kingis makith mencioun of alle the kingis of Israel, and of Juda, from Ocozie, sone of Achab, in to Sedechie, king of Juda, that was in the secounde transmygracioun of the men of Juda and of Jerusalem, whanne the cite of Jerusalem was taken and brent, with the temple of the Lord, and maad desolat, either forlete, bi seuenti зeer, after the wordis of Jeremye, profete.

— ◆ —

*The fourthe of Kingus*ᵃ.

CAP. I.

1 MOAB forsothe trespasside in Yrael, 2 aftir that Acab was deed. And Ochosias felle thoruз the wyndowes of his soupynge place, that he hade in Samarye, and he wexe seeke; and he sente messangers, seiynge to hem, Gooth, and counselith Belzabub, the god of Accharon, whether I may lyue fro this myn 3 infirmyte. The aungel forsothe of the Lord spak to Helias Thesbytes, seyinge, Riys, and go doun in to the aзein commynge of the messagers of the kynge of Samarie; and thou schalt scye to hem, Whether God is not in Yrael, that зe goon to counseylen Belzabub, the god of 4 Accharon? Wherfore these thingis seith the Lord, Fro the bed, upon the whiche thou steyзidist up, thou schalt not goo doun, bot bi deth thou schalt dyen. And 5 Helias went. And the messagers ben turned aзeyn to Ochosias. 'The whicheᵇ seyde to hem, Why ben зe turned aзeyn? 6 And thei answerden to hym, A man

*Here biginneth the ferthe book of Kingis*ᵇ.

CAP. I.

FORSOTHE Moab trespasside aзens Is- 1 raelᵗ, after that Achab was deed. And 2 Ocozie felde thorou the aleris of his soler, which he hadde in Samarie, and was sijk; and he sente messangeris, and seide to hem, Go зe, and councele Belzebub, god of Acharon, whether Y may lyue after this sijknesse of me. Forsothe the aungel 3 of the Lord spak to Elye of Thesbi, and seide, Rise thou, and go doun into the metynge of the messangeris of the kyng of Samarie; and thou schalt seie to hem, Whether God is not in Israel, that зe go to counsel Belzebub, god of Acharon? For 4 which thingᵗ the Lord seith these thingis, Thou schalt not go doun of the bed, on which thou stiedist. And Elie зede. And 5 the messangeris turneden aзen to Ocozie. And he seide to hem, Whi turneden зe aзen? And thei answeriden to hym, A 6 man mette vs, and seide to vs, Go зe, turne зe aзen to the kyng, that sente зou; and зe schulen seie to him, The Lord seith

† *Moab tres-passide aзeuus Israel;* for the king of Moab swoor for him and his rewms, to serue the king of Israel vndur tribute, and he rebell-ide, and brak this ooth. *Lire here.* c.

‡ *for which thing;* that is, for vnfeithful-nesse. *Lire here.* c.

ᵃ *Here bigynneth the fourthe book of Kyngis* E. No initial rubric in ᴀᴄꜰʜ. From the commencement of IV. Kings to the end of II. Chronicles the text is taken from ʙ. ᵇ *that* E *pr. m.*

ᵃ This prologue is from ᴍ. ᵇ From ᴍç. *The iiij. of Kinges.* ᴘ. No initial rubric in the other Mss.

aʒein came to us, and seyde to us, Gooth, and turneth aʒein to the kynge, that sente ʒou; and ʒe schuln to hym seyn, These thingis seith the Lord, Whether for there was not God in Yrael, thou sentist, that Belzabub be counseyled, the god of Aacharonᶜ? Therfore fro the bed upon the whiche thou steiʒedist up, thou schalt noo doun, bot by deth thou 7 schalt dye. The whiche seyde to hem, Of what fygure and habyte is that man, that aʒeyn came to ʒou, and spake to ʒou 8 these wordis? And thei seyden, A rowʒ man, and with an hery gyrdyl gyrd to the reenys. The whiche seith, Helyas 9 Thesbytes it is. And he sente to hym the prince of fyftye, and the fyfty men that with hym weren. The whiche steiʒiden up to hym, and to hym syttynge in the cop of the hill seith, Man of God, the kynge comaundid, that thou come doun. 10 And Helyas answerynge seith to the quynquagenarye, ʒif the man of God I am, come doun fijr fro heuen, and deuoure thee and thi fyfty men. Than fijr came doun fro heuen, and deuouride hym, and the fyfty that weren with hym. 11 Eft he sente to hym another prynce of fyfty, and fyfty with hym, the whiche spac to hym, Man of God, these thinges 12 seth the kynge, Hyʒe, come doun. Answerynge Helyas seith, ʒif the man of God I am, come doun fijr fro heuen, and deuoure thee and thi fyfty. Than the fijr of God came doun fro heuen, and de-13 uouride hym and his fyfty. Eft soonys he sente the thridd prynce of fyfty, and the fyfty that weren with hym. The whiche whan was commen, bowed the kneeʒis aʒeins Hely, and preyede him, and seith, Man of God, wylle thou not dispijse my lijf, and the lijues of thi seruauntis that 14 ben with me. Loo! fijre came doun fro heuen, and deuourede the two first princis of fyfty, and the fyftees that weren with hem; and now, I beseche, that thou haue 15 mercye to my lijf. The aungel forsothe

these thingis, Whether for God was not in Israel, thou sendist, that Belzebub, god of Acharon, be counselid? Therfor thou schalt not go doun of the bed, on which thou stiedist, but thou schalt die bi deeth. Which Ocozie seide to hem, Of what 7 figure and abite is that man, that mette ʒou, and spak to ʒou these wordis? And 8 thei seiden, An heeri man, and gird with a girdil of skyn† in the reynes. Which 9 seide to hem, It is Elie of Thesbi. And he sente to Elie a prince of fifti, and fifti men that weren vndur hym. Which prince stiede to hym, and seide to hym, sittynge in the cop of the hil, Man of God, the kyng comaundith, that thou come doun. And Elie answeride, and seide to the 10 prince of fifti men, If Y am the man of God‡, fier come doun fro heuene, and deuoure thee and thi fifti men. Therfor fier cam doun fro heuene, and deuouride hym, and the fifti men that weren with hym. Eft he sente to Elie another prince of fifti, 11 and fifti men with hym, which spak to Helye, Man of God, the kyng seith these thingis, Haste thou, come thou doun. Elie 12 answeride, and seide, If Y am the man of God, fier come doun fro heuene, and deuoure thee and thi fifti men. Therfor the fier of God cam doun fro heuene, and deuouride hym and hise fifti men. Eft he 13 sente the thridde prince§ of fifti men, and fifti men that weren with hym. And whanne this prynce hadde come, he bowide the knees aʒens Elie, and preiede hym, and seide, Man of God, nyle thou dispise my lijf, and the lyues of thi seruauntis that ben with me. Lo! fier cam doun fro 14 heuene, and deuouride tweyne, the firste princis of fifti men, and the fifti men that weren with hem; but now, Y biseche, that thou haue mercy on my lijf. Forsotheᶜ 15 the aungel of the Lord spak to Helie of Thesbi, and seide, Go thou doun with hym; dredeᵈ thou not. Therfor Elie roos, and cam doun with hym to the kyng; and 16 he spak to the kyng, The Lord seith thes

† of skyn; in Ebreu it is, of lether. c.

‡ If Y am the man of God; verili and not scornefuly. Fier come doun, etc. Elie knew bi reuelacioun, that this prince clepide him in scorn the man of God, and that he consentide to the king in the synne of idolatrie and in the punyschinge of Elie, and so diden thei that weren with the prince; and herfor by Goddis sentence, they weren worthi to be punyschid; wherfor Elie pronounside Goddis sentence, and seide, If Y am the man of God, etc.; and so it is of the ij. prince, and hise fifti men. Lire here. c.

§ he sente the thridde prince, etc.; this thridde prince was Abdie, as Ebreis and Cristen doctours seyen comynly, and Abdie dredde God gretly, in iii. book of Kingis, xviii. c., and therfor he mekide him silf bifor God, and Elie his seruaunt. Lire here. c.

ᶜ Nacharon BFH.

ᶜ Forsothe lo A.   ᵈ and drede x.

of the Lord spak to Helyas Thesbytes, seyinge, Comme doun with hym; ne drede thou. Thanne he roose and came 16 doun with hym to the kynge; and spac to hym, These thingis seith the Lord, For thou sentist messagers to counseylen Belzabub, god of Accharon, as ther were not God in Yrael, of the whiche thou mi3tist not asken a worde; therfore fro thi bed, upon the whiche thou stey3idist up, thou schalt not goo doun, bot by deth 17 thou schalt dye. Thanne he is deed aftir the word of the Lord, that Helye spac; and Joram, his brothir, regnede for hym, the seconde 3eer of Joram, the sone of Josaphath, kyng of Jude; forsothe he 18 hade not a sone. The remnaunt forsothe of the wordis of Ochosie, 'the whiche[d] he wrou3t, whethir thei[e] ben not writen in the boke of the wordis of the days of the kyngis of Yrael?

thingis, For thou sentist messangeris to counsele Belzebub, god of Acharon, as if no God were in Israel, of whom thow my3tist axe a word; therfor thou schalt not go doun of the bed, on which thou stiedist, but thou schalt die bi deeth. Therfor he was deed bi the word of the 17 Lord, which word Elie spak; and Joram, hys brothir, regnyde for hym, in the secounde 3eer of Joram†, the[c] sone of Josephat, kyng of Juda; for Ocozie hadde no sone. Sotheli the residue of wordis of 18 Ocozie, whiche he wrou3te, whether these ben not writun in the book of wordis of daies of the kyngis of Israel?

† the ij. 3eer of Jorum; in which he regnede with his fadir, for he regnede vilj. 3eer with his fadir, for fro that tyme that Josophath was in perel of deth in Ramoth of Galaad, he ordeynede Joram, his sone, king, lest strivf weren among hise sones for the rewme, aftir his deth. Lire here. c.

CAP. II.

1 Done it is forsoth, whan the Lord wolde reren Helyas by a whyrlwynd in to henen, Helyas and Helyse wenten fro 2 Galgalis. And Helyas to Helyse seide, Sytt here, for the Lord hath sent me vnto Bethel. To whom seith Helese, the Lord liueth and thi soule liueth, for I schal not forsake thee. And whanne thei 3 weren goo doun fro Bethel, the sonys of prophetis, that weren in Bethel, wenten out to Helysee, and seyden to hym, Whether thou hast knowe, for the Lord to day schal taken thi lord fro thee? The whiche answerde, And I haue 4 knowen; beeth stylle. Helyas forsothe seide to Helise, Sytt heere, for the Lord hath sente me into Jericho. And he seith, The Lord liueth and thy soule liueth, for I schal not forsake thee. And when 5 thei weren commen to Jericho, the sonys of prophetis, that weren in Jericho, ney3iden to Helyse, and seyden to hym, Whether thou hast knowen, that the Lord schal taken to day thi lord fro thee?

CAP. II.

Forsothe it was don, whanne the Lord 1 wolde reise Elie bi a whirlewynd in to heuene, Elie and Elisee 3eden fro Galgalis. And Elie seide to Elisee, Sitte thou here, 2 for the Lord sente me til into Bethel. To whom Elisee seide, The Lord lyueth and thi soule lyueth, for Y schal not forsake thee. And whanne thei hadden come doun to[f] Bethel, the sones of prophetis, that 3 weren in Bethel, 3eden out to Elisee, and seiden to hym, Whether thou knowist, that the Lord schal take awey thi lord to dai fro thee? Which answeride, And I knowe[g]; be 3e stille. Forsothe Elie seide 4 to Elisee, Sitte thou here, for the Lord sente me into Jerico. And he seide, The Lord lyueth and thi soule lyueth, for Y schal not forsake thee. And whanne thei hadden come to Jerico, the sones of pro- 5 phetis, that weren in Jerico, nei3iden to Elisee, and seiden to hym, Whether thou knowist, that the Lord schal take awei thi lord to dai fro thee? And he seide, Y knowe; be 3e stille. Forsothe Elie seide 6

d that c pr. m.   e these cE.

e Om. x.   f in to cx.   g knowede s.

And he seith, I haue knowen ; beeth styll. 6 Helyas forsothe seyde to hym, Sytt here, for the Lord hath[f] sente me vnto Jordan. The whiche seith, The Lord liueth and thi soule lyueth, for I schal not forsake thee. Thanne both thei wenten to gydre ; 7 and fyfty men of the sonys of prophetis foloweden, the whiche and stoden forn a3eynst aferre ; thei forsothe stoden both 8 upon Jordane. And Helyas tooke his mantyll, and inwrappyde it, and smote the watirs ; the whiche ben deuydid in to eithir partye, and thei wenten both 9 thor3 the drye. And whanne thei weren goon ouer, Helyas seyde to Helise, Aske that thou wilt, that I doo to thee, er I be taken awey fro thee. And Helise seyde, I beseche, that ther be doo thi 10 spirite double in me. The whiche answerde, An hard thing thou hast askede ; neuer the later 3if thou seest me, whanne I schal be taken fro thee, it schal be that thou hast askyde ; 3if forsothe thou seest 11 not, it schal not be. And whanne thei wenten, and goynge speke wordis, loo ! the fijren chaare and the fijren hors deuyden euer either ; and Helyas stey3ide up by 'the whirlwynde[g] in to heuen. 12 Helise forsothe sawe, and criede, Fader myn ! fader myn ! the chaar of Yrael, and charieter[h] of it. And he saw3 hym no more. And he toke his clothis, and kutt 13 hem in to two partyes. And he rerede the mantyll of Helye, that hadde fallen to hym ; and, turned[i] a3ein, stode upon 14 the brynke of Jordan. And with the mantyll of Helye, that hadde fallen to hym, he smote the waters, and thei ben not deuydid. And he seide, Where is the God of Helye also nowe ? And he smote the watirs, and thei ben dyuydid hidre and thidre ; and Helisee passede 15 ouer. Forsothe the sonys of the prophetis that weren in Jericho, seeinge, a3einward seyden, The spirite of Helye hath restyde upon Helisee. And thei

to Elisee, Sitte thou here, for the Lord sente me 'til to[f] Jordan. Which seide, The Lord lyueth and thi soule lyueth, for Y schal not forsake thee. Therfor bothe 3eden togidere ; and fifti men of the sones 7 of prophetis sueden, which also stoden fer euen a3ens ; sothely thei bothe stoden ouer Jordan. And Elie took his mentil, and 8 wlappide it[g], and smoot the watris† ; whiche weren departid 'into[h] euer ethir part, and bothe 3eden bi the[i] drie. And 9 whanne thei hadden passid, Elie seide to Elisee, Axe thou that, that thou wolt that Y do to thee, bifor that Y be takun awey fro thee. And Elisee seide, Y biseche, that thi double spirit‡ be 'maad in[k] me. Which 10 Elie answeride, Thou axist an hard thing ; netheles if thou schalt se me, whanne Y schal be takun awei fro thee, that that thou axidist schal be ; sotheli, if thou schalt not se, it schal not be. And whanne 11 thei 3eden, and spaken goynge, lo ! a chare of fier and horsys of fier departiden euer either ; and Elie stiede bi a whirlewynd in to heuene§. Forsothe Elise si3, and 12 criede, My fadir ! my fadir ! the chare of Israel‖, and the charietere therof. And he si3 no more Elie. And he took hise clothis, and to-rente tho in to twei partis. And he reiside the mentil of Elie, that 13 felde doun to hym ; and he turnede a3en, and stood ouer the ryuer of Jordan. And 14 with the mentil of Elie, that felde doun to hym, he smoot the watris, whiche weren not departid¶. And he seide, Where is God of Elie also now ? And he smoot the watris, and tho weren departid hidur and thidur ; and Elisee passide. Sotheli the 15 sones of prophetis, that weren in Jerico euene a3ens, si3en, and seiden, The spirit of Elie restide on Elisee. And thei camen in to the meetyng of hym, and worschipiden hym lowli to erthe. And thei seiden 16 to hym, Lo ! with thi seruauntis ben fifti stronge men, that moun go, and seke thi lord, lest perauenture the Spirit of the

† smoot the watris ; the watris weren departid, not bi ony vertu that was in the mentil, but bi Goddis vertu, bi which he wolde schewe the merit of Elie. Lire here. c.
‡ that thi double spirit ; Elisee axide not the spirit in double proporcioun in comparisoun of Elie, that he schulde be set so bifor Elie, but he axide that the double grace that was in Elie, that is, the grace of myraclis, and the grace of profecie, schulde be in him, that so he schulde be maad lijk the maister. Lire here. c.
§ in to heuene ; not in to heuene of sterris, nether of brihtnesse in blis, but in to heuene of the eir ; and bi the eir Elie was borun in to erthely paradiys, whidur Enok was translatid bifore ; and aboute the ende of the world bothe schulen come forth fram thennus, to preeche a3enus the falsnesse of Auntecrist. Lire here. c.
‖ the chare of Israel ; a chare berith up, and a charietere rulith, so Elie bar up the puple of Israel, in sillinge other amendinge defautis, as in ɪɪ. book. xviii. c°., in the gruinge of watir to the puple bringe in perel ; also Elie rulide the puple, and brou3te it a3en to the veri feith of o God, by geting of fier fro heuene on his brent sacrifice, to declaringe of veri Godhed, wherfor the puple

f Om. ᴇ pr. m. g whirlwynde ʙ. the wirlynge wynde ɪɪ. h the charieter ᴀ. i he turned ᴀ.

f til in to ᴇʟᴘ. to x. g Om. s. h in c. i Om. ᴇʟ. k with ᴇʟ.

commynge in to aʒein commynge of hym,
honoureden hym redye in to the erth.
16 And thei seyden to hym, Loo! with thi
seruauntis ben fyfty stronge men, that
mown goon, and seechen thi lord, lest
perauenture the Spirite of the Lord
haue taken hym, and throwen hym in
oon of the hillis, or in oon of the valeys.
The whiche seithe, Wylle ʒe not senden.
17 And they constreyniden hym, to tyme that
he assentide to hem, and seyde, Sendith.
And thei senten fyfty men; whiche
whanne hadden souʒt three days, founden
18 not. And thei turneden aʒeyn to hym;
and he dwellyde in Jericho. And he
seyde to hem, Whether I seyde not to
19 ʒou, Willith not senden? Than the men
of the cytee seyden to Helyse, Lo! the
dwellynge of this cytee is best, as thou
thi silf, lord, byholdist; bot and the watirs
20 ben werst, and the erth bareyn. And he
seith, Bringith to me a newe vessel, and
puttith in it salt. The whiche whan
21 they hadden brouʒte, goon oute to the
welle of watirs, he putte in to it salt,
and seith, These thingis seith the Lord,
I haue heelide these watirs, and there
schal be no more in hem deth, ne ba-
22 reynte. Thanne the watirs ben helyde
into this day, aftir the word of Helise,
23 that he spac. Forsothe Helise steyʒide
up thens in to Bethel; and whanne he
schulde stey up by the weye, lytyl children wenten out fro the cyte, and scorneden to hym seyinge, Stey up, ballard!
24 stey up, ballard! The whiche whan he
byheld, sawʒe hem, and cursed to hem
in name of the Lord. And two beris
wente oute fro the wyild wode, and to-
tereden[k] of hem two and fourty chyl-
25 dren. Forsothe he wente thens in to the
hill of Carmele, and thens turnede aʒein
in to Samarye.

Lord hath take hym, and hath cast forth
hym in oon of the hillis, ethir in oon of
the valeys. Which[l] seide, 'Nyle ʒe sende[m]. 17
And thei constreyneden hym, til he assentide to hem, and seide, Sende ʒe. And
thei senten fifti men; and whanne thei
hadden souʒt[n] bi thre daies, thei founden[o]
not. And thei turneden aʒen to hym[p]; 18
and he dwelide in Jerico. And he seide
to hem, Whether Y seide not to ʒou, Nyle
ʒe sende? Therfor the[q] men of the citee 19
seiden to Elisee, Lo! the dwellyng† of
this cite is ful good, as thou thi silf, lord,
seest; but the watris ben ful[r] yuele, and
the lond is bareyn. And he[s] seide, Brynge 20
ʒe to me a newe vessel, and sende[t] ʒe salt
in to it. And whanne thei hadden brouʒt
it[u], he ʒede out to the welle of watris, and 21
sente[v] salt in to it[vv], and seide, The Lord
seith these thingis, Y haue helid these[w]
watris, and nethir deeth, nether[x] bareyn-
esse, schal be more in tho[y]. Therfor the 22
watris weren heelid til[z] in to this dai, bi
the word of Elisee, which[a] he spak. For-23
sothe Elisee stiede[b] fro thennus in to
Bethel; and whanne he stiede[c] bi the
weie, litle children ʒeden out of the citee,
and scorneden hym, and seiden, Stie[d], thou
ballard! stie[d], thou ballard! And whanne 24
he hadde biholde, he siʒ hem, and curside
hem‡ in the name of the Lord. And
twey beeris ʒeden[e] out of the forest, and
to-rente fourti children of hem. Sotheli[f] 25
Elisee wente fro thennus in to the hil of
Carmele, and fro thennus he turnede 'aʒen
to[g] Samarie.

criede thanne, the Lord him silf is God. In Ebreu it is thus, the chare of Israel, and the chyualrie therof, that is, myʒtleres to defence of Israel, than chyualry with charis of intel, as Rabi Salomon expowneth. Lire here. c.

¶ *which weren not departid ; this was doon of God, that Elisee schulde not be reisid ouer mychte, of the geting of the spirit of Elie. Where is God of Elie? at this criyng the watris weren departid, that it were schewid, that he gat grace and kunning to professie and to do myraclis, not of hise owne meritis, but of Goddis fre ʒifte, and of the meritis of Elie. Lire here. c.*

† *the dwelling, etc.; that is, the setting of the citee was best for profetis, for it was couenable to contemplacioun ; and the erthe was not bareyne, not but for malice of the watir. Lire here. c.*

‡ *and curside hem; these children weren taust and stirid of her fadris and modris, idolatrouris, to scorne the profete of the Lord, and therfor he cursidc hem, that her fadris and modris schulden be punyschid, and that the children schulden no more be stirid, to the malice of fadris and modris; for he wiste bi God schewinge, that her deth ouʒte to come sone aftir his cursing, which he bruʒte forth bi the sentence of Goddis riʒtfulnesse. Lire here. c.*

k to-teeren CE pr. m.

l And Helizee 1. m Sende ʒe not 1. n souʒt *him* 1. o founden him 1. p Helizee 1. q Om. 1.
r moost 1. s Helizee 1. t putte 1. u it to him 1. v putte 1. vv the welle 1. w the L. x ne ELP.
y hem 1. z Om. 1. a that 1. b wente up 1. c wente up 1. d Stie up 1. e wenten 1. f Certis 1.
g aʒen into DI. to ELP.

CAP. III.

1 Joram forsoth, the sone of Acab, regnede upon Yrael, in Samarie, the ei3teenth
3eer of Josaphath, kyng of Juda. And
2 he regnyde twelue 3eer, and dyde yuel
bifore the Lord, bot not as his fadir
3 and modir ; forsothe he toke aweye the
ymagis of Baal, that his fadir hadde
maade, neuer the latir he cleeuyde in
the synnys of Jeroboam, the sone of Nabath, that made Yrael to synnen ; and
4 he wente not aweye fro hem. Forsothe
Mesa, the kyng of Moab, nuryschede
many beestis, and payed to the kyng of
Yrael an hundreth thousand of lombis,
and an hundreth thousand of [l] wetheris,
5 with their fleeses[m]. And whann Acab
was deed, he brake the bonde of pese
that he hade with the kyng of Yrael.
6 Thann kyng Joram wente out in that
day fro Samarie, and noumbrede alle
7 Yrael. And he sente to Josaphath, kyng
of Juda, seyinge, Kynge Moab is goon
aweye fro me ; comme with me a3eynst
hym to batayl. The whiche answerde,
I schal steyen up ; he that is myn, is
thyne ; my puple thi puple, and myn
8 hors thin hors. And he seyde, By what
weye schuln we stey3en up? And he an-
9 swerde, By the desert of Ydume. Thann
the kyng of Yrael, and the kyng of Juda,
and the kyng of Edom, wenten, and
3eeden aboute by the weye of seuene
days ; and ther was not watir to the
hoost, and to the beestis, that foleweden
10 hem. And the kyng of Yrael seide,
Allas ! allas ! allas ! the Lord hath gaderd us three kyngis, that he take[n] in
11 the hond of Moab. And Josaphath seith,
Is there not a prophete of the Lord, that
we preyen the Lord by hym? And oon
answerde of the seruuuntis of the[o] kynge
of Yrael, There is here Helisee, the sone

CAP. III.

Forsothe[b] Joram, sone[i] of Achab, regn- 1
ede on[j] Israel, in Samarie, in the ei3tenthe
3eer of Josephat, kyng of Juda. And he
regnede twelue 3eer, and he dide yuel bi- 2
for the Lord, but not as his[k] fader and
modir[l]† ; for[m] he took[n] awei the ymagis 3
of Baal, whiche his fadir hadde maad,
netheles in[o] the synnes of Jeroboam, sone[p]
of Nabath, that made Israel to do synne,
'he cleuyde[q], and 3ede[r] not awei fro tho[s].
Forsothe Mesa, kyng of Moab, nurschide 4
many beestis, and paiede[t] to the kyng of
Israel an hundrid thousynde of lambren,
and an hundrid thousynde of[u] wetheris,
with her fleesis[v]. And whanne Achab was 5
deed, he[w] brak the boond of pees, which[x]
he hadde with the kyng of Israel. Therfor 6
kyng Joram 3ede out of Samarie in that
dai, and noumbride[y] al Israel. And he 7
sente to Josephat, kyng of Juda, and seide,
The kyng of Moab 3ede[z] awei fro me ;
come thou with me a3ens him to batel.
Which[a] Josephat answeride, Y schal stie[b] ;
he that is myn, is thin ; my puple is thi
puple ; and myn horsis ben thin horsis.
And he[c] seide, Bi what weie schulen we 8
stie[d] ? And he[e] answeride, Bi the deseert
of Ydumee. Therfor the kyng of Israel, 9
and the kyng of Juda, and the kyng of
Edom, 3eden forth, and cumpassiden bi
the weie of seuene daies ; and 'watir was
not[f] to the oost, and to the beestis, that
sueden hem. And the kyng of Israel 10
seide, Alas ! alas ! alas ! the Lord hath
gaderide[g] vs thre kyngis to bitake vs[h] in
the hond of Moab. And Josephat seide, 11
Whether ony prophete of the Lord is
here, that we biseche the Lord bi hym?
And oon of the seruuntis of the kyng of
Israel answeride, Elisee, the sone of Saphat, is here, that schedde[i] watir on[k] the
hondis of Elie. And Josephat seide, Is 12

† not as his
fadir and mo-
dir ; for they
brou3ten in the
worschipinge
of the idol
Baal, and this
Joram re-
mouyde it ; but
he dwellide in
the worschip-
ing of calues,
whiche Jero-
boam made.
Lire here. C.

---

¹ Om. AB.   ᵐ flees CE.   ⁿ take vs A.   ᵒ Om. ABF.

ᵇ Certis ι.   ⁱ the sone ι.   ʲ upon ι.   ᵏ Om. DEMP℔.   ˡ his modir EL.   ᵐ forsothe ι.   ⁿ dide ι.
ᵒ he cleuyde to ι.   ᵖ the sone ι.   ᑫOm. ι.   ʳ he 3ede ι.   ˢ hem ι.   ᵗ he paiede ι.   ᵘ Om. ι.   ᵛ flees ELᵖb.
flees for tribute ι.   ʷ Mesa ι.   ˣ that ι.   ʸ he noumbride ι.   ᶻ hath gon ι.   ˢ And ι.   ᵇ stie up with
thee ι.   ᶜ Josephat ι.   ᵈ wende up ι.   ᵉ Joram ι.   ᶠ ther was not watir ι.   ᵍ gaderide to gidre ι.
ᵇ Om. plures.   ⁱ helde ι.   ᵏ upon ι.

of Saphath, that heelde watir vpon the
12 hondis of Helye. And Josaphath seith,
Is ther anentis hym the wordc of the
Lord? And the kyng of Yrael came
doun to hym, and Josaphath, kyng of
13 Juda, and the kyng of Edom. Forsothe
Helisee seyde to the kyng of Yrael, What
is to me and to thee? Goo to the prophetis of thi fadir and thi⁹ modir. And
the kyng of Yrael seith to hym, Why the
Lord hath gaderde these three kyngis,
that he take hem in to the hondis of
14 Moab? And Helyse seyde to hym, The
Lord of hoostis liueth, in whose siȝt I
stonde, that ȝif not the cheer of Josaphath, kyng of Juda, I schamyde, forsoth
I schulde not haue taken hede to thee, ne
15 haue byholden. Now forsothe bryngith
to me an sawtrer. And whanne the
sawtrer songe, the honde of the Lord is
16 don upon hym, and he seith, These
thingis seith the Lord, Makith the
wombe of this streme dychis and dychis.
17 Forsothe these thingis seith the Lord, ȝe
schuln not seen wynde, ne reyn, and this
wombe schal ben fulfilled with watirs,
and drynke schuln ȝe, and ȝoure meyne,
18 ȝoure beestis. Lytyll is this in the
siȝt of the Lord. Ferthermore also he
19 schal taken Moab in to ȝoure hondis; and
ȝe schul smyten alle streyngthid⁹ cytee,
and alle chosen cyte, and ȝe schuln hewen
doun eche tree berynge fruyt, and alle
the wellis of watirs ȝe schuln stoppen,
and alle noble feeld ȝe schuln coueren
20 with stonys. It is doo than erly, whann
sacrifice is wont to be offerd, and, loo!
watirs camen by the weye of Edom;
21 and the erth is fulfillid with watirs. Alle
forsothe Moabitis herynge, that kyngis
hadden steyȝiden up, that thei fiȝten
aȝeynus hem, thei clepiden to gydre alle
that weren gird abowen with knyȝtis
gyrdill, and thei stoden in the termys.
22 And first erly rijsynge, and nowe the

the word¹ of the Lord at hym? Whiche
seiden, 'It isᵐ. And the kyng of Israel,
and Josephat, kyng of Juda, and the kyng
of Edom, ȝeden doun to hym. Forsotheⁿ 13
Elise seide to the kyng of Israel, What is
to me and to theeᵒ? Go thou to the prophetis of thi fadir and of thi modir. And
the kyng of Israel seide to hym, Whi hath
the Lord gaderidᵖ these thre kyngis, to bitake hem into the hondis of Moab? And 14
Elisee seide to hym, The Lord of oostis
lyueth, in whos siȝt Y stonde, if Y were
not aschamed† of the cheer of Josephat,
king of Juda, treuli Y hadde not per-
seyued, nethir Y hadde biholde thee. Now 15
forsothe brynge ȝe to me a sautrere. And
whanne the sautrere song, the hond of the
Lord was maad on⁹ hymʳ, and he seide,
The Lord seith these thingis, Make ȝe 16
theˢ wombe, ether deptheᵗ, of this stronde
dichis and dichis. For the Lord seith 17
these thingis, Ȝe schulen not se wynd,
nethir reyn, and this depthe schal be fillid
with watris, and ȝe schulen drynke, and
ȝoure meynees, and ȝoure beestis. And 18
this is litilᵘ in the siȝt of the Lord. Ferthermore also he schal bitake Moab in to
ȝoure hondis; and ȝe schulen smyte ech 19
strengthid citee, and ech chosun citee, and
ȝe schulen kitte doun ech tre‡ berynge
fruyt, and ȝe schulen stoppe alle the wellis
of watris, and ȝe schulen hile with stonys
ech noble feeld. Therfor it was doon eerli; 20
whanne sacrifice is wont to be offrid, and,
lo! watris camen bi the weie of Edom,
and the lond was fillid with watris. So- 21
theli alle menᵛ of Moab herden, that
kyngisᵛᵛ hadden stiedʷ to fiȝte aȝens hem;
'and men of Moabˣ clepiden togidereʸ alle
men, that weren gird with girdilᶻ aboue,
and thei stoden in theᵃ termes. And men 22
of Moab risidenᵇ ful eerli, and whanne
the sunne was risun thanne euen aȝens
the watris, thei sien the watris reed as
blood euene aȝensᶜ. And thei seiden, It 23

† aschamed; in denyinge his axing to him, sithen he is feithful and deuout. Lire here. c.

‡ kitte doun ech tre, etc.; this is specialy doon for the malice of the puple of Moab, ether this myȝte wel be doon out of the lond of biheest. Lire here. c.

ᵖ of thi CE. Om. ʙ.   ⁹ the strengthid ᴀ.

¹ seruaunt ɪ.   ᵐ ȝhe ɪ.   ⁿ And ɪ.   ᵒ thee, an ydolatour ɪ.   ᵖ gaderid to gidre ɪ.   ⁹ upon ɪ.   ʳ Helizee ɪ.
ˢ Om. ᴇʟᴘ.   ᵗ the depthe ɪ.   ᵘ litil thing ɪ.   ᵛ the men x sec. m.   ᵛᵛ these kyngis ɪ.   ʷ stied up ɪ.
ˣ sum men of Moab c. and thei ɪ.   ʸ Om. ᴅᴇғɢᴋʟᴍᴏᴘǫʀsᴡxby.   ᶻ u knyȝtis girdil ɪ. u girdil ʀ.   ᵃ her ɪ.
ᵇ resen ɪ. risen ᴇʟᴘ.   ᶜ aȝens hem ɪ.

sunne sprungen forn aȝeinst of the watirs, Moabitis seen aȝenward rede watirs
23 as blode. And thei seiden, Blood of
swerde it is; the kyngis han fouȝten
aȝeynst hem seluen, and thei ben slayn
to gidre; nowe, Moab, goo to the praye.
24 And thei wenten in to the tentis of
Yrael; forsothe Yrael ryisynge smote
Moab, and thei flowen byfore hem.
Thanne camen thei that ouercomen, and
25 smyten Moab, and distruyden the cytees;
and alle the best feelde thei fulfilliden,
eche seendynge stoonys; and alle the
wellis of watirs thei stoppyden, and alle
the treese berynge fruyt thei heweden
doun, so that oonly the wallis made with
erthe laften; and the cyte is enuyround
of slyngers, and of grete partye smyten.
26 And whanne kyng Moab hadde seen, that
is, the enemyes to han the ouerhond, he
tooke with him seuen hundreth men
drawynge oute swerdis, that thei breken
oute to king Edom; and thei myȝten
27 not. And takynge his first goten sone,
that was to regnen for him, he offerd
brent sacrifice upon the wall; and greet
indignacioun is made in Yrael; and
anoon thei wenten aweye fro hym, and
turneden aȝeyn into their lond.

CAP. IV.

1 Forsothe a maner womman of the wiyuys
of prophetis cryede to Helise, seyinge,
Thy seruaunt, my man, is deed, and thou
hast knowen for thy seruaunt was dreedynge God; and loo! a creaunsure came,
that he take my two sonys to sernen to
2 hym. To whom seyde Helisee, What wilt
thou that I doo to² thee? sey to me, what
hast thou in thin hous? And sche answerde, I thi seruaunt haue not eny
thinge in my hous, bot a lytill of oyle,
3 by the whiche I be anoyntid. To whome
he seith, Goo, and aske by borwynge of
alle thi neyȝbours voyd vessellis not fewe.

is the[d] blood of swerd, *that is, sched out
bi swerd*[e]; kyngis fouȝten[f] aȝens hem silf,
and thei ben slayn togider; now go thou,
Moab, to the prey. And thei ȝeden in to 24
the castels of Israel; forsothe Israel roos,
and smoot Moab, and thei fledden bifor
men[g] of Israel. Therfor[h] thei that hadden
ouercome, camen[i], and smytiden[j] Moab,
and destrieden cytees[k]; and alle men send-25
ynge stoonys filliden ech beste feeld, and
stoppiden alle the wellis of watris, and
kittiden[l] doun alle trees[m] berynge fruyt,
so that oneli 'wallis maad of erthe[n] weren
left; and the citee was cumpassid of men
settinge engynes, and was[o] smytun bi greet
part[p]. And whanne the kyng of Moab 26
hadde seyn this, that is, that the[q] enemyes
hadden the maistrie, he took with hym
seuene hundrid men drawynge[r] swerdis,
that thei shulden breke in to the kyng of
Edom; and thei myȝten not. And he took 27
his firste gendrid sone, that schulde regne
for hym, and offride[s] brent sacrifice on the
wal; and greet indignacioun was[t] maad in
Israel†; and anoon thei ȝeden awei fro
hym, and turneden aȝen in to her lond.

CAP. IV.

Forsothe[u] sum[v] womman† of the wyues 1
of prophetys criede to Elisee, and seide,
Thi seruaunt, myn hosebonde, is deed, and
thou knowist that thi seruaunt dredde
God; and lo! the[w] creaunser, *that is, he
to whom the*[x] *dette is owid*[y], cometh to
take my two² sones to serue hym. To 2
whom Elisee seide, What wolt thou that
Y do to thee? seie thou to me, what hast
thou in thin hows? And she answeride,
Y thin handmayde haue not ony thing in
myn hows, no but a litil of oile, bi[z] which
Y schal be anoyntid§. To whom he seide, 3
Go thou, and axe bi borewyng of alle thi

† *greet indig-
nacioun was
maad in Is-
rael;* in Ebreu
it is, greet ire
was maad on
Israel, that is,
of God offendid
aȝenus the sones
of Israel, for
thanne her
wickidnesses
weren remem-
brid bifore God,
bi the aungel
that was prince
of Moabitis;
that is, that
the sones of
Israel hadden
do as grete
yuels ether
worse, in of-
frynge her sones
and douȝtris
to fendis, wher-
for thanne for
the veniaunce
of this yuel,
pestilence felde
in the oost of
Israel, and so
thei weren
compellid to go
awey fro the
sege, for her
synnes passid.
Lire here. c.
‡ *sum wom-
man;* bi Ebreys
and Latyn doc-
turis, this
womman was
the wiyf of
Abdie, that
was in dette,
for the feeding
of profitis, in
the tyme of
persecucioun of
Jesabel. *Lire
here.* c.
§ *anoyntid;*
that is, schal
be refreischid
a litil to the
sauering of
potage. *Lire
here.* c.

d Om. EIL.   e Om. CI.   f han fouȝten I.   g the men I.   h Thanne I.   i Om. L.   j smeten EILP.
k her cytees I.   l kitten J.   m the trees I.   n eerthen wallis I.   o it was I.   p part *therof* I.   q his I.
r drawynge out I.   s offride *him* a I.   t *of the Lord* wus I.   u Sothely I.   v a IM.   w a I.   x Om. CD
FGKLMNOPSXbg.   y Gloss omitted in I.   z Om. Q.   a with I.

I i 2

4 And goo in, and close thi dore, whanne thou and thi sonys weren with inne forth; and putte therof in to alle these vessellis; and whanne thei weren ful, thou schalt 5 take. And so the woman wente, and closede the dore vpon hir silf and vpon hir children, thei offerden vesselis, and 6 sche heelde in. And whanne the vesselis weren fulle, sche seyde to hire sone, Brynge to me ʒit a vessel. And he vnswerde, I haue not. And the oyle stode. 7 Sche forsothe came, and schewide to the man of God; and he, Goo, he seith, sylle the oyle, and ʒeelde to thi creaunser; thou forsothe and thi sonys liuith of the 8 remnaunt. Forsothe a maner day is done, and Helisee passed thorʒ Suna cyte; forsothe ther was there a grete womman, that heelde hym, that he ete brede. And whann oft sithes he passede thens, he turnede asyde to hyre, that he ete brede. 9 The whiche seyde to hyre man, I perceyue that this is an holy man, that oft 10 sithis passith bi us; thanne make we to hym a litill soupynge place, and putte we in it to hym a lityll bed, and a borde, and a lytyll seete, and a candilstyke; that whanne he comith to us, he dwelle ther. 11 Thann a maner day is done, and commynge he turnede asyde in to the soup-12 ynge place, and restyde there. And he seide to Gyazi, his child, Clepe this^f Sunamyte. The whiche whanne hade clepyd hyre, and sche hadde stonden beforn hym, 13 he seide to his childe, Speke to hire, Lo! bisily in alle thingis thou hast serued to us; what wilt thou that I do to thee? Whethir hast thou a nede, and wilt that I speke to the kyng, or to the prince of chyualrye? The whiche answerd, In the 14 mydil of my peple I dwelle. And he seith, What thanne sche wille that I do to hyre? And Giazi seide to hym, Ne

neiʒboris voide vessels not fewe^b. And 4 entre, and close thi dore, whanne thou art with ynne, thou and thi sones; and putte ʒe therof in to alle these vessels; and whanne tho schulen be ful, thou schalt take awei^c. Therfor the womman ʒede, 5 and closide the dore on^d hir silf and on^e hir sones, thei brouʒten vessels^f, and sche 'heldide in^g. And whanne the vessels weren 6 fulle, sche seide to hir sone, Brynge thou^h ʒit a vessel to me. And he answeride, Y haue not^i. And^k the oyle stood^l. For-7 sothe sche cam, and schewide^m to the man of God; and he seide, Go thou, sil thou^n the oile, and ʒelde to thi creauncer; forsothe^o thou and thi children lyue^p of the residue^q. Forsothe sum^r day was maad, 8 and Elisee passide bi a citee, Sunam^s; sotheli^t a greet womman was there, which helde hym+, that he schulde ete breed. And whanne he passide ofte therbi, 'he turnede to hir, that he schulde ete breed^u. 'Which womman^v seide to hir hosebonde, 9 Y perseyue that this is an hooli man of God, that passith ofte bi vs; therfor make 10 we a litil soler to hym, and putte we therynne a litil bed to hym, and a boord, and a chaier, and a candilstike; that whanne he cometh to vs, he dwelle there. Ther-11 for sum^w dai was maad, and he^x cam, and turnede in to the soler, and restide there. And he seide to Giezi, his child, Clepe 12 thou this Sunamyte^y. And whanne he hadde clepid hir, and sche hadde stonde^z bifor him, he seide to his child, Speke 13 thou to hir, Lo! thou hast mynystride^a to vs bisili in alle thingis; what wolt thou that Y do to thee? Whether thou hast a cause, and wolt that Y speke to the kyng, ether to the prince of the chyualrye? And sche answeride, I dwelle in the myddis of my puple. And he^b seide^c, What therfor^d 14 wole sche that Y do to hir? Giezi seide

+ *which helde him; that is, bisily preyude to mete. Lire here. c.*

---

f this seruaunt B. sec. m.

b a fewe I. c awei *thin hoond* I. d upon I. e Om. I. f the vessels R. g ʒotte in BC. ʒettide in X. helde in DFGIKMNOQSWbç. helde in tho R. Om. ELPU. h Om. EL. i noon I. k And *thanne* I. l stood, *encreessinge no more* I. m schewide it I. n Om. I. o and I. p lyue ʒe IS. q remenaunt I. r a I. s that hiʒt Sunam I. t and I. u that he wolde ete breed *with hir* I. v And sche I. w a I. x Helizee I. y womman of Sunam I. z come up I. a seruyd I. b Helizee I. c seide to him I. d thanne I.

aske thou, forsothe sche hath no sone,
15 and hyre man is olde. And so he comaundid, that he clepe hyre. The whiche
whanne was clepid, and hade stonden by-
16 fore the doore, he seyde to hyre, In this
tyme and in this same houre, ʒif the liyf
were leder, thou schalt haue a sone. in
thy wombe. And sche answerde, Wylle
thou not, I beseche, my lord, man of God,
wylle thou not lyʒen to thin hond wom-
17 man. And the womman conceyuede, and
bare a chiʒlde in tyme, and in the same
18 houre, that Helise hadde seyde. Forsothe
the child wexe; and whan ther was a
maner day, and he was gon oute to his
19 fadir, and to the repers, he seith to his
fadir, Myn heued 'I aakeᵍ, my hened 'I
aakeᵍ. And he seyde to a childe, Take,
20 and leed hym to his modir. The whiche
whanne he hadde taken, and lade to his
modir, sche putte hym upon hir knees
21 vnto the mydday, and he is deed. Forsothe sche steiʒede up, and leyde hym
vpon the bed of the man of God, and
closede the dore. And sche gon oute,
22 clepyde hyre man, and seith, Sende with
me, I bisech, oon of the childre, and a
sche asse, and I schal rennen oute vnto
23 the man of God, and turnen aʒein. The
whiche seith to hyre, For what cause
gost thou to him? to day ben not kalendis, ne sabot. The whiche answerde, I
24 schal goon. And sche greythede the sche
asse, and comaundid to the chiʒlde, Driyf,
and go forth; ne make thou to me abijdynge in goynge, and that doo that I co-
25 maunde to thee. Than sche wente forthe,
and came to the man of God, in to the
hill of Carmele. And whan the man of
God hade seen hyre forn aʒeynst, he seith
to Giazi, his chiʒld, Lo! that Sunamyte;
26 go than in to aʒein commynge of hyre,
and seye to hyre, Whethir riʒt it is don
aboute thee, and thi man, and thi chylde?

to hym, Axe thou not, forᶠ she hath no
15 sone, and hir hosebonde is eeld. Therfor
Elisee comaundide, that heᵍ schulde clepe
hir. And whanne sche was clepid, and
16 stood bifor the dore, heʰ seide to hir, In
this tyme† and in this same our, if lijf
schalⁱ be felowᵏ, thou schalt haue a sone
in theˡ wombe. And sche answeride, Nyle
thou, my lord, the man of God, Y biseche,
17 nyle thou lyeⱡ to thin hondmaide. And
the womman conseyuede, and childide a
sone in the tyme, and in the same our, in
18 which Elisee hadde seid. Sotheli the child
encreeside; and whanne summᵐ day was,
and the child was goon out, and ʒede to
19 his fadir, and to the repers, he seide to his
fadir, Myn heed akith, myn heed akith.
And heⁿ seide to a childᵒ, Take, and lede
20 hym to his modir. And whanne he hadde
take, and hadde brouʒt hym to his modir,
sche settideᵖ hym onq hir knees 'til toʳ
21 myddai, and he was deedˢ. Sotheliᵗ she
stiedeᵘ, and leide hym onᵛ the litil bed of
the man of God, and closide the dore.
22 And sche ʒede out, and clepide hir hosebonde, and seide, Y biseche, sende thou
with me oon of the children, and an asse,
and Y schal renne out 'til toʷ the man of
23 God, and Y schal turne aʒen. And he seide
to hir, For what cause goist thou to hym?
to dai benˣ not calendisʸ, nether sabatᶻ.
24 And she answeride, Y schal go. And scheᵃ
sadlideᵃ theᵇ asse, and comaundide to the
childᶜ, Dryue thou, and haasteᵈ; make
thou noteᵉ tariyng to me in goyng, and
do thou this thing whichᶠ Y comaunde
25 to thee. Therforᵍ sche ʒede forth, and
cam to the man of God, in to the hil of
Carmele. And whanne the man of God
hadde seyn hir euene aʒenʰ, he seide to
Giezi, his child, Lo! thilke Sunamyteⁱ;
26 go thou therfor in to the metyng of hir,
and seie thou to hir, Whether it is doon
riʒtfuli aboute thee, and aboute thin hose-

† in this tyme; in Ebreu it is thus, in this tyme as in tyme of liyf, thou schalt biclippe a sone, that is, in the ʒeer turned aboute thou schalt lyue hool as now, and thou schalt biclippe a sone borun thanne, as Rabi Salomon seith. Lire here. c.
‡ nyle thou lye; Ebreys seyen, nyle thou faile to thyn hand-maide, for the Ebrew word set here, signe-fieth bothe lye and faile; and this is the sen-tence, as Rabi Salomon seith; if thou axidist to me, that schal die soone, it were not matir of ioye to me, but of morenyng, and therfor Y preye, that thi word faile not, so that the sone that schal be ioun to me, dye not. Lire here. c.

ᵍ akith A.

ᶠ for whi 1. ᵍ Giezy 1. ʰ Helizee 1. ⁱ Om. 1. ᵏ felow, or if I lyue 1. ˡ thi 1. ᵐ a 1. ⁿ his fadir 1.
ᵒ seruaunt 1. ᵖ sette 1. q upon 1. ʳ vnto 1. ˢ deed thanne 1. ᵗ Certis 1. ᵘ stiede up 1. ᵛ upon 1.
ʷ vnto 1. ˣ ther ben 1. ʸ solempnytees 1. ᶻ haly day 1. ᵃ greythide 1. ᵇ an 1. ᶜ child or seruaunt 1.
ᵈ haaste thee 1. ᵉ no 1. ᶠ that 1. ᵍ Thanne 1. ʰ aʒens him 1. ⁱ womman of Sunam 1.

27 The whiche answerde, Riȝt. And whann
sche was commen to the man of God, in
to the hyll, sche cauȝte his feete; and
Giazi wente niȝ, for to meuen hyre aweye.
And the man of God seith, Lete hyr;
forsothe the liyf of hyre is in bytternesse, and the Lord hath hillid fro me,
28 and hath not schewed to me. The whiche
seyde to hym, Whethir I askide my sone
of my lord? Whethir I seyde not to
29 thee, Ne begijle thou me? And he seith
to Giazy, Gyrde thi reenys, and take my
staf in thin hond, and goo; ȝif eny[i] man
aȝein comme to thee, ne salute thou hym;
and ȝif eny man salutith thee, answere
thou not to hym; and putte my staf
30 vpon the face of the chylde. Bot the
moder of the chyld seith, The Lord
lyueth and thi soule lyueth, I schal not
leue thee. Thanne he roos, and folowed
31 hyre. Giazi forsothe wente before hem,
and putt the staf upon the face of the
chyld; and ther was not voice, ne witte.
And he turned aȝein in to 'aȝein commynge[j] of hym; and he tolde to hym,
32 seyinge, The child hath not rysen. Than
Helisee wente in to the hous, and lo!
the child laye deed in the bed of hym.
33 And goon in he closede the dore vpon
hym, and vpon the chyld; and he preyed
34 the Lord. And he steiȝide up, and laye
vpon the chyld; and he putte his mouth
vpon the mouth of hym, and his eeȝen
vpon the eeȝen of hym, and his hondis
vpon the hondis of hym. And he bowede
hym silf vpon hym; and made hoote is
35 the flesche of the chyld. And he eft
'turnede aȝein[k] in the hous oonys hydre
and thidre; and he steiȝide vp, and laye
vpon hym, and the chyld brethed seuen
36 sithes, and opnede the eeȝen. And he
clepide Giazi, and seyde to hym, Clepe
this Sunamyte. The whiche clepid wente
in to hym. The whiche seith, Take thi

bonde, and aboute thi sone? And sche
answeride, Riȝtfuli[k]. And whanne sche 27
hadde come to the man of God, in to the
hil, sche took his feet; and Giezi neiȝede,
that he schulde remoue hir[l]. And the
man of God seide, Suffre thou hir; for
hir soule is in bitternesse, and the Lord
helde[m] priuy fro me, and schewide[n] not to
me. And sche seide to hym, Whether I 28
axide my[o] sone of my[p] lord? Whether
Y seide not to thee, Scorne thou not me?
And he seide to Giezi, Girde thi leendis, 29
and take my staf in thin hond[pp], and go;
if[q] a man metith[qq] thee, grete thou not
hym†; and if ony man gretith thee, answere thou not hym; and putte thou my
staf on[r] the face of the child. Forsothe[s] 30
the 'modir of the child[t] seide, The Lord
lyueth and thi soule lyueth, Y schal not
leeue, '*ether forsake*[u], thee. Therfor[v] he
roos, and suede hir. Sotheli[w] Giezi ȝede 31
bifor hem, and puttide the staaf on[x] the
face of the child; and 'vois was not[y], nether wit. And Giezi turnede aȝen to[z] the
meetyng of hym; and telde to him, and
seyde, The child 'roos not[a]. Therfor Elisee 32
entride in to the hows, and, lo! the deed
child lai in his bed. And he[b] entride, and 33
closide the dore[c] on hym silf, and on[d] the
child; and preiede to the Lord. And he[e] 34
stiede[f], and lay on[g] the child; and he puttide his mouth on[h] the mouth of the child,
and hise iȝen on[h] the iȝen of the child,
and hise hondis on[h] the hondis of the
child. And he bouwide hym silf on[h] the
child; and the fleisch of the child was
maad hoot. And he[i] turnede aȝen, and 35
walkide in the hows onys hidur and
thidur; and[k] Elisee stiede[l], and lai on[m]
the child, and the child ȝoxide seuene
sithis, and openyde the iȝen. And he[n] 36
clepide Giezi, and seide to hym, Clepe
thou this Sunamyte[o]. And sche was
clepid, and entride to hym. And he seide,

† *greete thou not hym*: that is, meddle thou not with hym, wordis lettinge thee fro the weye, and bi sich maner Crist spekith in x. c°. of Luk to dissiplis sent to preche, Grete ȝe no man bi the weye. *Lire here.* c.

[i] a *ACEFH*. [j] the aȝen comyng *A*. [k] wente *E pr. m.*

[k] *it is don* riȝtfuli I. [l] hir *awey* I. [m] hath holde it I. [n] schewide it I. I. [p] *thee* my I. [pp] hondis L. [q] and if EL. [qq] mete L. [r] upon I. [s] And I. [t] childs modir I. [u] Om. CDGINOQSX *sec. m.* bç. [v] Thanne I. [w] And I. [x] upon I. [y] ther was not vois in him I. [z] in to I. [a] hath not risen I. [b] Helizee I. [c] upon I. [d] upon I. [e] Helizee I. [f] stiede up I. [g] upon I. [h] upon I. [i] Helizee I. [k] and eft I. [l] ȝede up I. [m] up I. [n] Helizee I. [o] womman of Sunam I.

37 sone. Sche came, and felle at hys feet, and honourede vpon the erthe; and sche 38 toke hyre sone, and wente oute. And Helisee turnede aȝein in to Galgala. Forsothe ther was hunger in the lond, and the sonys of prophetis dwelliden before hym. And Helisee seyde to oon of his childre, Sete a grete potte, and seethe 39 potage to the sonis of prophetes. And oon wente oute in to the feelde, that he gedre wijld herbis; and he foond as a wijld vyne, and he gederde of it wijld gourdis of the feeld. And he fulfillide his mantylle, and turnede aȝein, and¹ hewede^m to gydre in to the pott of potage; he wyst not forsothe what it was. 40 Thanne they helden in to felawis, that thei myȝten eten; and whanne thei haden tastyden of the seethinge, thei crieden oute, seyinge, Deth in the pott! deth in the pott! man of God. And thei myȝten 41 not eeten. And he, Bryngith to, he seith, mele. And whanne thei haden brouȝt, he putt in to the pott, and seith, Heeldith in to the puple, that thei eten; and there was no more eny thing of bytternesse in 42 the pott. Forsothe a maner man came fro Balsalisa, bryngynge to the man of God loouys of first fruytes, and tenue barly loouys, and newe whete, in his bagge. And he seide, Ȝeue to the puple, 43 that it ete. And his seruaunt answerde to hym, Howe mychc is this, that I putt before an hundreth men? Eft he seith, Ȝeue to the puple, that it ete; these thingis forsothe seith the Lord, Thei schul eten, and ther schal leuen ouer. 44 And so he sette before hem, the whiche eeten; and ther laft ouer, aftir the worde of the Lorde.

Take thi sone. She cam, and felde doun 37 to his feet, and worschipide on erthe^p; and sche took hir sone, and ȝede out. And 38 Elisee turnede aȝen in to Galgala. Forsothe hungur was in the loud, and the sones of prophetis dwelliden bifor hym. And Elisee seide to oon of his children, Set thou a greet pot, and sethe thou potage to the sones of prophetis†. And oon 39 ȝede^q out in to the feeld to gadere eerbis of the feeld; and he foond as a^r wilde vyne, and he gaderide therof gourdis of the feeld. And he fillide his mentil, and he turnede aȝen, and schredde^s in to the pot of potage; for^t he wiste not what it was. Therfor thei helden yn^a to felowis 40 to ete; and whanne thei hadden taastid of the sething, thei crieden out, and seiden, Deth^v in the pot! deeth^v in the pot! thou man of God. And thei miȝten not ete^w. And he^x seide, Brynge ȝe meele. And 41 whanne thei hadden brouȝt, he puttide^y in to the pot, and seide, Helde ȝe^yy to the cumpany, that thei ete; and ony thing of bitternesse was^z nomore in the pot. For-42 sothe^n sum^b man cam fro the pleyn of Salisa^c†, and bar to the man of God looues of the firste fruytis§, ten looues of barli, and newe wheete, in his scrippe. And the man of God seide, Ȝyue thou^d to the puple, that it ete. And his mynystre 43 answeride^f to hym, 'Hou myche^g is this, that Y sette bifor an hundrid men? Eft Elisee seide, Ȝyue thou to the puple, that it ete; for^h the Lord seith these thingis, Thei schulen ete, and it^i shal leeue. Ther-44 for^k he puttide^l bifor hem, whiche^m eeten; and it^n lefte^o, bi^p the word of the Lord.

† to the sones of prophetis; that is, disciplis of hem, for they lyueden religiously. Lire here. c.

‡ Salisa; Baal Salisa, is twey wordis in Ebreu, and Baal signefieth here pleyn, ether cuntrey, and Salisa is the propir name of a citee in that cuntrey. Lire here. c.
§ looues of the firste fruytis ben not takun here siche, as weren offrid in the temple of the Lord, but tho ben seid looues of the firste fruytis, for tho weren of the firste fruyth of that ȝeer; summe bokis laan, and x r. looues of barly, but this word and, is not in Ebreu, nether it is of the text, and newe wheete in Ebreu it is, thing maad of cornes, for the cornes of wheete weren not fully ripe, but tho myȝten be sengid and eten so. Lire here. c.

CAP. V.

1 Naaman, the prince of chyualrye of the kyng of Cyrye, was a grete man anentis

CAP. V.

Naaman, prince of the chyualrye of the 1 kyng of Syrie, was a greet man, and wor-

¹ Om. ce. ^m heewȝ ce.

p the erthe i. q wente i. r it were a i. s schredde tho i. t forsothe i. u yn theroff i. v Deth is i. w ete it i. x Helizee i. y putte it i. putte el. puttide it k. yy ȝe out i. z ther was i. a Certis i. Therfor kls. b a iniw. c Balsalisa a scc. m. d thou of tho looues i. e seruaunt i. f seide el. g What i. h forsothe i. i ther i. k Thanne i. l putte i. m the whiche i. n ther i. o lefte mete i. p aftir i.

his lord, and a wirschipide; by hym forsothe the Lord ȝaue helth to Cyrye;
forsothe he was a stronge man and riche,
2 but mesell. Forsothe fro Cyrye wenten
out lytyll theeues, and thei haden brouȝt
fro the lond of Yrael a lytill chyld womman caytife, that was in the seruyce of
3 the wiyf of Naaman. The whiche seith
to hir lady, Wolde God, my lord were
at a prophete that is in Samarye; forsothe he schulde han helyde hym fro the
4 lepre that he hath. And so Naaman
wente in to his lord, and tolde to hym,
seyinge, Thus and thus spake the chyld
5 womman of the lond of Yrael. And so
the kyng of Cyrye seyde to hym, Go,
and I schal sende letters to the kyng of
Yrael. The whiche whann was gon,
and hade take with hym tenn talentis of
syluer, and sexe thousand platis of gold,
and tenn chaungynge maner of clothis,
6 he tooke to the kyng of Yrael lettris in
to these wordis; Whanne thou takist this
lettre, wyte thou, that I haue sente to
thee Naaman my scruaunt, that thou
7 hele hym fro his lepre. And whanne
the kyng of Yrael hade red the letters,
he kutte his clothis, and seith, Whethir
a god I am, that I mow slen and quyck-
en, for he hath sente to me, that I hele
a man fro his lepre? Takith heed and
seeth, that occasiouns he sechith aȝeyns
8 me. The whiche whanne Helisee, the
man of God, hadde herde, that is, the
kyng of Yrael to han kutte his clothis,
he sente to hym, seyinge, Why hast thou
kutte thy clothis? come he to me, and
9 wyte a prophete to be in Yrael. Thanne
Naaman came with hors and chaaris, and
stood at the dore of the hous of Helisee.
10 And Helisee sente to hym a messanger,
seyinge, Goo, and be waschen seuen
sithis in Jordan; and thi flesche schal
receyuen helth, and thou schalt be
11 clensed. Naaman wroth wente aweye,

schipid anentis his lord; for bi hym the
Lord ȝaf helthe to Sirie; sotheli he was
a strong man and riche[q], but leprouse[r].
Forsothe theues ȝede out of Sirie, and led-2
den prisonere[s] fro the lond of Israel a litil
damysele[t], that was in the[u] seruyce of the
wijf of Naaman. 'Which damysele[v] seide 3
to hir ladi, 'Y wolde[w], that my lord hadde
be at the prophete which[x] is in Samarie;
sotheli the prophete schulde[y] haue curid
hym of the[z] lepre which[a] he hath. Ther-4
for Naaman entride to his lord, and telde
to hym, and seide, A damysel of the lond
of Israel spak[b] so and so. Therfor the 5
kyng of Syrie seide to hym, Go thou, and
Y schal sende lettris to the kyng of Israel.
And whanne he[c] hadde go forth, and hadde
take with hym ten talentis of siluer, and
sixe thousynde goldun platis, 'ether floreyns[d], and ten chaungyngis of clothis,
he brouȝte lettris to the kyng of Israel 6
bi these[e] wordis; Whanne thou hast take
this pistle, wite thou, that Y haue sent to
thee Naaman, my seruaunt, that thou cure
hym of his lepre. And whanne the kyng 7
of Israel hadde red the[f] lettris, he to-rente
his clothis, and seide, Whether Y am God,
that may[ff] sle and quykene, for this kyng
sente to me, that Y cure a man of his
lepre? Perseyue ȝe, and se[g], that he sekith
occasiouns aȝens me. And whanne Elisee, 8
the man of God, hadde herd this, that is,
that the kyng of Israel hadde to-rente hise
clothis, he sente to the kyng, and seide,
Whi to-rentist thou thi clothis? come he[h]
to me, and wite he, that a[i] prophete is[k] in
Israel. Therfor[l] Naaman cam with horsis 9
and charis, and stood at the dore of the
hows of Elisee. And Elisee sente to hym 10
a messanger, and seide, Go thou[m], and be
thou waischun[n] seuensithis in Jordan; and
thi fleisch shal resseyue helthe, and thou
schalt be clensid[o]. Naaman was wrooth, 11
and ȝede awei, and seide, Y gesside, that
he schulde[p] go[q] out to me, and that he

---

q a riche 1.   r he was leprouse 1.   s Om. 1.   t damysele prisoner 1.   u Om. 1.   v And sche 1.   w Wolde
God 1.   x that 1.   y wolde 1.   z Om. 1.   a that 1.   b haath spoke 1.   c Naaman 1.   d Om. пɕɪк pr. m.
мᴎᴏᴏѕᴡьç.   e these same 1.   f these 1.   ff Y may cç.   g seeth 1.   h Naaman 1.   i ther is a 1.   k Om. 1.
l Thanne 1.   m Om. 1.   n weische 1.   o clensid so 1.   p wolde 1.   q haue gon 1к.

seyinge, I wende that he schulde goon oute to me, and stondynge schulde inwardly clepen the name of his God, and touche with his hond the place of the 12 lepre, and helen me. Whethir not beter ben Abana and Pharphar, the floodis of Damask, thanne alle the waters of Yrael, that I be waschen in hem, and be clens- 13 ede? Whann thann he hadde turnyde hymsilf, and goon aweye endeynynge, wenten to hym his seruauntis, and speken to hym, Fader, and ȝif a grete thinge the prophete hadde seide to thee, certis thou owedist to done; myche more for nowe he seyde to thee, Be wasched, and thou 14 schalt be clansede. He wente doun, and wasche in Jordane seuen sithis, aftir the worde of the man of God; and the flesche of hym is restorid as the flesche of a litil 15 chyld, and he is clensed. And turned aȝein to the man of God with alle his felawschip came, and stood before hym; and seith, Vereyly I woot, that ther is noon other God in all erth[p], bot oonly the God of Yrael; also, I beseche, that thou take a blissynge of thi seruaunt. 16 And he answerde, The Lord lyueth before whom I stonde, for I schal not taken. And whanne forsynge he made, vtturly 17 he assentyde not. And so Naaman seide, As thou wilt; bot, I beseche, graunte to me, thi seruaunt, that I take two burdowns charge fro the lond; forsothe thi seruaunt schal no more make brent sacrifice, or slayn sacrifice, to alyen goddis, bot 18 to the Lord. This forsothe oonly is, of the whiche thou preye the Lord for thi seruaunt, whanne my lord goth in to the temple of Remmon, that he honoure, and hym lenynge vpon myn hond, ȝif I honoure in the temple of Remmon, he honouryng in the same place, that the Lord forȝeue to me, thi seruaunt, for this thing.

schulde[r] stonde[s], and clepe[t] the name of 'the Lord[u] his God, and that he schulde touche[v] with his hond the place of lepre[w], and schulde cure[x] me[y]. Whether Abana 12 and Pharphar, floodis[z] of Damask, ben not betere than alle the watris of Israel, that Y be waischun in tho[a], and be clensid? Therfor whanne he[b] hadde turned hym 13 silf, and ȝede[c] awei, hauynge indignacioun, hise seruauntis neiȝiden to hym, and spaken to hym, Fadir, thouȝ the prophete hadde seid to thee a greet thing, certis thou owist[d] to do[e]; hou myche more[f] for now he seide to thee, Be thou waischun, and thou schalt be clensid. He[g] 14 ȝede[h] doun, and waischide *hym* seuensithis in Jordan, bi[i] the word of the man of God; and his fleisch was restored as the fleisch of a litil child, and he was clensid. And 15 he turnede aȝen with al his felouschipe to the man of God, and cam, and stood bifor hym; and seide, Verili Y knowe, that noon other God is in al erthe, no but oneli God of Israel; therfor, Y biseche, that thou take blessyng[k]† of thi seruaunt. And he[l] 16 answeride, The Lord lyueth bifor whom Y stonde, for Y schal not take[m]. And whanne he made 'strengthe, *that is, greet preier*[n], Elisee assentide not outirli. Therfor[o] Naaman seide, As thou wolt; but, I 17 biseche, graunte thou to me, thi seruaunt, that Y take of 'the lond[p]‡ the birthun[q] of twei burdones§; for[r] thi seruaunt schal no more make brent sacrifice, èther slayn sacrifice, to alien goddis, no but to the Lord. Forsothe[s] this thing is[t] oneli, of 18 which thou schalt preic the Lord for thi seruaunt, whanne my lord schal entre into the temple of Remmon, that he worschipe[n], and while[v] he 'schal lene[w] on[x] myn hond, if Y worschipe in the temple of Remmon‖, while[y] he worschipith[z] in the same place, that the Lord forȝyue to[a]

† *blessing; that is, ȝiftis offrid wilfulli and deuoutly.*
‡ *Lire here. c.*
‡ *that Y take of the lond, etc.; this was of special dyuocioun of Naaman, thouȝ he were not boundun therto, and myȝte lawfully make an auter to God with out Jerusalem and offre theronne to God, for he was not boundun to Moises law. Lire here. c.*
§ *burdones be bestis gendrid of an hors and femal asse, as a mule is gendrid aȝenward of a mere and a male asse. Lire here. c.*
‖ *if Y worschepe in the temple of Remmon; Elisee declaride, that this was leueful to him, and to worschipe God, may as wel bee doon with out the temple of an ydol, as with ȝnne. Lire here. c.*

---

[p] the erthe ᴇ *pr. m.*

[r] wolde 1.   [s] haue stonde 1.   [t] ynwardly haue clepid 1. schulde clepe ɴ.   [u] Om. ᴀ *pr. m. et plures.*
[v] haue touchid 1.   [w] the lepre ᴇɪ.   [x] haue curid 1.   [y] me so 1.   [z] the floodis 1.   [a] hem 1.   [b] Naaman 1.
[c] wente 1.   [d] ouȝtist ʙᴄᴅᴇꜰɢɪᴋʟᴍɴᴏᴘQʀꜱᴇᴜᴡxQ.   [e] do it ᴇɪʟ.   [f] more *rather* 1.   [g] Thanne Naaman 1.
[b] wente 1.   [i] aftir 1.   [k] blessyng, *that is, a ȝift* 1.   [l] Helizee 1.   [m] take it *of thee* 1.   [n] *greet foors therto* 1.   [o] Thanne 1.   [p] this eerthe 1.   [q] charge 1.   [r] forsothe 1.   [s] Sothely 1.   [t] it is 1.   [u] worschipe *the ydole* 1.   [v] Om. 1.   [w] worschipinge lene 1.   [x] upon 1.   [y] Om. 1.   [z] wurschipinge 1.   [a] to me 1.

19 The whiche seide to hym, Goo in pese.
Thann he ȝeede fro hym the chosen tyme
20 of the lond. And Giazi, the childe of the
man of God, seide, My lord hath sparede
to this Naaman Cyro, that he take not of
hym that he brouȝte; the Lord liueth,
for I schal rennen aftir hym, and I schal
21 taken of hym sumwhate. And Giazi folowede aftir the bac of Naaman; whom
whan he hade seen rennynge to hym, he
'leep doun[q] of the chaar in to aȝein commynge of hym; and seith, Whether riȝt
22 ben alle thingis? And he seith, Riȝt;
my lord sente me to thee, seyinge, Nowe
ben commen to me two yonge men fro
the hyll of Effraym, of the sonys of prophetes; ȝeue to hem a talent of syluer,
23 and double chaungynge clothis. And
Naaman seyde, Beter it is that thou take
two talentis. And he constreyned hym;
and he boond two talentis of syluer in
two baggis, and double clothis, and putte
to his two chylder, the whiche and bern
24 before hym. And whanne he was commyn nowe at euen, he tooke fro the hond
of hem, and leyde up in the house; and
he laft the men, and they wenten aweye.
25 He forsothe goon in stode bifore his lord.
And Helisee seyde, Whenns comyst thou,
Giezi? The whiche answerde, Thi ser-
26 uaunt ȝeede not o whydre. And he seith,
Whether myn hert was not in present,
whanne the man turnede aȝein fro his
chaar in to aȝein commynge of thee?
Nowe thanne thou hast taken syluer,
and taken clothes, that thou bye olyuis,
and vinis, and scheep, and oxen, and ser-
27 uauntis, and hond wymmen; bot and the
leepre of Naaman schal cleue to thee,
and to thi seede in to euermore. And
he wente out from hym mesell as snowe.

thi seruaunt for this thing. Which[b] Elisee 19
seide to hym, Go thou in pees. 'Therfor
he[c] ȝede fro Elisee in a chosun tyme of
the lond. And Giezi, the child of the 20
man of God, seide[d], My lord sparide[e] this
Naaman[f] of Syrie, that he took not of
hym that, that he brouȝte; the Lord
lyueth, for Y schal renne aftir hym, and
Y schal take of hym sum thing. And 21
Giezi suede aftir the bak of Naaman;
and whanne Naaman hadde seyn Giezi
rennynge to hym, he skippide doun[g] of
the chare in to the metyng of Giezi; and
seide, Whether alle thingis ben riȝtfuli[h]?
And[i] he seide, Riȝtfuli[k]; my lord sente me 22
to thee, and seide, Twey ȝonge men of the
hille of Effraym, of the sones of prophetis,
camen now to me; ȝyue thou to hem a
talent of siluer, and double chaungyng
clothis. And Naaman seide, It is betere 23
that thou take twei talentis†. And Naaman constreynede hym; and Naaman
boond twei[l] talentis of siluer in twei
sackis[m], and double[n] clothis, and puttide[o]
on[p] his twey children, '*that is, seruauntis*[q], whiche[r] also baren[s] bifor Giezi.
And whanne he[ss] hadde come thanne in 24
the euentid, he took[t] fro the hond of hem,
and leide[u] vp in the hows; and he delyuerede the men, and thei ȝeden[v]. For- 25
sothe[w] Giezi entride, and stood bifor his
lord. And Elise seide, Giezi, fro whennus
comest thou? Which[x] answeride, Thi seruaunt ȝede not to ony place. And Elise 26
seide, Whether myn herte was not in[y] present[z], whanne the man turnede aȝen fro
his chare in to the metyng of thee? Now
therfor thou hast take siluer, and thou
hast take clothis, that thou bie[a] places of[b]
olyues, and vyneris, and scheep, and oxis[c],
and seruauntis, and handmaydis[d]; but also 27
the lepre of Naaman schal cleue to thee,
and to thi seed withouten ende. And Giezi
ȝede[e] leprouse as snow, 'fro hym[f].

† *it is betere that thou take twei talentis;* in Ebreu it is thus, swere thou, and take thou twey talentis, swere thou, that is, Elisee sente thee, and bi this he dide periurie. *Lire here.* c.

[q] stood doun stille E *pr. m.* wente doun stille E *sec. vice.* leep doun E *tertia vice.*

[b] And I. [c] And so Naaman I. [d] seide *in his herte* I. [e] hath sparid I. [f] man I. [g] adoun I. [h] riȝtful I. doon riȝtfuli X *sec. m.* [i] Om. I. [k] *Thei ben* riȝt riȝtfuli I. [l] the two I. [m] baggis I. [n] the double I. [o] he putte I. [p] *tho* upon I. [q] Om. I. [r] the whiche I. [s] baren *it* I. [ss] Giezy I. [t] took *it* I. [u] leide it I. [v] ȝeden forth I. [w] And *thanne* I. [x] The which I. [y] Om. I. [z] present *there* I. presence ELP. [a] bie *therwith* I. [b] and I. [c] oxen I. [d] handmaydens I. [e] ȝede out fro him I. [f] Om. I.

CAP. VI.

1 Seyden forsothe the sonys of prophetis to Helisee, Loo! the place in the whiche we dwellen before thee, is streyt to us; 2 goo we vnto Jordan, and taken eche fro the wood sundrye matteers, that we beelden to us there a place to dwellen. 3 The whiche seide, Gooth. And oon of hem seith, Comme thanne and thou with thi seruauntis. He answerde, I schal 4 commen. And he wente with hem. And whanne thei weren commen to Jordan, 5 they hewen treese. It fell forsothe, that whanne oon had hewen a mateer, felle the yren of the axe in to the watir; and he criede oute, and seith, Allas! allas! allas! my lord, and that same I tooke of 6 borowynge. Forsothe the man of God seyde, Where felle it? And he schewyde to hym the place. Thanne he hewede of a tree, and putte thidir; and the yren 7 swam. And he saith, Take. The whiche 8 strauȝt out the hoond, and took it. The kyng forsothe of Cyrye fauȝte aȝeynst Yrael; and wente in counseil with his seruauntis, seiynge, In this place and 9 that sette we buschementis. And so the man of God sente to the kynge of Yrael, seyinge, Be war, lest thou passe to that place, for ther ben Cyris in busche- 10 mentis. And so the kyng of Yrael sente to that place, the whicheʳ the man of God hade spoken to hym, and heˢ before occupiede it, and he weytyde hym there 11 not oonys, ne twyes. And the herte of the kyng of Cyrye is distourbled for this thing; and, the seruauntis clepid to gydre, seith, Whi han ȝe not schewed to me, who be my traitour anentis the kyng 12 of Yrael? And oon of the seruauntis of hym seyde, Nay, my lord kyng, bot Helisee, the prophete, that is in Yrael,

CAP. VI.

1 Forsotheᵍ the sones of prophetis seiden to Elisee, Lo! the place in which we dwellen bifor thee, is streiȝtʰ to vs; 2 go we¹ ‘til to⌉ Jordan, and ech man takeᵏ of the¹ wode ‘a materᵐ† for hym silf, that we bild to vs here a place to dwelleⁿ. 3 Whichᵒ Elisee seide, Go ȝe. And oon of hem seide, Therfor ‘and thou comeᵖ with thi scruauntis. He answeride, Y schal 4 come. Andᑫ he ȝede with hem. And whanne thei ‘hadden comeʳ to Jordan, thei hewiden trees. Sotheliˢ it bifelde, that 5 whanne ‘o manᵗ hadde kit doun materᵘ, the yrun of the axe felde in to the watir; and he criede, and seide, Alas! alas! alas! my lordᵛ, and Y hadde take this same thing bi borewing. Sotheli the man of God 6 seide, Where felde it? And he schewide to hym the place. Therfor heʷ kittide doun a tree, and senteˣ thidurʸ; and the yrun fletide. And heˣ seide, Take thouᵃ. 7 Whichᵇ helde forth the hond, and took it. Forsothe theᶜ kyng of Syrie fauȝte aȝens 8 Israel; and he took counseil with hise seruauntis, and seide, Sette we busche- mentis in this place and thatᵈ. Therforᵉ 9 the man of God sente to the kyng of Israel, and seide, Be war, lest thou passe to that place, for men of Sirie ben there 10 in buschementis. Therfor the kyng of Israel sente to the place, whichᶠ the man of God hadde seid to him, and biforᵍ ocu- piede‡ it, and kepte hym silf there not onys, nether twies§. And the herte of 11 the kyng of Sirie was disturblid for this thing; and whanne hise seruauntis weren clepide togidere, he seide, Whi schewen ȝe not to me, who is my tretour anentis the kyng of Israel? And oon of hise ser- 12 uauntis seide, Nay, my lord the¹ kyng, but Elisee, the prophete, whichᵏ is in

† a mater: that is, trees, that ben mater for howsis to be bildid. Lire here. c.

‡ bifor occupi- ede; in takinge the buysche- mentis. Lire here. c.
§ nether twies; vndurstonde thou onely but ofte. Lire here. c.

ʳ that c.   ˢ be v.

ᵍ Sothely 1. ʰ noyous 1. ¹ we therfore 1. ʲ to 1. ᵏ take a porsion 1. ˡ Om. 1. ᵐ Om. 1. ⁿ dwelle therin 1. ᵒ And 1. ᵖ come thou also 1. ᑫ And thanne 1. ʳ camen 1. ˢ And 1. ᵗ a man of hem 1. ᵘ mater or wode 1. ᵛ Lord God oq. ʷ Helizee 1. ˣ sente it 1. ʸ thidur where the iren was 1. ˣ Helizee 1. ᵃ thou it 1. ᵇ The which 1. ᶜ Om. 1. ᵈ in that 1. ᵉ And therfor A. ᶠ that 1. ᵍ the king of Israel bifor 1. ʰ twies, but eft 1. ¹ Om. 1. ᵏ that 1.

schewith to the kyng alle wordis, whateuer thou hast spoken in thy priue
13 chaumbre. And he seyde to hym, Gooth,
and seeth, wher he be, that I sende, and
take hym. And thei tolden to hym, sey-
14 inge, Loo! in Dotaym he dwellith. And
he sente thidre hors, and chaaris, and
the strengthe of the oost; the whiche,
when thei weren commen at ny3t, they
15 enuyrounden the cyte. The seruaunt
forsothe of the man of God rysynge erly
wente oute, and he sawe the hoost in
enuyroun of the cyte, and hors, and
chaaris. And he tolde to hym, seyinge,
Allas! allas! allas! my lord, what schal
16 we done? And he answerde, Wylle thou
not dreede; forsothe mo ben with us than
17 with hem. And whanne Helise hade
preyede, he seith, Lord, opyn the ee3en
of this chylde, that he see. And the
Lord opnede the ee3en of the chijld, and
he saw3. And loo! an hyll ful of hors,
and of fyren chaaris, in enuyroun of He-
18 lisee. Forsothe the enmyes camen doun
to hym; bot Helisee preyede to the Lord,
seyinge, Smyit, I beseche, this folc with
blyndnesse. And the Lord smoot hem,
lest thei see3en, after the worde of Helisee.
19 Forsothe Helisee seyde to hem, This is
not the weye, ne this is not[t] the cyte;
folowith me, and I schal schewe to 3ou
the man, whom 3e[u] seeken. And he ladde
20 hem in to Samarye. And whan thei
weren commen in to Samarie, Helisee
seyde, Lord, opne the ee3en of these, that
thei seen. And the Lord opnede the ee3en
of hem, and thei seen hem selfen to ben
21 in the mydill of Samarye. And the kynge
of Yrael seide to Helisee, whanne he
hadde seen hem, Whether I schal smyten
22 hem, fader myne? And he seith, Thou
schalt not smyten hem, ne forsoth thou
hast taken hem with swerde[v], and with
thi bowe, that thou smyte; bot putte

Israel, schewith to the kyng of Israel alle
thingis, what euer thingis thou spekist in
thi closet. And the kyng seide to hem, 13
'Go 3e[l], and se[m], where he is, that Y sende,
and take hym. And thei telden to him,
and seiden, Lo! he dwellith in Dothaym.
And the kyng sente thidur horsis, and 14
charis, and the strengthe of the oost;
whiche[n], whanne thei hadden come bi
ny3t, cumpassiden the citee. Sotheli the 15
mynystre of the man of God roos eerli,
and 3ede out, and he si3 an oost in the
cumpas of the citee, and horsis, and charis.
And he telde to the man of God, and
seide, Alas! alas! alas! my lord, what
schulen we do? And he[o] answeride, Nile 16
thou drede; for[p] mo ben with vs than
with hem. And whanne Elisee hadde 17
preied, he seide, Lord, opene thou the
i3en† of this child, that he se. And the
Lord openyde the i3en of the[q] child, and[r]
he si3. And, lo! the hil[s] ful of horsis,
and of charis of fier, in the cumpas of
Elisee. Sotheli[t] the enemyes camen doun 18
to hym; forsothe[u] Elisee preiede to the
Lord, and seide, Y biseche[v], smyte thou[w]
this folc with blyndenesse‡. And[ww] the
Lord smoot hem, that thei sien not, bi the
word of Elisee. Forsothe Elisee seide to 19
hem, This is not the weie, nether this is[x]
the citee[y]; sue 3e me, and Y schal schewe
to[z] 3ou the man, whom 3e seken. And he
ledde hem into Samarie. And whanne 20
thei hadden entrid into Samarie, Elisee
seide, Lord, opene thou[a] the i3en of these
men, that thei see[b]. And the Lord openyde her i3en, and thei si3en, that thei
weren in the[c] myddis of Samarie. And 21
the kyng of Israel, whanne he hadde seyn
hem, seide to Elisee, My fadir, whether
Y schal smyte hem? And he seide, Thou 22
schalt not smyte hem, for thou hast not
take hem bi thi[d] swerd and bouwe, that
thou smyte hem; but sette thou breed

† *opene thou the i3en, etc.*; that is, 3yue thou to hym vertu to se tho thingis, that moun not be seyn of him bi kynde. *Lire here.* c.

‡ *blyndnesse* is takun here for si3t with out discrecioun, ether knowing; and Sodomytis that wolden breke the dore of Loth, weren smytun in this maner. *Lire here.* c.

[t] Om. CE. [u] thou E *pr. v.* 3ee *sec. v.* [v] the swerde E.

[l] Goth I. [m] se 3e I. [n] the whiche I. [o] Helizee I. [p] forsothe I. [q] this CDEMPb. [r] and *thanne* I. [s] hil *appeeride* I. [t] And I. [u] but I. [v] biseche *thee* I. [w] Om. I. [ww] And *thanne* I. [x] is not EL. [y] citee *where Helizee dwellith* I. [z] Om. I. [a] Om. I. [b] see *now* I. [c] Om. I. [d] Om. I. the s.

brede and watir before hem, that thei
eten and drynken, and goon to their lord.
23 And there is putte to hem grete greith-
inge of metis ; and thei eeten, and drunk-
en. And he laft hem, and thei wenten
to their lord ; and no more camen the
theeuis of Cyrye in to the lond of Yrael.
24 It is done forsothe aftir these thingis,
Benadab, kyng of Cyrye, gaderde alle
his hoost, and stey3ede vp, and bescegide
25 Samarye. And there is maad grete hungre in Samarye ; and so long it is be-
seegide[w], to the tyme that the heued of
an asse were sold for foure scoor[x] platis
of syluer, and the ferth parte of a mesure of the dryt of culuers for fyue
26 platis of syluer. And whanne the kyng
of Yrael passed by the wall, a maner
womman criede to hym, seiynge, Saue
27 me, my lord kyng. The whiche seith,
Nay, saue thee the Lord ; wherof may
I saue thee? of the corn flore, or of the
presse? And the kyng seide to hire,
What wylt thou to thee? The whiche
28 answerde, Thys womman seide to me,
3eue thi sone, that we eten hym to day ;
and my sone we schal eten to morwe.
29 Thanne we seetheden my sone, and eeten.
And I seide to hire the tother day, 3eue
thi sone, that we eten hym ; the which
30 hyde hyre sone. The which thing whanne
the kyng hade herde, he kutt his clothis,
and passede by the wall ; and alle the
puple sawe an hayre, with whiche[y] the
kyng was clothid[z] at the flesch with in
31 forthe. And the kynge seith, Thes
thingis do to me God, and thes thingis
adde, 3if the heued of Helisee, the sone
of Saphath, schulde stonden vpon hym
32 to day. Helisee forsothe satt in his hous,
and olde men seeten with hym ; and so
he sente beforn a man, and er the messager came, he seide to the old men,
Whether 3e knowen, that the sone of a

and watir bifor hem, that thei ete and
drynke, and go to her lord[e]. And ʻgreet 23
makyng redi[f] of metis was set forth to
hem ; and thei eten, and drunken. And
the kyng lefte hem, and thei 3eden to her
lord ; and theues of Sirie camen no more
in to the lond of Israel[g]. Forsothe it was 24
don after these thingis, Benadab, king of
Sirie, gaderide alle his oost, and stiede[h],
and bisegide Samarie. And greet hungur 25
was maad in Samarie ; and so long it was
bisegid, til the heed of an asse were seeld
for fourescore platis of siluer, and the
fourthe part of a mesure clepid cabus of
the crawe† of culueris was seeld for fyue
platis of siluer. And whanne the kyng of 26
Israel passide bi the wal[i], sum[k] womman
criede to hym, and seide, My lord the[l]
kyng, saue thou me. Which[m] seide, Nai, 27
the Lord saue thee ; wherof may Y saue
thee? of cornfloor, ethir of pressour? And[n]
the kyng seide to hir, What wolt thou to[o]
thee? And sche answeride, This womman 28
seide to me, 3yue thi sone, that we ete
hym to dai, and we schulen ete my sone
to morewe. Therfor we setheden my sone, 29
and eten him[p]. And Y seide to hir in[pp] the
tother day, 3yue thi sone, that we ete
hym ; and she hidde hir sone. And 30
whanne the kyng hadde herd this, he
to-rente hise clothis, and passide[q] bi the
wal ; and al the puple si3 the heire, ʻwith
which[r] the kyng was clothid[s] at the[t]
fleisch with ynne. And the kyng seide, 31
God do to me these thingis, and adde these
thingis[u], if the heed of Elise[t], sone[n] of
Saphat, schal stonde on hym to dai. So- 32
theli Elisee sat in his hows, and elde men
saten with hym ; ʻtherfor he[v] biforsente a
man[w], and bifor that thilke messanger
cam, Elisee seide to the elde men, Whether 3e witen, that the[x] sone of manquellere[y] sente[z] hidur, that myn heed be gird
of? Therfor se 3e, whanne the messanger

† crawe ; in
Latyn it is seid
of the drit of
culuers ; but
drit is not
takun here
propirly, but
vnpropirly for
the throte,
where cornes,
etun of cul-
neris, ben ga-
derid, and cokis
of riche men
seldum these
cornes to the
pople, for hun-
gur. Lire here.
c.

‡ if the heed of
Elisee ; the
kyng arettide
this turment to
Elisee, for he
dide not awey
it bi hise prey-
eris, and the
kyng hilde the
preyeris of Eli-
see spedeful,
ether mystier
anentis God, to
gete this ; ne-
theles Elisee
abood herto
couenable
tyme, bi the
ordenaunce of
Goddis wille,
which he knew
bi the Hooly
Goost. Lire
here. c.

---

[w] to be seegide B.   [x] hundrid E pr. v. score sec. v.   [y] the whiche E pr. m.   [z] clad c.

[e] lord a3en I.   [f] myche greything I.   [g] Israel in the daies of Helizee I.   [h] stiede vp I.   [i] wal of the
citee I.   [k] a IM.   [l] Om. I.   [m] The which I.   [n] And eft I.   [o] that I do to I.   [p] Om. plures.   [pp] in to o.
[q] passide forth thens I.   [r] that I.   [s] clothid with I.   [t] his I.   [u] thingis to I.   [n] the sone I.   [v] thanne
the kyng I.   [w] man to Helizee I.   [x] Benadab the I.   [y] Achab a manquellere I.   [z] hath sent I.

man sleere hath sente hithir, that myn
heued be gyrd off? Seeʒith than, whanne
the messager commith, closeth the dore,
and suffreth hym not to commen in; lo!
forsothe the soun of the feet of his lord
33 is bihynde hym. And ʒit hym spekynge
to hem, apeeride the messager, that came
to hym; and seith, Loo! so myche yuel
of the Lord is; what more schal I abyden
of the Lord?

CAP. VII.

1 Helisee forsothe seide, Here ʒe the
word of the Lord; these thingis seith
the Lord, In this tyme to morwe a
buschell of tryid floure schal be at 'half
an ounce of monee^a, and two buschels of
barly for half an ounce of monee, in the
2 ʒate of Samarye. Answerynge forsothe
oon of the duykis, vpon whose hond the
kyng lenyde, to the man of God, seide,
ʒif the Lord make also the goters in
heuen to be opnyde, whether it schal
mow ben that thou spekist? The whiche
seith, Thou schalt seen with thin eeʒen,
3 and therof thou schalt not eten. Than
foure leprouse men weren byside the entree of the ʒate, the whiche seyden to
gydre, What wil we be here, to the tyme
4 that we dyen? Whether we wyln goon
in to the cyte, by hungre we schul dyen;
whethir we schuln dwellen here, to dyen
it is to us. Commith thann, and fleeʒe
we ouer to the tentis of Cyrie; ʒif thei
sparen to us, we schul lyuen; 'ʒif for-
sothe^b thei wiln slen, neuer the later we
5 schul dyen. Thanne they rysen at euen,
that thei comen to the tentis of Cirie;
and whanne thei weren commen to the
bigynnynge of the tentis of Cyrye, no
6 man there thei founden. Forsothe the
Lord hadde made^c to heren a^d soun in
the tentis of Cyrye of charis, and of hors,

cometh, close^a ʒe the dore, and 'suffre ʒe^b
not hym to entre; for, lo! the sown of
the feet of his lord† is bihynde hym^c.
And ʒit 'while he spak^d to hem, the mes-33
sanger that cam to hym apperide; and the
kyng seide, Lo! so greet yuel is of the
Lord; sotheli what more schal Y abide
of the Lord?

CAP. VII.

Forsothe Elisee seide, Here ʒe the word 1
of the Lord; the Lord seith these thingis,
In this tyme to morewe a buschel of flour
schal be*‡ for a stater^f, and twei buschels^g
of barli for a stater, in the ʒate of Samarie.
And oon of the^h duykis, on^i whos hond 2
the kyng lenyde, answeride to the man of
God, and seide, Thouʒ 'also the Lord make‡
the goteris of heuene to be openyd, whether that, that thou spekist, mai be§?
Which^k Elisee seide, Thou schalt se^m with
thin iʒen, and thou schalt not ete therof.
Therfor foure leprouse men weren bisidis 3
the entryng of the ʒate^n, whiche^o seiden
togidere, What wolen we be here, til we
dien? Whether we^p wolen entre in to the 4
citee, we schulen die for hungur; whether
we dwellen^q here, we schulen die. Therfor come ʒe, and fle we ouer to^{qq} the cas-
tels^r of Sirie; if thei schulen spare vs, we
schulen lyue; sotheli if thei wolen sle^s,
netheles^t we schulen die^u. Therfor^v thei 5
risiden^w in the euentide to come to the
castels^x of Sirie; and whanne thei hadden
come to the bigynnyng of the castels^y of
Sirie, thei founden not ony man there.
Forsothe the Lord hadde maad a sown of 6
charis, and of horsis, and of ful^z myche
oost to be herd in the castels^a of Sirie;
and thei^b seiden togidere, Lo! the kyng
of Israel hath hirid bi meede aʒens vs the

Margin notes:

† the feet of his lord; for aftir the going of the messanger, Joram repentide, and therfor he suede the messanger to aʒen clepe the comaundement. Lire here. c.

‡ schal be; that is, schal be ʒouun. Lire here. c.

§ may be; as if he seide, nay. Lire here. c.

---

^{a} thre schillyngis E pr. m. ^{b} for ʒif A. ^{c} made hem A. ^{d} such a c.

^{a} schette I. ^{b} suffreth I. ^{c} hym *to lette that dede* I. ^{d} whanne he spak s. Helizee spekinge *thus* I.
^{e} be soold I. ^{f} stater, *that is, v. pens* I *marg.* ^{g} buschel I. ^{h} Om. s. ^{i} vpon I. ^{j} the Lord make
also DEIKLMPвxbꝯ. ^{k} And I. ^{m} se *it* I. ^{n} *citees* gate I. ^{o} the whiche I. ^{p} that we I. ^{q} abiden I.
^{qq} Om. ELP. ^{r} tentis I. ^{s} sle *us* I. ^{t} neuerthelesse BCDGKMNOQRSUWxbꝯ. netheles ELP. ^{u} die *ellis
for hungre* I. ^{v} Thanne I. ^{w} resin ELP. resen up I. ^{x} tentis I. ^{y} tentis I. ^{z} a ful I. ^{a} tentis I.
^{b} men *of Sirie* I.

and of a[e] mych hoost; and thei seyden
to gydre, Loo! by meede the kyng of
Yrael hath hyred aȝeynst us the kyngis
of Etheis and of Egipciens; and thei
7 ben commen vpon us. Thanne thei risen,
and flowen in dercnessis, and laften their
tentis, and hors, and mulis, and asses, in
the tentis; and thei flowen, their lyuis
8 oonly coueitynge to sauen. Thann whanne
thoo[f] mesels weren commen to the bigynnynge of the tentis, thei wenten in to
oon tabernacle, and eten, and drunken;
and token thenns syluer, and gold, and
clothis; and thei wenten aweye, and
hydden; and eft thei ben turned aȝeyn
to another tabernacle, and thenns lyc
9 maner beerynge aweye, hydden. And
they seyden to gidir, We do not riȝt, this
is forsothe a day of good message; ȝif
we holden oure pese, and wyln not tellen
vnto the morowe, we schul be vndernum-
men of hydous gylt; commith, and goo
we, and tellen in the halle of the kyng.
10 And whanne thei weren commen to the
ȝate of the cytee, thei tolden to hem,
seyinge, We wenten to the tentis of Syrie, and no man ther we founden, bot
hors and assis bounden, and the piȝt
11 tentis. Thanne the porteris ȝeden, and
tolden in the paleys of the kyng with-
12 inne forth. The whiche rose at nyȝt,
and seith to his seruauntis, I sey to ȝou,
what to us Cyryes han done; thei wyten,
for[g] with hungre we traueylen, and therfore they ben goon oute of the tentis, and
lurken in the feeldis, seyinge, Whanne
thei weren goon oute of the cyte, we
schuln taken hem on lyue, and thann we
13 schuln mowe goon in to the cytee. Forsoth oon of his seruauntis answerde,
Take we the fyue hors, that ben laft in
the cytee; for thei oonly ben in alle the
multitude of Yrael, the tother forsothe
ben wastyde; and seendynge we schuln

kyngis[c] of Etheis and of Egipcians; and
thei camen[d] on[e] vs. Therfor thei risiden[f], 7
and fledden[g] in derknessis[h], and leften
her tentis, and horsis[i], and mulis, and
assis, in the castels; and thei fledden,
couetynge to saue her lyues oonli. Ther- 8
for whanne thilke leprouse men hadden
come to the bigynnyng of the castels[j], thei
entriden into o[k] tabernacle, and eetun,
and drunken; and thei token fro thennus
siluer, and gold, and clothis; and ȝeden[l],
and hidden[m]; and eft thei turneden aȝen
to anothir tabernacle, and in lijk maner
thei token awei fro thennus, and hidden.
And thei seiden togidere, We doen not 9
riȝtfuli, for[n] this is a dai of good message;
if we holden[o] stille, and nylen[p] telle til[q]
the morewtid, we schulen be repreued of
trespassyng; come ȝe, go we, and telle[r] in
the 'halle of the kyng[s]. And whanne thei 10
hadden come to the ȝate of the citee, thei
telden to hem, and seiden, We ȝeden to
the castels of Sirie, and we founden not
ony man there, no[ss] but horsis and assis
tied, and tentis fastned. Therfor[t] the por- 11
teris ȝeden, and telden[u] in the paleis of
the kyng with ynne. Which[v] king roos[w] 12
bi niȝt, and seide to hise seruauntis, Y seie
to ȝou, what the men of Sirie han do to
vs; thei witen, that we trauelen with
hungur, therfor thei ȝeden[x] out of the[y]
castels, and ben hid in the feeldis, and
seien, Whanne thei[z] schulen go out of the
citee, we schulen take hem quyk, and
thanne we schulen mowe entre in to the
citee. Forsothe[a] oon of his seruauntis an- 13
sweride, Take we fyue horsis, that leften
in the citee; for tho ben[b] oonli in al the
multitude of Israel, for othere *horsis*[c]
ben wastid; and we sendynge[d] moun
aspie. Therfor thei brouȝten forth twei 14
horsis; and the kyng sente in to the castels[e] of men[f] of Sirie, and seide, Go ȝe,
and se[g]. Whiche[h] ȝeden after hem 'til to[i] 15

[e] Om. E *pr. m.* [f] thoo ilke E *pr. m.* [g] therfor E *pr. m.*

[c] king E. [d] camen *sodeynly* I. [e] upon I. [f] resin ELP. resen up I. [g] fledden awey I. [h] dernesse L. [i] her horsis I. [j] *or tentis* I *marg.* [k] a I. [l] wenten I. [m] hidden *it* I. [n] certis I. [o] holden *it* I. [p] woln not I. [q] in al I. [r] telle *it* I. [s] kingis halle I. [ss] Om. I. [t] And so I. [u] telden these thingis I. [v] And the I. [w] roos up I. [x] han go I. [y] her I. [z] men *of Israel* I. [a] And I. [b] ben *left* I. [c] Om. I. [d] *thus* sendynge I. [e] tentis I. [f] the men I. [g] se *if thei ben go* I. [h] The whiche I. [i] vnto I.

14 mowe aspyen. Thanne thei brouʒten forthe two hors; and the kyng sente in to the tentis of Cyries, seyinge, Goth, 15 and seeth. The whiche wenten aftre hem vnto Jordan; and, lo! al the wey was ful of clothis, and of[h] vesselis, that the Cyryes hadden throwen aweye, whanne thei weren distourblid. And the messagers turnede aʒeyn, scheweden to 16 the kyng. And the puple goon oute, to-brast the tentis of Cyrye; and a buschel of floure is maad at 'half an ounce of monee[l], and two buschels of barly for half an ounce of monee, aftir the word 17 of the Lord. Forsothe the kynge that duyk, in whose hond he hade lenyd, he sett at the ʒate; whom the puple alto-trade in the entre of the ʒate, and is deed, aftir that, that the man of God hadde spoken, whanne the kyng came doun to 18 hym. And it is done aftir the word of the man of God, the whiche he hade seide to the kyng, whanne he seith, Two buschels of barly schuln ben at one half ounce of monee, and oon buschell of flour for oon half ounce of monee, this same tyme to morwe in the ʒate of Sa-19 marie; whanne the[k] duyk hadde an-swerde to the man of God, and hadde seyde, Also ʒif the Lord make the goters in heuen to be opnede, whether it schal mow[l] be done that thou spekist? and he seid, Thou schalt seen with thin eeʒen, 20 and therof thou schalt not eten. Thanne it felle to hym, as it was seyde beforn; and the puple to-trade him 'in the ʒate[m], and he is deed[n].

Jordan; lo! forsothe al the weie was ful of clothis, and of vessels, whiche the men of Sirie castiden forth, whanne thei weren disturblid. And the messangeris turneden aʒen, and schewiden[k] to the kyng. And 16 the puple ʒede out, and rauyschide the castels of Sirie; and a buyschel of flour[l] was maad[m] for o[n] stater†, and twei buyschels of barli for o[n] stater, bi[o] the word of the Lord. Forsothe[p] the kyng 17 ordeynede at the ʒate[q] that duyk, in whos hond the kyng lenyde; whom the cum-peny to-trad with her[r] feet, and he was deed, bi the word, which[s] the man of God spak, whanne the kyng cam doun to hym. And it was doon[t] bi the word of the man 18 of God, which[u] he seide to the kyng, whanne he seide, Twei buyschels of barli shulen be[v] for a[w] statir, and a buyschel of wheete[x] flour for a[w] stater, in this[y] same tyme to morewe in the ʒate of Sa-marie; whanne thilke duyk answeride to 19 the man of God, and seide, ʒhe, thouʒ the Lord schal make the goteris in heuene to be openyd, whether this that thou spekist may be? and *the man of God* seide, Thou schalt se[z] with thin iʒen, and thou schalt not ete therof. Therfore it bifelde to hym, 20 as it was biforseid; and the puple to-trad hym with feet[a] in the ʒate, and he was deed.

† *ether vun half ounce of money. X.*

CAP. VIII.

1 Helisee forsothe[o] spac to the womman, whose sone he made to lyue, seyinge, Rijs, goo, and thou and thin hous, in pil-grymage, whereuer thou schalt fynde; the Lord forsothe schal clepen hungre,

CAP. VIII.

Forsothe Elisee spak to the womman, 1 whose sone he made to lyue, and he[b] seide, Rise thou, and go, bothe thou and thin hows, and 'go in[c] pilgrimage, where euer thou schalt fynde[d]; for the Lord schal

---

ʰ Om. B.   ˡ thre schillyngis E *pr. m.*   ᵏ that CE.   ˡ not A.   ᵐ Om. CE *pr. m.*   ⁿ deed in the ʒate CE. ᵒ Om. E *pr. m.*

ᵏ schewiden *it* I.   ˡ tried flour I.   ᵐ maad *sold* I.   ᵃ a I.   ᵒ aftir I.   ᵖ Certis I.   ᑫ ʒate *of the citee* I. ʳ Om. BCDEFGIKLMNOPRSXbç.   ˢ that I.   ᵗ doon *so* I.   ᵘ that I.   ᵛ be *soold* I.   ʷ o *plures.*   ˣ tried wheete I.   ʸ the c.   ᶻ se it I.   ᵃ her feet I.   ᵇ Om. I.   ᶜ make I.   ᵈ fynde *it best* I.

and it schal commen vpon the lond seuen
2 ʒeer. The whiche rose, and dyde aftir
the word of the man of God; and gooynge with hyre hous pylgrymagid in
3 the lond of Phylisteis many dayes. And
whanne seuen ʒeer weren fynyschid, the
womman is turnede aʒein fro the lond
of Philisteis; and sche wente oute, that
sche preye the kyng for hyre hous, and
4 for hir feeldis. The kynge forsothe spak
with Giezi, the chijld of the man of God,
seyinge, Telle to me alle the grete thingis
5 that Helisee dide. And whanne he tolde
to the kynge, what maner wijse he hade
rered the deed, the womman apeeride,
whose sone he hade quyckenede, criynge
to the kyng for hyre hous, and for hyre
feeldis. And Giezi seide, My lord kyng,
this is the womman, and this is the sone
6 of hyre, that Helisee rerede. And the
kynge askyde the womman, the whiche
tolde to hym tho thingis to be soth. And
the kyng ʒaue to hyre an geldynge, seiynge, Restore to hyre alle thingis that
ben hyres, and alle the rentes of feeldis,
fro the day that sche laft the lond vnto
7 the tyme that is nowe. Forsothe Helisee cam to Damask, and Benadab, kyng
of Cyrye, wexe seeke; and thei tolden
to hym, seyinge, The man of God is com-
8 men hydre. And the kyng seith to Asael,
Take with thee ʒiftis, and goo in to aʒein
commynge of the man of God, and counseyle by hym the Lord, seyinge, ʒif I
schal mow ascapen of this myn enfir-
9 myte? Than[p] Asael wente in to aʒein
commynge of hym, hauynge with hym
ʒiftis, and alle the[q] goodis of Damaske,
fourty chamel[r] chaargis. And whanne he
hade stonden before hym, seith, Thi sone,
Benadab, kyng of Syrie, sente me to thee,
seyinge, ʒif I schal mowe be heelid of
10 this myn enfirmyte? And Helisee seide,
Goo, seye to hym, Thou schalt ben hoole;

clepe hungur, and it schal come on[e] the
lond bi[f] seuene ʒeer. And sche roos, and 2
dide bi[g] the word of the man of God; and
sche ʒede with hir hows, and was in pilgrimage[h] in the lond of Philistym[i] many
daies. And whanne seuene ʒeer weren 3
endid, the womman turnede aʒen fro the
lond of Philisteis; and sche ʒede out, to
axe the kyng for her hows, and hir[j]
feeldis. Sotheli[k] the kyng spak with 4
Giezi, child[l] of the man of God, and
seide, Telle thou to me alle the grete
dedis whiche[m] Elisee dide. And whanne 5
he telde to the kyng, hou Elisee hadde
reiside a deed man, the womman apperide,
whos sone he hadde maad to lyue, and
sche criede to the kyng for hir hows, and
for hir feeldis. And Giesi seide, My lord
the[n] king, this is the womman, and this
is hir sone, whom Elisee reiside. And 6
the kyng axide the womman, and sche
tolde to hym, that the thingis weren
sothe. And the kyng ʒaf[o] to hir o[p]
chaumburleyn, and seide, Restore thou
to[pp] hir alle thingis that ben hern[q], and
alle fruytis of the feeldis, fro the dai in
which she[r] left the lond 'til to[s] present
tyme. Also Elisee cam to Damask, and 7
Benadab, kyng[t] of Sirie, was sijk; and
thei[u] telden to hym, and seiden, The man
of God cam hidur. And the kyng seide 8
to Azael, Take with thee ʒiftis, and go
thou in to the meetyng of the man of
God, and counsele thou[v] bi hym the[vv]
Lord, and seie thou, Whether Y may
ascape fro this 'sikenesse of me[w]? Therfor 9
Azael ʒede[x] in to the meetyng of hym[y],
and hadde with hym silf[z] ʒiftis, and alle
the goodis of Damask, the burthuns of
fourti camels. And whanne he hadde
stonde bifor Elisee, he seide, Thi sone,
Benadab, kyng of Sirie, sente me to thee,
and seide, Whether Y may be helid of this
'sikenesse of me[a]? And Elisee seide, Go 10

---

p And than ᴀ sec. m.   q Om. ʙ.   r chamels ᴀ.

e upon ɪ.   f Om. ɪ.   g aftir ɪ.   h pilgrimage or fro hoome ɪ.   i Philistees ɪ.   j Om. s. sec. m.
k And ɪ.   l the child ɪ.   m that ɪ.   n Om. ɪ.   o ʒaf or assignyde ɪ.   p ᴀ ɪ.   pp Om. ᴋ.   q hers ɪ.
r he ᴀᴍᴜx pr. m.   s vnto this ɪ. til into this ᴋ.   t the kyng ʟ.   u men ɪ.   v axe thou counsel ᴇʟᴘ.
vv of the ᴇʟᴘ.   w my sikenesse ɪ.   x ʒede forth ɪ.   y Helizee ɪ.   z Om. ɪs.   a my sikenesse ɪ.

bot the Lord hath schewide to me for by
11 deth he schal dye. And he stode with
hym, and is distourbled, vnto the schedynge doun of the cheere; and the man
12 of God wepte. To whom Asael seith,
Why my lord weepith? And he answerde, For I wote what thou be to doo
to the sonis of Yrael euyls; the strengthide cytees of hem thou schalt brenne up
with fijr, and the ȝonge men of hem thou
schalt slee with swerde, and the lytyll
chyldre of hem thou schalt hurtlyn, and
the wymmen with chijlde thou schalt
13 deuyde. And Asael seyde, What forsothe am I, thi seruaunt, an hound, that
I doo this grete thinge? And Helisee
seith, The Lord hath schewide to me
14 thee to be kyng of Cyrye. The which
whanne hade goon aweye fro Helisee,
came to his lord; the which seith to
hym, What seide Helisee to thee? And
he answerde, He seide to me, Thou schalt
15 resseyue helth. And whanne the tother
day was commen, he toke an couerlyte,
and helte in with watir, and spradde
vpon his face; the whiche deed, Asael
16 regnede for hym. The fyft ȝeer of Joram,
the sone of Acab, kyng of Yrael, regnede
Joram, the sone of Josaphath, king of
17 Juda. Of two and thritty ȝeer he was
whanne he beganne to regnen, and eiȝte
18 ȝere he regnyde in Jerusalem. And he
wente in the weyes of the kyngis of
Yrael, as wente the hous of Acab; the
douȝter forsothe of Acab was his wiyf;
and he dydde that, that is yuel in the
19 siȝt of the Lord. And the Lord wolde
not scateren Juda, for Dauid, his seruaunt, as he hadde behoten to hym, that
he schulde ȝeue to hym a lanterne, and
20 to his sones⁵ alle days. In tho days
wente aweye Edom, that thei weren not
vndur Juda; and he sette to hym a kyng.

thou, and seye to hym, Thou schalt be
heelid; forsothe^b the Lord schewide to
me that he schal die bi deth. And he^c 11
stood with hym^d, and he was disturblid,
'til to^e the castyng doun of cheer^f; and
the man of God wepte. 'To whom^g Azael 12
seide, Whi wepith my lord? And he answeride, For Y woot what yuelis thou
schalt do to the sones of Israel; thou
schalt brenne bi fier the strengthid citees
of hem, and thou schalt sle bi swerd the
ȝonge men of hem, and thou schalt hurtle
doun the litle children of hem, and thou
schalt departe the women with^h childe.
And Azael seide, What sotheli am Y, thi 13
seruaunt, a dogge, that Y do this grete
thing? And Elisee seide, The Lord schew-
ideⁱ to me that thou schalt be kyng of
Sirie. And whanne he^k hadde departid 14
fro Elisee, he cam to his lord; which^l
seide to Azael, What seide Elisee to thee?
And he answeride, Elisee seide to me,
Thou schalt resseyue helthe. And whanne 15
'the tother^m day hadde come, Azael took
the cloth onⁿ the bed^o, and bischedde^p
with watir, and spredde^q abrood on^r the
face of hym^s; and whanne he was deed,
Azael regnede for hym. In the fyuethe 16
ȝeer of Joram, sone of Achab, kyng of
Israel, and of Josephat, kyng of Juda,
Joram, sone^t of Josephat, kyng of Juda,
regnede. He^u was of two and thretti 17
ȝeer whanne he bigan to regne, and he
regnede eiȝte ȝeer in Jerusalem. And he 18
ȝede in the weies of the kyngis^v of Israel,
as the hows of Achab hadde go; for the
douȝter of Achab was his wijf; and he
dide that, that is^w yuel in the siȝt of the
Lord. Forsothe the Lord nolde^x distrie 19
Juda, for Dauid, his seruaunt, as he 'hadde
bihiȝt^y to Dauid, that he schulde ȝyue to
hym a lanterne, and to hise sones in alle
daies^z. In tho daies Edom, 'that is, 20

---

⁵ sone ᴀʙꜰʜ.

^b certis ɪ.   ^c Azael ɪ.   ^d Helizee ɪ.   ^e vnto ɪ.   ^f his cheer ɪ.   ^g And ɪ.   ^h grete with ᴀ see. m.
ⁱ hath schewid ɪ.   ^k Azahel ɪ.   ^l the which ɪ.   ^m that oother ɪ.   ⁿ that lay on ɪ.   ^o bed of Benedab ɪ.
^p he bischedde it.   ^q spredede ᴇ. he spredde it ɪ.   ^r upon ɪ.   ^s Benedab. ɪ.   ^t the sone ɪ.   ^u This Joram ɪ.
^v king ᴇʟᴘ.   ^w was ɪ.   ^x wolde not ɪ.   ^y bihiȝte ᴅɪᴋsxb. hadde hiȝt ᴇʟ.   ^z daies, kepinge his seed upon
his trone ɪ.

21 And Joram came to Seyr, and alle the charis with hym; and he roose the ny3t, and smote Ydumes, that hym hadden enuyround, and the princis of the chaaris; the puple forsothe fleey3 in to their taber-22naclis. Than went Edom, that he were not vndur Juda vnto this day; thanne wente aweye Lobna and in that tyme. 23 The remnaunt forsothe of the wordis of Joram, and alle thingis that he dyde, whether not these ben writen in the booke of the wordis of the days of the 24 kyngis of Juda? And Joram slepte with his faders, and is byryed with hem in the cytee of Dauid; and Ochosias, his 25 sone, regnede for hym. The twelfith 3eer of Joram, the sone of kyng Achab, regnede Ochosias, the sone of kyng Joram, of 26 Jude. Of two and twenty 3eer was Ochosias, the sone of Joram, whanne he beganne to regnen, and oon 3eer he regned in Jerusalem; the name of his modir Athalia, the dou3ter of Amry, kyng of 27 Yrael. And he wente in the weyes of the hous of Achab, and dydde that, that is yuel before the Lord, as the hous of Acab; forsothe the sone in lawe of the 28 hous of Acab he was. Forsothe he wente with Joram, the sone of Acab, to fi3ten a3eyn Azael, kyng of Cyrie, in to Ramoth Galaad; and Cyries woundeden Jo-29ram. The whiche is turned a3eyn, that he were helyd in Jezrael; for Cyries woundeden hym in Ramoth, fi3tynge a3eynst Azael, kynge of Cyrie. Forsothe Ochozias, the sone of Joram, kyng of Juda, came doun to visyten Joram, the sone of Achab, in Jezrael, the whiche seekened there.

Ydumee[a], 3ede awei, that it schulde not be vndur Juda; and made a kyng to it silf. And Joram cam to Seira, and alle 21 the[b] charis with[bb] hym; and he roos bi ny3t; and smoot Ydumeis[c], that cumpassiden hym, and the princis of charis[d]; sotheli[e] the puple fledde in to her tabernaclis. Therfor Edom 3ede awei, that it 22 was not vndur[f] Juda 'til to[g] this day; thanne also Lobna 3ede awey in that tyme[h]. Forsothe[i] the residues[k] of wordis[l] 23 of Joram, and alle thingis whiche he dide, whether these ben not writun in the book of wordis of daies of the kingis of Juda? And Joram slepte with hise fadris, and 24 was biried with hem in the citee of Dauid; and Ocozie, his sone, regnede for hym. In the tweluethe 3eer of Joram, sone[m] of 25 Achab, kyng of Israel, Ocozie, sone[m] of Joram, kyng of Juda, regnede. Ocozie, 26 the sone of Joram, was of two and twenti 3eer whanne he bigan to regne, and he regnede o 3eer in Jerusalem; the name of his moder *was* Athalia, the dou3ter of Amry, kyng of Israel. And he 3ede in 27 the[n] waies of the hows of Achab, and dide that, that is yuel, bifor[o] the Lord, as the hows of Achab *dide*; for[p] he was hosebonde of a dou3ter of the hows of Achab. Also he 3ede with Joram, sone[q] of Achab, 28 to fi3t a3ens Azael, kyng of Sirie, in Ramoth of Galaad; and men of Sirie woundiden Joram. Which[r] turnede a3en, to be 29 heelid in Jezrael; for men of Sirie woundiden hym in Ramoth, fi3tynge a3ens Azael, kyng of Sirye. Forsothe[s] Ocozie, sone[t] of Joram, the kyng of Juda, cam doun to se Joram, sone[u] of Achab, in to Jezrael, that was sijk there.

CAP. IX.

1 Forsothe Helisee, the[u] prophete, clepide oon of the sonys of prophetis, and seith to hym, Gyrde thi reenys, and take this

CAP. IX.

Forsothe Elisee, the prophete, clepide 1 oon of the sones of prophetis, and seide to hym, Girde thi leendis, and take this

---

t Om. B. u Om. BF.

a *that is, men of Ydumee* 1 marg. Om. c. b hise 1. bb to EL. c the men of Edom 1. d her charis 1. e and 1. f *tributarie* vnder 1. g vnto 1. h tyme *fro Juda* 1. i Certis 1. k residue 1. l the wordis 1. m the sone 1. n Om. A. o in si3t of 1. p forsothe 1. q the sone 1. r The which 1. s And 1. t the sone 1. u the sone 1.

oynment vessel of oyle in thin hond, and
2 goo in to Ramoth Galaad. And whanne
thou commyst thidre, thou schalt seen
Hieu, the sone of Josaphath, the sone of
Nampsy; and goon in thou schalt reren
hym fro the mydill of his bretheren, and
thou schalt bryngen hym with inforth
3 in to the^v inner more^w bed place. And
holdinge an oynment vessel of oyle thou^x
schalt heelden vpon his heued, and seye,
These thingis seith the Lord, I haue
anoyntyde thee in to kynge vpon Yrael;
and thou schalt opne the dore, and flee3en,
4 and there thou schalt not abyden. Thanne
3eede a 3onge waxen child of the profete
5 in to Ramoth Galaad, and wente in
thidir. Lo! forsothe the princis of the
hoostis seeten; and he seith, A worde to
me anentis thee, O! prince. And Hieu
seide, To whom of us alle? And he
6 seide, To thee, O! prince. And he roos,
and wente in to the bede place. And
he helde oyle vpon his heuede, and
seith, These thingis seith the Lord God
of Ysrael, I haue anoyntyde thee in to
kyng vpon the puple of the Lord of
7 Yrael; and thou schalt smyten the hous
of Achab, thi lord, that I venge the blode
of my seruauntis prophetis, and the blode
of alle the seruauntis of the Lord, fro the
8 hond of Jezabel. And I schal distruy alle
the hous of Achab, and slen fro the hous
of Achab a pysser to the walle, and
9 closed, and the last in Yrael. And I
schal 3eue the hous of Achab as the hous
of Jeroboam, the sone of Nabath, and as
the hous of Basaa, the sone of Ahia.
10 Jezabel forsothe houndis schulen eten
in the feelde^y of Jezrael; and there
schal not ben that byrye hyre. And he
11 opnede the dore, and fley3. Hieu forsothe wente oute to the seruauntis of his
lord, the whiche seyden to hym, Whether

vessel of oile in thin hond, and go in to
Ramoth of Galaad. And whanne thou 2
schalt come thidur, thou schalt se Hieu,
sone^v of Josephat, sone^v of Namsi; and
thou schalt entre, and schalt^w reise hym
fro the myddis of hise britheren, and thou
schalt lede hym in to the^x ynnere closet.
And thou schalt holde the vessel of oile, 3
and schalt^y schede^z on his heed, and schalt^a
seie, The Lord seith these thingis, I haue
anoyntid thee in to kyng on^b Israel; and^c
thou schalt opene the dore, and schalt
flee^d, and schalt^e not abide there. Ther- 4
for the 3ong wexynge man, the child of
the prophete, 3ede in to Ramoth of Galaad, and entride thidur. Lo! sotheli the 5
princes of the oost saten^f; and he seide,
A^g! prince, Y haue a word to thee. And
Hieu seide, To whom of alle vs? And he
seide, To thee, thou prince. And he^h roos, 6
and entride into theⁱ closet. And thilk
child schedde^k oile on^l the heed of hym,
and seide, The Lord God of Israel seith
these thingis, Y haue anointid thee in to
kyng on^m the puple of the Lord of Israel;
and thou schalt smyte the hows of Achab, 7
thi lord, that Y venge the blood of my
seruauntis prophetis, and the blood of alle
theⁿ seruauntis of the Lord, of the hond
of Jezabel. And Y schal lese al the hows 8
of Achab, and Y schal sle of the hows of
Achab a pissere to the wal, and closid°†,
and the laste in Israel^p. And Y schal 3yue 9
the hows of Achab^q as the hows of Jeroboam, sone^r of Nabat, and as the hous of
Baasa, sone^r of Ahia. Also doggis schu- 10
len ete Jezabel in the feeld of Jezrael;
and 'noon schal be^s that schal birie hir.
And 'the child^t openyde the dore, and
fledde. Forsothe^u Hieu 3ede out to the 11
seruauntis of his lord, whiche seiden to
hym, Whether alle thingis ben^v ri3tfuli^w?
What cam this woodman‡ to thee? Which^x

† *closid*; in
prisoun. *Lire
here.* c.

‡ *wood man*;
profetis weren
arettid woode
men, for thei
dispisiden the
goodis of this
world, and for
thei spaken
ofte siche
thingis, that
semyden alien
to othere men.
Lire here. c.

v the sone I.   w thou schalt I.   x an I.   y thou schalt I.   z helde *it* I.   a thou schalt I.   b upon I.
c and *thanne* I.   d flee *thenns* I.   e thou schalt I.   f saten *there* I.   g O! I.   h Hien I.   i a I.   k helde I.
l upon I.   m upon I.   n Om. EL.   o the closid *in prisoun* I.   P Israel *of his hous* I.   q Achab *in lo
repreff* I.   r the sone I.   s ther schal be noon I.   t *whanne he hadde seid these thingis* he I.   u And I.
v ben don I.   w ri3tful EL.   x The which I.

riȝt ben alle thingis? What came this
wood man to thee? The whiche seith to
hem, ȝe han knowen the man, and what
12 he hath spoken. And thei answerden, It
is fals; but more telle thou to us. The
whiche seith to hem, These thingis and
these thingis he spac to me, and seith,
These thingis seith the Lord, I haue
13 anoyntide thee kynge vpon Ysrael. And
so thei hyȝeden, and echone, takynge his
mantylle, putten vndur his feet in lyck-
nesse of a kyngis chayer. And they
sungen with trumpe, and seyden, Hieu
14 schal regnen. Thanne Hieu, the sone of
Josaphath, the sone of Nampsy, coniured
aȝeynst Joram. Forsothe Joram hadde
byseegyd Ramoth Galaad, he and alle
Yrael, aȝeynst Azael, kyng of Cyrye.
15 And he was turned aȝeyn, that he were
helyd in Jezrael for the woundis; for Cyries hadden smyten hym fiȝtynge aȝeynst
Azael, kyng of Cyrie. And Hieu seide,
Ȝif it plese to ȝou, no man goo oute fugy-
tyue fro the cyte, lest he go, and tell in
16 Jezrael. And he steyȝide vp, and wente
forth into Jezrael; Joram forsothe laye
seeke there, and Ochosias, kyng of Juda, hadde goon doun to vysyte Joram.
17 Thanne the wayte, that stode vpon the
toure of Jezrael, see the glub of Hieu
commynge, and seith, I see a glub. And
Joram seide, Take the chare, and sende
in to aȝcyn commynge of hem; and the
gooer sey, Whether riȝt ben alle thingis?
18 Thanne ȝeede, that steyȝide up the chaare,
in to aȝeyn commynge of hym, and seith,
Thes thingis seith the kyng, Apayid ben
alle thingis? And Hieu seyde to hym,
What to thee and to pese? Go, and
folow me. The weyt forsothe tolde, seyinge, The messager cam to hem, and he
19 is not turned aȝeyn. Also he sent the
secounde chaar of hors, and he came to

seide to hem, ȝe knowen the man, and
what he spak. And thei answeriden, It is 12
fals; but more telle thou to us. Which
seide to hem, He spak these and these
thingis to me, and seide, The Lord seith
these thingis, Y haue anoyntid thee kyng
on Israel. Therfor thei hastiden, and ech 13
man took his mentil, and puttide vndir
hise feet bi the licnesse of a trone. And
thei sungen with a trumpe, and seiden,
Hieu schal regne. Therfor Hieu, sone 14
of Josephat, sone of Namsi, swoor to
gidere† aȝens Joram. Forsothe Joram
hadde bisegid Ramoth of Galaad, he and
al Israel, aȝens Azael, kyng of Sirie. And 15
he turnede aȝen to be heelid in Jezrael
for woundis; for men of Sirie hadden
smyte hym fiȝtynge aȝens Azael, kyng of
Sirie. And Hieu seide, If it plesith ȝou,
no man go out fleynge fro the citee, lest
he go, and telle in Jezrael. And he 16
stiede, and ȝede forth in to Jezrael; for
Joram was sijk there, and Ocozie, kyng
of Juda, cam doun to visite Joram. Ther- 17
for a spiere, that stood aboue a tour of
Jezrael, siȝ the multitude of Hieu comynge, and he seide, Y se a multitude. And
Joram seide, Take thou a chare, and sende
in to the metyng of hem; and seie the
goere, Whether alle thingis ben riȝtful?
Therfor he, that stiede on the chare, 18
ȝede in to the meetyng of hym, and seide,
The kyng seith these thingis, Whether alle
thingis ben peesid? And Hieu seide to
hym, What to thee and to pees? Passe
thou, and sue me. And the aspiere telde,
and seide, the messanger cam to hem, and
he turneth not aȝen. Also the kyng sente 19
the secounde chare of horsis, and he cam
to hem, and seide, The kyng seith these
thingis, Whether pees is? And Hieu
seide, What to thee and to pees? Passe
thou, and sue me. Sotheli the aspiere 20

† swoore to gi-
dere; with the
prynces beynge
with him, that
thei schulden
fille feithfully
Goddis heeste,
of the hows of
Achab to be
distried. Lire
here. c.

z the kyng E pr. m.

y more rather 1. z Om. 1. a vs what he seide 1. b The which 1. c these thingis 1. d Om. 1. e of 1.
f a 1. g the sone 1. h swoor with oothere 1. i Certis 1. k Joram 1. l woundis that he hadde 1.
m plese 1. n Hieu 1. o stiede up 1. p waitere 1. q sende it 1. go L. r goere thus 1. s riȝtful EL.
.don iustly 1. t Thanne 1. u ȝede 1. v vpon 1. w wente 1. x Hieu 1. y thou fro Joram 1.
z waitere 1. a telde to Joram 1. b Om. c. c is with ȝou 1. d thou forth 1. dd Om. EL. e And 1.

hem, and seith, These thingis seith the kyng, Where is there pese? And Hieu seith, What to thee and to pese? Passe, 20 and folowe me. Forsothe the weyt tolde, seyinge, He came vnto hem, and he turnith not aȝein; forsothe the goynge is as the goynge of Hieu, the sone of Nampsy; 21 ‘ful swyftlyche^a forsothe he^b goth. And Joram seith, Ioynith the chaar. And they ioyneden his chaar. And Joram, the kyng of Yrael, wente oute, and Ochosias, kyng of Juda, ech in their chaaris; and thei wenten oute into aȝeyncommynge of Hieu, and thei founden hym in the 22 feeld of Nabath Jezraelyte. And whanne Joram hadde seen Hieu, he seide, Pese is there, Hieu? And he answerde, What pese? Ȝit the fornycacions of Jezabel, thi modir, and hyr many venymyngis thrijuen. 23 Forsothe Joram turnede his hond, and fleeȝinge seith to Ochosie, Busschementis! 24 busschementis! Ochosie. Bot Hieu bente the bowe with the honde, and smote Joram bytwene the schulders, and the arewe is sent out thoruȝ his hert; and 25 anoon he felle in his chaare. And Hieu seith to duyke Badachar, Take, throwe hym in the feelde of Naboth Jezraelite; I haue mynde forsothe, when I and thow syttynge in the chaar foloweden Achab, his fadir, for the Lord hadde rerede out 26 this^d charge^e upon hym, seyinge, Whether not for the blode of Naboth, and for the blode of the sonys of hym, the whiche I sawe ȝisterday^f, seith the Lord, I schal ȝelden to thee in this feeld, seith the Lord. Nowe thanne take hym, and throwe hym in the feeld, aftir the word of the Lord. 27 Ochosias forsothe, kyng of Juda, seeinge this, fleeȝ by the weye of the hous of the gardyn; and Hieu folewede hym, and seith, Also this smytith in his chare.

telde^f, and seide, He cam ’til to^g hem, and he turneth not aȝen; forsothe the goyng^h is as the goyng of Hieu, sone of Namsi; sothelyⁱ he goith faste. And Joram seide, 21 Ioyn ȝe a chare. And thei ioyneden his chare. And Joram, kyng of Israel, ȝede out, and Ocozie, kyng of Juda^k, ȝede out, ech in his chare; and thei ȝeden out^l in to the meetyng of Hieu, and thei founden hym in the feeld of Naboth of Jezrael. And whanne Joram hadde seyn Hieu, he 22 seide, Hieu^m, ‘is peesⁿ? And he^o answeride, What pees? Ȝit the fornycaciouns† of Jezabel, thi modir, and many poisenyngis^p of hir ben in strengthe. Forsothe^q Joram 23 turnede his hond, and fledde, and seide to Ocozie, Tresouns! tresouns! Ocozie. For-24 sothe^r Hieu bente a bouwe with the^s hond, and smoot Joram bitwixe the schuldris, and the arowe ȝede out thoruȝ^t his^u herte; and anoon he felde doun in his chare. And 25 Hieu seide to Badacher duyk^v, Take thou awei^w, cast^x forth hym in the feeld of Naboth of Jezrael; for^y Y haue mynde, whanne Y and thou saten in the chare, and suede Achab, the fadir of hym^z, that the Lord reiside on^a hym^b this birthun, and seide, If^c not for the blood of Naboth, and for 26 the blood of hise sones, which^d Y siȝ ȝistirdai^e, seith the Lord, Y schal ȝeeld to thee in this feeld, seith the Lord. Now therfor do^f awei him^g, and cast forth him in the feeld, bi the word of the Lord. For-27 sothe Ocozie, king of Juda, siȝ this, and fledde bi the weie of the hows of the^h gardyn; and Hieu pursuede hym, and seide, Also smyte ȝe this man in his chare. And theiⁱ smytiden^k hym^l in the stiyng^m of Gaber, whichⁿ is bisidis Jeblaam; and he^o fledde into Mageddo, and was deed there. And hise seruauntis puttiden hym 28 on^p his chare, and brouȝten *hym*^q in to

† *fornyca-* *ciouns; that* *is, idolatries,* *whiche Jezabel,* *brouȝte yn.* *and poison-* *yngis; for sche* *poysonyde* *gostli; and* *therfor good* *pees may not* *be in Israel,* *as longe as* *these ben in* *strengthe.* *Lire here.* c.

---

^a a prince E pr. m.   ^b Om. E pr. m.   ^d his A.   ^e chaare FH.   ^f ȝistai c et E passim.

^f telde *to Joram* I.   ^g vnto I.   ^h goyng *of the duyk* I.   ⁱ certis I.   ^k Juda *with him* I.   ^l forth I. ^m Om. I.   ⁿ Is ther pees *with thee* I.   ^o Hieu I.   ^p venymyngis I.   ^q And I.   ^r Certis I.   ^s his I.   ^t and thoruȝ ELP. bi I.   ^u the M.   ^v the duyk I.   ^w awei *Joram* I.   ^x and cast I.   ^y for whi I.   ^z this *Joram* I. ^a bi Helie upon I.   ^b Achab I.   ^c Wher I.   ^d the which I.   ^e ȝistirdai sched out I.   ^f do thou I. ^g Joram I.   ^h a I.   ⁱ men I.   ^k smoten I. smiten EL. smetin P.   ^l Ocozie I.   ^m stiyng up I.   ⁿ that I. ^o Ocozie I.   ^p upon I.   ^q Om. *plures.*

And thei smyten hym in the steyinge up
of Gaber, that is besyde Jeblaam; the
whiche fley3 in to Magedo, and is deed
28 there. And his seruauntis putten hym
vpon his chaar, and token in to Jerusalem; and biriden hym in the sepulcre
with his fadirs, in the cytee of Dauith.
29 The elleuenth 3eer of Joram, the sone of
Achab, the kyng of Yrael, regnede Ocho-
30 sias vpon Judam. And Hieu came in
to Jezrael. Forsothe Jezabel, his entree
herde, peyntyde hyre ee3en with strum-
pettis oynment, and sche anournede hyre
heued; and sche byhelde thoru3 the wyn-
31 dowe Hieu commynge in by the 3ate,
and seith, Whether pese may be to Zamry
32 that hath slayn his lord? And Hieu
rerede up his face to the wyndowe, and
seith, What is sche this? And there
boweden hem to hym two or thre geldingis, and seyden to hym, This is sche,
33 that Jezabel. And he seyde to hem,
Tumblith hyre doun. And thei tum-
bliden hyre; and the wall is sprengid
with the blod, and the hors houes, that
34 treden hyre. And when he was goon in,
that he ete and drynke, he seith, Gooth,
and seeth that cursed, and burieth hyre,
35 for the dou3ter of a kyng sche is. And
when thei weren gon, that they biryen
hyre, thei founden not, no⁸ bot the scul,
and the feet, and gobitis of the hond;
36 and they turned a3ein, tolden to hym.
And Hieu seith, The word of the Lord
it is, the whiche he spak by his seruaunt
Helye Thesbyten, seyinge, In the feeld
of Jezrael houndis schulen eten the flesche
37 of Jezabel; and the flesche of Jezabel
schul be as drytt vpon the face of the
erthe in the feeld of Jezrael, so that men
passynge bysydis seyn, Whether sche this
is not that Jezabel?

Jerusalem; and thei birieden hym in a
sepulcre with hise fadris, in the citee of
Dauid. In the eleuenthe 3eer of Joram, 29
sone^r of Achab, kyng of Israel, Ocozie
regnede on^s Juda. And Hieu cam in to 30
Jezrael. Forsothe whanne his entryng
was herd, Jezabel peyntide hir i3en with
oynement of wymmen^t, and ournede hir
heed; and sche bihelde bi a wyndow Hieu 31
entrynge bi the 3ate, and sche seide, Whether pees may be to Zamri†, that kyllide^u
his lord? And Hieu reiside^v his face to 32
the wyndow, and seide, What womman
is this? And tweyne ether thre chaum-
birleyns bowiden hem silf to hym^w, and
seiden to hym, This is thilke Jezabel. And 33
he seide to hem, Caste 3e hir doun^x. And
thei 'castiden doun hir^y; and the wal was
bispreynt with^z blood, and the howues
of horsis, that 'to tredden^a hir. And 34
whanne he^b hadde entrid to ete and
drynke, he seide, Go 3e, and se^c thilke
cursid womman, and birie 3e hir, for sche
is^d a kyngis dou3ter. And whanne thei^e 35
hadden go^f to birie hir, thei founden not⁸,
no but the sculle, and the feet, and the
endis of hondis^h; and thei turneden a3en, 36
and telden to hym^i. And Hieu seide, It^k
is the word of the Lord, which^l he spak
bi his seruaunt, Elie 'of Thesbi^m, and seide,
Doggis schulen ete the fleisch of Jezabel
in the feeld of Jezrael; and the fleischis 37
of Jezabel schulen be as 'a toord^n on^o the
face of erthe^p in the feeld of Jezrael, so
that men passynge forth^q seie, Lo! this
is thilke Jezabel.

† wher pees
may be to
Zamry; oure
doctouris ex-
pownen this
comynly bi
negacioun
thus, as Zamry
hadde not pees,
so nether thou
schalt haue
pees; but this
exposicioun
acordith not to
the lettre bifor
goinge, therfor
Ebreis ex-
pownen thus,
wher pees may
be, that is, Y
preye, that thou
haue pees with
me. Zamry
killide his lord;
as if sche seide,
this is not
newe, that thou
killidist Joram
thi lord, for
Zamry dide in
liyk maner,
and netheles
Achab, his sone,
regnyde in pees
aftir hym; so
it may be to
thee. Lire
here. c.

⁸ Om. ACEFH.

^r the sone 1. ^s upon 1. ^t lecherouse wymmen 1. ^u slewe 1. ^v reiside up 1. ^w Hieu 1. ^x doun
heedling 1. ^y puttiden hir doun heedling 1. ^z of hir 1. ^a trodiden 1. ^b Hieu 1. ^c se 3e 1. ^d was 1.
^e men 1. ^f gon forth 1. ^g not of hir 1. ^h hir hondis 1. ^i Hieu 1. ^k This 1. ^l that 1. ^m Thesbiten 1.
^n dunge 1. ^o upon 1. ^p the erthe 1. ^q forth therby 1.

CAP. X.

1 Of Achab forsoth weren seuenty sonis
in Samary. Than Hieu wrote lettris, and
sente in to Samarye to the best of the
cytee, and to the more thoruȝ birth, and
2 to the nurischis of Achab, seyinge, Anoon
as ȝe taken thes lettres, ȝe that haue the
sonis of ȝoure lord, and chaaris, and hors,
3 and stronge cytees, and aarmys, chesith
the beter, and hym that to ȝou schal
plesen of the sonis of ȝour lord, and puttith hym vpon the see of his fadir, and
4 fiȝtith for the hous of ȝoure lord. And
thei dredden hugelye, and seyden, Loo!
two kyngis myȝten not stonden beforn
hym, and what maner wijse schuln we
5 mowen to withstonden hym? Thanne
the prouostis of the hous senten, and the
prefect of the cyte, and the more thoruȝ
birthe, and the nurischis to Hieu, seyinge, Thi seruauntis we ben; what euer
thingis thou schalt comaunde, we schul
done, and we schul not ordeyne to us a
kynge; what euer thinge to thee plesith,
6 do. Forsothe he wrote aȝein lettris to
hem the secounde tyme, seyinge, Ȝif myn
ȝe ben, and obeschen to me, takith the
heuedis of the sonis of ȝoure lord, and
commith to me this same houre to morowe
in to Jezrael. Forsothe the sonis of the
kyng, seuenty men, anentis the best of
7 the cytee weren nurischide. And when
lettris weren commen to hem, thei token
the sonis of the kyng, and slewen the
seuenty men, and putten the heuedis of
hem in cofynes; and senten to hym in
8 to Jezrael. Forsothe a messagere came
to hym, and schewede to hym, seyinge,
Thei han brouȝt the heuedis of the sonys
of the kyng. The whiche answerde, Puttith hem at the two stone hepis, besydis
the entre of the ȝate, vnto to morowe.
9 And when the day hadde liȝted, he wente
out, and stondynge seide to alle the puple, Riȝtwyse ȝe ben; ȝif I haue coniured

CAP. X.

Forsothe seuenti sones in Samarie weren 1
to Achab. Therfor Hieu wroot lettris, and
sente in to Samarie to the beste men of
the citee, and to the gretter men in birthe,
and to alle the nurschis of Achab†, and
seide, Anoon as ȝe han take these lettris, ȝe 2
that han the sones of ȝoure lord, and the
charis, and horsis, and stronge citees, and
armeris, chese[n] the beste, and hym that 3
plesith to ȝou of the sones of ȝoure lord[o],
and sette ȝe[p] him on[q] the trone of his
fadir, and fiȝte ȝe for the hows of ȝoure
lord. And thei[r] dredden greetli, and 4
seiden, Lo! twei kyngis myȝten not
stonde bifor hym, and how schulen we
mowe aȝenstonde hym? Therfor the 5
souereyns of the hows, and the prefect[s]
of the citee, and the grettere men in
birthe, and the nurschis senten to Hieu,
and seiden, We ben thi seruauntis; what
euer thingis thou comaundist, we schulen
do, and we schulen not make a kyng to
vs; do thou what euer thing plesith thee.
Forsothe he wroot aȝen to hem lettris the 6
secunde tyme, and seide, If ȝe ben myne,
and obeien to me, take ȝe the heedis of
the sones of ȝoure lord, and come ȝe to me
in this same our to morewe in to Jezrael.
Sotheli[t] the sones of the kyng, seuenti
men, weren nurschid at the beste men of
the citee. And whanne the lettris hadden 7
come to hem, thei token the sones of the
kyng, and killiden seuenti[u] men, and puttiden[v] the heedis of hem in coffyns; and
senten[w] to hym[x] in to Jezrael. Forsothe[y] 8
a messanger cam to hym, and schewide
to hym, and seide, Thei[z] han brouȝt the
heedis of the sones of the king. Which[a]
answeride, Putte ȝe tho[b] heedis to tweyne
hepis, bisidis the entring[c] of the ȝate, til[d]
the[e] morewtid. And whanne it was cleer 9
dai, he[f] ȝede out, and stood, and seide to
al the puple[g], Ȝe ben iust men; if Y conspiride aȝens my lord, and killide hym,

† *nursis of Achab;* that is, of the sones of Achab. *Lire here.* c.

[n] chese ȝe I. [o] lord *Achab* I. [p] Om. C. [q] upon I. [r] the men I. [s] provoustis *or bailies* I. [t] And I. [u] *tho* seuenti I. [v] thei puttiden I. [w] senten *tho* I. [x] Hieu I. [y] And I. [z] Men I. [a] The which N. [b] the I. [c] entris A. [d] vnto I. til to N. [e] Om. N. [f] Hieu I. [g] puple *of Samarie* I.

aȝeynus my lord, and slayn hym; who
10 smoot alle these? Seeth thann nowe, for
there hath not fallen of the wordis of the
Lord in the erthe, the whiche the Lord
spac vpon the hous of Achab; and the
Lord dydde that he spak in the hond
11 of Helye, his seruaunt. Thanneᵇ Hieu
smoot alle that weren laft of the hous of
Achab in Jezrael, and alle the best of
hym, and knowen, and prestis, to the
tyme that ther laft not of hym relykys.
12 And he roos, and came in to Samerye;
and when thei weren commen to the
13 chaumbre of scheperdis in the weye, he
fonde the bretheren of Ochosie, kyng of
Juda; and he seide to hem, Who forsothe ben ȝe? And thei answerden, The
bretheren of Ochosie we ben, and we ben
commen doun to saluten the sonis of the
14 kyng and the sonys of the qween. The
whiche seith, Takith hem on lyue. Whom
when thei hadden taken alyue, thei
throtyden hem in the cystern, besyde
the chaumbre, two and fourty men; and
15 he laft not of hem eny man. And when
he was goon thens, he foond Jonadah,
the sone of Reechab, in to aȝein commynge to hym, and blessede to hym.
And Hieu seith to hym, Whether is thin
hert riȝt with myne herte, as myn hert
with thin hert? And Jonadab seith, It
is. Ȝif it is, he seith, ȝeue me thin honde.
The whiche ȝaue to hym his hond; and
he rerede hym to hym in to the chaar.
16 And he seyde to hym, Comme with me,
and see my loue for the Lord. And
17 hym sett in his chaar, he ladde in to Samarye. And he smote alle that weren
laft of Achab in Samarye vnto oon, after
the word of the Lord, that he spac by
18 Helye. Than Hieu gaderd alle the puple, and seide to hem, Achab heryide
Baal a lytyl, I forsothe schal herye hym
19 more. Nowe than alle the prophetis of

who killide alle these? Therfor se ȝe 10
nowt, that noon of the wordis of the
Lord feldeʰ doun in to the erthe, whiche
the Lord spak on the hows of Achab;
and the Lord hath do that, that he spak
in the hond of his seruaunt, Elie. Therfor 11
Hieu smoot alle that weren residueⁱ of
the hows of Achab in Jezrael, and alle
the beste menᵏ of hymˡ, and knowunᵐ
men, and preestisⁿ, til no relikis of hym
leften. And heᵒ roosᵖ, and cam in to Sa- 12
marie; and whanne he hadde come to the
chaumbir of scheperdisᵠ in the weie, he 13
foondʳ the britherent of Ocozie, kyng of
Juda; and he seide to hem, Who ben ȝe?
And thei answeriden, We ben the britheren
of Ocozie, and we comen doun to grete
the sones of the kyng and the sones of
the queen. Whichˢ Hieu seide, Take ȝe 14
hem quyke. And whanne thei hadden
take hem quyke, thei strangliden hem in
theᵗ cisterne, bisidis the chaumbre, two and
fourti men; and he lefte not ony of hem.
And whanne heᵘ hadde go fro thennus, he 15
foond Jonadab, the sone of Rechab, in to
meetyng ofᵛ hym; and heʷ blesside hym.
And Hieu seide to hym, Whether thin
herte is riȝtful with myn herte, as myn
herte is with thin herte? And Jonadab
seide, It is. Hieuˣ seide, If 'it isʸ, ȝyueᶻ
thin hond. Whichᵃ ȝaf his hond to hym;
and heᵇ reiside hymᶜ to hym silfᵈ in to
theᵉ chare. And heᶠ seide to hym, Come 16
thou with me, and se my feruent loue for
the Lord. And he ledde hym, put in hys 17
chare, in to Samarie. And heᵍ killide alle
men that weren residueʰ of Achab in Samarie 'til toⁱ oon, bi the word of the Lord,
whichᵏ he spak bi Elie. Therfor Hieu 18
gaderide to gidere alle the puple, and seide
to hem, Achab worschipide Baal a litil,
but Y schalˡ worschipe hym more. Now 19
therfor clepe ȝe to me alle the prophetis
of Baal, and alle hise seruauntis, and alle

† therfor se ȝe now; as if he seide, nether Y in comaund-inge, nether ȝe in parform-ynge, ben blameful, but more iust and preisable, for it is doon bi the wille and co-maundement of the Lord, as it was bifor-seid by Elie, and was en-ioyned to me bi his disiȝde. Lire here. c.

‡ britheren; that is, kynnes-men, for they weren hise cosyns; in 11. book of Paralip. xxi. c°. Lire here. c.

ᵇ Om. AB pr. m. FII.

ʰ hath falle I. ⁱ left I. ᵏ men also I. ˡ Achab I. ᵐ his knowun I. ⁿ his preestis I. ᵒ Hieu I. ᵖ roos up I. ᵠ the scheperdis I. ʳ foond there I. ˢ And I. ᵗ a I. ᵘ Hieu I. ᵛ to DEIKLMPXbç. ʷ Jonadab I. ˣ And Hieu IS. ʸ thin herte is riȝtful I. ᶻ ȝyne me I. ᵃ The which I. ᵇ Hieu I. ᶜ hym up I. ᵈ Om. I. ᵉ his I. ᶠ Hieu I. ᵍ Hieu I. ʰ left I. ⁱ vnto I. ᵏ that I. ˡ Om. c.

Baal, and alle his seruauntis, and alle
the prestis of hem clepith to me; noon
be that cumme not, forsothe grete sacrifice is to me to Baal; who so euer be
aweye, he schal not lyuen. Forsothe
Hieu dydde this aspyingly, that he dis-
20 truye alle the heryeris of Baal. And he
seyde, Halowith a solempne day to Baal.
21 And he clepid, and sente in to al the
termes of Yrael; and ther camen alle
the seruauntis of Baal, and ther was
not lafte not oone forsothe that came
not. And thei wenten in to the temple
'of Baal; and the hous of Baal is fulfillid,
22 from the hee3ist to the hee3ist. And he
seide to hem that haden maistrye vpon
the clothes, Bryngith forth the vesty-
mentis to alle the seruauntis of Baal;
and thei brou3tyn to hym the clothis.
23 And Hieu wente in, and Jonadab, the
sone of Reechab, in to the temple of
Baal. And he seith to the herieris of
Baal, Enserchith, and seeth, lest eny man
perauenture be with 3ou of the seruauntis
of the Lord; bot that aloon ben the ser-
24 uauntis of Baal. Thanne thei wenten in,
that thei done slayne offryngis, and brent
sacrifices[i]. Hieu made redy forsothe with
oute forthe foure score men, and hadde
seyde to hem, Who so euer flee3ith of
alle these, 'the whiche[k] I schal brynge
in to 3oure hondis, his lijf schal ben for
25 the lijf of hym. It is do forsothe, when
the brent sacrifice was fulfillid, Hieu comaundide to the kny3tis and 'to his
duykis, Gooth in, and smytith hem, that
noon ascaape. And the kny3tis and the
duykis smyten hem in the mouthe of
the[l] swerd, and threwen aweye. And thei
wenten in to the cyte of the temple of
26 Baal, and thei brou3ten forthe the ymage
fro the temple of Baal, and thei brenden,
27 and distruyden it. Forsothe thei dis-

hise preestis; 'noon be[m] that come not,
for[n] grete sacrifice is of me to Baal; who
euer schal faile[o], he schal not lyue. Forsothe Hieu dide this bi tresoun, that he
schulde[p] distrie alle the worschipers of
Baal. And he seide[q], Halewe 3e a so- 20
lempne day to Baal. And he[r] clepide, and 21
sente in to alle the termes of Israel; and
alle the seruauntis of Baal camen[s], 'noon
was residue[t], and sotheli 'not oon was[u]
that cam not. And thei entriden in to
the temple of Baal; and the hows of Baal
was fillid, fro oon[v] ende 'til to[w] 'the tothir[x]. And he[y] seide to hem that weren 22
souereyns ouer the clothis[z], Bringe 3e[a]
forth clothis[b] to alle the seruauntis of
Baal; and thei brou3ten forth clothis[c] to
hem. And Hieu entride, and Jonadab, 23
the sone of Rechab, in to the temple of
Baal. And *Hieu* seide to the worschiperis
of Baal, Enquere 3e, and se, lest perauenture ony of the seruauntis of the Lord be
with 3ou; but that the seruauntis be aloone
of Baal. Therfor[d] thei entriden, to make 24
slayn sacrifices, and brent sacrifices. Sotheli[e] Hieu hadde maad redi to hym with
outforth foure scoore men, and hadde seid
to hem, Who euer schal fle[f] of alle these,
whiche Y schal brynge in to 3oure hondis,
the lijf of hym schal be† for the lijf of
hym *that ascapith.* Forsothe it was don, 25
whanne the brent sacrifice was fillid[g], Hieu
comaundide 'to hise kny3tis and duykis,
Entre 3e, and sle[h] hem, that noon ascape.
And the kny3tis and duykis smytiden[i]
'hem bi the[k] scharpnesse of swerd, and
castiden[l] forth. And 'thei 3eden[m] into
the citee of the temple of Baal, and thei 26
brou3ten forth the ymage[n] fro the temple
of Baal, and brenten it[o], and al to braken 27
it. Also thei destrieden the hows of Baal,
and maden priuyes‡ for it 'til in to[p] this
dai. Therfor[q] Hieu dide awei Baal fro 28

† *the lijf of him schal be, etc.; that suffrith ony ascape. c.*

‡ *maden priuyes; for abhomynacioun of idolatrie, and that thilke place schulde serue the comynte in this nede. Lire here. c.*

i sacrifice ABFH.   k that c *pr. m.*   l Om. AC *pr. m.*

m be ther noon I.   n forsothe I.   o faile *to come* I.   p wolde I.   q seide to hem I.   r Hieu I.   s camen
thidere I.   t and noon was left EL. ther was noon left thenns I. noon was left F.   u ther was not oon I.
v that oon I.   w to I.   x that oother I.   y Hieu I.   z prestis clothis I.   a Om. R.   b thi clothis c.
vestmentis I.   c vestmentis I.   d Thanne I.   e Certis I.   f fle awey I.   g fulfillid I.   h sleeth I.
i smiten EL *passim.* smyten F *passim.* smeten I. smetin P *passim.*   k with I.   l casten FI.   m 3eid A *sup.ras.*
n ymage of Baal I.   o Om. BIKLMPSXbc.   p vnto I.   q Thanne I.

troyeden the hous of Baal, and thei maden for it waardropis vnto this day.

28 And so Hieu dyde aweye Baal from Yrael;

29 neuerthelatre fro the synnes of Jeroboam, the sone of Naboth, that maad Yrael to synne, he 3eede not aweye, ne dyde aweye the golden caluis, that weren

30 in Bethel and in Dan . The Lord forsothe seyde to Hieu, For wysely thou hast done that that was ri3t, and it pleside in myn ce3en, and alle thingis that weren in myne herte thou dyddist a3eynst the hous of^m Achab, tbi sonys vnto the ferth generacioun schuln sytten vpon

31 the trone of Yrael . Bot Hieu kepte not, that he wente in the lawe of the Lord God of Yrael in al his herte; forsothe he wente not fro the synnes of Jeroboham, that maad Yrael to synnen

32 In tho days the Lord beganne to noy3en vpon Yrael, and Azael smote hem in^n

33 alle the coostis of Yrael, fro Jordane a3eyns the este coost, alle the lond of Galaad, and Gad, and Ruben, and Manasse, fro Aroer that is vpon the streme

34 of Arnon, and Galaad, and Basan The remnaunt forsothe of the wordis of Hieu, and alle thingis that he dide, and his strengthe, whether not thes ben wiiten in the boke of the wordis of the days of

35 the kyngis of Yrael? And Hieu slepte with his fadirs, and thei birieden hym in Samarie, and Joacath, his sone, regn-

36 ede for hym The days forsothe, the whiche^o Hieu regned vpon Yrael in Samarye, ben ei3t and twenty 3eer

Israel; netheles he 3ede not awei fro the

29 synnes of Jeroboam, sone^r of Nabath, that made Israel to do synne, nether he forsook the goldun caluys, that weren in Bethel and in Dan Forsothe the Lord

30 seide to Hieu, For thou didist bisili that that was ri3tful, and pleside^s in myn y3en, and hast do a3ens the hows of Achab alle thingis that weren in myn herte, thi sones 'til to^t the fourthe generacioun schulen sitte on^u the trone of Israel Forsothe^v

31 Hieu kepte not, that he 3ede in the lawe of the Lord God of Israel in al his herte; for he 3ede^vv not awei fro the synnes of Jeroboam, that made Israel to do synne

32 In tho daies the Lord bigan to be anoyed† on^w Israel; and Asahel smoot hem^x in alle the coostis of Israel), fro Jordan a3ens the

33 eest coost, al the lond of Galaad, and of Gad, and of Ruben, and of Manasses, fro Aroei which^z is on^a the stronde of Arnon, and Galaad, and Baasan Forsothe^b the

34 residue of wordis^c of Hieu, and alle thingis whiche^d he dide, and his strengthe, whether these ben not writun in the book of wordis of daies of the kyngis of Israel?

35 And Hieu slepte with hise fadris, and thei birieden hym in Samarie; and Joachaz, his sone, regnyde for hym. For-

36 sothe^e the daies, in whiche Hieu regnede on^f Israel in Samarie, ben ei3te and twenti 3eer

Margin note: 32 † the Lord bigan to be anoied, that is, to haue abbomynacioun of her dedis, for the worschiping of idols haddi durid longe thanne, and 34 many othere yuels camen forth with tho, and therfor that rewme was suffrid to be tormentid 35 bi Assel in many maneris. Iare here c

CAP XI

1 Athalia forsothe, the modir of Ochosie, see3inge hyre sone deed, roos, and slew3

2 alle the kyngis seede Forsothe Jozaba, the dou3tir of kyng Joram, the sistei of Ochosie, takynge Joas, the sone of Ochosie, staal hym fro the myddis of the sonis of the kyng, that weren slayn; and his

CAP XI

Forsothe Athalie, modir^g of Ocozie, si3

1 hii sone deed, and sche roos^h, and kilhde al the seed of the kyng^i Sotheli^h Josaha,

2 dou3ter^l of kyng Joiam, the sistir of Ocozie, took Joas, sone^m of Ocozie, and stal him fro the myddis of the sones of the kyng, that weren slayn, *and sche took*

---

m Om BF sec m   n and AB   o that c pr m

r the sone I   s plesidest E   that pleside I   t therfore vnto I   u upon I   v For A   vv wente I.   w upon I
x Israel I   y hem I   z that I   a upon I   b And I   c the wordis I   d that I   e Certis I   f upon I
g the modir I   h roos up I   i kyng of Juda I   k And I   l the dou3ter I   m the sone I

nurische fro the chaumbre of three beddis; and sche hydde hym fro the face of
3 Athalie, that he were not slayne. And
he was with hyre in the hous of the
Lord priuely sex ʒeer. Forsothe Athalie
4 regnede vpon the lond sex ʒeer. The seuenth forsothe ʒeer Joiada sente, and takynge rewlers of hundrethis, and knyʒtis,
and brouʒte in to hym in to the temple
of the Lord; and he couenauntyde with
hem a couenaunt of pese, and, adiurynge
hem in the temple of the Lord, schewide
5 to hem the sone of the kynge. And he
comaundide[p] to hem, seyinge, This is the
6 word, the whiche ʒe owe to done; the
thrydde partye of ʒou go in the saboth,
and keep he wele the watchis of the hous
of the kyng; the thrydde forsothe party
be at the ʒate of Scir; and the thridde
party be at the ʒate that is bihynde the
dwellynge place of the scheld bereris[q];
and ʒe schulen kepen the watchis of the
7 hous of Messa. Two forsothe partyes of
ʒou alle goynge oute the saboth, keepen
thei the watchis of the hous of the Lord
8 aboute the kynge. And ʒee schul 'setten
hym[r] aboute, hauynge aarmys in ʒoure
hondis; and ʒif eny man comme with in
the purseynt of the temple, be he slayn;
and ʒe schul ben with the kynge com-
9 mynge in and goynge out. And the
keepers of hundrethis dyden aftir alle
thingis that Joiada, the prest, hadde comaundide to hem; and ech takynge their
men that wenten in to the saboth, with hem
that wenten out fro the saboth, camen to
10 Joiada, the prest. The whiche ʒaue to hem
the speris, and the armys of kyng Dauid,
that weren in the hous of the Lord.
11 And eche stoden hauynge aarmys in
their hond, fro the riʒt partye of the
temple vnto the left paartye of the auter
12 and of the hous, aboute the kynge. And

the nursche of hym fro the hows of thre
stagis; and sche hidde hym fro the face
of Athalie, that he were not slayn. And 3
he was with hir in the hows of the Lord
priueli sixe ʒeer. Forsothe Athalia regnede on[n] the lond sixe ʒeer. Forsothe[o] in 4
the seuenthe ʒeer Joiada[p] sente, and took
centuriouns[q], and knyʒtis, and brouʒte[r] to[s]
hym in to the temple of the Lord; and
couenauntide with hem boond[t] of pees,
and he made hem to swere† in the temple
of the Lord, and schewide to hem the
sone of the kyng. And he[u] comaundide 5
to hem, and seide, This is the word, which[v]
ʒe owen to do; the thridde part of ʒou 6
entre in the sabat[w], and kepe the[x] wakyngis[y] of the 'hows of the kyng[z]; sothely[a]
the[b] thridde part be at the ʒate of Scir;
and the thridde part be at the ʒate which[c]
is bihynde the dwellyng place[cc] of the
makeris of scheeldis; and ʒe schulen kepe
the wakyngis of the hows of Messa. For- 7
sothe twei partis of ʒou alle goynge out in
the sabat, kepe ʒe[d] the wakyngis of the
hows of the Lord aboute the kyng. And 8
ʒe schulen cumpasse hym[e], and ʒe schulen
haue armeris in ʒoure hondis; and forsothe[f]
if ony man entrith[g] in to the closyng of
the temple, be he slayn; and ʒe schulen
be with the kyng goynge in and goynge
out. And the centuriouns[h] diden bi alle 9
thingis whiche[i] Joiada, the preest, hadde
comaundid to hem; and alle[k] takynge her
men that entriden to[l] the sabat[m], with
hem that ʒeden out fro the sabat[m], camen
to Joiada, the preest. Which[n] ʒaf to hem 10
speris, and armeris of kyng Dauid, that
weren in the hows of the Lord. And alle 11
stoden hauynge armeris in her hond, fro
the riʒt side of the temple 'til to[o] the left
side of the auter and of the hows, aboute
the kyng. And he[p] brouʒte forth the sone 12
of the kyng, and puttide[q] on[r] hym[s] a dia-

† *swere;* that
thei schulden
helpe him
feithfuly, in
the ordeynyng
of the du king,
which thing
thei diden
gladly in parti;
for ech man
kyndeli louyth
his vere lord,
in parti, for
the lordschip
of a whomman
displeside him.
Lire here. c.

---

[p] couenauntide *A*.   [q] berer *AB*.   [r] besetten c. behooldyn *E pr. m.*

---

[a] upon 1.   [o] But 1.   [p] Joiada the prest 1.   [q] chefteyns upon hundridis 1.   [r] he brouʒte *hem* 1.   [s] Om. *M.*
[t] a boond 1.   [u] Joiada 1.   [v] that 1.   [w] sabat day 1.   [x] ʒe *AI*.   [y] the watchis 1.   [z] kyngis hows 1.   [a] aad 1.
[b] another 1.   [c] that 1.   [cc] placis s.   [d] thei 1. Om. s.   [e] the kyng 1.   [f] and 1.   [g] entre 1.   [h] chefteyns
upon hundridis 1.   [i] that 1.   [k] thei alle 1.   [l] in to *A*.   [m] sabat day 1.   [n] The which 1.   [o] vnto 1.   [p] Joiada 1.
[q] putte 1.   [r] upon 1.   [s] his heed 1.

he brouȝt forthe the sone of the kyng, and putte vpon hym a dyademe, and witnessynge, and thei maden him kyng, and anoynteden; and, ioyinge with the hondis, 13 seyden, Lyue the kyng¹ Forsothe Athalia herde the voice of the puple rennynge, and goon in to the pephs in to 14 the temple of the Lord, sche sawȝ the kyng stondinge vpon the chayer aftir the manei, and syngers, and companyes besidis hym, and alle the puple of the lond glaadinge, and syngynge with trompis And sche kytt hyre clothis, and cryede, 15 Coniuiacioun¹ coniuracioun¹ Forsothe Joiada comaundide to the rewlers of hundrethis, that weren vpon the hoost, and seith to hem, Leedith hyre out of the purseyntis of the temple, and who so euer folewith hyre, be he smyten with a swerde Forsothe the prest hadde seyde, Be sche not slayn in the temple of the 16 Lord And thei putten to hyre hondis, and stykeden hyre by the weye of the entree of the hors besyde the paleys; and 17 sche is slayn there Than Joiada couenauntyde couenaunt of pese bytwen the the Lord and the kyng, and bytwene the puple, that ther weie a puple of the Lord; bytwene the king and the puple. 18 And alle the puple of the lond wente in to the temple of Baal, and thei distruyden his auters, and the ymagis broosiden to gydris miȝtily; Mathan forsothe, the prest of Baal, thei slewen befoie the auter. And the prest sette waardis in the hous of the Lord; and toke the rewlers of hundrethis, and the[s] legiouns of Cerethey and Ferethey, and 19 alle the puple of the lond And thei brouȝten the kyng fro the hous of the Lord; and thei camen by the weye of the ȝaat of the scheeld bereris in to the paleys; and he sate vpon the trone of

deme, and witnessyng[t]*; and thei maden hym kyng, and anoyntiden hym[u], and thei beeten[v] with the hoond, and seiden, The kyng lyue¹ Forsothe Athalia herde 13 the vois of the puple rennynge, and sche entride to the cumpenyes in to the temple of the Lord, and sche siȝ the kyng stond- 14 ynge on[w] the trone bi custom, and syngeris, and cumpenyes nyȝ hym, and al the puple of the lond beynge glad, and syngynge with trumpis And sche to-rente hir clothis, and criede,'Swerynge togidere¹ swerynge togidere[x]¹ *ether tresoun.* For- 15 sothe[y] Joiada comaundide to the centuriouns[z], that weren on[a] the oost, and seide to hem, Lede ȝe hir out of the closyngis of the temple, and who euer sueth† hir, be[b] smytun with swerd. Forsothe[c] the preest seide, Be sche not slayn in the temple of the Lord And thei[d] puttiden 16 hondis on[e] hir, and builiden[f] hir bi the weie of the entryng of horsis bisidis the paleis, and sche was slayn there. Thei- 17 for Joiada made boond of pees bitwixe the Lord and the kyng‡, and bitwixe the puple, that it schulde be the puple of the Lord§; and bitwixe the kyng and the puple[g]‖ Al the puple of the lond en- 18 tride in to the temple of Baal, and thei distrieden the auteris of hym, and al tobraken strongli the ymagis; and thei killiden bifore the auter Mathan, the preest of Baal And[h] the preest settide[i] kepyngis in the hows of the Lord, and he took centriouns[k], and the[l] legiouns of Cerethi[m]¶ and Pherethi[n], and al the puple of the lond And thei ledden forth the 19 kyng fro the hows of the Lord, and thei camen bi the weie of the ȝate of makeris[o] of scheldis in to the paleis, and he[p] sat on[q] the trone of kyngis And al the puple 20 of the lond was glad, and the citee restide. Forsothe[r] Athalia was slayn bi swerd in

Margin notes:

* witnessing, that is, the lawe of God, in which the king ordeyned owith to studie, and bithenke, and kepe it, and make it to be kept of othere men Lire here c

† sueth, to fauere hir Lire here c

‡ that he schulde kepe feithfuly the lawe of the Lord § the Lord, verily and not feynyngly Lire here. c ‖ bitwixe the kyng and the puple, that the puple schulde be feithful to the kyng, and that the kyng schulde do feithfuly tho thingis, that weren for the comyn proht of the puple Lire here c ¶ Cerethi is interpretid dis troieris, and Phelethi is interpretid woundurful, these weren wisiste weryours, as Katholicon seith c.

[s] Om D

[t] the witnessyng 1   [u] Om *plures*   [v] clappiden 1   [w] upon 1   [x] Coniuracioun, coniuracioun 1
[y] Certis 1   [z] chefteynes 1   [a] upon 1   [b] be he 1   [c] And 1   [d] men 1   [e] upon 1.   [f] thei hurliden 1
[g] puple he made pees 1   [h] and Joiada 1   [i] sette 1.   [k] chefteyns upon hundredis 1   [l] Om 1.
[m] archers 1   [n] alblasters 1   [o] the makeris 1   [p] Joas 1.   [q] upon 1   [r] Certis 1

20 kyngis[t]. And alle the puple of the lond glaadid[u], and alle the cytee restide in oon. Athalia forsothe is slayn with 21 swerde in the hous of the kyng. And of seuen ʒeer was Joas, when he beganne to regne.

the hows of the kyng. And Joas was of 21 seuen ʒeer, whanne he bigan to regne.

CAP. XII.

1 The seuenth ʒeer of Hieu regnede Joas; fourty ʒeer he regnede in Jerusalem; the name of his modir Sebia of 2 Bersabe. And Joas dyde riʒt beforn the Lord alle days, the whiche tauʒte hym 3 Joiada, the prest. Neuerthelater heeʒe thingis he dide not aweye; ʒit forsothe the puple offride, and brente encense in 4 heiʒtis. And Joias seide to the prestis, Al the monee of seyntis[v], 'the whiche[w] were brouʒt in to the temple of the Lord of men passynge, 'the whiche[w] is offred for the synne of the soule, and the whiche thei bryngen in wilfully, and by dome of their herte, in to the temple of the Lord, 5 the prestis taken thei it aftir their ordre. And enstoore thei the coueryngis of the hous, ʒif eny thinge thei seen necessarye 6 in the restorynge. Thanne vnto the three and twentithe ʒeer of kyng Joas, the prestis restooreden not the couer- 7 yngis of the temple. And kyng Joas clepide Joiada, the bischop, and the prestis, seyinge to hem, Why the coueryngis ʒe restoren not of the temple? Wille ʒe than not no more taken the monee aftir ʒoure ordre, bot to the re- 8 stooringe of the temple ʒeldith it. And the prestis ben forfendid to eny more takyn monee of the puple, and to re- 9 storen the coueryngis of the hous. And Joiada, the bischop, toke oon tresoringe place, and he opnede an hoole ther aboue, and putte it bisyde the auter, at the riʒt syde of men commynge in to the house of the Lord; and the prestis, that

CAP. XII.

1 Joas regnede in the seuenthe ʒeer of Hieu; Joas[s] regnede fourti ʒeer in Jerusalem; the name of his modir was Sebia of Bersabee. And Joas dide riʒtfulnesse 2 bifor the Lord in alle the daies, in whiche Joiada, the preest, tauʒte hym. Netheles 3 he dide noʒt awey hiʒ[t] thingis; for ʒit the puple made sacrifice, and brente encense in hiʒe thingis. And Joas seide to the 4 preestis, 'Preestis bi her ordre take[u] al that[v] money of hooli thingis, which[w] is brouʒt of men passyng forth in to the temple of the Lord, 'which money[x] is offrid for the prijs of soule[xx], and 'which money thei[y] bryngen wilfuli, and bi the[z] fredom of her herte, in to the temple of the Lord[a]. And 'the preestis[b] reparele 5 the hilyngis of the hows, if thei seen ony thing nedeful in reparelyng. Therfor[c] the 6 preestis repareliden not the hilyngis of the temple, 'til to[d] the thre and twentithe ʒeer of kyng Joas. And Joas, the kyng, clepide 7 Joiada, the bischop, and the prestis, and seide to hem, Whi han ʒe not reparelid the hilyngis of the temple? Therfor nyle ʒe more take money bi ʒoure ordre, but ʒelde[e] it to the reparacioun of the temple. And the prestis weren forbodun to take 8 more the[f] money of the puple, and to reparele the hilyngis of the hows. And 9 Joiada, the bischop, took a[g] cofere of[h] tresorie[i], and openyde an hole aboue, and settide it bisidis the auter, at the riʒtside of men entrynge in to the hows of the Lord; and preestis, that kepten the doris, senten[k] in[l] it al the money that was brouʒt

---

[t] the kyngis ᴀ.   [u] of Galaad ᴀ.   [v] the seyntis ᴀ.   [w] that c.

[s] he I.   [t] the hiʒ I.   [u] Om. I.   [v] the I.   [w] that I.   [x] and that I.   [xx] the soule s.   [y] that men I.   [z] Om. I.   [a] Lord, prestis bi her ordre take it I.   [b] Om. I.   [c] Sothly I.   [d] vnto I.   [e] ʒelde ʒe ᴀ sec. m.   [f] Om. I.   [g] o plures.   [h] of the ᴇɪʟ.   [i] tresour ᴋ.   [k] senten or putten I.   [l] in to I.

kepten the doris, putten in it al the monee that was brou3t to the temple of 10 the Lord. And when he sau3 to myche monee to be in the tresorye, a scribe of the kyngis^x stey3ide up, and a byschop, and thei heelden out, and noumbreden the monee that was foundun in the hous 11 of the Lord. And thei 3euen it aftir the noumbre and mesure in the hond of hem, that weren before to the masouns of the hous of the Lord, the whiche 3euen it in carpentaris, and in thes masouns, that 12 wrou3ten in the hous of the Lord, and the coueryngis maaden ; and in hem that^y hewyden^z stonys ; and that schulden byen treese and stonys, the whiche weren hewen out ; so that the enstor-ynge of the hous of the Lord were ful-fillid in alle thingis, 'the whiche^a nededen expensis to the hous to be warnyschid. 13 Neuerthelatre ther weren not maad of the same monee the stenys of the temple of the Lord, and the fleschookis, and the censeris, and the trompis, and all golden vessel^b and siluere_n, of the monee that was brou3t in to the temple of the Lord. 14 To thes forsothe that maden werk was 3euen, that the temple of the Lord were 15 enstooride^c. And no reknynge was maad to tho men that token the monee, that thei delen it to the craftyse men^d ; bot in 16 feith thei tretiden it. The monee for-sothe for trespasse, and the monee for synnes, thei brou3ten not in to the temple 17 of the Lord, for it was of prestis. Than Azael, kyng of Cyrye, stey3ide up, and fau3t a3eynus Geth ; and he took it, and he dresside his face, that he stey3e up in 18 to Jerusalem. For what thing Joas, king of Juda, took alle the halowed thingis, 'the whiche^e Josaphath, and Joram, and Ochosias, hise faders, kyngis of Juda, hadden sacred, and the whiche he hadde

to the temple of the Lord. And whanne 10 thei sien that ful myche money was in the tresorie, the scryuen of the kyng and the bischop stieden^m, and scheddenⁿ it^o out, and thei noumbriden the money that was founden in the hous of the Lord. And 11 thei 3auen it bi noumbre and mesure in the hond of hem, that weren souereyns to the masouns of the hows of the Lord, whiche^p spendiden that money^q in crafti men of trees^r, and in these masouns, that wrou3ten in the hous of the Lord, and 12 maden the hilyngis, and in these men that hewiden stoonys ; and that thei schulden bie trees and stoonys, that weren hewid^s doun ; so that the reparacioun of the hows of the Lord was fillid in alle thingis, that nediden^t cost to make strong the hows. Netheles water pottis of the temple of the 13 Lord weren not maad of the same money, and fleischokis, and censeris, and trumpis ; ech vessel of gold and of^{tt} siluer weren not maad of the money, that was brou3t in to the temple of the Lord. For it was 14 3ouun to hem that maden werk^u, that the temple of the Lord schulde be reparelid. And rekenyng was not maad to these men 15 that token monei^v, that thei schulden deele it to crafti men ; but thei tretiden^w it in feith. Sotheli thei brou3ten not in to the 16 temple of the Lord the money^x for tres-pas, and the money for synnes, for it was the preestis. Thanne† Asael, kyng of 17 Sirie, stiede^y, and fau3te a3en Geth ; and he took it, and dresside his face, that he schulde^z stie^a in to Jerusalem. Wherfor^b 18 Joas, kyng of Juda, took alle 'thingis ha-lewid^c, whiche^d Josephat hadde halewid, and Joram, and Ocozie, fadris^e of hym, kyngis of Juda, and whiche thingis he hadde offrid, and al the siluer, that my3te be foundun in the tresours of the temple of the Lord, and in the paleis of the kyng.

† Thanne; that is, aftir that Joas took to him Goddis onour, and killide in the temple Zacarie, the his prest, for he re-preuyde the kyng of his synne. Lire here. c.

x kyng AE.   y thei A.   z heewen c.   a that c pr. m.   b vessels A.   c restoryd A.   d crafty men A.   e that c pr. m.

m stieden up I.   n helden I.   o Om. plures.   p the whiche DIKMXç.   q 3auen it DKMSXç.   r carpen-ters DKMSXç. crafti men and trees ELP.   s hewen ELP.   t neden A.   tt Om. EL.   u the werk I.   v the monei I.   w tretiden or spendiden I.   x money offrid I.   y wente up I.   z wolde I.   a wende up I.   b Therfore I.   c the halewid thingis I.   d that I.   e the fadris I.

offred, and al the syluer and gold, that myȝt be founden in the tresouries of the temple of the Lord, and in paleys° of the kyng. And he sente to Azael, the kyng of Cyrye, and wente aweye fro Jerusalem.
19 The remnaunt forsothe of the wordis of Joas, and alle thingis that he dyde, whether thes ben not writen in the book of the wordis of the days of the kyngis of
20 Juda? Forsothe his seruauntis rysen, and coniureden bytwene hemseluen; and thei smyten Joas in the hous of Mello, in
21 the goynge doun of Sela. Josafath forsothe, the sone of Semath, and Joiadath, the sone of Somer, his seruauntis, smyten hym, and he is deed; and thei birieden hym with his faders in the cytee of Dauith; and Amazias, his sone, regnede for hym.

And he^f sente^g to Asael, kyng^gg of Sirie; 19 and^h he^i ȝede awei fro Jerusalem. Sotheli the residue^k of wordis^l of Joas, and alle thingis whiche^m he dide, whether these ben not writun in the book of wordis of daies of the kyngis of Juda? Forsothe^n 20 hise^o seruauntis^p risiden^q, and sworen togidere bitwixe hem silf, and smytiden^r Joas in the hows Mello^s, and in the goyng doun of Sela. For^t Jozachat, sone^u of Se-21 math, and Joiadath, sone^u of Soomer, hise seruauntis, smytiden^v him, and he was deed; and thei birieden hym with hise fadris in the citee of Dauid; and Amasie, his sone, regnyde for hym.

CAP. XIII.

1 The three and twentithe ȝeer of Joas, the sone of Ochasie, kyng of Juda, regnede Joachas, the sone of Hieu, vpon Yrael,
2 in^f Samarie seuentene ȝeer. And he dyde yuel before the Lord, and he folowide the synnes of Jeroboam, the sone of Nabath, that maad Yrael to synne; and he bow-
3 ide not aweye fro hem. And the woodnesse of the Lord is wroth aȝeynst Yrael, and he toke hem in to the hondis of Azael, kynge of Cyrye, and in the hond of Benadab, the sone of Azael, all days.
4 Forsothe Joachaz preyide the face of the Lord, and the Lord herde hym; he sawe forsothe the angwysche of Yrael, for the kyng of Cyrye hadde 'to troden^g hem.
5 And the Lord ȝaue a saueour to Yrael, and he is delyuerd fro the hond of the kyng of Cyrie; and the sonys of Yrael dwelliden in their tabernaclis, as ȝistirday
6 and the thrid day henns. Neuerthelatre thei wenten not aweye fro the synnes of the hous of Jeroboam, that made Yrael

CAP. XIII.

In the thre and twentithe ȝeer of Joas, 1 sone^w of Ocozie, kyng of Juda, Joachaz, sone^w of Hieu, regnede on^x Israel, in Samarie seuentene ȝeer. And he dide yuel 2 bifor the Lord, and he suede the synnes of Jeroboam, sone^y of Nabath, that made Israel to do synne; and he bowide not awei fro tho^z. And the strong^a veniaunce†3 of the Lord was wrooth aȝens Israel, and he bitook hem in to the hondis^b of Azael, kyng of Sirie, and in^c the hond of Benadab, sone of Asael^d, in alle daies. For-4 sothe Joachaz bisouȝte the face of the Lord, and the Lord herde hym; for he^e siȝ the anguysch of Israel, for the kyng of Sirie hadde al to brokun hem. And 5 the Lord ȝaf a sauyour‡ to Israel, and he was delyuered fro the hond of the kyng of Sirie; and the sones of Israel dwelliden in her tabernaclis, as ȝistirdai and the thridde dai ago. Netheles thei de- 6 partiden not fro the synnes of the hows of Jeroboam, that made Israel to do synne;

° the paleys CE.   ^f and B.   ^g troden B.

---

^f Joas I.   ^g sente *these* I.   ^gg the kyng M.   ^h Om. I.   ^i Azael I.   ^k remenaunt I.   ^l the wordis EIL.
^m that I.   ^n And I.   ^o the I.   ^p seruauntis of Joas I.   ^q risen EL. resen I. resin P.   ^r smeten I.
smetyn ELP.   ^s of Mello Is.   ^t Forsothe I.   ^u the sone I.   ^v smoten I. smetiu ELP.   ^w the sone I.
^x upon I.   ^y the sone I.   ^z tho *synnus* I.   ^a woodnesse or *strong* I.   ^b hoond I.   ^c to I.   ^d Asael, *kyng of Sirie* I.   ^e thi that the Lord I.

to synnen, and in hem thei ʒeden, forsothe
and the mawmett wode abood stylle in
7 Samarye And thei ben not laft to Joachas of the puple, bot fyue hundreth hors
men, and ten chaaris, and ten thousandis
of fote men, forsothe the kyng of Cyrye
hadde slayn hem, and hadde brouʒte hem
doun as powdre in the threschynge of the
scorn flore The remnaunt forsothe of the
wordis of Joachaz, and alle thingis that
he dyde, bot and his strengthe, whethei
not these thingis ben writen in the boke
of the wordis of the days of the kyngis
9 of Yrael? And Joachaz slepte with his
faders, and thei byryeden hym in Samarye; and Joas, his sone, regned for hym
10 The seuenth[h] and thrittithe[i] ʒeer of Joas,
kyng of Juda, regnede Joas, the sone of
Joachaz vpon Yrael in Samarye sextene
11 ʒeer And he dyde that, that is euyl in
the siʒt of the Lord; forsothe he bowide
not doun fro alle the synnes of Jeroboam,
the sone of Nabath, the whiche maad
12 Yrael to synne, in hem he wente The
remnaunt forsothe of the wordis of Joas,
and alle thingis that he dyde, bot and the
strength of hym, what maner wijse he
fauʒte aʒeynst Amaziam, kyng of Juda,
whether not these ben wryten in the
boke of the wordis of the days of the
13 kyngis of Yrael? And Joas slepte with
his fadirs, Jeroboam forsothe, his sone,
sate vpon his see. Bot Joas is byryed in
14 Samarye with the kyngis of Yrael Helise forsothe sykide in sijknesse, by the
whiche and he is deed; and Joas, the
kynge of Yrael, came doun to hym, and
wepte beforn hym, and seyde, Fader
myne' fadir myne' the chaar of Yrael,
15 and the charietere of it' And Helise
seith to hym, Brynge forthe a bowe and
arowis And whanne he hadde brouʒt
16 to hym a bowe and arowis, he seide to
the kyng of Yrael, Putte thin hond vpon

thei[f] ʒeden in tho synnes, sotheli also the
wodes†[g] dwellide[h] in Samarie And to
7 Joacham[i] weren not left of the puple, no[k]
but fyue hundrid knyʒtis, and ten chaais,
and ten thousynde of foot men; for the
kyng of Sirie hadde slayn hem, and hadde
dryue hem[l] as in to poudni in the thresch-
yng of a cornfloor. Forsothe the residue[m]
8 of wordis[n] of Joachaz, and alle thingis
whiche[o] he dide, and the strength of hym,
whethei these ben not wrytun in the book
of wordis of daies of the kyngis of Israel?
And Joachaz slepte with hise fadris, and
9 thei birieden hym in Samaie; and Joas,
his sone, regnyde for hym In the se-
10 uenthe[q] and threttithe[qq] ʒeer of Joas, king
of Juda, Joas, soner[r] of Joachaz, regnede
on[s] Israel in Samarie sixtene ʒeer And
11 he dide that, that is yuel in the[t] siʒt of
the Lord; for he bowide not awei fro alle
the synnes of Jeroboam, sone[u] of Nabath,
that made Israel to do synne; he[v] ʒede
in tho synnes Forsothe the residue[w] of
12 wordis[x] of Joas, and alle thingis whiche[y]
he dide, but also his strengthe, hou he
fauʒt aʒens Amasie, kyng of Juda, whethei these ben not writun in the book of
wordis of daies[z] of the kyngis of Israel?
And Joas slepte with hise fadris, forsothe
13 Jeroboam sat on[a] his trone Sotheh[b] Joas
was biried in Samarie with the kyngis of
14 Israel Forsothe Elisee was sijk in sikenesse[c], bi[d] which and[e] he was deed; and
Joas, kyng of Israel, ʒede doun to hym,
and wepte bifor hym, and seide, My fadir'
my fadu' the chare of Israel, and the
charietere therof' And Elisee seide to
15 hym, Brynge thou[f] a bouwe and arowis
And whanne he hadde brouʒte to Elisee
a bouwe and arowis, he[g] seide to the kyng
16 of Israel, Set thin hond on the bouwe And
whanne he hadde set[h] his hond, Elisee
settide[i] his hondis on[k] the hondis of the
17 kyng, and seide, Opene thou the eest

† the wode, this was of the relikis of the worschiping of Baal therin distriede the temple of Baal that was in Samarie, but the wode whee ynne lecherie was hauntid left stille, aʒenus the comaundement of the lawe Lire here

---

h seuene CF   i thretti A

f but thei ꞏ g thicke wode ꞏ h aboode stille ꞏ dwellide ful s ꞏ ' Joacham, *kyng of Israel* ꞏ k Om ꞏ
l Om *plures* ꞏ m remenaunt ꞏ n the woordis ꞏ o that ꞏ p men ꞏ q seuen EIIP ꞏ qq thretti L
r the sone ꞏ s upon ꞏ t Om ꞏ u the sone ꞏ v but he ꞏ w remenaunt ꞏ x the wordis ꞏ y that ꞏ
z the daies ꞏ a upon ꞏ b And ꞏ c a sikenesse ꞏ d in ꞏ e Om A ꞏ f thou *hidir* ꞏ g Heliʒee ꞏ
h set, *that is, whanne he had take the bowe in* ꞏ i sette ꞏ k upon ꞏ

VOL II   N n

the bowe. And whann he hadde putte
his hond, Helisee putte aboue his hondis
17 to the hondis of the kyng, and seith,
Opyn the eeste wyndowe. And whanne
he hade opnede, Helise seyde, Kast an
arowe; and he kest. And Helise seith,
The arowe of the help of the Lord, and
the arowe of helthe aʒeyns Cyrye; and
thou schalt smyten Cyrye in to Affeth,
18 to the tyme that thou waast it. And
he seith, Taak the arowis. The whiche
whanne he hadde taaken, eft he seyde to
hym, Smyte with a dart the erthe. And
whanne he hadde smyten thre sithis, and
19 hadde stonden, the man of God wrath-
thede aʒeyns hym, and seith, ʒif thou
haddist smyten fyue sithis, or sexe sithis,
or seuen sithis, thou haddist smyten Cyrye vnto the hool waastynge; nowe forsothe thou schalt smyten it three sithis.
20 Thanne Helise dyʒede, and thei birieden
hym. Forsothe the lityl theeuis of Moab
21 camen in to the lond in that ʒeer. Summe
forsothe byryinge a man, seeʒen the lytyl
theeuis, and kasten the careyn in the sepulcre of Helise; the whiche whanne
hadde touchid the boonis of Helisee, the
man quyckened aʒeyn, and stode vpon
22 his feet. Thanne Azael, kyng of Cyrie,
tourmentyde Yrael alle the days of Joa-
23 chaz. And the Lord hadde reuthe of hem,
and he turnede aʒeyn to hem for his couenaunt, that he hadde with Abraham,
Ysaac, and Jacob; and he wolde not sca-
tren hem, ne fully throwen aweye, into
24 the present tyme. Forsothe Azael, the
kyng of Cyrye, diede; and Benadab, his
25 sone, regnede for hym. Bot Joas, the
sone of Joachaz, toke the cytees fro the
hond of Benadab, the sone of Azael, 'the
whiche[k] he hadde taken fro the hond of
Joachas, his fadir, thorʒ riʒt of bateyl;
thre sithis Joas smoot hym, and he ʒeeldide the cytees to Yrael.

wyndow. And whanne he hadde openyd,
Elisee seide, Schete thou an arewe; and
he schete[l]. And Elisee seide, *It* is an arewe
of helthe of the Lord, and an arowe of
helthe aʒens Sirie; and thou schalt smyte
Sirie in Affeth, til thou waste it. And 18
Elisee seide, Take awei the arowis. And
whanne he hadde take awei, Elisee seide
eft[n] to him, Smyte thou the erthe with a
dart. And whanne he[o] hadde smyte thre
tymes, and hadde stonde[p], the man of God 19
was wrooth† aʒens hym[q], and seide, If thou
haddist smyte fyue sithis, ether sixe sithis,
ethir seuen sithis, thou schuldist haue
smyte Sirie 'til to[r] the endyng; now forsothe thou schalt smyte it thre sithis.
Therfor[s] Elisee was deed, and thei[t] biri- 20
eden hym. And the[u] theuys of Moab
camen in to the lond in that ʒeer. For- 21
sothe sum men birieden a man, and thei
siʒen the[v] theues[w], and thei castiden[x] forth
the deed bodi in[y] the sepulcre of Elisee;
and whanne it hadde touchid the bonys
of Elisee, the man lyuede aʒen, and stood
on[yy] his feet. Therfor[z] Azael, kyng of 22
Sirie, turmentide Israel in alle the daies
of Joachaz. And the Lord hadde merci 23
on[a] hem[b], and turnede aʒen to hem for
his[u] couenaunt, which[d] he hadde[e] with
Abraham, Isaac, and Jacob; and he nolde[f]
distrie hem, nether cast[g] awei outirli, til[h]
in to present[i] tyme. Forsothe[k] Azael, 24
kyng of Sirie, diede; and Benadad, his
sone, regnede for hym. Forsothe[l] Joas, 25
sone[m] of Joachas, took awei citees fro the
hond of Benadad‡, sone[n] of Azael, which[o]
he hadde take bi the riʒt of batel fro the
hoond of Joachaz, his fadir; Joas smoot
hym[p] thre tymes, and he ʒeldide the[q]
citees to Israel.

† the man of
God was
wrooth; for it
was schewid to
Elisee, that if
the kyng
smytide the
erthe ofte
without cess-
yng, he schulde
caste doun Si-
rie outirly;
netheles Elisee
hadde not li-
cence to seye to
the king the
reuelacioun,
sithis the Hooly
Goost touchith
the hertis of
profetis in that
maner bi which
he wole. First
it was schewid
to Elisee, that
if the king
smoot ofte the
erthe, he
schulde do
awey Sirie;
netheles it was
not schewid
hou ofte he
schulde smyte.
But aftir that
he smoot
thries and
ceesside, it was
schewid to
Elisee, that the
king schulde
smyte Sirie
thre sithis, and
in particuler
batails. *Lire
here.* c.
‡ *Benadad*;
Jerom seith,
that this sone
of Azael schal
be writun bi
d in the ende,
and so it is in
Ebreu; but
Benadab, that
ʒede bifor Aza-
el, is writun
bi ð in the
ende. *Lire
here.* c.

k that c pr. m.

l schotte 1. m *This* 1. n Om. ELP. o Joas 1. p stonde *stille* 1. q the kyng 1. r vnto 1. s Thanne 1.
t men 1. u Om. is. v Om. 1. w theues niʒ 1. x casten 1. y in to 1. yy upon 1. z Thanne 1.
a upon 1. b the sones of Israel 1. c the 1. d that 1. e hadde *maad* 1. f wolde not 1. g caste *hem* 1.
h Om. 1. i this present 1. k And 1. l Certis 1. m the sone 1. n the sone 2. o that 1. p Benadab 1.
q tho 1.

CAP. XIV.

1 In the secounde ʒeer of Joas, the sone of Joachas, kyng of Yrael, regnede Ama-2zias, the sone of Joas, kyng of Juda. Of fyue and twenty ʒeer he was, whanne he beganne to regnen ; twenty forsothe and nyne ʒeer he regnede in Jerusalem ; name 3of his modir, Joaden of Jerusalem. And he dyde riʒt before the Lord, neuerthe-latre not as Dauid, his fadir ; aftir alle thingis that Joas, his fadir, dyde he dide, 4bot that oonly, that heeʒe thingis he dydde not aweye ; ʒit forsothe the puple offrede, 5and brende encense in heiʒtis. And whan he hadde weldyde the rewme, he smoote his seruauntis, that hadden slayn the 6kyng, his fadre ; the sonys forsothe of hem that hadden slayn, he slewʒ not ; after that that is writen in the boke of the lawe of Moyses, as the Lord co-maundide to Moyses, seyinge, The fadirs schuln not dyʒen for the sonys, ne the souys for the fadirs, bot echone schal 7dyen in his synne. He smote Edom in the valey of placis of salt, tenn thousandis ; and he cauʒte the place, that hatte Petra, in bateyl ; and he clepide his name Jeze-8chel, vnto the day that is nowe. Thanne Amazias sente messagers to Joas, the sone of Joachas, the sone of Hieu, kyng of Yrael, seyinge, Comme, and see we us. 9And Joas, kyng of Yrael, sente aʒeyn to Amazias, kyng of Juda, seyinge, The thistill of Lybane sente to the cedre, that is in Libane, seyinge, ʒeue thi douʒtir to my sone wijf ; and the beestis of the wijlde wode, that ben in Lybane, wenten, 10and treden^m the thistill. And smytynge thou haddist the ouerhond vpon Edom, and thin herte arered thee ; be thou apayid^n with thi glorie, and sytt in thi hous ; why stirist thou euyl, that thou

CAP. XIV.

Yn the secounde ʒeer of Joas, sone^r of 1 Joachas, kyng of Israel, Amasie, sone^r of Joas, kyng of Juda, regnyde. *Amasie* 2 was of fyue and twenti ʒeer, whanne he bigan to regne ; forsothe^s he regnyde in Jerusalem nyne and twenti ʒeer ; the name of his modir was Joade of Jerusalem. And 3 he dide riʒtfulnesse bifor the Lord, nethe-les not as Dauid, his fadir^t ; he dide bi alle thingis whiche^u Joas, his fadir, dide, no but this oonli†, that he dide not a wei 4 hiʒ thingis ; for ʒit the puple made sacri-fice, and brent encence in hiʒ thingis. And 5 whanne he^uu hadde gete the rewme, he smoot hise seruauntis, that hadden killid the kyng, his fadir ; but he killide not the 6 sones of hem that hadden slayn '*the kyng*^v, bi that that is writun in the book of the lawe of Moyses, as the Lord comaundide to Moises, and seide, Fadris schulen not die for the^w sones, nethir the^x sones for the^w fadris, but eche man schal die in his owne synne. He^y smoot Edom in the 7 valey of makyngis of salt, '*he smoot*^z ten thousynde^a, and took '*the Stoon*^b in batel^c ; and he clepide the name therof Jethel‡, 'til in to^d present dai. Thanne§ Amasie sente 8 messangeris to Joas, sone^e of Joachaz, sone^e of Hieu, kyng of Israel, and seide, Come thou, and se we vs '*in batel*^f. And 9 Joas, kyng of Israel, sente aʒen to Amasie, kyng of Juda, and seide^g, The cardue^h, '*that is, a low cerbe, and ful of thornes*^i, of the Liban sente to the cedre, which^k is in the^l Liban, and seide, ʒyue thi douʒtir wijf to my sone ; and the beestis of the forest, that ben in the Liban, passiden^m, and tredden^n doun the cardue. Thou 10 hast smyte^o, and haddist the maistri on^p Edom^q, and thin herte hath^r reisid thee ; be thou apaied with glorie^s, and sitte in

† *this onely;* this may not by referrid to the lettre next bifore, but to this that is seid, he dide riʒtfulnesse bifor the Lord, no but this onely, etc. *Lire here.* c.

‡ *Jethel;* that is, sourenesse of teeth, for thei that weren slayn there gnastiden with teeth, for the orrour and so-rewe of deth. *Lire here.* c.

§ *Thanne;* that is, aftir pride, for the victorie aʒenus Idumeys, and aftir idola-trie, and aftir mannaasing of Goddis profete, in 11. book of Paralip. xxv. c°. God suf-fride him falle in to so greet presumpcioun, that he terride Joas, kyng of Israel, to batel, that his pride were brouʒt doun so. And this it is that is seid here *thanne,* that is, after the for-seid wickid-nesses doon of him. *Lire here.* c.

---

m treteden B.   n paʒid C.

r the sone I. s and I. t fadir dide I. u that I. uu Amasie I. v his fadir I. w her I. x Om. I.
y Amasie I. z Om. I. a thousynde of men I. b Om. I. c batel the noble Stoon, *a citee of Arabie* I.
d vnto this I. e the sone I. f Om. I. g seide mystily I. h cardue *or thistle* I. i Om. I. k that I.
l Om. I. m passiden forth I. n trooden I. o smyte Edom I. p vpon I. q it I. r therfore hath I.
s this glorie I.

11 falle, and Juda with thee? And Amazias assentyde not; and Joas, the kyng of Yrael, stey3ide up, and thei see3en hem silf, he and Amazias, the kyng of Juda, in Bethsames, the bour3toun of 12 Jude. And Juda is smyten beforn Vrael; and thei flowen echone in to their tabernaclis. 13 Joas, the kyng of Yrael, forsothe toke Amazie, the kynge of Juda, the sone of Joas, the sone of Ochosie, in Bethsames, and brou3te hym in to Jerusalem; and he to-brast the walle of Jerusalem, fro the 3aat of Effraym vnto the 3aat of the cornere, in foure hundreth 14 cubitis. And he toke al the gold and syluer, and alle the vessels, that ben foundun in the hous of the Lord, and in the tresories of the kyng, and prisoners, 15 and is turnede a3eyn in to Samarye. The remnaunt forsothe of the wordis of Joas, the whiche he dyde, and his strengthe, in the whiche he fau3te a3eynst Amazie, kyng of Juda, whether not thes ben writen in the boke of the wordis of the 16 days of the kyngis of Yrael? And Joas slepte with his fadirs, and is biryed in Samarye with the kyngis of Yrael; and Jeroboam, his sone, regnede for hym. 17 Forsothe Amazias, the sone of Joas, lyuede kyng of Juda, aftir that Joas, the sone of Joachas, kyng of Yrael, dy3ide, 18 fyue and twenty 3eer. The remnaunt forsothe of the wordis of Amazie, whether not thes ben writen in the boke of the wordis of the days of the kyngis of 19 Juda? And there is maad a3eyn hym coniuracyoun in Jerusalem, and he fleci3° in to Lachis; and thei senten aftir hym in to Lachis, and thei slewen hym there. 20 And brou3ten hym thennus in hors, and he is biryide in Jerusalem with his fa-21 dirs, in the cytee of Dauid. Forsothe alle the puple of Jude toke Azaria, 3eeris born sixteene; and thei ordeynde hym

thin hows; whi excitist[w] thou yuel, that thou falle, and Juda with thee? And 11 Amasie assentide not 'to be in pees[x]; and Joas, kyng[y] of Israel, stiede[z], and he and Amasie, kyng[a] of Juda, sien hem silf in[b] Bethsames, a citee of Juda. And Juda 12 was smytun bifor[c] Israel; and thei fledden ech man in to his tabernaclis. Sotheli 13 Joas, kyng[d] of Israel, took in Bethsames Amasie, kyng[d] of Juda, the sone of Joas, sone[e] of Ocozie, and brou3te hym in to Jerusalem; and he[f] brak the wal of Jerusalem, fro the 3ate of Effraym 'til to[g] the 3ate of the corner, bi foure hundrid cubitis. And he took al the gold and sil-14 uer, and alle vessels[h], that weren foundun in the hows of the Lord, and in the tresours of the kyng; and *he took* ostagis[†], and turnede a3en in to Samarie. Sotheli[k] 15 the resydue of wordis[l] of Joas, whiche[m] he dide, and his strengthe, bi which he fau3t a3ens Amasie, kyng of Juda, whether these ben not writun in the book of wordis of dayes of the[n] kyngis of Israel? And Joas slepte with hise fadris, and was 16 biried in Samarie with the kyngis of Israel; and Jeroboam, his sone, regnede for hym. Forsothe Amasie, sone[o] of Joas, 17 kyng[p] of Juda, lyuede fyue and twenti 3eer, after that Joas, sone[q] of Joachaz, kyng of Israel, was deed. Forsothe the 18 residue of wordis[r] of Amasie, whether these ben not writun in the book of wordis of daies of the kyngis of Juda? And 19 'sweryng[‡] togidir[s] in Jerusalem was maad a3ens hym, and he fledde in to Lachis; and thei senten[§] aftir hym in to Lachis, and killiden hym there. And thei baren 20 out hym[ss] in horsis, and he was biried in Jerusalem with hise fadris, in the citee of Dauid. Forsothe al the puple of Juda 21 took Azarie[t], hauynge sixtene 3eer; and maden hym king for his fadir Amasie. And[u] he bildide Ahila, and restoride it to 22

† *ostagis* : that is, the sones of noble men, that her fadris my3ten not rebelle a3euns hem. *Lire here.* C.

‡ *swering, etc.*; that is, conspirasie. *Lire here.* C.
§ *thei senten,* greet multitude of werriours. *Lire here.* C.

° fleeth B.

22 kyng for his fadır Amazie And he
bylde Ahılam, and restoorıde it to Jude,
aftır that the kyng hadde slepte with his
23 fadırs The fyftenth ȝeeı of Amazıas, the
sone of Joas, kyng of Juda, regned Jeıo-
boam, the sone of Joas, kyng of Yrael, in
24 Samarye oon and fourty ȝeeı ; and dydde
that, that is euyl before the Lord ; and
he wente not aweye fro alle the synnys
of Jeroboam, the sone of Nabath, that
25 maad Yıael to synne And he restoor-
ide the termys of Yrael, fro the entree of
Emath vnto the se of wyldıenesse, aftıı
the word of the Lord God of Yıael, that
he spak by his seruaunt Jonas, the sone
of Amathıe, prophete, that was of Geth,
26 that is ın Oofeı. Foısothe the Lord
sawe the tourmentynge of Yıael to myche
, bittır, and that theı weren waastıd vnto
the closed of the pıısone, and ıttırmostıs,
and ther was not the whıche myȝt helpen
27 Yıael And the Lord spac not, that he
schulde done aweye the name of Yrael
fıo vndır heuen, bot he sauede hem ın
the hond of Jeroboham, the sone of Joas
28 The remnaunt forsothe of the wordıs of
Jeroboam, and alle thıngıs that he dyde,
and his strengthe, ın the whıche he tauȝte,
and howe he restorıde Damask, and E-
math of Jude, ın Yıael, whether not thes
ben writen ın the boke of the wordis of
29 the dayes of the kyngıs of Yıael ? And
Jeroboam slepte with his fadırs, the
kyngıs of Yrael ; and Azarıas, his sone,
regnede for hym

Juda, afteᵛ that 'the kvngʷ slepte with
hise fadrıs In the fiftenethe ȝeer of Ama-23
sıe, soneˣ of Joas, kyng of Juda, Jeroboam,
soneˣ of Joas, kyng of Israel, ıegnyde ın
Samarıe oon and fourtı ȝeeı ; and dıde 24
that, that is ynel bifor the Lord , he ȝede
not aweı fıo alle the synnes of Jeroboam,
sone of Nabath, that made Isıael to do
synne He restorıde the teımes of Isıael, 25
fro the entryng of Emath 'tıl toʸ the see
of wildırnesse, bı the word of the Lord
God of Isıael, whichᶻ he spak bı his seruaunt Jonas, soneᵃ of Amathı, bı Jonas,
the prophete, that was of Jetht, 'which
Jethᵇ ıs in Ophır For the Lord sıȝ the 26
ful bittir tuıment of Isıael, and that theı
weren wastıd 'til toᶜ the closıd men of
pıısonn, and theᵈ laste men, and 'noon
wasᵉ that helpıde Israel And the Lord 27
spak not, that he schulde do aweı Israel
fro vndur heuene, but he sauyde hem ın
the hond of Jeroboam, soneᶠ of Joas For-28
sothe the reıidue of wordısᵍ of Jeroboam,
and alle thıngıs whıcheʰ he dıde, and the
strengthe of hym, bı which he fauȝt, and
hou he restorıde Damask, and Emath of
Juda, ın Isıael, whether these ben not
wrytun ın the book of wordıs of daıes
of the kyngıs of Israel ? And Jeroboam 29
slepte with hıse fadrıs, the kyngıs of Israel , and Azarıeʰʰ, his sone, ıegnede foı
hym

CAP XV

1 The seuen and twentithe ȝeer of Jeroboam, kyng of Yrael, regned Azarıe, the
2 sone of Amazıe, kyng of Juda , of sextene ȝeer he was, whanne he begane to
regnen, and two and fyfty ȝeer he ıegnede ın Jerusalem , name of his modır,
3 Jecelıa of Jerusalem And he dyde that,
that was plesaunt befoın the Lord, aftir
alle thıngıs that Amazıas, his fadır, hadde

CAP XV.

In the seuenthe¹ and twentithe) ȝeer of 1
Jeroboam, kıng of Israel, Azarie, soneᵏ of
Amasıe, kyng of Juda, regncde , he was 2
of sıxtene ȝeeı, whanne he bıgan to regne,
and he regnede two and fifti ȝeer ın Jeıusalem ; the name of his modır was Jecelıa
of Jerusalem And he dıde that, that was 3
plesaunt bifor the Lord, bı alle thıngıs
whıch¹ Amasıe, his fadır, hadde do; ne-4

4 done; neuer the latre the heeȝe thingis he distruyde not; ȝit the puple sacri-5 fiside, and brent encense in heiȝtis. The Lord forsothe smoote the kyng, and he was messel vnto the day of his deth; and he dwellede in the hous freely asyde. Jonthas forsoth, the kyngis sone, go-uernde the paleys, and he demyde the 6 puple of the lond. The remnaunt for-sothe of the wordis of Azarie, and alle thingis that he dyde, whether not thes ben writen in the boke of the wordis of 7 the⁹ days of kyngis of Juda? And Aza-rie slepte with his fadirs; and they biri-eden hym with his morisᵠᵠ in the cytee of Dauith; and Joathas, his sone, regnede 8 for hym. The eiȝt and thrittithe ȝeer of Azaria, kyng of Juda, regnede Zacharie, the sone of Jeroboam, vpon Yrael in Sa-9 marie sexe monethis. And he dyde that, that was euyl beforn the Lord, as his fadirs dyden; he wente not aweye fro the synnes of Jeroboam, the sone of Na-10 bath, that maad Yrael to synnen. For-sothe Sellum, the sone of Jabes, in Sa-marye coniurede aȝenus hym; and he smoot hym opynly, and slewȝ, and regn-11 ede for hym. The remnaunt forsothe of the wordis of Zacharie, whether not thes ben writen in the boke of the wordis of 12 the days of theʳ kyngis of Yrael? This is the word of the Lord, that he spake to Hieu, seyinge, Thi sonys vnto the ferth generacioun schul sytten of thee vpon the trone of Ysrael; and it is done so. 13 Sellum, the sone of Jabes, regnede the nyne and thrittithe ȝeere of Azarie, kyng of Juda; he regnede forsothe oon monethe 14 in Samarye. And Manaheu, the sone of Gaddy, steyȝide up fro Tharsa, and came in to Samarie; and smoot Sellum, the sone of Jabes, in Samaryc, and slewȝ 15 hym, and regnede for hym. The rem-naunt forsothe of the wordis of Sellum,

theles he distriede not hiȝ thingis; ȝitᵐ the puple made sacrifice, and brente en-cense in hiȝe thingis. Forsothe the Lord 5 smoot the kyng, and he was leprouse† til in to the day of his deeth; and he dwell-ide in an hous freli bi hym silf. Sotheli Joathas, sone of the kyng, gouernde the palis, and demyde the puple of the lond. Forsothe the residue of theⁿ wordis of 6 Azarie, and alle thingis whicheᵒ he dide, whether these ben not writun in the book of wordis of daies of theᵖ kyngis of Juda? And Azarie slepte with hise fadris; and 7 thei birieden hym with hise eldre men in the citee of Dauid; and Joathas, his sone, regnede for hym. In the eiȝte and thret-8 tithe ȝeer of Azarie, kyng of Juda, Za-charie, soneᵠ of Jeroboam, regnede onʳ Israel in Samarie sixe monethis. And he 9 dide that, that was yuel bifor the Lord, as his fadris diden; he departide not fro the synnes of Jeroboam, soneˢ of Nabath, that made Israel to do synne. Forsothe† 10 Sellum, the sone of Jabes, conspiride aȝens hym in Samarie; and *Sellum* smoot hym opynli‡, and killide *hym*ᵘ, and regnede for hym. Sotheliᵛ the residue ofʷ theˣ wordis 11 of Zacharie, whethir these ben not writun in the book of wordis of daies of the kyngis of Israel? Thilkeʸ is the word of 12 the Lord, whichˣ he spak to Hieu, and seide, 'Thi sonesᵃ 'til toᵇ the fourthe gene-racioun schulen sitte 'of thee on the troneᶜ of Israel; and it was doon so. Sellumᵈ, 13 soneᵉ of Jabes, regnede in the nytheᶠ and thritty ȝeer of Azarie, kyng of Juda; sotheli he reguyde o monethe in Samarie. And Manaheu, the sone of Gaddi, styedeᵍ 14 fro Thersa, and cam in to Samarie; and he smoot Sellum, soneʰ of Jabes, in Sa-marie, and killide hym, and regnede for hym. Sotheli the residue of wordisⁱ of 15 Sellum, and his conspirasie, bi which he settide tresouns, whether these ben not

† *was leprouse; for bi pride he wolde mystake to him the office of prest, and entride in to the temple, to offre en-cense; and whanne the prestis seiden, that this per-teynede not to his office, he manasside hem, and helde the censere; wherfor he was smytun su-deynly and opinli with lepre. And therfor anoon the prestis putciden him out of the temple, and he feelide the ven-isaunce of the Lord; and he ȝede out wil-fulie, dredinge lest it schulde bifalle worse to him, as it is had in 11. book of Paralip. xxvi. cᵉ. Lire here. c.*
‡ *opynly; in Ebreu it is bi-for the peple, and bi this it is signefied, that he hadde myche part of the puple con-sentinge with him; for this Zacarie was ful yuel. Lire here. c.*

ᵐ but ȝit ɪ.　ⁿ Om. ʙᴄғɢᴋᴍɴᴏᴘQʀsᴜᴡbᴄ.　ᵒ that ɪ.　ᵖ Om. ᴇʟ.　ᵠ the sone ɪ.　ʳ upon ɪ.　ˢ the sone ɪ.　ᵗ Certis ɪ.　ᵘ Om. *plures*.　ᵛ And ɪ.　ʷOm. ɢ.　ˣ Om. ʙᴄᴅᴇғɢᴋʟᴍɴᴏᴘsxᴄ.　ʸ That ɪ, This ᴇʟ.　ˣ the which ɪ.　ᵃ Sones of thee ɪ.　ᵇ vnto ɪ.　ᶜ on the trone of thee ᴇʟ.　ᵈ And Sellum ɪ.　ᵉ the sone ɪ.　ᶠ nyne ɪ.　ᵍ styede up ɪ.　ʰ the sone ɪ.　ⁱ the wordis ɪ.

and his coniuracyoun, by the whiche he bente buschementis, whether not thes ben writen in the boke of the wordis of the 16 days of the kyngis of Yrael? Than Manaheu smoot Thersam, and alle that weren in it, and his termys fro Thersa, forsothe they wolden not openen to hym, and he slew3 alle the wymmen of it with 17 childe, and kutte hem The nyne and thrittithe 3eer of Azarie, kyng of Juda, regnede Manaheu, the sone of Gaddi, 18 vpon Yrael tenn 3eer in Samarie And he dydde that, that was euyl beforn the Lord, and he wente not aweye fro the synnes of Jeroboam, the sone of Nabath, 19 that maad Yrael to synnen Alle the days of hym came Phul, the kyng of Assiries, in Thersa And Manaheu gaue to Phul a thousand talentis of syluer, that he were to hym in to help, and that 20 he fasten his rewme; and Manaheu comaundid syluer vpon Yrael to alle the my3ti and to the ryche, that he schulde 3eue to the kyng of Assiries, fyfty ciclis of syluer, thoru3 oute alle 3eeris, and the kyng of Assiries is turned a3ein, and 21 dwellide not in Therse The remnaunt forsothe of the wordis of Manaheu, and alle thingis that he dide, whether not these ben writen in the boke of the wordis of the days of the kyngis of 22 Yrael? And Manaheu slepte with his fadris; and Phasaya, his sone, regnede for 23 hym The fyftythe 3eer of Azaria, kyng of Juda, regnede Phasaye, the sone of Manaheu, vpon Yrael in Samarye two 24 3eer And he dyde that, that was euyl before the Lord; and he wente not aweye fro the synnes of Jeroboam, the sone of 25 Nabath, that maad Yrael to synnen Forsothe Phacee, the sone of Romelie, duyk of his hoost, coniurede a3eyn hym, and smoote hym in Samarye, in the toure of the kyngis hous, bisydis Argoh, and bisidis Arib, and with hym fyfty men of the sonis of Galaditis; and he slew3 hym,

writun in the book of wordis of daies of 16 the kyngis of Israel Thanne Manaheu smoot Capham, and alle men that weren there ynne, and the termes therof froThersa, for thei nolden opyn to hym†; and he killide alle wymmen therof with child, and 17 karf hym In the nynthe and thrittithe 3eer of Azarie, kyng of Juda, Manaheu, sone of Gaddi, regnede on Israel ten 3eer 18 in Samarie And he dide that that was yuel bifor the Lord, he departide not fro the synnes of Jeroboam, sone of Nabath, 19 that made Israel to do synne In alle‡ the daies of hym Phul, the kyng of Assiries, cam in to Thersa And Manaheu 3af to Phul a thousynde talentis of siluei, that he schulde be to hym in to help, and 20 schulde make stidefast his rewme, and Manaheu settide taliage of siluer on Israel to alle my3ti men and riche, that he schulde§ 3yue to the kyng of Assiries, he settide fifti siclis of siluer bi alle men§ , and the king of Assiries turnede a3en, and 21 dwellide not in Thersa Forsothe the residue of wordis of Manaheu, and alle thingis whiche he dide, whether these ben not wi3tun in the book of wordis of daies of the kyngis of Israel? And Mana- 22 heu slepte with hise fadris, and Phaceia, his sone, regnyde for hym. In the fiftithe 23 3eer of Azarie, kyng of Juda, Phaceia, sone of Manaheu, regnede on Israel in Samarie twei 3eer And he dide that, that 24 was yuel bifor the Lord, he departide not fro the synnes of Jeroboam, sone of Nabath, that made Israel to do synne For- 25 sothe Phacee, sone of Romelie, duyk of his oost, conspiride a3ens hym, and smoot hym in Samarie, and the tour of the kyngis hous, bisidis Argob, and bisidis Arib||; and he smoot hym with fifti men of the sones of Galaditis; and Phacee killide hym, and regnede for hym Sotheli the 26 residue of wordis of Phacee, and alle thingis whiche he dide, whether these ben not writun in the book of wordis of daies

---

† to hym that is, resseyue hym in the citee as king Lire here

‡ In alle, etc, whanne Manaheu preiede him to conferme his rewme Lire here

§ bi alle men, that is, riche men In Ebreu it is to o man that is, to ech man, bi maner of spekinge of Ebreu, therfor bokis that han here bi alle 3eris, ben false, for the Ebreu bokis, and oure bokis amendid, han not 3eris Lire here

|| Arib, that is, the palis, as Rabi Salomon seith Lire here. Arib, in Ebreu it is bisidis Arie, that signefieth a houn, for a goldun houn was there, to noble and fairnesse, as Rabi Salomon seith Lire here

---

k smoot *the citee* 1   l the men 1   m wolden not 1   n opyn *her 3atis* 1   o keruyde 1   p nyne 1   q the sone 1   r upon 1   s the sone 1   t upon 1   u wolde 1   v *sette* 1   w *thu* men 1   x the wordis 1   y that 1   z the sone 1   a the sone 1   b the 1   c oost of Phacea 1   d with fifty men of the sones of Galaditis in 1   e Oui 1   f Phacea 1   g the wordis 1   h that 1

26 and regnede for hym. The remnaunt forsothe of the wordis of Phasaye, and alle thingis that he dyde, whether thes ben not writen in the boke of the wordis of 27 the days of the kyngis of Yrael? The two and fyftithe[a] ʒeer of Azarie, kyng of Jude, regnede Phacee, the sone of Romelie, vpon Yrael in Samarye twenty ʒeer. 28 And dydde that, that was euyl beforn the Lord; and he wente not aweye fro the synnes of Jeroboam, the sone of Nabath, 29 that maad Yrael to synnen. In the days of Phacee, kyng of Yrael, canne Theglath Falasar, the kyng of Assur, and toke Ayon, and Aybel, the hous of Maacha, and Janoe, and Cedes, and Asor, and Ga- laad, and Galilee, and al the lond of Neptalym; and translatyde hem in to 30 Assiries. Forsothe Osee, the sone of Hela, coniurede, and bende busschementis aʒeyns Phacee, the sone of Romelie, and smoote hym and slew ʒ; and for hym regned, the twentithe ʒeer of Jonathan, 31 the sone of Osee. The remnaunt forsothe of the wordis of Phacee, and alle thingis that he dyde, whether thes ben not writen in the boke of the wordis of 32 the days of the kyngis of Yrael? The secounde ʒeer of Phacee, the sone of Ro- melye, kyng of Yrael, regnede Joathan, 33 the sone of Osee, kyng of Juda; of fyue and twenti ʒeer he was, whanne he by- ganne to regnen, and sixtene ʒeer he regned in Jerusalem; name of his modir 34 Cerusa, the douʒtir of Sadoch. And he dyde that, that was plesaunt beforn the Lord; aftir alle thingis that hadde done 35 Oseas, his fadir, he wrouʒt; neuerthelatre the heiʒtis he dyde not aweye; ʒitt the puple offred, and brent encense in heiʒtis; he bylde up the altherheeʒist ʒaat of the 36 hous of the Lord. The remnaunt forsothe of the wordis of Joathan, and alle the thingis that he dyde, whether thes ben not writen in the boke of the wordis 37 of the days of the kyngis of Juda? In

of the kyngis of Israel? In the two and 27 fiftithe ʒeer of Azarie, kyng of Juda, Phasee, sone[j] of Romelie, regnyde in Sa- marie twenti ʒeer. And he dide that, that 28 was yuel bifor the Lord; and[k] he departide not fro the synnes of Jeroboam, sone[l] of Nabath, that made Israel to do synne. In 29 the daies of Phacee, kyng of Israel, Teglat Phalasar, kyng of Assur, cam, and took Aion, and Aibel, the hows of Maacha, and Janoe, and Cedes, and Asor, and Galaad, and Galilee, and al the lond of Neptalym; and translatide hem in to Assiriens. For- 30 sothe Osee, sone[l] of Hela, conspiride, and settide[m] tresouns aʒens Phasee, sone[l] of Romelie, and smoot hym, and killide hym[n]; and he regnyde for hym, in the twentithe ʒeer of Joathan, sone[o] of Ozie. Forsothe 31 the residue of wordis[p] of Phacee, and alle thingis whiche[q] he dide, whether these ben not writun in the book of wordis of daies of the[r] kyngis of Israel? In the 32 secounde ʒeer of Phacee, sone[s] of Romelie, kyng of Israel, Joathan, sone[s] of Ozie, kyng[t] of Juda, regnyde; he was of fyue 33 and twenti ʒeer, whanne he bigan to regne, and he regnede sixtene ʒeer in Je- rusalem; the name of his modir was Jerusa, the douʒter of Sadoch. And he[u] 34 dide that, that was plesaunt bifor the Lord; he wrouʒte bi alle thingis†, whiche[v] his fadir Ozie hadde do; netheles he dide 35 not awey hiʒ thingis; ʒit[w] the puple made sacrifice, and brente incense in hiʒ thingis; he bildide the hiʒeste ʒate of the hows of the Lord. Forsothe the residue[x] of wordis[y] 36 of Joathan, and alle thingis whiche[z] he dide, whether these ben not writun in the book of wordis of daies of the kyngis of Juda? In tho daies the Lord bigan to 37 sende in to Juda Rasyn‡, the kyng of Sirie, and Phacee, the sone of Romelie. And Joathan slepte with hise fadris, and 38 was biried with hem in the citee of Dauid, his fadir; and Achaz, his sone, regnyde for hym.

† bi alle thingis; in synge him in goode werkis, not in yuele werkis, as in II. book of Paralip. xxvii. c⁰. Lire here. c.

‡ Rasyn; to punysche the yuels that weren doon in the rewme of Juda; for of long tyme the puple made sacrifice in hiʒe thingis, that was vnleueful fro the making of the temple, and dide many othere yuels, for the malice of Achaz. Lire here. c.

ᵃ fifti A.

ⁱ the sone I.   ᵏ Om. BCDF sec. m. GIMNOQRSUWXb.   ˡ the sone I.   ᵐ sette EL.   ⁿ Om. BCFKLOQRSUWç. ᵒ the sone I.   ᵖ the wordis I.   �q that I.   ʳ Om. E.   ˢ the sone L.   ᵗ the kyng I.   ᵘ Joathan I.   ᵛ that I. ʷ but ʒit I.   ˣ remenaunt I.   ʸ the wordis I.   ᶻ that I.

tho days byganne the Lord to senden
into Judam Rasym, the kyng of Cyrye;
38 and Phacee, the sone of Romelie. And
Joathan slepte with his fadirs, and is
biryed with hem in the cytee of Dauid,
his fadir; and Achaz, his sone, regnede
for hym.

CAP. XVI.

1 The seuententhe[t] ʒeer of Phacee, the
sone of Romelie, regned Achaz, the sone
2 of Joathan, kyng of Juda. Of twenty
ʒeer was Achaz, whan he began to regnen, and sexteen ʒeer he regned in Jerusalem; he dyde not that was plesaunt in
the siʒt of the Lord his God, as Dauith,
3 his fadir, bot ʒeede in the weye[n] of the
kyngis of Yrael. Forthermore and his
sone he sacrid, ouer berynge thoruʒ fyre,
aftir the mawmettis of heithen men, the
whiche the Lord scatered beforn the
4 sonys of Yrael. Forsothe he offred slayn
sacrifices, and brende encense in heiʒtis,
and in hillis, and vnder ech tree ful of
5 braunchis. Than Rasyn, kyng of Cyryc,
steyʒide up, and Phacee, the sone of Romelie, kyng of Yrael, in to Jerusalem to
fiʒten; and whanne thei bysegiden Achaz,
6 they myʒten not ouercomme hym. In
that tyme Rasyn, kyng of Cyrye, restoride Ahilam to Cyrye, and kest out
the Jewis fro Ahyla; and Ydumeis and
Cyries camen in to Ahilam, and dwelten
7 there vnto this day. Forsothe Achaz
sente messagers to Teglath Falasar, kyng
of Assurye, seyinge, Thi seruaunt and
thi sone I am; steyʒe up, and make me
safe fro the hond of the kyng of Cyrye,
and fro the hond of the kyng of Yrael,
8 that han rysen to gyther aʒeynus me. And
whan Achaz hadde gedrede to gydre syluer and gold, that myʒt ben foundun in
the hous of the Lord, and in the tresuries
of the kyng, and sente to the kyng of
9 Assuries ʒiftis; the whiche and assentide

CAP. XVI.

In the seuententhe ʒeer of Phacee, sone[a] 1
of Romelie, Achaz, the sone of Joathan,
kyng of Juda, regnyde. Achaz was of 2
twenti ʒeer, whanne he bigan to regne,
and he regnyde sixtene ʒeer in Jerusalem;
he dide not that, that was plesaunt in the
siʒt of his[b] Lord God, as Dauid, his fadir
dide, but he ʒede in the weie of the kyngis
of Israel. Ferthermore and he halewide 3
his sone, and bar[c] thorouʒ the fier, bi[d] the
idols of hethene men, whiche the Lord
distriede bifore the sones of Israel. And 4
he offride sacrifices[e], and brente encense
in hiʒ placis, and in hillis, and vndur ech
tree ful of bowis. Thanne Rasyn, kyng 5
of Sirye, and Phacee, sone[f] of Romelie,
kyng of Israel, stiede[g] in to Jerusalem to
fiʒte[h]; and whanne thei bisegide Achaz,
thei miʒten not ouercome hym. In that 6
tyme Rasyn, kyng of Sirie, restoride Ahila
to Sirie, and castide out Jewis[l] fro Ahila;
and Ydumeis and men of Sirie camen into[k]
Ahila, and dwelliden there til in to this
dai. Forsothe Achaz sente messangeris 7
to Teglat Phalasar, kyng of Assiriens, and
seide, Y am thi seruaunt and thi sone;
stie thou[l], and make me saaf fro the hond
of the kyng of Sirie, and fro the hond of
the kyng of Israel, that han rise togidere
aʒens me. And whanne Achaz hadde ga- 8
deride togidere siluer and gold, that myʒte
be foundun in the hows of the Lord, and
in the tresours of the kyng, he sente ʒiftis
to the kyng of Assiriens; whiche[m] as- 9
sentide to his wille. Sotheli the kyng of
Asseriens stiede[n] in to Damask, and wast-

---

[t] seuenth A. seuentithe BII.   [u] ways A.

[a] the sone L.   [b] the L.   [c] bar or drewe him L.   [d] aftir L.   [e] sacrifice ELP.   [f] the sone L.   [g] stieden up L.
[h] fiʒte with Achaz L.   [l] the Jewis L.   [k] in A.   [l] thou up L.   [m] and he L.   [n] ʒede up L.

to the wylle of hym. The kyng forsothe of Assuries steyȝide up in to Damasc, and waastyde it, and brouȝt ouer the dwellers of it to[v] Cyryuen[w]; Rasyn forsothe he 10 slewȝ. And kyng Achas wente in to aȝein commyng to Teglath Phalasar, kyng of Assirie, in to Damask; and whanne he hadde seen the auter of Damasc, kyng Achaz sente to Vrias, the prest, the exsaumpler[x] of it, and the licensse, aftir al 11 the werk of it. And Vrias, the prest, maad vp the auter aftir alle thingis that king Achas hadde comaundide of Damasc, so dyde the prest Vrias, to the tyme that kyng Achaz came from Da- 12 mask. And whanne the kyng schuld commen fro Damask, he sawȝ the auter, and wirschipide it; and he steiȝid up, and offred brent sacrificis, and his sacri- 13 fice; and he offrede sacrificis of licours, and held the blode of pesyble thingis, 'the whiche[y] he[x] hadde offred vpon the 14 auter. Forsothe the brasen auter, that was beforn the Lord, he bare ouer fro the face of the temple, and fro the place of the auter, and fro the place of the temple of the Lord; and putte it on syde 15 of the auter at the north. King forsothe Achaz comaundide to Vrie, the prest, seyinge, Vpon the more auter offre the morowtyde brent sacrifice, and the euentyde sacrifice, and the brent sacrifice of the kyng, and his sacrifice, and the brent sacrificis of al the puple of the lond, and the sacrificis of hem, and the sacrificis of the licours of hem; and al the blode of the brent sacrifice, and al the blode of the slayn sacrifyce, vpon it thou schalt heelden; forsothe the brasen auter schal be maad redye at my wylle. 16 Than Vrias, the prest, dyde aftir alle thingis that kyng Achaz hadde comaund- 17 yde to hym. Forsothe kyng Achaz toke

ide it, and translatide the dwelleris therof to Sirenen; sotheli he killide Rasyn. And 10 kyng Achaz ȝede in to metyng[o] to Teglat Phalasaar, kyng of Assiriens[p]; and whanne kyng Achaz hadde seyn the auter of Damask, he sent[q] to Vrie, the preest, the saumpler and licnesse therof, bi al the werk[r] therof. And Vrie, the preest, bild- 11 ide an auter bi alle thingis whiche[s] king Achaz hadde comaundid fro Damask, so dide the preest Vrie, til kyng Achaz cam fro Damask. And whanne the king cam 12 fro Damask, he siȝ the auter[t], and worschipide it; and he stiede[u], and offride brent sacrifices, and his sacrifice; and he 13 offride moist sacrifices, and he schedde[v] the blood of pesible thingis, which[w] he hadde offrid on the auter. Forsothe he[x] 14 dide awei the brasun auter[y], that was bifor the Lord, fro the face of the temple, and fro the place[z] of the auter, and fro[a] the place of the temple of the Lord; and[b] settide[c] it[d] on[e] the side[f] of the[g] auter 'at the north[h]. Also kyng Achaz comaundide to 15 Vrie, the preest, and seide, Offre thou on[i] the more auter† thei[j] brent sacrifice of the morewtid, and the sacrifice[k] of euentid[l], and the brent sacrifice of the king, and the sacrifice of hym, and the brent sacrifice of al the puple of the lond, and the sacrifices of hem, and the moist sacrifices of hem; and thou schalt schede[m] out on[n] that[o] al the blood of brent sacrifice, and al the blood of slayn sacrifice; sotheli the brasun auter schal be redi at my wille. Therfor Vrie, the preest, dide bi alle 16 thingis whiche[p] kyng Achaz hadde comaundid to hym. Forsothe kyng Achaz 17 took the peyntid foundementis[q], and the waischyng vessel, that was[r] aboue, and he puttide[s] doun the see, that is, the waischung vessel 'for preestis[t], fro the brasun oxis[u], that[v] susteyneden it, and he settide[w]

† the more auter; that is, on the newe auter, which he arettide more in hoolynesse, thouȝ it was cursid. Lire here. c.

° the metyng i.   P Assiriens in to Damask i.   q sent into Jerusalem i.   r werkis A.   s that i.   t auter fair and curious i.   u stlede up i.   v helde i.   w the which i.   x Achaz i.   y auter that Moises made i.   z propre place i.   a Om. A.   b and he i.   c sette i.   d Goddis auter i.   e at i.   f north side i.   g his i.   h Om. i.   i upon i.   j Om. GINQWXb.   k sacrifyses s. brent sacrifice X.   l the euentid CEINVç.   m helde i.   n upon i.   o that newe auter i.   P that i.   q foundementis of pileris i.   r was sett i.   s putte i.   t Om. i.   u oxen i.   v the whiche i.   w sette i.

v into FH.   w Cyrenen CZ.   x exsaumple A.   y that C.   z Om. ABFH.

grauen feete, and the watir[a] vessel, that
was there aboue, and the se he putte
doun of the brasen oxen, that susteyneden it, and he putte vpon the pament
18 greithid with stoon Forsothe the place
where the kingis offrynge was leyd of
the saboth, that he hadde bylde in the
temple, and the commynge in of the
kyng withouten forth, he turnede in to
the temple of the Lord for the kyng of
19 Assiries The remnaunt forsothe of the
wordis of Achaz, and alle thingis that
he dyde, whether not thes ben writen in
the boke of the wordis of the days of the
20 kyngis of Juda? And Achaz slepte with
his fadirs, and is biried with hem in the
cytee of Dauid, and Ezechias, his sone,
regned for hym

on[x] the pawment araied with stoon Also 18
he[y] turnede the tresorie[z] of sabat[a], which[b]
he hadde[c] bildid in the temple, and '*he*
turnede[d] the entiyng of the kyng with
outforth, in to the temple of the Lord for
the[e] kyng† of Assiriens[f] Forsothe[g] the re- 19
sidue of wordis[h] of Achaz, and alle thingis
whiche[i] he dide, whether these ben not
writun in the book of wordis of daies of
the kyngis of Juda? And Achaz slepte 20
with hise fadris, and was biried with hem
in the citee of Dauid, and Ezechie, his
sone, regnede for hym.

† *the king*, that the king of Assiriens if he cam thidir schulde se, hou he hadde do awey the worschiping of God, and that Achaz passide to the worschiping ether religioun of the king of Assiriens *Lire here* c

CAP. XVII

1 The twelfthe ʒeer of Achaz, kyng of
Juda, regnede Osee, the sone of Hela, in
2 Samarie vpon Yrael nyne ʒeer. And he
dyde euyl before the Lord, bot not as the
kyngis of Yrael, that weren beforn hym
3 Aʒeynus this steyʒide up Salmanaser, kyng
of Assiries, and Osee is maad to hym
seruaunt, and ʒeeldide to hym tributis.
4 And whanne the kyng of Assiries hadde
perceyued, that Osee enforcede to rebellen, and that he hadde sente messagers to Sua, kyng of Egipt, lest he
schulde ʒeuen tributis to the kyng of
Assiries, as eche ʒeer he was wont, he
bysegyde hym, and bounden he putte in
5 to prysoun And he wente thoruʒ out
al the lond, and steyʒynge to Samarie he
6 bysegide it thre ʒeer The nynethe ʒeer
forsoth of Osee, the kyng of Assiries
toke Samarie, and translatyde Ysrael into
Assiries, and he sett hem in Hela, and
in Thabor, besyde the flode of Gozam,
7 in the cytees of Medis It is done for-

CAP XVII

Yn the twelthe ʒeer‡ of Achaz, kyng 1
of Juda, Osee, sone[k] of Hela, regnyde in
Samarie on[l] Israel nyne ʒeer And he dide 2
yuel bifor the Lord, but not as the[m] kyngis
of Israel, that weren bifor hym Salma- 3
nasar, kyng of Assiriens, stiede[n] aʒens this[o]
Osee, and Osee was maad seruaunt to
hym, and ʒildide tributis to hym And 4
whanne the kyng of Assiriens hadde per-
seyued, that Osee he[p] enforside[q] to be[r] rebelle, and hadde sent messangeris to Sua,
kyng of Egipt, that he schulde not ʒyue
tributis to the kyng of Assiriens, as he
was wont bi alle ʒeeris, '*the kyng of*
Assiriens[s] bisegide hym[t], and sente *him*[u]
boundun in to prisoun. And he[v] ʒede 5
thoruʒ al the lond, and he stiede[w] to Samarie, and bisegide it bi[x] thre ʒeer. For- 6
sothe in the nynthe ʒeer of Osee, the kyng
of Assiriens took Samarie, and translatide
Israel in to Assiriens; and he puttide[y]
hem[z] in Hela, and in Thabor, bisidis the
flood Gozam, in the citee[a] of Medeis For- 7

‡ *In the xii ʒeer* Osee bigan to regne in the fourthe ʒeer of Achaz, but he hadde not the rewme in pees, til to the xii ʒeer of Achaz, therfor it is seid that he regnede in the xii ʒeer of Achaz, that is, in pees, ether in viii ʒeer he seruede vndir tribute to the king of Assiriens, and in the laste ʒeer that was the twelfthe ʒeer of Achaz he bigan to regne fre fro tribute *Lire here* c

[a] licour F *pr m*

[x] *tho* on I [y] Achaz I [z] kyngis tresorie I [a] the sabat I [b] that I [c] Om I [d] Om I.
[e] Om A *sec m* [f] Assirie I [g] Certis I [h] the wordis I [i] that I [k] the sone I [l] upon I [m] Om I.
[n] wente up I [o] Om IS [p] Om CGIKMNOSWç hed L [q] enforside *him self* I [r] Om. W. [s] he I.
[t] *king Ozee* I [u] Om *plures* [v] *Salmanaser* I [w] stiede up I [x] Om. I [y] putte I [z] Om EL.
[a] citees IS

sothe, whanne the sonys of Yrael hadden
synned beforn the Lord their God, that
ladde hem out fro[b] the lond of Egipt,
fro the hond of Pharao, kyng of Egipte,
8 thei heryeden alyen goddis; and wenten
aftir the custom of heithene, whom the
Lord hadde waastyde in the siȝt of the
sonys of Yrael, and of the kyngis of
Yrael, for lijk maner thei hadden done.
9 And the sonys of Yrael offendiden with
wordis not riȝt the Lord their God, and
thei bildiden to hem heeȝe thingis in alle
their cytees, fro the toure of kepers vnto
10 the strengthid cytee. And thei maden
to hem ymagis, and mawmett wodis, in
all heeȝe hill, and vndir al braunchy[c]
11 tree; and they brenden there encense
vpon the auters in maner of heithen,
whom the Lord hade translatide fro the
face of hem. And thei diden the warst
12 wordis, terryng the Lord; and they
heryeden the vnclennesse[d], of the whiche
the Lord comaundide to hem, that thei
13 schulden not done that worde. And the
Lord witnesside in Yrael and in Juda,
by the hond of alle prophetis, and the
seeȝers, seyinge, Turnith aȝeyn[e] fro ȝoure
warst weyes, and kepith myn hestis, and
my cerymonyes, aftir al the lawe 'the
whiche[f] I haue comaundide to ȝoure fadirs, and as I sente to ȝou in the hond
14 of my seruauntis prophetis. The whiche
herden not, bot hardeneden their noll aftir the noll of their fadirs, that wolden
not obeyschen to the Lord their God.
15 And thei kasten aweye the lawful thingis
of hym, and the couenaunt that he couenauntyde with the fadirs of hem, and the
witnessingis by the whiche he wytness-
ede hem[g]; and thei foloweden vanytes,
and vaynly thei diden; and thei foloweden heithen folc, that weren by the
enuyroun of hem; vpon the whiche the
Lord had comaundyde to hem, that thei

sothe it was don, whanne the sones of Israel hadden synned bifor her[b] Lord God,
that ledde hem out of the lond of Egipt,
fro the hond of Farao, kyng of Egipt,
thei worschipeden alien goddis; and ȝeden[c] 8
bi the custom of hethene men, whiche the
Lord hadde wastid in the siȝt of the sones
of Israel, and of the kyngis of Israel, for
thei hadden do in lijk maner. And the 9
sones of Israel offendiden her Lord God
bi wordis not riȝtful, and thei bildiden to
hem silf hiȝ thingis in alle her citees, fro[d]
the tour† of keperis 'til to[e] a strengthid
citee. And thei maden to hem ymagis, 10
and wodis[f], in ech hiȝ hil, and vndur ech
tree ful of bowis; and thei[g] brenten there 11
encence on[h] the auteris bi the custom of
hethene men, whiche the Lord hadde
translatid fro the face of hem. And thei
diden[i] werste[j] wordis‡, and thei wraththiden the Lord; and worschipiden vn- 12
clenesses, of whiche the Lord comaundide
to hem, that thei schulden not do this
word. And the Lord witnesside in Israel 13
and in[k] Juda, bi the hond of alle prophetis
and seeris, and seide, Turne ȝe aȝen fro
ȝoure werste[l] weies, and kepe ȝe[m] myn[n]
comaundementis, and ceremonyes, bi al the
lawe whiche[o] Y comaundide to ȝoure fadris, and as Y sente to ȝou in the hond of
my seruauntis prophetis. Whiche[p] herden 14
not, but maden hard her nol bi[q] the nol[r]
of her fadris, that nolden[s] obeie to her
Lord God. And thei castiden awei the 15
lawful thingis§ of hym[t], and the couenaunt
which[u] he couenauntide with her fadris,
and the witnessyngis bi whiche he witnesside to hem; and thei sueden vanytees,
'*that is, idols*[v], and diden veynli; and
sueden hethene men, that weren 'bi the
cumpas of[w] hem; of whiche *vanytees*[x]
the Lord comaundide to hem, that thei
schulden not do as[y] also tho[z] *hethene men*[a]
diden. And thei[b] forsoken alle the co- 16

† *fro the tour*; that is, fro a forselet, in which fewe men dwelliden; this is the sentence, fro the leeste town til to the moste, idolatrie hadde strengthe in alle. *Lire here.* c.

‡ that is, worste werkis. *Lire here.* c.

§ *the lawful thingis*; that is, cerymonyes; *the couenaunt*; that is, moral hestis; *witnessingis*; that is, iudicial comaundementis, ether peynes manassid in the lawe to trespasseris. *Lire here.* c.

[b] of A. [c] braunchid H. [d] vnclennessis ABCFH. [e] awey A. [f] that C. [g] to hem E *pr. m.*

[b] the I. [c] wenten forth I. [d] for AS. [e] vnto I. [f] mawmett wodis I. [g] the sones *of Israel* I. [h] upon I. [i] diden *or spaken* I. [j] ful wicked I. [k] Om. A. [l] ful yuel I. [m] Om. S. [n] Om. I. [o] that I. [p] The whiche I. [q] aftir I. [r] *hard* nol I. [s] wolden not I. [t] the Lord I. [u] that I. [v] Om. I. [w] about I. [x] *thingis* I. [y] Om. EIL. [z] Om. ELP. thilke I. [a] *folk* I. [b] the sones *of Israel* I.

schulden not done as and[h] thei dyden
16 And thei forsoken alle the hestis of the
Lord then God, and thei maaden to hem
two ʒoten calues, and maw mette wodis¹,
and thei honoureden alle the knyʒthode
17 of heuen ; and thei serueden to Baal, and
thei sacreden to it their sonys and their
douʒtris thoruʒ fyer, and to dyuynynge
thei inwardly serueden, and to dyuynynge in chiterynge of briddis ; and thei
bitauʒten hem seluen that thei done euyl
byforn the Lord, and thei terreden hym
18 And the Lord is wrothe hydously to
Yrael, and he toke hem aweye fro his
siʒt, and ther laft not bot the lynage of
19 Juda aloon Bot and not he, Juda, kepte
the hestis of the Lord his God, neuer the
later he errid, and went in the errours
of Yrael, the ˙whiche he hadde wrouʒt
20 And the Lord threwe aweye al the seed
of Yrael, and tourmentyde hem, and he
toke hem in the hond of distriers[k]; to the
tyme that he cast hem aweye fro his
21 face, fro that nowe tyme fro the whiche
Yrael was kutt of fro the hous of Dauid,
and thei ordeyneden to hem a kyng, Jeroboam, the sone of Nabath Forsothe
Jeroboam seuerede Yrael fro the Lord,
and made hem to synnen a grete synne
22 And the sonys of Yrael wenten in alle
the[l] synnes of Jeroboam, ˋthe whiche[m] he
hadde done, and thei wenten not aweye
23 fro hem, for to the Lord dyde Yrael
awey fro his face, as he hadde spoken in
the hond of alle his seruauntis prophetis,
and Yrael is translatyd fro his lond in to
24 Assiries vnto this day Forsothe the
kyng of Assiries brouʒt the puple fro
Babiloyne, and fro Cutha, and fro Hay-
lath, and fro Emath, and fro Sepharuaym,
and he sette hem in the cytees of Samarye for the sonys of Yrael ; the whiche
weeldiden Samarie, and dwelliden in the
25 cytees of it And whanne there thei had-

maundementis of her Lord God, and thei
maden to hem twei ʒotun calues, and
wodis[c], and worschipiden[d] al the knyʒthod of heuene[e]†, and thei seruyden Baal,
and halewiden to hym her sones, and hei 17
douʒtris thoruʒ[f] fier, and thei seruyden to
fals dyuynyng[g], and to dyuynyng bi chiterynge of briddis, and thei ʒauen hem‡
silf to do yuel bifor the Lord, and thei
wraththiden hym And the Lord was 18
wrooth greeth to Israel ; and he took
awei hem fro his siʒt, and noon[h] lefte, no
but the lynage of Juda oneli But nethei 19
Juda hym silf kepte the heestis of ˈhis
Lord God[i], netheles[k] he erride, and ʒede
in the erroui of Israel, whiche[l] it wrouʒte
And the Lord castide awei al the seed of 20
Israel, and turmentide hem, and bitook
hem in the hond of rauynouris ; til he
castide[m] awei hem fro his face, fro that 21
tyme§ in which Israel was departid fio
the hous of Dauid, and maden to hem a
kyng, Jeroboam, sone[n] of Nabath For Jeroboam departide Israel fro the Lord, and
made hem to do a[o] greet synne. And the 22
sones of Israel ʒeden in alle.the synnes of
Jeroboam, whiche[p] he hadde do, and thei
departiden not fro tho *synnes*, til the 23
Lord dide awei Israel fro his face, as he
spak in the hond of alle hise seruauntis
prophetis, and Israel was translatid[q] fio
his lond in to Assiriens til in to this dai
Forsothe the kyng of Assiriens brouʒte 24
puple[r] fro Babiloyne, and fro Cutha, and
fro Hailath, and fro Emath, and fro Sepharuaym, and settide[s] hem in the citees[t]
of Samarie for the sones of Israel, whiche[u]
hadden in possessioun Samarie, and dwelliden[v] in the citees therof And whanne 25
thei bigunnen to dwelle there, thei dredden not the Lord ; and the Lord sente to
hem louns, that[w] killiden hem And it 26
was told to the kyng of Assiriens, and
was seid, The folkis[x] whiche[y] thou trans-

† *the knyʒhode
of heuene, that
is, sunne and
moone, and
othre planetis
Lire here* c

‡ *thei ʒauen
hem in as
sentence to the
wille of the
deuel in alle
thingis Lire
here* c

§ *fro that
tyme, for fro
that tyme Is-
rael bowede
awey, fro the
veri religioun
of God bi
vnlike Jero
boam Lire
here* c

h Om *ABFH*   ¹ templis *E pr m*   k the destriers *ADFH*   l Om *A*   m that c *pr m*

c mawmett wodis 1   d thei worschipiden 1   e heuene *or of the firmament* 1   f bi 1   g dyuynyng *or
witchecraft* 1   h noon *of hem* 1   i the Lord his God 1   k *but* netheles 1   l that 1   m had cast 1   n the
sone 1   o Om 1   p that 1   q brouʒt ouer 1   r the puple 1   s sette *EIL*   t citee 1   u and these 1
v thei dwelliden 1   w the whiche 1   x folk 1   y that 1

den begunne to dwellen, thei dredden not the Lord ; and the Lord sente to hem 26 lyouns, that slewen hem. And it is told to the kyng of Assiries, and seide, The folc that thou hast translatyde, and maad to dwellen in the cytees of Samarye, knowen not the lawful thingis of the God of the lond ; and the Lord sente in to hem lyouns, and loo ! thei schuln slen hem ; for thy that thei knowen not the 27 custum of the God of the lond. The^n kyng forsothe of Assiries comaundyde, seyinge, Bringith hidre oon of the prestis, 'the whiche^o in to caytyfte ȝe han brouȝt, that he goo, and dwelle with hem, and teche hem the lawful thingis of God of 28 the lond. Thanne whanne oon of thes prestis, that weren ladde caytyfe fro Samarie, was commen, he dwellide in Bethel, and tauȝte hem, in what maner wyse thei 29 schulden herie the Lord. And ech folc forgid his god, and putten hem in heeȝe templis, 'the whiche^o Samaritis maden, folc and folc in their cytees, in the whiche 30 thei dwelliden. Forsothe Babyloynes men maden Socoth Benoth ; forsothe Cutheny men maaden Vergel ; and the men of E- 31 math maaden Asma ; bot Euey maaden Nabaath and Tharcha ; thes forsothe that weren of Sepharuaym brenten their sonys with fyre to Adramalech and Ara- 32 malech^p, goddis of Sepharuaym. And ne- uer the latere thei herieden the Lord ; thei maaden forsothe to hem prestis of the most newe thingis of heeȝe thingis, and thei putten hem in heeȝe heithen templis. 33 And whanne thei schulden heryen God, forsothe to their goddis^q thei serueden, aftir the vsage of heithen men, fro the whiche thei were translatyde to Samarye ; 34 vnto the day that is nowe thei folow- eden^r the old maner ; they dredden not the Lord, ne keepen his cerymonyes, and domys, and lawe, and maundement, that

latidist^r, and madist to dwelle in the citees of Samarie, kunnen not the lawful thingis of God of the^r lond ; and the Lord sente^a liouns in to hem, and lo ! *liouns*^{b} sleen hem ; for thei kunnen not the custom of God of the lond. Sotheli the kyng of 27 Assirieus comaundide, and seide, Lede ȝe thidur oon of the preestis, whiche^c ȝe brouȝten^d prisoneris fro thennus, that he go, and dwelle with hem, and teche hem the lawful thingis of God of the lond. Therfor whanne oon of these preestis hade^e 28 come^f, that weren led prisoneris fro Sa- marie, he dwellide in Bethel, and tauȝte hem^g, how thei schulden worschipe the Lord†. And ech folk^h made his god, and 29 thei settiden tho goddis in the^i hiȝ tem- plis, whiche^k the^l men of Samarie hadden maad, folk^m and folk^n in her^o citees, in whiche thei dwelliden^p. For men of Ba- 30 biloyne maden^q Socoth Benoth‡ ; forsothe^r men of Cutha maden Vergel^s ; and men of Emath maden Asyma ; forsothe^t Eueis 31 maden Nabaath and Tharcha^u ; sotheli thei that weren of Sepharuaym brenten her sones in fier to Adramelech and Aname- lech, goddis^r of Sepharuaym. And ne- 32 theles thei worschipiden the Lord ; for- sothe of the laste men§ thei maden preestis of the hiȝe thingis, and settiden hem in hiȝe templis. And whanne thei worschip- 33 iden God, thei serueden also her goddis, bi the custom of hethene men, fro whiche thei weren translatid to Samarie ; 'til in 34 to^w present dai thei suen^x the^y eld cus- tom ; thei dredden not‖ the Lord, nethir thei kepen hise cerymonyes, and domes, and lawe, and comaundement, which^z the Lord comaundide to the sones of Jacob, whom he nemyde^a Israel ; and he^b smoot 35 a couenaunt with hem, and comaundide to hem, and seide, Nyle ȝe drede alien goddis, and onoure ȝe not outwardli hem, nethir worschipe ȝe inwardli hem, and

† *worschipe the Lord* ; not perfitly, for he was of the prestis of Sa- marie, and not of Jerusalem. *Lire here.* c.

‡ *Sochot Benoth*; that signefieth in Ebreu the tabernacle of sones. *Lire here.* c.

§ *the laste men*; that is, of vile per- sones, that weren not of prestis kyn, bi the lawe of Moyses. *Lire here.* c.

‖ *dredden not*; that is, per- fitly, as it is comaundid in the lawe. *Lire here.* c.

^{u} And the *ABFH*. ^{o} that c *pr. m.* ^{p} Amalech b. ^{q} goodis b. ^{r} folewen e.

^{y} hast translatid i. ^{z} that s. ^{a} hath sent i. ^{b} thoo i. ^{c} that i. ^{d} ladden el. ^{e} hadden a. ^{f} come *thidere* i. ^{g} men i. ^{h} *of tho v.* folk i. ^{l} Om. bl. ^{k} that i. ^{l} Om. is. ^{m} that folk *his god* i. ^{n} that folk *his* i. ^{o} the i. ^{p} dwelten i. ^{q} maden *her god* i. ^{r} and i. ^{s} Vergel *her god* i. ^{t} and i. ^{u} Tharcha *here goddis* i. ^{v} the goddis i. ^{w} til to this i. ^{x} sueden i. ^{y} Om. i. ^{z} the whiche t. ^{a} clepide l. ^{b} the Lord i.

the Lord hadde comaundide to the sonys
35 of Jacob, whome he clepide Yrael , and
hadde smyten with hem couenaunt, and
hadde comaundide to hem, seyinge, Wylle
ȝe not dreeden alyen goddis and honourith not hem, ne herieth hem, and offre
36 ȝe not to hem , bot the Lord ȝoure God,
that ladde ȝou out fro the lond of Egipt
in grete strengthe, and in aarme strauȝte
out, hym dreedith, and hym[a] honourith,
37 and to him ofirith   The ceirymonyes forsothe, and the domys, and the lawe, and
the maundement that he wioote to ȝou,
keepith, that ȝe done alle days , and dreed
38 ȝe not alyen goddis.   And the couenaunt
that he smoote with ȝou, wilhth not for-
39 ȝeten, ne herie ȝee alyen goddis; bot the
Lord ȝoure God dreedith, and he schal
delyuere ȝou fro the hond of alle ȝoure
40 enmyes   Thei forsothe herden not, bot
aftir their vsage beforn hadde thei diden
41 euyl   Thanne thes gentylis forsothe
weren dreedynge God , bot neuer the
later and[t] to their mawmettis seiuynge,
for and the sonys of hem and the sonys
sonys so done, as dyden thei fadirs, vnto
the present day.

make ȝe not sacrifice to hem ; but ȝoure 36
Lord God, that ledde ȝou out of the lond
of Egipt in greet stiengthe, and in arme
holdun[d] forth[e], drede ȝe hym, and worschipe ȝe hym, and make ȝe saciifice to
hym   Also kepe ȝe the cerymonyes, and 37
domes, and the lawe, and comaundement[f],
whichȝ[g] he wroot to ȝou, that ȝe do[h] in alle
daies , and drede ȝe not alien goddis   And 38
nyle ȝe foiȝete the couenaunt, which[i] he[k]
smoot with ȝou, nether worschipe ȝe alien
goddis , but drede ȝe ȝoure Lord God, and 39
he schal delyuere ȝou fro the hond of alle
ȝoure enemyes   Forsothe thei heiden not[l], 40
but diden bi her formere custom[m]   Thei-41
for[n] these hethene men diedden sotheli[o]
God ; but netheles thei serueden also her
idols, for bothe her sones and the sones of
sones[p] doen so, til in to present[q] dai, as
her fadris diden

CAP XVIII.

1   The thrid ȝeer of Osce, the sone of
Hela, kyng of Yrael, regned Ezechias,
2 the sone of Achaz, kyng of Juda   Of
fyue and twenty ȝeer he was, whanne he
beganne to regnen, and twenty and nyne
ȝeer he regnede in Jeiusalem , name of
his modir, Abisa, douȝtir of Zacharie
3 And he dyde that[u], that was good beforn
the Lord, aftir alle thingis that Dauith,
4 his fadir, hadde done   And he scatered
the heeȝe thingis, and to-brusede the
ymagis, and hewȝ doun the mawmett
wodis, and he to-braste the brasen ad-
dcie, that Moyses hadde maad ; forsothe
vnto that tyme the sonys of Yrael

CAP XVIII.

In the thridde ȝeer of Osee, sone[r] of 1
Hela, kyng of Isiael, regnyde Ezechie,
sone of Achaz, kyng of Juda.   He was of 2
fyue and twenti ȝeei, whanne he bigan to
regne, and he regnyde in Jerusalem nyne
and twenti ȝeer , the name of his modir
was Abisa, douȝtei[w] of Zacharie.   And 3
he[x] dide that, that was good bifor the
Lord, bi alle thingis, which[y] Dauid, his
fadii, hadde do   And he distiiede hiȝe 4
places[z], and al to-brak ymagis, and kittide[a] doun wodis, and he brak the brasin
serpent, whom Moyses hadde maad , for
'til to[b] that tyme the sones of Israel
brenten encense to it , and he[c] clepide the

---

[a] to hym *A*   [t] Om *E pr m in B*   [u] Om *BFH*

[c] an arm 1   [d] streȝit 1   [e] out 1   [f] the comaundment 1   [g] that 1   [h] do *sl* 1   [i] that 1   [k] the Lord 1
[l] not the Lord 1   [m] customes *FLP*   [n] Therfor sothly 1   [o] Om. 1   [p] her sones 1   [q] this presint 1
[r] the sone 1   [w] the douȝter 1   [x] Ezechie 1   [y] that 1   [z] places of mawmetrie 1   [a] kitte 1   [b] vnto 1
[c] Ezechie 1

brenden to it encense; and he clepide
5 the name of it Noestam. And in the
Lord God of Yrael he hoopide; also aftir
hym was not lijk to hym of alle the
kyngis of Juda, bot nouther in hem that
6 weren beforn hym. And he cleeuede to
the Lord, and he wente not aweye fro
the steppis of hym, and he dyde his
heestis, the whiche the Lord hadde co-
7 maundide to Moyses; wherfore and the
Lord was with hym, and in alle thingis
to the whiche he went forth, wysely he
had hym silf. Forsothe he rebellide
a3eynus the king of Assiries, and therfore
8 he serued not to hym; and he smoote
the Philisteis vnto Gasam, and alle the
ternys of hem, fro the toure of keepers
9 vnto the strengthid cytee. The ferth
3eer of kyng Ezechie, the whiche was
the seuenthe 3eer of Osee, the sone of
Hela, kyng of Yrael, Salmanazer, kyng
of Assirie, stey3ide vp to Samarie, and
10 ouercame it, and toke[v]. For aftir three
3eer, the sext 3eer of Ezechie, that is
nynthe 3eer of Osee, kyng of Yrael,
11 taken is Samarie; and the kyng of Assiries translatyde Yrael in to Assiries,
and sette hem in Haila, and in Habor,
flodis of Gosam, in the cytees of Medis;
12 for thei herden not the voice of the Lord
their God, bot wenten besyde the couenaunt
of hym; alle thingis that Moyses, the
sernaunt of the Lord, hadde comaundide,
13 thei herden not, ne dyden. The fourtenthe
3eer of kyng Ezekie, stey3ide vp Senacherub, kyng of Assiries, to alle the
strengthid cytees of Juda, and toke hem.
14 Than Ezechias, kyng of Juda, sente messagers to the kyng of Assiries in Lachis,
seyinge, I haue synned; go aweye fro
me, and al that thou puttist on to me,
I schale beren. And so the kyng of
Assiries comaundide to Ezechie, kyng
of Juda, thre[w] hundreth talentis of syl-

name therof[d] Noestam[e]†. And he[f] hopide
in the Lord God of Israel; therfor aftir
hym[g] noon was lijk hym‡ of alle the
kyngis of Juda, but 'and nether[h] in tho[i]
kyngis that weren bifor hym. And he
cleuyde to the Lord, and 3ede not awei
fro hise steppis, and he dide the comaundementis of the Lord, whiche the Lord comaundide to Moises; wherfor and the
Lord was with hym, and he gouernede
wiseli hym silf in alle thingis, to whiche[k]
he 3ede forth. Also he[l] rebellide§ a3ens the
kyng of Assiriens, and therfor he serucde
not to 'that *kyng of Asseriens*[m]; and he[n]
smoot Philisteis[o] 'til to[p] Gazam, and alle
the termes of hem, fro the tour of keperis[q]
'til to[r] a citee maad strong. In the fourthe
3eer of kyng Ezechie, that was the seuenthe 3eer of Osee, sone[s] of Hela, kyng
of Israel, Salmanazar, kyng of Assiriens,
stiede[t] to Samarie, and fau3t a3ens it, and
took it[u]. For after thre 3eer, in the sixte
3eer of Ezechie, that is, in the nynthe
3eer of Osee, kyng of Israel, Samarie was
takun; and the kyng of Assiriens translatide Israel in to Assiriens, and settyde[v]
hem in Haila, and in Habor, ryueris of
Gozam, in the citees[w] of Medeis; for thei
herden not the vois of her Lord God, but
thei braken his couenaunt; thei herden not,
nether diden alle thingis, whiche Moises,
the seruaunt of the Lord, comaundide. In
the fourtenthe 3eer of kyng Ezechie, Senacherub, kyng[x] of Assiryens, stiede[y] to alle
the strengthide citees of Juda, and took
tho[z]. Thanne Ezechie, kyng of Juda,
sente messangeris to the kyng of Assiriens in to Lachis, and seide, Y haue syn-
ned‖; go awei fro me, and Y schal bere
'al thing[a], which[b] thou schalt putte to me.
Therfor the kyng of Asseriens puttide on[c]
Ezechie, kyng of Juda, thre hundrid talentis[d] of siluer, and thretti talentis of
gold. And Ezechie 3af al the siluer, that

Marginal notes (right):

† *Noestam; that is, copir; ether of copir; as if he seide, no thing of Godhed was in it, as symple men bileuyden, and weren disseyued bi errour, no but copir was there. c.*

‡ *noon was lijk him; not that he was hooliere than Dauyth, that was bifor him, ether than Josie, that was aftir him; as also the chirche singith of ech confessour, noon is found un Ilyk him, and this for sum preroga-tif ether ex-celence, which is not foundun so in othere men, thou3 he falle in many prerogatyues that thei han. So it is seid of Ezechie, noon was lijk him, etc. in parti, for he distriede lije places, and the brasun serpent, in parti; for at the preyeris of him, an aungel smoot the oost of Senacherib, and the sunne 3ede abak bi ten lynes, and these were ful special thingis. Lire here. c.*

§ *he rebellide, etc.; that is, resseyuede not him as lord, as many kingis diden. Lire here. c.*

‖ *Y haue syn-ned; a3enus the Lord, he aret-tide the synne of his fadir, and of the pu-ple, his synne in this. Lire here. c.*

v toke it A.   w foure B pr. m.

d of it I.   e Noestam, *that is, copir* A *et plures.*   f Ezechie I.   g Ezechie I.   h nether also I.
the I.   k the whiche I.   l Ezechie I.   m him I.   n Ezechie I.   o the Philisteis I.   p vnto I.   q the
keperis I.   r vnto I.   s the sone I.   t stiede up I.   u Om. *plures.*   v he sette I.   w citee I.   x the
kyng I.   y stiede up I.   z hem I.   a alle thingis I.   b that I.   c upon I.   d of talentis s.

15 uer, and thritty talentis of gold. And Ezechias 3aue alle the syluer, that was founden in the hous of the Lord, and in 16 the kingis tresouries. In that tyme Ezechias brake the doris of the temple of the Lord, and the platis of gold, the whiche he hadde affitchide, and he 3aue 17 hem to the kyng of Assiries. Forsothe the kyng of Assiries sente Thercam and Rapsacem fro Lachis to kyng Ezechie, with stronge bond to Jerusalem; the whiche whanne hadden stey3ide up, thei camen to Jerusalem, and stoden bysydis the kundyte of watir of the ouer fysch poond, that is in the weye of the fullers 18 feeld. And thei clepide the kyng; forsothe Eliachym, the sone of Elchie, prouost of the hous, wente out to hem, and Sobna, scribe, and Joache, the sone of 19 Azaf, chauncelere. And Rapsaces seide to hem, Spekith to Ezechie, Thes thingis seith the grete kyng, kyng of Assiries, What is this trust, in the whiche thou 20 leuist? Perauenture thou hast goon in counseil, that thou greithe thee to batayl. In what tristist thou, that thou be hardy 21 to rebellen? Whether hopist thou in the reeden staf and broken×, Egipt, vpon whiche 3if a man lene, to-broken it schal goon in to his hond, and thrillen it? So is Pharao, the kyng of Egipt, to alle that 22 trusten in hym. And 3if thou seist to me, In the Lord oure God we han trust; whether not he is, of whome Ezechie toke aweye the hee3e thingis and the auters, and comaundide to Jude and to Jerusalem, Beforn this auter 3e schuln honouren in 23 Jerusalem? Nowe thanne gooth to my lord, king of Assiries, and I schal 3eue to 3ou two thousand of hors, and see3ith, whether 3e mown han stey3ers vpon 24 hem? And what maner wijse mowen 3e with stonden beforn oon prince^y of

was foundun in the hows of the Lord, and in the kyngis tresories^d. In that tyme 16 Ezechie brak the 3atis† of the temple of the Lord, and the platis of gold, whiche^e he hadde^f fastned, and he 3af tho to the kyng of Assiriens. Forsothe the kyng of 17 Assiriens sente Thercha and Rabsaces fro Lachis to kyng Ezechie, with strong hond‡ to Jerusalem; and whanne thei hadden stied^g, thei camen to Jerusalem, and stoden bisidis the water cundijt of the hi3ere cisterne, which^h is in the weie of the^i fullere, `ethir toukere^j`. And thei 18 clepiden the^k kyng^l; sotheli Eliachym, sone^m of Elchie, the souereyn^n of the hows^o, and Sobna, scryueyn^p, and Joahe, chaunseler, the sone of Asaph, 3eden out to hem. And Rabsaces seide to hem, 19 Speke 3e to Ezechie, The grete kyng, the kyng of Assiriens, seith these thingis, What is this trist, in which thou enforsist^q? In hap thou hast take counsel, 20 that thou woldist make thee redi to batel. In whom tristist thou, that thou be hardi to rebelle^r? Whethir thou hopist in a ˈstaf 21 of rehed^s and brokun, Egipt^t, on^u which^v, if a man lenith, it schal be brokun, and schal^w entre in to hys hond, and schal peerse it? So is Farao, kyng of Egipt, to alle men that tristen on^x hym. That if 22 thou seist to me, We han trist in ˈoure Lord God^y; whether this is not he, whos hi3e thingis^yy and auteris^z Ezechie took awei, and comaundide to Juda and to Jerusalem, 3e^a schulen worschipe bifor this auter in Jerusalem? Now therfor passe 3e^b§ to my 23 lord, the kyng of Assiriens, and Y schal 3yue to^c 3ou twei thousynde^cc of horsis, and se 3e, whether 3e moun haue rideris of ˈtho horsis^d? And hou moun 3e with-24 stonde bifor o prince of the leste seruauntis of my lord? Whether thou hast trist in Egipt, for charis and kny3tis^e?

† Ezechie brak the 3atis; Ezechie wiste, the puple suget to him, and Achaz, his fadir, hadden offendid God in many maneris, and therfor he dredde skilefuly, lest for veniaunce of the forseid 3uels the king of Assiriens schulde be suffrid to come on his rewme; and therfor to kepe the citee of Jerusalem, where Goddis worschip was, in strengthe, and the puple as myche as he my3te fro distriyng, he spendide the riches of the temple and of the king, as the text here seith. Brak the 3atis of the temple; in whiche myche gold was fastned bi kingis biforgoinge and bi him, to fairnesse in worschip; and bi nede he was compellid to do this, for he hadde noon other thing, wherof he my3te paie so greet a summe. Of this is had an argument ether preef, that princes in nede moun take of the tresours of the chirche, for the sauyng of the comyn puple. Lire here. c. Ambrose and Decrees in XII. cause, ii. question, c°. aurum, and Gregorie in his Registre, in VII. book, xiii. c°. and xxxiij. c°. and ix. book, xvi. c°.

× the broken E pr. m.   y satrape E pr. m.

d tresours EKLMX. tresories to the kyng of Assiriens I.   e that I.   f Om. I.   g gon up I.   h that I.
i Om. L.   j or of toukere ELP.   k Om. I.   l kyng Ezechie I.   m the sone I.   n souereyn or bischop I.
o hows of the Lord I.   P the scryueyn I.   q enforsist thee I.   r rebelle a3ens Senacherib I.   s reedy staf I.
t O! Egypt I.   u upon I.   v the which staff I.   w the splyndre or speel therof schal I.   x in I.   y the Lord
oure God I.   yy ymagis s.   z auteris of offence I.   a seiyinge, 3e I.   b 3e forth I.   c Om. I.   cc thousendis s.   d hem I.   e kny3tis therof I.

the lest seruauntis of my lord? Whether hast thou trust in Egipt, for the chaaris 25 and hors men? Whether with oute the wille of God I haue stey₃ide up to this place, that I distruye it? The Lord seide to me, Stey₃e ₃eˣ up to this lond, and dis- 26 truye it. Forsothe Eliachym, the sone of Elchie, and Sobna, and Joache, seyden to Rapsace, We preyen, that thou speke to us, thi seruauntis, Ciriely; forsothe we vndirstonden that tong; and speke thou not to us Jewly, heerynge the puple, that 27 is vpon the walle. And Rapsaces an- swerde to hym, seyinge, Whether to thi lord and to thee sente me my lord, that I schulde speken thes wordis, and not more to the men that sytten vpon the wall, that thei eten their dritt, and 28 drynken their vryne with ₃ou? And so Rapsaces stode, and cryede out with a grete voyce Jewly, and seith, Heerith the wordis of the grete kyng, kyng of As- 29 siries. Thes thingis seith the kyng, 'Disceyue not ₃ouᵃ Ezechie; forsothe he schal not mowen delyuer ₃ou fro myn 30 hond; ne ₃yue he trust to ₃ou vpon the Lord, seying, Delyuerynge schal dely- ueren us the Lord, and this cyte schal not be taken in the hond of the kyng of 31 Assiries; wille ₃e not heeren Ezechias. Thes thingis forsothe seith the kyng of Assiries, Dooth with me that to ₃ou is profytable, and comith out to me; and ete ech oon of his vijne, and of his fijge tree, and ₃e schuln drynke watirs of ₃oure 32 cisternys, to the tyme that I come, and translate ₃ou in to the lond that is lijc to ₃our lond, in to the lond berynge fruyt, and plenteuows of wijne, the lond of brede, and of vynys, the lond of olyues, 'and of oyleᵇ, and of hony; and ₃e schulen lyuen, and not dy₃en. Wylle ₃e not heeren Ezechie, that ₃ou disceyueth, seyinge, 33 The Lord schal delyueren us. Whether delyuerden the goddis of Gentylis their

Whether Y stiedeᶠ with outen 'Goddis 25 willeᵍ to this place, that Y schulde dis- trie it? 'The Lordʰ seide to me, 'Stie thouⁱ to this lond, and distrie thou it. Forsothe 26 Eliachym, soneᵏ of Elchie, and Sobna, and Joahe, seiden to Rabsaces, We preienˡ, that thou speke bi the langage of Sirie to vs, thi seruauntis; for we vndirstondun this langage; and thatᵐ thou speke not* to vs bi the langage of Juwis, while the puple herith, which is onⁿ the wal. And Rab- 27 saces answeride, 'and seideᵒ, Whethir my lord sente me to thi lord and to thee, that Y schulde speke these wordis, and not rather to the men 'that sittenᵖ onᑫ the wal, that thei ete her toordis, and drynke her pisse with ₃ou? Therfor Rabsaces 28 stood, and criede with greet vois bi lan- gage of Jewis, and seide, Here ₃e the wordis of the greet kyng, the kyng of Assiriens. The kyng seith these thingis, 29 Ezechie disceyue not ₃ou, for he may not delyuere ₃ou fro myn hond; netherᵣ ₃yue 30 heᵣ trist to ₃ou onˢ the Lordᵗ, and seie, The Lord delyuerynge schal delyuere vs, and this citee shal not be bitakunⁿ in the hond of the kyng of Assiriens; nyle ₃e 31 here Ezechie. For the kyng of Assiriens seith these thingis, Do ₃e with me that, that is profitable to ₃ou, and go ₃e out to me; and eche man schal ete of his vyner, and of his fige tree, and ₃e schulen drynke watris of ₃oure cisternes, tilᵛ Y come, and 32 translateʷ ₃ouˣ in to a lond whichʸ is lijk ₃oure lond, in to a fruytful lond, and plen- teuouseᶻ of wyn, a lond of breed, and of vineris, a lond of olyue trees, and ofᵃ oile, and of hony; and ₃e schulen lyue, and ₃e schulen not die. Nyle ₃e here Ezechie, that disseyueth ₃ou, and seith, The Lord schal delyuere ₃ow. Whether the goddis 33 of hethene men delyueriden her lond fro the hond of the kyng of Assiriens? Where 34 is god of Emath, and of Arphat? Where is god of Sapharuaym, of Ana, and of

(marginal notes, right column)

²⁵ witnessen this pleynly. And king Richard dide this in dede, as Sis- trense seith, in vii. book, xxviii. cᵒ. c. ‡ with strong hond; for whanne he hadde maad couenaunt, and take gold, to suffre the rewme of Eze- chie in pees, he brak the
²⁷ couenaunt vnfeithfuly, and sente oost to take Jeru- salem, and lede the puple in to Assi- riens. Lire here. c.
§ passe ₃e; in Ebreu it is, ₃yue ₃o weddie, that is, for ij. thousynde of torsis. Lire here. c.
* and that thou speke not; lest
²⁹ the peple were aferd of the wordis of Rab-
³⁰ saces, and for he mediide wordis of blas- fomye in his wordis. Of this place both Ebreys and Cristen doc- tours seyen, that this Rab- saces was a Jew of birthe, but he forsook the lawe, and was pervertid to hethennesse. Lire here. c.

ᶻ Om. CEH.　ᵃ Lede not ₃ou doun E pr. m.　ᵇ Om. A.

ᶠ stiede up I.　ᵍ the wille of my lord I.　ʰ My lord I.　ⁱ Wende thou up I.　ᵏ the sone I.　ˡ preien thee I. ᵐ Om. IS.　ⁿ upon I.　ᵘ seiynge I.　ᵖ sittinge I.　ᑫ upon I.　ᵣ ₃e I.　ˢ upon I.　ᵗ Lord God I. ᵘ takun CEIK pr. m. L.　ᵛ til that I.　ʷ bere I.　ˣ ₃ou ouer I.　ʸ that I.　ᶻ a plenteuouse I.　ᵃ Om. I.

lond fro the hond of the kyng of Assi-
34 ries? Where is the god of Emath, and
Arfath? Where is the god of Sapharuaym, Ana, and Aua[a]? Whether thei de-
35 lyuerden Samarie fro myn hond? Who
forsothe ben thes in alle the goddis of
londis, 'the whiche[b] delyuerden their regyoun fro my hond, that the Lord may
36 delyueren Jerusalem fro myn hond? And
so the puple was styll, and answerde not
to hym eny thinge; forsothe maundement of the kyng thei hadde taken, that
37 thei schulden not answeren to hym[c]. And
Eliachym, the sone of Elchie, the prouost of the hous, came, and Sobna, scribe,
and Joache, the sone of Azaf, chauncelere, to Ezechie, the clothis kutt, and
thei tolden to hym the wordis of Rapsaces.

CAP. XIX

1 The whiche thingis whanne kyng Ezechie hadde herde, he cutte his clothis, and
is couerde with a sac, and he wente in to
2 the hous of the Lord And he sente Eliachym, the prouost of the hous, and[d] Sobna,
scribe, and the olde men of the prestis,
couerd with sackis, to Ysay, the prophete,
3 the sone of Amos The whiche seyden,
Thes thingis seith Ezechias, Days of tri-
bulacyoun, and of blamynge, and of blasfemye thes days; ther ben commyn sonys
to the birthe, and strengthis hath not the
4 childe berere 3if perauenture heere the
Lord thi God alle the wordis of Rapsaces,
whom sente the kynge of Assiries, his
loid, that he repreue the Lord lyuynge,
and vndernym with wordis, the whiche
herde the Lord thi God; and make orysoun for thes relikis, that ben founden
5 Thanne the seruauntis of kyng Ezechie
6 camen to Ysay; and Ysay seith to hem,
Thes thingis seith to 3oure[e] lord, Thes
thingis seith the[e] Lord, Wille 3e not

Aua? Whether thei delyueriden Samarie
fro myn hond? For[b] who ben thei in alle 35
goddis of londis, that delyueriden her cuntrey fro myn hond, that the Lord may
delyuere Jerusalem fro myn hoond?
Therfor the puple was stille, and answer- 36
ide nott† ony thing to hym, for thei hadden
take comaundement of the kyng, that thei
schulden not answere to hym And Elia- 37
chym, sone[c] of Elchie, the souereyn of the
hows[d], and Sobna, scryuen[e], and Joahe,
chaunceler[f], the sone of Asaph, camen
with to-rent clothis to Ezechie; and telden
to hym the wordis of Rabsaces

*† and answer-
ide not, bi co
maundement
of the king,
lest Rabsaces
were sterid iit
to sue blas
femyes of God,
if he were an-
swerid Lire
here c*

CAP XIX

And whanne kyng Ezechie hadde herd 1
these thingis, he to-rente his clothist,‡ and
was hilid with a sak; and he entride in
to the hous of the Lord. And he sente 2
Eliachym, souereyn of the hous[g], and
Sobna, scryueyn[h], and elde men of the
preestis, hilid with sackis, to Ysaie, the
prophete, sone[i] of Amos Whiche[k] seiden[l], 3
Ezechie seith these thingis, This dai is a
dai of tribulacioun, and of blamyng, and
of blasfemye; sones camen 'til to[m] the
childberyng[n]§, and the 'traueler of childe[o]
hath not strengthis? If perauenture thi 4
Lord God here alle the wordis of Rabsaces, whom the kyng of Assiryens, his
lord sente[pp], that he schulde dispise the
Lord lyuynge, and repreue[q] bi wordis,
whiche[r] thi Lord God herde, and make
thou preier for these relikis[s], that ben
foundun Therfor[t] the seruauntis of kyng 5
Ezechie camen to Isaie; and Isaie seide 6
to hem, See 3e these thingis to 3oure lord,
The Lord seith these thingis, Nyle thou

*‡ to rente his
clothis, for
wordis of blas-
femye seid
ajenus God
Lire here c*

*§ childbering,
that is, we ben
set in so greet
affliccioun as a
womman that
is set in afflic
cioun of child-
bering, where
strengthis to
bere the child
fallen Lire
here c*

---

a Ayra *ABC sec m FII.*   b that *c pr m.*   c hym any thyng *F pr m*   d to *ABFII*   e 3oure *A*

b For whi I   c the sone I   d *Lordus* hows I   e the scryuen I   f the chaunceler I   g *Iordus* hous I
h the scrvueyn I   i the sone I   k The whiche I   l seiden to him I   m vnto I   n birthe I   o modir
trauailinge I   P strengthe *therto* I   PP hath sent I   q repreue *him* I   r that I   s remenauntis *of the*
peple I   t *Heere* therfor I

dreeden fro the face of the wordis that
ȝe han herde, with the whiche the children of the kyng of Assiries han blas-
7 femyden me. Loo! I schal senden in
to hym a spirit, and he schal here a messager, and he schal 'be turned[f] aȝeyn in
to his lond; and I schal throwen hym
8 doun by swerd in his owne lond. Thanne
Rapsaces is turned aȝeyn, and foond the
kyng of Assiries ouercommynge Lob-
nam; forsothe he hade herde, that he
9 was goon aweye fro Lachis. And
whanne he hade herd of kyng Thea-
racha of Ethcope, messager[g] seyinge, Lo!
he is goon out, that he fiȝt aȝeynus thee;
that he goo aȝeynus hym, he sente mes-
10 sagers to Ezechie, seyinge, Thes thingis
seyith to Ezekie, kyng of Juda, Leede
thee not asyde[h] the[i] Lord thi God, in
the whiche thou hast trust, ne sey thou,
Jerusalem schal not be taken in to the
11 hondis of the kyng of Assiries; thou
forsothe thi silf hast herd what thingis
the kyngis of Assiries han done in alle[k]
londis, what maner thei han waastiden
hem; whether than aloon thou schalt
12 mowen ben delyuered? Whether the
goddis of Gentylis delyuerden alle whom
my faders waastyden, Gozam, that is,
and Aran, and Reseph, and the sonys of
13 Eden, that weren in Thelassar? Wher
is the kyng of Emath, and the kyng of
Arfath? and the kyng of the cytee of
14 Cepharuaym, Ana, and Aua? And so
whanne Ezechias hade taken the lettres
fro the hond of the messagers, and hadde
rad hem, he steyȝide up in to the hous
of the Lord, and he spradde hym out
15 beforn the Lord; and preyide in his siȝt,
seyinge, Lord God of Yrael, that syttyst
vpon cherubyn, thou ert aloon God of
alle kyngis of the[l] erth; thou maadist

drede of the face[u]† of wordis[v] whiche[w]
thou herdist, bi whiche the children of the
kyng of Assiriens blasfemeden me. Lo!7
Y schal sende to hym a spirit, and he
schal here a messanger, and he schal turne
aȝen in to his lond; and Y schal caste
hym doun bi swerd in his owne lond.
Therfor[x] Rabsaces turnede aȝen[y], and 8
foond the kyng of Assiriens fiȝtynge aȝens
Lobna; for he[z] hadde herd, that *the kyng*
hadde go awei fro Lachis. And whanne 9
he[a] hadde herd of Theracha[b], kyng of
Ethiope, 'men seyynge[c], Lo! he[d] ȝede[e]
out, that he fiȝte aȝens thee; that he[f]
schulde go aȝens 'that *kyng*[g], he sente
messangeris to Ezechie, and seide, Seie ȝe 10
these thingis to Ezechie, kyng of Juda,
Thi Lord God, in whom thou hast trist,
disseyue not thee, nether seie thou, Jerusalem schal not be 'bitakun[l] in to the
hondis of the kyng of Assiriens; for thou 11
thi silf herdist[k] what thingis the kyngis
of Assiriens diden[l] in alle londis, hou thei
wastiden[m] tho[n]; whether therfor thou
aloone maist be delyuered? Whether the 12
goddis of hethene men[o] delyueriden[p] alle
men[q] whiche my fadris distrieden, that is,
Gozam[r], and Aran[s], and Reseph[t], and the
sones of Eden, that weren in Thelassar?
Where is the kyng of Emath[u], and the 13
kyng of Arphat? and the kyng of the
cytee of Sepharuaym, of Ana, and of
Aua? Therfor whanne Ezechie hadde 14
take the lettris fro the hond of messangeris[w], and hadde red tho[x], he stiede[y] in
to the hows of the Lord, and spredde
abrood tho[z] bifor the Lord; and preiede 15
in his siȝt, and seide, Lord God of Israel,
that sittist on[a] cherubym‡, thou art God
aloone of alle kyngis of erthe; thou madist
heuene and erthe. Bowe thin eere, and 16
here; opyn thin iȝen, Lord, and se; and

† that is, for
the wordis.
Lire here. c.

‡ that is, art
souereyn of ech
creature, ȝhe, of
auugel. *Lire
here.* c.

---

[f] turnyn E *pr. m.*   [g] message A.   [h] doun E *pr. m.*   [i] that H.   [k] the B.   [l] Om. AC.

[u] face *or schewyng* I.   [v] the wordis I.   [w] what I.   [x] Thanne I.   [y] aȝen *fro Jerusalem* I.   [z] Rabsaces I.
[a] the king of Assiriens I.   [b] men tellinge *it of the comynge* of Theracha I.   [c] Om. I.   [d] Theracha I.
[e] hath go I.   [f] the king *of Assiriens* I.   [g] Theracha I.   [h] takun CEK *pr. m.* L.   [k] hast herd I.
[l] han do I.   [m] han wastid I.   [n] hem I.   [o] folk I.   [p] han delyuered I.   [q] the men I.   [r] the men of
Gozam I.   [s] of Aran I.   [t] of Reseph I.   [u] *the citee* of Emath I.   [w] the messangeris BCEIL.   [x] hem I.
[y] stiede up I.   [z] tho *lettris* I.   [a] upon I.

16 heuen and erthe Bowe doun thin ere,
and here; opyn thin eeʒen, Lord, and
see; and here thou alle the wordis of
Senacherub, that sente, that he repreue
17 to us the lyuynge God Forsothe, Lord,
the kyngis of Assiries scatirden the Gen-
16 tylis, and the londis of alle, and senten
the goddis of hem in to fyre; forsothe
they weren not goddis, bot the wercis
of the hondis of men, of tree and stoon,
19 and thei distruyeden hem Now than,
Lord oure God, maake vs saaf fro the
hond of hem, that alle rewmys of the
erth knowen for thou ert Lord God
20 aloon Forsothe Ysayas, the sone of
Amos, sente to Ezechie, seyinge, Thes
thingis seith the Lord God of Yrael,
What thingis thou preyedist me vpon
Senacherub, kyng of Assiries, I haue
21 herde. This is the word, that the Lord
hath spoken of hym; He hath dispiside
thee, and scorned thee, thou meyden
douʒtir of Syon; aftir thi bac the heued
he meuede, thou douʒtir of Jerusalem
22 To whom hast thou repreued, and whom
hast thou blasfemede? Aʒeynus whome
hast thou enhauncid thi voice, and hast
reride in to heeiʒ thin eeʒen? Aʒenus the
23 hooly of Yrael Bi the hond^m of thi
seruauntes thou hast putte reprofe to
the Lord, and seidist, In the^n multitude
of my chaaris I steiʒide up the heiʒtis of
hillis, in the ouermost of Lybane, and I
hewʒ doun the heeʒe cedris of it, and the
chosen firris of it; and I wente in vnto
the termys of it, and the wyldc wode of
24 the Carmele of it I haue hewen doun,
and I haue dronken alyen watirs, and
haue dryed with the steppis of my feet
25 alle the closed watirs Whether hast
thou not herde, what I haue done fro the

here alle the wordis of Senacherib, which^b
sente^c, that he schulde^d dispise 'to vs^e
'God lyuynge^f Verili^g, Lord, the kynges^h 17
of Assiriens distrieden^i hethene men, and
the londis of alle men, and senten^k the 18
goddis of hem in to fier; for^l thei weren
not goddis, but werkis of 'hondis of men^m,
of tre and stoon^n; and thei losten^o 'tho
goddis^p† Now therfor, oure Lord God, 19 † not for zeel
make vs saaf fro the hond of hem, that
alle rewmes^q of erthe wite that thou art
the^r Lord God aloone Forsothe Isaie, 20
sone^s of Amos, sente to Ezechie, and seide,
The Lord God of Israel seith these thingis,
Y haue herd 'tho thingis, whiche^t thou
preidist me on^u Sennacherib, king of Assiriens This is the word, which' the 21
Lord spak^w of hym, Thou virgyn douʒtir^x
of Syon‡, he^y dispiside^z thee, and scornyde thee, thou douʒter of Jerusalem, he
mouyde his heed aftir thi bak Senna- 22
cherib^a, whom 'dispisidist thou^b, and whom
'blasfemedist thou^c? Aʒens whom hast thou
reisid thi vois, and hast reisid thin iʒen
an^d hiʒe? Aʒens the hooli of Israel. Bi 23
the hond of thi seruauntis thou dispisidist^e
the Lord, and seidist, In the multitude of
my chaiys Y stiede^f in to the^g hiʒe thingis
of hillis, in the hiʒnesse of Liban §, and
kittide^h doun the hiʒe cedris therof', and
the chosyn beechis therof, and Y entride
'til to^k the termes^l therof, and Y kittide 24
doun the forest^m of Carmele therof; and
Y drank alien watris, and Y made drie
with^n the^o steppis of 'the feet of myn^p‖ 'alle
watris closid^q Whether thou herdist not, 25
what Y made at the bigynnyng? Fro elde
daies Y made it^r, and now Y haue brouʒt^s
forth, and strengthid citees^t of fiʒteris^u
schulen be in to fallyng of hillis^v And 26
thei that sitten meke of^w hond in tho^x,

† not for zeel
of God, but in
her pride,
enuye, and co
ueitise I

‡ virgyn, the
douʒtir of Sion,
that is, Jeru-
salem, which
is seid a vir-
gyn, for the
hoolnesse of
feith, that
dwellide euere
there In sum
men It is seid
the douʒter of
Sion, for that
a douʒter is de-
fendid of the
modir, so the
citee of Jeru-
salem was de
fendid of the
stronge hold,
that was in the
hil of Sion
I vse here c
§ of Liban;
that is, of the
temple maad
of the trees of
Liban Lire
here c
‖ of myne;
that is, of men
of myn oost,
and of beestis
Lire here c

m hondis ABFH   n Om ABFH

b the which I   c hath sent to us I   d wolde I   e Om I   f the lyuynge God I   g Treuli I
h kyng A pr m   i han destried I   k thei han sent I   l forsothe I   m mennus hondis I   n of stoon I
o forbiden I   p hem I   q the rewmes I   r Om I   s the sone I   t that I   u upon I   v that I
w hath spoke I   x the douʒtir I   y the king of Assirie I   z hath dispisid I   a O' Sennacherib I   b hast
thou dispisid I   c hast thou blasfemed I   d on I   e hast dispisid I   f went up I   g Om E   h I kittide IK   i Om I   k vnto I   l termes or vttermost coostis I   m or the sautre I marg   n all the closid
watris with I   o Om GKL   p my feet A sec m   K sec m   x sec m   feet of myne seruauntis c sec m Q
the feet o   sec m   the feet of men U   q Om I   r that thing I   s brouʒt it I   t the citees ELP.
u hillis A sec m I   v fiʒteris A sec m I   w in I   x tho citees I

bigynnynge? Fro^p the olde days I haue fourmyd it, and nowe I haue brou3t to; and the streyngthid cytees schuln ben in 26 to fallynge of the fi3tynge hyllis. And thilk that sytten in hem meeke in hond, han tremblyd to gydre, and ben confoundyd; thei ben maad as hey of the feeld, and as greene herbe of rofys, the whiche is maad drye, er it my3t comme 27 to rijpnesse. And thi dwellynge place, and thi goynge oute, and thi commynge in, and thi weye I knewe beforn, and thi 28 woodnesse a3eynus me. Thou wexe wood in me, and thi pride stey3ide up in to my eris; and so I schal putten a cercle in thyn noos thrillis, and a bernacle in thi lippis, and I schal brynge thee a3eyn by 29 the weye that thou came. To thee forsothe, Ezechie, this schal ben a tokne; ete this 3ere that thou fyndist; in the secounde forsothe 3ere that freely growen; bot in the thrid 3eer sowith, and repith, and plauntith vynes, and etith the fruyt 30 of hem. And what euer were laft of the hous of Juda, it schal putten the rote 31 benethe, and maken fruyt abouen. Fro^q Jerusalem forsoth schuln goon out relykis, and that schal ben saued of the hyll of Syon; the zeel of the Lord of 32 hoostis schal done that. For what thing thes thinges seith the Lord of the kyng of Assiries, He schal not commen in to this^r cytee, ne senden arowe in to it, and targett schal not ocupien it, and warn- 33 yschynge schal not enuyroun it. By the weye that he came he schal be turned a3eyn, and this cytee he schal not comme 34 in, seith the Lord; and I schal defenden this cytee, and sauen it for me, and for 35 Dauid, my seruaunt. · It is done thanne, the aungel of the Lord came in that ny3t, and smoote in the tentis of Assiries an hundreth fourescoore and fyue thousandis.

trembliden togidere, and ben schent; thei ben maad as the hei of the^y feeld, and as grene^z eerbe of roouys^a, which^b is^c dried^d, bifor that it cam to ripenesse. And Y 27 bifor^e knew thi dwellyng, and thi goyng out, and thin entryng^f, and thi weie, and thi woodnesse a3ens me. Thou were wood 28 a3ens me, and thi pride stide^g in to myn eeris; therfor Y schal putte a cercle^h in thi nosethirlis, and a bernacle in thi lippis, and Y schal lede thee a3en in toⁱ the weie bi which thou camest. Forsothe, Ezechie, 29 this^k schal be a signe^l 'to thee^m; ete thou in this 3eer that, that thou fyndist; forsothe in the secounde 3eer tho thingis, that growen bi her owne wille; sotheli in the thridde 3eer sowe 3e, and repe 3e, plaunteⁿ 3e vyneris, and ete^o the fruytis of tho. And what euer thing schal be residue^p 30 of the hows of Juda, it schal sende root^q dounward, and schal^r make fruyt^{rr} vpward. For relikis^s schulen go out of Jerusalem, 31 and that, that schal be sauyd, 'schal go out^t of the hil of Syon; the feruent loue of the Lord of oostis schal do this^u. Wher- 32 for the Lord seith these thingis of the kyng of Assiriens, He schal not entre in to this citee^v, nethir he schal sende an arowe in to it, nether scheeld^w schal occupie it, nether strengthing, ethir bisegyng, schal cumpasse it. He schal turne a3en 33 bi the weie 'bi which^x he cam^y, and he schal not entre in to this citee, seith the Lord; and Y schal defende this citee, and 34 Y schal saue it for me^z, and for Dauid, my seruaunt. Therfor it was don, in that 3i ni3t the aungel† of the Lord cam, and smoot in the castels of Assiryens an hundrid foure^a score and fyue thousynde. And whanne *Sennacherib* hadde rise eerli, he si3 alle bodies^b of deed men; and he departide, and 3ede awei^c. And Senna- 36 cherib, the^d kyng of Assiriens, turnede

† in that ny3t the aungel, etc.; not in the next ny3t aftir that Ysaie bifor seide these thingis, for twey 3ere werrin bitwixe, but aftir ij. 3eer Sennacherib cam toward Jerusalem, whanne his oost was in Nobe, which is not ful fer fro Jerusalem; and in that ny3t the aungel took this veniaunce on his oost. Lire here. c.

p For n.   q For A.   r the AII. thi n.

y n E.   z a grene I.   a the *hous riggis* I.   b the which I.   c Om. I.   d dried or *welewide* I.   e Om. I. f go3ng in I.   g stiede up I.   h ry3g IV.   i Om. I.   k to thee this I.   l tokne I.   m Om. I.   n and plaunte EL.   o ete 3e I.   p left ouer I.   q the root I.   r it schal I.   rr the fruyt I.   s the relikis or *folk left* I.   t Om. I.   u this *thing* I.   v citee *Jerusalem* I.   w scheeld *of him* I.   x that I.   y cam by I. z my selff I.   a and foure I.   b the bodies x *sec. m.*   c awei *thenns* I.   d Om. I.

And whanne erly he hade rysen, he saw3
alle the bodies of the deed; and a3eyn
30 gooynge wente aweye. And Senacherub,
the^r kyng of Assiries, is turned a3eyn,
37 and dwellide in Nynyue And whanne
he schulde honouren in the temple of
Nesarath, his god, Toramelech and Cirasar,
the sonys of hym, smyten hym with
swerd; and thei flowen in to the lond
of Armeneys; and Asseraddon, his sone,
regnede for hym

a3en, and dwellide in Nynyue. And 37
wh.nne he worschipide in the temple
Nestrach his god, Adramelech and Sira-
sar, his sones†, killide hym with swerde^e;
and thei fledden in to the lond of Ar-
menyes; and Asaradon, his sone, regnyde
for hym

† haue sones,
etc , for he
wolde haue
slayn hem in to
sacrifice to his
God Lire
here c

CAP. XX

1 In tho dayes syjknede Ezechias vnto
the deeth; and there cam to hym Ysayas,
the sone of Amos, prophete, and seyde^s
to hym, Thes thingis seith the Lord God,
Comaunde to thin hous, forsothe thou
2 schalt dyen, and not lyuen The whiche
turned his face to the wall, and honourede
3 the Lord, seyinge, I beseche, Lord, haue
mynde, how I haue goon before thee in
treuthe, and in perfyte herte, and that is
plesaunt before thee haue^t done And
so Ezechias wepte with grete weepynge
4 And ere Ysay were gon out the half
partye of the porche, the word of the
5 Lord is done to hym, seyinge, Turne
a3eyn, and sey to Ezechie, the duke of
my puple, Thes thingis seith the Lord
of Dauid, thi fadre, I haue herd thi
preyer, and seen thi tere, and, loo^l I have
helid thee The thrid day thou schalt
stey3en up to the temple of the Lord,
6 and I schal adden to thy days fyueteen
3eer; bot and fro the hond of the kyng
of Assiries I schal delyueren thee, and
this cytee, and I schal defenden this cyte
7 for me, and for Dauid, my seruaunt And
Ysay seyde, Bryngith to me a masse of
fijgis The whiche whan thei hadden
brou3t to, and putte vpon his botche, he
8 is heelid. Ezechie forsothe seide to Ysay,
What schal ben the tokne, for the Lord
schal helyn me, and for the thrid day

CAP XX

In tho daies Ezechie was sijk 'til to^f the 1
deeth; and Isaie, the prophete, sones^g of
Amos, cam to hym, and seide to hym, The
Lord God seith these thingis, Comaunde^h ‡
to thin hows, for thou schalt die, and thou
schalt not lyue§ Which^i Ezechie turnyde 2
his face to the wal, and worschipide the
Lord, and seide, Y biseche, Lord, haue^j
mynde, hou Y 3edej bifor thee in treuthe,
and in a^k parfit herte, and Y dide that, that
was plesaunt bifor thee Therfor^l Ezechie
wepte bi^m greet^n wepyng. And bifor that 4
Ysaie 3ede out half the part of the court,
the word of the Lord was maad to Isaie,
and seide, Turne thou a3en, and seie to 5
Ezechie, duyk^o of my puple, The Lord
God of Dauid, thi fadir, seith thes thingis,
Y herde^p thi preiere, and Y si3 thi teer,
and, lo^l Y heelide^q thee In the thridde
dai thou schalt stie^r in to the temple of the
Lord, and Y schal adde^s fiftene 3eer to thi 6
daies , but also Y schal delyuere thee and
this citee fro the hond of the kyng of
Assiriens, and Y schal defende this citee
for me, and for Dauid, my seruaunt And 7
Ysaie seide, Bry nge 3e to me a gobet of
figis. And whanne thei hadden brou3te it,
and hadde putte^t on 'his botche^u, he was
heelid Forsothe^v Ezechie seide to Isaie, 8
What schal be the signe^w ‖, that the Lord
schal heele me, and that^x in the thridde
dai Y schal stie^y in to the temple of the

‡ Comaunde,
that is, make
thi testament.
Lire here c
§ schalt not
lyue , that is,
thou maist not
ascape by weye
of kynde , and
bi this maner it
was schewid to
the profete,
netheles, bi
Goddis grace
aboue kynde,
he my3te be
heelid, but this
was schewid
thanne to the
profete. Lire
here c

‖ Ezechie
axide not this
in vnfeithful-
nesse, ethei
dispeir, but
more bi Goddis
tried, that his
glorie schulde
appere, bi the
wonderful heel-
ing Lire
here c

^{r} Om _A_ ^{s} seith _A._ ^{t} I haue _AC pr m_

^{e} a swerd 1 ^{f} vnto 1 ^{g} the sone 1 ^{h} Dispose 1 ^{i} And 1 ^{j} haue go 1 ^{k} Om _A pr m_
^{l} Thanne 1 ^{m} with r11 ^{n} a greet 1 ^{o} the duyk 1 ^{p} haue herd 1 ^{q} haue heelid 1 ^{r} stie up 1
^{s} adde to 1 ^{t} putte it 1 ^{u} the booche of Ezechie 1 ^{v} And 1 ^{w} tokne 1. ^{x} also that 1 ^{y} stie up 1

I am to stey3en up the temple of the
9 Lord? To whom seith Ysay, This schal
ben the tokne fro the Lord, that the Lord
be to do the word that he spac; wylt
thou, that vmbre stey3e up tenn lynys, or
that it be turned a3eyn as fele grees?
10 And Ezechie seith, It is li3t vmbre to
cresen tenn lynis, ne this I wylle that be
done, bot that it be turned a3eyn bac-
11 ward tenn degrees. And so Ysay, the
prophete, inwardly clepyde the Lord, and
brou3t a3eyn the vmbre by the lynys, with
the whiche nowe it hadde goon doun in
the orloge of Achaz, bacward tenn degrees.
12 In that tyme sente Berodachaladam, the
sone of Baladam, kyng of Babyloyne,
lettris and 3iftis to Ezechie; forsothe he
hadde herd, that Ezechie was sijk, and
13 hadde couerde. And Ezechias gladide in
the commynge of hem, and schewide to
hem the hous of swote spycis[u], and gold,
and siluer, and dyuerse pymentis, and
oynementis, and the hous of his vessels,
and alle thingis that he my3t han in his
tresouries; ther was not a word, that
Ezechie schewide not to hem in his hous,
14 and in alle his power. Forsothe Ysay,
the prophete, came to kynge[v] Ezechie, and
seide to hym, What seyden thes men, or
whenns camen thei to thee? To whome
seith Ezechie, Fro a ferre lond thei camen
15 to me, fro Babyloyne. And he answerde,
What see3en thei in thin hous? Ezechie
seith, Alle thingis, what euer ben in myn
hous, thei see3en; no thing is that I haue
not schewide to hem in my tresuries.
16 And so Ysay seyde to Ezechie, Heere
17 thou the word of the Lord. Lo! days
commen, and alle thingis that ben in thi
hous schuln be taken aweye, and the
whiche thi fadirs hydden vnto this day, in
to Babyloyne; ther schal not leuen eny
18 thinge, seith the Lord. Bot and of thi
sonys, that schul goon out of thee, the

Lord? To whom Ysaie seide, This schal 9
be 'a signe[z] of the Lord, that the Lord
schal do the word which[a] he spak; wolt
thou, that the schadewe[b] stie[c]† by ten lynes,
ethir turne a3en bi so many degrees? And 10
Ezechie seide, It is esy[d] that the schadewe
encreesse bi ten lynes[e], nethir Y wole that
this be doon, but that it[f] turne a3en bacward bi ten degrees. Therfor[g] Ysaie, the 11
prophete, clepide inwardli[h] the Lord, and
brou3te a3en bacward bi ten degrees the
schadewe bi lynes[i], bi whiche it hadde
go doun thanne in the orologie of Achaz.
In that tyme Beradacbaladan, sone[k] of 12
Baladam, the[l] kyng of Babiloyne, sente
lettris and 3iftis to Ezechie; for he hadde
herd that Ezechie was[m] sijk, and hadde
couerid[n]. Forsothe[o] Ezechie was glad‡ in 13
the comyng of hem, and he schewide to
hem the hows of spyceries, and gold, and
siluer, and dyuerse pymentis, also oynementis, and the hows of hise vessels, and
alle thingis whiche[p] he my3te haue in
hise tresouris; 'no word was[q], 'which Ezechie schewide not to hem[r] in his hows,
and in al his power[s]. Sotheli Ysaie, the 14
prophete, cam to the[t] kyng Ezechie, and
seide to hym, What seiden these men,
ether fro whennus camen thei to the?
To whom Ezechie seide, Thei camen to
me fro a fer lond, fro Babiloyne. And he[u] 15
answeride, What 'sien thei[v] in thin hows?
Ezechie seide, Thei sien[w] alle thingis, what
euer thingis ben in myn hows; no thing is
in my tresouris, which Y schewide not to
hem. Therfor Isaie seide to Ezechie, 16
Here thou the word of the Lord. Lo! 17
dayes comen, and alle thingis that ben in
thin hows, and 'whiche thingis[x] thi fadris
maden til in to this dai, schulen be takun
awey into Babiloyne; 'not ony thing schal
dwelle[y], seith the Lord. But also of thi 18
sones, that schulen go out of thee, whiche
thou schalt gendere[z], schulen be takun, and

† stie; that is,
go ferthere:
and so it is in
Ebreu. Lire
here. c.

‡ glad; bi vn-
resonable glad-
nesse and pride,
for so greet a
kyng hadde
sent to hym
messangeris
fro so fer a
lond. Lire
here. c.

---

[u] oynementis E pr. m.   [v] the kynge B.

[z] the tokne I.   [a] that I.   [b] schadewe of the sunne I.   [c] stie up I.   [d] li3t or esy I.   [e] lynes or houris I.
[f] the sunne I.   [g] Thanne I.   [h] ynly I.   [i] the same lynes I.   [k] the sone I.   [l] Om. I.   [m] had be I.
[n] rekonerid I.   [o] And I.   [p] that I.   [q] ther was not ony word I text. or thing I marg.   [r] Om. I.   [s] power,
that Ezechie schewide not to hem I.   [t] Om. I.   [u] Ysaie I.   [v] han thei seen I.   [w] han seie I.   [x] that I.
[y] ther schal not ony thing therof dwelle or abijde I.   [z] bigete I.

whiche thou schalt geten schul ben taken
aweye, and thei schul ben geldyngis in
the paleys of the kyng of Babyloyne
19 Ezechie seide to Ysay, Good is the word
of the Lord, that he spac; be oonly pees
20 and treuthe in my days   The remnaunt
forsothe of the wordis of Ezechie, and alle
his streyngthe, and howe he maad the
fische poond, and the watre cundite, and
brou3ten in watirs in to the cytee, whether
not thes ben writen in the boke of the
wordys of the days of kyngis of Juda?

CAP XXI

21 And Ezechie slepte with his fadirs,
and Manasses, his sone, regnede for hym
1 Of twelue 3eer was Manasses, whanne he
begunne to regnen, and fyue and fourty
3eer he regnede in Jerusalem; the name
2 of his modir, Asiba   And he dide euyl in
the si3t of the Lord, after the mawmettis
of Gentilis, the whiche the Lord dide aweye
3 fro the face of the sonys of Yrael   And
he is turned, and bylde^w up hee3e thingis,
the whiche Ezechie, his fadir, scatirde,
and he rerede up the auters of Baal, and
maad mawmett woddis, as dyde Achab,
kyng of Yrael; and he honourede al the
4 kny3thod of heuen, and heryede it   And
he maad up autirs in the hous of the Lord,
of the whiche the Lord seide, In Jeru-
5 salem I schal putten my name. And he
maad up autirs of alle the kny3thode of
heuen in^x two poorchis of the temple of
6 the Lord, and he ouerladde his sone thor3
fijr, and he dyuynede, and he wey tide the
dyuynynge of chiterynge of briddis; and
maad enchaunteris, and clepers of deuyls
he multiplied, that he dide euyl beforn
7 the Lord, and terrede hym   And he
putte the mawmett of the mawmett
wodde, that he hadde maad, in to the
temple of the Lord, vpon the whiche the
Lord spac to Dauid, and to Salomon, his

thei schulen be geldyngis in the paleis of
the king of Babiloyne   Ezechie^a seide to 19
Isaie, The word of the Lord, 'which he
spak, is good^b†; oonely pees and treuthe be
in my daies   Forsothe the residue^c of 20
wordis^d of Ezechie, and al his strengthe,
and hou he made a cisterne, and a watir
cundijt, and brou3te watris^e, 'in to^f the
citee, whether these ben not writun in the
book of wordis of daies of the^g kyngis of
Juda?

CAP XXI

And Ezechie slepte with hise fadris, and 21
Manasses, his sone, regnyde for hym
Manasses was of twelue 3eer, whanne he
bigan to regne, and he regnyde fyue and
fifti 3eer in Jerusalem; the name of his
modir was Asiba   And he dide yuel in 2
the si3t of the Lord, bi^h the idolsⁱ of hethene
men, 'whiche hethene^k men the Lord dide
awei fro the face of the sones of Israel
And he^l was turned^m, and bildide li3e 3
thingis, whiche Ezechie, his fadir, distriede,
and he reisideⁿ autoris of Baal, and he
made woodis^o, as Achab kyng of Israel
hadde do; and he worschipide 'with out
forth^p al the kny3thod of heuene^q, and
worschipide^r it in herte   And he bildide 4
auteris‡ in the hows of the Lord, of which^{rr}
the Lord seide, Y schal sette my name in
Jerusalem   And he bildide auteris to al 5
the kny3thod of heuene^s in the^t twei large
places of the temple of the Lord, and he 6
'ledde ouer^u his sone thorou3^v the fier, and
he vside false dyuynyngis in auteris, on^w
whiche^x sacrifice was maad to feendis, and
he kepte false dyuynyngis bi chiteryng
of bryddis; and he made men to haue yuele
spiritis spekynge in the^{xx} wombe^y, and he
multipliede false dyuynours in entraylis^z of
beestis sacrified^a to feendis, that he schulde^b
do yuel bifor the Lord, and terre hym to

† The word of
the Lord, which
he spak, is
good, Ezechie
repentide, and
so took the
sentence of the
Lord on him
and his rewme,
wherfor and
this pevne was
not brou3t in in
hise tymes, but
it was dilaued,
til to the tyme
of Joachym and
Sedechie, and
whanne this
was seid in
Isaye to him,
he seide, one'ly
pees, etc   Iare
here c

‡ auteris, to
do ydolatrie c

---

^w bieldide A   ^x and A

^a And Ezechie is   ^b is good, that he hath spoke 1   ^c remenaunt 1   ^d the wordis 1   · ^e water 1
^f and to 1   ^g Om 1   ^h after 1   ⁱ yuels 1   ^k the whiche 1   ^l Manasses 1   ^m turned awei 1
ⁿ reiside up 1   ^o mawmett wodis 1   ^p Om 1   ^q the firmament 1   ^r loutide 1   ^{rr} which hous 1
^s heuene or firmament 1   ^t Om disxb_ç   ^u drow3e 1   ^v bi EL   ^w upon 1   ^x the whiche 1   ^{xx} her 1
^y wombis BCDFGIKLMNOPQRSUVWXb_ç   ^z the entraylis 1   ^a sacrifisid DKMDst_ç   ^b wolde 1

sone, In this temple, and in Jerusalem that I haue chosen of alle the lynagis of Yrael, I schal putte my name vnto euer-8 more. And I schal make no more to be styred the fote of Yrael fro the lond that I ȝaue to the fadirs of hem; so neuer the later ȝif thei kepen in dede alle thingis that I bad hem, and al the lawe that Moyses, my seruaunt, comaundyde to 9 hem. Thei forsothe herden not, bot ben bouȝt doun of Manasse, that thei don euyl ouer the Gentilis, the whiche the Lord to-trade fro the face of the sonys of 10 Yrael. And the Lord spac in the hond 11 of his seruauntis prophetis, seyinge, For Manasses, king of Juda, dyde alle thes abomynacyouns most euylouer alle thingis the whiche dyden Amorreis beforn hym, and also he maad Juda to synnen in his 12 vnclennessis[z]; therfore thes thingis seith the Lord God of Yrael, Lo! I schal bryngen in euyls vpon Jerusalem and Judam, that who so euer heerith, bothe the eris of hym 13 schal tynclyn; and I schal stretchen out vpon Jerusalem the lytyl coord of Sama-rye, and the birthen of the hous of Achab, and I schal don aweye Jerusalem, as tablis ben wont to ben don aweye; doynge aweye I schal turnen, and bryngyn 14 ofte[a] the poyntel vpon his face. For-sothe I schal leuen the relikis of myn herytage[b], and schal taken hem in to the hond of his enmyes; and thei schul ben in waastite, and in rauyne to alle their 15 aduersaries; for thi that thei dyden euyl beforn me, and dwelliden stedfast ter-rynge me, fro the day that their fadirs 16 wenten out of Egipt vnto this day. Fer-thermore and Manasses schad myche gyltlesse blode ouer gretely, to the tyme that Jerusalem wer fulfyld vp to the mouthe, with oute his synnes in whiche he maad Judam to synnen, that he do yuel 17 beforn the Lord. The remnaunt for-

ire. And he settide[c] an ydol of wode, 7 which[d] he hadde maad, in[e] the temple of the Lord, 'of which *temple*[f] the Lord spak[g] to Dauid, and to Salomon, his sone[h], Y schal sette my name withouten ende in this temple, and in Jerusalem which[i] Y chees of alle the lynagis of Israel. And Y 8 schal nomore make the foot of Israel to be moued fro the lond which[k] Y ȝaf to the fadris of hem; so netheles if thei kepen in werk alle thingis whiche[k] Y comaundide[l] to hem, and al the lawe whiche[m] Moises, my seruaunt, comaundide to hem. Sotheli 9 thei[n] herden not, but weren disseyued of Manasses, that thei diden yuel ouer hethene men, whiche the Lord al to-brak fro the face of the sones of Israel. And the Lord 10 spak in the hond of his seruauntis pro-phetis, and seide, For Manasses, kyng of 11 Juda, dide these worste abhomynaciouns ouer alle thingis which[o] Ammorreis[p] diden bifor hym, and maden also the puple of Juda to do synne in hise vnclennessis[pp]; therfor the Lord God of Israel seith these 12 thingis, Lo! Y schal brynge in yuelis on[q] Jerusalem and Juda, that[r] who euer herith[s], bothe hise eeris tynglc[t] †; and Y 13 schal holde forth on[u] Jerusalem the corde of Samarie, and the birthun of the hows of Achab‡, and Y schal do awei Jerusalem, as tablis ben wont to be doon awei; and[v] Y schal do awey and turne[vv] *it*[w], and Y schal lede ful ofte the[x] poyntel on[y] the face therof. Forsothe Y schal leeue relikis[z] 14 of myn eritage, and Y schal bitake hem in to[a] the hond of enemyes therof; and thei schulen be in distriynge, and in raueyn to alle her aduersaries; for thei diden yuel 15 bifor me, and thei continueden terrynge[b] me to ire, fro the dai in which her fadris ȝeden out of the lond of Egipt 'til to[c] this day. Ferthermore also Manasses schedde 16 ful myche ynnocent[d] blood, til he fillide Jerusalem 'til to[e] the mouth, with outen

[13] *+ his eeris tyngle;* for drede and won-dring of the greetnesse of yuel, that schal come on Jeru-salem. *Lire here.* c.

‡ the birthun of the hows of Achab; that is, 14 in the same mesure and in the same weiȝte Y schal pun-ysche the rewme of Juda, in which Y 15 punyschide the rewme of Israel. *as ta-blis;* in whiche no thing ap-perith of these thingis that 16 weren writun, so Nabuzardon dide awey Je-rusalem, and breute alle the housis. *Lire here.* c.

[x] vnclennesse D.　[a] efte D.　[b] eritages E.

[c] sette EI.　[d] that I.　[e] upon I.　[f] that I.　[g] spak of I.　[h] sone, *seiynge* I.　[i] the which *citee* I.
[k] that I.　[l] have comaundid I.　[m] that I.　[n] the sones of Israel I.　[o] that I.　[p] *hethen* men of Ammorey I.
[pp] vnclannesse LX.　[q] upon I.　[r] and I.　[s] berith *these yuelis* I.　[t] tyncle *or* ringe I.　[u] upon I.
[v] Om. BCDEFIKLMPXbç.　[vv] ouer turne I.　[w] Om. KL.　[x] a I.　[y] upon I.　[z] remenauntis I.　[a] Om. I.
[b] in terrynge I.　[c] til into EL. vnto I. to X.　[d] giltlees I.　[e] vnto I.

sothe of the wordis of Manasse, and alle
thingis that he dyde, and his synne that
he synned, whether thes ben not wryten
in the boke of the wordis of the days
18 of kyngis of Juda ?   And Manasses slept
with his fadirs, and is byryed in the
gardyne of his hous, in the gardyn of
Azam; and Amon, his sone, regned for
19 hym   Of two and twenty ӡeer he was,
whanne he beganne to regnen; two
forsothe ӡeer he regned in Jerusalem;
name of his modir, Messalometh, douӡtir
20 of Arus of Jethaba   And he dyde euyl
in the siӡt of the Lord, as dydde Ma-
21 nasses, his fadir   And he wente in al
the weye, by the whiche his fadir wente,
and he seruede in the vnclennessis° in
whiche serued his fadir, and honourede
22 hem, and forsoke the Lord God of his
fadirs, and wente not in the weye of the
23 Lord   And his seruauntis benten to hym
buschementis, and slewen the kyng in his
24 hous.   The^d puple forsothe of the lond
smoote alle, that coniureden aӡeinus king
Amon, and thei setten to hem king, Jo-
25 siam, his sone, for him   The remnaunt
forsothe of the wordis of Amon, that he
dide, whether not thes ben writen in the
boke of the wordes of the days of kyngis
26 of Juda ?   And thei birneden him in his
sepulcre in the gardyn of Aza; and Josias,
his sone, regnede for hym

hise synnes bi whiche he made Juda to do
synne, to^f do yuel bifor the Lord   Forsothe 17
the residue^g of the^h wordis of Manasses,
and alle thingis whiche^i he dide, and his
synne whiche^k he synnede^l, whether these
ben not writun in the book of wordis of
daies of the kyngis of Juda ?   And Ma-18
nasses slepte with hise fadris, and was
biried in the gardyn of his hows, in the
gardyn of Azam, and Amon, his sone,
regnyde for hym   He^m was of two and 19
twenti ӡeer, whanne he bigan to regne;
and he regnede twei ӡeer in Jerusalem, the
name of his modir was Mesalamech, the
douӡter of Arus of Gethela.   And he^n dide 20
yuel in the siӡt of the Lord, as Manasses,
his fader, hadde do   And he ӡede in al the 21
weie, bi which his fader hadde go, and he
seruide to vnclennessis†, to whiche his fadir
hadde seruyd, and he worschipide tho;
and he forsook the Lord God of hise fadris, 22
and he ӡede not in the weye of the Lord
And hise seruauntis settiden tresouns to 23
hym, and killiden the kyng in hise hows
Sothely the puple of the Lord smoot alle 24
men°, that hadden conspirid aӡens kyng
Amon, and thei ordeyneden to hem a kyng,
Josias, 'his sone^p, for hym   Forsothe^q 25
the residue of wordis^r of Amon, whiche
he dide, whether these ben not writun in
the book of wordis of daies of the kyngis
of Juda ?   And he slepte with hise fadris, 26
and thei birneden hym in his sepulcre in .
the gardyn of Azam, and Josias, his sone,
regnede for him

† vnclennessis,
that is, vdolis.
Lire here ι

CAP. XXII

1 Of eyӡt ӡeere was Josias, whann he
byganne to regnen, and oon and thrytty
ӡeer he regnede in Jerusalem, name of
his modir, Ydida, the douӡtir of Fadaya
2 of Besocath   And he dyde that, that was
plesaunt beforn the Lord, and he wente
by alle the wayes of Dauid, his fadir, and
bowede not, neither to the riӡt, ne to the

CAP XXII.

Josias^s was of eiӡte ӡeer, whanne he 1
bigan to regne, and he regnyde oon and
thritti ӡeer in Jerusalem; the name of his
modir was Ydida, the douӡtir of Phadaia
of Besechath.   And he^t dide that, that 2
was plesaunt bifor the Lord, and he ӡede
be alle the wayes‡ of Dauid, his fadir; he
bowide not, nethir to the riӡtside, nethir^u

‡ in good, and
not in yuel
Lire here ς

ς vnclennesse в   d And the л

f and to 1   g remenaunt 1   h Om 1.   i that 1   k that 1   l dede вL.   m Amon 1   n Amon 1
o the men 1   p the sone of Amon 1   q Sothly 1   r the wordis 1   s Josias, his sone DEL   t Jozias 1
u ne EILF.

Q q 2

3 left. Forsothe the eyȝtenthe ȝeer of kyng
Josie, sente the kyng Safan, the sone of
Asua, the sone of Mesulam, the scribe of
the temple of the Lord, seyinge to hym,
4 Goo to Elchiam, the grete preest, that the
monee, that is brouȝt in to the temple of
the Lord, be blowen to gydre, the whiche
the porteris of the temple gaderden of
5 the puple; and be it ȝeuen to wriȝtis by
the prouostis of the hous of the Lord;
the whiche and delen it to hem that
wirchen in the temple of the Lord, to
the coueryngis of the temple of the Lord
6 to ben enstorid, that is, to the mayster
carpenters, and masouns, and to hem
that maken to gydre the bytwene[e] broken,
and that there be bouȝt trees and stonys
of the quarrees, to the enstorynge of the
7 temple of the Lord; neuer the later the
syluer be not tolde to hem, that thei
taken, bot in power haue[f] thei, and in
8 feith. Forsothe Elchias, the bischop,
seide to Sapham, scribe, The boke of
the lawe I haue founden in the hous of
the Lord. And Elchias ȝaue the volym
to Sapham, scribe, the whiche and radde
9 it. Forsothe Sapham, scribe, came to the
kyng, and told to hym what thingis he
hade comaundide, and seith, Thi seruauntis blewen to gydre the monee, that
is founden in the hous of the Lord, and
han ȝeuen, that it be delid to the wriȝtis
of the prefectis of the werkis of the
10 temple of the Lord. Forsothe Sapham,
scribe, tolde to the kyng, seyinge, Elchias, the prest of God, ȝaue to me a
boke; the whiche whanne Sapham hade
11 radde before the kyng, and the king had
herd the wordis of the boke of the lawe
12 of the Lord, he kutte his clothis. And
he comaundyde to Elchie, the prest, and
to Aychan, the sone of Saphan, and to
Achabor, the sone of Mycha, and to Sapham, scribe, and to Achic, seruaunt of

of the leftside. Forsothe in the eiȝtenthe 3
ȝeer of kyng Josias, the kyng[q] sente Saphan, sone[r] of Asua, the sone of Mesulam, scryueyn, *ethir doctour*, of the temple of the Lord, and seide to him, Go 4
thou to Elchie, the grete preest, that the
money, which[s] is borun in to the temple
of the Lord, be spendid[t], which[u] *money*
the porteris of the temple han gaderid[v] of
the puple; and that it be ȝouun to crafti 5
men bi the souereyns of the hows of the
Lord; which[w] also departide that money
to hem that worchen in the temple of the
Lord, to reparele the rooues[x] of the temple of the Lord, that is[xx], to[y] carpenteris, 6
and to masouns, and to hem that maken
brokun thingis, and that trees and stoonus
of quarieris be bouȝt[yy], to reparele the
temple of the Lord; netheles siluer[z], 7
which[a] thei[b] taken, be not rekynyd to
hem, but haue thei[c] in power, and in
feith. Forsothe[d] Helchie, the bischop, 8
seide to Saphan, the scryuen, Y haue
founde the[e] book of the lawe in the hows
of the Lord. And Elchie ȝaf the[f] book to
Saphan, the scryuen, which[g] also redde it.
Also Saphan, the scryuen, cam to the 9
kyng, and telde to hym tho thingis, whiche
Elchie hadde comaundid, and he seide,
Thi seruauntis han spendid the monei,
which[h] was foundun in the hows of the
Lord, and ȝauen[i], that it schulde be departid to crafti men of the souereyns of
werkis of the temple of the Lord. Also 10
Saphan, the scriueyn, telde to the kyng,
and seide, Helchie, the preest of God, ȝaf[k]
to me a book; and whanne Saphan hadde
red that book bifor the kyng, and the 11
kyng hadde herd the wordis of the[l] book
of the[m] lawe of the Lord, he to-rente
hise clothis. And he comaundide to Elchie, 12
the preest, and to Aicham, sone[n] of Saphan, and to Achabor, sone[n] of Mycha,
and to Saphan, the scryuen, and to Achia,

[e] betwix *A.* [f] ha *E.*

[q] kyng Jozias I. [r] the sone I. [s] that I. [t] molten togidere I. [u] the which I. [v] gaderid togidere I. [w] the which I. [x] hilyngis I. [xx] his L. [y] Om. EL. [yy] brouȝt A *pr. m.* [z] the siluer I. [a] that I. [b] the work men I. [c] thei it I. [d] And I. [e] a I. [f] that I. [g] the which I. [h] that I. [i] thei han ȝouen I. [k] hath ȝoue I. [l] that I. [m] Om. I. [n] the sone I.

13 the kyng, seyinge, Gooth, and counseilith
the Lord vpon me, and vpon the puple,
and vpon al Juda, of the wordis of this
volyme, that is founden; grete forsothe
wrathe of the Lord is tende up aʒeynus
us, for oure fadirs herden not the wordis
of this boke, that thei schulde done al
14 that is writen to us And so Elchias,
the prest, and Aycham, and Achabor,
and Saphan, and Asia, wenten to Oldam,
prophetisse, wyf of Sellum, sone of Thechue, sone of Aras, keper of the clothes,
the whiche dwellede in Jerusalem, in
'the secounde wallynge[g], and thei speken
15 to hire And sche answerd to hem, Thes
thingis seith the Lord God of Yrael,
Seith to the man, that sente ʒou to me,
16 Thes thingis seith the Lord God of
Ysrael, Loo! I schal bringe forth euyls
vpon this place, and vpon the dwellers of
it, alle the wordis of the lawe, the whiche
17 the kyng of Juda radde, for thei forsoken me, and sacrifiden to alyen goddis,
terrynge me in alle the werkis of then
hondis, and myn indignacioun schal be
tend up in this place, and schal not ben
18 qweynt To the kyng forsothe of Juda
that sente ʒou, that ʒe counseylen the
Lord, thus seith, Thes thingis seith the
Lord God of Yrael, For thy that thou
19 herdyst the wordis of the volyme, and
thi herte is gaastyde, and thou ert
meeked beforn the Lord, the werdis herd
aʒeyn this place and the dwellers of it,
that is, that schulden ben maad in to
stoneynge, and into cursidhed, and thou
kuttist thy clothis, and thou weptist beforn me, and I herde, seith the Lord,
20 therfore I schal gedere thee to thi fadirs,
and thou schalt be gadred to thy sepulcre
in pese, that thin eeʒen seen not alle the
euylis, the whiche I am to brynge in
vpon this place

seruaunt of the kyng, and seide, Go ʒe, 13
and 'counsele ʒe[o] the Lord[p] on[q] me, and
on[r] the puple[s], and on[t] al Juda, of the[u]
wordis of this book, which[v] is foundun,
for[w] greet ire of the Lord is kyndlid aʒens
vs, for oure fadris herden not the wordis
of this book, to do al thing which[x] is
writun to vs Therfor Helchie, the preest, 14
and Aicham, and Achabor, and Saphan,
and Asia, ʒeden to Olda, the prophetesse,
the wijf of Sellum, sone[y] of Thecue, sone[y]
of Aras, kepere of the[z] clothis, which[a]
Olda dwellide in Jerusalem, in the secounde *dwellyng*[b]; and thei spaken to hir
And sche answeride to hem, The Lord 15
God of Israel seith these thingis, Seie ʒe
to the man, that sente ʒou to me, The 16
Lord God of Israel seith these thingis,
Lo! Y schal brynge yuelis on[c] this place,
and on[c] the dwelleris therof, alle[d] the
wordis 'of the lawe[e], whiche the kyng of
Juda redde; for thei forsoken me, and 17
maden sacrifice to alien goddis, and terriden me to ire in alle the werkis of her
hondis; and myn indignacioun schal be
kyndlid in this place, and schal[f] not be
quenchid Sotheli to the kyng of Juda, 18
that sente ʒou, that ʒe schulen 'counsele
the Lord[g], ʒe schulen seie thus, The Lord
God of Israel seith these thingis, For
thou[h] herdist the wordis of the book, and 19
thin herte was aferd, and thou were maad
meke bifor the Lord, whanne the[i] wordis
weren herd aʒens this place and aʒens
the dwelleris therof, that is, that thei
schulden be maad in to wondiyng, and
in to cursyng, and thou to-rentist thi
clothis, and weptist bifor me, and Y herde,
seith the Lord; herfor Y schal gadere 20
thee to thi fadris, and thou schalt be gaderid to thi sepulcre in pees, that thin
iʒen se not alle the yuelis, whiche Y schal
brynge yn on[k] this place

[g] welsum fortune E *scc m sup ras* the secounde wallyng *tert m*

[o] axe ELP [p] Lord councel EIP [q] upon I [r] upon I [s] puple *of this citee* I [t] upon I [u] Om FL
[v] that I [w] forsothe I [x] that I [y] the sone I [z] Om DEKIMPXsbç [a] the which I [b] enuyronynge
of the wall I [c] upon I [d] and alle ELb *and I schal fulfille* alle I [e] Om I [f] it schal I [g] axe the
Lord councel FIP [h] thou, Josias I [i] *his* I [k] upon I

CAP. XXIII.

1 And thei tolden to the kyng that sche hadde seide; the whiche sent, and ben gadred to hym alle the olde men of Juda, 2 and of Jerusalem. And the kyng steyʒide up the temple of the Lord, and alle the men of Juda, and alle that dwelliden in Jerusalem with hym, prestis, and prophetis, and alle the puple, fro lytyl vnto mychil; and he radde, alle men heerynge, alle the wordis of the boke of the pese couenaunt of the Lord, the whiche 3 is founden in the hous of the Lord. And the kyng stood vpon a gree; and he smote pese couenaunt before the Lord, that thei goon after the Lord, and keepen his heestis and witnessyngis and cerymoynes in al herte and in al soule, that thei reren the wordis of this pese couenaunt, that weren wryten in that boke; and the puple assentyde to the couenaunt. And the kyng comaundyde to 4 Elchie, the bischop, and to the prestis of the secound ordre, and to the ʒate kepers, that thei throwen forthe fro the temple of the Lord alle the vessels, that weren maad to Baal, and in the mawmett wodde, and to al the knyʒthod of heuen; and he brende hem with outen forth Jerusalem, in the valey of Cedron, 5 and he toke the poudre of hem in to Bethel. And he dyde aweye the deuyl clepers, whome the kyngis of Juda hadden sett to sacrifien in heiʒtis by the cytees of Juda, and the enuyroun of Jerusalem, and hem that brenden encense to Baal, and to the sunne, and to the mone, and to the twelue syngnys, and to alle the knyʒthode of heuen. 6 And he comaundyde to ben born out the mawmett wodde fro the hous of the Lord with out forth Jerusalem in the

CAP. XXIII.

And thei telden to the kyng that, that 1 sche seide; ʼwhich kyng[m] sente, and alle the elde men of Juda, and of Jerusalem, weren gaderid[n] to hym. And the kyng 2 stiede[o] in to the temple of the Lord, and alle the[p] men of Juda, and alle men[q] that dwelliden in Jerusalem with hym, the preestis, and the prophetis, and al the puple, fro litil ʼtil to[r] greet; and he[s] redde, while alle men herden, alle the wordis of the book of boond of pees of the Lord, which[t] book[u] was foundun in the hows of the Lord. And the kyng stood on[v] the 3 grees; and he[w] smoot boond[x] of pees bifor the Lord, that thei schulden[y] go aftir the Lord, and kepe hise comaundementis and witnessyngis and cerymonyes in al the[z] herte and in al the[a] soule, that[b] thei schulden reise[c] the wordis of this boond of pees, that weren writun in that book; and the puple assentide to the[d] couenaunt. And the kyng comaundide to Helchie, the 4 bischop, and to the preestis of the secounde ordre, and to the porteris, that thei schulden caste out of the temple alle the vesselis, that weren maad to Baal, and in the wode[e], and to al the knyʒthod of heuene; and he[f] brente tho *vessels* with out Jerusalem, in the euene valey of Cedron, and he bar the poudir of tho ʼ*vessels*[g] in to Bethel. And he[h] dide awei false dy- 5 uynours ʼthat dyuynyden in the entrailis of beestis sacrified[i] to idols[k], whiche the kingis of Juda hadden sett to make sacrifice in hiʒ thingis bi the citees of Juda, and in the cumpas of Jerusalem; and *he* *dide away* hem that brenten encense to Baal, and to the sunne, and to the moone, and to twelue signes, and to al the knyʒthod of heuene[l]. And he[m] made the wode[n] 6 to be borun out of the hows of the Lord

---

h that E. i place E pr. m. k in the CE.

m and he I. n gaderid togidere I. o wente up I. p Om. I. q the men I. r vnto I. s the kyng I. t the which I. u Om. I. v upon I. w Om. I. x a boond I. y wolden I. z her I. a her I. b and that I. c reise up I. d that I. e mawmet wode I. f the king I. g Om. c. h the kyng I. i sacrifisid DKMXbʠ. 'k Om. I. l heuene *or of the firmament* I. m the kyng I. n wode *of mawmetrie* I.

valey of Cedron, and brende^m it there,
and brou3t it^n in to poudre, and threw3
forth vpon the sepulcris of the comun.
7 Forsothe he distruy3ide the lytyl housis
of the wommannysch maad men, that
weren in the hous of the Lord; for the
whiche wymmen weueden as lytyll houses
8 of the mawmett wodde. And he gadrede
alle the prestis of the° cytees of Juda,
and he defoulide the hey3tis, where the
prestis sacrifieden, fro Gaba vnto Bersabe; and he distruyed the auters of the
3atis in the entree of the dore of Josie,
prince of the^p cytee, that was at the left
9 syde of the 3ate of the cytee. Neuer
the latre the prestis of the hee3e thingis
stey3iden not vp to the auter of the Lord
in Jerusalem, bot oonly eten therfe loouys
10 in the mydill of their bretheren. Forsothe he defoulide Topheth, that is in
the valeye of the sone of Ennon, that
no man schuld sacryn his sone or his
11 dou3tre thor3 fyr to Moloch. Forsothe
he toke awey the hors, the whiche the
kingis of Jude hadden 3euen to the sunne,
in the entree of the temple of the Lord,
besijdis the chayer of Nathanmylech,
geldynge, that was in Faturym; the
chaare forsothe of the sunne he brende
12 with fijr. And the auters, that weren
vpon the rooues of the soupynge place
of Achath, the whiche the kyngis of
Juda hadden maad, and the auters that
Manasses hadde maad in the two poorchis
of the temple of the Lord, the kyng de-
struyede; and he ran to Jude, and he
scatrede the askis^q of hem in to the
13 streme of Cedron. The hee3e thingis
forsothe, that weren in Jerusalem at the
ri3t partye of the hyll of the offencyoun,
the whiche Salomon, kyng of Yrael,
hadde bylde, and Astaroth, the mawmett
of Sydonyes, and Camos, of the offencyoun of^r Moab, and Melchon, the abomy-

without Jerusalem in the euene valey of
Cedron, and he brente it there; and he
droof it in to poudir, and castide it° forth
on^p the sepulcris of the comyn puple. Also 7
he distriede the litle housis of 'men turnyd
into wommens condiciouns^q, whiche^r housis
weren in the hows of the Lord; for whiche^s
the^t wymmen 'maden^u as litil howsis of
the wode. And he^v gaderide the 8
preestis fro^w the citees of Juda, and he
defoulide the hi3e thingis, where the^x
preestis maden sacrifice, fro Gabaa 'til to^y
Bersabee; and he distriede the^z auters of
3atis^a in the entryng of the dore of Josie,
prince^b of a citee, which^c dore was at the
lift half of the 3ate of the cytee. Netheles 9
the preestis of hi3e thingis stieden not^d to
the auter of the Lord in Jerusalem, but
oneli thei eten therf looues in the myddis
of her britheren. Also he^d defoulide To- 10
phet†, which^f is in the euene valey of the
sone of Ennon, that no man schulde halewe his sone ether his 'dou3tir bi fier to
Moloch. Also he dide awei horsis, whiche^g 11
the kyngis of Juda hadden 3oue to the
sunne, in the entryng of the temple of the
Lord, bisidis the chaumbir of Nathanma-
lech, geldyng^h, that was in Pharurym;
forsothe he^i brente bi fier the charis of the
sunne. Also the kyng distriede the au- 12
teris, that weren on^k the roouys^l of the
soler of Achaz, whiche auteris^m the kyngis
of Juda hadden maad; and the kyng distriede the auteris, whiche Manasses hadde
maad in the^n twei grete placis of° the
temple of the Lord; and he^p ran fro
thennus, and scateride the askis of tho^q
in to the strond of Cedron. Also the 13
kyng defoulide the hi3e thingis, that weren
in Jerusalem at the ri3t part^r of the hil of
offenciount‡, whiche^s Salomon, kyng of Israel, hadde bildid to Astroth, the ydol of
Sidoneis, and to Chamos, the offencioun
of Moab, and to Melchon, abhominacioun^t

† *Tophet*; that is, idolatrie. The idol of Moloch that was clepid To-phet, signefieth tympan, ether sown of tym-pan, for the preestis of this idol, maden noyse with timpans, lest fadris and mo-dris schulden here the cry of her sones, dyynge bi fier in the hondis of the idol; as it was seid in xvi. c°. bifore, and in xviii. c°. of Leuyt. *Lire here.* c.

‡ *offencioun*; that is, the hil of Olynete, for Salomon of-fendide God there, in bild-inge templis of idelis for his wyues. *Lire here.* c.

---

^m brenne ʙ.   ^n Om. *ABFII.*   ° Om. *ABFII.*   ^p Om. ʙ.   ^q ashen *A.*   ^r and *ABF.* Om. *c.*

° Om. *plures.*   ^p upon ɪ.   ^q wommannysche men ɪ.   ^r the whiche ɪ.   ^s the whiche *housis* ɪ.   ^t Om. ɪ.
^u weuyden *or watleden* ɪ.   ^v the king ɪ.   ^w of ɪ.   ^x Om. *ᴇʟ.*   ^y vnto ɪ.   ^z Om. ɪ.   ^a the 3atis *ᴇɪʟ.*
^b the prince ɪ.   ^c the which ɪ.   ^d not up ɪ.   ^e the kyng ɪ.   ^f that ɪ.   ^g that ɪ.   ^h the geldyng ɪ.   ^i the
king ɪ.   ^k upon ɪ.   ^l flatt roouys ɪ.   ^m Om. ɪ.   ^n Om. ɪ.   ^o jn ɪ.   ^p the kyng ɪ.   ^q tho *auters* ɪ.
^r halff ɪ.   ^s that ɪ.   ^t the abhominacioun ɪ.

nacyouns of the sonys of Amon, the
14 kyng defoulide; and broosede the ymagis,
and hewȝ doun the mawmett woodis, and
fulfillide the places of hem with the
15 boonis of deed men. Ferthermore and
the auter that was in Bethel, and the
heeȝe thinge, that Jeroboam, the sone of
Nabath, hadde maad, the whiche maad
Yrael to synnen; and that heeȝ auter he
distruyede, and brende, and mynuschede
in to poudre, and also[s] brende up the
16 mawmett woode. And Josias turned,
sauȝ there sepulcris that weren in the
hyll; and he sente, and toke the boonys
fro the sepulcris, and brende hem vpon
the auter, and putte it aftir the word of
the Lord, that the man of God spac, the
whiche hadde before seide these wordis.
17 And he seith, Whose is this towmbe that
I see? And the cyteȝeens of that cyte
answerden to hym, The sepulcre it is of
the man of God, that came fro Juda, and
before seide thes wordis, 'the whiche[t]
thou hast done vpon the auter of Bethel.
18 And he seith, Lefe hym; no man styrre
the boonys of hym. And vntouchid
laften [u] the boonys of hym with the
boonis of the prophete, that came fro
19 Samarye. Ferthermore and alle the
mawmett templis of the heeȝe thingis,
that weren in the cytees of Samarye, the
whiche the kyngis of Yrael hadden maad
to terre the Lord, Josias toke aweye;
and he dyde to hem aftir alle the werkis
20 that he hadde done in Bethel. And he
slewȝ alle the prestis of the heeȝe thingis,
that weren ther vpon the auteres[w], and he
brende mens boonys vpon thoo[x]; and he
21 turnede aȝeyn to Jerusalem. And he
comaundide to al[y] the puple, seyinge,
Makith pask to the Lord ȝoure God, aftir
that is writen in the boke of this pese

of the sones of Amon; and he[u] al to-brak 14
ymagis[v], and kittide doun[w] wodis[x], and
fillide[y] the places of tho with the boonys
of deed men. Ferthermore also *he dis-* 15
triede the auter that was in Bethel, and
'*he distriede*[z] the hiȝe thing[a], which Jeroboam, sone[b] of Nabath, hadde maad, that
made Israel to do synne; and he[c] distriede that hiȝ autir[d], and brente *it*[e], and al
to brak *it*[e] in to poudir, and kittide[f] doun
also[ff] the[g] wode[h]. And Josias[i] turnyde, 16
and siȝ there sepulcris that weren[k] in the
hil; and he sente, and took the boonys fro[l]
the sepulcris, and brente[m] tho on[n] the
auter[o], and defoulide[p] it[q] bi[r] the word of
the Lord, which[s] word[t] the man of God
spak, that biforseide these wordis. And 17
the kyng seide, What is this biriel, which[u]
Y se? And the citeseyns of that citee
answeriden to hym, It is the sepulcre of
the man of God, that cam fro Juda, and
biforseide these wordis, whiche thou hast
doon on[v] the auter of Bethel. And *the* 18
kyng seide, Suffre ȝe hym; no man moue[w]
hise boonys. And[x] hise boonys dwelliden[y]
vntouchid with the boones of the prophete,
that cam fro Samarie. Ferthermore also 19
Josias dide awei alle the templis[z] of hiȝe
thingis[a], that weren in the citees of Samarie, whiche[aa] the kyngis of Israel hadden
maad to terre the Lord to ire; and he
dide to tho[b] *templis* bi alle thingis whiche
he hadde do in Bethel. And he killide 20
alle the preestis of hiȝe thingis, that
weren there on[c] the auteris, and he brente
mennus boonus on[c] tho *auteris*[d]; and he[e]
turnede aȝen to Jerusalem; and co- 21
maundide[f] to al the puple, and seide,
Make ȝe pask to 'ȝoure Lord God[g], vp[h]
that, that is writun in the book of this
boond of pees. Forsothe[i] sich pask[k] was 22
not maad, fro the daies of iugis that

[s] al *A*. [t] whiche *A*. that c. [u] thei laften *A*. [w] waters *ABH*. [x] it *E pr. m.* [y] Om. *A*.

[u] the king *Jozias* I. [v] the ymagis I. [w] adoun I. [x] mawmett wodis I. [y] he fillide I. [z] Om. I.
[a] *solempne* thing I. [b] the sone IB. [c] Jozias I. [d] autir *in Bethel* I. [e] Om. *plures*. [f] he kittide I.
[ff] al A. [g] Om. I. [h] mawmett wode of it I. [i] he I. [k] weren *bildid* I. [l] of I. [m] he brente I. [n] upon I.
[o] auter *in Bethel* I. [p] he defoulide I. [q] that *auter* I. [r] aftir I. [s] that I. [t] Om. I. [u] that I.
[v] upon I. [w] moue awey I. [x] And *so* I. [y] leften stille I. [z] *mawmett* templis I. [a] *solempne* thingis I.
[aa] that I. [b] the EL. [c] upon I. [d] Om. I. [e] the king I. [f] he comaundide I. [g] the Lord youre God I.
[h] aftir I. [i] Certis I. [k] a pask I.

22 of couenaunt   Ne forsothe ther is maad siche a pask fio the days of iugis, that demeden Yrael, and of alle the days of the kyngis of Yrael, and of the kyngis of 23 Juda, as in the eiȝtenthe ȝeer of kyng Josie this pasch is maad to the Lord in 24 Jerusalem   Bot and the clepers of de- uyls, and deuynours, and the fyguris of mawmettis, and the vnclennessesʸ, and abomynacyounsᶻ, that weren in the lond of Juda and of Jerusalem, Josias dyde aweye, that he make stable the wordis of the lawe, that ben writen in the boke, that Elchias, the prest, fonde in the temple 25 of the Lord   Lijk hym was not beforn hym a kyng, that was turned aȝeyn to the Lord in al his herte, and in alle his soule, and in al his vertue, aftir al the lawe of Moyses ; ne aftir hym rose lijke 26 to hym   Neuerthelatre the Lord is not turned aweye fro the wrath of his grete woodnes, in the whiche his wodnes is wrothe aȝeynus Juda, foi the teriyngisᵃ in the whiche Manasses hadde terred hym. 27 And so the Lord seide, Also Judam I schal taken aweye fro my face, as I toke aweye Yrael ; and I schal throwen aweye this cytee, that I chees, Jerusalem, and the hous of the whiche I seide, My name 28 schal ben there   The remnaunt forsothe of the wordis of Josie, and alle thingis that he dyde, whether not thes ben writen in the boke of the wordis of the 29 days of the kyngis of Juda ?   In his days steyȝide up Pharao Nechao, kyng of Egipt, aȝeynus the kyng of Assiries, at the flode of Eufraten ; and Josias, kyng of Juda, wente in to aȝein commynge of hym, 30 and is slayn in Magedo, whanne he had seen hym.   And his seruauntis beeren hym deed fro Magedo, and brouȝten hym in to Jerusalem, and byryeden hym in his sepulcre ; and the puple of the lond

demyden Israel, and of alle daiesᶠ of the kyngis of Israel and of Juda, as this pask 23 was maad to the Lord in Jerusalem in the ciȝtenthe ȝeei of kyng Josias   But 24 also Josias dide awei men hauynge fendis spekinge in herᵐ wombisⁿ, andᵒ false di- uinouris in auteris, and 'he dide aweiᵖ the figuris of�q idols, and alleʳ vnclennessis, and abhomynaciouns, that weren in the lond of Juda and inˢ Jerusalem, that he schulde do the woidis of the lawe, that weren writtin in the book, 'which bookᵗ Elchie, the preest, foond in the temple of the Lord   No kyng bifor himⁿ was 25 lijk hymᵛ, 'that turnede aȝenⁿ to the Lord in al his herte, and in al his soule, and in al his vertu, biˣ al the lawe of Moises ; nether aftir hym roos ony lijkʲ hym Netheles the Lord was not turned awei 26 fro the ire of his greet veniunce, bi which his strong veniaunceᶻ was wrooth aȝens Juda, foi the terryngis toᵃ ne by whiche Manasses hadde terrid hym to ireᵇ   Ther- 27 for the Lord seideᶜ, Y schal do awei also Juda fio my face, as Y dide awei Israel ; and Y schal caste awei this citeeᵈ, whichᵉ Y chees, Jerusalemᶠ, and the hows 'of whichᵍ Y seideʰ, My name schal be there. Forsothe the residue of wordisᵗ of Josias, 28 and alle thingis whicheᵏ he dide, whethei these ben not writun in the book of woidis of daies of the kyngis of Juda ?   In the 29 daies of hymˡ Farao Nechao, kyngᵐ of Egipt, stiedeⁿ aȝens the kyng of Assiriens, to the flood Eufrates ; and Josias, kyng of Juda, ȝede in to metyngᵒ of hymᵖ, and Josias was slayn in Magedo, whanne he hadde seyn hymq   And 'hise seruauntisʳ 30 baren hym deed fio Magedo, and brouȝte him in to Jeiusalem, and birieden hym in his sepulcre ; and the puple of the lond took Joachaz, soneˢ of Josias, and anoynt- iden hym, and maden hym kyng foi his

---

ʸ vnclennesse ᴀⁿ   ᶻ the abhomynaciouns c.   ᵃ terryngt ᴅ

ˡ the daies ɪ   ᵐ the ᴇʟᴍᴘ   ⁿ wombe ᴍ   ᵒ and wicchis and ᴍ   ᵖ Om ɪ   q in ɪ   ʳ Om plures
ˢ of ɪ   ᵗ that ɪ   ᵘ him in Juda ɪ   ᵛ hymselff ɪ   ᵂ Om ɪ   ˣ aftir ɪ   ʸ lijk to ɪ   ᶻ woodnesse ɪ
ᵃ of ɪ   ᵇ wraththe ɪ   ᶜ seith ɪ   ᵈ citee Jerusalem ɪ   ᵉ that ɪ   ᶠ Om ɪ   ᵍ that ɪ   ʰ seide off ɪ
ⁱ the wordis ɪ   ᵏ that ɪ   ˡ Josias ɪ   ᵐ the kyng ɪ   ⁿ ȝede up ɪ   ᵒ the metyng ᴇɪᴋʟᴍᴘˣᵇ   ᵖ Pharao,
to forbede him to passe thorouȝ Juda ɪ   q Pharao ɪ   ʳ the seruauntis of Jozias ɪ   ˢ the sone ɪ

toke Joachas, the sone of Josie, and anoyntyden hym, and setten hym kyng ³¹for his fadir. Of three and twenty ʒeer was Joachaz, whanne he hadde begunne to regnen, and thre monethis he regned in Jerusalem; name of his modir, Amychael, ³²douʒter of Jeremye of Lobna. And he dyde euyl beforn the Lord, aftir alle thingis that the fadirs of hym hadden ³³done. And Pharao Nechao bond[b] hym in Reblatha, that is in the lond of Emath, that he 'regne not[c] in Jerusalem; and he putte vpon a multynge to the lond, in an hundreth talentis of syluer, and a talent ³⁴of gold. And Pharao Nechao ordeynde kyng Eliachym, the sone of Josias, for Josias, his fadir; and he turnede his name Joachym; forsothe Joachaz[d] he toke, ³⁵and ladde in to Egipt. Forsothe Joachym ʒaue to Pharao syluer and gold, whanne he hadde comauncide to the lond by alle ʒeeris, that it were brouʒt, aftir the heest of Pharao; and echon aftir their strengthis he askyde bothe syluer and gold, of the puple of the lond, that he ³⁶myʒte ʒeue to Pharao Nechao. Of fyue and twenty ʒeer was Joachym, whanne he hadde begunne to regnen, and elleuen ʒeer he regnede in Jerusalem; the name of his modir, Zebida, douʒter of Fadaya ³⁷of Ruma. And he dyde euyl before the Lord, aftir alle thingis that his fadirs haden done.

CAP. XXIV.

₁   In his days of steyʒide up Nabugo-donosor, kyng of Babyloyne, and Joa-chym is maad to hym seruaunt three ʒeer; and eft he rebellide aʒeynus hym. ₂And the Lord sente in to hym lytyll theuis of Caldeys, and lytyll theuis of Cyrye, and lytyl theuis of Moab, and lytil theuis of the sonys of Amon; and

fadir. Joachaz was of thre and twenti ³¹ ʒeer, whanne he bigan to regne, and he regnede thre monethis in Jerusalem; the name of his modir was Amychal, douʒter[t] of Jeremye of Lobna. And he dide yuel ³² bifor the Lord, bi alle thingis which hise fadris hadden do. And Farao Nechao ³³ boond hym[u] in Reblatha, which[v] is in the lond of Emath, that he schulde not regne in Jerusalem; and he[w] settide[x] 'peyne[y], ether[z] raunsum[a], to the lond[b], in an hundrid talentis of siluer, and in a[c] talent of gold. And Farao Nechao made kyng Eliachim, ³⁴ sone[d] of Josias, for Josias, his fadir; and he[e] turnede the name of hym[f] Joachym[g]; forsothe *Farao* took Joachaz, and ledde *hym*[h] in to Egipt. Sotheli Joachym ʒaf ³⁵ siluer and gold to Farao, whanne he hadde comaundid to the lond bi alle ʒeeris, that it schulde be brouʒt, bi[i] the comaundement[k] of Farao; and he[l] reiside of ech man bi[m] hise myʒtis[n] bothe siluer and gold, of the puple of the lond[o], that he[p] schulde ʒyue[q] to Pharao Nechao. Joachym was of fyue ³⁶ and twenti ʒeer, whanne he bigan to regne, and he regnede eleuene ʒeer in Jerusalem; the name of his modir was Zebida, douʒter[r] of Phadaia of Ruma. And he dide yuel ³⁷ bifor the Lord, bi alle thingis which hise fadris hadden do.

CAP. XXIV.

In the daies of hym[s] Nabugodonosor, ᵢ kyng of Babiloyne, stiede[t], and Joachym was maad seruaunt to hym by thre ʒeeris; and eft *Joachym*[u] rebellide aʒens hym. And the Lord[v] sente to hym[w] theuys of ₂ Caldeis, and theuys of Sirie, and theuys of Moab, and theuys of the sones of Amon; and he[x] sente hem 'in to[y] Juda, that he

---

[b] enoyntide ε *pr. m.*   [c] schulde regne ε *pr. m.*   [d] Om. ε *pr. m.*

[t] the douʒtir ι.   [u] hym *in prisoun* ι.   [v] that ι.   [w] Pharao ι.   [x] sette ι.   [y] a peyne ι.   [z] Om. c.
[a] *a fijn* ι.   [b] lond *of Juda* ι.   [c] oo ι.   [d] the sone ι.   [e] Pharao ι.   [f] Heliachym ι.   [g] to Joachym ι.
[h] Om. *plures.*   [i] aftir ι.   [k] heest ι.   [l] Joachim ι.   [m] aftir ι.   [n] power ι.   [o] lond *of Juda* ι.
[p] Om. εʟ.   [q] ʒyue it ι.   [r] the douʒtir ι.   [s] Joachim ι.   [t] stiede up in to Juda ι.   [u] he ι.   [v] Lord *God* ι.
[w] Joachim ι.   [x] the Lord ι.   [y] to εʟ.

he int sente hem in to Judam, that he
scatere hym, aftir the word of the Lord,
that he hadde spoken bi his seruauntis
3 prophetis This forsothe is done by the
word of the Lord azeyns Judam, that he
do it aweye beforne hym, for the synnes
of Manasses, and alle thingis that he
4 dyde, and for the gyltles blode that he
schedde, and he fulfillide Jerusalem with
the blode of innocentis, and for this thing
5 the Lord wolde not be plesid The remnaunt forsothe of the wordis of Joachym,
and alle thingis that he dyde, whether
thes ben not writen in the boke of the
6 wordis of days of kyngis of Juda? And
Joachym slepte with his fadris, and
Joachym, his sone, regned fore hym
7 And the kyng of Egipt addide no more,
that he schulde goon out fro his lond;
forsothe the kynge of Babyloyne hadde
taken, fro the ryuer of Egipt vnto the
flode of Eufraten, alle thingis that weren
8 of the kyng of Egipt Of tenn and eizt
zeer was Joachym, whanne he hade begunne to regnen, and three monethis he
regned in Jerusalem; name of his modir,
Naessa, douzter of Elnathan of Jerusalem
9 And he dyde euyl beforn the Lord, aftir
alle thingis that his fadir hadde done
10 In that tyme steyzide up the seruauntis
of Nabugodonosor, kyng of Babyloyne, in
to Jerusalem, and the cyte is enuyround
11 with streyngthingis And Nabugodonosor came, the kyng of Babiloyne, to
the cyte with his seruauntis, that they
12 ouercommen it And Joachym, kyng of
Juda, wente out to the kyng of Babiloyne, he, and his modir, and his
seruauntis, and his princis, and his
geldyngis, and the kyng of Babyloyne
toke hym, the eiztithe zeer of his regne
13 And he brouzte thens alle the tresoures

schulde destrie it, bi the word of the Lord,
which^z he spak bi^{zz} hise seruauntis prophetis Forsothe this was doon bi the 3
word of the Lord azens Juda, that heⁿ
schulde^b do awei it bifor him silf^c, for the
synnes of Manasses, and alle^d thingis
whiche^e he dide, and for the giltles blood 4
which^f he schied out, and he filhde Jerusalem with the blood of innocentis, and
for this thing the Lord nolde^g do mercy^h
Forsothe the residueⁱ of wordis^k of Joa- 5
chim, and alle thingis whiche he dide,
whether these ben not writun in the book
of wordis of daies of the kyngis of Juda?
And Joachym slept with hise fadris, and 6
Joakyn, his sone, regnyde for him And 7
the kyng of Egipt addide^l no more to go
out of hys lond, for the kyng of Babiloyne
hadde take alle thingis that weren the
kyngis of Egipt, fro the strond of Egipt
'til to^m the flood Eufrates Joakyn was 8
of eiztene zeer, whanne he bigan to regne,
and he regnyde thre monethis in Jerusalem; the name of his modir was Nahesta,
douztirⁿ of Helnathan of Jerusalem And 9
he^o dide yuel bifor the Lord, bi alle thingis
whiche^p hise fadir hadde do In that 10
tyme the seruauntis of Nabugodonosor,
kyng of Babiloyne, stieden^q in to^r Jerusalem, and the citee was cumpassid with
bisegyngis And Nabugodonosor, kyng of 11
Babiloyne, cam to the citee with hise seruauntis, that he schulde fizte azens it
And Joakyn, kyng of Juda, zede out 12
to the kyng of Babiloyne, he, and his
modir, and hise seruauntis, and hise
princis, and hise chaumburleyns, and
the kyng of Babiloyne resseyuede hym^s, in
the eizthe zeer of 'his rewme' And he^u 13
brouzte forth^v fro thens^w alle the tresours
of the 'hous of the Lord^x, and the tresouis
of the kingis hous, and he beet^y togider

z that 1   zz to 4   a the Lord 1   b wolde 1   c Om ΔΕΙΚΛΧΡÇ sec m   d for alle 1   e that 1
f that 1   g wolde not 1   h mercy to Juda 1   i remenaunt 1   k the wordis 1   l addide to 1   m vnto 1
n the douztir 1   o Joachim 1   P that 1   q stiede A wenten up 1   r azens 1   s Joachim 1   t the
rewme of Nabugodonosor 1   u Nabugodonosor 1   v Om 1   w Jerusalem 1   x Lordus hous 1
y betide 1

of the hous of the Lord, and the tresoures of the kingis hous; and he heew3
to gydre alle the golden vessels, that Salomon, kyng of Yrael, hade maad in the
temple of the Lord, aftir the word of the
14 Lord. And he translatide al Jerusalem,
and alle the princis, and alle the stronge
men of the hoost, tenn thousand, in to
caytyfte, and alle craftise men, and en-
closere; no thinge is laft, out take the
15 pore puple of the lond. Joachym forsothe he translatyde in to Babyloyne,
and the kyngis modir, and the kyngis
wijf, and the kyngis geldyngis; and the
domysmen of the lond he ladde in to
caytifte fro Jerusalem in to Babiloyne;
16 and alle the stronge men, seuen thousand; and craftise men and enclosers, a
thousand; alle stronge men and fi3ters;
and the kynge of Babiloyne ladde hem
17 caytyfe in to Babyloyne. And he sette
Mathathiam, his vncle, for hym; and he
18 putte on a name to hym Sedechie. The
oon and twentithe[f] 3eer of age hadde
Sedechias, whanne he hadde begunne to
regnen, and elleuen 3eer he reguede in
Jerusalem; name of his modir was Amy-
19 chal, dou3tir of Jeremye of Lobna. And
he dyde euyl byfore the Lord, aftir alle
20 thingis that Joachym hadde done. Forsothe the Lord wrathede a3einus Jerusalem and Judam, to the tyme that he
threw3 hem aweye fro his face; and
Sedechie wente aweye fro the kyng of
Babiloyne.

alle the[z] goldun vessels, whiche Salomon,
king[a] of Israel, hadde maad in the temple
of the Lord, bi the 'word of the Lord[b].
And he[c] translatide al Jerusalem[d], and 14
alle the princis, and alle the strong men
of the oost, ten thousynde, in to caitiftee,
and ech crafti man, and goldsmy3t[e]; and
no thing was left[f], outakun the[g] pore puplis[h] of the lond. Also he[hh] translatide 15
Joakyn in to Babiloyne, and the moder of
the king, 'the wyues[i] of the king, and the
chaumburleyns[j] of the king; and he ledde
the iugis[k] of the lond[kk] in to caitifte fro
Jerusalem in to Babiloyne; and alle 16
stronge[l] men, seuene thousynde; and
crafti men and goldsmy3this, a thousynde; alle stronge men and werriouris;
and the king of Babiloyne ledde hem prisoners in to Babiloyne. And he ordeyn- 17
ede Mathanye, the brother of his[m] fadir,
for hym; and puttide[n] to hym the name
Sedechie†. Sedechie hadde the[o] oon and 18 †Sedechie, is
twentithe[p] 3eer of age, whanne he bigan   interpretid the
to regne, and he regnyde eleuene 3eer in   ri3tfulnesse of
Jerusalem; the name of his modir was   the Lord. c.
Amychal, dou3ter[q] of Jeremye of Lobna.
And he[r] dide yuel bifor the Lord, bi alle 19
thingis which[s] Joachym hadde[t] do. For[n] 20
the Lord was wrooth a3ens Jerusalem,
and a3ens Juda, til[v] he caste[w] hem awey
fro his face; and Sedechie 3ede awei fro
the king of Babiloyne.

CAP. XXV.

1 It is done forsothe the nynthe 3eer
of his regne, the tenthe monethe,
the tenthe day of the monethe, Nabugodonosor, kyng of Babyloyne, came, he,
and al his hoost, in to Jerusalem; and

CAP. XXV.

Forsothe it was don in the nynthe 3eer 1
of his[ww] rewme[x], in the tenthe moneth, in
the tenthe dai of the moneth, Nabugodonosor, kyng of Babiloyne, cam, he, and al
his oost, in to Jerusalem; and thei cum-

[f] twenti A.

z Om. EL.   a the king 1.   b Lordis word 1.   c Nabugodonosor 1.   d Israel plures.   e goldsmy3t, also 1.
f left vntranslatid 1.   g Om. 1.   h peple 1.   hh Nabugodonosor 1.   i and the wijf s.   j children s.
k thingis EL.   kk lond of Juda 1.   l the stronge 1.   m Joachym 1.   n he puttide 1.   o Om. 1.   P twenti 1.
q the dou3ter 1.   r Sedechie 1.   s that 1.   t his fadir hadde 1.   u Forsothe 1.   v til that 1.   w castide 1.
ww the 1.   x rewme of Sedechie 1.

thei enuyrounden it, and maden up in
2 his enuyroun streyngthingis And the
cyte is closede, and palid, vnto the elle-
3 uenthe ʒeer of kyng Sedechie, the nynthe
day of the monethe, and hungir wexe
grete in the cyte, and ther was not brede
4 to the puple of the lond And the cyte
is to-broken, and alle men fiʒters flowen
the nyʒt by the weue of the ʒate, that is
bytwene the double wall, at the spring-
ynge of the kyng; forsothe Caldeis be-
segyden in enuyroun the cyte And so
Sedechias fleiʒ by the weye that ledith
5 to the wijld feeldis of wyldirnesse, and
the hoost of Caldeis pursueden the kyng,
and he cauʒte hym in the pleyn of Jericho; and alle the fiʒters, that weren with
hym, ben scaterd, and forsoken hym
6 Thanne they ladden the taken kyng to
the kyng of Babyloyne, in Reblatha, the
7 whiche spake with[g] hym dome The
sonys forsothe of Sedechie he slewʒ before hym, and his eʒen he putte out, and
boond hym with cheynys and brouʒte
8 hym in to Babyloyne The fyfthe moneth, the seuenth day of the moneth, it
is the nyntenthe ʒeer of the kyng of
Babiloyne, came Nabusardam, prince of
the hoost, the seruaunt of the kyng of
9 Babyloyne, in to Jerusalem, and brende
up the hous of the Lord, and the hous of
the kyng, and the housis of Jerusalem,
10 and eche hous he brende with fijre, and
the wallis of Jerusalem in enuyroun de-
struyede al the hoost of Caldeys, that
11 was with the prince[h] of knyʒtis The
tother forsothe partye of the puple, that
laft in the cyte, and the thorʒ fleers, that
ouerflowen to the kyng of Babiloyn, and
the laft comoun, Nabusardan, prince of
12 knyʒthode, translatyde, and of the pore
men of the lond he laft wyne[i] makers,

passiden it, and bildiden 'stronge thingis[y]
in the cumpass[z] therof And the citee[2]
was closid, and cumpassid, 'til to[a] the[b]
eleuenthe ʒeer of king Sedechie[c], in the[3]
nynthe day of the monethe, and hungur
'hadde maistrie[d] in the citee, and 'breed
was not[e] to the[ee] puple of the lond And[4]
the citee was brokun, and alle men werriours fledden in the niʒt bi the weie of
the[ee] ʒate, which[f] is bitwixe the double
wal, to[g] the gardyn of the kyng; sotheli
Caldeis[h] bisegiden the citee 'bi cumpas[i]
Therfor Sedechie fledde[k] bi the weie that
ledith to the feeldi placis of the wildirnesse, and the oost of Caldeis pursuede[5]
the king, and it[l] took[m] him in the pleyn
of Jerico : and alle the werriours, that
weren with him[n], weren scaterid[o], and
leften him Therfor thei ledden the king[6]
takun to the king of Babiloyne, in to Reblatha, which[p] spak dom with him[q], 'that
is, with Sedechie[r] Sotheli he killide the[7]
sones of Sedechie bifor him, and puttide[s]
out his iʒen, and boond[t] him with chaynes,
and ledde him[u] in to Babiloyne In the[8]
fifthe monethe, in the seuenthe dai of the
monethe, thilke is the nyntenthe ʒeer of
the king of Babiloyne, Nabuzardan, prince
of the oost, seruaunt of the king of Babiloyne, cam in to Jerusalem; and he brente[9]
the hows of the Lord, and the hows of the
king, and the housis of Jerusalem, and he
brente bi fier ech hows[v]; and al the oost[10]
of Caldeis, that was with the prince of
knyʒtis, distriede the wallis of Jerusalem
'in cumpas[w] Forsothe Nabuzardan, prince[11]
of the chyyualrie, translatide the tother
part of the puple, that dwellide in the
citee[x], and the fleeris, that hadden fled
ouer to the king of Babiloyne, and the
residue[v] comyn puple, and he lefte of the[12]
pore men of the lond vyntilieris, and erthe

　　　g to *ABFH*　h princis *A*　i viyn *A*

y strengthingis *BIKLMPXb*　z cumpas *aboute I*　a vnto I　b Om[r] I　c Ezechie I　d wexide ouer
myʒt I　e ther was not bred I　ee Om *BL*　f that I　g towardo I　h the Caldeis I　i in cumpas *plures* aboute I　k fledde *fro Jerusalem* I　l Om *A pr m* I　m token I　n Sedechie I　o scaterid
abrood I　p the which I　q Sedechie I　r Om I　s he putte I　t he boond I　u Om *plures*　v hows
therof I　w aboute I　x citee *of Jerusalem* I　y remenaunt *BI* P

¹³ and erthtiliers Forsothe the brasen pylers, that weren in the temple of the
Lord, and the feet, and the biasen se,
that was in the hous of the Lord, Caldeis
breeken to gydre; and al the biasse thei
¹⁴ beeren ouei in to Babiloyne And brasen
pottis, trowels, and fleschokis, and cuppis,
and morters, and alle the brasen[h] vessels,
in whiche thei mynystriden, thei token,
¹⁵ also and encenseeris, and violis The
whiche forsothe weren golden, and
whiche sylueren, toke the prince of the
¹⁶ knyзthod, that is, two pylers, oon se,
and the feet, that Salomon hade maad
in to the temple of the Lord, and ther
was not peys of the biasse of alle the
¹⁷ vessels Tenn and eiзt cubitis of heiзt
hadde oon pyler, and a brasen heued
couerynge vpon hym of heyзt of thie
cubitis, and a calle, and poumgarnetis
vpon the heued couerynge of the pylei,
all biasen, and lijc honourynge hadde
¹⁸ the secound pylei Forsothe the[l] prince
of the knyзthode toke Sarayam, the first
pieste, and Sophonyam, the secound
¹⁹ preste, and the thre porters, and oon
geldynge of the cyte, that was prefect
vpon the fiзtynge men, and iyue men of
hem that stoden before the kyng, the
whiche he foond in the cyte, and Sophei, the prince of the hoost, that prouede
the newe knyзtis of the puple of the lond,
and sixe men of the comoun, that weren
²⁰ founden in the cyte, the whiche Nabusardan, prince of the knyзthode, takynge
ladde to the kyng of Babyloyne, in Reb-
²¹ latha And the kyng of Babiloyne smote
hem, and slewз hem in Reblatha, in the
lond of Emath and Juda is tianslatyd
²² fro his lond To the puple forsothe
that was laft in the lond of Juda, the
whiche Nabugodonosoi, kyng of Baby-

tiheris Sotheli Caldeis[z] braken the bra-¹³
sun pilers, that weren in the temple, and
the foundementis, and the see of bras,
that was in the hous of the Loid, and
thei tianslatiden[a] al the metal in to Babiloyne And thei token the pottis of bras,¹⁴
and trulhs, and fleisch hokis, and cuppis,
and morteris, and alle brasun vessels, in
whiche thei[b] mynystriden[c], also[d] and cen-¹⁵
seris[e], and violis The prince of the chyualiie took tho[f] that weien of gold, and
tho that weren of siluei, that is[g], twei pi-¹⁶
leris, o see, and the foundementis[h], whiche
king Salomon hadde maad 'in to' the temple of the Lord; and[k] no weiзte[l] was[m] of
metal of alle the vessels O piler hadde¹⁷
eiзten cubitis of hiзte, and a biasun pomel
on[n] it of the heiзte of thre cubitis, and a
weik lijk a net, and pomgarnadis on[n] the
pomel of the piler, alle thingis of bias;
and the secounde pilei hadde[o] lijk ournyng Also the prince of the[p] chyualiie¹⁸
took Saraie, the firste preest, and Sophony,
the secunde prest, and thre poiteris, and¹⁹
oon[q] onest seruaunt of the citee, that was
a[r] souereyn ouer men weriiours, and fyue
men 'of hem[s] that stoden bifoi the king,
whiche he[t] foond in the citee[u], and *he
took* Sophei, the[v] prince of the oost[w], that
preuide зonge knyзtis, '*ethei men able to
batel*', of the puple of the lond, and sixe
men of the comyns, that weien foundyn
in the citee, whiche[a] Nabuzardan, prince²⁰
of the chyualiie, took, and ledde to the
king of Babiloyne, in to Reblatha And²¹
the kyng of Babiloyne smoot hem, and
kilhde hem in Reblatha, in the lond of
Emath, and Juda was tianslatid fio his
lond Sotheli he[b] made souereyn[c] Godolie,²²
sone[d] of Aicham, sone[d] of Saphan, to[e] the
puple that was left in the lond of Juda,
whiɔh[f] puple Nabugodonosor, king of Ba-

---

k goldene E pr m   l of the B

---

z men of Caldei i   a baren ouer i   b men i   c mynystriden *in the temple* i   d Om i   e censeris
also i   f tho thingis i   g is *to* nite i   h foundementis oi basis i   i to A see in b pr m   k and
ther was i   l cerleyn weiзte i   m Om i   n upon i   o hadde *also* i   p Om s   q an i
r Om A pr m EL   s Om. R   t Nabuzardan i   u citee *of Jerusalem* i   v Om i   w oost *of Sedechie* i
з Om i   a the whiche i   b Nabugodonosor i.   c Om i   d the sone i   e souereyn to i   f the
which i

loyne, hadde laft, he made rewler Godo-
lyam, the sone of Aycham, the sone of
23 Safan The whiche thingis whanne alle
the duykis of kny3tis, they, and alle the
men that weren with hem haden herd,
that is, that the kyng of Babyloyne
hadde ordeynd Godolie, camen to Godolie, in^m Maspha, Ismael, the sone of Nathanye, and Johannan, the sone of Charee,
and Saraye the sone of Tenameth Ne-
thophathite, and Jechonias, the sone of
Mechati, thei, and Machath, and the fe-
24 lawis of hem And Godolias swore to
hem, and to the felawis of hem, seyinge,
Wylle 3e not dreden to seruen to the Caldeis, dwellith in the lond, and seiuith to
the kyng of Babiloyne, and wele it schal
25 be to 3ou It is done forsothe in the
seuenth moneth, came Ismael, the sone of
Nathanye, the sone of Elisama, of the
kyngis seed, and ten men with hym, and
smyten Godolie, the whiche is deed, bot
and the Jewis and the Caldeis, that weren
26 with him in Maspha. And al the puple
rijsynge to gydre fro litil vnto mychil,
and the princis of kny3tis, camen in to
27 Egipt, dreedynge the Caldeis It is done
thanne in the seuen and thrittithe 3eer of
the transmygracioun of Joachym, kyng
of Jude, the twelfthe monethe, the seuen
and twentithe day of the monethe, Euil-
meredoch, kyng of Babiloyne, the 3eer
that he beganne to regnen, rerede up the
heued of Joachym, kyng of Juda, fro
28 prisone, and he spac to hym benyngly,
and he putte his trone vpon the trone of
kyngis, that weren with hym in Babi-
29 loyne And he chaungide his clothis,
that he hadde in prisoun; and he eet
breed euermore in his si3t, alle days of
30 his lyfe 3eer fruyt forsothe he ordeynde
to hym withoute cesynge, the whiche

biloyne, hadde left8 And whanne alle 23
the duykis of kny3tis^h hadde herd these
thingis, thei^i, and the men that weren
with hem, that is^k, that the king of Babiloyne hadde ordeyned Godolie^l, thei camen^m
'to Godolie^n, in^nn Maspha, Ismael, sone^o of
Nathanye, and Johannan, sone^o of Charee,
and Saraie, sone^o of Thenameth of Necho-
phat, and Jeconye, sone^o of Machati, thei,
and Machat, and^p the felowis of hem.
And Godolie swoor to hem, and to the 24
felowis of hem, and seide, Nyle 3e drede
to serue the^q Caldeis, dwelle 3e in the
lond, and serue 3e^r the king of Babiloyne,
and it schal be wel to 3ou Forsothe it 25
was don in the seuenthe monethe, 'that is,
sithen^s Godolie was maad souereyn^t, Hismael, the sone of Nathanye, sone^u of Elysama, of the 'kyngis seed^v, cam, and ten
men with hym, and thei smytiden^w Godolie, which^x diede, but also thei smytiden^v
Jewis and Caldeis, that weren with hym^x
in Maspha And al the puple roos fro 26,
litil^a 'til to^b greet^c, and the prynces of
kny3tis, and camen^d in to Egipt, and
dredden Caldeis^e Therfor it was doon 27
in^ee the seuenthe^f and thrittithe 3eer of
transmigracioun^g, 'ether passyng oure^h, of
Joakyn, kyng of Juda, in the tweluethe
monethe, in the seuene and twentithe dai
of the monethe, Euylmeradach, kyng of
Babiloyne, in the 3eer in which he bigan
to regne, reiside^i the heed of Joakyn, kyng
of Juda, fro prisoun, and spak to hym 28
benygneli, and he settide^k the trone of
Joakyn aboue the trone of kyngis, that
weren with hym in Babilonye And he^l 29
chaungide 'hise clothis^m, whiche^n he hadde
in prisoun, and he eet breed euer in the
si3t of Euylmeradach, in alle the daies of
his lijf Also Euylmeradach ordeynede 30
sustenaunce 'to hym^o with out ceessyng,

m and B

g left in Juda 1 h kny3tis of Sedechie 1 i Om 1 k is to mite 1 l Godolie to be souereyn in Juda 1
m camen togidere 1 n Om 1 nn into K o the sone 1 P Om 1 q to FILP r 3e to 1K s that G
't after the souereyntee of Godolie 1 u the sone 1 v seed of king Sedechie 1 w smoten 1 smeten ELP
x that 1 y smyten 1 smetin EI P z Godolie 1 a the litil 1 b vnto 1 c the greet 1 d thei camen
or fledden 1 e the Caldeis 1 ee Om K f senen EIALS g the transmigracioun 1 h Om 1 i ne
reiside 1 k sette 1 l Euylmeradach 1 m the clothis of Joachin 1. n that 1 o for Joachin 1

and was ȝouen to hym of the kyng by
eche days, alle the days of his lijf.

Here eendith the fourthe boke of
Kingus, and bigynneth the prolog in the
first boke of Paralipomenon[n]

which[p] sustenaunce also was ȝouun of the
kyng to hym bi alle daies, and[q] in alle
the daies of his lijf.   .

Here endith the fourthe book of
Kingis; and here bigynneth the firste
book of Paralipomenon, that is, of wordis
of daies[r]

---

[n] *Here endith the fourth book of Kyngis, and now bigynneth the proloog of twey bookis of Paralipomenon* A *Explicit quartus liber Regum* E *Here endith the fourt bok Kyngis* F No final rubric in CII

[p] the which I   [q] Om EI   [r] *Here endith the fourthe book of Kingis, and here bigynneth the firste book of Paralipomynon* CN *Here endith the fourthe book of Kyngis, and begynneth a protog on the firste bok of Paulipominon* GM *Heere eendith the fourthe book of Kinges, se now the prolog bifore Paralipomenon.* K *Here endith the fourthe book of Kyngis, and here bigynneth the prolog on the firste book of Paralipomenon* O *Heere eendith the fourthe book of Kynges, and bigynneth the firste of Parlipominon* R *Here eendith the III book of Kingis, and biginneth the Paralipomynon* S *Here endith the fourthe boot of Kingis, and bigynneth the boot of the firste Paralipomynon* X *Here eendith the fourthe book of Kingis, and heere bigynneth the seeunde book of Paralipomenon* ҫ No final rubric in ELPQVb

I. PARALIPOMENON.

[*Prologue on the First book of Paralipomenon*[a].]

THIS book of Paralipomenon, the firste, bigynneth at Adam, rehersynge the riȝt lyne of generacioun in to Abraham, and alle the sones of Abraham, and the sones of hem, touchinge schortli of Saul king, and afterward of Dauith; rehersinge many thingis whiche ben not writen in the book of Kingis before, til to the regne of kyng Salomon. *Here endith the prologe, and here bigynneth the firste book of Paralipomenon.*

The Prolog in the first boke of Paralipomenon[a].

ȜIF the makynge of the seuenty remenours abyde styll pure, and as it is turned of hem in to Greek, my Chromati, holiest and wysest of byschopis, in veyn thou schuldist bydden me that I translate to thee Ebreu volymes in Latyn word. Forsothe that hath ocupied onys the eris of men, and hath streynthid the feith of the waxynge chirche, riȝtwijs was also with oure sylence to be apreued. Nowe forsothe whan dyuerse saumplers ben born for the dyuersite of regyouns, and thilk[b] olde germeyn translacyoun is corrupt and defoulid, thou wenyst[c] of oure dome to ben, outher to schewen of manye[d] whiche be verrey, outher[e] a new werk to maken in old werk, the Jewis forsothe scornynge, that, as it is seid, to fytche to gyder eeȝen[f] of curluris[g]. Alisaunder and Egipt in their seuenty preysen auctour Eusichy; Constantynople vnto Antioche apreuith the saumpleris of martir Lucyan; the mene prouynces by-

[*Prologue on the first book of Paralipomenon*[b].]

IFF the makynge of the seuenti interpretours dwelle stille cleene, and as it is turned of hem in to Greek, than thi silf, my Cromat, hoolyeste and wysest of bisschopis, shuldest in veyn bidde me, that I shulde translate to thee Ebrew volyms in to Latyn word. For it was riȝtwise, that sich thing that hath occupied ones the eeris of men, and hath strengthid the feith of the wexynge chirche, shulde be appreued with oure silence. Now forsothe sith dyuerse saumpleris ben born aboute for diuersite of regions, and sith thilke old translacioun of german is corrupt and defoulid, thou trowist that it be of oure owne doom, ethir to schewe of many draweris of hooly writ which is verie and trewe, eithir to make a newe werk on the oolde werk, and thouȝ the Jewis scorne, and, as me semeth, hem to ficche to gideris the iȝen of kurlewis. Alisaundre and Egipt among her seuenti translatours preisen Eusichic, her auctour;

---

[a] *Prologus Paralipomenon.* c. *Here 'bigynneth the prolog on Paralipomynon.* E. *Here bigynneth the prolong of Paralipomenon.* F. *Prologus.* II. [b] that K. [c] wentist II. [d] manye workis A. [e] or K. [f] aȝen A. eȝȝn E. [g] crowis E pr. m.

[a] This prologue is from M. [b] This prologue is from O.

twene[h] thes reden Palestynes bokis, the
whiche out tranayld of Origene, Eusebe
and Pamphilie pupplischeden, and al the
world bytwene[i] hem selue in this thre
maner dyuersite fiȝtith[k] to gyder   And
certis Origenes not oonly exsaumplis[l]
maad in oon of foure makyngis, 'forn
aȝeyn[m] alle the wordis discryuynge, that
the oon discordynge, the tothei betwene[n]
hem silf acordynge, anoon be vndernomyn, bot, that is of more hardynesse,
in the makynge of the seuenty he mengide
the makynge of Theodocioun, that is,
markynge that weren to lytyl with
sygnys of a sterre, and that weren seen
ouermych leid to, with[o] lityl ȝerdis. Ȝif
thanne to othei it was leful not to holden
that oons thei hadden taken; and aftir
seuenty lytyll sellis, the whiche with
outen auctour of the comoun ben boostid,
thei[p] opneden alle the sellis, that forsothe
in the chirche is rad that the seuenty
knewyn not, why[q] me taken not my
Latyn men, the whiche han maad so the
newe with[r] the olde makynge vndc-
fouhd, that[s] my traueyl I preue with the[t]
Ebrewis, and, that is more than these,
with the Apostlis auctours   I wrote not
ȝore a boke of the best maner of remenynge[u], schewynge[v] tho thingis of the
euangely[w], Fro Egipt I haue clepide[x] myn
sone, and, That Naȝare he schal be clepid[y],
and, Thei schul seen in whome thei hau
pungid; and that of the apostle, That eeȝe
hath not seen, ne eie hath herde, ne in to the
heit of man hath steyȝide up, the whiche
God hath maad redye before to the
louynge hym; and other liȝe to thes, in
the bokis of Ebrewis to ben founden
Certis the apostlis and the euaungehstis
hadden known the seuenty remenours,
and whenns that to hem to seyn tho
thingis that in the seuenty ben not had ?
Crist, oure God, is makei of eithei testament, in[z] euangelie aftir Joon, Who[a]
leuith[b], he seith[c], in me, as seith the

Constantynoble vnto Antioche appreueth
the sampleris of martir Lucian; the
meene pronencis bytwene these reden Pa-
lestinys bookes, whiche Eusebie and Pamphilie puplichiden, whanne thei hadden
traueyld it out of Origene, and al the
world stryuen to gideres withynne hem
silf in thes thie manere of dyuersitees
And certis Origene not oonly made to
gideres the ensamplis of foure drawyngis
out of hooly wiit, in to oon discriuynge
alle the wordes of the cuntrey, so that
oon discordynge be vndurnome anoon of
the othir bookis acordynge to gyderes,
but that is of more hardynesse, in the
makynge of seuenty translatouris he medlide the markynge of Theodocion, that is
to wite, markynge with the signes of a
sterre siche thingis that weren to litle, and
siche thingis that weren addid to of
superfluyte, he markyde with litil ȝerdis,
eithir sygnes of an arowe   Therfor if it
was leefful to othir not to holden that thei
hadden onys toke, and aftir the seuenty
selles, which of the selles, which of the
comynte ben bostid to be, with out auctor
thei openyde alle the selles, also that that
seuenty interpretours knowen not is red
in chirches; whi thanne my Latyn men
accepten not me, sithen I haue maad the
newe drawynge with the olde makyng
vndefoulid, that I preue my trauel with
the Ebrewis, and also with the Apostlis,
auctoritees that ben more worthi than
thei   I wioot a book not ful longe ago,
mye beste manere of drawyng out of
hooly wiit, shewynge thes tixtis of the
gospel folewynge to be in the bookes of
Ebrewes, as this tixt, Fio Egipt I haue
clepid my sone, and also this tixt, He
shal be clepid Nazaiey; and also the
tixt, Thei shulen se into whom thei han
thouȝ persed, also this tixt of the pistle,
That ȝe hath not seen, ne eere herd, ne it
hath not stied vp in to the herte of men,
the whiche God hath maad redy byfore to

---

[h] butwixe A   [i] bitwixe AA   [k] fiȝten K   [l] ensaumphs K   [m] for aȝeyn A   fro the regiown E pr m
[n] bitwixe K   [o] Om K   [p] that K   [q] with K   [r] that K   [s] with A   [t] Om A   [u] the remenyng A
[v] the shewinge K   [w] aungel A   [x] cald A   [y] called A   [z] in the EK   [a] whose K   [b] bileuith A   [c] he
seith K

scripture, flodis d of his wombe schul flowen 'quyke waters e Forsothe it is writen, that the Saueoure witnessith to ben wiiten ; wheie it is wiiten, the scuenty han not ; the hyd thingis know- ith not the chirche To the Ebrewis than it is to turnen a3eyn, wherof f and the Lord spekith, and the disciplis befoin taken exsaumplis Thes thingis bi pese of olde men I speke, and to my bacbyters oonly I answei, the whiche 'gnawen me with 'a dogge s tothe in opyn bacbytynge, reed- ynge in corners, i and h acusatours and defendours, whann in other men they aprenen that in me thei repreuen , as vertue and vice ben not in the thingis, bot with the autour ben chaungid Bot I haue had mynde the makyng of the seuenty translatours, sumtyme fro Greke amendid, me to haue 3euen to 3oure l, and not enmye of hem owyn to ben eymed, whome in the couent of bietheren euer- more I schal expownen And that De- bregemyn, that is, the wordis of days, I haue remened, therfore I haue don that I my3te hryng k to ri3t the insolible lettyngis and the wodis l of namys, the whiche, thor3 vice of writers, ben con- foundid, and m the dulnes of wittis, more opynly, and by distyncciouns of verse, to me my silf and to my wrytynge n aftir Hismenyum o, 3if eris of other ben dowmbe

hem that louen him And othir textes that ben li3k these, ben fonden in the book of Ebrewis Certis the apostlis and the euangelistis hadden knowe the seuenti interpretouis, and fro whennus come that grace to hem to seie tho thingis that ben not had among the seuenti interpretours ? Crist, our God, maker of euere eithu testament, in the gospel aftir Joones writynge 'seith thus, Who euere byleueth in me, as seith hooly scripturis floodis of a quyk watir schulen folewe of his wombe. Forsothe that thing that oure Sauyour witnessith to be write, it is sikirliche writen , but the seuenti interpretouis han no mencioun 'where it is writun , the chirche knowith not hid thingis Therfor it is to turne a3en to Ebrews, wher of oure Lord spekith, and the disciplis bifoi takun ensaumplis I speke thes thingis with the pees of olde men, and I answere oonly to my bacbiteis, which gnawen me with a doggi tooth, bagbitynge me in open, red- ynge the same in corneris, and also ac- cusours and defenderis thei ben, sithen thei appiouen in othir men that thei re- preuen in me ; as thou3 vertues and vyces ben not in thingis, but ben chaungid with the auctoure Feithermore I have remem- brid me, that I haue 3oue to 3oure scrip- turis the makynge of the seuenty transla- ture, that was suntyme amendid fro Greek, and therfor I ou3te not to be gessid an enemy of hem, which euere more I shal expowne to the couent of briththren And that book that is now clepid Debia- yamyn, that is, the wordis of dayes, I haue translatid , therfor I haue doon it that I my3te brynge to ri3t thilke betyngis, that ben tul hard to be opened, and to opene the woidis of names, the which thour3 vice of writeris ben confoundid, and more opynly by dulnesse of wittis, and by destyncciouns of uerse, to my silf and to my writynge aftir Hismenyum, thou3 the eeris of other inen be doumb

---

d flodis of quyk watris A   c Om A.   f wherfore II   g doggis A   h the same both A the same and cE see m FIIK that is and E pr m   i 3ou A   k bryngynge D   l wordis D   m in K,   n writingis K   o his meenyng K

An other Prolog[p].

The boke of Paralipomenon, that[q] is, the breggyng of the Olde Testament, siche and so myche is[r], that with outen it who so wyll by pride sechen to hym the kunnynge of scriptures, scorne he hym silf Forsothe by alle the[s] namys and iuncturis of wordis, and the laft stories in the bokis of Kyngis ben touchid, and vnowmbrable questiouns of the euaungelies[t] ben soyled.

Here eendith the prolog in the first boke of Paralipomenon, and bygynneth the first boke of Paralipomenon[u]

Another Prolog on the Firste book of Paralipomenon

The book of Paralipomenon, that is, the bregging of the Olde Testament, is such and so moche, that withouten it who so wole bi pride seche to him the kunnyng of scripturis, scorne he him silf. Forsothe bi alle the namys of ioynturis of wordis, and the laste stories ben touchid in the bookis of Kingis, and vnnoumbrable questiouns of the euangelies ben soylid

Here enden the prologis, and begynneth the book

Here bigynneth the bok of Paralipomenon[v].

CAP I

1
2 Adam, Seth, Enos, Chaynan, Malaleel,
3 Jared, Enoch, Matusale, Lameth, Noe,
4
5 Sem, Cham, and Japheth. The sones of Japheth, Gomor, Magday, Magog, and
6 Jauan, Tubal, Mosoch, and Tyras. Bot the sones of Gomer, Ascenez, and Ry-
7 phat, and Togorma The sones forsothe of Jauan, Helisa, and Tharsis, Cethym,
8 and Dodonym The sonys of Cham, Chus, and Mesraym, Phuth, and Cha-
9 naan The sonys forsothe of Chus, Saba, and Euila, Sabatha, and Regma, and Sabathaca Bot the sonys of Regma; Saba,

Here bigynneth the firste book of Paralipominon, that is, of words of daies[b].

CAP I.

1
2 Adam gendride[c] Seth; Enos[d], Chaynan[e], Malaleel[ee], Jared[f], Enoch[g], Matus-
sale[h], Lameth[i]; Noe[k] gendride[l] Sem,
4 Cham, and Japhet The sones of Japhat
5 weren Gomer, Magog, Magdai, and[m] Jauan, Tubal, Mosoch, and Tiras Forsothe
6 the sones of Gomer weren Asceneth, and[n]
Riphat, and Thogorma Sotheli[o] the sones
7 of Jauan weren Helisa, and Tharsis, Cethym, and Dodanym The sones of Cham
8 weren Chus, and[p] Mesraym, Phuth, and
Chanaan Sotheli[q] the sones of Chus weren
9 Saba, and Euila, Sabatha, and Regma, and

---

[p]Om c[b] H K Prologus [A] [q]Om K [r]it is [k] [s]Om. K [t]euangelistis K [u]Here eendith the proloog of Parra-lypomenon, and now bigynneth the first book [A] Here endeth the prologis, and bigynneth the firste Parali-pomynon [b] Here eendeth the prolog, se now the firste book of Paralipomenon K No final rubric in c[r] [u] [v]From [r] No initial rubric in [A] B C K H

[b]From E sec m L[r]b No initial rubric in the other Mss [c]bignat 1 [d]and Seth, Enos 1 [e]and Enos, Chaynan 1 [ee]and Caynan, Malaleel 1 [f]and Malaleel, Jared 1 [g]and Jared bignat Enoch 1 [h]and Enok Matusale 1 [i]and Matusale, Lameth 1 [k]and Lameth Noe, and Noe 1 [l]Om 1 [m]Om 1 [n]Om 1 [o]And is [p]Om 1 [q]And is

10 and Adan. Chus forsothe gat Nemroth; this byganne to ben myȝty in the lond. 11 Mesraym forsothe gat Ludym, and Ana-12 nym, and Labaym, and Nepthoym, Fe-trusym forsothe, and Chasluym, of the whiche wenten oute Phylisteis and Cap-13 thurym. Chanaan forsothe gat Sydon, 14 his first goten, and Ethee, Jebusee[b] for-15 sothe, and Amorre, and Jergese, Euee, 16 and Arache, and Cyne, Aradyum for-17 sothe, and Samarie, and Amathe. The sonys of Sem; Elam, and Assur, and Ar-faxath, and Luth, and Aram. The sonys forsothe of Aram; Hus, and Hul, and 18 Gothor, and Mosoch. Arfaxath forsothe gate Sale; the whiche and he gat Heber. 19 Forsothe to Heber ben born two sonys; name to the toon Phaleg, for in his days the erth is deuydid; and the name of his 20 brother Jectan. Jectan forsothe gat Hel-modad, and Salech, and Azelmod, and 21 Jare, Adoram forsothe, and Vsal, and 22 Deda, Hebal, and Ameth, and Abymael, 23 and Saba, also and Oofer, and Euila, and Jobab; alle thes the sonys of Jectan. 24,25 Sem, Arfaxath, Sale, Heber, Phalech, 26 Ragan, Seruth, Nachor, Thare, Abram; 27,28 this forsothe is Abraham. The sonys of 29 Abraham; Ysaac and Ysmael. And thes the generaciouns of hem; the first goten of Ismael Nabaioth, and Cedar, and Ab-30 dehel, and Mapsam, and Masma, and Duma, and Massa, Adad, and Thema, 31 Jahur, Naphis, Cedma; thes ben the 32 sonys of Ysmael. The sonys forsothe of Cethure, the secoundarie wijf of Abra-ham, 'the whiche[c] sche gat; Zamram, Jer-san, Madan, Madian, Jesboch, Sue. For-sothe the sones of Jersan; Saba, and Da-dan. The sones forsothe of Dadan; Assu-

Sabathaca. Forsothe[r] the sones of Regma weren Saba, and Dadan. Sotheli[s] Chus 10 gendride[t] Nemroth; this *Nemroth* bigan to be myȝti in erthe. Forsothe[u] Mes-11 raym gendride[v] Ludym, and Ananyn, and Labaym, and Neptoym, and Phetrusym,12 and Casluym, of whiche[w] the Philisteis and Capthureis ȝeden out[x]. Sotheli[y] Cha-13 naan gendride[z] Sidon his first gendrid[a] sone, and Ethei, and Jebusei, and Am-14 morrei, and Gergesei, and Euei, and Ara-15 chei, and Synei, and Aradye, and Sama-16 thei, and Emathei. The sones of Sem 17 weren Elam, and Assur, and Arphaxat, and Luth, and Aram. Forsothe[b] the sones of Aram weren Hus, and Hul, and Go-thor, and Mosoch. Forsothe[c] Arphaxat 18 gendride[d] Sale; which hym silf gendride Heber. Sotheli[e] to Heber weren borun 19 twei sones; name[ee] of[f] oon *was* Phaleg, for the lond was departid in hise daies; and the name of his brother *was* Jectan. For-20 sothe[g] Jectan gendride[h] Elmodad, and Sa-lech, and Aselmod, and Jare, and Adoram, 21 and Vzal, and Deda, Hebal, and Ameth, 22 and Abymael, and Saba, also and Ophir, 23 and Euila, and Jobab; alle these *weren* the sones of Jectan. Sem[i], Arphaxat[k], 24 Sale[l], Heber[m], Phalech[n], Ragau[o], Seruth[p], 25,26 Nachor[q], Thare[r], Abram; forsothe[s] this 27 is Abraham[ss]. The sones of Abraham 28 weren Isaac and Ismael. And these[t] the[u] 29 generaciouns of hem; the firste gendrid[v] of Ismael Nabioth[w], and[x] Cedar, and Ab-dahel, and Mapsam, and Masma, and 30 Duma, and Massa, Adad[xx], and Themar, Jahur, Naphis, Cedma[y]; these ben the 31 sones of Ismael. Forsothe[x] the[a] sones of 32 Cethure[b], secoundarie[c] wijf of Abraham, whiche[d] sche gendride[e], *weren* Zamram,

---

[b] and Jebusee ɪ.   [c] that *c pr. m.*

[r] And ɪs. [s] And ɪs. [t] bigaat ɪ. [u] And ɪs. [v] bigaat ɪ. [w] the whiche *sones* ɪ. [x] out *or camen* ɪ. out *or weren gendride* s. [y] And ɪs. [z] bigaat ɪ. [a] goten ɪ. [b] And ɪs. [c] And ɪs. [d] bigaat ɪ. [e] And ɪs. [ee] the name ɪ0. [f] to *plures.* to the ɢ. [g] And ɪs. [h] gaat ɪ. [i] And Sem gat Arphaxat ɪ. and Sem gendride Arphaxat s. [k] and Arphaxat, Sale ɪs. [l] and Sale, Heber ɪs. [m] and Heber, Phalech ɪs. [n] and Phalech, Ragau ɪs. [o] and Ragau, Seruth ɪs. [p] and Seruth, Nachor ɪs. [q] and Nachor, Thare ɪs. [r] and Thare ɪs. [s] Om. ɪs. [ss] Abraham, *the greet patriark* s. [t] these ben ᴅᴏɪʀs. 'these *weren* x. [u] Om. c. [v] goten ɪ. [w] was Nabioth ɪs. [x] and thanne ɪ. and after Nabioth he gendride Cedar s. [xx] and Adad s. [y] and Cedma ɪs. [z] And ɪs. [a] Om. c. [b] the sones of Cethure ɪ. [c] the secoundarie ɪs. [d] the whiche ɪ. [e] gendride *or conceyuyde* ɪ.

33 ym, and Latusym, and Laomym. The
sonys forsothe of Madian; Epha, Oter,
Etnoch, and Abida, and Eldaa. Alle thes
34 the sons of Cethure. Abraham forsothe
gat Ysaac, whos sones weren Esau and
35 Yrael The sones of Esau, Eliphath,
Rahuel, Seir[c], Jaus, Zelam, and Chore
36 The sonys of Eliphath; Theman, Omer,
Sephi, Gethem, Genez, Cenez, Thanna,
37 Amalech The sones of Rahuel, Naab,
38 Gazera, Samma, Masa The sonys of
Seir, Lothan, Sobal, Zebeon, Ana, Dy-
39 son, Eser, Dysan The sones of Lothan;
Horry, Huma; the syster forsothe of
40 Lothan was Thanna The sones of Sobal, Alian, and Manaath, and Ebal, and
Cephi, and Onam The sones of Sebeon;
Aia, and Ana The sones of Ana; Dy-
41 son, and Oolibama The sonys of Dyson;
Amaram, and Hesebam, and Lecram, and
42 Caram The sonys of Eser; Balaam, and
Jaban, and Jasan The sones of Dysan;
43 Hus, and Aram Thes ben the kyngis
that comaundiden in the lond of Edom,
before that there was kyng vpon the
sones of Yrael Baale, the sone of Beor,
44 and the name of his cytee Denaba Forsothe Bale is deed; and for hym regned
45 Joab, the sone of Zare, of Bosra And
whanne Joab was deed, regned for hym
46 Husam of the lond of Themanyas Forsothe Husam dyed; and for hym regned
Adad, the sone of Badad, that smote
Madyan in the lond of Moab; and the
47 name of his cyte Abyud And whan
Adad was deed, regned for hym Semela
48 of Maseracha Bot and Semela died, and
for hym regned Saul of Robooth, the
49 whiche bisides Amnem is sett Forsothe
Saul deed[d], regned[e] for hym Balanan the
50 sone of Achobor Bot and this dyed, and
for hym regnede Adad, of whos cyte the
name was Phou; and his wijf is clepid

Jersan, Madan, Madian, Jelboe, Sue[f] So-
theli[g] the sones of Jersan *weren* Saba, and
Dadan Forsothe[h] the sones of Dadan
weren Assurym, and Latusym, and Lao-
mym Sotheli[i] the sones of Madian *weren* 33
Epha, Ether[j], and[k] Enoch, and Abdia,
and Heldaa Alle these *weren* the sones
of Cethure Forsothe Abraham gendride[l] 34
Isaac; whose sones weren Esau and Israel
The sones of Esau *weren* Eliphat, Rahuel, 35
Semyaus, and Elam, and Chore The 36
sones of Eliphath *weren* Theman, Omer,
Sephi, Gethem, Genez, Cenez Thanna,
Amalech[m]. The sones of Rahuel *weren* 37
Naab, Gazara, Samma, Masa[n] The sones 38
of Seir *weren* Lothan, Sobal, Sebeon, Ana,
Dison, Eser, Disan[o] The sones of Lo- 39
than *weren* Horry, Huma[p]; sotheli the
sistir of Lothan was Thanna The sones 40
of Sobal *weren* Alian, and Manaath, and
Ebal, and Sephi, and Onam The sones of
Sebeon *weren* Ana, and Anna The[q] sone of
Ana *was* Dison The sones of Dison *weren* 41
Amaram, and Hesabam, and Lecram, and
Caram The sones of Eser *weren* Balaam, 42
and Jaban, and Jesan The sones of Disan *weren* Hus and Aram These ben 43
the kyngis that regneden in the lond of
Edom, bifor that a kyng was on the sones
of Israel Bale, the sone of Beor; and the
name of his citee *was* Danaba Sotheli[r] 44
Bale was deed, and Jobab, sone[w] of Zare
of Basra, regnyde for hym And whanne 45
Jobab was deed, Husam of the lond of
Themayns regnede for hym And Hu- 46
sam diede, and Adad, sone[x] of Badad,
that smoot Madian in the lond of Moab,
regnyde[y] for hym; and the name of the
citee of hym, *that is, of*[z] *Adad, was*
Abyud And whanne Adad was deed, 47
Semela of Maserecha, regnede for hym
But also Semela was deed, and Saul of 48
Roboth[a], which is set bisidis the[b] ryuer,

[c] Sen B [d] is deed A [e] regned and A

[f] and Sue I [g] and IS [h] And IS [i] And IS [j] and Ether C [k] Om S [l] gaat I [m] and Amalech IS [n] and Masa IS [o] and Disan IS [p] and Huma IS [q] And the S [r] And whanne IS. [w] the sone IS [x] the sone IS [y] and regnede S [z] Om IS [a] *the citee* Roboth I *the citee of Roboth* S [b] a IS

Methetabel, douȝter of Mathred, the douȝ-
51 ter of Mesaab. Adad forsothe deed, duykis
for the kyngis in Edom begunne to ben;
duyk Thanna, duyk Alia, duyk Jetheth,
52 duyk Oolibama, duyk Ela, duyk Philion,
53 duyk Cenez, duyk Theman, duyk Mab-
54 sar, duyk Magdyel, duyk Yran. Thes
the duykis of Edom.

regnyde for hym. Also whanne Saul was 49
deed, Balanam, the sone of Achabor, regnyde for him. But also he was deed, and 50
Adad, the name of whos citee was Phou,
regnede for hym; and his wijf was clepid
Methesael, the douȝter of Mathred, douȝter[c] of Mezaab. Forsothe[d] whanne Adad 51
was deed, dukis bigunnen to be in Edom
for kyngis; duyk Thanna, duyk Alia,
duyk Jetheth, duyk Olibama, duyk Ela, 52
duyk Phynon, duik Ceneth, duyk Theman, 53
duyk Mabsar, duyk Magdiel, duyk[e] Iram. 54
These *weren* the duykis of Edom.

CAP. II.

1 The sones forsothe of Yrael; Ruben,
Leuy, Semeon, Juda, Isachar, and Zabu-
2 lon, Dan, and[f] Joseph, Beniamyn, Nep-
3 talym, Gad, Aser. The sones of Juda;
Her, Onam, Sela; thes thre ben born to
hym of Sue, the douȝtir of[g] Chananytidis.
Forsothe Her was the first goten of Juda,
euyl before the Lord, and he slewȝ hym.
4 Thamar forsothe his douȝtir in lawe bare
to hym Phares and Saram; alle thann
5 the sonys of Juda, fyue. The sonys forsothe of Phares; Esrom and Thamul.
6 The sonys forsothe of Zare; Zamry, and
Ethan, and Eman, and Calchol, and Dar-
7 dam; togydre fyue. The sones of Zamri;
Achar, that distourblide Yrael, and syn-
8 nede in the theft of cursedhode. The
9 sones of Ethan; Azarias. The sonys forsothe of Esrom, that ben born to hym;
Jeramahel, and Aram, and Chaluby.
10 Forsothe Aram gat Amynadab. Amynadab forsothe gat Naason, prince of the
11 sones of Juda. Naason forsothe gat Sal-
12 mon; of whom is born Booz. Booz forsothe gat Obeth; the whiche and he gat
13 Ysay. Ysay forsothe gat the first goten,
Heliab; the secound, Amynadab; the thrid,
14 Samaa; the ferthe, Nathanael; the fyft, Sa-
15 day; the sixt, Asom; the seuenth, Dauid;

CAP. II.

Forsothe the sones of Israel *weren* Ru- 1
ben, Symeon, Leuy, Juda, Isachar, and
Zabulon, Dan, Joseph, Beniamyn[ce], Nep- 2
talym, Gad, Aser[f]. The sones of Juda 3
weren Her, Onam, Sela[g]; these thre weren
borun to hym of Sue, a[h] douȝter of Canaan. Sotheli[i] Her, the first gendrid[k]
sone of Juda, was yuel bifor the Lord,
and he[l] killide hym. Forsothe[m] Thamar, 4
wijf[n] of the sone of Judas, childide to
hym[o] Phares, and Zaram; therfor[p] alle
the sones of Judas *weren* fyue. Sotheli[q] 5
the sones of Phares *weren* Esrom, and
Chamul. And the sones of Zare *weren* 6
Zamry, and Ethen, and Eman, and Cal-
chab, and Dardan; fyue togidere. The 7
sone of Charmy was Achar, that disturblide Israel, and synnede in the[qq] theft of
thing halewid to the Lord. The sone of 8
Ethan was Azarie. Sotheli[r] the sones of 9
Esrom, that weren borun to hym, *weren*
Jeramael, and Aram, and Calubi. For- 10
sothe[s] Aram gendryde[t] Amynadab. Sotheli[u] Amynadab gendride[v] Naason, the[w]
prince of the sones of Juda. And Naason 11
gendride[x] Salmon; of which[y] Salmon[z] Booz
was borun. Sotheli[a] Booz gendride[b] O- 12
beth; which hym silf gendride[b] Ysay.
Forsothe[c] Ysai gendride[d] the[e] firste gen- 13

c the douȝter is.   d And is.   e and duyk is.   ce and Beniamyn s.   f and Aser is.   g and Sela is.
h the is.   i And is.   k goten i.   l the Lord is.   m And is.   n the wijf is.   o Judas is.   p and is.   q And i.
qq Om. s.   r And is.   s And is.   t gaat i.   u And is.   v gaat i.   w Om. is.   x gaat i.   y whom is.
z Om. is.   a And is.   b gaat i.   c And is.   d gaat i.   e his is.

16 whos systers weren Saruya and Abigail. The sones of Saruye; Abisay, Joab, and 17 Asael; thre. Abigail forsothe gat Amasa, 18 whos fadir was Jether Ysmaelyte. Caleph forsothe, the sone of Esrom, toke a wijf, Azuba by name, of whom he gat Jereoth; there weren forsothe sonys of 19 hym, Jesar, and Sobab, and Ardon. And whanne Azuba was deed, he toke a wijf of Caleph, Effrata, the whiche bare to 20 hym Hur. Forsothe Hur gat Hury; 21 Hury gat Beselael. Aftir thes thingis Esrom wente in to the douȝtir of Machir, the fadir of Galaad, and he toke hire, whann sche was of sexty ȝeer; the whiche 22 bare to hym Segub. Bot and Segub gat Jair, and weeldide foure and twenty 23 cytees in the lond of Galaad; and he toke Jessur, and Arym, the bourȝ tounnes of Jair, and Canath, and the lytyl townes of it, of seuenty cytees. Alle thes the 24 sonys of Machir, fadir of Galaad. Whann forsothe Esrom was deed, Caleph wente in to Effrata. Esrom forsothe hade a wijf Abia, the whiche bare to hym As- 25 sur, fadir of Thecue. Ther ben born forsothe sonys of Jezrameel, the first goten of Esrom; Ram his[h] first goten, and Hyma, and Aran, and Ason, and 26 Achia. Forsothe Jezramel weddide an- other wijf, Athara by name, the whiche 27 was the modir of Onam. Bot and of Onam, the sone of Ram, the first goten of Jezramael, weren Mohos, and Lamyn, 28 and Achas. Onam forsothe gat sones, Semei, and Juda. The sones forsothe of 29 Semei; Nadal, and Abiser; name forsothe · of the wijf of Abiser, Abigail, that bare 30 to hym Haaobban, and Molid. The sonys forsothe of Nadab weren Saled, and Apfaym. Forsothe Saled dyȝed with oute 31 fre childre. The sone[i] forsothe of Ap- phaym, Jesi; the whiche Jesi[j] gat Sesan.

dride[f] sone, Elyab, the secounde, Amyna- 14 dab; the thridde, Samaa; the fourthe, Nathanael; the fyuethe, Sadai; the sixte, 15 Asom; the[g] seuenthe, Dauyd; whose sis- 16 tris weren Saruya, and Abigail. The sones of Saruye *weren* thre, Abisai, Joab, and Asahel. Forsothe[h] Abigail childide Ama- 17 sa, whos fadir was Gether Hismaelite. Sotheli[i] Caleph, sone[k] of Esrom, took a 18 wijf, Azuba bi name, of whom he gen- dride[l] Jerioth; and hise sones weren Je- sar, and Sobab, and Ardon. And whanne 19 Azuba was deed, Caleph took a wijf Ef- frata, whiche[m] childide Hur to hym. For- 20 `sothe[n] Hur gendride[o] Hury; Hury gen- dride[o] Beseleel. After these thingis Esrom 21 entride to the douȝtir of Machir, fadir[p] of Galaad†, and he took hir[q], whanne he was of sixti ȝeer; and sche childide Segub to 22 hym. But also Segub gendride[r] Jair; and he hadde in possessioun thre and twenti citees in[s] the lond of Galaad; and he took 23 Gessur, and Aran, the citees of Jair, and Chanath, and the townes therof of[t] seuenti citees. Alle these *weren* the sones of Ma- chir, fadir[u] of Galaad. Sotheli[v] whanne 24 Esrom was deed, Caleph entride‡ in to Effrata. And Esrom hadde a wijf Abia, which[w] childide to hym Assir, fadir[x] of Thecue. Forsothe[y] sones weren borun of 25 Jezrameel, the firste gendrid[z] of Esrom; Ram[a], the first gendrid[b] of hym, and[c] Aran, and Ason, and Achia. Also Jez- 26 rameel weddide anothir wijf, Athara bi name, that was the modir of Onam. But 27 and the sones of Ram, the firste gendrid[d] of Jezrameel, weren Mohas, and Jamyn, and Achaz. Forsothe[e] Onam gendride[f] 28 sones, Semey, and Juda. Sotheli[g] the sones of Semei weren Nadab, and Abisur; for- 29 sothe[h] the name of the wijf of Abisur was Abigail, that[i] childide to hym Haaobban, and Molid. Sotheli[j] the sones of Nadab 30

† *of Galaad;* that is, lord of Galaad. c.

‡ *entride;* as eir. Effrata; bi another name it is Bethleem. *Lire here.* c.

h the *H.*   i sonys *FH.*   j Om. c *pr. m.*

f Om. is.   g and the is.   h And is.   i And is.   k the sone is.   l gnat i.   m the whiche i.   n And is. o gnat i.   p the fadir is.   q hir *to wijf* is.   r gaat i.   s of i.   t Om. oxм.   u the fadir is.   v And is. w the which i.   x the fadir is.   y And is.   z goten i.   a Ram *was* is.   b goten sone i. gendrid sone s. c and *thanne* i.   d goten i.   e And is.   f gaat i.   g and is.   h and is.   i and that s.   j And is.

32 bot Sesan gat Oholi. The sones forsothe of Jada, brother of Semei; Jether and Jonathan; bot Jether died without fre
33 childre; bot Jonatha gat Phales, and Cya. Thes ben the sones of Jezramael.
34 Cesan forsothe hadde no sones, bot douȝters, and Egipcian seruaunt, Gera by
35 name; and he ȝaue to hym his douȝter wijf, the whiche bare to hym Ethei.
36 Ethei forsothe gat Nathan, and Nathan
37 gat Zadab. Zadab forsothe gat Ophial,
38 and Ophial gat Obed. Obed gat Hieu,
39 Hieu gat Azariam, Azarias gat Helles,
40 Helles gat Elasa, Elasa gat Sesamoi,
41 Sesamoi gat Sellum, Sellum gat Jecho-
42 mya, Jechomya gat Elisama. The sones forsothe of Caleph, brother of Jeramael; Mosa his first goten; he is the fadir of ȝiph; and the sonys of Meresa, fadir of
43 Ebron. Forsothe the sonys of Ebron; Chore, and Raphu, Recem, and Samma.
44 Samma forsothe gat Raam, fadir of Jere-
45 haham; and Recem gat Semei. The sone of Semei, Maon; and Maon, the fadir of
46 Bethsur. Epha forsothe, the secoundarie wijf of Caleb, bare Arram, and Musa, and Theser; bot Arram gat Jezen.
47 The sonis of Jadai; Regon, and Jethan, and Zesun, and Phales, and Epha, and
48 Saaph. The secoundarie wijf of Caleb,
49 Maacha, bare Zaber, and Therana. Forsothe Saaph, the fadir of Madmenas, gat Sue, the fadir of Magbena, and the fadir of Gabaa; the douȝter forsothe of Ca-
50 leph was Axa. Thes weren the sones of Caleph. The sones of Hur, first goten of Effrata; Sobal, the fadir of Cariathiarym;
51 Salma, the fadir of Bethleem; Ariph, the
52 fadir of Bethgader. Forsothe ther weren sonys of Sobal, fadir of Cariathiarym, the whiche deuydiden the half of the rest-
53 yngis; and of the kynrede of Cariathiarym, Jethrei, and Afutei, and Samathei, and Maccerathei. Of thes wenten out
54 Saraitis and Eschaolitis. The sones of

weren Saled and Apphaym; forsothe[k] Saled diede without children. Sotheli[l] the 31 sone of Apphaym was Jesi, which[m] Jesi gendride[n] Sesan; sotheli[o] Sesan gendride[p] Oholi. Forsothe[q] the sones of Jada, bro- 32 ther[r] of Semei, weren Jether and Jonathan; but Jether diede with out sones; treuli[s] Jonathan gendride[t] Phalech, and 33 Ziza. These ben[u] the sones of Jeramecl. Forsothe[v] Sesan hadde not sones, but 34 douȝtris, and a seruaunt of Egipt, Jeraa bi name; and he ȝaf his douȝter to wijf to 35 Jeraa, whiche[w] childide Ethei to hym. Forsothe[x] Ethei gendride[y] Nathan, and 36 Nathan gendride[z] Zadab. Also Zadab 37 gendride[z] Ophial, and Ophial gendride[z] Obed. Obed gendride[z] Yeu, Yeu gendride[z] 38 Azarie, Azarie gendride[z] Helles, Helles 39 gendride[z] Elasa, Elasa gendride[z] Sesa- 40 moy, Sesamoy[a] gendride[b] Sellum, Sellum 41 gendride[b] Jecamya, Jecamia gendride[b] Elisama. Forsothe[c] the sones of Caleph, 42 brothir[d] of Jerameel, weren Mosa, the firste gendride[e] sone of hym; thilke is the fadir of Ziph; and[ee] the sones of Maresa, the fadir of Hebron. Certis the sones of 43 Ebron weren Chore, and Raphu, Recem, and Samma. Forsothe[f] Samma gendride[g] 44 Raam, the fadir of Jerechaam; and Recem gendride[g] Semei. The sone of Semei was 45 Maon; and Maon was the fadir[h] of Bethsur. Sotheli[i] Epha, the secundarie wijf 46 of Caleph, childide Aram, and Musa, and Theser; forsothe[k] Aram gendride[l] Jezen. The sones of Jadai weren[m] Regon, and 47 Jethon, and Zesum, Phalez[n], and Epha, and Saaph. Matha, the secoundarie wijf 48 of Caleph, childide Zaber, and Tharana. Forsothe[o] Saaph, the fadir of Madmenas, 49 gendride[p] Sue, the fadir of Magbena, and the fader of Gabaa; sotheli[q] the douȝter of Caleph was Axa. These weren the sones 50 of Caleph. The sones of Hur, the firste gendrid[r] sone of Effrata, weren Sobal, the fader of Cariathiarim; Salma, the fader 51

k and 18. l And 18. m the which 1. n gaat 1. o certis BCDEFGIKLMNOPQRSUWXb. p gaat 1. q And 18. r the brother 18. s and 18. t gaat 1. u weren 18. v And 18. w the whiche 1. x And 18. y gaat 1. z gaat 1. a And Sesamoy 1. b gaat 1. c And 18. d the brothir 18. e bigoten 1. ee Om. s. f And 18. g gaat 1. h sone 1. i And 18. k and 18. l gaat 1. m Om. c. n and Phalez DELPSW. o And 18. p gaat 1. q and 18. r goten 1.

Salma, 'fadir of[k] Bethlem, and Netho-
phatite, crownys of the hous of Joab,
55 and half of the restyng of Saray. The
kynredis forsothe of scribis, dwellynge in
Jabes, syngynge, and aȝein sounnynge,
and in tabernaclis dwellynge togider.
Thes ben Cynei, the whiche camen of the
feruour of the hous of the fadir of
Rechab.

of Bethleem; Ariph, the fader of Bethgader. Sotheli[s] the sones of Sobal, fader[t] 52
of Cariatiarim, that siȝ the myddil of
restingis, and was of the kynrede of Cary- 53
athiarym, weren Jethrey, and Aphutei, and
Samathei, and Maserathei. Of these weren
borun Sarytis, and Eschaolitis. The sones 54
of Salma, fadir[u] of Bethleem, and of Ne-
tophati, *weren* the corouns of the hows of
Joab, and the[v] half of restyng[w] of Sarai.
And the kynredis of scryuens, dwellynge 55
in Jabes, syngynge, and sownynge, and
dwellynge in tabernaclis. These ben Cy-
neis, that camen of the heete[†] of the fadir
of the hows of Rechab.

CAP. III.

1 Dauith forsothe hadde thes sonis, the
whiche ben born to hym in Ebron; the
first goten, Amon, of Achynoen Jezraelite;
the seconde, Danyel, of Abigail Carmel-
2 ite; the thrid, Absalon, the sone of
Maacha, douȝter[l] of[m] Tholomei, kyng of
Jessur; the ferth, Adonye, the sone of
3 Agith; the fyfthe, Saphathie, of Abithal;
4 the sixt, Jethraan, of Egla his wijf. Sixe
thann ben born to hym in Ebron, where
he regnede seuen ȝeer and sixe monethis;
forsothe thre and thritty ȝere he regned
5 in Jerusalem. Bot in Jerusalem ben
born to hym sonys, Sama, and Sobab, and
Nathan, and Salomon, foure, of Bersabee,
6 douȝtir of Amyhel; Jabaar forsothe, and
7 Elizama, and Elipheloch, and Noge, and
8 Napheth, and Japhee, also and Elizama,
9 and Eliade, and Eliphalech, nyne. Alle
thes sonys of Dauith, with oute sonis of
the secoundarie wijfis; and thei hadden
10 a syster, Thamar. The sone forsothe of
Salomon, Roboam, whos sone Abia gat
Asa; of this forsothe is born Josaphat,
11 the fadir of Joram; the whiche Joram
gat Ochosie, of whome is born Joas.

CAP. III.

Forsothe Dauid hadde these sones, that 1
weren borun to hym in Ebron; the firste
gendrid[x] sone[y], Amon, of Achynoem of
Jezrael; the secounde sone, Danyel[z], of
Abigail of Carmele; the thridde, Absolon, 2
the sone of Maacha, douȝter[b] of Tolomei,
kyng of Gessuri; the fourthe, Adonye,
sone[c] of Agith; the fyuethe, Saphacie, of 3
Abithal; the sixte, Jethraan, of[cc] Egla his
wijf. Therfor sixe sones weren borun to 4
hym[d] in Ebron, where he regnede seuene
ȝeer and sixe monethis; sotheli[e] he regnyde
thre and thritti ȝeer in Jerusalem. For- 5
sothe foure sones[‡], Sama[f], and Sobab, and
Nathan, and Salomon, weren borun of
Bersabee, the douȝter of Amyhel, to hym[g]
in Jerusalem; also Jabaar, and Elisama, 6
and Eliphalech, and Noge, and Napheth, 7
and Japhie, also and[h] Elisama, and Eli- 8
ade, and Eliphalech, nyne[i]. Alle these 9
weren the sones of David, with out the
sones of secoundarie[k] wyues; and thei
hadden a sistir, Thamar. Sotheli the sone 10
of Salomon *was* Roboam, whos sone Abia
gendride[l] Asa; and Josaphat, the fadir 11
of Joram, was borun of this Asa; which[m]

k Om. K *pr. m.*   l the douȝtir II.   m Om. II.

x And IS.   t the fader IS.   u the fadir IS.   v Om. IS.   w the restyng IS.   x goten I.   y sone *of him was* IS.
z hiȝt Danyel IS.   a *born of* IS.   b the douȝtir IS.   c the sone IS.   cc *Dauid hadde of* s.   d Dauid IS.
e and IS.   f *that ben,* Sama I. *that is,* Sama s.   g Dauid IS.   h Om. IS.   i nyne *sones* IS.   k the
secoundarie CM. his secoundarie IS.   l gaat I.   m the which I.

12 And of this the sone Amazias gat Azarie; bot Azarie, the sone of Jonathan,
13 brouȝte forth Achaz, the fadir of Ezechie;
14 of whome is born Manasses. Bot and
Manasses gat Amon, the fadir of Josie.
15 The sonys forsothe of Josie weren, the
first goten, Johannan; the secound, Joachym; the thrid, Sedechie; the ferth,
16 Sellum. Of Joachym is born Jechonyas,
17 and Sedechie. The sonys of Jechonye,
18 weren Asir, Salathiel, Melchiram, Fadaia, Sennaser, and Jeth, Semai, Sama,
19 and Nadabia. Of Phadaia ben born
Zorobabel, and Semei. Zorobabel gat
Mosollam, Ananyam, and Salomyth, the
20 syster of hem; and Asabam, and Ochol,
and Barachie, and Asadie, Josabesed,
21 fyue. The sone forsothe of Ananye,
Falciar, the fadir of Jeseie, whos sone
Raphaia. Of this forsothe the sone
Arnan, of the whiche is born Abdia,
22 whos sone was Sechenya. The sone of
Sechenye, Semeia, whos sonys, Archus,
and Jegal, and Baaria, and Naaria, and
23 Saphath; sixe in noumbre. The sonys
of Naarie; Elioenai, and Ezechiaz, and
24 Zicram, thre. Sonys of Elioenai; Odyna,
and Eliazub, and Pheleia, and Acub,
and Johannan, and Dalaia, and Anani,
seuen.

CAP. IV.

1 　Sones of Juda; Phares, and Esrom, and
2 Carmy, and Hur, and Sobal. Reya forsothe, the sone of Sobal, gat Jeth; of
whom ben born Achymay, and Laed.
3 Thes the kynredis of Sarathy. This
forsothe the lynage of Ethan; Jesrael,
Jezema, and Jedeboz; name forsothe of
4 the syster of hem Azalelfuny. Funyel
forsothe the fadir of Jedor, and Ezer,
the fadir of Osa; thes ben the sones of
Hur, first goten of Effrata, the fadir of
5 Bethleem. Of Asur forsothe, fader of

Joram gendride[n] Ocozie, of whom[nn] Joas
was borun[o]. And Amasie, the sone of 12
this Joas, gendride[p] Azarie; sotheli[q] Azarie, the[r] sone of Joathan, gendride[s] Achaz, 13
the fadir of Ezechie; of whom Manasses
was borun. But also Manasses gendride[s] 14
Amon, the fadir of Josias. Forsothe[t] the 15
sones of Josias weren[u], the firste gendrid[y]
sone, Johannan[w]; the secounde, Joachym[ww];
the thridde, Sedechie; the[x] fourthe, Sellum.
Of Joachym was borun[y] Jechonye, and 16
Sedechie. The sones of Jechonye weren 17
Asir, Salatiel, Melchiram, Phadaie, Sen- 18
naser, and Jech, Semma, Sama, and Nadabia. Of Phadaie weren borun Zorobabel, 19
and Semey. Zorobabel gendryde[z] Mosolla,
Ananye, and Salomyth, the sister of hem;
and Asaba, nnd Ochol, and Barachie, and 20
Asadaie, and Josabesed, fyue[a]. Forsothe[b] 21
the sone of Ananye was Falcias, the fadir
of Jeseie, whose sone was Raphaie. And
the sone of him was Arnan, of whom was
borun Abdia, whos sone was Sechema.
The sone of Sechema was Semeia, whose 22
sones weren Archus, and Gegal, and Baaria, and Naaria, and Saphat, and Sela;
sixe[c] in noumbre. The sones of Naaria 23
weren thre, Helionai, and Ezechie, and
Zichram. The sones of Helionai weren 24
seuene, Odyna, and Eliasub, and Pheleia,
and Accub, and Johannan, and Dalaia,
and Anani.

CAP. IV.

1 　The sones of Juda weren Phares, and 1
Esrom, and Carmy, and Hur, and Sobal.
Forsothe[d] Reaia, the sone of Sobal, gen- 2
dride[e] Geth; of whom weren borun Achy-
mai, and Laed. These weren the kynredis
of Sarathi. And this is the generacioun 3
of Ethan; Jesrael, Jezema, and[f] Jedebos;
and the name of the sistir of hem was
Asaelphumy. Sotheli[ff] Phunyel was the 4
fadir† of Gedor, and Ezer was the fadir of
Osa; these ben the sones of Hur, the firste
gendrid[g] sone of Effrata, the fadir of Beth-

† fadir; that
is, fadir of sich
a town, and so
it is expownyd
of Usa. Lire
here. c.

ᵇ gaat I.　ⁿⁿ which s.　ᵒ borun or goten I. born or gendride s.　ᵖ gaat I.　ۑ forsothe BCDEFGKLNOPQ
RUW. and Is.　ʳ Om. D.　ˢ gaat I.　ᵗ And Is.　ᵘ weren there Is.　ᵛ goten I.　ʷ was Johannan Is.
ʷʷ was Joachim s.　ˣ and the I.　ʸ goten I. gendrid s.　ᶻ gaat I.　ᵃ fyue sones Is.　ᵇ And Is.　ᶜ sixe
sones Is.　ᵈ And Is.　ᵉ gaat I.　ᶠ Om. c.　ᶠᶠ And Is.　ᵍ goten I.

Techue, weren two wiues, Hala, and
6 Naara; foisothe Naara bare to hym
Chosam, and Epher, and Theman, and
Aschari; thes ben the sonys of Naara.
7 Forsothe the sones of Hala, Cereth,
8 Ysaai, and Ethan Chus forsothe gat
Anob, and Sobaba, and the cognaciouns
9 of Aiab, sone of Aiym Jabes forsothe
was noble befoin alle his[n] bretheren;
and his modii clepide the name of hym
Jabes, seyinge, Foi I bare hym in so-
10 row. Foisothe Jabes inwardly clepyde
the God of Yrael, seyinge, ʒif blessynge
thou schalt blessen to me, and largen
my teimys, and thin hond were with me,
and makist me not to[o] ben oppiessed of
malice And the Lord ʒaue to hym that
11 he preyed. Caleph forsothe, brothei of
Sua, gat Machir, that was the fadii of
12 Eston, forsothe Eston gat Bechus, Rapha, aud Phese, and Thena, the fadii of
the cyte of Naas Thes ben the men of
13 Recha The sonys forsothe of Cenes,
Othonyel, and Saraia Foisothe the
14 sonys of Othonyel, Othiath, and Mao-
nathi, the whiche gat Ofra Saraias foisothe gat Joab, fadir of the valcy of
ciaftis men, ther forsothe weren ciaftise
15 men. Sonys forsothe of Caleph, sone of
Jephone, Hyn, and Hela, and Nahem
16 The sonys forsothe of Hela, Jalael, and
Cenes The sonys forsothe of Jalael,
Ceph, and Cipha, and Thiira, and Asia-
17 hech And the sonys of Esia, Jethei,
and Merid, and Epher, and Jason, and
he gat Mariam, and Semoi, and Jesba,
18 the fadir of Eschamo The wijf forsothe
of hym, Judaia, gat Jaied fadir of Jedor,
and Eber, fadir of Socho, and Hieutiel,
fadei of Zanon These forsothe the sonys
of Bethie, douʒtir of Pharao, the whiche
19 Meied toke And the sonys of the wijf
of Odoye, syster of Nathan, fadir of

leem Sotheli[h] Assur, the fadii of Thecue, 5
hadde twei wyues, Haala, and Naara; for- 6
sothe[i] Naara childide to hym Oozam, and
Epher, and Theman, and Aschaii, these
ben the sones of Naara. Forsothe[k] the 7
sones of Haala *ueren* Sereth, Isaar, and
Ethan Forsothe[l] Chus gendride[m] Anob, 8
and Sobala, and the kynredis of Arab
sone[n] of Aiym Forsothe[o] Jabes was noble 9
byfor alle hise britheren, and his modir
clepide his name Jabes, and seide, Foi Y
childide hym in sorewe Sotheli[p] Jabes 10
clepide inwardli[q] God of Israel, and seide,
Yf thou[qq] blessynge schal[r] blesse me, and
schalt alarge[s] my termes, and if thin hond
schal be with me, and thou schalt make
me to be not oppressid of malice And
God ʒaf to hym that thing, that he pieiede.
Forsothe[t] Caleph, the biother of Sua, gen- 11
dride[u] Machir, that was the fadir of
Eston; sotheli[v] Eston gendride[w] Beth, 12
Rapha, and Phese, and Thena, the fadir of
the citee Naas. These ben the sones of
Recha Forsothe[x] the sones of Cenez 13
ueren Othonyel, and Saraia Sotheli[y] the 14
sones of Othonyel *weren* Athiath, and Mao-
naththa, that gendride[z] Opham Forsothe[a] Saraia gendride[b] Joab, the fadir of
the valey of crafti men; for there weren
ciafti men Sotheli[c] the sones of Caleph, 15
sone[d] of Jephone, *weien* Hyn, and Helam,
and Nahem And the sones of Helam
weien Cenez Also the sones of Jaleel 16
weien Zeph, and Zipha, Tiiia, and Asiiel
And the sones of Esra *weien* Chether, and 17
Merid, and Epher, and Jalon; and he
gendride[e] Marie, and Semmai, and Jesba,
the fadir of Eschamo Also Judaia, hys 18
wijf, childide Jared, the fadii of Gedoi;
and Heber, the fadir of Zocho †, and
Hieutihel, the fadir of Janon Sotheli[f]
these *weren* the sones of Bethie, the douʒter
of Pharao, whom Meied took *to wijf* And 19

† *the fadir of
Zocho*, that is,
the fadir of
such a toun,
and so of Ja
non *Lire
here* (

[n] Om ABCFII [o] Om A

[h] And is [i] and is [k] And is [l] And is [m] gaat i [n] the sone i [o] Sotheli BCDLFGKLMNOPQ
RUUXb And is [p] And is [q] ynli i [qq] thou, *Lord* R [r] schalt is. [s] enlarge is [t] And is [u] gaat i
[v] and is [w] gaat i [x] And is [y] And is [z] gaat i [a] And is [b] gaat i [c] And is [d] the sone is
[e] gaat i [f] And is

Seila; Garmy, and Escamo, that was of
20 Machathi. The sonys forsothe of Symeon,
Amon, and Rena; the sone of Aman,
Chilon; and the sonys of Jeci, Zoeth, and
21 Benzoeth. The sonys of Cela, sone of
Juda; Her, fadir of Lecha, and Laada,
fadir of Marasa; and the kynredis of the
hous of men wirchynge bijs in the hous
22 of oth; and the whiche maad the sonne
to stonden, and men of lesynge, and
syker, and goynge, the whiche weren
princis in Moab, and the whiche ben
turned aȝeyn in Leem; thes forsothe ben
23 the olde wordis. Thes ben potters dwellynge in plauntyngis, and in cratchis,
anentis kyngis in their werkis; and thei
24 dwelliden there. The sonys of Symeon;
Namyel, and Jamyn, Jarib, Zara, Saul.
25 Sellum, the sone of hym; Mapsan, the
sone of hym; and[p] Masma, the sone
26 of hym. The sonys of Masma; Accuel,
the sone of hym; and Zaccur, the sone of
27 hym; and Semei, the sone of hym. The
sonys of Semei sixtene, and douȝtris sixe;
the bretheren forsothe of hym hadden
not many sonys, and al the kynrede
myȝte not maken euen to the soumme of
28 the sonys of Juda. Forsothe thei dwelliden in Bethsabe, and Molada, and
29 Asersual, and in Balaa, and in Asometh,
30 and in Tholoth, and in Bathuel, and
31 Orma, and in Sichelech, and in Beth,
and Mathaboth, and in Archasusyn, and
in Bethberai, and in Saarym; thes the
32 cytees of hem, vnto kyng Dauid. The
touns forsothe of hem; Ethan, and Aen,
and Remmon, and Techen, and Azan;
33 fyue cytees. And alle the lityll touns
of hem by enuyroun of thes cytees, vnto
Baal; this is the dwellynge of hem, and
34 the delynge of setis[q]. Mosobali forsothe,
and Jenyleth, and Josa, the sone of Ama-
35 sie, and Joel, and Jeu, the sone of Josabie, and the sonys of Saraie, the sone[r]

the sones of the wijf of Odoie, sister[g] of
Nathan, fadir of Ceila, *weren* Garmy, and
Escamo, that was of Machati. Also the 20
sones of Symeon *weren* Amon and Rena;
the sone of Anam *was* Chilon; and the
sones of Gesi *weren* Zoeth, and Benzoeth.
The sones of Cela, sone[h] of Juda, *weren* 21
Her, the fadir of Lecha, and Laada, the
fadir of Marasa; and these *weren* the kynredis of the hows of men worchynge biys
in the hows of an ooth, and which made 22
the sunne to stonde, and the men of
leesyng, sikir, and goynge, that weren
princes in Moab, and that turneden aȝen
in to Bethleem; forsothe[i] these ben elde
wordis. These ben potteris dwellinge in 23
plauntyngis, and in heggis, anentis kyngis
in her werkis; and thei dwelliden there.
The sones of Symeon *weren* Namyhel, and 24
Jamyn, Jarib, Zara, Saul. Sellum *was* his 25
sone; Mapsan *was* his sone; Masma *was*
his sone. The sones of Masma; Amuel[j], 26
his sone; and Zaccur, his sone; Semey[k], his
sone. The sones of Semey *weren* sixtene, 27
and sixe douȝtris; sotheli[kk] hise britheren
hadden not many sones, and al the kynrede myȝte not be euene[l] to the[m] summe[mm]
of the sones of Juda. Forsothe[n] thei 28
dwelliden in Bersabee, and in Molada, and
in Asarsual, and in Balaa, and in Aason, 29
and in Tholat, and in Bathuel, and in 30
Horma, and in Sicheloch, and in Betmar- 31
chaboth, and in Archasusym, and in Beth-
baray, and in Saarym; these *weren* the
citees of hem, 'til to[o] the[p] kyng Dauid.
Also the townes of hem *weren* Ethan, and 32
Aen, and Remmon, and Techen, and
Asan; fyue citees. And alle the vilagis 33
of hem bi the[q] cumpas of these citees[r], 'til
to[s] Baal[t]; this is the dwellyng of hem,
and[u] the departyng of seetis[v]. Also Mo- 34
sobaly, and Jemlech, and Josa, the sone
of Amasie, and Johel, and Jehu, the sone 35
of Josabie, and the sones of Saraie, the

p Om. CEFH. q citees ABH. r sonys H.

g the sister IS. h the sone IS. i and IS. j *was* Amuel S. k and Semey S. kk and IS. l eeuened IS. m Om. A. mm summe *or noumbre* S. n And IS. o vnto I. vnto *the time of* S. p Om. IS. q Om. I. r citees *weren hers* IS. s vnto IS. to X. t *the tyme of* Baal IS. u in S. v her citees IS.

36 of Aziel, and Elioneay, and Jamcoba,
aud Sycua, and Azaia, and Adiel, and
37 Isemeel, and Banaya, Sisa forsothe, the
sone of Cephei, the sone of Allon, sone
of Adaia, sone of Semri, sone of Samaia
38 Thes ben the princis nempnyd in their
kynredis, and in the hous of ther assyny-
39 tese thei ben multiplied hugely And thei
wenten that thei camen in to Gador, vnto
the este of the valey, and for to sechen
40 lesewes to their scheep And thei founden
most plenteuows leswes, and ful good,
and most large lond, and quyete, and
bryngynge fruyt, in the whiche beforn
hadden dwellid of⁵ the lynage of Cam
41 Thes than camen, the whiche beforn we
han discryued name by name in the dais
of Ezechie, kyng of Juda, and thei
smyten the tabernaclis of hem, and the
dwellers that ben founden there; and thei
dyden hem aweye vnto the present day;
and thei dwelliden for hem, for most
plenteuows leswes weren founden there
42 Of the sonys forsothe of Symeon wenten
in to the hil of Seir fyue hundreth men,
hauynge princis Phalsie, and Nariam,
and Raphayam, and Osiel, the sonys of
43 Jesy; and thei smyten the relikis, that
mi3ten not ascapyn of Amalachytes; and
thei dwelliden for hem there vnto this
day

CAP. V

1 The sonys forsothe of Ruben, the first
goten of Yrael; he forsothe was his first
goten, bot for he hadde defoulid the bed
of his fadir, the 113tis of his first getynge
ben 3euen to the sonys of Joseph, the
sone of Yrael; and he is not holden in to
2 the first goten. Forsothe Judas, that was
the strengist amonge his bietheren, of
his stok princis ben buriounned; and the
ri3tis of the first getyng forsothe ben
3 acountyde to Joseph. Than the sonys

36 sones of Asiel, and Helioneai, and Jacoba,
and Sucua, and Asaia, and Adihel, and
37 Hisemeel, and Banaia, and Ziza, the^u sone
of Sephei, the sone of Allon, sone^v of Ab-
daia, sone^v of Semry, sone^v of Samaia
38 These ben princis^w nemyd in her kynredis, and ben multiplied greetli in the
39 hows^x of her alies And thei 3eden forth
to entre in to Gador, 'til to^y the eest of
the valei, and to seke pastuiis to her
40 scheep And thei fonden pastuiis ful
plenteuouse, and ful goode, and a ful large
lond, and restful^z, and plenteuouse, wherynne men of the generacioun of Cham
41 hadden dwellid bifore Therfor these men,
whiche we discryueden^a bifore 'bi name^{aa},
camen in the daies of Ezechie, kyng of
Juda, and smytiden^b the tabernaclis of
hem, and the dwelleiis that weren foundun
there; and thei 'diden awei^{bb} hem 'til in to^c
present^d dai; and thei dwelliden for hem,
for thei founden there ful plenteuouse pas-
42 turis Also fyue hundrid men of the
sones of Symeon 3eden in i to the hil of
Seir, and thei hadden princes Faltias, and
Narias, and Raphaias, and Oziel, the
43 sones of Jesi; and thei smytiden^e the re-
lifs^f of Amalechites, that my3ten ascape;
and thei dwelliden there for hem 'til to^g
this day.

CAP V

1 Also the sones of Ruben, the firste gen-
drid^h sone of Israel; for he was the first
gendrid^h sone of Israel, but whanne he
hadde defoulid the bed of his fadir, the
dignitye of his firste gendryng^i was 3onun
to the sones of Joseph, the sone of Israel,
and Ruben was not arettid in to the firste
2 gendrid^k sone Forsothe Judas; that was
the^l strongeste among hise britheren,
prynces weren gaderid of his generacioun, forsothe the '113t of^m firste^n gen-

ˢ Om A

---

u and the ˢ   ᵛ the sone is   ʷ the princis CFK *sec m* MS   ˣ hows *or* meynee i houce *or in the*
meynee s   ʸ vnto is to λ   ᶻ ful restful c   ᵃ han discryued i haue discriued *or toold* s   ᵃᵃ Om s
ᵇ smytiden *or distrueden* s smeten ELP   ᵇᵇ fordiden i   ᶜ vnto i til to x   ᵈ this present i the present s
ᵉ smeten EILP   ᶠ remenauntis i reliks b   ᵍ into CELPII vnto i to x   ʰ goten i   ⁱ bigetynge i
ᵏ goten i   ˡ Om x   ᵐ Om EI   ⁿ his firste CD *pr m* b the firste KX

of Ruben, the firste goten of Yrael; E-
noch, and Fallu, Esrom, and Charmy.
4 The sonys of Joel; Samaia, the sone of
hym; Gog, the sone of hym; Semei, the
5 sone of hym; Mycha, the sone of hym;
Rema, the sone of hym; Baal, the sone
6 of hym; Bera, the sone of hym; whome
caytijf ladde Teglat Falasar, kyng of Assiries; and he was a prince in the lynage
7 of Ruben. The bretheren forsothe of
hym, and al the kynrede, whan thei
weren noumbred by their meines, hadden
8 princis Jeihel, and Zacharie. Forsothe
Baala, the sone of Achaz, sone of Sama,
sone of Johel, he dwellide in Aroer vnto
9 Nebo and Beelmeon; aȝeynst the eest
forsothe coost he dwellide, vnto the entre
of Heremy, and the flode of Eufraten.
Myche forsothe noumbre of bestis he
10 weldide in the lond of Galaad. In the
days forsothe of Saul thei fouȝten aȝeynus
Agarienis, and slewen hem; and dwelliden for hem in their tabernaclis, in al
the coost that beholdith to the este of
11 Galaad. The sonys forsothe of Gad forn
aȝeynst hem dwelliden in the lond of Ba-
12 san vnto Selcha; Joel in the heued, and
Sapham the secounde; Janay forsothe and
13 Sapha in Basan. And the bretheren of
hem aftir the houses of their kynredis,
Mychael, and Mosollam, and Sebe, and
Jore, and Joachan, and Zie, and Heber,
14 seuen. Thes the sones of Abiel, sone of
Vri, sone of Jaro, sone of Galaad, sone
of Michael, sone of Jesesi, sone of Jeddo,
15 sone of Bus. The bretheren forsothe of
the sone of Abdiel, sone of Gummy,
16 prince of the hous in their meynes. And
thei dwelliden in Galaad, and in Baasan,
and in the lityl tounes of it, in alle the
17 suburbis of Arnon, vnto the termys. Alle
thes ben noumbred in the days of Joathan, kyng of Juda, and in the days of
18 Jeroboam, kyng of Yrael. The sonys of
Ruben, and of Gad, and of the half lynage
of ᵗ Manasse, men fiȝters berynge sheeldis
and swerdis, and bendynge bowe, and

dryng° was arettid to Joseph. Therfor ₃
the sones of Ruben, the firste gendrid ᵖ
sone of Israel, weren Enoch, and Phallu,
Esrom, and Charmy. The sones of Johel ₄
weren ᑫ Samaie; his sone, Gog; his sone,
Semey; his sone, Mycha; his sone, Rema; ₅
his sone, Baal; his sone, Bera; whom Theg- ₆
latphalassar, kyng of Assyriens, ledde prisoner; and he was prince in the lynage of
Ruben. Sotheli hise britheren, and al the ₇
kynrede, whanne thei weren noumbrid bi
her meynees, hadden princes Jehiel, and
Zacharie. Forsothe Bala, the sone of ₈
Achaz, sone of Sama, sone of Johel, he
dwellide in Aroer til to Nebo and Beel-
moon; and ʳ he dwellide aȝens the eest ₉
coost, til to the ende ˢ of deseert, 'and to ᵗ
the flood Eufrates. And he hadde in possessioun myche noumbre of beestis in the
lond of Galaad. Forsothe in the daies of 10
Saul the sones of Ruben fouȝten aȝens
Agarenus, and killide hem; and dwelliden
for hem in the tabernaclis of hem, in al
the coost that biholdith to the eest of
Galaad. Sotheli the sones of Gad euene 11
aȝens hem dwelliden in the lond of Basan
til to Selca; Johel was in the bygynnyng, and 12
Saphan was the secounde; also Janahi and
Saphan weren in Basan. Also her bri- 13
theren bi the housis of her kynredis, Mychael, and Mosollam, and Sebe, and Jore,
and Jachan, and Zie, and Heber, seuene.
These weren the sones of Abiahel, the 14
sone of Vry, sone of Jaro, sone of Galaad,
sone of Mychael, sone of Esesi, sone of
Jeddo, sone of Buz. Also the britheren 15
of the sone of Abdiel, sone of Gumy, was
prince ᵘ of the hows in hise meynees. And 16
thei dwelliden in Galaad, and in Basan,
and in the townes therof, in alle the subarbis of Arnon, til to the endis. Alle 17
these weren noumbrid in the daies of
Joathan, kyng of Juda, and in the daies
of Jeroboam, kyng of Israel. The sones 18
of Ruben, and of Gad, and of half the
lynage of Manasses, weren men werriours,
berynge scheeldis and swerdis, and beend-

ᵗ Om. ᴀ.

° getyng ı. ᵖ goten ı. ᑫ Om. ı. ʳ Om. x sec. m. ˢ entring new. ᵗ in to ı. ᵘ the prince ᴀ.

tau3t to batailis, foure and fouɪety thou-
sandɪs seuen hundreth and sɪxty, goynge
19 forthe to fi3t, fou3ten a3eynus Aganens
Ethɪu eɪs forsothe, and Naphɪ, and Nadab,
20 3euen to heɪn help, and Aganens ben
taken ɪn to the hondɪs of hem, and alle
that weren wɪth hem; for the Lord theɪ
ɪnwaɪdly clepɪden, whɪl thei fou3ten, and
he herde hem, forthi that theɪ hadden
21 leened[u] ɪn hɪm And theɪ token alle
thingɪs that they hadden weldɪd, of chamels fyfty thousand, and of scheep two
hundreth and fyfty thousand, and of
assɪs two thousand, and lyues of men an
22 hundreth thousand; and many woundɪd
fellen, forsothe the batayl of the Lord ɪt
was Theɪ dwellɪden foɪ hem ɪnto the
23 transmygɪacɪoun The sonɪs forsothe of
the half lynage of Manasse weldeden the
lond, fro the coostɪs of Basan ɪnto Baal
Hermon, and Sanɪr, and the hyl of Hermon; a grete foɪsothe noumbre ther
24 was And thes weren the pryncɪs of the
hous of the kynrede of hem; Efer, and
Jesɪ, and Hehel, and Esɪɪel, and Jeremye, and Odoye, and Jedehel, men most
strong aud my3ty, and duykɪs nemned in
25 theɪɪ meynes Forsothe theɪ foɪsoken the
God of their fadɪrs, and dyden fornycacioun aftɪr goddɪs of the puphɪs of the
lond, the whɪche the Lord toke aweye
26 beforn hem And the Lord God of Yrael
reɪed the spɪrɪt of Phul, the kyng of As-
sɪrɪes, and the spɪrɪt of Teglat Falasar,
kyng of Assur, and tɪanslatyde Ruben,
and Gad, and the half lynage of Manasse,
and he brou3te hem ɪn to Ale, and Abor,
and Aram, and the flode of Gosam, ɪnto
1 thɪs day The sonys of Leuy, Jerson,
2 Caath, and Mereɪɪ The sonɪs of Caath,
3 Amram, Isaar, Ebron, and Ozɪel The
sonys of Amram; Aaron, Moyses, and
Marɪa The sonys of Aaɪon, Nadab,
4 and Abyu, Elɪazar, and Ythamaɪ Elɪa-
zaɪ gat Phynees, and Phynees gat Abɪ-
5 sue; Abɪsue gat Boccɪ, and Boccɪ gat
6 Osy, Osy gat Zarɪaɪas, Zaraɪas gat Me-

ynge bouwe, and tau3t to[u] batels, foure
and fourtɪ thousynde seuene huɪdrɪd and
sɪxti, and theɪ 3eden forth to batel, and 19
fou3ten a3ens Agarenus Forsothe Ethu-
reɪs, and Napheɪs, and Nadab, 3auen help 20
to hem, and Agarenus, and alle men that
weren wɪth hem, weɪen bɪtakun ɪn to the
hondɪs of Ruben, and Gad, and Manasses;
for theɪ clepɪden ɪnwardlɪ the Loɪd, whɪle
theɪ fou3ten, and the Lord herde hem, for
theɪ 'hadden bɪleuyd[v] ɪn to him And theɪ 21
token alle thingɪs whiche Agarenus hadden ɪn possessɪoun, fiftɪ thousynde of camels, and tweɪ hundrɪd and fifty thousynde of scheep, tweɪ thousynde of assɪs,
and an hundrɪd thousynde persoones[w] of
men; foɪ many men weren woundɪd and 22
felden doun; for ɪt was the batel of the
Lord And thei dwelhɪden for Agarenus
tɪl to the conquest Also the sones of the 23
half lynage of Manasses hadden ɪn possessɪoun the lond, fro the endɪs of Basan tɪl
to Baal Hermon, and Sanyr, and the hɪl
of Hermon, for ɪt was a greet noumbre
And these weren the prɪnces of the hows 24
of her kynrede; Epher, and Jesɪ, and Hehel, and Esryel, and Jeremye, and Odoɪe,
and Jedhel, strongeste[x] men and my3tɪ,
and nemyd duykɪs ɪn her meynees. For- 25
sothe theɪ forsoken the God of her fadrɪs,
and dɪden fornycacɪoun after the goddɪs
of puphɪs of the lond, whɪche the Lord
took aweɪ bɪfor hem And the Lord God 26
of Israel reɪsɪde the spɪrɪt of Phul, kyng
of Assɪrɪens, and the spɪɪɪt† of Theglat-
phalasser, kyng of Assur, and he trans-
latɪde Ruben, and Gad, and the half lynage
of Manasses, and brou3te hem ɪn to Ale,
and Abor, and Aram, and ɪn to the ryuer
of Gozam, tɪl to thɪs daɪ

† the spɪrɪt
that ɪs, wɪlle
to fɪ3te a3ens
the chɪldryn of
Israel. Lɪre
here c

CAP VI

The sones of Leuy *weren* Gerson, Caath, 1
and Merary The sones of Chaath *weɪen* 2
Amram, Isaar, Ebron, and Ozɪel The 3
sones of Amram *weɪen*[y] Aaron, Moyses,
and Marɪe. The sones of Aaron *weren*[y]

u bɪleued A   v thousend Fʜ.

u ɪn I   v bɪleuyden c   w of persones I   x ful stronge I   y Om I.

7 royoth. Forsothe Meroyoth gat Amaryas,
8 Amaryas gat Achytob, Achitob gat Sa-
9 doch, Sadoch gat Achimas, Achimas gat
10 Azarias, Azarias gat Johannam, Johannam gat Azarias ; he is Azarias, the
prest of the kynde of Aaron, the which
vside in the hous presthod, that Salamon
11 bylde in Jerusalem. Forsothe Azarias
gat Amarias, and Amarias gat Achitob,
12 Achitob gat Sadoch, Sadoch gat Sellum,
13 Sellum gat Elchias, Elchias gat Azari-
14 am[w], Azarias[w] gat Sarayam, Sarayam
15 gat Josedech. Forsothe Josedech ȝede
out, whanne the Lord translatyde Judam
and Jerusalem by the hondis of Nabugodonosor kyng.

CAP. VI.

16   The sonis than of Leuy ; Jersan, Caath,
17 and Merery. And thes the namys of the
18 sonys of Jersan ; Lobeni, and Semei. The
sonys of Caath; Amram, and Ysachar, and
19 Ebron, and Osiel. The sonys of Merery;
Mooli, and Musi. Thes forsothe the kynredis of Leuy aftir the meynees of hem ;
20 Jersan ; Lobeni, the sone of hym ; Jaath, the
21 sone of hym; Sama, the sone of hym; Joath,
the sone of hym ; Addo, the sone of hym ;
Zara, the sone of hym ; Jethrai, the sone
22 of hym. The sonys of Caath; Amynadab,
the sone of hym ; Chore, the sone of hym ;
23 Asura, the sone of hym ; Elchana, the
sone of hym ; Abiasaf, the sone of hym ;
24 Aser, the sone of hym ; Caath, the sone
of hym ; Vriel, the sone of hym ; Osias,
the sone of hym ; Saul, the sone of hym.
25 The sonys of Helchana ; Amasay, Achy-
26 mooth, and Helchana. The sonys of Helchana ; Sophai, the sone of hym ; Naath,
27 the sone of hym ; Eliab, the sone of hym ;
Heroan, the sone of hym ; Elchana, the
28 sone of hym. The sonys of Samuel ; the
29 first goten Nasen, and Abiam. The sonys
forsothe of Mereri ; Moli, the sone of
30 hym ; Lobeny, the sone of hym ; Semey,
the sone of hym ; Osa, the sone of hym ;

Nadab, and Abyu, Eleazar, and Ythamar. 4
Eleazar gendride[z] Phynees, and Phynees
gendride[z] Abisue, Abisue gendride[z] Bocci, 5
and Bocci gendride[z] Ozi, Ozi gendride[z] 6
Zaraie, and Zaraie gendride Meraioth.
Forsothe Meraioth gendride[z] Amarie, A- 7
marie gendride[z] Achitob, Achitob gen- 8
dride[z] Sadoch, Sadoch gendride[z] Achymaas, Achymaas gendride[z] Azarie, Aza- 9
rie gendride[z] Johannam, Johannam gen- 10
dride[z] Azarie ; he it is that was set in
preesthod, in the hows which[a] Salomon
bildide in Jerusalem. Forsothe Azarie 11
gendride[b] Amarye, and Amarie gendride[b]
Achitob, Achitob gendride[b] Sadoch, Sa- 12
doch gendride[b] Sellum, Sellum gendride[b] 13
Helchie, Helchie gendride[b] Azarie, Azarie 14
gendride[b] Saraie, Saraie gendride[b] Josedech. Forsothe Josedech ȝede out, whanne 15
the Lord translatide Juda and Jerusalem
bi the hondis of Nabugodonosor kyng[c].
Therfor the sones of Leuy weren Gerson, 16
Caath, and Merary. And these weren the 17
names of the sones of Gerson ; Lobeni, and
Semei. The sones of Caath weren Am- 18
ram, and Isaar, and Ebron, and Oziel.
The sones of Merari weren Moli, and 19
Musi. Sotheli these weren the kynredis
of Leuy bi the meynees of hem ; Gerson ; 20
Lobony, his sone ; Jaath, his sone; Zama, his
sone ; Joaith, his sone; Addo, his sone; Zara, 21
his sone ; Jethrai, his sone. The sones of 22
Caath ; Amynadab, his sone ; Chore, his
sone ; Azyra, his sone ; Helcana, his sone ; 23
Abiasaph, his sone ; Aser, his sone ; Caath, 24
his sone ; Vriel, his sone ; Azias, his sone ;
Saul, his sone. The sones of Helchana 25
weren Amasay, and Achymoth, and Helcana. The sones of Helcana ; Saphay, his 26
sone ; Naath, his sone ; Heliab, his sone; 27
Heroam, his sone ; Helcana, his sone. The 28
sones of Samuel ; the firste gendrid[d] Nasen, and Abia. Sotheli the sones of Me- 29
rari ; Moli, his sone ; Lobeny, his sone ;
Semey, his sone ; Oza, his sone ; Sama, his 30
sone ; Aggias, his sone ; Azaya, his sone ;

w Zacharias ε.

[z] gaat 1.   [a] that 1.   [b] gaut 1.   [c] the kyng 1.   [d] goten 1.

Sama, the sone of hym; Aggias, the sone
31 of hym; Azaia, the sone of hym Thes
ben the whiche Dauid ordeynde vpon the
syngers of the hous of the Lord, sithen
32 the arke was brou3t to, and thei mynystreden before the tabernacle of witnessynge syngynge, to the tyme that Salomon hadde byld the hous of the Lord
in Jerusalem; thei stoden forsothe aftir
33 their oider in their seruyse Thes forsothe ben that stoden to with their sonys
Of the sonys of Caath, Eman syngere,
34 the sone of Joel, sone of Samuel, sone of
Elchana, sone of Jeroam, sone of Heliel,
35 sone of Thou, sone of Suph, sone of Elchana, sone of Meath, sone of Amazi,
36 sone of Elchana, sone of Johel, sone of
37 Azarie, sone of Sophonie, sone of Caath,
sone of Aser, sone of Abiesaf, sone of
38 Chore, sone of Ysaar, sone of Caath,
39 sone of Leuy, sone of Yrael And the
brother of hym, Asaf, that stode on the
ri3t syde of hym, Asaf, the sone of Bara-
40 chie, sone of Samaa, sone ot Mychael,
41 sone of Basie, sone of Melchie, sone of
42 Attay, sone of Zara, sone of Adala, sone
of Edan, sone of Zama, sone of Semei,
43 sone of 'Jeth, sone of Jersan, sone of
44 Leuy The sonys foisothe of Mereri,
the bretheren of hem, at the left; Ethan,
the sone of Cusy, sone of Abdi, sone of
45 Moloch, sone of Asabie, sone of Amasie,
46 sone of Elchie, sone of Amasai, sone of
47 Bonny, sone of Somer, sone of Mooly,
sone of Musy, sone of Meiari, sone of
48 Leuy The bretheren forsothe of hem,
Leuytis, that ben ordeynd in to al the
seruyse of the tabernacle of the hous of
49 the Lord Aaron forsothe and his sonys
brenden encense vpon the auter of brent
sacrifices, and vpon the auter of the maad
encense, in to al the werk of the holy
of halowes, and that they preyen for
Yrael, aftir alle thingis that Moyses, the
50 seruaunt of God, comaundyde Thes forsothe ben the sonys of Aaron, Eliazar,
the sone of hym; Phynees, the sone of

These it ben whiche^e Dauid ordeynede on 31
the syngeris of the hows of the Lord,
sithen^f the arke of the Lord was set, and 32
thei mynystriden bifor the tabernacle ot
witnessyng, and sungun, til Salomon bildide the hows of the Lord in Jerusalem,
forsothe thei stoden bi her ordre in seruyce Sotheli^g thes it ben that stoden ny3 33
with her sones Of the sones of Caath, Heman the chauntor, the sone of Joel, sone
of Samuel, sone of Helcana, sone of Jo- 34
roam, sone of Heliel, sone of Thou, sone 35
of Suph, sone of Helcana, sone of Mabath, 36
sone of Amasi, sone of Helcana, sone^h of
Joel, sone of Azarie, sone^h of Sophonye,
sone^h of Caath, sone of Asyr,' sone^h of 37
Abiasaph, sone of Chore, sone^h of Isaar, 38
sone^h of Caath, sone of Leuy, sone^h of
Israel. And hise britheren; Asaph, that 39
stood at the ri3thalf of hym, Asaph, the
sone of Barachie, sone^h of Saman, sone^h 40
of Mychael, sone^h of Basye, sone of Melchie, sone of Atthay, sone of Zaia, sone 41
of Adala, sone of Edan, sone^h of Zama, 42
sone^h of Semey, sone^h of Geth, sone of 43
Gerson, sone^h of Leuy Forsothe the 44
sones of Merary, the britheren of hem,
weren at the leftside; Ethan, the sone of
Chusi, sone^h of Abdi, sone^h of Moloch,
sone of Asabie, sone of Amasie, sone^h of 45
Helchie, sone^h of Amasay, sone^h of Bonny, 46
sone of Soomer, sone of Moli, sone of 47
Musi, sone^h of Merarie, sone of Leuy.
And dekenes, the britheren of hem, that 48
weren ordeyned in to al the seruyce of
the tabeinacle of the hows of the Lord
Forsothe Aaron and hise sones brenten 49
encense on^i the auter of brent sacrifices,
and on^i the auter of encense, in to al the
werk 'of the hooli ot^k hooli thingis; and
that thei schulden preie for Israel, by alle
thingis whiche^l Moises, the seruaunt of
God, comaundide. Sotheli^m these ben the 50
sones of Aaron, Eleazar, his sone; Phynees, his sone, Abisue, his sone; Bocci, 51
his sone; Ogzi, his sone, Zaia, his sone,
Meraioth, his sone; Amarias, his sone, 52

---

e that 1 f sith 1 g And 18 h the sone 1 i upon 1 j Om 1 of holi Israel s k bi s l bi whiche 1
m And 1 Om s

51 hym ; Abisue, the sone of hym ; Boccy, the sone of hym ; Ogzi, the sone of hym ; 52 Zara, the sone of hym ; Meraioth, the sone of hym ; Amarias, the sone of hym ; 53 Achitob, the sone of hym ; Sadoch, the sone of hym ; Achymaas, the sone of hym. 54 And thes the dwellynge placis of hem, by tounnes and neeȝ coostis, of thilk sones, that is, of Aaron, aftir the kynredis of Caathitis ; to hem forsothe by lott thei 55 fellen. Thanne thei ȝeuen to hem Ebron in the lond of Juda, and the suburbis of 56 it by ennyroun ; the feeldis forsothe of the cyte, and the touns, to Caleph, the 57 sone of Jephone. Forsothe to the sonys of Aaron thei ȝeuen cytees to fleen to ; Ebron, and Lobna, and the suburbis of 58 it, Jether forsothe, and Escamo with his suburbis, and Helon, and Aber, with their 59 suburbis, Aaron forsothe, and Bethsames, 60 and the suburbis of hem. Of the lynage forsothe of Benjamyn, Gabee, and the suburbis of it, and Alamath with his suburbis, Anathoth forsothe with his suburbis ; alle the cytees thrittene with 61 their suburbis, by their kynredis. To the sonys forsothe of Caph, residue of ther[x] kynrede, thei ȝeuen of the half lynage of Manasse in to possessioun tenn cytees. 62 Forsothe to[y] the sonys of Jersan bi their kynredis, of the lynage of Ysachar, and of the lynage of Aser, and of the lynage of Neptalym, and of the lynage of Ma-63 nasse in Basan, fouretene cytees. To the sonys forsothe of Merery by their kyn-redis, of the lynage of Ruben, of the lynage of Gad, of the lynage of Zabulon 64 thei ȝeuen lottis, twelue cytees. For-sothe the sonys of Yrael ȝeuen to the Leuytis cytees and the suburbis of hem ; 65 and thei ȝeuen by lott, of the lynage of the sonys of Juda, and of the lynage of the sones of Symeon, and of the lynage of the sonys of Benjamyn, thes cytees 66 that thei clepen of their namys ; and of hem that weren of the kynrede of the

Achitob, his sone ; Sadoch, his sone ; Achi-53 maas, his sone. And these weren the 54 dwelling places, bi the townes and coostis of hem, that is, of the sones of Aaron, bi the kynredis of Caathitis ; for tho bifelden to hem bi lot. Therfor the children of 55 Israel ȝauen to hem Ebron in the lond of Juda, and the subarbis therof bi cum-pas ; sotheli[n] thei ȝauen the feeldis and 56 townes of the citees to Caleph, sone[o] of Jephone. Forsothe[p] thei ȝauen citees to 57 the sones of Aaron, Ebron to refuyt ; and thei ȝauen Lobna, with hise subarbis, and 58 Jether, and Escamo, with her subarbis, but also Helon, and Dabir, with her sub-arbis ; also thei ȝauen Asan, and Beth-59 sames, and the subarbis of tho. Sotheli[q] 60 of the lynage of Beniamyn thei ȝauen Gabee, and the subarbis therof, and Ala-mach with hise subarbis, Anathot also[r] with hise subarbis ; alle the citees weren threttene with her subarbis, bi the kyn-redis of hem. Forsothe[s] to[t] the sones of 61 Caath, residues[u] of her kynrede, thei ȝauen of the half lynage of Manasses ten citees 'in to possessioun[v]'. Sotheli[w] to the sones 62 of Gerson bi her kynredis thei ȝauen four-tene citees in Basan, of the lynage of Ysa-car, and of the lynage of Aser, and of the lynage of Neptalym, and of the lynage of Manasses. Forsothe[x] to the sones of Me-63 rary by her kynredis thei ȝauen bi lottis twelue citees, of the lynage of Ruben, of the lynage of Gad, and of the lynage of Zabulon. And the sones of Israel ȝauen 64 to dekenes citees and subarbis of tho ; and 65 thei ȝauen bi lot, of the sones of the lynage of Juda, and of the lynage of the sones of Symeon, and of the lynage of the sones of Beniamyn, these citees, which the dekenes clepiden bi her names ; and of hem that 66 weren of the kynrede[y] of the sones of Caath, and in the termes of hem weren the citees of the lynage of Effraym. And 67 the sones of Israel ȝauen to hem citees of refuyt ; Sichem with hise subarbis in the

---

x the n.   y of n.

n and is.   o the sone is.   P And is.   q And is.   r Om. x.   s And i.   t Om. i. to his and s sec. m.
u the residues i.   v Om. x.   w And is.   x And is.   y kinredis s.

sonys of Caath, and there weren cytees in the termys of hem of the lynage of 67 Effraym. And thei 3euen to hem cytees to fleen to, Sychym with his suburbis in the mount of Effraym, and Gasa with 68 his suburbis, Hiemaan forsothe with his 69 suburbis, and Betheron also Also of the lynage of Dan, Ebethe, Jebethor, and Heielan, and Helon with his suburbis, and Jethremon into the same maner. 70 Forsothe of the half lynage of Manasse, Aner, and the suburbis of it, Balaham, and the suburbis of it, to thes, that is, that of the kynrede of the sonys of Caath 71 weren laft To the sonys forsothe of Jerson, of the kynrede of the half lynage of Manasse, Gawlon in Basan, and the suburbis of it, and Astaroth with his sub- 72 urbis Of the lynage of Ysachar, Cedes, and the suburbis of it, and Daberith with 73 his suburbis, Samoth forsothe, and his suburbis, and Anen with his suburbis 74 Of the lynage forsothe of Aser, Masal with his suburbis, and Adon lijc maner, 75 Asach forsothe, and the suburbis of it, 76 and Roob with his suburbis Bot of the lynage of Neptalym, Cedes in Galilee, and the suburbis of it, Amon with his sub- urbis, and Cariathiarym, and the suburbis 77 of it To the sonys forsothe of Mereri residue, of the lond of Zabulon, Remon, and the suburbis of it, and Thabor with 78 his suburbis Be3onde Jordan forsothe, forn a3eynst Jericho, a3einus the est of Jordan; of the lynage of Ruben, Bozor in wildirnesse with his suburbis, and 79 Jaza with his suburbis, Cademoth forsothe, and the suburbis of it, and My- 80 phaath with his suburbis Also of the lynage of Gad, Ramoth in Galaad, and the suburbis of it, Manaym with his 81 suburbis, bot and Esebon with his sub- urbis, and Jezer with his suburbis

lul of Effiaym, and Gazer with hise sub- arbis, also Hicmaan with hise suburbis, 68 and Betheron also Also of the lynage of 69 Dan thei 3auen Ebethe, Gebethoi, and Heialan, and Helon, with hei suburbis, and Gethremon bi the same maner Foi- 70 sothe of the half lynage of Manasses thei 3auen Aner, and the suburbis therof, Ba- laam, and the suburbis therof, that is, to hem that weren residue of the kynrede of the sones of Caath Sotheli to the sones 71 of Gerson thei 3auen of the kynrede of half the lynage of Manasses, Gaulon in Ba- san, and the suburbis therof, and Astoroth with hise suburbis Of the lynage of Isa- 72 char thei 3auen Cedes, and the suburbis therof, and Daberith with hise suburbis, also Samoth, and his suburbis, and Anem 73 with hise suburbis Also of the linage 74 of Aser thei 3auen Masal with hise sub- arbis, and Abdon also, and Asach, and 75 the suburbis therof, and Roob with hise subarbis Sotheli of the lynage of Nep- 76 talym thei 3auen Cedes in Galilee and the subarbis therof, Amon with hise suburbis, and Cariathiarym, and subarbis therof. Sotheli to the residue sones of Merary 77 thei 3auen of the lynage of Zabulon, Re- mon and subarbis therof, and Thabor with hise suburbis Also bi3ende Jordan, 78 euene a3ens Jerico, a3ens the cest of Jor- dan, thei 3auen of the lynage of Ruben, Bosor in thei wildirnesse with hise sub- arbis, and Jasa with hise subarbis, also 79 Cademoth, and hise suburbis, and My- phaat with hise suburbis. Also and of 80 the lynage of Gad thei 3auen Ramoth in Galaath, and the subarbis therof, Manaym with hise suburbis, but also Esebon with 81 hise suburbis, and Jezer with hise sub- arbis

CAP VII

1 Forsothe the sonys of Ysachar, Thola, and Fua Jazub, and Zameron, foure 2 The sonis of Thola; Ozi, and Raphaya,

CAP VII

Forsothe the sones of Isachar weren 1 foure; Thola, and Phua, Jasub, and Sa- meron. The sones of Thola weren Ozi, 2

---

x And is a left r b And is c Om r d And r Om s e the subarbis IKX sec m s f Om r
K Om r h to is i the subarbis FKSX j Om is k Om N.

and Jerehel, and Jemay, and Jepsen, and
Samuel, princes by the houses of their
cognaciouns. Of the lynage of Thola,
most strouge men ben noumbred in the
days of Dauid, two and twenty thousand
3 and sixe hundreth. The sonis of Ozi,
Jesraya; of whome ben born Michael,
and Obadia, and Johel, and Jesay, fyue,
4 alle princes. And with hem by mcynees,
and ther puplis, gird to batail most
stronge men sixe and thritty thousand;
forsothe thei hadden many wijues and
5 sonys. And the bretheren of hem by
alle the kynredis of Ysachar most stronge
to fiȝten seuen and eyȝty thousand ben
6 noumbred. The sonys of Benjamyn;
7 Bale, and Bochor, and Adiel, thre. The
sonis of Bale; Esbon, and Ozi, and Osiel,
and Jerimoth, and Uray, fyue, princis of
the mcynees, to fiȝten most stronge; the
noumbre forsothe of hem two and twenty
8 thousand and foure and thritty. Bot the
sonys of Bochor; Samyra, and Joas,
and Eliazer, and Elioenay, and Zamry,
and Jerimoth, and Abia, and Anathot,
and Anathan; alle thes the sonys of
9 Bochor. There ben noumbred forsothe
by their meynes princis of kynredis to
batayls most stronge twenty thousand
10 and two hundreth. Forsothe the sonys
of Ledyel, Baalan; the sonys forsothe of
Baalan, Jheus, and Beniamyn, and Aoth,
and Canana, and Jotham, and Thassis,
11 and Thasaar. Alle thes the sonys of
Ledyel, princes of ther^z kynredis most
stronge men, seuentene thousand and two
12 hundreth, to batayl goynge forthe. Saphan forsothe and Akham, thes the sonis
13 of Hyr; and Asyn, the sone of Asir. The
sonys forsothe of Neptalym; Jasiel, and
Gunny, and Azer, and Sellum; the sonys
14 of Bale. Forsothe the sone^a of Manasse,
Ezriel; and the secoundary wijf of hym
Cira gat Machir, the fadir of Galaad.
15 Machir forsothe toke wijues to his sonys
Huphyn and Suphyn; and he hadde a

and Raphaia, and^k Jerihel, and Jemay,
and Jepsen, and Samuel, princis bi the
housis of her kynredis. Of the gene-
raciouu of Thola, weren noumbrid strongeste men in the daies of Dauid, two and
twenti thousynde and sixe hundrid. The 3
sones of Ozi *weren* Jezraie; of whom
weren borun Mychael, and Obadia, and
Johel, and Jezray, fyue, alle princes. And 4
with hem *weren* bi her meynees and
puplis, sixe and thretti thousynde strong-
este^l men gird to batel; for thei hadden
many wyues and sones. And her bri- 5
theren by alle the^m kynredis of Isachar
'moost stronge^n to fiȝte weren noumbrid
foure scoore and seuene thousynde. The 6
sones of Beniamyn *weren* Bale, and Bo-
thor, and Adiel, thre. The sones of Bale 7
weren Esbon, and Ozi, and Oziel, and
Jerymoth, and Vray, fyue, princes of
meynees, mooste stronge to fiȝte; for the
noumbre of hem was two and twenti
thousynde and foure and thretti. For- 8
sothe^o the sones of Bochor *weren* Samara,
and Joas, and Eliezer, and Elioenai, and
Zamri, and Jerimoth, and Abia, and Anathoth, and Almachan; alle these *weren* the
sones of Bochor. Sotheli^p the princes of 9
kynredis weren noumbrid bi her meynees
twenti thousynde and two hundrid moost
stronge men to batels. Forsothe^q the 10
sones of Ledihel *weren* Balan; sotheli
the sones of Balan *weren*^{r} Jheus, and Beniamyn, and Aoth, and Camana, and Jo-
than, and Tharsis, and Thasaar. Alle 11
these the sones of Ledihel *weren* princes
of her meynees, seuentene thousynde and
two hundrid, strongeste men goynge forth
to batel. Also Saphan and Apham *weren* 12
the sones of Hir; and Basym *was* the
sone of Aser. Forsothe^s the sones of 13
Neptalym *weren* Jasiel, and Guny, and
Aser, and Sellum; the sones of Bale.
Sotheli^t the sone of Manasses *was* Esriel; 14
and Sira his secundarie wijf childide Machir, the fadir of Galaad. And Machir 15

^{z} the *ABFH*. ^{a} sonys *FH*.

^{k} Om. s. ^{l} moost strong I. ^{m} Om. N. ^{n} strengist I. ^{o} And IS. ^{p} And IS. ^{q} And IS. ^{r} Om. I.
^{s} And IS. ^{t} And IS.

sustei Maacha by name; and name of
the secounde sone Salphaath, and there
16 ben boin to Salphaath douꝫtirs And
Maacha, the wijf of Machir, baie a sone,
and clepide the name of hym Phares,
forsothe the name of his biother Sares,
and the sonis of hym, Vlam and Recem
17 The sone forsothe of Vlam, Baldan Thes
the sonys of Galaad, sone of Machir, sone
18 of Manasse; the systei forsothe of hym
Regma, a fayr man sche bare, Abiezer,
19 and Moola Forsothe thei weren the
sonys of Semeida; Abyin, and Cychyin,
20 and Liey, and Anynam The sonys forsothe of Effraym, Suchaba, Bareth, the
sone of hym; Caath, the sone of hym;
Elida, the sone of hym, and Caath, the
sone of hym, and of this the sone, Zedaba;
21 and of this the sone, Suthala, and of this
the sone, Ezer, and Elad Forsothe thei
slewen hem the men of Geth thenns
goten, for thei camen doun that thei
22 assailen the possessiouns of hem Thanne
weylid Effiaym, the fadir of hem, many
days; and there camen his britheren,
23 that thei comforten hym And he wente
in to his wijf, the whiche conceyued, and
bare a sone, and clepyde his name Berya,
for thi that in the euyls of his hous he
24 was born The douꝫtir forsothe of hym
was Saia; the wniche bildide up Beth-
cron, the nether and the ouei, and Ozen,
25 and Sara Forsothe the sone of hir,
Rapha, and Receph, and Thale, of the
26 whiche is born Thaan, the whiche gat
Laadon; of this forsothe the sone, Amyud,
27 gat Elizama, of the whiche is born Nun,
28 the whiche hadde a sone Josue The
possessioun forsothe of hem and dwellynge, Bethel with his douꝫtirs, and aꝫeyns
the este of Noram; at the west plage of
Gazer, and the douꝫtirs of it, Sychem
with his douꝫtirs, and Aza with his
29 douꝫtirs. Besydis forsothe the sonys of
Manasse, Bethsan, and the douꝫtirs of it,

took wyues to hise sones Huphyn and
Suphyn, and he hadde a sister Maacha bi
name; and the name of the secounde sone
was Salphaath, and douꝫtris weren borun
to Salphaath And[t] Maacha, the wijf of 16
Machii, childide a sone, and clepide his
name Phares, forsothe[u] the name of his
brotlir *was* Saies; and hise sones *weren*
Vlam and Recem Sotheli[v] the sone of 17
Vlam *was* Baldan These weren the
sones of Galaad, sone of Machir, sone of
Manasses: forsothe[w] Regma his sistir 18
childide a feir man, Abiezer, and Mola
Forsothe[x] the sones of Semyda weren 19
Abym, and Sichem, and Liey, and Amany
Sotheli[y] the sones of Effiaym *weren* Su- 20
chaba, Baieth, his sone; Caath, his sone,
Elda, his sone; and Thaath, his sone, and
Zadaba, his sone; and Suthala, his sone, and 21
Ezei, and Elad, his sones Forsothe[z] men
of Geth borun in the lond killiden hem,
for thei ꝫeden doun to assaile hei possessiouns Thei for Effraym, the fadir of 22
hem, weilide bi many daies, and hise britheren camen to coumforte hym And he 23
entiide to his wijf, which[a] conseyuede, and
childide a sone; and he clepide his name
Beria, for he was borun in the yuehs of
his hows. Sotheli[b] his douꝫtir was[c] Sara; 24
that bildide Betheron, the lowere and the
hiꝫere, and Ozen, and Sara Foisothe[d] 25
his sone *was* Rapha, and Reseph, and[f]
Thale, of whom was borun Thaan, that 26
gendride Laodon, and Amyud, the sone
of hym, gendrides[g] Elysama, of whom was 27
boiun Nun, that hadde a sone Josue
Sotheli[h] the possessioun and dwellyng 28
place[i] of hem *was* Bethil with hise villagis,
and aꝫens the eest, Noram; at the west
coost. Gazei, and hise villagis, also Sichem
with hise villagis, and Aꝫa with hise villagis Also bisidis the sones of Manasses, 29
Bethsan, and hise townes, Thanach and
hise townes, Maggeddo, and hise townes,
Doi, and hise townes, the[j] sones of Joseph

[t] Om s [u] and is [v] And is [w] and is [x] And is [y] And is [z] And is [a] the which 1
[b] And is [c] was *clepide* s [d] And is [e] *hiꝫi* is [f] Roph, and A *sec* m [g] gaat 1 [h] And is [i] the dwelling placis s [j] and the D

Thauach, and the douȝtirs of it, Magedo, and the douȝtirs of it, Dor, and the douȝtirs of it; in thes dwelliden the sonys of 30 Joseph, sone of Yrael. The sonys of Aser; Jerona, and Jesua, and Ysni, and 31 Baria; and Sara, the syster of hem. The sonys forsothe of Baria; Heber, and Melchiel; 32 he is the fadir of Barsath. Heber forsothe gat Jeflath, and Somer, and 33 Otham, and Sua, the syster of hem. The sonys forsothe of Jeflath; Phosech, and Camaal, and Jasoph; thes the sonys of 34 Jeflath. Bot the sonys of Somer; Aachi, 35 and Roaga, and Jaba, and Aram. The sonys forsothe of Helem, his brother; Supha, and Jemma, and Selles, and 36 Amal. The sonys of Supha; Sue, Arnapheth, and Sual, and Bery, and Jamra, 37 and Bozor, and Odor, and Sama, and 38 Salusa, and Jethram, and Beram. The sonis of Ether; Jephone, and Phaspha, 39 and Ara. The sonys forsothe of Ollaa; 40 Areth, and Anyel, and Resya. Alle thes the sonys of Azer, princes[d] of the kynredis, chosen and most stronge duykis of duykis; the noumber forsothe, of the age of hem that was able to batayl, sixe and twenty thousand.

sone[k] of Israel dwelliden in these townes. The sones of Aser weren Sona, and Jesua, 30 and Isuy, and Baria; and Sara was the sister of hem. Sotheli[l] the sones of Baria 31 weren Heber, and Melchiel; he is the fadir of Barsath. Sotheli[m] Heber gendride 32 Ephiath, and Soomer, and Otham, and Sua, the sister of hem. Forsothe[n] the 33 sones of Jephiath weren Phosech, and Camaal, and Jasoph; these weren the sones of Jephiath. Sotheli[o] the sones of 34 Soomer weren Achi, and Roaga, and Jaba, and Aram. Sotheli[o] the sones of Helem, 35 his brother, weren Supha, and Jema, and Selles, and Amal. The sones of Supha 36 weren Sue, Arnapheth[p], and Sual, and Bery, and Jamra, and Bosor, and Ador, 37 and Sama, and Salusa, and Jethram, and Beram. The sones of Ether weren Je- 38 phone, and Phaspha, and Ara. Sotheli[q] 39 the sones of Ollaa weren Areth, and Aniel, and Resia. Alle these weren the sones of 40 Aser, princes of kynredis, chosun men and strongeste[r] duykis of duykis; forsothe[s] the noumbre, of the age of hem that weren[t] abel to[u] batel, was sixe and twenti thousynde.

CAP. VIII.

1 Beniamyn forsothe gat Baale his first goten, Asbaal the secounde, Othora the 2 thrid, Naua the ferthe, and Rapha the 3 fyft. And the sonys of Baale weren 4 Addoar, and Jera, and Abiud, Abisue 5 forsothe, and Noemany, and Achoe, Zed, and Jera, and Sephusam, and Vram. 6 Thes ben the sonys of Adoth, princis of the kynredis dwellyng in Gabaa, the 7 whiche ben translatid in Manath. Naaman forsothe, and Achia, and Jera, he translatide hem, and gat Osa, and Abyud; 8 bot Saarym he gat in the regioun of Moab, aftir that he laft Vrym and Bara, 9 his wijues; forsothe he gat of Edes, his

CAP. VIII.

1 Forsothe Beniamyn gendride[v] Bale his firste gendrid[w] sone, Asbaal the secounde, Othora the thridde, Naua the fourthe, and 2 Rapha the fyuethe. And the sones of 3 Bale weren Addoar, and Jera, and Abyud, and Abisue, and Noemany, and Acte, but 5 also Gera, and Sophupham, and Vram. These ben the sones of Haoth, princes of 6 kynredis dwellynge in Gabaa, that weren translatid in to Manath. Forsothe[x] Noa- 7 man, and Achia, and Jera, 'he translatide[y] hem, and gendride[z] Oza and Abyud; for- 8 sothe[a] 'Saarym gendride[b] in the cuntrey of Moab, aftir that he lefte Vrym and Bara, hise wyues; sotheli[c] he gendride[d] of Edes, 9

---

[d] prince ABFH.

[k] Om. A et plures. [l] And is. [m] And is. [n] And is. [o] And is. [p] and Arnapheth s. [q] And is. [r] ful stronge I. [s] and is. [t] was AELS. [u] in A pr. m. [v] gaat I. [w] goten I. [x] And is. [y] translatiden A sec. m. [z] he gaat I. he gendride s. [a] and is. [b] he gaat I. he gendride s. [c] and is. [d] gaat I.

wijf, Jobab, and Sebia, and Mosa, and
10 Molchom, Jebus forsothe, and Sechia, and
Marma , thes ben the sonys of hym,
11 princis in their meynees   Meusym for-
12 sothe gat Achytob, and Elphaal   Forsothe the sonys of Elphaal , Ebei, and
Mysaam, and Samaath , this bilde Ono,
13 and Lod, and the douȝtirs of it , Bara
forsothe and Sama, princis of the kynredis dwellynge in Haylon ; thes dryuen
14 aweye the dwellers of Geth , and Hayo,
15 and Sesach, and Jeiymoth, and Sadabia,
16 and Arod, and Eder, Mychael forsothe,
and Jespha, and Joaa, the sonys of Ba-
17 ria , Sadabia, and Mosollam, and Elethi,
18 and Hebei, and Jezamai, and Jesua,
19 and Jobab, sonys of Elphaal , Rachym,
20 and Zecri, and Zabdi, and Helioenai, and
21 Selectai, and Henelech, and Adaya, and
Baraza, and Samarath, the sonys of Se-
22 mei , Jesfan, and Heber, Esiel, and
Abyon, and Zechii, and Abdi, and He-
23 hoenai, and Saiai, and Heliel, and Abdon,
24 and Zechri, and Chanaan, and Ananya,
25 and Phanuel, the sonys of Sesnach ,
26 27 Sampsaii and Scoiia, and Otholia, and
Jersia, and Helia, and Zechri, the sonys
28 of Jeroaur   Thes patriarkis and princis
of kynredis, that dwelliden in Jerusalem
29 In Gabaon forsothe dwelliden Abigabaon,
30 and name of his wijf Maacha , the sone
forsothe of hym, the first goten Abdon,
and Sui, and Ciz, and Baal, and Ner,
31 and Nadab, Jeddo forsothe, and Hayo,
32 and Zacher and Machellot. And Machellot gat Samaa ; and thei dwelliden
foru aȝeins thei bretheren in Jeiusalem
33 with their bretheren   Nei forsothe gat
Ciz, and Ciz gat Saul   Forsothe Saul
gat Jonathan, and Melchisue, and Abyna-
34 dab, and Vbaal   The sone forsothe of
Jonathan, Myphybaal , and Myphibaal
35 gat Mycham. The sonys of Mycha ,
Pluton, and Meleth, and Thaia, and
36 Achaz   And Achaz gat Joiada , and
Joiada gat Almoth, and Azymoth, and
Zamry   Forsothe Zamry gat Mosa ;

his wijf, Jodab, and Sebia, and Mosa, and
Molchon, also Jebus, and Sechia, and Ma- 10
ryna , tho ben the sones of hym, prynces
in her meynees   Forsothe[e] Musyn gen- 11
dride[f] Achitob, and Elphaal   Sotheli[g] the 12
sones of Elphaal *weren* Hebei, and Mu-
saam, and Samaath ; he bildide Ono, and
Lod, and hise villagis ; forsothe[h] Baia and 13
Sama *weren* princes of kynredis dwellynge in Hailon ; these dryueden[i] awei the
dwelleris of Geth , and Haio, and Sesath, 14
and Jerymoth, and Zadabia, and Arod, 15
and Heder, and Mychael, and Jespha[k] 16
helpiden hem 'aȝens men of Geth' , the
sones of Abaria, and Zadabia, and Mo- 17
sollam, and Ezethi, and Hebei, and Jesa- 18
mary, and Jeȝha, and Jobab *helpiden[m] 'in
this tui ney aȝens men of Geth[n]*   The
sones of Elphaal *weien* Jachym, and 19
Jechii, and Zabdi, and Helioenay, and 20
Selettay, and Henelech, and Adaia, and 21
Baiasa, and Samarath , the sones of Semcy
wei en Jesphan, and Hebei, and Esiel, and 22
23
Abdon, and Zechry, and Cauaan   and 24
Anany, and Jalam, and Anathotia, and
Jephdma, and Phanuel ; the sones of Sesac 25
wei en Sampsaray, and Scoiia, and Otholia, 26
and Jersia, and Helia, and Zechri, the 27
sones of Jeream   These *weren* patriarkis 28
and princes of kynredis, that dwelliden in
Jerusalem   Forsothe[o] in Gabaon dwelliden 29
Abigaboon, and Maacha the name of his
wijf ; and his firste gendrid[p] sone Abdon, 30
and Sui, and Cys, and Baal, and Nei, and
Nadab, and Geddo, and Haio, and Zacher, 31
and Macelloth. Forsothe[q] Marcelloth gen- 32
dride[r] Samaa , and thei dwelliden euene
aȝens hei biitheren in Jeiusalem with her
britheren   Forsothe[s] Ner gendride[t] Cys, 33
and Cys gendride[t] Saul , forsothe[u] Saul
gendride[v] Jonathan, and Melchisue, and
Abynadab, and Isbaal   Sotheli[x] the sone 34
of Jonathan was Myphibaal ; and Myphibaal gendride[x] Micha   The sones of 35
Micha *wei en* Pluton, and Melech, and
Thara, and Abaz   And Ahaz gendride[y] 36
Joiada , and Joiada gendiide[v] Almoth, and

e And is f gaat 1 g And is h And is i dreuen 1 k Jespha and Joha ꭗ sec m l Om 1
m *helpiden also* 1 n Om 1 o And 1 p goten 1 q And is r gaat 1 s Aud is t gaat 1
u and ais v gaat 1 w And 1 x gaat 1 y gaat 1

37 and Moosa gat Banaa, whos sone was Raphaia, of the whiche is born Elesa, 38 the whiche gat Esel. Forsothe of Esel sixe sonys weren with thes namys, Esricham, Bocheu, Ismael, Saraia, Abadia, 39 Aman; alle thes the sonys of Ezel. The sonys forsothe of Aza, brother of hym; Vlam, the first goten, and Hus, the 40 secounde, and Eliphales, the thrid. And the sonys of Vlam weren most strong men, and with grete streyngthe beendynge bowe, and many sonys hauynge, and sonys sones, vnto an hundreth and fyfty thousand. Alle thes the sonys of Beniamyn.

CAP. IX.

1 Thanne alle[e] Yrael is noumbred, and the summe of hem writen in the boke of the kyngis of Yrael and of Juda; and thei ben translatid in to Babyloyne for 2 their trespasse. Whiche forsothe dwelliden first in their cytees, and in the possessiouns of Yrael, and prestis, and Le-3 uytis, and Nacheneis, dwelliden in Jerusalem. Of the sonys of Juda, and of the sonys of Beniamyn, of the sonys forsothe 4 of Effraym, and of Manasse; Ose, the sone of Ameud, sone of Zemri, sone of Omroy, sone of Bonny, of the sonys of 5 Phares, sone of Juda; and of Cilon, Josia, the first goten, and the sonys of 6 hym; of the sonis forsothe of Saray, Heuel, and the bretheren of hem; sexe 7 hundreth and nynty. Forsothe of the sonys of Beniamyn; Salo, the sone of Mosollam, sone[f] of Odoia, sone of Azana, 8 and Jobanya, sone of Jeroam, and Ela, the sone of Osy, sone of Mochosy, and Mosollam, the sone of Safazie, sone of 9 Rahuel, sone of Jebanye, and the bretheren of hem, bi their meynes; nyne hundreth and sixe and fyfty. Alle thes the princis of their kynredis by the housis of

Azimoth, and Zamry. Forsothe[x] Zamri 37 gendride[a] Moosa, and Moosa gendride[a] Banaa, whos sone was Raphaia, of whom was gendrid[b] Elesa, that gendride[c] Asel. Sotheli[d] Asel hadde sixe sones bi these 38 names, Esricham, Bochru, Ismael, Saria, Abadia, Aman[e]; alle these weren the sones of Asel. Forsothe[f] the sones of Asa, his 39 brothir, weren Vlam, the firste gendride[g] sone, and Hus, the secounde, and Eliphales, the thridde. And the sones of Vlam weren 40 strongeste[h] men, and beendynge a[i] bouwe with greef strength, and hauynge many sones, and sones of sones, til to an hundrid and fifti. Alle[k] these weren the sones of Beniamyn.

CAP. IX.

Therfor al Israel was noumbrid, and 1 the summe of hem was writun in the book of kyngis of Israel and of Juda; and thei weren translatid in to Babiloyne for her synne. Sotheli[l] thei that dwelliden first in 2 her citees, and in the possessiouns of Israel, and the preestis, and the dekenes, and Natyneys[m] †, dwelliden in Jerusalem. Of 3 the sones of Juda, and of the sones of Beniamyn, also of the sones of Effraym, and of Manasses; Othi, the sone of Amyud, 4 sone[n] of Semry, sone[n] of Omroy, sone[n] of Bonny, of the sones of Phares, the sone[o] of Juda; and of Sylom, Asia, the firste 5 gendrid[p], and his sones[q]; sotheli[r] of[s] the 6 sones of Zaray, Heuel, and hise britheren; sixe hundrid fourescore and ten. For-7 sothe[t] of the sones of Beniamyn; Salo, the sone of Mosollam, the sones of Odoia, the sones of Asana, and Jobanya, the sone of 8 Jerobam, and Ela, the sone of Ozi, the sones of Mochozi, and Mosollam, the sone of Saphacie, sone[u] of Rahuel, sone of Jebanye, and the britheren of hem, bi her 9 meynees; nyne hundrid sixe and fifti. Alle these weren princes of her kynredis by the housis of her fadris. Forsothe[v] of the 10

(marginal note right): † Natyneys; thes weren men of Gabaon, that weren conuertid to the feith and religioun of Jewes, and they weren ordeyned to bere wode and water to the place of Goddis worschiping, as it is had in ix. e°. of Josue. Lire here. c.

---

e Om. e pr. m.   f the sone 11.

z And 18.   a guat 1.   b goten 1.   c guat 1.   d Om. 1.   e and Aman 8.   f And 18.   g goten 1.   h ful stronge 1.   i Om. f sec. m. 1KLMSXb.   k And alle sx.   l And 18.   m Natynes a. Nathinuims, that is, a kind of peple 18.   n the sone 18.   o sones a et plures.   p goten 1.   q sone a et plures.   r and 18.   s Om. 18.   t And 18.   u the sone 1.   v And 18.

10 their fadirs. Of the prestis forsothe,
11 Joiada^g, Josarib, and Jachym; Azarias^h
forsothe, the sone of Elchie, sone of Mo-
sollam, sone of Sadoch, sone of Maraioth,
sone of Achitob, the bischop of the hous
12 of the Lord. Forsothe Adayas, the sone
of Jeroam, sone of Fasor, sone of Melchia, and Mazaya, the sone of Adihel,
sone of Jezra, sone of Mosollam, sone
13 of Mosellamoth, sone of Emyner, the
bretheren forsothe of hem, princis bi
their meynes, a thousand seuen hundrith and seuenty, most stronge men bi
streyngth, to don the werc of the seruyse
14 in the hous of the Lord. Of the Leuytis
forsothe, Semeia, the sone of Assub, sone
of Ezricham, sone of Azebny, of the sonys
15 of Merery; Bathacar forsothe carpenter,
and Galabeth, and Machama, the sone of
Mycha, soneⁱ of Zechry, sone of Asaph,
16 and Obdias, the sone of Semeie, sone of
Calaal, sone of Ydytym, and Barachia,
the sone of Asa, sone of Helchana, that
dwellide in the porchis of Methofatite.
17 The porters forsothe, Sellum, and Acub,
and Thelmon, and Achymam, and the
18 bretheren of hem; Sellum prince; vnto
that tyme in the ʒate of the kyng at the
est, thei kepten by ther whilis of the
19 sonys of Leuy. Sellum forsothe, the
sone of Chore, sone of Abiasaph, sone of
Chore, with his britheren, and the hous
of his fadir; thes ben Choritis vpon the
werkis of the seruyce, kepers of the
vestiaryes of the tabernacle, and the
meynees of hem be whilis kepynge the
20 entre of the tentis of the Lord. Phynees
forsothe, the sone of Eliazar, was duyke
21 of hem beforn the Lord. Forsothe Zacharye, the sone of Mosollam, portere
of the ʒate of the tabernacle of witness-
22 ynge. Alle thes chosun 'in to^k vsscheris
by ʒatis two hundrith and twelue, and
discryued in propre townys, whome ordeyneden Dauid and Samuel, seeynge in

preestis, Joiada, Jozarib, and Jachym; and 11
Azarie, the sone of Helchie, sone of Mo-
sollam, sone^v of Sadoch, sone^v of Maraioth,
sone of Achitob, was bischop of the hows
of the Lord. Forsothe^w Adaias, sone of 12
Jeroam, sone^x of Phasor, sone of Melchia,
and Masnia, sone of Adihel, sone of Jezra,
sone^x of Mosollam, sone of Mosselamoth,
sone of Emyner, also her britheren, 13
prynces hi her meynees, weren a thousynde
seuene hundrid and fourescoore, men strong-
este^y in bodili myʒt, to make the werk of
seruyce in the hows of the Lord. For- 14
sothe^z of dekenes^a, Semeya, the sone of
Assub, sone^b of Ezricam, sone^b of Asebyn,
of the sones of Merary; also Balthasar 15
the carpenter†, and Galebeth, and Machama, sone^c of Mycha, sone of Zechri,
sone of Asaph, and Obdias, sone^c of Semey, 16
sone of Calaal, sone^c of Idithum, and Barachie, the sone of Asa, sone^c of Helcana,
that dwellide in the porchis of Methophati.
Sotheli^d the porteris weren Sellum, and 17
Achub, and Thelmon, and Achyman, and
the britheren of hem; Sellum was the
prince; til to that tyme thei kepten bi her 18
whilis in the ʒate of the kyng at the eest,
of the sones of Leuy. Sellum forsothe, 19
the sone of Chore, sone^c of Abiasaph, sone^c
of Chore, with hise britheren, and with the
hows of his fadir; these ben the sones of
Chore on^f the werkis of the seruyce,
keperis of the porchis of the tabernacle,
and the meynees of hem kepten bi whilis^c
the entryng of the castelis of the Lord.
Forsothe^h Phynees, the sone of Eleazar, 20
was the duyk of hem bifor the Lord.
Sotheliⁱ Zacarie, the sone of Mosollam, 21
was porter of the ʒate of the tabernacle of
witnessyng. Alle these chosun in to 22
porteris bi ʒatis weren twei hundrid and
twelue, and weren^k discryued^l in her
owne townes, which^m dekenesⁿ Dauid and
Samuel, the prophete, ordeyneden in her
feith, both hem and the sones of hem in 23

† carpenter; that is, ouer-
seere of the car-
pentors, for
dekenes weren
hisy aboute the
seruyce of God,
of the temple.
Lire here. c.

---

^g of Joiada ABCE pr. m. FII.   ^h and Azarias II.   ⁱ the sone II.   ^k vnto II.

^v the sone I.   ^w Om. IS.   ^x the sone I.   ^y ful stronge I.   ^z And IS.   ^a the dekenesse s.   ^b the
sone IS.   ^c the sone I.   ^d And IS.   ^e the sone I.   ^f upon I.   ^g whilis or tymes I.   ^h And IS.   ⁱ And IS.
^k thei weren IS.   ^l discryued or presentid IS.   ^m the which I.   ⁿ dekenys or mynestris s.

23 his feith, bothe hem and the sonys of hem in the dores of the hous of the Lord, and in the tabernacle of witnessyng, be their 24 whilis. By foure wyndis weren the vsscheris, that is, at the este, and at the weste, and at the northe, and at the 25 southe. The bretheren forsothe of hem dwellide in lityl townys, and thei camen 26 in their sabotis fro tyme vnto tyme. To thes foure Leuytis was bitaken al the noumbre of porters, and thei weren kepinge pryue housis, and¹ the tresours of 27 the hous of the Lord. By enuyroun forsothe `of the temple of the Lord thei dweliden in their wardis, that whanne tyme were, thei erly schulden opynen the 28 ȝatis. And of the kynrede of hem weren vpon the vesselis of the seruyse; at noumbre forsothe the vesselis weren brouȝt in, 29 and of hem brouȝt out. And the whiche hadden be tauȝt alle the necessaries of the seyntuarye, weren bifore to the tried flour, and to the wijne, and to the oyle, and to the encense, and to the swote 30 spycesᵐ. The sonys forsothe of prestis 31 maden oynamentis of swote spices. And Mathatias Leuyte, the first goten of Sellum Chorite, was maystir of alle thingis that weren fryed in the fryinge panne. 32 Forsothe of the sonis of Caath, the bretheren of hem, weren vpon the loouys of proposicyoun, that euermore newe by eche sabot thei schulden maken redy. 33 Thes ben the princis of syngers by the meynes of Leuytis, that dwelliden in priue chaumbris, so that day and nyȝt contynuely thei seruen in therⁿ seruyseᵒ. 34 The heuedis of Leuytis bi their meynes, 35 princis, dwelliden in Jerusalem. In Gabaon forsothe thei dwelliden to gydre; the fadir of Gabaon, Rayelᵖ, and the 36 name of his wijf, Macha; the first goten sone of hym Abdon, and Sur, and Ciz, 37 and Baal, and Ner, and Nadab, Jedor

the doris of the hows of the Lord, and in tho tabernacle of witnessyng, bi her whiles. Porteris weren bi foure coostis, that is, at 24 the eest, andᑫ at the west, andᑫ at the north, and at the south. Forsotheʳ her 25 britheren dwelliden in townes, and camen in her sabatis fro tyme til to tyme. Al 26 the noumbre of porteris was bitakun to these foure dekenes, and thei kepten the chaumbris, and the tresours of the hows of the Lord. Also thei dwelliden in her 27 kepyngis bi the cumpas of the temple of the Lord, that whanne tyme were, thei schulden opene the ȝatis eerli. Men of 28 her kyn weren also on the vessels of seruyce; for the vessels weren borun in at noumbreˢ, and weren borun out of hem. And thei that hadden the vesselis of seyn- 29 tuarieᵗ bitakun to herᵘ kepyng, weren souereyns onᵛ flour, and wyn, and oile, and encense, andʷ swete smellinge spyceries. Sotheliˣ the sones of preestis maden 30 oynementis of swete smellynge spiceries. And Mathatias dekene, the firste gendridʸ 31 sone of Sellum of the kynrede of Chore, was the souereyn of alle thingis that weren fried in the friyng panne. Sotheliᶻ 32 menᵃ of the sones of Caath, the britheren of hem, weren on the looues of settyng forth, that thei schulden make redi euere newe looues bi ech sabat. These ben the 33 princis of chauntourisᵇ bi the meynees of Leuytis, that dwelliden in chaumbris, soᶜ that thei schulden serue contynueli dai and nyȝt in her seruyce. The heedis of 34 Leuitis bi her meynees, the princes, dwelliden in Jerusalem. Forsotheᵈ there dwell- 35 iden in Gabaon; Jaiel, the fadir of Gabaon, and the name of his wijf Maacha; Abdon, 36 his firste gendrideᵉ sone, and Sur, and Cys, and Baal, and Ner, and Nadab, and Gedor, 37 and Ahaio, and Zacharie, and Macelloth; forsotheᶠ Macelloth gendrideᵍ Semmaa; 38 these dwelliden euene aȝens her britheren

---

l in *FH.*   ᵐ oynementis *E pr. m.*   ⁿ the *ABFH.*   ᵒ seruyses c.   ᵖ Israel *n.*

ᑫ Om. s.   ʳ And ıs.   ˢ the noumbre ı.   ᵗ the seyntwarie s.   ᵘ Om. A.   ᵛ upon ı. of s.   ʷ Om. s. ˣ And ıs.   ʸ goten ı.   ᶻ And ıs.   ᵃ Om. ı.   ᵇ syngers ı.   ᶜ for ı.   ᵈ And ıs.   ᵉ goten ı.   ᶠ and ıs. ᵍ gaat ı.

forsoth, and Hayo, and Zacharias, and
38 Macelloth; forsothe Macelloth gat Cem-
maa; thes dwelliden for aȝeynst their
bretheren in Jerusalem, with their bre-
39 theren. Ner forsothe gat Ciz, and Ciz
gat Saul, and Saul gat Jonathan, and
Melchisue, and Abynadab, and Hisbaal.
40 The sone forsothe of Jonathan, Miribaal,
41 and Miribaal gat Mycha. Forsothe the
sonys of Mycha; Phiton, and Maleth⁹,
42 and Thara; Aaz forsothe gat Jara, and
Jara gat Alamath, Asmoth, and Zamry;
43 and Zamri^r gat Moosa, Moosa gat Baana,
whos sone Rephaya gat Elesa, of whome
44 is borne Hezel. Forsothe Hezel hadde
sixe sonys in thes names, Hezricham,
Bothru, Hizmael, Saria, Obdia, Anan;
thes the sonys of Hezel.

in Jerusalem, with her britheren. Sotheli^h 39
Ner gendride^l Cys, and Cys gendride^k
Saul, and Saul gendride^k Jonathan, and
Melchisue, and Abynadab, and Hisbaal.
Forsothe^l the sone of Jonathan *was* Myri- 40
baal, and Myribaal gendride^m Mycha.
Sotheli^n the sones of Micha *weren* Phiton, 41
and Malech, and Thara; forsothe^o Aaz 42
gendride^p Jara, and Jara gendride^p Ala-
math, and Azmoth, and Zamri; and Zamri
gendride^p Moosa, sotheli⁹ Moosa gendride^r 43
Baana, whose sone Raphaia gendride^r Eli-
sa, of whom Esel was gendrid^s. Forsothe^t 44
Esel hadde sixe sones bi these names,
Ezricam, Bochru, Hismael, Saria, Obdia,
Anan; these *weren* the sones of Hesel.

CAP. X.

1 Philisteis forsothe fouȝten aȝeinus Yrael,
and the sonys of Yrael flowen Palestynes,
and woundide thei fellen in the hil of
2 Jesboe. And whenn Philisteis hadden
neyȝid pursuynge Saul and his sonys,
thei smyten Jonathan, and Abynadab,
3 and Melchisue, the sonys of Saul. And
the batayle is agreggid aȝeins Saul; and
ther founden hym men scheters, and
4 woundiden with dartis. And Saul seyde
to his squyer, Drawȝe out thi swerd, and
slee me, lest perauenture the vncircumcidid commen, and scorne to me. Forsothe his squyer wolde not done that,
by dreed agast; thanne Saul cauȝte a
5 swerde, and felle in it. The whiche
whanne his squyer hadde seen, that is,
Saul to ben deed, also he felle in to his
6 swerde, and is deed. Thanne Saul died,
and his thre sonys, and al the hous of
hym to gydre fel. The whiche thing
whan the men of Yrael hadden seen, that
dwelliden in the wijlde feeldis, flowen;
and Saul and his sonys deed, they for-

CAP. X.

Forsothe Filisteis^u fouȝten aȝens Israel, 1
and the sones of Israel fledden Palestyns^v,
and felden doun woundid in the hil of
Gelboe. And whanne Filisteis^w hadde 2
neiȝed pursuynge Saul and hise sones,
thei killiden Jonathan, and Abynadab, and
Melchisue, the sones of Saul. And the 3
batel was agreggid aȝens Saul; and men
archeris foundun hym, and woundiden
hym^x with dartis. And Saul seide to his 4
squiere, Drawe out thi swerd, and sle me,
leste these vncircumcidid men come, and
scorne me. Sothli^y his squyer was aferd
bi drede, and nolde^z do this; therfor Saul^a
took a swerd, and felde on^b it^c. And 5
whanne his squyer hadde seyn this, that
is, that Saul was deed, he felde also on
his swerd, and was deed. Therfor Saul 6
perischide, and hise thre sones, and al his
hows felde doun togidere. And whanne 7
the men of Israel, that dwelliden in feeldi
places, hadden seyn this, thei fledden; and
whanne Saul and hise sones weren deed,
thei forsoken her citees, and weren sca-

^h And is.   ^i gaat i.   ^k gaat i.   ^l And i.   ^m gaat i.   ^n And s.   ^o and is.   ^p gaat i.   ⁹ and is.
gaat i.   ^s goten i.   ^t And s.   ^u the Filisteis i.   ^v the Philistees i. Fylistyns s.   ^w the Philistees i.
Om. *plures*.   ^y But is.   ^z wolde not i.   ^a Saul *him silf* s.   ^b upon is.   ^c it, *and slowe him silf* s.

soken their cytees, and[a] hidir and thidir ben scatered; and Philisteis camen, and dwelliden in hem. Thanne the tother day the Philisteis drawynge aweye the spuylis of the slayn men, founden Saul and his sones lyinge in the hil of Jelboe. And whanne thei haden spuylid hym, and gird of the heued, and nakenyd[t] fro armys, thei senten in to their lond, that he schuld be born about, and be schewid to the templis of mawmetis and peplis; the armys forsothe of hym thei sacriden in the temple of their god, and the heued thei fitchiden in the temple of Dagon. That thing whan the men of Jabes Galaad hadden herd, that is, alle thingis that the Philisteis dyden vpon Saul, echon of the stronge men rysen to gyder, and token the careyns of Saul and his sonys, and brou3ten hem in to Jabes, and birieden the bones of hem vndir an ook, that was in Jabes; and thei fastiden seuen days. Thanne Saul is deed for his wickidnessis[u], for thi that he brake the maundement of the Lord, that he hadde comaundide, and kept it not, bot ouermore also he councelide a wytche, and hopid not in the Lord; and for the whiche thing he slew3 hym, and translatyde the rewme of hym to Dauid, the sone of Ysay.

CAP. XI.

1 Thanne al Yrael is gaderid to gider to Dauid in Ebron, seyinge, Thi boon and thi flesche we ben; 3isterday[v] forsothe and the thrid day hennus, whanne 3it regned Saul vpon Yrael, thou wer that laddist out and brou3tist in Yrael; to thee forsothe the Lord thi God seide, Thou schal feden my puple Yrael, and thou schalt ben prince vpon it. Thanne al the more thoru3 birthe of Yrael camen to the kyng in Ebron; and Dauid wente in with hem pese couenaunt beforn the

teríd hidur and thidur; and Filisteis camen, and dwelliden in tho. Therfor in the tother day Filisteis[d] drowen awei the spuylis of slayn men, and founden Saul and hise sones liggynge in the hil of Gelboe. And whanne thei hadden spuylid hym, and hadden gird of the heed, and hadden[e] maad hym[f] nakid of[g] armeris, thei senten[h] in to her lond, that it schulde be borun aboute, and schulde[i] be schewid in the templis of idols and to puplis; forsothe[k] thei halewiden his armeris in the temple of her god, and thei settiden the heed in the temple of Dagon. Whanne men of Jabes of Galad hadden herd this, that is, alle thingis whiche the Filisteis diden on Saul, alle stronge men risiden[l] togidere, and took[m] the deed bodies of Saul and of hise sones, and brou3ten tho in to Jabes; and thei birieden the boonus of hem vndur an ook, that was in Jabes; and thei[n] fastiden seuene daies. Therfor Saul was deed for hise wickidnessis, for he brak the comaundement[o] of the Lord, whiche he comaundide, and kepte not it, but ferthirmore also he took counsel at a womman hauynge a feend spekynge in the wombe, and he hopide not in the Lord; for which thing bothe the Lord killide hym, and translatide his rewme to Dauid, sone[p] of Ysay.

CAP. XI.

1 Therfor al Israel was gaderid to Dauid in Ebron, and seide, We ben thi boon and thi fleisch; also 3isterdai and the thridde dai ago, whanne Saul regnede 3it on[q] Israel, thou it were[r] that leddist out and leddist in Israel; for 'thi Lord God[s] seide to thee, Thou schalt fede my puple Israel, and thou schalt be prince on[t] it. Therfor alle the gretter[u] in birthe of Israel camen to the kyng in Ebron; and Dauid maad with hem a boond of pees bifor the Lord, and thei anoyntiden hym kyng on[v] Israel,

---

[a] Om. H.   [t] nakyd II.   [u] wickidnes A.   [v] 3istai CE.

[d] the Philistees I.   [e] Om. G.   [f] Om. plures.   [g] the IS.   [h] senten the heed I. sente his heed S.   [i] it shuld S.   [k] and IS.   [l] resen EIL.   [m] token plures.   [n] Om. S.   [o] heest IS.   [p] Om. A.   [q] upou IS.   [r] was I.   [s] the Lord thi God I.   [t] upon IS.   [u] gretter men IS.   [v] upon IS.

Lord, and thei anoyntiden hym king vpon Yrael, aftir the word of the Lord, that he spac in the hond of Samuel 4 Thanne Dauid zede, and al Ysrael, in to Jerusalem; this is Jebus, where weren 5 Jebuseis dwellers of the lond And thei that dwelliden at Jebus seiden to Dauyd, Thou schalt not commen in hydre For- sothe Dauid toke the toure of Syon, that 6 is the cytee of Dauid, and he seide, Eche that smytith Jebuse first, schal ben a prince and duyke Thanne Joab, the sone of Saruye, steyzide up first, and is 7 maad a prince Dauid forsothe dwellid in the tour, and therfore it is clepid the 8 cytee of Dauid, and he bildex up a cytee in enuyroun fro Mello vnto Gyrum; Joab forsothe the tother partye of the cytee 9 made out And Dauith profitide goynge and waxynge, and the Lord of hoostis 10 was with hym Thes the princis of the stronge men of Dauid, the whiche help- iden hym, that he wer kyng vpon al Ysrael, aftir the word of the Lord that 11 he spac to Yrael And this the noumbre of the stronge men of Dauid; Jesbaam, the sone of Achamony, prince amonge thritty, he rerede his spere vpon thre 12 hundrith woundide oon while And aftir hym Eliazar, the sone of his vncle Ahoi- 13 tes, that was among the threz myzty This was with Dauid in Aphedomyn, whanne Philisteis ben gederd to oon place in to batail; and thei was a feeld of that regyoun full of barly, and the puple fleizn 14 fro the face of Philisteis This stode in the mydil of the feeld, and defendid hym; and whanne he hadde smyten the Phi- listeis, the Lord zaue grete helthe to his 15 puple. Thereb wenten doun forsothe thre of the thritty princis to the petra, in the whiche was Dauid, at the denn of Odolla, whanne Philisteis hadden sett tentis in 16 the valey of Raphaym Forsothe Dauid

bi the word of the Lord, which he spak in the hond of Samuel Therfor Dauid 4 zede, and al Israel, in to Jerusalem, this *Jerusalem* is Jebus, where Jebuseis enha- biteris of the lond weren And thei thats dwelliden at Jebus seiden to Dauid, Thou schalt not entrew hidur Forsothe Dauid took the hiz tour of Syon, which is thex citee of Dauid; and he seide, Ech man 6 that 'sleeth firsty Jebusei, schal be prince and duyk Therfor Joab, sonez of Saruye, stiedea first, and was maad prince So- 7 theli b Dauid dwellide in the hiz tour, and therfor it was clepid the cytee of Dauid; and he bildide the citee in cumpas fro 8 Mello til to the cumpas; forsothec Joab bildide the tother part of the citee And 9 Dauid profitide goyngd and wexynge, and the Lord of oostis was with hym These 10 *ben* thee princes of the stronge men of Dauid, thatf helpiden hym, that he schulde be kyng ong al Israel, bi the word of the Lord which he spak to Israel And this 11 *is* the noumbre of the stronge men of Dauid, Jesbaam, the sone of Achamony, *was* prince among thretti; this reisideh his schaft *ethir spere* oni thre hundrid woundid men in o tyme And after hym 12 *was* Eleazai, the sone of his fadris brothir, andk *was* 'a man' of Ahoitm, whichn *Ele- azar* was among thre mizti men This 13 was with Dauid in Aphesdomyn, whanne Filisteis weren gaderid to o place in to batel; and a feeld of that cuntrey was ful of baili, and the puple fledde fro the face of Filisteis Thiso *Eleazai* stood in the 14 myddis of the feeld, and defendide it, and whanne he hadde slayn Filisteisp, the Lord zaf greet helthe to his puple So- 15 theli thre ofq thritti princes zeden doun to the stoon, wher ynne Dauid was, to the denne of Odolla, whanne Filisteisr settiden tentis in the valey of Raphaym Forsothes 16 Dauid was in a strong hold, and the sta-

x byldide A y and A z Om A a fleeth H b And there ABCH

w entre in s x in the A y first shal smyte s z the sone is a stiede up is b And is c and is
d in going s e Om I f whiche is g upon is h reiside up is i upon is k that is l Om I
m *a cuntrey, or of citee that hizt* Ahoit s n the which I o *Thanne* this is. p the Philistees I q and A pr m
CHILNSb r the Philisteis I s And is

was in the streyngthe, and the stacyoun
17 of Philisteis in Bethlem. Thanne Dauid
desiride watir, and seide, O! ȝif eny wolde
ȝeuen to me water of the sisterne of Beth-
18 lem, that is in the ȝate. Thanne thes
thre by the mydil tentis of the Philisteis
wenten, and drewen watir of the cysterne
of Bethlem, that was in the ȝate, and
brouȝten to Dauid, that he schuld drynk-
en; the whiche wolde not, bot more
19 offride it to the Lord, seyinge, God
scheelde, that in the siȝt of my God I do
this, and the blood of thes men I drynke,
for in perele of their lijues thei brouȝten
to me water; and for this cause he wolde
not drynke. Thes thingus diden the three
20 strengeste. Abisay forsothe, the brother
of Joab, he was prince of thre, and he
rerede his spere aȝeynus thre hundrith
woundid; and he was amonge thre most
21 nemned, and among the seconde
counde, noble, and a prince of hem; neuerthelater vnto the thre first he came
22 not. Banayas, the sone of Joiade, most
stronge man, the whiche many werkis
dyde, of Capseel; he smote two, Aryel,
Moab; and he descendide, and slowȝ a
lyoun in the mydil cisterne, in tyme of
23 snowȝ; and he smote an Egipcien man,
whos stature was of fyue cubitis, and
hadde a spere as the beem of websters;
thanne he came doun to hym with a
ȝerde, and cauȝte the spere, that he helde
in hond[d], and slowȝ hym with his spere.
24 Thes thingus dyde Bananyas, the sone of
Joiade, that was amonge the thre stronge
25 most named, and among the thritty the
first; neuer the later vnto the thre he
came not; Dauid forsothe putte hym at
26 his litil ere. Forsothe the most stronge
men in the hoost; Azahel, the brother of
Joab, and Eleanan, the sone of his vncle
27 of Bethlem, Semynoth Arorithes, Helles
28 Phalonythes, Iras, the sone of Acces The-

cioun, 'that is, the oost gaderid[t], of Filisteis was in Bethleem. Therfor Dauid de- 17
siride watir, and seide, Y wolde, that sum
man ȝaf to me water of the cisterne of
Bethleem, which is in the ȝate. Therfor 18
these thre ȝeden thoruȝ the myddil of the
castelis[u] of Filisteis, and drowen[v] watir
of the cisterne of Bethleem, that was in
the ȝate, and thei brouȝten to Dauid, that
he schulde drynke; and Dauid nolde[w]
'drynke it[x], but rather he offride it to the
Lord, and seide, Fer be it, that Y do this 19
thing in the siȝt of my God, and that Y
drynke the blood of these men, for in the
perel of her lynes thei brouȝten[y] watir to
me; and for this cause he nolde[z] drynke.
Thre strongeste[a] men diden these thingis.
Also Abisai, the brother of Joab, he was 20
the[b] prince of thre[c] men, and he reiside[d]
his schafte[e] aȝens thre hundrid woundid
men; and he[f] was moost named among
thre, among the secounde thre he was 21
noble, and the prince of hem; netheles he
cam not til[g] to the[h] firste thre. Banaye, 22
the sone of Joiada, strongest[i] man of Cap-
sael, that dide many werkis; he killide two
stronge men of Moab; and he ȝede doun,
and killide a lioun in the myddil[j] of a cisterne, in the tyme of snow; and he killide 23
a man of Egipt, whos stature was of fyue
cubitis, and he hadde a spere as the beem
of webbis; therfor Banaye ȝede[k] doun to
hym with a ȝerde, and rauyschide[l] the
spere, which[m] he held[n] in the[o] hond, and
killide hym with his owne spere. Banaye, 24
the sone of Joiada, dide these thingis, that
was moost named among thre stronge
men, and was[p] the firste among thretti; 25
netheles he cam not til[q] to the thre; sotheli[r] Dauid settide[s] hym at his eere[t]. For- 26
sothe[u] the strongeste men 'in the oost[v]
weren Asael, the brother of Joab, and
Eleanan, the sone of his fadris brothir of
Bethleem, Semynoth Arorites, Helles Phal- 27

---

c Om. A.   d his hond AF pr. m.

t Om. W. u castels or of the oostis s. v thei drowen IS. w wolde not I. x Om. I. y han brouȝt IS.
z wolde not I. a the strongeste I. b Om. BCDEFGIKLMNOSXb. c these thre IS. d reiside up IS. e spere I.
shaft or spere S. f Om. A. g Om. I. h Om. S. i the strongest IS. j middis S. k wente I. l rauyschide
fro him IS. m that IS. n hadde IS. o his C. p he was IS. q Om. X. r and IS. s sette I. t eere for
a good counselour IS. u Certis I. v Om. I.

29 cuytes, Abieser Anothotites, Sobachai
30 Sotlutes, Ilay Achoites, Marai Nethophatites, Heles, the sone of Bana, Netho-
31 phatites, and Hay, the sone of Relay, of
Gabaoth of the sonys of Beniamyn; Ba-
32 naya Pharathonytes, men of the strem
of Gaaz, Abiel Arabathites, Azynoth
33 Baruanythes, Ehaba Salaonythes, the
sonys of Assem Jesonythes, Jonathan,
34 the sone of Saga, Araiites, Achiam, the
35 sone of Achar, Ararithes, Eliphal, the
36 sone of Vri, Efer Mechurathites, Ahia
37 Philonytes, Aziai Carmelites, Joamy, the
38 sone of Eyrabay, Joel, the brother of
Nathan Mybahur, the sone of Agaiay,
39 Selech Amonytes, Noorai Berothites, the
40 squyer of Joab, sone of Saruye, Yras
41 Jethreus, Gareb Jethreus, Vrias Etheus,
42 Sabab, the sone of Choli, Abyna, the
sone of Segar Rubenyte, prince of Ru-
43 benytis, and with hym thiitty, Hanan,
the sone of Macha, and Josephath Ma-
44 thanytes, Osias Astorothites, Semma, and
45 Rahel, sonys of Otayn Arociites, Le-
diel, the sone of Zamry, and Joa, his bro-
46 ther, Thosaites, Heliel Mannytes, Jeribai
and Josia, sonys of Elnaen, Jethma Moabites, Heliel, and Obed, and Jasiel of
Mosobia

CAP XII

1 Thes forsothe camen to Dauid in Sichelech, whanne 3it he fleiz Saul, the sone
of Ciz, the whiche weren most stronge
2 and noble. fizters, bendynge bowe, and
with either hond throwynge stones with
slyngis, and diessynge arewis; of the bre-
3 theren of Saul of Beniamyn, prynce
Achieser, and Joas, the sone of Samaa
Gabatites, and Jasahel, and Phalleg,
sonys of Asmod, and Barachia, and Jeu
4 Anothothites, also Samayas Gabaonytes,
most stronge among thritty and vpon
thritty; Jeremyas, and Jezihel, and Jo-
5 hannan, and Zebadga Zeruthites, Elusai,
and Jerymuth, and Baalia, and Samaria,
6 and Saphia Araphites, Helchana, and
Jesia, and Azrael, and Jeser, and Jes-

lonytes, Iias[w], the sone of Acces of Thecue, 28
Abiesei of Anathot, Sobochay Sochites, 29
Ylai Achoytes, Maray Nethophatithes, 30
Heles, the sone of Banaa, Nethophatithes,
Ethaa, the sone of Rabai, of Gabaath of 31
the sones of Beniamyn, Banaye Phaia-
tonythes, men of the stronde Gaas, Abihel 32
Aiabatithes, Azmoth Baruanythes, Eliaba
Salaonythes, the sones of Assem Gesony- 33
thes, Jonathan, the sone of Saga, Aiarithes,
Achiaiu, the sone of Achai, Ararites, Eli- 34, 35
phal, the sone of Mapher, Mechoratithes, 36
Ahya Phellonythes, Asiahi Carmelites, 37
Neoray, the sone of Thasbi, Johel, the bro- 38
thei of Nathan, Mabar, the sone of Ag-
garay, Selech Ammonythes, Nooiay Beio- 39
thites, the squyer of Joab, sone of Saruye,
Iras Jetreus, Gareb Jethreus, Vrie Ethei, 40, 41
Sabab, the sone of Ooli, Adyna, the sone 42
of Segar Rubenytes, prince of Rubenytis,
and thritti men with hym, Hanan, the 43
sone of Macha, and Josaphath Mathany-
thes, Ozias Astarothites, Semma and Ja- 44
hel, the sones of Hotayn Aroerites, Ledi- 45
hel, the sone of Zamri, and Joha, his brother, Thosaythes, Heliel Maanytes, Jery- 46
bay and Josia, the sones of Helnaen, Jethma Moabites, Heliel, and Obed, and Jasihel of Masobia

CAP. XII

Also these[x] camen to Dauid in Sichelech, 1
whanne he fledde 3it fio Saul, the sone of
Cys; whiche[y] weren strongeste[z] men and
noble fizterys, beendynge bouwe, and cast- 2
ynge stoonys with slyngis with euer either
hond, and dressynge arowis, of the britheren of Saul of Beniamyn, the prince 3
Achieser[a], and Joas, the sones of Samaa of[b]
Gabaath, and Jazachel, and Phallech, the
sones of Azmod, and Barachie, and Jehu
of Anathot; also Samay of Gabaon was 4
the strongeste among thretti and aboue
thretti, Jeremy, and Jezihel, and Johannan, and Zebadga Zerothites, Elusay, and 5
Jerymoth, and Baalia, and Samaria, and
Saphia Araphites, Elchana, and Jesia, 6
and Azrahel, and Jezer, and Jesbaam of

---

[w] and Iras s   [x] these *men* s   [y] the whiche i   [z] ful stronge i   [a] of Thieser A *pr m*   [b] and s

7 baam of Tharemy, Joelam forsothe, and
8 Sabadia, sonys of Jeroam of Jedor. But
and of Gaddi ouerflowen to Dauid, whanne
he lurkide in desert, most[e] stronge men,
and best fiȝters, holdynge target and
spere; the faces of hem as faces of a
lyoun, and swyft as capretis in hillis;
9 Ozer prince, Obdias the secound, Eliab
10 the thridde, Masmana the ferth, Hiere-
11 myes the fyfte, Becchi the sixte, Heliel
12 the seuenth, Johannan the ciȝte[f], Elzadad
13 the nynthe, Jeremyas the tenthe, Bachana
14 the elleuenth; thes of the sonys of Gad,
princes of the hoost; the last was before
to an hundrith knyȝtis, and the[g] most to
15 a thousand. Thes ben that passeden
ouer Jordan the first moneth, whanne it
was wont to flowen vpon his brynkis;
and thei dryuen alle that dwelliden in
the valeys at the este coost and at the
16 west. Forsothe and there camen of Beniamyn and of Juda to the strengthe, in
17 the whiche dwellide Dauid. And Dauid
wente out to meet with hem, and seith,
ȝif pesybly ȝe ben commen to me, that ȝe
helpen to me, myn herte be joyned to
ȝou; ȝif forsothe ȝe weyten to me for
myn aduersaries, whanne I wickidnesse
haue not in myn hondis, God of oure
18 fadirs see and deme. The spirit forsothe
clothed Abisay, the prince among thritty,
and seith, Thine we ben, O Dauid, and
with thee, the sone[h] of Ysay; pese, pese
to thee, and pese to thyn helpers, thee
forsothe helpith the Lord thi God. Than
Dauid toke hem, and sette hem princis of
19 the cumpanye. Forsothe of Manasses
ouerflowen to Dauid, whanne he came
with Philisteis to fiȝten aȝenus Saul, and
he fauȝte not with hem, for, the counseil
goon in, the princis of Philisteis senten
him aȝein, seyinge, In perele of ȝoure[i]
heued be he turned aȝeyn to his lord
20 Saul. Whanne thanne[j] he is turned
aȝein in to Sichelech, ouerflowen to hym

Taremy, and Joelam, and Sabadia, the 7
sones of Jeroam of Jedor. But also of 8
Gaddi* strongeste men, and beste fiȝteris,
holdynge scheld and spere, fledden ouer
to Dauid, whanne he was hid in deseert;
the faces of hem as the face of a lioun,
and thei weren swift as capretis in hillis.
Ozer was the prince, Obdias the secounde, 9
Eliab the thridde, Masmana the fourthe, 10
Jeremye the fyuethe, Becchi the sixte, 11
Heliel the seuenthe, Johannan the eiȝthe, 12
Helzedad the nynthe, Jeremye the tenthe, 13
Bachana the euleuenthe; these of the sones 14
of Gad weren princes of the oost†; the[e]
laste‡ was souereyn ouer an hundrid
knyȝtis, and the moost was souereyn[f]
ouer a thousynde. These ben that pass- 15
iden ouer Jordan in the firste monethe,
whanne it was wont to flowe ouer hise
brynkis; and thei dryueden[g] awei alle
menh§ that dwelliden in the valeis at the
eest coost and west coost. Sotheli[l] also 16
men of Beniamyn and of Juda camen to
the stronge hoold, whereyn Dauid dwellide.
And Dauid ȝede out aȝens hem, and seide, 17
If ȝe 'ben comyn[j] pesible to me, for to helpe
me, myn herte be ioyned to ȝou; forsothe[k] if ȝe setten aspies to me for myn
aduersaries, sithen[l] Y haue not wickidnesse in the hondis, God of our fadris se
and deme. Forsothe[m] the spirit‖ clothide 18
Amasay¶, the prynce among thritti, and he
seide, A[n]! Dauid, we ben thin, and thou,
sone of Ysai, we schulen be with thee;
pees, pees to thee, and pees to thin helperis,
for thi Lord God helpith thee. Therfor
Dauid resseyuede hem, and made[o] princes
of the cumpeny. Forsothe[p] men of Ma- 19
nasses fledden ouer to Dauid, whanne he
cam with Filisteis to fiȝte aȝens Saul, and
he fauȝte not with hem, for after that the
princes of Filisteis hadden take counsel,
thei senten hym[q] aȝen, and seiden, With
perel of oure heed he schal turne aȝen[r] to
Saul his lord. Therfor whanne[s] Dauid 20

*Gaddi; that
is, of the lynage
of Gad. Lire
here. Plures.

†after that
Dauid hadde
the rewme.
Lire here. GKL
OPSB.
‡the last is he
that leest power
hadde. Lyre
gloos. B.

§men; thes
weren hethen
men, that occu-
pieden a part of
the lond of the
sones of Israel.
Lire here. CG
KOB.

‖spirit; that
is, stedefast-
nesse and
hardynesse to
speke. Lire
here. C et
plures.
¶In Ebreu it
is Amasay, and
this was Ama-
sa, as Ebreus
seien. Lire
here. KOB.

---

e amonge FII.   f eiȝthe C. eiȝtethe E. eyȝtith H.   g Om. F.   h sonys F pr. m. H.   i oure C.   j Om. A.

e and the IS.   f Om. I.   g dreuen I.   h that is, hethen men LP.   l And IS.   j comen I.   k and IS.
l sith I.   m And I.   n O IS.   o he made IS.   p And IS.   q Dauid IS.   r Om. X.   s Om. A.

fro Manasse, Eduas, and Josadab, and Jedielech, Mychael, and Naaz, and Jozabath, and Helieu, and Salathy, princis of 21 kny3tis in Manasse. Thes 3euen help to Dauid a3eyns the lityl theeues; alle forsothe weren most stronge men, and ben 22 maad princis in the hoost. Bot and by eche days thei camen to Dauith, to helpen to hym, vnto the time that there were maad a grete noumbre as the hoost of God. 23 This forsothe is the noumbre of the princis of the hoost that camen to Dauid, whan he was in Ebron, that thei translate^k the rewme of Saul to hym, aftir the word 24 of the Lord; the sonys of Juda, berynge target and spere, sexe thousand and ei3t 25 hundrith, redy to batail; of the sonys of Symeon, most stronge men to fi3ten, 26 seuen thousand and an hundrith; of the sonys of Leuy, foure thousand and sixe 27 hundrith; and Joiada, prince of the stok of Aaron, and with hem thre thousand 28 and seuen hundrith; Sadoch also, a chijld of noble preuynge, and the hous of his 29 fadir, princis two and twenty; of the sonys forsothe of Beniamyn, the^l bretheren of Saul, thre thousand; forsothe a grete partye of hem 3it folowede the 30 hous of Saul; but of^m the sonys of Effraym, twenty thousand and ei3t hundrith, most stronge in streyngthe, men 31 namyd in their kynredis; and of the half partye of the lynage of Manasse, ei3teene thousand; eche bi their names camen, 32 that thei ordeyn kyng Dauith; of the sonys also of Ysachar, men tau3t, that knewen alle tymes to comaunden what Yrael schuld done, princis two hundreth; al forsothe the tother lynage folowede 33 the counseils of hem; bot of Zabulon that wenten out to bateil, and stoden in the scheltrun, enfourmed in armys of batail, fyfty thousand camen in to help, 34 not in double hert; and of Neptalym, princis of kny3thode, and with hem

turnede a3en in to Sichelech, men of Manasses fledden ouer to hym, Eduas, and Jozabad, Jedihel, and Mychael, and Naas, and Jozabath, and Helyu, and Salathi, princes of kny3tis in Manasses^t. These 21 men 3auen help to Dauid a3ens theues; for alle weren strongeste^u men^v, and thei^w weren maad prynces in the oost. But also 22 bi ech dai men camen to Dauid, for to helpe hym, til that the noumbre was maad greet as the oost of God. Also this 23 is the noumbre of princes of the oost that camen to Dauid, whanne he was in Ebron, that thei schulden translate the rewme of Saul to hym, bi the^x word of the Lord; the sones of Juda, berynge scheeld and 24 spere, sixe thousynde and ei3te hundrid, redi to batel; of the sones of Simeon, 25 seuene thousinde and an hundrid, of strongeste men to fi3te; of the sones of Leuy, 26 foure thousynde and sixe hundrid; also 27 Joiada, prince of the generacioun of Aaron, and thre thousynd and seuene hundrid with hym; also Sadoch, a child of noble 28 wit, and the hows of his fadir, twei and twenti princes; forsothe^y of the sones of 29 Beniamyn, britheren^z of Saul, thre thousynde; for a greet part of hem suede 3it the hows of Saul; forsothe^a of the sones 30 of Effraym, twenti thousynde and ei3te hundrid, strongeste^b men in bodili my3t, men named in her meynees; and of the 31 half part of the lynage of Manasses, ei3tene thousynde; alle camen bi her names, to make Dauid kyng; also of the sones of 32 Ysacar, two hundrid princes, lernd men, that knewen ech tyme to comaunde what the puple of Israel ou3t to do; sotheli^c al the residue^d lynage^e suede the counseils of hem; forsothe^f of Zabulon camen fifti 33 thousynde in to helpe^g, not in double herte, which^h 3eden^i out to batel, and stoden in the scheltrun, and weren maad redi with armuris of batel; and of Neptalym a 34 thousynde prynces, and with hem *camen*^k

---

^k translatyde μ.   ^l Om. A.   ^m Om. FH.

^t Manasses *lynage* 18.   ^u ful stronge 1.   ^v Om. 1.   ^w Om. 1.   ^x Om. 1.   ^y and 18.   ^z the britheren s.   ^a and 18.   ^b ful stronge 1.   ^c and 18.   ^d remenaunt 1. residue *or* remenaunt s.   ^e *of the* lynage 18.   ^f and 18.   ^g his helpe 1. helpe *of Dauith* s.   ^h the which 1.   ^i wenten 1.   ^k Om. 1.

enfourmed in scheelde and spere, seuen 35 and thritty thousand; of Dan also, redy to bateil, ey3t and twenty thousand and 36 sexe hundreth; and of Aser, goynge out[n] to fi3ten in the scheltrun egre, fourty 37 thousand. Be3ond Jordan forsothe, of the sonys of Ruben, and of Gad, and of the half lynage of Manasse, enfourmed in armes of batel, an hundreth and 38 twenty thousand. Alle thes men fi3ters and redy to fi3ten, with perfijt hert camen in to Ebron, that thei setten Dauid kyng vpon al[o] Yrael; bot and al the remnaunt of Ysrael weren in oon hert, that Dauith 39 wer maad kyng vpon al[p] Yrael. And thei weren there anentis Dauith thre days, etinge and drynkynge; forsothe the bretheren[q] of hem hadde beforne 40 maad redy to hem; bot and thilk that weren besidis hem, vnto Ysachar and Zabulon and Neptalym, brou3ten looues to eten, in assis, and chamoilis, and mulis, and oxen; mele, and chargis of fijgis, and dried grapis, wijne, oyle, oxen, and wethers, at al plente; ioye forsothe was in Yrael.

CAP. XIII.

1 Dauith forsothe wente in to counseil with the maystirs of thousandis, and maystirs of hundrithes, and with al the 2 princis. And he seith to al the companye of the sonys of Yrael, 3if it plesith to 3ou, and of the Lord oure[r] God goth out the word that I speke, sende we to oure other bretheren in[s] alle the regyouns of Yrael, and to the prestis and Leuytis that dwellen in the suburbis of cytees, 3 that thei ben gedered to us, and we bryngen a3eyn the arke of God to us; forsothe we sou3ten it not in the days of 4 Saul. And al the multitude answerd, that it so schuld be done; forsothe the 5 word pleside to al the puple. Thanne Dauide gederide al Ysrael, fro Seor of

seuene[l] and thritti thousynde men,[m] arayed with scheeld and speere; also of Dan, ei3te 35 and twenti thousynde and sixe hundrid men, maad[n] redi to batel; and of Aser 36 fourti thousynde men, goynge out to batel, and stirynge[o] to batel in the scheltrun. Forsothe[p] bi3ende Jordan, of the sones of 37 Ruben, and of Gad, and of the half part of the lynage of Manasses, sixe scoore thousynde men, araied with armuris of[q] batel. Alle these men werriouris and redi to batel 38 camen with perfit herte in to Ebron, to make Dauid kyng on[r] al Israel; but also alle the residue[s] of Israel weren of oon herte, that Dauid schulde be maad king on[t] al Israel. And thei weren ther at 39 Dauid thre daies, and eten and drunken; for her britheren hadden maad redi to hem; but also thei that weren ni3 hem, 40 til to Isacar and Zabulon and Neptalym, brou3ten looues on assis, and camelis, and mulis, and oxis[u], for to ete; mele, bundelis of pressid figis, dried[v] grapis, wyn, oile[w], oxis[x] and wetheres, to al plentee; for[y] ioy was in Israel.

CAP. XIII.

Forsothe[z] Dauid took counsel with tri- 1 bunes, and centuriouns, and alle princes; and seide[a] to alle the cumpeny of the 2 sones of Israel, If it plesith 3ou, and if the word which[b] Y speke goith out fro oure[c] Lord God[d], sende we to 'oure residue[e] britheren to alle the cuntrees of Israel, and to preestis and dekenes[f] that dwellen in the subarbis of citees, that thei be gaderid to vs, and[g] that we brynge a3en to vs the arke 3 of oure God; for[h] we sou3ten not it in the daies of Saul. And al the multitude 4 answeride, that it schulde be don so; for the word pleside al the puple. Therfor 5 Dauid gaderide togidere al Israel, fro Sior of Egipt til[i] thou entre in to Emath, that he schulde brynge the arke of God fro

---

n Om. FH.   o Om. F.   p Om. ABCFH.   q brether FH.   r 3oure H.   s Om. BCFH.

l two 1 pr. m. ei3te 1 sec. m.   m of men x.   n men maad I.   o of stirynge c. stirid D.   p And 1s.
q to s.   r upon 1s.   s remenaunt 1s.   t upon 1s.   u oxen s.   v and dried cx.   w and oile x.   x oxen 1s.
y forsothe 1s.   z Sothely 1s.   a he seide 1.   b that 1s.   c the 1s. 3oure x.   d oure God 1s.   e the
remenaunt of oure 1. the remenaunt our s.   f to dekenes plures.   g Om. s.   h certis 1s.   i til that 1s.

Egipt vnto the tyme that thou go in to
Emath, that he brynge the arke of God
6 fro Cariathiarym. And Dauid steyȝide up,
and alle the men of Yrael, to the hill of
Cariathiarym, that is in Juda, that he
brynge the arke of the Lord God syttynge
vpon cherubyn, wher inwardly is clepid
7 the name of hym. And thei putten the
arke of the Lord God vpon a newe wayn
of the hous of Amynadab; Osa forsothe
and the bretheren of hym dryuen the
8 wayne. Bot Dauid and al Ysrael pleyden
beforn the Lord, in al vertue, in songis,
and in harpis, and in sawtrees, and in
tymbris, and in cymbalis, and inᵗ trumpis.
9 And whanne thei weren commen to the
cornflore of Chydon, Osa strauȝt out his
hond, that he susteyne the arke; forsothe
the oxe pleyinge a litill wiȝt bowede it
10 doun. And so the Lord is wroth aȝeinus
Osam, and smote hym, forthi that he
hadde touchid the arke; and he is deed
11 there beforn the Lord. And Dauid is
sory, for thi that the Lord hadde deuydid
Osam; and he clepid that place The
Deuydynge of Ose vnto the present day.
12 And he dredde the Lord that tyme, seyinge, What maner wise may I bryngen
13 in to me the ark of the Lord? And
for this cause he brouȝt it not to hym,
that is, in the cyte of Dauid, bot turnede
it asyde in to the hous of Obededom
14 Jethei. Thanne the arke of God dwellide
in the hous of Obededom Jethei thre
monethis; and the Lord blesside to the
hous of hym, and to alle thingis that he
hadde.

CAP. XIV.

1 Iram forsothe, kyng of Tyri, sent messagers to Dauid, and cedre trees, and
crafty men of wallis, and of trees, that
2 thei bylden to hymᵘ an hous. And
Dauid knewȝ that the Lord hadde con-

Cariathiarim. And Dauid stiedeᵏ, and 6
alle the men of Israel, to the hil of Cariathiarym, whichˡ is in Juda, that he schulde
brynge fro thennus the arke of the Lord
God sittynge on cherubyn, where his name
was clepidᵐ. And thei puttiden the arke 7
of the Lord Godⁿ on a newe wayn fro the
hous of Amynadab; forsotheᵒ Oza and
hise britheren driuedenᵖ the wayn. For- 8
sotheᑫ Dauid and al Israel pleiedenʳ bifor
the Lord, with al miȝt, in songis, and in
harpis, and sautries, and tympansˢ, and
cymbalisᵗ, and trumpis. Forsotheᵘ whanne 9
thei hadden come to the cornfloor of Chi-
don, Oza strechide forth his hond to sus-
teyneᵛ the arke; forʷ the oxeˣ wexynge
wieldeʸ hadde bowidᶻ itᵃ a litil. Therfor 10
the Lord was wrooth aȝens Oza, and
smoot hym, for he haddeᵇ touchide the
ark; and he was deed there bifor the
Lord. And Dauid was sori, for the Lord 11
hadde departidᶜ Oza; and heᵈ clepide that
place The Departyng of Oza 'til in toᵉ
presentᶠ dai. And Dauid dredde the Lord 12
in that tyme, and seide, How may Y brynge
in to me the arke of the Lord? And for 13
this cause he brouȝte not it toᵍ hym, that
is, in to the citee of Dauid, but he turnede it in to the hows of Obededom of Geth.
Therfor the arke of God dwellide in the 14
hous of Obededom of Geth thre monethis;
and the Lord blessid his hows, and 'alle
thingisʰ that he hadde.

CAP. XIV.

And Iram, the kyng of Tyre, sente mes- 1
sageris to Dauid, and 'he senteⁱ trees of
cedre, and werk men of wallis and of trees,
that thei schulden bilde to hym an hows.
And Dauid knewe that the Lord haddeᵈ 2

ᵗ Om. ᴇ.   ᵘ God ᴇ pr. m.

ᵏ stiede up ɪꜱ.   ˡ that ɪꜱ.   ᵐ ynwardly clepid ɪꜱ.   ⁿ upon ɪꜱ.   ᵒ and ɪ. Om. ꜱ.   ᵖ dreuen ᴇɪ. dreuyn ʟᴘ.
ᑫ And ɪꜱ. Sotheli ᴋᴍxb.   ʳ pleiden *or gladedin* ꜱ.   ˢ in tympans ꜱ.   ᵗ in cymbalis ꜱ.   ᵘ And ɪꜱ.   ᵛ susteyne *or stable* ꜱ.   ʷ certis ɪꜱ.   ˣ oxen ɪꜱ.   ʸ wilide *either pleying for welinesse* ꜱ.   ᶻ bowid asijde ɪꜱ.
ᵃ the arke ɪꜱ.   ᵇ Om. ɪꜱ.   ᶜ departid *or sleyne* ꜱ.   ᵈ Dauith ꜱ.   ᵉ vnto ɪ. into x.   ᶠ this present ɪᴋꜱ *pr. m.*
ᵍ into ɪꜱ.   ʰ al thing ꜱ.   ⁱ Om. ɪ. *he sent to him* ꜱ.

fermed hym in to kyng vpon Yrael; and
his rewme was putt up vpon Yrael his
3 puple. And Dauid toke other wijues in
Jerusalem, and gat sonis and dou3tirs.
4 And thes the names of hem that ben
born to hym in Jerusalem; Sammu, and
5 Sobab, and Nathan, and Salomon, Jeber,
and Elisu, and Heeli, and Eliphalech,
6 also Noga, and Napheg, and Japhie,
7 and Elisama, and Baliada, and Eliphe-
8 lech. Forsothe Philisteis heerynge, for
thi that Dauith was anoynt in to kyng
vpon al Yrael, thei stey3eden up alle for to
sechen hym. The whiche thing whanne
Dauid hadde 3ede, he wente out to
9 meeten with hem. Bot the Philisteis
commynge ben held out in the valey of
10 Raphaym; and Dauith counseilide the
Lord, seyinge, 3if I schal steyen up to
the Philisteis? and 3if thou schalt taken
hem in to myne hondis? And the Lord
seide to hym, Stey3e up, and I schal
11 taken hem in thin hond. And whanne
thei hadden stey3eden up in to Baal
Farasym, Dauid smote hem there, and
seide, God hath deuydide myne enemyse
by myne hond, as watirs ben deuydide.
And therfore the name of that place was
12 clepid Baal Pharasym; and there thei
forsoken their goddis, the whiche Dauith
13 comaundide to be brent. Another while
forsothe Philisteis fellen on, and ben
14 helde out in the valey; and eft Dauith
counseilede the Lord, and the Lord seide
to hym, Thou schalt not stey3en up aftir
hem; go thou awey fro hem, and thou
schalt fynden hem forn a3cynus the pere
15 trees. And whanne thou heerist the
sown of goynge in the cop of the pere
trees, thanne thou schalt gon out to
batail; forsothe God is gon out beforne
thee, that he smyte the tentis of the
16 Philisteis. Than Dauid dyde as God

confermyd hym in to kyng on j Israel;
and that his rewme was reisid on j his
puple Israel. And Dauid took othere 3
wyues in Jerusalem, and gendride k sones
and dou3tris. And these ben the names 4
of hem that weren borun to hym in Jerusalem; Sammu, and Sobab, Nathan, and
Salomon, Jeber, and Elisu, and Heli, and 5
Eliphalech, and Noga, and Napheg, and 6
Japhie, and Elisama, and Baliada, and 7
Eliphelech. Forsothe l the Filisteis herden 8
that Dauid was anoyntid m 'in to n kyng on o
al Israel, and alle p stieden q to seke Dauid r.
And whanne Dauid hadde herd this thing,
he 3ede out a3ens hem. Forsothe s Filisteis 9
camen, and weren spred abrood in the
valey of Raphaym; and Dauid counselide 10
the Lord t, and seide, Whether Y schal
stie u to Filisteis v? and whether thou schalt
bitake hem in to myn hondis? And the
Lord seide to hym w, Stie thou x, and Y schal
bitake hem in y thin hond. And whanne 11
thei z hadden styed a in to Baal Pharasym,
Dauid smoot hem there, and seide, God hath
departid myn enemyes bi myn hond, as
watris ben departid. And therfor the name
of that place was clepid Baal Pharasym;
and thei leften there her goddis, which b 12
Dauid comaundide to be brent. Forsothe c 13
another tyme Filisteis d felden in, and
weren spred abrood in the valei; and eft 14
Dauid counseilide e the Lord, and the Lord
seide to hym, Thou schalt not stie f aftir
hem; go awei fro hem, and thou schalt
come a3ens hem euen a3ens the pere trees.
And whanne thou schalt here the sowun 15
of a goere in the cop g of the pere trees,
thanne thou schalt go out to batel; for the
Lord is go out byfor h thee, to smyte the
castels i of Filisteis. Therfor Dauid dide 16
as God comaundide to hym, and he smoot
the castels i of Filisteis fro Gabaon 'til to k
Gazara. And the name of Dauid was 17

v Om. A.

j upon 1s. k he gaat 1. he gendride s. l And 1s. m anoynd A. n Om. G. o upon 1s. p alle thei 1s.
q 3eden up 1. stieden vp s. r Dauith to fi3t with him. s. s And 1s. t Lord, that is, he took counsel of the
Lord s. u stie up 1s. v the Filisteis 1. w Dauid 1s. x thou up 1s. y into FKLxb. z the Philistees 1.
Filisteis s. a styed up 1s. b the which 1. c And 1s. d the Filisteis 1s. e was counselid be s.
f stie up 1s. g cop or hei3t s. h to fore s. i powers 1s. k to x.

hadde comaundide to hym, and he smote
the tentis of Philisteis fro Gabaon vnto
17 Gazera   And the name of Dauid is
puplischid in alle regiouns, and the Lord
3aue the drede of hym vpon alle gentilis

puplischid in¹ alle cuntreis, and the Lord
3af his drede^m on^n alle folkis ·   -   ^r

CAP XV

1   And he maad houses to hym in the
cyte of Dauid, and he bilde up the place
of the ark of God, and he strau3t out to
2 it a tabernacle   Thanne Dauid seide,
Vnleeful it is, that of eny man be born
the arke of God bot of Leuytis, whome
the Lord hath chosen to bern^w it, and to
mynystre to hym vnto with outen eend
3 And he gadered al Yrael in to Jerusalem,
that the arke of God were born in to hys
place, the whiche he hadde redy before
4 made to it ; also and the sonys of Aaron
5 and Leuytes ; of the sonys of Caath
Vriel was prince, and the brethren of
6 hym two hundrith and twenty ; of the
sonys of Merery, Azaia prince, and the
bretheren of hym two hundrith and
7 thritty, of the sonys of Jersam, Joel
prince, and the brethren of hym an hun-
8 drith and thritty ; of the sonis of Elisaphan, Semeias prince, and the brethren
9 of hym two hundrith, of the sonys of
Ebron, Helyel prince, and the bretheren
10 of hym ey3tye^x, of the sonys of Osiel,
Amynadab prince, and the bretheren of
11 hym an hundrith and twelue. And Dauid clepide Sadoch and Abiathar prestis,
and Leuytis Vriel, Azaia, Johel, Seme-
12 yam, Eliel, and Amynadab. And he
seide to hem, 3e that ben princes of Leuytis meynees, be 3e halowed with 3our
bretheren, and bryng ith the arke of the
Lord God of Yrael to the place, the
13 whiche is maad redy to it, lest, as at
the bigynnynge, for 3e weren not present, the Lord smote us, so and nowe it
be done, us doynge eny thinge vnleeful

CAP. XV

And he^o made to hym housis in the 1
citee of Dauid, and he bildide 'a place^p to
the arke of the Lord, and araiede a tabernacle to it. Thanne Dauid seide, It is 2
vnleueful, that the arke of God be borun^q
of 'ony 'thing no^r but of the dekenes,
whiche the Lord chees to bere it, and 'for
to mynystre^s to hym 'til in to^t with outen
ende   And he^u gaderide togidere al Israel 3
in to Jerusalem, that the arke of God
schulde be brou3t in to 'his place^v, which^n
he hadde maad redy to it; also and he 4
gaderide togidere the sones of Aaron,
and the dekenes , of the sones of Caath 5
Vriel was prince, and hise britheren two
hundrid and twenti^x; of the sones of Me- 6
rari Asaya *uas* prince, and hise britheren
two hundrid and thritti, of the sones of 7
Gerson the prince *uas* Johel, and hise
britheren an hundrid and thritti; of the 8
sones of Elisaphan Semei *was* prynce,
and hise britheren two hundrid; of the 9
sones of Ebroun Heliel *was* prince, and
hise britheren foure score , of the sones of 10
Oziel Amynadab *was* prince, and 'hise
britheren an hundrid and twelue   And 11
Dauid 'clepide Sadoch 'and Abiathar
priestis, and the dekenes Vriel, Asaie^z,
Johel^a, Semeie^b, Eliel, and Amynadab;
and seide^c to hem, 3e that ben princes of 12
the meynees of Leuy, be^d halewid with'
3oure britheren, and brynge 3e the arke of
the Lord God of Israel to the place, which^e
is maad redi to it , lest, as^f at the bigyn- 13
nyng, for 3e weren not present, the Lord
smoot vs, and^g now· it be don, if we don'
ony vnleueful thing† Therfor the preestis 14

† *Glose* It was
a custum in
Israel whan
env greet thing
shuld be do,
that thei shul-
den absteyne
hem bifore that
tyme fro al
vnleful thing
and lustis, and
specialli fro
lecherie. s

          ^w bren H   ^x ei3te H

¹ in to 18   ^m the drede of Dauid is   ^n upon 1   ^o Dauid is   ^p an hous 18   ^q borun aboute 15
^r oother 1 eny othere no s   ^s for the mynisterie K forte ministre L   ^t til to IK pr m in to x   ^u Dauid 19
^v the place of itis   ^w the which 1   ^x twenti men s   ^y Om s   ^z and Asaie 19   ^a and Johel x   ^b and
Semeie s   ^c he seide is   ^d be 3e is   ^e that is   ^f Om CDEFIKLMPQRSUWXb   ^g so and is

14 Thanne the prestis ben halowed, and the
Leuytis, that thei beren the ark of the
15 Lord God of Yrael. And the sonys of
Leuy token the arke of God, as Moyses
hadde comaundide aftir the word of God,
with their schulderis in berynge staues.
16 And Dauid seide to the pryncis of Leuytis, that thei schulden ordeynen of
their bretheren syngers in[y] orgnes of
musikis, that is, in sawtrees, and syngynge instrumentis, and cymbalis; that
the sown of gladnesse sowne aȝeyn in
17 heiȝtis. And thei ordeynden Leuytes,
Heeman, the sone of Joel, and of his
bretheren, Asaph, the sone of Barachie;
of the sonis forsothe of Merery, the bretheren of hem, Ethan, the sone of Cha-
18 saie, and with hem their bretheren; in
the secounde ordre, Zacharie, and Ben,
and Jasiel, and Semmyramoth, and Jahiel, and Anysey, and Heliab, and Banayam, and Elifalu, and Macenyam, and
19 Obededon, and Johiel, porters; forsothe
the chauntours[z] Eman, Asaph, and E-
20 than, in brasen cymbalis syngynge; Zacharie forsothe, and Osiel, and Semyramoth, and Jayhel, and Ham, and Eliab,
and Maazias, and Banaias, in orgnys[a]
21 sungyn priue thingis; forsothe Mathatias, and Eliphalu, and Macenyas, and
Ebededom, and Jehiel, and Ozasyn, in
harpis for the eyȝtethe sungyn cyny-
chyon, that is, to the God ouercomer vic-
22 torie and preysynge; Chononyas forsothe,
prynce of the Leuytis, was beforne to the
prophecie, and to the melodye to be
sungyn before, he was forsothe fulwijs;
23 and Barachias, and Helchana, porters of
24 the arke; bot Sebenyas, and Josaphath,
and Mathanael, and Amazai, and Zacharias, and Banayas, and Eliezer, prestis,
sowneden with trumpis beforne the arke
of the Lord; and Ebededom, and Achy-
25 maas, weren porters of the arke. Thanne

and dekenes weren halewid, that thei
schulden bere the arke of the Lord God
of Israel. And the sones of Leuy token 15
the arke of God with barris on[h] her
schuldris, as Moises comaundide bi the[i]
word of the Lord. And Dauid seide to 16
the princes[k] of dekenes, that thei schulden
ordeyne of her britheren syngeris in orguns of musikis, that is, in gitemes, and
harpis, and symbalis; that the sown of
gladnesse schulde sowne an hiȝ. And thei 17
ordeyneden dekenes, Heman, the sone of
Johel, and of hise britheren, Asaph, the
sone of Barachie; sotheli of the sones of
Merary, britheren of hem, *thei ordeyneden*
Ethan, the sone of Casaye, and the bri- 18
theren of hem with hem; in the secunde
ordre ˋ*thei ordeyneden*ˊ[l] Zacarie, and Ben,
and Jazihel, and Semyramoth, and Jahiel,
ˋand Am, Heliabˊ[m], and Benaye, and Maasie, and Mathathie, and Eliphalu, and
Mathenye, and Obededon, and Jehiel, porteris; forsothe[n] ˋ*thei ordeyneden*ˊ[o] the 19
syngeris Eman, Asaph, and Ethan, sownynge in brasun cymbalis; sotheli[p] Zaca- 20
rie, and Oziel, and Semyramoth, and Ja-
hihel, and Ham, and Eliab, and Maasie,
and Banaie, sungun[q] pryuetees[r] in gi-
ternes; forsothe[s] Mathathie, and Eliphalu, 21
and Mathenye, and Obededom, and Jehiel, and Ozazym, sungen in harpis for
the eiȝthe†, and epynychion, ˋ*that is,*
*victorie*ˋ*be to*ˊ[t] *God ouercomere*ˊ[u]; forsothe[v] 22
Chinonye, the prince of dekenes, and of
profecie, was souereyn to biforsynge melodie, for he was ful wijs; and Barachie, 23
and Elchana, *weren* porters of the arke;
forsothe[x] Sebenye, and Josaphath, and 24
Mathanael, and Amasaye, and Zacarie,
and Banaye, and Eliezer, preestis, sowneden with trumpis bifor the arke of the
Lord; and Obededom, and Achymaas,
weren[y] porteris of the arke. Therfor 25
Dauid, and[z] the[a] grettere men in birthe

† that is, for Cristis risynge aȝen in the eiȝthe dai, that was figurid bi that song. Lire here. Plures.

[y] and in A. and H. [z] chauntour B. [a] orglis H.

[h] upon IS. [i] Om. I. [k] prince S. [l] Om. I. [m] and Am, and Heliab EFLMSXb. and Aheliab K *sec. m.* [n] and IS. [o] Om. I. [p] and IS. [q] these sungun S. [r] pryuyli D. [s] and IS. [t] *to be* EFKLMNOXb. ˋ[u] *that is, thankingis that owen to be do to God, ouercomere and victour* IS. [u] *ouer mere* AFMNO. *euer more* DGQb. *ouer come* L. [v] and IS. [x] and I. [y] weren also S. [z] and alle BCW. [a] Om ELX.

Dauid, and alle the more thoru; birthe
of Yiael, and the maystris of thousandis,
wenten to the arke of pesc[b] couenaunt of
the Lord, to ben born fro the hous of
26 Obededom with[c] ioye   And whanne God
hadde holpen the Leuytes that beeren
the ark of the pese couenaunt of the
Lord, 'then weren[d] offride[e] seuen boolis
27 and seuen wethers   Forsothe Dauid was
clothed with a bijs stole, and alle the
Leuytis that beeren the arke, and the
syngeis, and Chononyas, the prince of
the piophecie amonge the syngers ; Dauid forsothe also was clothed with a sur-
28 plees   And al Yrael brou;ten the arke of
the pese couenaunt of the Lord in ioye,
and in sowne of trumpe, and in trumpis,
and cymbalis, and sawtiees, and harpis,
29 to gider syngynge   And whanne the
arke of the pese couenaunt of the Lord
was commen vnto the cytee of Dauith,
Mychol, the dou;tir of Saul, beholdynge
thoru; the wyndowe, saw; kyng Dauith
lepynge and pleyinge , and sche dispisede
him in her herte

of Isiael, and the tribunes, ;eden to brynge
the arke of boond of pees of the Lord fro
the hows of Obededom with gladnesse.
And whanne God hadde helpid the de-26
kenes that baien the arke of boond of
pees of the Lord, seuene bolis and seuene
rainnes weren offrid   Forsothe[b] Dauid 27.
was clothid with a white stole†, and alle
the dekenes that baren the arke, and the
syngeris, and Chononye, the[c] prince of
profecie[d] among syngeris, *weien clothid
in white stolis ;* forsothe[e] also Dauid was
clothid with a lynun surphjs. And al 28
Israel ledden forth the arke of boond of
pees of the Lord, and sowneden[f] in ioiful
song, and in sown of clariouns, and in
trumpis, and cymbalis[g], and giternis[h], and
harpis   And whanne the aike of boond 29
of pees of the Lord hadde come to[i] the
citee of Dauid, Mychol, the dou;tii of
Saul, bihelde foith bi a wyndowe, and
sche[k] si; king Dauyd daunsynge and pleiynge , and sche dispiside hym in hir herte

† A stole is
an honest gar-
ment s

CAP XVI

1 Thanne thei brou;ten in the aike of
of God, and setten it in the mydil of the
taberuacle, that Dauith hadde stiau;te
oute to it ; and thei offreden bient sacri-
2 fices and pesible before the Lord   And
whanne Dauid offrynge hadde fulfillide
brent sacrifices and pesible, he blessede
3 the puple in name of the Lord ; and he
deuydide to alle thoru; oute echone fro
man vnto wouiinan a kike of brede, and a
partye of roostyd flesche of a bugle, and
4 tried floure fryed in oyle   And he sette
beforn the arke of the Lord, of the Leuytis, that schulden mynystren, and re-
corden of the werkis of hym, and glorifien and pieysen the Lord God of Yrael ,
5 Asaph prince, and his secound Zacharie,

CAP. XVI

Therfor thei brou;ten the arke of God, 1
and settiden it in the[i] myddis of the tabernacle, that Dauid hadde araied[m] therto ;
and thei offiiden brent sacrifices and pesible sacrifices bifor the Lord   And whanne 2
Dauid offiynge brent saciifices and pesible
sacrifices hadde fillid[n], he blesside the puple in the[o] name of the Lord , and de-3
partide[p] to alle[q] to ech[r] bi hym silf fio a[s]
man til[t] to a[u] wommau o[v] cake of breed,
and a part of rostid fleisch of a bugle, and
flour fiied in oile   And he ordeynede bi-4
for the arke of the Lord, of the Leuytis[w]‡,
that schulden mynystre[x], and haue mynde
of the weikis of the Lord, and glorifie and
preyse the Lord God of Israel ; 'he or-5
deynede[y] Asaph the[z] prince, and Zacharie

‡ *Leuytis,*
that is, de-
kenes c

[b] And is   [c] Om is   [d] the profecie is   [e] and i Om s for x   [f] thei sowneden is   [g] in cymbalis is   [h] in giternis i   [i] in to is.   [k] Om a   [l] Om i   [m] araid is   [n] fulfillid is   [o] Om i
[p] he departide is   [q] alle men s   [r] ech man s   [s] Om is   [t] Om isx   [u] Om is   [v] a is   [w] dekenes is
[x] *that is, serue* K *marg*   [y] Om i of these *he ordeyned* s   [z] he ordeynede to be the i to be s

forsothe Jaihel, and Semyramoth, and
Jeihel, and Mathatiam, and Eliab, and
Banaya, and Obededom, and Jeiel, vpon
orgnys of sawtree, and syngynge instrumentis; Asaph forsothe schuld syngyn
6 in cymbalis; Bananyam forsothe and
Asiel, prestis, sungen in trumpe besily
beforne the arke of the pese couenaunt
7 of the Lord. In that day Dauith maad
prince, to knowlachen to the Lord, Asaph,
8 and his britheren. Knowlechith to the
Lord, and inwardly clepith his name;
knowen make ȝe in puplis the fyndyngis
9 of hym. Syngith to hym, and doth
psalmes to hym, and tellith alle his mer-
10 ueyls. Preyseth his holy name; ioye the
11 hert of men sechynge the Lord. Secheth
the Lord in his vertue; sechith his face
12 euermore. Recordith of his merueyles
that he dide; of the syngnes of hym, and
13 of the domes of his mouth; Ȝe seed of
Yrael, his seruaunt; ȝe[f] sones of Jacob,
14 his chosen. He the Lord oure God; in
15 al erthe the domes of hym. Recordith
vnto euermore of his couenaunt; of the
word that he comaundide in to a thou-
16 sand generaciouns. The whiche he couenauntide with Abraham; and of the
17 ooth of hym to Ysaac. And to Jacob
he sette it in to heste[g]; and to Yrael in
18 to euere[h] couenaunt[i]. Seyinge, To thee
I schal ȝeuen the lond of Chanaan; the
19 lytyl cord of ȝoure eritage. Whanne thei
weren fewe in noumbre; lytyl, and[k] tyly-
20 eris of it. And thei passeden fro folk
vnto folk; and fro regne to another pu-
21 ple. He suffrede not eny man to chal-
lengen hem; bot he blamede for hem
22 kyngis. Wyle ȝe not touchen my cristis;
and in my prophetis wyle ȝe not don
23 malice. Syngith to the Lord, al the
erth; tellith fro day 'in to[l] day the ȝeuer
24 of his helth. Tellith in gentylis his glo-

his secounde; forsothe '*he ordeynede*[a] Jahiel, and Semiramoth, and Jahel, and Mathathie, and Eliab, and Banaye, and Obededom, and Jehiel, on the orguns, on[b] the
sautrie, and on the harpis; but *he ordeynede* Asaph to sowne with cymbalis; so- 6
theli[c] *he ordeynede* Banaye and Aziel,
preestis, bifor the arke of the[d] boond of
pees of the Lord, for to trumpe contynueli†.
In that dai Dauid made Asaph prince, and[e] 7
hise britheren, for to knowleche 'to the
Lord[f]. Knowleche ȝe to the Lord, and 8
inwardli clepe ȝe his name; make ȝe hise
fyndyngis‡ knowun among puplis. Synge 9
ȝe to hym, and seie ȝe salm to hym, and
telle ȝe alle his merueylis. Preise ȝe his 10
hooli name; the herte of men sekynge the
Lord be glad[g]. Seke ȝe the Lord and[h] his 11
vertu; seke ȝe euere his face. Haue ȝe 12
mynde of hise merueilis whiche[i] he dide[k];
of hise signes, and of the domes of his
mouth. The seed of Israel, his seruaunt, 13
preise thou God; the sones of Jacob, his
chosun, *preise ȝe God.* He *is* 'oure Lord 14
God[l]; hise domes *ben* in ech lond. Haue 15
ȝe mynde with outen ende of his couenaunt; of the word whiche[m] he couenauntide 'in to[n] a thousynde generaciouns.
Which[o] word he couenauntide with Abra- 16
ham; and of his ooth to Ysaac. And he 17
ordeynede that[p] to Jacob in to a[q] comaundement; and to Israel in to euerlastynge couenaunt. And seide[r], To thee 18
Y schal ȝyue the lond of Canaan; the
part of ȝoure erytage. Whanne thei weren 19
fewe in noumbre; litle, and pilgrims therof[s]. And thei passiden fro folk in to the[t] 20
folk; and fro a rewme to[u] another puple.
He[v] suffride not ony man falseli[w] chalenge 21
hem; but he blamyde kyngis for hem[x].
Nyle ȝe touche my cristis§; and nyle ȝe 22
do wickidli aȝens my prophetis. Al erthe||, 23
singe ȝe to the Lord; telle ȝe fro dai into

† *contynuely*; that is, whanne the contynuel sacrifice was offrid, in the morewtid and euentid. *Lire here.* c.

‡ *fyndingis*; that is, hou by a wondirful maner and vnherd, he sauede the peple of Israel fro Egipt. *Lire here.* c.

§ *cristis*; that is, patriarkis anoyntid with the anoynting of grace. *Lire here.* c.

|| *al erthe*; that is, alle men dwellinge in erthe. *Lire here.* c.

[f] the A. [g] the heste H. [h] euermore H. [i] witnessynge E *pr. m.* [k] in H. [l] vnto C.

[a] Om. *plures.* [b] of BCW. [c] and IS. [d] Om. IS. [e] of C. [f] to the Lord, *seiyinge* I. preisyng to the Lord, and seying S. [g] it glad IS. [h] in A. [i] that IS. [k] hath do IS. [l] the Lord oure God IS. [m] that IS. [n] Om. S. [o] The which I. [p] that *word* IS. [q] Om. CDELNPS. [r] he seide IS. [s] therof, *he behiȝte hem this lond* S. [t] Om. BCEIKLPS. [u] in to X. [v] God IS. [w] wrongfully IS. [x] hem, *and seide* IS.

rie; and in alle puplis his merucylis.
25 For the Lord grete, and preysable ful
myche; and horrible vpon alle goddis.
26 Alle forsothe goddis mawmettis of puplis; the Lord forsothe heuens maad.
27 Knowlechynge and grete doynge beforn
hym; streyngthe and ioye in his place.
28 Bryngith to the Lord, ȝe meynes of puples; bryngith to the Lord glorie and
29 empyre. Ȝeuith glorie to the name of
hym, rereth sacrifice, and commith in his
siȝt; and honourith the Lord in holy
30 fairnesse. Be meued fro the siȝt of hym
al erth; he forsothe foundide the world
31 vnmeuable. Joyen heuens, and the^m erth
glade; and sey thei in naciouns, The
32 Lord schal regnen. Doone the se, and
the^n plente of it; ioyen the feeldis, and
33 alle thingis that in hem ben. Thann
schal preysen the trees of the wijlde wood
before the Lord; for he came to demen
34 the erthe. Knowlechith to the Lord, for
good^o he is; for with oute ende the
35 mercy of hym. And seith, Saue us, God
oure Saueoure, and gader vs, and delyuer
fro gentilis; that we knowlechen to thin
holy name, and ioyen in thi dytees.
36 Blessid^p the Lord God of Yrael fro with
out ende vnto with out ende; and sey
alle puple, Amen, and an hympne to God.
37 And so he laft there, beforn the arke of
the pese couenaunt of the Lord, Asaph
and his bretheren, that they schulden
mynystren in the siȝt of the arke besily
38 bi alle days and^q ther whilis. Forsothe
Obededom and his bretheren, eyȝt and
sexty, and Obededom, the sone of Ydi-
39 tym, and Osa, he ordeynede porters. Sadoch forsothe prest, and the bretheren of
hym, prestis before the tabernacle of the
Lord, in the heiȝt that was in Gabaon,
40 that thei offren brent sacrifices to the

dai his helthe^y. Telle ȝe among hethen 24
men his glorie; hise^z merueylis among
alle puplis. For the Lord is greet, and 25
worthi to be preisid ful myche; and he is
orible, 'ethir griseful^a, ouer alle goddis.
For alle the goddis of puplis ben idols; 26
but the Lord made^b heuenes. Knoulech-27
yng and greet doyng ben bifor hym;
strengthe and ioy ben in the place of
hym. Ȝe meynees of puplis, 'bringe ȝe^c 28
to the Lord; brynge ȝe to the Lord glorie
and empire. Ȝyue ȝe glorie^d to his name, 29
reise ȝe^e sacrifice, and come ȝe in his siȝt;
and worschipe ȝe the Lord in hooli fairnesse. Al erthe be mouyd fro his face; 30
for he foundide^f the world vnmouable.
Heuenes be^g glad, and the erthe 'ioy 31
fulli^h; and seie thei among naciouns, The
Lord schal^i regne. The see thundre, and 32
his fulnesse; the feeldis fulli ioye^k, and
alle thingis that ben in tho. Thanne the 33
trees of the forest schulen preyse bifor the
Lord; for he cometh to deme the erthe.
Knouleche ȝe^l to the Lord, for he is good; 34
for his mersi is withouten ende. And seie 35
ȝe, Thou God oure^m sauyour, saue vs, and
gadere vs^n, and delyuere^o vs^p fro hethen
men; that we knowleche to thin hooli
name, and be fulli glade in thi songis.
Blessid be the Lord God of Israel fro 36
with oute bigynnyng and til^q 'in to^r with
outen ende; and al the^s puple seie^t, Amen,
and seie heriyng to God. Therfor Dauid 37
lefte there, bifor the arke of boond of pees
of the Lord, Asaph and hise britheren, for
to mynystre in the siȝt of the arke^u contynueli bi alle daies and^w her whilis^x.
Forsothe^y he^z ordeynede porteris, Obed-38
edom and hise britheren, eiȝte and sixti,
and Obededom, the sone of Idithum, and
Oza. Sotheli^a 'he ordeynede^b Sadoch 39
preest, and hise britheren, preestis bifor

---

^m Om. *A*.   ^n Om. *FH*.   ^o gode *F.* God *H.*   ^p Blessid be *A*.   ^q in *AH*.

^y helthe ȝeue 1. helthe ȝeuer s.   ^z and his s.   ^a *that is, ferful* 1s.   ^b he made 1.   ^c bringe *plures*.
bringeth *EP*.   ^d the glorie s.   ^e ȝe up 1s.   ^f hath foundid 1s.   ^g be ȝe 1s.   ^h ioy it fulli *A sec. m.* s.
gladful *EL*. make ful out ioie *K sec. m.* ioyeful *NP*.   ^i Om. *EL*.   ^k ioye they 1s.   ^l Om. 1s.   ^m of oure 1s.
^n vs togidere 1s.   ^o delyuere thou 1s.   ^p Om. *plures*.   ^q Om. *x*.   ^r vnto 1. vnto into s.   ^s Om. 1s.
^t schal seie *x*.   ^u arke, *or bifore the arke* 1s.   ^w and bi 1s.   ^x whilis, *that is, now oon and eft anoother* 1.
whilis, *that is, oon of hem o while or sesun, and another anoother while or sesun* s.   ^y And 1.   ^z Dauid 1.
^a And 1s.   ^b Om. 1.

Lord vpon the auter of brent sacrifice
bisily, erly and at euen, aftir alle thingis
that ben writen in the lawe of the Lord,
41 that he comaundide to Yrael. And aftir
hym Eman, and Iditym, and the tother
chosen, echon bi his name, to knowlachen to the Lord; for with oute ende
42 the mercy of hym. Heman also, and Iditym, synginge in trumpe, and smytynge
cymbalis, and alle orgnys of musikis, to
syngyn to God; the sonis forsothe of
43 Yditym he made to ben porters. And
al the puple is turned aȝein in to his
hous, and Dauid, that also he schuld
blessen to his hous.

CAP. XVII.

1 Whanne forsothe Dauid dwellid in his
hous, he seyde to Nathan, the prophete,
Loo! I dwelle in a cedre hous; the arke
forsothe of the pese couenaunt of the
2 Lord is vndir skynnes. And Nathan
seith to Dauith, Alle thingis that ben
in thi hert do, God forsothe is with thee.
3 Than that nyȝt is maad the word of the
4 Lord to Nathan, seyinge, Go, and speke
to Dauith, my seruaunt, Thes thingis
seith the Lord, Thou schalt not bylde
5 to me an hows to dwellen[r]; ne forsothe
I dwellede in hous, fro that tyme that I
ladde out Yrael fro the lond of Egipt 'in
to[s] this day, bot was euermore chaungynge the places[t] of tabernacle, and in
6 tent with al Yrael dwellynge. Whether
I spake oonly to oon of the iugis of
Yrael, to whome I hadde comaundid,
that he schulde feden my puple, and
seyde, Why hast thou not bildid[u] up 'to
7 me[v] a cedre hous? Nowe also thus thou
schalt speken to my seruaunt Dauid,

the tabernacle of the Lord, in the hiȝ
place that was in Gabaon, for to offre 40
brent sacrifices to the Lord on[c] the auter
of brent sacrifice contynueli, in the morwetid and euentid, bi alle thingis that ben
writun in the lawe of the Lord, which he
comaundide to Israel. And aftir hym[d] 41
Dauyd ordeynede Eman, and Idithum,
and other chosene[e], ech man bi his name,
for to knowleche to the Lord; for his
mercy is withouten ende. Also[f] *he or-* 42
deynede Eman, and Idithum, trumpynge,
and schakynge cymbalis, and alle orguns
of musikis, for to synge to God; forsothe[g]
he made the sones of Idithum to be portours[h], '*ether bereris*[i]. And al the puple 43
turnede aȝen in to her hows, and Dauid
turnede aȝen, to blesse† also his hows.

† *blesse*; that is, to do good to his meynee. *Lire here.* COQ.

CAP. XVII.

Forsothe whanne Dauid dwellide in his 1
hows, he seide to Nathan, the prophete,
Lo! Y dwelle in an hows of cedris[k]; sotheli[l] the arke of boond of pees of the
Lord is[m] vndur skynnys. And Nathan 2
seide to Dauid, Do thou alle thingis that
ben in thin herte, for God is with thee.
Therfor in that nyȝt the word of the Lord 3
was maad to Nathan, and seide, Go thou, 4
and speke to Dauid, my seruaunt, The
Lord seith these thingis, Thou schalt not
bilde to me an hows to dwelle in[n]; for[o] Y 5
'dwellide not[p] in an hows, fro that tyme
in which Y ledde Israel out of the lond
of Egipt til[q] to this dai, but euere Y
chaungide[r] places[s] of tabernacle[t], and
dwellide[u] in a tente with al Israel. Where 6
I spak[v] nameli to oon of the iugis of Israel, to which I comaundide[w] that thei
schulde fede my puple, and seide, Whi
'bildidist thou not[x] to me an hous of
cedre? Now therfor thou schalt speke 7
thus to my seruaunt Dauid, The Lord of

[r] dwelle yn *A.* [s] vnto *E.* [t] place *A.* [u] bild *ACEFH.* [v] Om. *B.*

[c] in IS. [d] Sadoch IS. [e] chosene men IS. [f] And X. [g] and IS. [h] portours *of thingis perteynynge to the tabernacle* I. porters *or berers of necessari thingis perteynyng to the tabernacle* S. [i] Om. DIS. [k] cedris, *that is, ful perdurable* S. [l] and IS. [m] is *hilid* IS. [n] Om. *plures.* [o] certis IS. [p] haue not dwellid I. [q] Om. X. [r] haue chaungid IS. [s] place X. [t] the tabernacle IS. [u] haue dwellid IS. [v] haue spoke I. haue not spoke S. spac not X. [w] comaunde A. [x] hast thou not bildid IS.

Thes thingis seith the Lord of hoostis,
I toke thee, when in lesewes thou folow-
edist the flok, that thou were duyke of
8 my puple Yrael, and I was with thee
whither euer thou wentist, and I slew3
alle thin enmyes beforn thee, and I maad
to thee a name as of oon of the grete
men that ben oft wirschipid in᙮ the˟
9 erthe And I 3aue a place to my puple
Yrael, it schal be plauntid, and he schal
dwelle in it, and no more he schal be
meued, ne the sonis of wickidnesse schuln
10 to-tein hem, as fro the begynnynge of
the days inʸ whiche I 3aue iuges to my
puple Yrael; and I haue inekid alle thin
enmyes. I telle than to thee, that the
11 Lord be to belden to thee an hous And
whanne thou hast fulfillid thy days, that
thou go to thi fadirs, I schal reren thi
seed aftir thee, that schal ben of thi
sonys, and I schal stablen the rewme of
12 hym, he schal beelde to me an hous,
and I schal fastnen his see˟ vnto with
13 outen ende I schal ben to hym in to
fadin, and he schal ben to me in to sone;
and my mercy I schal not don awey fro
hym, as I toke aweye fro hym that was
14 bifoie thee, and I schal setten hym in
my hous and in my regne vnto euermore; and the trone of hym schal be
15 most fast vnto with oute ende Aftie
alle thes wordis, and aftir al this visioun,
16 thus spak Nathan to Dauid And whanne
kyng Dauid was commen, and hadde sytten before the Lord, he seide, Who am I,
Lord God, and what my hous, that thou
17 schuldist 3euen to me syche thingis ? Bot
and that lityl is seen in thi si3te, and
theifore thou speke on the hous of thi
seruaunt, also in to comyn, and thou
hast maad me hee3 vpon alle men Lord
18 God, what more ouer may Dauid adden,
whanne thus thou hast glorified thi ser-
19 uaunt, and knowen hym? Lord, for thi

oostis seith these thingis, Y took thee,
whanne thou suedist theʸ floc in the lesewis, that thou schuldist be duyk on˟ my
puple Israel; and Y was with thee whidur 8
euere thou 3edist, and Y killide alle thin
enemyes bifor thee, and Y made to thee
an name as of oon of the giete men that
ben maad worschipful, ether˟ ʼfamouse, in
ertheᵇ And Y 3af a place to my puple Is- 9
rael; it schal be plauntid, and schalᶜ dwelle
there ynne, and it schal no more be moued,
and the sones of wickydnesse schulen not
defoule hem, as fro the bigynnyng, fro the 10
daies in whiche Y 3af iugis to my puple
Israel, and Y made lowe alle thin enemyes Therfor Y telle to theeᵈ, that the
Lord schal bilde an hows to thee And 11
whanne thou hast fillidᵉ thi daies, that
thou go to thi fadris, Y schal reiseᶠ thi
seed after thee, that schal be of thi sones,
and Y schal stablische his rewme, he schal 12
bilde to me an hows, and Y schal make
stidefast his seete tilᵍ in to with outen
ende Yʰ schal be to hym in to a fadir, 13
and he schal be to me in to a sone; and
Y schal not doᵗ myᵏ mersi fro hym, as
Y tookˡ awei fro hymᵐ that was bifore
thee; and Y schal oideyne hymⁿ in mynᵗ⁴
hows and in my rewme tilᵒ in to with
outen ende; and his trone schal be moost
stidefast with outen ende Bi alle these 15
wordis, and bi al this ieuelacioun, so Nathan spak to Dauid And whanne kyng 16
Dauid hadde come, and hadde sete bifore
the Lord, he seide, Lord God, who am Y,
and what is myn hows, that thou schuldist
3yue siche thingis to me ? But also this is 17
seyn litil in thi si3t, and therfor thou
spakestᵖ onᑫ the hows of thi seruaunt, 3he,
in to tyme to comynge, and hastʳ maad
me worthi to be biholdunˢ ouer alle men
My Lord God, whatᵗ may Dauid addeⁿ 18
more, sithen thou hast so glorified thi seruaunt, and hast knowe hym? Lord, for 19

ʷ heere in *FH*   ˟ Om *FH*   ᵛ the *EF*   ˣ seed *A*

ʸ a is   ˣ upon I   ᵃ *and* ᴅ Om cɪ   ᵇ Om cɪ   ᶜ it schal ɪ Israel shal s Y schal w   ᵈ thee,
Dauith s   ᵉ fulfillid is   ᶠ reise up is   ᵍ Om x   ʰ And I s   ⁱ do awey new   ᵏ Om ᾽   ˡ took it is
ᵐ *Saul* is   ⁿ him, *that is, thi sone* s   ᵒ Om ᾽   ᵖ hast spoke is   ᑫ of is   ʳ thou hast is   ˢ holden s
ᵗ what thing is   ᵘ adde to is

seruaunt aftir thi herte thou hast done
al this grete doynge, and al thi grete
woundirs thou woldist to ben knowen.
20 Lord, ther is noon lije thee, and ther
is noon other God with oute thee, of al
the whiche we han herd with oure eris.
21 Who forsothe is an other as thi puple
Yrael, oon folk of kynde in the lond, to
the whiche God wente, that he delyuere
and make a peple to him, and by his
gretnesse and grysynges he caste out nacyouns fro his face, the whiche he hadde
22 delyuerd fro Egipt? And thou hast
putte thy puple Ysrael to thee in to a
puple in to with oute eend, and thou,
23 Lord, art maad his God. Now thann,
Lord, the word that thou hast spoken to
thi seruaunt, and vpon his hous, be confermed in to with outen eend, and do, as
24 thou hast spoken; and thi name abijde
stille, and be magnyfied in to euermore;
and be it seid, The Lord of hoostis, God
of Yrael, and the hous of Dauid, his ser-
25 uaunt, abijdynge stille beforn hym. Thou
forsothe, Lord my God, hast told opynly
the lityl ere of thi seruaunt, that thou
schuldist bilden to hym an hous; and
therfore thi seruaunt hath founden trust,
26 that he preye before thee. Nowe thanne,
Lord, thou ert God, and thou hast spoken
27 to thi seruaunt so fele benfetis; and thou
hast begunnen to blessen to the hous of
thi seruaunt, that it be euer more before
thee; thee forsothe blessynge, blessid it
schal ben in to with outen end.

thi seruaunt thou hast do bi thin herte al
this grete doyng, and woldist[v] that alle
grete thingis be knowun. Lord, noon is 20
lijk thee, and noon other God is with oute
thee, of alle whiche we herden[w] with oure
eeris. For who is anothir[x] as[y] thi[z] puple 21
Israel, o folc in erthe, to whom God ȝede,
to delyuere and make[a] a puple to hym
silf, and to caste out bi his greetnesse and
dredis naciouns fro the face therof, which[b]
he delyuerede fro Egipt? And thou[c] hast 22
set thi puple Israel in to a puple to thee
til[d] in to with outen ende, and thou, Lord,
art maad the God therof. Now therfor, 23
Lord, the word which thou hast spoke to
thi seruaunt, and on his hows, be[e] confermed with outen ende, and do, as thou
spake[f]; and thi name dwelle[g], and be 24
magnefied[h] 'with outen[i] ende; and be it
seid, The Lord of oostis is God of Israel,
and the hous of Dauid, his seruaunt, dwellynge bifor hym. For thou, my Lord God, 25
hast maad reuelacioun to[k] the eere of thi
seruaunt, that thou woldist bilde to hym
an hous; and therfor[l] thi seruaunt foond[m]
trist, that he preie bifor thee. Now ther- 26
for, Lord, thou art God, and hast spoke
to thi seruaunt so grete benefices; and 27
thou hast bigunne to blesse the hous of
thi seruaunt, that it be euer bifore thee;
for[n], Lord, for thou blessist, it schal be
blessid with outen ende.

CAP. XVIII.

1 Done it is forsothe aftir thes thingis,
that Dauid schuld smijten Philisteis, and
meeken hem, and taken Geth and the
douȝtirs of it fro the hond of Philisteis,
2 and smijten Moab; and Moabitis schulden
ben maad the seruauntis of Dauid, of-
3 fringe to hym ȝiftis. That tyme also

CAP. XVIII.

Forsothe[o] it was doon aftir these thingis, 1
that Dauid smoot Filisteis[p], and made hem
lowe, and took[q] awey Geth and vilagis[r]
therof fro the hond of Filisteis; and that[s] 2
he smoot Moab; and Moabitis weren maad
seruauntis[t] of Dauid, and brouȝten[u] ȝiftis
to hym. In that tyme Dauid smoot also 3

---

[v] thou woldist 1s.　　[w] han herd 1s.　　[x] sich anothir 1. another soche peple s.　　[y] as is 1s.　　[z] the s.
[a] to make 1s.　　[b] the which puple 1. which puple s.　　[c] thou, Lord 1s.　　[d] Om. x.　　[e] be it 1s.　　[f] hast
spoke BCDFIKLMNOPQRSTUWXb.　　[g] dwelle worshepful s.　　[h] it maad greet 1s.　　[i] anentis thi seruaunt withouten s.　　[k] into 1. in s.　　[l] therfor, Lord 1. herfor KMXb. herfor, Lord s.　　[m] huth founde 1s.　　[n] certis 1s.
[o] Sothely 1s.　　[p] the Philistees 1s.　　[q] he took 1s.　　[r] the vilagis 1s.　　[s] Om. 1s.　　[t] the seruauntis 1s.　　[u] thei
brouȝten 1s.

Dauid smote Adadeser, kyng of Soba, of
the regyoun of Emath, whanne he wente
for to largen his empyre vnto the flode
4 of Eufraten. Thanne Dauid toke a thousand foure whelid cartis of hym, and
seuen thousand of hors men, and twenty
thousand of fote men; and he kutte the
knee senewis of alle the hors of the
chaaris, out taken an hundrith foure
whelid cartis, the whiche he reseruede to
5 hym silf. Forsothe and Cyre Damascen
came ouer, that he ȝeue helpe to Adadeser, kyng of Soba, bot and of this Dauid
6 smote twenty thousand of men; and he
putte knyȝtis in Damasc, that Cyrie also[a]
schuld seruen to hym, and offre ȝiftis.
And the Lord herde hym in alle thingis
7 to the whiche he wente. Also Dauid
toke the golden arewe cases, that the
seruauntes of Adadezer hadden, and
8 brouȝte hem in to Jerusalem; also and
fro Thebath and Cum[b], cytees of Adadezer, myche of brasse, of the[c] whiche
Salomon made the brasen se, and pylers,
9 and brasen vessels. The whiche thing
whanne Thou, kyng of Emath, hadde
herd, that is, Dauith to han smyten al
10 the hoost of Adadeser, kyng of Soba, he
sente Aduram, his sone, to kyng Dauid,
that he aske of[d] hym pese, and thanckide
to hym, for thi that he hadde ouercommen and smyten Adadezer; forsothe
kyng Adadezer was aduersarie to Thou.
11 Bot and alle the golden vesselis, and sylueren, and brasen kyng Dauid sacride to
the Lord; and the syluer, and the gold,
that the kyng hadde taken fro alle gentiles, as wele of Ydume and Moab, and
the sonys of Amon, as of the Philisteis
12 and Amalech. Forsothe Abisai, the sone
of Saruye, smote Edom in the valey of
13 salt placis, ten and eyȝt thousand. And
he sett in Edom a streyngthe, that Ydu-

Adadezer, kyng of Soba, of the cuntrey
of Emath, whanne he ȝede for[v] to alarge
his empire til to the flood Eufrates. Ther- 4
for Dauid took a thousynde foure[w] horsid
cartis of his, and seuene thousynde of
horsmen, and twenti thousynde of foot
men; and he hoxide[x] alle the horsis of
charis[y], outakun an hundrid foure horsid
cartis, whiche[z] he kepte to hym silf. For- 5
sothe[a] also Sirus of[b] Damask cam aboue,
to ȝyue help to Adadezer, kyng of Soba,
but Dauid smoot also of hise[c] two and
twenti thousynde of men; and he[d] set- 6
tide[e] kniȝtis in Damask, that Sirie also
schulde serue hym, and brynge[f] ȝiftis. And
the Lord helpide hym[g] in alle thingis to
whiche he ȝede. And Dauid took goldun 7
arowe caasis, whiche the seruauntis of
Adadezer hadden, and he brouȝte[h] tho in
to Jerusalem; also and[i] of Thebath and 8
of Chum, the citees of Adadezer, *he took*
ful myche of bras, wherof Salomon made
the brasun see, '*that is, waischynge ves-*
sel[k], and pileris, and[l] brasun vessels. And 9
whanne Thou, kyng of Emath, hadde
herd this thing, 'that is[m], that Dauid
hadde smyte al the oost of Adadezer,
kyng of Soba, he sente Aduram, his sone, 10
to Dauid the kyng, for to axe of hym
pees, and for to thanke hym, for he hadde
ouercome and hadde[n] smyte Adadezer; for
whi king Adadezer was aduersarie of
Thou. But also kyng Dauid halewide 11
to the Lord alle the vessels of gold, and
of siluer, and of bras; and the siluer, and
the gold, which the kyng hadde take of
alle folkis, as wel of Idumee and Moab[o],
and of the[p] sones of Amon, as of Filisteis
and Amalech[q]. Forsothe[r] Abisai, the sone 12
of Saruye, smoot Edom in the valei of salt
pittis, 'ten and eiȝte[s] thousynde. And he[t] 13
settide[u] strong hold in Edom, that Ydumei
schulde serue Dauid. And the Lord sauide

[a] Om. H. [b] sum ABFH. [c] Om. CFH.

[v] Om. S. [w] of foure IS. [x] oxide, *that is, he kitte asonder the houȝ sennes of* S. [y] the charis IS. [z] the whiche I. [a] And IS. [b] *prince* of IS. [c] *Syrus* IS. [d] Dauid IS. [e] sette IS. [f] bryng *to him* S. [g] Dauid IS. [h] brouȝt in S. [i] Om. S. [k] Om. I. *that is, wasshing vesselis for vse of the tabernacle* S. [l] and othere diuers S. [m] Om. S. [n] Om. IS. [o] of Moab C. [p] alle the IS. [q] of Amalech C. [r] And IS. [s] eiȝtene IX. [t] Abisay S. [u] sette IS.

me schulde seruen to Dauid. And the Lord sauede Dauid in alle thingis, to the 14 whiche he wente. Thann Dauid regned vpon al Yrael, and dide dome and riȝt- 15 wisnesse to al his puple. Bot Joab, the sone of Saruye, was vpon the hoost; and Josephath, the sone of Ailuth, chaun- 16 celer; Sadoch forsothe, the sone of Achitob, and Achymalech, the sone of 17 Abither, prestis; and Susa, scribe; Ba- nanyas also, the sone of Joiade, vpon the legiouns Cerethi and Pherethi; forsothe the sonys of Dauid first at the kyngis hond.

CAP. XIX.

1 It fel forsothe, that Naas, the kynge of the sonys of Amon, schulde dyen, and his sone regnen for hym. And Dauid seide, I schal do mercy with Hanon, the sone of Naas; forsothe his fadir ȝaue to 2 me mercy. And Dauid sente messagers, to coumforten hym vpon the deth of his fadir. The whiche whan weren commen in to the lond of the sonys of Amon, that 3 thei coumforten Hanon, the princis of the sonys of Amon seiden to Hanon, Thou perauenture weenest, that Dauid by che- soun[e] of wirschip vnto thi fadir sente, that he coumforten thee; and thou takist no heed, that that[f] thei aspyen, and sechen, and enserchen thi lond, ben commen to thee 4 the seruauntis of hym. Therfore Hanon maad ballid and schoofe[g] the childre[h] of Dauid, and kutte the kootis of hem fro the ers of hem vnto the feet; and he laft 5 hem. The whiche when weren gone awey, and that hadden sente to Dauid, he sente in to aȝein commynge of hem; forsothe grete despyte thei hadden suf- fred; and he comaundyde, that thei schul- den dwellen in Jericho, to the tyme that the berd of hem weren sprongen, and 6 thanne they schulden turnen aȝeyn. For- sothe the sonis of Amon, seeynge that

Dauid in alle thingis, to whiche he ȝede. Therfor Dauid regnede on[v] al Israel, and 14 dide[w] doom and[x] riȝtwisnesse[y] to al his puple. Forsothe[z] Joab, the sone of Saruye, 15 was[a] 'on the[b] oost; and Josaphat, the sone of Ayluth, was chaunceler[c]; forsothe[d] Sa- 16 doch, the sone of Achitob, and Achyma- lech, the sone of Abyathar, weren preestis; and Susa was scribe; and Banaye, the sone 17 of Joiada, was on[e] the legiouns Cerethi and Phelethi†; sotheli the sones of Dauid weren the firste at the[f] hond of the kyng.

† Glose. Cere- thie and Phele- thie weren moost tauȝt fiȝters, and thei werin kepers of Da- uith heed.

CAP. XIX.

1 Forsothe it bifelde, that Naas, kyng of the sones of Amon, diede, and his sone 2 regnyde for him. And Dauid seide, Y schal do mercy with Anoon, the sone of Naas; for his fadir ȝaf merci to me. And Dauid sente messageris, to coumforte hym on the deeth of his fadir. And whanne thei weren comen in[g] to the lond of the sones of Amon, for to coumforte Anon, the 3 princes of the sones of Amon seiden to Anon, In hap thou gessist, that Dauid for cause of onour in to thi fadir sente men, that schulden coumforte thee; and thou perseyuest not, that hise seruauntis ben comen to thee to aspie, and enquere, and seche[h] thi lond. Therfor Anoon made 4 ballid and schauyde the children of Dauid, and kittide[i] the cootis of hem fro the hut- tokis of hem til to the feet; and lefte[k] hem. And whanne thei hadden go[l], and hadden 5 sent this[m] to Dauid, he[n] sente in to the meting of hem; for thei hadden suffrid greet dispit; and he comaundide, that thei schulden dwelle in Gerico, til her berde wexide, and thanne thei schulden turne aȝen. Forsothe[o] the sones of Amon sien, 6 that thei hadden do wrong to Dauid, bothe Anoon and the tother[p] puple, and thei senten a thousynde talentis of siluer, for

---

e enchesoun AC.　f Om. A.　g choof II.　h children A.

v upon IS.　w he diðe S.　x in D.　y riȝtfulnesse plures.　z And S.　a was duke S.　b vpon Dauith S. c Dauith chaunseler S.　d and S.　e souereyne vpon S.　f Om. S.　g Om. IS.　h to seche IS.　i thei kittiden IS.　k so thei leften IS.　l go forth IS.　m and shewed this S.　n Dauid IS.　o And IS. p oother IS.

thei hadden don wronge to Dauith, bothe Hanon and the tother puple, thei senten a thousand talentis of syluer, that thei hiren to hem fro Mesopotanye and Ciria, Maacha and from Soba, charis and hors-7 men; and thei hyreden two and thritty thousand of charis, and the kyng of Maacha with his puple. The whiche, whan weren commen, setten tentis forn aʒeynus Medaba; also the sonys of Amon gaderd fro their cytees, camen to bateil. 8 The whiche thing whanne Dauid hadde herde, he sente Joab, and al the hoost of 9 stronge men. And the sonys of Amon gon out, dresseden scheltrun bysidis the ʒate of the cytee; the kyngis forsothe, that weren commen to helpe, stoden a-10 part in the feld. Than Joab vndirstond-ynge the bateil forn aʒeynst and behynde the bac aʒeynst hym to be maad, he chees most stronge men of al Yrael, and 11 wente aʒein Cyrum; the tother forsothe part of the puple he ʒaue vndir the hond of Abisay, his brother; and thei wenten 12 aʒein the sonys of Amon. And he seide, ʒif Cyries ouercommen me, thou schalt ben in helpe to me; ʒif forsothe the sonys of Amon ouercommen thee, I schal 13 ben to thee in to socour; take coumfort, and do we manly for oure puple, and for the cytees of oure God; the Lord for-14 sothe, that in his siʒt is good, do. Thanne Joab, and the puple that was with hym, wente aʒeyn Cyrus to bateil, and drofe 15 hem. Bot the sonis of Amon seeynge that Cyres hadden flowen, thei also flowen Abisay, his brother, and wenten in to the cytee; and Joab is turned aʒeyn 16 in to Jernsalem. Seeynge forsothe Cy-res, that they hadden falle beforn Yrael, senten messagers, and brouʒten forthe Cyre, that was beʒond the flode; Sophat forsothe, prince of the knyʒthode of Adad-17 ezer, was the duyke of hem. The whiche

to hire to hem charis and horsmen of Mesopotanye and Sirie⁹, of ʳ Maacha and of ˢ Soba; and thei hiriden to hem two 7 and thretti thousynde of charis †, and the kyng of Maacha with his puple. And whanne thei weren comen, thei settiden ᵗ tentis ᵘ euene aʒens Medaba; and the sones of Amon weren gaderid ᵛ fro her citees, and camen to batel. And whanne Dauid 8 'hadde herd ʷ this, he sente ˣ Joab, and al the oost of stronge men. And the sones 9 of Amon ʒeden out, and dressiden ʸ schel-trun ˣ bisidis the ʒate of the citee; but the kyngis, that weren comen to helpe ᶻ, stoden asidis half in the feeld. Therfor Joab vn-10 durstood, that batel was maad aʒens hym 'euene aʒens ᵇ and bihynde thee ᶜ bak, and he chees ᵈ the strongeste men of al Israel, and ʒede ᵉ aʒens Sirus; sotheli ᶠ he ʒaf the 11 residue ᵍ part of the puple vnder the hond of Abisai, his brother; and thei ʒeden ʰ aʒens the sones of Amon. And Joab seide ⁱ, 12 If Sirus schal ouercome me, thou schalt helpe me; sotheli ᵏ if the sones of Amon schulen ouercome thee, Y schal helpe thee; be thou coumfortid, and do we manli for 13 oure puple, and for the citees ˡ of oure God; forsothe ᵐ the Lord do ⁿ that, that is good in his siʒt. Therfor Joab ʒede ᵒ, and 14 the puple that was with hym, aʒens Sirus to batel, and he ᵖ droof hem awei. Sotheli ᵠ 15 the sones of Amon sien, that Sirus hadde fled, and thei fledden fro Abisay, his bro-ther, and entriden ʳ in to ˢ the ᵗ citee; and Joab turnede aʒen in to Jerusalem. For-16 sothe ᵘ Sirus siʒ, that he felde ᵛ doun bi-for Israel, and he sente messageris, and brouʒte ʷ Sirus, that was biʒende the flood; sotheli ˣ Sophath, the prynce of chyualrie of Adadezer, was the duyk of hem. And 17 whanne this was teld to Dauid, he gader-ide ʸ al Israel, and passide ᶻ Jordan; and he felde in on ᵃ hem, and dresside ᵇ scheltrun euene aʒens hem, fiʒtynge aʒenward. 'For-18

† of charis; that is, xxxii. thousand of men fiʒtinge in charis, and of footmen; in the secunde book of Kingis, x. cᵒ. Lire here. cx ɪpᴑᵇ.

ᵠ of Sirie ɪꜱ. ʳ and of s. ˢ Om. cn. ᵗ setten s. ᵘ her tentis ɪꜱ. ᵛ gaderid togidere ɪꜱ. ʷ herde ɪ. ˣ sente forth ɪꜱ; ʸ thei dressiden ɪ. ᶻ her scheltrun ɪꜱ. ᵃ helpe him ɪ. helpe Anon s. ᵇ Om. c. euene aʒens him s. ᶜ his ɪꜱ. ᵈ chese oute s. ᵉ he ʒede s. ᶠ and ɪꜱ. ᵍ remenaunt ɪꜱ. ʰ wenten forth ɪ. ʒeden forth s. ⁱ seide to Abisay ɪꜱ. ᵏ and ɪꜱ. ˡ citees s. ᵐ and ɪꜱ. ⁿ do hem ɪ. do he s. ᵒ ʒede forth ɪꜱ. ᵖ Joab ɪꜱ. ᵠ And ɪꜱ. ʳ thei entriden ɪꜱ. ˢ Om. s. ᵗ her s. ᵘ And ɪꜱ. ᵛ had falle ɪꜱ. ʷ brouʒten to him ɪꜱ. ˣ and ɪꜱ. ʸ gaderide togidere ɪꜱ. ᶻ he passide ɪꜱ. ᵃ upon ɪꜱ. ᵇ he dresside ɪꜱ.

thing whan was tolde to Dauid, he gaderde al Yrael, and passede Jordán, and
fel in to hem, and dresside forn aȝeyns
18 scheltrun, hem aȝeyn fiȝtynge. Forsothe
Cyres fleyȝ Yrael, and Dauith slowȝ of
Cyres seuen thousand of charis, and
fourty thousand of foote men, and So-
19 phat, the prince of the[l] hoost. Seeynge
forsothe the seruauntis of Adadezer hem
silf of Yrael to be ouercommen, ouerflowen to Dauith, and serueden to hym ;
and[k] Cyre wolde no more ȝeuen help to
the sonys of Amon.

sothe[c] Sirus fledde fro Israel, and Dauid
killide of men[d] of Sirie seuene thousynde
of charis†, and fourti thousynde of foot
men, and[e] Sophath, the[f] prince of the oost.
Sotheli[g] the seruauntis of Adadezer siȝen, 19
that thei weren ouercomun of Israel, and
thei fledden ouer to Dauid, and seruiden[h]
hym ; and Sirie wolde no more ȝyue helpe
to the sones of Amon.

† of charis ;
that is, vii.
thousind men
fiȝtinge in
charis, for they
weren vii. hun-
drid of charis,
in the secunde
book of Kingis
x. c°., and in
ech chare weren
x. men, and
these maken
vii. thousynd
men fiȝtinge in
charis. Lire
here. CKLOb.

CAP. XX.

1 Done it is forsothe aftir the cercle of
a[l] ȝeer, that tyme that kyngis ben wont
to gon forth to batelis, Joab gaderde the
hoost, and the streyngthe of knyȝthode,
and waastide the lond of the sonys of
Amon, and wente, and besegide Rabath ;
bot Dauid abood in Jerusalem, whan Joab
2 smote Rabath, and distroyede it. Dauith
forsothe toke the crowne of Melchon fro
his heued, and foonde in it a talent of
gold weiȝt, and most precious gemmes,
and maad therof to hym a dyademe ;
also manye spoylis of the cytee he toke.
3 The puple forsothe that was in it he
ladde out, and maad vpon hem pestelis,
and sledis, and prowd yren charis, to gon
ouer, so that thei weren al to-kut and to-
brosed alle ; thus dide Dauid to alle the
cytees of the sonys of Amon, and he is[m]
turned aȝeyn with alle his puple in to
4 Jerusalem. Aftir thes[n] thingis bateil is
gon in in Gaser aȝeinus Philisteis, in the
whiche smote Sobachai Vsachites Saphai
of the kynrede of Raphaym, and
5 lowede[o] hem. Another also bateil is
don aȝeynus the Philisteis, in the whiche
Adeodate, the sone of Saltus, Bethlamyte, smote the brother of Goliath Je-

CAP. XX.

Forsothe[i] it was doon after the ende of 1
a[k] ȝeer, in that tyme wherinne kyngis ben
wont to go forth to batels, Joab gederide[l]
the oost, and the strengthe of chyualrie,
and he wastide the lond of the sones of
Amon, and ȝede[m], and bisegide Rabath ;
forsothe[n] Dauid dwellide in Jerusalem,
whanne Joab smoot Rabath, and distriede
it. Forsothe[o] Dauid took the coroun of 2
Melchon[p] fro his heed, and foond[q] therynne the weiȝt of gold a talent, and moost
precious iemmes, and he made therof a
diademe to hym silf ; also he took ful
many spuylis of the citee. Sotheli[r] he 3
ledde out the puple that was therynne,
and made[s] breris, 'ethir instrumentis bi
whiche cornes ben brokun[t], and sleddis[u],
and irone charis, to passe on[v] hem[w], so
that alle men weren kit[x] in to dyuerse
partis, and weren al to-brokun ; Dauid[y]
dide thus to alle the cytees of the[yy] sones
of Amon, and turnede[z] aȝen with al his
puple in to Jerusalem. Aftir these thingis 4
a batel was maad in Gazer aȝens Filisteis,
wherynne Sobochai Vsachites slow Saphai
of the kyn of Raphym‡, and mekide[n] hem.
Also another batel was don aȝens Filisteis[b], 5
in which a man ȝouun of God, the[c] sone

‡ Raphaym ;
that is, of the
kynde of
giauntis. Lire
here. CNOsb.

i his B.   k Om. B.   l o A.   m Om. AB.   n ther F. her U.   o bowide A.

c And Is.   d the men s.   e also s.   f Om. Is.   g and Is.   h strengthed s.   i Sothely I.   k oo Is.
l gederide togidere Is.   m he ȝede forth Is.   n und Is.   o And Is.   p Melchon, and distriede it s.   q he
foond Is.   r And I. Om. s sec. m.   s he made there Is.   t that ben instrumentis with whiche cornes ben
broke and destried Is.   u he made sleddus s.   v vpon Is.   w hem for to waaste I. hem for to waste hem s.
x kit doun Is.   y and Dauid c.   yy Om. A.   z he turnede Is.   a he mekide Is.   b the Filisteis s.   c Om. Is.

thee, whos spere schaft was as the beme
6 of websters. Bot and another bateil fell
in Geth, in⁹ the whiche 'a most' longe
man was, hauynge sexe fyngers, that is,
to gider foure and twenty, the whiche and
he was of Raphaym lynage goten; this
7 blasfemede Yrael, and⁸ Jonathan, the sone
of Sama, brother of Dauid, smote hym.
Thes ben the sonys of Raphaym in Jeth,
the whiche fellen in the hond of Dauid
and of the seruauntis of hym.

of forest⁴, a man of Bethleem, killide Goliath of Geth, the brother *of giauntis*, of
whos schaft⁶ the tre was as the beem of
webbis. But also another batel bifelde in 6
Geth, in which a ful long man was⁶, hauynge sixe fyngris, that is, togidere⁸ foure
and twenti, and he was gendrid⁶ of the
generacioun of Raphaym; he¹ blasfemyde 7
Israel, and Jonathan, the sone of Samaa,
brother of Dauid, killide hym. These
ben the sones of Raphaym in Geth, that
felden doun in the hond of Dauid and of
hise seruauntis.

CAP. XXI.

1 Sathan forsothe rose a3ein Yrael, and
2 stired Dauith for to noumbre Yrael. And
Dauid seid to Joab, and to the princes
of the puple, Goth, and noumbrith Yrael
fro Bersabe vnto Dan, and bryngith to
3 me the noumbre, that I knowe. And
Joab answerd, The Lord encrese his puple an hundrith fold thann⁶ thei ben;
whether not, my lord kyng, thi seruauntis thei ben alle? Why this thing
sechith my lord, that in to synne it be
4 rettid⁶ to Yrael? Bot the word of the
kyng more hadde the maistrie; and Joab
wente out, and enuyrouned al Yrael, and
5 is turned a3ein in to Jerusalem. And he
3aue to Dauid the noumbre of hem, the
whiche he hadde enuyrownede; and al
the noumbre of Yrael is founden a thousand thousandes, and⁶ an hundrith thousand of men, drawynge oute swerd; of
Juda forsothe thre hundrith and seuenty
6 thousand of fi3tynge men. Forsothe Leuy
and Beniamyn he noumbride not, for thi
that constreyned he folowede out the
7 kyngis hest. Forsothe that was comaundid displeside to the Lord, and he
8 smote Yrael. And Dauid seid to God,
I haue synned ful myche for to do this;
I biseche, do awey the wickidnesse of thi

CAP. XXI.

Sotheli Sathan roos a3ens Israel, and 1
stiride Dauid for to noumbre Israel. And 2
Dauid seide to Joab, and to the princes
of the puple, Go 3e, and noumbre Israel⁶
fro Bersabe til to Dan, and brynge 3e the
noumbre to me, that Y wite¹. And Joab 3
answeride, The Lord encresse his puple
an hundrid fold more than thei ben; my
lord the⁶ kyng, whether alle ben not thi
seruauntis? Whi sekith my lord this thing,
that⁶ schal be arettid in to synne to Israel?
But the word of the kyng hadde more the 4
maistrie; and Joab 3ede out⁶, and cumpasside al Israel, and turnede⁶ a3en in to
Jerusalem. And he 3af to Dauid the 5
noumbre of hem, which he hadde cumpassid; and al the noumbre of Israel was
foundun a thousynde thousande, and an
hundrid thousynde of men, drawynge out
swerd; forsothe of Juda⁹ weren thre hundrid thousynde, and seuenti thousynde of⁶
werriouris. For⁸ Joab noumbride not Leuy 6
and Beniamyn, for a3ens his wille he dide
the comaundement of the kyng. Forsothe 7
that⁶ that was comaundid displeside the
Lord, and⁶ he smoot Israel. And Dauid 8
seide to God, Y synnede⁶ greetli that Y
wolde do this⁶; Y biseche⁶, do thou awey
the wickidnesse of thi seruaunt, for Y dide

---

⁹ and BEF.   ʳ among H.   ˢ Om. B.   ᵗ that E *pr. m.*   ᵘ holden E *pr. m.*   ᵛ Om. AB.

ᵈ the forest IS.   ᵉ shafte *or spere* S.   ᶠ that was IS.   ᵍ al togidere IS.   ʰ goten I.   ¹ and he CELP.
ᵏ *al* Israel A.   ˡ wite *what it is* I.   ᵐ Om. S.   ⁿ whiche IS.   ᵒ forth IS.   ᵖ he turnede IS.   ⁹ Juda
linage S.   ʳ Om. X.   ˢ but IS.   ᵗ that thing IS.   ᵘ therfor S.   ᵛ haue synned IS.   ʷ this thing IS.
ˣ biseche the, Lord S.

9 seruaunt, for vnwijsly I dide. And the Lord spac to Gad, seere of Dauid, sey-
10 inge, Go, and speke to Dauid, and sey to hym, Thes thingis seith the Lord, Of thre thingis to thee I ȝeue chois; oon that
11 thou wylt, chees, that I doo to thee. And whann Gad was commen to Dauid, he seide to hym, Thes thingis seith the
12 Lord, Chees that thou wilt, or three ȝeer pestilence, or thee thre monethis to flee thi enmyes and the swerd of hem not to mowen ascapyn, or thre days the swerd of the Lord and deth to be turned aboute in the lond, and the aungel of the Lord to slen in alle the cytees[v] of Yrael. Nowe thanne see, what I schal answere
13 to hym that sente me. And Dauith seid to Gad, On alle sijdes angwyschis thresten me doun, bot beter it is to me, that I falle in to the hondis of the Lord, for many ben the mercyes of hym, thanne
14 in to the hondis of men. Thanne the Lord sente pestilence in to Yrael, and ther fellen of Yrael seuenty thousand of
15 men. And he sente the aungel in to Jerusalem, that he smyte it; and whanne it schulde ben smyten, the Lord sawȝ, and hadde rewthe vpon the mykilnesse[w] of euyl; and he comaundide to the aun- gel that smote, It sufficith, nowe cese thi hond. Forsothe the aungel of the Lord stode besides the corn flore of Ornam
16 Jebusei. And Dauid, rerynge his eeȝen up, sawe the aungel of the Lord stond- ynge bitwene[x] heuene and erthe, and a drawn swerd in his hond, and turned aȝeinus Jerusalem. And there fellen downe as wele he as the more thoruȝ birthe, clothid with heyris, bowed doun in to
17 the erth. And Dauid seide to the Lord, Whether not I am the whiche haue co- maundide that the puple be noumbrid? I that haue synned, I the whiche dyde euyl; this floc what hath[y] deserued?

folili. And the Lord spak to Gad, the 9 profete of Dauid, and seide, Go thou, and 10 speke to Dauid, and seie to him, The Lord seith these thingis, Y ȝeue to thee the[y] chesyng of thre thingis; chese thou oon which thou wolt, that Y do to thee. And 11 whanne Gad was comen to Dauid, he seide to Dauid, The Lord seith these thingis, Chese thou that that thou wolt[z], ether pestilence thre ȝeer[a], ether that thre 12 monethis thou fle thin enemyes and mow not ascape her swerd, ether that the swerd of the Lord and deeth regne thre daies in the lond, and that the aungel of the Lord slee[b] in alle the coostis of Israel. Now therfor se thou, what Y schal answere to hym that sente me[c]. And Dauid seide to 13 Gad, Angwischis oppresse me on ech part, but it is betere to me, that Y falle in to the hondis of the Lord, for his merciful doynges ben manye, than in to the hondis of men. Therfor the Lord sente pestilence 14 in to Israel, and seuenti thousynde of men felden doun of Israel. Also he[d] sente an 15 aungel in to Jerusalem, that he schulde smyte it; and whanne it was smytun, the Lord siȝ, and hadde merci on[e] the greet- nesse of yuel; and comaundide[f] to the aungel that smoot[g], It suffisith, now thin hond ceesse. Forsothe[h] the aungel of the Lord stood bisidis the cornfloor of Ornam Jebusey. And Dauid reiside[i] hise iȝen, 16 and siȝ[k] the aungel of the Lord stondynge bitwixe heuene and erthe, and a[l] drawun swerd in his hond, and[m] turnede[n] aȝens Jerusalem. And bothe he[o] and the grettere men in birthe weren clothid with heiris, and felden[p] doun lowe[q] on[r] the erthe. And 17 Dauid seide to the Lord, Whether Y am not[s] that comaundide that the puple schulde be noumbrid? Y it am that synnede, Y it am that dide yuel; what[t] disscruid this floc[u]? My Lord God, Y bische[v], thin hond be[w] turned 'in to[x] me, and 'in to[x]

---

v lynagis E pr. m.   w mychnes A.   x betwixe A.   y day H.

y Om. is.   z wolt of these is.   a ȝeer to be in thi rewme s.   b sle the peple s.   c me to thee s.   d the Lord s.   e upon is.   f he comaundide is.   g smoot, seiynge i, smote and scide s.   h And is.   i reiside up is.   k he siȝ is.   l Om. s.   m Om. i.   n he was turned s.   o the king i, king s.   p thei fellen is.   q Om. is.   r upon is.   s not he is.   t what of yuel s.   u hath this floc deserued i, hath this folk dis- seruid s.   v bische thee s.   w be it s.   x aȝens is.

Lord my God, be turned, I biseche, thi hond in to me, and in to the hous of my fadir; thi puple forsothe be not smyten. 18 The aungel forsothe of the Lord comaundide to Gad, that he schuld seyn to Dauith, that he schuld steyȝe up, and maken out an auter to the Lord God in 19 the corne flore of Ornam Jebuse. Than Dauid steyȝide up aftir the word of Gad, that to hym he hadde spoken of the word 20 of the Lord. Bot Ornam whanne he hadde beholden and seen the aungel, and his foure sonys with hym, hidden hem silf, for why that tyme he tradde corn 21 in the flore. Thanne whanne Dauid came to Ornam, Ornam byheld hym, and wente forth to meeten hym fro the flore, and honouride hym, bowed in to the 22 erthe. And Dauid seide to hym, ȝeue to me a place of thy flore, that I bild in it an auter to the Lord; so that howe myche it is worth of syluer thou take, and the veniaunce cese fro the puple. 23 And Ornam seyde to Dauid, Take, and my lord the kyng do what euer thing plese[z] to hym; bot and oxen I ȝeue in to brent sacrifice, and the pestels in to wode, and the whete in to sacrifice; alle thingis 24 gladly I ȝeue. And kyng Dauith seide to hym, It schal not ben so, bot syluer I schal ȝeuen as myche as it be[a] worth; ne forsothe I owe to taken awey to thee, and so to offren to the Lord free brent 25 sacrifices. Than Dauid ȝaue to Ornam for the place ownces of gold of most just 26 weiȝt sixe hundrith. And he bilde there an auter to the Lord, and offride brent sacrifices and pesible, and inwardly clepid God; and he herd hym in fyre fro heuen 27 vpon the auter of brent sacrifice. And the Lord comaundide to the aungel, and he turned the swerd in to the schethe.

the hows of my fadir; but thi puple be[y] not smytun. Forsothe[z] an[a] aungel of the 18 Lord comaundide[b] Gad, that he schulde seie to Dauid, that he schulde[c] stic[d], and[e] bilde an auter to the Lord God in the cornfloor of Ornam Jebusei. Therfor Da-19 uid stiede[f] bi the word of Gad, which[g] he spak to hym bi the word of the Lord. Forsothe[h] whanne Ornam hadde biholde, 20 and[i] hadde[k] seyn the aungel, and hise[l] foure sones with hym[m] hadde seyn[n], thei hidden hem, for in that tyme he[o] threischide whete in the cornfloor. Therfor whanne 21 Dauid cam to Ornam, Ornam bihelde Da- uid, and ȝede[p] forth fro the cornfloor aȝens hym, and worschipide hym, lowli on[q] the ground. And Dauid seide to hym, ȝyue 22 the place of[r] thi[s] cornfloor to me, that Y bilde ther ynne an auter to the Lord; so that thou take[t] as myche siluer as it is worth, and that the veniaunce cesse fro the puple. Forsothe[u] Ornam seide to 23 Dauid, Take thou[v], and my lord the[w] kyng do[x] what euer[y] thing plesith hym; but also Y ȝyue oxis[z] in to brent sacrifice, and instrumentis of tree, wherbi cornes ben throischun, in[a] to trees[b], and wheete in to sacrifice[c]; Y ȝyue[d] alle thingis[e] wil- fully[f]. And Dauid the kyng[g] seide to 24 hym, It schal not be don so, but Y schal ȝyue[h] siluer[i] as myche as it is worth; for Y owe not take[k] awei fro thee, and offre so to the Lord brent sacrifices freli[l] ȝouun. Therfor Dauid ȝaf to Ornam for the[m] place 25 sixe hundrid siclis of gold of most[n] iust weiȝte. And he[o] bildide there an[p] auter 26 to the Lord, and he[q] offride[r] brent sacri- fice[s] and pesible sacrifices, and[t] he inwardli clepide God; and God herde hym in fier fro heuene on[u] the auter of brent sacrifice[v]. And the Lord comaundide to the aungel, 27 and he turnede his swerd[w] in to the

---

[z] pleseth A.   [a] is A.

[y] be it s. [z] And 1s. [a] the s. [b] comaundide to c. [c] Om. s. [d] stie vp 1s. [e] Om. s. [f] wente up 1. stiede vp s. [g] the which 1s. [h] And 1s. [i] Om. s. [k] Om. 1s. [l] Om. 1. when Ornam s. [m] Om. s. [n] Om. 1. had seien the aungel s. [o] Ornam s. [p] he ȝede 1s. [q] upon 1s. [r] Om. AELMb. [s] the s. [t] take therfore 1s. [u] And 1s. [v] thou it 1s. [w] Om. 1. [x] do he 1s. [y] Om. c. [z] oxen 1s. [a] I ȝeue hem in s. [b] stikkis to be brent 1. trees to be brent s. [c] sacrifice to be maad s. [d] ȝyue gladly 1. [e] these thingis 1s. [f] Om. 1. [g] kyng Dauid 1. Dauith s. [h] ȝyue to thee 1s. [i] therfor siluer s. [k] to take CEGILNQ. to take it s. [l] kyndely 1. [m] that 1s. [n] ful 1. [o] Dauid 1s. [p] the s. [q] Om. 1. [r] offride theron 1. offrid therupon s. [s] sacrifices A sec. m. s. [t] and there s. [u] upon 1s. [v] sacrifices s. [w] swerd aȝen 1s.

28 Thanne Dauid anoon seeynge, that the Lord hadde herde hym in the corn flore of Ornam Jebusei, he offride there slayne 29 sacrifices. Forsothe the tabernacle of the Lord, that Moyses hadde maad in desert, and[b] the auter of brent sacrifices, was in 30 that tempest in the heiȝt of Gabaon; and Dauid myȝt not gon to the auter, that there he beseche God, forsothe he was with to myche gastnesse aferd, seeinge the swerd of the aungel of the Lord.

CAP. XXII.

1 And Dauid seide, This is the hous of God[c], and this the auter in to brent sacri- 2 fice in Irael. And he comaundide that alle the comlyngis of the lond of Yrael schulden be gaderd; and he ordeynede of hem masouns to stoonis to ben hewen and polischit, that the hous of the Lord 3 be bild up; and myche yren to the naylis of the ȝatis, and to endentyngis and ioyn- yngis Dauid made redy, and weiȝt vn- 4 noumbreable of brasse; also cedre trees myȝten not ben cymed, the whiche Cy- doynes and Tyres brouȝten to Dauid. 5 And Dauid seid, Salomon, my sone, is a lityl child and delicate; the hous forsothe, that I wyll to ben bildid[d] to the Lord, siche owith to ben, that in alle regyouns it ben nemmyd; I schal grethe[e] than to hym necessaryes. And for this cause be- 6 forn his death he made redy alle the dispensis. And he clepide Salomon, his sone, and he comaundide to hym, that he schulde bilden an hous to the Lord 7 God of Yrael. And Dauid seide to Salo- mon, My sone, of my wille it was, that I schuld bilden an hous to the name of 8 the Lord my God; bot the word of the Lord is done to me, seyinge, Myche blode thou hast sched, and many bateils thou hast fouȝten; thou schalt not mown[f]

schethe. Therfor[x] anoon Dauid siȝ, that 28 the Lord hadde herd hym in the corn floor of Ornam Jebusey, and he offride there slayn sacrifices. Forsothe[y] the taber- 29 nacle of the Lord, that Moyses hadde maad in the[z] descert, and the auter of brent sacrifices, was in that[a] tempest[b] in the hiȝ place of Gabaon; and Dauid 30 myȝte not go to the auter, to biseche God there, for he was aferd bi[c] ful greet drede, seynge the swerd of the aungel of the Lord[d].

CAP. XXII.

And Dauid seide, This is the hows of 1 God, and this auter is in to brent sacrifice[e] of Israel. And he[f] comaundide that alle 2 conuersis[g] fro hethenesse to the lawe of Israel schulden be[h] gaderid[i] of the lond of Israel[k]; and he ordeynede of hem ma- souns for to kytte[l] stoonys and for[m] to polische[n], that[o] the hows of the Lord schulde be bildid; also Dauid made redy 3 ful myche yrun to the[p] nailes of the ȝatis, and to the medlyngis and[q] ioyntouris, and[r] vnnoumbrable weiȝte of bras; also 4 the trees of cedre myȝten not be gessid, whiche the men of Sidonye and the men of Tyre brouȝten to Dauid. And Dauid 5 seide, Salomon, my sone, is a litil child and delicate[†]; sotheli[s] the hows, which Y wole be bildid to the Lord, owith to be sich, that it be named in alle cuntrees; therfor Y schal make redi necessaries to hym. And for this cause Dauid bifor his deeth made redi alle costis[‡]. And he[t] cle- 6 pide Salomon, his sone, and comaundide[u] to hym, that he schulde bilde an hows to the Lord God of Israel. And Dauid seide 7 to Salomon, My sone, it was my wille to bilde an hows to the name of my Lord God[v]; but the word of the Lord was made 8 to me, and seide, Thou hast sched out myche blood, and thou hast fouȝt ful many

+ Glos. Salo-mon is seide delicate for tendernesse of age, not hav-ing vse of ma-ners. s.

‡ Glos. that is, sum of al coostis, for no doute Salomon addide to ouer dauty purui-aunce many coostis. Lire. s.

---

b in B.   c the Lord E pr. m.   d bild CE.   e ordeynde A.   f Om. H.

x Thanne I.   y And IS.   z Om. IS.   a the s.   b tempest of veniaunce I. tempest of veniaunce takyng s.   c with IS.   d Lordis aungel I.   e sacrifices A.   f Dauid IS.   g men turned IS.   h weren X.   I gaderid togidere ISX.   k Om. X.   l kytte or hewe IS.   m Om. I.   n polische hem IS.   o and that IS. p Om. IS.   q of s.   r and he made redy s.   s forsothe I.   t Dauid IS.   u he comaundide A pr. m. IS. v the Lord my God I.

bild up an hous to my name, so myche
9 blode schad out before me; the sone that
schal ben born to thee, schal ben a man
most quyete, I schal maken forsothe hym
to resten fro alle his enmyes by enuyroun, and for this cause pesible he schal
be clepid, and pese and rest I schal ȝeue
10 in Yrael alle the days of hym. He schal
bilden up an hous to my name; and he
schal ben to me in to a sone, and I schal
ben to hym in to a fadir, and I schal
fastne the see of his regne vpon Yrael
11 vnto with oute eende. Now thann, my
sone, the Lord be with thee, and do welsumly, and bilde up an hous to the Lord
12 thi God, as he hath spoken of thee. Also
the Lord ȝeue to thee prudence and wytt,
that thou mowe gouerne Yrael, and keep
13 the lawe of the Lord thi God. Thanne
forsothe thou schalt mown profyten, ȝif
thou kepist the hestis and domes, the
whiche the Lord comaundyde to Moyses,
that he schulde techen Yrael; take coumfort and do manly, ne drede thou, ne
14 take fer. Loo! I in my lytyl pornesse
haue mad redy before the expenses of
the hous of the Lord; of gold an hundreth thousand talentis, and of talentis
of syluer a thousand thousandis; of
brasse forsothe and of yren there is no
weiȝt, forsothe the noumbre is ouer passed
by mychilnesse; trees and stoonis I haue
maad redye before to alle the expenses.
15 Thou hast also many craftise men, masouns, and leyers, and craftisemen of
trees, and of alle craftis, most wijs to
16 dou werk, in gold, and syluer, brasse,
and yren, of the whiche is no noumbre;
rijs than, and make, and the Lord schal
17 be with thee. And Dauid comaundide
to alle the princis of Yrael, that thei
18 schulden helpen Salomon, his sone, seyinge, Ȝe seen, that the Lord oure God is
with us, and hath ȝcuen to us rest by

batels; thou mayst not bilde an hows to
my name, for thou hast sched out so
myche blood bifor me; the sone that schal 9
be borun to thee, schal be a man most
pesible, for Y schal make hym to haue
reste of alle hise enemyes bi cumpas, and
for this cause he schal be clepid pesible,
and Y schal ȝyue pees and reste in Israel
in alle hise daies. He schal bilde an hows 10
to my name; he schal be to me in to a
sone, and Y schal be to hym in to a fadir,
and Y schal make stidefast the seete of his
rewme on^w Israel withouten ende. Now 11
therfor, my sone, the Lord be with thee,
and haue thou prosperite, and bilde thou
an hows to 'thi Lord God^x, as he spak^y
of^z thee^a. And the Lord ȝyue to thee 12
prudence and wit, that thou mow gouerne
Israel, and kepe the lawe of 'thi Lord
God^b. For thanne thou maist profite, if 13
thou kepist the comaundementis^c and
domes, whiche the Lord comaundide to
Moises, that he schulde teche Israel; be
thou coumfortid, and do^d manli, drede thou
not 'with outforth^e, nether drede thou
'with ynne^f. Lo! in my pouert Y haue 14
maad redi the costis of the hows of the
Lord; an hundrid thousinde talentis of
gold, and a thousynde thousynde talentis^g
of siluer; sotheli^h of bras and irun is no
weiȝte, for the noumbre is ouercomun^i bi^j
greetnesse^k; Y haue maad redi trees and
stoonys to^l alle costis. Also thou hast ful 15
many crafti men, masouns, and leggeris
of stonys, and crafti men of trees, and of
alle craftis, most prudent to make werk, in 16
gold, and siluer, and bras^m, and in yrun,
of which is no noumbre; therfor rise
thou^n, and make^o, and the Lord schal be
with thee. Also Dauid comaundide to 17
alle the princis of Israel, that thei schulden helpe Salomon, his sone, and seide^p, 18
Ȝe seen, that 'ȝoure Lord God^q is with ȝou,
and hath^r ȝoue to ȝou reste 'by cumpas^s,

---

^{w} in s. ^{x} the Lord thi God i. thi Lord thi God s. ^{y} hath spoke is. ^{z} to CDEFGKLMNOPQRSUXb.
^{a} me N. ^{b} the Lord thi God is. ^{c} heestis is. ^{d} do thou s. ^{e} outward i. ^{f} with ynne forth is. ^{g} of
talentis NCDF sec. m. MN pr. m. OUXb. ^{h} and is. ^{i} ouer comun weiȝt is. ^{j} with L. ^{k} gretenesse thereof s.
^{l} at i. ^{m} in brasse s. ^{n} thou up is. ^{o} make it i. make this houce s. ^{p} he seide is. ^{q} the Lord ȝoure
God s. ^{r} he hath is. ^{s} abowte i.

enuyroun, and hath ȝeuen alle thes[g] enmyes in oure hond, that the lond be
suget before the Lord, and beforn his
19 puple. Ȝeueth therefore ȝoure hertis and
ȝoure soules, that ȝe sechen the Lord
ȝoure God; and rijsith to gidre, and bildith up a seyntuarye to the Lord ȝoure
God, that the arke of the pese couenaunt
of the Lord be brouȝt in, and the sacrid
vessels to the Lord in to the hous, that is
byld to the name of the Lord.

CAP. XXIII.

1 Thanne Dauid olde and ful of days
ordeynede Salomon, his sone, king vpon
2 Yrael. And he gaderde alle the princis
3 of Irael, and prestis, and Leuytis; and
the Leuytis ben noumbred fro twenty
ȝeer and aboue, and there ben founde
4 eyȝt and thritty thousand of men. Of
thes ben chosen, delid in to the seruyse
of the house of the Lord, foure and
twenty thousand; of prouostes forsothe,
5 and of domesmen, sixe thousand; bot
foure thousand porters, and as fele saw-
trers, syngynge in orgnys, that Dauith
6 maad to syngyn. And Dauith departyde
hem by whiles of the sonys of Leuy, that
7 is, Jersan, and Caath, and Merary, and
8 Jersam, and Leadan, and Semei. The
sones of Leadan; prince Jehiel, and E-
9 than, and Joel, thre. The sonys of Semei; Salomyth, and Osiel, and Aram,
thre; thes the princes of the meynes of
10 Leadan. Bot the sonys of Semei; Leeth,
and Sisa, and Jaus, and Baria, thes the
11 sonys of Semei, foure. Forsothe Leeth
was the rather, and Sisa the secounde;
bot[h] Jaus and Baria hadden no mo
sonys, and therfore in oon meyne and in
12 oon hous thei ben countid. The sonys
of Caath; Amram, and Ysaar, Ebron,
13 and Osiel, foure. The sonis of Amram;

and hath[t] bitake alle enemyes in[u] ȝoure
hoond, and the erthe is suget bifor the
Lord, and bifor his puple. Therfor ȝyue[v] 19
ȝoure hertis and ȝoure soulis, that ȝe seke
'ȝoure Lord God[w]; and rise ȝe[x] togidere,
and bilde ȝe a seyntuarie to 'ȝoure Lord
God[y], that the arke of boond of pees of
the Lord be brouȝt in[z], and that vessels
halewid to the Lord *be brouȝt* in to[a] the
hows, which[b] is bildid to the name of the
Lord.

CAP. XXIII.

Therfor[c] Dauid was eld and ful of daies, 1
and ordeynede[d] Salomon, his sone, kyng
on[e] Israel. And he[f] gaderide togidere alle 2
the[g] princes of Israel, and the[h] preestis, and
dekenes; and the dekenes weren noum- 3
brid fro twenti ȝeer and[i] aboue, and eiȝte
and thretti[k] thousynde of men weren
foundun[l]. And foure and twenty thou- 4
synde men weren chosun of hem, and
weren[m] departid in to the seruyce of the
hows of the Lord; sotheli[n] of souereyns,
and iugis, sixe thousynde[o]; forsothe[p] foure 5
thousynde 'porteris weren[q], and so many
syngeris, syngynge to the Lord in orguns,
whiche[r] Dauid hadde maad for to synge[s].
And Dauid departide hem[t] bi the[u] whilis 6
of the sones of Leuy, that is, of Gerson,
and of[v] Caath, and Merary. And the sones 7
of Gerson *weren* Leedan and Semeye. The 8
sones of Leedan *weren* thre, the prince
Jehiel, and Ethan, and Johel. The sones 9
of Semei *weren* thre, Salamyth, and Oziel,
and Aram; these *weren* the[v] princes of
the meynees of Leedan. Forsothe[w] the 10
sones of Semeye *weren* Leeth, and Ziza,
and Yaus, and Baria, these foure *weren*
the sones of Semei. Sotheli[x] Leeth was 11
the formere, and Ziza the secounde; forsothe[y] Yaus and Baria hadden not ful
many sones, and therfor thei weren rikenyd

[g] Om. *A*. [h] lo *H*.

[t] he hath IS. [u] vndir X. [v] ȝyue ȝe IS. [w] the Lord ȝoure God IS. [x] ȝe up IS. [y] the Lord oure God IS. [z] in theder S. [a] Om. S. [b] that IS. [c] Thanne I. [d] he ordeynede I. [e] upon IS. [f] Dauid IS. [g] Om. S. [h] Om. IS. [i] Om. S. [k] twenti I *pr. m.* S. [l] foundun of hem IS. [m] thei weren IS. [n] and IS. [o] thousynde *weren ordeyned to be in the hous of the Lord* IS. [p] and ther weren I. and S. [q] porteris I. that weren porters of ȝatis and doris S. [r] that I. [s] syng with S. [t] these syngers S. [u] Om. IS. [v] Om. S. [w] And IS. [x] and IS. [y] and IS.

Aaron and Moyses; and Aaron is seuerd, that he mynystre in to the holy of
halowis, he and the souys of hym in to
euermore, and that thei brennen encens
to the Lord aftir his riȝt, and blessen to[i]
14 his name vnto[k] with oute eend.   The
sonis also of Moises, the man of God,
ben noumbred in the lynage of Leuy.
15 The sonys of Moysi; Jersan, and Eliazar.
16 The sonys of Jersan; Sobuel the first.
17 There weren forsothe sonys of Eliasar,
Roboia the first, and ther weren not of
Eliasar other sonys; bot the[l] sonis of
18 Robie ben multiplied ful myche.   The
19 sonys of Ysaar; Salomyth the first.   The
sonis of Ebron; Jeriahu the first, Amarias the secounde, Jasiel the thrid, Jehe-
20 mehan the firth.   The sonis of Osiel;
21 Mycha the first, Josia the secound.   The
sonis of Mereri; Mooli and Musi.   The
22 sonys of Mooly; Eliasar, and Cis.   Eliasar forsothe is deed, and hadde no sonis,
bot douȝters; and the sonis of Cis token
23 hem, and the bretheren of hem.   The
sonys of Musi; Mooli, and Heder, and
24 Jeremyth, thre.   Thes the sonis of Leuy
in kynredis, and in[m] their meynese,
princis be whilis, and noumbre of alle
the heuedis, the whiche dyden the bysy-
nesse of the seruyse of the hous of the
25 Lord, fro twenty ȝeer and aboue.   Dauid
forsothe seid, The Lord God of Yrael
hath ȝeuen rest to his puple, and a dwellynge in Jerusalem in to with outen eend;
26 ne it schal ben of the office of Leuytis,
that eny more thei beren the tabernacle,
and alle the vessels of it to mynystren.
27 And aftir the laste hestis[n] of Dauith
there schal ben countid a noumbre of
the sonys of Leuy fro twenty ȝeer and
28 aboue; and thei schul ben vndir the hond
of the sonys of Aaron, in to heriynge of
the hous of the Lord, in vestiaries, and
in chaumbres, and in place of purify-

in o meynee and oon[z] hows.   The sones 12
of Caath weren foure, Amram, and Ysaac,
Ebron, and Oziel.   The sones of Amram 13
weren Aaron and Moyses; and Aaron
was departid[a], that he schulde mynystre
in the hooli thing[b] of hooli thingis, he and
hise sones with outen ende, and to brenne
encense to the Lord bi his custom, and[c]
to[d] blesse his name with outen ende.   Also 14
the sones of Moyses, man[e] of God, weren
noumbrid in the lynage of Leuy.   The 15
sones of Moises weren Gerson and Elieser.   The sones of Gerson; 'Subuhel the 16
firste[f].   Sotheli[g] the sones of Eliezer weren 17
Roboya the firste, and othere sones weren
not to Eliezer; forsothe[h] the sones of
Roboia weren multipliede ful miche.   The 18
sones of Isaar; 'Salumuth the firste[i].   The 19
sones of Ebron; 'Jerian the firste[k], Amarias the secounde, Jaziel the thridde, Je-
thamaan the fourthe.   The sones of Oziel; 20
'Mycha the firste[l], Jesia the secounde.   The 21
sones of Merari weren Mooli and Musi.
The sones of Mooli weren Eleazar, and
Cys.   Sotheli[m] Eleazar was deed, and 22
hadde[n] not sones, but douȝtris; and the
sones of Cys, the britheren[†] of hem, weddiden hem.   The sones of Musi weren 23
thre, Mooli, and Heder, and Jerymuth.
These weren the sones of Leuy in her 24
kynredis and meynees, prynces[o] bi whilis,
and noumbre[p] of alle heedis[q], that diden
the trauel of the seruyce of the hows of
the Lord, fro twenti ȝeer and[r] aboue.   For 25
Dauid seide, The Lord God of Israel hath
ȝoue reste to his puple, and a dwellyng in
Jerusalem til[s] in to with outen ende; and 26
it schal not be the office of dekenes for to
bere more the tabernacle, and alle vessels[t]
therof for to mynystre[u].   Also bi the laste 27
comaundementis[v] of Dauid the noumbre
of the sones of Leuy schulen be rikened
fro twenti ȝeer and aboue; and thei schu- 28
len be vndir the hond of the sones of

† that is, co-
syns germayns.
Lire. GKP.

i vnto II.   k into A.   l Om. A.   m Om. E.   n heste FH.

z in o s.   a departid or ordeyned IS.   b Om. I.   c Om. D.   d Om. c.   e the man IS.   f the firste was
Subuhel IS.   g And IS.   h and IS.   i the firste was Salumuth IS.   k the firste was Jerian I. Jerian
the first rerid s.   l the firste was Mycha IS.   m And IS.   n he hadde s.   o and thei weren prynces IS.
p the noumbre IS.   q the heedis I.   r Om. S.   s Om. X.   t the vessels IS.   u mynystre therynne IS.
v heestis IS.

inge, and in the° seyntuarye, and in alle
werkis of the seruyce of the temple of
29 the Lord. The prestis forsothe vpon the
looues of proposicioun, and^p to the sacrifice of tryed floure, and to the thynne
kakis, and to the therf looues, and to
the fryinge panne, and the boylynge
tryed floure, and to turnen, and vpon
30 the weiȝt and mesure. The Leuytes forsothe, that thei^q stoden^r erly, to knowlechen and syngen to the Lord, and lijc
31 maner at euen, as wele in offrynge of
brent sacrifices of the hous of the Lord,
as in sabotis, and kalendis, and other
solempnytese, aftir the noumbre and cerymonyes of eche thing besily before the
32 Lord; and kepe thei the obseruauncis
of the tabernacle of the pese couenaunt,
and the rijt of the seyntuarye, and the
obseruauncis of the sonys of Aaron, their
bretheren, that they mynystren in the
hows of the Lord.

Aaron in to the^w worschipe of the hows
of the Lord, in porchis, and in chaumbris,
and in the place of clensyng, and in the
seyntuarie, and in alle werkis of the^x seruyce of the temple of the Lord. Forsothe^y 29
preestis *schulen* be ouer the looues of pro-
posicioun^{yy}, and to the sacrifice of flour,
and to the^z pastis sodun in watir, and to
the^z therf looues, and friyng^a panne, and
to hoot flour, and to seenge^b, and ouer al
weiȝte and mesure. Forsothe^c the dekenes 30
schulen be, that thei stonde eerli, for to
knowleche and synge to the Lord, and
lijk^d maner at euentide, as wel in the^e 31
offryng of brent sacrifices of the Lord, as
in sabatis, and kalendis, and othere solempnytees, bi the noumbre and^f cerymonyes of eche thing contynueli bifor the
Lord†; and that thei kepe the obser- 32
uaunces of the tabernacle of the^g boond
of pees of the Lord, and the custum of
the seyntuarie, and the obseruaunce of the
sones of Aaron, her britheren, that thei
mynystre in the hows of the Lord.

† that is, to the
prestis of Aa-
rons kyn. *Lire
here.* LOQ.

CAP. XXIV.

1 Forsothe to the sonis of Aaron thes
porciouns schul ben; the sonis of Aaron,
Nadab, and Abiud, Eleasar, and Ytha-
2 mar; forsothe Nadab and Abiud ben
deed before their fadir, with oute free
chyldre, and Eleasar vsede presthode,
3 and Dauid deuydide hem,
that is, Sadoch, fro the sonys of Eleasar,
and Achymalech, fro the sonis of Ytha-
4 mar, aftir their whilis and seruyse; and
there ben founden manye mo sonys of
Eleasar in the men princis, thanne the
sonys of Ythamar. He deuydide forsothe
to hem, that is, the sonys of Eleasar,
princes by meynes sextene; and to the
sonys of Ythamar by meynes and their
5 houses eyȝt. Bot he deuydide either
meynes between hem selue by lottis;

CAP. XXIV.

Forsothe to the sones of Aaron these 1
porciouns schulen be; the sones of Aaron
weren Nadab, and Abyud, Eleazar, and
Ythamar; but Nadab and Abyud weren 2
deed with out fre children bifor her fadir^i,
and Eleazar and Ythamar weren set in
presthod. And Dauith departide hem, 3
that is, Sadoch, of^k the sones of Eleazar,
and Achymelech, of the sones of Ithamar,
by her whilis and seruyce^l; and the sones 4
of Eleazar weren founden many mo in
the men princes, than^m the sones of Ythamar. Forsothe^n he^o departide to hem,
that is, to the sones of^p Eleazar, sixtene
prynces bi meynees^q; and to the sones of
Ythamar eiȝte^r *prynces* bi her meynees
and howsis. Sotheli^s he departide euer 5
eithir meynees among hem silf bi lottis;

° Om. *ABFIL.* P in *A.* q Om. *ABFH.* r stonde *c.*

w Om. s. x Om. 1s. y And 1s. yy proposicioun, *that is, settynge forth* KOQ. proposicioun, *ether of
settynge forth* Ns. z Om. FIKLMQSXB. a to the friyng 1s. b seynge s. c And 1s. d in lijk 1Q. e Om. 1SX.
f of s. g Om. 1s. i fadir *diede* 1s. k and N. l her seruyce 1s. m than *weren* 1s. n And 1s.
o Dauid 1s. p of Israel s. q her meynees 1s. r *he departid* eiȝte s. s And 1s.

forsothe there weren princis of the seyntuarye, and princis of the hous of God, as wele of the sonys of Eleasar as of the 6 sonys of Ythamar. And Semeyas, the sone of Nathanael, Leuyte scribe, discryuede hem beforn the kyng and the princes, and before Sadoch, the prest, and Achymalech, the sone of Abiather, also before the princis of the prestis meynes and of Leuytis ; oon hous, the whiche beforn was to the tother, of Eleasar, and another hous, the whiche vndir hym silf 7 hadde the tother, of Ythamar. And the first lott wente out of Joiarib, the secound 8 of Jedeie, the thrid of Harym, the ferth 9 of Seosym, the fyfthe of Melchia, the 10 sixt of Mayman, the seuenth of Acchos, 11 the eiȝthe of Abia, the nynthe of Jesu, 12 the tenthe of Sethema, the elleuenth of 13 Eliazub, the twelfthe of Jacym, the thrittenthe of Oofa, ther fouretenthe of Isbaal, 14 the fyftenthe of Abelgaa, the sixtenthe 15 of Emmer, the seuententhes of Ezir, the 16 eiȝtenthe of Ahapses, the nyntenthe of 17 Pheceia, the twentethe of Zechel, the oon and twentithe of Joachym, the two and 18 twentethe of Gamul, the thre and twentethe of Dalayan, the foure and twen- 19 tithe of Mazian. Thes the whiles of hem aftir their seruyse, that thei gon in the hous of the Lord, and aftir ther rijt vndir the hond of Aaron, their fader, as 20 the Lord God of Yrael comaundide. Forsothe of the sonys of Leuy that weren laft, of the sonys of Amram, Sebahel was prynce ; and of the sonys of Sebahel, Je- 21 deia ; of the sonys of Robie, prince Je- 22 sias. Of Isaaris forsothe Salemoth ; also 23 the sone of Salemoth, Jonadiath ; and the sone of hym, Gerueanus the first, Aman the secound, Azihelv the thrid, Jethmoam 24 the ferthe. The sone of Ozihel, Mycha ; 25 the sone of Mycha, Samur ; the brother of Mycha, Jezia ; and the sone of Jezie, Za-

for there weren princes of the seyntuarye, and princes of the hows of God, as wel of the sones of Eleazar ast of the sones of 6 Ithamar. And Semeye, the sone of Na- thanael, a scribe of the lynage of Leuy, discriuedeu hem bifore the king and pryncisv, and bifor Sadoch, the preest, and Achymelechw, the sone of Ablathar, and to the prynces of meyneesx of ther preestis and ofz the dekenes ; he discriuyde oon hows of Eleazar, that was souereyn to othere, and 'the tothera hows of Itha- mar, that hadde othereb vndir hym. For- 7 sothec the firste lot ȝede out to Joiarib, the secounde to Jedeie, the thridde to Aha- 8 rym, the fourthe to Seorym, the fyuethe to Melchie, the sixte to Maynan, the se- 10 uenthe to Accos, the eiȝthe to Abia, the 11 nynthe to Hieusu, the tenthe to Sechema, the elleuenthe to Eliasib, the tweluethe 12 to Jacyn, the thrittenthe to Opha, the 13 fourtenthe to Isbaal, the fiftenthe to Abel- 14 ga, the sixtenthe to Emmer, the seuen- 15 tenthe to Ezir, the eiȝtenthe to Ahapses, the nyntenthe to Pheseye, the twentithe 16 to Jezechel, the oon and twentithe to Ja- 17 chym, the two and tweutithe to Gamul, the thre and twentithe to Dalayam, thed 18 foure and twentithe to Mazzian. These 19 weren the whilise of hem bi her mynysteriesf, that thei entre in to the hows of God, and bi her customg vndur the hond of Aaron, her fadir, as the Lord God of Israel comaundide. Forsothe Sebahel was 20 prince of the sones of Leuy that weren resydueh, of the sones of Amram ; and the sone of Sebahel was Jedeie ; also Jesie 21 was prince of the sones of Roobie. Sotheli 22 Salomoth was prince of Isaaris ; and the sone of Salamoth was Jonadiath ; and his 23 firste sone was Jeriuans, 'Amarie the secoundek, Azihel the thridde, 'Jethmoan the fourthel. The sone of Ozihel was My- 24 cha ; the sone of Mycha was Samyr ; the 25

---

r and E.   s seuentith B.   t the ABCFH.   v Azihe B.

t and A.   u discryued, *ordeyned or presentid* s.   v of princes s.   w bifore Achimalech s.   x the
meyncees c.   y Om. is.   z Om. s.   a that other i.   b othere *prestis and dekens* is.   c Certis is.   d and
the is.   e whilis *or tymes* is.   f seruyces i s.   g custom *do her office* i. custom *use her office* s.   h left is.
i And is.   k the secounde sone *was* Amarie is.   l and the fourthe Jethmoan i.

26 charie. The sonis of Mereri; Mooli and
27 Musi; the sone of Jozan, Bennon; the
sone also of Musi; Orian, and Soem, and
28 Saccur, and Ebri. Bot the sone of Mooli,
29 Eliazar, that hadde no free childre; the
30 sone forsothe of Ciz, Jeremyel; the sonis
of Musi; Mooli, Jeremuth. Thes the sonys
of Leuy, aftir the houses of their meynese.
31 Leyden also and thei lottis aȝeyn their
bretheren, sonys^w of Aaron, before Dauid
the kyng, and Sadoch, and Achymalech,
and the princis of the prestis meynese,
and Leuytis; as wele the more as the
lasse, alle the lott euenlyche^x deuydide.

CAP. XXV.

1 Dauith than, and the maysterhed of
the hoost, deseuereden^y in to the seruyce
the sonys of Asaph, and Eman, and Ydi-
tym, the whiche schulden prophecien in
harpis, and sawtrees, and cymbalis, aftir
their noumbre, seruynge to the office ha-
2 lowed to hem. Of the sonis of Asaph;
Zacur, and Joseph, and Nathanye, and
Azarela; the sonis of Asaph vndir the
hond of Azaph prophecyinge beside the
3 kyng. Forsothe of Yditym the sonis;
Yditym, Godolias, Soori, Jesias, and Sa-
baias, and Mathatias, sixe; vndir the
hond of his fadir Yditym, the whiche
propheciede in harpe vpon men know-
4 lechyng and preysynge the Lord. Of
Heman also the sonys; Heman, Buccian,
Mathania, Ezihel, Subuel, and^z Geriy-
moth, and^z Ananya, Anam, Eliatha, Gaeldothi, and Romenthi, Ezer, and Jesba-
5 chasi, Melothiathir, Mazioth; alle thes
the sonys of Heman, the seeris of the
kyng in the wordis of God, that the
horne he enhaunce^a. And God ȝaf to
Eman sonis fouretene, and douȝtirs thre.

brother of Mycha *was* Jesia; and^m the
sone of Jesia *was* Zacharie. The sones of 26
Merary *weren* Mooli and Musi; the sone
of Josyan *was* Bennon; and the sone of 27
Merarie *was* Ozian, and Soen, and Zac-
cur, and Hebri. Sotheliⁿ the sone of Mooli 28
was Eleazar, that^o hadde not fre sones;
forsothe^p the sone of Cys *was* Jeremybel; 29
the sones of Musy *weren* Mooli, Eder, 30
Jerymuth^q. These *weren* the sones of Leuy,
bi the housis of her meynees. Also and 31
thei senten lottis aȝens her britheren, the
sones of Aaron, bifor Dauid the^r kyng,
and bifor Sadoch, and Achymelech, and
the^s princes of meynees^t of preestis and of
dekenes; lot departide euenli alle^u, bothe
the^v gretter and the^v lesse.

CAP. XXV.

1 Therfor Dauid, and the magestratis of 1
the oost, departiden in^w to the seruyce
the sones of Asaph, and of Eman, and of
Idithum, whiche^x schulden profecye† in
harpis, and sawtrees^y, and cymbalis^z, bi her
noumbre, and serue the office halewid^a to
2 hem. Of the sones of Asaph; Zaccur, and 2
Joseph, and Nathania, and Asarela; so-
theli^b the sones of Asaph vndir the hond
of Asaph profesieden bisidis the kyng.
3 Forsothe^c the sones of Idithum *weren* 3
these; Idithum^d, Godolie, Sori, Jesie, and
Sabaie, and Mathatie, sixe; vndur the
hond of hir fadir Idithum, that profesiede
in an harpe on^e men knowlechynge and
4 preysynge the Lord. Also the sones of 4
Heman *weren* Heman, Boccia, Mathanya,
Oziel, Subuhel, and Jerymoth, Ananye,
Anan^f, Elyatha, Gaeldothi, and Romenthi,
Ezer, and Jesbacasi, Melothy, Othir, Ma-
5 zioth^g; alle these sones^h of Heman *weren* 5
profetis‡ of the kyng in the wordisⁱ of
God, that he schulde enhaunse the horn^k§.
And God ȝaf to Heman fourtene sones, and
6 thre douȝtris. Alle^l vndur the hond of 6

† that is, seien
profecies, either
with this thei
hadden the
spiryt of pro-
fecie, as Ebrais
seien. *Lire*
here. ᴏxʟᴘᴏs.
‡ thes weren
seide profetis,
for thei sungen
profecies, ether
for thei hadden
the spiritis of
profecie; thei
weren seide the
profetes of the
king, for thei
preisiden for
the king and
his reume.
ᴏxᴏs.
§ that he shulde
enhaunce the
horn; that is,
herfore thei
preisiden God,
that he shulde
enhaunce the
strengthe and
power of the
rewme of
Dauith. ᴏxᴏs.
that is,
strengthe and
power of the
rewme of Da-
uith. *Lire here.*
ʟᴘ.

^w the sonys ᴀ.   ^x euenli ᴀᴄᴇ.   ^y deserueden ꜰᴜ.   ^z Om. ᴀʙᴄᴜ.   ^a enhaunced ʙ sec. m.

^m Om. ʟᴍsxb.   ⁿ And ɪs.   ^o the whiche ɪ. whiche s.   ^p and ɪs,   ^q and Jerymuth ɪs.   ^r Om. s.
^s bifore the ɪ. bifore s.   ^t the meynees s.   ^u alle *thingis* ɪs.   ^v to ɪs.   ^w Om. ɪs.   ^x the whiche ɪ.   ^y in
sawtrees ɪs.   ^z in cymbalis ɪs.   ^a halewid *or enioyned* ɪs.   ^b and ɪs.   ^c And ɪs.   ^d Om. s.   ^e upon ɪs.
^f and Anan ɪs.   ^g and Mazioth ɪ.   ^h the sones x.   ⁱ word s.   ^k horn *or* strengthe ɪs.   ^l Al these s.

6 alle vndir the hond of their fadir, to
syngyn in the temple of the Lord thei
weren assygned, in cymbalis, and sawtrees, and harpis, in to the[b] seruyces[c] of
the hous of the Lord besyde the kyng,
Asaph that is, and Yditym, and Eman.
7 Forsothe the noumbre of hem with their
bretheren, that tauȝten the song[d] of the
Lord, alle doctours, was two hundrith
8 and foure score and eiȝt. And thei leyden lottis by their whilis euenly, as wele
more as lasse, the tauȝt and vntauȝt[e] to
9 gyder. And the first lott of Joseph is
gone out, that was of Asaph; the secounde of Godolie, to hym, and to his
10 sonis and to his britheren twelue; the
thridde of Zaccus, to his sonys and to
11 his britheren twelue; the ferthe of Ysan,
to his sonis and to his[f] bretheren twelue;
12 the fyfte of Nathanye, to the sonys and
13 his[g] bretheren twelue; the sixte of Bec-
cian, to the sonys and his bretheren,
14 twelue; the seuenthe of Ysraela, to the
15 sonys and his bretheren twelue; the
eiȝthe of Ysaye, to the sonys and his
16 bretheren twelue; the nynthe of Mathanye, to the sonys and his bretheren
17 twelue; the tenthe of Semeie, to the
18 sonys and his bretheren twelue; the
elleuenthe of Esrael, to the sonis and
19 his bretheren twelue; the twelfthe of
Asabie, to the sonis and his bretheren
20 twelue; the thrittenthe of Subahul, to
21 the sonys and his bretheren twelue; the
fouretenthe of Mathatie, to the sonis and
22 his bretheren twelue; the fyftenthe of
Jerymoth, to the sonis and his bretheren
23 twelue; the sextenthe of Ananye, to the
24 sonys and his bretheren twelue; the
seuententhe[h] of Jesbocase, to the sonys and
25 his bretheren twelue; the eyȝtenthe of
Amyham, to the sonys and his bretheren
26 twelue; the nyntenthe of Mellochu, to
27 the sonys and his bretheren twelue; the
twentithe of Eliatha, to the sonys and

her fadir weren 'delid, *ethir*[m] *asigned*, to
synge in the temple of the Lord, in cymbalis, and sawtrees, and harpis[n], in to the[o]
seruyces[p] of the hows of the Lord nyȝ the
kyng, that is to seie, Asaph, and Idithum,
and Heman. Sotheli[q] the noumbre of hem 7
with her britheren, that tauȝten the songe
of the Lord, alle the techeris, was[r] twey
hundrid 'foure scoor and eiȝte[s]. And thei 8
senten lottis bi her whiles euenli, as wel
the gretter as the lesse, also a wijs man
and vnwijs[t]. And the firste lot ȝede out 9
to Joseph, that was of Asaph; the secounde[u] to Godolie, to hym, and hise[v]
sones and hise[v] britheren twelue; the 10
thridde to Zaccur, to hise sones and hise[w]
bretheren twelue; the fourthe to Isary, 11
to hise sones and *hise*[x] britheren twelue;
the fyuethe to Nathanye, to hise sones 12
and *hise* britheren twelue; the sixte to 13
Boccian, to hise sones and hise britheren
twelue; the seuenthe to Israhela, to hise 14
sones and britheren[y] twelue; the eiȝthe 15
to Isaie, to his sones and britheren[y]
twelue; the nynthe to Mathany, to his 16
sones and britheren[y] twelue; the tenthe 17
to Semei, to his sones and britheren[y]
twelue; the elleuenthe to Ezrahel, to 18
hise sones and britheren[y] twelue; the 19
twelnethe to Asabie, to his sones and
britheren[y] twelue; the thrittenthe to 20
Subahel, to hise sones and britheren[y]
twelue; the fourtenthe to Mathathatie, 21
to hise sones and britheren[y] twelue;
the fiftenthe to Jerymoth, to hise sones 22
and britheren[y] twelue; the sixtenthe to 23
Ananye, to hise sones and britheren[y]
twelue; the seuententhe to Jesbocase, 24
to hise sones and britheren[z] twelue; the 25
eiȝtenthe to Annam, to hise sones and
britheren[z] twelue; the nyntenthe to Mol- 26
lothi, to hise sones and britheren[z] twelue;
the twentithe to Eliatha, to hise sones and 27
britheren[z] twelue; the oon and twentithe 28
to Othir, to hise sones and britheren[a]

[b] Om. A. [c] seruyse H. [d] songis A. [e] the vntauȝt H. [f] the CEFH. [g] to the AH. to B. [h] seuentethe B.

[m] Om. C. [n] in harpis IS. [o] Om. CDEFGIKLMOPQRSUX. [p] seruyse W. [q] And IS. [r] weren IS. [s] eiȝte and eiȝteti N. eiȝti and eiȝte MW. [t] an vnwijs I. a vnwise man S. [u] secounde lot S. [v] to hise IS. [w] to his S. [x] Om. *plures*. to his S. [y] to hise bretheren IS. [z] to his bretheren S. [a] to his bretheren S.

28 his bretheren twelue; the oon and twentithe of Other, to the sonys and his bre-
29 theren twelue; the two and twentithe
of Godoliathi, to the sonis and his bre-
30 theren twelue; the thre and twentithe
of Masuyth, to the sonys and his bre-
31 theren twelue; the foure and twentithe
of Romanathiezer, to the sonys and his
bretheren twelue.

twelue; the two and twentithe to Godo- 29
liathi, to hise sones and britheren[a] twelue;
the thre and twentithe to Mazioth, to hise 30
sones and britheren[b] twelue; the foure 31
and twentithe to Romonathiezer, to his
sones and britheren[a] twelue.

CAP. XXVI.

1 Dyuysiouns forsothe of the porters;
of the Chorites, Mellesemya, the sone of
2 Chory, of the sonys of Asaph. The sonis
of Mellezemie; Zacharias the first goten,
Jodiel the secounde, Sabadias the thrid,
3 Ythamael the ferth, Aylam the fyfthe,
Johannam the sixte, Elionenai the se-
4 uenthe. The sonis forsothe of Obed-
edome; Semeias the first goten, Josadad[i]
the secounde, Joncha the thrid, Saccar
5 the ferth, Athanael the fyft, Amyhel the
sixt, Isachar the seuenth, Pollathi the
ey3the, for to hym the Lord blessede.
6 To Semei forsothe, his sone, ben born
sonys, prefectis of their meynes; forsothe
7 thei weren most strong men. The sonys
than of Semei; Othyn, and Raphael, and
Obedihel, and Zabad; and the bretheren
of hym most strong men; Helyu also,
8 and Samachias. Alle thes of the sonys
of Obededom; thei, and the sonys, and the
bretheren of hem, most strong men to
mynystren, two and sexty of Obededom.
9 Bot of Meellymye the sonis and bretheren, most strong men and most
10 my3ty, ei3tene. Of Hosa forsothe, that
is, of the sonis of Merery, Sechary
prince; forsothe he hadde not a first
goten, and therfor his fadir putte hym
11 in to a prynce; Helchias the secounde,
Thebelias the thrid, Zacharias the ferth;
alle thes sonys and bretheren of Hosa,

CAP. XXVI.

Forsothe these weren the departingis 1
of porteris; of the sones of Chore, Mel-
lesemye was the sone of Chore, of[c] the
sones of Asaph. The sones of Mellesemie 2
weren Zacharie the firste gendrid[d], Jedihel the[e] secounde, Zabadie the thridde,
Yathanyel the fourthe, Aylam the fifthe, 3
Johannan the sixte, Helioenay[f] the seuenthe. Forsothe[g] the sones of Ebed- 4
edom weren these; Semey the firste gendrid[h], Jozabab the secounde, Joaha the
thridde, Seccar the fourthe, Nathanael
the fyuethe, Amyhel the sixte, Isachar 5
the seuenthe, Pollathi[i] the ei3the, for the
Lord blesside hym[k]. Forsothe[l] to Semeye, 6
his sone, weren borun sones, souereyns of
her meynees; for thei weren ful stronge
men. Therfor the sones of Semeye weren 7
Othyn, and Raphael, and Obediel, and
Zadab; and hise britheren, ful stronge
men; also Helyu, and Samathie. Alle these 8
weren of the sones of Obededom; thei
and her sones and britheren[m], ful stronge
men for to serue, two and sixti of[n] Obededom. Sotheli[o] of Mellesemeye[p], the[q] sones 9
and britheren[r], ful stronge[s], weren ei3tene[t].
Forsothe[n] of Oza, that is, of the sones of 10
Merarie, Sechri was prince; for[v] he hadde
no[w] firste gendrid[x]†, and[y] therfor his fadir
settide[z] hym in to prince; and Elchias 11
the[n] secounde, Thebelias[b] the thridde, Zacarie[c] the fourthe; alle these threttene

† that was of eny valu either reputacioun; therfor he made Sechri to be prince. Lire here. GXQSB.

i Josadab c.

a to hise bretheren 18. 　 b to his bretheren 8. 　 c and he was souereya of 18. 　 d goten 1. 　 e was the 18.
f and Helioenay 18. 　 g And 18. 　 h goten 1. 　 i and Pollathi 18. 　 k him, that is, encresid him 8. 　 l And 18.
m her britheren 18x. 　 n weren of 18. 　 o And 18. 　 p Mellesemeye weren ei3tene 18. 　 q Om. 18. 　 r the
britheren c. 　 s stronge men 1318. 　 t Om. 18. ei3tene M. 　 u And 18. 　 v and c. and for 18. 　 w not G.
x goten sone 1. gendrid sone 8. 　 y Om. 18. 　 z ordeynede 18. 　 a was the 18. 　 b and Thebelias 18. 　 c and
Zacarie 18.

12 thrittene. Thes ben deuydid in to the
porters, that euermore the princis of the
wardis, as and the bretheren of hem,
mynystren in the hous of the Lord.
13 Thanne the lottis ben leyd of euen, and
to the lytyll and to the grete, by their
14 meynes, in to echone of the ʒatis. Thanne
the este lott fell to Jemelie; forsothe to
Zachary, the sone of hym, most wijs man
and tauʒt, fel thoruʒ lott the northe coost;
15 to Obededom forsothe and his sonys at the
south, in whiche partye of the hous was
16 the counseil of the[i] elderis; to Sephyma
and Chosa at the west, besyde the ʒate
that ledith to the weye of the steyʒinge
17 up, warde aʒein warde. At the este forsothe Leuytis sixe, and at the north foure
bi day; and at the south also in[k] the[l]
day foure; and wher was the counseil,
18 two and two. In the lityl cellis forsothe
of the porters at the west, foure in the
19 weye, and two by the litill cellis. Thes
ben the dyuysiouns of porters, of the sonis
20 of Chory and of Merery. Forsothe Achias
was vpon the tresoures of the hous of the
Lord, and the vesselis of the halewis.
21 The sonis of Leadan, the sonys of Jer-
sony; of Leadan, prince of the meynes
22 of Leadan, and of Jersan, Jeihely. The
sonys of Jeihely; Jethan, and Joel, his
brother, vpon the tresoures of the hous
23 of the Lord, Amyramytis, and Isaaritis,
24 and Ebronytis, and Esielitis. Subahul
forsothe, the sone of Jerson, sone of
25 Moysi, prouost of the tresoure; and the
brother of hym, Eliezer; whos sone
Raabia; and of this the sone Asaias; of
this the sone Joram; and of this the
sone Zechri; bot and of this the sone
26 Selemyth. He, Selemyth, and the bretheren of hym, vpon the tresoures of
hooly thingis, the whiche kyng Dauith

weren the sones and britheren of Osa.
These weren departid in to porteris, that 12
euere the[d] princes of kepyngis[e], as also her
britheren, schulden mynystre in the hows
of the Lord. Therfor lottis weren sent[f] 13
euenly, bothe to the[g] litle and to the[g]
grete, bi her meyneeis, in to ech of the
ʒatis. Therfor the lot of the eest[h] bifelde 14
to Semelie; forsothe[i] the north coost bifelde bi lot to Zacarie, his sone, a ful prudent man and lernd[k]; sotheli[l] to Obed- 15
edom and hise[m] sones at[n] the southe[o], in
which part of the hows the[p] counsel of
the eldre men was[q]; Sephyma and Thosa 16
weren at the west[r], bisidis the ʒate that
ledith to the weie of stiyng[s], kepyng aʒens
kepyng. Sotheli[t] at the eest[u] *weren* sixe 17
dekenes, and at the north weren foure bi
dai; and at the south also weren foure
at the[v] myddai; and, where[w] the counsel
was, *weren* tweyne and tweyne. And in 18
the[x] sellis[y], *ethir*[z] *litle housis*[a], of porteris
at the west[b], *weren* foure in the weie, and
tweyne bi the sellis. These weren the[c] 19
departyngis of porteris[d], of the sones of
Chore and of Merary. Forsothe[e] Achias 20
was ouer the tresours of the hows of the
Lord, and ouer the[f] vessels of hooli[g]
thingis. The sones of Leedan, the sone 21
of Gerson; of Leedan *weren* the[h] princis
of meynees[i] of Leedan, and of Gerson, and
of Jehiel. The sones of Jehiel *weren*, Ze- 22
than, and Johel, his brother, ouer the[k] tresours of the hows of the Lord, Amram- 23
ytis, and Isaaritis, and Ebronytis, and
Ezielitis. Forsothe[l] Subahel, the sone of 24
Gerson, sone of Moises, *was* souereyn of
the tresour[m]; and his brother, Eliezer; 25
whos sone *was*[n] Raabia; and his sone *was*
Asaye; his[o] sone *was* Joram; and his sone
was Zechry; but and[p] his sone *was* Selemith.
Thilke Selemith, and his britheren, *weren* 26

[i] Om. B. [k] by H. [l] Om. H.

[d] Om. I. [e] the kepyngis I. [f] sent *or casten* S. [g] Om. IS. [h] eest *coost* IS. [i] and IS. [k] wel lernd IS. [l] and I. [m] to hise IS. [n] *lott fell* at IS. [o] southe *coost* IS. [p] was the IS. [q] Om. IS. [r] west *coost* IS. [s] steyng up IS. [t] And IS. [u] eest *part* IS. [v] Om. IS. [w] where that IS. [x] Om. IS. [y] Om. C. [z] Om. I. of W. [a] Om. I. [b] west *side* IS. [c] Om. IS. [d] the porteris IS. [e] And IS. [f] Om. IS. [g] the hooli IS. [h] Om. IS. [i] the meynees CIS. [k] Om. IS. [l] And IS. [m] tresouris S. [n] Om. X. [o] and his IS. [p] Om. A.

halowide, and the princis of meynes, and
the leders of thousandis, and the leders
27 of hundriths, and duykis of the hoost, of
bateilis, and of the spoilis of bateils, the
whiche thei sacreden to the restorynge
and to the necessaries of the temple of
28 the Lord. Forsothe alle thes thingis halowed Samuel, seer, and᷈ Saul, the sone
of Ciz, and Abner, the sone of Ner, and
Joab, the sone of Saruye; and thei alle
haloweden hem bi the hond of Salomyth
29 and his bretheren. To Ysaarites forsothe
befor was Chononyas and his sonis, to
the werkis with out forth vpon Yrael,
30 to techen and to demen hem. ʼBot of
Ebronytis°, Asabias, and Sabayas, and his
britheren, most stronge men, a thousand
and seuen hundrith, beforn weren to Yrael
beȝond Jordan aȝein the west, in alle the
werkis of the Lord, and in᷈ to the ser-
31 uyse of the kyng. Of Ebronytis forsothe
prince was Herias, aftir the meynes and
kynredis of hem. The fouretithe ȝeer of
kyng Dauid ben noumbred and founden
32 most strong men in Jaser Galaad; and
the bretheren of hem, of more stronge
age, two thousand seuen hundrith, princis
of meynes. Forsothe kyng Dauid beforn
putte hem to Rubenytis and Gadditis,
and to the half lynage of Manasse, in to
alle the seruyce of God and of the kyng.

ouer the tresours of hooliꝗ thingis, whiche
ʼDauid the kyngʳ halewide, and the princes
of meynees, and the tribunes, and the centuriouns, and the duykis of the oost, of 27
the᷉ batels, and of the ᵗ spuylis of batels,
whiche thei halewiden to the reparacioun
and purtenaunceᵘ of the temple of the
Lord. Forsotheᵛ Samuel, the prophete, 28
halewide† alle these thingis, and Saul, the
sone of Cys, and Abner, the sone of Ner,
and Joab, the sone of Saruye; and alleʷ
halewiden tho thingis bi the hond of Sale-
myth, and of his britheren. Sotheliˣ Cho- 29
nenye was souereyn and hise sones to
Isaaritis, toʸ the˟ werkis with outforth onᵃ
Israel, to teche‡ and to deme hem. Sotheliᵇ 30
of Ebronytis, Asabie, and Sabie, and hise
britheren, ful stronge men, a thousynde
and᷉ seuene hundrid, weren souereyns on᷉
Israel biȝende Jordan aȝens the weste, in
alle the᷉ werkis of the Lord, and in to
the ᶠ seruyce of the kyng. Forsothe᷉ Herie 31
was prynce of Ebronytis, bi her meynees
and kynredis. In the fourtithe ʰ ȝeer of
the rewme of Dauid there weren noumbred and foundun ᶦ ful stronge men in Jazer Galaad; and hise britheren, of strongere 32
age, twei thousynde and seuene hundrid,
princes of meynees. Sotheliᵏ ʼDauid the
kyng ˡ made hem souereyns of Rubenytis
and Gaditisᵐ, and of the᷉ half lynage° of
Manasses, ʼin to ᴾ al the seruyce of God
and of the kyng.

† Glose: hal-
wed; that is,
presentid or
offrid. s.

‡ to teche: for
summe of the
dekenes, that
kouden the
lawe, weren
ordeyned to
teche the peple
in places fer
fro Jerusalem,
and to deter-
myne doutis,
in whiche sim-
ple men douti-
den. Lire
here. CKQSB.

CAP. XXVII.

1 The sonis forsothe of Yrael aftir their
noumbre, princis of meynes, leders of
thousandis, and leders of hundrithes, and
the prefectis, that serueden to the kyng
aftir their companyes, commynge in᷈ and
goynge out bi alle the monethes in the
ȝeer, alle before weren to foure and
2 twenty thousand. To the first company
in the first moneth Isiboam, the sone of

CAP. XXVII.

Forsothe᷈ the sones of Israel bi her 1
noumbre, the princes of meynees, the tribunes, and centuriouns, and prefectis, that
mynystriden to ͬ the kyng bi her cum-
penyes§, entrynge᷈ and goynge out bi ech
monethe in the ȝeer, weren souereyns, ech
bi hym silf, on ᵗ foure and twenti thousynde. Isiboam, the sone of Zabdihel, 2
was souereyn of the firste cumpenye in

§ cumpenyes;
that is, cum-
penyes of
knyȝtis. Lire
here. c.

ᵃ of ABCFH.　ᵒ Of Ebronytis forsothe A.　ᴾ Om. H.　ꝗ Om. F pr. m. H.

ꝗ the holi s.　ʳ king Dauid is.　ˢ Om. is.　ᵗ Om. s.　ᵘ to the purtenaunce is.　ᵛ And is.　ʷ alle
these is.　ˣ And is.　ʸ and to is.　ᶻ Om. is.　ᵃ in is.　ᵇ And is.　ᶜ Om. s.　ᵈ upon is.　ᵉ Om. is.
ᶠ Om. is.　ᵍ And is.　ʰ fourtenthe s.　ᶦ wore foundun s.　ᵏ And is.　ˡ king Dauid is.　ᵐ of Gaditis is.
ⁿ Om. t.　ᵒ the lynage i.　ᴾ vnto is.　ꝗ Sothely is.　ʳ bifore to s.　ˢ entrynge in is.　ᵗ upon is.

Sobdiel was beforn, and vndir hym foure
3 and twenty thousand ; of the sonis[r] of
Phares, prince of alle the princis in the
4 hoost, the first moneth Of the secounde
moneth hadde the companye Didi Achoites, and aftir hym an other, Machilot
by name, the whiche gouernede a partye of the hoost of the foure and twenty
5 thousand Duyke also of the thrid companye in the thrid moneth was Bananyas, the sone of Joiade, prest, and in
his diuysioun foure and twenty thou-
6 sand , he is Bananyas, most strong
among thritty, and vpon thritty , forsothe Amyzadath, his sone, before was to
7 the companye of hym The ferth moneth,
the ferth, Asael, the brothei of Joab, and
Sabadias, his sone, aftir hym, and in[r] his
companye foure and twenty thousand
8 The fyfthe, the[s] fyfthe moneth, prince
Samoth Jesraites, and in his companye
9 foure and twenty thousand The sixte,
in the sixte moneth, Ira, the sone of
Acces, Techuytes[t], and in his companye
10 foure and twenty thousand The seuenth, in the seuenth moneth, Helles
Phalonytes, of the sonis of Effiaym, and
11 in his companye foure and twenty thousand. The eyзt, the[r] eyзt moneth, Sobochai Asathites, of the stok of Saray, and
in his companye foure and twenty thou-
12 sand The nynthe, the[v] nynthe moneth,
Abiesei Anothotites, of the stok of Gemyny, and in his companye foure and
13 twenty thousand The tenth, the[v] tenth
moneth, Marai, and he Neophatites, of
the stok of Saray, and in his companye
14 foure and twenty thousand The elleuenth, the[v] elleuenth moneth, Banas Pha-
ionytes, of the sones of Effraym, and in
his companye foure and twenty thousand
15 The[v] twelfthe, the twelfthe moneth, Holdia Nethofatites, of the stok of Gothonyel, and in his companye foure and
16 twenty thousand Forsothe ther stoden
beforn to the lynagis of Yrael, to Ru-

the firste monethe, and vndur hym *weren*
foure and twenti thousynde , of the sones[u] 3
of Fares *was* the prince of alle princes in
the oost, in the firste monethe Didi 4
Achoites hadde the cumpany of the secounde monethe, and aftir hym silf *he
hadde* anothei man, Macelloth bi name,
that gouernede a part of the oost of foure
and twenti thousynde And Bananye, the 5
sone of Joiada, the preest, was duyk of[v]
the thridde cumpenye in the thridde
monethe, and foui and twenti thousynde
in[w] his departyng , thilke is Bananye, 6
the strongest[x] among thritti, and aboue
thritti , forsothe[y] Amyzadath, his sone,
was souereyn of his cumpenye In the 7
fourthe monethe, the fourthe *prince was*
Asahel, the brother of Joab, and Zabadie,
his sone, aftir hym, and foure and twenti
thousynde iu[z] his cumpeny. In the fifthe 8
monethe, the fifthe *prince was* Samoth
Jezarites, and foure and twenti thousynde
in[z] his cumpenye In the sixte monethe, 9
the sixte *prince was* Ira, the sone of Actes,
Techuytes, and foure and twenti thousynde in[z] his cumpeny In the seuenthe 10
monethe, the seuenthe *prince was* Helles
Phallonites, of the sones of Effraym, and[a]
foure and twenti thousynde in[b] his cumpeny In the eiзthe monethe, the eiзthe 11
prince was Sobothai Assothites, of the
generacioun of Zarai, and foure and twenti
thousynde in[b] his cumpeny In the nynthe 12
monethe, the nynthe *prince uas* Abiezer
Anathotites, of the generacioun of Gemyny, and foure and tweynti thousynde
in[b] his cumpeny In the tenthe monethe, 13
the tenthe *prince was* Maray, and he *was*
Neophatites, of the generacioun of Zaray,
and foure and twenti thousynde in[b] his
cumpany In the elleuenthe monethe, the 14
elleuenthe *prince was* Banaas Pharonytes,
of the sones of Effraym, and foure and
twenti thousynde in[c] his cumpeny. In 15
the tweluethe monethe, the tweluethe
prince was Holdia Nethophatites, of the

r Om H.   s in the A.   t Om H   v in the A

u houce s   v on x   w *weren* in 1s   x strongest man 1s   y and 1s   z *weren* in 1s   a Om. IFMS
x sec m b   b *weren* in 1s   c *werin* in s

benytis, duyke Eliezer, the sone of Zechry; to Symeonitis, duke Saphathias, the sone 17 of Maacha; to Leuytis, Azabias, the sone 18 of Chamuel; to Aaronytes, Sadoch; to Judaites, Elyu, the brother of Dauith; to Ysacharites, Amri, the sone of My-19 chael; to Zabulonytes, Jesmaias, the sone of Abdie; to Neptalonytes, Jerymuth, 20 the sone of Oziel; to the sonis of Ef-fraym, Osee, the sone of Ozazyn; to the half lynage of Manasse, Johel, the sone 21 of Phathae; and to the half lynage of Manasse in^w Galaad, Jaddo, the sone of Zacharie; to Beniamyn forsothe, Zazi-22 hel, the sone of Abner; to Dan forsothe, Ezriel, the sone of Jeroam; thes the 23 princis of the sonis of Israel. Dauith forsothe wolde noumbre hem fro twenty ʒeer and benethen, for the Lord hadde seide, that he schuld multiplie Yrael as 24 the sterres of heuen. Joab, the sone of Saruye, beganne to noumbren, and fulfilde not; for vpon that wrath felle doun in to Yrael, and therfore the noumber of hem, that weren noumbred, is not told in to the worthi cronyclis of kyng Dauid. 25 Vpon the tresoures forsothe of the kyng was Azimoth, the sone of Adiel; to thes forsothe tresoures, that weren in cytees, and in touns, and in toures, Jonathan, 26 the sone of Ozie, satte vpon. To the churlische werk forsothe, and to the erth tilieris, that wrouʒten the erth, Esri, the 27 sone of Chebul, was vpon; and to the vyne tiliers, Semeias Roenatites; to the 28 wijne celeris, Zabdyas Aphonytes; for-sothe vpon the olyues, and the fijge trees, that weren in the wijld feeldis, Balanan Gadarites; on the leyinge up places for-29 sothe of oyle, Joas; bot to the droues, that weren fed in Sarona, prouost was Cetheray Ceronytes; and vpon the oxen in valeys, Saphat, the sone of Abdi;

generacioun of Gothonyel, and foure and twenti thousynde in^c his cumpeny. For-16 sothe *these* weren souereyns[d] of the ly-nages of Israel; duyk[e] Eliezer, sone[f] of Zechri, *was souereyn* to Rubenytis; duyk Saphacie, sone[g] of Maacha, *was souereyn* to Symeonytis; Asabie, the sone of Cha-17 muel, *was souereyn* to Leuytis[h]; Sadoch 'was souereyn[i] to Aaronytis; Elyu, the 18 brothir of Dauid, 'was souereyn[i] to the lynage of Juda; Amry, the sone of My-chael, 'was souereyn[i] to Isacharitis; Jes-19 maye, the sone of Abdie, *was souereyn* to Zabulonytis; Jerymuth, the sone of Oziel, 'was souereyn[i] to Neptalitis; Ozee, the 20 sone of Ozazym, 'was souereyn[i] to the sones of Effraym; Johel, the sone of Pha-tae, *was souereyn* to the half lynage of Manasses; and Jaddo, the sone of Zacarie, 21 'was souereyn[i] to the half lynage of Ma-nasses in Galaad; sotheli[j] Jasihel, the sone of Abner, 'was souereyn[k] to Benia-myn; forsothe[l] Ezriel, the sone of Je-22 roam, *was souereyn* to Dan; these *weren* the princes of the sones of Israel. For-23 sothe[m] Dauid nolde[n] noumbre hem with[o] ynne twenti ʒeer, for the Lord seide, that he wolde multiplie Israel as the sterris of heuene[p]. Joab, the sone of Saruye, bigan 24 for to noumbre[q], and[r] he fillide[s] not[t]; for ire[u] fel on[v] Israel for this thing, and ther-for the noumbre of hem, that weren noum-brid, was not teld[w] in to[x] the bookis of cronyclis of kyng Dauid. Forsothe[y] Azy-25 moth, the sone of Adihel, was on[z] the[a] tresouris[b] of the kyng; but Jonathan, the sone of Ozie, was souereyn of[c] these tre-sours, that weren in cytees, and in townes, and in touris. Sotheli[d] Ezri, the sone of 26 Chelub, was souereyn on[e] the werk of hosebondrie, and on[e] erthe tiliers, that til-iden the lond; and Semeye Ramathites 27 *was souereyn* on[e] tilieris of vyneris; so-

30 vpon the camels forsothe, Ubil Ismaelit;
and vpon the assis, Judas Meranathites;
31 vpon the scheep also, Jasir Agarene; alle
thes princis of the substaunce of Dauith
32 the kyng. Jonathas forsothe, the vncle[x]
of Dauid, counseyler, man my3ty, and
slee3, and lettred; he and Jahiel, the sone
of Achamony, weren with the sonis of
33 the kyng. Achitofel also the counceylere
of the king; and Chusi Archites, the
34 freend of the kyng. Aftir Achitofel was
Joiada, the sone of Banaye, and Abiathar; prince forsothe of the hoost of the
kyng was Joab.

theli[f] Zabdie Aphonytes *was souereyn* on[g]
the[h] wyn celeris; for Balanam Gadaritis 28
was[i] on the olyue placis, and fige[k] places,
that weren in the feeldi[l] places; sotheli[m]
Joas *was* on[n] the schoppis, '*ether celeris*[o],
of oile; forsothe[p] Cethray Saronytis '*was* 29
souereyn[q] of[r] the droues, that weren le-
sewid in Sarena; and Saphat, the sone of
Abdi, *was* ouer the oxis[s] in valeys; sotheli[t] 30
Vbil of Ismael *was* ouer the camelis; and
Jadye Meronathites *was* ouer the assis;
and Jazir Aggarene *was* ouer the scheep; 31
alle these *weren* princes of the[n] catel of
kyng Dauid. Forsothe[v] Jonathas, brother[w] 32
of 'Dauithis fader[x], *was* a councelour, a
my3ti man, and prudent, and lettrid[y]; he
and Jahiel, the sone of Achamony, weren
with the sones of the kyng. Also Achito- 33
fel *was* a counselour of the kyng; and
Chusi Arachites *was* a frend of the kyng.
Aftir Achitofel was Joiada, the sone of 34
Banaye, and Abyathar; but Joab was
prince of the oost of the kyng.

CAP. XXVIII.

1 Dauith thanne clepide to gider alle the
princis of Israel, duykis of lynagis, and
prouostis of companyes, the whiche mynystreden to the kyng, also leders of
thousandis, and leders of hundrithes, and
that before weren to the substaunce and
to the possessiouns of the kyng, and her
sonis, with the geldyngis, and the my3ty,
and alle the most strong in the hoost of
2 Jerusalem. And whanne the kyng hadde
rysen, and stonden, he seith, Herith me,
my bretheren and my puple. I thou3te
for to maken an hous, in the whiche
schulde resten the arke of the pese couenaunt of the Lord, and the stole of the
feet of oure God; and to beelden alle
3 thingis I haue made redy. God forsothe
seide to me, Thou schalt not bilden an

CAP. XXVIII.

Therfor Dauid clepide togidere alle the 1
princes of Israel, the duykis of lynagis,
and the souereyns of cumpenyes, that
'mynystriden to[z] the kyng, also[a] the tribunes, and centuriouns, and hem that
weren souereyns ouer the catel and possessiouns[b] of the kyng, and[c] hise sones,
with 'nurchis[†], and techeris[d], and alle the
my3ti[e] and strongeste[f] men[g] in the oost
of Jerusalem[h]. And whanne the kyng 2
hadde rise, and 'hadde stonde[i], he seide,
My britheren and my puple, here 3e me.
Y thou3te for to bilde an hows, wherynne the arke of boond of pees of the
Lord, and the stool of the feet of oure
God schulde reste; and Y made[k] redi alle[‡]
thingis to bilde[l]. But God seide to me, 3
Thou schalt not bilde an hows to my

† The Latyn
word here
eunuchis, is
propirly geld-
ingis, but here
it is takun for
nurscheris and
techeris, that
ben seid geld-
ingis, for they
weren chast
and onest. *Lire
here.* co̅ab.

‡ *alle;* that is,
summe of alle.
Lire here. cx
ob.

f and 1s. g upon 1s. of x. h Om. x. i Om. 1. k the fige s. l feeld As. m and 1s. n *souereyn*
upon 1s. o Om. 1. p and 1s. q Om. 1. r upon 1s. on m. s oxen 1s. t and 1s. u Om. s. v And 1s.
w the brother 1s. x the fadir of Dauid 1. y lettrid *or vnderstondyng* s. z serueden 1s. a also Dauid
clepide 1s. b the possessiouns 1s. c and *he clepide* 1. and *Dauith clepide* s. d the geldingis 1. the
gyldyngis, *which were chast honest uishers and techers* s. e my3ti men 1s. f stronge 1sx. g Om. 1s.
h Jerusalem *werin clepid* s. i stode up 1s. k haue maad 1s. l bilde it 1. bilde with this houce s.

hous to my name, for thi that thou be^y a man fiȝter, and blood thou hast schad. 4 Bot the Lord God of Yrael hath chosen me of al the hous of my fadir, that I wer kyng vpon Yrael in to euer more; of Juda forsothe he chees princis, bot of the hous of Juda the hous of my fadir, and of the sonis of my fadir it pleside to hym, that me he schulde chosen kyng 5 vpon al Israel. Bot many sonys the Lord ȝaue to me; and of my sonis he chees Salomon, my sone, that he schulde sytten in the trone of the rewme of the 6 Lord on Israel. And he seide to me, Salomon, thi sone, schal bilde myn hous, and myn auters; hym forsothe I haue chosen to me in to sone, and I schal be 7 to hym in to fadir; and I schal fastne his rewme in to with outen eend, ȝif he be stedfast to do my domys and myn 8 hestis, as and to day. Nowe thanne be-forn al the companye of Yrael, heerynge my God, kepith and sechith alle the maundementis of the Lord oure God, that ȝe welden a good lond, and leuen it to ȝoure sonis aftir ȝou in to euermore. 9 Thou forsothe, Salomon, my sone, knowe thou the God of thi fadir, and serue thou to hym in perfijt herte, and with wilful inwit; alle forsothe hertis the Lord serchith, and alle thouȝtis of myndis he vndirstondith; ȝif thou sechist hym, thou schalt fynden; ȝif forsothe thou forsakist hym, he schal throwen thee aweye into 10 with outen eend. Nowe thanne, for the Lord chees thee, that thou schuldist bilden the hous of the seyntuarie, take 11 coumfort,‘and perfourme. Forsothe Da-uith ȝaue to Salomon, his sone, the dis-cryuynge of the ȝate hous, and of the temple, and of celers^z, and of the soup-ynge place, and of the bed placis in pryue housis beside the auter, and of the

name, for thou art a man werriour, and hast sched^m blood. But the Lord God of 4 Israel chees^n me of al the hows of my fadir, that Y schulde be kyng on^o Israel with outen ende; for of Juda he^p chees^q princes, sotheli of the hows of Juda he chees^q the hows of my fadir, and^r of the sones of my fadir it pleside hym^s to chese me kyng on^t al^u Israel. But also of my 5 sones, for the Lord ȝaf^v to me many sones, he chees^w Salomon, my sone, that he schulde sitte in the troone of the rewme of the Lord on^x Israel. And he^y seide to 6 me, Salomon, thi sone, schal bilde myn hows, and myn auters; for Y haue chose hym to me in to a sone, and Y schal be to hym in to a fadir; and Y schal make 7 stidefast his rewme til^r in to with outen ende, if he schal contynue to do myn heestis and domes, as and^a to dai^b. Now 8 therfor bifor al the cumpeny of Israel, ‘Y seie these thingis that suen in the^c heryng of God^d, kepe ȝe and seke ȝe^e alle the^f comaundementis^g of ‘ȝoure Lord God^h, that ȝe haue in possessioun a good lond, and that ȝe leeue it^i to ȝoure sones aftir ȝou til^k in to with outen ende. But thou, 9 Salomon, my sone, knowe the God of thi fadir, and serue thou hym with perfit herte, and wilful^l soule^m; for^n the Lord serchith alle hertis, and vndirstondith^o alle thouȝtis^p of soulis; if thou sekist hym, thou schalt fynde hym^q; forsothe if thou forsakist hym, he schal caste thee awei with outen ende. Now therfor, for^r the 10 Lord chees^s thee, for to bilde the hows of seyntuarie, be thou coumfortid, and par-forme^t. Forsothe^u Dauid ȝaf to Salomon, 11 his sone, the discryuyng, ‘ether ensaum-ple^v, of the porche, and^w of the temple, and of celeris, and of the soler†, and of closetis in pryuy places, and of the hows of propiciacioun‡, ‘that is, of mersi^x; also 12

† soler; that is, of thre dwellingis of the temple. co κab.
‡ propicia-cioun; that is, of the hooly of hooly thingis, where the pro-piciatorie was. Lire here. co

^{y} art A. ^{z} the celers EF.

^{m} sched out IS. ^{n} hath chose IS. ^{o} upon IS. ^{p} the Lord S. ^{q} hath chose IS. ^{r} also X. ^{s} the Lord S. ^{t} upon IS. ^{u} Om. I. ^{v} hath ȝoue IS. ^{w} hath chose IS. ^{x} upon IS. ^{y} the Lord S. ^{z} Om. X. ^{a} also I. ^{b} daȝ I witnesse IS. ^{c} Om. o. ^{d} God heringe, I sey, I. ^{e} Om. BCDEFGIKLNOPRUWb. ^{f} Om. GQ. ^{g} heestis IS. ^{h} the Lord ȝoure God I. ^{i} it in maundement to be kept S. ^{k} Om. X. ^{l} with a wilful IS. ^{m} soule or mynde S. ^{n} forsothe I. ^{o} he vndirstondith IS. ^{p} the thouȝtis IS. ^{q} Om. plures. ^{r} Om. S. ^{s} hath chosun IS. ^{t} performe it IS. ^{u} And IS. ^{v} Om. I. either the ensaumple S. ^{w} Om. S. ^{x} Om. B. or of merci doyng IS.

12 hous of Goddis plesaunce; and also of alle the porches, the whiche he hadde cast, and of the pryue chaumbris by enuyroun, in to the tresoures of the hous of the Lord, and in to the tresours of the 13 hous of hooly^a thingis, and of the prestis and Lenytis dyuysiouns, in to alle the werkis of the hous of the Lord, and alle the vessels of the seruyse of the temple 14 of the Lord. Of gold in weiȝt thoruȝ alle the vesselis of the seruyse, also of syluer, for the dyuerste of vessels, and of werkis; 15 bot and to the golden chaundelers, and to the lanternes of hem, gold, for the mesure of eche chaundeler and of lanternes; and also in the silueren chaundelers, and in the lanternes of hem, for the dyuerste 16 of mesure weiȝt of syluer he toke. Also gold he ȝaue in to the boordis of proposicioun, for the dyuerste of mesure, and also siluer in to othere syluleren boordis; 17 also to the fleschokis, and violes, and encenseris of most pure gold; and to golden litil lyouns, for the qualite of mesure, weiȝte he delid in to litil lyoun and litil lyoun; and lijc maner in to the^b siluleren lyouns dyuerse weiȝte of syluer he se- 18 uerede. To the auter forsothe, in the whiche was brend encense, most pure gold he ȝaue, that of it were maad the licnesse of the cart of cherubyn, stretchynge out the weengis, and couerynge the arke of the pese couenaunt of the Lord. 19 Alle thingis, he seith, camen writen by the hond of the Lord to me, that I schuld vndurstonde alle the werkis of 20 the saumpler. And Dauith seide to Salomon, his sone, Do manly, and take coumfort, and make; ne dreed thou, and take thou no ferd; the Lord forsothe my God schal be with thee, and he schal not leue thee, ne forsake thee, to the tyme that thou perfourme al the werk of the

and^y of alle thingis whiche he thouȝte of the large places, and of^z chaumbris bi cumpas, in to the tresours of the hows of the Lord, and 'in to the^a tresours of holi thingis, and of the departyngis of preestis 13 and of^b dekenes, in to alle the werkis of the hows of the Lord, and alle vessels of the^c seruyce of the temple of the Lord. Of gold in weiȝte bi ech vessel of the^c ser- 14 uyce, and of siluer, for dyuersitee of vessels, and of werkis; but also to goldun 15 candilstikis, and to her lanternes, *he ȝaf* gold, for the mesure of ech candilstike and lanternes^d; also and^e in siluuren candilstikis, and in her lanternes, he bitook^f the weiȝte of siluer, for the dyuersite of mesure^g. Also^h and he ȝaf gold in to the 16 bord of settyng forth, for the^i dyuersite of mesure, also and *he ȝaf* siluer in to othere siluerne boordis^k; also^l to fleisch hookis, 17 and viols^m, and censeris^n of pureste gold; and to^o litle goldun lyouns†, for the maner of mesure, he departide a weiȝte in to a litil lyoun and a litil lioun; also and^p in to siluerne lions he departide dyuerse weiȝte of siluer. Forsothe^q he ȝaf pureste^r 18 gold to the auter, wherynne^s encense was brent, that a lickenesse of the^t cart of cherubyns, holdinge forth wyngis^u, and^v hilynge the arke of boond of pees of the Lord, schulde be maad therof. Dauid^w 19 seide, Alle thingis camen writun bi the hond of the Lord to me, that Y schulde vndirstonde alle the^x werkis of the saumpler^y. And Dauid seide to Salomon, his 20 sone, Do thou manli, and be thou coumfortid, and make^z; drede thou not 'with outforth^a, nether drede thou 'with ynne^b; for 'my Lord God^c schal be with thee, and he schal not leeue thee, nether schal^d forsake thee, til thou perfourme al the werk of the seruyce of the hows of the Lord. Lo! the departyngis^e of prestis and of^f de- 21

† where we han *litle goldoun lions,* in Ebreu it is, goldun clensyng vessels; that is, goldun baasyns, in which the blood was borun in to the hooly of hooli thingis, in day of clensing; also where we han *lions,* in Ebreu it is, *in to siluerne clensing vessels,* that is, siluerne baasyns. *Lire here.* COKLPAB.

^a the hooly ε.   ^b Om. ι.

y and *he ȝaaf him ensaumple* 1s.   z Om. s.   a Om. 1.   b Om. s.   c Om. 1s.   d of lanternes 1s.   e Om. s. f *bitook to hem* s.   g mesure *of tho* s.   h Om. 1s.   i Om. 1s.   k bourdis *to be maade* s.   l and c.   m to viols 1s.   n to censeris 1s.   o in to s.   p Om. s.   q And s.   r most fyne s.   s wherinne *or* whervpon s. t a s.   u his wingis s.   v Om. s.   w *And* Dauid 1s.   x Om. *plures.*   y ensaumpler 1s.   z make *it* 1. make this thing s.   a outward 1.   b withinne forthe s.   c the Lord my God 1s.   d he schal 1s. Om. x. e departing s.   f Om. s.

21 seruyse of the hous of the Lord. Loo!
the dyuysiouns of prestis and of Leuytis,
in to al the werk of the seruyse of the
hous of the Lord, schul stonden neeȝ to
thee; and bothe the princis and the puple
ben redy, and han knowen to don alle
thin hestis.

CAP. XXIX.

1 Kyng Dauid spac to al the chirche,
God hath chosen Salomon, my sone, ȝit
child and tendre; forsothe a grete werk
is, ne to man is greithed[c] a dwellynge
2 bot to God. I forsothe with alle my
streyngthes haue maad redy the expensis
of the hous of my God; gold to the
golden vessels, and syluer to the silueren[d], brasse in to the brasen, yryn in
to the yryn[e], trees in to the treenen,
onychyne stones, and as cleer whijt, and
alle precious stone of dyuerse coloures,
and dyuerse marbil, most plenteuously.
3 And vpon thes thingis gold and syluer
I ȝeue into the temple of my God, the
whiche I offred in to the hous of my
God of myn owne tresor, out take thes
thingis the whiche I made redy in to
4 the hooly hous, thre thousand talentis of
gold, of the gold of Oofer, and seuen
thousand of talentis of syluer most fyne,
to the wallis of the temple, to ben gildid;
5 and wher euer nede is gold, of[f] gold,
and wher euer nede is syluer, of syluer,
the werkis ben maad by the hondis of
craftise men; and ȝif eny man wilfully
offreth, fulfylle he his hond to day, and
6 offre he that he wille to the Lord. And
so byheeten the princis of the meynes,
and 'noble men[g] of the lynagis of Israel,
also the leders of thousandis, and the
maisters of hundrethis, and the princis
7 of the possessiouns of the kyng; and
thei ȝeuen in to the werkis of the hous
of the Lord, fyue thousand talentis of

kenes, in to al the werk of the seruyce of
the hows of the Lord, schulen stonde niȝ
thee; and thei ben redi[g], and bothe the
princes and the puple kunnen do alle thi
comaundementis[h].

CAP. XXIX.

And kyng Dauid spak to al the chirche, 1
God hath chose Salomon, my sone, ȝit a
child† and tendre; forsothe the werk is
greet[i], and a dwellyng is not maad redi[k]
to man[l] but to God. Sotheli[m] Y in alle 2
my myȝtis haue maad redi the costis of
the hows of my God; gold to goldun
vessels, siluer in[n] to siluerne vessels, bras
in[o] to brasun vessels, irun in to irun vessels, tre[p] in[q] to trenun[r] vessels, onychyn‡
stonys, and stonys as of the colour of
wymmens oynement, and ech precious
stoon of dyuerse colouris, and marbil of
dyuerse colouris, most plenteuously. And 3
ouer these thingis Y ȝyue gold and siluer
in to the temple of my God, whiche[s] Y
offride[t] of my propir catel in to the hows
of my God, outakun these thingis whiche§
Y made[u] redi in to the hooli hows, thre 4
thousynde talentis of gold, of the gold of
Ophir, and seuene thousynde of talentis of
siluer most preuyd, to ouergilde the wallis
of the temple; and werkis be maad bi the 5
hondis of crafti men, where euere gold is
nedeful, of[v] gold, and where euere siluer
is nedeful, of[w] siluer; and if ony man
offrith bi his fre wille, fille[x] he his hond
to dai[y], and offre he that that he wole to
the Lord. Therfor the princes of meynees, 6
and the duykis of the lynagis of Israel,
and the tribunes, and the centuriouns,
and the princes of the possessiouns of the
kyng, bihiȝten[z]; and thei ȝauen in to the 7
werkis of the hows of the Lord, fyue
thousynde talentis of gold, and ten thou-

† *a child*; not of xii. ȝeer, but tendir in comparisoun of so greet a werk. *Lire here*. C O X Q b.

‡ *onychym*; thei haue the licnesse of mannus nail. C.

§ whiche he hadde take of the preyes of enemyes. *Lire here*. G X Q S.

[c] ordeynd *A*. [d] silueren vessels *A*. [e] yrenen *EH*. [f] and *A*. [g] the noblemen *A*.

[g] redi *to do her seruice* S. [h] hestis I. [i] grete, *that he is ordeyned to do* S. [k] redi *therynne* I. [l] man only S. [m] Certis IS. [n] Om. ISX. [o] Om. IS. [p] and trees I. [q] Om. S. [r] treen IMSX. [s] the whiche I. [t] haue offrid IS. [u] haue maad IS. [v] *be the werk maad* of IS. [w] *be it maad of* S. [x] fulfille IS. [y] dai, *that is, take he now his offring* S. [z] bihiȝten *to ȝiue therto* I. bihiȝten *to ȝeue ȝiftis to the temple* S.

gold, and tenn thousand schillyngis; of
syluer tenn thousand talentis, and of
brasse ey3tene thousand talentis, also of
yren an hundrith thousand of talentis.
8 And anentis whom so euer the stonys
ben founden, thei 3euen in to the tresour
of the hous of the Lord, by the hond of
9 Johiel Jersonyte. And the puple gladide,
whanne vowis wilfully thei schulden behoten, for with al the herte thei offreden
hem to the Lord. Bot and Dauid the
10 kyng gladide with grete ioye, and blesside to the Lord beforn al the multitude,
and seith, Blessed ert thou, Lord God
of Yrael, oure fadir, fro with oute eend
11 and in to with oute eend; thin is, Lord,
grete doynge, and power, and glorie, and
victorie, and to thee preisynge; alle thingis
forsothe that ben in heuen and in erth
ben thine; thin, Lord, kyngdam¹, and
12 thou ert vpon alle princis; thin richch-
esses, and thin is glorie; thou lordschipist ofʲ alle thingis; in thin hond
vertue, and my3t, andᵏ inˡ thin hond
mykilnesse and empyre of alle thingis.
13 Nowe thanne, oure God, we knowlechen
to thee, and we preysen thi noble name.
14 Who Iᵐ, and who my puple, that we
mowen to thee alle thes thingis behoten?
Thin ben alle thingis, and the whiche of
thin hond we han taken, we han 3euen
15 to thee. Pilgrymes forsothe we ben beforn thee, and comlyngis, as alle oure
fadirs; oure days as schndowe vpon the
16 erth, and ther is no tariynge. Lord
oure God, al this plente that we han
maad redy, that an hous schulde ben bild
up to thi holy name, of thin hond is;
17 and thin ben alle thingis. My God, I
wote, that thou prouest hertis, and that
symplenes of herte thou louest; wherfore and I, in symplenesse of myn herte,
glaad haue offred alle thes thingis; and
thi peple, that here is founden, I saw3

synde schyllyngis; tenᵃ thousynde talentis
of siluer, and ei3tene thousynde talentis of
bras, and an hundrid thousynde ofᵇ talentis of irun. And at whom euereᵍ
stoonysᶜ were foundun, thei 3auen in to
theᵈ tresoureᵉ of the hows of the Lord, bi
the hond of Jehiel Gersonyte. And the 9
puple was glad, whanne thei hihi3ten
avowis bi her fre wille, for with al the
herte thei offridenᵗ thoᶠ to the Lord. But
also kyng Dauid was glad with greet ioye,
and blessideᵍ the Lord bifor al the multi- 10
tude, and seide, Lord God of Israel, oure
fadir, thou art blessid fro with outen bigynnyng in to with outen eude; Lord, 11
worthi doyng is thinʰ, and power, and
glorie, and victorie, and heriyng is to
thee; for alle thingis that ben in heuene
and in erthe ben thine; Lord, theⁱ rewme
is thin, and thou art ouer alle princes;
ritchessis ben thin, and glorie is thin; 12
thou art Lord of alle; in thin hond is
vertu, and power, and in thin hond is
greetnesse, and lordschipe of alle. Now 13
therfor, oure God, we knoulechen to thee,
and we herienᵏ thi noble name. Who am 14
Y, and who is my puple, that we moun
bihete alle these thingis to thee? Alle
thingis ben thine, and we han 3oue to
thee tho thingis, whiche we tokenˡ of thin
hond. Forᵐ we ben pilgrimes and come- 15
lyngis bifor thee, as alle oure fadrisⁿ;
oure daies ben as schadewe onᵒ theᵖ erthe,
and 'no dwellyng isᑫ. Oure Lord God, al 16
this plenteeʳ whichˢ we han maad redi,
that an hows schulde be byldid to thin
hooli name, is of thin hond; and alle
thingis ben thin. My God, Y woot, that 17
thou preuest hertis, and louestᵗ symple-
nesseᵘ of herte; wherfor andᵛ Yʷ, in theˣ
symplenesse of myn herte, haueʸ offrid
gladli alle these thingis; and Y si3ᶻ with
greet ioye thi puple, which is foundun
here, offreᵃ 3iftis to thee. Lord God of 18

ⁱ is the kyngdom ᴀ. ʲ vpon ᴀ.   ᵏ is ᴀ.   ˡ Om. ʜ.   ᵐ am I ᴀ.

ᵃ and ten ᴄᴅᴘǫʀ.   ᵇ Om. ɪsх.   ᶜ presious stones s.   ᵈ Om. ɪ.   ᵉ tresori s.   ᶠ Om. ɪ.   ᵍ he blesside ɪs.
ʰ thin, *that is, thi doyng is worthi and greet* s.   ⁱ Om. *plures.*   ᵏ herien, *that is, we preisyn* s.   ˡ han
take ɪs.   ᵐ Forsothe ɪ.   ⁿ fadris *weren* ɪs.   ᵒ upon ɪs.   ᵖ Om. ɪ.   ᑫ ther is no tarying ɪ.   ʳ plentee *of
diuers goodis* s.   ˢ the which ɪ.   ᵗ that thou louest ɪs.   ᵘ symplenesse, *that is, lownesse or mekenesse* s.
ᵛ Om. s.   ʷ Om. ɪs.   ˣ Om. sb.   ʸ I haue ɪs.   ᶻ haue seen ɪ.   ᵃ to offre ɪs.

with grete ioye to thee offren ʒiftis.
18 Lord God of Abraham, and of Ysaac, and
Yrael[n], oure fadirs, in to with oute eend
keepe this wille of the herte of hem ; and
euermore in to the[o] worschipynge of thee
19 this mynde abijde stylle. And to Salomon, my sone, ʒeue a perfijt herte, that
he keepe thin hestis, and[p] witnessyngis,
and thi cerymonyes ; and that he do alle
thingis, and bijld an hous, whos expenses
20 I haue maad redy. Dauid forsothe comaundide to al the chirche, Blesse ʒe to
the Lord oure God. And al the chirche
blessed to the Lord God of their fadirs,
and thei boweden hem seluen, and honoureden God, and thanne aftirwarde the
21 kyng. And thei slowen sacrifises to the
Lord, and offreden brent sacrifices the
day folowynge ; boolis a thousand, and
wethers a thousand, and[q] lombes a thousand, with their sacrifices of licours[r], and
al the rijt, most plenteuously, in to al
22 Yrael. And thei eeten and dronken before the Lord in that day, in greet gladnesse. And thei anoyntide the secounde,
Salomon, the sone of Dauid ; thei anoynteden forsothe to the Lord in to a prince,
23 and Sadoch in to a bischop. And Salomon satt vpon the see of the Lord in to
kyng, for Dauid, his fadir ; and to alle
men it pleside, and al Irael obeischide
24 to hym. Bot and alle the princes, and
myʒty, and alle sonys of kyng Dauid,
ʒeuen hond, and weren suget to kyng
25 Salomon. Than the Lord magnyfied
Salomon vpon al Irael, and ʒaue to hym
glorie of the kingdom, what maner no
kyng of Yrael hadden beforn hym.
26 Thanne Dauid, the sone of Ysay, regned
27 vpon al Irael ; and the days the whiche
he regned vpon Yrael weren fourty ʒeer ;
in Ebron he regned seuen ʒeer, and in
28 Jerusalem thre and thirty. He[s] is deed

Abraham, and of Ysaac, and of Israel, oure
fadris, kepe thou with outen ende this
wille of her hertis ; and this mynde dwelle
euere in to the worschipyng of thee. Also[h] 19
ʒyue thou to Salomon, my sone, a perfit
herte, that he kepe thin heestis, and witnessyngis[e], and thi ceremonyes ; and do
alle thingis[d], and that he bilde the[e] hows,
whose costis Y haue maad redi. Forsothe[f] 20
Dauid comaundide to al the chirche[g],
Blesse ʒe 'oure Lord God[h]. And al the
chirche[i] blesside the Lord God[k] of her
fadris, and thei bowiden hem silf, and
worschipiden God, aftirward[l] the[m] kyng.
And thei offriden slayn sacrifices to the 21
Lord, and thei offriden brent sacrifices in
the dai suynge ; a thousynde boolis, and a
thousynde rammes, and a thousynde lambren, with her fletynge sacrifices, and al[n]
the custom, most plenteuously, in to[o] al
Israel. And thei eten and drunken bifor 22
the Lord in that dai, with greet gladnesse.
And thei anoyntiden the secounde tyme
Salomon, the sone of Dauid ; and thei
anoyntiden hym in to prince to the Lord,
and Sadoch in[p] to bischop. And Salomon 23
sat on[q] the trone of the Lord in[r] to kyng,
for Dauid, his fadir ; and it pleside alle
men, and al Israel obeiede to hym. But 24
also alle princes, and myʒti men, and alle[n]
the sones of kyng Dauid, ʒauen hond[t]†,
and weren suget to 'Salomon the kyng[u].
Therfor the Lord magnefiede[v] Salomon 25
on[w] al Israel, and ʒaue[x] to hym glorie of
the rewme, what maner glorie no kyng of
Israel hadde bifor hym. Therfor[y] Dauid, 26
the sone of Ysai, regnede on[z] al Israel ;
and the daies in whiche he regnede on[z] 27
Israel weren fourti ʒeer ; in Ebron he
regnede seuene ʒeer, and in Jerusalem thre
and thretti ʒeer. And he diede in good 28
eelde, and was ful of daies, and richessis[a],
and glorie[b] ; and Salomon, his sone, regnede

† hond ; that
is, bihiʒten
feith, either
sworen, that
thei schulden
be suget feith-
fuly to Salo-
mon. Lire
here. CEG ab.
Gloss. ʒening 26
of hondis here
shewith swer-
ing or stidfast
bihetyng to be
feithful and
suget to the
king. Lire, s.

---

[b] Also, Lord s.   [c] thi witnessyngis 1s.   [d] these thingis 1s.   [e] thi b.   [f] Sothely 1s.   [g] chirche, that is, al the peple gaderid togidre s.   [h] the Lord oure God 1.   ʒoure Lord God sx.   [i] chirch, that is, the peple s.   [k] Om. s.   [l] and aftirward 1s.   [m] thei worschipiden the s.   [n] with al 1.   [o] Om. b.   [p] thei anoynteden in s.   [q] upon 1s.   [r] chosun in 1s.   [s] also 1s.   [t] her hondis 1s.   [u] kyng Salomon 1s.   [v] magnefied or made greet s.   [w] upon 1s.   [x] he ʒaue 1.   [y] And 1. Therfor and s.   [z] upon 1s.   [a] of richessis 1s.   [b] of glorie s.

in a good elde, full of days, and rytch-
esses, and glorie ; and Salomon, his sone,
29 regnede for hym.   Forsothe the rather
dedis of kyng Dauid, and the last, ben
writen in the boke of Samuel, seer, and
in the boke of Nathan, the prophete, and
30 in the volyme of Gad, seere ; and of al his
rewme, and streyngthe, and tymes, that
passiden vndur hym, or in[t] Yrael, or in
alle rewmes of londis.

*Here eendith the first book of Para-
lipomenon, and now bigynneth the proloog of the secounde book[u].*

for hym. Forsothe the formere and the 29
laste dedis[c] of Dauid[d] ben writun in the
book of Samuel, the prophete, and in the
book of Nathan, prophete[e], and in the
book of Gad, the[f] prophete ; and of al his 30
rewme, and strengthe[g], and tymes, that[h]
passiden vndur hym, ethir in Israel, ethir
in alle rewmes[i] of londis.

*Here endith the firste booke of Para-
lipomenon, and here bigynneth the secounde book of Paralipomenon[k].*

[t] Om. B.   [u] From A.   *Explicit primus liber Paralipomenon* E.   No final rubric in BCFH.

[c] daies s.   [d] kyng Dauid now.   [e] the prophete IKSX.   [f] Om. b.   [g] strengthis X.   [h] whiche IS.   [i] *oothere*
rewmes IS.   [k] *Here endith the firste book of Paralipomenon, and here bigynneth the secounde.* FNQSB. *Here
endith the firste book of Paralipominon, and biginnith a prolog.* G. *Heere endith the firste book of Paralipomynon.* I. *Here endeth the firste book of Paralipomenon, se now the secounde.* K. *Here endith the firste book
of Paralipomenon, and bigynneth prolog to the ije.* O. *Here endith Paralipomenon the firste, and here
biginneth the secounde.* W. *Explicit primus liber Paralipomenon ; incipit prologus libri secundi.* Z.   No final
rubric in ELP.

II. PARALIPOMENON.

Here bigynneth the Prologe in the secounde Paralipomenon[a].

EUSEBIUS, Jerome[b] senden gretynge to theirs in Crist Jhesu, Domynyon and Rogacian. What maner wijse thei beter vndirstonden the stories of Grekis, the whiche
han seen Athenas; and the thrid boke of Virgilie, the whiche han seiled fro Troye bi
Lewchaten, and fro Acroceranya to Cicilie, and thennys to the doris of Tibre; so
hooly Scripture he schal more clerly beholden, that Jude hath seen with ee3en, and
the myndis[c] of olde[d] cytees, and placis knowith names, or the same, or chaungid[e].
Wherfore and to us it was fors[f] with the most tau3te men of Ebruys this traucil[g] to
vndirgone, that we gon aboute the prouynce, that alle the chirchis of Crist sownen.
Forsothe, my Domynyon and Rogacian, most dere, I knowleche me neuer in Goddis
volymes to han 3euen feith to my propre strengthis, ne[h] to han had myne opynyoun
a mayster, bot also tho thingis of the whiche I demede me to kunnen, me wont to
han asked; myche more of tho thingis, vpon the whiche I was a fowler[i]. Forsothe
whanne of me 3e hadden asked sumtyme bi lettris, that to 3ou I schulde translatyn
Paralipomenon in Latyn sermoun, I toke of Tiberyades sumtyme autour of lawe,
the[k] whiche anentis the Ebrewis was had in wondryngis, and I disputed with hym
fro the top, as thei seyn, vnto the laste nayl; and so confermyd, I am hardy to don
that 3e comaundiden[l]. Forsothe frely to 3ou I speke; so in Greek and in Latyn bokis,
this boke of namys is vicious, that not oonly Ebrue namys, but straunge sum and
addid cast to gider it be to demyn. Ne that to the seuenty remenours, the whiche ful
of the Hooly Goost tho thinges that weren sothe translatiden, bot to the blame of
wrijters it is to wijten, while of the vnamendid thei wrijten vnamendide thingis; and
oft sithes thre namys, silables with drawen fro the mydil, thei drijuen in to oon name;
or a3einward, for[m] the brede, thei deuyden[n] in two or in[o] thre namys. Bot and thilk[p]
nemenyngis, not[q] men, as many eymen, bot cytees, and regiouns, and wodis, and prouynces sownen; and aside, vndur the remenynge and the figure of hem, sum stories
ben told, of the whiche in the boke of Kyngis[r] it is seyde, Loo! whether not thes ben
writen in the bokis[s] of the wordis of the[t] days of kyngis[u] of Juda; the whiche forsothe in oure bokis ben not had. This first is to wyten, that anentis the Ebruys
Paralipomenon be a boke, and anentis hem be clepid Dabregemyn, that is, the wordis
of days; the whiche for mychilnesse anentis us is deuydid. The whiche thing sum
men also in the Brute, dialog[v] of Citheron, don, that it[w] in thre parties thei deuyden,
whanne oon of his[x] autour it be maad. Ther aftir also that thei taken heede, that oft
sithes names sownen not names of men, bot, as I haue seide[y], betokenyngis of thingis.

a *Incipit prologus in librum secundum.* E. *The prolong of secounde Paralipomenon.* F. *Prologus.* H. No
initial rubric in AC. b and Jerome o. c myddis oz. d the olde o. e chaungynge ABFH. f forsothe BH.
g Om. E pr.m. h Om. o. i defouler o. k Om. o. l comunden co. m fro o. n deuydiden B.
o Om. o. P thoo c. q ben not E pr.m. r the Kyngis o. s bok ACF sec.m.o. t Om. c. u the kyngis c.
v dialos ABEFH. w Om. o. x its o. y sien o.

At the last, that al lernynge of scripturis in this boke is conteenyd; and the stories other that ben laft in their placis, other liȝtly touched, here by sum maner schort sentencis of wordis ben opned. And so I, holpen with help of ȝoure preyers, haue sente the boke to plesen to wele willid men; neuer the later I doute not, it to ben to displesen to enuyous men. Forsothe, as seith Plynye, sum men han leuere alle best thingis seen to dispisen, thanne to lernen. Ȝif eny man in this remenyng wille eny thing repreuen, aske he the Ebrues, remembre he his conscience, see he the order and the text of the word; and thanne, ȝif he may, putte he blame to oure traueil. Than wher euer ȝe seen asterichos, that is, sterres, to schynen in this volume, there wijte ȝe of Ebrue added, that in Latyne bokis is not had; wher forsothe obelus ouerturned, that is, a ȝerde, is sette before, there is betokened what the seuenty remenours addeden, or for grace of feyrnesse, or for autorite of the Hooly Goost; and in Ebrue volumes it is not rad.

Here eendith the prologe in the ij. Paralipomenon, and bigynneth the bok in the ij. Paralipomenon[x].

Here bigynneth the secounde bok of Paralipominon[a].

CAP. I.

1 SALOMON thanne, the sone of Dauid, is coumfortid in his rewme, and the Lord was with hym, and magnyfiede hym in 2 to an heeȝ. And Salomon comaundyde to al Yrael, to leders of thousandis, and maystirs of hundrethis, and to domys-men, and to[b] the duykis of al Yrael, and 3 to princis of meynes; and wente with al the multitude in to the heiȝt of Gabaon, where was the tabernacle of the[c] pese couenaunt of the Lord, that Moyses, the seruaunt of God, made in wyldirnesse. 4 Dauid forsothe hadde lad the arke of God fro Cariathiarym in to the place that he hadde made redi to it, and wher he hadde piȝt to it a tabernacle, that is, 5 in Jerusalem. Also a brasen auter, the whiche Beseleel, the sone of Vri, sone of Ur, hadde forgid, there was beforn the tabernacle of the Lord; the whiche and 6 Salomon souȝt and al the chirche. And

Heere biginnith the secounde book of Paralipomynon[a].

CAP. I.

THERFOR Salomon, the sone of Dauid, 1 was coumfortid in his rewme, and the Lord was with hym, and magnefiede hym an hiȝ. And Salomon comaundide 2 to al Israel, to tribunes, and centuriouns, and to duykis, and domesmen[b] of al Israel, and to the princes of meynees; and he[c] 3 ȝede with al the multitude in to the hiȝ place of Gabaon, where the tabernacle of boond of pees of the Lord was, which[d] tabernacle[e] Moyses, the seruaunt of the Lord, made in wildirnesse. Forsothe[f] 4 Dauid hadde brouȝt the arke of God fro Cariathiarym in to the place which he hadde[g] maad redy[h] to it, and where he hadde set a tabernacle to it, that is, in to[i] Jerusalem. And the brasun auter, which 5 Beseleel, the sone of Vri, sone[k] of Vr, hadde maad, was there bifor the taber-nacle of the Lord; whiche[l] also Salomon and al the chirche[m] souȝte. And Salomon 6

---

x *Here eendith the proloog, and now bigynneth the book* A. No final rubric in CEFHZ. a From F. No initial rubric in ANCEII. b in to ABFH. c Om. BFH.

a From CGI. *The secounde book of Parolypomynon.* L. *The secounde of Paralipominon.* P. No initial rubric in the other Mss. b to domis men S. c Salomon INS. d the which I. e Om. I. f And INS. g Om. X. h Om. A. i Om. CEILNS. k the sone INS. l the whiche *brasen auter* IN. whiche *brasyn auter* S. m chirche *of Israel* INS.

Salomon stei3ede up to the brasen auter, before the tabernacle of the pese couenaunt of the Lord, and offride in it a 7 thousand hoostis. Lo! forsothe in that ny3t God apeerid to hym, seyinge, Ask 8 that thou wylt, that I 3eue to thee. And Salomon seide to God, Thou didist with Dauith, my fadir, grete mercy, and set- 9 tist me kyng for hym. Nowe thanne, Lord God, thi word be fulfild, that thou bihi3tist to Dauid, my fadir ; thou forsothe hast made me kyng vpon thi grete puple, the whiche is as vnnoumbreable 10 as the poudre of the erth. 3eue to me wysdam and vndirstondynge, that I go in and go out beforn thi puple ; who forsothe may this thi puple, that is so greet, 11 worthily deemyn ? God forsothe seide to Salomon, For this more pleside to thin herte, and askidist not rychesses, and substaunce, and glorie, ne the lijues of hem that hatiden thee, ne many days of lijf ; but forsothe thou askidist wisdam and kunnynge, that thou my3tist deme puple[d], vpon the whiche I haue sett thee 12 kyng, wisdom and kunnynge ben 3euen to thee ; ritchesses forsothe, and substaunces, and glorie I schal 3euen to thee, so that no man in kyngis, ne before 13 thee ne aftir thee, were lijc thee. Than Salomon came fro the hei3t of [e] Gabaon in to Jerusalem, beforn the tabernacle of the pese couenaunt, and regned vpon 14 Yrael. And he gadirde to hym charis and hors men, and ther ben maad to hym a thousand and foure hundrith chaaris, and twelue thousand of horse men ; and he maad hem to ben in the citees of plowes of foure hors, and with 15 the kyng in Jerusalem. And the kyng 3aue in to Jerusalem syluer and gold as stonys, and cedres as long mulberies[f], that

stiede[r] to the brasun autir, bifor the tabernacle of boond[s] of pees of the Lord, and offride[t] in it a thousynde sacrifices. Lo[w]! 7 'forsothe in that ny3t[x] God apperide to hym[y], 'and seide[z], Axe that[a] that thou wolt, that Y 3yue[b] to thee. And Salomon 8 seide to God, Thou hast do greet mersi with Dauid, my fadir, and hast ordeyned me kyng for hym. Now therfor, Lord 9 God, thi word be fillid[c], which thou bihi3tist to Dauid, my fadir ; for thou hast maad me kyng on[d] thi greet puple, which[e] is so vnnoumbrable as the dust of erthe. 3iue thou to me wisdom and vndurstond- 10 yng, that Y go in and go out bifor thi puple ; for who may deme worthili this thi puple, which is so greet ? Sotheli[f] God 11 seide to Salomon, For[g] this thing pleside more thin herte, and thou axidist not richessis, and catel, and glorie, nether the lyues of them that hatiden[h] thee, but nether ful many daies of lijf[i] ; but thou axidist[k] wisdom and kunnyng, that thou maist deme my puple, on[l] which Y ordeynede[m] thee kyng, wisdom and kun- 12 nyng ben[n] 3ouun to thee ; forsothe[o] Y schal 3yue to thee richessis, and catel, and glorie, so that noon among kyngis, nether bifor thee nethir[p] aftir thee, be lijk thee. Therfor[q] Salomon cam fro the hi3 place 13 of Gabaon in to Jerusalem, bifor the tabernacle of boond[r] of pees, and he[s] regnede on[t] Israel. And he[u] gaderide[v] to hym 14 chaaris and kny3tis, and a thousynde and foure hundrid chaaris weren maad to hym, and twelue thousynde of[w] kny3tis ; and he made hem to be in the[x] citees of cartis, and with the kyng in Jerusalem. And 15 the kyng 3af in Jerusalem gold and siluer as stoonys[y], and cedris[z] as sicomoris, that comen forth in feeldi places in greet multitude. Forsothe[a] horsis weren brou3t to 16

---

d my puple c.   e fro c.   f mulberie trees c pr. m.

---

r stiede up 1NS.   s the boond 1NS.   t he offrede 1NS.   w And lo! 1NS.   x Om. 1NS.   y hym in that ni3t 1N. hym that ni3t s.   a that thing 1NS.   b 3yue it 1NS.   c fulfillid 1NS.   d upon 1S.   e the which 1.   f And 1NS.   g For thi that 1S. For that N.   h haten s.   i thi lijf 1NS.   k hast axid 1NS.   l upon 1S.   m haue ordeyned 1NS.   n therfore ben 1S.   o and ouer this 1NS.   p ne 1NS.   q Thanne 1.   r the boond 1N.   s Om. c.   t upon 1S.   u Salomon 1NS.   v gaderide togidere 1NS.   w Om. s.   x Om. c.   y stones in plentith s.   z he 3aue cedre trees s.   a And 1NS.

3 D 2

growen in wijld feeldis in myche multi-
16 tude. Forsothe ther weren brou3t to
hym hors fro Egipt, and fro Ohoa, of the
marchaundis of the kyng, that wenten
17 and bo3ten^f bi^g prijs, a plow3 of hors for
sixe hundrith platis of syluer, and an
hors for an hundrith and fyfty. Lijc
maner of alle the rewmes of Cetheys,
and of the kyngis of Cirie, the bying
was solemply don.

fro Egipt, and fro Choa, bi the marchauntis of the kyng, whiche^b 3eden, and
bou3ten^c bi^d prijs, 'a foure^e 'horsid carte^f 17
for sixe hundrid platis of siluer, and an^g
hors for an hundrid and fifti^h. In lijk maner biyng was maad of alle the rewmes of
citees, and of the kingis of Sirie.

CAP. II.

1 Forsothe Salomon demed to bilden up
an hous to the name of the Lord, and a
2 paleys to hym silf. And he noumbrede
seuenty thousand of men berynge in
schulderis, and ei3li^h thousand that schulden hewen stones in hillis ; and the prouostes of hem thre thousand and sixe
3 hundrith. Also he sente to Yram, kyng
of Tiry, seyinge, As thou hast don with
my fadir Dauid, and hast sente to hym
cedre trees, that he bilde to hym an hous,
4 in the whiche and he dwellide ; so do
with me, that I bilde an hous to the
name of the Lord my God, and that I
sacre it, to brennen encense beforn hym,
and to swote thingis to ben out smokid,
and to the euermore propocicioun of
looues, and to the brent sacrifices erly
and at euen, also to the sabotis, and to
the newe monesⁱ, and solempnytes of the
Lord oure God in to euermore, that ben
5 comaundid to Yrael. The hous forsothe,
that I coueite to bilden up, is greet ; forsothe the Lord oure God is grete vpon
6 alle goddis. Who than schal mowen ben
my3ty, that he bilde up to hym an worthi
hous ? 3if forsothe heuen and heuens of
heuens mown not taken hym, how myche
am I, that I may to hym bilden up an

CAP. II.

Forsothe Salomon demydeⁱ to bilde an 1
hows to the name of the Lord, and a
paleis to hym silf. And he noumbride 2
seuenti thousynde of men berynge^k in
schuldris^l, and fourescore thousynde^m that
schulden kitteⁿ stoonys in hillis ; and the
souereyns of hem thre^o thousynde and
sixe hundrid. And he^p sente to Iram, 3
kyng^q of Tire, and seide, As thou didist
with^r my fadir Dauid, and sentist to^s hym
trees of cedre, that he schulde bilde to hym
an hows, in which also he dwellide ; so 4
do thou with^t me, that Y bilde an hows
to the name of 'my Lord God^u, and that
Y halewe it, to brenne^v encense^w bifor hym,
and to make^x odour of swete smellynge^y
spiceries, and to^z euerlastynge settynge forth
of looues, and to^a brent sacrifices^b in the
morewtid and euentid, and in sabatis, and
neomenyes^c, and solempnytees^d of 'oure
Lord God^e in to with outen ende, that^f
ben comaundid to Israel. For^g the hows 5
which^h Y coueyteⁱ to bilde is greet ; for^k
'oure Lord God^l is greet ouer alle goddis.
Who therfor may haue my3t to bilde a 6
worthi hows to hym ? For if heuene and
the^m heuenes of heuenes moun not takeⁿ
hym^o, hou greet am Y, that Y may bilde
'an hows^p to hym, but to this thing^q

f brou3ten BH.   g for c.   h cy3t D.   i monethes D.

b the whiche I.   c brou3ten EL.   d aftir bi INS.   e aftir CDEFGLPQRUb¢.   a charre o. and foure s.   f of
horsis o.   g thei bou3ten an NS.   h fifti platis INS.   i demede or purposide NS.   k berynge stones INS.
l her schuldris INS.   m thousynde men INS.   n kitte or hewe IS. hewe N.   o weren thre INS.   p Salomon INS.
q the kyng IN.   r to IN. goodlich to s.   s Om. s.   t to x.   u the Lord my God s.   v brenne yne s.
w incense therynne IN.   x make there I. make therynne s.   y welle smelling s.   z to serne to s.   a to
make therynne IS. Om. N.   b sacrifice IN.   c in feestis in the bigynayng of monthis EILNS. that is, feestis
in the bigynnyngis of monethis GKOQb.   d in solempnitees s.   e the Lord oure God INS.   f the whiche
[whiche NS] obsernauncis and halewyngis INS.   g Certis INS.   h that IS.   i coueytide A.   k forsothe IXS.
l the Lord oure God NS.   m Om. INS.   n take or holde IN.   o him, or holde the Lord our God s.
P a couenable houce s.   q thing or seruise s.

hous, bot to thes thingis al oonly, that
7 encense be brent beforn hym? Sende
thann to me an tauȝt man, that kann
wirchen in gold, and siluer, brasse, and
yren, purpur, cocco, and iacynte; and
that kanne grauen in craft of grauyng
with these craftise men, 'the whiche[k] I
haue with me in Jewrie and Jerusalem[l],
the whiche Dauid, my fadir, made redy
8 before. Bot and cedre trees senden to
me, and tyne trees, and pyne trees of
Lyban; I knowe forsothe, that thi seruauntis kunnen hewen trees of the wode;
and my seruauntis schuln ben with thi
9 seruauntis, that ther ben made redy to
me many trees; the hous forsothe that
I coueite to bilden up is ful myche grete,
10 and ful glorious. Forthermore to werk
men, that ben to hewen trees, to thi seruauntis, I schal ȝeuen in to metis choris
of whete twenti thousand, and choris of
barly as fele, and of oyle twenti thou-
11 sand mesures, as of twelue galouns. Forsothe Iram, kyng of Tyry, seide bi the
lettres that he sente to Salomon, For the
Lord hath louede his puple, therfore thee
12 he maad regnen vpon it. And he addid,
seyinge, Blessid the Lord God of Yrael,
that made heuen and erth, that ȝaue to
kyng Dauid a wijs sone, and tauȝt, and
witty, and sleeȝ, that he bilde up an hous
to the Lord, and a paleis to hym silf.
13 Therfore I haue sente to thee a sleeiȝ
man and most kunnyng, Yram, my fadir,
14 sone of a womman of the lynage of Dan,
whos fadir was Tyrus; the whiche kouthe
wirchen in gold, and in siluer, brasse,
and yren, and marbil, and trees, in purpur also, and jacynct, and bijse, and
cocko; and that kanne grauen al grauynge, and fynde sleeȝly what euer thing

oonli, that encense be brent[r] bifor hym[s]?
Therfor sende[t] thou to me a lernd man, 7
that can worche in gold, and siuer[u], bras[v],
and yrun, purpur[w], rede[x] silke, and in-
cynct[y]; and that can graue in grauyng
with these crafti men, which Y haue with
me in Judee and Jerusalem[z], whiche[a] Dauid, my fadir, made[b] redi. But also sende 8
thou to me cedre trees, and pyne trees, and
thyne trees of the Liban[c]; for Y woot, that
thi seruauntis kunnen kitte[d] trees of the[e]
Liban; and my seruauntis schulen be with
thi seruauntis, that[f] ful many trees be[g] 9
maad redi to me; for[h] the hows which[i]
Y coueyte to bilde is ful greet and noble.
Ferthermore to thi seruauntis, werk men 10
that schulen kitte trees, Y schal ȝyue in to[k]
meetis twenti thousynde chorus† of whete,
and so many chorus of barli‡, and twenti
thousynde mesuris of oile, that ben clepid
sata[l]. Forsothe[m] Iram, king of Tire, seide 11
bi lettris whiche he sente to Salomon,
For[n] the Lord louyde his puple, therfor
he made[o] thee to regne on[p] it. And he[q] 12
addide[r], seiynge, Blessid be the Lord God
of Israel, that[s] made heuene and erthe,
which ȝaf[t] to 'Dauid the kyng[u] a wijs
sone, and lernd, and witti, and prudent,
that he schulde bilde an hows to the Lord,
and a paleis to hym silf. Therfor[v] Y sente[w] 13
to thee a prudent man and moost kunnynge, Iram, my fadir, the sone of a wom- 14
man of the lynage of Dan, whos fadir was
a man of Tire; whiche[x] Iram can worche
in gold, and siluer, bras[y], and irun[z], and
marble[a], and trees[b], also in purpur, and
iacynct, and bijs, and rede[c] silke; and
which[d] Iram can graue al[e] grauyng, and
fynde[f] prudentli, what euer thing is nedeful in werk with thi crafti men, and with
the crafti men of my lord Dauid, thi fadir.

† chorus con-
teyneth xxx.
buyschels;
bathus con-
teyneth iii.
buyschelis,
that is, as
myche as
xxiiii. galouns;
satum con-
teyneth a
buyschel and
half. CGKLOPQ
9b.
‡ aftir barly it
is set in Ebreu
xx. thousynde
mesuris of
wyu, that is
[ben GK] clepid
bathus. Lire
here. CGKQ.

---

k that c pr. m.   l in Jerusalem c.

---

r brent *there* 1. brent *therynne* s.   s hym, *Y purpose to make an houce* s.   t Hiram, sende 1s.   u in
siluer 1N.   v in bras 1N. and in brasse s.   w in purpur 1Ns.   x and in rede 1. in rede Ns. and rede v.
y in iacynct 1Ns.   z in Jerusalem 1Ns.   a the whiche men 1. which crafti werkmen s.   b bifore made 1Ns.
c *hill of* Liban 1. *mounteyn of* Liban Ns.   d kitte *or* hewe s.   e Om. Ns.   f and Ns.   g Om. s.   h certis Ns.
i that Ns.   k her N.   l sata, *that is, xij. galouns* N.   m And 1Ns.   n For that N. Forthi that s.   o hath
maad Ns.   p upon 1s.   q Yram 1Ns.   r addide to 1Ns.   s which *plures*.   t hath ȝoue 1Ns.   u kyng Dauid 1Ns.
v Therfor *Salomon* 1s pr. m.   w haue sent 1Ns.   x the whiche 1.   y in bras 1Ns.   z in irun 1N.   a in
marble 1Ns.   b in trees 1Ne.   c in rede 1Ns.   d the which 1.   e in al s.   f can fynde s.

is nedeful in werk with thi craftise men,
and with the craftise men of my lord
15 Dauid, thi fadir. Thanne the whete, and
the barly, and the oyle, and the wijne,
'the whiche^m, my lord, thou hast behoten,
16 sende to thi seruauntis. We forsothe
hewen the trees from the wode, as fele
as thou schalt han need ; and we schulen
applyen hem in names bi the se in to
Joppe ; thin forsothe schal ben to leeden
17 hem ouer in to Jerusalem. Than Salomon noumbride alle the men comlyngis,
that weren in the lond of Yrael, aftir the
noumbrynge that Dauid, his fadir, noumbred ; and ther ben founden an hundrith and fyfty thousand and thre thou-
18 sand and sixe hundrith. And he maad
of hem seuenty thousand, that schulde
beren birthens with schuldirs, and eiȝty
thousand, that stoonys in hillis schulden
hewen ; thre forsothe thousand and sex
hundrith prouostis of the werkis of the
puple^n.

CAP. III.

1 And Salomon beganne to bilden up
an hous of the Lord in Jerusalem, in the
hill of Moria, the whiche was schewed to
Dauid, his fader, in the place that Dauid
hadde maad redy in the corne flor^o of
2 Ornam Jebusei. He beganne forsothe
to bilden up the secounde moneth, in the
3 ferth ȝeer of his regne. And thes ben
the foundementis, 'the whiche^p Salomon
leide, that he bilde up the hous of God ;
of lengthe cubitis in the first mesure
4 sexty, of brede cubitis twenty. The ȝate
hous forsothe beforne the frount, the
whiche was strauȝt out in to leyngthe
aftir mesure of brede of the hous, of cubitis twenty, bot the heiȝte was of an
hundrith and twenty cubitis ; and he
gildide it with in forth with most cleen

Therfor, my lord, sende thou to thi ser- 15
nauntis the whete, and barli, and oyle, and
wyn, whiche^g thou bihiȝtist^h. Sotheli^i we 16
schulen kitte trees of the Liban, how
many euere thou hast nedeful^k ; and we
schulen bryuge tho^l in schippis bi the see
in to Joppe ; forsothe^m it schal be thin^n
to lede tho ouer in to Jerusalem. Ther- 17
for^o Salomon noumbride alle men conuertid fro hethenesse, that weren in the
lond of Israel, aftir the noumbryng which^p
Dauid, his fadir, noumbride^q ; and an hundrid thousynde and thre and fifti thousynde and sixe hundrid weren foundun^r.
And he^s made^t of hem seuenti thousynde, 18
that schulden bere birthuns in^u schuldris^v,
and 'foure score^w thousynde, that schulden
kitte^x stonys in hillis ; sotheli^y he made
thre thousynde and sixe hundrid souereyns of werkis of the puple.

CAP. III.

And Salomon bigan to bilde the hows 1
of the Lord in Jerusalem, in the hil of
Moria†, that^a was schewid to Dauid, his
fadir, in the place which^b Dauid hadde
maad redi in the corn floor of Ornam Je-
busei^c. Forsothe^d he^e bigan to bilde in 2
the secounde monethe‡, in the fourthe ȝeer
of his rewme. And these weren the foun- 3
dementis, whiche Salomon settide, that he
schulde bilde the hous of God ; sixti^f cubitis of lengthe in the firste mesure§,
twenti^h cubitis of breede. Forsothe^i he 4
bildide a porche bifor the frount, that was
stretchid forth along bisidis the^k mesure
of the breede of the hows, of twenti cubitis, sotheli^l the hiȝnesse was of an hundrid and twenti cubitis ; and he ouer-
gilde^m it with inne with clennest gold.

† *Moria;* that is, of siȝt. *Lire here.* CGIKLN OPQSb.

‡ *moneth;* in Ebreu it is, in the ii. day of the moneth. *Lire here.* CGK QQb.

§ *mesure;* that is, in the mesure ȝouun of Da- uith to hym. CKLOPQb.

---

^m that c pr. m. ^n puplis ABFII. ^o feeld ABFH. ^p that c.

^g that I. ^h hast bihiȝt INS. ^i And INS. ^k need of I. ^l tho trees INS. ^m and INS. ^n thin *doyng* INS.
^o Thanne I. ^p that IS. of N. ^q had noumbrid INS. ^r founden *of hem* IS. ^s Salomon INS. ^t *made or ordeyned* IS. ^u on I. ^v her schuldris INS. ^w eiȝti BCELW. ^x hewe INS. ^y and INS. ^a the whiche *hill* I.
which N. which *hill* s. ^b that INS. ^c Jebusei, *where he bildide an auter to the Lord* IS. ^d And INS.
^e Salomon INS. ^f six N. ^g mesure *ȝouen to him of his fader Dauith* s. ^h and twenti INS. ^i And INS.
^k *or at* the IS. ^l and INS. ^m ouergildide s.

5 gold. Also the more hous he couerede with firre tablis, and he fitchide platis of briȝt gold thoruȝ out; and he graued in it hondis, and as cheynes catchynge hem 6 silf to gydre. And he couerde the pawment of the temple with most preciouse 7 marble, in myche feyrnesse. Forsothe the gold was most fyne, of whos platis he couerde the hous, and his bemys, and postis, and wallis, and dores; and he 8 graued cherubyn in the wallis. Also he maad an hous to the holies of halowes, in leyngthe aftir the brede of the hous, of cubitis twenty, and the breed lijc maner of cubitis twenty; and with golden platis couerde it, as with sixe hundrith 9 talentis. Bot and golden naylis he maad, so that eche naylis peyseden fyfty ounces; also the soupynge place he couerde with 10 gold. And he maad in the hous of holies of halowis two cherubyn in ymage werke, 11 and couerde hem with gold. The weengis of cherubyn in twenty cubitis weren strauȝt out, so that oo wenge hadde cubitis fyue, and schulde touchen the wall of the hous; and the tother wenge hauynge fyue cubitis touche the wenge of 12 the tother cherub. Lijc mauer of the tother cherub the wenge hadde fyue cubitis, and touchid the wall, and his othere weeng of fyue cubitis touched the weeng 13 of the tother cherub. Thanne the weengis of either cherub weren sprad and strauȝt out bi cubitis twenty; thei forsothe stoden riȝt up the feet, and the faces of hem weren turned to the vttirmore hous. 14 And he maad a veyl of jacinct, and purpur, and cocko^r, and bijs; and thei 15 weueden to it cherubyn. Before the ȝatis also of the temple two pylers, 'the whiche^s thritty and fyue cubitis hadden of heiȝt; forsothe the heuedis of hem of fyue cu-16 bitis. Also and as litil cheynes in Goddis

Also he hilide the gretter hows with 5 tablis of beech, and he fastnede platis of gold of besteⁿ colour al aboute^o; and he grauyde therynne palmtrees, and as smale chaynes biclipynge hem silf togidere. And 6 he arayede the pawment of the temple with most preciouse marble, in^p myche fairenesse. Forsothe^q the gold was moost 7 preued, of whose platis he hilide the hows, and the beemys therof, and the postis, and the wallis, and the doris; and he grauyde cherubyns^r in the wallis. Also he made 8 an hows to the holi of holi thingis, in lengthe bi the breede of the hows, of twenti cubitis, and the breed also^t of twenti cubitis; and he hilide it with goldun platis, as with sixe hundrid talentis^u. But^v also 9 he made goldun nailis, so that ech nail peiside fifti siclis; and he hilide the solers with gold. Also he made in the hows of 10 the hooli of hooli thingis twei cherubyns bi the werk of an ymage makere, and hilide^w hem with gold. The wyngis of 11 cherubyns weren holdun forth bi twenti cubitis, so that o wynge hadde fyue cubitis, and touchide^x the wal of the hows; and the tother wynge hadde fyue cubitis, and touchide^y the wynge of the tother^z cherub. In lijk maner the wynge^a of the 12 tother^b cherub hadde fyue cubitis, and touchide^c the wal, and the tother^d wynge therof of^e fyue cubitis touchide the wynge of the tothir^f cherub. Therfor the wyngis 13 of euer eithir cherub weren spred abrood, and weren^g holdun forth bi twenti cubitis; sotheli^h thilke cherubyns stoden onⁱ the^k feet reisid^l, and her faces weren turned to the outermere hows^m. Also he made a 14 veil of iacynct and purpurⁿ, of^o reed seelk and bijs^p; and weuyde^q cherubyns^r therynne. Also bifor the ȝate^s of the temple 15 he made twei pilers, that^t hadden fyue and thretti^u cubitis of heiȝthe; forsothe^v

n the beste I.   o aboute it s.   p and s.   q And INS.   r cherubyns, *that is, aungels* s.   s made *ther* s.
t Om. I.   u talentis *in valu* s.   v And INS.   w he hilide IN.   x it touchide INS.   y it touchide INS.
z oother IS.   a oo wyng I. to wyng NS.   b oother IS.   c it touchide INS.   d oother I.   e *that was of* NS.
f oother IS.   g thei weren INS.   h and INS.   i upon IS.   k Om. INS.   l reisid up IN. reised vp *or enhancid
fro the thing thei stoden vpon* s.   m housis N.   n of purpur INS.   o and of INS.   p of bijs INS.   q he
weuyde INS.   r aungels NS.   s ȝatis INS.   t the whiche I. whiche NS.   u twenti X.   v and INS.

answerynge place, and he putte hem vpon the heuedes of the pilers; also an hundrith powngaruettis, the whiche he 17 putte among to the litil cheynes. And thilk^t pilers he putte in the vestiarye of the temple, oon fro the ri3t, an other fro the left; it that was fro the ri3t he clepide Jachym, and that to the lift he clepid Booz.

the heedis of tho^w *weren* of fyue cubitis^x. Also *he made* and^y as^z litle chaynes in 16 Goddis answeryng place†, and puttide^a tho^b on^c the heedis of the pilers; also *he made* an hundrid pumgarnadis, whiche^d he settide bitwixe the litle chaynes. And he 17 settide tho pilers in the porche of the temple, oon at the ri3tside, and the tother^e at the leftside; he clepide that^f that was at the ri3tside Jachym^g, and that that was at the leftside he^h clepide Boozⁱ.

† *answeryng plone; that is, in the porche of Salomon, as dictnuris seien here. Lire here. c.*

CAP. IV.

1 And he maad a brasen auter of twenty cubitis of lengthe, and of twenty cubitis of breed, and of tenn cubitis of hei3te; 2 also a 3oten se of tenn cubitis fro brynke vnto brynk, round bi ennyrouu; fyue cubitis he hadde of hei3te; and a litil coord of thritty cubitis enuyrounde the compas 3 of it. And licnesse of oxen was vndur it, and in the ten cubitis maner grauyngis with oute forth as with two vers wente aboute the brynke of the se; the oxen 4 forsothe weren 3oten. And that se was put vpon the twelue oxen^u, of the whiche thre biheelden to the north, and other thre to the west, bot the^v thre other the^w south, and the thre that weren laft the^w este, hauynge the se put aboue; the hyndirmore forsothe of the oxen 5 weren with in forth vndur the se. Bot the thicnesse of it hadde the mesure of a spanne, and the lippe of it was as the lippe of a chalice, or as of a lilie a3ein crokid, and it toke of mesure thre thou-6 sand potels. Also he maad tenn watir vessels, and he putte fyue fro the ri3t, and fyue fro the lift, that they schulden waschen in hem alle thingis that in

CAP. IV.

Also^k he^l made a brasun auter of twenti 1 cubitis of lengthe, and of twenti cubitis of breede, and of ten cubitis of hei3the; *he* 2 *made* also a 3otun see^m‡ of ten cubitis fro brynke tilⁿ to brynke, round bi cumpas; it hadde fyue cubitis of hei3the; and a coorde of thritti cubitis cumpasside the cumpas therof. And the licnesse^o of oxis^p 3 was vndur it, and bi ten cubitis summe grauyngis with outforth cumpassiden the brynke of the see as with tweyne ordris; sotheli^q the oxis^r weren 3otun. And thilke 4 see was set on^s twelue oxis^t, of whiche^u oxis^t thre bihelden to the north, and othere thre to the west, sotheli^v thre othere *bihelden*^w the^x south, and thre 'that weren residue^y *bihelden*^z the^a eest, and hadden^b the see set aboue^c; but the hyndrere^d partis of the oxis^e weren with ynne^f vndur the see. Sotheli^g the thicknesse 5 therof^h hadde the mesure of aⁱ pawm of the^j hond, and the brynke therof was^k as the brynke of a cuppe, ethir^l of a^m lilie crokid a3en, and itⁿ took^o thre thousynde metretis^p of mesure. Also he^q made ten 6 holowe vessels, and settide^r fyue at the ri3tside, and fyue at the leftside^s, that thei^t

‡ *see; that is, a greet wuschlng vessel for prestis. c.*

---

t thoo c.　u of oxen B.　v to B.　w to the A.

w tho *pilers* IS.　x cubitis in hei3the NS.　y Om. IS.　z as it were I. as and S.　a he puttide INS.　b tho chaynes IE. hem N.　c upon IS.　d the whiche I.　e oother I.　f that *piler* INS.　g *that is, a biforc ordeynyng* I *marg.* Jachym, *that is, a bifore ordeyner or before ordeynyng* S *text.*　h Salomon INS.　i Booz, *that is, in whom is strengthe* I. Booz, *that is, in whom is strength of vertu* S.　k And INS.　l Salomon INS.　m see, *that is, a weischinge vessel* INS.　n Om. I.　o licnessis X.　p oxen INS.　q and INS.　r oxen INS.　s upon IS.　t oxen INS.　u the whiche I.　v and INS.　w Om. IN.　x to the INS.　y the remenaunt INS.　z Om. I.　a to the I.　b *these* hadden IN.　c aboue *hem* INS.　d hyndere CSX.　e oxen INS.　f ynne forth INS.　g And INS.　h of the see INS.　i the INS.　j an INS.　k Om. A.　l ethir *as* IS.　m Om. c.　n the see INS.　o heeld N. tooke *or* heeld S.　p *that is, mesuris of wijn* K *marg.*　q Salomon INS.　r he sette INS.　s leftside *of the see* IS.　t *the dekens* INS.

brent sacrifices thei weren to offren; bot in the se the prestis weren waschen. 7 Forsothe he maad tenn golden chaun-delers aftir the fourme 'the whiche^x he hadde comaundide to be maad, and he put hem in the temple, fyue fro the ri3t 8 and fyue fro the left; also and tenn boordes, and putte hem in the temple, fyue fro the ri3t and fyue fro the left; 9 and golden violis an hundrith. And he made the porche of prestis, and a greet hous, and the dores in the hous, the 10 whiche he couerde with brasse. But the se he putte in the ri3t sijde a3einus the 11 este at the south. Also Yram made caudrowns, and fleschhokis, and violis, and he fulfilde al the werk of the kyng 12 in the hous of God, that is, two pilers, and heued coueryngis, and heuedes, and as maner nettis, the whiche the heuedis 13 schulden coueryn vpon the heued couer-yngis; also powngarnetis fourty, and two callis, so that two ordris of poungarnetis to alle the callis schulden ben ioyned, the whiche schulden coueren the heued coueryngis, and the heuedis of the pilers. 14 Also feet he maad, and water vessels, the 15 whiche he putte vpon the feet; oon se, 16 and oxen twelue vndir the se, and caw-drouns, and fleschhookis, and viols. Yram, his fadir, made alle the vesselis to Salo-mon, in the hous of the Lord, of most 17 clene brasse. In the regioun of Jordan the kyng 3eetide hem, in the cley^y lond 18 bitween Socoth and Saradatha. Forsothe ther was a multitude of vessels vnnoum-breable, so that the wei3te of brasse was 19 vnknowen. And Salomon maad alle the vessels of the hous of God, the golden auter, and boordis, and vpon hem the 20 looues of proposicioun; and candilstikis with their lanternes, that thei 3cuen li3t

schulden waische in tho alle thingis, whiche thei schulden offre in to brent sacrifice; sotheli^u the preestis weren waischun in the see^v. Sotheli^w he made ten goldun 7 candilstikis bi the licknesse which^x he^y hadde comaundid to^z be maad, and he set-tide tho in the temple, fyue at the ri3tside and fyue at the leftsid. And he made 8 also ten boordis^a, and settide^b tho in the temple, fyue at the ri3tside and fyue at the leftside. Also he made an hundrid 9 goldun viols. 'Also he made^c a large place of preestis^d, and a greet hows, and doris in the greet hows, which he hilide with bras. Forsothe^e he settide the see in 10 the ri3tsyde^f a3ens the eest at the south^g. Also Iram made cawdruns, and fleischokis, 11 and viols†, and he fillide^h al the werk of the kyng in the hows of God, that is, twei^i 12 pilers, and pomels^k, and heedis, and^l as summe nettis, that hiliden the heedis aboue the pomels; also he made fourti pum- 13 garnadis, and twei werkis lijk nettis, so that two^m ordris of pumgarnadis weren ioyned to ech werk like nettis, which^n hiliden the pomels, and heedis^o of the pilers. He made also foundementis, and 14 holow vessels, whiche^p he settide^q on^r the^s foundementis; he made o^t see, and twelue 15 oxis^u vndur the see, and caudruns, and 16 fleischookis, and viols. Iram, the fadir‡ of Salomon, made to hym alle vessels^v in the hows of the Lord of clennest bras. The kyng 3etide^w tho^x in the cuntrey of 17 Jordan, in cleiy^y lond bitwixe^z Socoth and Saredata. Forsothe^a the multitude of ves- 18 sels was vnnoumbrable, so that the wei3te of bras was not knowun. And Salomon 19 made alle the vessels of Goddis hows^b, the goldun auter, 'and bordis^c, and loouys^d of settyng forth on^e tho; and candilstikis of 20 purest gold, with her lanternes, that tho

† viols; in Ebren it is, bacyns. c.

‡ fadir; that is, for resoun of age, ether of excelence of craft. Lire here. c.

x that c pr. m.   y cleiy ʙ.

u And ɪɴꜱ. v see, or thei entreden in to the seintuarie ɪꜱ. w And ɪɴꜱ. x that ɪ. y Dauid ɪɴꜱ. z Om. ɴ. a tablis ɴꜱ. b sette ᴇʟ. he settide ɴꜱx. c and ɪ. d preestis, or far prcestis ꜱ. e And ɴꜱ. f ri3t syde of the porche ɪɴꜱ. g south coast ɪꜱ. h fulfillide ɪɴ. i he made twei ɴꜱ. k her pomels ɪꜱ. l and he made ꜱ. m tho two ɪɴ. the two ꜱ. n the which ɪ. o the heedis x sec. m. p the whiche ɪ. q sette ɪɴꜱ. r vpon ɪꜱ. s tho ɪꜱ. t a ɪɴꜱ. u oxen ɪɴꜱ. v necesarie vessels ꜱ. the vessels x sec. m. w did 3eete ɴꜱ. x tho vessels ɪɴꜱ. y cley ɪ. z bitwene ɪ. a Certis ɪɴꜱ. b hows, that is, to wite [seie ꜱ] ɪꜱ. c the mete tablis ɪɴꜱ. d the loouys ɪɴꜱ. e upon ɪɴꜱ.

before Goddis answeryng place aftir the
21 rijt, of most pure gold; and sum floures,
and lanterns, and golden snytters; alle of
22 most clene gold ben maad; also the maad
encense vessels, and censeres, and violis,
and morters, of most pure gold. And he
graued the doris of the innermore temple, that is, in[z] the hoolyes of halowes,
and the doris of the temple without forth
golden; and so is fulfild al the werk that
Salomon made in the hous of the Lord.

CAP. V.

1 Salomon thanne brou₃te in alle thingis,
that Dauid, his fadir, hadde vowed; syluer, and gold, and al the vessels, he putte
in the tresores of the hous of the Lord.
2 After the[a] whiche thingis he gadride the
more thoru₃ birthe of Irael, and al the
princis of lynagis, and the heuedis of
meynes, of the sonys of Yrael, in to Jerusalem, that thei bryngin the ark of the
pese couenaunt of the Lord fro the cyte
3 of Dauid, that is Syon. And so camen
to the kyng alle the men of Yrael, in
the solempne day of the seuenth moneth.
4 And whanne weren commen alle of the
elder of Yrael, the Leuytes beren the
5 arke, and brou₃ten it in, and al the aray
of the tabernacle. Bot the vessels of the
seyntuarye, that weren in the tabernacle,
the prestis beeren with the Leuytis.
6 Kyng Salomon forsothe, and al the companye of Irael, and alle that weren gadered beforn the arke, offreden wethers
and oxen with oute eny noumbre; so
myche forsothe was the multitude of
7 slayn offryngus. And the prestis brou₃ten
in the arke of the pese couenaunt of the
Lord in to his place, that is, to Goddis
answerynge place of the temple, in to the
holies of halowes, vndre the weengis of

schulden schyne bifor Goddis answering
place bi the[f] custom; and *he made* summe 21
werkis lijk flouris, and lanternes, and
goldun tongis; alle thingis[g] weren maad
of clennest gold; also *he made* pannes for 22
colis to brenne[h] encense, and censeris, and
viols, and morters, of pureste gold. And[i]
he grauyde doris[k] of the yunere temple,
that is, in the hooli of hooli thingis, and
the goldun doris of the temple with out
forth; and so al the werk was fillid[l] that
Salomon made in the hows of the Lord.

CAP. V.

Therfor Salomon brou₃te in[m] alle thingis, 1
siluer[n] and gold, whiche Dauid, his fadir,
hadde avowid; and he puttide alle vesselis[o] in[p] the[q] tresouris of the hows of the
Lord. After whiche thingis he gaderide 2
togidere alle the grettere men in birthe of
Israel, and alle the princes of lynagis, and
the heedis of meynees, of the sones[r] of Israel, in to Jerusalem, that thei schulden
brynge the arke of boond of pees of the
Lord fro the citee of Dauid, which[s] is
Syon. Therfor alle men of Israel camen 3
to the kyng, in the solempne dai of the
seuenthe monethe. And whanne alle the 4
eldre men of Israel 'weren comen[t], the dekenes baren the arke, and brou₃ten[u] it in[v], 5
and al the aray of the tabernacle[w]. Forsothe[x] the[y] preestis with the dekenes baren
the vessels of seyntuarie[z], that weren in
the tabernacle. Sotheli[a] kyng Salomon, 6
and alle the cumpenyes of Israel, and alle[b]
that weren gaderid to gidere, offriden bifor
the arke wetheris and oxis[c] with outen
ony[d] noumbre; for the multitude of slayn
sacrifices was 'so greet[e]. And preestis 7
brou₃ten the arke of boond of pees of the
Lord in to his[f] place[g], that is, to Goddis
answeryng place of the temple, in to the
hooli of hooli thingis, vndur the wyngis of

---

[f] Om. ins.   [g] these thingis ins.   [h] brenne ynne ins.   [i] Om. ax.   [k] the doris ins.   [l] fulfillid ins.
[m] forth ns.   [n] that is, siluer ins.   [o] the vesselis ins.   [p] in to ns.   [q] Om. s.   [r] hous n.   [s] that ins.
[t] camen a.   [u] thei brou₃ten ins.   [v] Om. ins.   [w] tabernacle *in to the temple of Jerusalem* is. tabernacle
in to the temple n.   [x] And ins.   [y] Om. in.   [z] the seyntuarie ins.   [a] And ins.   [b] alle men ins.
[c] oxen ins.   [d] Om. ins.   [e] so greet that it my₃te not be noumbrid ins.   [f] the ins.   [g] place
therof ins.

8 cherubyn; so that cherubyn spreden out
their weengis vpon the place, in the
whiche the ark was sett, and that arke
thei schulden coueren with their beryng
9 staues. Of the berynge staues forsothe,
with the whiche the ark was born, for a
litil wiȝt lengere thei weren, the heuedis
weren opene beforn Goddis answerynge
place; ȝif forsothe eny a[b] litil wiȝt were
with out forth, hem he myȝte not seen.
And so the arke was there vnto the pre-
10 sent day; and noon other thing was in
the ark, bot the two tablis that Moyses
hadde putte in Oreb, whanne he ȝaue the
lawe to the sonis of Yrael goyng out fro
11 Egipt. Forsothe the prestis goon out
fro the seyntuarye, alle forsothe prestis,
that there myȝt ben founden, ben halowed, ne ȝit in that tyme the whijlis,
and the order of seruyses betwene hem
12 seluen was deuydid; bothe Leuytis and
syngers, that is, and that vndur Asaph
weren, and that vndur Eman, and that
vndir Idythum, sonis and bretheren of
hem, clothed[c] with surples, in cymbalis
and sawtres and harpis sungyn, stondynge at the eest coost of the auter, and
with hem prestis an hundrith and twenty,
13 syngynge with trumpis. Thanne alle to
gyder, in trumpis, and voice, and cymbalis, and orgnys, and of dyuerse kynde
of musikis, sownynge to gydre, and the
voice berynge vp an heeiȝ, afer the sown
was hard, so that whanne the Lord thei
hadden begunnen to preysen, and seyn,
Knowlecheth to the Lord, for 'he is[d]
good, for in to the world the mercy of
hym; the hous of God was fulfillid with
14 a clowde, and the prestis myȝten not
stonden and mynystren for the derknessis; forsothe the glorie of the Lord
hadde fulfild the hous of God.

cherubyns[h]; so that cherubyns spredden[i] 8
forth her wyngis ouer the place, in which
the arke was put, and hiliden thilke arke
with hise barris[k]. Sotheli the heedis[l], by[m] 9
which the arke was borun, weren opyn[n]
bifor Goddis answeryng place, for tho
heedis weren a litil lengere[o]; but if a
man hadde be a litil with out forth, he
myȝt not se[p] tho barris[q]. Therfor the
arke was there til in to present[r] dai; and[s] 10
noon other thing was[t] in the arke, no[u]
but twei tablis, whiche[v] Moyses hadde
put[w] in Oreb, whanne the Lord ȝaf the
lawe to the sones of Israel goynge out of
Egipt. Forsothe[x] the[y] prestis ȝeden out 11
of the seyntuarie, for alle preestis[z], that
myȝten be foundun there, weren halewid[a],
and the whiles[b], and the ordre of seruyces[c]
among hem[d] was not departid ȝit in that
tyme; bothe[e] dekenes and syngeris, that 12
is, bothe thei that weren vndur Asaph,
and thei that weren vndur Eman, and thei
that weren vndur Idithum, her sones and
britheren, clothid[f] with white lynun clothis,
sownyden with cymbalis and sautrees and
harpis[g], and stoden[h] at the west coost[i] of
the auter, and with hem *weren* sixe score
preestis trumpynge. Therfor whanne alle[k] 13
sungen togidur both with trumpis, and
vois[l], and cymbalis[m], and orguns, and of
dyuerse kynde[n] of musikis, and reisiden[o]
the[p] vois an hiȝ, the sown was herd fer,
so that whanne thei hadden bigunne to
preyse the Lord, and to seie, Knouleche ȝe
to the Lord, for he is good, for[q] his mercy
is in to the world, '*ether, with outen ende*[r];
the hows of God was[s] fillid[t] with a cloude,
and the preestis miȝten not stonde and[u] 14
serue[v] for the[w] derknesse; for[x] the glorie
of the Lord hadde fillid[y] the hows of the
Lord.

[b] Om. ABFH. [c] clad C. [d] Om. E *pr. m.*

[h] cherubis E. [i] spredinge NS. [k] barynge barris INS. [l] heedis *or pomels* INS. [m] with I. [n] opyn *or vnhelid* IS. [o] lengere *than the streiching of cherubus wyngis* IS. [p] haue seen INS. [q] barynge barris INS. [r] the present I. [s] and ther was I. [t] Om. I. [u] Om. IS. [v] that I. [w] put therynne INS. [x] And *aftir this* IS. And N. [y] Om. I. [z] the preestis INS. [a] halwed, *or put in office to mynistre there before the Lord* S. [b] whilis, *or certeyn tymes* S. [c] seruyce X. [d] prestis INS. [e] *and* bothe IS. [f] *werin* clothid S. [g] with harpis INS. [h] thei stoden INS. [i] coost *or corner* S. [k] thei alle INS. [l] with vois INS. [m] with cymbalis INS. [n] kyndis NS. [o] thei reisiden I. [p] her INS. [q] and S. [r] Om. CIN. *ether in to withouten ende* X. [s] was than S. [t] fulfillid INS. [u] to A. [v] serue *in her office* S. [w] Om. N. [x] forsothe INS. [y] fulfillid INS.

CAP. VI.

1 Thanne Salomon seith, The Lord be-
hi3te, that he schulde dwellen in the
2 dirkenesse; I forsothe haue bilde up an
hous to the name of hym, that he schulde
3 dwellen there in to with oute eende. And
the kyng turnede his face, and blesside
to al the multitude of Israel; for why al
the puple stood, inwardly takynge heede;
4 and he seith, Blessed the Lord God of
Yrael, for that he spake to Dauid, my
fadir, in deede he hath fulfillide, sey-
5 inge, Fro the day that I ladde my puple
fro the lond of Egipt, I chees not a cytee
of alle the lynagis of Yrael, that there
schulde be bilde up in it an hous to my
name, ne eny othere man I chees, that he
6 were duyke vpon my puple Yrael; bot I
chees Jerusalem, that my name be in it,
and I chees Dauid, that I ordeyn hym
7 vpon my puple Yrael. And whanne it
was of the wille of Dauid, my fadir, that
he bilde an hous to the name of the Lord
8 God of Yrael, the Lord seid to hym, For
this was thi wille, that thou schuldist
bylden an hous to my name, forsothe
thou didyst wele, hauynge such a maner
9 wille, bot thou schalt not bylden vp an
hous to me; neuerthelater⁰ the sone, that
gooth out of thi reynes, he schal bylden
10 up an hous to my name. Thanne the
Lord fulfillide his word, that he hadde
spoken; and I roos for Dauid, my fadir,
and sat vpon the trone of Ysrael, as the
Lord spac, and bilde up an hous to the
11 name of the Lord God of Yrael; and
putte in it the arke, in the' whiche is the
couenaunt of the Lord, that he coue-
12 nauntide with the sonis of Yrael. Thanne
he stode before the auter of the Lord forn
a3eynst of al the multitude of Yrael, and
13 strau3t out his hondis. Forsothe Salomon hadde maad the brasyn stondynge,

CAP. VI.

Thanne Salomon seide, The Lord bi- 1
hi3te, that he wolde dwelle in derknesse²;
forsothe ⁿ I haue bilde an hows to his 2
name, that he schulde dwelle there ᵇ with
outen ende. And Salomon turnede his 3
face, and blesside⁰ al the multitude of Israel; for al the cumpeny stood ententif ᵈ;
and he⁰ seide, Blessid be the Lord God of 4
Israel, for he fillide' in werk that thing,
that he spak to Dauid, my fadir, and
seide, Fro⁵ the dai in which Y ledde my 5
puple out of the lond of Egipt, Y chees
not a citee of alle the lynagis ʰ of Israel,
that an hows schulde be bildid therynne
to my name, nether Y chees ony other
man, that he schulde be duyk on ⁱ my puple Israel; but Y chees Jerusalem, that ᵏ 6
my name be therynne, and Y chees Dauid,
to ordeyne hym on ⁱ my puple Israel. And 7
whanne it was of the wille of Dauid, my
fadir, to bilde an hows to the name of the
Lord God of Israel, the Lord seide to hym, 8
For this was thi wille, 'that thou woldist'
bilde ᵐ an hows to my name, sotheli thou
didist wel, hauynge suche a wil, but ⁿ thou 9
schalt not bilde an hows to me; netheles
the sone, that schal go out of ⁰ thi leendis,
he schal bilde an hows to my name. Ther- 10
for the Lord hath fillid ᵖ his word, which ᵠ
he spak; and Y roos' for Dauid, my fader,
and Y sat on⁵ the trone of Israel, as the
Lord spak, and Y bildide ᵗ an hous to the
name of the Lord God of Israel; and I 11
haue put therynne the arke, in which is
the couenaunt of the Lord, which he 'coue-
nenauntide with ⁿ the sones of Israel. Ther- 12
for Salomon stood bifor the auter of the
Lord euene a3ens al the multitude of Israel, and stretchide ᵛ forth his hondis. For ʷ 13
Salomon hadde maad a brasun founde-
ment, and hadde ˣ set it in the myddis of
the greet hows, and it hadde fyue cubitis

ᵉ nerthelatere c passim.　ᶠ Om. c.

ᶻ derknesses c.　ᵃ and ɪɴꜱ.　ᵇ there ynne ɪɴꜱ.　ᶜ he blesside ɪɴꜱ.　ᵈ ententif, or takinge tent ɪ.
ententife, that is, taking heed bisili s.　ᵉ Salomon ɪɴꜱ.　ᶠ hath fulfillid ɪɴꜱ.　ᵍ For ɴꜱ.　ʰ linage ꜱ.
ⁱ upon ɪꜱ.　ᵏ that and ꜱ.　ˡ to ꜱ.　ᵐ haue bilde ɪɴ.　ⁿ but 3it ɴꜱ.　⁰ at ꜱ.　ᵖ fulfillid ɪɴꜱ.　ᵠ that ɪɴꜱ.
ʳ roos up ɪɴꜱ.　ˢ upon ɪꜱ.　ᵗ haue bildid ɪɴꜱ.　ᵘ comaundide to ꜱ.　ᵛ he stretchide ɪɴꜱ.　ʷ And ɪɴꜱ.
ˣ he hadde ɪɴꜱ.

and hadde putte it in the mydil of the grete hous, hauynge fyue cubitis of lengthe, and fyue of brede, and thre cubitis of heiȝt, and he stode vpon it; and theraftir the knees bowed aȝeinus al the multitude of Yrael, and the hondis in to 14 heuen rered, seith, Lord God of Yrael, ther is not lijc thee, God in heuen and in erth, 'the whiche^g kepist couenaunt and mercy with thi seruauntis, that goon 15 before thee in al their herte; the whiche hast ȝeuen to Dauid thi seruaunt, my fa- dir, whateuer thingis thou haddist spoken to hym, and that with mouthe thou by- heetist, in deed thou hast fulfylde, as 16 and the present tyme preueth. Now thanne, Lord God of Yrael, fulfille to thi seruaunt my fadir Dauid, whateuer thingis thou hast spoken, seyinge, Ther schal not faylen of thee a man beforn me, that sytt vpon the trone of Yrael; so neuer the later ȝif thi sonis kepen my weies, and goon in my lawe, as and thou 17 wentist before me. And nowe, Lord God of Yrael, be fastned thi word, that thou 18 speke to thi seruaunt Dauid. Thanne whethir leeuable it be, that the Lord dwelle with men vpon erth? ȝif heuen and heuens of heuens thee taken not, how myche more this hous, that I haue 19 bylde? Bot to this oonly it is maad, that thou beholde the orisoun of thi seruaunt, and his bisechynge, Lord my God, and thou here the preyers, that thi seruaunt 20 heldith out before thee; that thou opene thi eeȝen vpon this hows dais and nyȝtis, vpon the place in the whiche thou hast behoten, that thy name schulde be in- 21 wardly clepid, and thou schuldist heeren the orisoun, that thi seruaunt preieth in it. Heere thou the preyers of thi ser- uaunt, and of thi^h puple Yrael; who so

of lengthe, and fyue of breede, and thre cubitis of heiȝthe, and he stood theron^y; and fro that tyme he knelide^z aȝens al the multitude of Israel, and reiside^a the^b hondis in to heuene, and seide, Lord God of Is- 14 rael, noon is lijk thee^c; 'thou art^d God in heuene and in erthe, whiche^e kepist coue- naunt and mercy with thi seruauntis, that^f goon bifor thee in al her herte; which^g 15 hast ȝoue to Dauid thi seruaunt, my fadir, what euer thingis^h thou hast spoke^i to hym, and^k thow hast fillid^l in werk tho thingis, whiche thou bihiȝtist bi mouth, as also present^m tyme preueth. Now therfor, 16 Lord God of Israel, fille^n thou to thi ser- uaunt my fadir Dauid, what euer thingis thou hast spoke, seiynge, A man of thee schal not faile bifor me, that schal sitte on^o the trone of Israel; so netheles if^p thi sones kepen my weies, and goon in my lawe†, as and thou^q hast go bifor me. And now, Lord God of Israel, thi word 17 be^r maad stidefast^s, which thou spakist to thi seruaunt Dauid. Therfor whether^t it 18 is leueful^u, that the Lord dwelle with men on^v erthe? If heuene and the^w heuenes of heuenes 'taken not thee^x, how myche more this hows, which Y haue bildid? But 19 herto oneli it is maad, that thou, my Lord God, biholde^y the preier of thi seruaunt, and the bisechyng of hym, and that thou^z here the preieris, whiche thi seruaunt schedith^a bifor thee; that thou opyne thin^b 20 iȝen on^c this hows bi dayes and nyȝtis, on^c the place in which thou bihiȝtist, that thi name schulde be clepid^d, and that 21 thou woldist here the preier, which thi seruaunt preieth therynne. Here thou^e the preieris of thi seruaunt, and of thi puple Israel; who euer preieth in this place, here thou^f fro thi dwellyng place, that is, fro heuenes^g, and do thou merci^h. If ony 22

†Lo! how God spekith condiscions! *Lire. s.*

g that c.   h the s.

y here upon ins.   z knelide on s.   a he reiside up ins.   b hise ins.   c thee *in power, kunnyng, ne in goodnesse* s.   d Om. n.   e the which i.   f whiche ins.   g thou ins.   h thing ins.   i spoke *or bihiȝte* s. k and *Lord* is.   l fulfillid ins.   m this present ins.   n fulfille ins.   o upon is.   p that ins.   q thou, Dauith ns.   r be it ins.   s stidfast, *or fulfillid* s.   t Om. in.   u bileueful BCDEGIKLMNOPQUVWXç. bileeue- ful, *that is, able or liȝt to bileue* s.   v upon is.   w Om. i.   x taken ethir moun not holde thee, Lord ns. y biholde there i. biholde *there* ine s.   z thou Lord s.   a heeldith i. shedith oute s.   b the x.   c upon is. d inclepid is.   e thou, Lord ins.   f thou *him* ins.   g heuene ns.   h merci *to him* ins.

euer preye[h] in this place, here fro thi dwellynge place, that is fro heuens, and 22 be thou maad plesed. 3if eny man synne[i] in to his nei3bour, and redi comme to sweren a3einus hym, and by curse bynde 23 hym before the auter in this hous, thou schalt heeren fro heuen, and thou schalt do dome of thi seruauntis; so that thou 3elde to the wickide[k] his weie in to his owne heued, and venge the ri3twijs, and 3eldynge[l] to hym aftir his ri3twisnesse. 24 3if thi puple Yrael were ouercomen of enmyes, forsothe thei schul synnen to thee, and turned done[m] penaunce, and besechen thi name, and preyen in this 25 place, thou schalt heeren fro heuen, and haue thou mercy to the synne of thi puple Yrael, and brynge hem a3ein in to the lond, that thou 3eue to hem, and to 26 their fadirs. 3if, heuen closed, reyn flowe not for synne of thi puple, and thei preyen thee in this place, and knowlechen to thi name, and turned fro their synnes, whanne hem thou tormentist, 27 here, Lord, fro heuen, and for3eue the synnes to thi seruauntis, and to thi puple Yrael, and teche hem a good wei, by the[n] whiche thei goon in, and 3eue reyn to the erth, that thou hast 3euen to thi 28 puple to weelden. 3if hunger were sprungyn in the lond, and pestilence, and rust, and weder rootynge tilth, and locust, and werm, and enmyes, the regyouns wasted, besee3en the 3atis of the cytee, and alle veniaunce and infirmyte 29 thrist doun; 3if any of thi puple Irael preye, knowynge the veniaunce, and his infirmyte, stretche out his hondis in this 30 hous, thou schalt heeren fro heuen, that is, fro thin hee3 dwellynge place, and be thou plesed, and 3eeld to eche man aftir

man synneth a3ens his nei3bore, and cometh redi to swere a3ens him, and byndith hym silf with cursyng bifor the auter in[l] this hows[k], thou schalt[l] here[m] fro heuene, and 23 schalt[n] do the doom of thi seruauntis[o]; so that thou 3elde to the wickid man his weie in to his owne heed, and that thou venge the iust man, and 3elde to hym after his ri3tfulnesse[p]. If thi puple Israel is ouer-24 comen of enemyes, for thei[q] schulen do synne a3ens thee, and if thei[r] conuertid[s] doen penaunce, and bisechen thi name, and preien in this place, thou schalt[t] here[u] 25 fro heuene, and do thou mercy to the synne of thi puple Israel, and brynge hem a3en 'in to[v] the lond, which thou hast 3oue to hem, and to 'the fadris of hem[w]. If 26 whanne heuene is closid, reyn come[x] not doun for the synne of thi puple, and thei bisechen thee in this place, and knowlechen to thi name, and ben turned[y] fro her synnes, whanne thou hast turmentid hem, here thou[z], Lord[a], fro heuene, and 27 for3yue thou synnes[b] to thi seruauntis, and to thi puple Israel, and teche[c] thou hem a good weie, bi which thei schulen entre[d], and 3yue thou reyn to the lond, which[e] thou hast 3oue to thi puple to haue in possessioun. If[f] hungur risith in the lond, 28 and pestilence, and rust, and wynd distriynge cornes, and a[g] locuste, and bruke[h] cometh[i], and if enemyes bisegen the 3atis of the citee, aftir that the cuntreis ben distried, and[k] al[l] veniaunce[m] and sikenesse oppressith[n]; if ony of thi puple Israel[o] 29 bisechith, and knowith his veniaunce[p] and sikenesse, and if he spredith abrood hise hondis in this hows, thou[q] schalt here[r] fro 30 heuene, that is, fro thin hi3e dwellyng place, and[s] do thou mercy, and 3elde thou to ech man aftir hise weies, whiche thou

h honoureth ε pr. m.　i synneth ce.　k wicke c.　l 3elde ε pr. m.　m schulden don ε pr. m.　n Om. c.

i of ns.　k house, that is, that his quarrel is iust s.　l shalt, Lord s.　m here him ins.　n thou schalt ins. o seruaunt n.　p ri3twisnesse ins.　q that thi peple ins.　r thi peple ins.　s conuertid fro her synne is. t shalt, Lord s.　u here hem ins.　v to ins.　w her fadris ins.　x cometh a sec. m.　y turned al togidre ins. z thou hem thanne in.　a Lord, hem s.　b the synnes ins.　c Lord, teche ns.　d entre to thee s. e that ins.　f If that ns.　g if that a ins.　h a bruke c.　i comen [comith s] freiynge cornes is.　k and if in. and if al, that is s.　l ouy mauer i. al the n. if eny of al the s.　m veniauncis biforseid s.　n oppressith thi puple is.　o of Israel ins.　p veniaunce, that is, his synne wherfore he hath disserued veniaunce s.　q Lord, thou is.　r here him ins.　s Om. s.

his weies[o], the whiche thou hast knowen
hym to han in his hert; thou forsothe
aloone hast knowen the hertis of the
31 sonis of men; that thei dreeden thee, and
goon in thi weies alle days, 'the whiche[p]
thei lyuen vpon the face of the erth,
32 that thou hast ȝeuen to oure fadirs. A
straunger also that is not of thy puple
Yrael, ȝif he come fro a ferre lond for
thi grete name, and for thi strong hond,
and for thi strauȝt out arme, and honour
33 in this place, thou schalt heeren fro heuen, thi most fast place; and thou schalt
don alle thingis, for the whiche that pilgryme inwardly clepith thee, that alle
puplis of erth knowen thi name, and
dreeden thee, as thi puple Yrael; and
knowen thei, for thi name is inwardly
clepide vpon this hous, that I haue bilde
34 to thi name. Ȝif thi puple weren goon
out to bataile aȝeinus ther aduersaries, by
the weye in to the[q] whiche thou sentist
hem, thei schuln honouren thee aȝeinus
the weye in the[q] whiche is the cytee
that thou hast chosen, and the hous that
35 I haue bylde to thi name, that thou here
fro heuen the preyers of hem and the
36 besechynge, and thou do veniaunce. Ȝif
forsothe thei synnen to thee, and forsothe
ther is no man that synneth not, and
thou were wroth to hem, and takist hem
to the enmyes; and caytijf thei leeden
hem in to a ferre lond, or certis that is
37 niȝ; and turned in al their herte in the
lond, to the whiche thei weren ladde
caytijf, done penaunce, and preyen thee
in the lond of their caytijfte, seyinge,
We han synned, wickidly[r] we han
38 wrouȝt, vnriȝtwisely we han done; and
weren torned to thee in al their herte,
and in al their soule, in the lond of their

knowist, that he hath in his herte; for
thou[t] aloone knowist the hertis of the
sones of men; that[u] thei drede thee, and 31
go in thi weies in alle daies, in which
thei lyuen on[v] the face of erthe, which
thou hast ȝoue to oure fadris. Also[w] thou 32
schalt here fro heuene, thi moost stidfast
dwellyng place, a straunger, which[x] is not
of thi puple Israel, if he cometh fro a fer
lond for[y] thi greet name, and for thi
stronge hond, and arm[z] holdun[a] forth, 'and
preye[b] in this place[c]; and[d] thou schalt do 33
alle thingis, for which thilke pilgrym 'inwardli clepith[e] thee, that[f] alle the[g] puplis[h]
of erthe knowe[i] thi name, and drede[k] thee,
as thi puple Israel *doith;* and that thei
knowe, that thi name is clepid[l] on[m] this
hows, which[n] Y haue bildid to thi name.
If thi puple goith out to batel aȝens hise 34
aduersaries[o], bi the weie in which thou
sendist hem, thei schulen worschipe thee
aȝens the weie in which this citee is[p],
which[q] thou hast chose, and[r] the hows
which[q] Y bildide[s] to thi name, that thou 35
here fro heuene her preieris and bisechyng[t], and do[u] veniaunce[v]. Forsothe[w] if 36
thei synnen aȝens thee, for no man is[x] that
synneth not, and if thou art wrooth to[y]
hem, and bitakist hem to enemyes[z]; and
enemyes[a] leden hem prisoneris in to a fer
lond, ether certis which[b] lond is nyȝ; and 37
if thei ben conuertid in her herte in the
lond, to[c] which thei ben led prisoneris,
and thei don penaunce[d], and bisechen thee
in the lond of her caitifte, and seien, We
han synned, we haue[e] do wickidly, we
diden vniustli; and[f] if thei turnen aȝen[g] 38
to thee in al her[h] herte, and in al her[i]
soule, in the lond of her[k] caitifte, to which
thei ben led, thei[l] schulen worschipe thee
aȝens the weie of her lond, which thou

[o] weie ABFH. [p] that C *pr. m.* [q] Om. C. [r] wickeli C.

[t] Lord, thou S. [u] *therfore* thei NS. [v] upon IS. [w] Also, *Lord* INS. [x] that INS. [y] and preieth in this place for INS. [z] thin arm INS. [a] streiȝt I. holdinge NS. [b] preieth BCDEFGKLMPQRUVWXbç. here thou him S. [c] 'Om. IN. [d] and, Lord S. [e] ynclepith IN. inwardli clepide S. [f] and INS. [g] Om. NS. [h] peple X. [i] knowe thei INS. [k] drede thei NS. [l] ynwardly clepid INS. [m] upon IS. [n] the which I. [o] aduersarie NS. [p] is *sett* NS. [q] that INS. [r] aȝens S. [s] haue bildid INS. [t] her bisechyng IN. her bisechingis S. [u] do thou INS. [v] veniaunce *to her aduersaries* S. [w] And INS. [x] is alyue S. [y] with S. [z] her enmyes NS. [a] if enmyes NS. [b] the which I. [c] in S. [d] *verei* penaunce I. [e] haue IS. [f] and, Lord S. [g] Om. I. [h] Om. INS. [i] Om. N. [k] Om. S. [l] *and if* thei INS.

caytyfte, to the whiche thei ben lad, thei schuln honouren thee aȝeinus the weie of their lond, that thou hast ȝeuen to their fadirs, and of the cytee that thou hast chosen, and of the hous that I haue bilde 39 to thi name ; that thou heere fro heuen, that is, fro thi fast dwellynge place, the preyers of hem, and do dome, and for-40 ȝyue to thi puple, thof synful ; thou ert forsothe my God ; I biseche, thin eeȝen ben opened, and thin eeris ben takynge heed to the orisoun that is don in this 41 place. Nowe thanne, Lord God, arijs[s] in to thi rest, thou and the ark of thi strength ; thi prestis, Lord God, ben clothed[t] helth, and thin halowes glaaden 42 thei in goodes. Lord God, ne turne thou awey the face of thi crist ; haue mynde of the mercyes of Dauid thi seruaunt. 1 And whanne Salomon hadde fulfilde heeldynge out preyers, fijr cam doun fro heuen, and deuoured the brent sacrifices, and the slayn offrynges ; and the mageste of the Lord fulfilde the hous. 2 And the prestis myȝten not goon in to the temple of the Lord ; forthi that the mageste of the Lord hadde fulfilde the 3 temple of the Lord. Bot and alle the sonis of Ysrael sawen fijr goyng doun, and the glorie of the Lord vpon the hous, and fallynge doun bowed in to the erth vpon the pament paued with stoon, honourden, and preyseden the Lord, For 'he is[u] good, for in to the world the 4 mercy of hym. The kyng forsothe, and al the puple offreden slayn offryngis beforn the Lord.

CAP. VII.

5 Kyng Salomon thanne slowȝ hoostis of oxen two and twenty thousand, of we-

hast ȝoue to the fadris of hem, and[m] of[n] the citee which thou hast chose, and[o] of the hows which[p] Y bildide to thi name ; that thou here fro heuene, that is, fro thi 39 stidefast dwellyng place, the preieris of hem, and that thou make dom, and forȝyue to thi puple, thouȝ ʻit be[q] synful ; for[r] thou art my God ; Y biseche[s], be thin 40 iȝen openyd, and thin[t] eeris be[u] ententif[v] to the preier which[w] is maad in this place. Now therfor[x], Lord God, rise[y] in to thi 41 reste, thou and the arke of thi strengthe ; Lord God, thi preestis be clothid with helthe, and thi hooli men be glad in goodis[z]. Lord God[a], turne thou not a weie 42 the face of thi crist[b] ; haue thou mynde on[c] the[d] mercyes[e] of Dauid thi seruaunt.

CAP. VII.

1 And whanne Salomon schedynge[f] prey-eris hadde fillid[g], fier cam doun fro heuene, and deuouride[h] brent[i] sacrifices, and slayn[k] sacrifices ; and the maieste[l] of the Lord fillide[m] the hows. And preestis[n] 2 myȝten not entre in to the temple of the Lord ; for the maieste[o] of the Lord hadde fillid[p] the temple of the Lord. But also 3 alle the sones of Israel sien fier comynge doun, and the glorie of the Lord on[q] the hows, and thei felden doun lowe to[r] the erthe on[q] the pawment araied[s] with stoon, and thei worschipiden, and preisiden the Lord, For he is good, for his merci is in to al[t] the world. Forsothe[u] 4 the kyng and al the puple offriden slayn sacrifices bifor the Lord. Therfor king 5 Salomon killide sacrifices of oxis[v] two and twenti thousynd, of wetheris sixe score thousynde ; and the kyng and al the puple halewiden the hows of God. Forsothe[w] 6 the preestis stoden in her offices, and de-

---

[s] ris c.   [t] clad c.   [u] Om. ᴇ pr. m.

[m] and aȝens the wey 1. and if thei shuln worshepe thee aȝens the wei s.   [n] Om. ɴ.   [o] Om. s.   [p] that ɪɴꜱ. [q] thei ben ᴇʟ. thei be ᴘ. it haue be ɪɴꜱ. Om. ʙᴄᴅꜰᴍᴏǫʀᴜᴠᴡxbꜱ.   [r] certis ɪɴꜱ.   [s] biseche thee 1. biseche thee, Lord ɴꜱ.   [t] be thin ɪɴx.   [u] Om. ɪɴx.   [v] ententif or takinge tent [heed s.] 1s.   [w] that 1.   [x] Om. ɪɴꜱ. [y] rise up ɪɴꜱ.   [z] gode thingis ɪɴꜱ.   [a] Om. s.   [b] that is, thi mercy doyng 1. marg. s. text.   [c] of ɪɴꜱb. [d] thi s.   [e] merci doyngis ɴꜱ.   [f] schedynge out his 1s. scheding out ɴ.   [g] ful eendid hem 1. fulfillid ɴ. [h] it deuouride ɪɴꜱ.   [i] the brent 1.   [k] the slayn ɪɴ.   [l] mageste or shinyng s.   [m] fulfillide ɪɴꜱ.   [n] the preestis s.   [o] miȝty schynyng ɪɴꜱ.   [p] fulfillid ɪɴꜱ.   [q] upon 1. seien vpon s.   [r] vpon s.   [s] arayed or paued s.   [t] Om. plures.   [u] And ɪɴꜱ.   [v] oxen ɪɴꜱ.   [w] And ɪɴꜱ.

thers an hundreth and twenty thousand; and the kyng bilde up the hous of God, 6 and al the puple. The prestis forsothe stooden in their offices, and the Leuytes in orgnys of dytees of the Lord, the whiche kyng Dauid maad to preysen the Lord, For in to world the mercy of hym, syngynge the ympnes of Dauid bi their hondis; bot the prestis sungyn in trumpis beforne hem, and al the puple of 7 Yrael stood. And Salomon halowed the myddil of the porche beforn the temple of the Lord; forsothe he hadde offrede there brent sacrifices, and talwes of peysible thingis, for the brasen auter that he hadde maad my3te not susteynen the brent sacrifices, and sacrifices, and talwes 8 of peysible thingus. Thanne Salamon made solempnyte in that tyme seuen days, and al Yrael with hym, a ful grete chirche, fro the entre of Emath vnto the 9 streme of Egipt. And the ey3the day he maad a collect, for thi that he halowed the auter seuen dais, and hadde halowede 10 the solempnyte seuen days. Thanne in the thre and twentithe day of the seuenth moneth he laft the puplis to their tabernaclis, ioyinge and gladynge vpon the good that God hadde don to Dauid, and 11 to Salomon, and to his puple Israel. And Salomon ful eendid the hous of the Lord, and the hous of the kyng, and alle thingus that he hadde disposed in his hert, that he do in the hous of the Lord and in his 12 owne hous; and he is maad welsum. Forsothe the Lord aperde to hym the ny3t, and seith, I haue herde thi preier, and chosen this place to me in to an hous of 13 sacrifice. 3if I schal closen heuen, and reyn flowe not, and schul senden, and comaunden to the locust, that he deuoure the lond, and schul sende pestilence in 14 to my puple; forsothe my puple turned,

kenes in[x] orguns of songis of the Lord, whiche[y] kyng Dauid made to preise the Lord, For his merci is in to the world; and thei sungen the ympnes of Dauid bi her hondis[z]; sotheli[a] the prestis sungen with trumpis bifor hem, and al the puple of Israel stood[b]. Therfor Salomon halew- 7 ide the myddil of the large[c] place bifor the temple of the Lord; for he hadde offrid there brent sacrifices, and the ynnere fatnesses[d] of pesible sacrifices, for the brasun auter which[e] he hadde maad my3te not susteyne[f] the brent sacrifices, and sacrifices[g], and the innere fatnessis[h] of pesible sacrifices. Therfor Salomon made a so- 8 lempnyte in that tyme in seuene dayes, and al[i] Israel with hym, a ful greete chirche[k], fro the entryng of Emath 'til to[l] the stronde of Egipt. And in the ei3the 9 dai he made a gaderyng of money, 'that is[m], for necessaries of the temple[n], for he hadde halewid the auter in seuene daies, and 'hadde maad[o] solempnytee[p] in seuene daies[q]. Therfor in the thre and 10 twentithe dai of the seuenthe monethe he lete the puplis go to her tabernaclis, ioiynge and gladynge on[r] the good[s] that God hadde do to Dauid, and to Salomon, and to his puple Israel. And Salomon parformyde 11 the hows of the Lord, and the hows of the kyng, and alle thingis which he hadde disposid in his herte for to do in the hows of the Lord and in his owne hows; and he hadde prosperite. Forsothe the Lord aper- 12 ide to hym in the ny3t, and seide, Y haue herd thi preiere, and Y haue chose this place to me in[t] to an hows of sacrifice. If 13 Y close heuene, and reyn cometh not doun, and if Y sende, and comaunde to a[u] locuste, that he deuoure the lond, and if Y send pestilence in[v] to my puple; for- 14 sothe[w] if my puple is conuertid[x], on[y] whiche[z] my name is clepid[a], and if it

x werin ocupied in s.   y the whiche *orgouns* i. whiche *orgons* s.   z hondis in orgons and othere instrumentis s.   a and ins.   b stood *and herde hem* is.   c greet ins.   d fatnesse ins.   e that ins.   f susteyne or *hold* s.   g sleyn sacrifices i. *othere* sacrifices ns.   h fatnesse cins.   i of n.   k chirche or *congregacioun* i. chirche or *ful miche gaderyng to gidre of peple* s.   l vnto ins.   m Om. s.   n Om. n.   o he made ins. p the solempnytee ins.   q daies, *that is, bi the space of seuen daies* s.   r vpon is.   s goodnesse s.   t and i. u the ins.   v Om. s.   w and ins.   x conuertide, *that is, al to gidre turned to me fro her vices* s.   y vpon is. z the whiche *puple* i. whiche *peple* s.   a ynwardly clepid ins.

vpon whom inwardly clepid is my name, me han preyed, and souȝt my face, and done penaunce fro their werst weyes, I schal heere fro heuen, and ben mercyable to the synnes of hem, and helyn their 15 lond. Also myn eeȝen schul ben opened, and my eeris rerid up to the horisoun of 16 hym, that in this place schal preie; for-sothe I haue chosen, and halowed this place, that my name be there in to euer-more, and my eeȝen and myn herte 17 abiden stille there alle days. Thou also, ȝif thou go before me, as ȝeede Dauid thi fadir, and dost aftir alle thingus that I haue comaundide to thee, and my riȝt-18 wisnesse and domes kepist, I schal areren the trone of thi rewme, as I behiȝte to Dauid thi fadir, seyinge, There schal not ben don awei fro thi lynage a man, that 19 be prince in Ysrael. Ȝif forsothe ȝe[v] weren turned aweiward, and forsaken myn riȝt-wisnesses and myn hestis that I haue purposed to ȝou, and goynge awey ȝe seruen to alyen goddis, and honouren 20 hem, I schal pullen ȝou vp fro my lond, that I haue ȝeuen to ȝou, and this hous that I haue bilde to my name I schal throwen awey fro my face, and taken it in to a parable, and in to exsaumple to 21 alle puplis. And this hous schal ben in 22 to a prouerbe to alle weye goeris; and thei schuln seyn, wondrynge, Why thus dide the Lord to this lond, and to this hous? And thei schuln answeryn, For thei forsoken the Lord God of their fa-ders, 'the whiche[w] lad hem out fro the lond of Egipt, and han taken alyen god-dis, and honoureden hem, and hery-eden; therfor camen vpon them alle thes euels.

bisechith me, and sekith my face, and doith penaunce of hise werste[b] weies, Y schal here[c] fro heuene, and Y schal be merciful to the synnes of hem, and Y schal heele the lond of hem. And myn 15 iȝen schulen be openyd, and myn eeren[d] schulen be reisid[e] to the preiere[f] of hym, that preieth in this place; for Y haue 16 chose, and halewid this place, that[g] my name be[h] there with outen ende, and that[i] myn iȝen and myn herte dwelle[k] there in[l] alle daies. Also if thou gost bifore me, 17 as Dauid thi fadir ȝede, and doist bi alle thingis[m] whiche Y comaundide[n] to thee, and kepist my riȝtwisnessis[o] and domes[p], Y schal reise[q] the trone of thi rewme, as 18 Y bihiȝte to Dauid thi fadir, and seide, A man of thi generacioun schal not be takun awei, that schal be prince in[r] Israel. But if ȝe turnen awey, and forsake my 19 riȝtwisnessis[s] and my comaundementis[t] whiche[u] Y settide[v] forth to ȝou, and ȝe[w] goen, and scruen alien goddis, and wor-schipen hem, Y schal drawe ȝou awey fro 20 my lond, which[x] Y ȝaf[y] to ȝou, and Y schal caste awey fro my face this hows which[z] Y haue bildid to my name, and Y schal ȝyue it in to a parable, and in to ensaum-ple to alle puplis. And this hows schal 21 be in to a prouerbe to alle men passynge forth[a]; and thei schulen seie, wondringe[b], Whi dide the Lord so to this lond, and to this hows? And thei schulen answere, 22 For thei forsoken the Lord God of her fadris, that ledde hem out of the lond of Egipt, and thei token alien goddis, and worschipiden, and herieden hem; therfor alle these yuelis camen on[c] hem.

---

[v] thou ᴇ pr. m.   [w] that c.

[b] ful yuel ɪ.   [c] here *him* ɪs.   [d] eeris ɪɴs.   [e] reisid up ɪɴs.   [f] preiers s.   [g] and s.   [h] be preisid ɴs. [i] Om. s.   [k] dwelle perfitely ɪɴs.   [l] hi ɪɴ.   [m] tho thingis ɪɴ.   [n] comaunde ɪ.   [o] riȝtfulnessis ʙᴄᴅᴇꜰɢɪᴋʟ. ᴍɴᴏᴘǫʀsᴜᴠᴡxbç.   [p] my domes ɪɴs.   [q] reise up ɪs.   [r] of ᴀ.   [s] riȝtfulnessis ʙᴄᴅᴇꜰɢᴋʟᴍᴏᴘǫʀᴜᴠᴡxbç. [t] heestis ɪɴs.   [u] the whiche ɪ.   [v] haue sett ɪɴs.   [w] *if* ȝe ɪs.   [x] that ɪ.   [y] befor ȝaue s.   [z] that ɪɴs. [a] forth *therby* ɪs.   [b] wondringe *in hem silf* ɴs.   [c] upon ɪs.

CAP. VIII.

1 Fulfild forsothe twenty ʒeer, aftir the whiche Salomon hadde bilde up the hous 2 of the Lord, and his own hous, and the citees, 'the whiche* Yram ʒaue to Salomon, he bylde up, and made the sonys of 3 Yrael to dwellen there. Also he wente 4 in to Emath Sobba, and weeldide it. And he bilde up Palmyram in desert, and othere citees most strengthid he bilde up 5 in Emath. And he maad up the oouer Betheron and the nether Betheron, citees most strengthed, hauynge ʒatis and lockis 6 and barres; Balaath also, and al the most fast cytees that weren of Salamon, and alle the cytees of plowes, and the cytees of horsmen; alle whateuer thingus he wolde, maad kyng Salamon, and disposede he bilde in Jerusalem, and in Lyban, and 7 in alle the lond of his power. Al the puple that was laft of Etheis, and Amorreis, and Phereseis, and Eueis, and Jebuseis, 8 that weren not of the stoc of Yrael, and of their sonis, and of ther after comers, 'the whiche* the sonis of Yrael hadde not slayn, Salamon vndirʒokede into* tribu- 9 tarijs vnto this day. Bot of the sonis of Yrael he vndirputte not, that thei schulden seruen to the werkis of the kyng; thei forsothe weren men fiʒters, and the first leders, and princis of plowes, 10 and of the horse men of hym; alle forsothe princes of the hoost of kyng Salamon weren two hundrith and fyfty, that 11 tauʒten the puple. The douʒter forsothe of Pharao he translatide fro the cite of Dauid in to the hous, that he hadde bilde to hyre; forsothe the kyng seide, My wijf schal not dwelle in the hous of Dauid, kyng of Yrael, forthi that it is halowed, for the ark of the Lord wente 12 in to it. Than Salamon offride brent

CAP. VIII.

Forsothe whanne twenti ʒeer weren 1 fillid[d], aftir that Salomon bildide[e] the hows of the Lord, and his owne hows, he bildide 2 the citees[f], whiche[g] Iram hadde ʒoue to Salomon; and he made the sones of Israel to dwelle there. Also he ʒede in to Emath 3 of Suba, and gat it. And he bildide Pal- 4 myram in deseert, and he bildide othere 'citees maad ful stronge[h] in Emath. And 5 he bildide the hiʒere Betheron and the lowere Betheron, wallid[l] citees, hauynge ʒatis and lockis and barris; also *he bildide* 6 Balaath, and alle 'citees ful stronge[k] that weren of Salomon; and alle the citees of cartis, and the citees of knyʒtis kyng[l] Salomon bildide, and disposide alle thingis whiche euere he wolde, in Jerusalem, and in the[m] Liban, and in al the lond of his power. Salomon[n] made suget in to tribu- 7 taries til in to this dai al the puple that was left of Etheis, and Amorreis, and Phereseis, and Eueis, and of[o] Jebuseis, that weren not of the generacioun[p] of Israel, and of the sones of hem, and of the 8 aftircomers of hem, whiche the sones of Israel hadden not slayn. Sotheli[q] of the 9 sones of Israel he[r] settide[s] not, that thei schulden serue the werkis[t] of the kyng; for thei[u] weren men werriours, and the firste[v] duykis, and princes of charis[w], and of hise knyʒtis; forsothe[x] alle the[y] princes 10 of the oost of kyng Salomon weren two hundrid and fifti, that tauʒten[z] the puple. Sotheli[a] he[b] translatide the[c] douʒter of Fa- 11 rao fro the citee of Dauid in to the[d] hows, which[e] he hadde bildid[f] to hir; for the kyng seide, My wijf schal not dwelle in the hows of Dauid, kyng of Israel, for it is halewid, for the arke of the Lord entride in to that hows. Thanne Salomon 12 offride brent sacrifices[g] to the Lord on[h]

x that c. y that c *pr. m.* z Om. c.

d fulfillid ɪɴs. e had bildid ɪɴs. f citee ɴs. g that ɪ. h ful stronge citees ɪɴs. l and made hem stronge ɪɴs. k the stronge citees ɪɴs. l and kyng x. m Om. ɪɴs. n And Salomon ɪɴs. o Om. cn. p generaciouns ɪɴs. q For ɪɴs. r Salomon ɪɴs. s sette ɪɴ. sette *or ordeined* s. t werkis *or nedis* s. u the sones of Israel s. v firste *or cheef* ɪɴ. firste of cheef s. w hise charis ɪɴs. x and ɪɴs. y Om. ɴs. z tauʒten *or ruleden* ɴs. a And ɪɴs. b Salomon ɪɴs. c his wife, the s. d an ɪɴs. e that ɪɴs. f bildide ɪɴs. g sacrifice ɪɴ. h upon ɪs.

sacrifices to the Lord vpon the auter of
the Lord, that he hadde maad up beforn
13 the ȝate hous, that by eche days wer
offrid in it, aftir the heest of Moises, in
sabotis, and in kalendis, and in feste dais,
thries bi the ȝer, that is, in the solempnyte of therfe looues, and in the solempnyte of wijkis, and in the solempnyte of
14 tabernaclis. And he sette aftir the disposicioun of Dauid, his fadir, officis of
prestis in their seruyses, and Leuytis in
their ordre, that thei preisen and mynystren beforn the prestis aftir the rijt of
eche day, and the porters in their dyui-
siouns by ȝate and ȝate. Thus forsothe
Dauid, the man of God, hadde co-
15 maundide; ne thei wenten beside fro
the maundementis of the kyng, bothe
prestis and Leuytis, of alle thingus that
he hadde comaundide. And in the wardis
16 of the tresoures alle the expensis maad
redy hadde Salomon, fro that day that
he foundide the hous of the Lord vnto
17 that day that he perfourmede it. Thanne
wente Salomon in to Asyongober, and in
to Hailath, to the mouth of the rede se,
18 that is in the lond of Edom. Thanne
Yram sente to hym, by the hondis of his
seruauntis, schippis, and wijs schipmen
of the see, and thei wenten with the seruauntis of Salomon in to Oofer, and thei
token thennis foure hundrithe and fyfty
talentis of gold, and brouȝten to kyng
Salamon.

CAP. IX.

1 And the quen of Saba, whanne sche
hadde herde the loos of Salamon, sche
cam, that sche tempte hym in dotous
questiouns in Jerusalem, with grete rychessis, and camels that beren swote spices,
and myche of gold, and precious gemmes.
And whanne sche was commen to Salamon, sche spak to hym whateuer thingis

the auter of the Lord, which[i] he hadde
bildid bifor the porche, that bi[k] alle daies 13
me[l] schulde offre[m] in[n] it, bi the comaundement[o] of Moises, in sabatis, and in kalendis, and in feeste daies, thries bi the ȝeer,
that is, in the[p] solempnyte of the[q] therf-
looues, and in[r] the solempnyte of woukis,
and in the solempnyte[s] of tabernaclis. And 14
he ordeynede bi the ordynaunce of Dauid,
his fadir, the officis of preestis in her seruyces, and the dekenes in her ordre, that
thei schulden preise[t] and mynystre bifor
preestis bi the custom of ech dai; and he
ordeynede porteris in her departyngis bi
ȝate and ȝate. For Dauid, the man of God,
hadde comaundid so; and bothe preestis 15
and dekenes passiden not fro the comaundementis[u] of the kyng of alle thingis
whiche he hadde comaundid. And Salo- 16
mon hadde alle costis[v] maad redi in the
kepingis[w] of tresouris, fro that dai in
whiche he foundide the hows of the Lord
til in to the dai in which he perfourmyde
it. Thanne Salomon ȝede in to Asion- 17
gaber, and in to Hailath, at the brynke of
the reed see, which[x] is in the lond of
Edom. Therfor Iram sente to hym[y], by 18
the hondis of his seruauntis, schippis, and
schippe men kunnyng of the see, and thei
ȝeden with the seruauntis of Salomon in
to Ophir, and thei token fro thennus foure
hundrid and fifti talentis of gold, and
brouȝten[z] to kyng Salomon.

CAP. IX.

Also[a] the queen of Saba, whanne sche 1
hadde herd the fame of Salomon, cam to[b]
tempte[c] hym in derk figuris[d]† 'in to Jerusalem[e], with[f] grete ritchessis, and camels[g],
that baren swete smellynge spices, and ful
myche of gold, and preciouse[h] iemmes,
'ether peerlis[i]. And whanne sche was
comun to Salomon, sche spak to hym what

† Figuratyf
speche is to
speke oon
thing, and to
vndirstonde
another. x s.

ᵃ Om. CE.

i that INS.   k in AS.   l men BELMX. offryng INS.   m be offrid INS.   n to S.   o heest INS.   p Om. N.
q Om. INS.   r Om. I.   s solempnytees IX pr. m.   t preise the Lord IS.   u heest INS.   v coostis or dis-
pences S.   w keping NS.   x that INS.   y Salomon S.   z thei brouȝten it IN. thei brouȝten there S.
ᵃ And b.   b in to Jerusalem for to INS.   c assaie INS.   d figuris or licknessis S.   e Om. INS.   f she cam
with S.   g with camels INS.   h of preciouse N.   i Om. IN.

2 weren in hyre herte. And Salamon expownede to hyre alle thingus that sche
purposede, ne eny thing was, that cleer
3 he maad not to hyre. The whiche aftir
that sche sawȝ, the wisdam, that is, of
Salamon, and the hous that he hadde
4 made, also and the meetis of his boord,
and the dwellyng place of his seruauntis,
and the office of his mynystris, and the
clothingis of hem, also the botelers, and
their clothis, and the slayn sacrifices that
he offride in the hous of the Lord, ther
was no more in hyre spyrite for stone-
5 ynge. And sche seide to the kyng, Sothe
is the sermoun, that I haue herde in my
6 lond, of vertues and of thi wijsdam; and
I trowed not to the tellers, to the tyme
that I my silf were comen, and myn
eeȝen hadden seen, and I hadde preued
vnneth the half of thi wijsdam to han
ben told to me; thou hast ouerpassed the
7 los in thi vertues. Blessed thi men, and
blessed thi seruauntis, and thei that
stonden neeȝ beforn thee in[b] al tyme,
8 and heeren thi wisdam. The Lord thi
God be blessid, 'the whiche[c] wolde ordeynen thee vpon his trone kyng of the
puple of the Lord thi God; forsothe for
God loueth Yrael, and wille sauyn it in
to with outen eend, therfor he putte thee
kyng vpon it, that thou do domes and
9 riȝtwisnesse. Forsothe sche ȝaue to the
kyng an hundrith and twenty talentis of
gold, and many swote spices ful myche,
and most precyous gemmes; and ther
weren not siche swote spices, as thes that
10 qween Saba ȝaue to kyng Salamon. Bot
and the seruauntis of Yram with the seruauntis of Salamon brouȝten gold fro
Oofer, and tyne trees, and gemmes most
11 precious; of the whiche the kyng made,
that is, of tyne trees, grees in the hous of

euer thingis weren in hir herte. And 2
Salomon expownede to hir alle thingis
whiche sche hadde put forth[k], and no
thing was, which[l] he made not opyn[m] to
hir. And aftir that sche siȝ these thingis, 3
that is, the wisdom of Salomon, and the
hows which[n] he hadde bildid, also and the 4
metis of his boord[o], and the dwellyng
places of seruauntis[p], and the offices of
hise[q] mynystris, and the clothis of hem,
and the boteleris, and[r] her clothis, and the
sacrifices whiche he offride in the hows of
the Lord, spirit[s] was no more[t] in hir for
wondryng[u]. And sche seide to the kyng, 5
The word[v] 'is trewe[w], which[x] Y[y] herde in
my lond[z], of thi vertues and wisdom; Y 6
bileuyde not to telleris, til Y my silf hadde
come, and myn[a] yȝen hadden seyn[b], and
Y[c] hadde preued[d] that vnnethis[e] the half
of thi wisdom was teld to me; thou hast
ouercome[f] the[g] fame bi thi vertues. Blessid 7
ben thi men, and[h] blessid ben thi seruauntis, these that stonden bifor thee in
al tyme, and heren thi wisdom. Blessid 8
be 'thi Lord God[i], that wolde ordeyne thee
on[k] his trone kyng of the puple of 'thi
Lord God[l]; treuli[m] for[n] God[o] loueth Israel, and wole[p] saue hym with outen ende,
therfor he hath set thee kyng on[q] hym[r],
that thou do domes and riȝtfulnesse[s]. For- 9
sothe[t] sche ȝaf to the kyng sixe scoore
talentis of gold, and ful many swete smellynge spices, and moost preciouse iemmes;
ther weren not siche swete smellynge
spices, as these whiche the queen of Saba
ȝaf 'to kyng[w] Salomon. But also the ser- 10
uauntis of Iram with the seruauntis of
Salomon brouȝten gold fro Ophir, and
trees of thyne, and most preciouse iemmes;
of whiche, that is, of the trees of thyne[x], 11
the kyng made grees[y] in the hows of the
Lord, and in the hows of the kyng, 'harpis

[b] Om. c. [c] that c.

[k] forth *to him* IS. [l] that INS. [m] opyn *or knowen* IS. [n] that INS. [o] tablis INS. [p] hise seruauntis INS. [q] Om. c. [r] of CELPU. [s] ther I. [t] more spirit I. [u] wondryng, *for these thingis passeden hir vnderstondyng* S. [v] word *or fame* S. [w] Om. I. [x] that INS. [y] is N. [z] lond is trewe I. [a] til myn IN. [b] sein, *that is, til Y had vndirstonde these thingis of thi self* S. [c] til that Y INS. [d] preued *it* I. [e] vnnethe I. [f] ouercome *or passid* INS. [g] thi INS. [h] Om. S. [i] the Lord thi God INS. [k] upon IS. [l] the Lord thi God INS. [m] Om. IN. [n] certis INS. [o] the Lord God N. [p] he wole INS. [q] upon IS. [r] Israel INS. [s] riȝtwisnesse INS. [t] And INS. [w] Om. NS. [x] thyn trees NS. [y] greecis NS.

the Lord, and in the hous of the kyng,
also harpis, and sawtrees to syngers;
neuer ben seen in the lond of Juda siche
12 trees. Kyng forsothe Salamon ȝaue to
the qween of Saba alle thingus that sche
wolde, and that sche asked, many mo
than sche brouȝte to hym. The whiche
turnede aȝein wente into hyre lond with
13 hyre seruauntis. Forsothe the weiȝt of
gold, that was offerd to Salamon by ech
ȝeer, was sixe hundrith and sixe and
14 sixty talentis of gold, outaken that soum
that legatis of dyuerse gentylis, and mer-
chauntis weren wont to 'bryngen to[d], and
alle the kyngis of Arabie, and satrapis
of londis, that brouȝten gold and syluer
15 to Salamon. Thanne kyng Salamon maad
two hundrith golden speris of the soum
of sixe hundrith golde platis, the whiche
16 in alle the speris weren spred abrod; also
thre hundrith golden scheldis of thre hundrith gold platis, with the whiche alle
the scheldis weren couerd; and the kyng
putte hem in the armerie place, that was
17 sett[e] in the wode. Also kyng Salomon
made a grete yuere sete, and clothed it
18 with most clene gold; and sixe grees, in
the[f] whiche men steyȝede up to the sete,
and a golden stole, and two lytyll armys,
either aȝeinus other, and two lyouns stond-
19 ynge besides the litil aarmes, bot and
other twelue litil lyouns stondynge vpon
the sixe grees on either party. There
was not siche a kyngis see in alle rewmes.
20 And alle the vessels of the kyngis feste
weren golden, and the vessels of the hous
of saltus Liban of most pure gold; syluer forsothe in tho days for nouȝt was
21 countid. Forsothe and the schippis of
the kyng wenten in Tharsis with the
seruauntis of Yram oones in thre ȝeer,

'also[z], and sautrees to syngeris; siche trees
weren neuere seyn in the lond of Juda.
Forsothe[a] Salomon ȝaf to the queen of 12
Saba alle thingis whiche sche wolde, and
whiche sche axide, many moo than sche
hadde[b] brouȝt to hym. And sche turnede
aȝen, and ȝede in to hir lond with hir seruauntis. Forsothe[c] the weiȝt of gold, that 13
was brouȝt to Salomon bi ech ȝeer, was
sixe hundrid and sixe and sixti talentis of
gold, outakun that summe whiche[d] the[e] 14
legatis of dyuerse folkis, and marchauntis
weren wont to brynge, and[f] alle the kyngis
of Arabie, and the[g] princes of londis[h], that[i]
brouȝten togidere gold and siluer to Salomon. Therfor[j] kyng Salomon made two 15
hundrid goldun speris of the summe of
sixe hundrid 'floreyns, *ether peesis of
gold*[k], that[l] weren spendid in ech spere;
and he made thre hundrid goldun scheeldis 16
of thre hundrid floreyns[m], with whiche ech
scheeld[n] was hilid; and the kyng puttide
tho[o] in the armure place, that was set[p] in
the[q] wode. Also the kyng made a greet 17
seete[r] of yuer, and clothide[s] it with clennest[t] gold; and *he made* sixe grees[u], bi 18
whiche me[v] stiede[w] to[x] the seete, and a[y]
goldun stool, and tweyne armes, oon aȝens
'the tother[z], and twei liouns stondynge bisidis the armes; but also *he made* twelue 19
othere[a] litle liouns stondynge on[b] sixe
grees[c] on euer either side[d]. Siche a seete[e]
was not in alle rewmes[f]. And 'alle the 20
vessels of the feeste of the kyng weren of
gold, and the vessels of the hows of the
forest of the[g] Liban *weren* of pureste[h]
gold; for siluer in tho daies was arettid
for[i] nouȝt. For[k] also the schippis of the 21
kyng ȝeden in to Tharsis with the seruauntis of Iram onys in thre ȝeer, and
brouȝten[l] fro thennus gold, and siluer, and

[d] offren E *pr. m.* [e] planed E *pr. m.* [f] Om. c.

[z] and also he made harpis INS. [a] And INS. [b] Om. S. [c] And INS. [d] that INS. [e] Om. INS. [f] and *outaken that* that I. and *withouten the summe* that S. [g] Om. INS. [h] *othere* londis I. diuers londis S. [i] the whiche I. whiche NS. [j] For N. [k] scutis *or floryns* [*peesis* N. *floryns or pecis* S.] *of gold* INS. Om. CD. [l] whiche INS. [m] peesis of gold INS. [n] spere INS. [o] tho *speris* IS. [p] ordeyned N. set *or ordeyned* S. [q] a INS. [r] seete *or a trone* IS. seete *or trone* N. [s] he hilide INS. [t] moost clene I. [u] greecis NS. [v] men ELS. [w] stiede up INS. [x] into K. [y] he made therto a NS. [z] that oother I. [a] Om. A *pr. m. et plures.* [b] upon INS. [c] greecis NS. [d] side of the trone INS. [e] trone INS. [f] rewmes, *that is, in noon of al the rewmes of the world* S. [g] Om. INS. [h] moost pure INS. [i] at S. [k] Om. INS. [l] thei brouȝten INS.

and thei brouȝten thennus gold, and syl-
22 uer, and yuer, and apis, and poos. Thanne
Salamon is magnified vpon alle the kyngis
23 of erth for rychesse and glorie. And
alle the kyngis of londis desireden to seen
the face of Salamon, that thei heeren the
wijsdam that God hadde ȝeuen in the
24 herte of hym; and thei brouȝten to hym
ȝiftes, sylueren vessels and golden, clothes
and armes, and spices, hors and mulis,
25 by alle ȝeeris. And Salamon hadde fourty
thousand of hors in his stallis, and of
charis and of horsmen twelue thousand;
and he sette hem in the cytees of 'foure
horsid carris[g], and where the kyng was
26 in Jerusalem. Forsothe he enhauntide
power vpon alle the kyngis, fro the flode
of Eufrate vnto the lond of Philisteis, and
27 vnto the termes of Egipt. And so myche
plente of syluer he ȝaue in Jerusalem, as
of stoones, and of cedres so myche multitude, as of wijlde mulberye trees that
28 ben sprungyn in wijld feeldis. Forsothe
ther weren brouȝt hors fro Egipt, and
29 of alle regyouns. The remnaunt forsothe
of the rather werkis of Salamon and of
the last ben wrijten in the wordis of Nathan, the prophete, and in the wordis of
Achie Sylonyte, and in the visioun of
Addo, scar, aȝeins Jeroboam, the sone of
30 Nabath. Salamon forsothe regnede in
Jerusalem vpon al Yrael fourety ȝere,
and he slepte with his fadirs; and thei
birieden hym in the cytee of Dauid, and
Roboam, his sone, regned for hym.

CAP. X.

1 Roboam forsothe wente in to Sychem;
thidre forsothe al Yrael was comen to
2 gydre that thei setten hym kyng. The
whiche thing whan Jeroboam, the sone
of Nabath, that was in Egypt, hadde
herd; forsothe he hadde flowen thidre

yuer[m], and[n] apis, and pokokis[o]. Therfor[p] 22
kyng Salomon was magnyfied ouer alle
kyngis of erthe[q] for richessis[r] and glorie.
And alle the kyngis of londis desireden to 23
se the face of Salomon, for to here the wisdom which[s] God hadde ȝoue in his herte;
and thei brouȝten to hym ȝiftis, vessels of 24
siluer and of gold, clothis and armuris,
and swete smellynge spices, horsis and
mulis, bi ech ȝeer. Also[t] Salomon hadde 25
fourti thousynde of horsis in stablis[u], and
twelue thousynde of charis and of[v]
knyȝtis; and 'he ordeynede[w] hem[x] in the
citees of charis, and where[y] the kyng was
in Jerusalem. Forsothe[z] he[a] vside power 26
on[b] alle the kyngis[c], fro the flood Eufrates[d]
'til to[e] the lond of Filisteis, and 'til to[f] the
termes[g] of Egipt. And he ȝaf so greet 27
plente of siluer in Jerusalem, as of stoonys,
and so greet multitude of cedris[h], as[i] of
sycomoris that growen in feeldi places.
Forsothe[k] horsis weren brouȝt[l] fro Egipt, 28
and fro alle cuntreis. Sotheli the residue[m] 29
of the formere werkis and the[n] laste of
Salomon ben writun in the wordis of Nathan, the prophete, and in the wordis[o] of
Achie of Silo, and in the visioun, '*ether
prophesie*[p], of Addo, the prophete[q], aȝens
Jeroboam, sone[r] of Nabath. Sotheli[s] Sa- 30
lomon regnede in Jerusalem on[t] al Israel
fourti ȝeer, and he slepte with his fadris;
and thei birieden hym in the citee of Dauid, and Roboam, his sone, regnyde for
hym.

CAP. X.

Forsothe Roboam ȝede forth in to Si- 1
chem; for al Israel came togidere thidur to
make hym kyng. And whanne Jeroboam, 2
the[u] sone of Nabath, that was in Egipt[w],
'for he[x] fledde thidur[y] bifor Salomon, hadde
herd this[z], he turnyde aȝen anoon. And 3

[g] ploowes E.

[m] Om. S. [n] Om. IS. [o] pekokis INS. [p] And INS. [q] the erthe S. [r] *hise* richessis INS. [s] that INS. [t] And INS. [u] his stablis S. [v] Om. S. [w] ordeyne N. [x] hem *to dwelle* I. tho kniȝtis *to dwelle* S. [y] *there* where I. [z] And INS. [a] Salomon INS. [b] upon IS. [c] knyȝtis V. [d] of Eufrates INS. [e] vnto IN. [f] vnto INS. [g] termes *or coostis* S. [h] cedre trees IN. there was of cedre trees S. [i] *was* as I. [k] And INS. [l] brouȝt to Salomon S. [m] remenaunt INS. [n] of the INS. [o] word S. [p] Om. IN. [q] prophete *propheciynge* IS. [r] the sone I. [s] Certis INS. [t] upon INS. [u] Om. NX. [w] Egipt, had herd this INS. [x] the whiche I. whiche NS. [y] in to Egipt INS. [z] *the deeth of* Salamon I. Salamon diede N. Salomon deiyng S.

beforn Salomon; anoon he is turned
3 aȝeyn. And thei clepiden hym, and he
came with al Ysrael, and thei speeken to
4 Roboam, seiynge, Thi fadir with most
harde ȝok oppressed us; thou comaunde
liȝter than thi fadir, 'the whiche^h putte
to us a grete seruage; and a litil wiȝt of
the charge put off, that we seruen to thee.
5 The whiche seith, Aftir thre days turneth
aȝein to me. And whan the puple was
6 gone aweie, he wente in counseil with
the olde men, that stoden beforn his fadir
Salamon, while ȝit he lyuede, seyinge,
What ȝeue ȝe of counseil, that I answer
7 to the puple? The whiche seyden to
hym, ȝif thou plese to this puple, and
soften hem with mercyable wordis, thei
8 schulen seruen to thee al tyme. And he
laft the counceil of olde men, and with
ȝonge men begunne to treeten, that with
hym were nurischid, and weren in the
9 felawschip of hym. And he seide to hem,
What to ȝou semeth? or what schal I answeren to this puple, that seide to me,
Hene of the ȝok, that thi fader putte vnto
10 us? And thei answerden, as ȝonge men
and nurschid with hym in delices, and
seiden, Thus thou schalt answeren to the
puple that seide to thee, Thi fadir ag-
gregide oure ȝok, thou putte off; thus
thou schalt answeren to hem, My lest
fynger is gretter than the reynes of my
11 fadir; my fadir putte to ȝou a grete ȝok,
and I schal putten to a more weiȝte; my
fader beet ȝou with scourgis, I forsothe
12 schal beten ȝou with scorpiouns. Thanne
Jeroboam came and al the puple the
thidde day to Roboam, as he hadde co-
13 maundide to hem. And the kyng answerde hard thingus, the counseil laft of
14 the eldre^i, spokyn aftir the will of ȝong

thei clepiden hym, and he cam with al
Israel, and thei spaken to Roboam, and
seiden, Thi fadir oppresside vs with ful^a 4
hard ȝok; comaunde thou liȝtere thingis^b
than thi fadir^c, that^d settide^e on^f vs a
greuouse seruage^g; and releese thou a litil
of 'the birthun^h, that we serue thee. And
he^i seide, After thre daies turne ȝe aȝen
to me. And whanne the puple was goon,
he took counsel with^k elde men, that^l 6
stoden bifor his fadir Salomon, while he
lyuyde ȝit, and seide^m, What counsel
ȝyuen ȝe, that Y answere to the puple?
And thei seiden to hym, If thou plesist 7
this puple, and makist hem softe^n bi meke
wordis, thei schulen serue thee in al tyme.
And^o he^p forsook the^q counsel of elde^r men, 8
and bigan^s to trete^t with ȝonge men, that^u
weren nurischid with hym, and weren in
his cumpenye. And he seide to hem, 9
What semeth to ȝou? ether what^w owe Y
answere^x to this puple, that seide to me,
Releese thou the ȝok, which^y thi fadir
puttide^z on^a vs? And thei answeriden, as 10
ȝonge men^b and nurschyd with hym in
delicis, and seiden^c, Thus thou schalt speke
to the puple that seide to thee, Thi fadir
made^d greuouse oure ȝok, releese thou^e;
and thus^f thou schalt answere to hem, My
leeste fyngur is gretter than the leendis of
my fader; my fadir puttide^g on^h ȝou a 11
greuouse ȝok, and Y schal leie to a gretter
birthun; my fadir beet^i ȝou with scourgis,
forsothe^k Y schal bete ȝou with 'scorpiouns, that is^l, hard knottid roopis^ll.
Therfor^m Jeroboam and^n al the puple cam 12
to Roboam in the thridde dai, as he hadde
comaundid to hem. And 'the kyng an- 13
sweride harde thingis^o, after that he^p hadde
forsake the counsel of the^q eldere men, and^r 14
he spak bi the wille of the^s ȝonge men^t,

---

h that c.   i elders c.

a a ful INS.   b thingis on us I. thingis to be don to vs S.   c fadir dide S.   d the whiche I. which NS.
c sette I. hath sett NS.   f vpon IS.   g seruage or charge S.   h oure charge I. oure burthun NS.   i Roboam INS.   k of S.   l whiche INS.   m he seide INS.   n softe or esye I. softe or quietest hem S.   o Om. S.
P Roboam INS.   q this S.   r the elde BCEFLMORVWh. the eldere P.   s he bigan N.   t trete and councele N.
trete a consel S.   u the whiche I. whiche NS.   w what thing INS.   x to answere S.   y that INS.   z hath
putt INS.   a upon IS.   b Om. S.   c thei seiden INS.   d hath mnad IN.   e thou it IN.   f Om. EFKLMNSXbç.
g hath put I. put S.   h vpon S.   i betide I.   k but INS.   l Om. IN.   ll roopis, that ben scorpiouns I.
m And INS.   n with INS.   o Om. INS.   P the kyng INS.   q Om. INSX.   r Om. S.   s Om. INS.   t men, he
answeride hard thingis to the peple INS.

meu; My fadir putte an heuy ȝok to ȝou, and I schal maken heuyar; my fadir beet ȝou with scourgis, I forsothe schal becten 15 ȝou with scorpiouns. And he assentide not to the preyers of the puple; forsothe the wille of God was, that his word schuld ben fulfild, that he hadde spoken by the hond of Achie Sylonyte to Jero- 16 boam, the sone of Nabath. Al the puple forsothe, the kyng seyinge harder thingus, thus spak to hym, There is not to us part in Dauid, ne heritage in the sone of Ysay; turne aȝein in to thi tabernaclis, Yrael, thou forsothe feed thin hons, Dauith. And Yrael wente in to their 17 tabernaclis. Vpon forsothe the sonis of Yrael, that dwelleden in the cytees of 18 Juda, regnede Roboam ᵏ. And kyng Roboam seute Aduram, that stode vpon the tributis; and the sones of Yrael stooneden hym, and he is deed. Bot kyng Roboam heeȝede to steyȝen up the 19 chaar, and fleiȝ in to Jerusalem. And Yrael wente awey fro the hous of Da- uid vnto this day. It is done forsothe, whanne al Yrael hadde herd, that Jero- boam was turned aȝein, thei senten, and clepeden hym, the companye gederd, and setten kyng vpon al Yrael; ne any man folowed the hous of Dauid, saue the lynage of Juda and Beniamyn allon.

Myᵘ fadir puttideʳ onʷ ȝou a greuouse ȝok, which Y schal make greuousere; my fadir beetˣ ȝou with scourgisʸ, sotheliᶻ Y schal bete ȝou with scorpiounsᵃ. And heᵇ 15 assentide not to theᶜ preieris of the puple; forᵈ it was the wille of God, that his word schulde be fillidᵉ, whichᶠ he hadde spoke bi the hond of Ahie ofᵍ Silo to Jeroboam, soneʰ of Nabath. Sotheliⁱ whanne the kyng 16 seideᵏ hardereˡ thingis, al the puple spak thus to hym, No part isᵐ to vs in Dauidⁿ, nether critage in the sone of Isaiᵒ; Israel, turne thou aȝen in to thi tabernaclis, so- theliᵖ thou, Dauid, feede thin�q howsʳ. And Israel ȝede in to hise tabernaclis. For- 17 sotheˢ Roboam regnede onᵗ the sones of Israel, thatᵘ dwelliden in the citees of Juda. And kyngʸ Roboam sente Adhu- 18 ram, that was souereyn ouerʷ the tributis; and the sones of Israel stonyden hym, and he was deed. Certisˣ kyngʸ Roboam hastideᶻ to stieⁿ in to theᵇ chare, and fleddeᶜ in to Jerusalem. And Israel ȝede 19 awei fro the hows of Dauid 'til toᵈ this dai. Forsotheᵉ† it was doon, whanne al Israel hadde herd, that Jeroboam turnede aȝen, thei senten, and clepiden hym, whanne the cumpeny was gaderidᶠ, and thei or- deyneden him king onᵍ al Israel; and noʰ man, outakun the lynageⁱ of Judaᵏ aloone, suede 'the hows of Dauidˡ.

† *Forsothe;* fro this place to the ende of this chapitre it is not of the text, for it is not in Ebreu, ne- ther in bokis amendid, but is takun of the thridde book of Kyngis, xii. cᵒ. *Lire here.* c,

CAP. XI.

1 Roboam forsothe came into Jerusalem, and clepide al the hous of Juda and of Beniamyn, vnto an hundrith and eiȝty thousand of chosen fiȝtynge men, that he fiȝte aȝeynus Ysrael, and turne to hym his 2 rewme. And the word of the Lord is maad toˡ Semyam, the man of God, sey- 3 inge, Speke to Roboam, the sone of Sala-

CAP. XI.

Forsotheᵐ Roboam cam in to Jerusalem, 1 and clepidenⁿ togidere al the howsᵒ of Juda and of Beniamyn, 'til toᵖ nyne scoore thousynde of chosen men andq werriouris, for to fiȝte aȝens Israel, and for to turneʳ his rewme to hym. And the word of the 2 Lord was maad to Semeye, the man of God, and seide, Speke thou to Roboam, 3

ᵏ Jeroboam ʙ *pr. m.* ˡ Om. ʙ.

ᵘ *and seide,* My ɴs. ᵛ hath putt ɪɴs. ʷ upon ɪs. ˣ betide ɪ. ʸ pleyn scourgis s. ᶻ but ɪɴs. ᵃ plumbid cordis ɪɴs. ᵇ Roboam ɪɴs. ᶜ Om. ɴs. ᵈ certis ɪɴs. ᵉ fulfillid ɪɴs. ᶠ that ɪɴs. ᵍ and s. ʰ the sone ɪ.ɴsbc. ⁱ And ɪɴs. ᵏ had seid ɪɴs. ˡ *these* hardere ɪs. ᵐ Om. ɪ. be ɴs. ⁿ *the lynage* of Dauid ɪ. Dauith *linage* s. ᵒ Ysay be among vs s. ᵖ and ɪɴs. q thin owen ɪɴs. ʳ meynee ɪɴs. ˢ And ɪɴs. ᵗ upon ɪs. ᵘ the whiche ɪ. whiche ɴs. ᵛ the kyng ɪ. ʷ of s. ˣ And ɪɴs. ʸ the kyng ɪ. ᶻ hastide him ɪs. ᵃ stie up ɪs. ᵇ his ɪɴs. ᶜ he fledde ɪɴs. ᵈ vnto ɪɴs. to x. ᵉ And ɪɴs. ᶠ gaderid togidre ɪɴs. ᵍ upon ɪs. ʰ eueri s. ⁱ linagis s. ᵏ Juda and of Beniamyn x *sec. m.* ˡ hym s. ᵐ Sothely ɪɴs. ⁿ he clepide ɪɴs. ᵒ meynee ɪɴs. ᵖ vnto ɪɴs. to x. q Om. ɪs. ʳ turne aȝen ɪɴs.

mon, kyng of Juda, and to al Yrael, that
4 is in Juda and Beniamyn; Thes thingis
seith the Lord, ȝe schul not steyȝen up,
ne fiȝten aȝeyn ȝoure bretheren; turne
aȝein ech oon[m] in to his hous, for this is
doon by my wille. The whiche whan
hadden herd the word of the Lord, ben
torned aȝeiu, ne thei wenten aȝeinus kyng
5 Jeroboam. Roboam forsothe dwellide in
Jerusalem, and he bilde up wallid cytees
6 in Juda; and he maad out Bethleem, and
7 Ethan, and Thecue, and Bethsur; also
8 and Sochot, and Odollam; also and Jeth,
9 and Mareza, and Ciph; but and Huram,
10 and Lachis, and Arecha; Saraa also, and
Haylon, and Ebron, that weren in Juda
and Beniamyn, cytees most strengthed.
11 And whanne he hadde closed hem with
wallis, he putte in hem princes of metis,
and bernes, that is, of oyle and of wijne.
12 Bot and to alle the cytees he maad armour places of scheeldis, and of speris,
and he fastnede hem with most diligence,
and comaundide vpon Judam, and vpon
13 Benjamin. The prestis forsothe and Leuytis, that weren in al Ysrael, camen to
14 hym fro al their seetis, forsakyng suburbis and their possessiouns, and goynge
ouer to Juda and to[n] Jerusalem; forthi
that Jeroboam hadde cast hem awey, and
his aftir comers, that thei vsen not the
15 presthood of the Lord; the whiche ordeynede to hym silf prestis of heeȝe
thingis, and of deuyls, and of calues, 'the
16 whiche[o] he hadde made. Bot and of al
the lynagis of Yrael, whiche euer hadde
ȝeuen their herte that thei sechen the
Lord God of Yrael, came to Jerusalem to
offryn their slayn sacrificis before the
17 Lord God of their faders. And thei
strengtheden the kyngdam of Juda, and
to gither strengtheden Roboam, the sone
of Salamon bi thre ȝeer; forsothe thei
wenten in the weies of Dauid, and of

the sone of Salomon, kyng of Juda, and to
al Israel, which[s] is in Juda and Beniamyn; The Lord seith these thingis, ȝe 4
schulen not stie[t], nethir ȝe schulen[u] fiȝte
aȝens ȝoure britheren; ech man turne aȝen
in[v] to his hows, for this thing is doon bi
my wille. And whanne thei hadden herd
the word of the Lord, thei turneden aȝen,
and ȝeden not aȝens kyng[w] Jeroboam.
Forsothe[x] Roboam dwellide in Jerusalem, 5
and he bildide wallid citees in Juda; and 6
bildide[y] Bethleem, and Ethan, and Thecue,
and Bethsur; and Sochot, and Odollam; 7
also and Jeth, and Maresa, and Ziph; but[8][9]
also Huram[z], and Lachis, and Azecha; and 10
Saraa, and Hailon, and Ebron, that[a] weren
in Juda and Beniamyn, ful strong citees.
And whanne he hadde closid tho with 11
wallis, he settide[b] 'in tho citees princes[c],
and[d] bernes of metis, that is, of oile, and
of wyn. But also in ech citee he made 12
placis of armuris of scheeldis, and speris,
and he made tho strong with most diligence; and he regnyde on Juda and Beniamyn. Sotheli[e] the preestis and dekenes[f], 13
that[g] weren in al Israel, camen to hym[h]
fro alle her seetis[i], and forsoken[k] her sub- 14
arbis and possessiouns[l], and thei passiden
to[m] Juda and to Jerusalem; for Jeroboam
and hise aftir comeris hadden cast hem
awey, that thei schulden not be set in
preesthod[n] of the Lord; which[o] Jeroboam 15
made to hym preestis of hiȝe places, and
of feendis, and of caluys, which he hadde
maad. But also of alle the linagis of Is- 16
rael, whiche euer ȝauen her herte to seke
the Lord God of Israel, thei camen to Jerusalem for to offre her sacrifices bifor the
Lord God of her fadris. And thei strength- 17
iden the rewme of Juda, and strengthiden[p] Roboam, the sone of Salomon, bi thre
ȝeer; for thei ȝeden in the weies of Dauid,
and of Salomon, oneli bi thre ȝeer. For- 18
sothe Roboam weddide a wijf Malaoth,

m Om. c.　n Om. ACEF. in H.　o that c pr. m.

s that INS.　t stie up INS.　u shuln not s.　v Om. s.　w the kyng I.　x And INS.　y he bildide INS.
x he bildide Huram INS.　a whiche INS.　b sette INS.　c princes in hem I.　d and he ordeyned in hem s.
e And INS.　f the dekenes s.　g which s.　h Roboam NS.　i citees N.　k thei forsoken INS.　l her possessiouns INS.　m in to s.　n the presthood s.　o the which I.　p thei strengthiden INS.

18 Salomon, al oonly thre ʒeer. Forsothe Roboam weddide a wijf Malaoth, the douʒter of Jerymuth, sone of Dauid, and Abiail, the douʒter of Heliab, sone of 19 Ysaye; the whiche bare to hym sonis, 20 Jeus, and Somoriam, and Jereum. And aftir this he toke Maacham, the douʒtir of Absalon, that bare to hym Abia, and 21 Thai, and Sisa, and Salomyth. Forsothe Roboam louede Maacham, the douʒter of Absalon, ouer alle his wijues and secundaries. Forsothe eiʒtene wijues he weddide, secundarie wijues forsothe sixty; and he gate eiʒte and twenty sonis, and 22 sixty douʒters. Forsothe he sette in the heued Abiam, the sone of Maacha, duke ouer alle his bretheren; he thouʒte for-23 sothe to makyn hym kyng, for wijser and myʒtyer ouer alle his sonis, and in alle the coostis of Juda and of Beniamyn, and in alle the walled cytees; and he ʒaue to hem many metis, and he hadde many wijues.

the douʒtir of Jerymuth, sone^q of Dauid, and^r Abiail, the douʒtir of Heliab, sone^s of Ysaye; and sche childide to hym sones, 19 Yeus, and Somorie, and Zerei. Also after 20 this *wijf* he took Maacha, the douʒter of Abissalon, and sche childide to hym Abia, and Thai, and Ziza, and Salomyth. For-21 sothe^t Roboam louyde Maacha, the douʒtir of Abissalon, aboue alle hise wyues and secundarie^u wyues. Forsothe^v he hadde weddid eiʒtene wyues, sotheli^w sixti secundarie wyues; and he gendride^x eiʒte and twenti sones, and sixti douʒtris. Sotheli^y 22 he ordeynede Abia, the sone of Maacha, in^z the heed, duyk ouer^a alle hise britheren; for^b he thouʒte to make Abia kyng, for *he* 23 *was* wiscre and myʒtiere ouer alle hise sones, and in alle the coostis of Juda and of Beniamyn, and in alle wallid^c citees^d; and he ʒaf to hem ful many metis^e, and he^f had^g many^h wyues.

CAP. XII.

1 And whanne the rewme of Roboam was strengthed and confermed, he for-soke the lawe of the Lord, and al Yrael 2 with hym. The fyfthe ʒeer forsothe of the regne of Roboam steyʒede up Sesach, the kyng of Egypt, in to Jerusalem, for 3 thei hadden synned to the Lord; with a thousand and two hundrith chaaris, and sixty thousand horsmen, and ther was no noumbre of the comoun, that came with hym fro Egipt, Libies, that is, and 4 Erogodite, and Ethiopes. And he tok the most strengthed cytees in Juda, and 5 came vnto Jerusalem. Semeias forsothe, the prophete, wente in to Roboam, and the princes of Juda, that weren gadered in to Jerusalem, fleeʒyng Sesach. And he seide to hem, Thes thinges seith the Lord, ʒe han forsaken me, and I haue

CAP. XII.

And whanne the rewme of Roboam was 1 maad strong and coumfortid, he forsook the lawe of the Lord, and al Israel with hym. Sotheliⁱ in the fyuethe ʒeer of the 2 rewme of Roboam Sesach, the^k kyng of Egipt, stiede^l in to Jerusalem, for thei^m synneden aʒens the Lord; and *he*ⁿ *stiede*^o 3 with a thousynde and two hundrid charys, and with^p sixti thousynde of^q horse men, and no noumbre was of the comyn puple, that cam with hym fro Egipt, that is, Libiens, and Trogoditis, and Ethiopiens. And he^r took ful stronge citees in Juda, 4 and he cam 'til to^s Jerusalem. Forsothe^t 5 Semei, the prophete, entride to Roboam, and to the princes of Juda, whiche^u fleynge fro Sesach weren gaderid togidere 'in to^v Jerusalem. And he seide to hem, The Lord seith these thingis, ʒe han forsake

q the sone I.   r Om. N.   s the sone INS.   t And INS.   u hise secoundarie INS.   v and INS.   w and he hadde INS.   x gaat I.   y And INS.   z Om. S.   a among ouer S.   b and INS.   c the wallid S.   d citees *he sette his sones* I. citees *Roboam ordeined his sones* S.   e Om. NS.   f Om. A.   g hadden I. took to hem NS.   h ful many CEL.   i And INS.   k Om. INS.   l stiede up INS.   m thei, *that is, the men of Jerusalem* S.   n Sesach INS.   o stiede up I. stiede up thidir NS.   p Om. ᴄᴅᴇꜰɢᴋʟᴍᴏᴘǫʀᴜxʙꞓ.   q Om. W.   r Sesach INS.   s vnto IN. into S. to X.   t And INS.   u the whiche I.   v in NS.

6 forsaken 30u in the hond of Sesach. And
the princis of Yrael and the kyng aferd
7 seyden, Ri3twijs is the Lord. And
whanne the Lord hadde seen that thei
weren meked, the word of the Lord is
doon to Semeiam, seyinge, For thei ben
meekid, I schal not leesen hem, and I
schal 3euen to hem a lytyll of help, and
my woodnesse schal not droppen upon
8 Jerusalem by the hond of Sesach. Neuer
the later thei schul serue to hym, that
thei knowen the distaunce of my seruyce
and of the seruyse of the rewme of londis.
9 And so Sesach, kyng of Egipt, wente
awei fro Jerusalem, the tresoures taken
awei of the hous of the Lord, and of the
hous of the kyng; and alle thingis he
toke with hym, and the golden tergetis
10 'the whiche[P] Salamon hadde maad, for
the whiche the kyng made brasen, and
toke hem to the princis of the tergeteris,
'the whiche[q] kepten the vestiarie of the
11 paleis. And whanne the kyng schulde
goone in to the house of the Lord, the
tergeters camen, and token hem, and eft
beeren hem a3ein to his armorie place.
12 Neuer the later for thei ben meekid, the
wrath of the Lord is torned awey fro
hem, and thei ben not don awei al oute;
forsothe and in Juda ben founden good
13 werkis. Thanne Roboam is coumfortid
in Jerusalem, and regnede. Forsothe of
oon and fourty 3eer he was, whanne he
beganne to regnen, and ei3tene 3eer he
regnede in Jerusalem, the citee that the
Lord chees that he conferme his name
there, of alle the lynagis of Yrael. The
name forsothe of his moder Naama
14 Amanyte. And he dide euyl, and he
greithede not his herte for[r] to sechen
15 God. The werkis forsothe of Roboam,
the first and the last, ben writen in the
bokis of Semei the prophete, and of

me, and Y haue forsake 30u in the hond
of Sesach. And the princes of Israel and 6
the kyng weren astonyed, and seiden, The
Lord is iust. And whanne the Lord hadde 7
seyn that thei weren mekid, the word of the
Lord was maad to Semey, and seide, For
thei ben mekid, Y schal not distrie hem,
and Y schal 3yue to hem a litil help, and
my stronge veniaunce schal not droppe[w]
on[x] Jerusalem[y] bi the hond of Sesach.
Netheles thei schulen serue hym, that thei 8
knowe the dyuersitee of my seruyce and
of the seruyce of the rewme of londis.
Therfor Sesach, the kyng of Egipt, 3ede 9
awey fro Jerusalem, aftir that he hadde
take awei the tresouris of the hows of the
Lord, and of the kyngis hows; and he
took alle thingis with hym, and the goldun
scheeldis whiche Salomon hadde maad, for 10
whiche[z] the[a] kyng[b] made brasun scheeldis,
and took[c] tho to the princes of scheeld
makeris, that kepten the porche of the
paleis. And[d] whanne the kyng entride 11
in to the hows of the Lord, the scheeld-
makeris camen, and token tho[e], and eft
brou3ten[f] tho[g] to[h] his[i] armure place. Ne- 12
theles for thei weren mekid, the ire of the
Lord was turned awei fro hem, and thei
weren not don awei outirli; for good
werkis weren foundyn also in Juda. Ther- 13
for kyng[k] Roboam was coumfortid in Jerusalem, and regnede[l]. Forsothe[m] he was
of oon and fourti 3eer, whanne he bigan
to regne, and he reguyde seuentene 3eer
in Jerusalem, the citee which[n] the Lord
chees of alle the lynagis of Israel, that he
schulde conferme his name there. Forsothe[o] the name of his modir was Naama
Amanytis. And he[p] dide yuel, and he 14
made not redi his herte to seke God. So- 15
theli[q] the firste and the laste werkis of
Roboam ben writun, and diligentli de-
clarid in the bookis of Semei the profete,

P that c pr. m. q that c. r Om. c.

w distrie w. x in ELP. upon INS. Om. w. y Israel A pr. m. z whiche scheldis I. whiche goldun
scheeldis NS. a Om. NS. b king Roboam NS. c he bitoke INS. d Om. S. e tho scheldus I. tho
brasun sheeldis S. f thei brou3ten INS. g hem IN. h a3en to INS. i the kyngis NS. k the kyng I.
l regnede there INS. m And INS. n that INS. o And INS. P Roboam INS. q And INS.

16 Abdo sear, and besily expownede. And Roboam and Jeroboam fou3ten a3einus hem seluen alle days. And Roboam slepte with his fadirs, and is biried in the cyte of Dauid; and Abia, his sone, regnede for hym.

and of Abdo the profete. And Roboam 16 and Jeroboam fou3ten in alle daies a3ens hem silf. And Roboam slepte with hise fadris, and was[r] biried in the citee of Dauid; and Abia, his sone, regnede for hym.

CAP. XIII.

1 The ei3tene[a] 3eer of kyng Jeroboam 2 regnede Abia vpon Judam; thre 3eer he regnede in Jerusalem; and name of his modir Machaia, the dou3ter of Vriel of Gabaa. And ther was bataile betwene[t] 3 Abiam and Jeroboam. And whanne Abia hadde gon in strijf, and hadde most best fi3tynge men, and of chosen foure hundrith thousand, Jeroboam ordeynde a3einward scheltrun of ei3t hundrith thousand of men, the whiche and thei weren chosen 4 and to batails most stronge. Thann Abia stood vpon the hil of Semeron, that was in Effram, and seith, Heere, Jeroboam 5 and al Yrael; whether 3e knowe not, that the Lord God of Yrael 3aue the rewme to Dauid vpon Yrael in to euermore, to hym and to his sonis into couenaunt of 6 salte[u]? And Jeroboam, the sone of Nabath, the seruaunt of Salamon, sone of Dauith, ros, and rebellide a3einus his lord. 7 And ther ben gaderd to hym most vein men and the sonis of Belial, and thei hadden the ouer hond a3einus Roboam, the sone of Salamon. Bot Roboam was rude, and with ferde herte, and my3t not 8 a3einstonden to hem. Now thann 3e sayn, that 3e schul mown withstonde to the rewme of the Lord, that he weldith by the sonis of Dauid; and 3e han a gret multitude of puple, and golden calues, 'the whiche[v] Jeroboam hath made to 3ou 9 in to goddis. And 3e han throwen awei the prestis of the Lord, the sonys of Aaron, and Leuytis, and han maad to

CAP. XIII.

Yn the ei3tenthe 3eer of kyng Jeroboam 1 Abia regnede on[s] Juda; he[t] regnede thre 2 3eer in Jerusalem; and the name of hise modir *was* Mychaie, the dou3ter·of Vriel of Gabaa. And batel was bitwixe Abia and Jeroboam. And whanne Abia hadde 3 bigunne batel, and hadde[u] most chyualrouse men, and four hundrid thousynde of chosun men, Jeroboam arayede a3enward the scheltroun with ei3te hundrid thousynde of men, and thei weren chosun men and most stronge[v] to batels[w]. Therfor[x] 4 Abia stood on[y] the hil Semeron, that was in Effraym, and seide[z], Here thou, Jeroboam and al Israel; whether 3e knowen 5 not, that the Lord God of Israel 3af to Dauid the rewme on[a] Israel with outen ende, to hym and to hise sones in to the[b] couenaunt of salt, 'that is, stidefast and stable[c]? And[d] Jeroboam, the sone of Nabath, the seruaunt of Salomon, sone[e] of Dauid, roos[f], and rebellide[g] a3ens his lord. And most veyn men and[h] the sones of 7 Belial weren gaderid[i] to hym, and thei hadden my3t a3ens Roboam, the sone of Salomon. Certis Roboam was buystuouse, 'ether sonne[k], and of feerdful herte, and my3te[l] not a3enstonde hem. Now therfor 8 3e seien, that 3e moun a3enstonde the rewme of the Lord, which[m] he holdith in possessioun bi the sones of Dauid; and 3e han[n] a greet multitude of puple, and[o] goldun caluys, whiche[p] Jeroboam made[q] in to goddis to 3ou. And 3e han caste 9 awei[r] the preestis of the Lord, the sones

---

[s] ei3tenthe *ACEFH*. [t] betwe c *passim*. [u] Salti *ABFH*. [v] that c.

[r] he was INS. [s] upon INS. [t] and he c. [u] hadde *with him* INS. [v] stronge men INS. [w] batel s. [x] And INS. [y] upon INS. [z] he seide INS. [a] of NS. [b] Om. INS. [c] *that is, stidefast* N. [d] And now s, [e] the sone I. [f] hath risen up INS. [g] he rebellide I. hath rebellid s. [h] Om. INS. [i] gaderid togidre INS, [k] Om. IN. *ethir formed* MW. *or* ontau3l s. [l] he my3te INS. [m] that INS. [n] haue IN. [o] and 3e han s, [p] the whiche I. [q] hath maad INS. [r] awey *fro* 3ou NS.

3ou prestes, as alle the puplis of londis; whosoeuer commith and sacrith his hond in bool, in oxen and in seuen wethers, anoon he is maad the^w preste of hem that 10 ben not goddis. Our forsothe Lord is God, whom we han not forsaken; and the prestis mynistriden^x to the Lord of the sonis of Aaron, and Leuytis ben in their 11 ordre; also brent sacrifices thei offren to the Lord by ech days, erly and at euen, and the encense maad aftir the hestis of the lawe; and there ben leid forth looues in the most clene borde; and there is anentis us a golden chaundeler, and the lantern of it, that it be tend euermore at euen; we forsothe kepen the hestis of 12 oure God, whom 3e han forsaken. Thanne duke in oure hoost is God, and the prestis of hym, that crien in trumpis and sownen a3eins 3ou; 3e sonis of Yrael, willith not fi3ten a3einus the Lord God of oure fadirs, 13 for it spedith not to 3ou. Thes thingis hym spekyng, Jeroboam bihynde kaste buschementis; and whanne he schulde stonden forn a3einus of the hoostis, he enuyrounde with his hoost Judam vn- 14 knowynge. And Juda biholdynge saw3 to stonden in bataile forn a3einst, and bi- hynde the bac; and he criede to the Lord, and the prestis with trumpis be- 15 gunnen to syngen. And alle the men of Juda crieden out, and loo! hem criynge out, God ferid Jeroboam and al Ysrael, that stood forn a3eynst Juda and Abia. 16 And the men of Yrael flowen Judam, and the Lord tok hem in to the hondis of hem. 17 Than smote hem Abia and his puple in a grete veniaunce, and ther fellen of hem woundid fyue hundrith^y thousand 18 of stronge men. And the sonis of Yrael ben mekid in that tyme, and the sonis

of Aaron, and dekenes^t, and 3e han maad preestis to 3ou, as alle the puplis^u of londis^v han^w preestis^x; who^y euer cometh and halewith his^z hond in a bole, in oxis^a, and^b in seuene wetheris^c, anoon he is maad preest of hem that^d ben not^e goddis^f. But 10 oure Lord is God, whom we forsaken not; and preestis of the sones of Aaron mynys- tren^g to the Lord, and dekenes ben in her ordre; and thei offren^h brent sacrifices 11 to the Lord bi^i ech dai in the morewtid and euentid, and^k encense maad bi co- maundementis of the lawe; and loues ben^l set forth in a moost^m clene boord; and at vs is the goldun candilstik and his^n lan- terne^o, that^p it be teendid^q euere at euen- tid; forsothe^r we kepen the comaunde- mentis^s of our God, whom 3e han forsake. Therfor God is duyk in oure oost, and 12 hise^t preestis, that^u trumpen and sownen a3ens 3ou; nyle 3e, sones of Israel, fi3te a3ens the Lord God of 3oure fadris, for it spedith not to 3ou. While he^v spak these 13 thingis, Jeroboam made redi tresouns bi- hynde^w; and whanne he^x stood euene a3ens the^y enemyes, he cumpasside with his oost Juda vnwitynge. And Juda bihelde, and 14 si3^z batel nei3 euene a3ens^a, and^b bihynde the^c bak; and he criede to the Lord, and preestis bigunnen for^d to trumpe. And 15 alle the men of Juda crieden^e, and, lo! while thei crieden^f, God made aferd Jero- boam and al Israel, that^g stood euen^h a3ens Juda and Abia. And the^i men of Israel 16 fledden fro Juda, and God bitook hem in to the hondis of men^k of^l Juda. Therfor 17 Abia and his puple smoot^m hem^n with a greet wounde, and there felden doun of hem fyue hundrid thousynde of stronge men woundid. And the sones of Israel 18 weren maad lowe in that tyme, and the

w Om. *ABFH.*   x mynystren c.   y Om. E pr. m.

t the dekenes s.   u prestis EFKLMNSxbç.   v londis, *that is, after custum of other londis* s.   w han maad 1. Om. NS.   x Om. INS.   y and who s.   z the kyngis INS.   a oxen INS.   b or INS.   c wetheris, *offringe hem to hym* NS.   d whiche NS.   e Om. N.   f of goddis s.   g mynystriden AELxbç.   h offriden 1.   i Om. 1.   k and *also* 1, and *thei offriden* N. and *thei offren* s.   l hen there s.   m ful 1.   n the INS.   o lanterne therof INS.   P and s.   q tend N.   r and INS.   s heestis INS.   t thei ben hise 1.   u whiche NS.   v Abia INS.   w behynde forth INS.   x Jeroboam INS.   y hise NS.   z he si3 NS.   a a3ens bifore 18.   b hem and s.   c her INS.   d Om. N.   e crieden out 1. crieden an hi3 NS.   f crieden an hi3 1.   g whiche NS.   h Om. INS.   i Om. A.   k the men c. Om. s.   l Om. s.   m smeten 1.   n Israel INS.

of Juda most hugely coumfortid, forthi that thei hadden hopide in the Lord God 19 of their fadirs. Forsothe Abia pursued Jeroboam fleeȝinge, and toke citees of him, Bethel and the douȝtirs of it, and Jesana with his douȝtirs, Efron also and 20 the douȝtirs of it; and miȝt no more withstonde Jeroboam in the days of Abia, 21 whome the Lord smote, and is deed. Than Abia, comfortid his empyre, toke fouretene wiȝues and gat two and twenty sonis, 22 and sixtene douȝters. And² the remnaunt of the wordis of Abia and of the weies and of his werkis, ben writen most bisily in the boke of Abdo, prophete.

CAP. XIV.

1 Forsothe Abia slepte[a] with his fadirs, and thei birieden hym in the cytee of Dauith; and Aza, his sone, regnede for hym. In whos days restide the londe 2 tenn ȝeer. And Aza dide that good and plesaunt was in the siȝte of his God, and he turned vpsadoun the auters of straunge 3 heryinge, and the heeȝ thingis, and to-brac the ymagis, and the mawmet woodis 4 hewȝ doun; and he comaundide to Jude, that he schulde sechen the Lord God of their fadirs, and done the lawe, and alle 5 the maundementis. And he toke awei fro alle the cytees of Juda auters and mawmet templis, and regned in pese. 6 Also he bylde up strengthed cytees in Juda; for quyete he was, and noon in his tyme batails risen, the Lord grauntynge 7 pese. Forsothe he seide to Jude, Bilde we up thes cytees, and enuyrown we with wallis, and strengthe we with touris and ȝatis and lockis, the whilis fro batails alle thingis ben quyete; forthi that we han souȝt the Lord God of oure fadirs, and he hath ȝeuen to us pese by enuyrown.

sones of Juda weren coumfortid ful greetli, for° thei hadden hopid in the Lord God of her fadris. Forsothe[p] Abia pursuede Je- 19 roboam fleynge, and took[q] hise cytees, Bethel[r] and hise vilagis, and Jesana with hise vilagis, and[s] Ephron and hise vilagis; and Jeroboam miȝte no more aȝenstonde[r] 20 smoot†, and he was deed. Therfor Abia, 21 whanne his empire was coumforted, took fourtene wyues, and he gendride[v] two and twenti sones, and sixtene douȝtris. The 22 residue[w] of wordis[x] of Abia and of his weyes and werkis[y], ben writun ful dili-gentli in the book of Abdo, the profete.

CAP. XIV.

Forsothe[z] Abia slepte with hise fadris, 1 and thei birieden hym in the citee of Da-uid; and Asa, his sone, regnede for hym. In whos daies the lond restide[a] ten ȝeer. And Asa dide that[b], that was good and 2 plesaunt in the siȝt of his God, and he destriede the auteris of straunge worschip-yng‡, and `he destriede[c] hiȝ[d] places, and 3 brak° ymagis, and kittide[f] doun woodis[g]; and he comaundide Juda to seke the Lord 4 God of her fadris, and to do the lawe and alle comaundementis[h]. And he[i] took awei 5 fro alle the citees of Juda auteris[k] and templis of idols, and he regnede in pees. And he bildide stronge cytees in Juda; for 6 he was in reste, and no batels risiden[l] in his tymes, for the Lord ȝaf[m] pees. For- 7 sothe[n] he° seide to Juda, Bilde we these cytees, and cumpasse we[p] with wallis, and strengthe we[p] with touris and ȝatis and lockis, as longe as alle thingis ben restful fro[q] batel[r]; for we han souȝte the Lord God of oure fadris, and he hath ȝoue to vs pees[s] bi cumpas. Therfor thei bildiden[t], and no[u] lettyng was[v] in bildyng[w]. So- 8

21 † smoot; for he dide idolatrie, in the thridde book of Kingis, xv. c°. Lire here. c.

‡ worschiping; that is, of idel-atrie; hiȝe placis where idoils weren wor-schepid. Lire here. c.

z Om. c.   a sleep c.

° forthi that IN.   P And INS.   q he took INS.   r that is, Bethel INS.   s Om. CDEFGKLMOPQRUXbᶜ.   t withstonde Juda IS. withstonde N.   u the whiche Jeroboam I. which N. which Jeroboam S.   v ȝaat I.   w reme-naunt INS.   x the wordis INS.   y hise werkis INS.   z And INS.   a restide in pees INS.   b that thing INS.   c Om. I.   d the hiȝ I.   e brake togidre the I. brake togidere NS.   f he hewide I. he kettide S.   g mawmet woodis INS.   h the heestis IN. the hestis thereof S.   i the kyng INS.   k the auteris INS.   l risen IS.   m ȝaue him S.   n And INS.   o Asa INS.   p we hem IS.   q for w.   r batels DCKOW.   s rest S.   t bildiden her citees NS.   u there was no I.   v Om. I.   w the bildyng IN. the bijlding of hem S.

Thanne thei beelden up, and no lettynge
8 was in the out makynge. Aza forsothe
hadde in his enuyrown of bereris scheeldis
and speris of Juda thre hundrith thousand, of Beniamyn forsothe of scheld
berers and archers two huudrith and seuenty thousand; alle thes most stronge
9 men. Forsothe aȝeinus hem went out
Zara Ethiope with his hoost tenn hundrith thousand, and with chaaris thre
hundrith, and he came vnto Mazara.
10 Forsothe Aza wente to mete with hym,
and maad a scheltrun to bataile in the
valei of Sophata, that is beside Mazera.
And he inwardly clepide the Lord God,
11 and seith, Lord, ther is not anentis thee
eny distaunce, whether in fewe thou helpist, or in many; help us, Lord oure God,
in thee forsothe and in thi name hauynge
trust we ben comen aȝeinus this multitude;
Lord, oure God thou ert, haue not the
12 ouerhand aȝeins thee a man. And so
the Lord fered Ethiopis beforn Asa and
13 Juda, and Ethiopis flowen; and Asa
pursued hem, and the peple that was with
hym, vnto Jerare. And Ethiopis fellyn
vnto deth, for the Lord smiȝtynge thei
ben to-hewen, and with the hoost of hym
fyȝtyng. Thanne thei token many spoylis,
14 and smijten alle the cytees by enuyrown
of Jerare; forsothe a grete fere assayl-
ede alle. And thei to-brosten cytees, and
15 beren aweic mych preye; bot and the
foldis of scheep distruynge token of beestis
a multitude withoute eende, and of camels, and ben torned aȝein in to Jerusalem.

CAP. XV.

1 Azarias forsothe, the sone of Obed,
2 the spirite of God maad in hym, wente
out in to aȝein comynge of Aza; and seide
to hym, Heere ȝe me, Aza and al Juda
and Beniamyn; the Lord with ȝou, for ȝe
weren with hym; ȝif ȝe sechen hym, ȝe

theli[x] Asa hadde in his oost thre hundrid
thousynde of men of Juda berynge scheldis
and speris, sotheli[y] of Beniamyn he hadde
two hundrid thousynde and fourscoore
thousynde of scheeld beeris and of arch-
cris; alle these *weren* ful stronge men.
Forsothe Zara of Ethiop[z] ȝede out aȝens 9
hem with his oost ten 'sithis an[a] hundrid
thousynde, and with thre hundrid charis,
and cam[b] 'til to[c] Masera. Certis Aza ȝede[d] 10
aȝens *hem*, and araiede[e] scheltrun[f] to batel
in the valei Sephata[g], which[h] is bisidis
Masera. And he[i] inwardli clepide the Lord
God, and seide, Lord, no dyuersitee is 11
anentis[k] thee, whether thou helpe in fewe,
ethir in manye; oure Lord God, helpe
thou vs, for we han trist in thee and in
thi name, and camen[l] aȝens this multitude; Lord, thou art oure God, a man
haue not the[m] maistrye aȝens thee. Ther- 12
for the Lord made aferd Ethiopens[n] bifor
Asa and Juda, and Ethiopens[o] fledden;
and Asa and his puple, that was with 13
hym, pursuede hem 'til to[p] Gerare. And
Ethiopens[q] felden doun 'til to[r] deeth, for
thei weren al to-brokun bi the Lord sleynge, and bi his oost fiȝtynge[s]. Therfor[t]
thei[u] token many spuylis, and[v] smitiden[w] 14
alle the citees 'bi the cumpas of[x] Gerare;
for greet drede hadde assailid alle men[y].
And thei[z] rifliden[a] cytees[b], and baren aweye
myche prey; but[c] also thei destrieden 15
the fooldis of scheep, and token[d] multitude without noumbre of scheep and of
camels, and turneden[e] aȝen in to Jerusalem.

CAP. XV.

Forsothe Azarie, the sone of Obeth, 1
whanne the spirit of the Lord was comyn
in to hym, ȝede[f] out[g] in to the metyng of 2
Asa; and seide[h] to hym, Asa and al Juda
and Beniamyn, here ȝe me; the Lord *is*
with ȝou, for ȝe weren with hym; if ȝe

x And ins.　y and ins.　z Ethiope ins.　a Om. 1.　b he cam s.　c vnto ins.　d ȝede forth ins.
e he araiede ins.　f the scheltrun 1.　his scheltrun ns.　g of Sephata c pr. m. imns.　h that ins.　i Asa ins.
k aȝens s.　l therfore camen 1.　we camen n. forthi we camen s.　m Om. ns.　n the men of Ethiope ins.
o the men of Ethiopie ins.　p vnto ins.　q the men of Ethiopie ins.　r vnto ins. to x.　s fyȝting aȝens
hem s.　t Thanne 1.　u men of Juda ns.　v and thei ins.　w smeten 1. smiteden or *distrcyeden* s.
x abonte 1. bi cumpas ns.　y men aduersaries to Juda s.　z men of Juda s.　a spuyliden 1.　b the
citees ins.　c and ins.　d thei token ins.　e thei turneden ins.　f he ȝede s.　g Om. x.　h he seide ins.

schul fynden; ȝif forsothe ȝe forsaken
3 hym, he schal forsaken ȝou. Forsothe
ther schul passen many days in Yrael
with oute verre God, and with oute prest,
and with out doctour, and with oute lawe.
4 And whanne thei weren turned aȝein in
their anguysch, and schul crien to the
Lord God of Yrael, and sechen hym, thei
5 schul fynden hym. In that tyme ther
schal not ben pese of goyng out and commynge in, bot feris on al sijde in alle
6 dwellers of londis. Forsothe folc schal
fiȝten aȝeinus folc, and cyte aȝeinus cytee,
for the Lord schal distourblen hem in al
7 anguysch; ȝe forsothe takith comfort,
and ȝoure hondis ben not febled; forsothe
8 meed schal ben to ȝoure werk. The
whiche thing whann Aza hadde herd,
that is, the wordis and the prophecie of
Azarie, sone of Obed, prophete, is comfortid, and toke aweie alle the mawmetis
of al the lond of Juda and of Beniamyn,
and of the cytees that he hadd taken of
the hill of Effraym. And he halowede
an auter of the Lord, that was before the
9 ȝate hous of the hous of the Lord. And
he gadride al Juda and Beniamyn, and
the comlyngis with hern of Effraym, and
of Manasse, and of Symeon; forsothe
many hadde flowen to hym of Ysrael,
seeynge that the Lord God of hym was
10 with hym. And whanne 'thei weren[b]
commen in to Jerusalem, the thrid moneth,
the fiftenthe ȝeer of the regne of Aza,
11 thei offreden to the Lord in that day, and
of the hondis and pray, that thei hadden
brouȝt, oxen seuen hundrith, and wethers
12 seuen thousand. And he wente in of
maner to strengthen the pese couenaunt,
that thei schulden seche the Lord God of
their fadirs in al herte, and in al their
13 soule. Ȝif any forsothe sechith not, he

seken hym, ȝe schulen fynde *hym*[i]; sotheli[k] if ȝe forsaken hym, he schal forsake
ȝou. Forsothe many daies schulen passe 3
in Israel with outen veri God, and without preest, and without techere, and without lawe. And whanne thei[l] turnen aȝen 4
in her angwisch, and crien to the Lord
God of Israel, and seken hym, thei schulen
fynde hym. In that tyme schal not be 5
pees to go out and to go in, but dredis[m]
on al[n] side on[o] alle the dwelleris of londis.
For a[p] folk schal fiȝte aȝens folk[q], and a[r] 6
citee aȝens a citee, for the Lord schal
disturble hem in al anguysch[s]; but be ȝe 7
coumfortid[t], and ȝoure hondis be[u] not
slakid[v]; for mede schal be to ȝoure werk.
And[w] whanne Asa hadde herd this thing, 8
that is, the wordis and profesye of Asarie,
the sone of Obed, the profete, he was
coumfortid, and he dide a wei alle the
idols fro al[x] the lond of Juda and of Beniamyn, and fro[y] the citees whiche[z] he
hadde take of the hil of Effraym. And he
halewide the auter of the Lord, that was
bifor the porche of the hows of the Lord.
And he[a] gaderide togidere al Juda and 9
Beniamyn, and with hem the comelyngis
of Effraym, and of Manasses, and of Symeon; for manye[b] of Israel, seynge that
his[c] Lord God was with hym[d], fledden
ouer to hym. And whanne thei[e] hadden 10
comun[f] in to Jerusalem, in the thridde
monethe, in the fiftenthe ȝeer of the rewme
of Asa, thei[g] offriden 'to the Lord[h] in that 11
dai, bothe of the spuylis and of the prey,
which thei hadden brouȝt, seuene[i] hundrid
oxis[k], and seuene thousynde wetheris. And 12
Asa entride[l] bi custom to[m] make strong
the boond of pees, that thei[n] schulden seke
the Lord God of her fadris in al her herte,
and in al her soule. Sotheli[o] he[p] seide, If 13
ony man sekith not the Lord God of Is-

---

[b] he was E *pr. m.*

---

[i] Om. *plures.*   [k] and INS.   [l] thei, *that is, there forcseid lawe* . . . . S.   [m] dredis *schul be* IS. dredis *be* N.
[n] eche I.   [o] in EIKLNO. and in S.   [p] Om. INS.   [q] a folk X *sec. m.*   [r] Om. N.   [s] anguishe, *for her synne* S.
[t] coumfortid *in ȝour soulis* S.   [u] be thei NS.   [v] slakid *fro gode werkis* IS.   [w] Om. S.   [x] Om. CNS.   [y] of S.
[z] that I.   [a] the kyng INS.   [b] manye men INS.   [c] the NS.   [d] hym Asa S.   [e] *Asa and his oost* N. *his oost* S.
[f] comen aȝene S.   [g] he and his peple S.   [h] Om. W.   [i] *that is,* seuene S.   [k] oxen INS.   [l] entride *among
the peple* S.   [m] *among the peple,* for to I. for to N.   [n] his peple S.   [o] And INS.   [p] the kyng INS.

seith, the Lord God of Yrael, be he deed, fro the leste vnto° the most, fro 14 man vnto womman. And thei sworen to the Lord with a grete voice, in ioye, and in crie of trumpe, and in sown of 15 clariowns, alle that weren in Jewrye, with execracioun ; in alle forsothe their herte thei sworen, and in alle wil thei souȝten hym, and founden ; and the Lord ȝaue to 16 hem reste by enuyroun. Bot and Maacha, the modir of kyng Aza, he put doun of hyre anguyschynge empyre, forthi that sche had maad a symulacre of a mans ȝeerde in the mawmet wode ; the whiche al he distroyede, and in to gobetis munyschynge, he brent in to the streem 17 of Cedron. Forsothe the heeȝe thingis ben laft^d stylle in Yrael ; neuer the later the herte of Aza was perfijt alle the days 18 of hym. Tho thingis that his fadir hadde avowed and he brouȝt in to the hous of the Lord, syluer and gold, and of vessels 19 dyuerse purtenauncis ; bataile forsothe was not vnto the thrittithe ȝeer of the regne of Aza.

rael, die he, fro the leeste 'til to^q the mooste, fro man 'til to^r womman^s. And alle^t that^u 14 weren in Juda sworen^v with cursyng^w† to^x the Lord^y, with greet vois, in^z hertli song, and^a in sown of trumpe, and in sown of clariouns^b; for^c thei sworen in al 15 her herte, and in al the^d wille thei souȝten hym^e, and founden hym^f; and the Lord ȝaf to hem reste bi cumpas. But also he 16 puttide^g doun Maacha, the modir of 'Asa the kyng^h, fro^i the streit empire, for sche hadde made in a wode the^k symylacre, 'ether licnesse^l, of a mannus ȝerde ; and he al to-brak al^m 'that symylacre^n, and pown- ede it^o in to gobetis, and^p 'brente it^q in^r the stronde of Cedron. But^s hiȝ places^t weren 17 left in Israel ; netheles the herte of Asa was riȝtful in alle hise daies. And he 18 brouȝte in to the hows of the Lord tho thingis that^u his fadir avowide^v, siluer and gold, and dyuerse purtenaunce of ves- sels ; sotheli^w batel was not 'til to^x the 19 thrittithe‡ ȝeer of the rewme of Asa.

† cursing; that is, obilschinge hem silf to cursing and peyne of deth, if they diden aȝenus the ooth, Lire here. c.

‡ thrittithe; in Ebreu is is, til to the xxxv. ȝeere. Lire here. c.

CAP. XVI.

1 The sixe and thrittithe ȝeer forsothe of his regne Baza, kyng of Yrael, steiȝide up in to Judam, and with a wal he en- uyrounde Rama, that no man sikirly myȝte gon oute or comme in fro the 2 rewme of Aza. Forsothe Aza brouȝt forth gold and syluer fro the tresories of the hous of the Lord, and fro the kyngis tresories ; and sente to Benadab, kyng of Cyrie, that dwellid in Damasch, seyinge, 3 Couenaunt of pese is betwene me and thee, forsothe my fadir and thi fader hadden acord ; for what thing I haue

CAP. XVI.

Forsothe^y in the sixe and thrittithe ȝeer 1 of his rewme Baasa, the^z kyng of Israel, stiede^a in to Juda, and cumpasside^b Rama with a wal, that no man of the rewme of Asa myȝte go out ether^c entre^d sikirli. So- 2 theli^e Asa brouȝte forth gold and siluer fro the tresours of the hows of the Lord, and fro the kyngis tresouris ; and sente^f to Benadab, kyng of Sirie, that dwellide in Damask, and seide^g, Boond of pees is^h bi- 3 twixe me and thee, and my fadir and thi fadir hadden acordyng^i; wherfor Y sente^j to thee siluer and gold, that whanne thou

c to ABFH. d forsaken B pr. m.

q vnto IN. to 8x pr. m.   r vnto INS.   s woman, be noon spared S.   t alle thei I. al men and wemen S.
u whiche NS.   v Om. INS.   w cursynge, that is, bindinge hem with curs IS.   x sworen to INS.   y Lord
God NS.   z Om. N.   a Om. C.   b clariouns to obeie herto INS.   c certis INS.   d her INS.   e the Lord NS.
f Om. plures.   g putte I.   h the kyng Asa I. king Asa NS.   i that is, his owen moder fro INS.   k a INS.
l or a licnesse I. Om. N.   m Om. S.   n it I.   o Om. plures.   p and he I.   q it brent N. brente S.   r and
threwe it into I. and he threw into NS.   s But ȝit INS.   t places of mawmetrie IS.   u whiche INS.
v avoued iustli S.   w and INS.   x vnto INS.   y Sothely INS.   z Om. INS.   a stiede up INS.   b he cumpasside INS.   c and A.   d entre yn INS.   e And INS.   f he sente tho INS.   g seide to him IS.   h Om. S.
i accord togidre I. concoord togidre NS.   j haue sent INS.

sente to thee syluer and gold, that the pese couenaunt broken, that thou hast with Baza, kyng of Yrael, thou make 4 hym gon awey fro me   The whiche thing founden, Benadab sente the princis[f] of his hoostis to the cytees of Yrael, the whiche smyten Achyon, and Dan, and Abelmaym, and alle the walled cytees of 5 Neptalym. The whiche thing whanne Baaza hadde herd, he cesede to bylden 6 up Rama, and he laft of his weik   Bot kyng Aza toke al Judam, and thei token the stoones of Rama, and the trees, that Baaza had maad redy to bildyng[g]; and he bilde up of hem Gaha, and Maspha 7 In that tyme came Ananye, the prophete, to Aza, kyng of Juda, and seide to hym, For thou haddist trust in the kyng of Cyrye, and not in the Lord thi God, therfore the hoost of the kyng of Cyrie 8 is scapid fro thin hond   Whether Ethiopes and Libies weren not many mo 'with carris of foure hors[h], and the horsmen, and the ful grete multitude; the whiche whanne thou haddist trowed to 9 the Lord, he toke in to thin hondis? The eeჳen forsothe of the Lord beholden al the erth, and ჳeuen strengthe to hem, that in perfiჟte herte bileeuen 'in to[i] hym   Folily thanne thou didist, and for that also in the present tyme aჳeins thee 10 batailes schul rijsen   And Aza is wroth aჳeinus the sear, and comaundide hym to be putt in the stockis   Forsothe myche vpon that was the Lord stered to indignacioun, and he slewჳ of[k] the puple in 11 that tyme manye   The werkis forsothe of Aza, the first and the last, ben writen in the boke of the kyngis of Juda and of 12 Yrael   Forsothe Aza was seeke the nyne and thrittithe ჳeer of his regne, most hi-

hast broke the boond of pees, which[k] thou hast with Baasa, king of Israel, thou make hym to go awei fro me. And whanne 4 this[l] was[m] foundun[n], Benadab sente princes[o] · of hise oostis to[p] the citees of Israel, whiche[q] smytiden[r] Ahion, and Dan, and Abelmaym, and alle the wallid citees of Neptalym   And whanne Baasa hadde herd this, he 5 ceesside to bilde Rama, and left[s] his weik   Forsothe[t] kyng Asa took al Juda, and 6 thei token fro Rama the[u] stonys and trees, whiche[v] Baasa hadde maad redi to bildyng, and he[w] bildide of tho Gabaa, and Maspha   In that tyme Anany, the pro- 7 fete, cam to Asa, kyng of Juda, and seide to hym, For[x] thou haddist trist in the kyng of Sirie, and not in 'thi Lord God[y], herfor the oost of 'the kyng of[z] Sirie aschapide[a] fro thin hond   Whether 'Ethio- 8 piens and Libiens[b] weren not many mo[c] in charis, and[d] knyჳtis, and[e] ful[f] greet multitude, whiche[g] whanne thou haddist bileuyd to the Lord, he bitook[h] in to thin hondis? For the ჳen[i] of the Lord biholden 9 al the[j] erthe, and ჳyuen[k] strengthe to hem, that with perfit herte bileuen in to hym   Therfor thou hast do folili, and[l] for this[m], ჳhe, in present[n] tyme batels schulen rise aჳens thee   And Asa was wrooth aჳens 10 the prophete, and comaundide hym[o] to be sent in to stockis[p]. Forsothe the Lord[q] hadde indignacioun greeth on[r] this thing, and killide[s] ful many of the[t] puple in that tyme   Sotheli the firste and the laste 11 werkis of Asa ben writun in the book of kyngis of Juda and of Israel   Forsothe[u] 12 Asa was sijk ful greth in the[v] akynge of feet[w], in the nyne and thrittithe ჳeer of his reume; and nether in his sikenesse[x] he souჳte the Lord, but tristide[y] more in the craft ot lechis   And Asa slepte with hise 13

---

[f] prince ACH   [g] the bilding c   [h] thin the ploowes E *pr m*   [i] to ABFH   [k] Om ABFH

[k] that INS   [l] this thing BCDLFGIKLMNOPQRUWXbç these thingis s   [m] werin s   [n] foundun *sooth* IS
[o] the princes INS   P in to s   q the whiche I   which *oostes* s   [r] smetyn I. II. smiteden *or distroyeden* s
[s] he lefte IN   [t] And INS   [u] *alle* the INS   [v] the whiche I   [w] *Aza* s   [x] Forth that INS   [y] the Lord
thi God INS   [z] Om NS   [a] ascapide, *that is, [the oost of Sirie* s] *made the king of Israel to ascape* NS
[b] the men of [*or the oost of* s] Ethiope and [of N] Libie INS   [c] mo *than Israel* is   [d] in INS   [e] Om N
[f] in ful INS   [g] the whiche I   whiche *greet oost and multitude* s   [h] bitook hem s   [i] iჳe N   [j] Om INS.
[k] ჳyueth c   thei ჳyuen INS   [l] Om s   [m] this *trist in men* I   this *thi mistrusting in the Lord* s.   [n] *this*
present INS   [o] to him EL.   P the stockis CNOS   q Lord *God* NS   [r] upon INS   [s] he killide INS   [t] his I
Azais N   *Aza* s.   [u] And INS   [v] Om I   [w] *his* feet INS   [x] sikenessis s   [y] he tristide INS

dously in sorowe of feet; and nether in the infirmyte he souȝte the Lord, bot more in the craft of lechis he trustide. 13 And Aza slepte[l] with his fadirs, and is deed the oon and fouretithe ȝeer of his 14 regne. And thei birieden hym in his sepulcre, that he hadde maad to hym in the cytee of Dauith; and thei putten hym vpon his bed ful of swote spices and strumpetis oynementis, that weren maad by the craft of pyment makers, and thei brenden vpon hym in a ful myche mouynge to lust.

fadris, and he[z] was deed in the oon and fourtithe ȝeer of his rewme. And thei 14 birieden him in his sepulcre, which[a] he hadde maad to hym silf in the cytee of Dauid; and thei puttiden[b] hym[c] on[d] his bed ful of swete smellynge spices and oynementis[e] of hooris[f], that[g] weren maad togidere[h] bi the craft of oynement makeris, and thei brenten on[i] hym with ful greet cost.

CAP. XVII.

1 Josaphath forsothe, his sone, regnede for hym; and he wexe stronge aȝeinus 2 Yrael. And he sette nonmbris of knyȝtis in alle the cytees of Juda, that weren enuyrounde with wallis, and he disposede strengthes in the lond of Juda, and in the cytees of Effraym, that Aza, his fadir, 3 hadde taken. And the Lord was with Josaphath, the whiche wente in the weies of Dauith, his fadir, in the first; he hoop-4 ide not in Baalym, bot in the Lord God of Dauid, his fadir, and he wente in the heestis of hym, and not aftir the synnes 5 of Yrael. And the Lord confermede the rewme in his hond, and al Juda ȝaue ȝiftis to Josaphath, and with oute noumber rychessis ben maad to hym, and 6 myche glorie. And whanne his herte hadde taken hardynesse for the weies of the Lord, also heeȝ thingis and mawmete 7 wodus he toke awei fro Juda. The thrid forsothe ȝeer of his regne[m] he sente of his[n] princis Banayl, and Abdyam, and Zachyam, and Nathanael, and Mychiam, that thei schulden techen in the cytees 8 of Juda; and with hem Leuytis, Semeyam, and Nathanyam, and Zabadyam, Azahil also, and Semyramoth, and Jona-

CAP. XVII.

Forsothe[k] Josaphat, his sone, regnyde 1 for hym; and he hadde the maistrye aȝens Israel. And he settide[l] noumbris[m] of 2 knyȝtis in[n] alle the citees of Juda, that[o] weren cumpassid with wallis, and he disposide strong holdis in the lond of Juda, and in the citees of Effraym, whiche[p] Asa, his fadir, hadde take. And the Lord was 3 with Josaphat, whiche[q] ȝede in the firste[r] weies of Dauid, his fadir; he hopide not in Baalym, but in[s] the Lord God of Dauid, 4 his fadir, and he ȝede in the comaundementis[t] of God, and not bi[u] the synnes of Israel. And the Lord confermyde the 5 rewme in his hond; and al Juda ȝaf ȝiftis to Josaphat, and ritchessis with outen noumbre, and myche glorie weren[v] maad to hym. And whanne his herte 6 hadde take hardynesse for the weies[w] of the Lord, he took[x] awei also hiȝ[y] placis and wodis[z] fro Juda. Forsothe[a] in the 7 thridde ȝeer of his rewme he sente of hise princes Benail, and Abdie, and Zacarie, and Nathanye, and Mychee, that thei schulden teche in the citees of Juda[b]; and 8 with hem *he sente* dekenes[c] Semeye[d], and[e] Nathanye, and Zabadie, and Azahel, and Semyramoth, and Jonathan, and Adonye,

---

[l] sleep c.　[m] rewme E pr. m.　[n] the E pr. m.

[z] Om. INS.　[a] that INS.　[b] putten I.　[c] him, or *leiden him* s.　[d] upon INS.　[e] of oynementis IN.
[f] strumpetis INS.　[g] the whiche I.　whiche NS.　[h] ul togidre maad INS.　[i] *these* upon INS.　[k] Certis INS.
[l] sette I.　[m] noumbre N. in noumbre s.　[n] of s.　[o] whiche INS.　[p] that I.　[q] that INS.　[r] first *or best* s.
[s] *he hopide* in IS.　[t] heestis INS.　[u] aftir I.　[v] was EFGIKLMNSxbç.　[w] weies *which he kepte* s.　[x] took
thanne INS.　[y] the hiȝ I.　[z] wodis *of mawmetrie* INS.　[a] And INS.　[b] Juda *Goddis lawe* NS.　[c] *nyne*
dekenes, *that is* s.　[d] *that is to wite*, Semcye I.　[e] Om. c.

than, and Adonyam, and Tobiam, and
Abadonyam, Leuytis; and with hem
9 Eliżama and Joram, prestis; and they
tauȝten the puple in Juda, hauynge the
boke of the lawe of the Lord; and thei
enuyrouneden alle the cytees of Juda,
10 and tauȝten al the puple. And so the
ferd of the Lord is maad vpon alle
rewmes of londis, that weren by ennyroun of Juda; and thei weren not hardy
11 to fiȝten aȝein Josaphath. Bot and the
Philisteis brouȝten ȝiftis to Josaphath,
and tribute of syluer; also Arabes
brouȝten beestis, of wethers seuen thousand and seuen hundrith, and geet as
12 feele. Than Josaphath wexe, and is
magnyfied vnto in heiȝte, and bilde up
in Juda houses at licenesse of touris, and
13 strengthed cytees; and many werkis
made redy in the cytees of Juda. And
men fiȝters and strong weren in Jerusa-
14 lem; of whome this is the noumbre, by
houses and meynes of echone. In Juda
prince of the hoost, duyk Eduas, and
with hym most stronge men thre hun-
15 drith thousand. After this Johannan
prynce, and with hym two hundrith and
16 eiȝtye thousand. Aftir hym also Amazias, the sone of Zechri, sacrid to the
Lord, and with hym two hundrith thou-
17 sand of stronge men. This folowede a
stronge man to batails, Eliada, and with
hym of holdynge bowe and terget two
18 hundrith thousand. Aftir hym also Josa-
bath, and with hym an hundrith and
19 eiȝtye thousand of al redy knyȝtis. Alle
thes weren at the hond of the kyng,
outake othere, 'the whiche⁰ he hadde
sette forth in wallid citees and in al
Juda.

and Thobie, and Abadonye, dekenes; and
with hem 'he sente^f Elisama and Joram,
preestis; and thei tauȝten the puple in 9
Juda, and hadden^g the book of the lawe
of the Lord; and thei cumpassiden alle
the citees of Juda, and tauȝten^h al the
puple. Therfor the drede of the Lord 10
was maad on^i al the rewmes^k of londis,
that weren 'bi cumpas of^l Juda; and tho
dursten not fiȝte aȝens Josaphat. But 11
also Filisteis brouȝten ȝiftis to Josaphat,
and tol^m of siluer; and men of Arabie
brouȝten^n scheep seuene thousynde, and
seuene hundrid of^o wetheris, and so
many buckis of geet. Therfor^p Josaphat 12
encreesside, and was^q magnyfied 'til in to^r
an^s hiȝ^t; and he bildide in Juda housis at
the licnesse of touris, and stronge^u citees;
and he made redi many werkis in the 13
citees of Juda. Also men werriouris and
stronge men weren in Jerusalem; of 14
whiche^v this is the noumbre, 'bi the^w
housis and meynees of alle^x in Juda^y.
Duyk Eduas *was* prince of the oost, and
with hym *weren* thre hundrid thousynde
ful stronge men. Aftir^z hym was Johan- 15
nan prince, and with hym *weren* two
hundrid thousynde and foure scoore thou-
synde^a. After this also Amasye, the sone 16
of Zechri, *was* halewid to the Lord, and
with hym *weren* two hundrid thousynde
of stronge men. Eliada myȝti^b to batels 17
suede this *Amasie*, and with hym *weren*
two hundrid thousynde of men holdynge
bouwe and scheeld. Aftir this^c *was* also 18
Josaphat, and with hym *weren* an hundrid thousynde and foure scoore thousynde of redi knyȝtis. Alle these weren 19
at the hond of the kyng, outakun othere,
whiche he hadde put in wallid cytees and^d
in al Juda.

⁰ that c *pr. m.*

f Om. N. *sente* s.   g thei hadden INS.   h thei tauȝten INS.   i upon INS.   k rewme EKL.   l bi the
cumpas of BCDEFGKLMNOPQRSUVWXbç. aboute I.   m tribute INS.   n brouȝten *to him* s.   o Om. INS.
P Thanne I.   q he was IN.   r vnto I. til to Nb. unto into s.   s ful INS.   t hiȝ *wirschipe* INS.   u ful
stronge s.   v whiche *men* INS.   w of s.   x alle *men* IN. alle *men that there werin* s.   y *the meynee of*
Juda INS.   z And after s.   a thousand *men* NS.   b a myȝti *man* INS.   c *Eliada* INS.   d Om. s.

CAP. XVIII.

1 Josaphath thanne was ryche and myche glorious[p], and in affynite ioyned is[q] to 2 Achab. And he wente doun aftir ȝeeris to hym in to Samarie; at whos commynge Achab slewȝ wethers and many oxen, and made to hym a feeste, and to the puple that was commen with hym; and he mouede to hym that he schulde 3 steiȝe up in to Ramoth-galaad. And Achab, kyng of Yrael, seid to Josaphath, kyng of Juda, Comme with me in to Ramoth-galaad. To whome he answerde, As I, and thou; as thi puple, so and my puple; and with thee we schul ben in 4 bataile. And Josaphath seide to the kyng of Yrael, Counseile, I beseche, now the 5 word of the Lord. Than the kyng of Yrael gadrede of prophetis four hundrith men, and seide to hem, In Ramoth-galaad to fiȝten schul we gon, or cesen? And thei, Steiȝith up, thei seyn, and God schal take 6 hem in the hond of the kyng. And Josaphath seide, Whether is ther[r] not heere a prophete of the Lord, that of hym also 7 we asken? And the kyng of Yrael seith to Josaphath, Ther is oon man, of the which we mown asken the wille of the Lord, bot and I hatide hym, for he prophecieth not to me good, bot euyl al tyme; he is forsothe Mychias, the sone of Jemla[s]. And Josaphath seide to hym, 8 Ne speke thou, kyng, this maner. Thanne the kyng of Yrael clepide oon of his geldyngis, and seide to hym, Clepe[t] anoon 9 Mychyam, the sone of Jemla[u]. Bot the kyng of Yrael and Josaphath, kyng of

CAP. XVIII.

1 Therfor[e] Josaphat was riche[f] and ful[g] noble, and bi affynyte, 'ethir alie', he was ioyned to Achab. And aftir ȝeeris he[k] 2 cam doun to hym[l] in to Samarie; at whos comyng Achab killide ful many wetheris and oxis[m], and to the puple that cam with hym; and he[n] counseilide hym[o] to stie[p] in to Ramoth of Galaad. And[q] Achab, 3 the[r] kyng of Israel, seide to Josaphat, kyng of Juda, Come thou with me in to Ramoth of Galaad. To whom he answeride, As and Y am[s], thou[t] art[u]; as[v] thi puple[w], so and[x] my puple[y]; and we schulen be with thee in batel. And[z] Josaphat seide to the 4 kyng of Israel, Y biseche[a], counsele thou in present[b] tyme the word of the Lord. Therfor[c] the kyng of Israel gaderide togi- 5 dere foure hundrid 'men of [d] prophetis, and seide[e] hem, Owen we to go in to Ramath of Galaad for to fiȝte, ethir 'take reste[f]? And thei[g] seiden, Stie ȝe[h], and God schal bitake[i] in[k] the hond of the king. And Josaphat seide, Whether no profete 6 of the Lord is[l] here, that we 'axe also[m] of hym? And the kyng of Israel seide to 7 Josaphat, O man is[n], of whom we 'moun axe[p] the wille of the Lord, but and[q] Y hate hym, for he prophecieth not good[r], but yuel[s] to me in al tyme; sothely[t] it is Mychee, the sone of Jebla. And Josaphat seide to hym, Kyng, speke thou not in this maner. Therfor[u] the kyng of Israel cle- 8 pide oon of the[v] geldyngis[w], and seide to hym, Clepe thou soone[x] Mychee, the sone of Jebla. Forsothe[y] the kyng of Israel 9 and Josaphat, the[z] kyng of Juda, saten[a]

---

[p] glorious of knyȝtis E pr. m.   [q] Om. E pr. m.   [r] Om. ADFH.   [s] Jebla E pr. m.   [t] Clepe to me E pr. m.   [u] Jebla E.

[e] Forsothe INS.   [f] ful riche INS.   [g] Om. INS.   [h] Om. INS.   [i] certeyn ȝeeris INS.   [k] Josaphat INS.   [l] Achab INS.   [m] oxen INS.   [n] Achab NS.   [o] Josaphat INS.   [p] wende up with him I. stie with him N. stie vp with him s.   [q] Om. s.   [r] Om. INS.   [s] am ioyned to thee I. am bi affinyte ioyned to the in frenshepe s.   [t] so and thou NS.   [u] art also to me I. art to me s.   [v] and as IN. and as bi our affinyte s.   [w] peple is my peple s.   [x] also I.   [y] peple is thi peple s.   [z] And eft I. And ouer this s.   [a] biseche thee IS.   [b] this present IS.   [c] Thunne I.   [d] Om. c.   [e] he seide INS.   [f] reste at hoom I. shuln we take reste and cum not there s.   [g] the prophetis INS.   [h] ȝe up thidere I. ȝe vp N. up thidere s.   [i] bitake it INS.   [k] in to INS.   [l] be IS.   [m] may also axe I. axe this also s.   [n] ther is I. is niȝ here s.   [p] may wite I. moun wite NS.   [q] Om. IS.   [r] good thing IN. good thing to my lykyng s.   [s] yuel thing IN. he profecieth yuel thing s.   [t] and INS.   [u] Thanne I.   [v] hise INS.   [w] geldingis or chast seruauntis I. chaast seruauntis NS.   [x] anoon IN. to me anoon s.   [y] And INS.   [z] Om. INS.   [a] saten thanne I. saten this tyme s.

Juda, either seeten in their see, clothed[v]
with kyngis honournyng[w]; forsothe thei
seeten in the corn flore bysidis the ʒate
of Samarye; and alle the prophetis pro-
10 phecieden beforn hem. Sedechias forsothe, the sone of Chanane, made to hym
yren hornes, and seith, Thes thingus
seith the Lord, With thes thou schalt
wynewen Cyrie, to the tyme that thou
11 'to-trede[x] it. And alle the prophetis prophecieden lijc maner, and seiden, Steiʒe
up in to Ramoth-galaad, and thou schalt
welsumly done; and the Lord schal take
12 hem in to the hondis of the kyng. The
messager forsothe, that wente to clepen
Mychie, seith to hym, Lo! the wordis of
alle the[y] prophetis with oon mouthe good
thingus tellen to the kyng; thanne, I beseche thee, that thi word fro hem dis-
sente not, and speke thou welsum thingis.
13 To whome answerd Mychias, The Lord
liuith, for what euer thingis my Lord
schal seyn, thes I schal speken. Thanne
14 he came to the kyng. To whom the king
seith, Mychie, schul we gon into Ramoth-
galaad to fiʒten, or resten? To whom he
answerde, Steiʒith up, alle thingus forsothe welsum schul fallen, and the enmyes schul ben taken into ʒoure hondis.
15 And the kyng seide, Eft and eft I adiure
thee, that thou speke not to me bot that[z]
16 is sothe in the name of the Lord. And
he seith, I sawe al Yrael scatered in
hyllis, as scheep with oute schepherde.
And the Lord seid, Thes han not lordis;
be turned aʒein ech man in to his house
17 in pees. The kyng of Yrael seith to Josaphath, Whether I seide not to thee, that
this schulde not prophecien to me eny

euer eithir in his seete, and weren[b] clothid
in kyngis aray; forsothe[c] thei saten in the
cornfloor, 'ether large hows[d], bisidis the
ʒate of Samarie[e]; and alle the prophetis[f]
profesieden bifor hem. Forsothe[g] Sede- 10
chie, the sone of Cananee, made to hym
yrone hornes, and seide[h], The Lord seith
these thingis, With these[i] thou schalt wyndewe[k] Sirie[l], til thou al to-brake it[m]. And 11
alle prophetis[n] profesieden in lijk maner,
and seiden[o], Stie thou[p] in to Ramoth of
Galaad, and thou schalt haue prosperite;
and the Lord schal bitake hem in to the
hondis of the kyng. Forsothe[q] the mes- 12
sanger, that ʒede to clepe Mychee, seide
to hym, Lo! the wordis of alle prophetis[r]
tellen with o mouth goodis[s] to the kyng;
therfor, Y preye thee, that thi word di-
sente[t] not fro hem, and that thou speke
prosperitees[u]. To whom Mychee answer- 13
ide, The Lord lyueth, for what euer thingis
my Lord[v] spekith to me, Y schal speke[w]
these[x] thingis. Therfor[y] he[z] cam to the
kyng. To whom the kyng seide, Mychee, 14
owen we go in to Ramoth of Galaad to
fiʒte, ether take[a] reste[b]? To whom he[c]
answeride, Stie ʒe[d], for alle prosperitees
schulen come[e], and enemyes schulen be bitakun[f] in to ʒoure hondis[g]. And the kyng 15
seide[h], Eft and eft Y charge thee, that thou
speke not to me no but that[i] that is soth
in the name of the Lord. And he[k] seide, 16
Y siʒ al Israel scaterid[l] in the[m] hillis, as
scheep with out scheepherde[n]. And the
Lord seide, These men han not lordis;
ech man[o] turne aʒen in to his hows in
pees. The kyng of Israel seide to Josa- 17
phat, Whether Y seide not to[p] thee, that
he profesiede not ony good[q] to me, but

[v] clad c.   [w] onourynge π.   [x] trede B.   [y] Om. ABFH.   [z] the thing that c.

[b] thei weren INS.   [c] sotheli BCDEFGKLMOPQRUVWxbç. and INS.   [d] Om. IN. ether in a large house s.   [e] the seyntuarie IN.   [f] kingis profetis s.   [g] Oon of hem I. And N. And oo greet profeet of hem s.   [h] he seide to Achab I. he seide to king Achab s.   [i] these hornes IS.   [k] wyndewe or scatere abrood IS.   [l] the men of Sirie INS.   [m] that loond IS. hem N.   [n] the prophetis IN. the kingis profectis s.   [o] thei seiden to Achab IS. thei seiden N.   [p] thou up INS.   [q] And INS.   [r] the prophetis IS.   [s] goode thingis INS.   [t] discorde I. dissent or discord s.   [u] prosperitees to him L. prosperite to the king s.   [v] Lord God INS.   [w] sey INS.   [x] tho I.   [y] And INS.   [z] Mychee INS.   [a] to take INS.   [b] reste, and not to go thidere INS.   [c] Mychee INS.   [d] ʒe up thider INS.   [e] come to ʒou I. come there to ʒou NS.   [f] takun NSX.   [g] hondis, as ʒour profetis to whom ʒe bilenen, profecien to ʒou s.   [h] seide to him s.   [i] that thing INS.   [k] Mychee INS.   [l] scaterid abrood INS.   [m] Om. NS.   [n] a scheepherde IS.   [o] man therfor IS.   [p] Om. s.   [q] good thing NS.

thing of good, bot tho thingis that ben
18 euyl? And he therfore seith, Herith the
word of the Lord. I sawȝ the Lord syttynge in his seete, and al the hoost of
heuen stondynge neeȝ to hym fro the
19 riȝt and fro the left. And the Lord seide,
Who schal deceyuen Achab, kyng of
Yrael, that he steiȝe up, and falle in Ramoth-galaad? And whanne oon seide in
20 this maner, and another in[a] another, a[b]
spirite went forth, and stood before the
Lord, and seith, I schal deceyuen hym.
To whome the Lord, In what thanne, he
21 seith, thou schalt deceyuen? And he answerd, I schal goon out, and I schal ben
a[c] spirite lier in the mouth of alle the
prophetis of hym. And the Lord seide,
Thou schalt deceyuen, and han the oouer
22 hond; go out, and do so. Nowe thanne,
lo! the Lord ȝaue a spirite of lesynge in
the mouthe of alle thi[d] prophetis, and the
23 Lord spac of thee euyl thingis. Forsothe
Sedechias, the sone of Chanane, wente to,
and smote the cheek boon of Mychie,
and seith, Bi what weie passede ouer the
Spirite of the Lord fro me, that he schulde
24 speke to thee? And Mychias seide, Thou
thi silf schal seen in that day, whanne
thou schalt gon in the bed fro the bed,
25 that thou be hid. Forsothe the kyng of
Yrael comaundide, seyinge, Takith Myche,
and ledith hym to Amon, the prince of
the cyte, and to Joas, the sone of Ama-
26 lech; and ȝe schul seyn, Thes thingis
seith the kyng, Puttith this in to prisone,
and ȝeuith to hym a litill of brede, and a
lityll of water, to the tyme that I be
27 turned aȝeyn in pese. And Mychias seide,
Ȝif thou schal be torned aȝein in peese,
the Lord hath not spoken in me. And

tho thingis that ben yuele? And therfor[r] 18
Mychee seide, Here ȝe the word of the
Lord. Y siȝ the Lord sittynge in his
trone, and al the oost[s] of heuene stondynge nyȝ him at the riȝtside and[t] 'leftside[u]. And the Lord seide, Who schal 19
disseyue Achab, the[v] kyng of Israel, that
he stie[w], and falle doun[x] in Ramoth of
Galaad? And whanne oon seide in[y] this
maner, and another seide in[y] another maner, a spirit cam forth, and stood bifor 20
the Lord, and seide, Y schal disseyue hym[z].
To whom the Lord seide, 'Wherynne,
therfor[a] schalt thou disseyue[b]? And he 21
answeride, Y schal[c] go out, and Y schal
be a 'fals spirit[d] in the mouth of alle hise
profetis. And the Lord seide[e], Thou schalt
disseyue[f], and thou schalt haue the may-
stri; go thou out, and do so. Now[g] ther- 22
for, lo! the Lord hath ȝoue a spirit of
leesyng in the mouth of alle thi prophetis,
and the Lord spak[h] yuels[i] of thee[k]. For- 23
sothe[l] Sedechie[m], the sone of Chananee,
neiȝide[n], and smoot[o] 'the cheke of Mychee[p],
and seide, Bi what weye passide[q] the Spirit
of the Lord[r] fro me to speke to[s] thee?
And Mychee[t] seide[u], Thou thi silf schalt 24
se in that dai, whanne thou schalt entre
fro closet in to closet, that thou be hid[v].
Sotheli[w] the kyng of Israel comaundide, 25
seiynge, Take ȝe Mychee, and lede ȝe hym
to Amon, prince of the citee, and to Joas,
the sone of Amalech; and ȝe schulen seie[x], 26
The kyng seith these thingis, Sende ȝe[y]
this man in to prisoun, and ȝyue ȝe to[z]
hym a litil of breed, and a litil of[a] watir,
til[b] Y turne aȝen in pees. And Mychee 27
seide, If thou turnest aȝen in pees, the
Lord spak not in[c] me[d]. And[e] he[f] seide,
Alle 'puplis here ȝe[g]. Therfor[h] the kyng 28

[a] Om. C. [b] o *AH*. oo *B*. [c] Om. C. [d] the *ABFH*.

[r] thanne I. [s] oost *or cumpany* S. [t] and *at the* INS. [u] left NS. [v] Om. INS. [w] stie up INS. [x] doun *bi deth* S. [y] *he shuld disseiue him* in S. [z] *Achab* INS. [a] Wherynne B. And wherynne INS. [b] disseyue *him* INS. [c] shal, *he seith* S. [d] lyȝinge spirit N. spirit leȝinge S. [e] seide *to him* NS. [f] disseyue *him* I. disseyue *Achab* NS. [g] Om. NS. [h] hath spoken INS. [i] yuel thingis INS. [k] thee *to come* I. thee, *that is, he hath seid yuel thingis to come to thee* S. [l] And IN. [m] Sedechie, *the kingis propheet* IS. [n] neiȝede nyȝ NS. [o] he smoot INS. [p] Mychee upon the cheeke INS. [q] hath INS. [r] Lord passid INS. [s] with I. [t] Mychee, *the propheet* I. Mychee, *the prophete of God* S. [u] seide *to him* S. [v] hid *for drede* I. hid, *that thou hast disseiued the king bi lesyng* S. [w] And INS. [x] seie *to hem* NS. [y] ȝe *or put ȝe* S. [z] Om. NS. [a] Om. K. [b] til that IN. til the tyme that S. [c] to NSX. [d] me *these thingis* S. [e] And *eft* I. [f] *Myche* S. [g] peplis, *that ben here present,* here ȝe, *that is, vnderstonde ȝe, these thingis that ben seid* S. [h] Thanne I.

28 he seith, Herith, alle puplis. Thanne steiȝeden up the kyng of Yrael, and Josaphath, kyng of Juda, in to Ramoth-
29 galaad. And the kyng of Yrael seide to Josaphath, I schal chaungen habite, and so I schal gone to fiȝten; thou forsothe be clothed[e] with thi clothes. And, the habite chaungid, the kyng of Yrael came
30 to bataile. The kyng forsothe of Cyrie hadde comaundid to the dukis of his chyualrye, seyinge, Fiȝtith not aȝeyn the lest, or aȝein the moste; bot aȝeins
31 aloone the kyng of Yrael. And so whanne the princes of the chyualrye hadden seen Josaphath, thei seiden, Kyng of Yrael is this; and thei enuyrouneden hym, fiȝtynge. And he cried to the Lord; and he 'helpide to[f] hym, and he torned
32 hem awei fro hym. And whanne the duykis of the chyualrye hadden herd, that it was not the kyng of Yrael, thei
33 laften hym. It felle forsothe, that oon of the puple in to vncerteyn kast an arowe, and smote the kyng of Yrael betwen the hatreel and the schulders. And he to his chariotere seith, Turne thin hond, and leede out me fro the scheltrun; for I am
34 woundid. And the fiȝt is eendid in that day. Bot the kyng of Yrael stode in his[g] chaar aȝeinus Cyries vnto euen, and is deed, the sone goynge doun.

CAP. XIX.

1 Josaphath, the kyng of Juda, is turned aȝein pesibly in to his house in to
2 Jerusalem. To whome Hieu, the sone of Ananye, sear, aȝein came, and seith to hym, To the vnpiteuous man thou ȝeuist helpe, and to hem that haten the Lord by frenschip thou ert ioyned; and therfore the wrath forsothe of the Lord thou

of Israel, and Josaphat, the kyng of Juda, stieden[i] in to Ramoth of Galaad. And the 29 kyng of Israel seide to Josaphat, Y schal chaunge[k] clothing[l], and so Y schal go to fiȝte; but be thou clothid in thi clothis[m]. Therfor[n] whanne the kyng of Israel hadde chaungid clothing[o], he cam[p] to batel. For-30 sothe[q] the kyng of Sirie comaundide to the duykis of his[r] multitude of knyȝtis[s], and seide[t], Fiȝte ȝe not aȝens the leeste, nether[u] aȝens the mooste; no[v] but aȝens the kyng aloone of Israel. Therfor whanne the 31 princes of the multitude of knyȝtis hadden seyn Josaphat[w], thei seiden, This is the kyng of Israel; and thei cumpassiden hym, and fouȝten[x]. And he[y] criede to the Lord; and the Lord helpide hym, and turnede hem[z] awey fro hym. Sotheli[a] whanne the 32 duykis of the multitude of knyȝtis hadden herd[b], that it was not the kyng of Israel, thei leften hym. Forsothe[c] it bifelde[i], that 33 oon[e] of the puple[f] schette an arewe in to vncerteyn[g], and smooth[h] the[i] kyng of Israel bitwixe the necke and the schuldris. And he[k] seide to his charietere, Turne thin hond, and lede me out of the scheltrun; for Y am woundид. And the batel was 34 endid in that dai. Certis the[l] kyng of Israel stood in his chare aȝens[m] men of Sirye 'til to[n] euentid[o], and he diede, whanne the sunne ȝede doun.

CAP. XIX.

Forsothe Josaphat, kyng of Juda, turn-1 ede aȝen pesibli in to his hows in to Jerusalem. Whom the profete Hieu, the sone 2 of Ananye, mette, and seide[p] to hym, Thou ȝyuest help to a wickid man, and thou art ioyned bi frendschip to hem that haten the Lord; and therfor sotheli thou deseruedist[q] the wraththe of the Lord; but 3

---

[e] clad c. [f] halp c. [g] Om. *ABFH.*

[i] stieden up INS. [k] chaunge *or do of* S. [l] *my* clothing I. *my kingis* clothes S. [m] clothis, *that is, in thi kingis aray* NS. [n] And INS. [o] *his* clothing INS. [p] cam forth INS. [q] And INS. [r] the NS. [s] his knyȝtis NS. [t] seide *to hem* S. [u] ne S. [v] Om, I. [w] Josaphat, *kyng of Juda* IS. [x] fouȝten *aȝens him* IS. [y] Josaphat INS. [z] hem *that feersly assayled him* S. [a] And INS. [b] herd *or vndirstonde* IS. [c] And INS. [d] bifelle *thanne* I. bifille *ther thanne* S. [e] a man I. oo man NS. [f] puple *of Sirie* IS. [g] vncerteyn *or to gesse* I. vncerteynte *amonge the oost of Israel* S. [h] he smoot INS. [i] *Achab* the IS. [k] *Achab* NS. [l] *Achab* the N. *Achab* S. [m] forn aȝens *the oost of* INF. [n] vnto INS. [o] the euentid INS. [p] he seide INS. [q] hast disserued INS.

₃haddist deserued; bot good werkis ben
founden in thee, for thi that thou toke
awey the mawmete wodis fro the lond of
Juda, and haddist maad redy thin hert,
that thou seche aȝein the Lord God of
₄thi fadirs. Than Josaphath dwellide in
Jerusalem; and eft he wente out to the
puple fro Bersabee vnto the hill of Effraym, and he clepide hem aȝein to
₅the Lord God of their fadirs. And he
sette domesmen of the lond in alle the
strengthed citees of Juda, by alle placis.
₆And comaundyng to the iugis, Seeith,
he seith, what ȝe done; forsothe ȝe enhaunten not dome of man, ᵇot of the
Lord; and what euer ȝe schul demyn,
₇in to ȝou it schal redoundyn; be the
drede of the Lord with ȝou, and with
diligence alle thingus doith; forsothe
ther is not anentis the Lord oure God
wyckidnesseʰ, ne acceptynge of persones,
₈ne couetise of ȝiftis. And Josaphath in
Jerusalemⁱ sette Leuytis, and prestis, and
princes of the meynees of Yrael, that
dome and the cause of the Lord thei
schulden deemyn to the dwellers of it.
₉And he comaundide to hem, seyinge,
Thus ȝe schul doon in drede of the Lord,
₁₀feithfully and in perfijte herte. Al cause
that comith to ȝou of ȝoure bretheren,
that dwellen in theirᵏ cytees, bitwen kynrede and kynrede, wher euer questioun is
of the lawe, of the maundement, of cerymonyes, ofˡ justyfyingis, scheweth to hem,
that thei synnen not in to the Lord, and
wrath come not vpon ȝou and on ȝoure
faders. So thanne doynge ȝe schul not
₁₁synnen. Amarias forsothe, preste and
ȝoure bischop, in thes thingis that to
God pertenen, schal sytten vpon. Bot Za-
badias, the sone of Ysmael, ʼthe whicheᵐ

good werkis ben foundyn in thee, for
thou didistʳ awey wodisˢ fro the lond of
Juda, andᵗ thou hast maad redi thin herte,
for to seke the Lord God of thi fadris.
Therfor Josaphat dwellide in Jerusalem; ₄
and eft he ȝede out to the puple fro Bersabee tilᵘ to the hil of Effraym, and he
clepide hem aȝen to the Lord God of her
fadris. And he ordeynede iugis of the ₅
lond in alle the strengthid citees of Juda,
bi ech placeᵛ. And he comaundide to the ₆
iugis, and seideʷ, Se ȝeˣ, what ȝe doen;
for ȝe vsen not the doom of man, butʸ of
the Lord; and what euere thing ȝe demenᶻ,
schalᵃ turne ʼin toᵇ ȝou; the drede of the ₇
Lord be with ȝou, and do ȝeᶜ alle thingis
with diligenceᵈ; forᵉ anentis ʼȝoure Lord
Godᶠ is no wickidnesse, netherᵍ takyngeʰ
of persoones, netherⁱ coueitise of ȝiftisᵏ.
Alsoˡ in Jerusalem Josaphat ordeynede ₈
dekenes, and preestis, and the princes of
meyneesᵐ of Israel, that thei schulden
deme the doom and causeⁿ of the Lord to
the dwellers of itᵒ. And he comaundide ₉
to hem, and seide, Thus ȝe schulen do in
the drede of the Lord, feithfuli and in perfite herte. Ech cause that cometh to ȝou ₁₀
ofᵖ ȝoure bretheren, thatᵠ dwellen in her
citees, bitwixe kynrede and kynrede, where
euere is questioun of the lawe, ofʳ ʼthe co-
maundementˢ, ofᵗ cerymonyes, ʼether sacrifices ᵘ, ofᵛ iustifyingis, schewe ȝe to hemʷ,
that thei do not synne aȝens the Lord, and
that wraththeˣ com not onʸ ȝou and onʸ
ȝoure bretheren. Therfor ȝe doyngeᶻ thusᵃ
schulen not do synne. Forsotheᵇ Amarie, ₁₁
ȝoure preest and bischop, schal be souereyn
in these thingis, that perteynen to God.
Sotheliᶜ Zabadie, the sone of Ismael, whichᵈ
is duyk in the hows of Juda, schal be onᵉ
thoᶠ werkis that perteynen to the office of

ʰ wickenesse c.   ⁱ Irael c.   ᵏ ȝoure ᴇ pr. m.   ˡ and ᴮ.   ᵐ that c.

ʳ hast don ɪɴꜱ.   ˢ mawmet wodis ɪɴꜱ.   ᵗ and also ɪꜱ.   ⁿ Om. ɪɴꜱx.   ᵛ place or cuntrey therof ɪꜱ.
place or cuntre ɴ.   ʷ seide to hem ɪɴꜱ.   ˣ ȝe, that is, be ȝe ware ꜱ.   ʸ but dome ꜱ.   ᶻ demen vniustly ɪɴꜱ.
ᵃ it schal ɪ.   ᵇ aȝens ɪ. aȝen ɴꜱ.   ᶜ Om. ꜱ.   ᵈ diligens, that is, with discrecioun ꜱ.   ᵉ forsothe ɪɴꜱ.   ᶠ the
Lord ȝoure God ɪɴꜱ.   ᵍ ne ꜱ.   ʰ he is a taker ɪ. he is acceptinge ɴ. he is taking or accepting ꜱ.   ⁱ ne ɪɴꜱ.
ᵏ ȝiftis ouer cometh him ɪɴꜱ.   ˡ And also ꜱ.   ᵐ the meynees ɴꜱ.   ⁿ the cause ɪɴꜱ.   ᵒ Jerusalem ɪɴꜱ.
ᵖ fro ᴀ.   ᵠ whiche ɴꜱ.   ʳ or of ɴꜱ.   ˢ heest ɪɴꜱ.   ᵗ or of ɪɴꜱ.   ᵘ Om. ɪɴ. or of sacrifices ꜱ.   ᵛ or of ɪ.
or ɴꜱ.   ʷ hem the trewthe ꜱ.   ˣ wraththe of the Lord ɪꜱ. his wraththe ɴ.   ʸ upon ɪɴꜱ.   ᶻ doynge or
demynge ɴꜱ.   ᵃ thus iustly ɪɴꜱ.   ᵇ And ɪɴꜱ.   ᶜ And ɪɴꜱ.   ᵈ that ɪɴꜱ.   ᵉ souereyn upon ɪꜱ. vpon ɴ.
ᶠ the ɪɴᴏꜱxᴮ.

is duyk in the hous of Juda, schal ben
vpon tho[n] werkis that pertenen to the
office of the kyng; and ȝe han maistris
and Leuytis before ȝou; takith coumfort,
and doith diligently, and the Lord schal
ben with ȝou in goodis.

the kyng, and ȝe han maistris[g] dekenes
bifor ȝou; be ȝe coumfortid, and do ȝe diligentli[h], and the Lord schal be with ȝou in
goodis[i].

CAP. XX.

1 Aftir these thinges ben gedered the
sonis of Moab, and the sonis of Amon, and
with hem of the Ydumes, to Josaphath,
2 that thei fiȝten aȝeinus hym. And messagers camen, and scheweden to Josaphath, seying, Ther is comen aȝeins thee
a grete multitude fro thes places that ben
beȝonde the see, and of Cyrie; and, lo!
thei ben in Azozonthamar, that is of
3 Engaddi. Josaphath forsothe, for drede
agast, al ȝaf hym self to preyen the Lord,
4 and prechide fastyng to al Juda. And
Juda is gadered to preye the Lord, bot
and alle of their cytees camen to be-
5 sechen hym. And whanne Josaphath
hadde stonden in the mydil company of
Jude and Jerusalem, in the hous of the
6 Lord, before the newe porche, and seith,
Lord God of oure fadirs, thou art God
in heuen, and thou lordschipist to alle
rewmes of gentilis; in thin hond is
strengthe and myȝt, ne eny man may to
7 thee aȝeyn stonden. Whether not thou,
oure God, hast slayn alle the dwellers of
this lond before thi puple Irael, and
hast ȝeuen it to the seed of Abraham, thi
8 freinde, in to euermore? And thei dwelliden in it, and maden out in it a seyn-
9 tuarie to thi name, seyinge, ȝif euyls
commen vpon us, swerde of dome, of
pestilence, and hungur, we schul stonden
before this hous in to euermore in thi
siȝte, in the[o] whiche is inwardly clepid
thi name, and we schul crien to thee

CAP. XX.

Aftir these thingis the sones of Moab, 1
and the sones of Amon, and with hem of[k]
Idumeis[l], weren gaderid togidere to[m] Josaphat, for to fiȝte aȝens hym. And mes- 2
sangeris camen, and schewiden[n] to Josaphat, and seiden, A greet multitude of tho
placis that[o] ben biȝondis the see, and[p] of
Sirie, is comun aȝens thee; and, lo! thei
stonden[q] in Asasonthamar, which[r] is Engaddi[s]. Forsothe[t] Josaphat was aferd by 3
drede, and ȝaf hym silf al for[u] to preye
the Lord[v], and prechide[w] fastynge to al
Juda. And Juda was gaderid togidere[x] 4
for to preye the Lord, but[y] also alle men
camen fro her citees for to b",
bisech hym[z].
And whanne Josaphat hadde stonde in the 5
myddis of the cumpeny of Juda and of Jerusalem, in[a] the hows of the Lord, bifor
the newe large place[b], he seide, Lord God 6
of oure fadris, thou art God in heuene,
and thou art lord of alle rewmes of folkis;
strengthe and power ben in thin hond,
and noon[c] may aȝenstonde thee. Whe- 7
ther not thou, oure God, hast slayn alle
the dwelleris of this lond bifor thi puple
Israel, and hast[d] ȝoue it to the seed of
Abraham, thi freend, withouten ende? And 8
thei[e] dwelliden[f] therynne, and bildiden[g]
therinne a seyntuarie to thi name, and
seiden, If yuelis comen on[h] vs, the[i] swerd 9
of doom, pestilence, and[k] hungur, we
schulen stonde bifor this hows withouten
ende in thi siȝt, in which hows thi name
is clepid[l], and we[m] schulen crie[n] to thee

---

[n] to the A. the B.　[o] Om. c pr. m.

---

[g] maistir INS. 　[b] diligentli, that is, studiously or bisili S. 　[i] gode thingis INS. 　[k] Om. CIN. 　[l] men of
Ydumee INS. 　[m] and thei camen to INS. 　[n] schewiden this IS. 　[o] whiche NS. 　[p] Om. S. 　[q] stonden
togidre INS. 　[r] that INS. 　[s] clepid Engaddi INS. 　[t] And INS. 　[u] al him selff he ȝaf INS. 　[v] to the Lord
of help S. 　[w] he prechide IN. he prechide, that is, he comaundid S. 　[x] Om. INS. 　[y] and INS. 　[z] hym of
help NS. 　[a] and in A. 　[b] place of the temple NS. 　[c] ne ony thing INS. 　[d] thou hast INS. 　[e] thei, that is,
the after comers of Abraham S. 　[f] han dwellid INS. 　[g] thei bildiden INS. 　[b] to INS. 　[i] or the INS.
[k] or INS. 　[l] ynclepid IN. 　[m] Om. A. 　[n] crie there IS.

in oure tribulaciouns ; and thou schalt
10 heeren us, and maken us saaf. Nowe
thanne see, sonus of Amon and of Moab
and the hil of Seyr, by whome thou
grauntidist not to the sonus of Irael that
thei schulden passe, whann they wenten
out fro Egipt, bot thei boweden aside fro
11 hem, and thei slowen hem not, aȝein-
ward thei don, and enforsen to kasten us
12 out fro the possessyoun[p], that thou, oure
God, hast taken to us ; thanne schalt thou
not demen hem ? In us forsothe is not so
myche strengthe, that we mown to this
multitude with stonden, that fallith vpon
us ; bot whanne we vnknowen what we
owen to don, that oonly we han of residue, that oure eeȝen we dressen up to
13 thee. Al forsothe Juda stood before the
Lord, with litil childre and wijues and
14 their free childre. Forsothe there was
Yaziel, the sone of Sacharie, sone of Ananye, sone of Hieyel, sone of Machanye,
Leuyte, and of the sonus of Asaph, vpon
whome is maad the Spirit of the Lord in
15 mydil of the puple, and seith, Takith
heede, al Juda, and that dwellen in Jerusalem, and thou, kyng Josaphath, thes
thingus seith the Lord to ȝou, Willith not
dreeden this multitude, ne taken ferd, it
16 is not forsothe ȝour fiȝt, bot of God. To
morowe ȝe schul steyȝen up aȝeinus hem ;
forsothe thei ben to steiȝen up bi the
pich hil, Cis by name, and ȝe schul
fynden hem in the ouermest of the
streme, that is aȝeinus the wildernesse of
17 Jheruel. Forsothe ȝe schul not ben, the
whiche schul fiȝten ; bot onely tristely
stondith, and ȝe schul seen the help of
the Lord vpon ȝou. O Juda and Jerusalem, willith not dreeden, ne takith ferd ;
to morowe ȝe schul goon out aȝeynus hem,

in oure tribulaciouns; and thou schalt here
vs, and schalt[o] make vs saaf. Now ther-10
for[p] lo ! the sones of Amon and of[q] Moab
and the hil of Seir, bi whiche[r] thou grauntidist not to the sones of Israel for to passe,
whanne thei ȝeden out of Egipt, but thei
bowiden awei fro hem, and killiden[s] not
hem, thei[t] doon[u] aȝenward, and enforsen[v]11
to caste vs out of the possessioun, which[w]
thou, oure God, hast ȝoue to vs ; therfor 12
whether thou[x] schalt not deme hem[y] ?
Treuli in vs is not so greet strengthe, that
we moun aȝenstonde this multitude, that
felde[z] yn on[a] vs ; but sithen[b] we witen
not what[c] we owen to do, we 'han oneli
this residue[d], that we dresse oure iȝen to
thee[e]. Sotheli[f] al Juda stood bifor the[g] 13
Lord, with her litle children and wyues[h]
and fre[i] children. Forsothe[k] Hiaziel, the 14
sone of Zacarie, sone[l] of Ananye, sone[l] of
Hieyel, sone[l] of Machanye, was a dekene,
and of[m] the sones of Asaph, on[n] whom
the Spirit of the Lord was maad in the[o]
myddis of the cumpeny[p], and he[q] seide, 15
Al Juda, and ȝe that dwellen in Jerusalem,
and thou, king Josaphat, perseyne ȝe[r], the
Lord seith these thingis to ȝou, Nyle ȝe
drede, nether be ȝe aferd of this multitude,
for it is not ȝoure batel, but Goddis batel.
To morewe ȝe schulen stie[s] 'aȝens hem ; for 16
thei schulen[t] stie[u] bi the side of the hil, 'bi
name Seys[v], and ȝe schulen fynde hem in
the hiȝnesse[w] of the stronde, which[x] is
aȝens the wildirnesse of Jheruhel. For[y] 17
it schulen[z] not be ȝe, that schulen fiȝte ;
but oncli stonde ȝe trustili, and ȝe schulen
se the help of the Lord on[a] ȝou. A[b]! Juda
and Jerusalem, nyle ȝe drede, nether be ȝe
aferd ; to morewe ȝe schulen go out aȝens
hem, and the Lord schal be with ȝou.
Therfor Josaphat, and Juda, and alle the 18

[p] possyoun _B._

[o] Om. INS.   [p] therfor _Lord_ INS.   [q] _the sones_ of s.   [r] whom I. whiche _peplis_ s.   [s] thei killiden INS.
[t] Om. A. _but_ thei I. _Lord,_ thei s.   [u] doon _yuel for good_ s.   [v] thei enforsen _hem_ I. thei enforsen NS.
[w] that I.   [x] thou, _Lord_ IS.   [y] hem _gilti of greet trispace_ s.   [z] fallith I. fallen N.   [a] upon I. now vpon s.
[b] sith INS.   [c] that what s.   [d] the peple that is left han _cause_ I. the residue han _this_ oonly N. the residue,
or the remenauntis, of the peple han _this trust_ oonli in the s.   [e] bifor thee D.   [f] And INS.   [g] thee I.
[h] her wyues INS.   [i] with her fre INS.   [k] And INS.   [l] the sone INS.   [m] _he was_ of IS.   [n] upon INS.
[o] Om. IN.   [p] cumpeny _of Juda_ IS.   [q] Om. I.   [r] ȝe _or taketh heede_ IS.   [s] stiȝe vp NS.   [t] Om. I.   [u] stiȝe
vp NS. Om. I.   [v] clepid Sey bi name INS.   [w] heiȝthe INS.   [x] that INS.   [y] Certis INS.   [z] schal IN.
[a] upon IS.   [b] O INS. al o.

18 and the Lord schal ben with ȝou. Josaphath thanne, and Juda, and alle the
dwellers of Jerusalem, fellen bowed in to
the erth before the Lord, and honoureden
19 hym. Bot the Leuytis of the sonus of
Caath, and of the sonus of Chore, preyseden the Lord God of Yrael with a grete
20 voice in to heiȝt. And whann erly thei
hadden risen, they wenten out by the desert of Thecue; and, hem goon forth, Josaphath stonding in the mydil of hem,
seide, Heerith me, Juda and alle the
dwellers of Jerusalem; beleeuith in the
Lord ȝoure God, and ȝe schul ben syker;
leeuith to the prophetis of hym, and alle
21 thingus schul commen welsum. And he
ȝaf counseil to the puple, and he sette
the syngers of the Lord, that they schulden preysen hym in their companyes, and
that thei schulden gon before the hoost,
and with cordaunt voice thei schulden
seyn, Knowlecheth[q] to the Lord for good[r];
for in to the world the mercy of hym.
22 And whanne thei hadden begunne preysyngis to syngyn, the Lord turned the
buschementis of hem in to hem silf, of
the sonus, that is, of Amon and Moab and
of the hil of Seyr, the whiche wenten out
to fiȝten aȝeinus Judam, and ben smyten.
23 Forsothe the sonus of Amon and of Moab
rysen to gydre aȝeinus the dwellers of the
hyl of Seyr, that they schulden slen, and
done awey hem; and whanne that in dede
thei hadden fulfild, also in to hem selue
turned thei smyten to gider in woundes
24 either in other. Bot whanne Juda was
commen to the denn, that beholdith wildernesse, he sawȝ aferre al the regyoun
abrood ful of careyns, ne to ben ouer laft
eny man, ‘the whiche[s] hadde mouȝt[t] to[u]
25 scapen the deth. Thanne Josaphath came,
and al the puple with hym, to the spoylis
of the[v] deed to ben drawen awey, and

dwelleris of Jerusalem, felden[c] lowli on[d]
the erthe bifor the Lord, and worschypiden
hym. Forsothe[e] the dekenes of the sones 19
of Caath, and of the sones of Chore, herieden the Lord God of Israel with greet
vois an hiȝ. And whanne[f] thei hadden 20
rise eerli, thei ȝeden not bi the deseert of
Thecue; and whanne thei ‘hadden goun[g]
forth, Josaphat[h] stood in the myddis of
hem, and seide, Juda and alle the dwelleris of Jerusalem, here ȝe me; bileue ȝe in
‘ȝoure Lord God[i], and ȝe schulen be sikur;
bileue ȝe to hise prophetis, and alle prosperitees schulen come[k]. And he[l] ȝaf coun- 21
sel to the puple, and he ordeynede the
syngeris of the Lord, that thei schulden
herye hym[m] in her cumpanyes, and that[n]
thei schulden go bifor the oost, and seie
with acordynge vois, Knouleche ȝe to the
Lord, for he is good; for his merci is ‘in
to the world[o]. And whanne thei bigun- 22
nen to synge heriyngis, the Lord turnede
the buyschementis of hem ‘in to[p] hem silf,
that is, of the sones of Amon and of Moab
and of[q] the hil of Seir, that[r] ȝeden out to
fiȝte aȝens Juda; and thei weren slayn[s].
For whi the sones of Amon and of Moab 23
risiden[t] togidere aȝens the dwelleris of the
hil of Seir, to[u] sle, and to[v] do awey hem;
and whanne thei hadden do this[w] in werk,
thei weren ‘turned also[x] ‘in to[y] hem silf,
and felden[z] doun togidere bi woundis ech
of[a] othere. Certis whanne Juda was comun 24
to the denne, that biholdith[b] the wildirnesse, he siȝ afer al the large cuntrei[c] ful
of deed bodies, and that noon was left,
that miȝte ascape deeth. Therfor Josa- 25
phat cam, and al the puple with hym, to
drawe awey the spuylis of deed men, and
thei founden among the deed bodies dyuerse purtenaunce of houshold, and clothis,
and ful[d] preciouse vessels; and thei ra-
uyischiden[e] in dyuerse maneres, so that

[q] Knowleche *D.* [r] he is good *A.* [s] that *C.* [t] not *H.* [u] Om. *C.* [v] Om. *B.*

[c] fellen I. felden doun NS. [d] upon IS. [e] And INS. [f] whanne *vpon the morewe* S. [g] weren go INS. [h] *king* Josaphat INS. [i] the Lord ȝoure God INS. [k] come *to ȝou* NS. [l] the kyng INS. [m] the Lord INS. [n] Om. S. [o] withouten eend S. [p] aȝens INS. [q] *of men* of I. *of the men* of S. [r] the whiche I. whiche NS. [s] slayn *eche of oother* INS. [t] risen EFIL. [u] and to S. [v] Om. C. [w] this thing INS. [x] *thanne* also turned IS. [y] aȝen INS. [z] fellen I. thei fellen NS. [a] *sleiynge* INS. [b] biholdith *or is forn aȝens* IS. [c] place S. [d] ful of S. [e] rauyschiden *or toke tho thingis awey* IS.

thei founden[w] betwene the careynes dyuerse necessarie, and clothes, and vessels
most precious; and thei breeken on two,
so that alle they mi ȝten not beren, ne bi
thre days the spoyles taken awey, for the
26 mychilnesse of the preye. The ferth forsothe day thei ben gadered in the valey
of Blessynge; forsothe for ther thei blissiden to the Lord, thei clepiden that place
the valey of Blessynge in to the present
27 day. And eche man of Juda is turned
aȝein, and the dwellers of Jerusalem, and
Josaphath beforn hem, in to Jerusalem
with grete ioye; forthi that the Lord
hadde ȝeuen to hem ioye of their enmyes.
28 And thei wenten in to Jerusalem with
sawtrees, and harpis, and trumpis, in to
29 the hous of the Lord. Forsothe inward
ferd of the Lord fel vpon alle the rewmes
of londis, whanne thei hadden herd, that
the Lord hadde fouȝten aȝeinus the enmyes
30 of Irael. And the rewme of Josaphath
hadde reste; and the Lord ȝaue to hym
31 pese by enuyroun. Thanne Josaphath
regnede vpon Judam; and he was of fyue
and thritty ȝeer, whanne he beganne to
regnen; forsothe twenty and fyue ȝeer
he regned in Jerusalem; and name of
his modir Azuba, the douȝter of Selathy.
32 And he wente in the wey of his fadir
Aza, and he bowide not fro it, doynge
what euer thingus weren plesaunt before
33 the Lord. Neuer the later the heeȝe
thingus he dide not awey; ȝit the puple
hadden not dressid their hert to the Lord
34 God of their fadirs. The remnaunt forsothe of the deedis of Josaphath, of the
rather and of the last, ben writen in the
bokis of Hieu, the[x] sone of Anany, the
whiche he discriued in the boke of the[y]

thei myȝten not bere[f] alle thingis, nether
thei myȝten[g] take awei the spuylis bi thre
daies, for the[h] greetnesse of prey. Sotheli[i] 26
in the fourthe dai thei[k] weren gaderid togidere in the valey of Blessyng; 'forsothe
for[l] thei blessiden the Lord there, thei
clepiden that place the valei of Blessyng
'til in to[m] present[n] dai. And ech man of 27
Juda turnede aȝen, and the dwelleris of
Jerusalem, and Josaphat[o] bifor hem, in to
Jerusalem with greet gladnesse; for the
Lord God hadde ȝoue to hem ioye of her
enemyes. And thei entriden[p] in to Jeru- 28
salem with sawtrees, and harpis, and trumpis, in[q] to the hows of the Lord. Forsothe 29
the[r] drede of the Lord felde on[s] alle the
rewmes of londis, whanne thei hadden
herd, that[t] the Lord hadde fouȝte aȝens
the enemies of Israel. And the rewme of 30
Josaphat restide[u]; and the Lord ȝaf 'pees
to hym[v] 'bi cumpas[w]. Therfor[x] Josaphat 31
regnede on[y] Juda; and he was of fyue
and thritti ȝeer, whanne he bigan to regne;
sotheli[z] he regnede fyue and twenti ȝeer in
Jerusalem; and the name of his modir *was*
Azuba, the[a] douȝtir of Selathi. And he[b] 32
ȝede in the weie of Asa his fadir, and
bowide[c] not fro it, and he dide what euer
thingis weren plesaunt bifor the Lord.
Netheles he dide not awei hiȝ[d] thingis[e]†; 33
ȝit[f] the puple hadde not dressid her herte
to the Lord God of her fadris. Forsothe[g] 34
the residue[h] of the formere and the[i] laste
dedis of Josaphat ben writun in the book
of Hieu, the[k] sone of Anany, which[l] he
ordeynede[m] in the book[n] of kyngis[o] of
Israel. After these thingis Josaphat, kyng 35
of Juda, made frendschipis with Ocozie,
kyng of Israel, whose werkis weren ful[p]
yuele; and he[q] was parcener[r] that[s] thei[t] 36

† *hiȝe place;* in the xvii. c°. the Scripture spekith of hiȝe places, in whiche men offride to idolis and not to God; here the Scripture [spekith] of hiȝe placis, in whiche men offride to God; and this was suffrid of many kyngis, to eschewe more yuel. *Lire here.* C.

[w] ben founden *B.* [x] Om. C. [y] Om. *B.*

[f] *thanne* bere *thens* S. [g] myȝten not C. [h] Om. INS. [i] And INS. [k] the men of Juda INS. [l] for forthi that I. for therfore that N. for forthi S. [m] vnto I. in to N. vnto into S. [n] this present IS. [o] Josaphat ȝ*ede* INS. [p] turneden aȝen INS. [q] goynge in I. Om. NS. [r] Om. IS. [s] upon IS. [t] how that S. [u] restide *fro werre* INS. [v] him pees S. [w] al aboute I. [x] And INS. [y] upon I. *wilsumli* vpon S. [z] and INS. [a] Om. C. [b] Josaphat IS. [c] he bowide INS. [d] the hiȝ EIL. [e] placis BCDEFGKLMNOPQRS UWXbç. *mawmett* placis I. [f] *and* ȝit INS. [g] And INS. [h] remenaunt INS. [i] of the INS. Om. BCDGKO QNUWXb. [k] Om. C. [l] the whiche *deedis* I. whiche *dedis* NS. [m] ordeynede *to be writen* INS. [n] bookis X. [o] the kyngis CIS. the king N. [p] moost INS. [q] Josaphat S. [r] parcener *with Ochozie* I. parcener *to him* N. parcener *in wille and werke* S. [s] and N. so that S. [t] Ocozie and he *bi oon assent* S.

35 kyngis of Yrael. After thes thingus Josaphath, kyng of Juda, wente in frenschippes with Ochosie, the king of Yrael, 36 whos werkes weren werst, and parcener was that thei schulden maken schippis, that schulden gon in to Tharsis; and 37 thei maden a nauee in Aziongaber. Forsothe Heliezer, the sone of Doden, of Mareza, prophecyede to Josaphath, seyinge, For thou haddist couenaunt of pese with Ochosia, the Lord smote thi werkes; and the schippes ben to-broken, and they my3ten not gon in to Tharsis.

maden schippis, that^u schulden^v go^w in to Tharsis ; and thei maden o schip^x in to Asiongaber. Sotheli^y Eliezer, sone^z of 37 Dodan, of Maresa, profesiede to Josaphat, and seide, For thou haddist^a boond of pees with Ocozie, the Lord smoot^b thi werkis ; and the schippis^c ben brokun^d, and my3ten^e not go in to Tharsis.

CAP. XXI.

1 Josaphath forsothe slepte^z with his faders, and is biryed with hem in the cite of Dauid ; and Joram, his sone, regned 2 for hym. The whiche hadde bretheren, sonus of Josaphath, Azaryam, Jahiel, and Zacharie, and^a Azarie, and Mychael, and Saphaciam ; alle thes the sonis of Josa-3 phath, kyng of Juda. And his fadir 3aue to hem many 3iftis of gold and of syluer, and pensyouns, with the most strengthed citees in Juda ; the rewme forsothe he toke to Joram, for thi that he was the 4 first goten. Joram forsothe roos vpon the rewme of his fadir ; and whanne he hadde confermede him selue, he slew3 alle his bretheren with swerde, and sum of 5 the princis of Juda. Of two and thritty 3eer Joram was, whanne he beganne to regnen ; and ei3t^b 3eer he regnede in Je-6 rusalem. And he wente in the weyes of the kyngis of Irael, as the hous of Achab hadde don, the dou3ter forsothe of Achab was his wijf ; and he dide euyl in 7 the si3t of the Lord. Forsothe the Lord wolde not distruyen the hous of Dauid, for the couenaunt that he hadde gon in with hym, and for he hadde behoten

CAP. XXI.

Forsothe^f Josaphat slepte with hise fa-1 dris, and was^g biried with hem in the citee of Dauid ; and Joram, his sone, regnede for hym. And he^h hadde britheren, the 2 sones of Josaphat, Azarie^i, Jahiel, and Zacarie, Anany^k, and Mychael, and Saphatie ; alle these weren the sones of Josaphat, kyng of Juda. And her fadir 3af to hem 3 many 3iftis of gold and of^l siluer, and^m rentis^n, with strongeste^o citees in Juda ; but he 3af the rewme to Joram, for he was the^p firste gendrid^q. Forsothe^r Joram roos 4 on^t the rewme of his fadir ; and whanne he hadde confermyd hym silf^u, he killide^v alle hise britheren bi swerd, and summe^w of the princes of Juda. Joram was of two 5 and thritti 3eer, whanne he bigan to regne ; and he regnede ei3te 3eer in Jerusalem. And he 3ede in the weies^x of the kyngis 6 of Israel, as the hows of Achab hadde do, for^y the dou3ter of Achab was his wijf ; and he dide yuel in the si3t of the Lord. But the Lord nolde^z distrie the hows of 7 Dauid, for the couenaunt^a which^b he 'hadde maad^c with Dauid, and for^d he 'hadde bi-hi3te^e to 3yue to hym^f a lanterne, and to hise sones^g in al tyme. In tho daies Edom 8

---

z sleep c.　ᵃ Om. ABFH.　ᵇ seuene E.

---

^{u} the whiche ι. whiche NS.　^{v} thei schulden c.　^{w} wende ι.　^{x} schip to go ι. shippe go E.　^{y} And INS. ^{z} the sone INS.　ᵃ hast had INS.　ᵇ hath smyte or destried IS. hath distried N.　^{c} schippis whiche he consentide to make INS.　ᵈ al to-brokun INS.　^{e} thei my3ten INS.　f And INS.　ᵍ he was NS.　ʰ Joram INS. ^{l} that is to wite, Azarie ι. that is, Azarie s.　^{k} and Ananie s.　^{l} Om. N.　^{m} and he 3af hem pencioues INS. ^{n} or rentis IS. Om. N.　^{o} ful stronge ι.　ᴾ his INS.　^{q} goten zone ι.　ʳ And INS.　^{s} roos and wexide [wexe s] my3ti NS.　^{t} upon IS.　ᵘ silf in the [his s] rewme IS.　^{v} slew3 INS.　^{w} also summe ι.　^{x} yuel weies s.　^{y} certis INS.　^{z} wolde not ι.　ᵃ couenaunt of pees s.　ᵇ that INS.　^{c} made INS.　ᵈ that N. forthi that s.　^{e} hi3te INS.　f Dauid INS.　ᵍ Om. N. sones after him s.

that he schulde ʒeuen to hym a lantern, 8 and to his souns in al tyme. In tho days Edom rebellide, that he were not suget to Jude, and he sette to hym a kyng. 9 And whanne Joram was passed with his princis, and with al the chyualrie, that was with hym, he ros the niʒt, and smote Edom, 'the whiche[c] hadde enuyrounde hym, and alle the duykis of his chyualrye. 10 Neuer the later Edom rebellide, that he were not vnder the comaundinge of Juda vnto this day. That tyme and Lobna wente awey, that he were not vnder the hond of hym; forsothe he hadde for- 11 saken the Lord God of their fadirs. Forthermore he forgide heeʒe thingus in the cytees of Juda, and he maad the dwellers of Jerusalem to do fornycacioun, and 12 Juda to breken the lawe. Forsothe ther ben brouʒt to hym lettris fro Helia, the prophete, in the whiche was writen, Thes thingus seith the Lord God of Dauid, thi 13 fadir, For thou wentist not in the weies of Josaphath, thi fadir, and in the wei of Aza, kyng of Juda, bot and thou wentist bi the wey of the kyngis of Irael, and thou madist Judam and the dwellers of Jerusalem to don fornycacioun, folewynge the fornycacioun of the hous of[d] Achab; ferthermore and thi bretheren and the hous of thi fadir, beter thanne thi silf, 14 thou hast sleyn; loo! the Lord schal smyten thee with a grete veniaunce, with thi puple, and sonus, and thi wyues, and 15 with al thi substaunce; thou forsothe schalt waxen seek the most warst langour of wombe, to the tyme that thi guttis gon out lityl melum by sundre 16 days. Thanne the Lord rerede aʒeinus Joram the spirite of Philisteis, and of Arabes, the which ben neeʒ coostis to

rebellide, that[h] it was not suget to Juda, and it ordeynede a kyng to it silf. And 9 whanne Joram hadde passide[i] with hise princes, and al[k] the multitude of knyʒtis, that was with hym, he roos[l] bi niʒt, and smoot Edom†, that cumpasside him, and[m] alle hise[n] duykis of his multitude of knyʒtis. Netheles Edom rebellide[o], that it was not 10 vndir the lordschip of Juda 'til to[p] this dai. In that tyme also Lobna[q] ʒede awei[r], that[s] it was not vndur the hond[t] of hym; for[u] he[v] hadde forsake the Lord God of hise fadris. Ferthermore he made hiʒe 11 places[w] in the citees of Juda, and made[x] the dwelleris of Jerusalem to do fornyca- cioun, 'that is, idolatrie[y], and Juda[z] to breke the lawe[a]. Forsothe[b] lettris weren 12 brouʒt to hym fro Elie, the prophete, in whiche it was writun, The Lord God of Dauid, thi fadir, seith these thingis, For[c] 13 thou 'ʒedist not[d] in the weies of Josaphat, thi fadir, and in the weie of Asa, kyng of Juda, but thou ʒediste[e] bi the weie of the kyngis of Israel, and madist[f] Juda and the dwelleris of Jerusalem to do fornicacioun, and suedist[g] the fornicacioun[h] of the hows of Achab; ferthermore and thou hast slayn thi britheren and[i] the hows of thi fadir[k], 'that weren[l] betere than thou; lo[m]! 14 the Lord schal smyte thee with a greet veniaunce, and thi puple, and thi sones, and wyues[n], and al thi catel; sotheli[o] thou 15 schalt be sijk 'with the[p] worste sorewe of wombe[q], til[r] thin entrailis go out litil[s] and litil bi[t] ech dai. Therfor the Lord reiside[u] 16 aʒens Joram the spirit of Filisteis and Arabeis[v], that[w] marchen with Ethiopiens; and thei[x] stieden[y] in to the lond of Juda, 17 and wastiden[z] it, and thei token awei al the catel[a], that was foundun in the hows of the kyng, ferthermore and hise sones,

† Edom; that is, he killide sudeynly Vdumeys that weren in his oost, lest they wolden go to helpe Ydumeys, that rebelliden aʒens him. Lire here. c.

---

[c] that c.　[d] Om. ꜰ.

[h] so that ꜱ. [i] passid forth aʒens Edom ɪɴꜱ. [k] with al ɪɴꜱ. [l] roos up ɪɴꜱ. [m] and Joram vencushide ɴꜱ. [n] the ɪɴꜱ. [o] rebellid so aʒens Juda ꜱ. [p] vnto ɪɴꜱ. to x. [q] the cuntrey of Lobna ɪɴꜱ. [r] awei fro Joram ɪꜱ. [s] so that ɪꜱ. [t] power ɪɴꜱ. [u] certis ɪɴꜱ. [v] Joram ɪɴꜱ. [w] placis of ydolatrie ɪꜱ. [x] he made ɪɴꜱ. [y] Om. ɪ. [z] he made Juda ɴꜱ. [a] lawe of God ɴꜱ. [b] And ɪɴꜱ. [c] For that ɪɴ. Forthi that ꜱ. [d] hast not go ɪɴꜱ. [e] hast go ɪɴꜱ. [f] thou hast maad ɪɴꜱ. [g] thou hast sued ɪɴꜱ. [h] leccherie ɴꜱ. [i] in ꜱ. [k] fader, that is, princis of the house of thi fader ꜱ. [l] Om. ɴ. which werin ꜱ. [m] lo! that is, wite thou for thi ꜱ. [n] thi wyues ɪɴꜱ. [o] and ɪɴꜱ. [p] Om. ꜱ. [q] thi wombe ɪꜱ. [r] til that ɪɴꜱ. [s] bi litil ɪɴꜱ. [t] Om. ɪɴꜱ. [u] reiside up ɪɴꜱ. [v] of Arabeis ᴄɪɴꜱ. [w] the whiche ɪ. whiche ɴꜱ. [x] these ɪɴꜱ. [y] stieden up ɪᴡꜱ. [z] thei wasteden ɪɴꜱ. [a] substaunce ɪɴꜱ.

17 Ethiopes; and thei stey3eden up in to the lond of Juda, and thei wastiden it, and thei distruyeden al the substaunce, that is founden in the hous of the kyng; ferthermore and the sonus of hym, and the[e] wijues; and ther laft not to hym a sone bot Joacha, that was leste thoru3 18 birth. And vpon alle thes thingus the Lord smote hym with vncurable sorowe of 19 wombe. And whanne to the day schulde folowen day, and the spacis of tymes weren turned ouer, of two 3eer the cercle is fulfild; and so with longe langour he is wastid, so that he schot out also his guttis, and so he wantide the langour to gydre and lijf[f], and he is deed in warst infirmyte. And the puple dide not to hym the deedis office after the maner of brennynge, as it hadde done to the more of 20 hym. Of two and thritty 3eer he was, whanne he beganne to regnen, and ei3t 3eer he regnede in Jerusalem, and he wente not ri3t; and thei biryeden hym in the cyte of Dauid, neuer the later not in the sepulcre of kyngis.

and wyues[b]; and no sone was left to hym, no[c] but Joachaz, that was the[d] leeste[e] in[f] birthe. And ouer alle these thingis the 18 Lord smoot hym[g] with vncurable sorewe of the[h] wombe. And whanne dai cam 19 aftir a[i] dai, and the spaces of tymes weren turned aboute, the[k] cours of twey 3eer was fillid[l]; and so[m] he[n] was wastid 'bi long[o] rot[p], so that he castide[q] out also his[r] entrailis, and so[s] he wantide sorewe[t] and liyf[u] togidere, and he was deed in the werste sikenesse. And the puple dide not to hym seruyce of deed men bi the custom of brennyng, as it[v] hadde do to hise grettere, 'ether auncetris[w]. He[x] was of two 20 and thritti 3eer whanne he bigan to regne, and he regnede ei3te 3eer in Jerusalem, and he 3ede not ri3tfuli[y]; and thei birieden hym in the citee of Dauid, netheles not in the sepulcre of kingis.

CAP. XXII.

1 The dwellers forsothe of Jerusalem setten Ochosiam, his leste sone, kyng for hym; alle forsothe the more thoru3 birthe, that beforn hym weren, theeues of Arabes hadden slayn, the whiche hadden fallyn in to the tentis. And regnede Ochosias, the sone of Joram, kyng of 2 Juda. Of two and fourty 3eer was Ochosias, whanne he hadde begunne to regnen, and oon 3eer he regnede in Jerusalem; name of his modir, Athalia, dou3ter 3 of Amry. And he wente in by the weye of the hous of Achab; forsothe his modir putte hym in, that he vnpitously schulde

CAP. XXII.

Forsothe the dwelleris of Jerusalem or-1 deyneden Ocozie, 'his leeste sone[z], kyng[a] for hym; for theues[b] of Arabeis[c], that[d] felden[e] in to the castels[f], hadden[g] slayn alle the[h] grettere[i] 'in birthe[k], that[l] weren[m] bifor hym. And Ocozie, the sone of Joram, kyng of Juda, regnede[n]. Ocozie was 2 of two and fourti 3eer, whanne he bigan to regne, and he regnede o 3eer in Jerusalem; the name of his modir was Athalia, the dou3ter of Amry. But[o] he en- 3 tride[p] bi the weie of the hows[q] of Achab; for his modir compellide hym to do yuele. Therfor[r] he dide yuel in the si3t of the 4

---

[e] Om. CE. [f] the lif c.

[b] hise wyues _thei taken awey_ INS. [c] Om. I. [d] his INS. [e] leeste _sone_ IS. [f] _or_ 3oungest _sone_ in s. [g] Joram INS. [h] his INS. [i] Om. BCDIM _pr. m._ NOSX. [k] and the IS. [l] fulfillid INS. [m] Om. INS. [n] _the_ kyng I. king Joram s. [o] of vile s. [p] langwschyng IN. [q] defiede _or_ delyuerde out I. defiede N. defied _or_ voyded out s. [r] his owne P. [s] Om. INS. [t] sorwe _or_ peyne s. [u] his liyf INS. [v] he x. [w] Om. IN. [x] Joram INS. [y] ri3tfuli _in the_ [Goddis s] _lawe_ IS. [z] the 3oungist sone of Joram INS. [a] _to be_ kyng INS. [b] the theues INS. [c] Arabie NS. [d] whiche NS. [e] fillen feersly s. [f] castels _of Juda_ INS. [g] and hadden N. [h] hise INS. [i] grettere _or_ eldre bretheren IS. [k] Om. I. [l] whiche INS. [m] weren goten I. werin gendrid S. [n] regned _king_ s. [o] And INS. [p] entride and 3ede s. [q] meynee INS. [r] Certis INS.

4 done. Thanne he dyde yuel in the siʒt of the Lord, as the hous of Achab; thei forsothe weren to hym counseilers after the deth of his fadir, in to his own deth; 5 and he wente in the counseyle of hem. And he wente with Joram, sone of Achab, king of Yrael, in to bataile aʒeinus Asael, kyng of Cyrie, in Ramoth-galaad. And 6 Cyres woundiden Joram; the whiche is turned aʒein, that he were helid in Jezrael; forsothe many woundis he hadde taken in the forseid strijf. Thanne Ochosias, king of Juda, the sone of Joram, came doun for to visiten Joram, the sone of 7 Achab, seeke in Jezrael; the wille forsothe of God was aʒeinus Ochosiam, that he were commyn to Joram. And whanne he were commen, that he schulde gon in with hym aʒeinus Hieu, the sone of Nampsy, whome God anoyntide, that he schulde don awey the hous of Achab. 8 Thanne whanne Hieu schulde ouerturnen[g] the hous of Achab, he fonde the princis of Juda, and the sonus of the bretheren of Ochosie, that mynystreden to hym; and 9 he slewʒ hem. And hym Ochosie sechynge, he toke lurkyng in Samarie, and brouʒt forth to hym he slewʒ; and thei birieden hym, forthi that he was the sone of Josaphath, the whiche hadde souʒte God in al his herte. And ther was no more eny hope, that eny schulde regnen 10 of the stoc of Ochosie. Forsothe Athalia, his modir, seeynge that hire sone was deed, ros, and slewʒ al the kingus stoc 11 of the hous of Joram. Bot Josabeth, the douʒter of the kyng, toke Joas, the sone of Ochosie, and sche staale hym fro the myddis of the sonus of the kyng, whanne thei schulde ben slayn; and sche hidde hym with his nursche in the bed place of lityl beddis. Josabeth forsothe, that hadde hydde hym, was the douʒter of

Lord, as[a] the hows of Achab; for thei[t] weren counselouris to hym[u] in to his perischyng[v], aftir the deth of his fadir; and[w] he ʒede in the counsele of hem. 5 And he[x] ʒede with Joram, the sone of Achab, kyng of Israel, in to batel aʒens Azahel, kyng of Sirye, in to Ramoth of Galaad. And men of Sirie woundiden Jo- 6 ram; which[y] turnede aʒen for to be heelid in Jezrahel; for he hadde take many woundis in the forseid batel. Therfor Ocozie, kyng of Juda, the sone of Joram, ʒede doun[z] to visite Joram, the[a] sone of Achab, sijk[b] in Jezrahel; for[c] it was 7 Goddis wille aʒens Ocozie, that he cam to Joram. And whanne he was comun[d], he ʒede out with hym aʒens Hieu, the sone of Namsi, whom God anoyntide[e], that he schulde do awey the hows of Achab. Therfor whanne Hieu destriede the hows 8 of Achab, he foond[f] the[g] princis of Juda, and the sones of the britheren of Ocozie, that[h] mynystriden to hym[i]; and he[k] killide hem. And he souʒte thilke Ocozie, and 9 cauʒte[l] him hid in Samarie, and after that he was brouʒt to Hieu, Hieu killide hym; and thei birieden hym, for he was the sone of Josaphat, that hadde souʒt God in al his herte. And noon hope was more, that ony of the generacioun of Ocozie schulde regne. For[m] Athalia, his[n] modir[o], 10 siʒ, that hir sone was deed, and sche roos[p], and killide alle the kyngis generacioun of the hows of Joram. Forsothe[q] Josabeth, 11 the douʒter of the[r] kyng[s], took Joas, the sone of Ocozie, and stal[t] hym fro the myddis of the sones of the kyng, whanne thei weren slayn; and sche hidde hym with his nurse in the[u] closet of beddis. Forsothe[v] Josabeth, that hadde hid[w] hym, was the[x] douʒtir of kyng Joram, and wijf of Joiada, the bischop, and the sister of Ocozie; and therfor Athalia killide not

g ouertrowen B.

a as *dide* INS.   t his meynees I. the meynee of Achab S.   u Ochozie IS.   v spillyng I.   w Om. S. x Ochozie INS.   y the which I.   z out X.   a Om. X.   b *that was* sijk IS.   c forsothe INS.   d comun *to Joram* INS.   e anoyntide *king upon Israel* IS.   f foond *there* INS.   g Om. C.   h the whiche I. whiche NS. i seruyden Ochozie INS.   k Hieu INS.   l he cauʒte INS.   m And INS.   n the INS.   o modir of Ochozie INS. p roos vp NS.   q And INS.   r Om. INS.   s kyng *Joram* INS.   t sche stal INS.   u a NS.   v And NS. For X. w hidde AS.   x Om. INS.

kyng Joram, wijf of Joiade, bischop, sister of Ochosie; and therfore Athalie slew3
12 hym^h not. Thanne he was with hem in
the hous of God hid sexe 3eer, in the
whiche Athalie regnede vpon the lond.

hir. Therfor^y he^z was hid with hem in 12
the hows of God sixe 3eer, in whiche^a
Athalia regnede on^b the lond^c.

CAP. XXIII.

1   Joiada forsothe the seuenth 3eer comfortide, toke the maisters of hundrithes,
Azariam, that is, the sone of Jeroboam,
and Ismael, the sone of Johannan, also
Azariam, the sone of Obed, and Maaziam, the sone of Adaye, and Elisaphath,
the sone of Ysecry; and he wente in with
2 hem counseyl and pese couenaunt. The
whiche enuyrounynge Judam, gaderden
Leuytis of alle the cytees of Juda, and
the princis of the meynes of Irael, and
3 camen 'in to^j Jerusalem. Thanne wente
in couenaunt al the multitude in the hous
of the Lord with the kyng. And Joiada
seide to hem, Loo! the sone of the kyng
schal regnen, as the Lord spake vpon the
4 sonus of Dauid. This is thanne the word
5 that 3e schul done. The thridde part of
3ou that ben commen to the saboth, of
prestis, and of Leuytis, and of porters,
schal ben in the 3aatis; the thrid forsothe part at the hous of the kyng; and
the thrid part at the 3aate, that is clepid
of the foundement. Al forsothe the tother
comoun be in the porches of the hous of
6 the Lord; ne eny other man comme in
to the hous of the Lord, bot the prestis,
and that mynystren of Leuytis; thei
aloonly commen in, that ben halowed,
and alle the tother comoun keepe wele
7 the wardis of the Lord. The Leuytis
forsothe enuyroun thei the kyng, eche
hauynge their armes; 3if eny other^k schal
commyn in to the temple, be he slayn;

CAP. XXIII.

Forsothe in the seuenthe 3eer Joiada^d 1
was coumfortid, and took^e centuriouns,
that is^f, Azarie, sone^g of Jeroboam, and
Ismael, the sone of Johannam, and Aza-
rie, the sone of Obeth, and Maasie, the
sone of Adaie, and Elisaphat, the sone of
Zcchri; and he made with hem a^h counsel
and a boond of pees. Whichⁱ cumpassiden 2
Juda, and gaderiden^k togidere dekenes of
alle the citees of Juda, and^l the princes of
the meynees of Israel, and camen^m in to
Jerusalem. Therforⁿ al the multitude 3
made^o couenaunt in the hows of the Lord
with the kyng. And Joinda^p seide to hem,
Lo^q! the^r sone of the kyng schal regne,
as the Lord spak on the sones of Dauid.
Therfor this is the word^s, which^t 3e schu- 4
len do. The thridde part of 3ou thatⁿ ben 5
comun to the sabat, of preestis, and of
dekenes, and of porterys, schal be in the
3atis^v; sotheli^w the^x thridde part schal be^y
at the hous of the kyng; and the thridde^z
part schal be at the 3ate, which^a is clepid
of the foundement. Forsothe^b al the tother^c
comyn puple be^d in the large places^e of
the hows of the Lord; and noon other 6
man entre in to the hows of the Lord, no
but preestis, and thei that mynystren^f of^g
the^h dekenesⁱ; oneli entre thei, that ben
halewid^k, and al the tother^l comyn puple
kepe^m the kepyngis of the Lord. For- 7
sotheⁿ the dekenes cumpasse^o the kyng,
and ech man haue^p hise armuris; and if
ony othere man^q entrith^r in to the temple,

---

^h hir ʀ pr. m.   ⁱ to ᴀʙꜰʜ.   ^k other man c.

^y And ɪɴꜱ.   ^z Joas ɪɴꜱ.   ^a which 3eris ɪꜱ.   ^b upon ɪɴꜱ.   ^c lond *of Juda* ɪꜱ.   ^d Joiada *the bischop* ɪɴꜱ.
^e he took *to him* ɪɴꜱ.   ^f is *to wite* ɪ.   ^g the sone ɪɴꜱ.   ^h Om. ɪɴꜱ.   ⁱ The which ɪ.   ^k thei gaderiden ɪɴꜱ.
^l and *thei gaderiden togidere* ɪꜱ.   ^m thei camen ɪɴꜱ.   ⁿ And ɪɴꜱ.   ^o maade *togidre* ꜱ.   ^p Joiada *the
bishope* ꜱ.   ^q Lo! *Joas* ɪɴꜱ.   ^r Om. ɴꜱ.   ^s word *either heest* ꜱ.   ^t that ɪɴꜱ.   ^u whiche ɴꜱ.   ^v 3atis
kepyng ꜱ.   ^w and ɪɴꜱ.   ^x a ɴ.   ^y be *macchyng* ꜱ.   ^z oother thridde ɪꜱ.   ^a that ɪɴꜱ.   ^b And ɪɴꜱ.
^c oother ɪꜱ.   ^d be *it* ꜱ.   ^e place ꜱ.   ^f seruen ɪɴꜱ.   ^g or ꜱ.   ^h Om. ɪ.   ⁱ dekenes *in the temple* ɪꜱ.
^k halewid *in to the temple* ɪꜱ.   ^l oother ɪꜱ.   ^m kepe *thei* ɪɴꜱ.   ⁿ And ɪɴꜱ.   ^o cumpasse *thei* ɪɴꜱ.   ^p haue
he ɪɴꜱ.   ^q Om. ɴ.   ^r entre ɪɴꜱ.

and be thei with the kyng commynge in
8 and goinge out. Thanne the Leuytis
diden, and al Juda, after alle thingis that
Joiada, the bischop, hadde comaundide;
and alle thei token the men, that weren
vndir hem, and thei camen by ordre of
the saboth with hem, that nowe hadden
fulfild the saboth, and weren gon out.
9 Forsothe Joiade, the bischop, hadde not
leetyn the cumpanyes to[1] gon awey, the
whiche weren wont by sundre weekis to
comme after to hem selue. And Joiada,
the prest, ȝaf to the leders of hundrithis
speres, and tergetis, and bokelers of kyng
Dauid, the whiche he hadde sacride in
10 to the hous of the Lord. And he sette
al the puple, of holdyng daggers, fro the
riȝt partie of the temple vnto the left
part of the temple, before the auter and
the temple, by enuyroun of the kyng.
11 And thei ladden out the kingus sone, and
putten on to hym a dyademe; and ȝeuen
to hym in his hond the lawe to ben
holden, and thei setten hym kyng. And
Joiada, the byschop, enoyntide hym, and
his sonus; and thei inwardly preyden,
12 and seyden, Lyue the kyng! That
whanne Athalia hadde herde, that is, the
voice of men rennyng and preysyng the
kyng, sche wente in to the puple, into
13 the temple of the Lord. And whanne
sche had seen the kyng stondynge upon
the grec in the entre, and princis and
companyes abouten hym, and al the puple
of the lond ioyinge, and criynge in
trumpis, and orgnys of dyuerse maner,
syngynge to gydir, and the voice of men
preysynge, sche kutte hir clothis, and
14 seith, Aspyes! aspyes! Forsothe Joiada,
the bischop, gon out to the leeders of

be he slayn; and be thei[s] with the kyng
entrynge[t] and goynge out. Therfor the 8
dekenes and al Juda diden bi alle thingis,
which Joiada, the bischop, hadde comaundid[u];
and alle[v] token the men, that
weren with hem, and camen[w] bi the ordre
of sabat[x] with hem, that hadden 'fillid
now[y] the sabat, and schulen go[z] out[a]. For 9
Joiada, the bischop, suffride not the cumpenyes
to go awei[b], that[c] weren wont[d] to
come[e] oon after 'the tother[f] bi ech wouke.
And Joiada, the preest, ȝaf to the centurionns
speris, and scheeldis, and bokeleris
of kyng Dauid, whiche[g] he[h] hadde halewid
in to[i] the hows of the Lord. And he[k] or- 10
deynede al the puple, of hem 'that helden[l]
swerdis, at[m] the riȝt side of the temple
'til to[n] the left side of the temple, bifor the
auter and[o] the temple, bi cumpas[p] of the
king. And thei ledden out[q] the sone of 11
the kyng, and[r] settiden[s] a diademe on[t]
hym[u]; and thei ȝauen to hym in his hond
the lawe[v] to be holdun, and thei maden
hym kyng. And Joiada, the bischop, and
his sones anoyntiden hym; and thei preiden[w]
hertli, and seiden, The kyng lyue[x]!
And whanne Athalia hadde herd this 12
thing, that is, the vois of men rennynge
and preisynge the[y] kyng, sche entride to[z]
the puple, in to the temple of the Lord.
And whanne sche hadde seyn the kyng 13
stondynge on[a] the grees in the entryng[b],
and the[c] princes and cumpenyes[d] of knyȝtis
aboute hym, and al the puple of the lond
ioiynge, and sownynge[e] with trumpis, and
syngynge togidere with orguns of dyuerse
kynde, and the vois of men preisynge[f],
sche to-rente hir clothis, and seide, Tresouns!
tresouns! Sotheli[g] Joiada, the bi- 14
schop, ȝede out to the centuriouns, and

[1] Om. c.

[s] *the dekens* INS. [t] entrynge ynne INS. [u] comaundid *to hem* s. [v] alle thei IS. [w] thei camen *to Jerusalem* IS. [x] the sabat INS. [y] now fulfillid INS. [z] haue go IS. han go N. [a] out *thenns* IS. [b] awei *fro the temple* INS. [c] whiche INS. [d] woned I. [e] come *thidur* N. [f] an oother INS. [g] the whiche *weepyns* I. which *weepens* s. [h] Dauid IN. king Dauith s. [i] Om. N. [k] Joiada INS. [l] whiche hadden NS. that holden o. [m] *to be* at NS. [n] vnto I. *lastinge* vnto NS. to X. [o] of AS. [p] the enuyroun INS. the cumpas *plures*. [q] out *Joas* INS. [r] and thei INS. [s] setten IS. [t] upon IS. [u] his heed INS. [v] lawe *of God* NS. [w] preieden *to God* s. [x] liue *he welsumli* s. [y] a NS. [z] into s. [a] at INS. [b] entryng *of the temple* I. entryng *of the temple of God* s. [c] Om. INS. [d] the cumpenyes ç. [e] sownyng *to gidre* s. [f] preisynge *a kyng* IS. [g] And IS.

hundrithes, and princis of the hoost, seide to hem, Ledith hir out of the purseyntis of the temple, and be sche slayn with out forth with swerd; and the prest comaundid, that sche shuld not be slayn in 15 the hous of the Lord. And he putte on hondis to the nollis of hyre; and whanne sche had gon in the ʒate of the hors, of the hous of the king, thei slewen hir 16 there. Forsothe Joiada couenauntide couenaunt of pese betwene hym and al the puple and the kyng, that ther were a 17 puple of the Lord. And so al the puple wente ʼin toᵐ the hous of Baal, and thei distroyeden it; and auters, and mawmetis of it thei to-breeken; Mathan also, the preste of Baal, thei slewen before the 18 auters. Forsothe Joiada sette prouostis in the hous of the Lord, that vndir the hondis of prestis, and Leuytis, the whiche Dauid delide in the hous of the Lord, that thei schulden offeren brent sacrifices to the Lord, as it is writen in the boke of Moysy, in ioye and songus, after the 19 disposicyoun of Dauid. Also he sette porters in the ʒatis of the hous of the Lord, that ther schulde not gon in to 20 it vnclene in eny thing. And he toke leeders of hundrithes, and most stronge men, and princis of the puple, and al the comoun of the lond. And thei maden the kyng to comme doun fro the hous of the Lord, and gon in by the mydil of the ouerʒate in to the hous of the kyng; and thei setten hym in the kyngus see. 21 And al the puple of the lond gladide, and the cytee restyde; bot Athalia is slayn with swerde.

princesʰ of the oost, and seideⁱ to hem, Lede ʒe hir with out the ʼpurseyntis, ethirᵏ closyngis, of the temple, and be sche slayn with outforth bi swerd; and the preest comaundide, that sche schulde not be slayn in the hows of the Lord. And theiˡ set- 15 tiden hondis onᵐ hir nol; and whanne she hadde entrid in to the ʒate of the horsis, of the kyngis hows, thei killiden hir there. Forsothe Joiada couenanntide a boond of 16 pees bitwixe him silf and al the puple and the kyng, that it schulde be the puple of the Lord. Therfor al the puple entride 17 in to the hows of Baal, and distriedenⁿ it, and brakenᵒ the auteris and symylacrisᵖ therof; but thei killiden bifor the auteris Mathan, the preest of Baal. Forsotheᑫ 18 Joiada ordeynede souereyns in the hows of the Lord, that vndur the hondis of preestis, and of dekenes, whicheʳ Dauid departide inˢ the hows of the Lord, theiᵗ schulden offre brent sacrifices to the Lord, as it is writun in the book of Moises, in ioie and songisⁿ, by the ordynaunce of Dauid. Also heᵛ ordeynede porteris in 19 the ʒatis of the hows of the Lord, that an vnclene man in ony thing schulde not entre in to it. And heʷ took theˣ centu- 20 riouns, andʸ strongeste men, and princes of the puple, and al the comyn puple of the lond. And thei maden the kyng to go doun froᶻ the hows of the Lord, and to entre bi the myddis of the hiʒere ʒate in to the hows of the kyng; and thei set- tidenᵃ hym in the kyngis trone. And alᵃ 21 the puple of the lond was glad, and the citee restideᵇ; forsotheᶜ Athalia was slayn bi swerd.

CAP. XXIV.

1 Of seuenⁿ ʒeer was Joas, whanne he hadde begunne to regnen, and fourtye ʒeer he regnede in Jerusalem; name of 2 his modir Sebia of Bersabe. And he dyde that was good before the Lord, alle

CAP. XXIV.

Joas was of seuene ʒeer, whanne he 1 bigan to regne, and he regnyde fourti ʒeer in Jerusalem; the name of his modir was Sebia of Bersabee. And he dide that, 2 that was good bifor the Lord, in alle the

ʰ to princes IN. to the princis s.   ⁱ he seide IN.   ᵏ Om. INS.   ˡ men INS.   ᵐ upon IS.   ⁿ thei distrieden INS.   ᵒ thei braken INS.   ᵖ the symulacris INS.   ᑫ And INS.   ʳ the whiche I.   ˢ into s. ᵗ men INS.   ᵘ in songis INS.   ᵛ Joiada INS.   ʷ Joiada INS.   ˣ Om. IN. to him s.   ʸ the strongeste I. ᶻ of s.   ᵃ setten I.   ᵇ restide fro werris IS.   ᶜ and N3.

3 the days of Joiada, the preste. Forsothe and Joas took two wijues, of the whiche 4 he gat sones and douȝters. After whiche thingus it pleside to Joas, that he schulde 5 enstore the hous of the Lord. And he gadirde the prestis and Leuytis, and seyde to hem, Goth out to the cytees of Juda, and gadereth of al Irael monee, to the reparaciouns of the temple of the Lord oure God, by alle ȝeers; and swijth doth it. Bot the Leuytis diden it more 6 necgligently. And the kyng clepide Joiada, prince, and seyde to hym, Why was not to thee bisynesse, that thou constreyn Leuytis to brengyn in fro Juda and Jerusalem monee, the whiche is ordeynd of Moyses, the seruaunt of the Lord, that al the multitude of Irael schulde bryngyn it⁰ in to the tabernacle of wytnessynge? 7 Athalia forsothe most vnpitous, and hir sonus, distruyeden the hous of God; and of alle thingus, that weren halowed to the temple of the Lord, sche enournede the 8 templeᵖ of Baalym. Thann the kyng comaundide, and thei maaden the ark, and putten it beside the ȝate of the Lord 9 with outeforth. And it is prechid in Juda and in Jerusalem, that alle schulden bere pris to the Lord, that Moyses ordeynde to the seruauntis of God vpon al 10 Irael, in deserte. And alle the princis and alle the puple gladedyn, and goon in, thei ȝeuen in to the ark of the Lord, 11 and putten, so that it was ful. And whanne tyme was, that thei schulden bern the arke bifore the kyng bi the hondis of Leuytis, forsothe thei seen myche monee; and ther wente in a scribe of lawe, whom the firste preste hadde ordeyned, and thei heelden oute the monee, that was in the arke; forsothe the arke thei bern aȝein to his place. And so thei diden bi sundre days,

daies of Joiada, theᵈ preest. Sotheliᵉ and 3 Joas took twei wyues, of whyche he gendrideᶠ sones and douȝtris. Afterᵍ whiche 4 thingis it pleside Joasʰ toⁱ reparele the hows of the Lord. And he gaderide to-5 gidere preestis and dekenes, and seide to hem, Go ȝe out to the citees of Juda, and gadere ȝe of al Israel money, to theᵏ reparelyng of the temple of 'ȝoure Lord Godˡ, bi ech ȝeer; and do ȝe thisᵐ hiȝyngliⁿ. Certis the dekenes didenᵒ necgligentli. And 6 the kyng clepide Joiada, the princeᵖ, and seide to hym, Whi was it not charge to thee, to constreyne the dekenes to brynge yn money of Juda and of Jerusalem, whichᑫ money was ordeyned of Moises, the seruaunt of 'the Lordʳ, that al the multitude of Israel schulde brynge it in to the tabernacle of witnessyng? For the 7 worsteˢ Athalia, and hir sones, distrieden the hows of God; and of alle thingisᵗ, weren halewid to the temple of the Lord, thei ourneden the temple of Baalym. Ther-8 for the kyng comaundide, andᵛ thei maaden an arke, and settidenʷ it bisidis the ȝate of the Lord with out forth. And it wasᵍ 9 prechid in Juda and Jerusalemˣ, that ech man schulde brynge to the Lord theʸ prijs, whichᶻ Moyses, the seruaunt of Godᵃ, ordeynede onᵇ al Israel, in descert. And alle 10 the princes andᶜ al the puple weren glad, and thei entriden, and brouȝten, and sentenᵈ in to the arke of the Lord, so that it was fillidᵉ. And whanne it was tyme, that thei 11 schulden bere the arke bifor the kyng bi the hondis of dekenes, forᶠ thei sienᵍ myche moneyʰ, theⁱ clerk of the kyngᵏ entride, and he whom the firsteˡ preest haddeᵐ ordeynede, and thei scheddenⁿ out the money, that was in the arke; sotheliᵒ thei beren aȝen the arke to 'his placeᵖ. And so thei diden bi alle daies, and money with out noumbre was gaderid togidere; which 12

⁰ Om. ABFII.　ᵖ aunswering place E pr. m.

ᵈ Om. cN.　ᵉ Om. INS.　ᶠ gaat I.　ᵍ And after s.　ʰ to Joas I.　ⁱ for to INS.　ᵏ Om. N.　ˡ the Lord ȝoure God INS.　ᵐ this thing INS.　ⁿ hastily I.　ᵒ diden this thing INS.　ᵖ prince of prestis IS.　ᑫ the which I.　ʳ God s.　ˢ wickid womman IS.　ᵗ the thingis IN.　ᵘ whiche NS.　ᵛ that s.　ʷ thei settiden INS.　ˣ in Jerusalem INS.　ʸ his s.　ᶻ that INS.　ᵃ the Lord NS.　ᵇ vpon IS.　ᶜ of N.　ᵈ senten freli hir ȝiftis s.　ᵉ fillid with tresour s.　ᶠ forthi that IS. for that N.　ᵍ sien or perseyuedin s.　ʰ money in the arke I.　ⁱ money to be in the arke s.　ⁱ a INS.　ᵏ kyngis INS.　ˡ firste or cheef IS.　ᵐ Om. N.　ⁿ helden I.　ᵒ and INS.　ᵖ the place therof INS.

and ther is gadird monee with oute
12 noumbre; the whiche the kyng and
Joiada ȝeuen to hem that stoden vpon
the werkis of the hous of the Lord And
thei hireden of it hewers of stoones, and
craftise men of alle werkis, that thei restoren the hous of the Lord; also forgers
of yren, and of brasse, that that, that
hadde begunne to fallen, were susteyned
13 And thes that wrouȝten diden wijsly, and
the gap of the wallis was hillid bi the
hondis of hem; and thei rereden the hous
of the Lord in to the rather state, and
14 thei maaden it to stonden fast And
whanne thei hadden fulfild alle the
werkis, thei brouȝten before the kyng
and Joiada the tother part of the monee,
of the whiche ben maad the vessels of
the temple in to the seruyse, and to brent
sacrifices; also violis, and other golden
vessels and sylueren And ther weren
offrid brent sacrifices in the hous of the
Lord contynuly, alle the days of Joiade.
15 Forsothe Joiada eeldide ful of days, and
dyed, whanne he was of an hundrith and
16 thrittiᵖ ȝeer, and thei birieden hym in
the cytee of Dauid with kingus, forthi
that he hadde done good with Irael, and
17 with his hous Forsothe after that Joiada died, the princis of Jude wenten in,
and honoureden the kyng, the whiche
pleside by the seruyses of hem, assentide
18 to hem And thei forsoken the temple[q]
of the Lord God of their fadirs, and thei
serueden to mawmette woodis, and grauen
thingus, and ther is don the wrath of
the Lord aȝeynus Judam and Jerusalem
19 for this synne. And he sente to hem
prophetis, that thei schulden turnen aȝein
to the Lord; whom beforen witnessynge
20 thei wolden not heeren And so the Spirite of the Lord clothed Zacharie, the
sone of Joiade, preste, and he stode in

the kyng and Joiada ȝauen to hem that
weren souereyns of the werkis of the hows
of the Lord ' And[q] thei hiriden therof[r]
kitteris of stonys, and crafti men of alle
werkis, that thei schulden reparele the
hows of the Lord, also *thei hiriden*
smythis of yrun, and of bras, that[s] that
thing schulde be vndurset, that[t] bigan to
falle Thei that wrouȝten diden craftili, 13
and the[u] crasyng of the wallis was stoppid bi the hondis of hem, and thei reisiden
the hows of the Lord in to[v] the formere
staat, and maden[w] it to stonde stidfastli
And whanne thei hadden fillid[x] alle werkis[y], 14
thei brouȝten bifor the kyng and Joiada
the tother part of the money, of which
money vessels weren maad in to the[z] seruyce of the temple, and to brent sacrifices[a], also viols, and othere vessels of
gold and of siluer '*weren maad therof*[b]
And brent sacrifices weren offrid in the
hows of the Lord contynueli, in alle the
daies of Joiada Forsothe[c] Joiada ful of 15
daies wexide eld, and he was deed, whanne
he was of an hundrid ȝeer and thritti,
and thei birieden hym in the citee of 16
Dauid with kyngis, for he hadde do good[d]
with Israel, and with his hows. But[e] 17
aftir that[f] Joiada diede[g], the princes of
Juda entriden, and worschipiden the kyng,
which[h] was flaterid with her seruices, and
assentide[i] to hem. And thei forsoken the 18
temple of the Lord God of her fadris,
and seruyden[k] idols in wodis, and grauen
ymagis; and the ire of the Lord was
maad aȝens Juda and Jerusalem for this
synne And he[l] sente to hem profetis, that 19
thei schulen turne aȝen to[m] the Lord,
whiche[n] profetis witnessynge[o] thei nolden[p]
here Therfor[q] the Spirit of the Lord 20
clothide[r] Zacharie, the preest, the sone of
Joiada, and he stood in the[s] siȝt of the
puple, and seide to hem, The Lord seith

[p] thrittith *B* [q] couenaunt *E pr m*

[q] And of that money INS [r] Om INS [s] and S [t] the whiche I [u] of the S [v] Om S [w] thei maden INS [x] fulfillid INS [y] the werkis IN [z] Om INS [a] sacrifice NS. [b] Om N [c] And INS [d] gode *thingis* IN many good *thingis* S [e] And NS [f] Om I [g] was deed IN [h] that I [i] he consentide INS [k] thei seruyden INS [l] *God* IS [m] to *him* IS [n] the whiche I [o] witnessinge *the truthe* NS [p] wolden not I [q] Thanne I [r] clothide *or enuyrounde* IS [s] Om IN

the siȝte of the puple, and seyde, Thes thingus seith the Lord, Why ouerpasse ȝe the heeste of the Lord, that schal not profiten to ȝou, and ȝe han forsaken the 21 Lord, that he forsake ȝou? The whiche gadered aȝeynus hym, senten stoones, after the heste of the kyng, in the hall of the 22 hous of the Lord. And king Joas is not recordid of the mercy that Joiada, the fadir of hym, hadde done with hym; bot he[r] slewȝ his sone. The whiche, whanne he schulde dyen, seith, The Lord see, and 23 requyre. And whanne the ȝeer was ouerturned, the hoost of Cirie steiȝede up aȝeinus hym, and came in to Judam and Jerusalem, and slewȝ alle the princis of the puple; and al the pray thei senten 24 to the king, to Damasc. And certis whanne ther was commen a litil noumbre of Ciries, the Lord toke in[s] the hondis of hem vnnoumbreable multitude, forthy that thei hadde forsaken the Lord God of their fadris. In to Joas also thei enhauntiden schenschipful domys; 25 and goynge awey thei laften hym in grete langours. Forsothe his seruauntis arisen aȝeinus hym, in to vengyng of the blode of the sone of Joiade, prest; and thei slewen hym in his bed, and he is deed. And thei birieden hym in the cytee of Dauid, bot not in the sepulcris 26 of kingis. Forsothe ther aweytiden to hym Zabath, the sone of Semath Amanytidis, and Josabeth, the sone of Se-27 marith, Moabitidis. Bot the sonus of hym, and the soume of monee that was leyd to gydre vndir hym, and the enstorynge of the hous of God, ben writen more diligently in the boke of Kyngis.

these thingis, Whi breken ȝe the co-maundement[t] of the Lord, 'which thing[u] schal not profite to ȝou, and ȝe han forsake the Lord, that he schulde forsake ȝou? Whiche[v] weren[w] gaderide togidere 21 aȝens hym[x], and[y] senten[z] stonys[a], bi[b] co-maundement[c] 'of the kyng[d], in the large place of the hows of the Lord. And kyng 22 Joas hadde not mynde on[e] the merci[f] which[g] Joiada, the fadir of Zacharie, hadde doon with hym; but he killide the soue of Joiada. And whanne Zacharie diede, he seide, The Lord se[h], and seke[i]. And 23 whanne a ȝeer was turned[k] aboute, 'ether endid[l], the oost of Sirie stiede[m] aȝens Joas, and it cam in to Juda and in to Jerusalem, and it killide alle the princes of the puple; and thei[n] senten al the prey to the kyng, to[p] Damask[q]. And certeyn, 24 whanne a ful litle noumbre of men of Sirie was comun[r], the Lord bitook in her hondis a multitude[s] with out noumbre, for thei hadden forsake the Lord God of her fadris. Also thei vsiden[t] schameful[u] domes in[v] Joas; and thei ȝeden[w] awei[x], and leften[y] 25 hym in grete sorewis. Sotheli[z] hise seruauntis risiden[a] aȝens hym, in to veniaunce of the blood of the sone of Joiada, preest; and killiden[b] hym in his bed, and he was deed. And thei[c] birieden hym in the citee of Dauid, but not in the sepulcris[d] of kyngis. Forsothe[e] Sabath, the sone of 26 Semath of Amon, and Josabeth, the sone of Semarith of Moab, settiden tresouns to hym[f]. Sotheli[g] hise sones, and the summe 27 of money that was gaderid vndur hym, and the reparelyng of the hows of God, ben writun diligentli in the book of Kyngis.

---

[r] Om. ABCFH.   [s] in to E pr. m.

---

[t] heest INS.   [u] the whiche thing I. that N.   [v] And the peple INS.   [w] wus I.   [x] the prophet I. the profeet of God S.   [y] and thei INS.   [z] threwen I. castiden N. senten, that is, thei threwen S.   [a] stonys at him INS.   [b] bi the kyngis I.   [c] heest INS.   [d] Om. I.   [e] of INS.   [f] merci or goodnesse S.   [g] that INS.   [h] se this thing I. se or take heede to this thing S.   [i] aȝen seke it I. aȝen seke N. aȝen seke he it S.   [k] brouȝt I.   [l] Om. IN.   [m] stiede up INS.   [n] the men of Sirie is. the men N.   [p] of A.   [q] Sirie INS.   [r] comun in to Juda INS.   [s] multitude of Jewis is.   [t] vsiden or diden s.   [u] shaamful or dispiteful s.   [v] aȝens INS.   [w] wenten I.   [x] awei fro him S.   [y] thei leften S.   [z] And INS.   [a] resen up INS.   [b] thei killiden INS.   [c] men INS.   [d] sepulcre S.   [e] And INS.   [f] Joas INS.   [g] Certis INS.

CAP. XXV.

1 Amasias forsothe, his sone, regnede for hym; of fyue and twenty ȝeer was Amasias, whanne he hadde begunne to regnen, and nyne and twenty ȝeer he regnede in Jerusalem; name of his modir Joiaden, 2 of Jerusalem. And he dide good in the siȝte of the Lord, neuer the later not in 3 perfijt herte. And whanne he sawȝ the empyre strengthed to hym, he kutte the seruauntis throtis, that slewen his fadir 4 the kyng; bot the sonus of hem he slewȝ not; as it is writen in the boke of the lawe of Moyses, where the Lord comaundide, seyinge, The fadirs schul not ben slayn for the sonus, ne the sonus for their fadirs; bot echone[t] in his synne 5 schal dyen. Thanne Amazias gaderde Judam, and ordeynede hem by meynees leders of thousandis and maystris of hundrithis, in al Juda and Beniamyn; and he tolde fro twentye ȝeer and aboue, and he fonde thritty thousande of ȝonge men, that myȝten gon out to fiȝten, and holden 6 spere and terget. Also by meed he hyred of Irael an hundrith thousand of stronge men, for an hundrith talentis of syluer, that thei schulden fiȝten aȝeinus the sonus 7 of Edom. There came forsothe to hym a man of God, and seith, O! kyng, go not out with thee the hoost of Irael; forsothe the Lord is not with Irael and 8 with alle the sonus of Effraym; that ȝif thou weenist that strengthe of hoost batails to stonden, the Lord schal maken thee to ben ouercommen of ennnyes; of God forsothe is to helpen, and in to fliȝt to 9 turnen. And Amazias seide to the man of God, What thanne schal be done of the hundrith talentis, that I ȝaf to the knyȝtis of Irael? And the man of God

CAP. XXV.

Forsothe[h] Amasie, 'his sone[i], regnede for 1 hym; Amasie was of fyue and twenti ȝeer, whanne he bigan to regne, and he regnyde nyne and twenti ȝeer in Jerusalem; the name of his modir *was* Joiaden, of Jerusalem. And he dide good in the siȝt of 2 the Lord, netheles not in perfit herte. And whanne he siȝ the empire strengthid 3 to hym silf, he stranglide the seruauntis, that[j] killiden the kyng, his fadir; but he 4 killide not the sones of hem; as it is writun in the book of the lawe of Moises, where the Lord comaundide, seiynge[k], Fadris schulen not be slayn for the[l] sones, nether the[m] sones for her fadris; but ech man schal die in[n] his owne synne. Ther- 5 for[o] Amasie gaderide togidere[p] Juda[q], and ordeynede[r] hem bi meynees and[s] tribunes and centuriouns, in[t] al Juda and Beniamyn; and he noumbride[u] fro twenti ȝeer and aboue, and he foonde thritti thousynde of ȝonge[v] men, that ȝeden out to batel, and helden spere and scheeld. Also 6 for mede he hiride of Israel an hundrid thousynde of stronge men, for an hundrid talentis of siluer, that thei schulden fiȝte aȝens the sones of Edom. Forsothe[w] a 7 man of God cam to hym[x], and seide, A[y]! kyng[z], the oost of Israel go[a] not out with thee, for[b] the Lord is not with Israel and with alle the sones of Effraym; for if[a] thou gessist that batels stonden in the[c] myȝt of oost[d], the Lord schal make thee to be ouercomun of enemyes[e], for[f] it is of God for to helpe, and to turne[g] in to fliȝt. And Amasie seide to the man of God, 9 What therfor[h] schal be doon of the hundrid talentis, which Y ȝaf to the knyȝtis of Israel? And the man of God answeride to hym, The Lord hath[i], wherof he

---

[t] eche c.

[h] And INS. [i] the sone of Joas I. sone of Joas N. Joas sone s. [j] whiche NS. [k] seiynge *thus* I. [l] her NS. [m] Om. INS. [n] in or for s. [o] And INS. [p] Om. IN. thanne s. [q] the men of Juda INS. [r] he ordeynede INS. [s] Om. I. and *he ordeyned* s. [t] and I. [u] noumbride *hem* IN. noumbrid *the peple* s. [v] *able* ȝoung s. [w] And INS. [x] Amasie INS. [y] A! A! v. [z] thou kyng INS. [a] go it s. [b] certis INS. [c] Om. INS. [d] an oost INS. the oost xb. [e] thin enemyes IN. [f] forsothe INS. [g] turne *men* INS. [h] thanne s. [i] haue s.

answerde, The Lord hath, wherof he may
10 зeue to thee many mo thanne these. And
so Amazias seuered theᵘ hoost that came
to hym of Effraym, that he schulde
turnen aзeyn in to his place; and thei,
aзeinus Judam hugely wratthedᵛ, ben turn-
11 ede aзein in to their regyoun. Bot Amazias trustily ladde out his puple, and
wente in to the valeye of salt places, and
he smote the sonus of Seyr, tenn thou-
12 sand. And other tenn thousand of men
token the sonus of Juda, and brouзten to
an heeзe fallynge place of a maner stoon;
and thei tumbleden hem doun fro the
cop in to the lowest; the whiche al to-
13 brosten. And that hoost thatᵂ Amazie
sente aзein, that it зeede not with hym
in to batayle, is helde out in the cytees of
Juda fro Samarie and to Betheron; and,
thre thousand sleen, he deuydideˣ myche
14 preye. Amazias also after the slauзter
of Ydumes, the brouзt to goddis of the
sonis of Seyr, he sette hem in to goddis
to hym, and he honourede hem, and to
15 hem he brende ensence. For what thing
the Lord wroth aзeynst Amazie, he sente
to hym a prophete, that schulde sey to
hym, Why hast thou honourede goddis
that han not delyuerde their puple fro
16 thin hond? And whanne these thingus
he schulde speken, he answerde to hym,
Whether ert thou the counseylere of the
kyng? rest, lest perauenture I slee thee.
And so the prophete goynge aweye, I
woote, he seith, that the Lord hath
thouзte to sleen thee; for thou hast don
this yuel, and ferthermore thou hast not
17 assentide to my counseyle. Thanne Amazias, king of Juda, the werst counseil gon
in, sente to Joas, the sone of Joachas, sone
of Hieu, the king of Irael, seyinge, Cum,

may зelde to thee mycheᵏ mo thingis
than these. Therfor Amasie departide the 10
oost that cam to hym fro Effraym, that
it schulde turne aзen in to his place; and
theiˡ weren wrooth greetli aзens Juda, and
turnedenᵐ aзen in to her cuntrei. For- 11
sotheⁿ Amasie ledde out tristili his puple,
and зedeᵒ in to the valei of makyngis of
salt, and he killide of the sones of Seir
ten thousynde. And the sones of Juda 12
token othere ten thousynde of men, and
brouзtenᵖ to the hiз scarre of summeq
stoon; andʳ castidenˢ hem doun fro the
hiзesteᵗ in to theᵘ pit; whicheᵛ alleᵂ
brakenˣ. And thilke oost whomʸ Amasie 13
hadde sent aзen, that it schulde not go
with him to batel, was spred abrood in
the citees of Juda fro Samarie 'til toˣ
Betheron; and aftir 'that itᵃ hadde slayn
thre thousyndeᵇ, it took aweyᶜ a greet
preie. And Amasie, after the sleyng of 14
Idumeis, and after that he hadde brouзtᵈ
the goddis of the sones of Seir, ordeynedeᵉ
hem 'in toᶠ goddis to hym silf, and wor-
schipideᵍ hem, and brente enceuse to hem.
Wherfor the Lord was wrooth aзeus Ama- 15
sie, and senteʰ to hym a profete, that seide
to hym, Whi worschipist thou goddis thatⁱ
'delyueriden notᵏ her puple fro thin hond?
Whanneˡ the profete spak these thingis, 16
Amasie answeride to hym, Whether thou
art a counselour of the king? ceesse thouᵐ,
lest perauenture Y sle thee. Therforⁿ the
profete зede aweiᵒ, and seide, Y woot, that
the Lord thouзteᵖ to sle thee; for thou
didistq this yuel, and ferthermore thouʳ
assentidistˢ not to my counsel. Therfor 17
Amasie, the king of Juda, whanne he
hadde takeᵗ a ful yuel counsel, senteᵘ to
the kyng of Israel Joas, the sone of Joachaz, the sone of Hieu, and seideᵛ, Come

---

ᵘ that c. ᵛ wratthith BH. ᵂ that abode stille F. ˣ deuide c.

ᵏ many I. ˡ the men INS. ᵐ thei turneden INS. ⁿ And INS. ᵒ he зede INS. ᵖ thei brouзten hem INS.
q u IM pr. m. ʳ and thei INS. ˢ casten I. ᵗ hiзeste part I. ᵘ a I. ᵛ the whiche I. ᵂ al in her
fallyng s. ˣ to-braken I. to-brasten N. to-braste s. ʸ that I. ᶻ vnto INS. ᵃ the oost of Israel IS.
it N. ᵇ thousynde of Juda I. thousynde men of Juda NS. ᶜ awei with it s. ᵈ brouзt thens with him s.
ᵉ he ordeynede INS. ᶠ to be into I. ᵍ he worschipide INS. ʰ he sente INS. ⁱ the whiche I. whiche NS.
ᵏ han not delyuered INS. ˡ And whanne INS. ᵐ thou to speke thus to me NS. ⁿ And INS. ᵒ awei
fro him s. ᵖ hath thouзt INS. q hast do INS. ʳ for thou s. ˢ assentist NS. ᵗ Om. INS. ᵘ he
sente INS. ᵛ he seide IN. he seide to him s.

18 see we[z] us to gyder. And he sente aȝein
messagers, seyinge, The thistil that is in
Liban sente to the cedre of Liban, seyinge, Ȝeue thi douȝter wijf to my sone;
and loo! the bestis that weren in the
wode of Liban wenten and to-treden the
19 thistil. Thou seidist, I haue smyten E-
dom, and therfore thin hert is rered in to
prid; sitt in thi hous; why enyl stirrist
thou aȝeinus thee, that thou falle, and
20 Juda with thee? Amazias wolde not
heeren, for thi that the wille of the Lord
was, that he schulde ben taken in the
hondes of the enmyes, for the goddis of
21 Edom. Thanne Joas, kyng of Irael,
steiȝide up, and thei ȝenen to hem silf
beholdingis either to other. Amazias
forsothe, kyng of Juda, was in Beth-
22 sames of Juda; and Juda felle beforn
23 Irael, and fleiȝ in to his tabernaclis. Forsothe Joas, kyng of Irael, toke Amaziam,
kyng of Juda, sone of Joas, sone of Ochosie, in Bethsames, and brouȝt in to Jerusalem; and distruyde the wallis of it fro
the ȝate of Effraym vnto the ȝate of the[a]
24 corner, in foure hundrith cubitis. And
al the gold and the[b] syluer, and alle the
vessels that he founde in the hous of the
Lord, and anentis Obededom, in the tresories and of the kyngis hous, also and
the sonus of taken to prisoun he brouȝte
25 in to Samarie. Forsothe Amazias, the
sone of Joas, kyng of Juda, lyuede, after
that Joas, the sone of Joachaz, kyng of
26 Irael, is deed, fyfteen ȝeer. The remnaunt forsothe of the wordis of Amazie,
the rather and the last, ben writen in the
boke of the kingus of Juda and of Irael.
27 The whiche after that he wente awei fro

thou[w], se we[x] vs togidere. And he[y] sente 18
aȝen[z] messangeris[a], and seide, A 'cardue,
ether a tasil[b], which[c] is in[d] the Liban[e]
sente to the[f] cedre[g] of the Liban, and
seide, Ȝyue thi douȝter a[h] wijf to my
sone; and lo! beestis that weren in the[i]
wode of the[j] Liban ȝeden and defouliden
the cardue[k]. Thou seidist, Y haue smyte[l] 19
Edom, and therfor thin herte is reysid in
to pride; sitte thou[m] in thin hows; whi
stirist thou yuel aȝens thee[n], that thou
falle[o], and Juda with thee? Amasie nolde[p] 20
here[q], for it was the wille of the Lord,
that he schulde be bitakun[r] in to the
hondis of enemyes[s], for the goddis of
Edom[t]. Therfor Joas, kyng[u] of Israel, 21
stiede[v], and thei[w] siȝen hem silf togidere.
Sotheli[x] Amasie, the[y] kyng of Juda, was
in Bethsames of[z] Juda; and Juda felde 22
doun bifor Israel, and fledde[a] in to his
tabernaclis. Certis[b] the kyng of Israel 23
took in Bethsames Amasie, the[c] kyng of
Juda, the[d] sone of Joas, sone[e] of Joachaz,
and[f] brouȝte[g] in to Jerusalem; and he[h]
destriede the wallis therof fro the ȝate of
Effraym 'til to[i] the ȝate of the corner, bi
foure hundrid cubitis[k]. And he ledde 24
aȝen in to Samarie al the gold and siluer,
and alle vessels[l] whiche[m] he foond in the
hows of the Lord, and at Obededom, in
the tresouris also of the kyngis hows,
also and the sones of ostagis[n]. Forsothe[o] 25
Amasie, kyng[p] of Juda, the[q] sone of
Joas, lyuede fiftene ȝeer aftir that Joas,
kyng[r] of Israel, the[rr] sone of Joachaz,
was deed. Sotheli[s] the residue[t] of[u] the 26
formere and the laste wordis of Amasie
ben writun in the book of kyngis of Juda
and of Israel. And aftir that he ȝede[v] 27

[z] seew *or ioyne* A. [a] Om. B. [b] Om. ACH.

[w] thou *to me* S. [x] and se we IN. and se thow we S. [y] *the kyng of Israel* IS. [z] Om. I. [a] messageris *to him* S. [b] thystil I. tasil N. [c] that INS. [d] Om. S. [e] Liban *or mount* S. [f] a INS. [g] cedre tree INS. [h] Om. INS. [i] Om. N. [j] Om. I. [k] thistil I. tasil NS. [l] smetyn *or distroyed* S. [m] thou *stille* I. thou *or abide* S. [n] thi selff INS. [o] falle *or perische* IS. [p] wolde not I. [q] here *this* I. here *these wordis* NS. [r] takun X. [s] hise enemyes NS. [t] Edom *whiche he wirschipide* IS. [u] the kyng INS. [v] wente up *aȝens Juda* I. stiede *aȝens Juda* N. stiede up *aȝens Juda* S. [w] he and Amasie INS. [x] And INS. [y] Om. S. [z] *a citee* of IS. [a] he fledde INS. [b] And INS. [c] Om. S. [d] Om. NS. [e] the sone IN. [f] and he INS. [g] brouȝte *hin* NS. [h] Joas IN. [i] vnto INS. to X. [k] cubitis *of lengthe* S. [l] the vessels INS. [m] that I. [n] ostagis *he took awei with him* S. [o] And INS. [p] the kyng INX. [q] and the A. [r] the kyng IN. [rr] and the A *pr. m.* [s] And INS. [t] remenaunt INS. [u] and INS. [v] had gon INS.

the Lord benten to hym buschmentis in Jerusalem ; and whanne he hadde flowen to Lachis, thei senten and slewen hym 28 there ; and bryngynge aȝein vpon hors, biryeden hym with his faders in the citee of Dauid.

awei fro the Lord, thei settiden[w] to hym tresouns in Jerusalem ; and whanne he hadde fledde to Lachis, thei senten[x] and killiden hym there ; and thei brouȝten[y] 28 aȝen on[z] horsis, and birieden[a] hym with his fadris in the citee of Dauid.

CAP. XXVI.

1 Forsothe al the puple of Juda his sone, Osie, of sexteen ȝeer, setten kyng for his 2 fadir Amazie. He bild up Aylath, and restored it to the lordschip of Juda, aftir 3 that the kyng slepte with his fadirs. Of sexteen ȝeer Osias was, whanne he hadde begunne to regnen ; and two and fyfty ȝeer he regned in Jerusalem ; name of his 4 modre, Yechelya, of Jerusalem. And he dide that was riȝt in the siȝt of the Lord, aftir alle thingus that Amazias, his fader, 5 hadde done. And he souȝte the Lord in the days of Zacharie, vndirstondinge and seeing God ; and whanne he schuld sechen 6 God, he louede hym in alle thingus. Aftirward he wente out, and fauȝte aȝeinus Philisteis, and he[e] distruyede the wall of Geth, and the wall of Jabnye, and the wal of Azoty ; and he bilde up burȝ 7 towns in Azote of Phylisteym. And the Lord halpe hym aȝeynus Philisteym, and aȝenus Arabas that dwelliden in Garba- 8 hal, and aȝenus Amonytis. And Amonytis spendiden the ȝiftis to Ozie, and his name is puplischit vnto the entre of Egipt for 9 his oft victories. And Ozias bilde up toures in Jerusalem vpon the ȝate of the corner, and vpon the ȝate of the valey, and other in the same side of the wall ; 10 and he fastnede hem. And he bilde out also toures in wildirnesse, and dalf out many cysternes ; forthi that he hadde many heestis bothe in the wijlde feeldis and in the wastite of desert. Also vynes he hadde and wyne makers in hillis, and

CAP. XXVI.

Forsothe al the puple of Juda made 1 kyng[b], Ozie, his sone, of sixtene[c] ȝeer[d], for[e] his fader Amasie. He bildide Hailath, and 2 restoride it to the lordschipe of Juda, after that the[f] kyng[g] slepte with hise fadris. Ozie was of sixtene[h] ȝeer, whanne he bi- 3 gan to regne ; and he regnede two and fifti ȝeer in Jerusalem ; the[i] name of his modir was Hiechelia, of Jerusalem. And 4 he dide that[k], that was riȝtful in the siȝt of the Lord, bi alle thingis whiche Amasie, his fadir, hadde do. And he souȝte the 5 Lord in the daies of Zacarie, vndurstond- ynge and seynge God ; and whanne he souȝte God, God reulide hym in alle thingis. Forsothe[l] he ȝede out, and fauȝt 6 aȝens Filisteis, and distriede the wal of Geth[m], and the wal of Jabyne, and the wal of Azotus ; and he bildide stronge places in Azotus and in Filistiym. And the 7 Lord helpide hym bothe aȝens Filisteis, and aȝens[n] Arabeis that dwelliden in Gar- bahal, and[o] aȝenus Amonytis. Amonytis 8 paieden ȝiftis to Ozie, and his name was pupplischid 'til to[p] the entryng of Egipt for ofte[q] victories. And Ozie bildide touris[r] 9 in Jerusalem ouer the ȝate of the corner, and ouer the ȝate of the valey, and[s] othere[t] touris[u] in the same side of the wal ; and made[v] tho stidefast[w]. Also he bildide touris 10 in the[x] wildirnesse, and he[y] diggide ful many cisternes ; for he hadde many[z] beestis as wel in the[a] feeldi places as in the[b] wast- nesse of deseert. Also he hadde vyneris and tiliers of vynes in the[c] hilles, and in

[c] Om. c.

[w] setten 1.   [x] senten *thider* s.   [y] brouȝten *him* ins.   [z] vpon s.   [a] thei birieden ins.   [b] Om. ins. [c] of fyftene N. *that was* of fiftene s.   [d] ȝeer *age* is.   [e] kyng for ins.   [f] Om. ins.   [g] kyng *Amasie* ins. [h] fyftene N.   [i] and the s.   [k] that *thing* ins.   [l] And ins.   [m] *strength of* Geth s.   [n] Om. s.   [o] Om. s. [p] vnto ins. to x.   [q] *hise* ofte is.   [r] ȝatis s.   [s] and *he made* ns.   [t] *mo* othere 1.   [u] Om. 1.   [v] he made ins.   [w] stidfast *or strong* s.   [x] Om. ins.   [y] Om. n.   [z] ful many ins.   [a] Om. insx.   [b] Om. cs. [c] Om. ins.

in Carmele; forsothe he was a man ȝeuen
11 to erth tyllyinge[d]. The hoost forsothe of
the fyȝtynge men of hym, that wenten
forth to batayles, was vndir the hond of
Heiel, scribe, and Mazie, doctour, and vndir the hond of Ananye that was of the
duykis of the kyng; and al the noumbre
of princis, by their meynees, of stronge
men two thousand and sexe hundrith.
13 And vndir hem al the hoost of thre hundrith and seuen thousand and fyne hundrith, that weren able to batail, and for
14 the king aȝeinus the enmyes fouȝten. And
Ozias maad redy to hem, that is, to al
the hoost, tergetis, and speres, and hel-
mes, and hauberiouns, and bowes, and
15 slyngis to stones to ben throwen. And
he maad in Jerusalem engynes of dyuerse maner, the whiche he sette in
toures, and in the corners of wallis, that
thei schulden casten arewes and grete
stones; and his name is gon out aferre,
for thi that the Lord halpe hym, and
16 hadde strengthede hym. Bot whanne he
was strengthed, his hert is arered[e] in to
his deth; and he dispisede the Lord his
God; and gon in to the temple of the
Lord, he wolde brenne encense vpon the
17 autir of maad encense. And anoon aftir
hym wente in Azarias, the preste, and
with hym prestis of the Lord, seuenty
18 men most worthi; and thei withstoden
to the kyng, and seyden, Ozia, it is not
of thin office, that thou brenne encense to
the Lord, bot of the prestis of the Lord,
that is, of the sonus of Aaron, that ben
sacrid to syche of maner seruyse; go out
fro the seyntuarye, ne dispise thou; for
it schal not ben wijtyd to thee in to glo-
19 rie of the Lord God. And Ozias is
wroth, and holdinge in the hond a censere, that he brenne encense, he 'thratt to[g]
the prestis; and anoon ther is sprungen

Carmele[d]; for he was a man ȝouun to
erthetilthe. Forsothe[e] the oost of hise 11
werriours, that ȝeden forth to batels, vndur
the hond of Heiel, scribe, and of Masie,
techere[f], and vndur the hond of Ananye
that was of[g] the[h] duykis of the kyng; and
al the noumbre of princes, by her meynees,
was of stronge men two thousynde and
sixe hundrid. And vndur hem was al the 13
oost, thre[i] hundrid thousynde and seuen
thousynde and fyue hundrid, that[j] weren
able[k] to batel, and fouȝten[l] for the king
aȝens aduersaries[m]. And Ozie made redi 14
to hem, that is, to al the oost, scheldis,
and speris, and basynetis, and haburiouns,
and bouwis, and slyngis to caste stonys.
And he made in Jerusalem eugynes of dy- 15
uerse kynde, which he settide[n] in touris,
and in the[o] corneris of wallis, that tho
schulden caste[p] arowis and grete stoonys;
and his name ȝede out fer, for the Lord
helpide hym, and hadde maad him strong.
But whanne he was maad strong, his herte 16
was reisid[q] in to his perischyng; and he[r]
dispiside 'his Lord God[s]; and he entride
in to the temple of the Lord, and wolde
brenne encense on[t] the auter of encense.
And anoon Azarie, the preest, entride after 17
hym, and with hym the[u] preestis of the
Lord, seuenti[v] 'men ful noble[w]; whiche[x] 18
aȝenstoden the kyng, and seiden[y], Ozie, it
is not of thin office, that thou brenne encense to the Lord, but[z] of the[a] preestis of
the Lord, that is, of the sones of Aaron,
that[b] ben halewid to siche seruyce; go
thou out of the[c] seyntuarye; dispise[d] thou
not[e]; for this thing schal not be arettid of
the Lord God to thee in to glorie. And 19
Ozie was wrooth[f], and he[g] helde in the[h]
hond the censere for to offre encence, and
manaasside[i] the preestis[j]; and anoon lepre
was sprungun forth in his forheed, bifor
the preestis in the hows of the Lord on[k]

[d] tilthynge E. [e] rerid c. [f] Om. DCFII. [g] was dryuen of E pr. m.

[d] the greet mounteyne INS. Carmele I marg. [e] And IN. [f] the techere INS. [g] souereyn of INS.
[h] Om. INS. [i] that is, thre IS. [j] the whiche I. whiche NS. [k] able men INS. [l] these fouȝten IS. [m] hise
aduersaries IS. [n] sette INS. [o] Om. A. [p] caste out INS. [q] reisid up INS. [r] Om. S. [s] the Lord his
God INS. [t] upon IS. [u] sixty INS. [v] Om. INS. [w] of ful noble men S. [x] the whiche I. [y] seiden to
him S. [z] but it is I. but this office is S. [a] Om. I. [b] whiche NS. [c] Om. I. [d] and dispise INS. [e] not
God IS. [f] wroth therfor S. [g] Om. CELP. [h] his IS. [i] he manasside INS. [j] preestis for that thei vnder-
nemyn him S. [k] upon IN.

a lepre in his forhede, before the prestis in
the hous of the Lord vpon the auter of maad
20 encense. And whanne Azaria, the bischop,
hadde beholden hym, and alle the tother
prestis seen a lepre in his forhede, hastely
thei puttyn hym out; and he aferd hyȝede
to gon out; forthi that he hadde feelid
21 anoon the veniaunce of the Lord. Thanne
Ozias was mesel vnto the day of his deth,
and dwellide in an hous seuered, ful of
lepre; for the whiche he was throwen out
fro the hous of the Lord. Bot Joathan,
his sone, gouernede the hous of the kyng,
22 and demede the puple of the lond. The
remnaunt forsothe of the wordis of Ozie,
of the rather and of the last, wrote
Ysayas, the sone of Amos, prophete.
23 And Ozias slepte with his fadirs, and
thei biryeden hym not in the feeld of
kyngis sepulcres, forthi that he was lee-
prous; and Joathan, his sone, regnede
for hym.

CAP. XXVII.

1   Of fyue and twenty ȝeer was Joathan,
whanne he hadde begunne to regnen, and
sixteen ȝeer he regnede in Jerusalem;
name of his moder Jerusa, the douȝter of
2 Sadoch. And he dide that was riȝt before the Lord, aftir alle thingus that Ozias,
his fadir, hadde don; out take that he
wente not in to the temple of the Lord,
3 and ȝit the puple trespasside. He bild
up the heeȝ ȝate of the hous of the Lord,
and in the wal of Ophel many thingus
4 maad[h]; and citees bilde in the hillis of
Juda, and in heeȝ wodis, castels, and
5 toures. And he fauȝt aȝeinus the kyng of
the sonus of Amon, and ouercame hym;
and the sonus of Amon ȝeuen to hym in
that tyme an hundrith talentis of syluer,
and tenn thousand choris of barly, and as
fele of whete; thes thingus ȝeuen to hym
the sonus of Amon the secound ȝeer and
6 the thrid. And Joathan is strengthed,

the auter of encense. And whanne Azarie, 20
the bischop, hadde biholde hym, and[l] alle
othere[m] preestis ʼhadden biholde him[n], thei
sien lepre in his forheed, and hyyngli[o] thei
puttiden hym[p] out[q]; but also he was aferd,
and hastide to go out; for he feelide anoon
the veniaunce of the Lord. Therfor kyng 21
Ozie was leprouse ʼtil to[r] the[s] dai of his
deeth, and dwellide[t] in an hows bi it silf,
and he was ful of lepre; ʼfor which[u] he
was cast out of the hows of the Lord.
Forsothe[v] Joathan, his sone, gouernyde the
hows[w] of the kyng, and demyde[x] the puple
of the lond. Sotheli[y] Ysaie, the prophete, 22
the sone of Amos, wroot the residue[z] ʼof
the[a] formere and of[b] the laste wordis of
Ozie. And Ozie slepte with hise fadris, 23
and thei birieden not hym in the feeld of
the kyngis sepulcris, for he was leprouse;
and Joathan, his sone, regnyde for hym.

CAP. XXVII.

Joathan[d] was of fyue and twenti ȝeer, 1
whanne he bigan to regne, and he regnede
sixtene ȝeer in Jerusalem; the name of his
modir was[e] Jerusa, the douȝter of Sadoch.
He[f] dide that, that was riȝtful bifor the 2
Lord, bi alle thingis whiche Ozie, his fadir,
hadde do; outakun that he entride not in
to the temple of the Lord, and the puple
trespasside ȝit[g]. He bildide the hiȝ ȝate 3
of the hous of the Lord, and he bildide
manye thingis in the wal of Ophel; also 4
he bildide citees in the hillis of Juda, and
he bildide castels and touris in forestis.
He[h] fauȝt aȝens the kyng of the sones of 5
Amon, and ouercam hym; and the sones
of Amon ȝauen to hym in that tyme an
hundrid talentis of siluer, and ten thousynde choris of barli, and so manye of
wheete; the sones of Amon ȝauen these
thingis to hym in the secounde and in[i]
the[k] thridde ȝeer. And Joathan[l] was maad 6

---

[h] he maad c.

[l] and also INS.   [m] Om. A. the othere INS.   [n] Om. INS.   [o] anoon I.   [p] the kyng INS.   [q] out of the
temple s.   [r] vnto INS. to X.   [s] Om. A.   [t] he dwellide INS.   [u] wherfor I. for which lepre s.   [v] And INS.
[w] house or meyne s.   [x] he demyde INS.   [y] And INS.   [z] remenaunt IW. Om. s.   [a] Om. s.   [b] Om. s.
[d] Jonathan XS.   [e] Om. N.   [f] Joathan I. Jonathan XS.   [g] ȝit theryune IN.   [h] And he INS.   [i] Om. XS.
[k] Om. s.   [l] Jonathan XS.

forthi that he hadde dresside his weys
7 before the Lord his God. The remnaunt
forsothe of the wordis of Joathan, and
alle the fiʒtyngis of hym, and werkes,
ben writen in the boke of kingus of Irael
8 and of Juda. Of fyue and twenty ʒeer
he was, whanne he hadde begunne to
regnen, and sixtene ʒeer he regnede in
9 Jerusalem. And Joathan slepte with his
faders, and thei birieden hym in the citee
of Dauid; and Achaz, his sone, regned
for hym.

CAP. XXVIII.

1　Of fyue and twenty ʒeer was Achaz,
whanne he hadde begunne to regnen,
and sexteene ʒeer he regnede in Jerusalem; and he dide not riʒt in the siʒt of
2 the Lord, as Dauid, his fadir; bot wente
in the weyes of the kyngis of Irael. Forthermore and he ʒeetyde ymagis to Ba-
3 alym. He is that brende encense in the
valey of Bennon, and he enuyrounde his
sonus in fiʒr aftir the riʒt of gentilis, the
whiche the Lord slowʒ in the commynge
4 of the sonus of Irael. Also he sacrified,
and brende maad encense in heiʒtis, and
in hillis, and vnder alle braunchid tree.
5 And the Lord his God toke hym in the
hond of the kyng of Cyrie, the whiche
smote hym, and a gret prey of his empyre toke, and brouʒt in to Damasc. And
he is taken to the hondis of the kyng of
Irael, and smyten with a grete veniaunce.
6 And Phacee, the sone of Romelie, slewʒ
of Juda an hundrith and twenty thousand in oo day, and alle men fiʒters; for
thi that thei hadden forsake the Lord
7 God of their fadirs. The same tyme
Jechry, a myʒty man of Effraym, slewʒ
Maaziam, the sone of the kyng, and Esricham, duyke of his hous, also Elchanan,
8 the secounde fro the kyng. And the
sonus of Irael token of their bretheren
two hundrith thousand of wymmen and
of knaue childre and of mayde childre,

strong, for he hadde dressid hise weies bifor 'his Lord God[m]. Forsothe[n] the resi- 7
due[o] of wordis[p] of Joathan[q], and alle hise
batels, and werkis, ben writun in the book
of kyngis[r] of Israel and of Juda. He was 8
of fyue and twenti ʒeer, whanne he bigan
to regne, and he regnede sixtene ʒeer in
Jerusalem. And Joathan[s] slepte with hise 9
fadris, and thei birieden hym in the citee
of Dauid; and Achaz, his sone, regnede
for him.

CAP. XXVIII.

　Achaz was of twenti ʒeer, whanne he 1
bigan to regne, and he regnede sixtene
ʒeer in Jerusalem; he dide not riʒtfulnesse[t] in the siʒt of the Lord, as Dauid,
his fadir, dide[u]; but he ʒede in the weies 2
of the kyngis of Israel. Ferthermore and
he ʒetyde[v] ymagis to Baalym. He it is 3
that brente encense in the valey of Beennon, and[w] purgide[x] hise sones bi fier bi
the custom of hethene men, whiche[y] the
Lord killide in the comyng of the sones
of Israel[z]. Also he[a] made sacrifice, and 4
brente encense in hiʒ places, and in hillis,
and vndur ech tree ful of bowis. And 'his 5
Lord God[b] bitook hym in the hond of the[c]
kyng of Sirie, which[d] smoot[e] Achaz, and
took[f] a greet preie of his empire, and
brouʒten[g] in to Damask. Also Achaz was
bitakun to the hondis of the kyng of
Israel, and was[h] smytun[i] with a greet
wounde. And Facee, the sone of Romelie, 6
killide of[k] Juda sixe scoore thousynde in
o dai, alle the men werriours; for thei
hadden forsake the Lord God of her fadris. In the same tyme Zechry, a myʒti 7
man of Effraym, killide Maasie, the sone
of Rogloth, the kyng; and 'he killide[l]
Ezrica, the duyk of his hows, and El-
cana, the secounde[m] fro the kyng. And 8
the sones of Israel token of her britheren
two hundrid thousynde of wymmen and
of children and of damysels, and prey

[m] the Lord his God INS.　[n] And INS.　[o] remenaunt INS.　[p] the wordis INS.　[q] Jonathan NS.　[r] the
kyngis IN.　[s] Jonathan NS.　[t] riʒtwisnesse I.　[u] Om. N.　[v] ʒetyde out IN.　[w] or S.　[x] purgide or
breni S.　[y] whom I.　[z] Israel fro Egipt I. Israel towardus the lond of bikest S.　[a] Achaz INS.　[b] the
Lord his God NS.　[c] Om. S.　[d] the which I.　[e] smoot or ouercame S.　[f] he took IS.　[g] he brouʒte it INS.
[h] he was INS.　[i] smytun of him IS.　[k] of the men of INS.　[l] Om. IN.　[m] secounde persone S.

and a pray with out noumbre ; and thei
9 brou3ten it in to Samarie. In that tempest was ther a prophete of the Lord,
Obed by name, the whiche gon out meetyng to the hoost commyng to Samarie,
seide to hem, Lo! the Lord God of oure
fadirs is wrooth a3einus Judam, and toke
hem in 3our hondis ; and 3e han sleen
hem cruely, so that in to heuen 3oure
10 cruelte schulde commen. Forthermore
the sonis of Juda and of Jerusalem 3ee
wiln subjecten to 3ou seruauntis and
hond wymmen ; that 'indeede is no nede¹;
3e han synned vpon this to the Lord
11 3oure God. Bot heerith my counseil, and
bringith a3ein the caytyues, the whiche
3e han lad awey of 3oure bretheren ; for
grete woodnesse of the Lord stant ouer
12 to 3ou. And so the men of the princis
of the sonus of Effraym stodyn, Azarias,
the sone of Johannan, Barachias, the
sone of Mosollamoth, Jezechias, the sone
of Sellum, and Amazias, the sone of
Adaly, a3eyn hem that camen fro the
13 bataile ; and seyden to hem, 3e schul
not bryngen in hydre the caytifes, lest
we synnen to the Lord ; why wille 3e
casten to vpon 3oure synnes, and hepen
olde synnes ? Grete forsothe synne it is ;
and the wrath of the wodnesse of the
14 Lord stant vpon Yrael. And the fi3tynge
men laften the pray, and alle thingis that
thei hadden taken, before the princis and
15 al the multitude. And the men, the
whiche aboue we myndedyn, stoden, and,
takynge the caityues, clothedyn of the
spoylis alle that weren nakyd ; and
whanne thei hadden clothede^k hem, and
schod, and fyld hem with mete and
drynk, and anoyntide for the^l trauayle,

with out noumbre ; and baren^n it in to
Samarie. In that tempest^o a profete of 9
the Lord, Obed bi name, was there, which^p
3ede out a3ens the oost^q comynge in to Samarie, and seide^r to hem, Lo! the Lord
God of 3oure fadris was wrooth a3ens Juda,
and bitook^s hem in 3oure hondis ; and 3e
han slayn hem crueli, so that 3oure cruelte
stretchide^t forth in to heuene. Ferther-10
more^u 3e wolen make suget to 3ou the
sones of Juda and of Jerusalem in to seruauntis and handmaidis^v ; which thing is
not nedeful to be doon ; for^w 3e han synned on^x this thing to '3oure Lord God^y.
But here^z 3e my councel, and lede^a a3en 11
the prisounneris, whyche^b 3e han brou3t^c of
3oure britheren ; for greet veniaunce of the
Lord nei3ith^d to 3ou. Therfor men^e of the 12
princes of the sones of Effraym, Azarie,
the sone of Johannan, Barachie^f, the sone
of Mosollamoth, Jesechie^g, the sone of Sellum, and Amasie, the sone of Adali, stoden
a3ens hem that^h camen fro the batel ; and 13
seiden to hem, 3e schulen not brynge in
hidur the^l prisoneris, lest we^k doen synne
a3ens the Lord ; whi wolen^l 3e 'ley to^m on
3oure synnes, and heepe elde^n trespassis ?
For^o it^p is greet synne ; the^q ire^r of the
strong veniaunce of the Lord nei3eth on^s
Israel. And the men werriouris^t leften 14
the prey, and alle thingis whiche thei
hadden take, bifor the princes and al the
multitude. And the men stoden^u, whiche 15
we remembriden^v bifore, and thei token
the prisounneris, and clothiden^w of the
spuylis alle that weren nakid ; and whanne
thei hadden clothid hem, and hadden^x
schod^y, and hadden^z refreschid^a with mete
and drynke^b, and hadden^c anoyntid^d for
trauel^e, and hadden^f 3oue cure, 'ether me-

---

¹ is were to a wicked deede E pr. m.   ^k clad c.   ^l that c.

ⁿ thei baren INS.   ^o tempest or veniaunce IS.   ^p the which I. which profeet s.   ^q oost of Israel INS.
^r he seide INS.   ^s he hath bitake INS.   ^t stretchith INS.   ^u And N. Ferthermore and s.   ^v hond
maidenes s.   ^w certis INS.   ^x vpon N. in s.   ^y the Lord 3oure God NS.   ^z herith s.   ^a ledeth INS.
^b that I.   ^c brou3t thenns IS.   ^d ny3ith ni3 s.   ^e men of Israel s.   ^f and Barachie s.   ^g and Jesechie s.
^h the whiche I. whiche NS.   ^i tho NS.   ^k we consentinge to 3ou I. we concenie to 3ou to s.   ^l wil I.
^m caste up more yuel I. leyn to more yuel vp s.   ^n 3oure olde IS.   ^o Certis INS.   ^p this INS.   ^q and
the IN. therfor the s.   ^r wraththe IN.   ^s upon IS.   ^t werriouris of Israel IS.   ^u stoden there IS.
^v remembreden and rehersiden s.   ^w thei clothiden INS.   ^x Om. INS.   ^y schod hem INS.   ^z Om. INS.
^a refreschid hem INS.   ^b with dryuke IN.   ^c Om. N.   ^d anointid hem INS.   ^e her trauel I. her greet
trauelle s.   ^f Om. INS.

and ȝeuen to hem besynesse; who so
euer myȝten not gon, and weren with
feble body, thei putten hem on bestis,
and ladden to Jericho, the citee of palmes,
to their bretheren; and thei ben turned
16 aȝein in to Samarie. That tyme kyng
Achaz sente to the kyng of Assiries, ask-
17 ynge helpe. And Ydumeis camen, and
smyten many of Juda, and token grete
18 pray. And the Philisteis ben held out
by wijld feeldy cytees, and at the south
of Juda; and thei token Bethsames, and
Hailon, and Gaderoth, Socoth also, and
Thannan, and Zamro, with their litil
19 touns; and thei dwelliden in hem. Forsothe the Lord hadde meekide Judam for
Achaz, kyng of Juda; forthi that he
hadde nakyd hym fro helpe, and hadde
20 the Lord to dispyte. And the Lord
brouȝt aȝeinus hym Teglat Falasar, king
of Assiries, the whiche tourmentyde hym,
and no man withstondinge, waastide.
21 Thanne Achaz, the hous of the Lord
spoylide, and the hous of kingus and
princis, ȝaf to the kyng of Assiries ȝiftis,
and neuer the latre it profitide no thing
22 to hym. Forthermore and in tyme of
his anguysch he echide dispite in to the
23 Lord; he by hym silf kyng Achaz offrede
to the goddis of Damasc slayn sacrifices,
to his smyters, and seyde, The goddis
of the kingus of Cyrie helpen to hem,
the which I schal plesen with hoostis,
and thei schul stonden to to me; whanne
aȝeenward thei weren fallyng to hym,
24 and to al Irael. And so Achaz, alle the
vessels of the hous of God taken awey,
and broken to gydre, closede the ȝatis of
the temple of God, and maad to hym
auters in alle the corners of Jerusalem.
25 Also in alle the cytees of Juda he maad
up auters to brennen encense, and he ter-

decyn[g], to hem; 'thei puttiden hem on
horsis[h], whiche euere[i] 'myȝten not go, and
weren feble[k] 'of bodi[l], and brouȝten[m] to
Jerico, a[n] citee of palmes, to 'the britheren
of hem[o]; and thei turneden aȝen in to
Samarie. In that tyme kyng Achaz sente 16
to the kyng of Assiriens, and axide help[p].
And Ydumeis[q] camen, and killiden[r] many[s] 17
men of Juda, and token greet prey. Also 18
Filisteis weren spred abrood bi citees of
the feeldis, and at the south[t] of Juda; and
thei token Bethsames, and Hailon, and
Gaderoth, and Socoth, and Thannan, and
Zamro, with her villagis; and dwelliden[u]
in tho. For[v] the Lord made low Juda for 19
Achaz, the kyng of Juda; for[w] he hadde
maad him[x] nakid of help, and hadde[y] dispisid the Lord. And the Lord brouȝte 20
aȝens him[z] Teglat Phalasar, kyng[a] of Assiriens, that[b] turmentide hym[c], and waastide *hym*[d], while[e] no man aȝenstood. Ther- 21
for Achaz, after that he hadde spuylid the
hows of the Lord, and the hows of the
kyng and of princes[f], ȝaf[g] ȝiftis to the
kyng of Assiriens, and netheles it profitide
'no thing[h] to hym. Ferthermore also in 22
the tyme of his angwisch he encreesside
dispit aȝens God†; thilke[i] kyng Achaz bi[k]
hym silf offride sacrifices to the goddis of 23
Damask, hise smyteris[l], and seide[m], The
goddis of the kyngis of Sirie helpen hem,
whiche[n] goddis Y schal plese bi sacrifices,
and thei schulen help me; whanne aȝenward thei weren fallyng[o] to hym, and to[p]
al Israel. Therfor aftir that Achaz hadde 24
take awei, and broke alle the vessels of the
hows of God, he closide the ȝatis of Goddis
temple, and made[r] auteris to hym silf in
alle the corneris of Jerusalem. And in 25
alle citees[s] of Juda he bildide auteris to
brenne[t] encence, and he stiride[u] the Lord
God of hise fadris to[v] wrathfulnesse. So- 26

† As men doen now, gruching in her sijknessis and in other dissecis. s.

g Om. IS. h Om. INS. i euere *of hem* INS. k *weren feble* and miȝt not go S. l of bodi thei putten [puttiden N] *hem* on horsis IN. thei puttiden on horsis S. m thei brouȝten *hem* INS. n the INS. o her britheren INS. p help *of him* IS. q men of Ydumee I. men of Edom NS. r thei killiden IN. s Om. S. t south *cost* INS. u thei dwelliden INS. v Sothly IN. Forsoth S. w for thi that IN. for that that S. x him self INS. y Om. INS. z *Achaz* INS. a the king NS. b which NS. c Om. INS. d Om. *plures*. e the while IS. f the princes INS. g he ȝaf INS. h not S. i *for* thilke INS. k Om. NS. l smyteris *or destriers* IS. m he seide INS. n the whiche I. o falling *and hindring* S. p Om. S. r he made INS. s the citees INS. t brenne *upon* S. u stiride *therbi* IS. v in to S.

rede to wrath the Lord God of their
26 fadirs. The remnaunt forsothe of his
wordis and of alle his werkes, of the rather and of the last, ben writen in the
boke of the kyngis of Juda and of Irael.
27 And Achaz slepte with his[m] fadirs, and
thei birieden hym in the cyte of Dauid
of Jerusalem; ne forsothe thei receyueden
hym in the sepulcres of the kingus of
Irael; and Ezechias, his sone, regnede
for hym.

CAP. XXIX.

1 Ezechias thanne beganne to regnen,
whanne he was of fyue and twenty ȝeer,
and nyne and twenty ȝeer he regnede in
Jerusalém; name of his modir, Abia, the
2 douȝter of Zacharye. And he dide that
was plesaunt in the siȝt of the Lord, aftir
alle thingus that Dauid, his fadir, hadde
3 done. In that ȝeer and the first moneth
of his regne he opnede the ȝate leues of
the hous of the Lord, and he enstorede
4 hem; and brouȝte to the prestis and the
Leuytis, and gaderede hem in to the
5 este strete, and seide to hem, Heerith
me, Leuytis, and beth halowed; clensith
the hous of the Lord God of oure faders,
and doth awey alle vnclennesse fro the
6 seyntuarye. Oure fadirs synneden, and
diden euyl in the siȝte of the Lord oure
God, forsakyng hym; thei turneden awei
their faces fro the tabernacle of the Lord
7 oure God, and ȝeuen bac. Thei closeden
the dores that weren in the ȝate hous,
and quencheden the lanterns; and encense thei brenneden not, and brent sacrifices thei offreden not in the seyn-
8 tuarye of God of Irael. And so the
woodnesse of the Lord is sterid vpon
Judam and Jerusalem; and he toke hem
in to distourblynge, and into deth, and
in to whistlyng, as ȝe beholden with

theli[w] the residue[x] of hise[y] wordis and of
alle hise werkis, the formere and the laste,
ben writun in the book of kyngis of Juda
and of Israel. And Achaz slepte with 27
hise fadris, and thei birieden hym in the
citee of Jerusalem; for thei resseyueden
not hym in[z] the sepulcris of the kyngis of
Israel; and Ezechie, his sone, regnede for
hym.

CAP. XXIX.

Therfor[a] Ezechie bigan to regne, whanne 1
he was of fyue and twenti ȝeer, and he
regnede in Jerusalem nyne and twenti
ȝeer; the name of his modir *was* Abia, the
douȝtir of Zacharie. And he[b] dide that, 2
that[c] was pleasaunt[d] in the siȝt of the
Lord, bi alle thingis whiche[e] Dauid, his
fadir, hadde do. In that ȝeer and the[f] 3
firste monethe of his rewme he openyde
the ȝatis of the hows of the Lord, and
restoride[g] tho[h]; and he brouȝte[i] the[k] 4
preestis and dekenes, and gaderide[l] hem[m]
in to the eest strete, and seide[n] to hem, 5
Sones of Leuy, here ȝe me, and be ȝe halewid[o]; clense ȝe the hows of the Lord
God of ȝoure fadris; do[p] ȝe awei al vnclennesse fro the seyntuarie. Oure fadris 6
synneden[q], and diden[r] yuel in the siȝt of
'oure Lord God[s], and forsoken[t] hym; thei
turneden awei her faces[u] fro the tabernacle
of 'oure Lord God[v], and ȝauen[w] the[x] bak.
Thei closiden the doris that weren in the 7
porche, and quenchiden the lanternes[y]; and
thei brenten[z] not[a] encense, and thei offriden
not brent sacrifices in the seyntuarie of
God of Israel. Therfor the stronge ven- 8
iaunce of the Lord was reisid on[b] Juda
and Jerusalem; and he ȝaf hem in to
stiryng[c], and in to perischyng, and in to
'hisshing, *ether*[d] *scornyng*, as ȝe seen[e] with

[m] Om. B.

[w] And INS. [x] remenaunt INS. [y] Achaz INS. [z] in to INS. [a] And INS. [b] Ezechie INS. [c] thinge S. [d] plesynge INS. [e] that I. [f] in the INS. [g] restoride *or repereilide* IS. [h] tho *ȝatis* NS. [i] brouȝt hider S. [k] Om. INS. [l] he gaderide INS. [m] hem *to gidre* INS. [n] he seide INS. [o] halwed *to serue the Lord* S. [p] and do INS. [q] han synned INS. [r] han don I. don NS. [s] the Lord oure God N. the Lord ȝour God S. ȝoure Lord God X. [t] thei forsoken INS. [u] face S. [v] the Lord oure God INS. [w] thei ȝauen *therto* IN. thei ȝauen *or turned therto* S. [x] her INS. [y] lanterns therof S. [z] brouȝten NS. [a] not *thider* S. [b] upon IS. [c] mouyng IN. mouyng *or vnstablenesse* S. [d] Om. INS. [e] siȝen *now* S.

9 зoure eeзen Lo' oure fadirs fellen with swerdis, oure sonus, and oure douзters, and oure wiues ben lad caityf for this 10 hidous gilt Nowe thanne it plesith to me, that we gon in pese couenaunt with the Lord God of Irael, and he do awey 11 fro us the woodnesse of his wrath My sonus, williht not dispisen, the Lord chees зou, that зe stonden beforn hym, and mynystren to hym, and heiзen hym, 12 and brennen to hym enceuse Thanne the Leuytis rysen, Maath, the sone of Amazie, and Joel, the sone of Azarie, of the sonis of Caath, bot of the sonus of Merery, Ciz, the sone of Abday, and Azarias, the sone of Jalalael, of the sonus forsothe of Jeisan, Joha, the sone of Zemma and Hedem, the sone ot Joha, 13 and forsothe of the sonus of Elizaphan, Zamry, and Jahiel, of the sonus also of 14 Asaph, Zacharias, and Mathanyas, also of the sonus of Heman, Jahiel, and Semei, bot and of the sonus of Yditum, Semeyas, 15 and Oziel And thei gadreden their bretheren, and ben halowed, and gon in, after the maundement of the kyng, and the heste of the Lord, that thei clensen the 16 hous of the Lord And the prestis gon in to the temple of the Lord, that thei halowen it, beeren out al the vnclennesse, that with inne thei hadden foundyn in the vestiarie of the hous of the Lord; the whiche token the Leuytis, and beeien out with out forth to the streme of Cedron 17 And thei begunnen the first day of the first moneth to clensen, and in the eзthe day of the same moneth thei wenten in to the зate hous of the temple of the Lord, and thei purgedyn the temple eiзte days, and in the sixtenthe day of the same moneth, that thei hadden begunnen, 18 thei fulfilden And thei wenten in to Ezechie, the kyng, and seyden to hym,

9 зoure 13en Lo' oure fadris felden[f] doun bi swerdis, oure sones, and[g] oure douзtris, and wyues[h] ben led[i] prisouneris for this greet trespas 10 Now therfor it plesith me, that we make a boond of pees with the Lord God of Israel, and that he turne fro vs the stronge veniaunce of his ire[k] 11 My sones, nyle зe be[l] reccheles, the Lord hath chose зou, that зe stonde bifor hym, and serue hym, that зe herie hym, and brenne[m] encense to hym Therfor the dekenes ris-12 iden[n], Mahat, the sone of Amasie, and Johel, the sone of Azarie, of the sones of Caath; sotheli[o] of the sones of Merarye[p], Cys, the sone of Abdai, and Azarie, the sone of Jelaleel, forsothe[q] of the sones of Jerson[r], Joha, the sone of Zemma, and Hedem, the sone of Johaa; and sotheli[s] 13 of the sones of Elisaphan[t], Samri, and Jahiel, and of the sones of Asaph[u], Zacharie, and Mathanye, also of[v] the sones of He-14 man[w], Jahiel, and Semei, but also of the sones of Iditum[x], Semei and Oziel And 15 thei gaderiden to gidere hei britheren, and weren[y] halewid; and thei entriden[z] bi[a] comaundement[b] of the kyng, and bi co-maundement of the Lord, for to clense the hows of the Lord Also preestis entriden 16 in to the temple of the Lord, for to halewe it and thei baren out al vnclennesse[c], which[d] thei founden ther ynne in the porche, `ethir large place[e], of the hows of the Lord, which vnclennesse the dekenes token, and baren[f] out[g] to[h] the stronde of Cedron with outforth Sotheli[i] 17 thei bigunnen to clense[k] in the firste dai of the firste monethe, and in the eiзte dai of the same monethe thei entriden in to the porche of the hows of the Lord, and thei clensiden the temple eiзte[l] daies; and in the sixtenthe dai of the same monethe thei filliden[m] that[n], that thei hadden bigunne And thei entriden to Ezechie, the[o] 18

f han falle INS g Om INS h oure wyues INS i ledde *fro vs* s k wraththe INS l *here ynne* be s m that зe brenne INS n resen up I risiden up NS o and INS p Merarye *resen up* I Merarye *riseden vp* s q and INS r Jerson *resen up* I Jerson *riseden vp* s s Om INS t Elisaphan *resen up* I Elisaphan *riseden vp* s u Aeaph *riseden vp* s v Om N w Heman *resen vp* I Heman *riseden vp* s x Iditum *risiden vp* NS y thei weren INS z entriden *into the temple* I marg NS text a bi the CI b heest INS c the vnclennesse INS d that INS e Om INS f thei baren *it* IN barin *it* s g Om s h into A i And INS k clense *it* I clense *the temple* s l in eiзte INS m fulfilhden INS n the thinge s. o Om N

We han halowed al the hous of the Lord, and the auter of brent[n] sacrifice of hym, and his vessels, also and the borde of pro-19 posicyoun with alle his vessels, and alle the[o] purtenauncis of the temple, that kyng Achaz in his rewme hadde polutide, after that he hadde trespassede; and loo! leid out ben alle thingus before the auter of 20 the Lord. And Ezechie, the kyng, rijsyng erly, gadered in oon alle princis[p] of the cytee, and he stei3ede up in to the hous 21 of the Lord; and thei offreden to gyder boolis seuen, and wetheris seuen, and[q] lombis seuen, and geet seuen, for the synne, for the rewme, for the seyntuarye, for Juda. And he seide to the prestis, sonis of Aaron, that thei schulden offren 22 vpon the auter of the Lord. Thanne thei slewen boolis, and the prestis token the blood, and heldyn it vpon the auter; also thei slewen wethers, and of hem the blood thei heldyn vpon the auter; and thei offreden lombis, and helden vpon the 23 auter the blood. And thei applieden the geet for the synne before the kyng and al the multitude, and thei putten their 24 hondis vpon hem; and the prestis of-freden hem, and thei sprengden the blood of hem beforn the auter, for the synne of al Irael. Forsothe for al Irael the kyng hadde comaundide, that there schulde be 25 don brent sacrifice, and for synne. And he ordeynde Leuytis in the hous of the Lord, with cymbales, and sawtrees, and harpis, aftir the disposicyoun of king Dauid, and of Gad, seear, and of Nathan, the prophete; forsothe the beste of the Lord it was bi the hond of his prophetis. 26 And the Leuytis stoden, holdyng the orgnys of Dauid; and prestis the trumpis. 27 And Ezechias comaundide, that ther

king, and seiden to hym, We han halewid[p] al the hows of the Lord, and the auter of brent sacrifice therof, and the vessels ther-of, also and the boord of settyngforth with alle hise vessels, and al the purtenaunce 19 of the temple, 'which purtenaunce[q] king Achaz hadde defoulid in his rewme, aftir that he brak[r] the lawe[s]; and lo! alle thingis ben set forth bifor the auter of the Lord. And Ezechie, the kyng, roos[t] in the 20 morwetid, and gaderide[u] togidere alle the princes of the citee, and stiede[v] in[w] to the hows of the Lord; and[x] thei offriden to-21 gidere seuene bolis, and seuene rammes, seuene lambren, and seuene buckis of geet, for synne[y], for[z] the rewme†, for the seyn-tuarye, and for Juda. And he[a] seide to preestis, the sones of Aaron, that thei schulden offre[b] on[c] the auter of the Lord. Therfor thei[d] killiden bolis, and 'the 22 preestis[e] tooken the blood, and schedden[f] it on[g] the auter; also thei killiden rammes, and 'the preestis[h] schedden[i] the blood of tho on[k] the auter; thei[l] offriden lambren, and 'the preestis[m] schedden[n] the blood on[o] the auter. And thei[p] brou3ten buckis of 23 geet 'for synne[q] bifor the kyng and al the multitude, and thei[r] settiden[s] her[t] hondis on[u] tho[v]; and the preestis offriden 24 tho[w], and spreynten[x] the blood of[y] tho[z] bifor the auter, for the clensyng of al Is-rael. For[a] the king comaundide, that brent sacrifice shulde be made for al Israel, and for synne[b]. Also he[c] ordeynede dekenes 25 in the hows of the Lord, with cymbalis, and sawtrees, and harpis, bi the orde-naunce of 'Dauid the kyng[d], and of[e] Gad, the profete, and of Nathan, the profete; for[f] it[g] was the comaundement of the Lord bi the hond of hise prophetis. And the[h] 26 dekenes stoden, and helden[i] the orguns of

+ for the rewme; that is, for the princes, for the seyn-tuarye, that is, for preestis and dekenes my-nystringe there, for Juda, that is, for al the peple. Lire here. c.

ⁿ his brent ᴇ *pr. m.*   ᵒ Om. c.   ᵖ the princis cᴇ *pr. m.*   ᑫ Om. ᴀᴄʜ.

ᵖ halewid *or* clensid ɪꜱ.   ᑫ that ɪɴꜱ.   ʳ had broke ꜱ.   ˢ lawe *of God* ꜱ.   ᵗ roos up ɪɴꜱ.   ᵘ he gaderide ɪɴꜱ.   ᵛ he stiede up ɪꜱ. he stiede ɴ.   ʷ *with hem* in ꜱ.   ˣ *and there* ɪꜱ.   ʸ *her owne* synne ɪɴꜱ. ᶻ and for ɪɴꜱ.   ᵃ the kyng ɪɴꜱ.   ᵇ offre *sacrifices* ɴꜱ.   ᶜ upon ɪꜱ.   ᵈ the prestis ɴꜱ.   ᵉ thei ɪɴꜱ. ᶠ helden ɪ.   ᵍ upon ɪꜱ.   ʰ thei ɪɴꜱ.   ⁱ helden ɪ.   ᵏ upon ɪꜱ.   ˡ and thei ɪɴꜱ.   ᵐ thei ɪɴꜱ.   ⁿ helden ɪ. ᵒ upon ɪꜱ.   ᵖ prestis *for synne* ɪɴ. prestis *also for synne* ꜱ.   ᑫ Om. ɪɴꜱ.   ʳ the prestis ɪɴꜱ.   ˢ setten ɪ. ᵗ Om. ꜱ.   ᵘ upon ɪꜱ.   ᵛ tho, *and killiden hem* ɪɴꜱ.   ʷ hem ɪ.   ˣ thei spreynten ɪɴꜱ.   ʸ Om. ꜱ.   ᶻ hem ɪ. Om. ꜱ.   ᵃ Forsothe ɪɴꜱ.   ᵇ synne *therof* ɪɴꜱ.   ᶜ *the kyng* ɪɴꜱ.   ᵈ kyng Dauid ɪɴꜱ.   ᵉ bi ꜱ.   ᶠ certis ɪɴꜱ. ᵍ this ɪɴꜱ.   ʰ Om. ɪɴꜱ.   ⁱ heeld *in her hondis* ꜱ.

schulden ben offred brent sacrifices vpon
the auter; and whanne thei schulden
offren brent sacrifices, thei begunnen to
syngen preysyngis to the Lord, and sown
with trumpis, and in dyuerse orgnys, that
Dauid, king of Irael, hadde maad redy to
28 sown with. Al the puple forsothe honourynge, the syngers and tho that
helden trumpis weren in their offices[r], to
the tyme that the brent sacrifices weren
29 ful eendid. And whanne the offryng was
eendid, the kyng is ful bowed, and alle
that weren with hym, and thei honour-
30 eden. And Ezechias comaundide and the
princis to Leuytis, that thei schulden
preysen the Lord with the wordis of
Dauid, and of Asaph, seear; the whiche
preyseden with grete gladnesse, and the
31 knee ful bowede, thei honourden. Ezechias forsothe thes[s] also addide, Зе han
fulfild зoure hondis to the Lord; committ
neeз, and offrith sacrifices and preysingis
32 in the hous of the Lord. Thanne al the
multitude offride oostis, and preysingis,
and brent sacrifices, with deuout mynde.
Forsothe the noumbre of the brent sacrifices, that the multitude offride, was
this; boolis seuenty, wethers an hundrith,
33 lombis two hundrith. Also thei haloweden to the Lord oxes[t] sexe hundrith,
34 and scheep thre thousand. The prestis
forsothe weren fewe, and myзten not suffice that thei drawen of the skynnes of
the brent sacrifices; wherfore and the
Leuitis their bretheren helpiden[u] hem, to
the tyme that the werc were fulfild, and
the bischopis weren halowed; the Leuytis forsothe with liзter rijt ben ha-
35 lowed thanne the prestis. Ther weren
thanne many brent sacrifices, and talowes
of pesible thingus, and liquours offryngis

Dauid; and preestis *helden* trumpis. And 27
Ezechie comaundide, that thei schulden
offre brent sacrifices on[k] the auter; and
whanne brent sacrifices weren offrid, thei
bigunnen to synge preisyngis to the Lord,
and to sowne with trumpis, and in[l] dyuerse orguns, whiche Dauid, the[m] kyng of
Israel, hadde maad redi for[n] to sowne[o].
Forsothe[p] whanne al the cumpenye wor-28
schipide[q], syngeris and thei that helden
trumpis weren in her office, til the brent
sacrifice was fillid. And whanne the of-29
fryng was endid, the kyng was bowid[r],
and alle that weren with hym, and thei
worschipiden *God*[s]. And Ezechie[t] and 30
the princes comaundiden to the dekenes,
that thei schulden preise the Lord with[u]
the wordis[r] of Dauith, and of Asaph, the
profete; whiche[w] preisiden *hym*[x] with greet
gladnesse, and kneliden[y], and worschipiden[z]. Sothely[a] Ezechie addide[b] also these 31
thingis, Зe han[c] fillid зoure hondis[d] to the
Lord; neiзe зe, and offre[e] sacrifices and
preisyngis in the hows of the Lord. Ther-32
for al the multitude offride with denoute
soule sacrifices[f], and preisyngis, and brent
sacrifices. Sotheli[g] this was the noumbre
of brent sacrifices, whiche the multitude
offride; seuenti[h] bolis, and[i] an[k] hundrid
rammes, two[l] hundrid lambren. Also thei 33
halewiden to the Lord sixe hundrid oxis[m],
and thre thousynde sheep. Forsothe[n] the 34
preestis weren fewe, and myзten[o] not suffice for to 'drawe awei[p] the skynnes of
brent sacrifices; wherfor and the dekenes
her britheren helpiden hem, til the werk
was fillid, and the preestis weren halewid[q];
for[r] the dekenes ben halewid bi liзtere custom[s] than[t] the[u] preestis. Therfor there 35
weren ful[v] many brent sacrifices, ynnere[w]
fatnessis[x] of pesible sacrifices, and the[y]

---

[r] offis cii.   [s] this c.   [t] oxen Acii.   [u] holpen c.

[k] upon is.   [l] with s.   [m] Om. ns.   [n] Om. s.   [o] sowne *with* ins.   [p] And ins.   [q] worschepid *the Lord* s.
[r] bowid *doun* in.   bowed *doun lowe* s.   [s] Om. n.   *God mekeli* s.   [t] the king ins.   [u] in s.   [v] wordis *or the*
salmus i.   wordis *or psalmes* n.   wordis *of salmes* s.   [w] the whiche *dekens* in.   which *dekenes* s.   [x] *the*
Lord ins.   [y] thei kneliden in.   thei kneliden *low* s.   [z] worschipiden *him* i.   worschipiden *him gladli* ns.
[a] And ins.   [b] addide to ins.   [c] han, *he seide* s.   [d] hondis *with blessyngis* is.   [e] offrith in.   [f] sacrifices
to ouercome her enemyes ns.   [g] And ins.   [h] seuene ns.   [i] Om. in.   [k] Om. s.   [l] and two ins.
[m] oxen ins.   [n] And ins.   [o] thei myзten ins.   [p] drawe awei *or hilde* i marg.   drawe *or fle of* s. *text.*
[q] halwed *bi vertu of her besy and wilful trauel* s.   [r] and ins.   [s] custom *of trauell* ins.   [t] than *ben* ins.
[u] Om. Δ.   [v] Om. s.   [w] and ynnere ins.   [x] fatnesse s.   [y] Om. n.

of brent sacrifices, and the heryng of the
36 hous of the Lord is ful eendid. And
Ezechie is glad, and al the puple with
hym, forthi that the seruyce of the
Lord was ful eendid; forsothe of sodenly
it pleside that to ben don.

CAP. XXX.

1 Ezechie also sente to al Irael and Juda,
and he wroote letters to Effraym and
Manassen, that thei schulden commen in
to the hous of the Lord in Jerusalem,
and do pasch to the Lord God of Irael.
2 Thanne gon in the counsele of the kyng,
and of the princis, and of al the companye of Irael, thei deemedyn that they
schulden don pasch the secounde moneth.
3 Forsothe thei camen not to gydre to don
in his tyme; for the prestis that my3ten
suffisen weren not halowed, and the puple not 3it was gadered in to Jerusalem.
4 And the word pleside to the kyng, and
5 to al the multitude. And they deemeden
for to senden messagers in to al Irael,
fro Bersabe vnto Dan, that thei schulden
commen, and don pasch to the Lord God
of Irael in Jerusalem; manye forsothe
hadden not done, as in the lawe it is
6 beforn writen. And curours wenten with
letters, of the heste of the kyng and of
his princis, in to al Irael and Juda, after
the whiche thing the kyng hadde comaundide prechours, Sonis of Irael,
turnith a3ein to the Lord God of Abraham, and of Ysaac, and of Irael; and he
schal be turned a3ein to the releuys, that
scapeden the hondis of the kyng of As-
7 siries. Willith not ben maad as 3oure
fadirs and bretheren, that wenten awey
fro the Lord God of their fadirs; and he
8 toke hem in to deth, as 3e seen. Willith
not ful hardne 3our nollis, as 3oure fadirs;

moyste sacrifices of brent sacrifices, and^z
the worschip^a, 'ethir ournyng^b, of the
'Lordis hows^c was fillid. And Ezechie 36
was glad, and al the puple, for the seruyce of the Lord was fillid^d; for^e it
pleside^f, that this was doon sodeynly^g.

CAP. XXX.

1 And Ezechie sente to al Israel and to
Juda, and he wroot pistlis to Effraym and
to Manasses, that thei schulden come in
to the hous of the Lord in Jerusalem, and
make^h paske to the Lord God of Israel.
2 Therfor whanne counseil was takun of
the kyng, and of princes, and of al the
cumpeny of Jerusalem, thei demyden^i to
make paske in the secounde moneth. For 3
thei demyden^k not to^l do^m in his tyme†;
for the preestis that^o my3ten suffice^p weren
not^q halewid^r, and the puple was not 3it
gaderid in to Jerusalem. And the^s word 4
pleside the king, and al the multitude.
And thei demyden^u to sende messangeris 5
in to al Israel, fro Bersabee 'til to^v Dan,
that thei schulden come, and make pask
to the Lord God of Israel in Jerusalem;
for many men hadden not^w do^x, as it is
bifor writun in the lawe. And corouris 6
3eden forth with pistlis, bi comaundement^y
of the kyng and of hise princis, in to al
Israel and Juda, and prechiden^z hi that,
that the kyng hadde comaundid^a, Sones of
Israel, turne 3e a3en to the Lord God of
Abraham, and of Isaac, and of Israel; and
he schal turne a3en to the residue^b men,
that^c ascapiden the hondis of the kyng of
Assiriens. Nyle 3e be maad^d as 3oure fa- 7
dris and britheren^e, that^f 3eden^g awei fro
the Lord God of her fadris; and he^h 3aue^i
hem in to perischyng, as 3e seen^k. Nyle 8
3e make hard 3oure nollis, as 3oure fadris
diden; 3yue 3e hondis^l‡ to^m the Lord, and

† tyme; that is, the firste monethe. Lire here. c.

‡ hondis; in bihetinge that 3e schulen serue ham feithfuly. Lire here. c.

z and herbi 1s. a worschiping x. b Om. 1NS. c hows of the Lord 1. d fulfillid 1N. fulfillid preisabli s.
e certis 1NS. f pleside the kyng 1NS. g hastily 1. sodeynli or hastili, and with good wille s. h make
there 1s. i demed or purposide s. k demyden or gessiden 1s. l to mowe 1NS. m do this N. do this hi3e
solempnite s. o whiche 1NS. p suffice herto 1N. suffice therto s. q not 3it NS. r halwed, chosen, or
ordeyned s. s this 1NS. t word or counseil 1NS. u demed as worthi thing to preisyng of the Lord s.
v vnto 1s. into N. to x. w not long tyme bifore NS. x do it 1. do this N. do this thing s. y the heest 1.
heest NS. z Om. 1NS. a comaundid, thei prechiden, and seiden 1. comaundid, thei prechiden N. comaundide,
thei precheden a grect solempnite of pask, and seiden s. b remenaunt of 1NS. c whiche N. d maad
rebel NS. e 3oure britheren 1NS. f whiche NS. g wenten 1. h the Lord 1NS. i therfor 3aue s. k now
seen 1s. l 3oure hondis 1NS. m or bihote 3e to s.

takıth hondıs[v] to the Lord, and commıth
to the seyntuarye of hym, that he halowed[w] wıth out eende; seruith to the
Lord God of ȝour fadırs, and schal ben
turned awey fro ȝou the wrath of hıs
9 woodnesse   Ȝıf forsothe ȝe weren turned
aȝeın to the Lord, ȝour bretheren and
ȝour sonus schul haue mercy, wıth theır
lordıs that hem laddyn caıtıjf, and theı
schul ben turned aȝeın ınto thıs lond   Forsothe pytouse and mercyable ıs the Lord
oure God, and he schal not turnen awey
hıs face fro ȝou, ȝif ȝe weren turned aȝeın
10 to hym.   Thanne currours wente swıftly
fro cyte vnto cıte thoruȝ the lond of Ef-
frayn and Manasse vnto Zabulon, hem
11 scoornynge and vndermowynge hem   Ne-
uertbelater sum men of Aseı, and of
Manasse, and of Zabulon, assentynge to
12 the counseıle, camen ın to Jerusalem   In
Juda forsothe ıs done the hond of the
Lord, that he schulde ȝeuen to hem oon
heıte, and theı schulden don, after the
heste of the kyng and prıncıs, the word
13 of the Loıd   And there ben gadered ınto
Jerusalem many puplıs, that theı don the
solempnyte of therf looucs ın the se-
14 counde moneth   And rıjsyng theı dıs-
truyden the auters, that weren in Jerusalem; and alle thıngus ın the whıche to
mawmetıs was brend encense, tuınynge
vpsadoun, theı threwen ın to the streıne
15 of Cedron   Theı offrıden forsothe pasch
the fourtenth day of the secound moneth;
the prestıs also and Leuytıs at the last
halowed, offreden brent sacrifice ın the
16 hous of the Lord   And theı stoden ın
theır ordre, aftır the dısposıcyoun and the
lawe of Moyses, the man of God   The
prestıs forsothe hadden taken the blood
to ben sched of the hondıs of Leuytıs,
17 forthı that myche puple was not ha-

come ȝe to hıs seyntuarie, whıch he halew-
ıde[n] wıthouten ende, serue ȝe the Lord
God[o] of ȝoure fadrıs, and the ıre[p] of hıs
strong venıaunce schal 'be turned[q] awey
fro ȝou   For[r] ıf ȝe turnen aȝen to the[9]
Lord, ȝoure brıtheren and ȝoure sones
schulen haue mercy, bıfor her lordıs that[s]
ledden[t] hem[u] prısonerıs, and theı schulen
turne aȝen ın to thıs lond   For 'oure Lord
God[v] ıs pıtouse, 'ethır benygne[w], and merciful, and he schal[x] not turne awey hıs
face fro ȝou, ıf ȝe turne[y] aȝen to hym
Therfor the corours ȝeden swıftlı fro cytee 10
in to cıtee thorou the lond of Effıaym and
of Manasses 'tıl to[z] Zabulon, whıle theı[a]
scoınıden and[b] bımowıden hem   Netheles 11
snm men of Aser, and of Manasses, and of
Zabulon, assentıden[c] to the[d] counsel, and
camen ın to Jeıusalem   Forsothe[e] the 12
hond of the[f] Lord was maad ın Juda, that
he ȝaf to hem oon herte, and that theı
dıden the word of the Lord, bı the comaundement[g] of the kyng and of the
princes   And many puplıs weren gaderıd 13
ın to Jeıusalem, for to make the solempnyte of therf looues[h] ın the secounde
monethe   And theı rısıden[i], and destrı- 14
eden[k] the auterıs[l], that[m] weren ın Jerusalem, and 'theı destrıynge[n] alle thingıs ın
whıche encense was brent to idols, castıden[o] forth ın to the stronde of Cedron[p]
Forsothe[q] theı offrıden pask ın the four- 15
tenthe daı of the secounde monethe; also
the preestıs and the[r] dekenes weren halewıd at the laste[s], and offrıden[t] brent sacrifices ın the hows of the Lord   And 16
theı stoden ın her ordre, bı the ordynaunce
and lawe of Moıses, the man of God   Sothely[u] the preestıs token of the hondıs of
dekenes† the blood[v] to be sched out, foı 17
myche cumpeny was not[w] halewıd, and
therfor the dekenes offrıden pask foı hem,

+ of dekenes,
far bı co
maundement
of the kyng
the dekenes
offreden pask
for hem that
weren not fully
elensıd I ire
here c

---

       [v] hondıth B   beede AFH   [w] halowe B sec M

    [n] hath halewıd INS   [o] Om FGIKLMNXbç   [p] wrath INS   [q] turne N   [r] Forsothe INS   [s] whıche INS
[t] han led INS   [u] hem *out of her lond* S   [v] the Lord oure God INS   [w] Om INS   [x] wole INS   [y] turne
ȝou INS   [z] vnto INS   [a] the men I   the men *of tho cuntreıs* NS   [b] or N   [c] consentıden INS   [d] thıs NS
[e] Certıs INS   [f] *grace of* the S   [g] heest INS   [h] looues, *that ıs, pask* INS   [i] resen EL   resen up I
rısıden up NS   [k] theı destrıeden INS   [l] auterıs *of ydolıs* INS   [m] whıche NS   [n] dıstroyeden S   [o] theı
castıden *hem* INS   [p] cedrıs A *pr m* EKLMXbç   [q] And INS   [r] Om N   [s] last *or whan the peple had*
sacrificıd S   [t] theı offrıden INS   [u] And INS   [v] blood *of bestıs* INS   [w] not ȝıt INS

lowed ; and therfore the Leuytis schulden offren pasch to hem, that 'came not to 18 gydre^x to ben halowed to the Lord. A grete also part of the puple of Effraym, and Manasse, and Ysachar, and Zabulon, the whiche was not halowed, eetyn pasch not after that it is writen. And Ezechie preyede for hem, seyinge, The good 19 Lord schal haue mercy to alle, that in al herte sechen the Lord God of ther fadirs ; and it schal not ben wijtid to hem, 20 that thei ben not halowed. Whome the Lord herde, and is plesid to the puple. 21 And the sonus of Irael, that ben founden in Jerusalem, diden the solempnyte of therf looues seuen days in grete ioye, preisynge^y the Lord bi eche dais ; the Leuytis also and the prestis by orgnys, 22 that to their office fellen. And Ezechias spac to the herte of alle the Leuytis, that hadden good vndirstondynge vpon the Lord ; and thei eeten seuen days of the solempnyte, offrynge slayn sacrifice^z of pesyble thingus, and preysyng the Lord 23 God of their fadirs. And it pleside to al the multitude, that thei schulden also halowen other seuen days ; the whiche 24 and thei diden with ful grete ioy. Ezechias forsothe, king of Juda, 3af to the multitude a thousand boolis, and seuen thousand of scheep ; the princis forsothe 3euen to the puple a thousand boolis, and scheep tenn thousand. Thanne is halowed a more multitude of prestis ; 25 and gladnesse thoru3 held al the puple of Juda, both of prestis and of Leuytis, and of al the besy commyng, that weren commen of Irael, and of the comlyngis of the lond of Irael, and of the dwellers 26 of Juda. And ther is don a grete solempnyte in Jerusalem, whiche^a maner

that^x my3ten not^y be halewid to the Lord. Also a greet part of the puple of Effraym, 18 and Manasses^z, and of Ysachar, and of Zabulon, that was not halewid, eet pask not bi that that is writun. And Ezechie preyde for hem, and seide, The good Lord schal do mercy to alle men, that^a seken in 19 al the^b herte the Lord God of her fadris ; and it schal not be arettid to hem^c, that thei ben not halewid^d. And^e the Lord 20 herde hym^f, and was^g plesid to the puple. And the sones of Israel, that^h weren 21 founden in Jerusalem, maden solempnyteⁱ of therf looues seuene daies in greet gladnesse, and herieden^k the Lord bi ech dai ; and dekenes^l and preestis^m 'preisiden the Lordⁿ bi orguns, that^o acordiden to her offices^p. And Ezechie^q spak to the herte 22 of alle the dekenes, that^r hadden good vndurstondyng of the Lord ; and thei eeten^s bi seuene daies of the solempnyte, offrynge^t sacrifices^u of pesible thingis, and heriynge the Lord God of her fadris. And 23 it pleside al the multitude to halewe also othere seuene daies ; which thing^v also thei diden with greet ioye. Forsothe^w 24 Ezechie, kyng of Juda, 3af to the multitude a thousynde bolis, and seuene thousynde of scheep ; sotheli^x the princes^y 3auen to the puple a thousynde bolis, and ten thousynde scheep. Therfor ful^z greet multitude of preestis was halewid† ; and 25 al the cumpany of Juda was fillid with gladnesse, as wel of^a preestis and dekenes, as of al the multitude, that camen fro Israel, and 'of conuersis^b of the lond of Israel, and of dwelleris^c in^d Juda^e. And 26 greet solempnytee was maad in Jerusalem, which^f maner^g solempnyte^h was not in that citee fro the daies of Salomon, soneⁱ of Dauid, kyng of Israel. Sotheli^k preestis 27

† that is, or-deyned to kille and offre to the Lord thes beestis. 18.

---

^x remembredyn not s pr. m.   ^y preyinge v.   ^z sacrifices c.   ^a the whiche s.

---

^x whiche INS.   ^y not *thanne* NS.   ^z of Manasses s.   ^a whiche INS.   ^b her INS.   ^c hem *into synne* IS. ^d halwed *bi offring of 3iftis* IS.   ^e Om. s.   ^f the kyng INS.   ^g he was INS.   ^h which s.   ⁱ the solempnyte INS.   ^k thei herieden INS.   ^l the dekenes IN.   ^m the prestis s.   ⁿ *herieden him* I.   ^o whiche INS. ^p office NS.   ^q the kyng INS.   ^r whiche INS.   ^s eeten *bi tho sacrifices* I. eeten *of tho* N. eten *of tho sacrifices of the peple* s.   ^t offryng *to the Lord* s.   ^u the sacrifices s.   ^v Om. s.   ^w And INS.   ^x and INS. ^y princes *of Juda* IS.   ^z a ful INS.   ^a *the cumpenye* of I. *the multitude* of s.   ^b of men conuertid I. *the multitude* of men conuertid NS.   ^c the dwelleris INS.   ^d of NS.   ^e Juda *was glad in the Lord* NS.   ^f what INS. ^g kynd NS.   ^h Om. INS.   ⁱ the sone INS.   ^k And INS.

was not in the same cyte fro the days of Salomon, sone of Dauid, kyng of Irael. 27 Forsothe the prestis and Leuytis risen, blessyng to the puple; and the voyce of hem is herd, and the preyer ful came into the hooly dwellinge place of heuen.

and dekenes rysyden[l], and blessiden the puple; and the vois of hem was herd, and the[m] preier cam in to the hooli dwelling place of heuene.

CAP. XXXI.

1 And whanne thes thingus weren manerly ful halowed, al Irael wente out, that was founden in the citees of Juda; and thei breeken the mawmetis, and hewen doun mawmete wodis, and the heeʒe thingus thei wastiden, and the auters distruyden, not onely of al Juda and Beniamyn, bot and of Effraym also and of Manasse, to the tyme that fully thei weren don awey. And alle the sonus of Irael ben torned aʒein in to posses-2 siouns, and their citees. Ezechias forsothe sette prestis companyes and Leuytis bi their deuysions, echone[b] in propre office, bothe of prestis, that is, and of Leuytis, to brent sacrifices and pesible, that thei seruen, and knowlechen, and syngen in the ʒatis of the tentis of the 3 Lord. A paartye forsothe of the kyng was, that of his propre substaunce schulde ben offrid brent sacrifice erly and at euen, the sabothis also, and kalendis, and other solempnytes, as it is writen in the lawe of 4 Moyses. Also he comaundide to the puple of the dwellers in Jerusalem, that thei ʒeuen partis to prestis and Leuytis, that thei mown taken tent to the lawe of the 5 Lord. The whiche whanne was puplischt in the[c] eris of the multitude, the sonus of Irael offreden manye first fruytis of whete, aud of wyne, and of oyle, also of hony; and of alle thingus that the erth 6 getith, thei offreden dymys. Bot and the sonus of Irael and of Juda, that dwelliden

CAP. XXXI.

And whanne these thingis weren doon 1 riʒtfuli, al Israel ʒede out, that was foundun in the citees of Juda; and thei braken simylacris, and kittiden[n] doun woodis, and wastiden[o] hiʒ[p] places, and distrieden[q] auteris[r], not[s] oneli of al Juda and Beniamyn[t], but also and[u] of Effraym and Manasses[v], til[w] thei distrieden[x] outirli[y]. And[z] alle the sones of Israel turneden aʒen in to her possessiouns and citees. Forsothe[a] Eze-2 chie ordeynede cumpenyes of preestis and of[b] dekenes bi her departyngis, ech man in his owne office, that is, as wel of preestis as of dekenes, to[c] brent sacrifices and pesible sacrifices, that thei schulden mynystre[d], and knowleche, and synge in the ʒatis of the castels† of the Lord. Sotheli[e] the 3 part of the kyng[f] was, that of his owne catel[g] brent sacrifice schulde be offrid euere[h] in the morewtid and euentide[i], also in sabatis[k], and calendis, and othere[l] solempnytees, as it is writun in the lawe of Moises. Also he[m] comaundide to the pu-4 ple of hem that dwelliden in Jerusalem, to ʒyue partis[n] to the preestis and dekenes, that thei myʒten ʒyue tent to the lawe of the Lord. And[o] whanne[p] this[q] was knowun 5 in the eeris of the multitude, the sones of Israel offriden ful many firste fruytis of wheete, of wyn, of oyle, and of hony; and of alle thingis whiche the erthe bringith forth, thei offriden tithis. But also the 6 sones of Israel and of Juda, that[r] dwelliden in the citees of Juda, offriden tithis

† castels; that is, of the large places of prestis and dekenes. Lire here. c.

b eche c.   c Om. ABFH.

l risen EL. resen up I. riseden up NS.   m her INS.   n thei kittiden INS.   o thei wastiden INS.   p hiʒ, *that is, solempne* s.   q thei destrieden INS.   r the auteris IN. *there* the auteris s.   s and not IN.   t of Beniamyn N.   u Om. INS.   v of Manasses IMNSX.   w til that INS.   x had destried INS.   y *tho auters* outirli I. *her ydols* outirli NS.   z And *thanne* I.   a And INS.   b Om. s.   c *the king ordeined* to s.   d serue INS.   e And INS.   f *kyngis sacrifice* IN. *kingis sacrifices* s.   g substaunce INS.   h euermore s.   i in the euentide IN.   k sabot I.   l in othere INS.   m *the king* INS.   n *part of* lyuclood INS.   o Om. s.   p Om. N.   q this thing INS.   r whiche NS.

in the cytees of Juda offreden dymes of
oxen and scheep, and dymes of hooly
thingus, that thei hadden vowed to the
Lord ther God, and, alle thingus beerynge,
7 maaden many heepils. The thrid moneth
thei begunne to castyn groundis of the
heepils, and the seuenth moneth thei
8 eendiden hem. And whanne Ezechias
and his princis weren commen in, thei
seen the heepils, and thei blesseden to the
9 Lord, and to the puple of Irael. And
Ezechias askide the prestis and Leuytis,
10 why the heepils schulden so lyen. Aza-
zie, the prest, first of the stoc of Sadoch,
answerde to hym, seyinge, Sithen the
first fruytis begunne to ben offrid in the
hous of the Lord, we eetyn and ben fulfild, and there ben laft many thingus;
forthi that the Lord hath blessid to his
puple; of the releuys forsothe this is the
11 plente, that thou seest. Thanne Ezechias
comaundide, that thei schulden make
redy bernes in the hous of the Lord; the
whiche thing whan thei hadden don,
12 thei brou3ten in bothe first fruytis, and
dymes, and what euer thingus thei hadden vowed feithfully. Forsothe the prefect of hem was Chonenyas, Leuyte; and
13 Semeye, his brother, the secounde; aftir
whome Jehiel, and Azarias, and Naath,
and Azabel, and Jerymoth, Jozabad also,
and Helieel, and Jesmahias, and Maath,
and Banayas, prouostis vndir the hondis
of Chonenye and Semeye, his brother, of
the maundement of kyng Ezechie, and of
Azarie, the bischop of the hous of the
Lord, to whom alle thingus perteyneden.
14 Chore forsothe, the sone of Jemna, Leuyte, and porter of the este 3ate, was
prouost to thes that wilfully offreden to

of oxis[s] and of scheep, and the[t] tithis of
holi thingis, whiche thei avowiden to 'her
Lord God[u], and thei brou3ten alle[v] thingis[w],
and[x] maden[y] ful[z] many heepis. In[a] the 7
thridde monethe thei bigunnen to leie the[b]
foundementis of the[c] heepis, and in the
seuenthe monethe thei filliden[d] tho[e] heepis.
And whanne[f] Ezechie and hise princes 8
hadden entrid[g], thei si3en the[h] heepis[i],
and blessiden[k] the Lord, and the puple
of Israel. And Ezechie[l] axide the preestis 9
and dekenes[m], whi the[n] heepis laien so.
Azarie[o], the firste[p] preest of the genera- 10
cioun of Sadoch, answeride to hym, and
seide, Sithen[q] the firste fruytis bigunnen
to be offrid in the hows of the Lord, we
han ete[r] and ben fillid[s], and ful many
thingis ben left[t]; for the Lord hath blessid[u]
his puple; sotheli[v] this plentee, which[w]
thou seest, is of the relifs[x]. Therfor Eze- 11
chie[y] comaundide, that thei schulden make
redi bernes in the hows of the Lord; and
whanne thei hadden do this thing, thei[z] 12
brou3ten in[a] feithfuly bothe the[b] firste
fruytis, and tithis, and what euere thingis
thei hadden avowid. Forsothe[c] Chonenye,
the dekene, was the[d] souereyn[e] of tho[f]; and
Semei his brother was the secounde[g]; aftir 13
whom Jehiel, and Azarie, and Nabath, and
Asahel, and Jerimoth, 'and Jozabad[h], and
Helyel, and Jesmahie, and Maath, and
Banaie, weren souereyns vndur the hondis[i]
of Chonenye and Semei, his brother, bi[k]
the comaundement[l] of 'Ezechie the kyng[m],
and of Azarie, the bischop of the hows of
the Lord, to whiche[o] alle thingis perteyneden[o]. But Chore, the sone of Jemnya, 14
dekene and portere of the eest 3ate, was
souereyn of tho thingis that[p] weren offrid bi fre wille to the Lord, and[q] of the[r]

[s] oxen INS. [t] Om. I. *thei offriden* NS. [u] the Lord her God S. [v] alle *these* S. [w] thingis *into the temple* INS. [x] *to prestis and dekenes to be susteyned with*, and S. [y] thei maden INS. [z] Om. IN. *Of these thingis* S. [a] Om. S. [b] Om. INS. [c] Om. *plures.* [d] filliden *or* endiden IS. [e] the A. [f] whanne that INS. [g] entrid *in thider* S. [h] tho DV. [i] heep C. heepis *of sacrifices* IS. [k] thei blessiden INS. [l] the kyng INS. [m] the dekenes INS. [n] tho INS. [o] And Azarie INS. [p] first *or* cheef IS. [q] Sith I. [r] ete *of tho* I. ete *of tho fruytis* S. [s] fulfillid INS. [t] left *3it here* S. [u] blessid, *that is, he hath encrexid* I.
blessid, *that is, with diuers goodis he hath encreside* S. [v] and INS. [w] that INS. [x] remenauntis *ouer* I.
remenauntis N. remnauntis *ouer our lyfelood* S. [y] the kyng INS. [z] men INS. [a] in *thider* S. [b] her INS.
[c] And INS. [d] Om. INS. [e] souereyn *keper* S. [f] tho thingis INS. [g] secounde *next him* INS. [h] Om. N.
[i] hondis *or* poweris S. [k] *these weren* souereyns bi S. [l] heest INS. [m] king Ezechie NS. [n] whom I.
[o] perteyneden *to be ordeyned* S. [p] whiche NS. [q] Om. N. *Also he was souereyn* S. [r] alle the A *pr. m.*
EGIKLMNSXb̧c̦.

the Lord, and to the first fruytis, and to
15 the sacred in to the holy of halowes, and
vndir hit cure Eden, and Beniamyn, Jesue, and Semeyas, Amarias also, and Sechenyas, in the citees of prestis, that
feithfully thei delen to their bretheren
16 parties, to the lesse and to the more, out
taken the men fro thre ʒeei and abouen,
thes thingus to alle that wenten in to the
temple of the Lord, and what euer thing
bi eche dais was hired in the seruyse and
17 keepyngis after their deuysiouns   To
prestis bi meynes, and to Leuytis fro
twenty ʒeer and aboue by ordres and
18 their companyes, and to al the multitude,
bothe to wyues and .to the^d fre childre
of hem of either kynde, feithfully of mete
of thes thingus that weren halowed weren
19 ʒeuen   Bot and of the sonus of Aaron
bi feeldis and suburbis of eche cytees
ther weren disposid men, that by partis
schulden delen to al male kynde of prestis
20 and Leuytis.   Thanne Ezechias dide alle
thingus, that we han seide, in al Juda, and
wrouʒte riʒt and gode and soth thing be-
21 fore the Lord his God, in al heryng of
the seruyse of the hous of the Lord,
after the lawe and cerymonyes, willynge
to sechen the Lord his God in al his
herte, and he dide, and is maad welsum

.

CAP XXXII.

1   After the^e whiche thingis and siche
a maner treuth, came Senacherub, king
of Assiries, and gon in to Judam, be-
seegide strengthed cytees, wilnynge to
2 taken hem.   The whiche thing whanne
Ezechias hadde herd, that is^f, Senacherub
to han commen, and al the bure of the^g

firste fruytis, and of thingis halewid in
to hooli thingis *of the noumbre* of hooli
thingis, and vndur his cure *weren* Eden, 15
and Beniamyn, Jesue, and Semeye, and
Amarie, and Sechenye, in the citees of
preestis, that thei schulden departe feithfuli to her britheren the partis^t, to the
lesse and the^u grettere, outakun malis 16
fro^v three ʒeer and aboue, these thingis
to^w alle that entriden in to the temple of
the Lord, and what euer thing bi ech dai
was hirid in the seruyce and obseruaunces^x
bi her departyngis   To preestis bi mey- 17
nees^y, and to^z dekenes fro 'the twentithe^a
ʒeer and aboue bi her ordris and cumpenyes, and to alle the multitude, bothe^b 18
to the^c wyues and fre^d children of hem
of euer either kynde^e, metis weren ʒouun
feithfuli^f of these thingis that^g weren ha-
lewid^h   But also men of the sones of 19
Aaron weren ordeyned bi the feeldis and
suharbis^i of alle citees^k, whyche^l men^m
schulden dele partis^n to al the male kynde
of preestis and dekenes^o   Therfor^p Eze- 20
chie^q dide alle thingis^r, whiche we seiden^s,
in al Juda, and he wrouʒte that, that was
riʒtful and good and trewe bifor 'his Lord
God^t, in al the^u religioun of the^v seruyce 21
of the hows of the Lord, bi the lawe^w and
ceiymonyes^x, and he wolde seke his^v Lord
God in^z al his herte, and he dide^a, and
hadde prosperite

CAP XXXII

1   Aftir whiche thingis and sich treuthe,
Senacheiib, the kyng of Assiriens, cam
and entride in to Juda; and he bisegide
stronge citees, and wolde take^b tho   And 2
whanne Ezechie hadde herd this thing,
that is, that Senacherib was^c comun, and
that al the^d fersnesse of batel^c was turned

^d Om. n   ^e Om c   ^f is, in n   ^g Om c *pr m*

^a the holi s   ^t partis, *that weren lymytid to hem for lyflode* is   ^u to the ins   ^v of x   ^w *weren do to* ins
^x obseruaunces *of the temple* is   ^y *her* meynees ins   ^z Om n *sec m* s   ^a twenty ins   ^b *that is,* bothe s
^c Om *plures.*   ^d to the fre is   to fre nx   ^e kynde, *that is, male and female* s   ^f freli ns   ^g whiche ins
^h halewid *or offrid in the temple* is   ^i bi subarbis ins   ^k the citees i   the citee vs   ^l the whiche i
^m Om ins   ^n in the partis ins   ^o of dekenes s   ^p Certis ins   ^q kyng i zechie is   ^r thes thingis ins
^s han seid ins   ^t the Lord his God ins   ^u Om in   ^v Om in   ^w lawe *of God* is   ^x bi the cerymonyes
therof is   bi the eerymonyes n   ^v the ins   ^z of v   ^a dide *so* ins   ^b haue take ins   ^c had ins
^d his s   ^e his batel ins

batayl to ben turned aȝeinus Jerusalem, 3 gon in counseile with the princis and most stronge men, that thei schulden stoppyn the heuedis of wellis, that weren with oute the cyte; and, that deemyng 4 the sentence of alle, he gaderede a myche multitude, and thei stoppiden alle the wellis, and the ryuer, that flowede in the myddis of the lond; seyinge, Lest there commen kingis of Assiries, and fynde[h] 5 aboundaunce of watirs. And doyng tauȝtly he bilde up al the wal that was scatered, and maad out touris ther vpon, and with oute forth another wall. And he enstored Mello in the cyte of Dauid; 6 and maad armour of al maner, and ter-gettis. And he sette princis of fiȝters in the hoost; and he togider clepide alle in the strete of the ȝate of the citee, and he 7 spac to the herte of hem, seyinge, Doth manly, and takith coumfort; willith not taken ferd, ne dreeden the kyng of Assiries, and al the multitude that is with hym; forsothe many mo ben with us 8 thanne with hym. With hym is the fleschely arm; with us the Lord oure God, the which is oure help and fiȝter for us. And the puple is comfortide with siche maner wordis of Ezechie, 9 kyng of Juda. The whiche thingus after that ben don, Senacherub, the king of Assiries, sente his seruauntis vnto Jeru-salem; he forsothe with al his host be-segide Lachis; to Ezechie, kyng of Juda, and to al the puple that was in the cytee, 10 seyinge, Thes thingus seith Senacherub, king of Assiries, In whome hauing trust 11 ȝe sitten bisegid in Jerusalem? For why Ezechias deceyuith ȝou, that he take to deth in hungur and thirst, affermynge that the Lord ȝoure God delyuer ȝou fro

aȝens Jerusalem, he took counsel with the[f] 3 princes and[g] strongest[h] men, that thei schulden stoppe the heedis of wellis, that[i] weren without the citee; and whanne the sentence of alle men demyde this, he ga- 4 deride togidere a ful greet multitude[k], and thei stoppiden alle the wellis, and the[l] ryuer, that flowide[m] in the[n] myddis of the lond; and[o] seiden[p], Lest the kyngis of As-siriens comen, and fynden abundance of watris. Also he[q] dide wittili, and bildide[r] 5 al the wal that was distride, and he bild-ide touris aboue[s], and an other wal with-outforth. And he reparilide Mello in[t] the citee of Dauid; and made[u] armure[v] of al kynde, and scheldis. And he ordeynede 6 princes[w] of werriouris in[x] the oost; and he clepide togidere alle men in the street of the ȝate of the citee, and spake[y] to the herte of hem[z], and seide, Do ȝe manli, and 7 be ȝe coumfortid; nyle ȝe drede, nether be ȝe[n] aferd of the kyng of Assiriens, and[b] of al the multitude which[c] is with him; for[d] many mo[†] ben with vs than with him. Fleischli[e] arm[f] is with him; ʻoure Lord[g] God[s] is with vs, which[h] is oure helpere, and schal[i] fiȝte for vs. And the puple was coumfortid with sich wordis of Ezechie, kyng of Juda. And aftir that these thingis 9 weren doon[k], Sennacherib sente hise ser-uauntis to Jerusalem; for he[l] ʻwith al the oost[m] bisegide Lachis. *He ʼsente* to Eze-chie, kyng of Juda, and to al the puple that was in the citee[n], and seide[o], Sen- 10 nacherib, the[p] kyng of Assiriens, seith these thingis, In whom han ȝe trist, and sitten bisegid in Jerusalem? Whether[q] 11 Ezechie disseyueth ȝou, that he[r] bitake ȝou[s] to deeth in hungur and thirst, and[t] affermeth[u], that[v] ʻȝoure Lord God[w] schal delyuere ȝou fro the hond of the kyng of

[h] fynde thei ᴇ *pr. m.*

[f] Om. ɪɴѕ.   [g] and with ɪѕ.   [h] moost stronge ɪɴѕ.   [i] whiche ɴѕ.   [j] this *profitable* ɪ. this *to be pro-fitable* ɴѕ.   [k] multitude *of men* ɪѕ.   [l] a ɪɴѕ.   [m] was ѕ.   [n] Om. ɴ.   [o] and thei ɪɴѕ.   [p] seiden *the cause whi* ɪ. seiden, *Stopping of the cours of watris is speedful,* ɴѕ.   [q] Ezechie ɪɴѕ.   [r] he bildide ɪɴѕ.   [s] aboue *the wal* ɴ. on *the walle* ѕ.   [t] Om. ɪɴѕ.   [u] he made ɪɴѕ.   [v] *to be ther inne* armure ѕ.   [w] Om. ɴ.   [x] to be in ѕ.   [y] he spake ɪɴѕ.   [z] *his men* ɪɴѕ.   [a] Om. ѕ.   [b] ne ɪɴѕ.   [c] that ɪɴѕ.   [d] forsothe ɪɴ.   [e] a fleischli ɪɴѕ.   [f] arm *or power* ɪɴѕ.   [g] and the Lord oure God ɪɴѕ.   [h] that ɪ.   [i] he schal ɪɴѕ.   [k] doon *and spoken* ѕ.   [l] he himself ɪɴѕ.   [m] Om. ɴ.   [n] citee *of Jerusalem* ɪɴѕ.   [o] he seide ɪɴѕ.   [p] Om. ɪɴѕ.   [q] Whether not ɪɴѕ.   [r] ȝe ɴ.   [s] Om. *plures.*   [t] and he ɪɴѕ.   [u] affermeth *or bihotith* ɪ.   [v] ȝou that ѕ.   [w] the Lord ȝoure God ɪɴѕ.

12 the hond ot the kyng of Assiies? Whether this is Ezechie, that distruyede his heeze thingus and auters, and comaundide to Jude and Jerusalem, seyinge, Before oon auter ze schul honouren, and in[1] it ze

13 schul brenne encense? Whether ze vnknowen what I haue don, and my fadirs, to alle puphs of londis? Whether the goddis of Gentilis and of alle londis myzten delyueren their iegyoun fro my

14 hond? Who is of alle the goddis ot Gentilis, whom my fadirs waastiden, that myzte delyueren his puple of myn hond, that also zoure God myzte delyueren zou

15 of this hond? Thanne zou deceyue not Ezechie, ne by veyn mouynge begile, ne trowe ze to hym, zif forsothe no God of alle Gentilis and of regzouns myzte delyueren his puple of my hond, and ot the hond ot my fadirs, folowyngly ne zour God schal mown delyuei zou of this myn

16 hond Bot and many other thingus his seruauntis speeken azeinus the Loid God,

17 and azeinus Ezechie, his seruaunt Also letters he wroot ful of blastemy in to the Lord God of Iiael, and he spac azeinus hym, As the goddis of Gentilis of othei londis myzten not delyueren their puple fro myn hond, so and the God of Ezechie schal not mowen delyuei his puple fro

18 this hond Forthermore and with a grete crie in Jews tunge azeinus the puple, that sat in the wallis of Jeiusalem, he ful out sounnede, that he agaste[m] hem, and take

19 the cite. And he spac azein the God of Irael, as azeinus the goddis of the[n] puplis of the erth, the werkis of menus hondis

20 Thanne preyden Ezechias, king, and Isaias, the[o] sone of Amos, prophete, azeynus this blasfemye, and thei ciyeden

21 out vnto heuen And the Loid sente his aungel, that smote eche stronge man and fizter, and the prince of the hoost of the kyng of Assiries, and he is turned azeyn with schenschip in to his lond And

12 Assyriens? Whether not[x] this is[y] Ezechie, 12 that distriede hiz[z] places, and auters[a] of hym[b], and comaundide to Juda and to[c] Jerusalem, and seide, ze schulen worschipe[d] bifoi oon autei, and therynne ze schulen brenne encense? Whether ze witen not

13 what thingis Y haue do, and my fadir[e], to alle the puplis of londis? Whether the goddis of folkis and of alle londis myzten delyuere hei cuntrei fio myn hond[f]?

14 Who is of alle goddis[g] of folkis, whiche my fadris distrieden, that myzte delyueie his puple fro myn hond, that also zouie God may delyuere zou fro this[h] hond? Therfor

15 Ezechie disseyue not zou, nethei scorne[i] bi veyn couniselyng, nethii bileue ze to hym, for if no god of alle folkis and cuntreis myzte delyuere his puple fro myn hond, and fro the hond[k] of my fadris, suyngh nethei zoure God schal mowe delyuere zou fro this myn hond But also

16 hise seruauntis spaken many othii thingis azenus the Lord God, and azens Ezechie, his seruaunte Also he wroot epistlis ful

17 of blasfemye azeus the Loid God of Israel, and he spak azens God[l], As the goddis of othere folkis myzten not delyuere her puple fro myn hond, so and the God of Ezechie may not delyuere his puple[e] fro myn hond Feithermore and with greet

18 cry in the langage ot Jewis he sownede azens the puple, that sat on[m] the wallis of Jerusalem, to make hem aferd, and to take the citee And he spake azens God of Is-

19 rael, as azens the goddis of the[n] puplis of erthe, the weikis of mennus hondis Ther-

20 foi Ezechie, the kyng, and Ysaie, the profete, the sone of Amos, preieden azens this blasfemye, and crieden[o] til in to heuene

21 And the Lord sente his aungel, that killide ech strong man and werrioui, and the prince of the oost of the kyng of Assiriens; and he[q] turnede azen with schenschip in to[r] his lond And whanne he hadde entrid in to the hows of his god,

[l]Om D   [m]gaste ACEF gatt H   [n]Om AB   [o]Om C

[x] Om IS   [y] IS not DINS   [z] hiz solempne S   [a] the auteris INS   [b] it INS   [c] Om S   [d] worschipe the Lord God INS   [e] fadris S   [f] hondis NS   [g] the goddis INS   [h] myn INS   [i] scorne he zou IN   scorne he not zou S   [k] hondis NS   [l] God, and seide INS   [m] upon INS   [n] Om INS   [o] thei crieden INS   [P] the whiche I   [q] Senacherib INS   [r] to C

whanne he was gon in to the hous of his god, the sonus, that weren gon out of ²² his wombe, slewen hym with swerd. And the Lord sauede Ezechie, and the dwellers of Jerusalem, fro the hond of Senacherub, kyng of Assiries, and fro the hond of alle men; and ȝaue to hem reste ²³ by enuyroun. Many also beeren hoostis and sacrifices to the Lord in to Jerusalem, and ȝiftis to Ezechie, kyng of Juda; the whiche is enhaunsid after thes thingus ²⁴ before alle folkis of kynde. In tho dais siknede Ezechie vnto the deth, and he preyde the Lord; and he herde hym, and ²⁵ ȝaue to hym a sygne; bot not after the benefetis that he hadde taken, he ȝeeld-ide[P], for arered is his herte; and ther is don aȝeinus hym wrath, and aȝeinus Ju- ²⁶ dam, and aȝeinus Jerusalem. And he is mekide aftirward, forthi that his herte was arered[q], bothe he and the dwellers of Jerusalem; and therfore came not vpon hem the wrath of the Lord in the ²⁷ dais of Ezechie. Forsothe Ezechias was riche, and ful glorious, and he gaderede to hym many tresoures of syluer, of gold, and of precious stone, of swote spices, and of alle maner armour, and of vessels ²⁸ of grete prise. And leyinge places of whete, and of wyne, and of oyle, and cratchis of alle bestis, and foldes to feeld ²⁹ bestis, and sixe cytees he bilde. He hadde forsothe flockis of scheep, and of droues vnnoumbreable; forthi that the Lord hadde ȝeuen to hym ful mych sub- ³⁰ staunce. He is Ezechie, that stoppide the ouer well of the waters of Gyon, and he turnede hem awey vndirnethe toward the west of the citee of Dauid; in[r] alle his werkis he dide welsumly, that he ³¹ wolde. Neuerthelater in the message of the princis of Babyloyne, that weren

the sones, that[s] ȝeden out of his wombe, killiden hym[t] with swerd. And the Lord ²² sauyde Ezechie, and the dwelleris of Jerusalem, fro the hond of Senacherib, kyng of Assiriens, and fro the hond of alle men; and ȝaf[u] to hem reste bi cumpas. Also ²³ many men brouȝten offryngis and sacrifices to the Lord in[v] to Jerusalem, and ȝiftis to Ezechie, kyng of Juda; which[w] was enhaunsid aftir these thingis bifor alle folkis. In tho daies Ezechie was sijk ²⁴ 'til to[x] the deth, and he preiede the Lord; and he herde hym, and ȝaf[y] to hym a signe[z]; but he ȝeldide not[a] bi[b] the bene- ²⁵ fices[c] whiche[d] he hadde take, for his herte was reisid[e]; and ire[f] was maad aȝens hym, and aȝens Juda, and aȝens Jerusalem. And he was mekid aftirward, for[g] his ²⁶ herte was reisid; bothe[h] he *was mekid*, and the dwelleris of Jerusalem; and therfor the ire[i] of the Lord cam not[j] on hem in the daies of Ezechie. Forsothe[k] Ezechie ²⁷ was riche, and ful noble, and gaderide[l] to hym silf ful many tresours of siluer, of[m] gold, and of preciouse stoon[n], of[o] swete smellynge spices, and of armuris of[p] al kynde, and[q] of vessels of greet prijs. Also he bildide large housis of wheete, of ²⁸ wyn, and of oile, and cratchis of alle beestis, and fooldis to scheep, and sixe[r] ²⁹ citees. For[s] he hadde vnnoumbrable flockis of scheep and of grete beestis; for the Lord hadde ȝoue to hym ful myche catel. Thilke is Ezechie, that stoppide the hiȝere ³⁰ welle of the watris of Gion, and turnede[t] tho awei vndur *the erthe* at the west[u] of the citee of Dauid; in alle hise werkis he dide 'bi prosperite[v], what euer[w] thing[x] he wolde. Netheles in the message of the ³¹ princes of Babiloyne, that[y] weren sent to hym for to axe of the grete wondir, that bifelde on[z] the lond[a], God forsook hym,

<hr>

[P] ȝeld c. [q] rerid c. [r] and B.

sente to hym, that thei schulden asken
of the wonder, that hadde fallen vpon the
erth, God forsoke hym, that he schulde
be temptid, and alle thingus schulden ben
maad knowen that weren in his herte

32 The remnaunt forsothe of the wordis of
Ezechie, and of his mercyes, ben writen
in the visioun of Ysay, the sone of Amos,
prophete, and in the boke of kingus of

33 Juda and of Irael   And Ezechie slepte
with his fadirs, and thei birieden hym
vpon the sepulcies[a] of the sonus of Dauid
And al Juda maad solempne his deed offices, and alle the dwelleres of Jeiusalem,
and Manasses, his sone, regnede for hym

that he were temptid[b], and that alle
thingis weren knowun that weren[c] in his
herte   Sotheli[d] the residue[e] of wordis[f] of 32
Ezechie, and of hise mercies, ben writun
in the profesie[g] of Ysaie, the profete, sone[h]
of Amos, and[i] in the book of kyngis of
Juda and of Israel.   And Ezechie slepte 33
with hise fadris, and thei birieden hym
aboue the sepulcris of the sones of Dauid
And al Juda and alle the dwelleris of Jerusalem maden solempne the seruyces[k] of
his biriyng, and Manasses, his sone, reg-
nide for him.

CAP XXXIII

1 Of twelue 3eer was Manasses, whanne
he hadde begunne to regnen, and fyue
and fyfty 3eer he regned in Jerusalem.

2 Forsothe he dide euyl befoie the Lord
aftir the abomynacyouns of Gentilis, the
whiche the Lord tuinede vpsadoun be-

3 fore the sonus of Irael   And turnede he
enstored the hee3e thingus, 'the whiche[t]
Ezechie, his fadir, hadde distruyede
And he sette up auters of Baalym, and
maad mawmete wodus, and honourede al
the kny3thode of heuen, and hemede it

4 And he bilde up auters in the hous of
the Lord, of the whiche the Loid hadde
seyde, In Jerusalem schal ben my name

5 without eend   Forsothe he bilde up
hem to al the hoost of heuen in the two

6 porchis of the hous of the Lord   And
he made his sonus to passen thoru3 fiji
in the valey of Hennon, and he weytide
sweuens, and he folowede deuynynge in
briddes, and he enseiuede to enchaunt-
yng craftis, and he hadde with hym de-
uynouis and enchaunters, and many
euyls wrou3t[u] before the Lord, that he

7 terre hym   Grauen also and 3oten tookne

CAP XXXIII

Manasses was of twelue 3eer, whanne 1
he bygan to regne, and he iegnyde in Jerusalem fyue and fifti 3eer   Forsothe[l] he 2
dide yuel bifor the Lord bi[m] abhomynaciouns[n] of hethene men, whiche[o] the Lord
destriede bifor the sones of Israel   And 3
he tuinede[p], and restoride the hi3e places[q],
whiche Ezechie, his fadir, hadde destried
And he bildide[r] auteris to Baalym, and
made[s] wodis[t], and worschipide[u] al the
kny3thod of heuene, and hemede it   And 4
he bildide auteris in the hows of the Loid,
of which[v] the Lord hadde[w] seid, My name
schal be[x] in Jerusalem with outen ende
Sotheli[y] he[z] bildide tho auteris to al the 5
kny3thod of heuene in[a] the[b] twei laige
places of the hows of the Lord   And 6
he made hise sones to passe thorou3 the
fier in the valei 'of Beennon; he kepte[c]
dremes[d]; he suede fals diuynyng bi chiteryng of briddis, he[e] seruyde witche
craftis, he[f] hadde with hym astronomy-
eris and enchaunteris, 'ethir trigetouis s[g],
that[h] disseyuen[i] mennus wittis[j], and he
wrou3te many yuelis bifor the Lord to
terre hym to wraththe   Also[k] he settide[l] 7

a sepulcre c   t that c.   u he wro3te c

b assaied INS   c was s.   d And INS   e remenaunt INS   f the wordis INS   g prophecies INS   h the
sone INS   i and also NS   k seruice s.   l And INS   m aftir I   n al abhomynaciouns o the abhominaciouns I   o whom I   p turnede a3en INS   q solempne places IS   r bildide up INS   s he made INS
t mawmet wodis INS   u he worschipide INS   v which hous INS   w Om INS   x he inclepid IS
y And INS   z Manasses INS   a and I   b Om cis to v   c kepte or waitide IS   d aftir dremes INS
e and he INS   f and he s   g trechetouris B   h which s   i deceiueden EI M   'J Gloss omitted in IN
k And INS   l sette I settide or ordeynede s

he putte in the hous of the Lord, of the[v] whiche God spac to Dauid, and to Salomon, his sone, seyinge, In this hous and in Jerusalem, that I chees of alle the lynagis of Irael, I schal putte my name 8 in to euermore; and I schal not maken to meuen the fote of Irael fro the lond that I toke to[w] the fadirs of hem, so oonly 3if thei kepyn to don that I comaundide to hem, and al the lawe, and cerymonyes, and domys, by the hond of Moyses. 9 Thanne Manasses deceyuede Judam, and the dwellers of Jerusalem, that thei diden euyl ouer alle Gentylis, 'the whiche[x] the Lord ouerturnede fro the face of the sonus 10 of Irael. And the Lord spac to hym, and to his puple; and thei wolden not taken 11 heede. Therfore he ouerladde in to hem princis and hoostis of the kyng of Assiries; and thei tooken Manassen, and bounden with cheynes and with gyues 12 thei brou3ten hym in to Babyloyne. The which aftir that he was to gydre anguyscht, he preyde the Lord his God, and dide penaunce gretely before the God 13 of his fadirs. And he preyede hym, and halsende[y] ententijfly; and he herde the orisoun of hym, and he brou3te hym a3ein in to Jerusalem in to his kyngdam; and Manasses knew3, that the Lord he is 14 God. After thes thingus he bilde a wal withoute the cytee of Dauid, at the west of Gyon, in the grete valey, fro the entre of the 3ate of fischis, bi enuyroun vnto Ofel; and he enhauncide it hugeli; and he sette princis of the hoost in alle the 15 strengthed cytees of Juda. And he toke awey alien goddis and symulacres fro the hous of the Lord; the auters also that he hadde maad in the hil of the hous of the Lord and in Jerusalem, and al he threw3 16 aferre out of the cite. Bot he enstorede the auter of the Lord, and offrede vpon

a grauum[m] signe[n] and a 3otun signe[o] in the hows of the Lord, of which[p] hows God spak to Dauid, and to Salomon, his sone, and seide, Y schal sette my name with outen ende in this hows and in Jerusalem, which[q] Y chees of alle the lynagis of Israel; and Y schal not make the foot 8 of Israel to moue fro the lond which[r] Y 3af to her fadris, so oneli if[s] thei kepen[t] to do tho thingis whiche[u] Y comaundide[v] to hem, and al[w] the lawe[x], and cerymonyes, and domes, bi the hond[y] of Moises. Therfor[z] Manasses disseyuede Juda[a], and 9 the dwelleris of Jerusalem, that[b] thei diden yuel, more than alle hethene men, whiche the Lord hadde distriede fro the face[c] of the sones of Israel. And the Lord spak 10 to hym, and to his puple; and thei nolden[d] take heed[e]. Therfor the Lord brou3te on[f] 11 hem the princes of the oost of the kyng of Assiriens†; and thei token Manasses, and bounden hym with chaynes, and stockis, and ledden[g] hym in to Babiloyne. And aftir that he was augwischid, 12 he preiede 'his Lord God[h], and[i] dide[k] penaunce gretli bifor the God of hise fadris. And he preiede God, and bisechide[l] en- 13 tentifli; and God herde his preier, and brou3te[m] hym a3en 'in to[n] Jerusalem in[o] to his rewme; and[p] Manasses knew, that the Lord hym silf is God[q]. Aftir these thingis 14 he[r] bildide the wal with out the citee of Dauid, at the west[s] of Gion, in the valei, fro the entryng of the 3ate of fischis, bi cumpas 'til to[t] Ophel; and he reiside it[u] gretli[v]; and he ordeynede princes of the oost in alle ' the stronge citees of Juda. And he dide awei alien goddis and symy- 15 lacris fro the hows of the Lord; and he dide awei the auteris, whiche he hadde maad in the hil[w] of the hows of the Lord, and in Jerusalem, and he castide[x] awei alle[y] with out the citee. Certis he restoride 16

† Assiriens; that is, hem that weren princes of the oost of Assiriens, whanne the king of Babiloyne was suget to Assiriens, for thanne the king of Babiloyne and hise princes, weren of the oost of the king of Assiriens, but now the king of Babiloyne was not suget to Assiriens, as Josephus and othre cronycleris seyen, therfor they ledden him in to Babiloyne. Lire here. c.

---

[m] 3otun NS.   [n] Om. I.   [o] Om. NS.   [p] the which I.   [q] the which I. which citee s.   [r] that INS. [s] that INS.   [t] taken hede INS.   [u] that I.   [v] haue comaundid INS.   [w] alle I.   [x] lawis I.   [y] hond or heest s.   [z] But INS.   [a] the men of Juda INS.   [b] so that s.   [c] faces A pr. m.   [d] wolden not I.   [e] heed to him e.   [f] upon is.   [g] thei ledden INS.   [h] the Lord his God INS.   [i] of merci and s.   [k] he dide INS. [l] bisechide him INS.   [m] he brou3te IN.   [n] to IN.   [o] and I.   [p] and thanne INS.   [q] God aloone I. God oonli NS.   [r] Manasses INS.   [s] west side INS.   [t] vnto INS. to x.   [u] it up I. up NS.   [v] gretli that wal NS. [w] hil or hei3the I. hil or the hei3the s.   [x] castide hem INS.   [y] Om s.

it slayn sacrifices, and pesible, and preysynge, and he comaundede to Jude, that 17 he schulde seruen to God of Irael Neuer the latei ȝit the puple offiede in heeȝe 18 thingus to the Lord his God The remnaunt forsothe of the dedis of Manasse, and the obseuraioun of hym to his God, the wordis also of the seearis, that speeken to hym in the name of the Lord God of Irael, ben conteenede in the wordis of the 19 kingus of Liael The preyer also of hym, and heering, and alle the synnes, and dispitis, also the places in the whiche he bilde up heeȝe thingus, and maad mawmeteˣ wodis and ymagis, before that he dide penaunce, ben wiiten in the wordis 20 of Ozai. Forsothe Manasses slepte with his faders. and they birieden hym in his hous; and Amon, his sone, regnede for 21 hym Of two and twenty ȝeer was Amon, whanne he hadde begunne to iegnen, and 22 two ȝeer he regnede in Jerusalem And he dide euyl in the siȝte of the Lord, as hadde done Manasses, his fader, and to alle the mawmetis, that Manasses hadde 23 foi gide, he offride, and seiuede And he dradde not the face of the Lord, as dradde Manasses, his fadir; and manye 24 more thingus trespasside And whanne his seruauntis hadden sworn to gydre aȝeinus hym, thei slowen hym in his hous 25 But the tothei multitude of the puple, hem slayn that hadden smyten Amon, thei setten Joziam, his sone, kyng for hym

CAP XXXIV

1 Of eiȝt ȝeer was Jozias, whanne he hadde begunne to iegnen, and oon and thritty ȝeer he regnede in Jerusalem 2 And he dide that was riȝt in the siȝt of the Lord, and he wente in the weies of

the auter of the Lord, and offiideᶻ theronneˣ slayn sacrifices, and pesible sacrifices, and preisyngᵇ, and he comaundide Judaᶜ to serue the Lord God of Israel Netheles 17 the pupleᵈ offride ȝit in hiȝᶜ places to 'her Lord Godᶠ. Forsotheᵍ the residueʰ of 18 dedisⁱ of Manasses, and his bisechyng to 'his Lord Godᵏ, and the wordis of piofetis, thatˡ spaken to hym in theᵐ name of the Lord God of Isiael, ben conteyned in the wordis of the kyngis of Isiael. And his 19 preierⁿ, and theᵒ heryngᵖ, and alle synnesᑫ, and dispisyngʳ, alsoˢ the places in whiche he bildide hiȝ thingis, and made wodisᵗ and ymagis, bifor that he dide penaunce, benᵘ writun in the bokis' of Ozaiʷ For-20 sotheˣ Manasses slepte with hise fadiis, and thei birieden hym in his hows, and Amon, his sone, regnyde foi hym. Amon 21 was of two and twenti ȝeer, whanne he bigan to regne, and he regnyde twei ȝeei in Jerusalem. And he dide yuel in the 22 siȝt of the Lord, as Manasses, his fadii, hadde doʸ, and he offiide, and seiuyde to alle theˣ idols, whiche Manassesᵃ hadde maad And he reuerenside not the face 23 of the Loid, as Manasses, 'his fadirᵇ, reuerensideᶜ, and he dide mych grettei trespassisᵈ And whanne his seruauntis 24 'hadden swore to gyderᵉ aȝens hym, thei killiden hym in his hows Sotheliᶠ the 25 residueᵍ multitude of the pupleʰ, aftir that thei hadden slaynⁱ hem that 'hadden slaynᵏ Amon, ordeynedenˡ Josie, his sone, kyng for hym

CAP. XXXIV.

1 Josie was of eiȝte ȝeer, whanne he bigan to regne, and he regnede in Jerusalem oon and thritti ȝeer And he dide that, thatᵐ 2 was riȝtful in the siȝt of the Lord, and ȝedeⁿ in the waies of Dauid his fadii, and

ᶻ he offride ɪɴꜱ   ᵃ ther upon ɪꜱ   ᵇ preisyng *to the Lord* ꜱ   ᶜ *the men of* Juda ɪɴꜱ   ᵈ peple ȝit *after her own fyndyngs* ꜱ   ᵉ hiȝ solempne ɪꜱ   ᶠ the Lord her God ɪɴꜱ   ᵍ And ɪɴꜱ   ʰ remenaunt ɪɴꜱ   ⁱ the dedis ɪɴꜱ   ᵏ the Lord his God ɪɴꜱ   ˡ whiche ɴꜱ   ᵐ Om ɴꜱ   ⁿ preier *to God* ꜱ   ᵒ Om ɪ   ᵖ herying *that the Lord herd him* ꜱ   ᑫ his synnes ɪɴꜱ   ʳ *al* his dispisyng ꜱ   ˢ and also ɪɴꜱ   ᵗ mawmet wodis ɪɴꜱ   ᵘ these ben ꜱ   ᵛ book ɪɴꜱ   ʷ Yzaye ꜱ   ˣ And ɪɴꜱ   ʸ *first* do ꜱ   ᶻ Om ɪ   ᵃ *at his beginnyug* Manasses ꜱ   ᵇ Om. ꜱ.   ᶜ reuerenside not *first* ɪ reuerenside not ɴ *first* reuerencid him not ꜱ   ᵈ trespassis *than his fadir* ɪɴ trespassis *than his fader* dide ꜱ   ᵉ in conspiracioun had sworn ꜱ   ᶠ And ɪɴꜱ   ᵍ remenaunt ɪɴꜱ.   ᵇ puple *that consentide not to the deth of Amon* ɪꜱ puple *that consentide not to his deeth* ɴ   ⁱ killiden ꜱ   ᵏ killiden ɪɴꜱ   ˡ thei ordeyneden ɪɴꜱ   ᵐ Om ꜱ   ⁿ he ȝede ɪɴꜱ

Dauid, his fadir, and he bowede not to
3 the ri3t ne to the left. The ei3the 3eer
forsothe of his empyre, whanne 3it he was
a child, he beganne to sechen the God of
his fadir Dauid ; and the twelfthe 3eer
aftir that he hadde begunnen, he clensede Judeam and Jerusalem fro hee3e
thingus, and mawmete wodis, and symu-
4 lacres, and grauen thingus. And thei
distruy3eden before hym the auters of
Baalym, and the symulacres that weren
sett vpon ; thei waastiden also the mawmete wodis. And grauen thingus he
hew3 doun, and mynuscht ; and vpon the
toumbis of hem, that weren wount to
5 offren, he scatercde the releuys. Forthermore the boones of prestis he brende
in the auters of mawmetis, and he clensed
6 Judam and Jerusalem. Bot and in the
citees of Manasse, and of Effraym, and
of Semeon, vnto Neptalym, alle thingus
7 he turnede vpsadoun. And whanne the
auters he hadde 'to-scaterede[a], and the
mawmete wodus and grauen thingus he
hadde to-bray3ide in to gobetis, and al
the wasching templis he hadde waastide
fro al the lond of Irael, he is turnede
8 a3ein in to Jerusalem. Thanne the
ei3tenthe 3eer of his regne, the lond now
clensede and the temple of the Lord, he
sente Saphan, the sone of Elchie, and
Maazian, prince of the cytee, and Joa,
the sone of Joachas, chauncelere, that
thei schulden enstore the hous of the
9 Lord their God. The whiche camyn to
Elchyam, the grete preste ; and monee
taken of hym, that was brou3t into the
hous of the Lord, and that gadereden
Leuytis and porters, of Manasse, and of
Effraym, and of alle the tother of Irael,

bowide[o] not to the ri3t side nether to the
left side. Forsothe[p] in the ei3tethe 3eer 3
of the rewme of his empire, whanne he
was 3it a child, he bigan to seke God[q] of
his fadir Dauid ; and in[r] the tweluethe
3eer after[s] that he bigan[t], he clenside Juda
and Jerusalem fro[u] hi3[v] places, and wodis[w],
and similacris[x], and grauun[y] ymagis. And 4
thei[z] destrieden bifor hym the auteris of
Baalym, and thei destrieden the symy-
lacris, that weren put aboue[a]. Also he
hewide doun the wodis[b], and grauun[c]
ymagis, and brak[d] to[e] smale gobetis ; and
scateride[f] abrood 'the smale gobetis[g] on[h]
the[i] birielis of hem, that[k] weren wont to
offre 'to tho[l]. Ferthermore he[m] brente the 5
boonys of preestis in[n] the auteris of idols,
and he clenside Juda and Jerusalem[o]. But 6
also he destriede alle idols[p] in[q] the citees[r]
of Manasses, and of Effraym, and of Symeon, 'til to[s] Neptalym. And whanne he[t] 7
hadde scateride the[n] auteris, and hadde[v]
al to[w]-broke in to gobetis the wodis[x], and
grauun[y] ymagis, and hadde[z] destried alle
templis[a] of ydols fro al the lond of Israel,
he turnede a3en in to Jerusalem. Therfor 8
in the ei3tenthe 3eer of his rewme, whanne
the lond and temple[b] 'of the Lord[c] was
clensid nowe[d], he sente Saphan, the sone
of Helchie, and Masie, the prince of the
citee, and Joa, the sone of Joachaz, chaunceler[e], that thei schulden reparele the hous
'of his Lord God[f]. Whiche[g] camen to Hel- 9
chie, the grete preest ; and whanne thei
hadden take of hym the money, which[h]
was brou3t in to the hows of the Lord ;
and[i] which monei the dekenes and porteris hadden gaderid of Manasses[k], and of
Effraym, and of alle the residue[l] men[m] of
Israel, and of al[n] Juda and Beniamyn[o],

---

[a] scattered c.

[o] he bowide INS.　[p] And INS.　[q] the God s.　[r] aftir INS.　[s] Om. INS.　[t] bigan to regne INS.　[u] of INS.
[v] hi3 solempne INS.　[w] of mawmet wodis INS.　[x] of similacris INS.　[y] of grauun INS.　[z] the men of
Jorie INS.　[a] aboue tho auters IS.　[b] mawmett wodis INS.　[c] the grauen s.　[d] he brak IS.　[e] thes into INS.
[f] tho smale gobetis he scateride INS.　[g] Om. INS.　[h] vpon IS.　[i] Om. c.　[k] whiche INS.　[l] to the ymagis
of ydolatrie I marg. to tho ymagis NS.　[m] the kyng INS.　[n] upon IS. on N.　[o] Jerusalem of ydolatrie NS.
[p] the idols INS.　[q] of s.　[r] citee AS.　[s] vnto INS.　[t] kyng Josias INS.　[u] thes INS.　[v] Om. INS.　[w] Om. I.
[x] mawmett wodis INS.　[y] the grauun INS.　[z] whanne he hadde INS.　[a] the temples INS.　[b] the temple INS.
[c] Om. s.　[d] Om. N.　[e] his chaunceler INS.　[f] the Lord his God INS.　[g] The whiche men I. Which men s.
[h] that IN.　[i] Om. A pr. m. INS.　[k] men of Manasses INS.　[l] remenaunt INS.　[m] of men s.　[n] Om. INS.
[o] of Beniamyn INS.

also of al Juda and Beniamyn, and the
10 dwellers of Jerusalem, thei token in the
hondis of hem that stoden vpon to the
werkmen in the hous of the Lord, that
thei enstoren the temple, and eche feble
11 thingus thei bocthyn And thei ʒeuen it
to the craftise men, and to masouns, that
thei schulden bien hewen stones of the
quarers, and trees to the iunctours of the
bildynge, and to the ioynynge of the
houses, that the kingus of Irael hadden
12 distruyede The whiche feithfully alle
thingus diden. Forsothe prouostis of the
werkmen weren Jabath, and Abdias, of
the sonus of Mereiy; Zacharias, and Mosollam, of the sonis of Caath; that streyn-
eden the werk, alle Leuytis, cunnynge in
13 orgnys to syngyn Vpon hem forsothe
that to dyuerse vses beeren birthens weren
scribis, and maisters, the porters of the
14 Leuytis And whanne thei schulden offeren the monee, that was brouʒt in to
the temple of the Lord, Elchias, the
preste, fonde a boke of the lawe of the
15 Lord by the hond of Moisy, and seith
to Saphan, scribe, The boke of the lawe
I haue founden in the hous of the Lord
16 And he toke to hym, and he brouʒt in
the volume to the kyng, and tolde to
hym, seyinge, Alle thingus that thou hast
ʒeuen in to the hondis of thi seruauntis,
17 loo! thei ben fulfild. The syluer that is
founden in the hous of the Lord thei
han ʒotyn; and it is ʒeuen to the prefectis
of craftise men, and forgynge dyuerse
18 werkis, forthermore Elchias, the preste,
toke to me this boke. The whiche whanne
19 the kyng present, he hadde reherside, and
he hadde herd the wordis of the lawe, he
20 kutte his clothes, and he comaundide to
Elchie, and to Aichan, the sone of Saphan, and to Abdon, the sone of Micha,
also to Saphan, scribe, and to Asie, the
21 seruaunt of the kyng, seyinge, Goth, and

and of the dwelleris of Jerusalem, thei 10
ʒauen it in[p] the hondis of hem that[q] weren
souereyns of the werk men in the hows of
the Lord, that thei schulden restore the
temple, and reparele alle feble[r] thingis[s]
And thei ʒauen that monei to the[t] crafti 11
men and masouns, for to bie stoonys hewid
out of the ⸢delues, *ether*[u] *quarreris*[w], and
trees[x] to the[y] ioynyngis of the bildyng[z], and
to the coupling of housis, whiche the kingis
of Juda hadden destried Whiche[a] men[b] 12
diden feithfuli alle thingis Sotheli[c] the
souereyns of worcheris weren Jabath, and
Abdie, of the sones of Merari, Zacarie[d],
and Mosallam, of the sones of Caath,
whiche hastiden the werk, alle[e] *weren*
dekenes, kunnynge[f] to synge with orguns
Sotheli[g] ouer them that baren birthuns to 13
dyuerse vsis weren the[h] scribis, and maistris of the[i] dekenes, and porteris And 14
whanne thei baren out the monei, that
was borun[k] in to the temple of the Lord,
Helchie, ⸢the preest[l], foond the[m] book of
the lawe of the Lord bi the hond[n] of
Moises And he[o] seide to Saphan, the 15
writere, Y haue founde the[p] book of the
lawe in the hows of the Lord And Hel- 16
chie took[q] to Saphan, and he bar in the[r]
book to the king, and telde[s] to hym, and
seide, Lo! alle thingis ben fillid[t], whiche
thou hast ʒoue in to the hondis of thi seruauntis Thei[u] han wellyd togidere the[v] 17
siluere, which is foundun in the hous of
the Lord, and it is ʒouun to the souereyns of the[w] crafti men, and makynge
dyuerse werkis, ferthermore Helchie, the 18
preest, took to me this book And whanne
he hadde rehersid this book in the[x] presence of the kyng, and he[y] hadde herd the 19
wordis of the lawe, he to-rente hise clothis,
and he comaundide to Helchie, and to Ai- 20
chan, the sone of Saphan, and to Abdon,
the sone of Mycha, and to Saphan, the
scryuen, and to Asaie, the seruaunt of the

[p] in to S. [q] whiche INS [r] the feble INS [s] thingis *therof* INS [t] Om INS [u] Om INS [w] quarreis A [x] *to bie* trees INS [y] Om INS [z] bildingis I [a] The whiche I [b] werk men INS [c] And INS [d] and Zacarie NS [e] alle *thes* INS [f] kunnynge *men* INS [g] And INS [h] Om IN *sec. m.* S [i] Om INS. [k] broʒt INS [l] Om S [m] a INS [n] hond *or* *loor* S [o] *Helchie* INS [p] a INS [q] took *it* INS [r] that INS [s] he telde INS [t] fulfillid IN fulfillid *or* *endide* S [u] And thei S [v] thi N [w] Om INS [x] Om INS [y] *whanne the kyng* INS

preyeth the Lord for me, and for the remnaunt of Irael and of Juda, vpon alle the wordis of this boke, that is founden. Forsothe grete woodnesse of the Lord droppide vpon us, forthi that oure fadirs han not kept the wordis of the Lord, that thei schulden don alle thingus that 22 ben writen in this volume. Thanne wente Elchias, and thes that to gider of the kyng weren sent, to Oldam, prophetisse, wijf of Sellum, sone of Thecuath, sone of Azia, keper of the clothes, 'the whiche[b] dwellide in Jerusalem in 'the secounde wallynge[c]; and thei speekyn to hyr the 23 wordis, that we han aboue told. And sche answerde to hem, Thes thingus seith the Lord God of Irael, Seith to the man, 24 that sente 30u to me, Thes thingus seith the Lord, Loo! I schal bryngyn in euyls vpon this place, and vpon the dwellers of it, and alle the cursingus that ben writen in this boke, that thei radden beforn the 25 kyng of Juda. For thei forsoken me, and sacrifieden to alien goddis, that me to wrath thei schulden terren in alle the werkis of their hondus; and therfor my woodnesse schal droppen vpon this place, 26 and it schal not ben queynt. To the kyng forsothe of Juda, that sente 30u for the Lord to ben preyede, thus spekith, Thes thingus seith the Lord God of Irael, For thou hast herd the word of this 27 volume, and thin hert is tempered, and thou ert meekid in the si3t of the Lord vpon thes thingus that ben seid a3ein this place and the dwellers of Jerusalem, and thou dreedist reuerently my face, and cuttist thi clothes, and weptist before me; I forsothe haue herd thee, seith the 28 Lord. Nowe forsothe I schal gedre thee to thi faders, and thou schalt be brout in to thi sepulcre in pese; and thin ee3en

kyng, and seide[z], Go 3e, and preie[a] the 21 Lord for me, and for the resydue[b] men[c] of Israel and of Juda, on alle the wordis of this book, which[d] is[e] foundun. For[f] greet veniaunce of the Lord hath droppid on[g] vs, for oure fadris kepten not the wordis of the Lord, to do alle thingis that[h] ben writun in this book. Therfor Helchie 22 3ede[i], and thei that weren sent togidere of[k] the king, to[l] Olda, the prophetesse, the wijf of Sellum, sone[m] of Thecuath, sone[m] of Asra, kepere of clothis[n], which[o] Olda dwellide in Jerusalem in the secounde warde; and thei spaken to hir the wordis, whiche we telden bifore. And sche an- 23 sweride to hem, The Lord God of Israel seith these thingis, Seie 3e to the[p] man, that sente 30u to me, The Lord seith 24 these thingis, Lo! Y schal brynge ynne[q] yuels on[r] this place, and on[s] the dwelleris therof, and alle the cursyngis that ben writun in this book, which[t] thei redden[u] bifor the kyng of Juda. For thei han 25 forsake me, and han sacrified[v] to alien goddis, for to terre me to wrathfulnesse in alle the werkis of her hondis; therfor my strong veniaunce schal droppe on[w] this place, and it schal not be quenchid[x]. But 26 speke 3e thus to the kyng of Juda, that sente 30u to preye the Lord, The Lord God of Israel seith these thingis, For thou herdist the wordis of the book[y], and thin 27 herte[z] is maad neisch[a], and thou art mekid in the si3t of the Lord of[b] these thingis that[c] ben seide a3ens this place and the[d] dwelleris of Jerusalem, and thou hast re-uerensid my face, and hast to-rente thi clothis, and hast wepte bifor me; also Y haue[e] herd thee, seith the Lord. For[f] 28 now Y schal gadere thee to thi fadris, and thou schalt be borun in to thi sepulcre in pees; and thin i3en schulen not se al yuels,

---

schul not seen al the euyl, that I am to
biᵧngyn in vpon this place, and vpon the
dwellers of it   And so thei tolden to the
kyng alle thingus, that sche hadde seᵧde
29 And he, clepide to gidre alle the more
thoruᵹ birthe of Juda and of Jerusalem,
30 steiᵹede up in to the hous of the Lord,
and also togydre alle the men of Juda,
and the dwellers of Jerusalem, prestis,
and Leuytis, and al the puple, fro the
leste vnto the moste ; the whiche heeryng
in the hous of the Lord, the kyng radde
31 alle the wordis of the volume ; and stondyng in his chayere smote pese couenaunt
before the Lord, that he schulde gon aftir
hym, and keepyn the heestis, and witnessyngus, and iustifiyngus, in al his herte and
in al his soule , and he schulde done that
ben writen in that volume, that he hadde
32 radde   Also he adiurede vpon this alle,
that ben founden in Jerusalem and Beniamyn ; and the dwellers of Jerusalem
diden after the couenaunt of the Lord
33 God of their fadirs   Thanne Jozias dide
aweye alle the abomynaciouns of alle the
regyouns of the sonus of Irael , and maad
alle, that weren laft in Jerusalem, to seruen
to the Lord their God ; alle the dais of
his lijf thei wenten not awey fro the
Lord God of their fadirs.

CAP XXXV

1 Forsothe Jozias maad in Jerusalem
pasch to the Lord, that was offred the
2 fourtenthe day of the first moneth ; and
he sette prestis in their offices , and he
meuede hem louely, that thei schulden
3 mynystren in the hous of the Lord   Also
to the Leuytis, at whos techinge al Irael
was halowed to the Lord, he spak, Put-
titth the ark in the seyntuarie of the

whichᵇ Y schal brynge yn onⁱ this place,
and onᵏ the dwelleris therof   Therfoⁱ
thei telden to the king alle thingis,
whicheᵐ Olda hadde seid   And aftir that 29
heⁿ hadde clepid togidere alle the eldere
men of Juda and of Jerusalem, he stiedeⁿ 30
in to the hows of the Lord, andᵖ togidereᑫ
alleʳ theˢ men of Juda, ˋand the dwelleris
of Jerusalemᵗ, preestis, and dekenes, and
al the puple, fio the leeste ˋtil toⁿ the
moste ; to whicheᵛ herynge in the hows of
the Lord, the kyng redde alle the wordis
of the bookʷ   And he stood in hisˣ trone, 31
and smootʸ a boond of pees bifor the Lord,
foi to ˋgo aftirᶻ hym, and to kepe the
comaundementisᵃ, and witnessyngisᵇ, and
iustifiyngisᶜ of hym, in al his herte and
in al his soule ; and to do tho thingis
thatᵈ weren writun in that book, whicheᵉ
he hadde red   And he chargide greeth 32
onᶠ this thing alle men, that weren foundun
in Jerusalem and Beniamynᵍ , and the
dwelleis of Jerusalem didenʰ aftur the
couenauntⁱ of the Lord God of her fadris
Therfor Josie dide awei alle abhomyna-33
ciounsᵏ fro alle the cuntreis of the sones
of Israel ; and heˡ made alle men, that
weren residueᵐ in Isiael, to serue heiⁿ
Lord God ; inᵒ alle theᵖ daies of his lijf
thei ᵹeden not awei fro the Lord God of
her fadris

CAP. XXXV.

Forsotheᑫ Josie made pask to the Lord 1
in Jerusalem, thatʳ was offridˢ in the fourtenthe dai of the firste monethe ; and he 2
ordeynede prestis in hei offices ; and heᵗ
comaundide hem for to mynystreⁿ in the
hows of the Lord   And he spak to theᵛ 3
dekenes, at whos techyng al Isiael was
halewid to the Lord, Sette ᵹeʷ the arkeˣ
in the seyntuarie of the temple, whichʸ

h that INS   ⁱ upon 18   ᵏ upon is   ˡ Thanne I   ᵐ that I   ⁿ *the kyng* INS   ᵒ stiede up INS
ᵖ and *ther stieden up* I   ᑫ togidere *with him* INS   ʳ *stied vp* al s   ˢ Om N   ᵗ Om INS
ᵘ vnto IN to sx   ᵛ whos INS   ʷ *forseide* book s   ˣ the N   ʸ smote *or made* s   ᶻ suc INS
ᵃ heestis INS   ᵇ the witnessyngis INS   ᶜ the iustifyingis NS   ᵈ which s   ᵉ that INS   ᶠ upon INS
ᵍ in Beniamyn IN   ʰ *bi heest of the king* diden s   ⁱ heest INS   ᵏ the abhomynacionns I   ˡ Om. s.
ᵐ left INS   ⁿ the INS.   ᵒ and in NS   ᵖ Om I   ᑫ Certis INS   ʳ the whiche *pask* I whiche *pask* NS
ˢ offrid *or maad* IS.   ᵗ Om *plures*   ᵘ serue INS   ᵛ Om A   ʷ ᵹe, *he seide* I6   ˣ arke *of the lord* NS
ʸ that INS

temple, that Salomon, the sone of Dauid, kyng of Irael, bilde up; forsothe ȝe schul bern it namore. Nowe forsothe mynystreth to the Lord oure God and to his 4 puple Irael, and makith ȝou redy by houses and ȝoure kynredis in the deuysiouns of eche oon, as Dauid, king of Irael, comaundide, and Salomon, his sone, 5 discriuede; and mynystreth in the seyntuarie bi ȝour meynees and Leuytis com6 panyes, and, halowed, offreth pasch; also ȝoure bretheren, that thei mowen aftir the wordis that the Lord spac in the hond of Moyses don, makith redy before. 7 Forthermore Jozias ȝaue to al the puple, that was founden in to the solempnyte of pasch, lombis, and kides of the flockes, and of other feeld beestis thritty thousand, of oxen forsothe, thre thousand; thes thingus of al the substaunce of the 8 kyng. Also his duykis wilfully that thei voweden offreden, bothe to the puple and prestis and Leuytis. Bot Elchias, and Zacharias, and Jehiel, princis of the hous of the Lord, ȝeuen to the prestis, to don pasch, feeld bestis mengyngly, two thousand and sexe hundrith, and oxen thre 9 hundrith. Choneyas forsothe, and Semeyas, also Nathanael and his bretheren, also Azabias, Jahiel, and Josabas, princis of Leuytis, ȝeuen to other Lenytis, to halowen the pasch, fyue thousand of feeld 10 beestis, and oxen fyue hundrith. And the seruyse is maad redy beforn; and the prestis stoden in their office[e], also Leuytis in companyes, after the kingis comaunde11 ment; and offred is pasch. And the prestis sprengeden their hondis with blood, and Leuytis drewen of skynnes 12 of brent sacrifices, and seuerden hem, that thei schulden ȝeuen by houses and mey-

Salomon, kyng[z] of Israel, the sone of Dauid, bildide; for[a] ȝe schulen no more bere it[b]. But now serue[c] 'ȝoure Lord God[d] and his puple Israel, and make[e] ȝou redi 4 bi ȝoure housis and meynees in the departyngis of ech bi hym silf, as Dauid, king of Israel, comaundide, and[f] Salomon, his sone, discryuede[g]; and serue ȝe in the 5 seyntuarie bi the[h] meynees and cumpenyes of dekenes, and be ȝe halewid, and offre 6 ȝe pask; also 'make redi[i] ȝoure britheren[k], that thei moun 'do bi[l] the wordis, whiche the Lord spak in[m] the hond of Moyses. Ferthermore Josie ȝaf to al the puple[n], 7 that was foundun there in the solempnytee† of pask, lambren, and kidis of the flockis, and of residue[o] scheep 'he ȝaf[p] thritti thousynde, and of oxis[q] thre thousynde; these thingis of[r] al[s] the catel[t] of the kyng. And hise duykis offriden tho 8 thingis whiche thei avowiden bi fre[u] wille, as wel to the puple as to prestis and dekenes. Forsothe[v] Elchie, and Zacharie, and Jehiel, princes of the hows of the Lord, ȝauen to[w] preestis, to make pask in comyn, two thousynde and sixe hundrid scheep, and thre hundrid oxis[x]. Forsothe[y] Cho9 nonye, and Semei, and Nathanael and hise britheren, also[z] Asabie, Jahiel, and[a] Josabaz, princis[b] of dekenes, ȝauen to othere dekenes, to make pask, fyue thousynde of scheep, and fyue hundrid oxis[c]. And the seruyce was maad redi; and 10 preestis stoden in her office, and dekenes in cumpenyes[d], bi[e] comaundement[f] of the kyng; and pask was offrid[g]. And preestis 11 spreynten her hondis with blood, and dekenes drowen of the[h] skynnes of sacrifices[i], and departiden[k] tho sacrificis, for to 12 ȝyue[l] bi the[m] housis and meyneis of alle men[n]; and that tho[o] schulden be offrid to

† solempnytee; that is, to make the solempnyte. Lire here. c.

---

e offices c.

z the kyng IN. a certis INS. b it aboute NS. c serue ȝe IMNSX. d the Lord ȝoure God INS. e make ȝe INS. f and as INS. g ordeynede INS. h Om. INS. i make ȝe redi c. sec. m. he made redi DEGKLMOᴘ QRᴜᴡxbç. Om. INS. k britheren, be thei maad redi INS. l do aftir I. do her seruyce bi NS. m bi INS. n multitude IS. o the remenaunt of INS. ᴘ Om. N. q oxen INS. r weren ȝoue of INS. s Om. s. t substaunce INS. u her fre INS. v And INS. w Om. EFGKLMxbç. x oxen INS. y And INS. z and also INS. a Om. N. b the princis INS. c oxen INS. d her cumpanyes NS. e bi the c. f heest INS. g offrid or maad IS. h Om. INS. i the sacrified bestis INS. k thei departiden INS. l ȝyue hem INS. m Om. IN. n men that weren come thidere to make pask IS. o tho sacrifices IS.

nees of echon, and thei schulden ben offred to the Loid, as it is writen in the
boke of Moyses, and of oxen thei diden
13 lijc maner And thei roosteden pasch
vpon the fiyi, after that it is wriyten in
the lawe Forsothe pesible hoostis thei
seetheden in posnettis, and cawdrones,
and pottis, and hastily thei deleden to al
14 the puple, to hem selue forsothe, and to
the prestis aftirward[f] thei maden redy,
for in the offrynge of brent sacrifices and
talewis, vnto the nyзt the prestis weren
ocupied Wherfore the Leuytis to hem
silf and to the prestis, sonus of Aaron,
15 greitheden last Bot the syngers, sonus
of Asaph, stoden in their ordre, aftii the
heste of Dauid, and Asaph, and Eman,
and Ydytyin, of the prophetis of the
kyng; the porters forsothe bi alle the
зatis keptyn al about, so that in no poynt
forsothe thei wenten fro the seruyse;
wherfore and the bretheren of hem, Le-
16 uytis, greitheden to hem metis Thanne
al the heryinge of the Lord lawfuly is
fulfild in that day, that thei do pasch,
and offren brent sacrifice vpon the auter
of the Lord, aftii the heste of the kyng
17 Jozie And the sonus of Irael, that weren
founden, diden ther pasch in that tyme,
and the[g] solempnyte of therf looues seuen
18 days. Ther was not a pasch lijc to this
in Irael, fro the days of Samuel, prophete; bot ne eny of the kingus of Irael
maad pasch as Jozias, to the prestis and
Leuytis, and to al Jude and Irael, that
was founden, and to the dwellers of Je-
19 rusalem The eiзtenthe зeer of the kyng-
20 dam of Jozie this pasch is halewed. After
that Jozias hadde enstored the temple,
Nechao, kyng of Egipt, steiзede up to
fiзten in Charchamys beside Eufraten,

the Lord, as it is wiitun in the book of
Moises, and of oxis[p] thei diden in[q] lijk
maner And thei ioostiden pask[r] on[s] the 13
fiei, bi[t] that[u] that is writun in the lawe.
Sotheli[v] thei setliden pesible sacrifices in
pannes, and cawdruns[w], and pottis[x], and
in haste thei deliden[y] to al the puple; but 14
thei[z] maden redi aftiiward to hem silf,
and to prestis, for preestis[a] weien occupied 'til to[b] nyзt in[c] the offryng of brent
sacrifices and of ynnere[d] fatnessis[e] Wherfor dekenes[f] maden redi[g] to hem silf and
to preestis[h], the sones of Aaion, 'the laste[i]
Forsothe[k] syngeris, the sones of Asaph, 15
stoden in her ordre, bi the comaundement[l]
of Dauid, and of Asaph, and of Eman,
and of Yditun, the profetis of the kyng,
but the porteiis kepten[m] bi ech зate, so
that thei зeden not awei fro the[n] seruice,
sotheli in a poynt[o]; wherfor and dekenes[p],
her britheren, maden redi metis[q] to hem.
Therfor al the religioun of the Lord was 16
fillid[r] riзtfuli in that day, that thei maden
pask, and offriden brent saciifices on[s] the
auter of the Lord, bi the[t] comaundement[u]
of kyng[v] Josie And the sones of Israel, 17
that weren foundun there, maden pask in
that tyme, and the solempnite of therf
looues seuene[w] daies No pask was lijk 18
this in Israel, fro the daies of Samuel, the
prophete, but nethii ony of the kyngis[†]
of Israel made pask as Josie dide[x], to
preestis and dekenes, and to al Juda and
Israel, that was foundun[v], and to the
dwelleris of Jerusalem This pask was 19
halewid in the eiзtenthe зeer of 'the rewme
of[z] Josie[a] Aftir[b] that Josie hadde re- 20
parelid the temple, Nechao, the kyng of
Egipt, stiede[c] to fiзte in Carcainys bisidis
Eufrates; and Josie зede forth in to his
metyng And he[d] seide bi messangeris 21

† kyngis, not
as to multitude
of puple, for in
the tyme of
Dauyth and
of Salomon,
more multi-
tude of puple
cam to the so-
lempnyte ot
pask, but this
excelence is
vndurstondun
as to the fre
зifte of Josie,
that зaf more
to the puple
than Dauyth
and Salomon,
that weren
richere Lire
here c

f aftir c   g in the з pr m

P oxen INS   q of s   r the pask lomb is   s upon INS   t aftir I   u that *biddyng* s   v And INS
w in cawdruns INS   x in pottis INS   y deliden it INS   z *the dekens* INS   a the prestis INS   b vnto Iн
to s   c to s   d the ynnere INS   e fatnesse s   f the dekenes INS   g redi *her part* at the laste INS
h the preestis INS   i Om INS   k And INS   l heest INS   m kepten *her office* is   n her INS   o poynt,
no tyme cessynge *therof* i poynt, *that is, thei weren in no tyme absent fro hei office* s   P the dekenes INS
q her metis INS   r fulfillid INS   s upon is   t Om NS   u heest INS.   v the kyng INS   w bi seuene INS
x Om i   y foundun *there* is   z Om s   a *kung* Josie INS   b And aftir NS   c stiede up INS
d *Nechao* INS

and Jozias wente forth in to aȝein com-
21 mynge of hym. And he, messangers sent
to hym, seith, What to me and to thee,
kyng of Juda? To day not aȝeinus thee I
comme, bot aȝeinus an other hous I fyȝte,
to whom God comaundide me hastely to
gon; leue aȝeinus God to don, that is with
22 me, lest he slee thee. Jozias wolde not
ben turned aȝein, bot greithede aȝein hym
bataile; and he[h] assentide not to the
wordis of Nechao, of the mouth of God,
bot wente for to fiȝten in the feeld of
23 Magedo. And there woundid of the
scheters, seide to his childre, Ledith me
out of the bataile, for gretely I am
24 woundid. The whiche beeren hym ouer
fro oon chaar to an other, that folowede
hym, in kingus maner, and beeren hym
awey in to Jerusalem; and he is deed,
and beried in the costeuous toumbe of
his fadirs. And al Juda and Jerusalem
25 weileden hym, Jeremyas most, whos alle
the syngers and syngeresses in to the
present day lamentaciouns vpon Jozie re-
plyen; and as lawe it is hadde in Irael,
Loo! it is told writen in the Lamenta-
26 ciouns. The remnaunt forsothe of the
wordis of Jozie, and of his mercyes, the
whiche in the lawe of the Lord ben comaundide, also the werkis of hym, the
first and the last, ben writen in the bok
of the kyngus of Irael and of Juda.

CAP. XXXVI.

1 Toke thanne the puple of the lond
Joachaz, the sone of Jozie, and setten
2 king for his fader in Jerusalem. Of thre
and twenty ȝeer was Joachaz, whanne
he hadde begunne to reguen, and thre
3 monethis he regnede in Jerusalem. Forsothe the king of Egipt, whanne he was

sent to hym[e], Kyng of Juda, what is[f] to
me and to thee? Y come not aȝens thee
to dai, but Y fiȝte aȝens another hows[g], to
which[h] God bad me go in haste; ceesse
thou to do[i] aȝens God, which[k] is with me,
lest he sle thee. Josie[l] nolde[m] turne aȝen, 22
but made[n] redi batel aȝens hym; and he
assentide not to the wordis of Nechao, bi[u]
Goddis mouth, but he ȝede for to fiȝte in
the feeld of Magedo. And there he was 23
woundide of archeris, and seide[p] to hise
children, 'Lede ȝe[q] me out of the batel,
for Y am woundid greetli. Whiche[r] baren 24
hym ouer fro the[s] chare in to an other
chare, that suede hym, bi custom of the
kyng, and 'baren out[t] hym[u] in to Jerusalem; and he diede[r], and was[w] biried in
the sepulcre of hise fadris. And al Juda
and Jerusalem biweiliden hym, Jeremye[x] 25
moost[y], of whom alle syngeris and syngeressis[z] 'til in to[a] present[b] dai rehersen
'lamentaciouns, ether[c] weilyngis[d], on[e] Josie; and it[f] cam forth as a lawe in Israel,
Lo! it is seid writun[g] in Lamentaciouns[h].
Forsothe[i] the residue[k] of wordis[l] of Jo- 26
sie, and of hise[m] mercies[n], that[o] ben comaundid[p] in the lawe of the Lord, and
hise werkis[q], 'the firste[r] and the laste, ben
wryten in the book of kyngis[s] of Israel
and of Juda.

CAP. XXXVI.

Therfor the puple of the lond[t] took 1
Joachaz, the sone of Josie, and ordeynede
hym kyng for his fadir in Jerusalem.
Joachaz was of thre and twenti ȝeer, 2
whanne he bigan to regne, and he regnede
thre monethis in Jerusalem. Sotheli[u] the 3
kyng of Egipt, 'whan he[v] hadde come

e Josie INS.   f cause of strijf is IS.   g meyne INS.   h the which I.   i do thus NS.   k that INS.   l And Josie c. But Josias NS.   m wolde not I.   n he made INS.   o spokyn bi S.   p Josias seide INS.   q Lede plures. Ledeth INS.   r And thei INS.   s that INS.   t thei broȝten INS.   u hym forth INS.   v diede there INS. w he was NS.   x but Jeremye INS.   y biweilide him moost NS.   z syngsteris I.   a vnto I.   b this present INS. c Om. INS.   d the weilyngis INS.   e of INS.   f this weilyng INS.   g writyn to haue in mynde S. h Weilyngis INS.   i Certis INS.   k remenaunt INS.   l the wordis INS.   m the INS.   n mercies of Josie S. o whiche NS.   p boden INS.   q firste werkis INS.   r Om. INS.   s the kyngis INS.   t lond of Juda IS. u And whanne INS.   v Om. INS.

commen to Jerusalem^b, remeuede hym,
and condempnede the lond in an hundrith
talentis of syluer and a talent of gold
4 And he sette king for hym Elyachim,
his brother, vpon Judam and Jerusalem;
and he turnede his name Joachym Hym
forsothe Joachaz he toke with hym, and
5 brou3t in to Egipt Of fyue and twenty
3eer was Joachym, whanne he hadde begunne to regnen, and elleuen 3eer he regnede in Jerusalem, and he dide euyl be-
6 forn the Lord his God A3eins this ster3id
up Nabugodonosor, king of Caldeis, and
bounden with cheynes ladde in to Baby-
7 loyne To the whiche and the vessels of
the Lord he translatide, and putte hem
8 in' his temple The remnaunt forsothe
of the wordis of Joachym, and his
ahomynaciouns that he wrou3te, and that
ben founden in hym, ben contened in the
boke of the kingus of Irael and of Juda
Thanne Joachym, his sone, regnede for
9 hym Of ei3t 3eer was Joachym, whanne
he hadde begunn to regnen, and thre
monethis and tenn days he regned in
Jerusalem, and he dide euyl in the si3t
10 of the Lord And whanne the cercle of
oo 3eer were turned, king Nabugodonosor
sente hem, the whiche and brou3ten hym
into Babiloyne, born awey togider the
most precious vessels of the hous of the
Lord Forsothe he sette Sedechie, his
vncle, kyng vpon Judam and Jerusalem
11 And of oon and twenty 3eer was Sedechias, whanne he hadde begunne to regnen, and elleuen 3eer he regned in Jeru-
12 salem And he dide euyl in the ee3en of
the Lord his God, ne he schamyde the
face of Jeremye, the prophete, spekinge to
13 hym of the mouth of the Lord Also
fro king Nabugodonosor he wente awei,
the whiche hadde adiurede hym bi God;

to Jerusalem, remouyde^w hym, and con-
dempnede^x the lond^y in an hundrid talentis of siluer and in a^z talent of gold.
And he ordeynede for hym Eliachim his 4
brother, kyng on^a Juda and Jerusalem^b;
and turnede^c his name Joakym^d Sotheli^e
he took thilk Joachaz with hym silf, and
brou3te^f in to Egipt Joakym^g was of 5
fyue and twenti 3eer, whanne he bigan to
regne, and he regnyde eleuene 3eer in Jerusalem, and he dide yuel bifor 'his Lord
God^h Nabugodonosor^i, kyng of Caldeis, 6
styede^k a3ens this Joakym, and ledde^l hym
boundun with chaynes in to Babiloyne
To which^m Babiloyne^n he translatide also 7
the vessels of the^o Lord, and settide^p tho
in his temple Sotheli the residue^q of a
wordis^r of Joakym, and of hise abhomynaciouns whiche he wrou3te, and that^s
weren foundun in hym, ben conteyned in
the book of kyngis of Israel and of Juda
Therfor^t Joachym, his sone, regnede for
hym Joachym was of ei3te 3eer, whanne 9
he bigan to regne, and he regnede thre
monethis and ten daies in Jerusalem, and
he dide yuel in the si3t of the Lord And 10
whanne the cercle of the^u 3eer was turned
aboute, Nabugodonosor the^v kynge^w sente
men^x, whiche also brou3ten hym in to
Babiloyne, whanne the moost preciouse
vessels of the hows of the Lord weren
borun out togidir^y Sotheli he^z ordeynede Sedechie, his fadris brother, kyng on^b
Juda and Jerusalem Sedechie was of oon 11
and twenti 3eer, whanne he bigan to regne,
and he regnede eleuene 3eer in Jerusalem
And he dide yuel in the si3t of 'his Lord 12
God^c, and he was not aschamed of the face
of Jeremye, the prophete, spekynge^d to
hym bi the mouth of the Lord Also he 13
3ede awey^e fro the^f kyng Nabugodonosor,
that^g hadde^h made hym to swere bi God';

b Irael n   i in to n

w he remouyde ins   x he condempnede ins   y lond of Juda is,   z oo s   a upon is   b upon
Jerusalem i on Jerusalem n   c he turnede ins   d and clepide him Joakym is   e And ins   f he
brou3te him ins   g And Joak3m c   h the Lord his God ins   i And Nabugodonosor ns   k wente up i
sti3ede up ns   l he ledde ins   m the which i   n citee is   o the hous of the n   P he sette ins
q remenaunt ins   r the wordis ins   s the whiche i   whiche ns   t And ins   u thre a pr m   v Om ins
w kynge of Babiloyn i3   x men in to Juda is   y togidre then s   z And iv Oin s   a Nabugodonosor ins   b upon is   c the Lord his God ins   d that spake ins   e Om ins   f Om ns   g whiche ins
h Om ins   i God, that is [to bihote stidfastly i]   to be trewe to him ins

and he endurede his nolle and herte, that
he were not turnede aȝein to the Lord
14 God of Irael. Bot and alle the princis of
prestis and the puple trespaseden wickid-
ly^k, after alle the abomynaciouns of gentilis ; and thei defouleden the hous of the
Lord, that he halowede to hym in Jeru-
15 salem. The Lord forsothe God of their
fadirs sente to hem bi the hond of his
messagers, fro nyȝt rijsyng, and eche
day togydre monestynge ; forthi that he
wolde sparen to the puple, and to his
16 dwellynge place. And thei vndremow-
eden the messagers of God, and^l dis-
piseden his wordis, and scorneden to the
prophetis ; to the tyme that schulde steiȝ
vp the woodnesse of the Lord vpon his
17 puple, and were no medecyne. And he
brouȝt vpon hem the king of Caldeis ;
and he slowȝ the ȝong men of hem with
swerd in the hous of the seyntuarye ; and
he hadde not reuth of the ȝong waxe
man, and of the meyden, and of the olde
man, ne forsothe of the ful feble for eeld,
18 bot alle he toke in his hondis. And alle
the vessels of the hous of the Lord, bothe
more and lasse, and the tresores of the
temple, and of the kyng, and of the
princis, he bare ouer in to Babiloyne.
19 Enmyes brenden up the hous of the
Lord, distruyeden the wal of Jerusalem,
alle the toures brenden, and whateuer
20 was precyous thei waastiden. Ȝif eny
hadde scapid the swerd, lad in to Babyloyne, seruede to the king and his sonus ;
to the tyme that the kyng of Persis
21 hadde empyre, and were fulfild the word
of the Lord of the mouth of Jeremye,
and the lond schulde halowen their holy

and he^k made hard his nol and herte^l, that
he nolde^m turne aȝen to the Lordⁿ of Israel. But also alle the princes of preestis 14
and the puple trespassiden wickidli, bi alle
abhomynaciouns^o of hethene men ; and
thei defouliden the hows of the Lord,
which he halewide^p to hym silf in Jerusalem. Forsothe^q the Lord God of her 15
fadris sente to hem bi the hond^r of hise
messangeris, and^s roos^t bi nyȝt^u, and
amonestide^v ech day ; for^w he sparide^x
his puple and dwellyng^y place. And thei 16
scorneden^z the messangeris of God, and
dispisiden^a hise wordis, and scorneden^b
hise prophetis ; til the greet veniaunce of
the Lord stiede on^c his puple, and noon^d
heelynge^e were^f. And he brouȝte on^g hem 17
the kyng of Caldeis ; and killide^h the ȝonge
men of hem 'bi swerdⁱ in the hows of
seyntuarie^k ; 'he hadde not merci^l of^m a
ȝong 'man, and of aⁿ vergyn, and of an eld
manⁿⁿ, and sotheli^o nether of^p a^q man niȝ
the deth for eldnesse^r, but he bitook alle^s
in^t the hond of that^u *king of Caldeis*.
And he translatide in to Babiloyne alle 18
the vessels of the hows of the Lord, bothe
the grettere and the lasse vessels, and the
tresours of the temple, and of the kyng^v,
and of the princes^w. Enemyes^x brenten 19
the hows of the Lord ; thei^y distrieden the
wal of Jerusalem ; thei brenten alle the
touris ; and thei distrieden what euer thing
was preciouse^z. If ony man ascapide the 20
swerd^a, he was led^b in to Babiloyne, and
seruyde^c the kyng and hise sones^d ; til
the kyng of Peersis regnyde, and^e the 21
word of the Lord bi the mouth of Jere-
mye was fillid^f, and til the lond halewide
hise sabatis. For^g in^h alle the daies of

k wickeli c.   l and at litil π pr. m.

k *Sedechie* ιאs.   l his herte ιאs.   m wolde not ι.   n Lord *God* ιאs.   o the abhomynaciouns ιאs.
p hadde halewid אs.   q And ιאs.   r hond *or bifore warning* s.   s and the Lord אs.   t roos up ιאs.
u nyȝt, *that is, whanne thei weren blyndid bi derknesse of synne, he profride his grace to hem* ιs.   v he
amonestide *hem* ιאs.   w forthi that ι. for that א. for that that s.   x wolde spare ιאs.   y his dwellyng ιאs.
v vndremowiden *in scorn* ι. vndirmowiden אs.   a thei dispisiden ιאs.   b thei scorneden ιאs.   c up
upon ι. vpon s.   d no אs.   e cure *or heelyng* ιs. cure א.   f were *to hem* s.   g upon ιs.   h with swerd
he killide ι. bi swerd he killide אs.   i Om. ιאs.   k the seyntuarie ιאs.   l Om. ιאs.   m on c. and π.   n Om. a.
nn man he had not thanne mercy ιאs.   o certis ιאs.   p Om. ιאs.   q he sparide a ιאs.   r age ιאs.   s alle
men ιאs.   t in to ιאs.   u the אs. Om. ι.   v kyng *of Juda* ιאs.   w princes *theroff* ιאs.   x *And* enemyes אs.
y *and* thei ιאs.   z preciouse *therynne* ιאs.   a swerd *and was not slayn* s.   b taken and led ιאs.   c seruede
there s.   d sones, *this subieccioun was upon the men of Juda* ι. sones, *this subieccion or thraldom con-
tegned vpon the men of Juda* s.   e and til ιאs.   f fulfillid ιאs.   g Sothely ιאs.   h *Juda* in ιs.

days. Forsothe alle the days of desolacioun he dide saboth, vnto the whijl
22 seuenty ȝeer weren fulfild. Forsothe the
first ȝeer of Cirus, kyng of Persis, to fulfille the word of the Lord, that he hadde
spoken by the mouth of Jeremye, the
Lord stired the spirite of Cirus, kyng of
Persis, that comaundide to ben prechide
to al his rewme also by scripture, sey-
23 inge, Thes thingus seith Cirus, kyng of
Persis, Alle the rewmes of the erth ȝaf
to me the Lord God of heuen, and he
comaundide to me, that I schulde bilde
up to hym an hous in Jerusalem, the
whiche is in Jude. Who of ȝou is in al
the puple of hym? be the Lord his God
with hym, and steiȝe he up. Lord God† Almyȝty of our faders, Abraham, Ysaac, and Jacob, and to the riȝtwise seede of hem, the whiche madist heuen and erth with al the ournynge of hem, 'the whiche[m] markedist the se with the word of thin heste, whiche[n] closedist the depnesse, and merkedist to thi ferful and preysable name, that alle inwardly dreeden, and tremblen fro thi chere of thi vertue, and vnsuffrable wrath vpon the synnful of thi thretynge. Forsothe with oute mesure grete and vnserchable the mercy of thi beheste; for thou art Lord altherheeȝest vpon al erth, long abidyng and miche mercyful, and othinkyng vpon the malices of men. Thou forsothe, Lord, after thi goodnesse hast bihoten penaunce of remissioun of synnes; and thou, God of riȝtwijs men, hast not putte penaunce to the riȝtwijse, Abraham, Ysaac, and Jacob, to hem that to thee synnede not. For I haue synnede ouer the noumbre of grauel of the see; multiplied ben my

† This preyere of Manasses is not in Ebrue. AEII.

desolacioun[i] it[k] made sabat, til that seuenti ȝeer weren fillid[l]. Forsothe[m] in the 22
firste ȝeer of Cyrus, kyng[n] of Persis, to
fille[o] the word of the Lord, which he
hadde spoke bi the mouth of Jeremye, the
Lord reiside the spirit of Cirus, king[p] of
Persis, that[q] comaundide to be prechid in
al his rewme, ȝhe, bi scripture[r], and seide,
Cirus, the[s] king of Persis, seith these 23
thingis, The Lord God of heuene ȝaf[t] to
me alle the rewmes of erthe, and he comaundide to me, that Y schulde bilde to
hym an hows in Jerusalem, which[u] is in
Judee. Who of ȝou is in al his puple[v]?
'his Lord God[w] be with hym, and stie he[x]
'*in to Jerusalem*[y].

CAP. XXXVII.

Lord God† Almyȝti of our fadris, Abraham, Isaac, and Jacob[z], and of her iust seed, which[a] madist heuene and erthe with[b] al the ournyng of tho[c], which hast markid the see bi the word of 'thi comaundement[d], which hast closid togidere the depthe[e] of watris, and hast markid[f] to thi ferdful[g] and preysable name, which[h] alle men dreden, 'and tremblen[i] of the cheer of thi vertu, and the ire[k] of thi manassyng on[l] synneris 'is vnsuffrable[m], '*ether may not be susteyned*[n]. Sotheli[o] the merci of thi biheest is fulgreet and[p] 'vnserchable, *ether*[q] *may not be comprehendid* '*bi mannus wit*[r]; for 'thou art the[s] Lord moost[t] hiȝ ouer al erthe; *thou art* pacient[u], and myche[v] merciful, and 'doynge penaunce[w] on the malices[x] of men. Treuli[y], Lord, thou[z] bi thi goodnesse hast[a] bihiȝt penaunce‡ of forȝyuenesse of synnes; and thou, God[b] of iust men, hast not set penaunce to iust men, to Abraham, Ysaac[c],

† This is the preyere of Manasses, but it is not in Ebreu, nether it is of the text. *Lire here.* C.

‡ *penaunce*; that is, forȝyuynge synnes for repenting of men. C.

[m] that C. [n] that C. the whiche E.

[i] desolacioun *or of the distrying or forsaking therof* S. [k] Om. I. [l] fulfillid INS. [m] Sothli INS. [n] the kyng INS. [o] fulfille INS. [p] the king NS. [q] whiche INS. [r] writing IN. writing *he sente out hise lettris* S. [s] Om. INS. [t] hath ȝouen INS. [u] that INS. [v] puple, *that wil go wirschipe him there* INS. [w] the Lord his God NS. [x] he up I. he up *thidur* NS. [y] Om. INS. [z] of Jacob S. [a] that I. [b] and INS. [c] hem INS. [d] thin heest INS. [e] depnesse INS. [f] markid *hem* IS. [g] stidefast INS. [h] the which *name* I. which *name* NS. [i] Om. NS. [k] wraththe INS. [l] upon IS. [m] may not be suffrid INS. [n] Om. INS. [o] Sotheli *to hem that verili forthenk her synne* S. [p] and it INS. [q] Om. INS. [r] bi mannus wickidnesse D. Om. IN. [s] Om. INS. [t] thou art moost INS. [u] longe abidynge INS. [v] ful INS. [w] forthinkynge INS. [x] malice INS. [y] certis INS. [z] Om. INS. [a] thou hast INS. [b] *Lord, that art* God I. *Lord, which art* God NS. [c] to Ysaac S.

wickidnesses[o]. I am myche croked with myche bond of yren, and there is not aȝeyn brething to me; for I stirede thi wrath, and euyl before thee I dide, settyng abomynacyouns and multiplying offenciouns. And nowe I bowe the knees of myn herte, preyinge of thee goodnesse, Lord. I synnede, Lord, I synnede, and my wickidnesse[p] I knowe. I aske, preyinge thee, Lord; forȝeue to me, forȝeue to me, ne togidre leese thou me with my wickidnesses[q], ne without eend reserue thou euyls to me. For[r] vnworthi thou schalt sauen me[s] after thi grete mercy, and I schal preysen thee euermore alle the days of my lyue; for thee preyseth al the vertue of heuens, and to thee is glorie in to world[t] of worldis. Amen.

Here eendith the secounde boke of Paralipomenon. Blesside be the Holy Trynyte[u].

and Jacob[d], to hem that synneden not aȝens thee[e]. For[f] Y haue synned more than the noumbre is of the grauel of the see; my wickidnessis ben multiplied. Y am bowid[g] with myche[h] boond of yrun, and no brething is to me; for Y haue stirid thi wrathfulnesse, and Y haue doon yuel bifor thee,'and Y haue set[i] abhomynacious, and 'Y haue multiplied[k] offensiouns[l]. And now Y bowe the knees of myn herte, and biseche[m] goodnesse[n] of thee, Lord. Y haue synned[o], Lord; Y haue synned[p], and Y knowleche[q] my wickidnesse. Y axe[r], and preye[s] thee, Lord; forȝyue thou to me[t], forȝyue thou[u] to me[v]; leese thou me not togidire with my wickidnessis, nether reserue[w] thou[x] yuels to me withouten ende. For, Lord, bi[y] thi greet merci thou[z] schalt saue me vnworthi[a], and[b] Y schal herie thee euere in alle the daies of my lijf; for al the vertu† of heuenes herieth[c] thee, and to thee is glorie in to worldis of worldis. Amen.

† *vertu; that is, alle tho ordris of aungels. Lire here. c.*

Here endith the secounde book of Paralipomenon, and here bigynneth the firste book of Esdre[d].

o wickenessis c. P wickenesse c. ꝗ wickenessis c. ʳ For me E pr. m. ˢ Om. H. ᵗ worldus c. ᵘ *Here endith the secounde book of Paralypomenon, and now bigynneth the prolog on the three bookis of Esdre. A. Here endith the secounde booc of Paralipomynon, and bigynneth the booc of Esdre the firste. E.* No final rubric in cFH.

ᵈ to Jacob s. ᵉ thee *thou settist not penaunce, ut* NS. ᶠ *But* for I. For that N. Forthi that s. ᵍ bound s. ʰ a greet INS. ⁱ settyng in *me* IS. settinge N. ᵏ multipliynge *thin* IN. multipliyng *aȝens me thi* s. ˡ confessiouns s. ᵐ I biseche INS. ⁿ the goodnesse INS. ᵒ synned *greetli* s. ᵖ synned *greuousli in thi siȝt* s. ꝗ knowleche *to thee* s. ʳ axe *mercy* IS. ˢ I preie NS. ᵗ me *my synne* IS. ᵘ thou *it* INS. ᵛ me *for thi holi name, Lord* s. ʷ kepe INS. ˣ Om. D. ʸ aftir INS. ᶻ *I trist that* thou s. ᵃ moost vnworthi *wrecche* s. ᵇ Om. s. ᶜ preisith INS. ᵈ *Here endith the secunde book of Paralipomenon, and bigynnith a prolog on Esdras the I. G. Heere endith the secounde book of Paralipomynon.* IꝖ. *Here endeth the seconde book of Paralipomenon; se now the prolog of Esdre.* K. *Here endith the secounde book of Paralipomenon, and here bigynneth a prologe on the firste book of Esdre.* M. *Here endith the secounde book of Paralipomenon, and bigynneth the prologe on the bookis of Esdre and Neome.* O. *Here endith Parilypomynon, and biginneth Esdre the Firste.* s. No final rubric in ELP.

I. ESDRAS.

[*Prologue on the First book of Esdras*ᵃ.]

THIS firste book of Esdre, whiche was a wurthi man among Jewis, and writer of the lawe of God, tellith, that Cyrus, the king of Persis, stirid by the Spirit of God, ordeynde Esdre, the scryuein, ledere to al the peple of Juda, that was translatid in to Babiloyne, to bringe hem aʒen in to her lond, with alle the vessels that weren of the hous of the Lord, and ʒaf gold and siluer in greet plente, to make sacrifise to the Lord in Jerusalem.

[*Prologue to the books of Esdras*ᵃ]

WHETHER it be hardere to do that ʒee asken, or to denyen, I haue not ʒyt demed, for nouther to ʒou any thing comaundende is of sentence to forsaken, and the gretnesse of charge put vpon oure nollis bereth doun, that rathere it be to fallen doun vndir the berthene, than to reren The studies of enuyouse men neʒhen to this, that alle thing that we wryten, weenen repref wrthi, and other while concience repugnende aʒen hem-self, opinli thei to-tern that thei reden priueli; in so myche that I am constreyned to crien, and sein, Lord, deliuere my soule fro wickeᵇ lippis, and fro a trecherous tunge The thridde ʒer is that euer mor ʒee wryten and aʒeen wryten, that the boc of Esdre and Ester I translateᶜ to ʒou fro Ebrue, as thofᵈ ʒee han not Grekisᵉ andᶠ Latynesᵍ volumus, or what euere thing that is that of vs is turned, not anon of alle men it be to be dispisid In vein forsothe, as seith sum man, to euforcen, neʰ other thing in trauailing sechen¹ but hate, is of vttermost wodnesse And so, I beseche ʒou, my derworthest Domynyon and Rogacian, that ʒe apaʒed bi priuat lessoun, ber not out the bokisin to comun, lest ʒee profre metis to vggli men; and eschewe ʒee the pride of hem, that onli to demen of othere, and thei themselue knewen no thing to do If any forsothe of brethern ben, to whom ouren displesen not, to them ʒiueth a saumpler, amonestende that the Ebrue namus, of the whiche in this volume is gret plente, distinctli and bi spacis thei transcryue, forsothe no thing it profitde to han amendid bokis, but the amending be kept bi diligence of writeris. Ne any man moue it, that o boc is maad of vs, ne delite he in the sweuenes of the writen thingus withoute autorite of the thridde and of the ferthe boc, for and anentis the Ebrues the woordis of Esdre and of Noemye in o volume ben togidere drawen, and thoo thingus that ben not had anentis hem, 'ne ben notᵏ of the foure and twenti olde men, ben worthi to be cast awei aferr If any man forsothe aʒen legge to vs the seuenti remenoures, of whom the saumpleris the diuersete shewith hem to-torn and turned vpsodoun, ne forsothe it mai not ben

ᵃ This prologue is from M

ᵃ *Prologus* FH No initial rubric in ACI ᵇ wickid AHI *et* K *passim* ᶜ translatide K ᵈ ʒof F ᵉ Grues H ne K ᵍ Latin c ʰ Om K ¹ sechyng K ᵏ nethir ben K

afermed soth that that is diuers, sendeth hym to the euangelies, in the whiche many thingus ben put of the olde testament, the[l] whiche anent the seuenti remenoures ben not had, as that, For Nazare he shal ben clepid ; and, Fro Egipt I clepede my sone ; and, They shul seen in whom thei pungeden ; and manye othere thingus, the whiche we reseruen to a braddere were ; and asketh of hym, where thei ben writen ; and whan thei schul not moun tellen, rede ȝee of thoo saumpleris, the whiche, sum time maad of vs, ben stikid eche dai with the tungus of euele spekeris. But that to short tretee I come ; certis that I 'am to concluden[m] is most riȝtwis ; haue I maand any thing that is not had in Greec, or that otherwise is had than off me is turned ? Wherto the remenour thei to-tern ? Aske thei the Ebrues, and bi thoo[n] autouris, to my translacioun or ȝiue thei feith or withdrawe. Certis another is, for thei wiln myssein to me, that it[o] is seid, with closid eȝen, and thei folewen not the studie and the weel willing of Greekis, the whiche aftir the seuenty remenoures, now shinende the euangelie of Crist, and curiousli reden Jewis and Hebionytis, remenoures of the olde lawe, Aquilam, that is, Symachum[p], and Theodocian, and bi the trauaile of Origenes thei halewiden to[q] chirchis in sixe maner translaciouns. Myche more Latin men aȝten to be kinde, that thei beholden Grece gladende of hem any thing to borewen. The firste forsothe is of gret costis and of difficulte withoute ende, to moun han alle the exsaumpleris ; also theraftir thei that han, and ben vnkunnende of Ebrue speche, more shuln erren, vnknowende who of manye trewliere seith. The whiche also fel sum time to a most wis man amongis the Grekis, that otherwhile leuende the sens[r] of scripture he folewide the errour of eche remenour. Wee forsothe that[s] nameli of Ebru tunge han a litil kunnyng, and Latin speche ȝit hider to failith not to vs, that of othere more we moun demen, and thoo thingus that wee vsself[t] vnderstonden, in oure owne tunge shewin. And so thof the serpentt hisse and the ouercomere if he throwe not brennyngus vp, neuer my speche shal be stille, Crist helpende ; also the tunge kut of it shal blaberen. Rede thei that wiln ; that wiln not, caste thei awei. And serche thei out the letteris, and falsli acuse thei the lettris ; more bi ȝoure charite I shal ben stirid to studie, than I shal ben agast bi the hate and the[u] bachiting of hem.

Another prolog[v].

Esdras and Neemye, belpere[w], that is, and[x] coumfortour fro the Lord, in o volume ben drawen. Thei enstoren the temple ; the wallis of the cite thei maken vp. And al that cumpanye of the puple turnende aȝeen in to the kuntre, and the descripcioun of prestus, and of Leuitus, and of the conuertide to the folc of Israel, and by alle the meynes of the[y] wallis and touris the werkis deuidid, other thing bern[z] in the rinde, other thing they holdin in the marȝ.

Here folewith the comendacioun of Esdre.

This[a] aftir Jude brend vp of the Caldeis, wbil the Jewis weren turned aȝeen into Jerusalem, alle the bokis of the olde testament reparaileide, and enspirid with Godis Spirit alle the volumys of profetis, that weren of the Jentilis corupt amendide ; wherfore it is writen, Esdras steȝide vp fro Babiloyne, and he a swift scribe in the lawe of Moises, swift, that is, for more redi figuris of lettris, than the Ebrues beforhond hadden, he fond.

Here eendeth the prolog of Esdre ; se now the book[b].

[l] Om. κ.   [m] haue seid κ.   [n] thilke ΑΕΓΗΚ.   [o] Om. κ.   [p] Smachum c.   [q] the κ.   [r] sentense Α. [s] Om. Α.   [t] oure silf κ.   [u] Om. κ.   [v] Prologus Α. The prolong. Γ. Another prolog ou Esdre. κ. No rubric in CHI.   [w] help H.   [x] Om. CHK.   [y] Om. κ.   [z] thei beren κ.   [a] This Esdre κ.   [b] From κ. No final rubric in the other Mss.

Here begynneth the fyrst book of Esdre[c]

CAP I

1 IN the firste ȝer ot Ciri, king of Persis, that the woord of the Lord of the mouth of Jeremye were fulfild, the Lord rerede the spirit of Ciri, king of Persis, and ladde ouer the vois in al his rewme also 2 bi scripture, seiende, These thingus seith Cirus, king of Persis, Alle the reumes of 'the erthe the Lord God of heuene and of[d] erthe hath ȝiue to me, and he comanndede to me, that I shulde bilde to hym an hous in Jerusalem, that is in 3 Jude Who is in ȝou of al the puple of hym? be the God of hym with hym ; steȝe he vp in to Jerusalem, that is in Jude, and bilde he vp an hous of the Lord God of Irael ; he is God, that is in Jerusalem 4 And alle the othere in alle placis, wher euere thei dwellen, helpe thei hym , the men of his place, with siluer, and gold, and substaunce, and bestis, out take that wilfulli thei ofire to the temple of God, 5 that is in Jerusalem And the princis of the fadris of Juda and of Beniamyn, and prestis, and Leuitus, eche whos spirit God rerede, risen, that thei steȝen vp to[e] bilden the temple of the Lord, that was in Je- 6 rusalem And alle that weren in the enuyroun helpiden the hondis of hem, in siluerene, and goldene vesselis, in sub- staunce, in necessarie thing, in bestis, out take thoo thingus that thei hadden offrid 7 wilfully   Forsothe king Cirus broȝte forth the vesselis of the temple of the Lord, the whiche Nabugodonosor hadde

Here bigynneth the firste book of Esdre[a]

CAP I.

IN the firste ȝeer of Cirus, kyng of 1 Persis, that the word of the Lord bi the mouth of Jeremye schulde be fillid[b], the Lord reiside the spirit of Cyrus, kyng ot Persis , and he pupplischide a vois in al his rewme, ȝe, bi the[c] scripture[d], and[e] seide, Cirus, the kyng of Persis, seith these 2 thingis, The Lord God of heuene ȝaf[f] to me alle the rewmes of erthe, and he co- maundide[g] to me, that Y schulde bilde to hym an hows in Jerusalem, which[h] is in Judee[i] Who is among ȝou of al his pu-3 ple[j] ? his God be with hym , stie[h] he[l] in to Jerusalem, which[m] is in Judee[n], and bilde he the hows of the Lord God of Israel , he is God, which is in Jerusalem. And[o] 4 alle othere[p] men, 'that dwellen[q] where euere[r] in alle places, helpe[s] hym[t], the[u] men of her place *helpe*[v] in[w] siluer, and gold, and catel[x], and scheep, outakun[y] that that thei offren wilfulli to the temple of God, which[z] is in Jerusalem And[a] the[b] 5 princis of fadris[c] of Juda and of Benia- myn risiden[d], and the preestis, and de- kenes[e], and ech man whos spirit God reiside, for to stie[f] to[g] bilde the temple of the Lord, that was in Jerusalem. And 6 alle men that weren 'in cumpas[h] helpiden the hondis of hem[i], in[k] vesselis of siluer, and of gold, 'in catel[l], in[m] purtenaunce of houshold, and in[n] alle[o] weik beestis, outakun[p] these thingis which thei of- friden bi fre[q] wille. Forsothe[r] kyng Cyrus 7 broȝte forth the vessels of the temple of

---

[c] From *A*.   No initial rubric in the other Mss   [d] Om *c*   [e] that thei *AH*

[a] From HIM *The firste book of Esdras* ENP *Of Esdre Book* o No initial rubric in the other Mss   [b] ful- hllid INS.   [c] Om *A sec m* s   [d] writyng INS   [e] *he sente* and I *he sente out hise lettris* and s   [f] hath ȝoue INS   [g] he comaundide s   [h] that INS   [i] Juda INS   [j] peple, *that hath wille to help this byldyng* s [k] and stye s   [l] he up INS   [m] that INS   [n] Juda NS   [o] *helpful to his peple*, and s   [p] the othere c [q] Om INS   [r] euere *thei dwellen* INS   [s] helpe thei INS   [t] hym *that bildith* I him that wold bylde the house of the Lord s   [u] Om IN   [v] helpe thei INS   [w] with INS   [x] with catel INS   [y] outakin *or* ouer s   [z] that INS   [a] And *thanne* I Om N And *whanne the king had ȝoue this coumfort to the peple* s [b] Om INS   [c] the fadris INS   [d] resen up I risiden up NS   [e] the dekenis s   [f] stie up INS   [g] to *Jeru- salem* for to IN in *to Jerusalem* for to s   [h] in cumpas *aboute* IN dwelling bi cumpas *about Jerusalem* s. [i] hem *that bildiden the temple* s   [k] with INS   [l] with her substaunce INS   [m] with INS and LLO [n] with INS   [o] Om BCISVW   [p] withoute I outakin *or* ouer s   [q] *her* fre INS   [r] And INS

taken fro Jerusalem, and hadde put hem
8 in the temple of his god. Forsothe Cirus,
king of Persis, broȝte them forth bi the
hond of Mitridatis, sone of Gazabar; and
he noumbride hem to Zazabazar, prince
9 of Jude. And this is the noumbre of
hem; goldene violis, thretti; siluerenn
violis, a thousend; knyues, nyne and
10 twenti; goldenn cuppis, thretti; siluerenn
cuppis, two thousend foure hundrid and
11 ten; othere vesselis, a thousend; alle the
vesselis, goldene and siluerene, fiue thousend
and foure hundrid. Alle Zazebazar
toc, with hem that steȝeden vp fro the
transmygracioun of Babiloyne, in to Jerusalem.

CAP. II.

1 These forsothe ben the men, sonus of
the prouynce, that steȝeden vp fro the[f]
caitifte, that Nabugodonosor, king of Babiloyne,
hadde taken ouer in to Babiloine;
and thei ben turned aȝeen in to Jerusa-
2 lem and Jude, eche[g] in to his cite, the
whiche camen with Zorobabel; Jesua,
Neemya, Saraia, Rahelaia, Mordochaa,
Belsan, Mesfar, Begnai, Reum, Baana.
The noumbre of the men of the puple of
3 Irael; sones of Fares, two thousend an
hundrid and two and seuenti; the sonus
of Arethi, seuene hundrid fiue and se-
4 uenti; the sonus of Sefesia, thre hundrid
5 and two and seuenti; the sonus of Aria,
6 seuene hundrid and fiue and seuenti; the
sonus of Fee and of Moab, sones of Josue
and of Joab, two thousend nyne hundrid
7 and twelue; the sones of Elam, a thousend
two hundrid and foure and fifti;
8 the sonus of Sechua, nyne hundrid and
9 fiue and fourty; the sonis of Zaahai,

the Lord, whiche[s] Nabugodonosor hadde
take fro Jerusalem, and hadde set tho[t] in
the temple of his god. Sotheli[u] Cyrus, 8
the kyng of Persis, brouȝte forth tho[v] bi
the hond of Mytridatis, sone[w] of Gazabar;
and[x] noumbride tho to[y] Sasabazar, the
prince of Juda. And[z] this is the noumbre 9
of tho[a] *vessels;* goldun violis, thritti; siluerne
viols, a thousynde; 'grete knyues,
nyne and twenti[b]; goldun[c] cuppis†, thritti[d];
siluerne cuppis, two[e] thousynde foure 10
hundrid and ten; othere[f] vessels[g], a thousynde;
alle the vessels of gold and sil- 11
uere[h] *weren* fyue thousynde foure[i] hundrid.
Sasabazar[k] took alle *vessels*[l], with
hem that stieden[m] fro the transmygracioun[n]
of Babiloyne, in to Jerusalem.

CAP. II.

Forsothe[o] these ben the sones of pro- 1
uynce[p]‡, that[q] stieden[r] fro the caitifte,
which Nabugodonosor, kyng[s] of Babiloyne,
hadde translatid in to Babiloyne;
and thei turneden aȝen in to Jerusalem
and in to Juda, ech man in to his citee,
that camen with Zorobabel; Jesua[t], Nee- 2
mie, Saray, Rahelaie, Mardochaa, Belsan,
Mesfar, Begnay, Reum, Baana[u]. *This is*
the noumbre of men of the sones of Israel;
the sones of Phares[v], two[w] thou- 3
synde an hundrid and two and seuenti;
the sones of Arethi, seuene[x] hundrid and
fyue and seuenti; the sones of Sephezie, 4
thre[y] hundrid and two and seuenti; the 5
sones of Area, seuene[z] hundrid and fyue
and seuenti; the sones of Phe and of 6
Moab, sones[a] of Josue and of Joab, twei[b]
thousynde nyne[c] hundrid and twelue; the 7
sones of Helam, a[d] thousynde two hundrid
and foure and fifti; the sones of 8
Zechua, nyne[e] hundrid and fyue and

† *goldun cuppis;* in Ebreu it is basyns. *Lire here.* c.

‡ *prouynce;* that is, of Judee. *Lire here.* c.

[f] Om. c. [g] eche one E. echon CFH.

[s] the whiche I. [t] hem INS. [u] And INS. [v] tho *vessels* IS. [w] the sone INS. [x] and *the kyng* IN. [y] in to X. Om. S. [z] Om. S. [a] the I. [b] a thousand and nyne and thritti grete knyues NS. [c] thritti goldun INS. [d] Om. IN. [e] and two S. [f] and othere INS. [g] violis, vesselis S. [h] of siluere INS. [i] and foure INS. [k] *And* Sasabazar INS. [l] *thes* vessels IN. the vesselis S. [m] stieden up INS. [n] transmygracioun *either ouer passing* S. [o] And INS. [p] the prouynce INS. [q] whiche INS. [r] ȝeden up I. stieden up NS. [s] the kyng BCDEFGHKLMOPQRUWb. [t] *that is,* Jesua IS. [u] and Baana INS. [v] *the lynage of* Phares IS. [w] *weren* two INS. [x] *weren* seuene INS. [y] *weren* thre N. [z] *weren* seuene IN. [a] *and* the sones NS. [b] *weren* two INS. [c] and nyne A. [d] *weren* a NS. [e] *weren* nyne NS.

10 seuene hundrid and sixti, the sonus of
Baany, sixe hundrid and two and fourti,
11 sonus of Bebai, sixe hundrid and thre and
12 twenti, sonus of Asgad, a thousend two
13 hundrid and two and twenti; sonus of
Adonycam, sixe hundrid and sixe and
14 sixti, sonus of Beguai, two thousend and
15 sixe and fifti; sonus of Adin, foure hun-
16 drid and foure and fifti; sonys of Aser,
that weren of Ezechie, nynti and eizte,
17 sonus of Besai, thre hundrid and thre and
18 twenti; sonus of Jora, an hundrid and
19 twelue, sonus of Ason, two hundrid and
20 thre and twenti, sonus of Jebar, nynti
21 and fiue, sonus of Bethlem, an hundrid
22 and thre and twenti, the men of Necofa,
23 sixe and fifti; the men of Anatot, an
24 hundrid and eizte and twenti; sonus of
25 Asmoneth, two[h] and fourti; sonus of Cariathiarym, Cefiara, and Berhoc, seuene
26 hundrid and thre and fourti; sonus of
Arama and of Gaba, sixe hundrid and
27 oon and twenti, men of Machinas, an
28 hundrid and two and twenti; men of
Bethel and of Gai, two hundrid and thre
29 and twenti, sonus of Nebo, two and fifti,
30 sonys of Megbis, an hundrid and sixe
31 and fifti; the sonus of the tothei Elam,
a thousend two hundrid and foure and
32 fifti; the sonus of Aiym, thre hundrid
33 and twenti, the sonus of Ladadin and of
Ono, seuen hundrid and fiue and twenti,
34 sonus of Jericho, thre hundrid and fiue
35 and fourti, sonus of Sanaa, thre thou-
36 send sixe hundrid and thritti, prestus,
sonus of Idaia, in the hous of Jesue, nyne
37 hundrid seuenti[k] and thre, sonus of Em-
38 meor, a thousend and two and fifti, sonus
of Fesur, a thousend two hundrid and
39 seuene fourti, sonus of Aiym, a thou-
40 send and seuentene; Lenitus, the sonus of
Jesue and of Cedinyel, sonus of Odonia,

fourti; the sones of Zahai, seuene[f] hun- 9
drid and sixti, the sones of Bany, sixe[g] 10
hundrid and two and fourti, the sones of 11
Bebai, sixe[h] hundrid and thre and twenti,
the sones[i] of Azgad, a[k] thousynde two[l] 12
hundrid and two and twenti, the sones 13
of Adonycam, sixe[m] hundrid and sixe and
sixti; the sones of Beguai, two[n] thou- 14
synde two hundrid and[o] sixe and fifti,
the sones of Adyn, foure[p] hundrid and 15
foure and fifti; the sones of Ather, that[q] 16
weren of Ezechie, nynti[r] and eizte, the 17
sones of Besai, thre[s] hundrid and thie and
twenti; the sones of Jora, an[t] hundrid 18
and twelue; the sones of Asom, two[u] hun- 19
drid and thre and thritti', the sones of 20
Gebar *weren* nynti and fyue, the sones 21
of Bethleem *weren*[w] an hundrid and eizte
and twenti, the men[x] of Nechopha, sixe[y] 22
and fifti; the men of Anathot, an[z] hun- 23
drid and eizte and twenti; the sones of 24
Asmaneth, two[a] and fourti; the sones of 25
Cariathiarym, Cephiara[b], and Berhoc, seuene[c] hundrid and thre and fourti[d]; the 26
sones of Arama and of Gaba, sixe[e] hundrid and oon and twenti, men of 'Math- 27
mas, an hundrid and two and twenti;
men of[f] Bethel and of Gay, two[g] hundrid 28
and thre and twenti; the sones of Nebo, 29
two[h] and fifti, the sones of Nebgis, an[i] 30
hundrid and sixe and fifti, the sones of 31
the tother Helam, a[k] thousynde two hundrid and foure and fifti; the sones of 32
Arym, thre[l] hundrid and twenti, the sones 33
of Loradid and of Ono, seuene[m] hundrid
and fyue and twenti, the sones of Jerico, 34
thie[n] hundrid[o] and fyue and fourti, the 35
sones of Sanaa, thre[p] thousynde sixe hundrid and thritti; preestis, the sones of 36
Idaie, in the hows of Jesue, nyne[q] hundrid and thie and seuenti; the sones of 37
Emmeor, a[r] thousynde and two and fifti;

h an hundrid and two *A* i and sixe *AII* k and seuenti *AII*

f *weren* seuene NS g *weren* sixe INS h *weren* sixe NS sones *weren* N k *weren* a S l and two C
m *weren* sixe NS n *weren* two NS o Om IS p *weren* foure INS q whiche NS r *weren* nynti NS
s *weren* thre NS t *weren* an NS u *weren* two NS v twenti no see m xxiii v w Om I x sones NS
y *weren* sixe NS z *weren* an NS a *weren* two NS b of Cephiara INS c *weren* seuene INS d fyfti N.
e *weren* sixe NS f Om IN g *weren* two INS h *weren* two NS i *weren* an NS k *weren* a NS.
l *weren* thre NS m *weren* seuene INS. n *weren* thre NS o thousand N p *weren* thre NS q *weren*
nynti INS r *weren* a NS

41 seuenti and foure; chauntoures, sonus of
Asaf, an hundrid and eizte and twenti;
42 the sonus of the[1] porteris, sones of Sellum, the sonus of Ather, sonus of Thelmon, the sonus of Accub, 'the sonus[m] of
Aritha, the sonus of Sobar, the sonus of
Sobai, alle, an hundrid and eizte and
43 thretti; sodeknys, sonus of Ozai, the
sonus of Azufa, the sonus of Thebaoth,
44 the sonus of Ceros, the sonus of Cisaa, the
45 sonus of Fadon, the sonus of Jebona, the
46 sonus of Agoba, the sonus of Accub, the
sonus of Accab, the sonus of Selmai, the
47 sonus of Annan, the sonus of Gaddei, the
48 sonus of Gaer, the sonus of Rahaia, the
sonus of Jasin, the sonus of Nethoda, the
49 sonus of Gasem, the sonus of Asa, the
50 sonus of Fasea, the sonus of Besee, the
sonus of Asennaa, the sonus of Numyn,
51 the sonus of Nechusym, the sonus of Be-
chne, the sonus of Accufa, the sonus of
52 Assur, the sonus of Besuth, the sonus of
53 Maida, the sonus of Arsa, the sonus of
Berchos, the sonus of Cizara, the sonus
54 of Thema, the sonus of Nazia, the sonus
55 of Acufa, the sonus of the[n] seruauns of
Salamon, the sonus of Sothelthei, the
sonus of Sofereth, the sonus of Feruda,
56 the sonus of Jala, the sonus of Derchon,
57 the sonus of Jedel, the sonus of Safatha,
the sonus of Athil, the sonus of Fesore-
thei, that weren of Azebam, the sonus
58 of Ammy; alle the sodeknys, and the
sonus of the seruauns of Salamon, thre
59 hundrid and nynti and two. And these
that stezeden vp fro Thelmela, and Thelersa, Cherub, and Don, and Mer, and
thei myzten not shewe the hous of ther
faders and ther sed, whether of Irael
60 thei weren; the sonus of Delain, the sonus
of Tobia, the sonus of Nechoda, sixe hun-
61 drid and two and fifti; and of the sonus
of prestus, the sonus of Obia, the sonus of

the sones of Phesur, a[s] thousynde two 38
hundrid and seuene and fourti; the sones 39
of Arym, a[t] thousynde and seuentene;
dekenes, the sones of Jesue and of Cedy- 40
nyel, sones[u] of Odonye, foure[v] and seuenti;
syngeris, the sones of Asaph, an[w] hundrid 41
and eizte and twenti; the sones of por- 42
teris, sones[x] of Sellum, sones of Ather,
sones of Thelmon, sones[y] of Accub, sones
of Aritha, sones of Sobar, sones of Sobai,
alle[z] weren an hundrid and eizte and
thritty; Nathynneis†, the sones of Osai, 43
sones[a] of Asupha, sones[a] of Thebaoth,
sones[a] of Ceros, sones[a] of Sisaa, sones[a] of 44
Phadon, sones[a] of Jebana, sones[a] of Agaba, 45
sones[a] of Accub, sones[a] of Accab, sones[a] of 46
Selmai, sones[a] of Annam, sones[a] of Gad- 47
del, sones[a] of Gaer, sones[a] of Rahaia, sones[a] 48
of Rasyn, sones[a] of Nethoda, sones[a] of Ga-
zem, sones[a] of Asa, sones[a] of Phasea, sones[a] 49
of Besee, sones[a] of Asennaa, sones[a] of Nu- 50
myn, sones[a] of Nethusym, sones[a] of Beth- 51
uth, sones[a] of Acupha, sones[a] of Aryn,
sones[a] of Besluth, sones[a] of Maida, sones[a] 52
of Arsa, sones[a] of Bercos, sones[a] of Sisara, 53
sones[a] of Thema, sones[a] of Nasia, sones[a] of 54
Acupha, the sones of the seruauntis‡ of 55
Salomon, the sones of Sothelthei, the
sones of Soforeth, the sones of Pharuda,
the sones of Asa, the sones of Delcon, the 56
sones of Gedeb, the sones of Saphata, the 57
sones of Atil, the sones of Phecerethi,
that[b] weren of Asebam, the sones of
Ammy; alle the Nathyneis, and the sones 58
of the[c] seruauntis of Salomon weren[d] thre
hundrid nynti and tweyne. And thei that 59
stieden[e] fro Thelmela, Thelersa[f], Cherub[g],
and[h] Don, and Mey[i], and myzten not
schewe the hows[k] of her fadris and her
seed[l], whether thei weren of Irael[m]; the 60
sones of Delaya, the sones of Thobie, the
sones of Nethoda, sixe[n] hundrid and two
and fifti; and of the sones of prestis, the[o] 61

43 † Nathynneis; these baren wole and water to the hows of Goddis religioun. Lire here. c.

55 ‡ seruauntis; they weren the seruauntis of Salomon, that weren assigned to the keping of the bildingis of the temple, and to reparele tho thingis that weren worthy to be reparelid. Lire here. c.

---

[1] Om. A.   [m] sone A.   [n] Om. A.

---

[s] weren a NS.   [t] weren a NS.   [u] the sones INS.   [v] weren foure NS.   [w] weren an NS.   [x] the sones INS.
[y] the sones NS.   [z] alle thes IS.   [a] the sones INS.   [b] whiche N.   [c] Om. N.   [d] Om. I.   [e] stieden up INS.
[f] and Thelersa c. fro Thelersa INS.   [g] fro Cherub INS.   [h] fro INS.   [i] fro Mey INS.   [k] hows or meynee IS.
[l] seed or progeny s.   [m] Israel, weren thes IS.   [n] that weren sixe I. whiche weren sixe NS.   [o] weren the INS.

Accos, the sonus of Bersellai, that toc a
wif of the doȝtris of Bersellai Galaditis,
and he is clepid bi the name of hem;
62 these soȝten the scripture of ther genelogie and founden not, and thei ben cast
63 awei fro presthod And Athersatha seide
to them, that thei shulde not eten of the
holi of halewis, to the time that ther
64 shulde risen a taȝt prest and perfit[o]. Al
the multitude as o man, two and fourti
65 thousend thre hundrid and sixti, out take
the seruauntis of hem and hand maidenes, that weren seuen thousend thre
hundrid seuene and thretti, and in hem
singeres and singeressis, two hundrid
66 The hors of hem, sixe hundrid and sixe
and thretti; the mulis of hem, foure hun-
67 drid and fiue and fourti; the camailis of
hem, foure hundrid and fiue and thretti;
the assis of hem, sixe thousend seuene
68 hundrid and twenti. And of the princis
of the[p] fadris, whan thei shulden gon in
to the temple of the Lord, that is in Jerusalem, wilfulli thei offriden in to the
hous of God, to it to be maad out in his
69 place; after ther strengthis thei ȝeuen[q]
the costis of the werk, of gold, shillingis
fourti thousend and a thousend, of siluer, besauntus fiue thousent; and prestus
70 clothis an hundrid Thanne dwelten the
prestus and the Leuitus of the puple, and
the singeres, and porteris, and sodeknys
in ther cites, and al Israel in their cytees

CAP III

1 And now was comen the seuenthe
monyth, and the sonus of Irael weren in
ther cites Thanne is gedered the puple
2 as oon in to Jerusalem And thei ros
Josue, the sone of Josedech, and the brethern of hym, prestus, and Sorobabel,

sones of Obia, sones[p] of Accos, sones[q] of
Berzellai, which[r] took a wijf of the douȝtris of Bersellai Galadite, and was[s] clepid
bi the name of hem, these souȝten the 62
scripture of her genologie*, and founden[t]
not, and thei weren cast[u] out of preesthod And Attersatha† seide to hem, that 63
thei schulden not ete of the hooli of hooli‡
thingis, til a wijs[v] preest and perfit roos[w].
Al[x] the multitude as[y] o man[z]§, two[a] and 64
fourti thousynde thre hundrid and sixti[b],
outakun[c] the seruauntis of hem and the 65
handmaydis[d], that[e] weren seuene thousynde thre hundrid and seuene and thretti,
and[f] among hem *weren*[g] syngeris and
syngeressis[h] twei hundrid. The horsis of 66
hem *weren* sixe hundrid and sixe and
thritti, the mulis of hem *weren*[i] foure
hundrid and fyue and fourti, the camels 67
of hem *weren*[k] foure hundrid and fyue
and thritti; the assis of hem *weren*[l] sixe
thousynde seuene hundrid and twenti
And of the princes of fadris, whanne thei 68
entriden in to the temple‖ of the Lord
which[m] is in Jerusalem, thei offriden[n] of
fre[o] wille in to the hows of God, to bilde
it in his[p] place[q], thei[r] ȝauen bi her myȝtes[s] 69
the costis of the werk, oon and fourti
thousynde platis of gold; fyue[t] thousynde
besauntis of siluer; and preestis clothis an
hundrid Therfor preestis and dekenes of 70
the puple, and syngeris, and porteris, and
Nathynneis[u] dwelliden in her citees, and
al Israel[v] in her cytees

CAP. III

And thanne[w] the seuenthe monethe was 1
comun, and the sones of Israel weren in
her citees Therfor[x] the puple was ga- 2
derid as o man¶ in to Jerusalem And
Josue, the sone of Josedech, roos[y], and
hise britheren, preestis, and Zorobabel,

* *genologie*; that is, kynrede c

† *Attersatha*, that is, Neomye c.

‡ *of the hooly of hooly*, that is, of metis grauntid to prestis aloone *Lire here* c

§ *o man*, that is, of o purpos and wille, to bilde the temple *Lire here* c

‖ *temple* that is, the place, where the temple was *Lire here* c

¶ *o man*, that is, of o wille and purpos, to the reising of the auter, and of the foundement of the temple *Lire here* c

[o] a perfijt A [p] Om A [q] ȝeuen to c

[p] the sones CINS [q] and the sones IS [r] the which I and the sones which N [s] he was INS [t] founden it INS [u] *therfore* cast IS [v] a perfit IS a perfit *man* N [w] roos up IN roos up *among hem* S [x] And al C [y] *beynge* as I *was* as N [z] man *consentide hereto* S [a] *weren* two I *and ther weren* two NS [b] sixti *men* S [c] withoute I [d] her handmaydens INS [e] whiche INS [f] Om S [g] Om N [h] syngsteres I [i] Om I [k] Om I [l] Om I [m] that INS [n] offriden there S [o] *her* fre INS [p] the INS [q] place *where it was arst* IS [r] aftir her power thei INS [s] Om INS. [t] and fyue INS [u] the men of Nathynny INS [v] Israel *dwelliden* S [w] whanne AINS [x] And INS [y] roos up INS

the sone of Salatiel, and the brethern of hym, and thei bilden[r] vp an[s] auter of God of Irael, that thei offre in it brent sacrifises, as it is writen in the lawe off 3 Moises, man of God. Forsothe thei setten an[t] auter vpon his feet, the puplis of londis ferende hem by enuyroun, and thei offriden vpon it brent sacrifise to the 4 Lord erli and at euen. And thei maden the solempnete of tabernaclis[u], as it is writen, and brent sacrifise alle daȝes bi order, after the comaundid were of the 5 dai in his dai; and after this, contynuel brent sacrifise, bothe in calendis and in alle solempnetes of the Lord that weren halewid, and in alle thingis in the whiche 6 ȝifte was freli offrid to God. The firste dai of the seuenthe monyth thei begunne to offre brent sacrifise to the Lord; forsothe the temple of God was not ȝit 7 founded. And thei ȝeue money to heweris of stonus, and to leieris[v], and mete, and drink, and oile, to Sidones and Tires, that thei shulde bringen ceder trees fro Liban to the se of Joppen, after that Cirus, the king of Persis, had comaundid 8 to them. The secunde forsothe ȝer of the comyng of hem to the temple of God in to Jerusalem, the secunde monyth, be- 9 gunne Sorababel, the sone of Salatiel, and Josue, the sone of Josedech, and othere of the brethern of hem, prestus and Leuitus, and alle that weren comen fro the caitifte in to Jerusalem; and thei ordeineden Leuitus, fro twenti ȝer and aboue, that thei shulden heeȝen the werk of the Lord; and Josue stod, and his sonus and his brethern, Cediniel and his sonus, and the sonus of Juda, as o man, that thei shulden stonden in vpon hem that diden werk in the temple of God; the sones of Benadab, sonus of hem and brethern of

the ṣone of Salatiel, and hise britheren, and thei bildiden the auter of God of Israel for to offre therynne[z] brent sacrifices, as it is writun in the lawe of Moises, the man of God. Forsothe[a] thei settiden the 3 auter on[b] his foundementis, while the puplis of londis[c] bi cumpas maden hem aferd, and thei offriden on[d] that auter brent sacrifice[e] to the Lord in the morewtid and euentid. And thei maden solempnytee[f] of 4 tabernaclis, as it is writun, and[g] brent sacrifice[h] ech dai bi ordre, 'bi the werk of the dai comaundid in his dai[i]. And after 5 this thei offriden contynuel[k] brent sacrifice, bothe in calendis and in alle solempnytees of the Lord, that weren halewid, and[l] in alle solempnytees[m], in whiche ȝifte[n] was offrid to the Lord bi fre wille. In 6 the firste dai of the seuenthe monethe thei bigunnen to offre brent sacrifice to the Lord; certis the temple of God was not foundid ȝit. But thei ȝauen monei to 7 heweris[o] of stoon, and to[p] liggeris[q] of stoon, and thei ȝauen mete, and drynke, and oile, to men of Sidon, and 'to men[r] of Tire, that thei schulden brynge cedre trees fro the Liban[s] to the see of Joppe, bi that that Cirus, kyng[t] of Persis, hadde comaundid to hem. Forsothe[u] in the se- 8 counde ȝeer of her comyng to the temple of God in Jerusalem, in the secounde monethe, Zorobabel, the sone of Salatiel, and Josue, the sone of Josedech, and 9 othere of her britheren, preestis and dekenes, and alle that camen fro the caitifte[v] in to Jerusalem, bigunnen[w]; and thei ordeyneden dekenes, fro twenti ȝeer and aboue, for to haste the werk of the Lord; and Josue stood, and hise sones, and hise britheren, Cedynyel[x] and hise sones, and the sones of Juda[y], as o man, to be bisi ouer hem that maden the werk in[z] the

---

[r] bildiden ᴀ.   [s] Om. c.   [t] Om. c.   [u] the tabernacles c.   [v] leggeris ᴀᴇꜰɪɪ.

[z] therupon ɪɴꜱ.   [a] And ɪɴꜱ.   [b] upon ɪɴꜱ.   [c] othere londis ɪɴꜱ.   [d] upon ɪɴꜱ.   [e] sacrifices ɴꜱ.   [f] the solempnytee ɪɴꜱ.   [g] and thei offriden ɪꜱ.   [h] sacrifices bi ꜱ.   [i] and in the day bi the heest of the lawe thei wrouȝten the werk of the day ɪꜱ. and in the day bi heest thei wrouȝten the werk of the day ɴ.   [k] the contynuel ɪɴꜱ.   [l] and this thei diden ꜱ.   [m] Om. ɴ. the solempnitees ꜱ.   [n] eny ȝift ꜱ.   [o] the heweris ɪꜱ.   [p] Om. ᴀ.   [q] the liggeris ɪɴ.   [r] Om. ꜱ.   [s] mounteyne ɪɴꜱ.   [t] the kyng ɪɴ.   [u] And ɪɴꜱ.   [v] caitifte of Babiloyne ɪꜱ.   [w] bigunnen the werk of Goddis temple ɪꜱ.   [x] and Cedynyel ɴꜱ.   [y] Juda togidre ɪ. Juda; alle these stoden togidere ꜱ.   [z] of ɪɴꜱ.

10 hem, Leuitus Thanne groundid of the
masonus the temple of the Lord, prestus
stoden in ther arm with trumpis, and
Leuitus, sonus of Asaf, in cimbalis, that
thei preise God bi the hond of Dauid,
11 king of Irael And thei sungen togidere
in ympnes and knoulechng to the Lord,
For 'he is[v] good, for in to withoute ende
the merci of hym vpon Irael. Also al
the puple criede out with a gret cry, in
preisinge the Lord, for thi that the tem-
12 ple of the Lord was founded Manie
also of the prestis, and Leuitus, and the
princis of fadris, and the eldere, that
hadden seen the rathere temple, whan it
was foundid, and this temple in the e3en
of hem, wepten with a gret vois, and
manye criende out in gladnesse iereden
13 vp a vois, ne any man my3te knowen
the vois of the cri of men gladende, and
the vois of the wepíng of the puple,
forsothe mengíngli togidere the puple
criede out with a gret cri, and the vois
1 was herd aferr Forsothe the enemys of
Jude and of Beniamyn herden, for the
sonus of caitifte shulden bilden vp the
2 temple to the Lord God of Irael, and,
ne3hende to Sorobabel, and to the princis
of fadris, seiden to hem, Bilde wee vp
with 3ou, for so as 3ee, wee sechen 3our
God; lo' wee offren slain sacrifises fro
the da3es of Assoroddon, king of Assur,
3 that bro3te vs hider. And Sorobabel
seide to them and Josue, and the tothere
princis of the fadris of Irael, It is not to
vs and to 3ou, that wee bilde vp an hous
to oure God; but wee vsself alone shul
bilden vp to the Lord oure God, as to vs
4 Cirus, king of Persis, comaundede It is
do forsothe, that the puple of the lond
shulde lette the hondis of the puple of
Jude, and disturben[w] them in bildíng

temple of God; the[a] sones of Benadab, her
sones and her britheren, dekenes[b], 'weren
bisy[c]. Therfor whanne the temple 'of 10
the Lord[d] was foundid of stoon leggeris,
prestis stoden in her ournement[e] with
trumpis, and dekenes, the sones of Asaph,
in[f] cymbalis, for to her ie[g] God bi the hond[h]
of Dauid, kyng of Israel And thei sungen 11
togidere in ympnes and knoulechyng[i] to
the Lord, For he is good, for his merci is
with outen ende on[k] Israel. And al the
puple criede with greet[l] cry, in preisynge
the Lord, for the temple of the Lord was
foundid Also ful manye of the preestis, 12
and of the dekenes, and the princes of fadris, and the eldre men, that hadden seyn
the formere temple, whanne it was foundid,
and this[m] temple bifor her i3en, wepten[n]
with greet vois[o], and many men criynge
in gladnesse[p] reisiden[q] the vois[r], and no 13
man my3te knowe the vois of cry[s] of men[t]
beynge glad, and the vois of wepyng of
the puple; for[u] the[v] puple[w] criede togidere
with greet cry, and the vois[x] was herd
afer

CAP IV.

Forsothe[y] the enemyes of Juda and of 1
Beniamyn herden, that the sones of caitifte bildiden[z] a temple to the Lord God
of Israel, and thei nei3eden[a] to Zorobabel, 2
and to the princes of fadris, and seiden[b]
to hem[c], Bilde we with 3ou, for so as 3e[d],
we seken 3oure God, lo' we han offrid
sacrificis fro the daies of Assoraddon, kyng
of Assur, that brou3te vs hidur[e] And Zo- 3
robabel, and Josue, and the[f] othere princes
of the fadris of Israel, seiden to hem, It is
not to vs and to 3ou, that we bilde[g] an
hows to oure God; but we vs silf aloone
schulen bilde[h] to 'oure Lord God[i], as Cirus,
the[l] kyng of Persis, comaundide to[m] vs
Forsothe[n] it was doon, that the puple of 4

[a] and the INS [b] dekenes also I Om s [c] Om IN weren bisi there aboute s [d] Om N [e] ournementis s [f] stoden syngínge in INS [g] preise INS [h] hond or ordynaunce s [i] in knowlechyng I in deuout
knowlechíag s [k] upon IS [l] Om NS [m] si3en this NS [n] thei wepten I [o] vois for ioye IS [p] greet
gladnesse N [q] reisiden up INS [r] voice of preisyng s [s] crying s [t] the men IN [u] and INS [v] al
the I [w] peple bothe ioyíng and wepíng s [x] voice of hem s [y] And INS [z] a erin commyn a3en in to
Jerusalem and byldide there s [a] camen INS [b] thei seiden INS [c] hem in gile IVS [d] 3e don INS
[e] hidur in to this lond IS [f] Om INS [g] bilde togidre INS [h] bilde an hous IS [i] the Lord oure God IVS
[l] Om s [m] Om IN [n] And IVS

5 Forsothe thei hadden hirid aȝen hem counseileris, that thei shulden destroȝe the conseil of hem, alle the daȝes of Ciri, king of Persis, and vnto the regne of Daryi, king of Persis, two ȝeer thei ben lettid.

CAP. IV.

6 In the regne forsothe of Assueri, he is Artaxerses, in the begynning of his regne, thei writen accusacioun aȝen the 7 dwelleris of Jude and of Jerusalem; and in the daȝis of Artaxerses, Besellam Mitridates wrot, and Thabel, and the tothere that weren in the counscil of hem, to Artaxerses, king of Persis. Forsothe the epistil of accusacioun is writen Cire maner, and it was rad in Cire 8 speche. Reum, Bethlem, and Sansai, scribe, writen oon epistil fro Jerusalem to Artaxerse the king 'on this maner^x; 9 Reum, Bethlem, and Sansai, scribe, and the tothere counseilourys of hem, Dinaei, Farsarei, Therfalei, Arfasei, Arthuei, Babiloynys, Susannathaneis, Daceis, Elam- 10 ytis, and the tothere of the Jentilis, whom translatide the grete and glorious Assennafar, and made them to dwellen in the cites of Samarie, and in othere re- 11 giouns beȝunde the flod, in pes. This is the saumpler of the epistil, that thei senten to hym. To Artaxersi, king, thi seruauns, men that ben beȝunde the flod, 12 greting sein. Be it knowen to the king, for Jewis that steȝeden vp fro thee to vs, camen in to Jerusalem, cite rebel and werst, the whiche thei bilden vp, makende vp the stonene wallis of it, and 13 makende wowis^y. Now thanne be it knowe to the king, for if that cite were bild vp, and the wallis of it enstorid, tribute, and pedage, and ȝeris rentus thei shul not ȝiue, and vnto the king this

the lond lettide the hondis of the puple of Juda, and trobliden hem in^o bildyng. And 5 thei hiriden counselouris^p aȝens the Jewis, that thei schulden destrie the counseil^q of the^r Jewis, in alle the daies of Cirus, king of Persis, and 'til to^s the rewme of Darius, king of Persis. Forsothe^t in the rewme 6 of Assueris, he is^u Artaxersis†, in^v the bigynnyng of his rewme, thei writiden accusing aȝens the dwellers of Juda and of Jerusalem; and in the daies of Ar- 7 taxarses, Besellam wroot^w, Mytridates^x, and Thabel, and othere, that weren in the counsel of hem, to^y Artaxarses, kyng of Persis. For^z the pistle of accusyng was writun in langage^a of Sirie, and was^b red in word^c of Sirie. Reum^d, Beel, Theem, 8 and Samsai, the scryuen^e, writen^f sich oon^g epistle^h fro Jerusalem to the^i kyng Artaxerses; Reum^k, Beel, Theem, and Samsai, 9 the writere^l, and othere counselouris of hem^m, Dyney, Pharsathei, and Therphalei, Arphasei, Harthuei, men of Babiloyne, Susanne^n, Thanei, Dacei^o, men of Helam, and othere of hethene men, 10 whiche the grete and gloriouse^p Asennaphar translatide, and made hem to dwelle^q in the citees of Samarie, and in othere cuntrees biȝonde the flood, 'in pees^r. This 11 is the saumplere of the pistle, which^s thei senten to the kyng. 'To Artaxerses, king^t, thi seruauntis, men 'that ben^u biȝende the flood, seyn helthe^v. Be it knowun to the 12 kyng, that the^w Jewis, that^x stieden^y fro thee, ben comun to vs 'in to^z Jerusalem, the^a rebel and worste^b citee, which thei bilden, and thei maken the ground wallis therof, and arayen^c the wallis^d aboue. Nou therfor be it knowun to the kyng, 13 that if thilke citee be bildid, and^e the wallis therof be restorid, thei^f schulen not ȝyue^g tribut, and tol, and annuel rentis,

† This clause, he is Artaxerses, is not in Ebrea, nether is of the text, but first sum doctour bi the maner of a glos, and aftirward bi vnkunning of writers, it was set in the text. Lire here, c.

x of this matere E pr. m. y vowis AC sec. m.

o and her 1. in her NS. p the councelours x. q counseil or purpos 1S. r Om. c. s vnto 1NS. to x. t And 1NS. u is clepid NS. v and in s. w wroot this accusing of Jewis 1NS. x and Mytridates NS. y writiden to s. z And 1NS. a the langage s. b it was 1NS. c the word 1NS. d And Reum NS. e writere 1NS. f writide N. g a 1NS. h pistle NS. l Om. NS. k and Reum NS. l scryneyn x. m hem that is to mite 1. hem, that is NS. n and Susanne NS. o and Dacei 1NS. p gloriouse kyng 1S. q dwelle in pees 1NS. r Om. 1NS. s that 1NS. t Om. s. u Om. 1. dwellinge NS. v helthe to thee 1N. w Om. x. x whiche 1N. Om. s. y stieden up 1NS. z in s. a a 1NS. b fal yuel 1. the worste NS. c thei arayen 1NS. d wallis therof s. e and if 1NS. f Jewis 1NS. g thanne ȝyue NS.

14 blame shal come Wee thanne mynde
hauende of the salt, that in the paleis
wee eeten, and for the harmys of the
king to seen vnleeful wee holden^z, therfore wee han sent and told to the king;
15 that thou enserche in the bokis of the
stories of thi fadris, and thou shalt finde
write in armaries, and knowen, for that
cite is a rebel cite, and noȝende to kingus
and to prouincis^b, and batailis ben sterid
vp in it of old daȝes, for what thing and
16 that cite is destroȝid Wee tellen to the
king, for if that cite were bild vp, and
his wallis enstorid, thou shalt not han
17 possessioun beȝunde the flod The king
sente woord to Reum, Bethlem, and to
Sansay, scribe, and to the tothere that
weren in the counseil of hem, dwelleris
of Samarie, and to the tothere beȝunde
the flod, Greetinge, seiende, and pes
18 The acusacioun, that ȝee senten to vs,
19 openli is rad befor me; and of me it
is comaundid, and thei ensercheden, and
founden, for that cite of olde daȝes aȝen
kingus rebellith, and descenciouns and
20 batailis ben rerid vp in it; for and most
stronge kingis weren in Jerusalem, the
whiche and^c lordshipeden to al the regioun that is beȝunde the flod, tribute
also, and pedage, and rentis, thei token
21 Now thanne hereth the sentence, that ȝee
forfende 'thoo men^d, and that cite be not
bild vp, to the time if perauenture of me it
22 were comaundid Seeth, lest necgligentli
this be fulfild, and htilmelum growe euel
23 aȝen kingys And so the saumple of the
maundement of Artaxerses, king, is rad
befor Reum, Bethlem, and Sansai, scribe,
and the counseileris of hem; and thei
wenten hastif in to Jerusalem to the
Jewis, and thei forfendeden^e them in

and this trespas^h schal come 'til to^i the
kyng Therfor we ben myndeful of the 14
salt†, which^k we eeten in the^l paleis, and^m
for we holden it vnleueful to se the harmes
of the kyng^n, therfor we han sent and teld
to the kyng; that thou acounte^o in the^p 15
bokis of stories of thi fadris, and thou
schalt fynde writun in cronyclis, and thou
schalt wite, that thilke citee^q is a rebel
citee, and that it anoieth kyngis and prouynces, and batels^r ben reisid therynne of
elde daies; wherfor also thilke citee was
distried We tellen to the kyng, that if 16
thilke^s citee be bildid, and^t the^u wallis
therof be restorid, thou schalt not haue
possessioun biȝende^v the flood. The^w kyng 17
sente word^x to Reum, Beel^y, Theem^z, and^a
to Samsai, the scryuen^b, and to othere
that weren in the counsel of hem, to^c the
dwelleris of Samarie, and to othere biȝendis the flood, and seide^d, Helthe and
pees^e The accusyng^f, which^g ȝe senten to 18
vs, was red opynli bifor me; and it was 19
comaundid of me^h, and thei rekenyden, and
thei^k foundun, that thilke citee^l rebellith^m
of elde daies aȝens kyngis, and dissen-
ciouns and batels ben reisid therynne; for 20
whi 'and ful stronge kyngis weren in
Jerusalem^n, which also weren lordis of al
the cuntrei which^p is biȝende the flood;
also thei^q token tribut, and tol, and rentis
Now therfor here ȝe the sentence^r, that ȝe 21
forbede tho men^s, and that thilke citee^t be
not bildid, til if^u perauenture it be comaundid of me Se ȝe, that this^v be not 22
fillid^w necgligentli, and yuel^x encreesse^y
litil 'and litil^z aȝens kyngis. Therfor the 23
saumple of the comaundement^a of kyng^b
Artaxarses was red bifor Reum, Beel^c,
Theem^d, and Samsai, the scryueyn^e, and
her^f counseleris; and thei ȝeden hastili^g in

† salt, that is,
of metis maad
sauery, with
salt Lire
here c

---

z sevn z pr m   a the A   b the prouyncis A.   c Om c   d to me A the men n   e forfenden A

h trespas or harm NS   i to INS.   k that INS   l thi INS   m Om S   n king, and to certifie him not
of tho S.   o acounte and seke IS   P thi M   q citee Jerusalem INS   r that batels INS   s that S   t and
if INS   u Om INS   v ȝendis D   W And the NS   x word aȝen IS   Y to Beel INS   z to Theem INS
a Om N   b writere INS   c and to INS   d he seide IN he seide to hem S   e pees be to ȝou INS
f accusynge of Jewis IS   g that INS   h me to be souȝt I me to seke out the cronyclis NS   i men INS
k Om INS   l citee Jerusalem IS   m rebelled S   n ther weren in Jerusalem ful stronge kyngis I
P that INS   q tho kyngis NS   r sentence of rie INS   s men to bilde INS   t Om N   u Om A   v this
heest INS   w fulfillid INS   x yuel fro thens S   Y encreesse so I encrecid X   z Om N   a heest INS
b the kyng X   c and Beel INS   d and Theem INS.   e writere INS   f bifore her INS   g in haast I

24 power and strengthe. Thanne is laft of the werc of the hous of God in Jerusalem, and it was not maad vnto the secunde 3er of the regne of Darii, king of Persis.

CAP. V.

1 Forsothe ther profecieden Aggeus, profete, and Zacharias, profete, the sone of Addo, propheciende to the Jewis that weren in Jude and Jerusalem, in the 2 name of God of Irael. Thanne risen Sorobabel, the sone of Salatiel, and Josue, the sone of Josedech, and thei begunnen to bilden vp the temple of God in Jerusalem; and with hem profetis, helpende 3 hem. In that forsothe time cam to hem Thathannai, that was duk be3unde the flod, and Starbusannai, and the counseiloures of hem; and thus thei seiden to hem, Who 3af to 3ou counseil, that this hous 3ee shulden bilden vp, and these 4 wallis enstoren? To the whiche wee answerden to hem, whiche weren the namys 5 of men, autouris of that bilding. The e3e forsothe of the God of hem is don vpon the olde men of Jewis, and thei my3te not forfenden hem; and it pleside that the thing were told to Darie, and thanne thei shulden don aseeth a3en 6 that acusing. The saumpler of the epistil, that sente Thathannai, duk of the regioun be3unde the flod, and Starbusannai, and the counseileris of hym, Arfarsacei, that weren be3unde the flod, to 7 Darie, the king. The woord that thei senten to hym thus was writen; To 8 Darie, the king, alle pes. Be it knowen to the king, wee to han go to Jude prouynce, to the hous of the grete God, that is bild vp with ston vnpolisht, and trees ben sett in the wowis[f], and that were

to Jerusalem to the Jewis, and[h] forbediden[i] hem[k] with arm and my3t[†]. Thanne 24 the werk of Goddis hows in Jerusalem was left, and it was not maad til[l] to the secounde 3eer of Darius[m], king[n] of Persis.

CAP. V.

Forsothe Aggei, the prophete, and Za-1 charie, the prophete, the sone of Ado, prophesieden[o], prophesiynge in the name of God of Israel, to the Jewis that weren in Juda and Jerusalem. Thanne Zoroba-2 bel, the sone of Salatiel, and Josue, the sone of Josedech, risiden[p], and bigunnen[q] to bilde the temple of God in Jerusalem; and with hem rysyden[r] the prophetis of God, helpynge hem. Forsothe[s] in that 3 tyme Tatannai, that was duyk bi3ende the flood, and Starbusannay, and the counselouris of hem, camen to hem[t], and seiden thus to hem, Who 3af counsel to 3ou to bilde this hows, and to restore these wallis? To which[u] thing[v] we answeriden 4 to hem[w], whiche weren the names of men, autours of that bildyng. Forsothe the i3e[‡] 5 of God of hem[x] was maad on the elde[y] men of Jewis, and thei my3ten not forbede[z] the Jewis[a]; and it pleside that the thing schulde be teld to Darius, and[b] thanne thei schulden make satisfaccioun a3ens that accusyng. *This is* the saum-6 pler of the pistle, which Tatannai, duyk of the cuntrey bi3ende the flood, and Starbursannai, and hise counselouris, Arphasacei, that[c] weren bi3ende the flood, senten to kyng Darius. The word which[d] thei 7 senten to hym was writun thus; Al pees be to the[e] kyng Darius. Be it knowun 8 to the kyng, that we 3eden to the prouince of Judee, to the hows of greet God, which[f] is bildid with stoon vnpolischid, and trees ben set[g] in the wallis[h], and

† my3t; that with strengthe of oost, which the Jewis my3ten not a3en stonde. Lire here. c.

‡ the i3e; that is the biholding of Goddis mercy and help. Lire here. c.

f vowis H.

h and thei INS. i forbeden I. k hem *to bilde* INS. l Om. ANS. m *the rewme of* Darius INS. n the king INS. o profecieden *thanne and thei weren* S. P resin E *et* L pass. resen up I. risiden up NS. q thei begunnen INS. r risen EL. resen up I. risiden up NS. s And IN. Om. S. t *the Jewis* INS. u the which I. v axing N. axynd S. w hem *and tolden* IN. hem *and telden hem* S. x Jewis N. the Jewis S. y eldre GHIKNSX. olde EL. z forbede *or lette* IS. a Jewis *to bilde* I. Jewis *to bilde the house of God* S. b and that INS. c whiche NS. d that IN. e Om. N. f that I. g sent *or leide* S. h wallis *theroff* IS.

diligentli is maad upᵍ, and waxeth in the
9 hondis of hem Wee axeden thanne thoo
olde men, and thus we seiden to them,
Who ȝaf to ȝou power that this hous ȝee
shulden bilden, and the wallis enstoren ?
10 But and the names of hem we han soȝt
of hem, that wee telle to thee ; and we
han write the namus of theᵇ men that
11 ben princis in hem Forsothe such woord
thei answerden to vs, seiende, We ben
the seruauns of God of heuene and of ˙
erthe , and we bilden vp the temple that
was maad out befor these ȝeris manye, and
the whiche the grete king of Irael hadde
12 bild, and maad out Forsothe aftir that
to wrathe oure fadris hadden terred the
God of heuene, he toc hem in the hond
of Nabugodonosor, king of Babiloyne,
Caldeis , and this hous he destroȝede,
and the puple of it he translatide in to
13 Babiloine Forsothe the firste ȝer of Ciri,
king of Babiloine, Cirus, king of Babiloyne, purposide a maundement, that the
14 hous of God shulde be maad vp For
and the vesselis of the temple of God,
goldene and siluerene, that Nabugodonosor hadde take fro the temple, that was
in Jerusalem, and hadde born hem awei
in to the temple of Babiloyne, king Cirus
broȝte forth fro the temple of Babyloyne,
and ben ȝiue to Zazabazar bi name, whom
15 and he ordeynede prince And he seide
to hym, These vesselis tac, and go, and
put hem in the temple, that is in Jerusalem ; and theᵗ hous of God be bild vp
16 in his place And so thanne thilkeʲ Zazabazar cam, and sette the groundis of
the temple of God in Jerusalem , and fro
that time vnto now it is bild, and ȝit is
17 not fulfild. Now thanne if it seme to the
king good, enserche he in the librarie of
the king, that is in Babiloyne, whether

thilke werk is bildid diligently, andᵗ en-
creessith in the hondis of hemᵏ Therfor 9
we axiden tho elde men, and thus we
seiden to hem, Who ȝaf to ȝou powei to
bilde this hows, and to restore these
wallis ? But also we axiden of hem theˡ 10
names ˙of hemᵐ, that we schulden telle
to thee , and we han write the names of
menⁿ, whiche thei ben, that ben princes
among hem Sotheliᵒ thei answeriden bi 11
sich wordᵖ, and seiden�q, We ben the seruauntis of God of heuene and of erthe ,
and we bilden the temple thatʳ was bildid
bifor these many ȝeeris, and ˙whiche templeˢ
theᵗ greet kyng of Israel ˙hadde bildidᵘ,
and maadᵛ. But aftir that oure fadris 12
strydenʷ God of heuene and of erthe to
wrathfulnesse, botheˣ he bitook hem in
the hond of Nabugodonosor, Caldeyʸ, kyng
of Babiloyne ; and he distriede this howsᶻ,
and translatideᵃ the puple therof in to
Babiloyne Forsotheᵇ in the firste ȝeer of 13
Cirus, king of Babiloyne, Cirusᶜ, theᵈ king
of Babiloyne, settideᵉ forth ˙a comaunde-
mentᶠ, that the hows of God schulde be
bildid For whi kyng Cirus brouȝte forth 14
˙fro the temple of Babiloyneᵍ also the
goldun and siluerne vessels of Goddis temple, whiche Nabugodonosor hadde take fro
the temple, that was in Jerusalem, and
hadde bore tho awei in to the temple of
Babiloyne ; and tho vessels weren ȝouun
to Sasabazai bi name, whom ˙he madeᵇ
alsoⁱ princeᵏ And Cirus seide to hym,
Take these vessels, and go, and sette thoˡ 15
in the temple, whichᵐ is in Jerusalem ,
and theⁿ hows of God beᵒ bildid in ˙his
placeᵖ. Therfor thanne thilke Sasabazar 16
camq, and settideʳ the foundementis of˙
Goddis temple in Jerusalem ; and fro that
tyme ˙til toˢ now it is bildid, and isᵗ not
ȝit fillidᵘ. Now therfor if it ˙semeth goodᵛ 17

ᵍ Om c   ᵇ Om ᴀ   ⁱ this ᴀ   ʲ that c sec m

ⁱ and it ɪɴs   ᵏ Jewis ɴs   ˡ her ɪ   ᵐ Om ᴀ   ⁿ tho men ɪɴs   ᵒ And ɪɴs   ᵖ werdis ɴs   q seiden
to vs ᵍ   ʳ whiche ɪɴs   ˢ the temple which ɪɴs   ᵗ Salomon the ɪɴs   ᵘ bildide ɪɴ   ᵛ hadde maad x
ʷ hadden stiriid ɪɴs   ˣ Om ɪɴs   ʸ of Caldey ɪɴ   of the cuntrey of Caldey s   ᶻ hows of God is   ᵃ he
translatide ɴs.   ᵇ And ɪɴs   ᶜ this Cirus ɪs   ᵈ Om ɪɴ   ᵉ puttide ɪ settide or puttide ɴs   ᶠ an
heeste ɴs   ᵍ Om ɴ   ᵇ Om ɪɴs   ⁱ also Cirus had maad ɪɴs   ᵏ prince upon the lond of Juda ɪs
ˡ hem ɪɴs   ᵐ that ɪɴs   ⁿ be the ɪɴs   ᵒ Om ɪɴs   ᵖ the place where it was [erst s] ɴs   q cam in to
Juda ɪs   ʳ he settide ɪɴs   ˢ vnto ɪɴs   ᵗ it is ɪɴs   ᵘ fulfillid ɪɴs   ᵛ semeth good or plesith ɴ semeth
or plesith s

forsothe of king Cire it be comaunded, that the hous of God shulde be bilde vp in Jerusalem; and the wil of the king vpon this thing sende he to vs.

to the king, rikene^w he^x in the biblet^y of the kyng, which^z is in Babiloyne, whether it be^a comaundid of kyng Cyrus, that Goddis hows schulde be bildid in^b Jerusalem^c; and sende^d he to vs the wille of the kyng `on this thing^e.

CAP. VI.

1 Thanne king Darie comaunded, and thei enscrchiden in the tresorie of the bokis, that weren leid vp in Babiloine. 2 And there is founde in Egbadonys, that is a castel in Medene prouynce, o volume, and such a sentence was writen in it. 3 The firste ʒer of Ciri king, Cirus the king demede, that the hous of God, that^k is in Jerusalem, shulde be bild vp in the place where thei offren ostus, and that thei putte groundis vnderberende the heiʒte of sixti cubitus, and the breede of 4 sixti cubitus, and thre ordris of vnpolisht stonis, and so ordris of uewe trees. Costis forsothe of the hous of the king 5 shulden ben ʒiue. But and the vesselis, goldene and siluerene of the temple of God, that Nabugodonosor hadde take of the^l temple of Jerusalem, and broʒt hem in to Babiloine, be thei ʒolden, and born aʒeen in to the temple of Jerusalem, and in to ther place, the whiche and ben 6 put in^m the temple of God. Now thanne Thathannai, duke of the regioun that is beʒunde the flod, and Scarbusannai, and ʒoure counseileris, Arfasacei, that ben beʒunde the flod, aferr goth awei fro them; 7 and leteth toⁿ be maad that^o temple of God of the duke of Jewis, and of the elders of hem; and that hous of God 8 bilde thei in his place. But and of me it is comaundid, that it behoueth to be maad of thoo prestus of Jewis, that the

CAP. VI.

Thanne^f kyng Darius comaundide, and 1 thei rekenyden^g in the biblet of bokis, that^h weren kept in Babiloyne. And oⁱ 2 book was foundun in Egbatanys, which is a castel in the prouynce of Medena, and sich a sentence of the kyng was writun therynne. In the first ʒeer of kyng 3 Cirus, Cirus the kyng demyde^k, that, 'Goddis hows^l, which^m is in Jerusalem, schulde be bildid in the place where thei offren sacrifices, and that thei sette foundementisⁿ supportynge^o the heiʒthe^p of sixti cubitis, and the lengthe of sixti cubitis, thre^q ordris of stonys vnpolischid, 4 and so ordris^r of newe trees. Sotheli^s costis^t schulen be ʒouun of the kyngis hows. But also the goldun and siluerne 5 vessels of Goddis temple, whiche Nabugodonosor took fro the temple of Jerusalem, and brouʒte tho^u in^v to Babiloyne, be^w ʒoldun, and borun aʒen in to the temple of Jerusalem, and in to her place, whiche^x also^y be^z set in the temple of God. Now 6 therfor Tathannai, duyk of the cuntrei which^a is biʒende the flood, and^b Starbusannai, and ʒoure counseleris, Arphasacei, that^c ben byʒende the flood, departe ʒe fer fro hem^d; and suffre ʒe, that thilke 7 temple of God be maad of the duyk of Jewis, and of the eldre men of hem; and that thei bilde that hows of God in his place. But also it is comaundid of me, 8 that that bihoueth to be maad of tho

k the which *AH*. l Om. *A*. m in to *E pr. m.* n Om. *C*. o the *A*.

w rekene *or se* N. x he *diligently* I. he *or seke he diligently* S. y biblet, *that is, the book of cronicling* I. biblet *of cronyclis* N. biblet, *that is, in the book of cronyclis* S. z the which I. which *book* S. a is INS. b or in S. c Jerusalem *or nat* I. Jerusalem *or nay* S. d upon this thing sende IS. e Om. IS. f Whanne A. g rekenyden *or souʒten* INS. h whiche *bokis* INS. i that INS. k demede *or ordeyned* S. l the hous of God INS. m that INS. n foundement *EL.* o beringe up I. up beringe NS. p heiʒthe *of the werk* I. heiʒthe *of werk* NS. q and sette *thei* thre INS. r the ordris INS. s And INS. t costis *herto* IS. u hem INS. v Om. IS. w be thei INS. x the whiche I. y vessels *also* INS. z be thei IN. a that INS. b of S. c whiche NS. d the Jewis INS.

hous of God be bild vp, that is, that of
the kingis cofre, that is, of tributis, that
ben ʒiue of the regioun beʒunde the flod,
besih costys be ʒiue to thoo men, lest be
ᵍlettid the werk. That if nede were, andᵖ
caluis, and lombis, and kidis in to brent
sacrifise to the God of henene; whete,
salt, and win, and oile, aftir the custum
of piestus that ben in Jerusalem, be ther
ʒiue to them bi alle daʒis, lest ther be in
10 any thing pleynyng And offre thei offringus to the God of heuene, and preʒe
thei for the lif of the king and of his
11 sonus Of me thanne is sett a decree,
that eche man that this comaundement
chaungith, be don awei the tree of the
hous of hym, and be he rerid vp, and to-
brosid in it, the hous forsothe of hym
12 be forfetidq God forsothe, that maketh
to dwellen his name there, scatere alle
reumys and puple, that strecchith out
ther hond, that thei withstonde and scatere that hous of God, that is in Jerusalem I Darie haue ordeined a decre, the
13 whiche bisih I wile to be fulfild Therfore Thathannai, duk of the regioun be-
ʒonde the flod, and Scarbusannay, and
the conseileris of hym, after that king
Darie hadde comaunded so diligentli,
14 folewiden out The eldere forsothe of
Jewis bilden vp, and hadden prosperite,
after the profecie of Aggei, the profete,
and of Zacarie, sone of Addo, and thei
bilden, and maden, the God of Irael
comaundende, and comaundende Ciro, and
Darie, and Artaxerse, kingus of Persis;
15 and thei fulfilden thisʳ hous of God vnto
the thridde dai of the monyth of Adar,
that is the sixte ʒer of the regne of
16 king Darie Forsothe the sonus of Irael,
prestus and Leuitus, and the tothere of
the sonus of transmygracioun, maden the

preestis of Jewys, that the hows of God
be bildid, that is, that costis be ʒouun
bisih to tho men of the arke of the kyng,
that is, of tributisᵉ, that ben ʒouun of the
contrei biʒende the flood, lest the werk be
lettid That if it be nede, ʒyue thei botheʒ9
calues, and lambren, and kidis in to brent
sacrificé to God†il of heuene, wheeteᶠ, salt,
and wyn, and oile, in the custom of
preestis that ben in Jerusalem, be ʒouun
to hem bi ech dai, that no pleynt be in
ony thing And offre thei offryngis to 10
God of heuene, and preye thei for theˢ
lijf of the kyng and of hise sones Ther- 11
for theʰ sentence is setⁱ of me, that if ony
man chaungithᵏ this comaundementˡ, a tre
be takun of his hows, and be reisidᵐ, and
be heⁿ hangid theiynneᵒ; sotheliᵖ his
hows beq forfetid Forsotheʳ God, that 12
makith his name to dwelle there, distrie
alle rewmesˢ and puple, that holdithᵗ forth
her hond to impugne and destrie thilke
hows of God, whichᵘ is in Jerusalem. I
Dariusᵛ haue demyd the sentenceʷ, which
Y wole be filhdˣ diligentli Therfor Ta- 13
thannai, duyk of the cuntrei biʒende the
flood, andʸ Starbusannai, and hise coun-
seleiris, diden execucioun, 'ether filhdenᶻ,
soᵃ diligentli, bi that thatᵇ kyng Darius
hadde comaundid Sotheliᶜ the eldre men 14
of Jewis bildidenᵈ, and haddenᵉ prosperite,
bi the profesie of Aggey, the profcte, and
of Zacarie, the sone of Ado; and thei
bildiden, and madenᶠ, for God of Israel
comaundideᵍ, and forʰ Cirus, and Darius,
and Aitaxerses, kyngis of Persis, co-
maundidenⁱ; and thei performyden this 15
hows of God 'til toⱼ the thridde dai of
the monethe Adarᵏ‡, whichˡ is the sixte
ʒeer of the rewine of king Darius For- 16
sotheᵐ the sones of Israel, theⁿ preestis
and dekenes, and theoᵒ otheie of the sones

ᵖ both A   q opynli destroʒed F pr m   r the A

ᵉ the tributis is   ᶠ also wheete INS   ᵍ Om INS   ʰ this c   ⁱ boden INS   ᵏ chaunge INS   ˡ heest INS
ᵐ it reisid up INS   ⁿ Om is   ᵒ ther upon is   theron N   ᵖ and be INS   q Om INS   ʳ And INS   ˢ the
rewmes s   ᵗ holden xç   ᵘ that INS   ᵛ Darius the kyng I   Darius king NS   ʷ forseid sentence NS
ˣ fulfillid INS   ʸ flood biʒonde the s   ᶻ ether fulfilliden c   Om INS   ᵃ Om INS   ᵇ heest that q
ᶜ And INS   ᵈ bildiden Goddis temple INS   ᵉ thei hadden I s   ᶠ maden the temple INS   ᵍ comaundide
so INS   ʰ also INS   ⁱ comaundiden this thing INS   ⱼ vnto INS   ᵏ Adar or Marche INS   ˡ that INS
ᵐ And INS   ⁿ Om INS   ᵒ Om INS

dedicacioun of the hous of God in ioȝe;
17 and offriden, in the dedicacioun of the
hous of God, caluys an hundrid, wetheris
two hundrid, lambys foure hundrid, get
buckis for the synne of al the puple
twelue, after the noumbre of the linagis
18 of Irael. And thei ordeyneden prestus in
ther ordris, and Leuitus in ther whilis,
vp on the werkis of God in Jerusalem,
as it is write in the boc of Moises.
19 Forsothe the sonus of transmygracioun
maden pasch, the fourtenthe dai of the
20 firste monyth. Forsothe the prestus and
Leuitus as oon weren purified, alle clene
to offren pasch to alle the sonus of
transmygracioun, and to their brethern
21 prestus, and to themself. And the sonus
of Irael, that weren turned aȝeen of the
transmygracioun, eeten, and alle[s] that
hadden seuered hemself fro al[t] defouling
of Jentilis of the lond to them, that thei
22 seche the Lord God of Irael. And thei
maden the solempnete of therue louys
seuen daȝes in gladnesse; for the Lord
hadde gladid hem, and conuertid the
herte of king Assur to hem, that he
helpe the hondis of hem in the werk of
the hous of the Lord God of Irael.

CAP. VII.

1 Aftir these woordis forsothe, in the
regne of Artaxerses, king of Persis, Esdras, the sone of Saraie, sone of Azarie,
2 sone of Elchie, sone of Sellum, sone of
3 Sadoch, sone of Achitob, sone of Amarie,
4 sone of Azarie, sone of Maraioth, sone
5 of Saraie, sone of Osi, sone of Bocci, sone
of Abisue, sone of Finees, sone of Eleasar, sone of Aron, prest fro the begyn-
6 nyng; this Esdras steȝede vp fro Babiloine, and he a swift scribe in the lawe

of transmygracioun, '*that is, that*[p] *camen
fro transmigracioun*[q], '*ether caitifte*[r],
maden the halewyng of Goddis hows in
ioie; and offriden[s], 'in the halewyng of 17
Goddis hows[t], an hundrid caluys, twei[u]
hundryd wetheris, foure[v] hundrid lambren, twelue[w] buckis of geet for the
synne of al Israel, bi the[x] noumbre of
lynagis[y] of Israel. And thei ordeyneden 18
preestis in her ordris, and dekenes in her
whilis, on[z] the werkis of God in Jerusalem, as it is writun in the book of Moises.
Forsothe[a] the sones of transmygracioun 19
maden pask, in the fourtenthe dai of the
firste monethe. For[b] the[c] preestis and 20
dekenes[d] as o man weren clensid, alle[e]
weren clene for[f] to offre pask to alle the
sones of transmygracioun, and to her britheren preestis, and to hem silf. And the 21
sones of Israel eeten, that turneden aȝen
fro transmygracioun[g], and ech man *eet*,
that hadde departid hym silf fro al[h] the[i]
defoulyng of hethene men of the[k] lond,
for to seke the Lord God of Israel. And 22
thei maden solempnyte[l] of therf looues
seuene daies in gladnesse; for the Lord
hadde maad hem glad, and hadde[m] turned
the herte of the kyng of Assur to hem,
that he wolde helpe 'her hondis[n] in the
werk of the hows of the Lord God of
Israel.

CAP. VII.

Forsothe[o] aftir these wordis Esdras, the 1
sone of Saraie, sone of Azarie, sone of
Helchie, sone of Sellum, sone of Sadoch, 2
sone of Achitob, sone of Amarie, sone of 3
Azarie, sone of Maraioth, sone of Saraie, 4
sone of Ozi, sone of Bocci, sone of Abisue, 5
sone of Phynees, sone of Eleazar, sone of
Aaron, preest at the bigynnyng, was[p] in
the rewme of Artaxerses, king of Persis;
thilke Esdras stiede[q] fro Babiloyne, and 6
he was a swift writere† in the lawe of

† *writere*; for he reparelide the lawe brent by Caldeis, and for he foond newe lettris, bi whiche the wordis of Ebreu ben writun spedlyere and betere. *Lire here.* C.

[s] eche E *pr. m.* [t] Om. C.

[p] *of hem that* S. [q] *the transmygracioun* S. [r] Om. S. 'Gloss omitted in IX. [s] thei offriden NS. [t] Om. S. [u] two I. and two NS. [v] and foure S. [w] and twelue NS. [x] Om. NS. [y] the lynagis BCENPV *pr. m.* the lynage L. [z] vpon S. [a] And INS. [b] Forsothe INS. [c] Om. I. [d] dekenes *of the first* S. [e] alle thei INS. [f] Om. INS. [g] the transmygracioun S. [h] Om. S. [i] Om. X. [k] that INS. [l] the solempnyte INS. [m] he hadde INS. [n] the hondis of hem INS. [o] And INS. [p] he was I. this was N. this *Esdras* was S. [q] stiede up INS.

of Moises, the whiche the Lord God of
Irael ʒaf, and the king ʒaf to hym, after
the goode hond of the Lord his God
7 vpon hym, al his asking And ther
steʒeden vp of the sonus of Irael, and of
the sonus of prestus, and of the sonus of
Leuitus, and of the singeres, and of the
porteris, and of the sodeknys, in Jerusalem the seuenthe ʒer of Artaxerses, king
8 And thei camen in to Jerusalem the fifte
monyth; this is the seuenthe ʒer of the
9 king For in the firste dai of the firste
monyth thei begunnen to steʒen vp fro
Babiloine, and in the firste dai of the
fitte monyth he cam in to Jerusalem,
after the goode hond of his God vpon
10 hym Esdras forsothe greithede his
herte, that he enserche the lawe of the
Lord, and do, and teche in Irael maun-
11 dement and dom. This is forsothe the
saumpler of the epistil of the maundement, that king Artaxerses ʒaf to Esdre,
preest, wis scribe in woordis and in
maundemens of the Lord, and his ceri-
12 moines in Irael Artaxerses, king of
kingus, to Esdre, the prest, most wis
scribe of the lawe of God of heuene,
13 greting Of me is a decre, that to whom-
soeuer it plese in my rewme of the puple
of Irael, and of his prestus, and of the
Leuitus, to gon in to Jerusalem, go he
14 with thee Forsothe fro the face of the
king and of the seuene counseilers of
hym thou art sent, that thou visite Jude
and Jerusalem in the lawe of thi God,
15 that is in thi hond, and that thou bere
siluer and gold, that the king and his
counseileris wilfulli offriden to the God
of Irael, whos tabernacle is in Jerusalem
16 And al the siluer and gold, what euere
thou findist in al the prouince of Babiloine, and the puple wile offren, and of
·the prestus that wilfulli offriden to the

Moises, which the Lord God of Israel
ʒat's; and the kyng ʒaf to hym al his
axyng, by the goode hoond of his Lord
God on hym. And there stieden of 7
the sones of Israel, and of the sones of
preestis, and of the sones of dekenes, and
of the syngers, and of the porteris, and
of Nathyneis, 'in to Jerusalem in the seuenthe ʒeer of Artaxerses, kyng And 8
thei camen in to Jerusalem in the fyuethe
monethe; thilke is the seuenthe of the
kyng. For in the firste dai of the firste 9
monethe he bigan to stie fro Babiloyne, and in the firste dai of the fyuethe
monethe he cam in to Jerusalem, bi the
good hond of his God on hym Forsothe Esdras made redi his herte to en- 10
quere the lawe of the Lord, and to do,
and teche in Israel the comaundement
and doom Sotheli this is the saum- 11
pler of the pistle of the comaundement,
which the kyng Artaxerses ʒaf to Esdras,
preest, writere lerud in the woidis and
comaundementis of the Lord, and in hise
cerymonyes in Israel Artaxerses, kyng 12
of kyngis, desirith helthe to Esdras, the
preest, moost wijs writere of the lawe of
God of heuene It is demyd of me, that 13
whom euer it plesith in my rewme of the
puple of Israel, and of hise preestis, and
dekenes, to go in to Jerusalem, go he with
thee. For thou art sent fro the face † of 14
the kyng and of hise seuene counselers,
that thou visite Judee and Jerusalem in
the lawe of thi God, which is in thin
hond; and that thou bere siluer and gold, 15
which the kyng and hise counselers han
offrid bi fre wille to God of Israel, whos
tabernacle is in Jerusalem And take thou 16
freli al siluer and gold, which euer thou
fyndist in al the prouynce of Babiloyne,
and the puple wole offre, and of preestis
that offriden bi fre wille to the hows of

† *face* that is, presence and ordenaunce *Lire here* c

r that 1   which *lawe* 8   s ʒaue *to his peple* 8   t Esdras INS   u hond *or* mouyng 18   v the INS
w of INS   x in the seuenthe ʒeer of Artaxerxes kyng there INS   y stieden up into Jerusalem men INS
z Om INS   a Om INS   b seuenthe ʒeer A *sec* m seuenthe *monthe* INS   c And INS   d Esdras INS
e stie up INS   f hond *or help* 18   g the INS   h Lord God s   l of INS   k And INS   l do it 1 do it in
dede s   m to teche 18   n huest INS   o doom *of the Lord* INS   p And INS   q epistle IN   r Om s
s that 1   t Om NS   u the preest INS   v a writere INS *that was* a writere s   w lerned N   w heestis INS
x the moost INS   y heuenes s   z presens IN   a *the lond of* Judee INS   b the whiche *lawe* 1   c the
siluer INS   d what 1   e that that the INS   f *take* of 1 take *thou* of NS   g that that thei INS

hous of ther God, that is in Jerusalem,
17 freli to taken; and bisili bie of that
monei calues, wetheris, lombis, and sacrifises, and the offring of likouris of hem;
and offre them vpon the auter of the
temple of ȝour God, that is in Jerusalem.
18 But and if any thing to thee, and to thi
brethern plese, of the remnaunt of siluer
and of gold that ȝee do, after the wil of
19 ȝoure God doth; also the vesselis that ben
ȝiue in the seruise of the hous of thi God,
tac in the siȝte of God in to Jerusalem.
20 But and othere thingus the whiche nede
were in the hous of thi God, hou miche
euere is nede, that thou spende, thou shalt
ȝiue of the tresor of the king and of the
21 comun bagge, and of me. I, Artaxerses,
king, haue ordeined, and demed to alle
the keperis of the comun cofre, that ben
beȝonde the flod, that what euer aske of
ȝou Esdras, prest, scribe[u] of the lawe of
God of heuene, withoute tariyng ȝiue
22 ȝee, vnto an hundrid talentus of siluir,
and vnto an hundrid batus of win, and
vnto an hundrid choris of whete, and
vnto an hundrid batus of oile, salt for-
23 sothe withoute mesure. Al that to the
rit of God of heuene perteneth, be it ȝiue
bisili in the hous of God of heuene, lest
perauenture he be wroth aȝen the reume
24 of the king and of his sonus. To ȝou
also we maken knowen of alle the prestus,
and Leuitus, singeres, porteris, sodeknys,
and mynystris of the hous of this God,
and[v] pedage and tribute and ȝeris frutus
haue ȝee no power of putting ʻvpon[w]
25 hem. Thou forsothe, Esdra, after the
wisdam of thi God, that is in thin hond,
ordeine thou domysmen and gouernoures,
that thei deme to al the puple, that is

her[h] God, which[i] is in Jerusalem; and bie 17
thou bisili of this monei calues, rammes,
lambren[k], and sacrifices[l], and moiste sacrifices of tho; and offre thou tho on[m] the
auter of the temple of ȝoure God, which[n]
temple is in Jerusalem. But also[o] if oný 18
thing plesith to thee, and to thi britheren,
for[p] to do of the residue[q] siluer and gold[r],
do ȝe[s] bi the wille of ȝoure God; also bi- 19
take[t] thou in the siȝt of God in Jerusalem
the vessels, that[u] ben ȝonun in to the seruyce of the hows of thi God. But also 20
thou schalt ȝyue of ʻ the tresouris[w] of the
kyng, and of the comyn arke[x], ʻethir
purse[y], and of me ʻothere thingis, that
ben nedeful in the hows of thi God[z], as
myche euere as is[a] nedeful, that thou
spende. Y Artaxerses, kyng, haue or- 21
deyned, and demyd to alle the keperis of
the comyn arke[b], that ben biȝende the
flood, that what euer thing Esdras, the
preest, writere[c] of the lawe of God of
heuene, axith of ȝou, ȝe ȝyue[d] with out
tariyng, ʻtil to[e] an[f] hundrid talentis of sil- 22
uer, and to[g] an hundrid ʻmesuris clepid[h]
chorus† of wheete, and til[l] an hundrid
mesuris[j] clepid[k] bathus of wyn, and ʻtil
to[l] an hundrid ʻmesuris clepid[m] bathus of
oile, salt[u] forsothe[o] without mesure. Al 23
thing that perteyneth to the custom[p], ʻethir
religioun[q], of God of heuene, be[r] ȝonun
diligentli in the hows of God of heuene,
lest perauenture he[s] be wrooth aȝens the
rewme of the kyng and of hise sones.
Also we make knowun to ȝou of ʻ alle the 24
preestis, and dekenes, syngeris[u], and[v] porteris[w], and[x] Nathyncis[y], and[z] mynystris
of the hows of this[a] God, ʻthat ȝe han not
power[b] to put on[c] hem tol, and tribute, and
costis[d] for keperis[e] of the lond. Forsothe[f] 25

† a chore is
xx. buschels. 1.
a choor is
thrittí bus-
shels. s.

[u] and scribe c.   [v] Om. A.   [w] on c.

[h] Om. N.   [i] that INS.   [k] and lambren INS.   [l] othere offryngis INS.   [m] upon IS.   [n] the which I.   [o] ouer
this also IS.   [p] Om. NS.   [q] Om. INS.   [r] gold that leuith INS.   [s] ȝe it IS.   [t] bitake or ordeyne IS.
[u] whiche NS.   [v] Om. G.   [w] tresour BC.   [x] hucche NS.   [y] Om. NS.   [z] take s.   [a] it is N.   [b] hucche INS.
or arke I marg.   [c] and writere s.   [d] ȝyue it I. ȝoue that thing to him s.   [e] vnto INS. til K pr. m.
[f] the summe of an s.   [g] til FGHK pr. m. MNSXB.   [h] Om. INS.   [i] vnto INS.   [j] Om. s.   [k] of INS.
[l] vnto INS. til K pr. m. to x.   [m] Om. INS.   [n] and ȝeueth him salt I. and salt N. and ȝeue ȝe to him salt s.
[o] Om. INS.   [p] wirschip INS.   [q] Om. INS.   [r] be it INS.   [s] God INS.   [t] that ȝe haue not power of noon
of INS.   [u] of syngeris I. ne of syngeris NS.   [v] ne of INS.   [w] the porteris I. porteris of Goddis house s.
[x] ne INS.   [y] of the men of Nathyneis INS.   [z] ne of the INS.   [a] Om. INS.   [b] Om. INS.   [c] upon IS.
[d] othere costis INS.   [e] kepyng INS.   [f] But INS.

beȝonde the flod, to hem, that is, that
knewen the lawe of thi God, and the
lawe of the king; but and vnwise men
26 techeth freely. And eche that doth not
the lawe of thi God, and the lawe of the
king bisili, dom shal ben of hym, or[x] in
to deth, or[x] in to outlawe, or in to con-
dempnacioun of his substaunce, or certis
in to prisoun And Esdras, scribe, seide,
27 Blessid the Lord God of oure fadris, that
ȝaf this in the herte of the king, that he
shulde glorifie the hous of the Lord, that
28 is in Jerusalem, and in me hath in bowid
his merci befor the king, and his counseileris, and alle the myȝti princis of the
king And I, coumfortid bi the hond of
the Lord, of my God, that was in me,
I gaderede of the sonus of Irael princis,
that steȝeden vp with me

thou[g], Esdras, bi the wisdom of thi[h] God,
which[i] is in thin hond, ordeyne[k] iugis and
gouernouris, that thei deme to[l] the puple,
which[m] is biȝende the flood, that is[n], to[o]
hem that kunnen[p] the lawe of thi God,
and the lawe of the kyng; but also teche
ȝe freli vnkunnynge men And ech man, 26
that doth not[q] the lawe of thi God, and
the lawe of the kyng diligentli[r], doom[s]
schal be of hym, ethir[t] in[u] to the[v] deeth,
ethir in to exilyng[w], ethir in to condemp-
nyng[x] of his catel, ethir certis in to prisoun. And Esdras, the writere, seide[y],
Blissid be the Lord God of oure fadris, 27
that ȝaf this thing[z] in[a] the[b] herte of the
kyng, that he schulde glorifie the hows of
the Lord, which[c] is in Jerusalem, and 28
bowide[d] his mercy in to me bifor the
kyng, and hise counseleris, and bifore alle
the[e] myȝti princes of the kyng And Y was
coumfortid bi the hond[f] of my Lord[g]
God[h], that was in me, and Y gederide of[i]
the sones of Israel princes[k], that[l] stieden[m]
with me[n]

CAP VIII

1 These thanne ben the princis of meines,
and this the genelogie of hem, that steȝeden vp with me in the reume of Ar-
2 taxerses, king, fro Babiloine Of the sonus
of Finees, Jerson; of the sonus of Ithamar, Danyel, of the sonus of Dauid,
3 Archus; of the sonus of Sechemye and of
the sonus of Faros, Zacharias, and with
hym ben noumbrid an hundrid and fifti
4 men; of the sonus of Fethmoab and of
Eleoenai, sone of Zacharie, and with
5 hym two hundrid men; of the sonus of
Sechemye, sone of Jesechiel, and with
6 hym thre hundrid men, of the sonus of

CAP VIII.

Therfor[o] these ben the princes of mey- 1
nees, and this is the genologie[p] of hem,
whiche[q] *beynge*[r] in the rewme of Artaxerses, kyng[s], stieden[t] with[u] me fro
Babiloyne Of the sones of Phynees, Ger- 2
son[v]; of the sones of Ythamar, Danyel,
of the sones of Dauid, Arcus, of the 3
sones of Sechemye and of the sones of
Pharos, Zacarie[w], and with hym weren
noumbrid an hundrid and fifti men; of 4
the sones of Phet, Moab, and[x] Elioneay,
the sone of Zacharie[y], and with hym[z] two
hundrid men; of the sones of Sechemye, 5
the sone of Ezechiel[a], and with hym[b] thre

[x] outher AEFH

[g] Om IS [h] Om I [i] that INS [k] ordeyne thou INS [l] Om INS [m] that INS [n] is, *that thei reule iustly* I is, that *thei reule and deme trewli* S [o] Om IN [p] knowen INS [q] not diligently INS [r] Om INS [s] this doom INS [t] ethir *he schal go* INS [u] Om INS [v] Om BCINSVW [w] outlawyng INS [x] leesing INS [y] seide *to the king* NS [z] *counseil* INS [a] in to INS [b] Om N [c] that INS [d] that bowide IN *be the Lord preised* that bowid S [e] Om I [f] hond *or the goodnesse* S [g] the Lord IN the Lord God S [h] my God I [i] togidre princis of INS [k] Om INS [l] the whiche I whiche NS [m] stieden up INS [n] me [*in* S] *to Jerusalem* IS. [o] Forsothe INS [p] generacioun INS [q] that INS [r] *weren* INS [s] the kyng I [t] *and* stieden INS [u] up with IN. [v] Gerson *was prince* INS. [w] Zacarie *was prince* IS [x] Om NS [y] Zacarie *was prince* IS [z] hym *ȝeden up* I him *stieden vp* S [a] Ezechiel *was prince* IS [b] hym *ȝeden up* I him *stieden vp* S

Addaenebeth, sone of Jonathan, and with
7 hym fifti men; of the sonys of Elam,
Isaias, the sone of Italie, and with hym
8 seuenti men; of the sonus of Safacie, Ze-
bedias, the sone of Mychael, and with
9 hym eiȝteti men; of the sonus of Joab,
Obedia, the sone of Jehiel, and with hym
10 two hundrid and eiȝtetene men; of the
sonus of Salomyth, the sone of Josfie,
and with hym an hundrid and sixti
11 men; of the sonus of Belbai, Zacharias,
the sone of Bebai, and with hym twenti
12 and eiȝte men; of the sonus of Esiad,
Johannan, the sone of Esethan, and with
hym an hundrid and ten men; of the
13 sonus of Odonycham, that last weren,
and these the namus of hem, Elifilech,
and Heiel, and Samaias, and with hem
14 sixti men; of the sonus of Beguy, Vthai,
and Saccur, and with hem seuenti men.
15 I gederede hem forsothe to the flod, that
renneth to Hanna; and wee dwelten
there thre daȝis. And I soȝte in the puple,
and in the prestus of the sonus of Leuy,
16 and I fond not there. And so I sente
Elizer, and Arihel, and Semeiam, and
Elnathan, and Jaubeth, and an other
Elnathan, and Nathan, and Zacharie, and
Mesollam, princis; and Joarib, and El-
17 nathan, wise men; and I sente hem to
Heldo, the whiche is the firste in the
place off Casfee, and I putte in the mouth
of hem woordis, that thei shulden speken
to Eldo, and to the brethern of hym,
sodeknys, in the place of Casfee, that
thei shulden bringe to vs mynystris of
18 the hous of oure God. And thei broȝten
to vs, bi the goode hond of oure God
vpon vs, a most wis man of the sonus of
Mooli, sone of Leui, sone of Irael; and
Sarabiam, and the sonus of hym, twenti,
19 and the brethern of hym, eiȝtetene; and
Azabie, and with hym, Isaie, of the sonys

hundrid men; of the sones of Addam, 6
Nabeth, the sone of Jonathan[c], and with
hym[d] fifti men; of the sones of Elam, 7
Ysaie, the sone of Italie, and with him
seuenti men; of the sones of Saphacie, 8
Zebedie, the sone of Mycael, and with
him fourescore men; of the sones of Joab, 9
Obedie, the sone of Jehiel, and with him
two hundrid and eiȝtene men; of[e] the 10
sones of Salomyth, the sone of Josphie,
and with hym an hundrid and sixti men;
of the sones of Belbai, Zacarie, the sone 11
of Belbai, and with hym twenti and eiȝte
men; of the sones of Ezcad, Johannam[f], 12
the sone of Ezethan, and with hym an
hundrid and ten men; of the sones of 13
Adonycam, that weren[g] the[h] laste, and
these ben[i] the names of hem, Eliphelech,
and Eihel, and Samaie, and with hem
weren[k] sexti men; of the sones of Beguy, 14
Vtai, and Zaccur[l], and with hem weren[m]
seuenti men. Forsothe[n] Y[o] gaderide hem[p] 15
togidere[q] at the flood, that renneth doun
to Hanna; and we dwelliden there thre
daies. And 'Y souȝte[r] in[s] the puple, and in[t]
the prestis of the sonus of Leuy†, and Y 16
fonde not there. Therfor Y sente Eliezer,
and Ariehel, and Semeam, and Helnathan,
and Jaubeth, and an other Helnathan,
and Nathan, and Zacharie, and Mesollam,
princes[v]; and[w] Joarib, and Elnathan, wise[x]
men; and[y] Y sente hem[z] to Heldo, which[a] 17
is 'the firste[b] in the place of Casphie, and
Y puttide[c] in the mouth of hem wordis[d],
whiche thei schulden speke to Heldo, and
to hise britheren, Natynneis, in the place
of Casphie, for to brynge to vs the mynystris of the hows of oure God. And 'thei 18
brouȝten to vs[e], bi the good hoond[f] of oure
God on[g] vs, a[h] ful wijs man of the sones
of Mooli, the sone of Leuy, sone[i] of Israel;
and[j] Sarabie, and his sones twenti, and
his britheren eiȝtene[k]; and Azabie, and 19

† Leuy; that is, dekenes symply and not prestis. Lire here. c.

---

[c] Jonathan *was prince* s.   [d] hym *weren* INS.   [e] *and of* s.   [f] Johannam Adonyca s.   [g] weren in B.
[h] that U.   [i] Om. *plures.*   [k] ȝeden up ɪ. Om. N. *stieden vp* s.   [l] Zaccur *weren princes* ɪs.   [m] Om. N.
[n] And INS.   [o] Y *Esdras* ɪs.   [p] *alle* hem ɪ. *alle* these *men* Ns.   [q] Om. INS.   [r] Om. ɪ.   [s] among INS.
[t] Om. INS.   [u] Leuy I souȝte INS.   [v] *which alle weren* princis s.   [w] *and with hem* ɪ. *and with hem I
sente* s.   [x] *which weren* wise s.   [y] *and these* ɪ. *and alle these* s.   [z] Om. INS.   [a] *that* INS.   [b] cheef ɪ.
the first or chefe man s.   [c] putte INS.   [d] *the wordis* INS.   [e] Om. INS.   [f] *hond or loue* s.   [g] vpon INS.
[h] thei brouȝten a INS.   [i] *the sone* INS.   [j] *and thei brouȝten* INS.   [k] *weren* eiȝtene INS.

of Merari, the brethern of hym, and the
20 sonys of hym, twenti; and of the sodeknys, that^y Dauid hadde ʒiue and princis
to the seruise of Leuitys, sodeknys two
hundrid and twenti; alle these bi ther
21 namys weren clepid   And I prechide
there fasting beside the flod of Hanna,
that we shulden ben trauailid in penaunce befor the Lord oure God, and
asken of hym a riʒt weie to vs, and to
oure sonus, and to al oure substaunce.
22 Forsothe I was ashamyd to asken the
king helpe, and horse men, that myʒten
defenden vs fro the enemy in the weie,
for wee hadden seid to the king, The
hond of oure God is vpon alle that sechen
hym in goodnesse; and the empire of
hym, and the strengthe of hym, and
wodnesse vpon alle that forsaken hym
23 Wee fasteden forsothe, and preʒeden oure
God for this, and it cam to vs welsumli
24 And I seuerede of the princis of prestis
twelue, Sarabiam, Sazabiam, and with hem
25 of the brethern of hem, ten, and I peisede
to hem the siluer and gold, and the sacride vesselis of the hous of oure God, the
whiche the king hadde offrid, and the
counseleris of hym, and the princis of
hym, and al Irael, of hem that weren
26 founden. And I peisede in the hondis of
hem of siluer talentis sixe hundrid and
fifti, and siluerene vesselys an hundrid;
27 of gold an hundrid talentus, and goldene
chalicis twenti, the whiche hadden a
thousend shillingus, and two faire ves-
28 selis of best shinende bras as gold   And
I seide to hem, ʒee halewis of the Lord,
and the holy vesselis, and^x siluer and
gold, that wilfulli is offrid to the Lord
29 God^a of oure fadris, waketh, and kepith,
to the time that ʒee peisen vp befor the
princis of prestis, and of Leuitus, and

Isaie, with^l him of the sones of Merari,
thei brouʒten his britheren, and his sones,
twenti; and of Nathynneis, whiche^m Dauid 20
and theⁿ princis hadden ʒone to the seruyces of dekenes, thei brouʒten two hundrid and twenti Nathynneis; alle these
weren clepid bi her names   And 'Y 21
prechide^o there fastyng^p bisidis the flood
of Hanna^q, that we schulden be^r turmentid bifor 'oure Lord God^s, and that
we schulden axe of him the riʒtful^t weie
to vs, and to oure sones, and to al oure
catel^u   For^v Y schamede to axe of the 22
kyng help, and horse men, that^w schulden
defende vs fro enemyes^x in the weie, for
we hadden seid to the king, The hond^y of
oure God is on^z alle men that seken hym
in goodnesse; and his lordschip, and his
strengthe, and strong^a veniaunce ben on
alle men that forsaken^b hym   Forsothe^c 23
we fastiden, and preieden oure God for
this thing, and it bifelde to vs 'bi pros-
peiite^d. And 'Y departide^e twelue of the 24
princes of prestis, Sarabie^f, and Asabie
and ten of her britheren with hem; and 25
Y bitook vndui certeyn weiʒte and noumbre to hem the siluer and gold, and the
halewid vessels of the hows of oure God,
whiche the kyng hadde ofirid, and hise
counseleris, and hise princes, and 'al Israel, of hem that weren foundun^g. And 26
Y bitook vndur certeyn weiʒte and noumbre in^h the hondis of hem sixe hundrid
and fifti talentis of siluer, and an hundrid siluerne vessels; an hundrid talentis
of gold, and twenti goldun cuppis, thatⁱ 27
hadden^k a thousynde peesis of gold, and
twei^l faire vessels of best^m bras, schynynge as gold   And Y seide to hem, ʒe 28
benⁿ the hooli men of the Lord, andⁿ wake 29
ʒe, and kepe^o the hooli vessels, and^p siluer^q
and gold^r, which^s is offrid bi fre wille to

---

^l *camen* with 19   ^m that 1   ⁿ othere INS   ^o Om INS   ^p Om INS   ^q Hanna I prechide *or*
comaundide fastyng 1S   I prechide fasting N   ^r be *so* 1   *in doyng penaunce* be s   ^s the Lord oure
God INS   ^t riʒt INS   ^u substaunce INS   ^v Certis INS   ^w whiche INS   ^x enemy *A sec m* our enemyes s
^y hond *or help* s   ^z vpon INS   ^a his strong INS   ^b forsakith N   ^c And INS   ^d welsumly INS   ^e we
departiden s   ^f *that is*, Sarabie 19   ^g alle the men that weren founden of Israel IN   ^h into s   ⁱ the
whiche I   whiche N8   ^k hadden *in weiʒt* 1S   ^l I bitoke hem two I   I toke to hem two s   ^m ful good 1
ⁿ and *therfor* 1S   ^o kepeth INS   ^p of ACS   ^q the siluer IN   ^r of gold s.   ^s that 1

dukis of meines of Irael in Jerusalem, in
30 to the tresor[b] of the hous of God. Forsothe the prestus and Leuitus token the
peis of siluer, and of gold, and of vesselis,
that thei bringe in to Jerusalem, in to the
31 hous of ther God. Thanne we moueden
forth fro the flod of Hanna, the twelfthe
dai of the firste monyth, that we go in
to Jerusalem ; and the hond of oure God
was vpon vs, and deliuerede vs fro the
hond of the enemy and of the spiere in
32 the weie. And wee camen to Jerusalem,
33 and wee dwelten there thre daȝis. The
ferthe forsothe dai peisid vp is the siluer
and gold, and the vesselis, in the hous of
oure God, bi the hond of Remmoth, sone[c]
of Vrie, prest ; and with hym Eleazar, the
sone of Fynees, and with hem Josaded,
the sone of Josue, and Noadoia, the sone
of Bennoi, Leuite, aftir the noumbre and
34 weiȝte of alle thingus ; and al the weiȝte
35 is descriued in that time. But the sonus
of transmygracioun, that weren come fro
caitifte, offriden brent sacrifises to the
Lord God of Irael, caluys twelue for
al the puple of Irael, wetheris nynti
and sixe, lambis seuenti and seuene, got
buckis for synne twelue ; alle in to brent
36 sacrifise to the Lord. Thei ȝeuen forsothe maundemens of the king to the
satrapis, that weren of the siȝte of the
king, and to the dukis beȝonde the flod ;
and thei rereden vp a puple, and[d] the
hous of God.

the Lord God of oure fadris, til[t] ȝe ȝelde[u]
vndur certeyn weiȝte and noumbre bifor
th princes of prestis, and of dekenes, and
bifor the[v] duykis of meynees of Israel in
Jerusalem, in to the tresour of Goddis
hows. Sotheli[x] the preestis and dekenes 30
token the weiȝte of siluer, and of gold,
and of vessels, for to bere[y] in to Jerusalem, in to the hows of oure God. Therfor[z] 31
we mouyden[a] forth fro the flood of Hanna,
in the tweluethe dai of the firste monethe,
for to go in to Jerusalem ; and the hond[b]
of oure God was on[c] vs, and delyuerde vs
fro the hond of enemye[d] and of aspiere[e]
in the weie. And we camen to Jerusalem, 32
and we dwelliden there thre daies. For- 33
sothe[f] in the fourthe dai[g] the siluer was
ȝoldun[h] vndur certeyn weiȝte and noumbre, and the gold, and the[i] vessels, in the
hows of oure God[k], by the noumbre and
weiȝte of alle thingis, bi the hond of Remmoth, sone of Vrie[l], preest ; and with him
was Eleazar, the sone of Phynees, and
with him weren Jozaded, the sone of
Josue, and Noadaie, the sone of Bennoy,
dekenes[m] ; and al the weiȝte was discriued 34
in that tyme. But also the sones of 35
transmygracioun, that camen fro caitifte,
offriden brent sacrifices[n] to the Lord God
of Israel, twelue calues[o] for al the puple
of Israel[p], nynti[q] and sixe rammes, seuene[r] and seuenti lambren, twelue[s] buckis
of geet for synne ; alle thingis[t] in to brent
sacrifice to the Lord. Forsothe[u] thei ȝauen 36
the comaundementis[v] of the kyng to the
princes[w], that weren of [x] the siȝt of the
king, and to the[y] duykis[z] biȝende[a] the
flood ; and[b] thei reisiden[c] the puple, and
the hows of God.

t vnto the tyme that INS.   u ȝelde it aȝen INS.   v Om. INS.   x And INS.   y bere hem IS.   z Thanne INS.
a remoueden INS.   b hond or grace S.   c upon INS.   d oure enemy NS.   e the aspiere INS.   f And INS.
g dai in the hous of oure God INS.   h ȝoldun up INS.   i Om. S.   k Om. INS.   l the sone of Urie I.
Om. NS.   m which weren dekenes S.   n sacrifice IN.   o Om. INS.   P Israel weren offrid twelue calues IS.
Israel twelue calues N.   q and nynti INS.   r and seuene INS.   s and twelue INS.   t weren offrid I. these weren
offrid NS.   u And INS.   v heestis INS.   w wise men INS.   x in S.   y Om. INS.   z duykis that weren S.
a of biȝende INS.   b and into heriyng of God IS.   c reisiden up IN.

CAP IX

1 Aftir forsothe that these thingis ben fulfild, neȝheden to me the princis, sciende, The puple of Irael is not seuered, and piestus, and Leuitus, fro the puplis of londis, and fro the abhomynaciouns^e of hem, of Cananei, that is, of Ethei, and of Feresei, and of Jebusei, and of Amonitus, and of Moabitus, and 2 of Egipcienus, and of Amoriees Forsothe thei token of the doȝtris of hem to hem, and to ther sonus, wiues, and thei mengden hoh sed with the puplis of londis; the hond also of princis and of maistris was in this firste trespasing 3 And whan I hadde herd this woord, I cutte my mantil and cote, and pullide out the heris of myn hed and berd, and 4 sat weilende Forsothe ther camen to me alle that dradden the woord of God of Irael, for the trespasing of hem that weren come fro the caitifte, and I sat 5 dreri vnto the euctid sacrifise. And in the euctid sacrifise I ros fro myn afflicioun, and^f the mantil cut^g and cote, I bowide my knes, and spradde out myn hondis to 6 the Lord my God, and seide, Mi God, I am confoundid and ashamed to reren my face to thee, for oure wickenessis^h ben multiplied vponⁱ oure hed, and oure 7 giltis ben sprungen vnto heuene, fro the daȝis of oure fadris; but and wee vsself han synned greuoush vnto this dai, and in oure wickenessis we ben taken, wee, and oure kingus, and oure prestus, in the hondis of kingus of londis, and in to swerd, and in to caitifte, and in to rauein, and in to confusioun of chere, as 8 and in this dai And now as at^k litil

CAP IX

Forsothe^d after that these thingis weren 1 filhde^e, the princes neiȝeden to me^f, and seiden, The puple of Israel, and the prestis, and dekenes, ben not depertid fro the 'puplis of^g londis, and^h fro abhominaciounsⁱ of hem, that is, of Cananei, of Ethei, and of Pheresei, and of Jebusei, and of Amonyts and of Moabitis, and of Egipcians, and of^k Ammorreis For thei 2 han take 'of her douȝtris^m wyues to hem silf, and to her sones, and thei han medlid hoohⁿ seed with the puplis of londis^o, also^p the hond^q of princes^r and of magistratis^s was the^t firste in this trespassyng And 3 whanne Y^u hadde herd this word, Y torente my mentil and coote^v, and Y pullide awei the heeris of myn heed and berd^w, and Y sat morenynge Forsothe^x alle that 4 dredden the word of God of Israel camen togidere to me, for the trespassyng of hem that weren comun fro caitifte^z, and Y sat sori 'til to^a the sacrifice of euentid And in 5 the sacrifice of euentid Y roos^b fro myn afflicioun, and aftir that Y to-rente^c the^d mentil and coote^e, Y^f bowide my knees, and I^g spredde abrood myn hondis to 'my Lord God^h, and Y seide, My God, Y am 6 confoundid and aschamed to reiseⁱ my face to thee, for oure^k wickidnessis ben multiplied 'on myn heed^l, and oure trespassis encreessiden^m 'til toⁿ heuene, fro the daies 7 of oure fadris^o; but^p also we vs^q silf han synned greuoush 'til to^r this dai, and for our wickidnessis we, and oure kyngis, and oure prestis ben bitakun in^s the hondis of kyngis of londis^t, bothe in to swerd, and in to caitifte, in to raueyn, and in to schenship of cheer, as also in this dai^u

^e domynaciouns E pr m   ^f Om c   ^g knit A   ^h wickidnes A   ⁱ vp c   ^k a c

^d And INS   ^e fulfillid INS   ^f me, Esdras I me that is, to Esdras B   ^g peple and ritis of othere N peple and ritis and othere S   ^h ne INS   ⁱ the abhomynaciouns INS   ^k Om A   ^l of the douȝtris of thes peplis thei INS   ^m Om INS   ⁿ her hooh NS   ^o hethen londis INS   ^p and INS   ^q hond or the doyng S ^r the pryncis NS   ^s maistir men INS   ^t Om NS   ^u Y, Esdras S   ^v my coote INS   ^w of my beerd INS ^x Certis INS   ^y thei that NS   ^z the caitifte INS   ^a vnto IN on to S til X   ^b roos up INS   ^c hadde to-rente INS   ^d my INS   ^e mi coote INS   ^f and A   ^g Om A   ^h the Lord mi God INS   ⁱ reise up IN ^k upon myn heed or ouer myn vnderstondyng oure IS upon myn heed oure N   ^l Om INS   ^m han encressid INS   ⁿ vnto IN in to S   ^o fadris hidere to IS.   ^p and INS   ^q oure NS   ^r vnto INS to T ^s in to INS   ^t hethen londis INS   ^u dai is schenvid IS

and at a moment is don oure preȝere
anent the Lord our God, that the rem-
nauntus ben forȝiue[l] to vs, and the pes of
hyȝn be ȝiuen in his holi place, and oure
God liȝte oure eȝen, and ȝiue to vs a litil
9 lif in oure seruise. For seruauns wee ben,
and in oure oure seruise our God forsoc not
vs; and he bowide in vpon vs mercy befor the king of Persis, that he[m] ȝeue to
vs lijf, and rere the hous of oure God,
and make out the wildernessis[n] of it, and
ȝeue to vs hope in Juda and in[o] Jerusa-
10 lem. And now what shul wee sein, Lord
oure God, after these thingus? For wee
11 han forsake thin hestus, that thou hast
comaundid in the hond of thi seruauns
prophetis, seiende, The lond, to the
whiche ȝee shul gon out, that ȝee welden
it, is a lond vnclene, after the vnclenesse
of puplis, and of othere londis, the whiche
fulfilden it with the[p] abhomynaciouns of
hem, fro mouth vnto mouth in ther de-
12 fouling. Now thanne ȝoure doȝtris ne
ȝiue ȝe to the sonus of hem, and the doȝtris of hem taketh not to ȝour sonus; and
seketh not pes of hem and prosperite of
hem vnto euermor; that ȝee be coumfortid, and eten that ben goode thingus
of the lond, and eiris ȝee haue ȝoure
13 sonus vnto the world. And after alle
thingus that camen vpon vs in oure
werste werkis, and in oure grete gilte,
for thou, oure God, deliueredist vs fro
oure wickenesse, and ȝeue to vs helthe,
14 as is to dai, that we be not turned, and
make thin hestis in vein, ne bi matrimoyne we ben joyned with the puplis
of these abhomynaciouns. Whether thou
art wroth to vs vnto the ending, lest thou
15 leue to vs relikis and helthe? Lord God

And now as at a litil[v] and at a moment[s]
oure preier is maad anentis 'oure Lord
God[w], that relikis[x] schulden be left to vs,
and that 'his pees[y]† schulde[z] be ȝouun in
his hooli place, and that oure God schulde[a]
liȝtne oure iȝen, and ȝyue to vs a litil lijf
in oure seruage. For we ben seruauntis, 9
and oure God forsoke vs not in oure seruage[b]; and he bowide[c] merci[d] on[e] vs bifor
the king of Persis, that he schulde ȝyue
lijf to vs, and enhaunse the hows of oure
God, and that he schulde bilde the wil-
dernessis‡ therof[f], and ȝyue to vs hope[g]
in Juda and in Jerusalem. And now, 10
'oure Lord God[h], what schulen we seie
after these thingis? For[i] we han forsake
thi comaundementis[k], whiche thou co- 11
maundidist in the hond of thi seruauntis
profetis, and seidist[l], The lond, to[m] which
ȝe schulen entre, to holde it in possessioun,
is an vnclene lond, bi the vnclennesse of
puplis, and of othere[n] londis[o], in the abhomynaciouns of hem, that filliden[p] it with
her defoulyng, fro the mouth[q] 'til to[r] the
mouth[s]. Now therfor[t] ȝiue ȝe not ȝoure 12
douȝtris to her sones, and[u] take ȝe not her
douȝtris to ȝoure sones; and[v] seke ȝe not
the pees of hem and[w] the[x] prosperite 'of
hem[y] 'til in to[z] with outen ende; that ȝe
be coumfortid, and ete the goodis[a], that
ben of the lond[b], and that ȝe haue eiris[c],
ȝoure sones[d], 'til in to[e] 'the world[f]. And 13
after alle thingis[g] that camen on[h] vs in
oure werste werkis, and in[i] oure grete
trespas, for[k] thou, oure God, hast delyuered vs fro oure wickidnesse, and hast[l]
ȝoue helthe to vs, as 'it is[m] to[n] dai, that 14
we schulden not be turned[o], and make
voide thi comaundementis[p], and[q] that we
schulden not ioyne matrimonyes with the

† Pees; in
summe bokis
is a litil stake,
that is sum set-
ting and stable-
nesse in Jeru-
salem. Lire
here. c.

‡ wildirnesses;
that is, the
temple turned
in to wildir-
nesse. c.

l forsakyn A.　m ȝe A.　n wildirnes A.　o Om. c.　p Om. A.

v litil tyme is.　w the Lord oure God INS.　x relikis, that is, a fewe men c. marg. relikis, or remenauntis I.
relifs N. relikis, that is, after cummers s.　y pees of the Lord INS.　z Om. INS.　a Om. INS.　b thraldom I.
seruage or caitifte s.　c bowide doun INS.　d his merci s.　e upon INS.　f therof or the desolat things
therof s.　g hope or merci s.　h Lord oure God NS.　i Sotheli NS.　k hecstis NS.　l thou seidist NS.
m Om. s.　n othere hethen IS.　o londis it is defoulid INS.　p han fulfillid INS.　q mouth of fadris INS.
r vnto INS.　s mouth of her sones INS.　t therfor ȝe Jewis IS.　u ne INS.　v ne INS.　w ne INS.　x her INS.
y Om. INS.　z vnto I.　a gode thingis INS.　b erthe INS.　c Om. INS.　d sones ȝoure ciris INS.　e vnto I.
in to x.　f withouten ende INS.　g disesis IS.　h upon INS.　i Om. INS.　k Om. INS.　l thou hast INS.
m Om. N.　n schewid to IS.　o turned awei I. turned awey fro thee N.　p hestis INS.　q Om. N.

of Irael, riȝtwis thou art, for wee ben forsaken, the whiche shulden ben saaf as bi this dai, lo! befor thee we ben in oure gilte; forsothe it mai not ben stonden befor thee vpon this

puplis of these abhomynacouns Whether^r thou art wrooth to vs 'til to^s the^t endyng, that thou schuldist not leeue to us reme- nauntis^u†, and^v helthe? Lord God of Is-15 rael, thou art iust, for we ben left, that schulden be sauyd as in this day^w, lo! we ben bifor thee in oure synne, for^x me^y may 'not^z stonde^a bifor thee on^b this‡ thing^c

† remenauntis, that is, a fewe men c

‡ on this, that is, to excuse ether defende I ire here c.

CAP. X

1 So thanne Esdre preȝende, and besech- ende God, and wepende, and liende befor the temple of God, ther is gedered to hym a ful myche cumpanye gret of men, aud of wymmen, and childer, and the 2 puple wepte with myche weping And Sechenyas, the sone of Jaiel, of the sonus of Elam, answerde, and seide to Esdre, Wee han trespasid in oure God, and wee han weddid aliene wiues of the puplis of the lond And now, for ther is penaunce 3 in Irael vpon this, smyte wee couenaunt of pes with the Lord oure God, and throwe awei alle oure wiues, and hem that of hem ben born, after the wil of the Lord, and of hem that dreden the maundement of oure God, after the lawe 4 be it don. Ris, thin it is to demen, and wee shul be with thee, tac coumfort, 5 and do Thanne Esdras ros, and ad- iurede the princis of prestus, and of Le- uitus, and al Irael, that thei shulden do 6 after this woord; and thei sworen And Esdras ros befor the hous of God, and wente awei to the bed place of Johannan, sone of Eliasif, and he wente in thider; bred he eet not, and water he dranc not; forsothe he weilede the trespasing of hem, 7 that fro the caitife weren comen And ther is sent a vois in Juda and Jerusa- lem, to alle the sonus of transmygracioun,

CAP. X.

Therfor while Esdras preiede so, and 1 bisouȝte God^d, and wepte, and lai bifor the temple of God, a ful greet cumpenye of Israel, of men, and of wymmen, and of children, was gaderid^e to him, and the puple wepte bi^f myche weping And Se- 2 chenye§, the sone of Jehiel, of the sones of Helam, answerde, and seide to Esdras, We han^g trespasside aȝens oure God, and^h han^i weddid wyues, alien wymmen, of 'the puplis of^k the lond^l And now, for pe- naunce^m is in Israel on this thing, smyte^n 3 we boond of pees with 'oure Lord God^o, and caste we awei alle 'wyues aliens^p, and hem that ben borun of tho wyues^q, bi^r the wille of the Lord, and of hem that dreden the comaundement^s of oure God,'be it don bi the lawe^t Rise thou^u, it 'is thin^y office^w 4 to deme^x, and we schulen be with thee; be thou coumfortid, and do^v Therfor^z 5 Esdras roos^a, and chargide^b greeth the princes of prestis, and of^c dekenes, and of^d al Israel, to do after this word; and thei sworen^e And Esdras roos^f bifor the 6 hows of God, and he ȝede to the bed of Johannan, sone^g of Eliasiph, and entride^h thidur, he eet not^i breed, and^k drank not^l watir, for^m he biweilide^n the trespassing^o of hem, that weren comun fro the caitife And a vois of hem was sent in to Juda 7 and Jerusalem, to alle the sones of trans-

§ Sechenye, he was of the princypalis of the puple, and seide this in the name of him silf, and of othere prin- cipals I ire here c

r Lord, whether is.   s vnto ins into x   t Om 1   u the remenauntis of thi peple 1   remenauntis of thi peple 8   v to ins   w day thou schewist 18   x sothly ins   y no thing ins   men hx   z Om ins
a be sett ins   b upon 18   c ground ins   d God for the peple 18   e gaderid togidre ins   f with 1
g haue 1   h and we ins   i haue 1   k Om ins   l lond of hethen peplis ins   m penaunce or ponishing 8
n make ins   o the Lord oure God ins   p oure alien wyues ins   q wyues, and ns   r be this don bi the lawe, bi ins   s heest ins.   t Om ins   u thou up ins   v perteyneth to thee i   w Om plures   x deme this thing ns   y do thus 18   z Thanne 1   a roos np ins   b he chargide ins   c Om x   d Om EFHI KLMNPb   e sworen herto 18   f roos up ins   g the sone ns   h he entride ins   i not in this tyme 8.
k ne ins   l Om ins   m certis ins   n weilide ins   o trispacis 8

that thei shulden be gedered in to Jeru-
8 salem ; and alle that cometh not in thre
daȝis, aftir the counseil of the princis and
of the elders, al his substaunce shal be
taken awei, and he shal be cast awei
fro the cumpanye of transmygracioun.
9 Thanne alle the men of Juda and of
Beniamyn camyn togidre in Jerusalem
thre daȝes ; it is the nynthe monyth, in
the twentithe dai of the monyth ; and al
the puple sat in the strete of the hous of
God, tremblende for synne and reynes.
10 And Esdras, the prest, ros, and seide
to hem, ȝee han trespasid, and wedded
aliene wiues, that ȝee adden vp on the
11 gilte of Irael. And now ȝiueth confessioun to the Lord God of oure fadris,
and doth the plesaunce of hym, and beth
seuered fro the puplis of the lond, and
12 fro alien wiues. And al the multitude
answerde, and seide with a gret vois,
13 After thi woord to vs, so be it do. Nerthelatere for the puple is myche, and
the time of rein, and we sustene not to
stonde with oute forth, and it is not
the werc of o dai, or of two ; forsothe
hidousli we han synned in this woord ;
14 be ther sett princis in al the multitude,
and alle in oure cites, that han wedded
aliene wiues, come thei in the time set,
and with hem the elders, bi cite and cite,
and the domesmen of it, to the time that
the wrathe of oure God be turned awei
15 fro vs vpon this synne. Thanne Jonathan, the sone of Azahel, and Jasia, the
. sone of Thechue, stoden vpon this ; and
Mosollam, and Sebethai, Leuitus, holpen
16 hem. And so diden the sonus of trans-
mygracoun. And Esdras, prest, and the
men, princis of the meynes, wenten awei
in to the housis of ther fadris, and alle

mygracioun[p], that thei schulden be gaderid[q] in to[r] Jerusalem ; and ech man 8
that cometh not[s] in thre daies, bi the[t]
counsel of the[u] princes and of eldre men,
al his catel schal be takun awey fro him,
and he schal be cast awei fro the cumpeny of transmygracioun. Therfor alle 9
the men of Juda and of Beniamyn camen
togidere in to Jerusalem in thre daies ;
thilke is the nynthe monethe, in the twentithe dai of the monethe ; and al the puple sat in the street[v] of Goddis hows, and
trembliden[w] for synne and reyn[x]. And 10
Esdras, the preest, roos[y], and seide to hem,
ȝe han trespassid, and han[z] weddid wyues,
alien wymmen, that ȝe[a] schulden leie to[b]
on[c] the trespas of Israel. And[d] now[e] ȝyue 11
ȝe knowlechyng to the Lord God[f] of oure
fadris, and do ȝe his pleasaunce, and be ȝe
departid fro the puplis of the lond[g], and
fro wynes aliens[h]. And al the multitude 12
answeride, and seide with greet vois, Bi[i]
thi word to[k] vs[l], so[m] be it doon. Netheles 13
for[n] the puple[o] is myche, and the tyme of
reyn[p] is[q], and we suffren[r] not to stonde
withoutforth, and it[s] is not werk[t] of o
dai, nether of tweyne ; for we han synned
greetli in this word[u] ; princes be[v] or-14
deyned in al the multitude[w], and alle men
in oure citees, that han weddid wyues
aliens[x], come[y] in[z] tymes[a] ordeyned, and
with hem come the eldere men, bi citee
and citee, and the iugis therof[b], til the
ire[c] of oure God be turned awei fro vs
on[d] this synne. Therfor Jonathan, the 15
sone of Asahel, and Jaazie, the sone of
Thecue, stoden on[e] this thing ; and Mosollam, and Sebethai, dekenes, helpiden
hem. And the sones of transmygracioun 16
diden so[f]. And Esdras, the prest, and
men[g], princes[h] of meynees, ȝeden into the

P caitiftee 1NS.   q gaderid togidre 1NS.   r Om. N.   s not thidere 1s.   t Om. 1NS.   u Om. CGINQS.
v a large place 1NS.   w thei trembliden 1NS.   x for reyn that thanne felle 1s. for reyn N.   y roos up 1NS.
z ȝe han 1NS.   a thei A pr. m.   b leie to or encresse 1s.   c upon 1NS.   d Om. s.   e now therfore 1s.
f Om. 1.   g hethen 1NS.   h ȝoure alien wyues 1s. alien wyues N.   i Aftir 1. Be N.   k seid to 1. word to N8.
l us stidefast N. vs ferm and stable s.   m and so NS.   n for that 1. for that that s.   o multitude 1xs.
P reyn now 1NS.   q is gret 1NS.   r susteinen 1. sufficen N8.   s this 1NS.   t the werk 1NS.   u word that
thou schewist to us 1s.   v be therfor princes 1s.   w multitude to iustifie this synne 1s.   x alien wyues 1N.
y come thei 1NS.   z to here princis in 1s.   a tyme 1NS.   b of the peple do thei iust execucioun 1s.
of the peple N.   c wrath 1NS.   d of 1. upon NS.   c upon 1NS.   f so as it was ordeyned 1s.   g the men 1N.
h that weren princes 1NS.

bi ther namys; and thei seten in the
firste dai of the tenthe monith, that thei
17 enserche the thing   And alle the men
that hadden weddid alien wiues ben
endid, vn to the firste dai of the firste
18 moneth   And ther ben founden of the
sonus of prestus, that weddeden hethene
wiues, of the sonus of Josue, the sones
of ꝙ Josedech, and the brethern of hym,
Maasia, and Eliezer, and Jarib, and Go-
19 dolia   And thei ʒeuen ther hondis, that
thei shulden casten awei thei wiues,
and for ther gilte thei shulden offren a
20 wether of the shep   And of the sonus
21 of Semmer; Anam and Sebedia. And of
the sonus of Seerim; Maazia, and Helia,
22 and Semeia, and Jehiel, and Osias   And
of the sonus of Fessui; Helioenai, Maazia, Hismael, Nathanael, and Josabeth,
23 and Elasa   And of the sones of Leuitus, Josabeth, and Semei, and Eliaia;
he is Calithafathaia, Juda, and Elieser
24 And of the singeris, Eliazub; and of the
porteris, Sellum, and Thellem, and Vri
25 And of Irael, of the sonus of Faros; Remea, and Ezia, and Melchia, and Bua-
nym, and Eliezer, and Melchia, and
26 Banya   And of the sonus of Elam, Mathanya, and Zacharias, and Jehil, and
27 Abdi, and Rimoth, and Helia   And of
the sonus of Secua, Heheonai, Heliazub,
Mathanya, and Jerymuth, and Saeth,
28 and Aziza   And of the sonus of Bebai,
29 Johannan, Ananya, Zabbai, Athalia   And
of the sonys of Beny; Mosollam, and Melue, and ꭨ Azaia, Jasub, and Saal, and Ja-
30 moth   And of the sonus of Faeth; Moab,
Edua, and Calal, Banaias, and Massias,
Mathanyas, Beseleel, and Bemym, and
31 Manasse   And of the sonus of Erem;
Elieer, Jesue, Melchias, Semeias, Symeon,
32
33 Beniamyn, Maloth, Samarias   And of
the sonus of Asom, Mathanai, Mathetha,

howsis¹ of hei fadris, and alle ᵏ men¹ bi
hei names, and thei saten in the firste dai
of the tenthe monethe, for to seke ᵐ the
thing ⁿ   And alle men weren endid ᵒ, that 17
hadden weddid ʻwyues aliens ᵖ, ʻtil to ꝙ the
firste dai of the firste monethe   And there 18
weren foundun of the sones of preestis,
that weddiden ʳ ʻwyues aliens ᵃ; of the sones
of Josue, the sone of Josedech, and hise
britheren, Maasie, and Eliezer, and Jarib,
and Godolie ᵗ   And thei ʒauen her hondis ᵘ†, 19
that thei schulden caste out hei wyues,
and offre ᵛ for her trespas a ram of the ˣ
scheep   And of the sones of Semmer, 20
Anam, and Zebedie   And of the sones of 21
Serym; Maasie, and Helie, and Semeie,
and Jehiel, and Ozie   And of the sones of 22
Phessur; Helioneai Maasie, Hismael, Nathanael, and Jozabet, and Elasa   And of 23
the sones of dekenes, Josabeth, and Semey,
and Elaie, he is ˣ Calithaphataie, Juda,
and Elezei   And of syngeris, Eliazub; 24
and of porteris, Sellum, and Thellem, and
Vry   And of ʸ Israel, of the sones of Pha- 25
ros, Remea, and Ezia, and Melchia, and
Vnanym, and Eliezer, and Melchia, and
Banea   And of the sones of Elam; Ma- 26
thanye, and Zacharie, and Jehil, and Abdi,
and Rymoth, and Helia   And of the sones 27
of Zechua, Helioneay, Heliasib, Mathanye,
and Jerymuth, and Zaeth, and Aziza   And 28
of the sones of Bebai, Johannan, Ananye,
Zabbai, Athalia ᶻ   And of the sones of Beny; 29
Mosallam, and Melue, and Azaie, Jasub ᵃ,
and Saal, and Ramoth   And of the sones 30
of Phaeth; Moab, Edua, and Calal, Banaie,
and Massie, Mathanye, Beseleel, and Ben-
nun, and Manasse   And of the sones of 31
Erem; Elieer, Jesue, Melchie, Semeye, Symeon, Beniamyn, Maloth, Samarie ᵇ   And ¹²
of the sones of Asom, Mathanai, Mathe- ₄₃
tha, Zabeth, Eliphelech, Jermai, Manasse,
Semei ᶜ. Of the sones of Bany, Maddi, 34

(marginal note, right side): † her hondis; that is, con fermeden with a solempne ooth Lire here c.

ꝙ Om c   ꭨ Om ᴀ

¹ hous ᴋ   ᵏ alle the eldre is   ˡ men and iugis is Om ᴋ   ᵐ enquere ins   ⁿ thing that was amysse s
ᵒ that is, here causis weren determyned ɪ marg endid, that [is], the caucis of alle men weren determyned s
ᵖ alien wyues ɪᴀs   ꝙ vnto ins   ʳ hadden wedded ins   ᵃ alien wyues ins   ᵗ Godolie weren foundun ɪ
Godolie weren foundun gilt s   ᵘ hondis, that is, thei assuriden is   ᵛ thei schulden offre ɪ shulden
offre ᴋ that thei shulden offre s   ʷ Om ins   ˣ is clepid is   ʸ of the men of ᴀs   ᶻ and Thalia ins
ᵃ and Jasub ɪᴠs   ᵇ and Samarie ɪᴠs   ᶜ and Semei ɪᴠ s

Zabeth, Elifelech, Jermai, Manasse, Se-
34 mei. And of h sonus of Bany; Maddi,
35 Amram, and Huel, Baneas, and Badaias,
36 Cheilian, Bianna, Marimuth, and Elia-
$^{37}_{38}$ sif, Mathanyas, Mathanay, and Jasi, and
39 Lany, and Bennan, and Semei, and Sal-
40 myes, and Nathan, and Daias, Mesuede-
41 bai, Susai, Sarai, Esriel, and^t Seloman,
$^{42}_{43}$ Semeria, Sellum, Amaria, Joseph. Of the
sonus of Nebny; Aiel, Mathathias, Zabed,
44 Zabina, Jebdu, and Joel, Banai. Alle
these hadden taken hethene wiues, and
ther weren of these wymmen, that hadden born souys.

*Explicit liber primus. Incipit liber
secundus*^{u}.

Amram, and Huel, Baneas, and Badaie, 35
Cheilian^d, Biamna, Marymuth, and Elia- 36
sipb, Mathanye^e, and Jasy, and Bany, and $^{37}_{38}$
Bennan, and Semei, and Salymas, and Na- 39
than, and Daias, Metuedabai, Sisai, Sarai, 40
Ezrel, and Seloman, Semerie, Sellum, Ama- $^{41}_{42}$
rie, Joseph^f. Of the sones of Nebny; Aiel, 43
Mathatie, Zabed, Zabina, Jebdu, and^g Johel, Banai^h. Alle these hadden take 'wyues 44
aliens^i, and of hem weren wymmen, that
hadden bore children.

*Here eendith the firste book of Esdras,
and here bigynneth the secound book*^{k}.

---

^{t} Om. *AH*. ^{u} *Here eendith the first book of Esdre, and nom begynneth the secounde.* A. *Explicit liber
Esdre primus, incipit secundus.* E. *Here endith Esdre the first, and now bygyneth Esdre the secounde.* F.
No final rubric in *H*.

^{d} and Cheilian c. ^{e} Mathanye, and Mathanay BC. Mathanye, Mathanay v. ^{f} and Joseph IN. ^{g} Om. INS.
^{h} and Banai INS. ^{i} alien wyues IN. alien *or hethen* wiues s. ^{k} From BDFOUW. *Here endith the firste
book of Esdras, and bigynneth a prologe on the ij. book.* GM. *Here endeth the firste book of Esdre, and
here bigynneth the ij. book of Esdre.* HX. *Heere endith the firste book of Esdras, and the secounde biginnith.* I.
Heere eendeth the firste book of Esdre; see now the seconde book of Esdre or Neemye. K. *Here endith the
firste book of Esdras, and bigynneth the secunde.* NRSV. *Here endith the firste book of Esdre, and bigynneth
the secunde book.* Qb. No final rubric in ACELP.

II. ESDRAS.

[*Prologue on the Second book of Esdras*ᵃ.]

Iɴ this secounde book of Esdre is contened the actis of Neemye, duyk and gouernour of the peple of Juda, which made aȝen the wallis and ȝatis of Jerusalem, and the hous of the Lord, and heeld smal houshold, and oppiesside not the peple, but dredde God, and kepte hise comaundementis, in so myche that he suffiide not the peple to bringe yn burthuns in to the cite neither ledinge out, in the dai of sabat; therfor he wiouȝte alle thingis with prosperite, and God was with him.

The second book of Esdrasᵃ	Here bigynneth the secounde book of Esdreᵇ.
CAP I	**CAP. I**

1 THE woordis of Neemye, sone of Elchie And it is do in the monith of December, the twentithe ȝer, and I was 2 in the burȝ toun of Susis; and thei cam to me Annam, oon of my brethern, he and the men of Juda; and I askide hem of Jewisᵇ, that abiden stille, and laften ouei of the caitifte, and of Jerusalem 3 And thei seiden to me, Thei that abiden stille, and ben laft of the caitifte there in the prouynce, ben in gret affliccioun, and in repref, and the wal of Jerusalem is scatered, and his ȝatis ben brendᶜ with 4 fiȝr And whan I hadde herd such maner woordis, I sat and wepte, and weilide manye daȝes, and fastide, and preȝede be-5 for the face of God of heuene , and seide, I beseche, Lord God of heuene, strong,

THEᶜ wordis of Neemye, the sone of 1 Helchie And it was doon in the monetheᵈ Casleuᵉ, in the twentitheᶠ ȝeer, and Y was in the castel Susisᵍ; and Ananye, oon of 2 my britheren, cam to me, he and men of Juda , and Y axide hem of the Jewis, that weren left, and weren alyue of the caitifte, and of Jerusalem And thei seiden to me, 3 Thei that 'dwelliden, andʰ ben left of the caitifteⁱ thereᵏ inˡ the prouynce, ben in greet turment, and inᵐ schenship; and the walⁿ of Jerusalem is destried, and the ȝatis therofᵒ ben brent with fier And whanne 4 Y hadde heid siche wordis, Y sat and wepteᵖ, and morenedeᑫ many daies, and Y fastide, and pieiedeʳ bifor the face of God of heuene , and Y seide, Y biseches, 5 Lord God of heuene, strongᵗ, greet, and

---

ᵃ No initial rubric in the Mss but in c, *Neemye*, as a running title   ᵇ the Jewis *AII*   ᶜ brend vp *AC*

ᵃ This prologue is from ᴍ   ᵇ *Here endith the prologe, and bigynneth the secunde book of Esdras* ᴌ *Here bigynneth the ii book of Esdras, that is clepid Neeme* ᴌᴘ No initial rubric in ꜰɪɪɪɴᴏsᴠxʙ   ᶜ *These ben the* ɪs   ᵈ monethe of ɪɴs   ᵉ *that is, Nouembre* ɪ *marg* s *text*   ᶠ twenti ɴ   ᵍ of Susis ɪɴs   ʰ Om ɪɴs   ⁱ caitifte, and that dwelleden ɪɴs   ᵏ Om ɴ   ˡ stille in ɪɴs   ᵐ Om s   ⁿ wallis s   ᵒ of it ɪɴs   ᵖ I wepte ɪɴs   ᑫ I morenede *herfore* ɪɴs   ʳ I preiede ɪɴs   s biseche *thee* ɴs   ᵗ *that art* strong ɪɴs

gret, and ferful, that^d kepist couenaunt
and merci with hem, that loouen thee,
6 and kepen thi maundemens; be thi ere
maad herknende, and thi eȝen opeued,
that thou here the orisoun of thi seruaunt, in the whiche I preyȝe befor^e thee
to dai, nyȝt and dai, for the sonys of
Irael, thi seruauns, and I knowleche for
the synnes of the sones of Irael, in the
whiche thei synneden to thee; and I and
7 the hous of my fader han synned; bi
vanyte wee ben born doun, and wee han
not kept the heste, and cerimoines, and
domus, that thou comaundedest^f to Moises,
8 thi seruaunt. Haue mynde of the^g woord,
that thou comaundedest^f to thi seruaunt,
seiende, Whan ȝee han trespasid, I shal
9 scatere ȝou in to puplis; and if ȝee be
turned aȝeen to me, that ȝee kepe myn
hestus, and don hem, also if ȝee weren
lad awei to the endis of heuene, thennus
I shal gadere ȝou togidere, and leden in
to the place, that I ches, that my name
10 dwelle there. And wee^h thi seruauns,
and thi puple, whom thou hast boȝt in
thi grete strengthe, and in thi stronge
11 hond. I beseche, Lord, be thin ere takende heede to the orisoun of thi seruaunt,
and to the orisoun of thi seruauns, that
wiln dreden thi name; and dresse thi
seruaunt to dai, and ȝif to hym merci
befor this man. I forsothe was theⁱ
booteler of the king.

CAP. II.

1 It is do forsothe in the monith of
Aprill, the twentithe ȝer of Artaxerses,
the^k king, and win was befor hym, and
I heuede vp the win, and ȝaf to the king,
2 and I was astoneid beform his face. And
the king seide to me, Whi is thi chere
dreri, sithen I see thee not sijk? That is

ferdful, which^u kepist couenaunt and merci
with hem, that louen thee, and kepen thin
heestis; thin eere be maad herknynge^v, 6
and thin iȝen openyd^w, that thou here the
preier of thi seruaunt, bi^x which^y Y preie
bifor thee `to dai^z, bi^a nyȝt and dai^b, for the
sones of Israel, thi seruauntis, and ꞌY knou-
leche^c for the synnes of the sones of Israel,
bi which thei han synned to thee; bothe^d
Y and the hows of my fadir han synned^e;
we weren disscyued bi vanyte, and we 7
ꞌkepten not^f ꞌthi comaundement^g, and cerymonyes, and domes, which thou comaund-
idist^h to Moises, thi seruaunt. Haue mynde 8
of the word, which thou comaundidist to
thi seruaunt Moises, and seidist, Whanne
ȝe han trespassid, Y schal scatere ȝou
in to puplis; and if ȝe turnen aȝen to 9
me, that ȝe kepe myn heestis, and do tho,
ȝhe, thouȝ ȝe ben led awei to the fertheste
thingis of heuene, fro thennus Y schal gadere ȝou togidere, and Y schal brynge ȝou
in to the place, whichⁱ Y chees^k, that my
name schulde dwelle there. And^l we ben 10
thi seruauntis, and thi puple, whiche thou
ꞌaȝen bouȝtist^m in thi greet strengthe, and
in thi strong hond. Lord, Y bisecheⁿ, 11
ꞌthin eere be^o ententif^p to the preier of
thi seruaunt, and to the preier^q of thi
seruauntis, that wolen drede thi name;
and dresse^r thi seruaunt to dai, and ȝiue
thou^s merci to him^t bifor this man^u†. For^v
Y was the boteler of the kyng.

CAP. II.

Forsothe^w it was doon in the monethe 1
Nysan^x†, in the twentithe ȝeer of Artaxerses, kyng^y, and wyn was bifor hym, and
Y reyside^z the wyn, and ȝaf^a to the kyng,
and Y was as langwischynge bifor his face.
And the kyng seide to me, Whi is thi 2
cheer sory^b, sithen^c Y se not thee sijk?

† this man;
that is, Artax-
erses, king.
Lire here. c.
‡ Nysan; the
comyn opyn-
youn of Jewes
is this, that
the world was
maad of nouȝt
in the monethe
which is clepid
Tissery, and it
answerith in
party to oure
Septembre, and
in party to
Octobre; and
this monethe
is seid ouirly
the firste anen-
tis Ebreys, and
by maner of
rekenyng
Casleu is the
thirde monethe,
and Nysan in
the vii. mo-
nethe, and
these fallen in
the same ȝeer,
and thus is
rekenyng maad
here; but for
the Jewis ȝeden
out of Egipt in
the monethe
Nysan, therfor
thilke monethe
is clepid the
firste, in xii. c°,
of Exody, and
in rikenynge
in this maner,
Casleu and Ny-
san suynge, ben
not in the same
ȝeer, but Cas-
leu is the ix.
monethe of the
ȝeer bifor-
goynge, and
Nysan suynge
is the bigyn-
nyng of the
ȝeer suynge.
Lire here. c.

d the which A H. e to A. f comanndist A II. g thi A. h we ben A. i Om. c. k Om. c.

u that INS. v herkenyng to me s. w be openyd N. x with I. y the which I. which preier s.
x Om. INS. a now bi INS. b bi dai I. c Om. INS. d I knowleche that bothe INS. e synned to thee IS.
f haue not kept INS. g thin heest IN. thin heestis s. h hast comanndid INS. i that IN. k haue
chosen INS. l And, Lord, I. Lord, s. m hast aȝen bouȝt INS. n biseche thee IS. o be thin eere INS.
p takynge hede INS. q preiers s. r dresse thou IN. dresse thou me s. s Om. INS. t him, that is, to me s.
u man Artaxerses INS. v Certis INS. w And INS. x of Nysan, that is, Aprel INS. y the kyng I.
z toke vp INS. a I ȝaf it INS. b drury or heuy I. drery NS. c sith I.

not in vein , but I wot not the euel that
is in thin herte And I dradde ful myche ;
3 and I seide to the king, King, with outen
ende liue , whi shulde not my chere so-
rew in priueli ? for the cite of the hous of
the sepulcris of my fader¹ is desert, and
4 his ȝatus ben brent with fiir And the
king seith to me, For what thing askist
thou? And I preȝede the God of heuene,
5 and seide to the king, If it is seen good
to the king, and if it plese to thi seruauns befor thi face, that thou sende me
in to Jude, I beseche, to the cite of the
sepulcre of my fader, and I shal bilden
6 it. And the king seide to me and the
quen that sat biside hym, Vnto what
time shal be thi wei, and 'whanne shaltᵐ
thou come aȝeen? And I pleside befor
the chere of the king, and he sente me,
7 and I sette hym a time ; and seide to the
king, If to the king it is seen good, lettris
ȝiue he to me to the dukis of the regioun
beȝonde the flod, that thei lede me ouer,
8 to the time Iⁿ come in to Jude, and a
lettre to Asaf, kepere of the wilde wode
of the king, that he ȝiue to me trees, that
I mowe couere the ȝatis of the tour of
the hous, and of the wal of the cite, and
the hous that I shal come in And the
king ȝaf to me, after the goode hond of
9 my God with me And I cam to the
dukis of the regioun beȝunde the flod,
and I ȝaf to hym the epistolis of the
king Forsothe the king hadde sent with
10 me prinsis of kniȝtus, and horsemen And
Sanaballath Oronyte, and Tobie, seruaunt Amonyte, herden, and ben euele
paȝid bi gret sorewe, that a man was
come, that shulde seche the prosperite of
11 the sonus of Irael And I cam in to Jerusalem, and Iᵒ was there thre daȝes

Thisᵈ is not without cause , but 'yuel, Y
not whatᵉ, is in thin herte And'ᶠ Y dredde
3 ful greetli ; and seideᵍ to the kyng, Kyng,
lyue thou withouten ende : whi morenethʰ
not' my cheerᵏ ? for the citee of the hows
of the sepulcris of my fadir is desert,
'ether forsakun¹, and the ȝatis therof ben
4 brent with fier And the kyng seide to
me, Foi what thing axist thou ? And Y
preiede God of heuene, and seideᵐ to the
5 kyng, If it semeth good to the kyng, and
if it plesith thi seruauntis biforⁿ thi face,
Y bischeᵒ, that thou sende me in to Judee,
to the citee of the sepulcre of my fadir,
6 and Y schal bilde it. And the kyng seide
to me, and the queen† sat bisidis hun,
'Til toᵖ what tyme schal thi weie be, and
whanne schalt thou turne aȝen ? And Yᵠ
pleside 'bifor the cheer ofʳ the kyng, and
he sente meˢ, and Y ordeynedeᵗ to hymᵘ a
7 timeᵛ, and Y seide to 'the kyngʷ, If it
semeth good to the kyng, ȝyue he pistlisˣ
to me to the duykis of the cuntrey biȝende
the flood, that thei lede me ouer, til Y
8 come in to Judee , 'and a pistleʸ to Asaph,
kepereᶻ of the kyngis forest, that he ȝyue
trees to me, that Y may hile the ȝatis of
the tour of the hows, and of the wal of
the citee, and the hows, into which Y
schal entre‡ And 'the kyng ȝaf to meᵃ,
bi the good hondᵇ of my God withᶜ meᵈ
9 And Y cam to the duykis of the cuntrei
biȝende the flood, and Y ȝaf to hem the
pistlisᵉ of the kyng Sotheliᶠ the kyng
'hadde sentᵍ with me theʰ princes of
10 knyȝtis', and horsemen And Sanaballath Oronythes, and Tobie, the seruaunt
Amanytesᵏ, herden¹, and thei weren soreuful bi greet turmentᵐ, forⁿ a man was
comun, that souȝte prosperite of the sones
11 of Israel And Y cam in to Jerusalem,

† quene, thus it is in Ebreu, and bi this the king, and not queen, spak to Neemye this that sieth Lire here c

‡ entre, that is, the hows which Y purpose to bilde for my dwelling place Lire here c

¹ fadris ᴀ ᵐ what wolt ᴀ ⁿ that I ᴀн. ᵒ Om ᴀ

ᵈ It 1 This dreriuesse s ᵉ I woot not what yuel ɪɴs ᶠ And thanne 1 ᵍ I seide ɪɴs ʰ Om ɪɴs.
ⁱ schulde not ɪɴs ᵏ cheer moarne ɪɴs ¹ Om cɪɴs ᵐ I seide ɪɴs ⁿ which ben bifore s ᵒ biseche
thee s ᵖ Vnto ɪɴs Til x ᵠ it ɪɴ ʳ to ɴs ˢ me forth ɪɴs ᵗ sette ɪɴs ᵘ the kvng ɪɴs ᵛ tyme
of comyng aȝen ɴ tyme of myn aȝen comyng s ʷ him ɪɴs ˣ pistlis or lettres ɪs ʸ a lettre also 1 and
a lettre ɴ also sende the king a lettre s ᶻ the kepere ɪɴ ᵃ Om ɪɴs ᵇ hond or help 1 hond or
grace ɴs ᶜ beynge with 1 that was with ɴs ᵈ me the kyng ȝaaf to me myn axyng ɪɴs ᵉ lettres ɪɴs
ᶠ And ɪɴs ᵍ sente ɪɴs ʰ Om ɪɴs ⁱ his knyȝtis ɪɴs ᵏ of Amanytes 1 ¹ herden of my comyng ɪʙ
ᵐ turment of herte 1 ⁿ for cause that 1 that ɴ for that that s

12 And I ros the ny3t, and fewe men with me, and I shewide to no man, what God hadde 3iuen in myn herte, that I shulde do in Jerusalem; and there was noon helpely beeste to me, but the beeste that 13 I sat on. And I wente out bi the 3ate of the valei the ny3t, and beforn the welle of the dragoun, and at the drit 3ate; and I beheeld the wal of Jerusalem scaterid, 14 and his 3atis wastid with fijr. And I passide ouer to the 3ate of the welle, and to the watir cundict of the king, and ther was no place to the beeste, that I 15 sat on that he my3te passen ouer; and I ste3ide vp bi the strem the ny3t, and I beheeld the wal, and᷎ turned a3een I᷈ cam to the 3ate of the valei, and am 16 comen a3een. The maister iuges forsothe wisten not, whider I was go, or what I wolde do; but and to the Jewis, and to the prestus, and to the most worshipeful men, and to the maister iuges, and to the tothere that maden the were, vnto that of the placis no thing I hadde shewid. 17 And I seide to hem, 3ee han knowen the affliccioun, in whiche we ben, for Jerusalem is desert, and his 3atis ben wastid with fijr; cometh, and bilde we vp the wallis of Jerusalem, and be we no more 18 represf. And I shewide to hem the hond of my God, that it was good with me, and the woordis of the king, that he spac to me; and I sey, Rise we, and bilde we; and the hondis of hem ben coumfortid 19 in goode. Forsothe Sanballath Oronyte, and Tobias, seruaunt Amonyte, and Gosem Arabs, herden, and scorneden vs, and despiseden; and seiden, What is this thing that 3ee don? whether a3en 20 the king 3ee rebellen? And I 3eld᷈ to them a woord, and seide to them, God

and Y was there thre daies. And Y roos᷍ 12 bi ny3t, Y and a fewe men with me, and Y schewide not to ony man, what thing God hadde 3oue in myn herte, that Y wolde do in Jerusalem; and no᷎ werk beest was᷈ with me, no᷍ but the beeste, ʿon which᷈ Y sat᷇. And Y 3ede out bi the 13 3ate of the valei bi ny3t, and bifor the welle of dragoun᷈, and to᷍ the 3at᷍ of drit᷍; and Y bihelde the wal of Jerusalem distried, and the 3atis therof wastid bi fier. And Y passid᷍ to the 3ate of the 14 welle, and to the watir cundit of the kyng, and no᷍ place was᷈ to᷈ the hors,ʿon which᷈ Y sat᷍ ʿfor to passe᷈; and᷈ Y stiede᷈ bi the 15 stronde ʿin ny3t᷈, and Y᷈ bihelde the wal᷈, and Y᷈ turnede a3en, and cam᷈ to the 3ate of the valei, and Y 3ede a3en. Forsothe᷈ 16 the magistratis᷍ wisten not, whidir Y hadde go, ethir what Y wolde do; but also Y hadde not schewid ony thing to the Jewis, and prestis, and᷎ to the best men, and magestratis᷈, and᷍ to othere men that maden the werk, ʿtil to᷈ that ʿplace, *that is, til to that*᷇ *tyme*᷈. And Y seide 17 to hem, 3e knowen the turment᷍, in which we᷍ ben, for Jerusalem is deseert, and the 3atis therof ben wastid with fier; come 3e, bilde we the wallis of Jerusalem, and be we no more schenship᷍. And Y schewide 18 to hem the hond᷍ of my God, that it was good with me, and the wordis᷍ of the kyng, whiche he spak to me; and Y seide, Rise we᷈, and bilde we; and the hondis of hem weren coumfortid in good᷈. Forsothe᷈ Sanballath Oronytes, and Tobie, the 19 seruaunt Amanytes᷈, and Gosem Arabs, herden᷈, and scorneden᷈ vs, and dispisiden; and seiden, What is this thing, which᷈ 3e doon? whether 3e rebellen a3ens the kyng? And Y 3eldide᷈ to hem a word, and seide᷈ 20

ᴾ I ᴀ.   ᑫ and I ᴀ.   ʳ 3eldide ᴀᴇ *sec. m.* ꜰʜ.

᷍ roos up ɪɴs.   ᵖ ther was no ɪ.   ᑫ Om. ɪ.   ʳ Om. ɪ.   ˢ that ɪ.   ᵗ sat on ɪ.   ᵘ the dragoun ɪ.
ᵛ *I wente* to ɪs.   ʷ 3ate *that is clepid the* 3ate s.   ˣ dunge ɪɴs.   ʸ passide forth ɪɴs.   ᶻ ther was no ɪ.
ᵃ Om. ɪɴs.   ᵇ for to passe to ɪ. for to passe was to ɴs.   ᶜ that ɪ. upon which ɴs.   ᵈ sat upon ɪ.
ᵉ Om. ɪɴs.   ᶠ and in the ni3t ɪɴs.   ᵍ wente up ɪ. stiede up ɴs.   ʰ Om. ɪɴs.   ⁱ Om. s.   ᵏ wallis s.
ˡ Om. s.   ᵐ I cam ɪɴs.   ⁿ And ɪɴs.   ᵒ maistir men ɪɴs.   ᵖ ne ɪɴs.   ᑫ maistir men ɪɴs.   ʳ ne ɪɴs.
ˢ vnto ɪɴs. til x.   ᵗ Om. x.   ᵘ Gloss omitted in ɪɴs.   ᵛ turmentis c.   ʷ we *Jewis* ɪ. we *the Jewis* s.
ˣ in schenschip ɪɴs.   ʸ hond or *the help* ɪ. hond or *cumfort* s.   ᶻ word s.   ᵃ we up ɪɴs.   ᵇ God ɴs.
ᶜ And ɪɴs.   ᵈ of Amanytes ɪ.   ᵉ herden *this* ɪ. herd *oure purpose* s.   ᶠ thei scorneden ɪɴs.   ᵍ that ɪɴs.
ʰ answeride ɪɴs.   ⁱ I seide ɪɴs.

of heuene, he helpith vs, and wee his seruauns ben; rise wee, and bilde wee, to 3ou forsothe is no* part and ri3twisnesse and mynde in Jerusalem

CAP III

1 And Eliasif, the grete prest, ros^t, and his brethern, and prestus, and thei bilden^u vp the 3atis of the floc, thei^v halewiden it, and setten the 3ate leuys of it, and vn to the tour of an hundrid cubitus thei halewiden it, vn to the tour of Anane-2hel And beside hym the men of Jericho bilden, and biside hem bilde Zaccur, the 3sone of Amri The 3ate forsothe of fisshis^w bilden vp the sonus of Azanaa; thei coueieden it^x, and setten his 3ate leues, and lokis, and heengis And biside hem bilde Marimuth, the sone of Vri, 4sone of Accus And biside hym bilde Mosolla, the sone of Barachie, sone of Mesezebeel And biside hym bilde Sa-5doc, the sone of Baana And biside hym bilden Thecuenus, forsothe the more wirshipeful men of hem vnder putten not ther neckis in the were of the Lord 6ther God And the olde 3ate bilden vp ' Joiada, the sone of Fasia, and Mosollam, the sone of Besoida, and thei couereden it, and setten his 3ate leuis, and lokis, 7aud heengis And biside hem bilden Melchia Gabonite, and Jaddon Metho-nothite, men of Gabaon and Masfa, for the duk that was in the regioun be3onde 8the flod And biside hym bilde Eziel, the sone of Aria, goldsmith, and biside hym bilde Annany, the sone of a piment makere, and thei laften Jerusalem vnto 9the wal of the braddere strete And bi-side hym bilde Rafaia, the sone of Hahul, 10prince of a toun of Jerusalem And bi-side hym bilde Jeieda, the sone of Ra-

to hem, God hym silf of heuene helpith vs, and we ben hise seruauntis; rise we^k, and bilde^l, forsothe part and ri3tfulnesse^m and mynde in Jerusalem is not to 3ou^n

CAP III

And Eliasiph, the greet preest, roos^o, 1 and hise britheren, and prestis, and thei bildiden the 3ate of the floc; thei maden it^p stidfast^q; and^r settiden^s the 3atis therof, and 'til to^t the tour of an hundrid cubitis, thei maden it^u stidfast^r, 'til to^w the tour of Ananehel And bisidis hym the 2 men of Jeiico bildiden; and bisidis hem^x Zaccur, the sone of Amry, bildide^y For-3 sothe^z the sones of Asamaa bildiden^a the 3atis of fischis, thei^b hiliden it, and set-tiden^c the 3atis therof, and lockis^d, and barris And Marymuth, sone^e of Vrye, the sone of Accus, bildide bisidis hem And 4 Mosolla, sone^f of Barachie, the sone of Meseze, bildide bisidis hym And Sadoch, the sone of Baana, bildide bisidis him And men of Thecue bildiden bisidis hym, 5 but the principal men of hem puttiden^g not her neckis vndur^h in the werk of her Lord God And Joiada, the sone of Pha-6 sea, and Mosollam, the sone of Besoyda, bildiden the elde 3ate, thei hiliden^i it, and settiden^k the 3atis therof, and lockis^l, and barris And Melchie Gabaonyte, and Jad-7 don Methonatite, men of Gabaon and of Maspha, bildiden bisidis hem, for the duyk that was in the cuntrei bi3ende the flood And Eziel, goldsmy3t^m, the sone 8 of Araie, bildide bisidis hym; and An-nany, the sone of a makere of oynement^n, bildide bisidis him; and thei leften Jeru-salem^o 'til to^p the wal of the largere^q street And Raphaie, the sone of Hahul, 9 prince of a street of Jerusalem, bildide bi-sidis him And Jeieda, the sone of Ara-10

---

s not ⊿   t aroos ⊿   u bildiden ⊿   v and ⊿   w the fisshis c   x Om c

---

k we up IN   we vp in his name s   l bilde we it I   bilde we N   bilde we *this place* s   m ri3twisnesse I
n 3ou *that gruechen her a3ens* IS   o roos up INS   p Om EFGHKLMNOPSXb   q stidfast *werk* NS   r and thei INS   s setten up I   settiden up NS   t vnto INS   til L   to X   u Om LFGIIIKLMNOPSXb   v stidfast *werk* IS   w vnto IN   and vnto s   to X   x hem bildide INS   y Om INS   z And INS   a bilden ∿
b and thei INS   c settiden up INS   d *maden* lockis I   *thei maden therto* lockis S   e the sone CKILNSX
f the sone INS   g vndirputtiden INS   h Om INS   i bildiden NS   k settiden up INS   l the lockis INS
m the goldsmy3t INS   n an oynement makere INS   o Jerusalem *bild* I, Jerusalem *bildid* NS   p vnto INS
til X   q large INSb *lengere* A

math, aȝen his hous ; and biside hym
11 bilde Accus, the sone of Azebonie. The
myddel forsothe partᵞ of the toun bilde
Melchias, the sone of Herem, and Asub,
the sone of Feth Moab ; and the tour of
12 ouenus. Biside hym bilde Sellum, the
sone of Aloes, prince of the myddel part
of a toun of Jerusalem, and he and his
13 sonus. And the ȝate of the valei bilde
Annun, and the dwelleris of Sanoe ; thei
bilden it, and setten his ȝate leuis, and
lokis, and henglisᶻ, and a thousend cubitus in the wal vnto the ȝate of the
14 dunge hil. And the ȝate of the dunge
hil bilde Melchias, the sone of Recab,
prince of the toun of Bethacharem ; he
bilde it, and sette his ȝate leues, and
15 lokis, and henglisᵃ. And the ȝate of the
welle bilde Sellum, the sone of Colosai,
prince of the toun of Masfa ; he bilde it,
and couerede, and sette his ȝate leuis,
and lockis, and heengisᵇ ; and the wallis
of the fish pond of Siloe in to the ȝerd
of the king, and vn to the grees of the
king, that comen doun fro the cite of
16 Dauid. After hym bilde Neemyas, the
sone of Asboc, the prince of the half
partᶜ of the toun of Bethsuri, vnto aȝen
the sepulcre of Dauid, and vnto the fish
pond, that bi gret were is maad, and vnto
17 the hous of stronge men. After hym
bilden Leuitus ; and after hem Reum,
the sone of Benny. After hym bilde
Azebias, prince of the half part of the
18 toun of Cheile, in his toun. After hym
bilden the brethern of hem, Bethin, the
sone of Enadad, prince of the half partᶜ
19 of Cheila. And Aser, the sonn of Josue,
prince of Masfa, bilde beside hym the
secunde mesure aȝen the steȝing vp of
20 the most fast corner. After hym in the
hil bilde Baruch, the sone of Sachaie, the

math, bildide bisidis him aȝensʳ his owne
hous ; and Accusᵃ, the sone of Asebonye,
bildide bisidis hym. Forsotheᵗ Melchie, 11
the sone of Herem, and Asub, the sone of
Phet Moabᵘ, bildiden theᵛ half part of
theʷ street, and the tour of ouenys. Sel- 12
lum, the sone of Aloes, princeˣ of theʸ
half part of a street of Jerusalem, bildide
bisidis hym, he and hise sones. And Am- 13
ram, and the dwelleris of Zanoe, bildiden
the ȝate of the valei ; thei bildidenᶻ it, and
settidenᵃ the ȝatis therof, and lockisᵇ, and
barris therofᶜ ; and *thei bildidenᵈ* a thousynde cubitis in the wal 'til toᵉ the ȝate
of the dunghil. And Melchie, the sone of 14
Rechab, prynce of a street of Bethacarem,
bildide the ȝate of the dunghil ; he bildide
it, and settideᶠ, and hilide the ȝatis therof,
and lockisᵍ, and barrisʰ. And Sellum, the 15
sone of Colozai, prince of a toun Masphaⁱ,
bildide the ȝate of the welle ; he bildide it,
and hilideᵏ, andˡ settideᵐ the ȝatis therof,
and lockis, and barris ; and *he bildide* the
wallis of the cisterne of Ciloe 'til in toⁿ
the orchard of the kyng, and 'til toᵒ the
greces of the kyng, thatᵖ comen doun fro
the citee of Dauid. Nemyeˢ, the sone of 16
Azboch, prince of the half part of the
street of Bethsury, bildide after hym tilʳ
aȝensˢ the sepulcre of Dauid, and 'til toᵗ
the cisterne, whichᵘ is bildide with greet
werk, and 'til toᵛ the hous of stronge men.
Dekenesʷ bildiden after hym ; and Reum, 17
the sone of Beny, bildide aftir hemˣ. Ase-
bieʸ, theᶻ prince of half part of the street
of Cheile, bildide in his street aftir hym.
Theᵃ britheren of hemᵇ, Bethynᶜ, the sone 18
of Enadab, prince of theᵈ half part of
Cheyla, bildiden after hymᶜ. And Aser, the 19
sone of Josue, prince of Maspha, bildide
bisidis hym the secounde† mesure aȝens
the stiyngᶠ of the 'moost stidefastᵍ corner.

† *secounde ;
that is, his por-
cioun in the
secounde wal.
Lire here. c.*

ᵞ partie ᴀ*ɴ*.   ᶻ heengis ᴀʜ.   ᵃ heengys ᴀᴇʜ.   ᵇ heenglis ꜰ.   ᶜ partie ᴀʜ.

ʳ ouer aȝens ɪ. forn aȝens ɴꜱ.   ˢ Accub ɴꜱ.   ᵗ And ɪɴꜱ.   ᵘ of Moab ɴꜱ.   ᵛ Om. ɪɴ.   ʷ a ɪɴꜱ.   ˣ *and
prince* ɪꜱ. *and* the prince ɴ.   ʸ Om. ꜱ.   ᶻ bilden ᴄᴅʜᴏꜱxʙ.   ᵃ settiden up ɪɴꜱ.   ᵇ the lockis ɪɴꜱ.   ᶜ therof
thei ordeyneden ꜱ.   ᵈ *bilden* ᴄ.   ᵉ vnto ɪɴꜱ. to x.   ᶠ settide it up ɪɴꜱ.   ᵍ *ordeyned* lockis ɪ.   ʰ barris
he ordeyned to hem ꜱ.   ⁱ of Maspha ɪɴꜱ.   ᵏ hilide it ɪɴꜱ.   ˡ and he ɪɴꜱ.   ᵐ sette up ɪ. settide up ɴꜱ.
ⁿ vnto ɪɴꜱ. into x.   ᵒ vnto ɪɴꜱ. til x.   ᵖ whiche ɪɴꜱ.   𐞥 And Neemye ɪɴꜱ.   ʳ vnto ɪɴꜱ.   ˢ ouer aȝens ɪ.
forn aȝens ɴꜱ.   ᵗ vnto ɪɴꜱ. til x *pr. m.*   ᵘ that ɪɴꜱ.   ᵛ vnto ɪɴꜱ. to x.   ʷ And dekenes ɪɴꜱ.   ˣ him ɴꜱ.
ʸ And Asebie ɪɴꜱ.   ᶻ Om. ꜱ.   ᵃ And the ɪɴꜱ.   ᵇ him *bildiden aftir him* ɪɴꜱ.   ᶜ and Bethyn ɪɴꜱ.
ᵈ Om. ɪꜱ.   ᶜ hem ɪ.   ᶠ stiyng up ɪɴꜱ.   ᵍ strengest ɪ. mooste staliworthe ɴꜱ.

secunde mesure fro the corner vnto the
ȝate of the hous of Eliazif, grete prest
21 After hym bilde Marimuth, the sone of
Vrie, sone of Accur, the secunde mesure
fro the ȝate of the hous of Eliasif, to the
time that the hous of Eliasif were straȝt
22 out. And aftir hym bildeden[d] the[e] prestus,
23 men of the wilde feldis of Jordan. After
hym[f] bilden Beniamyn and Asub aȝen
ther hous ; and after hym bilde Asarias,
the sone of Moosie, sone of Ananye, aȝen
24 his hous. Aftir hym bilde Benni, the
sone of Senadad, the secunde mesure fro
the hous of Azarie vnto the bowing and
25 vnto the corner   Falel, the sone of Osi,
aȝen the bowing, and the tour that stant
aboue, fro the heȝe hous of the king, that
is in the porche of the prisoun ; and after
26 hym Fadaia, the sone of Feros   Gabon-
ites, water bereris forsothe dwelten in
Ofel aȝen the ȝate of watris at the est,
27 and the tour that aboue semede   After
hym bilden Thecuynes the secunde mesure forn aȝen, tro the grete tour and
stondende aboue vnto the wal of the
28 temple   Aboue forsothe at the horse
ȝate bildeden the prestus, eche aȝen his
hous. Aftir hem bilde Seddo, the sone
29 of Enner, aȝen his hous   After hym bilde
Semeia, the sone of Sechenye, kepere of
30 the est ȝate.   After hym bilde Ananye,
the sone of Selemye, and Anon, the sone
of Selon, the sixte, the secunde mesure.
After hym bilde Mosollam, the sone of
Barachie, aȝen his tresorie   After hym
bilde Melchias, the sone of a goldsmith,
vnto the hous of sodeknys, and of the
men sellende sheldis aȝen the iudicial
ȝate, and vnto the supping place of the
31 corner.   And withinne the supping place
of the corner in to the ȝate of the king
1 bilden craftusmen and marchandus   It

Baruch[h], the sone of Zachay, bildide aftir 20
hym in the hil the secounde mesure fro
the corner 'til to[i] the ȝate of the hows of
Eliasiph, the greet prest.   Marymuth[k], 21
the sone of Vrie, sone of Zaccur, bildide
after hym the secounde mesure fro the
ȝate of Eliasiph, as fer as the hows of
Eliasiph was stretchid[l] forth. And prestis, 22
men[m] of the[n] feeldi places of Jordan, bildiden aftir hym.   Beniamyn[o] and Asub 23
bildiden[p] aftei hem[q] aȝens[r] her hows , and
Azarie, the sone of Maasie, sone of Ananye, bildide aftir hym aȝens[s] his owne
hows.   Bennuy[t], the sone of Senadad, bild- 24
ide after hym the secounde mesure fro
the hows of Azarie 'til to[u] the bowyng
and 'til to[v] the corner   Phalel[w], the sone 25
of Ozi, bildide aȝens[x] the bowyng, and
the tour that stondith[y] forth, fro the hiȝ
hows of the kyng, that is in the large
place of the[x] prisoun ; Phadaie[a], the sone
of Pheros, bildide after hym   Forsothe[b] 26
Nathynneis dwelliden in Ophel til aȝens
the ȝate of watris at the eest, and[c] the
tour that apperide[d].   Aftir hym men of 27
Thecue bildiden the secounde mesure
euene aȝens[e], fro the greet tour and[f] apperynge 'til to[g] the wal of the temple
Forsothe[h] prestis bildiden aboue at the 28
ȝate of horsis, ech man aȝens[i] his hows
Seddo[k], the sone of Enner, bildide aȝens[l]
his hows aftir hem.   And Semeie, the 29
sone of Sechenye, the kepere of the eest
ȝate, bildide after hym.   Ananye[m], the 30
sone of Selemye, and Anon, the sixte sone
of Selon, bildide[n] aftir hym the secounde
mesure   Mosallam[o], the sone of Barachie,
bildide aȝenus[p] his tresorie after hym
Melchie[q], the sone of a goldsmiȝt, bildide
aftir hym 'til to[r] the hows of Nathynneis,
and of men sillynge scheldis aȝens[s] the
ȝate of iugis, and 'til to[t] the[u] soler of the

---

[d] bylden _u_   [e] Om _u_   [f] hem _d_

[h] And Baruch INS   [i] vnto INS   [k] And Marymuth INS   [l] streiȝt I.   [m] the men INS   [n] Om INS.
[o] And Beniamyn INS   [p] bilden c   [q] hym EFGHKLMNSX   [r] forn aȝens INS   [s] ouer aȝens I forn aȝens NS
[t] And Bennuy INS   [u] vnto INS to X   [v] vnto INS til X   [w] And Phalel INS   [x] forn aȝens INS
[y] strecchith INS   [z] a INS   [a] and Phadaie INS   [b] And INS.   [c] coost and forn aȝens s   [d] apperide
ouer other   And s   [e] forn aȝens s   [f] Om s   [g] vnto NS   [h] And NS   [i] forn aȝens NS   [k] And N   And
Seddo s   [l] forn aȝens NS   [m] And Ananye INS   [n] bildiden N   [o] And Mosallam INS   [p] forn aȝens INS
[q] And Milchie INS   [r] vnto INS   [s] ouer aȝens I forn aȝens NS   [t] vnto INS   [u] a IN

is do forsothe, whan Sanaballath hadde
herd, that we schulden bilde the wal, he
wrathide gretli, and^g, moued ful myche,
2 scornede the Jewis. And he seide beforn
his brethern, and the court of Samari-
tanys^h, What do the Jewis ful feble?
Whether shuln leuen hem the Jentilis?
Whether shul thei sacrifien and fulfillen
in o dai? Whether thei shuln moun
bilden vp stonis of the hillokis of pouder,
3 that ben brent? But and Tobias Amonite seith to his neȝhebores, Bilde thei;
if ther steȝe vp a fox, he shal lepe ouer
4 ther ston wal. And Neemie seide, Here
thou, oure God, for we ben maad despit;
turne the repref vp on the hed of hem,
and ȝif hem in to despising in the lond
5 of caitifte; ne couere thou the wickenesse
of hem, and the synnus of hem befor thi
face be not don awei; for thei scorneden
6 the bilders. And so we bilden the wal,
and al we ioyneden togidere vnto the
half partⁱ, and the herte of the puple is
stirid to werken.

CAP. IV.

7   It is do forsothe, whan Sanaballath
hadde herd, and^k Tobias, and Arabes,
and Amanytes, and Azozie, that the gap
of the wal of Jerusalem was maad al hol,
and that the chinys^l 'or crauasis^m begunnen to be closid, thei ben ful myche
8 wroth. And alle thei ben gedered togidere, that thei comen and fiȝte aȝen Jeru-
9 salem, and casten busshemens. And we
preȝeden the Lord oure God, and we setten keperis vp on the wal dai and nyȝt
10 aȝen hem. Forsothe Judas seide, The
strengthe of the berere is feblid, and
there is to miche erthe, and we shul not
11 moun bilden vp the wal. And oure ene-

corner. And crafti men and marchauntis 31
bildiden with ynne the soler of the corner
and^v the ȝate of the kyng.

CAP. IV.

Forsothe^w it was doon, whanne Sana- 1
ballath hadde herd, that we bildiden the
wal, he^x was ful wrooth, and he was stirid
greetli, and scornede^y the Jewis. And he 2
seide bifor hise britheren, and the^z multitude of Samaritans, What doen the feble
Jewis? Whether hethene men schulen suf-
fre hem^a? Whether thei schulen fille^b, and
make sacrifice in o dai? Whether thei
moun bilde stonys of^c the^d heepis of the^e
dust, that^f ben brent? But^g also Tobie 3
Amanytes, his neiȝbore, seide, Bilde thei;
if a fox stieth^h, he schal 'skippe ouerⁱ the^k
stony^l wal 'of hem^m. And Neemye seide, 4
Oure God, here thou, for we ben maad
dispising; turne thou the schenschip onⁿ
her^o heed, and ȝyue thou hem in to dispisyng in the lond of caytifte; hile thou 5
not the wickidnesse of hem, and her synnes
be^p not doon awei bifor thi face; for thei
scorneden bilderis^q. Therfor^r we bildiden^s 6
the wal, and ioyneden^t togidere al 'til to^u
the half part, and the herte of the puple
was exitid to worche. Forsothe^v it was 7
doon, whanne Sanaballat 'hadde herd^w,
and Tobie, and^x Arabiens^y, and Amanytys,
and men of Azotus *hadden herd*, that the
brekyng of the wal of Jerusalem was
stoppid, and that the crasyngis hadden
bigunne to be closid togidere, thei weren
ful wrothe. And alle^z weren gaderid to- 8
gidere to come and fiȝte aȝens Jerusalem,
and to caste tresouns^a. And we preieden 9
oure^b Lord God^c, and we settiden keperis
on the wal bi^d dai and niȝt aȝens hem.
Forsothe^e Juda^f† seide^g, The strengthe of 10

---

g Om. c.   h the Samaritanys *A*.   i partie *AH*.   k Om. *A*.   l chynys *A*. chynes *EF*. chenes *H*.   m of
crauasis F. Om. E pr. m.

. v and *thei bildiden* 1s.   w And 1ns.   x and he ns.   y he scornede 1ns.   z *bifore* the 1ns.   a hem
thus s.   b fulfille *this cuntrey* 1ns.   c upon 1ns.   d Om. 1ns.   e Om. 1ns.   f whiche 1ns.   g And 1ns.
h go up 1. stie up n. shal stie vp s.   i ouerlepe 1ns.   k her 1ns.   l stonen 1.   m Om. 1ns.   n upon 1ns.
o her owne 1ns.   p ben cd.   q the bilders n. the bilders *of thi citee* 1s.   r Thanne 1.   s bildiden up 1n.
bilden vp s.   t we ioyneden *it* 1ns.   u vnto 1s. in to n.   v And 1ns.   w Om. 1ns.   x Om. s.
y Arabietis ns.   z *thei* alle 1ns.   a tresouns *aȝens it* ns.   b the 1ns.   c oure God 1ns.   d Om. 1.
e And 1ns.   f men of Juda 1n.   g seiden 1ns.

mis seiden, Wite thei not, and vnknowe
thei, to the time that we comen in to the
middel of hem, and slen hem, and make
12 the werc to cesen. It is do forsothe, the
Jewis comende, that dwelten bisides hem,
and seiende to vs ten sithis, of alle the
placis fro whiche[n] thei weren come to vs,
13 I sette in a place behinde the wal bi
enuyroun a puple in order, with ther
14 swerdis, and speris, and bowis. I[o] beheeld, and ros, and seide[oo] to the more
wrshipeful men, and maister iugis, and to
the tother part of the comun, Wilith not
dreden fro the face of hem ; of the grete
Lord and ferful hath mynde, and fiȝteth
for ȝour brethern, and ȝour[p] sonus, and
15 ȝour doȝtris, ȝour wiues, and housis. It
is do forsothe, whan oure enemys hadden
herd to be told to vs, God scaterede the
conseil of hem ; and alle wee ben turned
aȝeen to the wallis, eche to his werk.
16 And it is do fro that dai, the half part
of the ȝunge men maden the werk, and
the half part was redi to bataile ; and
speris, and sheeldis, and bowis, and ha-
beriones, and princis bihinde them, in al
17 the hous of Juda, of bilders in the wal,
and of bereris berthenus, and of leieris
on ; with ther oon hond thei maden the
werc, and with the tother thei heelden
18 swerd. Forsothe of the bilders eche was
gird aboute the hipis with a swerd ; and
thei bilden, and crieden with trumpe bi-
19 syde me. And I seide to the most wrshipeful men, and to the maister iugis,
and to the tother part of the comun,
A gret werc it is, and brod, and we ben
scuered in the wal aferr, an other fro
20 an other ; in what euere place ȝee shul
here the criyng of the trumpe, thider

the berere[h] is[l] maad feble, and the erthe[k]†
is ful[l] myche, and we moun not bilde[m] the
wal. And oure enemyes seiden[n], Wite thei 11
not, and knowe thei not, til we comen in
to the myddil of hem, and sleen hem, and
maken the werk to ceesse. Forsothe[o] it 12
was doon, whanne[q] Jewis came[q], that[r]
dwelliden bisidis hem[s], and seiden to vs[t]
'bi ten tymes[u], fro[v] alle places[w] fro whiche
thei camen to vs, Y ordeynede the puple 13
in ordre, with her swerdis, and speris, and
bouwis, in a place bihynde the wal[x] bi
cumpas. Y[y] bihelde, and roos[z], and seide[a] 14
to the principal men[b], and magistratis[c], and
to 'the tother[d] part of the comyn puple,
Nyle ȝe drede of her face ; haue ȝe mynde
of the greet Lord, and ferdful, and fiȝte
ȝe for ȝoure britheren, and ȝoure[f] sones,
and ȝoure[g] douȝtris, for[h] ȝoure wyues, and
housis[i]. Forsothe[k] it was doon, whanne 15
oure enemyes hadden herd that it was
teld to vs, God distriede her counsel ; and[l]
alle we turneden aȝen to the wallis, ech
man to his werk. And it was doon fro 16
that dai, the half part of ȝonge[m] men made
werk[n], and the half part was redi to batel ;
'and speris, and scheldis, and bouwis, and
harburiouns, and princes[o] aftir hem, in al
the hows of men of Juda, bildynge in the 17
wal, and berynge birthuns, and puttynge
on ; with[p] her[q] oon hond thei maden werk[r],
and with the[s] tother[t] thei helden swerd[u].
For ech of the bilderis was[v] gird with the[w] 18
swerd on[x] thei[y] reynes ; and thei bildiden[z],
and sowneden[a] with clariouns bisidis me.
And Y seide to the principal men[b], and 19
magistratis[c], and to the tothir[d] part of the
comyn puple, The werk is greet and brood,
and we ben departid fer in the wal, oon
from anothir ; in[e] what euer place ȝe[f] heren 20

† the erthe ;
that is, grauel
and schalk,
that ben nede-
ful to make
morter, ben re-
quirid in greet
quantite, so
that we mowen
not haue It.
Lire here. c.

---

n the whiche AEFH.   o And I A.   oo sei c   P for ȝour A.

h kepere INS.   i of the wal is IS.   k erthe aboute it I. erthe in cumpas of the wal s.   l Om. INS.
m bilde on I. bilde up NS.   n han seid INS.   o And INS.   P whanne that INS.   q Om. INS.   r the whiche I.
s hem camen ten tymes INS.   t us her purpos INS.   u Om. INS.   v and fro INS.   w the places INS.   x wallis c.
y And Y INS.   z I roos up INS.   a I seide N.   b Om. INS.   c maister men INS.   d that oother I.   e but
haue INS.   f for ȝoure IN.   g for ȝour s.   h and for INS.   i meynees INS.   k And INS.   l and thanne IS.
m the ȝonge INS.   n the werk c.   o princes weren redi I. princes weren born s.   p and in al the hous of
men of Juda bildinge in the wal, and of hem that beeren birthuns, and of hem that puttiden birthuns upon
hem that shulden bere hem, aftir her pryncis, speris, and sheeldis, and boowis, and haburionns ; and with N.
q the s.   r the werk c.   s that B.   t other BIS.   u her swerd IN.   v weren N.   w a INS.   x upon INS.
y his INS.   z bildeden the wal INS.   a thei sowneden INS.   b Om. IN.   c maistir men INS.   d oother IS.
e therfore in I. for ther in s.   f that ȝe INS.

renneth togidere to vs; forsothe oure
21 God shal fiȝte for vs. And we vsself ꟼ
shul make the werk, and the half part
of vs holde speris, fro the steȝing vp of
the morutid to the time that the sterris
22 gon out. Also that ʳ time I seide to the
puple, Eche with his child dwelle in the
middel of Jerusalem, and be ther to ȝou
23 whilis by nyȝt and dai to werken. I
forsothe, and my brethern, and the keperis, and my childer, that weren bihinde
me, diden ˢ not of oure clothis; eche ᵗ onli
was nakid to baptem.

CAP. V.

1 And ther is maad a cri of the puple
and of ther wiues, a gret, aȝen Jewis,
2 ther brethern. And ther weren that
seiden, Oure sonus and oure doȝtris ben
ful manye; take we for the pris of hem
3 whete, and ete we, and liue wee. And
ther weren that seiden, Oure feldis, and
vines, and oure housis lei wee to ᵘ, and
4 take wee whete in hunger. And othere
seiden, Borewe wee monei in to the tributus of the king, and ȝiue wee oure feldis,
5 and oure vines. And now as the flesh of
oure brethern, so oure flesh ben; and as
the sonys of hem, so and oure sonus; lo!
we han vnder ȝokid our sonus and oure
doȝtris in to seruage, and of oure doȝtris
ben thrallis, and we han not, wherof thei
moun be boȝt; and our feldus, and oure
6 vines other men welden. And I wrathide
ful myche, whan I hadde herd the cri of
7 hem after these woordys. And myn herte
thoȝte with me, and I blamede the most
wrshipeful men and maister iugis; and
seide to hem, Echone aske ȝee not vsuris
of ȝoure brethern. And I gederede aȝen

the ᵍ sown of the ʰ trumpe, renne ȝe togidere
thidur to vs; for ⁱ oure God schal fiȝte for
vs. And we 'vs silf ᵏ schal make the werk, 21
and the half part ˡ of vs holde ᵐ speris, fro
'the stiyng ⁿ of the moreutid til ᵒ that sterris
go out. And 'in that tyme ᵖ Y seide to the 22
puple, Ech man with his child ꟼ dwelle ʳ in
the myddil ˢ of Jerusalem, and whilis ᵗ be ⁿ
to vs 'bi nyȝt† and dai ᵛ to worche ʷ. But 23
Y, and my britheren, and my ˣ keperis, and ʸ
children ᶻ, that ᵃ weren ᵇ after me, diden not
of oure clothis; ech ᶜ man ᵈ was maad nakid
oneli to waischyng.

CAP. V.

And greet cry of the puple and of her 1
wyues was maad aȝens her britheren Jewis.
And there weren ᵉ that seiden, Oure sones 2
and oure douȝtris ᶠ ben ful manye; take we
wheete for the prijs of hem, and ete we,
and lyue. And ᵍ there weren that seiden, 3
Sette we ‡ forth ʰ oure feeldis, and vyneris,
and oure howsis, and take we wheete ⁱ in
hungur ᵏ. And othere men ˡ seiden, Take 4
we money bi borewyng§ in ᵐ to the ⁿ tributis of the kyng, and ȝyue ᵒ oure feeldis
and vyneris ᵖ. And now as the fleischis ꟼ ‖ 5
of oure britheren ben ʳ, so ˢ and ᵗ oure ᵘ
fleischis ᵛ ben ʷ; and as ben ˣ the sones of
hem, so ʸ and ᶻ oure ᵃ sones ᵇ ben ᶜ; lo! we
han maad suget ᵈ oure sones and oure douȝtris ᶜ in to seruage, and seruauntissis ᶠ ben ᵍ
of oure douȝtris ʰ, and we han not wherof
thei moun be aȝenbouȝt; and othere men
han in possessioun oure feeldis, and oure
vyneris. And Y was ful wrooth, whanne 6
Y hadde herde the cry of hem bi these
wordis. And myn herte thouȝte with me, 7
and Y blamede the principal men ⁱ and
magistratis ᵏ; and Y seide to hem, Axe ˡ ȝe

23 † *by nyȝt ; not
to worche bi
the nyȝt, but
summe weren
ordeyned bi
whilis to wake
bi nyȝt, for
keping of the
cytee. Lire
here. c.*

3 *Sette we ; to
silling ether to
lenyng to wed-
dis. Lire here.
c.*

§ *boreuyng ;
for vsure. Lire
here. c.*

‖ *fleischis ;
that is, as oure
britheren in
Babiloyne ben
in tarment, so
and we here,
and as here
children ben
seruauntis of
hethen men, so
oure children
ben here boonde
to Jewis.
Lire here. c.*

ꟼ oure silf ᴀ.   ʳ in that ᴀ ɪɪ.   ˢ we diden ᴇ pr. m.   ᵗ eche oon ᴀᴇꜰɴ.   ᵘ Om. c.

ᵍ Om. ɪɴꜱ.   ʰ a ɪɴꜱ.   ⁱ forsothe ɪɴꜱ.   ᵏ oure self ɴꜱ.   ˡ Om. ɪɴꜱ.   ᵐ holde we ɪɴ. holde we *in our
hondis* ꜱ.   ⁿ spryngyng up ɪ. stiȝyng up ɴꜱ.   ᵒ til *niȝt* ɪꜱ.   ᵖ Om. ɴꜱ pr. m.   ꟼ sheeld ꜱ.   ʳ dwelle he ɪɴ.
dwelle he *stille* ꜱ.   ˢ myddis ᴄꜱ.   ᵗ niȝt and day be ther *dyuerse* whilis ɪ. [bi ꜱ] niȝt and dai while melis
ɴꜱ.   ᵘ Om. ɪ.   ᵛ Om. ɪɴꜱ.   ʷ worche ynne ɪ.   ˣ the ɪɴꜱ.   ʸ of ɴ.   ᶻ my children ɪɴꜱ.   ᵃ whiche ɴꜱ.
ᵇ weren *goynge* ɪɴꜱ.   ᶜ *but* ech ɪɴꜱ.   ᵈ of us ɪɴꜱ.   ᵉ weren *of hem* ɪꜱ.   ᶠ douȝtren ɪꜱ.   ᵍ Also ɪɴꜱ.
ʰ forth *to sele* ɪ. forth *to selle* ɴꜱ.   ⁱ wheete *to ete* ɴꜱ.   ᵏ *this* hungur ɪɴꜱ.   ˡ of hem ɪꜱ.   ᵐ *oblischinge
us* in ɪꜱ.   ⁿ Om. ɪꜱ.   ᵒ ȝyue we *to him* ɪꜱ.   ᵖ our vyners ꜱ.   ꟼ bodies ɪꜱ.   ʳ ben *maad thral* ɪ. ben *made thral or
wastid* ꜱ.   ˢ *riȝt* so ɪ.   ᵗ Om. ɪ.   ᵘ be oure ɪ.   ᵛ bodies ɪꜱ.   ʷ Om. ɪ.   ˣ ben *in caitiflee* ꜱ.   ʸ *riȝt* so ɪ.
ᶻ Om. ɪ.   ᵃ be oure ɪ.   ᵇ *in caitiflee* ɪ marg.   ᶜ Om. ɪ.   ᵈ Om. ɪꜱ.   ᵉ douȝtris sugettis ɪꜱ.   ᶠ seruauntis ɴ.
Om. ɪꜱ.   ᵍ Om. ɪꜱ.   ʰ douȝtren ben *maad* seruauntessis ɪ. douȝtren ben seruauntessis ꜱ.   ⁱ Om. ɪꜱ.   ᵏ maistir men ɪꜱ.   ˡ Eche of ȝou axe ɪꜱ.

8 hem a gret connocacioun, and seide to
them, Wee, as ȝee witen, han forboȝt oure
brethern Jewis, that weren sold to the
Jentilis, after oure power , and ȝee thanne
sellen ȝoure brethern, and wee shul bien^v
hem aȝeen　And thei heelden ther pes,
ne founden not what thei shulden an-
9 swern　And I seide to hem, This is no
good thing, that ȝee don ; whi in the
drede of oure God ȝee gon not, lest it be
repreued to vs of the Jentilis, oure ene-
10 mys ? And I and my brethern, and my
childei, lenten to manye men monei and
whete, ne wee askeden not aȝen this in
to comun ; and othei thing that is aȝt^w to
11 vs graunte wee　ȝeldeth to them to dai
ther feldis, and ther vines, their oliues,
and ther housis , but more and the hundrid part of monee of whete, and of wyn,
⟨ and oile, that ȝee weren wont to asken of
12 hem, ȝiueth for hem　And thei seiden,
Wee shal ȝelden, and of hem nothing we
sechen^x, and thus wee shul do as thou
spekist　And I clepide the prestis, and
' adiurede hem, that thei shulde do aftir
13 that I hadde seid　Ferthei mor I shakide
out my bosum, and seide, Thus God shake
out eche man, that fulfillith not this woord
of his hous, and of his trauailis , and be
he shaken out, and maad voide　And al
the multitude seide, Amen , and preiseden God.　Thanne dide the puple, as it
14 was seid　Forsothe fro that dai that the
king hadde comaunded to me, that I were
duke in the lond of Juda, fro the twentithe ȝer vn to the^y two and threttithe
ȝer of king Artaxerses, bi twelue ȝei,
I and my brethern the ȝeris frutus, that
15 weren due to dukis, wee eeten not　Forsothe the firste dukis that weren befor
me greueden the puple, and token of hem
in bred, and win, and in mone, eche dai

not vsuris^m, 'ech manⁿ of ȝoure britheren
And Y gaderide togidire a greet cumpeny
aȝens hem, and Y seide to hem, As ȝe s
witen, we^o bi oure power aȝenbouȝten^p oure
britheren Jewis, that weren seeld to he-
thene men ; and ȝe therfor^q sillen ȝoure
britheren, and schulen we aȝenbie hem^r ?
And thei holden silence, and founden not
what thei schulen answere　And Y seide 9
to hem, It is not good thing, which^s ȝe
doon , whi goen ȝe not in the drede of
oure God, and repreef be not seid to vs of
hethene men, oure enemyes ?　Bothe Y 10
and my britheren, and my childien, han
lent to ful many men monei and wheete , in
comyn† axe we not this aȝen , foi ȝyue^t
we alien money^u, which is due to vs^v
ȝelde^w ȝe to hem to dai her feeldis, and 11
her vyneris, her olyue places, and her
housis , but^x rather ȝyue ȝe for hem bothe^y
the hundrid part 'of money^z of wheete, of
wyn, and of oile, which weⁿ weren wont
to^b take of hem.　And thei seiden, We 12
schulen ȝelde^c, and we schulen axe no
thing of hem , and we schulen do so as
thou spekist　And Y clepide the prestis,
and Y made hem to^d swere, that thei
schulden do aftir that^e, that Y hadde^f seid
Feithermore^g Y schook^h my bosum, and 13
Y seide, So God schake awei ech man,
'that fillith not this wordⁱ fro his hows,
and hise^k trauels^l, and be he schakun
awei, and be he maad voide　And al the
multitude seide, Amen , and herieden
God　Therfoi^m the puple dide, as it was
seid　Forsotheⁿ fro that dai in which the 14
kyng hadde comaundid to me, that Y
schulde be duyk in the lond of Juda, fro
the twentithe ȝeer 'til to^o the two and
threttithe ȝeer of Artaxeises kyng, bi^p
twelue ȝeer, Y and my britheien eeten not
sustenauncis^q, that^r weren due to duykis

† in comyn
that is, consente
we in comyn,
that these
thingis be not
axid aȝen
Lire here ⟨

---

^v forbyen c pr m　^w owid AEFH　^x shul sechen E pr m　^y Om A

^m vseris or encrece s　ⁿ Om 18　^o we haue i　^p aȝenbouȝt i　^q now 18　^r hem of ȝou 18　^s that is
^t but forȝyue 18　^u money or vsure 18　^v bi couenaunt i　marg vs bi the graunt of hem thai hiȝten u s
^w And aȝen ȝelde 18　^x and 18　^y Om 18　^z Om BCEFHNPRUVX of the monei κ　of money and o
^a ȝe neisv　^b bi vse to s　^c ȝelde tho godis to hem i　ȝelden her goodis to hem s　^d Om i　^e this is
^f haue ix　^g And ferthermore 18　^h shoke or made empit s　ⁱ Om 18　^k fro hise 18　^l trauels, that
fulfillith not this word 18　^m And 18　ⁿ Sothly 18　^o vnto 18　^p that is bi 18　^q the sustenauncis 18
^r the whiche i　which s

fourti ouncis; but and the seruauns of hem presseden doun the puple. I forsothe dide not so, for the drede of God; 16 but rathere in the werk of the wal bildede, and feeld I boȝte not, and alle my 17 childer gedered weren to the werc. Also Jewisᶻ and the maister iugis of hem weren an hundrid men and fifti; and thoo that camen to vs. of the Jentilis, that ben in oure ennyroun, weren in my 18 bord. Forsoth there wasᵃ greithid to me bi alle daȝis an oxe, sixe chosen wetheris, out take volatilis, and betweᵇ ten daȝes diuerse wines; and othere manye thingus I ȝaf; ferthermor and the ȝeris frutis of my duchie I soȝte not; forsothe the puple gretli was poueresht. 19 My God, haue mynde of me in to goode, after alle thingis that I haue do to this puple.

But the firste duykis, that weren bifor me, 15 greuyden the puple, and tokenᵃ of hem in breed, andᵗ inᵘ wiyn, and inᵛ monei, ech dai fourti siclis; butᵂ also her mynistris oppressiden the puple. Forsotheˣ Y dide not so, for the drede of God; but rather 16 Yʸ bildide in the werk of the wal, and Y bouȝte no feeld, and alle my children weren gaderidᶻ to theᵃ werk. Also 'Jewis and the 17 magistratis of hemᵇ, an hundrid and fifti menᶜ; and thei that camen to me fro hethene men, that ben in oure cumpas, werenᵈ in my table. Forsotheᵉ bifᶠ ech 18 dai oonˢ oxe was maad redi to meʰ, sixeˡ chosun wetheris, outakun volatils, and withynne ten daies dyuerseᵏ wynes; and Yˡ ȝaf many othere thingisᵐ; ferthermore and Y axide not the sustenauncis of my duchee; for the puple was maad ful pore. My God, haue thou mynde ofⁿ me 19 in to good, bi alle thingis whiche Y dideᵘ to this puple.

CAP. VI.

1 It is do forsothe, whan Sanaballath hadde herd, and Thobias, and Gosem Arabsᶜ, and oure othere enemys, that I hadde bild the wal, and ther was not in it laft brosure among; forsothe vnto that time I hadde not put ȝate leues in 2 the ȝate; Sanaballath, and Thobias, and Gosem Arabs senten to me, seiende, Cum, and smite wee pes couenaunt togidere in litle tounus, in a feeld; thei forsothe thoȝten, that thei do to me euel. 3 Thanne I sente to hem messageris, seiende, A gret werc I do, and I mai not come doun, lest parauenture it be laft, whan I shulde comen, and descende to 4 ȝou. Forsothe thei senten to me after this woord bi foure sithes, and I answerde to hem after the rathere woord. 5 And Sanaballath sente to me after the

CAP. VI.

Forsothe it was doon, whanne Sana-1 ballath hadde herd, and Tobieᵖ, and Gosem of Arabie, and oure other enemyes, that Y hadde bildideᑫ the walʳ, andⁿ nomore brekyng was therynne; sotheliᵗ 'til toᵘ that tyme Y hadde not setᵛ leeuysᵂ of schittyng inˣ the ȝatis; Sanaballathʸ, and 2 Tobie, and Gosem of Arabie senten to me, and seiden, Come thouᶻ, and smyte we boond of pecs in caluesᵃ, 'in o feeldᵇ; forsotheᶜ thei thouȝten forᵈ to do ynel to me. Therfor Y sente messangeris to hem, 3 and Y seide, Y make a greet werk, and Y mai not go dounᵉ, lest perauenture it be doon retcheleslif, whanne Y come, and go doun to ȝou. Sotheliˢ thei senten to me 4 'bi this woordʰ bi foure tymes, and Y answeride toˡ hem by the formere word. And Sanaballath sente to me the fyuethe 5

ᶻ the Jewis ᴀ.   ᵃ weren ᴀ.   ᵇ betwixe ᴀ. betwen ᴇ pass. bytwene ꜰʜ.   ᶜ Arabes ᴀ.

ˢ thei token ɪ.   ᵗ Om. ɴ.   ᵘ Om. ꜱx.   ᵛ Om. ꜱ.   ᵂ and ɪꜱ.   ˣ But ɪꜱ.   ʸ I sugettide my self and Y ɪꜱ.   ᶻ gatherid togidre with me ɪꜱ.   ᵃ Om. ɪꜱ.   ᵇ Om. ɪꜱ.   ᶜ men [of ꜱ] Jewis and maistir men ɪꜱ.   ᵈ weren etynge ɪ.   ᵉ And ɪꜱ.   ᶠ Om. ɪ.   ᵍ an ɪꜱ.   ʰ me in myn houshold ɪꜱ.   ⁱ und sixe ɪꜱ.   ᵏ I hadde dynerse ɪꜱ.   ˡ Om. ꜱ.   ᵐ thingis to diuers men ɪꜱ.   ⁿ on ɪx.   ᵒ haue do ɪꜱ.   ᵖ also Tobie ɪꜱ.   ᑫ bildide also up ɪꜱ.   ʳ wal of Jerusalem ɪꜱ.   ˢ and that ɪꜱ.   ᵗ and ɪꜱ.   ᵘ vn to ɪꜱ. to x.   ᵛ set up ɪꜱ.   ᵂ the leeuys ɪ.   ˣ of ɪꜱ.   ʸ and Sanballath ɪꜱ.   ᶻ thou in to a feeld ɪꜱ.   ᵃ vilagis ꜱ.   ᵇ Om. ɪꜱ.   ᶜ certis ɪꜱ.   ᵈ Om. ɪꜱ.   ᵉ doun iherfro ɪꜱ.   ᶠ necgligently ɪꜱ.   ᵍ And aftir this word ɪ. And bi this word ꜱ.   ʰ Om. ɪꜱ.   ˡ Om. ɪꜱ.

ıathere woord the fifte sıthe hıs chıld; and he hadde a lettre ın hıs hond wrıten ⁶ın thıs maner, In Gentılıs ıt ıs herd, and Gosem seıde, for thou and the Jewıs thenken to rebellen, and therfore 3ee bilden, and thou wılt rere vp on hem ⁷kıng, foı what cause and profetus thou hast sett, that prechen of thee ın Jerusalem, seıende, A king ın Jerusalem is; the kıng ıs to here these woordıs, therfore cum now, that wee go ın counseil ⁸togidere And I sente to hem, seıende, It ıs not don after these woordıs that thou spekıst, forsothe of thın herte thou ⁹makıst these thıngıs Alle these fereden ⱱs, thenkende that our hondıs shulden cesen fro werkıs, and resten a3ecn; for what cause more I confortıd myn hond ¹⁰And I wente ın to the hous of Samaie, sone of Dalıe, sone of Methabehel, prınylı, the whıche seith, Trete wee with ⱱs ın the hous of God, ın the mıddel of the temple, and close we the 3atus of the hous; for theı ben to come that theı sle thee, and the ny3t theı ben to come that ¹¹theı sle thee And I seıde, Whethır any man lıc me fleeth, and who as I shal go ın to the temple, and lıuen? I shal not ¹²gon in And I vnderstod that God hadde not sent hym, but as profecıende he hadde spoke to me, and Thobias and Sanaballath ¹³lath bi mede hadden hırıd hym. Forsothe he hadde take pııs, that aferd I shulde don, and synnen, and theı my3te ¹⁴han cuel, that theı repreue to me. Haue mynde of me, Lord, for Tobıas and Sanaballath, after^d suche werkus of hem; but and of Nadıe, profete, and of othere pro-

tyme bı the foımere word his chıld; and he hadde ın his hond a pıstle^k wrıtun ın thıs maner, It ıs herd among hethene c men, and Gosem seıde^l, that thou and the^m Jewıs thenken for to rebelle, and therfoı 3e bilden^n, and thou^o wolt reıse thee^p kıng on^q hem^r, for whıch^s cause also thou hast set 7 profetıs, that^t prechen of thee ın Jerusalem, and seıen^tt, A kıng ıs ın Jerusalem, the kıng schal here these wordıs; therfor come thou now, that we take counsel^u togidere And Y sente to hem, and seıde,8 It ıs not doon bı^ᵛ these wordıs whıche^w thou spekıst; for of thın^x herte thou makıst these thıngıs Alle these men maden 9 vs aferd, and thou3ten that oure hondıs schulden ceesse fro^y werkıs^z, that^a we schulden reste^b; for whıch cause Y coumfortide more myn honde^c And Y entrıde 10 prıueh in to the hows of Samaıe, sone^d of Dalie, the sone of Methabehel, whıch^e seıde^f, Trete we^g wıth vs^h sılf ın the hows of God, in the myddıs^ı of the temple, and close we the 3atıs of the hows, for theı schulen come to sle thee, 'and theı schulen^k come 'bı nı3t^ıt to sle thee. And Y seıde, 11 Whether ony man lıjk^m me† fledde^n, and who as Y schal entre ın to the temple, and schal lyue^o? Y schal^p not entre^q 12 And Y vndurstood^r that God 'hadde not sent^s hym^t, but 'he spak as profesıynge to me; and^u Tobıe and Sanaballath 'hadden hıııd^ᵛ hym for meede^w For he hadde 13 take^x prıjs, that Y schulde be aferd, and do^ᵛ, and^z that Y schulde^a do^b synne^c; and theı^d schulden^e hauef yuel^g, whıch theı schulden^h putte to me wıth schenschıp Lord, haue mynde of me, for^ı Tobye and 14

† lıjk me . that ıs, tristinge so to God, as Y do. schal lyue, as ıf he seide, ıf ony man trısting so myche of Goddıs defendıng, as Y do, fledde to the temple for mannıs drede, God ou3te takı awey his lıvf Lıre here c

d Om ı

k lettere ıs   l hath seıd ıs   m Om ıs   n bılden *the wal* ı bılden *the wal of Jerusalem* s   o that thou s   p enhaunce thi self ıs   q upon ıs   r the Jewıs ı Jewıs s   s the whıch ı   t whıche ıs   tt Om ʌ   u counsel *heroff* ıs   ᵛ aftır ı   w that ı ın whıch s   x thın owne ı   y of s   oure werkıs ıs her werkıs x   a and that ıs   b reste *fro bıldıng* ı reste *fro bıldyng of Jerusalem* s   c hond *therto* ı honde *ın wırchıng* s   d the sone ıs   e the whıche ı   f seıde *to me* ıs   g we theıe s   h our s   ı myddıl ı   k 3he and bı nı3t theı wıl ı 3ea bı nı3t theı shuln s   l Om ıs   m lıjk to ıs   n hath fled *for nch a thıng* ı hath fled *for such a lawe* s   o lyue *or be sawıd there* ıs   p wıl ı   q entre thıdere ı entre thıder *to take grıth* s   r haue vndırstonde ıs   s sente not ıs   t thıs man ı thıs messager s   u Om ıs   ᵛ hınden ıs   w meede, and he hath spoke to me as propheciynge ıs   x take of hem ıs   y do her wıll ıs   z Om ı and theı *enforsyn hem to proue* s   a schulde so ı   b Om ı   c synne *a3ens God and the kıng ın bıldınge [of Jerusalem* s] ıs   d that theı ı   e wolden ı   f ın thıs haue ıs   g yuel *a3ens me* ı yuel *or quarel a3ens me* s   h wolden ı   ı that for ıs

15 fetus, that fereden me. Forsothe the wal
is fulfild the fiue and twentithe dai of
the sixte moneth, in two and fifti daȝes.
16 It is do thanne, whan alle oure enemys
hadden herd, that alle the Jentilis that
weren in oure enuyroun dredden, and
fellen togidere with inne themself, and
knewen, that of the Lord was do this
17 were. But and in tho daȝes manye epistolis of the moste wrthi men of Jewis
weren sent to Tobie, and fro Tobie camen
18 to them. Manye forsothe weren in Jude,
hauende his oth ; for he was the sone in
lawe of Sechenye, sone of Jorel ; and Johannan, his sone, hadde taken the doȝter
19 of Mosollam, sone of Barachie. But and
thei preseden hym befor me, and my
woordis thei tolden to hym ; and Thobias sente lettris, that he shulde fere me.

Sanaballath, biᵏ siche werkis 'of hem¹; but
also of ᵐ Noodie, the profete, and of othere
profetis, that maden ᵘ me aferd. Forsothe° ¹⁵
the wal was fillidᵖ in the fyue and twentithe dai of the monethe Ebulᑫ†, in two
and fifti daies. Sotheliʳ it was doon, ¹⁶
whanne alle oure enemyes hadden herd,
that alle hethene men dreddenˢ, that weren
in oure cumpas, and thei felden doun with
ynne hem silf, and wisteᵗ, that this work
was maad of God. But also in tho daies ¹⁷
many pistlisᵘ of the principal men of Jewis
weren sent to Tobie, and camenᵛ fro Tobie
to hem. For many men weren in Judee, ¹⁸
andʷ hadden his oothˣ‡ ; for he hadde
weddid the douȝter of Sechenye, the sone
of Rote*ʸ ; and Johannam, his sone, hadde
take the douȝter of Mosallam, soneᶻ of
Barachie. Butᵃ also thei preisiden hymᵇ ¹⁹
bifor me, and teiden my° wordisᵈ to°
hym ; and Tobie sente lettris, for to make
me aferd.

† Ebul; Ebul
is the sixte
¹⁶ monethe anen-
tis Ebreis, and
it answerith in
parti to oure
August, and in
party to Sep-
tembre. Lire
here. c.

‡ ooth; that is,
bond of pees
with him, con-
fermed with an
ooth. Lire
here. c.

CAP. VII.

1 Aftir forsothe that the wal is maad
vp, and I sette the ȝate leuys, and noumbride the porteres, and the singeris, and
2 the Leuitis, I comaundede to Aneny, my
brother, and to Ananye, prince of the
hous of Jerusalem ; he forsothe as a sothfast man, and dredende God more than
3 othere was seen ; and I seide to hem,
The ȝatis of Jerusalem be thei not opened
vnto the hete of the sunne ; and whan ȝit
I stod neeȝh, the ȝatis ben closid and
stoppid. And I sette keperis of the
dwelleris of Jerusalem, eche bi ther
4 whilis, and eche aȝen his hous. Forsothe
the cite was myche brod and gret, and
the puple litil in the middel of it, and
5 ther weren not housis bild. God forsothe ȝaf in myn herte, and I gaderede
togidere the most wrshipeful men, and

CAP. VII.

Forsotheᵍ aftir that the wal of Jerusa- 1
lem was bildid, and Y hadde setʰ ȝatisⁱ,
and Yᵏ hadde noumbrid porters¹, and
syngeris, and dekenys, Y comaunndide toᵐ 2
Aneny, my brother, and to Ananye, theⁿ
prince of the hows of Jerusalem ; for he°
semyde a sothefast man, and dredynge
God more than othere men *diden;* 'andᵖ 3
Y seide 'to hemᴾ, The ȝatis of Jerusalem
ben not openyd 'til toᑫ the heete of the
sunne ; and, whanne Y was ȝit present,
the ȝatis weren closid, and lockid. And
Y settideʳ keperisˢ of the dwelleris of Jerusalem, alle men bi her whilisᵗ, and ech
man aȝensᵘ hisᵛ hows. Sotheliʷ the citee 4
was ful brood and greet, and litil puple
wns in myddisˣ therof, and housisʸ weren
not bildidᶻ§. Forsotheᵃ God ȝafᵇ in myn 5
herte, and Y gaderide togidere the prin-

§ housis weren
not bildid to
enhabite, but
hulkis and
pentisis weren
maad bisidis
the wallis in
the ynnere
part, in whiche
they mysten
abide for a
litil tyme, til
the citee were
bildid. Lire
here. c.

ᵏ han troublid, and aftir her 18.   ¹ ȝelde to hem 18.   ᵐ haue thou mynde of 8.   ⁿ han maad 18.
° And 18.   ᴾ endid 1. fillid or endid 8.   ᑫ of Ebul, that is, August 1. of Ebul 8.   ʳ And 1.   ˢ dredden
us 1. dredden of vs 8.   ᵗ thei wisten 1. thei wisten thanne 8.   ᵘ lettris 18.   ᵛ camen also 18.   ʷ that 18.
ˣ ooth, that is, weren sworen to him 1. ooth, and weren asurid to him bi ooth 8.   ʸ Rotel, a greet potes-
tate 8.   ᶻ the sone 18.   ᵃ And 18.   ᵇ this Tobie 18.   ° to me 18.   ᵈ feerful wordis 8.   ° of 18.   ᶠ Om. 18.
ᵍ And 18.   ʰ set up 18.   ⁱ the ȝatis therof 18.   ᵏ Om. 18.   ¹ the porters 18.   ᵐ Om. 8.   ⁿ Om. 8.   ° this
prince 8.   ᴾ Om. 8.   ᑫ vnto 8.   ʳ sett 8.   ˢ kepers therof 8.   ᵗ whilis or tymes 1.   ᵘ forn aȝens 18.   ᵛ his
owne 18.   ʷ And 18.   ˣ the myddis 18.   ʸ the housis 18.   ᶻ ȝitt bildid 18.   ᵃ And 18.   ᵇ ȝaue
to me 8.

the maister iugis, and the comun, that I noumbre hem, and I fond the boc of the noumbring of hem, that hadden steȝid vp first And it is founde[e] writen in it, 6 These[f] the sones of the prouince, that steȝeden vp fro the caitifte of transmigiacioun, the whiche Nabugodonosor, king of Babiloine, hadde tianslatid, and thei ben turned aȝeen in to Jeiusalem and in 7 to Jude, eche in to his cite, that camen with Sorobabel; Josue, Neemias, Azarias, Raamias, Naanum, Mardocheus, Bethsar, Mesfarath, Beggai, Naum, Banaa The noumbre of the men of the puple of 8 Irael; the sones of Faros, two thousend 9 and hundrid and two and seuenti, the sonus of Safaie, thre hundrid foure score 10 and two; the sonus of Area, sixe hundrid 11 two and fifti, the sonus of Faeth Moab, of the sonus of Josue and of Joab, two thousend eiȝte[g] hundrid and eiȝtetene, 12 the sonus of Elam, a thousend eiȝte hun-13 drid and foure and fifti; the sonus of Zechua, eiȝte hundrid and fiue and fourti; 14 the sonus of Zachai, senene hundrid and 15 sixty; the sonus of Bennui, sixe hundrid 16 and eiȝte and fourti, the sonus of Ebai, 17 sixe hundiid 'and eiȝte[h] and twenti, the sonus of Asgad, two thousend thre hun-18 drid and two and twenti, the sonus of Asonycham, sixe hundrid and seuene and 19 sixti; the sonus of Bagoamy, two thou-20 send and seuene and sixti; the sonus of Adin, sixe hundrid and fiue and fifti; 21 the sonus of Aser, sone of Ezechie, eiȝte 22 and twenti, the sonus of Asem, thre hun-23 drid and eiȝte and twenti, the sonus of Bethsai, thre hundiid and foure and 24 twenti, the sonus of Aref, an hundrid 25 and seuene and twenti; the sonus of Sa-26 laon fiue and nynti; the men of Beth-lem and of Nethufa, an hundrid foure

cipal men[c], and magistratis[d], and the comyn puple, foi to noumbre hem, and Y foond the[e] book of the noumbre of hem, that hadden stied[f] firsts And it was foundun writun thei ynne, These ben the sones of[g] the prouynce, 'that stieden[h] fro the caitifte of men passynge ouei[i], whiche Nabugodonosor, the kyng of Babiloyne, hadde 'translatid, etheii led ouer[k], and thei that 7 weren comun with Zorobabel turneden aȝen in to Jerusalem and in to Judee, ech man in[l] to his citee; Josue[m], Neemye, Azarie, Raanye, Naanum, Mardochee, Bethsar, Mespharath, Beggaay, Naum, Baann[n] The[o] noumbre of men[p] of the puple of Israel[q]; the sones of Pharos, two[r] 8 thousynde an hundrid and two and se-uenti; the sones of Saphaie, thre[s] hun-9 drid and two and seuenti, the sones of 10 Area, sixe[t] hundrid and two and fifti, the sones of Phaeth Moab, of the sones 11 of Josue and of Joab, two[u] thousynde eiȝte hundrid and eiȝtene; the sones of 12 Helam, a[v] thousynde eiȝte hundrid and foure and fifti, the sones of Ezecua, eiȝte[w] 13 hundrid and fyue and fourti, the sones 14 of Zachai, seuene[x] hundrid and sixti, the 15 sones of Bennuy, sixe[y] hundrid and eiȝte and fourti, the sones of Hebahi, sixe[z] 16 hundrid and eiȝte and twenti · the sones 17 of Degad, two[z] thousynde thre hundrid ' and two and twenti; the sones of Azo-18 nicam, sixe[a] hundrid and seuene and ' sixti; the sones of Bagoamy, two[b] thou-19 synde and seuene and sixti, the sones 20 of Adyn, sixe[c] hundiid and fiue and ' fifti; the sones of Azer, sone[d] of Eze-21 chie, eiȝte[e] and twenti; the sones of A-22 sem, thre[f] hundiid and eiȝte and tventi; the sones of Bethsai, thre[g] hundrid and 23 foure and twenti; the sones of Areph, 24 an[h] hundrid and seuene and twenti, the 25

---

       e Om E pr m   f These ben A   g sexe A   b Om A

c Om is   d maistir men is   e a is   f stied up i   g first fro the caitiftee is   h whiche ȝeden up i which stieden vp s   i ouer fro Babiloyne to Jerusalem is   J Om is   k ouer into Babiloyne is l Om is   m that is to uite, Josue i that is to seie, Josue s   n and Baana is   o And the is   p the men s   q Israel is this is   r weren two is   s weren thre s   t weren sixe s   u weren two is v weren n is   w weren eiȝte is   x weren seuene is   Y weren sixe is   z weren two is   a weren sixe is b weren two is   c weren sixe is   d the sone is   e weren eiȝte is   f weren thre is.   g weren thre is h weren an is

27 score and eiȝte; men of Anatot, an hun-
28 drid and eiȝte and twenti; men of Beth-
29 samoth, two and fourti; men of Cariathiarim, Sefira, and Beroth, seuene hundrid
30 and thre and fourti; men of Ramaa and
of Gabaa, sixe hundrid and oon and
31 twenti; men of Machinas, two hundrid
32 and two and twenti; men of Bethel and
of Hai, an hundrid and thre and twenti;
33 men of the tother Nebo, two and fifti;
34 men of the tother Elam, a thousend two
35 hundrid and foure and fifti; the sonus
36 of Arem, thre hundrid and twenti; the
sonus of Jericho, thre hundrid and fiue
37 and fourti; the sonus of Joiadid and of
Anon, seuene hundrid and oon and
38 twenti; the sonus of Senaa, thre thou-
39 send nyne hundrid and thretti; prestus,
the sonus of Joiada, in the hous of Josue,
40 nyne hundrid and foure and seuenti; the
sonys of Emmer, a thousend and two and
41 fifti; the sonus of Fassur, a thousend two
42 hundrid seuene and fourti; the sones of
Arem, a thousend and seuentene; Le-
43
44 uitus, sonus of Josue and of Gadimel, sonus
of Odina, seuenti and foure; singeres,
45 sonus of Asaf, an hundrid and seuene and
46 fourti; porteres, sonus of Sellum, sonus of
Ather, sonus of Thelmon, sonus of Accub,
sonus of Accita, sonus of Sobai, an hun-
47 drid and eiȝte and thretti; sodeknes,
sonus of Soa, sonus of Asfa, sonus of The-
48 baoth, sonus of Cheros, sonus of Sicca,
sonus of Fado, sonus of Lebana, sonus of
49 Agaba, sonus of Selmon, sonus of Anon,
50 sonus of Jeddel, sonys of Gair, sonus of
Raaia, sonus of Rasym, sonus of Nechoda,
51 sonus of Jesem, sonus of Asa, sonus of
52 Fascha, sonus of Besai, sonus of Minum,
53 sonus of Nefusym, sonis of Bechue, sonus
54 of Acufa, sonus of Assur, sonus of Belloth,
55 sonus of Meida, sonus of Arsa, sonus of
Berchos, sonus of Cizara, sonus of Thema,
56
57 sonus of Nezia, sonus of Athifa, sonus of
the seruauns of Salomon, sonus of Sothai,

sones of Zabaon, fyue[l] and twenti; the 26
men of Bethleem and of Necupha, an[k]
hundrid foure score and eiȝte; the men 27
of Anatoth, an[k] hundrid and eiȝte and
twenti; the men of Bethamoth, two[l] and 28
fourti; the men of Cariathiarym, of Ce- 29
phura, and Beroth[m], seuene[n] hundrid and
thre and fourti; the men of Rama and of 30
Gabaa, sixe[o] hundrid and oon and twenti;
the men of Machimas, two[p] hundrid and 31
two and twenti; the men of Bethel and 32
of Hay, an[q] hundrid and thre and twenti;
the men of the tother[r] Nebo, two[s] and 33
fifti; the men of the tother[t] Helam, an[u] 34
thousynde two hundrid and foure and
fifti; the sones of Arem, thre[v] hundrid 35
and twenti; the sones of Jerico, thre[w] 36
hundrid and fyue and fourti; the sones 37
of Joiadid and Anon[x], seuene[y] hundrid
and oon and twenti; the sones of Senaa, 38
thre[z] thousynde nyne hundrid and thritti;
preestis, the sones of Idaic, in the hous of 39
Josua, nyne[a] hundrid and foure and seuenti; the sones of Emmer, a[b] thousynde 40
and two and fifti; the sones of Phassur, 41
a[b] thousynd two[c] hundrid and 'seuene and
fourti[d]; the sones of Arem, a[b] thousynde 42
and eiȝtene; dekenes, the sones of Josue 43
and of Gadymel, sones[e] of Odyna, foure[f] 44
and seuenti; syngeris, the[g] sones of Asaph, 45
an[h] hundrid and seuene and fourti; por- 46
teris, the sones of Sellum, sones[i] of Ater,
sones[i] of Thelmon, sones [i] of Accub, sones [i]
of Accita, sones [i] of Sobai, an[k] hundrid
and eiȝte and thretti; Nathynneis, sones[l] 47
of Soa, sones[l] of Aspha, sones[l] of Thebaoth, sones[l] of Cheros, sones[l] of Sicca, sones[l] 48
of Phado, sones[l] of Lebana, sones[l] of Agaba, sones[l] of Selmon, sones[l] of Anau, sones[l] 49
of Geddel, sones[l] of Gaer, sones[l] of Raaie, 50
sones[l] of Rasym, sones[l] of Necuda, sones[l] 51
of Jezem, sones[l] of Asa, sones[l] of Phascha,
sones[l] of Besai, sones[l] of Mynum, sones of 52
Nephusym, sones of Bechue, sones of Acu- 53
pha, sones of Assur, sones of Belloth, sones 54

---

i *weren* fyue 1s.   k *weren* an 1s.   l *weren* two 1s.   m *of Beroth* 1s.   n *weren* seuene 1s.   o *weren*
sixe 1s.   p *weren* two 1s.   q *weren* an 1s.   r *oother* 1s.   s *weren* two 1s.   t *oother* 1s.   u *weren* a 1s.
v *weren* thre 1s.   w *weren* thre 1s.   x *of Anon* 1s.   y *weren* seuene 1s.   z *weren* thre 1s.   a *weren*
nyne 1s.   b *weren* a 1s.   c *and two* K.   d *seuenti and foure* A *pr. m.* sixti and seuene A *sec. m.*   e *the*
sones 1s.   f *weren foure* s.   g *of the* 1s.   h *weren* an s.   i *the sones* 1s.   k *weren* an 1s.   l *the sones* 1s.

58 sonus of Soforeth, sonus of Ferida, sonus of Jachala, sonus of Dalchon, sonns of 59 Jeddel, sonus of Safacia, sonus of Atchil, sonus of Focereth, that was boin of 60 Abaim, sone of Amon, alle the sodek-nes, and the sonus of the thiallis of Sala-mon, thre hundiid and two and twenti 61 These ben that steʒeden vp of Themelath, Thelarsa, Cherub, Addo, and Emmer, and thei myʒten not shewe the hous of ther fadnis, and ther sed, whether of 62 Israel thei weren, sonus of Dalaia, sonus of Thobia, sonus of Nethoda, sixe hun-63 drid and two and fouiti, and of the prestis, sonus of Abia sonus of Achos, sonus of Beisellai, that toc a wif of the doʒtris of Bersellai Galadite, and is cle-64 pid bi the name of hem, these soʒten the scripture of ther genelogie, and founde 65 not, and ben cast out fro presthod. And Athersatha seide to them, that thei shul-den not eten of the holi thingus of ha-lewis, to the time that ther rijse a taʒt 66 and lerned prest Al the multitude as o man, two and fouiti thousend thre hun-67 drid and sixti, with oute the seruauns and the hand wymmen of hem, that weren seuen thousend thre hundrid and seuene and thretti, and among hem sing-eres and singressis two hundrid and fiue 68 and fourti The hors of hem, seuene 69 hundrid and thie and thretti; the ca-mailis of hem, foure hundrid and fiue and thretti; the assis of hem, sixe thousend seuene hundred and thretti, 'the mulis of hem, two hundrid and fiue and fourti[l] 70 Summe forsothe of the princis of the meynes ʒeuen expensis in to the werc of God, Athersatha ʒaf in to the tresorie, of gold, dragmys a thousend, fifty violis, prestus cotus fiue hundrid and thretti

55 of Meida, sones of Arsa, sones of Berchos, 56 sones of Sisara, sones of Thema, sones of 57 Nesia, sones of Atipha, sones of the ser-uauntis of Salomon, sones of Sothai, sones of Sophoreth, sones of Pherida, sones of 58 Jacala, sones of Dalcon, sones of Geddel, sones of Saphatie, sones of Atthal, the[m] 59 sones of Phetereth, 'that was[n] borun of Abaim, sone[o] of Amon, alle Natynneis, 60 and the sones of the seruauntis of Salo-mon, ueren thre hundrid and two and twenti[p]. Forsothe[q] these it[r] ben[s] that 61 stieden[t], Dethemel[u], Mela[v], Thelarsa[w], Cherub[x], Addo[y], and Emmer[z], and[a] myʒten not schewe the hows of her fadris, and[b] her seed, whether thei weren of[c] Israel[d], the sones of Dalaic, the sones of Tobie, 62 the[o] sones of Nethoda, sixe[f] hundrid and two and fourti; and of prestis[g], the sones 63 of Abia, the sones of Achos, the sones of Berzellai, that took a wijf of the douʒtris of Berzellai of Galaad, and was[h] clepid bi the name of hem, these[i] souʒten the scrip-64 ture of her genelogie[k], and founden[l] not, and weren[m] cast out of presthod. And 65 Athersata seide to hem, that thei schulden not eete of the hooli thingis of hooli men, til[n] a wis prest 'and lerud[o] roos[p] Al the 66 multitude as[q] o man, two[r] and fourti thou-synde sixe hundrid and sixti[s], outakun[t] 67 the[n] seruauntis and handmaidis[v] of hem, that[w] weren seuene thousynde thre hun-drid and seuene and thretti; and[x] among 68 the syngeris and syngeressis[y], sixe[z] hun-drid and fyue and fourti The horsis of 68 hem, sixe[b] hundrid and sixe and thritti; the mulis of hem, two[c] hundrid and fyue and fourti, the camels of hem, foure[d] 69 hundrid and fyue and thritti, the assis of hem, sixe[e] thousynde eiʒte hundrid and thritti Forsothe[f] summe of the princes 70

[l] Om ACFH

[m] Om is   [n] whiche weren is   [o] the sone is   [p] seuenti sx   [q] And is   [r] that suen is   [s] ben thei is   [t] stieden up of the euntrey is   [u] of Dethemel ix pr m   of Themel s   [v] Om is   [w] of Thelarsa is   [x] of Cherub is   [y] of Addo is   [z] of Emmer is   [a] the whiche i   which s   [b] ne is   [c] of the lynage of is   [d] Israel or no i   Israel or nay s   [e] Om i   [f] weren sixe is   [g] the prestis is   [h] he wns is   [i] these men s   [k] generacioun is   [l] thei founden it is   [m] thei weren therfore is   [n] til that is   [o] lerned EM Om is   [p] rise [ros s] up among the peple is.   [q] was as i   was gaderid togidre as s   [r] and ther weren of hem two s   [s] sixti men is   [t] withoute i   [u] Om i   [v] handmaidens is   [w] whiche is   [x] Om x   [y] syngsteres i   [z] weren sixe is   [a] fourti seruauntis and hondmaydens s   [b] weren sixe is   [c] weren two is   [d] weren foure is   [e] weren sixe is   [f] Sothely is

71 And of the princis of the[k] meines ther
3euen in to the tresorie of the werk, of
gold, dragmis twenti thousend, and of
siluer, two thousend besauntus and two
72 hundrid.   And that that 3af the tother
puple, of gold, dragmis twenti thousend,
and of siluer, besauntus two thousend, and
prestus cotus sixti and seuenn. Forsothe
the prestus, and Leuitus, and the porteris,
and singeris, and the tother comun, and
the sodeknys, and al Irael dwelten in
ther cites.

of meynees[g] 3auen costis in to the werk
of God ; Athersata 3af in to the tresour,
a thousynde dragmes of gold, fifti[h] viols,
fyue[i] hundrid and thritti cootis of prestis.
And of the prynces of meynees thei 3auen 71
in to the tresour of the werk, twenti thousynde dragmes of gold, and two thousynde
and two hundrid besauntis of siluer. And 72
that that the residue[k] puple 3af, twenti[l]
thousynde dragmes of gold, and two thousynde besauntis of siluer, and seuene and
sixti cootis of prestis. Sotheli[m] prestis,
and dekenes, and porteris, and syngeris,
and the residue[n] puple, and Natynneis,
and al Israel dwelliden[o] in her citees.

CAP. VIII.

1   And the seuenthe monethe of the feste
of tabernaclis was comen vnder Esdra
and Neemie ; the sonus forsothe of Irael
weren in ther cites. And al the puple is
gedered as oo man, at the strete that is
befor the 3ate of watris. And thei seiden
to Esdra, scribe, that he shulde bringe
forth the boc of the lawe of Moises, that
the Lord hadde comaundid to Irael.
2 Thanne Esdras, the preest, bro3te forth
the lawe, befor the multitude of men and
wymmen, and to alle that my3ten vnderstonde, in the firste dai of the seuenthe
3 monyth. And he radde in it apertli in
the strete that was befor the 3ate of
watris, fro the morutid vnto the[l] middai,
in the si3te of men and wymmen and of
wise men ; and the eris of al the puple
4 weren ri3t to the boc. Forsothe Esdras
scribe stod vpon a treene gree[m], the
whiche he hadde maad to speken in ; and
ther stoden beside hym, Mathathias,
and Semma, and Anania, and Vria, and
Elchia, and Maasia, at his ri3t side ; and
at his left[n], Fadaia, Misael, and Melchia,
Assum, and Asef, Dana, and Acharia,

CAP. VIII.

And[p] the seuenthe monethe[q]† `was comun[r] 1
vndur Esdras[s] and Neemye[t] ; sotheli the
sones of Israel weren in her cytees. And al
the puple was gaderid togydere as o man,
to[u] the[v] street which[w] is bifor the 3ate of
watris. And thei seiden to Esdras, the
scribe[x], that he schulde brynge[y] the book
of the lawe of Moises, which[z] the Lord
hadde comaundid to Israel. Therfor[a] 2
Esdras, the preest, brou3te[b] the lawe bifor
the multitude of men and of wymmen, and
bifor alle[c] that my3ten vndurstonde[d], `in
the firste day of the seuenth monethe[e].
And he[f] redde in it opynli in the street 3
that was bifor the 3ate of watris, fro the
morewtid `til to[g] myddai, in the si3t of men
and of wymmen and of wise men ; and the
eeris of al the puple weren reisid[h] to the
book[i]. Forsothe[k] Esdras the writere stood 4
on the[l] grees of tree, which[m] he hadde
maad to speke theron[n] ; and Mathatie, and
Semma, and Ananye, and Vrie, and Elchie, and Maasie stoden bisidis hym at his
ri3t half ; and Phadaie, Mysael, and Melchie, Assum, and Asepb, Dana, and Zacharie, and Mosollam stoden at the left

† this word
synagogie is not
in Ebreu, ne-
ther is of the
text, nether is
vndurstandun ;
for senofegie
and the feste
of tabernaclis
is al oon, that
was maad in
the xv. day.
Lire here. c.

k Om. A.   l Om. EFII.   m grece AFII.   n left side A.

g the meynees is.   h and fifti s.   i and fyue is.   k remenaunt is.   l was twenti is.   m And is.   n remenaunt
is.   o dwelliden there aftir is.   p And whanne is.   q monethe of the feest of tabernaclis is.   r had come is.
s the office of Esdras is.   t of Neemye is.   u into is.   v a is.   w that is.   x writer is.   y brynge forth is.
z whiche lawe is.   a Therfor in the firste day of the seuenthe monthe is.   b brou3te forth is.   c alle men is.
d vndirstonde it is.   e Om. is.   f Om. s.   g vnto is.   h reisid up is.   i book to here the lawe s.
k And is.   l a s.   m that i.   n upon i, vpon to the peple s.

5 and Mosollam   And Esdras openede the boc beforn al the puple ; vp on al the puple forsothe he stod ouer , and whan he 6 hadde opened it, al the puple stod   And Esdras blesside to the Lord God with a gret vois ; and al the puple answerde, Amen, Amen, reiend vp ther hondus. And thei ben ful bowid, and bowid in to 7 the erthe thei honoureden God   But Josue, and Baani, and Serebia, Jamyn, Accub, Sefai, Odia, Maasia, Celitha, Azarias, Josabeth, Anan, Fallaia, Leuitus, maden silence in the puple to the lawe to ben herd   The puple forsothe 8 stod in his gree   And thei radden in the boc of the lawe distincth and aperth to vnderstonde , and thei vnderstoden, whan 9 it schulde be rad   Forsothe Neemias, he is Athersata, seide, and Esdras, prest and scribe, and the Leuitus, remenyng to al the puple, A dai is halewid to the Lord oure God , wileth not weilen, and wileth not wepen   Forsothe al the puple wepte, when he herde the woordis of the lawe 10 And he seide to them, Goth, and eteth fatte thingis, and drinketh meth, and sendeth for hem, that han not maad redi to them self, for it is the holi dai of the Lord , wileth not be dreri, forsothe the 11 ioɜe of the Lord is ɜoure strengthe.   Also Leuitus maden silence in al the puple, seiende, Holdeth ɜour pes, for it is hali- 12 dai, and wileth not sorewen   And so al the puple wente to ete, and drinken, and to sende partis, and to make gret glad- nesse , for thei vnderstoden the woordis, 13 that he hadde taɜt hem.   In the secunde dai ben gedered the princis of meynes, and al the puple, prestus, and Leuitus, to Esdra, scribe, that he remene to them the

half   And Esdras openyde the book[o] bifor 5 al the puple , for he[p] apperide ouer al the puple ; and whanne he hadde openyd the book, al the puple stood[q]   And Esdras 6 blesside the Lord God with greet vois , and al the puple answeride, Amen, Amen[r], reisynge[a] her hondis   And thei weren bowid, and thei worschipiden God, lowli on[t] the erthe Forsothe[u] Josue, and Baany, 7 and Serebie, Jamyn[v], Acub, Septhai, Odia, Maasie, Celitha, Aɜarie, Jorabeth, Anan, Phallaie, dekenes, maden silence in the puple for to here the lawe   Sotheli[w] the 8 puple stood in her degree. And thei[x] 8 redden in the book of Goddis lawe dis- tincth, 'ether atreet[y], and opynli to[z] vnder- stonde[a] ; 'and thei vnderstoden[b], whanne it was red[c]   Forsothe[d] Neemye seide[e], he 9 is[f] Athersata[g], and Esdras, the preest and writere, and the dekenes, expownynge[h] to al the puple, It[i] is a dai halewid to 'oure Lord God[k] ; nyle ɜe moine[l], and nyle ɜe wepe‡   For[m] al the puple wepte, whanne it herde the wordis of the[n] lawe   And 10 he seide to hem, Go ɜe, and 'ete ɜe[p] fatte thingis, and drynke ɜe wiyn 'maad swete with hony[q], and sende ɜe partis[r] to hem, that maden[s] not redi[t] to hem silf, for it is an hooli dai of the Lord ; 'nyle ɜe be sory[a], for[v] the ioye§ of the Lord is ɜoure strengthe. Sotheli[w] the dekenes maden 11 silence in al the puple, and seiden[x], Be ɜe stille, for it[y] is an hooli dai, and 'nyle ɜe make sorewe[z]   Therfor[a] al the puple[b] 12 ɜede for to ete, and drynke, and to sende partis[c], and 'to make[d] greet gladnesse ; for thei vndurstoden the wordis||[e], whiche[f] he[g] hadde tauɜt hem   And in the second dai 13 the princes of meynees, alle[h] the[i] puplis, prestis, and dekenes, weren gaderid to-

‡ To mourne and wepe in the holi dai, is to consent to synne, whrch is cause of mourn- yng and wep- ing s

§ ioie , that is, goostly ioye, bi which ɜe owen to haue ioye in this solemp- nyte, is ɜoure counfort, mak- inge ɜou stronge to goodnesse. Lire here c

|| To a feithful man the ioye of the Lord is to vnderstonde his lawe, and do therafter s

ᵛ thei H   ᴾ Om A   ᑫ for to AFFH

ᵒ book of Goddis lawe s   ᴾ he stondyng on the greeee s   ᑫ stood to here I   ʳ that is, be it doon, be it doon, κ marg   ˢ reisynge up is   ᵗ upon I   ᵘ And is   ᵛ and Jamyn is   ʷ And is   ˣ prestis s   ʸ atreed ᴀ Om I or atreet s   ᶻ to be is   ᵃ vndurstonde it I   ᵇ Om I and men vnderstode it s   ᶜ ther redde s   ᵈ And is   ᵉ Om is   ᶠ is clepid is   ᵍ Athersata seide is,   ʰ expowninge the lame is   ˡ This is   ᵏ the Lord oure God is   ˡ now morne s   ᵐ Sothly is   ⁿ Goddis s   ᵒ Neemye I the preist s   ᴾ etith s   ᑫ or meeth I or water maad swete with hony s   ʳ part therof I part of ɜour mete and drynke s   ˢ han is   ᵗ wherof to make redi s   ᵘ therfor be ɜe not sory I nyle ɜe now therfor be sori s   ᵛ Sothly is,   ʷ And is   ˣ thei seiden is   ʸ this is   ᶻ make ɜe no sorewe I   ᵃ Thanne I   ᵇ multitude is   ᶜ partis therof to the nedy I part therof to pore men s   ᵈ thei maden is   ᵉ wordis of Goddis lawe s   ᶠ that I   ᵍ the techere s   ʰ and alle is   ˡ Om s

3 x 2

14 woordis of the lawe. And thei founde writen in the lawe, the Lord to han comaundid in the hond of Moises, that the sonus of Irael dwelle in tabernaclis in the
15 solempne dai, the seuenthe moneth; and that thei prechen, and pupplishen vois in alle ther cites, and in Jerusalem; seiende, Goth out in to the hil, and bringeth braunchis of oliues, and braunchis of the most fair tree, and the braunchis of myrt^r tree, and bowis of palmys, and braunchis of a wodi tree, that ther be
16 made tabernaclis, as it is write. And al the puple wente out, and broȝten, and maden tabernaclis to them, eche in his hous, and in ther porchis, and in the porchis of the hous of God, and in the strete of the ȝate of watris, and in the strete of
17 the ȝate of Effraym. Thanne al the chirche of hem, that ben turned aȝeen fro the caitifte, made tabernaclis, and thei dwelten in tabernaclis. Forsothe the sonus of Irael hadden nott maad suche thingis fro the dai of Josue, sone of Nun, vnto that dai; and ther was a gret
18 gladnesse riȝt miche. Forsothe he radde in the boc of the lawe bi eche daȝes, fro the firste dai vn to the laste dai; and thei maden solempnete seuene daȝes, and in the eiȝthe a colect, after the custum.

CAP. IX.

1 In the foure and twentithe dai forsothe of this monith, the sonus of Irael camen togidere in fasting, and in sackis, and
2 erthe vpon^s hem. And the sed of the sonus of Irael is seuered fro eche alien sone. And thei stoden befor the Lord, and thei knoulecheden ther synnes, and

gidere to Esdras, the writere, that he schulde expowne to hem the wordis of the
14 lawe. And thei foundun writun in the lawe, that the Lord comaundide 'in the hond^k of Moyses, that the sones of Israel dwelle^l in tabernaclis^m in the solempue dai, in the seuenthe moneth; and that thei
15 preche, and pupplische a vois in alle her citees, and in Jerusalem; and seie, Go ȝe out in to the hil, and brynge ȝe bowis of olyue^n, and bowis of the faireste tree, the bowis of a myrte^o tree, and the braunchis of a^p palm tree^q, and the bowis of a 'tree ful of wode^r, that tabernaclis be maad^s, as it is writun. And^t al the puple ȝede out,
16 and thei brouȝten^u, and maden^v to hem silf^w tabernaclis, 'ech man in^x 'his hows roof^y, and in^z her stretis, 'ether forȝerdis^a, and in the large placis^b of Goddis hows, and in the street of the ȝate of watris, and in the street of the ȝate of Effraym. Ther-
17 for al the chirche^c of hem, that camen aȝen^d fro caytifte^e, made^f tabernaclis, and thei dwelliden in tabernaclis^g. For^h the sones of Israel hadden not do siche thingis fro the daies of Josue, sone^i of Nun, 'til to^k that dai; and ful greet gladnesse was^l. Forsothe^m
18 Esdras radde in the book of Goddis lawe bi alle daies^n, fro the firste dai 'til to^o the laste dai; and thei maden solempnytee^p bi seuene daies, and in the eiȝte day^q thei maden a gaderyng† of siluer^r, 'bi the custom^s.

CAP. IX.

Forsothe^t in the foure and twentithe
1 dai of this monethe, the sones of Israel camen togidere in fastyng^u, and in^2 sackis, and 'erthe was^v on^w hem^x. And the seed^y of the sones of Israel was departid fro ech alien sone^z. And thei stoden^a bifor the Lord, and knoulechi-

† a gaderyng; thas is, for necessaries of the temple. Lire here. c.

---

^r myr f.   ^s vp c.

^k hond or bi the doyng s.   ^l dwelle stille is.   ^m the tabernaclis i. her tabernaclis s.   ^n the olyue tree is.
^o mirre s.   ^p Om. is.   ^q trees is.   ^r wody tree is.   ^s maad of the bowis is.   ^t Om. s.   ^u brouȝten with hem bowis is.   ^v thei maden is.   ^w Om. s.   ^x Om. s.   ^y her hilid place i. Om. s.   ^z Om. s.   ^a Om. is.
^b strect is.   ^c that is, the congregacioun of inst folk i marg. chirche, that is, the gaderyng togidre s.
^d togidre s.   ^e the caitifte s.   ^f made to hem silf s.   ^g tho tabernaclis is.   ^h Certis is.   ^i the sone is.
^k vnto is.   ^l was there among hem i. was ther among the peple s.   ^m And is.   ^n dayes of the solempnite s.
^o vnto is. to x.   ^p the solempnytee s.   ^q day bi custom is.   ^r siluer to do withal charitable werkis after the lawe s.   ^s Om. is.   ^t Sothely is.   ^u fastyngis is.   ^v ther was erthe i. thei castiden erthe s.
^w upon is.   ^x hem silf s.   ^y lynage is.   ^z man is.   ^a stoden up is.

ꝺ the wickednesses of thei fadiis And thei risen togidere to stonden, and thei radden in the volum of the lawe of the Loid thei God foure sithes in the dai, and foure sithes in the nyȝt, thei knou-lecheden, and preiseden the Lord ther 4 God Forsothe ther risen vp on the gree, of Leuitus Jesue, and Baani, and Cedmiel, Remm, Abany, Sarabias, Baani 5 And the Leuitus crieden with a giet vois to the Lord thei God And Jesue and Sedeniel, Bonni, Assebia, Serebia Aiabia, Odaia, Sebua, Fachaia, seiden, Riseth, and blesseth to the Lord oure God fio withouten ende and vn to with oute ende; and blesse thei to the heȝe name of thi glorie in alle blessing and preising. 6 And Esdras seide, Thou thi self, Lord, alone, thou madist heuene of heuenus, and al the ost of hem, the eithe and alle thingus that in it ben, ses aud alle thingus that in hem ben, and thou quikenest alle these thingus, and the ost of heuene 7 honoureth thee Thou thi self Lord God, that chesedest Abraham, and laddest hym out fro the fijr of Caldeis, and ssettist his name Abiaham, and foundist his herte trewe befor thee, and smite with hym pes couuenaunt, that thou ȝeue to hym the lond of Cananee, Ethei, and Euei, and Amorrei, and Feiesei, and Je-busei, and Jeigesei, that thou ȝeue to his sed, and thou hast fulfild thi woordis, 9 for thou art riȝtwis And thou hast seen the affliccioun of oure fadris in Egipt, and the cri of hem thou hast herd vpon 10 the rede se And thou ȝeue tocnes and wndris in Faiao, and in alle his seruauuis, and in al the puple of that lond, for-sothe thou hast knowen, for proudli thei diden aȝen hem, and thou madist to thee 11 a name as in this dai And the see thou

den her synnes, and the wickidnessis of hei fadris And theit† risiden togidere to stonde, and thei redden in the book of the lawe of 'her Loid God fouresiths in the dai, and fouresithis in the niȝt; thei knoulechiden, and he-rieden 'her Lord God Forsothe 4 'thei risiden on the degree, of dekenes, Jesuy, and Bany, Cedynyel, Remmy, Abany, Sarabie, Bany, and Chanany. 'And the dekenes crieden with grete vois 5 to her Lord God And Jesue, and Cedy-niel, Bonny, Assebie, Serebie, Aiabie, Odaie, Sebua, and Facaia, seiden, Rise ȝe, and blesse ȝe ȝoure Lord God fio without bigynnyng and til in to with outen ende, and blesse thei the liȝe name of thi glorie in al blessyng and preysyng And Esdras 6 seide‡, Thou thi silf, Lord, art aloone, thou madist heuene and the heuene of heuenes, and al the ostȝ of tho heuenes, thou madist the erthe and alle thingis that ben theie ynne, 'thou madist the sees and alle thingis that ben in tho; and thou quikenyst alle these thingis; and the oost|| of heuene worschipith thee Thou thi silf 7 art the Loid God, that chesidist Abiam, and leddist hym out of the fier of Caldeis, and settidist his name Abraham, and 8 foundist his heite feithful bifor thee, and thou hast smyte with hym a boond of pees, that thou woldist ȝyue to hym the lond of Cananei, of Ethei, of Euey, and of Animorrei, and of Pheiezei, and of Je-buzei, and of Gergesei, that thou woldist ȝyue it to his seed; and thou hast fillid thi wordis, for thou art iust And thou hast 10 seyn the turment of oure fadris in Egipt, and thou heidist the cry of hem on the reed see. And thou hast ȝoue signes and grete wondris in Farao, and in alle hise seruauntis, and in al the puple of that

† and they, that is, dekenes I ire here c

‡ this word and Esdras seide, is not in Ebreu, nether is of the text, for it is not the word of Esdras aloone, but also of othere men knoulechinge that God is cre-atoure of alle heuenly thingis and erthely thingis Lire here c

§ oost, that is, sterris ard liȝtis. Lire herr c.

|| oost, for aun-gels worschi-pen God bi propir wor-schip, and sterris and liȝtis worschepen him, bi wor-schip seid largely, in as myche as in the iſtis of her liȝtis, the good-nesse and wis-dom of God is knowun, and in thin reson-able creaturis ben sturned to worschape God bi propir wor-schip Lire here c

ꝺ resen 1 risen ꝗ1 c stonde bifore the Lord s d the Lord her God 1ꝗ e And 1s f Om 1s g and Cedynyel 1ꝗ h and Abany 1s Om 1 k Chanany residen up [to reed Goddis lawe s] upon the degree of dekenes 1ꝗ Om 1s m And the dekenes s n Facaia, dekens, crieden with gret voice to the Lord her God, and 1 Facaia crieden with a greet voice to the Lord her God, and s o the Lord ȝoure God 1s p Lord, blesse 1ꝗ q alone God s r Om 1 and 1 and thou madist s t hem 1s u thou settidist 1 thou settidest or clepidist s v thou foundist 1s w and s x Om 1 y and that 1s z fulfil-lid 1ꝗ a upon 1ꝗ b tokens 1s

deuidedest beforn hem, and thei passeden ouer thur3 the middel of the se in drie ; the pursueris forsothe of hem thou threwe aferr in to the depnesse, as a ston in 12 stronge watris. And in a pileer of a cloude ledere of hem thou were bi dai, and in a piler of fijr bi ny3t, that the weie aperede to them, bi whiche thei 13 wenten in. Also to the hil of Sinai thou came doun, and speke to hem fro heuene, and 3eue to them ri3te domus, and the lawe of treuthe, cerimoines, and gode 14 hestis. And halewid sabot thou shewedest to them ; and maundemens, and cerimoines, and lawe, thou comaundedist[u] to them, in the hond of Moises, 15 thi seruaunt. Bred also fro heuene thou 3eue to them in ther hunger ; and water of a ston thou bro3tist out to hem threstende ; and thou seidest to them, that thei shulden gon in, and welde the lond, vp on the whiche thou reredist thin hond, 16 that thou take it to hem. Thei forsothe and ther fadris proudli diden, and inwardli hardeden ther nollis, and thei 17 herden not thi maundemens. And thei wolden not heren ; and thei recordeden not of thi merueilis, that thou haddest do to them ; and thei inwardli hardeden ther nollis ; and thei 3euen hed[v], that thei were turned togidere to ther thraldam ; thou forsothe God merciful, and noble, and benigne, longe abidende, and of myche mercy, and thou forsoke not 18 hem ; and forsothe whan thei hadden maad to them a calf, as bi strif 3oten, and sciden, This is thi God that ladde thee out fro Egipt, and thei diden grete 19 blasfemys. Thou forsothe in thi manie mercies lafttist them not in desert ; a piler of a cloude wente not awei fro hem bi

lond ; for thou knowist, that thei[c] diden proudli a3ens oure fadris ; and[d] thou madist to thee a name[e], as also in this dai[f]. And thou departidist the see bifor 11 hem[g], and thei passiden thorou the 'myddis of the see[h] in the[i] drie place ; forsothe[k] thou castidist doun the pursueris of hem into[l] depthe[m], as a stoon in strong watris. And in a piler of cloude thou were the 12 ledere of hem bi dai, and in a piler of fier bi ny3t, that the weie, bi which thei entriden, schulde appere to hem. Also thou 13 camest doun at[n] the hil of Synai, and spakist[o] with[p] hem[q] fro heuene, and thou 3auest to hem ri3tful domes, and the lawe of trewthe, cerymonyes[r], and goode comaundementis[s]. And thou schewidist to 14 hem an halewid sabat ; and thou comaundidist 'to hem[t] comaundementis[u], and cerymonyes[v], and lawe[w], in the hond of Moises, thi seruaunt. Also[x] thou 3auest 15 to hem breed fro[y] heuene in her hungur ; and thou leddist out of the stoon watir[z] to hem thirstinge ; and thou seidist to hem, that thei schulden entre, and haue in possessioun the[a] lond[b], on[c] which[d] *lond* thou reisidist[e] thin hond, that thou schuldist 3yue it[f] to hem. But[g] 'thei and[h] oure fa- 16 dris diden proudli[i], and maden[k] hard her nollis, and herden[l] not thi comaundementis[m]. And thei nolden[n] here ; and 17 thei hadden not mynde of[o] thi merueils, which thou haddist do to hem ; and thei maden hard her nollis ; and thei 3auen the[p] heed[q], that[r] thei 'weren als turned[t] to her seruage as bi strijf; but thou *art* God[u] helpful[v], meke, and merciful, abidynge longe, '*ether pacient*[w], and of myche merciful doyng, and forsokist[x] not hem ; and 18 sotheli[y] whanne thei hadden maad to hem a 3otun calf, as bi strijf, and hadden seid,

u comaundist A. v heued EFH. hede A.

c men of Egipt 1S. d and in the destruccioun of Farao and his seruauntis S. e gloryous name 1S. f day it is knowe S. g thi peple 1S. h Om. 1S. i a 1S. k and 1S. l vnto S. m the depthe BCISV. n to I. fro hence to S. o thou spakist 1S. p there with S. q oure fadris 1S. r and cerymonyes S. s heestis 1S t Om. 1S. u thin heestis to hem 1S. v thi cerymonyes 1S. w thi lawe 1S. x And 1S. y of A. to HU pr. m. z watris S. a a good S. b of bihest 1 marg. c upon 1S. d the which 1. e residist up 1. f Om. FGHMX. g But 3it 1. h Om. 1. that peple and S. i proudli a3ens thee S. k thei maden 1S. l thei herden 1S. m hestis 1S. n wolden not 1. o on plures. p her 1S. q heed takinge counsel togidre 1. heed takinge togidre wickid counsel S. r so that S. s wolden be 1. t turned awei togidre 1. togidre turned S. u Om. 1S. v an helpful God 1S. w Om. 1S. x thou forsakist 1S. y Om. 1S.

daı, that ıt lede hem ın to the weıe, and
a pıler of fıjr bı nyȝt, that he shewe to
them the weıe, bı whıche^x theı shulden
20 gon ıu   And thı goode Spırıt thou ȝeue
to hem, that shulde teche them ; and thı
aungelıs mete thou forfendedest^y not fro
the mouth of hem, and watır thou ȝeue
21 to hem ın thrıst   Fourtı ȝer thou feddıst
hem ın desert, and no thıng to hem faıl-
ede, the clothıs of hem eeldeden not, and
22 the feet of hem ben not ouertroden   And
thou ȝeue to hem reumys, and puplıs ; and
partıdıst to them lotıs, and theı weldıden
the lond of Seon, and the lond of the
kıng of Esebon, and the lond of Og, kıng
23 of Basan   And the sonus of hem thou
multeplıedest, as the sternıs of heuene,
and broȝtıst hem to the lond, of the
whıche thou haddest seıd to ther fadrıs,
that theı shulden gon ın, and welden ıt.
24 And the sonus of Iraeel eamen, and weldeden the lond, and thou mekedest beforn
hem the Cananees, dwellırıs of the lond,
and thou ȝeue hem ın to theı hondıs,
and the kıngus of hem, and the puplıs of
the lond, that theı do to hem as ıt plesıde
25 to them   And theı token strengthıd cıtes,
and fat erthe, and weldeden honsıs ful
of alle goodıs, cısternes^z of otheı men
forgıd, vınes, and olıues, and manıe appıl
trees   And theı eeten, and ben fulfıld,
and ben maad fatte, and theı abound-
eden in rıchessıs ın thı grete goodnesse
26 Theı terreden forsothe thee to wrathe,
and wenten aweı fro thee, and threwen
aweı thı lawe bıhınde ther backes ; and
thı profetus slowen, that wıtnesseden to
them, that theı shulden turne aȝeen to
thee, and theı dıden grete blasfemys
27 And thou ȝeue them ınto the hond of
ther enemıs, and theı tormenteden hem,
and in tıme^a of ther trıbulacıoun theı
crıeden to thee ; and thou fro heuene

Thıs ıs thı God^z, that 'ledde thee out of
Egıpt, and theı dıden grete blasfemyes^a.
But thou^b ın thı many mercyes leftıst^c 19
not hem^d ın deseert ; for a pıler of cloude
ȝede not aweı fıo hem bı the daı, that ıt
schulde lede hem ın to the weıe^e ; and a^f
pıleı of fier ȝede not aweı 'fro hem^s bı
nyȝt, that ıt schulde schewe to hem the
weıe, bı which theı schulden entre   And 20
thou ȝauest to hem thı good Spırıt, that
tauȝte hem ; and thou forbedıst not thın
aungelıs^h mete fro her mouth, and thou
ȝauest to hem water ın thırst^ı   Fourtı 21
ȝeer thou feddıst hem ın deseert, and no
thıng faılıde to hem^k, her clothıs^ı wexiden
not elde^m, and her feet weren not hirt
And thou ȝauest to hem rewmes, and pu- 22
plıs ; and thou departıdıst lottıs, 'ether
erıtagısⁿ, to hem, and theı hadden in possessıoun the lond of Seon, and the lond
of the kyng of Esebon, and the lond of
Og^o, kyng^p of Basan   And thou multı- 23
plıedist the sones of hem, as the sternıs of
heuene^q, and thou brouȝtıst hem to the
lond, of which thou seıdıst to her fadrıs,
that theı schulden entre, and holde ıt ın
possessıoun   And the sones of Israel 24
eamen^r, and hadden^s the^t lond ın possessıoun ; and bifor hem thou madıst low^u
the^v dwellers of the^w lond, Cananeıs^x, and
thou ȝauest hem ın to the hondıs of the
sones of Israel, and the kyngıs of hem,
and the puplıs of the lond, that theı dıden
to hem, as ıt plesıde hem   And theı token 25
cıtees^y maad^z strong^a, and fat^h eıthe ; and
theı hadden ın possessıoun housıs fulle of
alle goodıs, cısternes^c maad of othere men,
vınerıs^d, and places of olyues, and many
apple trees   And theı eeten, and weıen
fillıd^e, and weren maad fat, and hadden^f
plentee of rıtchessıs 'ın thı greet good-
nesse   Sothelı^g theı terııden thee to 26
wrathfulnesse, and ȝeden^h aweı fro thee,

---

^x the whıche *AEFH*   ^y forfendıst *AII pr m*   ^z and cısternvs *A*   ^a that tıme c

^z God, *Israel* ıs   ^a blasfemȝe *to thın name* s.   ^b thou, *I ord* s   ^c leftıst *or forsokıst* s   ^d hem *herfor* s   ^e weıe *wheder theı weren to go* s   ^f the s   ^g Om ı   ^h aungel s   ^ı *her* thırst ıs   ^k hem *al that tyme* s   ^l clothıng ı   ^m elde ıs   ⁿ Om ı   ^o Om ıs   ^p the kyng ıs   ^q the firmament ı ^r comen *thıdere* ıs   ^s theı hadden ıs   ^t that ıs   ^u low [the s] men of Chananyc ıs   ^v Om ıs   ^w that ı ^x Om ı   ^y her cıtees ıs   ^z *whıche weren* maad ıs   ^a and also ıs   ^b fat *or plentuous* s   ^c and cısternes ıs   ^d and vınerıs ıs   ^e fulfillıd ıs   ^f *in thı greet goodnesses* [goodnesse s] theı hadden ıs ^g And ȝıt ıs   ^h wenten ı

herdest hem, and aftir thi manie deedis of mercy thou ȝeue to hem saueoures, that shulden sauen hem fro the hond of ther 28 enemis. And whan thei hadden restid, thei ben turned aȝen that thei do euel in thi siȝte; and thou forsoke hem in the hond of ther enemys, and thei weld-eden hem; and thei ben conuertyd, and thei crieden to thee; thou forsothe fro heuene herdist, and deliueredest hem in 29 thi mercies manie times. And thou wit-nessedest to them, that thei shulden turnen aȝeen to thi lawe; thei forsothe proudli diden, and thei herden not thi maundementus, and in thi domys thei synneden, the whiche what man doth shal liuen in hem; and thei ȝeuen a going awey shulder, and ther nol thei 30 inwardli hardeden. And thou drowe afer vpon hem manie ȝeris, and thou witness-edist hem in thi Spirit bi the hond of thi profetus; and thei herden not; and thou toke them in to the hond of the puplis 31 of londis. Forsothe in thi manie mer-cies thou madist not hem in to wasting, ne forsoke them; for God of mysera-32 ciouns, and benigne thou art. And so now, Lord oure God, grete God, strong, and ferful, kepende couenaunt and merci, ne turne thou awei thi face in al the tra-uaile that hath founden vs, oure kingis, and oure princis, and oure fadris, and oure prestis, and oure profetis, and al thi puple, fro the daȝis of king Assur vnto 33 this dai. And thou art riȝtwis in alle thingus, that camen vpon vs; for treuthe thou didist to vs; wee forsothe vnpitousli 34 diden. Oure kingus, and oure princis, oure prestis, and oure fadris, diden not thi lawe, and tentiden not to thin hestis, and thy witnessis that thou witnessedist 35 in hem. And thei in their goode reumis, and in thi miche goodnesse that thou

and castiden[k] awei thi lawe bihynde her backis[l]; and thei killiden thi prophetis, that witnessiden to hem, that thei schul-den turne aȝen to thee; and thei diden grete blasfemyes. And thou ȝauest hem 27 in to the hond of her enemyes; and thei turmentiden hem; and in the tyme of her tribulacioun thei crieden to thee; and thou herdist them fro heuyn, and bi thi many merciful doyngis thou ȝauest hem[m] sauy-ours, that sauyden hem fro the hond of her enemyes. And whanne thei hadden 28 restid, thei turneden aȝen to do yuel in thi siȝt; and thou forsokist hem in the hond of her enemyes, and enemyes hadden hem in possessioun; and[n] thei weren con-uertid[o], and thei[p] crieden to thee; forsothe[q] thou herdist hem fro heuene, and[r] dely-ueridist[s] hem 'in thi mercies[t] in[tt] many tymes. And thou witnessidist to hem, 29 that thei schulden turne aȝen to thi lawe; but thei diden proudli, and herden not thin heestis, and synneden[u] in thi domes, whiche[v] a[w] man that schal do[x] schal lyue in tho; and[y] thei ȝauen the[z] schuldre goynge[a] awei, and thei maden hard her nol[b]. And thou drowist along many 3 ȝeeris on[c] hem[d], and thou witnessidist to hem in thi Spirit bi the honde[e] of thi pro-phetis[f]; and thei herden[g] not; and[h] thou ȝauest hem in to the hond of the[i] puplis of londis[k]. But in thi mercies[l] ful manye[m] 31 thou madist not hem in[n] to wastyng, ne-thir thou forsokist hem; for[o] thou art God of merciful doynges, and meke. Now ther-32 for, oure Lord God, greet God, strong, and ferdful[p], kepynge couenaunt and merci, turne thou not awei thi face[q] in al the trauel that foond[r] vs, oure[s] kyngis, and oure princes, and oure fadris, and oure preestis, and oure profetis, and al thi pu-ple, fro the daies of kyng Assur til to this dai[t]. And thou[u] art iust in alle thingis, 33

k thei castiden 18. 	l bak 18. 	m to hem plures. 	n than s. 	o turned aȝen 1. turned aȝen to thee s. p Om. 18. 	q and 18. 	r and in thi mercy doyng thou 18. 	s delyueryst AC. 	t Om. 18. 	tt bi 18. 	u thei synneden 18. 	v the whiche domes 1. which domes s. 	w the s. 	x do hem 18. 	y but 1. but here aȝens s. z her 18. 	a and ȝeden 18. 	b nollis and wolden not obei to thi domes s. 	c upon 18. 	d hem, suffryng hem s. 	e honde or ȝoude 1. honde or tellynge s. 	f profetis that thei weren lawe brekers s. 	g herden hem 18. 	h and therfor 18. 	i Om. 18. 	k strange londis 18. 	l Om. 18. 	m manye merciful doyngis 18. n to be in 18. 	o sothely 18. 	p stidefast 18. 	q face fro vs s. 	r hath found 18. 	s and oure 18. 	t present tyme 18. 	u Lord, thou 18.

haddest ʒiue to hem, and in^c the most large lond and fat, that thou haddest taken in the siʒte of hem, thei serueden not to thee, ne ben turned aʒeen fro ther 36 werste studies. Lo! wee vsself to dai ben thrallis ; and^d the lond that thou ʒeue to oure fadris, that thei shulden ete the bred of it, and tho thingus that ben goode of 37 it ; and we vsself^e ben thrallis in it. And the frutus of hem ben multiplied to kingis, that^f thou hast put vp on vs for oure synnes ; and thei lordshipen to oure bo- dies, and to oure bestis, aftir ther wil, 38 and in gret tribulacioun we ben. Thanne vp on alle these thingus wee vsself^g smijten pes couenaunt, and wrijten, and oure princis, oure Leuitis, oure prestis sette marke.

that camen on^v vs, for^w thou didist trewthe to vs ; but^x we han do wickidliʃ. Oure^z 34 kyngis, and oure princes, oure^a prestis, and fadris^b 'diden not^c thi lawe ; and thei perseyueden not thin heestis and witness- yngis^d, whiche^e thou witnessidist^f in hem^g. And thei in her good rewmes, and in thi 35 myche goodnesse, which thou ʒauest^h to hem, and in the largestⁱ lond and fat, whych thou haddist ʒoue in the siʒt of hem, serueden not thee, nether turneden aʒen fro her werste studies. Lo^k ! we 'vs 36 silf^l ben thrallis to dai ; and the lond^m whichⁿ thou ʒauest^o to oure fadris, that thei shulden ete the breed therof, and the goodis that ben therof, 'is thral^p'; and we 'vs silf^q ben thrallis, 'ethir boonde men^r', in that lond. And the fruytis therof 37 ben multiplied to kyngis, whiche^s thou hast set on^t vs for oure synnes ; and thei ben lordis of oure bodies, and of oure beestis, bi her wille, and we ben in greet tribulacioun.

CAP. X.

1 Selers forsothe weren Neemias, Ather- 2 sata, sone of Achelai, and Sedechias, Sa- 3 raias, Azarias, Jeremias, Fasur, Amaria, 4,5 Melchia, Accus, Sebenia, Mellucharem, 6 Nerimuth, Oddias, Daniel, Jenthon, Ba- 7,8 ruch, Mosollam, Abia, Mianymy, Mazia, 9 Belga, Semein ; these preestis. But the Leuitus ; Jesue, sone of Azarie, Bennuy, 10 of the sonus of Ennadab, Cediniel, and the brether of hem, Sechenia, Odomia, 11 Thelitha, Falaia, Anam, Micha, Roob, 12,13 Azabia, Zaccur, Zerebias, Zabanya, Odi- 14 as, Bani, Hanyim. The hedis of the puple, Fethos, Moab, Elam, Zecu, Banni, 15,16 Bonni, Asgad, Bebai, Donai, Bagoai, 17,18 Adin, Ather, Azothia, Asin, Adonia, 19 Asuyn, Bessaia, Ares, Anathoth, Nebay,

CAP. X.

Therfor on alle these thingis† we 'vs 38 † thingis ; that is, synnes passid silf^u smyten^v and writen boond^w of pees, to be eschewid outirly. Lire and^x oure princes, oure^y dekenes, and oure here. c. prestis ascelen^z. Forsothe^a the seeleris 1 weren Neemye, Athersata^b, the sone of Achilai, and Sedechie, Saraie, Azarie, Je- 2 remye, Phasur, Amarie, Melchie, Accus, 3,4 Sebenye, Mellucarem, Nerymuth, Oddie, 5 Danyel, Genton, Baruc, Mosollam, Abia, 6,7 Minynymy, Mazie, Belga, and Semeie ; these 8 weren prestis. Forsothe^c dekenes weren 9 Josue, the sone of Azarie, Bennuy^d, of the sones of Ennadab, Cedinyel^e, and hise bri- 10 theren, Sethenye, Odenmye, Telita, Pha- laie, Anam, Myca, Roob, Asebie, Zaccur, 11,12 Serebie, Sabanye, Odias, Bany, Hamyn^f. 13 The^g heedis^h of the puple, Phetosⁱ, Moab, 14

^c Om. *A.* ^d in *A.* ^e oureself *A.* ^f the whiche *AEFH.* ^g oureself *A.*

^v to 1s. ^w for *euer* s. ^x and 1s. ^y wickidli *aʒens thee* 1s. ^z And oure 1s. ^a and oure 1s. ^b oure fadris 1s. ^c han not don 1s. ^d thi witnessyngis 1s. ^e that 1. ^f hast witnessid 1s. ^g thin heestis 1s. ^h hast ʒoue 1s. ⁱ ful large 1. ^k Lo ! *therfore* 1s. ^l oure self EILPs. ^m lond *also* 1. ⁿ that 1s. ^o hast ʒouen 1s. ^p Om. 1. ^q oure self EILPs. ^r Om. CIs. ^s that 1. ^t upon 1s. ^u oure self E *pass.* L *pass.* ^s *pass.* ^v maken 1s. ^w a boond 1s. ^x *bitwixe the Lord our God and vs* and s. ^y and oure 1s. ^z ascelen *it* 1. ascelen *this obligacioun on our side* s. ^a And 1s. ^b *that is,* Athersata 1. *that is clepid* Athersata s. ^c And the 1s. ^d and Benny s. ^e *weren* Cydyniel s. ^f and Hamyn 1s. ^g And the 1s. ^h cheef men 1. heedis men s. ⁱ *weren* Phetos 1s.

20 Methpia, Mosollam, Azir, Meisabel, Sa-
21,22 doc, Reddua, Felthia, Anania, Ozee, Ana-
23,24 nia, Azub, Aloes, Faleam, Sobeth, Reu,
25,26 Azebina, Mathsia, Ethaia, Anam, Mel-
27,28 lucharem, Baana; and othere of the puple, prestus, Leuitus, porteres, and singeres, sodeknes, and alle that seuereden
hemself fro the puplis of londis to the
lawe of God, ther wiues, and ther sonus,
29 and ther doȝtris; alle that myȝten sa-
uouren, behotende for ther brethern,
ther most wrshipeful men, and thei that
camen to behoten, and sweru, that thei
shulden gon in the lawe of the Lord,
that he hadde ȝiue in the hond of Moises,
his seruaunt, that thei shulde don and
kepe alle the maundemens of the Lord
ther God, and his domys, his[h] cerymo-
30 nies; and that wee shulden not ȝiuen
oure doȝtris to the puple of the lond, and
there doȝtris wee shulde not take to oure
31 sones. The puplis forsothe of the lond,
that bringen in chaffaris, and alle thingus
to vsen bi the dai of sabot, that thei selle,
wee shul not taken of hem in the sabot,
and in the halewid dai; and wee shuln
forȝiue the seuenthe ȝer, and exaccioun of
32 alle hond. And we shul setten vp on vs
hestus, that we ȝiue the thridde part of
an ounce bi the ȝer to the werc of the
33 Lord oure God, to the loues of proposicioun, and to the sacrifise euermor durende, and in to brent sacryfise euermor
lastende, in sabatis, in calendis, in so-
lempnetees, in halewid daȝis, and for
synne, that it be preȝed for Irael, and
in to alle vse of the hous of oure[i] God.
34 Thanne we leiden lotis vp on the offring
of trees, betwe[k] prestis and Leuitis and
the puple, that thei shulden bringen in

Elam, Zecu, Banny, Bonny, Azgad, Be-15,16
bay, Donai, Bogoia, Adyn, Ather, Azo-17
chie, Azur, Odenye, Assuyn, Bessaie, Ares,18,19
Anatoth, Nebai, Methpie, Mosollam, Azir,20,21
Meizabel, Sadoch, Reddua, Pheltie, Ana-22,23
nye, Osee, Anaie, Azub, Aloes, Phalenm,24,25,26
Sobeth, Reu, Asebyne, Mathsie, Ethaie,
Anam, Mellucarem, Baana; and othere of27,28
the puple, prestis[k], dekenes[l], porteris, and
syngeris, Natynneis[m], and alle men that
departiden hem silf fro the[n] puplis[o] of
londis[p] to[q] the lawe of God, the wynes of
hem, and[r] 'the sones of hem, and the douȝtris of hem[s]; alle[t] that myȝten vndur-29
stonde, bihetynge[u] for her britheren, the[v]
principal men of hem, 'and thei[w] that
camen[x] to bihecte, and to swere, that[y]
thei schulden go in the lawe of the Lord,
which he 'hadde ȝoue[z] bi the hond of
Moyses, his seruaunt, that[a] thei schulden
do and kepe alle the hcestis of 'oure
Lord God[b], and hise domes, and hise cerymonyes; and[c] that we schulden not ȝyue30
oure douȝtris to the[d] puple of the lond,
and that we schulden not take her douȝtris to oure sones. Also[e] the puplis[f] of31
the lond, 'that bryngen in thingis set to
sale, and alle thingis to vss, bi[g] the dai of
sabat, for to sille[i], we schulen not[k] take[l]
of hem in the sabat[n], and in a[n] dai
halewid[o]; and[p] we schulen leeue[q]† the seuenthe ȝer, and the[r] axynge of al hond[s].
And[t] we schulen ordeyne[u] comaunde-32
mentis 'on vs[v], that[w] we ȝyue the thridde
part of a sicle 'bi the ȝeer[x] to the werk of
'oure Lord God[y], to[z] the looues of settyng-33
forth, and to the euerlastynge sacrifice[a],
'and in to brent sacrifice euerlastynge[b], in[c]
sabatis, in[d] calendis[e], 'that is, bigynnyngis
of monethis[f], in[g] solempnytees, in[h] halewid

† leeue; with
out tilthe and
sowing and
gadering, ga-
yng; that is,
release dettis,
and delynere
Ebrew ser-
uauntis. Lire
here. c.

---

h and his _A._   i the Lord oure _A._   k betwixe _A._ betwen _E pass._ bytwene _F et II pass._

k and preestis 1s.   l and dekenes 1s.   m and Natynneis c. _tho ben suddekns E et L marg._
a _hethen_ 1s.   o _peple_ s.   p _othere_ londis 1. _diuers_ londis s.   q _turnynge_ to 1. 'and camen to s.   r Om. s.
s Om. 1.   t and alle s.   u _maden_ bihetynge 1s.   v and the s.   w Om. s.   x _camen thidere_ 1s.   y _bihotiden
and sworen_ that s.   z ȝaf 1s.   a and that 1s.   b the Lord oure God 1s.   c also _we sworen_ that s.
d _hethen_ 1s.   e Also _we sworen_ that if 1s.   f _peple_ 1s.   g _brynge_ yn bi 1. bryng ynne among vs bi s.
i _sille_ thingis_ sett to sale and alle thingis _perteynynge_ to vss 1s.   k _not in ony wise_ 1s.   l take _ony thing_ 1s.
m sabat dai 1s.   n the 1s.   o _that is_ halewed 1. _that is_ halwede _bi the lawe of God_ s.   p and also 1s.
q _leeue or release_ 1s.   r Om. 1s.   s _maner_ hoond _of deit_ 1. hond _and of ech dettour_ s.   t And also s.
u ordeyne _upon_ us 1s.   v Om. 1s.   w that bi ech ȝeer 1s.   x Om. 1s.   y the Lord our God s.   z and to 1s.
a brent _sacrifice_ s.   b _which sacrifices_ s.   c _to be offrid_ in 1. _shulu be offrid_ in s.   d and in 1.   e the firste
dnies of the monethis 1s.   f Om. 1s.   g and in 1s.   h and in 1s.

to the hous of oure God, bi the housis of oure fadris bi times, fro times of the ӡer vn to a ӡer, that thei shulden brennen vp on the auter of the Lord oure God, as it is writen in the lawe of Moises; 35 and that we bringe forth oure firste goten of oure lond, and the first of alle frut of eche tree, fro ӡer in to ӡer, in to 36 the hous of the Lord, and the firste of oure childer, and of oure bestus, as it is writen in the lawe, and the firste of oure oxen, and of oure shep, that thei be offrid in the hous of oure God, to prestis that seruen in the hous of oure God; 37 and the firste of oure^m metus, and of oure sacrifises of likouris, and appilis of eche tree, also of vindage, and of oile, bringe wee to prestis^n, to the tresorie of the Lord, and the tenthe part of oure lond to Leuitus; thoo Leuitis shul take dimes 38 of alle the cites of oure werkis. Forsothe the sone of Aron, prest, shal be with the Leuitus in the dimes of Leuitis; and Leuitus shuln offre the tenthe part of ther dime in the hous of oure God, to the tresorie, in the hous of the tresor. 39 To the tresorie forsothe shul bern the sonus of Israel and the sonus of Leui the firste of whete, and of win, and of oile; and there shul ben the halewid vesselis and prestus, and singeris, and porteris, and seruauns; and we shul not leue the hous of oure God.

daies, and for synne, that 'me preie^i for Israel, and^k in to al the vss of the hows of oure God. 'Therfor we senten^l 'lottis on 34 the offryng of trees^m, bitwixe^n prestis and dekenes and the puple^o, that tho schulden be brouӡt in to the hows of oure God, bi the housis^p of oure fadris bi^q tymes, fro the tymes of a ӡeer 'til to^r a ӡeer, that 'tho schulden^s brenne on^t the auter of 'oure Lord God^n, as it is writun in the lawe of Moyses; and that we bringe the firste gen- 35 drid thingis of oure lond, and the firste fruytis of al fruyt of ech tree, fro ӡeer in to ӡeer, in to the hows of the Lord, and 36 the firste gendrid^v thingis of oure sones, and of oure beestis^w, as it is writun in the lawe, and the firste gendrid^x thingis of oure oxis^y, and of oure scheep, that tho be offrid in the hows of oure God, to prestis^z that mynystren^a in the hows of oure God; and^b we schulen brynge the 37 firste fruytis of oure metis, and of oure moiste sacrifices, and the applis^c of ech tre, and of^d vendage, and of oile, to^e 'prestis, at^f the treserie of the Lord^g, and the tenthe part of oure lond to^h dekenes; thilke dekenes schulen take tithis of alle the citees of oure werkis. Sotheli^i a prest, 38 the sone of Aaron, schal be with the dekenes in the tithis of dekenes; and the dekenes schulen offre the tenthe^k part of her tithe in the hows of oure God^l, 'at the tresorie, in the hows of tresour^n. For^n the 39 sones of Israel and the sones of Leuy schulen brynge^o the firste fruytis of wheete, of wiyn, and of oile^p; and halewid vessels schulen be there, and prestis, and syngeris, and porteris, and mynystris^q; and we^r schulen not forsake the hows of 'oure God^s.

^i Om. _a._ ^m Om. _a._ ^n the preestis _a._

^l men preie ниx. preier be maad is. ^k and _be that moneth putt_ 1. and _be the forseide moneth put_ s. ^l Also we castiden s. Om. 1. ^m Om. 1. ^n Also bitwixe 1. ^o puple we castiden lottis on the offryng of trees 1. ^p meynees 1s. ^q _in certeyn_ 1s. ^r _sufficient_ unto 1s. til x. ^s thilke _wode_ schulde 1. that _wode_ shulde s. ^t upon 1s. ^u the Lord oure God 1s. ^v goten 1. ^w beestis, _brynge we thider_ s. ^x goten 1. ^y oxen 1s. ^z the preestis s. ^a seruen 1s. ^b _and also_ 1. and _al_ s. ^c fruytis s. ^d _the fruytis_ of 1s. ^e _these shuln be bronӡt_ to s. ^f Om. 1s. ^g Lord, and [ӡouen s] to prestis 1s. ^h _we schul ӡiue_ to 1. ^i And 1s. ^k tithe 1s. ^l God _to prestis_ 1. Lord _to prestis_ s. ^m Om. 1. ^n And 1s. ^o brynge _thidere_ 1. ^e oyle _to thilk place_ s. ^q mynystris _also_ 1s. ^r thei 1s. ^s the Lord 1. our Lord, _absenting hem thens_ s.

CAP. XI.

1 Forsothe the princis of the puple dwelten in Jerusalem ; the most wrshipeful men with oute lot in the middel of the puple dwelten ; the tother forsothe puple leide lot, that it take o part of ten°, that weren to dwellen in Jerusalem, in the holi cite ; the tenthe part of the puple is rerid, that it dwelle in Jerusalem, for the cite was voide ; nyne forsothe 2 partis in cites. Forsothe the puple blesside to alle men, that hadden offrid hemself wilfulli, that thei dwelle in Jerusa- 3 lem. And so these ben the princis of the prouince, that dwelten in Jerusalem, and in the cites of Juda ; forsothe eche dwelte in his possessioun, in ther cites, Irael, prestis, Lenitis, sodeknis, and the sonus 4 of the^p thrallis of Salomon. And in Jerusalem dwelten of the sonus of Juda, and of the sonus of Beniamyn ; of the sonus of Juda, Athaias, 'the sone^q of Azian, the sonus of Zacharie, the sonus of Amarie, the sonus of Safaie, the sonus of 5 Malalele ; of the sonus of Fares, Amasia, the sone of Baruch, the sone of Cholosai, the sone of Asia, the sone of Adaia, the sone of Josarib, the sone of Zacharie, the 6 sone of Salonites ; alle the sonus of Fares, that dwelten in Jerusalem, foure hundrid 7 sixti and eiȝte, stronge men. These ben forsothe the sonus of Beniamyn ; Sellum, the sone of Mosollam, the sone of Joadi, the sone of Sadaia, the sone of Cholaia, the sone of Maisia, the sone of Ethel, the 8 sone of Saia ; and aftir hym Gabai, Sellai, nyne hundrid and eiȝte and twenti ; and Joel, the sone of Secry, the prouost of hem, and Judas, the sone of Sennua, 10 vpon the cite the secunde. And of the prestis ; Idaia, the sone of Joarib, Jachim,

CAP. XI.

Forsothe the princis of the puple dwell- 1 iden in Jerusalem ; the^t principal† men dwelliden in the myddis of the puple with out lot^u ; but the residue^v puple^w sente lot, for to take o part of ten, 'whiche schulden dwelle in Jerusalem, in the hooli citee^x ; the^y tenthe part of the puple is^z chosun for to dwelle in Jerusalem, for the citee was voide^a ; forsothe^b the nyne partis dwelliden in citees^c. Forsothe^d the puple 2 blesside alle men, that profriden hem silf bi fre wille to dwelle in Jerusalem. And 3 so these ben the princes of prouynce^e, that dwelliden in Jerusalem, and in the citees of Juda ; sothely^f ech man dwellide in his possessioun, in her citees of Israel, prestis^g, dekenes, Nathynneis, and the sones of the seruauntis of Salomon. And men of the 4 sones of Juda, and of the sones of Beniamyn dwelliden in Jerusalem ; of the sones of Juda, Athaie, the sone of Aziam, sone of Zacarie, sone of Amarie, sone of Saphie, sone of Malaleel ; of the sones of 5 Phares, Amasie, the sone of Baruch, the^h sone of Colozay, the^i sone of Azie, the^k sone of Adaie, the^l sone of Jozarib, the^m sone of Zacarie, the^n sone of Salonytes ; alle the sones of Phares, that dwelliden in 6 Jerusalem, weren foure hundrid eiȝte° and sixti, stronge men. Sotheli^p these ben the 7 sones of Beniamyn ; Sellum, the sone of Mosollam, the sone of Joedi, the^r sone of Sadaie, the^s sone of Colaie, the^s sone of Masie, the^s sone of Ethel, the^u sone of Saie ; and aftir hym^t Gabai, Sellai, nynti 8 and eiȝte and twenti^u ; and Johel, the sone of Zechri, was the souereyn of hem, and Judas, the sone of Semyna, was the secounde man on^v the citee^w. And of prestis ; 10 Idaie, sone^x of Joarib, Jachyn, Saraie, the^y 11

† the principal; this resoun is not in Ebreu, nether is of the text, to this word with out lot be passid; also this resoun the tenthe part and so forth til thidir was void, is not in Ebren. Lire here. c.

° the ten *AFH.*   P Om. *A.*   q of the sones *A.*

t *and the* 1s.   u lot *of ony part limytid to hem* 1s.   v remenaunt 1s.   w puple, that schulde dwelle in Jerusalem, the hooly citee 1s.   x Om. 1s.   y *for the* 1s.   z was 1s.   a voide *of dwellers* s.   b and 1s.   c *othere* citees 1s.   d And 1s.   e that prouynce 1. the prouince s.   f and 1s.   G *that is*, prestis 1s.   h Om. 1s.   i Om. 1s.   k Om. 1s.   l Om. 1s.   m Om. 1s.   n Om. 1s.   o and eiȝte c.   P And 1s.   q Om. 1s.   r Om. 1s.   s Om. 1s.   t hym *dwelliden there* 1s.   u twenti *men* 1s.   v upon 1s.   w citee *of Jerusalem* 1s.   x the sone 1s.   y Om. 1s.

11 Saraia, the sone of Elchie, the sone of Mosollam, the sone of Sadoch, the sone of Meraioth, the sone of Achitob, princis of 12 the hous of God, and the brethern of hem, doende the^r werkis of the temple ; ei3te hundrid and two and twenti. And Adaia, the sone of Jeroam, the sone of Feler, the sone of Ampsi, the sone of Zacharie, the sone of Fessur, the sone of Melchie, 13 and the brethern of hem, princis of fadris ; two hundrid and two and fourty. And Amazie, the sone of Azriel, the sone of Azi, the sone of Mosollamoth, the sone 14 of Seminer, and the brether of hem, ful mi3ti, an hundrid and ei3te and twenti ; and the prouost of hem, Zebdiel, the sone 15 of mi3ti men. And of the Leuitus ; Zechenia, the sone of Azab, the sone of Azarie, 16 the sone of Azabie, the sone of Boni, and of Sabathai, and Josabel ; and vp on alle the werkis that weren with oute forth in the hous of God, fro^a the princis of 17 Leuitus. And Mathania, the sone of Micha, the sone of Sebdai, the sone of Asaf, prince, to preisen, and to knoulechen in orisoun ; and Bethechias the secunde of his brethern, and Abdia, the sone of Sammia, the sone of Galai, the sone of 18 Iditum. Alle the Leuitus in the holi cite, 19 two hundrid foure score and foure. And the porteris ; Accub, Thelmon, and the brethern of hem, that kepten the doris ; 20 an hundrid seuenti^t and two. And the tothere of Irael, prestis, and Leuitus, in alle the cites of Juda, eche in his posses-21 sioun. And the sodeknis, that^{tt} dwelten in Ofel, and Ciacha, and Gaffa, of the 22 sodekins. And bisshopis of Leuitus in Jerusalem ; Aazi, the sone of Bani, the sone of Azabie, the sone of Mathanie, the sone of Miche. Of the sonus of Asaf, singeres in the seruise of the hous of God. 23 Forsothe the beste of the king was vpon

sone of Helchie, the^y sone of Mossollam, the^y sone of Sadoch, the^y sone of Meraioth, the^r sone of Achitob, the princis^z of 'Goddis hows^a, and her britheren, makynge the 12 werkis of the temple, weren ei3te hundrid and two and twenti. And Adaie, the sone of Jeroam, the^b sone of Pheler, the^b sone of Amsi, the^b sone of Zacarie, the^b sone of Phessur, the^b sone of Melchie, and the 13 britheren of hem, the^c princes of fadris, weren two hundrid and two and fourti. And Amasie, the sone of Azrihel, the^d sone of Azi, the^d sone of Mosollamoth, the^d sone of Semyner, and her britheren, ful my3ti 14 men, weren an hundrid and ei3te and twenti ; and the souereyn of hem was Zebdiel, the sone of^e my3ty men. And of 15 dekenes ; Sechenye, the sone of Azab, the sone of Azarie, the sone of Azabie, the sone of Bone, and Sabathai ; and Jozabed 16 was ordened of the princes of dekenes, on^f alle the werkis that weren^g with out forth in Goddis hows. And Mathanye, the sone 17 of Mycha, the^h sone of Zebdai, the^h sone of Asaph, was prince^i, to herie^k and to^l knowleche^m in preier^n ; and Bethechie was the secounde of hise britheren, and Abdie, the sone of Sammya, the^o sone of Galal, the^o sone of Iditum^p. Alle the dekenes 18 in the hooli citee^q, weren two hundrid and^r foure score and foure. And the por-19 teris, Accub, Thelmon, and the britheren of hem, that kepten the doris^s, weren an hundrid 'and two and seuenti^t. And othere 20 men of Israel, prestis, and dekenes, in alle the citees of Juda, ech man in his posses-sioun. And Natynneis, that dwelliden in 21 Ophel, and^u Siacha, and^u Gaspha^v ; of^w Natynneis. And^x bischopis^y† of dekenes^z 22 in Jerusalem ; Azi^a, the sone of Bany, the sone of Asabie, the sone of Mathanye, the sone of Mychee. Of the sones of Asaph, syngeris^b in the seruyce of Goddis hows.

† bischopis; in Ebreu it is, and souereyns of dekenes, for prestis aloone weren bischops bi propir speche, and hadden aboue hem onely oon hi3este bischop; therfor this Avi is seid here bischop of dekenes, bi large myche as he was souereyn of hem ; for a bischop is seid, as hauynge cure aboue othere men. Lire here. c.

^{r} Om. ACFH. ^{s} for A. ^{t} and seuenti A. ^{tt} that that C.

^{y} Om. IS. ^{z} thes weren princis IS. ^{a} the hous of God IS. ^{b} Om. IS. ^{c} Om. IS. ^{d} Om. IS. ^{e} of cosyn of S. ^{f} upon IS. ^{g} weren don I. ^{h} Om. IS. ^{i} prince in Goddus hous IS. ^{k} herie God S. ^{l} Om. I. ^{m} knowleche to him IS. ^{n} preier in hise merciful doyngis S. ^{o} Om. IS. ^{p} Iditum, weren the dekenes S. ^{q} citee Jerusalem I. citee of Jerusalem S. ^{r} Om. plures. ^{s} doris of the temple IS. ^{t} four score and two S, ^{u} in S. ^{v} Gaspha hadden her possessioun IS. ^{w} And of IS. And K. ^{x} and of BIS. ^{y} bischop plures. ^{z} the dekenes IS. ^{a} weren Azi IS. ^{b} weren syngeris IS.

hem, and ordre in the singeris bi alle
24 daȝis; and Afataia, the sone of Mosese-
hel, of the sonus of Zara, sone of Juda, in
the hond of the king, aftir al[u] the woord
25 of the puple; and in the housis bi alle
the[v] regiouns of hem. Of the sonis of Juda
dwelten in Cariatharbe, and in the doȝtris
of it, and in Dibon, and in the doȝtris of
it, and in Capceel, and in the litle tounus
26 of it; and in Jesue, and in Molada, and
27 in Bethfeleth, and in Asersual, and in
28 Bersabe, and in the doȝtris of it; and in
Sichelech, and in Mochone, and in the
29 doȝtris of it; and in Remon, and in Sara,
30 and in Jerimuth, Sonocha, Odollam, and
in the litle tounus of hem; in Lachis, in
the regiouns of it; Azecha, and in the
doȝtris of it; and thei dwelten in Ber-
31 sabe vn to the valei of Ennon. The sonus
forsothe of Beniamyn; Areba, Mechinas,
and Aia, and Bethel, and in the doȝtris
32 of it; Anatot, Nob, Anania, Nazor, Rama,
33 34 Jetheem, Adid, Zoboim, Nebollaloth, and
35 36 Onam, in the valei of craftis men. And
of Leuitus, the porceouns of Jude and of
Beniamyn.

CAP. XII.

1 These forsothe ben the prestus and the
Leuitis, that steȝeden vp with Sorobabel,
the sone of Salatiel, and Josue; Saraia,
2 Jeremia, Esdras, Amaria, Melluch, Accus,
3 4 Sechenia, Reum, Merimuth, Addo, Je-
5 thom, Miomin, Abia, Meldaa, Belga,
6 Semeia, and Joarib, Adaia, Sellum, A-
7 moe, Elceia, Idaia; these the princis of
prestys, and the brethern of hem, in the
8 daȝes of Josue. But Leuitus; Jesua, Bennui, Cediniel, Serabia, Juda, Mathanias,
vp on the ympnes, thei and the brether

For the comaundement[c] of the kyng was 23
on[d] hem[e], and ordre[f] *was* in syngeris bi
alle daies; and Aphataie, the sone of Mo- 24
sezchel, of the sones of Zara, sone[g] of Juda,
in the hond† of the kyng[h], bi ech word of
the puple[i]; and in the housis bi alle the 25
cuntreis of hem. Of the sones of Juda
dwelliden in Cariatharbe, and in the vilagis
therof, and in Dibon, and in the vilagis
therof, and in Capseel, and in the[k] townes
therof; and in Jesue, and in Molada, and 26
in Bethpheleth, and in Asersual, and in 27
Bersabee, and in[l] the vilagis therof; and 28
in Sicheleg, and in Mochone, and in the[m]
vilagis therof; and in Remmon, and in 29
Sara, and in Jerymuth, Zonocha[n], Odol- 30
lam[o], and in the townes `of tho[p]; in Lachis,
and in the cuntreis[q] therof; in Azecha and
the[r] vilagis therof; and[s] thei[t] dwelliden in
Bersabee `til to[u] the valei of Ennon. For- 31
sothe[v] the sones of Beniamyn *dwelliden* in
Areba, Mechynas[w], and Aia[x], and Bethel[y]
and vilagis[z] therof; in Anatoth, Nob[a], 32
Ananya[b], Asor[c], Rama[d], Jethaym[e], Adid[f], 33 34
Soboym[g], Nebollaloth[h], and in Onam, the 35
valei of crafti men. And of dekenes[i], `the 36
porciouns[k]‡ of Juda and of[l] Beniamyn[m].

CAP. XII.

Sotheli[n] these *weren* prestis[o] and de- 1
kenes, that stieden[p] with Zorobabel, the
sone of Salatiel, and with Josue; Saraie,
Jeremye, Esdras, Amarie, Melluch, Accus, 2
Sechenye, Reum, Merymucth, Addo, Je- 3 4
thon, Myomyn, Abia, Meldaa, Belga, Se- 5
meie, and Joarib, Adaie, Sellum, Amoo, 6
Elceia, and Jadie[q]; these *weren* the princes 7
of[r] prestis `and her britheren, in the daies
of Josue[s]. Certis[t] dekenes[u]; Jesua, Ben- 8
nuy, Cedynyel, Serabie, Juda, Mathanye[v],
`*weren* ouer the[w] ympnes, `thei and her

† *in the hond*; that is, bi the ordenaunce of the kyng. *Lire here.* c.

‡ *porciouns*; that is, summe of the lynage of Leuy dwelliden with out Jerusalem in euer either part, that is, in the part of Juda, and in the part of Beniamyn, for they hadden no propir part assigned to hem. *Lire here.* c.

[u] Om. c. [v] Om. c.

[c] heest IS. [d] upon IS. [e] hem, *that thei shulden be syngers* S. [f] an ordre IS. [g] the sone IS. [h] king *or bi the heest of him* S. [i] peple *dide his office* S. [k] Om. I. [l] Om. S. [m] Om. S. [n] in Zonoche IS. [o] in Odollam IS. [p] therof IS. [q] cuntrei A *pr. m. et plures.* [r] in the IS. [s] also S. [t] thei *of Juda* I. *the sones of Juda* S. [u] vnto IS. [v] And IS. [w] in Mechynas IS. [x] in Aia IS. [y] in Bethel IS. [z] in the vilagis IS. [a] in Nob IS. [b] in Ananya IS. [c] in Asor IS. [d] in Rama IS. [e] in Jethaym IS. [f] in Adid IS. [g] in Soboym IS. [h] in Nebollaloth IS. [i] the dekenes I. [k] Om. IS. [l] Om. S. [m] Beniamyn *thes weren* the porciouns IS. [n] Certis IS. [o] the prestis IS. [p] stieden up I. stieden vp *into Jerusalem and into Juda* S. [q] Jadie, in the daies of Josue IS. [r] and [of S] the bretheren of IS. [s] Om. IS. [t] And I. Om. S. [u] Om. IS. [v] Mathanye, *thes weren* dekens IS. [w] and thei and her bretheren weren *souereyns* ouer the IS.

9 of hem, in the daȝis of Josue ; and Bese-
chia, and Ezamith, and the brethern of
10 hem, eche in his offis. Josue forsothe gat
Joachim, and Joachim gat Eliazub, and
11 Eliazub gat Joiada, and Joiada gat Jona-
12 than, and Jonathan gat Jedaia. In the^w
daȝis forsothe of Joachim weren prestus,
and the princis of meines, Saraie, Amarie,
13 Jeremie, Ananie, Esdre, Mosollam, Ama-
14 rie, Johannan, Milicho, Jonathan, Sebe-
15 nie, Josef, Aram, Edua, Maraioth, Elchi,
16,17 Adaie, Zacharie, Jenthon, Mosollam, A-
bie, Zecarie, Miamin, and Moadie, Fel-
18 thi, Belge, Sannia, Semeie, Jonathan,
19,20 Joarib, Mathania, Jodaie, Asi, Sellaie,
21 Celaie, Mochebor, Elchie, Azebias, Idaie,
22 Nathaneel. Leuitus in the daȝes of Eliazub, and of Joiada, and Jonan, and Jed-
doa, writen princis of meines, and prestis
23 in the regne of Darie of^x Persis. The
sonus of Leui, princis of meines, writen
in the boc of the woordis of daȝes, and
vn to the daȝes of Jonathan, sone of Elia-
24 zub. And the princis of Leuitys ; Aze-
bia, Zerebia, and Jesue, sone of Cediniel ;
and the brethern of hem bi ther whilis,
that thei shulden preisen and knoulechen,
aftir the heste of king Dauid, man of
God, and waiten aboute euene bi ordre.
25 Mathania, Belthbecia, and Obedia, Mosollam, Thelmon, Accub, keperis of ȝatis,
26 and of vestiaries befor the ȝatus. These
in the daȝes of Joachim, sone of Josue,
sone of Josedech, and in the daȝes of
Neemie, duke, and Esdre, prest and
27 scribe. In the dedicacioun forsothe of
the wal of Jerusalem thei soȝten Leuites
fro alle ther placis, that thei bringen
them in to Jerusalem, and do the dedicacioun in gladnesse, and in doing of gracis,
and in song, and in cimbalis, and in sau-
28 trees, and in harpis. Forsothe the sonus

britheren^x ; and Bezechie, and Ezanny, 9
and the britheren of hem, ech man in his
office^y. Sotheli^z Josue gendride^a Joachym, 10
and Joachym gendride^b Eliasib, and Elia-
sib gendride^b Joiada, and Joiada gendride^b 11
Jonathan, and Jonathan gendride^b Jed-
daia. Forsothe^c in the daies of Joachym 12
weren^d prestis^e, and princis^f of meynees^g
of prestis, Saraie^h, Amarie, Jeremye, Ana-
nye, Esdre, Mosollam, Amarie, Johannam, 13
Mylico, Jonathan, Sebenye, Joseph, Aram, 14
Edua, Maraioth, Elchie, Addaie, Zacharie, 16
Genthon, Mosollam, Abie, Zecherie, Mya- 17
myn, andⁱ Moadie, Phelti, Belge, Sannya, 18
Semeie, Jonathan, Joarib, Mathanye, Jo- 19
daie, Azi, Sellaye, Mochebor, Helchie, Ase- 20,21
bie, Idaie, Nathanael^k. Dekenes^l in the daies 22
of Eliasib, and of Joiada, and of Jonam,
and of Jedda, weren^m writun princes of
meynees, and prestisⁿ in the rewme of
Darius of^o Persis. The sones of Leuy, 23
princes of meynees, weren writun in the
book of wordis^p of daies, and til to^q the
daies of Jonathan, sone^r of Eliasib. And 24
the princes of dekenes weren^s Asebie, Serebie, and^t Jesue, the sone of Cedynyel ;
and the britheren of hem bi her whiles^u,
that thei schulden berie^v and knowleche^w
bi^x the comaundement^y of kyng Dauid,
the man of God, and^z thei schulden kepe^a
euenli bi ordre. Mathanye^b, and Bethbecie, 25
and Obedie, Mosollam^c, Thelmon, Accub^d,
weren keperis of the ȝatis, and of the
porchis bifor the ȝatis. These^e weren in 26
the daies of Joachym, sone^f of Josue, sone
of Josedech, and in the daies of Neemye,
duyk^g, and of Esdras, the prest and
writere. Forsothe^h in the halewyng of 27
the wal of Jerusalem theiⁱ souȝten dekenes
of alle her places, to bryng hem in to Jerusalem, and to make the halewyng in gladnesse, in the^k doyng of thankyngis, and in

x Om. 1s.   y office had his charge s.   z And 1s.   a gaat 1.   b gaat 1.   c And 1s.   d Om. 1. these
weren s.   e the prestis 1s.   f the princis 1s.   g the meynes s.   h weren Saraie 1.   i Om. 1.   k and
Nathanael 1s.   l Om. 1. And s.   m dekens and prestis weren 1s.   n Om. 1s.   o kyng of 1s.   p the
wordis 1s.   q vnto 1s.   r the sone 1s.   s These weren the princis of dekenes s.   t Om. s.   u whilis or
tymes 1.   v herie God 1s.   w knowleche him 1. knowlech in her preier the beneficis of the Lord s.   x weren
ordeyned bi s.   y heest 1s.   z and that 1s.   a kepe her office 1. kepe her whilis in her office s.   b And
Mathanye 1s.   c and Mosollam 1s.   d and Accub 1s.   e These men 1s.   f the sone 1s.   g the duyk 1s.
h And 1s.   i men 1s.   k Om. 1s.

of singeris ben gadered and of the wilde
feldis aboute Jerusalem, and of the tounus
29 of Nethofati, and of the hous of Galgal,
and of the regiouns of Jebes, and of[y]
Amanech ; for tounes the singeris bilden
to hemself in the enuiroun of Jerusalem.
30 And the prestus and Leuitus ben clensid,
and thei clenseden the puple, and the
31 ӡatus of the wal. Forsothe I made the
princis[z] of Juda to steӡen vp vpon the
wal, and I sette two grete querus of preis-
eris ; and thei wenten at the riӡt side vpon
32 the wal, at the ӡate of the[a] dunghil. And
ther wenten after hem Osias, and the
33 half part[b] of princis of Juda, and Azaria, Esdras[c], and Mosollam, Juda[d], and
Beniamyn, and Semeia, and Jeremia.
34 And of the sonus of prestis, in trumpis ;
Zacharias, the sone of Jonathan, the sone
of Semeie, the sone of Mathanie, the sone
of Machaie, the sone of Seecur, the sone
35 of Asaf. And the brethern of hym ;
Semein, and Azarel, Malalai, Galalay,
Mai, Nathanael, and Juda, and Amaui,
in the vesselis of the song of Dauid, man
of God ; and Esdras, scribe, beforn hem, in
36 the welle ӡate. And aӡen hem steӡeden
vp in the gres of the cite of Dauid, in
the steӡing vp of the wal, vp on the hous
of Dauid, and vn to the ӡate of watris at
37 the est. And the secunde quer of men
tellende gracis wente forn aӡen, and I
after it ; and the half part of the puple vp
on the wal, and vp on the tour of ouenus,
38 and vn to the most large wal ; and vp on
the ӡate of Effraym, and vp on the olde
ӡate, and vp on the ӡate of fisshis, and the
tour of Ananehel, and the tour of Emath,
39 and vn to the floc ӡate ; and thei stoden in
the warde ӡate. And two queris of men
preisende stoden in the hous of God, and

song, and in cymbalis, and in sautrees, and
in harpis. Sotheli[l] the sones of syngeris 28
weren gaderid[m] bothe fro the feeldi places
aboute Jerusalem, and fro the townes of
Nethophati, and fro the hows of Galgal, 29
and fro the cuntreis[n] of Gebez, and of Amanech ; for syngeris[o] hadden bildid townes
to hem silf in the cumpas of Jerusalem.
And prestis and dekenes weren clensid, 30
and[p] thei[q] clensiden the puple, and the
ӡatis, and the wal. Forsothe[r] Y made the 31
princes of Juda to stic on[s] the wal, and
Y ordeynede twei greete queris[t] of men
heriynge[u] ; and thei ӡeden to the riӡt side[v]
on the wal, to the ӡate of the dunghil.
And Osaie ӡede aftir hem, and the half 32
part of prynces[w] of Juda, and Azarie, 33
Esdras, and Mosollam, Juda, and Beniamyn, and Semeye, and Jeremye 'ӡeden
aftir hem[x]. And of the sones of prestis 34
syngynge in trumpis ; Zacharie, the sone
of Jonathan, the sone of Semeie, the[y] sone
of Mathanye, the[y] sone of Machaie, the[y]
sone of Zeccur, the[y] sone of Asaph. And 35
hise britheren ; Semcie, and Azarel, Malalai, Galalai, Maai, Nathanael, and Juda,
and Amany, in[z] the[a] instrumentis of
song of Dauid, the man of God ; and Esdras, the wrytere, bifor[c] hem, in the ӡate of
the welle. And thei[d] sticden[e] aӡens hem 36
in the greis of the citee of Dauid, in the[f]
stiyng[g] of the[h] wal, on[i] the hows of Dauid,
and 'til to[k] the ӡate of watris[l] at the eest[m].
And the secounde queer[n] of men tellynge[o] 37
thankyngis ӡede euene aӡens[p], and Y[q] aftir
hym[r] ; and the[s] half part of the puple was
on[t] the wal, and on[u] the tour[v] of ouenys,
and 'til to[w] the broddeste wal ; and on[x] the 38
ӡate of Effraym, and[y] on[z] the elde ӡate,
and on[a] the ӡate of fischis, and on[b] the
toure of Ananeel, and on[c] the tour of

---

[y] Om. c.   [z] preestis A.   [a] Om. EH.   [b] partie AII.   [c] and Esdras A.   [d] and Juda A.

[l] And is.   [m] gaderid togidre is.   [n] cuntrey is.   [o] the syngeris is.   [p] and thanne i.   [q] Om. c.
[r] And is.   [s] upon is.   [t] queris or cumpanyes s.   [u] heriynge the Lord is.   [v] half is.   [w] the princis s.
[x] Om. i. ӡeden also after hem s.   [y] Om. is.   [z] weren presyng the Lord in s.   [a] Om. is.   [c] was
bifor is.   [d] men is.   [e] stieden up is.   [f] Om. is.   [g] stiyng up is.   [h] Om. s.   [i] ouer is.   [k] vnto is.
[l] the watris is.   [m] eest coost is.   [n] quere of processioun s.   [o] tellynge out is.   [p] ouer aӡens i.   ouer
aӡens or on the other side s.   [q] Y ӡede is.   [r] it i, hem s.   [s] Om. is.   [t] upon is.   [u] upon is.
[v] toure ӡate, that is clepid the toure s.   [w] thei ӡeden vnto is.   [x] ouer is.   [y] Om. s.   [z] ouer i. Om. s.
[a] ouer is.   [b] ouer is.   [c] ouer is.

I and the half part of maister iugis with
40 me. And the prestus, Eliachim, Maazia,
Myamin, Michia, Elioenai, Zacharia,
41 Anania, in trumpis; and Maazia, and
Senea, and Eleazar, and Azi, and Johannan, and Melchia, and Elam, and Ezer;
and clerli sungen[e] the singeris, and Je-
42 sraia, the prouost. And thei offreden in
that dai grete slaine sacrifises, and thei
gladeden; God forsothe hadde gladid hem
in gret gladnesse. But and the wiues of
hem and the fre childer ioȝeden, and the
gladnesse of Jerusalem is herd aferre.
43 Also thei noumbreden in that dai men
vpon the tresories of the tresor, to sacrifise of likour, and to the[f] firste frutis, and
dimes, that the princis of the cite, in fairnesse of doing of gracis, shulden bringen
in to the prestis and Leuitus bi hem; for
Juda gladede in the prestus and Leuitus
44 stondende to. And thei kepten the ob-
seruacioun of ther God, and the besinesse
of clensing; and singeris, and porteris,
after the heste of Dauid and of Salamon,
45 his sone; for in the daȝis of Dauid and of
Asaph from the beginnyng weren princis
ordeined of singeris in dite, of men prei-
46 sende and knoulechende to[g] God. And
al Irael, in the daȝes of Sorobabel, and in
the daȝes of Neemie, ȝeuen partus to singeris and porteris bi alle daȝes; and thei
halewiden the Leuitus, and the[h] Leuitis
halewiden the sonys of Aaron.

Emath, and thei camen 'til to[d] the ȝate of
the[e] floc; and thei stoden[f] in the ȝate of 39
kepyng. And twei[g] queeris of[h] men heriynge[i] stoden in the hows of God, and Y
and the half part of magistratis[k] with me.
And the prestis, Eliachym, Maasie, Mya- 40
myn, Mychea, Helioneai, Zacharie, Ananye, in[l] trumpis; and Maasie, and Senea, 41
and Eleazar, and Azi, and Johannan, and
Melchia, and Elam, and Ezer; and the
syngeris sungen clereli, and Jezraie, the[m]
souereyn[n]. And thei[o] offriden in that dai 42
grete sacrifices[p], and weren glad; 'for God[q]
'hadde maad hem glad[r] with grete gladnesse. But also her wyues and lawful[s]
childre weren ioiful, and the gladnesse of
Jerusalem was herd fer. Also thei noum- 43
briden in that dai men[t] ouer[u] the keping
places of tresour[v], to[w] moiste sacrifices, and
to[x] the[y] firste fruytis, and to[z] tithis, that
the[a] princes[b] of the citee schulden brynge
in bi hem, 'in the fairenesse of doyng of
thankyngis[c], prestis and dekenes; for Juda
was glad in prestis and dekenes present[d].
And thei[e] kepten the kepyng of her God, 44
the[f] kepyng of clensyng[g]; and syngeris[h],
and porteris[i], bi the comaundement[k] of
Dauid and of[l] Salomon, his sone; for in 45
the daies of Dauid and of Asaph fro the
bigynnyng princes of syngeris weren ordeyned, heriyng[m] in[n] song[o], and knou-
lechynge to God[p]. And al Israel, in the 46
daies of Zorobabel, and in the daies of
Neemye, ȝauen partis[q] to syngeris and to
porteris bi alle 'the daies[r]; and[s] thei[t]† halewiden dekenes, and the dekenes halewiden
the sones of Aaron.

† *and thei*; that is, the peple payede tithis to the dekenes, and the dekenes payede tithis to the prestis. *Lire here.* c.

CAP. XIII.

1 In the dai forsothe is rad in the volum
of Moises, herende the puple; and ther

CAP. XIII.

Forsothe in that dai it was red in the 1
book of Moises, in heryng of the puple;

[e] syngen *A*. [f] Om. *AH*. [g] Om. *A*. [h] Om. *AH*.

[d] vnto IS. [e] Om. IS. [f] stoden stille IS. [g] the two IS. [h] *of the other processiouns* of S. [i] heriynge *the Lord* S. [k] maistir men IS. [l] *herieden* in I. *sunge* in S. [m] her IS. [n] souereyn *also* IS. [o] men IS. [p] sacrifices *of victorie* IS. [q] sothely the Lord I. Om. S. [r] Om. S. [s] her lawful IS. [t] the men IS. [u] *that weren* ouer I. *which weren* ouer S. [v] the tresour IS. [w] to *resceyue* IS. [x] Om. IS. [y] Om. S. [z] Om. IS. [a] Om. IS. [b] in seemlynesse of doyng of thankyngis *to the Lord* princes IS. [c] Om. IS. [d] beinge present I. [e] *thes souereyns* IS. [f] and the IS. [g] the clensyng IS. [h] *thei kepten or reuliden* the syngeris I. [i] the porteris IS. [k] heest IS. [l] Om. S. [m] Om. IS. [n] to be in IS. [o] song heriynge *the Lord* IS. [p] God *his wonderfulnesse and his merciful doyng* S. [q] partis *of diuers fruytis* S. [r] tymes IS. [s] Om. S. [t] thes prestis IS.

is founde writen in it, that Amonites
and Moabitis aȝten not to gon in to the
2 chirche of God vnto withoute ende ; for
thi that thei aȝen camen not to the sonus
of Irael with bred and watir, and thei
hireden aȝen hem[i] Balam to cursen to
hem ; and oure God turnede the cursing
3 in to blessing. It is do forsothe, whan thei
hadden herd the lawe, thei seuereden alle
4 alien fro Irael. And vpon these thingus
was Eliasub, the prest, that was prouost
in the 'tresorie of the hous[k] of oure God,
5 and neȝhebore to Tobie. Thanne he
made to hym a gret tresorie ; and thero
weren beforn hym leiende vp ȝiftis, and
encens, and vesselis, and the dime of
whete, win, and of[l] oile, partis of Leuitis, and of singeris, and of porteris, and
6 the preestus firste frutis. In alle these
thingus forsothe I was not in Jerusalem ; for in the two and threttithe ȝer
of Artaxerses, king of Babiloine, I cam
to the king, and in the ende of daȝis I
7 preȝide the king. And I cam into Jerusalem, and I vnderstod the[m] euel, that
Eliazub hadde do to Tobie, that he make
to hym a tresor in the vestiaries of the
8 hous off God ; and euel it is seen to me
gretli. And I threw out the vesselis of
9 the hous of Tobie fro the tresorie ; and I
comaundede, and thei clenseden the tresories ; and I bar aȝeen thider the vesselis of the hous of God, sacrifise, and
10 encens. And I knewȝ for the partis of
Leuitus weren not ȝiuen, and that eche
was in to his regioun of the Leuitus, and
of the singerys, and of hem that ministre-
11 den ; and I pursuede the cause aȝen the
master iugis, and seide, Whi han wee
forsake the hous of God ? And I gede-

and it was foundun writun ther ynne, that
Amonytis and Moabitis owen not entre[u]
in to the chirche of God til[v] in to with
outen ende ; for thei metten not the sones 2
of Israel with bred and watir[w], and thei
hiriden aȝens the sones of Israel Balaam,
for to curse hem ; and oure God turnede
the cursyng in to blessyng. Sotheli[x] itȝ
was doon, whanne 'thei hadden[y] herd the
lawe, thei departiden ech alien[z] fro Israel.
And upon[n] these thingis Eliasib[b], the prest, 4
'was blameful[c], that[d] was the[e] souereyn in
the tresorie of the hows of oure God, and
was[f] the[g] neiȝboret[†] of[h] Tobie. Therfor[i] 5
he[k] made to him[l] a grete treserie, 'that is[m],
in the hows of God[n] ; and men[o] kepynge[p]
ȝiftis[q], and encence, and vessels[r], and the
tithe of wheete, of[s] wyn, and of oile, the[t]
partis of dekenes, and of syngeris, and of
porteris, and the firste fruytis of prestis,
'weren there[‡] bifor him[u]. Forsothe[v] in 6
alle these thingis Y was not in Jerusalem ;
for in the two and thrittithe ȝeer of Artaxerses, kyng of Babiloyne, Y cam to the
kyng, and in the ende of daies[w] Y preiede
the[x] kyng. And[y] Y cam in to Jerusalem, 7
and Y vndurstood the yuel, which[z] Eliasib
hadde do to Tobie, to make to hym a
tresour in the porchis of Goddis hows ;
and to me it[a] semede ful yuel. And Y 8
castide forth[b] the vessels of the hows of
Tobie out of the tresorie ; and Y co- 9
maundide[c], and thei clensiden the tresories ; and Y brouȝte aȝen there the vessels
of Goddis hous, sacrifice[d], and encence[e].
And Y knew that the partes of dekenes[f] 10
weren not ȝouun[g], and that[h] ech man[i] of
the dekenes and of the syngeris, and of
hem that mynystriden[k] hadde fledde[l] in to
his cuntrei ; and Y dide the cause[m] aȝens 11

† the neiȝbore ;
that is, frend,
by the matri-
monye of his
cosyn that
hadde weddid
the douȝter of
Sanaballath.
Lire here. c.

‡ weren there ;
that is, tho
thingis that
weren halewid
to Goddis re-
ligioun weren
remoued fro
thennus that the
vessels of Tobie
schulden be
put there.
Lire here. c.

[l] Om. A. 　[k] hous tresorie z pr. m. 　[l] Om. A. 　[m] that A.

[u] to entre is. 　[v] Om. K. 　[w] goynge toward the loond of biheest I marg. s text. 　[x] And is. 　[y] the peple
had is. 　[z] alien man that was no Jewe is. 　[a] oon of A pr. m. FH. one of EL. on DC sec. man. EV. 　[b] was
Eliasib is. 　[c] Om. I. blameful s. 　[d] whiche I. 　[e] Om. is. 　[f] he was is. 　[g] Om. is. 　[h] to is. 　[i] And is.
[k] Eliasib is. 　[l] him self is. 　[m] Om. I. 　[n] oure God L. 　[o] there bifore him weren men is. 　[p] that kepten
the is. 　[q] ȝiftis offrid I. ȝiftis that weren offrid s. 　[r] dyuerse vessels is. 　[s] and of X. 　[t] and the I. and s.
[u] Om. is. 　[v] And is. 　[w] daies of him is. 　[x] to the is. 　[y] And than s. 　[z] that is. 　[a] this thing is.
[b] out s. 　[c] comaundide the mynystris is. 　[d] and the sacrifice therof is. 　[e] the encense is. 　[f] the dekenes I.
[g] ȝouun to hem is. 　[h] that therfor s. 　[i] Om. R. 　[k] mynystriden in the temple is. 　[l] gon awey is. 　[m] cause
or execucioun I. cause, that is, execucioun or dome s.

rede hem, and made to stonde in ther 12 staciouns. And al Juda broȝte to[n] the dime of whete, and of win, and of oile, in 13 to bernes. And wee setten vpon the bernes, Selemiam, prest, and Sadoch, scribe, and Fadaiam, of the Leuitus, and biside hem, Anan, the sone of Saccur, the sone of Mathanie ; for feithful thei ben preued, and to them ben take to 14 kepe the partis of ther brethren. My God, haue mynde of me for this, and do thou not awei my mercies, that I dide in the hous of my God, and in his cerimoines.

CAP. XIV.

15 In thoo daȝes I saȝ in Juda tredende pressours in the sabot, hipelis berende, and chargende vpon assis win, and grapis, and figis, and eche charge, and berende in to Jerusalem in the dai of sabot ; and I witnessede vpon hem, that in the dai, in whiche it was not leeful to 16 sellen, thei solden. And Tiris dwelten[o] in it, berende in fisshis and alle chaffaris, and thei solden in the sabatis to the sonus 17 of Juda and of Jerusalem. And I repreuede the most wrshipeful men of Juda, and seide to hem, What is this euele thing that ȝee don, and defoulen 18 the dai of sabot ? Whether nott these thingus diden oure fadris, and oure God broȝte vp on vs al this euel, and vpon this cite ? and ȝee adden wrathe vpon Israel, 19 defoulende the sabot. It is do forsothe, whan the ȝatis of Jerusalem hadden restid in the sabot dai, I seide, Closeth the ȝatis ;

magistratis[n]†, and[o] Y seide, Whi ꞌforsaken we[p] the hous of God ? And Y gaderide hem[q] togidere, ꞌthat is[r], dekenes and mynystris[s] ꞌthat hadden go awei[t], and Y made hem[u] to stonde in her stondyngis. And 12 al Juda brouȝte the[v] tithe of wheete, of wiyn, and of oile, in to bernes[w]. And we 13 ordeyneden on the[x] bernes, Selemye, the prest, and Sadoch, the writere, and Phadaie, of[y] the dekenes, and bisidis hem[z], Anan, the sone of Zaccur, the sone of Mathanye ; for thei[a] weren preued feithful men, and the partis of her britheren weren bitakun to hem. My God, haue 14 mynde of me for this thing, and do thou not awei my merciful doyngis, whiche Y dide[b] in the hows of my God, and in hise cerymonyes.

CAP. XIV.

Yn tho daies Y siȝ in Juda men tredinge 15 pressours in the sabat[c], ꞌmen bryngynge[d] hepis[e], and chargynge[f] on assis wiyn, and grapis, and figis, and al birthun[g], and ꞌbringynge in to Jerusalem[h] in the dai of sabat[i] ; and Y witnesside to hem, that thei schulden sille[k] in the[l] dai, in which it was leueful to sille[m]. And[n] men of Tire dwell- 16 iden ꞌin it[o], and brouȝten[p] in[q] fischis, and alle thingis set to sale, and[r] thei selden[s] ꞌin the sabatis[t] to the sones of Juda and of Jerusalem. And Y rebuykide[u] the prin- 17 cipal men of Juda, and Y seide to hem, What is this yuel thing which[v] ȝe doen[x], and maken vnhooli the daie of the sabat ? Whether oure fadris diden not these 18 thingis, and oure God[y] brouȝte[z] on[a] vs al this yuel, and on[b] this citee ? and ȝe encreessen[c] wrathfulnesse[d] on[e] Israel, in defoulynge the[f] sabat. Forsothe[g] it was 19 doon, whanne the ȝatis of Jerusalem

† magistratis ; that is, the hiȝeste preest and othere principal men faneringe him. Lire here. c.

---

[n] to me A. [o] dwelleden ABFH.

[n] maistir men 18. [o] that suffriden this yuel, and 8. [p] forsaken ȝe plures. haue ȝe forsake 18. [q] Om. 18. [r] the 18. [s] the mynystris 18. [t] Om. 1. [u] Om. plures. [v] Om. 18. [w] the bernes 8. [x] thes 18. [y] oon of 18. [z] hem we ordeyneden 1. [a] thes 18. [b] haue do 18. [c] sabat day 18. [d] and thei brouȝten 18. [e] hepis or birthins 18. [f] thei chargiden up 1. [g] othere charge 18. [h] Om. 18. [i] sabat, and thei brouȝten thes thingis in to Jerusalem 18. [k] sille thes thingis 18. [l] that 18. [m] sille thingis 18. [n] And in Jerusalem 18. [o] Om. 18. [p] thei brouȝten 18. [q] ther ynne thydre 8. [r] and in the sabot day 18. [s] selden thes thingis 18. [t] Om. 18. [u] rebuykide herfore 18. [v] that 18. [x] done in the ȝatis 8. [y] God herfore 18. [z] hath brouȝt 18. [a] upon 18. [b] upon 18. [c] Om. 19. [d] the wrathfulnesse of God 18. [e] ȝe encressen upon 18. [f] thus the 8. [g] And 18.

and thei closeden the ȝatis; and I comaundede, that thei shulden not opene
them vnto after the sabot. And of my
childer I ordeinede noumbris vp on the
ȝatis, that no man shulde bern in^p charge
20 vp on the sabot dai. And the marchaundis dwelten, aud sellende al ther chaffaris,
21 withoute Jerusalem ones and twies. And
I witnessede to them, and seide to hem,
Whi dwelle ȝee forn aȝen of^q the wal? If
the secunde this ȝee do, hond I shal lein
in ȝou. And so fro that time thei camen
22 not in the sabot. Also I seide to the
Leuitis, that thei shulden be clensid,
and comen to the ȝatis to be kept, and
to halewen the sabat dai. And bi this
thanne haue mynde of me, my God, and
spare to me aftir the multitude of thi^r
myseraciouns.

CAP. XV.

23 But in thoo dayes Y saȝ the Jewis
weddinge^s wiues, Azotitis, Amonitis, and
24 Moabitis. And the sonus of hem speeken
of the half part^t Azotitis maner, and thei
couthen not speken Jeuli, and thei speken
after the tunge of puple and of puple.
25 And I repreuede hem, and curside; and
I felde of hem men, and made hem ballid,
and made hem swern in the Lord, that
thei shulde not ȝiue ther doȝtris to the
sonus of hem, and thei shulden not take of
the doȝtris of hem to ther sonus and to
26 hemself; seiende, Whether not in such
maner thing synnede Salamon, the^u king
of Irael? And certis in manie Jentilis
was ther no king of Irael lic hym, and
he was derworthe to his God, and hys
God sette hym king vpon al Irael, and
hym thanne ladden to synne aliene wym-
27 men. Whether and wee vnbuxhum shul
don al this grete euel, that wee trespa-

hadden restid in the dai of sabat, Y^h
seideⁱ, Schitte ȝe the ȝatis; and thei schit-
tiden the ȝatis; and I comaundide^k, that
thei schuden not opene tho ȝatis til aftir
the sabat. And of my children^l Y ordeynede
noumbris on the ȝatis^m, that no manⁿ
schulde brynge in a birthun in the dai of
sabat. And^o marchauntis, and men sil- 20
linge alle thingis set to sale dwelliden with
out Jerusalem onys and^p twies^q. And Y 21
aresonyde hem, and Y^r seide to hem, Whi
dwellen ȝe^s euene aȝens^t the wal? If ȝe
doon this^u the secounde tyme, Y schal^v
sette hond† on^w ȝou. Therfor fro that
tyme^x thei camen not^y in^z the sabat. Also 22
Y seide to dekenes^a, that thei schulden be
clensid, and that thei schulden come to
kepe the ȝatis, and to halowe^b the dai of
sabat^c. And therfor for this thing, my
God, haue mynde of me, and spare^d me
bi^e the mychilnesse of thi merciful doyngis. But also in tho daies Y siȝ Jewys 23
weddinge wyues, wymmen of Azotus, and
wymmen of Amonytis, and wymmen of
Moabitis. And her children spaken half 24
part bi the speche of Aȝotus, and kouden^f
not speke bi the speche of Jewis, and thei
spaken biȝ the langage of puple^h and of
pupleⁱ. And Y rebuykide hem, and Y^k 25
curside^l; and Y beet the men^m 'of hemⁿ,
and Y made hem ballid^o, and Y made
hem to^p swere bi the Lord, that thei
schulden not ȝyue her douȝtris to the sones
of 'tho aliens^q, and that thei schulden not
take of the douȝtris of 'tho aliens^r to her
sones, and to hem silf; and Y seide, Whe- 26
ther Salomon, the kyng of Israel, synnede
not in siche a^s thing^t? And certis in many
folkis was^u no kyng lijk hym, and he was
loued of his God, and God settide hym
kyng on^v al Israel, and therfor^w alien
wymmen brouȝten hym to synne. Whe- 27

† hond ; for to
prisone and
22 bete ȝou.
Lire here. cv.

---

^p Om. A.   ^q Om. AC pr. m.   ^r the F.   ^s wending c.   ^t partie AEFH.   ^u Om. A.

^h and Y is.   ⁱ seide to the porters is.   ^k comaundide hem s.   ^l children or seruauntis is.   ^m ȝatis to
kepe hem i. ȝatis to kepe shitte s.   ⁿ man bi hem s.   ^o And than s.   ^p or is.   ^q tweyes in the sabot
day s.   ^r Om. i.   ^s ȝe there is.   ^t anentis or on the other side of s.   ^u this thing is.   ^v shal bi foors s.
^w upon is.   ^x tyme forth is.   ^y not thidere is.   ^z to sille eny thing in s.   ^a the dekenes s.   ^b halwe or
shewe s.   ^c sabot to be holi s.   ^d spare thou is.   ^e in is.   ^f thei kouden is.   ^g aftir i.   ^h that puple is.
ⁱ that i. that, that was not leeful s.   ^k Om. is.   ^l curside hem i.   ^m housbondis is.   ⁿ Om. i. of the
wymmen s.   ^o ballid or aschamed is.   ^p Om. is.   ^q hem i text. aliens i marg.   ^r hem i.   ^s Om. is.
^t thingis s.   ^u ther was i.   ^v vpon is.   ^w Om. i.

sen in the Lord oure God, and wedden
28 straunge wiues. Of[v] the sonus forsothe
of Joiada, sone of the grete prest, Eliazib, sone in lawe was Sanaballath Oro-
29 nite, whom I drof fro me. Recorde thou,
Lord my God, aȝen hem, that defoulen
presthod, and the prestus and Leuitus riȝt.
30 Thanne I clensede hem fro alle alienes,
and ordeinede ordris of prestis and of
31 Leuitis, eche in his seruise, and in offring
of trees in ordeincd times, and in firste
frutis. Haue mynde of me, mi God, in
to goode.

ther also we vnobedient schulden do al
this grete yuel, that we trespasse aȝens
'oure Lord God[x], and wedde alien wyues?
Forsothe[y] Sanabalath Horonyte hadde 28
weddid a douȝter of the sones of Joiada,
sone of Eliasib, the grete prest, which[z]
Sanaballath Y droof[a] awei fro me. My 29
Lord God, haue mynde aȝens hem†, that
defoulen presthod, and the riȝt of prestis
and of dekenes. Therfor I clenside hem[b]
fro alle aliens, and I ordeynede ordris[c] of
prestis and of dekenes, ech man in his ser- 30
uice, and in[d] the[e] offring, *that is, dressing,* 31
of trees[f] in tymes ordeyned, and in the
firste fruytis. My God, haue mynde of
me in to good.

† aȝenus hem *
in punysching
hem orribly
and greuously,
to the drede
of othere men.
Lire here. c.

Explicit liber secundus Esdre[w].   *Here eendith the secunde book of Esdre,
and here bigynneth the book of Tobie[g].*

    [v] And of *A.*   [w] *Here endith the secounde book of Esdre, and now begynneth the 3. A. Explicit liber
secundus Esdre, incipit tertius.* E.   *Here endeth Esdre secundo, and now bygynneth Esdre tercio.* F.
No final rubric in *H.*

    [x] the Lord oure God 18.   [y] Sothely 18.   [z] the which 1.   [a] drofe *therfor* 8.   [b] the prestis 18.   [c] the
ordris 16.   [d] *to be in* 18.   [e] Om. 18.   [f] trees *or of wode to brenne with offrid sacrifices* 8.   [g] From
BCDFQUVWXb. *Here endith the secounde book of Esdras, and bigynneth a prologe on the book of Thobie.* G.
Here endeth the secounde book of Esdre, and here bygynneth Tobic. Has. *Heere endith the secounde book of
Esdre, and heere biginnyth the thridde book of Esdre.* I. *Here endeth the seconde book of Esdre, or Neemye;
se now the prolog of Tobie.* K. *Here endith the secounde book of Esdre, and here bigynneth a prologe on the
book of Tobie.* M. *Here endith the secunde book of Esdre, and bigynneth a storie of an hooly man Tobie,
that bifelde in the sixte ȝeer of Ezechie, king of Juda* N. *Here endith the secounde book of Esdre, and bigynneth the prolog on the book of Tobie.* o. No final rubric in the other Mss.

III. ESDRAS.[a]

CAP. I.

1 AND Josias made pasch in Jerusalem
to the Lord, and he offride pasch the
fourtenthe dai of the moone of the firste
2 monith, ordeinende prestis bi whilis of
daȝis, clothid in stolis, in the temple of
3 the Lord. And he seide to the Leuitus, the
holi seruauns of Irael, that thei shulden
halewe them self to the Lord, in setting
of the holi arke of the Lord in the hous,
that king Salamon, the sone of Dauid,
4 bilde; It shal not be to ȝou to taken it
vp on shuldris; and now serueth to oure
Lord, and doth the cure of that folc of
Irael, of parti aftir tounis, and[b] ther
5 linagis, aftir the writing of Dauid, king
of Irael, and aftir the grete wrshipeful
doing of Salamon, his sone, alle in the
temple, and aftir ȝoure litil fader partie
of princehod of hem, that stonden in the
siȝte of the brethern of the sonus of Irael.
6 Offrith pasch, and maketh redi sacrifises
to ȝoure brethern; and doth aftir the
heste of the Lord, that[c] is ȝiue to Moises.
7 And Josias ȝaf in to the folc that is
founde, shep, of lombis, and of kidis, and
of she got, thretti thousend; calues thre
8 thousend. These thingus of the kingus
thingus ben ȝiuen aftir beheste to the
puple, and to prestis, in to pasch; shep
in noumbre two thousend, and caluis an

CAP. I.

AND Josias made pask in Jerusalem 1
to the Lord, and he offride pask the fourtenthe day of the monthe of the first
monthe, ordeynynge prestis bi *her* whiles 2
of daies, clothid in stolis, *or longe clothis*,
in the temple of the Lord. And he seide 3
to the dekens, the holy seruauntis of Israel,
that thei schulden halewe hem self to the
Lord, in settynge of the holy arke of the
Lord in the hous, that kyng Salomon, the
sone of Dauid, bildide; It schal not be to 4
ȝou *no more* to take it upon schuldris;
and now serueth to oure Lord, and do ȝe
cure of that folk of Israel, of the part aftir
townes, and her lynagis, aftir the writyng 5
of Dauid, kyng of Israel, and aftir the
greet wirschipful doyng of Salomon, his
sone, in al the temple, and aftir ȝoure litil
fadris part of princehood of hem, that
stonden in the siȝt of the bretheren of the
sones of Israel. Offre ȝe pask, and maketh 6
redy the sacrifices to ȝoure bretheren; and
do ȝe aftir the heest of the Lord, that is
ȝouen to Moyses. And Josias ȝaf to the 7
folc that was founden *there*, scheep, of
lombis, and of kides, and of sche geet,
thritti thousynd; calues, thre thousynd.
Thes ȝiftis ben ȝouen of the kingis owne 8
thingis aftir the heest *of the Lord* to the
peple, and to prestis, in to pask; scheep

---

9 hundrid. And Jechonias, and Semeias, and Nathanael, brother, and Azabias, and Oziel, and Coraba, in to pasch, shep, 10 fiue thousend; caluis, fiue hundrid. And whan these thingis weren do nobli, the prestis and Leuitus stoden, hauende 11 therue loues bi linagys. And aftir the parties of the princehod of fadris in the si3te of the puple thei offriden to the Lord, aftir thoo thingus that in the boc 12 of Moises ben writen. And thei rosteden pasch with fijr, as it behouede; and ostus thei soden in sething vesselis and pottis, 13 with weel willing. And thei bro3ten to alle that weren of the folc; and aftir these thingus thei maden redi to hemself 14 and to prestis. The prestus forsothe offriden talewis, vnto the hour was endid; and Leuitus maden redi to hemself, and to ther bretheren, and to the sonys of 15 Aron. And the sacrifieris[d] offriden do3-tris, after ordre, and after the heste of Dauid; and Azaf, and Zacharias, and 16 Jeddinus, that was of the king; and the ussheris bi alle the 3atis, so that noon ouerpasside his. Forsothe the brethern 17 of hem gretheden to hem. And thoo thingis, that perteneden to the sacrifise 18 of the Lord, ben ended. In that dai thei dide pasch, and offriden ostis vp on the sacrifise of the Lord, after the heste of 19 king Josie. And the sonus of Irael, that ben founde, diden in that time pasch, and the feste dai of therue loues bi seuene 20 da3es. And there is not solempnisid such a pasch in Irael, fro the times of Samuel, 21 the profete. And alle the kingus of Irael haleweden not such a pasch, as dide Josias, and the prestus, and Leuitis, and Jewis, and al Irael, that ben founden in 22 the commemoracioun at Jerusalem. The ei3etenthe 3er, regnende Josias, is halewid 23 pasch. And the werkis of Josie ben made ri3te in the si3te of his Lord, in ful herte 24 dredende; and thoo thingus forsothe that abouten hym ben writen, in the rathere times of hem that sinneden, who so euere weren vnreligious a3en the Lord, befor

in noumbre two thousynd, and calues an hundrid. And Jechonyas, and Semeias, 9 and Nathanael, *his* brother, and Azabias, and Oziel, and Coroba, 3auen in to pask, fyue thousynd scheep, and fyue hundrid calues. And whanne thes thingis weren nobly 10 don, the prestis and dekens stoden, hau-ynge therf looues bi lynages. And aftir 11 the partis of the princehood of fadris thei offriden to the Lord in the si3t of the peple, after tho thingis that ben writen in the book of Moyses. And thei rostiden 12 the pask with fijr, as it bihouyde; and thei soden oostis in sethinge vessels and in pottis, with wel willyng. And thei 13 brou3ten *it* to alle that ther weren of the folk; and aftir thes thingis thei maden redy to hem self and to prestis. Forsothe 14 the prestis offriden ynner fatnesse, vnto the hour was endid; and dekens grey-thiden to hem self, and to her bretheren, and to the sones of Aaron. And men 15 sacrifiynge offriden *her* dou3tris, aftir the oordre and the heestis of Dauid; and Azaph, and Zacharie, and Jeddynus, that was of the king; and the porters bi alle 16 the 3atis *offriden,* so that noon passide his 3ate. Forsothe her bretheren greythiden to hem. And *so* tho thingis, that per-17 teynyden to the sacrifice of the Lord, ben endid. In that day thei diden pask, and 18 offriden ostis upon the sacrifice of the Lord, aftir the heest of kyng Josie. And 19 the sones of Israel, that weren founden *present,* diden in that tyme pask, and the feest day of therf looues bi seuen daies. And ther was not solempnyzed sich a 20 paske in Israel, fro the tymes of Samuel, the prophet. And alle the kyngis of 21 Israel halewiden not sich a pask, as diden Josias, and the prestis, and dekens, and Jewis, and al Israel, that weren founden in the commemoracioun, *or mynde mak-ing,* at Jerusalem. In the ei3tenthe 3er, 22 Josie regnynge, *this* pask was halewid. And the werkis of Josie ben maad ri3t in 23 the si3t of his Lord, in ful dredynge herte; and tho thingis forsothe that *weren* aboute 24

alle folc, and that soȝten not the woordis
25 of the Lord vp on Irael. And aftir al
this deede of Josie, Farao, king of Egipt,
steȝede vp, comende to casten awei in
Carcamys vpon Eufraten; and Josias
26 wente in to meeting to hym. And the
king of Egipt sente to Josiam, seiende,
What is to me and to thee, king of Jude?
27 I am not sent of the Lord, vpon Eufraten
forsothe is mi bataile; heeȝende go doun.
28 And Josias is not turned aȝeen vp on
the char, but enforcide to ouercomyn hym,
not takende heede to the woord of the
29 profete, of the mouth of the Lord; but
he sette to hym bataile in the feld of
Mecedan; and princis descendeden to
30 king Josiam. And the king seide to his
childer, Moueth me awei fro the bataile;
forsothe I am gretli maad sijk. And anoon
his childre moueden hym awei fro the
31 sheltrun. And he steȝede vp vpon his
secunde^e char; and comende to Jerusalem, diede, and is biried in the fader se-
32 pulcre. And in al Jude thei weileden
Josie, and thei that befor seten with
wiues, weilede hym vnto this dai; and
this is ȝiue to be don euermor in to al
33 the kinrede of Irael. These thingus forsothe ben beforn writen in the boc of
stories of kingus of Juda, and 'in to^f alle
iestis, the deede of Josie, the glorie of
hym, and his vnderstonding in the lawe
of God; for euenli ben don of hym, and
thoo thingus that ben not writen in the
34 boc of kingus of Irael and of Juda. And
thei that weren of the kinrede, takende
Jechoniam, the sone of Josie, setten king
for Josie, his fadir, whan he was of thre
35 and thretti ȝer. And he regnede vp on
Irael thre monethis; and the king of
Egipt putte hym awei, that he regne not
36 in Jerusalem. And he pilde^g the folc of
an hundrid talentus of siluer, and a talent
37 of gold. And the king of Egipt sette
Joachym, his brother, king of Jude and
38 of Jerusalem; and he bond the maister
iugis of Joachim; Saracel, his brother,
39 takende, he broȝte aȝeen to Egipt. Joa-

him ben writen, in the rathere tymes of
hem that synnyden, and the whiche weren
vnreligious aȝen the Lord, bifore *or more
than* al hethen folk, and the whiche synners souȝten not the wordis of the Lord
upon Israel. And aftir al this deede of 25
Josie, Pharao, king of Egipt, ȝede up,
comynge to casten awey in Carcamys upon
Eufraten; and Josias wente in to metyng
to him. And the king of Egipt sente to 26
Josiam, seiynge, What is to me and to
thee, kyng of Jude? I am not sent of the 27
Lord, upon Eufraten forsothe is my bataile; hastily *therfor* go doun. And Jo- 28
sias was not turned aȝen upon the chare,
but he enforside him *self* to ouercome
Pharao, not takinge hede to the word of
the prophet, fro the mouth of the Lord;
but he sette to him bataile in the feeld of 29
Mecedan; and princis camen doun to kyng
Josiam. And *thanne* the king seide to his 30
children, *or seruauntes*, Moueth me awey
fro the bataile; forsothe I am gretly maad
sijk. And anoon his children moueden
him awey fro the scheltrun. And he 31
stiede upon his secoundarie chare; and
comynge to Jerusalem, he diede, and was
biried in *his* fadris sepulcre. And in al 32
Jude thei biweiliden Josie, and thei that
bifore seten with wyues, weiliden him vnto
this day; and this is grauntid to be don
euer more in al the kynrede of Israel.
Thes thingis forsothe ben writen in the 33
book of stories of kyngis of Juda, and the
glorie of Josie, and his vndirstonding in
the lawe of God, bi alle dedes of the doyng
of him; for euenly tho weren don of hym,
and the whiche ben not writun in the
book of kingis of Israel and of Juda. And 34
thei that weren of the kynrede token Jeconye, the sone of Josie, and setten him
king for Josie, his fadir, whanne he was
of thre and thritty ȝeer. And he regnyde 35
upon Israel thre monethis; and *thanne* the
kyng of Egipt putte him awey, that he
regnyde not in Jerusalem. And he pilide 36
the folk of an hundrid talentis of siluer,
and of a talent of gold. And the kyng of 37

---

chim was of fiue and twenti ʒer, whan
he regnede in the lond of Juda and of
Jerusalem; and he dide euel in the siʒte
40 of the Lord. Aftir this forsothe Nabugodonosor, king of Babiloine, steʒede vp,
and bindende hym[h] in a strong[i] bond,
41 broʒte in to Babiloine; and the holi vesselis of God Nabugodonosor toc and
broʒte, and sacride in his temple in Babi-
42 loine. Forsothe of his vnclennesse and
vnreligiosite it is writen in the boc of
43 the times of kingus. And Joachim, his
sone, regnede for hym; whan forsothe he
44 was of ordeined, he was of eiʒte ʒer. Forsothe he regnede thre monethis and ten
daʒes in Jerusalem; and dideJ euel in the
45 siʒte of the Lord. And aftir a ʒer Nabugodonosor sendende broʒte hym ouer in
to Babiloine, togidere with the sacride
46 vesselis of the Lord. And he sette Sede-
chiam king of Juda and of Jerusalem,
47 whan he was of oon and twenti ʒer. Forsothe he regnede elleuen ʒer; and dide
euel in the siʒte of the Lord, and was not
adrad of the woordis that ben seid of Jeremie, the profete, of the mouth of the
48 Lord; and adiurid of king Nabugodonosor, forsworn wente awei, and his[k] hard-
ned nol, and with his herte trespaside the
lawful thingus of the Lord God of Irael.
49 And the dukis of the puple of the Lord
manie thingus wickeli beeren, and vnpitousli diden ouer alle the vnclennessis of
Jentilis; and thei defouleden the temple
of the Lord, that was holi[l] in Jerusalem.
50 And God of ther fadris sente bi his
aungil to aʒeen clepen hem, for the
whiche thing he sparede to hem, and to
51 ther tabernacle. Thei forsothe scorneden in ther corneris, and that dai that
the Lord spac, thei weren bobbende his
52 profetus. The whiche vnto wrathe is
stirid vp on his folc[m], for ther irreligi-
osite. Comaundende and steʒende vp the
53 kingus of Caldeis, thei slowen the ʒunge
men of hem in swerd, in the enuyroun of
the holi temple of hem; and thei spareden
not to ʒung man, and to maiden, and to

Egipt sette Joachim, his brother, kyng of
Jude and of Jerusalem; and he bonde the
maistir iuges of Joachim, and takynge Saracel, his brother, he brouʒte him aʒen to
Egipt. Joachim was of fyue and twenty 39
ʒeer, whanne he regnyde in the loond of
Juda and of Jerusalem; and he dide yuel
thing in the siʒt of the Lord. Aftir this 40
forsothe Nabugodonosor, kyng of Babiloyne, stiede up, and byndynge Joachim
in a strong boond, brouʒte him in to
Babiloyne; and Nabugodonosor toke and 41
brouʒte the holy vessels of God, and sacride *tho* in his temple in Babiloyne. For- 42
sothe of his vncleunesse and his vnreli-
gioustee it is writen in the book of the
tymes of kyngis. And Joachim, his sone, 43
regnyde for him; whanne forsothe he was
ordeyned *king*, he was of eiʒte ʒeer. For- 44
sothe he regnyde thre monthis and ten
daies in Jerusalem; and dide yuel in siʒt
of the Lord. And aftir a ʒer Nabugodo- 45
nosor sente, and brouʒte him ouer in to
Babiloyne, togidre with the sacrid vessels
of the Lord. And he sette Sedechie kyng 46
of Juda and of Jerusalem, whanne he was
of oon and twenti ʒeer. Forsothe he reg- 47
nyde elleuen ʒeer; and he dide yuel in siʒt
of the Lord, and was not adred of the
wordis that ben seid of Jeremye, the prophet, fro the mouth of the Lord. And he 48
adiurid, *or chargid bi ooth*, of kyng Nabugodonosor, forsworn wente awey, and his
noll made hard, he ouerpasside the laweful thingis of the Lord God of Israel.
And the duykis of the Lordis peple baren 49
hem wickidly many thingis, and thei diden
vnpitously ouer alle the wickidnessis of
Gentiles; and thei defouliden the temple
of the Lord, that was hooly in Jerusalem.
And God of her fadris sente bi his aungel 50
to aʒenclepe hem, for the whiche thing he
sparide to hem, and to her tabernaclis.
Thei forsothe scornyden in her corners, 51
and that dai that the Lord spake, thei
weren bobbynge his prophetis. The whiche 52
Lord is stirid to wraththe upon his folk,
for their irreligiositee. *And* the kyngis

---

[h] Om. c pr. m.   [i] deuynyd ᴇ pr. m.   [j] he dide ᴀ.   [k] with his ᴇ pr. m.   [l] Om. c.   [m] puple c nr. m.

54 old man, and to ful waxen man; but and alle thei ben taken in to the hondus of hem ; and alle the sacride vesselis of the Lord, and the kingis cofrys takende, thei 55 bro₃ten in to Babiloine. And thei brenden vp the hous of the Lord, and distrieden the wallis of Jerusalem, and his touris 56 brenden with fijr. And thei wasteden alle the wrshipeful thingus, and to no₃t bro₃ten ; and the laft fro swerd thei 57 bro₃ten in to Babiloine. And thei weren his thrallis, vnto the time that Persis regneden, in the fulfilling of the woord of 58 the Lord, in the mouth of Jeremie ; for to the lond wolde do benigneli ther sabatis, al the time of ther forsaking he sabatisede, in the apliyng of seuenti° ₃er.

of Caldeis comaundiden, and sti₃eden up, thei slowen the ₃ounge men of hem with 53 swerd, aboute the hooly temple of hem ; and thei spariden not to ₃onge man, ne to maiden, ne to old man, and to ful woxen man ; but also alle thei ben taken in to 54 the hondis of hem ; and thei token alle the sacrid vessels of the Lord, and the kyngis coffres, and brou₃ten tho in to Ba- 55 biloyne. And thei brenden up the hous of the Lord, and destroieden the wallis of Jerusalem, and thei brenden his touris with fijr. And thei wastiden alle the 56 wurschipful thingis, and brou₃ten hem to nou₃t ; and thei brou₃ten *the peple* lefte of the swerd in to Babiloyne. And thei 57 weren his thrallis, vn to the tyme that Peersis regnyden, in the fulfillynge of the word of the Lord, in the mouth of Je- remye ; til that the loond wolde do be- 58 nyngnely their sabotis, he sabatisode al the tyme of their forsakyng, in the appliynge of scuenti ₃er.

CAP. II.

1   Regnende Ciro, king of Persis, in the fulfilling of the woord of the Lord, in 2 the mouth of Jeremie, the Lord rerede the spirit of Ciri, king of Persis ; and prechide in al his reume togidere bi 3 scripture, seiende, These thingus seith Cirus, king of Persis, Me hath ordeined king to the world of erthis the Lord of 4 Irael, the hee₃e Lord ; and he signefiede to me to bilde to hym an hous in Jeru- 5 salem, that is in Juda. If ani man is of ₃oure kinrede, his Lord ste₃e vp with 6 hym in to Jerusalem. Hou fele euere thanne aboute placis dwellen, helpe thei hym that ben in that place, in gold and 7 siluer, in ₃iftis, with hors, and bestis, and with othere thingus, that aftir vouwis ben leid vp in to the hous of the Lord, 8 that is in Jerusalem. And the stondende princis of linagis of tounus of Jude, of the linage of Beniamyn, and prestis and Leuitis, whom the Lord stiride to ste₃en vp, and to bilden vp the hous of the

CAP. II.

Regnynge Cyro, kyng of Peersis, in the 1 fulfillyng of the word of the Lord, in the mouth of Jeremye, the Lord reiside up 2 the spirit of Ciry, kyng of Persis ; and he prechide in al his rewme togidre bi scrip- ture, seiynge, Thes thingis seith Cirus, 3 kyng of Persis, The Lord of Israel, the hi₃e Lord, hath ordeyned me kyng to the world of erthis ; and he signyfiede to me 4 to bilde to him an hous in Jerusalem, that is in Juda. If ther is ony man of ₃oure 5 kynrede, his Lord stie up with him in to Jerusalem. Therfor hou many euer 6 dwellen in places aboute, helpe thei hem that dwellen in that place, in gold and siluer, in ₃iftis, with hors, and bestis, and 7 with othere thingis, the whiche aftir vowes ben leid up in to the hous of the Lord, that is in Jerusalem. And the stondynge 8 princis of lynages of townes of Jude, of the lynage of Beniamyn, and prestis and dekens, whom the Lord stiride to wende up, and to bilde up the hous of the Lord,

---

° the seuenti *AH.*

Lord, that is in Jerusalem; and thoo, that weren in the enuyroun of hem, 9 shulden helpe[P] in alle siluer and gold of it, and in bestis, and in manie vouwis; 10 manie, of whom the wit is stirid. And king Cirus broȝte forth the sacride vesselis of the Lord, that Nabugodonosor translatide fro Jerusalem, and sacride 11 hem in his maumet. And bringende forth hem Cirus, king of Persis, toc to Mitridate, that was vp on the tresoris of 12 hym. Bi hym forsothe thei ben taken 13 to Salmanasar, gouernour of Jude. Of these forsothe this[q] the noumbre; siluer sacrid vesselis of likouris, two thousend and foure hundrid; siluerene drinking vesselis, thretti; goldene violis, thretti; also siluerene, two thousend and foure hundrid; and othere vesselis, a thousend. 14 Alle forsothe goldene vesselis and siluerene, four thousend foure hundrid and 15 eiȝte and sixti. And thei ben deliuerd out to Salmanasar, togidere with hem, that of the caytifte of Babiloine weren 16 comen in to Jerusalem. Forsothe in the times of Artaxerses, king of Persis, writen to hym[r], of these that dwelten in Jude and in Jerusalem, Balsamus, and Mitridatus, and Sabellius, and Ratinius, Balteneus, Samelius, scribe, and othere dwellende in Samarie, and in othere placis, the vnderset lettre to king Artaxersi. 17 Lord, thi childer, Ratinus, and Sabelius, scribe, and othere domysmen of thi cort, of thingus that fallen in to Coelem Siriem, 18 and Fenicem. And now be it knowen to the lord the king, for Jewis, that steȝeden vp fro ȝou to vs, comende in to Jerusalem, cite aȝeen flowen to, and werst[s], bilden up[t] the ouenus of it, and setten the 19 wallis, and reren the temple. That if this cite and wallis weren ful endid, thei shul not suffre to ȝelde tributis, but also 20 thei shuln aȝen stonde to kingus. And for that that is do aboute the temple, to han riȝtli wee han demyd to not despisen 21 that same thing, but 'to maken knowen[u] to the lord the king, that if[v] it shal

that is in Jerusalem; and thei, that weren in the enuyroun, *or in cumpas,* of hem, schulden helpe in al siluer and gold of it, 9 and in bestis, and in many vowis; *and* many *othere,* of whom the witt is stirid, *helpe thei also.* And kyng Cirus brouȝte 10 forth the sacrid vessels of the Lord, the whiche Nabugodonosor translatide fro Jerusalem, and sacride hem in his mawmett. And Cirus, king of Persis, bryngynge hem 11 forth, toke *tho* to Mitridate, that was upon the tresours of him. Forsothe bi him thei 12 ben taken to Salmanasar, gouernour of Jude. Of thes thinges forsothe this is 13 the noumbre; silueren halewid vessels of licours, two thousynd and foure hundrid; thritti silueren drinkynge vessels; thritty goldene violes; and two thousynd and foure hundrid silueren *violes;* and a thousynd othere vessels. Forsothe alle the golden 14 and silueren vessels *weren* foure thousynd and foure hundrid and eiȝt and sixty. And 15 thei ben delyuered out to Salmanasar, togidere with hem, that weren comen in to Jerusalem of the caytiftee *or thraldom* of Babiloyne. Forsothe in the tyme of Ar- 16 taxerses, kyng of Persis, ther wreten to him, of thes that dwelliden in Judee and in Jerusalem, Balsamus, and Mitridatus, and Sabelius, and Ratymus, Baltheneus, and Samelius, the scribe, and othere dwellinge in Samarie, and in othere placis, *thei writen this* subiect lettre to the kyng Artaxersy. Lord, thi children, Ratymus, 17 and Sabelius, the scribe, and othere domes men of thi court, of thingis that fallen in Coelem Siriem, and Fenycen. And now 18 be it knowen to the lord the kyng, that Jewis, the whiche stieden up fro ȝou to us, comynge in to Jerusalem, a citee of fleers awei, and a ful yuel *citee,* thei bilden up the ouenes of it, and thei setten the wallis, and reren the temple. That if this 19 citee and wallis weren maad up, thei shul not suffre to ȝelde tributis, but also thei shul aȝenstonde to kyngis. And for cause 20 that that thing is done aboute the temple, to haue *it* riȝtly we haue demed to not

P helpe them c. q this is A. r ben A. s ferst II. t Om. c. u anon to don E pr. m. v Om. II.

4 A 2

seme, O[v]! thee[w] king, be it soȝt in the[x]
22 bokis of thi fadris; and thou shalt finde in
the remembrauncis writen of hem, and
thou shalt knowen, for that cite was
aȝeen floun, and kingis and cites smitende
23 togidere, and Jewis aȝeen fleende, and
makende batailis in it fro euermor; for
24 what cause this cite is desert. Now
thanne knowen we maken, lord[y] king[z],
for if this cite were bild vp, and of this
the wallis weren rerid[a], comyng doun
shal not be to thee in to Coelem Ciriem
25 and Fenicem. Thanne the king wrot
aȝee to Ratinum, that wrot the fallende
thingus, and to Bellumym, and to Sabellio,
scribe, and to othire ordeined, and dwelleris in Cirie and Fenyce, thoo thingus
26 that ben sett vnder. I ha[b] rad the lettre[c],
that thou sentist to me. Thanne[d] I comaundide to be soȝt; and it is founde,
for that cite is fro alwei withstondende
27 to kingus, and the men aȝeen fugitif, and
batailis in it makende; and most stronge
kingus han ben in Jerusalem lordship-
ende, and tributus askende of Cele Cirie
28 and Fenice. Now thanne I comaundede
to forfende thoo men to bilden vp the
cite, and to puruein, lest ani thing more
29 this thing be maad; but go thei not forth
in to more, sithen thei ben of malice, so
that to kingis greeues ben[e] born in.

despise that same thing, but to make 21
knowen to the lord kyng, that if it schal
be seen *plesyng* to the king, be it souȝt in
the bookis of thi fadris; and thou schalt 22
fynde in remembrauncis writen of hem,
and thou schalt knowe, that thilke citee
was aȝen flowun, and kyngis and citees
smytinge togidre, and Jewis fleynge aȝen, 23
and makinge bateilis in it alwey; for the
whiche cause this citee was forsake. Now 24
therfor we maken knowen to the lord
king, that if this citee were bild up, and
the wallis of it weren arerid, ther schal be
no comyng doun to thee in to Choelem
Cyriem and Fenycen. Thanne the kyng 25
wroot aȝen to Ratimym, that wroot *tho*
thingis that bifellen, and to Bellumym,
and to Sabellio, the scribe, and to othere
ordeyned *souereyns*, and dwellinge in
Cirye and in Fenyce, *he wrot to hem* thes
thingis that ben sett vndir. I haue rad 26
the lettre, that thou sentist to me. Therfor I comaundide *it* to be souȝt; and it was
founden, that thilke citee was alwey with-
stondynge to kyngis, and men aȝen fugi- 27
tijf, and makynge bateilis in it; and moost
stronge kingis han ben lordschipinge in
Jerusalem, and askinge tributis of Chole
Cirie and Fenycem. Now therfore I co- 28
maunde to forfende tho men to bilde up
the citee, and to loke, that ony thing be
not maad her aftir; but that thei passe 29
not in to ful myche, sith thei ben of
malice, so that greuauncis be not brouȝt
ther to kinges.

CAP. III.

30 Thanne these thingus rehersid, that of
king Artaxerse weren writen, Rathinus,
and Sabellius, scribe, and that with hem
weren ordeined, ioynende[f], heeȝendeli[g]
camen in to Jerusalem, with horse men,
31 and puple, and cumpanie; and begunnen
to forfenden the bilders. And thei voided-
en fro the bilding of the temple in Jerusalem, vnto the secunde ȝer of the regne
1 of Darie, king of Persis. King Darie

CAP. III.

Thanne aftir thes thingis weren re- 30
hersid, that weren writen of Artaxerses,
the kyng, Rathinus, and Sabellius, the
scribe, and thei that weren with hem ordeyned, ioynynge, hyingly camen in to
Jerusalem, with horse men, and peple, and
with cumpanye; and thei bigunnen to for- 31
fende the buylders. And thei voididen
thanne fro the bildyng of the temple, vnto
the secounde ȝeer of the rewme of Darij,

---

[v] of A.   [w] the A. Om. E pr. m.   [x] Om. A.   [y] the lord A.   [z] the kyng A.   [a] arered AEFH.
[b] haue AEFH.   [c] thingis E pr. m.   [d] That A.   [e] ben not c pr. m.   [f] runnynge E pr. m.   [g] heeȝyngli EF.

made a gret soper to alle his seruauns,
and to alle the maister iugis of Meedis
2 and of Persis, and to alle that wereden^h
purper, and to gouernoures, and to coun-
seilens, and to prefectis vnder hym, fro
Ynde vnto Ethiope, to an hundrid and
3 seuene and twenti piouincis And whan
they hadden eten and drunken, and fulfild, turneden aȝeen, thanne king Darie
steȝede vp in his litil bed place, and sleep^l,
4 and is wakid^k. Thanne thoo thre ȝunge
men, keperis of the body, that kepten the
bodi of the king, seiden the tothir to the
5 tother, Seie wee eche of vs a woord, that
befor passe ; and whos euere woord ȝeme
wisere of the tother, king Darie shal
6 ȝiue to hym grete ȝiftus, and to be couered
with purper, and to drinken in gold, and
vpon gold to slepen, and a goldene char,
with bridel, and a bys mytre, and a beȝe
7 aboute the necke ; and in the secunde
place he shal sitte fro Darie, for his wisdam ; and the cosin of Darie he shal be
8 clepid Thanne eche writende his woord,
seleden, and putten vnder the pilwe
9 of king Darie , and seiden, Whan the
king hadde rise^l, thei shul ȝiue to hym
ther thingus writen, and what euere
thing the king shal demen of thre, and
the maister iugis of Persis, for the woord
of hym is wisere, to hym shal be ȝiue the
10 victorie, as it is write Oon wrot, Strong
11 is win The tother wrot, Strengere is
12 the king The thridde wrot, Strengere
ben wymmen , ouer alle thingus forsothe
13 ouercometh treuthe And whan the king
hadde risen, thei token ther writen
thingis, and ȝeuen to hym, and he radde
14 And sendende he clepide alle the maister
iugis of Persis, and of Meedis, and the
clothed in purper, and the reuleris of
15 prouincis, and prefectis , and thei seten
in conseil, and ben rad write befor them.
16 And he seide, Clepeth the ȝunge men, and
thei shul shewe ther woordis And thei
17 ben clepid^m, and camen in And he seide
to hem, Shewith to vs of these thingus that
ben writen. And the rathere, that hadde

kyng of Persis Kyng Darius made a 1
gret soper to alle his seruauntis, and to
alle the maistei iuges of Medes and of
Persis, and to alle that wereden purpre, 2
and to gouernours, and to counselers, and
to prefectis vndir him, fro Ynde vn to
Ethiope, to an hundrid and seuen and
twenty prouyncis. And whanne thei 3
hadden eten and drunken, and weren fulfillid, thei turneden aȝen Thanne kyng
Darius stiede vp in his litil bed place, and
slepte, and was waken Thaune thilke 4
thre ȝounge men, kepers of the bodi, the
whiche kepten the bodi of the kyng,
seiden oon to an oother, Sey we ech of us 5
a word, that bifore passe *in kunnyng*, and
whos euer word seme wiser *than* of an
oother, kyng Darius schal ȝiue to him
grete ȝiftis, and to be kouered with pur- 6
pie, and to drynke in gold, and to slepe
upon gold ; *and he schal ȝiue him* a golden
chare, with the bridil, and a mytre of bijs,
and a bie aboute the necke ; and he schal 7
sitte in the secounde place fro Darius, for
his wisdom ; and he schal be clepid Daryus
cosyn Thanne ech *of hem thre* writinge 8
his word, seleden, and putten *tho* vndir the /
pelewe of kyng Daryus, and seiden, 9
Whanne the king hath risen, thei wil take
to him her thingis writen, and what euer
thing the kyng shall deme of thre, and the
maistir iuges of Persis, forsothe the word
of him is wiser, *than of the othere*, to him
schal be ȝouen the victoiie, as it is wiiten
Oon wiot, Wyn is strong An oother ^10
wrot, The kyng is strenger The thridde ^12
wrot, Wymmen ben strengiste ; treuthe
ouercomith forsothe ouer alle thingis And 13
whanne the kyng had resen up, thei token
her thingis writen, and ȝouen *tho* to him,
and he radde And he sende and clepede 14
alle the maistre iuges of Persis, and of *the
lond* Medis, and the clothid men in purpre, and the rewleris of prouynces, and
prefectis ; and thei seten in counsel, and 15
the writingis weren red bifore hem And 16
the kyng seide, Clepeth the ȝounge men,
and thei schul schewe her wordis. And

---

18 seid of the strengthe of win, began, and
seide, Men! hou miche win is passende
strong; to alle men that drinken it it
19 berth doun the mynde; also of king and
of faderles child it maketh the minde
vein; also of seruaunt and of freman, of
20 pore and of riche; and alle minde it[a]
turneth in to sikyrnesse, and in to gladnesse; and it remembreth not of[o] any
21 sorewe and dette; and alle the entrailis
it makith onest; and it remembrith not
king, ne maister iuge; and alle thingis
22 bi talent it maketh to speke; and thei
remembre not, whan thei han drunke,
frendshipe ne brotherhed, and after not
23 miche thei taken swerdis; and whan of
win thei drownyn, and rijsen, thei han
24 no mynde that thei diden. O men!
whether win is not passendeli strong,
that thus constreineth to do? And this
seid, he held his pes.

thei weren clepid, and thei camen yn.
And Darius seide to hem, Schewe ȝe to us 17
of thes thingis that ben writen. And the
firste, that had scid of the strengthe of
wyn, he biganne, and seide *to hem*, Men! 18
ful passynge strong is wyn; to alle men
that drynken it it berith doun the mynde;
also it makith the mynde veyn, bothe of 19
kyng and of the fadirles child; also of seruaunt and of fre men, of pore and of riche;
and it turnith al the mynde in to sikir- 20
nesse, and to gladnesse; and it remembrith
not ony serewe and dette; and it makith 21
alle the entrailes honest; and it remembrith not kyng, ne maistir iuge; and alle
thingis it makith speke bi talent; and 22
whanne thei han drunken, thei remembren not frendschip ne brotherhed, and
not longe aftir thei taken swerdis; and 23
whanne thei han be drowned of wyn,
and rijsen, thei han no mynde what
thinges thei diden. O men! whether wyn 24
is not passyngly strong, that thus con-
streynith *men* to do? And this thing seid,
he hilde his pes.

CAP. IV.

1 And the folewere began to sein, that
2 seith of the strengthe of king, O men!
whether men ben not passendely strong,
that erthe and se holden, and alle thingus
3 that in hem ben? The king forsothe ouer
alle thingus passith, and hath lordshipe
of hem, and alle thing, what euere he shal
4 sei to them, thei don. And if[p] he sende
hem to fiȝteres, thei gon, and destroȝen
5 hillis, and wallis, and touris; thei ben
slain, and slen, and the woord of the
king thei passe not; for if thei ouercomen, thei bringe to the king alle
thingus, whateuere thingus thei han spoil-
6 id euermor, and alle othere thingus.
And[q] hou fele euere bern not[r] kniȝthod,
ne fiȝten, but eren the lond, eftsone whan
thei weren repende, thei bringe tributus
7 to the king. And he oon alone; and if he
seie to slen, thei slen; and if he seie to
8 forȝiuen, thei forȝiuen; and if he seie to

CAP. IV.

And the *nexte* folewer biganne to sey, 1
that seide of the strengthe of a kyng, O 2
men! whether men ben not passyngly
stronge, the whiche holden loond and see,
and alle thingis that ben in hem? The kyng 3
forsothe passith aboue alle thingis, and he
hath lordschip of hem, and thei don al
thing, what euer he wil sey to hem. And 4
if he sende hem to fiȝters, thei gon, and
destroyen hillis, and walles, and toures;
thei ben sleyn, and slen, and thei passen 5
not the word of the kyng; for if thei ouercomen, thei bryngen to the king alle
thingis, what euer thingis thei han spoil-
ed euermore, and all othere thingis. And 6
hou fele euer beren not knyȝthod, ne fiȝten,
but eren the loond, eftsone whanne thei
schul repe, thei bringen tributis to the
king. And he *is* oon aloone; and if he 7
bidde to sle, thei sleen; and if he bidde
hem to forȝiue, thei forȝiuen; and if he s

n he *A.*   o Om. *AEFH.*   P Om. *c.*   q Om. *A.*   r up E pr. *m.*

smyten, thei smite; if he seie to outlawen, thei outlawen ; if he seie to bilden,
9 thei bilden ; if he seie to fallenᵃ of, thei
fallenˢ of; if he seie to plaunten, thei
10 plaunten ; and alle folc and vertues hym
obeshen ; and ouer theseᵗ thingus he shal
11 sitte, and drinke, and slepen. These
forsothe in enuyroun kepen hym, and
moun not go eche, and do ther werkis,
but and in woord men ben obeshende to
12 hym. What maner wise the king passeth not befor, that thus is losid ᵘ ? And
13 he heeld his pes. The thridde, that
hadde seid of wymmen, and of treuthe ;
14 this is Sorobabel ; began to speke, Men !
not gret the king, and manie men, ne win
passeth beforn ; who is thanne that hath
15 lordshipe of hem ? Whether not wymmen
geetcᵘᵘ king, and al the puple, that lordshipe to the se, and toᵛ the erthe, and of
16 hem ben born? And thei broʒten forth
hem that plaunteden vines, of the whiche
17 win is maad. And thei maken the stolis
of alle men, and thei don glorie to men,
and men moun not ben seuered fro wym-
18 men. If thei gedere togidere gold and
seluer, and alle fair thing, and seen a
womman in good abite, and in good fair-
19 nesse, alle these thingis forsakende, in to
hir thei taken heede, and the mouth
opened, beholden, andʷ hir drawenˣ to
more than gold orʸ siluer, or any precious
20 thingʸʸ. A man hys fader shal forsaken,
that nurshide hym, and his regioun, and
21 to a womman ioyneth togidere, and with
a womman leueth the lif, and nouther
fader remembreth, ne moder, ne regioun.
22 And therfore it behoueth vs to knowen,
for wymmen han lordshipe of vs. Whe-
23 ther sorewe ʒee not ? And a man take
his swerd, and goth in the weie to do
theftis, and manslaʒterisᶻ, and to seilen
24 ouer the se and flodis ; and a leounᵃ he
seeth, and in dercnesseᵇ he goth in ; and
whan he hath don thefte, and gilis, and
25 raueincs, he bringeth to his leef. And
eft a man looueth his wif mor than fader

sey hem to smyten, thei smyten ; if he sey
to outlawe, thei outlawen ; if he bidde
hem to bilden, thei bilden ; if he bidde to 9
throwe doun, thei throwen adoun ; if he
bidde to plaunte, thei plaunten ; and alle 10
folk and vertues obeishen to him ; and ouer
alle thes thingis he schal sitte, and drynke,
and slepe. Thes forsothe kepen him 11
aboute, and moun not gon echoon, and do
her owne werkis, but in his word men
obeishen to him. What maner wise pass- 12
ith not the kyng bifore oothere, that thus
is loosid ? And he helde his pes. The 13
thridde, that had seid of wymmen, and of
treuthe ; this is seid Sorobabel ; he biganne to speke, O men ! the kyng is not 14
greet, neither many othere men, ne wyn
passith biforn ; who is it thanne that hath
lordschip of hem ? Whether not wymmen, 15
that han goten kyngis, and al the peple,
the whiche kingis han lordschip bothe of
see and of loond, and of wymmen thei ben
born ? And thei brouʒten forth hem that 16
plauntiden vynes, of the whiche wyn is
maad. And thei maken the stoles, or 17
longe clothis, of alle men, and thei don
glorie to men, and men moun not be seuered fro wymmen. If thei gedere togidere 18
gold and siluer, and al fair thing, and
seen a womman in good aray, and in good
fairnesse, thei, forsakynge alle thes thingis, 19
taken heede to here, and the mouth opened, thei biholden hir, and thei drawen
more to hir than to gold and siluer, or
ony precious thing. A man schal forsake 20
his fadir, that norishide him, and his
owne loond, and to a womman he ioynith him togidre, and with a womman he 21
lyuith his lijf, and noither remembrith
fadir, ne modir, ne the lond of his birthe.
And therfor it bihouith us to knowen, that 22
wymmen han lordschip of us. Whether
ʒe serewen not? And also a man takith 23
his swerd, and goth in the wey to don
theftis, and man slauʒtris, and to seilen
ouer the see, and ouer flodes ; and he 24
seeth a lioun, and he goth in derkenessis ;

ˢ hewen E pr. m.   ᵗ alle these c pr. m. E pr. m.   ᵘ defamed E pr. m.   ᵘᵘ geten the A. geeten E.
ᵛ Om. A. al E pr. m.   ʷ in c.   ˣ and drawen c.   ʸ and AH.   ʸʸ ston c pr. m.   ᶻ manslaʒtis cH.
ᵃ lioun AFH.   ᵇ dirknessis A.

26 or modir; and manie woode men ben
maade for ther wiues, and thrallis ben
27 made for hem; and manie pershiden, and
ben stranglid, and synneden for wymmen.
28 And now leeueth to^c me; for gret is the
king in his power, for alle regiouns^d ben
29 aferd to touchen hym. I saȝ ner the
latere Apemen, the doȝter of wndirful man
Besacis, the secundarie wif of the king,
sittende biside the king at the riȝt side;
30 and takende awei the diademe fro his
hed, and puttende on to hirself^e, and with
the hondis she smot the king of ^f the lift
31 hond. And ouer these thingus, the mouth
opened, he beheeld hir, and if she loowe
to hym, he looȝ^g, and if she were wroth
to hym, he glosith, to the time that he be
32 recounsilid 'in to^h grace. O men! whi
ben not wymmen strengere? Gret is the
erthe, and heeȝ is heuene, that these
33 thingus don. And thanne the king and
the purprid men beheelden either in to
other; and heⁱ began to speken of
34 treuthe. O men! whether stronge ben
not wymmen? Gret is the erthe, and heȝ
is heuene, and swift is the cours of the
sunne; it is turned in the cumpas of heuene, and eft it renneth aȝeen in to the
35 same place o dai. Whether not a gret
doere is he, that maketh these thingus?
and treuthe gret, and strengere beforn
36 alle thingis? Al erthe treuthe inwardli
clepeth, heuene also it blesseth, and alle
werkus ben moued and dreden it; and
ther is not with it any thing wicked^j.
37 Wicked^j king, wicked^j wymmen, and
wicked^j alle the sonis of men, and wicked^j
alle the werkis of hem, and ther is not
in hem treuthe, and in ther wickednessis^k
38 thei shuln pershen; and treuthe dwellith,
and waxeth in to with oute ende, and
lineth, and weldeth, in to worldis of
39 worldis. And to taken persones and
differencis is not anent it; but thoo
thingis that ben riȝtwis it doth, to alle
vnriȝtwise and euele men; and alle men
40 ben maad benigne in his werkis. And

and whanne he hath don *his* thefte, and
gijles, and raueynes, he bringith it to his
leef. And efte a man louith his wijf more 25
than fadir or modir; and many men ben 26
maad woode for their wyues, and *many*
ben maad thrallis for hem; and many 27
perischiden, and weren stranglid, and many
han synned for wymmen. And now leeu- 28
eth me; forsothe a kyng is greet, and
his power, for alle regiouns, *or kingdoms
aboute*, ben aferd to touche him. I sawȝe 29
neuer the latter Apeemen, the douȝter of
Besacis, the wondirful man, the secoundarie wijf of the kyng, sittynge biside the
kyng at the riȝt side; and takynge awey 30
the diademe fro his heed, and puttynge it
on hir self, and with the pawme of hir lift
hoond she smote the kyng. And ouer 31
thes thingis, the mouth opened, he bihilde
hir, and if sche lowȝe to him, he lowȝe, and
if sche were wrooth to him, he glosith *or
plesith*, vnto the tyme that he be recounsilid to grace. O men! whi ben not 32
wymmen strengist? Greet is the erthe,
and heuen is hiȝ, that don thes thingis.
Thanne the kyng and the purpred men 33
bihelden either in to oothere; and he biganne to speke of treuthe. O men! wher 34
wymmen ben not stronge? Greet is the
eerthe, and heuen is hiȝ, and the cours of
the sunne is swift; it is turned in the
cumpas of heuen, and eft it renneth aȝen
in to the same place in a day. Wher he 35
is not a greet doer, that makith thes
thingis? and treuthe greet, and strenger
biforn alle thingis? All erthe clepith in- 36
wardly trouthe, also it blessith heuene,
and alle werkis ben moued and dreden it;
and ther is no wickid thing with it.
Wickid kyng, *and* wickid wymmen, and 37
alle the sones of men *ben* wickid, and ther
is not treuthe in hem, and in her wickidnesse thei schul perische; and treuthe 38
dwellith, and wexith in to withouten ende,
and it lyuith, and weldith, into worldus of
worldis. It is not anentis treuthe to out- 39
take persoones, and differencis; but it doth

---

ther is not in his dom wickednesse[k], but
strengthe, and reume, and power, and
mageste of alle duringis aboue time.
41 Blessid be the God of treuthe ! And he
lafte in speking. And alle puplis crieden,
and seiden, Gret is treuthe, and beforn
42 passeth. Thanne the king seith to hym,
Aske, if any thing thou wilt more ouer,
than .ther ben[l] writen, and I shal ȝiue to
thee, aftir that thou art founde wisere ;
and next to[m] me thou shalt sitte, and my
43 cosin thou shalt be clepid. Thanne he
seith to the king, Be thou myndeful of
the vou, that thou vouwidist, to bilde[n]
Jerusalem, in the dai that[o] thou toke the
44 reume ; and alle the vesselis, that ben
taken of Jerusalem, to senden aȝeen, the
whiche Cirus seuerede, whan he sloȝ Babiloine, and wolde senden aȝeen thoo
45 thingus thider. And thou woldist bilden
vp the temple, that Idumeis brenden vp[p],
for Jude is put out of termes fro Caldeis.
46 And now this is that I aske, lord, and
that I bidde ; this is maieste that of thee
I aske, that thou do the vou, that thou
vouwedist to the king of heuene, of thi
47 mouth. Thanne Darie, the king, risende
kiste hym, and wrot epistolis to alle the
dispensatouris, and prefectis, and purprid
men, that thei shulden leden hym forth,
and hem that with hym weren, alle steȝ-
48 ende vp to bilde Jerusalem. And to alle
the prefectis that weren in Cirie, and[q]
Fenice, and Liban, he wrot epistolis, that
thei shulden drawe cedre trees fro Liban
in to Jerusalem, that thei bilde vp with
49 hem the cite. And he wrot to alle the
Jewis, that steȝeden vp fro the reume in
Jude, for fredam, alle myȝti man, and
maister iuge, and prefect, to not comen
50 ouer to the ȝatus of hem, and eche regioun, that thei hadden weldid, to be free
fro hem ; and Idumeis laften the castelis,
51 that thei weldeden of the Jewis, and in
to the making of the temple to[r] ȝiue bi
ȝeris twenti talentis, vnto the time that
52 it be ful bildid ; and to offren ostis eche

tho thingis that ben riȝtful, to alle vnriȝtwise and yuel men ; and alle men ben
maad benyngne in his werkis. And ther 40
is not wickidnesse in his doom, but *ther is*
strengthe, and rewme, and power, and
magestee of alle duryngis aboue tyme.
Blessid be the God of treuthe ! And 41
thanne he lefte in spekynge. And alle
the peplis crieden, and seiden, Greet is
treuthe, and it passith bifore *alle othere*.
Thanne the kyng seide to him, Aske, if 42
thou wilt, ony thing more ouer, than ther
ben writen, and I schal ȝiue to thee, aftir
that thou art founden wiser ; and next to
me thou schalt sitte, and thou schalt be
clepid my cosyn. Thanne seide he to the 43
king, Be thou myndeful of the vowȝ, that
thou vowidist, to bilden up Jerusalem, in
the day in whiche thou toke the rewme ;
and to senden aȝen alle the vessels, that 44
ben taken fro Jerusalem, the whiche Cyrus departide, whanne he slouȝ Babiloyne,
and wolde sende aȝen thoo thingis thidere.
And thou woldist bilde up the temple, that 45
Ydumes brenden, for Judee is put out of
her termes, *or marchis*, of the Caldeis.
And now, lord, this it is that I aske, and 46
that I bidde ; this is the mageste that I
aske of thee, that thou do the vow that
thou vowidist to the kyng of heuen, of thi
mouth. Thanne Darius, the kyng, risynge 47
kisside him, and wroot epistlis to alle the
dispensatours, and prefectis, and to men
clothid in purpre, that thei schulden lede
him forth, and hem that weren with him,
alle wendynge up to bilde Jerusalem. And 48
to alle the prefectis that weren in Sirie,
and Fenyce, and Libau, he wroot epistles,
that thei schulden drawe cedre trees fro
the *hill* Liban in to Jerusalem, that thei
bilde up the citee with hem. And he 49
wroot to alle the Jewis, that steyden up
fro the rewme in Judee, for fredam, that
ony man of power, or maistir iuge, and
prefect, schulden not come ouer to the
ȝatis of hem, and eche regioun, that thei 50
hadden holde, to be fre fro hem ; and that

---

[k] wickenesse c. [l] is A. [m] Om. A. [n] bilde in c. [o] in whiche AH. [p] Om. A. [q] Om. c.
[r] thei A.

dai vp on the place of sacrid thingus, as thei han heste; othere ten talentus to of-
53 fren bi alle ȝeris; and to alle men, that gon forth fro Babiloine, to make cite⁵, as fredam were, bothe to hem, and to the sonus of hem, and to alle the prestis that
54 gon beforn. Forsothe he wrot and the quantite; and the sacrid stole he co-maundede to be ȝiue, in the whiche thei
55 shulden serue; and to the Leuitis he wrot to ȝiue wagis, vnto the dai that the hous shulde be fulli endid, and Jerusalem
56 maad out; and to alle men kepende the cite he wrot, to ȝiue to hem lotis and
57 wagis. And he lafte alle the vesselis, that Cirus hadde seuered fro Babiloine; and alle thingis, whateuere Cirus seide, also he comaundede to be don, and to be
58 sent to Jerusalem. And whan that ȝunge man hadde go forth, rerende the face in to Jerusalem, he⁵⁵ blesside the king of he-
59 uene, and seide, Of thee is victorie, and of thee is wisdam, and clernesse, and I
60 am thy seruaunt. Blessid thou art, for thou hast ȝiue to me wisdam, and I knou-
61 leche to thee, Lord of oure fadris. And he toc the epistolis, and wente forth in to Babiloine; and cam, and tolde to alle his
62 brethern that weren in Babiloine. And thei blesseden the God of ther fadris, that ȝaf to hem forȝiuenesse and refresh-
63 ing, that thei steȝen vp, and bilde Jeru-salem, and the temple, where is his name nemnyd in it; and thei ioȝeden ful out with musikis and gladnessys ᵗ seuene daȝes.

Ydumeis leue up the castels of Jewis, that thei withholden, and to ȝiue ȝer bi ȝer
51 twenty talentis, in to making of the tem-ple, vnto the tyme that it be ful bildid; and ech day to offre ostis upon the place
52 of sacrid thingis, as thei ben comaundid; to offre, bi alle ȝeris, othere ten talentis; and to alle men, that gon forth fro Babi-
53 loyne, to make the citee, as fredom were, bothe to hem, and to the sones of hem, and to the prestis that gon bifore. For-
54 sothe also he wroot the quantitee; and he comaundide the sacrid stole, *or vestyment,* to be ȝouen, in whiche thei schulden serue; and he wroot wagis to be ȝouen to the
55 dekens, vnto the day that the hous schulde be fully endid, and Jerusalem maad out; and he wrot to alle men kepinge the citee,
56 to ȝiue to the bilders lottis and wagis. And he lefte hem alle the vessels, that
57 Cirus had partid fro Babiloyn; and alle thingis, what euer Cyrus seide, he co-maundide *it* to be don, and to be sent to Jerusalem. And whanne that ȝounge man
58 had gon forth, reisynge his face toward Jerusalem, he blesside the kyng of heuen, and seide, Of thee, *Lord,* is victorie, and
59 of thee is wisdom, and clernesse, and I am thi seruaunt. Thou art blessid, for thou
60 hast ȝouen to me wisdom, and I know-leche to thee, Lord of oure fadris. And
61 he toke the epistlis, *or lettres,* and wente forth in to Babiloyne; and he came, and tolde to alle his bretheren, that weren in Babyloyne. And thei blessiden the God of
62 her fadris, that ȝaf to hem forȝiuenesse and refreschyng, that thei schulden stye up,
63 and bilde Jerusalem, and the temple, where his name is nemned in it; and thei ioy-eden with musikis and with gladnesse seuen daies.

CAP. V.

1 Aftir these thingus forsothe ben chosen, that thei steȝen vp, the princis of tounns, bi housis, bi ther linagis, and the wiues of hem, and sones and doȝtris of hem, and seruauns and hand wymmen of hem,

CAP. V.

1 Aftir thes thingis forsothe ther weren pryncis chosen of townus, that thei schul-den wende up, bi housis, bi her lynagis, and the wyues of hem, and the sonus and douȝtris of hem, and seruauntis and hand

ˢ cytees *A.* ⁵⁵ Om. *CEFH.* ᵗ gladnes *A.*

2 and bestis of hem. And king Darie sente togidere with hem a thousend horse men, to the time that thei broȝten hem in to Jerusalem, with pes, and with musikis, and timbres, and trunpis; and alle the 3 brethern weren pleiende. And he made 4 hem to steȝen vp togidere with hem. And these ben the namis of the᷎ men that steȝeden vp, bi their tounus, in to linagis, and in to part of the princehod of hem. 5 Prestus; the sonus of Finces, the sonus of Aron, Jesus, the sone of Josedech, Jachim, the sone of Sorobabel, sone of Solatiel, of the hous of Dauid, of the progenie of Fares, of the linage forsothe of Juda, 6 that spac vnder Darie, king of Persis, merucilous doende woordis, in the secunde ȝer of his regneᵛ, in Aprill, the 7 firste moneth. Forsothe these ben, that of Juda steȝeden vp fro the caitifte of transmigracioun, whom Nabugodonosor, king of Babiloine, translatide into Babiloine; and is turned aȝeen in to Jerusa- 8 lem, and in to alle the cites of Jude, eche in to his cite, that camen with Sorobabel and Jesu; Neemias, Ariores, Elimeo, Emanio, Mardocheo, Beelsuro, Methsatothor, Olioro, Eboma, oon of the princis 9 of hem. And the noumbre fro the Jentilis of hem, fro the prouostis of hem; the sonus of Fares, two thousend an hundrid 10 and seuenti and two; the sonus of Ares, 11 thre thousend fifti and seuene; the sonus of Femo, an hundrid and two and fourti; in the sonus of Jese and Joabes, a thou- 12 send thre hundrid and two; the sonus of Denny, two thousend foure hundrid and seuenti; the sones of Choraba, two hundrid and fiue; the sonus of Banycha, an 13 hundrid and sixti and eiȝte; the sonus of Bebeth, foureʷ hundrid and thre; the sonus of Archad, foure hundrid and se- 14 uene and twenti; the sonus of Hau, seuene and thretti; the sonus of Sozaar, two thousend sixti and seuene; the sonus of Adymy, foure hundrid and oon and 15 sixti; the sonus of Azeroectis, an hundrid and eiȝte; the sonus of Ziazo and Zelas,

maydens of hem, and her bestis. And 2 kyng Darye sende togidre with hem a thousynd hors men, to the tyme that thei brouȝte hem in to Jerusalem, with pees, and with musikis, and tymbres, and trum- pis; and alle the britheren weren pleiynge. And he made hem to stie up togidre with 3 hem. And thes ben the names of the men, 4 that ȝeden up, bi her tounnes, in to lynagis, and in to part of the princehod of hem. Prestis; the sones of Fynees, the sones of 5 Aaron, Jesus, the sone of Josedech, Joa- chim, the sone of Sorobabel, sone of Sala- thiel, of the hous of Dauid, of the pro- genye of Phares, of the lynage forsothe of Juda, that spac vndir Darij, king of 6 Persis, mcrucylous doynge wordis, in the secounde ȝeer of his rewme, in Aprel, the firste monthe. Forsothe thes it ben, that 7 stieden up of Juda fro the caitiftee, *or thraldom*, of the transmygracioun, whom Nabugodonosor, kyng of Babiloyne, trans- latide in to Babiloyne; and ech is turned aȝen in to Jerusalem, and in to alle the 8 citees of Judee, ech in to his owne citee, that camen with Sorobabel, and with Jesu; Neemyas, Ariores, and Elymeo, Emmanyo, Mardocheo, Beelsuro, Methsatothor, Olioro, Eboma, oon of the princis of hem. And 9 the noumbre fro the Gentiles of hem, fro the prouostis, *or reeuys*, of hem; the sones of Phares, two thousynd an hundrid se- uenty and two; the sones of Ares, thre 10 thousynd and fifty and seuen; the sones 11 of Phemo, an hundrid and two and fourty·; the sones of Jesu and of Joabes, a thou- synd thre hundrid and two; the sones of 12 Denny, two thousynd foure hundrid and senenty; the sones of Choroba, two hun- drid and fyue; the sones of Banycha, an hundrid and sixty and eiȝte; the sones of 13 Bebeth, foure hundrid and thre; the sones of Arcad, foure hundrid and seuen and twenty; the sones of Thau, seuen and 14 thritty; the sones of Zozaar, two thou- synd sixty and seuen; the sones of Ady- my, foure hundrid and oon and sixty; the 15 sones of Azeroectis, an hundrid and eiȝte;

an hundrid and seuene ; the sonus of Azoroch, foure hundrid and nyne and thretty;
16 the sonus of Jebdarbone, an hundrid and
two and thretti ; the sonus of Ananie, an
hundrid and thretti ; 'the sonus of Arsom^w;
17 the sonus of Marsar, foure hundrid and
two and twenti^x ; the sonus of Saberus,
ninti and fiue ; the sonus of Sofelomon,
18 an hundrid and thre and twenti ; the
sonus of Nepobai, fiue and fifti ; the sonus
of Echanatus, an hundrid and eiʒte and
fifti ; the sonus of Ebcathamus, an hun-
19 drid and two and thretti ; the sonus of
Octatarpatros, the whiche Enechades
and Modie, foure hundrid and two and
twenti ; the whiche of Gramas and Ga-
20 bia, an hundrid and oon and twenti ; the
whiche of Besellon and of^y Agie, fiue and
sixti ; the whiche of Bascharo, an hun-
21 drid and two and twenti ; the whiche of
Bethonobes, fiue and fifti ; the sones of
Lyptis, an hundred and fyue and fifty ;
the sonus of Jabomy, thre hundrid and
22 seuene and fifti ; the sonus of Sichem, thre
hundrid and seuenti ; the sonus of Sanadon and Chomus, thre hundrid and se-
23 uenti and eiʒte ; the sonus of Ericus, two
thousend an hundrid and fiue and fifti ;
the sonus of Anaas, thre hundrid and se-
24 uenti. Prestis ; the sonus of Jeddus, the
sonus of Enitem, the sonus of Eliazib, thre
hundrid and two and seuenti ; the sonus
of Emmechus, two hundrid and two and
25 fifti ; the sonus of Sasurij, thre hundrid
and seuene and fifti ; the sonus of Caree,
26 two hundrid and seuene and twenti. Leuitis ; the sonus of Jesu, in Caduel, and
Banus, and Serebias, and Edias, foure
and seuenti ; al the noumbre fro the two^z
and twenti^a ʒer, thretti thousend foure
27 hundrid and two and sixti ; sones, and
doʒtris, and wiues, al the noumbring,
sixti^b thousend two hundrid and two and
28 fourti. Sonus of prestis, that sungen in
the temple ; the sonus of Asaf, an hundrid
29 and eiʒte and twenti. Ussheris forsothe ;
the^c sonus of Esuem, the sonus of Ather,
the sonus of Amon, the sonus of Accuba

the sonus of Ziazo and Zelas, an hundrid
and seuene ; the sones of Azoroch, foure
hundrid and nyne and thritty ; the sones 16
of Jebdarbone, an hundrid and two and
thritty ; the sones of Ananye, an hundrid
and thritty ; the sones of Arsom ; the 17
sones of Marsar, foure hundrid and two
and twenty ; the sones of Saberus, nynty
and fyue ; the sones of Sophelemon, an
hundrid and thre and twenty ; the sones 18
of Nepobai, fyue and fifty ; the sones of
Ecbanatus, an hundrid and eiʒt and fifty ;
the sones of Ebethamus, an hundrid and
two and thritty ; the sones of Octatarpa- 19
tros, the whiche weren clepid Enochadies
and Modie, foure hundrid and two and
twenti ; thei that weren of Gramas and
Gabia, an hundrid and oon and twenti ;
the whiche weren of Besellon and of Agie, 20
fyue and sixty ; thei that 'weren of Bascharo, an hundrid and two and twenty ;
the whiche of Bethonobes, fyue and fifty ; 21
the sones of Lippis, an hundrid and fyue
and fifty ; the sones of Jabomy, thre hundrid and seuen and fifty ; the sones of 22
Sichem, thre hundrid and seuenty ; the
sones of Sanadon and of Chamus, thre
hundrid and seuenty and eiʒte ; the sones 23
of Ericus, two thousynd an hundrid and
fyue and fifty ; the sones of Anaas, thre
hundrid and seuenty. Prestis ; the sones 24
of Jeddus, the sones of Enytem, the sones
of Eliazib, thre hundrid and two and seuenty ; the sones of Emmechus, two hundrid and two and fifty ; the sones of Sa- 25
surij, thre hundrid and seuen and fifty ;
the sones of Charee, two hundrid and seuen
and twenty. Dekens ; the sonus of Jesu, 26
in Caduel, and Banus, and Serebias, and
Edias, foure and seuenty ; al the noumbre
fro the two and twenty ʒeer, thritti thousynd foure hundrid and two and sixty ;
sones, and douʒtris, and wyues, al the 27
noumbryng, sixty thousynd two hundrid
and two and fourty. The sones of prestis, 28
that sungen in the temple ; the sones of
Asaph, an hundrid and eiʒt and twenty.
Vschers forsothe ; the sones of Esueum, 29

---

^w Om. *A*.   ^x thretti *A*.   ^y Om. *A*.   ^z twelfthe *E pr. m.*   ^a twentithe *E*.   ^b fourti *E pr. m.*   ^c of the *A*.

Copa, the sonus of Tobi, alle an hundrid 30 and nyne and thretti. Prestis, seruende in the temple; sonus of Sel, the sonus of Gasipa, the sonus of Tabloth, the sonus of Carie, the sonus of Su, the sonus of Fellu, the sonus of Labana, the sonus of Acmatha, the sones of Accub, the sonus of Vta, the sonus of Ceta, the sonus of Agab, the sonus of Obai, the sonus of Anan, the sonus 31 of Caima, the sonus of Juddu, the sonus of An, the sonus of Radin, the sonus of Desamyn, the sonus of Nechoba, the sonus of Saseba, the sonus of Gaze, the sonus of Osin, the sonus of Finoe, the sonus of Atren, the sonus of Baseem, the sonus of Aziana, the sonus of Manai, the sonus of Nafisim, the sones of Accufn, the sonus of Agista, the sonus of Aria Faucin[d], the 32 sonus of Fasalon, the sonus of Meedda, the sonus of Fusia, the sonus of Careth, the sonus of Barchus, the sonus of Caree, the sonus of Thoesi, the sonus of Nasith, the 33 sonys of Agisti, the sonus of Pedon. Salmon, the sonus of hym, the sonus of Asoffoth, the sonus of Farida, the sonus of Theli, the sonus of Dedon, the sonus of 34 Gaddahel, the sonus of Cefegi, the sonus of Aggia, the sonus of Facareth, the sonus of Sabathan, the sonus of Saranoth, the sonus of Malcie, the sones of Amee, the sonus of Safuy, the sonus of Addus, the sonus of Suba, the sonus of Eyra, the sonus of Rabatis, the sonus of Fasofath, 35 the sonus of Malmon. Alle in holi seruende; and the childer of Salomon, foure 36 hundrid foure score and two. These ben the sonus, that steȝeden vp Atheemel and Thersas; the princis of hem, Carmellam 37 and Careth; and thei myȝten not tellen out ther cites, and progenies, what maner thei ben; and of Irael, the sonus of Dalarij, the sonus of Tubam, the sonus of 38 Nechodaici. And of the prestis, that vseden presthod, and ben not founde; the sonus of Obia, the sonus of Achisos, the sonus of Addin, that toc Vnim wif, of 39 the doȝtris of Fargelen, and ben clepid bi the name of hir; and of these is soȝt the

the sones of Ather, the sones of Amon, the sones of Accuba Copa, the sones of Thoby, alle an hundrid and nyne and thritty. Prestis, seruynge in the temple; sones of 30 Sel, the sones of Gasipa, the sones of Tabloth, the sones of Carie, the sones of Su, the sones of Phellu, the sones of Labana, the sones of Acmathi, the sones of Accub, the sones of Vta, the sonus of Cetha, the sones of Agab, the sones of Obay, the sones of Anan, the sones of Chayma, the sones of Jeddu, the sones of An, the sones 31 of Radyn, the sones of Desamyn, the sones of Nechoba, the sones of Caseba, the sones of Gase, the sones of Osyn, the sones of Phynoe, the sones of Atren, the sones of Bascem, the sones of Aziana, the sones of Manay, the sones of Naphisym, the sones of Accuphu, the sones of Agista, the sonus of Aria Phausym, the sones of Phasaluon, the sones of Meeda, the sones of Phusia, 32 the sones of Careth, the sones of Barthus, the sones of Caree, the sones of Thoesy, the sones of Nasith, the sones of Agisty, the sones of Pedon. Salmon, the sones of 33 hym, the sones of Asophoth, the sones of Pharida, the sones of Thely, the sones of Dedon, the sones of Gaddahel, the sones of Cephegy, the sones of Aggya, the sones 34 of Phacareth, the sones of Sabathan, the sones of Saroneth, the sones of Malcie, the sones of Ame, the sones of Saphuy, the sones of Addus, the sones of Suba, the sones of Eirra, the sones of Rabatis, the sones of Phasophat, the sonus of Malmon. Alle *thes weren* in holy seruyng; and the 35 children of Salmon *weren* foure hundrid foure score and two. These ben the sones 36 that ȝeden up to Athemel and Thersas; the princis of hem *weren* Carmellam and Careth; and thei myȝten not telle out her citees, 37 and her progenyes, what manere thei ben; and of Israel, the sones of Dalarij, the sones of Tubam, the sones of Nechodaicy. And 38 of the prestis, that vsiden presthod, and weren founden; the sones of Obia, the sones of Achisos, the sones of Addyn, that token Vmyn wijf, of the douȝtris of Phar-

write genelogie of kinrede, and it is not founden, and thei ben forfendid to vse 40 presthod. And Neemie seide to hem, and Ascaras^e, that thei take not part of the holi thingus, to the time that ther rise^f a taȝt bisshop, in to shewing and 41 treuthe. Al^g forsothe Irael was twelue thousend, out take seruauns and hand wymmen, two and fourti thousend thre 42 hundrid and sixti. The seruauns of hem and hand wymmen, seuene thousend three hundrid and seuene and thretti; singeres and singeressis, two hundrid and fiue and 43 sixti^h; camailis, foure hundrid and fiue and thretti; hors, seuen thousend sixe^i and thretti; mulis, two hundrid thousend and fiue and fourti; bestis vnder ȝoc, fiue 44 thousend and fiue and twenti. And of thoo prouostis bi tounus, whil thei shulden come in to the temple of God, that was in Jerusalem, to ben auouwid to rere the temple in his place, after ther 45 vertue; and to be ȝiue in to the temple the^k holi tresorie of werkis, eleue thousend besauns, and prestis stolis an hun- 46 drid. And ther dwelten prestus, and Leuitus, and that weren of the folc in Jerusalem, and in the regioun; and the holi singeres, vssheris, and al Irael, in 47 ther regiouns. In stondende forsothe the seuenthe moneth, and whan the sonus of Irael weren eche in his owne thingus, thei camen togidere of oon acord in to the porche, that was befor the est ȝate. 48 And stondende Jesus, the sone of Jose-dech, and his brether, prestis, and So-robabel, the sone of Salatiel, and of this 49 the brether, maden redi an auter, that thei offre vpon it brent sacrifises, aftir thoo^l thingus that in the boc of Moises, 50 man of God, ben writen. And ther camen to hem of othere naciouns of the lond, and rereden the holi tresorie in his place, alle the folc of the lond; and thei offriden ostis, and morutide brent sacri- 51 fises to the Lord. And thei diden the feste of tabernaclis, and a solempne dai, as it is write in the lawe, and sacrifises

gelen, and thei ben clepid bi the name of 39 hir; and of thes is souȝt the genologie writen of the kynrede, and thei ben for-fendid to vsen presthode. And Neemye 40 seide to hem, and Astaras, that thei take not part of the hooly thingis, til the tyme that ther arijse a tauȝt bischop, in to schewyng and treuthe. Al Israel forsothe 41 was twelff thousynd, out take seruauntis and hand maidens, two and fourty thou-synd thre hundrid and sixti. The ser- 42 uauntis of hand maidens weren seuen thousynd thre hundrid and seuen and thritty; syngers and singsters, two hun-drid and fyue and sixty; cameils, foure 43 hundrid and fyue and thritty; horsis, seuen thousind sixe and thritti; mules, two hundrid thousynd and fyue and fourty; bestis vndir ȝok, fyue thousynd and fyue and twenty. And of tho prouostis, or 44 reeues, bi tounnes, while thei schulden come in to the temple of God, that was in Jerusalem, to ben avowid to rere up the temple in his place, aftir her vertue; and 45 the hooly tresorie to be ȝouen in to the temple of werkis, weren elleuen thousynd besauntis, and an hundrid prestis stolis. And ther dwelliden prestis, and dekens, 46 and othere, that weren of the peple, in Jerusalem, and in the rewme; and the hooly syngers, and vsshers, and al Israel, in her regiouns. While the seuenthe 47 monthe ȝilt lastide, and whanne the sonus of Israel weren ech in his owne thingis, thei camen togidre of oon accord in to the porche, that was bifore the eest ȝate. And while Jesus, the sone of Jose- 48 dech, and his bretheren, prestis, stoden, and Sorobabel, the sone of Salatiel, and his bretheren, thei maden redy an auter, that thei wolden offre on it brent sacri- 49 fices, aftir tho thingis that ben writen in the book of Moyses, the man of God. And 50 ther camen to hem of othere naciouns of the loond, and reriden the holy tresorie in his place, alle the folk of the lond; and thei offriden oostis, and brent sacrifises of the morutijd to the Lord. And thei diden 51

³²eche dai, as it behouede^m.   And aftir these thingus the^n ordeined offringus, and ostus of sabatis, and of newe mones, and ⁵³of alle halewid solempne daȝes.   And hou fele euere vouweden to the Lord, fro the newe mone of the seuenthe moneth, token° ostis to offre to God;   and the temple of the Lord ȝit was not bild vp. ⁵⁴And thei ȝeue monee to masonus, and to wriȝtus, and drink and metus with ioȝe. ⁵⁵And thei ȝeue carris to Sidonyes and to Tires, that thei shulden carien ouer to hem fro Liban wode cedre bemus, and maken a naue in to Joppe hauene, aftir the decre that was write to them fro ⁵⁶Ciro, king of Persis.   And in the secunde ȝer thei comende in to the temple of God, in to Jerusalem, the secunde moneth began Sorobabel, the sone of Salatiel, and Jesus, the sone of Josedech, and the brethern of hem, and prestis, and Leuitus, and alle that camen fro the ⁵⁷caitifte in to Jerusalem ; and foundeden the temple of God, in the newe mone of the secunde moneth of the secunde ȝer, whan thei hadde comen in to Jude and ⁵⁸Jerusalem ; and setten^P Leuitus fro twenti ȝer vpon the werkis of the Lord.   And Jesus stod, his sone, and brethern, alle Leuitus togidere castende, and foleweris out of the lawe, and doende werkis in ⁵⁹the hous of the Lord.   And ther stoden prestys, hauende stolis, with trumpis, and Leuitus, the sonus of Asaf, hauende ⁶⁰cymbalis, togidere preisende the Lord, and blessende, aftir Dauid, king of Irael. ⁶¹And thei sungen a song to the Lord, for his swetnesse and wrshipe in to worldis ⁶²vp on al Irael.   And al the puple with trumpe sungen, and crieden with gret vois, preisende togidere the Lord, in the ⁶³rering of the hous of the Lord.   And ther camen of prestus, and of Leuitus, and of presidentus aftir the tounus, to the^q elders that hadden seen the rathere ⁶⁴hous, and at the bilding vp of this, with cri, and with gret weiling ; and manye ⁶⁵with trumpis, and gret ioȝe, so that

the feest of tabernaclis, and a solempne dai, as it is writen in the lawe, and sacrifises ech day, as it bihouyde.   And aftir ⁵²thes thingis thei ordeyneden offryngis, and oostis of sabotis, and of newe mones, and of alle solempne daies halewid.   And hou ⁵³many euere vowiden to the Lord, fro the *tyme of the* newe moone of the seuenthe monthe, thei token oostis to offren to God ; and the temple of the Lord was not ȝitt bildid up.   And thei ȝauen money to ma-⁵⁴souns, and to wriȝtis, and drynkis and metis with ioye.   And thei ȝauen carris ⁵⁵to Sydonyes and to Tyres, that thei shulden carie ouer to hem fro Lyban wode cedre beemes, and to make a nauee in to the hauuen of Joppe, aftir the decree that was writen to hem fro Cyro, kyng of Persis.   And in the secounde ȝeer thei ⁵⁶camen in to the temple of God, in to Jerusalem ; the secunde monthe Sorobabel biganne, the sone of Salatiel, and Jesus, the sone of Josedech, and the bretheren of hem, and prestis, and Leuytis, and alle thei that camen fro the caitiftee in to Jerusalem ; and founden the temple of God,⁵⁷ in the newe moone of the secunde monthe of the secunde ȝeer, whanne thei hadden come in to Judee and to Jerusalem ; and ⁵⁸setten dekens fro *the age of* twenty ȝeer upon the werkis of the Lord.   And Jesus stode, his sone, and his bretheren, alle the dekens togidre castynge, and executours, *or folewers*, of the lawe, and doynge werkis in the hous of the Lord.   And ther stoden ⁵⁹prestis, hauynge stoles, *or longe clothis*, with trumpis, and Leuytis, the sones of Asaph, hauynge cymbals, togidre preis-⁶⁰yng the Lord, and blessynge *him*, aftir *the maner of* Dauid, kyng of Israel.   And ⁶¹thei sungen a song to the Lord, for his swetnesse and his worschip in to worldis, *or euer*, upon al Israel.   And al the peple ⁶² sungen with trumpe, and crieden with gret vois, preisynge togidre the Lord, in the rerynge of the Lordus hous.   And ⁶³ther camen *many* of the prestis, and of dekens, and of presidentis aftir tounnes,

---

^m is behouede c *sec. m. II*.   ^n thei *A Π*.   ° thei token ɛ *pr. m*.   ^P senten *A*.   ^q Om. *A*.

the puple herde not the trumpis, for
the weiliug of the puple. Forsothe a
cumpanye was singende wrshipefulli in
66 trumpe, so that afer it was herd. And
the enemis herden the linagis of Juda
and of Beniamyn, and camen to wite,
67 what was the vois of the trumpes. And
thei knewen, for thei that weren of the
caitifte bilden the temple to the Lord
68 God of Irael. And comende nee3 to Sorobabel, and to Jesu, and to the prouostis
of tounus, seiden to hem, Wee shul bilde
69 togidere with 3ou. Lic maner forsothe
wee han herd of[r] oure Lord, and we togidere han go fro the da3es of Asbasareth, king of Assiries, that wente ouer
70 hennus. And seide to hem Sorobabel,
and Jesue, and the princis of the tounus
71 of Irael, It is not to vs and to 3ou to
bilden vp the hous of oure God; we forsothe alone shul bilden the hous of oure
God, aftir thoo thingus, that Cirus, king
72 of Persis, comaundede. The Jentilis forsothe of the lond leuende to them that
ben in Jude, and rerende vp the werk of
the[a] bilding, and aspies and puple bringende forth, forfendeden hem to bilden
73 vp; and letteden the men, hauntende the
goingus to, that the bilding shulde not
ben endid al the time of the lif of king
Ciri; and thei drowen along the making
vp bi two 3er, vn to the regne of Darie.

to the eldris that hadden seen the rather
hous, and at the bildyng up of this *hous,* 64
with cry, and with greet weilyng; and
many with trumpis, and gret ioye, so that 65
the peple herde not the trumpis, for the
gret weilyng of the peple. Forsothe ther
was a cumpeny syngynge wirschipfully in
trumpe, so that it was herd a ferr. And 66
the enmyes herden the lynagis of Juda
and of Beniamyn, and camen to wite,
what was this vois of trumpis. And thei 67
knewen, that thei that weren of the caitiftee bildiden the temple to the Lord God
of Israel. And *the enmyes* comynge ni3 68
to Sorobabel, and to Jesu, and to the
reeues of tounnes, thei seiden to hem, We
schul bilde togidre with 3ou. In lijk 69
maner forsothe we haue herd oure Lord,
and we haue gon togidre from the daies of
Asbasareth, kyng of Assiriens, that ouer
passide fro hennes. And Sorobabel, and 70
Jesus, and the princis of the tounnus of
Israel seiden to hem, It longith not to us 71
and to 3ou *togidere* to bilde up the hous
of oure God; forsothe we aloone shul bilde
the hous of oure God, aftir tho thingis,
that Cyrus, kyng of Persis, comaundide.
The Gentiles forsothe of the loond leuynge 72
with hem that ben in Judee, and rerynge
up the werk of bildyng, and bringynge
forth bothe aspies and peple, thei for-
fendiden hem to bilden up; and thei let- 73
tiden men, hauntynge the goynges to, that
the bildyng shulde not be endid in al the
tyme of the lijf of the kyng Ciry; and
thei drowen along the makyng up bi two
3eer, vnto the regne of Darij.

CAP. VI.

1 In the secunde forsothe 3er of the regne
of Darie profeciede Agge, and Sacharie,
the sone of Addiu, profete, anent Jude
and in Jerusalem, in the name of the
2 Lord God of Irael, vpon hem. Thane
stondende Sorobabel, the sone of Salatiel,
and Jesus, the sone of Jesedech, begunnen to bilden vp the hous of the Lord,
3 that is in Jerusalem; whan ther weren

CAP. VI.

Forsothe in the secounde 3eer of the 1
rewme of Darij, Agge propheciede, and
Zacharias, the sone of Addyn, a prophete,
anentis Judee and in Jerusalem, in the
name of the Lord God of Israel, upon
hem. Thanne stondynge Sorobabel, the 2
sone of Salathiel, and Jesus, the sone of
Josedech, *thei* bigunnen to bilde up the
hous of the Lord, that is in Jerusalem;

[r] Om. *AH.*   [a] Om. *AH.*

nee3 to hem profetis of the Lord, and
holpen[t] hem. In that time cam to hem
Cisennes, the vnder litil king of Cirie and
of Fenices, and Satrabosones, and ther
4 felawis. And thei seiden to hem, Who
comaundende to 3ou, this hous 3e bilden,
and this rof, and othere manie thingus
3ee parformen? and who ben the bilders,
5 that these thingus bilden vp? And the
visiting don vp on hem that weren of the
caitifte, hadden grace of the Lord the
6 elders of Irael; and thei ben not lettid
to bilden vp, to the time that it were
signefied to Darie of alle these thingus,
7 and an answere were taken. The saumple of the epistil, that to Darie senten
Cisennes, vnder king of Cirie and of
Fenyces, and Satrobosanes, and ther
felawis, in Cirie and in Fenice reuleris.
8 To king Darie, greeting. Alle thingus
knowen be thei to the lord the king; for
whan we camen in to the regioun of
Jude, and wenten in to Jerusalem, wee
founde men bildende a gret hous of God,
9 and a temple of grete poolisht stones,
10 and of precious materes in wallis; and
thoo werkis besili to be maad, and to
helpe, and[u] to make welsum in the
hondis of hem, and in alle glorie, as most
11 diligentli to be parformed. Thanne wee
askeden the eldere men, seiende, Who
suffrende 3ee suffre to 3ou this hous, and
12 these werkus founden? Therfore forsothe wee askeden hem, that knowen
wee my3ten make to thee the men, and
the prouostis; and the writing of the
namis of the prouostus wee askeden hem.
13 And thei answerden to vs, seiende, We
ben the seruauns of the Lord, that made
14 heuene and erthe; and this hous was
bild beforn these manie 3eris of the king
of Irael, gret, and most strong, and it is
15 ful endid. And for oure fadris weren
terrende and synneden[v] in the God of
Irael, he[w] toc hem in to the hondus of
Nabugodonosor, king of Babiloine, king
16 of Caldeis; and this hous destro3ende
brenden vp, and the puple caitif bro3ten

whanne ther weren ni3 to hem prophetis 3
of the Lord, and helpiden hem. In that
tyme came to hem Cysennes, the vndir
litil kyng of Ciryе and of Fenycis, and
Satrabozanes, and her felawis. And thei 4
seiden to hem, Who comaundide to 3ou,
that 3e bilden this hows, and this roof,
and many othere thingis 3e perfourmen?
and who ben tho bilders, that bilden up
thes thingis? And the eldre men of Is- 5
rael hadden grace of the Lord, whanne
the visitacioun of hem was maad upon
hem that weren of the caitifte; and thei 6
weren not lettid to bilden up, to the tyme
that it were signified to Darij of alle thes
thingis, and an answere were taken a3en.
This is the ensaumple of the lettre, that 7
Cysennes, the vndir kyng of Cyrie and of
Fenyces, and Satrobosanes, and her felawis, rewlers in Sirye and in Fenyce,
senden to the king. To kyng Darye,
gretyng. Alle thingis be thei knowen to 8
the lord the kyng; forsothe whanne we
camen in to the regioun of Judee, and
wenten in to Jerusalem, we founden men
bildynge a greet hous of God, and a temple 9
of gret polishid stones, and of precious
maters in the wallis; and tho werkis besily 10
in makynge, and to help, and to make welsum in the hondis of hem, and in al glorie,
ful diligently to be perfourmyd. Thanne 11
we askiden the eldre men, seiynge, Who
suffride 3ou to bilde this hous, and to bilde
thes werkis? Therfor forsothe we askiden 12
hem, that we my3ten make knowen to thee
the men, and the prouostis, or reuys; and
we askiden hem the writyng of the names
of the maistris of the werk. And thei an- 13
sweriden to vs, seiynge, We ben seruauntis
of the Lord, that made bothe heuen and
erthe; and this hous was bild bifore thes 14
many 3eris of the kyng of Israel, that was
greet, and a ful strong kyng, and it was
destried a3en. And for oure fadris terriden 15
and synneden a3en God of Israel, he bitook
hem in to the hondis of Nabugodonosor,
kyng of Babiloyne, kyng of Caldeis; and 16
thei destrieden and brenden up this hous,

---

　　　t helpeden *AH*.　u Om. *A*.　v thei synneden *A*.　w and he *A*.

17 in to Babiloyne. In the firste ȝer regnende Ciro, king of Babiloine, king Cirus
18 wrot to bilden vp this hous; and thoo[x]
holi goldene vesselis and siluerene, that
Nabugodonosor hadde born awei fro the
hous, that is in Jerusalem, and hadde
sacrid hem in his temple, eft king Cirus
broȝte them forth fro the temple that
was in Babiloyne, and ben take to Sorobabel, and to Salmanasar, vndir litil king.
19 And it is comaundid to hem, that thei
offren these vesselis, and lein vp in the
temple, that was in Jerusalem, and that
temple of God to bilden vp in that place.
20 Thanne Salmanasar vnder leide the foundemens of the hous of the Lord, that is
in Jerusalem; and fro thennus vn to now
21 is bild vp, and toe no ful ending. Now
thanne, if it is demed of thee, O king! be
it parfitli soȝt in the kingis libraries of
22 king Ciri, that ben in Babiloine; and if
it were founden in the counseil of king
Ciri, to ben begunne the making of the
hous of the Lord, that is in Jerusalem,
and it shal be shewid of the lord oure
king, wrijte he of these thingus to vs.
23 Thanne king Darie comaundede to ben
inwardli soȝt in the librarijs; and ther
is founde in Egbatenis, burȝtoun, that
is in the myddel regioun, o place, in the
24 whiche weren writen these thingus. The
firste ȝer regnende Ciro king, Cirus comaundede the hous of the Lord, that is
in Jerusalem, to bilden vp, where thei
25 brenden with[y] contynuel fijr; whos heiȝte
is maad of ten cubitis, and breede of
fourti cubitus, squarid with thre polisht
stonus, and with soleer tree of the same
regioun, and with oon newe soleer; and
costus to be ȝiuen of the hous of king
26 Cirus; and the holi vesselis of the hous
of the Lord, both goldene and siluerene,
that Nabugodonosor bar awei, that thei
be put thider in to[r] the hous, that is in
27 Jerusalem, where thei weren put. And
he comaundede besinesse to don Cisen-
nem, vnder litil king of Cirie and Fenice, and Satrabusanam, and his felawis,

and thei brouȝten the peple maad thral in
to Babiloyne. In the first ȝeer regnynge 17
Cyro, kyng of Babiloyne, kyng Cyrus
wroot to bilden up this hous; and tho 18
hooly golden vessels and silueren, that
Nabugodonosor had born awey fro the
hous *of God*, that is in Jerusalem, and
had sacrid hem in his temple, efte kyng
Cyrus brouȝte hem forth fro the temple
that was in Babiloyn, and thei weren bitake to Sorobabel, and to Salmanasar, the
vndir litil kyng. And it was comaundid 19
to hem, that thei offre thes vessels, and
thei schulde ley hem up in the temple,
that was in Jerusalem, and to bilde up
that temple of God in that place. Thanne 20
Salmanasar vndirleide the foundementis of
the hous of the Lord, that is in Jerusalem;
and fro thennes vn to now is a bildynge,
and hath take no ful endyng. Now thanne, 21
O kyng! if it is demed of thee, that it be
perfitly souȝt in the kyngis libraries of
kyng Cyry, that ben in Babiloyne; and if 22
it were founden in the counseil of kyng
Ciry, the makyng of the hous of the Lord,
that is in Jerusalem, to be bigunnen, and
if it schal be schewid of the lord oure
kyng, write he to vs of thes thingis.
Thanne kyng Darie comaundid to ben 23
ynwardly souȝt in the libraries; and ther
was founden in Egbathanys, a borouȝ
town, that is in the myddil regioun, a
place, in the whiche weren wreten thes
thingis. The firste ȝer regnynge Cyro 24
kyng, Cyrus comaundide to bilden up the
hous of the Lord, that is in Jerusalem,
where thei brenden with contynuel fijr;
whos heiȝt was maad of lx. cubitis, and 25
the brede of sixty cubitis, squarid with
thre polischid stones, and with soler tree
of the same regioun, and with o newe
soler; and costis to be ȝouen of the hous
of kyng Cyrus; and the holy vessels of 26
the hous of the Lord, bothe golden and
silueren, that Nabugodonosor bare awey,
that tho be putt thidere in to the hous,
that is in Jerusalem, where thei weren
put. And he comaundide Cysennem, the 27

and thei that weren in Cirie and in Fenice ordeineden reuleris, that thei ab-
28 stene them fro the same place. And I
also comaundede al to maken vp, and
forth lookide, that thei helpe them that
ben of the caitifte of Jewis, to the time
that the temple of the hous of the Lord
29 be ful endid; and of the trauaile of the
tributus of Cirie Choeles and Fenices diligentli a quantite to be ӡiue to these men,
to the sacrifise of the Lord, to Sorobabel, prefect, to bolis, and wetheris, and
30 lambis; also forsothe and whete, and
salt, and win, and oile, besili bi alle ӡeris,
as the prestus, that ben in Jerusalem, ordeineden to be fulfild eche dai, with oute
31 any delai; that ther ben offrid offringus
of likourus to the heiӡeste God, for the
king, and his childer, and preӡe for the
32 lif of hem. And be it denounsid, that
whoso euere ouer passen[a] any thing of
these thingus that ben writen, or despisen,
be ther taken a tree of ther own proper, and be thei hangid, and the goodis
33 of hem to the king be eschetid. Therfore
and the Lord, whos name is inwardli
clepid there, outlawe eche king and folc,
that strecchen out ther hond to forfenden,
or to euele treten that hous of the Lord,
34 that is in Jerusalem. I, king Darie, haue
maad a decre, to be don as most diligentli aftir these thingis.

CAP. VII.

1 Thanne Cisennes, vnder litil king of
Choelem Cirie and Fenicem, and Satra-
busanes, and the felawis, obesheden' to
these thingus, that of king Darye weren
2 demed, stoden in to the holi werkis most
diligentli, togidere werkende with the
eldere men of Jewis, princis of Cirie.
3 And the sacrid holi werkis ben maad
welsum, profeciende Agge and Sacarie,
4 profetus. And alle thingus thei fulfilden,
bi the heste of the Lord God of Irael,
and of the counseil of Ciri, and of Darie,

vndir litil kyng of Cyrie and Fenyce, and
Satrabusanam, and his felawis, to do *her*
bisynesse, and thei that weren in Sirie
and Fenyce ordeyneden rewlers, that thei
schulden absteyne them fro the same place.
And I also comaundide to make *it* up al, 28
and I lokide forth, that thei help them
that ben of the caitiftee of Jewis, vnto the
tyme that the temple of the hous of the
Lord be full endid; and a quantitee to be 29
ӡouen diligently to these men of the tra-
ueile of the tributis of Sirye Choles and
Fenyces, to the sacrifice of the Lord, to
Sorobabel, the prefect, to bolis, and wetheris, and to lombis; also forsothe bothe 30
whete, and salt, wyn, and oile, bisily bi
alle ӡeris, as the prestis, that ben in Jerusalem, ordeyneden to be fulfillid eche day,
withoute ony delay; *also* that ther be 31
offrid offryngis of licours to the hiӡest
God, for the kyng, and for his children,
and preie thei for the lijf of hem. And 32
be it denounsid, that who so euer ouer
passen ony thing of these thingis that ben
wreten, outher despisen, be ther taken a
tree of her owne, and be thei hangid
theron, and her goodes be ethchetid to
the kyng. Therfor also the Lord, whos 33
name is ynwardly clepid there, outlawe
he eche kyng and folk, that strecchen out
her hoond to offende, or to yuele trete
that hous of the Lord, that is in Jerusalem. I, kyng Darie, haue maad a decree, 34
to be don as moost diligently after thes
thingis.

CAP. VII.

Thanne Cysennes, the litil vndir kyng 1
of Choelem Cyrie and Fenycen, and Satra-
busanes, and *her* felawis, obeisheden to
these thingis, that weren demyd of kyng
Darie, and stoden ful diligently in to the 2
hooly werkis, wirchinge togidre with the
eldre men of Jewis, princis of Cirie. And 3
the hooly werkis ben maad welsum, as
the prophetes Agge and Zacharie prophecieden. And thei fulfilliden alle thingis, 4
aftir the heest of the Lord God of Israel,
and aftir the counseil of Cyri, and of

⁵and of Artaxerse, king of Persis. And oure hous is endyd, vnto the thre and twentithe dai of the moneth of March, ⁶the sixte ȝer of king Darie. And the sonus of Irael diden, and the prestis, and Lcuitus, and othere that weren of the caitifte, that ben set to, after thoo thingus that ben writen in the boc of Moises. ⁷And thei offriden in to the dedicacioun of the temple of the Lord, bolis, an hundrid; wetheris, two hundrid; lambis, ⁸foure hundrid; kidis for the synnes of al Irael, twelue, after the noumbre of the ⁹linagis of Irael. And the prestus stoden, and Lenitus, clad^c the stolis, bi the linagis, vpon the werc of the Lord God of Irael, after the boc of Moises; and vssheris bi ¹⁰alle the ȝatis. And the sonus of Irael diden, with hem that weren of the caitifte, that pasch, the mone of the firste moneth, fourtene, whan ben halewid the ¹¹prestis and the Leuitus. And alle the sonus of caitifte ben not togidere halewid, for alle the Lenitus ben togidere halewid. ¹²And thei offriden pasch to alle the sonus of caitifte, and to ther brethern, prestis, ¹³and to hemself. And the sonus of Irael eeten, that weren in^d the caitifte, alle that hadden laft fro alle the cursidnessis of the Jentilis of the erthe, sechende the ¹⁴Lord; and thei haleweden the feste dai of therue loues, seuene daȝes etende in ¹⁵the siȝte of the Lord; for he conuertide the counseil of the king of Assiris in hem, to coumforte the hondus of hem to the werkis of the Lord God of Irael. ¹And after this, regnende Artaxerse, king of Persis, wente to Esdras, the sone of Azarie, sone of Elchie, sone of Salome, ²sone of Sadduch, sone of Achitob, sone of Ameri, sone of Azaei, sone of Bocce, sone of Abisae, sone of Finees, sone of Eleasar, sone of Aron, firste preest. ³This Esdras steȝede vp fro Babiloine, whan he was scribe, and witti in the lawe of Moises, that is ȝiuen of the Lord ⁴of Irael, to sein and to do. And the king ȝaf to hym glorie, that he hadde

Darij, and of Artaxersis, kyng of Persis. And oure hous is endid, in the three and⁵ twentithe dai of the monthe of Marche, in the sixte ȝeer of kyng Darij. And the⁶ sones of Israel, and the prestis, and dekens, and othere that weren of the caitiftee, the whiche ben sett to, diden aftir thoo thingis that ben writen in the book of Moyses. And thei offreden in to the dedi-⁷ catioun of the temple of the Lord, an hundrid bolis, two hundrid wetheris, foure hundrid lambren, twelue kides, for the⁸ synnes of al Israel, after the noumbre of the xij. lynages of Israel. And the prestis⁹ and dekens stoden, clothid with the stolis, bi *her* lynagis, upon the werkis of the Lord God of Israel, aftir the book of Moyses; and *ther weren* porters bi alle the ȝatis. And the sones of Israel diden¹⁰ that pask, with hem that weren of the caitiftee, in the moone of the first monthe, the fourtenthe *day*, whanne the prestis and dekens ben halewid. And alle the¹¹ sones of caitiftee thei ben not halewid togidre, for alle the Leuytis ben halewid togidere. And thei offreden pask to alle¹² the sones of caitiftee, and to her bretheren, prestis, and to them selff. And the sonus¹³ of Israel, the whiche weren of the caitiftee, alle thei that hadden left fro alle the cursidnessis of Gentiles, *or hethen folk,* of the eerthe, eeten, and souȝten the Lord; and thei balewiden the feest day of therff¹⁴ looues, seuene daies etynge in siȝt of the Lord; for he conuertide the counseil of¹⁵ the kyng of Assirijs in hem, to coumforte the hondis of hem to the werkis of the Lord God of Israel. And aftir this, while¹ Artaxerse, kyng of Persis, regnyde, ther wente to Esdras, *a man that was* the sone of Azarie, sone of Elchie, sone of Salome, sone of Sadduch, sone of Achitob, sone of² Amarie, sone of Aza, sone of Bocce, sone of Abisae, sone of Phynees, sone of Eleazar, sone of Aaron, the first preest. This³ Esdras stiede up fro Babiloyne, whanne he was scribe, and witty in the lawe of Moyses, the whiche was ȝouen of the Lord

---

^c clothede *AEFH.*   ^d of *E pr. m.*

founde grace in alle dignete, and desijr, 5 in the sijte of hym[e]. And ther stejeden vp togidere with hym of the sonus of Irael, and prestis, and Leuitus, and holi singeres of the temple, aud vssheris, and sernauns of the temple, in to Jerusalem. 6 The seuenthe jer regnende Artaxerse, in the fifte monyth, this is the seuenthe jer of the regne, goende out forsothe fro Babiloine in the newe mone of the fifte 7 moneth, thei camen to Jerusalem, after the[f] hestus of hym, after the jiuen prosperite of the weie to hem of that Lord. 8 In these thingys forsothe Esdras weldede gret discipline, lest he passide biside any thing of thoo thingis that weren of the lawe of the Lord, and hestus, and in techende al Irael alle rijtwesnesse and 9 dom. Comende forsothe neej thei that writen the writen thingus of king Artaxerses, token writen that, that cam fro king Artaxerses to Esdras, prest, and redere of the lawe of the Lord, of whiche thinge the exsaumple is leid vnder.

of Israel, to sey *it* and do *it*. And the 4 kyng jaaf to him glorie, that he hadde founden grace in al dignytee, and in desijr, in the sijt of him. And ther stiede 5 up with him in to Jerusalem of the sones of Israel, bothe prestis, and dekens, and holy syngers of the temple, and vsshers, and seruauntis of the temple. In the se- 6 uenthe jeer regnynge Artaxerse, in the fifthe monthe, this is the seuenthe jeer of the rewme, goynge out forsothe fro Babiloyne in the newe moone of the fifte monthe, thei camen to Jerusalem, aftir 7 the heestis of him, whanne the prosperitee of the wey was grauntid to hem of that Lord. In these thingis forsothe Esdras 8 weldide greet discipline, lest he passide ony thing of tho thingis that weren of the lawe of the Lord, and of the heestis, and in techynge al Israel al rijtwisnesse and doom. Thei forsothe that writen the 9 writyngis of kyng Artaxerses, comynge nij[a], token writen that, that came from kyng Artaxerses to Esdras, the prest, and redere of the lawe of the Lord, the ensaumple of the whiche thing *writen* is sett next aftir.

CAP. VIII.

10 King Artaxerse to Esdre, prest, and redere of the lawe of the Lord, greeting. 11 More benygne I demende also to benefetus, comandede to hem that desiren of the folc of Jewis ther owne thingus wilfulli, and of the prestis, and Leuits, that ben in my reume, to felashipen with thee 12 in to Jerusalem. Thane if any couetten to go with thee, come thei togidere, and go thei forth, as it pleseth to me, and to 13 my seuene frendis counseileris; that thei visite thoo thingus, that ben don after Jude and Jerusalem, kepende the[g] lawe, as thou hast in the lawe of the Lord; 14 and bere thei jiftus to the Lord of Irael, the whiche I knewj, and the frendis of Jerusalem, and al the gold and siluer,

CAP. VIII.

Kyng Artaxerses to Esdre, the prest, 10 and redere of the lawe of the Lord, *sendith* gretyng. More benygne I demynge also 11 to benefetis, comaundide to hem that desiren of the folke of Jewis their owne thingis wilfully, and of the prestis, and of dekens, that ben in my rewme, to felawschipe with thee in to Jerusalem. Thanne 12 if ony coueiten to gon with thee, come thei togidre, and go thei forth, as it plesith to me, and to my seuene frendis counseilers; that thei visite tho thingis, that 13 ben don aftir Jude and Jerusalem, kepinge *the lawe*, as thou hast in the lawe of the Lord; and bere thei jiftis to the Lord of 14 Israel, whom I knew, and the frendis of Jerusalem, and al the gold and the siluer,

---

[e] hem *c pr. m.*　[f] Om. *A.*　[g] in the *c.*

[a] nij to Esdras 1 *pr. m.*

that were founden in the regioun of Babiloine, to the Lord in Jerusalem, with
15 that that is ȝiuen of that folc in the
temple of the Lord, of hem that is in
Jerusalem ; that be gedered this gold and
siluer, and to bolis, and wetheris, and
lambis, and kidis, and that to these ben
16 couenable ; that thei offre ostis to the
Lord, vp on the auter of the Lord of hem,
17 that is in Jerusalem. And alle thingus
what euere thou wilt with[h] thi brethern
don, with gold and siluer parforme, for
the wil, after the heste of the Lord thi
18 God. And the sacride holi vesselis, that
ben ȝiue to thee, to the werkis of the
hous of the Lord thi God, that is in Je-
19 rusalem, and othere thingus, what euere
to thee wiln helpen to the werkis of the
temple of thi God, thou shalt ȝiue of the
20 kingis tresorie, whan thou wilt with thi
brethern maken, with gold and siluer ;
and parforme thou aftir the wil of thi
21 Lord. And I, king Artaxerses, haue comaundid to the keperis of the tresories
of Cirie and of Fenice, that what euere
thingus Esdras, prest, and redere of the
lawe of the Lord, write fore, besili be it
ȝiue to hym, vnto an hundrid talentis of
22 siluer, lic maner and of gold ; and vnto
an hundrid busshelis of whete, and an
hundrid vesselis of win, and othere
thingis, what euere abounden, with oute
23 taxing. Alle thingus after the lawe of
God be don to the heiȝeste God, lest parauenture rise[i] vp wrathe in the reume of
the king, and of the sone, and of] the sones
24 of hym. To ȝou forsothe is seid, that to
alle the prestis, and Leuitus, and holi
singeres, and seruauns of the temple, and
25 scribis of this temple, no tribute, ne any
other forfending be born to, ne haue
any man power to aȝen casten any thing
26 to hem. Thou forsothe, Esdras, aftir the
wisdam of God ordeine domesmen and
arbitrouris, in al Cirie and Fenice, and
alle that the lawe of thi God knewen,
27 teche ; that hou fele euere ouerpasse the
lawe, bisili be thei punshid, or bi deth,

that weren founde in the rewme of Babiloyne, *be it born* to the Lord in Jerusalem,
with that that is ȝouen of thilke folk in 15
the temple of the Lord, of hem that is in
Jerusalem ; that this gold be gederid and
siluer, to bolis, and wetheris, and to lambis,
and kides, and that to these ben couenable;
that thei offren oostes to the Lord, upon 16
the auter of the Lord of hem, that is in
Jerusalem. And alle thingis what euer 17
thou wilt do with thi bretheren, perfourme
it with gold and siluer, for *thi* will, aftir
the heest of the Lord thi God. And the 18
sacrid hooly vessels, the whiche weren
ȝouen to thee, to the werkis of the Lordis
hous, thi God, that is in Jerusalem, and 19
othere thingis, what euere woln helpe to
the werkis of the temple of thi God, thou
schalt ȝiuen *it* of the kyngis tresorie,
whanne thou wilt maken *the werk* with 20
thi bretheren, with gold and siluer ; and
parfourme thou *al thing* aftir the will of
thi Lord. And I, kyng Artaxerses, haue 21
comaundid to kepers of the tresours of
Cirye and of Fenyce, that what euer
thingis Esdras, the preest, and redere of
the lawe of the Lord, wrijte fore, bisily
be it ȝouen to him, vn to an hundrid talentis of siluer, also and of gold ; and vnto 22
an hundrid busshelis of whete, and an
hundrid vessels of wyn, and othere thingis,
what euer abounden, withoute taxynge.
Alle thingis be don to the hiest God, aftir 23
the lawe of God, lest perauenture wraththe
arijse up in the rewme of the kyng, and
of his sone, and of the sones of him. To 24
ȝou forsothe it was seid, that to alle the
prestis, and dekens, and to holy syngers,
and seruauntis of the temple, and to scribis
of this temple, no tribute, no ony oother 25
forfendyng be born to *hem*, ne haue ther
ony man power to aȝen caste ony thing
to hem. Thou forsothe, Esdras, aftir the 26
wisdom of God ordeyne domesmen and
arbitrours, in al Cirye and Fenyce, and
teche alle that knowen the lawe of thi
God ; that hou fele euere passen the lawe, 27
thei be besely punyshid, or bi deth, or bi

or bi torment, or also bi multing of
28 monee, or bi seuering awei. And Esdras,
scribe, seide, Blessid be the Lord God of
oure fadris, that ʒaf this wil in to the
herte of the king, to clarifien his hous,
29 that is in Jerusalem ; and me hath
wrshipid ·in the siʒte of the king, and
counseileris, and his frendis, and of his
30 purprid men. And I am mand stedefast
in inwit, after the helping of the Lord
oure God ; and I gederede of Irael men,
that thei shulden steʒen vp togidere with
31 me. And these ben the prouostis, after
ther kuntres, and porciounelis ʲ prince-
hodis of hem, that with me steʒeden vp
fro Babiloine, in the reume of Artaxersis.
32 Of the sonus of Fares, Jersomus ; of the
sonus of Ciameruth, Amenus ; of the sonus
33 of Dauid, Accus, the sone of Cecelie ; of
the sonus of Fares, Zacharie, and with
hym ben turned aʒeen an hundrid men
34 and fifti ; of the sonus of Ductor, Moabilonys, Zaraei, and with hym two hun-
35 drid men and fifti ; of the sonus of Sa-
cues, Jechonie, Cetheeli, and with hym
36 two hundrid men and fifti ; of the sones
of Solomosias, Gotholie, and with hym
37 seuenti men ; of the sones of Sofocie,
Zarias, Micheli, and with hym foure
38 score men ; of the sonus of Jobab, Dias,
Jeseli, and with hym two hundrid men
39 and twelue ; of the sonus of Banie, Sal-
imoth, the sone of Josafie, and with hym
40 an hundrid men and sixti ; of the sonus
of Beer, Zacharias, Bebei, and with hym
41 two hundrid men and eiʒte ; of the sones
of Azachie, Channes, Acharie, and with
42 hym an hundrid men and ten ; of the
sonus of Adonicam, hem last, and these
ben the namus of hem, Elifalam, the sone
of Jebel, and Semeias, and with hym se-
43 uenti men. And I gederede hem to the
flod, that is seid Thia and Methati ;
there wee weren thre daʒis, and I knewʒ
44 hem. And of the sonus of prestis and
45 of Leuitus I fond not there. And I sente
to Eleasar, and to Acccbam, and Masman,
and Malolan, and Enathan, and Samea,
and Joribum, Nathan, Ennagan, Zacharie,

tonrment, or also bi multyng, *or punysch-*
ing, of money, or bi departyng awey. And 28
Esdras, the scribe, seide, Blessid be the
Lord God of oure fadris, that ʒaaf this
will in to the herte of the kyng, to clarifie
his hous, that is in Jerusalem ; and hath 29
wirschipid me in siʒt of the kyng, and of
hise counselours, and of hise frendis, and
of hise purpred men. And I am mand 30
stidefast in inwitt, aftir the helpyng of
the Lord oure God ; and I gadride of Israel men, that thei schulden stie up togidre with me. And these ben the pro- 31
uostis, aftir their cuntrees, and porcionel
princehedis of hem, that with me stieden
up fro Babiloyne, in the rewme of Artaxerses. Of the sones of Phares *was* Jer- 32
somus ; of the sones of Cyemarith, Amenus ; of the sones of Dauid, Accus, the
sone of Cecelie ; of the sones of Phares, 33
Zacharie, and with him ben turned aʒen
an hundrid men and fifty ; of the sonus of 34
Ductor, Moabilonys, Zaraey, and with him
two hundrid men and fifty ; of the sonus 35
of Sacnes, Jechonye, Thetheely, and with
him two hundrid men and fifty ; of the 36
sones of Salomosias, Gotholie, and with
him scuenty men ; of the sones of Sapha- 37
cye, Zarias, Mychely, and with him foure
score men ; of the sones of Jobab, Dias, 38
Jesely, and with him two hundrid men
and twelue ; of the sones of Banye, Saly- 39
moth, the sone of Josaphie, and with him
an hundrid men and sixty ; of the sones 40
of Beer, Zacharie, Bebey, and with him
two hundrid men and eiʒte ; of the sones 41
of Azachie, Channes, Acharie, and with
him an hundrid men and ten ; of the sones 42
of Adonycam, *that ben* the laste, and thes
ben the names of hem, Elyphalam, the
sone of Jebel, and Semeas, and with him
seuenty men. And I gedride hem to the 43
flood, that is seid Thia and Methaty ;
there we weren thre daies, and I knewe
hem. And of the sones of prestis and of 44
Leuytis I fonde not there. And I sente 45
to Eleazar, and to Eccelom, and Masman,
and Malolan, and Enaathan, and Sanea,
and Joribum, Nathan, Ennagan, Zacharie,

ʲ porciounel *c pr. m.*

and Mosollamym, hem leders and wise
46 men. And I seide to hem, that thei
shulden come to Luddyum, that was at
47 the place of the tresorie. And I sente to
them, that thei shulden sei to Luddium,
and his brethern, and to hem that weren
in the tresorie, that thei shulden sende to
vs hem that shulden vse presthod in the
48 hous of the Lord oure God. And thei
broȝten to vs, after the stronge hond of
the Lord oure God, wise men of the
sonus of Mooli, sone of Leuy, sone of
Irael, Sebebian, and sonus, and brethern,
49 that weren eiȝtetene; Asbiam, and A-
mum, of the sonus of Cananei; and the
50 sonus of hem, twenti men. And of hem
that in the temple serueden, the whiche
Dauid ȝaf, and thei princis, to the werking to the Leuitus, to the temple, of men
seruende, two hundrid and twenti. The[k]
namys of alle ben signefied in scripturis.
51 And I vouwede there fasting to ȝunge
men, in the siȝte of the Lord, that I
shulde sechen of hym good weie to vs,
and that weren with vs, of sonus, and
52 bestus, for aspies. Forsothe I shamede
to asken of the king foot men and horse
men, in felashipe of grace, of keping aȝen
53 oure aduersaries. Forsothe we seiden to
the king, For the vertue of the Lord shal
be with hem, that inwardli sechen hym
54 in alle efect. And eft we preȝeden the
Lord oure God, after these thingis, whom
and benigne we hadden; and hol wee
55 ben maad to oure God. And I seuerede
of the pronostis of the folc, and of the
prestus of the puple, twelue men, and
Sedebian, and Affamian, and with hem of
56 ther brethern ten men. And I peisede
to hem siluer and gold, and prestis
vesselis, of the hous of the Lord oure
God, the whiche the king hadde ȝinen,
and his counseileris, and princis, and al
57 Irael. And whan I hadde peisid, I toc
talentus of siluer an hundrid and fifti,
and siluerene vesselis of an hundrid talentis, and of gold talentus an hundrid,
58 and of goldene vesselis seue score, and
brasene vesselis of good metal shinende,

Mosollamym, *the whiche* weren leders and
wise men. And I seide to hem, that thei 46
schulden come to Luddium, that was at
the place of the tresorie. And I sente to 47
hem, that they schulden sey to Luddyum,
and his bretheren, and to hem that weren
in the tresorie, that thei schulden sende to
vs hem that schulden vse presthod in the
hous of the Lord oure God. And thei 48
brouȝten to us, aftir the strong hoond of
the Lord oure God, wise men of the sones
of Mooly, sone of Leuy, sone of Israel,
Sebebian, and sones, and bretheren, that
weren eiȝtene; Asbiam, and Ammum, of 49
the sones of Chananey; and the sonus of
hem *weren* twenti men. And of hem that 50
seruyden in the temple, the whiche Dauid
and thei princis ȝauen, to the wirching to
the Leuytis, to the temple, of men seruynge, two hundrid and twenty. The
names of alle ben signyfied in scripturis.
And I vowide there fastyng to ȝonge men, 51
in the siȝt of the Lord, that I schulde
seche of hym a good wey to us, and *to*
hem that weren with us, of sones, and
bestis, for aspies. Forsothe I schamyde 52
to aske of the kyng foot men and hors
men, in felauschipe of grace, of keping
aȝen oure aduersaries. Forsothe we seiden 53
to the kyng, For the vertue of the Lord
schal be with hem, that inwardly sechen
him in al effect. And efte we preieden 54
the Lord oure God, aftir thes thingis,
whom also we hadden benyngly; and we
ben maad hool to oure God. And I de- 55
partide of the prouostis of the folc, and of
the prestis of the temple, xij men, and
Sedebian, and Affamyan, and ten men with
hem of her bretheren. And I weiede to 56
hem siluer and gold, and prestis vessels, of
the hous of the Lord oure God, the whiche
the kyng had ȝouen, and his counseilers,
and princis, and al Israel. And whanne 57
I hadde peisid *it*, I toke an hundrid talentis of siluer and fifty, and silueren
vessels of an hundrid talentis, and of gold
an hundrid talentis, and of golden vessels 58
seuen score, and twelue brasen vessels of
good schynynge metal, ȝeldinge the lik-

---

[k] And the c.

twelue, ȝeldende the licnesse of gold.
59 And I seide to hem, And ȝee ben holi to
the Lord, and the vesselis ben holi, and
the gold and the seluer is of the auou to
60 the Lord God of oure fadris. Waketh,
and kepeth, to the time that ȝee take of
the prouostis of the puple, and of the
prestis, and of the Leuitis, and princis of
the cites of Irael, in Jerusalem, in the
priue chaumbre of the hous of oure God.
61 And these prestis and Leuitus, that token
gold and siluer, and vesselis, that weren
in Jerusalem, broȝten in to the temple of
62 the Lord. And we moueden forth fro
the flod of Thia, the twelfthe dai of the
firste moneth, for to we ȝiden in to Jeru-
63 salem. And whan the thridde dai was
don, the ferthe forsothe dai the peisid
gold and siluer is taken in the hous of
the Lord oure God, to Marymoth, the
64 sone of Jori, prest; and with hym was
Eleasar, the sone of Finees; and ther
weren with hem Josabdus, the soue of
Jesu, and Medias, and Banny, the sone
of a Leuite; at noumbre and weiȝte alle
65 thingus. And the peis of hem is writen
66 in the same hour. Thoo forsothe, that
camen fro the caitifte, offriden sacrifise
of the Lord of Irael, bolis, twelue for al
Irael; wetheres, foure score and sixe;
67 lambis, two and scuenti; get for synne
twelue, and for helthe twelue kijn; alle
68 in to the sacrifise of the Lord. And thei
eft radden the hestis of the king to the
kingis dispensatouris, and to the litle
vnder kingus of Choele, and Cirie, and
Fenice; and thei wrshipeden the folc
69 and the temple of the Lord. And these
thingis ful endid, thei camen to me,
seiende, The kinrede of Irael, and the
70 princis, and prestys, and Leuitis, and
aliene folkis, and naciouns of the lond,
han not seuered ther vnclennesses fro
Cananeis, and Etheis, and Fereseis, and
Jebuseis, and Moabitis, and Egipcienes,
71 and Idumeis; forsothe thei ben ioyned to

nesse of gold. And I seide to hem, Bothe 59
ȝe ben holy to the Lord, and the vessels
ben holy, and the gold and the siluer is of
the avowe to the Lord God of oure fadris.
Wake ȝe, and kepe *it*, til the tyme that 60
ȝe take *it* of the prouostes of the peple,
and of the prestis, and of the dekens, and
of princis of the citees of Israel and Jerusalem, in the priuey chaumbre of the hous
of oure God. And thes prestis and de- 61
kens, that token gold and siluer, and vessels, that weren in Jerusalem, thei broȝten
thoo in to the temple of the Lord. And 62
we moeueden forth fro the flood of Thya,
the twelfthe day of the firste monthe, til
that we ȝeden in to Jerusalem. And 63
whanne the thrid day was don, the firthe
day forsothe the peisid gold and siluer
was bitaken in to the hous of the Lord
oure God, to Marymoth, the sone of Jory,
the prest; and with him was Eleazar, the 64
sone of Phynees; and ther weren with
him Josabdus, the sone of Jesu, and Medias, and Banny, the sone of a deken;
alle thingis at noumbre and weiȝt. And 65
the weiȝt of hem is writen in the same
hour. Thoo forsothe, that camen fro the 66
caitifte, offriden sacrifice of the Lord of
Israel, twelue bolis for alle Israel, foure
score wetheris and sixe, two and seuenty 67
lambren, twelue geet for synne, and twelue
kiyn for helthe; alle in to the sacrifice of
the Lord. And eft thei redden the hestis 68
of the kyng to the kyngis dispensatours,
and to the litle vndir kyngis of Choele,
and of Cirye, and of Fenyce; and thei
wirschipiden the folc and the temple of
the Lord. And aftir thes thingis weren 69
endid[b], thei camen to me, seiynge, The
kynrede of Israel, and the princis, and the
prestis, and Leuytis, and alien folkis, and 70
naciouns of the lond, han not partid awey
her vnclennessis fro the Chananeis, and
Etheis, and fro Pheriseis, and Jebuseis,
and fro the Moabitis, and Egipcians, and
Ydumeis; forsothe thei weren ioyned to 71

[b] fillid endid 1.

the doȝtris of hem, and thei and ther sonis; and the holi sed is[1] mengd togidere to the hethene folc of the lond; and parceneres weren the prouostus and maistir iugis of this wickednesse, fro the 72 begynnyng of that reume. And anon as I herde these thingis, I cutte the clothis, and the sacrid cote, and to-terende the heris of the hed, and the berd, I sat so-73 rewende, and dreri. And ther camen to me as fele as euere weren thanne moued in the woord of the Lord God of Irael, me weilende vp on this[m] wickenesse[n]; and I sat soreweful vnto the 74 euentid sacrifise. And risende fro fasting, hauende the clothis cut, miche knelende, and strecchende out the hondis 75 to the Lord, I seide, Lord, I am confoundid, and I am adrad befor thi face. 76 Forsothe oure synnes ben multiplied vp on oure hedis, and oure wickednessis ben 77 enhauncid vnto heuene; for fro the time of oure fadris we ben in gret synne vn 78 to this day. And for oure synnes, and of oure fadris we ben taken, with oure brethern, and with oure prestus, and kingus of the lond, in to swerd, and caitiftc, and in to prei, with confusion, vn 79 to the dai that is now. And now hou myche is, that falleth to vs the merci of thee, Lord God; lef to vs a roote and a 80 name, in to the place of thin halewing, to vnkoueren oure ȝiuere of liȝt in the hous of the Lord oure God, to ȝiue to vs mete 81 in the time of oure seruage. And whan wee seruen, wee ben not forsaken of the Lord oure God; but he sette vs in grace, puttende to vs kingus of Persis to ȝine mete, 82 and to clarifien the temple of the Lord oure God, and to edefie the desertis of Sion, and to ȝiue to vs stablenesse in Jude 83 and Jerusalem. And now what sei wee, Lord, hauende these thingus? We han ouyr passid thin hestis, 'the whiche[o] thou ȝeue in to the hondis of thi childer, pro-84 fetus, seiende, For the lond, in the

the douȝtris of hem, bothe thei and their sones; and the hooly seed was mengid togidre with the hethene folk of the loond; and the prouostis and maistre iuges weren parceners of this wickidnesse, fro the bi-72 gynnyng of that rewme. And anoon as I herde thes thingis, I kitte *my* clothis, and the halewid coote, and I taar the heris of myn hed, and the berd, *and* I sate serew-73 ynge, and drury. And ther camen to me thanne as many as euer weren moued in the word of the Lord God of Israel, weil-ynge me upon this wickidnesse; and I saat serewful vnto the euentijd sacrifice. And *thanne* I risynge fro fastyng, hau-74 ynge my clothis kitt, knelide myche, and strecchinge out *myn* hondis to the Lord, I 75 seide, Lord, I am confoundid, and I am adred bifore thi face. Forsothe oure 76 synnes ben multiplied upon oure hedis, and oure wickidnessis ben enhaunsid vnto heuen; for fro the tyme of oure fadris we 77 haue be in gret synne vnto this dai. And for oure owne synnes, and *for the* 78 *synne* of oure fadris we ben taken, with oure bretheren, and with oure prestis, and with kyngis of the loond, in to swerd, and caitiftee, and in to prey, with confusion, vnto the dai that is now. And now hou 79 myche is *it*, that the mercy of thee, Lord God, fallith to us; leue thou to us a roote and a name, in to the place of thin halew-yng, to vnkoueren oure ȝyuere of liȝt in 80 the hous of the Lord oure God, to ȝiue to us mete in the tyme of oure seruage. And 81 whanne we seruyden, we weren not forsa-ken of the Lord oure God; but he sette us in grace, puttynge to us kyngis of Persis to ȝiue *us* mete, and to clarifie the temple 82 of the Lord oure God, and to bilde the deseertis of Syon, and to ȝiue to us stable-nesse in Judee and in Jerusalem. And 83 now, Lord, what sey we, hauynge thes thingis? We haue ouerpassid thin hestis, the whiche thou ȝiue in to the hondis of thi children, prophetis, that seiden, For-84

---

[1] and *A*.   [m] the *H*.   [n] wickidnes *AH*.   [o] that *c pr. m.*

whiche ȝee wenten in, to welden his eritage, is a defoulid lond with filthes of
the° hethene men of the lond, and the
vnclennessis of hem han fulfild it al in
85 his vnclennesse. And now ȝoure doȝtris
ȝee shul not ioyne to ther sonus, and ther
doȝtris ȝee shul not take to ȝouré sonus ;
86 and ȝee shul not seche to han pès with
hem alle time, that comende aboue ȝee
ete the beste thingus of the lond, and the
eritage ȝee delen to ȝoure sonus, in to the
87 during aboue time. And thoo thingus
that fallen to vs, alle ben do for oure
shrewde werkis, and oure grete synnes.
88 And thou hast ȝiue to vs such a roote,
and eft wee ben turned aȝeen to ouer
passe thi laweful thingis, that the vn-
clennessisᵖ of the hethene folc of this
89 lond weren mengd. Whether thou shalt
not wrathen to vs, to leesen vs, for to the
90 roote be forsaken, and oure sed ? Lord
God of Irael, thou art sothfast ; forsothe
the roote is forsaken, vnto the dai that is
91 now. Lo ! now we ben in thi siȝte in
oure wickenessisq ; forsothe it is not ȝit
to stonde befor thee in these thingus.
92 And whan honourende Esdras knou-
lechede, wepende, falleʳ doun to the erthe
befor the temple, ben gedered beforn
hym of Jerusalem a ful gret cumpanye,
men, and wemmen, and ȝunge men, and
ȝunge wymmen ; forsothe the weping
93 was gret in that multitude. And whan
Jechonias, the sone of Jeeli, of the sonus
of Irael, hadde cried, Esdras seide, Wee
han synned aȝen the Lord, that wee han
sett with vs in to matrimoyne hethene
wymmen, of the Jentilis of the lond.
94 And now who so euere is ouer al Irael
in these thingus, be ther to vs an oth of
the Lord, to putten awei alle oure wiues,
that of the hethene ben, with ther sonus ;
95 as to thee is demed of the more, aftir the
lawe of the Lord. Risendeˢ vp, shen
96 out ; to thee forsothe abideth this nede,
97 and wee ben with thee ; do manli. And
risendeˢ vp Esdras, he made the princis

sothe the lond, in whiche ȝe haue entrid, to
welde the heritage of it, is a defoulid lond
with the filthis of hethen men of the lond,
and the vnclennessis of hem han fulfillid
al it in his vnclennesse. And now *therfor* 85
ȝe schul not ioyne ȝoure douȝtris to her
sones, and her douȝtris ȝe schul not take
to ȝoure sones ; and ȝe schul not seche to 86
haue pes with hem al tyme, that comynge
aboue ȝe ete thé beste thingis of the lond,
and that ȝe dele the heritage to ȝoure
sones, for euere. And thoo thingis that 87
fallen to us, be thei alle don for oure
schrewid werkis, and oure grete synnes.
And thou hast ȝouen to us sich a roote, 88
and eft we ben turned aȝen to ouerpasse
thi laweful thingis, that the vnclennessis
of the hethen folc of this lond weren
mengid. Whether thou schalt not wrath- 89
then to us, to lese us, for til the roote be
forsaken, and oure seed ? Lord God of 90
Israel, thou art sothfast ; forsothe the root
is forsaken, vnto the day that is now. Lo ! 91
now we ben in thi siȝt in oure wickidnessis ; forsothe it is not ȝitt to stonde
bifore thee in thes thingis. And whanne 92
Esdras honouringe knowlechide, wepinge,
he fel doun to the erthe bifore the temple,
ther ben gederid bifore him a ful gret
multitude of Jerusalem, men, and wymmen, and ȝounge men, and ȝounge wymmen ; forsothe the wepynge was gret in
that multitude. And whanne Jechonyas, 93
the sone of Jeely, of the sones of Israel,
hadde cried, Esdras seide, We haue synned
aȝen the Lord, *for* that we haue sett with
us in to matrimonye hethen wymmen, of
the Gentiles of the lond. And now who 94
so euer is ouer al Israel in thes thingis, be
ther to us an ooth of the Lord, to putten
awey alle oure wyues, that ben, with her
sones, of the hethene folk ; as it is demed 95
to thee of the grettere men, aftir the lawe
of the Lord. Arijse *now* up, and schewe
thi will ; forsothe to thee abijdith this 96
nede, and we ben with thee ; do manly.
And Esdras arisynge up, made the princis 97

° Om. *A.*   ᵖ vnclennes *A.*   q wickidnessis *A et* ᴨ *passim.*   ʳ fallid *AEFH.*   ˢ Arijsynge *AEFH.*

off prestis, and the Leuitus, and al Irael, to swere to don aftir these alle these thingis; and thei sworen.

CAP. IX.

1 And risende^t vp Esdras fro 'the beforn^u porche of the temple, wente in to the 2 celle of Jonathe, sone of Nazabi. And herberewid there, he tastede no bred, ne water^v dranc, vp on the wickednesses of 3 the multitude. And ther is maad a preching in al Jude and in Jerusalem, to alle that weren of the caitifte gedered in 4 Jerusalem, Whosoeuere a3een cometh not to the secunde or the thridde dai, aftir the dom of the eldere men sittende, his facultees shul ben taken awei, and he alien demed fro the multitude of caitifte^w. 5 And alle ben gedered togidere, that weren of the linage of Juda and of Beniamyn, thre da3es in Jerusalem; this is the nynthe moneth, the twentithe dai of the 6 monyth. And al the multitude sat in the flor of the temple, tremblende for 7 the present winter. Esdras risende vp, seide to Irael, 3ee wickedeli diden, set-tende^x 3ou in to matrimoine hethene wiues, that 3ee adde to the synnes of 8 Irael. And now 3iueth shrifte, and gret doing to the Lord God of oure fadris; 9 and parformeth his wil, and goth awei fro the hethene folc of the lond, and fro 10 hethene wiues. And al the multitude criede, and seiden with a gret vois, As 11 thou hast seid, wee^y shul do. But for the multitude is gret, and the time win-ter, and wee moun not vnholpen^z stonde, and this were is not to vs of o dai, ne of two; myche in these thingus wee han 12 synned; stonde the prouostus of the mul-titude, and alle that with vs dwellen, and hou fele euere han 'anent them^a hethene 13 wiues; and stonde thei ne3 in the accept time of alle place, prestis, and domes men, for to thei losne the wrathe of the 14 Lord, of this nede. Jonathas forsothe,

of prestes, and the dekens, and al Israel, to swere to do aftir alle thes thingis; and thei sworen.

CAP. IX.

And Esdras risynge up fro the fore 1 porche of the temple, wente in to the celle of Jonathe, the sone of Nazaby. And he 2 herbowrewid there, tastide no bred, ne dronke watir, for the wickidnessis of the multitude. And ther was maad a prech-3 yng in al Judee and in Jerusalem, to alle that weren of the caitiftee gederid in Je-rusalem, Who so euer a3en comith not to 4 the secounde or the thrid day, aftir the doom of the eldre men sittynge, his facultees schul be taken awey, and he be demed alien fro the multitude of the caitiftee. And 5 alle, that weren of the lynage of Judee and of Beniamyn, weren gedrid togidre, thre daies in Jerusalem; this is the nynthe monthe, the twentithe day of the monthe. And al the multitude saat in the floor of 6 the temple, tremblynge for wyntir *thanne* beynge. *And* Esdras risynge up, seide to 7 Israel, 3e han do wickidly, settynge to 3ou in to matrimonye hethen wyues, that 3e adde to the synnes of Israel. And now 3iue 8 3e to the Lord God of oure fadris confes-sioun, and gret worthynesse; and per-9 fourme 3e his will, and goth awey fro the hethene folc of the lond, and fro hethene wyues. And al the multitude criede, and 10 thei seiden with a gret voice, We schul do, as thou hast seid. But for the multitude is 11 gret, and the tyme is wyntir, and we mowen not stonde vnholpen, and this werk is not to us of oo day, ne of two; myche we haue synned in thes thingis; *therfor* 12 stonde the prouostis of the multitude, and alle that dwellen with us, and hou many euere han anentis hem hethen wijues; and 13 stonde thei ny3 in the tyme that is take, prestis, and domesmen, til that thei lousen the wraththe of the Lord, of this nede. Jonathas forsothe, the sone of Ezely, and 14

---

^{t} arisynge *A*. ^{u} before the *A*. ^{v} no water *A*. ^{w} the caitifte c *pr. m.* H. ^{x} settynge *AEFH*. sentende c.
^{y} so wee E *pr. m.* ^{z} vnhelpid *AH*. ^{a} anentis vs *A*.

the sone of Ezeli, and Ozias, Thethan, token aftir these thingus, and Bosoramus, and Leuys[b], and Satheus togidere wroȝten 15 with hem. And ther stoden aftir alle these thingus, alle that weren of the cai-16 tifte. And Esdras, prest, chees to hym men, grete princis, of the fadris of hem, after the names; and thei seten togidere, in the newe mone of the tenthe moneth, 17 to examyne this nede. And it is deter-myned of the men, that hadden hethene wiues, vnto the newe mones of the firste 18 moneth. And there ben founden mengd among of the prestis, that hadden he-19 thene wiues; of the sonus of Jesu, the sonus of Josedech, and of his brethern, Maseas, and Eleeserus, and Joribus, and 20 Joadeus. And thei leiden[c] hondis, that thei shulden putten awei ther wiues, and to sacrifien, in to preieere for ther 21 ignoraunce. And of the sonus of Sem-mery, Masseas, and Esses, and Geleth, 22 Azarias; and of the sones of Fosore, Leomasias, Hismaeius, and Nathanias, 23 Jussio, Leddus, and Talsas. And of the Lenitus, Josabdus, and Semeis, and Cho-litus, and Calitas, and Facceas, and Colu-24 as, and Elionas. And of the sacrid syng-25 eres, Eliazub, Zaccurus. And of the 26 vssheris, Salumus, and Tholbanes. And of Irael, of the sonus of Forchosi, and Remias, and Jeddias, and Melchias, and Michelus, and Eliasarus, and Jemebias, 27 and Bannas. And of the sonis of Jola-mani, Anias, and Zacharias, Jerselus, and[d] 28 Jobdius, and Erirmoth, and Elias. And of the sonus of Sachon, Eliadas, and Elia-sumus, and Othias, and Jarimoth and 29 Zabdis, and Thebedias. And of the sones of Bede, Johannes, and Amanyas, 30 and Zabdias, and Emetis. And of the sonis of Baun, Olamus, and Mallucus, and Jeddeus, and Jasub, and Azabus, 31 and Jerimoth. And of the sonis of Ad-din, Nathns and Moosias, and Caalemus, and Raanas, and Baseas, Mathatias, and Bethsel, and Bonnus, and Manasses.

Ozias, Thethan, token aftir thes thingis, and Bosoramus, and Leuys, and Satheus wrouȝten togidre with hem. And alle 15 that weren of the caitiftee stoden there, aftir alle thes thingis. And Esdras, prest, 16 chees to him men, grete princis, of the fadris of hem, aftir the names; and thei seten togidre, in the newe moone of the tenthe monthe, to examyne this nede. And it is determyned of the men, that 17 hadden hethen wyues, vnto the newe mones of the firste monthe. And ther 18 ben founden mengid among of the prestis, that hadden hethen wiues; of the sones of 19 Jesu, the sone of Josedech, and of his brotheren, Maseas, and Eleeserus, and Joribus, and Joadeus. And thei leiden 20 her hoondis, that thei schuldn putte awey their wyues, and for to sacrifie a ram, in to preier for their ignoraunce. And of 21 the sones of Semmery, Masseas, and Esses, and Geley, Azarias; and of the sonus of 22 Phosore, Leomasias, Hismaenis, and Na-thanae, Jussio, Jeddus, and Talsas. And 23 of the dekens, Josabdus, and Semeis, and Cholitus, and Calitas, and Phacceas, and Coluas, and Elionas. And of the halewid 24 syngers, Eliazub, Zacturus. And of the 25 vsschers, Salumus, and Thosbanes. And 26 of Israel, of the sones of Phorcosy, and Remyas, and Jeddias, and Melchias, and Mychelus, and Eleazarus, and Jemebias, and Bannus. And of the sones of Jol-27 amani, Anias, and Zacharias, Jerselus, and Jobdius, and Erymath, and Elias. And of the sonns of Sachon, Eleadas, and 28 Eleasumus, and Othias, and Jarymoth, and Zabdis, and Thebedias. And of the 29 sones of Bedo, Johannes, and Amanyas, and Zabdias, and Emetis. And of the 30 sonus of Banny, Olamus, and Mallucus, and Jeddeus, and Jazub, and Azabus, and Jerymoth. And of the sones of Addyn, 31 Naathus, and Moosias, and Calemus, and Raanas, and Baseas, Mathatias, and Beth-sel, and Bonnus, and Manasses. And of 32 the sones of Myaie, Nenyas, and Apheas,

32 And of the sonus of Miaie, Nenyas, and
Afeas, and Melcheas, and Sameas, and
Simon, Beniamyn, and Malchus, and
33 Marias. Of the sonus of Azom, Cartaneus,
Mathatias, and Bannus, and Elifalath,
34 and Manasses, and Semeth. And of the
sonus of Banny, Jeremias, and Modias,
and Abramus, and Johel, and Baneas,
and Pelias, and Jonas, and Marymoth,
and Eliazub, and Mathaneus, and Ele-
asis, and Orisas, and Dielus, and Same-
35 dius, and Zambris, and Josefus. And of
the sonus of Nobei, Idelus, and Mathatias, and Zabadus, and Cetheda, Seduni,
36 and Jessei, Baneas. Alle these ioineden
to hem hethene wines, and laften hem,
37 with the sones. And prestis, and Leuitus, and that weren of Irael, dwelten in
Jerusalem in oon hol regioun, the newe
mone of the seuenthe moneth; and the
sonus of Irael weren in ther abidingus.
38 And al the multitude is gedered togidere
in to the flor, that is fro the est of the
39 sacrid ȝate. And thei seiden to Esdre,
bisshop and redere, that he shulde bringe
forth the lawe of Moises, that is ȝiuen
40 of the Lord God of Irael. And Esdras,
bisshop, broȝte forth the lawe to al the
multitude of hem, fro man vnto womman, and to alle the prestus, to heren the
lawe, in the newe mone of the seuenthe
41 moneth. And he radde in the flor, that
is befor the holi ȝate of the temple, fro
the firste liȝt vnto euen, befor men and
wymmen; and alle thei ȝeuen wit to the
42 lawe. And Esdras, prest, and redere of
the lawe, stod vp on the treene chaȝer,
43 that was forgid. And there stoden to
hym Mathatias, and Samus, and Ananyas, Azarias, Vrias, Ezechias, and Bal-
44 samus, at the riȝt; and at the lift, Faldeus,
and[e] Misael, Malachias, Abustas, Sabus,
45 Nabadias, and Zacharias. And[f] Esdras
toc a boc beforn al the multitude; forsothe he sat beforn in glorie, in the siȝte[g]
46 of alle. And whan he hadde asoilid the
lawe, alle stoden vp riȝt. And Esdras

and Melcheas, and Sameas, and Symon,
Beniamyn, and Malchus, and Marias. Of 33
the sones of Azom, Cartaneus, Mathatias,
and Bannus, and Eliphalath, and Manasses, and Semey. Of the sones of 34
Banny, Jeremias, and Moodias, and Abramus, and Johel, and Baneas, and Pelias,
and Jonas, and Marymoth, and Eliazub,
and Mathaneus, and Eleazis, and Ozias,
and Dielus, and Samedius, and Zambris,
and Josephus. And of the sones of Nobey, 35
Ydelus, and Mathatias, and Zaladus, and
Setheda, Sedym, and Jessei, Baneas. Alle 36
these ioyneden to hem hethen wyues, and
leften hem, with her sones. And prestis, 37
and dekens, and thei that weren of Israel,
dwelliden in Jerusalem in an oo regioun,
the newe moone of the seuenthe monthe;
and the sones of Israel weren in their
abidyngis. And al the multitude gedride 38
togidre in the floor, that is fro the eest of
the halewid ȝate. And thei seiden to 39
Esdre, bisschop and reder, that he schulde
brynge forth the lawe of Moises, that was
ȝouen of the Lord God of Israel. And 40
Esdras, the bisschop, brouȝte forth the lawe
to al the multitude of hem, fro man vn to
womman, and to alle the prestis, to here
the lawe, in the newe moone of the seuenthe monthe. And he radde in the 41
floor, that is bifore the hooly ȝate of the
temple, fro the firste liȝt of the daie vnto
euyn, bifore men and wymmen; and alle
thei ȝauen witt to the lawe. And Esdras, 42
the prest, and redere of the lawe, stood
upon the treen chaier, that was maad
therfore. And ther stoden with him 43
Mathatins, and Samus, and Ananyas,
Azarias, Vrias, Ezechias, and Balsamus,
at the riȝt side; and at the left side, Pha- 44
leleus, Mysael, Malachias, Abustas, Sabus,
Nabadias, and Zacharias. And Esdras 45
took a book bifore al the multitude; forsothe he sate bifore in worschip, in the
siȝt of alle. And whanne he hadde as- 46
soilid the lawe, alle thei stoden upright.
And Esdras blesside the Lord God, alther

---

[e] Om. AH.   [f] Om. A.   [g] multitude E pr. m.

blesside the Lord God, al ther heiȝest
47 God of Sabaoth, al myȝti. And al the
puple answerde, Amen. And eft, the
hondis rerid vp, thei, fallende doun in to
48 the erthe, honoureden the Lord. And
Esdras comaundede, that ther shulden
teche the lawe, Jesus, and Banaeus, and
Sarabias, and Jadinus, and Accubus, and
Sabatheus, and Calithes, and Azarias,
and Joradus, and Ananias, and Filas,
49 Leuite. The whiche taȝten the lawe of
the Lord, and in[h] the multitude radden
the lawe of the Lord ; and eche putten
beforn hem, that vndirstoden the lessoun.
50 And Atharathes seide to Esdre, the bisshop and redere, and to the Leuitus that
51 taȝten the multitude, seiende, This dai is
holi to the Lord. And alle wepten,
52 whan thei hadden herd the lawe. And
Esdras seide, ȝee thanne, gon atwynne,
eteth alle most fatte thingys, and drinketh alle most sweete, and sendeth ȝiftus
53 to hem that han not ; forsothe holi is
this dai of the Lord ; and wileth not ben
sori, the Lord forsothe shal clarifien vs.
54 And the Leuitus denounceden in opene
to alle men, seiende, This dai is holi ;
55 wileth not ben sori. And alle wenten
awei, to eten, and to drinken, and to han
plente of mete, and to ȝiue ȝiftus to hem
that han not, that thei plenteuousli eten.
Gret doingli forsothe thei ben enhauncid
in the woordis, with the whiche thei ben
56 taȝt. And alle thei ben gedered in to
Jerusalem, to make solempne the gladnesse, after the testament of the Lord
God of Irael.

*Here endith the thridde book of
Esdre, and now begynneth the prolog
of the book of Tobie[l].*

hiȝest God of Sabaoth, al myȝti. And al 47
the peple answeride, Amen. And efte
thei reisyden up *her* hondis, and fallynge
doun vnto the erthe, thei honouriden the
Lord. And Esdras comaundide, that these 48
schulden teche the lawe, Jesus, and Banaeus, and Sarabias, and Jadmus, and
Accubus, and Sabatheus, and Calithes,
and Azarias, and Joradus, and Ananyas,
and Philas, dekens. The whiche tauȝten 49
the lawe of the Lord, and in the multitude
thei radden the lawe of the Lord ; and
eche bi him self, that vndirstoden the
lesson, tolde *it* before hem. And Atha- 50
rathes seide to Esdre, the bisschop and
redere, and to the Leuytis that tauȝten
the multitude, seiynge, This day is hooly 51
to the Lord. And alle thei wepten,
whanne thei hadden herd the lawe. And 52
Esdras seide, ȝe therfore, aftir ȝe ben
gon atwynne, eteth alle moost fatte thingis,
and drynketh alle mooste swete, and sende
ȝe ȝiftis to hem that han not ; forsothe this 53
day of the Lord is hooly ; and be ȝe not
sory, the Lord forsothe schal clarifie vs.
And the dekens denounciden, *or schew-* 54
iden, openly to alle men, seiynge, This
day is hooly ; wille ȝe not be sory. And 55
thanne alle thei wenten awey, to ete, and
to drynke, and to haue plentee of mete,
and to ȝiue ȝiftis to hem that han not,
wheroff to ete plenteuously. Gretly forsothe thei ben enhaunsid in the wordis,
with the whiche thei ben tauȝt. And alle 56
thei weren gadrid in to Jerusalem, to
make solempne the gladnesse, aftir the
testament of the Lord God of Israel.

*Heere endith the thridde book of
Esdre, and bigynnith Thobie.*

h Om. *A.*   l From *A.* *Explicit liber Esdre tertius.* E. *Here endith the thrid bok of Esdre.* F. No final
rubric in *CII.*

TOBIT.

―――

[Prologue on the book of Tobit[a].]

I<small>N</small> this book of Tobie ben contened the seuen dedis of merci, whiche Tobie wrouȝte
with his peple of the sones of Israel, that weren in caitifte, acordinge to the gospel of
Crist, seiynge, Blessid ben thei that ben merciful, for thei schullen haue merci ; wherfor
Tobie doinge merci hadde merci of God, which sente his aungel to comforte him, and
to do merci to him, as he hadde do bifore to his peple of Israel.

―――

Here begynneth proloug of Tobie[a].

T<small>O</small> Cromacio and Eliodre, bisshopys, Jerome, prest, in the Lord sendeth greeting.
To merueilen I cese not the instaunce of ȝoure asking ; forsothe ȝee asken of me, that
the boc, writen in Caldee sermoun, in to Latin writing I drawe, the boc of Tobie that
is, the whiche Ebrues, seuerende fro the noumbre of Godis scripturis, to these that holi
scriptures remembren[b] casten to. I haue don a seeth to ȝoure desijr, ner the latere
not to my studie. Forsothe the studies of Ebrues vndernymyn vs, and wijten to vs
these thingis to translaten to the[c] Latin eris aȝen ther[d] bible. But I demeude to be
betere to desplesen to the dom of Farisees, and to serue to the bisshopis maundemens,
bisiede[e] as I myȝte ; and, for the tunge of Caldeis is neeȝ to Ebrue sermoun, findende a
most wijs spekere of[f] either tunge, I toc to the trauaile of o dai ; and what euere thing
he to me expressede in Ebrue woordis, thoo thingus I, clepid to a notorie, expounede
in Latin woordis. To ȝoure prieeris the meede of this werk[g] I shal ȝelde, whan
I lerne me to han fulfild this werc to ben acceptid of[h] ȝou that[i] voucheden saaf to
comaunden.

Heere endith the prolog of Tobie, and now begynneth the book[j].

<hr>

ᵃ This prologue is from M.

ᵃ From F. *Incipit prologus Jeronimi in librum Thobie.* E. *Prologus.* H. No initial rubric in ACIO.
ᵇ be remembren E *pr. m.* ᶜ Om. AI. ᵈ the HK. ᵉ bisiede me E *pr. m.* ᶠ to o. ᵍ werk.
man A. ʰ to o. ⁱ the whiche AEFH. ʲ From AF. *Here endeth the prolog of Tobie, se now the booc.* I.
Here endith the prolog, and bigynneth the book. O. No final rubric in CEH.

Tobie[k].

CAP. I.

1 TOBIE, of the linage and of the cite of Neptalim, that is in the ouere partis of Galilee, aboue Nason, after the weie that ledith to the west, in the left 2 hauende the cite of Sofeth, whan he was caȝt in the daȝes of Salmanasar, king of Assiries, ner the latere in caitifte[l] sett, 3 the weie of treuthe he forsoc not, so that alle thingus that he myȝte han, eche dai to the caityue brethern that weren of 4 his kinrede he delede. And whan he was alle ȝungere in the linage of Neptalim, ner the latere no childli thing he 5 dide in deede. After whan alle wenten to the goldene calues, the whiche Jeroboam, king of Irael, made, this alone fleiȝ 6 the cumpanye of alle; and wente to Jerusalem, to the temple of the Lord, and there honourede the Lord God of Irael, alle his firste frutis and his dymys treuli 7 offrende; so that in the thredde[m] ȝer to the conuertid fro Jentilis and to come- 8 lingus he mynystrede alle tithing. These thingus, and to these lic, after the lawe of 9 God a litil child he kepte wel. Whan forsothe he was maad a man, he toc a wif, Anne, of his linage; and he gat of hir a sone, his own name puttende to 10 hym; whom fro the time that he began to speken, he taȝte to dreden God, and to 11 abstenen[n] fro alle synne. Thanne whan by caytifte he was come, with his wif and sone, in to the cite Nynyue, with al his 12 linage, and alle eeten of the metis of Jentilis, this kepte his soule, and neuere is

Here bigynneth the book of Tobie[b].

CAP. I.

TOBIE† was of the lynage and[bb] citee of 1 Neptalym, which[c] is in the hiȝere partis of Galilee, aboue Naason, bihynde the weie that ledith to the west, and hath[d] in the lefte side the citee of Sapheth, whanne[e] he[f] 2 was takun in the daies of Salmanazar, kyng of Assiriens, netheles he set in caytifte, 'ether takun prisoner[g], forsook not the weie of treuthe, so that he depart- 3 ide ech dai alle thingis whiche he myȝte[h] haue[i], with caitif[k] britheren that weren of his kyn. And whanne he was ȝongere 4 than alle[l]‡ in the lynage of Neptalym, netheles he dide no childische[m] thing in werk[n]. Forsothe[o] whanne alle Jewis[p] 5 ȝeden to the[q] goldun calues, whiche Jeroboam, the kyng of Israel, made[r], this Tobie aloone fledde the[s] cumpenyes[t] of alle[u] men[v]; and[w] he ȝede[x] to Jerusalem, to 6 the temple of the Lord, and there he worschipide the Lord God[y] of Israel; and he offride feithfuly alle hise firste fruytis, and hise tithis; so that in the thridde ȝer he 7 mynystride[z] al the[a] tithe to conuersis[b] and comlyngis[c]. The[d] ȝonge man[e] kepte[f] these 8 thingis, and thingis[g] lijk[h] these, bi[i] the lawe of God of heuene. Sotheli[k] whanne he 9 was maad a man[l], he took a wijf, Anne[m], of his lynage; and he gendride[n] of hir a sone, and puttide[o] his owne name to hym; whom he tauȝte fro ȝong childhed for[p] to 10 drede God, and for to absteyne[q] fro al synne. Therfor whanne bi caitifte he[r] 11 was comun, with his wijf and sone[s], in to the citee Nynyue[t], with al his lynage, and 12

† This storie of Tobie bifelde in the sixte ȝeer of king Ezechie. Lire here. A et plures.

‡ than alle; notable persoyns. Lire here. CV.

---

k Running title in c. *Incipit liber.* E. No initial rubric in the other Mss.   l the caitifte CE pr. m.
m firste E pr. m.   n abstenen hym E pr. m.

b *The book of Tobie.* ELP. *Here bigynneth Tobie.* ag. No initial rubric in the other Mss.   bb and of the 18.   c the which 1.   d it hath 18.   e and whanne 18.   f Thobie 18.   g either maad thral 18. h myȝte leuefully 18.   i haue or gete 18.   k his thral 1. his caitif 8.   l alle othere 1.   m Om. 18.   n werk childely 18.   o Certis 18.   p *the Jewis* DELag. *othere* 1.   q worshepe the 8.   r had made 8.   s al the 8. t cumpany 8.   u Om. 8.   v *thilke Jewis* 1. *Jewis* 8.   w Om. A.   x wente 1.   y Om. A.   z ȝaaf 18. a his 1.   b men that weren turned to the bileue 1. men turned to the bileue 8.   c to comlyngis 1. comlyngis come fro other cuntreis 8.   d This 18.   e man Thobie 18.   f kepte in doynge 1. kept or dide 8. g othere thingis 1.   h lijk to 18.   i aftir 1.   k And 18.   l man hauyng discresioun 8.   m Anne bi name 18. n gaat 1.   o he putte 1. he puttide 8.   p Om. 18X.   q absteyne him 8.   r Thobie 18.   s his sone A. t of Nynyue BCG18.

13 defoulid in metis of hem. And for he
was myndeful of the Lord in al his herte,
God ȝaf to hym grace in the siȝte of king
14 Salamanasar; and ȝaf to hym power to
go whider euere he wolde, hauende fredam to do what euere he hadde wold.
15 Thanne he wente bi alle that weren in
the caitifte, and monestingus of helthe he
16 ȝaf to hem. Whan forsothe he was
come in to Ragis, cite of Medis, and of
these thingus with the whiche he was
wrshipid of the king, hadde ten talentis of
17 siluer; and with myche cumpanye of his
kinrede, he saȝ Gabel nedi, that was of
his linage, he ȝaf to hym the seid[o] peis
18 of siluer, vndir writing. Forsothe[p] after
miche of time king Salmanasar dead,
whan his sone Senacherub regnede for
hym, and hadde the sonus of Irael hate-
19 sum in his siȝte, Tobie wente eche dai bi
al hys kinrede, and coumfortide hem, and
deuidede[q] to eche, as he myȝte, of his fa-
20 cultees; the hungri men he fedde, and to
the nakide he ȝaf clothis, and to the
deade and the slaine besi[r] he fond sepul-
21 ture. After whan king Senacherub was
turned aȝeen, fleende fro Jude the veniaunce that abouten hym God hadde do
for his blasfemye, and wroth sloȝ manie
of the sonus of Irael, Tobie biriede the
22 bodies of hem. And wher it was told to
the king, he comandide hym to be slain,
23 and toc al his substaunce. Tobie forsothe with his sone and with wif[s] fleende,
nakid lurkide, for manie loueden hym.
24 After forsothe fiue and fourti daȝes, the
25 king his sonus slowen; and Tobie is
turned aȝeen to his hous, and al his fa-
culte[t] restorid to hym.

alle *men*[u] eeten[v] of the meetis of hethene
men, this Tobie kepte his soule[w], and
was[x] neuere defoulid in the metis† of hem.
And[y] for he was myndeful of the Lord in 13
al his herte, God ȝaf grace to hym in the
siȝt of Salamanazar, the kyng; and he ȝaf 14
to Tobie power to go whidur euer he
wolde, and he hadde fredom to do what
euer thingis he wolde. Therfor he[z] ȝede 15
bi alle men[a] that weren in caitifte[b], and
ȝaf[c] to hem the[d] heestis of helthe[e]. So- 16
theli[f] whanne he was comyn in to Rages,
a citee of[g] Medeis, and hadde[h] ten talentis
of siluer, of these thingis bi whiche he was
onourid of the kyng[i]; and siȝ[k] Gabelus 17
nedi, that was of[l] his lynage[m], with myche
cumpeny of his kyn[n], Tobie[o] ȝaf to hym,
vndur an obligacioun, the forseid weiȝte
of siluer. Forsothe[p] after myche tyme, 18
aftir[q] that Salamanazar, the kyng, was
deed, whanne Senacherib, his sone, regnyde for hym, and hadde[r] the sones of
Israel hateful in his siȝt, Tobie ȝede ech 19
dai bi al his kynrede, and coumfortide
hem, and departide[s] of hise catels[t] to ech
man, as he myȝte; he fedde hungri men, 20
and ȝaf clothis to nakid men, and he ˋȝaf
bisili[u] sepulture to deed men and slayn.
Sotheli[v] whanne the[w] kyng Senacherib 21
turnede aȝen, fleynge fro Judee the[x] veniaunce that God ˋhadde do[y] aboute[z] hym
for his blasfemye, and he[a] was wrooth, and
killide many of the sones of Israel, Tobie
biriede ˋthe bodies of hem[b]. And aftir 22
that it[c] was teld to the kyng, he comaundide Tobie to be slayn, and he took awei[d]
al his catel. Sotheli[e] Tobie fledde with 23
his sone and with his wijf, and was[f] hid
nakid‡, for many men loueden hym. For- 24
sothe[g] after[h] fyue and fourti daies[i], the
sones of the kyng kyilliden the kyng;
and[k] Tobie turnede aȝen to his hows, and 25
al his catel was restorid to hym.

† *metis*; forbedun to Jewis bi Moises lawe. *Lire here.* c.

‡ *nakid*; that is, spuylid of alle catelis. *Lire here.* cv.

[o] forseid A. [p] Not E *pr. m.* [q] deuyde A. [r] bisili A. [s] his wijf A. [t] facultees A.

[u] Om. I. [v] eeten *there* IS. [w] soule *or his consience cleene* S. [x] he was I. [y] Om. S. [z] Thobie IS. [a] the men I. [b] thraldom I. [c] he ȝaf IS. [d] Om. IS. [e] helth, *to be pacient in her disese* S. [f] And IS. [g] *of the cuntree* of I. [h] he hadde IS. [i] kyng, *to haue fredom of his owne good* IS. [k] he siȝ IS. [l] *a man* of IS. [m] seyn IS. [n] lynage I. [o] and I. and Tobie S. [p] And IS. [q] Om. S. [r] he hadde I. [s] he departide IS. [t] catel IS. [u] bisili ordeynede I. [v] And IS. [w] Om. S. [x] for the IS. [y] dide *there* IS. [z] to IS. [a] Om. I. [b] her bodies IS. [c] this IS. [d] fro him IS. [e] And IS. [f] he was IS. [g] And IS. [h] Om. IS. [i] daies aftir *this* IS. [k] and *thanne* IS.

CAP. II.

1 Aftir these thingus forsothe, whan was the feste dai of the Lord, and shulde be maad a good meteshipe in the hous of 2 Tobie, he seide to his sone, Go, and bring summe men of oure linage, dred-3 end God, and ete thei with vs. And whan he shulde gon, turned aȝeen he tolde to hym, oon of the sonus of Irael slain[u] to lyn in the strete; and anoon stertende out fro his mete sete, leuende 4 the mete, fastende cam to the bodi; and takende it, he bar to his hous priueli, that whil the sunne were go doun, sleeȝli he 5 shulde birien it. And whan he hadde hid the bodi, he eet bred with weiling 6 and trembrende that[v] woord, that the Lord seide by Amos, the pro-fete, ȝoure feste daȝes shul be turned in 7 to weiling and sorewing. Whan forsothe the sunne hadde go doun, he wente, and 8 biriede it. Forsothe alle hise neȝheboris vndernomyn hym, seiende, Now bi cause of this thing thou art comaundid to be slain, and vnnethe thou hast scapid the maundement of deth, and eft thou biriest 9 the deade? But Tobye, more dredende God than the king, caȝte the bodies of the slaine, and hidde in his hous, and in 10 the mydnyȝtus biriede[w] hem. It fel for-sothe, that on a dai weri[x] of biriyng, co-mende hom, he hadde cast hymself beside 11 the wal, and hadde faste slept; and fro the nest of swalewis to hym slepende hote toordis fellen in vp on his eȝen; 12 and was[y] maad blind. This forsothe temptacioun therfore the Lord suffride to come to hym, that to the[x] after-comeres shulde exsaumple be ȝiuen of his 13 pacience, as and of holi Job. And whan fro his time that he began to speke,

CAP. II.

Forsothe[l] aftir these thingis, whanne a 1 feeste dai of the Lord was, and a[m] good meete was maad in the hows of Tobie, he seide to his sone, Go thou, and brynge[n] 2 sum men of oure lynage[o], 'that dreden[p] God, that thei ete with vs. And whanne 3 he[q] was goon[r], he turnede aȝen, and telde to hym[s], that oon of the sones of Israel lai stranglid in the street; and anoon 'he skippide[t] fro his sittyng place, and lefte[u] the[v] mete, and cam fastynge to the bodi[w]; and he took it[x], and bar[y] to[z] his hows pry-4 uely, for to birie hym warli, whanne the sunne was[a] go[b] doun. And whanne he 5 hadde hid the bodi, he eet breed[c] with morenyng and tremblyng[d], and remem-6 bride[e] that[f] word, which[g] the Lord seide bi Amos, the prophete, ȝoure feeste daies schulen be turned in to morenyng and 'lamentacioun, ether[h] weilyng. Sotheli[i] 7 whanne the sunne was go doun, Tobie ȝede, and biriede hym. Forsothe[k] alle hise 8 neiȝboris blameden hym, and seiden, Now for the[l] cause of this thing thou were co-maundid to be slayn, and vnnethis thou ascapidist[m] the comaundement[n] of deeth, and eft 'hiriest thou[o] deed men? But 9 Tobie dredde more God than the kyng, and took[p] awei the bodies of slayn men, and hidde[q] in his hows, and biriede[r] tho in the myddil of nyȝtis. Sotheli[s] it bi-10 felde, that in sum[t] day he[u] was maad wery of biriyng[v]; and he cam hoom, and leide hym silf bisidis a wal, and slepte[w]; and 11 while he slepte, hoote[x] ordures[y] 'fellen doun[z] fro the nest of swalewis on[a] hise iȝen; and[b] he was maad blynd. Forsothe[c] 12 herfor the Lord suffride this temptacioun bifalle[d] to hym, that the saumple[e] of his pacience, 'as also of seynt Job[f], schulde be

---

[u] Om. A. [v] the AII. [w] he biriede A. [x] trauailid E pr. m. [y] he was c pr. m. [z] Om. AII.

[l] Certis IS. [m] Om. IS. [n] brynge yn hidere IS. [o] kyn IS. [p] dredyng S. [q] ȝoung Thobie IS. [r] gone forth S. [s] his fadtr IS. [t] Tobie rose up IS. [u] he lefte IS. [v] hiis IS. [w] ded bodi I. [x] it up IS. [y] bar it ISg. [z] in to S. [a] were I. [b] Om. g. [c] the breed AB pr. m. [d] with tremblyng IS. [e] he hadde in' mynde IS. [f] the g. [g] that IS. [h] Om. IS. [i] And IS. [k] Sothely IS. [l] Om. IS. [m] hast ascapid S. [n] hoest IS. [o] thou biriest IS. [p] he took IS. [q] hidde hem I. he hidde hem S. [r] he hidde I. he biriede S. [s] And IS. [t] a I. [u] Tobie IS. [v] biriyng deed bodies IS. [w] he slepte there I. slepte there S. [x] ther fell doun hoote I. [y] toordis BCDEFGKLMNOPQRUVWXabfh. drit II sec. m. dounge I. filthe S. [z] Om. I. [a] upon IS. [b] and so I. [c] And IS. [d] to bifalle IS. [e] ensaumple IS. [f] Om. IS.

4 E 2

cuermore he dredde God, and kepte his
hestis, he sorewide not aȝen God, that
the veniaunce of blindnesse cam to hym ;
14 but vnmouable in the drede of God abod
stille, gracis doende to God alle the daȝes
15 of his lif. For as to blisful Job asail-
eden the kingus, so to this fader and
moder and his cosynes scorneden his lif,
16 seiende, Where is thin hope, for the whiche
almesse deede and sepulturis thou didist ?
17 Tobie forsothe blamede hem, seiende,
18 Wileth not so speken, for the sonus of
halewis wee ben, and that lif wee abijden,
that God is to ȝiue to hem that ther
19 feith neuermor chaungen fro hym. Anne
forsothe, his wif, wente to weuyng werc
eche dai, and of the trauaile of hir hondis
the liflode, that she myȝte gete, she broȝte.
20 And it is do, that takende a kide of she
21 get, she broȝte hom. Of the whiche ble-
tende the vois whan hir man hadde herd,
seide^a, Looketh, lest parauenture it be
stoln, but ȝeldeth it to his lordis ; for it
is not leeful to vs, or^b to eten of stelthe
22 any thing or to touchen. At these
thingis his wif wroth answerde, Openli
vein is maad thin hope, and thine almesse
23 deedis now han aperid. And in these
and in othere suche maner woordis she
putte reprof to hym.

CAP. III.

1 Thanne Tobie inwardli weilede, and
2 began to preȝe with teres, seyende, Riȝtwis thou art, Lord, and alle thi domes
ben^c riȝtwise, and alle thi weies merci,

ȝouun to 'after comeris^g. For whi whanne 13
he^h dredde God euere fro his ȝong childhed,
and kepte hise comaundementis^i, he was
not sory^k aȝens God, for^l the sikenesse of
blyndnesse cam to hym ; but he dwellide 14
vnmouable in the drede of God, and dide^m
thankyngis to God in alle the dais of his
lijf. For whi as kyngis vpbreididen^n 15
seynt^o Job, so it bifelde to this Tobie,
hise^p eldris and kynesmen^q scorneden his
lijf, and seiden^r, Where is^s thin hope†, for 16
which thou didist almes dedis and biri-
yngis^t? Sotheli^u Tobie blamyde hem^v, 17
and seide^w, Nyle ȝe speke so, for we ben 18
the sones of hooli men, and we abiden
that lijf, which^x God schal ȝyue to hem
that^y chaungen^z neuere her feith fro hym.
Forsothe^a Anne, his wijf, ȝede ech dai to 19
the 'werk of weuyng^b, and brouȝte^c lyue-
lode^d, which^e sche myȝte gete of the trauel
of hir hondis. Wherof^f it 'was doon^g, that 20
sche took a kide of geet^h, and brouȝte^i
hoom. And whanne^k hir hosebonde hadde^l 21
herd the vois of this kide bletynge, he
seide, Se^m ȝe, lest perauenture it^n be^o of
thefte, but^p 'ȝelde ȝe^q it^r to 'hise lordis^s ;
for it is not leueful 'to vs^t, ethir to ete
ether to touche ony thing of thefte. At 22
these thingis^u his^v wijf^w was wrooth, and
answeride^x, Opynli^y thin hope is^z maad
veyn, and thin almes dedis apperiden^a‡
now^b. And bi these^c and 'othere siche 23
wordis^d sche seide schenschip to hym^e.

CAP. III.

Thanne Tobie inwardli sorewide, and 1
bigan^f to preye with teeris, and seide^g,
Lord, thou art iust, and alle thi domes 2
ben iust, and alle thi weies ben mercy, and

† hope; these bileuyden the rewarding of good and of yuel is onely in present lijf, as the frendis of Joob diden. Lire here. c.

‡ apperiden; that is, feyned and void, as doon for hpocrisie. Lire here. c.

---

a he seide A.   b for AII.   c Om. AH.

g after comeris, as also it is of hooly Job 1. aftercomeris, as also the paciens of seint Job s. h Tobie 1s.
i hestis 1s. k sory or heuy 1. sori or gruching s. l for that 1. for that that s. m he dide 1s.
n upbreiden c1x. o blessid 1s. p that hise 1s. q his kynesmen 1. r seiden to him s. s is nowe 1s.
t madist sepulcris to deed men 1s. u And 1s. v hem that thus spaken s. w he seide 1. he seide to hem s.
x that 1s. y whiche s. z chaungiden s. a And 1s. b weuynge craft H sec. m. c sche brouȝte hom 1s.
d the lyuelode 1s. e that 1s. f Wherfor s. Where x. g bifelle 1s. h geet, for her weuyng s. i sche
brouȝte it 1s. k whanne Tobie 1s. l Om. s. m Loke 1. n this kide 1s. o be gotun 1s. p but if it so
be 1. but thanne s. q ȝeldeth 1. r it aȝen 1s. s hem that onȝten it 1s. t Om. 1. u wordis 1. v the 1.
w wijf of Tobie 1. x sche answeride to him 1s. y Now is opynli 1. Now apertli s. z Om. 1. a han
apeerid 1. b Om. 1s. c these wordis 1. these wordis of malice s. d bi siche othere 1s. e hir husbonde 1s.
f he bigan 1s. g he seide s.

3 and treuthe, and dom. And now, Lord, haue mynde of me, ne take thou veniaunce of my synnes, ne remembre thou my giltis, or of my fader and moder. 4 For wee han not obeshid to thin hestis, and wee ben taken in to wasting, and caitifte, and deth, and in to fable, and in to reprof to[d] alle naciouns, in the 5 whiche thou hast scatered vs. And now, Lord, grete ben thi domys; for wee han not don aftir thin hestis, and wee han 6 not go cleerli befor thee. And now, Lord, after thi wille do with me merci, and comaunde in pes my spirit to be resceiued; it is spedful forsothe to me 7 more to dien than to liuen. And so the same dai fel, that Sara, the dozter of Raguel, in Ragis, cite of Medis, and she herde the repref of oon of the handwym- 8 men of hir fadir; for she was take to seuene men, and a deuel, Asmodius bi name, slo3 hem, anoon as thei weren gon 9 in to hir. Thanne whan she blamede the child womman for hir gilte, she an- swerde to hir, seiende, See wee no more of thee sone or[e] do3ter vp on erthe, thou 10 sleeresse of thi men; whether and slen thou wilt me, as and thou slowe seuene men? At this vois she wente in to the ouere bed place of hir hous, and thre da3is and thre ny3t she eet not, ne dranc; 11 but in orisoun abidende stille, with teres she pre3ede God, that fro this reprof he 12 shulde deliueren hir. It is do forsothe the thridde dai, whil she fulfilde the 13 orisoun, blessende the Lord, she seide, Blessid is thi name, God of oure fadris, that whan thou were wrathid, thou shalt do merci, and in time of tribulacioun synnes thou for3iuest to hem, that in- 14 wardli clepen thee. To thee, Lord, I turne my face, and to thee myn e3en I

treuthe, and doom. And now, Lord, haue 3 thou[h] mynde of me, and take thou not[i] veniaunce of my synnes, nether haue thou mynde of my trespassis, ethir[k] of my fa- dris[l]. For we 'obeieden not[m] to 'thi co- 4 maundementis[n], and[o] we ben takun in to rifelyng, and in to caitifte, and in to deth, and in to 'a fable[p], and in to schenschip to alle naciouns, among whiche thou hast scaterid vs. And now, Lord, thi domes 5 ben grete[q]; for we han not do aftir 'thi comaundementis[r], and we han not go clenli bifor thee. And now, Lord, bi[s] thi wille 6 do thou merci[t] with me, and comaunde thou my spirit to be resseyued in pees; for[u] it spedith more to me to die than to lyue. And so[v] it bifelde in[w] the same dai, 7 that Sare, the dou3ter of Raguel, was in Rages, a citee of Medeis, and sche herd schenschip of[x] oon of the handmaidis[y] of hir fadir; for sche[z] was 3ouun to scuene 8 hosebondis, and a feend, Asmodeus bi name, killide hem[a], anoon as thei hadden entrid to hir[b]. Therfor[c] whanne sche[d] 9 blamyde 'the damyscle[e] for her gilt, the damisele answeride to hir, and seide, Thou sleeresse[f] of thin hosebondis, se we 'no more a[g] sone ether a[h] dou3ter of thee 'on erthe[i]; whether also thou wolt sle me, as 10 also thou hast slayn seuene men? At this vois[k] sche[l] 3ede in to the hi3ere closet of hir hows, and thre daies and thre ny3tis sche eet not, nether drank; but sche con- 11 tynuede in preier[m] with teeris, and bi- sou3te[n] God, that he schulde delyuere hir fro this schenschip. Forsothe[o] it was doon 12 in the thridde dai, while sche hadde fillid[p] the[q] preier, sche blesside the Lord, and 13 seide, God of oure fadris, thi name is blessid, which[r] whanne thou hast be wrooth, schalt do[s] merci, and in tyme of tribulacioun for3yuest[t] synnes[u] to hem,

d of A.   e ne A.

b Om. I.   i not withoute eend s.   k neither is.   l fadris trespassis I.   m haue not obeied is.   n thin hestis is.   o and therfor is.   P langlyng is.   q grete and dredeful is.   r thin hestis is.   s aftir is.   t Om. I.   u forsothe is.   v also is.   w that in s.   x spoken of I. seide to hir silf of s.   y hoond maidens isx.   z Sara is.   a hem alle s.   b hir, wilnyng hir for hir fleshli lust s.   c And is.   d Sara is.   e hir maide is.   f sleestere i. quellere ii sec. m.   g neuere upon erthe i. no more vpon erthe s.   h Om. is.   i Om. is.   k word s.   l Sara s.   m holi preier s.   n sche bisou3te is.   o And is.   p fulfillid is.   q hir is.   r the which i.   s of thi goodnesse do s.   t thou for3yuest is.   u synne s.

15 rere. I aske, Lord, that fro the bond of
this repref thou asoile me, or certis fro
16 aboue the[f] erthe thou delyuere me. Thou
wost, Lord, for neuere I coueitide man,
and clene I haue kept my soule fro alle
17 lust. Neuere with pleieres I mengde me,
ne with hem that in liȝtnesse gon par-
18 cener I ȝaf me. An husbonde forsothe
with thi drede, not with my lust, I con-
19 sentide to taken. And or[g] I was vnwrthi
to hem, or thei parauenture to me weren
not wrthi; for parauenture to an other
20 man thou hast kept me. Forsothe in
21 mannys power is not thi counseil. That
forsothe for certein hath eche man that
herieth thee, for his lif, if in prouyng[h]
it were, shal ben crouned; if forsothe in
tribulacioun it were, it shal be deliuered;
and if in chastising it were, it shal ben
22 leful to come to thi merci. Forsothe thou
hast not delit in oure leesingus; for after
tempest thou makist reste, and after
teres sheding and weiling[i], ful out ioȝing
23 thou heeldest in. Be thi name, God of
24 Irael, blessid in to worldus. In that time
ben herd ful the preȝeeris of bothe in the
siȝte of the glorie of the most good God;
25 and ther is sent an aungil of the Lord,
the holi Rafael, that he shulde curen hem
bothe, whos orisouns o time in the siȝte
of the Lord ben rehersid.

that inwardli clepen thee. Lord, to thee 14
Y turne togidere[v] my face; to[w] thee 'Y
reise[x] 'myn iȝen[xx]. Lord, Y axe[y], that thou 15
assoile[z] me[a] fro[b] the boond of this schenschip, ether certis that thou take me awei
fro aboue the[c] erthe. Lord, thou wost, 16
that Y neuere coueitide man[d], and Y[e] haue
kept my soule cleene fro al coueitise[f]. Y 17
medlide me neuere with pleieris†, nether
Y ȝaf me[g] parcener[h] with hem that goon
in vnstablenesse. But[i] Y consentide to 18
take an hosebonde with thi drede, not
with my lust. And ether Y was vnworthi 19
to hem, ether thei perauenture weren not
worthi to me; for in hap thou hast kept
me to another hosebonde. For[k] thi coun- 20
cel is not in the power of man[l]. Forsothe[m] 21
ech[n] that worschipith thee hath this[o] for
a[p] certeyn, that[q] if his lijf is[r] in preuyng,
he schal be corowned[s]; sotheli[t] if he is in
tribulacioun, he schal be delyuerid[u]; and
if he is in chastisyng‡, it schal be leueful[v]
to come to thi merci. For[w] thou delitist 22
not in oure lossis; for after tempest thou
makist pesible[x], and after morenyng and
wepyng thou bryngist yn ful ioye[y]. God 23
of Israel, thi name be[z] blessid 'in to
worldis, *that is, til[a] in to[b] withouten ende.*
In that tyme the preieris of bothe[c] weren 24
herd in the[d] siȝt of glorie[e] of hiȝeste[f] God;
and Raphael, the hooli aungel of the Lord, 25
was sent for[g] to heele hem bothe, whose
preyeris weren[h] rehersid in o tyme in the[i]
siȝt of the Lord.

† *pleieris*; dissolutly and vnonestly. *Lire here.* c.

‡ *in chastisyng*; an other lettre hath *in corupcioun*, that is, synneth bi ignoraunce ether freelte. *Lire here.* c.

CAP. IV.

1 Thanne whan Tobie wende his preȝeere to ben herd, that he myȝte dien, he
2 clepide to hym Tobie, his sone, and seide
to hym, Here, my sone, the woordis of
my mouth, and hem in thi herte as foun-
3 demens mak togidere. Whan God shal

CAP. IV.

Therfor whanne Tobie gesside his preier 1
to be herd, that he myȝte die, he clepide
Tobie, his sone, to hym silf[k], and seide to 2
hym, My sone, here thou the wordis of
my mouth, and bilde[l] thou tho[m] as foundementis[n] in thin herte. Whanne God 3

[f] Om. c. [g] other AEFH. [h] reprouynge AH. [i] wepinge AH.

[v] al togidre s. [w] and I lifte up [myn iȝen s] to IS. [x] Om. IS. [xx] Om. s. [y] axe *of thee* s. [z] louse IS. [a] me *out* IS. [b] of s. [c] Om. IS. [d] man *for fleshli lust* s. [e] that Y IS. [f] *vnleeful* coueitise IS. [g] myself IS. [h] *to be* parcener IS. [i] But, *Lord* IS. [k] Certis IS. [l] man *to knowe it* s. [m] But IS. [n] ech *man* IS. [o] this *thing* IS. [p] Om. ISg. [q] *as bileue* that s. [r] is *here* IS. [s] crowned, *if he continue pacientli* s. [t] and IS. [u] delyuerid *whan best tyme is* s. [v] leueful *to him* IS. [w] Certis IS. [x] pesible *wedre* IS. [y] outioiynge IS. [z] is g. [a] Om. x. [b] Om. IS. [c] bothe *Tobie and Sara* IS. [d] Om. IS. [e] the glorie IS. [f] the hiȝest s. [g] Om. IS. [h] *of holi aungels* weren s. [i] Om. I. [k] Om. IS. [l] grounde IS. [m] hem IS. [n] a foundement IS.

take my soule, my bodi birie; and wrshipe
thou shalt han to thi moder alle the daȝes
4 of thi lif; forsothe myndeful thou owist
to be, what and hou grete she suffride
5 perilis for thee in hir wombe. Whan
forsothe and she haue fulfild the time of
hir lif, thou shalt birien hir aboute me.
6 Alle forsothe the daȝes of thi lif in mynde
haue thou^k God, and bewar, lest any time
to synne thou consente, and leie aside the
7 hestis of oure God. Of thi substaunce do
almesse deede, and wile thou not turne
awei thi face fro any pore man; so forsothe it shal be do, that neither fro thee
he turned awei the face of the Lord.
8 What maner wise thou shalt moun, so
9 be thou merciful. If myche were to thee,
abundauntli ȝif; if litil ther were, also
10 litil gladli studie to parten. Forsothe a
good meede to thee thou tresorist in the
11 dai of nede; for almesse deede fro alle
synne and fro deth delyuereth, and shal
not suffre the soule to gon in to derc-
12 nesses. Gret trost shal ben almesse deede
befor the most goode God to alle men
13 doende it. Tac heede to thee, sone, fro
alle fornicacioun, and, beside thi wif, neuer
suffre thou synne of euel-los to knowen.
14 Pride neuer in thi wit or in thi woord
suffre thou to han lordshipe; in it for-
15 sothe al perdicioun toe begynnyng. Who
so euere^l any thing to thee wercheth,
anoon ȝeeld his meede, and the meed of
thin hiryd man algate anent thee abijde
16 not. That of an other thou hatist to be
do to thee, looke thou, that any time thou
17 do^m not to an other. Thi bred with the
hungri and with the nedi ett, and of thi
18 clothis nakide men couere. Thi bred
and thi win vp on the sepulture of the
riȝtwise ordeyne, and wile thou not of

hath take my soule, byrie thou my bodi;
and 'thou schal haue onour to thi modir^o
in alle the daies of hir^p lijf^q; for^r thou
owist to be myndeful, what perels and
how grete^s sche suffride for thee in hir
wombe. Forsothe^t whanne also sche hath
fillid^u the tyme of hir lijf, thou schalt
birie hir bisidis me. Sotheli^v in alle the
daies of thi lijf haue thou God in mynde,
and be thou war, lest ony tyme thou consente to synne, and forsake the heestis of
oure God. Of^w thi^x catel do thou almes,
and nyle thou turne awei thi face fro ony
pore† man; for^y so it schal be doon, that
the face of the Lord be not turned awei
fro thee. As thou maist^z, so^a be thou
merciful. If thou hast myche^b, ȝyue thou^c
plenteuousli; if^d thou hast a litil, also be
thou bisi to departe wilfuli^e a^f litil. For^g
thou tresorist to thee a good meede in the
dai of nede; for whi almes delyuereth fro
al synne and fro deeth^h, and schal^i not
suffre the soule to go in to^k derknessis^l.
Almes schal be grete^m trist bifor the hiȝeste God to alle men doynge it^o. Sone,
take heede to thi silf, and^p fle fro al fornicacioun, and, 'outakun thi wijf^r, suffre
thou neuere^s to know^t synne^u. Suffre^v
thou neuere pride to haue lordschip in thi
wit, nether in thi word; for al 'los, ether^w
dampnacioun, took biginnyng in that^x
pride. Who euere worchith ony thing to
thee, ȝelde thou anoon his mede, and outirli
the hire of 'thin hirid man^y dwelle^z not at^a
thee. That^b that thou hatist to be doon
to thee of another man, se^c thou^d, lest ony
tyme thou do^e to another man. Ete thi
breed^f with hungri men and nedi, and
with thi clothis hile thou nakid men. Ordeyne thi breed and thi wiyn on the sepul-
ture^g‡ of a iust man, and nyle thou ete

† any pore; if thou maist not ȝyue catel, ȝyue thou wille and signe of com-passioun. Lire here. c.

‡ on the sepul-cre; not to sette medis on the sepulcris of deed men, as if deed men hadden nede to bodily metis, nether to make grete feestis for prideether veyn glorie, in the deth of myȝty men; but that pore men be fed in the deth of iust men, for the soulis of hem. Lire here. c.

k Om. A.   l Om. A.   m do it A.

o Om. is.   p thi is.   q lijf thou schalt do honour to thi modir is.   r forsothe is.   s grete perels i.
t And is.   u endid is.   v And is.   w And of s.   x thi owne is.   y and is.   z maist, (that is, after thi power s.   a Om. is.   b myche catel is.   c it is.   d and if is.   e gladly is.   f that is.   g Certis thanne i.
Certis if thou thus doist s.   h deeth of helle B.   i it schal is.   k Om. cx.   l depenesse D. derknesse EL.
m the gret s.   o it as God techith i. it after Goddis heste s.   P Om. e.   q fle thou awey i. fle thou s.
r Om. is.   s neuere thee i. neuer eny s.   t know of thee s.   u that hidous synne, outaken thi wijf is.
v And suffre is.   w Om. is.   x Om. is.   y thi werk man is.   z dwelle it is.   a with s.   b That thing is.
c loke i.   d thou waarly i. thou, or bewar s.   e do that thing is.   f mete i.   g biriyng is.

19 it eten and drinke with the sinful. Coun-
20 seil euermor of the wise man seek. Alle
time blesse God, and aske of hym, that
thi weies he make redi, and alle thi coun-
21 seilis in hym abijde stille. I shewe also to
thee, my sone, me to han ʒiue ten talentus
of seluer, whil ʒit thou were a litil faunt,
to Gabel, in Ragis, cite of Medis; and
22 the writ of it anent me I haue; and
therfore enserche, what maner to hym
thou come, and resceyue of hym the
aboue membrid weiʒte of siluer, and re-
23 store to hym his writ. Wile thou not
dreden, sone myn; a pore lijf forsothe
wee bern, but manye goodis wee shul
han, if wee drede God, and gon awei fro
alle synne, and do wel.

CAP. V.

1 Thanne answerde Tobie to his fader,
and seide, Alle thingus, what euere thou
hast comaundid to me, fader, I shal do ;
2 thou forsothe this monei I shal enserche,
I knowe not ; he me knowith not, and I
hym vnknowe ; what tocne shal I ʒiue to
hym ? but neither the weie, bi the whiche
3 me goth thider, any time I knew. Thanne
his fader answerde to hym, and seide,
Forsothe his writ anent me I haue, the
whiche whanne thou to hym shewist,
4 anoon he shal ʒelde the monee. But go
now, and enserche to thee sum feithful
man, that go with thee, saued his meede,
whil ʒit I liue, that thou resceyue it.
5 Thanne Tobie gon out, fond a ʒung man
stondende, ful fair, gird, and as redi to
6 gon ; and vnknowende that an aungil
of God he was, grette hym, and seide,
Whennus han wee thee, goode ʒunge
7 man? And he answerde, Of the sonus
of Irael. And Tobie seide to hym, Hast
thou knowen the weie, that ledeth in to
8 the regioun of Medis ? To whom[n] he
answerde, I haue knowen, and alle the

and drynke therof with synneris. Euere 19
seke thou perfitli a[h] counsel of a wijs man.
Al[l] tyme blesse thou God, and axe thou 20
of hym, that he dresse thi weies, and alle
thi counsels dwelle[k] in hym. Also, my 21
sone, Y schewe to thee, that the[l] while
thou were ʒit a litil child, Y ʒaf ten talentis of siluer to Gabelus, in[m] Rages, a
citee of Medeis[n] ; and Y[o] haue his obligacioun anentis me ; and[p] therfor perfitli[q] 22
enquere thou[r], hou thou schalt come to
hym, and resseyue[s] of hym the forseid
weiʒte of siluer, and restore to hym his
obligacioun. My sone, nyle thou drede ; 23
forsothe we leden a pore lijf, but we schulen haue many goodis, if we dreden God,
and goen[t] awei fro al synne†, and doen
wel.

CAP. V.

Thanne Tobie answeride to his fadir, 1
and seide, Fadir, Y schal do alle thingis,
which euer thou comaundidist to me ; but 2
Y noot, hou Y schal gete this money ; he[u]
knowith not me, and Y knowe not him ;
what tokyn schal Y ʒyue to hym? but
nether Y knew ony tyme the weie, bi
which me goith thidur. Thanne his fadir 3
answerid to hym, and seide, Sotheli[v] Y
haue this[w] obligacioun at[x] me, which the
while thou schewist[y] to him, he schal restore anoon the monei. But go[z] now, and 4
enquere to thee sum feithful man, that
schal go with thee for his hire saf, ʻthe
while Y lyue ʒit[a], that[b] thou resseyue that
monei[c]. Thanne Tobie ʒede out[d], and 5
foond[e] a[f] ʒong‡ oon[g] stondynge, ʻschyn-
ynge, and gird[h], and as redi to go ; and 6
he[i] wiste not, that it[k] was the angel of
God. And he grette[l] the ʒong oon[m], and
seide, Of whennus han we thee, goode[n]
ʒonge man? And he answeride, Of[o] the 7
sones of Israel§. And Tobie seide to hym,
Knowist thou the weie, that ledith in to
the cuntrei of Medeis? To whom he an- 8

† al synne ;
dedly, for we
moun not
outirly eschewe
al venyal in
this liyf. Lire
here. c.

‡ a ʒong ; that
is, an aungel
apperinge in
the licnesse of
a ʒong man.
schynynge ;
that is, ful
faire in the
face. Lire
here. c.
§ of Israel ;
the aungel
seide soth,
thouʒ he were
no man, for
tho thingis that
ben doon of
aungels among
men, ben
thingis of
fygure, and by
this speche he
signefieth the
ioynyng to
gidere of cha-
rite, by which
hooly aungels
ben ioyned with
deuout feithful
men. Lire
here. c.

n the whiche E pr. m.

h Om. 1s.   i In al 1s.   k dwelle thei perfjily 1s.   l Om. 1.   m that dwellith in 1s.   n the cuntrey of
Medeis s.   o Om. H.   p Om. 1s.   q Om. 1s.   r thou bisily 1s.   s resseyne thou 1.   t if we goen 1.
u Gabelus 1s.   v Certis 1s.   w his 1.   x here anentis 1s.   y schewist it 1s.   z go thou s.   a Om. 1s.
b and that s.   c monei ʒit while I liue 1s.   d forth 1s.   e he foond 1s.   f a schynynge 1s.   g man 1s.
h tuckid up 1s.   i Tobie s.   k he 1.   l saluede 1. salutide s.   m man 1s.   n Om. g.   o I am of 1s.

weies of it oftesithes I haue go, and haue
dwellid anent Gabel, ȝoure brother, that
dwelleth in Ragis, cite of Medis, that is
9 sett in the hil of Exbatenys.   To whom
Tobie seith, Suffre me, I beseche, to the
time these thingus I telle to my fader.
10 Thanne Tobie, gon in, shewide° alle these
thingus to his fader ; vpe the whiche the
fader, wundrid, preȝede, that he shulde
11 comen in to hym ; and so gon in, salutide hym, and seide, Ioȝe to thee euer-
12 mor be ! And Tobie seith, What ioȝe to
me shal be, thatᴾ in derknesses sitte, and
13 the liȝt of heuene see not ? To whom
seith the ȝunge man, In strong inwit be
thou ; ful neeȝ it is that of God thou be
14 curid. And so seide Tobie to hym, Whether shalt thou mown ful lede my sone
to Gabel in to Ragis, cite of Medis, and
whan thou comest aȝeen, I shal ȝelde thee
15 thi meede ? And the aungil seide to hym,
I shal leden, and aȝeen lede hym to thee
16 hol. To whom answerde Tobie, I preȝe
thee, shew to me, of what hous, and of
17 what linage thou art ? To whom Rafael,
the aungil, seide, The kinrede thou askist
of the hirid man, or that hirid man, that
18 with thi sone go ? But lest parauenture
I make thee stirid, I am Azarie, the sone
19 of greteᑫ Ananye. And Tobie answerde,
Of gret kinrede thou art ; but I aske, be
thou not wroth, for I wolde knowe thi
20 kinrede. Forsothe the aungil seide to
hym, I sound shal lede, and sound shalʳ
21 aȝeen bringe to thee thi sone. Forsothe
Tobie answerende seide, Wel go ȝee,
and the Lord be in ȝoure weie, and his
22 aungil folewe with ȝou. Thanne alle
thingus maad redi, that weren to be born
in the weie, Tobie dide farewel to his
fader and to his moder ; and thei wente
23 bothe togidere. And whan thei weren

sweride, Y knoweᴾ, and Y haue go ofte
alle the weies therof, and Y haue dwellid
atᑫ Gabelus, ȝoure brotherʳ, thatˢ dwellith
in Rages, a citee of Medeis, whichᵗ is set
in 'the hil ofᵘ Echbathanis.   To whom 9
Tobie seide, Y bisecheᵛ, abide thou meᵂ,
til Y telle these thingis to my fader.
Thanne Tobie entride, and teldeˣ alle 10
these thingis to his fader ; on whichʸ
thingis theᶻ fader wondrideᵃ, and preiedeᵇ,
that he wolde entreᶜ to him. Therforᵈ he 11
entride, and gretteᵉ Tobie, and seideᶠ, Ioie
be euere to thee ! And Tobie seide, What 12
maner† ioie schal be to me, that sitte in
derknessis, and se not 'the liȝtˢ of he-
ueneʰ ? To whom the ȝong oonˡ seide, Be 13
thou of strong witᵏ ; it is in the nexteˡ
that thou be heelid of God. Therforᵐ 14
Tobie seide to hym, Whether thou maist
lede my sone to Gabelus in to Rages, theⁿ
citee of Medeis, and whanne thou comest
aȝen, Y schal restore thi mede to thee?
And the aungel seide to hym, Y schal 15
ledeᵒ, andᴾ bringeᑫ aȝen him hool to thee.
To whom Tobie answeride, Y preie thee, 16
schewe to me, of what hows, ethir of what
lynage thou art ? To whom Raphael, the 17
aungel, seide, Axist thou the kyn ofʳ the
hirid man, ethirˢ the hirid man hym silf,
that schal go with thi sone ? But lest 18
perauenture Y make thee douteful, Y am
Azarieᵗ, the sone of greteᵗ Ananye. And 19
Tobie answeride, Thou art of greet kyn ;
but Y axeⁿ, that thou be not wrooth, that
Y wolde knowe thi kyn. Forsotheᵛ the 20
aungel seide to hym, Y schal ledeᵂ thi
sone hool, and Y schal bring aȝenʸ to
thee 'thi sone hoolᶻ. Sotheliᵃ Tobie an- 21
sweride, and seide, Wel 'go ȝeᵇ, and the
Lord be in ȝoure weie, and his aungel go
with ȝou. Thanne whanne alle thingis 22
weren redi, that schulden be borunᶜ in

† what maner ;
he seide not
this by vnpa-
cience of his
blyndnesse, but
dispisinge the
ioye of present
lijf, and hop-
inge the ioye
of lijf to com-
ynge. Lire
here. c.

‡ Azarie ; the
aungel seide
soth, for his
speche was
fyguratif. Aza-
rie is inter-
pretid the hel-
pere of God ;
treuly goode
aungels ben
the helperis of
God, in as
myche as eho-
sun men ben
dressid in to
helthe bi the
seruyce of hem ;
and thus seith
Poul of him
silf and othere
prechouris in
the firste pistle
to Cor. iij. c⁰.
We ben the
helperis of
God. Ananye
is interpretid
the grace of
God, whos
sones aungels
ben in that
maner, bi which
they ben seid
the sones of
glorie, which is
grace fully
endid, ethir
perfit ; but
Tobie vndur-
stood that he
was a man, the
sone of sum
noble man of
Israel, but the
aungel dis-
seyuede not
Tobie in this,
for Tobie hadde
thus before his
purpos. Lire
here. c.

º and shewide ᴀɪɪ.   ᴾ the whiche ᴀᴇꜰɪɪ.   ᑫ the greet preest ᴀ. ᵣ I shal ᴀ.

ᴾ knowe it ɪꜱ.   ᑫ with ɪꜱ.   ʳ cosyn ɪꜱ.   ˢ which ꜱ.   ᵗ the which citee ɪ. which cite ꜱ.   ⁿ Om. ɪꜱ.   ᵛ biseche
thee ꜱ.   ᵂ me here ꜱ.   ˣ he telde ɪ.   ʸ the which ɪ.   ᶻ his ɪ.   ᵃ a wondride how he had ꜱo soon geten him a
felowe ꜱ.   ᵇ he preiede the ȝounge man ɪ.   ᶜ entre yn ꜱ.   ᵈ Thanne ɪ.   ᵉ saluede ɪ. salutide ꜱ.   ᶠ seide to
him ɪꜱ.   ᵍ Om. ꜱ.   ʰ the eir ɪ.   ˡ man ɪꜱ.   ᵏ inwitt ɪɪɪ.   ˡ moost niȝ tyme ɪꜱ. ful nyȝ ɪɪ sec. m.   ᵐ Thanne ɪ.
ⁿ n ɪꜱ.   ᵒ lede him ɪɪ sec. m. lede him thidere ɪꜱ.   ᴾ and I schal ɪꜱ.   ᑫ lede plures.   ʳ of me ꜱ.   ˢ ethir
axist thou who is ɪꜱ.   ᵗ the grete ɪ.   ᵘ axe [thee ꜱ] or preie thee ɪꜱ.   ᵛ And ɪꜱ.   ᵂ lede forth ɪꜱ.
ˣ lede plures.   ʸ him aȝen hool ɪꜱ.   ᶻ Om. ɪɪ.   ᵃ And ɪ.   ᵇ mote ȝe go ɪɪ sec. m.   ᶜ borne with him ꜱ.

go forth, his moder began to wepen, and sein, The staf of oure elde thou hast taken awei, and hast sent ouer fro vs; 24 neuere hadde be that monee, for the 25 whiche thou sentist hym; forsothe oure porenesse suffiside to vs, that richessis wee shulden counte that, that oure sone 26 wee sezen. And Tobie seide to hir, Wile thou not wepen; saf shal comen oure sone, and saf shal azeen turne to vs, and thin 27 ezen shul seen hym. I leeue forsothe, that the goode aungil of God folewes[s] hym, and wel shal disposen alle thingus, that ben don aboute hym, so that with ioze 28 he be turned azeen to vs. At this vois ceside his modir to wepen, and was stille.

the weie[d], Tobie made 'farewel to[e] his fadir and his[f] modir[g]; and 'bothe zeden[h] togidere. And whanne thei[i] weren goon 23 forth, his modir bigan to wepe, and to seie[k], Thou hast take the staf[l]† of oure eelde, and hast sent[m] awey fro vs; 'Y 24 wolde[n] thilke[o] monei were[p] neuere[q], 'for which[r] thou sentist[s] him[t]; oure pouert 25 sufficide to vs, that we schulden arette[u] this[v] richessis[w], that we sien[x] oure sone[y]. And Tobie seide to hir, 'Nyle thou wepe[a]; 26 oure sone schal come saaf[b], and he schal turne azen saaf to vs, and thin izen schulen se hym. For[c] Y bileue, that the good 27 aungel of God[d] goith with him, and he[e] schal dispose wel alle thingis, that ben doon aboute hym, so that he turne azen with ioie to vs. At this vois[f] his moder 28 ceesside to wepe, and was stille.

† the staf that is, the susteyn-yng, for chil-dren owen to fadris and mo-dris the ser-uyce of re-uerence, and of nedeful purnyaunce, if they han nede. Lire here. c.

CAP. VI.

1 Tobie forsothe wente forth, and an hound folewide hym, and he abod the firste abiding biside the flod of Tigris. 2 And he wente out for[t] to wasshen his feet; and lo! a gret fish wente out for[t] 3 to denouren hym. Whom dredende Tobie criede out[u] with a gret vois, seiende, 4 Lord, he asaileth[v] me. And the aungil seide to hym, Cach his fin, and draz it to thee. The whiche thing whan he hadde do, he droz it in to the drie, and 5 it began to quappe befor his feet. Thanne the aungil seide to hym, Opene this fish, and his herte and galle and mawe lei vp to thee; these thingus forsothe ben pro-6 fitabli necessarie to medicynes. The whiche thingus whan he hadde do, he

CAP. VI.

Forsothe[g] Tobie zede forth, and 'a dogge[h] 1 suede hym, and he[i] dwellide[k] in the firste dwellyng[l] bisidis the flood of[m] Tigrys. And he 'zede out[n] to waische hise feet; 2 and lo! a greet fisch zede out' to deuoure hym. Which[p] fisch Tobie dredde, and 3 criede[q] with greet vois, and seide, Sire, he[r] assailith me. And the aungel seide 4 to hym, Take 'thou his[s] gile, 'ether iowe[t], and drawe hym to thee. And whanne he[u] hadde do this thing, he drow it[v] in to the[w] drie place, and it bigan to spranle bifor[x] hise[y] feet[z]. Thanne the aungel seide to 5 hym[a], Drawe out the entrails of this fisch, and kepe to thee his herte and[b] galle and mawe[c]; for[d] these thingis ben nedeful to[e] medicyns profitabli[f]. And whanne he[g] 6

s folewith *A.*   t Om. *c.*   u Om. *AU.*   v coometh on *E pr. m.*

d weie *with hem* 1.   e Om. s.   f Om. g.   g moder to fare wel s.   h thei walkiden forth bothe 1.   i the aungel and Tobie 1s.   k seie *to cold Tobie* 1. seie *to Tobie hir husbond* s.   l staf *or the sustynaunce* 1. m sent *him* 1s.   n Om. A *pr. m. et plures.* wolde God H *sec. m.*   o that 11s. that that 1.   p had H1s. q neuere ben 1118.   r that 1.   s hast sent 1s.   t him fore 1.   u haue arettid 1s.   v this thing *to be* 1. w richessis *to us* 1s.   x han seen 1s.   y sone *bisidis vs* s.   z Wepe thou not 1.   b saaf *thidere* 1s. c Sothly 1s.   d the Lord s.   e *that aungel* 1. *that the aungel* s.   f vois *or word* 1s.   g And 1s.   h an hound 1s.   i Tobie 1s.   k abood 1. duellide *or abood* s.   l dwellyng *of his iourney* 1. duellyng *or restyng of her first iorney* s.   m Om. BCEF *pr. m.* 11 *pr. m.* LPUVX.   n wente forth 1. zede forth s.   o out azens *him* s.   p The which 1.   q therfor he criede 1s.   r this *fisch* 1s.   s the fisch bi the 1s.   t Om. 1. *or bi the iowe* s.   u Tobie 1s.   v the fisch 1s.   w a 1s.   x to fore g.   y the 1. Om. s.   z feet of Tobie 1. Tobie 8. a Tobie 1s.   b his 1s.   c his mawe 1s.   d certis 1s.   e and to s.   f thei *helpen* profitabli 1. thei *wolen help* profitabli s.   g Tobie 1s.

rostide his flesh^w, and beren with hem
in the weie ; the tother thei saltiden, that
shulden suffise to them in the weie, to
the time that thei shulden ful come in to
7 Ragis, cite of Medis. Thanne Tobie askide the aungil, and seide to hym, I beseche, Asarie, brother, that thou sei to
me, what remedie shuln han these
thingus, that of the fish thou hast co-
8 maundid to be kept. And the aungil
answerende seide to hym, A parcel of
his herte if thou putte vp on the^x colis,
his smoke putteth out al the kinde of
deuelis, outher fro man or fro womman,
so that he come no more nee3 to hem.
9 And the galle is worth to e3en to ben
enointid, in the whiche were rime, and
10 thei shul ben hol. And Tobie seide to
hym, Where wilt thou, that wee dwelle?
11 And the aungil answerende seith, Heer
is a man, Raguel bi name, nee3 of thi
linage, and this hath a do3ter, Sara bi
name; but any other he hath saue hir,
12 neither male ne femele. To thee is due
al his substaunce ; and thee behoueth to
13 han hir wif. Aske thanne bir of hir
fader ; and he shal 3iue to thee hir wif.
14 Thanne answerde Tobie, and seide, I haue
herd, for she hath ben take to seuene men,
and thei ben deade; but and these thingus
15 I haue herd, for a deuel slo3 hem. I drede
thanne, lest parauenture and these thingus
fallen to me ; and sithen I am alone to
my fader and moder, I putte doun the
16 eelde of hem wyth sorewe to helle. Thanne
aungil Rafael seide to hym, Here me,
and I shal shewe to thee, who ben, to
17 whom mai the deuel han maistrie; in
hem, that wedloc so taken, that God fro
them and fro ther mynde thei closen

hadde do this^h thing^i, he rostide 'hise
fleischis^k, and thei token^l 'with hem in
the weie^m ; thei^n saltiden othere thingis^o,
that schulde suffice to hem in the weie,
til thei camen in to Rages, the^p citee of
Medeis. Thanne Tobie axide the aungel, 7
and seide to hym, Azarie, brother, Y biseche thee, that thou seie to me, what re-
medie^q these thingis schulen haue, whiche^r
thou comaundidist^s to be kept of the fisch.
And the aungel answeride, and seide to 8
hym, If thou puttist a lytil part of his
herte on^t the^u coolis^v, the smoke therof
dryueth awei+ al the^w kynde of feendis,
ethir fro man ether fro womman, so that
it nei3e^x no more to hem. And the galle^y 9
is myche worth to anoynte^z i3en, in whiche
is a web, and tho^a schulen be^b heelid. And 10
Tobie seide to him, Where wolt thou, that
we dwelle^c? And the aungel answeride, 11
and seide, Here is a man, Raguel bi name,
a ny3^d man of thi lynage, and he hath a
dou3tir, Sare bi name; but nether he hath
male^e nethir ony other femal^f, outakun hir.
Al his catel is due to thee ; and it bihoueth 12
thee^g haue hir to wijf^h. Therfor axe thou 13
hir of hir fadir ; and he schal 3yue 'hir a^i
wijf to thee^k. Thanne Tobie answeride^l, 14
and seide, Y haue herd, that sche^m was
3ouun to seuene hosebondis, and thei^n ben
deed ; but also^o Y herde^p this^q, that a fend
killide hem. Therfor^r Y dredde, lest per- 15
auenture also^s these^t thingis bifalle to me;
and sithen^u Y am con^v aloone^w to my fadir and modir^x, Y putte^y doun 'with sorewe her eelde to hellis^z+. Thanne the 16
aungel Raphael seide to hym^a, Here thou
me, and Y schal schewe to thee, 'whiche
it^b ben, ouer whiche^c the fend hath maistrie ; ouer^d hem, that taken so weddyngys^e, 17

† dryueth awey; that is, figurith the putting awey of feendis, for the dedis of the aungel aboute Tobie weren figuratif in many thingis; therfor thilke smoke figuride the virtu of preyer of 3ongere Tobie and of Sare, hi whos merit the aungel Raphael puttide awey the fend fro Sare; wherfor it is seid in viij. c°. that not thilke smoke droof awey the fend, but that Raphael took him, and boond him in the hi3ere partis of Egipt; for sithen aungels ben outirly creaturis of vndurstonding, and han no bodies kyndly to hem, no material creature may make othir prenting in hem, wherfor this smoke puttide not awey the fend, but figuride his putting awey. Lire here. c.

‡ hellis; he dredde lest if he were deed, that his fadir and modir schulden be vnpacient for sorewe, and so die bothe bodily and goostly. Lire here. c.

w fish A H.   x Om. A H.

h these B C. the g.   i thingis B.   k the fleisch therof IS. hise flesch R. the fleisch of the fisch A.   l token
that fleisch and baren it forth IS.   m in the weie with hem IS.   n and thei IS.   o thingis of that fiske I.
thingis or remenauntis of that fissh S.   P a S.   q remedies S.   r which thingis S.   s hast comaundid IS.
comaundist fg.   t upon IS.   u Om. IS.   v hoot coolis IS.   w Om. IS.   x schal nei3e I.   y galle of the
[this S] fisch IS.   z anoynte with IS.   a thei I.   b be ther thur3 S.   c abiden I. duelle or abyde S.   d Om. I.
e knaue child I. male childe S.   f maide child I.   g thou moste I.   h thi wijf I.   i Om. S.   k thee hir to
wijf n sec. m.   l answerede to him IS.   m this Sara IS.   n alle thei IS.   o Om. I.   P haue herd IS.   q this
also I.   r and therfor IS.   s Om. S.   t Om. I.   u sith I.   v an IS.   w oonly soue IS.   x to my modir B.
y drede to putte IS.   z to helle her eelde with drurynesse IS.   a Tobie IS.   b who thei IS.   c whom IS.
d certis ouer I. certis the feend hath power ouer S.   e her weddyngis IS.

out, and to ther lustis so thei taken
heede, as an hors and a mule, in the
whiche is not vnderstonding, hath vpon
18 hem the deuel power. Thou forsothe,
whan thou shalt taken hir, gon in to the
bed place, bi thre dazes be thou continent
fro hir, and no thing other but to prei-
19 eeris thou shalt stonde in with hir. That
nyzt forsothe the mawe of the fish brent,
20 the deuel shal be dryuen awei. The secunde forsothe nyzt in the coupling[y] of
holi patriarkis thou shalt ben admittid.
21 The thridde forsothe nyzt blessing thou
shalt gete, that sonus be goten of zou
22 sounde. The thridde forsothe nyzt ouerpassid, thou shalt take the maiden with
the drede of the Lord, and for looue of
sonus more than of lust lad, that in the
sed of Abraham thou gete blessing in
sonus.

that thei close out God fro hem and fro
her mynde; 'the fend hath power ouer
hem[f], that[g] zyuen so tent[h] to her[i] letcherie,
as an[k] hors[l] and mule[m] *doon*[n], 'that han[o]
noon vndurstondyng[p]. But whanne thou 18
hast take hir[q], entre thou[r] in to the[s] bed[t],
and bi thre daies be thou continent[u] 'fro
hir[v], and to noon other thing[w] thou schalt
zyue tent[x] with hir, no[y] but[z] to preieris.
Forsothe[a] in that[b] *firste* nizt, whanne the 19
mawe of the fisch is[c] brent, the fend[d] schal
be dryuun awei[e]. Sotheli[f] in the secounde 20
nyzt thou[g] schalt be resseyued in the[h] couplyng[i] of hooli patriarkis[k]. Forsothe[l] in 21
the thridde nyzt thou[m] schalt gete blessyng[n], that hoole sones[o] be gendrid of zou.
But whanne the thridde nizt is passid, 22
thou schalt take the virgyn with the[p]
drede of the Lord, and thou[q] schalt be
led[r] more bi the loue of children[s] than
of[t] lust[u], that in the seed of Abraham
thou gete blessyng in sones[v].

CAP. VII.

1 Forsothe thei wenten in to Raguel;
and Raguel resceyuede hem with ioze.
2 And Raguel, beholdende Tobie, seide to
Anne, his wif, Hou lic is this zunge man
3 to oure auntis sone. And whan these
thingus he hadde seid, he seith, Whennus
be zee, zunge men, my brethern? And
thei seiden, Of the linage of Neptalim
4 wee ben, of the caitifte of Nynyue. Raguel
seide to them, Knowe zee Tobie, my brother? The whiche answerden, Wee han
5 knowen. And whan he spac of[z] hym
manye goode thingus, the aungil seide to
Raguel, Tobie, of the[a] whiche thou askest,
6 is thisis fader. And Raguel putte hym

CAP. VII.

'Forsothe thei[w] entriden to Raguel; and 1
Raguel[x] resseyuede hem with ioie. And 2
Raguel bihelde Tobie, and seide[y] to Anne,
his wijf, This zong man is ful lijk my
sister sone. And whanne he[z] hadde seid 3
these thingis[a], he seide, Of whennus ben
ze, zonge men, oure britheren? And thei
seiden, We ben of the lynage of Neptalym, of the caitifte of Nynyue. And Ra- 4
guel seide to hem, Knowen ze Tobi, my
brother? Whiche[b] answeriden, We knowen
him[c]. And 'whanne he spak[d] manye good 5
thingis of Tobie, the aungel seide to Raguel[e], Tobie, of whom thou axist, is the
fadir of this man. Thanne Raguel bow- 6

[y] counseilynge AH. [z] to A. [a] Om. C.

[f] Om. IS. [g] and that IS. [h] her bisinesse S. [i] Om. S. [k] Om. I. [l] hors *doith* S. [m] a mule S. [n] Om. IS. [o] in whom is S. [p] vndirstondyng, *ouer hem the feend hath maistrie* I. [q] hir *to wijf* S. [r] Om. S. [s] thi S. [t] bed place S. [u] chast IS. [v] absteynyng thee from hir *in al fleshli lust* S. [w] thing *in that* [*this* S] *tyme* IS. [x] thi bisynesse I. the bisinesse S. [y] Om. I. [z] but oonly I. [a] Certis IS. [b] the IS. [c] schal be IS. [d] fend *therbi* IS. [e] awei *fro zou* S. [f] And IS. [g] *bi holi preier and bisi mynde* thou S. [h] Om. IS. [i] couplyng *or mariage* IS. [k] patriarkis, *whose mynde is withouten ende* S. [l] And IS. [m] *thurz thi holi preier and good purpose* thou S. [n] the blessyng *of God* IS. [o] sones *in rizt feith and other vertues* S. [p] Om. IS. [q] *in thi wil* thou S. [r] led *and moued* S. [s] *geting of* children IS. [t] bi IS. [u] lust *of flessh* S. [v] thi sones I. sones *bryngyng forth* S. [w] Thanne *the aungel and Tobie* IS. [x] he I. [y] he seide IS. [z] Raguel IS. [a] thingis *to his wijf* IS. [b] And thei IS. [c] Om. *plures*. [d] Raguel spekynge I. whan Raguel spake S. [e] him IS.

self, and with teres kiste hym, and wep-
7 ende vp on his necke, seide, Blessing be
to thee, sone myn; for of good and of the
8 beste man thou art sone[b]. And Anne,
his wif, and Sara, the doȝter of hem,
9 wepten. After forsothe that thei hadden
spoken, Raguel comaundede a wether to
be slain, and to be maad redi a feste.
And whan he besoȝte them to sitte doun
10 to the mete, Tobie seith, Heer I to dai
shal not ete, ne drinke, but if first myn
asking thou conferme, and thou behote
11 to ȝiue to me Sara, thi doȝter. The
whiche woord herd, Raguel dradde, witende what fel to thoo[c] seuene men; and
he began to dreden, lest parauenture lic
maner to this[d] shulde fallen, and he die.
And whan he doutede, and ȝaf not any
12 answere to the askere, the aungil seide
to hym, Wile thou not dreden to ȝiuen
hir to this; for to this dredende God
wif thi doȝtir is due; therfore an other
13 myȝte not han hir. Thanne seide Raguel, I doute not, that God preieeris[e] and
14 my teres in his siȝte hath taken. And
I trowe, for the Lord therfore made ȝou
to come to me, that and this shulde be
ioyned to hir kin after the lawe of
Moises; and now wile thou not bern
15 doute, for to thee hir I shal take[f]. And
takende the riȝt hond of his doȝter toc to
the riȝt hond of Tobie, seiende, God of
Abraham, and God of Isaac, and God of
Jacob, be with ȝou, and he[g] ioine ȝou,
16 and fulfille his blissing in ȝou. And the
chartre taken, thei maden the conscrip-
17 cioun of the wedloc. And after these
thingus thei plenteuousli eeten, blessende
18 God. And Raguel clepede to hym Anna,
his wif, and comaundede to hir, that she
19 shulde make redi an other bed place. And
he broȝte in to it Sara, his doȝter, and

ede[f] doun hym silf, and with teeris he
kisside Tobie, and he[g] wepte on[h] his
necke, and seide, My sone, blessyng be to 7
thee; for thou art the sone of a good[l] and
'a ful noble[k] man. And Anne, 'his wijf[l], 8
and Sare[m], 'the douȝtir of hem[n], wepten[o].
Forsothe[p] after that thei hadden spoke[q], 9
Raguel comaundide a wethir to be slayn,
and a feeste to be maad redi. And whanne
he[r] excitide[s] hem to sitte doun to mete,
Tobie seide, Y schal not ete, nethir drynke 10
here to dai, no[t] but thou conferme first
myn axyng, and biheete[u] to ȝyue to me
Sare, thi douȝter[v]. And whanne this word 11
was herd, Raguel dredde, witynge what
bifelde to tho[w] seuene men; and he[x] bigan for[y] to drede, lest perauenture it
schulde bifalle in lijk maner to this Tobie. And whanne he doutide[z], and ȝaf noou
answere to the axere, the aungel seide to 12
hym[a], Nyle thou drede to ȝyue hir to this
man; for thi douȝter 'is due wiyf[b] to this
man dredynge God; therfor another man
myȝte not haue hir. Thanne Raguel seide, 13
Y doute not, that[c] God hath resseyued my
preieris and teeris[d] in his siȝt. And Y 14
bileue, that herfor[e] the Lord made ȝou
come[f] to me, that also this womman
schulde be ioyned to her kynrede bi the
lawe of Moises; and now[g] nyle thou bere
doute[h], that Y schal ȝyue hir to thee.
And he[i] took the riȝt hond of his douȝter, 15
and ȝaf[k] to the riȝt hond of Tobie, and
seide, God of Abraham, and God of Isaac,
and God of Jacob, be with ȝou, and he
ioyne ȝou togidere, and 'he fille[l] his blessyng in ȝou. And whanne[m] a chartere 16
'was takun[n], thei[o] maden 'writyng togidere[p] of[q] the mariage. And aftir these 17
thingis thei eten, and blessiden God. And 18
Raguel clepide to hym Anne, his wijf,
and comaundide[r] hir to make redi another

---

[b] the sone c.   [c] the ᴀ.   [d] this man ᴀ.   [e] my preiers ᴀ.   [f] ȝyue ᴀ.   [g] Om. ᴀ.

[f] sente ᴇɴ pr. m. ʟxg.   [g] Raguel 18.   [h] upon 18.   [i] ful good 8.   [k] the best ʙᴇʟᴘᴜᴠxg. ful noble c pr. m. a noble 11 sec. m. noble 8.   [l] the wijf of Raguel 1. Raguelis wife 8.   [m] Om. 8.   [n] her douȝtir 18.   [o] wepten bothe 18.   [p] And 1.   [q] spoke thus 1. spoken thus togidre 8.   [r] Raguel 18.   [s] mourde 18. excite b.   [t] Om. 1.   [u] bihote 18.   [v] douȝter to wiif 18.   [w] the 18.   [x] Raguel 18.   [y] Om. 18.   [z] doutid or musyd in this mater 8.   [a] Raguel 18.   [b] owith to be ȝouen 18.   [c] that ne 18.   [d] my teeris 8.   [v] therfor 8.   [f] to come 1.   [g] now, Tobie 18.   [h] ony doute 1. douȝt in thin herte 8.   [i] Raguel 18.   [k] he ȝaf hir 1. ȝaue hir 8.   [l] fulfille he 18.   [m] thei token 18.   [n] Om. 18.   [o] and thei 18.   [p] togidere a writyng 18.   [q] of witnessyng of 18.   [r] he comaundide 18.

she wepte; and he seith to hir, In strong
inwit be thou, do3ter myn; the Lord of
heuene 3iue to thee io3e, for the no3e that
thou hast suffrid.

CAP. VIII.

1 Aftir forsothe that thei suppeden, thei
2 bro3ten the 3unge man in to hir. And
so Tobie recordid of the woordis of the
aungil, bro3te forth of his bagge a part
of the mawe, and putte it vp on the
3 quike colis. Thanne aungil Rafael ca3te
the deuel, and bond hym in the^h desert
4 of the ouere Egipt. Thanne Tobie be-
so3te the maiden, and seide to hir, Sara,
rijs, and pre3ee wee to dai toⁱ God, and
to moru, and the secunde moru; for
these thre ny3tis wee shul be ioined to
God; the thridde forsothe ny3t passid
5 ouer, wee shul ben in oure wedloc; sonus
forsothe of halewis wee ben, and wee
moun not so be ioyned as and Jentilis,
6 that vnknowen God. Risende forsothe
togidere, bisili thei pre3eden bothe togidere, that helthe shulde be 3iue to hem.
7 And Tobie seide, Lord God of oure fadris, blesse thee heuenus, and érthis, and
se, and wellis, and flodis, and eche thi
8 creature, that is in hem; thou^k madist
Adam of the slim of erthe^l, and thou 3eue
9 to hym helpe, Eue. And now, Lord, thou
wost, for not bicause of leccherie I take
my sister, but for onli loue of bringing
forth of childre, in the^m whiche be blessid
10 thi name in to worldis 'of worldisⁿ. Also
seide Sara, Haue merci to vs, Lord, haue
merci to vs, and eelde wee bothe togidere
11 hole. And it is do aboute chykenys^o crow-

---

bed. And sche ledde Sare, hir dou3tir, in 19
to it, and sche^s wepte; and Anne seide to
hir, My dou3ter, be thou of strong^t wit^u;
the Lord of heuene 3yue to^v thee ioie, for
the anoie that thou suffridist^w.

CAP. VIII.

1 Forsothe^x aftir that thei hadden soupid,
thei brou3ten in^y the 3ong man to^z hir.
2 Therfor^a Tobie^b bithou3te^c of^d the wordis
of the aungel, and 'brou3te forth^e of his
scrippe a part of the mawe^f, and puttide^g
3 it on^h quikeⁱ coolis. Thanne^k Raphael, the
aungel, took the fend, and boond^l hym^m in
4 theⁿ desert of hi3ere Egipte. Thanne^o
Tobie monestide^p the virgyn, and seide^q
to hir, Sare, rise vp, and preye we God to
dai, and to morewe, and 'the secounde^r
morewe; for in these thre ny3tis we ben
ioyned^s† to God^t; sotheli^u whanne the
thridde ny3t is passid, we schulen be^v 'in
5 oure mariage^w; for^x we ben the children
of hooli men, and we moun not so^y be
ioyned^z togidere^a as also^b hethene men^c,
6 that knowen not God. Sotheli thei ris-
iden^d togidere, and bothe^e preyeden togidere bisili, that helthe^f schulde be 3ouun
7 to hem. And Tobie seide, Lord God of
oure fadris, heuenes, and londis^g, and the
see, and wellis, and floodis, and ech crea-
8 ture of thin, which^h is in tho, blesse theeⁱ;
thou madist Adam of the sliym of erthe,
9 and 3auest^k to hym an help, Eue. And
now, Lord, thou woost, that Y take my
sistir^l not for cause of letcherie, but for
loue aloone of eeris^m, inⁿ whiche^o thi name
10 be blessid in to worldis^p of worldis. Ther-
for^q Sare seide, Lord, haue thou mercy on
vs, haue thou merci on vs, and waxe we

† ioyned; that
is, owen to be
ioyned to God
bi deuocioun
and preyer,
bifor that we
go to the dede
of matrimonye.
Lire here. c.

---

^h Om. AII.   ⁱ Om. AII.   ^k thou forsothe A.   ^l the erthe E pr. m.   ^m Om. AII.   ⁿ Om. c.
^o cokkis A.

^s Sare IS.   ^t a strong A pr. m.   ^u ynwitt H sec. m. IS.   ^v Om. EFGHIKLMSxafgh.   ^w hast suffrid IS.
^x And IS.   ^y Om. IS.   ^z Tobic in to IS.   ^a And I. And thanne S.   ^b he g.   ^c bithou3te him IS.   ^d Om. g.
^e he drewe out IS.   ^f mawe of the fische IS.   ^g he puttide IS.   ^h upon IS.   ⁱ the quyke g.   ^k And than S.
^l he a3en boond IS.   ^m hym faste IS.   ⁿ Om. sx.   ^o And than S.   ^p warnyde I. amonestide S.   ^q he
seide I.   ^r aftir to I.   ^s ioyned togidre s.   ^t God, to preie him hertli to dresse alle our waies s.   ^u and IS.
^v be ooned IS.   ^w mariage thorou drede and loue of the Lord s.   ^x certis IS.   ^y Om. IS.   ^z couplid IS.
^a togidre in wedlok s.   ^b Om. I.   ^c men ben s.   ^d resen EL. resen up I. riseden vp s.   ^e thei bothe IS.
^f helthe of body and of soule s.   ^g erthes I. alle londis s.   ^h that IS.   ⁱ it to thee I. to thee s.   ^k thou
3auest IS.   ^l sistir to wiif IS.   ^m getyng of children IS.   ⁿ into x.   ^o the whiche children getyng IS.
^p world cFHMQUVWxbfgh. the world EILOPRa. the worldis s.   ^q And thanne IS.

ing, Raguel comaundede his seruauns to
be clepid, and thei wenten[p] with hym
12 that thei delue a biriel[q]. Forsothe he
dradde, lest lic maner shulde falle to
hym, that and to the tothere seuene, that
13 wenten in to hir. And whan thei hadden
maad redi the pit, Raguel gon a3een to
14 his wif, seide to hir, Send oon of thin
hand wimmen, and see she, if he is dead,
15 that I birie hym, befor it waxe li3t. And
she sente oon of hir hand wimmen, the
whiche gon in to the bed place, fond hem
saue and sounde, slepende togidere with
16 hem self. And she, turned a3een, told
good message. And thei blesseden the
Lord, Raguel, that is, and Anna, his wif,
17 and seiden, Wee blessen thee, Lord God
of Irael, for it falleth not to vs, as we
18 wenden ; forsothe thou hast do with vs
thi mercy, and hast closid out fro vs the
19 enemy pursuende vs. Don thou hast
mercy to thi two alone. Mac hem, my
Lord, to bless thee more fulli, and to
offre to thee sacrifise of thi preising, and
of ther helthe, that the vnyuersite of
Jentilis knowe, for thou art God alone in
20 al erthe. And anoon Raguel comaundede
to his seruauntis, that thei shulden fille
the pit, that thei hadden maad, befor that
21 it waxe li3t. To his wif forsothe he
seide, that she shulde ordeyne a feste,
and make redi alle thingus, that in to
metis weren necessarie to weie goeris.
22 Also two fatte kijn, and foure wethcres he
made to be slain, and plenteuous metus to
ben maad redi to alle his ne3hebores, and
23 to alle his frendis. And Raguel adiurede Tobie, that two wikis he shulde
24 dwelle anent hym. Of alle thingus forsothe that Raguel weldede, the half part
he 3af to Tobie ; and he made this scrip-

bothe eelde togidere hoole[r]. And it was 11
doon aboute the 'cockis crowyng[s], Raguel
made hise seruauntis to be clepid, and
thei 3eden with hym to digge a sepulcre[t].
For[u] he dredde, lest it bifelde[v] in lijk 12
maner to hym[w], that bifelde also to 'seuene othere[x] men, that[y] entriden[z] to hir[a].
And whanne thei[b] hadden maad redi a 13
pit, Raguel 3ede a3en to his[c] wijf, and
seide[d] to hir, Sende oon of thin hand- 14
maydis[e], and se[f] sche, whether 'he is[g]
deed, that Y byrie hym, bifor that the[h]
li3t[i] come. And sche sente oon of hir 15
handmaidis[k], which[l] entride in to[m] the
closet[n], and foond[o] hem saaf[p] and sounde,
slepynge togidir with[q] hem silf. And sche 16
turnede a3en, and teld good massage. And
thei blessiden the Lord, that is, Raguel
and Anne, his wijf, and seiden, Lord God 17
of Israel, we blessen thee, for it 'bifelde
not[r] to vs, as we gessiden ; for[s] thou hast 18
do thi[t] merci with vs, and[u] hast schit out
fro vs the enemy pursuynge vs. Sotheli 19
thou hast do merci 'to tweyne[v] aloone.
My Lord, make thou hem to blesse thee
fullicre, and for to offre to thee the sacrifice of thi preisyng, and of her helthe, that
the vnyuersite[w] of folkis knowe, that thou
art God aloone in al erthe. And anoon 20
Raguel comaundide hise seruauntis, that
fille[x] the pit, which[y] thei hadden maad,
bifor that the[z] li3t[a] cam. 'Forsothe he[b] 21
seide to his wijf, that sche schulde araie a
feeste, and make[c] redi alle thingis, that
weren nedeful to men makynge iournei.
Also he[d] made to be slayn twei[e] fatte 22
kien, and foure wetheris, and metis[f] to be
maad redi to alle hise nei3boris, and alle[g]
hise frendis. And Raguel made Tobie 23
to swere[h], that he schulde 'dwelle twei
woukis at Raguel[i]. Sotheli[k] of[l] alle 24

P weren A. q birielis cz sec. m.

r hoole *in body and soule* 1s. s crowyng of cockis 1s. t graue 1s. u Forsothe 1s. v had bifalle 1s.
w Tobie 1s. x the oothere seuene 1s. y which s. z entriden *in to wedlok* s. a Sare *bifore* 1. Sare s.
b Raguel and his seruauntis 1s. c *Anne,* his s. d he seide 1s. e hoond maydens 1sxf. f loke 1. g Tobie
be 1 Tobie is s. h Om. 1msx. i li3t of day 1. li3t of day time s. k handmaydens 1sx. l the which 1.
m Om. s. n closet *or bed chaumbre* 1s. o sche foond 1s. P hool 1s. q bi 1. r hath not bifalle 1s.
s certis 1s. t Om. EGHIKLMsxafgh. u thou 1s. v with two 1s. w vnyuersite *or al manere* 1. vniuersitee
or the multitude s. x fille a3en 1s. y that 1s. z Om. 1s. a li3t of day 1s. b And Raguel 1s. c *that sche
schulde make* 1s. d Raguel 1s. e two 1. f *he made* metis 1s. g to alle 1s. h bihote him 1s. i abijde
with him two wokis 1s. k And 1s. l Om. 1s.

ture, that the half part that lafte ouer, after ther^r deth shulde come to the hous of Tobie.

CAP. IX.

1 Thanne Tobie clepide to hym the aun-gil, whom forsothe he wende a man ; and seide to hym, Azarie, brother, I aske, 2 that thou herkne my woordis. If myself I take to thee a seruaunt, I shal not ben 3 euene worthi to thi prouidence. Ner the latere I beseche thee, that thou take to thee bestis, or^s sernyses, and go to Gabel in to Ragis, cite of Medis, and 3eld to hym his writ; and thou shalt re-sceyuen of hym mone, and pre3e hym to 4 comen to my bridalis. Forsothe thiself wost, that my fadir noumbreth the da3is, and if I^t shul tarien o dai more, his lijf 5 shal be maad sori. And certis thou seest, hou Raguel hath coniurid me, whos 6 adiurement I mai not dispisen. Thanne Rafael, takende foure of the seruauns of Raguel, and two camailis, wente in to Ragis, cite of Medis, and findende Gabel 3af to hym his writ, and resceyuede of 7 hym al the monee ; and shewede to hym of Tobie, the sone of Tobie, alle thingus that ben don. And he made hym to 8 come with hym to the bridalis. And whan he was come in to the hous of Ra-guel, he fonde Tobie sittende ; and stir- 9 tende thei kisten hem togidere. And Gabel wepte, and blesside God, and seide, Blesse thee the Lord God of Irael, for the sone thou art of the beste man, and ri3twis, and dredende God, and 10 doende almesse deedis ; and be ther seid blessing vp on thi wif, and vp on 3oure

thingis, whiche^m Raguel hadde in posses-sioun, he 3af the half part^n to Tobie ; and he^n made this scripture^p, that the half part, that was left^q, schulde come to the lordschip of Tobie aftir the deeth of hem^r.

CAP. IX.

Thanne Tobie clepide to hym the aun- 1 gel, whom sotheli he gesside a man. And Tobie seide to hym, Azarie, brother, Y axe^n, that thou herkne^t my wordis. Thou3^u 2 Y bitake^v my silf seruaunt to thee, Y^w schal not^x be euene worthi to thi puruy-aunce^y. Netheles Y biseche thee^z, that thou 3 take to thee beestis, ethir sernyces^a†, and go^b thou^c to Gabelus 'in to^d Rages, a^n citee of Medeis, and 3elde^f to hym his obliga-cioun ; and take of hym the money^g, and preie hym to come^h to my weddyngis. For thou woost, that my fadir noumbrith 4 the daies^i, and yf Y tarie o dai more^k, his soule^l schal be maad sorie^m. And certis 5 thou seest, hou Raguel hath chargid me^n, whos chargyng^n Y mai not dispise. Thanne Raphael took foure of the ser- 6 uauntis of Raguel, and twei camels, and 3ede^p in to Rages, a citee of Medeis, and he foond^q Gabelus, and 3af^r to hym his obligacioun, and resseyuede^s of hym al the monei ; and he^t schewide to hym^u of^v 7 Tobie, the sone of Tobie, alle^w thingis that weren doon^x. And he made Gabelus come^y with hym to the weddyngis^z. And whanne 8 he^n entride^b in to the hows of Raguel, he foond Tobie sittynge at the mete ; and 'he skippide^c vp, and thei kissiden hem silf togidere. And Gabelus wepte, and blesside^d 9 God, and seide, The Lord God of Israel blesse thee, for thou art the sone of a ful good man, and iust^e, and dredynge God, and doynge almesdedis ; and blessing^f be 10

† *seruyces ; that is, seru-auntis able to go with thee. Lire here.* c.

---

^{r} the c. ^{s} and E pr. m. ^{t} Om. F.

^{m} that 1S. ^{n} part therof 8. ^{o} Raguel 1S. ^{p} obligacioun writen 1S. ^{q} left *of his catel* 1S. ^{r} him and of his wijf 1S, ^{s} axe *of thee* 1S. ^{t} herke 1. ^{u} If 1S. ^{v} schal bitake 1S. ^{w} 3itt Y 1. ^{x} not *bi mi kunnyng* 8. ^{y} purueyaunce *or wisdom* 1S. ^{z} Om. 1. ^{a} seruauntis 1S. ^{b} go in B pr. m. K. ^{c} Om. *plures.* ^{d} in F. ^{e} the 1S. ^{f} bitake thou 1S. ^{g} money *that he owith to my fader* 8. ^{h} com bedir s. ^{i} daies *of our iourney* 1. daies *whilis I am out in this iorney* 8. ^{k} more *ouer* 1. more *ouer than he hath set to me* s. ^{l} lijf 1S. ^{m} heuy 1S. ^{n} me *to dwelle stille* 1. me *to dwelle here with him* s. ^{o} biheest 1S. ^{p} he 3ede 1S. ^{q} foond *there* 1S. ^{r} he 3af 1S. ^{s} he resseyued 1S. ^{t} Raphael 1S. ^{u} Gabelus 1S. ^{v} Om. s. ^{w} and alle 1S. ^{x} doon *to him* s. ^{y} to come 1S. ^{z} weddyngs *of Tobie* 1S. ^{a} Gabelus 1S. ^{b} hadde entrid x. ^{c} Tobie roos [risede s] up anoon 1S. ^{d} he blesside s. ^{e} a iust 1S. ^{f} blessing *or eneeressyng* 1. the blessing *of God* s.

11 fadris and modris, and see ȝee ȝoure
sonus, and sonus of ȝoure sonus, vn to the
thridde and ferthe[u] ieneracioun ; and be
ȝour seed blessid of God of Irael, that
12 regneth in to worldys of worldis. And
whan alle hadden seid Amen, thei wenten
to the feste ; but and with drede[v] of the
Lord thei enhaunteden the feste of bridalis.

CAP. X.

1   Whan forsothe Tobie made abidingus[w]
bi enchesoun of the bridalis, his fadir
Tobie was stirid, seiende, Wenest thou,
whi my sone abit[x], and whi he is with-
2 holden there ? Wenest thou, lest Gabel
be dead, and no man ȝelde to hym the
3 monei ? Forsothe he began to be sori,
and Anna, his wif, with hym ; and thei
begunne bothe togidyr[y] to wepe, for thi
that the[z] sett dai ther sone was not
4 turned aȝeen to hem. Thanne wepte his
modir with vnremediable teris, and seide,
Allas me ! my sone, wherto sente wee
thee to pilgrimagen, the liȝt of oure eȝen,
the[a] staf of oure eelde, solace of oure lif,
hope of oure after bringing forth of
5 childer ? Alle thingis togidere in thee oon
hauende, wee shulden not lete thee goa
6 fro vs. To whom seide Tobie, Be stille,
and wile thou not be disturbid ; hol is
oure sone ; feithful inow[b] is that man,
7 with the whiche wee senten hym. She
forsothe no wise myȝte take coumfort,
but eche dai stertende out, beheeld aboute,
and wente aboute alle the weies, bi the[c]
whiche semede hope of turnyng aȝeen,
that afer she myȝte seen hym comende[d],

seid[g] on[h] thi wijf, and on[i] ȝoure fadris
and modris, and se ȝe ȝoure sones, and the 11
sones of ȝoure sones, til[k] in to the thridde
and the fourthe generacioun ; and ȝoure
seed be blessid of God of Israel, that
regneth in 'to the worldis of worldis[l].
And whanne alle men hadden seid Amen, 12
thei ȝeden to 'the feeste[m] ; but[n] also[o] thei
vsiden the feeste of weddyngis[p] with the[q]
drede of the Lord.

CAP. X.

  Sotheli whanne Tobie made tariyngis[r] 1
for 'the cause[s] of weddyngis[t], 'Tobie his[u]
fadir was angwisched[v], seiynge[w], Gessist[x]
thou, whi[y] my[z] sone tarieth[a], ethir whi he
is 'witholdun there[b] ? Gessist thou, whe- 2
ther Gabelus is[c] deed, and no man ȝeldith
to hym the monei ? 'Forsothe he[d] bigan to 3
be 'sorie ful myche[e], and[f] Anne, his wijf,
with hym ; and bothe[g] bigunnen to wepe
togidere, for[h] her sone turnede not[i] aȝen to
hem 'in the[j] dai set. Therfor[k] his modir 4
wepte with teeris withouten remedie, and
seide, Alas to me ! my sone, whi senten
we thee[l] a[ll] pilgrimage, the[m] liȝt of oure
iȝen, the staf† of oure eelde, the solace of
oure lijf, the[n] hope of oure eiris[o] ? Wc[p] had- 5
den alle thingis togidere in[q] thee oon[r], and[s]
ouȝte[t] not leete[u] thee go fro vs. To whom 6
Tobie seide, Be stille[v], and nyle thou be
troblid ; oure sone is hool[w] ; thilke[x] man
is feithful ynow, with whom we senten
hym[y]. Forsothe[z] sche[zz] myȝte not be coum- 7
fortid in ony maner, but ech dai sche
'skippide forthe[a], and lokide aboute[b], and
cumpassidc[c] alle the weies, bi whiche the
hope of 'comyng aȝen was seyn[e], to[f] se
hym comynge afer, if it myȝte be doon.

† the staf ; for
as a siyk man
is sustoyned bi
a staf, so fadir
and modir in
eelde owen to
be susteyned of
sones. Lire
here. c.

---

[u] the ferthe AII. [v] the drede E. [w] abidyng A. [x] abideth A. [y] Om. c pr. m. [z] at the AFII. [a] Om. AII.
[b] ynowȝ AEF. and trewe II. [c] Om. c. [d] lyuynge E pr. m.

[g] brouȝt I. brouȝt or come s. [h] vpon s. [i] upon is. Om. g. [k] Om. x. [l] worldis of worldis BCRVBFG withouten ende ra. world of worldis x. to worldis of worldis a. [m] mete is. [n] and is. [o] Om. is. [p] tho weddyngis is. [q] Om. is. [r] tariyng e. [s] cause is. bicause g. [t] his weddyngis is. [u] Tobies g. [v] houyed is.
[w] and he [Om. s] seide to his wijf is. [x] Whi gessist is. [y] Om. is. [z] that my s. [a] tarieth thus is. [b] holden
there thus longe is. [c] be is. [d] Certis Tobie is. [e] ful sory is. [f] and also is. [g] bothe thei is. [h] for
that I. for that that s. [i] not hoom is. [j] Om. g. in that s. [k] Thanne I. [l] thee for [Om. s] to go
sich is. [ll] Om. s. [m] thou art the I. sith thou art the s. [n] and the is. [o] aftir comera is. [p] Whan we s.
[q] into x. [r] aloone I. [s] and therfor I. [t] we ouȝte is. [u] to haue leet is. [v] stille, wijf is. [w] hool and
saaf I. hool and in good quert s. [x] for thilke is. [y] hym forth is. [z] But ȝit I. But s. [zz] his modir is.
[a] wente out is. [b] aboute after him I. abouȝt after hir sone s. [c] sche cumpesside is. [e] his aȝen comyng
semyde [was sein s] to hir is. [f] for to I.

⁸if it my3te be do. But forsothe Raguel seide to his sone in lawe, Dwel heer, and I shal senden a messager of helthe ⁹fro thee to Tobie, thi fader. To whom Tobie seide, I knew, that my fader and my moder now counten the da3es, and ¹⁰ther spirit is tormentid in hem. And whan withᵉ manye woordis Raguel pre3ede Tobie, and he hym bi no resoun wolde heren, he toc to hym Sara, and the half part of al his substaunce, in childer, in hand wymmen, in bestis, in camailis, and in kijn, and myche monee; and saaf and io3ende he lafte hym fro ¹¹hym, seiende, The holi aungil of the Lord be in 3oure weie, and ful bringe 3ou sound, and finde 3ee alle thingus ri3te aboute 3oure fadris and modris, and see myn e3en 3oure sonus, rathere than I die. ¹²And the fader and moder, takende ther do3ter, kisten hyr, and laften hir to gon, ¹³monestende hirᶠ to wrshipen hir fader and moder in lawe, to looue the husbonde, to reule the meyne, to gouerne the hous, to 3iue hirself vnreprefable.

And sotheliᵍ Raguel seideʰ to¹ 'the hose-⁸ bonde of his dou3tir^j, Dwelleᵏ thou here¹, and Y schal sende a messangerᵐ of heltheⁿ 'of thee° to Tobie, thi fadir. To whom⁹ Tobie seide, Y knowe, that my fadir and my modir rekynen now the daies^p, and her spirit is turmentid in hem^q. And¹⁰ whanne Raguel preicdeʳ Tobie with many wordisˢ, and he 'nolde here Raguel bi onyᵗ resounᵘ, Raguel bitookᵛ to hym Sareʷ, and half 'the part of al his catelˣ, in children^y and damysels^z, in scheep and camelsᵃ, andᵇ in kiyn, and in myche monei; andᶜ heᵈ delyueride fro hym silfᶜ Tobie saafᶠ and io3ynge, and seideᵍ, The hooli aungel¹¹ of the Lord be in 3oure weie, and brynge 3ou soundeʰ, and fynde 3e alle thingis ri3tfuli aboute 3oure fadir and modir^i, and myn¹² i3en se 3oure sones, bifor that Y die. And theᵏ fadir and modir¹ tokenᵏ 'her dou3terᵐ, and kissiden hirⁿ, and leeten hir go°, and¹³ monestiden^p hir to onour the fader and modir of hir hosebonde, to^q loue theʳ hosebonde, to^s reule^t the^u meynce, to^v gonerneʷ the^x hows, and to schewe hir self vnrepreuable.

CAP. XI.

¹ And whan thei weren turned a3een, thei camen to Carre, that is in myddel wei a3en Nynyuen, the elleuenthe dai. ²And the aungil seide, Tobie brother, thou wost, what maner thou laftist thi ³fader. And so if it plese to thee, go wee beforn; and with softe pas the meyne, togidere with thi wif and with the bestys, ⁴folewe thei oure wei. And whan that hadde plesid, that thei shulden go, Rafael

CAP. XI.

And whanne 'thei turneden a3en^y, thei¹ camen to Carram, which^z is^a in the myddil of the weie a3ens Nynyue, 'in the eleuenthe dai†ᵇ. Andᶜ the aungel seideᵈ, Tobie² brother, thou woost, hou thou leftist thi fadirᶜ. Therfor if it plesith thee^f, go we³ bifore; and the meineis, with thi wijf togidere and^g with the beestis, sueᵇ oure weie with soft goynge. And whanne this^i⁴ plesideᵏ, that thei¹ schulden go^m, Raphael

† the eleuenthe day; fro departing fro the hows of Raguel. Lire here. c.

ᵉ that c.   ᶠ Om. All.

ᵍ But certis 1s.   ʰ seide *thanne* 1s.   ¹ to *Tobie* s.   ^j his dou3ter housbonde 1.   ᵏ Abijde 1.   ¹ here *with me* 1s.   ᵐ messenger *to telle* 1s.   ⁿ thin helthe 1s.   ° Om. 1s.   ^p daies *of myn absens fro hem* s.   ^q hem *for my long duellyng* s.   ʳ had preied 1s.   ˢ wordis *to abijde* 1. wordis *to abide with him* s.   ᵗ wolde not consente to him for no 1. nold concente to him for no s.   ᵘ resoun *that he shewid,* thanne s.   ᵛ bitook thanne 1.   ʷ Sare, *his dou3ter* s.   ˣ his good 1s.   ^y seruauntis 1s.   ^z hand maydens 1s.   ᵃ in camels 1s.   ᵇ Om. 1s.   ᶜ and so 1.   ᵈ Raguel 1s.   ᵉ Om. 1s.   ᶠ saaf *in good helthe* s.   ᵍ *Raguel* seide 1s.   ʰ sounde *hoom* 1. sounde *to 3our freendis* s.   ^i 3oure modir 1s.   ᵏ *Raguel* the s.   ¹ moder *of Sare* s.   ᵐ Om. 1s.   ⁿ her dou3tir 1. Sare, her dou3ter s.   ° go *with him* 1. go *forth with Tobie hir husbonde* s.   ^p thei commaundiden 1s.   ^q and to 1s.   ʳ hir 1s.   ˢ and to 1s.   ᵗ reule *wel* 1s.   ᵘ hir 1s.   ᵛ and to 1s.   ʷ gouerne *wiseli* s.   ˣ hir 1s.   ^y Tobie and his wijf weren turned *to go* [*thennus* 1] [*hoom to his fader and moder* s] in the elleuenthe day 1s.   ^z that 1.   ᵃ is a place s.   ᵇ Om. 1s.   ᶜ And *there* s.   ᵈ seide *to Tobie* 1s.   ᵉ fader *heuy in thi departyng fro him* s.   ᶠ to thee 1s.   ᵍ Om. 1.   ʰ sue thei 1s.   ^i this thing 1s.   ᵏ pleside *Tobie* 1. pleside *to Tobie* s.   ¹ thei *two* s.   ᵐ go *bifore* 1s.

seide to Tobie, Tac with thee of the galle
of the fish, forsothe it shal be necessarie.
And so Tobie toc of that galle, and thei
5 wenten. Anne forsothe sat beside the
weie eche dai in the euese of the hil, fro
whennus she myȝte beholden fro aferr.
6 And whil fro the same place she beheeld
his comyng, she saȝ aferr, and anoon she
knewȝ hir sone comende; and rennende
she tolde to hir husbonde, seiende, Lo!
7 thi sone cometh. And Rafael seide to
Tobie, But wher thou shalt gon in to
thin hous, anoon honoure the Lord thi
God, and gracis doende to hym, neȝhe to
8 thi fader, and kis hym. And anoon
anointe vp on hys eȝen of that galle of
the fish, that thou berest with thee;
wite thou forsothe, for anoon his eȝen
shul ben opened, and thi fader shal seen
the liȝt of heuene, and in thi siȝte he
9 shal ioȝen. Thanne the hound ran beforn, that togidere was in the weie, and,
as a messager comende neiȝ[g], with the
10 faunyng of his tail he ioȝede. And risende vp the blinde fader, stumblende
with the feet, began to rennen, and, the
hond ȝiuen to the child, he cam aȝen to
11 meete with his sone. And takende he
kiste hym, with his wijf, and thei be-
12 gunnen bothe to wepe with ioȝe. And
whan thei hadden honourid God, and do
13 gracys, thei seten togidere. Thanne Tobie,
takende of the galle of the fish, enointede
14 the eȝen of his fadir. And he suffrede
as almost half an hour, and the ryme of
his eȝen began, as the fellis of an ey, to
15 gon out. The whiche Tobie takende,
droȝ fro his eȝen, and anoon he resceyuede

seide to Tobie, Take with thee of the galle
of the[n] fisch, for it schal be nedeful.
Therfor[o] Tobie took[p] of that galle, and
thei[q] ȝeden forth[r]. Forsothe[s] Anne[ss] sat 5
bisidis the weie ech dai in the cop of the[t]
hil, fro whennus sche myȝte biholde fro
afer[u]. And while[v] sche biheld fro the 6
same place the comyng of hym, sche siȝ
a fer, and knew[w] anoon hir sone comynge;
and[x] sche ran[y], and telde to[z] hir hosebonde, and seide[a], Lo[b]! thi sone cometh.
And Raphael seide to Tobie[c], And[d] whanne 7
thou hast entrid in to thin hows, anoon
worschipe[e] ˹thi Lord God[f], and do thou
thankyngis to hym, and[g] neiȝe to thi fadir,
and kisse hym. And anoon anoynte on[h] 8
hise iȝen of this galle of the fisch, which[i]
galle[k] thou berist with thee; for ˹whi wite
thou[l], that[m] anoon[n] hise iȝen schulen be
openyd, and ˹thi fadir[o] schal se the liȝt of
heuene, and he schal be ioiful in thi siȝt.
Thanne the[p] dogge[q] ˹ran bifore[r], ˹that was 9
togidere in the weie[s], and made[t] ioie with
the[u] faunyng of his tail[v], as a[w] messanger
comynge[x]. And his[y] blynde fadir[z] roos 10
vp, and bigan[a] to renne, hirtynge[b] ˹in the[c]
feet, and whanne he[d] hadde ȝoue hond[e] to
a child[f], he ran aȝens his sone. And he[g] 11
resseyuede[h] and kisside hym, ˹with his
wijf[i], and bothe[k] bigunnen to wepe for
ioie. And whanne thei hadden worschipid 12
God, and hadden[l] do thankyngis[m], thei
saten[n] togidere. Thanne[o] Tobie took of 13
the galle of the fisch, and anoyntide[p] the
iȝen of his fadir. And[q] he abood[r] as[s] half[t] 14
an our almest[u], and[v] the[w] web, as the litil
skyn of an ey, bigan to go out of hise iȝen.
Which[x] web Tobie[y] took, and drow[z] fro 15

[g] Om. c.

[n] *thi* I. [o] Thanne I. [p] toke *with him* S. [q] *he and Raphael* IS. [r] forth *togidre* IS. [s] And IS. [ss] Anne, *the moder of Tobie* S. [t] an IS. [u] ferr *to loke aftir him* I. ferre *to loke after hir sone* S. [v] the whilis S. [w] she knewe S. [x] and *for ioye* S. [y] ran *hoom* IS. [z] Om. IS. [a] sche seide *to him* IS. [b] Lo! *now* IS. [c] *ȝoung* Tobie IS. [d] Om. I. [e] worschipe thou IS. [f] the Lord thi God IS. [g] and *thanne* IS. [h] thou upon IS. [i] the which I. [k] Om. S. [l] thou schalt wite IS. [m] that *herbi* IS. [n] Om. S. [o] he IS. [p] a g. [q] hound that ȝede forth in the wey IS. [r] for hem ran hoom bifore S. [s] Om. IS. [t] he made IS. [u] Om. IS. [v] taile *to old Tobie and his wife* S. [w] Om. S. [x] coming *bifore* I. comyng *and bryngyng good tithings* S. [y] the IS. [z] fadir of Tobie IS. [a] he bigan IS. [b] stumblynge I. shoueling forth S. hirtynge *ethir stumblinge* x *sec. m.* [c] with his IS. [d] Tobie IS. [e] his hond IS. [f] child *to lede him* IS. [g] Tobie with his wijf IS. [h] resseyuede *her sone* IS. [i] Om. IS. [k] bothe *he and his sone* IS. [l] Om. I. [m] thankyngis *to him* S. [n] saten doun IS. [o] And thanne IS. [p] he anoyntide *therwith* IS. [q] And *thanne* I. [r] abood *the wirching of that medicyne* S. [s] as *it were* I. [t] almoost half IS. [u] Om. IS. [v] and *than* S. [w] a *plures.* [x] The which I. [y] *ȝoung* Tobie I. Tobie *his sone* S. [z] drewe *it* S.

16 siȝt. And thei glorifieden God, he, that is, and his wif, and alle that knewen
17 hym. And Tobie seide, I blesse thee, Lord God of Irael, for thou hast chastisid me, and thou hast sauyd me; and
18 lo! I see Tobie, my sone. Also after seuen daȝes Sara, the wif of his sone, cam in, and al the meyne, and the bestis hole, and the camailis, and myche monee of the wif, but and the monee that he
19 hadde taken of Gabel. And he tolde to his fader and moder alle the benefetus of God, that he hadde don abouten hym bi
20 the man, that hym hadde lad. And ther camen Achior and Nabath, 'cosynes to[h] Tobie, ioȝende to Tobie, togidere thank-ende to hym of alle goodis, that God
21 hadde shewid abouten hym. And bi seuene daȝes etende, with[i] gret ioȝe thei gladeden.

CAP. XII.

1 Thanne Tobie clepide to hym his sone, and seide to hym, What moun wee ȝiue to this holi man, that with thee cam?
2 Tobie answerende seide to his fadir, Fader, what meede shul wee ȝiue to hym, or what thing wrthi mai ben to the bene-
3 fetis of hym? Me he hath led, and aȝein broȝt hol; the monee fro Gabel he toc; a wif he me made to han, and the deuel fro hir he refreynede; ioȝe he dide to hir fader and to hir moder; me myself fro the deuouring of the fish he delyuerede; thee also to seen the liȝt of heuene he made; and with alle goodis bi hym wee ben fulfild; what to hym to these thingus
4 wrthi wee shuln moun ȝiue? But I aske thee, fader, that thou preȝe hym, if par-

hise iȝen, and anoon he resseyuede siȝt[a]. And thei glorifieden God, that is[b], he[c],
16 and his wijf, and alle that knewen hym. And Tobie seide, Lord God of Israel, Y
17 blesse thee, for thou hast chastisid me, and thou[d] hast saued me; and lo[e]! Y se Tobie, my sone. Also[f] Sare, the wijf of his[g]
18 sone, entride[h] aftir seuene daies, and alle the meynees[i], and the[k] beestis hoole[l], and camels[m], and[n] miche monei of the[o] wijf, but[p] also the money which[q] 'he hadde res-seyued[r] of Gabelus[s]. And he[t] telde to his
19 fadir and modir alle the benefices[u] of God, whiche he hadde do aboute hym bi the man, that hadde led[v] hym[w]. And Achior
20 and Nabath, the 'sistir sones[x] of Tobie[z], camen ioifuly to Tobie[z], and thankiden[a] hym[b] of alle the 'goodis, whiche[c] God hadde schewid aboute hym. And bi
21 seuene daies thei eeten[d], and ioyden[e] with greet ioye.

CAP. XII.

1 Thanne Tobie clepide to hym his sone, and seide to hym, What[f] moun we ȝyue to this hooli man, that cam with thee?
2 Tobie[g] answeride, and seide to his fadir, Fadir, what meede schulen we ȝyue[h] to hym, ether what[i] mai be worthi to hise benefices[k]? He ledde[l], and 'brouȝte me hool aȝen[m]; he[n] resseyuede of Gabelus the monei[o]; he[p] made me to haue a wijf, and he droof awei the feend fro hir; he[q] made[r] ioie to hir fadir and moder; he[s] delyuerede 'my silf[t] fro the[u] deuouryng of a fisch; and he made[v] thee to se the liȝt of heuene; and we ben fillid[w] with[x] alle goodis bi hym; what thing[y] worthi to these thingis moun we ȝyue to hym? But, fadir, Y
4 axe thee[z], that thou preie hym, if perauen-

---

[h] and the childre of E pr. m.   [i] with hym c pr. m.

[a] his siȝt 18.   [b] is to wite 1.   [c] Tobie 18.   [d] Om. 18.   [e] lo! now 1.   [f] Thanne also 18.   [g] Tobie his s.
[h] entride or cam hoom 8.   [i] meynee 18.   [k] Om. 18X.   [l] Om. 18.   [m] camels hool with hir 1.   camels camen with hir hool and sounde s.   [n] and also s.   [o] Tobies 1.   [p] and 1.   [q] that 1.   [r] Tobie resceynyde 1.
[s] Gabelus was brouȝt with hem 1.   [t] Tobie 18.   [u] goodnessis 1, good s.   [v] led and felonshipid s.
[w] hym in the mey 1.   [x] niȝ cosyns 18.   [y] Om. 18.   [z] Tobie, and weren ioyful with him 18.   [a] thei thankiden 18.   [b] God with hym 18.   [c] goodnessis that 1. goodnessis which s.   [d] eeten there s.   [e] thei ioyeden 18.   [f] What thing 18.   [g] And Tobie 18.   [h] moun ȝyue 18.   [i] what thing 18.   [k] goodnessis 18.
[l] ledde me forth 18.   [m] he hath brouȝt me aȝen hool 18. ledde aȝen me hool nxg.   [n] and he 18.   [o] monei that he hiȝte [ouȝt s] to thee 18.   [p] and he 18.   [q] and he 18X.   [r] hath maad 18.   [s] he also s.   [t] me 18.
[u] Om. c.   [v] hath maad 18.   [w] fulfillid 18.   [x] of x.   [y] thing therfore 18.   [z] thee, that is, I beseche thee s.

auenture he shal vouche saf the half of
alle thingus, what euere ben bro3t, to take
6 to hym. And clepende hym his fader
and the sone, token hym apart, and thei
begunne to pre3en, that he vouche saf
the^k half part of alle thingus, that thei
6 bro3ten, acceptid to han. Thanne he
seide to hem priueli, Blesseth God of
heuene, and beforn alle thingus liuende
knoulecheth to hym, for he hath don his
7 merci with 3ou. Forsothe the sacrament
of the king to hiden is good; the werkis
forsothe of God to shewen and to know-
8 lechen is wrshipeful. Good is orisoun
with fasting, and almesse deede more
9 than tresores of gold to hiden; for almes
deede fro deth deliuereth, and it is that
purgeth synnes, and shal make to finde
10 euere lastende lif. Thei forsothe that
don synne and wickenesse^l, ben enemys
11 of ther soule. Thanne I opene to 3ou
the trenthe, and shal not hide fro 3ou the
12 priue woord. Whan thou pre3edest with
teris, and thou biriedest the deade, and
laftist the mete, and the deade bi dai
thou hiddest in thin hous, and the^m ny3t
thou biriedest, I offride thin orisoun to
13 the Lord. And for thou were acceptid
to God, it was nedful that temptacioun
14 shulde preue thee. And now the Lord
sente me, that I shulde hele thee, and
Sara, the wif of thi sone, fro the deuel
15 deliueren. I forsothe am Rafael, aungil,
oon of the seuene that stonden befor the
16 Lord. And whan these thingus thei
hadden herd, thei ben disturbid, and fellen doun tremblende vp on ther face.
17 And the aungil seide to hem, Pes to 3ou,
18 wileth not dreden; forsothe whan I
was with 3ou, I was bi the wil of God.
19 Forsothe I was seen with 3ou to eten and

ture he schal vouche saaf to take to hym
the half^a of alle thingis, what^b euer thingis
ben bro3t^c. And the^d fadir and the^e 5
sone clepiden hym^f, and token^g hym asidis
half, and bigunnen^h to^i preie^k, that he
wolde vouche saaf to haue acceptable the
half part of alle thingis, whiche thei hadden
bro3t^l. Thanne he^m seide to hem priueli, 6
Blesse 3e God of heuene, and knouleche
3e to hym bifor alle men lyuynge, for he
hath do his^n merci with 3ou. For^o it is 7
good^p to hide the priuyte of a^q kyng^r; but
it is^s worschipful to schewe and know-
leche^t the werkis of God. Preier is good 8
with fastyng, and almes^u, more^v than to
hide tresouris of gold; for whi almes de- 9
lyuereth fro deth, and thilke^w almes it^x
is^y that purgith synnes, and makith^z to
fynde euerlastynge lijf. Forsothe thei 10
that doon synne and wickidnesse, ben
enemyes of her soule. Therfor Y schewe 11
trewthe to 3ou, and Y schal not hide fro
3ou a pryuy word. Whane thou^a prey- 12
edist with teeris, and biryedist deed men,
and forsokist the^b meete, and hiddist deed^d
men bi dai in thin hows, and biriedist^d in
the^o ny3t, Y^f offride† thi preier^g to the
Lord. And for thou were acceptable to 13
God^h, it was nedeful that temptacioun
schulde preue thee. And now the Lord 14
sente^i me for to^k cure thee, and to^l delyuere Sare, the wijf of thi sone, fro the
fend. For^m Y am Raphael, the aungel, 15
oon of the seuene† that ben present bifor
the Lord. And whanne thei^n hadden herd 16
this, thei weren disturblid° §, and felden^p
tremblynge on^q her face. And the^r aungel 17
seide to hem, Pees be to 3ou, nyle 3e
drede; for^s whanne Y was with 3ou^t, Y 18
was^u bi Goddis wille^v. Blesse 3e hym^x,
and synge 3e to hym^y. Sotheli^z Y semyde 19

Margin note:

† offride: aun-
gels offren to
God the prey-
eris of iust men,
not to schewe
ony thing to
him, for alle
thingis ben
nakid and opyn
to hise i3en,
she bifor that
tho be doon,
but to take
counsel of this
thing at Goddis
counceil, what
owith to be
doon of this
thing aboute
iust men; for
aungels ben
spiritis of ser-
uyce sent in
to seruyce, for
hem that taken
the eritage of
helthe; to
Ebrewis in the
firste chaptire.
Lire here. c.
§ seuene; that
is, the vnyuer-
site of aungels.
Lire here. c.
§ disturblid;
that is, they
wondriden and
weren astonyed
of Goddis belog
neij aboute
hem. Lire
here. c.

k Om. AU.   l wickednesse AEFIt.   m in the A.

a half part HIMsfg.   b whiche 1s.   c bro3t hidere 1s.   d Tobie the 1s.   e his 1s.   f Raphael 1. to hem
Raphael s.   g thei token 1s.   h thei bigunnen 1s.   i for to s.   k preie him 1s.   l bro3t thidre s.
m Raphael 1s.   n Om. cs.   o Sotheli 1s.   p good conneel s.   q an erthely 1s.   r king, for bodeli pereile o.
s is euer s.   t knowe 1s.   u with almes 1. almes doyng s.   v more worth 1. 3ea it is more worthi s.
w thilke thing 1s.   x Om. 1s.   y Om. 1s.   z makith man s.   a thou, Tobie s.   b leftist thi 1s.   c tho
deed 1s.   d biriedist hem 1s.   e bi s.   f thaune Y 1s.   g preiers 1s.   h the Lord 1s.   i hath sent 1s.
k that I schulde 1s.   l for to 1.   m Forsothe 1s.   n Tobie and his sone 1s.   o disturblid or astoneyed 1s.
p thei fellen doun 1s.   q upon 1s.   r Raphael the s.   s forsothe 1s.   t 3ou in the likenesse of a man s.
u was thanne s.   v wille, doyng so his biddyng. s.   w Therfore blesse 1.   x him in hert and word s.   y him
in holi werkis s.   z Certis 1s.

to drinken; but I inuysible mete, and drink that of men mai not ben seen, vse.
20 Tinne is thanne, that I turne aȝen to hym, that ine sente; ȝee forsothe blesseth God, and telleth out alle his meruelis;
21 hym blisseth, and syngeth to hym. And whan these thingus he hadde seid, he is born awei fro the siȝte of hem; and thei
22 inyȝten seen hym no mor. Thanne thei, throwen doun bi thre houris in to the face, blessiden[n] God.

CAP. XIII.

And risende thei tolden alle his mer-
1 ueilis. Forsothe the[o] eldere Tobie, open- ende his mouth, blesside God, and seide, Lord, thou art gret in to with oute ende,
2 and in to alle worldis thi reume; for thou scourgist, and sauest; ledest to hellis, and aȝeen bringist; and ther is not that
3 ascape[p] thin hond. Knoulecheth to the Lord, ȝee sonus of Irael, and in the siȝte
4 of Jentilis preiseth hym; for therfore he scaterede ȝou among Jentilis, that vn- knowen God, that ȝee tellen out his mer- ueilis, and maken[q] hem to knowen, for there is noon other God almyȝti biside
5 hym. He chastiseth vs for oure wicked- nesse; and he shal sauen vs for his mercy.
6 Beholdeth thanne, what thingis he hath do with vs, and with drede and trem- bling knoulecheth to hym; and the king of worldis enhaunseth in ȝoure werkus.
7 I forsothe in the lond of my caitifte shal knouleche to hym; for he hath shewid
8 his mageste in to a[r] synful folc. Beth conuertid also, ȝee synful men, and doth riȝtwisnesse befor God, leeuende that he
9 doth mercy with vs. I forsothe and my

---

to ete[†] and drynke[a] with ȝou; but Y vse vnuysible meete, and drynk that mai not be seyn of men. Therfor it is tyme, that[b]
20 Y turne[‡] aȝen to hym, that sente me[c]; but blesse ȝe God, and telle ȝe out alle hise meruels; blesse ȝe hym[d], and synge ȝe to hym[e]. And whanne he[f] hadde seide
21 these thingis[g], he was takun awei fro her siȝt; and thei[h] myȝten no more se hym. Thanne[i] thei felden doun 'bi thre ouris[k]
22 on[l] the[m] face[n], and blessiden[o] God; and thei risynge vp telden alle hise meruels.

CAP. XIII.

Forsothe[p] the eldere Tobie openyde[q] his
1 mouth, and[r] blesside God, and seide, Lord, thou art greet with outen ende, and thi rewme is in to[s] 'alle worldis[t]; for[u] thou
2 betist[v], and makist saaf[w]; thou ledist[x] doun to hellis[y], and 'ledist aȝen[z]; and[a] noon is that ascapith thin hoond. Sones of Israel, knowleche ȝe to the Lord, and herye ȝe hym in the siȝt of hethene men[b]; for herfor he[c] scateride[d] ȝou among he-
4 thene men, that[e] knowen not God, that ȝe telle out his meruels, and make[f] hem to wite, that[g] noon othere God is[h] almyȝti outakun hym[i]. He chastiside[k] vs for oure
5 wickidnessis; and he schal saue vs for his mercy. Therfor biholde ȝe, what thingis[o] he hath do with ȝou, and knowleche[l] ȝe[m] to hym with drede and tremblyng; and enhaunse ȝe the kyng of worldis in ȝoure werkis. Forsothe[n] Y in the lond of my
7 caitifte schal knowleche[o] to hym; for he schewide[p] his maieste[q] on[r] 'a synful folc. Therfor, synneris[s], be ȝe conuertid[t], and do
8 ȝe riȝtfulnesse bifor God, and[u] bileue ȝe, that he schal do his merci with ȝou.
9 Sotheli Y[§] and my soule schulen be glad in

[n] thei blessiden ε pr. m. [o] Om. c. [p] ascapith A. [q] maketh AII. [r] Om. AII.

[a] to drynke is. [b] Om. s. [c] me to ȝou s. [d] hym in word is. [e] him in werk s. [f] the aungel is. thei g. [g] wordis g. [h] thei thanne s. [i] And thanne s. [k] Om. is. [l] upon is. [m] her is. [n] face the space of thre ouris i. face, and leien there the space of thre ouris s. [o] thei blessiden is. [p] Sothely is. [q] opnynge is. [r] Om. is. [s] Om. s. [t] withouten ende is. [u] for, Lord s. [v] betist men s. [w] hem saaf is. [x] ledist hem is. [y] hellis, which continuen her synnes to her end s. [z] thou aȝen ledist hem is. [a] for i. to thee that bileuen in thee, and kepyn thin heestis; for s. [b] men, to ȝeue good ensaumple to hem s. [c] the Lord is. [d] hath scatrid is. [e] whiche is. [f] that ȝe make is. [g] that ther is is. [h] Om. is. [i] he x. [k] hath chastisid is. [l] schryue is. [m] ȝe ȝou s. [n] Sothely is. [o] schryue me is. [p] hath schewid is. [q] worshepe or dignyte s. [r] upon is. [s] ȝe synneris is. [t] connertid, that is, be ȝe altogidre in hert and word and deed turned fro ȝour synne s. [u] and thanne s.

[† sample to ete; aungels apperinge in bodies takun, moun take mete and drynke, and drawe in to the wombes, for this is doon bi bodily mouyng, and bodily kynde obeyeth to aungels as to bodily mouyng; but aungels han mete and drynke in to the kynde of body as takun by the vertu of nurschinge; for siche bodies ben not onyd kyndly to hem, and therfor tho bodies ben not able to be nurschid. Lire here. c.

‡ Y turne; not that aungels goen awey fro God, but the turnyng aȝen is disapering, vanysching awey fro mennus siȝt. Lire here. c.

§ Y; that is, the ynner man, and my soule, that is, sensualite, ethir the lowere myȝt of the soule. Lire here. c.]

10 soule in hym shuln gladen. Blesseth the Lord, ȝee alle chosen of hym; doth daȝes of gladnesse, and knoulecheth to hym. 11 Jerusalem, cite of God, the Lord hath chastisid thee in the werkis of thin hondis. 12 Knouleche thou to God in thi goodis, and blesse God of worldys, that he bilde aȝeen in thee his tabernacle, and clepe aȝeen to thee alle thi caitiues; and thou ioȝe into 13 alle worldis of worldis. With shynende liȝt thou shalt shyne, and alle the costus 14 of erthe shuln honoure thee. Naciouns fro aferr shuln come to thee, and bringende ȝiftus shuln honouren in thee the Lord, and thi lond in to halewing thei 15 shuln han; forsothe a gret name thei 16 shul inwardli clepen in thee. And cursid shuln ben, that despise thee, and dampned shul be, that blasfemen thee; and blessid 17 shul be that bilden vp thee. Thou forsothe shalt gladen in thi sonns, for alle shul be blessyd, and be gedered togidere 18 to the Lord. Blessid[s] alle that loouen 19 thee, and that ioȝen vp on thi pes. My soule, blesse the Lord, for he hath delyuered Jerusalem, his cite, fro alle his 20 tribulaciouns, the Lord oure God. Blessid I shal be, if ther weren relikis of my[t] sed to be seen the clerte of Jerusalem. 21 The ȝatus of Jerusalem of safijr and of smaragd shul be bild, and of precious 22 ston al the cumpas of his wallis. And[u] of whyit ston and clene gold alle his streetis shul ben pauyd; bi his tounus 23 alleluia shal be sungen. Blessid the Lord that enhauncide it, that his reume be in to worldys of worldys vp on it. Amen.

hym[v]. Alle chosun[w] of the Lord, blesse 10 ȝe hym; make[x] ȝe the[y] daies of gladnesse, and knouleche[z] ȝe[a] to hym. Jerusalem, 11 the citee of God, the Lord hath chastisid[*] thee for the werkis of thin hondis[b]. Knouleche[c] thou[d] to God in thi goodis[e], 12 and blesse thou God of worldis[f], that he bilde aȝen in thee his tabernacle, and aȝen clepe to thee alle thi prisoneris; and that thou haue ioie in to alle worldis of worldis. Thou[g] schalt schyne with briȝt liȝt[†], and 13 alle the[h] coostis of erthe[i] schulen worschipe thee. Naciouns[k] schulen come fro 14 fer to thee, and thei schulen brynge ȝiftis[l], and schulen worschipe the Lord in thee, and thei schulen haue thi lond[m] in to halewyng; for[n] thei schulen 'clepe in thee[o] 15 the grete name[p]. And thei schulen be 16 cursid, that dispisen thee, and thei schulen be dampned, that blasfemen thee[q]; and thei schulen be blessid, that bilden thee. Forsothe[r] thou schalt be glad in thi sones, 17 for alle[s] schulen be blessid, and schulen[t] be gaderid togidere to the Lord. Blessid 18 ben alle[u] that louen thee, and that han ioie on[v] thi pees. My soule, blesse thou 19 the Lord, for 'oure Lord God[w] hath delyuered Jerusalem[t], his citee, fro alle tribulaciouns therof. Y schal be blessid, if the 20 relikis[x] of my seed schulen be[y] to se the clerenesse of Jerusalem. The ȝatis of Je- 21 rusalem schulen be bildid of saphire§ and smaragde[z], and of preciouse stoon; al the cumpas of wallis[a] therof schal be of white and clene stoon. Alle[b] the stretis therof 22 schulen be strewid; and alleluya, 'that is, the heriyng of God[c], schal be sungun bi[d] the stretis therof. Blessid be the Lord, 23 that enhaunside[e] it, that his rewme[f] be on[g] it in to worldis of worldis. Amen.

hath chastisid; that is, schal chastise, for it was not distried in the tyme of Tobie. Lire here. c.

† liȝt; this list was Crist offrid in the temple. Lire here. c.

‡ This is seid of heuenly Jerusalem, which is in blis. Lire here. c.

§ of saphire; bi this bilding of preciouse stones, ben vndurstoudun meritis of vertues, with whiche the chosun men of God han entring to dyuerse dwellingis of heuenli Jerusalem bi dyuersites of meritis. Lire here. c.

[s] Blessid ben A. [t] thi E pr.m. [u] Om c.

[v] him outward and inwarde s. [w] chosun men is. [x] do A pr.m. BC sup. ras. EHPUVX. and do L. do make a.
[y] Om. EIL. here in holinesse the s. [z] schryue is. [a] ȝe ȝou is. [b] hondis weren synful s. [c] Schryue is.
[d] thou thee s. [e] goodis whilis thou maist do good s. [f] worldis, that is, withouten cudyng s. [g] Thanne thou is. [h] Om. I. [i] the erthe g. [k] Naciouns, that is, many men fro dyuers cuntreis s. [l] ȝiftis to thee s.
[m] lond, that is, the lond that Jerusalem is in thanne s. [n] and in thee, Jerusalem is. [o] ynwardly clepe is. [p] name of the Lord is. [q] thee, that is, thei that baebityn or wrongfulli repreuen thee s. [r] Forsothe, Jerusalem is. [s] alle thei is. [t] thei schulen is. [u] alle thei is. [v] upon is. [w] the Lord oure God is. [x] aftircomers is. [y] be abidinge is. [z] of smaragde is. [a] the wallis is. [b] and alle is.
[c] Om. IX. [d] thorouȝ is. [e] hath enhaunsid is. [f] rewme or gouernaunce is. [g] upon is.

CAP. XIV.

1 And the woordis of Tobie ben ful endid; and after that he is liȝtid to seen, he linede two and fourti ȝer, and he saȝ 2 the sonus of his sonus sonus. And so fulfild an hundrid ȝer and twelue^v, he is 3 biryed^w wrshipefulli in Nynyue. Of sixe and fifti ȝer forsothe he lafte the liȝt of eȝen; forsothe in the sixtithe ȝeer of age 4 he resceynede. The remnaunt forsothe of his lif was in ioȝe, and with good profit of the drede of God he passide in pes. 5 In the hour forsothe of his deth he clepide to hym Tobie, his sone, and seuene ȝunge sonus of hym, his sonus sonus, and 6 seide to hem, Neeȝh shal be the destruccioun of Nynyue, forsothe the woord of God falleth not of; and oure brethern, that ben scaterid fro the lond of Irael, 7 shul be turned aȝeen to it. Al forsothe the desert lond of it shal be fulfild, and the hous of God, that in it was brent, shal be bild aȝeen, and thider shul turne aȝeen 8 alle men dredende God. And Jentilis shuln leue there maumetus, and thei shul come to Jerusalem, and dwellen in it. 9 And ther shul ioȝen in it alle kingus of erthe, honourende the king^x of Irael. 10 Hereth thanne, my sonus, ȝoure fader; serueth to the Lord in drede and in treuthe; and inwardli secheth, that ȝee 11 do that ben plesaunt to hym. And to ȝoure sonus comaundeth, that thei do riȝtwisnessis and almesse deedis; that thei be myndeful of God, and blesse God in alle time, in treuthe and in al his vertue. 12 Now thanne, my sonus, hereth me, and wileth not dwellen heer, but what euere dai ȝee birie ȝoure moder aboute me in o

CAP. XIV.

And^h the wordis of Tobie † weren 1 endid; and aftir that he was liȝtned^l, he lyuede two and fourti ȝeer, and siȝ^k the sones of hise sones sones. For^l whanne 2 an hundrid ȝeer and tweyn weren fillid^m, he was biried worschipfuli in Nynyue. 'For he^n of sixe and fifti ȝeer loste^o the 3 liȝt of iȝen^p; sotheli^q her sixti^s ȝeer eeld^t resseyuede^u 'that liȝt^v. Forsothe^w the resi- 4 due^x of his lijf was in ioie, and he ȝede^y in pees^z with good encresyng of Goddis drede. Forsothe^a in the our of his deeth 5 he clepide to hym Tobie, his sone, and seuene ȝonge sones of hym, hise sones sones, and seide^h to hem, The perischyng^e 6 of Nynyue schal be niȝ, for^d the word of God schal not falle doun^e‡; and ȝoure britheren, that^f ben scaterid fro the lond of Israel, schulen turne aȝen to it. Sotheli^q 7 al deseert^h lond therof^i schal be fillid^k, and the hows of God, which^l is brent ther ynne, schal be bildid aȝen, and alle^m that dreden God schulen turne aȝen thidur. And hethene men schulen forsake her 8 idols§, and schulen^n come to Jerusalem, and schulen^o 'enhabite it^p. And alle the 9 kyngis of erthe schulen haue ioie ther ynne, and schulen^q worschipe the kyng of Israel. Therfor, my sones, here ȝe ȝoure 10 fadir; serue ȝe the Lord in drede and treuthe^r; and enquere ȝe to do tho thingis that ben plesaunt to hym. And comaunde 11 ȝe ȝoure sones to do riȝtfulnessis^s and almesdedis; that^t thei be myndeful of God, and blesse^u God in al tyme, in treuthe and in al her^v vertu^w. Now therfor, my sones, 12 here ȝe me, and nyle ȝe dwelle here^x, but in what euer dai ȝe han biried ȝoure modir

† Tobie knowleching and propheciynge of heuenli Jerusalem. 1. The preisable knowleching of Tobie, and his profecie of heuenli Jerusalem. 2.

‡ falle doun; sum is profesie of mannas, and this is chaungid, as the meritis of men chaungen; and in this maner Jonas profeciede the distriyng of Nynyue, but for thei diden penaunce, this peyne was delayed; and whanne thei turneden aȝen to her synnes, God ȝaf ful doom of distriynge of Nynyue bi profesie of predestynacioun ether of ful doom, as it is in Goddis knowyng, and this profesie ether doom is neuere chaungid. Lire here. c.

§ forsake her idols; this profesie was fillid in part, whanne the Jewis turneden aȝen fro Babiloyne; but more perfitly it was fillid in the tyme of Crist and hise apostlis, whanne hethen men forsoken her idols, and camen to cristen feith, and serueden Crist truly, King of Israel. Lire here. c.

---

^v two E pr. m.   ^w deed and biried A.   ^x kingis E pr. m.

^h And *thus* 1s.   ^i liȝtned *of his blyndnesse* s.   ^k he siȝ 1s.   ^l And 1s.   ^m endid 1s.   ^n Sothely *whanne Tobie was* 1s.   ^o he loste 1s.   ^p his iȝen 1s.   ^q and *whanne* 1s.   ^r he *was* 1s.   ^s of sixti s.   ^t age 1s.   ^u he resseyuede 1s.   ^v *his siȝt aȝen* 1s.   ^w Sothely 1s.   ^x remenaunt 1s.   ^y ȝede *or* lyuede s.   ^z pees *to his [lyues s] ende* 1s.   ^a And 1s.   ^b he seide 1s.   ^c pereshing *or* destruccioun s.   ^d certis 1s.   ^e awey void 1. awei voide, *that neuer it schal be fulfillid* s.   ^f which s.   ^g And 1s.   ^h the desert 1s.   ^i of it 1s.   ^k fulfillid 1s.   ^l that 1s.   ^m alle men 1s.   ^n thei schulen 1s.   ^o thei schulen 1s.   ^p dwelle therynne 1s.   ^q thei schulen 1s.   ^r in treuthe 1. riȝtwisnesses 1. riȝtfulnesse s.   ^t and that 1s.   ^u that thei blesse s.   ^v Om. g.   ^w power 1s.   ^x here in *Nynyue* s.

biriele, fro that tyme dresseth ȝoure go-
13 ingus, that ȝee go hennus; forsothe I see
that his wickednesse ende shal ȝiue to it.
14 It is do forsothe after the deth of his
moder, Tobie wente awei fro Nynyue,
with his wif, and sonus[y], and sonus of
sonus[y], and is turned aȝeen to his fader
15 and moder in lawe. And he fond hem
sound in good eelde. And the cure of
hem he bar, and he closide the eȝen of
hem; and al the eritage of the hous of
Raguel he perceyuede, and he saȝ the
fifte ieneracioun, the sonus of his sonus.
16 And fulfild nynti and nyne ȝer in the
drede of the Lord, with ioȝe thei birieden
17 hym. Al forsothe his kinrede, and al his
ieneracioun, in good lif, and in holy conuersacioun, abod stille, so that thei weren
acceptid bothe to God and to men, and to
alle dwellende in the lond.

Here endith the book of Tobie, and now begynneth the prologe of Judith[z].

bisideʸ me in o[z] sepulcre, fro that dai
dresse ȝe ȝoure steppis, that ȝe go out fro
hennus; for[a] Y se that the wickidnesse 13
therof[b] schal ȝyue an ende[c] therto. For- 14
sothe[d] it was doon aftir the deeth of his[e]
modir, Tobie ȝede awei fro Nynyue, with
his wijf, and sones[f], and with the sones of
sones[g], and turnede[h] aȝen to the fadir and
modir of his wijf. And he foond hem 15
sounde[i] in[k] good eelde. And he dide the
cure of hem[l], and he closide her iȝen;
and[m] he took al the erytage of the hows
of Raguel, and he[n] siȝ the fyuethe generacioun, the sones of hise sones. And 16
whanne nynti ȝeer and nyne weren fillid[o]
in the drede of the Lord, thei birieden
hym[p] with ioie. Forsothe al his kynrede, 17
and al his generacioun, dwellide perfitli in
good lijf, and in hooli conuersacioun, so
that thei weren acceptable bothe[q] to God
and to men, and[r] to alle enhabitynge[s] the[t]
erthe.

Here endith the book of Tobie, and here bigynneth the book of Judith[u].

[y] his sones A. [z] From A. *Explicit liber Tobie.* E. No final rubric in CFH.

[y] bisidis I. here bisidis S. [z] a IS. [a] sothely IS. [b] *of Nynyue* IS. [c] bringe destruccioun IS. [d] And IS. [e] *ȝounger Tobie* S. [f] his sones IS. [g] his sones IS. [h] he turnede IS. [i] sounde *and hool* IS. [k] and in S. [l] hem, *beringe hir charge while thei lyuyden* IS. [m] and after that S. [n] *Tobie* IS. [o] fulfillid IS. [p] *Tobie* IS. [q] Om. X. [r] Om. C. [s] that dwelliden in IS. [t] Om. IS. [u] *Here eendith Tobye, and bigynneth the book of Judith.* B. *Here endith Tobie, and here bigynneth Judith.* CDHQSUb. *Here endith Thobie, and bigynneth a prologe on Judith.* GOa. *Heere endith Thobie, and bigynnith Judith.* I. *Here endeth the book of Thobie; se now the prolog of Judith.* K. *Here endith the book of Tobie, and here bigynneth a prologe on the book of Judith.* M. *Here endith the book of Tobie, and bigynneth the book of Judith.* NVX. *Heere eendith the book of Thobie, and bigynneth the book of Judicum.* R. *Explicit Tobie.* f. *Here endith Tobie.* g. *Here endith the blessid book of Tobie.* h. No final rubric in ELP.

JUDITH.

[*Prologue on the book of Judith*ª.]

THIS book of Judith, the holi widewe, ȝyueth vs ensaumple to be of holi conuersacioun, and to triste hoolliche in the help of Almyȝti God, as Judith dide, which
ouercam oonli bi the help of God the grete prince Olofernes, tristinge in the strengthe
of fleschli arm, and not in the help of God.

*Prologus*ª.

Anentus the Ebrues the boc of Judith is rad among thoo scriptures, whos autour is
vnknowen, whos autorite to be strengthid thoo thingus that in to strijf comen lasse
couenable isᵇ demed; ner the latere in Caldeis sermoun writen among the stories it
is countid. But for this boc Nyceneᶜ synodᵈ in the noumbre of holi scripturis is rad
to hanᵉ countid, I assentide to ȝoure asking, ȝhe, to ȝoure stedefast asking; and the
occupaciouns leid aside, with whicheᶠ hugeli I was artid, to thys thing o litil waking
whileᵍ I ȝaf, more sence of sence than woord of woord translatende. Of manye bokis
the most vicious diuersete Iʰ kutte awei, onli thoo thingus that with parfitⁱ vnderstondinge I myȝte finde in Caldeis woordis, in Latin I expressede. Taketh Judith, widewe,
saumple of chastyte, and declareth in perpetewel wrshipeful tellingus with the preising
of victorie. This forsothe not oneli to wymmen, but also to men, wrthi to ben folewid
he ȝaf, that, ȝeldere of hir chastite, such a vertue ȝaf to hir, that the vnouercomen of
alle men she ouercam, and the vnouerpassable she ouerpassede.

An *nother prolog of Judith*ᵏ.

Judith, widewe, the doȝter of Merari, of the linage of Symeon, ful miche gret in
glorie, and of men the parfitere; the whiche in figure of the churche girde of the
deuel in the hed, ne she dradde deth for the helthe of the puple, ne the kingus wodnesse quakide; for whi the slepende prince she sloȝ, and, saued the chastite, to hir
citeseynus she broȝte aȝeen the principal victorie; forsothe she liuede an hundrid ȝer
and fiue, and is biried in the spelunke of hir husbonde Manasse, in Betulia.

*Here endith the prolog of Judith, and now begynneth the book*ˡ.

ª This prologue is from M.

ª From U. No initial rubric in the other Mss. ᵇ ben AFHLO. ᶜ in Nicenys LO. ᵈ sene AFHLO.
ᵉ haue be LO. ᶠ the whiche AFHI. ᵍ Om. LO. ʰ Om. LO. ⁱ profyt LO. ᵏ From A. No rubric in the
other Mss. ˡ From A. Here endeth the prolog of Judith, se now the booc. I. Here endith the prolog of
Judith, and bygynneth the book of hir. LO. No final rubric in the other Mss.

Here beginneth the bok of Judith^m.

CAP. I.

1 ARFAXATH forsothe, king of Meedis, hadde put vnder 30e manie Jentilis to his empire; and he bilde vp a cite most 2 my3ti, that he clepede Egbatenys. Of square stones and hewen he made his wallis, in hei3te of seuenti cubitus, and in breede of thretti cubitus. His tourys forsothe he sette in hei3te of an hundrid 3 cubitis. Bi square forsothe of hem either side was strecchid, iu space of twenti feet; and he putte his 3atis in the hei3te of the 4 touris. And he gloriede, as my3ti in my3t of his ost, and in glorie of his 5 foure horsid carrisⁿ. The twelfthe 3er therfore of his regne, Nabugodonosor, king of Assiries, that regnede in the grete cite of Nynyue, fa3t a3en Arfaxath, 6 and waan hym in the grete feld, that is clepid Ragau, aboute Eufraten, and Tigre, and Jodasan, in the feld of Erioth, king 7 of Elikis^o. Thanne is enhauncid vp the reume of Nabugodonosor, and his herte is rerid^p; and he sente to alle, that dwelten in Cicilie, and Damasch, and Lyban, 8 and to the Jentilis, that ben in Carmel and Cedar, and to the dwelleris in Gali-lee, and in the grete feld of Esdrelon, 9 and to alle, that weren in Samarie, and be3onde Jordan flod, vnto Jerusalem; and to al the lond of Jesse, to that me cometh 10 to the hillis of Ethiope. To alle these Nabugodonosor, king of Assiries, sente 11 messageres; the whiche alle with o wil withseiden, and thei senten hem a3cen voide, and with oute wrshipe casten 12 awei. Thanne endeyned king^q Nabugo-donosor to al that lond, swor bi the

Here biginneth the bok of Judith^a.

CAP. I.

'AND so^b Arphaxat, kyng† of Medcis, 1 hadde maad suget many folkis to his em-pire; and he bildide a ful my3ti citee, which he clepide Egbathanys. Of squarid^c 2 stonys and korfe^d he made the wallis ther-of, in the hei3the of thre score cubitis and ten, and^e in the^f breede of^g thritti cubitis. Sotheli^h he settideⁱ the touris therof in the hei3the of an hundrid cubitis. For-3 sothe^k bi the square^l of tho^m touris euer either sideⁿ was stretchid forth, in the space of twenti feet; and he settide^o the 3atis of that *citee* in the hei3the of the^p touris. And he hadde glorie, as mi3ti^q in 4 the power of his oost, and in the glorie of hise charis. Therfor Nabugodonosor‡, 5 kyng of Assyriens, that regnede in the grete citee Nynyue, fau3t^r in the tweluethe 3eer of his rewme a3ens^s Arphaxat, and gat^t him^u in the^v greet feeld, 'which is^w 6 clepid Ragau, bisidis Eufrates^x, and Ti-gris^y, and Jadasa^z, in the feeld of Erioch, kyng^a of Elichoris. Thanne the rewme of 7 Nabugodonosor was enhaunsid, and his herte was reisid^b; and he sente to alle men, that dwelliden in Cilicie, and in Damask, and in Liban, and to folkis, that weren in 8 Carmele, and in Cedar, and to men dwell-ynge in Galile, and in the grete feeld of Es-drolon, and to alle men, that weren in Sama-9 rie, and bi3ende the flood Jordan^c, 'til to^d Jerusalem; and to al the lond of Jesse, til^e me come to the hillis of Ethiope. Nabugo-10 donosor^f, kyng of Assiriens, sente messan-geris^g to alle these men^g; 'which alle^h a3en-11 seidenⁱ with o wille, and senten^k a3en hem^l voide, and castiden^m aweiⁿ with out onour.

^m From F. No initial rubric in the other Mss.   ⁿ cartis AFH.   ^o Elibis AFH.   ^p arered AFH.   ^q the kyng A.

^a From ELMP. No initial rubric in the other Mss.   ^b Certis IS.   ^c squaar IS.   ^d kit BCEHILPUVX. of keruen IKS.   ^e Om. c.   ^f Om. S.   ^g *the wallis weren* of S.   ^h And IS.   ⁱ sette IS.   ^k And IS.   ^l squaar-nesse I. square werk s.   ^m the IM.   ⁿ side *of hem* S.   ^o sette IS.   ^p tho ISX.   ^q a mi3ti man IS.   ^r Om. IS.   ^s he fau3te a3ens IS.   ^t he gat I. he gat *or* toke S.   ^u *Arphaxat* IS.   ^v a AIS.   ^w that was IS.   ^x *the flood of* Eufrates IS.   ^y of Tigris IS.   ^z of Jadasa IS.   ^a the kyng IS.   ^b reisid *into pride* S.   ^c of Jordan IS.   ^d vn to IS.   ^e til that IS.   ^f To alle thes men Nabugodonosor IS.   ^g Om. IS.   ^h and alle thes IS.   ⁱ a3enseiden *and withstoden his maundement* S.   ^k thei senten IS.   ^l *his messaugeris* IS.   ^m thei castiden *hem* IS.   ⁿ awei *fro hem* S.

rewme and his trone, that he shulde defenden hym fro alle thoo regiounus.

CAP. II.

1 The threttenthe ȝer of Nabugodonosor
king, the two and twentithe dai of the
firste moneth, ther is don a woord in
the hous off Nabugodonosor, king of As-
2 siries, that he shulde defenden hym. And
he clepede to hym alle the more thurȝ
birthe, and alle the dukis, his fiȝteres;
and he hadde with hem the priuyte of
3 his counseil. And he seide his thenking in hym to ben, that al the erthe he
4 shulde vnder ȝoke to his empire. The
whiche sawe whan it pleside to alle men,
king Nabugodonosor clepede Olofernes,
5 prince of his chiualrie, and seide to hym,
Go out aȝen eche reume of the west, and
aȝen hem nameli, that despiseden myn
6 empire. And thi eȝe spare not to any
reume, and alle strengthid cite thou shalt
7 vnderȝoke to me. Thanne Olofernes clepyde dukis and the maister domys men
of the vertue of Assiries, and noumbrede
men in to the speding, as the king comaundede to hym, an hundrid and twenti
thousend of fiȝtende foot men, and horse
8 men and archeris twelf thousend. And
al his ost redi he made to go before in
multitude of vnnoumbrable camailis, with
thoo that shulden suffisen plenteuousli
to the ostis, of oxen also droues, and
flockis of shep, of the whiche was no
9 noumbre. Whete of al Ciric in his going
10 he ordeynede to be maad redi. Myche
forsothe gold and siluer of the hous of
11 the king he toc ful myche. And he wente
forth, he, and al the ost, with foure horsid
cartis, and horse men, and archeris, that

Thanne kyng[o] Nabugodonosor was wrooth 12
to al that[p] lond[q], and swoor[r] bi his rewme
and trone[s], that he wolde defende† him
fro alle these cuntreis.

† *defende*; that is, assaile alle tho cuntreys. *Lire here.* c.

CAP. II.

In the thrittenthe ȝeer of kyng Nabu- 1
godonosor, in the two and twentithe dai
of the firste monethe, a word was maad
in[t] the hows of Nabugodonosor, kyng of
Assiriens, that he wolde defende hym[u].
And he clepide to hym alle the[v] eldere 2
men, and alle duykis[w], hise[x] werriouris;
and hadde[y] with hem the priuete of his
counsel. And he seide, that his thouȝte[z] 3
was[a] in[b] that thing, to make suget ech lond
to his empire. And whanne this seiyng[c] 4
hadde plesid[d] alle men[e], 'kyng Nabugodonosor[f] clepide Holofernes, prince[g] of his
chyualrie, and seide[h] to hym, Go thou out 5
aȝens ech rewme of[i] the west[k], and aȝens
hem principali, that dispisiden[l] 'my comaundement[m]. Thin iȝen[n] schal not spare 6
ony rewme, and thou schalt make suget
to me ech strengthid citee. Thanne Holo- 7
fernes clepide the duykis and magistratis[o]
of the vertu[p] of Assiriens, and he noumbride men in to the makyng redi[q], as the
kyng 'comaundide to[r] hym, sixe[s] score
thousynde of foot men fiȝteris, and twelue
thousynde horse men and archeris. And 8
he made al his puruyaunce to go bifore[t]
in multitude of vnnoumbrable camels, with
these[u] thingis that suffisiden plenteuousli
to the[v] oostis, and[w] droues of oxis[x], and
flockis of scheep, of which was noon
noumbre. He[y] ordeynede[z] whete to be 9
maad redi of al[a] Sirie 'in his passage[b]. And 10
he took[c] ful[d] myche gold and siluer of the
kyngis hows. And he[e], and al his oost, 11
ȝede forth with charis, and horse men, and
archeris, whiche[f] hiliden the face[g] of the

[o] Om. IS. [p] the X. [q] lond, *that aȝenstoden his heest* S. [r] he swoor IS. [s] bi his trone IS. [t] in to S. [u] him *fro his enemyes* S. [v] hise S. [w] the duykis IS. [x] *which weren* hise S. [y] he hadde IS. [z] thouȝt *and his entent* S. [a] was *sett* IS. [b] on C. [c] seiyng *of* [*the king* S] *Nabugodonsor* IS. [d] plesid to IS. [e] the men I. *hise* men S. [f] he IS. [g] the prince I. [h] *he* seide IS. [i] at S. [k] west *coost* S. [l] dispisyn S. [m] myn heest IS. [n] iȝe BCDEFHIKLMNOPQRSVWXab. [o] the maistir men IS. [p] power IS. [q] redi *of batail* S. [r] had boden IS. [s] *he noumbride* sixe S. [t] bifore *him* IS. [u] tho IS. [v] his IS. [w] and *he sente* I. and *he sente bifore him* S. [x] oxen IS. [y] And in his pasage he IS. [z] ordeyne NO. [a] alle *the men of* IS. [b] Om. IS. [c] took *with him* IS. [d] Om. I. [e] *Holofernes* IS. [f] the whiche I. [g] ouer part IS.

couereden the face of the erthe, as lo-
12 custus. And whan he hadde ouerpassid
the coostus of Assiries, he cam to the
grete hillis of Auge, that ben fro the lift
side of Cicilie; and he steȝede vp alle the
castelis of hem, and weldede eche hold
13 strengthid. Forsothe he brac out the
most riche cite Melothi, and spoilide alle
the sonus of Tarsis, and the sonus of Ismael, that weren aȝen the face of desert,
and at the south of the lond of Celeon.
14 And he passide ouer Eufraten, and cam
in to Mesopotanee, and brac alle the heȝe
cites that weren there, fro the strem of
Mambre vn to it be ful come to the se.
15 And he ocupiede the termes of it fro
Cicilie vn to the coostus of Jafeth, that
16 ben to the south. And he broȝte alle
the sonus of Madian, and spoilide alle the
richessis of hem; and alle with stondende
to hym he sloȝ in the mouth of the^q swerd.
17 And after these thingus he cam doun in
to the feldis of Damasch, in the daȝes of
rep, and he brende vp alle the sowen
thingus, and alle trees and vynes he made
18 to ben hewen doun; and the drede of
hym fel vp alle the dwelleris in the lond.

erthe, as locustis _doon_^h. And whanne he 12
hadde passid the endisⁱ of Assiriens, he
came to the^k grete hillis Auge^l, that^m ben
at the lift half of Cilicie; and he stiedeⁿ in
to alle the castels of hem, and he gat ech
strong place^o. Forsothe^p he brak^q the 13
richeste^r, _ethir_^s _famouse_^t, citee Melothi^u,
and robbide^v alle the sones of Tharsis,
and^{vv} the sones of Ismael†, that weren^w
aȝens the face of desert, and at the south^x
of the lond Celeon^y. And he passide Eu- 14
frates, and cam^z in to Mesopotanye, and
he brak^a alle hiȝe^b citees^c that weren there,
fro the stronde Manbre^d til 'me come^e to
the see. And he occupiede the endis^f 15
therof^g fro Cilicie 'til to^h the endis of
Japhet, thatⁱ ben at the south. And he 16
brouȝte^k alle the sones of Madian, and he
'robbide al the richessis of hem^l; and he
killide 'bi the^m scharpnesse of swerd alle
men aȝenstondynge hym. And after 17
these thingis heⁿ cam doun in to the
feeldis of Damask, in the daies of ripe
corn^o, and he brente alle cornes^p, and he
made alle trees^q and vynes to be kit doun;
and his drede 'felde on^r alle men 'enhabit- 18
ynge the lond^s.

+ Summe bokes
han _of Israel_;
but elde bokis
han _Ismael_,
and this the
veriere lettre.
Lire here.

CAP. III.

1　Thanne thei senten ther legatus of alle
cites and prouyncis, the kingus and the
princis of Cirie, that is, of Mesopotanie,
and of Cirie Sobal, and of Libie, and of
Cicilie. The whiche comende to Olofer-
2 nen, seiden, Cese thin indignacioun aboute
vs; betere forsothe it is that liuende wee
serue to Nabugodonosor, the grete king,
and soget wee be to thee, than diende
with oure deth wee vsself^r suffre the
3 harmys of oure seruyse. Al oure cite,

CAP. III.

Thanne kyngis^t and princes of alle 1
citees and prouynces, that is, of Cirie, of
Mesopotanye, and of Sirie Sobal, and of
Libie, and of Cilicie, sente her messan-
geris^u. 'Whiche comynge^v to Holofernes,
seiden^w, Thin indignacioun ceesse aboute 2
vs; for it is betere, that we lyue and serue
Nabugodonosor, the grete kyng, and be^x
suget to thee, than that we die, and suffre with oure perischyng^y the harmes‡ of
oure seruage^z. Ech citee of oure^a, al^b 3

‡ _harmes_; that
is, suffre more
harmes than is
seruage. _Lire
here._ c.

q Om. c pr. m.　　r ouresilf AFH.

h Om. I.　i coostis s.　k Om. s.　l clepid Auge I.　that weren clepid Auge s.　m which s.　n stiede up 1s.
o place there I. place of that cuntrei s.　P And 1s.　q brak and destriede 1s.　r moost strong 1s.　s Om. 1s.
t famousiste B. Om. 1s.　u clepid Melothi 1s.　v he robbide 1s.　vv and spoilid s.　w weren duelling s.　x south
coost 1s.　y of Celeon 1s.　z he cam 1s.　a brake and wastid s.　b the hiȝe 1s.　c cheef citees s.　d of
Mambre I.　e that men comen 1s.　f coostis 1s.　g of that cuntrey s.　h vn to 1s.　i the whiche endis I.
which endis or coostis s.　k brouȝte with him s.　l toke fro hem alle her richessis 1s.　m with I.
n Holofernes 1s.　o corn, that is, in haruest s.　P thilke cornes I. tho cornes s.　q the trees 1s.　r felle
upon 1s.　s dwellynge on erthe I. duelling ypon al erthe s.　t the kyngis 1s.　u messagers to Holofernes s.
v and whanne thei camen 1s.　w thei seiden 1s.　x to be 1s.　y greet perishing s.　z thraldom 1s.
a ouris 1s.　b and al s.

al[s] oure possessioun, alle hillis, and litle hillis, and feldis, and droues of oxen, and flockis of shep, and of she get, and of hors, and of camailis, and alle oure facul-[4]tees and meynes in thi siȝte ben; alle [5]thingus ben vndir thi lawe. Wee also [6]and oure sonus ben thy seruauns. Cum to vs a pesible lord, and vse oure ser-[7]uyse, as it pleseth to thee. Thanne he cam doun fro the hillis, with horsmen in gret vertue, and weldede eche cite, and [8]alle men[t] dwellende in the lond. Of alle forsothe cites he toc to hym helperis, [9]stronge men and chosen to bataile. And so myche drede to that prouynce fel in, that of alle cites the dwelleris, princys and wrshipeful men, togidre with the puple wenten out in to meeting to hym [10]comende, resceyuende hym *with crounus and laumpis, ledende dauncis in trumpis* [11]and timbris. And ȝit ner the latere these thingus doende thei myȝten not [12]swagen the feerste of his brest; for and ther cites he destroȝede, and ther mau-[13]met wodus he heew doun. Forsothe king Nabugodonosor hadde comaundid to hym, that alle the goddis of the lond he shulde outlawen, that is, that he god alone were seid of these naciouns, that myȝten ben vnderȝokid bi the myȝt of Olofernes. [14]Passende forsothe Cirie Sobal, and al Ap-panyam, and al Mesopotanye, cam to Idu-[15]mes in[n] the lond of Gabaa; and he toc the cites of hem, and sat there bi thretti daȝes, in whiche[v] daȝes he comaundede to be gedered togidere al the ost of his vertue.

possessioun[c], alle munteyns[d], and litle hillis, and feeldis[e], and droues of oxes[f], and flockis[g] of scheep, and of geet, and of horsis, and of camels, and alle oure richessis and meyneis[h] ben in thi siȝt; alle thingis[i] be vndur thi lawe. Also we[s], and oure children ben thi seruauntis. Come thou a[k] pesible lord to vs, and vse[e] thou oure seruyce, as it plesith thee[l]. Thanne he[m] cam doun fro the hillis, with[7] knyȝtis in greet 'vertu, *that is[n], strengthe,* and gat[o] ech citee, and ech man 'enhabit-ynge the[p] lond[q]. Forsothe[r] of alle citees[s] he[t] took to hym helperis, stronge men and chosun to batel[u]. And so grete drede[u] lay[9] on[v] alle prouynces, that enhabiteris[w] of alle citees, princes[x] and 'onourid men[y], ȝeden togidere out with puplis[z] to meete hym comynge[a], and 'resseyueden hym[b][10] with corouns and laumpis[c], and ledden[d] daunsis[e] with pipis and tympans. Nethe-[11]les thei doynge these thingis myȝten not swage the fersnesse of his herte; for whi[12] bothe[f] he distriede her citees, and hew[g] doun her wodis. For[h] kyng Nabugodo-[13]nosor hadde comaundid to hym[k], that he schulde distrie alle the goddis of erthe, that is, that he aloone schulde be seid god of alle these naciouns, that[l] myȝten be maad suget[m] bi the power[n] of Holofernes. Forsothe[o] he[p] passide[q] al Sirie Sobal[r], and[14] al[s] Appanye, and al Mesopotanye, and cam[t] to Idumeis 'in to[n] the lond of Gabaa; and[15] he took the citees of hem, and dwellide[w] there[w] bi thritti daies, in whiche daies he comaundide al the oost of his power[x] to be gaderid togidere[y].

---

[s] and al ᴢ. of II. [t] man c. [u] in to AII. [v] the whiche AFH.

[c] oure possessioun 18. [d] oure mounteyns 18. [e] oure feeldis 18. [f] oxen 18. [g] oure flockis 18. [h] oure meyneis 18. [i] our thingis s. [k] and be thou a s. [l] to thee 18. [m] Holofernes 18. [n] Om. 18. [o] he gat 18. [p] that dwellide in that 18. [q] lond *where he came* 1. lond *that he came to* s. [r] And 18. [s] the citees 18. [t] *that he came to,* he s. [u] drede *of Holofernes* 18. [v] upon 18. [w] the dwellers 18. [x] *and* the princes 18. [y] men of honour 18. [z] her peplis s. [a] comyng *towardis hem* s. [b] Om. 18. [c] with [ȝit s] laumpis thei resseyueden him 18. [d] thei ledden 18. [e] dauuces *before him* s. [f] Om. s. [g] he hewide ᵗ. hewide s. [h] Certis 18. [i] Om. 18. [k] Holofernes 18. [l] which s. [m] sugettis 18. [n] powers s. [o] And 18. [p] Holofernes 18. [q] passide ouer 18. [r] of Sobal s. [s] al *the cuntrey of* s. [t] he cam 18. [u] in x. [v] he dwellide 18. [w] Om. 18. [x] vertu BEJLPUVX. [y] togidere *to him* 18.

CAP. IV.

1 Thanne herende the sonus of Irael
these thingus, that dwelten in the lond
of Juda, dredden gretli fro the face of
2 hym. Drede also and orrour assailede
the wittus of hem, lest that he shulde do
to Jerusalem and to the temple of the
Lord, that he hadde do to othere cites
3 and to ther templis. And thei senten
in to al Samarie, bi enuyroun vnto Jericho, and thei ocupieden beforn alle the
4 coppis of hillis; and with wallis thei
enuyrouneden ther tounus, and gedereden
whetis in to the befor greithing of fiȝt.
5 The prest also Eliachym wrot to alle,
that weren aboute Esdrelon, that is aȝen
the face of the grete feld biside Dotaym,
and to alle bi whom passing myȝte be,
6 that thei welde the steȝingus vp of hillis,
bi whiche weie myȝte be to Jerusalem,
and there thei shulden kepe, where myȝte
7 be streit weie betwen hillis. And the
sonus of Irael diden after that Eleachym,
the prest of the Lord, hadde ordeined to
8 hem. And al the puple criede to the
Lord with gret instaunce, and mekeden
ther soulis in fastingus, thei and ther
9 wymmen. And the prestus clothiden
hemselue with heiris, and the ȝunge childer threwen hemself doun befor the face
of the temple of the Lord, and the auter
of the Lord thei couereden with an heire.
10 And thei crieden to the Lord God of
Irael alle togidere, lest weren ȝyuen ther
childer in to prei, and ther wyues in to
deuyseoun, and ther cites in to destruccioun, and the holi thingus of hem in to
11 pollucioun. Thanne Eleachym, the grete
prest of the Lord, enuyrounede al Irael,
12 and spac to hem, seiende, Witeth, for the
Lord hath herd oure preȝceris, if dwell-

CAP. IV.

Thanne the sones of Israel, that dwell-1
iden in the lond of Juda, herden these
thingis, and dredden[z] greetli of 'his face[a].
Also tremblyng and hidousnesse asailide 2
the wittis of hem, lest he schulde do this
thing[b] to Jerusalem and to the temple of
the Lord, which thing he hadde do to
othere citees and templis of tho[c]. And 3
thei[d] senten in to al Samarie, bi cumpas
'til to Jerico[e], and bifore[f] ocupieden alle
the coppis[g] of hillis[h]; and thei cumpass-4
iden her townes with wallis, and gaderiden[i] togidere wheete in to making[k] redi
of batel. Also the prest[l] Eliachym wroot 5
to alle men, 'that weren[m] aȝenus Esdrelon,
which is aȝenus[n] the face of the grete
feeld bisidis Dotaym, and to[o] alle men bi
whiche[p] passage[q] myȝte be, that[r] thei 6
schulden holde the stiyngis of[s] hillis, bi
whiche weie[t] myȝte[u] be to Jerusalem, and
that[v] thei schulden kepe[w] there, where
streyt weie miȝte be among[x] hillis[y]. And 7
the sones of Israel diden aftir this[z], that
Eliachym, prest[a] of the Lord, hadde ordeyned to[b] hem. And al the puple[c] criede 8
to the Lord with greet instaunce[d], and
thei and the wymmen of hem mekiden
her soulis in fastyngis. And the prestis 9
clothiden hem silf with heyris, and ȝonge[e]
children boweden hem silf aȝens[f] the face[g]
of the temple of the Lord, and thei[h] hiliden the auter of the Lord with an heire.
And thei crieden togidere to the Lord 10
God of Israel, lest the children of hem
schulden be ȝouun in[i] to prey, and the
wyues of hem in to departyng†, and her
citees in to distriyng, and her hooli thingis
in to defoulyng. Thanne Eliachym, the 11
grete[k] prest of the Lord, cumpasside al
Israel, and spak[l] to hem, and seide, Wite 12

† departing :
bi violence of
ranyscherie.
Lire here. c.

[z] thei dredden 18. [a] the face of Holofernes 18. [b] these thingis 8. [c] hem 1. hem the which he had
distried 8. [d] vn to Jericho the Jewis 18. [e] Om. 18. [f] thei bifore 18. [g] heiȝtis 18. [h] the hillis 18. [i] thei
gaderiden 18. [k] the making ᴄᴅꜰɢʜɪᴋᴍɴᴏQʀsᴜᴠᴡxab. [l] hiȝ cheef preest 8. [m] dwellinge 1. that weren
wonyng 8. [n] euen aȝenus 18. [o] he wroot to 18. [p] whom 1. [q] thanne as passage 8. [r] and he bad that 8.
[s] up of the 18. [t] hillis a weie 18. [u] to her enemyes miȝten 8. [v] he bad hem that 8. [w] kepe wele 8.
[x] perceyued among 18. [y] the hillis 18. [z] this heest 18. [a] the prest 18. [b] for 8. [c] peple of Jewis 8.
[d] instaunce or hertli biseeching 8. [e] the ȝonge c. [f] lowli aȝens 8. [g] biholding 18. [h] the prestis 18.
[i] Om. 8. [k] greet or cheif 8. [l] he spake 8.

ende ʒee abijde stille in fastingus and in
11 preʒeeris in the siʒte of the Lord Beth
myndeful of Moises, the seruaunt of the
Lord, thatⁿ cast doun Amalech trost-
ende in his vertue, and in his myʒt, and
in his ost, and in his targetis, and in his
charis, and in his horsemen, not with
iryn fiʒtende, but with holi preʒeeris
14 preʒende, so shul ben born doun alle
the enemys of Irael, if ʒee stedefastli
abijden in this weik, that ʒee han be-
15 gunne Therfore at this exhortacioun of
hym thei, preʒende the Lord, abiden stille
16 in the siʒte of the Lord, so that also
these, that brent sacrifises offriden to the
Lord, gird with heiris offriden sacrifise
to the Lord, and ther was askis vpon
17 the hed of hem And of al ther herte
alle preʒeden God, that he shulde visiten
his puple Irael

ʒe, that the Lord schal here ʒoure preieris,
if ʒe dwellinge dwellenᵐ perfith in fastyngis and preierisⁿ in the siʒt of the
Lord Be ʒe myndful of Moises, the ser- 13
uaunt of the Lord, whichᵒ not in fiʒtynge
with irun, but in preiynge with hooli
preieris, castide doun Amalech tristinge
in his vertuᴾ, and in his power, and in
his oost, and in hise scheldis, and in hise
charis, and in hise knyʒtis; soq alle the 14
enemyes of Israel schulenʳ be castˢ doun,
if ʒe continuen in this weik, whichᵗ ʒe
han bigunne Therfoi at this excityngᵘ 15
of hymᵛ theiʷ preieden herth theˣ Lord,
'and dwelliden in the siʒt of the Lordy,
so that also thei, that offriden brent sacri- 16
ficesᶻ to the Lord, weren gird with heiris,
and thei offriden sacrifices to the Lord,
and 'aische wasᵃ onᵇ hei heedis And alle 17
men of al hei heite preieden Godᶜ, that
he wolde visite his puple Israel

CAP V

1 And it is told to Olofernes, prince of
the chiualrie of Assiries, that the sonus
of Irael maden hem redi to withstonden,
and that thei hadden closid the weies of
2 hillis And with ful myche wodnesse he
brende out in to gret wiathe, and he
clepide alle the princis of Moab, and dukis
3 of Amon, and seide to hem, Seith to me,
who ben thisc puple, that the hillis segen;
and what maner, and hou fele ben the
cites of hem, what also be the veitue of
hem, or what be the multitude of hem,
or who be the king of the chiualrie of
4 hem, whi beforn alle, that dwellen in the
est, these dispisidenˣ me, and wenten not
oute to meeten with vs, that thei shulden
5 taken vs with pes? Thanne Achior, duke
of alle the sonus of Amon, answerende
seith, If thou vouche saaf to here, my

CAP. V.

And it was teld to Holofeines, prince 1
of the chiualrie of Assiriensᵈ, that the
childrenᵉ of Israel maden redi hem silf to
aʒenstondeᶠ, and that thei hadden closid
togidere the weies of hillisᵍ Andʰ bi 2
ouer greet woodnesse heⁱ brente out in to
greet wiathfulnesse; and he clepide alle
the princes of Moab, and the duykis of
Amon, and seideʲ to hem, Seie ʒe to me, 3
who this puple is, that bisegith the hilli
places, ethii whiche, and what maner, and
hou grete ben her citees; alsoᵏ what is the
vertuˡ of hem, ether what is the multitude of hem, ethir who is the kyng of her
chyualrie, and whi bifor alle men, that 4
dwellen in the eest, han these men dispisid me, andᵐ thei han not go out to
resseyue vs with pees? Than Achior, 5
duyk of alle the sones of Amon, answerde

ʷ the whiche AFH   ˣ dispisen AH

ᵐ in bileue shuln duelle s   ⁿ in preieris A pr m s   ᵒ the which I   ᴾ strengthe is   q and so schul I
and so as Amalech was cast doun so shuln s   ʳ Om is   ˢ casten is   ᵗ that is   ᵘ excityng or stiring s
ᵛ Eliakim the preest s   ʷ men of Israel s   ˣ to the s   y Om b   ᶻ sacrifice s   ᵃ askis weren EL asschis
was F askis was P asske or pouder was s   ᵇ putt upon is   ᶜ the Lord is   ᵈ men of Assirie is
ᵉ sones is   ᶠ aʒenstonde him is   ᵍ the hillis is   ʰ And Olofernes I   And herfor Holofernes s   ⁱ Om is
ʲ be seide is   ᵏ also telle ʒe me s   ˡ strengthe is   ᵐ and nhi is

lord, I shal sei the treuthe in thi[y] siȝt of
this puple that in the mountaynes dwellith, and ther shal not go out a fals
6 woord of my mouth. This puple is of
7 the progenye of Caldeis; this first in
Mesopotanye dwelte; for thei wolde not
folewe the godis of ther fadris, that
8 weren in the lond of Caldeis. And so
forsakende the cerimoynes of ther fadris, that with the multitude of godis
9 weren, o God of heuene thei herieden,
the whiche and comaundede to hem, that
thei shulden gon out thennus, and dwelle
in Carram. And whan hungir hadde ouercouered al the lond, thei wenten doun
into Egipt, and there bi foure hundrid
ȝer so ben multiplied, that the ost of hem
10 myȝte not ben noumbrid. And whan the
king of Egipt hadde greued hem, and in
bildingus[z] of his cites in clei and tijl
hadde vnderȝokid hem, thei crieden to
ther God, and he smot al the lond of
11 Egipt with diuerse veniauncis. And
whan Egipcyenus hadden cast hem out
fro hem, and veniaunce hadde cesid fro
hem, and eft thei wolden hem taken, and
12 to their seruise aȝeen clepen, hem fleende,
God of heuene openede the se, so that on
either side the watris as wallis weren
maad sad, and thei drie foot the ground
13 of the se goende passeden ouer. In the
whiche place whil the vnnoumbrable ost
of Egipcienus them shulde pursuen, so
with watris it is couered, that ther lafte
not ne[a] oon, that the deede to after
14 comeres shulde telle. Also, gon out the
Rede Se, thei wenten aȝen the desertus of
the mountus of Sina, in the whiche neuere man myȝte dwellen, or sone of man
15 restide. There bitter wellis ben maad
swete to them to drinke; and bi fourti ȝer

and seide, My lord, if thou vouchist saaf
to here[n], Y schal seie treuthe[o] in thi siȝt
of this puple that dwellith in the hilli
places, and a fals word schal not go out
of my mouth. This puple is of the gene- 6
racioun of Caldeis; this[p] puple dwellide 7
firste in Mesopotanye; for thei nolden[q]
sue the goddis of her fadris, that[r] weren[s]
in the lond of Caldeis. Therfor thei for- 8
soken the cerymonyes of her fadris, that[t]
weren with[u] the multitude of goddis, and 9
worschipiden[v] o God of heuene, which
also comaundide to hem to go out fro
thennus†, and to dwelle in Carram. And
whanne hungur hadde hilid al the lond[w],
thei ȝeden doun in to Egipt, and there
thei weren so multiplied bi foure hundrid
ȝeer, that the oost of hem myȝte not be
noumbrid‡. And whanne the kyng of 10
Egipt hadde greuyd hem, and hadde[x]
maad hem sugetis in the bildyngis of hise
citees in cley and tijl[y] stoon, thei crieden
to her God, and he[z] smoot al the lond
of Egipt with dyuerse veniaunces. And 11
whanne Egipcians[a] hadden castid[b] out
'hem fro hem silf[c], and the veniaunce
hadde ceessid fro hem[d], and efte[e] wolden[f]
take hem[g], and aȝen clepe[h] to her seruyce, God[i] of heuene openyde the see to 12
these men[k] fleynge[l], so that on this side
and that[m] side the[n] watris weren maad
sad as wallis, and[o] these men with dry
foot[p] passiden 'in walkynge bi[q] the depthe[r]
of the see. In which place the while[s] 13
vnnoumbrable oost of Egipcians[t] pursuede
hem[u], it was so kyueryd[v] with watris,
that there dwellide not nameli oon[w], that
schulde telle the dede to aftir comeris.
Also[x] thei[y] ȝeden out of the Reed See, and 14
ocupieden[z] the desertis of the hil Sina[a], in
whiche[b] 'neuere man myȝte[c] dwelle, nethir

† *that is, fro Mesopotanye.* I.

‡ This natyuyte bigynnyth at Isaac, and endith in the goyng out of Egipt. *Lire here.* C.

[y] the AH. [z] bieldynge A. [a] Om. A.

[n] here me IS. [o] the treuthe I. [p] and this S. [q] wolden not I. [r] which S. [s] weren *worshepid* S. [t] [the S] whiche *cerymonyes* IS. [u] in IS. [v] thei worschipiden IS. [w] lond *of Carran* IS. [x] Om. IS. [y] in tijl IS. [z] God IS. [a] the men of Egipt IS. [b] cast IS. [c] fro hem the men of Israel IS. [d] the men of Egipt IS. [e] eftsoons IS. [f] *whanne* thei wolden IS. [g] the men of Israel IS. [h] clepe *hem* I. [i] *thanne* God IS. [k] men *of Israel* IS. [l] fleynge *awei* I. [m] on that IS. [n] *where this peple wentyn ouer the see*, the S. [o] and in her walkynge IS. [p] feet I. [q] Om. IS. [r] depnesse IS. [s] whilis S. [t] men of Egipt IS. [u] Israel IS. [v] hilid IS. [w] oo man *alyue* IS. [x] *Thanne* also S. [y] the men of Israel IS. [z] thei ocupieden IS. [a] of Sina CS. [b] [the S] whiche *desertis* IS. [c] ther myȝte neuer man I.

16 ȝeris frute fro heuene thei geeten. Wher
euere thei wenten in, with oute bowe and
arwe, and with oute sheld and swerd
ther God faȝt for hem, and ouercam.
17 And ther was not that shulde asailen to
that puple, but whan it wente awei fro
18 the heriyng of the Lord his God. As
ofte sithes forsothe biside hym ther God
an other thei herieden, thei ben ȝiuen in
to prei[b], and in to swerd, and in to re-
19 pref. As ofte sithes forsothe thei othoȝten
themself to han gon awey fro the heriyng
of ther God, God of heuene[c] ȝaf to hem
20 vertue of withstonding. Ferthermore king
Cananee, and Jebusee, and Feresee, and
Ethee, and Euee, and Amorree, and alle
the myȝti men in Esebon thei threwe
doun, and the londis of hem, and the
21 citees of hem thei weldeden; and vnto
the time that thei hadden synned in the
siȝte of ther God, goodis weren with
hem, the God forsothe of hem hateth
22 wickenesse[d]. For and befor these ȝerys,
whan thei hadden gon awei fro the weie
that God hadde ȝiue to them, that thei
shulden gon in it, thei ben destroȝid with
manye batailis of naciouns, and manye of
hem ben lad caitif in to a lond not theris.
23 Forsothe not ȝore[e] ago, turned aȝeen to
the Lord ther God, fro the scatering that
thei weren scaterid, thei ben gedered in
to oon; and thei steȝeden vp alle these
mounteynes, and eft welden[f] Jerusalem,
wher ben the holi thingus of halewis.
24 Now thanne, my lord, enserche, if ther
is any wickednesse of hem in the siȝte
of ther God, and steȝe wee vp to hem;
for takende he shal taken hem ther God
to thee, and vnderȝokid shul[g] ben vnder
25 the ȝoc of thi myȝt. If forsothe ther is
noon offencioun of this puple befor ther

the[d] sone of man restyde[e]. There bittir 15
wellis weren maad swete to hem for to
drynke; and bi fourti ȝeer thei gaten[f]
lyuelode[g] fro heuene. Where[h] euere[i] thei 16
entriden, her God fauȝt for hem, and ouer
cam[k] with[l] out bouwe and arowe, and
without scheld and swerd. And ʼnoon 17
was[m] that castide doun this puple, no[n]
but whanne it ȝede awey fro the worschipyng of her[o] Lord God[p]. Sotheli as 18
ofte euere as thei worschipiden an[q] other[r]
outakun thilke her[s] God, thei weren ȝouun
in to preye, and in to swerd, and in to
schenschip. But as ofte euere as thei 19
repentiden that thei hadden go awei fro
the worschipyng of her God, God of heuene ȝaf to hem vertue to aȝenstonde[t].
Forsothe[u] thei castiden[v] doun the kyng 20
Cananei[w], and Jebusei[x], and Pheresei[y], and
Ethei[z], and Euey[a], and Ammorrei[b], and
alle the myȝti men of Esebon, and thei
hadden in possessioun the londis of hem,
and the citees of hem; and[c] til that[d] thei 21
hadden synned in the siȝt of her God,
good thingis[e] weren with hem, for[f] the
God of hem hatith wickidnesse. For whi 22
and bifor these ȝeeris, whanne thei hadden
go awei fro the weie which[g] God hadde
ȝoue to hem, that thei schulden go ther
ynne, thei weren distried of naciouns[h] bi
many batels, and ful many of hem weren
led prisoneris in to a lond not hern. For- 23
sothe[i] a while agoon[k] thei turneden aȝen
to ʼher Lord God[l], and weren[m] gaderid
togidere fro the scateryng, in which thei
weren scaterid; and[n] thei stieden[o] in to
alle these hilli places, and[p] eft thei han
Jerusalem in possessioun, where the hooli
of hooli thingis ben. Now therfor, my 24
lord, enquere thou perfitli, if ony wickidnesse of hem is in the siȝt of her God,

[b] the praye *A.* [c] hem *A.* [d] wickedenesse *AEFH.* [e] a ȝeer *A.* [f] weeldiden *A.* [g] thei shulen *A.*

[d] *ony* I. [e] *there* restyde I. rest *there* S. [f] gaten hem I. [g] the liuelode S. [h] And where IS. [i] euer *in to what cuntrey* S. [k] he ouercam IS. [l] *her aduersaries* with S. [m] ther was no man I. no man was S. [n] Om. I. [o] the IS. [p] God theroff IS. [q] ony I. [r] other *God* S. [s] her owne IS. [t] aȝenstonde *her enemyes* S. [u] Certis IS. For U. [v] caste A. [w] of Cananei IS. [x] of Jebusei IS. [y] of Pheresei IS. [z] of Ethei IS. [a] of Euey IS. [b] of Amorrei IS. [c] Om. S. [d] Om. IS. [e] thingis *and prosperite* S. [f] sothely I. [g] that I. [h] *diuers* naciouns S. [i] But IS. [k] ago IS. [l] the Lord her God IS. [m] thei weren IS. [n] and *now* IS. [o] han stied up IS. [p] and also S.

God, wee shul not moun withstonde to them; for ther God shal defende them, and wee shul ben in to repref of al 26 erthe. And it is do, whan Achior hadde cesid to speken these woordis, alle[h] the grete men of Olofernes ben wrothe, and tho3ten to slen hym, seiende, either to 27 other, Who is he[i] this that seith, the sonus of Irael to moun withstonde to king Nabugodonosor and to his ostus, men with oute armys, and with oute vertue, and with oute wisdam of the craft of fi3ting? 28 That thanne Achior knowe, for[k] he bigileth vs, ste3e wee vp in to the mountaines; and whan the my3ti men of hem weren taken, thanne with the same he 29 shal ben smyte thur3 with swerd; that alle folc knowen, for[l] Nabugodonosor is god vpon erthe, and bisides hym ys not an othir.

and stie we[q] to hem; for her God bitakynge schal bitake hem to thee, and thei schulen be maad suget vndur the 3ok of thi my3t. Trewli if noon offense of this 25 puple is bifor her God, we moun not a3enstonde hem; for the God of hem schal defende hem, and we schulen be in to schenschip to al erthe. And it was doon, 26 whanne Achior hadde ceessid to speke these wordis, alle the grete men of Holofernes weren wrothe[r], and thei thou3ten to sle hym, and seiden[s] togidere, Who is 27 this that seith, that the sones of Israel, men[t] with outen armure, and with out vertu[u], and with out kunnyng of the craft of fi3tynge, moun a3enstonde kyng Nabugodonosor and hise oostis? Therfor that 28 Achior[v] knowe, that he disseyueth vs, stie we[w] in to the hilli places; and whanne the my3ti men of hem[x] ben takun, thanne he schal be persid with swerd[y] with the same men; 'that ech[z] folk knowe, that 29 Nabugodonosor is god of erthe, and outakun hym 'noon other is[a].

CAP. VI.

1 It is do forsothe, whan thei hadden cesid to speken, Olofernes, endeyned 2 hugeli, seide to Achior, For thou hast profecied to vs, seiende, that the folc of Irael was defendid of ther God, that I shewe to thee, that ther is no god but 3 Nabugodonosor; whan wee han smyte them alle as o man, thanne and thiself with hem with the swerd of Assiries shalt dien, and al Irael with thee shal 4 dispershen in perdicioun; and thou shalt preue, for Nabugodonosor be lord of al erthe; and thanne the swerd of my kny3thod shal passe thur3 thi sidis, and stikid thou shalt fallen among the woundid men of Irael, and thou shalt no mor take breth, to the time that thou be put out of the

CAP. VI.

1 Forsothe[b] it was doon, whanne thei hadden ceessid to speke, Holofernes hadde dedeyn 'gretli, and seide[c] to Achior, For 2 thou propheciedist[d] to vs, and seidist, that the folk of Israel is defendid of her God, that[e] Y schewe to thee, that no god is no[f] but Nabugodonosor; whanne we[g] han 3 slayn 'hem alle as o man[h], thanne also thou schalt perische with hem bi[i] the swerd of Assiriens[k], and al Israel schal perische dyuerseli with thee in perdicioun; and thou schalt preue, that Nabu- 4 godonosor is lord of al erthe; and thanne the swerd of my chyualric schal passe thorou3 thi sidis, and thou schalt be persid[l], and schalt[m] falle among the woundid men of Israel, and thou schalt

h and alle A II.   i Om. A.   k that A.   l that A II.

q we thanne up IS.   r wroth a3ens him S.   s thei seiden IS.   t the whiche ben men I. which ben men S. u strengthe IS.   v this Achior S.   w we up IS.   x Jewis IS.   y a swerd IS.   z and al I.   a ther is noon other I. noon other god is I.   b And IS.   c he seide IS.   d hast prophecied IS.   e and that IS.   f Om. I. g we as oo man IS.   h alle the sones of Israel IS.   i with I.   k men of Assirie IS.   l perischid A. m thou schalt IS.

5 lond with hem. But forsothe if thi profecie soth^m thou weene^n, falle not doun
thi chere; and the palenesse that with-
holdeth thi face, go awei fro thee, if
these my woordis thou weenest not to
6 moun be fulfild. Forsothe that thou
knowe, for togidere with them that thou
shalt knowe bi experiense, lo! fro this
hour thou shalt be felashipid to the puple of hem, and whan wrthi peynes of
my swerd thei han taken, thiself shalt
7 vnderlin to lie veniaunce. Thanne Olofernes comaundide to his seruauns, that
thei shulden taken Achior, and leden
hym in to Betulie, and taken hym in
8 the hond of the sonus of Irael. And
the seruauns of Olofernes, takende hym,
wenten bi the wilde feldis, but whan
thei hadden ne3hed to the mounteynes,
9 wenten out a3en hem slingeres. Thei
forsothe, turnende aside fro the side of
the hil, bounden Achior to a tree hondus
and feet, and so bounden of cordis thei
laften hym, and ben turned a3een to
10 ther lord. But the sonus of Irael, comende doun fro Betulie, camen to hym,
whom loosende thei^o ladden to Betulie,
and in to the myddel of the puple hym
settende askeden hym, what of thingus
it were, that hym bounde the Assiries
11 hadden laft. In thoo da3es weren there
princis, Osias, the sone of Myca, of the
linage of Symeon, and Carmy, the whiche
12 and Gothonyel. And so in the myddel
of the elders, and in the si3te of alle
men, Achior seide alle thingus, that he
askid of Olofernes hadde spoken, and
what maner the puple of Olofernes
13 wolde for this woord slen hym, and what
maner he Olofernes wroth comaundede
hym to be take to the men of Irael for

no more brethe a3en^n, til thou be distried
with hem. But certis if thou gessist thi 5
profecie sothe, thi cheer falle^o not doun;
and the palenesse that hath gete thi face,
go^p awey fro thee, if thou gessist that
these my wordis moun not 'be fillid^q.
But that thou knowe, that thou schalt 6
feele this thing togidere with hem^r, lo^s!
fro this our thou schalt be felouschipid
to the puple of hem, that whanne thei
han take^t worthi peynes of my swerd,
thou be suget to lijk veniaunce. Thanne 7
Olofernes comaundide hise^u seruauntis to
take Achior, and to lede hym in to Bethulia, and to bitake hym in to the hondis
of the sones of Israel. And the seruauntis 8
of Olofernes token him, and 3eden^v forth
bi the feeldi places, but whanne thei hadden nei3id to the hilli places, slingeris^w
3eden out a3ens hem. Sotheli^x thei turn- 9
eden awei^y fro the side of the hil, and
bounden^z Achior to a tre bi hondis^a and
feet, and so thei leften hym houndun with
withthis^b, and turneden^c a3en to her lord.
Certis^d the sones of Israel 3eden doun 10
fro Bethulia, and camen^e to hym^f, whom
thei vnhounden, and ledden^g to Bethulia,
and thei settiden^h hym^i in to^k the^l myddis
of the puple, and axiden^m, what manere^n
of^o thinges bifel^p, that Assiriens^q hadden
left hym boundun. In tho daies princes^r 11
weren there, Ozias^s, the sone of Mycha,
of the lynage of Symeon, and Charmy^t,
which is also^u Gothonyel. Therfor in the^v 12
myddis of eldere men, and in the si3t
of alle men, Achior seide alle^w thingis^x,
whiche he was axid of Holofernes, and
hadde^y spoke^z, and hou the puple of Holofernes wolde sle hym for this word^n, and 13
hou Holofernes hym silf was wrooth, and
comaundide hym to be bitakun for this

---

m be soth _A._   n wenyst _AEFH._   o Om. _AEFH._

n Om. s.   o falle _it_ 1s.   P go _it_ 1s.   q ben fulfillid 1s.   r the children of Israel 1s.   s lo! _now_ 1s.
t takin _or suffrid_ s.   u to hise s.   V thei 3eden 1s.   w men throwynge stones with slyngis 1s.   x And 1s.
Y a3en _A._   z thei bounden 1s.   a _hise_ hondis s.   b ropis 1.   c thei turneden 1s.   d And 1. And thanne s.
e thei camen 1s.   f Achior 1s.   g ledden hhm 1s.   h setten 1. settiden _or_ brou3t s.   i Om. s.   k Om. 1x.
l Om. s.   m thei axiden 1. axiden _him_ s.   n Om. BCHLFUVX.   o Om. 1.   P was BCEHLPUVX.   q the men
of Assirie 1s.   r thes princes 1. _these_ princis _of Jewis_ s.   s _that is,_ Ozias s.   t Charmy, _the prince_ s.
u also _clepid_ 1s.   V Om. 1s.   w thes x.   x the thingis 1s.   y _which thingis_ he had s.   z told _to Holo-
fernes_ 1s.   a word _that he had seid_ 1s.

this cause, that whil he shulde ouercome the sonus of Israel, thanne and that Achior he comaunde[p] with dyuers tormentus to dien, for that that he hadde seid, God of 14 heuene is the defendere of hem. And whan alle thingus Achior hadde expouned, al the puple fel in to the face, honourende the Lord ; and with comun lamenting[q] and weping alle of o wil ther 15 pre3eeris to the Lord helden out, seiende, Lord God of heuene and of erthe, see the pride of hem, and beholde to oure meknesse, and to the face of thi halewis tac heede, and shew3 for thou forsakist not that befor alle thingus taken trost of[r] thee, and principally takende trost of hemself, and of ther vertue gloriende 16 thou meekist. And so the weping endid, and bi al the dai the orisoun of the pu-17 ple fulfild, thei coumforteden Achior, seiende, God of oure fadris, whos vertue thou hast prechid, he 3eldere to thee this recompensacioun shal 3iue, that thou ra-18 there see[a] the deth of hem. Whan forsothe the Lord oure God shal 3iue this fredam to his seruauns, be and the Lord with thee in the myddel of vs, that as it shal plese to thee, so with alle thine thou 19 dwelle. Thanne Osias, the counseil eudid, toc hym in to his hous, and made a gret 20 soper. And, alle the prestus clepid togi-21 dere, the fasting fulfild, thei eeten. After forsothe, al the puple clepid togidere, thur3 out al the ny3t withinne the chirche thei pre3eden, askende helpe of the God of Israel.

cause to men[b] of Israel, that the while he[c] ouercam the sones of Israel, thanne he comaundide that also thilk Achior perische[d] bi[e] dyuerse turmentis, for[r] this[g] that he hadde seid, God of heuene is the defendere of hem[h]. And whanne Achior 14 hadde expowned alle thingis[i], al the puple felde doun on[k] the[l] face, and worschipide the Lord ; and with comyn weilyng and wepyng thei schedden out to the Lord her preyeris of[m] o wille, seiynge[n], 15 Lord God of heuene and of erthe, biholde the pride of hem[o], and biholde thou to oure mekenesse, and perseyue[p] the face of thi seyntis, and schewe[q] that thou forsakist[r] not men tristynge of[s] thee, and thou[t] makist low men tristynge of hem silf, and 'men hauynge[u] glorie of her' vertu[v]. Therfor whanne the wepyng[x] was endid, 16 and the preier of the puple bi al the dai was fillid[y], thei coumfortiden Achior, and 17 seiden, God of oure fadris, whos vertu[z] thou prechidist[a], he is rewardere[b], and schal[c] 3yue to[d] thee this[e] while, that thou se more the perischyng of hem. Forsothe[f] 18 whanne 'oure Lord God[g] hath 3oue this fredom to hise seruauntis[h], also the Lord be[l] with thee in the myddis[k] of vs, that as it plesith[l] thee, so thou lyue with 'alle thi thingis[m]. Thanne after that the[n] coun-19 sel was endid, Ozias[o] resseyuede hym[p] in to his hows, and made a greet soper to hym. And whanne alle the prestis weren 20 clepid togidere, aftir[r] that the fastyng was fillid[s], thei refreischiden Achior 'and hem silf[t]. Forsothe[u] aftirward al the puple 21 was clepid togidere, and thei preieden bi al the ni3t with ynne the chirche, and axiden[v] help of God of Israel.

---

[p] comaundide A.　　[q] weymentyng A.　　[r] to A.　　[s] shal se A.

[b] the men 1s.　　[c] Holofernes 1s.　　[d] to perishe s.　　[e] with 1s.　　[f] and for s.　　[g] this thing 1s.　　[h] his peple 1s.　　[i] thes thingis 1s.　　[k] vpon s.　　[l] her 1s.　　[m] and of s.　　[n] thei seiden 1s.　　[o] thin enmyes 1s.　　[p] take thou hede to 1s.　　[q] schewe thou n. schewe we c pr. m. DFHIMORX pr. m. ab. shewe we bi verre bileue, and good werkus s.　　[r] forsokist w.　　[s] in 1s.　　[t] that thou 1s.　　[u] hem that han 1s.　　[v] her owne 1s.　　[w] vertu or strengthe s.　　[x] weping of the men of Israel s.　　[y] fulfillid 1s.　　[z] power 1s.　　[a] hast prechid 1s.　　[b] rewarder of al goodnesse s.　　[c] he schal 1s.　　[d] Om. 1s.　　[e] grace for this 1s.　　[f] And 1s.　　[g] the Lord oure God 1s.　　[h] seruauntis, that we han oucreome our enemyes s.　　[i] be thanne 1s.　　[k] myddle 1s.　　[l] schal plese 1. thanne plese s.　　[m] al thi thing 1. al thi thing among vs s.　　[n] this 1s.　　[o] Ozias, the cheef preest 1s.　　[p] Achior 1s.　　[r] and after s.　　[s] fulfillid 1s.　　[t] Om. 1. and hemsilf bi some recreacioun s.　　[u] And 1s.　　[v] thei axiden 1s.

CAP. VII.

1 Olofernes forsothe that[t] tother dai comaundide to his[u] ostus, that thei shulden
2 steȝe vp aȝen Betulie. Ther weren forsothe footmen of fiȝteres an hundrid and
twenti thousend, and horse men twelue
thousend, biside the redi cumpanyes of
thoo[v] men, whom caitifte hadde ocupied,
and weren broȝt fro prouyncis and cites,
3 of alle ȝouthe. Alle togidere maden themself redi to the fiȝt aȝen the sones of Irael ;
and thei camen bi the brinke of the hil
vnto the cop, that beholdeth Dotaym, fro
the place that is seid Belena vnto Sel-
4 mon, that is aȝen Esdrelon. The sones
forsothe of Irael, as thei seȝen the multitude of hem, thei threwen themself doun
vpon the erthe, puttende askis vpon ther
hedis, togidere of o wil preȝende, that
God of Irael his merci shewe vp on his
5 puple. And takende ther armys of bataile, seten bi the placis that leden the
path of streit weie betwe[w] the hilli placis,
and thei weren kepende them al dai and
6 nyȝt. But Olofernes, whil he goth aboute
bi cumpas, fond that a welle, that flowide
in to the watir condute of them, fro the
south partie out of the cite diuersli reulide, and comaundede[x] to ben hewe doun
7 the water cundute of hem. Ner the
latere ther weren not fer from the wallis
wellis, of the whiche theefli thei weren
seen to drawe water, rathere to refreshen
8 than to drinken. But the sonus of Amon
and of Moab wenten to Olofernes, seiende, The sones of Irael not in spere and
arewe trosten, but the mountaynes defenden hem, and strengthen hem the litle

Forsothe in 'the tother[w] dai Holofernes 1
comaundide hise oostis to stie[x] aȝens Bethulia. Forsothe[y] there weren[z] six score 2
thousynde 'foot men of fiȝteris[a], and twelue
thousynde knyȝtis, 'outakun the makyng
redi of tho men[b], whiche caitifte[c] hadde
ocupied[d], and weren brouȝt fro prouynces
and citees, of alle ȝongthe[e]. Alle[f] togidere 3
maden hem redi to batel aȝens the sones
of Israel ; and thei camen bi the side of
the[h] hil 'til to[i] the cop[k], that biholdith
Dothaym, fro the place which[l] is seid
Belma 'til to[m] Selmon, which is aȝens
Esdrolon. Forsothe[n] the sones of Israel, 4
as[o] thei sien the multitude of hem, bowiden[p] doun hem silf on[q] the erthe, and
senten[r] aische[s] on[t] her heedis, and preiden[u]
with o wille, that God of Israel schulde
schewe his merci on[v] his puple. And thei 5
token her armuris of batel, and saten[w]
bi the places 'that dressen[x] the path of
streyt[y] weie bitwixe hilli[z] places[a], and
thei kepten tho places al the dai and
nyȝt[b]. Certis Holofernes, the while[c] he 6
ȝede aboute bi cumpas, foonde that the
welle, that flowide in to the watir cundit
of hem[d], was dressid[e] at the south part
with out the citee, and he comaundide her
watir cundit to be kit[f]. Netheles[g] wellis 7
weren not fer fro the wallis[h], of whiche[i]
wellis thei[k] weren seyn to drawe watir
bi thefte[l], rather to refreische[m] than to
drynke. But the sones of Amon and of 8
Moab neiȝiden to Holofernes, and seiden[n],
The sones of Israel tristen not in spere
and arowe[o], but hillis defenden hem, and
litle hillis set in the rooche of stoon maken

---

[t] the *AEFH.*   [u] Om. *AII.*   [v] Om. *AII.*   [w] bitwix *A.* betwen *E.* bitwene *H.*   [x] he comaundide *AII.*

[w] that oother 1. the other s.   [x] stie up 1s.   [y] And 1s.   [z] weren *with hem* s.   [a] of footmen fiȝteris B.
fiȝters of footmen *with him* 1. fiȝters of footmen s.   [b] withoute thilke men, that weren *there* redy 1.
outakyn tho men, which weren *there* redy s.   [c] the caitifte 1. the caitifte *of Holofernes* s.   [d] ocupied
or made thral s.   [e] ȝongthe *or of able fiȝters* 1s.   [f] And alle 1. And alle *there* s.   [h] an 1s.   [i] vn to 1s.
[k] heiȝte *theroff* 1s.   [l] that 1.   [m] vnto 1s.   [n] And 1s.   [o] as soon as s.   [p] thei bowiden 1s.   [q] upon 1s.
[r] threwen 1s.   [s] asshe *or poudre* s.   [t] up on 1s.   [u] thei preieden 1s.   [v] vpon 1s.   [w] thei saten 1s.   [x] bi
whiche 1s. that dressiden x.   [y] the streyt 1s.   [z] the hilli 1s.   [a] places is dressid 1s.   [b] al nyȝt 1.   [c] whilis s.
[d] men of Israel 1s.   [e] dressid *or ordeyned* s.   [f] kit at two 1. kitte sonder s.   [g] And netheles 1s.   [h] wallis
of the citee s.   [i] the whiche 1. which *wellis* s.   [k] men of Israel 1s.   [l] stelthe 1. stelthe *or priueli* s.
[m] refreische *hem* 1s.   [n] thei seiden *to him* 1s.   [o] in arowe 1s.

9 hillis sett in a dich broken beforn. Thanne that with oute going to fiȝtʸ thou mowe ouercome them, put keperis of wellis, that thei drawe not of hem; and with oute swerd thou shalt slen hem, or certis weried thei shuln take ther cite, the whiche thei wecnen in the hillis to moun 10 not ben ouercome. And these woordis pleseden beforn Olofernes, and beforn alle his cruel knyȝtus; and he sette bi enuy-11 roun hundredis bi alle the wellis. And whan this warde bi twenti daȝis was ful ended, faileden the cisternes and the gederingis of watris to alle the dwelleris in Betulie, so that ther was not with inne the cite, wher of thei myȝten han ynowȝ or for o dai, for at mesure watirᶻ was ȝiue 12 to the puplis eche dai. Thanne to Osias alle men and wymmen, and ȝunge men, and litle childer, gadered togidere, alle 13 togidere with o vois seiden, The Lord deme betwenᵃ vs and thee, for thou hast don in to vs euelys, not willende to speken pesibli with the Assiries, and for that God hath sold vs in the hondis of hem. 14 And therfore ther is not that helpeth, whan wee ben throwe doun befor the eȝen of hem in thrist, and in gret perdi-15 cioun. And now gedereth alle men, that ben in this citee, that wilfulli wee of al 16 the puple taken vs to Olofernes. Betere it is that caitif wee blisse God liuende, than wee die, and be repref to alle flesh, whan wee seen oure wiues and oure chil-17 der dienᵇ beforn oure eȝen. Wee taken to witnesse to dai heuene and erthe, and God of oure fadris, that doth veniaunce on vs after oure synnes, that now ȝee take the cite in the hond of the chiualrie of Olofernes, that oure ende be short in the mouth of swerd, that lengere is maad

hem stronge. Therfor that thou maist 9 ouercome hem without asailyng of batel, sette thou keperis of wellisᵖ, that thei drawe notᑫ of tho; and thou schalt sle hem without swerd, ethir certis theirʳ maad feyntˢ schulent bitakeᵘ her citee, whichᵛ thei gessen 'to mowᵂ notˣ be ouercomun 'in the hillisʸ. And these wordis plesiden 10 bifor Holofernes, and bifor alle hise knyȝtis; and he ordeynede bi cumpas bi ech welle an hundrid men. And whanne 'this kep-11 yng was fillidᶻ bi twenti daiesᵃ, cisternesᵇ and gaderyngisᶜ of watris fayliden to alle menᵈ dwellynge in Bethulia, so that there was notᵉ with ynne the citee, wherof thei schulden be fillidᶠ, nameli o dai, for the watir was ȝouun atᵍ mesure to the puplisʰ ech dai. Thanne alle men and wymmen, 12 ȝonge men and elde, and litle children, weren gaderid togidere to Ozieⁱ, and alle *thei* seiden to gidere with o voisᵏ, The 13 Lord deme bitwixe vs and thee, for thou, not wyllyngeˡ spekeᵐ pesibli with Assi-riensⁿ, hast 'do yuelsᵒ aȝenus vs, and for this thing God hath seld vs inᵖ the hondis of hem. Andᑫ therfor 'noon isʳ that help-14 ithˢ, whanne we ben cast doun in thirst, and in greet los bifor her iȝen. Andᵗ 15 nowᵘ gadere ȝe togidere alle men, that ben in theᵛ citee, that alle we puplis bi-take vsᵂ bi fre wille to Holofernes. It is 16 betere that weˣ prisoneris blesseʸ God and lyue, than that we dieᶻ, and beᵃ schenschip to ech man, sithenᵇ we seen thatᶜ oure wyues and oure ȝonge children dienᵈ bifor oure iȝen. We clepen in to witnessyng to 17 dai heuene and erthe, and the God of oure fadris, thatᵉ punischith vs aftir oure synnes, thatᶠ nowe ȝe bitake theᵍ citee in to the hondis of the chyualrie of Holo-fernes, and oureʰ ende beⁱ schort in the

---

ʸ the fiȝt c.　ᶻ the water *A*.　ᵃ betwixe *A*. bitwene *H*.　ᵇ to dien *All*.

ᵖ *her* wellis 18.　ᑫ *not watir* 18.　ʳ *whanne thei ben* 18.　ˢ feynt *for defaute* 1. feynt *for defaute of watir* 8.　ᵗ *thei schulen* 18.　ᵘ bitake *to thee* 18.　ᵛ *the which* citee, *for it is sett in the hillis* 18.　ᵂ Om. 1. it mow 8. ˣ it may not 1. -ʸ Om. 18.　ᶻ Om. 18.　ᵃ daies the kepyng *of the wellis* was fulfillid 18.　ᵇ *the* cisternes 18.　ᶜ *the* gaderyngis 18.　ᵈ the men *of Israel* 18.　ᵉ not *of water* 8.　ᶠ fulfillid 1.　ᵍ bi 18.　ʰ peple 18x.　ⁱ Ozie, *the cheef prest* 18.　ᵏ voice *to him* 8.　ˡ wilnynge 18.　ᵐ to speke 18.　ⁿ *the men of Assirie* 18.　ᵒ don yuele thingis 18.　ᵖ in to 18.　ᑫ Om. 8.　ʳ ther is noon 1.　ˢ helpith *vs* 8.　ᵗ Om. 8. ᵘ now *therfore* 18.　ᵛ *this* 18.　ᵂ *vs* self 18.　ˣ we *ben maad* 18.　ʸ *and* blesse 18.　ᶻ die *thus* 1. die *bi defaute or bi the honde of our enemyes* 8.　ᵃ we be 1. *so* he 8.　ᵇ *and sith* 18.　ᶜ Om. 18.　ᵈ dien *for defaute* 18. ᵉ which 8.　ᶠ and 8.　ᵍ *this* 18.　ʰ *that* oure 18.　ⁱ *be maad* 18.

18in droȝte of thiist And whan these thingis thei hadden seid, weping and gret ȝelling is maad in a gret chirche of alle men, and bi manye houris with o vois thei crieden to the Lord, seiende, 19Wee han synned with oure fadris, vn-riȝtwisli wee han don, wickednesse wee 20han maad For thou art piteuous, haue merci on vs, and in thi scourge venge oure wickednessis, and wile thou not taken men knoulechende thee to the pu-21ple that knowith not thee, that thei sei not among Jentilis, Whe1e is the God of 22hem? And whan, tiauailid with these cries and these wepingis, thei weren 23weri, Osias risende, the teiis inshed, seide, Euene inwit beth, brethern, 'and these fiue daȝes bijde wee of the Lord 24mercy; par auenture forsothe his indignacioun he shal putten awei, and ȝiue 25gloiie to his name If forsothe, fiue daȝes passid ouei, helpe cometh^c not, wee shul do these woordis that ȝee han spoken

CAP. VIII

1 And it is do, whan these wooidis hadde herd Judit, widewe, that was the doȝtei of Meiari, sone of Idor, sone of Joseph, sone of Ozie, sone of Elai, sone of Jamnoi, sone of Jedeon, sone of Rafoni, sone of Achitob, sone of Melchie, sone of Euam, sone of Mathanye, sone of Salathiel, sone 2of Symeon, sone of Ruben. And hii husbonde was Manasses, that diede in the 3daȝes of baili rip; forsothe he stod ouer the^d men bindende sheues in the feld, and ther cam hete vp on his hed, and he diede in Betulie his cite, and is biried 4there with his fadris Forsothe Judit vas the laft widue of hym now thre ȝer 5and sixe monethis And in the ouere^e partis of hii hous she made to hir a

scharpnesse of swerd, which^k *ende* is^l maad lengere in the diynesse of thirst. And 18 whanne thei hadden seid these thingis, greet wepyng and ȝellyng was maad of alle men in the giete chirche, and bi many ouris thei crieden 'with o vois^m to the Loid, and seiden, We and oure fadris 19 han synned, we han do vniusth, we^n diden^o wickidnesse Thou^p, for thou ait merciful, 20 haue meicy on vs, and venge^q oure wickidnessis^r in^s thi scourge; and^t nyle thou bitake men^u knoulechinge^v thee to a^w puple that knowith not thee, that thei scie not 21 amonge hethene men, Where is the God of hem? And whanne thei^x weren maad 22 feynt with these ciies, and weren maad very with these wepyngis, and weren stille, Ozie roos up, bisched^y with teeris, 23 and seide, Britheren, be ȝe pacient, and bi these fyue daies abide we meicy^z of the Lord; for in hap he schal kitte awei his 24 indignacioun, and schal^a ȝyue glorie to his name Sotheli if whanne these fyue daies 25 ben passid, help cometh^b not, we schulen do these wordis whiche ȝe han spoke

CAP VIII

And it was doon, whanne Judith, the 1 widowe, had herd these wordis, whiche *Judith*^{c} was the douȝtei of Meiaiy, the sone of Idor, the sone of Joseph, the sone of Ozie, the sone of Elai, the sone of Jamnor, the sone of Jedeon, the sone of Raphony, the sone of Achitob, the sone of Melchie, the sone of Euam, the sone of Mathanye, the sone of Salatiel, the sone of Symeon, the^d sone of Ruben And hir 2 hosebonde was^e Manasses, that was deed in the daies of baili heiuest, for^f he stood 3 bisili ouer men byndynge togidere reepis in the feeld, and heete cam on^g his heed, and he was deed in Bethulia his citee, and was^h biried theie with hise fadris So- 4 theh^i Judith left of hym^k was widewe

---

c coome AEFII   d Om AII,   e corner A

k the which 1   l is *now* is   m Om 1   n and we 1   o haue do 1   p Thou, *Lord* 1   q avenge c
r wickidnesse c1   s with a   t and, *Iord* 1   u me c   v schryuynge to 1   w Om 1   x *the sones of*
Israel 1   y al bisched 1   z the mercy cuiq   a he schal 1   b come is   c Om 1   d and the 1   e was
clepid 1   f certis 1   g upon 1   h he was 1   i And 1   k hym *or lynynge aftir him* 1

priue bed place, in whiche[f] with hir
6 hand wymmen closid she dwelte ; and,
hauende vp on hir lendis an heire, fastide
alle the da3es of hir lif, saue sabatis, and
newe mones, and the festis of the hous
7 of Irael. Forsothe she was with fair beholding ful myche, to whom hir husbonde
hadde laft myche richesse, and plenteuous
meyne, and possessiouns ful with droues
8 of oxen, and flockis of shep. And this
was in alle thingus most famous ; for she
dradde God gretli, ne ther was that shulde
9 speken of hir euel woord. And so this
whan she hadde herd, for Osias hadde
behoten, that, the fifte dai passid ouer, he
shulde take the cite, she sente to the
10 prestis of Cambre and of Carmy. And
thei camen to hir ; and she seide to them,
What is this woord, in the[g] whiche Osias
consentide that he take the cite to Assiries, if with inne fiue da3es ther come
11 not helpe to vs? And who ben 3ee that
12 tempten the Lord? This woord is not
that stire mercy ; but rathere that rere[h]
13 wrathe, and teende woodnesse. 3ee han
sett a time of mercy[i] doing of the Lord,
and in 3oure dom 3ee han ordeyned a dai
14 to hym. But for the Lord is pacient, in
this synne othinke wee, and his for3iue-
15 nesse with teres aske wee ; ne forsothe as
a man so God shal threten[k], ne as the
sone of man to wrathe he shal ben en-
16 flaumed. And therfore meke wee to hym
oure soulis, and in contrit spirit and
17 mekid serue wee to hym ; and sei wee
wepende to the Lord, that aftir his wil
so he do with vs his mercy ; and as oure
herte is disturbid[l] in the pride of hem,
18 so also of oure mecnesse wee glorien, For
wee han not folewid the synnes of oure
fadris, that forsoken ther God, and
19 honoureden alien godis ; for the whiche
hidous gilte thei ben 3iuen in to swerd,

thanne thre 3eer and sixe monethis. And
in the hi3ere partis of hir hows sche made
to hir a priuy closet, in which sche dwellide cloos with hir damesels ; and sche 6
hadde an heire on[l] her leendis, and fastide[m]
alle the daies of hir lijf, outakun sabatis[n],
and the 'bigynnyngis of monethis[o], and the
feestis of the hows[p] of Israel. Sotheli[q] 7
sche was of[r] ful[s] semeli biholdyng[t], to
whom hir hosebonde hadde left many
richessis, and plenteuouse meynee, and
possessiouns ful of droues of oxis[u], and
of[v] flockis of scheep. And this *Judith*[a] 8
was moost famouse among alle men ; for
sche dredde God greetli, nethir ony was
that spak of hir an yuel word. Therfor[o] 9
whanne this Judith hadde herd, that Ozie
hadde bihi3te, that whanne the fyuethe
day was passid, he wolde bitake the citee[w],
sche sente to the prestis† Cambri and
Carmy. And thei camen to hir ; and sche 10
seide to hem, What is this word, in which
Ozie consentide[x] to bitake the[y] citee to
Assiriens[z], if with ynne fyue daies help
cometh[a] not[b] to vs? And who ben 3e that 11
tempten the Lord? This 'word is not[c] 12
that stirith merci ; but rather that[d] stirith
ire[e], and kyndlith woodnesse[f]. Han 3e set 13
tyme[g] of the merciful[h] doynge of the Lord,
and in 3oure wille '3e han[l] set a dai to
hym? But for the Lord is pacient, do we 14
penaunce for this synne, and axe we with
teeris his for3yuenesse ; for[k] God schal not 15
manaasse so as man, nethir as 'a sone of
man[l] he schal be enflawmed to wrathfulnesse. And therfor meke we oure soulis 16
to hym, and in contrit[m] spirit and maad[n]
meke serue we[o] hym ; and seie we wepynge 17
to the Lord, that aftir his wille so he do
his merci with vs ; and as oure herte is
troblid in the pride of hem[p], so haue we
glorie 'also of[q] oure mekenesse. For we 18
'sueden not[r] the synnes of oure fadris,

† *the prestis ;* Judith spak to the prestis more coupable, far of that consent suede the distriyng of Goddis worschip, for which the prestis ou3ten for to loue more feruently, than the princes, for by taking of this citee the weye was redy to enemyes to go to Jerusalem, and distrie Goddis worschip, wher- for they ou3ten defende that cytee, as longe as they my3ten, she, in most turment. *Lire here.* c.

---

f the whiche *AEFII*. g Om. *AII*. h arere *AEFII*. i the mercy E *pr. m.* k threten vs *A*. l disturblid *AH*.

l upon 1. m sche fastide 1. n the sabot daies 1. o firste daies of the mone 1. P hows *or temple* 1.
q And 1. r Om. o. s a ful o. t in byholdynge o. u oxen 1. v Om. c. w citee *to Holofernes* 1.
x hath consentid 1. y this 1. z men of Assirie 1. a coune 1. b nat 1. c is no word 1. d it 1.
e *Goddis* wraththe 1. f *his* woodnesse 1. g a tyme 1. h mercy 1. l haue 3e 1. k certis 1. l the sone of
man c. mannus sone 1. m a contrit 1. n ymaad 1. o we to 1. P *oure enmyes* 1. q in 1. r haue not
sued 1.

and in to rauein, and in to confusioun to
ther^m enemys; wee forsothe other God
20 knowen not saue hym. Abijde wee meke
the coumforting of hym, and he shal
sechen out oure blod fro the torment-
ingis^n of oure enemys; and he shal meken
alle Jentilis, who so euere rijsen^o a3en
vs; and he shal make them with oute
21 wrshipe, the Lord oure God. And now,
brethern, for 3ee that ben prestis in the
puple of God, of 3ou hangeth the lif of
hem at 3oure speche, rereth vp the hertis
of hem, that myndeful 3ee be, for 3oure
fadris ben temptid, for thei shulden be
preued, if verreli thei herieden ther^p
22 God. Myndeful owen thei to ben, what
maner oure fader Abraham is temptid,
and, bi manye tribulaciouns preuyd, the
23 frend of God is maad. So Isaac, so Jacob, so Moises, and alle that pleseden to
the Lord, bi manye tribulaciouns pass-
24 eden feithful. Thei forsothe that temptaciouns resseyueden not with the^q drede
of God, and bro3ten forth ther vnpacience, and the repref of ther grucching
25 a3en the Lord, ben exilid of the exilere,
26 and of serpentis^r pershiden. And wee
thanne venge we not vsself^s for these
27 thingus that wee suffren; but, wijtende
to oure synnes these same lasse tormentis
to ben, the scourgis of the Lord, as seruauns of the Lord that ben chastisid, to
amendement, and not to han come to
28 oure perdicioun, wee leeuen^t. And Osias
and the prestis seiden to hir, Alle thingus,
that thou hast spoke, ben sothe, and ther
is not in thi woordis any repreuyng.
29 Now thanne prei thou for vs, for thou
art an holi womman, and dredende God.
30 And Judit seide to them, As that, that
I my3te speken, 3ee knowen to ben of
31 God, so that I purposide to do, preueth,

that^s forsoken her God, and worschipiden
alien goddis; for which^t greet trespas thei^u 19
weren 3ouun to her enemyes in to swerd,
and in to raueyn, and in to confusioun;
but we knowen not an othir God outakun
hym. 'Abide we meke^v his coumfort, and 20
he schal seke^w oure blood of the turmentis
of oure enemies; and he schal make meke
alle folkis, whiche euer risen^x a3ens vs';
and oure^y Lord God schal make hem without onour. And now, britheren, for 3e 21
ben prestis in the puple of God, and the
soule of hem^z hangith of 3ou, reise 3e^a her
hertis^b at 3oure speche, that thei be myndeful, that oure fadris weren temptid, that
thei schulden be preued, whethir thei worschipiden God verili. Thei owen to be 22
myndeful, hou oure fadir Abraham was
temptid^c, and^d he was preuyd bi mauy
tribulaciouns, and^e was maad the frend of
God. So Isaac, so Jacob, so^f Moyses, and 23
alle that plesiden 'the Lord^g, passiden^h
feithful^i bi many tribulaciouns. Sotheli^j 24
thei that resseyueden not temptaciouns
with the^k drede of the Lord, and bro3ten^l
forth her vnpacience, and the schenschip
of her grutchyng 'a3ens the Lord^m, weren^n 25
distried of a distriere, and perischiden^o of
serpentis. And therfor venge we not vs 26
for these thingis whiche^p we suffren; but 27
arette we, that these same turmentis ben
lesse than oure synnes, and bileue we, as
seruauntis of the Lord that^q ben chastisid,
that the betyngis^r of the Lord ben comun
to amendyng^s, and not to oure perdicioun.
And Ozie and the prestis seiden to hir^t, 28
Alle thingis^u, whiche^v thou hast spoke,
ben sothe, and no repreuyng is in thi
wordis. Now therfor preie thou for vs, 29
for thou art an hooli womman, and dredynge God. And Judith seide to hem, As 30
3e knowen, that this^w, that Y my3te speke,

---

^m alle there E pr. m.   ^n tormenting c.   ^o arijsen AEFH.   ^p Om. AH.   ^q Om. AH.   ^r the serpentis c.
^s oureself AH.   ^t bileuen A.

---

^a the whiche I.   ^t the which I.   ^u oure fadris I.   ^v Therfore, we beynge meke, abide we I.   ^w seke or
venge I.   ^x han risen I.   ^y the I.   ^z the peple I.   ^a 3e up I.   ^b hertis to God I.   ^c assaied I.   ^d and
hou I.   ^e and so he I.   ^f and so I.   ^g to God I.   ^h passiden forth I.   ^i feithfuli A pr. m. s.
^j And I.   ^k Om. I.   ^l a3ens the Lord bro3ten I.   ^m Om. I.   ^n thei weren I.   ^o thei perischiden I.
^p that I.   ^q whiche I.   ^r tourmentis I.   ^s oure amendyng I.   ^t Judith I.   ^u thes thingis I.   ^v that I.
^w this thing I.

if it is of God; and preȝeth, that God
32 stedefast make my counseil. Ȝee shul
stonden at the ȝate this nyȝt, and I shal
gon out with my fre handmaiden; and
preȝeth, that, as ȝee han seid, the^u Lord
33 in fiue daȝes beholde his puple Irael. Ȝou
forsothe I wile, that ȝee serche my deede,
and vnto the time that I bringe aȝeen
woord to ȝou, noon other thing be don,
but orisoun for me to the Lord oure God.
34 And Osias, the prince of Jude, seide to
hir, Go in pes, and the Lord be with
thee in^v the veniynge of oure enemys.
And, turnende aȝeen, thei wenten awei.

CAP. IX.

1 The whiche goende awei, Judit wente
in to hir oratorie, and, clothende hir with
an heire, putte askes^w vp on hir hed;
and, throwende hirself doun to the Lord,
2 criede to the Lord, sciende, Lord God of
my fader Symeon, that ȝeue to hym a
swerd in to defending of alienes, that
weren defouleris in ther defouling, and
nakeden the hipe of the maiden in to
3 confusioun; and thou ȝeue the wymmen
of hem in to prei, the doȝtris of hem in
to caitifte, and al the prei in to deui-
sioun to thi seruauns, that looueden thi
looue; help, I beseche, Lord, to me
4 widewe. Thou forsothe didist rathere
thingis, and thoo after thoo thou thoȝtist,
and this deede is, that thi self woldist.
5 Alle forsothe thi weies ben maad redi,
and thi domes in thi prouidence thou
6 hast put. Beholde the tentis of Assiries
now, as thanne the tentis of Egipcienus
thou vouchedest saf to beholde, whan after thi seruauns thei runnen armed, trost-
ende in ther foure horsid cartis, and in
ther horsing, and in the multitude of
7 fiȝteres. But thou beheelde vp on the

is of God, so preue ȝe, if this that Y pur- 31
poside^x to do, is of God; and preie ȝe, that
God make stidfast my counsel. Ȝe schulen 32
stonde at the ȝate this niȝt, and Y schal go
out^y with my fre handmayde; and preie ȝe,
that, as ȝe seiden, the Lord biholde his puple
Israel in^z fyue daies. But Y nyle^a, that 33
ȝe enquere my doyng, and til that^b Y telle
*to ȝou, noon othir thing be doon, no^c but
preier for me to oure Lord God. And 34
Ozie, the prince of Juda, seide to hir, Go
thou in pees, and the Lord be with thee
in the veniaunce of oure enemyes. And
thei^d turneden aȝen^e, and ȝeden awey.

CAP. IX.

And while thei ȝeden awei, Judith en- 1
tride in to hir oratorie, and sche clothide
hir silf with an heire, and puttide^f aische^g
on^h hir heed; and sche bowide doun hir
silf to the Lord, and criedeⁱ to the Lord,
and seide, Lord God of my fadir Symeon, 2
which^k ȝanest to hym a swerd in to de-
fence† of aliens, that^l weren defouleris in^m
her defoulyng, and maden nakid the hipe
of a virgyn in to confusiounⁿ; and thou 3
ȝauest the wymmen of hem in to prey,
the^o douȝtris of hem in to caitifte, and^p al
the prey in to departyng to thi seruauntis,
that loueden feruentli thi feruent louet‡;
Lord, Y bische^q, helpe thou me a widewe.
For^r thou madist the^s formere thingis, and 4
thouȝtist^t tho thingis aftir^u tho^v, and this
thing is maad^w, which thou woldist. For^x 5
alle thi weies ben redi, and thou has set
thi domes in thi^y puruyaunce. Biholde 6
thou the castels^z of Assiriens^a now^b, as
thou^c vouchidist saaf to biholde thanne^d
the castels^e of Egipcians^f, whanne thei
runnen^g armed after thi seruauntis, and
tristiden in charis^h, and in multitudeⁱ of
her knyȝtis, and in multitude^k of wer-

† *defence ; that is, in defending of hlm silf fro aliens ; defence here is seid the sleing of Siche-mytis, for the violent oppress-ing of Dyna, the doughter of Jacob. Lire here. c.*
‡ *thy ferueni loue ; the con-trarie semeth, for Jacob re-preuyde that doing of Sy-myon and of Leuy in xxiiij. c⁰. and in xlix. c⁰. of Genesis ; the soiling is this ; the fer-uent loue to avenge the de-fouling of a virgyn, was leueful and inst, for they hadden no iuge that wolde punysche the dede, of which the prince of the citee was auctour, and his puple was fautour; and thus spekith Judith here, and Jacob re-preuyde the yuel and trai-terouse maner of venging, in as myche as the sones of Jacob braken couenaunt maad with Si-chemytis. Lire here. c.*

---

^u that the A. ^v and in c sec. m. ^w asshen A. asken H.

^x haue purposid I. ^y forth I. ^z thes I. ^a wile not I. ^b Om. I. ^c be ther don noon othir thing of ȝou I. ^d Ozias and the prestis I. ^e Om. I. ^f sche puttide I. ^g ashen s. ^h upon I. ⁱ sche criede I.
^k that I. ^l the whiche I. ^m of I. ⁿ her owne confusioun I. ^o and the I. ^p and thou ȝauest I.
^q biseche thee I. ^r Certis I. ^s Om. I. ^t thouȝtis BCEFPS. Om. I. ^u and I. ^v tho thou thouȝtist to make aftirward I. ^w maad to us I. ^x Sothely I. ^y thi owne I. ^z strengthis I. ^a the men of Assirie I.
^b Om. I. ^c thanne thou I. ^d Om. I. ^e strengthis I. ^f the men of Egipt I. ^g camen I. ^h her charis I.
ⁱ the multitude I. ^k the multitude I.

tentis of hem, and dercnesses ouertrauaileden hem; the se heeld the feet of
hem, and watris couereden hem. So,
Lord, and these be maad, that trosten in
ther multitude; and in ther charis, and
in wepnys, and in ther arewis, and in
speris glorien; and thei knowen not, for
thou thi self art oure God, that to-tredest
batailis fro the bigynnyng, and Lord
name is to thee. Rere vp thin arm as
fro the begynnyng, and hurtle the vertue
of hem in thi vertue; falle the vertue of
hem in thi wrathe, that behoten themself to defoule thin holi thingus, and to
polluten the tabernacle of thi name, and
to throwe doun with swerd the horne of
thin auter. Do, Lord, that the pride of
hem be cut awei with ther owne swerd;
be he taken with the grane of his eȝen
in me; and thou shalt smyten hym of
the lippis of my charite. Ȝif to me in
wil stedefastnesse, that I dispise hym
and his vertue, and I turne hym vp so
doun. Forsothe he shal be the memorial
of thi name, whan the hondis of a womman han throwen hym doun. Forsothe,
Lord, not in multitude is thi vertue, ne
in strengthys of hors thi wil; ne proude
men pleseden to thee fro the begynnyng,
but of meke men and of buxum euermor to thee pleside the preȝeere. God
of heuenes, makere of watris, and Lord
of eche creature, here me wrecche preȝende and of thi merci principali takende
trost. Haue mynde, Lord, of thi testament, and ȝif woord in my mouth, and
strengthe the counseil in myn herte, that
thin hous in thin halewinge abijde stille;
and alle Jentilis knowen, for thou art
God, and ther is noon other biside thee.

riours¹. But thou biheldist on the castels^m 7
of hem, and derknessis maden hem feynt;
the botme of the see helde her feet, and 8
watris hiliden hem. Lord, ʼalso these men 9
be maad so, that^n tristen in her multitude,
and in her charis, and in scharp° schaftis
with oute irun, and in her arowis; and
han glorie^p in her speris; and witen^q not, 10
that thou thi silf art oure^r God, that^s ʼal
to-brekist batels^t fro the bigynnyng^u, and
the^v Lord is name to thee. Reise^w thin 11
arm† as^x at the bigynnyng, and^y hurle^z
doun the power^a of hem ʼin thi vertu^b; the
power^c of hem falle^d doun in thi wrath-
fulnesse^e, whiche biheten hem to defoule
ʼthin hooli thingis, and to defoule^f the
tabernacle of thi name, and to cast doun
with her swerd the horn^g of thin auter.
Lord, make thou that the pride of hem 12
be kit of with her owne swerd; be^h he^i 13
takun with the snare of hise iȝen in me;
and thou schalt smyte hym with the lippis
of my charite‡. Ȝyue^k thou to^l me stid-14
fastnesse in soule, that Y dispise hym^m
and his vertu^n, and distrie° hym. For^p it 15
schal be a memorial^q of ^r thi name, whanne
the hondis of a womman han cast hym doun.
For whi, Lord, thi vertu^s is not in multi-16
tude, nether thi wille is in the strengthis
of horsis; and^t proude spiritis plesiden not
thee at the bigynnyng, but the preier of
meke men and mylde ʼpleside euere^u thee.
God of heuenes, the^v creatour of watris, 17
and Lord of alle^w creature, here thou me
wretchid *womman* preiynge^x and tristynge
of thi merci. Lord, haue thou mynde of 18
thi testament, and ȝyue thou a word in
my mouth^y, and make thou strong the
counsel^z in myn herte, that thin hows
dwelle perfitly in thin halewyng; and 19
that alle folkis knowe, that thou art God,
and^a noon other is outakun thee.

*† arm; that is,
thi power.
Lire here. c.*

*‡ my charite;
that is, by my
swete wordis
and schewinge
loue. Lire
here. c.*

x Om. AH.

¹ *her* werriouris I.   ^m powers I.   ^n be thes men maad also in lijk manere, whiche I.   ° *her* scharp I.
^p veyn glorie I.   ^q thei witen I.   ^r Om. s.   ^s whiche I.   ^t Om. I.   ^u bigynnyng hast alto broke batailis I.
^v Om. I.   ^w Reise up I.   ^x as *thou didist* I.   ^y and in thi vertu I.   ^z hurledist I. hurtle R.   ^a vertu BEII
sec. m. LPUVX.   ^b Om. I.   ^c vertu GKLMXa.   ^d falle it I.   ^e riȝtfulnesse I.   ^f Om. I.   ^g myȝt I.
^h *and* be I.   ^i *Holofernes* I.   ^k ȝyue, Lord I.   ^l Om. s.   ^m *Holofernes* I.   ^n power U sec. m. I.   ° *make
me to distrie* I.   ^p Certis I.   ^q myndfulnesse I.   ^r to B pr. m.   ^s power I.   ^t and, Lord I.   ^u hath euer
plesid I.   ^v thou art I.   ^w ech I.   ^x Om. I.   ^y mouth *to speke* I.   ^z counsel *of thee* I.   ^a and that I.

CAP. X.

1 It is do forsothe, whan she hadde cesid
to crien to the Lord, she ros fro the place,
in whiche she lai throwe doun to[y] the
2 Lord. And she clepide hir fre maiden,
and cam doun in to hir hous; she[z] dide
awei fro hir the heire, and clothide hyrself out of the clothing of hir widewehed.
3 And she wesh hir bodi, and oyntide hirself with the beste myrre, and she platte
the her of hir hed, and putte a mytre
vp on hir hed, and she clothide hir with
the clothis of hir jolite, and clothide hirself gaȝe shon to hir feet; and she toc
armes onournemens[a], and lilies, and ere
ringus, and finger ringys, and with alle
hir onournemens[b] she onournede hir.
4 To whom also the Lord ȝaf briȝtnesse,
for al this composicioun not of lust, but
of vertue heeng[c]; and therfore the Lord
made more this fairnesse in to hir, that
she aperede to the eȝen of alle men with
5 fairnesse vncomparable. And so she putte
on to hir fre maiden a botel of wijn, and
ʽa vessel[d] of oile, and potage, and dried
figes, and loues, and chese, and wente
6 forth. And whan thei weren come to
the ȝate of the cite, thei founden Osiam
7 abidende, and the prestis of the cite. The
whiche whan thei hadden seen hir, stone-
ȝende merueileden ful miche the fairnesse
8 of hir. No thing ner the latere askende
hir laften to passen, seiende, God of oure
fadris ȝiue to thee grace, and al the
counseil of thin herte with his vertue
strengthe, and glorie vp on thee Jerusalem, and be thi name in the noumbre

CAP. X.

Forsothe[b] it was doon, whanne sche[c] hadde 1
ceessid to crie to the Lord, sche roos[d] fro
the place, in which sche lay bowid doun to
the Lord. And sche clepide hir fre hand- 2
maide, and cam[e] doun in to hir hows; and
sche took awei fro hir[f] the heire, and[g] vnclothide hir silf[i] fro the clothing of hir widewehod. And sche waischide hir bodi, and 3
anoyntide[k] hir with beste[l] myrre†, and sche
schedide[m] the heer of hir heed, and settide[n]
a mytre[o] on[p] hir heed, and sche clothide
hir with the clothis of hyr gladnesse, and
clothide[q] hir feet with sandalies[r]; and sche
took ournementis[s] of the[t] armes, and lilies,
and eeryngis, and ryngis[u], and ournede[v]
hir silf[w] with alle hir ournementis. To 4
whom also[x] the Lord ȝaf briȝtnesse[y], for al
this ourenement[z] hangide[a] not[b] of letcherie,
but of[c] vertu[d]; and[e] therfor[f] the Lord
ʽmade large[g] this fairnesse on[h] hir, that[i]
bi ʽvncomparable fairnesse[k] sche apperide[l]
to the iȝen of alle men. Therfor[m] sche 5
puttide on[n] hir fre handmaide a botel of
wyn[o], and a vessel of oile, and meet maad
of meele, and dried[p] figus, and looues[q], and
cheese, and ȝeden[r] forth. And whanne 6
thei weren comen to the ȝate[s] of the citee,
thei founden[t] Ozie and the prestis of the
citee abidynge *hir*[u]. And whanne thei 7
hadden seyn hir, thei weren astonyed, and
wondriden[v] ful myche on hir fairnesse.
Netheles thei axiden hir no thing, and 8
leeten[w] passe[x], and seiden[y], The[z] God of
oure fadris ȝyue grace to thee, and make[a]
strong with his vertu al the counsel of
thin herte, and Jerusalem haue[b] glorie on[c]

† *myrre*; that is, oynement maad of myrre for greet part. *Lire here*. c.

[y] into E *pr. m.* [z] and sue A. [a] honournementis E. ournementis F. [b] honournementis E. ourne-mentis AF. [c] hangide AEFH. [d] vessels AH.

[b] And I. [c] *Judith* I. [d] roos up I. [e] *Judith* cam I. [f] hir self IS. [g] and sche IS. [i] Om. I. [k] sche anoyntide IS. [l] ful good I. [m] schedde IS. schoddide MX. [n] sche settide IS. [o] mytre, *that is, a semely ournement* IS. [p] upon IS. [q] sche hilide IS. [r] sandalies, *that is, an ournement of feet, which was vsid in the old tyme* S. [s] the ournementis IS. [t] Om. IS. [u] *othere* ryngis IS. [v] sche ournede IS. [w] Om. IS. [x] also *ouer al this* I. also *ouer al her owrnement* S. [y] fairnesse IS. [z] ournement, *that is, noon of al this ournement* S. [a] Om. I. [b] not *upon hir bicause* S. [c] *bicause* of S. [d] vertu hangide *on hir* I. [e] Om. S. [f] therfor *in hir* IS. [g] made large *or encresside* IS. [h] upon IS. [i] so that IS. [k] fairnesse that myȝte not be comparisound IS. [l] apperide *semely* IS. [m] And thanne IS. [n] upon IS. [o] wyne *to bere with hir* S. [p] of dried IS. [q] *sche toke to hir* looues IS. [r] thei ȝeden IS. [s] ȝatis IS. [t] founden *there* IS. [u] *Judith* IS. [v] thei wondriden IS. [w] thei leeten *hir* IS. [x] passe forth IS. [y] seiden *to hir* S. [z] Om. I. [a] make he IS. [b] haue it IS. [c] upon IS.

9 of seintus and of riʒtwis men. And these, that ther weren, alle with o vois seiden, 10 Be it do! be it do! Thanne Judit preʒende the Lord, passede thurʒ the ʒatis, 11 she and hir fre maiden. It is do forsothe, whan she cam doun the hil aboute spring of the dai, aʒen camen to hir the aspies of the[c] Assiries, and heelden hir, seiende, Whennes comest thou, or whider gost 12 thou? The whiche answerde, A doʒter I am of Ebrues, and therfore I fleiʒ fro the face of hem, for to comen I knew, that thei shul ben to ʒou in to prei taking, for thi that despisende ʒou wolden not freeli taken themself, that thei shulden 13 finde mercy in ʒoure siʒte. For this cause I thoʒte with myself, seiende, I shal go to the face off Olofernes prince, that I shewe to hym the priuites of hem, and I shal shewe to hym, bi what entre he mai wynne hem, so that ther falle 14 not oon man of his ost. And whan thoo men hadden herd hir woordis, thei beheelden hir face, and she was in ther eʒen stoneyng, for thei merueileden ful 15 myche the fairnesse of hir. And thei seiden to hir, Thou hast kept thi lif, for thi that such a counseil thou hast founde, 16 that thou come doun to oure lord. This forsothe wite thou, that, whan thou stondist in his siʒte, he shal wel do to thee, and thou shalt be most acceptid in his herte. And thei ladden hir to the tabernacle of Olofernes, and shewiden hir. 17 And whan she was comen in beforn his face, anoon Olofernes is caʒt in his eʒen. 18 And hise tyraunt knyʒtis seiden to hym, Who despisede the puple of Jewis, that han so faire wymmen, that not for hem bi riʒt aʒen hem wee owen to fiʒten? 19 And so Judit seande Olofernes sittende in the canope, that was of purper, and

thee, and thi name be in the noumbre of hooli and iust men. And alle thei, that 9 weren there, seiden with o vois, Be it doon! be it doon! Therfor[d] Judith preiede 10 the Lord, and passide[e] thorouʒ the ʒatis, sche[f] and hir fre[g] handmayde[h]. Forsothe[i] 11 it was doon, whanne sche cam doun of the hil aboute the risynge[k] of the dai, the aspieris[l] of Assiriens[m] metten hir, and helden[n] hir, and seiden, Fro whennus comest thou, ether whidur goist thou? And sche[o] answeride, Y am a douʒter of 12 Ebreis[p], and therfor Y fledde[q] fro the face of hem, for Y knew[r]†, that it[s] schal come, that thei schulen be ʒouun to ʒou in to prey, for thei dispisiden[t] ʒou, and nolde[u] bitake[v] hem silf wilfuli[w], that thei schulden fynde[x] grace in ʒoure siʒt. For[y] this 13 cause Y thouʒte with[z] men[a], and seide[b], Y schal go to the face[c] of the prynce Holofernes, for to schewe to hym the priuytees of hem[d], and Y schal schewe to hym, bi what entryng[e] he mai gete hem, so that not o man of his oost falle doun[f]. And whanne tho men hadden herd the 14 wordis of hir[g], thei bihelden hir face, and wondryng was in hir iʒen, for thei wondriden greetli on hir fairnesse. And thei 15 seiden to hir, Thou hast kept thi lijf, for[h] thou hast founde sich a counsel, that thou woldist come doun to oure lord. Sotheli[i] 16 wite thou this[k], that, whanne thou 'hast stonde[l] in his siʒt, he schal do wel to thee, and thou schalt be moost acceptable in his herte. And thei ledden hir to the tabernacle of Holofernes, and thei schewiden hir to hym. And whanne sche hadde en- 17 trid bifor his face, anoon Holofernes was takun bi hise iʒen[m]. And hise knyʒtis 18 seiden to hym, Who schal dispise[n] the puple of Jewis, whiche[o] han so faire wymmen, that we owen not to fiʒte skilfuli

[o] Om. AH.

[d] Certis 13.   [e] sche passide forth 18.   [f] Om. 18.   [g] Om. 1.   [h] handmayde with hir 18.   [i] And 18. [k] spryngyng 18.   [l] spieris 18.   [m] the men of Assiric 18.   [n] thei helden 1.   [o] Judith 18.   [p] the men of Ebreis 18.   [q] haue fled 18.   [r] knowe 1.   [s] this thing 18.   [t] han dispisid 18.   [u] for thei wolden not 1. for thei mulden 8.   [v] take c.   [w] wilfuli to ʒou 18.   [x] haue founden 18.   [y] And for 8.   [z] with ynne 1.   [a] me in my herte 8.   [b] I seide 18.   [c] presence 18.   [d] the men of Israel 18.   [e] entre x.   [f] doun bi deeth 8. [g] Judith 13.   [h] for thi that 18.   [i] And 18.   [k] this thing 18.   [l] stondist 1.   [m] iʒen with lust 18.   [n] dispise to destrie 1. dispise or leue to distrie s.   [o] that 1.

of gold, and of smaragd, and of most
20 precious stones with inne wouen, and
whan 'in to^f his face she hadde lokid,
she honourede hym, fallende hyrself doun
vpon the erthe; and the seruauns of Olofernes rereden hir vp, ther^g lord comaundende.

a3enus hem for these wymmen? Therfor^p 19
Judith si3 Holofernes sittynge in^q a cur-
teyn†, round^r bynethe and scharp^s abouc,
that^t was wouun of^u purpur, and gold^v,
and smaragde^w, and moost^x preciouse
stoonys^y, and whanne sche hadde lokid 20
in to^z his face, sche worschipide hym, and
bowide^a doun hir silf on the erthe; and
the seruauntis of Holofernes reisiden hir^b,
for her lord comaundide^c.

† a curtyn; that is, in a chayer, hilid with siche a curtyn. Lire here. c.

CAP. XI.

1　Thanne Olofernes seide to hir, Euene
inwit be thou, and wile thou not dreden
in thin herte, for I neuere no3ede man,
that wolde serue to king Nabugodonosor.
2 Thi puple forsothe, if it hadde not despisid me, I hadde not rerid myn hond
3 vp on it. Now forsothe sei to me, of^h
what cause thou wentist awei fro them,
and it pleside to thee that thou hast come
4 to vs. And Judit seide, Tac the woordis
of thin hand maiden; for, if thou folewist
the woordis of thin hand maiden, a parfit
5 thing the Lord shal don with thee. Forsothe Nabugodonosor liueth, king of theⁱ
erthe, and his vertue liueth, that is in
thee to the chastising of alle liues er-
rende^k; for not onli men shul serue to
hym bi thee, but and bestis of the feld
6 obeshen to hym. Forsothe the redynesse
of thin inwit is told to alle folkis; and
it is open to al the world, for thou alone
good and my3ti art in al his reume; and
thi discipline to alle prouyncis is prechid.
7 Ne that is vnknowen, that Achior spac,
ne that is vnwist, that hym thou hast
8 comaundid to fallen. Forsothe it is
knoweu so oure God offendid to synnes,
that he hath sent by his profetis to the
puple, that he shal taken it for ther
9 synnes. And for the sones of Irael witen
them to han offendid the Lord ther God,

CAP. XI.

　Thanne Holofernes seide to hir^d, Be 1
thou coumfortid, and nyle thou drede in
thin herte, for Y neuere anoyede^e man, that
wolde serue Nabugodonosor, the^f kyng^g.
Sotheli^h if thi puple hadde not dispisid 2
me, Y hadde not reisid 'myn hondⁱ on it.
But 'now seie^k to me, for what cause 3
3edist thou awei fro hem, and^l it pleside
thee to come to vs. And Judith seide, 4
Take^m thou the wordis of thin hand-
maide; for, if thou suestⁿ the^o wordis of
thin handmaide, the Lord schal make a
perfit thing with thee. Forsothe Nabu- 5
godonosor, the kyng of erthe, lyueth, and
his vertu^p lyueth, which is in thee to the
chastisyng of alle soulis^q errynge; for not
oneli^r men schulen serue hym^s 'bi thee^t,
but also beestis of the feeld obeien^u to
hym^v. For the prudence of thi soule^w is 6
teld to alle folkis; and it is schewid to al
the world, that thou aloon art good and
my3ti in al his rewme; and thi techyng
is prechid in alle prouyncis. Nether this 7
thing is hid, which^y Achior spak^z, nether
that thing is vnknowun, which thou co-
maundidist^a to bifalle to hym. For^b it is 8
knowun, that oure God is so offendid bi
synnes, that he sente^c bi hise profetis to
the puple^d, that he wolde bitake hem^e for
her synnes. And for the sones of Israel 9
witen, that thei han offendid 'her Lord

^f Om. *A.*　^g tho *A.*　^h for *A.*　ⁱ Om. *AII.*　^k lyuynge *E pr. m.* errynge *sec. m.*

^p And 18.　^q withynne 18.　^r that was wijd 18.　^s narou3 18.　^t the whiche 1. which 8.　^u with 8.
^v of gold 18.　^w of smaragde 1.　^x of moost 1.　^y stoones *weren fretie ther vpon* 8.　^z Om. 18.　^a she
bowide 18.　^b hir up 18.　^c comaundide *so* 18.　^d *Judith* 18.　^e noiede 18.　^f Om. 8.　^g kyng *of Assirie* 18.
^h And 18.　ⁱ my power up 18.　^k seie thou now 18.　^l and *whi* 1. whi 8.　^m Take *to herte* 18.　ⁿ schalt
sue 18.　^o *and do after* the 8.　^p power 18.　^q lyues 1.　^r oneli bi thee 18.　^s *Nabugodonosor* 18.　^t Om. 18.
^u shul obeie 18.　^v hym *bi thee* 18.　^w soule *or wit* 8.　^y that 1.　^z hath spoke 18.　^a comaundist 18.
^b Forsothe 18.　^c hath sent 18.　^d peple *of vs* 8.　^e hem *to her ennyes* 18.

10 his trembling is vp on hem. Ferthermor also hungir hath asailid hem, and of the dro3te of water now among deade men 11 ben countid. Therfore this thei ordeynen, that ther bestis thei slen, and the blod 12 of hem thei drinken; and the holi thingis of ther Lord, that God comaundide not to be touchid, in^l whete, win, and oile, these thingus thei han tho3t to 3iuen out, and wiln waste thoo thingus, that with hondus thei shulden not touche; thanne for these thingys thei don, it is certcin 13 that in to leesing thei shul be 3iue. The whiche thing I, thin hand maiden, knowende, flei3 fro them, and the Lord sente 14 me these same thingus to telle thee. I forsothe, thin hand maiden, herie God, also now anent thee; and thin hand maiden shal gon out, and I shal pre3en 15 God; and he shal sei to me, for he shal 3elde to them ther synne; and comende I shal telle to thee, so that I shal bringe thee bi the myddel of Jerusalem, and thou shalt han al the puple of Irael as shep to whiche^m is no shepperde, and ther shal not berken or^n oon a3en thee; 16 for these thingis to me ben seid bi the 17 prouidence of God. And for God is wroth to them, I am sent these same thingus to 18 telle thee^o. Forsothe alle these woordis pleseden beforn Olofernes, and beforn his childer; and thei merueileden at the wisdam of hir; and the tother^p seide to the 19 tother, Ther is not such a womman vpon erthe in si3te, in fairnesse, and^q in wit of 20 woordis. And Olofernes seide to hir, God hath do wel, that sente thee befor the puple, that thou 3eue it in oure hondis; 21 and for good is thi beheste, if thi God do to me these thingus, he shal ben and my God, and thou in the hous of Nabugodonosor shalt be gret, and thi name shal be nemned in al erthe.

God^f, the tremblyng of hym^g is on^h hem. Ferthermore also hungur hath asailid hem, 10 and for drynesse of watir thei ben rikenyd now among deed men. Forsothe^i thei or- 11 deynen this^k, that thei sle her beestis, and drynke her blood; and thei thou3ten^l to 12 3yue these hooli thingis 'of her Lord in^m wheete, wyn, and oile, whiche^n God comaundide to be not touchid, and thei wolen waste the^{nn} thingis, which thei ou3ten^o not touche^p with hondis; therfor for thei doen these thingis, it is certeyn that thei schulen be 3ouun in to perdicioun. Which thing Y, thin handmaide, 13 knew^q, and^r fledde fro hem, and the Lord sente^s me to telle these same thingis to thee. For^t Y, thin handmaide, worschipe 14 God, also now at^u thee; and thin handmaide schal go out^v, and Y schal preie God; and he schal seie to me, whanne he 15 schal 3elde to hem^w her synne; and Y schal come, and telle to^x thee, so that Y brynge thee thorou3 the myddis of Jerusalem, and thou schalt haue al the puple of Israel as scheep 'to whiche is^y no scheepherde^z, and ther schal not berke^a a3ens thee nameli oon; for these thingis ben seid to me bi 16 the puruyaunce of God. And for God is 17 wrooth to hem, Y am sente to telle to^b thee these same thingis. Sotheli^c alle 18 these wordis plesiden bifor Holofernes, and bifore hise children^d; and thei wondriden at the wisdom of hir^e; and oon^f seide to another, Ther is not sich a womman on^g 19 erthe in si3t, in fairenesse, and in wit of wordis. And Holofernes seide to hir, God 20 dide wel, that sente thee bifor the puple, that thou 3yue^h it in^i myn hondis; and^k 21 for thi biheest is good, if thi God doith these thingis to me, he schal be also my God, and thow schalt be greet in the hows of Nabugodonosor, and thi name schal be nemyd in al erthe.

^{l} Om. A. ^{m} the whiche A. ^{n} Om. A. ^{o} to thee C. ^{p} toon A. ^{q} Om. A.

^{f} the Lord her God is. ^{g} hem i. ^{h} upon is. ^{i} And this thing is. ^{k} now is. ^{l} han thou3t i. ^{m} to bie with i. of her Lord to bie with s. ^{n} the whiche i. ^{nn} tho As. ^{o} owen iRs. ^{p} to touche a. ^{q} knowe is. ^{r} and therfor I i. and herefor I s. ^{s} hath sent is. ^{t} Sothely is. ^{u} anentis i. ^{v} forth is. ^{w} the Jewis s. ^{x} Om. i. ^{y} that i. ^{z} schepherde is to i. ^{a} chide i. chide either speke foul s. ^{b} Om. i. ^{c} Certis is. ^{d} seruauntis is. ^{e} Judith is. ^{f} oon of hem s. ^{g} upon is. ^{h} bitake is. ^{i} in to s. ^{k} Om. s.

CAP. XII.

1 Thanne he comaundede hir to gon in, wher his tresories[r] weren leid vp, and he comaundide hir to dwelle there; and he ordeynede, what shulde be ʒiue to hir of 2 his feste. To whom answerde Judit, and seide, Now I shal not moun ete of these thingus, that thou comaundist to me to be ʒolden, lest ther come vp on me gilte; of thoo thingis forsothe that with me I 3 haue broʒt, I shal ete. To whom seith Olofernes, If these thingis failen to thee, that with thee thou hast broʒt, what shul 4 wee do to thee? And Judit seide, Lord, thi soule liueth, for thin hand maide shal not spende alle these thingus, to the time that God shul do in myn hond thoo thingus that I haue thoʒt. And his ser-5 uauns ladden hir in to the tabernacle, wher he hadde comaundede. And she askide, whil she shulde gon in, that ther shulde be ʒiue to hir fredam, the nyʒt, and beforn the liʒt[s], of going out to ori-6 soun, and of preʒing the Lord. And he comaundede to his cubicularies, that, as it pleside to hir, she shulde gon out, and comen in, to preʒen hir God bi thre daʒes. 7 And she wente out on nyʒtis in to the valei of Betulie, and baptiside hirself in 8 to the welle of watir. And as she steʒede vp, she preʒede the Lord God of Irael, that he shulde gouerne hir wei to the[t] 9 deliueryng of hir puple. And goende in, clen she dwelte in the tabernacle, vnto 10 the time she toc hir mete vnto euen. And it is don the ferthe dai, Olofernes made a soper to his seruauns, and seide to Vagio, gelding, Go, and sweteli moue this Ebru, that wilfulli she sente[u] to dwelle with 11 me. Forsothe a foul thing it is anent Assiries, if a womman scorne a man, doende that she passe fro hym withoute

CAP. XII.

1 Thanne Holofernes comaundide hir[l] to entre, where his tresouris weren kept, and he comaundide hir to dwelle there; and he ordeynede, what[m] schulde be ʒouun to hir of his feeste. To whom Judith answeride, 2 and seide, Now Y may not ete of these thingis, which thou comaundidist to be ʒouun to me, lest offence come on me; but Y schal ete of these thingis, whiche 3 Y brouʒte[n] with me. To whom Holofernes seide, If these thingis failen[nn], whiche thou brouʒtist[o] with thee, what schulen we[p] do to thee? And Judith seide, Lord, thi soule 4 lyueth, for thin handmaide schal not spende alle these thingis, til God schal do in myn hondis these thingis which Y thouʒte[q]. And hise seruauntis ledden hir in to the tabernacle, whidur he hadde comaundid. And sche axide[r], the[s] while sche entride[t], 5 that fredom schulde be ʒouun to hir to go out to preier, in the nyʒt, and bifor the liʒt[u], and[v] to biseche the Lord. And he[vv] 6 comaundide to his chaumberleyns, that, as it pleside hir, sche schulde go out, and entre[w], for to preie hir God bi thre daies. And sche ʒede out[x] in nyʒtis in to the 7 valei of Bethulia, and waischide[y] hir silf[z] in the[a] welle of watir. And as sche 8 stiede[b], sche preiede the Lord God of Is-rael, that he wolde dresse hir weie to the delyueraunce of his puple. And sche en-9 tride[c], and dwellide clene in the taber-nacle, til that sche took hir mete in the euentid. And it was doon in the fourthe[†] 10 dai, Holofernes made a soper to hise ser-uauntis, and he seide to Vagao, the[d] chaumburleyn, Go thou, and counsele[e] that[f] Ebrew womman, that sche consente wilfuli to dwelle with me. For it is foul[g] 11 anentis Assiriens[h], if a womman scorne[i] a man, in doynge[k] that[l] sche passe 'with

[†] *fourthe; fro the entringe of Judith fro the cytee of Bithu-lia. Lire here. c.*

---

r tresours A. tresour II.   s while E pr. m.   t Om. A.   u asente A.

l *Judith* 18.   m what thing 18.   n haue brouʒt 18.   nn failen *to thee* 18.   o hast brouʒt 18.   p we thanne 18.   q haue thouʒt *to do* 18.   r axide *of Holofernes* s.   s Om. 1.   t entride *in to the tabernacle* 8. u liʒt *of [the s] dai came* 18.   v Om. 1.   vv *Holofernes* 18.   w yn 1.   x forth 18.   y sche waischide 18. z Om. 1. there s.   a a 18.   b stiede up 1. stiede vp *there* 8.   c entride yn 18.   d his 18.   e counsel *thou* 8. f *Judith* the 18.   g a foul thing 18.   h men of Assirie 18.   i scorne *or desceyue* 1.   k hir doynge 1. l and that 18.

12 hir offis. Thanne wente in Vagio to Judit, and seide, Be not adrad, thou goode child maide[v], to gon in to my lord, that she be maad wrshipeful beforn his face, and ete she with hym, and drinke win 13 with gladnesse. To whom Judit answerde, What am I, that I a3enseie to 14 my lord? Alle thing, that shal ben beforn his e3en good and best, I shal do. What euere forsothe to hym shulde plese, that to me shal be best alle da3es[w] of my 15 lif. And she ros, and enournede hirself with hir clothis, and gon in she stod 16 beforn his face. Forsothe the herte of Olofernes is smyten; forsothe he was 17 brennende in the lust of hir. And Olofernes seide to hir, Drink now, and sitt doun in io3e; for thou hast founde grace 18 befor me. And Judit seide, I shal drinke, lord, for my lif is magnyfied to dai be-19 forn alle the da3es of my liuyng. And she toc, and eet, and dranc beforn hym thoo thingis, that hir hond maiden hadde 20 maad redi to hir. And Olofernes is maad myrie 'to hir[x], and myche win he dranc ful myche, hou myche in o dai neucre he hadde drunken in his lyue.

CAP. XIII.

1 As forsothe euetid[y] is do, his seruauns he3eden to ther herbergeries; and Vagio closide the dores of the priue chaumbre, 2 and wente. Forsothe alle weren ouer-3 trauailid of win; and Judit was alone 4 in the priue chaumbre. But Olofernes lai in the bed, with to myche drunk-5 enesse aslepe. And Judit seide to hir child womman, that she shulde stonde with oute forthe befor the dore of the 6 priue chaumbre, and waiten aboute. And Judit stod befor the bed, pre3ende with teres, and with moouyng of lippis in

out part[m] fro hym. Thanne Vagao en-12 tride[n] to Judith, and seide[o], A good damesele be not aschamed to entre[p] to my lord, that sche be onourid bifor his face, and that sche eete with hym, and drynke wiyn with gladnesse. To whom Judith 13 answeryde, Who am Y, that Y a3enseie my lord? Y schal do al thing, that schal 14 be good and best bifor hise i3en. Sotheli[q] what euer thing plesith hym, this[r] schal be best to me in alle the daies of my lijf. And sche roos[s], and ournede hir silf[t] with 15 hir clothis, and entride[u], and stood bifor 'his face[v]. Forsothe[w] the herte of Holo-16 fernes was stirid[x]; for he was brennynge in the[y] coueitise of hir. And Holofernes 17 seide to hir, Drynke thou now, and take[z] mete in[a] gladnesse; for thou hast founde grace bifor me. And Judith seide, Lord, 18 Y schal drynke, for my soule is magnyfied to dai bifor alle the daies of my lijf. And sche took, and eet, and drank bifor 19 hym tho thingis, whiche hir handmayde hadde maad redi to hir. And Holofernes 20 was maad glad 'to hir[b], and he drank[c] ful myche wiyn, hou myche he hadde neuere drank in o dai in his lijf.

CAP. XIII.

Forsothe as[d] euentid was maad, hise[e] 1 seruauntis[f] hastideng[g] to her ynnest†; and Vagao[h] closid togidere the doris of the closet[i], and 3ede[j] forth. For alle men 2 weren maad feynt[k] of wiyn; and Judith 3 aloone was[l] in[m] the closet. Certis Holo-4 fernes lai[n] in the[n] bed, aslepid with ful myche drunkenesse. And Judith seide to 5 hir damesele, that sche schulde stonde with outforth bifor the dore of the closet, and aspie[p]. And Judith stood bifor the 6 bed[q], preiynge[r] with teeris, and with stir-yng[s] of lippis[t] 'in silence, seiynge[u], Lord 7

† *ynnes; that is, tentis. Liue here.* c.

---

[v] womman c pr. m.   [w] the dais AII.   [x] Om. A.   [y] eueutide AII.

---

[m] free I.   [n] entride yn is.   [o] he seide *to hir* is.   [p] entre yn is.   [q] And is.   [r] this thing is.   [s] roos up is.   [t] Om. is.   [u] sche entride yn is.   [v] the face of Holofernes is.   [w] And is.   [x] stiride *to lust* s.   [y] *fleishly* I.   [z] take *thou* s.   [a] with s.   [b] toward hir I. to hir wardus s.   [c] drank *thanne* is.   [d] *as soone . as* is.   [e] the is.   [f] seruauntis of Holofernes is.   [g] hastiden hem is.   [h] Vages, *chamberleyne* I. Vagao, *his chaunmberleyne* s.   [i] closet *where Holofernes lay* is.   [j] he 3ede is.   [k] feynt *or drunken* is.   [l] was there is.   [m] withynne I.   [n] lai *there* is.   [o] a is.   [p] aspie *that no man were ni3* s.   [q] bed *of him* I. bed *of Holofernes* s.   [r] and she preiede is.   [s] mouyng is.   [t] hir lippis is.   [u] sche seide in silence is.

7 silence, seiende, Conferme me, Lord God
of Irael, and behold in this hour to the
werkis of myn hondis, that thou rere vp
thi cite Jerusalem, as thou hast behoten;
and that, that I leeuende to moun be don
8 bi thee tho3te, I parforme. And whan
that she hadde seid, she wente to the
piler that was at the hed of his bed, and
his swerd, that in it bounden heeng[z], she
9 losede. And whan she hadde drawen it
out, she toc the her of his hed, and seith,
Conferme me, God of Irael, in this hour.
10 And she smot twies in to his haterel,
and she cutte of his hed; and she toc
awei his canope fro the pileris, and she
11 turnede out his body behedid[a]. And
after a litil while she wente out, and toc
the hed of Olofernes to hir hand maiden,
and comaundede, that she shulde putten
12 it in to hir scrippe. And thei two wenten
out after ther vsage as to pre3eere, and
thei passeden the tentis, and, goende
aboute the valei, camen[b] to the 3ate of
13 the cite. And Judit seide aferre to the
keperis of the wallis, Openeth the 3atis,
for with vs is God, that dide gret vertue
14 in Irael. And it is do, whan the men
hadden herd hir vois, thei clepeden the
15 prestis of the cite. And alle runnen a3en
hir fro the leste to the moste; for thei
16 hopeden hir no mor to be to come. And,
teendende li3tis, alle wenten abouten hir.
She forsothe ste3ende vp in to an hei3ere
place, comaundede to be maad silence.
And whan alle hadden holden ther pes,
17 Judit seide, Preiseth the Lord oure God,
that forsaketh not men hopende in hym,
18 and in me, his hand womman, hath[c] fulfild his merci, that he behi3te to the hous
of Irael, and hath slain in myn hond the
19 enemy of his puple this ny3t. And bring-

God of Israel, conferme me[v], and biholde[w]
in this our[x] to[y] the werkis of myn hondis,
that, as thou bihi3tist[z], thou reise[a] Jerusalem thi citee; and that[b] Y performe this
thing, which thing Y bileuynge thou3te
to mow be doon bi thee. And whanne 8
sche hadde seid this[c], sche nei3ede to the[d]
piler that was at the heed of his[e] bed[f],
and sche loside his swerd, that hangide[g]
boundun 'ther ynne[h]. And whanne sche 9
hadde drawe out of the scheeth thilke
swerd, sche took the heer of his heed; and
seide, Lord God of Israel, conferme me in
this our[i]. And sche smoot twies on[k] his 10
necke, and kittide[l] awei[m] his heed; and
sche took awei his curteyn fro the pileris,
and walewide[n] awei his bodi heedles. And 11
aftir a litil sche 3ede out, and bitook[o] the
heed of Holofernes to hir handmaide, and
comaundide[p], that sche schulde putte it in
to hir scrippe. And[q] the twei wymmen 12
3eden out[r] 'bi her custom[s] as[t] to preier[u],
and passiden[v] the castels[w]† *of Assiriens*[x],
and thei cumpassiden[y] the valei, and camen[z]
to the 3ate of the citee. And Judith seide 13
afer to the keperis of the wallis, 'Opene 3e[a]
the 3atis, for God is with vs, that hath do
greet vertu in Israel. And it was doon, 14
whanne the[b] men hadden herd 'her vois[c],
thei clepiden the prestis of the citee. And 15
alle men fro the leest 'til to[d] the mooste
runnen to hir[e]; for thei hopiden not, that
sche schulde come[f] now. And thei teend- 16
iden[g] li3tis, and alle men cumpassiden
aboute hir. Sotheli[h] sche stiede[i] in to an
hi3ere place, and[k] comaundide[l] silence to
be maad. And whanne alle men weren
stille, Judith seide, Herie 3e 'oure Lord 17
God[m], that hath not forsake hem that
hopen[n] in hym, and bi me, his handmaide, 18
he hath fillid[o] his merci, which he bihi3te

† *casteis*; that is, oost. CV.

[z] hangede EF. [a] beheueded AEFH. [b] thei camen C. [c] he hath A.

[v] me, or *make me stable* I. me, *that is, make me stable in this doyng* S. [w] Om. IS. [x] tyme IS. [y] biholde thou to IS. [z] hast bihi3t IS. [a] reise up IS. [b] *helpe me* that S. [c] this thing IS. [d] Om. N. [e] the AI. [f] bed of Holofernes I. [g] hangide *there* I. [h] on the piler I. [i] tyme I. [k] in I. [l] sche kittide I. [m] off I. [n] sche walewide I. [o] sche bitook I. [p] *Judith* comaundide *hir* I. [q] And bi her custom I. [r] forth I. [s] Om. I. [t] as *it were* I. [u] *her* preier I. [v] thei passiden I. [w] tentis I. [x] *the men of Assirie* I. [y] 3eden aboute I. [z] thei camen I. [a] Openeth I. [b] tho I. [c] the vois of Judith I. [d] vnto I. [e] Judith I. [f] hane come I. [g] teenden C. teendiden up I. [h] And I. [i] stiede up I. [k] and sche I. [l] comaunde A. [m] the Lord oure God I. [n] tristen I. [o] fulfillid I.

ende forth of the scripp the hed of Olofernes, shewide to them, seiende, Lo! the hed of Olofernes, prince of the chiualrie of Assiries; and, lo! the canope of hym, in whiche he lai in his drunkinhed, wher and bi the hond of a womman smot hym 20 the Lord our God. Forsothe the Lord God lineth, for his aungil kepte me, and hennus goende, and there dwellende, and thennus hider turnende a3een; and the Lord suffride not me his hand womman to be defoulid, but with oute pollucioun of synne hath a3een clepid me to 3ou, io3ende in his victorie, in myn ascaping, 21 in 3oure deliueraunce. Knoulecheth to hym alle, for good, for in to the world 22 his merci. Alle forsothe, houourende the Lord, seiden to hir, The Lord blesside thee in his vertue, for bi thee to no3t he 23 hath bro3t oure[d] enemys. But Osias, the prince of the puple of Irael, seide to hir, Blessid thou art, do3ter, of the Lord, the be3e God, befor alle wymmen vp on 24 erthe. Blessid the Lord, that made heuene and erthe, and that hath dressid thee in to the woundis of the hed of 25 prince of oure enemys; for to dai so thi name he hath magnefied, that thi preising go not awei fro the mouth of men, that weren myndeful of the vertue of the Lord in to with oute ende; for the whiche thingus[e] thou sparedest not to thi lif for anguysshis and tribulaciouns of thi kinrede, but holpedist to the falling 26 befor the si3te of oure God. And al the 27 puple seide, So be it! so be it! Forsothe Achior clepid cam; and Judit seide to hym, God of Irael, to the whiche witnessing thou hast 3iue, that he be vengid of his enemys, he the hed of alle mysbeleeued men hath hewen of in this ny3t 28 in myn hond. And that thou preue for

to the hows of Israel, and[p] hath slayn in myn hond the enemye of his puple in this ni3t[q]. And sche bro3te forth[r] of the 19 scrippe the heed of Holofernes, and[t] schewide[u] it to hem, and seide, Lo! the heed of Holofernes, prince of the chiualrie of Assiriens[v]; and, lo! his curteyn, in[w] which he lay in his drunkenesse, where also oure[x] Lord God[y] killide hym bi the hond of a womman. Forsothe the Lord 20 God lyueth, for his aungel kepte[z] me, bothe goynge fro hennus, and dwellynge there, and turnynge a3en fro thennus hidur; and the Lord suffride not[a] his handmaide to be defoulid, but with out defoulyng of synne he a3en[b] clepid me to 3ou, and Y haue ioie in his[c] victorie[d], and in my scapyng[e], and in 3oure delyueraunce. Knouleche 3e alle to hym[f], for he 21 is good, for his mercy is in to the worldis[g]. Sotheli alle men worschipiden the Lord, 22 and seiden to hir[h], The Lord hath blessid thee in his vertu, for bi thee he hath brou3t to nou3t oure enemyes. Certis[i] 23 Ozie, prince[k] of the puple of Israel, seide to hir[l], Dou3tir, thou art blessid of the hi3 Lord God, bifor alle wymmen on[m] erthe. Blessid be the Lord[n], that made 24 heuene and erthe, and that dresside thee in to the woundis of the heed of the prince of oure enemyes; for to dai he 25 hath magnefied so thi name, that thi preisyng go not awei fro the mouth of men, that[o] schulen be myndeful of the vertu of the Lord with outen ende; for whiche[p] thou sparidist not thi lijf for[q] the angwischis and tribulaciouns of thi kyn, but[r] helpidist[s] the fallinge[t] bifor the si3t of oure God. And al the puple seide, 26 'Be it! be it[u]! Forsothe[v] Achior was 27 clepid, and cam[w]; and Judith seide to hym, Thilke God of Israel, to whom thou

---

[d] his κ pr. m.   [e] thing AII.

[p] and in this ni3t he I.   [q] Om. I.   [r] toke out I.   [s] hir s.   [t] Om. s.   [u] sche shewide I.   [v] men of Assirie I.   [w] withynne I.   [x] the I.   [y] oure God I.   [z] hath kept I.   [a] hath not suffrid I.   [b] hath a3en I.   [c] Om. I.   [d] victorie of the Lord I.   [e] my schapyng A. myn ascapyng I.   [f] the Lord I.   [g] withouten ende I.   [h] Judith I.   [i] And thanne I.   [k] the prince I.   [l] Judith I.   [m] upon I.   [n] Lord God AD pr. m.   [o] the whiche I.   [P] whiche men I.   [q] but puttidist it for I.   [r] and thou I.   [s] hast holpen I.   [t] fallinge of the peple I.   [u] Be it thus don, be it thus don I. Amen! amen! that is, be it, be it K. Be it s.   [v] And thanne I.   [w] he cam I.

so it is, lo! the hed of Olofernes, that in the despising of his pride God of Israel dispiside, and to thee deth thratte, seiende, Whan the puple of Irael were taken, I shal comaunde with a swerd to 29 stiken hym thur₃ the sides. Seende forsothe Achior the hed of Olofernes, anguysht for inward drede, fel in to his face vpon the erthe, and his lif quap-30 pide. After forsothe that, the spirit taken a₃een, he is reformed, he fel doun to hir 31 feet, and honourede hir, and seide, Blessid be thou of thi God in al the tabernacle of Jacob; for in alle folc, that hereth thi name, shal be magnefied vp on thee God of Irael.

₃auest witnessyng, that he auengith hym of hise enemyes, hath kit of the heed of alle vnbileueful men in this ni₃t bi myn hond. And that[x] thou preue that it is[28] so, lo[y]! the heed of Holofernes, which[z] in the dispit of his pride dispiside God of Israel, and manaasside[a] deth to thee, and seide, Whanne the puple of Israel is takun, Y schal comaunde thi sidis to be persid with a swerd. Sotheli[b] Achior si₃ the[29] heed of Holofernes, and[c] was angwischid for drede, and felde[d] doun on his face on[e] the erthe, and his soule suffride eneyntisyng[f]. Sotheli[g] aftir that he hadde[30] take a₃en spirit[h], and was coumfortid, he felde doun at 'hir feet[i], and worschipide[k] hir, and seide, Blessid art thou of thi God[31] in al[l] the tabernacle[m]† of Jacob; for in ech[n] folk, that schal here thi name, God of Israel schal be magnyfied in thee.

† al the tabernacle; that is, of alle men dwellinge in the tabernaclis of Ehreys, comyng forth of Jacob. Lire here. c.

CAP. XIV.

1 Judit forsothe seide to al the puple, Hereth, brethern; hangeth vp this hed 2 vp on the wallis. And it shal be, whan the sunne goth out, eche man take his armes, and goth out with bure, not that ₃ee go doun benethe, but as buref doende. 3 Thanne it shal nede ben, that the spieres of the lond flen to ther prince to be rerid 4 vp to the fi₃t. And whan the dukis of hem comen to gidere to the tabernaclis of Olofernes, and finden hym heded[h], in his blod wrappid, drede shal fal doun 5 vpon hem. And whan ₃ee knowen them to fleen, goth after hem siker, for God shal to-trede them vnder ₃oure feet. 6 Thanne Achior seande the vertue that God of Irael hadde do, laft the custum of his hethenenesse, leeuede[i] to God; and circumcidede the flesh of his ₃erde, and is put to the puple of Irael, and al the successioun of his kinrede vnto the dai

CAP. XIV.

Forsothe Judith seide to al the puple,[1] Britheren, here ₃e; hang ₃e[o] this heed on[p] ₃oure wallis. And it schal be[q], whanne[2] the sunne 'goith out[r], ech man take hise armuris, and go ₃e out with feersnesse, not that ₃e go[s] doun binethe[t], but as makyng[u] asau₃t. Thanne[v] it schal be[3] nede; that the spieris of the lond fle to reise[w] her prynce to batel. And whanne[4] the duykis of hem rennen[x] togidere to the tabernacle of Holofernes, and fynden[y] hym heedles, waltrid in his blood, dreed schal falle doun on[z] hem. And whanne[5] ₃e knowen that thei fleen, go ₃e sikirli aftir hem, for God schal al to-breke hem vndur ₃oure feet. Thanne Achior si₃ the[6] vertu that God of Israel hadde do, and he forsook the custom of hethenesse, and bileuede[a] to God; and he circumcidede the fleisch of his ₃erde, and he was put to the puple of Israel, and al the aftircomyng

---

[f] woodnesse E pr. m. [g] spies c. [h] heuedid EFJJ. [i] and bileuede A.

[x] Om. s. [y]o ! here 1. [z] the which 1. [a] he manaasside 1. [b] And whanne 1. [c] he 1. [d] he fille 1. [e] upon 1. [f] that is, swonnyng 1 marg. [g] And 1. [h] his spirit 1. [i] the feet of Judith 1. [k] he worschipide 1. [l] alle 1. [m] tabernaclis 1. [n] al 1. [o] ₃e up 1. [p] upon 1. in s. [q] he don that 1. [r] risith 1. [s] go al 1. [t] binethe the hill 1. [u] men makynge 1. [v] And thanne 1. [w] reise up 1. [x] schal renne 1. [y] thei schal fynde 1. [z] upon 1. [a] he bilenede 1.

7 that is now. Anon forsothe that sprungen is dai, thei heengen^k vpon the wallis the hed of Olofernes; and eche^l toc his armes, and thei wenten out with gret noise and 8 ȝelling. Whiche thing seande, the aspies runnen togidere to the tabernacle of Olo-9fernes. Forsothe thei, that weren comende in the tabernacle, and befor the incomyng of the priue chaumbre makende noise, for ende to reren^m hym, bi craft casten vn-reste, that not of the rereres^n, but of the noise makeris Olofernes shulde waken^o. 10 No man forsothe was hardi the taber-nacle of the vertue of Assiries knockende 11 or entrende to openen. But whan his dukis hadden come, and the leders of thousendis, and alle the more of the ost of the king of Assiries, thei seiden to the 12 priue chaumberleynes, Goth, and rereth^p hym; for myis gon out of ther caues ben hardi to clepen forth^q vs to bataile. 13 Thanne Vagio, gon in to his priue chaumbre, stod befor the curtin, and made fawnyng with his hondis; for-sothe he trowide hym with Judit to 14 slepen. But whan no mouyng of hym liende with the wit of eris parceiuede, he wente to neȝhende to the curtin, and rerende^r it, and seande the carein of Olofernes withouten hed to lin roten in his blod vpon the^s erthe, criede out with a gret vois with weeping, and cutte his 15 clothis. And gon in to the tabernacle of Judit, fond her not, and he out sterte 16 with oute to the puple, and seide, An Ebru womman hath do confusioun in the hous of king Nabugodonosor; lo! forsothe Olofernes lith in the erthe, and 17 his hed is not in hym. The whiche

of his kyn 'til in to^b this dai^c. Forsothe^d 7 anoon as the dai roos^e, thei hangiden the heed of Holofernes on^f the^g wallis^h; and^i ech man took his armuris, and thei ȝeden out with grete noise and ȝellyng. Which 8 thing the aspieris sien, and runnen^k to the tabernacle of Holofernes. Certis^l thei, that 9 weren in the tabernacle, camen, and maden noise bifore the entryng of the bed^m, and^n ymagyneden by craft vnrestfulnesse for cause of reisyng^o, that Holofernes schulde awake not of the reiseris, but of sowneris^p. For^q no man was hardi to opene the taber- 10 nacle of the vertu^r† of Assiriens^s bi knock-yng ethir bi entryng. But whanne hise 11 duykis, and tribunes^t, and alle the grettere men of the oost of the kyng of Assiriens^u weren comen^v, thei seiden to the chaum-burleyns^w, Entre ȝe^x, and reise ȝe hym^y; 12 for myis ben goon out of her caues, and doren^z excite^a vs to batel. Thanne Vagao^b 13 entride in to his closet, and stood^c bifor the curtyn^d, and made^e betyng togidere with hise hondis; for^f he supposide hym to slepe with Judith. But whanne^g he 14 perseyuede not 'with wit of eeris^h ony stiryng of Holofernes liggynge^i, he cam neiȝynge^k to the curtyn, and he 'reiside it^l, and siȝ^m the deed bodi^n with out the^o heed 'of Holofernes^p 'maad slow^q in his^r blood ligge^s on the erthe, and he criede bi^t grete vois with weping, and to-rente^u hise clothis. And he^v entride in to the taber- 15 nacle of Judith, and foond^w not hir, and^x he skippide^y out to the puple, and seide, 16 Oon^z Ebrew womman hath maad^a confu-sioun in the hows of kyng Nabugodono-sor; for^b lo^c! Holofernes liggith^d in the erthe, and his heed is not in^e hym. And 17

† the vertu; that is, of the chyualry, in whom the strengthe of the oost stond-ith by vertu. Like here. c.

k hungyden AEFH. l eche one AEFH. m arere AEFH. n arereris AEFH. o awaken AEFH. p arereth AEFH. q Om. c. r arerynge E. s Om. c.

b vnto I. c tyme I. d Certis I. e spronge I. f upon I. g her I. h wal s. i and thanne I. k thei runnen I. l And I. m bed of Holofernes I. n and thei I. o upreisyng I. p the noise of sowneris I. the sowneris CMR. q Certis I. r power or cheef prince I. s men of Assirie I. t his tribunes I. u Assirie I. v comen togidere I. w chaumberleyns of Holofernes I. x ȝe in to him I. y hym up I. z thei doren I. a moeue I. b Vagao, the chamburleyne I. c he stood I. d curteyn of his bed I. e he made I. f sothely I. g whanne bi the witt or listnyng of his eeris I. h Om. I. i liggynge there I. k niȝ and neiȝide I. l drewȝ it up I. m he siȝ I. a bodi of Holofernes I. o Om. I. p Om. I. s defoulid I. r Om. I. s and liggynge up I. t with IS. u he to-rente I. v Vagao I. w he foond I. x and anoon I. y wente I. x An I. a do I. b Om. I. c lo! certis I. d lijth I. e with I.

thing whan hadden herd the princis of
the vertue of Assiries, alle cutten ther
clothis, and vntolerable drede and trembling fel vp on hem, and ther inwittis
18 ben disturbid[t] gretly. And ther is maad
an vntolerable cry in to the middel tentis.

CAP. XV.

1 And whan al the ost hadde herd Olofernes of hedid[u], fleiʒ mynde and counscil
fro[v] them, and with onli trembling and
2 drede stirid token socour of fliʒt, so that
noon wolde speke with his neʒhebore;
but, the hed bowid doun, alle thingus
laft, to scape[w] the Ebrues, whom armed
vp on hem to come thei hadden herd,
thei enforceden, fleende bi weies of feldis,
3 and bi sties of ful litle hillis. And so
the sonus of Irael, seande them fleende,
folewiden, goende doun, and criende with
4 trumpis, and ʒellende after hem. And
for Assiries not togidere in oon wenten
fallende doun in to fliʒt, the sonus forsothe
of Irael with o cumpany pursuende fe-
5 bleden alle, that thei myʒten finde. And
Osias sente messageres bi alle the cites
6 and regiouns of Irael. And so alle regioun and alle cite sente a chosen ʒouthe[x]
armed after hem; and thei pursueden hem
in mouth of swerd, to the time that thei
7 came to the vtmost of ther costis. The
tothere men forsothe, that weren in Betulia, wenten in to the tentis of Assiries,
and the prei, that Assiries fleende hadden
laft, thei token with them, and thei ben
8 wrshipid gretli. Thei forsothe that hadden ben ouercomeres, ben turned aʒeen to
Betulie, alle thingis whateuere weren of

whanne the prynces of the[f] vertu[g] of Assiriens[h] hadden herd this thing, alle thei
to-renten her clothis, and vnsuffrable drede
and tremblyng felde doun on[l] hem, and
her soulis[j] weren troblid greetli. And 18
'vncomparable cry[k] was maad 'bi the
myddil of[l] her tentis.

CAP. XV.

And whanne al the oost hadde herd 1
Holofernes bihcedid[n], mynde and councel
fledde fro hem, and thei 'schakun bi[o]
tremblyng and drede aloone[p] token the
help of fliʒt, so that no man spak with 2
his neiʒbore; but 'whanne the heed was
bowid doun[q], and alle thingis[r] 'weren forsakun[s], thei weren bisy to ascape Ebreis[t],
which thei hadden herd to come armed
on[u] hem; and thei fledden bi the weies
of feeldis, and bi the pathis of litle hillis.
Therfor the sones of Israel siʒen *Assi-*3
riens[v] fleynge[w], and sueden[x] hem, and
camen[y] doun, and sowneden[z] with trumpis, and ʒelliden[a] aftir hem. And for 4
Assiriens[b] not gaderid togidere ʒeden[c]
heedlyng[d] in to fliʒt, forsothe[e] the sones
of Israel pursuynge with o[f] cumpeny
maden feble alle[g], whiche thei myʒten
fynde[h]. And Ozie[i] sente[k] messangeris 5
bi alle the[l] citees and cuntreis of Israel.
Therfor ech cuntrei and ech citee sente[m] 6
chosun ʒonge men armed after hem; and
thei[n] pursueden 'thilke Assiriens[o] with
the[p] scharpnesse of swerd, til thei camen
to the laste part of her[q] coostis[r]. Forsothe[s] 7
the residue[t] men[u], that weren[v] in[w] Bethulia, entriden in to the tentis of Assiriens[x],
and token[y] awey with hem the[z] prey,
which[b] Assiriens fleynge[c] hadden left, and

---

[t] disturblid *AH.*   [u] heueded *EFU.*   [v] of *A.*   [w] ascapyn *AEFH.*   [x] ʒong *A.*

[f] Om. 1.   [g] power 1.   [h] men of Assirie 1.   [l] upon 1.   [j] ynwittis 1.   [k] cry that myʒte not be comparisound 1.   [l] thorowe out 1.   [n] to be biheedid 1.   [o] stirid with oonly 1.   [p] Om. 1.   [q] ech man bowynge
doun his heed 1.   [r] her thingis 1.   [s] yleft bihynde hem 1.   [t] the Jewis 1.   [u] upon 1.   [v] *the men of
Assirie* 1.   [w] fleynge awey 1.   [x] thei sueden aftir 1.   [y] *men of Israel* camen 1.   [z] thei sowneden 1.
[a] maden noyse 1.   [b] the men of Assirie 1.   [c] but ʒeden 1.   [d] heedlingis EL. hedlingis P.   [e] therfor 1.
[f] a 1.   [g] alle the men *of* hem 1.   [h] fynde *or* take 1.   [i] Ozie, her prince 1.   [k] sente forth 1.   [l] Om. 1.
[m] sente forth 1.   [n] the Jewis 1.   [o] the men of Assirie 1.   [p] Om. c.   [q] the 1.   [r] coostis of Israel 1.
[s] And 1.   [t] remenaunt 1.   [u] of the sones of Israel 1.   [v] weren *left* 1.   [w] in *the citee of* 1.   [x] the men of
Assirie 1.   [y] thei token 1.   [z] Om. 1.   [b] that 1.   [c] fleynge awey 1.

hem, thei token awei with them, so that ther was no noumbre in feld bestis, and in hous bestis, and in alle the mouable thingus of hem, that fro the leste vnto the myche alle weren made riche of 'the 9 'prei takingusᵞ of hem. Joachym forsothe, the heȝe bisshop of Jerusalem, cam in to Betulie with alle the prestis, that he see 10 Judit. The whiche whan hadde gon out to hym, alle blessiden hir with o vois, seiende, Thou glorie of Jerusalem, thou gladnesse of Irael, thou the wrshipe 11 doende of oure puple, that didist manli, and thin herte is coumfortid, for thi that chastite thou loouedest, and aftir thi man an other thou knewe not; and therfore the hond of the Lord coumfortide thee, and therfore thou shalt be blissid in to 12 with oute ende. And al the puple seide, 13 Be it do! be it do! Forsothe bi thretti daȝes vnnethe ben gedered the spoilis of 14 the Assiries of the puple of Irael. But alle the proper richessis of Olofernes, that ben proued to han ben, thei ȝeue to Judit, in gold, and siluer, and clothis, and iemmes, and in alle purtenaunces to household; and alle thingus ben taken 15 to hir of the puple. And alle puplis ioȝeden, with wymmen, and maidenes, and 1 ȝunge men, in orgnys and harpis. Thanne Judit song this song to the Lord, seiende, 2 Begynneth in timbris; singeth to the Lord in cimbalis; manerly singeth to hym a new salm; ful out ioȝeth, and in- 3 wardli clepeth his name. The Lord to- tredende batailis, Lord name is to hym. 4 That putte his tentis in the middel off his puple. that he deliuere vs fro the 5 hond of alle oure enemys. Assur cam fro hillis, fro the north, in multitude of

theiᵈ weren chargid gretliᵉ. Butᶠ thei that 8 weren ouercomerys, turnedenᵍ aȝen to Be- thuliaʰ, and thei token awei with hem alle thingis whichⁱ euer weren of tho Assi- riensʲ, so that noᵏ noumbre wasˡ in scheep, and beestis, and in alle mouable thingis of hem, thatᵐ fro the leeste 'til toⁿ the mooste alle menᵒ weren maad riche of herᵖ preies. Forsothe Joachym, the hiȝeste bischop, 9 cam fro Jerusalem in to Bethulia with alle the�q prestis, to se Judith. And whanne 10 sche hadde goon outʳ to hym, alleˢ bless- iden hir with o vois, and seiden, Thou art the glorie† of Jerusalem, and thou art the gladnesse of Israel, thou art the onour of oure puple, whichᵗ hast do manli, andᵘ 11 thin herte was coumfortidᵛ, for thou loued- ist chastite, and aftir thin hosebonde thou knowistʷ not anotherˣ; therfor and the hond of the Lord counfortide thee, and therfor thou schalt be blessid with outen ende. And al theʸ puple seide, 'Be it! be 12 itᶻ! Forsothe bi thritti daies vnnethis theᵃ 13 spuylis of Assiriensᵇ werenᶜ gaderidᵈ of the pupleᵉ of Israel. Certis thei ȝauen to 14 Judith alle thingis, that weren preued to be propir, 'ether syngulerᶠ, of Holofernes, in gold, andᵍ siluer, and in clothis, and in gemmes, and in alle purtenaunce of hous- hold; and alle thingis weren ȝouun to hir of the puple. And alle puplis 'maden ioyeʰ, 15 with wymmen, and vergynes, and ȝongeⁱ menʲ, in organs and harpis.

CAP. XVI.

Thanne Judith song 'this songᵏ to the 1 Lord, and seide, Bigynne ȝeᵐ in tympans; 2 synge ȝeⁿ to the Lord in cymbalis; synge ȝe swetli a newe salm to hym; fulli make ȝe ioye, and inwardli clepe ȝe his name. The 3

† the glorie; for sche kepte the worschip- yng of God that was in Jerusalem, of which wor- schiping the Jewes hadden most glorie, and in sleynge Holofernes, that wolde distrie Goddis wor- schiping, sche ȝaf mater of onour and of gladnesse to the peple of Israel. Lire here. c.

ᵞ pray takynge ᴀɪɪ.

ᵈ men of Israel ɪ. ᵉ gretli chargid with catel ɪ. ᶠ And ɪ. ᵍ in her pursuyt turneden ɪ. ʰ the citee Bethulia ɪ. ⁱ what ɪ. ʲ mennus of Assirie ɪ. ᵏ ther was no ɪ. ˡ Om. ɪ. ᵐ so that ɪ. ⁿ vnto ɪ. to x. ᵒ men of Israel ɪ. ᵖ the ɪ. �q hise ɪ. ʳ forth ɪ. ˢ alle thei ɪ. ᵗ the which ɪ. ᵘ and certis ɪ. ᵛ coumfortid in God ɪ. ʷ knewe ɪ. ˣ another man ɪ. ʸ Om. s. ᶻ Be it don, be it don ɪ. Amen! Amen! that is, be it, be it ᴋ. ᵃ weren the ɪ. ᵇ men of Assirie ɪ. ᶜ Om. ɪ. ᵈ gaderid up ɪ. ᵉ men ɪ. ᶠ Om. ɪ. ᵍ in ɪ. ʰ Om. ɪ. ⁱ with ȝonge ɪ. ʲ men maden ioye ɪ. ᵏ Om. s. ᵐ ȝe to preise God ɪ. ⁿ Om. c.

his strengthe; whos multitude stoppide
the stremes[z], and the hors of hem couer-
6 eden the valeis. And he seide hymself
to brennen vp oure costis, and oure ȝunge
men to slen with swerd, my fauntis to
ȝiue in to prei, and maidenes in to cai-
7 tifte. The Lord forsothe Almyȝti noȝede
hym, and toc[n] to the hondis of a wom-
8 man, and confoundede hym. Forsothe
the myȝti of hem fel not of ȝunge men,
ne the sonus of a tiraunt smyten hym, ne
heȝe ieauntus putten hem to hym; but
Judit, wydewe, the doȝter of Merari, in
the fairnesse of hir face vnloside hym.
9 Forsothe she clothide hir fro the cloth
of hyr widewehed, and clothide hir in
the cloth of gladnesse, in[b] ful out ioȝing
10 to the sonus of Irael. She oyntide[c] hir
face with an[d] oynement, and she bond
togidere hir crisp heris with a mitre, to
11 desceiuen hym. Hir gaȝe shon rauesh-
eden his eȝen, hir fairnesse made his lif
caitif; sche girde of with a swerd his
12 haterel. The Persis grisiden hir stedefastnesse, and Medis hir hardynesse.
13 Thanne ȝelleden the tentis of Assiries,
whan apereden my meke, drie waxende
14 in thrist. The sonus of child wymmen
pungeden them, and as childer fleende
slowen hem; thei persheden in bataile fro
15 the face of my Lord. A newe ympne
16 singe wee to the Lord oure God. Lord
Adonai, a gret God thou art, and beforn
alle cleer in thi vertue, and whom no
17 man mai ouercome. To thee serue alle
thi creature[e], for thou hast seid, and
thei ben maad; thou sentist thi spirit,
and thei ben formed; and ther is not
18 that withstonde to thi comanding. Hillis

Lord al to-brekith batels, the[o] Lord is name
to hym; that[p] hath set hise castels[q]† in the[r] 4
myddis of his puple, for to deliuere vs fro
the hond of alle oure enemyes. Assur 5
cam fro the[s] hillis, fro[t] the north, in the
multitude of his strengthe; whose multitude stoppide strondis, and the horsis of
hem hiliden valeis. And he seide, that[u] 6
he schulde brenne my coostis[v], and sle my
ȝonge men bi[w] swerd, to[x] ȝiue my ȝonge
children in to prei, virgyns[y] in to caitifte.
But the Lord Almyȝti anoiede hym, and 7
bitook hym in to the hondis of a womman, and schente[z] hym. For the myȝti[a] 8
of hem felde not doun[b] of ȝonge men, nether the sones of giauntis killiden hym,
nether hiȝe[c] giauntis puttiden hem silf to
hym; but Judith, the douȝtir of Merari,
ouercam hym bi the fairnesse of hir face.
For sche vnclothide hir fro the cloth of 9
widewehod, and clothide[d] hir with the
cloth of gladnesse, in[e] the[f] ful[g] ioiyng of
the sones of Israel. Sche anoyntide hir 10
face with oynement, and boond[h] togidere
the tressis of hir heeris with a coronal,
disseyue‡ hym[i]. 'Hir sandalies[ii] rauysch- 11
iden hise iȝen, hir fairnesse made his soule
caitif; with a swerd sche kittide[j] of his
necke. Men of[k] Persis hadden hidousnesse of hir stidfastnesse, and Medeis[l] of
hyr hardynesse. Thanne the castels[m] of 13
Assiriens[n] ȝelliden[o], whanne my meke men[p],
wexinge drie for thirst, apperiden[q]. The 14
sones of damesels[r] prickiden[s] hem, and
killiden[t] hem as children fleynge; thei
perischiden in batel fro the face of my
God. 'Synge we an ympne to the Lord[u], 15
synge[v] we a newe[w] ympne to oure God[x].
Lord[y], Lord[z] God, thou art grete[a], and ful 16

† castels; that
is, aungels.
Lire here. c.

‡ disseyue; not
that sche pur-
poside to bringe
him to dedly
synne, but that
he schulde de-
sire to haue hir
to wyf, and bi
this thing Ju-
dith schulde
haue homely
nehing to him,
bi which sche
myȝte sle him.
Lire here. c.

z sterris A.   aternesse H.   n toc him AE pr. m.   b and of A pr. m.   c enoyntide AEFH.   d Om. AH.
e creaturis A.

o Om. I.   p whiche I.   q strengthis I.   r Om. I.   s Om. I.   t and fro I.   u Om. I.   v coostis of Israel I.
w with I.   x he thouȝte to I.   y and the virgyns therof I.   z sche schente I.   a myȝti prince I. miȝte x.
b doun bi strengthe I.   c cheef I.   d sche clothide I.   e in to I.   f Om. 18.   g ful out I.   h sche boond I.
i Holofernes I.   ii The ournement of hir feet I.   j kitte I.   k of the cuntrey of I.   l men of Medeis I.
m stronge powers I.   n the men of Assirie I.   o ȝelliden for drede I.   p men of Israel I.   q apperiden
to hem I.   r ȝoung wymmen I.   s han prickid I.   t thei han killid I.   u Om. s.   v and synge I.
w Om. cs.   x Om. s.   y Om. ia.   z Om. s.   a grete Lord I.

fro foundemens shuln[f] ben moued with watris; stonus as wax shul melte befor 19 thi face. Who forsothe dreden thee, gret 20 shul be anentis thee bi alle thingus. Wo to the folc risende vp on my kinrede; the Lord forsothe Almyȝti shal venge in hem, in the dai of dom he shal visite 21 them. Forsothe he shal ȝiue fijr and wormes in ther flesh, that thei be brend, and lyuen, and feelen vnto enermore. 22 And it is do after these thingus, al the puple after the victorie cam to Jerusalem to honoure the Lord; and anoon as thei weren purified, alle offreden brent sacrifises, and vouwis, and ther behestis. 23 Forsothe Judit alle the armes of bataile of Olofernes, that the puple ȝaf to hir, and the canope, that she hadde taken, 24 she toc in to the curs of forȝeting. Forsothe al the puple was ioȝeful after the face of seintis; and bi thre monethis the ioȝe of this victorie is solempnysid with 25 Judit. After thoo daȝes forsothe eche wente aȝeen in to his owne; and Judit is maad gret in Betulie, and was more 26 cler to alle men of the lond of Irael. Forsothe she was ioyned to the vertue of chastite, so that she knew no man alle the daȝis of hir lif, sithen is dead Manasses, hir husbonde. 27 Forsothe she was in feste daȝes forth goende with gret 28 glorie. Forsothe she dwelte in the hous of hir man an hundrid ȝer and fiue; and she lafte hir damesele free[g]. And she is dead, and biriede with hir husbonde in 29 Betulie; and al the puple weilide hir 30 seuen daȝes. In al the space forsothe of hir lif was not that disturbide[h] Irael, 31 and after hir deth manye ȝer. The daȝes forsothe of this feste of victorie of the[i]

cleer[b] in thi vertu, and[c] whom no man may ouercome. Ech creature of thin serue[d] 17 thee, for thou seidist, and thingis[e] weren maad; thou sentist thi spirit, and thingis[f] weren maad of nouȝt; and noon[g] is that aȝenstondith thi comaundement[h]. Hillis[i] 18 schulen be moued fro foundementis[k] with watris; stonys[l] schulen flete abrood as wex bifor thi face. Sotheli[m] thei that 19 dreden thee, schulen be grete anentis thee bi alle thingis. Woo to the folk rysynge 20 on[n] my kyn; for[o] the Lord Almyȝti schal take veniaunce in hem, in[p] the dai of doom he schal visite hem. For[q] he schal 21 ȝyue fier and wormes in the fleischis of hem, that thei be brent, and lyue, and feele[r] til in to with outen ende. And it 22 was doon aftir these thingis, al the puple[s] aftir the victorie[t] cam to Jerusalem to worschipe[u] the Lord; and anoon as thei weren clensid[v], alle men offriden brent sacrifices, and avowis, and her biheestis. Certis[w] Judith ȝaf[x]† in to the[y] cursyng 23 of forȝetyng[z] alle the armuris of batel of Holofernes, whiche the[a] puple ȝaf[b] to hir, and[c] the curteyn, which sche hadde take awei. Forsothe[d] al the puple was myrie 24 aftir the face of hooli men; and bi thre monethis the ioye of this victorie was halewid with Judith. Sotheli[e] aftir tho 25 daies ech man ȝede aȝen[f] in to his owne[g]; and Judith was maad greet in Bethulia, and sche was more cleer thanne alle wymmen[h] of the lond of Israel. For[i] chastite 26 was ioyned to hir vertu‡, so that sche knewe not[k] man[l] alle the daies of hir lijf, sithen[m] Manasses, hir hosebonde, was deed. Sotheli[n] in 'feeste daies[o] sche[p] cam forth 27 with[q] greet glorie[r]. Forsothe[s] sche dwell- 28 ide in the hows of hir hosebonde an hun-

Margin notes:

† Judith ȝaf; to prestis alle these thingis, that no man schulde vse tho affirwaris, but the schulden be kept in the place of Goddis worschiping, to the mynde of Goddis benefice. Lire here. c.

‡ vertu; of stidefastnesse, bi which sche hadde cast doun Holofernes. Lire here.

---

f Om. A.   g freest AII.   h disturblide AII.   i Om. A.

b cleer art thou I.   c Om. CIOA.   d serue it to I.   e so alle thingis I.   f thanne alle thingis I.   g no creature I.   h comaundement fynaly I.   i For hillis I.   k the foundementis I.   l and stonys I.   m And I. n up upon I.   o forsothe I.   p and in I.   q Sothely I.   r thei feele the feersnesse therof I.   s puple of Israel I.   t victorie of Holofernes I.   u worschipe there I.   v clensid after the lawe I.   w Forsothe I. x ȝaf thanne I.   y Om. plures.   z fiȝting c.   a Om. c.   b had ȝouen I.   c also I.   d Certis I.   e And I. f awey ELPR.   g thingis BCDEGKLMNOPQRSUVWXab. owne dwellynge place I.   h the wymmen I.   i Certis I. k no I.   l man fleishly I.   m sith I.   n Om. I.   o solempne halidaies I.   p Judith I.   q and with I. r glorie sche was wirschipid bifore othere wymmen I.   s And I.

Ebrues in the noumbre of holi daȝes is acceptid, and heried of the Jewis fro that time vnto the present day.

Explicit liber Judith[k].

drid ȝeer and fyue; and sche lefte[t] hir handmaide fre. And[u] sche[v] was deed, and biried[w] with hir hosebonde in Bethulia; and al the puple biweilide hir sceuene 29 daies. Forsothe[x] in al the space of her lijf 30 noon[y] 'was disturblide[z] Israel, and many ȝeeris aftir hir deeth. Sotheli[a] the day of 31 the[b] victorie of this feeste is takun of Ebreis[c] in the noumbre of hooli daies, and it is worschipid of the Jewis fro that tyme til in to present[d] day.

Here endith the book of Judith[e].

---

[k] *Here endith the book of Judith, and now bigynneth the prolog of the book of Hester.* A. *Here endith the bok of Judith, and now the bok of Ester.* F.

---

[t] lefte *or* made I.   [u] And *thanne* I.   [v] Judith I.   [w] sche was biried I.   [x] For so s.   [y] ther was noon I. [z] that ouercame I. was that disturblide s.   [a] And I.   [b] Om. A.   [c] Ebreis, *and rekenyd* I.   [d] this present I. [e] *Here eendith the book of Judith, and here bigynneth Hester.* BDUB. *Here endith the book of Judith, and here biginneth the book of Hester.* CRW. *Here endith Judith, and bigynnith the prolog of Hester.* G. *Here endeth Judith, and here bigynneth Hester.* H. *Heere endith the book of Judith, and bigynnith Ester.* IQ. *Here endeth the book of Judith, se now the prolog of Hester.* K. *Here endith the book of Judith, and here bigynneth a prologe on the book of Hester.* M. *Here endith the book of Judith, and bigynneth the book of Hester.* NV. *Here endith the book of Judith, and bigyn[neth] the prolog on the book of Hester.* O. *Here endith Judith, and bigynneth the booc of Hester.* X. *Here endith the book of Judith.* ɔ. No final rubric in ELPS.

ESTHER.

[Prologue on the book of Esther[a].]

THIS book of Hester, the qween, makith mynde of the riȝtful Mardochee, and of the wickide man Aman, how he castide the deeth of Mardochee, and also of alle Jewis, for hate that he hadde to Mardochee; wherfor thoruȝ the help of God and of the qween Hester his wickidnesse was retourned in to his owne heed; for God helpith hem that tristen in him, and lyuen iustli in the drede of him.

Here bigynneth a prolog on the booc of Ester[a].

'The boc of Ester to be maad vicious of dyuerse translatoures is knowen[b], whom I, of the libraries of Ebrues takende vp, woord bi woord more openli translatide; the whiche boc the comun making drawith along hider and thider with the torne draȝtis, addende thoo[c] thingis, that 'of tyme[d] myȝten ben seid and herd; as it is wont to scoleris disciplines, and a theme taken, to out thenke what woordis he myȝte vsen, he that suffride wrong, or he that dide wrong. Ȝee forsothe, O! Paule and Eustache, that onli han studied to gon in to the libraries of Ebrues, and the striues of interpretoures han knowen, holdende Ester[e] an Ebru boc, beholdeth bi alle the woordis oure translacioun; that ȝee moun knowen me no thing also to han encresid addende, but with trewe witnessing simpleli[f], as it is had in Ebreu, the Ebru storie to han taken to[g] Latin tunge. Ne we desiren the preisingus[h] of men, ne blamingus wee dreden. Forsothe wee besiende to plesen to God, vtterli wee drede not the thretis of men; for God scatereth the bones of hem that desiren to plesen to men, and[i], after the apostil, they, that suche men ben, moun not ben the[k] seruauns of Crist. Ferthermor in the boc of Ester wee han maad an abece of red colour vnto the eiȝthe[l] lettre in diuers placis, willende, that is, the order of the seuenti interpretoures bi these thingus to[m] shewen a[n] wijs redere; we forsothe after the maner han leuere, and[o] in the making of the[p] seuenti remenoures, to pursue the order of Ebrues.

Here endith the prolog of Hester, and now bigynneth the book[q].

ª This prologue is from M.

ª From E. *Prologus.* A. *Here bigynneth the prolog on the book of Hester.* L. No initial rubric in CFHIO. ᵇ It is knowun the book of Hester to be maad visions of dyuerse translatours LO. ᶜ the LO. ᵈ ofte tymes L. ᵉ after AHLO. ᶠ sympli AHLO. ᵍ in to L. ʰ preisyng LO. ⁱ Om. L. ᵏ Om. L. ˡ eiȝteenthe AHILO. ᵐ Om. C. ⁿ to a CI. ᵒ Om. I. ᵖ Om. H. ᑫ From A. *Here endith the prolog, and bigynneth the booc of Ester.* E. *Here endeth the prolog of Hester, ȝe now the book.* I. *Here eendith the prolog of Hester, and bigynneth i.* Cᵒ. L. *Here endith the prolog on Hester, and bigynneth the book.* O. No rubric in CFH.

Hesther[a].

CAP. I.

CAP. I.

1 In the daȝes of king Assueri, that regnede fro Jude vnto Ethiope, vp on an hundrid and seuene and twenti pro- 2 uynces, whan he sat in the see of his regne, Susa cyte was the begynnyng of 3 his rewme. The thridde thanne ȝer of his empire he made a gret feste to alle the princis, and to his most strong chil- dre of Persis, and of Meedis, to the noble men, and to the prefectus of prouincis, be- 4 forn hym, that he shewe the richesses of the glorie of his regne, and the mykil- nesse, and the bost of his power myche tyme, an hundrid, that is, and foure score 5 daȝes. And whan the daȝes of the feste weren ful endid, he bad al the puple that is founde in Susys, fro the moste vnto the leste; and he comaundede seuene daȝes a feste to be maad redi in the vestiarie of the ȝerd and of the wode, that was sett togidere with the kingis enournyng and 6 hond. And ther heengen[b] on eche side tentis of the colour of the eir, and of goldene colour, and of incinctin, sustened with bijs cordis, and purper, that weren inset with yuer cerclis, and thei weren vnderset with marbil pileeris; also goldene setis and siluerene vp on the raied[c] pa- ment smaragd and pario stones[d] weren disposid; the whiche thing the peynteur 7 with wonder diuersete made fair. For- sothe thei, that weren biden, drunken of goldene cuppis, and with other and othere vesselis metis weren broȝt in; win also, as it was wrthi for the kingis grete doing,

In the daies of kyng Assuerus, that 1 regnede fro Ynde 'til to[b] Ethiopie, on[c] an hundrid and seuene and twenti prouynces, whanne he sat in the seete of his rewme, 2 the citee Susa[d] was the bigynnyng of his rewme. Therfor[e] in the thridde ȝeer of 3 his empire he made a greet feeste to alle hise princes and[f] children[g], the[h] strongeste men of Persis, and to the noble men of Medeis, and to the prefectis[i] of prouynces, bifor him silf, to[j] schewe the richessis of 4 the glorie of his rewme, and the gretnesse, and boost[k] of his power in[l] myche tyme, that is, an hundrid and 'foure scoor[m] daies[n]. And whanne the daies of the 5 feeste weren fillid[o], he[p] clepide to feeste[q] al the puple that was foundun in Susa[r], fro the moost 'til to[s] the leeste; and he[t] comaundide the[n] feeste to be maad redi bi seuene daies in the porche† of the[v] orcherd and wode[w], that was set[x] with the kyngis ournement and hond[r]‡. And tentis of 'the 6 colour of[z] the eir, and of gold, and of iacynct, susteyned[a] with coordis of[aa] bijs, and of purpur[b], hangiden[c] on ech side, whiche[d] weren set in cerclis[e] of yuer[f], and[g] weren vndur set with pilers of marble; also[h] seetis[i] at the maner of beddis of gold and of siluer 'weren disposid[k] on[l] the pawment arayede with smaragde and dy- uerse[m] stoon[n]; which[o] pawment peynture made fair bi wondurful dyuersite. So- 7 theli[p] thei, that weren clepid to meet, drunkun in goldun cuppis, and metes weren borun in[q] with othere[r] 'and othere[s]

† porche; that is, aley. Lire here. c.

‡ hond; that is, werkis. Lire here. c.

---

[a] No initial rubric, but only this running title in the Mss. [b] hongeden AEFH. [c] Om. AE pr. m. FII. [d] strate stones E pr. m.

[a] Here bigynneth Hester. ELP. No initial rubric in BNOQRSVXB. [b] vnto I. to X. [c] vpon I. [d] of Susa CM. [e] And I. [f] and to olle his I. [g] children or sernauntis I. [h] to the I. [i] cheef men I. [j] for to I. [k] the boost I. [l] and in I. [m] lxxx. BDEIILO. eiȝti CNVW. seuenti M. [n] daies this feste lastide I. [o] endid I. [p] the emperour I. [q] his feeste I. [r] the citee of Susa I. [s] vnto I. [t] Om. B. [u] this I. [v] an I. [w] of a wode I. [x] set aboute I. [y] with his hond I. [z] Om. S. [a] weren holden up I. [aa] and X. [b] purpel I. purpul LP. [c] and thei hangiden I. [d] the whiche tentis I. [e] the cercles A pr. m. [f] yuorie I. [g] and thei I. [h] and X. [l] ther weren ordeyned seetis I. [k] Om. I. [l] upon I. [m] with othere dyuerse I. [n] and precious stones I. [o] the which I. [p] And I. [q] in to hem I. [r] oon I. [s] Om. S.

8 plente and chef was set. And ther was not that constreynede to drinke hem that wolden not; but so the king hadde ordeyned, befor settende sunder men of his princis to the bord, that eche man shulde 9 take that he wolde. Also Vasthi, the quen, made a feste of wymmen in the paleis, wher king Assuer was wont to 10 dwelle. And so the seuenthe dai, whan he was gladere cherid, and after to myche drinking was chaufid with win, he comaundede to Naumam, and Baracha, and Arbana, and Gabatha, and Zarath, and Abgatha, and Carthas, seuene geldingis, 11 that in his siʒte mynystreden, that thei shulden bringen in Vasthi, the quen, befor the king, put vp on hir hed a diademe, that he shewe to alle ʼprincis and puplisᵉ the fairnesse of hir; forsothe she 12 was ful fair. The whiche forsoc, and at the kings heste, that bi the geldingis he hadde comaundid, she dispiside to comen. Wherfore the king wroth, and ᶠ with 13 myche wodnesse tend, askide the wise men, that of the kingis maner euermor weren neeʒ to hym, and dide alle thingus bi the counseil of hem, kunnende the 14 lawe and the riʒtis of more men; forsothe the firste and the nexte weren Carcena, and Secaba, Admatha, and Tharsis, and Mares, and Marsana, and Mamucha, seuene dukis of Persis and of Medis, that seʒen the face of the king, and first after 15 hym weren wont to sitten; to what sentence quenᵍ Vasthi shulden vnderlyn, that the heste of king Assuer, the whiche bi geldingis he hadde sent, she wolde not 16 do. And Manucha answerde, herende the king and the princis, Not onli quen Vasthi hath greued the king, but alle the princis and puplis, that ben in alle 17 the prouyncis of king Assuer. Forsothe

vessels; also plenteuouse wiyn, and ʼthe bestᵗ was setᵘ, as it was worthi to the greet doyngᵛ of the kyng. And ʼnoon ₈ wasʷ that constreynede ʼmen not willynge toˣ drynke; but soʸ the kyng hadde ordeyned, ʼmakynge souereyns ᶻ of hise princesᵃ ʼto alle boordisᵇ, that ech man schulde take that, that he wolde. Also ₉ Vasthi, the queen, made a feeste of wymmen in the paleis, where kyng Assuerus was wontᵈ to dwelle. Therfor in the se- 10 uenthe dai, whanne the kyng was gladereᵉ, and wasᶠ hoot of wiyn aftir ful myche drinkyng, he comaundideᵍ Nauman, andʰ Baracha, andʰ Arbana, andʰ Gabatha, andʰ Zarath, andʰ Abgatha, andʰ Charchas, seuene oneste and chast seruauntis, ʼthat mynistridenⁱ in his siʒt, that 11 thei schulden brynge in bifor the kyng the queen Vasti, with a diademe set onᵏ hir heed, to schewe hir fairnesse to alle the puplis and prynces; forˡ sche was ful fair. And sche forsook, and dispiside to 12 come at the comaundement of the kyng, whichᵐ he hadde sentⁿ bi theᵒ oneste and chast seruauntes. Wherfor the kyng was wrooth, and kyndlidᵖ biᑫ fulgreet woodnesse; and he axide the wise men, whiche 13 bi theʳ ʼkyngis custom ˢ weren euere with hym, and he dide alle thingis bi the counsel of hem, kunnyngeᵗ the lawisᵘ and ritisᵛ of gretereʷ men; forsotheˣ theʸ firsteᶻ 14 and theᵃ nexte weren Carsena, and Sechaaba, Admatha, and Tharsis, and Mares, and Marsana, and Manucha, seuene duykis of Persis and of Medeis, thatᵇ sien the face of the kyng, and weren wont to sitte the firste aftir hym; ʼthe kyngᶜ axide hem, 15 to what sentence the queen Vasthi schulde be suget, that noldeᵈ do the comaundement of kyng Assuerus, whichᵉ he hadde sentᶠ bi theᵍ onest and chast seruauntis.

ᵉ the puplis and princis ᴀ. puplis and princis ᴇ.   ᶠ Om. c.   ᵍ the quene ᴇ pr. m.

ᵗ ful good ɪ. ᵘ set *forth bifore hem* ɪ. ᵛ preisyng ɪ. ʷ ther was no man ɪ. ˣ hem to drynke that wolden not ɪ. ʸ to alle the bordis ɪ. ᶻ Om. ɪ. ᵃ princes to be soueregnes ɪ. ᵇ Om. ɪ. ᵈ woned ɪ. ᵉ gladdere *than bifore* ɪ. ᶠ *whanne* he was ɪ. ᵍ comaundide to ɪ. ʰ and to ɪ. ⁱ the whiche seruyden ɪ. ᵏ upon ɪ. ˡ certis ɪ. ᵐ the which *comaundement* ɪ. ⁿ sent *to hir* ɪ. ᵒ his ɪ. ᵖ he kyndlid *or* tend ɪ. ᑫ with ɪ. ʳ Om. ɪ. ˢ custom of the kyng ɪ. ᵗ that knewen ɪ. ᵘ lawe ɪ. ᵛ the ritis ɪ. ʷ grettist ɪ. ˣ and ɪ. ʸ Om. c. ᶻ firste *men* ɪ. ᵃ Om. ɪ. ᵇ the whiche ɪ. ᶜ *and he* ɪ. ᵈ wolde not ɪ. ᵉ the which *comaundement* ɪ. ᶠ sent *to hir* ɪ. ᵍ his ɪ.

the woord of the quen shal gon out to
alle wymmen, that thei dispise ther husbondis, and seyn, King Assuer comaundide, that Vasthi, the quen, shulde gon in
18 to hym, and she wolde not. And bi this
exsaumple alle the wiues of princis of
Persis and of Medis shuln dispise the
hestis of ther husbondis; wherfore riȝt-
19 wis is the kingis indignacioun. If it
plese to thee, go ther out a maundement[h] fro thi face, and be it writen after
the lawe of Persis and of Medis, the
whiche to ouerpassen is vnleeful, that
no more Vasthi go in to the king, but
his reume an other, that is betere than
20 she, take. And this be puplishid in eche[i]
empire of thi prouynce, that is most brod,
that alle wyues, bothe of[k] more and of[k]
lasse, bere to ther husbondis wrshipe.
21 And his counseil pleside to the king and
to the princis; and the king dide after
22 the counseil of Manucha, and sente epistelis bi alle prouyncis of his reume, that
eche folc heren and reden myȝte, with
diuerse tungis and lettris, men to be
princis and more men in ther[l] housis;
and that bi alle puplis to be pupplisht.

And Manucha answeride, in audience of 16
the kyng and of the pryncis, The queen
Vasthi hath not oneli dispisid the kyng,
but[h] alle the pryncis and puplis, that ben
in alle prouynces[i] of kyng Assuerus. For 17
the word of the queen schal go out to alle
wymmen, that thei[k] dispise her hosebondis, and seie, Kyng Assuerus comaundide, that the queen Vasthi schulde
entre[l] to hym, and sche nolde[m]. And bi 18
this saumple[n] alle the wyues of prynces[o]
of Persis and of Medeis schulen dispise the comaundementis[p] of hosebondis[q];
wherfor the indignacioun of the kyng[r] is
iust[s]. If it plesith[t] to thee, 'a comaunde- 19
ment go out fro thi face[u], and 'be writun[v]
bi the lawe of Persis and of Medeis, which[w]
it[x] is vnleueful to be passid[y], that[z] Vasthi[a]
entre[b] no more to the kyng, but anothir
womman, which is betere than sche, take
'the rewme of hir[c]. And be this[d] puplischid 20
in to al the empire of thi prouynces, which
is ful large, that alle wyues, both of grettere[e] men and of lesse, ȝyue onour to her
hosebondis. His[f] counsel[g] pleside[h] the 21
kyng and the[i] prynces, and the kyng dide
bi the counsel of Manucha; and he sente[k] 22
pistlis[l] bi alle the prouyncis of his rewme,
as ech folk myȝte here and rede, in dyuerse
langagis[m] and lettris, that hosebondis ben
prynces and the[n] grettere[o] in her housis;
and '*he sente*[p], that this[q] be pupplischid bi
alle puplis.

CAP. II.

1 And so these thingus don, after that
the indignacioun of king Assuer fro feruour hadde passid, he recordide of Vasthi,
and what she hadde do, and what she
2 hadde suffrid. And the childer and his
mynystris seiden to the king, Be ther

CAP. II.

Therfor whanne these thingis weren 1
doon, aftir that the indignacioun of kyng[r]
Assuerus was coold[rr]†, he bithouȝte[s] of
Vasthi, and what thingis sche hadde do,
ethir[t] what thingis sche suffride[u]. And[v] 2
the children and the mynystris of the

† *was coold*; that is, the passioun of ire, and of trobling was passid. *Lire here*. C.

[h] comaundement *A*. [i] alle *E pr. m.* [k] Om. *E pr. m.* [l] ther owne C.

[h] but *sche hath dispisid* I. [i] the prouynces I. [k] thei *also* I. [l] haue come I. [m] wolde not I. [n] ensaumple I. [o] the prynces I. [p] heestis I. [q] her hosebondis I. [r] kyng *aȝens hir* I. [s] iust *therfore* I. [t] plese I. [u] go ther out a comaundement fro thi face I. [v] Om. I. [w] the which *lawe* I. [x] Om. I. [y] ouer passid *or broke* I. [z] *be it writen* that I. [a] Vasthi *the queen* I. [b] come I. [c] hir rewme I. [d] this *heest* I. [e] the grettere C. [f] And the I. [g] counsel *of this duyk* I. [h] pleside to I. [i] to the I. [k] sente out I. [l] lettris I. [m] langis C. [n] Om. I. [o] grettere men I. [p] Om. I. [q] this thing I. [r] the kyng CN. [rr] swagid I. [s] bithouȝte *him* I. [t] and I. [u] had suffrid I. [v] And *thanne* I.

soȝt to the king child wymmen, maidenes
3 and faire; and be ther sent, that beholden
biᵐ alle prouyncis faire child wymmen
and maidenes; and bringe thei hem to
Susa cite, and take thei in to the hous of
wymmen, vnder the hond of Egei, gelding, that is prouost and kepere of the
kingus wymmen; and take thei wym-
menusⁿ ournemens°, and othere thingus
4 to vse necessarie. And who euere among
alle to the eȝen of the king shal plese,
she regne for Vasthi. The woord pleside
to the king; and so as thei hadden
5 moued, he comaundide to be do. Ther
was forsothe a Jew man in the cite of
Susis, Mardoche bi name, the sone of
Jair, sone of Semei, sone of Cis, of the
6 linage of Gemyny; that was translatid
fro Jerusalem that time that Nabugodonosor, king of Babiloyne, hadde trans-
7 latid Jeconye, theᵖ king of Juda; the
whiche was the nurse of the doȝter of
his brother, Edisse, that bi an other name
was clepid Ester, and either fader and
moder hadde laft, ful myche fair, and
semeli in face; and hir fader and moder
dead, Mardoche clepid hir to hym in to
8 doȝter. And whanne the maundement of
the king more wex knowen, and after his
heste manye faire maidenes were broȝt to
Susem, and to Egeo, gelding, wer taken,
Ester also among othere child maidenes
is take to hym, that she wer kept in
9 the noumbre of wymmen. The whiche
pleside to hym, and fond grace in his
siȝte, that he shulde heȝen the wymmen
enournyng, and ȝeue to hir hir partis
and seuene most faire child wymmen of
the hous of the king; and bothe hir and
hir dameselis she shulde enournen and
10 araȝen. The whiche wolde not to hym

kyng seiden to 'the kyngʷ, Damyselisˣ,
virgynsʸ 'and faireᶻ, be souȝt to the kyng;
and 'men benᵃ sentᵇ, thatᶜ schulen biholde 3
bi alle prouinces damesels faire and virgyns; and brynge thei hem to the citee
Susaᵈ, and bitake theiᵉ in to the hows of
wymmen, vndur the hondᶠ of Egei, the
onest seruaunt and chast, whichᵍ is the
soucreyn and kepere of the kyngis wymmen; and take theʰ damesels ournement
of wymmen, and other thingis nedeful to
vsisⁱ. And which euer damesele amongᵏ 4
alleˡ plesithᵐ the iȝen of the kyng, regne
sche for Vasti. Theⁿ word pleside the
kyng; and he comaundide to be don so,
as thei counceliden. Forsothe° a man, a 5
Jew, was in the citee Susaᵖ, Mardoche bi
name, the sone of Jair, soneq of Semei,
soneq of Cys, of the generacioun of Gemyny; that was translatid fro Jerusalem 6
in that tyme, wherynneʳ Nabugodonosor,
kyng of Babiloyne, hadde translatid Jechonye, kyng of Juda; whichˢ *Mardoche* 7
was the nurschere of Edissa, the douȝter
of his brothir, whichᵗ *douȝtir*ᵘ was clepid
Hester bi anothir name, and scheᵛ haddeʷ
lostˣ bothe fadirʸ and modirᶻ; scheᵃ *was*
ful fair, and semeli of face; and whanne
hir fadir and modir weren deed, Mardoche
'purchaside hir in to a douȝtir to hym-
silfᵇ. And whanne the comaundement ofᵇ 8
the kyng was ofte pupplischid, and bi his
comaundementᶜ many faire virgyns weren
brouȝt to Susa, and werenᵈ bitakun to
Egey, the onest seruaunt and chast, also
Hester among othere damesels was by-
takun to hym, that sche schulde be kept
in the noumbre of wymmenᵉ. And scheᶠ 9
pleside hymᵍ, and foondʰ grace in his siȝt,
thatⁱ he hastideᵏ theˡ ournement of wymmen, and bitookᵐ to hirⁿ her partis°, and

---

ᵐ Om. AH.   ⁿ wymmen AH.   ° enourmentis AEFH.   ᵖ Om. AH.

ʷ him I.   ˣ Faire damyselis I.   ʸ and virgyns I.   ᶻ Om. I.   ᵃ be ther men I.   ᵇ sent forth I.
ᶜ whiche I.   ᵈ of Susa I.   ᵉ thei *hem* I.   ᶠ kepyng I.   ᵍ the which I.   ʰ tho I.   ⁱ her vsis I.   ᵏ of c.
ˡ alle *hem* I.   ᵐ plesith *moost* I.   ⁿ And this I.   ° And I.   ᵖ of Susa IX *sec. m.*   q the sone IS.   ʳ in
whiche I.   ˢ the which IS.   ᵗ the which I.   ᵘ *Edissa* IS.   ᵛ *bi deth* sche IS.   ʷ Om. IS.   ˣ left or
forȝede I. forȝede S.   ʸ hir fadir IS.   ᶻ hir modir IS.   ᵃ *and sche* IS.   ᵇ toke hir to him, and he made hir
his douȝter IS.   ᶜ heest IS.   ᵈ thei weren I.   ᵉ *thilke* wymmen I. *tho* wymmen s.   ᶠ Hester IS.   ᵍ Egey IS.
ʰ sche foond IS.   ⁱ so that S.   ᵏ hastide *to take to hir* IS.   ˡ an I.   ᵐ he bitook IS.   ⁿ Hester IS.   ° partis
of alle thingis nedeful to hir s.

shewe the puple and hir kuntre; forsothe
Mardoche hadde comaundid to hir, that
of this thing vtterli she shulde holde hir
11 pes. The whiche wente eche dai befor
the vestiarie of the hous, in the whiche
chosene maidenes weren kept, doende
cure of the helthe of Ester, and willende
12 to witen, what to hir shulde falle. And
whan tyme was comen of alle the child
wymmen by order, that thei shulden gon
in to the king, alle thingus fulfild that
to wymmenys^q enournyng^r pertende, the
twelfthe moneth was turned ouer; so onli
that sixe monethis thei shulde ben enoynt
with myrtine oile, and othere sixe thei
shulden vse maner pimentis and swote
13 spice. And goende in to the king, whateuere thei hadden askid pertenende to
ournyng, thei token; and, as it to them
hadde plesid, enourned, of the chaumbre
of wymmen to the kingus priue chaumbre
14 wenten. And she that cam in at euen,
wente oute at morn^s; and thennes in to
the secounde housis weren broȝt, that
weren vnder the hond of gelding Zagazi,
that stod before to the secoundarie wyues
of the king; and she hadde no power of
turnyng aȝeen more to the king, but if
the king wolde, and hir hadde comaundid
15 to come bi name. Forsothe the tyme
turned ouer bi order, the dai stood, in
that Ester, the doȝter of Abihael, brother
of Mardoche, whom to hym he hadde
clepid in to doȝter, shulde gon in to the
king; the whiche soȝte not wymmenes
enournyng, but whateuere thing wolde
Egee, gelding, the kepere of maidenes,
thoo thingis to hir to enournyng he ȝaf;
forsothe she was ful semeli, and with
vntrouable fairnesse, and to the eȝen of

seuene the faireste damesels of the kyngis
hows; and^p he^q ournede and araiede bothe
hir and damesels^r suynge hir feet. And 10
'sche nolde^s schewe to hym^t hir puple
and^u hir cuntrei; for Mardoche hadde comaundid to^v hir, that in al maner sche
schulde be stille of this thing. And he^w 11
walkide ech dai bifor the porche of the
dore, in which the chosun virgyns weren
kept, and he dide the cure of the^x helthe
of Hester^y, and wolde^z wite, what bifelde
to hyr. And whanne the tyme of alle^a 12
damesels bi ordre was comun, that thei
schulden entre^b to the kyng, whanne^c alle
thingis weren fillid^d that^e perteyneden to
wymmens atire, the^f tweluethe monethe^g
was turned^h; so oneli that^i thei weren
anoyntid with oile^k of 'myrte tre^l bi sixe
monethis, and bi othere sixe monethis
'thei vsiden summe^m pymentis^n and swete-
smellynge oynementis. And thei entriden 13
to the kyng, and what euer thing perteynynge to ournement^o thei axiden, thei
token^p; and thei weren araied as it
pleside^q hem, and^r passiden^s fro the chaumbre of wymmen to the kyngis bed. And 14
sche that hadde entrid^t in the euentid,
ȝede out^u in the morwetid; and fro thennus
thei weren led forth in to the secounde
housis, that^v weren vndur the hond^w of
Sagazi, onest^x seruaunt and chast, that
was gouernour of the kyngis concubyns†;
and sche^y hadde not power to go aȝen
more to the kyng, no^z but the kyng wolde,
'and had comaundid hir to come^a bi name^b.
Sotheli^c whanne the tyme was turned 15
aboute bi ordre, the^d dai neiȝede, wherynne Hester, the douȝter of Abiahel, bro-
ther^e of Mardoche, 'whom he hadde purchasid in to a douȝter to hym silf^f, ouȝte

† concubyns: ȝe is licly that these that entriden to the kyngis bed, weren hise wyues, netheles they weren seid concubyns, for they weren not principal wyues. *Lire here.* c.

---

q wimmen A.   r honournyng EFH.   s morwen A. morewen EFH.

---

p and *in most honest maner to plese the king with* s.   q Egey 1s.   r *thilke* dameseils 1. *tho* damyseils s.
s Hester wolde not 1. Hester nuld s.   t Egey 1s.   u neither 1s.   v Om. 1s.   w Mardocheus 1s.   x Om. A.
y hir, *of ony maner infirmytee* 1. hir, *if ony infirmyte took hir* s.   z he wolde 1s.   a alle the 1s.   b go yn 1s.
c and whanne 1s.   d fulfillid 1s.   e which s.   f and the 1s.   g monethe *of the ȝeer* 1. moneth *which tho
damysels sholden apere bifore the king* s.   h brouȝt aboute 1. turned *or endid* s.   i Om. s.   k the oile 1s.
l myrre 1sb. myrre tree HX. mirre tree x.   m summe vsiden s.   n pymentis, *that is, delicious drinkis* s.
o her ournement 1s.   p token *it* 1. token *it with hem* s.   q pleside to 1s.   r and *thanne* s.   s thei passiden
forth 1s.   t entrid *thidir* 1s.   u forth 1s.   v whiche 1s.   w kepyng 1s.   x the onest 1s.   y sche *that ȝede
fro the kyng* 1s.   z Om. 1.   a haue hir to come to him s.   b name to him 1.   c And 1s.   d and the 1s.
e the brother 1s.   f [the s] whiche Hester Mardoche hadde take to him, and made hir his douȝter 1s.

alle men gracious and loouesum was seen.
16 And so she is lad to the priue chaumbre
of king Assuer, the tenthe moneth, that
is clepid Thebeth, that is, Januer, the
17 seuenthe 3er of his regne. And the king
loouede hir more than alle the wymmen,
and she hadde grace and mercy befor
hym ouer alle the wymmen; and he putte
the diademe of the reume vp on hir hed,
and he made her to regnen in the stede
18 of Vasthi. And he comaundide a ful
glorious feste to be maad redi to alle the
princis and to his seruauns, for the coupling and the bridalis of Ester; and he
3af reste to alle prouyncis, and grauntide
large 3iftis aftir principal gret doing.
19 And whan the seconde maidenes weren
so3t, and gedered togidere, Mardoche
20 dwelte at the kingis 3ate. And 3it not
Ester hadde told out the kuntre and hir
puple, after the heste of hym; what euere
thing forsothe he comaundide, Ester kepte
wel, and so alle thingus she dide, as she
was wont that tyme, that he nurshide
21 hir a litil child. That time thanne that
Mardoche at the kingus 3ate dwelte, ben
wrothe Bagathan and Thares, two geldingis of the king, that weren porteres,
and in the firste entre of the paleis
dwelten; and wolden a3en risen in to the
22 king, and slen hym. The whiche thing
was not vnknowen to Mardoche, and anoon
he tolde to quen Ester, and she to the
king, of name of Mardoche, that to hir
23 the thing hadde told. It is so3t, and is
founde, and either of hem is hangid in the
iebet; and it is comaundid to the stories,
and taken to the bokis of 3eris deedis,
befor the king.

entre to the kyng; and sche axide not
wymmenus ournement, but what euer
thingis Egei, the onest seruaunt and chast,
kepere of virgyns, wolde, he 3af these
thingis to hir to ournement; for sche
was ful schapli, and of fairnesse that may
not li3tli be bileuyd, and sche semyde
graciouse and amyable to the i3en of alle
men. Therfor sche was lad to the bed 16
of kyng Assuerus, in the tenthe monethe,
which is clepid Cebeth, in the seuenthe
3eer of his rewme. And the kyng fer- 17
uentlir louyde hir more than alle wymmen, and sche hadde grace and mercy
bifor hym ouer alle wymmen; and he
settide the diademe of rewme on hir
heed, and he made hir to regne in the
stide of Vasthi. And he comaundide a 18
ful worschipful feeste to be maad redi to
alle hise princes and seruauntis, for the
ioynyng togidere and the weddyngis of
Hester; and he 3af rest† to alle prouynces,
and 3af 3iftis aftir the worschipful doyng
of a prynce. And whanne virgyns weren 19
sou3t also the secounde tyme, and weren
gaderid togidere, Mardochee dwellide at
the 3ate of the kyng. Hester hadde not 20
3it schewid hir cuntrei and puple, bi comaundement of hym; for whi what
euer thing he comaundide, Hester kepte,
and sche dide so alle thingis, as sche was
wont in that tyme, in which he nurschide
hir a litil child. Therfor in that tyme, 21
wherynne Mardochee dwellide at the
3ate of the kyng, Bagathan and Thares,
twei seruauntis of the kyng, weren
wrothe, that weren porteris×‡, and
saten in the first threisfold of the paleis;
and thei wolden rise a3ens the kyng,

† reste; that is, relessing of tribut. Lire here. c.

‡ porteris; for al this sentence, porteris til thidir, of the paleys, in Ebrew it is, keperis of pertenaunce of houshold, and this acordith more to the lettre suyuge. The cause of this dyuersite is this, that the Ebrew word here signefieth bothe threisfold, and pertenaunce of houshold, and oure translacioun useth the firste signyfycacioun, and Ebreys usen the secunde. Lire here. c.

t the queen A.   u it is AII.   v the 3eris A.

g to entre 18. h and kepere 18. i the virgyns 1. the kings virgyns 8. k Hester 18. l hir ournement 18.
m certis 18. n was seen 18. o in to 8. p that 1. q Feuer3eer A marg. Tebeth, that is, Januyer 18× marg.
r Om. 1. s Hester 18. t more feruently 1. u othere wymmen 1. v she L. w sette upon hir heed 18.
× a 1. y diademe or crowne 1. diademe, that is, coroun 8. z the rewme CEKL. his rewme 18. a Om. 18.
b Om. 18. c conplyng 18. d he 3af CIK sec. m. 8. e tyme to the kyng 18. f dwellide thanne 18. g kyng,
a porter 1. king, and was a porter 8. h And Hester 18. i hir puple 18. k the heest 18. l Mardoche 18.
m Om. 1. n comaundide hir 18. o sche 18. p kepte it 18. q so thanne 18. r woned 1. s Thanne 8.
t in whiche 18. u dwellide porter 18. v kyngis gate 18. w wrothe a3ens the kyng 18. × Om. 1. thei
weren his porteris 8. y and thei 18. z threisfold as cheef porters 1. threshfoold, or upon the cheef porters
sect 8. a haue risen 18.

and sle^b hym. Which^c thing was not hid fro Mardochee, and anoon he^d telde^e to the queen Hester, and sche^f to the kyng, bi^g the name of Mardochee, that hadde teld the^h thing to hir. Itⁱ was souȝt, and it was foundun^k, and ech^l of hem was hangid in a iebat; and 'it was sent to^m storyes, and wasⁿ bitakun^o to bookis^p of ȝeeris, 'bifor the^q kyng^r.

CAP. III.

Aftir these thingus king Assuer enhauncide Aaman, the^w sone of Amadathi, that was of the linage of Agag, and putte his sete ouer alle the princis that ʒhe hadde. And alle the seruauns of the king, that withinne the paleis ȝatis dwelten, boweden kne^x, and honoureden Aaman ; so forsothe the emperour hadde comaundid to hem ; onli Mardoche bowede not kne^x, ne honourede hym. To whom seiden the childer of the king, that to the ȝatis of the paleys seten before, Whi beside other men thou kepist not ʒthe hestis of the king? Whan these thingus more often thei seiden, and he^y wolde not heren, thei tolden to Aman, coucitende to witen, whether he wolde stonde stedefast in the sentence ; forsothe he hadde seid to them, hym to ben a Jew. ʒThe whiche thing whan Aman hadde herd, and bi experience proued, that Mardoche bowide not kne to hym, he honourede, he is wroth ful gretli, and for noȝt tolde in to Mardoche on to^z putte hondis ; forsothe he hadde herd, that he was of Jew kinrede, and more wolde leesen al the nacioun of Jewis, that weren

CAP. III.

Aftir these thingis kyng Assuerus enhaunside Aaman, the sone of Amadathi, that was of the kynrede of Agag, and^s settide^t his trone aboue alle the princes whiche^u he hadde. And alle the seruauntis of the kyng, that lyuyden^v in the ȝatis of the paleis, kneliden, and worschipiden Aaman ; for^w the emperour hadde comaundid so^x to hem ; Mardochee^y aloone howide not the^z knees^a†, nethir worschipide hym. 'To whom^b the children^c of the kyng seiden^d, that^e saten bifore^f at the ȝatis of the paleis^g, Whi kepist 'thou not^h the comaundementisⁱ of the kyng, othere wise^k than othere men^l? And whanne⁴ thei seiden ful ofte^m these thingis, and he noldeⁿ here^o, thei tolden^p to Aaman, 'and wolden^q wite, whether he contynuede^r in sentence^s ; for he hadde seid to hem, that he was a Jew. And whanne Aaman hadde herd this thing, and hadde^t preued 'bi experience^u, that Mardochee bowide not the^v kne to hym, nethir worschipide hym, he was ful wrooth, and he^w ledde^x for nouȝt^y to sette hise hondis on^z Mardochee aloone^a; for he^b hadde herd, that Mardochee was of the folc of Jewis, and more^c he wolde

^w Om. ᴀ. ^x the knee ᴀ. ^y Om. ᴀʜ. ^z Om. ʜ.

^b haue sleyn ɪꜱ. ^c The which ɪ. ^d Mardoche ɪꜱ. ^e telde this ɪ. toold this tresoun ꜱ. ^f sche tolde it ɪꜱ. ^g in ɪꜱ. ^h that ɪꜱ. ⁱ And it ɪꜱ. ^k foundun sooth ɪꜱ. ^l either ɪꜱ. ^m this was comaundid to be writen in ɪ. his tresoun was set to be writyn in ꜱ. ⁿ it was ɪ. ^o bitakyn bifore the king ꜱ. ^p the bookis ɪꜱ. ^q Om. ꜱ. ^r kyng, to be entrid ɪ, to be entrid in hem, to haue in mynde this tresoun, and to dreed the king ꜱ. ^s and the kyng ɪꜱ. ^t sette ɪꜱ. ^u that ɪ. ^v seruyden ɪ. ^w for so ɪ. ^x Om. ɪ. ^y but Mardochee ɪꜱ. ^z his ɪꜱ. ^a knees to him ɪ. knees to Aaman ꜱ. ^b And ɪꜱ. ^c seruauntis ɪꜱ. ^d Om. ɪꜱ. ^e which ꜱ. ^f aboue ɪ. Om. x. ^g paleis, seiden to Mardochie ɪꜱ. ^h not thou, sith thou art a Jew ꜱ. ⁱ heestis ɪꜱ. ^k wise, that is, more dilygently ꜱ. ^l men don ɪꜱ. ^m ofte to him ɪꜱ. ⁿ wolde nat ɪ. ^o here hem ɪ. ^p tolden thes thingis thanne ɪ. ^q for thei coueitiden to ɪꜱ. ^r wolde contynue ᴋꜱᴇᴄ.ᴍ.ᴡᴀ. ^s the sentence schewid to hem ɪ. the sentence that he had shewed to hem ꜱ. the sentence x sᴇᴄ.ᴍ. ^t whanne he hadde ɪ. Om. ꜱ. ^u the soth bi knowyng of the trenthe theroff ɪꜱ. ^v his ɪꜱ. ^w Aaman ɪꜱ. ^x arettide it ɪ. rettid ꜱ. ^y nouȝt, or for no veniaunce ꜱ. ^z upon ɪꜱ. ^a aloone, to sle him ɪ. aloone, to kille him ꜱ. ^b Aaman ɪꜱ. ^c the more rathir ɪ. more herfor ꜱ.

7 in the reume of Assuer. The^zz firste
moneth, whos name is Nysan, the twelfthe
3er of the regne of Assuer, lot is leid in
to a vessel, that Ebruli is seid fur, beforn Aman, what dai and what moneth
the folc of Jewis shulde be slayn; and
8 clepid Adar. And Aman seide to king
Assuer, Ther is a puple bi alle the
prouyncis of thi reume scaterid, and fro
themself^a togidere seuered, newe vsende
lawis and cerimoynes, ferthermor and the
statutis of the king dispisende; and best
thou hast knowen, that it spedeth not to
thi reume, that ouercustomed it waxe
9 proud bi leeue. If to thee it plese, deme
that it pershe, and ten thousend of ta-
10 lentis I shal lei to tresories of thi rich-
esse^b. Thanne the king toc of his hond
the ring that he vside, and 3af it to the
enemys of Jewys, Aman, sone of Ama-
11 dathi, of the kinrede of Agag. And he
seide to hym, The siluer that thou be-
hotist, be thin; of the puple do that to
12 thee plesith. And the scribis of the king
ben clepid the firste moneth of Nysan,
the threttenthe dai of the same moneth;
and it is writen, as Aman hadde comaundid, to alle the satrapis of the king,
and domysmen of dyuerse prouyncis and
folkis, that alle folc^c my3ten rede and
heren, for the diuersite of tungis, of the
name of king Assuer. And the lettris
13 selid^d with his ring ben sent bi the corouris of the king to alle his prouyncis,
that thei shulde slen and don awei alle
the Jewis, fro child vn to old man, litle
childer and wymmen, o dai, that is, the

leese^d al the nacioun of Jewis, that^e weren
in the rewme of Assuerus. In^f the firste 7
monethe, whos nam is^g Nysan^h, in the
tweluethe 3eer of the rewme of Assuerus,
lot was sent^i in to a vessel, which^k lot is
seid in Ebrew phurf, 'bifor Aaman^l, in
what dai and in what monethe the folk
of Jewis ou3te to be slayn; and^m the
tweluethe monethe 3ede out, which^n is
clepid Adar^o. And^p Aaman seide to the^q 8
king Assuerus, A puple is scaterid bi alle
the^r prouynces of thi rewme, and is^r departid fro it^t silf togidere^u, and^uu vsith^v
newe lawis and cerymonyes, and ferther-
more^x it^y dispisith also^z the comaunde-
mentis^zz of the kyng; and thou knowest
best, that it spedith not to thi rewme,
'that it encreesse in malice^a bi licence^b. If^a
it plesith^c thee^d, 'deme thou^e that it^f pe-
rissh, and Y schal paie ten thousynde of^g
talentis^h to the keperis of thi tresour.
Therfor^i the kyng took 'fro his hond the 10
ryng^k which he vside^l, and 3af^m it to
Aaman, the sone of Amadathi, of the
kynrede of Agag, to^n the enemy of Jewis.
And the kyng seide to hym^o, The siluer, 11
which^p thou bihi3tist^q, be^r thin^s; do^t thou
of the^u puple that^v, that plesith^w thee.
And^x the^y scryuens^z of the kyng weren 12
clepid in the firste monethe Nysan^a, in the
threttenthe dai of the same monethe; and
it was writun, as Aaman hadde comaundid,
to alle prynces^b of the kyng, and to' domesmen of prouynces^c and of dyuerse^d folkis,
that^e ech folk my3te rede^f and here^g, 'for
dyuersite of langagis^h, bi^i the name of
kyng Assuerus. And^k lettris ascelid^l with
the ring of the kyng weren sent bi the 13

† phur, is no
word of Ebrew,
but of Persis,
and therfor in
Ebreu it is
seid phur, go-
ral, so that
goral is an
Ebreu word,
and signefieth
lot. Lire here.
c.

---

zz In the c pr. m. a hym silf AH. b ritchessis A. c folkis AH. d aselid B pr. m.

d fordo 1. e the whiche 1. whiche s. f Thanne in 18. g was 8. h Nysan, that is, Aprel 18.
i caste 18. k the which 1. l bifore him, to wite 1. this lot Aaman, which bileued in wicheke craft, did caste
bifore him to wite s. m and bi the lott 18. n that 1. o March A. marg. Adar, that is, Marche 18. p And
thanne 18. q Om. 18. r Om. 8. s it is 18. t thi s. u Om. 1. uu and as a peple without propre or
certeyn abydinge 8. v this peple vsith 1. this peple ysen s. x ferthermore also 1. y Om. 8. z Om. 9.
zz hestis 18. ' a to be infect bi vnwisdom of proude folk and yuele manered 18. b thi licence 1. licence of
thee s. c pleese 8. d to thee 1. e deeme and comaunde 8. f this peple 18. g Om. 01s. h talentis of
siluer 1. i Thanne therfor 1. Therfor than s. k his ryng fro his fyngir s. l vside for a sygnet s. m he
3af 18. n Om. 1. o Aaman 18. p that 18. q hast bihi3t 1. hast bihi3t io me s. r be it 18. s thin owne 18.
t and do 18. u that s. v that thing 18. w plesith to 18. x And thanne 18. y bi the heeste of Aaman,
the s. z writers 1. a of Nysan, that is, Aprel 18. b the prynces 18. c dyuerse prouynces 18. d Om. 18.
e that for dyuers [of s] langage 18. f rede hem 1. rede thise lettris 8. g here hem 18. h Om. 18.
i in 1. to be sent in s. k And thus 18. l enselid 1.

threttenthe^e dai of the twelfthe moneth, that is clepid Adar, that is, March ; and 14 ther goodis thei shulden forfeten. The sentence forsothe of the^f epistelis^g was this, that alle prouyncis shulden knowe, and go themself to the forseide dai. And thei, that weren sent, hee3eden to fulfillen out the heste of the king; and anoon in Susis hoeng^h the maundement froⁱ the king, and Aman solempneli makende a feste, and alle the Jewis, that in the cite weren, wepende.

corouris of the kyng to alle hise prouynces, that thei schulden sle, and 'do awei^m alle Jewisⁿ, fro a^o child to^p an eld man, litle^q children and wymmen, in o dai, that is, in the thrittenthe dai of the tweluethe monethe, which^r is clepid Adar^s; and^t that thei schulden take awei the goodis of Jewis^u. Forsothe^v the sentence 14 'in schort^w of the^x pistlis^y was this^z, that alle prouyncis schulden wite, and make hem redi to the forseid dai. And the coroures, that weren sent^a, hastiden^b to fille^c the comaundement^d of the kyng; and anoon the comaundement^e hangide^f in Susa^g, 'while the kyng^h and Aaman madenⁱ feeste, and 'the while^k that^l alle Jewis^m wepten, that weren in theⁿ citee.

CAP. IV.

1 The whiche thingis^k whan Mardocheus hadde herd, he cutte his clothis, and is clad^l with a sac, sprengende askis^m to his hed, and in the strete of the myddil cite with gret vois criede, shewende the bit- 2 ternesse of his inwit, and with this weping vnto the 3atis of the paleis goende; forsothe it was not leful a man cladⁿ with a sac to entre the kingis halle. 3 Also in alle prouyncis, bur3 townes, and placis, to the whiche the cruel bidding of the king hadde ful comyn, gret weiling was anentis the Jewis fastende, and 3ellende, and wepende, manye men vsende 4 for bed sac and askis^o. Forsothe the childer^p wymmen of Ester, and the geldingus, wenten in, and tolden to hir; the whiche herende is stoneid^q, and sente a cloth, that the sac don awei, he shulde clothin hym; the whiche taken he wolde 5 not. And Athac, gelding, clepid, whom the king hadde 3iue to hir seruaunt, she

CAP. IV.

And whanne Mardochee hadde herd 1 these thingis, he to-rente hise clothis, and he was clothid in a sak, and spreynt^o aische on^p the^q heed, and he criede with greet vois in the street of the myddis of the citee, and schewide^r the bitternesse of his soule, and he 3ede with this 3ellyng 'til 2 to^s the 3atis of the paleis; for^t it was not leueful a man clothid with a sak to entre in to the halle of the kyng. Also in alle 3 prouynces, citees^u, and places^v, to which the cruel sentence of the king was comun, was^w greet weilyng, fastyng, 3ellyng^x, and wepyng^y anentis the Jewis, and many Jewis vsiden sak^z and aische for bed^a. Sotheli^b the dameselis and onest^c seruauntis and chast of Hester entriden^d, and telden^e to hir^f; which thing sche herde, and was^g astonyed; and sche sente a cloth *to Mardochee*, that whanne the sak was^h takun a wei, he schulde clothe hym therynne; whichⁱ cloth he nolde^k

---

^e threttithe *AII.*   ^f Om. *H.*   ^g epistil *AE.*   ^h hongide out *A.* hangide *EFH.*   ⁱ of *A.*   ^k thing c. ^l clothid *AII.*   ^m asshen *A.*   ⁿ clothid *AII.*   ^o asshen *A.*   ^p child *AII.*   ^q astoneyd *AEFII.*

^m fordo I.   ⁿ the Jewis I.   ^o Om. cI.   ^p vnto I.   ^q and litle I.   ^r that I.   ^s *March* A. *marg.* Adar *or Marche* I.   ^t and *thei weren also comanudid* I.   ^u the Jewis Is.   ^v And I.   ^w Om. I.   ^x Om. c. ^y epistolis EILFRa. lettris I.   ^z this, writen in a fewe wordis I.   ^a sent forth I.   ^b hastiden *hem self* I. ^c fulfille I.   ^d heest I.   ^e heest *of the kyng* I. commaundement *of the king* s.   ^f was hangid up I.   ^g *the citee of* Susa I.   ^h Om. I.   ⁱ made a I.   ^k Om. KI.   ^l Om. *plures.*   ^m the Jewis Is.   ⁿ that I.   ^o he spreynt I. ^p upon I.   ^q his I.   ^r he schewide I.   ^s vnto I, to x.   ^t sothely I.   ^u in citees I.   ^v in places I.   ^w ther was I.   ^x Om. I.   ^y wepyng and 3ellyng I.   ^z a sak I.   ^a her bed I.   ^b And I.   ^c the onest I. ^d entriden yn I.   ^e telden *this thing* I.   ^f Hester I.   ^g sche was I.   ^h were I.   ⁱ the which I.   ^k wolde not I.

comaundide, that he shulde go to Mardoche, and lernen of hym, whi that thing
6 he dide. And Athac gon out, wente to Mardoche stondende in the strete of the
7 cyte, beforn the dore of the paleis ; the whiche shewide to hym alle thingus that hadden falle, hou Aman hadde behoten, that he shulde bringe siluer in to the tresories of the king for the Jewis deth.
8 Also the saumple of the maundement, that heeng[r] in Susis, he ʒaf to hym, that to the quen he shulde shewen, and warnen hir, that she go in to the king,
9 and preʒe hym for hir puple. And Athac, gon out, tolde Ester alle thingus,
10 that Mardoche hadde seid. The whiche auswerde to hym, and seide, that he
11 shulde sey to Mardoche, Alle the[s] seruauns of the king, and alle prouyncis that ben vnder his comaunding, knowen, that outher[t] man or womman not clepid entre the innermor porche of the king, withoute aʒeen cleping[u] anoon he be[v] slain, but if perauenture the king 'the goldene ʒerde to hym streeche for signe of mercy, and so he may lyuen ; I thanne what maner shal moun entre to the king, that now thretti daʒis am not clepid to
12 hym? The whiche thing whan Mardoche
13 hadde herd, eft he sente to Ester, seiende, Ne wene thou, that thi lif onli thou deliuere, for in the hous of the king thou art,
14 for alle Jewis ; if thou holde[w] thi pes, bi an other ocasioun the Jewis shul be deliuered, and thou and the hous of thi fader shul pershen ; and who knew, whether therfore to the reume thou came[x], that in such a time thou shuldest be redi?
15 And eft Ester these woordis sente to
16 Mardoche, Go, and gedere alle the Jewis, that in Susis thou findist, and preʒeth

take. And aftir that[l] Athac, the[m] onest 5 seruaunt and chast[n], 'was clepid[o], whom the kyng hadde ʒoue a mynystre[p] to hir[q], sche[r] comaundide, that he schulde go to Mardochee, and lerne of hym, whi he dide this thing. And Athac ʒede out[s], and ʒede[t] 6 to Mardochee stondynge in the street of the citee, bifor the dore[u] of the paleis ; which[v] 7 schewide to Athac alle thingis that bifelden[w], hou Aaman hadde bihiʒt to bryng siluer in to tresours[x] of the kyng for the[y] deeth of Jewis[z]. Also he[a] ʒaf to Athac 8 the copie of the comaundement[b], that hangide in Susa[c], to[d] schewe to the queen, and to moneste[e] hir for to entre[f] to the kyng, and to biseche hym for hir puple. And Athac ʒede aʒen, and telde to Hester 9 alle thingis, whiche[g] Mardochee hadde seid[h]. And sche answeryde to hym[i], and 10 seide, that he schulde seie[k] to Mardochee, Alle[l] the seruauntis of the kyng, and alle 11 prouyncis[m] that[n] ben vndur his lordschip, knowen, that whether a[o] man ether a[p] womman not clepid[q] entrith in to the ynnere halle of the kyng, he schal be slayn anoon with outen ony tariyng, no[r] but[s] in hap the kyng holdith[t] forth[u] the goldun ʒerde 'to hym[v] for 'the signe[w] of merci, and[x] he mai lyue so ; therfor hou mai Y entre to the kyng, which[y] am not clepid to hym now bi thritti daies ? And 12 whanne Mardochee hadde herd 'this thing[z], he sente efte to Hester, and seide, Gesse 13 thou not, that thou schalt delyuer oonli thi lijf, for[a] thou art in the hows of the kyng, bifor alle Jewis[b] ; for if thou art 14 stille now, Jewis[c] schulen be delyuered bi another occasioun[d]†, and thou and the hows of thi fadir schulen perische‡ ; and who knowith, whether herfor thou camist to the rewme, that thou schuldist be maad

† bi another occasioun ; for God hath many maneris to deliyuere hise seruauntis. Lire here. c.

‡ schule perische ; bi Goddis riʒtfulnesse, for thou hast dispisid thi puple. Lire here. c.

---

r hangede AEFH.   s Om. A.   t or AEFH.   u aclepyng F.   v shal be A.   w holdist AEFH.
x come AEFH.

l this thing, was clepid I. m an I. n a chast I. o Om. I. p seruaunt I. q Hester I. r and sche I.
s forth I. t he came I. u ʒate I. v and he I. w hadden bifalle I. x the tresours I. y Om. I. z the
Jewis I. a Mardochee I. b kingis heest I. c the citee of Susa I. d for to I. e moue I. f entre yn I.
g that I. h seid to him I. i Athac I. k seie this thing I. l that alle I. m the prouyncis I. n whiche I.
o Om. I. p Om. I. q clepid of the kyng I. r Om. I. s but if I. t holde I. u forth to him I.
v Om. I. w n token I. x and that I. y that I. z thes thingis I. a for thi that I. b the Jewis I.
c the Jewis I. d wey I.

for me; ne eteth, ne drinkith thre daȝes
and thre nyȝt, and I with myn hond
wymmen lic maner shal fasten; and
thanne not clepid I shal gon in to the
king, aȝen the lawe doende, takende me
17 to deth and to perile. And so Mardoche
wente, and dide alle thingus, that Ester
hadde comaundid to hym.

redi in sich a[e] tyme[f]? And eft Hester sente 15
these wordis to Mardochee[g], Go thou, and 16
gadere togidere alle Jewis[h], whiche thou
fyndist in Susa, and preie ȝe for me; ete
ȝe not†, nether drynke ȝe in thre daies and
thre nyȝtis, and Y with myn handmaydis[i]
schal fast in lijk maner; and thanne Y
not clepid schal entre[k] to the kyng, and
Y schal do aȝens the lawe, and Y[l] schal
bitake me to deth and to perel. Therfor 17
Mardochee ȝede[m], and dide alle thingis,
whiche[n] Hester hadde comaundid to hym.

† ete ȝe not; that is, faste ȝe, and ete onyȝ onely in the day, for it were vndiscreet abstynence to ete no thing nether to drynke in thre dayes, and thre nyȝtis. Lire here. c.

CAP. V.

1 Forsothe the thridde dai Ester was
clad[y] with kingus clothis, and stod in the
porche of the kingus hous, that was withinne forth aȝen the kingis hous; and[z]
he sat vp on his see, in the constorie of
the paleis, aȝen the dore of the hous.
2 And whan he hadde seen Ester, the
quen, stondende, she pleside to his eȝen,
and he straȝte out aȝen hir a goldene
ȝerde, that he heeld with hond; the
whiche neȝhende kiste the ouermor[a] of
3 his ȝerde. And the kyng seide to hir,
What wilt thou, quen Ester? what is
thin asking? Also if the half part of the
reume thou aske, it shal ben ȝiue to thee.
4 And she answerde, If to the king it plese,
I beseche, that thou come to me to dai,
and Aman with thee, to the feste, that
5 I haue greithid. And anoon the king
Clepeth, he seith, Aman anon, that he
obeȝhe to the wil of Ester. Aud so the
king and Aman camen to the feste, that
6 the quen hadde maad redi to hem. And
the king seide to hir, after that he hadde
drunke win plenteuously; What askist
thou, that be ȝiue to thee, and for what
thing preȝist thou? Also if the half part
of my reume thou aske, thou shalt gete.

CAP. V.

Forsothe[o] in the thridde dai Hester was 1
clothid in 'the kyngis[p] clothis, and stood[q]
in the porche of the kyngis hows, that
was 'the ynnere aȝens[r] the kyngis halle;
and he[s] sat on[t] his trone, in the consistorie
of the[u] paleis, aȝens the dore of the hows.
And whanne he hadde seyn Hester, the 2
queen, stondynge[v], sche pleside[w] hise iȝen,
and he helde forth aȝens hir the goldun
ȝerde, which[x] he helde in the[y] hond; and
sche[z] neiȝide[a], and kisside[b] the hiȝnesse[c]
of his ȝerde. And the king seide to hir, 3
Hester, the queen, what 'wolt thou[d]? what
is thin axyng? ȝhe, thouȝ[e] thou axist[f] the
half part of my rewme, it schal be ȝouun
to thee. And sche answeride, If it plesith[g] 4
the kyng, Y biseche, that thou come to
me to dai, and Aaman with thee, to the
feeste, which[h] Y haue maad redi. And 5
anoon the king seide, Clepe ȝe[i] Aaman
soone[k], that he obeie to the wille of Hester.
Therfor[l] the kyng and Aaman camen to
the feeste, which the queen hadde maad
redi to hem. And the king seide to hir[m], 6
aftir that he hadde drunk[n] wiyn[o] plenteuousli, What[p] axist thou[q], that it be
ȝouun to thee, and for what thing axist
thou[r]? ȝhe, thouȝ thou axist[s] the half

[y] clothed AEFH. [z] Om. c. [a] ouermost AEFH.

[e] Om. o. [f] tyme to helpe I. [g] Mardochee, seiynge I. [h] the Jewis IX sec. m. [l] handmaidens I.
[k] entre yn I. [l] Om. plures. [m] ȝede forth I. [n] that I. [o] Certis I. [p] real I. [q] sche stood I.
[r] withynneforth forn aȝens I. [s] the kyng I. [t] upon I. [u] his I. [v] stondynge there I. [w] pleside to I.
[x] that I. [y] his I. [z] Hester I. [a] neiȝide niȝ I. [b] sche kisside I. [c] ende I. [d] woltow n. seist thou EL.
wilt thou IP. [e] ȝif EL. Om. P. [f] axe CDI. [g] plesith to I. [h] that I. [i] ȝe anoon I. [k] Om. I. [l] And
thanne I. [m] Hester I. [n] drunken I. [o] Om. I. [p] What thing is. [q] thou of me s. [r] thou now s.
[s] axe I. axedist s.

7 To whom auswerde Ester, Myn asking 8 and my preȝeeris ben these. If I haue founde grace in the siȝte of the king, and if to the king it plese, that he ȝiue to me that I preȝe fore, and fulfille myn asking, come the king and Aman to the feste, that I haue maad redi to hem; and to morn I shal opene to the king my wil. 9 And so Aman wente out that dai glad and merie. And whan he hadde seen Mardoche sittende at the ȝatis of the paleis, and not onli not to[b] han rise to hym, but ne moued forsothe of the place 10 of his sitting, he endeynede gretli; and the wrathe feyned, turnede aȝeen in to his hous, clepide to gidere to hym frendis, 11 and Sares, his wif, and expounede to hem the mychilnesse of his richessis, and the cumpanye of sones, and with 'hou myche[c] glorie vp on alle the princis and his seruauns the king hym hadde rerid. 12 And after these thingus he seith, The quen also Ester noon other man clepeth with the king to the feste, saue me, anent whom also to morn with the king I am 13 to ete. And whan alle these thingus I haue, no thing I wene me to han, as longe as I see Mardoche, Jeu, sittende at the 14 kingis ȝatis. And Sares, his wif, and othere frendis answerden,Comaunde to ben maad redi an heiȝ bem, hauende of heiȝte fifti cubitis; and sei erli to the king, that Mardoche be hangid vp on it; and so thou shalt go with the king glad to the 15 feste. And the counseil pleside, and he comaundide to be maad redi an heiȝ cros.

part of my rewme, thou schalt[t] gete[u]. To 7 whom Hester answeride[v], My axyng and preieris ben these. If Y haue founde grace 8 in the siȝt of the kyng, and if it plesith the kyng, that he ȝyue to me that[w], that Y axe, and that he fille[x] myn axyng, the kyng and Aaman come[y] to[z] the feeste, which[a] Y haue maad redi to hem; and to morewe Y schal opene my wille to the kyng. Therfor[b] Aaman[c] ȝede out[d] glad 9 and swift 'in that dai[e]. And whanne he hadde seyn Mardochee sittynge bifor the ȝatis of the paleys, and not oneli to haue not[f] rise[g] to hym, but sotheli nether moued[h] fro[i] the place of his sittyng, he[k] was[l] ful wrooth; and 'whanne the ire was 10 dissymelid, he[m] turnede aȝen in to his hows, and he clepide togidire 'to him[n] silf[o] frendis[p], and Zares, his wijf; and he de- 11 clarid[q] to hem the greetnesse of his richessis, and the cumpeny of children[r], and with hou greet glorie the kyng hadde enhaunsid hym aboue alle hise princis and seruauntis. And he seide after these 12 thinges[s], Also the queen Hester clepide noon other man with the kyng to the feeste, outakun me, anentis 'which *queen*[u] Y schal ete also to morewe with the kyng. And whanne[v] Y haue alle these thingis, 13 Y gesse that Y haue no thing, as long as Y se Mardochee, Jew[w], sittynge bifor the 'kyngis ȝatis[x]. And Zares, his wijf, and 14 othere[y] frendis answeriden to hym, Comaunde thou an hiȝ beem[z] to be maad redi, hauynge fifti cubitis of heiȝthe; and seie[a] thou eerly[b] to the kyng[c], that Mardochee be hangid theronne[d]; and so thou schalt go glad with the kyng to the feeste[e]. And the counsel[f] plesyde him, and he co- 15 maundide an hiȝ cros[g] to be maad redi.

---

[b] Om. c.   [c] what ᴇ pr. m.

[t] sholdest s.   [u] gete it ɪs.   [v] seyde s.   [w] that thing ɪs.   [x] fulfille ɪs.   [y] come thei to morewe ɪs. [z] aȝeyn to s.   [a] that ɪ.   [b] Thanne ɪ.   [c] Aaman that dai ɪ.   [d] forth thens ɪ. thens s.   [e] Om. ɪ.   [f] Om. s. [g] risen up ɪs.   [h] he moued him ɪs.   [i] ones fro s.   [k] Aaaman ɪs.   [l] herfore was.   [m] Aaman feynyde him as not wrooth herfore, and ɪs.   [n] Om. s.   [o] Om. ɪs.   [p] hise frendis cɪs.   [q] tolde ɪs.   [r] his children ɪs. [s] thingis to hem ɪs.   [t] hir ɪs.   [u] whom ɪs.   [v] thouȝ ɪs.   [w] the Jew ɪs.   [x] ȝatis of the kyng ɪs.   [y] his s. [z] beem or a galewe tre s.   [a] speke ɪs.   [b] to morewe eerly s.   [c] kyng, preiynge him ɪ. kyng, and axe of him s.   [d] ther upon ɪ.   [e] queens feeste s.   [f] counsel of hem ɪ. counceil of these s.   [g] cros, that is, a jebet s.

CAP. VI.

1 That ny3t the king ladde withoute slep, and he comaundide to be bro3t to hym stories, and the bokis of 3eris deedis of rathere times. The whiche thingus whan, 2 hym present, weren rad, it is come to that place, wher was write, hou Mardoche hadde told the aspies of Gabathan and Thares, geldingis, coueitende to sle 3 king Assuer. The whiche thing whan the king hadde herd, he[d] seith, What for this feith of wrshipe or of mede Mardoche hath goten? And his seruans and mynestres seiden to hym, No thing of 4 mede vtterli he toc. And anoon the king, Who is, he seith, in the porche? Aman forsothe wente in the innere[e] porche of the kingus hous, that he make suggestioun to the king, that he comaunde Mardoche to be ficchid on the iebet, that 5 to hym was maad redi beforn. And the childer answerden, Aman stant[f] in the porche. And the king seide, Come he in. 6 And whan he was comyn, he seide to hym, What owith to be do to the man, whom the king desireth to honouren? Aman thenkende in his herte, and trowende, that noon other man but[g] hym the 7 king wolde honouren, answerde, The man, whom the king coueitith to honouren, 8 owith to be clad[h] with kingus clothis, and to be put vpon an hors that is of the kingus sadil, and to take the kingus 9 diademe vp on his hed; and the firste of the kingus princis and kny3tis holde his hors, and bi the stretis of the cite goende, crie he, and seie, Thus shal ben honoured, 10 whom euere[i] the king wile honoure. And so the king seide to hym, Hee3e[j], and,

CAP. VI.

The kyng ledde[h] that ny3t with out 1 sleep, and he comaundide the stories and the bookis of 3eeris 'of formere tymes[i] to be bro3t to hym. And whanne tho[k] weren red in his presense, me cam to 2 the[l] place, where it was writun, hou Mardochee hadde teld the tresouns of Gabathan and Thares[m], oneste[n] seruauntis[o], couetynge to strangle[p] kyng Assuerus. And whanne the kyng hadde herd this[q], 3 he seide, What onour and meede gat Mardochee for this feithfulnesse? And hise seruauntis and mynystris[r] seiden[s] to hym[t], Outirli he took[u] no meede. And anoon 4 the kyng seide, Who is in the halle? Sotheli[v] Aaman hadde entrid in to the ynnere halle of the kyngis hows, to make suggestioun to the kyng, that he[w] schulde comaunde Mardochee to be hangid on[x] the[y] iebat, which[z] was[a] maad redi[b] to him. And the children[c] answeriden[d], Aaman 5 stondith in the halle. And the kyng 6 seide, Entre he[e]. And whanne he[f] was comun yn, the kyng seide to hym, What owith to be don to the man, whom the kyng desirith to onoure[g]? Aaman[h] thou3te in his herte, and gesside[i], that the kyng wolde onoure noon othere man no[k] but hym silf[l]; and[m] he answeride[n], The man, 7 whom the kyng couetith to onoure, owith 8 to be clothid with[o] the kyngis clothis†, and[p] to be set on[q] the horst‡ which[r] is of the kyngis sadel, and to take the kyngis diademe[s]§ on[t] his heed; and the firste[n] of 9 the[v] princes and stronge[w] men of the kyng holde[x] his hors[y], and go[z] bi the stretis of the citee, and crie[a], and seie, Thus he schal be onourid, whom ener[b] the kyng wole

d Om. AEFH.　e nere AH.　f stoondith A.　g than AH.　h clothed AEFH.　i whom so euere A.　j Hei3 thee A.

h wakide 1s.　i bifore passid 1. passid bifore hoond s.　k tho bokis 1s.　l that B sup. ras. c sec. m. v. m of Thares 1.　n priuey 1s.　o seruauntis of the king 1s.　p haue stranglid 1s.　q this story red s.　r his mynistris 1s.　s more and lesse seiden s.　t the kyng 1s.　u took of the herfore s.　v Certis 1s.　w the kyng 1s.　x upon 1s.　y a 1s.　z that 1.　a is m.　b redi of Aaman 1s.　c children of the kyng 1s. d answeriden to him 1. seyden to him s.　e he yn 1. he inne to me s.　f Aaman 1s.　g to onoure A see. m. s. h And Aaman s.　i he gesside 1s.　k Om. 1s.　l silf Aaman 1s.　m and therfore s.　n answeride thus s. o in s.　p and him owith 1s.　q upon 1s.　r the which 1.　s diademe, that is, his coroun s.　t upon 1s. u cheef 1.　firste or cheef s.　v Om. s.　w of the stronge 1s.　x he holde 1s.　y hors, ledinge him 1. hors, ledinge his bridil s.　z go he 1. go this cheef prince s.　a crie he 1s.　b Om. 1s.

† kyngis clothis; that is, whiche it is not leueful to ony man to vse, no but to the kyng. c.
‡ on the hors, etc.; that is, whom no man rood, no but the kyng. c.
§ the kyngis diademe, etc.; of whiche thingis it is opyn ynow, that Aaman aspiride to the rewme. Lire here. c.

the stole taken and an hors, do, as thou hast spoke, to Mardoche, Jew, that sit^k befor the ʒatis of the paleis; bewar, lest any thing of tho, that thou hast spoken, 11 thou leue of. And so Aman toc a stole and an hors, and Mardoche clad^l in the strete of the cite, and set vp on the^m hors, wente beforn, and criede, This wrshipe he is wrthi, whom euere the king wile 12 honoure. And Mardoche is turned aʒeen to the ʒate of the paleys, and Aman heeʒede to gon in to his hous, weilende, 13 and the hed couered. And he tolde to Sari, his wif, and to frendis, alle thingus that hadden falle to hym. To whom answerden the wise men, whom he hadde in counseil, and his wif, If of the sed of Jewis is Mardoche, befor whom thou begunne to fallen, thou shalt not moun withstonde to hym, but thou shalt falle 14 in his siʒt. ʒit hem spekende, the geldingis of the king camen, and anon hym to the feste, that the quen hadde maad redi, thei constreyneden to^n gon.

CAP. VII.

1 And so the king cam in^o and Aman to the feste, that thei shulde drinke with 2 the quen. And the king seide to hir also in the seconde day, aftir that he was chaufid with wyn, What is thin asking, Ester, that it be ʒiue to thee, and what wilt thou^oo to be do^p? Also if the half part of my reume thou aske, thou shalt gete. 3 To whom she answerd, If I haue founde grace in thin eʒen, O! king, and if to thee it plese, ʒif to me my lif, for the

onoure. Therfor^c the kyng seide to hym^d, 10 Haste thou^e, and whanne `a stoole^f† and hors^g is takun^h, do thou, as thou hast spoke, to Mardochee the Jew, that sittith bifor the ʒatis of the paleis; be^i thou war, that thou leeue not out^k ony thing of these^l, whiche thou hast spoke^m. Ther-11 for^n Aaman took `a stoole and hors^o, and ʒede^p, and criede bifor Mardochee clothid^q in the strete^r of the citee, and set ou^s `the hors^t, He is worthi this onour, whom euer the kyng wole onoure. And^u Mardochee 12 turnede aʒen to the ʒate of the paleis, and Aaman hastide to go in to his hows, morenynge, and with the^v heed hilid. And 13 he teld to Zares, his wijf, and to frendis^w alle thingis that hadden bifelde^x to hym. To whom the wise men‡, whiche^y he hadde^z in counsel^a, and his wijf, answeriden, If Mardochee, bifor whom thou hast^b bigunne to falle, is of the seed of Jewis, thou^c schalt not^d mowe^e aʒenstonde hym, but thou schalt falle^f in his siʒt. ʒit while 14 thei spaken^g, the oneste seruauntis and chast of the kyng camen^h, and compelliden^i hym to go soone^k to the feeste, which the queen hadde maad redi.

CAP. VII.

Therfor^l the kyng and Aaman entriden^m 1 to the feeste, to^n drynke with the queen. And the kyng seide^p to hir^q, ʒhe^r, in the 2 secounde dai, aftir that he was hoot^s of the^t wiyn^u, Hester, what is thin axyng^v, that it be ʒouun to thee, and what wolt^w thou be doon? ʒhe, thouʒ thou axist^x the half part of my rewme, thou schalt gete^y. To whom sche answeride, A^z! king^a, if Y^ʒ haue founde grace in thin iʒen, and if it plesith^b thee, ʒyue thou my lijf to me, for

† a stoole; that is, the kyngis cloth, and the kyngis hors; he spekith not of the diademe, for it was not semely that another man than the king schulde bere it. Lire here. c.

‡ wise men; an Ebreu glos seith here, that these wise men hadden seyn the bokis of Moyses lawe, for summe Jewis, takun prisoneris, hadden translatid thanne the bokis in to language of Persis; and there they hadden seyn, that Ebreys ben comparisond ether liened to the steris of heuene, and to the dust of erthe, as it is had in xii. c^o. and xxxv. c^o. of Genesis; and therfor they seiden, whanne Ebreys bigynnen to falle, they ben brouʒt to nouʒt as dust, and whanne they bigynnen to haue the maistry, thei stien as the steris of heuene, and therfor thou maist not aʒenstonde hem. Lire here. c.

k sittith AII. l clothed EF. m an AII. n hym to E pr. m. o Om. c. oo that c. P do to thee c pr. vice.

c And thanne IS. d Aaman IS. e thou thee IS. f the kyngis clothing IS. g his hors IS. h take to thee IS. i and bo IS. k oute vndon S. l these vndon I. m now spoke IS. n And thanne IS. o the kyngis cloth and his palfrey IS. P he ʒede farth IS. q clothid in the kyngis clothinge S. r cheef strete IS. s upon IS. t his palfrey IS. u And aftir this IS. v his IS. w his frendis IS. x bifalle IIIS. y the whiche I. z hadde towardis him S. a his counsel I. b hast now S. c doynge thi seruyse to him, thou I. doinge to him this hiʒ seruise, thou S. d not thanne IS. e Om. IS. f falle schamefully I. falle shamly S. g spaken thes thingis IS. h camen oftir Aaman IS. i thei compelliden IS. k anoon IS. l And thanne IS. m entriden yn I. n and to IS. P seide also I. q Hester IS. r Om. IS. s hoot or chaufed S. t Om. CIS. u wyn drinkinge S. v axyng of me IS. w wilt I. x axe IS. y haue it IS. z O! I. a my lord kyng S. b plesith to IS.

whiche I preȝe, and my puple, for the
4 whiche I beseche. Forsothe wee ben
taken, I and my puple, that wee be to-
treden, slainᵖ, and pershen; and wolde God
in to thrallis and thrallessis wee were
sold, and it were tolerable euel, and
weilende I shulde holden my pes; now
forsothe oure enemy is, whos cruelte
5 reboundeth in to the king. And king
Assuer answerende seith, Who is he
this, and of what power, that these
6 thingus he be hardi to do? And Ester
seide, Enemy and oure werste enemy is
this Aman. The whiche thing he herende
anoon stoneȝede, not suffrende to bern the
7 chere of the king and of the quen. Forsothe the king ros wroth, and fro the
place of the feste wente in to a ȝerd set
with trees. Also Aman ros for to preȝen
Ester, the quen, for his lif; forsothe he
vnderstod euel maad redi to hym of the
8 king. The whiche whan was comen
aȝeen fro the ȝerd set with wodis, and
he hadde comyn in to the place of the
feste, he fond Aman vpon the bed to han
fallen doun, in the whiche lai Ester; and
seith, Also the quen he wile opresse, me
present, in myn hous. Ne ȝit the woord
of the kingus mouth hadde gon out, and
anon couereden his face the seruauns of
9 the king. And Arbona, oon of the geldingus that stoden in the seruyse of the
king, seide, Lo! the tree that he hadde
maad redi to Mardoche, that spac for
the king, stantᵍ in the hous of Aman,
hauende of heiȝte fifti cubitis. To whom
10 seide the king, Hangeth hym in it. And
so Aman is hangid in the iebet, that he

whichᵉ Y preiedᵈ, and myᵉ puple, for whichᶠ
Yᵍ biescheʰ. Forⁱ Y and my puple ben
4 ȝouunᵏ, that we be defoulid, and strangild,
and that we perische; ᴵand Y wolde, that
we weren seeldᴵ in to seruauntis and seruauntessis, ᴵand theᵐ yuel ᴵwere suffrableⁿ,
and Y ᴵwere stille weilyngeᵒ; but now
oure enemy isᵖ, whos cruelte turneth ᴵin
toᑫ the kyngᵗ. And kyngⁿ Assuerus an-
5 sweride, and seide, Who is thisᵇ, and of
what power, that he be hardi to do theseᶜ
thingis? And Hester seide, Oure worsteᶜ
aduersarie and enemy is this Aaman.
Whichᵈ thing heᵉ herdeᶠ, andᵍ was aston-
yde anoon, and ᴵsuffride notʰ to bere the
semelauntⁱ of the kyng and of the queen.
Forsotheᵏ the kyng roosᴵ wrooth, and fro
7 the place of the feeste he entride in to
a gardyn bisetᵐ with trees. And Aaman
roosⁿ for to preie Hester, the queen, for
his lijf; for he vndurstood yuel maadᵒ
redi of the kyng to hym. And whanne
8 the kyng turnede aȝen fro the gardyn
ᴵbiset with wodeᵖ, and hadde entrid in to
the place of feesteᑫ he foond that Aaman
feldeʳ doun onˢ the bed, wherynne Hester
lai. And the king seide, ᴵAlso he woleᵗ
oppresse theⁿ queen, while Y am present,
in myn hows. Theᵛ word was not ȝitʷ
goon outˣ of the kyngis mouth, and anoon
theiʸ hiliden hisᶻ faceᵃ. And Arbona seideᵇ,
9 oon of the onest seruauntis and chast, that
stoden in theᶜ seruyce of the kyngᵈ, Lo!
theᵉ tre hauynge fifti cubitis of heiȝthe
stondith in the hows of Aaman, whichᶠ
treᵍ he hadde maad redi to Mardochee,
that spak for the kyngʰ. To whom the
kyng seide, Hange ȝeⁱ Aaman in that treᵏ.

† is to the kyng; for whanne we ben slayn, he schal sette tresoun to the kingis lijf, as it is seid in xvi. cᵒ. Lire here. c.

ᵖ and slain c.   ᑫ stondith a.

ᶜ the which thing i.   ᵈ preie thee now i8.   ᵉ also the lijf of my i. also, lord, I biseche thee hertly to ȝeue to me the lijf of my s.   ᶠ the which i. Om. s.   ᵍ Om. s.   ʰ biseche thee i. Om. s.   ⁱ Certis i8.
ᵏ demed i.   ᴵ O! whi ne had we rather be sold i. O lord! whi ne hadde we bi thin heste ben sold s.   ᵐ for that i8.   ⁿ myȝte haue be suffrid i8.   ᵒ weilynge schulde haue be stille i. now wepinge shulde haue be stille, and suffrid mekly my thraldam s.   ᵖ is present i8.   ᑫ aȝeus i8.   ᵃ the kyng i.   ᵇ this enemy 8.
ᶜ siche i8.   ᵈ The which i.   ᵉ whanne he i.   ᶠ hadde herd 8.   ᵍ he i8.   ʰ he was nat sufficient i8.
ⁱ semblaunt i. semblaunt or the indignacioun 8.   ᵏ And i8.   ᴵ roos up i8.   ᵐ biset aboute i8.   ⁿ roos up i8.   ⁿ to be maad i8.   ᵖ Om. i8.   ᑫ the feeste CEIL. feeste holding i. hoolding of the feste 8.   ʳ had falle i8.   ˢ upon i8.   ᵗ Aaman wole also i8.   ⁿ Hester the 8.   ᵛ And the i8.   ʷ Om. c.   ˣ out fulli 8.
ʸ men i8.   ᶻ the i8.   ᵃ face of Aaman i8.   ᵇ Om. i8.   ᶜ Om. i.   ᵈ kyng, seide i8.   ᵉ a i8.   ᶠ the which i.
ᵍ Om. i8.   ʰ king, and made knowe his traytours 8.   ⁱ ȝe up i8.   ᵏ gebett i8.

hadde maad redi to Mardoche, and the
kingis wrathe restide.

CAP. VIII.

1 That dai king Assuer ȝaf to Ester, the
quen, the hous of Aman, aduersarie of
Jewis. And Mardoche wente in befor
the face of the king; Ester forsothe
knoulechide to hym, that he was hir
2 em[r]. And so the king toc the ring, the
whiche of Aman he hadde comaundid to
be resceiued, and toc to Mardoche. Ester
forsothe sette Mardoche vp on hir hous.
3 Ne with these thingus paȝed, she fel doun
at the feet of the king, and wepte, and
spac to hym, and preȝede, that the malice
of Aman Agachite, and his werste castis,
that he hadde thoȝt out aȝen the Jewis,
4 he comaunde to be maad voide. And
he of maner the kingus goldene septre
strauȝte out with the[s] hond, with the
whiche a tocne of the kingys mercy was
shewid. And so she risende stod before
5 hym, and seith, If it plese to the king,
and if I haue founde grace in his eȝen,
and my preȝcere be not seen to ben contrarie to hym, I beseche, that with newe
epistelis the olde lettris of Aman, spiere
and enemye of Jewis, with the whiche
he hadde comaundid them to pershen in
6 alle the kingus prouyncis, be mendid; hou
forsothe shal I moun suffre the deth and
7 the slaȝter of my puple? And king Assuer answerde to Ester, the quen, and to
Mardoche, Jew, The hous of Aman I haue
grauntid to Ester, the quen, and hym I
haue comaundid[t] to be ficchid on the cros,
for he was hardi to putte hond in to the
8 Jewis. Thanne writeth to the Jewis, as

Therfor[l] Aaman was hangid in the iebat[m], 10
which he hadde maad redi to Mardochee,
and[n] the ire[o] of the kyng restide[p].

CAP. VIII.

In that dai kyng Assuerus ȝaf to Hester, 1
the queen, the hows† of Aaman, aduersarie[q] of Jewis[r]. And Mardochee entride[s]
bifor the face of the kyng; for[t] Hester
knoulechide to[u] hym, that he was ˋhir
fadris brother[v]. Therfor the kyng took 2
the ryng, which he hadde comaundid to
be resseyued fro[w] Aaman, and ȝaf[x] to
Mardochee. Forsothe[y] Hester ordeynede
Mardochee ouer[z] hir hows[a]. And Hester 3
was not appaied with these thingis[b], and
felde[c] doun to the feet of the kyng, and
wepte[d], and spak to hym[e], and preiede[f],
that he schulde[g] *comaunde*[h] *the malice of*
Aaman of Agag[i], and hise worste castis,
whiche he hadde thouȝte out aȝens Jewis[l],
ˋto be maad voide[m]. And the kyng bi 4
custom helde forth the goldun ȝerde of
the kyng with his hond, bi which the
signe[n] of merci[o] was[p] schewid. ˋTherfor
sche[q] roos vp, and stood bifor hym[r], and 5
seide, If it plesith[s] the kyng, and if Y
haue founde grace bifor hise iȝen, and if
my preier is not seyn ˋto be[t] contrarie to
hym, Y biseche[u], that the elde lettris of
Aaman, traitour[v] and enemy of Jewis, by
whiche[w] he hadde comaundid hem to perische in alle the prouynces of the kyng,
be amendid bi newe pistlis[x]; for hou schal 6
Y mowe suffre the deth, and the sleyng
of my puple? And kyng Assuerus an- 7
sweride to Hester, the queen, and to Mardochee, Jew[y], Y[z] grauntide[a] the hows of
Aaman to Hester, the queen, and Y comaundide hym to be hangid ˋon the[b] cros,

† *howes*; that is, alle his castels. *Lire here.*

[r] vncle *AH*. encle *F*. [s] Om. *A*. [t] sent *E pr. m.*

[l] And so IS. [m] *same* iebat I. [n] and *thanne* I. and *so thanne* S. [o] wraththe IS. [p] restide *aȝens the Jewis* IS. [q] enmye IS. [r] the Jewis CS. [s] entride yn IS. [t] certis IS. [u] Om. IS. [v] the brother of hir fadir IS. [w] of IS. [x] he ȝaf *it* IS. [y] And IS. [z] *to be* ouer I. *to be souerein* ouer S. [a] meynee I. meynees S. [b] thingis *whiche Aaman had conspirid* [*aȝens the Jewis* S] IS. [c] and *therfor* felle I. and *therfore Hester* felle S. [d] sche wepte IS. [e] the kyng IS. [f] preiede *him* IS. [g] wolde I. [h] comaunde to be maad void IS. [i] *the lynage of* Agag IS. [l] the Jewis IS. [m] Om. IS. [n] token IS. [o] his merci S. [p] is S. [q] And *thanne* Hester IS. [r] the kyng IS. [s] plesith *to* IS. [t] Om. S. [u] biseche *the, lord* S. [v] the traitour IS. [w] the whiche *lettres* I. which *lettris* S. [x] lettres IS. [y] the Jew IS. [z] *and seide*, I S. [a] haue grauntid IS. [b] upon a I. on a S.

it plesith to ȝou, in the kingus name, selende the lettris with my ring. Forsothe this was the custum, that to the epistolis, the whiche of the kingus name weren sent, and weren selid with his ring, no man shulde ben hardi to with-9 seyn. And the scribis and the librarijs of the king clepid; forsothe time was of the thridde moneth, that is clepid Ciban, that is, June, the thre and twentithe dai of it; ben write the epistolis, as Mardoche wolde, to the Jewis, and to the princis, and procuratoures, and iugis, that in an hundrid and seuene and twenti prouyncis, fro Ynde vnto Ethiope, befor seten, to pro-uynce and prouynce, to puple and puple, aftir tungis and ther lettris, and to the Jewis, that thei myȝte reden and heren. 10 And tho epistolis, that in the kingus name wer sent, with his ryng ben selid, and sent bi messageris, that bi alle the prouyncis rennende shulde come before the olde lettris with the newe messageris. 11 To whom the king comaundide, that thei shulden gadere togidere the Jewis bi alle the cites, and thei shulden comaunden in oon to be gedered, that thei stonde for ther liues; and alle their enemys, with ther wiues and fre childer, and alle ther housis, thei shulden slen, and don 12 awei. And ther is set^u bi^v alle prouyncis^w o dai of veniaunce, that is, the thrittenthe dai of Adar, the twelfthe 13 moneth. And the shorte sentence of the epistil was this, that in alle londis and puplis, the whiche vnderleȝen to the empire of king Assuer, it shulde be maad knowen, Jewis to be redi to be take 14 veniaunce of ther enemys. And ther wenten out messageris, berende beforn messagis; and the maundement of the king

for^e he was hardi to sette hond aȝens the Jewis. Therfor^d write ȝe to Jewis^e, as it 8 plesith to ȝou, 'bi the^ee name of the kyng^f, and aseele ȝe the lettris with my ring. For this was the^g custom, that no man durste aȝenseie the pistlis^h, that^i weren sente in the kyngis name, and weren aseelid^k with his ryng. And whanne the 9 dyteris^i and 'writeris of the kyng^m weren clepid; 'sotheli it was^n the tyme of the thridde monethe, which^o is clepid Siban^p, in the thre and twentithe dai of that^q monethe; pistlis^r weren writun, as Mardochee wolde, to Jewis, and to princes, and to procuratouris, and to iugis, that weren souereyns of^s an hundrid and se-uene and twenti prouynces, fro Iynde 'til to^t Ethiope, to^u prouynce and to pro-uynce^v, to puple^w and to puple^y, bi her langagis and lettris^z, and to Jewis^a, that thei myȝten rede and here^b. And tho^c 10 pistlis^d, that weren sent 'bi the kyngis name^e, weren aseelid with his ryng, and sent^f bi messangeris^g, whiche^h runnen aboute bi alle prouynces, and camen^i with newe messagis bifor^k the elde lettris^l. To 11 whiche^m the kyng comaundide, that thei schulden clepe togidere the Jewis^n bi alle citees, 'and comaunde to be gaderid togi-dere^o, that^p thei schulden stonde^q for her lyues; and schulden^r sle, and do awei alle her enemyes, with her wyues and chil-dren^s, and alle^t howsis^n. And o dai of 12 veniaunce, that is, in^v the thrittenthe dai of the tweluethe monethe Adar^w, was or-deined bi alle prouynces. And the schort 13 sentence of the pistle^x was this^y, that it were maad knowun in alle londis and puplis, that weren suget to the empire of kyng Assuerus, that the Jewis ben redi^z to take veniaunce of her enemyes. And 14

---

^u sent A. ^v in A. ^w the prouyncis AF. ^x Om. A.

^c for thi that I. for thi s. ^d Therfor in the name of the king IS. ^e the Jewis IS. ^ee Om. A. ^f Om. IS. ^g a s. ^h lettres IS. ^i which s. ^k seelid I. ^l araiers of the kyngis lettris I. endyters s. ^m his writeris I. ^n it was thanne I. ^o that I. ^p May, A marg. Siban, that is, June I. ^q the I. ^r lettres I. epistlis s. ^s ouer M. ^t vnto I. ^u thei weren writen to that I. ^v that I. ^w that puple I. ^y that I. ^z bi her lettris I. ^a the Jewis I. ^b here hem I. ^c thilke I. ^d lettres I. epistelis s. ^e in the name of the kyng I. ^f weren sent forth I. ^g his messangeris I. ^h the whiche I. ^i thei camen I. ^k bifor that I. ^l lettris weren exsecutid I. ^m whom I. ^n Jewis, and comaunde hem to be gaderid togidre I. ^o Om. I. ^p and that I. ^q storde togidere I. ^r that thei schulden I. ^s with her children I. ^t with alle I. ^u her housholdis I. ^v Om. I. ^w March, A marg. Adar, that is, Marche I. of Adar x sec. m. ^x epistle s. ^y Om. I. ^z redi that day I.

15 heng^y in Susis. Mardoche forsothe of the paleis and of the siȝte of the king goende out, schynede in kingis clothis, incinctine, that is, and^z of eir^a colour, berende a goldene coroun in the hed, and wrappid with a silkene pal and purper; and al 16 the cite ful out ioȝede, and is glad. For-sothe to the Jewis is seen to ben sprungen a newe liȝt, ioȝe, wrshiping, and daunc-17 ing, anentis alle puplis, cites, and alle prouyncis, whider euere the kingus maun-demens camen, meruelouse out ioȝingis^b, metys plenteuous, and festis, and feste daȝes, in so myche, that manye of the tother folc and sect to ther religioun and cerimoynes weren ioyned; gret for-sothe drede of Jewis name alle men hadde asalid.

the^a messangeris ȝeden out^b, bifor berynge swift messages; and the^c comaundement^d of the kyng hangide in Susa^e. Sotheli^f 15 Mardochee ȝede out of the paleis^g and^h of the kyngis siȝt, and schynede^i in the kyngis clothis, that is^k, of^l iacynet^m and of^n colour of the eir, and he^o bar a goldun coroun in^p his heed, and was^q clothid^r with a mentil of selk^s and of purpur^t; and al the citee fulli ioiede^u, and was glad. For- 16 sothe^v a newe liȝt semede to rise^w to the Jewis, ioie^x, onour^y, and daunsyng, at^z alle 17 puplis, citees^a, and alle^aa prouynces, whidur euere the comaundementis^b of the kyng camen, a^c wondurful ioie, metis^d, and feestis, and an hooli dai, in so myche, that many^e of an^f other folk and sect^g weren ioyned to the religioun and cerymonyes^h of hem^i; for^k the^l greet drede of the name of Jewis ʼhadde asaylid^m alle hem^n.

CAP. IX.

1 Thanne of^c the twelfthe moneth, whom Adar to be clepid now beforn wee seiden, the threttenthe day, whanne to alle the Jewis slaȝter was greithid, and enemys waiteden to the blod of hem, the while turned, the Jewis begunne to ben ouer heiȝere, and hem of the aduersaries to 2 venge. And ther ben gedered bi alle cites^d, burȝ^e tounys, and placis, that thei shulde streechen out hond aȝen enemys and ther pursueris; and no man was hardi to withstonde, for thi that the fer of the gretnesse of hem alle puplis hadde 3 persid. For and of prouyncis the iugis, dukis, and procuratoures, and al dignete, that to alle placis and werkis weren be-forn, ful out enhauncide the Jewis, for 4 drede of Mardoche, whom to be prince of the paleis and of myche power thei

CAP. IX.

Therfor in the thrittenthe dai of the 1 tweluethe monethe, which^o we seiden now bifore to be clepid Adar, whanne sleyng was maad redi to alle Jewis^p, and her enemyes settiden tresoun to blood^q, aȝen-ward Jewes^r bigunnen^s to be the hiȝere^t, and to venge hem of aduersaries^u. And 2 thei^v weren gaderid togidere bi alle citees, castels, and places, to stretche forth hond^w aȝens her enemyes and pursueris^x; and no man was hardi to aȝenstonde^y, for the drede of her gretnesse hadde persid^z alle puplis. For whi bothe the^a iugis, duykis, 3 and procuratouris of prouynces, and ech dignyte, that weren souereyns of alle places and werkis^b, enhaunsiden Jewis^c, for the^d drede of Mardochee, whom thei knewen^e 4 to be prince of the paleis^f, and to mow do ful myche; and the fame of his name en-

---

ʸ henged AEFH. ᶻ Om. AH. ᵃ feir H. ᵇ ioȝing AEFH. ᶜ Om. A. ᵈ the citees H. ᵉ and burȝ AC.

ᵃ Om. I. ᵇ forth I. ᶜ this same I. ᵈ heest I. ᵉ the citee of Susa I. ᶠ And I. ᵍ kyngis paleis I. ʰ Om. CN. ⁱ he schynede I. ᵏ is to sey I. ˡ in I. ᵐ iacynet clothis I. ⁿ in clothis hauynge I. ᵒ Mardochie I. ᵖ on GHIX. q he was I. ʳ hilid I. ˢ siluer s. ᵗ purpul s. ᵘ out ioiede I. ᵛ Certis thanne I. ʷ rise up I. ˣ and ioie I. ʸ and onour I. ᶻ was at I. ᵃ and citees I. ᵃᵃ at alle I. ᵇ heestis I. ᶜ among hem was a I. ᵈ and metis I. ᵉ many men I. ᶠ Om. I. ᵍ of an oother sect I. ʰ to the cerymonyes I. ˡ Jewis I. ᵏ sothely I. ˡ Om. I. ᵐ assailide I. ⁿ men plures. ᵒ the which I. ᵖ the Jewis bi Aaman I. q her blood I. ʳ the Jewis I. ˢ now bigunnen I. ᵗ hiȝere part I. ᵘ her aduersaries CI. ᵛ the Jewis I. ʷ her honde I. ˣ her pursueris I. ʸ aȝenstonde hem I. ᶻ peerschid I. ᵃ Om. I. ᵇ of werkis I. ᶜ the Jewis I. ᵈ Om. I. ᵉ knowen O. ᶠ kingis paleis I.

knewen ; also the fame of his name wex eche dai, and bi the^f mouthis of alle men softe flei₃. And so the Jewis smyten ther enemys with a gret veniaunce, and slowen hem, ₃eldende to hem that thei to them ₆hadden maad redi to do^g, in so miche, that also in Susis fiue hundrid men thei slowen, with oute the ten sonys of Aman Agagite, enemy of the Jewis, of whom ₇these ben the namys; Fasondatha, Delᵃfon, and Esfata, and Forata, and Dalia, ₉and Aridatha, and Efermesta, and Arisai, ₁₀and Aridai, and Vaisatha. Whom whan thei hadde slain, thei wolden not pursue ₁₁praies^h of the substauncis^i of hem. And anon the noumbre of hem, that weren ₁₂slain in Susis, is told to the king. The whiche seide to the quen, In the cite of Susis the Jewis slowen fiue hundrid men, and othere ten sones of Aman ; hou myche sla₃ter wenest thou them to enhaunten^k in alle prouyncis? what more askist thou? and what wilt thou, that I ₁₃comaunde to be don? To whom she ansuerde, If to the king it plese, be ther ₃iue power to the Jewis, that as thei diden to day in Susis, so and do thei to morn, and the ten sones of Aman be ₁₄thei haugid in iebetis. And the king comaundide, that so it shulde be do ; and anon in Susis heeng^l a maundement, and ₁₅the ten sonus of Aman ben hangid. The Jewis gederede togidere, the fourtenthe dai of the monyth of Adar, and ther be slain in Susis thre hundrid men, ne ther substaunce fro them is raueshid ₁₆awei. But and bi alle the^m prouyncis, that vnder le₃en to the maundement of the king, the Jewis stoden for ther liues, the enemys slain and ther pursueris, in so miche, that fiue and seuenti thousend of slaine men weren fulfild, and no man

creeside ech dai, and flei^g bi the mouthis of alle men. Therfor the Jewis smytiden^h ⁵ her enemyes with greet veniaunce, and killiden hem, and ₃eldiden to tho^i enemyes that, that^k thei hadden maad redi to do to ᶜthe Jewis^l, in so myche, that also in Susa^m ⁶ thei^n killiden fyue hundrid men, with out the ten sones of Aaman of Agag^o, the enemye of Jewis, of whiche^p these ben the names; Phasandatha, Delphon, and^q ⁷ Esphata, and^q Phorata, and^q Adalia, and^q ⁸ Aridatha, and^q Ephermesta, and^q Arisai, ⁹ and^q Aridai, and Vaizatha. And whanne ₁₀ the Jewis hadden slayn hem^r, thei nolden^s take^t preies^u of the catels^v of hem. And ₁₁ anoon the noumbre of hem, that weren slayn in Susa^w, was teld to the kyng. Which^x seide to the queen, Jewis^y han ₁₂ slayn fyue hundrid men in the citee of Susa, and othere^z ten sones of Aaman ; hou grete sleyng gessist thou, that thei haunten in alle prouynces? what axist thou more? and what wolt^a thou, that Y comaunde to be doon? To whom sche^b ₁₃ answeride, If it plesith^c the kyng, power be ₃ouun to the Jewis, that as thei han do to dai in Susa^d, so do thei also to morewe, and that the ten sones of Aaman be hangid vp in iebatis. And the kyng comaundide, ₁₄ that it schulde be doon so ; and anoon the comaundement^e hangide in Susa, and the ten sones of Aaman weren hangid. Ther-₁₅ for^f whanne the Jewis weren gaderid togidere, in the fourtenthe dai of the monethe Adar^g, thre hundrid men weren slayn^h in Susa^i, and the Jewis token not awei the catel of tho^k men. But also bi alle the ₁₆ prouynces, that weren suget to the lordschip of the kyng, Jewis^l stoden for her lyues, whanne her enemyes and pursueris^m weren slayn, in^n so myche, that^o fyue and seuenti thousynde of slayn men ᶜweren

---

^{f} Om. A. ^{g} han don E pr. m. ^{h} pris c. ^{i} substaunce AII. ^{k} haunten A. ^{l} hangede AEFH. ^{m} Om. AII.

^{g} it passide I. ^{h} smeten EII.P. smetin s. ^{i} her I. the N. ^{k} Om. AS. ^{l} hem I. ^{m} the citee of Susa I. ^{n} the Jewis I. ^{o} the kynrede of Agag I. ^{p} the whiche sones I. ^{q} Om. I. ^{r} the sones of Aaman I. ^{s} wolden not I. ^{t} do BCDEFGHILMNOPQRSUVWXab. touche K sec. m. ^{u} the preies K sec. m. ^{v} substaunce I. castels GORXa. catel I.PS. batailes N. ^{w} the citee of Susa I. ^{x} And he I. ^{y} the Jewis I. ^{z} the I. ^{a} wilt I. ^{b} Hester I. ^{c} plesith to I. ^{d} the citee of Susa I. ^{e} heest of the kyng I. ^{f} And I. ^{g} of Marche I. ^{h} slayn that day I. ^{i} the citee of Susa I. ^{k} thilke sleyin I. ^{l} the Jewis I. ^{m} her pursueris I. ^{n} and in I. ^{o} that thei fulfilliden the noumbre of I.

, of ther substaunce any thing touchide.
17 Forsothe the threttenthe dai of the
monyth Adar[n] was of o sla3ter anentis
alle, and the fourtenthe dai thei lafte to
slen; whom thei ordeyneden to be solempne, that in that time eche 3er therafter thei shulden voiden to plenteuous
18 metis, aud to io3e, and to festis. And
these, that in the cite of Susys hadden
hauntid the[o] sla3ter, the threttenthe and
the fourtenthe dai of the same moneth
ben ocupied in the sla3ter. The fiftenthe
forsothe dai thei laften to smyte; and
therfore the same dai thei ordeyneden
solempne of plenteuous metis and of
19 gladnesse. These forsothe Jewis, that
in bur3 tounys not wallid and tounes
duelten, the fourtenthe daie of the
moneth of Adar, of festis, and of io3e
demeden, so that thei ful[p] out gladen in
it, and senden to hemself togidere partis
20 of plentes and of metis. And so Mardoche wrot alle these thingus, and comprehendid in lettris sente[q] to the Jewis,
that in alle the[r] prouyncis of the king
21 dwelten, bothe in nee3h set and afer, that
the fourtenthe and the fiftenthe dai of
the moneth of[s] Adar thei shulden take
for festis, and euermor, the 3er turnende
a3een, with solempne wrshipe thei shul-
22 den halewe; for in tho da3is the Jewis
vengide them of ther enemys, and weiling and sorewe in to io3e and gladnesse
ben turned; and these da3es shulde ben
da3es of plentenous metis, and of gladnesse, and thei shulden sende to themself partis togidere of the[t] metis, and to
pore men thei shulden graunt litle 3iftis.
23 Forsothe the Jewis token in to a solempne custum alle thingus, that thei
hadde begunne that time to do, and that

fillid[p], and no man[q] touchide ony thing of
the catelis[r] of hem. Forsothe[s] the thrit- 17
tenthe dai of the moncthe Adar[t] was o[u]
dai of sleyng at[v] alle *Jewis*[w], and in the
fourtenthe dai thei ceessiden to sle; which[x]
thei ordeyneden to be solempne[y], that[z]
therynne in ech tyme aftirward thei
schulden[a] 3yue tent to metis, to ioye, and
to feestis. And thei[b], that hauntiden[c] 18
sleyng in the citee of Susa, 'lyueden in[d]
sleyng in the thrittenthe and[e] fourtenthe[f]
dai of the same monethe. But in the fiftenthe dai thei ceessiden to sle; and[g]
therfor thei ordeyneden the same dai solempne[h] of feestis and of gladnesse. For- 19
sothe[i] these Jewis, that dwelliden in borow
townes not wallid and vilagis[k], demeden
the fourtenthe dai of the monethe Adar
of[l] feestis, and of ioie, so that thei[m] be
ioiful therynne, and sende ech to other
partis of feestis[n] and of metis[o]. Therfor[p] 20
Mardochee wroot alle these thingis, and
sente[q] these thingis comprehendid[r] bi lettris to the Jewis, that dwelliden in alle
prouynces[s] of the kyng, as wel to Jewis
set[t] ny3 as fer, that thei schulden res- 21
seyue[u] the fourtenthe and the[v] fiftenthe
dai of the monethe Adar 'for feestis[w], and
euer whanne the 3cer turneth a3en, 'thei
schulden[x] halowe[y] with solempne onour;
for in tho daies the Jewis vengiden hem 22
silf of her enemyes, and morenyng[z] and
sorewe[a] weren turned in to gladnesse and
ioie; and[b] these daies schulden be daies of
feestis, and of gladnesse, and 'that thei[c]
schulden sende ech to other partis of
metis[e], and '3yue litle 3iftis[f] to pore men.
Forsothe[g] the Jewis resseyueden in to 23
solempne[h] custom alle thingis[i], whiche
thei bigunnen to do in that tyme, and
whiche thingis Mardochee hadde co-

---

[n] of Adar *AH*. [o] Om. c. [p] fulli *AEFH*. [q] and sente *A*. [r] Om. *A*. [s] Om. *AEFH*. [t] Om. *A*.

[p] Om. I. [q] Jewe I. [r] goodis I. [s] Certis I. [t] of Marche I. [u] the I. [v] anentis I. [w] hem I. [x] and that *dai* I. [y] solempne *at hem* I. [z] so that I. [a] schulden *thanne* I. [b] tho *Jewis* I. [c] vsiden the I. [d] contynueden her I. [e] and in I. *dai* and a. [f] the fourtenthe CDFGHIKMNOPQSUVab. [g] Om. A. [h] to be solempne I. [i] And I. [k] in vilagis I. [l] to be solempne of I. [m] alle the Jewis I. [n] her feestis I. [o] her metis I. [p] And I. [q] he sente *alle* I. [r] writen I. [s] the prouyncis IX *see. m.* [t] dwellinge I. [u] resseyue and holde for *here* feeste daies I. [v] Om. A. [w] Om. I. [x] to I. [y] halowe *thes daies* I. [z] *thanne* her morenyng I. [a] her sorewe I. [b] and *therfor* I. [c] the Jewis I. [e] her metis I. [f] that thei departe of her godis I. [g] And I. For the sothe s. [h] the solempne co *pr. m.* a solempne I. [i] *tho* thingis I.

Mardoche in lettris hadde sent to be do.
24 Aman forsothe, the sone of Amadathi,
stoc of Agag, enemy and aduersarie of
Jewis, tho3te a3en hem euel, that he
shulde sle them and don awei, and leide
fur, that in oure tunge is turned in to lot.
25 And afterward Ester wente in to the
king, besechende, that his ententis with
the[n] lettris of the king shulden be maad
voide, and the euel, that a3en Jewis he
hadde tho3t, shulde be turned a3een in to
his hed. Afterward and[v] hym and his
26 sonus thei fiecheden to[w] the cros. And
fro that time these da3is be clepid Furim,
that is, of lotis, forthi that fur, that is,
lot, in to a pot was put; and alle thingus
that ben don ben contened in the volume
27 of the epistil, that is, of this boc; alle
thingus that thei suffreden, and that
ther after ben chaungid, Jewis and
ther sed token vp on hem, and vp on
alle that wolden to ther religioun be
couplid, that to no man it be leful these
two da3is with oute solempnete to ouerpasse, whom scripture witnesseth, and
othere tymes asken, the 3eres to them-
28 self continueli comende aftir other. These
ben the da3is, whom neuer any for3eting
shal don awei, and bi sunder ieneraciouns alle prouyncis, that in alle the
world ben, shuln halewen; ne ther is
any cite, in the whiche da3is of Furim,
that is, of lotis, be not kept of the[x]
Jewis, and of ther progenye, that with
29 these cerimoynes is oblisht. And Ester,
quen, the do3tir of Abihael, and Mardoche, Jeu, writen also the secounde
epistil, that with alle besynesse this dai
30 solempneli shulde ben halewid ther afterward. And thei sente to the[y] Jewis,
that in an hundrid and seuene and twenti

maundid bi lettris to be doon. Sotheli[k] 24
Aaman, the sone of Amadathi, of the
kynrede of Agag, the enemy and aduersarie of Jewis, thou3te yuel a3ens hem, to
sle hem and to do[l] awei, and he sente[m]
phur, which[n] is interpretid[o] in[p] oure langage[q] 'in to[r] lot[s]. And afterward[t] Hester 25
entride[u] to the kyng, and bisou3te[v], that
'hise enforsyngis[w] schulden be maad voide
bi the lettris of the kyng, and that the
yuel, which[x] he hadde thou3t a3enus the
Jewis, schulde turne a3en in to his heed.
'Forsothe thei[y] hangiden[z] on[a] the[b] cros
'bothe hym[c] and hise sones[d]. And fro 26
that tyme[e] these daies weren clepid 'Phurym, that is, of lottis[f], for 'phur, that is[g],
lot, was sent[h] in to a vessel; and the
Jewis resseyueden on[i] hem silf, and on[k]
her seed, and on[l] alle men that wolden
be couplid to her religioun, alle thingis
that weren doon[m], and ben[n] conteyned in
the volym[o] of the pistle[p], 'that is, of this
book[q], and whiche[r] thingis thei[s] suffriden, 27
and whiche[t] thingis weren chaungid aftirward, that[u] it be not leneful to ony man
to passe[v] with out solempnyte these[w] 'daies,
which[x] the scripture witnessith, and certeyn tymes axen, while the[y] 3eeris comen
contynuely oon aftir an other. These 28
ben the daies, whiche neuer ony for3et-
yng schal do awei, and[z] bi alle generaciouns alle prouynces[a], that ben in al the
world, schulen halewe[b]; nether 'ony citee
is[c], in which the daies of Phurym[d], that
is, of lottis[e], schulen not be kept of Jewis,
and of the generacioun of hem, which is
bounden to these cerymonyes. And Hes- 29
ter, the queen, the dou3ter of Abiahel,
and Mardochee, the Jew, writiden[f] also
the secounde pistle[g], that this solempne
dai schulde be halewid aftirward with al

---

[n] Om. A.　　[v] bothe A.　　[w] on A.　　[x] Om. All.　　[y] hem All.

---

[k] For I.　　[l] do hem I.　　[m] caste I.　　[n] that I.　　[o] to, sey I.　　[p] on N.　　[q] langagis D. lange PS.　　[r] Om. I.
[s] lot to do it I.　　[t] aftir this I.　　[u] entride yn I.　　[v] sche bisou3te the kyng I.　　[w] the enforsyngis of
Aaman I.　　[x] that I.　　[y] and so the Jewis I.　　[z] hangiden Aaman I.　　[a] upon I.　　[b] a I.　　[c] Om. I.　　[d] sones
also I.　　[e] tyme forth I.　　[f] the daies of lott I.　　[g] Om. I.　　[h] cast I.　　[l] upon I.　　[k] upon I.　　[l] upon I.
[m] doon bi Hester and Mardochie I.　　[n] alle thingis that ben I.　　[o] book I.　　[p] epistle s.　　[q] Om. I.　　[r] the
whiche I.　　[s] the Jewis I.　　[t] the whiche I.　　[u] so that I.　　[v] passe thes two daies I.　　[w] Om. I.　　[x] which
daies I.　　[y] that I.　　[z] but I.　　[a] the prouynces I.　　[b] halowe hem I.　　[c] ther is ony citee I.　　[d] Phur I.
[e] lott I.　　[f] wroten I.　　writin s.　　[g] epistle s.

prouyncis of king Assuer dwelten, that thei shulden han pes, and resceyue treuthe,
31 kepende wel the daȝes of lotis, and in ther tyme with ioȝe shulden halewe; as hadden ordeyned Mardoche and Ester, thei to be kept hadden taken, of hemself and of ther sed, fastingis², and clamoures,
32 and daȝes of lotis, and alle thingus that ben contened in the storie of this boc, that is clepid Ester.

CAP. X.

1 King forsothe Assuer al the lond and alle the ilis of the se made tributaries;
2 whos strengthe and empire and dignete and heiȝnesse, that he enhauncide Mardoche in, ben writen in the bokis of
3 Medis and of Persis; and hou Mardoche of Jeu kinrede were the secounde fro king Assuer, and gret anentis the Jewis, and acceptable to the folc of ther brethern, sechende goodis to his puple, and spekende tho thingus, that to the pes of his sed shulden pertene. *The whiche ben had in Ebru in pleyn feith I expressede; these thingus forsothe, that folewen, I fond write in the comun making, the whiche in Grekis tunge and lettris ben contened; and eft after the ende of the boc this chapitre was seid, that after oure consuetude with obelo, that is, with 'a stric², wee han be-*
4 *for notid.* And Mardoche seide, Of God
5 these thingus ben don. I am recordid of a sweuene, that I saȝ, magnefiende these same thingus, ne of tho any thing was
6 voide. A litil welle, that grew in to a flod, and in to liȝt and sunne is turned,

bisynesse. Andᵇ thei seuten to thoˡ Jewis, 30 that dwelliden in an hundrid and seuene and twenti prouynces of kyng Assuerus, that thei schulden haue pees†, and res-31 seyue the trewthe‡, and kepeᵏ the daies of lottisˡ, and haleweᵐ with ioie in her tyme, as Mardochee and Hester hadden ordeyned; and theiⁿ ressciueden the fastyngis, and the criesº, and the daies of lottisᑫ, to be kept of hem silf and of her seed, *and 'that thei* 32 *schulden resseyue among hooli bookis*ʳ alle thingis that ben conteyned in the storie of this book, whichˢ is clepid Hester.

CAP X.

Forsothe kyng Assuerus made tribu-1 tarye ech lond, and alle the ilis of the see; whos strengthe and empire andᵗ dig-2 nyte and hiȝnesse, by which he enhaunside Mardochee, ben writun in the bookis of Medeis and of Persis; and howᵘ Mar-3 dochee ofᵛ the kyn of Jewis was the secoundeʷ fro king Assuerus, andˣ *was greet anentis Jewis*ʸ*, and acceptable*ᶻ *to the puple of hise britheren, and he souȝte goodis*ᵃ *to his puple, and spak*ᵇ *tho thingis, that*º *perteyneden to the pees of his seed. Here endith the text of Ebrew*ᵈ*. I haue set opynli with ful feith tho thingis, that ben had in Ebrew; but Y foond these thingis, that suen, writun*ᵉ *in the comyn translacioun, that ben conteyned in the langage*ᶠ *and lettris of Grekis; and in the meene tyme this chapitre was seid after the ende of the book, 'which chapitre we bi oure custom han bifor markid*ᵍ *'with a*ʰ *spite*ⁱ*.* And Mardochee seide, These 4 thingis ben doon of God. Y haue myndeˢ onᵏ theˡ dreem, whichᵐ 'Y siȝ, signifiyngeⁿ these same thingiso, and no thing of tho was voide. Aᵖ litil welle, thatᑫ wexide 5

[margin:] † haue pees; that is, dwelle pesibly among hethen men, and be not wantoun as traistinge of the power of Hes-ter and of Mardoche. Lire here. c.
‡ and resseyue the treuthe, of this book among hooly bokis. Lire here. c.

ᶻ fastynge *a.*   ᵃ *a stirke n.*

ʰ And also I.   ⁱ thilke I.   ᵏ that thei schulden kepe I.   ˡ lott I.   ᵐ halewe hem I.   ⁿ the Jewis I.
º solempne cries I.   ᑫ lott I.   ʳ thei resceyueden I.   ˢ that I.   ᵗ his dignyte I.   ᵘ how that I.   ᵛ the whiche was of I.   ʷ secounde man I.   ˣ and Mardochie I.   ʸ the Jewis I.   ˣ he was acceptable I.
ᵃ gode thingis I.   ᵇ he spak I.   ᶜ whiche I.   ᵈ Ebrew, and this is a rubrich n text c marg.   ᵉ Om. n.
ᶠ langagis w.   ᵍ Om. n.   ʰ Om. m.   ˡ dispite D. spite, ether a spere ᴇɢʟɴᴘꞯʀx. spite, ether a finger m.
spite, ether a sterr o. spite, ether a sui a. Om. ɪʙ.   ᵏ of I.   ˡ a I.   ᵐ the which I.   ⁿ schewide I.
º thingis that now appeeren I.   ᵖ I siȝ a I.   ᑫ the whiche I.

and in to manye watris reboundide, is
Ester, that the king toc wif, and wolde
7 to be quen. Two forsothe dragounes, I
8 am and Aman; the folc that camen togidere, these ben, that enforceden to don
9 awei the name of Jewis. Forsothe my
folc is Irael, that criede to the Lord; and
the Lord made saaf his puple, and deliuerede vs fro alle euelis, and made grete
signes and wondris among the Jentilis;
10 and comaundide two lotis to ben, oon of
the puple of God, and an other of alle
11 Jentilis. And either lot cam in to the
set dai befor God now fro that time to
12 alle Jentilis. And the Lord recordide of
13 his puple, and rewide of his eritage. And
these da3es shul be kept in the moneth
of Adar, the fourtenthe and the[b] fiftenthe
dai of the same moneth, with alle bisynesse and io3e of the puple gedered in to
o cumpanye, in to alle ther aftirward
ieneraciouns of the puple of Irael.

CAP. XI.

1   The ferthe 3er, regnende Ptholome and
Cleopatra, Dositheus, that a prest and of
Leuy kinrede seide hymself to be, and
Ptholome, his sone, bro3ten this epistil
of furim, the whiche thei seiden, Silima-
cum, the sone of Ptholome, in Jerusalem
to han remened. *This forsothe was the
begynnyng in the comun translacioun,
that nouther in Ebru, ne anent any of*
2 *the[c] remenours is told.* The secounde
3er, regnyng Artaxerse the moste, the
firste dai of the moneth Nysan, Mardoche, the sone of Jari, sone of Semei,
sone of Cis, of the linage of Beniamyn,
3 a man Jeu, that dwelte in the cite of

in to a flood, and was[r] turned in to the[s]
li3t and[t] sunne[u], and turnede[v] a3en in to
ful many watris, is[w] Hester, whom the
kyng took in to wijf, and wolde[x] that
sche were his queen. Sotheli[y] twei[z] dra- 7
gouns, Y am and Aaman; folkis[a] that 8
camen togidere, ben these, that enforsiden[b]
to do a wei the name of Jewis. Sotheli[c] 9
my folk Israel it is, that criede to the
Lord; and the Lord made saaf his puple,
and delyueride[d] vs fro alle yuels, and dide[e]
grete signes[f] and wondris among hethene
men; and he comaundide[g] twei[h] lottis to 10
be, oon of Goddis puple, and the tother[i]
of alle hethene men. And[k] euer either lot 11
cam in to 'determynd dai thanne[l] fro that
tyme bifor God and alle folkis. And the 12
Lord hadde mynde on[m] his puple, and
hadde[n] merci on[o] his eritage. And these 13
daies[p] schulen be kept in the monethe
Adar[q], in the fourtenthe 'and the[r] fiftenthe[s] dai of the same monethe, with al
bisynesse and ioie of the puple gaderid
in to o cumpenye, in to alle generaciouns[t]
of the puple of Israel aftirward.

CAP. XI.

1   In the fourthe 3eer, whanne Ptolome
and Cleopatra regneden, Dositheus, that
seide hym silf to be a prest and of the
kyn of Leuy, and Ptolome, his sone,
brou3ten this pistle[u] of lottis[v] in to Jerusalem, which[w] pistle[x] thei seiden, that
Lysimachus, the sone of Ptolome, translatide. *Also[y] this bigynnyng was in the
comyn translacioun, which[z] bigynnyng is
not teld in Ebreu, nethir at ony of
the[a] translatouris.* In the secounde 3eer, 2
whanne Artaxerses the moost[b] regnyde,
Mardochee, the sone of Jairy, sone[c] of
Semei, sone[d] of Cys, of the lynage of Beniamyn, si3 a dreem in the firste dai of the

b Om. A.   c Om. AU.

r it was 1.   s Om. BEIL.   t of EL.   u in to the sunne 1.   v it turnede 1.   w *this welle* is 1.   x he
wolde 1.   y And 1.   z the two 1.   a and *many* folkis 1.   b enforsiden *hem* 1.   c But 1.   d he hath
delyuered 1.   e he hath do 1.   f tokenes 1.   g hath comaundid 1.   h two 1.   i oother 1.   k And thanne 1.
l a dai ordeyned 1.   m of 1.   n he hadde 1.   o of 1.   p *solempne* daies 1.   q of Marche 1.   r Om. IX.
's Om. s.   t the generaciouns 1.   u epistle s.   v lott 1.   w the which 1.   x epistle s.   y *This is a rubrich;*
for B.   z *the which* A.   a *tho* W.   b my3tiest *king* 1.   c the sone 1.   d the sone 1.

Susis, a gret man, and among the firste
4 of the kingus halle, saȝ a sweuene. Forsothe he was of the noumbre of caityues,
whom Nabugodonosor, king of Babiloyne,
hadde translatid fro Jerusalem with Je-
5 conye, king of Jude. And this was his
sweuene. There semeden voisis, and noisis,
and thundris, and erthe quaues, and dis-
6 turbing[d] vp on the erthe. And lo! two
grete dragounes, redi aȝen hemself in to
7 bataile; at whos cri alle naciouns ben
stirid togidere, that thei fiȝte aȝen the
8 folc off riȝtwis men. And that dai was of
dercnessis, and of perile, of tribulacioun,
and of anguysh, and gret fer vp on erthe.
9 And disturbid[d] is the folc of riȝtwis men,
dredende ther euelis, and maad redi to
10 the deth. Thei crieden to God; and hem
criende out, a litle welle wex in to the
moste flod, and in to manye watris re-
11 dundede. Liȝt and the sunne is sprungen; and meke men ben euhauncid,
12 and thei deuoureden the gloriouse. The
whiche thing whan Mardoche hadde seen,
and risen of the bed, he thoȝte, what God
wolde do, and ficchid he hadde in the
inwit, coueitende to wite, what the sue-
uene shulde betocne.

CAP. XII.

1 Forsothe he dwelte that time in the
halle of the king, with Bagatha and
Thara, geldingus of the king, that por-
2 teris weren of the paleis. And whan he
hadde vnderstonde the thoȝtis of hem,
and the besynessis mor diligentli hadde
seen before, he lernede that thei enfor-
ciden to putten hond in to king Artax-
ersen, and tolde vp on it to the king.

monethe Nysan[e]; and *Mardochee was* a[3]
man Jew[f], that dwellide in the citee of
Susa, a[g] grete man, and[h] amonge the
firste[i] men of the kyngis halle. Sotheli[j] 4
he was of that noumbre of prisoneris,
which Nabugodonosor, the[k] kyng of Babiloyn, hadde translatid fro Jerusalem with
Jeconye, kyng of Judee. And this was[3]
'his dreem[l]. Voices[m] and noises and thundris and erthemouyngis and troblyug[n]
apperiden on[o] the erthe. And[p] lo! twei[6]
grete dragouns, and maad[q] redi aȝens hem
silf in to batel; at the[r] cry 'of which[s] alle[7]
naciouns weren stirid togidere, to fiȝte
aȝens the folc of iust men. And that was[8]
a day of derknessis, and of perel, of tribulacioun, and of angwisch, and grete drede
was on[t] erthe. And the folc of iust men[9]
dredynge 'her yuels[u] was[v] disturblid, and
maad redi to deeth. And thei crieden to[10]
God; and whanne thei crieden, a[w] litil
welle encreesside in to a ful greet flood,
and turnede[x] aȝen in to ful many watris.
The[y] liȝt and[z] the sunne roos[a]; and meke[11]
men weren enhaunsid, and deuouriden[b]
noble men. And whanne Mardochee[c] 12
hadde seyn this thing, and hadde rise fro
the[d] bed, he thouȝte, what God wolde do,
and he hadde fast set in soule[e], and couetide[f] to wite, what the dreem signyfiede[g].

CAP. XII.

Forsothe[h] Mardochee dwellide that tyme 1
in the halle of the kyng, with Bagatha and
Thara, oneste[i] seruauntis[k] of the kyng,
that weren porteris of the paleis[l]. And[2]
whanne he hadde vndurstonde the thouȝtis
of hem[m], and hadde[n] bifor seyn ful diligentli the[o] bisynessis, he lurnyde that
thei enforsiden[p] to set hond[q] on[r] kyng[s]
Artaxerses, and he telde of that thing to

---

[d] disturbling *All.*

c Nysan, *that is, June* 1.   f a Jew BCDEFGHKLMNOPQRSUVWXab.   g and *he was* a 1.   h Om. 1.   i cheef 1.
j And 1.   k Om. 1.   l the dreem of Mardochie 1.   m *He siȝ that* voices 1.   n *greet* troblyng 1.   o upon 1.
p Om. c.   q *thei weren* maad 1.   r whos 1.   s Om. 1.   t *thanne* upon 1.   u the *yuel of her enmyes* 1.
v weren 1.   w I sawȝe a 1.   x it turnede 1.   y *And thanne* the 1.   z of ox.   a roos np 1.   b thei
denouriden *and ouereamen* 1.   c Mardochee *in his sleep* 1.   d his 1.   e his soule *this visioun* 1.   f he
coueitide 1.   g bitokenyde 1.   h Certis 1.   i the oneste 1.   k seruauntis and chaast 1.   l *kyngis* paleis 1.
m these men 1.   n he hadde 1.   o her 1.   p enforsiden hem 1.   q her hond 1.   r upon 1.   s the
kyng 1.

3 The whiche, of either questioun had confessid, he comaundede to ben had to deth. 4 The king forsothe that was don, wrot in librarijes, but and Mardoche the mynde 5 of the thing toc to lettris. And the king comaundide to hym, that in the halle of the paleis he shulde duelle, ʒiftis ʒiue to 6 hym for the telling. Aman forsothe, the sone of Amadathy, gelding, was most glorious befor the king, and wolde noʒen to Mardoche, and his puple, for the two geldingus of the king that weren slain. *Hider to the prohemy; thoo thingus, that folewen, in that place weren put, wher is write in the volume,* And thei wasteden the goodis or ther substauncis; *the whiche onli in the comun translacioun we han* founden. Of the epistil forsothe this was the saumpler.*

the kyng. And whanne enqueryng was 3 had of euer cithir, the kyng comanndide hem, 'that knoulechiden, to be led to deth. Forsothe the kyng wroot in bookis 4 that, that was doon, but also Mardochee bitook the mynde of the thing to lettris. And the kyng comaundide hym, that he 5 schulde dwelle in the halle of the paleis, and ʒaf to hym ʒiftis for the tellynge. Forsothe Aaman, the sone of Amadathi, 6 a bugei, was moost glorius bifor the kyng, and he wolde anoye Mardochee, and his puple, for the 'tweyne onestc seruauntis of the king 'that weren slayn. *Hidur to is the prohemye; tho thingis, that suen, weren set in that place, where it was writun in the book,* And thei token awey the goodis, ether the catels of hem; *whiche thingis we founden in the comyn translacioun. Sotheli this was the saumpler of the pistle.*

CAP. XIII.

1 The moste king Artaxerses, fro Ynde vnto Ethiope, of an hundrid and seuene and twenti prouyncis, to princis and dukis, that to his empire ben soget, 2 greting seith. Whan to manye folkis I shulde comaunden, and al the world hadde sogetid to my comaunding, I wolde not the mykilnesse of my power mysvsen, but with mercy and softenesse gouerne the sogetis, that, with oute any drede ouerpassende the lif in silence, thei shulden vse the pes desirid to alle deadli 3 men. Me forsothe sechende of my counseileris, hou that myʒte be fulfild, oon, that in wisdam and feith othere men passide, and was after the king the se-4 conde, Aaman bi name, tolde to me in al the world of londis to ben a puple scaterid, that newe shulde vsen lawis, and, aʒen the custum of alle Jentilis

CAP. XIII.

The gretteste kyng Artaxerses, fro 1 Iynde 'til to Ethiope, seith helthe to the princes and duykys of an hundrid and seuene and twenti pronynces, whiche *princes and duykis* ben suget to his empire. Whanne Y was lord of ful many 2 folkis, and Y hadde maad suget al the world to my lordschip, Y wolde not mysuse the greetnesse of power, but gouerne sugetis bi merci and softnesse, that thei, ledynge lijf in silence with outen ony drede, schulden vse pees couetid of alle deedli men. Sotheli whanne Y axide of 3 my counselours, hou this myʒte be fillid, ooni, Aaman bi name, that passide othere men in wisdom and 'feithfulnesse, and was the secounde aftir the kyng, schewide to 4 me, that a puple was scaterid in al the roundnesse of londis, which *puple* vside newe lawis, and dide aʒens the custom of

---

e which iche c.　　　f Om. c pr. m.

t either *of hem* 1.　　u knowlechinge *her tresoun* 1.　　v the deth 1.　　w And 1.　　x that thing 1.　　y and 1.
z toke 1.　　a Om. 1.　　b this 1.　　c *be writen in lettris* 1.　　d Mardochie 1.　　e he ʒaf 1.　　f And 1.　　g was
thanne 1.　　h haue anoied 1.　　i two princy 1.　　k *whiche Aaman louyde myche* 1.　　l *writun* x.　　m *is* 1.
n *epistle* KHLV.　　o vnto 1.　　p the whiche 1.　　q sugettis 1.　　r lord, *he seide,* 1.　　s and *whanne* 1.　　t *my*
sugetis 1.　　u *her lijf* 1.　　v And 1.　　w this *governaile* 1.　　x *best fulfillid* 1.　　y oo *prinze* 1.　　z in feithfulnesse, the whiche 1.　　a the which 1.　　b *that this peple dide* 1.

doende, the hestis of the kingis dispise,
and the 'oon acord^f of diuerse naciouns
5 with ther descencioun defoule. The
whiche thing whan we hadden lerned,
seande o folc rebel aȝen alle kinde of men
to vse shreude lawis, and to oure hestis
to gon aȝen, and to disturbe the pes and
the acord of the prouyncis soget to vs,
6 wee comaundeden, that who so euere
Aman, that is prouost to alle prouyncis,
and secounde fro the king, and whom
in stede of a fader wee wrshipen, shal
shewyn, with wiues and fre childer be
thei don awci of ther enemys, and no
man haue mercy of^g them, the fourtenthe dai of the twelfthe moneth Adar,
7 of the ȝer present; that wicke^h men, o dai
to helle goende doun, ȝelde to oure em-
pire the pes, that thei han disturbidⁱ.
Hider to the saumple of the epistil;
thoo thingus, that folewen, after that
place writen^j *I fond, wher is rad,*
And goende Mardoche dide alle thingus,
that Ester hadde comaundid to hym;
and ner the latere thei ben not had
in Ebru, and anent no man of the re-
8 *menoures thei ben vtterli told.* Mardoche forsothe preȝede the Lord, mynde-
9 ful of alle his werkis, and scide, Lord,
Lord, king almyȝti, in thi power alle
thingis hen set, and ther is not, that
mai withstonde to thy wil; if thou deme
to sauen Irael, anoon wee shul be dely-
10 uered. Thou madist heuene and erthe,
and alle thing that is conteued in the
11 cumpas of heuene. Lord of alle thingus
thou art, ne ther is that withstonde^k to
12 thi mageste. Alle thingus thou knewe,
and wost, that not for pride and strif
and any^l coueitise of glorie I do this,
that I honoure not the most proud
13 Aman; forsothe gladli for the helthe of

alle folkis, and dispiside^c the comaunde-
mentis^d of kyngis, and defoulide^e hi his
discencioun the acordyng of alle naciouns.
And whanne we hadden lerned this thing, 5
and sien, that o^f folk rebel aȝens al the
kynde of men vside^g weiward lawis, and^h
was contrarie to oure comaundementisⁱ,
and disturblide^k the pees and acording
of prouynces suget to vs, 'we comaund- 6
iden, that whiche euere^l Aaman 'schewide,
which^m is souereyn of alle prouynces, and
isⁿ the secounde fro^o the kyng, and^p whom
we onouren in 'the place^q of fadir^r, thei^s
with her wiues and children^t be^u doon
awei of her enemyes, and noon^v haue
merci on^w hem, in^x the fourtenthe dai of
the twelfithe monethe Adar^y, of present^z
ȝeer; that cursid men go doun to hellis^a 7
in o dai, and ȝelde^b pees to oure empire,
which thei hadden troblid. *Hidur^c to is*
the saumpler^d of the pistle^e; these thingis,
that suen, Y foond writun aftir that place,
where it is red^f, And Mardochee ȝede, and
dide alle thingis, whiche Hester hadde comaundide to hym; *netheles tho thingis*
ben not hadde in Ebrew, and^g outirli tho
ben not seid at ony of the translatours.
Forsothe^h Mardochee bisouȝte the Lerd, 8
and wasⁱ myndeful of alle 'hise werkys^k,
and seide^l, Lord God, kyng almyȝti, alle 9
thingis ben set in thi lordschip, 'ethir
power^m, and 'noon isⁿ, that may aȝenstonde thi wille; if thou demest for to
saue Israel, we schulen be delyuered anoon.
Thou madist heuene and erthe, and what 10
euer thing is conteyned in the cumpas of
heuene. Thou *art* Lord of alle thingis, 11
and 'noon is^o that aȝenstondith thi maieste.
Thou knowist alle thingis, and woost, that 12
not for pride and dispit and^p ony coneytise
of glorie^q Y dide this^r thing, that^s Y wor-
schipide^t not Aaman moost^u proud^v; for^w 13

---

f concord *AII*. g on *A*. h wickede *AFFH*. i disturblid *A*. j wher writen *AC*. k withstondith *A*. l my *AII*.

c it dispiside 1. d heestis 1. e it defoulide 1. f ther was a 1. g and that it vside 1. h that it was 1.
i heestis 1. k that it disturblide 1. l thanne sith 1. m Om. 1. n he is 1. o persoone aftir 1. p Om. 1.
q stede 1. r a fudir 1. s therfor we comaunden that whiche euer that Aaman hath schewid, be thei 1.
t her children 1. u Om. 1. v no man 1. w upon 1. x be this veniaunce don 1. y of Marche 1. z this
present 1. a helle 1. b ȝelde thei so 1. c A rubrich. *Hidur* BC. d ensaumpler ELP. e epistle EHL.
f seid K. g Om. K. h Certis 1. i he was 1. k the werkys of the Lord 1. l he seide 1. m Om. 1.
n ther is noon 1. o ther is noon 1. p neither for 1. q veyn glorie 1. r ony R. s and that A.
t worschip D. u the moost 1. v proud man 1. w forsothe 1.

Irael also the steppis of his feet I were
14 redi to kisse, but I dradde, lest the
wrshipe of my God I shulde bern ouer
to man, and lest any man I shulde ho-
15 noure out take my God. And now, Lord
king, God of Abraham, haue mercy of
thi puple, for oure enemys wiln leesen
16 vs, and thin eritage don awei ; ne dispise
thou thi part, that thou hast aȝcen boȝt
17 fro Egipt. Heere my preȝeere, and merciful be thou to the lot, and the litle
corde of thin eritage ; and turne oure
weiling in to ioȝe, that liuende we preise
thi name, Lord ; and ne close thou the
18 mouthis of men preisende thee. And al
Irael lie mynde and beseching criede to
the Lord, for thi that to hem shulde
hange in certeyn deth.

CAP. XIV.

1 Ester also the quen fleiȝ to the Lord,
dredende the perile, that wex aboue.
2 And whan she hadde do doun hir kingus
clothis, she toc couenable clothis to wepingis and to weiling ; and for diuers
oynemens with askis and drit she fulfilde the hed, and hir bodi mekide with
fastingus ; and alle placis, in the whiche
she was wont to gladen, with to-tering
3 of heris she fulfilde. And she preȝede
the Lord God of Irael, seiende, My Lord,
that art king alone, help me solitarie,
and of whom saue thee is noon other
4 helpere ; my perile is in myn hondis.
5 I haue herd of my fader, that thou
shuldest han taken Irael fro alle Jentilis, and oure fadris fro alle ther more
behinde, that thou shuldist welde the
euermor durende eritage ; and thou didist
6 to hem, as thou speke. Wee han synned
in thi siȝte, and therfore thou hast taken
7 vs in to the houdis of oure enemys ; forsothe wee han heried the godis of hem.

Y was redi 'wilfuli to kissc[x], ȝhe, the
steppis of hise feet for the helthe of Israel,
but Y dredde, lest Y schulde bere ouerc to 14
a[y] man the onour of my God, and lest Y
schulde worschipe ony man outakun my
God. And now, Lord kyng, God of Abra- 15
ham, haue thou merci on thi puple, for
oure enemyes wolen lecse vs, and do awei
thin eritage ; dispise not thi part, which[z] 16
thou aȝenhouȝtist fro Egipt. Here thou 17
my preier, and be thou merciful to the
lot, and the[a] part of thin eritage ; and
turne thou oure morenyng in to ioie, that
we lyuynge herie thi name, Lord ; and
close thou[b] not the mouthis of men
heriynge thee. And al Israel with lijk[c] 18
mynde and bisechyng criede to the Lord,
for[d] certeyn deeth neiȝede to hem.

CAP. XIV.

Also the[e] queen Hester fledde to the 1
Lord[f], and dredde[g] the perel, that neiȝede.
And whanne sche hadde put awei the 2
kyngis clothis[h], sche took[i] clothis couenable to wepyngis and morenyng[k] ; and for
dyuerse oynementis[l] sche 'fillide the[m] heed
with nische and dust[n], and 'made meke[o]
hir bodi with fastyngys ; and with to-
breidyng awei of heeris[q], sche fillide[r] alle
places[s], in which[t] sche was wont to be
glad ; and bisouȝte[u] the Lord God of 3
Israel, and seide, My Lord, which[v] aloone
art oure kyng, helpe me a womman left
aloone, and of whom noon othere helpere
is outakun thee ; my perel is in my hondis. 4
Y haue herd of my fadir, that thou, **Lord,** 5
tokist[w] awei Israel fro alle folkis, and[x]
oure fadris fro alle her grettere men bifore, that thou schuldist welde euerlastynge[y] eritage ; and thou hast do to hem,
as thou hast spoke[z]. We synneden[a] in 6
thi siȝt, and therfor thou hast bitake vs
in to the hondis of oure enemyes ; for[b] 7

x to haue kissid wilfuli 1.   y Om. 1.   z the which *part* 1.   a to the 1x.   b Om. s.   c sich maner 1.
d for cause that 1.   e Om. 1.   f Lord God 1.   g sche dredde .   h clothis *that perteyneden to the queen* 1.
i took *thanne* 1.   k to morenyng 1.   l oynementis *that sche had vsid bifore* 1.   m fulfillide hir 1.
n drit *plures.* vile poudre *or dust* 1.   o sche mekide 1.   p Om. 1.   q hir heer 1.   r fulfillide 1.   s the
places *of hir heed* 1.   t which *placis* 1.   u sche bisouȝte 1.   v that 1.   w hast take 1.   x and *thou hast
taken or chosen* 1.   y an euerlastynge 1.   z spoke *or hiȝt* 1.   a haue synned 1.   b forsothe 1.

8 Riȝtwis thou art, Lord; and now it suf-
fiseth not to them, that with most hard
sernyse they oppressen vs, but, the
strengthe of ther hondis wijtende to
9 the power of maumetis, wiln chaunge
thin hestis^m, and don awei thin eritage,
and close the mouthis of men preisende
thee, and quenchen out the glorie of the
10 temple and of thin auter, that thei opene
the mouthis of Jentilis, and preise the
strengthe of maumetis, and prechen a
11 fleshli king in to euermor. Ne take thou,
Lord, thi kingus dignete to them, that
ben not, lest thei laȝhen at oure falling;
but turne the counseil of hem vp on
hem^n, and hym that in vs began to waxe
12 feers, scatere. Haue mynde, Lord, and
sheuȝ thee to vs in time of oure tribulacioun; and ȝif to me trost, Lord, king
13 of Jewis and of alle power; ȝif a semeli
woord in my mouth in the siȝte of the
leoun, and ber ouer the herte of hym in
to the hate of oure enemy, that and he
pershe, and othere that consenten to hym.
14 Vs also deliuere in thin hond, and help
me, noon other hauende helpe but thee,
Lord, that hast kunnyng of alle thingis.
15 And thou hast knowen for I hatide the
glorie of wicke^o men, and wlate the bed
of vncircumcidide men, and of alle he-
16 thene. Thou knowist infirmyte and my
nede, that I wlate the signe of pride and
of my glorie, that is vpon myn hed in
the daȝis of my shewing, and I wlate it
as the cloth of the womman in flux of
blod, and I bere not in the daȝis of my
17 silence, and that I eet not in the bord of
Aman, ne to me pleside the feste of the
king, and I dranc nott win of sacrifises;
18 and neuere gladide thin hond womman,

we worschipiden^e the goddis of hem.
Lord^d, thou art iust; and now it suffisith 8
not to hem^e, that thei oppressen vs with
hardeste^f sernage, but thei aretten the
strengthe of her hondis to the power of
idols, and^g wolen chaunge thi biheestis, 9
and do^h awei thin eritage, and close the
mouthis of men heriynge thee, and quenche^i
the glorie of thi^k temple and auter^l, that^m 10
thei opene^n the mouthis of hethene men,
and preise^o the strengthe of ydols, and
preche a fleischli^p kyng with outen ende.
Lord, ȝyue thou not thi kyngis ȝerde^q to 11
hem, that ben noȝt^r, lest^s thei leiȝen^t at
oure fallyng; but turne thou the councel
of hem on^u hem^v, and distrie thou hym,
that bigan to be cruel aȝens vs. Lord, 12
haue thou mynde, and schewe thee to vs
in the tyme of tribulacioun; and, Lord,
kyng of goddis and^w of al power, ȝyue
thou trist to me; ȝyue thou a word wel 13
dressid in my mouth in the^x siȝt of the
lioun^y, and turne^z ouer his herte in to
the hatrede of oure enemy, that bothe he
perische, and othere men that consenten^a
to hym. But^b delyuere vs in thin hond, 14
and helpe me, hauynge noon othere help
no^c but thee, Lord, that hast the kunnyng
of alle thingis; and knowist^d that Y hate 15
the glorie of wickid men, and that Y wlate
the bed of vncircumcidid men, and of ech
alien. Thou^e knowist my freelte and nede^f, 16
that Y holde abhomynable the signe^g of
my pride and glorie^h, which is on myn
heed in the daies^i of my schewyng, and
that Y wlate it `as the cloth of a womman
hauynge vncleene blood^k, and Y bere not^l
in the daies of my stillenesse^m, and that^n 17
Y eet not in the boord of Aaman, nether
the feeste of the kyng pleside me, and Y

---

m behestis E. n us E pr. m. o wickede AEFH.

c haue wirschipid I. d And s. e oure enmyes I. f ful hard I. g and therfor thei I. h thei
woln do I. i thei woln quenche I. k the plures. l of the auter I. m and I. n woln opene I. o thei
woln preise I. p fleischi ACHNOU. fleischli man to the I. q ȝerde or gouernaile I. r not plures. not of
thi sort I. s that I. t leȝe not I. u upon I. v hemself I. w and kyng I. x Om. I. y lioun
Assuerus I. z turne thou I. a consentiden I. b But, Lord I. c Om. I. d Lord, thou knowist I. e And,
Lord, thou I. f my nede I. g signe or schenyng I. h of my glorie I. i day I. k Om. I sec. m.
as the blodi skin of wommans infirmytee s. l not, or vse it I. not, that is, I vse not swich pride s.
m stilnesse, oute of the kingis presence s. n thou wost, Lord, that s.

sithen hider I am translatid vnto the present dai, but in thee, Lord God of Abra-
19 ham. Strong God ouer alle, heere the
vois of hem, that noon other hope[p] han,
and delyuere vs fro the hond of wicke[q]
men, and pul out me fro my drede.
These thingus also addid I fond in the
comun translacionu.

CAP. XV.

1   And no doute that Mardoche sente to
hir, that Ester shulde gon in to the king,
and preʒe for hir puple, and for hir kuntre.
2 Myndeful, he seith, be thou of the daʒes
of thi mecnesse, hou thou art nurshid
in myn hond ; for Aman, ordeined the
secounde of the king, spac aʒen vs in to
3 deth ; and thou inwardli clep the Lord,
and spec to the king for vs, and deliuere
vs fro deth. *Also and these thingus, that*
ben vnderleid, in the comun translacioun
4 *I fond.* Forsothe the thridde dai she dide
doun the clothis of hir enournyng, and
5 hir owne glorie is don abonte. And
whan with the kingis abite she schyned,
and inwardli hadde clepid the Gouernour
of alle thingus and sauere God, she toc
6 two seruauntes, and vp on the oon[r] forsothe she lenede, as for delicis and ful
myche tendernesse not suffrynde to bern
7 hir owne bodi ; the tother forsothe of the
dameselis folewede the ladi, berende vp
the clothys flowende doun in to the erthe.
8 She forsothe thurʒshed the chere with
rose colour, and freeli, and with briʒte
eʒen she couerede the dreri inwit, and

---

drank not the wiyn of moiste sacrifices,
and[o] that thin[p] handmayde 'was neuere 18
glad[q], sithen[r] Y was translatid hidur til
in to present[s] dai[t], no[n] but in thee[v], Lord
God of Abraham. 'God stronge[w] aboue 19
alle[x], here thou[y] the vois of hem, that han
noon othere hope[z], and delyuere thou vs
fro the hond of wickid men, and delyuere
thou me fro my drede. *Also Y foond*
'these wordis[n] in the comyn translacioun.

CAP. XV.

And 'he sente to hir[b], no doute that 1
ne Mardochee sente to Hester, that sche
schulde entre[c] to the kyng, and preie for
hir puple, and for hir cuntrei. He[d] seide[e], 2
Be thou myndeful of the daies of thi
mekenesse, hou thou were nurschid in
myn hond ; for[f] Aaman, ordeyned[g] the secounde[h] fro the kyng, spak[i] aʒens vs in to
deth ; and[k] thou inwardli clepe the Lord[l], 3
and speke[m] to the kyng for vs, and delyuere vs fro deeth. *And[n] also Y foond*
these thingis, that suen, in the comyn
translacioun. Forsothe[o] in the thridde 4
dai sche[p] 'puttide of[q] the[r] clothis of hir
ournyng[s], and was[t] cumpassid with hir
glorie[u]. And whanne sche 'schinede in 5
the kyngis clothing, and[v] hadde inwardli
clepid the Gouernour of alle thingis and
the sauyour God[w], sche took[x] twei seruauntis[y], and sotheli[z] sche[n] leenyde on[b] 6
oon[c], as not[d] susteynynge[e] to bere hir[f]
body, for delices and ful[g] greet tendir-
nesse ; but the tother[h] 'of the seruaunt- 7
essis[i] suede the ladi, and bar vp the[k] clothis
fletinge[l] doun 'in to[m] the erthe. 'Sotheli 8
sche was bisched[n] with 'colour of roosis[o]

---

[p] helpe *AH.*   [q] wickede *AEFU.*   [r] toon *A.*

[o] and *thou woost* I. and *Lord, thou wost* s.   [p] I thin 1s.   [q] Om. 1s.   [r] sith 1.   [s] this present 1s.   [t] dai
was neuer glad 1s.   [u] Om. 1.   [v] the *ARU.*   [w] A I stronge God 1. *That art* a stronge God s.   [x] alle *other* s.
[y] thou, *Lord* s.   [z] hope *than thee* 1. hope *than in thee* s.   [a] *these thingis addid* n. *these addid plures.*
this addid c *pr. m. this thingis addid* c *sec. m.*   [b] Om. *A sec. m.* s.   [c] entre yn 1s.   [d] And Mardochie 1s.
[e] seide *to hir* 1s.   [f] forsothe 1s.   [g] which is s.   [h] secounde *persone in power* s.   [i] hath spoke 1s.
[k] *therfor* 1. *forthi* s.   [l] Lord *God to help* s.   [m] speke thou 1s.   [n] Om. *GQWX.*   [o] Certis 1s.   [p] Hester 1s.
[q] ordeynede 1s.   [r] hir s.   [s] enournyng x *sec. m.*   [t] sche was 1s.   [u] glorie *in ful riche araie* s.   [v] Om. 1s.
[w] God, and schynyde in the kingis clothing 1s.   [x] took *to hir* 1s.   [y] scruauntessis *BCEISVX sec. m.*
[z] Om. 1s.   [a] Hester 1s.   [b] upon 1s.   [c] oon *of hem* 1s.   [d] if sche had not 1s.   [e] suffisid 1s.   [f] hir owne 1s.
[g] for ful 1s.   [h] oother 1.   [i] seruauntesse 1s.   [k] hir 1s.   [l] trailinge *A sup. ras. F sup. ras.* 1s.   [m] upon 1s. on a.
[n] And Hester in hir face was colourid 1s.   [o] roose colouris s.

drawe togidere with ful myche drede.

9 Thanne she gon in alle the doris bi ordre, stod aȝen the king, wher he sat vp on the see of his regne, clothid with kingus clothis, and shinende with gold and precious stones; and he was ferful in siȝte.

10 And whan he hadde rerid vp the face, and with brennende eȝen the wodnesse of the brest hadde shewid, the quen fel doun ; and the colour chaungid in to palenesse, the weeri hed vpon the hond maide^s

11 she bowide doun. And God turnede the spirit of the king in to debonernesse, and heeȝende and dredende he stirte out of the see; and sustenende hir with his armys, to the tyme she turnede aȝeen to

12 hirself, with these woordis gloside, What hast thou, Ester ? I am thi brother ; wile

13 thou not drede, thou shalt not die ; forsothe not for thee, but for alle this^ss lawe

14 is^t ordeyned. Cum hider thanne, and

15 touche the kingus ȝerde. And whan she heeld hir pes, he toc the kingus ȝerde, and putte vp on hir necke, and kiste hir, and seith, Whi to me spekist thou not ?

16 The whiche answerde, I saȝ thee, lord, as the angil of God, and myn herte is dis-

17 turbid^u for drede of thi glorie ; forsothe, lord, thou art gretli merueilous, and thi

18 face is ful of graeis. And whan he spac, eft she fel doun, and uttirli swounede.

19 The king forsothe was disturbid^u, and alle his mynestris coumfortiden hym. *The saumple of the epistil of king Artaxerses, that for the Jewis he sente to alle the prouyncis of his reume ; the whiche and it is not had in Ebrue volume.*

'in the cheer^p, and with pleasaunt^q and schynynge iȝen sche hilide the^r soreuful soule, and^s drawun togidere with ful myche drede. Therfor^t sche entride^u tho-

9 rouȝ^v alle the doris bi ordre^w, and stood^x aȝens^y the kyng, where he sat on^z the seete of his rewme, and was^a clothid in the^b kyngis clothis^c, and schynyde^d in gold and^e preciouse stoonys, and was^f dredeful in siȝt. And whanne he hadde

10 reisid^g the^h face, and hadde schewid the woodnesse^i of herte^k with brennynge iȝen, the queen felde doun^m ; and whanne the^n colour was chaungid in to palenesse, sche restide the^o heed slidun^p on^q the^r handmaide. And God turnede the spirit of

11 the kyng in to myldenesse, and he^s hastide^t, and dredde^u, 'and skippyde out^v of the^w scete ; and he^x 'susteynede hir^y with hise armes, til sche cam aȝen to hir self; and he spak faire^z bi these wordis, Hester,

12 what^a hast thou ? Y am thi brother ; nyle thou drede, thou schalt not die^b ; for this

13 lawe is not maad for^c thee, but^d for alle men^e. Therfor neiȝe thou^f, and touche

14 the^g ceptre, '*that is, the kyngis ȝerde*^h. And whanne sche^i was stille^k, he^l took

15 the^m goldun ȝerde, and 'puttide on^n hir necke; and he kisside hir, and seide, Why spekist thou not to me? And sche an-

16 sweride, Lord, Y siȝ thee as an^o aungel of God, and myn herte was troblid for^oo the^p drede of thi glorye ; for, lord, thou art ful

17 wondurful, and thi face is ful of graces. And whanne sche spak^q, eft sche felde

18 doun^r, and was^s almest deed. Sotheli^t the

19 kyng was troblid^u, and alle hise mynystris^v coumfortiden hir. *The^w saumpler*

---

^s maiden *AEH*.   ^ss is this c *pr. m.*   ^t Om. c.   ^u disturblid *AH*.

^p Om. IS.   ^q hir plesaunt IS.   ^r hir IS.   ^s that was IS.   ^t And I.   ^u entride yn IS.   ^v bi S.   ^w rewe IS. ^x sche stood IS.   ^y euen anentes S.   ^z upon IS.   ^a *the king* was IS.   ^b Om. IS.   ^c aray IS.   ^d he schynyde IS.   ^e and in S.   ^f he was IS.   ^g reisid up IS.   ^h his IS.   ^i austernesse IS.   ^k his herte IAS. ^m down *bifore him* IS.   ^n hir I.   ^o hir I. and hir S.   ^p bowid doun IS.   ^q upon IS.   ^r hir IS. ^s the kyng IS.   ^t hasty I. hastinge S.   ^u dredynge IS.   ^v rose up anoon IS.   ^w his IS.   ^x Om. c.   ^y helde up the queen IS.   ^z *faire to hir* IS.   ^a what *greef* IS.   ^b die *for this comyng thus to me* I. die *for thi cummynge to me withouten clepinge* S.   ^c oonly for S.   ^d but *it is maad* IS.   ^e othere, *that thei* [*wymmen* S] *be buxum to her husbondis* IS.   ^f thou hidere IS.   ^g my IS.   ^h or ȝerde I.   ^i Hester IS.   ^k coumfortid IS. ^l the kyng IS.   ^m his IS.   ^n touchide *therwith* IS.   ^o the c.   ^oo fro A.   ^p Om. S.   ^q had thus spoke IS. ^r doun *in a swoun* S.   ^s sche was IS.   ^t And IS.   ^u troblid *herfore* IS.   ^v seruauntis IS.   ^w *This swinge is the* K. *This is the* R.

of 'the lettre of[x] the[y] kyng Artaxerses,
which he sente for[z] the Jewis to alle
the[a] prouynces of his rewme; and[b] the[c]
same[d] saumpler[e] is not had in the book
of Ebreu.

CAP. XVI.

1 Artaxerses, the grete king, fro Ynde
vnto Ethiope, of an hundrid and seuene
and twenti prouyncis, to dukis and
princis, that to oure comaunding obe-
2 shen, seith greeting. Manye the goodnesse of princis and wrshipe, that in to
hem is ʒiuen, han mys vsid in to pride;
3 and not onli enforcen to opresse the
sogetis to the king, but the glorie ʒiue
to hem not berende, in to them that ʒiuen
4 waiten aspies; ne ben not paʒid to not
do gracis to benefetis, and defoule the
riʒtus of humanyte in to them; but also
demen hemself to moun flee the sentence
5 of God demende alle thingus. And in so
myche to wodnesse breken out, that to
hem that besili kepen the offis taken to
hem, and so alle thingus don, that thei
ben wrthi the preising[u] of alle men, with
the'priue and sotile flateringus[v] of lesingus
6 thei enforsen to turne vp so doun, whil
the symple eris of princis and of ther
kinde other men eymende with fel gile
7 desceyuen. The whiche thing and of olde
stories is proued, and of these thingus
that ben don eche dai; hou bi euele so-
gestiouns of summe men the studies of
8 kingus ben depraued. Wherfore it is to
9 purueye to the pes of alle prouyucis. Ne
ʒee shul not wene, if diuers thingus we
comaunde, to come of liʒtnesse of oure
inwit; but for qualite and necessite of
tymes, as the profit of the comun thing
10 asketh, to do sentence. And that ʒee

CAP. XVI.

The grete kyng Artaxerses, fro[f] Yinde 1
'til to[g] Ethiopie, seith helthe to the duykis
and pryncis of an hundrid and seuene and
twenti prouynces, that[h] obeien to oure comaundement. Many men mysusen in to 2
pride the goodnesse and onour[i] of princes,
which[j] is ʒouun[k] to hem; and not oneli ʒ
thei[l] enforsen[m] to oppresse sugetis to
kyngis, but thei beren not[n] glorie[o] ʒouun[p]
to hem, and maken[q] redy tresouns aʒens
hem, that ʒauen the[r] glorie[s]. And thei 4
ben not apaied to do not thankyngis for
benefices[t], and to defoule in hem silf the
lawis of curtesie; but also thei demen,
that thei moun fle the sentence of God
seynge alle thingis. And thei breken out 5
in to so mych woodnesse, that thei enforsen[u] with the[v] roopis of leesyngis to
distrie hem, that kepen diligentli offices[w]
bitakun to hem, and doen so alle thingis,
that thei ben worthi the[x] preisyng of alle
men; while[y] bi sutil fraude 'false men[z] 6
disseyuen the symple[a] eeris of kyngis[b],
'and gessynge othere men bi her owne
kynde[c]. Which thing is preuyd bothe bi 7
elde stories, and bi these thingis that ben
doen ech dai; hou the studies of kyngis
ben maad schrewid[d] bi yuele suggestiouns
of summen. Wherfor it is to purueye for 8
the pees of alle prouynces. And thouʒ we 9
comaunden dyuerse thingis[e], ʒe owen not
to gesse, that it[f] cometh of the[g] vnstablenesse of oure[h] soule[i]; but that we ʒyuen
sentence[k] for the maner and nede of tymes,

---

[u] preuing c.   [v] litle cordis E pr. m.

[x] Om. AREDIUV. *the pistle of* F. [y] Om. GKMNOSWA. [z] *fro* OA. [a] Om. X. [b] *also* F. [c] *this* K. [d] Om. C.
[e] *saumpler hereof* S. [f] *beynge lord* fro I. *whos lordship was* fro S. [g] *to* FX. *vnto* IS. [h] *the whiche* I.
which S. [i] *the honour* S. [j] *that* IS. [k] *taken* IS. [l] *swich men* S. [m] *enforsen hem* IS. [n] *not dewly* I.
not ether vsen not duly S. [o] *the glorie* IS. [p] *taken* IS. [q] *thes maken* IS. [r] *her* IS. [s] *glorie to hem* IS.
[t] *goodnessis* IS. [u] *enforsen hem* IS. [v] Om. IS. [w] *the offices* IS. [x] Om. IS. [y] *and while malicious men*
gessynge othere men bi her owen kynde blameful IS. [z] *thei* I. *smiche* S. [a] *sotel* S. [b] *the king* S.
[c] Om. IS. [d] *ful contrarious* IS. [e] *thingis, as now we bidden oo thing to be don, and now rec forbeden the*
same S. [f] *this* IS. [g] Om. DCIKB. [h] Om. R. [i] *herte* IS. [k] *sentence bi oure counseil* IS.

4 Q 2

more openli vndirstonde that wee han
seid ; Aaman, the sone of Amadathi, wille
and kinrede of Macedo, and alien fro the
blod of Persis, and oure pite with his
cruelte defouleude, a pilgrim is taken of
11 vs ; and so myche humanyte expert in
hymself, that oure fader he were clepid,
and honoured of alle men the secounde
12 after the king ; the whiche in so myche
swelling of pride is born, that he enforcide to prinen vs the reume and spirit.
13 For Mardoche, bi whos feith and benefetis wee liuen, and the felawe of oure
reume Ester, with al hir folc, with newe
maner and vnherd engynes ful out askide
14 in to deth; these thingus thenkende, that,
hem slain, he shulde aspie^w to oure onli-
hed, and the reume of Persis to ouerbern
15 in to Macedoynes. Wee forsothe outerli
finden in no blame the Jewis, ordeyned
to deth of the werste man of deadli men ;
16 but a3eenward vsende ri3te lawis, and
the sones of the he3est, and the moste,
and euermor liuende God, thur3 whos
benefet and to oure fadris and to vs the
reume ys taken, and vnto to dai is kept.
17 Wherfore tho lettris, that vnder oure name
18 he 3af forth, witeth to ben as none. For
the whiche hidous gilte befor the 3atis of
this cite, that is, Susis, and he that caste,
and al his kinrede, hangeth in iebetis^x ;
not vs, but God to hym 3eldende that he
19 deseruede. This forsothe maundement,
that wee now senden, in alle cites be
purposid, that it be leful to Jewis to vse
20 ther lawis. To whom 3ee shul be to
helpe, that tho men, the whiche hemself
to ther deth hadden maad redi, thei
moun slen, the fourtenthe dai of the
twelfthe moneth, that is clepid Adar ;

as the profit of the^l comyn thing axith.
And that 3e vndurstonde opynliere^m that^n, 10
that we seyen ; Aaman, the soue of Amadathi, a man of Macedoyne bi^o soule^p and
folk^q, and an^r alien fro the blood^s of Persis, and^t defoulynge oure pitee with his
cruelte, was a pilgrym, _ethir^u a^v straun-
ger_, and was^w resseyned of vs^x ; and he 11
feelide in hym silf so grete curtesie _of vs_,
that he was clepid oure fadir, and was^y
worschipid of alle men the^x secounde^a
aftir the kyng ; which^b Aaman was reisid 12
in to so greet bolnyng of pride, that he
enforside^c to pryue us of the rewme and
spirit^d. For bi summe newe and vnherd 13
castis he axide in to deeth Mardochee, bi
whos feith and benefices we liuen, and^e
the felowe of oure rewme Hester, with al^f
hir folk^g ; and he thou3te these thingis, 14
that whanne thei^h weren slayn, he schulde
sette tresoun to^i 'oure aloonenesse^k †, and
that he schulde^l translate the rewme of
Persis in to Macedoynes^m. Forsothe^n we 15
founden not the Jewis in ony gilt outirli,
that^o weren ordeyned to deth^p by the^q
worste of deedli men ; but a3enward that^r
thei^s ysen iust lawis, and ben the sones of 16
the hi3este and moste God^t, and 'euere
lyuynge^u, bi whos benefice^v the^w rewme
was 3ouun bothe to oure fadris and to vs,
and is kept 'til to^x dai^y. Wherfor wyte 3e, 17
that tho lettris ben voide, whiche^z thilke
Aaman sente vndur oure name. For which 18
greet trespas bothe he^a that ymagynede^b,
and al his kynrede, hangith in iebātis bifor
the 3atis of this^c citee, 'that is^d, Susa ; for
not we, but God 3eldide to hym that, that
he desseruyde. Forsothe^e this comaunde- 19
ment^f, which^g we senden^h now, be^i set
forth^k in alle citees, that it be leueful to

† _to oure_
aloonenesse ;
that is, to vs
self aloone. c.

w enspien _AFH._　　x the iebetis _A._

l Om. i. m more openly 1s. n that thing 1. that that thing s. o bothe bi 1s. p kynde 1s. q bi folk 1s.
r Om. 1s. s blood or _kynde_ 1. blood _of kynrede_ s. t and he 1s. u or 1s. v Om. c. w he was 1s. x vs _moost_
favourably s. y he was 1s. z _as_ the 1s. a secounde _persoone_ 1s. b the which 1. c enforside _him_ 1s.
d _lijf_ A. _sec. m._ of oure lijf 1s. e and _also_ 1. f Om. s. g folk _he wolde haue distrioied_ s. h thes 1s. i a3ens s.
k oure onlinesse A _sec. m._ us _so_ maad aloone 1. oure aloonesse, _that is, to the kyngis persone_ s. l wolde
thanne 1. m _the rewme of_ Macedoynes 1. _the rewme of_ Macedonie s. n And forsothe 1s. o the whiche
netheles 1. which s. p the deth 1. q _him that_ is 1. r _we founden_ that 1s. s the Jewis 1s. t Om. 1s.
u of euerlastynge God 1s. v benefices c. goodnesse 1s. w this 1s. x vn to 1. in to s. y this dai 1.
this dai _bi his grace_ s. z the whiche 1. a Aaman s. b ymagynede _it_ 1. ymagynide _this yuel_ s. c the s.
d of s. e Therfor 1. For thi s. f heest 1s. g that 1s. h senden forth 1s. i be _it_ 1s. k up 1s.

21 this forsothe dai of sorewe and of weiling the Almy3ti God turnede to hem in
22 to io3e. Wherfore and 3ee among othcr
feste da3is this dai haueth[y], and halewith
23 it with alle gladnesse; and herafter alle
men knowe, that feithful obeshen to Persis, for feith to take wrthi mede; thei forsothe that waiten to the regne of hem, to
24 pershe for the[z] hidous gilte. Eche[a] forsothe prouynce and cite, that wil not of
this solempncte ben parcener, bi swerd
and fyr pershe he; and so be he don
awei, that not onli to men but to bestis
with oute wei 'be in to[b] euer mor, for exsaumple of dispising and vnobeisaunce.

Explicit[c].

Jewis[l] to vse her lawis. 'Whyche Jewis[m] 20
3e owen[n] helpe[o], that thei moun sle hem,
that maden hem silf redi[p] to the deeth
of Jewis, in the thrittenthe dai of the
twelucthe monethe, which[q] is clepyd A-
dar[r]; for Almy3ti God turneth[s] this dai 21
of weilyng and morenyng[t] in to ioye to
hem[u]. Wherfor and 3e[v] han[w] this dai 22
among othere feeste daies, and halowe[x] it
with al[y] gladnesse; that it be knowun
aftirward, that alle men, that obeien feith- 23
fuli to Persis[z], resseyuen worthi meed for
feith[a]; sotheli[b] that thei, that setten[c] tresoun to the rewme of hem, perischen[d] for
the[e] felony. Forsothe[f] ech prouynce and 24
citee, that wole not be parcenere of this
solempnytee, perische[g] bi swerd and fier[h];
and be it 'doon awey[i] so[k], that not oneli
it be with out weie to men but also to
heestis with outen ende, for ensaumple[l] of
dispisyng[m] and vnobedience.

*Here endith the book of Hester, and
here bygynneth the book of Job*[n].

[y] hath ΛΗ. [z] Om. ΛΗ. [a] Alle E pr. m. [b] be it in Λ. be it euere in to π. [c] *Here endith the book of Hester, and now bigynneth the prolog of the book of Job. Λ. Explicit liber Ester. E.* No final rubric in Fπ.

[l] the Jewis ι. [m] Whom *also* ι. [n] owen *also* s. [o] to helpe ιs. [p] to be redi s. [q] that ι. [r] Adar, *or Marche* ιs. [s] hath turned ιs. [t] of morenyng ιs. [u] the Jewis ιs. [v] *we comaunden* that 3e ιs. [w] haue *plures.* [x] halewe 3e ιs. [y] Om. ιs. [z] *the kyngis of* Persis ιs. [a] her feith ιs. [b] and ιs. [c] senten w. settiden v. [d] perishe ι. [e] her ιs. [f] And ιs. [g] perische *it* ι. [h] bi fier ιs. [i] Om. ι. [k] so fordon ι. [l] the ensaumple ιs. [m] her dispisyng ιs. [n] *Here endith the book of Hester, and bigynneth a prolog on the book of Job.* G. *Heere endith Hester.* ι. *Heere eendeth the book of Hester, se now the prolog of Joob.* K. *Here endith the book of Hester, and here bigynneth the prologe on the book of Joob.* MO. *Here endith the book of Hester, and bigynneth the book of Joob.* NVX. *Here eendith Hester, and bigynneth the first prolog of Joob.* R. *Here endith Hester, and bigynneth the book of Job.* s. *Here eendith the book of Hester.* Q. No final rubric in ELP.

J O B.

I<small>N</small> this book of Joob is contened, first, the possessioun and prosperite of the iust man Joob; and, aftirward, how God suffride him to be temptid of Sathan, by los of hise worldli goodis, and of hise children; and afterward bi sijknesse of his owne flesch, and bi repreef of hise frendis, and of his owne wijf; and ensaumple to vs, that no man is temptid more than he mai withstonde, if he be iust and pacient, with preier of the help of God.

Incipit prologus in libro Job^a.

I am constreyned bi alle the bokis of Godis scripture to answern to the euele sawis of aduersaries, that sinfulli putten to me, that my remenyng I shulde make into^b the^c vndernymyng of the^d Seuenti remenoures; as tho3e^e, anent the Grekis, Aquila, Simacus, and Theodocian, or woord^f of^g woord, or sens of^g sens, or of either mengd, and tempred maner of mene translacioun tolden out; and Origenes alle the volumes of the Olde Testament markide with signe of a 3erde, 'and with signe of a sterre^h, the whiche or addid, or taken of Theodocian, sette in to the olde translacioun, prouende to han failid that is added. Thanne lerne my bacbiteres to resceyuen in the hoole, that in parcelis thei resceyueden, or to shauen awey my remenyng with ther sterre signes. Ne forsothe it may be do, thatⁱ whom they beheelde manye thingus to han lafte of, not the same men also in summe thingus to han errid thei knowlechen, nameli, in Job, to the whiche that if tho thingus, that vnder sterre signe ben addid, thou withdrawe, the most part of thi volume shal be kut of; and that only anent the Grekis. But and^k anent the Latynes, befor that translacioun, that vnder sterre signes and 3erde signes not 3ore we maden out, seuene hundrid almest or ei3te hundrid vers failen; with the whiche the boc shortid, and to-torn and to-bite, sheweth openli to the rederes his foule defaute. This forsothe translacioun non remenour of the olde folewith, but of that^l Ebru and Arabik woord, and other while Cire, now woordis, now sens, now either togidere shal tellen out. Also forsothe al the boc anent the Ebrues is seid^m derc and slideryⁿ, and that the cheef spekeris of Grekis clepen defaute of comun maner of speche, whil other thing

---

^a This prologue is from M.

is spoken and other thing is don ; as if thou woldest an eel or a laumprun holde with streite hondis, how myche strengerli° thou thristis, so myche the[p] sunnere it shal sliden awey. I haue remembrid me, Liddium, a maner doctour, that anent the Ebruis the firste was weened to ben had, for the vnderstonding of this volume not with fewe penys to han hirid, with whos doctrine if any thing I profitede, I wot neuere ; this oon I wot wel, me not to han mo3t[q] remenc, but that before I hadde vnderstonde. And so fro the begynnyng of the volume vnto the woordis of Job, anent the Ebruys the enditing[r] is prose ; but fro the woordis of Job, in the[s] whiche he seith, Pershe the dai in the whiche I am born, and the ny3t, in[t] whiche[u] it is seid, a man is conseiued, vnto that place wher befor the end of the volume it is write, Therfor I myself reproue, and do penaunce in colis and asken[v], ben vers of sixe feet, rennende with dactile and sponde feet, and for the langage of the tunge ofte takende and othere feet, not of the same silablis, but of the same times. Otherwhile also that sweete rym and sweteli sounende is told with noumbris[w] loosid with lawe ; the whiche thing versifioures more than a symple redere vnderstonden. Fro the foreseide vers forsothe vnto the ende of the boc, the litle distinccioun that leueth with prose enditing is wouen[x]. The whiche thing if[y] to[z] any man is seen vntrouable, metre, that is, to be anent the Ebrues, and in maner of oure Flacci, and Graccy, Pindarie, and Alchei, and Saffo, that weren Grek poetis, or the Sauter, or the[a] Lamentaciouns[b] of Jeremie, or alle almest the Kanticulis of scripturis to[c] ben comprehendid, that is to seye, in metre, rede he Filonem, Josefum, Origenem, Cesariensem Eusebeum, and bi the witnesse of hem he shal proue me to sey soth. Here therfore myn houndis, therfore me in this volume to han trauailid, not that the olde remenyng I reproue, but that tho thingis, that in it or ben derc, or ben laft of, or certis bi the[d] vice of writeres depraued, shulden be maad more open bi oure remenyng ; the whiche and the[e] Ebrues sermoun a parti wee han lerned, and in Latin fulli fro the[f] cradelis among gramarienes[g], and retorikis, and filosofres wee ben defoulid. That if anent the Grekis, aftir the making of the Seuenti, now the euangelie of Crist shynende, Jew Aquila, and Simacus, and Theodocian, Jewinge eretikis, ben founde, that manye mysterijs of the Saueour bi treccherous remenyng hidden, and nerthelatere in sixe exaumpleris[h] ben had[i] anent the chirches, and ben expouned of chirchemen ; myche more I, a Cristene man, born of fader and moder Cristene, and the baner of the cros in my forhed berende, whos studie was to telle a3een laft of thingus, and to amende the depraued, and the sacramens of the chirche with pure and trewe sermounes to openen, or of proude men or of shreude reders I a3te not to be repreued. Haue[k] that wiln olde bokis, and in rede skynnes with gold and siluer writen, or with capital lettris, as comunli men sein, chargis grauen out more than bokis, so that to me and to myne thei suffre to han pore scrowis, and not as myche faire bokis as amendid. Eithir forsothe translacioun, and the Seuenti after Grekis, and myn after the Ebrues, in Latin bi my trauaile is translatid ; chese eche man that he wile, and proue he[l] hymself more studious than euel willid.

Anothir prolog[m].

If forsothe a iunket[n] with resshe I shulde make, or the leues of palmys I shulde platte°, that in the[p] swot of my chere I shulde ete bred, and the were of the wombe with besi mynde treten, no man shulde bite, no man shulde repreue. Now forsothe for after the sentence of the Saueour, I wile werke the mete that persheth not, the olde weie of Godys volumys to purgen fro thornes and busshis, double errour^q is piȝt in to me; a fals corectour^r of vices I am clepid, and erroures not to taken awei, but to sowen. So myche forsothe is the custum of oldnesse, that also other while confesid vicis plesen, whil more faire bokis they wiln han than amendid. Wherfore, O! moost^s looued brethern, oon. exsaumpler^t of noblehed for the werelis, lepis, basketis, and litle ȝiftis of munkis, these spirituél and ȝiftis to dwelle taketh; and blisful Job, that ȝit anent Latynes lai in the drit, and with wermes of erroures brac out, hool and withoute wem ioȝeth. What maner. forsothe, after prouyng and victorie, double to hym alle thingus ben ȝolden, so I^u in to ȝoure tunge, that hardili I speke, haue maad hym to han that^v he hadde lost. Therfor and^w ȝou and eche redere I warne 'to gidere^x with besy before telling, and in the begynnyngus of bokis the same thingus euermor ioynende, I preȝe, 'that wher euermor^y litle ȝerdis goende beforn ȝee shul see, witeth tho thingis that ben vnder leid in Ebru volumys not to^z ben^a had; but wher the image of a sterre shyneth beforn, of Ebru in oure sermoun ben added. Also and thoo thingus weren^b seen to ben had^c in Grek, and so weren corupt, that the^d wit to^e the reders thei token awei, ȝou preȝende, with gret trauaile I amendide; wenende more what profitable thing to comyn of myn hate to the chirchis of Crist, than of other meunnys besinesse.

Here endeth the prolog of Job, and now bigynneth the book^f.

Incipit liber Job^a.

CAP. I.

1 THER was a man in the lond of Hus, Job by name; and that man was simple, and riȝt, and dredende God, and goende 2 awei fro euel. And ther ben born to 3 hym seue sones, and thre douȝtris; and his possessioun was seuen thousend of shep, and thre thousend of camailis, also fiue^b hundrid ȝokis of oxen, and fiue hundryd assis, and ful myche meyne; and that man was gret among alle the men 4 of the est. And his sones wenten, and maden festis bi housis, eche in his day; and sendende thei clepeden ther thre sistris, that thei shulden ete, and drinke win

Here bigynnith the bok of Joob^a.

CAP. I.

'A man, Joob† bi name, was^b in the 1 lond of Hus^c; and thilke man^d was symple^e†, and riȝtful^f, and dredynge God, and goynge awey fro yuel. And^g seuene sones 2 and thre douȝtris weren^h borun to hym; and his possessioun was seuene thousynde 3 of scheep, and thre thousynde ofⁱ camels, and fyue hundrid ȝockis of oxis^k, and fyue hundrid of femal assis, and ful myche meynee; and 'thilke man^l was grete^m among alle menⁿ of the eest. And hise 4 sones ȝeden, and maden feestis bi housis^o, ech man^p in his day; and thei^q senten, and clepiden her thre sistris, 'that thei schul-

q errours OR. r coniectour OR. s ȝe most OR. t exsaumple H. u that R. v that that R. w Om. I. x Om. R. y euermore, that wher euere OR. z Om. AUOR. a Om. I. b that weren OR. c hid H. d ȝe A. sche H. e of R. f From A. *Here endeth the prolog of Joob, se now the booc.* I. *Here eendith the prologis, and bigynneth the boke of Joob.* R. No final rubric in CEFHO. g *Incipit liber.* E. *Here begynneth the bok of Job.* F. No initial rubric in the other Mss. h fifty E pr. m.

a From LMOPF. *Heere biginnith Job.* IU. No initial rubric in the other Mss. b Om. IS. c Hus was a man that hiȝte Job IS. d Job IS. e a symple man I. a symple man, that is, he was withouten doublenesse and variaunce S. f he was riȝtful IS. g And ther weren I. h Om. I. i Om. IS. k oxen IS. l this Job IS. m a grete man IS. n the men S. o her housis IS. p man of hem S. q in her feeste daies thei S.

5 with hem. And whan the daȝes of the feste hadden passid aboute, Job sente to them, and haliwide them, and risende erli, offride brent sacrifise bi alle. Forsothe he seide, Lest perauenture my sonys synnen, and blisse to God in ther hertis.
6 So Job dide alle daȝis. On a dai forsothe, whan the sones of God wer come, that thei shulde stonde neeȝ before God, was
7 neeȝ among hem and Sathan. To whom seide the Lord, Whennus[e] comest thou? The whiche answerende seith, I haue enuyround the erthe, and thurȝ gon it.
8 And the Lord seide to hym, Whether hast thou not beholde my seruaunt Job, that ther be not lic to hym in the[d] erthe, a man simple, and riȝt, and[e] dredende
9 God, and goende awei fro euel. To whom answerde Sathan, Whether in vein Job
10 dredith God? Whether hast thou not strengthid hym, and his hous, and al his substaunce bi enuyroun? To the werkis of his hondis thou hast blissid, and his
11 possessioun wex in the[f] erthe. But strecche out a litil thin hond, and touche alle thingus that he weldeth; but in the
12 face he blesse to thee. Thanne the Lord seide to Sathan, Lo! alle thingus, that he hath, in thin hond ben; onli in hym ne strecche thou out thin hond. And Sathan is gon out fro the face of the Lord.
13 Whan forsothe on a dai the sones and his doȝtris shulden ete, and drinke win in the hous of ther firste gote brother,
14 a messager cam to Job, that shulde sein, Oxen ereden, and she assis weren fed
15 beside them; and Sabeis feerly fellen to, and token alle thingis, and smyte the

den[r] ete, and drynke[s] wiyn with hem. And
5 whanne the daies of feeste[t] hadden passid in to the world[u]†, Joob sente to hem, and halewide hem[w], and[x] he[y] roos[z] eerli, and offride[a] brent sacrifices 'bi alle[b]. For[c] he seide‡, Lest perauenture my sones do synne, and curse God in her hertis. Joob[f]
6 dide so in alle daies[g]. Forsothe[h] in sum[i] day, whanne the sones of God§ 'weren comun[k] to be present bifor the Lord[l], also Sathan cam[m] among hem[n]. To whom the
7 Lord seide, Fro whennus comest thou? Which[o] answeride, and seide, Y haue cumpassid the erthe, and Y haue walkid thorouȝ
8 it. And the Lord seide to hym, Whether[q] thou hast biholde my seruaunt Joob, that[r] noon[s] in erthe is[t] lyik hym[u]; he is
9 a[w] symple man[x], and riȝtful, and dredynge God, and goynge awei fro yuel? To whom
10 Sathan answeride, Whether Joob dredith God veynli[y]‖? Whethir thou hast not[z] cumpassid hym, and his hows, and al his catel bi cumpas[z]? Thou hast blessid the
11 werkis of hise hondis, and hise possessioun encreesside[a] in[b] erthe. But stretche[c] forth thin hond a litil, and touche thou alle thingis whiche[d] he hath in possessioun[e]; if[f] he cursith[g] not thee 'in the face[h], bileue not to me[i]. Therfor[k] the Lord seide to
12 Sathan, Lo! alle thingis, whiche[l] he[m] hath, ben in thin hond[n]; oneli[o] stretche thou not forth thin hond in to hym[p]. And[q] Sathan ȝede out fro the face of the Lord.
13 Sotheli[r] whanne in sum[s] dai 'hise sones[t] and douȝtris[u] eeten, and drunken wiyn in the hows of her firste gendrid[w] brothir, a
14 messanger cam to Job, 'whiche messanger[x] seide[y], Oxis[z] eriden[a], and[b] femal assis

† in to the world: that is, in the ende of the wouke. Lire here. c.
‡ seide; that is, thouȝte. Lire here. c.
§ sones of God: that is, holi aungels, to be present: hiȝere aungels ben propirli present to God, that ben not [sent] out to outermere seruyces, othere that ben sent out for to serue God. In large maner of spekinge, alle aungels and myngels and aungels ben seid to be present to God, in as myche as thei seen God clerely; thus spekith Danyel in vii. c°., seiynge, a thousinde thousinde sueden him, and tensithis an hundrid thousinde weren present to him. In the largeste maner, fendis ben seid to be present to God, in as myche as thei and her dedis ben opyn to Goddis siȝt, and thus spekith the scripture here. Lire here. c.
‖ Wher Joob dredith God veynli: as if he seye nay, for Joob serueth thee for the loue of temperal thingis. eum passid: so him and hise thingis with thi proteccioun, that Y may not terapte hym. Lire here. c.

e Whenne EFH. d Om. A. e Om. A. f Om. AH.

r to 18. s to drynke 18. t her feeste 18. u world bi greet fame 18. w hem or mouyde hem to holynesse I. hem, that is, he meuid hem to holynesse 8. x and bi alle her feest daies 18. y Job 18. z roos up 18. a he offride 18. b for hem I. for his children 8. c And 18. e hertis, I shal do peuannce for hem 8. f And Job 18. g her feest daies 1. h And 18. i a plures. oo 8. k camen 8. l Lord, makinge sacrifice 1. Lord, to maken her sacrifice 8. m cam niȝ 18. n hem to disturble hem 8. o And Sathan 18. q Wher plures passim. r that ther is 1. s no man 18. t Om. 1. u to him 8. w Om. 18. x Om. 18. y veynli or in ydel 1. veynli withouten cause 8. z enuyroun 18 a hath encressid 1. is encresed 8. b on 8. c holde BCEFHLPUVX. d that 1. e possessioun takynge hem awey 1. possessioun anentischinge hem 8. f and if 18. g curse 18. h thane 8. i he is verily synple and riȝtuis [and dreding thee 8] 18. bileue thou not to me K. k Thanne 1. l that 1. m Job 18. n hond or power 1. hond or in thi power be my suffraunce 8. o but oneli 18. p his persoone 18. q And thanne 8. r And 18. Forsothe N. s a plures. t the sones of Job 18. u his douȝtris 18. w goten 1. x and 18. y seide to him 18. z Thin oxen 18. a that eriden thi loond 8. b and thi 18.

childer^g with swerd ; and I alone scapide^h
16 that I shulde telle to thee. And whan
ʒit he spac, cam an other, and seide, The
fyr of God cam doun fro heuene, and the
shep touchid, and the childer wastide ;
and I alone fleiʒ awei that I telle to thee.
17 But ʒit hym spekende, cam and an other,
and seide, Caldeis maden thre cumpanyes,
and asailiden the camailis, and token
hem, also and the childer thei smyten
with swerd ; and I alone fleiʒ awei that
18 I telle to thee. And ʒit he spac, and lo !
an other cam inne, and seide, Thi sones
and doʒtris etende, and drinkende win in
the hous of therⁱ firste goten brother,
19 feerli an hidous wind fel in fro the re-
gioun^k of desert, and smot togidere the
foure corneres of the hous, the whiche
fallende opresside thi^l fre childer, and
ben deade ; and I alone fleiʒ awei that I
20 telle to thee. Thanne Job ros, and kutte
his clothis, and his hed shauen fel in to
21 the erthe, and honourede, and seide, Nakid
I wente out fro the wombe of my moder,
and nakid I shal gon aʒeen thider ; the
Lord ʒaf, the Lord toc awei ; as to the
Lord pleside, so^m it is do ; be the name
22 of the Lord blissid. In alle thes thingusⁿ
Job synnede not with his lippis, ne any
foli thing aʒen God spac.

'weren lesewid^c bisidis^d tho^e ; and Sabeis^f 15
felden yn, and token^g awey^h alle thingisⁱ,
and 'smytiden the children^k with swerd^l ;
and Y aloone ascapide for^m to telle toⁿ
thee. And whanne^o he^p spak ʒit^q, anothir^r 16
cam, and seide^s, Fier of God cam doun fro
heuene, and wastide^t scheep^u, and 'children
touchid^w ; and Y aloone ascapide^x for^y to
telle 'to thee^z. But ʒit the^a while he^b 17
spak, also anothir cam, and seide, Caldeis^c
maden^d thre cumpenyes, and^e assailiden
the^f camels, and token^g tho^h awei, and
thei smytidenⁱ 'also the children^k with^l
swerd ; and Y aloone ascapide^m to telle
toⁿ thee^o. And^p ʒit^q he spak, and^r, lo ! 18
anothir entride^s, and seide, While thi
sones and douʒtris^t eeten, and drunken
wiyn in the hows of her firste gendrid^u
brothir, a^w greet wynde felde yn sudenli 19
fro the coost of desert, and schook^x foure
corneris of the hows, 'which felde^y doun,
and^z oppresside thi^a children, and thei ben
deed ; and Y aloone fledde to 'telle to^b
thee. Thanne Joob roos^c, and^d to-rente 20
hise clothis, and 'with pollid heed^e he
felde doun on^f the erthe, and^g worschip-
ide^h God, and seide, Y ʒede nakid out of 21
the wombe of my modir, Yⁱ schal turne
aʒen nakid^k thidur^l ; the Lord ʒaf, the^m
Lord tookⁿ awei ; as it pleside the Lord,
so 'it is^o doon ; the name of the Lord be
blessid. In alle these thingis Joob syn- 22
nede not in hise lippis, nether spak^p ony
fonned^q thing aʒens^r God.

CAP. II.

1 It is do forsothe, whan on a dai hadden
comen the sones of God, and stoden be-

CAP. II.

Forsothe^s it was doon, whanne^t in sum^u 1
dai the sones of God 'weren comun^w, and^x

---

^g children A passim. ^h ascaped E. ⁱ the A. ^k regiouns A. ^l the c. ^m Om. AH. ⁿ thing c. Om. H.

^c lesewiden 1s. ^d there bisidis s. ^e hem 1s. ^f men of the cuntrey of Sabey 1s. ^g thei token 1s.
^h awey with hem s. ⁱ thi godis 1s. ^k Om. 1s. ^l swerd thei han sleyn thi seruauntis 1s. ^m Om. 1.
ⁿ this to 1. these thingis to s. ^o while 1. whilis s. ^p this messanger 1s. ^q Om. s. ^r also anothir 1.
^s seide to Job s. ^t it hath wastid 1s. ^u thi scheep 1s. ^w smeten thi children 1. sleyn thi children s.
^x scapid s. ^y Om. 1s. ^z it 1. thee these thingis s. ^a Om. 1s. ^b this messanger 1s. ^c Men of the
cuntrey of Caldey 1s. ^d han maad 1s. ^e and thei 1s. ^f thi 1. ^g han take 1s. ^h hem 1s. ⁱ han
killid 1s. smiten F. ^k Om. 1. ^l thi seruauntis with 1s. ^m scapide s. ⁿ Om. 1s. ^o thee these thingis s.
^p Om. BEHLX. ^q ʒit while 1. ʒit the while that s. ^r Om. 1s. ^s entride yn to Job 1s. ^t thi douʒtris 1s.
^u goten 1. ^w and a 1. and s. ^x it stroke 1. ^y and the hous felle 1. ^z and it 1. ^a the s. ^b Om. 1.
^c roos up 1. ^d and he 1. ^e whanne his heed was polled 1. ^f upon 1. in to s. ^g and he 1. ^h worschip s.
ⁱ and nakid Y 1. and nakid s. ^k Om. 1s. ^l Om. s. ^m and the 1. ⁿ hath taken 1. takyt s. ^o be it s.
^p he spak L. ^q foly 1s. ^r to 1. ^s And 1. ^t Om. 1. ^u the sum c sec. m. a 1. ^w weren come to kerie
him 1. shulden come s. ^x and thei 1.

fore the Lord, and Sathan hadde comen
2 among hem, and stod in his siȝt, that the
Lord seide to Sathan, Whennes comest
thou? The whiche answerende seith, I
haue gon aboute the erthe, and thurȝ
3 passid it. And the Lord seide to Sathan,
Whether hast thou beholde my seruaunt
Job, that ther be not to hym lic in the
erthe, a man simple, and riȝt, and dredende God, and goende awei fro euel, and
ȝit withholdende innocence? Thou forsothe hast stirid me aȝen hym, that I
4 scourge hym in vein. To whom answerde Sathan, and seith, Fel for fel,
and alle thingus that a man hath he
5 shulde ȝiue for his soule; ellis put thin
hond, and touche his bon and flesh, and
thanne thou shalt see, that in to the face
6 he blisse to thee. Thanne the Lord seide
to Sathan, Lo! in thin hond he is;
7 nerthelater his lif kep. Thanne Sathan, gon out fro the face of the Lord,
he smot Job 'with the° werste stinkende
bleyne fro the sole of the fot vnto the
8 nol; the whiche with a sherd scrapide
awei the quyture, sittende in the dung-
9 hil. His wif forsothe seide to hym, Ȝit
forsothe thou abidist stille in thi sym-
10 plete. Blisse to God, and die. The whiche
seith to hir, As oon of the fool wymmen
thou speeke; if goodis wee han taken of
the hond of the Lord, euelis forsothe
why shulde wee not suffre? In alle these
thingis Job synnede not with his lippis.
11 Thanne thre° frendus of Job, herende al
the euel that hadde fallen to hym, alle
camen fro ther place, Elifath Themanites,
and Baldach Suytes, and Sofar Naamatites; forsothe thei hadden seid togidere
to themself, that comende togidere thei
shulden visiten hym, and coumforten.

stoden^y bifor the Lord, and Sathan 'was
comun^z among hem, and^a stood in his^b
siȝt^c, that^d the Lord seide^e to Sathan, Fro 2
whennus comest thou? Which^f answeride,
and seide, Y haue cumpassid the erthe,
'and Y haue go thurȝ it^g. And the Lord 3
seide to Sathan, Whethir thou hast bi-
holde^h my seruaunt Joob, that^i noon^k in
erthe is^l lijk^m hym; *he is* a^n symple
man°, and^p riȝtful, and dredynge God, and
goynge^q awei fro yuel, and ȝit holdynge^r
innocence? 'But thou^s hast moued me
aȝens him, that 'Y schulde turmente^t hym
in veyn. To whom Sathan answeride, 4
and seide^n, 'A man schal ȝyue skyn for
skyn^v, and alle thingis that he hath for
his lijf^w; 'ellis sende^x thin hond, and 5
touche his boon and^y fleisch, and thanne
thou schalt se, that he schal curse thee in
the^z face. Therfor^a the Lord seide to 6
Sathan, Lo! he^b is^c in 'thin hond^d; netheles kepe thou his lijf. Therfor Sathan 7
ȝede out fro the face of the Lord, and^e
smoot Joob with 'a ful wickid^f botche fro
the sole of the^g foot 'til to^h his top;
which^i *Joob*^k schanyde^l the quytere with^m 8
a schelle, 'and sat in the dunghill^n. For- 9
sothe his wijf seide to hym, Dwellist thou
ȝit in thi symplenesse†? Curse thou God,
and die°. And Joob seide^p, Thou hast 10
spoke as oon of the fonned wymmen; if
we han take goodis^q of the hond of the
Lord, whi forsothe^r suffren we not yuels^s?
In alle these thingis Joob synnede not in
hise lippis. Therfor^t thre^u frendis of Joob 11
herden al the yuel, that hadde bifelde^w
to hym, and camen^x ech many^y fro his
place, Eliphath Temanytes, and Baldach
Suythes, and Sophar Naamathites; for^z
thei 'hadden seide^a togidere to hem silf,
that thei wolden come togidere, and visite

† *symplenesse;
that is, fonned-
nesse. Lire
here. c.*

° Om. *All.* ᴾ the thre *c.*

ʸ stonde s. ᶻ come s. ᵃ and he ɪ. ᵇ Om. ɪ. ᶜ siȝt of the Lord ɪ. ᵈ and ɪ. ᵉ shuld say s. ᶠ The
which ɪ. ᵍ Om. s. ʰ not considerd s. ⁱ that ther is s. ᵏ no man ɪ. ˡ Om. s. ᵐ lijk to ɪs. ⁿ Om. s.
° Om. s. ᵖ and a ɪ. ᑫ departyng s. ʳ he holdith ɪ. ˢ And thou forther s. ᵗ thou vex hym s. ᵘ seide
to the Lord s. ᵛ Om. s. ʷ soule ɪ. ˣ therfor putte to ɪ. ʸ and his ɪ. ᶻ thi ɪ. ᵃ Thanne ɪ. ᵇ Job ɪ.
ᶜ is *now* ɪ. ᵈ thi power ɪ. ᵉ and he ɪ. ᶠ the worste stynkynge ɪ. ᵍ his s. ʰ vnto ɪ. to x. ⁱ and ɪ.
ᵏ Job sate in a dunge hill ɪ. ˡ and he schanyde awey ɪ. ᵐ of him with ɪ. ⁿ Om. ɪ. ° die *as the lame
wole* ɪ. ᵖ seide *to hir* ɪs. ᑫ gode thingis ɪ. ʳ thanne ɪ. ˢ *gladly* yuel thingis ɪ. ᵗ And thanne ɪ.
ᵘ then the s. ʷ bifalle ɪs. ˣ thei camen *to him* ɪ. ʸ of hem ɪ. ᶻ sothely ɪ. ᵃ seiden ɪ.

12 And whan thei hadden rerid up aferr ther eȝen, thei kneweu hym not; and criende out thei wepten, and, the clothis kitt, thei sprengden poudre vpon ther hed
13 in to heuene. And thei seten with hym in the erthe seuen daȝis and seuen nyȝt, and no man spac to hym woord; forsothe thei seȝen the sorewe to ben hydous.

CAP. III.

1 Aftir these thingus Job openede his
2 mouth, and curside to his dai, and seide,
3 Pershe the dai in the whiche I am born, and the nyȝt in the whiche it is seid, A
4 man is conceyued. That dai be turned in to derenessis; God seche it not from aboue, and be it not in recording, ne be
5 it liȝtid with liȝt. Derenesses derene it, and the shadewe of deth ocupie it in derenesse; and be it with inne wrappid
6 with bitternesse. A dere whirlewind welde that nyȝt; and be it not countid in the daȝes of the ȝer, ne noumbrid in
7 monethis. Be that nyȝt solitarie, and not
8 preise wrthi. Curse thei to it, that cursen to the dai, that ben redi to rere Leui-
9 ethan. The sterris be thei derkid with the derenesse of it; abide it liȝt, and se not, ne the springing of the risende
10 morwetid. For it closide not the doris of the wombe, that bar me, ne toc awei
11 euelis fro myn eyen. Whi not in the wombe I am dead? gon out of the wombe
12 not anoon It perslide? Whi taken out of
13 the knes? whi soukid the tetis? Now forsothe slepende I sholde holde my pes,
14 and with my slep resten, with kingus and counseileris of the erthe, that bilden
15 to hem solitarie dwellingus; or with princis that welde gold, and fulfillen
16 ther housis with siluer; or as abortif

hym, and coumforte. And whanne thei
12 hadden reisid afer her iȝen, thei knewen not hym; and theij crieden, and wepten, and to-renten her clothis, and spreynten dust on her heed in to heuene. And
13 thei saten with hym in the erthe seuene daies and seuene nyȝtis, and no man spak a word to hym; for thei sien, that his sorewe was greet.

CAP. III.

Aftir these thingis Joob openyde his
1 mouth, and curside his dai, and seide, 2 Perische the dai in which Y was borun, 3 and the nyȝt in which it was seid, The man is conceyued. Thilke dai be turnede 4 in to derknessis; God seke not it aboue, and be it not in mynde; nethir be it liȝt-ned with liȝt. Derknessis make it derk, 5 and the schadewe of deeth and myist ocupie it; and be it wlappid with bittir-nesse. Derk whirlwynde holde that nyȝt; 6 be it not rikynyd among the daies of the ȝeer, nethir be it noumbrid among the monethes. Thilke nyȝt be soleyn, and not 7 worthi of preisyng. Curse thei it, that 8 cursen the dai, that ben redi to reise Le-uyathan§. Sterris be maad derk with 9 the derknesse therof; abide it liȝt, and se it not, nethir the bigynnyng of the morwetid risyng vp. For it closide not 10 the doris of the wombe, that bar me, ne-thir took awei yuels fro min iȝen. Whi 11 was not Y deed in the wombe? whi ȝede Y out of the wombe, and perischide not anoon? Whi was Y takun on knees? 12 whi was Y suelid with teetis? For now 13 Y slepynge schulde be stille, and schulde reste in my sleep, with kyngis, and con- 14 suls of erthe, that bilden to hem soleyn places; ethir with pryuces that han gold 15 in possessioun, and fillen her housis with

12 † Perische the day: Greg. in iii. book of Moralis seith, that Joob spekith in parable, ethir to goostly 13 vndurstonding, and not to the lettre; for many wordis here takun to the lettre ben vnresonable and vnpossible, and of a man vnpacient and dispeiringe, and blasfemynge God; but Joob was not siche a man, as God witnessith in the ende. Netheles Tomas Alquyn here expowneth this proces to the lettre, and seith, that Joob spekith here aftir the sensualite, ethir fleisly lust, and bi the resoun of soule be suffride wilfully and paciently his disese. But for it sueth heraf that Joob and hise freendis disputiden to dyuerse wittis, and not to the purpos, therfor it may be seid betere, that these freendis seiden paynysching only for synne passid, and rewarding onely in this lijf for goode werkis passid. Therfor Joob argueth aȝenus hem, that it sueth of her errour, that Joob schulde skilfuly curse the day of his birthe, and othere thing's, as the text sowneth, and Joob spekith of day passid, bi wordis of tyme to comynge, but in truth Joob curside not his

---

q derened *AEFH*.   r sprynge *A*.   s is close *H*.   t Om. *C*.   u Om. *AH*.

b Job I.   c coumforte *him* I.   d thei afer I.   e reisid up I.   f Om. I. afore s.   g hem ȝet s.
h knowen A.   i Job I.   j *thanne* thei I.   k and thei I.   l and thei I.   m upon I.   n heedis I.   o *biholdynge in to* I.   p heuenward I.   q Job I.   r upon I.   s forsothe I.   t the curside I.   u lie seide I.   w A I.
x Derkenes s.   y make thei I.   z of myist I.   a wrappid s.   b Om. I.   c Om. s.   d he it not I.   e Om. I.
f whiche I.   g Leuyathan, *that is, a venym watir eddre* I.   h Sterris of that niȝt I.   i be thei I.   k nethir se it I.   l it took I.   m yuel I.   n fro I.   o upon I.   p ȝiue souke I.   q Forsothe I.   qq I schulde I.
r with worthi men of counseil I.   s the erthe I.   t whiche I.   u *I schulde reste* with I.

hid I shulde not abide, or that conceyued
17 se3en not li3t. There vnpitous men cesiden
fro noise, and there resteden the wery in
18 strengthe. And sum time togidere ioyned
withoute gref thei herden not the vois of
19 the askere with strif. Litil and gret ther
ben, and seruaunt and fre man fro ther
20 lord. Whi to the wrecche is 3iue li3t,
and lif to hem that ben in bitternesse of
21 soule? The whiche abiden deth, and^v
cometh not; as men deluende out tresor
22 and io3en hugely, whan thei finde the
23 sepulcre? To the man whos weie is hid,
and God hath cumpassid hym with derc-
24 nessis? Er I shul ete, I si3he; and as of
25 flowende water, so my roring. For the
drede, that I dradde, ys ful out come to
me; and that I shamede of, is falle.
26 Whether I feynede not? whether^w I
heeld not my pes? whether I restide
not? and ther is comen vp on me indignacioun.

siluer; ethir as a 'thing hid not borun^w 16
Y schulde not stonde^x, ethir whiche^y conseyued sien^z not li3t. There wickid men 17
ceessiden of noise, and there men maad
wery of strengthe restiden. And sum 18
tyme boundun^a togidere with out disese
thei herden not the voys of the wrongful
axere. A litil man and greet^b man be^c 19
there, and a seruaunt^d free^e fro his lord.
Whi is li3t 3ouun to the wretche, and lijf 20
to hem that ben in bitternesse of soule?
Whiche^f abiden deeth, and it cometh not; 21
as men diggynge^g out tresour and ioien 22
greetly, whanne thei han founde a sepulcre? *Whi is li3t 3ouun* to a man, whos 23
weie is hid, and God hath cumpassid hym
with derknessis? Bifore that Y ete, Y 24
si3he; and as of watir flowynge, so is my
roryng. For^h the drede, which^i Y dredde, 25
cam^k to me; and that^l, that Y schamede,
bifelde^m. Whether Y dissymilide^n not? 26
whether Y was not stille? whether Y
restide not? and^o indignacioun cometh^p
on me.

[margin:] 16 day of birthe, but paciently suffride his disese, and held ri3tful sentence, as God witnessith in the ende. *Lire here.* c.
: This word, be not in mynde, is not in Ebreu, nether in bokis amendid. *Lire here.* c.
§ *Leuyathan;* that is, the deuel, as Alquyn seith. *Lire here.* c.
21 that is, the fend. v.

CAP. IV.

1 Answerende forsothe Elifath Thema-
2 nythes seide, If wee begynne to speke to
thee, perauenture greuously thou shalt
taken; but the conceiuede woord who
3 shal moun holde? Lo! thou hast ta3t
manye men, and thou hast strengthid
4 the weri hondis. Thi woordis hau maad
stable the vnstedefast, and the tremblende
5 knes thou hast coumfortid. Now forsothe is comen vp on thee veniaunce, and
thou hast failid; it hath touchid thee,
6 and thou art disturbid^x. Wher is thi
drede, thi strengthe, and thi pacience,
7 and the perfeccioun of thi weies? Recorde, I beseche thee, who euere innocent pershide, or whanne 'ri3twis men^y
8 ben don awei? But rathere I haue seen
hem, that werken wickidnesse, and sowen

CAP. IV.

Forsothe^q Eliphat Themanytes answer- 1
ide, and seide^r, If we bigynnen to^s speke 2
to thee, in hap thou schalt take it heuyli;
but who may holde^t a word conseyued?
Lo! thou hast tau3t ful many men, and 3
thou hast strengthid hondis maad feynt.
Thi wordis confermyden^u men doutynge, 4
and thou coumfortidist^w knees tremblynge.
But now a wounde^x is comun on^y thee, 5
and thou hast failid; it touchide^z thee,
and thou art disturblid. Where is thi 6
drede, thi strengthe, and thi pacience, and
the perfeccioun of thi weies? Y biseche 7
thee, haue thou mynde, what innocent
man perischide euere, ethir whanne ri3t-
ful men weren doon awei? Certis rathir 8
Y si3 hem, that worchen wickidnesse, and
sowen^a sorewis, and repen tho, to haue 9

---

^{v} as *All.* ^{w} Om. *All.* ^{x} distourblid *A.* ^{y} the ri3twise *A.* ri3twise *B.*

^{w} *child or a beest* born bifore the tyme and hid 1. ^{x} haue ben 1. ^{y} as thei that ben 1. ^{z} and sien 1.
^{a} *men* bounden 1. ^{b} a greet 1. ^{c} be he 1. ^{d} seruaunt be he there 1. ^{e} fer D. ^{f} The whiche 1. ^{g} that
diggen 1. ^{h} Certis 1. ^{i} that 1. ^{k} hath come 1. ^{l} that *thing* 1. ^{m} hath bifalle to me 1. ^{n} feynyde 1.
^{o} and 3itt 1. ^{p} hath comen 1. ^{q} Thanne 1. ^{r} seide *to Job* 1. ^{s} aud 1. ^{t} holde *in silence* 1. ^{u} han
confermyd 1. ^{w} hast coumfortid 1. ^{x} wounde *or sijknesse* 1. ^{y} upon 1. ^{z} hath touchid 1. ^{a} that
sowen 1.

9 sorewis, and repen hem, God blowende,
to han pershid, and᷾ thur₃ the spirit of
10 his wrathe to be wastid. The roring
of a leoun, and the vois of a leounesse,
and the teth of leoun whelpis ben to-
11 brosid. The tigre pershide, forthi that
he hadde no prei; and the leoun whelpis
12 ben scaterid. But to me is seid a woord
hid, and as theefli myn ere toc the veynes
13 of his gruching. In the orroure of the
ny₃t si₃te, whan slep is wont to ocupie
14 men, inward drede heeld me, and trembling; and alle my bones ben agast.
15 And whan the spirit me present shulde
passe, inwardli griseden the heris of my
16 flesh. Ther stod oon, whos chere I knew
not, an ymage befor myn e₃en; and a
17 vois as of a softe eir I herde. Whethir
aⁿ man of God shal be iustified bi comparisoun; and a man shal be more clene
18 than his Makere? Lo! that seruen to
hym ben not stable; and in his aungelis
19 he fond shreudenesse. Myche more theseᵇ
that dwellenᶜ cleyene housis, that han an
erthely foundement, shul be wastid as of
20 a mo₃heᵈ. Fro morutid vnto euen thei
shul ben hewe doun; and for no man
vnderstondith, with outen ende thei shul
21 pershe. Thei forsothe, that weren lafte,
shul be taken awei fro hem, and dien,
and not in wisdam.

CAP. V.

1 Clep thanne, if ther is that answere to
thee, and turne to summe of the seintis.
2 Wrathe sleth a man fol, and enuye sleth
3 a litil child. I sa₃ a fool with a stable
roote, and I curside to his fairnesse anoon.
4 Aferr shul be maade his sones fro helthe,
and shul be to-treden in the ₃ate, and
5 ther shal not be that deliuere. Whos
rep the hungri shal ete, and hym shal

perischid bi God blowynge ᵇ, and to be
wastid bi the spirit of his ire. The roryng 10
of a ᵉ lioun ᵈ†, and the vois of a ᵉ lionesse ᶠ,
and the teeth of ʻwhelpis of liouns ᵍ ben
al ʰ to-brokun. Tigris perischide, for sche 11
hadde not prey; and the ⁱ whelpis of a ᵏ
lioun ben distried. Certis an hid word 12
was seid to me, and myn eere took as ˡ
theueli the veynes of priuy ᵐ noise ⁿ therof.
In the hidousnesse of ʻny₃tis si₃t ᵒ, whanne 13
heuy sleep is wont to occupie men, drede ᵖ 14
and tremblyng helde ᑫ me; and alle my
boonys weren aferd. And whanne the 15
spirit ʻ₃ede in my presence ʳ, the heiris of
ʻmy fleisch ˢ hadden hidousnesse. Oon 16
stood, whos chere ᵗ Y knewe not, an ymage
bifor myn i₃en; and Y herde a ᵘ vois as ʷ
of softe ˣ wynd. Whether a man schal be 17
maad iust‡ in comparisoun of God? ethir
whethir ʸ a man schal be clennere than his
Makere? Lo! thei that seruen hym ben 18
not stidefast; and he findith ᶻ schrewid-
nesse in hise aungels. Hou myche more 19
thei that dwellen in housis of cley, that ᵇ
han an ertheli foundement, schulen be
wastyd as of a mou₃te. Fro ᶜ morewtid 20
til ᵈ to ᵉ enentid thei schulen be kit doun;
and for no man vndurstondith, thei schulen perische with outen ende. Sotheli ᶠ 21
thei, that ben residue ᵍ, schulen be takun
awei§; thei schulen die, and not in wisdom.

CAP. V.

Therfor ʰ clepe thou, if ʻony is ⁱ that schal 1
answere thee, and turne thou to summe of
seyntis. Wrathfulnesse sleeth ʻa fonned ᵏ 2
man, and enuye sleeth a litil child ˡ. Y si₃ 3
a fool with stidefast‖ rote, and Y curside
his feirnesse anoon. Hise sones schulen 4
be maad fer fro helthe, and thei schulen
be defoulid in the ₃ate, and ʻnoon schal
be ᵐ that schal delyuere hem ⁿ. Whos ᵒ ripe 5

† A glos. Bi a
lioun he vndur-
stondith Joob;
bi a lionesse
and tigris he
vndurstondith
his wijf; bi
the teeth of
liouns he vn-
durstondith
hise sones.
Lire here. c et
plures.

‡ maad iust;
this is the sen-
tence of Eli-
phat, althen no
man is ri₃t-
fulere nethir
clennere than
God, and a
ri₃tful iuge
dampneth not
an innocent
man, therfor
God punysch-
ith not a man
without his
synne bifor
doon. This re-
soun is not
worth; for
whanne a iuge
dampnyth an
innocent man,
he may not
rewarde him
aftir deth, but
God punysch-
ith a man here
with out gilt
for to encreesse
his meede in
blis, and to yiue
saumple of pa-
cience to othere
men. Lire
here. c.

§ awey; that
is, fro present
liyf. c.

‖ stidefast; that
is, sad in pros-
perite. Lire
here. c.

ᶻ Om. ᴀ. ᵃ the ᴀᴇꜰ. ᵇ the ᴀ. ᶜ dwellen in ᴀ. ᵈ mowghe ᴀᴇʜ. moughe ꜰ.

ᵇ sownynge a₃ens hem ɪ. ᶜ the ɪ. ᵈ lioun, that is, Job ɪ. ᵉ the ɪ. ᶠ lionesse, that is, his wijf ɪ.
ᵍ the liounis whelpis, that is, his children ɪ. ʰ al now ɪ. ⁱ Om. ɪ. ᵏ the ɪ. ˡ as it were ɪ. ᵐ the
priuey ɪ. ⁿ spekyng ɪ. ᵒ si₃t of the ni₃t ɪ. ᵖ and drede ɪ. ᑫ helden ɪ. ʳ passide me beynge present ɪ.
ˢ myn heed ɪ. ᵗ chere or lickenesse ɪ. ᵘ the ɪ. ʷ Om. ɪ. ˣ a softe ɪ. ʸ Om. ɪ. ᶻ hath founde ɪ.
ᵇ whiche ɪ. ᶜ Fro the ɪ. ᵈ vntil ɪ. ᵉ to the ɪ. ᶠ And ʳ. ᵍ left ɪ. ʰ Therfor, Job ɪ. ⁱ ther
is ony man ɪ. ᵏ an vnwise ɪ. ˡ child withouten witt ɪ. ᵐ ther schal be noon ɪ. ⁿ Om. plures.
ᵒ The ɪ.

raueshe the armed, and the thristi men
6 shul drinke his richessis. No thing in
the erthe is maad withoute cause, and of
7 the erthe shal not gon out sorewe. A
man to trauaile is born, and a brid to
8 fleen. For what thing I shal preȝe the
Lord, and to my God I shal putte my
9 speche. That doth grete thingus, and vnserchable, and merueilouse thingus with-
10 oute noumbre. That ȝiueth reyn vpon
the face of the erthe, and moysteth with
11 watris alle thingus. That setteth meke
men in to heiȝte, and weilende men
12 rereth[c] with helthe. That scatereth the
thoȝtis of euele men, that ther hondis
13 moun not fulfille that thei begunne. That
caccheth wise men in ther felnesse, and
14 the counseil of shrewis scattereth. Bi
the dai thei shul renne in to dercnessis,
and as in nyȝt so thei shul graspen in
15 mydday. But saf he shal make the nedi
fro the swerd of the mouth of hem, and
fro the hond doende violence the pore
16 man. And he shal be to the nédi man
hope, wickidnesse forsothe shal drawe to-
17 gidere his mouth. Blisful[f] the men that
is chastisid of the Lord ; thanne the
blamyng of the Lord ne repreue thou.
18 For he woundeth, and lecheth ; smyteth,
19 and his hondis shuln helen. In sixe tribulaciouns he shal deliuere thee, and in the
20 seuenthe shal not touche thee euel. In
hungir he shal deliuere thee fro deth,
and in bataile fro the hond of swerd.
21 Fro the scourge of tunge thou shalt ben
hid, and thou shalt not drede wrecchid-
22 nesse, whan it cometh. In wastite and
hunger thou shalt laȝwhin, and beste of
23 the erthe thou shalt not dreden. But
with stones of regiouns thi couenaunt,
and the bestis of erthe shul be pesible to
24 thee. And thou shalt wite, that thi tabernacle haue pes, and visitende thi kinde

corn[p] an hungri man schal ete, and an
armed man schal rauysche hym, and thei,
that thirsten, schulen drynke hise richessis.
6 No thing is doon in erthe with out cause,
and sorewe† schal not go out of the[q] erthe.
7 A man is borun to labour, and a brid to
8 fliȝt. Wherfor Y schal biseche the Lord,
and Y schal sette my speche to my God.
9 That makith grete thingis, and[r] that[s]
moun not be souȝt out, and wondurful
10 thingis with out noumbre. Which[t] ȝyueth
reyn on[u] the face of erthe[w], and moistith[x]
11 alle thingis with watris. Which[y] settith
meke men an biȝ, and[z] reisith with helthe
12 hem that morenen. Which distrieth the
thouȝtis of yuel willid men, that her hondis
moun not fille[a] tho thingis that thei bi-
13 gunnen[b]. Which takith cantelouse[c] men
in the[d] felnesse[e] 'of hem[f], and[g] distrieth
14 the counsel of schrewis. Bi dai[h] thei[i]
schulen renne in to derknessis, and as in
nyȝt so[k] thei schulen grope in myddai.
15 Certis God schal make saaf a nedi man‡
fro the[l] swerd of her[m] mouth, and a pore
man fro[n] the hond of the violent[o], 'ethir
rauynour[p]. And hope schal be to a nedi
16 man, but wickidnesse[q] schal drawe togidere his mouth. Blessid is the man,
17 which[r] is chastisid of the Lord ; therfor
repreue thou not the blamyng of the Lord.
18 For he woundith, and[s] doith medicyn ; he
smytith, and hise hondis schulen make
19 hool. In sixe tribulaciouns he schal delyuere thee, and in the seuenthe tribulacioun
yuel schal not touche thee. In hungur he
20 schal delyuere thee fro deeth, and in batel
fro the[t] power of swerd. Thou schalt be
21 hid fro the scourge of tunge[u], and thou
schalt not drede myseiste[w], 'ethir wretchid-
22 nesse[x], whanne it cometh. In distriyng
maad of enemyes and in hungur thou
schalt leiȝe, and thou schalt not drede the
23 beestis of erthe. But thi couenaunt schal

† sorewe; that is, aduersite bifallith not to ony man with out cause. Lire here. c.

‡ a nedy man; amendid of his trespassis bi nedynesse. Lire here. c.

[e] rerynge A. [f] Blessyd is A. Blessid II.

[p] corn of him I. [q] Om. I. [r] Om. IIC. [s] the whiche thingis I. [t] The which God I. [u] upon I. [w] the erthe I. [x] he moistith I. [y] The which I. [z] and he I. [a] fulfille I. [b] han bigunne I. [c] slie cantelouse I. [d] her owne I. [e] felnesse, ether wylynesse K marg. [f] Om. I. [g] and he I. [h] dai or openly I. [i] siche I. [k] Om. I. [l] Om. n. [m] the f. [n] God schal saue fro I. [o] violent man I. [p] ethir rauenoure N. Om. I. [q] wickidnesse of endurid men I. [r] that I. [s] and he I. [t] Om. I. [u] an yuel tunge I. [w] myseesnesse I. [x] Om. I.

²⁵ thou shalt not synne. And thou shalt
wite also, for manyfold shal be thi sed,
and thi progenye as the erbe of the^g
²⁶ erthe. Thou shalt go in to the sepulcre
in plenteuousnessis, as is born in an hep
²⁷ off whete in his tyme. Lo! this, as wee
han enserchid, so is; that is herd, in
mynde thur3 trete.

be with the^y stonys of erthe, and beestis
of erthe schulen be pesible to thee. And ²⁴
thou schalt wite, that thi tabernacle hath^z
pees, and thou visitynge† thi fairnesse
schalt not do^a synne. And thou schalt ²⁵
wite also, that thi seed schal be^b many
fold, and thi generacioun schal be as an
erbe of erthe. In abundaunce thou schalt ²⁶
go in to the sepulcre, as an heep of wheete
is borun in his tyme. Lo! this^c is so, as ²⁷
we han sou3t; which^d thing herd^e, trete
thou^f in^g minde.

† visityng; that is, biholding thi prosperite. schalt not do synne; for thou schalt not be reisid in to pride, but more in to preisinge of God. Lire here. c.

CAP. VI.

¹₂ Answerende forsothe Job seith, Wolde
God, my synnes weren we3ed, bi the
whiche wrathe I deseruede; and the^h
wreechidnesseⁱ that I suffre, in a ba-
³ launce. As the grauel of the se this
more greuous shulde seme; wherfore and
⁴ my woordis ben ful of sorewe. For the
arwis of the Lord ben in me, of the
whiche the indignacioun drinketh vp my
spirit; and the gastnessis of the Lord
⁵ fi3ten a3en me. Whethir an asse shal
roren, whan he hath erbe? Or an oxe
shul loowen, whan befor the fulle cracche
⁶ he shal stonde? Or shal moun ben eten
vnsauere thing, that is not with salt
poudrid? Or shal a man moun taste,
⁷ that tastid bringeth deth? Forsothe to
the hungrende lif, also bitter thingis
semen to be sweete; that beforn my soule
wolde not touche, now for anguysh ben
⁸ my metis. Who 3eue, that myn asking
come; and that I abijde, 3elde to me God?
⁹ And that began, he me to-trede; lose
¹⁰ his hond, and hewe me doun? And this
be to me a coumfort, that the tormentende me with sorewe pershe not, ne
withseie to the woordis of a seint. What

CAP. VI.

Forsothe^h Joob answeride, and seide, Y ¹₂
wolde, that my synnes, bi whiche Y des-
seruede ireⁱ, and the wretchidnesse which
Y suffre, weren peisid in a balaunce. As ³
the grauel of the see, this wretchidnesse
schulde appere greuousere^k; wherfor and
my wordis ben ful of sorewe‡. For the ⁴
arowis of the Lord ben in me, the indig-
nacioun^l of whiche^m drynkith vp my spirit; and the dredis of the Lord fi3ten a3ens
me. Whether a feeld asse schal roreⁿ, ⁵
whanne he hath gras^o? Ethir whether an
oxe schal lowe, whanne he stondith byfor
a 'ful cratche^p? Ether whethir a thing ⁶
vnsauery may be etun, which is not maad
sauery bi salt? Ether whether ony man
may taaste a thing, which^q tastid bryng-
ith^r deeth? For whi to an hungri soule, ⁷
3he^s, bittir thingis semen to be swete;
tho thingis whiche my soule nolde^t touche
bifore^u, ben now my meetis for angwisch.
Who 3yueth^w, that myn axyng come^x; and ⁸
that God 3yue^z to me that^a, that Y abide?
And he that bigan^b, al^c to-breke^d mee; re-⁹
leesse^f he his hond^g, and kitte^h me dounⁱ§?
And 'this be^k coumfort to me, that he^l tur-¹⁰
mente me with sorewe, and spare^m not,

‡ and my words, seid in lii. c^o. ben fulle of sorewe; resonably, If no rewarding is in liyf to comynge for peynes in this liyf, as Eliphath seide. Lire here. c.

§ doun, fro present liyf. Lire here. c.

---

g Om. *ACF.*   h my *A.*   i wrecchenesse *E.*

y Om. 1.   z schal haue 1.   a Om. 1.   b be *encressid* 1.   c *this thing* 1.   d *the which* 1.   e *whanne thou hast herd* 1.   f it 1.   g in thi 1.   h *And* 1.   i *haue deserued the wraththe of God* 1.   k *more greuous* 1.   l *indignaciouns* 1s.   m *thes arowis* 1s.   n *rore for hungre* 1s.   o *gras in plente* s.   p *cratche ful of mete* 1s.   q *which thing* 1s.   r *bryngith* yn 1s.   s Om. s.   t *wolde not* 1.   u *bifore hoond* s.   w 3yueth *or graunteth* 1. 3yueth s *pr. m.* graunteth s *sec. m.*   x *come to me* 1s.   z 3yueth o.   a *that thing* 1s.   b *hath bigunne* 1s.   c *to punyshe,* al 1. *iustly to punishe me for my synne* al s.   d *to-broke* he 1s.   e *me with diuers anoyes, til I be purgid of my filthe* s.   f *louse* 1s.   g *hond, which he hath long tide fro me* s.   h *kitte* he 1s.   i *doun, that I wex no more vp to synne* s.   k *be this thing* 1s.   l *the Lord* 1s.   m *spare me* 1s.

forsothe is my strengthe, that I suffre?
or what myn ende, that I pacientli do?
12 Ne the strengthe of stones my strengthe,
13 ne my flesh is brasene. Lo ! ther is not
helpe to me in me ; also my necessarie
14 men wenten awei fro me. He that taketh
awei fro his frend mercy, the drede of
15 the Lord forsaketh. My brethern passeden biside me, as a strem that raueshe-
16 melum^k passeth in valeis. That dreden
17 frost, snow3 shal falle vpon hem. The
time that thei wer scaterid, thei shul
pershe ; and as thei enchaufe, thei shul
18 be losid fro ther place. Withinne wrappid ben the sties of ther goingus ; thei
19 shul gon in vein, and pershen. Behold-
eth^l the sties of Theman, the weies of
20 Saba ; and abidith a litil while. Thei
ben confoundid, for I hopide ; thei camen
also to me, and with shame thei ben
21 ouercouered. Now 3ee han comen^m, and
now scande my veniaunce 3ee dreden.
22 Whether I seide, Bringeth to me, and of
23 3oure substaunce 3iueth to me ? or, Deliuere me fro the hond of the enemy, and
fro the hond of stronge men pullith out
24 me ? Techeth me, and I shal be stille ;
and if any thing perauenture I haue vn-
25 knowen, enformeth me. Whi han 3ee
bacbitid to the woordis of treuthe ? whan
of 3ou no man be, that mai vndernyme
26 me. To blamen^n onli spechis 3ee or-
deynyn, and a3en wind woordis 3ee
27 speken. Vpon the faderles child 3ee fallen
on, and enforsen 3oure frend to turne vp
28 so doun. Nerthelater^o that 3ee han begunne, fulfillith ; 3iueth ere, and seeth,

and that Y a3enseie not the wordis of the
hooli^n. For whi^o, what is my strengthe, 11
that Y suffre^p? ethir which is myn ende,
that Y do^q pacientli†? Nethir my strengthe 12 † *paciently ;
is the strengthe of stoonus, nether my
fleisch is of bras. Lo ! noon help is to me 13
in me^r ; also^s my meyneal^t frendis '3eden
awey^u fro me. He that takith awei merci 14
fro his frend, forsakith the drede of the
Lord. My britheren passiden me^w, as a 15
stronde *doith*, that passith^x ruschyngli^y in
grete valeis. Snow schal come on^z hem, 16
that dreden frost^a. In the tyme wherynne 17
thei ben^b scaterid, thei schulen perische ;
and as^c thei ben^d hoote, thei schulen be
vnknyt^e fro^f her place. The pathis of her 18
steppis ben wlappid^g ; thei schulen go in
veyn, and^h schulen perische. Biholde 3e 19
the pathis of Theman‡, and the weies of
Saba; and abide 3e a litil. Thei ben schent^i, 20
for Y hopide^k ; and thei camen 'til to^l me,
and thei ben hilid with schame. Now 3e 21
ben comun^m, and now 3e seen my wounde^n,
and^o dreden^p. Whether Y seide^q, Brynge 22
3e to me, and 3iue 3e of 3oure catel to me ?
ethir^r, Delyuere 3e me fro the hond of 23
enemy^s, and rausche^t 3e me fro the hond
of stronge men ? Teche 3e me^u, and Y 24
schal be stille ; and if in hap Y vnknew
ony thing^w, teche 3e^x me^y. Whi han 3e 25
depraued^z the wordis of trewthe ? sithen^a
noon is^b of 3ou, that may^c repreue me^d.
3e maken redi spechis^e oneli for to blame^f, 26
and^g 3e bryngen forth wordis^h in to wynde^i.
3e fallen in^k on^l a fadirles child, and^m en- 27
forsen to^n peruerte^o 3oure frend^p. Netheles 28
fille^q 3e that, that 3e han bigunne^r ; 3yue^s

bi the errour
of Eliphat, sei-
ynge, that no
meede is in
an other liyf for
aduersites suf-
frid in this
liyf, it is no
resoun to suf-
fre paciently.
15 *Lire here. c.*

‡ *the pathis of
Theman ; that
is, the comynge
of Eliphat The-
manytis, and
the comyng of
othere frendis,
that her com-
yng is not
coumfort ne-
ther help to
me. Lire here.*
c.

---

^k rauyshe meel *A*, raueshemeles *EF*. rauyschith mele *H*.   ^l Biholde *A*.   ^m comen to me *E sup. ras.*
^n blamen me *E sup. ras.*   ^o Neuerthelater *AEFH*.

^a *moost* hooli 1. holi *Lord* s.   ^o Om. 1s.   ^p suffre, Y *suffre the scourge that Y haue deserued* s.
^q suffre *it* s.   ^r my self̃ 1. me *as of my silf* s.   ^s *and also* 1s.   ^t nesessarie 1. necesearie *and home* s.
^u departiden 1s.   ^w fro me s.   ^x passith *or rennyth* s.   ^y ruschyngli *and hastily* 1s.   ^z vpon 1s.
^a frost, *that is, he that wile not suffre here, schal suffre more aftir* 1 marg. frost, *that is, who wole not
suffre here a lytil while, shal ellis where suffre longere* s.   ^b schul be 1s.   ^c whanne 1s.   ^d schul wexe 1s.
^e lousid 1s.   ^f *and removed fro* s.   ^g wlappid *with diuers diseeis* s.   ^h and thei 1s.   ^i aschamed 1s.
^k hopide *in the Lord* 1s.   ^l vnto 1s.   ^m comen hidre s.   ^n veniaunce 1s.   ^o *which I disseruide* and s.
^p 3e dreden 1s.   ^q seide *to 3ou* 1s.   ^r ethir *seide* 1. ethir *seide I to 3ow* e.   ^s myn enemy 1s.   ^t bynyme 1.
^u me *tremble* s.   ^w *thing of this that I speke* s.   ^x 3e *it* 1.   ^y me *hettir* s.   ^z contraried 1s.   ^a sith
ther is 1.   ^b Om̅. 1.   ^c *may iustly* s.   ^d me *for my suffringe* s.   ^e 3oure spechis s.   ^f blame *that thyng
that 3e sholden ioie of* s.   ^g and *so* 1s.   ^h 3oure wordis 1s.   ^i wynde *to be wastid* s.   ^k in here 1.
^l upon 1s.   ^m and 3e 1s.   ^n 3ou to 1s.   ^o turne 1s.   ^p frend *awey fro [the* s] *trenthe* 1s.   ^q fulfille 1s.
^r bigunne *to the merite of pacient men* s.   ^s and 3yue 1s.

29 whether I lie. Answerth, I beseche,
withoute strif, and spekende that, that is
30 riȝtwis, shewith. And ȝee shul not finde
in my tunge wickidnesse, ne in my chekis
folie shal thurȝ soune.

ȝe the' eere", and" se ȝe, whether Y lie.
Y biseche*, answere ȝe' with out strijf, 29
and speke ȝe", and deme ȝe that, that is
iust. And ȝe schulen not* fynde wickid- 30
nesse in my tunge", nethir foli schal sowne
in my chekis°.

CAP. VII.

1   Kniȝthod is the lif of man vpon erthe,
and as the daȝes of an hirid man, the
2 daȝis of hym. As an hert desireth shadewe, and as an hirid man abideth the
3 ende of his werc ; so and I hadde voide
monethis, and trauailous nyȝtis I noum-
4 bride out to me. If I shul slepen, I shal
sey, Whanne shal I rise ? and eft I shal
abide the euctid, and I shal be fulfild
5 with sorewis vnto dercnessis. My flesh
is clad^q with roting, and with filthis of
ponder ; my fel driede, and is drawen to-
6 gidere. My daȝes swiftliere passiden
than of the weuere the web is kut of ;
and thei ben wastid withoute any hope.
7 Haue mynde, for wind is my lif, and
myn eȝe shal not be turned aȝeen, that
8 I see goodis. Ne the siȝte of man shal
beholde me ; but thin eȝen in me, and I
9 shal not stonden. As a cloude is wastid,
and passeth, so that goth doun to helle,
10 shal not steȝen vp ; ne shal turne aȝeen
more in to his hous, ne his place shal
11 more ouer knowen hym. Wherfore and
I shal not spare to my mouth ; I shal
speke in the tribulacioun of my spirit,
and I shal talke with the bitternesse of
12 my soule. Whether am I the se, or a
whal, for ȝee han ennyround me with a
13 prisoun ? If I shal seyn, My bed shal
coumforte me, and I shal be releued

CAP. VII.

Knyȝthod^d is° lijf of man^f on^g erthe, 1
and his daies ben as the daies of an hired
man^h. As an hert desireth schadowe, and 2
as an hirede man abideth the ende of his
werk ; so and^i Y hadde^k voide† monethis, 3
and Y noumbrede^l trauailous niȝtes to me.
If Y schal slepe, Y schal seie, Whanne 4
schal Y rise ? and eft Y schal abide the
euentid, and Y schal be fillid^m with sorewis ʽtil to^n derknessis°. Mi fleisch is 5
clothid with rot, and filthis^p of dust ; my^q
skyn driede vp, and is^r drawun togidere.
My daies passiden^s swiftliere^t thanne a 6
web is kit doun^u ʽof a webstere^w ; and tho
daies ben wastid with outen ony hope^x.
God^y, haue thou mynde, for my lijf is 7
wynde^z, and myn iȝe schal net turne aȝen,
that it se goodis^a. Nethir the siȝt of man 8
schal biholde me ; but^b thin iȝen° ben in
me^d, and Y schal not ʽbe *in deedli lijf*^e.
As a cloude is wastid, and passith^f, so he 9
that goith doun to^g helle, schal not stie^h ;
nether schal^i turne aȝen more in to his 10
hows, and his place schal no more knowe
hym. Wherfor and Y schal not spare 11
my mouth ; Y schal speke in the tribulacioun of my spirit, Y^k schal talke togidere
with the bitternesse of my soule. Whether 12
Y am the^l see, ethir a whal, for thou hast^m
cumpassid me with prisoun^n ? If Y° seie^p, 13
My bed^q schal coumfort me, and Y schal

† *voide ;* that
is, not hauyng
the laste ende,
that is, blis.
Lire here. c.

q clothed *AEFH.*

t ȝoure 1s.   u eere or *hering* 1.   w *for to lystne the trewthe,* and s.   x biseche ȝou 1s.   y ȝe me 1s.
z ȝe *trewthe* s.   a not *thanne* s.   b tunge, *thou I decme my synne more thanne the veniaunce that I suffre* s.
c chekis, *thouȝ I couaite to be punyshid here, and sparid aftir* 1s.   d Knyȝthod, *that is, contynuel traueyle
and fyȝtinge aȝen vices* s.   e is the 1s.   f a man 1s.   g upon-1. *here on* s.   h man, *that bisely traueylith in
trewthe fro morewe til euen* s.   i Om. s.   k haue had 1s.   l haue noumbrid 1s.   m fulfillid 1s.   n vnto 1.
into s.   o derkuessis *come* 1s.   p with filthe 1s.   q and my 1s.   r it is 1s.   s han passid 1s.   t swifter 1.
u doun *fro the loomes* 1.   w Om. 1. of the webstere s.   x hope *of comyng aȝen* 1. hope *of aȝen cleping* s.
y Lord 1s.   z wynde, *that is, vnstable* 1s.   a goodis *of this lyf* s.   b Om. 1. but, *Lord* s.   c iȝen, *Lord* 1.
d me, *biholdynge me* s.   e abijde 1.   f passith *soone awey* 1s.   g into s.   h stie up 1. stie up *thennys* s.
l he schal 1s.   k and Y 1s.   l a 1.   m hast, *Lord* s.   n a prisoun 1s.   o Y schal 1s.   p seie *my feelynge* s.
q litil bed 1s.

14 spekende with me in my bed ; thou shalt
fere me bi sweuenys, and bi viscouns ;
thur3orrour thou shalt smyte me to gidere.
15 Wherfore my soule ches hangyng vp, and
16 my bones deth. I despeirede, now I shal
no mor liue ; spare to me, Lord, no thing
17 forsothe ben my da3es. What is a man,
for thou magnefiest hym ? or what thou
18 settis to a3en hym thin herte ? Thou
visitist hym the morutid, and feerli thou
19 prouest hym. Hou longe thou sparist
not to me, ne letist me, that I swolewe
20 my spotele ? I haue synned ; what shal
I don to thee, O ! kepere of men ? Whi
hast thou put me contrarie to thee, and
21 am maad to myself heuy ? Whi takist
thou not awei my synne, and⁴ whi dost
thou not awei my wickidnesse ? Lo !
nowe in pouder I slepe, and if erli thou
sche^r me, I shal not stonde stille.

CAP. VIII.

1   Answerende forsothe Baldach Suythes
2 seide, Hou longe shalt thou speke suche
thingus ? Ther is a manyfold spirit of the
3 woord of thi mouth. Whether God supplauntith dom, and the Almy3ti turneth
4 vpso doun, that is ri3twis ? Also if thi
sonys synneden to hym, and lafte them
5 in the hond of ther wickidnesse ; thou
nerthelatere³, if thou erli to gidere risist
to God, and the Almy3ti haddest pre3id,
6 if clene and ri3twis thou gost, anoon he
shal waken out to thee, and maad pesible
the dwelling place of thi ri3twisnesse he
7 shal 3elde ; in so myche that thi rather-
more weren litle, and thi laste thingis
8 shuln be multiplied ful myche. Forsothe
aske the rathermor ieneracioun, and bisili enserche the mynde of the faders.

be ʼreleeuyd^r, spekynge with me^s in my
bed^t ; thou schalt make me aferd bi dremys, 14
and thou^u schalt schake me with ʼorrour,
ethir^w hidousnesse, ʼbi si3tis^x. Wherfor† 15
my soule ʼchees hangyng^y, and my boonys
cheesiden^z deth. ʼY dispeiride^a, now Y schal 16
no more lyue ; Lord, spare‡ thou me, for^b
my daies ben nou3t. What is a man^c, for 17
thou ʼmagnefiest hym^d ? ether what settist
thou thin herte toward hym^e ? Thou^f 18
visitist hym eerly^g, and sudeynli thou
preuest hym. Hou long sparist thou not 19
me, nether suffrist^h me, that Y swolowe
my spotele ? Y haue synned ; A^i ! thou 20
kepere of men, what schal Y do to thee ?
Whi hast thou set me contrarie to thee,
and Y am maad greuouse to my silf ?
Whi doist thou not awei my sinne, and 21
whi takist thou not awei my wickidnesse ?
Lo ! now Y schal slepe in dust, and if
thou sekist me eerli, Y schal not abide^k.

CAP. VIII.

Sotheli^l Baldath Suytes answeride, and 1
seide^m, Hou longe schalt thou speke siche 2
thingis ? The spirit of the word of thi
mouth is manyfold. Whether God sup-3
plauntith^n, *ethir disseyueth^o,* doom, and
whether Almy3ti God districth that^p, that
is iust ? 3he^q, thou3 thi sones synneden 4
a3ens hym^r, and^s he lefte hem in the hond
of her wickidnesse ; netheles, if thou risist 5
eerli to God^t, and bisechist^u Almy3ti God^w,
if^x thou goist clene and ri3tful^y, anoon he 6
schal wake^z fulli to thee, and schal^a make
pesible the dwellyng place of thi ry3t-
fulnesse^b ; in so miche that thi formere 7
thingis weren litil, and that thi laste
thingis be multiplied greetli. For whic^c, axe 8
thou^d the^e formere generacioun^f, and seke
thou diligentli the mynde of fadris^g. For^h

⁴ Om. c.   ^r sechest *AEFH.*   ^s neuerthelater *AEFH.*

9 Forsothe wee ben as ʒistaiᵗ born, and wee han vnkunnyng; for as shadewe oure 10 daʒis ben vp on ertheᵘ. And thei shul teche thee, and speke to thee, and fro thin herte shul bringe forth spechis. 11 Whether a resshe may liuen withoute humour? or reeddi place growe with 12 oute water? Whanne ʒitᵛ it be in flour, and be it not taken with hond, beforn 13 alle erbis it waxeth drie. So the weies of alle men, that forʒeten God; and the hope 14 of an ipocrite shal pershe. To hym shal not plese his couwardise, and as the web 15 of attercoppis, his trost. He shal lene vp on his hous, and it shal not stonde; he shal vnder setten it, and it shal not 16 riseʷ. Moiste semeth the resshe, befor the sunne come; and in his springing 17 the buriownyng of it shal gon out. Vp on an hep of stones his rootis shul be maad thicke, and among the stonys it shal 18 dwelle. And if it pulle it vp fro his place, it shal denyen hym, and seyn, I 19 knewe not thee. This forsothe is the gladnesse of his weie, that eft fro the 20 erthe othere be buriouned. God shal not throwen aferr the symple, ne putten hond 21 to shrewis; to the time that thi mouth be fulfild with laʒhing, and thi lippis 22 with ioʒe. Thei that hateden thee shul be clad with confusioun; and the tabernacle of vnpitouse men shal not stonde stille.

CAP. IX.

1/2 Answerende Job seith, Verreli I wot, that so it is, and that a man comparisoun 3 to God shal not be iustified. If he wile striue with hym, he shal not moun answere to hym oon for a thousend. 4 Wisˣ in herte he is, and strong in strengthe; who withstodʸ to hym, and

we ben men of ʒistirdai¹, andᵏ 'kunnen notˡ; for oure daies ben as schadewe on the erthe. And theiᵐ schulen teche thee, 10 thei schulen speke to thee, and of herⁿ herte thei schulen bring forth spechis°†. 11 Whether a rusche may lyueᵖ with out moysture? cthir a spierq 'may wexeʳ with out watir? Whanneˢ itᵗ is ʒit in the flourᵘ, 12 nethir isʷ takunˣ with hond, it wexethʸ drie bifor alle erbis. Soᶻ the weies of alle 13 men, that forʒeten God; and the hope of an ypocrite schal perische. His cowardiseǂ 14 schal not plese hymᵃ, and his trist schal be as a web of yreynsᵇ. He schal leeneᶜ, 15 'ether resteᵈ, onᵉ his hows, and it schal not stonde; he schal vndursette it, and it schal not rise togidere. The rusche semeth 16 moist, bifor that the sunne comeᵍ; and iⁿ the risyng of the sunne the seed therof 17 schal go out. Rootisʰ therof schulen be maad thicke onˡ anᵏ heep of stoonys, and it schal dwelle among stoonys. If a man 18 drawith it out of 'his placeˡ, hisᵐ place schal denye it, and schalⁿ seie°, Y knowe 19 thee not. For this is the gladnesse of his weie, that eft othere ruschis springe out 20 of the erthe. Forsothe God schal not caste a wei a symple manſ, nethir schalᵖ dresse hondq to wickid men; til thi mouth be 21 fillidʳ with leiʒtir, and thi lippis with hertli song. Thei that haten thee schulen 22 be clothid with schenschip; and the tabernacle of wickid men schal not stonde°.

CAP. IX.

1/2 Joohᵗ answeride, and seide, Verili Y woot, that it is so‖, and that a man comparisound to God schal not be maad iust. 3 If he wole stryue with God, he may not answere to God oon¶ for a thousynde. 4 Heⁿ is wiys in herte, and strong in myʒt; who aʒenstoodʷ hym, and hadde pees?

+ spechis; here Baldath vndurstod, that hi dedis of fadris passid it schal not be foundun that ony weren punyschid, no but for her synnes passid, and thei that weren amendid throuʒ to temporal prosperite; but this is not soth generali. Lire here. c.

ǂ cowardise; Greg. seith here, no cowardise is gretere than for trauele strongly in Goddis heestie for mannus ʒelding; and sich cowardise displesith an ipocrite, whanne he fallith fro temporal good, ether fro mannus preising. Lire here. c.

§ God schal not caste away a simple man; enere this is soth in goostly goodis, that ben not takun fro iust men, but in temporal goodis it is not enere soth, for God with drawith temporal goodis fro many symple men and iust, and serueth to hem goostly goodis and euerlastinge. Lire here. c.

symple; that is, innocent man, that serueth God bi veri herte and not feyned. Lire here. c.

‖ so; that God dissineth not dom, and distrieth not a iust thing. Lire here. c.

¶ oon; that is, he mai seie no thing resonably aʒens Goddis doom. Lire here. c.

ᵗ ʒisterday ᴀɴ. ᵘ the erthe ᴀ. ᵛ Om. ᴀ. ʷ arijsen ᴀᴇꜰʜ. ˣ A wis ᴇ in ras. ʸ withstond ꜰ.

¹ ʒistirdai, that is, of late tyme s. ᵏ and therfor ɪ. Om. s. ˡ we vnknowen ɪ. Om. s. ᵐ thilke fadris ɪ. oolde fadris s. ⁿ Om. c. ° trewe spechis ɪs. ᵖ growe ɪs. q reed ɪs. ʳ Om. ɪs. ˢ And whanne ɪs. ᵗ the reed ɪs. ᵘ flour most quik s. ʷ it is ɪ. ˣ takun or neʒed s. ʸ wex s. ᶻ So ben s. ᵃ God ɪs. ᵇ spithers ɪ. nreyns, that soone faylith s. ᶜ leene him ɪs. ᵈ Om. ɪs. ᵉ upon ɪs. ꜰ rise up ɪs. ᵍ come theron ɪ. come ther vpon s. ʰ The rootis ɪs. ˡ npon ɪs. ᵏ the s. ˡ the place therof ɪs. ᵐ that ɪs. ⁿ it schal ɪ. ° seie in effect ɪs. ᵖ he schal ɪs. q his hond ɪs. ʳ fulfillid ɪs. ˢ stonde with hem s. ᵗ And Job ɪs. ᵘ The Lord ɪs. ʷ hath aʒenstonde ɪs.

5 pes hadde? That translatide hillis, and these wisten not; whom he turnede vpso 6 doun in his wodnesse. That stirith the erthe fro his place, and his pileris shul 7 be smyte togidere. That comaundith to the sunne, and springeth not; and closeth 8 the sterris, as vnder a sel. The whiche alone streccheth out heuenes, and goth 9 vp on the flodis of the se. That maketh the sterris, that is^z clepid Arthurus, and Orionas, and Iadas, and the innermor of 10 the south. That maketh grete thingus and vnserchable, and merueilouse thingus, 11 of whiche is no noumbre. If he come to me, I shal not seen hym; if he go awei, 12 I shal not vnderstonde. If feerli he aske, who shal answere to hym? or who may 13 sein to hym, Whi dost thou thus? God, to whos wrathe no man mai withstonde; vnder whom ben bowid, that bern the 14 world. Hou myche am I, that I answere to hym, and speke in my woordus with 15 hym? The whiche also, if I shul han any thing ri3t^a, shal not answern; but my 16 domys man I shal pre3en. And whan he hereth me inwardli clepende, I leue not, 17 that he shal here my vois. In a whirle-wiud forsothe he shal to-brose me, and multiplien my woundis also withoute 18 cause. He graunteth not my spirit to resten, and he fulfillith me with bitter-19 nessis. If strengthe is so3t, he is^b most strong^c; if euencnesse of dom, no man shal ben hardi for me to 3elde witnesse. 20 If I wile iustcfie me, my mouth shal condempne me; if innocent I shal shewe me, 21 a shrewe he shal proue me. Also iff symple I shul be, that same my soule shal vnknowe; and it shal no3e me of my 22 lif. O thing is, that I spac, also the innocent and the vnpitous he shal waste.

Which^x bar^y hillis^z fro o place to anothir, 5 and thei^a wisten not; whiche^b he^c driede in his strong veniaunce. Which stirith the 6 erthe fro his place, and the pilers therof schulen 'be schakun^d togidere. Which^e co-7 maundith to the sunne, and it risith not; and^f he closith the sterris, as vndur a sig-net. Which^g aloone stretchith forth he-8 uenes, and^h goith on^i the wawis of the see. Which^k makith Ariture†, and Ori-9 onas, and Hiadas, 'that is, seuene sterris^l, and the^m innere thingis of the south. Which^n makith grete thingis, and that 10 moun not be sou3t out, and^o wondurful thingis, of whiche is^p noon noumbre. If ^{q} 11 he cometh to me, 'that is, bi his grace^r, Y schal not se hym; if^s he goith awey^t, 'that is, in withdrawynge his grace^n, Y schal not vndurstonde. If he axith so-12 deynli^w, who schal answere to hym? ethir who may seie to hym, Whi doist thou so? 'God is he^x, whos wraththe no man may 13 withstonde; and vndur whom thei ben bowid, that beren the world. Hou greet^y 14 am Y^z, that Y answere to hym, and speke^a bi my wordis with hym? Which also schal 15 not answere^b, thou3 Y haue ony thing iust; but Y schal bisech my iuge^c. And whanne he hath herd me inwardli 16 clepynge^d, Y bileue not, that he hath herd my vois. For^e in a whirlewynd^f he schal 17 al to-breke me, and he schal multiplie my woundis, 3he, without cause. He graunt-18 ith not, that my spirit haue reste, and he fillith me with bittirnesses. If strengthe 19 is sou3t^g, 'he is^h moost strong; if^i equyte^k of doom is sou3t, no man dar 3elde wit-nessynge for me. If Y wole make me 20 iust‡, my^l mouth schal dampne me; if^m Y schal schewe me innocent^n, he schal preue me a schrewe. 3he, thou3 Y am^o 21

† *Ariture; is a gadering of sterris aboute the north.* Orion is a ga- dering of clere sterris, and the rising therof signefieth tem- pestis. *Lire here.* c.

‡ *me iust; bi my witnessing a3enus Goddis doom. Lire here.* c.

^{z} ben A. ^{a} of ri3t A. ^{b} Om. II. ^{c} Om. AII.

^{x} He IS. ^{y} it is that bar S. ^{z} ouer hillis IS. ^{a} men S. ^{b} whom I. which of hem S. ^{c} Om. A. ^{d} schake I. ^{e} He IS. ^{f} Om. IS. ^{g} He IS. ^{h} vnd he IS. ^{i} vpon IS. ^{k} He IS. ^{l} that is, the seuene sterris N. that ben ynner sterris, whiche sum men clepen the seuen sterris I marg. that is, innermore sterris, which summe men clepith the vii. sterris S. ^{m} Om. I. ^{n} He IS. ^{o} and also I. ^{p} ther is I. ^{q} If bi his grace S. ^{r} Om. IS. ^{s} and if bi withdrawyng his grace S. .^{t} fro me IS. ^{u} Om. IS. ^{w} sodeynli rekenyng S. ^{x} He is God IS. ^{y} greet thanne IS. ^{z} Y, seith Job S. ^{a} that I speke IS. ^{b} answere to him S. ^{c} iuge to spare me S. ^{d} clepynge him S. ^{e} Forsothe IS. ^{f} whirlewynd or sodeynli I. whirle-wynd, that is, sodeynly S. ^{g} sou3t than S. ^{h} is he S. ^{i} and if IS. ^{k} euenesse IS. ^{l} my owne IS. ^{m} and if IS. ^{n} an innocent IS. ^{o} be I.

23 If he scourgeth, sle he onys, and not of
24 the peynes of innocentis laȝhe. The erthe
is ȝiue in to the hondis of the vnpitous;
his dom couereth the chere; that if he is
25 not, who thanne is? My daȝis swiftere
weren than a corour; thei floun, and thei
26 seȝen no good. Thei passeden as shipis^d
berende appelis, as an egle fleende to
27 mete. Whan I shal sei, Nai, thus I shal
speke; I chaunge my face, and with
28 sorewe I am tormentid. I shamede alle
my werkis, witende that thou shuldist
29 not spare to the giltende. If forsothe and
so I am vnpitous, whi in vein haue I
30 trauailid? If I shul be wasshe as with
watris^e of snowȝ, and myn hondis as most
31 clene shyneden^f, nerthelatere^g with filthis
thou shalt weete me, and my clothis shul
32 wlaten me. Ne forsothe to the man that
is lic me, I shal answern; ne that with
33 me in dom euenli mai ben herd. Ther
is not, that either mai vndernyme, and
34 putten his hond in bothe. Do he awei
fro me his ȝerde, and his inward drede
35 fere me not. I shal speke, and I shal
not dreden hym; ne forsothe I mai
dredende answern.

CAP. X.

1 It noȝeth me of^h my lif; I shal leten
aȝen me my speche, I shal speke in bit-
2 ternesse to my soule. I^i shal sei to God,
Wile thou not me condempne; shew to
3 me, whi me so thou demest. Whether
good to thee it semeth, if thou chalenge
and opresse me, the werk of thin hondis;
and the counseil of vnpitous men thou

symple, my soule schal not knowe this
same thing; and it schal anoye me of my
lijf. O thing is, which Y spak^p†, he^q schal 22
waste `bi deth^r also^s the innocent and
wickid^t man. If^u he betith^w, sle he onys, 23
and leiȝe he not of the peynes of innocent
men. The erthe is ȝounn‡ in to the hondis 24
of the wickid^x; he^y hilith the face of
iugis^z; that if he^a is not, who therfor^b is?
Mi daies weren swiftere than a corour; 25
thei fledden^c, and sien not good^d. Thei 26
passiden^e as schippis^f berynge applis, as^g
an egle fleynge to mete. Whanne Y seie^h, 27
Y schal not speke so; Y chaunge my face,
and Y am turmentid with sorewe. Y drede 28
alle my werkis, witynge that thou `woldist
not spare^i the trespassour. Sotheli^k if Y 29
am also thus wickid§, whi haue Y trauelid
in veyn^l? Thouȝ Y am^m waischun as^n with 30
watris of snow, and thouȝ myn hondis^o
schynen^p as^q moost cleene^r, netheles thou 31
schalt dippe me in filthis^s, and my clothis,
`that is, werkis^t, schulen holde^u me abho-
mynable. Trewli Y schal not answere a 32
man, which^w is lijk^x me; nether that may
be herd euenli with me in doom. `Noon 33
is^y, that may repreue euer eithir, and sette
his hond in bothe. Do he awei his ȝerde 34
fro me, and his drede make not me aferd.
Y schal speke, and Y schal not drede hym; 35
for^z Y may not answere dredynge.

CAP. X.

Yt anoieth my soule of my lijf; Y schal 1
lete^a my speche aȝens me, Y schal speke
in the bitternesse of my soule. Y^b schal 2
seie to God, Nyle thou condempne me;
schewe thou to me^c, whi thou demest me
so. Whether it semeth good to thee, if 3
thou `falsli chalengist^d and oppressist me,
the werk of thin hondis; and^e if thou

† Y spak; that is, wole susteyne, that peynes in this lyif ben ȝouun of God, not onely for synne. Lire here. c.
‡ the erthe is ȝouun; if thou seist, that Satan is cause of wrongis doon to innocent men, for he hath power in erthe, and blyndith iugis bi iftis and fauour, that they ne not eqitie in condempnynge innocentis, this answere is nouȝt, for Satan may do no thing, no but he be suffrid of God; and therfor the peynes of innocentis moten be arettid to God, that if he, that is, Satan, is not the firste cause of the forseid peynes, who is, as if he seye, God suffrith. Lire here. c.
§ thus wickid; that Y disserueie so greet turment, whi haue Y trauelid in veyn; to kepe innocence so diligently. Lire here. c.

d the shipis c. e quyke watris E pr. v. f helpeden E pr. m. g neuerthelater AEFH. h Om. AFH.
i And I AHI.

p haue spoken IS. q the Lord IS. r Om. I. e Om. IS. t the wickid IS. u Also if IS. w betith or
punnishith S. x wickid man IS. y and it IS. z the iugis therof IS. a the Lord IS. b thanne IS.
c fledden awey I. d good thing IS. e passiden awey IS. f a ship S. g and as IS. h shal seie S.
i sparist not IS. k And IS. l veyn, gessynge me lesse yuel, than I knowe me now to be S. m schal be IS.
n Om. S. o hondis, that is, my werkis S. P schyne I. q Om. c. r cleene thing IS. s filthis, and
punnishe me as vnclene S. t Om. I. that is, my werkis S. u holde or schewe IS. w that IS. x lijk to S.
y Ther is noon I, z certis IS. a leue IS. b And I S. c me, Lord IS. d chalengist me as fals IS.
e as S.

4 helpe? Whether fleshly eʒen ben to thee,
or as seeth a mau, and thou shalt seen?
5 Whether as the daʒis of man, thi daʒes,
and thi ʒeris ben as mannys[k] tymes;
6 that thou seche my wickidnesse, and my
7 synne thou serche? And wite thou, for
no thing vnpitous I dide; sithen[l] ther is
no man, that of thin hond mai deliuere?
8 Thin hondis maden me, and formeden
me al in enuyroun; and so feerli thou
9 puttist me doun. Haue mynde, I beseche, that as clei thou madist me, and
in to pouder thou shalt aʒeen bringe me.
10 Whether not as mylc thou hast mylkid
me, and as chese thou hast crudded me?
11 With fel and flesh thou hast clad[m] me;
with bones and senewis thou hast togi-
12 dere ioyned me. Lif and mercy thou hast
ʒiue to me, and thi visiting kepte my
13 spirit. Al be it that these thingus thou
hidist in thin herte, nerthelatere[n] I wot, for
14 of alle thingus thou hast mynde. If I
synnede, and at an houre thou sparedest
to me; whi fro my wickidnesse thou suf-
15 frist not me to be clene? And if a wicke[nn]
man I shal be, wo is to me; and if riʒtwis, I shal not reren vp the hed, fulfild
16 with affliccioun and wrecchidnesse. And
for pride as a leounesse thou shalt take
me; and turned aʒeen, merueilously thou
17 tormentist me. Thou restorist thi witnessis aʒen me, and thou multipliest thi
wrathe aʒen me; and peynes fiʒten[o] in me.
18 Whi of the wombe thou broʒtist me out?
That wolde God I hadde be wastid, that
19 eʒe shulde not seen me. I hadde ben as
I were not, fro the wombe translatid to
20 the toumbe. Whether not the fewenesse
of my daʒis shal ben endid in short? Let
me thanne, that I weile a litil while my
21 sorewe, er I go, and turne not aʒeen, to

helpist the counsel of wickid men? Whe-4
thir fleischli iʒen ben to thee, ethir, as a
man seeth, also[f] ʻthou schalt[g] se? Whether 5
thi daies ben as the daies of man[h], and
ʻthi ʒeeris ben[i] as mannus tymes†; that thou 6
enquere my wickidnesse, and enserche my
synne? And[j] wite[k], that Y haue do no 7
ʻwickid thing[l]; sithen[m] no[n] man is[o], that
may delyuere fro thin hond? Thin hondis 8
han maad me, and han[p] formed me al in
cumpas; and thou castist[q] me doun so[r]
sodeynli. Y[s] preye[t], haue thou mynde, 9
that thou madist me as cley, and schalt[u]
brynge[w] me aʒen in to dust. Whether thou 10
hast not mylkid me as mylk, and hast[x]
cruddid me togidere as cheese? Thou 11
clothidist[y] me with skyn and fleisch[z];
thou[a] hast ioyned me togidere with boonys
and senewis. Thou hast ʒoue lijf and 12
mercy to me, and thi visiting hath kept
my spirit. Thouʒ[b] thou helist these 13
thingis in thin herte, netheles Y woot,
that thou hast mynde of alle thingis[c]. If[d] 14
Y dide synne, and[e] thou sparidist me at
an our; whi suffrist thou not me to be
cleene of my wickidnesse? And if[f] Y was 15
wickid, wo is to me‡; and if Y was iust,
Y fillid[g] with turment and[h] wretchiduesse
ʻschal not reise the heed[i]. And if Y reise[r] 16
ʻthe heed[j] for pride, thou schalt take
me as a lionesse; and thou turnest aʒen,
and turmentist me[k] wondirli[l]. Thou[m] ga- 17
derist in store thi[n] witnessis aʒens me, and
thou multipliest thin yre, ʻthat is, veniaunce[o], aʒens me; and peynes holden
knyʒthod[p]§ in me. Whi[q] hast thou led me 18
out of the wombe? ʻAnd Y wolde, that Y
were[r] wastid‖, lest[a] an iʒe ʻschulde set[i] me.
That Y hadde be, as if Y were not, and 19
ʻwere translatid, ethir borun ouer[u], fro the
wombe to the sepulcre. Whether[w] the 20

† as mannus tymes; God punyschith not an innocent man bi malice, as a tiraunt doth, nether bi vnkunnyng of truthe, as an erthely iuge doith. Lire here. c.

‡ wo is to me; that is, Y am and was in so greet tribula-cioun, that it ouʒte suffise to thee for peyne. Lire here. c.

§ holden knyʒt-hod; that is, holden me so suget, that in no maner Y may aʒenstonde. Lire here. c.

‖ that Y were wastid; here Joob preueth, that contradic-cioun sueth of the seiynge of hise aduersa-ries, for thei selden that mannus blis is in temporal prosperite; therof it sueth, that mannus liyf, solet to grete peynes, is hateful and hidouse, name-ly, whanne no releeoyng of peyne apperith, as it was of Joob; and they seiden also, that no thing of man dwellith aftir deth; ther-of it sueth, that deth puttith awey alle goodis outirly, and so it is most oritile; and therfor liyf, be it neuere so peyneful, owith to be coueitid skilefuly. Lire here. c.

---

[k] man A. many II.   [l] sin c.   [m] clothed AEFH.   [n] neuerthelater passim AEFH.   [na] wickid AEFH.
[o] enhaunten knyʒthod E pr. m.

[f] Om. s.   [g] schalt thou is.   [h] a man s.   [i] ben thi ʒeeris is.   [j] And, Lord i. And thou, Lord s.   [k] that
thou wite i.   [l] wickidnesse, ʒildinge me to thee s.   [m] sith is.   [n] ther is no i.   [o] Om. i.   [p] thei han is.
[q] hast cast is.   [r] Om. is.   [s] Lord, Y is.   [t] preye thee is.   [u] thou schalt is.   [w] lede is.   [x] thou hast is.
[y] hast clothid is.   [z] with fleisch s.   [a] and thou is.   [b] And thouʒ s.   [c] these thingis s.   [d] And if
whanne is.   [e] Om. is.   [f] Om. c. for s.   [g] schal not reise vp myn heed [to thee s], that am fulfillid is.
[h] and with i.   [i] Om. i.   [j] it i. vp myn heed s.   [k] me wilfulli s.   [l] wondirfully is.   [m] For thou L.
[n] the A.   [o] Om. is.   [p] the knyʒthod i.   [q] Lord, whi is.   [r] Whi ne had I erst ben is.   [s] that is.
[t] had not seen is.   [u] had ben ouer born is.   [w] Whether not is.

the derke erthe, and couered with the
dercnesse of deth the erthc of wrecchid-
22 nesse and of derenessis; wher shadewe
of deth^p, and noon ordcr, but fulli in-
dwellith euere durende orrour.

fewnesse of my daies schal not^x be endid
in schort^y? Therfor^z suffre thou me, that
Y biweile 'a litil^a my sorewe, bifor^b that 21
Y go, and turne not a3en, to^c the derk
lond, and hilid with the^d derknesse^e of
deth, to the lond of wrecchidnesse and of
derknessis; where *is* schadewe of deeth, 22
and noon ordre, but euerlastynge hidousnesse dwellith^f.

CAP. XI.

1 Answerende forsothe Sofar Naama-
2 tithes seide, Whether he, that manye
thingus spekith, whether and he shal
heren? or a man ful of woordis shal be
3 iustefied? To thee alone men shul holde
ther pes? and whan other men thou
scornest, of no man thou shalt be con-
4 foundid? Thou forsothe seidist, Pure is
my woord, and clene I am in thi si3te.
5 And wolde God, God shulde speke with
6 thee, and openen his lippis to thee; that
he shulde shewe to thee the priuytes of
wisdam, and that manyfold is his lawe,
and thou shuldest vnderstonde, that manye
lasse thingus thou art askid of hym, than
7 deserueth thi wickidnesse. Perauenture
the steppis of God thou shalt holde, and
vnto perfit the Almy3ti thou shalt finde.
8 Hei3ere than heuene he is, and what
shalt thou do? deppere than helle, and
9 whennys shalt thou knowen? Lengere
than the erthe the mesure of hym, and
10 braddere than the se. If he turne vpso
doun alle thingus, or in to oon drawe
togidere, who shal a3ensein to hym? Or
who shal moun sey to hym, Whi dost
11 thou so? He forsothe knew3 the vanyte
of men; and seande wickidnesse whether
12 he beholde not? A veyn man in to pride
is rerid; and as a colt of an asse, he
13 weeneth hymself born free. Thou forsothe hast fastned thin herte, and hast
14 sprad out to hym thin hondis. If the

CAP. XI.

Forsothe^g Sophar Naamathites answer- 1
ide, and seide^h, Whether he, that spekith 2
many thingis, schal not also here? ether
whethirⁱ a man ful of wordis schal be
maad iust? Schulen men be stille to thee 3
aloone? whanne^k thou hast scorned othere
men, schalt thou not be ouercomun of ony
man†? For^l thou seidist, My word is 4
cleene, and Y am cleene in thi si3t. And 5
'Y wolde, that God spak^m with thee, and
openyde hise lippis to thee; to scheweⁿ 6
to thee the priuetees of wisdom, and that
his lawe is manyfold, and thou schuldist^o
vndurstonde, that thou art requirid of
hym^p *to paie* myche lesse thingis, than
thi wickidnesse disserueth. In hap thou 7
schalt comprehende^q the steppis of God,
and thou schalt fynde Almy3ti God 'til to^r
perfeccioun. He is hi3ere than heuene, and 8
what schalt thou do? he is deppere than
helle, and wherof schalt thou knowe? His 9
mesure *is* lengere than erthe^s, and brodere
than the see. If he distrieth alle thingis, 10
ethir dryueth^t streitli 'in to^u oon, who schal
a3enseie hym? Ethir who may seie to
hym, Whi doest thou so? For^w he know- 11
ith the vanyte of men; and^x whether he
seynge byholdith not wickidnesse§? A veyn 12
man is reisid in to pride; and^y gessith hym
silf borun fre, as the colt of a wilde asse.
But^z thou hast maad stidefast thin herte‖, 13
and hast^a spred abroad thin hondis to
hym^b. If thou doest awei 'fro thee^c the 14

† *of ony man;*
as if he seye,
3is, certis Y
schal schewe
thi foly. *Lire*
here. c.

‡ *comprehende*
the steppis;
Sophar seith
this bi deny-
ing. *Lire*
here. c.

§ *biholdeth not*
wickidnesse;
in punyschinge
it, as if he seye,
3is. *Lire here.*
c.

‖ *stidefast thyn*
herte; in con-
tynuynge in
malice, and in
defendinge it.

spred abrood;
in veyn, for thi
malice lettith
the preyer.
Lire here. c.

x Om. 18.   y schort *tyme* 18.   z Therfor, *Lord* s.   a Om. s.   b or s.   c into s.   d Om. EILPS.   e derknessis NOV.   f *there* dwellinge 1. dwellynge s.   g Thanne 18.   h seide *to Job* s.   i Om. s.   k and
whanne 18.   l Forsothe 18.   m whi ne hadde God spoke 18.   n haue schewid 18.   o schuldist *thanne* 18.
P God 18.   q comprehende *or take* 18.   r vnto 1. into s.   s the erthe s.   t dryueth *hem* 18.   u til to s.
w Certis 18.   x Om. c.   y and he 18.   z But, *Job* s.   a thou hast 18.   b the Lord 18.   c Om. s.

wickidnesse, that is in thin hond, thou
takest awei fro thee, and vnriȝtwisnesse
15 abideth not stille in thi tabernacle, thanne
thou shalt moun rere thi face with oute
wem, and thou shalt be stable, and not
16 dreden. Of wrecchenesse⁹ also thou shalt
forȝete, and, as of watris that passeden,
17 thou shalt not recorde. And as myddai
liȝting it shal rise to thee at euen; and
whan thee wastid thou wenest, thou shalt
18 springe as the dai sterre. And thou shalt
han trost, purposid to thee^r hope; and
19 doun dolue, siker thou shalt slepe. Thou
shalt reste, and ther shal not be that
fere^s thee; and manye shul preȝe thi
20 face. The eȝen forsothe of vnpitous men
shul faile; and out fliȝt shal pershe fro
hem, and the hope of hem abhomyna-
cioun^t of soule.

CAP. XII.

1/2 Answerende forsothe Job seide, Thanne
ȝee ben men alone, that with ȝou dwelle
3 wisdam? And to me is an herte, as and
to ȝou, ne lowere I am than ȝee; who
forsothe these thingis, that ȝee knowen,
4 vnknoweth? Who is scorned of his frend,
as I, inwardli shal clepe God, and he shal
heren hym; forsothe the symplenesse of
5 the riȝtwise is scorned. A^n laumpe despisid anent the thoȝtis of riche men,
6 maad redi to the ordeyned time. The
tabernaclis of reueres abounden; and
hardili thei terren God, whan he ȝiueth
7 alle thingus in to the hondis of hem. No
wunder, aske the bestis, and thei shul
teche thee; and the foulis of heuene, and
8 thei shul shewc to thee. Spec to the
erthe, and it shal answer to thee; and
the fisshis of the se shul telle tho thingis.
9 Who vnknoweth, that alle these thingis
10 the hond of the Lord made? In whos
hond the soule of alle lyuynge, and the

wickidnesse, which^d is in thin hond, and^e
vnriȝtfulnesse^f dwellith not in thi tabernacle, thanne thou schalt mowe^g reise^h 15
thi face with out wem^i, and thou schalt
be stidefast, and thou schalt not drede.
And thou schalt forȝete wretchidnesse, and 16
thou schalt not thenke of^k it, as^l of watris
that han passid. And^m as myddai schyn- 17
ynge it^n schal reise^o to thee at^p euentid;
and whanne thou gessist thee wastid, thou
schalt rise vp as the dai sterre. And thou 18
schalt haue trist, while hope schal be set
forth to thee; and thou biried schalt slepe
sikurli. Thou schalt reste, and 'noon 19
schal be⁹ that schal make thee aferd;
and ful many men schulen bische thi
face. But the iȝen of wickid men schulen 20
faile; and socour schal perische fro hem,
and the hope of hem schal be abhomina-
cyioun of soule.

CAP. XII.

1/2 Sotheli Joob answeride, and seide; Ther-
for^r ben ȝe^s men aloone, that^t wisdom
dwelle with ȝou? And to me is an herte^t, 3
as and to ȝou, and Y am not lowcre than
ȝe^u; for who knowith not these thingis,
whiche ȝe knowen? He that is scorned 4
of his·frend, as Y am, schal inwardli clepe
God, and God schal here hym; for^w the
symplenesse of a iust man is scorned‡.
A^x laumpe is dispisid at the thouȝtis of 5
riche men, and^y the^z laumpe is maad redi
to a tyme ordeyned. The tabernaclis of 6
robberis ben plenteuouse, 'ether ful of
goodis^a; and boldli thei terren God to
wraththe, whanne he hath ȝoue alle thingis
in to her^b hondis. No wondur, ax thou 7
beestis§, and tho^c schulen teche thee; and
axe thou volatilis^d of the eir, and tho^e
schulen schewe to thee. Speke thou^f to 8
the erthe, and it schal answere^g thee; and
the fischis of the see schulen telle tho
thingis. Who knowith not that the hond 9

† And to me is an herte; that is, vndurstonding. Lire here. c.

‡ for the symplenesse etc.; that is, the liyf of hem that ben with out wryn[e]le of gile, is scornyd of worldly men, that setten her ende in temporal goodis, that ben getun ofte with fraudis and leesingis, therfor thei aretten iust men that ſleen siche goodis, foolis and vnkunnynge; at siche riche men the liyf of iust men is dispisid, thouȝ it be a a laumpe, that conteyneth liȝt of wisdom and brennynge of charite, maad redi to the blis of liyf to cumynge; bi the merit of liyf. Lire here. c.

§ A gloos. to axe creaturis, is to biholde the kyndis of tho, and the answer of creaturis is in this, that bi sich biholding a man rysith to the knowing of God, which is the firste cause of alle thingis. Lire here. c et plures.

---

⁹ wretchidnes AH. ^r thin AH. ^s afere AEFH. ^t the abomynacioun A. ^u And n AH.

d that 18. e and if 18. f vnriȝtwisnesse 1. g Om. 18. h reise up 18. i wem to the Lord s. k on 18.
l no more than 18. m Om. 8. n grace 1. Goddis grace 8. o rise up 1s. P at the 8. q ther schal be noon 1. ^r And ȝe therfor 1s. s Om. 18. t and 18. u be ȝe 8. w forsothe 18. x And a 18.
y Om. 18. z the whiche 18. a Om. 18. b his 8. c thei 18. d briddis 18. e thei 1. f Om. 1.
g answere to 8.

11 spirit of alle flesh of man. Whether not the ere demeth woordis, and the chekis 12 of the etere sauour? In olde men is wis- 13 dam, and in myche time prudence. Anent hym is wisdam and strengthe; he hath 14 destroʒe, no man is that bilde vp; if he in- 15 close a man, no man is that opene. If he holde togidere watris, alle thingus shul be maad drie; if he out sende them, thei shul 16 tnrne vpsodoun the erthe. Anent hym is strengthe and wisdam; he knew and[v] the begilere and hym that is begilid. 17 And he bringeth[w] forth the counseileris in to a fool ende, and domesmen in to 18 stoncing. The girdil of kingus he looside, and girte[x] with a corde the reenes of hem. 19 He bringeth[y] the prestis of hem vnglori- ous, and the beste men of wrshipe he 20 supplauntith; chaungende the lippe of trewe men, and the teching of olde men 21 doende awei. He heeldeth out despising[z] vp on princis, and hem, that weren opres- 22 sid, releueth. That sheweth[a] vp depe thingis fro dercnessis; and bringeth forth 23 in to liʒt the shadewe of deth. That mul- teplieth Jentilis, and leesith hem, and turned vpso doun in to the[b] hoole re- 24 storeth. That withinne chaungeth the herte of the prince of the puple of the erthe; and desceyueth hem, that in vein 25 thei go bi withoute weie. Thei shul graspen[c], as in dercnessis, and not in liʒt; and he shal make them to erren as drunken.

CAP. XIII.

1 Lo! alle thingus saʒ myn eʒe, and myn ere herde; and I vnderstod alle thingus. 2 Aftyr ʒoure kunnyng and I knewʒ, ne the

of the Lord made alle these thingis? In whos hond the soule is of ech lyuynge thing, and the spirit, 'that is, resonable soule[h], of ech fleisch of man. Whether 11 the eere demeth not wordis[i], and the chekis of the etere demen sauour[k]? Wisdom is 12 in elde men, and prudence is in myche tyme. Wisdom and strengthe is at God; 13 he[l] hath counsel and vndurstondyng. If 14 he districth, no[m] man is[n] that bildith; if[o] he schittith[p] in a man, 'noon is[q] that openith. If he holdith togidcre watris†, alle 15 thingis schulen be maad drie; if[r] he send- ith out tho watris, tho[s] schulen distrie the erthe. Strengthe and wisdom is at[t] God; 16 he knowith bothe hym that disseyueth and hym that is disseyued. And he bryng- 17 ith conseiours[u] in[w] to a fonned eende, and iugis in to wondryng, *ethir astonying*[x]. He vnbindith the girdil of kyngis‡, and[y] 18 girdith her reynes with a coorde. He 19 ledith her prestis with out glorie, and he disseyueth the principal men, '*ethir coun- selours*[x]; and he chaungith the lippis of 20 sothefast men§, and[a] takith awei the doc- trine of elde men. He schedith out dis- 21 pisyng on[b] princes, and[c] releeueth hem, that weren[d] oppressid. Which[e] schewith 22 depe thingis fro derknessis; and[f] bryngith forth in to liʒt the schadewe of deth‖. Which[g] multiplieth folkis, and[h] leesith 23 hem, and[i] restorith hem destried[k] in to the[l] hool[m]. Which[n] chaungith the herte 24 of princes of the puple of erthe; and[o] dis- seyueth hem¶, that thei go in veyn out of the weie[p]. Thei schulen grope, as in derk- 25 nessis, and not in liʒt; and he[q] schal make hem to erre as drunken men.

CAP. XIII.

Lo! myn iʒe siʒ[r] alle thingis, and myn 1 eere herde[s]; and Y vndurstood[t] alle thingis. Euene[u] with ʒoure kunnyng also[w] Y kan, 2

† *If he holdith togidere watris; so that reyn come not doun fro heuene. Lire here. c.*
‡ *He vnbyndith the girdil of kingis; that is, the myʒt of her chyualri and oost, whanne comian asous mennis herte. Lire here. c.*
§ *chaungith the lippe of sothfast men; that is, of hem that ben wont to speke truthis, as ben filoso- foris, fro whiche the liʒt of veri knaw- ing is with- drawun and tyme for her pride, and so they speken false thingis. and takith. awege, etc. in makinge hem foolis whanne he withdrawith his grace, and lutith hem tyne vnprofitable conncel ethir noyful, not that God sendith ony fals thing in to her vn- durstondingis, but for he withdrawith his liʒtnyng fro her tynne, and so they fallen fro tcuthe to her owne defaute. Lire here. c.*
‖ *the schadewe of deth; that is, men dwell- inge as in scha- dewe of deth, as ben men pri- amed, that dreden ech day to be slayn. Lire here. c.*
¶ *disseyueth hem; in wrap- pinge hem in her felnesis, and so they ʒyuen vnprofit- able ethir noyful counncol in the stide of good counnel; not that disseit is*

v bothe *A.* w broʒte E *pr. m.* x girdede *AEFH.* y broʒte E *pr. m.* z preyere E *pr. m.*
a arereth E *pr. m.* b Om. *A.* c grape *A.* gropen *H.*

h Om. 1. i the wordis s. k sauour *or the taast of mete* s. l and he 1s. m ther is no 1. n Om. 1. o and if 1s. p closith 1s. q ther is noon 1. r and if 1s. s thei 1. t anentis 1. u yuele counselours 1s. w Om. s. x Om. 1. y and he 1s. z Om. 1s. a and he 1s. b upon 1, of s. c and he 1s. d is wrong- fully s. e He 1s. f and he 1s. g He 1s. h and he 1s. i and he 1s. k whanne thei ben destried 1s. l Om. 1s. m hool *noumbre* 1s. n He 1s. o and he 1s. p riʒle weie s. q the Lord 1s. r iʒe, *seith Job* 1s. s hath seen 1s. t hath herd 1s. u Also euene 1s. w Om. 1s.

3 nethere of ȝou I am. But nerthelater
to the Almyȝty I shal speke, and to dis-
4 pute with God I coueite; rathere shewende ȝou forgeris of lesingus, and herieris
5 of shreude techingis. And wolde God,
ȝee heelde ȝoure pes, that ȝee weren
6 weened wise men to ben. Hereth thanne
my correcciouns; and to the dom of my
7 lippis taketh heede to. Whether God
nedeth ȝoure lesing, that for hym ȝee
8 speke treccheries? Whether his face ȝee
taken, and for God ȝee enforcen to deme?
9 Or^d it shal plese to hym, whom hide no
thing mai? Or he shal be desceiued, as
10 a man, with oure gilis? He ȝou shal vndernyme; for in hydelis his face ȝee take.
11 Anoon as he stereth hymself, he shal dis-
turbe^e ȝou; and his drede shal falle^f vp on
12 ȝou. Ȝoure mynde shal be comparisound
to askis; and ȝoure nollis shul be broȝt
13 aȝeen in to clei. Beth stille a litil while,
that I speke, what euere thing to me the
14 mynde moue to^g. Whi to-tere I my flesh
with my teth, and my soule I bere in
15 myn hondis? Also if he sle me, in hym
I shal hope; nerthelatere^h my weies in
16 his siȝte I shal vndernyme. And he shal
be my sauyoure; forsothe ther shal not
17 come in his siȝt eche ipocrite. Hereth
my woord, and the derke speches par-
18 ceyneth with ȝoure eris. If I shul be
demed, I wot that riȝtwis I shal be
19 founde. Who is he that be demed with
me? Come he; whi beende stille I am
20 wastid? Two thingus onli ne do thou to
me; and thanne fro thi face I shal not
21 ben hid. Thin hond fer do fro me; and
22 thi ferd gaste not me. Clep me, and I
shal answeren to thee; or certis I shal
23 speke, and thou answere^i to me. Hou
fele haue I wickidnessis and synnes? Myn
hidous trespasis and giltis sheu to me.
24 Whi thi face thou hidist, and demest me

and Y am not lowere than ȝe. But ne-3
theles Y schal speke to Almyȝti God, and
Y coueite to dispute with God^x†; and 4
firste Y schewe ȝou makeris of leesyng,
and louyeris^y of weyward techyngis. And 5
'Y wolde that ȝe weren^z stille, that ȝe
weren gessid to be wise men. Therfor 6
here ȝe my chastisyngis; and perseyue ȝe
the doom of my lippis. Whether God 7
hath nede to ȝoure leesyng^rz, that ȝe speke
gilis^a for hym? Whether ȝe taken his 8
face, and enforsen^b to deme for God? Ethir 9
it^c schal plese hym, fro whom no thing
mai be hid? Whether he as a man schal
be disseyued with^e ȝoure falsnessis? He 10
schal repreue ȝou; for ȝe taken his face in
hiddlis‡. Anoon as he schal stire^f hym, 11
he schal disturble ȝou; and his drede schal
falle on^g ȝou. Ȝoure mynde schal be com-12
parisound to aische; and ȝoure nollis
schulen be dryuun^h in to clei. Be ȝe stille 13
a litil, that Y speke, what euer thing the^i
mynde hath schewid to me. Whi to-rende 14
Y my fleischis^k with my teeth, and bere
my lijf in myn hondis? Ȝhe, thouȝ God 15
sleeth^l me, Y schal hope in hym; netheles
Y schal preue my weies in his siȝt. And 16
he schal be my sauyour; for whi ech
ypocrite schal not come in his siȝt. Here 17
ȝe my word, and perseyue ȝe with eeris
derke and harde figuratif^m spechis. Yf 18
Y schal be demed§, Y woot that^n Y schal
be foundun iust. Who is he that is demed 19
with me? Come he; whi am Y stille, and
am wastid? Do^o thou not to me twei 20
thingis oneli; and thanne Y schal not be
hid fro thi face. Make thin hond fer fro 21
me; and thi drede make^p not me aferd.
Clepe thou me, and Y schal answere thee; 22
ethir certis Y schal speke, and thou schalt
answere me^q. Hou grete synnes and wick-23
idnessis^r haue Y? Schewe thou to me my
felonyes^s, and^t trespassis. Whi hidist thou 24

Marginal notes:

sent of God euenly, but for by his iust doom he with-drawith his liȝt, and so a man fallith in to dissait. *Lire here. c.*

+ *dispute with God;* not folily repreuynge his dedis, but enqueringe mekely the truthe. *Lire here. c.*

‡ *for ȝe taken his face in hiddlis;* he takith in doom the face of a man in hiddlis, that spekith aȝenus conscience for that man; so diden these men, for they knewen his hooly liyf and innocence, and netheles they dampneden him, as to appreue Goddis riȝtfulnesse. *Lire here. c.* that is, spoken of him aȝenus conscience. v.

§ *if Y schal be demed;* that is, if doom be ȝouun of the sentence which Y susteyne as trewe, Y woot that it schal be appreued as trewe, as God seith in the ende of Joob. *Lire here. c.*

d Outher *AEFH.* e disturble *A.* f falle in *A.* g Om. *A.* h neuerthelatere *AEF et H ȝ assim.* i shalt answere *E pr. m.*

x God *my feelynge* s. y fautours is. z whi ne were ȝe is. rz leesyngis s. a gilful thingis is. b enforsen ȝou is. c whethir ȝoure gile s. e bi s. f moue is. g upon is. h driuen doun is. l my is. k fleishe is. l slee s. m priuey is. n Om. is. o Lord, do is. p make it is. q to me s. r wickidnesse s. s grete giltis is. t and my is.

25 thin enemy? Aȝen a lef, that is raueschid with the wind, thou shewist thi myȝt; 26 and drie stobil thou pursuest. Forsothe thou writist aȝen me bitternessis[k]; and waste me thou wilt with synnes of my 27 waxende ȝouthe. Thou hast[l] putte in the stoc my foot, and thou hast waitid alle my pathis; and the steppis of my 28 feet[m] thou hast beholde. The whiche as rotenesse am to be wastid, and as cloth-1 ing that is eten of a mowȝhe. A man born of a womman, short time liuende, is fulfild with many wrecchidnessis. 2 That as a flour goth out, and is to-treden; and fleth as shadewe, and ne-3 uere in the same state abit[n] stille. And wrthi thou bringist vpon such a man to opene thin eȝen; and to bringe hym with 4 thee in to dom? Who mai make clene the conceyued of vnclene sed? Whether not thou, that art alone?

CAP. XIV.

5 Shorte ben the daȝis of man, the noumbre of his monethis is anent thee; thou hast ordeyned his termes, that shul 6 not moun be passid ouer. Go awei thanne a litil fro hym, that he reste; to the time that the desirid dai come, and 7 as of an hirid man the dai of hym. A tree hath hope, if it be kut of; eft it wax-eth grene, and his braunchis springen. 8 If his roote waxe old in the erthe, and 9 in[o] pouder were out dead; his stoc at the smel of water shal burioune[p], and shal make an hep of leues, as whan first 10 it is plauntid. A man forsothe whan he shal be dead, and nakid, and wastid; 11 wher, I beseche, is he? What maner if watris gon awei fro the se, and flod voided 12 waxe drie, so a man, whan he slepeth, shal not rise, to the time that he be to-

thi face, and demest me thin enemy? Thou 25 schewist thi myȝt aȝens a leef, which[tt] is rauyschid[u] with the wynd; and thou pursuest drye stobil. For[w] thou writist bitter-26 nessis aȝens me; and[x] wolt[y] waste me with the[z] synnes of my ȝong wexynge age. Thou hast set my foot in[zz] a stok*, and 27 thou hast kept[a] alle my pathis; and thou hast biholde the steppis of my feet. And 28 Y schal be wastid as rot, and as a cloth, which[b] is etun of[c] a mouȝte.

CAP. XIV.

A man is[d] borun of a womman, and 1 lyueth[e] schort tyme, and[f] is[g] fillid[h] with many wretchidnessis. Which[i] goith out, 2 and is defoulid as a flour; and fleeth[k] as schadewe[l], and dwellith[m] neuere† perfitli in the same staat. And gessist thou it[n] 3 worthi[o] to opene thin iȝen on[p] siche a man; and to brynge hym in to doom with thee? Who may make a man clene[o] con-4 seyued of vnclene seed? Whether not thou[q], which[r] art aloone? The daies of man[s] ben 5 schorte, the[t] noumbre of his monethis is[u] at[w] thee; thou hast set‡, ethir ordeyned, hise termes, whiche[x] moun not be passid. Therfor go[y] thou awey fro hym a litil, 6 'that is, bi withdrawyng of bodili liif[z], that he haue reste; til the[a] meede coueitid come, and his dai is as the dai of an hirid man. A tree hath hope, if it is kit 7 doun; and eft it wexith greene, and hise braunches spreden forth. If the roote 8 therof is celd in the erthe, and the stok therof is[b] nyȝ deed in dust; it schal 9 buriowne at the odour[c] of watir, and it schal make heer[d]§, as whanne it was plauntid first. But whanne a man is 10 deed, and maad nakid, and wastid; Y preye[e], where[f] is he[g]? As if watris goen 11 awei fro the see, and a[h] ryuer maad

---

27 * that is, lawe of Goddis riȝtfulnesse. v.

† and dwellith neuere, etc.; not that a man is euere in chaungiȝg, as Eraclitus selde, but for he is not longe in the same disposicioun, nether bi bodil nether bi soule. Lire here. c.

‡ hast set; as this settyng is in Goddis ordenaunce, so the termes of mannus lyf moun not be passid bi schert-ing nether bi dilaying; set-tyng of mannus lyf also is in kyndly causis, sum schortere, sum lengere, bi dyuersite of complexioun, and bi this manere the terme of mannus lyf may be schortid, bi yuel gouer-nayle, and bi swerd and othere cause. Lire here. c.

§ heer; that is, leeuos and braunchis. Lire here. c.

---

[k] bittirnesse H.   [l] shalt c.   [m] foot E pr. m.   [n] abideth AEFH.   [o] in to A.   [p] out burioune c.

[tt] that I.   [u] rauyschid awey I.   [w] And IS.   [x] and thou IS.   [y] wilt I.   [z] Om. c.   [zz] Om. N.
[a] awaitid IS.   [b] the which I. that s.   [c] with cHV.   [d] Om. I.   [e] lyuynge I.   [f] Om. I.   [g] he is s.
[h] fulfillid IS.   [i] And he IS.   [k] he fleeth awey IS.   [l] a schadewe IS.   [m] he dwellith IS.   [n] Om. I.
[o] worthi thing I.   [p] vpon s.   [q] thou, Lord IS.   [r] that IS.   [s] a man s.   [t] and the IS.   [u] beth s.
[w] anentis IS.   [x] the whiche I.   [y] departe IS.   [z] Om. IV.   [a] his IS.   [b] Om. c.   [c] taast IS.   [d] heer or
smal roote I. heer or take roote s.   [e] preye thee IS.   [f] what IS.   [g] he thanne IS.   [h] as a IS.

treden ; heuene shal not wake⁹ out, ne he
13 shal rise fro his slep. Who ȝeue to me
that, that in helle thou defende me, and
hide me, to the time thi wodnesse ouerpasse ; and sette to me a time, in whiche
14 thou recorde of me? Whether weenest
thou not a dead man eft liue? Alle the
daȝis, in whiche now I fiȝte, I abide, to
the time myn inward chaunging come.
15 Thou shalt clepe me, and I shal answere
toʳ thee ; to the werc of thin hondis thou
16 shalt putte forth the riȝt hond. Thou
forsothe hast noumbrid my goingis ; but
17 spare to my synnes. Thou hast selid as
inˢ a litil sac my giltis, but thou hast
18 kurid my wickidnesse. A fallende hil
flowith doun, and a ston is born ouer
19 fro his place. Watris therlenᵗ out stones,
and of smyting of watris the erthe litle
mele is wastid ; thanne men lic maner
20 thou shalt leese. Thou hast strengthid
hym a litil, that in to euermor he shulde
21 passe ; thou shalt inchaungen his face,
and thou shalt senden hym out. If forsothe noble shul ben his sonys, orᵘ vn-
22 noble, he shal not vnderstonde. Nerthelatere his flesh whil it liueth, shal
sorewen, and his soule vp on himself shal
weilen.

voideⁱ wexe drie, so a man, whanne he 12
hath sleptᵏ, 'that is, deedˡ, he schal not
rise aȝen†, til heuene be brokun, 'that is,
beᵐ maad newe ; he schal not wake,
nether he schal ryse togidere fro his sleep.
Who ȝiueth thisⁿ to me, that thou de- 13
fende me in helle, and that thou hide me,
til thiᵒ greet veniaunce passe ; andᵖ thou
sette to me a tyme, in which thou haue
mynde onⁱ me ? Gessist thou, whethir a 14
deed man schal lyue aȝen ? Inʳ alle theˢ
daies, in whiche Y holde knyȝthod, nowᵗ Y
abide, til my chaungyng come‡. Thou 15
schalt clepe me, and Y schal answere thee ;
thou schalt dresse the riȝt half, 'that is,
blisᵘ, to theʷ werk of thin hondis. Sotheli 16
thou hast noumbrid my steppis ; butˣ
spare thou my synnes. Thou hast seelid 17
as inʸ a bagge my trespassis, but thou
hast curid my wickidnesse. An hil fall- 18
ynge droppith doun, and a rooche of stoon
is borun ouer fro his place. Watris 19
maken stoonys holowe, and the erthe is
wastid litil and litil bi waischyng awey of
watir ; and therforᶻ thou schalt leese men§
in lijk maner. Thou madist a man strong 20
a litil, that he schulde passe with outen
ende ; thou schalt chaunge his face, andᵃ
schalt sende hym outᵇ. Whether hise 21
sones ben noble, ether vnnoble, he schal
not vndurstonde. Netheles his fleisch, 22
while he lyueth, schal haue sorewe, and
his soule schal morne onᶜ hym silf.

(margin, right column)
† he schal not rise aȝen; that is, bi kyndly manere to this dedly lyf, but bi Goddis word he schal rise aȝen to lyf vndedly. Lire here. C.

‡ til my chaungynge come; that is, rising aȝen to the condicioun of goode men, that schulen haue blis. Lire here. C.

§ leese men etc.; that is, fro mennus mynde aftir her deth, sichen they ben lesse stable. Lire here. C.

CAP. XV.

1 Answerende forsothe Elifath Theman-
2 ythes seide; Whether a wis man shal
answere, as spekende in to wind, and he
shal fulfille with brennyng his stomac ?
3 Thou vndernemyst hym with woordis,
that is not euene to thee, and thou
4 spekist, that spedeth not to thee. As
myche as in thee is, thou hast voididᵛ
drede ; and taken awei preȝeeris befor

CAP. XV.

Forsotheᵈ Eliphat Themanytes answer- 1
ide, and seideᵉ, Whether a wise man schal 2
answere, as spekynge aȝens the wynd,
andᶠ schal fille his stomac with brennyngᵍ,
'that is, ire ? Forʰ thou repreuest hym bi 3
wordis, which is not lijk thee, and thou
spekist thatⁱ, that spedith not to thee. As 4
myche as is in thee, thou hast avoidid
drede ; and thou hast take awey preyerisᵏ

---

q waken him ᴢ super ras.   r Om. c.   s Om. ᴀᴠᴴ.   t thrillen ᴀᴴ.   u outher ᴇꜰᴴ.   v auoided ᴇꜰᴴ.

i voide of watris 1s.   k slept bi deth 1s.   l Om. ʙɪs.   m or 1s. ether v.   n this thing s.   o the s.   p and
that 1s.   q of 1.   r Now in 1s.   s Om. plures.   t Om. 1s.   u Om. 1. that is, eendlesse blisse s.   w thi s.
x but, Lord 1s.   y Om. s.   z Om. s.   a and thou 1s.   b with out s.   c upon 1s.   d Thanne 1s.   e seide
to Job s.   f and when he 1. and whether he s.   g brennynge wraththe 1e.   h Om. 1s.   i that thing 1s.
k thi preyeris 1s.

5 God. Forsothe thi wickidnesse tauȝte thi mouth, and^w thou folewist^x a tunge of 6 blasfemende men. Thi mouth shal condempne thee, and not I, and thi lippis 7 shul answer to thee. Whether the firste man thou art born, and beforn alle hillis 8 formed? Whether the counseil of God thou hast herd, and lowere^y than^z thou 9 shalt ben his wisdam? What knewe thou^a, that wee vnknowen? What^b vnder- 10 stondes^c thou, that wee wite not? And men of the laste age and of manye ȝeeris ben in vs, myche eldere than thi fadris. 11 Whether gret it is, that God coumforte thee? But thi shreude woordis forfenden 12 that. What rereth^d thee thin herte, and as grete thingis thenkende thou hast 13 stoneȝid eȝen? What aȝen God swelleth thi spirit, that thou speke of thi mouth 14 suche maner woordis? What is a man, that he be vndefoulid, and riȝtwis seme 15 born of a womman? Lo! among his seintus noon is vnchaungable, and heuenes 16 ben not clene in his siȝt. Hou myche more an abhominable and an vnprofitable man, that drinketh as watris wickid- 17 nesse? I shal shewe to thee, here me; 18 that I saȝ, I shal telle to thee. Wise men knoulechen, and shul not hide ther faders. 19 To whom alone is ȝiue the erthe, and 20 ther shal not passe an alien bi hem. Alle his daȝis the vnpitous man proudeth; and the noumbre of ȝeris of his tiraundise is 21 vncertein. The soun of ferd^e euermore in the eris of hym, and whan pes is, he 22 euermor troweth aspies. He beleueth^f not that he mai be turned aȝen fro derc- nesses vnto liȝt, beholdende swerd on alle 23 sides aboute^g. Whan he moueth hym- self to sechen bred, he knew, that dai of derenessis is maad redi in his hond. 24 Tribulacioun shal gasten hym, and an- guysh shal enuyroune hym, as a king

bifor God. For^l wickidnesse hath tauȝt 5 thi mouth, and thou suest the tunge of blasfemeris. Thi tunge, and not Y, schal 6 condempne thee, and thi lippis schulen answere thee. Whether thou art borun 7 the firste man, and^m art formed bifor alleⁿ little hillis? Whether thou herdist^o the 8 counsel of God, and^p his wisdom is lower than thou? What thing^q knowist thou, 9 whiche we knowen not? What^r thing vndurstondist thou, whiche we witen not? Bothe wise men and elde, myche eldre 10 than thi fadris, ben among vs. Whether 11 it is greet, that God coumforte^s thee? But thi schrewid wordis forbeden this. What 12 reisith thin herte thee, and thou as thenk- ynge grete thingis^t hast iȝen astonyed? What bolneth thi spirit aȝens God, that 13 thou brynge forth of thi mouth siche wordis? What is a man, that he be with 14 out wem, and that he borun of a womman appere iust? Lo! noon^u among hise 15 seyntis[†] is^w vnchaungable, and heuenes ben not cleene in his siȝt. How myche more^x 16 a^y man abhomynable‡ and vnprofitable, that drynkith wickidnesse as water? I 17 schal schewe to thee, here thou me; Y schal telle to thee that, that Y siȝ. Wise 18 men knoulechen, and hiden not her fadris. To whiche^z aloone^a the erthe is ȝouun, 19 and an alien schal not passe bi hem^b. A 20 wickid man is proud in alle hise daies; and the noumbre of hise ȝeeris and of his tirauntrie is vncerteyn. The sown of 21 drede is euere in hise eeris, and whanne pees is, he supposith euere tresouns. He 22 bileueth not that he may turne aȝen fro derknessis to liȝt; and^c biholdith aboute on ech side a swerd. Whanne he stirith^d 23 hym to seke breed, he woot,§ that the dai of derknessis is maad redi in his hond. Tri- 24 bulacioun schal make hym aferd, and angwisch schal cumpas hym, as a kyng

^w Om. E.   ^x folowedist AFH.   ^y the lowere E pr. m.   ^z Om. E pr. m.   ^a whether thou hast knowen E pr. m.   ^b Whether E pr. m.   ^c vndurstodist AII.   ^d arereth AEFH.   ^e his ferd E super ras.   ^f leueth E pr. m.   ^g abouten him E super ras.

^l Certis is.   ^m and wher thou i. and whether thou s.   ⁿ Om. s.   ^o hast herd is.   ^p and wher i. and whether s.   ^q thingis A.   ^r And what s.   ^s coumforte or turne is.   ^t thouȝtis s.   ^u ther is noon i.   ^w Om. i.   ^x Om. i.   ^y is a is.   ^z the whiche i.   ^a wyse men aloone is.   ^b hem, that is, shal not caste hem doun fro her prosperite v.   ^c and he is.   ^d moeneth is.

25 that is beforn maad redi to bataile. Forsothe he bende his hond a3en God, and
26 a3en the Almy3ti he is strengthid. He
ran a3en God the necke vpri3t, and he is
27 armed with a fat nol. Fatnesse couerde
his face, and of his sides grece hangeth.
28 He shall dwelle in desolat[h] cites, and in
desert housis, that ben bro3t in to toumbis.
29 He shal not be maad riche, ne his substaunce shal abide stille ; and he shal not
30 putte in the erthe his roote, ne gon
awei fro dercnessis. His braunchis flaume
shal make drie, and he shal be take awei
31 thur3 the spirit of his mouth. Trowe he
not in vein bi errour desceyued, that for
32 any pris he is to ben a3een bo3t. Er
his da3is ben fulfild, he shal pershe, and
33 his hondis shul waxe drie; he[i] shal 'ben
hurt[k] as a vine, in the firste flour his
cluster, and as an oliue throwende awei his
34 flour. Forsothe the gedering[l] of an ipocrite barein, and fyr shal denoure ther
35 tabernaclis, that gladli taken 3iftis. He
conceyuede sorewe, and bar wickidnesse,
and his wombe befor makith redi treccheries.

CAP. XVI.

1
2 Answerende forsothe Job seide, I haue
herd ofte sithes suche thingus ; alle 3ee
3 ben heuye coumfortoures. Whethir windi
woordis shul not[m] han ende? or any
thing is greuous to thee, if thou spekist?
4 And I my3te lie thingis of 3ou speken,
and wolde God 3oure lif were for my
5 lif ; and I shulde coumforte 3ou with
woordis, and moue myn hed vp on 3ou ;
6 I shulde strengthe 3ou with my mouth,
and moue the lippis as sparende to 3ou.

which[e] is maad redi to batel. For[f] he 25
helde forth his hond a3ens God, and he
was maad strong a3ens Almy3ti God. He 26
ran with[g] neck reisid[h] a3ens God, and he
was armed with[i] fat nol. Fatnesse, that[k] 27
is, pride 'comyng forth[l] of temporal
aboundaunce, hilide his face, 'that is[m], the[n]
knowyng[o] of[p] vndurstondyng, and outward fatnesse[q]† hangith doun of his sidis.
He schal dwelle in desolat citees, and in 28
deseert, 'ethir forsakun[r], housis[s], that ben
turned in to biriels. He schal not be 29
maad riche, nether his catel schal dwelle
stidefastli ; nether he schal sende his roote
in[t] the[u] erthe, nether he schal go awei 30
fro derknessis. Flawme‡ schal make drie
hise braunchis, and he schal be takun
a wey bi the spirit of his mouth. Bileue 31
he not veynli disseyued[w] bi errour, that he
schal be a3enbou3t bi ony prijs. Bifor 32
that hise daies ben[j] fillid, he schal perische,
and hise hondis schulen wexe drye ; he 33
schal be hirt as a vyne in the firste flour of
his grape, and as an olyue tre castinge
awei his flour. For[x] the gaderyng to- 34
gidere of an ipocrite is bareyn, and fier
schal denoure the tabernaclis of hem, that
taken[y] 3iftis wilfuli[z]. He conseyuede[a] § 35
sorewe, and[b] childide[c] wickidnesse, and his
wombe makith redi tretcheries.

CAP. XVI.

Forsothe[d] Joob answeride, and seide, 1
Y 'herde ofte[e] siche thingis ; alle[f] 3e ben 2
heuy coumfortouris. Whether wordis ful 3
of wynd schulen haue an ende ? ether ony
thing is diseseful to thee, if thou spekist ?
Also[g] Y my3te speke thingis lijk to 3ou, 4
and 'Y wolde, that 3oure soule‖ were[h] for
my soule ; and[i] Y wolde coumfort 3ou by[k] 5
wordis, and Y wolde moue myn heed on[l]
3ou ; Y wolde make 3ou stronge bi my 6
mouth, and Y wolde moue lippis[m] as

Right margin notes:

† fatnesse ; that is, pride comynge forth of temporal aboundance. c.

‡ flawme &c. ; that is, Goddis ri3tfulnesse schal sle hise sones and dou3tris. Lire here. c.

§ conseyuede sorewe ; that is, bifor thou3te to do ynel to othere men. and childide wickidnesse, bringinge to effect hise wickid thou3t, while he was in temporal powere. makith redi; that is, aftir his casting doun he hath 3it wille to anoye, if he my3te. Lire here. c.

‖ 3oure soule ; that is, in affliccioun and heuynesse in which Y am, and Y were delyuerid. Joo seide not this for dsmire of veniaunce, but for the loue of ri3tfulnesse, and that they set in turment, schulen asaye the truthe of his frenschip. c.

---

[h] the desolat A. [i] Om. c. [k] gladen, E pr. m. [l] gendrynge A. [m] Om. A.

[e] that is. [f] Forsothe is. [g] with his is. [h] reised vp s. [i] with a is. [k] Om. L. [l] Om. isv. [m] Om. iv.
[n] Om. cimrsv. [o] Om. isv. [p] and c. or i. his s. [q] fatnesse, that is, vaschamefastnesse is. [r] Om. is.
[s] in housis ACD pr. m. knu. [t] in to i. [u] Om s. [w] the whiche disseyued is i. whiche is disseyued s. [x] Forsothe is. [y] taken gladli i. [z] Om. i. [a] hath conseiued is. conseyueth s. [b] and he i. [c] hath childid is.
[d] Sothely is. [e] haue ofte herd is. [f] certis alle is. [g] And is. [h] whi ne were 3oure sowle s. [i] Om. is.
[k] with i. [l] upon is. [m] my lippis is.

7 But what shal I do? If I shal speke, my sorewe 'shal not reste[n]; and if I shul holde my pes, it 'shal not go[o] fro me awei. 8 Now forsothe my sorewe hath opressid me, and alle my lymes ben turned in 9 to no3t. My ryuelis seyn witnesse a3en me, and the false seiere is rered vp a3en 10 my face, withseiende to me. He gederede his wodnesse in me, and thretende to me gnastide vp on me with his teth; myn enemy with grisli e3en me beheld. 11 Thei openeden ther mouthis vp on me, aud mysseiende smyten my cheke; thei 12 ben fulfild with my peynes. God hath closid me anent the wicke, and to the 13 hondis of vnpitouse toe me. And I he sum tine plenteuouse, feerli am sorewid; he hath holde my nol; he hath to-brosid 14 me, and put me as in to a marke. He hath enuyround me with his speris, he woundede my leendis to gidere; he sparide not, and he dalf[p] out in to the erthe 15 my bowelis. And he heew3[q] me with wounde vp on wounde; and he fel in to 16 me as a ieaunt. I souwide a sac vpon my skin; and I couerede my flesh with askis. 17 My face to-swal for weping, and myn e3e 18 lidis daswiden. These thingus I suffride withoute wickidnesse of myn hond, whan 19 I hadde to God clene pre3eeris. Erthe, ne couere thou my blod, ne my cry finde 20 in thee place of lurking. Lo! forsothe in heuene is my witnesse; am I knowere 21 of myself in hei3tis? My woordi frendis, 22 myn e3e droppith to God. And wolde God, so a man shulde be demed with God, hou the sone of man is demed with 23 his felawe. Lo! forsothe shorte 3eris passen, and the sty, bi the[r] whiche I shal not be turned a3en, I go.

sparynge 3ou. But what schal Y do? If 7 Y speke, my sorewe restith not; and if Y am stille, it goith not awei fro me. But 8 now my sorewe hath oppressid me, and alle my lymes ben dryuun in to nou3t. 9 My[n] ryuelyngis[o] seien witnessyng a3ens me, and a fals spekere† is reisid[o] a3ens my face, and a3enseith me[q]. He gaderide[r] to- 10 gidere his woodnesse in[s] me, and he ma-naasside me, and[t] gnastide a3ens me with his teeth; myn enemye bihelde[u] me with ferdful i3en. Thei openyden‡ her mouthis 11 on[w] me, and thei seiden schenschip[x], and[y] smytiden[z] my cheke; and thei ben fillid 12 with my peynes. God hath closid me togidere at[a] the[b] wickid[c], and hath[d] 3oue 13 me to the hondis of wickid men. Y thilke riche man and famouse[e] sum tyme, am al to brokun sudeynli; 'he helde[f] my nol; he[g] hath broke me[h], and hath[i] set me as in 14 to a signe[k]. He[l] hath cumpasside me with hise speris, he woundide[m] togidere my leendis; he sparide not[n], and schedde[o] out 15 myn entrails in to the erthe. He beet[p] me with wounde on[q] wounde; he[r] as a 16 giaunt felde[s] in ou[t] me. Y sewide to- gidere a sak on[u] my skyn; and Y hilide 17 my fleisch with aische. My face bolnyde of wepynge, and myn i3eliddis§ wexiden 18 derke. Y suffride these thingis with out wickidnesse of myn hond, 'that is, werk[w], 19 whanne Y hadde cleene preieris to God. Erthe, hile thou not‖ my blood, and my 20 cry fynde[x] not in thee a place of hidyng. 'For, lo[y]! my witnesse is in heuene; and 21 the knowere of my cousience is in hi3e places. A[z]! my frendis, ful of wordis, myn 22 i3e droppith to God. And 'Y wolde, that a man were[a] demed so with God, as the sone of man is demed with his felowe. 23 'For lo[b]! schorte 3eeris passen, and Y go a path, bi which Y schal not turne a3en.

† a fals spek-ere; that is, the deuel, which is a liere, and the fadir of leesing. a3en seith me; bi my freudis, whiche he hath excitid a3enus me. Lire here. c.

‡ thei openyden; that is, the deuel and my freudis stirid bi him; the deuel, in defamynge me bifor God, as in i. c[e], and my freudis, in condemnynge me falsly. smytiden my cheke; that is, dispiliden me openly, as he is dispisid, that is smytun in the face. Lire here. c.

§ myn i3eliddis, etc.; that is, myn i3en con-teyned bitwixe the i3elidis; for si3t is maad derk, by greet and contynued weping. Lire here. c.

‖ Erthe, hile thou not etc.; Joob clepide erthe hise frendis, that seekiden his in erthely pros-perite. Thus seith Austin; if thou louest gold, thou art gold, if thou louest erthe, thou art erthe. Thei enforsiden to hile the blood of Joob and his turment, and selden, that he was punyschid for his gilt, and so Joob hadde lust tide to playne herof bi declaring of his innocense. Lire here. c.

---

[n] resteth not E pr. m.   [o] goth not E pr. m.   [p] deluede AEFH.   [q] bewide AEFH.   [r] Om. AEFH.

[a] The 1s. [o] ryuelyngis of my face 1s. [p] reisid up 1s. [q] bi mi frendis v marg. [r] hath gadrid 1s. [s] a3ens in s. [t] and he 1s. [u] hath biholde 1s. [w] upon 1s. [x] schenship to me 1s. [y] and thei 1s. [z] smeten 1. smyten s. [a] anentis 1. [b] n 1s. [c] wickid man 1s. [d] he hath 1s. [e] of greet fame 1s. [f] the Lord hath holden 1s. [g] and he 1s. [h] me togidre 1s. [i] he hath 1s. [k] token 1s. [l] And he 1s. [m] hath woundid 1s. [n] hath not sparid me 1s. [o] he hath sched 1s. [p] hath bete 1s. [q] upon 1s. [r] and he 1s. [s] hath fullen 1s. [t] upon 1s. [u] upon 1s. [w] Om. 1. or werk E. [x] fynde it 1s. [y] Forsothe 1s. [z] O 1s. [a] whi ne were a man s. [b] Lo! certis 1s.

CAP. XVII.

1 My spirit shal be maad thynne; my daȝis shul be shortid, and onli to me 2 leueth ouer a sepulcre. I synnede not, 3 and in bittirnessis abideth myn eȝe. Lord; deliuere me, and put me beside thee; and whos euere hond thou wilt, fiȝte aȝen me. 4 The herte of hem thou hast maad aferre[s] fro discipline; therfore thei shul not ben 5 enhauncid. A prei he behotith to felawis, 6 and his sones eȝen shul failen. He[t] putte me as in to a prouerbe of the comun, and 7 his exsaumple beforn hem. At the indignacioun daswide myn eȝe; and my 8 lymes as vnto noȝt ben broȝt. Riȝtwis men shul stoneȝen vp on that; and the innocent aȝen the ipocrite shal be stirid 9 vp. And the riȝtwis shal holden his weie, and with clene hondis adde strengthe. 10 Thanne alle ȝee beth conuertid, and cometh; and I shal not finde in ȝou any wis 11 man. My daȝis passeden; my thoȝtis ben 12 scatered, tormentende myn herte. Nyȝt thei turneden in to dai; and eft aftir 13 dercnessis I hope liȝt. If I shul sustene, helle is myn hous; and in dercnessis I 14 beddede my bed. To stinc I seide, Thou art my fader; My moder and my sister, 15 to wermes. Wher is thanne now myn abiding? and my pacience who beholdeth? 16 In to the most deppest helle shul falle doun alle myne; wenest thou nameli, whethir there shal ben reste to me?

CAP. XVIII.

1 Answerende forsothe Baldath Suythes 2 seide, In to what ende woordis thou shalt boste? Vnderstond rathere, and so speke 3 wee. Whi be wee holden as bestis, and

CAP. XVII.

1 Mi spirit[c] schal be maad feble; my 2 daies schulen be maad schort, and oneli the[d] sepulcre is left to me. Y have not 3 synned†, and myn iȝe dwellith in bittirnessis. Lord, delyuere thou me, and sette thou[e] me bisidis thee; and the hond of ech[f] fiȝte aȝens me. Thou[g] hast maad 4 the herte of hem fer fro doctryn, 'ethir knowyng of treuthe[h]; therfor[i] thei schulen not be enhaunsid. He bihetith‡ prey[k] to[l] 5 felowis, and the iȝen of hise sones schulen 6 faile. He hath set as in to a prouerbe[m] of[n] the comyn puple, and his saumple[o] bifor hem. Myn 'iȝe dasewide[p] at in-7 dignacioun[q]; and my membris ben dryuun as in to nouȝt. Iust men schulen wondre 8 on this thing; and an innocent schal be reisid[r] aȝens an ypocrite. And a iust man 9 schal holde his weie, and he schal adde strengthe[s] to clene hondis. Therfor alle 10 'ȝe be[t] conuertid, and come ȝe; and Y schal not fynde in ȝou ony wiys man. My 11 daies ben passid; my thouȝtis ben scaterid, turmentynge myn herte. Tho han turned 12 the nyȝt 'in to[u] day; and eft aftir derknessis 13 hope liȝt. If Y 'susteyne, ether[w] suffre pacientli[x], helle is myn hous§; and Y haue 14 arayede my bed in derknessis. Y seide to rot, Thou art my fadur; and to wormes, 15 ȝe ben my modir and my[y] sister. Therfor where is now myn abidyng? and who 16 biholdith my pacience? Alle my thingis schulen go doun in to deppeste helle; gessist thou, whether reste schal be to me, nameli there.

CAP. XVIII.

1 Forsothe[z] Baldach Suythes answeride, and seide[a], 'Til to[b] what ende schalt thou 2 booste with wordis? Vndurstonde thou[c] first, and so speke we[d]. Whi ben we 3

† Y haue not synned; thouȝ Joob passide not present liyf with out summe synnes, netheles tho waren not so greuouse, that sich peyne schulde be ȝouun to him for tho. *Lire here.* c.

‡ he biheteth; that is, Eliphat, that settide mannus blis in erthely prosperite. *biheteth prey to felowis;* that is, erthely prosperite for nieede to hem that weren of his opynyoun, *and the iȝen of hise sones,* that ben tauȝt of him in his errour, schulen faile fro geting of veri blis. *Lire here.* c.

§ helle, etc.; that is, biriyng with ynne the erthe, for Y abide no more erthely prosperite; in this place and othere of this book for helle, is an Ebreu word, that signefiath ofte a diche ether biriyng. *Lire here.* cx.

---

s ferre A.   t thei E pr. m.

c spirit, seith Job 1s.   d a 1s.   e Om. s.   f eche man 1s.   g Lord, thou 1s.   h Om. IV. that is, fro knowyng of treuthe s.   i and therfor 1s.   k to prey s.   l to hise 1s.   m prouerbe, or a lijknesse s.   n to 1s.   o ensaumple 1s.   p iȝen daȝewiden s.   q the indignacioun of vnwise men 1s.   r reisid up 1s.   s his strengthe s.   t ȝe s.   u in A pr. m.   w Om. 1s.   x Om. 1.   y Om. 1.   z Thanne 1s.   a seide to Job s.   b Vnto 1s.   c thou vs s.   d we to gidre 1s.

4 wee han waxe foul before thee? What lesist thou thi soule in thi wodnesse? Whether for thee the erthe shal be for-saken, and rochis shal be translatid fro 5 ther placis? Whether the liȝt of the wycke man shal not be quenchid; ne 6 the flaume of his fyr shal shyne? Liȝt shal waxe derk in his tabernacle; and the lanterne that is vpon hym shal be 7 quenchid. The goingis of his vertue shul be streitid; and his counseyl shal 8 putten hym doun. Forsothe he putte in his feet in to the nett; and in his 9 filthis he goth. His sole shal ben holde with a grene; and thrist shal brenne out 10 aȝen hym. His foot grene is hid in the erthe, and his desceyuende gyn vp on 11 the sty. Al aboute feris shul gasten hym, and withinne wrappen his feet. 12 His strengthe shal ben feblid with hunger; and scarsnesse of mete asaile his ribbis. 13 Deuoure it the fairnesse of hys skin; the firste goten deth waste the armys of hym. 14 His trost be pullid vp fro his tabernacle; and deth trede vp on hym, as a king al 15 aboue. Dwellen his felawis in the taber-nacle of hym that is not; brumston be 16 sprengd in his tabernacle. Doun be dried his rootis; aboue forsothe be to-17 treden his rip. The mynde of hym pershe fro the erthe; and his name be 18 not maad solempne in stretis. He shal putten hym out fro liȝt in to derenessis; and fro the roundnesse ouerbern hym. 19 His sed ne progenye shal ben in his puple, ne any remnaunt in the regions 20 of hym. In his daȝes the laste men shul stoneȝen; and grising shal asaile the firste. 21 These thanne ben the tabernaclis of the wicke man; and this his place, that vnknowith God.

arettid as beestis, and han we be foule 4 bifor thee? What leesist thou thi soule in thi woodnes? Whether the erthe* schal be forsakun 'for thee, and hard stoonys schulen be borun ouer fro her 5 place? Whethir the liȝt† of a wickid man schal not be quenchid; and the flawme 6 of his fier schal not schyne? Liȝt schal wexe derke in his tabernacle; and the lan-terne, which is on hym, schal be quenchid. The steppis of his vertu schulen be maad 7 streit; and his counsel schal caste hym doun. For he hath sent hise feet in to 8 a net; and he goith in the meschis therof. His foot schal be holdun with a snare‡; 9 and thirst schal brenne out aȝens hym. The foot trappe of hym is hid in the 10 erthe, and his snare on the path. Dredis 11 schulen make hym aferd on ech side, and schulen biwlappe hise feet. His strengthe 12 be maad feble bi hungur; and pouert asaile hise ribbis. Deuoure it the fairnesse of 13 his skyn; the firste§ gendrid deth waste hise armes. His trist be takun awei fro 14 his tabernacle; and perischyng, as a kyng, aboue trede on hym. The felowis of hym 15 that is not‖, dwelle in his tabernacle; brymston be spreynt in his tabernacle. The rootis of hym be maad drie bynethe; 16 sotheli his ripe corn be al to-brokun aboue. His mynde perische fro the erthe; 17 and his name be not maad solempne in stretis. He schal put hym out fro liȝt 18 in to derknessis; and he schal bere hym ouer fro the world. Nethir his seed 19 nether kynrede schal be in his puple, nether ony relifs in hise cuntreis. The laste 20 men schulen wondre in hise daies; and hidousnesse schal asaile the firste men. Therfor these ben the tabernaclis of a 21 wickid man: and this is the place of hym, that knowith not God.

Wher the erthe, etc.; that is, sadnesse of oure sentence for thyn vnresonable wordis. Lire here. c.

† the liȝt; that is, his temporal prosperite. Lire here. c.

‡ with a snare; that is, custom of synne. thirst; that is, brennyng and desire to do synne. c.

§ the firste etc.; that is, hasty deth, comynge bifor kyndly deth. Lire here. c.

‖ is not; that is, the felowis of the deed man, which is not now with lyuynge men, whos tabernacle is the sepulcre, where he hath no felowschipe no but worynes. Lire here. c.

¶ The laste; that is, the lesse men of the peple; and the firste, that is, the grettere men in the peple. Lire here. c. wondre in hise daies; the resouns of Baldath presen not his purpos, for the forseid aduersites bifallen not onely to wickid men in this lyf, but also ofte to iust men, that ben turmentid not onely in this lyf and in deth, but also aftir deth thei ben dispisid among men; as the bodies of martris weren forbedun to be biried, and weren left to be deuourid of wilde beestis and briddis, thouȝ this were lettid sum tyme by Goddis purueyaunce. Lire here. c.

---

u streit AⅡ.   v Om. ⅡH.   w Adoun AEFH.   x eft E pr. m.   y mouth E pr. m.

e of thee as I.   f whi haue I.   g Whar to I. What or whi s.   h Wherfore s.   i Om. s.   k and wher for thee I. and wherfore the s.   l and wher Is.   m that Is.   n putt Is.   o meshis or knyttingis I. meschis and in the knittingis s.   p is leid on Is.   q euery Is.   r and thei Is.   s bewrappe s.   t upon Is.   u and bronston Is.   w And the Is.   x be thei Is.   y and be Is.   z Om. Is.   a Om. s.   b his kynrede s.   c remenauntis of hem Is.   d lefte in I.   e thus s.

CAP. XIX.

¹
₂ Answerende forsothe Job seide, Hou
longe ȝee tormente my lif, and pownen^z
₃ me with woordis? Lo! ten sithes ȝee
confounde me, and ȝee shame not, opress-
₄ ende me. Forsothe if I am vnknowende,
₅ with me it shal be, myn vnkunnyng. And
ȝee aȝen me ben rerid, and vndernyme me
₆ with my repreues. Nameli now vnderstondeth, for God not with^a euene dom
tormentith me, and with his scourgis
₇ girdith me. Lo! I shal crie sufferende
fors, and no man shal here; I shal crien
₈ out, and ther is not that deme. My sty
he heggide aboute, and I mai not gon
ouer; and in my path he putte derc-
₉ nesses. He spoilide me my glorie, and he
₁₀ toc awei the croune fro myn hed. He de-
stroȝide me al aboute, and I pershe; and
as to a pullid vp tree he toc awey myn
₁₁ hope^b. His wodnesse is wroth aȝen me;
₁₂ and so me he hadde as his enemy. His
theues camen togidere, and maden to hem
a weie bi me; and besegiden in enuyroun
₁₃ my tabernacle. He made a ferr my brethren fro me; and my knowen as alienes
₁₄ wenten awei fro me. My neȝh men forsoken me; and that me hadden knowe
₁₅ forȝete me. The comelingus of myn hous
and myn hond wymen as an alien hadden
me ⁑; and as a pilgrim I^c was in the eȝen
₁₆ of hem. My seruaunt I clepide, and he
answerde not to me; with my propre
₁₇ mouth I preȝede hym. My wif agriside
my breth; and I^d preȝede the sones of my
₁₈ wombe. Foolys also despisiden me; and
whan I hadde gon awei fro them, thei
₁₉ bacbiten to^e me. Sum time my coun-
seyleris wlateden me; and whom I most
₂₀ loouede withstod me. My bon cleuede
to my skin, the flesh wastid; and onli

CAP. XIX.

Forsothe Joob answeride, and seide,₁
Hou long turmente ȝe my soule, and al₂
to-breken me with wordis? Lo! ten sithis₃
ȝe schenden^f me†, and ȝe ben not aschamed,
oppressynge me. Forsothe^g and if Y 'koude₄
not^h, myn vnkynnyng schal be with me.
And ȝe ben reisid aȝens me, andⁱ repreuen₅
me with my schenschipis. Nameli now₆
vndurstonde ȝe, that God hath turmentid
me not bi euene doom^k‡, and^l hath cumpassid me with hise betyngis. Lo! Y suf-₇
frynge violence schal crye, and no man
schal here^m; Y schal crye loude, and 'noon
isⁿ that demeth^o. He^p bisette^q aboute my₈
path, and Y may not go; and he settide^r
derknessis in my weie. He hath spuylid₉
me of my glorye, and^s hath take awey the
coroun fro myn heed. He hath distried₁₀
me on ech side, and Y perischide^t; and^u
he hath take awei myn hope^w, as fro a
tre pullid vp bi the roote. His stronge₁₁
veniaunce was wroothȝ aȝens me; and he
hadde me so as his enemye. Hise theues₁₂
camen^x togidere, and 'maden to^y hem a
wei bi me; and bisegiden^z my tabernacle
in^a cumpas. He^b made fer my britheren₁₃
fro me; and my knowun^c as aliens ȝeden
awei fro me. My neiȝboris forsoken^d me;₁₄
and thei that knewen me han forȝete me.
The tenauntis of myn hows, and myn₁₅
handmaydis^e hadden me as a straunger;
and Y was as a pilgrym bifor her iȝen.
Y clepide my seruaunt, and he answeride₁₆
not to me; with myn owne mouth Y preiede
hym^f. My wijf wlatide my breeth; and Y₁₇
preiede the sones‖ of my wombe. Also₁₈
foolis dispisiden me; and whanne Y was
goon awei fro hem, thei bacbitiden me.
Thei^g, that weren my counselouris sum₁₉
tyme, hadden abhomynacioun of me^h; and

---

^z ponen c. thralle E pr. m. pownen E sec. m.   ^a withouten A.   ^b fairnesse E pr. m.   ^c Om. c.
^d Om. AH.   ^e bacbitiden A. bacbiten H.

^f haue ȝchent 1S.   ^g Certis 1S.   ^h haue vnknowe 1S.   ⁱ and ȝe 1S.   ^k doom, for he sparid me s.   ^l and
he 1S.   ^m here me 1S.   ⁿ ther is noon 1.   ^o demeth me worthi to be herd 1S.   ^p The Lord 1S.   ^q hath
bisett 1S.   ^r luth sett 1S.   ^s and he 1S.   ^t perishe worthly s.   ^u Om. 1S.   ^w hope as ȝe gessen 1S.   ^x han
come 1.   ^y thei han maad 1S.   ^z thei han biseegid 1S.   ^a bi 1S.   ^b The Lord 1S.   ^c knowun men S.   ^d han
forsake 1S.   ^e handmaidens 1.   ^f hym, but he herde mee not s.   ^g And thei 1S.   ^h me aftirward 1S.

21 the lippis ben lafte aboute my teth. Haueth reuthe of me, haueth reuthe of me, nameli, ȝee my frendis ; for the hond of 22 the Lord hath touchid me. Whi pursue ȝee me, as God ; and with my flesh ȝee 23 be fulfild ? Who ȝiueth to me, that my woordis be writen ? Who ȝiueth to me 24 that thei be grauen in a boc with an iren pointel, or with a pece of led ; or with 25 a chisell thei be grauen in flint ? Forsothe I wot, that myn aȝeenbiere liueth, and in the laste dai I am to rise fro the 26 erthe ; and eft shal ben enuyround with my skin, and in my flesh I shal se God, 27 my sauere. Whom I myself am to seen, and myn eȝen ben to beholden, and noon other. This myn hope is led vp in my 28 bosum. Whi thanne now sey ȝee, Pursue wee hym, and the roote of woord finde 29 wee aȝen hym ? Fleeth thanne fro the face of swerd ; for vengere of wickidnesse is the swerd, and witeth dom to be.

CAP. XX.

1 Answerende forsothe Sofar Naamatites, 2 seide, Therfore my thoȝtis diuers comyn after other to them ; and my mynde in to 3 diuers thingus is raueshid. The doctrine that thou vndernemest me, I shal heren ; and the spirit of myn vnderstonding shal 4 answern to me. That I wot fro the begynnyng, sithen a man 'is sett vp on 5 erthe, that the preising of vnpitous men is short, and the ioȝe of an ipocrite at 6 the licnesse of a point. If his pride steȝe vp in to heuene, and the cloude touche 7 his hed, as a dunghil, in the ende he shal ben lost ; and thei that hadden seen hym,

he, whom Y louede moost, was aduersarie to me. Whanne fleischis weren wastid, my 20 boon cleuyde to my skyn ; and 'oneli lippis ben left aboute my teeth. Haue ȝe merci 21 on me, haue ȝe merci on me, nameli, ȝe my freudis ; for the hond of the Lord hath touchid me. Whi pursuen ȝe me, as God 22 pursueth ; and ben fillid with my fleischis† ? Who ȝyueth to me, that my 23 wordis be writun ? Who ȝyueth to me, that tho be writun in a book with an 24 yrun poyntil, ethir with a plate of leed ; ethir with a chisel be grauun in a flynt ? For Y woot, that myn aȝenbiere lyueth, 25 and in the laste dai Y schal rise fro the erthe ; and eft Y schal be cumpassid with 26 my skyn, and in my fleisch Y schal se God, my sauyour. Whom Y my silf schal 27 se, and myn iȝen schulen biholde, and not an other man†. This myn hope is kept in my bosum. Whi therfor seien ȝe now, 28 Pursue we hym, and fynde we the roote of a word aȝens hym ? Therfor fle ȝe fro 29 the face of the swerd§ ; for the swerd is the vengere of wickidnessi, and wite ȝe, that doom schal be.

CAP. XX.

Forsothe Sophar Naamathites answer- 1 ide, and seide, Therfor my thouȝtis dy- 2 uerse comen|| oon aftir anothir ; and the mynde is rauyischid in to dyuerse thingis. Y schal here the techyng, bi which thou 3 repreuest me ; and the spirit of myn vndurstondyng schal answere me. Y woot 4 this fro the bigynnyng, sithen man was set on erthe, that the preisyng of wickid 5 men is schort, and the ioie of an ypocrite is at the licnesse of a poynt. Thouȝ his 6 pride 'stieth in to heuene, and his heed touchith the cloudis, he schal be lost in 7 the ende, as a dunghil ; and, thei that

f Om. AEFH.   g me A.   h I am sett E pr. m.   i the erthe A.

l my fleischis is.   k lippis aloone i.   l of i.   m of i.   n Om. is.   o ȝe ben is.   p fulfilid i.   q ȝyueth or grauntith s.   r grauntith is.   s tho be i.   t Certis is.   u biholde him is.   w man, than I my self that now am is. man, but rich as I am now κ marg.   x bosum, or bileue i. bosum, or in my beleeue s. bosum, that is, in myn herte v.   y Om. is.   z And thanne is.   a seide to Job s.   b Certis is, my is.   c Om. s.   d this thing i.   e sith that is.   f upon is.   g poynt soone passinge i. poynt, that is, soone onerpassed s.   h And thouȝ s.   i stie up is.   k and if is.   l lost or forȝete s.   m of i.

† with my fleischis ; in hachitinge me, and affermynge that Y am iustly punyschid for synnes, for whi bac-biteris ben fillid with quyke fleschis. Lire here. c.

† not another man ; that is, Y schal be the same man in body and soule, that Y am now. Lire here. c.

§ fro the face of the swerd ; that is, fro the sentence of Goddis doom, of wickidnessis that ben not punyschid here. Lire here. c.

|| dyuerse comen, etc. ; whanne Sophar hadde heed the wordis of Job, he assentide of the doom to comynge and of vndedlynesse of soulis, but he dissentide fro Joob in prosperites of this lyf, for he helde that aduersites weren peynes of synnes, and prosperites weren meede of vertu. Lire here. c.

8 shul sein, Wher is he? As a sweuene
fleende awei he shal not be founde; he
9 shal passe as the ny3t si3te. The e3e that
hym sa3[k] shal not seen; and his place no
10 mor shul beholden hym. His sones shul
be to-trede with nede; and the hondis of
11 hym shul 3elde[l] to hym his sorewe. The
bones of hym shul be fulfild with vicis of
his· waxende 3outhe; and with hym in
12 pouder thei shul slepe. Whan forsothe
euel were sweete in his mouth, he hidde
13 it vnder his tunge. He shal spare to it,
and not forsaken it; and hiden in ·his
14 throte[m]. The bred of hym in his wombe
shal be turned in to galle of edderes
15 withinneforth. The richessis that he deuourede, he shal spewen out; and of his
16 wombe God shal drawe them out. The
hed of edderes shal rise; and the tunge
17 of the serpent shal slen hym. See he not
the litle ryueres of the flod, of the strem
18 of hony, and of buttere. He shal abie alle
thingus that he dide, and nerthelatere
he shal not be wastid; aftir the multitude of his findingus, so and[n] he shal
19 suffre. For brekende togidere he nakide
the hous of the pore man; raueshide, and
20 not bilde it. And his wombe is not fulfild; and whan he shal han, that he hadde
21 coueitid, he shal not moun welde. Ther
'lafte not[o] of his mete; and therfore no
22 thing shal leue of his goodus. Whan he
shal be fulfild, he shal be streyned, and
brenne; and alle sorewe shal falle in to
23 hym. Wolde God his wombe be fulfild,
that he sende out in to hym the wrathe
of his wodnesse, and reyne vp on hym
24 his bataile. He shal fleen iren armys;
and he shal falle in to the brasene bowe.

sien[n] hym, schulen seie, Where is he?
As a dreem fleynge awei[o] he schal not be
foundun; he schal passe as[p] 'a ny3tis si3t[q].
The i3e that si3[r] hym[s] schal not se[t]; and 9
his place schal no more biholde him. Hise 10
sones[u] schulen be 'al to-brokun[x] with
nedynesse; and hise hondis schulen 3elde
to hym his sorewe. Hise boonys† schulen 11
be fillid with the vices of his 3ong wexynge age; and[y] schulen slepe with hym in
dust. For[z] whanne yuel was swete in his 12
mouth, he hidde[a] it[b] vndur his tunge. He 13
schal spare it[c], and[d] schal not forsake it[e];
and[f] schal hide[g] in his throte[h]. His[i] breed‡ 14
in his wombe schal be turned in to galle[k]
of snakis withynne[l]. He schal spue[m] out 15
the richessis, whiche he deuouride[n]; and
God schal drawe tho ritchessis out of his
wombe. He schal souke the heed of snakis‖; 16
and the tunge of an addre schal sle hym.
Se he not the[o] stremys of the flood of the 17
stronde, of hony, and of botere. He schal 18
suffre peyne[p] for alle thingis whiche[q] he
hath do, netheles he schal not be wastid[r];
aftir[s] the multitude of his fyndyngis, so
and[t] 'he schal[u] suffre. For[w] he brake, and 19
made nakid the bows of a[x] pore man; he
rauyschide[y], and bildide it not[z]. And his 20
wombe was not[a] fillid; and whanne he
hath that, that he couetide, he may not
holde[b] in possessioun[c]. 'No thing lefte[d] 21
of his mete[e]; and therfor no thing schal
dwelle of his goodis[f]. Whanne he is fillid[g], 22
he[h] schal be maad streit[i]; he schal 'be
hoot[k], and alle sorewe schal falle in on[l]
hym. 'Y wolde, that[m] his wombe be[n] fillid, 23
that he sende out[o] in[p] to hym the ire[q] of
his strong veniaunce, and[r] reyne his hatel
on[s] hym. He schal fle yrun armuris, and 24

† hise boonys; that is, hise felowis 3yuynge strengthe to him. Lire here. c.

‡ his breed, etc.; that is, 3ynne in which he delitide and was fillid. of snakis; for the bitirnesse of peyne suynge. Lire here. c.

§ the heed of snakis. Tomas Alquyn and summe othere doctours expownen thus this lettre, The heed of snakis schal rise, that is, the deuel ether another my3ty man schal rise to asaile him, as the heed of a snake is reisid to bite. But this exposicioun acordith not with the Ebreu, where it is, schal souke; and where we han heed, in Ebreu it is ros, that signefieth bothe heed and galle; if it is takun in the lj. signeficacioun, that is, galle, it is pleyn ynow, seiynge thus, He schal souke the galle o snakis. Lire here. c.

‖ irone, etc.; that is, peynes of present lijf, that smyten visibly and ef ny3. brasun boue; that is, in to peynes of helle. Lire here. c.

---

k seeth AII. sei3 EF.   l 3elde them E.   m roote C.   n Om. A.   o shal not leuen E pr. m.

n han seen 18.   o awei or soone for3eten 8.   p Om. 8.   q the si3t of ni3tis 18.   r hath seie 8.   s Om. 8.
t se him eft 1. se him 8.   u sones also 18.   x broke 1. broke to gidere 8.   y and thei 18.   z Certis 18.
a hidde and kepte 18.   b Om. 8.   c it for a tyme 1. it to a tyme 8.   d and he 18.   e it, but hoolde it 8.   f and
he 18.   g hide it 18.   h throte; and 8.   i til he may anote, his 18.   k the galle 1.   l withynne him 18.
m vome or caste 18.   n hath denourid 18.   o Om. 18.   p peynes 18.   q that 1.   r wastid bi tho peynes, but
euer endure 8.   s and aftir 18.   t Om. 18.   u schal he 8.   w For whi 8.   x the 18.   y rauyschide it 18.
z not a3en 18.   a not 3itt 1. not 3it therbi 8.   b holde it 8.   c possessioun long tyme 8.   d Ther lefte
nothing 1.   e meete to poore men 8.   f goodis to his bihoue, but 8.   g fulfillid with richesse 1. fulfillid with
catel 8.   h 3itt he 1.   i streit in coueitise 1.   k brenne in it 1. brenne in coueytyse and malice 8.   l upon 1.
with 8.   m Whi ne were 18.   n Om. 18.   o out thanne 1.   p Om. 8.   q wraththe 18.   r and falle as 1.
s upon 18.

25 Broȝt out, and goende out fro his shethe, and leitinge in to his bitternesse; thei shul go, and come vp on hym alle grisful. 26 Hid dercnessis be in his priue thingus; fyr shal deuoure hym, that shal not be brend vp; laft in his tabernacle he shal be tor-27 mentid. Heuenys shul shewen his wickidnesse; and erthe shal rise aȝen hym. 28 The buriounyng of his hous shal ben opened; it[p] shal be to[q] drawen awei in 29 the dai of the wodnesse of the Lord. This is the part of the vnpitous man fro God, and the eritage of his woordis fro the Lord.

he schal falle in to a[t] brasun boowe. Led[u] 25 out[w], and[x] goynge out 'of his schethe[y], and schynynge, '*ether smytinge with leit*[z], 'in to his[a] bittirnesse; orrible *fendis*[b] schulen go, and schulen[c] come on[d] hym. Alle derk-26 nessis ben hid in hise priuytees; fier, which[e] is not teendid[f], schal deuoure hym; he schal be turmentid left[g] in his tabernacle. Heuenes schulen schewe his wickidnesse; 27 and erthe schal rise[b] togidere aȝens hym. The seed[i]† of his hows schal be[k] opyn; it[l] 28 schal be drawun doun in the dai of the[m] strong veniaunce of the Lord. This is the 29 part of a[n] wickid man, '*which part is*[o] ȝouun[p] of God, and the eritage of hise wordis[q] of[r] the Lord.

† *The seed, etc.: that is, the damnacioun of hise sones telling his synne, to encreessing of her owne damnacioun. Lire here. c.*

CAP. XXI.

1/2 Answerende forsothe Job seide, Hereth, I beseche, my woordis, and doth penaunce. 3 Suffreth me, and I shal speke; and after my woordus, if it shul be seen, laȝheth. 4 Whethir aȝen man is my disputesoun, that thurȝ desert I owe not to be maad 5 sory? Taketh heede to me, and becometh doumbe; and puttith vpon the finger to 6 ȝoure mouth. And[r] whan I shal recorde, drede and trembling shal smyte togidere 7 my flesh. Whi thanne vnpitous men liuen, and ben rered vp, and coumfortid with 8 richessis? The sed of hem abit[s] stille beforn hem; and the cumpanye of neeȝb men, and of cosynes in the siȝte of hem. 9 The housis of hem ben sikere, and pesible; and the ȝerde of God is not vp on hem. 10 The oxe of hem conceyuede, and bar not abortif; the kow bar, and is[t] not priued 11 the frut. The litle childer of hem gon out as flockis; and the fauntis of hem

CAP. XXI.

1/2 Forsothe[s] Joob answeride, and seide, Y preye[t], here ȝe my wordis, and do ȝe penaunce[u]. Suffre ȝe me, that Y speke; and 3 leiȝe ȝe aftir my wordis, if it schal seme[w] worthi[x]. Whether my disputyng is aȝens[a] man, that skilfuli Y owe not to be sori? 5 Perseyue ȝe me, and be ȝe astonyed; and sette ȝe[y] fyngur[z] on[a] ȝoure mouth. And[g] whanne Y bithenke[b], Y drede, and tremblyng schakith my fleisch. Whi therfor 7 lyuen wickid men? Thei ben enhaunsid, and[c] coumfortid with richessis. Her seed 8 dwellith bifor hem; the cumpeny of[d] kynesmen, and of[e] sones[f] of[g] sones *dwellith*[h] in her siȝt. Her housis ben sikur, and pesi-9 ble; and the ȝerde[i] of God is not on[k] hem. The cow of hem conceyuede[l], and caluede 10 not a deed calf[m]; the[n] cow caluyde, and[o] is not[p] priued[q] of hir calf. Her[r] litle chil-11 dren[s] goen out as flockis; and her ȝonge children 'maken fulli ioye[t] with pleies[u].

---

[p] and it *A*.   [q] Om. *H*.   [r] And I *AEF*.   [s] abideth *AH*.   [t] it is *E pr. m.*

[t] Om. I.   [u] The whiche is led I. Which is led or *taken* s.   [w] out of his schethe or *caas* I. ont of his shethe, *or out of the furel* s.   [x] and *this bowe* IS.   [y] Om. IS.   [z] *as leit* IS.   [a] schal smyte him in IS.   [b] *feerls* IS.   [c] Om. IS.   [d] upon IS.   [e] that IS.   [f] teendid *of man* IS.   [g] and left IS.   [h] rise up IS.   [i] generacioun IS.   [k] be *maad* I.   [l] and it s.   [m] Om. IS.   [n] the I.   [o] *antecrist* I. *which is* s.   [p] ȝouen to him IS.   [q] *disceyuable* wordis I.   [r] *ordeyned to him of* I. *is also of* s.   [s] Sothely IS.   [t] preye ȝou IS.   [u] penaunce *for ȝoure erringe* s.   [w] seme *to ȝou* s.   [x] worthi *to do so* s.   [y] the BCDEKLMPQRUWf.   [z] ȝoure fyngur IS.   [a] upon IS.   [b] bithenke *me* IS.   [c] or s.   [d] of her IS.   [e] Om. I.   [f] the sones *plures.*   [g] of her s.   [h] *lyuen* I.   [i] ȝerde *or skourge* I. ȝerde *or the chastisynge* s.   [k] upon IS.   [l] hath conceyued IS.   [m] calf, *but a quyk* s.   [n] her IS.   [o] and sche IS.   [p] now s.   [q] maad calflees I. calflees s.   [r] The IS.   [s] children of hem I. children of *wickid men* s.   [t] ful outioyen IS.   [u] pleynges s.

12 gladen out with pleies. They holden the
timbre, and the harpe; and ioȝen at the
13 soun of the" orgne. Thei^v leden in goodis
ther daȝis; and in a point to hellis thei
14 go doun. The whiche seiden to God,
Go awei fro vs; the kunnyng of thi^vv
15 weies wee wiln not. Who is the Almyȝti,
that wee serue to hym? and what pro-
16 fiteth to vs, if wee preȝen hym? Nerthelater for ther goodis ben not in the
hond of hem, the counseil of vnpitous
17 men be aferr fro me. Hou ofte sithes
the lanterne of vnpitouse men shal be
quenchid, and flowing ouercam to them,
and deuidede^w the sorewis of his wod-
18 nesse? Thei shul ben as chaf befor the
face of wind; and as a^x sparke, that the
19 cole scatereth. God shal kepe to the
sones of hym the sorewe of the fader;
and whan he shal ȝelde, thanne he shal
20 knowen. His eȝen shul seen his slaȝter;
and of the wodnesse of the Almyȝti he
21 shal drinke. What forsothe to hym perteneth of his hous aftir hym, and if the
noumbre of his monethis shal 'come to
22 the half^y? Whethir any man shal teche
God kunnyng, that demeth heȝe men?
23 This dieth stronge and hol, riche and wel-
24 sum. His bowelis ben ful of talȝ^y; and the
bones of hym ben moistid with marȝ.
25 Another forsothe dieth in the bitternesse
26 of his soule, withoute any richessis^x. And
nertbelater togidere in pouder ther shul
27 slepe, and wermes shul couere them. Certis I haue knowe ȝoure thoȝtis, and ȝoure
28 wicke^a sentencis aȝen me. Ȝee seyn forsothe, Wher is the hous of the prince?
and where the tabernaclis^b of vnpitous
29 men? Asketh any man of the weie goeris;
and these same thingis ȝee shul knowe
30 hym to vnderstonde. For the euele man

Thei holden tympan^w, and^x harpe^y; and 12
ioïen^z at the soun of^a orgun. Thei leden^b 13
in^c goodis^d her daies; and in a point^e thei
goen doun to hellis†. Whiche^f men seiden 14
to God^g, Go thou awei fro us; we nylen^h
the kunnyng of thi weies. Who is Almiȝti 15
God, that we serue him? and what profitith it^i to vs, if we preien^k him? Nethe- 16
les for^l her goodis‡ ben not in her houd^m,
'that is^n, power, the^o counsel of wickid men
be^p fer fro me. Hou ofte schal the lan- 17
terne of wickid men be quenchid, and
flowing schal come on^q hem, and God
schal departe^r the sorewis of his stronge
veniaunce? Thei schulen be as chaffis^s bi- 18
for the face of the wynd; and as a deed
sparcle, whiche^t the whirlewynd scaterith
abrood. God schal kepe the sorewe of the^u 19
fadir§ to hise sones; and whanne he hath
ȝoldun^w, thanne he schal wite^x. Hise iȝen 20
schulen se her^y sleyng^z; and he schal drynke
of the stronge veniaunce of Almyȝti God.
For whi what perteyneth it to hym of his 21
hows^a aftir hym, thouȝ the noumbre of his
monethis be half takun awey? Whether 22
ony man schal teche God kunnyng, which^b
demeth hem that ben hiȝe? This yuel 23
man dieth strong and hool, riche and bles-
ful^c, 'that is, myrie^d. Hise entrails ben 24
ful of fatnesse; and hise boonys ben moistid
with merowis^e. Sotheli^f anothir wickid^g 25
man dieth in the^h bittirnesse of his soule,
and with outen ony^i richessis. And^k ne- 26
theles thei schulen slepe togidere in dust,
and wormes schulen hile hem. Certis Y 27
knowe ȝoure wickid thouȝtis, and^l sen-
tensis^m aȝens me. For ȝe seien, Where is 28
the hows of the prince‖? and where ben
the tabernaclis of wickid men? Axe ȝe 29
ech^n of 'the weie goeris^o; and ȝe schulen
knowe, that he vndurstondith^p these same

shal be kept 'in to° the dai of perdicioun, and to the dai of wodnesse he shal be 31 broȝt. Who shal vndernyme beforn hym his weyes? and what he dide, who shal 32 ȝelde to hym? He shal be broȝt to the sepulcris; and in the hipil of deade men 33 shal wake. He was sweete to the greet of helle flod; and after hym alle men he 34 droȝ, and beforn hym vnnoumbrable. Hou thanne coumforte ȝee me in vein, whan ȝoure answeris ben shewid to repugne^d 'to the^e treuthe?

CAP. XXII.

1 Answerende forsothe Elifath Temanites 2 seide, Whether to God mai a man ben comparisound, also whan he shal be of 3 perfit kunnyng? What profitith to God, if thou shul be riȝtwis? or what to hym bringist thou, if thi lif were vnde- 4 foulid? Whether dredende he shal vndernyme thee, and come with thee in to 5 dom, and not for thi myche^f malice, and 6 thi wickidnessis vnendid? Forsothe thou hast take awei the wed of thi brethern with oute cause; and nakid men thou 7 hast spoilid fro clothis. Water to the weri thou ȝeue not; and to the hungri 8 thou withdrowe bred. In the strengthe of thin arm thou weldedest^g the erthe; 9 and most myȝti thou heelde it. Widewis thou laftist voide; and the brawnes of 10 moderles childer thou to-brosidist. Therfore thou art enuyround with granes; 11 and feerli dredeⁱ disturbide^k thee. Thou wendest thee not to seen derenessis; and thurȝ bire of rennynge watris not to 12 ben opressid. Whether thenkest thou, that God be heȝere than heuene, and 13 ouer the cop of sterres he be heȝed? And thou seist, What forsothe the Lord knewȝ? 14 and, As bi derenesse he demeth^l? A cloude

---

thingis, that^q an yuel man schal be kept 30 in to the dai of perdicioun, and^r schal be led to the dai of woodnesse. Who schal 31 repreue hise weies bifor hym? and who schal ȝelde to hym tho thingis, whiche he hath doon? He schal be led to the^s sepul- 32 cris; and he schal wake^t in the heep of deed men. He was swete† to the 'stoonys, 33 *ether filthis*, of helle^u; and^w drawith ech man aftir hym, and vnnoumbrable men^x bifor him. Hou therfor coumforten ȝe me 34 in veyn, sithen ȝoure answeris ben schewid to^y 'repugne to^z treuthe?

CAP. XXII.

Forsothe^a Eliphat Themanytes answer- 1 ide, and seide^b, Whether a man, ȝhe, whanne 2 he is of perfit kunnyng, mai be comparisound to God? What profitith it to God, 3 if thou art iust? ethir what schalt thou ȝyue to hym, if thi lijf is without^d wem? Whether he schal drede, and schal^{dd} re- 4 preue thee, and schal^e come with thee in to doom, and not for thi ful myche malice, 5 and thi^f wickidnessis with out noumbre, 'these peynes bifelden^g iustli to thee? For^h 6 thou hast take awei with out cause the wed of thi britheren; and^j hast spuylid nakid‡ men of clothis. Thou ȝauest not 7 watir to the feynt man; and thou withdrowist breed§ fro the hungri man. In 8 the strengthe of thin arm thou haddist the lond in possessioun; and thou moost myȝti heldist^k it. Thou leftist widewis 9 voide^l; and^m al to-brakist the schuldris of fadirles children. Therfor thou artⁿ cum- 10 passid with snaris; and sodeyn drede disturblith thee. And thou gessidist, that 11 thou schuldist not se derknessis; and that thou schuldist not be oppressid with the^p fersnesse of watris‖ flowyng. Whether 12 thou thenkist, that God is hiȝere than heuene^q¶, and is^r enhaunsid aboue the coppe

---

---

^c to *AH.*　^d repugnynge *A.* repreuynge *N.*　^e of *A.* of the *N.*　^f mychile *E.*　^g weeldist *A sec. m.*
ⁱ strengthe *E pr. m.*　^k disturblith *A.* distourbith *H.*　^l schewith *E pr. m.*

^q *that is*, that s.　^r and he ıs.　^s Om. ıs.　^t walke ıs.　^u filthi erthe, and to the stones of helle ıs.
^w and he ıs.　^x men ȝiden s.　^y the e.　^z contrarie the ıs.　^a Thanne ıs.　^b seide to *Job* s.
^d withouten ı *et* s *pass.*　^{dd} shal he s.　^e schal he ıs.　^f Om. c.　^g *this hath falle* ı. these peynes haue
fallen s.　^h Certis ıs.　ⁱ and thou ıs.　^k heeld s.　^l voide *or* vnkolpen ı. voide *withouten help* s.　^m and
thou ıs.　ⁿ art *now* ıs.　^p Om. cs.　^q heuenes s.　^r that he is s.

his hidelis, ne oure thingus he beholdeth, and aboute the vttermostis of heuene he 15 goth. Whether the sti of worldis thou coueitist to kepe, the whiche wicke[m] men 16 treden? The whiche ben rerid[n] befor ther time, and flod turnede vp so doun 17 the foundement of hem. The whiche seiden to God, Go awei fro vs; and as the Almy3ti mi3te do no thing, thei cymeden 18 hym, whan he hadde fulfild ther housis with goodis; whos sentence ferr be fro 19 me. Ri3twis men shul seen, and be glad; and the innocent shal scorne them. 20 Whether is nott hewe doun the rering vp of hem, and fyr shall deuoure ther relikis? 21 Assente thanne to hym, and haue pes; and bi these thingus thou shalt han best 22 frutis. Tac of his mouth the lawe, and 23 put his woordis in thin herte. If thou shul be turned a3een to the Almy3ti, thou shalt be bild vp; and aferr thou shalt make 24 the wickidnesse fro thi tabernacle. He shal 3iue for the erthe flint, and for the 25 flint goldene stremes. And the Almy3ti shal ben a3en thin enemys; and seluer 26 shal ben hepid to thee. Thanne vp on the Almy3ti delicis thou shalt flowen; and thou shalt reren vp to God thi face. 27 Thou shalt pre3en hym, and he shal here thee; and thi vouwis thou shalt 3elde. 28 Thou shalt beholden a thing, and it shal come to thee; and in thi weies li3t shal 29 shyne. He forsothe that shal be mekid, shal ben in glorie; and he that bowith 30 his e3en, shal be saued. The innocent shal be saued; forsothe he shal be saued bi the clennesse of hyse hondys.

of sterris? And thou[s] seist, What sotheli knowith God? and, He demeth as bi derk- 14 nesse. A cloude is[t] his hidyng place, and he biholdith not oure thingis, and he 15 'goith aboute[u] the herris of heuene. Whe- ther thou coueitist to kepe the path[w] of worldis†, which[x] wickid men han ofte 16 go? Whiche[y] weren takun awei bifor her tyme, and the flood‡ distriede the 17 foundement of hem. Whiche[z] seiden to God, Go thou awei fro vs; and as if Almy3ti God may[a] do no thing, thei 18 gessiden hym, whanne he hadde fillid[b] her housis with goodis; the sentence of whiche[c] men be fer fro me. Iust men 19 schulen se, and schulen be glad; and an innocent man schal scorne hem[d]. Whether 20 the reisyng[e] of hem is not kit doun, and fier schal deuoure the relifs[f] of hem? Ther- 21 for[g] assente thou to God, and haue thou pees; and bi these thingis thou schalt haue best fruytis. Take thou the lawe of 22 his mouth, and sette thou hise wordis in thin herte. If thou turnest a3en to Al- 23 my3ti God, thou schalt be bildid; and thou schalt make wickidnesse fer fro thi taber- nacle. He[h] schal[i] 3yue[k] a[l] flynt for erthe‡, 24 and goldun strondis for a flynt. And Al- 25 my3ti God schal be a3ens thin enemyes; and siluer schal be gaderid togidere to[m] thee. Thanne on Almy3ti God thou schalt 26 flowe with delicis; and thou schalt reise[n] thi face to God. Thou[o] schalt preye hym, 27 and he schal here thee; and thou schalt 3elde thi vowis[p]. Thou schalt deme[q] a 28 thing, and it schal come to thee; and ly3t schal schyne in[r] thi weies. For[s] he that is 29 mekid, schal be in glorie; and he that bowith doun hise i3en, schal be saued. An 30 innocent[t] schal be saued; sotheli he schal be saued in the clennesse of hise hondis.

Marginal notes:

13 filosofie, and for Eliphat gesside, that Joob was in this errour, he repreuede Joob, and seide also that[the]was

15 punyschid for his synne; but it was not so of Joob. Lire here. c.

16 † path of worldis; that is, the lyif of men lyuynge worldlyly and dissolutly. Lire here. c.

‡ the flood, etc.; that is, the firmnesse of tribulacious comynge on hem. foundement; that is, power and richessis, in whiche thei tristiden. Lire here. c.

24 ‡ a flynt for erthe; that is, myche betere thingis than thou haddist bifore, as a flynt is betere than symple erthe, and gold is betere than a flynt. Lire here. c.

---

m wickid AH.   n arered AEFH.

---

s 3ilt thou 1. t is in c. u cumpassith 18. w pathis 8. x the whiche 1. y The whiche men 18. z The whiche 1. a mi3t 8. b fulfillid 18. c the whiche 1. d wickid men 18. e up reisyng 18. f remenauntis 18. g Therfor, Job 18. h The Lord 18. i schal thanne 18. k 3yue thee 1. l Om. 1. the s. m for 8. n reise up 18. o And thou 18. p vowis to him 1. vois to him 8. q deme or axe 18. r to 18. s Certis 18. t innocent man 1.

CAP. XXIII.

1
2 Answerende forsothe Job seide, Now
also in bitternesse is my woord, and the
hond of my veniaunce is agreggid vp on
3 my weiling. Who to me ʒeneᵒ, that I
knowe, and finde hym, and come vnto
4 the seet of hym ? I shal setten beforn
hym dom, and my mouth I shal fille with
5 blamyngis ; that I wite the woordis, that
he answerth to me, and vnderstonde what
6 he speke to me. I wil not with myche
strengthe he striue with me, ne with
the pois of his mykilnesse he bere me
7 doun. He purpose eueneuesse aʒen me,
8 and myn dom come to victorie. If to
the est I shal go, he apereth not ; if to
the west, I shal not vnderstonde hym ;
9 if to the lift, what shal I do ? I shal not
otake hym ; if I turne me to the riʒt, I
10 shal not seen hym. He forsothe wot my
weie, and shal proue me as gold, that
11 thurʒ the fyr passeth. My foot folewide
his steppis ; his weie I kepte, and I
12 bowide not doun fro it. Fro the hestis
of his lippis I wente not awei ; and in
my bosum I hidde the woordis of his
13 mouth. He forsothe is alone, and no
man mai turne awey his thoʒtis ; and his
soule what thing euere it woldeᵖ, that it
14 dideᑫ. Whan it shal fulfille in me his
wil, and othere manye lie thingus ben
15 redi to hym. And therfore fro the face
of hym I am disturbidʳ, and beholdende
16 hym with drede I am bisy. God tem-
prede myn herte, and the Almyʒti dis-
17 turbideˢ me. Forsothe I pershide not for
the aboue comende derenessis ; and dusk-
nesseᵗ couerede my face.

CAP. XXIV.

1 Fro the Almyʒti ben not hid the times ;
thei forsothe that knewen hym, vnknow-
2 en his daʒis. Othere men translateden
termes, breeken atwynne the flockis,

CAP. XXIII.

1
2 Sotheliᵃ Joob answeride, and seide, Now
also my word is in bitternesse, and the
hond* of my wounde is agreggid on my
weilyng. Who ʒyueth to me, that Y knowe, 3
and fynde hym, and come 'til toʷ his trone?
4 Y schal sette doom bifor hym, and Y schal
fille my mouth with blamyngis*† ; that Y 5
kunne the wordis, whiche he schal answere
to me, and that Y vnderstonde, what he
schal speke to me. Y nyleʸ, that he stryue 6
with me bi greet strengthe, nether ᶻ oppresse me with the heuynesse of his greetnesse. Sette he forth equite aʒens me, and 7
my doom comeᵃ perfitli to victorie. If Y 8
go to the eest, God apperith notᵇ ; if Y go
to the west, Y schal not vndurstonde hym ;
if Y go to the left side, what schal Y do ? 9
Y schal not take hym ; if ᶜ Y turne me to
the riʒt side, Y schal not se hym. But he 10
knowith my weie, and he schal preue me
as gold‡, that passith thorouʒ fierᵈ. My 11
foot suede hise steppis ; Y kepte his weie,
and Y bowide not awey fro it. Y ʒede not 12
awei fro the comaundementisᵉ of hise lippis ;
and Y hidde in my bosum the wordis of
his mouth. Forᶠ he is aloone, and no man 13
may turne awei hise thouʒtis ; and what
euer thing he wolde, his wille§ dide this
thing. Whanne he hath fillid his wille in 14
me, also many othere lijk thingis ben redi
to hym. And therfor Y am disturblid of 15
his face, and Y biholdynge hym am an-
guyschid for drede. God hath maad 16
neische myn herte, and Almyʒti God hath
disturblid me. Forᵍ Y perischide not|| for 17
derknessis neiʒyngeʰ ; nethir myist hilide
my face.

CAP. XXIV.

1 Tymes ben not hid fro Almyʒti God ;
sotheli thei that knowen hym, knowen not
hise daies¶. Othere men turnedenⁱ ouer 2
the termes of neiʒboris eritageᵏ, thei tokenˡ

* the hond,
etc. ; that is,
the greuous-
nesse of beting.
Lire here. c.
† blamyngis ;
in Ebreu it is,
with argu-
mentis, as a
disciple makith
ofte argumentis
bifor the mais-
ter, not to stryf,
but to knowing
of truthe, that
he desirith to
here of the
maister ; thus
wolde Joob do
with God.
Lire here. c.

‡ gold ; the
fyer that preueth
gold, ʒyueth
not to it the
truthe of gold,
but declarith
it biforheynge ;
therfor Joob
seith, that the
fier of tribula-
cioun ʒaf not
ynnocence to
him, but de-
claride it bi
his pacience ;
and so God
preuede him,
not to knowe
his innocence
vnknowun to
him, but that
it schulde be
schewid to
othere men ; as
also he sayede
Abraham in
xxii. eᵗ. of
Genesis, that
his obedience
were knowun
to othere men.
Lire here. c.
§ his wille,
etc. ; in tur-
mentinge me
as his creature.
Lire here. c.
|| Y perischid
not, etc. ; that
is, Y suffride
not turmentis
for opyn
synnes, nether
for priuy
synnes. Lire
here. c.
¶ hise daies ;
that is, com-
prehenden not
the maner of
his euerlast-
ingenesse. Lire
here. c.

ᵒ ʒyueth ᴀ.   ᵖ wile ᴇ pr. m.   ᑫ doth ᴇ pr. m.
derknessis ʜ.

ʳ disturblid ᴀ.   ˢ disturblide ᴀ.   ᵗ dusknessis ᴀ.

ᵘ And ɪs.   ʷ vn to ɪ.   ˣ blamynge s.   ʸ wil not ɪ.   ᶻ nether that he ɪs.   ᵃ come it s.   ᵇ not there ɪs.
ᶜ and if ɪs.   ᵈ the fier ɪ.   ᵉ heestis ɪs.   ᶠ Certis ɪs.   ᵍ Certis ɪs.   ʰ neiʒynge to me ɪs.   ˡ han turned ɪs.
ᵏ Om. ɪs.   ˡ han take ɪs.

3 and fedden hem. Thei dryuen awei the asse[u] of moderles childer, and token awei for a wed the oxe of the widewe. 4 Thei turneden vp so doun the weie of pore men, and opresseden togidere the 5 debonere men of erthe[v]. Othere men as assis in desert gon out to ther were; and wakende at the prey, greithe bred to fre 6 childer. The feld not thers thei destroȝen, and his vine, whom bi violence thei opresseden, thei kutte the grapis. 7 Nakid thei leue men, takende awei clothis, 8 to whom is no koueryng in cold; whom wederes of hillis moisten, and not hauende 9 wrielys[w] clippe stones. Fors thei diden robbende moderles childer; and the comun 10 of pore men thei spoileden. To the nakide, and to the goende withoute clothing, and to the hungri thei token awei 11 eris. Among the hipilis of hem thei resteden in mydday, the whiche thresten, 12 the pressoures tredid. They maden men of citees to weilen, and the liues of woundid men shul crien; and God suffreth not vnuengid to gon awey. Thei 13 weren rebel to liȝt; thei knewen not his weies, ne thei be turned aȝeen bi his 14 sties. Erli first riseth[x] the mansleere, and he sleth the nedy, and the pore; bi the nyȝt forsothe he shal ben as a thef[y]. 15 The eȝe of the auoutrer waiteth derknesse, seiende, The eȝe shal not see me; 16 and he shal coueren his chere. Thei breeken thurȝ housis in dercnesses, as in the dai thei hadde scid togidere to themself; and thei vnknewe liȝt. If feerli apere 17 the morutid, thei deme the shadewe of deth; and so in dercnessis thei gon as in 18 liȝt. Liȝt he is vp on the face of the water; cursid be his part in the erthe, ne 19 go he bi the weie of vines. To[z] ful myche hete he shal passen fro the watris of

3 awei[m] flockis[n], and fedden tho[o]. Thei 3 driueden[p] awei the asse of fadirlesse children, and[q] token awei the cow of a widewe for a wed. Thei districden the weie of pore 4 men, and thei oppressiden togidere the mylde men of erthe. Othere men as 5 wielde assis in deseert goon out to her werk; and thei waken to prey, and bifor maken[r] redy breed to her children. Thei 6 kitten doun a feeld† not hern[s], and thei gaderen grapis of his vyner, whom thei han oppressid bi violence. Thei lecuen 7 men nakid, and taken awei the[t] clothis, to whiche[u] men is[w] noon[x] hiling in coold; whiche[y] men the[z] reynes[a] of munteyns 8 weeten, and thei han noon[b] hilyng, and[c] biclippen[d] stoonys‡. Thei diden violence, 9 and[e] robbiden fadirles and modirles children; and thei spuyliden, 'other robbiden[f]', the comynte of pore men. Thei token 10 awey eeris of corn fro nakid men, and goynge with out cloth, and fro hungry men. Thei weren hid in myddai among 11 the heepis of tho[g] men, that thirsten, whanne the presses[h] ben trodun. Thei 12 maden men of citees to weile, and the soulis of woundid men schulen crye; and God suffrith it[i] not to[k] go awei vnpunyschid. Thei weren rebel to liȝt; thei 13 knewen not the weyes therof, nether thei turneden aȝen bi the pathis therof. A 14 mansleere risith ful eerli, and sleeth a nedi man[l], and a pore man; sotheli[m] bi nyȝt he schal be as a nyȝt theef. The iȝe 15 of avouter kepith derknesse, and[n] seith, An yȝe schal not se me; and he schal hile his face. Thei§ mynen housis in 16 derknessis, as thei seiden togidere to hem silf in the dai; and thei knewen not liȝt. If the morewtid apperith sudeynli, thei 17 demen[o] the schadewe of deth; and so thei goon in derknessis as in liȝt. He[p] is vn- 18

† thei kitten doun a feeld, etc. ; that is, gaderen bi violence to hem silf othere mennus corn. Lire here. c.

‡ biclippen stoonys ; in puttinge hem silf with ynne eauys. Lire here. c.

§ They ; that is, auouter and auoateresse. Lire hers. c

---

u assis *AII.*   v the erthe *AEFII.*   w wriels *or* coueryngis *A.*   x ariseth *AEFH.*   y dai thef *E pr. m.*   z At *E pr. m.*

m Om. s.   n her flockis IS.   o hem self IS.   p han drijue IS.   q and thei IS.   r thei maken IS.   s heres s.   t her IS.   u the whiche I.   w ther is I.   x no IS.   y the whiche I.   z Om. I.   a reyn s.   b no IS.   c and thei IS.   d biclippiden s.   e and thei I.   f Om. ILS.   g thilke I.   h presses *of grapis* IS.   i Om. IS.   k that cry to IS.   l Om. s.   m and IS.   n and he IS.   o demen it IS.   p He this I. He that thus doth s.

snowis, and vnto helle the synne of hym.
20 His mercy be forʒeten; his swetnesse a
worm; be he not in recording, but be to-
21 trede as a tree vnfructuous. Forsothe he
fedde the barein, that^a bar not child, and
22 to the widewe he dide not wel^b. He^c
droʒ doun the stronge men in ther
strengthe; and whan he shulde stonde,
23 he shall not trowe to his lif. God to hym
a place of penaunce ʒaf, and he mysuseth
it in to pride; forsothe the eʒen of hym
24 ben in his weies. Thei ben rerid at a
litil, and thei shul not stonde stille; and
thei shul be mekid as alle thinges, and
be do awey; and as the ouermostis of
25 corneris thei shul ben to-broosid. That if
it is not so, who may me vndernyme to
han lowen, and to putte beforn God my
woordys?

CAP. XXV.

1 Answerende forsothe Baldac Suytes
2 seide, Power and fere anent hym is, that
maketh acord in ther heʒe put thingus.
3 Whether is ther noumbre of the knyʒtis
of hym? and vp on whom shyneth not
4 the liʒt of hym? Whether mai a man be
iustified comparisoun to God, or seme
5 clene born of a womman? Lo! also the
mone shineth not, and the sterris ben not
6 clene in the siʒte of hym; myche more
a man stink^d, and the sone of a man a
werm.

CAP. XXVI.

1
2 Answerende forsothe Job seide, Whos
helpere art thou? whether feble, and

stableret than the face of the¶ water; his
part in erthe be cursid^r, and go he not bi
the weie of vyneris. Passe he to^s ful greet 19
heete fro the watris of snowis, and the
synne of hym^t 'til to^u hellis. Merci forʒete 20
hym; his swetnesse be a worm; be he
not in^w mynde, but be he al to-brokun
as 'a tre vnfruytful^x. For he fedde the 21
bareyn‡, and hir that childith not, and he
dide not wel to the widewe. He drow 22
doun stronge men in his strengthe; and
whanne he stondith in 'greet state^y, he
schal not bileue to his lijf. God ʒaf to hym 23
place^z of penaunce, and he mysusith that
in to pride; for^a the iʒen of God ben^b
in the weies of that man. Their^c ben reisid 24
at^d a litil^e, and thei schulen not stonde;
and thei schulen be maad low as alle^f
thingis, and thei schulen be takun awei;
and as the hyʒnessis^g of eeris of corn thei
schulen be al to-brokun. That if it is not 25
so§, who may repreue‖ me, that Y liede,
and putte^h my^i wordis bifor^k God?

CAP. XXV.

1 Forsothe^l Baldach Suytes answeride, and
seide^m, Power and drede is anentis hym,
that is, God, that^n makith acordyng in
hise hiʒe thingis. Whether^o noumbre is^p of 3
hise knyʒtis? and on^q whom schyneth
not his liʒt? Whether a man compari- 4
sound to God mai be iustified, ether^r
borun of a womman mai appere cleene?
Lo! also the moone¶ schyneth not, and 5
sterris ben not cleene in 'his siʒt‡; hou 6
miche more a^t man^u rot, and the sone
of a^w man^x a worm, is vncleene 'and vile,
if he^y is^z comparisound^a to God.

CAP. XXVI.

1
2 Forsothe^b Joob answeride, and seide,
Whos helpere art thou? whether 'of the

^a and that A H. ^b welthe A. ^c And H. ^d is stynke A.

q Om. 18. r acursid 18. s to a 1. t hym passe 1. hym be it 8. u nn to 1. in to s. w in hooly 18.
x an unfruytful tre 18. y prosperitee 18. z heere a place 18. a sothly 18. b ben biholdinge s. c Thei that
ben suich men s. d up at 18. e litil while 1. f alle vile 18. g hiʒnesse 18. h haue putt forth 1. haue put s.
i folily my 18. k aʒens my s. l Then 18. m seide to Job s. n which s. o Wher ther be 1. Wher ther is s.
p Om. 18. q up on 18. r ether wher a man 1. ether a man s. s the siʒt of God 18. t Om. 1. u man that
is 18. w Om. A sec. m. x man that is s. y Om. 1. z Om. 18. a in comparisoun 1. b Sothely 18.

† he is vnsta-
blere, etc.; that
is, the avoter
sueth the fers-
nesse of his
lust, as the
hiʒere part of
the water sueth
the string of
ech wind. Lire
here. c.
‡ the bareyn;
that is, he
wastide hise
goodis in
veyn and vn-
fruytful werkis.
Lire here. c,
§ if it is not so,
as Y seide,
that is, that my
turment passith
my synnes, and
that Goddis
puruyaunce
strecchith forth
it silf to alle
thingis, and
dilayith sum
tyme the pun-
ysching of
synnes in pre-
sent tyme, and
reserueth hem
to the peyne of
helle, bi the
ordre of his
wisdom. and
putte my wordis
bi for God; as
brouʒt forth
with out reue-
rence, other with
blasfemye; as if
he seie, Noon
of ʒou may do
this. Lire here.
c.
‖ who may re-
preue, etc. ;
Eliphat con-
cludide not
aʒenus Joob, for
Joob affermede
not him silf
iust bi al maner,
nether in com-
parisoun to
God, but onely
that he haldie
not so grete
synnes, hou
grete turment
was ʒouun to
him of God;
but rathere
that he schulde
be rewardid of
God by the
ordre of his
wisdom in tyme
to comynge,
for the merit of
his pacience;
and so Baldath
seide seth to

sustenest the arm of hym, that is not
3 strong? To whom hast thou ȝiue counseil? Perauenture to hym that hath no
wisdam; and myche prudence thou hast
4 shewid. Or whom woldest thou techen?
whether not hym, that made space of^e
5 bretling? Lo! ieauntis weilen vnder wa-
^{a}tris, and that duellen with hem. Nakid
is helle beforn hym, and no coueryng is
7 to perdicioun. He that streccheth out the
north vp on vein, and hangeth vp the
8 erthe vp on noȝt. That^f bindeth watris
in his cloudis, that thei breke not out
9 togidere dounward. That holdeth the
chere of his sete, and streccheth out vp
10 on it his cloude. The terme he enuyrounde with watris, vn to the time that
11 ben fynysht liȝt and dercnessis. The
pileris of heuene togidere quaken, and^g
12 dreden at his bek. In the strengthe of
hym feerli ses ben gedered, and the pru-
13 dence of hym smot the proude man. His
spirit ournede heuenes, and his hond liȝtli
ledende out, the eche side krokende ed-
14 dere is led out. Lo! a part ben seid of
his weies; and whan vnnethe a litil drope
of his woord wee han herd, who shal
moun the thunder of his gretnesse beholde?

CAP. XXVII.

1 Also Job addede, takende his parable,
2 and seith, God liueth, that toc awei my
dom, and the Almyȝti, that to bitternesse
3 broȝte my lif. For whil ther leueth breth
in me, and the spirit of God in my nose
4 therlis, my lippis shul not speke wickidnesse, ne my tunge shal bethenke lesing.
5 Ferr be fro me, that I deme ȝou to be
riȝtwise; to the time I faile, I shal not
6 gon awei fro myn innocence. My iustifiyng, that I haue begunne to holde, I shal
not forsake; ne forsothe myn herte re-

feble^c, and^d susteyneste the^e arm of hym,
which^f is not strong? To whom hast thou ȝ
ȝoue counsel? In hap to hym that hath
not wisdom; and thou hast schewid ful
4 myche prudence. Ether whom woldist
thou teche? whether not hym, that made
bretling? Lo! giauntis* weilen vnder ȝ
watris, and thei^g that dwellen with hem.
Helle is nakid bifor hym, and noon hilyng ȝ
is to perdicioun. Which^h *God* stretchith 7
forth the north on^i voide thing, and^k hangith the erthe on^l nouȝt. `Which God^m ȝ
byndith watris in her cloudis, that tho
breke not out togidere dounward. `Whych 9
God^n holdith the cheer of his seete, and^o
spredith abrood therou^p his cloude. He 10
hath cumpassid a terme^q to watris, til that
liȝt and derknessis^r be endid. The pilers† 11
of heuene tremblen, and^s dreden at his
wille. In the strengthe of hym the sees 12
weren gaderid togidere sudeynly, and his
prudence smoot the proude^t. His spiryt^u 13
ournede heuenes, and the crokid serpent
was led out bi his hond, ledynge^w out as
a^x mydwijf ledith out a child. Lo! these 14
thingis ben seid in partie of `hise weyes^y;
and whanne we han herd vnnethis a litil
drope of his word, who may se the thundur of his greetnesse?

CAP. XXVII.

Also Joob addide^z, takynge his parable, 1
and^a seide, God lyueth, that hath take 2
awey‡ my doom^b, and Almyȝti God, that
hath brouȝt my soule^c to bitternesse^d. For 3
as long as breeth is in me, and the spirit
of God is^e in my nose thirlis, my lippis 4
schulen not speke wickidnesse, nether my
tunge schal thenke a leesyng. Fer be it 5
fro me, that Y deme ȝou iust^f; til Y faile§,
Y schal not go awei fro myn innocence.
Y schal not forsake my iustifiyng^h, which^i 6
Y bigan to holde; for myn herte repreueth

Marginal notes:

hise owne
boost, and not
to the purpos
aȝenus Joob.
Lire here. c.
¶ *Lo! also the
monne, etc.;*
ech creature
comparisound
to God is derk-
nesse and vn-
clene. *Lire
here. c.*
* *Lo! giauntis,
etc.;* that weren
bifor the flood
of Noe, and
weren dreynt
thanne in wa-
tris, weilen now
in the peynes
of helle. *Lire
here. c.*

† + *the pileris,
etc.;* that is,
aungels that
mynystren
ether rulen the
styringis of
heuene, doen
reuerence to
God. *Lire
here. c.*

‡ *take awei,
etc.;* bi the
errour of his
freendis, selynge
that peynes in
this lijf ben
iouun onely for
synnes pasid.
Lire here. c.

§ *til Y faile;*
that is, as longe
as Y lyue.
Lire here. c.

^{e} to A. ^{f} And AH. ^{g} Om. AH.

^{c} *thou be [art s] the helpere of a feble man* is. ^{d} *and whether thou* s. ^{e} *thou the* 1. ^{f} *that* is.
^{g} *thei also* is. ^{h} *The which* 1. ^{i} *upon* is. ^{k} *and he* is. ^{l} *upon* is. ^{m} *And he* is. ^{n} *He* is. ^{o} *and
he* is. ^{p} *ther upon* is. ^{q} *terme or an ende* 1. ^{r} *derknesse* 1. ^{s} *and thei* is. ^{t} *proud prince* s. ^{u} *spirit
hath* is. ^{w} *ledynge him* is. ^{x} Om. R. ^{y} *the weies of the Lord* is. ^{z} *addide to* is. ^{a} *and he* is.
^{b} *doom or dampnacioun* s. ^{c} *lijf* is. ^{d} *bitternesse of sorewe* s. ^{e} Om. is. ^{f} *iust counceylours* s.
^{g} *faile lijf* is. ^{h} *iustefiengis of the Lord* s. ^{i} *that* 1.

7 preude me in al my lif. As vnpitous myn enemye; myn aduersarie as wicke^h.
8 What is forsothe the hope of an ipocrite, if auerously he take, and God deliuere
9 not his soule? Whether God shal here the cri of hym, whan shal come vp on
10 hym anguysh? or shal moun in the Almy3ti delite, and inwardly clepe God in
11 alle tyme? I shal teche 3ou bi the hond of God, what thingus the Almy3ti hath;
12 and I shal not hide. Lo! alle 3ee han knowe, and what withoute cause veyne^l
13 thingis 3ee speken? This is the part of the vnpitous man anent God, and the eritage of the violent^k men^l, that of the
14 Almy3ti thei shul take. If his sones be multeplied, thei shul be in swerd; and his sones sones shul not be fulfild with
15 bred. That shul be laft of hym, shul be biried in deth; and his widewis shul not
16 wepe. If he shul bere togidere as erthe
17 siluer, and as clei make redi clothis; he greithede forsothe, but the ri3twise shal be clad^m with them, and the innocent
18 shall deuyde the siluer. He bilde vp his hous as a mow3he, and as a kepere he
19 made^n an hilet. The riche man, whan he shal slepe, no thing with hym shal bern; he shal opene his e3en, and no thing he
20 shal finde. Mysese shal caechen hym as water; in the ny3t shal opresse hym tem-
21 pest. Brennende wind shal take hym, and don awei; and as a whirlewind shal
22 raueshen hym fro his place. He shal senden out vp on hym, and not sparen;
23 fro his hond fleende he shal flee. He shal streyne vp on hym his hondis, and whistlen vpon hym, beholdende his place.

me* not^k in al my lijf. As my wickid 7 enemy** doth; myn aduersarie is as wickid.
For what is the hope of an ypocrite, if he 8 rauyschith gredili, and God delyuerith not his soule? Whether God schal here the 9 cry of hym, whanne angwisch† schal come on' hym? ether whether he may delite in 10 Almy3ti God, and inwardli clepe God in al tyme? Y schal teche 3ou bi the hond of 11 God, what thingis Almy3ti God hath; and Y schal not hide^m. Lo! alle 3e knowen^n, 12 and what^o speken 3e veyn thingis with out cause? This is the part of a wickid 13 man anentis God, and the eritage of vio-lent men, ether^p rauenours, whiche thei schulen take of Almy3ti God. If^q hise^r 14 children ben multiplied, thei schulen be slayn^t in^u swerd; and hise^w sones sones schulen not be fillid with breed‡. Their 15 that ben residue^y of hym^z, schulen be biried in perischyng; and the^a widewis of hym^b schulen not wepe. If he gaderith^c 16 togidere siluer as erthe, and^d makith redi clothis^e as cley; sotheli he made^f redi, 17 but a iust man schal be clothid in tho^g, and an innocent man schal departe the siluer. As a mou3te he^h hath bildid his 18 hous, and as a^i kepere^k he^l made a scha-dewyng place. A riche man, whanne he 19 schal die, schal bere no thing§ with hym; he schal opene hise i3en, and he schal fynde no thing. Pouert as water schal 20 take hym; and tempeste schal oppresse hym in the ny3t. Brennynge wynd schal 21 take hym, and schal^m do^n awei; and as a whirlewynd it schal rauysche hym fro 22 his place. He^o schal sende out turmentis on^p hym, and^q schal not spare^r; he fleynge schal 'fle fro his hond^s||. He^t schal streyne 23 hise hondis on^u him, and he schal hisse on^w hym^x, and^y schal biholde his^z place.

*myn herte repreueth me; that Y belde siche errours ether llyk. Lire here. c.
**say wickid enemy; Joob clepith hise frendis hise enemyes, in as myche as they ben con-tearie to him in the truthe of liyf, of feith, of teching, and of vertues. Lire here. c.
†Wher God schal here the cri of him, whanne an-gwisch of deth; as if he seie, Nay. This is seid anentis hem that con-tynuen her synnes, and thenken in the ende to crie to God bi pe-nuance, but they ben pryued of this hope, for thei re-penten not thanne, in this that al is with, a synnere in sinytun bi this peyne, that whanne he dieth, he forgete that schal; which the while he lyuede, forjat God; if he re-pentith, this is fire the dreede of peyne, and not for disples-ing of synne, ether delite; in his to comynge and clepe God in al tyme; as if he seie, Nay; and this is seide specialy anentis synneris, that maken hem silf sikur of his to comynge, and seyen, God made not vs to be dampned, but to be saued; for this is not soth, no but hi sup-posing of me-ritis. Lire here. c.

---

h wickid A.   i and veyn A.   k the violent ABFH.   l thingis E pr. m. man H.   m clothid ABFH.   n make A.

k not heere of s.   l upon 1s.   m hide hem 1s.   n knowen, that is, owen to knowe B. knowen discrescioun s.   o wherto thanne 1. what than s.   p or 1s.   q And if 1. And s.   r the 1s.   s children of siche men 1s.   t Om. plures. killed s.   u with 1s.   w her 1s.   x And thei 1s.   y the remnaunt 1s.   z sich a man 1s.   a tho s.   b hem s.   c gadere s.   d and if he 1s.   e dyuerse clothis 1s.   f made these thingis s.   g tho thingis 1.   h the wickid man s.   i an heerd 1.   k kepere of beestis s.   l he hath 1s.   m it shal 1.   n do hym A pr. m. 1s.   o The Lord 1s.   p upon 1.   q and he 1s.   r spare hym 1.   s enforse him to fle fro the hoond of the Lord 1s.   t But he s.   u upon 1s.   w upon 1s.   x hym in scorn 1. hym bi scorn s.   y and he 1s.   z his desert 1s.

CAP. XXVIII.

1 Siluer hath the principlis of his veynes;
and to gold is a place, in the whiche it is
2 blowe togidere. Iren[o] fro the erthe is
taken, and a ston losid bi hete, in to bras
3 is turned. Tyme he putte to dercnessis,
and the ende of alle thingus he beholdeth.
4 Also the strem deuydeth the ston of dusc-
nesse, and the shadewe of deth, fro the
puple pilgrimagende; hem[p], whom the
foot of the nedi man forȝat, in to men
5 withoute weies. The erthe, of the whiche
bred cam of in his place, with fyr is
6 turned vpsodoun. Place of a safyr is
7 stones, and the gluggis of hym gold. The
brid vnknewȝ the sty, ne the eȝe of the
8 gripe beheeld it. The sones of marchaundis treeden it not, ne the leounesse
9 thurȝ passide bi it. To the flint he straȝte
out his hond; he turnede vpsodoun fro
10 the rootis[q] the hillis. In stones riueres
he heewȝ[r] out; and alle precious thing
11 saȝ his eȝe. The depe thingus also of
flodis he enserchide; and hid thingus he
12 broȝte in to liȝt. Wisdam forsothe, wher
is it[s] founde, and what is the place of
13 vndirstonding? A man wot not the pris
of it, ne it is founde in the lond of
14 sweteli lyuende men. The depnessis[t] of
watris seith, It is not in me; and the se
15 speketh, It is not with me. Shynende
gold shal not be ȝiue for it, ne siluer shal
16 be peisid in the chaffaring of it. It shal
not be comparisound to the steyned coloures of Ynde, ne to the most precious
17 sardenyk ston, or[u] safyr. Ne shal be
maad euene to it gold, or glas; ne for it
18 shul be chaungid vesselis of gold, heȝe
and ouerstondende[v], ne shul be remembrid in the comparisoun of it. Wisdam
19 forsothe is drawen of hidde thingis; ne
ther shal be maad euene to it topasie of

CAP. XXVIII.

Siluer hath bigynnyngis[a] of his veynes; 1
and a place is to gold, in which it is
wellid* togidere. Irun is takun fro erthe[b], 2
and a stoon resolued, '*ethir meltid*[c],' bi
heete, is turned in[d] to money. God hath[e] 3
set tyme to derknessis, and he biholdith
the ende of alle thingis. Also a stronde 4
departith a stoon of[f] derknesse, and the
schadewe of deth, fro the puple goynge in[g]
pilgrymage; *it departith* tho *hillis*, whiche
the[h] foot of a nedi man forȝat, and *hillis*
with out weie. The erthe, wher of breed† 5
cam forth in his place, is destried bi fier.
The place of[i] saphir ben[k] stoonys therof, 6
and the clottis therof ben gold. A brid 7
knewe not the weie, and the iȝe of a vul-
tur[l], *ethir*[m] *rauenouse*[n] *brid*[o], bihelde it
not. The sones of marchauntis tretiden[p] 8
not on[q] it[r], and a lyonesse passide not
therbi. God stretchide forth his hond to[s] 9
a flynt; he distriede hillis fro the rootis[t].
He hewide doun ryuers in stoonys; and 10
his iȝe siȝ al precious thing[u]. And he 11
souȝte out the depthis[w] of floodis; and he
brouȝte forth hid thingis in to liȝt. But 12
where is wisdom‡ foundun, and which is
the place of vndurstondyng? A[x] man 13
noot[y] the prijs therof, nether it is foundun
in the lond of men lyuynge swetli[z], '*ether*
delicatli[a]. The depthe of watris seith, It 14
is not in me; and the see spekith, It is not
with me. Gold ful cleene schal not be 15
ȝouun for wisdom, nether siluer schal be
weied in the chaungyng therof. It[b] schal 16
not be comparysound to the died colours
of Iynde, not[c] to the moost preciouse stoon
of[d] sardius, nether to[e] saphir. Nether gold, 17
nether glas schal be maad[f] euene worth
therto[g]; and hiȝe and fer apperynge ves- 18
sels of gold schulen not be chaungid for
wisdom, nether[h] schulen be had in mynde

‡ *with breed*; that is, schulen die for hungur. *Lire here.* c.
§ *no thing, etc.*; of goodis of present liyf. *Lire here.* c.
and he schal fynde nothing; of goodis of present liyf, nether to comynge. *Lire here.* c.
‖ *schal fle fro his hond*; that is, schal desire to fle, if he myȝte. *Lire here.* c.
* *wellid*; that is, gendrid. c.
† *erthe, wher of breed*; that is, corn, wher of breed is maad. *Lire here.* c.

‡ *But wher is wisdom*; that is, the knowyng and loue of God, and so wisdom enclosith grace, and othere vertues ȝouun of God, and they that ben ȝouun to fleisly likyngis, ben not able to the reuelaciouns and coumfortis of God. *Lire here.* c.

[o] And yren A. [p] he A. [q] iudgis E *pr. m.* [r] hewide AH. [s] Om. A. [t] depnes AH. [u] of A.
[v] *or schynyng* A *et* E *marg.* F *text.*

[a] biginninge S. [b] the erthe IS. [c] Om. I. *or meltid* S. [d] Om. S. [e] shal S. [f] fro S. [g] in to IS.
[h] Om. S. [i] of a IS. [k] ben the IS. [l] vowtur *plures.* [m] *that is, a* BS. *or* I. Om. V. [n] Om. V. [o] *foul* S.
Om. V. [p] troden I. trededen SU. [q] upon IS. [r] that *wey* I. the *way* S. [s] in I. [t] rootis *therof* IS.
[u] thingis S. [w] depnesse I. [x] Om. I. [y] wot not I. [z] delicatly I. [a] Om. I. [b] Wisdom I. [c] ne IS.
[d] Om. I. [e] to the ISW. [f] Om. I. [g] to wisdom I. [h] nether thei I.

Ethiope, ne to the most clene steynyng
20 shal be comparisound^w. Whennes thanne
wisdam shal come, and what is the place
21 of vnderstonding? It is hid fro the eʒen
of alle liuende men; also to the foulis of
22 heuene it is vnknowen. Perdicioun and
deth seiden, With oure eris wee han herd
23 the fame of it. God vnderstaunt^x the weie
24 of it, and he knewʒ the place of it. He
forsothe looketh the endis of the world;
and alle thingus that ben vnder heuene
25 he beholdeth. That made to windis peis,
26 and watris heeng^y vp in mesure. Whan
he putte to reynes lawe, and weie to
27 sounende tempestis; thanne he saʒ it,
and tolde out, and made redi beforn, and
28 enserchide. And he seide to man, Lo!
the drede of God, it is wisdam; and to
gon awei fro euel, vnderstonding.

CAP. XXIX.

1 Also Job addede, takende to his para-
2 ble, and seide, Who ʒeue to me, that I
be after the rathere monethis, after the
daʒes in the whiche God kepte me?
3 Whanne shynede his lanterne vp on myn
hed, and at his liʒt I wente in derc-
4 nessis. As I was in the daʒes of my
waxende ʒouthe^z, whan priueli God was
5 in my tabernacle. Whan the Almyʒti
was with me, and in myn enuyroun my
6 childer; whan I wesh my feet with buttere, and the ston helde^a to me ryueres
7 of oile; whan I wente forth to the ʒate of
the cite, and in the strete thei maden
8 redy a chaʒer to me. Ʒunge men seʒen
me, and weren hid, and olde men risende
9 stoden; princis ceseden to speken, and
10 finger putten vpon to ther mouth; dukis
withdroweu ther vois, and the tunge of

in comparisoun therof. Forsothe wisdom
is drawunⁱ of pryuy thingis†; topasie of^k 19
Ethiope schal not be maad euene worth
to wisdom, and moost preciouse diyngis
schulen not be set togidere in prijs, ether
comparisound^l, therto. Therfor wherof 20
cometh wisdom, and which is the place
of vndurstondyng? It is hid fro the iʒen^m 21
of alle lyuynge men; alsoⁿ it is hid fro^o
briddis of heuene^p‡. Perdicioun and death§ 22
seiden, With oure eeris we herden^q the
fame therof^r. God vndurstondith the weye 23
therof, and he knowith the place therof.
For^s he biholdith the endis of the world, 24
and^u biholdith alle thingis that ben vndur
heuene. Which God^w made weiʒte to 25
wyndis, and^x weiede watris in mesure.
Whanne he settide^y lawe to reyn, and weie 26
to tempestis sownynge; thanne he siʒ^z 27
wisdom, and telde^a out, and^b made^c redi,
and souʒte^d out. And he seide to man, 28
Lo! the drede of the Lord, thilke^e is wisdom; and to go awei fro yuel, is vndurstondyng.

CAP. XXIX.

Also^f Joob addide^g, takynge his parable, 1
and^{gg} seide, Who ʒyueth to me, that I he 2
bisidis the elde monethis‖, bi the daies
in whiche God kepte me? Whanne his 3
lanterne schynede on myn heed, and Y
ʒede in derknessis at his liʒt. As Y was 4
in the daies of my ʒongthe, whanne in
priuete God was in my tabernacle. Whanne 5
Almyʒti God was with me, and my children weren^h in my cumpas; whanne Y 6
waischide my feet in botere, and theⁱ stoon
schedde out to me the stremes of oile;
whanne^k Y ʒede forth to the ʒate of the 7
citee, and in the street^l thei maden redi
a chaier to me. Ʒonge^m men, that is, wan- 8
tounⁿ, sien me, and weren hid, and elde
men risynge vp stoden; princes ceessiden 9
to speke, and^o puttiden the^p fyngur on^q
her mouth; duykis refreyneden her vois, 10

---

11 hem to ther throte cleuede. The herende
ere 'blisful maade[b] me, and the sennde
12 eȝe witnesse ȝeld to me ; forthi that I
hadde delyuered the pore man criende
out, and the moderles child, to the whiche
13 was noon helpere[c]. The blessing of hym,
that was to pershen, vp on me cam, and
the herte of the widewe I coumfortide.
14 Riȝtwisnesse[d] I am clad[e] ; and I clothide
me as a vestyment, and with a diademe
15 with[f] my dom. An eȝe I was to blinde,
16 and a foot to the halte. Fader I was of
pore men ; and the cause that I knew
17 not, most diligentli I enserchide. I to-
broside the chaulis of the wicke man,
and fro his teth I toc awei the prey.
18 And I seide, Die I in my litle nest ; and
19 as a palme I shal multiplie daȝis. My
roote is opened beside watris, and deu
20 shal abide in my reping. My glorie euermore shal be newid, and my bowe in
21 myn hond shal be reparailid. That herden
me, abiden my sentence ; and takende heede
22 thei heelde stille at my counseil. To my
woordis no thing to adden thei weren
hardi ; and vpon hem droppide my speche.
23 Thei biden as reyn my speche ; and
mouth[g] thei openeden as to the late co-
24 mende weder. If any time I loowȝ to
them, thei leeueden[h] not ; and the liȝt of my
25 chere fel not in to the erthe. If I wolde
go to them, I sat first ; and whan I sat as
a king, the ost aboute stondende, I was
neuerthelatere of dreri men the coum-
fortere.

CAP. XXX.

1 Now forsothe scorne me the ȝungere
in time, of whom I deynede not the fadris
2 to sitte with the hondis of my floc. Of
whom the vertue of hondis to me was
for noȝt, and thei weren trowid vnwrthi

---

11 and[r] her tunge cleuyde to her throte. An[s]
ecre herynge[t] blesside me, and an[u] iȝe se-
12 ynge[w] ȝeldide witnessyng to me ; for Y
hadde[x] delyueride a[y] pore man criynge,
and a[z] fadirles child, that hadde noon[a]
13 helpere. The blessyng of a[b] man 'to perische[c]† cam on[d] me, and Y coumfortide
14 the herte of a[e] widewe. Y was clothid
with riȝtfulnesse ; and Y clothide me as
with a cloth, and with my 'doom a[f] dia-
15 deme[g]. Y was iȝe[h] 'to a[i] blynde man, and[k]
16 foot to a[l] crokyd man. Y was a fadir of
pore men ; and Y enqueride most diligentli
the cause, which[m] Y knew not. Y al to-
17 brak the grete teeth of the wickid man‡,
18 and Y took awei prey[n] fro hise teeth. And
Y seide, Y schal die in my nest[o] ; and as a
19 palm tre Y schal multiplie daies[p]. My
roote is openyde bisidis watris, and deew
20 schal dwelle in my repyng. My glorie
schal euere be renulid, and my bouwe schal
21 be astorid in myn hond. Thei, that herden
me, abiden my sentence ; and thei weren
ententif[q], and[r] weren stille to[s] my counsel.
22 Thei dursten no thing adde[t] to my wordis ;
23 and my speche droppide on[u] hem. Thei
abididen[w] me as[x] reyn ; and thei openyden
her mouth as to the[y] softe[z] reyn 'comynge
24 late[a]. If ony tyme Y leiȝide to hem, thei
bileueden not ; and the liȝt of my cheer§
25 felde not doun in to erthe[b]. If Y wolde
go to hem, Y sat the firste ; and whanne
Y sat as kyng, while the oost stood
aboute[c], netheles Y was comfortour of
hem that morenyden.

CAP. XXX.

1 But[d] now ȝongere men in tyme scornen
me, whos fadris Y deynede[e]‖ not to sette
with the doggis[f] of my flok. Of whiche
2 men the vertu of[g] hondis was for[h] nouȝt
to me, and thei weren gessid vnworthi

† *to perische ;
that is, of him
that dredde to
perische anoon.
Lire here.* c.

‡ *Y al to-brak
the grete teeth
of the wickid
man ; that is,
mystis and vio-
lences ; and
Y took awei
prey ; for Y
constreynede
him to restore
things takun,
and to make
amendis for
wrongis. Lire
here.* c.

§ *and the liȝt
of my cheer ;
that is, the
gladnesse of
my face, felde
not doun ; as
aschamed for
the vncouena-
blete of glad-
nesse, nether for
sorewe of heuy-
nesse. Lire
here.* c.

‖ *Y deynede
not, etc. ; this
dedeyn cam not
of dispit nether
of pride, but of
worthi bihold-
ing of vilete.
Lire here.* c.

---

[b] gladide E *pr. m.* 　[c] helpe *AII.* 　[d] In riȝtwisnes *A.* 　[e] clothed *AEFH.* 　[f] to E *pr. m.* 　[g] her mouth *AII.*
[h] bileueden *A.*

[r] and *for stilnesse* I. 　[s] The I. 　[t] that herde *me* I. 　[u] the I. 　[w] that siȝe *me* I. 　[x] Om. I. 　[y] the I.
[z] the I. 　[a] no I. 　[b] the I. 　[c] that schulde haue perishid I. 　[d] upon I. 　[e] the I. 　[f] Om. I. 　[g] diademe in
my doom I. 　[h] the iȝe I. 　[i] of the I. 　[k] and the I. 　[l] the I. 　[m] that I. 　[n] the prei I. 　[o] litil nest A *sec. m.*
[p] my daies I. 　[q] takynge heede *to me* I. 　[r] and thei I. 　[s] at I. 　[t] putte I. 　[u] upon I. 　[w] abeden I.
abiden s. 　[x] as *men don* I. 　[y] a *sup. ras.* ADCV. 　[z] softe sesenable I. 　[a] Om. I. 　[b] the erthe IS. 　[c] aboute
me I. 　[d] Certis I. 　[e] vowchide not saaf I. 　[f] houndis I. 　[g] of her I. 　[h] Om. s.

3 that lif. And thurȝ nede and hunger
barein; that gnowen[l] in wildernesse, waxende foul with wrecchidnesse and sorewe.
4 And thei eeten erbis, and the rindis of trees;
and the[k] roote of iunypere trees was the
5 mete of hem. The whiche of the[l] valeis
these thingus takende; whan alle thingus
thei hadde founde, with cri thei runne to
6 thoo thingus. In desertis of stremys thei
dwelten, and in dennes of the erthe, or
7 vp on grauel[m]. The whiche among such
thingus gladeden, and to ben vnder busschis
8 counteden delicis. The sonus of foolis
and of vnnoble men, and in the lond not
9 fulli perende. Now forsothe I am turned
in to the song of hem, and I am maad to
10 hem a prouerbe. Thei wlaten me, and
ferr floun fro me, and to spute my face
11 they shame[n] not. Forsothe his arwe girdil
he openede, and tormentide me, and he
12 putte a bridil in to my mouth. At the
riȝt of the est my wrecchenesses[o] anoon
risen; thei turneden vpsodoun my feet,
and opresseden as with flodis bi ther
13 sties. Thei scatereden my weies, and
waiteden to me, and hadden the ouere
hond; and ther was not broȝte helpe.
14 As the wal broken and the ȝate opened
thei fellen in on me, and to my wrecchid-
15 nessis thei ben myche boowid to. I am
broȝt in to noȝt; as the wind he hath
taken awei my desyr, and as a cloude
16 passide myn helthe. Now forsothe in
myself welewith my lif, and welde me
17 the daȝis of tormentinge. In[p] the nyȝt
my mouth is thirlid thurȝ with sorewis;
18 and that eten me, slepen not. In the
multitude of hem my clothing is wastid,
and as with a coler of a kote thei girten
19 me. I am comparisound to clei, and am[q]
20 licned to a[r] sparke and to askis[s]. I shal
crie to thee, and thou shalt not heren;

to that lijf†. Thei weren bareyn for nedy- 3
nesse and hungur; that[l] gnawiden in
wildirnesse, and[k] weren[l] pale[m] for pouert
and[n] wretchidnesse; and[o] eeten eerbis, 4
aud the ryndis of trees; and the roote of
iunyperis was her mete. Whiche[p] men 5
rauyschiden these thingis fro grete valeis;
and whanne thei hadden foundun ony of
alle[q], thei runnen with cry to tho[r]. Thei 6
dwelliden in deseertis of strondis, and in
caues of erthe, ethir on[s] grauel, 'ethir on
cley[t]. Whiche weren glad among siche 7
thingis, and[u] arettiden delices[w] to be vndur
buschis. The[x] sones of foolis and of vn- 8
noble men, and outirli apperynge not in[y]
erthe. But now Y am turned in to the 9
song of hem, and Y am maad a prouerbe
to hem. Thei holden me abhomynable, 10
and[z] fleen fer fro me, and[a] dreden not to
spete on my face. For[b] God hath openyd 11
his arowe caas, and[c] hath turmentid me,
and[d] hath set[e] a bridil in to my mouth.
At the riȝtside of the eest my wretchid- 12
nessis risiden[f] anoon; thei turneden vpsedoun my feet, and[g] oppressiden with[h] her
pathis as with floodis. Thei destrieden my 13
weies; thei settiden tresoun to me, and[i]
hadden the maistri; and 'noon was[k] that
helpide[l]. Thei felden in on[m] me as bi a[n] 14
brokun wal, and bi ȝate[o] openyd, and[p]
weren[q] stretchid forth to my wretchidnessis. Y am dryuun in[r] to nouȝt; he[s] 15
took awei my desir as wynd, and myn
helpe passide awei as a cloude. But now 16
my soule fadith in my silf, and daies of
turment holden me stidfastly. In nyȝt my 17
boon is persid with sorewis; and thei, that
eten me‡, slepen[t] not. In the multitude of 18
tho my cloth is wastid, and thei han gird
me as with coler[n] of a coote. Y am com- 19
parisound to cley, and Y am maad lijk to
a deed sparcle and[w] aisch[x]. Y schal cry 20

† vnworthi to that lijf; as wickid men and makinge pestilence. Lire here. c.

‡ that eeten me; that is, wormes comynge forth of my bilis. Lire here. c.

l guewen AEH.   k Om. A.   l Om. A.   m the grauel A.   n shameden A.   o wrecchedenessis AEFH.
P And in A. And H.   q I am AFH.   r Om. c.   s asshen A.

i thei I.   k as becstis, and I.   l thei weren I.   m maad foule I.   n in I.   o and thei I.   P The whiche I.
q alle thes thiagis I.   r hem I.   s upon I.   t Om. I.   u and thei I.   w as delices I.   x Thes weren the I.
And the K sec. m. H.   y on s.   z and thei I.   a and thei I.   b Sotheli I.   c and he I.   d and he I.
e putt I.   f han risen up I.   g and thei I.   h me with I.   i and thei I.   k ther was noon I.   l helpide me I.
m upon I.   n Om. Bov.   o a ȝate A pr. m. x sec. m.   P and thei I.   q ben I.   r Om. s.   s the Lord I.
t slepten A. slepith L.   u the coler I.   a coler FX sec. m.   w and to I.   x aishen s.

I stonde, and thou beholdest^t not me.
21 Thou art chaungid to me in to cruel,
and in the hardnesse of thin hond thou
22 art aduersarie to me. Thou hast rered
me, and as vp on wind settende thou hast
23 hurtlid me doun my3tili. I wot, for thou
shalt take me to deth, wher is sett an
24 hous to alle liuende. Nerthelatere not
to the wasting of hem thou puttist out
thin hond; and if thei falle, thou thi self
25 shalt saue. I wepte sum time vp on hym
that was tormentid, and my soule hadde
26 compassioun to the pore. I abod goodis,
and ther camen to me euelis; I abod
li3t, and ther breeken oute dercnessis.
27 Myn entrailis brenden out with oute any
reste; befor wente me the da3es of tor-
28 ment. Dreri I wente withoute wodnesse,
29 risende in the puple I criede. Brother
I was of dragouns, and felawe of the half
30 beste half foul. My skin is bleckid vp on
31 me, and my bones drieden for hete. Myn
harpe is turned in to weiling^u, and myn
orgne in to the vois of weperis.

CAP. XXXI.

1 I couenauntide a pes couenaunt with
myn e3en, that forsothe I shulde not
2 thenke of^v a^w maiden. What forsothe part
God fro aboue shulde han in me, and the
3 Almy3ti eritage fro he3e thingus. Whethir not perdicioun is to the wicke,
and alienyng to men werkende wick-
4 enesse^x? Whether he beholdeth not my
weies, and alle my goingis noumbreth?
5 If I 3ide in vanyte, and my foot hee3ide
6 in treccherie^y, peise he me in a ri3twis
balauns, and wite God my symplenesse.
7 If my going bowide doun fro the weie;
if^z myn e3e folewide myn herte, and a
8 spot cleuede to myn hondis; I shal

to thee^y, and thou schalt not here me; Y
stonde^z†, and thou biholdist^a not me. Thou 21
art chaungid in to cruel^b‡ to me, and in
the hardnesse of thin hond thou art aduersarie to me. Thou hast reisid^c me, and 22
hast^d set^dd as on^e wynd; and^f hast hurtlid^g
me doun strongli. Y woot, that thow 23
schalt bitake me to deeth, where an hows
is ordeyned to ech lyuynge man. Netheles 24
thou sendist^h not out^i thin hond to the
wastyng of hem; and if thei fallen doun,
thou schalt saue^k. Y wepte sum tyme on 25
him, that was turmentid, and my soule
hadde compassioun on a pore man. Y 26
abood^l goodis^m, and yuelis^n ben comun to
me; Y abood li3t, and derknessis braken
out^o. Myn ynnere thingis buyliden out 27
with outen my reste; daies^p of turment
camen bifor me. Y 3ede morenynge, and 28
Y roos^q with out woodnesse in the cumpenye, and^r criede. Y was the brother of 29
dragouns§, and the felow of ostrigis. My 30
skyn was maad blak on^a me, and my
boonys drieden for heete. Myn harpe is 31
turned in to morenyng, and myn orgun in
to the vois of weperis.

CAP. XXXI.

1 I made couenaunt with myn i3en, that
Y schulde not thenke of^t a virgyn‖. For 2
what part schulde God aboue haue in
me, and^u eritage Almy3ti^w God of hi3e
thingis^x? Whether perdicioun is not to a 3
wickid^y man, and alienacioun of God is to
men worchynge wickidnesse? Whether 4
he^x biholdith not my weies, and noumbrith
alle my goyngis? If Y 3ede^a in vanyte, 5
and my foot^b hastide^c in gile, God weie 6
me in a iust balaunce, and knowe^d my
symplenesse. If my step^e bowide fro the 7
weie; if^f myn i3e¶ suede^g myn herte, and^h
a^i spotte cleuede^k to^l myn hondis; sowe Y^m, 8
and another ete^n, and my generacioun be

† Y stonde; contynuynge in preyer. Lire here. c.
‡ in to cruel etc.; thou3 God is not chaungable, nethelese he worchith chaungeble thingis, of whiche he is nemyd dyuersell; and so he is seid pitouse, whanne he 3yueth prosperites, hard, whanne he bringith in aduersitees; and this is seid by the comyn maner of speking of men, which maner Joob suede, thou3 he helde tidefastly, that alle lesingis ben wront of God, pitously and iustly. Lire here. c.
§ brother of dragouns; for they that ou3t loue me as bretheren, hiliden in her pouyschingis and bacbitingis as draguns. of ostrigis; for they that weren homely, and felowis to me, for3aten me as an ostrige for3etith his brid. Lire here. c.
‖ not thenke of a virgyne; lest thoro3 biholding Y schulde falle in to lyting ether consent of ony damesel, 3he, most fair. Lire here. c.
¶ what part; as if he seie, noon. A man, in whom God dwellith by grace, is the part and eritage of God, but he dwellith not in men defoulid bi lecherie, rathire he drawith silf fer fro hem. Lire here. c.
‖ if myn i3e; biholdinge vn-

^t beheeldlist A.   ^u cley E pr. m.   ^v on A.   ^w Om. H.   ^x wickidnesse AH.   ^y treccheries c pr. m.
^z of AH.

^y thee Lord I.   ^z stode I.   ^a biheldist I.   ^b a cruel venger I.   ^c up reisid I.   ^d thou hast I.
^dd set me A pr. m.   ^e upon I.   ^f and thou I.   ^g hurlid I.   ^h puttist I.   ^i forth I.   ^k saue hem I.
^l boode I.   ^m gode thingis I.   ^n yuel thingis I.   ^o out on me I.   ^p and daies I.   ^q roos up I.   ^r and I I.
^s upon I.   ^t on AC.   ^u and what I.   ^w schulde Almy3ti I.   ^x thingis haue in me I.   ^y my3ti s.   ^z God I.
^a haue gon I.   ^b foot hath I.   ^c hastide to go I.   ^d knowe he I.   ^e step haue I.   ^f and if I.   ^g haue
suede I.   ^b consentinge to lust, and I.   ^i if a I.   ^k haue cleuede I.   ^l on s.   ^m I the seed thanue I.
^n ete the fru3t I.

sowen, and an other ete, and my pro-
9 genye be drawe vp bi the roote. If myn^u
herte is desceyued vp on a womman, and
if at the dore of my frend I sette spies;
10 the strumpet of an other be my wif, and
vpon hir othere men be thei crookid.
11 This forsothe is vnleeful, and most wick-
12 idnesse. Fyr is deuouring vnto wasting,
and pullende vp bi the roote alle bur-
13 iounyngus. If I dispiside to gon vnder
dom with my seruaunt and hond maiden,
14 whan thei shulden pleten a3ens me. What
forsothe shal I do, whan God shal rise to
deme? and whan he shal aske, what shal
15 I answern to hym? Whether not in the
wombe he made me, the whiche and
hym wro3te, and oon formede me in the
16 wombe? If I denyede^b to pore men that
thei wolden, and made the e3en of a
17 widewe to abide; if I eet my morsel
alone, and the moderles child eet not of
18 it; for fro my 3outhe doing of mercy
wex with me, and fro the wombe of my
19 moder wente out with me; if I dispiside
the goere beside, for thi that he hadde
not clothing, and the pore withoute couer-
20 yng; if his sidis blessiden not to me, and
21 of the flees of my shep he is chaufid; if
I rerede vp on the moderles child myn^c
hond, also whan I sa3 me in the 3ate
22 the ouerhe3ere; my shulder falle fro his
ioynt, and myn arm with his bones be
23 to-brosid. Forsothe euermor as flodis
swellende vp on me, I dredde God; and
24 his peis I my3te not bern. If I wende^d
gold my strengthe, and to the shynende
25 gold I seide, My trost; if I gladede vp
on my manye richessis, and for myn
26 hond fond manye thingis; if I sa3 the
sunne, whan it shulde shyne, and the
27 mone goende clereli; and myn herte is
gladid in hid thing, and kiste myn hond
28 fro my mouth; the whiche is the moste

drawun out bi the root. If^o myn herte
9 was^p disseyued on a womman*, and if Y
settide^q aspies at the dore of my frend;
my wijf be^r the hoore^s of anothir man, 10
and othir men be bowid doun on^t hir. For^u
11 this^w† is vnleeful, and the moost wickidnesse. Fier^x is deourynge 'til to^y wastyng, 12
and drawynge^z vp bi the roote alle generaciouns. If Y dispiside to take doom with 13
my seruaunt and^a myn hand mayde, whanne
thei stryueden a3ens me. What sotheli 14
schal Y do, whanne God schal rise^b to
deme? and whanne he schal axe, what
schal Y answere to hym? Whether he, 15
that wrou3te also hym, made not me in the
wombe, and o God formede me in the
wombe? If Y denyede to pore men that, 16
that thei wolden‡, and if Y made the i3en
of a wydewe to abide; if^d Y aloone eet my 17
mussel, and^e a faderles child eet not therof;
for^f merciful doyng encreesside with me 18
fro my 3ong childhed, and^g 3ede out of
my modris wombe with me; if Y dis- 19
piside a man passynge forth^h, for he hadde
not a cloth, and a pore man with out
hilyng; if hise sidis blessiden not me, and 20
was^i not maad hoot of the fleeces^k of my
scheep; if Y reiside^l myn hond § on^m a 21
fadirles child, 3he, whanne Y si3^n me the
hi3ere in the 3ate; my schuldre^o falle fro 22
his ioynt, and myn arm with hise boonys
be al to-brokun. For^p euere Y dredde 23
God, as wawis wexynge gret on^q me; and^r
'Y my3te not bere his birthun^s. If Y gess- 24
ide gold my strengthe, and if Y seide to
purid gold, *Thou art* my trist; if Y was 25
glad on my many ritchessis, and for^t myn
hond foond ful many thingis^u ‖; if Y si3 26
the sunne, whanne it schynede, and the
moone goynge clereli; and if myn herte 27
was glad in priuyte, and if Y kisside¶
myn hond with my mouth; which^w is the 28
moost wickidnesse, and deniyng a3ens

chastly. *suche myn herte*; that is, sudeyn thou3tis of the leccherouse fleisch. *Lire here.* c.

* *on a womman*: ioyned in matrymonye, ethir trouthe pli3t to an other man, as the Ebreu word sowneth. *Lire here.* c.

† *For this*; that is, anoutrie. is most wickidnesse; in synnes a3ens the nei3bore. *Lire here.* c.

‡ *that thei wolden*; the while her wille was resonable. *Lire here.* c.

§ *myn hond*; that is, my power, vniustly. *Lire here.* c.

‖ *ful many thingis*; as if he seie, Goddis veniaunce come on me. *Lire here.* c.

¶ *if Y kisside* etc.; 3yuynge to it the reuerence due to God onely. *Lire here.* c.

^a cay A. ^b denie AH. ^c with myn A. ^d weendide H. weenyde A.

^o And if I. And s. ^p hath I. ^q haue sott I. sette s. ^r be *thanne* I. ^s strumpett I. ^t upon I.
^u Forsothe I. ^w this thing I. ^x *Fier of brennynge lust* I. ^y un to I. ^3 it drawith I. ^a and with I.
^b rise up I. ^c that thing I. ^d and if I. ^e and if I. ^f sothely I. ^g and *it* IS. ^h forth *bi me* I.
^i weron I. ^k flees IS. ^l reiside up I. reiside in s. ^m upon I. ^n saw3e: *pass.* ^o shuldren s. ^p Forsothe I. ^q upon I. ^r Om. L. ^s whos birthun I my3te not here I. ^t For cause that I. ^u richessis I.
^w the which I.

wickidnesse, and denyyng aȝen the heȝest
29 God ; if I ioȝide at his falling, that hatide
me, and ful out ioȝide, that euel hadde
30 founden hym ; forsothe I ȝaf not my
throte to synne, that I shulde abide
31 cursende his soule ; if the men of my
tabernacle seiden not, Who ȝiueth of his
32 fleshe, that we be fulfild ? without forth
abod not the pilgrim ; my dore was open
33 to the weie goere ; if I hidde as a man
my synne, and hilede in my bosum my
34 wickenesse ; if I dradde at the moste
multitude, and dispising of neeȝh men
ferede me ; and not more I heeld my pes,
35 and wente not out[e] the dore ; who ȝeue
to me an auditour[f], that my desyr heere
the Almyȝti ? that he that demeth write
36 the boc, that in my shulder I bere it,
37 and enuyroune it as[g] a crowne to me? Bi
alle my grees I shal pronouncen it, and as
38 to a prince I shal offre it. If aȝen me
myn erthe crie, and with it his forewis
39 bewepen[h] ; if his frutis I eet with oute
monee, and the soule of his erthe tilieris
40 I tormentide ; for whete be sprunge to
me a brimbil, and for barli a thorne.

CAP. XXXII.

1 These thre men laften forsothe to answern to Job, forthi that riȝtwis he is
2 seen to them. And Elyu, the sone of
Barachiel Busites, of the kynrede of
Ram, ys wroth, and endeyned ; he is wroth
aȝen Job, forthi that he shulde sein hym-
3 self to be riȝtwis befor God. But aȝen
the thre frendis of hym he dedeynede[i],
forthi that thei hadden not founde a
resounable answere, but onely thei shulden
4 han condempned Job. Thanne Eliu abod
Job spekende, forthi that eldere thei weren,
5 that speken. Whan forsothe he hadde
seen, that the thre myȝten not answern,
6 he wrathede hugeli. And answerende
Elyu, the sone of Barachiel Busites,
seide, I am ȝungere in time, ȝee forsothe

hiȝeste[x] God ; if Y hadde ioye at the fall- 29
yng of hym, that hatide me, and if Y ioide
fulli, that yuel hadde founde hym ; for[y] Y 30
ȝaf not my throte to do[z] synne, that Y
schulde asaile and curse his soule ; if the 31
men of my tabernacle seiden not, Who
ȝyueth, that we be fillid† of hise fleischis ?
a pilgryme dwellide not with outforth ; 32
my dore was opyn to a weiegoere[a] ; if Y 33
as man hidde my synne‡, and helide my
wickidnesse in my bosum[b] ; if Y dredde 34
at ful greet multitude, and if dispisyng of
neyȝboris made me aferd ; and not more[c]
Y was stille, and ȝede[d] not out of the
dore ; who ȝyueth[e] an helpere to me, that 35
Almyȝti God here my desire ? that he that
demeth, write a book§, that Y bere it in[f] my 36
schuldre, and cumpasse it as a coroun to
me ? Bi alle my degrees Y schal pronounce 37
it, and Y schal as[g] offre it to the prynce.
If my lond crieth‖ aȝens me, and hise 38
forewis wepen with it ; if[h] Y eet fruytis[i] 39
therof with out money, and[k] Y turmentide
the soule of[l] erthetileris of it ; a brere 40
growe to me for wheete, and a thorn for
barli.

CAP. XXXII.

Forsothe these thre men leften of to 1
answere Joob, for he semyde a iust man
to hem. And Helyu, the sone of Barachel 2
Buzites, of the kynrede of Ram, was
wrooth, and hadde indignacioun ; forsothe[m]
he was wrooth aȝens Joob, for he seide
hym silf to be iust bifor God. Sotheli[n] 3
Helyu hadde indignacioun aȝens the thre
frendis of hym[o], for thei hadden not
founde resonable[p] answere, but oneli hadde[q]
condempned Joob. Therfor Helyu abood 4
Joob spekynge, for thei, that spaken, weren
eldere men. But whanne he hadde seyn, 5
that thre[r] *men*[s] myȝten not answere[ss], he
was wrooth greetly. And[t] Helyu, the 6
sone of Barachel Buzites, answeride, and
seyde, Y am ȝongere in tyme, sotheli[u] ȝe

† *be fillid etc.*; that is, who ȝyueth that he be euere al present with vs, that we be fillid of his felouschipe. *Lire here.* C.

‡ *hidde my synne*; that is, in denyinge it vnduly, ethir in excusinge falsly. *in my bosum*; that is, herte, bi fals schewing of hoolynesse withoutforth. *Lire here.* C. *if Y dredde at ful greet multitude*; in goynge awey fro riȝtfulnesse, for the drede of many men. *and if dispising etc.*; so that Y ȝede awey fro truthe, and dredde lest Y schulde offende my neiȝbouris, willinge the contrarie. *and not more Y was stille*; heringe the blamyngis of my neiȝboris, for Y nolde assent to hem. *and ȝede not out*; to do any wickid thing for hem. *Lire here.* C.

§ *write a book*; in ȝyuynge the sentence for me. *Lire here.* C.

‖ *if my lond crieth etc.*; that is, if Y gaderide outrageouse fruytis therof, and if Y withdrow the hiris of erthetileris. *Lire here.* C.

[e] without A. [f] heerere E *pr. m.* helpere E *sec. m.* [g] Om. C. [h] floowen doun E *pr. m.* [i] deynede A.

[x] the hiȝeste I. [y] forsothe I. [z] do *that* I. [a] way ferynge man I. [b] bosum, *ether herte* V. [c] more *herfore* I. [d] Y ȝede C. [e] ȝyueth *thanne* I. [f] on IS. [g] as *offryng* I. [h] and if I. [i] the fruytis I. [k] and if I. [l] of the IS. [m] and I. [n] Certis BCDEFHKLMNOPQRSUVWXbf. And also I. [o] Job I. [p] no resonable S. [q] thei hadden I. [r] *thes* thre I. [s] Om. *plures*. [ss] answere *Job* I. [t] And *thanne* I. [u] and I.

eldere; therfore the hed leid doun I am
7 shamed to shewe to 30u my sentence. I
hopede forsothe that the lengere age
shulde speke, and the multitude of 3eeris
8 shulde techen wisdam. But as I see,
spirit is in men, and the inbrething of the
9 Almy3ti 3iueth vnderstonding. Wise men
ben not longe liuende, ne olde men vnder-
10 stonde dom. Therfore I shal seyn, Hereth
me, and also I shal shewe to 30u my kun-
11 nyng. Forsothe I haue abide 30ure woordis,
herde^k 30ure prudence, whil 3ee striuen in
12 30ure woordis. And whil I wende 30u
any thing to seyn, I beheeld; but as I
see, ther is not, that mai vnderneme Job,
13 and answern of 30u to his woordis; lest
perauenture 3ee seyn, Wee han founde^l
wisdam; God hath throwen hym aferr,
14 and not man. No thing he hath spoke to
me, and I after 30ure woordis shal not
15 answere to hym. Thei myche dradden,
and answerden no more, and token awey
16 speche fro themself. Thanne for I haue
abide, and thei speken not, stoden, and
17 answerden no more; shal and I answere
my partie, and shewen my kunnyng.
18 Forsothe I am ful of woordis, and the
19 spirit of my wombe artith me. Lo! my
wombe as must withoute venting^m, that
20 breketh newe litle win vesselys. I shal
speke, and brethen a3een a litil; I shal
21 opene my lippis, and answern. I shal not
taken persone of man, and God to man I
22 shal not euenen. I wot neuere forsothe
hou longe I shal stonde stille, and if after
a litil take me my Makere.

CAP. XXXIII.

1   Here thanne, Job, my spechis, and alle
2 my woordis herene. Lo! I haue opened
my mouth; my tunge in my chekis shal
3 speke. With symple herte my woordis,

ben eldere ; therfor with heed holdun
doun Y dredde to schewe to 30u my sentence. For Y hopide that lengere age 7
schulde speke^w, and that the multitude of
3eeris schulden teche wisdom. But as Y 8
se^x, spirit is in men†, and the enspiryng^y
'ether reuelacioun^z, of Almy3ti^a God 3yueth
vndurstondyng. Men of long lijf ben not 9
wise, and elde men vndurstonden not
doom. Therfor^b Y schal seie, Here 3e me, 10
and Y also schal schewe my kunnyug to
30u. For Y abood 30ure wordis, Y herde 11
30ure prudence, as long as 3e dispuytiden
in 30ure wordis. And as long as Y gesside 12
30u to seie ony thing, Y bihelde; but as
Y se^c, 'noon is^d of 30u, that may repreue
Joob, and answere to hise wordis; lest^e 13
perauenture 3e seien, We han founde wisdom; God, and not man, hath cast hym^f
awei. Joob spak no thing to me, and^g Y 14
not bi 30ure wordis‡ schal answere hym.
Thei dredden, and answeriden no more^h, 15
and ^{i} token awei speche fro hem silf.
Therfor for^k Y abood, and thei spaken 16
not, thei stoden, and answeriden no more ;
also^l Y schal answere my part, and Y 17
schal schewe my kunnyng. For Y am ful 18
of wordis§, and the spirit of my wombe,
'that is, mynde^m, constreyneth me^n‖. Lo ! 19
my wombe is as must with out 'spigot,
ether^o a ventyng,that brekith^p newe vessels.
Y schal speke, and brethe a3en a litil ; Y 20
schal opene my lippis, and Y schal answere^q.
Y^{qq} schal not take the persoone of^r man, and 21
Y schal not make God euene to man. For 22
Y woot not hou long Y schal abide^s, and
if my Makere take^t me awei 'after a^u litil
tyme.

CAP. XXXIII.

Therfor, Joob, here thou my spechis, and 1
herkene^w alle my wordis. Lo ! Y haue 2
openyd my mouth, my^x tunge schal speke
in my chekis. Of symple herte ben my 3

† spirit is in men ; as resonable in 3onge men, as in elde men. Lire here. c.

‡ bi 30ure wordis etc.; Helyu acordide with Joob in this, that he settide another punysching of yuel men and rewarding of good men, aftir deth, but he discordide in this, that he helde that aduersites of this lyf ben brou3t

§ in for synne, thou3 tho ben not euere al the peyne due for synne ; and so he arettide Joob vniust, and punyschid for synne ; also he made strongere resouns a3enus Joob than the thre diden. Lire here. c.

§ ful of wordis; that is, spedeful resouns a3enus Joob. c.

‖ constreyneth me ; as if he seye, The loue of truthe to be defendid, constreyneth me to speke. Lire here. c.

^{k} and herde A. ^{l} Om. AU. ^{m} auentinge $AEFH$.

^{w} haue spoke wisilier 1. ^{x} se now a 1. ^{y} inspiracioun x. ^{z} Om. 1. ^{a} Om. 1. ^{b} Of verry discrecioun therfor 1. ^{c} perceyue 1. ^{d} ther is noon 1. ^{e} but lest 1. ^{f} Job 1. ^{g} and therfor 1. ^{h} more to Job 1. ^{i} and thei 1. ^{k} sith 1. ^{l} therfor 1. ^{m} Om. 1. ^{n} me to speke 1. ^{o} Om. 1.   faucet ether v. ^{p} berstith 1. ^{q} answere Job 1. ^{qq} And Y s. ^{r} of a 1. ^{s} abide alijue 1. ^{t} wole take 1. ^{u} be s. ^{w} herkene thou 1. ^{x} and my 1.

and pure sentence my lippis shul speke.
4 The spirit of God made me, and the
brething space of the Almy3ti quykenede
5 me. If thou maist, answere to me, and
6 stond stille a3en my face. Lo! me as and
thee made God; and of the same cley
7 I also am formed. Nerthelatere my mi-
racle fere thee not, and my faire speche
8 be not to thee heuy. Thou seidest thanne
in myn eris, and the vois of thi woordis
9 I herde; Clene I am, and withoute gilte,
vnwemmed, and ther is not wickidnesse
10 in me. For pleintis in me he fond, ther-
11 fore he demede me enemy to hym. He
putte in the stockis my feet, and kepte
12 alle my stics. This is thanne, in the
whiche thou art not iustified; I shal answer to thee, for God is more than man.
13 A3en God thou striuest, that to alle
woordis he shal not answer to thee.
14 Ones God shal speke, and the secounde
15 that same he shal not eft seyn. Bi
sweuene in ny3t si3te, whan falle slep vp
on men, and thei slepen in the litle bed.
16 Thanne he openeth the eris of men, and
enformende[n] them techith[o] discipline;
17 that he turne awei a man fro tho thingus
that he dide, and deliuere hym fro pride;
18 and takende awei his soule fro corupcioun, and his lif, that he go not in to
19 swerd. He blameth also bi sorewe in the
litle bed, and alle his bones maketh to
20 become drie. Abhomynable to hym bred
is maad in his lif, and to the soule of
21 hym mete[p] beforn desirable. His flesh
shal become roten, and the bones, that
22 weren couered, shul be maad nakid. The
soule of hym shal ne3he to corupcioun,
23 and his lif to thingus berende deth. If
ther were for hym an aungil spekende
oon of the lic thingis, that he telle the
24 equite of man, he shal han reuthe, and
sein, Delyuere hym, that he go not doun

wordis, and my lippis schulen speke clene
sentence. The spirit of God made me, and 4
the brething of Almy3ti God quykenyde
me. If thou maist, answere thou to me, 5
and stoonde thou a3ens my face. Lo! 6
God made me as and thee; and also Y am
formyd of the same cley. Netheles my 7
myracle† make thee not afeerd, and myn
eloquence be[z] not greuouse to thee. Ther- 8
for[a] thou seidist in myn eeris[b], and Y herde
the vois of thi wordis; Y am cleene, and 9
with out gilt, and vnwemmed, and wickidnesse is not in me. 'For God foond querels[c] 10
in me, therfor he[d] demyde me enemy to
hym silf. He hath set my feet in a stok; 11
he[e] kepte alle my pathis. Therfor this 12
thing it is, in which thou art not maad
iust‡; Y schal answere to thee, that God
is more than man. Thou[f] stryuest a3enus 13
God, that not at alle[g] wordis he[h] answeride to thee. God spekith onys, and the 14
secounde tyme he rehersith not the same
thing. *God spekith* bi[i] a dreem in[k] the 15
visioun of ny3t, whanne sleep fallith on
men, and[l] thei slepen in the[m] bed[n]. Thanne 16
he openith the eeris of men, and he[o] techith hem[p], 'and techith prudence[q]; that he 17
turne awei a man fro these thingis whiche
he made[r], and delyuere hym fro pride;
delyuerynge[s] his soule fro corrupcioun§, 18
and his lijf, that it go not in to swerd.
Also *God* blameth *a synnere*[t] bi sorewe 19
in the[u] bed[w], and[x] makith alle the boonys
of hym 'to fade[y]. Breed is maad abho- 20
mynable to hym in his lijf, and[z] mete[a].
desirable[b] 'bifor to his soule[c]‖. His[d] fleisch 21
schal faile for rot, and hise boonys, that
weren hilid, schulen be maad nakid. His 22
soule schal nei3e to corrupcioun, and his
lijf to thingis[e] 'bryngynge deeth[f]. If an 23
aungel, oon of a thousynde, is[g] spekynge¶
for hym, that he telle[h] the equyte of man,
God schal haue mercy on[i] hym, and schal 24

† *myracle, etc.*; that is, kunnyng 3ouun of God, ether bi myracle to me. *Lire here.* c.

‡ *not maad iust*; that is, of these wordis Y shal conclude thee vniust; thou3 noon other thing were a3enus thee. *Lire here.* c.

§ *fro corrupcioun*; of synne. *Lire here.* c.

‖ *to his soule*; that is, is abomynable to him. c.

¶ *is speking*; that is, tellinge his penaunse to God. *Lire here.* c.

[n] enfourmeth *AH*. [o] and techith *A*. [p] mete forsothe *E pr. m.*

[z] be *it* I. [a] Om. I. [b] heeryng I. [c] And for cause that God hath founden playnyngis I. [d] he hath I. [e] and he I. [f] Thou, *Job* I. [g] alle *thi* I. [h] Om. I. [i] in S. [k] bi S. [l] and *whanne* I. [m] her I. [n] litil bed X *sec. m.* [o] he *techinge* I. [p] Om. S. [q] disciplyne, *that is, lore of chastisyng* I. [r] hath made I. [s] and that he delyuere I. [t] *man* I. [u] his I. [w] litil bed X *sec. m.* [x] and he I. [y] for to wexe rotun I. [z] and the I. [a] mete that bifore was to him I. [b] desiderable CQ. delitable R. [c] *wlatide* to his soule *after* I. bifor his soule LR. [d] Om. O. [e] deedly thingis I. [f] Om. I. [g] Om. S. [h] schewe I. [i] of I.

in to corupcioun ; I haue founde in what
23 I be plesid to hym. His flesh is wastid
of tormentis ; be he turned aȝeen to the
26 daȝes of his waxende ȝouthe. He shal
preȝe God, and be plesable to hym ; and
seen his face in ioȝe, and ȝelde to man
27 his riȝtwisnesse. He shal beholde men,
and sein, I haue synned, and vereli I
haue trespasid ; and as I was worthi, I
28 haue not resceyued. Forsothe he hath
deliuered his soule, that he go not in to
29 deth, but lyuende liȝt he shal seen. Lo !
alle these thingus wercheth God thre
30 sithes bi alle men ; that he aȝeen clepe
the soulis of hem fro corupcioun, and
31 liȝtne in the liȝt of liuende men. Tac
heede, Job, and here me, and be stille,
32 whil I speke. If forsothe thou hast what
thou speke, answere to me, spec ; I wile
33 forsothe thee to apere riȝtwis. That if
thou haue*q* not, here me ; be still, and I
shal teche thee wisdam.

seie*, Delyuere thou hym, that he go not
doun in to corrupcioun ; Y haue founde*k*
in what thing Y schal do merci to hym.
His fleisch is wastid of*l* turmentis ; turne*m* 25
he aȝen to the daies of his ȝonge wexynge
age. He schal biseche God, and he schal 26
be quemeful to hym ; and he schal se his
face in hertly*n* ioye, and he schal ȝelde to
man his riȝtfulnesse. He schal biholde 27
men, and he schal seie, Y haue synned,
and verili Y haue trespassid ; and Y haue
not resseyued, as Y was*o* worthi. For*p* 28
he*q* delyueride his soule, that it schulde
not go in to perischyng, but that he lyuynge schulde se liȝt. Lo ! God worchith 29
alle these thingis in thre tymes bi alle
men† ; that he aȝen clepe her soulis fro 30
corrupcioun, and liȝtne in*r* the liȝt of lyuynge men. Thou*s*, Joob, perseyue*t*, and 31
here*u* me, and be thou stille, the*w* while
Y speke. Sotheli* if thou hast*y* what†
thou schalt speke, answere thou to me,
speke thou*z* ; for Y wole §, that thou appere iust. That if thou hast*a*, here 33
thou me ; be thou stille, and Y schal teche
thee wisdom.

CAP. XXXIV.

1   Tellende forth forsothe Elyu, thes
2 thingis also spac, Hereth, wise men, my
3 woordis, and taȝt, herkneth me ; the ere
forsothe woordis proueth, and the throte
4 metis bi tast demeth. Dom chese we to
vs ; and among vs see wee what is betere.
5 For thou seidist, Job, Riȝtwis I am, and
6 God turnede vp so doun my dom. In*r*
demyng forsothe me is lesing, and violent
7 is myn arewe withoute any synne. Who
is a man, as is Job, that drinketh scorn-
8 yng as water? that goth with men wirkende wickidnesse, and wendeth with vn-
9 pytous men ? Forsothe he seide, A man
shal not plese to God, also if he shul

CAP. XXXIV.

And*b* Helyu pronounside*c*, and spak 1
also these thingis, Wise men, here ȝe my 2
wordis, and lerned*d* men, herkne*e* ȝe me ;
for*f* the eere preueth wordis, and the throte 3
demeth metis*g* bi taast. Chese we doom to 4
vs ; and se we among vs, what*h* is the*i*
betere*k*. For Job*l* seide*m*, Y am iust, and 5
God hath distried*n* my doom*o*‖. For whi 6
lesynge is in demynge me, and myn arowe ¶
is violent*p* with out ony*q* synne. Who is a 7
man, as Joob is, that drynkith scornyng** 8
as watir ? that*r* goith with men worchynge 8
wickidnesse, and goith*t* with vnfeithful
men ? For he*u* seide, A man schal not 9
plese God, ȝhe, thouȝ he renneth*w* with

q hast *AEFH.*   *r* And *H.*

k founde, *seith the Lord* I.   *l* with s.   *m* and turne c.   *n* perfijt I.   *o* were I.   *p* Forsothe I.   *q* he
hath I.   *r* *hem* in I.   *s* Om. I.   *t* take heede I.   *u* here *thou* I.   *w* Om. I.   *x* But I.   *y* hast *redy* I.
z Om. I.   *a* not *to answere* I.   *b* And *so f scc. m.*   *c* schewide forth I.   *d* lerud *A pr. m.* CDNOV.   *e* herke I.
f forsothe I.   *g* mete cs.   *h* what *thing* I.   *i* Om. I.   *k* betere *than oother* I.   *l* thou, Job *A pr. m.* s.
m seidest *A pr. m.* s.   *n* turned I.   *u* iustnesse upsodoun I.   *p* violent, *and doon* I.   *q* my I.   *r* the
whiche I.   *s* and he I.   *t* goith aboute I.   *u* Job I.   *w* renne I.

10 renne with hym. Therfore, herty men, hereth me; ferr be fro God vnpitous-nesse, and fro the Almyȝti wickenesse[s].
11 Forsothe the werk of man he shal ȝelde to hym; and after the weies of echone
12 he shal quite to them. Vereli forsothe God shal not condempne in veyn; ne the Almyȝti shal turne vpsodoun dom.
13 Whom other[t] sette he vp on erthe? or whom putte he vp on the world, that he
14 forgide? If he shul dresse to it his herte, the spirit of it and blast he shal drawe
15 to hym. Al flesh shal faile to gidere; and a man into askis shal be turned
16 aȝeen. If thou hast thanne vndirstond-inge, here that is seid, and herkne the
17 vois of my speche. Whether he that looueth not dom mai ben helid? and hou thou hym, that is riȝtwis, in so
18 myche condempnest? That seith to the king, Apostata; that clepeth dukys vn-
19 pitous. That taketh not the persoues of princis, ne knewȝ the tiraunt, whan he shulde striuen aȝen the pore; forsothe the werk of his hondis ben alle men.
20 Feerli[u] thei shul die, and in mydnyȝt puplis shul be boowid; and passen, and taken awei the violent withoute hond.
21 Forsothe the eȝen of hym vp on the weies of men, and alle the goingus of
22 hem he beholdeth. Ther ben not derc-nessis, and ther is not shadewe of deth, that ther ben hid there that werken
23 wickidnesse; ne forsothe more ouer in mannys power is, that he come to God
24 in to dom. He shal to-trede manye and vnnoumbrable; and make to stonden
25 othere men for hem. Forsothe he knew the werkis of hem; and therfore he shal bringe in nyȝt, and thei shul be to-trede.

God. Therfor ȝe men[x] hertid[y], 'that is, vndurstonde[z], here ȝe[a] me; vnpite, 'ethir cruelte[b], be[c] fer fro God, and[d] wickidnesse fro[e] Almyȝti God. For[f] he schal ȝelde the 11 werk of man to hym; and[g] bi the weies[h] of ech[i] man he schal restore to hym[k]. For 12 verili God schal not condempne with out cause; nether Almyȝti God schal distrie doom[l]. What othere man hath he ordeyned 13 on[m] the[n] lond[o]? ether whom hath he set on[p] the world, which[q] he made[r]? If God 14 dressith his[s] herte to hym, he schal drawe to hym silf[t] his spirit and[u] blast. Ech 15 fleisch schal faile togidere[w]; 'and a[x] man schal turne aȝen in to aisch. Therfor if 16 thou[y] hast[z] vndurstondyng, here thou that that is seid, and herkne the[a] vois of my speche. Whether he that loueth not doom[b] 17 may be maad hool? and hou[c] condempnest thou so myche him, that is iust? Which[d] seith to the[e] kyng, Thou art 18 apostata†; which[f] clepith the[g] duykis vn-pitouse[h],'ethir vnfeithful[i]. 'Which takith[k] 19 not the persoones of princes, nether knew[l] a tyraunt, whanne[m] he stryuede[n] aȝens a pore man; for[o] alle men ben the werk of hise hondis. Their[p] schulen die sudeynli, 20 and at mydnyȝt puplis schulen be troblid[q], 'ethir schulen be bowid, as[r] othere bookis han[s]; and[t] schulen passe, and[u] schulen take 'awei[w] 'a violent[x] man with out hond‡. For[y] the eȝen of God[z] ben[a] ou[a] the weies of 21 men, and[b] biholdith[c] alle[d] goyngis of hem. No derknessis ben, and[e] no schadewe of 22 deeth is, that thei, that worchen wickid-nesse, be hid there◊; for[f] it is 'no more 23 in the power of man[g], that he come to God in to doom‖. God schal al to-breke 24 many men and vnnoumbrable; and[b] schal make othere men to stonde for hem. For 25

10 other thing is to distrie doom, other thing is to take awey doom; for whi to distrie doom is euere yuel, and may not be doon wel, 12 and therfor it may not bifalle to God; but to take awey doom, is not 13 ellis no but to use not doom, and this may wel be doon, 14 whanne the iuge vsith mersy and not rigour. And therfor what euere thing Helyu con- 16 cludith in this cᵒ. aȝenus Joob, in put-tinge to him, that he seide 17 that God is vniust, ether distriere of riȝtfulnesse, it concludith not aȝenus him. 18 Lire here. c. ¶ and mῳ arowe; that is, aduersite which Y suffre, is brouȝt In to me bi the vio-lence of God, and may not riȝtfulnesse. 20 Lire here. c. ** scornyng, etc.; that is, scorneth with out bridil and mesure, Goddis doom. Lire here. c. 21 † apostata; thanne the kyng is apo-stata, ether brekere of re-ligioun,whanne he kepith not riȝtfulnesse and the comyn good. Lire here. c. 22 ‡ with out hond; that is, without power of aduersaries of the tyrauns. Lire here. c. 23 ◊ be hid there;

ˢ wickidnes ᴀɪɪ. ᵗ ouere ᴀ. ᵘ Sodeynli ᴇ sec. m.

ˣ wise men ɪ. ʸ Om. ɪ. ᶻ that is, vndirstondinge ʙ, Om. ɪᴠ. ᵃ Om. ɴᴏsᴠ. ᵇ Om. ɪ. ᶜ he it ɪ. ᵈ and also ɪ. ᵉ be fer fro ɪ. ᶠ Forsothe ɪ. ᵍ Om. c. ʰ werkis ᴅ. ⁱ Om. ʟ. ᵏ man ɪ. ˡ doom or riȝtwisnesse ɪ. ᵐ upon ɪ. ⁿ Om. ɪ. ᵒ erthe ɪ. ᵖ oother upon ɪ. ᵠ that ɪ. ʳ hath made ɪ. ˢ mennus ɪ. ᵗ Om. ɪ. ᵘ and his ɪ. ʷ togidere in diyng ɪ. ˣ and aftir ech ɪ. ʸ thou, Job ɪ. ᶻ hane s. ᵃ thou the ɪ. ᵇ iust doom ɪ. ᶜ hou thanne ɪ. ᵈ He it is that ɪ. ᵉ a ɪ. ᶠ he this ɪ. ᵍ Om. ɪ. ʰ vnpi-touse men ɪ. ⁱ Om. ɪ. ᵏ He acceptith ɪ. ˡ he knowith ɪ. ᵐ to spare him, whanne ɪ. ⁿ stryuith ɪ. ᵒ forsothe ɪ. ᵖ Men ɪ. ᵠ troblid ether bowid ᴠ. ʳ and as ᴄʀʜʟᴘᴜ. ˢ Gloss om. in ɪᴠx. ᵗ and aungels ɪ. ᵘ and thei ɪ. ʷ Om. s. ˣ the cruel ɪ. ʸ Sothely ɪ. ᶻ the Lord ɪ. ᵃ biholdynge upon ɪ. ᵇ and he ɪs. ᶜ biheldeth s. ᵈ alle the ɪs. ᵉ neither ɪ. ᶠ certis ɪ. ᵍ not ouer in mannus power ɪ. ʰ and he ɪ.

26 As vnpitous, he smot hem in the place of
27 men seende. The whiche as bi studie
wente awei fro hym, and alle his weies
28 thei wolde not vnderstonde. That thei
make to come to hym the cri of the nedi,
29 and he here the vois of pore men. Hym
forsothe grauntende pes, who is that con-
dempneth? Sithen he hath^v hid his chere,
who is that beholdeth hym? And vpon
30 Jentilis and vpon alle men, the whiche
maketh to regne an ipocrite man, for the
31 synnes of the puple. Thanne for I spac
32 to God, thee also I shal not forfende. If
I haue errid, thou teche me; if wickid-
33 nesse I spac, I shal adde no mor. Whether God of thee asketh it out, for he displeside to thee? Thou forsothe begunne
to speke, and not I; that if any thing
34 thou knewe betere, spec. Vnderstondende
men, speke thei to me; and a wis man,
35 here he me. Job forsothe folily spac, and
the woordis of hym soune not disciplyne.
36 Fader myn, be preued Job vnto the ende;
ne leue thou fro a man of wickidnesse,
37 that addeth vp on his synnes blasfemye.
Amongis vs euere^w among be he streyned; and thanne at the dom terre he God
with his woordis.

CAP. XXXV.

1 Thanne Eliu these thingus eft spac,
2 Whethir euene to thee seme thi thoзt,
that thou shuldest seyn, I am mor riзt-
3 wis than God? Thou seidest forsothe, It
'pleseth not^x to thee, that is good; or
what to thee shal profite, if I shul syn-
4 nen? Also I shal answern to thi woordis,
5 and to thi frendis with thee. Behold
heuene, and loke, and myndefulli see the

he knowith the werkis of hem; therfor^i
he schal brynge yn niзt^k†, and thei schulen be al to-brokun. He smoot hem, as 26
vnpitouse men, in the place of seinge men.
Whiche зeden awei fro hym bi 'castyng 27
afore^l, and nolden^m vndurstonde alle hise
weies. That thei schulden make the cry 28
of a nedi man to come to hym, and that
he schulde here the vois of pore men. For 29
whanne he grauntith pees^n, who is^o that
condempneth^p? Sithen^q he bidith his cheer,
who is that seeth hym? And on folkis
and on alle men 'he hath power^r 'to do
siche thingis^s. Which^t makith 'a man 30
ypocrite^w to regne, for the synnes of the
puple. Therfor for Y haue spoke to God, 31
also^x Y schal not forbede thee^y. If Y^z 32
erride, teche thou me; if Y spak^a wickidnesse, Y schal no more adde^b. Whether 33
God axith that wickidnesse of thee, for it
displeside thee? For^c thou hast bigunne to
speke, and not Y; that if thou knowist
ony thing betere, speke thou^d. Men vndur- 34
stondynge, speke^e to me; and a wise man,
here^f me. Forsothe Joob spak^g folili, and 35
hise wordis sownen not techyng^h. My fa- 36
dir, be Joob preuede 'til to^i the ende;
ceesse thou not fro the man of wickidnesse, 'that addith^k blasfemye^l ouer hise
synnes. Be he constreyned among vs in
the meene tyme; and^m thanne bi hise
wordis stire he God to the^n doom.

CAP. XXXV.

Therfor Helyu spak eft these thingis, 1
Whethir thi thouзt semeth euene, 'ether^o
riзtful^o, to thee, that thou schuldist seie,
Y am riзtfulere than God‡? For^p thou 2
seidist, That^q, that is good, plesith not^r
thee; ethir what profitith it to thee,
if^s Y do synne? Therfor Y schal an- 4
swere to thi wordis, and to thi frendis
with thee. Se thou, and biholde^t he- 5

that is, in Goddis knowing; netheles God is seid to knowe not hem bi knowing of appreuyng. Lire here. c.

‖ in to doom; aftir that he is damnyd bi ful sentence. Lire here. c.

† nyзt; that is, sudeyn deth. Lire here. c.

‡ Y am riзtfulere than God; Joob seide neuere this, but Helyu concludide this of fals vndirstondinge of Joobis wordis. That that is good pleuith not thee; Helyn took зtide this of that, that Joob seide, Thouз Y am iust, Y shal not reise myn heed. Here Helyu vndurstood him thus, that he seide, that riзtfulnesse plesith not God; and bi this that Joob seide to God, Whi suffrist thou me not to be cleene? Helyn vndurstood, that Joob menyde thus, that sun profit encresside to God bi this, that Joob was holdun in synne, ether in the peyne of synne. Lire here. c.

---

^v shal E pr. m.   ^w eft E pr. m.   ^x shal not plesen E pr. m.

^i and therfor s.   ^k niзt upon hem I.   ^l fore castynge I.   ^m wolden not I.   ^n hijf I.   ^o is it I.
^p condempnith him I.   ^q And sith I.   ^r Om. B.   ^s Om. BV.   ^t He I.   ^w an ypocrite man I.
^x Om. I.   ^y thee to speke I.   ^z Y han I.   ^a haue spoke I.   ^b adde to I.   ^c Certis I.   ^d thou that I.
^e speke thei I.   ^f here he I.   ^g hath spoke I.   ^h chastisyng I.   ^i unto I.   ^k the whiche puttith I.
^l blasfemye to God I.   ^m to knowe his blasfemy, and I.   ^n Om. I.   ^o Om. I.   ^p Forsothe I.   ^q that
thing I.   ^r not to s.   ^s if that s.   ^t biholde thou I.

6 cloudis, that is heȝere than thou. If thou
shalt synnen, what shalt thou noȝe to
hym? and if thi wickidnesses[y] be multiplied, what shalt thou don aȝen hym?
7 But if thou shalt do riȝtwisli, what shalt
thou ȝiue to hym; or what of thin hond
8 he shal take? To man that is lic thee,
thin vnpitousnesse shal noȝe; and the sone
9 of man thi riȝtwisnesse shal helpe. For
the multitude of chalengeres thei shul
crie, and ȝelle out for the fors of the arm
10 of tirauntis. And he seide not, Where is
God, that made me, and that ȝaf ditees
11 in the nyȝt? That techeth vs ouer the
bestis of the erthe, ouer the foulis of he-
12 uene shal lernen vs. There thei shul crie,
and he shal not heren, for the pride of
13 euele men. Forsothe not in veyn God
shal heren, and the Almyȝti beholde shal
14 the causis of alle men. Also whan thou
shal sein, He beholdith[z] not; be thou de-
15 med beforn hym, and abid hym. Now forsothe he bringeth not in his wodnesse,
ne the hydous gilte is vengid gretli.
16 Thanne Job in veiu openede his mouth,
and withoute kunnynge woordis multiplieth.

uene, and biholde thou the eir, that[u]
God is hiȝere than thou. If thou synnest 6
'aȝens hym[w], what schalt thou anoye hym?
and if thi wickidnessis ben multiplied,
what schalt thou do aȝens hym? Certis if 7
thou doist[x] iustli, what schalt thou ȝyue
to hym[y]; ether what schal he take of thin
hond? Thi wickidnesse schal anoie a man, 8
which[z] is lijk[a] thee; and thi riȝtfulnesse[b]
schal helpe the sone of a man. Thei[c] 9
schulen cry for the multitude of fals
chalengeris, and thei schulen weile for
the violence of the arm[d] of tirauntis. And 10
Joob seide not, Where is God, that made
me, and that ȝaf songis† in the nyȝt?
Which[e] God[f] techith vs aboue the beestis 11
of erthe, and he schal teche vs aboue the
briddis of heuene. There thei schulen 12
crye, and God schal not here[g], for the
pride of yuele men. For[h] God schal not 13
here with out cause, and Almyȝti God
schal biholde the causis of ech man. Ȝhe, 14
whanne thou seist, He biholdith not; be
thou[i] demed bifor hym, and abide thou
hym. For now he[k] bryngith not in his 15
strong veniaunce, nether[l] vengith 'greetli
felonye[m]. Therfor Joob openith his mouth 16
in veyn, and multiplieth wordis with out
kunnyng.

† *that ȝaf songis, etc.*; that is, reuelaciouns to the teching of men, which reuelaciouns ben writun ofte bi the maner of songis. *Lire here.* c.

CAP. XXXVI.

1 Also Eliu addende these thingus spac,
2 Sustene me a litil while, and I shal
shewen to thee; ȝit forsothe I haue that
3 for God I speke. I shal aȝeen aske my
kunnyng[a] fro the bygynnyng; and my
4 werkere I shal proue riȝtwis. Verili forsothe and withoute lesing my woordus,
and perfit kunnyng shal be preued to
5 thee. God myȝti men throwith not awei,
6 sithen he is myȝti; but he saueth not vnpitous men, and dom to pore men he
7 ȝyueth. He shal not take awei fro the[b]
riȝtwis his eȝen; and kingis in sete he
setteth in to euermor, and thider thei

CAP. XXXVI.

Also Helyu addide, and spak these 1
thingis, Suffre[n] thou me a litil, and Y 2
schal schewe to thee; for ȝit Y haue that,
that Y schal speke for God. Y schal 3
reherse my kunnyng fro the bigynnyng;
and Y schal[o] preue my worchere iust. For 4
verili my wordis ben with out leesyng,
and[p] perfit kunnyng schal be preued to
thee. God castith not awei myȝti men‡, 5
sithen he is myȝti; but he saueth not 6
wickid men, and he ȝyueth dom to pore
men. He takith not awei hise iȝen fro 7
a iust man; and he settith kyngis in[q] seete
with out ende, and thei ben reisid[r] there.

‡ *God castith not awei myȝti men*; fro her power, no but for synne. *Lire here.* c.

[y] wyckidnes A. [z] behalt C *pr. m.* [a] sentence E *pr. m.* [b] Om. AH.

[u] *and wile* that I. [w] Om. I. [x] do I. [y] God I. [z] that I. [a] lijk to I. [b] riȝtwisnesse I. [c] Men I. [d] power I. [e] And the which I. [f] Om. I. [g] here *hem* I. [h] Forsothe I. [i] thou *herfor* I. [k] the Lord I. [l] ether he I. [m] felonyes greetli *heere* I. [n] *Job*, suffre I. [o] Om. A *pr. m.* [p] and *bi hem* I. [q] in *her* I. [r] reisid up I.

8 ben rerid vp. And if thei shul ben in cheynes, and ben bounde with cordis of 9 poreuesse, he shal shewe to them ther werkis, and ther hidous giltis; for cruel 10 they weren. Also he shal opene the ere of hem, that he chastise; and he shal speke, that thei be turned a3een fro wick- 11 idnesse. If thei shuln here, and kepe wel, thei shul fille^b ther da3es in goode, 12 and ther 3eris in glorie. If forsothe thei shul not heren, they shul passe 13 bi swerd, and be wastid in folie. Feyn- eres and felle men terren the wrathe of God; and thei shul not crie, whan 14 thei shul be bounden. The soule of hem shal die in tempest; and the lif of hem 15 among wommanysh men. He shal de- liuere the pore man fro his anguysh; and he shal opene his ere in tribulacioun. 16 Therfore he shal saue thee fro the streite mouth most widly, not^e hauende a ground vnder itself^d; the reste forsothe 17 of thi bord shal be full of fatnesse. Thi cause as of an vnpitous man is demed; forsothe thi cause and dom thou shalt 18 finde. Thanne ouercome thee not wrathe, that any man thou opresse; ne the multi- 19 tude of 3iftis bowe thee. Do doun thi mykilnesse withoute tribulacioun, and 20 alle the stronge men in strengthe. Ne drawe thou along the ny3t, that puplis 21 ste3en vp for hem. Be war, ne bowe thou to wickidnesse; that forsothe thou hast begunne to folewe aftyr wrecchidnesse. 22 Lo! he3e God in his strengthe, and noon 23 to hym lic in lawe 3ineres. Who shall moun serchen his weies? or who is hardy to sei to hym, Thou wro3tist wickid- 24 nesse? Ha^e mynde, that thou vnknowist the werk of hym, of whiche^f men writen. 25 Alle men seen hym; eche shal beholde^g 26 aferr. Lo! God gret^h, ouercomende oure kunnyng; the noumbre of the 3eris of

And if thei ben in chaynes, and ben 8 boundun with the roopis of ponert, he schal 9 shewe to hem her werkis, and her grete trespassis; for thei weren violent, 'ethir rauenours^s. Also he schal opene her eere, 10 that he chastise^t; and he schal speke^u, that thei turne a3en fro^w wickidnesse. If thei 11 heren^x, and kepen^y, thei schulen fille^z her daies in good, and her 3eris in glorie. Sotheli if thei heren^a not, thei schulen 12 passe bi swerd, and thei schulen be wastid in foli. Feyneris and false men stiren the 13 ire^b of God; and thei schulen not crye†, whanne thei ben boundun. The soule of 14 hem schal die^c in tempest; and the lijf of hem among 'men of wymmens condi- ciouns^d‡. He^e schal delyuere a pore man 15 fro his angwisch; and he schal opene 'the eere of hym^f in tribulacioun. Therfor he 16 schal saue thee fro the streit mouth of the broddeste *tribulacioun*, and not hauynge a foundement vndur it; sotheli^s the rest of thi table schal be ful of fatnesse. Thi 17 cause is demed as *the cause* of a wickid man; forsothe^h thou schalt resseyue thi cause and^i doom. Therfor ire^k ouercome 18 thee not, that thou oppresse ony man; and the multitude of 3iftis bowe thee not. 19 Putte doun thi greetnesse^l§ with out tribu- lacioun, and *putte^m doun* alle stronge men bi strengthe^n. Dilaie thou not ny3t^o, that 20 puplis stie^p for hem. Be thou war, that 21 thou bowe not to wickidnesse; for^q thou hast bigunne to sue this *wickidnesse* aftir wretchidnesse. Lo! God is hi3 in his 22 strengthe, and noon is^r lijk^s hym among the 3yueris of lawe. Who mai seke out 23 the weies of God? ethir who dar seie to hym, Thou hast wrou3t^t wickidnesse? Haue thou mynde, that thou knowist not 24 his werk, of whom men^u sungun. Alle 25 men seen God; ech^w man biholdith afer. Lo! God *is* greet, ouercomynge oure kun- 26

† *and they schulen not orie*; *to God, and knouleche her gilt. Lire here.* c.

‡ *among men of wymmens condicioune*; *that is, among hem that moun not defende hem silf fro ynels fallinge on hem. Lire here.* c.

§ *Putte doun thi greetnesse*; *that is, pride. Lire here.* *without tribulacioun*; *that is, leste thou falle eft into tribulacioun. Lire here.* c. *bi strengthe*; *that is, bi sentence, fro opmen. Lire here.* c. *Dilaye thou not ny3t*; *that is, tyme to 3yue this sentence, for in sich dilaiyng strong men moun gardere to hem a multitude, bi which thou maist not v3e ri3tfulnesse. Lire here.* c.

^b fulfillen AEFU. ^c now E pr. m. and not AH. ^d himself E pr. m. ^e Haue AEFH. ^f the whiche AEFH. ^g beholde hym AH. ^h is greet A.

^s Om. I. ^t chastise hem I. ^u speke to hem I. ^w fro her I. ^x heren him I. ^y kepen his heestis I. ^z ful- fille I. ^a kepen s. ^b wraththe I. ^c be I. ^d wommanishe men I. ^e The Lord I. ^f his eere I. ^g and I. ^h and I. ^i and thi I. ^k wraththe I. ^l greetnesse wilfully I. greetnesse of pride v. ^m putte thou I. ^n strengthe, oppressinge pore men v. ^o the ny3t I. ^p stie up I. ^q forsothe I. ^r ther is I. ^s lijk to I. ^t wrou3t with c. ^u men han I. ^w and ech I.

27 hym vneymable. That doth awei the
dropis[i] of rein[k]; and heeldeth out we-
28 deres at the licnesse of swolewis, that
of the cloudis flowen, that before weuen
29 alle thingus therabouc. If he wile strecche
30 out cloudis as his tent, and leitne with
his liȝt fro aboue, also the vtmost[l] of the
31 se he shal couere. Bi these thingis forsothe he demeth puplis, and ȝiueth mete
32 to manye deadli thingus. In the hond he
hideth liȝt; and comaundeth to it, that
33 eft it come to. He tellith of[m] it to his
frend, that his possessioun it be; and to
it he mai steȝen vp.

CAP. XXXVII.

1 Vpon that mych dradde myn herte,
2 and is moued out fro[n] his place. He[o]
shal heren heringe in gastnesse[p] of his
vois, and the soun goende out of the
3 mouth of hym. Ouer alle heuenys he beholdeth; and the liȝt of hym vp on the
4 termes of the erthe. After hym shal rore
sounyng, he shal thunder with the vois
of his mykilnesse; and he shal not ben
enserchid, whan shal ben herd the vois
5 of hym. God shal thundre in his vois
merueilously, that doth grete thingus and
6 vnserchable. That comaundeth to the
snowȝ, that it ʻcome doun vp[q] on erthe[r],
and to reynes of winter, and to wederes
7 of his strengthe. That marketh in the
hond of alle men, that alle men arowe
8 shulden knowen his werkis. The beste
shal go in to his lurking place, and in his
9 dich he shal abide. Fro the innermor
shal gon out tempest[s], and fro the north
10 sterre cold. God blowende, waxeth togidere frost; and eft moost wide ben
11 shed out watris. Whete desirith cloudis;
12 and cloudis sprengen[t] ther liȝt. That gon
alle thingus bi enuyroun, whider euere
thou gost, the wil of the gouernere shal

nyng; the noumbre of hise ȝeeris is with
out noumbre. Which[x] takith awei[y] the 27
dropis of reyn; and schedith[z] out reynes at
the licnesse of floodȝatis, whiche[a] comen[b] 28
doun of the[c] cloudis, that hilen alle thingis
aboue. If he wole stretche forthe cloudis 29
as his teute, and leite with his liȝt fro 30
aboue, he schal hile, ȝhe, the herris of the 31
see. For[d] bi these thingis he demeth puplis,
and ȝyueth mete to many deedli men.

CAP. XXXVII.

In[e] hondis he[f] hidith liȝt†; and[g] co- 32
maundith it, that it come eft. He tellith of 33
it to his freend, that it is his possessioun;
and that he may stie[h] to it. Myn herte 1
dredde of this thing, and is[i] moued out[k] of
his place. It schal here an heryng in the 2
feerdfulnesse of his vois, and a sown
comynge forth of his mouth. He biholdith 3
ouere alle heuenes; and his liȝt *is* ouere the
termes of erthe[l]. Sown[m]‡ schal rore aftir 4
hym, he[n] schal thundre with the vois of
his greetnesse; and it schal not be souȝt
out, whanne his vois is herd. God schal 5
thundre in his vois wondurfulli, that[o]
makith grete thingis and[p] that moun not
be souȝt out. Which[q] comaundith to[r] the 6
snow to come doun on[s] erthe, and to the
reynes of wijntir, and to the reynes of his
strengthe. Which[t] markith in the hond of 7
alle men, that alle men knowe her werkis.
An vnresonable beeste schal go in to[u] his 8
denne, and schal dwelle in his caue, ʻ*ethir
derke place*[w]. Tempestis[x] schulen[y] go out 9
fro the ynnere thingis, and coold fro[z]
Arturus[a]. Whanne God makith blowyng, 10
frost[b] wexith togidere; and eft ful brood
watris ben sched[c] out[d]. Whete desirith 11
cloudis, and cloudis spreeden abrood her
liȝt. Whiche[e] cloudes cumpassen alle 12
thingis bi[f] cumpas, whidur euere the wil
of the gouernour ledith tho[g], to al thing

† *In hondis he hidith liȝt*; that is, bi the vertu and ordenaunce of God the liȝt of grace and of glorie is hid to summen, as to chosun men; and that this is vndirstondun of goostly liȝt, it is opyn bi this, that sueth. *And he tellith of it to his frend*; that is, to chosun men, for charite departith bitwixe the sones of rewme and of perdicioun. *he may stie to it*; that is, to the liȝt of glorie, to which a man may come with Goddis help, and bi meedeful werkis; this liȝt of glorie is maad redi onely to loued men; and therfor ech man owith for to drede, lest perauenture he be not of the noumbre of chosun men, for defaute of goode werkis. *Lire here.* C.

‡ *Sown*; that is, thundur. *Lire here.* C.

[i] droop *A.* [k] his reyne *A.* [l] vttermost *AEFH.* [m] Om. *AH.* [n] of *A.* [o] It *A.* [p] ferdnes *A.* [q] steye vp *E pr. m.* [r] the erthe *A.* [s] the tempest *AEF.* [t] sprongen *AH.*

[x] He I. [y] Om. I. [z] he heeldith I. [a] the whiche I. [b] camen C. cometh D. [c] Om. I. [d] Forsothe I. [e] In *his* I. [f] God I. [g] and he I. [h] stie up I. [i] it is IS. [k] *therfore* out I. [l] the erthe S. [m] *Greet* sown I. [n] and he I. [o] whiche I. [p] Om. I. [q] He *it is* that I. [r] Om. IS. [s] up on I. [t] He I. [u] Om. I. [w] Om. I. [x] Tempest I. [y] schal I. [z] fro the I. [a] *that is a signe of v. sterris in the north* I *marg.* [b] frost I. [c] held I. [d] out *therof* I. [e] The whiche I. [f] aboute bi I. [g] hem I.

lede, to alle thingus that he shal comaunde to them vp on the face of the round- 13 nesse of erthis; or in o lynage, or in his erthe, or in what euere place of his mercy hem he shal comaunde to be founde. 14 Herene these thingus, Job; and stond, 15 and behold the merueilis of God. Whe- ther thou wost, whan God comaundide to reynes, that thei shulden shewe the li3t of 16 the cloudis of hym? Whether thou hast knowen the sties of the cloudis, grete and 17 parfit kunnyngis? Whether thi clothis ben not hote, whan the erthe shal be 18 blowe thur3 with the south? Thou per- auenture with hym forgedist heuenes, that most sad, as with bras, ben foundid. 19 Shew3 to vs, what wee seyn to hym; wee 20 forsothe ben wrappid in dercnessis. Who shal telle to hym, that I speke? also if a man shal speke, he shal be deuourid. 21 And now thei see not li3t; feerli the eir shal be wro3t togidere in to cloudis, and 22 ouergoende wind shal driue them. Fro the north shal come gold, and fro God 23 dredful preising. Wrthili hym finde wee moun not; gret in strengthe, and dom, and ri3twisnesse, that he mai not þe told 24 out. Therfore men shul dreden hym; and alle that to themself ben sen[u] to be wise, shuln not ben hardy to beholden.

CAP. XXXVIII.

1 Answerende forsothe the Lord to Job 2 fro the whirlewind seide, Who is this, wrappende in sentencis with woordis vn- 3 wise? Gird as a man thi leendis; I shal 4 aske thee, and thou answere to me. Wher were thou, whan I sette the founde- mens of the erthe? sheu to me, if thou 5 hast vnderstonding. Who putte the me- suris of it, if thou hast knowen? or who 6 stra3te vp on it a line? Vp on what the feet of it ben sad? who dide doun the 7 corner ston of it, whan me shulden preise

---

which[h] he comaundith 'to tho[i] on[k] the face of the world; whether in o lynage, ethir in 13 his lond[l], ether in what euer place of his merci he comaundith tho to be foundun. Joob, herkene thou these thingis; stonde 14 thou, and biholde the meruels of God. Whethir thou woost, whanne God co- 15 maundide to the reynes, that tho schulen schewe the li3t of hise cloudis? Whether 16 thou knowist the grete weies of[m] cloudis, and[n] perfit kunnyngis[o]? Whether thi 17 cloothis ben not hoote, whanne the erthe is blowun[p] with the south? In hap thou 18 madist† with hym[q] heuenes, which moost sad ben foundid, as of bras. Schewe thou 19 to vs[r], what we schulen seie to hym; for[s] we ben wlappid in derknessis. Who schal 20 telle to hym[t], what thingis Y speke? 3he, if he spekith, a man schal be deuourid‡. And now men seen not li3t; the cir schal 21 be maad thicke sudenli in to cloudis, and wynd passynge schal dryue awei tho. Gold schal come fro the north, and[u] ferdful 22 preisyng of God. For[w] we moun[x] not 23 fynde him[y] worthili; he is greet in strengthe, and in doom, and in ri3tfulnesse, and[z] may not be teld out. Therfor men 24 schulen drede hym; and alle men, that semen to hem silf to be wise§, schulen not be hardi to biholde[a].

CAP. XXXVIII.

Forsothe[h] the Lord answeride fro the 1 whirlewynd to Joob, and seide, Who is 2 this man, wlappynge[c] sentences with vn- wise wordis? Girde thou as a man thi 3 leendis; Y schal axe thee, and answere thou to[d] me. Where were thou, whanne Y 4 settide[e] the foundementis of[f] erthe? schewe thou to me, if thou hast vnderstondyng. Who settide[g] mesures[h] therof, if thou 5 knowist[i]? ethir who stretchide forth a lyne theronne[k]? On[l] what thing ben the 6 foundementis therof maad fast? ether who 7

† in hap thou madist etc.; he seith this in scorn of Joob. Lire here. c.
‡ a man schal be deuourid; that is, schal not now suffre; as the peple seide to Moises in xx. c. of Exody; ether thus, 3he, if a man spekith, it schal be deuourid; that is, the word schal be deuourid of the greetnesse of matter, as a litil flood is de- uourid of the see. Lire here. c.
§ and alle men that semen to hem silf to be wise; of thingis bifor seid it is opyn, that He- lyu acordide with Joob in summe thingis, and in othere thingis he took not wel the vn- durstonding of Joob, and so he meddilide ofte dispisingis a3enus Joob, for whiche Joob nolde answere him, but more be stille, and chees to de- parte himsilf fro chidingis, bi the seying of Paul. Therfor God answeride for Joob, and seide, Who is this man wlap- pinge sentences, for thou3 he had seid many trewe thingis of the power and wisdom of God, netheles he seide not clerely, and he meddilide many dispitouse wordis a3enus Joob. And this Helyu took the side of deter- minynge the question of Goddis poray- nunce, and to this de- termynacioun God aloone is sufficient; and

---

[h] to which 1.   [i] hem 1.   [k] up on 1.   [l] hoond s.   [m] of the 1.   [n] and the 1.   [o] kunnyngis of tho 1.
[p] blowe 1.   [q] God 1.   [r] God 1.   [s] forsothe 1.   [t] God 1.   [u] and the 1.   [w] Om. A sec. m. Sothely 1.
[x] mowe 1.   [y] Om. A pr. m. DCEHLPUVX. if 1.   [z] and he 1.   [a] biholde God 1.   [b] Certis s.   [c] wlappynge togidre 1.   [d] Om. 1.   [e] sette 1.   [f] of the 1.   [g] hath sett 1.   [h] the mesures 1.   [i] knowist, telle thou 1.
[k] therupon 1. theronne, shewe thou to me s.   [l] Up on 1.

togidere the morutid sterris, and alle·the
8 sones of God shulden ioзen? Who closede
the se with doris, whan it brac out as
9 goende forth of the wombe? Whan I
shuld setten the cloude his clothing, and
with dercnesse it, as with clothis of vnspekende childhed, I wrappide aboute.
10 I enuyrounde it with my termes, and
11 sette the heenglis, and doris; and seide,
Vnto' hider thou shalt come, and no ferthere gon; and heer thou shalt breke to-
12 gidere thi swellende flodis. Whether aftir
thi rising thou comaundedist to the morutid, and hast shewid to the dai spring his
13 place? Whethir thou hast holde smyt-
ende togidere the vtmostis" of the erthe,
and hast smyten out the vnpitous men
14 of it? The litle marke shal be restorid
15 as cley, and shal stonde as clothing. His
liзt shal be take awei fro the vnpitous,
and the heзe arm shal be broke togidere.
16 Whether thou wentist in the depthe of the
se, and in the laste thingus of the derke
17 depthe' of the se thou hast ful go? Whether to thee ben opened the зatis of deth,
and the derke doris thou hast seen?
18 Whether thou hast beholde the breede of
the erthe? Sheu to me, if thou hast
19 knowen alle thingis, in what weie liзt
dwellith, and of dercnessis what is the
20 place; that thou lede eche man to hys
termes, and vnderstonde the sties of his
21 hous. Thou wistist thanne, that thou
were to be born, and the noumbre of thi
22 daзes thou haddest knowe? Whether
wentist thou in to the tresoris of snowз,
or the tresoris of hail thou hast beholde?
23 that I haue maad redi in to the time of
the enemy, in to the dai of fiзt, and of
24 bataile. Bi what weie is sprengd liзt,
25 deuyded is hete vp on erthe? Who зaf
to the most hidous weder cours, and weie
26 of the sounende thunder? That it shulde

sente doun the corner stoon therof, whanne 7
the morew sterris^m† herieden^n me togidere, and alle the sones of God sungun^o
ioyfuli? Who closide togidere the see with 8
doris, whanne it brak out comynge^p forth
as of the wombe? Whanne Y settide a 9
cloude the hilyng therof^q, and Y wlappide
it with derknesse, as with clothis of зong^r
childhed. Y cumpasside it^s with my termes, 10
and Y settide^t a barre, and doris^u; and Y 11
seide, 'Til hidur^w thou schalt come, and
thou schalt not go forth^x ferthere; and
here thou schalt breke togidere thi bol-
nynge wawis. Whethir aftir thi birthe 12
thou comaundist^y to the bigynnyng of
dai^z, and schewidist to the morewtid his
place? Whethir thou heldist schakynge 13
togidere the laste partis of erthe, and
schakedist awei wickid men therfro? A 14
seeling schal be restorid as cley, and it
schal stonde as a^a cloth. The liзt of wickid 15
men schal be takun^b awey fro hem, and
an hiз arm^c‡ schal be brokun. Whethir 16
thou entridist^d in to the depthe of the see,
and walkidist^e in the laste partis of the^f
occian^g? Whether the зatis of deeth ben 17
openyd to thee, and 'siest thou^h the derk
doris? Whethir thou hast biholde the 18
brede of erthe^i? Schewe thou to me, if
thou knowist alle thingis, in what weie 19
the liзt dwellith, and which is^k the
place of derknesse^l; that thou lede^m ech 20
thing to hise termes, and^n thou vndurstonde the weies of his hows. Wistist 21
thou thanne, that thou schuldist be borun,
and knew thou the noumbre of thi daies?
Whethir thou entridist in to the tresours 22
of snow, ether biheldist thou the tresours
of hail? whiche thingis Y made redy in to 23
the tyme of an enemy, in to the dai of
fiзtyng and of batel. Bi what weie is the 24
liзt spred abrood, heete^o is departid on^p
erthe? Who зaf cours to the strongeste 25

Right margin, verse 7: therfor God repreuesh his presumpcioun, and seith, *Who is this?* as if he seide, Helyu is vnsufficient to entremete herof. *Lire here.* c.
† *the morewe sterris*; that is, aungels, that weren maad at the begynnyng, with cleer heuene, bifor departing of elementis. *Lire here.* c.

Right margin, verse 16: ‡ *and an hiз arm etc.*; that is, the power of proude men, that ben borun doun sumtyme in the erthe-mouyng. *Lire here.* c.

' How longe E pr. m.   ʷ vttermostis AEFH.   ˣ depnesse AEFH.

ᵐ *that is, aungels* v marg.   ⁿ preiseden I.   ᵒ sungun *thanne* I.   ᵖ goyng I.   q of the see I.   ʳ Om. s.
ˢ the see I.   ᵗ puttide to it I.   ᵘ a dore I.   ʷ Hidurto I.   ˣ Om. I.   ʸ comaundidist wxf.   z the dai I.
ᵃ Om. I.   ᵇ don s.   ᶜ arm *or* proud power I. *that is, power of pryde* v marg.   ᵈ hast entrid I.   ᵉ hast
walked I.   ᶠ Om. s.   ᵍ depthe I. *the greet west see* v marg.   ʰ thou hast seen I.   ⁱ the erthe I.
ᵏ it is A pr. m.   ˡ derknessis EFHLMNOSVXbf.   ᵐ lede out s.   ⁿ and that I.   ᵒ *and bi what wey*
heete I.   ᵖ up on I.

reyne vp on erthe withoute man, in
desert wher noon of dedly men dwelleth?
27 That he shulde fulfille the space withoute wei and desolat, and bringe forth
28 grene erbis? Who is the fader of reyn,
29 or who gat dropis of deu? Fro whos
wombe wente out iys, and frost fro heuene
30 who gat? In the licnesse of a ston watris
ben hardid, and the vtmost^y of the se
31 is streyned togidere. Whether thou art
strong to ioyne the shynende seue^z sterres,
or thou shalt moun scatere the cumpas of
32 the north sterre? Whether thou bringist
forth the dai sterre in his time, and the
euetid sterre vp on the sones of the erthe
33 thou makist to rise? Whether thou hast
knowe the ordre of heuene, and shalt
34 putte his resoun in the erthe? Whether
thou shalt rere thi vois in to a lytil
cloude, and the bure of watris shal conere
35 thee? Whether thou shalt sende leitis,
and thei shul go, and turnende aȝeen
thei shul sey to thee, Wee be neeȝh?
36 Who putte in the entrailis of a man wisdam, and^a who ȝaf to the cok vnderstond-
37 ing? Who shal tellen out the resoun of
heuenus, and the singing of heuene who
38 shal make to slepe? Whanne was pouder
held in the erthe, and clottis weren
39 clunge togidere? Whether thou shalt
take the prei of the leounesse, and the
soule of hir whelpis thou shalt fulfille,
40 whan thei lyn in dichis, and in dennus
41 thei aspien? Who maketh redi to the
crowe his mete, whan his briddis crie to
God, hider and thider waggende, forthi
that thei han no metis?

CAP. XXXIX.

1 Whether thou hast knowen the time
of the berthe of wilde capretis in stonys,
or thou hast waitid hindis berende calf?
2 Thou hast noumbrid the monethis of con-

reyn, and weie of the thundur sownynge? 26
That it schulde reyne on the erthe with out
man in desert, where noon of^q deedli men
dwellith? That it schulde fille a lond with 27
out weie and desolat, and^r schulde brynge
forth greene eerbis? Who is fadir^s of 28
reyn, ether who gendride the dropis of
deew? Of whos wombe ȝede out iys, 29
and who gendride^t frost^u fro heuene? Wa- 30
tris ben maad hard in the licnesse of stoon,
and the ouer^w part of^x occian^y is streyned
togidere. Whether thou schalt mowe^z 31
ioyne togidere schynynge sterris Pliades^a,
ethir thou schalt mowe distrie the cumpas
of Arturis^b? Whether thou bryngist forth 32
Lucifer, 'that is^c, dai^d sterre^e, in his tyme,
and makist euene^f sterre to rise on^g the
sones of erthe? Whether thou knowist the 33
ordre of heuene, and schalt sette the resoun
therof in^h erthe? Whethir thou schalt 34
reise thi vois in to a cloude†, and the fersnesse of watris schal hile thee? Whethir 35
thou schalt sende^i leitis, and tho^k schulen
go^l, and tho schulen turne aȝen, and
schulen seie to thee, We ben present? Who 36
puttide^m wisdoom in^n the entrailist of man,
ethir who ȝaf vndurstondyng to the cok?
Who schal telle out the resoun of heuenes, 37
and who schal make acordyng of heuene
to sleep? Whanne dust was foundid^o in^p 38
the^q erthe, and^r clottis weren ioyned togidere? Whether thou schalt take prey to 39
the lionesse, and schalt fille the soulis^s of
hir whelpis, whanne tho^t liggen in caues, 40
and aspien in dennes? Who makith redi 41
for^u the crowe his mete, whanne hise
briddis crien to God, and wandren aboute,
for tho^w han not meetis?

CAP. XXXIX.

Whethir thou knowist the tyme of 1
birthe of wielde geet in stoonys, ethir
hast thou aspied hyndis bryngynge forth
calues? Hast thou noumbrid the monethis 2

*+ Wher thou
schalt reise thi
vois in to a
cloude; that is,
schalt make the
vois of thundur,
which is gedrid
in the cloude.
Liue here. c.
‡ entrailis;
that is, smile.
Liue here. t.*

---

^{y} vttermost *AEFH.* ^{z} seuen *AH.* ^{a} Om. c.

^{q} Om. s. ^{r} and *that it* I. ^{s} fadris I. ^{t} gaat I. ^{u} frost IS. ^{w} ouerer BCD. ^{x} Om. o. ^{y} depthe I.
^{z} Om. I. ^{a} *that is, the seuen sterris* I marg. ^{b} Arturis, *the whiche is cuen north* I. ^{c} or I. ^{d} a dai FSX,
the dai BR. ^{e} Gloss om. in v. ^{f} the euene IKS. ^{g} up on I. ^{h} on s. ^{i} seude out I. ^{k} thei I. ^{l} go forth I.
^{m} hath putt I. ^{n} to I. ^{o} foundun ELQU. ^{p} on DF. ^{q} Om. *plures.* ^{r} and *whanne* I. ^{s} gredynesse I.
^{t} thei I. ^{u} to s. ^{w} thei I.

ceyuyng of hem, and thou hast knowe
3 the time of the birthe of hem? Thei ben
bowid to the frut of kinde, and beren;
4 and 'roringus thei senden^b out. The sones
of hem ben seuered, and go to the feding;
thei gon out, and ben not turned aȝen
5 to them. Who lafte the asse fre, and
6 his bondis who looside? To whom I ȝaf
in wildernesse an hous, and his taber-
7 naclis in the lond of bareynte. He de-
spiseth the multitude of the cite; the cry
8 of the pletere he hereth not. He beholdeth aboute the hillis of hys leswe,
and alle grene growende thingis he
9 secheth. Whether the vnycorn shal wiln
serue to thee, or^c shal dwelle at thi
10 cracche? Whether shalt thou tie to eren
the vnycorn with thi bridil, or^d he shal
11 breke clottis of valeis after thee? Whether trost thou shalt han in the grete
strengthe of hym, and leuen to hym thi
12 trauailis? Whether takist thou to hym,
that seed he ȝeelde to thee, and thi corn
13 flor he gedere? The fether of a stru-
cioun is lic to the fetheris of a ierfakoun,
14 and of a goshauk; that leueth hir^n eiren
in the erthe, thou peranenture in pouder
15 shalt make them hot. She forȝet, that
the foot to-trede them, or beste of the
16 feeld to-brose. She is maad hard to hir
sones, as thoȝ thei be not hiris; in veyn
she trauailide, no drede constreynende.
17 God forsothe priuede hir wisdam, and
18 ȝaf not to hir vnderstonding. Whan time
were, in heiȝte she rerede out hir weengis;
scorneth the hors, and the steȝere vp of
19 it. Whether shalt thou ȝiue to the hors
strengthe, or don aboute his necke ney-
20 enge? Whether shalt thou reren hym as
locustis? The glorie of his nese therlis
21 ferd. The erthe the houe delueth, hardili
he gladeth out; in to the^f aȝencomyng

of her conseyuyng, and hast thou knowe
the tyme of her caluyng? Tho^x ben bowid^y 3
to the^z calf, and caluen^a; and senden^b out^c
roryngis. Her calues ben departid^d, and 4
goen^e to pasture; tho^f goen out, and
turnen^g not aȝen to 'tho *hyndis*^h. Who let^i 5
go the wielde asse fre, and who loside^k
the boondis of hym? To whom I haue 6
ȝoue an hows in wildirnesse, and the tabernacles of hym^l in the lond of saltnesse. He 7
dispisith the multitude of citee^m; he berith
not the cry of an^n axere. He lokith aboute 8
the hillis of his lesewe, and he sekith alle
greene thingis. Whether an vnycorn schal 9
wilne serue^o thee, ethir schal^p dwelle at
thi cratche? Whether thou schalt bynde 10
the vnicorn with thi chayne, for to ero^q,
ethir schal he breke the clottis of valeis^r
aftir thee? Whether thou schalt haue 11
trist in his grete strengthe, and schalt
thou leeue to hym thi traueils†? Whether 12
thou schalt bileue^s to hym, that he schal
ȝelde seed to thee, and schal^t gadere togidere thi cornfloor? The fethere of an 13
ostriche is lijk^u the fetheris of a gerfaw-
cun, and of an^w hauk; which^x *ostrige* 14
forsakith hise eirun in the erthe, in hap
thou schalt make tho hoot in the dust.
He^y forȝetith, that a foot tredith tho^z, 15
ethir that a beeste of the feeld al to-
brekith tho^a. He^b is maad hard to hise 16
briddis, as if thei ben^c not hise; he traueilide in veyn, while no drede con-
streynede^d. For^e God hath priued hym 17
fro wisdom, and 'ȝaf not^f vnderstondyng
to hym. Whanne tyme is, he reisith the 18
wengis an hiȝ; he scorneth the^g hors, and
his^h ridere^i. Whether thou schalt ȝyue 19
strengthe to an hors, ether schal^k ȝyue
neiyng 'aboute his necke^l? Whether thou 20
schalt reyse^m hym^n as locustis? The glorie
of hise nosethirlis *is* drede. He diggith 21

† *thi trauelis;
that is, fruytis
trauelid of thee,
for to kepe
tho. Lire
hers. C.*

---

^b beslly thei nurschen E *pr. m.* ^c outher *AEFH.* ^d outher *AII.* ^e his *AII.* ^f Om. *CII.*

^x Thei 1. ^y bowid doun 1. ^z Om. 1. ^a *so* caluen 1. ^b thei senden 1. ^c out *thanne* 1. ^d departid
fro hem 1. ^e goen forth 1. ^f thei 1. ^g thei turnen 1. ^h her modris 1. ^i hath let 1. ^k hath losid 1.
^l that *wijlde asse* ben 1. ^m *tame asses*, of a 1. ^n the 1. ^o to serue 18. ^p schal he 1. ^q erie *thi loond* 1.
^r the valeys s. ^s trowe 1. ^t that he schal 1. ^u lijk to 1. ^w an oother 1. ^x the which 1. ^y The
ostricche 1. ^z tho *eyren* 1. ^a *hem* 1. ^b The ostricche 1. ^c weren 1. ^d constreynede *him* 1. ^e Forsothe 1.
^f he hath not ȝouen 1. ^g an 1. ^h the IX. ^i ridere *upon him* 1. ^k schalt thou 1. ^l to his throte 1.
^m reyse up 1. ^n an hors 1.

22 he goth to the armed. He dispisith
dreede, and he ʒiueth not stede to the
23 swerd. Vp on hym the arewe girdil shal
sounen; the spere and the sheeld shal
24 braundishen. Feruent and gnastende he
soupeth the erthe; and rewarde he not
25 to the trumpe sounende trumping. Where
he shal here the trumpe, he shal seyn,
Fy! aferr he smellith bataile; the cleping
26 to of dukis, and ʒelling[g] of the[h] ost. Whether bi thi wisdam waxeth fetherid the
goshauk, strecchende out his weengus to
27 the south? Whether at thi comaundement shal be rerid the egle, and in heʒe
28 thingus shal putten his nest? In stones
he dwellith, and in heʒe sett scarri flintis
he bideth[i], and in rochis hard to come to.
29 Thennes he behalt[k] mete, and fro a ferr
30 his eʒen beholden. His briddes licken
blod, and wher euere shal be the careyn,
31 anoon he is neeʒh. And the Lord addede,
32 and spac to Job, Whether he that striueth
with God, so liʒtli shal reste? Forsothe
he, that vndernemeth God, owith to an-
33 swere to hym. Answerende forsothe Job
34 to the Lord seide, I that liʒtli spac, what
may I answern? Myn hond I shal putte
35 vp on my mouth. O thing I spac, that
wolde God I hadde not seid; and an
other, to the whiche thingus I shal
adden no more.

CAP. XL.

1 Answerende forsothe the Lord to Job
2 fro the whirlewind, seide, Gird as a man
thi leendis, and I shal aske thee, and
3 sheu thou to me. Whether vein thou
shalt make my dom, and condempne me,
4 that thou be iustified? And if thou hast
an arm as God, and with lic vois thun-

erthe with the[o] foot, he 'fulli ioietli
booldli[p]; he[q] goith aʒens[r] armed men.
He dispisith ferdfulnesse, and he ʒyueth 22
not stide to swerd. An arowe caas schal 23
sowne on[s] hym; a spere and scheeld[t] schal
florische[u]. He is hoot[v], and gnastith, and 24
swolewith the erthe†; and he arettith not
that the crie of the trumpe sowneth[w].
Whanne he herith a clarioun, he 'seith, 25
Joie[x]! he smellith batel afer[s]; the excityng
of duykis, and the ʒellyng of the oost.
Whether an hauk spredinge abrood hise 26
wyngis to the south, bigynneth to haue
fetheris bi thi wisdom? Whether an egle 27
schal be reisid[y] at thi comaundement, and
schal sette his nest in hiʒ places? He 28
dwellith in stoonys, and he dwellith[z] in
flyntis brokun bifor, and in rochis, to
whiche[a] 'me may[b] not neiʒe. Fro thennus 29
he[c] biholdith mete, and hise iʒen loken[d]
fro fer. Hise briddis souken blood, and 30
where euere a[n] careyn is, anoon he is
present. And the Lord addide[f], and spak 31
to Joob[g], Whether he, that stryueth with 32
God, schal haue rest so liʒtli? Sotheli he,
that repreueth God, owith for to answere
to hym. Forsothe[h] Joob answeride to the 33
Lord, and seide, What may Y answere, 34
which haue spoke liʒtli[i]‡? Y schal putte
myn hond on[k] my mouth. Y spak o[l] thing§,
which thing Y wold, that Y hadde not 35
seid; and Y spak anothir thing, to which[m]
Y schal no more adde.

CAP. XL.

Forsothe the Lord answeride to Joob 1
fro the whirlewynd, and seide, Girde thou 2
as a man thi leendis, and Y schal axe thee,
and schewe thou to me. Whether thou 3
schalt make voide my doom‖, and schalt[n]
condempne me, that thou be maad iust?
And if thou hast an arm[o], as God hath, 4

Marginal notes:

† gnastith, and swolewith the erthe; that is, neyeth, and semeth to swolewe the erthe, in digginge with feet. Lire here. c.

‡ which haue spoke liʒtli; that is, vndiscreetly and folily; for thouʒ he paside netheles the maner of speking. Lire here. c.

§ Y spak o thing; this was, whanne he seide, Y coueite to dispute with God; and anothir thing; this was, whanne in preisinge his riʒtfulnesse, he semyde to decreesse the riʒtfulnesse of God.

‖ Wher thou shalt make voide my doom; that is, owist thou to remembre thi riʒtfulnesse bi sich a maner, that therbi my doom seme voide, that is, fals to men, and therbi that Y se me condempnable, as if he seye, Nay; and netheles thou didist this, for by thi wordis, in whiche thou declaridist thi riʒtfulnesse, thi frendis vndurstoden so, that thou repreuedist my doom as vniust; therfor no man schal iustifie him silf bi sich a maner, bi which a man may gesse, that sich iustifiyng turneth into decreessing of Goddis riʒtfulnesse. Lire here. c.

[g] to ʒelling ᴇ pr. m.   [h] Om. ᴀꜰʜ.   [i] abideth ᴀꜰʜ.   [k] beholdeth ᴀᴇꜰʜ.

[o] his ɪ.   [p] ful ontioieth ɪ.   [q] and he ɪ.   [r] boldly aʒen ɪ.   [s] upon ɪ,   [t] a scheelde ɪ.   [u] schyne ɪ.
[v] feruent ɪ.   [w] sowneth to batteil ɪ.   [x] ioieth ɪ. seith, Joie; that is, make me a signe of ioye v.   [y] reisid
up ɪ.   [z] abidith ɪ.   [a] the whiche ɪ.   [b] men mowen ɪ.   [c] the egle ɪ.   [d] loken ther to ɪ.   [e] Om. ɪ.
[f] addide to ɪ.   [g] Joob, and seide ɪ.   [h] And ɪ.   [l] but liʒtli ɪ.   [k] upon ɪ.   [l] a ɪ.   [m] the which ɪ.   [n] schalt
thou ɪ.   [o] arm or power ɪ.

₅drist, do aboute to thee fairnesse, and
in to an¹ heiȝ be thou rerid, and be glorious, and be thou clad^m with faire
₆clothis. Scatere proude men in thi wodnesse, and beholdende eche enhaunsende
₇hymself meke thou. Behold alle proude
men, and confounde hem; and to-brose
₈vnpitouse men in ther place. Hijd hem
in pouder togidere^n, and the facis of hem
₉drenche in 'the diche°. And I shal knouleche, that thi riȝthond mai saue thee.
₁₀Lo! bemoth, that I made with thee, hey
₁₁as an oxe he shal ete. His strengthe in
his leendis, and his vertue in the nauele
₁₂of his wombe. He streyneth his tail as
a ceder; and the senewis of his ballokis
₁₃ben wrappid togidere. His bones as
pipis of bras; his gristil as irene platis.
₁₄He is the begynyng of the weies ᴾ of
God; that made hym, shal leiᑫ to his
₁₅swerd. To this hillis bern erbis; alle
₁₆the bestis of the feld pleien there. Vnder
shadewe he slepith, in the priue place of
₁₇reed, in moiste placis. Shadewis coueren
his vmbre; withiene trees of the strem
₁₈enuyrounen hym. He shal soupen vp the
flod, and he shal not wndre; he hath
trost, that Jordan flowe in to the mouth
₁₉of hym. In the eȝen of hym, as with an
hoc, he shal taken hym; and in stakys he
₂₀shal thirle thurȝ his nose therlis. Whether maist thou drawen out leuyethan
with an hoc, and with a corde thou
₂₁shalt binde his tunge? Whethir thou
shalt putte a sercle in his nose therlis,
or with a ring thou shalt therle thurȝ
₂₂his cheke bon? Whether he shal multiplie to thee preȝeeris, or speke to thee
₂₃softe thingus? Whether he shal smyte
with thee couenaunt, and thou shalt take
₂₄hym euermor seruaunt? Whether thou
shalt begile to hym as to a brid, or

and if thou thundrist with lijk vois,
'take thou fairnesse aboute theeᴾ, and be ₃
thou reisidᑫ an hiȝ, and be thou gloriouse,
and be thou clothid 'in faireʳ clothis. Dis- ₆
trieˢ thou proude men in thi woodnesseᵗ,
and biholde thouⁿ, and makeᵛ lowe ech
bostere. Biholde thou alle proude men, ₇
and schendeʷ thou hem; and al to-breke
thou wickid men in her place. Hide thou ₈
hem in dust† togidere, and drenche doun
her facesˣ in to a diche. Andʸ Y schal ₉
knowleche, that thi riȝt hond may saue
thee. Lo! behemotᶻ‡, whom Y made with ₁₀
thee, schal as an oxe ete hey. His strengthe ₁₁
is in hise leendis, and his vertuᵃ is in the
nawleᵇ of his wombe. He streyneth his ₁₂
tail as a cedreᶜ; the senewis of his 'stones
of gendrureᵈ ben foldid togidere. Hise ₁₃
boonys ben as theᵉ pipis of bras; the gristil
of hym is as platis of yrun. He is the ₁₄
bigynnyng of the weies of God; he, that
made hym, schal sette his swerdȝ to hym. ₁₅
Hillis beren cerbis to this behemot; alle ₁₅
the beestis of the feeld pleien there. He ₁₆
slepith vndur schadewe, in the pryuete of
rehedᶠ, in moiste places. Schadewis hilen ₁₇
his schadewe; the salewis of the ryuer
cumpassen hym. He schal soupe vp the ₁₈
flood, and he schal not wondre; he hath
trist, that Jordan schal flowe in to his
mouth. He schal take hem bi 'the iȝen ₁₉
of hymᵍ, as bi an hook; and bi scharpe
schaftis he schal perseʰ hise nosethirlis.
Whether thou schalt mowe drawe out ₂₀
leuyathanᵏ‖ with an hook, and schalt
bynde with a roop his tunge? Whethir ₂₁
thou schalt putte a ryng in hise nosethirlis, ethir schaltˡ perse hyse cheke
with 'an hookᵐ? Whether he schal mul- ₂₂
tiplie preieris to thee, ether schal speke
softe thingis to thee? Whether he schal ₂₃
make couenauntⁿ with thee, and 'thou

+ Hide thou
hem in dust;
in drynynge
her bodies in
to dust bi deth.
and her faces;
that is, soulis,
into a diche;
that is, in to
the depthe of
helle. Lire
here. c.

‡ Lo! behemot;
that is, an oli-
faunt, that sig-
nefieth the
deuel. Lire
here. Bi the
name of an
olifaunt and
of a whal God
descryueth the
power and ma-
lice of the fend,
and of his
membris, and
hou they ben
knyt togidere
in malice, and
hardid in
synne; and that
no man may
ouercome the
deuel and hise
membris bi
mannus vertu,
but only bi
Goddis vertu
and help. Lire
here. c.

ȝ his swerd; that
is, power to
anoye, which
he may not
vse, no but bi
Goddis suf-
fring. Lire
here. c.

‖ leuyathan;
that is, a whal,
that signefieth
the deuel. Lire
here. c.

¹ Om. ᴀɪɪ. ᵐ clothid ᴀᴇꜰɪɪ. ⁿ Om. ᴀ. ° dichis c. ᴾ weie c. ᑫ ioyne ᴀ.

ᴾ Environne thee with fairnesse ɪ. ᑫ reisid up ɪ. ʳ with semely ɪ. ˢ And distrie ɪ. ᵗ feers veniaunce ɪ.
ᵘ thou, or tak hede ɪ. ᵛ make thou ɪ. ʷ confound ɪ. ˣ face s. ʸ And thanne ɪ. ᶻ that is, an olifaunt,
that signefieth the fend v marg. ᵃ vertu of lusty appetyt ɪ. ᵇ nauil ɪ. ᶜ cedre tre ɪ. ᵈ ballokis ʙᴄᴇʜʟ
ᴘᴜᴠx. stones of gendruris ᴀ sec. m. ᴅᴍɴᴏsᴡbf. ᵉ Om. ɪ. ᶠ a rehed ɪ. ᵍ his iȝen ᴀ. ʰ perische cs.
ⁱ her ɪ. ᵏ that is, a whal, that signefieth the fend v marg. ˡ schalt thou ɪ. ᵐ a sercle ɪ. ⁿ a couenaunt ɪ.

25 binden hym with litle hokis? Frendis
shul hewen hym, marchaundis shul de-
26 uyden hym? Whether thou shalt fille^r
nettis with his skyn, and the lep of
27 fisshis with the hed of hym? Put vp on
hym thin hond; haue mynde of bataile,
28 and adde thou to speke no more. Lo!
the hope of hym shal ʻmaken hym^s
veyn; and alle men seende he shal ben
kast doun.

CAP. XLI.

1 Not as cruel I shal reren hym; who
forsothe mai withstonde to my chere?
2 And who befor ȝaf to me, that I ȝeelde to
hym? Alle thingus, that ben vnder heuene,
3 ben myne. I shal not spare to hym bi
myȝti woordis, and to preȝe sett togidere.
4 Who shal shewe the face of his clothing,
and in to the^t myddel of his mouth who
5 shal gon in? The ȝatis of his chere who
shal opene? bi cumpas of his teth drede.
6 His body as ȝoten sheeldis, and threst
togidere with scalis threstende doun hem-
7 self. Oon to oon is ioyned; and lest breth-
8 ing^u place forsothe go in bi them. Oon
shal cleue to the tother, and holdende
9 hemselue shul not ben seuered. His
nesing shynyug of fyr, and his eȝen as
10 eȝelidis of the morutid. Of his mouth
laumpis gon forth, as tend brondus of fyr.
11 Of his nose therlis goth forth smoke, as of
12 a tend pot and boilende. His breth
maketh colis to brenne, and flaume goth
13 out of hys mouth. In his necke shal
dwelle strengthe, and nede shal go be-
14 forn his face. The^v membris of his flesh
cleuende to themself; he shal senden aȝen
hym^w flodis, and to an other place thei
15 shul not be born. His herte shal ben inwardli harded as a ston; and shal be

schalt^o take him a seruaunt euerlastinge?
Whether thou schalt scorne hym as a 24
brid, ethir schalt^p bynde hym to thin
handmaidis^q? Schulen frendis^r ʻkerue 25
hym^s, schulen^t marchauntis departe hym?
Whether thou schalt fille nettis with his 26
skyn, and a ʻleep of fischis^u with his
heed? Schalt thou putte thin hond on^v 27
hym? haue thou mynde of the batel,
and adde^w no more to speke†. Lo! his 28
hope schal disseyue hym; and in the siȝt
of alle men he schal be cast doun^x.

CAP. XLI.

I not as cruel schal reise hym; for^y who^z 1
may aȝenstonde^a my face? And who ʻȝaf 2
to me^b bifore, that Y ȝelde^c to hym? Alle
thingis, that ben vndur heuene, ben myne.
Y schal not spare hym for^d myȝti wordis, 3
and maad faire to biseche^e. Who schal 4
schewe the face of his clothing, and who
schal entre in to the myddis of his mouth?
Who schal opene the ȝatis of his cheer? 5
ferdfulnesse *is* bi the cumpas of hise teeth.
His bodi *is* as ȝotun scheldys of bras, and 6
ioyned togidere with scalis ouerleiynge hem
silf. Oon is ioyned to another; and sotheli 7
brething goith not thorouȝ tho. Oon schal 8
cleue to anothir, and tho^f holdynge^g hem
silf schulen not be departid. His fnesynge^h 9
is as schynynge of fier, and hise iȝen *ben*
as iȝelidis of the morewtid‡. Laumpisⁱ 10
comen forth of his mouth, as trees^k of fier,
that ben kyndlid. Smoke cometh forth of 11
hise nosethirlis, as of^l a^m pot set onⁿ the
fier ʻand boilynge^o. His breeth makith 12
colis to brenne, and flawme goith out of
his mouth. Strengthe schal dwelle in his 13
necke, and nedynesse schal go bifor his
face. The membris of hise fleischis^p *ben* 14
cleuynge togidere to hem silf; God schal
sende floodis aȝens hym§, and tho schulen not be borun^q to an other place.

† and adde no more to speke; ony thing, that sowneth in to decreessing of Goddis riȝtfulnesse and wisdom. Lire here. c.

‡ ȝeeliddis of the morewtid; that is, briȝtnesse. c.

§ God schal sende floodis aȝenus him; that is, Goddis sentence of dampnacioun of the feend. c.

---

^r felle c.   ^s ben made E *pr. m.*   ^t Om. *AII.*   ^u brekynge π.   ^v Om. *AH.*   ^w hem *A.*

^o schalt thou I.   ^p schalt thou I.   ^q haud maidens I.   ^r thi frendis I.   ^s kitte him awey I.   ^t and schul I.
^u fische leep I.   ^v upon I.   ^w adde thou I.   ^x doun *hedlyng* I.   ^y Om. I.   ^z who *sothly* I.   ^a withstonde I.
^b hath ȝouen *auȝt* I.   ^c ȝeldide *it* I.   ^d for his I.   ^e bisoche *with* I.   ^f tho *platis* I.   ^g holdynge *togidere* I.
^h neesyng I.   ⁱ Liȝtis I.   ^k broudis I.   ^l Om. A *pr. m.* IS.   ^m a boilynge I.   ⁿ upon I.   ^o Om. I.
^p fleische I.   ^q borun ouer I.

streyned^x as the stithie of an hamer
16 betere. Whan he shal .be taken awei,
aungelis shul drede; and ferd thei shul
17 be purgid. Whan he shal cacchen hym,
swerd shal not moun stonde, ne spere, ne
18 brest plate. Forsothe he shal telle bi
iren as chaf, and bras as rotun^{xx} tree.
19 The man archer shal not driuen hym;
in to stobil ben turned to hym the stones
20 of the slinge. As stobil he shal eyme
the hamer; and scorne^y the man shakende
21 a spere. Vnder hym shul be the bemes of
the sunne; and he shal leyn vp gold to
22 hym as clei. He shal make the depthe
of the se to boilen as a pot; and sette, as
23 whan oynemens boilen. Aftir hym the
sty shal ȝiue liȝt; and he shal eymen
24 the se as an oldli^z man. Ther is not
vp on erthe power, that be comparisound
to hym; that is maad, that no man he
25 shulde drede. Alle heiȝ thing^a he seeth;
and he ys king vpon^b alle the sones of
pride.

His herte schal be maad hard[*] as a stoon; 15
and it schal be streyned togidere as the^r
anefeld^s of a smith. Whanne he schal be 16
takun awei, aungels schulen drede†; and
thei aferd schulen be purgid. Whanne 17
swerd takith hym, it^t may not stonde^u,
nethir spere, nether haburioun. For he 18
schal arette irun as chaffis^v, and bras as
rotun tre. A man archere schal not dryue 19
hym awei; stoonys of a slynge ben turned
in to stobil to hym. He schal arette an 20
hamer as stobil; and he schal scorne a
florischynge^w spere. The beemys of the 21
sunne schulen be vndur hym; and he schal
strewe to hym silf gold as cley. He schal 22
make the depe^x se to buyle as a pot; and
he schal putte^y, as whanne oynementis
buylen. A path schal schyne aftir hym; 23
he schal gesse the greet occian^z as wexynge
eld. No power is^a on erthe, that schal be 24
comparisound to hym; which is maad,
that he schulde drede noon^b. He seeth al 25
hiȝ thing; he is kyng ouer alle the sones
of pride.

CAP. XLII.

1 Answerende forsothe Job to the Lord,
2 seide, I wot, for alle thingus thou maist,
3 and no thoȝt is vnknowe to thee. Who is
this, that hilith counseil withoute kunnyng? Therfore vnwisly I spak, and tho
thingus that ouer^c maner shulden passe
4 my kunnyng. Heere thou, and I shal
speke; I shal aske thee, and answere
5 thou to me. Bi hering of ere I herde
thee, now forsothe myn eȝe seeth thee.
6 Therfore I myself repreue me, and do
7 penaunce in dead cole and askis^d. Aftir forsothe that the Lord spac these
woordis to Job, he seide to Elifath
Themanythen, My wodnesse is wroth

CAP. XLII.

Forsothe Joob answeride to the Lord, 1
and seide, Y woot, that thou maist alle 2
thingis, and^c no thouȝt^d is hid fro thee‡.
Who is^c this, that helith counsel with out 3
kunnyng? Therfor Y spak^f vnwiseli, and
tho thingis that passiden ouer mesure my
kunnyng. Here^g thou, and Y schal speke; 4
Y schal axe thee, and answere thou to
me. Bi heryng of eere Y herde^h thee, but 5
now myn iȝe seeth thee. Therfor Y re- 6
preueⁱ me^k, and do^l penaunce in^m deed
sparcle andⁿ aische. Forsothe^o aftir that 7
the Lord spak^p these wordis to Joob, he
seide to Eliphat Themanytes, My stronge
veniaunce is wrooth aȝens thee, and aȝens

*maad hard; the fend is obstynat, and is not bowid to good, bi ony smyting of Goddis ven-iaunce. c.
† aungels schulen drede; that is, wondre of Goddis vertu and riȝtful-nesse, in the casting doun, and panysching of the fend, which was doon in parti at the higynnyng of the fal fro houene, and schal be endid in the doom to comynge, whanne with sinful men dampned, he schal be cast doun into helle.
‡ schulen be purgid; not of vnclennesse, but of igno-raunse, in as myche as bi Goddis reue-lacioun, ether wonderful werkis, holy aungels schulen knowe summe thingis, which they knewen not bifore. Lire here. c.
‡ woot that thou maist alle thingis, and no thouȝt is hid fro thee; Joob wiste wel, that in remembringe his riȝtfulnesse he suffride sum stiring of veyn-glorie, which is wont to come liȝly in siche thingis, ȝhe, in men that ben parfiit. Y spak vnwiseli; In preisinge my riȝtfulnesse. that passiden ouer mesure; in enqueringe ouer myche the resouns of Goddis domes. c.

^x stryued c. ^{xx} rote c. ^y scornynge ΛII. ^z old ΛII. ^a thingis ΛII. ^b of II. ^c other II. ^d ashen Λ.

^r an I. ^s anfeeld, or stithie K. ^t ther I. ^u abyde I. ^v chaff I. ^w briȝt schynynge I. ^x grete s.
^y putte it I. ^z depthe of watir I. ^a ther is I. ^bno thing I. ^c and that I. ^d thing I. ^e iȝ he I.
^f haue spoke I. ^g Loord, here I. ^h haue herde I. ⁱ preue s. ^k myselff I. ^l I do I. ^m in Λ I.
ⁿ and in I. ^o And I. ^p had spoke I.

in to thee, and in to thi two frendis;
for ȝee han not spoke befor me riȝt,
8 as my seruaunt Job. Taketh therfore
to ȝou seuen bolis, and seuen wetheris;
and goth to my seruaunt Job, and
offreth for ȝou brent sacrifise. Job forsothe, my seruaunt, shal preȝen for ȝou;
his face I shal take, that folie be nott
witid to ȝou; ne forsothe ȝee han spoken
9 befor me riȝt, as my seruaunt Job. Thanne
Elyfath Themanythes, and Baldach Suythes, and Sofar Naamatites, wenten, and
diden, as the Lord hadde spoke to them;
10 and the Lord toc the face of Job. The
Lord also is turned to the penaunce of
Job, whan he shulde preȝe for his frendis.
And the Lord ȝaf to alle thingus, that
11 euere weren of Job, double. And ther
camen to hym alle his brethern, and alle
his sistris, and alle that hadden knowen
hym beforn; and thei ete with hym
bred in his hous, and moueden vpon hym
the hed; and coumforteden hym vp on al
the euel, that the Lord hadde broȝt in vp
on hym; and thei ȝeue to hym eche a shep,
12 and a golden ere ring. The Lord forsothe blisside to the laste thingus of Job,
more than to his begynnyng; and ther
ben maad to hym fourtene thousend of
shep, and sixe thousend of camailis, and
a thousend ȝokis of oxen, and a thou-
13 send she assis. And ther weren to hym
seue sones, and thre doȝtris; and he
clepide the name of the ton Diem, and
the name of the seconde Cassiam, and
14 the name of the thridde Cornu tibij. Ther
ben not forsothe founde so faire wymmen, as the doȝtris of Job, in al the
lond; and ther fader ȝaf to hem eri-
15 tage among ther brethern. Forsothe
Job lyuede aftir these scourgis an hundrid and fourti ȝeer, and saȝ his sones,
and the sones of his sones, in to the

thi twey frendis*; for ȝe 'spaken not[q] bifor
me riȝtful thing[r], as my seruaunt Joob
dide[s]. Therfor take ȝe to ȝou seuene bolis, 8
and seuene rammes; and go ȝe to my seruaunt Joob, and offre ȝe brent sacrifice for
ȝou. Forsothe[t] Joob, my seruaunt, schal
preie for ȝou; Y schal resseyue his face[u],
that foli be not arettid to ȝou†; for[v] ȝe
'spaken not[w] bifor me riȝtful thing, as[x]
my seruaunt Joob *dide*[y]. Therfor Eliphat 9
Themanytes, and Baldach Suythes, and
Sophar Naamathites, ȝeden, and[z] diden, as
the Lord hedde spoke to hem; and the
Lord resseyuede the face of Joob. Also 10
the Lord was conuertid[a] to the penaunce
of Joob, whanne he preiede for hise frendis.
And the Lord addide[b] alle thingis double,
whiche euere weren of Joob. Sotheli[c] alle 11
hise britheren, and alle hise sistris, and
alle that knewen hym bifore, camen to
hym; and thei eeten breed with hym in his
hows, and[d] moueden the[e] heed on[f] hym;
and thei coumfortiden hym of[g] al the yuel,
which[h] the Lord hadde brouȝt in on[i] hym;
and thei ȝauen to hym ech man o[k] scheep,
and o[k] goldun eere ring. Forsothe the 12
Lord blesside the laste thingis of Joob,
more than the bigynnyng of hym; and
fouretene thousynde of scheep weren maad
to hym, and sixe thousinde of camels,
and a thousynde ȝockis of oxis[l], and a
thousynde femal assis. And he hadde 13
seuene sones‡, and thre douȝtris; and he
clepide the name of o[m] douȝtir Dai, and the
name of the secounde douȝtir Cassia, and
the name of the thridde douȝtir 'An horn[n]
of wymmens oynement[o]. 'Sotheli no wym- 14
men weren foundun so faire[p] in al erthe[q],
as[r] the douȝtris of Joob; and her fadir ȝaf
eritage to hem among her britheren. For- 15
sothe[s] Joob lyuede aftir these betyngis[t] an
hundrid and fourti ȝeer, and 'siȝ hise[u]
sones, and[v] the sones of hise sones, 'til to[w]

* *aȝenus thee and thi twey frendis*; God seith not aȝenus Helyu, ether aȝenus Joob; for whi to do synne bi presumpcioun, ether bi vnwar speking, as Helyu and Joob diden, is not so greuouse synne as to do synne bi afermyng of falsnesse, which bifelde to these thre men. *Y schal resseyue his face*; for he synnede liȝtly, and dide penaunce therfor perfitly. *Lire here.* c.

† *be not arettid to ȝou*; to euerlastinge peyne. *Lire here.* c.

‡ *he hadde seuene sones etc.*; the formere sones and douȝtris weren in the weye of saluacioun, and so not deed outirly. *Lire here.* c.

[q] haue not spoke I. [r] thingis I. [s] Om. I. [t] Sothely I. [u] face *preiynge for ȝou* I. [v] certis I. [w] han not spoke I. [x] as *hath* I. [y] Om. I. [z] and thei I. [a] altogidere turned I. [b] addide to I. [c] And I. [d] and thei I. [e] her I. [f] upon I. [g] on K. [h] that I. [i] upon I. [k] a IS. [l] oxen IK. [m] the oo K. [n] *he clepide Cornu stibii, that is,* the horn I. [o] ournment I. [p] And ther weren not founde so faire wymmen I. [q] the loond I. [r] as *weren* I. [s] And I. [t] scourgyngis I. [u] he sauȝe the I. [v] of I. [w] unto I.

ferthe ieneracioun; and he^e diede old, and ful of daȝis.

Here endith the book of Job, and here begynneth the prolog of the Sauter^f.

the fourthe generacioun; and^x he was deed eld†, and ful of daies.

Here endith the book of Joob, and here bigynneth the Sauter, which is red comynli in chirchis^y.

† *he was deed eld; that is, he hadde lengthe and prosperite of lijf. Lire here. c.*

^e Om. ɪɪ. † From ᴀ. *Explicit liber Job.* ᴇ. No final rubric in cꜰɪɪ.

^x and *thanne* ɪ. ^y From ᴄᴅǫᴜ. *Here cendith the book of Joob, which book is an opin and autentick kalender to alle the children of God.* ʙ. *Here endith the book of Joob. Blessid be the hooly Trynyte. Amen.* ɪɪ. *Heere endith Job, and biginnith the Sauter.* ɪᴠ. *Heere eendeth the booc of Joob; se now the prolog of the Sauter.* ᴋ. *Here endith the book of Joob, and here bigynneth the prologe on the Sauter.* ᴍ. *Here endith Joob, and here bigynneth the . . . .* ɴ. *Here endith the book of Joob, and bigynneth the prolog on the Sauter.* ᴏ. *Here eendeth Joob, and bigynneth a prolog on the Sauter.* ʀ. *Here endith the booc of Job, and bigynneth the Sauter.* x. *Here endith Joob, and here bigynneth the Sauter, which is red comounli in the chirche.* b. *Explicit Joob.* f. No final rubric in ᴀᴇʟᴘsᴡ.

PSALMS.

[Prologue on the book of Psalms[a].]

THIS book Sauter is clepid, that is to seie, the book of songis of Dauith, and of Asaph, the channtour of the temple of the Lord; wherynne is conteyned profesie of the comynge of Crist, of his birthe, and of his power and teching; of his passioun and his rising aȝen fro deeth, and of his ascencioun and of his comynge aȝen in the laste doom; whiche songis ben red in holi cherche in to wurschiping and preising of the Lord, knoulechinge his heiȝ maieste, and hise grete werkis; and that he do merci to vs, whanne we trespasen aȝens him, brekinge hise comaundementis, that we perische not for oure synnes.

Incipit prologus in librum Psalterij[a].

Whan it is knowe, alle the profetis to han spoke bi reuelacioun of the Holi Gost, Dauid[b] most of profetis to han spoken sum[c] wise in wrthiere and ouer passende maner, as the trumpe of the Holi Gost, than othere profetis. Othere forsothe profetis profecieden bi sum maner ymagis of thingus, and withinne coueryngis of woordis, that is, bi sweuenes, and viseouns, and deedis, and sawis; Dauid forsothe, thurȝ stiring of the Holi Gost alone, withoute vttermor helpe his profecie made out. Wherfor couenabli this boc is seid, The boc of solitarie spechis. It is also seid a Sauter, the whiche name it toc of a musik instrument, that Ebruli is clepid nablum, Grekli a sauter, of this Grek woord sallim, that is, touching; Latinli is seid an[d] orgne, that is of ten cordis, and fro the ouere part ȝiueth soun, bi the touch of hondis. Of that forsothe instrument at the lettre therfore is[e] nemned 'this boc[f], for at the[g] vois of that instrument Dauid song salmys beforn the arke in the tabernacle of the Lord; and as alle the sweete songus of that instrument weren clepid salmys, so and alle the particlis of this boc, or clausis. Also[h] aftir the spirituel vnderstonding wel of that instrument it taketh name, for as that instrument is of ten cordis, so this boc techeth the al aboute keping[i] of the ten hestis; and as that instrument ȝiueth soun fro the ouere part bi the touch of hondis, so this boc techeth wel to werche, not for ertheli thingus, but for heuenli thingus, that ben

a This prologue is from M.

a From E. *Prolong.* F. *Prologus.* H. No initial rubric in AC. b *it is knowun* Dauid OR. c *in sum* c.
d *and* H. e *it is* R. f Om. R. g Om. H. h *And* R. i *the keping on.*

aboue. This boc stant[k] in an hundrid and fifti salmys, not biside the resoun of he3ere signefiyng; this forsothe noumbre is notid to most solempne mysteries. It stant[l] forsothe of ei3teti and seuenti. And ei3tety al oon signefieth that[m] ei3te, and seuenti the same that seuene. Ei3te forsothe signefieth the ei3tthe age of a3een rising; for sithen ther ben sixe agis of men liuende, and the seuenthe of men diende, the ei3the age shal ben of men a3een risende. Bi seuene forsothe is betocned the time of this lif, that is passid bi the oftesithes comyng of seuen da3es. Ri3tli thanne this boc is maad in such a noumbre of salmys, whos partyes signefien 'the beforseid[n] mysteries; for it techeth so vs in the seuenthe[o] of this lif to werken and to liuen, that in the ei3the[p] of a3een rising wee be not clad[q] with the doublefold cloth of confusioun, but with the stole of double glorifiyng. Or therfore in that noumbre of salmys it is maad, for, as wee han seid, this[r] noumbre stant[s] of ei3teti and seuenti, that al oon betocnen that[t] ei3te and seuene. Ei3te forsothe betocneth the newe testament, the fadris[u] forsothe of the newe testament to ogdoadi, that is, to ei3te descruen. Thei kepen[v] forsothe the ei3the dai of the resureccioun of Crist, that is, the sone dai, and the vtas of seintis, and abijden the ei3te of the a3een rising. Bi seuene forsothe[w] is betocned the olde testament therfore; for the fadris[x] of the olde testament serueden to ebdoady, that is, to seuene. Forsothe thei kepten[y] the seuenthe dai, and the seuenthe wike, the seuenthe moneth, the[z] 'seuenthe 3er[a], and the seuenthe 3er of the seuenthe, 'that is, the[b] fiftithe, that is seid iubile. Wherfore Salomon seith, " 3if partis seuene and also ei3te." And Mychias, " Wee shul reren 'vp on[c] hym seuen shepperdis, and ei3te primatis." Weel therfore this boc in that noumbre of salmys is maad, whos partis betocnen the doctrine of either testament, that bi that be[d] shewid the hestis of either testament to be contened in this boc. This boc forsothe is deuydid bi thre fifties; bi the whiche thre[e] statis of cristene religioun ben betocned. Of whiche the firste is in penaunce, the secounde in ri3twisnesse[f], the thridde in preising of the[g] euere lastende lif. Wherfore the firste fifti is endid in penaunce, that is, the salm that begynneth " Haue mercy of me, God;" the secounde in ri3twisnesse[h], that is, this salm, " Mercy and dom I shal singen to thee;" the thridde in preising of the[i] euere lastende lif, that is, this[k] woord " Eche[l] spirit preise God[m]." And for these thre thingus techeth Dauid in this boc, therfore this threfold distinccioun of salmys is maad. Also it is to be notid, this scripture mor than othere to ofte ben vsid in chirche[n] seruysis[o], that therfore is don, for in this boc is the fulle ending of the hole boc of Godis woord. Heer forsothe ben discriued the meedis of goode men, the tormentis of euele men, the pleyne techyngus[p] of begynende men, the forth going of profitende men, the perfeccioun of ful comynge[q] men, the lif of actif men, the[r] spirituel beholding of contemplatif men; heer also is ta3t what synne doth awei, what penaunce restoreth, what the gilti of synne othenkende[s] seye[t], that is, " Lord, in thi wodnesse vndernyme thou not me," and in an other place, " Haue mercy of me, God, aftir thy mychile[u] mercy;" and what bi penaunce be[v] purchasid, whan he vnderioyneth, " I shal teche wicke[w] men thi weies, and vnpitous men to thee shul be conuertid;" bi whiche is shewid to[x] no man, hou myche euere 'trespasinge to be[y], to[z] mystrosten of for3iuenesse, and of the merci of God, taken to the mecnesse of othenking[a]; whan forsothe

k stondith _AR._   l stondith _AI._   m _the same_ that _doith_ OR.   n parfite E _pr. m._   o seuenthe _age_ OR.
P ei3the _age_ OR.   q clothid _AEFHIOR._   r the O.   s stoondith _A._   t _that same_ that _doith_ O. _the same_ that
doith R.   u parties E _pr. m._   v kepten O.   w Om. R.   x parties E _pr. m._   y kepen E _pr. m._   z and
the _A sec. m._ Om. H.   a Om. H.   b Om. E _pr. m._   c vp OR.   d he OR.   e the thre R.   f ri3tfulnesse OR.
g Om. _AHOR._   h ri3tfulnesse O.   i Om. _A._   k the OR.   l alle E _pr. m._   m the Lord _AFHIOR._
n chirchemennys E _pr. m._ the chirchis OR.   o seruyse OR.   P techinge OR.   q kunnynge OR.   r and the OR.
s forthenkynge OR.   t seith _AHOR._   u miche IO.   v he OR.   w wickid _AIOR._   x that OR.   y be his
trespas OR.   z Om. OR.   a forthinking IOR.

VOL. II.   5 B

wee beholden Dauid, a man sleere and auoutrer, bi penaunce maad a doctour and a
profete, to no man doende penaunce is laft place of wanhope; as of[b] the conuerting of
Powil and his auaunsing in to apostil of the mercy of God pleynli wee ben certefied.
Wherfore the chirche vsith in offisis[c], as the profecie of Dauid, the epistolis[d] of hym
more than of[e] othere; and therfore this profecie is oftene[f] had in vse, for among
othere profecies it passith in openyng of sawys; tho forsothe thingus that othere profetis dercly and as bi figure seiden of the passion and the[g] resureccioun of Crist, and
of the euerlastende geteng, and of othere mysterijs, Dauid of profetis most excellent so
euydentli openede, that more he be seen to euangelisen than to profecien.

Another prolog[h].

Dauyd, the sone of Jesse, whan he was in his[i] reume, foure he ches that salmes
shulden maken, that is, Asaf, Eman, Ethan, and Iditym. Eiʒtety and eiʒte forsothe
seiden the salmys, and two hundrid the vndersinging, and[k] Abiud smot the harpe.
Whan Dauid hadde aʒen[l] broʒt the arke, aʒeen clepid fro Asotis in to Jerusalem aftir
twenti ʒer, and abod in the hous of Amynadab, this he putte[m] ou in a newe 'ʒokid
karte[n], and broʒte in to Jerusalem; men chosen of al the kinrede of the sonis of Israel,
seuenti thousend, of the lynage forsothe of Leuy, two hundrid seuenti and eiʒte
thousend men; of whiche foure princis he ordeynede to ben beforn to the songus, Asaf,
Eman, Ethan, and Iditym, to eche of hem deuydende two and seuenti men, vnder
criende preising of the songis to the Lord. And oon forsothe of hem smot the simbal,
an other the harpe, an other the hornene trumpe enhauncende. In the myddel forsothe of hem 'stod Dauid[o], holdende hymself[p] a sautre; forsothe[q] thei wenten befor
the arke in seuene queris, and the sacrifise, a[r] calf. Forsothe al the puple folewide
after the arke. Thanne alle the salmys of Dauid ben in noumbre an hundrid and
fifti, of whiche[s] alle forsothe nyne made Dauid himself, two and thretti han not super-
scripcioun, fifti and two and twenti in to Dauid, twelue in to Asaf, twelue in to
Iditym, nyne to the sones of Chori, oon to Moises, two[t] in to Salomon, two in to Aggie
and Zacharie. And[u] so alle the salmys of Dauid ben maad in noumbre of an hundrid
and fifti. The deuyseoun[v] of salmys that ben clepid diasalmys ben in noumbre[w] of
seuenti and fiue; the canticlis of grees ben in noumbre of fiftene. The firste salm to
no man is asigned, for it is of alle. Therfore what other man is vnderstonde in the
firste but the firste goten, that wrthili inscripcioun shul not be necessarie. Ferthermor for that salm maketh mencioun of Crist, as aʒen thi[x] Crist expouuende the persoue
'to ben inscriued[y], vttirli thei han not withinne chaungid the ordre of storie. Wee reden
and[z] in the titlis of salmys; but the salmys not after the storie, but aftir the profecie
hen rad, so the ordre of titlis mai not disturben[a] the order of salmys. Alle[b] the
salmys that ben inscriued to hym Dauid, pertenen to the sacrament of Crist, for Dauid
is seid Crist.

Explicit prologus super psalterium[c].

b Om. R.   c office OR.   d epistle O. pistil R.   e Om. AOR.   f ofter OR.   g of the A.   h From A. *Alius
prologus.* E. *Another prolog on the Sauter.* OR.   No rubric in CFHI.   i Om. O.   k on R.   l aʒee C.
m putted I.   n wayn C pr. m.   o Dauid himsilf stood OR.   p Om. OR.   q and sothely OR.   r of a R.
s the whiche AFHIOR.   t and two O.   u Om. O.   v diuisiouns IR.   w the noumbre ANOR.   x Om. AOR.
y transcryued R.   z Om. OR.   a distourblen HIOR.   b And alle OR.   c *Here endith the prolog.* A. *Here
endeth the prolog of the Sauter, se now the booc.* I. *Endith prolog.* O. *This seith seint Jerom, in his prologis on the Sauter.* R.   No rubric in EFH.

The boc begynneth of ympnes and solitarie spechis of the[a] profete Dauyd, of Cryst[b].

PSALM I.

1 BLISFUL the man, that went not awei
in the counseil of vnpitouse, and in the
wei off sinful stod not; and in the chaȝer
2 of pestilence sat not. But in the lawe
of the Lord his wil; and in the lawe of
hym he shal sweteli thenke dai and nyȝt.
3 And he shal ben as a tree, that is plauntid
biside the doun rennyngis[c] of watris; that
his frut shal ȝiue in his time. And the
lef of hym shal not fade; and alle thingus
what euere he shal don shul waxe wel-
4 sum. Not so the vnpitouse, not so; but as
poudre, that aferr throwith the wind fro
5 the face of the erthe. Therfore eft rijsen
not the vnpitouse in dom; ne sinful in the
6 counseil of riȝtwise. For the Lord hath
knowe the weie of the riȝtwise; and the
goyng of the vnpitouse shal pershen.

Here bigynneth the Sauter, which is red comynly in chirchis[b].

PSALM I.

The firste salm[c].

Blessid *is* the man, that ȝede[d] not in the 1
councel of wickid men; and stood not in
the weie of synneris, and sat not in the
chaier of pestilence. But his wille *is* in 2
the lawe of the Lord; and he schal bithenke in the lawe of hym dai and nyȝt.
And he schal be[e] as a tree, which[f] is 3
plauntid bisidis the rennyngis of watris;
which[g] *tre*[h] schal ȝyue his fruyt in his
tyme. And his leef schal not falle doun;
and alle thingis which euere he schal do
schulen haue prosperite. Not so wickid 4
men, not so; but *thei ben* as dust, which
the[i] wynd castith awei fro the face of
erthe[k]. Therfor wickid men risen not aȝen 5
in doom[l]; nethir synneres in the councel of
iust men. For the Lord knowith[m] the 6
weie of iust men; and the weie of wickid
men schal perische.

PSALM II.

The salm of Dauyd.

1 Whi gruccheden Jentilis; and puplys
sweteli thoȝten inwardli veyne thingus?
2 Ther stode neeȝh the kingus of the[d]
erthe; and princis kamen togidere in to
oon, aȝen the Lord, and aȝen his Crist.
3 To-breke we the bondis of hem; and aferr
4 throwe we fro vs the ȝoc of hem. That
dwelleth in heuenes shal scorne them;
5 and the Lord shal bemowe[e] them. Thanne
he shal speke to hem in his wrathe; and
in his wodnesse disturbe[f] them togidere.
6 I forsothe am sett king fro hym vpon
Sion, the holi mount of hym; prechende

PSALM II.

The secounde salm[n]†.

Whi gnastiden with teeth hethene men; 1
and puplis thouȝten veyn thingis? The 2
kyngis of erthe stoden togidere; and
princes camen togidere aȝens the Lord,
and aȝens his Crist? Breke we the bondis 3
of hem; and cast we awei the ȝok of
hem fro vs. He that dwellith in heuenes 4
schal scorne hem; and the Lord schal
bimowe hem. Thanne he schal speke to 5
hem in his ire[o]; and he schal disturble
hem in his stronge veniaunce. Forsothe[p] 6
Y am maad[q] of hym a kyng on[r] Syon, his
hooli hil; prechynge his comaundement.

† *A glos.* The secounde salm, that hath no title in Ebreu, and in Jeromes translacioun, was maad of Dauith, as the postlis witnessen in iiij. chapitre of Dedis. c *et alii.* *This secunde psalm is vndirstondun of Crist, God and man.* V.

[a] Om. E. [b] From ACE. No initial rubric in the other Mss. [c] rennyng AH. [d] Om. C. [e] mow A. [f] distourble A.

[b] From ALOP. *Here bigynneth first salm of the Sauter.* M. *Here biginneth the Sauter, the which ys red comunly in the chirche.* S. *Here bygynnyth the Psalmes of Dauith, that is clepid the Sauter.* k. No initial rubric in the other Mss. [c] *Psalmus i.* O. *The psalm of David.* V. Om. IMRS. [d] gooth S. [e] be maad K *sec. m.* [f] that I. [g] the which I. that KS. [h] Om IS. [i] Om. K. [k] the erthe CISIK [l] doom, *that is, to ther saluacion, but more to ther dampnacion* K *text.* that is, to han saluacioun, but to dampnacioun more V *marg.* [m] hath knowe I. [n] Om. IK. [o] wraththe I. [p] Sothely I. [q] ordeyned I. [r] up on I.

7 his heste. The Lord seide to me, My
8 sone thou art; I to day gat thee. Aske of
me, and I shal 3iue to thee Jentilis thin
eritage; and thi possessioun the termes of
9 erthe⁸. Thou shalt gouerne them in an
irene 3erde; and as a vessel of a crockere
10 breke them togidere. And now, kingus,
vnderstondeth; beth ta3t, that demen the
11 erthe. Serueth to the Lord in drede; and
ful out gladeth to hym with trembling.
12 Taketh discipline, lest any time be wrathid
the Lord; and 3ee pershe fro the ri3twis
13 weie. Whan his wrathe shal brenne out
in short; blisful alle that trosten in hym.

The Lord seide to me, Thou art my sone; 7
Y haue gendrid⁸ thee to dai. Axe thou of 8
me, and Y schal 3yue to thee hethene
men thin¹ eritage; and thi possessioun the
termes of erthe. Thou schalt gouerne hem 9
in an yrun 3erde; and thou schalt breke
hem" as the vessel of a pottere. And now, 10
3e kyngis, vndurstonde; 3e that demen
the erthe, be" lerud"". Serue 3e the Lord 11
with" drede; and make 3e fulˣ ioye to hym
with tremblyng. Take 3e loreʸ; lest the 12
Lord be wrooth² sumtyme, and lest˟ 3e
perischen fro iustᵇ waie. Whanne his ˋire 13
brennethᶜ out in schort tyme; blessed *hen*
alle thei, that tristen in hym.

PSALM III.

1 *Salm*ʰ *of*ⁱ *Dauid, whan he shulde flee
fro the face of Absolon, his sone.

The title of the thridde salm. ˋThe salm*d 1
of Dauid, whanne he fledde fro the
face of Absolon, his sone.*

quid. 2 Lord, wherto ben multiplied that trublen me? manye inwardli rijsen a3en me.
3 Manye seyn to my lifᵏ, Ther is not helthe
4 to hym in his God. Thou forsothe, Lord,
art myn vndirtakere; my gloric, and en-
5 hansende myn hed. With my vois to the
Lord I criede; and he ful out herde me
6 fro his holi hil. I sleep, and was a slepe,
and ful¹ out ros; for the Lord vndertoc
7 me. I shal not drede thousendis of puple
goende aboute me; rys vp, Lord; thou
8 me saf, my God. For thou hast smyte
alle doende aduersite to me with oute
cause; the teth of the sinful thou hast
9 to-brosid. Of the Lord is helthe; and
vpon thi puple thi blessing.

Lord, whi ben thei multiplied that dis- 2
turblen me? many men rysen a3ens me. 3
Many men seien ofᵉ my soule, Noon helthe
isᶠ to hym in his God. But thou, Lord, 4
art myn vptakere; my glorye, and en-
haunsyng myn heed. With my vois Y 5
criede to the Lord; and he berde me fro
his hooli hil. I slepte, and ˋwas quenchidᵍ, 6
and Y roos vp; for the Lord resseyuede
me. I schal not drede thousyndis of puple 7
cumpassynge me; Lord, riseʰ thou vp¹;
my God, make thouᵏ me saaf. For thou 8
hast smyte alle men beynge aduersaries
to me with out cause; thou hast al to-
broke the teeth of synneris. Helthe is 9
of the Lord; and thi blessyng, Lord¹, is
on thi puple.

PSALM IV.

1 *In to the ende, in ditees, the salm of
Dauid; or, In to the ende, the salm of
the song of Dauid.*

The title of the fourthe salm. ˋTo the vic- 1
torie in orguns*ᵐ; the salm of Dauid†.*

voca- 2 Whan I inwardli clepide, ful out herde
me the God of my ri3twisnesse; in tribu-

Whanne Y inwardli clepid", God of my 2
ri3twisnesseᵒ herdeᵖ me; in tribulacioun

† *A plos.* The
fourthe salm is
doynge of
thankingis to
God bi Dauid,
for God delyueride him fro
Saul, cumpassinge him with
his oost, that
he myste not
ascape in maanus weie, outakun the meruelouse help of
God. *c et alii.*

ᵍ the erthe *au.* ʰ *The salm a.* ⁱ *to k pr. m.* ᵏ soule *a.* ¹ Y ful *a.*

ᵏ goten ı. ᵗ to thin s. ⁿ hem to gidere ı. ᵛ be 3e ıᴋ. ᵂᵂ lerned ᴅ *et alii.* ᵂ in ı. ˟ ful out ᴋ *sec. m.*
ʸ lore of *chastisyng* ı. ᶻ wraththid ı. ᵃ Om. ı. ᵇ the iust ı. ᵒ wraththe shal brenne ı. ᵈ Om. ı.
ᵉ to ı. ᶠ ther is ı. ᵍ restide ı. ʰ arijse ı. ⁱ Om. ı. ᵏ Om. ıs. ¹ Om. ı. ᵐ *the ouercomere in
salmes* ᵛ. ⁿ clepid, *that is, preiede* ᵛ. ᵒ ri3tfulnesse *ceteri.* ᵖ full out herde ı.

3 lacioun thou spraddest out to me. Haue merci of me; and ful out here myn orisoun. Sones of men, hou longe with greuous herte? whereto looue зee vanyte, 4 and sechen lesing? And witeth, for the Lord hath maad merueilous his scynt; the Lord ful out shal here me, whan 5 I shal crie to hym. Wrathe зee, and wileth not synnen; that зee seyn in зoure hertis and in зoure couchis, haue 6 зee compunccioun. Sacrifiseth sacrifise of riзtwisnesse, and hopeth in the Lord; many seyn, Who shewith to vs goode 7 thingis? Markid is vpon vs the liзt of thi chere, Lord; thou зeue gladnesse in 8 myn herte. Of the frut of whete, win, 9 and oile of hem; thei ben multiplied. In pes into itself; I shal slepe, and reste. 10 For thou, Lord; singulerli in hope hast togidere set me.

PSALM V.

1 *Into the ende, for hir that getith the eritage.*

2 My woordis with eris parceyue thou, 3 Lord; vnderstond my cry. Tac heede to the vois of myn orisoun; my king, and 4 my God. For to thee I shal preзe, Lord; 5 erli thou ful out shalt here my vois. Erly I shal neeзh stonde to thee, and seen; for thou art God not willende wickid- 6 nesse. Ne shal dwelle beside thee the shrewe; ne shul dwelle stille the vn- 7 riзtwise before thin eзen. Thou hast hatid alle that wirken wickidnesse; thou shalt leesen alle that speken lesing. The man of blodis and trecherous the Lord 8 shal wlate; I forsothe in the multitude of thi mercy. I shal entre in to thin hous; I shal honouren at thin holi temple in thi 9 drede. Lord, bring forth me in thi riзt- wisnesse for myn enemys; mac redi in 10 thi siзte my weie. For ther is not in the mouth of hem treuthe; the herte of hem

---

thou hast alargid to me. Haue thou 3 mercy on me; and here[q] thou my preier. Sones of men, hou long *ben зe* of heuy herte? whi louen зe vanite, and seken[r] n[s] leesyng? And wite зe, that the Lord hath 4 maad merueilous his hooli man; the Lord schal here me, whanne Y schal crye to hym. Be зe wrothe, and nyle зe[t] do[u] ₅ synne; 'and *for tho thingis*[v] whiche зe seien in зoure hertis and in зoure beddis, be зe compunct. Sacrifie[w] зe 'the sacri- 6 fice[x] of riзtfulnesse, and hope зe in the Lord; many[y] seien, Who schewide goodis[z] to vs? Lord, the liзt of thi cheer is markid 7 on[a] vs; thou hast зoue gladnesse in myn herte. Thei ben multiplied of the fruit of[a] whete, *and*[b] of wyn; and of[c] her[d] oile. In 9 pees in the same thing; Y schal slepe, and take reste. For thou, Lord; hast set me 10 syngulerli[e] in hope.

PSALM V.

1 *The title of the fyuethe salm. To the ouercomere on the eritagis, the song[f] of Dauid †.*

2 Lord, perseyue thou my wordis with eeris; vndurstonde[g] thou my cry. Mi 3 kyng, and my God; зyue thou tent to the vois of my preier. For, Lord, Y schal 4 preie to thee; here thou eerly my vois. Eerli Y schal stonde nyз thee[b], and Y ₅ schal se; for thou art God not willyngei wickidnesse. Nethir an yuel willid man 6 schal dwelle bisidis thee; nethir vniust men schulen dwelle bifor thin iзen. Thou 7 hatist alle[k] that worchen wickidnesse; thou schalt leese[l] alle that speken leesyng. The Lord schal holde abhomynable a manquellere, and gilefuf[m] man. But[n], 8 *Lord*[o], in the multitude of thi merci Y schal entre in to thin hows; Y schal wor- schipe[p] to[q] thin hooli temple in thi drede. Lord, lede thou forth me in thi riзtful- 9 nesse[r] for myn enemyes; dresse thou my weie in thi siзt. For whi[s] treuthe is not 10

† *A glos.* Dauith made the fyuethe salm, for prestis and dekenes schulden synge it, to gete Goddis help aзenus enemyes of Goddis puple; and that God schulde defende his puple. c *et alii.*

q full out here I.   r seken зe s.   s Om. I.   t Om. c.   u Om. I.   v *tho yuelis to* I.   w Sacrifice IIKL MOSXbbhk. offre I.   x an offryng I.   y many *men* I.   z goode thingis I.   a up on I.   b Om. o. c Om. o. d Om. ILM.   e oonly I.   f *salm* x.   g *and* vnderstonde I.   h to thee I.   i wilnynge IS.   k alle *hem* I. l leese *hem* I.   m a gileful IK.   n But *I schal be* IKOS.   o Om. 10.   p worschip thee IKS.   q at IKS. r riзtwisnesse I.   s Om. I.

it is veyn. An open sepulcre is the throte of hem, with ther tungis treccherousli thei diden; deme them, thou God. Falle thei doun fro ther thoȝtis; after the multitude of the vnpitousnessis of hem, put hem awei; for thei han terrid thee, Lord. And glade thei alle, that hopen in thee; in to withoute ende thei shul ful out gladen; and thou shalt dwellen in hem. 12 And alle shul glorien in thee that loouen 13 thi name; for thou shalt blisse to the riȝtwise. Lord, as with the sheeld of thi goode wil, thou hast crouned vs.

PSALM VI.

1 *In to the ende, the salm of* ᵐ *Dauid, for the eiȝthe.*

ne in 2   Lord, in thi wodnesse vndernyme thou nott me; ne in thi wrathe chastise thou 3 me. Haue mercy of me, Lord, for I am syk; hele me, Lord, for disturbid ben 4 alle my bonys. And my soule is disturbid 5 gretli; but thou, Lord, hou longe? Be turned, Lord, and delyuere my soule; 6 mac me snaf, for thi grete mercy. For ther is not in deth, that be myndeful of thee; in helle forsothe who shal knou- 7 leche to thee? I haue trauailid in my weilinge, I shal wasshe bi alle nyȝtis my bed; and with my teres my bedding I 8 shal watrin. Disturbid is of wodnesse myn eȝe; I haue inwardli eldid amongis 9 alle myn enemys. Goth awei fro me, alle that werken wickidnesse; for the Lord ful out herde the vois of my weping. 10 The Lord ful out herde my louli preȝ- ing; the Lord myn orysoun hath vnder- taken. Shamen and be disturbid ⁿ hugely 11 alle myn enemys; be thei turned, and shame thei ful swiftli.

in her mouth; her herte is veyn. Her 11 throte ᵗ is an opyn sepulcre, thei diden gilefuli with ᵘ her tungis; God, deme thou hem. Falle thei doun fro her thouȝtis, vp ᵛ the multitude of her wickidnessis ʷ caste thou hem doun; for, Lord, thei han terrid thee to ire ˣ. And alle that hopen in thee, be ʸ glad; thei schulen make fulli ᶻ ioye with outen ende, and thou schalt dwelle in hem. And alle that louen thi name schulen 12 haue glorie in thee; for thou schalt blesse 13 a ᵃ iust man. Lord, thou hast corouned vs, as with the ᵇ scheeld of thi good wille.

PSALM VI.

The title of the sixte salm. To the ouer- 1 *comere in salmes, the salm of Dauid,* '*on the eiȝthe* ᶜ†.

Lord, repreue thou not me in thi stronge 2 veniaunce; nether chastice thou me in thin ire. Lord, haue thou merci on ᵈ me, for 3 Y am sijk; Lord, make thou me hool, for alle my boonys ben troblid. And my 4 soule is troblid greetli; but thou, Lord, hou long ᵉ? Lord, be thou conuertid ᶠ, and 5 delyuere my soule; make thou me snaf, for thi merci. For noon is ᵍ in deeth, which ʰ 6 is myndful of thee; but in helle who schal knouleche to thee? I traueilide in my 7 weilyng, Y schal waische my bed ⁱ bi ech nyȝt; Y schal moiste, '*ether make weet* ᵏ, my bedstre with my teeris. Myn iȝe is 8 disturblid of woodnesse; Y waxe ˡ eld among alle myn enemyes. Alle ȝe that 9 worchen wickidnesse, departe ᵐ fro me; for the Lord hath ⁿ herd the vois of my wepyng. The Lord hath herd my bi- 10 secbyng; the Lord hath resseyued ᵒ my preier ᵖ. Alle my enemyes be �q aschamed, 11 and be ʳ disturblid greetli; be thei turned togidere, and be thei aschamed ful swiftli.

† *A glos.* Dauide made the sixte salm, to axe merci for his offence, bi which he co- maundide the puple to be noumbrid for pride, and agens the lawe in xxx. chaptre of Exodi, with- out money as- signed there of God. א *et alii.*

ᵐ *to* ᴇ.   ⁿ distourblid ᴀ.

ᵗ herte ɪ. ᵘ in ɪ. ᵛ vpe c. after ɪ. ʷ vnpitenousnessis ɪ. ˣ wraththe ɪᴋs. ʸ be thei ɪ. ᶻ ful out s. ᵃ the ɪ. ᵇ a ᴋ. ᶜ Om. ᴋw. ᵈ of ɪ. ᵉ long *tariest* ɪ. ᶠ al to gidre turnid ɪ. ᵍ ther is ɪ. ʰ that ɪ. ⁱ bed, *or conscience* ɪ. ᵏ Om. ɪᴠ. ˡ haue wexe ɪ. wexide ᴋ. ᵐ departeth ɪ. departe ȝe s. ⁿ hath graciously ɪ. ᵒ vptaken ɪ. ᵖ orisoun ɪ. q be thei ᴋ. ʳ be thei ɪ.

PSALM VII.

1 *In to the ende; the salm to Dauid,
whom he song to the Lord for the
woordus of Cusi, sone*ⁿⁿ *of the riʒthalf,
'or Gemyny*°.

2 Lord, my God, in thee I hopide; mac
me saf fro alle men pursuende me, and
3 delyuere me.　Lest any time he raueshe
me as a leoun my soule; whil ther is not
4 that aʒeenhie, ne that make*ᵖ saf.　Lord
my God, if I dide this, if ther is wickid-
5 nesse in myn hondis; if I quitte to the
men ʒeldende to me euelis, I shal falle doun
thurʒ desert fro myn enemys inwardli
6 voide; pursue the enemy my lif, and
cacche, and to-trede in the erthe my lif;
and my glorie in to poudre bringe doun.
7 Rys vp, Lord, in thi wrathe; and be
thou enhauncid in the coostis of myn
8 enemys.　And ris vp, Lord my God, in
the heste that thou hast sent; and the
congregacioun of puplis shal enuyroun
9 thee.　And for it in to heiʒ go aʒeen; the
Lord demeth puplys.　Deme me, Lord,
aftir my riʒtwisnesse; and aftir my in-
10 nocence vpon me.　Shal ben endid the
shreudenesse of synneres, and thou shalt
dresse the riʒtwis; God serchende hertis
11 and reenes.　Riʒtwis myn helpe of the
Lord; that maketh saaf riʒte men in
12 herte.　God riʒtwis demere, strong andpa-
cient; whether he wrathith bi alle daʒes?
13 But ʒee shul ben conuertid, his swerd he
shal braundishen; his bowe he bende,
14 and made it redi.　And in it he maade
redi vesselis of deth; his arewis with
15 brennende thingus he made out.　Lo!
he withinne wroʒte vnriʒtwisnesse; con-
16 ceyuede sorewe, and bar wickidnesse.　A
lake he openede, and dalf⁹ it out; and

PSALM VII.

*The title of the*ˢ *seuenthe salm.　For the*ᵗ 1
*ignoraunce of Dauid, which he songe
to the Lord on the*ᵘ *wordis*ᵛ *of Ethi-
opien, the sone of Gemyny*†.

Mi Lord God, Y haue hopid in thee; 2
make thou me saaf fro*ʷ alle that pursuen me, and*ˣ delyuere thou me.　Lest ony 3
tyme he as a lioun rauysche my soule;
the*ʸ while noon is*ᶻ that aʒenbieth, nether
that makith saaf.　Mi Lord God, if Y 4
dide*ᵃ this thing*ᵇ, if wickidnesse*ᶜ is in myn
hondis*ᵈ; if Y 'ʒeldide to men ʒeldynge to 5
me yuels*ᵉ, falle Y 'bi disseruyng*ᶠ voide fro*ᵍ
myn enemyes; myn enemy pursue*ʰ my 6
soule, and take*ⁱ, and defoule my lijf in
erthe; and brynge my glorie in to dust.
Lord, rise thou vp in thin ire*ᵏ; and be 7
thou reysid*ˡ in the coostis of myn enemyes.
And, my Lord God, rise thou*ᵐ in the co- 8
maundement, which thou 'hast comaundid*ⁿ; and the synagoge of puplis schal cumpasse thee.　And for this go thou aʒen*° an 9
hiʒ; the Lord demeth puplis.　Lord, deme
thou me bi*ᵖ my riʒtfulnesse; and bi⁹ myn
innocence onʳ me.　The wickidnesse of 10
synneris be endid; and thou, God, sekyng
the hertis*ˢ and*ᵗ reynes*ᵘ, schalt dresse a
iust man.　Mi iust help *is* of the Lord; 11
that makith saaf riʒtful men in herte.
The Lord *is* a iust iuge, stronge and 12
pacient; whether*ᵛ he is*ʷ wrooth bi alle
daies?　If*ˣ ʒe ben 'not conuertid*ʸ, he 13
schal florische*ᶻ his swerd; he hath bent
his bouwe, and made it redi.　And ther- 14
ynne he hath maad redi the vessels of
deth; he*ᵃ hath fulli maad his arewis with
brennynge thingis.　Lo! he*ᵇ conseyuede 15
sorewe; he peynfuli brouʒte*ᶜ forth vnriʒtfulnesse, and childide*ᵈ wickidnesse.　He 16

† *A glos.* That
is, for the
synne of the
ignoraunce of
Dauid, bi which
he was occa-
sioun of the
deth of prestis
slayn of Saul,
and Doech, for
the helpyng of
Dauid. *A et alii.*

ⁿⁿ *the sone* AEH.　° Om. AII.　ᵖ make me *AE pr. m. H.*　⁹ deluyde *AEH.*

ˢ Om. Q.　ᵗ *the synne of the* K.　ᵘ Om. U.　ᵛ *word* BW.　ʷ and fro I.　ˣ Om. I.　ʸ Om. I.　ᶻ ther is I.
ᵃ haue do I.　ᵇ yuel I.　ᶜ wickidnesse, *that is, wille to do wickidnesse* K *text.* V *marg.*　ᵈ werkis I.
ᵉ haue ʒolden yuel thingis to hem that han ʒolde yuel thingis to me I.　ᶠ worthily I.　ᵍ fro *pacience of* I.
ʰ pursue he I.　ⁱ take he I.　ᵏ wraththe I.　ˡ enhaunsid I.　ᵐ thou up IKS.　ⁿ comaundidist K.
° Om. C.　ᵖ after I.　⁹ aftir I.　ʳ up on I.　ˢ hertis, *that is, thouʒtis* KV.　ᵗ and the I.　ᵘ reynes, *that is,
delitinges* K.　ᵛ wher *ceteri passim.*　ʷ be I.　ˣ But if I.　ʸ alle to gidre turnid I.　ᶻ make briʒt I.
florische, *that is, make redi to smyte* K *text.* V *marg.*　ᵃ and he I.　ᵇ *the wickid* hath I.　ᶜ hath brouʒt I.
ᵈ he hath childid I.

17 fel in to the dich that he made[r]. His sorewe shal be turned in to the hed of hym; and in to his nol the wickidnesse 18 of hym shal descenden. I shal knouleche to the Lord, after the riȝtwisnesse of hym; and I shal sein salm to the name of the heȝest Lord.

PSALM VIII.

1 *In to the ende, the salm of Dauid, for the pressis.*

Domine, Do-
minus.

2 Lord, oure Lord; hou myche merueilous is thi name in al the erthe. For rerid vp 3 is thi grete doing, ouer heuenes. Of the mouth of vnspekende[s] childer and souk-ende thou performedist preising, for thin enemys; that thou destroȝe the enemy 4 and the veniere. For I shal see thin heuenes, the werkis of thi fingris; the mone and the sterris, that thou hast 5 foundid. What is a man, that myndeful thou art of hym; or the son of man, for 6 thou visitist hym? Thou lassedest hym a litil lasse fro aungelis; with glorie and 7 worshipe thou crounedest hym, and set-tist hym ouer the werkis of thin hondys. 8 Alle thingus thou leidist vnder his feet, shep and oxen alle; ferthermor and the 9 bestis of the feeld; the foulis of heuene, and the fishis of the se; that thurȝ gon 10 the sties of the se. Lord, oure Lord; hou myche merueilous is thi name in al erthe[t].

PSALM IX.

1 *In to the ende, for the hid thingus of the sone, the salm of Dauid.*

Confitebor.

2 I shal knoulechen to thee, Lord, in al myn herte; and telle alle thi merueilis. 3 I shal gladen and ful out ioȝen in thee; I shal sey salm to thi name, thou heȝest. 4 In turnynge myn enemy bacward; thei shul be feblid, and pershe fro thi face.

---

openide a lake, and diggide it out; and he felde[c] in to the dich which he made. His 17 sorewe schal be turned in to his heed; and his wickidnesse schal come doun in to his necke. I schal knouleche to the Lord bi[f] 18 his riȝtfulnesse; and Y schal synge to the name of the hiȝeste Lord.

PSALM VIII.

1 *The title of the eiȝthe salm. To the ouercomere, for pressours, the salm of Dauid*†.

2 Lord, thou *art* oure Lord; thi name is ful[g] wonderful in al erthe. For thi greet doyng is reisid[h], aboue heuenes. Of the 3 mouth of ȝonge children, not spekynge and soukynge mylk, thou madist[i] per-fitil[k] heriyng, for thin enemys; that thou destrie the[l] enemy and avengere[m]. For Y 4 schal se thin heuenes, the werkis of thi fyngris; the moone and sterris[o], whiche thou hast foundid. What is a man[o], that 5 thou art myndeful of hym; ethir the sone of a virgyn, for thou visitist hym? Thou 6 hast maad hym a litil lesse than aungels; thou hast corouned hym with glorie and onour, and hast[p] ordeyned hym aboue the 7 werkis of thin hondis. Thou hast maad 8 suget alle thingis vndur hise feet; alle scheep and oxis[q], ferthermore and the beestis of the feeld; the briddis of the eir, 9 and the fischis of the see; that[r] passen bi the pathis of the see. Lord,'thou *art*[s] oure 10 Lord; thi[t] name 'is wondurful[u] in al erthe.

PALM IX.

1 *The title of the[v] nynthe salm. In to the ende, for the pryuytees of the sone, the salm of Dauid*‡.

2 Lord, Y schal knouleche to thee in al myn herte; Y schal telle alle thi merueils. 3 Thou hiȝeste[w], Y schal be glad, and Y schal be fulli ioieful in thee; Y[x] schal synge to thi name. For thou turnest myn 4 enemy abac; thei schulen be maad feble,

---

† *A glos.* That is, to Crist kyng ouer-comere, for the meritis of hise passiouns, bi whiche he hadde ful vic-torie, and coroun of glo-rie, and en-haunsyng aboue alle creaturis, this salm is maad of Dauid, to his glorie and onour. *A et al.*

‡ *A glos.* This salm was maad of Dauid for the pryuytees of the sones, that is, for the doom of dis-crecioun, bi which feithful men ben de-partid in meri-tis fro vnfeith-ful men, and for the doom of the last de-partyng of good men and yuel. *A et al.*

---

r hadde maad A.   s *the* vnspekynge A.   t the erthe AEH.

r felle I.   f aftir I.   g Om. K *pr. m.* L.   h reisid up I.   i hast maad I.   k perfijt I.   l an S.   m the avengere I.   n the sterris IS.   o man, *that is, mankinde, in comparisun of aungelis kinde* K *text.* V *marg.*   p thou hast I.   q oxen I.   r the whiche I.   s Om. I.   t hou wondurful is thi I.   u is ful won-durful *sec. m.* CK *sec. m.* ORxik. Om. I.   v Om. Q.   w hiȝeste Lord I.   x and Y I.

5 For thou didist my dom, and my cause; thou sittist vp on the trone, that demest 6 riȝtwisnesse. Thou feredist^u Jentilis^v, and the vnpitous pershide; the name of hem thou didist awei in to with oute ende, 7 and in to the world of world. Of the enemy failiden the swerdis in to the ende; and the cites of hem thou destroȝedist. Pershide the mynde of them with soun; 8 and the Lord in to withoute ende abit^w stille. He made redy in dom his trone; 9 and he shal deme the roundnesse of the erthe in equite; he shal deme puplis in 10 riȝtwisnesse. And 'maad is the Lord^x refut to the pore; helpere in tho thingus 11 that nede is, in tribulacioun. And hope thei in thee, that knewen thi name; for thou hast not forsake the sechende thee, 12 Lord. Singeth salmys to the Lord, that dwellith in Sion; telleth among Jentilis 13 the studies of hym. For aȝeen sechende the blod of hem he recordide; he forȝat 14 not the cry of pore men. Haue mercy of me, Lord; see my mecnesse fro myn 15 enemys. That enhauncist me fro the ȝatis of deth; that I telle alle thi preisingus in the ȝatis of the doȝter of Sion. 16 I shal ful out gladen in thi ȝiuere of helthe; ful ficchid ben the Jentilis in the deth, that thei maden. In this grene, that thei hidden, caȝt is the foot of hem. 17 The Lord shal be knowe doende domys; in the werkis of his hondis caȝt is the 18 sinful. Be turned the synneres in to helle; 19 alle Jentilis, that forȝeten God. For not into the ende forȝeting shal ben of the pore; the pacience of pore men shal not 20 pershen in to the ende. Rys, Lord, be not coumfortid a man; be demed the 21 Jentilis in thi siȝte. Sett, Lord, a lawe ȝiuere vp on hem; wite the Jentilis, for

1 they ben men. Wherto, Lord, wentist thou awei along? thou despisist in^y ned-

and^y schulen perische fro thi face. For 5 thou hast maad my doom and my cause; thou, that demest riȝtfulnesse, 'hast set^z on the^a trone. Thou blamedist^b hethene men, 6 and the wickid^c perischide; thou hast do awei the name of hem in to the world, and in to the world of world^d. The 7 swerdis of the enemy failiden^e in to the ende; and thou hast distried the citees of hem. The mynde of hem perischide^f with sown; and the Lord dwellith with outen 8 ende. He made^g redi his trone in doom; and he schal deme the world in equite, he 9 schal deme puplis in riȝtfulnesse. And the 10 Lord is maad refuyt^h, 'ether help^i, 'to a^k pore man; an^l helpere in couenable tymes in tribulacioun. And thei, that knowen 11 thi name, haue^m hope in thee; for thou, Lord, hast not forsake hem that seken thee. Synge ȝe to the Lord, that dwellith 12 in Syon; telle^n ȝe his studyes^o among hethene men. God forȝetith not the cry 13 of pore men; for he hath mynde^p, and^q sekith the blood of hem. Lord, haue thou 14 merci on^r me; se^s thou my mekenesse of myn enemyes. Which enhaunsist me fro 15 the ȝatis of deeth; that Y telle alle thi preisyngis in the ȝatis of the douȝter of Syon. Y schal 'be fulli ioyeful^t in thin 16 helthe; hethene men ben fast set in the perisching, which^u thei maden^v. In this snare, which thei hidden^w, the foot of hem 17 is kauȝt. The Lord makynge domes schal be knowun; the synnere is takun in the werkis of hise hondis. Synneris be turned 18 togidere in to helle; alle folkis, that forȝeten God. For the forȝetyng of a pore 19 man schal not be in to the ende; the pacience of pore men schal not perische in to the ende. Lord, rise thou vp, a man 20 be not coumfortid; folkis be demyd in thi siȝt. Lord, ordeine thou a lawe makere 21 on^x hem; wite folkis, that thei ben men.

---

^u blamedist E sec. m. sed postea expunxit.   ^v the Jentilis E.   ^w abijdeth A E π.   ^x he is maad the A. maad is the π.   ^y and A.

^y and thei π.   ^z sittist up π. sittist K.   ^a a π.   ^b hast blamid π.   ^c wickid man π.   ^d worldis s. ^e han failid π.   ^f perische A. hath perischid π.   ^g hath made π.   ^h the refuyt π.   ^i Om. π. ^k of the π.   ^l and his π.   ^m haue thei πK.   ^n and telle π.   ^o studies, that is, the gospel K.   ^p mynde of hem π.   ^q and he π.   ^r of π.   ^s and se π.   ^t ioye fully π.   ^u that π.   ^v han maad to oothere men π. ^w han hid π.   ^x upon π.

2 fultees in tribulacioun. Whil proudeth
the vnpitous with inne, tend is the pore
man; thei ben caȝt in the counseilis, bi
3 the whiche thei thenken. For preisid is
the synnere in the desiris of his soule;
4 and the wicke^z is blissid. The synnere
sharpli ful out terrede the Lord; after
the myculnesse^a of his wrathe he shal
5 not sechen. Ther is not God in his siȝt;
defoulid ben the weies of hym in alle
time. Thi domes be taken awei fro the
face of hym; of alle his enemys he shal
6 lordshipen. Forsothe he seide in his
herte, I shal not be moued, fro ieneracioun in to ieneracioun withoute euel.
7 Whos mouth is ful of cursing, and bitternesse, and treccherie; vnder his tunge
8 trauaile and sorewe. He sitt^b in aspies
with riche men in priuytes; that he sle
9 the innocent. The eȝen of hym beholden
in to the pore; he waitith in hid place,
as a leoun in his den. He waiteth, that
he raueshe the pore; to raueshe the pore,
10 whil he draweth hym to. In his grane
he shal meken hym; he shal bowen hymself and fallen; whan he shal lordshipen
11 of pore men. Forsothe he seide in his
herte, Forȝeten is God; he turneth awei
12 his face, lest he see in to the ende. Rys
up, Lord God, and be haunsid thin hond;
13 ne forȝete thou of^d the^e pore. For what
the vnpitouse terrede God? forsothe he
seide in his herte, He shal not aȝeen
14 sechen. Seest thou, for trauaile and
sorewe thou beholdist; that thou take
them in to thin hondis. To thee laft is
the pore; to the faderles child thou shalt
15 ben helpere. To-brose the arm of the
synnere, and of^f the malice doere; the
synne of hym shal be soȝt, and not be
16 founde. The Lord shal regne in to with
oute ende, and in to the world of world;
perishe shuln ȝee, Jentilis, fro the lond
17 of hym. The desyr of pore men ful out

Lord, whi hast thou go fer awei? thou 1
dispisist^y 'in couenable^z tymes^a in tribulacioun. While the wickid^b is^c proud, the 2
pore man is brent; thei ben taken in the
counsels^d, bi^e whiche thei thenken. For- 3
whi the synnere is preisid in the desiris
of his soule; and the wickid is blessid. The 4
synnere 'wraththide the Lord^f; vp^g the
multitude of his ire^h he schal not seke.
God is not in his siȝt; hise weies ben de- 5
foulid in al tyme. Godⁱ, thi domes ben
takun awei fro his face; he schal be lord
of alle hise enemyes. For^k he seide in his 6
herte, Y schal not be moued, fro generacioun in to generacioun without yuel.
'Whos mouth^l is ful of cursyng, and of 7
bitternesse, and of gyle; trauel^m and sorewe is vndur his tunge. He sittith in 8
aspies with ryche men in priuytees; to sle
the innocent man. Hise iȝen biholdenⁿ on 9
a^o pore man; he settith aspies in hid^p
place, as a lioun in his denne. He settith
aspies, for to rauysche a^q pore man; for to
rauysche a pore man, while he drawith
the^r pore man^s. In his snare he schal 10
make^t meke the pore man; he schal bowe
hym silf^u, and schal^v falle doun^w, whanne
he hath be lord of pore men. For^x he seide 11
in his herte, God hath forȝete^y; he hath
turned awei his face, that he se^z not in to
the ende. Lord God, rise thou vp, and 12
thin hond be enhaunsid; forȝete thou not
pore men. For what thing terride^a the 13
wickid^b man God to wraththe? for he
seide in his herte, God schal not^c seke.
Thou seest, for thou biholdist trauel and 14
sorewe; that thou take hem in to thin
hondis. The pore man is left to thee; thou
schalt be an helpere to the fadirles and
modirles^d. Al to-breke thou the arme of 15
the synnere, and yuel willid; his synne
schal be souȝt, and it schal not be foundun.
The Lord schal regne with onten ende, 16
and in to the world of world; folkis, ȝe

---

^z wickyd AEII.   ^a multitude c pr. m.   ^b sittith A. sett II.   ^d Om. A.   ^e Om. II.   ^f to AII.

^y dispisist vs I.   ^z couenably R.   ^a tyme A.   ^b wickid man I.   ^c wexith I.   ^d wickide counsels I.
^e Om. I.   ^f hath terrid the Lord to wraththe I.   ^g aftir I. on s.   ^h wraththe I.   ⁱ Om. I.   ^k Forsothe I.
^l The mouth of whom I.   ^m and trauel I.   ⁿ biholden cruelly I.   ^o the I.   ^p his I.   ^q the I.   ^r a I.
^s man to him I.   ^t Om. s.   ^u hym silf doun I.   ^v he schal I.   ^w Om. I.   ^x Forsothe I.   ^y forȝete the pore
man, and I.   ^z se him I.   ^a hath terrid I.   ^b vnpitous I.   ^c not aȝen I.   ^d moderles child s.

herde the Lord ; the befor rediyng of the
18 herte of hem herde thin ere. To deme to
the moderles child and to the meeke ;
that no more ley to[g] to magnefie hymself a man vp on erthe.

PSALM X.

1 *In to the ende, the[h] salm of Dauid.*

Domino nfido.

2 In the Lord I trostne[i] ; hou sey ȝee to
my soule, Passe forth in to the hil, as
3 a sparewe. For loo ! synneres benten[k]
bowe, maden redy ther arwis in the arwe
girdil ; that thei shete in derc the riȝte
4 men in herte. For thoo thingus that
thou parformedest, thei destroȝeden ; the
5 riȝtwis man what dide forsothe ? The
Lord in his holy temple ; the Lord, in
heuene the sete of hym. His eȝen in to
the pore beholden ; the eȝelidis of hym
6 asken the sones of men. The Lord asketh the riȝtwis man, and the vnpitous ;
he forsothe, that looueth wickidnesse,
7 hatith hys soule. He shal reyne vp on
synneres grenes ; fyr, brunston, and the
spiritis of tempestis, part of the chalis of
8 hem. For riȝtwis the Lord, and riȝtwisnesse he loouede ; equite saȝ the chere of
hym.

PSALM XI.

1 *In to the ende, the salm of Dauid, for the eiȝthe.*

alvum me ac.

2 Lord, mac me saf, for ther failith the
holy ; for mynusht ben treuthis fro the
3 sonys of men. Veyn thingus thei speeken,
eche to his neȝhebore ; ther[l] treccherous
4 lippis[m] in herte and herte speeken. The
Lord scatere alle trecherous lippis[n], and
5 the tunge gret speche[o]. That seiden,
Oure tunge wee shul magnefien ; oure
6 lippis of vs ben ; who is oure lord ? For

schulen perische fro the lond of hym. The 17
Lord hath herd the desir of pore men ;
thin eere hath herd the makyng redi of
her herte. To deme for[e] the[f] modirles 18
'and meke[g] ; that a man 'leie to[h] no more
to 'magnyfie hym silf[i] on erthe.

PSALM X.

The title of[k] the tenthe salm. To the victorie of Dauid. 1

I triste in the Lord ; hou seien ȝe to my 2
soule, Passe thou ouere in to an[l] hil, as
a sparowe *doith ?* For lo ! synneris han 3
bent a bouwe ; thei han maad redi her
arowis in an arowe caas ; 'for to[m] schete
in derknesse riȝtful[n] men in herte. For 4
thei han distryed, whom thou hast maad
perfit ; but what dide the riȝtful man ?
The Lord *is* in his hooli temple ; *he is* 5
Lord, his seete *is* in heuene. Hise iȝen biholden on a[o] pore man ; hise iȝelidis axen
the sones of men. The Lord axith a iust 6
man, and[p] vnfeithful man ; but he, that
loueth wickidnesse, hatith his[q] soule. He 7
schal reyne snaris on[r] 'synful men[s] ; fier,
brymston[t], and the spirit of tempestis *ben*
the part of the cuppe of hem. For the 8
Lord *is* riȝtful[u], and louede[v] riȝtfulnessis ;
his cheer siȝ[w] equite[x], '*ethir euennesse*[y].

PSALM XI.

The title of the[z] eleuenthe salm. To the victorie on the eiȝte[a], the[b] song of Dauid. 1

Lord, make thou me saaf, for the hooli 2
failide[c] ; for treuthis ben maad litle fro the
sones of men. Thei spaken veyn thingis, 3
ech man to hys neiȝbore ; *thei*[d] *han*[e] gileful lippis, thei[f] spaken in herte[g] and herte[h].
The Lord destrie alle gileful lippis ; and the 4
greet spekynge tunge. Whiche seiden, We 5
schulen magnyfie oure tunge, our lippis
ben of vs[i] ; who is oure lord ? For the 6

[g] Om. *H.* [h] Om. *H.* [i] triste *H.* [k] benden *AH.* [l] thei *ACH.* [m] Om. *H.* [n] tungis *E pr. m.* [o] spekynge *A.*

[e] fro KS. [f] the fadirles and I. [g] Om. I. [h] presume I. [i] make him selff greet I. [k] Om. A. [l] the I. [m] that thei I. [n] the riȝtful I. [o] the I. [p] and *eke* a I *pr. m.* and a I *sec. m.* and an K. [q] his *owne* I. [r] upon I. [s] synners I. [t] and brymston I. [u] iust EL. [v] he louede C. loueth EL. he louith I. [w] is EL. hath seen I. [x] euenesse I. [y] *ethir euenhede* ELP. Om. I. [z] Om. QR. [a] *eiȝthe* MXhi. [b] Om. OR. [c] hath failid I. [d] *and thei* I. [e] *hauynge* I. [f] Om. I. [g] her herte I. [h] with her herte I. [i] vs self I.

the wrecchidnesse of the[p] nedy, and the
weiling of the pore; now I shal vp rise,
seith the Lord. I shal putte in thin
helthe ʒiuere; trostily I shal don in hym.
7 The spechis of the Lord chaste spechis;
siluer examyned bi fyr, proued of the
8 erthe, purgid seuefold. Thou, Lord, shalt
withholden vs; and kepen vs fro this
9 ieneracioun and[q] in to withoute ende. In
enuyroun vnpitous men gon; aftir thin
heiʒnesse thou hast multiplied the sones
of men.

PSALM XII.

1   *In to the ende, the salm of Dauid.*

Usquequo, Domine.

Hou longe, Lord, thou forʒetist me in
to the ende? hou longe thou turnest
2 awei thi face fro me? Hou myche while
I shal putte counseilis in my soule; so-
3 rewe in myn herte bi day? Hou longe
shall ben enhauncid myn enemy vp on
4 me? Behold, and ful out here me, Lord
my God. Liʒte thou myn eʒen, lest any
5 tyme I slepe al doun in deth; lest sum
time sey myn enemy, I haue wonnen the
maistri aʒen hym. That trubblen me shul
6 ful out glade, if I shul be moued; I forsothe in thi mercy haue hopid. Myn
herte shal ful out gladen in thin helthe
ʒiuere; I shal singe to the Lord, that
goodis ʒaf to me; and do salm to the
name of the heiʒest Lord.

PSALM XIII.

1   *In to the ende, the salm of Dauid[r].*

Dixit insipiens.

The vnwise man seide in his herte,
Ther is not God. Corupt thei ben, and
abhominable ben maad in ther studies;
ther is not that do[s] good, ther is not
2 vnto oon. The Lord fro heuene forth beheeld vp on the sonus of men; that he
see, if ther is vnderstondende, or aʒeen
3 sechende God. Alle ben bowid doun, to-

wretchednesse[k] of nedy men, and for the
weilyng of pore men; now Y schal ryse
vp, seith the Lord. I schal sette[l] inhelt he[m];
Y schal do tristili in hym. The spechis7
of the Lord ben chast spechis; siluer examynyd[n] bi fier, preued fro erthe[o], purgid
seuen fold. Thou, Lord, schalt kepe vs;8
and[p] thou[q] 'schalt kepe' vs[s] fro this generacioun with[t] outen ende. Wickid[u] men9
goen[v] in cumpas; bi[w] thin hiʒnesse thou
hast multiplied the sones of men.

PSALM XII.

*The title of the[x] twelfthe salm. To the1
victorie of Dauid.*

Lord, hou long forʒetist thou me in to
the ende? hou long turnest thou[z] awei
thi face fro me? Hou long schal Y sette2
counsels[a] in my soule; sorewe in my herte
bi dai? Hou long schal myn enemy be3
reisid[b] on me? My Lord God, biholde4
thou, and here thou me. Liʒtne thou myn
iʒen, lest ony tyme Y slepe in deth; lest5
ony tyme myn enemye seie, Y hadde the
maistri aʒens hym. Thei, that troblen me,
schulen haue ioie, if Y schal be stirid;
forsothe[c] Y hopide in thi merei. Myn6
herte schal fulli haue ioie in thin helthe[d];
Y schal synge to the Lord, that ʒyueth
goodis to me, and Y schal seie salm[e] to
the name of the hiʒeste Lord.

PSALM XIII.

*The 'title of[f] the[g] threttenthe salm. To the1
victorie of Dauid.*

The vnwise man seide in his herte, God
is not. Thei ben corrupt, and[h] ben maad
abhomynable in her studies; noon is[i] that
doith good, noon is til to oon. The Lord2
bihelde fro heuene on the sones of men;
that he se, if ony[k] is[l] vndurstondynge, ethir
sekynge[m] God. Alle bowiden awei, togi-3
dere thei ben maad vnprofitable; noon is

---

[p] Om. *AEH sec. m.*   [q] Om. *AEH.*   [r] *Dauid, for the ciʒthe A.*   [s] doth *A.*

[k] wretchidnessis 1.   [l] putte *or* sette 1.   [m] the helthe ʒiuer, and 1.   [n] asaied 1.   [o] the erthe s.   [p] Om. s.
[q] Om. 1s.   [r] defende 1.   [s] Om. s.   [t] in to with 1.   [u] Vnpitouse 1.   [v] gon aboute 1.   [w] aftir 1.
[x] Om. coq.   [y] Om. ci.   [z] Om. 1.   [a] counceil s.   [b] reisid up 1.   [c] but 1.   [d] helthe ʒiuere, *Crist* 1.   [e] a salm s.
[f] Om. s.   [g] Om. qus.   [h] and thei 1.   [i] ther is 1.   [k] ony *man* s.   [l] ther is 1.   [m] aʒen sekynge 1.

gidere vnprofitable ben maad ; ther is not
that do good, ther is not vnto oon. A
sepulcre opened is the throte of hem, with
ther tungis treccherously thei diden ; the
venym of edderes vnder the lippis of hem.
Whos mouth of cursing and bitternesse
is ful ; swifte the feet of hem to sheden
out blod. To-brosing and vnwelsumnesse
in the weies of hem, and the weie of pes
thei knewen not ; ther is not the drede of
4 God befor ther eȝen. Whether alle shul
not knowen, that werken wickednesse ;
that deuoure my folc, as mete of bred ?
5 God they inwardli clepeden not ; there
thei trembliden bi drede, wher was not
6 drede. For the Lord is in a riȝtwis ieneracioun ; the counseil of the nedi ȝee
han confoundid, for the Lord is his hope.
7 Who shall ȝiue fro Sion the helthe ȝiuere
of Irael ? Whanne the Lord shal take awei
the caitifte of his puple ; Jacob ful out
shal ioȝen, and Irael shall gladen.

that doth good, noon is[n] 'til to[o] oon. The
throte of hem is an open sepulcre, thei
diden gilefuli with her tungis ; the venym
of snakis *is* vndur[p] her lippis. Whos mouth
is ful of cursyng and[q] bittirnesse ; her feet
ben swift to schede out blood. Sorewe
and cursidnesse *is* in the weies of hem,
and thei knewen not the weie of pees ;
the drede of God is not bifor her iȝen.
Whether alle men that worchen wickid- 4
nesse schulen not knowe ; that[r] deuowren
my puple, as mete of breed ? Thei cle- 5
peden[s] not the Lord ; thei trembliden there
for dreed, where was no drede ; for the 6
Lord is in a riȝtful generacioun. Thou
hast schent[t] the counsel of a[u] pore man ;
for the Lord is his hope. Who schal ȝyue 7
fro Syon helthe to Israel ? Whanne the
Lord hath turned awei the caitifte of his
puple ; Jacob schal 'fulli be ioiful[v], and
Israel schal be glad.

PSALM XIV.

The salm of Dauid.

PSALM XIV.

The title of the[w] fourtenthe salm. The salm of Dauid

omine, quis.   1   Lord, who shal duelle in thi tabernacle ; or who shal eft resten in thin
2 holy hil ? That goth in withoute wem ;
3 and werkith ryȝttwisnesse. That speketh
treuthe in his herte ; that dide not trecherie in his tunge. Ne dide to his neȝhebore euel ; and reprof toc not to aȝen hise
4 neȝhboris. To noȝt is broȝt doun in his
siȝt the malice doere ; forsothe the dredende the Lord he glorifieth. That swereth
to his neȝhebore, and desceyueth not ;
5 that his monee ȝaf not to vsure ; and
ȝiftis vp on the innocent toc not. He, that
doth these thingus, shal not be moued in
to without ende.

Lord, who schal dwelle in thi taber- 1
nacle ; ether who schal reste in thin hooli
hil ? He that entrith with out wem ; and 2
worchith riȝtfulnesse. Which[x] spekith 3
treuthe in his herte ; which dide not gile
in his tunge. Nethir[y] dide yuel to his
neiȝbore ; and took not schenschip[z] aȝens[a]
hise neiȝboris[b]. A wickid man is bronȝt to 4
nouȝt in his siȝt ; but he glorifieth hem
that dreden the Lord. Which[c] swerith to
his neiȝbore, and disseyueth not[d] ; which[e] 5
ȝaf not his money to vsure ; and took not
ȝiftis on[f] the innocent. He, that doith
these thingis, schal not be moued with
outen ende.

    [a] ther is I.   [o] unto I.   [p] vndirnethe s.   [q] and of I.   [r] whiche I.   [s] in clepeden A *sec. m.* clepen O.
[t] confoundid I.   [u] the I.   [v] ful out ioye I. fulli ioie K.   [w] Om. Q.   [x] He that I.   [y] Ne I.
[z] schenschipis D. repreef I.   [a] to V.   [b] neȝebore X.   [c] He that I.   [d] *him* not I.   [e] the which I.
[f] upon I.

PSALM XV.

*Of the title, the inscripcioun to hym
Danid.*

1 Kep me, Lord, for I hopide in thee;
2 I seide to the Lord, My God art thou;
3 for of my goodis thou nedist not. To the
seintis that ben in the lond of hym; he
made merueilous alle my willis in hem.
4 Ther ben multiplied the infirmytes of
hem; aftirward thei heeȝeden to. I shal
not gadere togidere the conuenticulis of
hem of blodis; ne I shal be myndeful of
5 the namys of hem bi my lippis. The Lord
the part of myn eritage, and of my chalis;
thou art, that shalt restore myn eritage
6 to me. Cordis fellen to me in ful cleer
thingis; forsothe myn eritage ful cler
7 is to me. I shal blisse the Lord, that
ȝaf to me vnderstondinge; ouermorᵗ ʾand
vntoⁿ the nyȝt mycheᵛ blameden me my
8 reenys. I purueiede the Lord in my siȝte
euermor; for fro the riȝt partis he is
9 to me, lest I be with moued. For that
gladede myn herte, and ful out ioȝede
my tunge; furthermor and my flesh shal
10 aȝeen resten in hope. For thou shalt not
forsake my soule in helle; ne ȝiue thin
halewe to seen corupcioun. Knowen to
me thou hast maad the weies of lif;
thou shalt fulfille me therto in gladnesse
with thi chere; delitingus in thi riȝtt
hond vnto the ende.

PSALM XVI.

1   *The orisoun of Dauid.*

Here, Lord, my riȝtwisnesse; vnderstond my lowe preȝing. With eris perceyue myn orisoun; not in treccherous
2 lippis. Fro thi chere my dom go forth;
3 thin eȝen see thei equites. Thou proued-
est myn herte, and visytedist in the nyȝt;

PSALM XV.

*The title of theᵍ fiuetenthe salm, ʾOf the
meke and sympleʰ, the salm of Dauid†.*

† A glos. This salm is maad of Dauid, to the preyȝyng of the meke and symple Crist. A et alii.

Lord, kepeˡ thou me, for Y haue hopid 1
in thee; Y seide to the Lord, Thou art 2
my God, for thou hast no nede of my
goodis. To the seyntis that ben in the 3
lond of hym; heᵏ made wondurful alle
my willis in hem. The sikenessis of hem 4
ben multiplied; aftirwardˡ thei hastiden.
I schal not gadire togidere theᵐ conuenticulis, ʾethir litleⁿ couentis, of hem of
bloodis; and Y schal not be myndeful of
her names bi my lippis. The Lord is 5
part of myn eritage, and of my passion;
thou artᵒ, that schalt restore myn eritage
to me. Coordis felden to me in ful clere 6
thingis; forᵖ myn eritage is ful cleer to me.
I schal blesse the Lord, that ȝafᑫ vndur- 7
stondyng to me; ferthermore and my
reynes blamedenʳ me ʾtil toˢ nyȝt. I pur- 8
ueideᵗ euere the Lord in my siȝt; for he
is onᵘ the riȝthalf to me, that Y be not
moued. For this thingᵛ myn herte was 9
glad, and my tunge ioyede fulli; ferthermore and my fleisch schal reste in hope.
For thou schalt not forsakeʷ my soule in 10
helle; nether thou schalt ȝyue thin hooli
to se corrupcioun. Thou hast maad knowun
to me the weies of lijf; thou schalt filleˣ
me ofʸ gladnesse with thi cheer; delit-
yngis *ben* in thi riȝthalf ʾtil in toᶻ the endeᵃ.

PSALM XVI.

1   *The title ofᵇ theᶜ sixtenthe salm. Theᵈ
preier of Dauid.*

Lord, here thou my riȝtfulnesse; biholde
thou my preier. Perseuyeᵉ thou with eeris
my preier; not *maad*ᶠ in gileful lippis.
Mi doom comesᵍ ʾforth ofʰ thi cheer; thin 2
iȝen seⁱ equite. Thou hast preued myn 3
herte, andᵏ hast visitidˡ in niȝt; thou hast

ᵗ euer more *AH.*   ᵘ in to *A.*   ᵛ Om. *A.*

ᵍ Om. Q.   ʰ *that he made to preising of the meek and symple Crist* V.   ⁱ to gidre kepe I.   ᵏ he hath I.
ˡ *and* aftirward I.   ᵐ Om. I.   ⁿ *or smale* I.   ᵒ it art I.   ᵖ forsothe I.   ᑫ hath ȝouen I.   ʳ han blamyd I.
ˢ unto the I.   ᵗ sawȝe bifore I.   ᵘ at I.   ᵛ thing, *that is, for my rising* aȝen K text V *marg.*   ʷ leue I.
ˣ fulfille I.   ʸ with S.   ᶻ unto I. til to K.   ᵃ eende, *ether til to wilhouten eende* K.   ᵇ on R.   ᶜ Om. L.
ᵈ Om. R.   ᵉ Parceyue I.   ᶠ *maad to me* I.   ᵍ cometh CKM. come it I.   ʰ bifore I.   ⁱ see thei K.   ᵏ and
thou I.   ˡ visited *it* I.

bi fyr thou examynedest me, and ther is
4 not founde in me wickidnesse. That my
mouth speke not the werkis of men; for
the woordis of thi lippis I kepte harde
5 weies. Parforme my goingus in thi sties;
6 that my steppis be not meued. I criede,
for thou, God, herdest me; bowe fully
thin ere, and ful out here my woordis.
7 Mac merueilouse thi mercyes; that makist
8 saf the hopende in thee. Fro the with-
stonderes to thi riȝthalf^w kep me, as the
appil of the^x eȝe. Vnder the shadewe of
9 thi weengis defend me; fro the face of
vnpitous men, that me han tormentid.
10 Myn enemys my soule cumpasiden; ther
talȝ thei closiden togidere; theyr mouth
11 hath spoken pride. Throwende me aferr
now thei enuyrounden me; ther eȝen thei
ordeyneden to bowe doun in to the erthe.
12 They toke me doun, as a leoun redy to
the prey; and as a leoun whelp dwell-
13 ende in hid placis. Rys vp, Lord, befor come hym, and supplaunte hym; tac
awei my soule fro the vnpitous; thy
14 swerd, fro the enemys of thin hond.
Lord, fro a fewe fro the lond deuyde hem
in ther lif; of thin hidde thingus fulfild
to^y is the wombe of hem. Thei ben fulfild with sones; and laften ther relikis to
15 ther childer. I forsothe in riȝtwisnesse
shal apere to thi siȝte; I shal be fulfild,
whan thi glorie shal apere.

examynyd^m me^n bi fier, and wickidnesse
is not foundun in me. That my mouth 4
speke not the werkis of men; for the
wordis of thi lippis Y haue kept harde
weies. Make thou perfit my goyngis in 5
thi pathis; that my steppis be not moned.
I criede, for thou, God, herdist^o me; bowe 6
doun thin eere to me, and here thou my
wordis. Make wondurful thi mercies; that 7
makist saaf 'men hopynge^p in thee. Kepe 8
thou me as the appil of the^q iȝe; fro^r 'men
aȝenstondynge^s thi riȝt hond. Keuere^t thou
me vndur the schadewe of thi wyngis; fro 9
the face of vnpitouse men, that han turmentid me. Myn enemyes han cumpassid
my soule; thei han closide togidere her fat-10
nesse; the^u mouth of hem spak pride. Thei 11
castiden^v me forth^w, and han cumpassid
me now; thei^x ordeyneden^y to bowe doun
her iȝen in to erthe. Thei, as a lioun 12
maad redi to prey^z, han take me; and as
the whelp of a lioun dwellynge in hid
places. Lord, rise thou vp, bifor come 13
thou hym^a, and disseyue^b thou hym; delyuere thou my lijf fro the 'vnpitouse,
delyuere^c thou thi^d swerd fro the ene-14
myes of thin hond. Lord, departe thou
hem fro a fewe men^e of 'the lond^f in the
lijf of hem; her wombe is fillid of thin
hid thingis. Thei ben fillid^g with sones;
and thei leften^h her relifis^i to her litle
children. But Y in riȝtfulnesse schal ap-15
pere to thi siȝt; Y schal be fillid, whanne
thi glorie schal appere.

PSALM XVII.

1 *In to the ende, to the child of the Lord,
Dauid; the whiche woordus of this^z
song he spac to the Lord, in the dai
that the Lord toe hym out fro the
hond^a of the enemys of hym, and fro
the hond of Saul; and seide:*

2 I shal looue thee, Lord, my strengthe;
the Lord my fastnyng, and my refut,

PSALM XVII.

*The title of the^k seuenetenthe salm. To 1
victorie^l, the word of the Lord to
Dauid; which^m spak the wordis of this
song, in the dai in^n which the Lord
delyuerede^o hym fro^p the^q hond^r of^s
alle hise enemyes, and fro the hond of
Saul; and he seide:*

Lord, my strengthe, Y schal loue thee; 2
the Lord is my stidfastnesse, and my re-

---

^w riȝt part AEH. ^x thyn E pr. m. ^y Om. c. ^z his AII. ^a hoondis A.

^m assaied I. ^n it I. ^o hast herd I. ^p hem that hopen I. ^q thin I. ^r and fro I. ^s hem that aȝen-
stonden I. ^t Hile I. ^u and the I. ^v han cast I. ^w out I. ^x and thei I. ^y han ordeyned I. ^z his
prey I. ^a Om. I. ^b ouerturne I. ^c vnpitouse *man, and delyuere* I. vnpitouse *man; delyuer* s. ^d the I.
^e *feithful* men I. ^f erthe I. ^g fulfillid I. ^h han left I. ^i relifs *ether residue* v. ^k Om. Q. ^l *the victorie* i.
^m *that* I. ^n *to* o. ^o *hadde delyuered* x. ^p Om. c. ^q Om. ci. ^r hondis n. Om. ci. ^s Om. i.

2 and my delyuerere. My God, myn helpere ; I shal hope in to hym. My defendere, and the horn of myn helthe; and
4 myn vndertakere. Preisende I shal inwardly clepe the Lord ; and fro myn
5 enemys I shal be saf. The sorewis of
deth enuyronnden me; and the stremes
of wickidnesse togidere sturbiden me.
6 The sorewis of helle wenten aboute me ;
befor ocupieden me the grenes of deth.
7 In my tribulacioun I inwardly clepide
the Lord ; and to my God I criede. And
he ful out herde fro his holi temple my
vois ; and my cry in his si3te wente in to
8 the eris of hym. Moued is togidere, and
togidere tremblide the erthe ; the foundemens of mounteynes ben togidere sturbid,
and togidere moued[b], for he wrathide to
9 them. Ther ste3ede vp smoke in his
wrathe, and fyr fro his face ful out
brente ; and colis ben vndertend of hym.
10 He ful bowide heuenes, and cam doun ;
11 and derenesse[c] vnder his feet. And he
ste3ede vpon cherubyn, and flei3 ; he flei3
12 on the pennes of windis. And he putte
dercnesses his hiding place, in the cumpas of hym his tabernacle ; derk watir[d]
13 in[e] the cloudis of the eir. Fro the li3ting
in the si3te of hym cloudis passeden ;
14 hail and the colis of fyr. And in thun-
drede fro heuene the Lord ; and the
he3est 3af his vois, hail and colis of fyr.
15 And he sente his arewis, and scaterede
hem ; leitis he multipliede, and togidere
16 sturbide hem. And ther apereden the
wellis of watris ; and ben opened the
foundemens of the roundnesse of erthis.
Of thi blamyng, Lord ; of the inbrething
17 of the spirit of thi wrathe. He sente fro
the he3est, and toc me ; and ca3te me fro
18 many watris. He toc me out fro my
most strong enemys ; and fro hem that
hatiden me, for thei ben coumfortid vpon
19 me. Thei befor camyn me in the dai of
my tormenting ; and the Lord is maad
20 my defendere. And he ladde out me in

fuyt, and mi deliuerere. Mi God *is* myn 3
helpere ; and Y schal hope in to[t] hym.
My defendere, and the horn of myn helthe;
and myn vptakere. I schal preise, and yn- 4
wardli clepe the Lord ; and Y schal be saaf
fro myn enemyes. The sorewis of deth 5
cumpassiden me; and the strondis of wickidnesse disturbliden[n] me. The sorewis of 6
helle cumpassiden[v] me; the snaris of deeth
'bifor ocupieden[w] me. In my tribulacioun 7
Y[x] inwardli clepide the Lord ; and Y criede
to my God. And he herde my vois fro his
hooli temple; and my cry in his si3t entride
in to hise eeris. The erthe was mouede 8
togidere, and tremblede togidere[y] ; the
foundementis of hillis weren troblid togidere, and weren[z] moued togidere ; for he[a]
was wrooth to hem. Smoke stiede[b] in the 9
ire of hym[c], and fier brente out fro his
face ; coolis weren kyndlid of hym. He 10
bowide doun heuenes, and cam doun ; and
derknesse *was* vndur hise feet. And he 11
stiede on cherubym, and flei[d] ; he fley
ouer the pennes of wyndis. And he set- 12
tide derknesses his hidyng place[e], his tabernacle 'in his cumpas[f]; derk[g] water *was*
in the cloudes of the lowere[h] eir. Ful 13
cleer cloudis passiden in his si3t; hail and
the coolis of fier. And the Lord thun- 14
drid fro heuene; and the hi3este 3af his
vois, hail and the[i] coolis of fier 'camen
doun[k]. And he sente hise arowis, and 15
distriede tho[l] men ; he multipliede leytis,
and disturblide tho men. And the wellis 16
of watris apperiden; and the foundementis
of the[m] erthe weren schewid. Lord, of thi
blamyng; of the brething of the spirit of
thin ire. He sente fro the hi3este place, 17
and took me; and he took me fro many
watris. He delyuerede me fro my strong- 18
este enemyes; and fro hem that hatiden
me, for thei weren coumfortid on me.
Thei camen bifor me in the dai of my 19
turment; and the Lord was maad my defendere. And he ledde out me in to breede; 20
he maad me saaf, for he wolde me. And 21

[b] ben moued π.　[c] darknessis ΛΠ.　[d] watris Λ.　[e] Om. Λ.

[t] Om. ɪ.　[u] han disturblid ɪ.　[v] han cumpassid ɪ.　[w] han bifor ocupied ɪ.　[x] Y haue ɪ.　[y] gretly ɪ.
[z] Om. ɪ.　[a] the Lord ɪ.　[b] stiede up ɪ.　[c] the Lord ɪ.　[d] he flei ɪ.　[e] place *of his maiestee*, and ɪ.
[f] O．．．．．．．．．．dn．．. ɪ.　[h] Om. ɪ.　[i] Om. ɪ.　[k] Om. ɪ.　[l] thilke ɪ.　[m] Om. κ.

to brodnesse; he made me saf, for he
21 wolde[f] me[g]. And the Lord shal ʒelde to
me after my riʒtwjsnesse; and after the
clennesse of myn hondis he shall ʒelde to
22 me. For I kepte the weies of the Lord;
23 ne vnpitously I dide fro. my God. For
alle the domys of hym in my siʒte; and
the riʒtwisnesses of hym I putte not fro
24 me awey. And I shal ben vndefoulid
with hym; and al abouten kepe me fro
25 my wickidnesse. And the Lord shal ʒelde
to me after my riʒtwisnesse; and after the
clennesse of myn hondis in the siʒte of
26 the eʒen of hym. With the holy, holy
thou shalt be; and with the innocent
27 man, an innocent thou shalt be. And
with the chosen, chosen thou shalt be;
and with the peruertid, thou shalt be per-
28 uertid. For thou a meke puple shalt
make saf; and the eʒen of proude men
29 thou shalt lowen. For thou liʒtist my
lanterne; Lord, my God, liʒte[h] my derc-
30 nessis. For in thee I shal be pullid out
fro temptacioun; and in my God I shal
31 gon ouer the wal. My God, vndefoulid
the weie of hym, the spechis of the Lord
bi fyr examyned; the defendere he is of
32 alle hoperis in hym. For who God but
the Lord? or who God but oure God?
33 God that befor girte[i] me with vertue;
34 and sette my weye vndefoulid. That parfitli made my feet as of hertes; and vp on
35 heʒe thingus settende me. That techeth
myn hondis to bataile; and thou[k] settist
36 as a brasene bowe myn armys. And
thou ʒeue to me the proteccioun of thin[l]
helthe; and thi riʒthond vndertoc me.
And thi discipline amendede me in to
the ende; and that thi discipline shal
37 teche me. Thou madest large my goingus
vnder me; and my steppis ben not feblid.
38 I shal pursue myn enemys, and taken
hem; and I shal not be turned, to the
39 time thei failen. I shal breke them togidere, ne thei myʒten stonde; thei shul
40 falle vnder my feet. And thou befor

the Lord schal ʒelde to me bi[n] my riʒtfulnesse; and he schal ʒelde to me bi[n] the
clennesse of myn hondis. For Y kepte the 22
weies of the Lord; and Y dide not vnfeithfuli fro my God. For alle hise domes ben 23
in my siʒt; and Y puttide not awei fro me
hise riʒtfulnessis. And Y schal be vnwem- 24
med with hym; and Y schal kepe me fro
my wickidnesse. And the Lord schal ʒelde 25
to me bi my riʒtfulnesse; and bi[n] the clennesse of myn hondis in the siʒt of hise
iʒen. With the hooli, thou schalt be hooli; 26
and with 'a man innocent[o], thou schalt be
innocent. And with a chosun man, thou 27
schalt be chosun; and with a weiward
man, thou schalt be weiward. For[p] thou 28
schalt make saaf a meke puple; and thou
schalt make meke the iʒen of proude men.
For thou, Lord, liʒtnest my lanterne; my 29
God, liʒtne thou my derknessis. For bi[q] 30
thee Y schal be delyuered fro temptacioun;
and in my God[r] Y schal 'go ouer[s] the wal.
Mi God, his weie is vndefoulid, the speches 31
of the Lord ben examyned bi fier; he is
defendere of alle men hopynge in hym.
For whi, who is God out takun the Lord? 32
ethir who is God outakun oure God? God 33
that hath gird me with vertu; and hath
set my weie vnwemmed. Which made per- 34
fit my feet as[t] of hertis; and ordeynynge[u]
me on hiʒe thingis. Which techith myn 35
hondis to batel; and thou hast set myn
armys as a brasun bouwe. And thou hast 36
ʒoue to me the kyueryng of thin helthe;
and thi riʒthond hath vptake me. And
thi chastisyng amendide me in to the
ende; and thilke chastisyng of thee schal
teche me. Thou alargidist my paaces[v] 37
vndur me; and my steppis ben not maad
vnstidefast. Y schal pursue myn enemyes, 38
and Y schal take hem[w]; and Y schal not
turne til thei failen. I schal al to-breke 39
hem, and thei schulen not mowe stonde;
thei schulen falle vndur my feet. And 40
thou hast gird me with vertu to batel;
and thou hast 'supplauntid, ether dis-

f welde ε. g Om. н. h liʒtne лɛн. i girde лн. k Om. л. l myn лн.

n aftir ι. o an innocent man ι. p For, Lord ι. q in ι. r God, that is, in the vertu of my God к text v marg. s passe ι. t as the feet ι. u ordeynede к. v pathis ι. w hem ultogidre ι.

girtist^m me with vertue to bataile; and
thou supplauntidist men risende in me
41 vnder me. And myn enemys thou ȝeuc
to me bac; and the hatende me thou
42 scateredest. Thei crieden, and ther was
not that shulde make saf; to the Lord,
43 and he ful out herde them not. And I
shal to-poone them into pouder befor the
face of the wind; as clei of stretis I shal
44 do them awei. Thou shalt take me out
fro the aȝen seiyngus of the puple; thou
shalt sette me in to the hed of Jentilis.
45 The puple, that I knewe not, seruede to
me; in heeringⁿ of ere it obeshede to me.
46 Alienes sones han lied to me, alienes
sonus ben elded; and haltiden^o fro thi
47 pathis. The Lord liueth, and blessid my
God; and God of myn helthe be en-
48 hauncid. God, that giuest veniauncis to
me, and sogetyst puplis vnder me; my
49 deliuerere fro my wratheful enemys. And
fro men risende in to me, thou shalt enhaunce me; fro the wicke^p man thou shalt
50 take me awei. Therfore, Lord, I shal
knouleche to thee in naciouns; and to thi
51 name a salm I shal seyn. Magnefiende
the helthis of his king; and doende
mercy to his crist Dauid, and to his sed
vnto the world.

PSALM XVIII.

1 *In to the ende, the salm of Dauid.*

*Celi enarrant
gloriam Dei.*

2 Heuenes tellen out the glorie of God;
and the werkis of his hondes tellith the
3 firmament. Dai to the^q dai bolketh out
woord; and nyȝt to the nyȝt shewith out
4 kunnyng. Ther ben not spechis, ne ser-
mownes; of the whiche ben not herd the
5 voises of hem. In to al the^r erthe wente
out the soun of hem; and in to the endis
of the roundnesse of erthe^s their woordis.
6 In the sunne he sette his tabernacle; and
he as a spouse goende forth fro his priue

scyued^x, vndur me men risynge aȝens me.
And thou hast ȝoue myn enemyes abac to 41
me; and thou hast distried 'men hatynge^y
me. Thei crieden, and noon was^z that 42
maad hem saaf; `thei crieden^a to the
Lord, and he herde not hem. And Y 43
schal al to-breke hem, as dust bifor the
face of wynd^b; Y schal do hem awei, as
the^c cley of stretis. Thou schalt dely- 44
uere me fro aȝenseiyngis of the puple;
thou schalt sette me in to the heed of
folkis^d. The puple, which Y knewe not, 45
seruede^e me; in the herynge of eere it
obeicde to me. Alien sones lieden to me, 46
alien sones wexiden elde; and^f crokiden
fro thi pathis. The Lord lyueth, and my 47
God *be* blessid; and the God of myn
helthe be^g enhaunsid. God, that ȝauest^h 48
veniaunces to me, andⁱ makist suget puplis vndur me; my^k delyuerere fro my
wrathful enemyes. And thou schalt en- 49
haunse me fro hem, that risen aȝens me;
thou schalt delyuere me fro a wickid man.
Therfor, Lord, Y schal knoulechc to thee 50
among naciouns; and Y schal seie salm to
thi name. Magnyfiynge the helthis of 51
his kyng; and doynge merci to his crist
Dauid, and to his seed til in to the world.

PSALM XVIII.

1 *The title of the^l eiȝtenthe salm. To victorie, the^m salm of Dauid.*

Heuenes tellen out the glorie of God; 2
and the firmament tellith the werkis of
hise hondis. The dai tellithⁿ out to the 3
dai a word; and the nyȝt schewith^o kunnyng to the nyȝt. No langagis ben, nether 4
wordis; of whiche the voices of hem ben
not herd. The soun of hem ȝede out in to 5
al erthe; and the wordis of hem `ȝeden out^p
in to the endis of the world. In the sunne 6
he hath set his tabernacle; and he as a
spouse comynge^q forth of his chaumbre.

---

^m girdist *AH.* girdedist *E.* ⁿ the heering *AEH.* ^o han haltid *A.* ^p wickid *H.* ^q Om. *A.* ^r Om. *AEH.*
^s the erthe *AEH.*

---

^x ouerturnid *I.* ^y hem that hatiden *I.* ^z ther was *I.* ^a Om. *I.* ^b the wynd *IKS.* ^c Om. *I.*
^d peplis *I.* ^e hath serued *I.* ^f and thei *I.* ^g *be* he *I.* ^h ȝyuest *plures.* ⁱ thou *I.* ^k *thou art* my *I.*
^l Om. *FQI.* ^m *of the* O. ⁿ tellith *ether* bolkith x *see. vi.* ^o sheweth out *K.* ^p Om. *I.* ^q *was*
comynge *I.*

chaumbre. He ful out gladide, as a ieaunt, 7 to be runne the weie; fro the heȝest heuene the going out of hym. And the aȝeencomyng of hym unto the heȝeste of hym; and ther is not that hide hymself 8 fro his hete. The lawe of the Lord vnwemmed, turnende soulis; the witnessing of the Lord feithful, wisdam ȝiuende 9 to litle childer. The riȝtwisnesses of the Lord euene, gladende hertis; the heste of 10 the Lord liȝtsum, liȝtende eȝen. The drede of the Lord holy, abit stille in to the world of world; the domes of the Lord 11 verre, iustefied in to themself. Desirable vp on gold, and precious ston myche; and swettere ouer the hony and the hony- 12 comb. Forsothe thi seruaunt kepeth hem; 13 in hem to be kept myche ȝelding. Giltis who vnderstandith? fro myn hid thingis 14 clense me; and fro alienes spare to thi seruaunt. If of me thei shul not lordshipen, thanne I shal ben vnwemmed; and ful out clensid fro the most gilte. 15 And the spechis of my mouth shul be, that thei plese; and the swete thenking of myn herte in thi siȝte euermore. Lord, myn helpere; and myn aȝeen biere.

He fulli ioyede, as a giaunt, to renne his weie; his goynge out was fro hiȝeste he- 7 uene. And his goyng aȝen was to the hiȝeste therof; and noon is that hidith hym silf fro his heet. The lawe of the 8 Lord is with out wem, and conuertith soulis; the witnessyng of the Lord is feithful, and ȝyueth wisdom to litle chil- dren. The riȝtfulnessis of the Lord ben 9 riȝtful, gladdynge hertis; the comaunde- ment of the Lord is cleere, liȝtnynge iȝen. The hooli drede of the Lord dwellith in to 10 world of world; the domes of the Lord ben trewe, iustified in to hem silf. De- 11 sirable more than gold, and a stoon myche preciouse; and swettere than hony and honycoomb. 'Forwhi thi seruaunt kepith 12 thoo; myche ȝeldyng is in tho to be kept. Who vndurstondith trespassis? make thou 13 me cleene fro my priuy synnes; and of 14 alien synnes spare thi seruaunt. 'If the forseid defautis ben not, Lord, of me, than Y schal be with out wem; and Y schal be clensid of the mooste synne. And the 15 spechis of my mouth schulen be, that tho plese; and the thenkynge of myn herte cuere in thi siȝt. Lord, myn helpere; and myn aȝenbiere.

PSALM XIX.

1 *In to the ende, the salm of Dauid.*

2 Ful out here thee the Lord in the dai of tribulacioun; defende thee the name 3 of the God of Jacob. Sende he to thee helpe fro the holy; and fro Sion defende 4 he thee. Myndeful be he of alle thi sacrifise; and thi brent sacrifise be maad 5 fat. Ȝelde he to thee after thin herte; 6 and alle thi counseil conferme. We shul gladen in thin helthe ȝiuere; and in the name of oure God wee shul be magnefied. 7 Fulfille the Lord alle thin askingus; now I haue knowe, for the Lord made saf his crist. He shal ful out heren hym fro his

PSALM XIX.

The title of the nyntenthe salm. To vic- 1 *torie, the salm of Dauid†.*

† A glos. This salm was maad of Dauid to gete victorie for his oost. A et alii.

The Lord here thee in the dai of tribu- 2 lacioun; the name of God of Jacob de- fende thee. Sende he helpe to thee fro 3 the hooli *place;* and fro Syon defende he thee. Be he myndeful of al thi sacrifice; 4 and thi brent sacrifice be maad fat. Ȝyue 5 he to thee aftir thin herte; and conferme he al thi counsel. We schulen be glad in 6 thin helthe; and we schulen be magnyfied in the name of oure God. The Lord fille 7 alle thin axyngis; nowe Y haue knowe, that the Lord hath maad saaf his crist. He schal here hym fro his hooly heuene;

---

holi heuene; in myȝtus the helthe of 8 his riȝthond. These in charis, and these in hors; wee forsothe in the name of the Lord oure God shul inwardli clepen. 9 Thei ben oblisht, and fellen; wee for-10 sothe risen, andʸ ben up riȝt. Lord, mac saaf the king; and here us in the day that wee shul inwardli clepe thee.

PSALM XX.

1 *In to the ende, the salm of Dauid.*

ne, in e.

2 Lord, in thi vertue shal the king gladen; and vpon thin helthe ȝiuere ful 3 out ioȝen hugely. The desyr of his herte thou ȝeue to hym; and in the wil of his 4 lippis thou begilidest not hym. For thou wentist beforn him in blessingus of swet-nesse; thou puttist in his hed a crowne 5 of precious ston. Lyf he askide of thee, and thou ȝeue to hym; lengthe of daȝis in to the world, and into the world of 6 world. Gret is his glorie in thin helthe giuere; glorie and gret fairnesse thou 7 shalt fulˣ putte vp on hym. For thou shalt ȝiuen hym in to blessing in to world of world; thou shalt gladen hym 8 in ioȝe with thi chere. For the king hopith in the Lord; and in the mercy 9 of the heȝest he shal not be moued. Be founde thin hond to alle thin enemys; thi riȝthond finde alle that thee hatiden. 10 Thou shalt putte them as aᵃ furneis of fyr in the time of thi chere; the Lord in his wrathe shal desturbe them, and 11 fyr shal deuoure them. The frute of hem fro the erthe thou shalt leese; and 12 the sed of hem fro the sones of men. For thei bowedeᵇ doun in to theeᶜ euelis; thei thoȝten counseilis, that thei myȝten not 13 stablen. For thou shalt putte them abac; in thi relikis thou shalt make beforn redi 14 the chere of hem. Be thou enhauncid, Lord, in thi vertue; wee shul synge, 'and with salm seynᵈ thi vertues.

the helthe of his riȝt hond *is* in poweris. Thesᵐ inⁿ charis, and these in horsis; butᵃ we schulen inwardli clepe in the name of oure Lord God. Thei ben boundun, and 9 felden doun; but we hanᵒ rise, and ben reisid. Lord, make thou saaf the kyng; 10 and here thou vs in the dai in which we inwardli clepen thee.

PSALM XX.

The title of theᵖ twentithe salm. To vic- 1 toric, the salm of Dauid.

Lord, the kyng schal be glad in thi 2 vertu; and he schal ful out haueᵍ ioye greetli onʳ thin helthe. Thou hast ȝoue 3 to hym the desire of his herte; and thou hast not defraudidˢ hym of theᵗ wille of hise lippis. For thou hastᵘ bifor comeᵛ hym in theᵛ blessyngis of swetnesse; thou hast setʷ onˣ his heed a coroun of pre-ciouse stoon. He axide of thee lijf, andᵇ 5 thou ȝauest toʸ hym; theᶻ lengthe of daies in to the world, 'and in to the worldⁿ of world. His glorie is greet in thin helthe; 6 thou schalt putte glorieᵇ, and greet fayr-nesse on hym. For thou schalt ȝyue hym 7 in to blessing in to the world of world; thou schalt make hym glad in ioye with thi cheer. For the kyng hopith in the 8 Lord; and in the merci of the hiȝeste he schal not be moued. Thyn hond be 9 foundun to alle thin enemyes; thi riȝthond fynde alle hem that haten thee. Thou 10 schalt putte hem as a furneis of fier in the tyme of thi cheer; the Lord schal dis-turble hem in his ire, and fier schal de-uoure hem. Thou schalt leese the fruyt 11 of hem fro ertheᶜ; and '*thou schalt leese*ᵈ the seed of hem fro the sones of men. For thei bowiden yuelsᵉ aȝens thee; thei 12 thoȝten counseils, whiche thei myȝten not stablische. For thou schalt putte hem abac; 13 in thi relifs thou schalt make redi the cheer of hem. Lord, be thou enhaunsid 14 in thi vertu; we schulen synge, and seie opinly thi vertues.

ʸ Om. Aɪɪ.　ˣ Om. A.　ᵃ Om. A.　ᵇ boowe E.　ᶜ the ɪɪ.　ᵈ and gladen out E pr. m.

ᵐ Thes, *that is, aduersaries, tristen* K.　ⁿ ben in ɪ.　ᵒ haue ɪ.　ᵖ Om. ʟQ.　ᵍ Om. ɪ.　ʳ of ɪ.
ˢ bigilid ɪ.　ᵗ thin s.　ᵘ Om. s.　ᵛ Om. ɪ.　ʷ put ɪ.　ˣ upon ɪ.　ʸ *it* to ɪ.　ᶻ and the ɪ.　ᵃ Om. ɪ.
ᵇ on hym the glorie v.　ᶜ the erthe ɪ.　ᵈ Om. v.　ᵉ yuel s.

PSALM XXI.

1 *In to the ende, the salm of Dauid, for that* ^e *taking to, or, for the morutid vndertaking, or, for the morutid hinde.*

Deus, Deus meus, respice.

2 God, my God, behold in me; whi hast thou forsake me? ferr fro myn helthe 3 the^f woordis of my giltis. My God, I shal crie bi dai, and thou shalt not ful out heren; and in the ny3t, and not to 4 vnwisdam to me. Thou forsothe in the 5 holi duellist, preising of Irael; in thee hopiden oure fadris, hopeden, and thou 6 deliueredest hem. To thee thei crieden, and thei ben maad saf; in thee thei 7 hopeden, and ben not confoundid. I forsothe am a werm, and not man; repref of 8 men, and the kasting out of folc. Alle seende me scorneden me; thei speeken 9 with lippis, and moueden the hed. He hopide in the Lord, 'deliuere he^g hym; make he hym saaf, for he wile hym. 10 For thou art that hast drawe me out from the wombe, myn hope fro the tetis 11 of my modir; in thee I am kast forth out^h fro the wombe. Fro the wombe of 12 my modir my God thou art; ne go thou awei fro me. For tribulacioun is 13 next; for ther is not that helpe. Ther han enuyround me manye calues; fatte 14 bolis besegeden me. Thei openeden vp on me ther mouth; as a leoun rampaunt 15 and rorende. As watir I am held out; and scatrid ben alle my bones. Maad is myn herte as wax meltende; in the myd- 16 del of my wombe. My vertue driede as aⁱ shord, and my tunge cleuede to my chekis; and in to pouder of deth thou 17 bro3tist doun me. For ther wenten aboute me manye houndis; the counseil of warieris besegide me. Thei dolue^k myn hondis 18 and my feet; and ful noumbrable maden alle my bones. Thei forsothe togidere lokeden, and inwardly beheelden me; 19 thei denydeden to themself my clothis,

PSALM XXI.

1 The ʻtitle ofⁱ the^g oon and twentithe salm. To ouercome^h, for ʻthe morewtidⁱ hynd^k; the salm of Dauid.

2 God^l, my God, biholde thou on me, whi hast thou forsake me? the wordis of my trespassis *ben* fer fro myn helthe. Mi God, 3 Y schal crye bi dai, and thou schalt not here; and bi ny3t, and not to vnwisdom to me. Forsothe thou, the preisyng of 4 Israel, dwellist in holynesse; oure fadris 5 hopiden in thee, thei hopiden, and thou delyueridist hem. Thei crieden to thee, 6 and thei weren maad saaf; thei hopiden in thee, and thei weren not schent. But 7 Y am a worm, and not man^m; the schenschip of men, and the outcastyng of the puple. Alle men seynge me scorneden 8 me; thei spaken with lippis, and stiridenⁿ the heed^o. He hopide in the Lord, dely- 9 uere he hym; make he hym saaf, for he wole hym. For thou it art that drowist 10 me out of the wombe, *thou art* myn hope fro the tetis of my modir; in to thee Y 11 am cast forth fro the wombe. Fro the wombe of my modir thou art my God; departe thou not fro me. For tribulacioun 12 is next; for noon is^p that helpith. Many 13 calues cumpassiden me; fatte bolis bisegiden me. Thei openyden her mouth 14 on me; as *doith*^q a lioun rauyschynge and rorynge. I am sched^r out as watir; and 15 alle my boonys ben scaterid^s. Myn herte is maad, as wex fletynge abrood; in the myddis of my wombe. Mi vertu driede 16 as a tiyl stoon, and my tunge cleuede to my chekis; and thou hast brou3t forth me in to the dust of deth. For many doggis 17 cumpassiden me; the counsel of wickid men bisegide me. Thei delueden myn hondis and my feet; thei noumbriden alle 18 my boonys. Sotheli thei lokiden, and bihelden me; thei departiden my clothis to 19 hem silf, and thei senten lot on my cloth.

^e the A*II*.   ^f Om. A*II*.   ^g that he deliuere E *pr. m.*   ^h Om. A.   ⁱ Om. A*II*.   ^k delueden AE*II*.

^f Om. X.   ^g Om. FQX.   ^h *ouercomere* L. *thi ouercomere* WX.   ⁱ Om. F.   ^k *hynd, that is, manheed of Crist, that roos a3en in the morontijd* KV. *hynd, that is, Cristis manhede* i.   ^l Lord H.   ^m a man I.   ⁿ *waggiden* I.   ^o *heed, and seiden* I.   ^p ther is I.   ^q Om. I.   ^r held I.   ^s *scaterid abrood* I.

20 and upon my cloth thei leiden lot. Thou
forsothe, Lord, ne awei longe thou thin
helpe fro me ; to my defending behold
21 anoon. Pul out fro the swerd my soule,
thou God; and fro the hond of the hound
22 myn only. Saue me fro the mouth of the
leoun; and fro the hornes of the¹ vny-
23 cornes^m my mecnesse. I shal telle thi
name to my brethern ; in the myddel of
24 the chirche I shal preise thee. ʒee that
dreden the Lord, preiseth hym ; al the
25 sed of Jacob, glorifieth hym. Drede hym
al the sed of Irael ; for he spornede not,
ne despiside the lowe preʒing of the pore.
Ne he turnede awei his face fro me; and
whan I shulde crie to hym, he ful out
26 herde me. Anent thee my preising in
the grete chirche ; my vouwes I shal
ʒelde in the siʒte of men dredende hym.
27 Pore men shul ete, and be fild^n, and
thei shul preise the Lord, that aʒeen
sechen hym; the hertis of hem shul liue
28 in to the world of world. Thei shul
recorde; and be conuertid to the Lord,
alle the coostis of erthe. And ther shuln
honoren in his siʒte; alle the meynes of
29 Jentilis. For of the Lord is reume^o;
30 and he shal lordshipen of Jentilis. Thei
eeten, and honoureden, alle fatte men of
erthe^p; in hys siʒte shul falle alle that
31 gon doun in to the erthe. And my soule
shal to him liue ; and my sed shal serue
32 to hym. Ther shal be told to the Lord
the ieneracioun to come ; and heuenes
shul telle the riʒtwisnesse of hym to the
puple that shal be born, the whiche the
Lord made.

But thou, Lord, delaie not thin help fro 20
me ; biholde thou to my defence. God, 21
delyuere thou my lijf fro swerd; and delyuere thou myn oon aloone fro the hond^t
of the dogge. Make thou me saaf fro the 22
mouth of a lioun; and my mekenesse fro
the hornes of vnycornes. I schal telle thi 23
name to my britheren ; Y schal preise thee
in the myddis of the chirche. ʒe that 24
dreden the Lord, herie^u hym ; alle the
seed^v of Jacob, glorifie ʒe^w hym. Al the 25
seed of Israel drede^x hym ; for he forsook
not, nethir dispiside the preier of a pore
man. Nethir he turnede awei his face fro
me; and whanne Y criede to hym, he herde
me. Mi preisyng is at^y thee in a greet 26
chirche ; Y schal ʒelde my vowis in the
siʒt of men dredynge hym. Pore men 27
schulen ete, and^z schulen be fillid, and
thei schulen herie the Lord, that seken
hym; the hertis of hem schulen lyue in
to the world of world. Alle the endis of 28
erthe schulen bithenke; and^z schulen be
conuertid to the Lord. And alle the meynees of hethene men; schulen worschipe in
his siʒt. For the rewme is the Lordis ; 29
and he schal be Lord of hethene men.
Alle the fatte men of erthe eeten and 30
worschipiden; alle men, that goen doun
in to erthe, schulen falle doun in his siʒt.
And my soule schal lyue to hym; and my 31
seed schal serue him. A generacioun to 32
comyng schal be teld to the Lord ; and
heuenes schulen telle his riʒtfulnesse to
the puple that schal be borun, whom the
Lord made.

PSALM XXII.

1　　*The^q salm of Dauid.*

Dominus regit.　The Lord gouerneth me, and^r no thing
2 to me shal lacke ; in the place of leswe
where he me ful sette. Ouer watir of
3 fulfilling he nurshide^s me ; my soule he

PSALM XXII.

The title of the^a two and twentithe salm. 1
'*The salm^b, ether^c the^d song^e of Dauid.*

The Lord gouerneth me, and no thing
schal faile to me ; in the place of pasture 2
there he hath set me. He nurschide me
on the watir of refreischyng; he conuert- 3

---

¹ Om. н.　^m vnycorn c.　^n fulfild л.　^o the reume лeн.　^p the erthe лeн.　^q Om. н.　^r Om. лн.
^s broʒte out e pr.m.

^t hond, *or power* 1.　^u herie ʒe 1.　^v seed, *that is, smers in feith and werk* к *text* v *marg.*　^w Om. s.
^x drede it 1.　^y anentis 1.　^z and thei 1.　^a Om. ғɢнрɋ.　^b Om. онsvх.　^c Om. cv.　^d Om. cɢ.
^e Om. c.

conuertide. He broȝte doun me vpon the
4 sties of riȝtwisnesse; for his name. For
whi and if I shal go in the myddel of the
shadewe of deth; I shal not dreden euelis,
for thou art with me. Thi ȝerde and thy
5 staf; tho han confortid me. Thou hast
maad redi in thi siȝte a bord; aȝen hem
that trublyn me. Thou hast myche fattid
in oile myn hed; and my chalis makende
6 ful drunken, hou riȝt cler it is. And thi
mercy shal vnderfolewe me; alle the daȝis
of my lif. And that I dwelle in the hous
of the Lord; in to the lengthe of daȝis.

PSALM XXIII.

1 *The salm of Dauid, in the first of the wike.*

est Off the Lord is the erthe, and the
plente of it; the roundnesse of londis,
2 and alle that duellen in it. For he vpon
the ses foundede it; and vp on the flodis
3 befor greithide it. Who shal steȝen vp
in to the hyl of the Lord; or who shal
4 stonde in his holy place? The innocent
in hondis, and in clene herte, that toc not
to[t] in veyn his soule; ne swor in trecherie
5 to hys neȝhebore. This shal take blessing
of the Lord; and mercy of God his helthe
6 ȝiuere. This is the ieneracioun of men
sechende God; of men sechende the face
7 of God of Jacob. Doth awei ȝoure ȝatus,
ȝee princis; and beth rerid out, ȝee euer
lastende ȝatis, and ther shal gon in the
8 king of glorie. Who is this king of
glorie? a Lord strong and myȝti, a
9 Lord myȝti in bataile. Doth awei ȝoure
ȝatis, ȝee princis; and beth rered vp, ȝee
euer lastende ȝatis, and ther shal gon in
10 the king of glorie. Who is this[u] king
of glorie? the Lord of vertues, he is
king of glorie.

ide my soule. He ledde me forth on the
pathis of riȝtfulnesse; for his name. For 4
whi thouȝ[f] Y schal go in the myddis of
schadewe of deeth; Y schal not drede yuels,
for thou art with me. Thi ȝerde and thi
staf; tho han counfortid me. Thou hast 5
maad redi a boord in my siȝt; aȝens hem
that troblen me. Thou hast maad fat myn
heed with oyle; and my cuppe, 'fillinge
greetli[g], is ful cleer. And thi merci schal 6
sue me; in alle the daies of my lijf. And
that Y dwelle in the hows of the Lord; in
to the[h] lengthe of daies.

PSALM XXIII.

The title of the[i] 'thre and twentithe[k] salm. 1
The song[l] of Dauid†.

The erthe and the fulnesse[m] therof is
'the Lordis[n]; the world, and alle that
dwellen therynne '*is the Lordis*[o]. For he 2
foundide it on the sees; and made it redi
on floodis. Who schal stie[p] in to the hil 3
of the Lord; ethir who schal stonde in
the hooli place of hym? The innocent in 4
hondis[q], and in cleene herte; which[r] took
not his soule in veyn, nether swoor in gile
to his neiȝbore. 'This man[s] schal take 5
blessyng of the Lord; and mercy of God
his helthe[t]. This is the generacioun of 6
men sekynge hym; of men sekynge the
face of God of Jacob. Ȝe princes, take vp 7
ȝoure ȝatis, and ȝe euerelastynge ȝatis, be[u]
reisid; and the kyng of glorie schal entre.
Who is this kyng of glorie? the Lord 8
strong and myȝti, the Lord myȝti in batel.
Ȝe princes, take vp ȝoure ȝatis, and ȝe 9
euerlastynge ȝatis, be[v] reisid; and the kyng
of glorie schal entre. Who is this kyng of 10
glorie? the Lord of vertues, he is the[w]
kyng of glorie.

† *A glos.* This salm is seid of the glorifiyng and risyng aȝen of Crist. A *et alii.*

[t] Om. *A*. [u] this the *A*.

[f] and thouȝ A *sec. m.* I. [g] that fillith me A *sec. m.* that filleth gretly S. [h] Om. I. [i] Om. CGHQb. [k] *twentithe and thridde* W. [l] *salm* X. [m] plentee I. [n] of the Lord I. [o] Om. I. *ben the Lordis* V. [p] stie up I. [q] hondis, *that is, in werkis* K *text* V *marg.* [r] the whiche I. [s] He, this I. [t] helthe ȝiuere I. [u] beth I. be ȝe K *sec. m.* [v] beth I. be ȝe K *sec. m.* [w] Om. GKV.

PSALM XXIV.

1 *In to the ende, the salm of Dauid.*

Ad te, Domine,
leuaui animam
meam.

2 To thee, Lord, I rerede my soule; my God, in thee I trostne[v], I shal not be- 3 comen ashamed. And scorne not me myn enemys; forsothe alle that sustene thee 4 shul not ben confonndid. Confoundid be alle doende wickid[w] thingus ouer veynly. Thi weies, Lord, shew thou[x] to me; and 5 thi sties teche ont[y] me. Dresse me in thi treuthe, and tech me, for thou art God, my sauere; and thee I sustenede all day. 6 Recorde of thi mercy deedis, Lord; and of thi mercies that fro the world ben. 7 The giltis of my ȝouthe[z]; and myn vn-kunnyngnessis[a], ne[b] wil thou not han in mynde. Aftir thi mercy haue mynde of[c] 8 me; for thi goodnesse, Lord. Swete and riȝt the Lord; for that lawe he shal ȝiue 9 to the[d] gilteris in the weie. He shal dresse debonere[e] men in dom; he shal 10 teche mylde men hys weies. Alle the weies of the Lord mercy and truthe; to the aȝeen sechende men, the testament of 11 hym and his witnessis. For thi name, Lord, thou shalt be merciful to my 12 synne; myche it is forsothe. Who is the man that dredeth the[f] Lord? lawe he sette to hym in the weie that he ches. 13 The soule of hym in goode thingus myche shal abide; and the sed of hym shal eri- 14 tage the erthe. Fastnesse is the Lord to men dredende hym; and the testament of 15 hym, that it be opened to them. Myn eȝen euermor to the Lord; for he shal 16 pullen up fro the grene[g] my foot. Loke aȝeen in me, and haue mercy of me; for 17 alone and a[f] pore man I am. Tribula-ciouns of myn herte ben multiplied; fro 18 my nedis delyuere me. See my mecnesse, and my trauaile; and forȝif alle my giltis.

PSALM XXIV.

The[x] title of the[y] foure and twentithe 1 salm. To[z] Dauid[a]†.

Lord, to thee Y haue reisid my soule; 2 my God, Y truste in thee, be Y not aschamed. Nethir myn enemyes scorne 3 me; for alle men that suffren thee[b] schu-len not be schent. Alle men doynge[c] 4 wickyd thingis superfluli[d]; be[e] schent. Lord, schewe thou thi weies to me; and teche thou me thi pathis. Dresse thou 5 me in thi treuthe, and teche thou[f] me, for thou art God my sauyour; and Y suf-fride[g] thee[h] al dai. Lord, haue thou 6 mynde of thi merciful doyngis; and of thi mercies that ben fro the world. Haue 7 thou not mynde on[i] the trespassis of my ȝongthe; and on myn vnkunnyngis. Thou, Lord, haue mynde on me bi thi merci; for thi goodnesse. The Lord *is* swete and 8 riȝtful; for this[k] he schal ȝyue a lawe to men trespassynge in the weie. He schal 9 dresse deboner men in doom[l]; he schal teche mylde men hise weies. Alle the 10 weies of the Lord ben mercy and treuthe; to men sekynge his testament, and hise witnessyngis. Lord, for thi name thou 11 schalt do merci to my synne; for it is myche. Who is a man, that dredith the 12 Lord? he ordeyneth to hym a lawe in the weie which he chees. His soule schal 13 dwelle in goodis; and his seed schal enerite the lond. The Lord is a[m] sadnesse to men 14 dredynge hym; and his testament is, that it be schewid to hem. Myn iȝen *ben* euere 15 to the Lord; for he schal breide awey my feet fro the snare. Biholde thou on[n] me, 16 and haue thou mercy on me; for Y am oon aloone and pore The tribulaciouns 17 of myn herte ben multiplied; delyuere thou me of my nedis. Se thou my mekenesse 18 and my trauel; and forȝyue thou alle my

---

[v] troste *AE.* trist *H.*   [w] wicke *E.*   [x] Om. *AH.*   [y] thou *A.*   [z] ȝongth *A.*   [a] vnkunnyngnes *A.* vnclen-nesse *H.*   [b] Om. *c.*   [c] thou of *E pr. m.*   [d] Om. *A.*   [e] the debonere *E.*   [f] Om. *c.*   [g] grane *c sec. m.*

[x] This s.   [y] Om. cgiiiq.   [z] The song of *F. Of* or.   [a] Dauid, for delyueraunce fro Saul *v.*   [b] thee, that is, persecucions for thee *k text v marg.*   [c] that don dgikmoqrswb.   [d] to veynli dgikmoqrwb. super-flui fhlpu. superflu *r.* Om. *s.*   [e] be thei ikqswb.   [f] Om. *i.*   [g] snsteynide *i.*   [h] thee, that is, for thee *k text v marg.*   [i] of *c.*   [k] this cause iosb.   [l] the doom *i.*   [m] Om. *i.*   [n] to *i.*

19 Behold myn enemys, for thei ben multiplied; and with wicke^g hate thei hateden
20 me. Kep my soule, and delyuere me;
I shal not become ashamed, for I hopide
21 in thee. Innocentis and ri3te cleueden to
22 me; for I sustenede thee. Deliuere, God,
Israel fro alle his tribulaciouns.

trespassis. Bihold thou myn enemyes, for 19
thei ben multiplied; and thei haten^o me bi
wickid hatrede. Kepe thou my soule, and 20
delyuere thou^p me; be Y not aschamed,
for Y hopide in thee. Innocent men and 21
ri3tful cleuyden to me; for Y suffride thee.
God, delyuere thou Israel; fro alle hise 22
tribulaciouns.

PSALM XXV.

1　　The salm of Dauid.

Deme me, Lord, for in myn innocence
I wente; and in the Lord hopende I shal
2 not ben vnfastned. Prof me, Lord, and
tempte me; brenne thou my reenys, and
3 myn herte. For thi mercy is befor myn
e3en; and I with pleside in thi treuthe.
4 I sat not with the counseil of vanyte; and
with berende wicke^h thingus I shal not
5 gon in. I hatide the chirche of wariende
men; and with the vnpitouse I shal not
6 sitte. I shal wasshe amongys innocentis
myn hondis; and I shal enuyroun thin
7 auter, Lord. That I here the vois of preis-
8 ing; and telle out alle thi merueilis. Lord,
I loouede the fairnesse of thin hous; and
the place off the dwelling of thi glorie.
9 Ne leese thou with the vnpitouse men,
God, my soule; and with men of blodis
10 my lif. In whos hondis wickidnessis ben;
the ri3thond of hem is fulfild with 3iftis.
11 I forsothe in myn innocence wente; a3een
12 bie me, and haue mercy of me. My foot
stod in ri3tⁱ; in chirchis I shal blisse thee,
Lord.

PSALM XXV.

The title of the^q fyue and twentithe salm. 1
`To Dauid^r†.

Lord^s, deme thou me, for Y entride in
myn innocens; and Y hopynge in the Lord
schal not be made vnstidfast. Lord, preue 2
thou me, and asaie me; brenne thou my
reynes, and myn herte. For whi thi merci 3
is bifor myn i3en; and Y pleside in thi
treuthe. I sat not with the counsel of 4
vanyte; and Y schal not entre with men
doynge wickid thingis. I hatide the 5
chirche of yuele men; and Y schal not sitte
with wickid men. I schal waische myn 6
hondis among innocentis; and, Lord, Y
schal cumpasse thin auter. That Y here 7
the vois of heriyng; and that Y telle out
alle thi merueils. Lord, Y haue loued the 8
fairnesse of thin hows^t; and the place of
the dwellyng of thi glorie. God, leese 9
thou not my soule with vnfeithful men;
and my lijf with men of bloodis. In whose 10
hondis wyckidnessis ben; the ri3thond of
hem is fillid^u with 3iftis. But Y entride in 11
myn innocens; a3enbie thou me, and haue
merci on me. Mi foot^v stood in ri3tfulnesse; 12
Lord, Y schal blesse thee in chirchis.

PSALM XXVI.

1 In to the ende, the salm of Dauid, befor that^k he was enoyntid.

The Lord my li3ting and myn helthe;
whom I shal dreden? The Lord defendere
2 of my lif; fro whom I shal quake? Whil
ne3hen vp on me no3eris; that thei ete
my flesh. That trublen me, myn enemys;

PSALM XXVI.

The title of the^w sixe and twentithe salm. 1
To Dauid^x‡.

The Lord is my li3tnyng, and myn
helthe; whom schal^y Y drede? The Lord
is defendere of my lijf; for whom schal Y
tremble? The while noiful men nei3en on 2
me; for to ete my fleischis. Myn enemyes,

---

g wickid AH.　h wickid A.　i euene ri3t E pr. m.　k Om. A.

o hatiden K sec. m.　p Om. 1.　q Om. CFGHQU.　r Om. K.　s God A.　t hous, that is, cristen mannes
soule K.　u fullid s.　v foot, that is, affection KPRSVi, foot, that is, affecciouns OQU.　w Om. CDFGHQh.
x Dauid. The holy preour of Dauy. R.　y schulde C.

3 thei arn[l] feblid and fellen. If they setten
aȝen me tentis; myn herte shal not drede.
If rijse out aȝen me bataile; in that I shal
4 hope. O thing I askide of the Lord, that
I shal ofte[m] sechen; that I duelle in the
hous of the Lord alle 'daȝis of[n] my lif.
That I see the wil of the Lord; and visite
5 his temple. For he hidde me in his tabernacle in the day of euelis; and defendede
me in the hidde place of hys tabernacle.
6 In the ston he enhauncide me; and now
he hath enhauucid myn hed vp on myn
enemys.   I haue gon aboute, and offrid
in his tabernacle an ost of criyng out ;
I shal singe, and seyn salm to the Lord.
7 Ful out here, Lord, my vois, that I criede
to thee; haue mercy of me, and ful out
8 here me.   To thee seide myn herte, Ful
out soȝte thee my face; thi face, Lord,
9 I shal ofte[o] seche.   Ne turne thou awei
thi face fro me; ne bowe thou doun in
wrathe fro thi seruaunt.   Myn helpere
be thou, Lord; ne forsake thou me, ne
despise thou[p] me, God, myn helthe ȝyuere.
10 For my fader and my moder forsoken me;
11 the Lord forsothe hath take me to. Lawe
set to me, Lord, in thi weie; and dresse
12 me in a riȝt path for myn enemys.   Ne
thou shalt take me in to the soulis of
men trublende me, for ther han in[q] risen
aȝen me wicke[r] witnessis; and wickid-
13 nesse hath lowe[s] to them[t]. I leeue to seen
the goodis of the Lord; in the lond of
14 lyueres.   Abiyd the Lord, manli do; and
be coumfortid thin herte, and sustene the
Lord.

that trobliden[z] me; thei weren maad sijk
and[a] felden doun. Thouȝ castels stonden 3
togidere aȝens me; myn herte schal not
drede. Thouȝ batel risith aȝens me; in
this thing Y schal haue hope. I axide of 4
the Lord o thing; Y schal seke this thing;
that Y dwelle in the hows of the Lord alle
the daies of my lijf. That Y se the wille of
the Lord; and that Y visite his temple.
For he hidde me in his tabernacle in the 5
dai of yuelis; he defendide me in the hid
place of his tabernacle.   He enhaunside 6
me in a stoon; and now he enhaunside
myn heed ouer myn enemyes. I cumpasside, and offride in his tabernacle a sacrifice
of criyng; Y schal synge, and Y schal seie
salm[b] to the Lord. Lord, here thou my 7
vois, bi which Y criede to thee; haue thou
merci on me, and here[c] me.   Myn herte 8
seide to thee, My face souȝte thee; Lord,
Y schal seke eft thi face. Turne thou not 9
awei thi face fro me; bouwe thou not awei
in ire[d] fro thi seruaunt. Lord, be thou
myn helpere, forsake thou not me; and,
God, myn helthe, dispise thou not me. For 10
my fadir and my modir han forsake me;
but the Lord hath take me. Lord, sette 11
thou a lawe to me in thi[e] weie; and dresse
thou me in thi[f] path[g] for[h] myn enemyes.
Bitake thou not me in to the soules of 12
hem, that troblen me; for wickid witnessis han rise aȝens me, and wickydnesse
liede to[i] it silf. I bileue to see the goodis 13
of the Lord; in the lond of 'hem that
lyuen[k]. Abide thou the Lord, do thou[l] 14
manli; and thin herte be coumfortid, and
suffre thou the Lord.

† A glos. Dauid
made this salm
of the persecu-
cioun of Abso-
lon aȝens him,
whanne Dauid
fledde fro Jeru-
salem for drede
of hym. A et
alii.
This salm is
the vois of Crist
him silf. Austin
here. v.

PSALM XXVII.

1   *The salm to this Dauid.*

12,   To thee, Lord, I shal crien; my God,
ne be thou stille fro me, lest 'any time
thou holde thi pes fro me[u]; and I shal be

PSALM XXVII.

The title of the[m] seuen and twentithe 1
salm. To Dauid[n]†.

     Lord, Y schal crye to thee; my God, be
thou not stille[o] fro me, be thou not stille
'ony tyme[p] fro me; and Y schal be maad

---

[l] ben *AEH*.   [m] eft *A*.   [n] the dais of *A*. Om. *H*.   [o] eft *A*.   [p] Om. *AEH*.   [q] Om. *C*.   [r] wyckid *AH*.
[s] flowen *H*.   [t] me *A*.   [u] sum tyme I be stille from thee *E pr. m.*

[z] troublen *K*.   [a] and thei *I*.   [b] a salm *S*.   [c] here thou *S*.   [d] wraththe *IKS*.   [e] the *S*.   [f] a riȝt *K sec. m.*
a riȝtful *I*.   [g] pathis *C sec. m.* *RSX*.   [h] and for *O*.   [i] on *S*.   [k] lifing men *K*.   [l] Om. *I*.   [m] Om. *A*.   [n] *Dauid,
and to eche selt in tribulacioun. v.*   [o] ony tyme *S*.   [p] Om. *S*.

2 lic to men fallende in to the dich. Ful
out here, Lord, the vois of my lowe preȝing, whil I preȝe to thee; whyl I poote
3 out myn hondis to thin holi temple. Ne
take thou me togidere with synneres;
and with men werkende wickidnesse ne
leese thou me. That speken pes with ther
neȝebore; euelis forsothe in the hertis of
4 hem. Ȝif to hem aftir ther werkis; and
after the wickidnesse of the findingus to[v]
of hem. Aftir the werkis of ther hondis
ȝif to hem; ȝelde ther ȝelding to hem.
5 For thei vnderstoden not the werkis of
the Lord; and in to the werkis of the
hondis of hym[w] thou shalt destroȝe them,
6 and not bilde them up. Blissid the Lord,
for he ful out herde the vois of my lowe
7 preiȝing. The Lord myn helpere, and my
defendere; in hym hopide myn herte, and
I am holpen. And aȝeen flourede myn
flesh; and of my wil I shal knoulechen
8 to hym. The Lord the strengthe of his
folc; and is the defendere of the saua-
9 ciouns of his crist. Lord, mac saf thi
puple, and blesse to thin eritage; and
gouerne them, and enhaunce them vnto
with oute ende.

PSALM XXVIII.

1 *The salm of Dauid, in the endynge of the tabernacle.*

Do-

Bringeth to the Lord, ȝee sones of
God[x]; bringeth to the Lord sones of
2 wetheres. Bringeth to the Lord glorie
and wrshipe; bringeth to the Lord
glorie to his name; honoureth the Lord
3 in his holi halle. The vois of the Lord
vp on watris, God of mageste in thun-
4 drede; the Lord vp on many watris. The
vois of the Lord in vertue; the vois of
5 the Lord in gret doing. The vois of the
Lord togidere brekende cedris[y]; and the
Lord shal to-breke the cedris of Liban.
6 And he shal to-poone them as the calf of
Liban; and the loouede as the sone of the

lijk to hem, that goen doun in to the lake.
Lord, here thou the vois of my bisechyng, 2
while Y preie to thee; whyle Y reise[q]
myn hondis to thin hooli temple. Bitake 3
thou not me togidere with synneris; and
leese thou not me with hem that worchen
wickidnesse. Whyche speken pees with[r]
her neiȝbore; but yuels *ben* in her hertis.
Ȝyue thou to hem vpe[s] the werkis of hem; 4
and vpe[s] the wickidnesse of her fyndyngis.
Ȝyue thou to hem vpe[s] the werkis of her
hondis; ȝelde thou her ȝeldyng to hem.
For thei vndurstoden not the werkis of 5
the Lord, and bi the werkis of hise hondis
thou schalt destrie hem; and thou schalt
not bilde hem. Blissid *be* the Lord; for 6
he herde the vois of my bisechyng. The 7
Lord *is* myn helpere and my defendere;
and myn herte hopide in hym, and Y am
helpid[u]. And my fleisch flouride aȝen; and
of my wille Y schal knowleche to hym.
The Lord *is* the strengthe of his puple; 8
and he is defendere[v] of the sauyngis of his
crist. Lord, make thou saaf thi puple, and 9
blesse thou thin eritage; and reule thou
hem, and enhaunse thou hem til in to
with outen ende.

PSALM XXVIII.

The title of the[w] eiȝt and twentithe salm. 1
The[x] salm[y], ethir[z] song[a] of Dauid†.

† *A glos.* Dauid made this salm in the endyng of the tabernacle, which he made to putte the arke therynne; as Jerom seith, on the prologe of the Sauter. A *et alii.*

Ȝe sones of God, brynge[b] to the Lord;
brynge ȝe to the Lord the sones of rammes.
Brynge ȝe to the Lord glorie and onour; 2
brynge ȝe to the Lord glorie to his name;
herie ȝe the[c] Lord in his hooli large place.
The vois of the Lord on[d] watris, God of 3
mageste thundride; the Lord on many watris. The vois of the Lord in vertu; the vois 4
of the Lord in greet doyng. The vois of 5
the Lord brekynge cedris[f]; and the Lord
schal breke the cedris of the[g] Liban. And 6
he schal al to-breke hem to[h] dust as a calf
of the Liban; and the derling *was* as the
sone of an vnycorn. The vois of the Lord 7

[v] Om. A. [w] Om. C. [x] men A. [y] cedre trees AH.

[q] reisede A. [r] to S. [s] aftir I. [u] holpen I. [v] the defendere S. [w] Om. DFGHQU. [x] Om. S. [y] Om. SV. [z] Om. CV. [a] Om. C. *the song* H. [b] bryngeth I. [c] to the S. [d] vpon S. [f] cedris, *that is, the princis of the Jewis* K *text* V *marg.* [g] Om. I. [h] as S.

7 vnycornes. The vois of the Lord betwe^z
8 brekende the flaume of fyr, the vois of
the Lord hurtlende togidere desert; and
the Lord shal to-stere the desert of Cades.
9 The vois of the Lord befor greithende
herttys, and he shal opene the derk
thingus; and in his temple alle shul sey
10 glorie. The Lord maketh the flod to
duellen in; and the Lord shal sitte king
11 with oute ende. The Lord shal ȝiuen
vertue to his puple; the Lord shal blisse
to his puple in pes.

PSALM XXIX.

1 *The salm of the song, in the dedicacioun*
of the hous of Dauyd.

le,   2 I shal enhaunce thee, Lord, for thou
vndertoke me; and thou hast not delitid
3 myn enemys vpon me. Lord, my God,
I criede to thee; and thou hast helid me.
4 Lord, thou broȝtist out of helle my soule;
thou sauedist me fro men fallende doun
5 in to the lake. Doth salmus to the Lord,
ȝee halewis of hym; and knoulecheth to
6 the mynde of his holynesse. For ire in
the indignacioun of hym; and lif in his
wil. At the euetid longe shal abide
7 weping; and at the morutid glading. I
forsothe seide in myn abundaunce; I shal
8 not be moued in to with oute ende. Lord,
in thi wil; thou ȝeue to my fairnesse vertue. Thou turnedist awei thi face fro me;
9 and I am maad disturbid. To thee, Lord,
I shal crie; and to my God I shal lowly
10 preȝe. What profit in my blod; whil I go
doun in to corupcioun? Whethir pouder
shal knouleche to thee; or tellen out thi
11 treuthe? The Lord herde, and rewede of
12 me; the Lord maad is myn helpere. Thou
turnedist my weiling in to ioȝe to me;
thou to-heewe^b my sac, and enuiroundest
13 me with gladnesse. That to thee singe
my glorie, and I shal not be pungid^c;
Lord my God, in to withouten ende I
shal knouleche to thee.

departynge the flawme of fier; the vois of 8
the Lord schakynge desert; and the Lord
schal stire togidere the desert of Cades.
The vois of the Lord makynge redi hertis, 9
and he schal schewe thicke thingis; and
in his temple alle men schulen seie glorie.
The Lord makith to enhabite the greet 10
flood; and the Lord schal sitte kyng with
outen ende. The Lord schal ȝyue vertu 11
to his puple; the Lord schal blesse his
puple in pees.

PSALM XXIX.

The title of the^i nyne and twentithe salm. 1
The salm of song, for the^k halewyng of
the hows of Dauid†.

Lord, Y schal enhaunse thee, for thou 2
hast vp take me; and thou delitidist not
myn enemyes on me. Mi Lord God, Y 3
criede to thee; and thou madist me hool.
Lord, thou leddist out my soule fro helle; 4
thou sauedist me fro hem that goen doun
into the lake. ȝe seyntis of the Lord, synge^m 5
to the Lord; and knowleche ȝe to the mynde
of his hoolynesse. For ire *is* in his indig- 6
nacioun^n; and lijf *is* in his wille. Wepyng
schal dwelle at^o euentid; and gladnesse at
the^p morewtid. Forsothe Y seide in my 7
plentee; Y schal not be moued with outen
ende. Lord, in thi wille; thou hast ȝoue^q 8
vertu to my fairnesse. Thou turnedist
awei thi face fro me; and Y am maad disturblid. Lord, Y schal crye to thee; and 9
Y schal preye to my God. What profit *is* 10
in my blood; while Y go doun in to corrupcioun? Whether dust schal knouleche
to thee; ethir schal^r telle thi treuthe? The 11
Lord herde, and hadde merci on me; the
Lord is maad myn helpere. Thou hast 12
turned my weilyng in to ioye to me; thou
hast to-rent my sak, and hast cumpassid
me with gladnesse. That my gloric synge 13
to thee, and Y be not compunct; my Lord
God, Y schal knouleche to thee with outen
ende.

† *A glos.* Dauid
made the xxix.
salm to preise
God of his
merci and
grace, for he
forȝaf the synne
of auoutrie and
of mansleynge,
for whiche he
disseruede to
be slayn and
dampned, outa-
kun Goddis
mercy. *A et alii.*

---

^{z} betwene *AH.* betwen *K.* ^{b} to-hewedist *AEH.* ^{c} to-pungid *AEH.*

^{i} Om. CDFGHPQUB. ^{k} Om. I. ^{m} syngeth I. ^{n} dignacioun A. ^{o} at the s. ^{p} Om. CEKL.
^{q} Om. K *pr. m.* land K *sec. m.* ^{r} it schal I.

PSALM XXX.

1 In to the ende, the salm of Dauid, for the ecces of mynde[d].

re, 2 In thee, Lord, I hopide; I shal not be confoundid in to withoute ende; in thi 3 riȝtwisnesse deliuere me. Bowe to me thin ere; heeȝe that thou delyuere me. Be thou to me in to God a defendere; and in to an hous of refut, that thou 4 make me saf. For my strengthe and my refut thou art; and[e] for thi name thou shal ful out lede me, and ful out nurshe 5 me. Thou shalt ful out lede me fro this grene, that thei hidden to me; for thou 6 art my defendere. In to thin hondis I take my spirit; thou boȝtist me, Lord 7 God of treuthe. Thou hatedist aboute 8 waiteris, vanytes ouer veynliche. I forsothe in the Lord hopide; ful out I shal ioȝen, and gladen in thi mercy. For thou hast beholde my mecnesse; and sauedest 9 fro nedis my soule. And thou closedest not me in the hondis of the enemy; thou 10 hast sett in large place my feet. Haue mercy of me, Lord, for I am trublid; disturbid is in wrathe myn eȝe, my soule, 11 and my wombe. For in sorewe hath failid my lif; and my ȝeris in weilingus. Enfeblid is in porenesse my vertue; and 12 my bones ben disturbid. Ouer alle myn enemys I am maad repref, and to my neȝhebores gretli; and drede to my knowen. That seȝen me, outfloun fro 13 me; to forȝeting I am ȝiue, as a[f] dead man fro herte. I am maad as a vessel 14 lost; for I herde blamyng of manye duellende in enuyroun. In that whyl thei shulde come togidere aȝen me; to 15 take my soule their counseileden. I forsothe in thee hopide, Lord, I seide, My 16 God thou art; in thin hondys my lottis. Tac me out fro the hondis of myn ene-17 mys; and fro men pursuende me. Liȝtne[g] thi face vp on thi seruaunt, mac me saaf

PSALM XXX.

The title of the[s] *thrittithe salm. To vic-1 torie, the salm of Dauid*†.

Lord, Y[t] hopide in thee, be Y not schent 2 with outen ende; delyuere thou me in thi riȝtfulnesse. Bouwe doun thin eere to me; 3 haaste thou to delyuere me. Be thou to[u] me in to[v] God defendere[w], and in to an hows of refuyt; that thou make me saaf. For thou art my strengthe and my refuyt; 4 and for thi name thou schalt lede me forth, and[x] schalt nurische me. Thou schalt lede 5 me out of the snarc, which thei hidden to me; for thou art my defendere. I bitake 6 my spirit in to thin hondis; Lord God of treuthe, thou hast aȝen bouȝt me. Thou 7 hatist[y] hem that kepen vanytees super-fluli[z]. Forsothe Y hopide in the Lord; Y 8 schal haue fulli ioie, and schal[a] be glad in thi merci. For thou byheldist my meke-nesse; thou sauedist my lijf fro nedis. And 9 thou closidist not me togidere withynne the hondis of the enemy; thou hast sett my feet in a large place. Lord, haue thou 10 merci on me, for Y am troblid; myn iȝe is troblid in ire, my soule and my wombe *'ben troblid*[b]. For whi my lijf failide in 11 sorewe; and my ȝeeris in weilynges. Mi vertu is maad feble in pouert; and my boonys ben disturblid. Ouer alle myn ene-12 myes Y am maad schenship greetli to my neiȝboris; and drede to my knowun. Thei that sien me with outforth, fledden fro me; Y am ȝouun to forȝetyng, as[c] a deed man 13 fro[d] herte[e]. I am maad as a lorun vessel; for Y herde dispisyng of many men dwell-14 ynge in cumpas. In that thing the[f] while thei camen togidere aȝens me; thei coun-celiden to take my lijf. But, Lord, Y 15 hopide in thee; Y seide, Thou art my God; my tymes *ben* in thin hondis. Delyuer 16 thou me fro the hondis of mynen enemyes; and fro hem that pursuen me. Make thou 17 cleer thi face on thi seruaunt; Lord, make

---

d Om. H. e Om. C. f Om. A. g Liȝt AH.

18 in thi mercy; Lord, I shal not be confoundid, for I inwardli clepide thee. Vnpitous men shame thei, and be thei broʒt
19 doun in to helle; doumbe be thei[h] made,
treccherous[i] lippis. That speken aʒen the
riʒtwis wickidnesse; in pride, and in abu-
20 sioun. Hou gret the multitude of thi
swetnesse, Lord; that thou hiddest to men
dredende thee. Thou performedist to hem,
that hopen in thee; in the siʒte of the
21 sones of men. Thou shalt hide them in
the hid place of thi face; fro the disturb-
ing[k] of men. Thou shalt defende them
in thi tabernacle; fro the aʒensciyng of
22 tungis. Blessid the Lord, for he[l] made
merueilous his mercy to me; in a strength-
23 id cite. I forsothe seide in exces of my
mynde; I am cast aferr fro the face of
thin eʒen. Therfore thou ful out herdist
the vois of myn orisoun; whil I shulde
24 crie to thee. Loooueth the Lord, alle ʒee
the seintus of hym; for the Lord shal
aʒeen seche the treuthe, and ʒelde plen-
25 teously to men doende pride. Manli
doth, and be counfortid ʒoure herte; alle
ʒee that hope in the Lord.

PSALM XXXI.

The vndirstondyng of Dauyd.

quorum. 1 Blissid of whom ben forʒiue the wickidnessis; and of whom couered ben the
2 synnes. Blessid the man, to whom witide
not the Lord synne; and ther is not in
3 the spirit of hym trecherie. For I heeld
my pes; inwardli eldeden my bones, whil
4 I shulde crie al dai. For dai and nyʒt
greued is on me thin hond; I am turned
in my myseise, whil with ficchid is the
5 thorn. My gilte knowen I made to thee;
and myn vnriʒtwisnesse I hidde not. I
seide, I shal knowleche aʒen me myn vnriʒtwisnesse to the Lord; and thou for-
6 ʒiue the vnpitousnesse of my synne. For
that shal preʒe to thee eche seint; in
nedful time. Neuerthelatere in the flod of

thou me saaf in thi merci; be Y not 18
schent, for Y inwardli clepide thee. Vnpitouse men be aschamed, and be[g] led forth
in to helle; gileful lippys be maad doumbe. 19
That speken wickidnesse aʒens a iust man;
in pride, and in mysusyng[h]. Lord, the 20
multitude of thi swetnesse *is* ful greet;
which thou hast hid to men dredynge
thee. Thou hast maad a perfit thing to
hem, that hopen in thee; in the siʒt of the
sones of men. Thou schalt hide hem in 21
the priuyte of thi face; fro disturblyng of
men. Thou schalt defende hem in thi tabernacle; fro aʒenseiyng of tungis. Blessid 22
be the Lord; for he hath maad wondurful
his merci to me in a strengthid citee. For- 23
sothe Y seide in the passyng[i] of my soule;
Y am cast out fro the face of thin iʒen.
Therfor thou herdist the vois of my preier;
while Y criede to thee. Alle ʒe hooli men 24
of the Lord, loue[k] hym; for the Lord
schal seke treuthe, and he schal ʒelde plenteuousli to hem that doen pride. Alle ʒe 25
that hopen in the Lord, do[l] manli; and
ʒoure herte be counfortid.

PSALM XXXI.

The title of the[m] oon and thrittithe salm. Lernyng to Dauid†.

† *A glos.* Dauid made this salm, whanne God schewide to hym, that his synne of auou-trie with Ber-sabee and of manquellyng of Vrie was for-ʒouun to hym. *A et alii.*

Blessid *ben* thei, whose wickidnessis ben 1
forʒouun; and whose synnes ben hilid.
Blessid *is* the man, to whom the Lord 2
arrettide not synne; nethir gile is in his
spirit. For Y was stille, my boonys wex- 3
iden elde; while Y criede al dai. For bi dai 4
and nyʒt thin `hond was[n] maad greuouse
on me; Y am turned in my wretchednesse,
while the thorn° is set in. I made my synne 5
knowun to thee; and Y hidde not my vnriʒtfulnesse. I seide, Y schal knouleche
aʒens me myn vnriʒtfulnesse to the Lord;
and thou hast forʒoue the wickidnesse of
my synne. For this thing ech hooli man 6
schal preye to thee; in couenable tyme.
Netheles in the greet flood of many watris;

---

h the *c pr. m.* Om. *sec. m.*   i the treccherous *E.*   k distourblynge *H.*   l that *E pr. m.*

g be thei 1.   h abusioun 1.   i out passyng 1.   k loueth 1.   l doth 1L. do ʒe K.   m Om. CDEFHQUWI.
n hondis weren A.   o thorn, *that is, of contricion* K.

manye watris; to hym thei shul not
7 neȝhen. Thou art my refute fro tribulacioun, that enuyrounde me; thou, my
ful out ioȝe, pul out me fro the^m enuy-
8 rounende me. Vnderstonding I shal ȝiue
to thee, and 'I shal^n enforme thee in that
weie, that thou shalt go; I shal fastne
9 vp on thee myn eȝe. Wileth not be maad
as an hors and a mule; to whom is not
vnderstonding. In bernacle and bridil
the chekis of hem constreyne; that neȝhen
10 not to thee. Manye scourgis of the synnere; the hopere forsothe in the Lord,
11 mercy shal enuyroune. Gladeth in the
Lord, and ful out ioȝeth, ȝee riȝtwise; and
glorieth, alle ȝee riȝt in herte.

PSALM XXXII.

In to the ende, the salm of Dauyd.

Exultate, iusti, in Domino.

1 Ful out ioȝeth, ȝee riȝtwise, in the Lord;
the riȝte men semeth togidere preising.
2 Knoulecheth to the Lord in an harpe; in
sautre of ten cordis doth salmys to hym.
3 Syngeth to hym a newe song; wel doth
4 salmys to hym in criende out. For riȝt
is the woord of the Lord; and alle his
5 werkis in feith. He loueth mercy and
dom; of° the mercy of the Lord ful is
6 the erthe. By the woord of the Lord
heuenes ben fastned; and bi the spirit of
7 his mouth al the vertu of hem. Gederende
as in a botel the watris of the se; and
8 puttende ses in tresoris. Alle the^P erthe
drede the Lord; of hym forsothe ben togidere moued alle the indwelleris the world.
9 For he seide, and thei ben maad; he
10 sente^q, and thei ben formed. The Lord
scatereth the counseilis of Jentilis, repreueth forsothe the thoȝtis of puplis;
and repreueth the counseilis of princis.
11 The counseill forsothe of the Lord withoute ende abit^r; the thoȝtus of his herte
in ieneracioun and in to ieneracioun.
12 Blisful the folc of kinde, of the whiche

tho^P schulen not neiȝe to thee. Thou art 7
my refuyt fro tribulacioun, that cumpasside me; thou, my fulli ioiyng, delyuere
me fro hem that cumpassen me. Y schal 8
ȝyue vnderstondyng to thee, and Y schal
teche thee; in this weie in which thou
schalt go, Y schal make stidefast myn iȝen
on thee. Nile ȝe be maad as an^q hors and 9
mule; to whiche^r is noon vndurstondyng.
Lord, constreyne thou the chekis of hem
with a bernacle and bridil; that neiȝen not
to thee. Many betyngis^s ben of the syn- 10
nere; but merci schal cumpasse hym that
hopith in the Lord. Ȝe iust men, be^t glad, 11
and make^u fulli ioie in the Lord; and alle
ȝe^v riȝtful^w of herte, haue glorie.

PSALM XXXII.

The two and threttithe salm hath no title.

Ȝe iust men, haue fulli ioye in the Lord; 1
presyng togidere bicometh riȝtful men.
Knouleche ȝe to the Lord in an harpe; 2
synge ȝe to hym in^x a sautre of ten
strengis. Synge ȝe to hym a newe song; 3
seie ȝe wel salm to hym in criyng. For 4
the word of the Lord is riȝtful; and alle
hise werkis *ben* in feithfulnesse. He loueth 5
merci and doom; the erthe is ful of the^y
merci of the Lord. Heuenes ben maad 6
stidfast bi the word of the Lord; and 'al
the^z vertu of tho bi the spirit of his mouth.
And he gaderith togidere the watris^a of 7
the see as in a bowge^b; and settith^c depe
watris in tresours. Al erthe drede the 8
Lord; sotheli alle men enhabitynge the^d
world ben mouyd of hym. For he seide, 9
and thingis weren maad; he comaundide,
and thingis weren maad^e of nouȝt. The 10
Lord distrieth the counsels of folkis, forsothe he repreueth the thouȝtis of puplis;
and he repreueth the counsels of prynces.
But the counsel of the Lord dwellith with 11
outen ende; the thouȝtis of his herte
dwellen in generacioun and into genera-

---

m Om. c.   n Om. *AII*.   o and of c.   P Om. *AEH*.   q sette *A*.   r abideth *AEH*.

P thei I.   q Om. I.   r the whiche I.   s scourgis s.   t beth IS.   u make ȝe I.   maketh s.   v the F. Om. U.
w riȝtful *men* CK *sec. m.* oBxi.   x Om. s.   y Om. I.   z alle *A*.   a wawis ELP.   b botel EL.   c he settith I.
d in the s.   e Om. s.

is the Lord his God; the puple that he
13 ches in to eritage to hym. Fro heuene
beheeld the Lord; he saʒ alle the sones of
14 men. Fro his duelling place befor maad
redi; he beheeld ouer alle, 'that duelle⁸ the
15 erthe. That made arowe the hertis of
hem; that vnderstondith alle ther werkis.
16 The king is not saued bi myche vertu;
and the ieaunt shal not be saued in the
17 multitude of his vertu. Desceyuable the
hors to helthe; forsothe in abundaunce⁸
18 of his vertu he shal not be saued. Lo!
the eʒen of the Lord vp on men dredende
hym; and in hem that hopen on his
19 mercy. That he pulle out fro deth the
soulis of hem; and fede them in hunger.
20 Oure soule suffreth the Lord; for helpere
21 and oure defendere he is. For in hym
shal gladen oure herte; and in his holi
22 name wee han hopid. Be do thi mercy,
Lord, vp on vs; as wee han hopid in thee.

PSALM XXXIII.

1 *The salm of Dauid, whan he chaungide*
his chere beforn Abymalech, and he
lafte hym, and he ʒide awey.

Benedicam
Dominum.

2 I shal blisse the Lord in alle time;
3 euermor his preising in my mouth. In
the Lord shal ben preisid my soule; here
4 the debonere, and glad thei. Magnefieth
the Lord with me; and enhaunce wee his
5 name in to itself. I soʒte out the Lord,
and he ful out herde me; and of alle my
6 tribulaciouns he caʒte me out. Neʒheth
to hym, and beth liʒtid; and ʒoure facis
7 shul not be confoundid. This pore man
criede, and the Lord ful out herde hym;
and of alle his tribulacions sauede hym.
8 The aungil of the Lord sendith in; in the
enuyroun of men dredende hym, and he
9 shal deliuere them. Tastith, and seeth,
for sweete is the Lord; blisful the man,
10 that hopith in hym. Dredeth the Lord,

cioun. Blessid *is* the folk, whose Lord is 12
his God; the puple which⁺ he chees into
eritage to hym silf. The Lord bihelde fro 13
heuene; he siʒ alle the sones of men. Fro 14
his dwellyng place maad redi bifor; he bihelde on alle men, that enhabiten the
erthe. Which made syngulerliᵍ the soules 15
of hem; which vndurstondith all the werkis
of hem. A kyng is not sauyd bi myche 16
vertuʰ; and a giaunt schal not be sauyd in
the mychilnesse of his vertu. An hors *is* 17
false to helthe; forsothe he schal not be
sauyd in theⁱ habundaunce, 'ether plenteeᵏ,
of his vertu. Lo! the iʒen of the Lord ben 18
on men dredynge hym; and in hem that
hopen onˡ his merci. That he delyuere her 19
soules fro deth; and feede hem in hungur.
Oure soule suffreth the Lordᵐ; for he is 20
oure helpere and defendere. For oure herte 21
schal be glad in him; and we schulen haue
hope in his hooli name. Lord, thi merci 22
be maad on vs; as we hopiden in thee.

PSALM XXXIII.

*The title of the*ⁿ *thre and thrittithe salm*ᵒ. 1
To Dauid, whanne he chaungide his
*mouth*ᵒᵒ *bifor Abymalech, and he* 'droof
*out*ᵖ *Dauid*ᑫ, 'and he ʒede forth*ʳ*.

I schal blesse the Lord in al⁸ tyme; 2
euere his heriyng *is*ᵗ in my mouth. Mi 3
soule schal be preisid in the Lord; mylde
men here, and beᵘ glad. Magnyfie ʒe the 4
Lord with me; and enhaunse we his name
into it silf. I souʒte the Lord, and he 5
herde me; and he delyueride me fro alle
my tribulaciouns. Neiʒe ʒe to him, and 6
be ʒe liʒtned; and ʒoure faces schulen not
be schent. This pore man criede, and the 7
Lord herde hym; andᵛ sauyde hym fro
alle hise tribulaciouns. The aungel of the 8
Lord sendith in the cumpas of men dredynge hym; and he schal delyuere hem.
Taaste ʒe, and se, for the Lord is swete; 9
blessid *is* the man, that hopith in hym.
Alle ʒe hooli men of the Lord, dredeᵂ 10

---

⁸ the dwelleris *A*.   ᵗ the haboundaunce *A*.

ᶠ that ɪ.   ᵍ singulerll, *ether ech bi himself* ᵥ.   ʰ vertu, *that is, strengthe* ᴋ *text* ᵥ *marg.*   ⁱ Om. c.
ᵏ Om. ɪʀ.   ˡ in ꜱ.   ᵐ Lord, *that is, abideth pacientli his wille* ᴋ *text* ᵥ *marg.*   ⁿ Om. cᴅᴘꜰɢᴏǫᵥɪ.
ᵒ Om. ʀǫ.   ᵒᵒ *mouth, or his word* ɪ.   ᵖ brouʒte ꜱ.   ᑫ Om. x.   ʳ Om. ᵥx.   ˢ eueri ᴋ.   ᵗ be ɪ. Om. *ceteri*.
ᵘ be thei ɪ.   ᵛ and he ɪ.   ᵂ drede ʒe ɪ.

alle ȝee seyntis[u] of hym ; for ther is not scarsnesse to the[v] men dredende hym. 11 Riche men nededen, and hungriden ; forsothe the inwardli sechende the Lord 12 shul not be mynusht alle goode. Cometh, sonys, hereth me ; the drede of the Lord 13 I shal techen ȝou. Who is the man that 14 wil lif ; looueth to seen goode daȝis ? Forfende thi tunge fro euel ; and thi lippis 15 that thei speke not treccherie. Turne awei fro euel, and do good ; inwardlyche 16 seek pes, and pursue it. The eȝen of the Lord vp on the[w] riȝtwise ; and the eris of 17 hym at 'the preȝeeris of hem[x]. The chere forsothe of the Lord vp on men doende euelis ; that he lese fro the erthe the me- 18 morie of hem. The riȝtwise crieden, and the Lord ful out herde hem ; and fro alle ther tribulaciouns he[y] deliuered hem. 19 Neȝh is the Lord to hem that ben with trublid herte ; and the meke in spirit he 20 shal sauen. Manye tribulaciouns of the riȝtwise ; and of alle these shal delyuere 21 them the Lord. The Lord kepeth alle the bones of hem ; oon of hem shal not 22 be to-brosid. The deth of synneres the werste ; and thei that hateden the riȝt- 23 wise shul gilten. The Lord shal aȝeen bie the soulis of his seruauns ; and ther shul not gilten alle, that hopen in hym.

hym ; for no nedynesse is to men dredynge hym. Riche men weren[x] nedi, and[y] weren 11 hungri ; but men that seken the Lord schulen not faile of al good. Come, ȝe 12 sones, here ȝe me ; Y[z] schal teche ȝou the drede of the Lord. Who is a[a] man, that 13 wole[b] lijf ; loueth[c] to se good daies ? For- 14 bede thi tunge fro yuel ; and thi lippis speke not gile. Turne thou awei fro yuel, 15 and do good ; seke thou pees, and perfitli sue thou it. The iȝen of the Lord ben on 16 iust men ; and hise eeren ben to her preiers. But the cheer of the Lord is on men do- 17 ynge yuels ; that he leese the mynde of hem fro erthe. Just men cryeden, and the 18 Lord herde hem ; and[d] delyueride hem fro alle her tribulaciouns. The Lord is nyȝ 19 hem that ben of troblid herte ; and he schal saue meke men in spirit. Many tribula- 20 ciouns ben of iust men ; and the Lord schal delyuere hem fro[e] alle these. The Lord 21 kepith alle the boonys of hem ; oon of tho schal not be brokun. The deth of syn- 22 neris is werst ; and thei that haten a iust man schulen trespasse. The Lord schal 23 aȝenbie the soulis of hise seruauntis ; and alle, that hopen in him, schulen not trespasse.

PSALM XXXIV.

[1] In to the ende, the salm 'to hym[z] Dauid.

Do-
centes.

Deme, Lord, the noȝende me ; out fiȝt 2 thou the inpugnende me. Tac armis and sheeld ; and ris vp in to helpe to me. 3 Heeld out swerd, and close aȝen hem that pursue me ; sei to my soule, I am thin 4 helthe. Be thei confoundid, and shamefully drede thei, sechende my soule. Be 5 thei turned awey bacward, and confounded, thenkende to me euelis. Be thei maad as pouder beforn the face of the wind ; and the aungil of the Lord to torment

PSALM XXXIV.

The title of the[f] foure and thrittithe salm. [1] 'To Dauid[g]†.

† A glos. Dauid made this salm aȝens the persecucioun of Saul. A et alii.

Lord, deme thou hem, that anoien me ; ouercome thou hem, that fiȝten aȝens me. Take thou armeris and scheeld ; and rise 2 vp into help to me. Schede[h] out the 3 swerd, and close togidere aȝens hem that pursuen me ; seie thou to my soule, Y am thin helthe. Thei that seken my lijf ; be 4 schent, and aschamed. Thei that thenken[i] yuels to me ; be turned awei bacward, and be[k] schent. Be thei maad as dust bifor 5 the face of the[l] wynd ; and the aungel of

u the seyntis E pr. m.   v Om. AEH.   w Om. A.   x her preyers AEH.   y Om. AE.   z of AH.

x han be I.   y and thei I.   z and Y I.   a the I.   b willith I.   c that loueth I.   d and he I.   e of G.
f Om. CDFHUb.   g Om. KL.   h Heelde I.   i seken c.   k be thei I.   l Om. K.

6 constreynende them. Be maad the weie
of hem dercnessis, and slideri; and the
7 aungel of the Lord pursuende hem. For
withoute cause thei hidden to me deth[a]
of ther grene; and ouer veynly thei
8 acuseden my soule. Come to hym the
grene that he knoweth not, and the taking that he hidde cacche hym; and in
9 the grene falle he in it. My soule forsothe ful out shal gladen in the Lord;
and shal deliten vp on his helthe 3iuere.
10 Alle my bones shul seyn Lord, who[b] lic
thee; takende out the helples fro the
hond of the strengere of hym; the[c] nedi
and the pore fro men brosende doun
11 hym? Risende wicke[d] witnessis; that I
12 knew not askeden me. Thei 3olden to
me euelis for goodis; bareynte to my
13 soule. I forsothe whan to me thei weren
heuy; was 'clad in[e] an heire. I mekide
in fastyng my soule; and my pre3eere in
14 my bosum shal be turned. As ne3hebore
and oure brother, so I with plesyde; as
weilende and sorewid, so I was mekid.
15 And a3en me thei gladiden, and came togidere; ther ben gedered vp on me scourgis,
16 and I knew not. Thei ben scaterid, and
not ficchid with sorewe; thei tempteden
me, thei vndermouwiden me[f] with vnder-
mouwing, and gnastiden vpon me with
17 ther teth. Lord, whan thou shalt beholde, restore my soule fro the malice
18 doing of hem; fro leouns myn one. I shal
knouleche to thee in a gret churche; in[g]
19 a sad puple I shal preisen thee. Ouer-
io3e[h] not to me that enemyen[i] to me
wickeli[k]; that hatiden me withoute cause,
20 and twincle with e3en. For to me forsothe pesibly thei speeken; and in the
wrathe of the erthe spekende, treccheries
21 thei tho3ten. And thei 3eneden their
mouth upon me; thei[l] seiden, Weu,
22 weu! oure e3en han seen. Thou hast
seen, Lord, ne be thou stille; Lord, ne

the Lord make hem streit. Her weie be 6
maad derknesse, and slydirnesse; and the
aungel of the Lord pursue hem. For 7
with out cause thei hidden to me the deth
of her snare; in veyn thei dispisiden my
soule. The snare which he knoweth not 8
come to hym, and the takyng which he
hidde take hym; and fall he in to the
snare in that thing. But my soule schal 9
fulli haue ioye in the Lord; and[m] schal
delite on[n] his helthe. Alle my boonys 10
schulen seie, Lord, who is lijk thee? Thou
delyuerist a pore man fro the hond of his
strengere; a nedi man and pore fro hem
that diuersely rauischen hym. Wickid 11
witnessis risynge axiden me thingis,
whiche Y knewe not. Thei 3eldiden[o] to 12
me yuels for goodis; hareynnesse to my
soule. But whanne thei weren diseseful 13
to me; Y was clothid in an heire. I mekide
my soule in fastyng; and my preier schal
be turned 'with ynne[p] my bosum. I pleside 14
so as oure nei3bore, as oure brother; Y
was 'maad meke[q] so as morenynge and
sorewful. And thei weren glad, and camen 15
togidere a3ens me; turmentis weren gaderid on me, and Y knew[r] not. Thei weren 16
scaterid, and not compunct, thei temptiden
me, thei scornyden me with mowyng; thei
gnastiden on me with her teeth. Lord, 17
whanne thou schalt biholde, restore thou
my soule fro the wickidnesse of hem;
'restore thou[s] myn oon[t] aloone[u] fro liouns.
I schal knowleche to thee in a greet 18
chirche; Y schal heric thee in a sad puple. Thei that ben aduersaries wickidli 19
to me, haue[r] not ioye on me; that haten
me with out cause, and bikenen with i3en.
For sotheli thei spaken pesibli to me; and 20
thei spekynge in wrathfulnesse of erthe
thou3ten giles. And thei maden large her 21
mouth on me; thei seiden, Wel, wel! oure
i3en han sien[w]. Lord, thou hast seen, be 22
thou not stille; Lord, departe thou not fro

---

[a] the deth E pr. m. [b] who is A. [c] and the c. [d] wickid A. [e] clothed with AEH. [f] vpon me A.
[g] and in A. [h] Ouerioyen thei AH. [i] enuyen H. [k] wickydli AH. [l] and thei A.

[m] and I I. [n] of I. [o] 3olden I. [p] in to s. [q] mekid s. [r] knew it I. [s] Om. IV. [t] oon lijf V.
[u] aloone lijf K. [v] haue thei I. [w] seie I.

23 go thou awei fro me. Ris, and see to
my dom; my God, my Lord, in to my
24 cause. Deme me aftir thi riʒtwisnesse,
Lord, my God; and ouer ioʒe thei not to
25 me. Sei thei not in ther hertis, Weu,
weu, to oure soule; ne sei thei, Wee
26 shul deuouren hym. Waxe thei ashamed,
and shamely drede thei togidere; that
thanken to myn euelis. Be thei clad[m]
with confusioun, and shamefast drede;
that deedis of malice thenken vp on me.
27 Ful out ioʒe thei, and glade that wiln
my riʒtwisnesse; and sei thei euermor,
The Lord be magnefied; that wiln the[n]
28 pes of his seruaunt. And my tunge shal
sweteli thenke thi riʒtwisnesse; al dai thi
preising.

me. Rise vp, and ʒyue tent to my doom; 23
my God and my Lord, biholde in[x] to my
cause. Mi Lord God, deme thou me bi 24
thi riʒtfulnesse; and haue thei not ioye on
me. Seie thei not in her hertis, Wel, wel, 25
to oure soule; nether seie thei, We schulen deuoure hym. Shame thei, and drede 26
thei togidere; that thanken[y] for myn yuels.
Be thei clothid with schame and drede;
that speken yuele thingis on me. Haue 27
thei ful ioie, and be thei glad that wolen[z]
my riʒtfulnesse; and seie thei euere, The
Lord be magnyfied, whiche wolen the pees
of his seruaunt. And my tunge schal 28
bithenke thi riʒtfulnesse; al day thin
heriyng.

PSALM XXXV.

1 *In to the ende, to the seruaunt of the
Lord, the salm of Dauid.*

PSALM XXXV.

'*The title[a] of the[b] fyue and thrittithe* 1
salm. '*To victorie[c], to Dauid[d],* '*the
seruaunt of the Lord*[o]†.

† *A glos.* Da-
uid made this
salm of hym
silf aʒens the
persecucioun of
Saul. A *et alii.*

niustns. 2 The vnriʒtwise seide, that he gilte[o] in
himself; ther is not the drede of God be-
3 forn the eʒen of hym. For treccherousli
he dide in his siʒte; that his wickidnesse
4 be founden at hate. The woordis of his
mouth wickidnesse and treccherie; he
wolde not vnderstonde that he do wel.
5 Wickidnesse he swetli thoʒte in his
couche[p]; he stod neʒh to eche wey not
good, malice forsothe he hatede not.
6 Lord, in heuene thi mercy; and thi
7 trenthe vnto the cloudis. Thi riʒtwisnesse as the mounteynes of God; thi
domes myche depnesse. Men and bestis
8 thou shalt saue, Lord; as thou, God, hast
multiplied thi mercy. The sones forsothe
of men; in the coueryng of thi wengis
9 shuln hopen. Thei shul ben inwardli
drunken of the plente of thin hous; and
of the strem of thi delit thou shalt ʒiue
10 them drinke. For anent thee is the welle
of lif; and in thi liʒt wee shul see liʒt.

The vniust man seide, that he trespasse 2
in hym silf; the drede of God is not bifor
hise iʒen. For he dide gilefuli in the siʒt 3
of God; that his wickidnesse be foundun
to hatrede. The wordis of his mouth ben 4
wickidnesse and gile, he nolde[f] vndirstonde
to do wel. He thouʒte wickidnesse in his 5
bed, he stood nyʒ al weie not good; forsothe he hatide not malice. Lord, thi 6
merci *is* in heuene; and thi trenthe *is* 'til
to[g] cloudis. Thi riʒtfulnesse *is* as the hillis 7
of God; thi domes ben myche depthe of
watris. Lord, thou schalt saue men and 8
beestis; as thou, God, hast multiplied thi
merci. But the sones of men; schulen hope
in the hilyng of thi wyngis. Thei schulen 9
be fillid gretli of the plentee of thin hows;
and thou schalt ʒyue drynke to hem with[h]
the steef stream of thi likyng. For the 10
wel of life is at[i] thee; and in thi liʒt we
schulen se liʒt. Lord, sette forth thi mercy 11
to hem, that knowen thee; and thi ryʒtful-

[m] clothed *AEH.* [n] Om. c. [o] gilte not *A.* [p] bed *AEN.*

[x] Om. c. [y] ioien I. [z] willen I. [a] Om. s. [b] Om. cDФGHOQs. [c] *In Ebrew thus, To victorie, to Dauith,
the seruaunt of the Lord. Jerom seith thus, For the victorie of Dauith, the seruaunt of the Lord, Dauith
made this salm of him silf* v. Om. consi. [d] Om. vi. [e] *aʒens the persecucioun of Saul* s. Om. v.
[f] wolde not I. [g] unto I. [h] of K. [i] anentis I.

11 Befor strecche thi mercy to men knowende thee; and thi riȝtwisnesse to hem
12 that ben in riȝt herte. Come not to me the foot of pride; and the hond of the
13 synnere moue not me. There fellen that^q werken wickidnesse; thei ben put out, and myghten not stonden.

PSALM XXXVI.

1   *The psalm of Dauyd.*

Noli emulari.   Wyle thou not folewe bi enuye in warieris; ne folewen bi looue men doende
2 wickidnesse. For as hei swiftli thei shuln waxe drie; and as wrtis of erbis soone
3 thei shul falle doun. Hope in the Lord, and do gooduesse; and indwelle thou the erthe, and thou shalt be fed in the
4 richesses of it. Delite in the Lord; and he shal ȝiue to thee the askingus of thin
5 herte. Opene to the Lord thi weie; and
6 hope in hym, and he shal do. And he shal bringen out as liȝt thi riȝtwisnesse,
7 and thi dom as mydday; soget be thou to the Lord, and preȝe hym. Wile thou not folewe bi enuye in hym that waxeth welsum in his weie; and in man^r doende
8 vnriȝtwisnessis^s. Lef of fro wrathe, and forsac wodnesse; wile thou not folewe bi enuye, that thou be maad malicious.
9 For thei, that ben maad malicious, shul ben outlawid; sustenende forsothe the
10 Lord, thei shuln eritagen the erthe. And ȝit a litil, and the synnere shal not ben; and thou shalt seche the place of hym,
11 and not finde. The debonere^t forsothe shuln eritagen the erthe; and deliten in
12 the multitude of pes. The synnere shal waite the riȝtwis; and gnaste vp on hym
13 with his teth. The Lord forsothe shal scorne hym; for he beheeld forth that
14 his day come. The synneres drowen out swerd; and benten^u ther bowe. That thei desceyue the pore and the helpeles; that

nesse to hem that ben of riȝtful herte. The foot of pryde come not to me; and
12 the hond of the synnere moue me not. There thei felden^k doun, that worchen
13 wickidnesse; thei ben cast out, and^l myȝten not stonde.

PSALM XXXVI.

The title of the^m sixe and thrittithe salm. 1
To Dauith.

Nile thou sue wickid men; nether loue thou men doynge wickidnesse. For thei
2 schulen wexe drie swiftli as hey; and thei schulen falle doun soone as the wortis of eerbis. Hope thou in the Lord, and do
3 thou goodnesse; and enhabite thou the lond, and thou schalt be fed with hise richessis. Delite thou in the Lord; and
4 he schal ȝyue to thee the axyngis of thin herte. Schewe thi weie to the Lord; and
5 hope thouⁿ in hym, and he schal do. And
6 he schal lede out thi riȝtfulnesse as liȝt, and thi doom as myddai; be thou suget
7 to the Lord, and preye thou hym. Nile thou sue hym, that hath prosperite in his weie; a man doynge vnriȝtfulnessis. Ceese
8 thou of ire, and forsake woodnesse; nyle thou sue, that thou do wickidli. For thei,
9 that doen wickidli, schulen be distried; but thei that suffren the Lordⁿⁿ, schulen enerite the lond. And ȝit a litil, and a
10 synnere schal not be; and thou schalt seke his place, and^o schalt not fynde^p. But
11 mylde men schulen enerite the lond; and^q schulen delite in the multitude of pees. A synnere schal aspie a^r riȝtful man; and
12 he schal gnaste with hise teeth on^s hym. But the Lord schal scorne the synnere;
13 for he biholdith that his day cometh. Synners drowen^t out swerd; thei benten^u
14 her bouwe. To disseyue a pore man and nedi^v; to strangle riȝtful men of herte. Her swerd entre^w in to the herte^x of hem
15

---

^q alle that c.   ^r a man *AII.*   ^s vnriȝtwisnes *AII.*   ^t bouere c.   ^u bende *AEH.*

^k han falle i.   ^l and thei IK.   ^m Om. DFGHPQU.   ⁿ Om. i.   ⁿⁿ Lord, *that is, mekeli his wille* K *text.*
^o and thou i.   ^p fynde *it* i.   ^q and thei i.   ^r the i.   ^s upon i.   ^t han drawe i.   ^u benden i.   ^v a nedi K.
^w entride cox.   ^x hertis DEGIKLMPQSVWbi.

15 thei to-hewe the riȝte men in herte. The swerd of hem entre in to ther hertes; and 16 the bowe of hem be to-broke. Betere is a litil to the riȝtwis; ouer manye richessis 17 of synneres. For the armys of synneres^v shul be to-brosid; forsothe the Lord con-18 firmeth riȝtwis men. The Lord knewȝ the daȝis of the vnwemmed; and the^w eritage of hem with oute ende shal be. 19 Thei shul not ben confoundid in an euel time, and in the daȝes of hungir thei 20 shul be fulfild; for synneres shul per-shen. The enemys forsothe of the Lord, anoon as thei shul be maad wrshipeful, and enhauncid; failende as smoke thei 21 shul faile. The synnere shal borewe, and not paȝen; the riȝtwis forsothe hath 22 merci, and shal ȝelde. For blessende to hym thei shuln eritage the erthe; curs-ende forsothe to hym shul doun pershe. 23 Anent the Lord the going of man shal be dressid^x; and the weie of hym he^y 24 shal wiln. Whan the riȝtwis shal fallen, he shal not ben hurtlid; for the Lord 25 vnderput^z his hond. Ȝungere I was, and forsothe I eldede; and I saȝ not the riȝt-wise forsake, ne his sed sechende bred. 26 Al dai he hath reuthe, and leeneth; and 27 his sed shal ben in blessing. Bowe doun fro euel, and do good; and indwelle in to 28 the world of world. For the Lord looueth dom, and he^a shal not forsake his seyntus; thei shul be togidere kept in to with oute ende. Vnriȝtwise shul be punshid; and 29 the sed of vnpitouse shal pershen. Riȝt-wise forsothe shuln eritagen the erthe; and indwelle in to the world of world 30 vp on it. The mouth of the riȝtwis shal sweteli thenke wisdam; and his tunge 31 speke dom. The lawe of his God in the herte of hym; and his goingus shul not be 32 supplauntid. The synnere beholdeth the 33 riȝtwise; and secheth to slen hym. The Lord forsothe shal not forsaken hym in

silf; and her bouwe be brokun. Betere is 16 a litil thing to a iust man; than many richessis of synneris. For the armes of 17 synneris schal^y be al to-brokun; but the Lord confermeth iust men. The Lord 18 knowith the daies of^z vnwemmed^a; and her heritage schal be withouten ende. Thei schulen not be schent in the yuel 19 tyme, and thei schulen be fillid in the dayes of hungur; for synneris schulen pe-20 rische. Forsothe anoon as the enemyes of the Lord ben onourid, and enhaunsid; thei failynge schulen faile as smoke. A syn-21 nere schal borewe, and^b schal not paie; but a iust man hath merci, and schal ȝyue. For thei that blessen the Lord schulen 22 enerite the lond; but thei that cursen hym schulen perische. The goyng of a man 23 schal be dressid anentis the Lord; and he schal wilne his weie. Whanne he fallith, 24 he schal not be hurtlid^c doun; for the Lord vndursettith^d his hond. I was 25 ȝongere, and sotheli Y wexide eld, and Y siȝ not a iust man forsakun; nethir his seed sekynge breed. Al dai he hath 26 merci, and leeneth; and his seed schal be in blessyng. Bouwe thou awei fro yuel, 27 and do good; and dwelle thou in to the^e world of world. For the Lord loueth 28 doom, and schal^f not forsake hise seyntis; thei schulen be kept with outen ende. Vniust men schulen be punyschid; and the seed of wickid men schal perische. But iust men schulen enerite the lond; 29 and^g schulen enabite theronne in to the world of world. The mouth of a iust 30 man schal bithenke wisdom; and his tunge schal speke doom^h. The lawe of his God 31 is in his herte; and hise steppis schulen not be disseyued. A synnere biholdith 32 a iust man; and^i sekith to sle hym. But 33 the Lord schal not forsake hym in hise hondis; nethir schal^k dampne hym, whanne it schal be demed aȝens hym. Abide thou 34

---

^v the synners A.   ^w Om. A.   ^x destruyed A.   ^y Om. c.   ^z vnderputtith AEH.   ^a Om. A.

^y shullen s.   ^z Om. A pr. m. FHOUX pr.m.   ^a men vnwemmed cIV. vnwemmed men DEGKLMPQRWbi. the vnwemmed x sec. m.   ^b and he I.   ^c hurlid I.   ^d under puttith I.   ^e Om. I.   ^f he wil I.   ^g and thei I. ^h riȝt doom I.   ^i and he I.   ^k he schal I.

his hondis; ne dampne him whan it[b] shal
34 be demed to hym. Abyd the Lord, and
kep his weie, and he shal enhaunce thee,
that bi eritage thou take the erthe; whan
35 synneres shul pershe, thou shalt see. I saȝ
the vnpitouse aboue hauncid; and rerid
36 vp as cedris of Liban. And I passide,
and lo! he was not; I soȝte hym[c], and
37 ther is not founden his place. Kep innocence, and see equite; for thei ben relikis
38 to a pesible man. The vnriȝtwise forsothe shul doun pershe togidere; the re-
39 likis of vnpitous men shul dien. The
helthe forsothe of the riȝtwis of the Lord;
and the defendere of hem he is in time
40 of tribulacioun. And the Lord shal
helpen hem, and delyueren hem, and
pullen hem out fro synneres; and sauen
hem, for thei hopeden in hym.

PSALM XXXVII.

Domine, ne in furore.

1 *The salm of Dauid, in remembring of*
the saboth.

2 Lord, in thi wodnesse ne vndernyme
thou me; ne in thi wrathe chastise thou
3 me. For thin arwis ben in ficchid to
me; and thou hast confermed thin hond
4 vp on me. Ther is not helthe in my
flesh fro the face of thi wrathe; ther is
not pes to my bones fro the face of my
5 synnes. For my wickidnesses ouerȝiden
myn hed; and as a greuous charge thei
6 ben heuyed vp on me. Myne woundis
stunken, and ben roten; fro the face of
7 myn vnwisdam[d]. A wrecche I am maad,
and am crookid vnto the ende; al dai al
8 dreri I wente in. For my leendis ben
fulfild with deceytis; and ther is not
9 helthe in my flesh. I am tormentid, and
I[e] am meked ful myche; I rorede from
10 the weiling of myn herte. Lord, befor
thee al my desyr; and my weiling fro
11 thee is not hid. Myn herte is al dis-

---

the Lord, and kepe thou his weie, and he
schal enhaunse thee, that bi eritage thou
take the lond; whanne synneris schulen
perische, thou schalt se. I siȝ a[l] wickid 35
man enhaunsid aboue; and reisid vp as
the cedris of Liban. And Y passide[m], and 36
lo! he was not; Y souȝte hym, and his
place is[n] not foundun. Kepe thou inno-37
cence, and se equite; for tho ben relikis
to a pesible man. Forsothe vniust men 38
schulen perische; the relifs[o] of wickid men
schulen perische togidere. But the helthe 39
of iust men is of the Lord; and he is her
defendere in the tyme of tribulacioun.
And the Lord schal helpe hem, and schal 40
make hem fre, and he schal delyuere hem
fro synneris; and he schal saue hem, for
thei hopiden in hym.

PSALM XXXVII.

The title of the[p] *seuene and thrittithe* 1
salm. '*The salm*[q] *of Dauid, to bythenke*
on[r] *the sabat.*

Lord, repreue thou not me in thi strong 2
veniaunce; nether chastice thou[s] me in
thin ire. For thin arowis ben fitchid in[t] 3
me; and thou hast confermed[u] thin hond
on me. Noon helthe is in my fleisch fro[v] 4
the face of thin ire; no pees is to my
boonys fro[w] the face of my synnes. For 5
my wickidnessis ben goon ouer[x] myn heed;
as an heuy birthun, tho ben maad heuy on
me. Myn heelid woundis weren rotun, 6
and ben[y] brokun; fro the face of myn vnwisdom. I am maad a wretche, and Y 7
am bowid doun til in to the ende; al dai
Y entride sorewful. For my leendis ben 8
fillid with scornyngis; and helthe is not
in my fleisch. I am turmentid, and maad 9
low ful greetli; Y roride for the weilyng
of myn herte. Lord, al my desire *is* bifor 10
thee; and my weilyng is not hid fro thee.
Myn herte is disturblid in me, my vertu 11

---

[b] he A.　[c] Om. c sec. m.　[d] wisdam AH.　[e] Om. A.

[1] the DEGIKLMPQbi. the a s.　[m] passide aboue c.　[n] was i.　[o] relikis CLMORXik.　[p] Om. DFGHIOPQU.
[q] Om. s.　[r] *of* i.　[s] thou not EGL.　[t] aȝens s.　[u] maad stidefast I.　[v] for c.　[w] for c.　[x] on K.
[y] han ben I.

turbid[f] in me; my vertu hath forsake me,
and li3t[g] of myn e3en, and it is not with
12 me. My frendis and my ne3hebores; a3en
me ne3heden and stoden. And that be-
13 siden me weren fro aferr stoden; and
fors thei maden that so3ten my soule.
And that inwardli so3ten euelis to me,
speeken vanytees; and treccheries al day
14 swetely thei tho3ten. I forsothe as def
herde not; and as doumb not openende
15 my[h] mouth. And I am maad as a man
not herende; and not havende in his
16 mouth a3en vndernemyngus. For in thee,
Lord, I hopede; thou shalt ful out heren
17 me, Lord, my God. For I seide, Lest any
time ouer io3en to me myn enemys; and
whil al to-stirid ben my feet vp on me,
18 grete thingus thei speeken. For I in to
scourgis am redi; and my sorewe in my
19 si3te euermor. For my wickidnesse I
shal telle out; and I shal thenken for my
20 synne. Forsothe myn enemys lyuen,
and ben confermed vpon me; and ben
multeplied, that wickeli[l] hateden me.
21 That 3elden euelis for goodis, bacbiteden
22 to me; for I folewede goodnesse. Ne forsake thou me, Lord, my God; ne go thou
23 awei fro me. Tac heede in to myn helpe;
Lord God of myn helthe.

forsook me; and the li3t of myn i3en *forsook me*[z], and it is not with me. My 12
frendis and my nei3boris nei3iden[a]; and
stoden a3ens me. And thei that weren
bisidis me stoden afer; and thei diden 13
violence, that sou3ten my lijf. And thei
that sou3ten yuels to me, spaken vanytees;
and thou3ten gilis al dai. But Y as a deef 14
man herde not; and as a doumb man not
openynge his mouth. And Y am maad 15
as a man not herynge; and not hauynge
repreuyngis in his mouth. For, Lord, 16
Y hopide in thee; my Lord God, thou
schalt here me. For Y seide, Lest ony 17
tyme myn enemyes haue ioye on me; and
the[b] while my feet ben[c] mouyd, thei
spaken grete thingis on me. For Y am 18
redi to betyngis; and my sorewe *is* euere
in my si3t. For Y schal telle my wickid- 19
nesse; and Y schal thenke for my synne.
But myn enemyes lyuen, and ben[d] con- 20
fermede on me; and thei ben multiplyed,
that haten[f] me wickidli. Thei that 3elden 21
yuels for goodis, backbitiden me; for Y
suede goodnesse. My Lord God, forsake 22
thou not me; go thou not awei fro me.
Lord God of myn helthe; biholde thou in 23
to myn help.

PSALM XXXVIII.

1 *In to the ende, the song*[k] *of Dauid, for
Yditym.*

2 I seide, I shal kepe my weies; that I
gilte not in my tunge. I putte to my
mouth warde; whan the synnere shulde
3 stonde a3en me. I becam doumb, and
am mekid, and heeld my pes fro[l] goodis;
4 and my sorewe is renewid. Myn herte
wex al hot with inne me; and in my
swete thenking ful out shal brenne fir.
5 I spac in my tunge; Lord, mac knowen
to me myn ende. And the noumbre of
my da3es, what it is; that I wite what
6 failith to me. Lo! mesurable thou hast

PSALM XXXVIII.

The title of the[g] *ei3te and threttithe salm*[h]. 1
For victorie, to[i] *Iditum*[k], *the song*[l] *of
Dauid* †.

† *A glos.* Da-
uid made this
salm for hym
silf, whanne he
was pursued of
Absolon, his
sone, aftir that
he herde the
displsyngis of
Semey. A *et
alii.*

I seide, Y schal kepe my weies; that Y 2
trespasse not in my tunge. I settide
kepyng to my mouth; whanne a synnere
stood a3ens me. I was doumb, and was[m] 3
mekid ful gretli, and was[m] stille fro goodis;
and my sorewe was renulid. Myn herte 4
was hoot with ynne me; and fier schal
brenne out in my thenkyng. I spak in 5
my tunge; Lord, make thou myn eende
knowun to me. And the noumbre of my
daies what it is; that Y wite, what failith
to me. Lo! thou hast set my daics 6

[f] distourblid II.   [g] the li3t AII.   [h] his A.   [l] wickidli AII.   [k] *the sones* A. sonis II.   [l] for A.

[z] Om. I.   [a] nei3en C.   [b] Om. I.   [c] weren I.   [d] thei ben I.   [e] confortid KL.   [f] hatiden K sce. m.
[g] Om. CFIIOPQU.   [h] Om. DEIIP.   [l] Om. o. *tolden* R.   [k] Om. R.   [l] *salm* A.   [m] I was I.

put my daȝes; and my substaunce as
noȝt befor thee. Neuerthelatere al vanyte;
7 eche man liuende. Neuerthelatere in
ymage passeth a man; but in veyn he
is al[m] disturbid. He tresoreth; and vnknowith, to whom he shal gedere tho
8 thingus. And now what is myn abiding?
whether not the Lord? and my sub-
9 staunce anent thee is. Fro alle my
wickidnessis[n] pul me awei; reprof to
10 the vnwise man thou hast ȝiue me. I
becam doumb, and openede not my
11 mouth, for thou didist; moue awei fro
12 me thi scourgis. Fro the strengthe of
thin hond I failide in blamyngus; for
wickednesse thou chastisidest[o] a man.
Thou madest to flowen awei as an ireyne
his soule; nerthelatere veynli is dis-
13 turbid[p] eche man. Ful out here myn
orisoun, Lord, and my lowe preȝing;
14 with eris perceyue my teris. Ne be
thou stille, for a comeling I am anent
thee; and a pilgrim as alle my fadris.
15 Forȝif to me, that I be refreshed, befor
that I go awei; and I shal be no more.

PSALM XXXIX.

1 *In to the ende, the salm of Dauid.*

Exspectans.   2 Abidende I abod the Lord; and he
3 beheeld to me. And he ful out herde
my preȝeeris; and broȝte out me fro the
lake of wrecchidnesse; and fro the[q] clei
of drestis. And he sette vp on a ston
4 my feet; and dresside my goingis. And
he ful putte in my mouth a newe song;
a ditee to oure God. Manye shul see,
and dreden; and hopen in the Lord.
5 Blisful the man, of whom the name of
the Lord is his hope; and aȝeen lokide
not in to vanytees, and in to false wod-
6 nessis[r]. Manye thi merueilis thou hast
do, Lord, my God; and in thi thoȝtis
ther is not, that be lic to thee. I tolde

mesurable; and my substaunce is as nouȝt
bifor thee. Netheles al vanytee; ech man
lyuynge. Netheles a man passith in[n]7
ymage[o]; but also he is disturblid veynli.
He tresorith; and he noot[p], to whom he
'schal gadere[q] tho thingis. And now 8
which is myn abiding? whether not the
Lord? and my substaunce is at thee.
Delyuere thou me fro[r] alle my wickid-9
nessis; thou hast ȝoue me schenschip to
the vnkunnynge. I was doumbe, and 10
openyde not my mouth; for thou hast
maad, remoue thou thi woundis fro me. 11
Fro the strengthe of thin hond Y failide 12
in blamyngis; for wickidnesse thou hast
chastisid man. And thou madist his lijf
to faile as an yreyne; netheles ech man
is disturblid in veyn. Lord, here thou 13
my preier and my bisechyng; perseyue
thou with ceris my teeris. Be thou not 14
stille, for Y am a comelyng at[s] thee; and
a pilgrime, as alle my fadris. Forȝyue 15
thou to me, that Y be refreischid, bifor
that Y go; and Y schal no more be.

PSALM XXXIX.

*The title of the[t] nyne and threttithe salm.*1
For victorie[u], the song[uu] of Dauid †.   † *A glos.
This salm is
expowned of
Crist.* a *et alii.*

Y abidynge abood[v] the Lord; and he ȝaf 2
tent to me. And he[w] herde my preieris; 3
and he ledde out me fro the lake of
wretchidnesse, and fro the filthe of draft[x].
And he ordeynede my feet on a stoon[y];
and he dresside my goyngis. And he 4
sente in to my mouth a newe song; a
song[z] to oure God. Many men schulen
se, and schulen[a] drede; and[b] schulen haue[c]
hope in the Lord. Blessid *is* the man, of 5
whom the name of the Lord is his hope;
and he bihelde not in to vanitees, and in
to false woodnesses. Mi Lord God, thou 6
hast maad thi merueils manye; and in thi
thouȝtis noon is[d], that is lijk[e] thee. I

---

[m] Om. *A.*   [n] wickenesse *E.* wickidnesse *H.*   [o] chastiside *AH.*   [p] distourblid *H.*   [q] Om. *A.*
[r] woodnes *AH.*

[n] in an I.   [o] ymage, *that is, derknesse* K *text* v *marg.*   [p] not CL. ne wot I. wot not K *sec. m. marg.*
[q] gaderith s.   [r] of I.   [s] anentis I.   [t] Om. HPQU.   [u] *the victorie* c.   [uu] *salm* v.   [v] haue abide I.   [w] Om. c.
[x] draftis I.   [y] stoon, *that is, Crist* K *text* v *marg.*   [z] song, *ether a ditee* K *sec. m.*   [a] Om. I.   [b] and thei I.
[c] Om. K *sec. m.*   [d] ther is I.   [e] lijk to I.

beforn, and spac; thei ben multiplied 7 ouer noumbre. Sacrifice and offring thou woldist not; eris forsothe thou parformedist to me. Brent sacrifise, and 8 for synne thou askidest not; thanne I seide, Lo! I come. In the hed of the 9 boc it is write of me, that I do thi wil; my God, I wolde; and thi lawe in 10 myddes of myn herte. I befortolde thi riȝtwisnesse in a gret chirche; lo! my lippis I shal not forfende, Lord, thou 11 hast knowen. Thi riȝtwisnesse I hidde not in myn herte; thi treuthe and thin helthe ȝyuere I seide. I hidde not thi mercy, and thi treuthe; fro myche 12 counseil. Thou, Lord, forsothe ne do thou aferr thi mercy doingus fro me; thi mercy and thi treuthe euer mor 13 vndertoken me. For ther enuyrounden me euelis, of the whiche is no noumbre; ther caȝten me my wickednessis, and I myȝte not, that I shulde see. Thei ben multiplied ouer the heris of myn hed; 14 and myn herte forsoc me. Holli plese it to thee, Lord, that thou delyuere me; 15 Lord, to helpen me looke aȝeen. Be thei confoundid, and shamefastli drede thei togidere; that sechen my soule, that thei do it awei. Be thei turned al bacward, and shamefastliche drede thei; 16 that wiln to me euelis. Bere they anoon ther confusioun; that seyn to me, Weu! 17 weu! Ful out ioȝe thei, and glade vpon me, alle that sechen thee; and that loouen thin helthe ȝiuere, sey thei, Euermor be 18 magnefied the Lord. I forsothe a beggere am and pore; the Lord is bisi of me. Myn helpere and my defendere thou art; my God, ne be thou tariende.

teld, and Y spak; and thei ben multiplied aboue noumbre. Thou noldist sacrifice 7 and offryng; but thou madist perfitli eeris to me. Thou axidist not brent sacrifice, and sacrifice for synne; thanne Y seide, 8 Lo! Y come. In the heed of the book it is writun of me, that Y schulde do thi 9 wille; my God, Y wolde; and thi lawe in the myddis of myn herte. I telde thi 10 riȝtfulnesse in a greet chirche; lo! Y schal not refreine my lippis, Lord, thou wistist. I hidde not thi riȝtfulnesse in myn 11 herte; Y seide thi treuthe and thin helthe. I hidde not thi mercy and thi treuthe; fro a myche counsel. But thou, 12 Lord, make not fer thi merciful doyngis fro me; thi mercy and treuthe euere token me vp. For whi yuels, of whiche 13 is no noumbre, cumpassiden me; my wickidnessis token me, and Y myȝte not, that Y schulde se. Tho ben multiplied aboue the heeris of myn heed; and myn herte forsook me. Lord, plese it to thee, 14 that thou delyuere me; Lord, biholde thou to helpe me. Be thei schent, and 15 aschamed togidere; that seken my lijf, to take awei it. Be thei turned abac, and be thei schamed; that wolen yuels to me. Bere thei her confusioun anoon; that seien 16 to me, Wel! wel! that is, in scorn. Alle 17 men that seken thee, be fulli ioyful, and be glad on thee; and seie thei, that louen thin helthe, The Lord be magnyfied euere. Forsothe Y am a beggere and pore; the 18 Lord is bisi of me. Thou arte myn helpere and my defendere; my God, tarie thou not.

PSALM XL.

1 *In to the ende, the salm of Dauid; or, in to the ende, the vnderstonding of Dauid.*

2 Blisful that vnderstant vp on the nedi and pore; in the euele dai shal de-

PSALM XL.

*The title of the fourtithe salm. For vic-*1 *torie, the song of Dauid†.*

Blessid is he that vndurstondith on a 2 nedi man and pore; the Lord schal de-

† *A glos.* This salm is expowned of Cristis passioun and rysyng aȝen. A et alii.

ˢ Om. c.   ᵗ doom A.   ᵘ taryed A.   ᵛ Om. A.   ʷ vnderstondeth AEH.

ᶠ tolde, *ether schewide* K.   ᵍ woldist not I.   ʰ and *oother* I.   ˡ wilnyde also *to do* IS.   ᵏ Om. IS.
ˡ han take I.   ᵐ aschamed HIKXI.   ⁿ wel! *in dispijt* KQ.   ᵒ Om. I.   ᵖ scorn, *in dispit* W.   ᑫ be thei I.
ʳ in S.   ˢ Om. CDGHOPQU.   ᵗ of the I. vpon a K.

3 lyueren hym the Lord. The Lord kepe[x] hym, and quykene hym, and blisful make hym in the erthe; and take hym not 'in 4 to[y] the soule of his enemys. The Lord helpe bere to hym vp on the bed of his sorewe; al his bedding thou turnedest in 5 his sicnesse. I seide, Lord, haue mercy of me; hele my soule, for I synnede to 6 thee. Myn enemys seiden euelis to me; Whanne shal dien, and pershen his name? 7 And if he wente in that he see, veyne thingus he spac; his herte shal gedere 8 wickidnessis[z] to hym. He wente forth outward; nud spac in to itself. Aȝen me priueli grucchiden alle myn enemys; 9 aȝen me thei thoȝten euelis to me. A wicke[a] woord thei setteden aȝen me; Whether he that slepeth, shal not kaste 10 to, that he ryse aȝeen? Forsothe the man of my pes, in whom I hopide; that eet my loues, magnefiede vp on me sup- 11 plaunting. Thou forsothe, Lord, haue mercy of me; and aȝeen rere me, and I 12 shal ȝelde to them. In that I knew, that thou woldist me; for ther shal not 13 ioȝe myn enemy ouer me. Me forsothe for innocence thou hast vndertaken; and confermedist me in thi siȝte in to with- 14 oute ende. Blessid[b] the Lord God of Irael; fro the world, and in to the world, be it do, be it do.

PSALM XLI.

1 *In to the ende, vnderstonding, or bi vnderstonding*[c], *to the sones of Chore.*

Quemadmo-
dum desiderat.

2 What maner desireth the hert to wellis[d] of watris; so desireth my soule 3 to thee, God. My soule thristide to God, the quyke welle; whan I shal comen, 4 and apere befor the face of God? Ther weren to me my teris, loues dai and nyȝt; whil it is seid to me eche day, 5 Wher is thi God? These thingus I re- cordide, and helde out in me my soule; for I shal passen in to the place of the ful merueylous tabernacle, vnto the hous

lyuere hym in the yuel dai. The Lord 3 kepe hym, and quykene hym, and make hym blesful in the lond; and bitake not hym in to the wille of his enemyes. The Lord 4 bere help to hym on the bed of his sorewe; thou hast ofte turned al his bed stre in his sijknesse. I seide, Lord, haue 5 thou mercy on me; heele thou my soule, for Y synnede aȝens thee. Myn enemyes 6 seiden yuels to me; Whanne schal he die, and his name schal perische? And if he 7 entride for to se, he spak veyn thingis; his herte gaderide wickidnesse to hym silf. He ȝede with out forth; and spak to the 8 same thing[u]. Alle myn enemyes bac- bitiden pryuyli aȝens me; aȝens me thei thouȝten yuels to me. Thei ordeineden 9 an yuel word aȝens me; Whether he that slepith, schal not leie to, that he rise aȝen? For whi the man of my pees, in whom Y 10 hopide, he that eet my looues; made greet disseit on me. But thou, Lord, haue 11 merci on me, and reise me aȝen; and Y schal ȝelde to hem. In this thing Y knew, 12 that thou woldist me; for myn enemye schal not haue ioye on me. Forsothe thou 13 hast take me vp for ynnocence; and hast confermed me in thi siȝt with outen ende. Blessid *be* the Lord God of Israel, fro the 14 world and[v] in to the[w] world; be it doon, be it doon.

PSALM XLI.

1 *The title of the*[x] *oon and fourtithe salm.*
To victorie[y]*, to the*[z] *sones of Chore*†.

As an hert desirith to the wellis of 2 watris; so thou[a], God, my soule desirith to thee. Mi soule thirstide[b] to God, 'that 3 is[c] a[d] 'quik welle[dd]; whanne schal Y come, and appere bifor the face of God? Mi teeris weren looues to me bi[e] dai and 4 nyȝt; while it is seid to me ech dai, Where is thi God? I bithouȝte of these thingis, 5 and Y schedde[f] out in me my soule; for Y schal passe in to the place of the won- durful tabernacle, til to the hows of God.

† *A glos.* This salm is expown- ed of the staat of the pupla of Israel, beynge in the caytifte of Babiloyne, and desirynge to come to Je- rusalem. A *et adil.*

[x] shall kepe E.   [y] in A.   [z] wickidnes A.   [a] wickede AEH.   [b] Blesful A.   [c] *the vnderstondynge* H. [d] the welles E pr. m.

[u] ende I.   [v] Om. GK. pr. m. i.   [w] Om. G.   [x] Om. CFHPQU.   [y] *victorie, the salm of Dauid* oxs. [z] Om. v.   [a] Om. I.   [b] thristid DUbik.   [c] Om. CEHLPUxik.   [d] Om. CHUVXbik. the ELP.   [dd] welle of liyf [e] *sup. ras.* H *sec. m.* ORxik. strong, quyk H *pr. m.* UV. *not welle* V *marg.*   [e] Om. I.   [f] helde I.

of God. In the vois of ful ont ioȝing
6 and confessioun; soun of the etere. Whi
dreri art thou, my soule; and whi al
disturbist thou me? Hope in God, for
ȝit I shal knoulechen to hym; the helthe
7 ȝiuere of my chere, and my God. To
myself my soule is al disturbid; therfore
I shal be myndeful of thee fro the lond
of Jordan, and fro Ermonyum, the litle
8 hil. The depnesse depnesse inwardli
clepeth; in the vois of thi gooteris. Alle
thin heȝe thingis; and thi flodis ouer me
9 passiden. In the dai the Lord sente his
10 mercy; and in the nyȝt his song. Anent
me orisoun to God of my lif; I shal sey
to God, Myn vndertakere thou art. Whi
forȝeete thou of⁵ me, and whi al sori I
go; whil the enemy tormenteth me?
11 Whil my bones ben to-broken; to me
repreueden myn enemys, that trublen
me. Whil thei seyn to me, bi alle daȝis,
12 Wher is thi God? My soule, whi art
thou dreri; and whi all sturbistᶠ thou
me? Hopeᵍ in God, for ȝit I shal
knoulechen to hym; the helthe ȝiuere of
my chere, and my God.

PSALM XLII.

Judica me,
Deus.

1   *In to the ende, the salm of Dauid.*

Deme me, God, and seuere my cause
fro folc not holy; fro a wickeʰ man, and
2 a treccherous pul me awei. For thou
art God, my strengthe; whi hast thou
put me abac, and whi dreri I go, whil
3 the enemye tormenteth me? Send out
thi liȝt, and thi treuthe; tho thingis
broȝten out me, and ladden to, in to thiⁱ
4 holi hil, and in to thi tabernaclis. And
I shal go in to the auter of God; to God
that gladeth my ȝouthe. I shal knouleche to thee in an harpe, God, my God;
5 whi dreri art thou, my soule, and whi
al to-sturbist thou me? Hope thou in
God, for ȝit I shal knoulechen to hym;
the helthe ȝyuere of my chere, and my
God.

In the vois of ful out ioiyng and knoulechyng; *is* the sown of the etere. Miⁿ
soule, whi art thou sory; and whi disturblist thouᵍ me? Hope thou in God,
for ȝit Y schal knouleche to hym; *he is*
the helthe of my cheer, and my God. 7
My soule is disturblid atʰ my silf; therfor,
God¹, Y schal be myndeful of thee fro
the lond of Jordan, and fro the litil hil
Hermonyimᵏ. Depthe clepith depthe¹; in 8
the vois of thi wyndows. Alle thin hiȝe
thingis and thi wawis; passiden ouer me.
The Lord sente his merci in the dai; and 9
his song in the nyȝt. Atᵐ me *is*ⁿ aᵒ preier 10
toᵖ theᵖ God of my lijf; Y schal seie to
God, Thou art my ᵗtakere vpʳ. Whi forȝetist thou me; and whi go Y sorewful,
while the enemy turmentith me? While 11
my boonys ben brokun togidereˢ; myn
enemyes, that troblen me, dispisedén me.
While thei seienᵗ to me, bi alle daies;
Where is thi God? Mi soule, whi art 12
thou sori; and whi disturblist thou me?
Hope thou in God, for ȝit Y schal knouleche to hym; ᵗ*he is*ᵘ theᵛ helthe of my
cheer, and my God.

PSALM XLII.

1   'The two and fourtithe salmʷ.

God, deme thou me, and departe thou
my cause fro a folc not hooli; delyuere
thou me fro a wickid man, and gileful.
For thou art God, my strengthe; whi 2
hast thou put me abac, and whi go Y
soreuful, while the enemy turmentith me?
Sende out thi liȝt, and thi treuthe; tho 3
ledden me forth, and broȝtenˣ in to thin
hooli hil, and in to thi tabernaclis. And 4
Y schal entre to the auter of God; to God,
that gladith my ȝongthe. God, my God,
Y schal knowleche to thee in an harpe;
my soule, whi art thou sory, and whi 5
troblist thou me? Hope thou in God,
for ȝit Y schal knouleche to hym; heʸ *is*
the helthe of my cheer, and my God.

ᵉ Om. *AII.*   ᶠ disturbist *A.*   ᵍ Hope thou *K pr. m.*   ʰ wickyd *AII.*   ⁱ the *A.*

ᵍ Om. ɪ.   ʰ anentis ɪ.   ⁱ *Lord* ɪ.   ᵏ of Hermonym ɪᴏs.   ¹ depthe, *that is, oon yuel bringith in another*
ᴋ *text* v *marg.*   ᵐ Anentis ɪ.   ⁿ Om. ᴏ.   ᵒ the ɪ.   ᵖ at ᴘ.   ᵖ Om. ᴄғɪxɪ. thee b.   ʳ vptakere.   ˢ al
togidere s.   ᵗ seiden ʀ.   ᵘ Om. ɪ.   ᵛ Om. b.   ʷ *The two and fourtithe salm and the oon and fourtithe
salm ben al oon in Ebrew, and therfore this hath no litle.* ᴋᴋᵛ.   ˣ broȝten *me* ɪᴋʟ.   ʸ *that* ɪ.

5 G 2

PSALM XLIII.

1 In to the ende, to the sones of Chore, to the vnderstonding.

Deus, auribus nostris.

2 God, with oure eris wee han herd; oure fadris befor tolden to vs. The werc that thou wroȝtist in the daȝis of hem; 3 and[k] in olde[l] daȝis. Thin hond Jentilis scaterede, and thou formedest hem; thou tormentidest puplis, and puttist out hem. 4 Ne forsothe in ther swerd thei weldeden the erthe; and their arm shal not sauen hem. But thi riȝthond, and thin arm, and the liȝting of thi chere; for holli 5 thou toke plesnunce in hem. Thou art he, my king and my God; that sendist 6 helthis to Jacob. In thee oure enemys we shul wynewe bi the horn; and in thi name we shul dispise inriseris in vs. 7 Forsothe[m] in my bowe I shal not hope; 8 and my swerd shal not saue me. Forsothe thou sauedist vs fro men tormentende vs; and the hatende vs thou con-9 foundedist. In God we shul be preisid al dai; and in thi name we shul knou-10 leche to thee in to the world. Nou forsothe thou hast put vs abac, and confoundid vs; and, God, thou shalt not 11 gon out in oure vertues. Thou turnedist vs awei bacward after oure enemys; and thei, that hatiden vs, dyuersly caȝten to 12 themself. Thou ȝeue vs as shep of metis; and in Jentilis[n] thou scateredist vs. 13 Thou soldist thi puple with oute pris; and ther was not multitude in the togi-14 dere chaungingus of hem. Thou hast put vs repref to oure neȝhebores; vnder mouwing 'and scorn[nn] to hem that ben in 15 oure enuyroun. Thou hast put vs in to licnesse to Jentilis; mouyng of the hed 16 in puplis. Al dai my shame is aȝen me; and the confusioun of my face ouer-17 couerede me. Fro the vois of repref[o] puttende, and euele spekende; fro the

PSALM XLIII.

The title of the[y] thre and fourtithe salm[z]. 1 *'To victorie, lernyng to the sones of Chore[n]†.*

† A glos. This salm was maad of the persecucioun, which the puple of Jewis suffride vndur Antiok, as the bokis of Machabeis tellen. A et alii.

God, we herden with oure[b] eeris; oure 2 fadris telden to vs. The werk, which thou wrouȝtist in the daies of hem; and in elde[c] daies. Thin hond lost[d] hethene men, and 3 thou plauntidist hem; thou turmentidist puplis, and castidist hem out. For the 4 *children of Israel* weldiden the lond not bi her swerd; and the arm[e] of hem sauyde not hem. But thi riȝt hond, and thin arm, and the[f] liȝtnyng of thi cheer[g]; for thou were plesid in hem. Thou art thi 5 silf, my kyng and my God; that sendist helthis to Jacob. Bi thee we schulen 6 wyndewe[h] oure enemyes with horn; and in thi name we schulen dispise hem, that risen aȝen vs. For Y schal not hope in 7 my bouwe; and my swerd schal not saue me. For thou hast saued vs fro men 8 turmentinge vs; and thou hast schent men hatinge vs. We schulen be preisid in 9 God al dai; and in thi name we schulen knouleche to thee in to the world. But 10 now thou hast put vs abac, and hast schent vs; and thou, God[i], schalt not go out in oure vertues. Thou hast turned 11 vs awei bihynde aftir oure enemyes; and thei, that hatiden vs, rauyschiden dyuerseli to hem silf. Thou hast ȝoue vs as[k] scheep 12 of meetis; and among hethene men thou hast scaterid vs. Thou hast seeld thi 13 puple with out prijs; and multitude was[l] not in the chaungyngis of hem. Thou 14 hast set vs[m] schenschip to oure neiȝboris; mouwyng[n] and scorn to hem that ben in oure cumpas. Thou hast set vs into 15 licnesse to hethene men; stiryng[o] of heed[p] among puplis. Al dai my schame is aȝens 16 me; and the schenschipe of my face hilide me. Fro the vois of dispisere, and yuele 17 spekere; fro the face of enemy[q], and pur-

---

k Om. A.   l the olde AEH.   m For A.   n the Gentilis AH.   nn Om. A.   o the repref c.

y Om. CDFGHQU.   z Om. AS.   n *lernyng to the victorie* o.   b Om. s.   c the oolde K. the eelde s.
d fordide I.   e arm *or strengthe* I.   f thi s. Om. v.   g cheer *sauede* v.   h wynewe I.   i Lord I.
k *to be* as I.   l ther was I.   m vs *to be* I.   n and mouwyng I.   o and waggyng I.   p the heed K *sec. m.*
q the enemy I.

face of the enemy, and the pursuere.
18 Alle these thingus camyn vpon vs; and
wee han not forȝete thee, and wickeli ᴾ
19 wee han not don in thi testament. And
oure herte wente not awei bacward; and
thou bowidist doun oure pathis fro thi
20 weie. For thou mekedist vs in the place
of tormenting; and ouercouerede vs the
21 shadewe of deth. If wee han forȝete the
name of oure God; and if wee han sprad
22 out oure hondis to an alien God. Whether God shal not aȝeen sechen thes
thingus? he forsothe knewȝ the hidde
thingis of the⁴ herte. For wee ben mor-
tefied for thee al dai; wee ben eymed as
23 shep of slaȝtir. Rys vp, whi alʳ slepist
thou, Lord? ris vp, and putte thou not
24 abac in to the ende. Whi thi face turnest thou awei? thou forȝetist of oure
25 myseise, and of oure tribulacioun. For
mekid in pouder is oure soule; oure
wombe is glued togidere in the erthe.
26 Ris vp, Lord, and help vs; and aȝeen
bie vs for thi name.

suere'. Alle these thingis camen on vs, 18
and we han⁸ not forȝete thee; and we
diden not wickidli in thi testament. And 19
oure herte ȝede not awei bihynde; and
thou hast bowid awei oure pathis fro thi'
weie. For thou hast maad vs lowe in 20
the place of turment; and the schadewe of
deth hilide vs. If we forȝaten the name 21
of oure God; and if we helden forth oure
hondis to an alien God. Whether God 22
schal not seke these thingis? for he knowith the hid thingis of herte. For whi we
ben slayn al dai for thee; we ben demed
as scheep of sleyng. Lord, rise vp, whi 23
slepist thou? rise vp, and putte not⁴ awei
in to the ende. Whi turnest thou awei 24
thi face? thou forȝetist oure pouert, and
oure tribulacioun. For oure lijf is maad 25
low in dust; oure wombe is glued togidere
in the erthe. Lord, rise vp thou, and 26
helpe vs; and aȝenbie vsᵛ for thi name.

PSALM XLIV.

cor

1 *In to the ende, for hem that shul ben*
with chaungid, to the sones of Chore,
to vndirstondyng, the song for the
loouede.

2   Myn herte bowide out a good woord;
I sey my werkis to the king. My tunge
the penne of a scribe, swiftli wrytende.
3 Fair in forme befor the sonus of men,
grace is held out in thi lippis; therfore
blesside thee God in to with oute ende.
4 Be thou gird to with thi swerd; vp on
5 thin hipe most myȝtili. In thi shap and
thi fairnesse behold; go forth welsumli,
and regne. For treuthe, and debonernesse, and riȝtwisnesse; and thi riȝthond
shal merueilously bringe thee thennes.
6 Thin arwis sharpe, puplis vnder thee
shul falle; in to the hertis of the enemys
7 of the king. Thy sete, God, in to the
world of world; the ȝerde of thi gouern-

PSALM XLIV.

*The title of the*ʷ *foure and fourtithe* 1
*salm*ˣ. *To the ouercomere for the lilies,*
*the most*ʸ *loued song of lernyng of the*
sones of Chore†.

Myn herte hath teldᶻ out⁴ a good word; 2
Y seie my workis 'to the kyng*ᵇ*. Mi tunge
is 'a penne of ᶜ a writere; writyuge swiftli.
Crist, thou art fairer in schap than the 3
sones of men; grace is spred abrood in
thi lippis; therfor God blessid thee withouten ende. Be thou gird with thi swerd; 4
on thi hipe most myȝtili. Biholde thou 5
in thi schaplynesse and thi fairnesse;
come thou forth with prosperite, and regne
thou. For treuthe, and myldenesse, and
riȝtfulnesse; and thi riȝt hond schal lede
forth thee wondurfuli. Thi scharpe ᶜ
arowis schulen falle in to the hertis of the
enemyes of the kyng; puplis *schulen be*
vndur thee. God, thi seete is in to the 7

† *A glos.* This
salm is seide of
Crist and of
hooli chirche,
moder and vir-
gyn; for Poul
in i. cᵒ. to
Ebreis, aleggith
this salm seid
of Crist, to the
letter. A *et alii.*

ᴾ wickidli *AII.*   ᑫ Om. *A.*   ʳ Om. *A.*

ʳ a pursuere ᴵ.   ˢ hane ᴵ.   ᵗ the s.   ᵘ not *us* ᴷ *sec. m.*   ᵛ thou vs ᴵ.   ʷ Om. ᴄᴅꜰᴄᴜꜰQᴜᴡ.   ˣ Om. ʟ.
ʸ *most lernyd* ɢ.   ᶻ teld, *ethir belkid* x *sec. m.*   ⁴ Om. ᴋ.   ᵇ Om. s.   ᶜ the penne of ᴵ. Om. s.

yng to euenenesse, the ȝerde of thi regne.
8 Thou loouedest riȝtwisnesse, and hated-
ist⁸ wickidnesse ; therfore enoyntide thee
God, 'thi God', with oile of gladnesse
9 befor thiⁿ felawis. Myrre, and the swote
gumme gutta, and the swote erbe casia,
fro thi clothis, fro the yuer housis ; of
10 the whiche deliteden thee the doȝtris
of kingus in thi wrshipe. The queen
stod neeȝh fro thi riȝt parties in clothing ouergilt ; enuyround with dyuersete.
11 Here, doȝter, and see, and inbowe thin
ere ; and forȝet thi puple, and the hous
12 of thi fader. And the king shal coueite
thi fairnesse ; for he is the Lord thi God,
13 and thei shul honouren hym. And the
doȝtris of Tiri in ȝiftis ; thi chere shul
louli preȝe alle the riche men of the
14 folc. Al the glorie of hym of the doȝter
of the king fro with inne, in goldene
15 hemmes ; abouteᵛ wrappid with diuerse-
tees. Ther shul ben broȝt to the king
maidenes aftir hir ; the neȝheboris of
16 hir shul be broȝt to thee. Thei shul be
broȝte in gladnesse, and ful out ioȝing ;
thei shul be lad to iu to the temple of
17 the king. For thi fadris ben born to
thee sones ; thou shalt sette them princis
18 vp on al erthe. Myndeful thei shul ben
of thi name, Lord ; in alle ieneracioun,
and in to ieneracioun. Therfor puplis
shul knoulechen to thee in to with oute
ende ; and in to the world of world.

world of world ; theᵈ ȝerde of thi rewme
is a ȝerde of riȝt reulyng, 'ethir of
equiteᵉ. Thou louedist riȝtfulnesse, and 8
hatidist wickidnesse ; therfor thou, God,
thi God, anoyntide thee with the oile of
gladnesse, more than thi felowis. Mirre, 9
and gumme, and cassia, of thi clothisᵍ, of
the 'housis yuerʰ ; of whiche the douȝtris of 10
kyngis delitiden theeⁱ. A queen stood nyȝ
on thiᵏ riȝt side in clothing ouergildid ;
cumpassid with dyuersitee. Douȝter, here 11
thou, and se, and bowe doun thin eere ;
and forȝete thi puple, and the hows of thi
fadir. And the kyng schal coueyte thi 12
fairnesse ; for he is thi Lord God, and thei
schulen worschipe hym. And the douȝtris 13
of Tire in ȝiftis ; alle the riche men of the
puple schulen biseche thi cheer. Al the 14
glorye of that douȝter of the kyng is with
ynne in goldun hemmes ; sche is clothid 15
aboute with dyuersitees. Virgyns schulen
be brouȝt to the kyng aftir hir ; hir neiȝ-
boressis schulen be brouȝt to thee. Thei 16
schulen be brouȝt in gladnesse, and ful
out ioiyng ; thei schulen be brouȝt in to
the temple of the kyng. Sones ben borun 17
to thee, for thi fadris ; thou schalt ordeyne
hem princes on al erthe. Lord, thei 18
schulen be myndeful of thi name ; in ech
generacioun, and in to generacioun. Therfor puplis schulen knouleche to thee withouten ende ; and in to the world of world.

PSALM XLV.

1 In to the ende, the salm of Dauid, for
the priue thingis.

2 Oure God refut, and vertue ; helpere
in tribulaciouns, that founden vs ful
3 myche. Therfore wee shul not drede,
whil the erthe shal be disturbid ; and
hillis shul be born ouer in to the herte
4 of the se. Ther souneden, and ben disturbid the watris of hem ; the hillis ben

PSALM XLV.

1 The title of theˡ fiue and fourtithe salm.
To the ouercomere, the song of theᵐ
sones 'of Choreⁿ, 'for ȝongthisᵒ †.

2 Oure God, thou art refuyt, and vertu ;
helpere in tribulacions, that hanᵖ founde
vs greetly. Therfor we schulen not drede, 3
while the erthe schal be troblid ; and the
hillis schulen be borun ouer in to the
herte of the see. The watris of hem 4
sowneden, and weren troblid ; hillis weren

† A glos. The
sones of Chore
maden this xlᵛ.
salm, whanne
thei weren
sauid by mira-
cle ; whiche
Chore, her fa-
der, perischide,
and many
othir ; in xvi.
cᵒ. of Numeri.
A et alii.

ᵃ hatist c.   ᵗ Om. c.   ᵘ alle thi ᴇ pr. m.   ᵛ al about A.

ᵈ thi ʀ.   ᵉ ethir equite cɢw. or of equite ɪ. Om. ᵛ.
ɪᴋᴍᴏᴜᵛxi. yuer housis ɢ. hous yuer ᴛs. hous of yuer ʀ.   ⁱ thee in thi honour ᴋ sec. m.   ᵏ the c.
ˡ Om. ᴄᴅꜰɢʜᴏᴘQᴜᵛ.   ᵐ Om. ᵛ.   ⁿ Om. ꜱ.   ᵒ Om. ᴋ.   ᵖ Om. ꜱ.   ᵍ clothingis ɪ.   ʰ housis of yuer c sec. m.

5 disturbid in the strengthe of it. The bure of the flod gladith the cite of God; the althcr hezist halewide his tabernacle. 6 God in the myddel of it shal not be stirid; God shal helpen it erli fro the 7 morutid. Jentilis ben disturbid, and reumes ben inbowid; he zaf his vois, 8 moued is the erthe. The Lord of vertues with vs; oure vndertakere God of 9 Jacob. Cometh, and seeth the werkis of the Lord; the whiche he sette wndris 10 vp on erth. Takende awei batailis vnto the ende of the erthe; the bowe he shal to-brose, and to-breke; armys and sheeldis he shal to-brenne with fyr. 11 Taketh heede, and seeth, for I am God; I shal ben enhauncid in Jentilis, and I 12 shal ben hauncid in the erthe. The Lord of vertues with vs; oure vndertakere[w] God of Jacob.

troblid togidere in the strengthe of hym. The feersnesse of flood makith glad the 5 citee of God; the hizeste God hath halewid his tabernacle. God in the myddis 6 therof schal not be moued; God schal helpe it eerli in the grey morewtid. He 7 thene men weren disturblid togidere, and rewmes weren bowid doun; God zaf his vois, the erthe was moued. The 8 Lord of vertues is with vs; God of Jacob is oure vptakere. Come ze, and se the 9 werkis of the Lord; whiche wondris he hath set on the[q] erthe. He doynge awei 10 batels til to the ende of the lond; schal al to-brese bouwe, and schal[r] breke togidere armuris, and schal[r] brenne scheldis bi[s] fier. Zyue[t] ze[u] tent, and se ze, that Y am 11 God; Y schal be enhaunsid among hethene men; and Y schal be enhaunsid in erthe. The Lord of vertues is with vs; 12 God of Jacob is oure vptakere.

PSALM XLVI.

1 In to the ende, the salm of Dauid, for the sonus of Chore.

Omnes gentes. 2 Alle Jentilis, iozc zcc with hondis; gladeth to God in vois of ful out iozing. 3 For the Lord heiz, ferful; a[x] grct king 4 ouer al the erthe. He vnder leide puplis to vs; and Jentylis vnder oure feet. 5 He ches to vs his eritage; the fairnesse 6 of Jacob, whom he louede. God stezide vp in ful ioze; and the Lord in vois of 7 trumpe. Doth salm to oure God, doth salm; doth salm to oure king, doth salm. 8 For the king of al erthe God; doth 9 salm wisli. God shal regne vp on Jentilis; God sit vp on his holy sete. 10 Princis of puplis ben gedered with God of Abraham; for the stronge godis of erthe[y] hugeli ben rerid.

PSALM XLVI.

1 The title of the[v] sixte and fourtithe salm. To victorie, a salm to[w] the sones of Chore†.

Alle ze folkis, make[x] ioie with hondis; 2 synge ze hertli to God in the vois of ful out ioiyng. For the Lord is hiz and 3 ferdful; a greet kyng on al erthe. He 4 made puplis suget to vs; and hethene men vndur oure feet. He chees his eri- 5 tage to vs; the fairnesse of Jacob, whom he louyde. God stiede in hertli song; 6 and the Lord in the vois of a trumpe. Synge ze to oure God, synge ze; synge ze 7 to oure kyng, synge ze. For God is kyng 8 of al erthe; synge ze wiseli. God schal 9 regne on[y] hethene men; God sittith on his hooli seete. The princes of puplis ben 10 gaderid togidere with God of Abraham; for the stronge goddis of erthe ben reisid greetli.

† A glos. The sones of Chore in this salm diden thankyngis to God, bi spirit of prophecie, for victorie to comynge, vndir Josue, of puplis enhabitynge the lond of Chanaan. A et alii.

w taker AII.   x and AII.   y the erthe AKII.

q Om. 1.   r he schal 1.   s with 1.   t zlueth 1.   u Om. c.   v Om. plures.   w of G.   x maketh 1.   y in 1.

PSALM XLVII.

1 *The salm, or*[a] *the preising of the song of the sones, or to the sones of Chore, the secounde*[b] *of the wike.*

Magnus Dominus.

2 The grete Lord, and preisable ful myche; in the citie of oure God, in his 3 holi hil. It is founded in ful out io3ing of al erthe; the mount of Sion, the side of the north, the cite of the grete king. 4 God in his housis shal be knowen; 5 whan he shal vndertaken it. For lo! the kingus of erthe ben gedered; thei 6 camen togidere in to oou. Thei seende thus gretli wndreden, thei ben alle dis- 7 turbid; thei ben togidere stirid, trem- bling ca3te hem. There sorewis as of 8 the berende child; in an hidous spirit thou shalt to-brose the shipis of Tharsis. 9 As wee han herd, so wee han seen, in the cite of the Lord of vertues, in the cite of oure God; God foundede it in to 10 with oute ende. God, wee han vndertake thi mercy; in the myddel of thi temple. 11 After thi name, God, so and thi preising in to the endis of the erthe; of ri3twis- 12 nesse ful is thi ri3thond. Glade the hil of Sion, and ful out io3e the do3tris of 13 Jude; for thi domes, Lord. Goth aboute Sion, and togidere biclippeth it; tellith 14 in the touris of it. Setteth 3oure hertes in the vertue of it; and delith the housis of it, that 3ee telle out in an other pro- 15 genye. For this is God, oure God, in to withoute ende, and in to the world of world; he shal gouerne vs in to worldis.

PSALM XLVII.

The title of the[z] *seuene and fourtithe* 1 *salm. The song of salm, of the sones of Chore†.*

† *A glos.* This salm is expowned of Crist, to the letture. A *et alii.*

The Lord *is* greet, and worthi to be 2 preisid ful myche; in the citee of oure God, in the hooli hil of hym. It is foundid 3 in the ful out ioiyng of al erthe; the hil of Syon; the sidis of the north, the citee of the greet kyng. God schal be knowun 4 in the housis therof; whanne he schal take it. For lo! the kyngis of erthe 5 weren gaderid togidere; thei camen into o place. Thei seynge so wondriden; 6 thei weren disturblid, thei weren mouyd togidere, tremblyng took hem. There[a] 7 sorewis as of a womman trauelynge[b] of child; in a greet spirit thou schalt al to- 8 breke the schippis of Tharsis. As we 9 herden, so we sien[c], in the citee of the Lord of vertues, in the citee of oure God; God hath foundid that citee with outen ende. God, we han[d] resseyued thi mercy; 10 in the myddis of thi temple. Aftir thi 11 name, God, so thin heriyng *is spred abrood* in to the endis of erthe; thi ri3t hond is ful of ri3tfulnesse[e]. The hil of 12 Sion be glad, and the dou3tris of Judee be fulli ioiful; for thi domes, Lord. Cum- 13 passe 3e Syon, and biclippe 3e it; telle 3e in the touris therof. Sette 3e 3oure hertis 14 in the vertu of him; and departe 3e the housis of hym, that 3e telle out in an other generacioun. For this is God, oure 15 God, in to withouten ende, and in to the world of world; he schal gouerne vs in to worldis.

PSALM XLVIII.

1 *In to the ende, to the sones of Chore, the salm of Dauyd.*

Audite hæc, omnes gentes.

2 Hereth these thingus, alle Jentilis; with eris perceyueth, alle that dwellen the 3 world. Alle 3ee ertheli geten, and the

PSALM XLVIII.

The title of the[f] *ei3te and fourtithe salm.* 1 *To victorie, a salm to the sones of Chore.*

Alle 3e folkis, here these thingis; alle 2 3e that dwellen in the world, perseyue 3 with eeris. Alle the sones of erthe and 3

---

[a] *of* H.   [b] *secounde day* A.

[z] Om. *plures.*   [a] There *weren* I.   [b] *childynge* I.   [c] *saw3en* I.   [d] *haue* I.   [e] *ri3twisnesse* I.   [f] Om.
plures.   [g] *perceyueth* I.

sones of men^c; togidere in to oon, the
4 riche and the pore. My mouth shal
speken wisdam; and the swete thenking
5 of myn herte prudence. I shal ful bowe
in to a parable myn ere; I shal opene
6 in a sauter my proposicioun. Whi shal
I drede in the euel dai? the wickidnesse
7 of myn heele shal ennyroune me. That
trosten in ther^d vertu; and in the mul-
8 titude of ther^d richessis glorien. A brother aȝeen-bieth not, shal a man aȝeen-
bieu? and he shal not ȝiue to God wher
9 of he be plesid. And the pris of the
aȝeen-biyng of his soule; and he shal
10 trauaile in to withoute ende, and liue
11 ȝit 'in to^e the ende. He shal not seen
deth, whan he shal seen wise men
diende; togidere the vnwise and the
fool shul pershe. And thei shul leue to
12 alienes their richessis; and the sepulcris
of hem the hous of hem withoute ende.
The tabernaclis of hem in progenye and
progenye; thei clepeden ther namys in
13 ther londis. A man, whan he was in
wrshipe, vnderstood^f not; he is comparisound to vnwise bestis, and lie is
14 maad to them. This weye of hem
sclaunder to^g them; and aftir in ther
15 mouth thei shul togidere plese. As shep
in helle thei ben set; and deth shal to-
gnawe them. And the riȝtwise shul
lordshipen of hem in the morutid; and
the helpe of hem shal waxen old in helle,
16 of the glorie of hem. Neuerthelatere God
shal aȝeen-bie my soule fro the hond of
17 helle; whan he shal take me to. Ne thou
shalt dreden, whan riche a man shal be
maad; and whan shal be multiplied the
18 glorie of his hous. For whan he shal
dien, he shal not take alle thingus; ne
19 shal go doun with hym his glorie. For
his^h soule in the lif of hym shal be
blessid; he shal knouleche to thee, whan
20 thou weel dost to hym. He shal gon in
to the progenyes of his fadris; and vnto

the sones of men; togidere the riche man
and the^h pore in to oon. Mi mouth schal 4
speke wisdom; and the thenkyng of myn
herte schal^i speke prudence. I schal 5
bouwe doun myn eere in to a parable; Y
schal opene my resoun set forth in a
sautree. Whi schal Y drede in the yuel 6
dai? the wickidnesse of myn heele^k schal
cumpasse me. Whiche^l tristen in her 7
owne vertu; and han glorie in the multitude of her richessis. A^m brother aȝen- 8
bieth not, schal a man aȝenbie? and he
schal not ȝyue to God his plesyng. And 9
he schal not ȝyue the prijs of raunsum
of^n his soule; and he schal trauele with
outen ende, and he schal lyue ȝit in to 10
the ende. He schal not se perischyng, 11
whanne he schal se wise men diynge;
the vnwise man and fool^o schulen perische
togidere. And thei schulen leeue her
richessis to aliens; and the sepulcris of 12
hem ben the housis of hem with outen
ende. The tabernaclis of hem ben in
generacioun^p and^q generacioun; thei clepiden her names in her londis. A^qq man, 13
whanne he was in honour, vndurstood
not; he is comparisound to vnwise beestis,
and he^r is maad lijk to tho. This weie 14
of hem is sclaundir to hem; and aftirward
thei schulen plese togidere in her mouth^s.
As scheep thei ben set^t in helle; deth schal 15
gnawe hem. And iust men schulen be
lordis of hem in the morewtid; and the
helpe of hem schal^u wexe eld^v in helle,
for^w the glorie of hem. Netheles God 16
schal aȝenbie my soule from the power of
helle; whanne he schal take me. Drede 17
thou not, whanne a man is maad riche;
and^x the glorie of his hows is multiplied.
For whanne he schal die, he schal not 18
take alle thingis^y; and his glorie schal not
go doun with him. For his soule schal 19
be blessid in his lijf; he schal knouleche
to thee, whanne thou hast do wel to hym.
He schal entre til in to the generaciouns 20

---

c man *All.* d thi *A.* e in *All.* f vnderstond c. g of *A.* h the *A.*

---

h Om. *plures.* i Om. *plures.* k heele, *that is, werk* KV. l The whiche I. m The I. n for I.
o the fool I. p generacions K. q and in I. qq Om. I. r Om. s. s mouth, *that is, bosting of lustful
lijf* K *text* V *marg.* t put I. u shal not R. v eld of hem o. w from K. fro LPV. x and whanne FKL.
y thingis with him I.

21 withoute ende he shal not see liȝt. A
man, whan he was in wrshipe, vnderstod
not; he is comparisouned to vnwise bestis,
and lic is maad to hem.

PSALM XLIX.

The salm to Asaph.

1

us deoruun. God of godis, Lord spac; and clepide
2 the erthe, fro the rising of the sunne vn
to the going doun. Fro Sion the shap of
3 his fairnesse, God openli shal come; oure
God, and he shal not be stille. Fyr in
his siȝt shal brenne out; and in his enuy-
4 roun strong tempest. He clepide to heuene fro aboue; and the erthe, to seueren
5 his puple. Gadereth to hym his seyntis;
that ordeynen his testament vp on sacri-
6 fises. And heuenes shuln his riȝtwisnes
7 before telle; for God is domesman. Here
thou, my puple, and I shal speke to
Irael; and I shal witnesse to thee, God,
8 thi God I am. Not in thi[i] sacrifisis I
shal vndernyme thee; forsothe thi brente
9 sacrifises in my siȝt ben euermor. I shal
not take to[k] of thin hous calues; ne of thi
10 flockis get. For myn ben alle the wilde
bestis of wodis; the tame bestis in hillis,
11 and oxen. I knewȝ alle the volatilis of
heuene; and the fairnesse of the feld is
12 with me. If I shal hungren, I shal not
sey to thee; myn is forsothe the round-
13 nesse of erthe[l], and his plente. Whethir
I shal ete flesh of bolis? or the blod
14 of get I shal drinke? Offre to God the
sacrifise of preising; and ȝeeld to the
15 heȝeste thi vouwis. And inwardli clep
me in the dai of tribulacioun; and I shal
pullen out thee, and thou shalt wrshipe
16 me. To the synnere forsothe God seide,
Whi tellist thou out my riȝtwisnessis;
and takist to my testament bi thi mouth?
17 Thou forsothe hatidist disciplyne; and

of hise fadris; and til in to with outen
ende he schal not se liȝt. A[x] man, whanne 21
he was in honour, vndurstood not; he is
comparisound to vnwise beestis, and is[a]
maad lijk to tho.

PSALM XLIX.

The title of the[b] nyne and fourtithe salm. 1
The salm of Asaph†.

† *A glose.* This
salm is expown-
ed of Crist to
the lettre. i.

God, the Lord[c] of goddis, spak; and
clepide the erthe, fro the risynge of the 2
sunne til to the goyng doun. The schap
of his fairnesse fro Syon, God schal come 3
opynli; oure God, and[d] he schal not be
stille. Fier schal brenne an hiȝe in his
siȝt; and a strong tempest in his cumpas.
He clepide heuene aboue; and the erthe, 4
to deme his puple. Gadere ȝe to hym hise 5
seyntis; that ordeynen his testament aboue
sacrifices. 'And heuenes schulen schewe[e] 6
his riȝtfulnesse[ee]; for God[f] is the[g] iuge[h].
Mi puple, here thou, and Y schal speke to 7
Israel; and Y schal witnesse to thee, Y am
God, thi God. I schal not repreue[i] thee[k] 8
in thi sacrifices; and[l] thi brent sacrifices
ben[ll] euere bifor me. I schal not take 9
calues of thin hows; nethir geet buckis of
thi flockis. For alle the[m] wyelde beestis 10
of wodis ben myne; werk beestis, and
oxis in hillis. I haue knowe alle the vola- 11
tils of heuene[n]; and the fairnesse of the
feeld is with me. If Y schal be hungry, 12
Y schal not seie to thee; for the world
and the fulnesse therof is myn. Whether 13
Y schal eete the fleischis[o] of boolis? ethir
schal Y drynke the blood of geet buckis?
Offre thou to God the sacrifice of heri- 14
yng[p]; and ȝelde thin avowis to the hiȝeste
God. And inwardli clepe thou me in the 15
dai of tribulacioun; and Y schal delyuere
thee, and thou schalt onoure me. But God 16
seide to the synnere, Whi tellist thou out
my riȝtfulnessis[q]; and takist my testament
bi thi mouth? Sotheli thou hatidist lore[r]; 17

---

[j] Om. c. [k] Om. *AH.* [l] the erthe *AEH.*

[z] Om. 1. [a] he was 1. [b] Om. *plures.* [c] God *EL.* [d] Om. s. [e] telle KRV. [ee] riȝtwisnesse X *sec. m.*
[f] he i. [g] Om. II *sec. m.* osx *sec. m.* [h] domesman II *sec. m.* i. 'h And heuenes shul telle the riȝtfulnesse
of him, that God is iustise ELP *marg.* Om. A *pr. m.* CFGII *pr. m.* IMOQUWX *pr. m.* [i] proue 1. [k] thee *iust* 1.
[l] forsothe 1. [ll] ben not A *pr. m.* [m] Om. s. [n] the firmament 1. [o] ficishe 1. [p] preisyng, *or of*
heriyng 1. [q] riȝtfulnesse 1. [r] lore *or discipline* 1.

18 threwe aferr my woordis hyndward. If
thou seȝe[m] a thef, thou runne with hym;
and with auoutereres[n] thi porcioun thou
19 leidist. Thi mouth aboundide in malice;
20 and thi tunge ordeynde treccheries. Sittende aȝen thi brother thou speeke, and
aȝen the sone of thi moder thou leidest
21 sclaunder; these thingus thou didist, and
I heeld my pees. Thou eymedest wickeli[o],
that I shal be lic thee; I shal vndernyme
22 thee, and sette thee aȝen thi face. Vnderstondeth this, ȝee that forȝeten God; lest
any tyme he raueshe, and ther be not
23 that deliuere. Sacrifise of preising shal
wrshipen me; and there the weie, bi the
whiche I shal shewe to hym the giuere
of the helthe of God.

PSALM L.

1
2 *The salm of Dauid; whan cam to hym Nathan the profete, whan or for he entride to Bersabee.*

Miserere mei.

3 Haue mercy of me, God; after thi grete
mercy. And after the multitude of thi
grete mercy doingus; do awey my wickid-
4 nesse. More ouer wash me fro wickenesse[p] myn; and fro my synne clense me.
5 For my wickidnesse I knowe; and my
6 synne aȝen me is euermor. To thee
alone I synnede, and euel befor thee I
dide; that thou be iustefied in thi woordis,
7 and ouercome whan thou art demed. Lo!
forsothe in wickidnessis[q] I am conceyued;
and in synnes conceyuede me my moder.
8 Lo! forsothe treuthe thou loouedist; vn-
certeyne and hidde thingis of thi wis-
9 dam thou madist open to me. Thou shal
sprenge me, Lord[r], with isope, and I shal
ben clensid; thou shalt washe me, and
10 aboue snowȝ I shal be maad al whit. To
myn heering thou shalt ȝiue ioȝe and gladnesse; and ful out shul ioȝe bones mekid.

and hast cast awey my wordis bihynde.
If thou siȝest a theef, thou 'hast runne[s] 18
with hym; and thou settidist thi part with
avowtreris. Thi mouth was plenteuouse 19
of malice; and thi tunge medlide togidere
giles. Thou sittynge spakist aȝens thi 20
brother, and[ss] thou settidist sclaundir aȝens
the sone of thi modir; thou didist these 21
thingis, and Y was stille. Thou gessidist
wickidli, that Y schal be lijk thee; Y schal
repreue thee, and Y schal sette aȝens thi
face. Ȝe that forȝeten God, vndurstonde[t] 22
these thingis; lest sum tyme he rauysche,
and noon be that schal delyuere. The 23
sacrifice of heriyng schal onoure me; and
there *is* the weie, where ynne Y schal
schewe to hym the helthe of God.

PSALM L.

The title of the[u] fiftithe salm. To victorie, 1
the salm of Dauid; 'whanne Nathan 2
the prophete cam to hym, whanne he
entride to Bersabee[v].

God, haue thou merci on me; bi[w] thi 3
greet merci. And bi the mychilnesse of
thi merciful doyngis; do thou awei my
wickidnesse[x]. More[y] waische thou me fro 4
my wickidnesse; and clense thou me fro
my synne. For Y knouleche my wickid- 5
nesse; and my synne is euere aȝens me.
I haue synned to thee aloone, and Y haue 6
do yuel bifor thee; that thou be iustified
in thi wordis, and ouercome whanne thou
art demed. For lo! Y was conseyued in 7
wickednessis; and my modir conceyuede
me in synnes. For lo! thou louedist[z] 8
treuthe; thou hast schewid to me the vncerteyn thingis, and pryuy thingis of thi
wisdom. Lord, sprenge thou[a] me with 9
ysope, and Y schal be clensid; waische
thou me, and Y schal be maad whijt more
than snow. Ȝyue thou ioie, and gladnesse 10
to myn heryng; and boonys maad meke

[m] seest *A.* [n] auouteres *C.* [o] wickidli *AH.* [p] wickidnes *AEH.* [q] wickidnes *A.* [r] Om. *C.*

[s] rennydist I. [ss] Om. C. [t] vndurstondeth I. [u] Om. *plures.* [v] *that is, whanne after the deeth of Vrie, Dauith weddide Bersabe* i. [w] aftir I. [x] wicknesse I. [y] More ouer I. [z] hast loued I. [a] Om. I.

11 Turne awey thi face fro my synnes; and
12 alle my wickidnesses do awei. A clene
herte forme in me, God; and a riȝt spirit
13 inwardli newe thou in my bowelis. Ne
throwe thou me aferr fro thi face; and
thin holy spirit ne do thou awei fro me.
14 Ȝeld to me the gladnesse of thin helthe
ȝiuere; and with the spirit principal con-
15 ferme thou me. I shal techen wicke^s men
thi weyes; and vnpitous men to thee shul
16 ben al turned. Deliuere me fro blodis^t,
God, God of^u myn helthe; and ful out
ioȝende shal my tunge telle thi riȝtwis-
17 nesse. Lord, my lippis thou shalt opene;
and my mouth shal beforn telle thi preis-
18 ing. For if thou haddest wold sacrifise,
I shulde han ȝiuen; but forsothe in^v brent
19 sacrifises^w thou woldest^x not deliten. Sacrifise to God, a spiritt holly trublid; a
contrit herte and mekid, God, thou shalt
20 not despise. Benygnely do, Lord, in thi
goode wil to Sion; that ful out be bild
21 the wallis of Jerusalem. Thanne thou
shalt taken at worth sacrifise of riȝtwisnesse, offringus, and brent sacrifises;
thanne thei shul putten in vp on thin
auter calues.

schulen ful out make ioye. Turne awei 11
thi face fro my synnes; and do^b awei alle
my wickidnesses. God, make thou a clene 12
herte in me; and make thou newe a riȝtful
spirit in my entrailis. Caste thou me not 13
awei fro thi face; and take thou not awei
fro me thin hooli spirit. Ȝiue thou to me 14
the gladnesse of thyn helthe; and conferme thou me with the principal spirit.
I schal teche wickid men thi weies; and 15
vnfeithful men schulen be conuertid to
thee. God, the God of myn helthe, dely- 16
uere thou me fro bloodis^c; and my tunge
schal ioyfuli synge thi riȝtfulnesse. Lord, 17
'opene thou^d my lippis; and my mouth
schal telle thi preysyng. For if thou had- 18
dist wold sacrifice, Y hadde ȝoue^c; treuli
thou schalt not delite in brent sacrifices^f.
A^g sacrifice to God is a spirit troblid^h; 19
God, thou schalt not dispise a contrit
herte and 'maad meke^i. Lord, do thou 20
benyngneli in thi good wille to Syon; that
the wallis of Jerusalem be bildid. Thanne 21
thou schalt take plesauntli the sacrifice
of riȝtfulnesse, offryngis, and brent sacrifices; thanne thei schulen putte calues on
thin auter.

PSALM LI.

1 *In to the ende, the vnderstonding of*
2 *Dauid, whan ther cam Doech Idume,*
and hadde told to Saul, Dauyd cam
in to the hous of Abymalech.

PSALM LI.

The title of the^k oon and fiftithe salm. 1
To victorie, the salm of Dauid, 'whanne 2
Doech Idumei cam, and telde to Saul,
and scide to him, Dauid cam in to the
hows of Abymelech^l.

3 What gloriest thou in malice; that
4 myȝti art in wickidnesse? Al dai vnriȝtwisnesse thoȝte thi tunge; as a sharp
5 rasour thou didist treccherie. Thou
loouedist malice ouer benygnete; wickid-
6 nesse mor than to speke equite. Thou
loouedest alle the woordis of kasting doun;
7 in a treccherous tunge. Therfore God
shal destroȝe thee in to the ende, he shal

What hast thou gloric in malice; which^m 3
art miȝti in wickidnesse? Al dai thi tunge 4
thoȝte vnriȝtfulnesse; as a scharp rasour
thou hast do gile. Thou louedist malice 5
more than benygnite; *'thou louedist^n*
wickidnesse more than to speke equite.
Thou louedist alle wordis of casting doun; 6
with a gileful tunge. Therfor God schal 7
distrie thee in to the ende, he schal drawe

---

^s wickid *AII.*   ^t blood *A.*   ^u Om. *A.*   ^v and *A.* Om. *C.*   ^w sacrifise *ACII.*   ^x shalt *AEII.*

^b do thou 1.   ^c bloodis *or synnes* 1.   ^d thou schalt opene κ.   ^e ȝoue *it* IX.   ^f sacrifice A.   ^g Om. V.
^h troblid, *that is, sori for synne* κ *text.* V *marg.*   ^i mekid 1.   ^k Om. *plures. Achymalech* U.   ^l Om. x.
^m that 1.   ^n and 1.

pulle thee out, and myne thee out fro thi tabernacle; and thi roote fro the lond of s liueres. Riʒtwis shul seen, and dreden; and vp on hym thei shul laʒen, and 9 seyn, Lo! the man that putte not God his helpere. But hopide[y] in the multitude of his richessis; and hadde 10 maistri in his vanyte. I forsothe as an olive berende frut in the hous of God; hopide in the merci of God in to with- 11 oute ende, and in to world[z] of world. I shal knouleche to thee in to the world, for thou hast don; and I shal abide thi name, for it is good in the siʒte of thi seyntys.

thee out bi the roote, and he schal make thee to passe awei fro thi tabernacle; and thi roote fro the lond of lyuynge men. Iust men schulen se, and[p] schulen drede ; s and thei schulen leiʒe on hym, and thei schulen seie, Lo! the man that settide[q] 9 not God his helpere. But he hopide in the multitude of his richessis; and hadde maistrie in his vanite. Forsothe Y, as a 10 fruytful olyue tre in the hous of God ; hopide in the merci of God with outen ende, and in to the world of world. Y 11 schal knowleche to thee in to the world, for thou hast do *mercy to me ;* and Y schal abide thi name, for it is good in the siʒt of thi seyntis.

PSALM LII.

1 *In to the ende, the vnderstonding of Dauid for Amalech.*

The vnwise man seide in his herte; 2 Ther is not God. Thei ben corupt, and thei ben made abhominable in ther wick- 3 idnessis; ther is not that do good. God fro heuene beheeld vp on the sones of men ; that he see, if ther is vnderstond- 4 ende, or aʒeen sechende God. Alle bow- eden doun togidere, thei ben maad vn- profitable; ther is not that do good, ther 5 is not vnto oon. Whether not alle shuln knowen, that werken wickidnesse; that deuouren my puple as mete of bred ? 6 God thei inwardli clepeden not ; there thei trembliden bi drede, where was not drede. For God scaterede the bones of hem, that plesen to men ; thei ben con- 7 foundid, for God dispiside them. Who shal ʒiue fro Sion the helthe ʒiuere to Irael ? whan the Lord shal holli turne the caitifte of his folc, Jacob shal ful out ioʒen, and Irael shal gladen.

PSALM LII.

The title of the[r] two and fiftithe salm. 1 *To the ouercomer bi the quere, the lernyng of Dauid.*

The vnwise man seide in his herte ; God is not. Thei ben 'corupt, and maad[s] 2 abhomynable in her wickidnessis; noon is that doith good. God bihelde fro heuene 3 on the sones of men; that he se, if 'ony is[t] vndurstondynge, ether sekynge God. Alle boweden awei, thei ben maad vn- 4 profitable togidre; noon is that doith good, ther is not til to oon. Whether alle men, 5 that worchen wickidnesse, schulen not wite; whiche deuouren my puple as the mete of breed ? Thei clepiden not God ; 6 there thei trembliden for drede, where no drede was. For God hath scaterid the boones of hem, that plesen men[u]; thei ben schent, for God hath forsake hem. Who schal ʒyue fro Syon helthe to Israel? 7 whanne the Lord hath turned the caitifte of his puple, Jacob schal 'ful out[v] make ioie, and Israel schal be glad.

[y] he hopide ᴀᴇ𝜫.   [z] the world ᴀ.

[p] and thei ɪ.   [q] puttide ɪ.   [r] Om. *plures.*   [s] maad corupt and s.   [t] ther is ony ɪ.   [u] to men ᴋ. [v] fulli v.

PSALM LIII.

1 *In to the ende in ditees or ympnes, in the titlis, or vnderstonding of Dauid,* 2 *whan ther hadden come Zifei to Saul, and hadden told to Saul, Whethir is not Dauyd hyd anentis vs?*

3 God, in thi name mac me saaf; and in 4 thi vertue deme me. God, ful out here thou[a] myn orisoun; with eris perceyue 5 the woordis of my mouth. For alienes inwardli risen aȝen me, and stronge men soȝten my soule; and thei purposide not 6 God befor ther siȝte. Lo! forsothe God helpeth me; and the Lord is vndertakere 7 of my soule. Turne awei euelis to myn enemys; and in thi treuthe scatere them. 8 Wilfulli I shal sacrifice[b] to thee; and I shal knoulechen to thi name, Lord, for 9 it is good. For fro alle tribulacioun thou hast deliuered me; and vpon myn enemys beheeld doun myn eȝe.

PSALM LIV.

1 *In to the ende, in ditees or ympnes, the vndirstonding of Dauid.*

2 Here thou, God, myn orisoun, and de-3 spise thou not my lowe preȝeere; tac heede to me, and ful out here me. I am maad al sory in myn enhaunting; and I 4 am al disturbid fro the vois of the enemy, and fro tribulacioun of the synnere. For thei bowiden doun in me wickidnessis; and in wrathe thei weren heuy to me. 5 Myn herte is al disturbid in me; and 6 ferd[c] of deth fel vp on me. Drede and trembling camen vp on me; and al couer-7 eden me derenesses. And I seide, Who shal ȝiue to me federes as of a culuer; 8 and I shal flee, and aȝeen resten? Lo! I droȝ out me along fleende; and I duelte 9 in wildernesse. I abod hym[d], that made

PSALM LIII.

The title of the[w] thre and fiftithe salm. 1 *To victorie[x] in orguns, ether in salmes, the lernyng of Dauid,* `whanne Zyfeys* 2 *camen, and seiden to Saul, Whethir Dauid is not hid at vs[y]?*

God, in thi name make thou me saaf; 3 and in thi vertu deme thou me. God, 4 here thou my preier; with ecris perseyue thou the wordis of my mouth. For aliens 5 han rise aȝens me, and stronge men souȝten my lijf; and thei settiden not God bifor her siȝt. For, lo! God helpith me; and 6 the Lord is vptaker[z] of my soule. Turne 7 thou awei yuelis to myn enemyes; and leese[a] thou hem in thi treuthe. Wilfuli 8 Y schal make sacrifice to thee; and, Lord, Y schal knouleche to thi name, for it is good. For thou delyueridist me fro al 9 tribulacioun; and myn iȝe dispiside on myn enemyes.

PSALM LIV.

The title of the[b] foure and fiftithe salm[c]. 1 `In Ebreu thus[d], To victorie in or-guns, the lernyng of Dauid.* `In Jeroms translacioun thus, To the ouercomer in salmes of Dauid lernid[e]†.*

God, here thou my preier, and dispise 2 thou[f] not my biseching; ȝyue thou tent 3 to me, and here thou me. I am sorewful in myn exercising[g]; and Y am disturblid of the face of the enemye, and of the tri-4 bulacioun of the synner. For thei bow-iden wickidnessis in to me; and in ire thei weren diseseful to me. Myn herte was 5 disturblid in me; and the drede of deth felde on[h] me. Drede[i] and trembling camen 6 on me; and derknessis hiliden me. And 7 Y scide, Who schal ȝyue to me fetheris, as of a[k] culuer; and Y schal fle, and schal[l] take rest? Lo! Y ȝede fer awei, and fledde; 8 and Y dwellide in wildirnesse. I abood 9 hym, that made me saaf fro the litilnesse,

† *A glos.* Dauith made this salm, doinge thankingis to God, whan he fledde fro Ceila, and was saued fro the hondis of Saul, that wolde biseye him in Ceila, and fro the hondis of the puple of Ceila, that disposide to bitraie him. LFQSbi.

---

[a] Om. ᴀ.   [b] sacrifie ᴀ.   [c] dreed ᴀ.   [d] hem c pr. m.

[w] Om. *plures.*   [x] *the victorie plures.*   [y] Om. x.   [z] the vptaker ɪ.   [a] fordo *or* leese ɪ.   [b] Om. *plures.* [c] Om. ᴅɢ.   [d] Om. *ceteri præter* ᴠ.   [e] Om. *ceteri præter* ᴠ.   [f] Om. ɪ.   [g] exercising *or* hauntyng ɪ.   [h] in ꜱ. [i] And drede ɪ. And dredinge ꜱ.   [k] Om. ꜱ.   [l] I schal ɪꜱ.

Deus, in no-mine tuo.

Exaudi, Deus, orationem meam.

me saf; fro to litil coraiouste of spirit, and fro tempest. Lord, put doun, and 10 deuyde the tungis of hem; for I saȝ wickidnesse and contradiccioun in the cite. Dai and nyȝt wickidnesse shal euuyroune 11 it vpon the wallis of it; and trauaile in the myddes of it, and vnriȝtwisnesse. 12 And ther failede not fro the stretis of it; vsure and treccherie. For if myn enemy 13 hadde cursid to me; I shulde also han suffrid. And if he, that hadde hatid me, ouer me grete thingis hadde spoken; I shulde han hid me perauenture fro hym. Thou forsothe a man of oon inwit; my 14 ledere, and my knowen. The whiche 15 togidere with me swete metis thou toke; in*e* the hous of God wee wente with consent. Deth come vp on hem; and 16 go they doun in to helle lyuende. For shreudenessys in the dwelling placis of hem; in the myddel of hem. I forsothe 17 to the Lord criede; and the Lord shal saue me. The euentid and the moru, 18 and at myddai, I shal seyn, and befor telle; and he shal ful out here my voys. He shal aȝeen bie my soule in pes fro 19 them, that neȝhen to me; for among manye thei weren with me. God shal 20 ful out heren, and meke them; that is befor worldis. Ther is not forsothe to them al hol chaunging, and thei dredde not God; he straȝte out his hond in 21 aȝeen ȝelding. Thei defouleden the testament of hym, thei ben deuydid fro the 22 wrathe of his chere; and the herte of hym neȝhede to. Softid ben the woordis of hym vp on oile; and thei ben speris. Throȝ vp on the Lord thi bisynesse, and 23 he shal nurshe thee out; and he shal not ȝiue in to with oute ende flotering to the riȝtwise. Thou forsothe, God, shalt 24 bringe them doun; in to the pit of deth. Men of blodis and treccherous shul not haluen ther daȝes; I forsothe shal hope in thee, Lord.

'ether drede, of spirit; and fro tempest. Lord, caste thou doun, departe thou the 10 tungis of hem; for Y siȝ wickidnesse aud aȝenseiyng in the citee. Bi dai and nyȝt 11 wickidnesse schal cumpasse it on the wallis therof; and trauel and vnriȝtful-12 nesse *ben* in the myddis therof. And vsure and gile failide not; fro the stretis therof. For if myn enemye hadde cursid 13 me; sotheli Y hadde suffride. And if he, that hatide me, hadde spoke greet thingis on me; in hap Y hadde hid me fro hym. But thou art a man of o wille; my leeder, 14 and my knowun. Which tokist togidere 15 swete meetis with me; we ȝeden with consent in the hous of God. Deth come on 16 hem; and go thei doun quyk in to helle. For weiwardnessis ben in the dwelling placis*m* of hem; in the myddis of hem. But Y criede to thee, Lord; and the Lord 17 sauede me. In the euentid and morewtid 18 and in myddai Y schal telle, and schewe; and he schal here my vois. He schal aȝen-19 bic my soule in pees fro hem, that neiȝen to me; for among manye thei weren with me. God schal here; and he that is bifore 20 the*n* worldis schal make hem low. For chaungyng*o* is not to hem, and thei dred-den not God; he holdith*p* forth his hoond 21 in ȝelding. Thei defouliden his testament, the cheris therof weren departid 22 fro ire; and his herte neiȝede. The wordis therof weren*q* softer than oyle; and tho*r* ben dartis. Caste thi cure*s* on the Lord, 23 and he schal fulli nurische thee; and he schal not ȝyue with outen ende flotering to a iust man. But thou, God, schalt lede 24 hem forth; in to the pit of deth. Men-quelleris and gilours schulen not haue half her daies; but, Lord, Y schal hope in thee.

e and in *All*.

PSALM LV.

1 *In to the ende, for the puple that fro
seintis is maad aferr, in the inscripcioun of the title to hym, Dauid, whan
ther shulden holden hym hethene men
in Jeth.*

Miserere mei. 2 Haue mercy of me, God, for a man
'to-trad[f] me; al day impugnende trublide
3 me. My enemys to-treeden me al day;
4 for manye fiȝtende aȝen me. Fro the
heiȝte of the dai I shal drede ; I forsothe
5 in thee shal hopen. In God I shal preise
my woordis ; in God I hopide, I shal not
6 drede what do to me the flesh. Al dai
thei cursiden my woordis ; aȝen me alle
7 thoȝtis of hem in to euel. Thei shul
duelle in and hiden ; thei myn heele shul
8 waite. As thei sustenedeu my soule for
noȝt ; thou shalt make them saf in wrathe
9 puplis thou shalt to-breke. God, my lif
I 'haue out told[g] to thee ; thou puttist
my teres in thi siȝte. As in thi beheste,
10 Lord ; thanne shul ben al turned myn
enemys bacward. In what euer dai I
shal inwardli clepe thee ; lo ! I knew, that
11 my God thou art. In God I shal preise
the woord ; in the Lord I shal preise the
sermoun. In God I hopede ; I shal not
12 drede what do to me a man. In me,
God, ben thi vouwis ; the whiche I shal
13 ȝelde preisingis to thee. For thou hast
deliuered my soule fro deth, and my
feet fro sliding ; that I plese befor God in
the liȝt[h] of liueres[i].

PSALM LV.

The title of the[t] fyue and fiftithe salm. 1
'In Ebreu thus[u], To the[v] ouercomyng
on the doumb culuer of fer drawing[w]
awei, the comely song of Dauid, whanne[x]
Filisteis[y] helden[z] hym in Geth. 'In
Jeroms translacioun thus, To the ouercomer for the doumb culuer, for it
ȝede awei fer. Dauid meke and symple
made[a] this salm, whanne Palesteyns
helden hym in Geth[b]†.*

God, haue thou merci on me, for a man 2
hath defoulid me ; al dai he impugnyde,
and troublide me. Myn enemyes defoul- 3
iden me al dai ; for manye fiȝteris *weren*
aȝens me. Of the hiȝnesse of dai Y schal 4
drede ; but God Y schal hope in thee. In 5
God Y schal preise my wordis ; Y hopide
in God, Y schal not drede what thing
fleisch[c] schal do to me. Al dai thei curs- 6
iden my wordis ; aȝens me alle her thouȝtis
weren in to yuel. Thei schulen dwelle, 7
and schulen[d] hide ; thei schulen aspie myn
heele. As thei abiden[e] my lijf, for nouȝt 8
schalt thou make hem saaf ; in ire thou
schalt breke togidre puplis. God, Y schew- 9
ide my lijf to thee ; thou hast set my teeris
in thi siȝt. As and in thi biheest, Lord ;
thanne myn enemyes schulen be turned 10
abak. In what euere dai Y schal inwardli
clepe thee ; lo ! Y haue knowe, that thou
art my God. In God Y schal preise a 11
word ; in the Lord Y schal preyse a word.
Y schal hope in God ; Y schal not drede
what thing a[f] man schal do to me. God, 12
thin auowis ben in me ; whiche Y schal
ȝelde heriyngis[g] to thee. For thou hast 13
delyuerid my lijf fro deth, and my feet
fro slidyng ; that Y plese bifore God in
the liȝt of hem that lyuen.

† *A glos.* Da-
uith made this
salm whanne
he fledde fro
the face of
Saul, and
came to Agis,
kyng of Geth ;
and whanne
thei wolden
kille Dauith,
he feynede him
wood, and so
he was sauyd.
c *et alii.*

[f] to-tredede *AEH.*   [g] shal tellen out *E pr. m.*   [h] siȝte *AH.*   [i] liues *H.*

[t] Om. DFGHOPQV.   [u] Om. *ceteri præter* v.   [v] Om. *plures.*   [w] *drawun* c.   [x] Om. x.   [y] *the
Filisteis* R.   [z] *hadden* v.   [a] *make plures.*   [b] Om. *ceteri præter* v.   [c] *fleisch or man* L.   [d] *thei schulen* I.
[e] *abideden* CFGHIKMOQRUVWXbi. abood ELP.   [f] Om. I.   [g] *heryinge* s.

PSALM LVI.

1 *In to the ende, ne destroȝe thou or shend[k]
Dauid, in the inscripcioun[l] of the title,
whan he fleiȝ fro the face of Saul in
the den.*

Miserere mei, Deus.

2 Haue merci of me, God, haue merci of
me; for in thee trosteth my soule. And
in the shadewe of thi wengis I shal hope;
to the tyme that wyckidnesse ouerpasse.
3 I shal crie to the heiȝest God; God that
4 dide weel to me. He sente fro heuene,
and deliuerede me; he ȝaf in to reprof
the tredende me. God sente his merci
5 and his treuthe, and toe awei my soule;
fro the myddel of the leonn whelpis, I
sleep[m] al disturbid. Sones of men, the
teth of hem armys and arwis; and the
6 tunge of hem a sharp swerd. Be thou
enhauncid, God, vpon heuenes; and vp on
7 alle erthe thi glorie. Thei maden redi a
grene to my feet; and thei myche crook-
eden my soule. Thei doluen[n] befor my
8 face a dich; and thei fellen in to it. Redi
myn herte, God, redi myn herte; I shal
9 singe and salm sein. Rys vp, my glorie;
ris vp, sautre and harpe; I shal risen vp
10 erly. I shal knouleche to thee in puplis,
Lord; and salm I shal sei to thee in
11 Jentylys. For magnefied is vnto heuenes
thi merci; and vnto the[o] cloudis thi
12 treuthe. Be thou enhauncid vp on heuenes, God; and ouer alle erthe thi
glorie.

PSALM LVI.

The title of the[h] sixte and fiftithe salm. 1
'*In Ebreu thus[i], To the victorie, lese
thou not the semeli song,* 'ether the[k]
'*swete song[l] of Dauid,* 'whanne he fledde
fro the face of Saul in to[m] the denne[n].
'*In Jeroms translacioun thus, For victorie, that thou lese not Dauid, meke
and simple, whanne he fledde fro the
face of Saul in to the denne[o].*

God, haue thou[p] merci on me, haue 2
thou merci on me; for my soule tristith
in thee. And Y schal hope in the schadewe
of thi wyngis; til wickidnesse passe. I 3
schal crye to God altherhiȝeste; to God
that dide wel to me. He sente fro he- 4
uene, and delyuerede me; he ȝaf in to
schenschip hem that defoulen[q] me. God
sente his merci and his treuthe, and 5
delyuerede my soule fro the myddis of
whelpis of liouns; Y slepte disturblid.
The sones of men, the teeth of hem *ben*
armuris and arowis; and her tunge *is* a[r]
scharp swerd. God, be thou enhaunsid 6
aboue heuenes; and thi glorie aboue al
erthe. Thei maden redi a[s] snare to my 7
feet; and thei greetly boweden my lijf.
Thei delueden a diche bifore my face; and
thei felden doun in to it. God, myn herte 8
is redi, myn herte *is* redi; Y schal singe,
and Y schal seie salm. Mi glorie, rise 9
thou vp; sautrie and harpe, rise thou
vp; Y schal rise vp[t] eerli. Lord, Y schal 10
knouleche to thee among puplis; and Y
schal seie salm among hethene men. For 11
thi merci is magnified til to[u] heuenes;
and thi treuthe til to cloudis[uu]. God, be 12
thou enhaunsid aboue heuenes; and thi
glorie ouer[v] al erthe.

h Om. *plures.* i Om. *ceteri præter* v. k *ether* cv. Om. s. l Om. s. m Om. Mb. 'n Om. x.
o Om. *ceteri præter* v. p Om. I. q defouleden K *sec. m.* r Om. s. s Om. s. t Om. I. u *in to* s.
uu the cloudis A *pr. m.* v aboue Is.

PSALM LVII.

1 *In to the ende, ne shende thou or destroȝe Dauid, in the inscripcioun of the title.*

vere utique. 2 If vereli also riȝtwisnesse ȝee speke;
3 euenli demeth, ȝee sones of men. Forsothe in the herte wickidnessis ȝee werken in the erthe; vnriȝtwisnesses ȝoure hondis
4 menge[p] togidere. Synneres ben aliened fro the wombe; thei erreden fro the
5 wombe, thei speeken false thingus. Wodnesse to them, after the licnesse of an eddere; as of a doumb eddere, and stop-
6 pende his eris. The whiche shal not ful out heren the vois of the enchaunteres; and of the venym makere enchauntende
7 wisly. God shal to-brose the teth of hem in the mouth of hem; and the wang teth
8 of leouns the Lord shal to-breke. To noȝt thei shul come, as water doun rennende; he bente[q] his bowe, to the time
9 that 'thei be[r] feblid. As wax that flowith, thei shul ben taken awei; fyr fel ouer,
10 and thei seȝen not the sunne. Befor that ȝoure thornes shulden vnderstonde the theue thorne; as the lyuende, so in
11 wrathe he shal soupe them vp. The riȝtwis shal glade, whan he seeth veniaunce; his hondis he shal washen in the
12 blod of the synnere. And a man shal seyn, If forsothe ther is frut to the riȝtwis; forsothe God is demende them in erthe.

PSALM LVII.

The title of the[w] *seuene and fiftithe* 1
salm. 'In Ebreu thus[x], *To victorie*[y]*;
'lese thou not the swete song, ether the semely salm*[a], *of Dauid*[b]. *'In Jeroms translacioun thus, To the ouercomere, that thou lese not Dauid, meke and simple*[c].

Forsothe if ȝe speken riȝtfulnesse verili; 2
ȝe sones of men, deme[d] riȝtfuli. For in 3
herte ȝe worchen wickidnesse in erthe; ȝoure hondis maken redi vnriȝtfulnessis[e].
Synneris weren maad aliens fro the 4
wombe; thei erriden fro the wombe, thei spaken false thingis. Woodnesse *is* to 5
hem, bi the licnesse of a serpent; as of a deef snake, and stoppynge hise eeris.
Which[f] schal not here the vois of charmeris; 6
and of a venym makere charmynge wiseli.
God schal al to-breke the teeth of hem in 7
her mouth; the Lord schal breke[g] togidere the greet teeth of liouns. Thei schulen 8
come to nouȝt, as water rennynge awei; he bente his bouwe, til thei ben[h] maad
sijk. As wexe that fletith awei, thei 9
schulen be takun awei; fier felle aboue, and thei siȝen not the sunne. Bifore that 10
ȝoure thornes vndurstoden the ramne[i]; he swolewith hem so in ire, as lyuynge men.
The iust man schal be glad, whanne he 11
schal se veniaunce; he schal waische hise hondis in the blood of a synner. And a 12
man schal seie treuli, For fruyt is to a iust man; treuli God is demynge hem in erthe.

† *A glos.* Dauith made this salm, whanne Saul, at the tellynge of Zipheis, ȝede out with thre thousynde of chosun men to seke Dauith, in firste book of Kyngis xxvi. c°. and Dauith took awei the spere and the cuppe of Saul slepynge. c *et alii.*

p mengeden *A.* q bende *AEH.* r he *A.*

w Om. *plures.* x Om. *ceteri præter* U. y *the ouercomere* V. a Om. K. *song ceteri.* 'b *that thou leese not Dauith, meek and symple.* V. c Om. *ceteri præter* U. d demeth IS. e vnriȝtfulnesse A. riȝtfulnessis RX. f The which I. g to-breke CP. al to-breke DESX. h weren I. i ramne, *ether theue thorn,* P *et plures.* the raveyne, *ether ramne* S.

PSALM LVIII.

1 *In to the ende, ne destroȝe thou or shend
Dauid, in the inscripcioun[s] of the title,
whan Saul sente, and kepte his hous,
that he shulde slen hym.*

Eripe me de inimicis.

2 Tac me out fro myn enemys, my God;
and fro the inrisende in me deliuere me.
3 Tac me out fro the werkende wickidnesse; and fro men of blodis saue me.
4 For lo! thei token my soule; ther fellen
5 in to me stronge men. Nouther my
wickidnesse, ne my synne; Lord, withoute wickidnesse I ran, and wel reulide.
6 Rys vp in to aȝen comyng to me, and see;
and thou, Lord God of vertues, God of
Irael. Tac heede to alle Jentilis to be
visited; haue thou not mercy to alle that
7 werken wickidnesse. Be thei conuertid
at euen, and hunger thei shul suffre as
houndys; and thei shul enuyroune the
8 cite. Lo! thei shuln speke in ther
mouth, and swerd in the lippis of hem;
9 for who herde? And thou, Lord, shalt
scorne them; to noȝt thou shalt bringe
10 alle Jentilis. My strengthe to thee I
11 shal kepe, for God myn vndertakere; my
12 God, his mercy shal befor come me. God
shewide to me vp on myn enemys, ne
sle thou hem; lest any time my puplis
forȝeten. Destroȝe them in thi vertu;
and put them doun, Lord, my defendere.
13 The gilte of the mouth of hem, and the
woord of ther lippis; and be thei caȝt
in ther pride. And of cursing and les-
14 ing[t] thei shul be told; in the full ending.
In the wrathe of hol eende, and thei shul
not ben; and they shul wite, for the
Lord shal lordshipen of Jacob, and of

PSALM LVIII.

The title of the[k] eiȝte and fiftithe salm. 1
*'In Jeroms translacioun thus[l], To the
ouercomer, that thou lese not Dauid,
meke and simple, 'whanne Saul sente
and kepte the hous, to slee hym[m]. 'In
Ebreu thus, To the ouercomyng, leese
thou not the semeli song of Dauid, and
so forth[n].*

Mi God, delyuer thou me fro myn 2
enemyes; and delyuer thou me fro hem
that risen aȝens me. Delyuer thou me 3
fro hem that worchen wickidnesse; and
saue thou me fro menquelleris. For lo! 4
thei han take my soule; stronge men fellen
in on me. Nethir my wickidnesse, nether 5
my synne; Lord, Y ran with out wickidnesse, and dresside '*my werkis*[o]. Rise vp 6
thou[p] in to[q] my meetyng, and se; and
thou, Lord God of vertues, *art* God of
Israel. Ȝyue thou tent to visite alle folkis;
do thou not merci to alle that worchen
wickidnesse. Thei schulen be turned at 7
euentid, and thei as doggis schulen suffre
hungir; and thei schulen cumpas[r] the
citee. Lo! thei schulen speke in her 8
mouth, and a[rr] swerd in her lippis; for
who herde? And thou, Lord, schalt 9
scorne hem; thou schalt bringe alle folkis
to nouȝt. I schal kepe my strengthe to 10
thee; for God *is* myn vptaker, my God, 11
his mercy schal come byfore me. God 12
schewide to me on myn enemyes, slee
thou not hem; lest ony tyme my puples
forȝete. Scatere thou hem in thi vertu;
and, Lord, my defender, putte thou hem
doun. *Putte thou*[s] *doun* the trespas of 13
her mouth, and the word of her lippis;
and be thei takun in her pride. And of
cursyng and of leesyng; thei schulen be
schewid in the endyng. In the[ss] ire of 14
ending, and thei schulen not be; and thei

[s] *scripcioun* H. [t] of lesing AEH.

[k] Om. *plures.* [l] Om. *ceteri præter* U. [m] Om. X. [n] Om. *ceteri præter* U. [o] Om. *plures. my werkis. Lire here.* Q *marg.* U *text.* [p] Om. A. [q] Om. C. [r] *that is, go a begging* K *marg.* [rr] Om. C. [s] Om. I. [ss] Om. I.

15 the coostis of the erthe. Thei shul be
conuertid at euen, and hunger thei shul
suffre, as houndis; and thei shul gon
16 aboute the cite. Thei shul be scaterid,
to eten; if forsothe thei shuln not be
17 fulfild, and thei shul grucche. I forsothe
shal singe thi strengthe; and enhauncen
vp erly thi mercy. For thou art maad
myn vndertakere; and my refute, in the
18 dai of my tribulacioun. Myn helpere, to
thee I shal do salm; for God, myn vndertakere, my God, my mercy.

PSALM LIX.

1 *In to the ende, for hem that shul ben
holli chaungid, in the inscripcioun of
the title, to hym Dauyd, in to lernyng*[u],
2 *whan he brende vp Mesopotanye of*[v]
*Cirie, or Ciric Sobal, and turnede
Joab, and smot Edom in the valei of
salt placis, twelue thousend.*

Deus, repulisti. 3 God, thou hast put vs abac, and de-
4 strozid vs; thou wrathedest vs. Thou
togidere mouedest erthe[w], and disturbidist
it; hele the to-tredingis of it, for it is to-
5 stirid. Thou hast shewid to thi puple
hard thingis; thou hast drunken vs with
6 wyn of compunccioun. Thou hast ziue
to the dredende thee toknyng; that thei
flee fro the face of the bowe. That thi
7 loouede be deliuered, mac saf in thi rizt
8 hond; and ful out here me. God spac in
his halewe; I shal gladen, and deuyde
Siccymam; and the valei of tabernaclis
9 I shal mesuren. Myn is Galaad, and
myn is Manasses; and Effraym the

schulen wite, that the Lord schal be Lord
of Jacob, and of the endis of erthe. Thei 15
schulen be turned at euentid, and thei as
doggis schulen suffre hungur; and thei
schulen cumpas[t] the citee. Thei schulen 16
be scaterid abrood, for to eete; sotheli if
thei ben not filltd, and thei schulen
grutche. But Y schal synge thi strengthe; 17
and eerli Y schal enhaunse thi merci.
For thou art maad myn vptaker; and my
refuyt, in the dai of my tribulacioun. Myn 18
helper, Y schal synge to thee; for *thou art*
God, myn vptaker, my God, my mercy.

PSALM LIX.

The title of the[v] *nyne and fiftithe salm*[w]. 1
'*In Ebreu thus*[x], *To victorie, on the
witnessyng of roose, the swete song
of Dauid, to teche*[y], '*whanne he fauzte* 2
*azens Aram of floodis, and Sirie of
Soba; and Joab turnede azen, and
smoot Edom in*[z] *the*[z] '*valei of salt
pittis, twelue*[a] *thousynde*[aa]. '*In Jeroms
translacioun thus, To the ouercomer
for lilies, the witnessing of meke and
parfit Dauid, to teche, whanne he fauzte
azens Sirie of Mesopotamye, and Soba,
and so forth*[b].

God, thou hast put awei vs, and thou 3
hast distried vs; thou were wrooth, and
thou hast do merci to vs. Thou moued- 4
ist the erthe, and thou disturblidist it;
make thou hool the sorewis therof, for it
is moued. Thou schewidist harde thingis 5
to thi puple; thou zauest drynk to vs with
the wyn of compunccioun. Thou hast 6
zoue a signefiyng to hem that dreden
thee; that thei fle fro the face of the
bouwe. That thi derlyngis be delyuered;
make thou saaf with thi rizt hond '*the* 7
puple of Israel[c], and here thou me. God 8
spak bi his hooli; Y schal be glad, and
Y schal departe Siccimam[d], and Y schal

---

[n] *the lernynge* u.   [v] *or of* AEH.   [w] the erthe AEH.

[t] *that is, gon a beggid* v marg.   [v] Om. *plures.*   [w] Om. F.   [x] Om. *ceteri præter* U.   [y] *teche men* D.
[z] Om. X.   [zz] Om. GX.   [a] Om. X.   [aa] thousandis v. Om. X.   [b] Om. *ceteri præter* U.   [c] Om. CEGHLPVXik.
the puple of Israel. Lire here. Q marg. U text.   [d] Siccimam, *that is, the lond of Sichem* K text v marg.

strengthe of myn hed. Juda, my king;
¹⁰Moab, the pot of myn hope. In to Idume
I shal strecche my shoing; to me alienus
¹¹ben soget. Who shal bringe me in to
strengthid˟ cite; who shal bringe me
¹²in to Idume? Whether not thou, God,
that hast put vs abac; and thou, God,
¹³shalt not gon out in oure vertues? ȝif
to vs helpe fro tribulacioun; for veyn is
¹⁴the helthe of man. In God wee shul do
vertu; and he to noȝt shal bringe doun
men trublende vs.

PSALM LX.

di, Deus.

¹ *In to the ende, in ympnes, the salm to˟*
Dauyd.

₂ Ful out here thou, God, my lowe
₃preȝing; tac heede to myn orisoun. Fro
the endis of the erthe to thee I criede,
whil myn herte shulde ben anguysht; in
₄a ston thou enhauncidist me. Thou
broȝtest me out, for thou art maad myn
hope; the tour of strengthe fro the face
₅of the enemy. I shal duelle in thi
tabernacle in to worldis; I shal be defendid in the coueryng of thi wengis.
₆For thou, my God, 'ful out˟ herdist myn
orisoun; thou ȝeue the eritage to men
₇dredende thi name. Daȝis vp on daȝis
of the king thou shalt caste to; his ȝeris
vnto the dai of ieneracioun and of iene-
₈racioun. He abit˟ stille into withoute
ende in the siȝte of God; the merci and
₉his treuthe who shal aȝeen sechen? Soo
salm I shal sey to thi name in to the
world of world; that I ȝelde my vouwis
fro dai in to dai.

PSALM LXI.

¹ *In to the ende, for Iditym, the salm of*
Dauyd.

e Deo.

₂ Whether not to God soget shal be my

meete the greet valei of tabernaclis. Ga-₉
laad is myn, and᷎ Manasses is myn; and
Effraym *is* the strengthe of myn heed.
Juda *is* my king; Moab *is* the᷎ pot of myn ₁₀
hope. In to Idumee Y schal stretche forth
my scho; aliens ben maad suget to me.
Who schal lede me in to a citee maad ₁₁
strong; who schal leede me til᷎ in to
Ydumee? Whether not thou, God, that᷎ ₁₂
hast put awei vs; and schalt thou not,
God, go out in oure vertues? Lord, ȝue ₁₃
thou to vs help of ᷎ tribulacioun; for the
heelthe᷎ of man is veyn. In God we ₁₄
schulen make vertu; and he schal bringe
to nouȝt hem that disturblen vs.

PSALM LX.

*The titil of the᷎ sixtithe salm. To the*ᵐ ₁
*victorie on orgun*ⁿ, *to Dauid hym silf*†.

† *A glos.* Da-
uith made this
salm aftir that
he hadde asca-
pid the hondis
of Saul, cum-
passinge him at
the maner of a
coroun. c *et alii.*

God, here thou my biseching; ȝyue ₂
thou tent to my preyer. Fro the endis of ₃
the lond Y criede to thee; the while myn
herte was angwischid, thou enhaunsidist
me inᵒ a stoon. Thou laddest me forth, ₄
for thou art maad myn hope; a tour of
strengthe fro the face of the enemye. I ₅
schal dwelle in thi tabernacle in to
worldis; Y schal be keuered in the hilyng of thi wengis. For thou, my God, ₆
hast herd my preier; thou hast ȝoue
eritage to hem that dreden thi name.
Thou schalt addeᴾ daies on the daies of ₇
the king; hise ȝeeris til in to the dai of
generacioun and of generacioun. He ₈
dwellith with outen ende in the siȝt of
God; who schal seke the merci and
treuthe of hym? So Y schal seie salm to ₉
thi name in to the�q world of world; that
Y ȝelde my vowis fro dai in to dai.

‡ *A glos.* Da-
uith made this
salm, whanne
he was in the
persecucioun of
Saul, and this
afcir that he
was coroun aȝen
fro the lond of
Moab to the
lond of Juda, at
the word of Gad
the profete.
Dauith made
the x. salm in
this comyng
aȝen, but he
made this salm
after that he
had dwellid
sumdel in the
lond of Juda.
c *et alii.*

PSALM LXI.

*The titil of the oon and sixtithe salm*ᶜ. ₁
*To the*ˢ *victorie on*ᵗ *Iditum, the salm of*
Dauid‡.

Whether my soule schal not be suget ₂

soule; of hym forsothe myn helthe
3 ʒiuere. Forwhi and he my God, myn
helthe ʒinere, myn vndertakere; I shal
4 be moued no more. Hou longe ʒee fallen
in to a man? ʒee slen alle ʒee; as to a
boowid woughe, 'and to^b a ston wal put
5 doun. Neuer the latere my pris thei
thoʒten to putte behinde, I ran in thrist;
with ther mouth thei blissiden, and with
6 ther herte cursiden. Neuer the latere to
God soget be thou, my soule; for of
7 hym my pacience. For lo! my God
and my saueour; myn helpere, I shal
8 not gon out. In God myn helthe ʒinere,
and my glorie; God of myn helpe, and
9 myn hope is in God. Hopeth in hym,
eche congregacioun of puple; heeldeth
out beforn hym ʒoure hertes, God oure
10 helpere in to withoute ende. Neuer the
latere veyne the sones of men; lieris the
sones of men in weiʒtis; that thei desceyue, thei of the vanyte in to itself.
11 Wileth not hopen in wickidnesse, raueynes
wileth not coueite; if richessis 'flowe to^c,
12 wileth not leyn to the herte. Oues God
spac, these two thingus I herde; for^d
13 the power of God is, and to thee, Lord,
mercy; for thou shalt ʒelde to eche man
aftir his werkis.

PSALM LXII.

1 *The salm of Dauyd, whan he was in
the^e desert of Ydume.*

2 God, my God, to thee fro liʒt I wake.
My soule thristide in thee; hou manyfold
3 to thee my flesh. In a desert erthe and
withoute weie, and with oute water, so
in holi I aperede to thee; that I shulde
4 see thi vertu, and thi glorie. For betere
is thi mercy vpon lyues; my lippis shul
5 preise thee. So I shal blesse thee in my
lif; and in thi name I shal reren vp myn
6 hondus. As bi talʒ and fatnesse be fulfild
my soule; and with lippis of ful out

to God; for myn heelthe *is* of hym.
For whi he *is* bothe my God, and myn 3
heelthe; my 'taker vp^u, Y schal no more
be moued. Hou longe fallen ʒe on a man? 4
alle ʒe sleen; as to a wal bowid, and^w a
wal of stoon with out morter cast doun.
Netheles thei thouʒten to putte awei my 5
prijs, Y ran in thirst; with her mouth
thei blessiden, and in her herte thei
cursiden. Netheles, my soule, be thou 6
suget to God; for my pacience *is* of hym.
For *he is* my God, and my saueour; myn 7
helpere, Y schal not passe out. Myn 8
helthe, and my glorie *is* in God; God *is*
the^x ʒyuer of myn help, and myn hope is
in God. Al the gaderyng togidere of the 9
puple, hope ʒe in God, schede^y ʒe out ʒoure
hertis bifore hym; God *is* oure helpere
with outen ende. Netheles the sones of men 10
ben veyne; the sones of men *ben* liers in
balauncis, that thei disseyue of vanytee in
to the same thing. Nile ʒe haue hope in 11
wickidnesse, and nyle ʒe coueyte raueyns;
if ritchessis be plenteuouse, nyle ʒe sette
the herte therto. God spak onys, Y herde 12
these twei thingis, that power *is* of God,
and, thou Lord, mercy *is* to thee; for 13
thou schalt ʒelde to ech man bi^z hise
werkis.

PSALM LXII.

1 *The titil of the^a two and sixtithe salm.
'The salm^b of Dauid, 'whanne he was
in the^c desert of Judee^d†.*

2 God, my God, Y wake to thee ful eerli.
Mi soule thirstide to thee; my fleisch
thirstide to thee ful many foold. In a 3
lond forsakun with out wei, and with out
water, so Y apperide to thee in hooli; that
Y schulde se thi vertu, and thi glorie.
For thi merci is betere than lyues; my 4
lippis schulen herie thee. So Y schal 5
blesse thee in my lijf; and in thi name
Y schal reise myn hondis. Mi soule be 6
fillid as with inner fatnesse and vttermere

† *A* ples. Da-
uith made this
salm, whanne
he was in the
pursuyng of
Saul, aftir that
he was turned
aʒen [fro the
lond of Moab
alii] in to the
lond of Judee,
and was in de-
sert of Judee.
c *et alii*.

---

^b in to *AII*.   ^c ouerflowen to *A*. flowen *II*.   ^d forsothe *AII*.   ^e Om. *A*.

^u vp taker 1.   ^w and *as* 1.   ^x Om. 1.   ^y helde 1.   ^z aftir 1.   ^a Om. *plures*.   ^b Om. oo.   ^c Om. *plures*.
^d Om. x.

7 iozing my mouth shal preise. So I was
myndeful of thee vp on my bedding, in
the morutidis I shal sweteli thenken in
8 thee; for thou were[f] myn helpere. And
in the coueryng of thi wengus I shal ful
9 out ioʒe, my soule cleuede to after thee;
10 me thi riʒthond vndirtoc. Thei forsothe
in to veyn soʒten my soule, they shul go
in to the nethermor partis of the erthe;
11 thei shul be taken in to the hond of
swerd, the partis of foxis thei shul be.
12 The king forsothe shal gladen in God,
and ther shul be preisid alle that swern
in hym; for stoppid is the mouth of men
spekende wicke thingus.

PSALM LXIII.

1 *In to the ende, the salm of Dauyd.*

Exaudi, Deus, orationem.

2 Ful out here thou, God, myn orisoun,
whan I louli preʒe; fro the drede of the
3 enemy tac awei my soule. Thou hast
defendid me fro the couent of warieris;
and fro the multitude of men wirkende
4 wickidnesse. For thei sharpiden out as
a swerd ther tungis; thei benten a
5 bowe, a bittere thing, that thei sheete in
6 hid thingus the vnwemmed. Sodeynly
thei shul sheten hym, and not dreden;
thei fastneden to hem a shreude woord.
Thei tolden, that thei shulden hide grenes;
7 thei seiden, Who shal see them? Thei
sercheden wickidnessis; thei serchende
faileden in serching. Ther shal neʒhen
8 a man to an heiʒ herte; and God shal
ben enhauncid. The arwis of litle childer
9 ben maad the veniauncis of hem; and
ther ben feblid aʒen hem the tungis of
hem. Alle that seʒen hem ben disturbid;
10 and eche man dredde. And thei beforn

fatnesse; and my mouth schal herie with
lippis of ful out ioiyng. So[e] Y hadde 7
mynde on[f] thee on[g] my bed[h], in morewtidis[i] Y shal thenke of[k] thee; for thou 8
were[l] myn helpere. And in the keueryng
of thi wyngis Y schal make ˋful out[m] ioye,
my soule cleuede after thee; thi riʒthond 9
took me vp. Forsothe thei souʒten in 10
veyn my lijf, thei schulen entre in to the
lower thingis of erthe; thei schulen be 11
bitakun in to the hondis of swerd, thei
schulen be maad the partis of foxis. But 12
the king schal be glad in God; and alle
men schulen be preysid that sweren in
hym, for the mouth of hem, that speken[n]
wickid thingis, is stoppid.

PSALM LXIII.

The titil of the[o] thre and sixtithe salm[p]. 1
*ˋIn Ebrewe thus[q], To the[r] victorie, the
salm of Dauid. ˋIn Jerom[s] ˋthus, To
the ouercomer, the song of Dauid[t].*

God, here thou my preier, whanne Y 2
biseche; delyuere thou my soule fro the[u]
drede of the enemy. Thou hast defendid 3
me fro the couent of yuele doers; fro the
multitude of hem that worchen wickidnesse. For thei scharpiden her tungis as 4
a[v] swerd, thei benten[w] a[x] bowe, a bittir
thing; for to schete in priuetees[y] hym that 5
is vnwemmed. Sodeynli thei schulen 6
schete hym, and thei schulen not drede;
thei maden stidefast to hem silf a wickid
word. Thei telden, that thei schulden
hide snaris; thei seiden, Who schal se hem?
Thei souʒten wickidnessis; thei souʒten, 7
and failiden in sekinge. A man neiʒhe[z]
to deep[a] herte; and God schal be en- 8
haunsid. The arowis of ˋlitle men[b] ben
maad the woundis of hem; and the tungis 9
of hem ben maad sijk aʒens hem. Alle
men ben[c] disturblid, that sien hem; and 10
ech man dredde. And thei telden the

[f] was *AH*.

[e] Lo V. [f] of IKLS. [g] upon K. [h] bedstree KO. [i] the morewtidis C. [k] on I. [l] hast be I. [m] fully I. [n] spaken C. [o] Om. *plures*. [p] Om. A. [q] Om. *ceteri præter* U. [r] Om. GLPQ. [s] *In Jeroms* U. Om. *ceteri*. [t] Om. *ceteri præter* U. [u] Om. IS. [v] Om. O. [w] benden I. [x] her I. [y] hiddels *or priuetees* I. [z] had neiʒe X *sec. m.* [a] a deep X. [b] litle men, *that is, enuiouse men* K *text* V *marg.* [c] weren *ceteri*.

tolden the werkis of God; and his deedis
11 thei vnderstoden. The riȝtwise shal
gladen in the Lord, and hopen in hym;
and alle riȝtwise in herte shul be preisid.

werkis of God; and[d] vndurstoden the dedis
of God[e]. The iust man schal be glad in 11
the Lord, and schal hope in hym; and alle
men of riȝtful herte schulen be preisid.

PSALM LXIV.

1 *In to the ende, the salm of Dauid, the
soug of Aggei, Jeremye, or Ezechiel,
of the woord of pilgrimagynge, or of[g]
the puple of transmygracioun, whan
thei shulden begynne to go forth.*

2   Thee semeth an ympne, thou God, in
Sion; and to thee shal ben ȝolden a
3 vou in Jerusalem. Ful out here thou
4 myn orisoun; to thee all flesh shal come.
The woordis of wicke[h] men hadden the
maistri ouer vs; and to oure vnpitous-
5 nessis thou shalt be plesid. Blisful whom
thou hast chosen, and take to; he shal
dwelle in thin hallis. Wee shul be fulfild in goodis of thin hous; holi is thi
6 temple, merueilous in equite. Ful out
here vs, God, oure helthe ȝiuere; hope of
alle the coostis of erthe, and in the se
7 afer. Greithende hillis in thi vertu, gird
8 to bi power; that disturbist the depthe
9 of the se, the soun of his flodis. Jentilis[i] shul ben sturbid[k], and dreden that
duellen the termes of thi toenes; the
goingus out of the morutid and the eue-
10 tid thou shalt make delitable. Thou hast
visitid the erthe, and maad it drunke;
and thou multipliedest in maken it riche.
The flod of God is fulfild with watris;
thou greithedest the mete of hem, for so
11 is the befor greithing of it. Thou inwardli makende drunke the ryueres of
it, multiplie his buriounys; and in his
drope fallingus shal glade the buri-
12 ounende. Thou shalt blesse to the
croune of the ȝer[l] of thi benyngnete;
and thi feldis shul be fulfild with plen-
13 teuouste. The faire thingus of desert
shul waxe fatte; and bi ful out ioȝing

God, heriyng bicometh thee in Syon; 2
and a vow schal be ȝolden to thee in Jerusalem. Here thou my preier; ech man 3
schal come to thee. The wordis of wickid 4
men hadden the maistrye ouer vs; and
thou schalt do merci to oure wickidnessis.
Blessid *is* he, whom thou hast chose, and 5
hast take; he schal dwelle in thin hallis[k].
We[l] schulen be fillid with the goodis of
thin hous; thi temple is hooli, wondurful 6
in equite. God, oure heelthe, here thou
vs; *thou art* hope of alle coostis of erthe,
and in the see afer. And thou makest 7
redi hillis in thi vertu, and art[m] gird with
power; which disturblist the depthe of 8
the see, the soun of the wawis therof.
Folkis schulen be disturblid, and thei that 9
dwellen in the endis schulen drede of thi
signes; thou schalt delite the outgoingis
of the morewtid and euentid. Thou hast 10
visitid the lond, and hast greetli fillid it;
thou hast multiplied to make it riche.
The flood of God was fillid with watris;
thou madist[n] redi the mete[o] of hem, for
the makyng redi therof is so. Thou fill- 11
yuge greetli the stremes therof, multiplic
the fruytis therof; *the lond* bringinge
forth[p] fruytis schal be glad in goteris[q] of
it. Thou schalt blesse the coroun[r] of the 12
ȝeer of thi good wille; and thi feeldis
schulen be fillid with plentee[s] of fruytis.
The feire thingis of desert schulen wexe 13
fatte; and litle hillis schulen be cumpassid

PSALM LXIV.

The titil of the[f] foure and sixtithe salm. 1
` To victorie[g], ` the salm[h] of[i] the song of
Dauid†.*

g *to* A.   h wickid H.   i The Gentilis A.   k disturbid A E H.   l erthe A.

d and thei 1.   e hIm K.   f Om. *plures.*   g Om. A.   h Om. FW.   i Om. F.   k forȝerdis *or hallis* 1 *marg.*
forȝerdis *ceteri.*   l ȝe L.   m thou art 1.   n hast maad 1.   o metis A.   p Om. K.   q the goteris *plures.*
r crowne *other serule* V.   s the plente V.

14 litle hillis shul be gird aboute. The wetheres of shep ben clad^m, and the valeis shuln abounde with whete ; thei shul crie, and forsothe seyn ympne.

PSALM LXV.

1 *In to the ende, the song of the salm of resureccioun.*

Deo.

2 Ioȝeth to God, al ertheⁿ, salm seith to his name ; ȝiueth gloric to his preising. 3 Seith to God, Hou ferful ben thi werkis, Lord ; in the multitude of thi vertu shuln 4 lie to thee thin enemys. Al erthe^o honoure thee, God, and do salm to thee ; and 5 sey salm to thi name. Cometh and seeth the werkis of God ; ferful in counseilis vp 6 on the sones of men. That al turneth the se in to drie, in the flod thei shul passe thurȝ afoote ; ther wee shul gladen 7 in hym. That lordshipeth in his vertu in to withoute ende ; his eȝen vp on Jentilis beholden, that ful out terren shul 8 not ben enhauncid in hemself. Blesseth, ȝee Jentylis, oure God ; and herd maketh 9 the vois of his preising. That putte my soule to lif, and ȝaf not in to togidere 10 stiring my feet. God, for thou hast proued vs ; bi fyr thou examynedest vs, as 11 siluer is examyned. Thou broȝtist vs in to the grene, thou puttist tribulaciouns^p 12 in oure rig ; thou puttist in men vpon oure hedis. Wee passiden thurȝ fyr and watir ; and thou broȝtist out vs in to re-13 freshing. I shal go in to thin hous in brent sacrifises ; I shal ȝelde to thee my 14 vowis, that determyneden my lippis. And my mouth spac in my tribulacioun ; 15 brent sacrifises ful of merȝ I shal offre to thee, with encens of wethers ; I shal 16 offre to thee oxen with get. Ȝee, alle that dreden God, cometh and hereth ; and I shal telle hou grete thingus he dede to 17 my soule. To hym with my mouth I criede ; and I ful out ioȝide vnder my

with ful out ioiyng. The wetheris of 14 scheep ben clothid, and valeis schulen be plenteuouse of wheete ; thei schulen crye, and sotheli thei schulen seye salm^t.

PSALM LXV.

The titil of the^u fyue and sixtithe salm. 1 To the^v victorie, the song of salm^w†.

Al the^x erthe, make ȝe ioie hertli to 2 God, seie ȝe salm to his name ; ȝyue ȝe glorie to his heriyng. Seie ȝe to God, 3 Lord, thi werkis ben dredeful^y ; in the^z multitude of thi vertu thin enemyes schulen lie to thee. God, al the^a erthe worschipe 4 thee, and synge^b to thee ; seie it salm to thi name. Come ȝe and se ȝe the werkis 5 of God ; ferdful in counseils on the sones of men. Which^c turnede the see in to 6 drie^d lond ; in the flood thei schulen passe with foot^e, there we schulen be glad in hym. Which^f is Lord in his vertu with-7 outen ende, hise iȝen biholden on folkis ; thei that maken scharp be not enhaunsid in hem silf. Ȝe hethen men, blesse^g oure 8 God ; and make ȝe herd the vois of his preising. That^h hath set my soule to lijf, 9 and ȝafⁱ not my feet in to stiryng. For 10 thou, God, hast preued vs ; thou hast examyned vs bi fier, as siluer is examyned. Thou leddist vs in to a snare, thou put-11 tidist^k tribulaciouns in oure bak ; thou 12 settidist men on oure heedis. We passiden bi fier and water ; and thou leddist^l vs out in to refreschyng. I schal entre in to thin 13 hous in brent sacrificis ; Y schal ȝelde to thee my vowis, which my lippis spaken 14 distinctly. And my mouth spake in my tribulacioun ; Y schal offre to thee brent 15 sacrificis ful of merow3, with the brennyng of rammes ; Y schal offre to thee oxis with buckis of geet. Alle ȝe that 16 dreden God, come^m and hereⁿ, and^o Y schal telle ; hou grete thingis he hath do to my soule. I criede to hym with my 17

† *A glos.* This salm is doyng of thankyng is for delyueraunce of the puple of Jewis fro Egipt. c *et alii.*

---

^m clothid *AEII.*　ⁿ the erthe *AEII.*　^o the erthe *AII.*　^p tribulacioun *AII.*

^t heriyng *ceteri.*　^u Om. *plures.*　^v Om. *plures.*　^w *Dauid, salm of thankingis* v.　^x Om. DW.
^y ful dredeful *ceteri.*　^z thi s.　^a Om. I.　^b synge it I.　^c The which I.　^d the drie I.　^e drie foot I.
^f The which I.　^g blesse ȝe I.　^h The whiche I.　ⁱ he ȝaf I.　^k hast putt I.　^l hast led I.　^m cometh I.
ⁿ here ȝe I.　^o Om. o.

18 tunge. Wickedenesse if I beheeld in myn herte; the Lord shal not ful out here. 19 Therfore ful out herde God; and toc heede to the vois of my lowe preȝing. 20 Blissid the God; that mouede not awei myn orisoun, and his merci fro me.

mouth; and Y ioyede fulli vndir my tunge. If Y bihelde wickidnesse in myn herte; 18 the Lord schal not here. Therfor God 19 herde; and[p] perseyuede the vois of my bisechyng. Blessid be God; that remeued 20 not my preyer, and[q] ʻtook not awei[r] his merci fro me.

PSALM LXVI.

1 *In to the ende, ʻin ympnes[q], the salm of the song to Dauyd.*

PSALM LXVI.

The titil of the[s] sixe and sixtithe salm. 1 *ʻIn Ebreu thus[t], To the[u] victorie in orguns, the salm of the[v] song[vv]. ʻIn Jerom[w] ʻthus, To the ouercomer in salmes, the song of writing of a delitable thing with metre[x].*

Deus misereatur nostri.

2 God haue merci of vs, and blisse to vs, liȝte to his chere vpon vs; and haue mercy 3 of vs. That wee knowe in the erthe thi weie; in alle Jentilis thi helthe ȝiuere. 4 Knouleche to thee puplis, God; knouleche 5 to thee alle puplis. Gladen and ful out ioȝe Jentilis, for thou demest puplis in equite; and Jentilis in the erthe thou 6 dressist. Knouleche to thee puplis, God, 7 knouleche to thee alle puplis; the erthe ȝaf his frut. Blesse vs God, oure God, 8 blesse vs God; and drede hym alle the coostus of erthe[r].

God haue merci on vs, and blesse 2 vs; liȝtne he his cheer on vs, and haue[z] merci on vs. That we knowe thi weie on[a] 3 erthe; thin heelthe in alle folkis. God, 4 puplis knowleche to thee; alle puplis knouleche to thee. Hethen men be glad, 5 and make[b] fulli ioye, for thou demest puplis in equite; and dressist hethene men in erthe. God, puplis knouleche to thee, 6 alle puplis knouleche to thee; the erthe 7 ȝaf[c] his fruyt. God, oure God blesse vs, God blesse vs; and alle the coostis of erthe drede hym.

PSALM LXVII.

1 *In to the ende, the salm of the[a] song of Dauyd.*

PSALM LXVII.

The titil of the[d] seuene and sixtithe salm. 1 *To the[e] victorie[f], the[g] salm ʻof the song[h] ʻof Dauid[i].*

Exurgat Deus.

2 Ryse vp God, and be scaterid his enemys; and flee thei that hatiden hym 3 fro his face. As faileth smoke, faile thei, as flowith wax fro the face of fyr; so pershe the synneres fro the face of God. 4 And the riȝtwise ete thei, and ful out glade thei in the siȝte of God; and delite 5 thei in gladnesse. Syngeth to God, salm seith to his name, maketh weie[t] to hym that steȝeth vp vp on the going doun; Lord name to hym. Ful out ioȝeth in

God rise vp, and hise enemyes be 2 scaterid; and thei that haten hym fle fro his face. As smoke failith, faile thei; as 3 wax fletith fro the face of fier, so perische synneris fro the face of God. And iust 4 men eete, and make[k] fulli ioye in the siȝt of God; and delite thei in gladnesse. Synge ȝe to God, seie ȝe salm to his name; 5 make ȝe weie to hym, that stieth on the goyng doun, the Lord is name to[l] hym. Make ȝe fulli ioye in his siȝt, *enemyes*

q Om. u.   r the erthe *AEH.*   s Om. H.   t a weye *A.*

P and he i.   q ne k̇.   r Om. *plures.* took not i. took not awei. Lire here. v.   s Om. *plures.*   t Om. *ceteri prater* v.   u Om. ELP.   v Om. *plures.*   vv *song, and is profecie of Cristis incarnacion* KV.   w *Jeroms* v. Om. *ceteri.*   x Om. *ceteri prater* v.   z haue he i.   a in KLs.   b make thei i.   c hath ȝoue i.   d Om. *plures.*   e Om. *plures.*   f *victorie in orgunis* s.   g Om. h.   h *of song plures.* Om. DF.   i Om. s.   k make thei i.   l of c.

his siȝte, thei shul be disturbid fro the
6 face of hym, fader of faderles childer; and
7 domes man of widewis. God in his holi
place ; God that maketh to indwelle of o
maner in an hous. The whiche bringeth
out the bounden men in strengthe; also
hem that terren, that dwellen in sepulcris.
8 God, whan thou shuldest gon out in the
siȝte of thi puple ; whan thou shuldist
9 passe in desert. The erthe is moued, forsothe heuenus droppeden doun fro the
face of God of Synay ; fro the face of God
10 of Irael. Wilful reyn thou shalt don a-
part, God, to thi eritage, and it is feblid ;
11 thou forsothe madist it parfit. Thi bestis
shul duelle in it, God ; thou madist redy
12 in thi swetnesse to the pore. The Lord
shal ȝiuen a‖ woord ; to the euangeliseris
13 in myche vertue. The king of vertues
of the looued of the looued ; and to deuyde
14 spoilis to the fairnesse of the hous. If
ȝee slepe betwe‧ the mene sortis, ȝee
shul be the siluerne pennes of the culuer ; and the hindermor of his ryg, in
15 the palenesse of gold. Whil the heueneli
deuydeth kingis vp on it with snowȝ, thei
16 shul ben maad whit in Selmon ; the hil
of God a fat hil. The hil cruddid to-
17 gidere a fat hil ; wherto ouer trowe ȝee,
the hillis cruddid togidere ? The hil in
whiche‧ is‧ wel plesid to God to duelle
in it ; forsothe the Lord shal dwelle in to
18 the ende. The charis of God manyfold
in ten thousendys, that ben thousandus of
men gladende ; the Lord in hem, in Syna,
19 in holi. Thou steȝcdest vp in to heiȝte,
thou toke caitifte ; thou toke to ȝiftis in
men. Forsothe men not beleeuende ; to
20 dwellen in the Lord God. Blessid the
Lord fro dai to eche dai ; welsum wei shal
make to vs the God‧ of oure helthe
21 ȝiueres. Oure God the God of makinge
men saf ; and of the Lord Lord the going
22 out of deth. Neuerthelatere God shal
to-breke the hedis of his enemys ; the top
of the her of men goende in ther giltus.

schulen be disturblid fro the face of hym,
which is the fadir of fadirles and modirles 6
children ; and the iuge of widewis. God 7
is in his hooli place ; God that makith men
of o wille to dwelle in the hous. Which
leedith out bi strengthe hem that ben
boundun ; in lijk maner hem that maken
scharp, that dwellen in sepulcris. God, 8
whanne thou ȝedist out in the siȝt of thi
puple ; whanne thou passidist forth in the
desert. The erthe was moued, for heuenes 9
droppiden doun fro the face of God of
Synay ; fro the face of God of Israel. God, 10
thou schalt departe wilful reyn to thin
eritage, and it was sijk ; but thou madist
it parfit. Thi beestis schulen dwelle ther- 11
ynne ; God, thou hast maad redi in thi
swetnesse to the pore man. The Lord 12
schal ȝyue a word ; to hem that prechen
the gospel with myche vertu. The kyngis 13
of vertues *ben maad* loued of the derlyng ;
and to the fairnesse of the hous to departe
spuylis. If ȝe slepen among‧ the myddil‧ 14
of‧ *eritagis‧*, the fetheris of the culuer
ben of siluer ; and the hyndrere thingis of
the bak therof *ben* in the shynyng of
gold. While *the king of* heuene demeth 15
kyngis theronne, thei schulen be maad
whitter then snow in Selmon ; the hille 16
of God *is* a fat hille. The cruddid hil *is*
a fat hil ; wherto bileuen ȝe falsli, cruddid 17
hillis? The hil in which it plesith wel
God to dwelle ther ynne ; for the Lord
schal dwelle `in to the‧ ende. The chare 18
of God is manyfoold with ten thousynde,
a thousynde of hem that ben glad ; the
Lord was in hem, in Syna, in the hooli.
Thou stiedist an hiȝ, thou tokist caitiftee ; 19
thou resseyuedist ȝiftis among men. For
whi *thou tokist* hem that bileueden not ;
for to dwelle in the Lord God. Blessid 20
be the Lord ech dai ; the God of oure
heelthis schal make an eesie wei to vs.
Oure God *is* God to make men saaf ; and 21
outgoyng fro deeth *is* of the Lord God.
Netheles God schal breke the heedis of 22

‧ Om. *all.*　‧ betwen *e passim.* betwene *a et n passim.*　‧ the whiche *e.*　‧ it *a.*　‧ Lord *a.*

‧ in *l.*　‧ middis s. myddil peple w.　‧ among *l.*　‧ sortis *ether eritagis plures.*　‧ with outen s.

23 The Lord seide, Fro Basan I shal al turne;
I shal al turne in to the depthe of the se.
24 That inwet^z be thi foot in blood; the tunge
of thin houndis fro hym of the enemys.
25 Thei seȝen thin ingoingus, God; the in-
going of my God, my king, that is in
26 holy. The princis camen befor ioyned
with the singeris; in the myddel of the
27 ȝunge wymmen tympanystris. In chirchis
blisseth to God; to the Lord of the wellis
28 of Irael. There Beniamyn, the ȝungling;
in the exces of mynde. Princis of Juda
the dukis of hem; princis of Zabulon,
29 the princis of Neptalym. Send, God, to
thi vertue; conferme thou, God, that that
30 thou hast wroȝt in vs. Fro thi temple,
that is in Jerusalem; to thee offre shul
31 kingus ȝiftis. Blame the wilde bestis of
the reed, the gedering togidere of bolis in
the kiyn of puplis; that thei close out
hem that ben preued bi siluer. Scatere
32 thou the Jentilis that wiln batailis, ther
shul come messageris fro Egipt; Ethiope
shal befor come his hondis to God.
33 Reumes of the erthe, singeth to God;
doth salm to the Lord. Doth salm to
34 God; that steȝeth vp vpon heuene 'of
heuenc^a at the est. Lo ! he shal ȝiue to
35 his vois vois of vertue; ȝiueth glorie to
God vp on Irael; his grete doing and
36 his vertue in cloudis. Merueilous God
in his halewis, God of Irael, he shal
ȝiue vertue, and strengthe of hys puple;
blessid be God.

hise enemyes; the cop of the heere of
hem that goen in her trespassis. The 23
Lord seide, Y schal turne fro Basan; Y
schal turne in to the depthe of the see.
That thi foot be deppid in blood; the tunge 24
of thi doggis *be dippid in blood* of the
enemyes of hym. God, thei sien thi go- 25
yngis yn; the goyngis yn of my God, of
my king, which is in the hooli. Prynces 26
ioyned with syngeris camen bifore; in the
myddil^r of ȝonge dameselis syngynge in
tympans. In chirchis blesse ȝe God; *blesse* 27
ȝe the Lord fro the wellis of Israel. There 28
Beniamyn, a ȝonge man; in the rauysch-
yng of mynde. The princis of Juda *weren*
the duykis of hem; the princis of Zabulon,
the princis of Neptalym. God, comaunde 29
thou to thi vertu; God, conferme thou this
thing, which^s thou hast wrouȝt in vs.
Fro thi temple, which is in Jerusalem; 30
kyngis schulen offre ȝiftis to thee. Blame 31
thou the wielde beestis of the^t reheed, the
gaderyng togidere of bolis is among the
kien of puplis; that thei exclude hem that
ben preuyd bi siluer. Distrie thou folkis
that wolen batels, legatis schulen come fro 32
Egipt; Ethiopie schal come bifore the
hondis therof to God. Rewmes of the^u 33
erthe, synge ȝe to God; seie ȝe salm to the
Lord. Singe ȝe to God; that stiede on the 34
heuene of heuene at the eest. Lo ! he
schal ȝyue to his vois the vois of vertu,
ȝyue ȝe glorie to God on Israel; his greet 35
doyng and his vertu *is* in the cloudis.
God *is* wondirful in hise seyntis; God of 36
Israel, he schal ȝyue vertu, and strengthe
to his puple; blessid be God.

PSALM LXVIII.

1 *In to the end, for hem that shuln ben
al chaungid, to hym Dauid.*

PSALM LXVIII.

The title of the^v eiȝte and sixtithe salm. 1
'*In Ebreu thus^w, To the^x victorie, on
the^y roosis^z of Dauid.* '*In Jerom thus,
To the ouercomer, for the sones of
Dauid^a.*

2 God, mac me saf; for watris camen in
3 vnto my soule. I am inficchid in the

God, make thou me saaf; for watris 2
'entriden til to^b my soule. I am set in 3

---

^{z} inweetid *AH.* ^{a} Om. *AH.*

^{r} myddis *plures.* ^{s} that 1. ^{t} Om. *plures.* ^{u} Om. *plures.* ^{v} Om. *plures.* ^{w} Om. *ceteri præter* v. ^{x} Om. cix.
^{y} Om. i. ^{z} roues M. roosis *for sonys* v. ^{a} Om. *ceteri præter* v. ^{b} han entrid vnto t. entriden to s.

slim of the depthe; and ther is not substaunce. I cam in to the hei3te of the
4 se; and tempest drenchide me doun. I
trauailide criende, horse[b] ben maad my
chekis; myn e3en failiden, whil I hope
5 in to my God. Thei ben multeplied ouer
the heris of myn hed; that hatiden me
withoute cause. Thei ben coumfortid
that pursueden me myn enemys vnri3t-
wisly; the[c] thingis that I raueshide not,
6 thanne I pa3ide out. God, thou knowest
myn vnwisdam; and my giltis fro thee
7 ben not hid. Lord, shame thei not in
me that abiden thee, Lord[d]; Lord of
vertues. Be thei not confoundid vp on me,
8 that sechen thee; God of Irael. For I
suffride for thee repref; shenshipe co-
9 uerede my face. Straunge I am maad
to my brethern; and a pilgrim to the
10 sonus of my modir. For loone of thin
hous eet me; and repreues of men re-
11 preuende thee fallen vp on me. And I
couerede in fasting my soul; and it is
12 maad in to repref to me. And I putte
my clothing an heire; and I am maad to
13 them in to a parable. A3en me speeken
that seeten in the 3ate; and in me diden
14 salm, that drunke win. I forsothe made
myn orisoun to thee, Lord; tyme is of
thi wel plesing, God. In the multitude
of thi mercy ful out here me; in the
15 treuthe of thin helthe. Tac me out fro
clei, that I be not inficchid; deliuere me
fro hem that hatiden me, and fro the
16 depthis of watris. Drenche me not doun
the tempest of water; ne soupe me awei
the depthe, ne threste vp on me the pit
17 his mouth. Ful out here me, Lord, for
benyngne is thi merci; after the multitude of thi merci doingus behoold in me.
18 And ne turne thou awei thi face fro thi
child; for I am trublid, swiftli ful out
19 here thou me. Loke in to my soule,
and deliuere it; for myn enemys tac out
20 me. Thou knowist my repref; and my

the sliym of the depthe; and 'substaunce
is not[c]. I cam in to the depthe of the
see; and the tempest drenchide me. I 4
traueilide criynge, my cheekis weren maad
hoose[d]; myn i3en failiden, the while Y
hope[e] in to my God. Thei that hatiden 5
me with out cause; weren multiplied aboue
the heeris of myn heed. Myn enemyes
that pursueden me vniustli weren coumfortid; Y paiede thanne tho thingis,
whiche Y rauischide not. God, thou 6
knowist myn vnkunnyng; and my trespassis ben not hid fro thee. Lord, Lord 7
of vertues; thei, that abiden thee, be not
aschamed in me. God of Israel; thei, that
seken thee, be not schent on me. For 8
Y suffride schenschipe for thee; schame
hilide my face. I am maad a straunger 9
to my brithcren; and a pilgryme to the
sones of my modir. For the feruent loue 10
of thin hous eet me; and the schenschipis
of men seiynge schenschipis to thee fellen
on me. And Y hilide my soule with fast- 11
yng; and it was maad in to schenschip to
me. And Y puttide my cloth an heire; 12
and Y am maad to hem in to a parable.
Thei, that saten in the 3ate, spaken a3ens 13
me; and thei, that drunken wien, sungen
of me. But Lord, Y dresse[ee] my preier 14
to thee; God, Y abide the tyme of good
plesaunce. Here thou me[f] in the multitude of thi mercy; in the treuthe of thin
heelthe. Delyuer thou me fro the cley, 15
that Y be not faste set in; delyuere thou
me fro hem that haten me, and fro depthe[g]
of watris. The tempest of watir drenche 16
not me, nethir the depthe swolowe me;
nethir the pit make streit his mouth on
me. Lord, here thou me, for thi merci is 17
benygne; vp the multitude of thi merciful doyngis biholde thou in to me. And 18
turne not awei thi face fro[h] thi child;
for Y am in tribulacioun, here thou me
swiftli. 3yue thou tente to my soule, and 19
delyuer thou it; for myn enemyes de-

b hoos *AE* sec. m. II.   c Om. *AH*.   d Om. *CE* pr. m.

c ther is no substaunce I.   d horse CDFSI. hoorse EGILOPRUX.   e hopide I.   ee *dresside* CDW.   f Om. a.
g depnesse I. depthis FKLS.   h fro me s.

21 confusioun, and my shame. In thi si3te ben alle that trublen me ; repref abod myn herte, and wrecchidnesse. And I suffride that summan togidere shulde with sorewen, and ther was not ; and that shulde coumforten, and I fond not. 22 And thei 3euen in to my mete galle ; and in my thrist thei drunke me with eisel. 23 Be mad the bord of hem in to a grene befor them ; and in to 3eldingus a3een, 24 and in to sclaunder. Be al to-dercned the e3en of hem, that thei see not ; and the rig of hem euermor crooke thou in. 25 Heeld out vp on hem thi wrathe ; and the 26 wodnesse of thi wrathe al take them. Be maad the dwelling of hem desert ; and in the tabernaclis of hem be ther not that 27 indwelle. For whom thou hast smyten, thei han pursued ; and vp on the sorewe 28 of my woundis thei addeden. Put to wickidnesse vp on the wickidnesse[e] of hem ; and entre thei not in to thi ri3twis- 29 nesse. Be thei do awei fro the boc of lyueres ; and with ri3twis men be thei not 30 write. I am a pore man, and sorewende ; 31 thin helthe, God, vndertoc me. I shal preise the name of God with song ; and 32 magnefien hym in preising. And he shal plese to God vp on a newe calf ; hornes 33 bringende forth, and cles. See the pore, and glade thei ; secheth God, and 3oure 34 soule shal liue. For the Lord ful out herde the pore ; and despiside not hise 35 bounden. Preise hym, heuenes and erthe ; the se, and alle crepende thingis in it. 36 For God shal make saf Sion ; and the cites of Jude shul be bild vp. And thei shuln induelle there ; and bi eritage thei 37 shul purchasen it. And the sed of his seruauns shal welden it ; and that loouen his name, shul duelle in it.

lyuere thou me. Thou knowist my 20 schenschip, and my dispysyng ; and my schame. Alle that troblen me ben in thi 21 si3t ; myn herte abood schendschipe, and wretchidnesse. And Y abood hym, that was sory togidere, and noon was[i] ; and that schulde coumforte[k], and Y foond not. And thei 3auen galle in to my meete ; and 22 in my thirst thei 3auen 'to me[l] drinke with vynegre. The boord of hem be maad bi- 23 fore hem in to a snare ; and in to 3eld- yngis, and in'to sclaundir. Her i3en be 24 maad derk, that thei se not ; and euere bouwe doun the bak of hem. Schede out 25 thin ire on hem ; and the strong veniaunce of thin ire take hem. The habitacioun of 26 hem be maad forsakun ; and 'noon be[m] that dwelle in the tabernaclis of hem. For thei 27 pursueden hym[n], whom thou hast smyte[n] ; and thei addiden[o] on the sorewe of my woundis. Adde thou wickidnesse on the 28 wickidnesse of hem ; and entre thei not in to thi ri3twisnesse[p]. Be thei don awei fro 29 the book of lyuynge men ; and be thei not writun with iust men. I am pore and 30 sorewful ; God, thin heelthe took me vp. I schal herye the name of God with song ; 31 and Y schal magnefye hym in[q] heriyng. And it schal plese God more than a newe 32 calf ; bryngynge forth hornes and clees. Pore men se, and be[r] glad ; seke 3e God, 33 and 3oure soule schal lyue. For the Lord 34 herde pore men ; and[s] dispiside not hise boundun men. Heuenes and erthe, herye[t] 35 hym ; the se, and alle crepynge bestis in[v] tho, herye hym. For God schal make 36 saaf Syon ; and the citees of Juda schulen be bildid. And thei schulen dwelle there ; and thei schulen gete it bi eritage. And 37 the seed of hise seruauntis schal haue it in possessioun ; and thei that louen his name, schulen dwelle ther ynne.

---

[e] wickenessis E. wickidnessis AH.

[i] ther was 1.   [k] coumforte *me* K.   [l] me to s.   [m] be ther noon 1.   [n] hem s.   [o] addiden to 1.   [p] ri3tfulnesse *ceteri*.   [q] with 1.   [r] be thei 1.   [s] and he 1.   [t] herie 3e s.   [v] in erthe s.

PSALM LXIX.

Deus, in adiu-
torium meum.

1 *In to the ende, the salm of Dauid, in*
remembring that the Lord made hym
saf.

2 God, in to myn helpe tac heed; Lord,
3 to helpen me heeʒe thou. Be thei confoundid, and shameli drede thei; that
4 sechen my soule. Be thei turned awei[f]
hindward, and waxe thei ashamed; that
wiln to me euelis. Be thei turned awei
anoon and shamende; that seyn to me,
5 Weu! weu! Ful out ioʒe thei, and glad
in thee, alle that sechen thee; and sey thei
euermor, The Lord be magnefied, that
6 loouen thi ʒiuere of helthe. I forsothe
a nedi and a pore man am; God, helpe
thou me. Myn helpere and my deliuerere, be thou; Lord, ne tarie thou.

PSALM LXX.

In te, Domine,
speraui.

1 *The salm of Dauid is of the sonys of*
Jonadab, and of the rathere caitiues.

In thee, Lord, I hopide; I shal not be
2 confoundid in to with oute ende; in thi
riʒtwisnesse deliuere me, and tac me awei.
Bowe thou in to me thin ere; and saue
3 me. Be thou to me in to God defendere,
and in to a strengthid place; that thou
make me saaf. For my fastnesse; and my
4 refute thou art. My God, tac me awey fro
the hond of the synnere; and fro the hond
of the doere aʒen the lawe, and of the wicke.
5 For thou art my pacience, Lord; Lord,
myn hope fro my ʒouthe. In thee I am
6 confermed fro the wombe; fro the wombe
7 of my moder thou art my defendere. In
thee my synging enermor; as wndring I
am maad to manye; and thou a strong
8 helpere. Be fulfild my mouth with preising, that I synge thi glorie; al dai thi
9 gretnesse. Ne throwe thou me aferr in

PSALM LXIX.

† A gios. Da-
uith made this
salm, whanne
he was in the
persecucioun of
Absolon, his
sone. Lire here,
c et abi.

1 *The titil of the[w] nyne and sixtithe salm.*
To the[x] victorie 'of Dauid[y], 'to haue
mynde[z]†.

2 God, biholde thou in to myn heelp;
Lord, hast thou to helpe me. Be thei
3 schent, and aschamed; that seken my lijf.
Be thei turned a bak; and schame thei,
that wolen yuels to me. Be thei turned
4 awei anoon, and schame thei; that seien
5 to me, Wel! wel! Alle men that seken
thee, make[a] fulli ioie, and be glad in thee;
and thei that louen thin heelthe, seie[b]
6 euere, The Lord be magnyfied. Forsothe
Y am a nedi man, and pore; God, helpe
thou me. Thou art myn helper and my
delyuerere[c]; Lord, tarye thou not.

PSALM LXX.

1 *The seuentithe salm hath no title[d].*

Lord, Y hopide in thee, be Y not schent
with outen ende; in thi riʒtwisnesse[f]
2 delyuere thou me, and rauysche me[g] out.
Bowe doun thin eere to me; and make
3 me saaf. Be thou to me in to God a defendere; and in to a strengthid place, that
thou make me saaf. For thou art my
stidefastnesse; and my refuit. My God,
4 delyuere thou me fro the hoond of the
synner; and fro the hoond of a man
doynge aʒens the lawe, and of the[h] wickid
5 man. For thou, Lord, art my pacience;
Lord, *thou art* myn hope fro my ʒongthe.
In thee Y am confermyd[i] fro the wombe;
6 thou art my defendere fro the wombe of
my modir. My syngyng *is* euere in thee;
7 Y am maad as a greet wonder to many
men; and thou *art* a strong helpere. My
8 mouth be fillid with heriyng; that Y synge

f Om. c.

w Om. *plures.* x Om. DWX. y Om. R. z Om. S. *to haue mynde on Dauith* o. a make thei I.
b seie thei K. c defendere S. d From KO. *The lxx. salm. plures. The titil of the lxx. salm.* A. *The*
lxx. salm of Dauid, whanne he was in persecucioun of Absolon, his sone. R. *The lxx. salm hath no tytle in*
Ebrew, nether in Jeroms translacioun. V. f riʒtfulnesse PQIRL. g Om. F. h the hond of the s.
i confermyd, *that is, defendid* K *text.* confermyd, *that is, not halewid but defendid* V *marg.*

time of elde ; whan shal faile my vertue,
10 ne forsake thou me. For myn enemys
seiden to me ; and thei that kepten my
11 soule counseil maden in to oon. Seiende,
God hath forsaken hym, pursueth, and
taketh hym ; for ther is not that take
12 awey. God, ne be thou longid awei fro
me ; my God, in to myn helpe behold.
13 Be thei confoundid, and faile thei, bacbitende to my soule ; be thei couered
with confusioun and shame, that sechen
14 euelis to me. I forsothe euermor shal
hopen ; and casten to vp on alle thi
15 preisiug. My mouth shal befor telle thi
riȝtwisnesse ; al dai thin helthe ȝiuere.
For I knew not lettrure, I shal gon in
16 to the poweris of the Lord ; Lord, I shal
17 han mynde of thi riȝtwisnesse alone. God,
thou hast taȝt me fro my ȝouthe, and vn
to now ; I shal telle forth thi meruellis.
18 And vn to the laste age, and the laste
ende of it ; God, ne forsake thou me. To
the time that I telle out thin arm ; to alle
ieneracioun that is to come. Thi power,
19 and thi riȝtwisnesse, God, vn to the heȝeste grete thingus that thou didist ;
20 God, who is lie to thee ? Hou grete thou
hast shewid to me tribulaciouns, manye
and euele, and al turned thou hast quykened me ; and fro the depnessis of the
21 erthe eft thou hast aȝeen broȝte me. Thou
hast multiplied thi grete doing ; and al
22 turned thou hast coumfortid me. For
and I shal knouleche to thee in vesselis
of salm thi treuthe, God ; I shal do salm
to thee in an harpe, thou holi of Irael.
23 Ful out shul ioȝe my lippis, whan I shal
synge to thee ; and my soule, that thou
24 aȝeen boȝtist. But and my tunge al dai
shal sweteli thenke thi riȝtwisnesse ; whan
confoundid and shamefastly aferd shul
ben that sechen euelis to me.

thi glorie, al dai thi greetnesse. Caste 9
thou not awei me in the[k] tyme of eldnesse[l] ; whanne my vertu failith, forsake
thou not me. For myn enemyes seiden of 10
me ; and thei that kepten my lijf maden
counsel togidere. Seiynge, God hath for-11
sake hym ; pursue ȝe, and take hym ; for
noon is[m] that schal delyuere. God, be 12
thou not maad afer fro me ; my God,
biholde thou in to myn help. Men that 13
bacbiten my soule, be schent, and faile
thei ; and be thei hilid with schenschip
and schame, that seken yuels to me. But 14
Y schal hope euere ; and Y schal adde[n]
euere ouer al thi preising. Mi mouth 15
schal telle thi riȝtfulnesse ; al dai thin
helthe. For Y knewe not lettrure[o], Y schal
entre in to the poweres of the Lord ; Lord, 16
Y schal bithenke on thi riȝtfulnesse aloone.
God, thou hast tauȝt me fro my ȝongthe, 17
and 'til to[p] now ; Y schal telle out thi
merneilis. And til in to 'the eldnesse[q] 18
and the laste age ; God, forsake thou not
me. Til Y telle thin arm[r] ; to eche generacioun, that schal come. *Til Y telle* thi
myȝt, and thi riȝtfulnesse, God, til in to 19
the hiȝeste grete dedis which[s] thou hast
do ; God, who is lijk thee ? Hou grete 20
tribulaciouns many and yuele hast thou
schewid to me ; and thou conuertid hast
quykenyd me, and hast eft brouȝt me aȝen
fro the depthis[t] of erthe. Thou hast mul-21
tiplied thi greet doyng ; and thou conuertid
hast coumfortid me. For whi and Y schal 22
knowleche to thee, thou God, thi treuthe
in the instrumentis of salm ; Y schal synge
in an harpe to thee, *that art* the hooli of
Israel. Mi lippis schulen make fulli ioye, 23
whanne Y schal synge to thee ; and my
soule, which thou aȝen bouȝtist. But and 24
my tunge schal thenke al dai on thi riȝtfulnesse ; whanne thei schulen be schent
and aschamed, that seken ynelis to me.

---

[k] Om. s.   [l] eelde i. ooldnesse k.   [m] ther is i.   [n] adde to i.   [o] lettrure, *that is, not bi mannes techyng, but bi Goddis reuelacion* k *text.* v *marg.*   [p] unto i.   [q] eelde i. ooldnesse k.   [r] arm *or power* i.   [s] that i.   [t] depnesse i.

PSALM LXXI.

In to Salomon.

1

Deus, iudi-
cium.

2 God, thi dom ȝif to the king; and thi
riȝtwysnesse to the sone of the king. To
demen thi puple[g] in riȝtwisnesse; and thi
3 pore men in dom. Vndertake mounteynes
pes to the puple; and the hillis riȝtwis-
4 nesse. He shal deme the pore men of
the puple; and saf he shal make the sonus
of pore men; and he shal meke the false
5 acusere. And he shal abide stille with
the sunne, and befor the mone; in ienera-
6 cioun and in to ieneracioun. He shal
come doun as reyn in to flees; and as
7 drope falling droppende vp on erthe[h]. In
his daȝis shal springe riȝtwisnesse, and
aboundaunce of pes; to the time that the
8 mone be don awei. And he shal lordshipen fro the se vn to the se; and fro
the flod vnto the termes of the round-
9 nesse of londis. Beforn hym shul falle
doun Ethiopis; and his enemys the erthe
10 shul licken. The kingis of Tharsis and
ylis shuln offre deserued ȝiftys; the kingus
of Arabs and Saba free ȝiftis shul bringe
11 to. And ther shuln honouren hym alle
kingus; alle Jentilis shul serue to hym.
12 For he shal deliuere the pore fro the
myȝti; and the pore to whom was not
13 an helpere. He shal spare to the pore,
and to the helpeles; and the soulis of
14 pore men he shal make saaf. Fro vsuris
and wickidnesse he shal aȝeen bie the
soulis of hem; and wrshipeful the name
15 of hem beforn hym. And he shal lyue,
and ther shal be ȝiue to hym of the[i] gold
of Arabie; and thei shul honouren of it,
16 al day thei shul blisse to hym. Ther shal
be fastnyng in the erthe, in the heȝest
thingis of mounteynes; ther[k] shal ben
aboue hauncyd aboue Liban his fruyt;

PSALM LXXI.

The title of the[u] oon and seuentithe salm[v]. 1
'To Salomon[w].

God, ȝyue[x] thi doom to the king; and 2
thi riȝtfulnesse to the sone of a king. To
deme thi puple in riȝtfulnesse; and thi
pore men in doom. Mounteyns resseyue 3
pees to the puple; and litle hillis resseyue
riȝtfulnesse. He schal deme the pore men 4
of the puple, and he schal make saaf the
sones of pore men; and he schal make low
the false chalengere. And he schal dwelle 5
with the sunne, and bifore the moone[y]; in
generacioun and in to generacioun. He 6
schal come doun as reyn in to a flees; and
as goteris droppinge on the erthe. Riȝt- 7
fulnesse schal come forth in hise dayes,
and the aboundaunce of pees[z]; til the moone
be takun awei. And he schal be lord fro 8
the see 'til to[a] the see; and fro the flood
til to the endis of the world. Ethiopiens 9
schulen falle doun bifore hym; and hise
enemyes[a] schulen licke the erthe. The 10
kyngis of Tarsis and ilis schulen offre
ȝiftis; the kyngis of Arabie and of Saba
schulen brynge ȝiftis. And alle kyngis 11
schulen worschipe hym; alle folkis schulen
serue hym. For he schal delyuer a pore 12
man fro the miȝti; and a pore man to
whom was[b] noon helpere. He schal spare 13
a pore man and nedi; and he schal make
saaf the soulis of pore men. He schal 14
aȝen the soulis of hem fro vsuris, and[c]
wickidnesse; and the name of hem is
onourable bifor hym. And he schal lyue, 15
and me schal ȝyue to hym of the gold of
Arabie; and thei schulen euere worschipe
of hym, al dai thei schulen blesse hym.
Stidefastnesse schal be in the erthe, in the 16
hiȝeste places[d] of mounteyns; the fruyt
therof schal be enhaunsid aboue the Liban;
and thei schulen blosme fro the citee, as

g puplis A.   b the erthe AEII.   i Om. A.   k thei A.

u Om. plures.   v Om. G.   w To Salomon, profecie of Crist, verrei king K. In Ebreu thus, To
Salamon; in Jerom thus, In to Salamon. U.   x ȝyue thou I.   y moone, that is, withoute bigynnyng
and eende KV.   z pees, that is, gostli pees K text V marg.   a unto I.   b ther was I.   c and fro I.
d place CKKLMPS.

and thei shul floure fro cite, as the hei of
17 erthe[l]. Be his name blissid in to worldis;
beforn the sunne abit stille his name.
And ther shul be blissid in hym alle the
linagis of erthe[m]; alle Jentilis shul mag-
18 nefien hym. Blissid be the Lord God of
Irael; that doth merueilous thingus alone.
19 And blissid be the name of his maieste
in to withoute ende; and ther shal be
fulfild with his maieste al erthe; be it
do, be it do.

20 *Ther faileden preisingis, or ympnes
of Dauid, sone[n] of Jesse.*

PSALM LXXII.

1 *The salm of Asaf.*

bonus.   Hou good the God of Irael; to hem
2 that ben in[o] rizt herte. My feet forsothe ben almost moued; almost ben held
3 doun[p] my goingis. For I enuyede vp on
wicke men; seande the pes of synneres.
4 For ther is not respit to the deth of hem;
5 and fastnyng in the wounde of hem. In
the trauaile of men thei ben not; and
with men thei shul not be scourgid.
6 Therfore heeld hem pride; thei ben couered with wickidnesse, and with ther
7 vnpitousnesse. Wente forth as of talz the
wickidnesse of hem; thei ouerpassiden in
8 to lust of herte. Thei thozten and speeke
shreudenesse; wickidnesse in heizte they
9 speeken. Thei putten[q] in to heuene ther
mouth; and the tunge of hem wente in[r]
10 the erthe. Therfore shal ben conuertid
my puple heer; and fulle dazis shul be
11 founden in hem. And thei selden, Hou
wot God; and whether is ther kunyng
12 in heizte? Lo! tho synneres, and[s] abun-
dende in the world; weldeden richessis.
13 And I seide, Thanne with oute eause I
iustefiede myn herte; and wesh among in-
14 nocentis myn hondis. And I was scourgid
al dai; and my chastising in the moru-

the hey of erthe doith. His name be 17
blessid in to worldis; his name dwelle[e]
bifore the sunne. And all the lynagis
of erthe schulen be blessid in hym; alle
folkis schulen magnyfie hym. Blessid be 18
the Lord God of Israel; which aloone
makith merueiylis. Blessid[f] be the name 19
of his maieste with outen ende; and al
erthe schal be fillid with[g] his maieste;
be it doon, be it doon.

'*The preieris of Dauid, the[h] sone of 20
Ysay, ben endid[i].*

PSALM LXXII.

The 'title of the[k] two and seuentithe salm. 1
'*The salm of Asaph[l]†.*

God of Israel is ful good; to hem that
ben of riztful herte. But my feet weren 2
moued almeest; my steppis weren sched
out almeest. For Y louede feruentli on 3
wickid men; seynge the pees of synneris.
For biholdyng is not to the deth of hem; 4
and stidefastnesse in the sikenesse of hem.
Thei ben not in the[m] trauel of men; and 5
thei schulen not be betun with men. Ther- 6
fore pride helde[n] hem; thei weren hilid
with her wickidnesse and[o] vnfeithfulnesse.
The wickidnesse of hem cam forth as of[p] 7
fatnesse; thei zeden in to desire of herte.
Thei thouzten and spaken weiwardnesse; 8
thei spaken wickidnesse[q] an hiz. Thei 9
puttiden her mouth in to heuene; and her
tunge passide in erthe. Therfor my puple 10
schal be conuertid here; and fulle daies
schulen be foundun in hem. And thei 11
seiden, How woot God; and whether
kunnyng is an heize, '*that is, in heuene*'?
Lo! thilke synneris and hauynge aboun- 12
dance in the world; helden richessis. And 13
Y seide, Therfor without cause Y iustifiede
myn herte; and[s] waischide myn hoondis
among innocentis. And Y was betun al 14
dai; and my chastisyng[t] *was* in morutidis.

† *A plas.* Asaph made this salm, to schewe the goodnesse of Goddis puruysunce. A *et alii.*

---

[l] the erthe AEU.   [m] the erthe AU.   [n] *the sone* A.   [o] of A.   [p] out A.   [q] puttiden AU.   [r] in to A.   [s] in A.

[e] dwellith A.   [f] And blessid CIKUVX *see. m.*   [g] of I.   [h] Om. PW.   [i] fillid HIKLMOPRUVWXbik. 'i Om. GQ.
[k] Om. A.   [l] Om. A. *The salm of Asaph; in Jerome thus, the song of Asaph.* IU.   [m] Om. I.   [n] hath holde I.
[o] and with I.   [p] Om. XI.   [q] wickidnesse, *that is, blasfemye ozens God* K *text.* blasfemyng ozens God
V *marg.*   [r] Om. *plures.*   [s] and I I.   [t] chastisyngis S.

15 tidis. If I seide, I shal telle thus; lo!
the nacioun^t of thi sones I haue repreued.
16 I eymede, that I shulde knowe that; tra-
17 uaile is befor me. To the tyme that I
entre in to the seyntuarie of God; and
vnderstonde in the laste thingus of hem.
18 Neuerthelatere for trecheries thou leidist
to hem; thou threwe hem doun, whil thei
19 weren rerid^u vp. What maner be thei
maad in to desolacioun; feerli thei faileden,
20 thei pershiden for ther wickidnesse. As
a sweuene of risende men; Lord, in thi
cite the ymage of hem to no3t thou shalt
21 bringe. For enflaumed is myn herte, and
22 my reenys ben al chaungid; and I to
23 no3t am bro3t, and I wiste not. As a
beeste I am maad anent thee; and I euer-
24 mor with thee. Thou heelde my ri3t
hond, and in thi wil thou bro3tist me
thennys; and with glorie thou vndertoke
25 me. What forsothe is to me in heuene;
and of thee what wolde I vp on erthe?
26 My flesh failide, and myn herte; God of
myn herte, and my part, God in to with-
27 oute ende. For loo! that longen hemself awei fro thee shul pershen; thou
lostist alle that don fornycacioun fro thee.
28 To me forsothe to cleue to God is good;
to^v putten in the Lord God myn hope.
That I telle out alle thi prechingus; in the
3atis of the do3ter of Sion.

PSALM LXXIII.

1 *The vnderstonding of Asaf.*

Vt quid, Deus. Wherto, God, hast thou put abac in to
the ende; thi wodnesse wrathide vpon the
2 shep of thi leswe? Myndeful be thou of
thi congregacioun; that thou weldedest
fro the begynnyng. Thou hast a3ene bo3t
the 3erde of thin eritage; the hil of Sion
3 in whiche thou dwellidist in^w it. Rere
vp thin hondis in to the pridis of hem in
to the ende; hou grete thingis wariede

If Y seide, Y schal telle thus; lo! Y re-15
preuede the nacioun of thi sones. I gess-16
ide, that Y schulde knowe this; trauel is
bifore me. Til Y entre in to the seyn-17
tuarie of God; and vndurstonde in the last
thingis of hem. Netheles for gilis thou 18
hast put to hem; thou castidist hem doun,
while thei weren reisid. Hou ben thei 19
maad into desolacioun^u; thei failiden sodeynli, thei perischiden for her wickid-
nesse^v. As the dreem of men that risen; 20
Lord, thou schalt dryue^w her ymage to
nou3t in thi citee. For myn herte is en-21
flaumed, and my reynes ben chaungid; and 22
Y am dryuun to nou3t, and Y wiste not.
As a werk beeste Y am maad at^x thee; and 23
Y am euere with thee. Thou heldist my 24
ri3thond, and in thi wille thou leddist me
forth; and with glorie thou tokist me vp.
For whi what is to me in heuene; and 25
what wolde Y of thee on erthe? Mi 26
fleische and myn herte failide; God of
myn herte, and my part *is* God withouten
ende. For lo! thei that drawen awei fer 27
hem silf fro thee, '*bi*^y *deedli*^z *synne*^a, schulen perische; thou hast lost alle men that
doen fornycacioun fro thee. But it is good 28
to me to cleue to God; and to sette myn
hope in the Lord God. That Y telle alle
thi prechyngis^b; in the 3atis of the dou3ter
of ^c Syon.

PSALM LXXIII.

The title of the^d thre and seuentithe salm. 1
The lernyng of Asaph^e.

God, whi hast thou put awei in to the
ende; thi strong veniaunce is wrooth on
the scheep of thi leesewe? Be thou 2
myndeful of thi gadering togidere; which
thou haddist in possessioun fro the bigynnyng. Thou a3enbou3tist the 3erde of thin
eritage; the hille of Syon in which thou
dwellidist ther ynne. Reise thin hondis 3
in to the prides of hem^f; hou grete thingis

---

t naciouns *AM.* u arered *EM.* v and *A sec. m.* w is in *c.*

a desolacioun, *ether discoumfort* c *et plures.* v weiwardnesse A. w al to-dryue I. x anentis I. y *that*
is, bi v. z *wilful* I. a *synne. Lire here.* u *marg.* 'a Om. CDEFGHIKLNOFQRSWXbi. b preisyngis I.
c Om. NX pr. m. i. d Om. *plures.* e *Asaph, of the caitifte of Babilon.* K. f hem into the ende x *sec. m.*

5 L 2

4 the enemy in the holi. And thei glo-
rieden that hateden thee; in the myddel
5 of thi solempnete. Thei putten^x ther
tocnes, tocnes; and thei knewe not as in
6 the going out vpon the he3ist. As in a
woode of trees with axis thei heewen
doun the 3atis of it in to itself; in axis
7 and hachet thei threwen it doun. Thei
brenden vp with fyr thi seintuarie; in
the erthe thei defouleden the tabernacle
8 of thi name. Thei seiden in ther herte,
the kinrede of hem togidere; To resten
make wee alle the feste da3is of God fro
9 the erthe. Oure signes wee han not seen,
now ther is not a profete; and he shal
10 knowen vs no more. Hou longe, God,
the enemye shal repreue? the aduersarie
vnlefulli taketh thi name in to the ende.
11 Wherto turnest thou awei thin hond, and
thi ri3thond fro thi myddel bosum in to
12 the ende? God forsothe oure king befor
worldis; wro3te helthe in the myddes of
13 erthe^y. Thou hast confermed in thi vertu
these; thou al to-trublidist the hedis of
14 dragounys^z in watris. Thou hast to-
broke the hedis of the dragoun; thou
hast 3iuen hym mete to the puplis of
15 Ethiope. Thou hast wastid the wellis,
and the stremes; thou hast dried the
16 flodis of Etham. Thin is the dai, and
thin is the ny3t; thou forgedist the
17 morutyd and the sunne. Thou madest
alle the termes of erthe^a; somer and ver
18 time, thou formedist hem. Myndeful be
thou of this, the enemy putte reprcf to
the Lord; and the vnwise puple terrede
19 thi name. Ne take thou to bestis soulis
knoulechende to thee; and the soulis of
thi pore men ne for3ete thou, in to the
20 ende. Behold in to thi testament; for
thei ben fulfild, that ben derened of erthe;
21 bi the housis of wickidnessis. Ne be
turned awei the meke maad confundid;
the pore and the helpelis shul prcise thi

the enemy dide wickidli in the hooli. And 4
thei that hatiden thee; hadden glorie in
the myddis of thi solempnete. Thei set-5
tiden her signes^g, 'ethir baneris', signes^k
on the hi3este, as in the outgoing; and
thei knewen not. As in a wode of trees 6
thei heweden doun with axis the 3atis
therof in to it silf; thei castiden doun it
with an ax, and a^m brood fallinge ax.
Thei brenten with fier thi seyntuarie; thei 7
defouliden the tabernacle of thi name in
erthe. The kynrede of hem seiden togidere 8
in her herte; Make we alle the feest daies
of God to cecsse fro^n the^o erthe. We han 9
not seyn oure signes, now 'no profete is^p;
and he schal no more knowe vs. God, hou 10
long schal the enemye seie dispit? the^q
aduersarie territh to ire thi name in to
the ende. Whi turnest thou awei thin 11
hoond, and^r 'to drawe out^s thi ri3thond
fro the myddis of thi bosum, til in^t to the
ende? Forsothe God oure kyng bifore 12
worldis; wrou3te heelthe in the mydis of
erthe. Thou madist sad the see bi^u thi 13
vertu; thou hast troblid^v the heedis of
dragouns^w in watris. Thou hast broke 14
the heedis of 'the dragoun^x; thou hast
3oue hym to^y mete to the puplis of E-
thiopiens. Thou hast broke wellis, and 15
strondis; thou madist drie the flodis of
Ethan. The dai is thin, and the ni3t is 16
thin; thou madist the morcutid and the
sunne. Thou madist alle the endis of 17
erthe^z; somer and veer tyme^a, thou fourm-
edist tho. Be thou myndeful of this thing, 18
the enemye hath seid schenschip to the
Lord; and the vnwijs puple hath excitid
to ire thi name. Bitake thou not to beestis 19
men knoulechenge to thee; and for3ete thou
not in to the ende the soulis of thi pore
men. Biholde in to thi testament; for thei 20
that ben maad derk of erthe, ben fillid
with the housis of wickidnessis. A meke 21
man be not turned awei maad aschamed;

---

x puttiden AH.   y the erthe E.   z dragoun A.   a the erthe AEH.

g baners x.   l Om. vx.   k to be signes I.   m with a I.   n in s.   o Om. plures.   p ther is
no profete I.   q thin A.   r Om. I.   s Om. v.   t Om. K.   u in I.   v troublid togidere K.
w the dragouns FL.   x dragons K.   y to be I. Om. K.   z the erthe K.   a tyme, either springinge
tyme I sec. in.

22 name. Rys vp, God, deme thou thi
cause, myndeful be thou of thi repreues
of hem; that of the vnwise man ben al
23 day. Ne forȝete thou the voisis of thin
enemys; the pride of hem that hateden
thee, steȝeth vp euermor.

a pore man and nedi schulen herie thi
name. God, rise vp, deme thou thi cause; 22
be thou myndeful of thin vpbreidyngis[b], of
tho that ben al dai of the vnwise man.
Forȝete thou not the voices of thin ene- 23
myes; the pride of hem that haten thee,
stieth euere.

PSALM LXXIV.

1 *In to the ende, the salm of the song of
Asaf, ne destroȝe thou, or shend.*

2 Wee shul knouleche to thee, God, we
shul knouleche; and inwardli wee shul
3 clepe thi name. Wee shul telle thi merueilis, whan I shal take tyme; I riȝtwis-
4 nessis shal deme. Molten is the erthe,
and alle that dwellen in it; I confermede
5 the pileeris of it. I seide to the wicke[b]
men, Wileth not wickidli don; and to
the gilteris, Ne wileth not reren[c] vp the
6 horn. Wileth not reren up in to heiȝte
ȝoure horn; wileth not speken aȝen God
7 wickidnesse. For nouther fro the est,
8 ne fro the west, ne fro[d] desert hillis; for
9 God is the domysman. This he mekith,
and this he enhaunceth; for the chalis
in the hond of the Lord of cler wyn, ful
of mengd. And he bowide[e] in of that
in to that; nerthelatere the dreste[f] of
it is not wastid out, ther shul drinke of
10 it alle the synneres of erthe[g]. I forsothe
shal telle out in to the world; I shal
11 synge to God of Jacob. And alle the
hornes of synneres I shal to-breke; and
the[h] hornes of the riȝtwis shul ben enhauncid.

PSALM LXXIV.

1 *The title of the[e] foure and seuentithe
salm. 'To the ouercomere; leese thou
not the salm of the song of Asaph[d].*

2 God, we schulen[e] knouleche to thee, 'we
schulen knouleche[f]; and[g] we schulen in-
3 wardli clepe thi name. We schulen telle
thi meruelis; whanne Y schal take tyme,
4 Y schal deme riȝtfulnesses. The erthe is
meltid, and alle that duellen ther ynne; Y
5 confermede the pileris therof. I seide to
wickid men, Nyle ȝe do wickidli; and to
trespassouris, Nyle ȝe enhaunce the horn.
6 Nyle ȝe reise an hiȝ ȝoure horn; nyle ȝe
speke wickidnesse aȝens God. For nether 7
fro the eest, nethir fro the west, nethir
8 fro desert hillis; for God is the iuge. He 9
mekith this[h] man, and enhaunsith hym;
for a cuppe of cleene wyn ful of meddling
is in the hoond of the Lord. And he bowide of this in to that; netheles the drast
therof is not anyntischid[i]; alle synneris
10 of erthe schulen drinke therof. Forsothe
Y schal telle in to the world; Y schal
synge to God of Jacob. And Y schal breke 11
alle the hornes of synneris; and the hornes
of the iust man schulen be enhaunsid.

PSALM LXXV.

1 *In to the ende, in ditees, the song to the[i]
Assiries, the salm of Asaf.*

2 Knowen is God in Jewerie; in Irael
3 gret is his name. And maad is in pes his
4 place; and his duelling in Sion. There

PSALM LXXV.

1 *The title of the[k] fyue and seuentithe salm.
To the[l] victorie in orguns, 'the salm
of[m] the[n] song of Asaph[o]†.*

2 God is knowun in Judee; his name is
3 greet in Israel. And his place is maad in
4 pees; and his dwellyng *is* in Syon. Ther

† *Agios.* Asaph
bi the spirit
of prophecie
made this salme
of the comyng
of the caitifte
of Babilone, and
of the ending
ther of. *Lire
here.* K.

b wickid II.   c areren EH.   d Om. A.   e bowith AII.   f drestis AEH.   g the erthe E.   h Om. A.
i Om. A.

b schenschipis, *ether vpbreidyngis* c *et plures.* shenshipis v.   c Om. CDFGHOQBI.   d Om. A.   e Om. D.
f Om. D.   g Om. C.   h his A.   i anyntishid, *either maad lesse* I *acc. m.*   k Om. *plures.*   l Om. K.
m Om. osxi.   n Om. K.   o *Asaph, bifor seynge the turment of Juda to come bi Sennacherib.* K.

he al to-brac poweris; bowe, sheld, swerd,
5 and bataile. Thou art listende merueilously fro the euere lastende mounteynes;
6 alle the vnwise men ben disturbid in herte.
Thei sleepen^k ther slep aslep, and no
thing founden; alle the men of richessis
7 in ther hondis. Fro thi blamyng, God
of Jacob; nappeden that stieseden vp
8 horsis^l. Ferful thou art, and who shal
withstonde to thee? fro thanne thi
9 wrathe. Fro heuene herd thou hast
maad dom; the erthe tremblide, and
10 restide. Whan God shulde rise vp^m 'in
to^n dom; that he make snaf alle^o the de-
11 bonere of erthe^p. For the thenking of a
man shal knouleche to thee; and the relikis of a^q thenking a feste dai shul do
12 to thee. Vouwith, and seldeth to the Lord
soure God; alle see that in his ennyroun
13 bringen to siftis. To the ferful, and to
hym that doth awey the spirit of princis;
to the ferful anent alle kingus^r of erthe^s.

PSALM LXXVI.

1 *In to the ende, for Iditym, the salm*
to^t Asaf.

Voce mea ad Dominum.

2 In my vois to the Lord I criede, in my
vois to God; and he tooc heede to me.
3 In the dai off my tribulacioun God I softe
out with myn hondis; the nyst forn asen
hym, and I am not deseyued. My soule
4 forsoc to be coumfortid; myndeful I was
of God, and dilitide, and am enhauntid^u,
5 and my spirit failide. Myn esen looke
'to forn^v wakingus; I am disturbid^w, and
6 I spac not. I thoste olde dasis; and euere
7 lastende seeris in mynde I hadde. And
I sweteli thoste in the nyst with myn
herte; and I was enhauntid^x, and 'I
8 swepte^y my spirit. Whether in to withoute ende God shal throwe aferr; or he
shall not lei to, that he be more plesid
9 sit? Or in to the ende his mercy he shal

he brak poweris; bowe, scheeld, swerd,
and batel. And thou, *God*, listnest won-
5 dirfuli fro euerlastynge hillis; alle vnwise
6 men of herte weren troblid. Thei slepten
her sleep^p; and alle men founden no thing
of richessis in her hondis. Thei that sti-
7 eden on horsis; slepten for thi blamyng,
thou God of Jacob. Thou art feerful^q, and
8 who schal asenstonde thee? fro that tyme
thin ire. Fro heuene thou madist doom
9 herd; the erthe tremblide, and restide.
Whanne God roos vp in to doom; to make
10 saaf al the^r mylde men of erthe. For the
11 thoust of man schal knouleche to thee; and
the relifs^s of thoust schulen make a feeste
dai to thee. Make se a vow, and selde se
12 to soure Lord God; alle that bringen siftis
in the cumpas of it. To God ferdful, and
13 to him that takith awei the spirit of
prynces; to the ferdful at the kyngis of
erthe.

PSALM LXXVI.

The 'title of the^t sixte and seuentithe
1 *salm^u. 'To the ouercomere^v on Ydi-*
tum, 'the salm of Asaph^{vv}†.

With^w my vois Y criede to the Lord;
2 with^x my vois to God, and he saf tent to
me. In the dai of my tribulacioun Y souste
3 God with myn hondis; in the nyst 'to fore^y
hym, and Y am not disscyued. Mi soule
4 forsook to be coumfortid; Y was myndeful
of God, and Y delitide, and Y was exercisid; and my spirit failide. Myn isen bi-
5 fore took wakyngis; Y was disturblid, and
6 Y^z spak not. I thouste elde daies; and Y
hadde in mynde euerlastinge seeris. And
7 Y thouste in the nyst with myn herte; and
Y was exercisid, and Y clensid my spirit.
Whether God schal caste awei with outen
8 ende; ether schal he not lei to, that he
be more plesid sit? Ethir schal he kitte
9 awei his merci into the ende^a; fro genera-

† Gostli this salme mai be expowned of ech feithful persone, wich is delyuered bi God wondir-fulli fro greet turment, temporal ether goostli, and for this is stired deuoutli to the heriing of God. *Lire here.* x.

---

k slepten *AEH.*   l hors c.   m Om. c.   n in c.   o Om. c.   p the erthe *AEH.*   q the *AH.*   r the kingis *AEH.*   s the erthe E *pr. m.*   t *of AH.*   u enhauncid *AH.*   v before *A.*   w distourblid *H.*   x enhauncyd *AH.*   y Y wepte *A.* swepte *H.*

p sleep, *that is, weren deed* v marg.   q ferdful FIKLMVxb.   r Om. I.   s leuyngis I.   t Om. A.   u Om. ORS.   v Om. A. *To the victorie* x.   vv Om. A.   Bi CDEGOPQRSUVWb.   x bi S.   y toward CDEFG HKLMOPQRSUVWxbi.   z Om. I.   a ende, *that is, holliche. Lire here.* U.

kutte awey; fro ieneracioun in to ienera-
10 cioun? Or God shal forȝete to han merci;
or he shal withholden in his wrathe his
11 mercies? Aud I seide, Now I haue begunne; this chaunging of the riȝthalf of
12 the heȝe. I was myndeful of the werkis
of the Lord; for I shal be myndeful fro
13 the begynnyng of thi merueilis. And I
shal sweteli thenke in alle thi werkis;
and in thi findingis I shal ben enhauntid[a].
14 God, in the holi thi wey; who gret God
15 as oure God? thou art God, that dost
merueilis. Knowen thou hast maad in
16 puplis thi vertu; thou hast aȝeen boȝt in
thin arm thi puple, the sones of Jacob
17 and of Joseph. Ther han seen thee watris, God, ther han seen thee watris,
and thei dredden; and disturbid ben the
18 depnessis. The multitude of the soun of
watris; a vois ȝeuen the cloudis. Forsothe
19 thin arwis passeden thurȝ; the vois of
thi thunder[b] in a whel. Thi shynyngus
liȝteden to the roundnesse of the erthe;
it is togidere moued; and the erthe togi-
20 dere tremblide. In the se thi weye; and
thi sties in manye watris; and thi steppis
21 shul not be knowen. Thou broȝtist out
as shep thi puple; in the hond of Moises
and Aaron[c].

cioun in to generacioun? Ethir schal God 10
forȝete to do mercy; ethir schal he withholde his mercies in his ire? And Y seide, 11
Now Y bigan; this *is* the chaunging of the
riȝthond of 'the hiȝe *God*[b]. I hadde mynde 12
on the werkis of the Lord; for Y schal
haue mynde fro the bigynnyng of thi merueilis. And Y schal thenke in[c] alle thi 13
werkis; and Y schal be occupied[d] in thi
fyndyngis. God, thi weie *was* in the 'hooli; 14
what God *is* greet as oure God? thou art 15
God, that doist merueilis. Thou madist
thi vertu knowun among puplis; thou 16
aȝenbouȝtist in thi arm thi puple, the sones
of Jacob and of Joseph. God, watris sien 17
thee, watris sien thee, and dredden; and
depthis[e] of watris weren disturblid. The 18
multitude of the soun of watris; cloudis
ȝauen vois. For whi thin arewis passen; the 19
vois of thi thundir *was* in a[f] wheel. Thi
liȝtnyngis schyneden[g] to the world; the
erthe was moued, and tremblid. Thi weie 20
in the see, and thi pathis in many watris;
and thi steppis schulen not be knowun.
Thou leddist forth thi puple as scheep; in 21
the hond of Moyses and of[h] Aaron.

PSALM LXXVII.

1　　*The vnderstonding of Asaf.*

po-　　Taketh tente, my puple, to my lawe;
inwardli bowith ȝoure ere in to the
2 woordis of my mouth. I shul opene in
parablis my mouth; I shal speke propo-
3 siciouns fro the begynnyng. Hou grete
thingis wee han herd, and han knowe
4 them; and oure fadris tolden to vs. Thei
ben not hid fro ther sones; in an other
ieneracioun. Tellende[d] the preisingus of
the Lord, and his vertues; and his mer-
5 ueilis, that he dide. And he rerede witnessing in Jacob; and lawe he putte in

PSALM LXXVII.

The 'title of the[i] seuene and seuentithe 1
salm. The lernyng of Asaph†.

Mi puple, perseyue ȝe my lawe; bowe[k]
ȝoure eere in to the wordis of my mouth.
I schal opene my mouth in parablis; Y 2
schal speke perfite resouns fro the bigynnyng. Hou grete thingis han we herd, 3
aud we han knowe tho; and oure fadris
telden to vs. Tho ben not hid fro the 4
sones of hem; in anothir generacioun. And
thei telden the heriyngis of the Lord, and
the vertues of hym; and hise merueilis,
whyche he dide. And he reiside witness- 5
yng in Jacob; and he settide lawe in Is-

† *A glos.* Asaph
made this salme
to shewe bi
scriptures and
oolde stories,
that the rewme
of Israel per-
teynede to Da-
uid and to hise
eris, bi Goddis
chesing. *Lire
here.* K.

a enhaunced *n.*　　b thundris *A.*　　c of Aaron *E.*　　d Tellith *A.*

b *God* hiȝe B.　　c on B.　　d exercised, *ether occupied* C *et plures.*　　e depnesse A.　　f the A *pr. m.*
g schewiden I.　　h Om. F *pr. m.*　　i Om. A.　　k bowe ȝe X.

Irael. Hou grete thingis he sente to
oure fadris, to make thoo thingus knowe
6 to ther sones; that the tother ieneracioun
knowe. The sonus, that shul be born,
and risen out; shul tellen out to ther
7 sones. That thei putte in God ther hope,
and thei forȝete not the werkis of God;
8 and his hestis thei out seche. Lest thei
be maad as ther fadris; a shreude ieneracioun and a terrende out. A ieneracioun
that dresside not his herte; and his spirit
9 is not take with God. The sones of Effraym lokende in, and sendende^e a bowe;
10 ben tnrned in the dai of bataile. Thei
kepten not the testament of God; and in
11 his lawe thei wolden not go. And thei
forȝeten his benefetis; and his merueylis,
12 that he shewide to them. Befor the fadris of hem he dide merueilis in the lond
13 of Egipt; in the feld of Tafneos. He
betwen vp brac the se, and thurȝ broȝte
them; and sette the watris as in a botel.
14 And he ladde hem thennes in the cloude
of the day; and al nyȝt in the liȝtnyng^f
15 of fyr. He betwe brac the ston in wildernesse; and watride hem as in a myche
16 deep water. And he broȝte out water of
the ston; and he ladde out watris as
17 flodis. And thei leide to ȝit to synnen
to hym; in to wrathe thei stiriden the
18 heȝe, in vnwatri place. And thei tempteden God in ther hertis; that thei nske
19 metis to ther soulis. And euele thei
speken of God; thei seiden, Whether God
shal moun make redi a bord in desert?
20 For he smot the ston, and ther floweden
watris; and the stremes maden to flowen.
Whether and bred he shal moun ȝiue;
21 or greithen a bord to his puple? Therfore the Lord herde, and lafte of; and
fyr is tend up in Jacob; and wrathe is
22 steȝed vp in Irael. For thei leeueden
not in God; ne hopiden in his helthe
23 ȝiuere. And he sente to the cloudes fro
aboue; and the ȝatis of heuene he openede.

rael. Hou grete thingis comaundide he to
oure fadris, to make tho knowun to her
sones; that another generacioun knowe. 6
Sones, that schulen be born, and schulen
rise vp; schulen telle out to her sones.
That thei sette her hope in God, and for- 7
ȝete not the werkis of God; and that thei
seke^l hise comaundementis. Lest thei be 8
maad a schrewid generacioun; and terrynge to wraththe, as the fadris of hem.
A generacioun that dresside not his herte;
and his spirit was not bileued with^m God.
The sones of Effraym, bendinge a bouwe 9
and sendynge *arowis*; weren turned in the
dai of batel. Thei kepten not the testa- 10
ment of God; and thei nolden^n go in his
lawe. And thei forȝaten hise benefices; and 11
hise merueils, whiche he schewide to hem.
He dide merueils bifore the fadris of hem 12
in the loond of Egipt; in the feeld of
Taphneos. He brak the see, and ledde 13
hem thorou; and^o he ordeynede the watris
as in a bouge. And he ledde hem forth 14
in^p a cloude of the dai; and al niȝt in the
liȝtnyng of fier. He brak a stoon in de- 15
seert; and he ȝaf watir to hem as in a
myche depthe. And he ledde watir out of 16
the stoon; and he ledde forth watris as
floodis. And thei 'leiden to^q ȝit to do 17
synne aȝens hym; thei excitiden hiȝe^r *God*
in to ire^s, in^t a place with out water. And 18
thei temptiden God in her hertis; that
thei axiden meetis to her lyues. And thei 19
spaken yuel of God; thei seiden, Whether
God may make redi a bord in desert? For 20
he smoot a stoon, and watris flowiden; and
streemys ȝeden out in aboundaunce. Whether also he may ȝyue breed; ether make
redi a bord to his puple? Therfor the 21
Lord herde, and delaiede; and fier was
kindelid in Jacob, and the ire of God
stiede on Israel. For thei bileueden not 22
in God; nether^u hopiden in his heelthe.
And he comaundide to the cloudis aboue; 23
and he openyde the ȝatis of heuene. And 24

---

e senden c. sendinge ΛΕΗ.   f lickenes Λ. lyȝtnesse H.

l serche I.   m in I.   n wolden not I.   o it, and I.   p as in I.   q puttiden I.   r the hiȝe I.   s the ire L.
t and in I.   u nether thei I.

24 And he reynede to hem manna to ete ; and the bred of heuene he ʒaf to hem. 25 Man eet the bred of aungelis ; metis he 26 sente to hem in abundaunce. He translatide the south fro heuene ; and broʒte 27 in his vertue the southerne wynd. And he reynede vp on hem flesh as pouder ; and federed volatilis, as the grauel of the 28 se. And thei fellen in the myddil of the tentys of hem ; aboute ther tabernaclis. 29 And thei eeten, and ben fulfild ful myche, 30 and ther desir he broʒte to them ; thei ben not bigilid fro ther desir. Ʒit their 31 'metis weren in the mouth[g] of hem ; and the wrathe of God steiʒide vp upon hem. And he sloʒ the fatte men of hem ; and 32 the chosen men of Irael he lettide. In alle these thingus thei synneden ʒit ; and 33 thei leeueden not in his merueilis. And the daʒis of hem failiden in vanytee ; and 34 the ʒeeris of hem in withheeʒing. Whan he shulde slen hem, thei soʒten him ; and weren turned aʒeen, and the morutid thei 35 camen to hym. And thei be remembrid, for God is ther helpere ; and the heʒe 36 God is the aʒeenbiere of hem. And thei looueden hym in ther mouth ; and in 37 ther tunge thei lieden to hym. The herte forsothe of hem was not riʒt with hym ; ne feithful thei ben had in the testament 38 of hym. He forsothe is merciful[h], and plesid shal be maad to the synnes of hem ; and he shal not scatere them. And he abundede, that he turne awei his wrathe ; and he teende not vp al his 39 wrathe. And he recordide, for thei ben flesh ; a spirit goende, and not turnende 40 aʒeen. Hou ofte sithis thei out terreden hym in desert ; in to wrathe thei to-41 stiriden hym in vnwatri place. And thei ben turned, and tempteden God ; and holy Irael thei ful out terreden. 42 Thei ben not recordid of his hond ; the dai that he boʒte hem fro the hond of

he reynede to hem manna for to eete ; and he ʒaf to hem breed of heuene. Man eet[v] 25 the[w] breed of aungels ; he sent to hem meetis in aboundance. He turnede ouere 26 the south wynde fro heuene ; and he brouʒte in bi his vertu the weste wynde. And he reynede fleischis as dust on hem ; 27 and[x] 'he reinede[y] volatils fethered, as the grauel of the see. And tho felden doun 28 in the myddis of her castels ; aboute the tabernaclis of hem. And thei eeten, and 29 weren fillid greetli, and he brouʒte her desire to hem ; thei weren not defraudid 30 of her desier. Ʒit her metis weren in her mouth ; and the ire[z] of God stiede on hem. 31 And he killide the fatte[a] men of hem ; and he lettide[b] the chosene men of Israel. In 32 alle these thingis thei synneden ʒit ; and[c] bileuede not in the merueils of God. And 33 the daies of hem failiden in vanytee ; and the ʒeeris of hem *faileden* with haste. Whanne he killide hem, thei souʒten hym ; 34 and[d] turneden aʒen, and eerli thei camen to hym. And thei bithouʒten, that God is 35 the helper of hem ; and 'the hiʒ God[e] is the aʒenbier of hem. And thei loueden 36 hym in her mouth ; and with her tunge thei lieden to hym. Forsothe the herte of 37 hem was not riʒtful with hym ; nethir thei weren had feithful in his testament. But 38 he is merciful, and he schal be maad merciful to the synnes of hem ; and he schal not destrie hem. And[f] he dide greetli, to turne awei his yre ; and he kyndelide not al his ire. And he bithouʒte, that thei ben 39 fleische ; a spirit goynge, and not turnynge aʒen. Hou oft maden thei hym wrooth in 40 desert ; thei stireden hym in to ire in a place with out watir. And thei weren 41 turned, and[g] temptiden God ; and thei wraththiden the hooli of Israel. Thei bi- 42 thouʒten not on his hond ; in the dai in the[h] which he aʒen bouʒte hem fro the hond of the trobler. As he settide hise 43

---

[g] mouthis *AH*.   [h] mercyable *AH*.

[v] hath eet 1.   [w] Om. 1.   [x] and *also* 1.   [y] Om. 1.   [z] wraththe 1.   [a] fatte, *that is, riche men* v.
[b] ledde s.   [c] and thei 1κ.   [d] and thei 1.   [e] he that is hiʒest 1.   [f] But 1.   [g] and thei CDEFGIKLOSVb.
[h] Om. 1s.

VOL. II.   5 M

43 the trublere. As he putte in Egipt his
signes; and his wunders in the feld of
44 Thaneos. And he turnede into blod the
flodis of hem; and ther cisternes, that
45 thei shulde not drinke. And he sente in
to them an hound fleȝe, and it eet hem;
and a frogge[i], and it destroȝede them.
46 And he ȝaf to rust the frutis of hem; and
47 ther trauailis to a locust. And he sloȝ in
hail the vynes of hem; and ther[k] mul-
48 berie trees in frost. And he toc to hail
the bestis of hem; and the possessioun of
49 hem to fyr. He sente in to them the
wrathe of his indignacioun; indignacioun[l], and wrathe, and tribulacioun, in
50 sendingus bi euele aungelis. A weie he
made to the path of his wrathe, and he
sparide not fro the deth of the lyues of
hem; and the bestis of hem in deth he
51 closide. And he smot alle the firste goten
in the lond of Egipt; the first frutis of
alle the trauayle of hem in the taber-
52 naclis[m] of Cham. And he toc awei as
shep his puple; and he ladde hem thurȝ
53 as a floc in desert. And he ladde hem
thennys in hope, and thei dreden not;
and the enemys of hem the se couerede.
54 And he inladde them in to the hil of his
halewing; the hil that his riȝthond purchaside. And he caste out fro the face
of hem Jentilis; and bi lot he deuydede
to hem the erthe in the litle corde of
55 deling. And he made to dwelle in the
tabernaclis of hem the linagis[n] of Irael.
56 And thei tempteden, and sharpli terreden
the heȝe God; and his witnessingus thei
57 kepten not. And they turneden themself
awei, and thei kepten not couenaunt; as
ther fadris ben turned in to a shreude
58 bowe. In to wrathe thei stiriden hym in
ther hillis; and in ther grauen thingis to
59 ielouste[nn] thei terreden hym. God herde,
and despiside; and to noȝt he broȝte gretli
60 Irael. And he putte abac the tabernacle
of Silo; his tabernacle wher he dwelte in

signes in Egipt; and hise grete wondris
in the feeld of Taphneos. And he turnede 44
the flodis of hem and the reynes of hem
in to blood; that thei schulden not drynke.
He sente a fleisch flie in to hem, and it 45
eet hem; and *he sente* a paddok, and it
loste hem. And he ȝaf the fruytis of hem 46
to rust; and *he ȝaf* the trauels of hem to
locustis. And he killide the vynes of hem 47
bi[i] hail; and the moore trees of hem bi[k] a[l]
frost[m]. And he bitook the beestis of hem 48
to[n] hail; and the possessioun of hem to fier.
He sente in to hem the ire of his indigna- 49
cioun; indignacioun, and ire, and tribulacioun, sendingis in bi iuel aungels. He 50
made weie to the path of his ire, and he
sparide not fro the deth of her lyues; and
he closide togidere in deth the beestis of
hem. And he smoot al the first gendrid 51
thing in the lond of Egipt; the first
fruytis of alle the trauel[o] of hem in the
tabernaclis of Cham. And he took awei 52
his puple as scheep; and he ledde hem
forth as a flok in desert. And he ledde 53
hem forth in hope, and thei dredden not;
and the see hilide the enemyes of hem.
And he brouȝte hem in to the hil of his 54
halewyng; in to the hil which his riȝthond gat. And he castide out hethene
men fro the face of hem; and bi lot he
departide to hem the lond in a cord of
delyng. And he made the lynagis of Is- 55
rael to dwelle in the tabernaclis of hem.
And thei temptiden, and wraththiden heiȝ[p] 56
God; and thei kepten not hise witnessyngis. And thei turneden awei hem silf, 57
and thei kepten not couenaunt; as her fadris weren turned in to a schrewid bouwe.
Thei stiriden him in to ire in her litle 58
hillis; and thei terriden hym to indignacioun of[q] her grauen ymagis. God herde, 59
and forsook; and brouȝte to nouȝt Israel
greetli. And he puttide awei the taber- 60
nacle of Sylo; his tabernacle where[r] he
dwellide among men. And he bitook the 61

[i] frosshe *A.* [k] the *A.* [l] Om. *A.* [m] tabernacle *AH.* [n] lynage *A.* [nn] the locuste *H.*

[i] with I. [k] with I. [l] Om. IKS *pr. m.* i. [m] forst CDFHKMQVWXb. [n] in to C. [o] trauels A.
[p] the heiȝ I. [q] in C *sup. ras.* EIKLOUV. [r] in whiche I.

61 men. And he toc into caitifte the vertu of hem ; and the fairnesse of hem in to 62 the hondus of the enemy. And he closide in swerd his puple ; and his eritage he⁰ 63 dispiside. ȝunge menᵖ of hem the fyr eet ; and the maidenes of hem ben not 64 weilid. The prestis of hem in swerd fellen ; and the widewis of hem weren 65 not wept. And the Lord is rerid vp, as 66 slepende ; as myȝti drunken of win. And he smot his enemys in to the hindermor partis ; euere lasting repref he ȝaf to 67 them. And he putte abac the tabernacle of Josep ; and . the linage of Effraym he 68 ches not. But he ches the linage of Juda ; 69 the hil of Sion, that he louuede. And he bilde vp as vnycorn his holi making ; in the lond, that he foundede in to worldus. 70 And he ches Dauid his seruaunt, and he bar hym vp fro the flockis of shep ; fro 71 the aftir berende blet he toc hym. To fede Jacob his seruaunt ; and Irael his 72 eritage. And he fedde hem in the innocence of his herte ; and in the vnderstondingus of ther hondis he ladde hem thenes.

PSALM LXXVIII.

1

The salm to Asaf.

Deus, uenerunt grates.

God, Jentilis camen in to thin eritage ; thei defouleden thin holi temple, thei putteᑫ Jerusalem in to the keping of applis. 2 Thei putte the smyten to deth of thi seruauntis, metis to the foulis of heuene ; flesh of thi seintis to the bestis of ertheʳ. 3 Thei shadden out the blod of hem, as water in the enuyroun of Jerusalem ; and 4 ther was not that ʻshulde birieˢ. Wee be maad repref to oure neȝheboris ; mouwing and scornyng to them, that ben 5 in oure cumpas. Hou longe, Lord, thou shalt wrathen in to the ende ? shal be 6 tendᵗ vp as fyr thi jelouste ? Heeld out thi wrathe in to Jentilis, that han not

vertu of hem. in to caitiftee ; and the fairnesse of hem in to the hondis of the ene- 62 mye. And he closide togidere his puple in swerd ; and he dispiside his crytage. Fier 63 eet the ȝonge men of hem ; and the virgyns of hem weren not biweilidˢ. The prestis 64 of hem fellen doun bi swerd ; and the widewis of hem weren not biwept. And the 65 Lord was reisid, as slepynge ; as miȝti greetli fillid of wiyn. And he smoot hise 66 enemyes on the hynderere partis ; he ȝaf to hem euerlastyng schenschipe. And he 67 puttide awei the tabernacle of Joseph ; and he chees not the lynage of Effraym. But 68 he chees the lynage of Juda ; *he chees* the hil of Syon, which he louede. Andᵗ he as 69 an vnicorn bildide his hooli place ; in the lond, which he foundide in to worldis. And he chees Dauid his seruaunt, and 70 took hym vp fro the flockis of scheep ; he took hym fro bihynde scheep with lam- bren. To feed Jacob his seruaunt ; and 71 Israel his eritage. Andᵘ he fedde hem in 72 the innocens of his herte ; and he ledde hem forth in the vndurstondyngis of his hondis.

PSALM LXXVIII.

The ʻtitle of theᵛ eiȝte and seuentithe 1 *salmʷ. Ofˣ Asaphʸ †.*

God, hethene men cam in to thin eri- tage ; thei defouliden thin hooli temple, thei settiden Jerusalem in to the keping of applis. Thei settiden the slayn bodies 2 of thi scruauntis, meetisˢ to the volatilis of heuenes ; the fleischis of thi seyntis to the beestis of theⁿ erthe. Thei schedden 3 out the blood of hem, as watir in the cumpas of Jerusalem ; and noon wasᵇ that biriede. We ben maad schenschipe to 4 oure neiȝboris ; mowynge and scornynge to hem, that ben in oure cumpas. Lord, 5 hou longe . schalt thou be wrooth in to the ende ? schal thi veniaunce be kyndelid as fier ? Schedeᶜ out thin ire in to he- 6

† Gostli this salm mai be expowned, that it be the preier of hooli chirche anentis vnfeithful men, de- fouling chirchis and hollc places, and sleing cris- ten puple, and destroiyng her lond. For which thing holi chirche in the liȝcrnyng of this salm bi- weyleth this distriyng, and the ij. tyme it biaecheth de- uoutell and mekeli for re- storing there shed out, and in biaeching Goddis riȝtful- nes aȝenus vn- feithful men, and his merci annotes feithful men, and at the laste it thank- eth God, in the hope of heriȝng there. Lire here. K.

⁰ Om. c.   ᵖ Om. c.   ᑫ puttiden ʌɪʀ.   ʳ the erthe ʌ.   ˢ biriede ʌᴇɪɪ.   ᵗ temptid ʌ.

ˢ biwepte ʟ. biweiled *or* wept ɪ.   ᵗ But ɪ.   ᵘ But ɪ.   ᵛ Om. ʌ.   ʷ Om. ɪɪᴘʀsx.   ˣ *The salm of* c *et plures*
ʸ Dauid s.   ᶻ *to be* meetis ɪ.   ᵃ Om. s.   ᵇ ther was ɪ.   ᶜ Heelde ɪ.

knowe thee; and in to reumes, that thi
7 name han not inwardli clepid. For thei
eete Jacob; and hys place thei han maad
8 desolat. Ne thou shalt han mynde of
oure olde wickidnessis, soone shul befor
taken vs thi mercies; for pore men wee
9 ben maad ful myche. Help vs, God,
oure helthe ʒiuere, and for the glorie of
thi name, Lord[u], deliuere vs; and plesid
be thou to oure synnes for thi name.
10 Lest parauenture thei sey in Jentilis,
Wher is the God of hem? and yt waxe
ful knowen in naciouns beforn oure eʒen.
The veniaunce of the blod of thi seruauns,
that is held out; go in to thi siʒte the
11 weiling of the[v] gyued men. After the
mykilnesse of thin arm; weld the sones
12 of the don to deth. And ʒeld to oure
neʒheboris seuefold in the bosum of hem;
the repref of them, that thei repreueden
13 thee, Lord. Wee forsothe thi puple, and
the shep of thi leswe; shul knouleche
to thee in to the world. In ieneracioun
aud in to ieneracioun; wee shul telle
out thi preising.

PSALM LXXIX.

1 *In to the ende, for hem that shul ben
al holli chaungid, the salm for the
Assiries; the witnessing of Asaph.*

*Qui regis Is-
rael, intende.*

2   Thou that gouernest Irael, tac heed;
that ledist as a shep Joseph. That sittist vp on cherubyn; be thou maad open
3 beforn Effraym, Beniamyn, and Manasse.
Rere vp thi myʒt, and cum; that saf thou
4 make vs. God, conuerte thou vs, and
sheu thi face; and wee shul be saf.
5 Lord God of vertues; hou longe shalt
thou wrathe vpon the orisoun of thi
6 seruaunt? Thou shalt feden vs with
bred of teris; and drinke thou shalt ʒiue
7 to vs in teris in mesure. Thou hast
put vs[w] in contradiccioun to oure neʒheboris; and oure enemys bemoweden vs.
8 God of vertues, conuerte thou vs; and

thene men, that knowen not thee; and in
to rewmes, that clepiden not thi name.
For thei eeten Jacob; and maden desolat 7
his place. Haue thou not mynde on oure 8
elde wickidnesses; thi mercies bifore take
vs soone, for we ben maad pore greetli.
God, oure heelthe, helpe thou vs, and, 9
Lord, for the glorie of thi name delyuer
thou vs; and be thou merciful to oure
synnes for thi name. Lest perauenture 10
thei seie among hethene men, Where is the
God of hem? and be he knowun among
naciouns bifore oure iʒen. The veniaunce
of the blood of thi seruauntis, which is
sched out[d]; the weilyng of feterid men
entre in[e] thi siʒt. Vpe[f] the greetnesse of 11
thin arm; welde thou the sones of slayn
men. And ʒelde thou to oure neiʒboris 12
seuenfoold in the bosum of hem; the
schenschip of hem, which thei diden
schenschipfuli to thee, thou Lord. But 13
we *that ben* thi puple, and the scheep of
thi leesewe; schulen knouleche to thee in
to the world. In generacioun and in to
generacioun; we schulen telle thin heriyng.

PSALM LXXIX.

1 *The title of the[g] nyne and seuentithe[1]
salm. To victorie; this salm is witnessing[h] of Asaph for lilies[i].*

2   Thou that gouernest Israel, ʒyue tent;
that leedist[k] forth Joseph as a scheep.
Thou that sittist on cherubym; be schewid
bifore Effraym, Beniamyn, and Manasses. 3
Stire thi power, and come thou; that thou
make vs saaf. God of vertues, turne thou 4
vs; and schewe thi face, and we schulen be
saaf. Lord God of vertues; hou longe 5
schalt thou be wrooth on the preier of thi
seruaunt? *Hou longe* schalt thou feede 6
vs with the breed of teeris; and schalt
ʒyue drynke to vs with teeris in mesure?
Thou hast set vs in to aʒenseiyng to oure 7
neiʒboris; and oure enemyes han scornyde
vs. God of vertues, turne thou vs; and 8

---

[u] Om. *c.*   [v] thi *c.*   [w] Om. *AH.*

---

[d] out, *he knowun among naciouns* CDEF *pr. m.* GHKLMOPQRSWXbi.   [e] *in to* S.   [f] *Aftir* 1.   [g] Om. *c et
plures.*   [h] *the witnessing* 1U.   [i] *lilies, that is, for Crist and his chirche.* X.   [k] *leddist* CDO.

sheu thi face, and wee shul be saf.

9 Thou translatidist a vyne fro Egipt; thou castidist^x out Jentilis, and plauntid-
10 ist it. Duke of the weie thou were in his siʒt ; and thou plauntidist his rootis,
11 and it fulfilde the erthe. His shadewe couerede hillis; and his shrubbis the
12 ceders of God. He straʒte out his braunchis vnto the se; and vnto the
13 flod his^y railingus. Wherto destroʒidist thou his wal; and pullen it alle that gon
14 beside the weie? The bor of the wode outlawide it; and the singuler wilde
15 beste destroʒide it. God of vertues, be thou turned, behold fro heuene, and see ;
16 and visite thou this vyne. And parfitli mac it, that thi riʒthond plauntide ; and
vp on the sone of man, whom thou hast
17 confermed to thee. The tend vp thingis with fyr, and the vnder doluen; of the
18 blamyng of thi chere shul pershen. Thin hond be don vp on the man of thi riʒthond ; and vp on the sone of man, whom
19 thou hast confermed to thee. And wee goon not awei fro thee ; thou shalt
quykene vs, and thi name wee shul in-
20 wardli clepe. Lord God of vertues, con-uerte vs; and sheu thou thi face, and wee shul be saf.

schewe thi face, and we schulen be saaf. Thou translatidist a vyne fro Egipt; thou 9 castidist out hethene men, and plauntidist it. Thou were leeder of the weie in the 10 siʒt therof; and thou plauntidist the rootis therof, and it fillide the lond. The scha-11 dewe therof hilide hillis; and the braunchis therof *filliden* the cedris of God. It 12 streiʒte forth hise siouns til to the see, and the generacioun^m ther of 'til toⁿ the flood. Whi hast thou destried the wal therof; 13 and alle men that goen forth bi the weie gaderiden^o awei the grapis therof? A 14 boor of the wode distriede it; and a sin-guler wielde beeste deuouride it. God of 15 vertues, be thou turned; biholde thou^p fro heuene, and se, and visite this vyne. And 16 make thou it perfit, which thi riʒthond plauntide; and *biholde thou* on the sone of man, which thou hast confermyd to thee. Thingis brent with fier, and vudur-17 myned; schulen perische for the blamyng of thi cheer. Thin hond be maad on the 18 man of thi riʒthond; and on the sone of man, whom thou hast confermed to thee. And we departiden not fro thee ; thou 19 schalt quykene vs, and we schulen in-wardli clepe thi name. Lord God of ver-20 tues, turne thou vs; and schewe thi face, and we schulen be saaf.

PSALM LXXX.

1 *In to the ende, for the pressis, salm^z to that Asaf, in the fifte dai of the wike.*

Exultate Deo.

2 Ful out ioʒith to God, oure helpere ;
3 ioʒeth to God of Jacob. Taketh salm, and ʒyueth timbre ; a merie sautre with
4 an harpe. Trumpeth in the newe mone ; with a trumpe in the noble dai of oure
5 solempnete. For comaundement in Jrael
6 it is; and dom to God of Jacob. Witness-ing in Joseph he putte it; whan he shulde gon out of the lond of Egipt, the tunge
7 that he hadde not knowe, he herde. He^a turnede awei fro birthenes^b his rig ; his

PSALM LXXX.

1 *The title of* ^q *the^r eiʒtetithe salm. To the ouercomer in* ^s *the pressours* ^{ss} *of Asaph†.*

2 Make ʒe fulli ioye to God, oure^t helpere ;
3 synge ʒe hertli to God of Jacob. Take ʒe a salm, and ʒyue ʒe a tympan ; a myrie sautere with^u a 4 harpe. Blowe ʒe with^u a trumpe in Neomenye‡; in the noble dai
5 of ʒoure solempnite. For whi comaunde-ment is in Israel; and doom *is* to God of
6 Jacob. He settide that witnessing in Joseph ; whanne he ʒede out of the lond of Egipt, he herde a langage, which^v he
7 knew not. He turnede a wei his bak fro

† *A glos.* This salm was or-deyned to be songen in the feest of trumpis, to doo thank-inges to God for the fruytis gederid thanne. *Lire heere.* K.
‡ *Neomenye* ; that is, the newe mone. AC.

x castist A*EH*.　　y is c.　　z *the salm* A.　　a Be *H*.　　b the birdens *H*.

m generaciouns FKL.　　n unto I.　　o gaderen IS.　　p Om. I.　　q Om. A.　　r Om. c *et alii.*　　s *on* Q.
ss *pressour* ELP.　　t Om. S.　　u *in* S.　　v *that* I.

ₐhondis in the cofin serueden. In tribulacioun thou inwardli clepidist me, and I deliuerede thee; I ful out herde thee in the hid place of tempest, I preuede thee[c] 9anentis the watir of contradiccioun. Here thou, my puple, and I shal witnesse to 10thee, Irael, if thou shalt here me, ther shall. not be in thee a[d] fresh God; ne 11thou[e] shalt honoure an alien God. I forsothe am the Lord thi God, that ladde thee out fro the lond of Egipt; spreed abrod thy mouth, and I shal fulfille it. 12And my puple herde not my vois; and 13Irael toc not[f] heed to me. And I lafte them after the desiris of ther herte; thei 14shul gon in ther findingus. If my puple hadde herde me; Irael, if[g] in my weies 15hadde go. For noȝt perauenture the enemys of hem I shulde han mekid; and vpon men trublende them I shulde han 16put myn hond. The enemys of the Lord lieden to hym; and the time of hem shal 17ben in to worldis. And he fedde them of the talȝ of whete; and of the ston with hony he fulfilde hem.

birthens; hise hondis serueden in a coffyn. In tribulacioun thou inwardli clepidist me, 8 and Y delyuerede thee; Y herde thee in the hid place of tempest, Y preuede thee at the water of aȝenseiyng. My puple, 9 here thou[w], and Y schal be witnesse aȝens thee; Israel, if thou herist me, a fresche 10 God schal not be in thee, and thou schalt not worschipe an alien god. For Y am 11 thi Lord God, that ladde thee out of the lond of Egipt; make large thi mouth, and Y schal fille it. And my puple herde 12 not my vois; and Israel ȝaue not tente to me. And Y lefte hem aftir the[x] desiris 13 of her[y] herte; thei schulen go in her fyndyngis. If my puple hadde[z] herde me; if 14 Israel hadde go in my weies. For nouȝt is 15 in hap Y hadde maad low her enemyes; and Y hadde send myn hond on men doynge tribulacioun to hem. The enemyes 16 of the Lord lieden to hym; and her tyme schal be in to worldis. And he fedde 17 hem of[a] the fatnesse of whete; and he fillide hem with hony of the stoon.

PSALM LXXXI.

The salm of Asaf.

1

Deus stetit in sinagoga.

God stod in the synagoge of godis; in the myddel forsothe godis he seuereth[h]. 2Hou longe ȝee demen wickidnesse; and 3the facis of synneres ȝce taken? Demeth to the nedy, and to the moderles child; 4the meke and the pore instefieth. Taketh awei the pore; and the nedi fro the hond 5of the synnere deliuereth. Thei knewen not, ne vnderstoden, in dercnessis thei gon; ther shul be moued alle the founde-6mens of erthe[i]. I scide, godis ȝee ben; 7and the sones of the heȝe alle. ȝee forsothe as men shul dien; and as oon of 8the princys shul falle. Rys, God, deme thou the erthe; for thou shalt eritagen in alle Jentilis.

PSALM LXXXI.

The title of the[b] oon and eiȝtetithe salm. 1   Of[c] Asaph.

God stood in the synagoge of goddis; forsothe[d] he demeth[e] goddis in the myddil. Hou longe demen ȝe wickidnesse; and 2 taken the facis[f] of synneris? Deme ȝe to 3 the nedi man, and to the modirles child; iustifie ȝe the meke man and pore. Raueische ȝe out a pore man; and de- 4 lyuere ȝe the[g] nedi man fro the hond of the synner. Thei knewen[h] not, nether 5 vndirstoden, thei goen in derknessis; alle the foundementis of erthe schulen be moued. I seide, ȝe ben goddis; and alle 6 ȝe ben the sones of hiȝ[k] God. But ȝe 7 schulen die as men; and ȝe schulen falle doun as oon of the princis. Ryse, thou 8 God, deme thou the erthe; for thou schalt haue eritage in alle folkis.

---

c Om. ₁₁.   d Om. A.   e Om. ₁₁.   f noon AEH.   g Om. A.   h seueride A.   i the erthe AEH.

w thou me s.   x Om. c et plures.   y Om. s.   z Om. s.   a with s.   b Om. c et alii.   c *The salm of* c et plures.   d and ₁.   e demeth more A pr. m. ₁.   f face ₁s.   g a ₁.   h knowen CDEFHLRS.   i vndurstonden CDELRS.   k the hiȝ s.

PSALM LXXXII.

1 *The song of the salm of Asaf.*

quis. 2 God, who shal be lic to thee? ne holde
thou thi pes, ne be thou refreyned, God.
3 For loo! thin enemys souneden; and thei
4 that hateden thee beeren vp the hed. Vp
on thi puple in malice ordeyneden a
counseyl; and thoȝten aȝen thi seyntis.
5 Thei seiden, Cometh, and scatere wee
them fro the folc; and be no mor remem-
6 brid the name of Irael. For thei thoȝten
alle of oon inwit; togidere aȝen thee a
7 testament disposiden the tabernaclis of
Ydumees and Ismaelitis. Moab, and Aga-
8 rienes, Jebal, and Amon, and Amelech;
alienes with the dwelleris of Tyrum.
9 Forsothe Assur cam with them; and
thei ben maad in to helpe to the sones
10 of Loth. Do to them as to Madian, and
Cisare; as to Jabyn in the strem of Cison.
11 Thei pershiden in Endor; thei ben maad
12 as the drit of erthe. Put the princis of
hem as Oreb and Zeb; and Zebie and
13 Zalmana. Alle the princis of hem, that
seiden; Bi eritage welde wee the sein-
14 tuarie of God. My God, put hem as a
wheel; and as stobil befor the face of
15 wind[k]. As fyr that brenneth a wode;
and as flaume togidere brennende hillis.
16 So thou shalt pursue them in thi tempest; and in thi wrathe thou shalt dis-
17 turbe them. Fulfil the facis of hem with
shenshipe; and thei shul seche thi name,
18 Lord. Waxe they ashamed, and be thei
al disturbid in to the world of world;
19 and be thei confoundid and pershe. And
knowe thei, for name to thee Lord; thou
onli heȝest in al the[l] erthe.

[k] the wynde *AH*. [l] Om. *AEH*.

PSALM LXXXII.

The title of the[l] two and eiȝtetithe salm. 1
The[m] song of the salm of[n] Asaph†.

God, who schal be lijk thee? God, be 2
thou not stille, nether be thou peesid.
For lo! thin enemyes sowneden; and thei 3
that haten[o] thee reisiden the heed. Thei 4
maden a wickid counsel on thi puple; and
thei thouȝten aȝens thi seyntis. Thei 5
seiden, Come ȝe, and leese we hem fro
the[p] folk; and the name of Israel be no
more hadde in mynde. For thei thouȝten 6
with oon acord; the tabernaclis of Ydu- 7
meys, and men of Ismael disposiden a
testament togidere aȝens thee. Moab, and
Agarenus, Jebal, and Amon, and Amalech; 8
alienys with hem that dwellen in Tyre.
For Assur cometh with hem; thei ben 9
maad in to help to the sones of Loth.
Make thou to hem as to Madian, and 10
Sisara; as to Jabyn in the stronde of
Sison. Thei perischiden in Endor; thei 11
weren maad as a toord of erthe. Putte 12
thou the prynces of hem as Oreb and Zeb;
and Zebee and Salmana. Alle the princis
of hem, that seiden; Holde[q] we bi eritage 13
the seyntuarie of God. My God, putte 14
thou hem as a[r] whele; and as stobil bifor
the face of the wynde. As fier that bren- 15
neth a wode; and as flawme brynnynge
hillis. So thou schalt pursue hem in thi 16
tempeste; and thou schalt disturble hem
in thin ire. Lord, fille thou the faces of 17
hem with schenschipe; and thei schulen
seke thi name. Be thei aschamed, and 18
be thei disturblid in to[s] world of world;
and[t] be thei schent and perische thei.
And knowe thei, that the[u] Lord is name 19
to thee; thou aloone *art* the[v] hiȝeste[w] in
ech[x] lond.

† *A glos.* Goostli this salm mai be the preier of holi chirche aȝens the enemyes of cristen men, that telleth mekely bifore God the wickidnesse of hem, and axith deuoutli Goddis veniaunse on this bi ensaumple of oolde wickide men punischid of God. *Lire here.* x.

[l] Om. c *et alii*. [m] *Of the* c. [n] *the song of* L. [o] hatiden IL. [p] Om. c *et plures*. [q] Helde A.
[r] Om. co. [s] to the c *et plures*. [t] Om. s. [u] Om. I. [v] Om. CI. [w] Om. c. [x] euery L.

PSALM LXXXIII.

1 *In to the ende, for the pressis, to the sonus of Chore, the*ᵃ *salm.*

Quam dileeta. 2 Hou looued ben thi tabernaclis, Lord 3 of vertues ; my soule coueiteth, and failith in to the hallis of the Lord. Myn herte and my flesh; ful out iozeden in to 4 God alyue. Forsothe the sparowe fonde to hym an hous; and the turtil a nest, wher he leye ⁿ vp his briddis. Thin auteres, Lord God of vertues; my king, 5 and my God. Blisful that dwellen in thin hous, Lord ; in to the worldis of 6 worldis thei shul preise thee. Blisful the man, whos helpe is of thee; stezingus 7 vp in his herte he disposide, in the valei of teris, in the place that he sette. 8 Forsothe blessingus shal ziue the lawe berere, thei shul go fro vertue in to vertue; God of godis shal ben seen in 9 Sion. Lord God of vertues, ful out here myn orisoun; with eris parceyue thou, 10 God of Jacobᵒ. Oure defendere, God, loke thou to, and behold in to the face of thi 11 crist. For betere is oo dai in thiu hallis; ouer thousendis. I ches to be cast awei in the hous of my God; more than to 12 duelle in the tabernaclis of synneres. For mercy and treuthe looueth God; grace 13 and glorie the Lord shal zyue. He shal not make them to be withoute goodis, that gon in innocence; Lord of vertues, blisful the man, that hopeth in thee.

PSALM LXXXIV.

1 *In to the ende, to the sonus of Chore.*

Benedixisti, Domine, terram tuam. 2 Lord, thou hast blissid thin erthe; thou hast turned awei the caitifte of 3 Jacob. Thou hast forziue the wickidnesse of thi folc; thou hast couered alle

PSALM LXXXIII.

*The title of the*ʸ *thre and eiztetithe salm*ᶻ. 1 *The salm of the sones of Chore†.*

Lord of vertues, thi tabernaclis ben 2 greetli loued ; my soule coueitith, and 3 failith in to the porchis of the Lord. Myn herte and my fleische ; ful out ioyeden in to quyk God. For whi a sparewe fyndith 4 an hous to it silf ; andᵃ a turtle *fyndith* a neste to it silf, where it ˋschal kepeᵇ hise bryddis. Lord of vertues, thin auteris ; my king, and my God. Lord, blessid ben 5 thei that dwellen in thin hous ; thei schulen preise thee in to theᶜ worldis of worldis. Blessid *is* the man, whos help 6 is of thee ; he hath disposidᵈ stiyngis in his herte, in the valei of teeris, in the place 7 whichᵉ he hath set. For the zyuer of the 8 lawe schal zyue blessyng, thei schulen go fro vertu in to vertu ; God of goddis schal be seyn in Sion. Lord God of ver- 9 tues, here thou my preier ; God of Jacob, perseyue thou with eeris. God, oure de- 10 fender, biholde thou ; and bihold eᶠ in to the face of thi crist. For whi o dai in 11 thin hallis is bettere ; than a thousynde. I chees to be ˋan out castᵍ in the hous of my God ; more than toʰ dwelle in the tabernaclis of synneris. For God loueth 12 merci and treuthe ; the Lord schal zyue grace and glorie. He schal not depriue ¹ 13 hem fro goodis, that gonᵏ inˡ innocence ; Lord of vertues, blessid *is* the man, that hopith in thee.

PSALM LXXXIV.

*The title of the*ᵐ *foure and eiztetithe salm.* 1 *Of*ⁿ *the*ᵒ *sones of Chore.*

Lord, thou hast blessid thi lond ; thou 2 hast turned awei the caitifte of Jacob. Thou hast forzoue the wickidnesse of thi 3 puple ; thou hast hilid alle the synnes of

† *A glos.* This salm declareth the desijr of holi men, liffing in this wickid world, to come to heuen blisse. *Lire here.* κ.

† *A glos.* This salm is deyng of thankinges for the turnyng agen of Jewis fro the caitifte of Babilon ; but principall it is profecie of the perfitt delyueraunce to be maad bi Crist, in his incarnacion and passion. *Lire here.* κ.

ᵐ Om. *A.*   ⁿ leyeth *A.*   ᵒ Israel *AH.*

ʸ Om. c *et alii.*   ᶻ salm, to victorie, on the pressours c *et plures.*   ᵃ Om. s.   ᵇ kepith ι.   ᶜ Om. ꜰʜιᴋᴍsxι.   ᵈ ordeyned ι.   ᵉ that ι.   ᶠ biholde thou s.   ᵍ abiect, *ether an outcast* c *et plures.*   ʰ for to κ *sec. m.*   ¹ bireue c *et plures.*   ᵏ gooth s.   ˡ Om. s.   ᵐ Om. c *et alii.*   ⁿ To the ouercomere, the song of c *et plures.*   ᵒ Om. ι.

4 the synnes of hem. Thou hast suagid al thi wrathe; thou hast turned awey fro the wrathe of thin indignacioun.
5 Conuerte vs, God, our helthe ȝiuere; and 6 turne awei thi wrathe fro us. Whether in to withoute ende thou shalt wrathe to vs; or thou shalt strecchen out thi wrathe fro ieneracioun in to ienera-7 cioun? God, thou turned shalt quykenen 8 vs; and thi folc shal gladen in thee. Sheu to vs, Lord, thi mercy; and thi helthe 9 ȝiuere ȝif thou to vs. I shal heren, what speke in me the Lord God; for he shal speke pees in to his folc. And vp on his seyntis; and in to them that ben con-10 uertid to the herte. Neuerthelatere neeȝh the dredende hym his helthe ȝiuere; 11 that indwelle gloric in oure erthe. Mercy and treuthe metten to themself; riȝtwis-12 nesse and pes ben kist. Treuthe of erthe is sprungen; and riȝtwisnesse fro heuene 13 beheeld forth. Forsothe the Lord shal ȝiue benygnete; and oure erthe shal ȝiue 14 his frute. Riȝtwysnesse beforn hym shal go; and he shal putte in the weie his goingus.

PSALM LXXXV.
The orisoun of Dauid.

1 Bowe in, Lord, thin ere, and ful out here me; for helpeles and a pore man I 2 am. Kepe thou my soule, for holi I am; mae saf thi seruaunt, my God, hopende 3 in thee. Haue mercy of me, Lord, for 4 to thee I criede al dai; glade thou the soule of thi seruaunt, for to thee, Lord, 5 my soule I rerede. For thou, Lord, sweete and mylde; and of myche mercy 6 to alle that inwardli clepen thee. With eris parceyue thou, Lord, myn orisoun; and tae heed to the vois of my lowe 7 preȝing. In the day of my tribulacioun I criede to thee; for thou ful out herdest 8 me. Ther is not lic thee in godis, Lord;

hem. Thou hast aswagid al thin ire; 4 thou hast turned awei fro the ire of thin indignacioun. God, oure helthe, conuerte 5 thou vs; and turne awei thin ire fro vs. Whether thou schalt be wrooth to vs 6 withouten ende; ether schalt thou holde forth thin ire fro generacioun in to gene-racioun? God, thou conuertid schalt 7 quykene vs; and thi puple schal be glad in thee. Lord, schewe thi merci to vs; 8 and ȝyue thin helthe to vs. I schal here 9 what the Lord God schal speke in me; for he schal speke pees on his puple. And on hise hooli men; and on hem that ben turned to herte. Netheles his helthe is 10 niȝ men dredynge him; that glorie dwelle in oure lond. Merci and trenthe metten 11 hem silf; riȝtwisnesse and pees weren kissid. Treuthe cam forth of erthe; and 12 riȝtfulnesse bihelde fro heuene. For the 13 Lord schal ȝyue benignyte; and oure erthe schal ȝyue his fruyt. Riȝtfulnesse schal 14 go bifore him; and schal sette hise steppis in the weie.

PSALM LXXXV.
The title of the fyne and eiȝtetithe salm. The preier of Dauid †.

Lord, bowe doun thin eere, and here 1 me; for Y am nedi and pore. Kepe thou 2 my lijf, for Y am holi; my God, make thou saaf thi seruaunt hopynge in thee. Lord, haue thou merci on me, for Y criede 3 al day to thee; make thou glad the soule 4 of thi seruaunt, for whi, Lord, Y haue reisid my soule to thee. For thou, Lord, 5 art swete and mylde; and of myche merci to alle men inwardli clepynge thee. Lord, 6 perseyue thou my preier with eeris; and ȝyue thou tente to the vois of my bisech-yng. In the dai of my tribulacioun Y 7 criede to thee; for thou herdist me. Lord, 8 noon among goddis is lijk thee; and noon

† A glos. Gostli this salme mai be expowned of ech Cristen man ȝett in tribulacien bodili excited of men, ether gostli turment maad of fendis, wich man prei-eth God de-uoutli for his delyueraunce, and aleyggeth first the wor-thynesse of Goddis heryng, and on his part he aleyggeth his nedynesse, in-nocence, and continuaunce of preier, and on Goddis part he aleyggeth mer-ci, and power, greet doyng, and henour; and ferther he formeth his axing there, Lord lede me forth, that I be kept in good werk, and be bifore kept fro the ȝuel of synne, and of peyne, so that he be crowned at the laste in the rewme of glorie. Lire here. K.

P the erthe AEH.   Q Om. H.   r Om. AH.   s to thee A.

P swagid I.   Q to I.   r riȝtfulnesse ceteri.   s of the I.   t Riȝtfulnesse, that is, Johan Baptist K text
v marg.   u and it I.   V Om. A.   w here thou I.   x mychil o.   y my s.

9 and ther is not aftir thi werkis. Alle Jentilis, what euere thou hast maad, shul come, and honoure befor thee[t], Lord; 10 and thei shul glorifie thi name. For gret art thou, and doende meruelis; 11 thou art God alone. Leed mee thencs, Lord, in thi weie, and I shal gon in thi treuthe; glad myn herte, that it drede 12 thi name. I shal knouleche to thee, Lord my God, in al myn herte; and I shal glorifie thi[u] name in to with oute ende. 13 For thi mercy great is vp on me; and thou toke out my soule fro[v] the nethere 14 helle. God, wicke[w] men inrisen vpon me; and the synagoge of my3ti men so3ten my soule; and thei purposiden not 15 thee in ther si3te. But thou, Lord God, ruwer, and mercyful; pacient, and of 16 myche merci, and verre. Behold in me, and haue mercy of me, 3if empire to thy child; and saf mae the sone of thin hand-17 maiden. Do with me a toene in good, that thei see, that hateden me, and be confounded; for thou, Lord, hast holpe me, and coumfortid me.

is euene to thi werkis. Lord, alle folkis, 9 whiche euere thou madist, schulen come, and worschipe bifore thee; and thei schulen glorifie thi name. For thou art ful greet, 10 and makinge merueils; thou art God aloone. Lord, lede thou me forth in thi weie, and 11 Y schal entre in thi treuthe; myn herte be glad, that it drede thi name. Mi Lord 12 God, Y schal knouleche to thee in al myn herte; and Y schal glorifie thi name with-outen ende. For thi merci is greet on 13 me; and thou deliueridist my soule fro the lower helle. God, wickid men han rise 14 vp on me; and the synagoge of my3ti men han sou3t my lijf; and thei han not set forth thee in her si3t. And thou, Lord 15 God, doynge merci, and merciful; pacient, and of myche merci, and sothefast. Bi- 16 holde on me, and haue mercy on me. 3yue thou the empire to thi[z] child; and make thou saaf the sone of thin hand-mayden[a]. Make thou with me a signe in 17 good, that thei se, that haten me, and be[b] aschamed; for thou, Lord, hast helpid[c] me, and hast coumfortid me.

PSALM LXXXVI.

1 *To the sonus of Chore, the salm of the song.*

Fundamenta eius in montibus.

The foundemens of hym in holi hillis; 2 the Lord looueth the 3atis of Syon, vp on 3 alle the tabernaclis of Jacob. Gloriouse thingus ben seid of thee; thou cite of 4 God. Myndeful I shal be of Raab, and of Babiloyne; knowende me. Lo! alienus, and Tiris, and the puple of Ethiopis; 5 these weren there. Whether a man shal sey to Sion, And[x] a man is born in it; 6 and he the most he3 foundede it? The Lord shal telle in the scripturis of puplis; 7 and of these princis, that weren in it. As of alle gladende; dwelling is in thee.

PSALM LXXXVI.

1 *The title of the[d] sixte and ei3tetithe salm[e]. `The salm of the song[f] of the sones of Chore.*

The foundementis therof *ben* in hooli hillis; the Lord loueth the 3atis of Sion, 2 more than alle the tabernaclis of Jacob. Thou citee of God, with outen ende; glo- 3 riouse thingis ben seide of thee. I schal 4 be myndeful of Raab, and[g] Babiloyne; knowynge[h] me. Lo! aliens, and Tyre, and the puple of Ethiopiens; thei weren there. Whether a man schal seie to Sion, 5 And[i] a man is born ther ynne; and that man altherhi3este foundide it? The Lord schal 6 telle in the scripturis of puplis; and of these princis, that weren ther ynne. As[k] 7 the dwellyng `of alle[l] that ben glad; is in thee.

---

[t] the *AII*. [u] in thi *A*. [v] of *AEII*. [w] wickid *A*. [x] Om. *A*.

[z] the s. [a] handmaide CDEFGHIKLMOPQRSUVWXbI. [b] be thei I. [c] holpen I. holpe K. [d] Om. C *et plures.* [e] Om. EFHILP. [f] Om. A. [g] and of I. [h] kunnynge L. [i] Om. A. [k] Om. I. [l] as of alle men I.

PSALM LXXXVII.

1 *The song of the salm, to the sonys of Chore, in to the ende, for Melech, to answern, the vnderstonding of Eman Israelyte, or Esrayte.*

Domine Deus salutis mee.

2 Lord God of myn helthe; in the dai I criede and in the nyȝte befor thee. 3 Entre in thi siȝte myn orisoun; bowe in 4 thin ere to my preȝeere. For fulfild is with euelis my soule; and my lif to helle 5 neȝhede. I am eymed with men goende doun in to the lake; I am maad as a man 6 withoute helpe, among deade men free. As woundid men slepende in sepulcris, of whom thou art no mor myndeful; and 7 thei of thin hond ben put aȝeen. They putten me in the nethere lake; in derke 8 thingus, and in shadeweᵞ of deth. Vp on me is confermyd thi wodnesse; and alle thi flodis thou broȝtist in vp on me. 9 Fer thou madest my knowen fro me; thei puttenᶻ me abhominacioun to them. 10 I am traȝidᵃ, and I wente not out; myn eȝen febleden for myseise. I criede to thee, Lord; al dai I spradde out to thee 11 myn hondis. Whether to deade men thouᵇ shal do merueilis; or lechis shul 12 reren, and knoulechen to thee? Whether sum man shal telle in sepulcris thi mercy; 13 and thi treuthe in to perdicioun? Whether shul be knowen in dercnessis thi merueilis; and thi riȝtwisnesse in the 14 lond of forȝeting? And I to thee, Lord, criede; and erli myn orisoun befor shal 15 come thee. Wherto, Lord, pootist thou abac myn orisoun; thou turnest awei thi 16 face fro me? A pore man I am, and in trauailis fro my ȝouthe; enhauncid, meekid forsothe I am, and al disturbid. 17 In me passiden thurȝ thi wrathis; and 18 thi feeris al disturbiden me. They enuy-rounden me as water al day; they enuy-19 rounden me togidere. Thou longedest awei fro me frend and neȝhebore; and my knowen fro wrechidnesse.

PSALM LXXXVII.

The title of theᵐ scuene and eiȝtetitheᵢ salm. Theⁿ song ofᵒ salm, to the sones of Chore, to victorie on Mahalat, for to answere, the lernyng of Heman Esraite.

Lord God of myn helthe; Y criede in 2 dai andᵖ nyȝt bifore thee. Mi preier entre 3 bifore thi siȝt; bowe doun thin eere to my preier. For my soule is fillid with yuels; 4 and my lijf neiȝede to helle. I am gessid 5 with hem that goon doun in to the lake; Y am maad as a man with outen help, and 6 fre among deed men. As men woundid slepinge in sepulcris, of whiche men noon is�q myndeful aftir; and thei ben put awei fro thin hond. Thei han put me in the 7 lower lake; in derke places, and in the schadewe of deth. Thi strong veniaunce 8 is confermed on me; and thou hast brouȝt in alle thi wawis on me. Thou hast maad 9 fer fro me my knowun; thei han set me abhomynacioun to hem silf. I am takun, and Y ȝede not out; myn iȝen weren sijk 10 for pouert. Lord, Y criede to thee; al dai Y spredde abrood myn hondis to thee. Whethir thou schalt do merueilis to deed 11 men; ether leechis schulen reise, and thei schulen knouleche to thee? Whether ony 12 man in sepulcre schal telle thi merci; and thi treuthe in perdicioun? Whether thi 13 merueilis schulen be knowun in derk-nessis; and thi riȝtfulnesse in the lond of forȝetyng? And, Lord, Y criede to thee; 14 and erli my preier schal bifor come to thee. Lord, whi puttist thou awei my 15 preier; turnestʳ awei thi face fro me? I 16 am pore, and in traueils fro my ȝongthe; sotheli Y am enhaunsid, and Y am maad low, and disturblid. Thi wraththis pass-17 iden on me; and thi dredis disturbliden me. Thei cumpassiden me as watir al 18 dai; thei cumpassiden me togidere. Thou 19 madist fer fro me a frend and neiȝbore; and my knowun fro wretchidnesse.

ᵞ the shadewe *AEII*.   ᶻ puttiden *AII*.   ᵃ trayed *A*. crathed *E*.   ᵇ he *E pr. m.*

ᵐ Om. c et alii.   ⁿ In Ebreu thus, the IU.   ᵒ of the BL.   ᵖ and in I.   q ther is I.   ʳ thou turnest IX sec. m. i sec. m.

PSALM LXXXVIII.

1 The vnderstondyng of Ethan, Israelite.

2 The mercies of the Lord ; 'in to[c] withoute ende I shal synge. In ieneracioun and in to ieneracioun ; I shal befortelle 3 thi treuthe in my mouth. For thou seidist, In to with oute ende mercy shal be bild 'out in[d] heuenes ; beforn shal be 4 maand redy thi treuthe in hem. I disposide testament to my chosene ; I swor 5 to Dauid, my seruaunt, In to withoute ende I shal beforgreithe thi seed. And I shal bilden out ; in ieneracioun and in to 6 ieneracioun thi sete. Lord, heuenus shul knouleche thi meruelis ; forsothe thi 7 treuthe in the chirche of halewis. For who in cloudis shal be maad euene to the[e] Lord ; lic shal ben to God in the 8 sonys of God ? God, that is glorified in the counseil of seyntis ; gret, and ferful 9 vp on alle that in his cumpas ben. Lord God of vertues, who lic[f] to thee ? my3ti thou art, Lord, and thi treuthe in thi 10 cumpas. Thou lordshipist of the power of the se ; forsothe the mouyngis of his 11 flodis thou suagist. Thou mekedist, as woundid, the proude ; in the arm of thi vertue thou destro3edist thin enemys. 12 Thine ben heuenes, and thin is the erthe ; the roundnesse of erthe, and hys plente 13 thou foundedest ; the north and the se thou formedist. Thabor and Ermon in 14 thi name shul ful out io3en ; thin arm with power. Be fastned thin hond, and 15 enhauncid be thi ri3thond ; ri3twisnesse and dom beforgreithing[g] of thi sete. Merci and treuthe shul beforgo thi face ; 16 blisful the puple that wot io3ing. Lord, 17 in the li3t of thi chere thei shul go ; and in thi name thei shul ful out io3en al day ; and in thi ri3twisnesse thei[h] shul be 18 enhauncid. For the glorie of the vertu of hem thou art ; and in thi wel plesing 19 shal ben enhauncid oure horn. For of

PSALM LXXXVIII.

The title of the[s] ei3te and ei3tetithe salm.
The lernyng of Ethan, Ezraite†.

I schal synge with outen ende ; the mer-2 cies of the Lord. In generacioun and in to generacioun ; Y schal telle thi treuthe with my mouth. For thou seidist, With 3 outen ende merci schal be bildid in heuenes ; thi treuthe schal be maad redi in tho. I disposide a testament to my 4 chosun men ; Y swoor to Dauid, my seruaunt, Til in to with outen ende I schal 5 make redi thi seed. And Y schal bilde thi seete ; in generacioun, and in to generacioun. Lord, heuenes schulen knoulcche 6 thi meruellis ; and thi treuthe in the chirche of seyntis. For who in the cloudis schal 7 be maad euene to the Lord ; schal be lijk God among the sones of God ? God, 8 which[t] is glorified in the counsel of seyntis ; *is* greet, and dreedful onere alle that ben in his cumpas. Lord[u] God of 9 vertues, who *is* lijk thee ? Lord, thou art mi3ti, and thi treuthe *is* in thi cumpas. Thou art Lord of the power of the see ; 10 forsothe thou aswagist the stiryng of the wawis therof. Thou madist lowe the 11 proude, as woundid ; in the arm of thi vertu thou hast scaterid thin enemyes. Heuenes ben thin, and erthe[v] is thin ; thou 12 hast foundid the world, and the fulnesse therof ; thou madist of nou3t the north 13 and the see. Thabor and Hermon schulen make ful out ioye in thi name ; thin arm 14 with power. Thin hond be maad stidefast, and thi ri3thond be enhaunsid ; ri3t-15 fulnesse and doom *is* the makyng redy of thi seete. Merci and treuthe schulen go bifore thi face ; blessid *is* the puple that 16 kan hertli[w] song. Lord, thei schulen go in the li3t of thi cheer ; and in thi name 17 thei schulen make ful out ioye al dai ; and thei schulen be enhaunsid in thi ri3tfulnesse. For thou art the glorie of the 18 vertu of hem ; and in thi good plesaunce

---

[e] Om. *A.* [d] vp and *A.* [e] thee *A.* [f] is lijk *A.* [g] before greithingis *A.* [h] Om. *ABH.*

[s] Om. *c et alii.* [t] that *I.* [u] For *I.* [v] the erthe *ceteri.* [w] herty *I.*

the Lord is oure taking vp ; and of the
20 holi of Irael oure king. Thanne thou
speeke in viseoun to thi seintis, and thou
seidist; I haue putt helpe in the myȝti,
and I haue enhauncid the chosen of my
21 folc. I haue founde Dauid, my seruaunt;
with myn holi oile I enoyntide hym.
22 Myn hond forsothe shal helpe to hym;
23 and myn arm shal conferme hym. No
thing shal profite the enemy in hym; and
the sone of wickednesse shal not sette toⁱ,
24 to noȝen hym. And I shal al to-hewe fro
the face of hym his enemys; and the
hatende hym in to fliȝt I shal al turne.
25 And my treuthe and my mercy with
hym; aud in my name shal ben en-
26 hauncid his horn. And I shal putte in
the se his hond ; and in flodis his riȝt
27 hond. He shal inwardli clepe me, My
fader thou art ; my God, and vndertakere
28 of myn helthe. And I the first goten
shal sette hym ; heȝ befor the kingis of
29 erthe. In to with onte ende I shal kepe
to hym my mercy; and my testament
30 feithful to hym. And I shall sette in to
worldᵏ of world his sed ; and his trone as
31 the daȝis of heuene. If forsothe his
sonys shal forsake my lawe ; and in my
32 domys shul not go. If my riȝtwisnessisˡ
thei poote ferr awei; and myn hestis shul
33 not kepe. I shal visite in a ȝerde the
wickidnessisᵐ of hem ; and in betingus
34 ther synnes. My mercy forsothe I shal
not don awei fro hym ; ne noȝen in my
35 treuthe. Ne I shal not defoule my testament; and that gon out of my lippis I
36 shal not make vein. Ones I swor in
37 myn holy, to Dauid I shal not lie; his sed
38 in to withoute ende shal duelle. And his
trone as the sunne in my siȝt; and as the
moone parfit in to withoute ende, and
39 the witnesse in henene feithful. Thou
forsothe hast put abac, and dispisid ;
40 tariedist thi crist. Thou turnedist awei
the testament of thi seruaunt; thou curs-
41 idist in the erthe his seintuarie. Thou

oure horn schal be enhaunsid. For oure 19
takyng vp is of the Lord ; and of the hooli
of Israel oure kyng. Thanne thou spakist 20
in reuelacioun to thi seyntis, and seidist,
Y haue set help in the myȝti ; and Y haue
enhaunsid the chosun man of my puple.
I foond Dauid, my seruaunt ; Yˣ anoyntide 21
hym with myn hooli oile. For myn hond 22
schal helpe him ; and myn arm schal conferme hym. The enemye schal no thing 23
profite in him ; and the sone of wickidnesse
schal not ˈley toʸ, for to anoye him. And 24
Y schal sle hise enemyes fro his face ; and
Y schal turne in to fliȝt hem that haten
hym. And my treuthe and mercy schal 25
be with him ; and his horn schal be enhaunsid in my name. And Y schal sette 26
his hond in the see ; and his riȝt hoond in
flodis. He schal inwardli clepe me, Thou 27
art my fadir ; my God, and theᶻ vptaker of
myn heelthe. And Y schal sette him the 28
firste gendridᵃ sone ; hiȝer than the kyngis
of erthe. With outen ende Y schal kepe 29
my merci to hym ; and my testament feithful to him. And Y schal sette his seed 30
in to the world of world ; and his trone as
the daies of heuene. Forsothe if hise 31
sones forsaken my lawe ; and goen not in
my domes. If thei maken vnhooli my 32
riȝtfulnessis; and kepen not my comaundementis. I schal visite in a ȝerde the wickid- 33
nessis of hem ; and in betyngis the synnes
of hem. But Y schal not scatere my 34
mercy fro hym ; and in my treuthe Y schal
not anoye hym. Nethir Y schal make 35
vnhooli my testament ; and Y schal not
make voide tho thingis that comen forth
of my lippis. Onys Y swoor in myn 36
hooli ; Y schal not lie to Dauid, his seed 37
schal dwelle with outen ende. And his 38
trone as sunne in my siȝt, and as a perfit
mone with outen ende ; and a feithful witnesse in heuene. But thou hast put awei, 39
and hastᵇ dispisid ; and hast dilaied thi
crist. Thou hast turned awei the tes- 40
tament of thi seruaunt ; thou madist

ⁱ Om. *н.*   ᵏ the world *A.*   ˡ riȝtwisnes *Aн.*   ᵐ wickenessis *E.*

ˣ and Y ɪᴋ.   ʸ putt to ɪ.   ᶻ myn ɪ.   ᵃ bigoten ɪ.   ᵇ Om. ɪ.

destroȝidist alle the heggis of hym; thou
42 puttist his fastnyng drede. Ther wasteden hym alle men passende the weie; he
43 is maad repref to his neȝheboris. Thou
enhauncidist the riȝthond of men berende
hym doun; thou gladedest alle his ene-
44 mys. Thou turnedest awei ⁿ the helpe
of his swerd; and thou helpedist hym not
45 in bataile. Thou destroȝidist hym fro
his out clensing; and his sete in the erthe
46 thou hurtlidist. Thou lassedist the daȝes
of hys time; thou ful heeldedest° hym
47 with confusion. Hou longe, Lord, thou
turnest awei in to the ende; shal brenne
48 out as fyr thi wrathe? Haue mynde
what my substaunce: whether forsothe
veyn thou hast ordeynd alle the sonus
49 of men? Who is a man, thatᵖ shal liue,
and shal not see deth; and shal pulle out
50 his soule fro the hond of helle? Wher
ben thin olde mercies, Lord; as thou hast
51 sworn to Dauid in thi treuthe? Myndeful be, Lord, of the repref of thi seruauns; that I withheldᵖᵖ in my bosum, of
52 many Jentilis. The whiche thin enemys
repreueden, Lord; that thei repreueden
53 the hole chaunging of thi crist. Blessid
the Lord in to with oute ende; be it do,
be it do.

PSALM LXXXIX.

1 *The orisoun of Moises, man of God.*

Domine, refu-
gium factus es.

Lord, refut thou art maad to vs; fro
2 ieneracioun in to ieneracioun. Befor that
hillis weren maad, or were formed the
erthe and the roundnesse; fro world 'and
3 vn toq world thou art God. Ne turne
thou a man in to mecnesse; and thou
seidist, Beth conuertid, ȝee sones of men.
4 For a thousend ȝeer befor thin eȝen; as
ȝisterdai that is passid. And the warde in
5 the nyȝt, that for noȝt ben had; the ȝeris
6 of hem shul ben. Erli as an erbe passe

vnhooli his seyntuarie in erthe. Thou 41
distriedist alle the heggis therof; thou
hast set the stidefastnesse therof drede.
Alle men passynge bi the weie rauyschiden 42
him; he is maad schenschipe to hise neiȝboris. Thou hast enhaunsid the riȝthond 43
of men oppressiuge him; thou hast gladid
alle hise enemyes. Thou hast turned awei 44
the help of his swerd; and thou helpidist
not hym in batel. Thou destriedist him 45
fro clensing; and thou hast hurtlidᶜ doun
his seete in erthe. Thou hast maad lesse 46
the daies of his time; thou hast bisched
him with schenschip. Lord, hou longe 47
turnest thou awei in to the ende; schal
thin ire brenne out as fier? Bithenke 48
thou what *is* my substaunce; for whether
thou hast ordeyned veynli alle the sones
of men? Who is a man, that schal lyue, 49
and schal not se deth; schalᵈ delyuere his
soule fro the hond of helle? Lord, where 50
ben thin elde mercies; as thou hast swore
to Dauid in thi treuthe? Lord, be thou 51
myndeful of the schenschipe of thi seruauntis, of many hethene men; whiche Y
helde togidere in my bosum. Whiche 52
thin enemyes, Lord, diden schenschipfuli;
for thei dispisiden the chaungyng of thi
crist. Blessid *be* the Lord with outen 53
ende; he it don, be it don.

PSALM LXXXIX.

The title of theᵉ nyne and eiȝtetithe salm. 1 †
The preier of Moises, the man of God †.

Lord, thou art maad help to vs; fro
generacioun in to generacioun. Bifore that 2
hillis weren maad, ether the erthe and the
world was formed; fro the world and in
to the world thou art God. Turne thou 3
not awei a man in to lownesse; and thou
seidist, Ȝe sones of men, be conuertid. For 4
a thousynde ȝeer *ben* bifore thin iȝen; as
ȝistirdai, which is passid, and as keping
in the niȝt. The ȝeeris of hem schulen be; 5
that ben had for nouȝt. Eerli passe he, as 6

† The preier of Moises, the man of God, to gete Goddis benefices to the puple of Israel, out of Egipt, to gette bene-fices in tyme to comyng. *Like here.* x.

ⁿ Om. c.   ° hilidist A.   ᵖ and AH.   ᵖᵖ withholde A.   q in to A. and in to EH.

ᶜ hurlid 1.   ᵈ *that* shal 1.   ᵉ Om. c *et alii.*

he, erli flurshe[r] he, and passe; at euen falle he doun, inwardli harde he, and waxe drie. 7 For we han failid in thi wrathe; and in 8 thi wodnesse wee ben disturbid. Thou hast put oure wickidnessis[s] in thi si3t; oure world in the li3ting of thi chere. 9 For alle oure da3is failleden; and in thi wrathe wee han failid. Oure 3eris, as an 10 ireyn, shul be betho3t; the da3is of oure 3eris in tho seuenti 3er[t]. If forsothe in my3tis ei3teti 3er; and the more ouer of them trauaile and sorewe. For ther ouer-cam debonernesse; and wee shul be chas-11 tisid. Who knew3 the power of thi wrathe; and for thi drede thi wrathe de-12 noumbren? Thi ri3thond so mac knowen; 13 and the ta3t with herte in wisdam. Be thou conuertid, Lord, hou longe; and louli preyable be thou vp on thi seruauns. 14 Wee ben fulfild erly with thi mercy; wee han ful out io3ed, and delitid in alle oure 15 da3is. Wee han io3id for the da3is in whiche thou hast mekid vs; the 3eris in 16 whiche wee han seen euelis. Behold, Lord, in to thi seruauns, and in to thi werkys; and reule forth the sones of hem. 17 And be the shynyng of the Lord oure God vp on vs; and the werkis of oure hondis ri3tforth reule 'vp on[u] vs; and the werk of oure hondis reule ri3tforth.

PSALM XC.

Qui habitat in adiutorio Altissimi.

1 *The preysing of the song, to hym Dauid.*

That woneth in the helpe of the hei3est; in the defending of God of heuene shal al 2 abide. He shal sei to the Lord, Myn vndertakere art thou, and my refut; my 3 God, I shal hope in to hym. For he deliuerede me fro the grene of hunteres; 4 and fro the sharpe woord. With his shuldris he shal al aboute shadewe to thee; and under his pennys thou shalt hopen. 5 With the sheld shal enuyroune thee his treuthe; thou shalt not drede fro the ny3t

---

an eerbe, eerli florische he, and passe; in the euentid falle he doun, be he hard, and wexe[f] drie. For we han failid in thin ire; 7 and we ben disturblid in thi strong ven-iaunce. Thou hast set oure wickidnessis 8 in thi si3t; oure world in the li3tning of thi cheer. For alle oure daies han failid; 9 and we han failid in thin ire. Oure 3eris schulen bithenke, as[g] an yreyn; the daies 10 of oure 3eeris *ben* in[h] tho seuenti 3eeris. Forsothe, if fourescoor[i] 3eer[k] *ben* in my3ti men; and the more[l] tyme of[m] hem is trauel and sorewe. For myldenesse cam aboue; and we schulen be chastisid. Who knew 11 the power of thin ire; and *durste* noumbre thin ire for thi drede? Make thi ri3thond 12 so knowun; and *make* men lerned[n] in herte bi wisdom. Lord, be thou conuertid sum-13 deel; and be thou able to be preied on[o] thi seruauntis. We weren fillid eerli with thi 14 merci; we maden ful out ioye, and we delitiden in alle oure daies. We weren glad 15 for the daies in whiche thou madist vs meke; for the 3eeris in whiche we si3en yuels. Lord, biholde thou into thi ser-16 uauntis, and in to thi werkis; and dresse thou the sones of hem. And the schynyng 17 of oure Lord God be on vs; and dresse thou the werkis of oure hondis on vs, and dresse thou the werk[p] of oure hondis.

PSALM XC.

1 `The nyntithe salm[q].

He that dwellith in the help of the hi3este *God*; schal dwelle in the proteccioun of God of heuene. He schal seie to 2 the Lord, Thou art myn vptaker, and my refuit; my God, Y schal hope in him. For 3 he delyuered me fro the snare of hunteris; and fro a scharp word. With hise schul-4 dris he schal make schadowe to thee; and thou schalt haue hope vnder hise fetheris. His treuthe schal cumpasse thee with a 5 scheld; thou schalt not drede of[r] ny3tis

---

r floure *AEH*.   s wickenessis *E*. wickidnesse *II*.   t 3eeris *AEH*.   u vp *A*.

f wexe he is.   g upon as i.   h Om. c.   i ei3ti c *et plures.*   k 3eeris i.   l Om. i.   m moreouer of i. n so leerned s.   o of i.   p werkis *A pr. m.*   q *The tijtle of the lxxxx. salm.* ioi. *The nyntithe salm Moises made also.* K. *The lxxxx. salm hath no title, nether in Ebrew, nether in Jerom.* uv.   r of the i.

6 drede. Fro the arwe fleende in dai^v, fro the nede goende in dercnessis thur3; fro the inrennyng, and the^w myddai deuel. 7 Ther shul falle fro thi side a thousend, and ten thousend^x fro thi ri3t sidis; to 8 thee forsothe he shal not ne3he. Neuerthelatere with thin e3en thou shalt beholde; and the 3elding of synnes thou 9 shalt see. For thou art^y, Lord, myn hope; he3est thou hast put thi^z refut. 10 Ther shal not come to thee euel; and scourge shal not ne3he^a to thi tabernacle. 11 For to his aungelis he comaundide of thee; that thei shulden kepen thee in alle 12 thi weies. In hondis thei shul bern thee; lest parauenture thou offende at the ston 13 thi foot. Vp on the eddere and the kokatrice thou shalt go; and thou shalt to-14 trede the leoun and the dragoun. For in me he hopide, I shal delyueren hym; I shal defende hym, for he knew3 my 15 name. He criede to me, and I ful out shal heren hym^b, with hym I am in tribulacioun; I^c shal taken hym out, and 16 glorifien hym. In lengthe of da3is I shal fulfillen hym; and shewen to hym myn helthe 3yuere.

PSALM XCI.

1 *The salm of the song, in the dai of sabot.*

Bonum est confiteri.

2 Good it is to knoulechen to the Lord; and to do salm to thi name, thou he3est. 3 To tellen out erly thi mercy; and thi 4 treuthe by the^d ny3t. In the ten cordid 5 sautre; with song in the harpe. For thou hast delitid me, Lord, in thi making; and in the werkis of thin hondis I 6 shal ful out io3en. Hou magnefied ben thi werkis, Lord; ful myche deep ben 7 maad thi tho3tys. The vnwise man shal not knowen; and the fool shal not vn-8 derstonde thes thingus. Whan full out sprunge shul ben the synneres, as hei; and shuln aperen alle, that wirken wicke-

drede. Of an arowe fliynge in^s the dai, 6 of^t a^n gobelyn goynge in derknessis; of asailing, and^v a myddai feend. A thou-7 synde schulen falle doun fro thi side, and ten thousynde fro thi ri3tside; forsothe it schal not nei3e to thee. Netheles thou 8 schalt biholde with thin i3en; and thou schalt se the 3elding of synneris. For 9 thou, Lord, art myn hope; thou hast set thin help altherhi3este. Yuel schal not 10 come to thee; and a scourge schal not nei3e to thi tabernacle. For *God* hath 11 comaundid to hise aungels of thee; that thei kepe thee in alle thi weies. Thei 12 schulen beere thee in the hondis; leste perauenture thou hirte thi foot at a stoon. Thou schalt go on^w a snake, and a^x coca-13 trice; and thou schalt defoule a lioun and a dragoun. For he hopide in me, Y schal 14 delyuere hym; Y schal defende him, for he knew my name. He criede to me, and 15 Y schal here him, Y am with him in tribulacioun; Y schal delyuere him, and Y schal glorifie hym. I schal fille hym with 16 the lengthe of daies; and Y schal schewe myn helthe to him.

PSALM XCI.

The `title of the^y oon and nyntithe salm. 1 `The salm^z of `song, in the dai of^a sabath.

It is good to knouleche to the Lord; 2 and to synge to thi name, thou^b hi3este. To schewe eerli thi merci; and thi treuthe 3 bi ny3t. In a sautrie of ten cordis; with 4 song in harpe. For thou, Lord, hast de-5 litid me in thi makyng; and Y schal make ful out ioye in the werkis of thin hondis. Lord, thi werkis ben magnefied greetli; 6 thi thou3tis ben maad ful depe. An vn-7 wise man schal not knowe; and a fool schal not vndirstonde these thingis. Whanne 8 synneris comen forth, as hey; and alle thei apperen, that worchen wickidnesse. That 9 thei perische in to the world of world;

v the dai ʌ II. w Om. ʌ. x thousandis ʌ. y Om. ʌ II. z my ʌ. a nei3e to ʌ. b Om. c. c and ʌ. d Om. ʌ II.

s on s. t and of c *et plures.* u Om. s. v and of m. of x. w upon k. x on a I. y Om. ʌ. z Om. c. a Om. ʌ. b *that art* I.

9 nesse[e]. That thei dien in to the world of world; thou forsothe he3est in to with-10 oute ende, Lord. For lo! thin enemys, Lord, for lo! thin enemys shul pershen; and alle shul be scaterid that werken 11 wickidnesse. And as an vnycorn shal ben enhauncyd myn horn; and my laste 12 age in 'plenteuous mercy[f]. And myn e3e lokide doun myn enemys; and to the in-riseris wariende in me shal here myn ere. 13 The ri3twis as palm shal floure; as the cedre of Liban he shal be multiplied. 14 The plauntid in the hous of the Lord; in the porchis of the hous of oure God 15 shul floure. 3it they shul be multiplied in the laste 'plenteuous age[g]; and wel suffrende thei shul be, that thei telle. For ri3t is the Lord oure God; and ther is not wickidnesse in hym.

forsothe thou, Lord, *art* the hi3est, with-outen ende. For lo! Lord, thin enemyes, 10 for lo! thin enemyes schulen perische; and alle [e] schulen be scaterid that worchen wickidnesse. And myn horn schal be 11 reisid as an vnicorn; and myn eelde in plenteuouse merci. And myn i3e dis- 12 piside myn enemyes; and whanne wickid men rysen a3ens me, myn eere schal here. A iust man schal floure as a palm tree; 13 he schal be multiplied as a cedre of Liban. Men plauntid in the hous of the Lord; 14 schulen floure in the porchis of the hous of oure God. 3it thei schulen be multi- 15 plied in plenteuouse elde; and thei schu-len be suffryng wel. That thei telle, that oure Lord God is ri3tful; and no wickid-nesse is in hym.

PSALM XCII.

The preising of the song of David, in the dai befor the sabat, whan foundid is the erthe.

1 The Lord regnede, fairnesse he is clad[h]; the Lord is clad[h] strengthe, and befor-2 girte[i] hymself. Forsothe he fastnede the roundnesse of erthe[k]; that shal not be to-3 gidere stirid. Greithid is thi sete, God, fro thanne; fro the world thou art. The flodis rereden vp, Lord; the flodis rereden vp ther vois. Flodis rereden vp ther flow-4 ingis; fro the voises[l] of manye watris. Merueilouse the wawis of the se; merueil-5 ous in he3e thingis the Lord. Thi wit-nessingis ben maad beleeuable ful myche; holynesse semeth thin hous, Lord, in to the lengthe of da3es.

PSALM XCII.

The two and nyntithe salm[d]†.

1 The Lord hath regned, he is clothid with fairnesse; the Lord is clothid with strengthe, and hath gird hym silf. For 2 he made stidefast the world; that schal not be móued. God, thi seete was maad 3 redi fro that tyme; thou art fro the world. Lord, the flodis han reisid; the flodis han reisid her vois. Flodis reisiden[e] her wawis; of the voicis[f] of many watris. The reisyngis 4 of the see *ben* wondurful; the Lord *is* wondurful in hi3e thingis. Thi witness- 5 ingis ben maad able to be hileued greetli; Lord, holynesse bicometh thin hous, in to the lengthe of daies.

†This salm hath no tijtle, nether in Ebreu, ne in Jerom, and E-bree3 seyn, that Moises made this salm. 1. The lettres of this salm is fillid in the rewme of Crist; and rewmes of the world ben suget to it bi feith. *Lyre here.* 1K.

PSALM XCIII.

The salm of Dauid, the ferthe dai of the wike.

1 God of veniauncis Lord; God of ven-2 iauncis freeli dide. Be thou enhauncid

PSALM XCIII.

The thre and nyntithe salm[g]†.

1 God *is* Lord of veniauncis; God of [h] veniauncis[i] dide freli. Be thou enhaunsid 2

‡ This salm hath no tijtle, neither in E-breu, ne in Jerom. 1. In this salm Moises a3en-clepith the pe-ple fro errour, about Goddis puruyannce, and schewith that Goddis puruyaunce streechith forth to alle thingis, and punischith iustli synners. *Lyre here.* 1K.

e wickedenesse AEH. f the mercy of the tete E pr. m. g age of the tete E pr. m. h clothed AEH. i he before girde A. k the erthe AEH. l vois A.

e alle thei 1. d The two and nyntithe salm, that Moizes made, hath no title. K. The lxxxxij. salm hath no title. U. e han reisiden L. f vois A. g The lxxxxij. A. The title of the lxxxxij. salm. G. The lxxxxij. salm hath no title. U. h Om. o sec. m. i veniaunce CDEFLSb.

that demest the erthe; ȝeld ȝelding to the
3 proude. Hou longe synneres, Lord; hou
4 longe synneres shul glorien? Thei shul
steringli seyn, and speke wickidnesse;
alle shul speke that wirchen vnriȝtwis-
5 nesse. Thi puple, Lord, thei mekeden;
6 and ouertrauaileden thin eritage. The
widewe and the comeling thei sloowen;
and the moderles childer thei killeden.
7 And thei seiden, The Lord shal not seen;
ne the God of Jacob shal vnderstonde.
8 Vnderstondeth, ȝee vnwise men in the
puple; and, ȝee foolis, sum tyme sa-
9 uoureth. He that plauntide the ere, shal
he not heren; or he that made the eȝe,
10 behalt[m] not? That chastiseth Jentilis,
shal he not vndirnyme; that techeth man
11 kunnyng? The Lord wot the thoȝtis of
12 men; for thei ben veyne. Blisful the
man, whom thou shalt euforme, Lord;
and of thi lawe thou shalt techen hym[n].
13 That thou suage hym fro euele daȝes; to
the time be dolue to the synnere a dich.
14 For the Lord shal not putte abac his
15 folc; and his eritage shal not forsake. For
to riȝtwisnesse be turned in to dom; and
who beside it, alle that ben riȝtwis in
16 herte. Who shal 'al rijsen[o] to me aȝen
the warieris; or who shal stonde with
me aȝen the werkende[p] wickidnesse?
17 But for the Lord halp[q] me; parauenture
18 my soule shulde han duellid in helle. If
I seide, Moued is my foot; thi mercy,
19 Lord, halp[q] me. After the multitude of
my sorewis in myn herte; thi coumfort-
20 ingis gladeden[r] my soule. Whether cleueth to thee the sete off wickidnesse; that
21 formest trauaile in the heste? Thei shul
cacchen in to the soule of the riȝtwis;
and the innocent blod thei shul con-
22 dempne. And the Lord is maad to me
in to refut; and my God in to the helpe
23 of myn hope. And he shal ȝeelde to hem
the wickidnesse of hem, and in the malice of hem he shal destroȝe them; shal
destroȝe them the Lord oure God.

that demest the erthe; ȝelde thou ȝeldinge
to proude men. Lord, hou longe synneris; 3
hou longe schulen synneris haue glorie?
Thei schulen telle out, and schulen speke 4
wickidnesse; alle men schulen speke that
worchen vnriȝtfulnesse. Lord, thei han 5
maad lowe thi puple; and thei han disesid
thin eritage. Thei killiden a widowe and 6
a comelyng; and thei han slayn fadirles
children and modirles. And thei seiden, 7
The Lord schal not se; and God of Jacob
schal not vndurstonde. Ȝe vnwise men in 8
the puple, vndirstonde[k]; and, ȝe foolis, lerne[l]
sum tyme. Schal not he here, that plaunt-9
ide the eere; ethere biholdith not he, that
made the iȝe? Schal not he repreue, that 10
chastisith folkis; which[m] techith man kunnyng? The Lord knowith the thouȝtis of 11
men; that tho ben veyne. Blessid is the[n] 12
man, whom thou, Lord, hast lerned[o]; and
hast tauȝt him of thi lawe. That thou 13
aswage hym fro yuele daies; til a diche
be diggid to the synner. For the Lord 14
schal not putte awei his puple; and he
schal not forsake his eritage. Til riȝtful-15
nesse be turned in to dom; and who ben
niȝ it, alle that ben of riȝtful herte. Who 16
schal rise with me aȝens mysdoeris; ether
who schal stonde with me aȝens hem that
worchen wickidnesse? No but for the 17
Lord helpide me; almest my soule hadde
dwellid in helle. If Y seide, My foot was 18
stirid; Lord, thi merci helpide me. Aftir 19
the multitude of my sorewis in myn herte;
thi coumfortis maden glad my soule. Whe-20
ther the seete of wickidnesse cleueth to
thee; that makist trauel[p] in comaundement? Thei schulen take aȝens the soule 21
of a iust man; and thei schulen condempne
innocent blood. And the Lord was maad 22
to me in to refuȝt; and my God was maad
in to[q] the help of myn hope. And he 23
schal ȝelde to hem the wickidnesse of hem;
and in the malice of hem he schal lese
hem, oure Lord God schal lese hem.

---

[m] beholdeth *ABH*.   [n] hem c.   [o] Arijse *AH*.   [p] worcher H.   [q] helpede *AEH*.   [r] gladen *H*.

[k] vndirstondeth I.   [l] lerneth I.   [m] the which I.   [n] that I.   [o] lered I.   [p] traueylis s.   [q] Om. LS.

PSALM XCIV.

The preising of the song, to hym Dauid.

exulte- 1 Cometh, ful out ioȝe wee to the Lord; inwardli ioȝe wee to God, our helthe 2 ȝiuere. Befor ocupie wee his face in knouleching; and in salmys inwardli ioȝe 3 wee to hym. For God a gret Lord, and a gret king ouer alle godis; for the Lord 4 shal not poote abac his folc. For in his hond ben alle the[s] coostis of erthe[t]; and 5 the heiȝtis of hillis ben of hym. For of hym is the se, and he made it; and the 6 drie his hondis formeden. Cometh, honoure wee, and falle wee doun before God, wepe wee befor the Lord, for he made 7 vs; for he is the Lord oure God. And wee the puple of his leswe; and the shep 8 of his hond. To dai if hys vois ȝee han 9 herd; wileth not[u] hardne ȝoure hertis. As in the terring, after the day; of tempting in desert. Where tempteden me ȝoure fadris; proueden and seȝen my werkis. 10 Fourti ȝeer offended I was to that ieneracioun; and I seide, Euermor these erren 11 in herte. And thes knewen not my weyes, to whom I swor in my wrathe; thei shul not entre in to my reste.

PSALM XCV.

1 *The salm of Dauid, whan the hous was bild vp after the caitifte.*

te Do- Syngeth to the Lord a newe song; 2 singeth to the Lord, al erthe. Syngeth to the Lord, and blesseth to his name; telleth fro dai in to dai his 'helthe ȝyuere[v]. 3 Tellith out among Jentilis his glorie; in 4 alle puplis his merueilis. For the·Lord gret[w], and preisable ful myche; ferful he 5 is ouer alle godis. For alle the godis off Jentilis deuelis; the Lord forsothe he-6 uens made. Knouleching and fairnesse in the siȝte of hym; holynesse and gret 7 doing in the halewing of hym. Bringeth

PSALM XCIV.

The foure and nyntithe salm[r]†.

Come ȝe, make we ful out ioie to the 1 Lord; hertli synge we to God, oure heelthe. Bifore ocupie we his face in knowleching; 2 and hertli synge we to him in salmes. For 3 God *is* a greet Lord, and a greet king aboue alle goddis; for the Lord schal not putte awei his puple. For alle the endis 4 of erthe ben in his hond; and the hiȝ-nesses[s] of hillis ben hise. For the see is 5 his, and he made it; and hise hondis form-eden the drie lond. Come ȝe, herie[t] we, 6 and falle we[u] doun bifore God, wepe we bifore the Lord that made vs; for he is 7 oure Lord God. And we *ben* the puple of his lesewe; and the scheep of his hond. If ȝe han herd his vois to dai; nyle ȝe make 8 hard ȝoure hertis. As in the terryng to 9 wraththe; bi the dai of temptacioun in de-sert. Where ȝoure fadris temptiden me; thei preueden and sien[v] my werkis. Fourti 10 ȝeer I was offendid to this generacioun; and Y seide, Euere thei erren in herte. And these men knewen not my weies; to 11 whiche[w] Y swoor in myn ire, thei schulen not entre in to my reste.

PSALM XCV.

The fyue and nyntithe salm hath no title[x]†. 1

Singe ȝe a newe song to the Lord; al erthe, synge ȝe to the Lord. Synge ȝe to 2 the Lord, and blesse ȝe his name; telle ȝe his heelthe fro dai in to dai. Telle ȝe his 3 glorie among hethene men; hise merueilis among alle puplis. For the Lord *is* greet, 4 and worthi to be preisid ful myche; he is ferdful aboue alle goddis. For alle the 5 goddis of hethene men *ben* feendis; but the Lord made heuenes. Knouleching 6 and fairnesse *is* in his siȝt; hoolynesse and worthi doyng *is* in his halewing. Ȝe 7 cuntrees of hethene men, brynge[y] to the

+ This salm hath no tijde, neither in E-breu, ne in Jerom. 1. Notheles in the Ej. and the lij. c°. to E-breies, Poul seith, that this salm was maad of Dauid, and it spekith not of the entring in to the lond of biheest vndir Josue, but of the entring in to the lond of lyuynge men, that schulde be opened bi Crist in the tyme of grace; for bi his blessid pas-sioun he re-mouyde the lettyng. *Lyre here.* 1x.

‡ *A glos.* This salm hath no tijde, neither in Ebreu, ne in Jerom. 1. This salm spek-ith of the tyme of Crist, that bigan propirly at the begyn-nyng of the preching of the gospel. *Lire here.* 1x.

---

[s] Om. *AEH.* [t] the erthe *E.* [u] not aȝeen *AEH.* [v] helthe *c.* [w] is greet *A.*

[r] *The* lxxxxiiij. *A. The foure and nyntithe salm hath no title, whanne Dauid made it.* K. *The* lxxxxiiij. *salm hath no title.* v. [s] hiȝnesse 1K. [t] and herie *s.* [u] Om. *s.* [v] sauȝen 1 *passim.* [w] whom 1. [x] From v. *The titil of the fyue and nyntithe salm.* c. *The* lxxxxv. *salm.* c *et plures. The fyue and nyntithe salm, the salm of Dauith, whanne the arke was brouȝt in to his hous.* K. [y] bryngeth 1.

to the Lord, ȝee kuntres of Jentilis; bringeth to the Lord glorie and wrshipe; 8 bringeth to the Lord glorie to hys name. Taketh ostis, and[x] entreth in to his 9 porchis; honoureth the Lord in his holi porche. Be to moued fro his face al 10 erthe; seith in Jentilis, for the Lord hath regned. Forsothe he hath amendid the roundnesse of erthe[y], that shal not be moued; he shal demen puplis in 11 equite. Gladen heuenes, and ful out ioȝe the erthe, be to moued the se, and his 12 pleute; feeldis shul ioȝen, and alle thingus that in hem ben. Thanne alle the[z] trees of wodis shul ful out ioȝen fro the face 13 of the Lord, for he cam; for he cam to demen the erthe. He shal demen the roundnesse of the[a] erthe in equite; and puplis in his treuthe.

PSALM XCVI.

1 The salm of Dauid, whan his lond is restorid to hym.

Dominus regnauit, exultet.

The Lord hath regned, the erthe ful 2 out ioȝe it; manye ilis glade thei. Cloude and derenesse in his cumpas; riȝtwisnesse 3 and dom the coreccioun of his sete. Fir beforn hym shal go; and enflaume in the 4 cumpas his enemys. His leitis liȝteden to the roundnesse of the erthe; he saȝ, 5 and the erthe is al to-moued. Hillis as wax floweden fro the face of the Lord; 6 fro the face of the Lord al erthe. Heuenes tolden out his riȝtwisnesse; and alle pu-7 plis seȝen his glorie. Be thei confoundid, alle that honouren grauen thingus; and that glorien in their maumetis. Honour-8 eth hym alle ȝee his aungelis; Sion herde, and gladdede. And the doȝtris of Jude ful 9 out gladeden; for thi domes, Lord. For thou, Lord, heȝest ouer alle erthe; ful myche thou art enhauncid ouer alle 10 goddis. ȝee that loouen the Lord, hatith euel; the Lord kepeth the soulis of hys

Lord, bringe ȝe glorye and onour to the Lord; bringe ȝe to the Lord glorie to hys 8 name. Take ȝe sacrificis, and entre ȝe in to the hallis of hym; herie ȝe the Lord in 9 his hooli halle. Al erthe be moued of his face; seie ȝe among hethene men, that the 10 Lord hath regned. And he hath amendid the world, that schal not be moued; he schal deme puplis in equite. Heuenes be 11 glad, and the erthe make ful out ioye, the see and the fulnesse therof be moued togi-dere; feeldis schulen make ioye, and alle 12 thingis that ben in tho. Thanne alle the trees of wodis schulen make ful out ioye, for the face of the Lord, for he cometh; 13 for he cometh to deme the erthe. He schal deme the world in equite; and pu-plis in his treuthe.

PSALM XCVI.

The sixe and nyntithe salm[z]†.

The Lord hath regned, the erthe make ful out ioye; many ilis be glad. Cloude 2 and derknesse in his cumpas; riȝtfulnesse and doom *is* amending of his secte. Fier 3 schal go bifore him; and[a] schal enflawme[b] hise enemyes in cumpas. Hise leitis schyn-4 eden to the world; the erthe siȝ, and was moued. Hillis as wax fletiden doun fro 5 the face of the Lord; al erthe fro the[c] face of the Lord. Heuenes telden his[d] 6 riȝtfulnesse; and alle puplis sien his glorie. Alle[e] that worschipen sculptilis[f]‡ be schent, 7 and thei that han glorie in her symelacris; alle ȝe[g] aungels of the Lord, worschipe[h] him. Sion herde, and was glad, and the 8 doȝtris of Juda maden ful out ioye; for 'thi domes, Lord[i]. For thou, Lord, art 9 the hiȝeste on al erthe; thou art greetli enhaunsid ouere alle goddis. ȝe that louen 10 the Lord, hate[k] yuel; the Lord kepith the soulis of hise seyntis; he schal delyuer

† This salm hath no titil, neither in Ebreu, ne in Jerom. It spekith of the comyng of Crist to the dome of discussioun, that is to reise gode men to blisse, and to caste doun wickid men to helle, as the salm bifore spekith of his comyng to the doom of discrecioun, that is, to clepe sum men to faith bi grace, and to forsake othere men in synne. *Lyre.* 1. ‡ That is, idols maad with hondis. *Austyn here,* x.

---

x Om. c.   y the erthe A.   z Om. AH.   a Om. A.

z *lxxxxvi.* A1. *The sixe and vyntithe salme hath no title, and it spekith of the comynge of Crist to the doom.* K. *The lxxxvi. salm hath no title.* V.   a and it 1.   b enflawme, either sette a fier c *et plures.* c Om. CF *pr. m.* ΠΚΡQWb.   d her A.   e Alle thei 1.   f grauen thingis *or* ymagis 1.   g the A. h worshipeth 1.   i the domes of the Lord s.   k hateth 1.

seintis; fro the hond of the synnere he 11'shal deliuere[b] them. Li3t is sprunge to the ri3twis; and gladnesse to the ri3t 12men in herte. Glade, 3ee ri3twise, in the Lord; and knoulecheth to the mynde of his halewing.

hem fro the hond of the[l] synner. Li3t is 11 risun to the ri3tful man; and gladnesse to ri3tful men of herte. Juste men, be 3e[m] 12 glad in the Lord; and knouleche 3e[n] to the mynde of his halewyng.

PSALM XCVII.

Cantate Dominico canticum nouum.

1   *The salm of Dauid.*

Singeth to the Lord a newe song; for merueilous thingus he dide. His ri3t hond sauede to hym; and the holi arm 2of hym. Knowen made the Lord his helthe 3euere; in the si3te of Jentilis he 3shewide his ri3twisnesse. He recordide of his mercy; and of his treuthe, to the hous of Irael. Alle the termes of erthe 4se3en; the helthe 3euere of oure God. Inwardli io3e 3ee to God, al erthe[c]; syng-eth, and ful out io3eth, and doth salm. 5Doth salm to the Lord in harpe, and in 6harpe and in vois of salm; in trumpis beten out, and in vois of the hornene trumpe. Inwardli io3eth in the si3te of 7the Lord king[d]; he moued the se, and his plente; the roundnesse of londis, and 8alle that dwellen in it. The flodis shul flappe for io3e with hond togidere; moun-9teynes shul ful out io3en fro the si3te of the Lord; for he cam to deme the erthe. He shal deme the roundnesse of the erthe in ri3twisnesse; and puplis in equitie.

PSALM XCVII.

The seuen and nyntithe salm hath no title[q]†. 1

Singe 3e a newe song to the Lord; for he hath do merueils. His ri3t hond and his hooli arm; hath maad heelthe to hym. The Lord hath maad knowun his heelthe; 2 in the si3t of hethene men he hath schewid his ri3tfulnesse. He bithou3te on his merci; 3 and on his treuthe, to the hous of Israel. Alle the endis of erthe; sien the heelthe of oure God. Al erthe, make 3e hertli ioye 4 to God; synge 3e, and make 3e ful out ioye, and seie 3e salm. Singe 3e to the 5 Lord in an harpe, in harpe and[r] vois of salm; in trumpis betun out[s] with hamer, 6 and in vois of a trumpe of horn. Hertli synge 3e in the si3t of the Lord, the king; the see and the fulnesse therof be moued; 7 the world, and thei that dwellen therynne. Flodis schulen make ioie with hond, to-8 gidere hillis schulen make ful out ioye, for[t] si3t of the Lord; for he cometh to 9 deme the erthe. He schal deme the world in ri3tfulnesse; and puplis in equite.

PSALM XCVIII.

Dominus regnauit, irascean-tur.

1   *The salm of Dauid.*

The Lord regnede, wrathen the puplis; thou that sittist vp on cherubyn, be moued 2the erthe. The Lord in Sion gret; and 3hey3 ouer alle puplis. Knouleche thei to thi gret name, for ferful and holi it is; 4and the wrshipe of the king looueth dom. Thou hast greithid ri3tforth reulingis; dom and ri3twisnesse in Jacob thou hast 5do. Enhaunce 3ee the Lord oure God,

PSALM XCVIII.

The ei3te and nyntithe salm[v]‡.

1

The Lord hath regned, puplis ben wrooth; thou that sittist on cherubyn, the erthe be moued. The Lord *is* greet 2 in Sion; and hi3 aboue alle puplis. Knou-3 leche thei to thi greet name, for it is ferd-ful and hooli; and the onour of the king 4 loueth doom. Thou hast maad redi dress-yngis; thou hast maad doom and ri3tful-nesse in Jacob. Enhaunse 3e oure Lord 5

---

[b] delyuered A. delyueren II.   [c] the erthe AEII.   [d] the king E *pr. m.*

[l] Om. 8.   [m] Om. A.   [n] Om. s.   [q] From K. *The titil of the seuen and nyntithe salm.* A. *The title of lxxxvii. salm; a salm* CDIIOQRSUX.   [r] and in I.   [s] Om. L.   [t] for the co *pr. m.* sx. fro K.   [u] *lxxxviii.* AI. *The ei3te and nyntithe salm, that Dauid made of the rewme of Crist, hath no title.* K. *The title lxxxviii. salm.* 8. *The lxxxviii. psalm hath no title, nether in Ebreu, nether in Jerom.* v.

and honoureth the litle steȝing vp place
6 of his feet, for it is holi. Moyses and
Aron in[e] the prestis of hym; and Samuel among hem that inwardli clepen
his name. Thei inwardli clepeden the
7 Lord, and he ful out herde them; in the
piler of a cloude he spac to them. Thei
kepten his witnessingus; and the heste
8 that he ȝaf to hem. Lord oure God, thou
'ful out[f] herdest hem; God, thou mèrciful
were to them, and veniende in to alle
9 the findingus of hem. Enhaunceth the
Lord oure God, and honoureth in the
holy hil of hym; for holi the Lord oure
God.

God; and worschipe ȝe the stool of hise
feet, for it is hooli. Moises and Aaron 6
weren among hise preestis; and Samuel
was among hem that inwardli clepen his
name. Thei inwardli clepiden the Lord,
and he herde hem; in a piler of cloude[o] 7
he spak to hem. Thei kepten hise witnessyngis; and the comaundement which
he ȝaf to hem. Oure Lord God[p], thou 8
herdist hem; God, thou were merciful to
hem, and thou tokist veniaunce on al her
fyndyngis. Enhaunse ȝe oure Lord God, 9
and worschipe ȝe in his hooli hil; for oure
Lord God *is* hooli.

PSALM XCIX.

1 *The salm in confessioun.*

Jubilate Deo.

2 Inwardli ioȝe ȝee to God, al erthe[g];
serueth to the Lord in gladnesse. En-
3 treth in his siȝte; in ful out ioȝing. Witeth,
for the Lord he is God; he made vs, and
we not vsself[h]. His puple, and the schep
4 of his leswe, goth in to his ȝatys in confessioun; his porchis in ympnes, 'knouleche ȝee[i] to hym. Preise ȝee his name,
5 for swete is the Lord, in to withouten
ende his mercy; and unto ieneracioun
and ieneracioun his treuthe.

PSALM XCIX.

The titil of the[q] nyne and nyntithe salm. 1
*'A salm[r] to knouleche; 'in Ebrew[s] 'thus,
A salm for knouleching[t]†.*

Al erthe, singe ȝe hertli to God; serue 2
ȝe the Lord in gladnesse. Entre ȝe in his
siȝt; in ful out ioiyng. Wite ȝe, that the 3
Lord hym silf is God; he made vs, and
not we maden vs. His puple, and the
scheep of his lesewe, entre ȝe in to hise 4
ȝatis in knoulechyng; *entre ȝe in to* hise
porchis, 'knouleche ȝe[u] to him in ympnes.
Herye ȝe his name, for the Lord is 5
swete, his merci *is* with outen ende; and
his treuthe *is* in generacioun and in to
generacioun.

PSALM C.

1 *The salm to hym Dauid.*

Misericordiam et iudicium.

Mercy and dom; I shal singe to thee,
2 Lord. I shal do salm, and vnderstonde in
the vndefoulid weie; whan thou shalt come
to me. I fulli ȝide in the innocence of
myn herte; in the myddel of myn hous.
3 I purposide not befor myn eȝen an vnriȝtwis thing; the doende the brekingus
of the lawe I hatide. Ther cleuede not
4 to me a shreude herte; the malice doere

PSALM C.

The titil of the hundrid salm. 'The salm[v] 1
of Dauid‡.

Lord[w], Y schal synge to thee; merci
and doom. I schal synge, and Y schal vn- 2
durstonde in a weie with out wem; whanne
thou schalt come to me. I ȝede perfitli in
the innocence of myn herte; in the myddil
of myn hous. I settide not forth bifore 3
myn iȝen an vniust thing; Y hatide hem
that maden trespassyngis. A schrewide 4
herte cleuede not to me; Y knewe not a

† *A glos.* This salm was maad to be songen in the offring of pesible sacrifices, that was offrid to God for sum benefice to be geten of him, to wiche the plesing of God is requyred bifore, ether for benefice now goten, to wich the doing of thankingis oweth to seve. *Lire here.* K.

‡ *A glos.* Dauith made this salm, whanne he knew that God hadde stabliyschid and confermed him in the rewme of Israel, and therfore he purposide thanne stidefastli to vse wel the power of king, thouȝ he felde fro this purpos bi his frelte and stiring of the deuel, in doing auowtrie, and mansleyng, and in the noumbring of the peple, ether summe othere synnes, for wiche he dide verrey penaunce. *Lire here.* K.

[e] and E. [f] Om. *AH.* [g] the erthe *AH.* [h] oure self *AH.* [i] knowlecheth ȝee *AEH.*

[o] a cloude K. [p] Om. K. [q] Om. c *et plures.* [r] Om. ELP. [s] *in Jerom* U. Om. c *et plures.*
[t] Om. c *et plures.* [u] knowlechynge D. [v] Om. S. [w] Lord God L.

5 bowende doun fro me I knew₃ not. The
bacbitende priueli to his ne₃hebore; thys
I pursuede. With the proude e₃e and the
6 vnfilable herte; with it I eet not. Myn
e₃en to the feithful men of the erthe, that
thei sytte with me; the man goende in
the vndefoulid weie, this seruede to me.
7 Ther shal not dwelle in the myddel of
myn house, that doth pride; that speketh
wicke^k thingus, reulide not ri₃t in the
8 si₃te of myn e₃en. In the morutid I slo₃
alle the synneres of erthe; that I shulde
destro₃e fro the cite of the Lord alle
men werkende wickidnesse.

PSALM CI.

1 *The orisoun of the pore man, whan he
was tormentid, also befor the Lord
he helde out his pre₃eere.*

ex- 2 Lord, ful out here myn orisoun; and
3 my cry to thee come. Ne turne thou
awei thi face fro me; in whateuere day
I am trublid, bowe in to me thin ere.
In what euere dai I shal inwardli clepe
4 thee; swiftli ful out here me. For my
da₃is han failid as smoke; and my bones
5 as croote han dried. I am smyten as
hei₃, and myn herte driede; for I haue
6 for₃ete to ete my bred. Fro the vois of
my weiling; cleuede to my bon to my
7 flesh. Lic I am maad to a pellican of
wildernesse; I am maad as a ny₃t rauen
8 in the hous euese. I wook^l; and am
9 maad as a spare solitare in the rof. Al
day putten^n to me repref myn enemys;
and thei that preisiden me a₃en me
10 sworen. For aske^o as bred I eet; and
11 my drinc with weping I mengde. Fro
the face of the wrathe of thin indignacioun; for rerende^p vp thou hurtledest
12 me. My da₃es as shadewe boweden doun;
13 and I as hey driede. Thou forsothe,
Lord, in to withoute ende^q abidist stille;
and thi memorial in to ieneracioun and

wickid man bowynge awei fro me. I pur-5
suede hym; that bacbitide priueli his nei₃-
bore. With the proude i₃e and an herte
vnable to be fillid; Y eet not with this.
Myn i₃en *weren* to the feithful men of 6
erthe, that thei sitte with me; he that
₃ede in a weie with out wem, mynystride
to me. He that doith pride, schal not 7
dwelle in the myddil of myn hous; he
that spekith wickid thingis, seruede not in
the si₃t of myn i₃en. In the morutid Y 8
killide alle the synners of erthe; that Y
schulde leese fro the citee of the Lord alle
men worchynge wickidnesse.

PSALM CI.

*The title of the 'hundrid and o^x salm. The 1
preier of a pore man, whanne he was
angwishid, and schedde out^y his speche
bifore the Lord†.*

Lord, here thou my preier; and my crie 2
come to thee. Turne not awei thi face fro 3
me; in what euere dai Y am troblid, bowe
doun thin eere to me. In what euere day
Y schal inwardli clepe thee; here thou me
swiftli. For my daies han failid as smoke; 4
and my boonus han^z dried vp^a as critouns^b‡.
I am smytun as hei, and myn herte dried 5
vp; for Y haue for₃ete to eete my breed.
Of the vois of my weilyng; my boon cleuede 6
to my fleische. I am maad lijk a pellican 7
of wildirnesse; Y am maad as a ni₃t crowe
in an hous. I wakide; and Y am maad as 8
a solitarie sparowe in the roof. Al dai 9
myn enemyes dispisiden me; and thei that
preisiden me sworen a₃ens me. For Y eet 10
aschis as breed; and Y meddlide my drinke
with weping. Fro the face of the ire of 11
thin indignacioun; for thou reisinge me
hast hurtlid me doun. Mi daies boweden 12
awei as a^c schadewe; and Y wexede drie
as hei. But, Lord, thou dwellist with 13
outen ende; and thi memorial in generacioun
and in to generacioun. Lord, thou 14
risinge vp schalt haue merci on Sion; for

† *A glos.* This salm speketh of the tyme of Crist, for in the firste chap. to Ebrewis, Poul aleggeth the lettre of this salm seid of Crist; to the lettre this salme speketh of the angwiss of the puple of Israel, preiing with desi₃r for the comyng of Crist; this angwiss felde most in the tyme of Antiok the noble. *Lire here.* x.
‡ *critouns;* that is, that that dwellith in the panne of the friyng. ob.

k wickid *AH.*   l wakede *AEH.*   n puttiden *A.*   o askes *AEH.*   p areryinge *AEH.*   q Om. *c.*

x *c.* and i. *A.* hundred and firste *ELP.*   y Om. *RX.*   z Om. *c.*   a Om. *I.*   b critouns, *ether leefing of friyng* K.   c Om. *c et plures.*

14 in to ieneracioun. Thou risende vp, Lord,
shalt han mercy of Sion; for time of his
15 rewing, for ther is comen time. For
ther pleseden to thi seruauns his stones;
and to his erthe they shuln han mercy.
16 And Jentilis shul dreden thi name, Lord;
17 and alle kingis of erthe thi glorie. For
the Lord hath bild vp Sion; and it shal
18 be seen in his glorie. He beheeld in to
the orisoun of the meke; and he despiside
19 not the prejeere of hem. These thingus
be thei write in an other iencracioun; and
the puple that shal be formed shal preise
20 the Lord. For he beheeld forth fro his
heje holy; the Lord fro heuene in to
21 erthe᷑ lokede. That he shulde here the
weilingus of the gyuede; and loosen the
22 sones of the slayne. That thei telle out
in Sion the name of the Lord; and his
23 preising in Jerusalem. In gedering togidere the puplis in to oon; and kingus,
24 that thei serue to the Lord. He answerde to hym in weie of his vertue;
Fewenesse of my dajis shewe thou to me.
25 Ne ajeen clepe thou me in the myddil of
my dajis; in iencracioun and in to iene-
26 racioun thi jeris. In the begynning thou,
Lord, the erthe foundedest; and the werkis
27 of thin hondis ben heuenus. Thei shul
pershen, thou forsothe abidist stille; and
alle as clothing shuln waxen old. And as
a couertour thou shalt channge them,
28 and thei shul be chaungid; thou forsothe
he the same art, and thi jeeris shul not
29 faile. The sones of thi seruauns shul
wone; and the sed of hem in to the world
shal be rijtforth reulid.

PSALM CII.

1
The salm to hym Dauid.

Benedic, anima mea.

Blesse thou, my soule, to the Lord;
and alle thingus that withinne me ben, to
2 his holi name. Blesse thou, my soule,
to the Lord; and wile thou not forjete

---

the tyme 'to haue᷑ merci therof cometh,
for the tyme cometh. For the stones ther- 15
of plesiden thi seruauntis; and thei schulen haue merci on the lond therof. And, 16
Lord, hethen men schulen drede thi name;
and alle kingis of erthe *schulen drede* thi
glori. For the Lord hath bildid᷑ Sion; 17
and he schal be seen in his glorie. He 18
bihelde on the preier of meke men; and
he dispiside not the preier of hem. Be 19
these thingis writun in an othere generacioun; and the puple that schal be maad
schal preise the Lord. For he bihelde fro 20
his hije hooli place; the Lord lokide fro
heuene in to erthe. For to here the weil- 21
ingis of feterid men; and for to vnbynde
the sones of slayn men. That thei telle in 22
Sion the name of the Lord; and his preising in Jerusalem. In gaderinge togidere 23
puplis in to oon; and kingis, that thei
serue the Lord. It᷑ answeride to hym in 24
the weie of his vertu; Telle thou to me
the fewnesse of my daies. Ajenclepe thou 25
not me in the myddil of my daies; thi
jeris *ben* in generacioun and in to generacioun. Lord, thou foundidist the erthe in 26
the bigynnyng; and heuenes ben the werkis
of thin hondis. Tho schulen perische, 27
but thou dwellist perfitli; and alle schulen
wexe eelde as a clooth. And thou schalt
chaunge hem as an hiling, and tho schulen
be chaungid; but thou art the same thi 28
silf, and thi jeeris schulen not faile. The 29
sones of thi seruauntis schulen dwelle; and
the seed of hem schal be dressid in to the
world.

PSALM CII.

The title of the ῾hundred and secoundeˢ 1
salm. ῾Of Dauid˟ †.

Mi soule, blesse thou the Lord; and alle
thingis that ben with ynne me, *blesse* his
hooli name. Mi soule, blesse thou the 2
Lord; and nyle thou forjete alle the jeld-

† *A glos.* Da-
uith made this
salme, for to
herie God; and
he exciteth men
and aungels
and ech crea-
ture, for to
herie God. *Lire
here.* ᴋ.

᷑ the erthe *EH.*

᷑ of hauyng ɪ. ᶜ bild ɪ. ᶠ It, *that is, the chirche of Crist* ᴋ. ᵍ *hundrid and tweithe* s. ʰ *A salm to
Dauid. c et plures. To Dauid.* ᴇʟᴘ. *A salm of Dauid.* ɪsᴜb. *A salm of Dauid to herie God.* ᴋ. *A song to
Dauid.* ɪ.

3 alle the ȝeldingus of hym. That hath mercy to alle thi wickidnessis; that 4 helith alle thin infirmytees. That aȝeen bieth fro deth thi lif; that crouneth thee 5 in mercy and mercy doingis. That fulfilleth in goode thingus thi diseyr; shal be renewid* as of an egle thi ȝouthe. 6 Doende mercies the Lord; and dom to 7 alle men suffrende wrong. Knowen he made his weies to Moises; and to the 8 sones of Irael his willis. Reewere, and merciful the Lord; long abidende, and 9 myche merciful. In to euermore he shal not wrathen; ne in to withoute ende he 10 shal threte. Aftir oure synnes he dide not to vs; ne aftir oure wickidnessis he 11 ȝelde† to vs. For after the heiȝte of heuene fro erthe; he strengthide his 12 mercy vpon men dredende hym. Hou myche the rising stant^u fro the going doun; aferr he made fro vs oure wickid- 13 nessis^v. What maner wise the fader hath mercy of the sonus, the Lord dide 14 mercy to men dredende hym; for he knew oure britil making. He recordide 15 for pouder wee be, a man as hey his daȝes; as the flour of the feld so he shal 16 floure out. For the spirit shal thurȝ passen in hym, and he shal not stonde stille; and he shal no more knowen his 17 place. The mercy forsothe of the Lord fro withoute ende, and vnto withoute ende; vpon men dredende hym. And the riȝtwisnesse of hym in to the sones of 18 sones; to hem that kepen his testament. And myndeful thei ben of his maunde- 19 mens; to do them. The Lord in heuene made redi his sete; and his reume to alle 20 shal lordshipen. Blisse ȝee to the Lord, alle his aungelis, miȝti bi vertue, doende the woord of hym; to ben herd the vois 21 of his sermounes. Blessith to the Lord, alle ȝee his vertues; ȝee his seruauns that 22 don his wil. Blessith to the Lord, alle ȝee his werkis, in alle place, ȝee his do- mynaciouns; blesse thou, my soule, to the Lord.

yngis of him. Which doith merci to alle 3 thi wickidnessis; which heelith alle thi sijknessis. Which aȝenbieth thi lijf fro 4 deth; which corowneth thee in merci and^i merciful doyngis. Which fillith thi desijr 5 in goodis; thi ȝongthe schal be renulid as *the ȝongthe* of an egle. The Lord doynge 6 mercies; and doom to alle men suffringe wrong. He^k made hise weies^l knowun to 7 Moises; hise willis to the sones of Israel. The Lord *is* a merciful doer, and merciful 8 in wille; longe abidinge, and myche merciful. He schal not be wrooth with outen 9 ende; and^m he schal not thretne with outen ende. He dide not to vs aftir oure synnes; 10 nether he ȝeldide to vs aftir oure wickid- nessis. For bi^n the hiȝnesse of heuene fro 11 erthe; he made strong his merci on men dredynge hym. As myche as the eest is 12 fer^o fro the west; he made fer oure wickid- nessis fro vs. As a fadir hath merci on^p 13 sones, the Lord hadde merci on men dred- ynge him; for he knewe oure makyng. 14 He bithouȝte that we ben dust, a man *is* 15 as hey; his dai schal flowre out so as a flour of the feeld. For the spirit schal passe in 16 hym, and^r schal not abide; and^s schal no more knowe his place. But the merci of 17 the Lord *is* fro with out bigynnyng, and til in to with outen ende; on men dredinge hym. And his riȝtfulnesse *is* in to the sones of sones; to hem that kepen his 18 testament. And ben myndeful of hise comaundementis; to do tho. The Lord 19 hath maad redi his seete in heuene; and his rewme schal be lord of alle. Aun- 20 gels of the Lord, blesse ȝe the Lord; ȝe myȝti in vertu, doynge his word, to here the vois of hise wordis. Alle vertues of 21 the Lord, blesse ȝe the Lord; ȝe mynys- tris of hym that doen his wille. Alle 22 werkis of the Lord, blesse ȝe the Lord, in ech place of his lordschipe; my soule, blesse thou the Lord.

* fulfild *E pr. m.* † ȝeldede *AEH.* ^u stoondith *A.* ^v wickidnes *A.*

^l and in *I.* ^k *Om. A pr. m.* CDHU. ^l weie G. ^m *Om. I.* ^n aftir *I.* ^o *Om. S.* ^p on *his I.* ^r and *it I.* ^s and *it I.*

PSALM CIII.

1   *The salm of Dauid.*

Blisse thou, my soule, to the Lord ;
Lord my God, thou art magnefied hugeli.
Confessioun and fairnesse thou hast
2 clad^w; wrappid with liȝt, as with cloth-
3 ing. Sreechende out heuene as skin; that
couerest with watris the onermoris of it. `
That potist the cloude thi steȝing vp;
that gost vp on the pennys of windis.
4 That makist thin aungelis spiritis; and
5 thi seruauns brennende fyr. That foundedest the erthe vpon hys stablenesse; it
shal not ben inbowid into the world of
6 world. The se as a clothing is his
wrapping; ouer mounteynes shul stonde
7 watris. Fro thi blamyng thei shul flee;
fro the vois of thi thunder thei shul
8 drede. Hillis steȝen vp, and the feldis
gon doun; in to the place that thou hast
9 foundid to hem. A terme thou hast set,
that thei shul not ouer passe; ne they
shul ben al turned, to couere the erthe. `
10 That sendist out wellis in valeis; betwe
the myddil of mounteynes shul passe
11 thurȝ watris. Alle the bestis of the feld
shul drinke; assis shul abide in ther
12 thrist. Vpon tho thingus the foulis of
heuene shul wone; fro the myddel of
13 stones thei shul ȝeue voisis. He watr-
ende the hillis fro thin ouermor; of the
frut of thy werkis shal be fulfild the
14 erthe. Bringende forth hei to hous
bestis; and erbe^x to the seruyse of men.
That thou bringe out bred fro the erthe ;
15 and wyn glade the herte of man. That
he make gladsum the face in oile; and
bred the herte of man make stable.
16 Ther shul ben fulfild the trees of the
feld, and the cedris of Liban that he
17 plauntede ; there sparewis shul make
nestis. The hous of the ierfaucoun
18 duke is of hem; the heȝe mounteynes to
19 herttis; the ston^y refut to irchounes. He

PSALM CIII.

1   *The^t hundrid and thridde salm^u†.*

Mi soule, blesse thou the Lord ; my
Lord God, thou art magnyfied greetli.
Thou hast clothid knouleching and fair-
2 nesse ; and thou art clothid with liȝt, as
with a cloth. And thou stretchist forth
3 heuene as a skyn ; and thou hilist with
watris the hiȝer partis therof. Which
settist a cloude thi stiyng ; which goest on
4 the fetheris of wyndis. Which makist
spiritis thin aungels; and thi mynystris
5 brennynge fier. Which hast foundid the
erthe on his stablenesse ; it schal not be
bowid in to the world of world. The
6 depthe of watris as a cloth is the clothing
therof ; watris schulen stonde on hillis.
7 Tho schulen fle fro thi blamyng ; men
schulen be aferd of the vois of thi thundur. Hillis stien vp, and feeldis goen
8 doun ; in to the place which thou hast `
foundid to tho. Thou hast set a terme,
9 which tho^v schulen not passe ; nether tho
schulen be turned, for to hile the erthe.
10 And thou sendist out wellis in^w grete
valeis ; watris schulen passe bitwix the
11 myddil^x of hillis. Alle the beestis of the
feeld schulen drynke; wielde assis schulen
abide in her thirst^y. Briddis of the eir
12 schulen dwelle on tho; fro the myddis
13 of^z stoonys thei schulen ȝyue voices. And
thou moistist hillis of her hiȝer thingis ;
the erthe schal be fillid of the fruyt of thi
14 werkis. And thou bringist forth hei to
beestis; and eerbe^a to the seruyce of men.
That thou bringe forth breed of the erthe;
15 and that wiyn make glad the herte of
men. That he make glad the face with
oile ; and that breed make stidefast the
16 herte of man. The trees of the feeld
schulen be fillid, and the cedris of the
17 Liban, whiche he plauntide; sparewis^b
schulen make nest there. The hous of
18 the gerfaukun is the leeder of tho; hiȝe

† The c. and iij. salm hath no tijtle, neither in Ebreu ne in Jerom. The salm maker inducith him self to herie God, and bringith resouns therto, and eft he rehersith the forseid heriyng. Lire. 1.
The same glos, that the salme bifore hath. x

---

^w clothid *AEH*.   ^x erbe be *AH*.   ^y stoon is *A*.

^t *The title of the* i.   ^u Om. 1. *salm hath no title.* KU.   ^v thei 1.   ^w in the c. in to 1.   ^x myddis
CDEFGHIKLMOPQRSWXbi.   ^y thirst, *that is, to be filled in her thirst* K.   ^z of the c.   ^a crbis 1.   ^b sparowen
CDPHMOQRSWbi.

made the mone in to times; the sunne
20 knew3 his going doun. Thou hast set
dercnessis, and maad is the ny3t; in it^z
shul thur3 passe alle the bestis of the
21 wode. The whelpis of leouns rorende
that thei raueshen; and sechen of God
22 mete to them. Sprungen is the sunne,
and thei ben gadered to gider; and in
ther ligging placis they shul be sett
23 togidere. A man shal go out to his
were; and to his werching, vn to euen.
24 Hou magncfied ben thi werkis, Lord,
alle thingus in wisdam thou hast maad;
fulfild is the erthe with thi posses-
25 sioun. This grete se and large to hondis;
there crepende bestis, of whiche is no
noumbre. Little bestis with the grete;
26 there shippis shul thur3 passe. This
dragoun that thou hast formed to begile
27 to hym; alle thingus of thee abijden,
that thou 3iue to them mete in tyme.
28 Thee 3yuende to them, thei shul gedere;
thee openende thin hond, alle thingis shul
29 be fulfild with goodnesse. Thee forsothe
turnende awei the face, thei shul be disturbid; thou shalt taken awei the spirit
of hem, and thei shul faile; and in to
30 ther pouder thei shul turne a3een. Send
out thi spirit, and thei shul be formed;
and thou shalt renewe the face of the
31 erthe. Be the glorie of the Lord in to
the world; glade shal the Lord in his
32 werkis. That behalt^a the erthe, and
maketh it to tremble; that toucheth the
mounteynes, and thei smoken. I shal
33 synge to the Lord in my lif; I shal do
salm to my God, as longe as I am.
34 Jo3eful be to hym my speche; I forsothe
35 shal deliten in the Lord. Faile the synneres fro the erthe, and wicke men, so
that thei be not; blesse thou, my soule,
to the Lord.

hillis *ben refute*^c to hertis; a^d stoon *is*
refutt to irchouns. He made the moone 10
in to tymes; the sunne knewe his goyng
doun. Thou hast set derknessis, and ny3t 20
is^e maad; alle beestis of the wode schulen
go ther yune. Liouns whelpis rorynge 21
for to rauysche; and to seke of God meete
to hem silf. The sunne is risun, and tho 22
ben gaderid togidere; and tho schulen be
set in her couchis. A man schal go out 23
to his werk; and to his worching, til to
the^f euentid. Lord, thi werkis ben mag- 24
nefiede ful myche, thou hast maad alle
thingis in wisdom; the erthe is fillid
with thi possessioun. This see *is* greet 25
and large to hondis; there *ben* crepinge
beestis, of which is noon^g noumbre. Litil
beestis with grete; schippis schulen passe 26
there. This dragoun which^h thou hast
formyd; for to scorne hym. Alle thingis 27
abiden^i of thee; that thou 3yue to hem
meete in tyme. Whanne thou schalt 3yue 28
to hem, thei schulen gadere; whanne thou
schalt opene thin hond, alle thingis schulen
be fillid with goodnesse. But whanne thou 29
schalt turne awey the^k face, thei schulen
be disturblid; thou schalt take awei the
spirit of them, and thei schulen faile; and
thei schulen turne a3en in to her dust.
Sende out thi spirit, and thei schulen be 30
formed^l of the^m newe; and thou schalt
renule the face of the erthe. The glorie 31
of the Lord be in to the world; the Lord
schal be glad in hise werkis. Which^n 32
biholdith the erthe, and makith it to
tremble; which^o touchith hillis, and tho
smoken. I schal singe to the Lord in my 33
lijf; Y schal seie salm to my God, as longe
as Y am. Mi speche be myrie^p to him; 34
forsothe Y schal delite in the Lord. Syn- 35
neris faile fro the^q erthe, and wickid men
faile, so that thei be not; my soule, blesse
thou the Lord.

z that *A*. a beholdeth *AEH*.

c *refuytis* c *et plures.* d the I. e *was* I. f Om. *ceteri fere omnes.* g no D *et plures.* h that I.
i abididen c. k thi I. l refourmed I. m Om. I. n The which I. o the which I. p myrthe I.
q Om. c *et plures.*

PSALM CIV.
Alleluia, Alleluia.

1 Knoulecheth to the Lord, and inwardly clepeth his name; telleth out among Jen-
2 tilis his werkis. Singeth to hym, and doth salm to hym, and tellith alle his
3 merueilis ; be ʒee preisid in his holi name. Glade the herte of ʒou sechende
4 the Lord ; secheth the Lord, and beth confermed ; secheth his face euermor.
5 Haneth[b] mynde of his merueilis, that he dide; his wonders, and the domes of his
6 mouth. The sed of Abraham, his ser-uaunt ; the sonus of Jacob, his chosen.
7 He the Lord oure God ; in al erthe his
8 domes. Myndeful he was in to the world of his testament; of the woord that
he sente in to a thousend ieneracious.
9 The whiche he disposide to Abraham ;
10 and of his oth to Isaac. And he sette it to Jacob in to an heste; and to Irael in
11 to euere lastende testament. Seiende, To thee I shal ʒeue the lond of Chanaan ; the
12 litle corde of ʒoure eritage. Whan thei weren in short noumbre; most fewe and
13 tilieris of it. And thei passiden thurʒ fro fole in to fole; and fro reume in to
14 an other puple. He lafte not a man to noʒe to them; and he chastiside for hem
15 kingis. Wileth not touche my cristis ; and in my profetis wileth not ben waried.
16 And he clepide hungir vp on the[d] erthe; and alle fastnesse of bred he to-ponede.
17 He sente beforn hem a man ; and[e] into a
18 thral Joseph is sold. Thei mekeden in stockis his feet, iren passide thurʒ hys
19 lif; to the time that his woord shulde come. The speche of the Lord en-
20 flaumede hym; the king sente and loosede hym, the prince of puplis and lafte hym.
21 He sette hym lord of his hous ; and
22 prince of all his possessioun. That he

PSALM CIV.
The title of the hundrid and fourthe salm.
Alleluya[r] †.

Knouleche ʒe to the Lord, and inwardli 1 clepe ʒe his name; telle ʒe hise werkis
among hethen men. Synge ʒe to hym, 2 and seie ʒe salm to him, and telle ʒe alle
hise merueylis ; be ʒe preisid in his hooli 3 name. The herte of men sekynge the
Lord be glad ; seke ʒe the Lord, and be 4 ʒe confermed ; seke ʒe euere his face.
Haue ʒe mynde on hise merueilis, whiche 5 he dide ; on his grete wondris, and domes
of his mouth. The seed of Abraham, his 6 seruaunt; the sones of Jacob, his chosun
man. He is oure Lord God; hise domes 7 ben in al the[s] erthe. He was myndeful 8
of his testament in to the world ; of the word which he comaundide in to a thousynde generaciouns. Which he disposide 9 to Abraham ; and of his ooth to Isaac.
And he ordeynede it to Jacob in to a 10 comaundement; and to Israel in to euerlastinge testament. And he seide, I shal 11 ʒiue to thee the lond of Canaan ; the cord
of ʒoure eritage. Whanne thei weren in 12 a litil noumbre; and the comelingis of
hem[t] weren ful fewe. And thei passiden 13 fro folk in to folk; and fro a rewme in to
another puple. He lefte not a man to 14 anoye hem ; and he chastiside kyngis for
hem. Nile ʒe touche my cristis; and nyle 15 ʒe do wickidli among my prophetis. And 16
God clepide hungir on erthe; and he wastide al the stidefastnesse of breed.
He sente a man bifore hem; Joseph was 17 seeld[u] in to a seruaunt. Thei maden lowe 18
hise feet in stockis[v], irun passide by his soule; til the word of him cam. The 19
speche of the Lord enflawmede him ; the 20 king sente and vnbond hym; the prince of
puplis sente and delyuerede him. He 21 ordeynede him the[w] lord of his hous; and

† A glos. This salm is a stir-yng to Goddis heriyng, and first the pro-phet excitith the puple for to herie God, and that this be don more spedely, he rehersith the mynde of Goddis bene-fiela. Lire here. IK.

---

[b] Hath AII. [d] Om. A. [e] Om. AH.

[r] Allelnya ; the salm of Dauith, whanne he hadde brouʒt the arke into his hous. K. Om. L. that is, herie ʒe God. I marg. [s] Om. c et plures. [t] him c et plures. [u] sold IKL. [v] feteris W. [w] Om. c et plures.

shulde enforme[f] his princis as hymself;
and his olde men prudence he shulde
23 teche. And Irael entride in to Egipt;
and Jacob a tiliere was in the lond of
24 Cham. And he encreeide his puple
hugely; and fastnede hym vpon his ene-
25 mys. He turned the herte of hem, that
thei hateden his puple; and treccherie
26 shulden do in to his seruauns. He sente
Moises, his seruaunt; and Aron, hym
27 whom he ches. And he putte in hem
the woordis of his tocnes; and of his
28 wonders in the lond of Cham. He sente
derenessis, and made dere; and vntymely
29 he fullfilde not his woordis. And he
turnede the watris of hem in to blod;
30 and sloȝ the fisshis of hem. And the
lond of hem ȝaf froggis; in the preue
31 chaumbris of ther kingus. He seide,
and ther cam an hound fleeȝe; and
32 gnattis in alle the coostis of hem. And
he putte the reynes of hem hayl; fyr
33 brennende in the lond of hem. And he
smot the vynes of hem, and the fige
placis of hem; and he to-broside the
34 wode of the coostis of hem. He seide,
and ther cam a locust; and worte werm
35 of the whiche was no nonmbre. And it
eet al the hei in the lond of hem; and eet
36 al the frut of the lond of hem. And he
smot alle the firste goten in the lond of
hem; the firste frutis of[g] alle the trauaile
37 of hem. And he broȝte hem out with
syluer and gold; and ther was not a[h] syk
38 man[i] in the linagis of hem. Egipt
gladede in ther forth going; for ther
39 drede lai in vp on hem. He straȝte out
a cloude, in to the proteccioun of hem;
and fyr, that he shulde liȝte to hem by
40 the nyȝt. Thei askeden, and ther kam a
kurlu[k]; and with the bred of heuene he
41 fulfilde hem. He to-brac the ston, and
ther flowiden watris; ther wenten awei
42 flodis in the drie. For myndeful he
was of his holi woord; that he hadde to

the[x] prince of al his possessioun. That he 22
schulde lerne hise princis as him silf; and
that he schulde teche hise elde men prudence. And Israel entride in to Egipt; 23
and Jacob was a comeling in the lond of
Cham. And God encreesside his puple 24
greetli; and made hym[y] stidefast on hise
enemyes. He turnede the herte of hem, 25
that thei hatiden his puple; and diden gile
aȝens hise seruauntis. He sent Moises, 26
his seruaunt; thilke Aaron, whom he chees.
He puttide in hem the wordis of hise 27
myraclis; and of hise grete wondris in the
lond of Cham. He sente derknessis, and 28
made derk; and he made not bitter hise
wordis. He turnede the watris of hem 29
in to blood; and he killide the fischis of
hem. And the lond of hem ȝaf paddoks; 30
in the priue places of the kyngis of hem.
God seide, and a fleische flie cam; and 31
gnattis in alle the coostis of hem. He 32
settide her reynes hail; fier brennynge in
the lond of hem. And he smoot the 33
vynes of hem, and the fige trees of hem;
and[z] al to-brak the tree[a] of the coostis
of hem. He seide, and a[b] locuste cam; 34
and a bruk of which was[c] noon[d] noumbre.
And it eet al the hey in the lond of hem; 35
and it eet al the fruyt of the lond of hem.
And he killide ech the firste gendrid thing 36
in the lond of hem; the firste fruitis of
alle the trauel of hem. And he ledde out 37
hem with siluer and gold; and noon was
sijk in the lynagis of hem. Egipt was 38
glad in the goyng forth[e] of hem; for the
drede of hem lai on Egipcians. He 39
spredde abrood a cloude, in to the hiling
of hem; and fier, that it schynede to hem
bi nyȝt. Thei axiden, and a curlew cam; 40
and he fillide hem with the breed of
heuene. He brak a[f] stoon, and watris 41
flowiden; floodis ȝeden forth in the[g] drye
place. For he was myndeful of his hooli 42
word; which he hadde to Abraham, his
child. And he ledde out his puple in ful 43

---

[f] techen ε pr. m.   [g] of hem ᴀ.   [h] an ʜ.   [i] Om. ᴀɪɪ.   [k] corlure ε.

[x] Om. ɪ.   [y] hem ɢ.   [z] and he c et plures.   [a] trees ᴀ.   [b] the ɪ.   [c] ther was ɪ.   [d] no c et plures.
[e] out ɪ.   [f] the ɪ.   [g] Om. ɪ.

43 Abraham, his child. And he broȝte out his puple in ful out ioȝing; and his 44 chosene in glading. And he ȝaf to them the regiouns of Jentilis; and the traualis 45 of puplis thei weldeden. That thei kepe his iustifiyngus; and his lawe they aȝeen seche.

PSALM CV.

Alleluia, Alleluia.

1 Knoulecheth to the Lord, for good; for in to the world the mercy of hym. 2 Who shal speke the poweris of the Lord; herd[1] shal make alle the preisingus of 3 hym? Blisful that kepen dom; and don 4 riȝtwissnesse in alle time. Haue mynde of vs, Lord, in the well willing[m] of thi puple; visite thou vs in thi helthe 5 ȝyuere. To seen in the goodnesse of thi chosene, to gladen in the gladnesse of thi folc; that thou be preisid with thin 6 eritage. Wee han synned with oure fadris, vnriȝtwisly wee han do; wickidnesse 7 wee han wroȝt. Oure fadris in Egipt vnderstoden not thi meruelis; thei weren not myndeful of the multitude of thi mercy. And thei in to the se steȝende vp, 8 the rede se, terreden; and he sauede them for his name, that knowen he 9 shulde make his power. And he in-bowiden the rede se, and it is dried; and he ladde hem in 'the se[o] depnessis as in 10 desert. And he sauede hem fro the hond of hateris; and he aȝeen boȝte them fro 11 the hond of the enemy. And water[p] couerede the men trublende them; oon 12 of hem lafte not. And thei leeueden to the woordis of hym; and thei preisiden 13 his preising. Soone thei diden, thei for-ȝeeten of the werkis of hym; and thei 14 susteneden not his counseil. And thei coueiteden coueiting in desert; and thei tempteden God in the place with oute 15 water. And he ȝaf to hem the asking

out ioiyng; and hise chosun men in gladnesse. And he ȝaf to hem the cuntreis of 44 hethen men; and thei hadden in possessioun the trauels of puplis. That thei 45 kepe hise iustifiyngis; and seke[h] his lawe.

PSALM CV.

The 'title of the[l] hundrid and fifthe salm[k].
Alleluya[l]†.

Kouleche ȝe to the Lord, for *he is* good; 1 for his mercy *is* with outen ende. Who 2 schal speke the powers of the Lord; schal make knowun alle hise preisyngis? Blessid 3 *ben* thei that kepen dom; and doon riȝtfulnesse in al tyme. Lord, haue thou mynde 4 on vs in the good plesaunce of thi puple; visite thou vs in thin heelthe. To se in 5 the goodnesse of thi chosun men, to be glad in the gladnes of thi folk; that thou be heried with thin eritage. We han 6 synned with oure fadris; we han do vniustli, we han do wickidnesse. Oure 7 fadris in Egipt vndirstoden not thi meruelis; thei weren not myndeful of the multitude of thi merci. And thei stiynge in to the see, in to the reed see, terreden to wraththe; and he sauede hem[m] for his 8 name, that 'he schulde[n] make knowun his[o] power. And he departide the reed 9 see, and it was dried; and he lede forth hem in the depthis of watris as in descert. And he sauede hem fro the hond of 10 hateris; and he aȝen bouȝte hem fro the hond of the enemye. And the watir[p] 11 hilide men troublynge hem; oon of hem abood not. And thei bileueden to hise 12 wordis; and thei preisiden the heriynge of hym. Thei hadden 'soone do[q], thei for-13 ȝaten hise werkis; and thei abididen[r] not his councel. And thei coueitiden coueitise 14 in descert; and[s] temptiden God in a place with out watir. And he ȝaf to hem the 15 axyng of hem; and he sente fulnesse in to

† *Alleluia* is sett oonus for Goddis heriyng in present tyme, and eft for his heriyng in heuen, i. First the prophet excitith men to herie God, the ij time he axith Goddus grace. IX.

[1] herd he E *pr. m.* [m] plesyng *AEH.* [n] deuydede E *pr. m.* [o] there *AH.* [p] the water *A.*

[h] kepe I. [l] Om. A. [k] Om. s. [l] *Alleluya, Alleluya.* CDGHIKMOQUVWXbi. [m] Om. L. [n] thei schulden A *pr. m.* [o] in his CDFGHMOP *pr. m.* QRWXbi. [p] watris A. [q] so do C. soone ido s. [r] abeden I. abood L. abiden RX. [s] and thei IK.

of hem; and he sente fulfilling in to the
16 soulis of hem. And thei terreden Moises
in the tentis; Aron, the holy of the Lord.
17 The erthe is opened, and it swolewid
doun Dathan; and it couerede vpon the
18 congregacioun of Abiron. And fyr brende
vp in the synagoge⁹ of hem; and flaume
19 al to-brende the synneres. And thei
maden a calf in Oreb; and thei ho-
20 noureden a grauen thing. And thei
chaungeden ther glorie; in to theʳ licnesse
21 of a calf etende hey. Thei forȝeeten God,
that sauede hem, that dide grete thingus
22 in Egipt, merueilous thingus in the lond
of Cam; ferful thingus in the rede se. And
23 he seide, that he shulde destroȝe them;
but Moises, his chosen, hadde stoden in
the to-breking in his siȝt. That he turne
awei hys wrathe, that he destroȝe them
24 not; and for noȝte they hadden the desirable erthe. They leeuede not to his
25 woord, and thei gruccheden in ther
tabernaclis; thei ful out herden not the
26 vois of the Lord. And he rerede vp his
hond vpon hem; that he shulde throwe
27 them doun in desert. And that he shulde
caste doun the sed of hem in naciouns;
28 and scatere them in regiouns. And thei
sacrifieden to Belfegor; and thei eete
29 the sacrifices of the deade. And thei
terreden hym in ther findingis; and
30 multiplied is in hem falling. And Fynees
stod, and pleside; and the brosing
31 ceside. And it is witid to hym to riȝtwisnesse; in ieneracioun and ieneracioun
32 vnto euermor. And thei terreden hymⁿ at
the watris of contradiccioun; and Moises
33 is ouertrauailid for hem, and thei to
myche sharpeden the spirit of hym. And
34 he ordeynede in his lippis; thei destroȝeden not the Jentilis, that the Lord seide
35 to them. And they be mengd togidere
among Jentilis, and thei lerneden ther
36 werkis, and serueden to the grauen
thingis of hem; and it is maad to them
37 in to sclaunder. And thei offreden ther

the soulis of hem. And thei wraththiden 16
Moyses in the castels; Aaron, the hooli of
the Lord. The erthe was opened, and 17
swolewid Datan; and hilide on the congregacioun of Abiron. And fier brente 18
an hiȝe in the synagoge of hem; flawme
brente synneris. And thei maden a calf 19
in Oreb; and worschipiden a ȝotun ymage.
And thei chaungiden her glorie; in to the 20
liknesse of a calf etynge hei. Thei for- 21
ȝaten God, that sauede hem, that dide
grete werkis in Egipt, merueils in the 22
lond of Cham; feerdful thingis in the reed
see. And God seide, that he wolde leeseᵗ 23
hem; if Moises, his chosun man, hadde not
stonde in the brekyng of ͧ his siȝt. That he
schulde turne awei his ire; lest he loste
hem. And thei hadden the desirable lond 24
for nouȝt, thei bileueden not to his word,
and thei grutchiden in her tabernaclis; 25
thei herden not the vois of the Lord.
And he reiside his hond on hem; to caste 26
doun hem in desert. And to caste awei her 27
seed in naciouns; and toᵛ leese hem in
cuntreis. And thei maden sacrifice to 28
Belfagor; and thei eeten the sacrificis of
deed beestis. And thei wraththiden God 29
in her fyndyngis; and fallyngʷ was multiplied in hem. And Fynees stood, and 30
pleeside God; and the veniaunce ceesside.
And it was arrettid to hym to riȝtfulnesse; 31
in generacioun and in to generacioun,
til in to with outen ende. And thei 32
wraththiden God at the watrisˣ of aȝenseiyng; and Moises was trauelid† for hem,
for thei maden bittere his spirit, and he 33
departide in his lippis. Thei losten not 34
hethen men; whiche the Lord seide to
hem. And thei weren meddlid among he- 35
thene men, andʸ lerneden the werkis of
hem, and serueden the grauen ymagis of 36
hem; and it was maad to hem in to
sclaundre. And thei offriden her sones; 37
and her douȝtris to feendis. And thei 38
schedden out innocent blood, the blood of
her sones and of her douȝtris; whiche thei

† *A glos.* That
is, disturblid in
soule; in so
miche that he
doutide lest
God wolde de-
nye hem water,
for her malice,
and so he bi-
leuede not fulli
to Goddis word.
Lire here. K.

ȹ synagogis ᴀ.   ʳ a ᴀ.   ˢ Om. c.

38 sones; and ther doȝtris to deuelis. And thei shadden out the innocent blod; the blod of ther sones and of ther doȝtris, that thei sacrifieden to the grauen thingus 39 of Canaan. And the lond is slayn in blodis, and defoulid is in the werkis of hem; and thei diden fornycacioun in 40 ther findingus. And the Lord wrathede in wodnesse in to his puple; and he 41 wlatide his eritage. And toc them in to the hondis of Jentilis; and thei lord-shipeden of hem, that hateden[t] hem. 42 And the enemys of them trobleden hem, and thei ben mekid vnder ther hondis; 43 ofte he delyuerede hem. Thei forsothe terreden hym in ther counseil; and ben 44 mekid in ther wickidnessis[u]. And he saȝ, whan thei weren trublid; and herde 45 the orisoun of hem. And myndeful he was of his testament; and it othoȝte hym 46 aftir the multitude of his mercy. And he ȝaf hem in to mercies; in the siȝte of 47 alle, that hadden take them. Mac vs saf, Lord oure God; and gadere vs fro na-ciouns. That wee knouleche to thin holi 48 name; and glorien in thi preising. Blessid be the Lord God of Irael fro world and unto world; and al the puple shal sey, Be it do, be it don.

sacrificiden to the grauun ymagis of Cha-naan. And the erthe was slayn in bloodis, 39 and was defoulid in the werkis of hem; and thei diden fornicacioun in her fynd-yngis. And the Lord was wrooth bi strong 40 veniaunce aȝens his puple; and[z] hadde abhominacioun of his eritage. And he 41 bitook[a] hem in to the hondis of hethene men; and thei that hatiden hem, weren lordis of hem. And her enemyes diden 42 tribulacioun to hem, and thei weren mekid vndir the hondis of enemyes; ofte he 43 delyuerede hem. But thei wraththiden hym in her counsel; and thei weren maad low in her wickidnessis. And he siȝe, 44 whanne thei weren set in tribulacioun; and he herde the preyer of hem. And he 45 was myndeful of his testament; and it repentide hym bi the multitude of his merci. And he ȝaf hem in to mercies; in 46 the siȝt of alle men, that hadden take hem. Oure Lord God, make thou vs saaf; and 47 gadere togidere vs fro naciouns. That we knouleche to thin hooli name; and haue glorie in thi preisyng. Blessid be the 48 Lord God of Israel fro the world and til[b] in to the world; and al the puple schal seye, Be it don, be it don.

PSALM CVI.
Alleluia, Alleluia.

Confitemini Domino, quo-niam bonus.

1 Knoulecheth to the Lord, for good; 2 for in to the world his mercy. Sei thei now, that ben aȝeen boȝt of the Lord, whom he aȝeen boȝte fro the hond of the enemy; fro regiouns he gederide hem. 3 Fro the sunne rising, and the going 4 doun; fro the north, and the se. Thei erreden in wildernesse, in vnwatri place; weie of dwelling place of a cite thei 5 founde not. Hungrende and thirstende; 6 the soule of hem in hem failide. And thei crieden to the Lord, whan thei weren

PSALM CVI.
The title of the[c] hundrid and sixte salm.
Alleluya[d].

Knouleche ȝe to the Lord[e], for he is 1 good; for his merci is in to the world. Sei[f] thei, that ben aȝen bouȝt of the Lord; 2 whiche he aȝen bouȝte fro the hond of the enemye, fro cuntreis he gaderide hem to-gidere. Fro the risyng of the sunne, and 3 fro the goyng doun; fro the north, and fro the see. Thei erriden in wildirnesse[g], 4 in a place with out watir; thei founden not weie of the citee of dwellyng place. Thei weren hungri and thirsti; her soule 5 failide in hem. And thei crieden to the 6

---

[t] sloowen E pr. m.   [u] wickidnes A.

[z] and he 1.   [a] took 1.   [b] Om. CEFGLPWX.   [c] Om. A. title of O.   [d] Alleluia. This is a stiring to doinge of thankinges of men delynerid by God fro perels and angwiȝsshis. K. Alleluia, Alleluia, U.   [e] Lord God S.   [f] Om. I.   [g] wildirnessis S.

trublid; and fro the nedis of hem he toc 7 hem out. And he broȝte hem thennus in to a riȝt weye; that thei shulde go in 8 to the cite of wonyng. Kuouleche to the Lord his mercies; and the merueilis 9 of hym to the sones of men. For he fulfilde the idil soule; and the hungri 10 soule he fulfilde with goodis. The sitteris in derenessis, and in the[v] vmbre of deth; and the bounden in beggeri and iren. 11 For thei maden egre the spechis of God; and the counseil of the heȝest thei ter- 12 reden. And mekid is in trauailes the herte of hem, and thei ben feblid; and 13 ther was not that wolde helpe. And thei crieden to the Lord, whan thei weren trublid; and fro the nedis of hem 14 he deliuerede hem. And he ladde hem out fro derenessis, and the shadewe of deth; and the bondis of hem he to-brac. 15 Knouleche[w] to the Lord his mercies; and 16 his merueilis to the sones of men. For he to-broside the irene ȝatis; and the 17 irene barris he to-brac. He toc hem fro the weie of wickidnesse of hem; for[x] ther vnriȝtwisnesses forsothe thei ben 18 mekid. Alle mete the soule of hem wlatide; and they neȝheden to the ȝatis 19 of deth. And thei crieden to the Lord, whan thei weren trublid; and fro the 20 nedis of hem he delyuerede hem. He sente his woord, and helide hem; and deliuerede hem fro the dethis of hem. 21 Knouleche to the Lord his mercies; and 22 his merueilis to the sonus of men. And sacrifise thei a sacrifise of preising; and telle thei out his werkis in ful out ioȝing. 23 That gon doun the se in shipis; doende 24 werching in many watris. Thei seȝen the werkis of the Lord; and his mer- 25 ueilis in depthe. He seide, and the spirit of tempest stod; and his flowingus ben 26 enhauncid. Thei steȝen vp`vn to[y] heuenes, and gon doun `vn to[y] depnessis; and the 27 soulis of hem in euelis failede. Thei ben

Lord, whanne thei weren set in tribula- cioun; and he delyuerede hem fro her nedynesses. And he ledde forth hem in 7 to the riȝt weie; that thei schulden go in to the citee of dwelling. The mercies of 8 the Lord knouleche to hym; and hise merueilis *knouleche* to the sones of men. For he fillide a voide man; and he fillide 9 with goodis an hungry man. *God de-* 10 *lyuerede* men sittynge in derknessis[h], and in the schadowe of deth; and men prisoned in beggerye and in yrun. For thei maden 11 bitter the spechis of God; and wraththiden the councel of the hiȝeste. And the herte 12 of hem was maad meke in trauelis; and thei weren sijk, and noon was that helpide. And thei crieden to the Lord, whanne thei 13 weren set in tribulacioun; and he dely- uerede hem from her nedynessis. And he 14 ledde hem out of derknessis, and schadowe of deth; and brak the boondis of hem. The mercies of the Lord knouleche to 15 hym; and hise merueils *knouleche* to the sones of men. For he al to-brak brasun 16 ȝatis; and he brak yrun barris. He vp- 17 took hem fro the weie of her wickidnesse; for thei weren maad lowe for her vnriȝt- fulnesses. The soule of hem wlatide al 18 mete; and thei neiȝeden `til to[i] the ȝatis of deth. And thei crieden to the Lord, 19 whanne thei weren set in tribulacioun; and he delyuerede hem fro her nedynessis. He sente his word, and heelide hem; and[k] 20 delyuerede hem fro the perischingis of hem. The mercies of the Lord knouleche 21 to hym; and hise merueils to the sones of men. And offre thei the sacrifice of heri- 22 yng; and telle thei hise werkis in[l] ful out ioiyng. Thei that gon doun in to the see 23 in schippis; and maken worching in many watris. Thei sien the werkis of the Lord; 24 and hise merueilis in[m] the depthe. He 25 seide, and the spirit of tempest stood; and the wawis therof weren arerid. Thei 26 stien til to heuenes, and goen doun `til to[n]

---

v Om. *A.*　w Knowlechith *A.*　x fro *A.*　y in to *A.*

h derknesse s.　i unto I.　k and he I.　l with s.　m into A.　n unto I.

disturbid, and ben moued as a drunke
man; and al the wisdam of hem is de-
28 nourid. And thei crieden to the Lord,
whan thei weren trublid; and of the
29 nedis of hem he broȝte hem out. And he
ordeynede his tempest in to fair^z weder;
30 and his flodis weren stille. And thei
gladeden, for thei were stille; and he
broȝte hem out in to the hauene of the
31 wil of hem. Knouleche to the Lord his
mercies; and his merueilis to the sonus
32 of men. And enhaunce thei hym in the
chirche of folc; and in the chaȝer of
33 elderis preise thei hym. He sette the
flodis of hem in to desert; and the^a issue
34 of watris in to thirst. The fructuous
erthe in to briyn^b; fro the malice of men
35 dwellende in it. He putte desert in to
pondis^c of watris; and the erthe withoute
36 water in to the^d issues of watris. And
he sette there the hungry men; and thei
37 ordeyneden a cite of wonyng. And thei
seewen^e feeldis, and plaunteden vines;
38 and maden the frut off birthe. And he
blisside to hem, and thei ben multiplied
ful myche; and the bestis of hem he
39 lasside not. And fewe thei ben maad,
and ben ouertrauailid; fro tribulacioun of
40 euelis and sorewe. Held out is strif vp
on the princis; and to erren he made
hem in withoute weye, and not in the
41 weie. And he halp^f the pore man fro
myseise; and putte as shep meynes.
42 Riȝt^g men shul seen, and gladen; and
alle wickidnesse shal stoppe ther mouth.
43 Who wis man, and shal kepe thes
thingus; and shal vnderstonde the mercies of the Lord?

the^o depthis; the soule of hem failide in
yuelis. Thei weren troblid, and thei 27
weren moued as a drunkun man; and al
the wisdom of hem was deuourid. And 28
thei crieden to the Lord, whanne thei
weren set in tribulacioun; and he ledde
hem out of^p her nedynessis^q. And he 29
ordeynede the tempest therof in to a^r soft
wynde^s; and the wawis therof weren stille.
And thei weren glad, for tho weren stille; 30
and he ladde hem forth in to the hauene
of her wille. The mercies of the Lord 31
knouleche to hym; and hise merueilis to
the sones of men. And enhaunse thei him 32
in the chirche of the puple; and preise
thei him in the chaier of eldre^t men. He 33
hath set floodis in to deseert; and the out
goingis of watris^u in to thirst. *He hath* 34
set fruytful lond in to saltnesse; for the
malice of men dwellyng ther ynne. He 35
hath set deseert in to pondis of watris;
and^v erthe with out watir in to^w out-
goyngis^x of watris. And he settide^y there 36
hungri men; and thei maden a citee of
dwelling. And thei sowiden feeldis, and 37
plauntiden vynes; and maden fruyt of
birthe. And he blesside hem, and thei 38
weren multiplied greetli; and he made not
lesse her werk beestis. And thei weren 39
maad fewe; and thei^z weren trauelid of
tribulacioun of yuelis and of sorewis^a.
Strijf was sched out on princes; and he 40
made hem for to erre without the weie,
and not in the weie. And he helpide the 41
pore man fro pouert; and^b settide meynees^c
as a^d scheep *bringynge forth lambren.*
Riȝtful men schulen se, and^e schulen be 42
glad; and al wickidnesse schal stoppe his
mouth. Who *is* wijs, and schal kepe 43
these thingis; and schal vndirstonde the
mercies of the Lord?

---

z a fayre AII. a in the AII. b salt making E pr. m. c stremes E pr. m. d Om. AEII. e soweden AEII. f helpede AEII. g ȝit AII.

o Om. L. p fro ceteri. q nedynesse w. r Om. ceteri. s wynde ether pesiblete CDEFGHKLMOPQSUVWXbi. t the elder s. u watir c. wawis M. v and the I. w to the F. x outgoinge ELP. y sette s. z Om. I. a sorewe ceteri. b and he I. c Om. A pr. m. I. d Om. I. e and thei I.

PSALM CVII.

1 *The song of the salm, to hym Dauid.*

2 Redi is myn herte, God, redy is myn herte ; I shal synge, 'and salm seyn[h] in 3 my glorie. Ris vp[i], sautre and harpe ; I 4 shal risen vp fro the morutid li3t. I shal knouleche to thee in puplis, Lord; and do 5 salm to thee in naciouns. For gret vp on heuenus thi mercy[k]; and vn to the cloudis 6 thi treuthe. Be thou enhaunid vp on heuenes, God ; and vp on alle erthe thi 7 glorie; that thi loouede be delyuered. Mac saf with thi ri3t hond, and ful out here 8 thou me ; God spac in his holi. I shal ful out io3en, and deuyde Syccymam ; and the grete valey of tabernaclis I shal me-9 sure. Myn is Galaad, and myn is Ma-nasses ; and Effraym the vndertaking of 10 myn hed. Juda my king; Moab the cau-droun of myn hope. In to Ydume I shal strecchen out my sho; to me alienes 11 frendis ben maad. Who shal bringe me thennus in to a strengthid cite; who shal bringe me thennus in to Idume ? 12 Whether not thou, God, that hast put us abac ; and thou shalt not gon out, God, 13 in oure vertues? 3if to vs helpe fro tri-bulacioun ; for vein is the helthe of man. 14 In God wee shuln do vertue; and he to no3t shal bringe doun oure enemys.

PSALM CVIII.

1 *In to the ende, the salm of Dauid.*

2 God, my preising holde thou not stille; for the mouth of the synnere, and the mouth of the treccherous vp on me is 3 opened. Thei speeken a3en me with a treccherous tunge, and with woordis of hate thei enuyrounden me; and thei 4 fo3ten me out with oute cause. For thi

PSALM CVII.

The ' title of the[f] hundrid and seuenthe i salm[g]. The song of ' the salm of [h] Dauid.

Min herte is redi, God, myn herte is 2 redi ; Y schal singe, and Y schal seie salm in my glorie. My glorie, ryse thou vp, 3 sautrie and harp, rise thou vp ; Y schal rise vp eerli. Lord, Y schal knouleche to 4 thee among puplis ; and Y schal seie salm to thee among naciouns. For whi, God, 5 thi merci *is* greet on heuenes ; and thi treuthe *is* til to the cloudis. God, be thou 6 enhaunsid aboue heuenes ; and thi glorie ouer al erthe. That thi derlingis be dely-7 uerid, make thou saaf with thi ri3thond, and here me ; God spak in his hooli. I 8 schal make ful out ioye, and Y schal de-parte Siccimam ; and Y schal mete the grete valei of tabernaclis. Galaad is myn, 9 and Manasses is myn ; and Effraym *is* the vptaking of myn heed. Juda *is* my king; Moab *is* the caudron of myn hope. In to 10 Ydume Y schal stretche forth[i] my scho ; aliens ben maad frendis to me. Who schal 11 lede me forth in to a stronge citee; who schal lede me forth til in to Idume ? Whe-12 ther not thou, God, that hast put vs awei; and, God, schalt thou not go out in oure vertues? 3yue thou help to vs of tribula-13 cioun ; for the heelthe[k] of man is veyn. We schulen make vertu in God ; and he 14 schal bringe oure enemyes to nou3t.

PSALM CVIII.

The title of the hundrid and ei3tthe salm[l]. i To victorye, the salm [m] of Dauid [n]†.

God, holde thou not stille my preisyng; 2 for the mouth of the synner, and the mouth of the gileful man is openyd on me. Thei 3 spaken a3ens me with a gileful tunge, and thei cumpassiden me with wordis of ha-trede ; and fou3ten a3ens me with out cause. For that thing that thei schulden 4

[h] to preie E *pr. m.* [i] vp, my glorie, ris up E *pr. m.* [k] mercy, God, AE *pr. m. II.*

[f] Om. A. [g] Om. A. [h] Om. i. [i] Om. c *et plures.* [k] help c. [l] salm ; in Ebreu thus IV.
[m] song vi. [n] Dauid ; in Jerom thus, For victorie, the salm [song U] of Dauid. IV. No rubric in s.

that me thei shulden loouen, thei bac-
6 biten[1] to me; I forsothe preȝede. And thei
setten[m] aȝen me euelis for goodis; and
6 hate for my louyng. Sett vp on hym a
synere ; and the deuell stonde at his riȝt
7 side. Whan he is demed, go he out con-
dempnèd ; and his orisoun be maad in to
8 synne. His daȝis be thei maad fewe; and
9 an other take his bishopriche. His sonus
be thei maad faderles; and his wif a
10 widewe. Wagerende be[n] translatid his
sones, and begge thei; and be they cast
11 out of ther wonyngus. Enserche the
vȝurer al the substaunce of hym[o]; and
12 alienus take thei awei his trauailis. Be
ther not to hym an helpere ; ne be ther
that haue mercy to his moderles childer.
13 His sones be thei maad in to deth ; in o
14 ieneracioun be don awei his name. In to
mynde turne aȝeen the wickidnesse of his
fadris in the siȝte of the Lord ; and the
15 synne of his moder be not don awei. Be
thei maad aȝen the Lord euermor, and
pershe awei fro the erthe the mynde of
16 hem; for thi that he hath not recordid to
17 do mercy. And he[p] pursuede an helpeles
man and a beggere ; and to slen the sory
18 in herte of synne[q]. And he loouede cursing, and it shal come to hym ; and he
wolde not blissing, and it shal be longid
awey fro hym. And he cladde[r] cursing
as clothing, and it wente in as water in
to his innermor partis; and as oile in hys
19 bones. Be it maad to hym as clothing,
with the[s] whiche he is couered; and as a
girdil, with the[s] whiche he is euermor
20 gird beforn. This the werc of hem that
bacbiten to me anent the Lord ; and that
21 speken euelis aȝen my soule. And thou,
Lord, Lord[t], do with me for thi name ;
22 for swete is thi mercy. Deliuere me, for
nedi and a pore man I am ; and myn
23 herte is al disturbid with inne me. As
shadewe, whan it bowith doun, I am
taken awei; and am shaken out as lo-

loue me, thei bacbitiden me; but Y preiede.
And thei settiden aȝens me yuelis for 5
goodis; and hatrede for my loue. Ordeyne 6
thou a synner on him ; and the deuel
stonde on his riȝt half. Whanne he is 7
demed, go he out condempned ; and his
preier† 'be maad[o] in to synne. Hise daies 8
be maad fewe ; and another take his bi-
schopriche. Hise sones be maad faderles ; 9
and his wijf a widewe. Hise sones trem- 10
blinge be born ouer, and begge ; and be[p]
cast out of her habitaciouns. An vsurere 11
seke al his catel ; and aliens rauysche hise
trauelis. Noon helpere be to him ; nether 12
ony be that haue mercy on hise modirles
children. Hise sones be maad in to pe- 13
risching; the name of him be don awei
in oon[q] generacioun. The wickidnesse of 14
hise fadris come aȝen in to mynde in the
siȝt of the Lord ; and the synne of his
modir be not don awei. Be thei maad 15
euere aȝens the Lord ; and the mynde of
hem perische fro erthe. For that thing 16
that[r] he thouȝte not to do merci, and he 17
pursuede a pore man and[s] beggere; and to
slee a man compunct in herte. And he 18
louede cursing, and it schal come to hym ;
and he nolde[t] blessing, and it schal be
maad fer fro him. And he clothide cursing
as a cloth, and it entride as water in to
hise ynnere thingis ; and as oile in hise
boonus. Be it maad to him as a cloth, 19
with which he is hilyd ; and as a girdil,
with which he is euere gird. This is the 20
werk of hem that bacbiten me anentis the
Lord ; and that speke yuels aȝens my lijf.
And thou, Lord, Lord[u], do with me for 21
thi name ; for thi merci is swete. Dely- 22
uere thou me, for Y am nedi and pore ;
and myn herte is disturblid with ynne
me. I am takun awei as a[v] schadowe, 23
whanne it bowith awei; and Y am schakun
awei as locustis. Mi knees ben maad[w] 24
feble of[x] fasting ; and my fleische was
chaungid for oile. And Y am maad schen- 25

† that is, the
reson of Judas
biȝrayiȝng Crist
to Jewis. κV.

---

[1] bacbiteden AEH.   [m] settiden AII.   [n] be thei A.   [o] hem c pr. m.   [p] Om. E.   [q] his synne E pr. m.
[r] clothede AEH.   [s] Om. AEH.   [t] Om. c.

[o] Om. L.   [p] be thei I.   [q] o CDEFLOVXb. oo GKS.   [r] Om. s.   [s] and a I.   [t] wolde not I.   [u] God onx.
[v] Om. c et plures.   [w] Om. I.   [x] with s.

24 custis. My knes ben feblid of fasting; and my flesh is 'chaungid to betere[u] for 25 oile. And I am maad repref to them; thei se3en me, and moueden ther hedis. 26 Help me, Lord my God; mac me saf 27 aftir thi mercy. And thei shul wite, for this is thin hond; and thou, Lord, hast 28 'maad it[v]. They shul curse, and thou shalt blesse, that rijsen a3en me, be thei confoundid; thi seruaunt forsothe shal 29 gladen. Be thei clad[w] with shame, that bacbiten to me; and be thei couered as with a double mantil with ther confusion. 30 I shal knouleche to the Lord ful myche in my mouth; and in the myddel of 31 manye I shal preisen hym. That stod ne3h fro the ri3t parties of the pore; that he make saf fro pursueris my soule.

schipe to hem; thei sien me, and moueden her heedis. Mi Lord God, helpe thou me; 26 make thou me saaf bi thi merci. And thei 27 schulen wite, that this is thin hond; and thou, Lord, hast do it. Thei[y] schulen 28 curse, and thou schalt blesse, thei that risen a3ens me, be schent; but thi seruaunt schal be glad. Thei that bacbiten me, be 29 clothid with schame; and be thei hilid with her schenschipe as with a double cloth. I schal knouleche to the Lord 30 greetli with my mouth; and Y schal herie hym in the myddil of many men. Which 31 stood ny3 on the ri3t half of a pore man; to make saaf my soule fro pursueris.

PSALM CIX.

1　　　*The salm of Dauid.*

Dixit Domi-
nus.

The Lord seide to my Lord; Sit thou[x] of [y] my ri3t parties. To the tyme that I poote thin enemys; the litle stee3ing vp 2 stol of thi[z] feet. The 3erde of thi vertue the Lord shal senden out fro Sion; lord-shipe thou in the myddel of thin enemys. 3 With thee[a] the begynnyng in the dai of thi[b] vertue, in shynyngis of seintis; fro the wombe befor the dai sterre I gat 4 thee. The Lord swor, and it shal not othinken hym; Thou art a prest in to withoute ende, after the order of Mel- 5 chisedech. The Lord fro thi ri3tsidis; to-broside[c] in the dai of his wrathe kingis. 6 He shal deme in naciouns; he shal fulfille fallingis; he shal to-brose hedis in the 7 lond of manye. Of the strem in the weie he drane; therfore he enhauncyde the hed.

PSALM CIX.

The 'title of the[z] hundrid and nynthe　1 salm. 'The salm of Dauith[a].

The Lord seide to my Lord; Sitte thou on my ri3t side. Til Y putte thin enemys; a stool of thi feet. The Lord schal sende 2 out fro Syon the 3erde of thi vertu; be thou lord in the myddis of thin ene-myes. The bigynnyng *is* with thee in 3 the dai of thi vertu, in the[b] bri3tnessis[c] of [d] seyntis; Y gendride[e] thee of the wombe before the dai sterre. The Lord swoor, 4 and it schal not repente him; Thou art a preest with outen ende, bi the ordre of Melchisedech. The Lord on thi ri3t side; 5 hath broke kyngis in the dai of his ven-iaunce. He schal deme among naciouns, 6 he schal fille fallyngis; he schal schake heedis in the lond of many men. He 7 dranke of the stronde in the weie; therfor he enhaunside the heed.

---

[u] gretly chaungid E pr. m.　[v] don these thingis E pr. m.　[w] clothid AEH.　[x] Om. A.　[y] at AH.　[z] my A.　[a] Om. H.　[b] Om. H.　[c] to-brac E pr. m.

[y] And thei I.　[z] Om. A.　[a] Om. A. *The salm of Dauith, seid of Crist.* v.　[b] Om. I.　[c] bri3tnesse A.　[d] of thi v.　[e] gnat I.

PSALM CX.

Alleluia.

Confitebor.

1 I shal knouleche to thee, Lord, in al myn herte; in counseil of riʒtwis men 2 and congregacioun. Grete the werkis of the Lord; ful out soʒt in to alle his willis. 3 Knoulechinge and gret doing the werc of hym; and his riʒtwisnesse woneth in 4 to world of world. Mynde he made of his merueilis the merciful and the re- 5 were Lord; mete he ʒaf to men dredende hym. Myndeful he shal ben in to the 6 world of his testament; the vertue of his werkis he shal befortelle to his 7 puple. That he ʒyue to them the eritage of Jentilis; the werkis of his hondis, 8 treuthe and dom. Feithful alle his man- demens, confermed in to world of world; 9 don in treuthe and equyte. Aʒeen biʒing the Lord sente to his puple; he sente in to withoute ende his testament. Holy and 10 ferful his name; the begynnyng of wis- dam, the drede of the Lord. Good vnder- stonding to alle men doende it; his preis- ing dwellith in to world[d] of world.

PSALM CXI.

Alleluia of the aʒeen turnyng of Aggee and of Zacarie.

Beatus vir qui timet Domi- num.

1 Blisful the man that dredeth the Lord; in his maundemens he shal wilne ful 2 myche. Myʒti in the erthe shal ben his sed; the ieneracioun of ryʒt men shal be 3 blissid. Glorie and richessis in his hous; and his riʒtwisnesse dwellith in to world[e] 4 of world. Ful out sprungen is in derc- nessis liʒt to the riʒte; the merciful, and 5 the mercy doere, and the riʒtwis. Joʒeful a man, that hath mercy, and leeneth; dis- 6 posith his woordis in dom; for in to 7 withoute ende he shal not be moued. In

PSALM CX.

The 'title of the[f] hundrid and tenthe salm. Alleluya[g].

Lord, Y schal knouleche to thee in al 1 myn herte; in the counsel and congrega- cioun of iust men. The werkis of the 2 Lord *ben* greete; souʒt out in to alle hise willis. His werk *is* knoulechyng and grete 3 doyng; and his riʒtfulnesse dwellith in to the[h] world of world. The Lord merciful[i] 4 in wille, and a merciful doere, hath maad a mynde of hise merueilis; he hath ʒoue 5 meete to men dredynge hym. He schal be myndeful of his testament in to the world; he schal telle to his puple the 6 vertu of hise werkis. That he ʒyue to 7 hem the eritage of folkis; the werkis of hise hondis *ben* treuthe and doom. Alle 8 hise comaundementis *ben* feithful, con- fermed in to the world of world; maad in treuthe and equite. The Lord sente re- 9 dempcioun to hys puple; he comaundide his testament with outen ende. His name *is* hooli and dreedful; the bigynnyng of 10 wisdom *is* the[k] drede of the Lord. Good vndirstondyng *is* to alle that doen it; his preising dwellith in to the world of world.

PSALM CXI.

The 'title of the[l] hundrid and enleuenthe salm[m]. Alleluya[n].

Blissid *is* the man that dredith the 1 Lord; he schal wilne ful myche in hise comaundementis. His seed schal be myʒti 2 in erthe; the generacioun of riʒtful men schal be blessid. Glorie and richessis *ben* 3 in his hous; and his riʒtfulnesse dwellith in to the world of world. Liʒt is risun 4 vp in derknessis to riʒtful men; *the Lord* is merciful in wille, and a merciful doere, and riʒtful. The man *is* merye, that 5 doith merci, and leeneth; he disposith hise wordis in dom; for he schal not be 6

---

d the world ᴀ.   e the world ᴀ.

f Om. ᴀ.   g *Alleluia, Alleluia.* ʟᴏᴘ.   h Om. ꜱ.   i *is* merciful ꜱ.   k Om. ɪ.   l Om. ᴀ.   m Om. ꜱ.
n *Alleluia. This salm shewith, that blisse shal be ʒolden for the werkis of merci, and peyne to hem that ben vnmerciful.* ᴋ.

euere lasting mynde shal be the riȝtwise;
of euel hering he shal not drede. Redi his
8 herte to hopen in the Lord; confermed
is his herte, he shal not be moued, to the
9 time that he looke doun his enemys. He
delede, he ȝaf to pore men; the riȝtwisnesse of hym dwellith in to world[f] of
world; the horn of hym shal ben en-
10 hauncid in glorie. The synnere shal
seen, and wrathen; with his teth he shal
gnasten, and wasten hymself; the desir
of synneres shal pershen.

moued with outen ende. A iust man schal 7
be in euerlastinge mynde; he schal not
drede of an yuel heryng. His herte *is* redi
for to hope in the Lord; his herte is con- 8
fermed, he schal not be moued, til he dispise hise enemyes. He spredde abroad, he 9
ȝaf to pore men; his riȝtwisnesse[n] dwellith
in to the world of world; his horn schal
be reisid in glorie. A synner schal se, and[o] 10
schal be wrooth; he schal gnaste with hise
teeth, and schal faile[p]; the desijr of synneris schal perische.

PSALM CXII.

Alleluia.

1 Preise, ȝee childer, the Lord; preise
2 ȝee the name of the Lord. Be the name
of the Lord blissid; fro this now 'and
3 vnto[g] the world. Fro the rising of the
sunne vn to the going doun; preisable the
4 name of the Lord. Heiȝ vp on alle Jentilis the Lord; and vp on heuenys his
5 glorie. Who as the Lord oure God,
6 that in heȝe thingus dwellith; and meke
thingus beholdith in heuene and in erthe?
7 Vnder rerende fro erthe[h] the helpeles; and
8 fro drit rerende vp the pore. That he
'sette hym[i] with princis; with the princis
9 of his puple. That maketh to wone the
bareyn in the hous; a moder of sonys
gladende.

PSALM CXII.

The 'title of the[q] hundrid and twelfthe salm[r]. Alleluya[†].

Children, preise ȝe the Lord; preise ȝe 1
the name of the Lord. The name of the 2
Lord be blessid; fro this tyme now and til
in to the world. Fro the risyng of the 3
sunne til to the goyng doun; the name of
the Lord *is* worthi to be preisid. The 4
Lord *is* hiȝ aboue alle folkis; and his glorie
is aboue heuenes. Who *is* as oure Lord 5
God, that dwellith in hiȝe thingis; and 6
biholdith meke thingis in heuene and in
erthe? Reisynge a nedi man fro the[s] 7
erthe; and enhaunsinge a pore man fro
drit. That he sette hym with princes; 8
with the princes of his puple. Which 9
makith a bareyn womman dwelle in the
hous; a glad modir of sones.

† This salm
stireth men to
herie God, for
his greet ex-
cellence, and
for he reiseth
hem, that ben
oppresside vn-
iustli, to greet
honour, sum-
tyme in this
world, and to
blisse of heuen,
if thei suffren
pacientli. *Lire
here.* K.

‡ *A glos.* Bi
allegorie this
salme is ex-
pouned of the
casting awei of
the peple of
Jewis, for vnbi-
leue, and of the
reising of he-
then peple in
the godis of
grace, for thei
resceyueden
deuoutli Cris-
ten feith; and
so the syna-
goge is maad
bareyne and
abiect, ether
cast out, and
holi chirche is
maad fruytful
in the feith of
hethen men
conuertid to
Cristen feith.
Lire here. K.

PSALM CXIII.

Alleluia.

1 In the going out of Irael fro Egipt;
of the hous of Jacob fro the straunge
2 puple. Maad is Jude his halewing; Irael
3 the power of it. The se saȝ, and fleiȝ;
4 Jordan is al turned hindward. Mounteynes ful[k] out ioȝeden as wetheris; and
5 hillys[l] as lombis of shep. What is to

PSALM CXIII.

The titil of the hundrid and thrittenthe salm. Alleluya[s]‡.

In the goyng out of Israel fro Egipt; of 1
the hous of Jacob fro the[u] hethene puple.
Judeeȝ was maad the halewyng of hym; 2
Israel the power of hym. The see siȝ, and 3
fledde; Jordan was turned abac. Mun- 4
teyns ful out ioyeden as rammes; and litle
hillis as the lambren of scheep. Thou see, 5

§ that is, the
lynage of Juda
was maad the
halowing of
him. *Lire
here.* K.

---

[f] the world *A.*   [g] and in to *A.* in to *H.*   [h] the erthe *AEH.*   [i] sitte *c.*   [k] ȝee ful *E pr. m.*   [l] ȝee
hillys *E pr. m.*

[n] riȝtfulnesse *ceteri.*   [o] and he *I.*   [p] faile, *ether* [shal s] *mexe rotun* CDEFGHIKLMOPQRSUWXBI.   [q] Om. *A.*
[r] Om. *A.*   [s] Om. *ceteri.*   [t] Alleluia. *Goostli, in this salm eche synnere, that hath greet merci, is excited to
herie God.* K. Om. i.   [u] Om. I.

thee, thou se, that thou flowe ; and thou
Jordan, for thou art al turned bacward ?
6 Hillis, ʒee ful out gladiden as wetheris ;
and ʒee hillis, as the lombis of sheep.
7 From the face of the Lord moued is the
erthe ; from the face of God of Jacob.
8 That turnede the ston in to poolis of
watris ; and the roche in to wellys of
1 watris. Not to vs, Lord, not to vs ; but
2 to thi name ʒif glorie. Vp on thi mercy
and thi treuthe ; lest any time sey then
3 Jentilis, Wher is the God of hem ? Oure
God forsothe in heuene ; alle thingus
4 what euere he wolde, dideᵒ. The maumetis of Jentilis syluer and gold ; the
5 werkis of the hondis of men. Mouth
thei han, and thei shul not speke ; eʒen
6 they han, and thei shul not see. Eris
thei han, and thei shul not heren ; nose
therlis thei han, and thei shul not smelle.
7 Hondis thei han, and thei shul not grope ;
feet thei han, and they shul not go ; thei
8 shul not crien in ther throte. Lyc to
them be thei maad, that don tho thingus ;
9 and alle that trosten in hem. The hous
of Israel hopide in the Lord ; he is the
helpere of hem, and theᵖ defendere of
10 hem. The hous of Aron hopide in the
Lord ; he is the helpere of hem, and the
11 defendere of hem. That dreden the Lord,
hopiden in the Lord ; he is the helpere
12 of hem, and the defendere of hem. The
Lord myndeful was of vs ; and blissede to
vs. He blissede to the hous of Irael ; he
13 blissede to the hous of Aaron. He blissede to alle men that dreden the Lord ;
14 to the litle with the more. The Lord
caste he to vp on ʒou ; vpon ʒou and vp on
15 ʒoure sones. Blessid be ʒee of the Lord ;
16 that made heuene and erthe. The heuene
of heuene to the Lord ; the erthe forsothe
17 he ʒaf to the sones of men. Not the
deade shul preise thee, Lord ; ne alle that
18 go doun into helle. But wee that lyuen,
blissen to the Lord ; fro this now and
vn to the world.

what was to thee, for thou fleddist ; and
thou, Jordan, for thou were turned abak ?
Munteyns, ʒe maden ful out ioye as 6
rammes ; and litle hillis, as the lambren
of scheep. The erthe was moued froᵛ the 7
face of 'the Lordᵂ ; fro the face of God
of Jacob. Which turnede a stoon in to 8
pondisˣ of watris ; and an hard rooch in to
wellis of watris. Lord, not to vs, not to 1
vs ; but ʒyue thou glorie to thi name. Onʸ 2
thi merci and thiᶻ treuthe ; lest ony tyme
hethene men seien, Where is the God of
hem ? Forsothe oure God in heuene ; dide 3
alle thingis, whiche euere he wolde. The 4
symulacris of hethene men *ben* siluer and
gold ; the werkis of mennus hondis. Thoᵃ 5
han mouth, and schulen not speke ; thoᵃ
han iʒen, and schulen not se. Thoᵃ han 6
eeris, and schulen not here ; thoᵃ han nose
thurls, and schulen not smelle. Thoᵃ han 7
hondis, and schulen not grope ; thoᵃ han
feet, and schulen not go ; thoᵃ schulen not
crye in her throte. Thei that maken thoᵇ 8
ben maad lijk tho ; and alle that triste in
thoᶜ. The hous of Israel hopide in the 9
Lord ; he is the helpere 'of hemᵈ, and the
defendere of hem. The hous of Aaron 10
hopide in the Lord ; he is the helpere of
hem, and the *defendere of hem*. *Thei that* 11
dreden the Lord, hopiden in the Lord ;
he is the helpere of hem, and the *defendere*
of hem. The Lord was myndeful of vs ; 12
and blesside vs. He blesside the hous of
Israel ; he blesside the hous of Aaron. He 13
blesside alle menᵉ that dreden the Lord ;
'he blessideᶠ litleᵍ 'men with thoʰ grettere.
The Lord encreesseⁱ on ʒou ; on ʒou and on 14
ʒoure sones. Blessid be ʒe of the Lord ; that 15
made heuene and erthe. Heuene of 'heuene 16
isᵏ to the Lord ; but he ʒaf ertheˡ to the
sones of men. Lord, not deed men schulen 17
herie thee ; nether alle men that goen doun
in to helle. But we that lyuen, blessen 18
the Lord ; fro this tyme now and til in to
the world.

ᵐ For *A*.   ⁿ Om. *A*.   ᵒ he dide *AH*.   ᵖ Om. *A*.

ᵛ for c.   ʷ God s.   ˣ a poond s.   ʸ Of ɪ. In ʟ.   ᶻ of thi ɪ.   ᵃ Thei ɪ.   ᵇ tho *symulacris* ɪ.   ᶜ hem ɪ.
ᵈ Om. ꜱ.   ᵉ Om. *A*.   ᶠ Om. ɪ.   ᵍ the litle cᴅᴇꜰʜᴋʟᴍᴏᴘʀꜱᴡxʰi. bothe litle ɪ.   ʰ and ɪ.   ⁱ adde *ether*
encrecse cᴅᴇꜰɢʜᴋᴍᴏᴘǫʀꜱᴜᴡxbi. adde to ɪ. addide *ether encrecede* ʟ.   ᵏ heuenys s.   ˡ the erthe ɪ.

PSALM CXIV.

Alleluia.

Dilexi quoniam exaudiet.

1 I loouede; for the Lord shal ful out 2 here the vois of myn orisoun. For he inbowide his ere to me; and in my daȝis 3 I shal inwardly clepe. Ther enuyrounden me sorewis of deth; and the perilis of 4 helle founden me. Trybulacioun and sorewe I fond; and the name of the Lord I inwardli clepede. Oᑫ! Lord, delyuere 5 thou myʳ soule; mercyful Lord, and riȝt- 6 wys, and oure God hath reuthe. The Lord kepende litil childer; I am meekid, 7 and he delinerede me. My soule, be thou al turned in to thi reste; for the Lord 8 hath wel do to thee. For he toc out my soule fro deth; myn eȝen fro teris, my 9 feet fro sliding. I shal plese to the Lord; in the regioun of men on lyne.

PSALM CXIV.

The titil of the hundrid and fourtenthe salm. Alleluiaᵐ.

I louede 'the Lordⁿ; for the Lord schal 1 here the vois of my preier. For he bowide 2 doun his ere to me; and Y schal inwardli clepeⁿⁿ in my daies. The sorewis of deth 3 cumpassiden me; and the perelis of helle founden me. I foond tribulacioun and 4 sorewe; and Y clepide inwardli the name of the Lord. Thou, Lord, delyuere my soule; the Lord is merciful, and iust; and 5 oure God doith merci. And the Lordₒ kepith litle children; Y was mekid, and he delyuerede me. Mi soule, turne thou 7 in to thi reste; for the Lord hath do wel to thee. For he hath delyuered my soule 8 fro deth; myn iȝen fro wepingis, myᵒ feet fro fallyng doun. I schal plese the Lord; 9 in the cuntrei of hem that lyuen.

PSALM CXV.

Alleluya.

Credidi propter quod.

10 I leeuede, wherfor I spac; I forsothe 11 am mekid ful myche. I seyde in myn 12 excesse; Eche man a liere. What shal I ȝeelde to the Lord; for alle thingus that 13 he ȝeldˢ to me? The chalis of the helthe ȝyuere I shal take; and the name of the 14 Lord I shal inwardli clepen. My vouwis to the Lord I shal ȝelde befor al his pu- 15 ple; precious in the siȝte of the Lord the 16 deth of his seintis. O! Lord, for I thi seruauut; I thi seruauut, and the sone of thin hond maiden. Thou hast broke 17 my bondis, to thee I shal sacrifien an ost of preising; and the name of the Lord 18 I shal inwardli clepe. My vouwis to the Lord I shal ȝelde, in the siȝte of al his 19 puple; in the porche of the hous of the Lord, in the myddil of thi Jerusalem.

PSALM CXV.

The titil of the hundrid and fiftenthe salm. Alleluyaᵖ.

I bileuede, for which thing Y spak; for- 10 soth Y was maad low ful myche. I seide 11 in my passing; Ech man is a lier. What 12 schal Y ȝelde to the Lord; for alle thingis which he ȝeldideᑫ to me? I schal take the 13 cuppeʳ of heelthe; and Y schal inwardli clepe the name of the Lord. I schal ȝelde 14 my vowis to the Lord bifor al his puple; the deth of seyntis of the Lord is precious 15 in his siȝt. Oˢ! Lord, forᵗ Y am thi ser- 16 uaut; Y am thi seruaunt, and the sone of thi handmaide. Thou hast broke my bondys, to thee Y schal offre a sacrifice 17 of heriyng; and Y schal inwardli clepe the name of the Lord. I schal ȝelde my vowis 18 to the Lord, in the siȝt of al his puple; inᵘ 19 the porchisᵛ of the hous of the Lord, in the myddilʷ of thee, Jerusalem.

ᑫ Om. н.   ʳ delyuere, delyuere my c.   ˢ ȝeeldede ʌɛн.

ᵐ Alleluia. Dauith made this salm for his delyueraunse fro pereis of Saul. к.   ᵒ Om. ı.   ⁿⁿ clepe him ꜱ.   ᵒ and my ꜱ.   ᵖ The hundrid and fiftenthe salm. cᴅꜰɢʜᴊᴏǫ ꜱxb. The titil of the hundrid and fiftenthe salm. ᴋʟᴘw. The c. and xv. salm hath no tiȝtle. ıv. The hundrid salm and fiftenthe hath no title, and it spekith of Dauith vndir Absolon, and he bihiȝie thankingis to God for delyueraunse. к.   ᑫ hath ȝolde ı.   ʳ cuppis o.   ˢ ʌ! ceteri.   ᵗ Om. c.   ᵘ and in ı.   ᵛ forȝerdis ceteri passim.   ʷ myd ʌ. middis cᴋ.

PSALM CXVI.

Alleluia.

Laudate Do-
minum, omnes.

1 Preise ȝee the Lord, alle Jentilis;
2 preise ȝee hym, alle puplis. For confermed is vp on vs the mercy of hym;
and the treuthe of the Lord dwellith in
to with oute ende.

PSALM CXVII.

Alleluya.

Confitemini
Domino.

1 Knoulecheth to the Lord, for he is
good; for in to the world the merci of
2 hym. Seye now Irael, for he is good;
for in to the world the mercy of hym.
3 Seie now the hons of Aron; for in to the
4 world the mercy of hym. Seye now thei
that dreden the Lord; for in to the world
5 the mercy of hym. Fro tribulacioun I inwardli clepide the Lord; and[t] ful out
6 herde me in breede the Lord. The Lord
to me an helpere; I[u] shal not drede what
7 do to me a man. The Lord to me an
helpere; and I shal despise myn enemys.
8 Good is to trostnen in the Lord; than to
9 trosten in man. Good is to hopen in the
10 Lord; than to hopen in princis. Alle Jen-
tilys ȝiden aboute me; and in the name
of the Lord, for I am vengid in hem.
11 Goende aboute thei ȝiden aboute me;
and in the name of the Lord, for I am
12 vengid in hem. Thei enuyrounden me
as bes[v], and wratheden out as fyr in
thornes; and in the name of the Lord,
13 for I am vengid in hem. Ful myche constreyned I am turned vp so doun, that I
shulde falle; and the Lord vndertoc me.
14 My strengthe, and my preising the Lord;
15 and he is maad to me in to helthe. The
vois of ful out ioȝing and of helthe; in
16 the tabernaclis of riȝtwis men. The riȝt
hond of the Lord dide vertue; the riȝt

PSALM CXVI.

The title of the hundrid and sixtenthe salm. Alleluya[x].

1 Alle hethen men, herie ȝe the Lord;
2 alle puplis, herie ȝe hym. For his merci
is confermyd on vs; and the treuthe of the
Lord dwellith with outen ende.

PSALM CXVII.

The titil of the[y] hundrid and seuententhe salm. Alleluia[z].

1 Knouleche ȝe to the Lord, for he is
good; for his merci is with outen ende.
2 Israel seie now, for he is good; for his
merci is with outen ende. The hous of[3]
Aaron seie now; for his merci is with
4 outen ende. Thei that dreden the Lord,
seie now; for his merci is withouten ende.
5 Of tribulacioun Y inwardli clepide the
Lord; and the Lord herde me in large-
6 nesse. The Lord is an helpere to me; Y
schal not drede what a[n] man schal do to
7 me. The Lord is an helpere to me; and
Y schal dispise myn enemyes. It is betere
8 for[b] to trist in the Lord; than for to triste
9 in man. It is betere for to hope in the
Lord; than for[c] to hope in princes. Alle
10 folkis cumpassiden me; and in the name
of the Lord it bifelde, for Y am auengide
11 on hem. Thei cumpassinge cumpassiden
me; and in the name of the Lord, for Y
12 am auengid on hem. Thei cumpassiden
me as been[d], and thei brenten out as fier
doith[a] among thornes; and in the name of
13 the Lord, for Y am avengid on hem. I
was hurlid, and turnede vpsedoun, that Y
schulde falle doun; and the Lord took me
14 vp. The Lord is my strengthe, and my
heryyng; and he is maad to me in to
15 heelthe. The vois of ful out ioiyng and is
of beelthe; be in the tabernaclis of iust
16 men. The riȝt hond of the Lord hath do

---

[t] and he A.   [u] and I c.   [v] been A.

[x] Om. A. salm. Alleluia, that is, to God do we heerijngis. K.   [y] Om. R.   [z] Alleluia. This salm inducith
men to herie God, and bringeth reson therto. K.   [3] Om. S.   [b] Om. IL.   [c] Om. I.   [d] bees CDEFGHKLMO
PQRSUWXbI.   [e] Om. I.

hond of the Lord enhauncide me; the
17 riȝt hond of the Lord dide vertue. I shal
not die, but liuen; and I shal telle the
18 werkis of the Lord. Chastisende chas-
tisede me the Lord; and to deth he toc
19 not me. Openeth to me the ȝatis of
riȝtwisnesse, and gon in to them I shal
20 knouleche to the Lord; this the ȝate of
the Lord, riȝtwis men shul gon in to it.
21 I shal knouleche to thee, for thou hast
ful out herd me; and thou art maad to
22 me in to helthe. The ston that hildende
thei repreueden; this is maad in to the
23 hed of the corner. Of the Lord this is
don; and it is merueilous in oure eȝen.
24 This is the dai that the Lord made; ful
25 out ioȝe wee, and glade wee in it. O! Lord,
mac me saf, O! Lord, weel be thou[w] wel-
26 sum; blissid that cometh in the name
of the Lord. Wee han blissid to ȝou fro
27 the hous of the Lord; God the Lord,
and he hath liȝtid to vs. Ordeyne ȝcc a
solempne dai in thicke thingis; vn to the
28 horn of the auter. My God thou art,
and I shal knouleche to thee; my God
thou art, and I shal enhaunce thee. I
shal knoulechen to thee, for thou hast ful
out herd me; and thou art maad to me
29 in to helthe. Knoulecheth to the Lord,
for he is good; for in to the world the
merci of hym.

vertu, the riȝt hond of the Lord enhaunside me; the riȝt hond of the Lord hath
do vertu. I schal not die, but Y schal 17
lyue; and Y schal telle the werkis of the
Lord. The Lord chastisinge hath chastisid 18
me; and he ȝaf not me to deth. Opene ȝe 19
to me the ȝatis of riȝtfulnesse, and Y schal
entre bi tho, and Y schal knouleche to the
Lord; this ȝate is of the Lord, and iust 20
men schulen entre bi it. I schal knou- 21
leche to thee, for thou herdist me; and art
maad to me in to heelthe. The stoon 22
which the bilderis repreueden; this is maad
in to the heed of the corner. This thing 23
is maad of the Lord; and it is wonderful
bifore oure iȝen. This is the dai which 24
the Lord made; make we ful out ioye,
and be we glad ther ynne. O[e]! Lord, make 25
thou me saaf, O[e]! Lord, make thou wel
prosperite; blessid is he that cometh in 26
the name of the Lord. We blesseden[f] ȝou
of the hous of the Lord; God is Lord, 27
and[g] hath ȝoue liȝt to vs. Ordeyne ȝe a
solempne dai in thicke puplis; til to the
horn of the auter. Thou art my God, and 28
Y schal knouleche to thee; thou art my
God, and Y schal enhaunse thee. I schal
knouleche to thee, for thou herdist me;
and thou art maad to me in to heelthe.
Knouleche ȝc to the Lord, for he is good; 29
for his merci is with outen ende.

PSALM CXVIII.

Alleluia.

Aleph.

inma-

1 Blisful[x] the vndefoulid in[y] the weie;
2 that gon in the lawe of the Lord. Blisful that enserche the witnessingus of
hym; in al the herte ful out sechen hym.
3 Forsothe not thei that wirken wickid-
4 nesse; in the weies of hym ȝiden. Thou
hast comaundid; thin hestis to be kept
5 ful myche. Wolde God weren dressid
my weies; to be kept thi iustifiyngus.
6 Thanne I shal not be confoundid; whan
I shal parfitli loken in alle thin hestis.

PSALM CXVIII.

'The titil of[h] the hundrid and eiȝtenthe salm. Alleluia†.

Blessid ben men with out wem in the 1
weie; that gon in the lawe of the Lord.
Blessid ben thei, that seken hise witness- 2
ingis; seken[i] him in al the herte. For thei 3
that worchen wickidnesse; ȝeden not in hise
weies. Thou hast comaundid; that thin 4
heestis be kept greetly. I wolde that my 5
weies be[k] dressid; to kepe thi iustifiyngis.
Thanne Y schal not be schent; whanne Y 6
schal biholde perfitli in alle thin heestis.
I schal knouleche to thee in the dressing 7

† A glos. This salm speketh of blisse; blisse is in truthe and dede, and thus it is bad confi in heuene; blisse is also in hope, and thus it is had in present liȝf, bi exercise of Goddis werkis; therfore this salue spekith of blisse, as it is had in present liȝf. Lire here. K.

---

[w] Om. c.   [x] Blessid ben A.   [y] that goon in n.

[e] A! ceteri fere omnes.   [f] blessen A pr. m. r.   [g] and he r.   [h] Om. s.   [i] and seken K.   [k] weren r.

7 I shal knouleche to thee in ri3t reuling of herte; in that that I haue lerned the 8 domes of thi ri3twisnesse. Thi justifiyngis I shal kepe; ne forsake thou mē on alle sydys.

Beth.

9 In what amendith the 3unge man more waxen his weye? in keping thi woordis. 10 In al myn herte I ful out so3te thee; ne 11 poote thou me abac fro thin hestis. In myn herte I hidde thi spechis[z]; that I 12 synne not to thee. Blissid thou art, 13 Lord; teche me thi iustifiyngus. In my lippis I tolde forth; alle the domes of thin 14 mouth. In the weie of thi witnessingis 15 I delitide; as in alle richesses. In thin hestys I shal ben enhauntid; and I shal 16 beholde thi weies. In thi iustefiyngus I shal swetcli thenken; and I shal not for-3ete thi woordis.

Gimel.

17 3eld to thi seruaunt; quikene[a] thou me, 18 and I shal kepe thi woordis. Opene myn e3en; and I shal beholde the merueilis of 19 thi lawe. A comeling wonere I am in the erthe; ne hide thou fro me thin 20 hestis. My soule coucitide to desire thi 21 iustefiyngus; in alle tyme. Thou blamedist proude men; cursid ben thei, that 22 bowen doun fro thi maundementis[b]. Do awei fro me repref and dispising; for 23 thi witnessingus I ful out so3te. For-sothe ther seten princis, and a3en me thei speeken; thi seruaunt forsothe was en-24 hauntid in thi iustefiyngus. For and[c] thi witnessingus is my swete thenking; and my counseil thi iustefiyngus.

Deleth.

25 Myn soule cleuede to the pament; 26 quykene thou me aftir thi woord. My weies I tolde out, and thou ful out herd-27 est me; teche me thi iustefiyngis. The weie of thi iustefiyngus enforme thou me; and I shal ben enhauntid in thi mer-

of[l] herte; in that that Y lernyde the domes of thi ri3tfulnesse[m]. I schal kepe thi iusti-8 fiyngis; forsake thou not me on ech side.

In what thing amendith a[n] 3ong wax-9 inge man his weie? in keping thi wordis. In al myn herte Y sou3te thee; putte thou 10 me not awei fro thin heestis. In myn 11 herte Y hidde thi spechis; that Y do not synne a3ens thee. Lord, thou art blessid; 12 teche thou me thi iustifiyngis. In my 13 lippis Y haue pronounsid; alle the domes of thi mouth. I delitide in the weie of 14 thi witnessingis; as in alle richessis. I 15 schal be ocupied[o] in thin heestis; and Y schal biholde thi weies. I schal bithenke 16 in thi iustifiyngis; Y schal not for3ete thi wordis.

3elde to thi seruaunt; quiken thou me, 17 and Y schal kepe thi wordis. Li3tne thou 18 myn i3en; and Y schal biholde the[p] mer-ueils of thi lawe. I am a comeling in 19 erthe; hide thou not thin heestis fro me. Mi soule coueitide to desire thi iustifiyngis; 20 in al tyme. Thou blamedist the proude; 21 thei ben cursid, that bowen awei fro thin heestis. Do thou awei 'fro me[q] schen-22 schipe and dispising; for Y sou3te thi witnessingis. For whi princis saten, and 23 spaken a3ens me; but thi seruaunt was exercisid in thi iustifiyngis. For whi and 24 thi witnessyngis[r] is my thenkyng; and my counsel is thi iustifiyngis.

Mi soule cleuede to the pawment; 25 quykine thou me bi thi word. I telde 26 out my weies, and thou herdist me; teche thou me thi iustifiyngis. Lerne thou me 27 the weie of thi iustifiyngis; and Y schal be exercisid in thi merueils. Mi soule nap-28

---

z speche A.   a quiyk A.   b heestis AEH. biddingis c pr. m.   c in H.

l of myn I.   m ri3tfulnessis s.   n the I.   o excercisid, *ether bisily ocupied* CDEFGHIKLMOPQRSTVWXb. p Om. ceteri.   q Om. s.   r witnessing FM. iustifiyngis IL pr. m.

28 ueilis. My soule nappide for noʒe ; con-
29 ferme thou me in thi woordis. The weie
of wickidnesse moue thou awey fro me ;
30 and in thi lawe hane mercy of me. The
weie of treuthe[d] I ches ; thi domes I haue
31 not forʒeten. I cleuede to thi witnessingus, Lord ; wile thou not me con-
32 founden. The weie of thin hestis I ran ;
whan thou spreddest abrod myn herte.

pide for anoye ; conferme thou me in thi
wordis. Remoue thou fro me the weie of 29
wickidnesse ; and in thi lawe haue thou
merci on me. I chees the weie of treuthe ; 30
Y forʒat not thi domes. Lord, Y cleuede 31
to thi witnessyngis ; nyle thou schende me.
I ran the[s] weie of thi comaundementis ; 32
whanne thou alargidist myn herte.

He.

Legem pone
michi.

33 Lawe set thou to me, Lord, the weie
of thi iustefiyngus ; and I shal seche out
34 it euermor. Ʒif to me vndirstonding, and
I shal enserche thi lawe ; and I shal kepen
35 it in al myn herte. Bring out me in the
36 sty of thin hestis ; for it I wolde. Bowe
in myn herte in to thi witnessyngus ; and
37 not in to coueitise. Turne awei myn eʒen,
lest thei see vanytee ; in thi weie quykene
38 thou me. Sett to thi seruaunt thi speche ;
39 in thi drede. Kut of my repref, that I
40 ouertrowide ; for thi domys ioʒeful. Lo !
I haue coueitid thin hestis ; in thin equite
quykene thou me.

Lord, sette thou to me a lawe, the weie 33
of thi iustifiyngis ; and Y schal seke it
euere. Ʒyue thou vndurstonding to me, 34
and Y schal seke thi lawe ; and Y schal
kepe it in al myn herte. Lede me forth 35
in the path of thin heestis ; for Y wolde it.
'Bowe thou[t] myn herte in to thi witness- 36
ingus ; and not in to aueryce. Turne thou 37
awei myn iʒen, that 'tho seen[u] not vanyte ;
quykene thou me in thi weie. Ordeyne 38
thi speche to thi seruaunt ; in thi drede.
Kitte awey my schenschip, which Y sup- 39
poside ; for thi domes ben myrie. Lo ! 40
Y coueitide thi comaundementis ; quikene
thou[v] me in thin equite.

Vau.

Et veniat
super me.

41 And thi mercy come vp on me, Lord ;
42 thin helthe ʒiuere after thi speche. And
I shal answere to the repreuende me a
woord ; for I hopide in thi sermounes.
43 And ne take thou awei fro my mouth a
woord of truthe on eche side ; for in thi
44 domes I ouer hopide. And I shal kepe
thi lawe euermor ; in to the world, and
45 in to the world of world. And I ʒide in
46 breede ; and thin hestis I out soʒte. And
I spac in thi witnessingus in the siʒte of
47 kingus ; and I was not confoundid. And
I sweteli thoʒte in thin hestis ; that I
48 loouede. And I rerede myn hondis to[e]
thin hestis, that I loouede ; and I shal
ben enhauntid in thi iustefiyngis.

And, Lord, thi merci come on me ; thin 41
heelthe come bi[w] thi speche. And Y schal 42
answere a word to men seiynge schenschipe to me ; for Y hopide in thi wordis.
And take thou not awei fro my mouth 43
the word of treuthe outerli ; for Y hopide
aboue in thi domes. And Y schal kepe 44
thi lawe euere ; in to the world, and in to
the world of[x] world. And Y ʒede in 45
largenesse ; for Y souʒte thi comaundementis. And Y spak of thi witnessyngis 46
in the siʒt of kingis ; and Y was not
schent. And Y bithouʒte in thin heestis ; 47
whiche Y louede. And Y reiside myn 48
hondis to thi comaundementis, whiche Y
louede ; and Y schal be excercisid in thi
iustifiyngis.

Zai.

Memor esto
verbi tui.

49 Myndeful be thou of thi woord to thi

Lord, haue thou mynde on thi word to 49

---

d thi trewth A.　　e in A.

* in the e.　　t Bowe thou doun κ. Bowe doun ΠLMsxi.　　u thei se I.　　v Om. I.　　w aftir I.　　x of
the e sec. m. ΓOΠQSUW.

seruaunt; in whiche to me hope thou
50 hast ȝiuen. This coumfortide me in my
mecnesse; for thi speche quykenede me.
51 Proude men wickidli deden on eche side;
fro thi lawe forsothe[f] I bowide not doun.
52 Myndeful I was of thi domes fro the
53 world, Lord; and I am coumfortid. Failing heeld me; for the synneres forsakende
54 thi lawe. Chauntable weren to me thi
iustefiyngus; in the place of my pilgrim-
55 aging[g]. Myndeful I was the nyȝt of thi
56 name, Lord; and I kepte thi lawe. This
is do to me; for thi iustefiyngis I out
soȝte.

Heth.

Porcio mea,
Domine.

57 My porcioun thou, Lord; I seide to
58 kepe thi lawe. I louli preȝede thi face
in al myn herte; haue mercy of me aftir
59 thi speche. I thoȝte my weies; and al
turnede my feet in to thi witnessingus.
60 I am redi, and am[h] not disturbid; that I
61 kepe thin hestys. The cordis of synneres
ben wounden aboute me; and thi lawe I
62 haue not forȝete. At myd nyȝt I ros to
knouleche to thee; vp on the domes of thi
63 iustefiyng. Parcener I am of alle men
dredende thee; and of kepende thin hestis.
64 Of thi mercy, Lord, ful is the erthe; thi
iustefiyngus teche thou me.

Teth.

Bonitatem
fecisti.

65 Goodnesse thou hast do to thi ser-
66 uaunt, Lord; aftir thi woord. Goodnesse,
and discipline, and kunnyng tech thou
67 me; for in thin hestys I leeuede. Beforn
that I was mekid, I trespaside; therfore
68 thi speche I kepte. Good art thou; and
in thi goodnesse tech me thi iustefiyngis.
69 Multeplied is vp on me the wickidnesse of
proude men[i]; I forsothe in al myn herte
70 shal enserche thin hestis. Cruddid is[k] as
mylc the herte of hem; I forsothe thi
71 lawe sweteli thoȝte. Good is to me, for
thou hast mekid me; that I lerne thi
72 iustefiyngus. Good is to me the lawe of

thi seruaunt; in which *word* thou hast
50 ȝoue hope to me. This coumfortide me
in my lownesse[y]; for thi word quikenede
me. Proude men diden wickidli bi alle[51]
thingis; but Y bowide not awei fro thi
lawe. Lord, Y was myndeful on[z] thi[52]
domes fro the world; and Y was coumfortid. Failing helde me; for synneris for-[53]
sakinge thi lawe. Thi iustifiyngis weren[54]
delitable to me to be sungun; in the place
of my pilgrimage. Lord, Y hadde mynde[55]
of thi name bi niȝt; and Y kepte thi lawe.
This thing was maad to me; for Y souȝte[56]
thi iustifiyngis.

Lord, my part; Y seide to kepe[a] thi[57]
lawe. I bisouȝte thi face in al myn herte;[58]
haue thou merci on me bi[b] thi speche. I[59]
bithouȝte my weies; and Y turnede my
feet in to thi witnessyngis. I am redi,[60]
and Y am not disturblid; to kepe thi comaundementis. The coordis of synneris[c][61]
han biclippid me; and Y haue not forȝete
thi lawe. At mydnyȝt Y roos to knou-[62]
leche to thee; on the domes of thi iustifiyngis. I am parcener of alle that dreden[63]
thee; and kepen thin heestis. Lord, the[64]
erthe is ful of thi merci; teche thou me
thi iustifiyngis.

Lord, thou hast do goodnesse with thi[65]
seruaunt; bi[d] thi word. Teche thou me[66]
goodnesse, and loore[e], and kunnyng; for
Y bileuede to thin heestis. Bifor that Y[67]
was maad meke, Y trespasside; therfor
Y kepte thi speche. Thou art good; and[68]
in thi goodnesse teche thou me thi iustifiyngis. The wickidnesse of hem that ben[69]
proude, is multiplied on me; but in al myn
herte Y schal[f] seke thin heestis. The herte[70]
of hem is cruddid[g] as mylk; but Y bithouȝte
thi lawe. It is good to me, that thou hast[71]
maad me meke; that Y lerne thi iustifiyngis. The lawe of thi mouth is betere[72]

---

[f] Om. c.   [g] pilgrymage *AH.*   [h] Y am *AH.*   [i] Om. E.   [k] Om. c.

[y] lownesse *maad bi turment* K. *that is, maad* [bi tor]ment v marg.   [z] of s.   [a] seke s.   [b] aftir I.
[c] synnes I.   [d] aftir I.   [e] loore, *ether chastiȝyng* c *et ceteri.*   [f] Om. c.   [g] cruddid, *ether maad*
hard v.

thi mouth; vp on thousendis of gold and of siluer.

to me; than thousyndis of gold and of [h] siluer.

Joth.

Manus tue fecerunt.

73 Thin hondus maden me, and formeden me; ȝif to me vnderstonding, that I lerne 74 thin hestis. That dreden thee shul see me, and gladen; for in thi wordis I ouer-75 hopide. I knewȝ, Lord, for equite thi domes; and in thi treuthe thou hast mekid 76 me. Be don thi mercy, that it coumforte me; after thi speche to thi seruaunt. 77 Come to me thi mercy doingus, and I shal liue; for thi lawe is my swete thenk-78 ing. Proude men be thei confoundid, for vnriȝtwisli wickidnesse thei diden aȝen me; I forsothe shal ben enhauntid in 79 thin hestis. The men dredende thee be thei al turned to me; and tho that knewe 80 thi wytnessingus. Be maad myn herte vndefoulyd in thi iustefiyngis; that I be not confoundid.

Thin hondis maden me, and fourmeden 73 me; ȝyue thou vndurstondyng to me, that Y lerne thin heestis. Thei that dreden 74 thee schulen se me, and[l] schulen be glad; for Y hopide more on thi wordis. Lord, 75 Y knewe, that thi domes *ben* equite; and in thi treuth thou hast maad me meke. Thi merci be maad, that it coumforte me; 76 bi[k] thi speche to thi seruaunt. Thi mer-77 ciful doyngis come to me, and Y schal lyue; for thi lawe is my thenkyng. Thei 78 that ben proude be schent, for vniustli thei diden wickidnesse aȝens me; but Y schal be exercisid in thin heestis. Thei 79 that dreden thee be turned to me; and thei that knowen[l] thi witnessyngis. Myn 80 herte be maad vnwemmed in thi iustifi-yngis; that Y be not schent.

Caf.

Defecit in sa-lutare tuum.

81 My soule failide in to thin helthe ȝiuere; and in to thi woord I ouerhopede. 82 Myn eȝen failede in to thin speche; seiende, Whanne shalt thou coumforte 83 me? For I am maad as a botel in hor frost; thi iustefiyngus I haue not forȝete. 84 Hou fele ben the daȝis of thi seruaunt; whanne shalt thou do of the pursuende 85 me dom? Wicke men tolden to me tal-86 ingus; but not as thi lawe. Alle thin maundemens treuthe; wicke men pursu-87 eden me, help thou me. A litel lasse thei wasteden me in the erthe; I forsothe 88 forsoc not thin hestis. After thi mercy quikene thou me; and I shal kepe the witnessingis of thi mouth.

Mi soule failide in to thin helthe; and 81 Y hopide more on[m] thi word. Myn iȝen 82 failiden in to thi[n] speche; seiynge, Whanne schalt thou coumforte me? For Y am 83 maad as a bowge in frost[o]; Y haue not forȝete thi iustifiyngis. Hou many ben 84 the daies of thi seruaunt; whanne thou schalt make doom of hem that pursuen me? Wickid men telden to me ianglyngis; 85 but not as thi lawe. Alle thi comaunde-86 mentis *ben* treuthe; wickid men han pur-sued me, helpe thou me. Almeest thei 87 endiden me in erthe; but I forsook not thi comaundementis. Bi[p] thi mersi quikene 88 thou me; and Y schal kepe the witness-ingis of thi mouth.

Lameth.

In eternum, Domine.

89 In to withoute ende, Lord; thi woord 90 abit[l] stille in heuene. In ieneracioun and to ieneracioun thi treuthe; thou foun-91 dedist the erthe, and it abit[l] stille. In thin ordynaunce[ll] abit[l] the day; for alle 92 thingus seruen to thee. But that thi

Lord, thi word dwellith in heuene; with 89 outen ende. Thi treuthe *dwellith* in gene-90 racioun, and in to generacioun; thou hast foundid the erthe, and it dwellith. The 91 dai lastith contynueli bi thi ordynaunce; for alle thingis seruen[q] to thee. No[r] but 92

---

[l] abideth *AEH*.　　[ll] ordeynynge *A*.

[h] Om. *Lox*.　[i] and thei *i*.　[k] aftir *i*.　[l] knoulechen *A*. knewen *i*.　[m] in *i*.　[n] my *i*.　[o] forst *c et plures*.
[p] Aftir *i*.　[q] schul serue *i*.　[r] Om. *i*.

lawe is my swete thenking; thanne parauenture I hadde pershid in my mecnesse.
93 In to withouten ende I shal not forȝete
thi iustefiyngis; for in hem thou hast
94 quykened me. Thin I am, mac me saf;
95 for thi iustefiyngis I haue out soȝt. Me
abiden synneres, that thei shulden destrie
96 me; thi witnessyngus I vnderstod. Of alle
ending I saȝ the ende; brod thin heste[m]
ful myche.

Men.

*Quomodo di-
lexi.*

97 What maner I loouede thi lawe, Lord;
98 al dai my swete thenking it is. Vp on
myn enemys prudent thou madist me
with thin heste; for in to withoute ende
99 it is to me. Vp on alle techende me I vnderstod; for thi witnessyngis[n] is my swete
100 thenking. Ouer olde men I vnderstod; for
101 thin hestis I soȝte. Fro alle cuel weie I
forfendede my feet; that I kepe thi woordus.
102 Fro thi domes I bowide not doun; for
103 lawe thou hast put to me. Hou swete to
myn chekis thi spechis; ouer hony to my
104 mouth. Of thin hestis I vnderstod; therfore I hatide eche weie of wickidnesse.

Nun.

*Lucerna pedi-
bus.*

105 Lanterne to my feet thi woord; and
106 liȝt to myn pathis. I swoor; and sette
to kepe the domes of thi riȝtwisnesse.
107 I am mekid on alle side; Lord, quykene
108 thou me aftir thi woord. The wilful
thingus of my mouth wel plesing mac
thou, Lord; and thi domys tech me.
109 My soule in myn[o] hondis euermor; and
110 thi lawe I haue not forȝeten. Synneres
setteden a grene to me; and fro thin
111 hestis I errede not. Bi eritage I purchaside thi witnessingus in to withoute
ende; for the ful out ioȝing of myn herte
112 thei ben. I bowede in myn herte to ben
don thi iustefiyngis; in to withoute ende
for ȝelding.

Sameth.

*Iniquos odio
habui.*

113 Wicke men to hate I hadde; and thi
114 lawe I loouede. Helpere, and myn vnder-

that[s] thi lawe was my thenking; thanne[t]
perauenture Y hadde perischid in my lownesse. With outen ende Y schal not for- 93
ȝete thi iustifiyngis; for in tho thou hast
quikened me. I am thin, make thou me 94
saaf; for Y haue souȝt thi iustifiyngis.
Synneris aboden[u] me, for to leese me; Y 95
vndurstood thi witnessingis. I siȝ the 96
ende of al ende; thi comaundement *is* ful
large.

Lord, hou louede Y thi lawe; al dai it 97
is my thenking. Aboue myn enemyes 98
thou madist me prudent bi thi comaundement; for it is to me with outen ende. I 99
vndurstood aboue[v] alle[w] men techinge me;
for thi witnessingis is my thenking. I vn- 100
dirstood aboue eelde men; for Y souȝte
thi comaundementis. I forbeed my feet 101
fro al euel weie; that Y kepe thi wordis.
I bowide not fro thi domes; for thou hast 102
set lawe to me. Thi spechis ben ful swete 103
to my cheekis; aboue hony to my mouth.
I vnderstood of thin heestis; therfor Y 104
hatide al[x] the weie[y] of wickidnesse.

Thi word *is* a lanterne to my feet; and 105
liȝt to my pathis. I swoor, and purposide 106
stidefastli; to kepe the domes of thi riȝtfulnesse. I am maad low bi alle thingis; 107
Lord, quykene thou me bi[z] thi word.
Lord, make thou wel plesinge the wilful 108
thingis of my mouth; and teche thou me
thi domes. Mi soule *is* euere in myn 109
hondis; and Y forȝat not thi lawe. Syn- 110
neris settiden a snare to me; and Y erride
not fro thi comaundementis. I pur- 111
chasside thi witnessyngis bi eritage with
outen ende; for tho ben the ful ioiyng
of myn herte. I bowide myn herte to 112
do thi iustifiyngis with outen ende; for
reward[a].

I[b] hatide wickid men; and Y louede thi 113
lawe. Thou art myn helpere, and my 114

---

[m] heestis *A.*   [n] witnessis c.   [o] thyn E.

[s] for I.   [t] thanne *ellis* I.   [u] abeden I.   [v] ouer I.   [w] olde L.   eelde s.   [x] alle s.   [y] weyes s.   [z] aftir I.
[a] ȝelding CDEFGHKLMOPQRSUVWXbi. the rewarding I.   [b] *Therfore* I I.

takere thou art; and in to thi woord I
115 hopide ouer. Boweth doun fro mee, ȝee
malice doeris; and I shal serche the
116 hestis of my God. Vndertac me aftir thi
speche, and I shal liue; and confounde
117 thou not me fro myn abiding. Help me,
and I shal ben saaf; and I shal sweteli
thenke in thi iustefiyngis euermor.
118 Thou hast despisid alle men goende doun
fro thi domes; for vnriȝtwis the thenk-
119 ing of hem. Trespasende I heeld alle
the synneres of erthe ͬ ; therfore I loouede
120 thi witnessingis. Pricke with thi drede
my flesh; forsothe fro thi domes I
dradde.

Ayn.

Feci iudicium. 121   I dide dom and riȝtwisnesse; tac thou
122 nott me to the akusende me. Vndertac
thi seruaunt in to good; chalenge me
123 not the proude. Myn eȝen faileden in to
thin helthe ȝiuere; and in to the speche
124 of thi riȝtwisnesse. Do with thi seruaunt
after thi mercy; and thi iustefiyngis teche
125 thou me. Thi seruaunt I am; ȝif to me
vnderstonding, that I wite thi witness-
126 ingis. Time of doing, Lord; thei han
127 scatered thi lawe. Therfore I loouede
thin hestis; ouer gold and topasion.
128 Therfore to alle thin hestis I was riȝtforth reulyd; alle wicke ͱ weie to hate I
hadde.

Phee.

Mirabilia. 129   Merueilous thi witnessingis, Lord;
130 therfore serchede them my soule. The
declaring of thi woordis liȝtneth; vnder-
131 stonding ȝiueth to litle childer. My
mouth I openede, and I droȝ to a spirit;
132 for thin hestis I desirede. Behold in me,
and haue mercy of me; after the dom of
133 men loouende thi name. My goingus
forth riȝt reule thou after thi speche;
that ther lordshipe not of me alle vnriȝt-
134 wisnesse. Aȝeen bie me fro the chalengis
135 of men; that I kepe thin hestis. Thi face
liȝtne ͬ thou ͤ vp on thi seruaunt; and

'taker vp ͨ ; and ͩ Y hopide more on ͤ thi
word. Ȝe ͬ wickide men, bowe ͦ awei fro 115
me; and Y schal seke ͪ the comaundementis of my God. Vp take thou me bi 116
thi word, and Y schal lyue; and schende
thou not me fro ͥ myn abydyng. Helpe 117
thou me, and Y schal be saaf; and Y schal
bithenke euere in thi iustifiyngis. Thou 118
hast forsake alle men goynge awey fro
thi domes; for the thouȝt of hem *is* vniust.
I arettide alle the synneris of erthe 119
brekeris of the ͪ lawe; therfor Y louede thi
witnessyngis. Naile thou my fleischis ͥ 120
with thi drede; for Y dredde of thi
domes.

I dide doom and riȝtwisnesse ͫ ; bitake 121
thou not me to hem that falsli chalengen
me. Take vp thi seruaunt in to ͫ good- 122
nesse; thei that ben proude chalenge not
me. Myn iȝen failiden in to thin helthe; 123
and in to the speche of thi riȝtfulnesse.
Do thou with thi seruaunt bi ͦ thi merci; 124
and teche thou me thi ͬ iustifiyngis. I am 125
thi seruaunt, ȝyue thou vndurstondyng to
me; that Y kunne thi witnessingis. Lord, 126
it is tyme to do; thei han distried thi
lawe. Therfor Y louede thi comaunde- 127
mentis; more than gold and topazion.
Therfor Y was dressid to alle thin heestis; 128
Y hatide al wickid weie.

Lord, thi witnessingis *ben* wondirful; 129
therfor my soule souȝte tho. Declaring 130
of thi wordis liȝtneth; and ͱ ȝyueth vnderstonding to meke men. I openede my 131
mouth, and drouȝ the spirit; for Y desiride thi comaundementis. Biholde thou 132
on me, and haue ͬ merci on me; bi the
dom of hem that louen thi name. Dresse 133
thou my goyingis bi ͮ thi speche; that al
vnriȝtfulnesse haue not lordschip on me.
Aȝeyn bie thou me fro the false chalengis 134
of men; that Y kepe thin heestis. Liȝtne ͭ 135
thi face on thi seruaunt; and teche thou

ͬ the erthe *AEH.*   ͱ wickid *AH.*   ͬ liȝt *H.*   ͤ Om. *A.*

ͨ vptakere s.   ͩ Om. o.   ͤ in I.   ͬ The s.   ͦ boweth I.   ͪ speke s.   ͥ for I.   ͪ Om. *plures.*
ͥ fleisch I.   ͫ riȝtfulnesse *ceteri.*   ͫ to *thi* I.   ͦ aftir I.   ͬ be thi s.   ͩ and *it* I.   ͬ haue thou s.
ͮ aftir I.   ͭ Liȝtne thou s.

136 tech me thi iustefiyngis. Issues of watris broʒten out myn eʒen; for thei kepten not thi lawe.

Sade.

Justus es, Do-mine.

137 Riʒtwis thou art, Lord; and riʒt is
138 thi dom. Thou hast comaundid riʒtwis-nesse, thi witnessingus; and thi treuthe
139 ful myche. My looue made me to dwyne¹; for myn enemys han forʒete thi
140 woordis. Fyrid is thi speche hugeli; and
141 thi seruaunt loouede it. A ʒung waxen man I am, and dispisid; thi iustefiyngis
142 I haue not forʒete. Thi riʒtwisnesse, Lord, riʒtwisnesse in to withoute ende;
143 and thi lawe treuthe. Tribulacioun and anguish founden me; thin hestis is my
144 swete thenking. Equite thi witnessingus in to withoute ende; vnderstonding ʒif thou to me, and I shal liue.

Cof.

Clamaui in toto corde.

145 I criede in al myn herte, full out here me, Lord; thi iustefiyngus I shal aʒeen
146 seche. I criede to thee, mac me saf;
147 that I kepe thin hestis. I cam beforn in cesounable time of werking, and I criede; in to thi woordis I ouer hopede.
148 Myn eʒen camen beforn to thee the morutid; that I shulde sweteli thenke
149 thi spechis. My vois here thou aftir thi mercy, Lord; and aftir thi dom quykene
150 thou me. Ther neʒheden the pursuende me to wickidnesse; fro thi lawe ferr thei
151 ben maad forsothe. Neeʒh thou art,
152 Lord; and alle thi weies treuthe. Fro the bigynnyng I knewʒ of thi witness-ingys; for in to withoute ende thou foundedest hem.

Res.

Vide humilita-tem meam.

153 See my mecnesse, and tac me out; for
154 thi lawe I haue not forʒete. Deme thou my dom, and aʒeen bie thou me; for thi
155 speche quikene thou me. Ferr fro syneres helthe; for thi iustefiyngus thei
156 out soʒten not. Thi mercies manye, Lord; and aftir thi dom quikene thou

me thi iustifiyngis. Myn iʒen ledden^u 136 forth the outgoynges of watris; for thei kepten not thi lawe.

Lord, thou art iust; and thi dom is 137 riʒtful. Thou hast comaundid riʒtfulnesse, 138 thi witnessingis; and thi treuthe greetli *to be kept^v*. Mi feruent loue made me to 139 be meltid^w; for myn enemys forʒaten thi wordis. Thi speche is greetli enflawmed^x; 140 and thi seruaunt louede it. I am ʒoug, 141 and dispisid; Y forʒat not thi iustifiyngis. Lord, thi riʒtfulnesse *is* riʒtfulnesse with 142 outen ende; and thi lawe *is* treuthe. Tri- 143 bulacioun and angwische founden^y me; thin heestis is my thenking. Thi wit- 144 nessyngis *is* equite with outen ende; ʒyue thou vndirstondyng to me, and Y schal lyue.

I criede in al myn herte, Lord, here 145 thou me; and^r Y schal seke thi iustifiyngis. I criede to thee, make thou me saaf; that 146 Y kepe thi comaundementis. I bifor cam 147 in ripenesse, and Y criede; Y hopide aboue on thi wordis. Myn iʒen bifor camen to 148 thee ful cerli; that Y schulde bithenke thi speches. Lord, here thou my vois bi^a thi 149 merci; and quykene thou me bi thi doom. Thei that pursuen me neiʒden to wickid- 150 nesse; forsothe thei ben maad fer fro thi lawe. Lord, thou art nyʒ; and alle thi 151 weies *ben* treuthe. In the bigynnyng Y 152 knewe of thi witnessingis; for thou hast foundid tho with outen ende.

Se thou my mekenesse, and delyuere 153 thou me; for Y forʒat not thi lawe. Deme 154 thou my dom, and aʒenbie thou me; quikene thou^b me for thi speche. Heelthe 155 *is* fer fro synners; for thei souʒten not thi iustifiyngis. Lord, thi mercies *ben* manye; 156 quykene thou me bi thi dom. *Thei ben* 157

---

¹ dwyyn *A.* dwynnen *E.* dwynen *H.*

u leden s. v kept. *Lire here.* ʋ text. w mekid ɢ. molte ɪ. *ether langwiʒeshid* ᴋ *marg.* x set a fire CDEGHIKLMOPQRSUVWXbl. y han founde ɪ. z Om. *ceteri.* a aftir ɪ. b Om. ɪ.

157 me. Manye that pursuen me, and trublen me; fro thi witnessingis I bowede
158 not doun. I saȝ lawe brekeris, and I
dwynede awei; for thei kepten not thi
159 spechis. See, for thi hestis I loouede,
Lord[u]; in thi mercy quikene[v] thou me.
160 The begynnyng of thi woordis treuthe;
into withoute ende alle the domes of thi
riȝtwisnesse.

Sin.

161 Princis pursueden me with oute cause;
162 and of thi woordis dradde myn herte. I
shal gladen vpon thine spechis; as he
163 that findeth manye spoilis. Wickidnesse
to hate I hadde, and wlatide; thi lawe
164 forsothe I loouede. Seuen sithes in the
dai preising I seide to thee; vp on the
165 domys of thi riȝtwisnesse. Myche pes
to the loouende thi lawe; and ther is
166 not to them sclaundre. I bod[w] thin
helthe ȝiuere, Lord; and thin hestis I
167 loouede. My soule kepte thy witness-
168 ingus; and loouede them hugeli. I kepte
thin hestis, and thi witnessingis; for alle
my weies in thi syȝt.

Tau.

169 Neȝhe my lowe preȝing in thi siȝte,
Lord; aftir thi speche ȝif to me vnder-
170 stonding. Entre myn asking in thin
171 sighte; aftir thi speche deliuere me. My
lippis shuln tellen out an impne; whan
172 thou shalt teche me thi iustefiyngus. My
tunge shal telle forth thi speche; for alle
173 thi maundemens equyte. Be maad thin
hond, that it saue me; for thi maunde-
174 mens I ches. I coueitide thin helthe
ȝiuere, Lord; and thi lawe is my sweete
175 thenking. Liue my soule, and it shal
preise thee; and thi domys shul helpe
176 me. I errede as a shep that pershede;
seche thi seruaunt, Lord, for thin hestis
I haue not forȝeten.

manye that pursuen me, and doen tribulacioun to me; Y bowide not awei fro thi
witnessingis. I siȝ brekers of the lawe, 158
and Y was meltid[e]; for thei kepten not thi
spechis. Lord, se thou, for Y louede thi 159
comaundementis; quikene thou me in thi
merci. The bigynnyng of thi wordis[d] *is* 160
treuthe; alle the domes of thi riȝtwisnesse[e]
ben withouten ende.

Princes pursueden me with outen cause; 161
and my herte dredde of thi wordis. I 162
schal be glad on thi spechis; as he that
fyndith many spuylis. I hatide and 163
wlatide[f] wickidnesse; forsothe Y louede
thi lawe. I seide heriyngis to thee seuene 164
sithis in the dai; on the domes of thi riȝtfulnesse. Miche pees *is* to hem that louen 165
thi lawe; and no sclaundir is to hem.
Lord, Y abood thin heelthe; and Y louede 166
thin heestis. Mi soule kepte thi witness- 167
yngis; and louede tho greetli. I kepte thi 168
'comaundementis, and thi[g] witnessingis; for
alle my weies *ben* in thi siȝt.

Lord, my biseching come niȝ in thi siȝt; 169
bi[h] thi[i] speche ȝyue thou vndurstonding
to me. Myn axing entre in[k] thi siȝt; bi 170
thi speche delyuere thou me. Mi lippis 171
schulen telle out an ympne; whanne thou
hast tauȝte me thi justifiyngis. Mi tunge 172
schal pronounce thi speche; for whi alle
thi comaundementis *ben* equite. Thin 173
hond be maad, that it saue me; for Y
haue chose thin heestis. Lord, Y coueitide 174
thin heelthe; and thi lawe is my thenking.
Mi soule schal lyue, and[l] schal herie thee; 175
and thi domes schulen helpe me. I erride 176
as a scheep that perischide; Lord, seke[m] thi
seruaunt, for Y forȝat not thi comaundementis.

u Om. c.　v quijk *A*.　w abood *A*.

e *ether langwiȝsshede* κ *marg.*　d word *A*.　e riȝtfulnesse s.　f Y wlatide *A pr. m.*　g Om. s.　h aftir i.
i the L.　k in to i.　l and *it* is.　m seke thou i.

PSALM CXIX.

The song of grees.

Ad Dominum, cum tribularer.

1 To the Lord, whan I was trublid, I 2 criede; and he ful out herde me. Lord, deliuere my soule fro wicke[x] lippys; and 3 fro the treccherous tunge. What be[xx] ʒiue to thee, or what be put to thee; aʒen the 4 treccherous tunge? Sharpe arewis of the 5 myʒti; with colis wastende. Allas to me! for my pilgrimaging is drawen along, I dwelte with men dwellende Cedar; 6 myche wonyng as a[y] comeling was my 7 soule. With hem that hateden pes I was pesible; whan I spac to them, thei impugneden me with oute cause.

PSALM CXX.

The song of grees[z].

Leuaui oculos meos.

1 I rered vp myn eʒen in to the[a] mounteynes; whennys shal come helpe to me. 2 Myn helpe of the Lord; that made 3 heuene and erthe. Ʒiue he not in to stiring thi foot; ne nappe he, that kep- 4 eth thee. Lo! he shal not nappen, ne 5 slepen; that kepeth Irael. The Lord kepeth thee, the Lord thi defending; vp 6 on thi riʒthond. By day the sunne shal not brenne thee; ne the mone bi the nyʒt. 7 The Lord kepeth thee fro alle euel; kepe 8 thi soule the Lord. The Lord kepe thin entre and thi issu; fro this now and vn to the world.

PSALM CXXI.

The song of grees.

Letatus sum in his.

1 I gladide in these thingus, that ben seid to me; In to the hous of the Lord wee

PSALM CXIX.

The 'title of the[n] hundrid and nyntenthe 1 salm[o]. The song of grees[p]†.

Whanne Y was set in tribulacioun, Y criede to the Lord; and he herde me. 2 Lord, delyuere thou my soule fro wickid lippis; and fro a gileful tunge. What 3 schal be ʒouun to thee, ether what schal be leid[q] to thee; to a gileful tunge? Scharpe arowis of the myʒti; with colis 4 that maken desolat. Allas to me! for my 5 dwelling in an alien lond is maad long, Y dwellide with men dwellinge in Cedar; my soule was myche a comelyng. I was 7 pesible with hem that hatiden pees; whanne Y spak to hem, thei aʒenseiden[r] me with outen cause.

PSALM CXX.

The 'title of the[s] hundrid and twentithe 1 salm[t]. The song[u] of grees[uu].

I reiside myn iʒen to the[v] hillis; fro whannus help schal come to me. Myn 2 help *is* of the Lord; that made heuene and erthe. The Lord ʒyue not thi foot in to 3 mouyng; nether he nappe, that kepith thee. Lo! he schal not nappe, nether 4 slepe; that kepith Isrnel. The Lord kep- 5 ith thee; the Lord is thi proteccioun aboue thi riʒthond. The sunne schal not brenne 6 thee bi dai; nether the moone bi nyʒt. The Lord kepe[w] thee fro al yuel; the 7 Lord kepe thi soule. The Lord kepe thi 8 goyng in and thi goyng out; fro this tyme now and in to the world.

PSALM CXXI.

The 'title of the[x] hundrid and oon and 1 twentithe salm[y]. The song of the[z] grecis of Dauid[a].

I am glad in these thingis, that ben seid to me; We schulen go in to the hous of

† *A plos.* Gostli this salm mai be expowned of ech feithful man sett in tribulacion, bodili ether gostli, by temptacion of fendis, of wich he axith deuoutli to be delyuerid, and the fendis bedryuen awey fro impugnyng of feithful men, and be closid doun in helle; and this man sieth for delaie of remedie. *Lire here.* K.

n Om. A. *title on the* HMQ. o Om. A. p greces, *either steyris.* IN. greces, ether steiers, *for delyueraunce of Israel fro caitifte.* K. greces, ether steyris, *for deliueraunce of the peple of Israel fro caityfte.* v. q ʒouen s. r empungneden *ether* aʒenseiden CDEFGHIKMOPQRSUVVWXb. impungneden L. s Om. A. t Om. A. u salm K. uu greces, *for the good state of the puple turned aʒen fro the caitifte of Babilone.* K. greces. *This is a preier for the peple turned aʒen fro the caitifte of Babiloyne.* v. v Om. CDEGIS. w kepith CDEGHIKLOPQRSUVVWXb. x Om. A. *title of* v. y Om. A. z Om. KLPRSWX. a *Dauid, ioiʒng in the Lord, for the bilding of the citee and the temple, that he bifore siʒ to be made bi Salomon.* K.

2 shul go. Stondende weren oure feet; in
3 thi porchis, O Jerusalem. Jerusalem,
that is bild as a cite; whos part taking
4 is in to itself. Thider forsothe steȝeden
vp lynagis, the linagis of the Lord; the
witnessing of Irael, to knouleche to the
5 name of the Lord. For ther seten the
setis in dom; the setis vpon[b] the hous of
6 Dauid. Preȝeth that to the pes ben of Jerusalem; and abundaunce to the loouende
7 thee. Be maad pes in thi vertue; and
8 abundaunce in thi touris. For my bretheren[c] and my neȝheboris; I spac pes of
9 thee. For the hous of the Lord oure
God; I soȝte goode thingus to thee.

the Lord. Oure feet weren stondynge; in 2
thi hallis[b], thou Jerusalem. Jerusalem, 3
which is bildid as a citee; whos part taking therof is in to the same thing. For 4
the lynagis, the lynagis of the Lord
stieden thidir, the witnessing of Israel;
to knouleche to the name of the Lord.
For thei saten there on seetis in doom; 5
seetis on the hous of Dauid. Preie ȝe tho 6
thingis, that ben to the pees of Jerusalem;
and abundaunce be to hem that louen
thee. Pees be maad in thi vertu; and 7
abundaunce in thi touris. For my bri- 8
theren and my neiȝboris; Y spak pees of
thee. For the hous of oure Lord[c] God; 9
Y souȝte goodis to thee.

PSALM CXXII.

1   *The song of grees.*

PSALM CXXII.

*The 'title of the[d] hundrid and two and 1
twentithe salm. 'The song of grecis[e].*

*Ad te leuaui
oculos.*

To thee I liftide myn eȝen; that dwell-
2 ist in heuenus. Lo! as the eȝen of the[d]
seruauns; in the hondis of ther lordis. As
the eȝen of the hondmaide[e], in the hondis
of hir ladi; so oure eȝen to the Lord oure
God[f], to the time he haue merci of vs.
3 Haue merci of vs, Lord, haue mercy of
vs; for myche wee be fulfild with dispis-
4 ing. For myche is fulfild oure soule; to
the abundaunt reproef, and to the proude
men dispising.

To thee Y haue reisid myn iȝen; that
dwellist in heuenes. Lo! as the iȝen of[f] 2
seruauntis; ben in the hondis of her lordis.
As the iȝen of the handmaide *ben* in the
hondis of her ladi; so oure iȝen *ben* to
oure Lord God, til he haue mercy on vs.
Lord, haue thou merci on vs, haue thou 3
merci on vs; for we ben myche fillid with
dispisyng. For oure soule is myche fillid; 4
we ben schenschipe to hem that ben
abundaunte *with richessis*, and dispising
to proude men.

PSALM CXXIII.

1   *The song of grees.*

PSALM CXXIII.

*The 'title of the[h] hundrid and thre and 1
twentithe 'salm. The song of[i] grecis[k]
'of Dauith[l].*

*Nisi quia Do-
minus erat.*

But for the Lord was in vs, seie now
2 Irael; but for the Lord was in vs. Whan
3 men shulden risen[ff] aȝen vs out; per
auenture aliue thei hadde swolewid vs.
Whan shulde wrathen the wodnesse of
4 hem in to vs; per auenture water hadde
5 vp sopen vs. Oure soule passide thurȝ

Israel seie now, No but for the Lord
was in vs; no[m] but for[n] 'the Lord[o] was 2
in vs. Whanne men risiden[p] vp aȝens vs;
in hap thei hadden swalewid vs quike. 3
Whanne the woodnesse of hem was wrooth
aȝens vs; in hap watir hadde sope vs vp. 4
Oure soule passide thoruȝ a stronde; in 5

     b vp *A*.   c brether c.   d Om. *AEH*.   e hond maydyn *AEH*.   f Om. c.   ff arisen *E*.

     b forȝerdis *ceteri passim*.   c Om. CIR.   d Om. A.   e Om. A. *The song of grecis; the preier of an holi
prophete for delyueraunce of the puple fro the turment of Antioche.* K. *The song of the grecis.* O.   f of the
con.   g Om. I.   h Om. A.   i Om. A.   k Om. A. *the grecis* IV.   l Om. A. *of Dauith, doing thankingis
for delyueraunce* [*of him and his peple* V.] *fro Filisteis 'stiȝnge aȝens* [*comynge on* V.] *him, 'whanne thei
knewen him* [*after he was* V.] *anoyntid king.* KV.   m Om. I.   n Om. L.   o he I.   p resen I. risen L.

the strem; per auenture oure soule shulde
han passid thur3 the vnsuffrable watir.
6 Blyssyd be the Lord; that 3aff not vs in
to the cacchynge to the teth of hem.
7 Oure soule, as a sparewe, is ca3t out; fro
the grene of hunteres[g]. The grene is
8 to-brosid; and wee be deliuered. Oure
helpe in the name of the Lord; that made
heuene and erthe.

PSALM CXXIV.

1   *The song of grees.*

Qui confidunt.   That trosten in the Lord as the mount
of Sion; he shal not be moued in to with-
2 oute ende, that dwellith in Jerusalem.
The mounteynes in his cumpas; and the
Lord in the cumpas of his puple, fro this
3 now and vnto the world. For the Lord
shal not lefe the 3erd of synneres vp on
the lot of ri3twis men; that the ri3twis
men strecche not out to wickidnesse ther
4 hondis. Wel do thou, Lord; to goode
5 men, and ri3t in herte. The boowende
doun forsothe in to oblishingis the Lord
shal bring to with werkende wickidnesse; pes vp on Irael.

PSALM CXXV.

1   *The song of grees.*

In conuer-
tendo.   Lord, in turnende the caitifte of Sion;
2 wee ben maad as coumfortid. Thanne
fild is our mouth with io3e; and oure
tunge in ful out io3ing. Thanne thei
shul seye among Jentilis; The Lord hath
3 magnefied to don with hem. The Lord
hath magnefied to do with vs; wee ben
4 maad gladende. Lord, al turne oure cai-
5 tifte; as a strem in the south. That
sowen in teris; in ful out io3ing shul repe.
6 Goende thei 3iden[h], and wepten; sendende
ther sedis. Comende forsothe thei shul
come; berende with ful out io3ing ther
handfullis.

hap oure soule hadde passide thoru3[q] a
watir vnsuffrable. Blessid be the Lord; 6
that '3af not[r] vs in[s] taking to[t] the teth of
hem. Oure soule, as a sparowe, is de-7
lyuered; fro the snare of hunters. The
snare is al to-brokun; and we ben delyuered. Oure helpe *is* in the name of 8
the Lord; that made heuene and erthe.

PSALM CXXIV.

The 'title of the[u] hundrid and foure and 1
. twentithe salm[v]. 'The song of grecis[w].

Thei that tristen in the Lord *ben* as
the hil of Syon; he schal not be moued
with outen ende, that dwellith in Jeru-2
salem. Hillis *ben* in the ·cumpas of it,
and the Lord *is* in the cumpas of his
puple; fro this tyme now and in to the
world. For the Lord schal not leeue the 3
3erde of synneris on the part of iust men;
that iust men holde not forth her hondis
to wickidnesse. Lord, do thou wel; to 4
good men, and of[x] ri3tful herte[y]. But 5
the Lord schal lede them that bowen in
to obligaciouns, with hem that worchen
wickidnesse; pees *be* on[z] Israel.

PSALM CXXV.

The 'title of the[a] hundrid and fyue and 1
twentithe 'salm. The song of grecis[b].

Whanne the Lord turnede the caitifte
of Sion; we weren maad as coumfortid.
Thanne oure mouth was fillid with ioye; 2
and oure tunge with ful out ioiyng. Thanne
thei schulen seie among hethene men; The
Lord magnefiede to do with hem. The 3
Lord magnefiede to do with vs; we ben
maad glad. Lord, turne thou[c] oure cai-4
tifte; as a stronde in the south. Thei that 5
sowen in teeris; schulen repe in ful out
ioiyng. Thei goynge 3eden, and wepten; 6
sendynge her seedis. But thei comynge
schulen come with ful out ioiyng; berynge
her handfullis.

g the hunteres E.   h wenten AEH.

q Om. 1.   r hath not 3oue 1.   s in to CX *sec. m.*   t of RX *pr. m.*   u Om. A.   v Om. AC.   w Om. A. *The*
song of greces of goostli Jerusalem, an holi citee and dwelling for cristen men bi feith of Crist. KV. *The*
song of Dauith. s. There is no title to this Psalm in LP.   x to 1.   y in herte 1.   z upon 1.   a Om. A.
b Om. A. *salm. The s. of g. and it speketh of the turnyng a3en of the puple of Israel fro the caitifte of*
Babiloyne. K. *salm. The s. of g. of the turnynge a3en fro Babiloyne.* V.   c thou awey 1.

PSALM CXXVI.

1 *The song of grees.*

Nisi Dominus.

But the Lord shulde bild the hous; in to veyn trauaileden that bilden it. But the Lord shul kepe the cite; in vein 2 waketh that kepeth it. Veyn it[l] is to 3ou befor li3t to risen; riseth aftir that 3ee seten, that[k] eten the bred of sorewe. Whan he shal 3iuen to his loouede a slep; 3 lo! the eritage of the Lord the sones, 4 the mede the frut of the wombe. As arewes in the hond of the my3ty; so the 5 sones off the out shaken. Blisful the man that fulfilde his desir of hem; he shal not be confoundid, whan he shal speke to his enemys in the 3ate.

PSALM CXXVII.

1 *The song of grees.*

Beati omnes.

Blisful alle that dreden the Lord; that 2 gon in his weies. The trauailis of thin hondis for thou shalt ete; blisful thou 3 art, and wel shal be to thee. Thi wif as a vine aboundende; in the sydes of thin hous. Thy sones as the newe braunchis 4 of oliues; in the cumpas of thi bord. Lo! thus shal be blissid the man; that dredeth 5 the Lord. Blisse to thee the Lord fro Sion; and see thou the goodis of Jerusa-6 lem alle the da3es of thi lif. And see thou the sones of thi sones; the[l] pes vp on Irael.

PSALM CXXVIII.

1 *The song of grees.*

Sepe expugna-cerunt.

Ofte thei han out fo3te me, fro my

PSALM CXXVI.

The 'title of the[d] hundrid and sixe and 1 *twentithe 'salm. The song of greces of Salomon[e].*

'No but[f] the Lord bilde[g] the hous; thei that bilden it han trauelid in veyn. No[h] but the Lord kepith the citee; he wakith in veyn that kepith it. It is veyn to 3ou 2 to rise bifore the li3t; rise 3e after that[l] 3e han sete, that eten the breed of sorewe. Whanne he schal 3yue sleep to his loued; lo! the[k] eritage of the Lord 'is sones, the 3 mede *is*[l] the[m] fruyt of[n] wombe. As 4 arowis *ben* in the hond of the mi3ti; so the sones of hem that ben schakun out. Blessid *is* the man, that hath fillid his 5 desier of tho; he schal not be schent, whanne he schal speke to hise enemyes in the 3ate.

PSALM CXXVII.

The title of the hundrid and seuene and 1 *twentithe salm[o]. The song of greces[p].*

Blessid *ben*[q] alle men, that dreden the Lord; that[r] gon in hise weies. For thou 2 schalt ete the trauels of thin hondis; thou art blessid, and it schal be wel to thee. Thi wijf as[s] a plenteous vyne; in the sidis 3 of thin hous. Thi sones as[t] the newe sprenges[u] of olyue trees; in the cumpas of thi bord. Lo! so[v] a man schal be blessid; 4 that dridith the Lord. The Lord blesse 5 thee fro Syon; and se thou the goodis of Jerusalem in alle the daies of thi lijf. And se thou the sones of thi sones; se thou 6 pees on Israel.

PSALM CXXVIII.

The 'title of the[w] hundrid and ci3te and 1 *twentithe 'salm. The song of greces[x].*

Israel seie now; Ofte thei fou3ten[y] a3ens

---

[l] Om. c. [k] and *AII.* [l] Om. *A.*

[d] Om. *A.* [e] Om. *A. salm. The s. of g. of S. and of Goddis help to bilding of his temple, and of holi chirche, bi teching of feith and vertues.* K. *salm. To Solomon.* s. *salm. The s. of g. of S. and of the bilding of his temple.* v. [f] *But if* 1. [g] *bildith* KLS. [h] Om. 1. [i] Om. 1. [k] *thanne the* 1. [l] *the meede of the sone* 1. [m] Om. L. [n] *of the* 1. [o] Om. s. [p] *greces of Dauid.* KLP. *greces, stiringe to Goddis drede, in biheting temporal prosperitees to hem that dreden God.* x. *greces, of Crist and hooly chirche.* v. In *A is no title, but only cxxvii.* [q] *be plures.* [r] *the whiche* 1. [s] *schal be as* 1. [t] *schul be as* 1. [u] *sprengingis* s. [v] *thus* 1. [w] Om. AS. *title of* v. [x] Om. *A. salm. The s. of g. for delyueraunse of the pnple of Israel fro her pursueris, wicke is offered.* K. [y] *han fou3te* 1.

2 ʒouthe, seye now Irael Ofte thei han out foʒte me fro my ʒouthe, forsothe 3 thei myʒte not to me Vpon my bac forgeden synneres, thei longeden aferr 4 thei wickidnessis^m The Lord riʒtwys 5 shal to-hewe the nollis of synneres; be thei confoundid, and al turned bacward, 6 that hateden Sion. Be thei maad as hei of roones; that beforn it be pullid out, 7 ful out driede Of the whiche he that repeth, shal not fulfille his hond; and hys bosum, that shal gedere handfullis. 8 And they seiden not that wenten biside, The blissing of the Lord vp on ʒou; wee han blissid to ʒou in the name of the Lord

PSALM CXXIX
The song of grees.

De profundis

Fro depthis I criede to thee, Lord, 2 Loid, full out here thou my vois Be maad thin eris vnderstondende; in to the 3 vois of my lowe preiyng If wickidnessis thou shalt 'al aboute^n kepe, Lord; Lord, 4 who shal sustene. For anent thee is mercy doyng; and for thi lawe I sustenede thee, Lord My soule sustenede 5 in the woord of hym, my soule hopide 6 in the Lord Fro the morutyd warde vnto the nyʒt; hope Irael in the Lord. 7 For anent the Lord mercy^o; and plen- 8 teous anentis hym aʒeen buyng. And he shal aʒeen bie Irael, fro alle the wickidnessis of hym

PSALM CXXX
The song of grees.

Domine, non

Loid, myn herte is not enhaunsid; ne rerid vp ben myn eʒen. Ne I wente in grete thingis, ne in merueilis ouer me 2 If not mekely I felede, but I^p enhaunced my soule As the wened vpon his mo-

me fro my ʒongth Ofte thei fouʒten 2 aʒens me fro my ʒongthe, and sotheli thei miʒten not to me Synneris forgeden 3 on my bak, thei maden long hei wickid- nesse The 'iust Loid^z schal beete^a the 4 nollis of synneris, alle that haten Sion 5 be^b schent, and turned abak Be thei 6 maad as the hey of hous coppis, that driede vp, bifoie that it be drawun vp Of which^c hei he that schal repe, schal not 7 fille his hond; and he that schal gadere hondfullis, schal not fille his bosum. And 8 thei that passiden forth seiden not, The blessing of the Lord be on ʒou, we bless- iden ʒou in the^d name of the Lord

PSALM CXXIX
The 'title of the^e hundrid and nyne and 1 twentithe 'salm The song of greecis^f.

Lord, Y criede to thee fro^g depthes; Lord, here thou mi vois Thin eeris be 2 maad ententif, in to the vois of my biseching Lord, if thou kepist wickidnessis^b, 3 Loid, who schal susteyne^i? For merci is 4 at thee, and, Lord, for thi lawe Y abood thee. Mi soule susteynede in his word; my soule hopide in the Lord Fro the 5 morewtid keping til to^k niʒt; Israel hope 6 in the Loid For whi merci is at the 7 Lord; and plenteous redempcioun is at hym And he schal aʒen bie Israel, fro alle 8 the wickidnessis therof

PSALM CXXX.
The title of the hundrid and thrittithe 1 salm The song of greeces, 'to Dauith^l himself^m.

Lord, myn heite is not enhaunsid, ne- ther myn iʒen ben reisid Nether Y ʒede 1 in the^n grete thingis, nether in merueilis aboue me. If Y feelide not mekely; but 2 enhaunside my soule As a childe wenyde

---

^m wickidnes AH ^n alboute c ^o is mercye A. ^p Om A

^z Lord is iust s ^a beete togidre 1 ^b be thei 1 ^c the which 1 ^d Om 1 ^e Om A title s ^f Om A salm The s of greces, for delyueraunce of synne and caitiftee K ^g fro the EL ^h wicked- nesse 1 ^i susteyne ether abide CDEFGHKLMOPQRSUVWXbi susteyne or abide 1 ^k to the c sec m FIR ^l Om D ^m Om DFO himself, for ceesing of vengeaunse K himself, for noumbringe of his peple v In A is no title, but only cxxx ^s Om is

3 der; so ȝelding in my soule. Hope Irael in the Lord; froᵠ this now and vn to the world.

PSALM CXXXI.
The song of grees.

1

Haue mynde, Lord, of Dauid; and of
2 al the debonernesse of hym. As he swor to the Lord; a vow he vouwide to the
3 God of Jacob. Iʳ shal not entre in to the tabernacle of myn hous; I shal not steȝen vp in to the bed of my bedding.
4 I shal not ȝine slep to myn eȝen; and to
5 my eȝe lidis napping. And reste to my times, to the time I finde a place to the Lord; a tabernacle to the God of Jacob.
6 Lo! wee han herd it in Effrata; wee han founden it in the feldis of the wode.
7 Wee shul entre in to the tabernacle of hym; wee shuln honouren in the place,
8 where stoden his feet. Ris, Lord, in to thi resting; thou and the arke of thin
9 halewing. Thi prestis be thei cladˢ riȝt- wisnesse; and thin halewis ful out ioȝe
10 they. For Dauid, thi seruaunt; turne
11 thou not awei the face of thi crist. The Lord swor to Dauid treuthe, and he shal not maken hymᵗ inᵘ vein; of the frute of thi wombe I shal putte vp on thi seete.
12 If thi sones shul kepe my testament; and my witnessingis, these that I shal teche themᵛ. And the sones of hem vn to the
13 world; shul sitte vp on thi sete. For the Lord ches Sion; he ches it in to dwelling
14 toʷ hym. This my reste in to the world of world; heer I shal dwelle, for I ches it.
15 His widewe blessende I shal blisse; his
16 poreˣ I shal fulfille with loues. Hise prestis I shal clothe with helthe ȝiuere; and his halewis with ful out ioȝing shuln
17 ful out ioȝen. Thider I shal bringe forth the horn of Dauid; I haue maad redi a

on his modir; so ȝelding beᵒ in my soule. Israel hope in the Lord; fro this tyme now 3 and inᴾ to the world.

PSALM CXXXI.
The title of the hundrid and oon and 1 *thrittithe salm. The song of grecesᵠ.*

Lord, haue thou mynde onʳ Dauid; and of al his myldenesse. As he swoor to the 2 Lord; he made a vowe to God of Jacob. I schal not entre in to the tabernacle of 3 myn hous; Y schal not stie in to the bed of mi restyng. I schal not ȝyue sleep to 4 myn iȝen; and napping to myn iȝe liddis. And rest to my templis, til Y fynde a place 5 to the Lord; a tabernacle to God of Jacob. Lo! we herden thatˢ *arke of testament* in 6 Effrata, `*that is, in Silo*ᵗ; we founden it in the feeldis of theᵘ wode. We schulen 7 entre in to the tabernacle of hym; we schulen worschipe in the place, where hise feet stoden. Lord, rise thou in to thi 8 reste; thou and the ark of thin halewing. Thi prestis be clothid with riȝtfulnesse; 9 and thi seyntis make ful out ioye. Forˡᵒ Dauid, thi seruaunt; turne thou not awei the face of thi crist. The Lord swoor 11 treuthe to Dauid, and he schal not make hym veyn; of the fruyt of thi wombe Y schal sette on thi seete. If thi sones 12 schulen kepe my testament; and my wit- nessingis, these whiche Y schal teche hem. And the sones of hem tilᵛ in to the world; 13 thei schulen sette on thi seete. For the Lord chees Sion; he chees it in to dwell- ing to hym silf. This *is* my reste in to 14 the world of world; Y schal dwelle here, for Y chees it. I blessynge schal blesse 15 the widewe of it; Y schal fille with looues the pore men of it. I schal clothe with 16 heelthe the preestis therof; and the hooli men therof schulen make ful out ioye inʷ fulˣ reioisingeʸ. Thidir Y schal bringe 17

ᵠ for *n.* ʳ If I c. ˢ clothid *AEII.* ᵗ Om. *AII.* ᵘ Om. *A.* ᵛ to them *E pr. m.* ʷ of *II.* ˣ pore men *AII.*

ᵒ Om. ʟ. ᴾ til in *ceteri.* ᵠ *greces, of deuocion that Dauith hadde, to bilde the temple, and of biheest of God to him, of eritage of the renvne.* ᴋ. In *A* is no title, but only *cxxxi.* ʳ of *CDEFGHIKLMOPQRUVWXbi.* ˢ the ᴋ. ᵗ Om. *CDEFGHK pr. m. LMOPQRSVWXbi. that is, in Silo, Lire here.* ᴜ. ᵘ Om. *ceteri.* ᵛ Om. x. ʷ in the c. ˣ *ful out ceteri.* ʸ ioiyng *CDEGHKLMOPQRSUVWXbi.*

18 lanterne to my crist. His enemys I shal clothe with shenshipe; vp on hym forsothe shal flouren out myn halewing.

forth the horn of Dauid; Y made redi a lanterne to my crist. I schal clothe hise 18 enemyes with schame; but myn halewing schal floure out on hym.

PSALM CXXXII.

1 *The song of grees.*

Ecce quam bonum.

Lo! hou good, and how iozeful; bre-2thern to dwellen in to᷎ oon. As an oynement in the hed; that goth doun in to the berd, the berd of Aaron. That goth doun in to the hemme of his cloth-3ing; as deu of Ermon, that goth doun in to the hil of Syon. For thider sente the Lord blessing; and lif vn to the world.

PSALM CXXXII.

The `title of the[a] *hundrid and two and* 1 *thrittithe salm*[a]. *The song of grecis*[b].

Lo! hou good and hou myrie *it is;* that britheren dwelle togidere. As oynement 2 in the heed; that goith doun in to the beerd, in to the beerd of Aaron. That goith doun in to the coler of his cloth; as the dew of Ermon, that goith doun in 3 to the hil of Sion. For there the Lord sente blessing; and lijf til[c] in to the world[d].

PSALM CXXXIII.

1 *The song of grees.*

Ecce nunc benedicite.

Lo! now blisseth the Lord; alle zee seruauns of the Lord. That stonden in the hous of the Lord; in the porchis of 2 the hous of oure God. In nyztes heueth vp zoure hondis in to holi thingis; and 3 blisseth to[z] the Lord. Blisse thee the Lord fro Sion; that made heuene and erthe.

PSALM CXXXIII.

The `title of the[e] *hundrid and thre and* 1 *thrittithe salm*[f]. *The song of greces*[g].

Lo! now blesse ze the Lord; alle the seruauntis of the Lord. Ze that stonden in the hous of the Lord; in the hallis[h] of `the hous of[i] oure God. In nyztis reise zoure 2 hondis in to hooli thingis; and blesse ze the Lord. The Lord blesse thee fro Syon; 3 which[k] *Lord* made heuene and erthe.

PSALM CXXXIV.

1 *Alleluya.*

Laudate nomen Domini.

Preise zee the name of the Lord; 2 preise zee, seruauns, the Lord. That stonden[a] in the hous of the Lord; in the porchis of the hous of oure God. 3 Preise zee the Lord, for good is the Lord; doth salm to his name, for it ys sweete. 4 For the Lord ches to hym Jacob; and 5 Irael in to possessioun to hym. For I knew, that gret is the Lord; and oure 6 God beforn alle godys. Alle thingis what euere the Lord wolde, he dide in heuene and in erthe; in the se, and in alle

PSALM CXXXIV.

The title of the hundrid and foure and 1 *thrittithe salm*[l]. *Alleluya*[m].

Herie ze the name of the Lord; ze seruauntis of the Lord, herie ze. Ze that 2 stonden in the hous of the Lord; in the hallis[n] of `the hous of[o] oure God. Herie 3 ze the Lord, for the Lord is good; singe ze to his name, for it is swete. For the 4 Lord chees Jacob to him silf; Israel in to possessioun to him silf. For Y haue 5 knowe, that the Lord is greet; and oure God bifore alle goddis. The Lord made 6 alle thingis, what euere thingis he wolde, in heuene and in erthe; in the see, and in

---

z Om. ʌʜ.   z Om. ʌɛʜ.   a stondith ʌ.

---

7 depnessis. Bringende out cloudis fro the vtmostis[b] of the erthe; leitis in to reyn he made. That bringeth forth windis 8 fro his tresores; that smot the first goten 9 of Egipt, fro man vn to beste. And he sente toenes and wndris in the myddel of thee, Egipt; in to Farao and in to alle 10 his seruauns. That smot manye Jentilis; 11 and sloȝ stronge kingis. Seon, the king of Amorreis; and Og the king of Basan, 12 and alle the reumys of Chanaan. And he ȝaf the lond of hem eritage; eritage 13 to Irael, his puple. Lord, thi name in to with oute ende; Lord, thi memorial 14 in ieneracioun and in to ieneracioun. For the Lord shal demen his puple; and in 15 his seruauns he shal be louly preȝid. The maumetis of Jentilis siluer and gold; the 16 werkis of the hondys of men. Mouth thei han, and thei shul not speke; eȝen 17 thei han, and thei shuln not see. Eris thei han, and thei shul not here; ne forsothe spirit is in the mouth of hem. 18 Lye to them be thei maad, that don tho thingis; and alle that trosten in hem. 19 Hous of Irael, blesse ȝee to the Lord; hous of Aron, blisse ȝee to the Lord. 20 Hous of Leuy, blisse ȝee to the Lord; ȝee that drede the Lord, blisseth[c] to the 21 Lord. Blissid be the Lord fro Sion; that dwellith in Jerusalem.

alle depthis of watris. He ledde out 7 cloudis fro the ferthest[p] part of erthe; and made leitis in to reyn. Which bringith forth wyndis fro hise tresours; which 8 killide the firste gendrid[q] thingis of Egipt, fro man 'til to[r] beeste. He sente out 9 signes and grete wondris, in the myddil of thee, thou Egipt; in to Farao and in to alle hise seruauntis. Which smoot many 10 folkis; and killide stronge kingis. Seon, 11 the king of Ammorreis, and Og, the king of Basan; and alle the rewmes of Chanaan. And he ȝaf the lond of[s] hem eritage; 12 eritage[t] to Israel, his puple. Lord, thi 13 name is[u] with outen ende; Lord, thi memorial[v] be in[w] generacioun and in to generacioun. For the Lord schal deme 14 his puple; and he schal be preied in hise seruauntis. The symulacris of hethene 15 men ben siluer and gold; the werkis of the hondis of men. Tho[x] han a mouth, 16 and schulen not speke; tho han iȝen, and schulen not se. Tho han eeris, and schulen 17 not here; for 'nether spirit is[y] in the mouth of tho[z]. Thei that maken tho, be 18 maad lijk tho[a]; and alle that tristen in tho[a]. The hous of Israel, blesse ȝe the[b] 19 Lord; the hous of Aaron, blesse ȝe the[c] Lord. The hous of Leuy, blesse ȝe the[d] 20 Lord; ȝe that dreden the Lord, 'blesse ȝe[e] the[f] Lord. Blessid be the Lord of Syon; 21 that dwellith in Jerusalem.

PSALM CXXXV.
Alleluya.

Confitemini Domino.

1 Knouleche ȝee to the Lord, for he is good; for in to the world the merci of 2 hym. Knoulecheth to the God of godis. ³ Knoulecheth to the Lord of lordis. That 4 5 maketh grete merueilis alone. That made 6 heuenes in vnderstonding. That fastnede 7 the erthe vp on watris. That made grete

PSALM CXXXV.
The title of the hundrid and fyue and thrittithe salm. Alleluya[g].

Knouleche ȝe to the Lord, for he is 1 good, for his merci is withouten ende. Knouleche ȝe to the[h] God of goddis[i]. 2 Knouleche ȝe to the Lord of lordis. Which ³4 aloone makith grete merueils. Which 5 made heuenes bi vndurstondyng. Which 6 made stidefast erthe on watris. Which 7

ᵇ vttermostis AII. ᶜ blesse ȝe AII.

P ferrest A. q gotun I. r vn to I. s to o. t to be heritage I. Om. R. u Om. ceteri. v memorial, or mynde I. w into s. x Tho ymagis I. y ther is no spirit I. z hem I. a hem I. b to the K sec. m. c to the K. d to the K sec. m. o. e blesse A pr. m. CDL sec. m. PRUXbi. blesseth I. f to the K sec. m. g Alleluya. This salm, as that that goith bifore, is a stiring to herie God, for he is good. K. In A is no title, but only cxxxv. h Om. ceteri. l that is, of hooli aungelis v marg.

8 liȝt ȝiueres. The sunne in to the^d power
9 of the dai. The mone and the sterris in to
10 the^d power of the nyȝt. That smot Egipt
11 with the first goten of hem. That broȝte
12 ounte Irael fro the myddel of hem. In
13 myghty hond; and in heiȝ arm. That de-
14 uydede^e the rede se in to^f deuyseouns. And
broȝte out Irael thurȝ the myddel of it.
15 And shoe out Farao and his vertue in the
16 rede se. That ladde ouer his puple thurȝ
17 the^g desert. That smot grete kingis. And
18
19 sloȝ stronge kingis. Seon, the king of
20 Amoreis. And Og, the king of Basan.
21 And he ȝaf the lond of hem eritage.
22
23 Eritage to Irael, his seruaunt. For in
oure mecnesse myndefull he was of vs.
24 And he aȝeen boȝte vs fro oure enemys.
25
26 That ȝiueth mete to alle flesh. Knoulecheth to God^h of heuene. Knoulecheth
to the Lord of lordis ; for in to withoute
ende the mercy of hym.

made grete liȝtis. The sunne in to the 8
power of the dai. The moone and sterris^k 9
in to the^l power of the^m niȝt. Which 10
smoot Egipt with the firste gendrid thingis
of hem. Which ledde out Israel fro the 11
myddil^n of hem. In a miȝti hond and in 12
an hiȝ arm. Whiche departide the reed see 13
in to departyngis. And ledde out Israel 14
thoruȝ the myddil^o therof. And he 'caste 15
a down^p Farao and his pouer^q in the reed
see. Which ledde ouer his puple thoruȝ 16
desert. Which smoot grete kingis. And 17
18
killide strong kingis. Seon, the king of 19
Amorreis. And Og, the king of Baasan. 20
And he ȝaf the lond of hem eritage^r. 21
Eritage to Israel, his seruaunt. For in 22
23
oure lownesse he hadde mynde on vs.
And he aȝenbouȝte vs fro oure enemyes. 24
Which ȝyueth mete^rr to ech fleisch. Knou- 25
26
leche ȝe to God^s of heuene. Knouleche ȝe
to the Lord of lordis ; for his merci is
with outen ende.

PSALM CXXXVI.

The salm of Dauid, for Jeremye.

Super flumina Babilonis.

1 Vp on the flodis of Babiloyne there wee
seten, and wepten ; whil wee recordeden
2 of Sion. In withies in the myddes of it ;
3 wee heengeu^l vp^k oure instrumens. For
there askeden vs that caityues broȝten vs;
the woordis of songis of despit. And thei
that 'ledden aweie^l vs ; An ympne sing-
4 eth^m to vs of the songis of Sion. Hou
shul wee singe the song of the Lord; in an
5 hethen^mm lond? If I shule forȝeten of thee,
Jerusalem ; to forȝeting be ȝiue my riȝt-
6 hond. Cleue my tunge to myn chekis ;
if I shul not han mynde of thee. If I
shul not purposen thee, Jerusalem ; in the
7 begynnyng of my gladnesse. Myndeful

PSALM CXXXVI.

The hundrid and sixe and thrittithe salm^ss.

On the floodis of Babiloyne there we 1
saten, and wepten ; while we bithouȝten
on Syon. In salewis in the myddil^t therof ; 2
we hangiden vp oure orguns. For thei 3
that ledden vs prisoners; axiden vs there
the wordis of songis. And thei that ledden
awei vs seiden; Synge ȝe to vs an ympne
of the songis of Syon. Hou schulen we 4
singe a songe of the Lord ; in an alien
lond? If Y forȝete thee, Jerusalem ; my 5
riȝt hond be ȝouun to forȝeting. Mi tunge 6
cleue to my chekis; if Y bithenke not on
thee. If Y purposide not of thee, Jerusalem ; in the bigynnyng of my gladnesse.
Lord, haue thou mynde on the sones of 7

---

d Om. A. e deuyde A. f Om. A. g Om. AII. h the God AE. i hangeden AII. k vpon II. l broȝten
K pr. m. m syngen A. mm alien C pr. m.

k the sterris IIIKSX. l Om. I. m Om. DEFIIKLM pr. m. i. n myddis I. o myddis ceteri. p schook
awei CDEF pr. m. GIIKLMOPQRSUVWXbi. q vertu CDEF pr. m. GHKLMOPQRSUVWXbi. r to be heritage I.
rr metis A pr. m. s the God A pr. m. ss The cxxxvi. A. The titil of the hundrid and xxxvi. salm. DEFL.
This salm haith no tijtle, neither [in] Ebren ne in Jerom; it spekith of destruccioun of the temple, and of the
caitiftee of Babiloyne. I. The hundrid and sixe and thrittithe salm hath no title, and it spekith of the destruccioun of the temple, and of the caitiftee of Babiloyne. K. The cxxxvi. salm hath no tytle ; it spekith of
the destruccioun of Jerusalem. v. The hundrid and xxxvi. salm hath no title, nethir in Ebreu nether in
Jerom. u. t myddis s.

be thou, Lord, of the sones of Edom; in
to the dai of Jerusalem. That seyn, Ful
out wasteth°, ful out wasteth°; vnto the
8 foundement in° it. The doȝtir of Babilon
wrecchid, blisful that shal ȝelde to thee
thi ȝelding; that thou hast ȝolde to vs.
9 Blisful that shal holden; and hurtlen his
litle childer to the ston.

PSALM CXXXVII.
The salm 'to hym° Dauid.

Confitebor.   1 I shal knoulechen to thee, Lord, in al
myn herte; for thou hast herd theᴾᴾ
woordis of my mouth. In the siȝte of
2 aungelis I shal don salm to thee, my God;
I shal honoure at�q thin holy temple, and
knouleche to thi namer. Vp on thi mercy
and thi treuthe; for thou hast magnefied
3 thi seynt ouer alle name. In what euere
day I shal inwardli clepe thee, ful out
here me; thou shalt multeplie in my soule
4 vertue. Knouleche to thee, Lord, alle
the kingis of erthe; for thei han herd alle
5 the woordys of thi mouth. And singe
thei in the weyes of the Lord; for gret
6 is the glorie of the Lord. For heiȝ the
Lord, and meke thingis he beholdeth; and
7 heȝe thingis fro a ferr he knowith. If I shul
go in the myddel of tribulacioun, thou
shalt quikene me; and vp on the wrathe
of myn enemys thou hast straȝt out thin
hond, and saf made me thi ryȝt hond.
8 The Lord shal ȝelde for me, Lord, thi
mercy in to the world; the werkis of
thin hondis ne despise thou.

PSALM CXXXVIII.
In to the ende, the salm of Dauid.

Domine, pro-   1 Lord, thou hast proued me, and knowen
basti.   2 me; thou hast knowe my sitting, and
3 myn aȝeen rising. Thou vnderstode my

Edom; for the dai of Jerusalem. Whiche
seien, Anyntische ȝe, anyntische ȝe; 'til toᵘ
the foundement ther ynne. Thou wretchid 8
douȝter of Babiloyne; he *is* blessid, that
'schal ȝeldeᵛ to thee thiʷ ȝelding, which
thou ȝeldidist to vs. He *is* blessid, that 9
schal holde; and hurtle doun hise litle
children at aˣ stoon.

PSALM CXXXVII.
*The 'title of theʸ hundrid and seuene and
thrittithe salm. 'To Dauith him silfᶻ.*

Lord, Y schal knouleche to thee in al 1
myn herte; for thou herdist the wordis of
my mouth. Mi God, Y schal singe to
thee in the siȝt of aungels; Y schal wor- 2
schipe toᵃ thin hooli temple, and Y schal
knouleche to thiᵇ name. On thi merci and
thi treuthe; for thou hast magnefied thin
hooli name aboue al thing. In what 3
euere dai Y schal inwardli clepe thee, here
thou me; thou schalt multipli vertu in
my soule. Lord, alle the kingis of erthe 4
knouleche to thee; for thei herden alle the
wordis of thi mouth. And singe thei in 5
the weies of the Lord; for the glorie of
the Lord is greet. For the Lord *is* hiȝ, 6
and biholdith meke thingis; and knowith
afer hiȝ thingis. If Y schal go inᶜ the 7
myddilᵈ of tribulacioun, thou schalt
quikene me; and thou stretchidistᵉ forth
thin hond on the ire of myn enemyes,
and thi riȝt hond made me saaf. The 8
Lord schal ȝelde for me, Lord, thi merci
*is*ᶠ with outen ende; dispise thou not the
werkis of thin hondis.

PSALM CXXXVIII.
*The 'title of theᵍ hundrid and eiȝte and
thrittithe salmʰ. 'To victorie, the salm
of Dauithⁱ.*

Lord, thou hast preued me, and hast 1
knowe me; thou hast knowe my sitting, 2
and my rising aȝen. Thou hast vndir- 3

ⁿ wastid ᴇ pr. m.   ° of ᴀ.   ᴾ of ᴨ.   ᴾᴾ alle the ᴄ pr. m.   q in ᴀ.   r holy name ᴇ pr. m.

ᵘ vn to ɪ.   ᵛ ȝeldith ɪ.   ʷ the ʟ.   ˣ the ɪ.   ʸ Om. ᴀ.   ᶻ Om. ᴀ. To Dauith him silf, the doing of
thankinges of Dauith, after delyueraunce of the persecucion of Saul. ᴋ. To Dauyth. 8. To Dauith him self,
doinge thankingis. ᵥ.   ᵃ at ɪ.   ᵇ thin hooly ɪ.   ᶜ in to x.   ᵈ myddis ceteri.   ᵉ strecchist 8.   ᶠ schal be ɪ.
ᵍ Om. ᴀ.   ʰ Om. ᴀʟ.   ⁱ Om. ᴀʟ. To victorie, the s. of D. This is a stiring to the knowleching of Goddis
herijng, thuruȝ biholding of his excellence. ᴋ.

tho3tis fro aferr; .my path and my litle
4 corde thou enserchedist. And alle my
weies thou beforn se3e; for ther is not
5 woord in my tunge. Lo! Lord, thou
hast knowen alle thingis, newest and
olde; thou hast formed me, and put vp
6 on me thin hond. Merueilous is maad
thy kunnyng of me; it is coumfortid, and
7 I shal not moun to it. Whidir shal I
go fro thi spirit; and whidur fro thi
8 face shal I flee? If I shul ste3en vp in
to heuene, thou art there; if I shul go
9 doun in to helle, thou art at. If I shul
take my pennys in the morutid; and shul
10 dwelle in the vtmostis^s of the se. Forsothe thider thin hond shal bringe me;
11 and shal holde me thi ri3t hond. And I
seide, Parauenture derenessis shul to-
trede me; and ny3t^t my li3ting in my
12 delicis. For derenesses shul not ben
derkid fro^u thee, and ny3t as day shal ben
li3tid; as his derenessis, so and the li3t of
13 it. For thou weldedest my reenes; thou
hast vndertake me fro the wombe of my
14 moder. I shal knouleche to thee, for
ferfulli thou art magnefied; merueilous
thi werkis; and my soule shal knouleche
15 ful myche. My mouth is not hid fro
thee, the whiche thou madest in priue;
and my substaunce is in the nethermoris^v
16 of the erthe. Myn vnparfit thing se3en
thin e3en, and in thi boc alle shul be
writen; da3es shul be formed, and no
17 man in hem. To me forsothe ful myche
ben maad wrshipeful thi frendis, God;
ful myche is coumfortid the princehed of
18 hem. I shal noumbre them atwynne,
and vpon grauel thei shul be multeplied;
I haue risen out, and 3it I am with thee.
19 God, for thou shalt sle synneres; 3ee men
20 of blodis, bowith doun fro me. For 3ee
seyn in tho3t; Take thei^w in vanyte ther
21 citees. Whethir not thoo^x that hateden
thee, Lord, I hatede; and vp on thin
22 enemys I dwynede? With parfyt hate

stonde my thou3tis fro fer; thou hast
enquerid my path and my corde. And 4
thou hast bifor seien alle my weies; for
no word is in my tunge. Lo! Lord, thou 5
hast knowe alle thingis, the laste^k thingis
and elde; thou hast formed me, and hast
set thin hond on me. Thi kunnyng is 6
maad wondirful of me; it is coumfortid,
and Y schal not mowe to it. Whidir 7
schal Y go fro thi spirit; and whider
schal Y fle fro thi face? If Y schal stie 8
in to heuene, thou art there; if Y schal
go doun to^l helle, thou art^m present. If 9
Y schal take my fetheris ful eerli; and
schal dwelle in the last partis of the see.
And sotheli thider thin hond^n schal leede 10
me forth; and thi ri3t hond schal holde
me. And Y seide, In hap derknessis 11
schulen defoule me; and the ny3t *is* my
li3tnyng in my delicis. For whi derk-12
nessis schulen not be maad derk fro thee,
aud the ni3t schal be li3tned as the dai; as
the derknessis therof, so and the li3t therof.
For thou haddist in possessioun my reines; 13
thou tokist^o me vp fro the wombe of my
modir. I schal knouleche to thee, for 14
thou art magnefied dreedfuli; thi werkis
ben wondirful, and my soule schal^p knou-
leche^q ful miche. Mi boon, which thou 15
madist in priuete, is not hyd fro thee; and
my substaunce in the lower partis of erthe.
Thin i3en sien^r myn vnperfit thing, and 16
alle men schulen be writun in thi book^s;
daies schulen be formed, and no man is^t
in tho. Forsothe, God, thi frendis ben 17
maad onourable ful myche to me; the
princeheed of hem is coumfortid ful
myche. I schal noumbre hem, and thei 18
schulen be multiplied aboue^{tt} grauel; Y
roos vp, and 3it Y am with thee. For 19
thou, God, schalt slee synneris; 3e men-
quelleris, bowe^u awei fro me. For 3e^v 20
seien in thou3t; Take thei her citees in
vanite. Lord, whether Y hatide not hem 21
that hatiden^w thee; and Y failide^x on thin

---

^{s} vttermostis *AH*. ^{t} the ny3t *AH*. ^{u} of *AH*. ^{v} nethermore *AH*. ^{w} 3e *A*. ^{x} that c.

^{k} newe I. ^{l} in to I. ^{m} art *there* I. ^{n} ri3thond s. ^{o} takeste R. ^{p} Om. i. ^{q} knowe CDEFGKLOPQ
Rsuvwxbi. ^{r} saw3en I *passim*. ^{s} book, *that is, in thi kunnyng* I. ^{t} Om. I. ^{tt} aboue the c. ^{u} boweth I.
^{v} thei I. ^{w} haten CDEFGLMOPQRSUVWb. ^{x} failide, *that is, mournyde gretly* IKV.

I hatede hem; enemys thei ben maad to
23 me. Proue me, God, and wite thou
myn herte; aske thou me, and knowe
24 thou my pathis. And see, if the weie of
wickidnesse is in me; and bring me
thennes in the euere lastende weie.

PSALM CXXXIX.

1   *In to the ende, the salm of Dauid.*

2   Tac me awei, Lord, fro an cuel man;
3 and fro a wicke^y man tac me awei. That
tho3ten wickidnessis in the herte; al dai
4 setteden batailis. Thei sharpeden ther
tungis as serpentis; the venym of edderes^z
5 vnder the lippis of hem. Kep thou me
fro the hond of the synnere; and fro
wicke^a men tac me awei. That tho3ten
6 to supplaunten my goingis; proude men
hidden a grene to me. And cordis thei
stra3ten out in to a grene; by side the
7 weie sclaunder thei putten^b to me. I
seide to the Lord, My God thou art; ful
out here thou, Lord, the vois of my lowe
8 pre3ing. Lord, Lord, the vertue of myn
helthe; thou al aboute shadewedest on
9 myn hed in the dai of bataile. Ne take
thou me, Lord, fro my desir to the synnere; they tho3ten a3en me, ne forsake
thou me, lest parauenture thei ben en-
10 hauncid. The hed of the cumpas of hem;
the trauayle of the lippis of hem shal
11 coueren hem. Colis shul fallen vp on
hem, in to fir thou shalt kaste them doun;
in wrecchidnessis thei shul not stonde.
12 A ianglende man shal not be ri3tforth
reulid in the erthe; an vnri3twis man
13 euelis shul take in deth. I knew3, for
the Lord shal do dom of the helpeles; and
14 veniaunce of the pore. Neuerthelatere
ri3twis shuln knoulechen to thi name; and
the ri3te shul wone with thi chere.

---

enemyes? Bi parfite hatercde Y hatide 22
hem; thei weren maad enemyes to me.
God, preue thou me, and knowe thou myn 23
herte; axe thou me, and knowe thou^y my
pathis. And^z se thou, if weie^a of wickid- 24
nesse is^{aa} in me; and lede thou me forth
in euerlastinge wei^b.

PSALM CXXXIX.

1   *The `title of the^c hundrid and nyne and*
thrittithe `salm. To victorie, the salm
of^d Dauith^e.

Lord, delyuere thou me fro an yuel 2
man; delyuere thou me fro a wickid man.
Whiche tho3ten wickidnesses^f in the^g 3
herte; al dai thei ordeyneden^h batels. Thei 4
scharpiden her tungis as serpentis; the
venym of snakis vndirⁱ the lippis of hem.
Lord, kepe thou me fro the hond of the 5
synnere; and delyuere thou me fro wickid
men. Which thou3ten to disseyue my goyngis; proude men hidden a snare to me. 6
And thei leiden forth cordis in to a snare;
thei settiden sclaundir to me bisidis the
weie. I seide to the Lord, Thou art mi 7
God; Lord, here thou the vois of my bisechiug. Lord, Lord, the vertu of myn 8
heelthe; thou madist schadowe on myn
heed in the dai of batel. Lord, bitake 9
thou not me fro my desire to the synnere;
thei thou3ten a3cus me, forsake thou not
me, lest perauenture thei ben enhaunsid.
The heed of the cumpas of hem; the trauel 10
of her lippis schal hile hem. Colis schulen 11
falle on hem, thou schalt caste hem doun
in to fier; in wretchidnessis thei schulen
not stonde. A man a^k greet inuglere schal 12
not be dressid in erthe; yuels schulen
take an vniust man in perisching. I haue 13
knowe, that the Lord schal make dom of
a^l nedi man; and the veniaunce of pore
men. Netheles iust men schulen knou- 14
leche to thi name; and ri3tful men schulen
dwelle with thi cheer.

---

y wickid *A*.   z eddre *AII*.   a wickid *A*.   b puttiden *AII*.

y Om. 1.   z Om. AIU.   a the weie *ceteri præter* IU.   aa ther is I.   b liyf CDEFGHIKLMOSVXbi.
c Om. A.   d Om. A.   e Om. A. *Dauith the king, axing to be delyuerid bi God of persecucion, whaune he was
pursued of Saul.* K. *Dauith, to be delynerid fro persecucioun of Saul.* V. *Dauith, the kyng.* i.   f wickidnesse s.   g Om. 1.   h ordeyne c.   i *was* vndir I. *is* vndir K.   k *that is* n 1.   l the I.

PSALM CXL.

1   *The salm of Dauid.*

Domine, cla-
mavi ad te.

Lord I criede to thee, ful out here
thou me; tac heede to my vois, whil I
2 shal crie to thee. Be forth riȝt reulid
myn orisoun as encens in thi siȝt; the
rering vp of myn hondis euentid sacri-
3 fise. Put, Lord, warde to my mouth;
and a dore of circumstaunce to my lippis.
4 Bowe thou not doun my herte in to the[c]
woordis of malice; to ben excusid excu-
saciouns in synnes. With men wirkende
wickidnesse; and I shal not comune with
5 the chosen of hem. The riȝtwis man
shal chastise me in mercy, and blamen
me; the oile forsothe of the synnere shal
not withinne fatten myn hed. For ȝit
and myn orisoun in the wel plesid thingus
6 of hem; the domes men of hem ioyned
to the stou ben sopen awey. Thei shuln
7 here my woordis, for thei myȝten; as the
fatnesse of erthe[d] is rerid vp 'vp on[e] the
erthe. Oure bones ben scaterid beside
8 helle, for to thee Lord, Lord, myn
eȝen; in thee I hopide, do not awei my
9 soule. Kep me fro the grene that thei
setteden to me; and fro sclaundris of men
10 wirkende wickidnesse. Synneres shuln
falle in the net of hym; syngulerli I am
to the time I passe.

PSALM CXLI.

1   *The vnderstonding of Dauid, whan he*
was in the spelunke.

Voce mea ad
Dominum.

2   With my vois to the Lord I criede;
with my vois to the Lord I louly preȝede.
3 I shede[f] out in his siȝt myn orisoun; and
my trybulacioun beforn hym I openli
4 telle. In failinge of me my spirit; and[g]
thou hast knowe my sties. In this weie

PSALM CXL.

1   *The 'title of the[m] hundrid and fourtithe*
salm. 'The salm[n] 'of Dauith[o].

Lord, Y criede to thee, here thou me;
ȝyue thou tent to my vois, whanne Y schal
2 crye to thee. Mi preier be dressid as
encense in thi siȝt; the reisyng[p] of myn
hondis *be as* the euentid sacrifice. Lord,
3 sette thou a keping to my mouth; and a
dore of stonding aboute to my lippis.
4 Bowe thou not myn herte in to wordis of
malice; to excuse excusingis in synne. With
men worchinge wickiduesse; and Y schal
not comyne with the chosun men of hem.
5 A iust man schal repreue me in mersi,
and[q] schal blame me; but the oile of a
synner make not fat myn heed. For whi
and ȝit my preier *is* in the wel plesaunt
6 thingis of hem; for the domesmen of hem
ioyned to the stoon weren sopun vp. Here
7 thei my wordis, for tho[r] weren myȝti.
As fatnesse is[s] brokun out on the erthe;
oure bonys ben scatered niȝ helle. Lord,
8 Lord, for myn iȝen ben to thee, Y hopide
in thee; take thou not awei my soule.
9 Kepe thou me fro the snare which thei
ordeyneden to me; and fro the sclaundris
of hem that worchen wickidnesse. Syn-
10 neris schulen falle in the nett therof; Y
am aloone[t] til Y passe.

PSALM CXLI.

1   *The 'title of the[u] hundrid and oon and*
fourtithe salm[v]. The lernyng of Da-
uid[w]; 'his preier[x], 'whanne he was in
the denne[y].

2   With my vois Y criede to the Lord;
with my vois Y preiede hertli to the Lord.
3 I schede out my preier in his siȝt; and Y
pronounce my tribulacioun bifor him.
4 While my spirit failith of me; and thou
hast knowe my pathis. In this weie in

c Om. ᴁʜ. d the erthe ᴬʜ. e vpon hem ᴀ. f helled ᴇ *pr. m.* g Om. ᴀ.

m Om. ᴀ. n Om. ᴀʟ. o Om. ᴀ. *of Dauith, preiyng to the Lord, that he shulde falle no more into*
the synne of tonge. ᴋ. *of Dauith, feelinge synne of his tunge.* ᴠ. *of Dauith, the kyng.* ɪ. p reisyng vp ɪ.
q and he ɪ. r thei c. s of the erthe is ᴀ *sec. m.* of erthe is ᴍ *sec. m.* s. t syngulerly ᴄᴅᴇꜰɢʜᴋʟɴᴏ
ᴩQᴿꜱᴡbi. aloone *bi my self* ɪ. syngulerli, *ether aloone bi my silf* ᴜᴠ. synguler x. u Om. ᴀ. v Om. ᴀ.
w *Dauithes* ᴋ. x Om. cꜰᴠ. y Om. ᴇʟᴩ.

that I ʒide ; proude men hidden a grene
5 to me. I beheeld at the riʒt hond, and
I[h] saʒ ; and ther was not that kneuʒ me.
Fliʒt pershede fro me ; and ther was not
6 that aʒeen soʒte my soule. I criede to
thee, Lord, I seide, Thou art myn hope ;
7 my porcioun in the lond of lyueres. Tac
heede to my lowe preʒing ; for I am
mekid ful myche. Deliuere me fro the
pursuende me ; for thei ben coumfortid
8 vpon me. Led out fro warde my soule
to knowleche to thi name ; me abijden the[l]
riʒtwise[k], to the time that thou ʒelde to
me.

which Y ʒede ; proude men hidden a snare
to me. I bihelde to the riʒt side, and Y[s]
siʒ ; and noon was[z] that knew me. Fliʒt
perischide fro me ; and noon is[a] that sekith
my soule. Lord, Y criede to thee, Y[c]
seide, Thou art myn hope ; my part in the
lond of lyueris. ʒyue thou tent to my 7
bisechiug ; for Y am maad low ful greetli.
Delyuere thou me fro hem that pursuen
me ; for thei ben coumfortid on me. Lede 8
my soule out of keping to knouleche to
thi name ; iust men abiden me, til thou
ʒelde to me.

PSALM CXLII.

1 *The orisoun of Dauid, whan pursuede*
hym Absolon, his sone.

Lord, ful out here myn orisoun, with
eris parceyue myn obsecracioun ; in thi
treuthe ful out here thou me, in thi riʒt-
2 wisnesse. And entre thou not into dom
with thi seruaunt ; for ther shal not be
3 iustified in thi siʒte eche lyuende. For
the enemy pursuede my soule ; mekede
in the erthe my lif. He sette me in
derke thingis, as the deade of the world,
4 and my spirit is anguysht vp on me ;
5 in me is disturbid myn herte. Myndeful
I was of olde daʒes, I thoʒte swetely in
alle thi werkis ; in the deedis of thin
6 hondis I sweteli thoʒte. I straʒte out
myn hondis to thee ; my soule as erthe
7 withoute water to thee. Swiftli full out
here thou me, Lord ; my spirit failide.
Turne thou not awei thi face fro me ;
and I shal ben lic to the goende doun in
8 to the lake. Herd mac thou to me erli[l]
thi mercy ; for in thee I hopide. Knowen
mac thou to me the weie, in the[m] whiche
9 go I ; for to thee I rerede my soule. Tac
awei me fro myn enemys, Lord, to thee
10 I fleiʒ, tech me to do thi wil ; for my
God thou art. Thi goode spirit shal

PSALM CXLII.

1 *The 'title of the[b] hundrid and two and*
fourtithe salm. The salm[c] of Dauid[d].

Lord, here thou my preier, with eeris
perseyue thou my bisechiug ; in thi treuthe
here thou me, in thi riʒtwisnesse[e]. And[f] 2
entre thou not in to dom with thi seruaunt ; for ech man lyuynge schal not be
maad iust in thi siʒt. For the enemy 3
pursuede my soule ; he made lowe my lijf
in erthe. He hath set me in derk placis,
as the deed men of the world, and my 4
spirit was angwischid on me ; myn herte
was disturblid in me. I was myndeful of 5
elde daies, Y bithouʒte in alle thi werkis ;
Y bithouʒte in the dedis of thin hondis.
I helde forth myn hondis to thee ; my 6
soule as erthe with out water to thee.
Lord, here thou me swiftli ; my spirit 7
failide. Turne thou not a wei thi face
fro me ; and Y schal be lijk to[g] hem that
gon doun in to the[h] lake. Make thou erli 8
thi merci herd to me ; for Y hopide in
thee. Make thou knowun to me the weie
in which Y schal go ; for Y rciside my
soule to thee. Delyuere thou me fro myn 9
enemyes, Lord, Y fledde to thee ; teche 10
thou me to do thi wille, for thou art my
God. Thi good spirit schal lede me forth

---

[h] Om. c. [i] Om. *AEII.* [k] riʒtwise men *A.* [l] Om. c. [m] Om. *AII.*

[z] ther was s. [a] ther is 1. [b] Om. A. [c] Om. ELP. [d] *Dauith, whanne Absolon, his sone, pursuede*
him, as a doclour tellith, for the lettre accordith wel therto. K. *Dauith, whanne Absolon, his sone, pursuede*
him. V. [e] riʒtfulnesse *ceteri.* [f] But 1. [g] Om. 1. [h] Om. CDFHMPRUW.

bringe me thennes in to the ryȝt lond; 11for thi name, Lord, thou shalt quykene me in thin equite. Thou shalt leden out 12of tribulacioun my soule; and in thi merci thou shalt destroȝen alle myn ene- mys. And thou shalt leesen alle, that trublen my soule; for I am thi seruaunt.

in to a riȝtful lond; Lord, for thi name 11 thou schalt quikene me in thin equite. Thou schalt lede my soule out of tribu- lacioun; and in thi merci thou schalt 12 scatere alle[l] myn enemyes. And thou schalt leese[k] alle them, that troublen my soule; for Y am thi seruaunt.

PSALM CXLIII.

1   *The salm of Dauid; aȝen Golie.*

Benedictus Dominus.

Blissed[n] the Lord my God, that techeth myn hondis to strif; and mi fingeris to 2bataile. My mercy, and my refut; myn vndertakere, and my delynerere. My de- fendere, and in hym I hopide; that vndir- 3pooteth[o] my puple vnder me. Lord, what is a man, for thou hast myche maad knowen to hym; or the sone of man, for 4thou eymest hym? A man to vanyte is maad lic; his daȝis as shadewe passen. 5Lord, bowe doun thin heuenes, and cum doun; touche the monteynes, and thei 6shuln smoken. Leite thou leitingis[p], and thou shalt scateren hem; send out thin arewis, and thou shalt al[pp] disturbe them. 7Send out thin hond fro an heiȝ, tac[q] me out, and deliuere me of many watris; and 8fro the hond of alien sones. Whos mouth spac vanyte; and the riȝthalf of hem the 9riȝthalf of wickidnesse. God, a newe song I shal singe to thee; in the ten cordid 10sautre I shal do salm to thee. That ȝiuest helthe to kingis; that aȝeen boȝtist Dauid, thi seruaunt, fro the malice do- 11inge swerd tac me awey. And pull me awei fro the hond of alienes sones, whos mouth spac vanyte; and the riȝthalf of 12hem the riȝthalf of wickidnesse. Whos sones; as newe plauntingis in ther ȝouthe. The doȝtris of hem maad semely; en- 13hourned aboute as the licnesse of the tem-

PSALM CXLIII.

The title of the hundrid and thre and 1 *fourtithe salm[l]. 'A salm[m].*

Blessid *be* my[n] Lord God, that techith myn hondis to werre[o]; and my fyngris to batel. Mi merci, and my refuyt; my 2 takere vp, and my delyuerer. Mi defender, and Y hopide in him; and thou makist suget my puple vnder me. Lord, what is 3 a man, for thou hast maad knowun to him; ether the sone of man, for thou aret- tist him of[p] sum valu? A man is maad 4 lijk vanyte; hise daies passen as schadow. Lord, bowe doun thin heuenes, and come 5 thou doun; touche[q] thou hillis, and[r] thei[s] schulen make smoke. Leite thou schyn- 6 yng, and thou schalt scatere hem; sende thou out thin arowis, and thou schalt dis- turble hem. Sende out thin hond fro an 7 hiȝ, rauysche[t] thou[u] me out, and delyuere thou me fro many watris; and fro the hond of alien sones. The mouth of which[v] 8 spak vanite; and the riȝthond of hem *is* the riȝt hond of wickidnesse. God, Y schal 9 synge to thee a new song; I schal seie salm[w] to thee[x] in a sautre of ten stringis. Which ȝyuest heelthe to kingis; which aȝen 10 bouȝtist Dauid, thi seruaunt, fro the wickid swerd rauische thou out me. And delyuere 11 thou[y] me fro 'the hond of[z] alien sones; the mouth of whiche[a] spak[b] vanyte, and the riȝthond of hem *is* the riȝt hond of wickid- nesse. Whose sones *ben;* as new plaunt- 12 ingis in her ȝongthe. The douȝtris of hem

---

[n] Blessid *is A.* [o] vndir puttist *A.* [p] leitynge *AII.* [pp] Om. c *pr. m.* [q] and tac c.

[l] Om. 1. [k] fordo 1. [l] Om. ʀ. [m] Om. ᴇɢʟᴍᴏᴘ. *The salm of Dauid.* ʏ. *The salm, whanne he stod aȝens Golie in batcil, bi stiring of the Holi Goost.* ᴋ. *A salm of Dauith.* s. *A salm, whanne he stod aȝenus Golie.* ᴠ. In ᴀ is no title but only, c *and xliij.* [n] the ʏ. [o] batel ᴀ. do werre ᴍ. [p] to 1. [q] and touche c. [r] Om. s. [s] tho 1. [t] and rauishe s. [u] Om. 1. [v] whom 1. [w] u salm s. [x] Om. 1. [y] out c. [z] Om. v. [a] whom 1. [b] hath spoke 1.

ple. The celeris of hem fulle; bowende out fro that into it. The shep of hem ful of 14 frut, aboundende in ther goingis; the oxen of hem fatte. Ther is not falling of wal, ne passing ouer; ne cry in the stretis of 15 hem. Blisful, thei sciden, the puple, to whom these thingis ben; blisful the puple, of the^r whiche the Lord is his God.

ben arayed; ourned about as the licnesse of the^c temple. The selers of hem *ben* fulle; 13 bringinge out fro this^d *vessel* in to that^e. The scheep of hem *ben* with lambre^f, plenteuouse in her^g goingis out; her kien *ben* 14 fatte. 'No falling of wal is^h, nether passing ouere; nether cry *is* in the stretis of hem. Thei seiden, 'The puple *is* blessidⁱ, 15 that hath^k these thingis; blessid^l *is* the puple, whos Lord is the^m God of itⁿ.

PSALM CXLIV.

1   *The preising to hym Dauid.*

I shal enhaunce thee, my God king; and I shal blesse to thi name in to the 2 world, and in to the world of world. Bi alle da3is I shal blissen to thee; and I shal preysen thi name in to the world, 3 and in to the world of world. Gret the Lord, and preisable full myche; and of 4 his mychilnesse is noon ende. Jeneracioun and ieneracioun shal preyse thi werkis; and thi power thei shul telle 5 forth. The grete doing of the glorie of thin holynesse thei shuln speke; and thi 6 merueylis thei shul telle. And the vertue of thi ferful thingis thei shul seyn; and 7 thi mykilnesse thei shuln telle. The mynde of the abundaunce of thi swetnesse thei shul bowen out; and in thi ri3twisnesse thei shul ful out io3en. 8 Mercy doere and mercyful the Lord; 9 pacient, and myche merciful. Swete the Lord to alle; and his mercy doingis vp 10 on alle his werkis. Knouleche to thee, Lord, alle thi werkys; and thin halewis 11 blisse thei to thee. The glorie of thi reume thei shul seyn; and thi my3t thei 12 shul speken. That knowen thei maken

PSALM CXLIV.

The title of the hundrid and foure and 1 *fourtithe salm.* ' *The ympne of Dauith*^o.

Mi God king, Y schal enhaunse thee; and Y schal blesse thi name in to the world, and in to the world of^p world. Bi 2 alle daies Y schal blesse thee; and Y schal herie thi name in to the world, and in to the^q world of the^r world. The Lord *is* 3 greet, and worthi to be preisid ful myche; and noon ende is^s of his greetnesse. Gene- 4 racioun and generacioun schal preise thi werkis; and thei schulen pronounse^t thi power. Thei schulen speke 'the greet 5 doyng^u of the glorie of thin holynesse; and thei schulen telle thi merueils. And 6 thei schulen seye the vertu of thi ferdful thingis; and thei schulen telle thi greetnesse. Thei schulen bringe forth the 7 mynde of the abundaunce of thi swetnesse; and thei schulen telle with ful out ioiyng thi ri3tfulnesse. The Lord *is* a 8 merciful doere, and merciful in wille; paciente, and myche merciful. The Lord *is* 9 swete in alle thingis; and hise merciful doyngis *ben* on^v alle hise werkis. Lord, 10 alle thi werkis knouleche to thee; and thi seyntis blesse thee. Thei schulen seie the 11 glorie of thi rewme; and thei schulen

^c a 1.   ^d one s.   ^e anothir s.   ^f eene CFGHIMOPQRVXbi. yn D. cne EL. 3eeene K. 3eene SU. 3ene w. ^g the s.   ^h Ther is no falling of her wal 1.   ⁱ hem a blessid puple 1. The puple blessid s.   ^k han 1.   ^l but blessid 1.   ^m Om. L.   ⁿ hem 1.   ^o *The salm of Dauith.* D. *The ympne of Dauith, to the heerijng of God, with song ether ful out ioiyng.* K. *Alleluia.* s. Om. ELP. In A *is no title, but only* cxliiij.   P of the CDFOP QRVW.   ^q Om. L.   ^r Om. IKS.   ^s ther is 1.   ^t pronounse, *ether telle fer* c *et ceteri.*   ^u the [thi IL] magneficence, *ether* [*or* I] *the greet doyng* CDEFOHIMOPQRUVWXb. the magneficence, *ether g. d.* EO. the magneficence K. thi magnificence, *ether thi grete worthinesse* s.   ^v aboue 1. of K.

to the sones of men[s] thi power, and the
glorie of the grete doing of thi reume
13 Thi reume reume of alle worldis, and
thi lordshiping in alle generacioun and
in to generacioun Feithful the Lord in
alle his woordis, and holy in alle his
14 werkis The Lord helpeth vp alle that
fallen, and rereth vp alle the hurthid
15 doun The eჳen of alle in thee hopen,
Lord, and thou ჳyuest the mete of hem
16 in the[t] behoffful[u] tyme Thou openest
thin hond; and fulfillist eche beste with
17 blissing Riჳtwis the Lord in alle his
18 weies, and holi in alle his werkis Neeჳh
is the Lord to alle inwardli clepende hym,
to alle inwardli clepende hym in treuthe
19 The wil of men dredende hym he shal
do, and the lowe preჳing of hem he shal
ful out heren, and saf he shal make them.
20 The Lord kepeth alle loouende hym; and
21 alle synneres he shal destroჳen The
preysing of the Lord my mouth shal
speke, and blisse alle flesh to his holi
name in to the world, and in to the
world of world ·

speke thi power That thei make thi power 12
knowun to the sones of men, and the
glorie of the greetnesse[w] of thi rewme
Thi rewme is the rewme of alle worldis, 13
and thi lordschipe is in al generacioun
and in to generacioun The Lord is feithful in alle hise wordis, and hooli in alle
hise werkis The Lord liftith vp alle that 14
fallen doun; and[x] reisith[y] alle men hurthid
doun Lord, the ჳen of alle beestis hopen 15
in thee; and thou ჳyuest the[z] mete of hem
in[a] couenable tyme Thou openest thin 16
hond, and thou fillist ech beeste with
blessing The Lord is iust in alle hise 17
weies; and hooli in alle hise werkis The 18
Lord is niჳ to alle that inwardli clepen
him, to[b] alle that inwardli[c] clepen him
in treuthe He schal do the wille of 19
hem, that dreden him, and he schal here
the biseching of hem, and he schal make
hem saaf. The Lord kepith alle men 20
louynge him, and he schal leese[d] alle synners Mi mouth schal speke the heriyng 21
of the Lord, and ech man blesse his hooli
name in to the world, and in to the world
of world ,

PSALM CXLV

1   *Alleluia*

Lauda, anima   2   Preise thou, my soule, the Lord, I
shal preise the Lord in my lif, I shal do
salm to my God as longe as I shal be
3 Wileth not trosten in princis; ne in the
sones of men, in whiche is not helthe
4 His spirit shal gon out, and turnen aჳeen
in to his lond, in that dai shuln pershe
5 alle the thoჳtus of hem Blisful, of whom
the God of Jacob is his helpere; his hope
6 in the Lord his God, that made heuene
and erthe, the se, and alle thingis that
7 ben in hem That kepeth treuthe in to
the world, doth dom to the suffrende
wrong; ჳyueth mete to the hungri The

PSALM CXLV

The `title of the[e] hundred and fyue and 1
foui tithe `salm Alleluya[f]

Mi soule, herie thou the Lord; Y schal 2
herie the Lord in my lijf, Y schal synge
to my God as longe as Y schal be Nile ჳe 3
triste in princis, nethei in the sones of
men, in whiche[g] is noon[h] helthe The 4
spirit of hym[i] schal go out, and he schal
turne aჳen in to his erthe, in that dai alle
the thouჳtis of hem schulen perische He 5
is blessid, of whom the God of Jacob is
his[k] helpere, his hope is in his Lord God,
that made heuene and erthe, the see, and 6
alle thingis that ben in tho Which kepith 7
treuthe in to the world, makith[l] dom to
hem that suffren wrong, ჳyueth[m] mete to

---

[s] hem *AII*.   [t] Om. *AII*.   [u] behool *II*

[w] magneficence CDEFGHIKLMOPQRSUVWXbi   [x] and he 1   [y] reisith up K   [z] Om c   [a] in a *plures*
[b] and to u   [c] Om D   [d] fordo 1   [e] Om A   [f] Om A *salm Alleluya, for to stire men to truste not in
men, but in God [oouli KO]* KORS *salm Alleluya, truste in God oonly* V   [g] whom 1 the whiche K.
[h] no 1 not K   [i] hem s   [k] the 1   [l] *he* makith 1   [m] *he* ჳyueth 1.

8 Lord losneth[u] the gyuede ; the Lord liȝtneth the blinde. The Lord rereth vp the
hurtlid doun ; the Lord riȝtforth reulith
9 the riȝtwise. The Lord kepeth the comelingis, the modirles child, and the widewe
he shal vndertake ; and the weies of syn-
10 neres he shal destroȝen. The Lord shal
regne in to worldis[v] ; thi God, Sion, in
ieneracioun and in to ieneracioun.

hem that ben hungri. The Lord vnbyndith feterid men ; the Lord liȝtneth blynde 8
men. The Lord reisith men hurtlid[n] doun ;
the[o] Lord loueth iust men. The Lord 9
kepith comelyngis, he schal take vp a
modirles child, and[p] widewe ; and he schal
distrie the weies of synners. The Lord 10
schal regne in to the[q] worldis ; Syon, thi
God schal regne in generacioun and in to
generacioun.

PSALM CXLVI.

Alleluia.

1

Preiseth the Lord, for good is a salm ;
to oure God be preising ioȝeful and fair.
2 The Lord bildende vp Jerusalem ; the
scateringis of Jerusalem shal gadere to-
3 gidere. That helith the contrit in herte ;
and bindeth the contriciouns[w] of hem.
4 That noumbreth the multitude of sterris ;
5 and to them alle clepeth names. Gret
oure Lord, and gret the vertue of hym ;
6 and of his wisdam is not noumbre. Vn-
dertakende debonere men the Lord ; mek-
ende forsothe synneres vn to the erthe.
7 Singeth beforn to the Lord in confessioun ;
8 doth salm to oure God in harpe. That
couereth heuene with cloudis ; and greith-
eth to the erthe reyn. That bringeth
forth in hillis hey ; and erbe to the seruise
9 of men. That ȝyueth to bestis the mete
of hem ; and to briddis of crowes inwardli
10 clepende hym. He shal not han wil in
the strengthe of hors ; ne in the leggis of
11 a man shall be wel plesid to hym. Wel
plesid thing is to the Lord vpon men
dredende hym ; and in hem that hopen
on[x] his mercy.

PSALM CXLVI.

*The `title of the[r] hundrid and sixe and 1
fourtithe salm. Alleluya[s].*

Herie ȝe the Lord, for the salm is good ;
heriyng be myrie, and fair to oure God.
The Lord schal bilde Jerusalem ; and[t] 2
schal gadere togidere the scateryngis of
Israel. Which[u] *Lord* makith hool men 3
contrit in herte ; and byndith togidere the
sorewes of hem. Which noumbrith the 4
multitude of sterris ; and clepith names to
alle tho. Oure Lord *is* greet, and his 5
vertu *is* greet ; and of his wisdom is[v] no
noumbre. The Lord takith vp mylde men ; 6
forsothe[w] he makith low synneris `til to
the[x] erthe. Bifore synge ȝe to the Lord 7
in knoulechyng ; seye ȝe salm to oure God
in an harpe. Which hilith heuene[y] with 8
cloudis ; and makith redi reyn to the erthe.
Which bryngith forth hei in hillis ; and
eerbe to the seruice of men. Which ȝyueth 9
mete to her werk beestis ; and to the briddys
of crowis clepinge[z] hym. He schal not 10
haue wille in[a] the strengthe of an hors ;
nether it schal be wel plesaunt to hym in
the leggis of a man. It is wel plesaunt 11
to the Lord on men that dreden hym ; and
in hem that hopen on[b] his mercy.

PSALM CXLVII.

Alleluia of Agge and Zacharye.

12　Preise thou, Jerusalem, the Lord ;

PSALM CXLVII.

*The[c] hundrid and seuene and fourtithe
salm[d].*

Jerusalem, herie thou the Lord ; Syon, 12

---

u loosith *A.*　v the worldis *AU.*　w contricioun *A.*　x in *A.*

n hurlid I.　o and the c.　p and a *ceteri.*　q Om. *ceteri.*　r Om. A.　s Om. A.　*Alleluya ; to induce men
to heerie God.* KORS. *Alleluya, that is, Herie ȝe God.* V.　t and he I.　u The which I.　v ther is I.　w and I.
x vn to I.　to the s.　y heuens s.　z ynclepynge I.　a in to s.　b in IL.　c *The title of the* FMORI.
d Om. A.　salm ; [this K] *spekith of the gostli bilding of Jerusalem.* KORS. *salm hath no title in Ebreu.* U
salm hath no tytle. This salm spekith of goostli Jerusalem. V.　In I. *is no title, but only cxlvii.*

13 preise thou thi God, Sion. For he coum-
fortede the lockis of thi ȝatis; he blissede
14 to thi sones in thee. That sette thi coostis
pes; and with talȝ of whete fillith thee.
15 That sendeth out his specheʸ to erthe;
16 swiftli renneth his word. That ȝiueth
snouȝ as wlle; the litle cloude as askeᶻ
17 he sprengeth. He sendeth his cristalⁿ as
musselisᵇ; befor the face of his cold who
18 shal susteynen? He shal sende out his
woord, and melte them; his spirit shal
19 blowen, and watris shul flowen. That
tellith out his woord to Jacob; riȝtwis-
20 nesses and his domes to Irael. He dide
not so to eche nacioun; and his domes
he openede not to them.

heric thou thi God. For he hath coum- 13
fortid the lockis of thi ȝatis; he hath
blessid thi sones in thee. Which hath set 14
thi coostis pees; and fillith thee with theᵉ
fatnesse of wheete. Which sendith out his 15
speche to the erthe; his word renneth
swiftli. Which ȝyueth snow as wolle; 16
spredithᶠ abrood a cloude as aische. He 17
sendith his cristal as mussels; who schalᵍ
suffre bifore the face of his cooldnesse?
He schal sende out his word, and schal 18
melte tho; his spirit schal blowe, and
watris schulen flowe. Which tellith his 19
word to Jacob; and hise riȝtfulnessis and
domes to Israel. He dide not so to ech 20
nacioun; and he schewide not hise domes
to hem.

PSALM CXLVIII.

Laudate Do-
minum de
celis.

1　*Alleluia of Aggee and Zacharie.*

The`title of theʰ hundrid and eiȝte and 1
fourtithe salm. Alleluyaⁱ.

Preise ȝee the Lord fro heuenes; preise
2 ȝee hym in heiȝtis. Preise ȝee hym, alle
his aungelis; preise ȝee hym, alle his ver-
3 tues. Preise ȝee hym, the sunne and the
moone; preise ȝee hym, alle the sterris
4 and liȝt. Preise ȝee hym, heuenes of heuenes; and watris that aboue heuenes
5 ben, preise thei the name of the Lord.
6 For he seide, and thei ben maad; he
sente, and thei ben formed. He sette them
in to withoute ende, and in to the world
of world; an heste he putte, and he shal
7 not beside passe. Preise ȝee the Lord, fro
the erthe; dragonnes, and alle depnessis.
8 Fyr, hail, snouȝ, iys, the spirit of tem-
9 pestis; that don the woord of hym. Mounteynes, and alle hillis; frut berende trees,
10 and alle cedris. Bestis, and alle vsable
bestis; serpentis, and fethered foulis.
11 Kyngis of ertheᶜ, and alle puplis; princis,
12 and alle domys men of erthe. Ȝung men,
and maidenes; olde men with the ȝungere,
13 preise theiᵈ the name of the Lord; for

Ȝe of heuenes, herieʲ the Lord; herie
ȝe hym in hiȝe thingis. Alle hise aungels, 2
herie ȝe hym; alle hise vertues, herye ȝe
hym. Sunne and moone, herie ȝe hym; 3
alle sterris and liȝt, herie ȝe hym. Heuenes 4
of heuenes, herie ȝe hym; and the watris
that ben aboue heuenesᵏ, herie ȝeˡ the 5
name of the Lord. For he seide, and 6
thingis weren maad; he comaundide, and
thingis weren maad of nouȝt. He ordeynede tho thingis in to the world, and in
to the world of world; he settide a comaundement, and it schal not passe. Ȝe 7
ofᵐ erthe, herieⁿ ȝeᵒ the Lord; dragouns,
and alle depthis of watris. Fier, hail, 8
snow, iys, spiritis of tempestis; that don
his word. Mounteyns, and alle litle hillis; 9
trees berynge fruyt, and alle cedris. Wielde 10
beestis, and alle tame beestis; serpentis,
and fetherid briddis. The kingis of erthe, 11
and alle puplis; the princis, and alle iugis
of erthe. Ȝonge men, and virgyns, elde 12
men with ȝongere, herie ȝeᵖ the name of

ʸ speches *A.*　ᶻ asken *A.*　ⁿ cristallis *AH.*　ᵇ morselis *AH.*　ᶜ the erthe *AH.*　ᵈ ȝe *A.*

ᵉ Om. ᴄɪ.　ᶠ he spredith ɪ.　ᵍ schal mowe ɪ.　ʰ Om. ᴀx.　ⁱ Om. ᴀᴏʀx. *Alleluya; [this* ᴋ] *exciteth
[alle* ᴋ] *men fulli to herie God.* ᴋᴏʀs. *Alleluya; of the firste comyng of Crist.* ᴠ.　ʲ herieth ɪ.　ᵏ heuene ᴋ.
ˡ thei ᴋ.　ᵐ of the ɢ.　ⁿ herieth ɪ.　ᵒ Om. ᴄᴅᴇғɢʜɪʟᴏᴘǫʀsᴠxⅠ.　ᵖ Om. ɢɪᴠ.

enhauncid is the name of hym alone. 14 The knouleching of hym vpon heuene and erthe; and he enhauncide the horn of his puple. Ympne to alle the seyntis of hym; to the sones of Irael, to the puple neʒhende to hym.

PSALM CXLIX.

1 *Alleluia.*

Cantate Domino canticum novum.

Singeth to the Lord a newe song; hys 2 preising in the chirche of halewis. Glade Irael in hym that made hym; and the doʒtris of Sion ful out ioʒe thei in ther 3 kyng. Preise thei the name of hym in quer; in timbre and sautre do they salm 4 to hym. For wel plesid is to the Lord in his puple; and he enhauncide the de- 5 bonere in to helthe. Halewys shul ful out ioʒen in glorie; thei shul gladen in 6 ther bed placis. The ful out ioʒingus of God in the throte of hem; and the swerdis on eithir side sharp in the hondis 7 of hem. To be do veniaunce in naciouns; 8 and blamyngis in puplis. To ben bounde the kingis of hem in fettris; and the noble 9 men of hem in irene manyclis. That thei do in hem dom writen; glorie this is to alle the seintis of hym".

PSALM CL.

1 *Alleluia.*

Laudate Dominum in sanctis.

Preise ʒee the Lord in his seintis; preise ʒee hym in the fastnyng of his 2 vertue. Preise ʒee hym in the vertues of hym; preise ʒee hym aftir the multi- 3 tude of the gretnesse of hym. Preise ʒee hym in the soun of trumpe; preiseth 4 hym in sautre and harpe. Preise ʒee hym in timbre and quer; preise ʒee hym

---

the Lord; for the name of hym aloone is 13 enhaunsid. His knouleching *be* on heuene 14 and erthe; and he hath enhaunsid the horn of his puple. An ympne *be* to alle hise seyntis; to the children of Israel, to a puple neiʒynge to hym.

PSALM CXLIX.

The `title of the*q* hundrid and nyne and*h* fourtithe salm. Alleluya*r*.

Synge ʒe to the Lord a newe song; hise 2 heriyng *be* in the chirche of seyntis. Is- rael be glad in hym that made hym; and the douʒtris of Syon make ful out ioye in her king. Herie thei his name in a queer; 3 seie thei the salm to hym in a tympan, and*s* sautre. For the Lord is wel plesid in his 4 puple; and he hath reisid mylde men in to heelthe. Seyntis schulen make ful out 5 ioye in glorie; thei schulen be glad in her beddis. The ful out ioiyngis of God in the 6 throte of hem; and swerdis scharp on*t* 'ech side" in the hondis of hem. To do ven- 7 iaunce in naciouns; blamyngis*v* in puplis. To bynde the kyngis of hem in stockis; 8 and the noble men of hem in yrun mana- clis. That thei make in hem doom writun; 9 this is glorye*w* to alle hise seyntis.

PSALM CL.

The title of the hundrid and fiftithe salm, 1 Alleluya*x*.

Herie ʒe*y* the Lord in hise seyntis; herie ʒe hym in the firmament of his vertu. Herie ʒe hym in hise vertues; herie*z* ʒe*a* 2 hym bi*b* the multitude of his greetnesse. Herie ʒe hym in the soun of *c* trumpe; 3 herie ʒe hym in a sautre and harpe. Herie 4 ʒe hym in a tympane and*d* queer; herie ʒe hym in strengis and orgun. Herie ʒe 5

c hem *A*.

5 in cordis and orgne. Preise ȝee hym in cymbalis wel sounende, preise ȝee hym 6 in cymbalis of huge ioȝing ; eche spirit, preise the Lord.

hym in cymbalis sownynge wel, herye ȝe hym in cymbalis of iubilacioun; ech spirit, 6 herye the Lord.

Here endith the Sawter; and now bigynneth the preface of Seynt Jerom in the book of Prouerbes[f].

Here endith the Sautere; and here bigynneth the Prouerbis of Salomon[e].

---

[f] From *A*. *Explicit. Here endith the Sauter*. E.   No final rubric in CH.

---

[e] *Here endith the Sauter, and here biginnen* [*bigynneth* U] *Prouerbis* [*Parablis* W] CFHQUW. *Here endith the Sautere*. D. *Here endith the Sauter, and bigynneth a prolog on Prouerbis*. G. *Heere endith the Sauter of Dauid, the prophete*. I. *Here endeth the book of Salmes; blessed be the Holi Trinyte. Amen. Amen*. K. *Here endith the Sauter, but mo salmes suwen, than ben writen in the Sauter, whiche ben writen in dyuerse chapitles of the bible bifore and after, whiche it is no nede to writen hem twies ; therfor we enden here, and here bigynneth a prologe vpon Prouerbis of Salomon*. M.   .   .   .   .   .   .   *and here bigynnen the Prouerbis of Salamon*. N.   *Here endith the book of Salmes, and bigynneth the prolog on the book of Prouerbis, ethir Parablis, as it sueth oftir*. O.   *Here endeth the Sauter, and bigynneth the prolog on the Prouerbis of Salomon*. R. *Here endith the Sauter, and bigynneth the book of Prouerbis*. V. *Here endith the Sauter, and bigynnen the Canticlis*. I.   No final rubric in P.

CPSIA information can be obtained
at www.ICGtesting.com
Printed in the USA
LVHW080209141020
668649LV00010BA/352